The Top 6000 Companies in The East Midlands

Companies with assets exceeding £9,000,000

John D Blackburn
Editor

dp

First Edition

Spring 2019

ISBN-13: 978-1-912736-20-1

ISBN-10: 1-912736-20-9

Printed in 8pt Nimbus Sans L

Designed by URW++ Design and Development GmbH

Dellam Publishing Limited

2 Heath Drive, Sutton, Surrey, SM2 5RP

Fax: 020 8770 7478 email: enquiries@dellam.com

SAN: 0177881 EAN/GLN: 5030670177882

Table of Contents

Acknowledgements

We appreciate your interest in our publications, and your comments and suggestions are always welcome. Please contact us at enquiries@dellam.com.

Scotland
Northern Ireland
North East (England)
North West (England)
Yorkshire and The Humber
East Midlands (England)
West Midlands (England)
East of England
Wales
See London Inset
South East (England)
South West (England)
Outer London East and North East
Outer London West and North West
Inner London East
Inner London West
Inner London East
Outer London East and North East
Outer London South

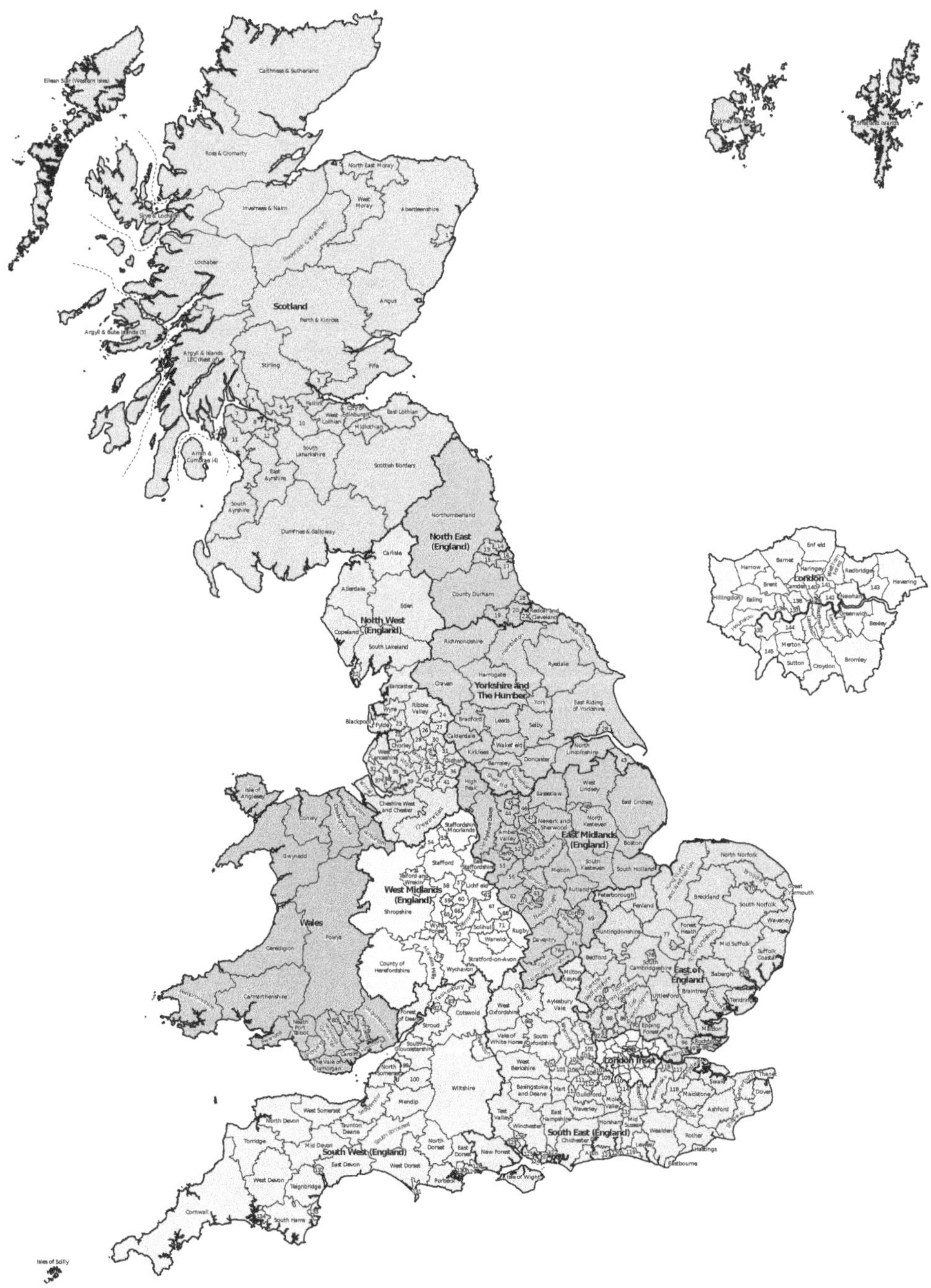
Scotland
North East (England)
North West (England)
Yorkshire and The Humber
East Midlands (England)
West Midlands (England)
Wales
East of England
London
South East (England)
South West (England)

Introduction

This study looks at all companies registered in the East Midlands and where their total assets are more than £9,000,000.

The East Midlands is a medium size region with a population of 4.8 million in 2017, out of 66 million for the UK .

The region comprises the counties of Derbyshire, Leicestershire, Lincolnshire, Northamptonshire, Nottinghamshire and Rutland. The main cities are Derby, Leicester, Lincoln, Northampton and Nottingham.

The aim of this study is to provide an overview of the key movers and shakers in the East Midlands corporate sector. Only key data has been isolated, particularly the company's net worth and total assets, but also its full name, date incorporated, registered office, activities, shareholders, directors (with date of birth, occupation and nationality) and number of employees.

Two indicators of size are used: net worth and total assets. These are preferable to turnover which is influenced by profit margins and whether the companies are capital or labour intensive.

A short summary of the corporate sector in the East Midlands:

Britain's hosiery and knitwear industry was largely based in the region, and in the 1980s it had more textile workers than any other British region. Derby was home to an important railway workshop. At its peak, Corby Steelworks was the largest in Britain.

The region is the UK's eighth largest region in terms of total output.

Total output (GVA), in 2016, was £100 billion (UK being £1,748 billion) while total output (GVA) per head, in 2016, was £21,185 (UK average £26,621).

The number employed, May-July 2018, was 2,278,000 out of UK total of 32,397,000 with an employment rate of 74.9% (UK being 75.5%).

Manufacturing accounts for 16.7%, making it the region with the second highest proportion of manufacturing output within the UK, after Wales. There were 12,210 manufacturing businesses in the region in 2017. The region's largest manufacturing sectors are food and drink, transport equipment, rubber, plastics and non-metallic minerals.

There were 294,000 manufacturing jobs in 2017 (12% of all jobs) while the public sector accounted for 15.6%.

In 2016, the region had around 173,000 VAT registered businesses, mainly SMEs. In 2017, there were 22,565 new businesses set up (up 12%) and 22,740 businesses ceased trading (up 12%). The number of businesses, in 2017, was 371,000 (UK total 5,695,000).

A new East Midlands Development Corporation (dev-corp) is currently being assembled.

Standard cataloguing guidelines for company names in the profile section have been used, but there will be occurrences when the name may not be strictly alphabetical. A certain licence was adopted where it was felt that strictly alphabetical could lead to improper cataloguing. Some company names have been shortened in the league tables for aesthetic reasons.

John D Blackburn
Editor

This page is intentionally left blank

Total Assets League Table

Company	Value
Green Planet Products Limited	£72,075,780,096
Jaguar Land Rover Automotive PLC	£26,780,000,256
Experian Finance PLC	£25,103,120,384
Jaguar Land Rover Limited	£24,846,000,128
National Farmers Union Mutual Insurance Society	£19,342,000,128
GUS 2000 Finance Unlimited	£17,997,971,456
Quadgas Holdco Limited	£17,127,000,064
Quadgas Midco Limited	£17,127,000,064
WIC (1) Limited	£16,552,205,312
Volkswagen Financial Services (UK) Limited	£14,847,398,912
Cemex UK	£14,785,547,264
Experian Investment Holdings Limited	£12,533,737,472
Nielsen Holdings PLC	£12,345,899,008
Godiva Mortgages Limited	£12,311,784,448
Osprey Holdco Limited	£11,413,799,936
Osprey Acquisitions Limited	£11,306,300,416
Experian Holdings (UK) Limited	£10,856,400,896
Anglian Water Services Limited	£10,790,700,032
Severn Trent Water Limited	£10,590,300,160
Experian (UK) Finance Limited	£10,532,550,656
Aldermore Bank PLC	£10,467,399,680
Cadent Gas Limited	£9,879,000,064
Severn Trent PLC	£9,421,800,448
GUS Holdings Unlimited	£7,850,981,888
Mercedes-Benz Financial Services UK Limited	£7,566,894,080
Anglian Water Services Financing PLC	£7,506,400,256
Barratt Developments P L C	£6,928,999,936
Severn Trent Draycote Limited	£6,453,899,776
Experian (UK) Holdings 2006 Limited	£6,428,568,064
Thomas Cook Group Treasury Limited	£5,947,229,184
AWG Parent Co Limited	£5,573,062,144
Jaguar Land Rover Holdings Limited	£5,514,299,904
BDW Trading Limited	£5,491,867,136
Travis Perkins PLC	£5,141,799,936
Experian Holdings Limited	£5,077,927,936
GUS Catalogues Unlimited	£4,974,806,528
RPC Group PLC	£4,783,399,936
Next Retail Limited	£4,591,239,168
Aldi Stores Limited	£4,331,130,880
Severn Trent Investment Holdings Limited	£4,064,699,904
Porterbrook Holdings I Limited	£3,921,875,968
Steris PLC	£3,917,389,056
Launchchange Holding Company	£3,902,550,016
Saint-Gobain Aldwych Limited	£3,853,967,872
Cemex UK Operations Limited	£3,840,877,056
Thomas Cook Investments (2) Limited	£3,789,469,184
Coventry Building Society Covered Bonds LLP	£3,785,728,000
VR Finance Company	£3,686,706,944
Severn Trent Utilities Finance PLC.	£3,589,700,096
Volkswagen Group United Kingdom Limited	£3,532,100,096
Boots UK Limited	£3,464,999,936
Porterbrook Leasing Company Limited	£3,403,115,008
T-Mobile Holdings Limited	£3,339,591,936
Experian US Holdings Unlimited	£3,338,498,048
Severn Trent Carsington Limited	£3,146,099,968
Travis Perkins Trading Company Limited	£3,065,400,064
Severn Trent Trimpley Limited	£3,046,700,032
Together Financial Services Limited	£2,979,200,000
Argos Limited	£2,905,533,952
Launchchange Instrumentation Limited	£2,891,536,896
TI Fluid Systems PLC	£2,863,465,472
Airtanker Holdings Limited	£2,851,141,120
Airtanker Limited	£2,850,868,992
Sports Direct International PLC	£2,849,600,000
BPB Limited	£2,837,552,896
Home Retail Group (UK) Limited	£2,790,338,048
E.On Energy Solutions Limited	£2,716,999,936
Cemex Investments Limited	£2,672,257,024
Vinters International Limited	£2,652,931,072
AWG Group Limited	£2,566,819,072
Sportsdirect.Com Retail Limited	£2,566,496,000
Next PLC	£2,561,499,904
Cummins Generator Technologies Limited	£2,536,200,960
Capital One (Europe) PLC	£2,533,635,072
BPB Group Finance Limited	£2,523,906,048
Airtanker Finance Limited	£2,482,470,912
Home Retail Group Limited	£2,453,499,904
Lubrizol Group, LLP	£2,421,948,928
Motor Insurers' Bureau	£2,400,355,072
Punch Taverns (PGE) Limited	£2,376,764,928
Rolls-Royce Overseas Investments Limited	£2,318,479,616
Redhill Famco Limited	£2,278,099,968
RPC 2017 Holding Company Limited	£2,271,000,064
Severn Trent (W & S) Limited	£2,257,999,872
BCA Marketplace PLC	£2,256,100,096
CEVA Limited	£2,210,174,720
Croda Investments No 3 Limited	£2,201,199,104
Pirelli International PLC	£2,200,726,016
Punch Taverns Limited	£2,190,899,968
Bombardier Transportation UK Ltd	£2,189,654,016
Mytravel Group Limited	£2,188,100,096
RPC Packaging Holdings Limited	£2,108,800,000
Argos Holdings Limited	£2,064,024,064
Pendragon PLC	£2,060,600,064
Saint-Gobain Limited	£2,026,028,032
Amtrust Europe Limited	£1,958,232,064
Porterbrook Leasing Asset Company Limited	£1,951,216,000
Thomas Cook UK Limited	£1,917,830,016
Holcim Participations (UK) Limited	£1,916,173,952
Rigid Plastic Containers Holdings Limited	£1,898,800,000
Amey UK PLC	£1,884,103,040
Amey Holdings Limited	£1,869,203,968
Center Parcs (Holdings 1) Limited	£1,841,200,000
DH Alpha Limited	£1,826,075,008
Together Commercial Finance Limited	£1,825,400,064
Admenta UK Limited	£1,821,915,008
Bloor Investments Limited	£1,814,712,064
Emerson Developments (Holdings) Limited	£1,813,374,976
Bloor Holdings Limited	£1,812,982,016
Heating Finance Limited	£1,727,757,056
Booker Limited	£1,700,300,032
British Business Bank PLC	£1,679,761,024
National House-Building Council	£1,674,989,952
Sytner Group Limited	£1,657,668,992
DH Omega Limited	£1,656,760,960
Croda International Public Limited Company	£1,648,700,032
Aston Martin Holdings (UK) Limited	£1,626,440,960
Anglian Water Services Holdings Limited	£1,609,092,992
Pets at Home No.1 Limited	£1,595,992,960
Sandbrook Overseas Investments Limited	£1,577,538,688
Aggregate Industries UK Limited	£1,570,253,056
Scoto Limited	£1,568,481,024
Launchchange Limited	£1,552,833,024
Next Holdings Limited	£1,523,399,936
Caterpillar UK Holdings Limited	£1,513,432,960
Commatone Limited	£1,504,935,936
Bloor Homes Limited	£1,495,132,032
B.L. Marketing Limited	£1,462,039,040
Severn Trent Finance Holdings Limited	£1,454,834,944
AGCO Services Limited	£1,446,155,392
Holland & Barrett Group Limited	£1,427,422,976
DPG Holdings Limited	£1,423,794,944
Mercedes-Benz Cars UK Limited	£1,414,178,048
Molson Coors (UK) Holdings LLP	£1,409,360,000
Booker Group Limited	£1,408,700,032
RPC Pisces Holdings Limited	£1,390,544,640
Ikea Properties Investments Limited	£1,384,669,056
Rolls-Royce Overseas Holdings Limited	£1,363,266,944
Global Payments U.K. Ltd	£1,358,274,944
Pets at Home Group PLC	£1,339,376,000
Launchchange Operations Limited	£1,332,269,056
Amey PLC	£1,308,209,024
NBH Holdco Limited	£1,301,528,704
Wolseley UK Limited	£1,301,063,936

Company	Value
NBCMH Holdings Limited	£1,297,876,736
Omega Acquisition Bidco Limited	£1,283,037,440
Avon Cosmetics Limited	£1,282,434,304
British Business Investments Ltd	£1,277,634,944
Travis Perkins Plumbing & Heating LLP	£1,277,200,000
BPB Group Operations Limited	£1,273,667,968
Essentra Finance Limited	£1,269,492,992
Duki (2006) Finance Limited	£1,269,117,952
Porterbrook Holdings II Limited	£1,262,193,024
Rigby Group (RG) PLC	£1,243,282,944
Essentra PLC	£1,239,699,968
BPB Investments Overseas Limited	£1,221,208,960
DHL Supply Chain Limited	£1,214,093,056
Holland & Barrett Retail Limited	£1,213,031,936
Jewson Limited	£1,212,049,024
GPUK LLP	£1,203,758,976
Bodycote International Limited	£1,188,212,992
Wickes Building Supplies Limited	£1,187,399,936
Center Parcs (Operating Company) Limited	£1,180,999,936
Telent Limited	£1,171,399,936
Booker Wholesale Holdings Limited	£1,168,700,032
Multi Packaging Solutions UK Limited	£1,162,897,024
Eco-Bat Technologies Limited	£1,158,886,016
Aston Martin Lagonda Limited	£1,157,005,056
Rampion Offshore Wind Limited	£1,145,164,032
Thomas Cook Group Hedging Limited	£1,137,655,040
Travis Perkins (Properties) Limited	£1,105,600,000
Thomas Cook Airlines Limited	£1,104,685,952
Ametek European Holdings Limited	£1,102,743,040
Blue Sea Overseas Investments Limited	£1,090,800,000
Canal & River Trust	£1,082,000,000
Dundee Holdco 4 Limited	£1,069,793,024
Multi Packaging Solutions Acquisitions 2 Limited	£1,067,397,696
PTS Group Limited	£1,065,400,000
Thomas Cook Continental Holdings Limited	£1,061,576,128
Cintra Infrastructures SE	£1,042,882,112
Pets at Home Ltd	£1,030,350,976
Dematic (Services) Limited	£1,028,694,400
Sophos Group PLC	£1,022,746,304
Punch Partnerships (PML) Limited	£1,022,707,968
Elsevier Limited	£1,022,680,000
Wabtec UK Holdings Limited	£1,011,732,352
Porterbrook Leasing Mid Company Limited	£1,010,468,992
AAH Pharmaceuticals Limited	£999,052,032
Doncasters Group Limited	£996,000,000
Rolls-Royce Power Engineering PLC	£988,800,000
Cognita BondCo Parent Limited	£988,616,000
Miller Homes Group Holdings PLC	£978,000,000
Experian Limited	£970,000,000
Thomas Cook Group UK Limited	£962,800,000
Bodycote PLC	£959,699,968
Full Moon Holdco 6 Limited	£954,200,000
Amtrust International Limited	£952,264,000
Doncasters Limited	£927,041,024
Baxi Holdings Limited	£924,073,984
Center Parcs (Holdings 3) Limited	£920,600,000
Cognita Holdings Limited	£907,203,008
Cognita UK Holdings Limited	£907,203,008
Golden Acquisition	£906,520,000
British Steel Holdings Limited	£897,830,976
Peugeot Motor Company PLC	£893,265,024
TI Automotive Limited	£892,684,224
Baxi Finance Limited	£882,812,992
Cambridge & Counties Bank Limited	£879,232,000
Molson Coors Brewing Company (UK) Limited	£878,267,008
Total Lindsey Oil Refinery Limited	£872,945,984
Telent Technology Services Limited	£868,499,968
Saint-Gobain Building Distribution Limited	£868,233,024
Saint-Gobain Construction Products UK Limited	£858,835,968
Arugani Limited	£850,376,448
Dundee Holdco 3 Limited	£848,078,016
Dyas UK Limited	£845,222,016

Company	Value
Bowmer and Kirkland Limited	£840,172,800
Sophos Holdings Limited	£839,215,360
Punch Taverns Holdco (B) Limited	£838,428,032
Daimler UK Limited	£836,051,968
Adient UK Financing International Ltd	£829,750,080
Albanwise Limited	£821,648,000
Multi Packaging Solutions Acquisitions 1 Limited	£821,265,216
Orbit Treasury Limited	£817,558,016
HBVB	£810,892,032
Travis Perkins P & H Partner Limited	£810,600,000
Full Moon Holdco 7 Limited	£810,099,968
Powergen International Limited	£805,467,008
Lloyds Pharmacy Limited	£805,225,024
Elli Finance (UK) PLC	£804,444,032
Multi Packaging Solutions Limited	£791,438,976
Langley Holdings PLC	£791,284,864
Home Retail Group Card Services Limited	£788,092,992
Office 1 Limited	£783,990,976
Life UK Healthcare Limited	£783,152,000
Caterpillar (U.K.) Limited	£780,827,008
Bodycote Finance Limited	£775,449,024
DFS Furniture PLC	£774,200,000
Scusi Limited	£769,230,016
Office Depot (Holdings) Limited	£768,821,184
CCF Limited	£767,400,000
Office Depot Europe Holdings Limited	£759,043,968
Weatherbys Bank Holdings Limited	£758,838,848
Weatherbys Bank Limited	£758,838,784
The Boots Company PLC	£753,000,000
Refresco Drinks UK Limited	£751,484,992
Severn Trent Holdings Limited	£749,216,000
Perkins Engines Company Limited	£748,249,984
Enterprise PLC	£745,878,976
Ibstock PLC	£744,843,008
BHL (UK) Holdings Ltd	£741,400,000
EMA Holdings UK Limited	£740,507,008
Firth Rixson Limited	£739,376,000
United Church Schools Foundation Ltd	£739,315,008
Jerrold Finco PLC	£739,092,672
Holland & Barrett Holdings Limited	£738,716,992
Sophos Limited	£732,288,000
Bracken Midco2 Limited	£731,699,968
Aggregate Industries Holdings Limited	£731,000,000
Adient UK Financing Ltd	£725,251,008
British Steel Limited	£724,134,016
AGCO International Limited	£722,129,024
Telent Communications Holdings Limited	£717,699,968
Arconic Limited	£717,590,720
GHP Midco Limited	£713,638,016
Holland & Barrett International Limited	£713,566,976
Doncasters UK Finance Limited	£709,664,704
Wabtec UK Investments Limited	£707,272,064
Thame and London Limited	£706,400,000
Baxi Global Limited	£705,094,016
Admenta Holdings Limited	£704,518,016
DFS Furniture Holdings PLC	£703,000,000
Welcome Break Group Limited	£701,206,016
Baxi Potterton Limited	£699,126,976
Millennium Inorganic Chemicals Overseas Holdings	£698,991,872
Charles Street Buildings (Leicester) Limited	£697,086,400
Adient Financing Ltd	£696,496,320
TI Automotive Euro Holdings Limited	£693,655,168
Volvo Group UK Limited	£693,393,024
Scania (Great Britain) Limited	£692,945,984
Travelodge Hotels Limited	£689,699,968
Emhart International Limited	£687,214,976
Paccar Financial PLC	£679,089,984
SIG Trading Limited	£676,000,000
Evonik UK Holdings Limited	£674,511,296
Oxford Sciences Innovation PLC	£668,587,008
Dematic Group Limited	£665,142,656
Peugeot Citroen Automobiles UK Limited	£663,350,976

Company	Value
Atlas Hotels Limited	£655,684,864
JHC Finance Company	£649,312,000
BGL (Holdings) Limited	£648,499,968
E.On Climate & Renewables UK Humber Wind Ltd	£645,260,992
FCC Recycling (UK) Limited	£644,808,000
Infinis Energy Group Holdings Limited	£642,665,024
SIG European Investments Limited	£635,296,000
SHV Energy Holdings UK Limited	£634,246,016
FCC Environment (UK) Limited	£631,352,000
Bombardier Transportation (Holdings) UK Ltd	£631,014,976
Citroen U.K. Limited	£630,558,976
FR Acquisitions Corporation (Europe) Limited	£628,000,000
Dawsongroup PLC	£625,916,032
Together Personal Finance Limited	£621,699,968
Dassault Systemes UK Limited	£620,798,976
XPO Holdings UK and Ireland Limited	£616,729,024
BISL Limited	£616,499,968
R P S Group PLC	£612,729,024
TI Automotive Holdings Limited	£610,521,792
Jeld-Wen Europe Ltd.	£604,894,016
Polypipe Group PLC	£602,800,000
Molson Coors Holdings Limited	£602,753,984
Tulip Limited	£601,492,992
Greencore Beechwood Limited	£599,827,968
Clinigen Group PLC	£594,351,360
Experian Europe Unlimited	£594,088,000
Arconic Manufacturing (GB) Limited	£589,929,984
Ikea Limited	£589,835,008
Ibstock Brick Limited	£585,729,024
Aston Martin Investments Limited	£585,558,016
Baxi Heating UK Limited	£576,209,024
Capital One Investments Limited	£567,590,976
Renewi European Holdings Limited	£567,320,000
Bodycote America Treasury Limited	£565,867,264
ITL Mortgages Limited	£561,296,000
Aviagen International Finance Limited	£559,744,640
Healthcare at Home Ltd	£553,518,976
United Learning Trust	£550,627,968
Geely UK Limited	£549,401,024
E.On Climate & Renewables UK London Array Ltd	£547,182,976
Thomas Cook Tour Operations Limited	£546,156,992
Custodian REIT PLC	£541,884,992
Stanley U.K. Holding Ltd.	£541,169,984
E.On Climate & Renewables UK Limited	£539,121,984
Keepmoat Limited	£538,776,000
Polypipe Limited	£537,100,032
Europcar Group UK Limited	£536,308,000
Croda Overseas Holdings Limited	£536,140,160
Rolls-Royce Leasing Limited	£535,630,016
RS Components Limited	£534,700,000
London EV Company Limited	£533,179,008
Aga Rangemaster Group Limited	£531,000,000
Cristal Pigment UK Limited	£528,820,000
Jewel UK Midco Limited	£527,827,008
Castle 1 Limited	£527,662,016
Young's Seafood Limited	£526,859,008
Giant Booker Limited	£524,000,000
Avant Homes (England) Limited	£521,600,992
CarnaudMetalbox Group UK Ltd.	£521,129,984
Mercedes-Benz Retail Group UK Limited	£519,217,984
Avant Homes Group Limited	£518,963,008
Infinis Energy Management Limited	£517,940,000
University of Derby	£517,323,008
Vaillant Holdings Limited	£515,036,000
Bakkavor Finance Limited	£514,768,000
Morris Homes Limited	£513,183,008
Croda Europe Limited	£513,164,992
Office Depot International (UK) Limited	£510,411,008
Benchmark Holdings PLC	£507,848,992
Cognita Midco Limited	£507,576,992
Keystone Midco Limited	£504,443,008
Weetabix Limited	£504,065,984
Vaillant Management Limited	£503,779,200
Keystone JVCO Limited	£503,755,008
Orbit Investments (Properties) Limited	£503,718,944
Methodist Homes	£503,104,000
Samworth Brothers (Holdings) Limited	£501,324,000
Enterprise Managed Services Limited	£500,051,008
Dundee Holdco 2 Limited	£500,012,000
Renewi Holdings Limited	£497,993,984
Harworth Group PLC	£496,958,016
BFSL Limited	£496,343,008
Lloyds Bank Commercial Finance Limited	£495,780,992
Wyn Overseas Operations Limited	£494,433,792
Perkins Holdings Limited	£490,375,008
Infinis Limited	£486,323,008
Sytner Limited	£484,305,984
Wyndham Holdings	£483,704,992
SG International Holdings Limited	£482,303,008
Essentra International Limited	£478,504,000
Samworth Brothers Limited	£478,072,000
Blemain Finance Limited	£476,400,000
Boketto Newco Limited	£476,193,984
Carlsberg UK Limited	£475,660,992
Experian Finance 2012 Limited	£475,067,072
Beeswax Dyson Farming Limited	£473,896,000
Croda Investments No 2 Limited	£470,505,952
Boketto Holdco Limited	£468,905,984
Halcyon Topco Limited	£467,729,984
WA Capital Limited	£466,599,200
Hazlewood Foods Limited	£466,135,008
Welcome Break No. 1 Limited	£466,100,000
Micromass Holdings Limited	£465,121,984
Dow Chemical Company Limited	£464,392,000
CP Woburn (Operating Company) Limited	£460,500,000
Unipart Group of Companies Limited	£458,500,000
Oxford Diocesan Board of Finance (The)	£456,952,000
RPC Containers Limited	£455,600,000
Multi Packaging Solutions Global Holdings Ltd	£455,382,880
Anglian Water (Osprey) Financing PLC	£455,227,008
Keepmoat Homes Limited	£452,708,000
Appia Europe Limited	£450,569,984
BPB Finance (No. 4) Limited	£449,071,040
Tunstall Healthcare Group Limited	£448,660,992
Doc Bidco Limited	£446,500,000
Doc Topco Limited	£445,800,000
Hunter Douglas (UK) Limited	£445,752,000
Alloga UK Limited	£442,500,992
Caterpillar UK Engines Company Limited	£441,944,992
Dunelm (Soft Furnishings) Ltd	£440,900,000
Ferrovial Services UK Ltd.	£439,264,480
BGL Group Limited	£439,000,000
A Shade Greener Tankersley LLP	£438,071,552
DB Cargo (UK) Limited	£437,000,000
Wilko Retail Limited	£435,607,008
Wilkinson Hardware Stores, Limited	£435,607,008
Calor Gas Limited	£433,800,000
Hilton Food Group PLC	£433,360,000
Cognita Financing PLC	£433,271,008
Millennium Inorganic Chemicals UK Holdings Ltd	£432,994,464
Watches of Switzerland Company Limited	£431,579,008
Henry Boot PLC	£428,059,008
TI Automotive USA Holdings Limited	£427,924,512
Crown UK Holdings Limited	£427,123,008
Loomis Investments US Limited	£426,816,288
Dunelm Group PLC	£425,000,000
Welcome Break Limited	£423,462,016
Severn Trent Leasing Limited	£422,240,992
Novoferm Europe Limited	£421,993,952
Morris Group Limited	£421,991,008
Boots Properties Limited	£420,800,000
Experian Latam Holdings Unlimited	£420,489,152
Ibstock Building Products Limited	£413,817,984
Ballyvesey Holdings Limited	£413,624,768

Company	Value
TNT GRS 2008 Limited	£412,756,608
Libra (Longhurst Group) Treasury PLC	£411,956,992
Greencore Food To Go Limited	£411,808,992
BASF Public Limited Company	£411,519,008
Baxi Overseas Holdings Limited	£410,859,008
Orbit Investments (Northern) Limited	£407,171,232
Diamond Light Source Limited	£404,731,616
Circassia Pharmaceuticals PLC	£402,400,000
Weatherford U.K. Limited	£402,358,016
TCGH Holdings Limited	£400,000,000
Tunstall Group Limited	£399,606,016
Faccenda Investments Limited	£398,034,688
Launchchange Holdings Limited	£397,692,992
BHFS One Limited	£392,724,992
Toyota Motor Manufacturing (UK) Limited	£392,552,576
Experian Group Limited	£390,820,352
Elsevier Life Sciences IP Limited	£389,050,304
Lavendon Group Limited	£386,055,008
Listers Group Limited	£385,247,008
Bauer Radio Limited	£384,135,008
Norcros Group (Holdings) Limited	£384,046,016
Gallagher Estates Limited	£383,724,096
Bracken Midco1 PLC	£383,700,000
Elliott Group Limited	£383,399,008
Domino's Pizza Group PLC	£380,900,000
Palm Paper Limited	£380,070,784
Thomas Cook Retail Limited	£379,560,992
Innspired (Cedar) Limited	£379,367,008
Tunstall Group Acquisition Limited	£377,736,992
Aggregate Industries Limited	£376,136,000
Logistics Acquisition Company (UK) Limited	£375,031,040
J.S.Bloor (Services) Limited	£374,988,000
Avant Homes (No.2) Limited	£374,716,000
CEF Holdings Limited	£370,702,016
Boketto Bidco Limited	£369,238,016
Tunstall Group Holdings Limited	£367,240,992
Croda Investments Limited	£366,340,000
TIFS Holdings Limited	£365,877,728
PAG International Limited	£363,934,016
Equity Solutions Asset Management Limited	£361,592,064
Thomas Cook Finance PLC	£361,270,912
Stripestar Limited	£360,457,984
Megaflo Limited	£358,404,992
BWSC Power Corporation Limited	£356,623,008
Wavin Limited	£353,940,992
Doc Midco Limited	£353,100,000
Doc Debtco Limited	£353,089,984
Spire Homes (LG) Limited	£351,399,008
UDG Healthcare (UK) Holdings Limited	£350,607,584
Jewel UK Bidco Limited	£350,400,512
Trafalgar Bidco Limited	£348,429,120
Office Depot UK Limited	£347,735,008
City Electrical Factors Limited	£347,552,032
Loomis UK Finance Company Limited	£347,518,464
East Midlands International Airport Limited	£346,347,008
Oxford Instruments PLC	£345,200,000
Topps Tiles (UK) Limited	£344,991,008
BHFS Two Limited	£344,417,984
TNT Holdings (UK) Limited	£343,652,000
Fifthgrange Limited	£342,580,992
Welcome Break Holdings Limited	£342,236,992
Whirlpool UK Appliances Limited	£341,740,000
AGCO Limited	£340,856,992
A-Plan Group Ltd	£340,239,104
Welcome Break No. 2 Limited	£339,100,992
Sofidel UK Limited	£338,875,008
Aviagen Limited	£338,387,008
Pirelli UK Tyres Limited	£337,968,992
AmeyCespa (AWRP) Holding Co Limited	£335,423,008
AmeyCespa (AWRP) SPV Limited	£335,423,008
Hexpol Finance UK Limited	£334,771,904
Nampak Holdings (UK) Limited	£333,298,176
Cape Industrial Services Group Limited	£330,820,992
Capital One Holdings Limited	£329,996,000
TNT UK Limited	£329,455,008
BPB Finance (No.2) Limited	£328,143,008
Thomas Cook West Investments Limited	£327,123,232
Sims Group UK Holdings Limited	£326,428,768
DFS Trading Limited	£326,100,000
Morris Homes (North) Limited	£325,529,984
Alliance Medical Group Limited	£324,400,000
Weatherford Eurasia Limited	£323,007,008
Caterpillar UK Group Limited	£322,132,992
Rigid Plastic Containers Finance Limited	£321,447,584
Welcome Break Holdings (1) Limited	£321,244,992
Amey LG Limited	£320,791,008
Wanfeng (UK) Aviation Co., Ltd	£319,532,864
Zonwering Holdings Limited	£318,734,016
Bodycote Investments	£317,319,744
Wienerberger Limited	£315,228,000
Norcros PLC	£313,000,000
Arconic UK Holdings Limited	£312,323,008
Bellotto Acquisition Limited	£312,235,008
Elliott Group Holdings (UK) Limited	£311,284,000
Travis Perkins Finance Company Limited	£310,095,008
Glid Wind Farms Topco Limited	£309,873,984
Caterpillar Overseas Limited	£308,056,992
Pendragon Stock Finance Limited	£306,244,992
Cristal Inorganic Chemicals UK Limited	£305,355,008
Welbeck Estates Company Limited (The)	£304,640,992
ESNT International Limited	£304,440,000
Dawsongroup Truck and Trailer Limited	£302,532,992
Greencore Northwood Limited	£300,446,016
Arconic UK Finance	£300,052,000
TGH Acquisitions Limited	£299,102,016
ENVA Topco Limited	£298,537,984
TGH Investments Limited	£298,462,016
Outokumpu Stainless Limited	£298,100,000
The MDS Estates Limited	£298,008,000
Breedon Southern Limited	£297,673,984
Trimas UK Aerospace Holdings Limited	£297,526,912
K & A Merger Limited	£297,492,992
New Terex Holdings UK Limited	£296,780,000
The Big Food Group Limited	£295,100,000
St Andrew's Healthcare	£293,900,000
Linx Acquisition Limited	£292,431,008
Indesit Company UK Holdings Limited	£291,823,264
Jelson Holdings Limited	£291,072,416
Irwin Mitchell LLP	£290,464,992
Eaton Holding (UK) II Limited	£290,412,000
Westmoreland Investments Limited	£287,797,728
Aurora Fashions Finance Limited	£287,300,000
Giant Midco Limited	£286,200,000
PSA Retail UK Limited	£285,931,008
Avant Homes Limited	£285,062,016
Triumph Motorcycles Limited	£284,680,992
Caledonia Venus Holdings Limited	£284,654,016
Multi-Tile Distribution Limited	£283,544,000
BDWZest Developments LLP	£281,496,000
Amey Birmingham Highways Limited	£280,692,000
Tunstall Healthcare (UK) Limited	£280,566,016
Frutarom (UK) Limited	£280,056,992
Forterra PLC	£279,300,000
The Extracare Charitable Trust	£278,743,008
Triplex Lloyd Limited	£277,272,000
CP Sherwood Village Limited	£276,800,000
Caledonia Venus Acquisitions Limited	£276,644,000
Severn Trent Finance Limited	£276,087,008
Leyland Trucks Limited	£275,276,000
W.L. Shareholding Company Limited	£275,150,016
Lucy Group Ltd	£275,097,984
CI Brite Limited	£274,212,864
Forterra Building Products Limited	£273,300,000
TRRG Holding Limited	£273,034,624

Company	Value
Terberg Rosroca Group Limited	£273,034,624
Harworth Estates Investments Limited	£272,420,992
Alliance Medical Acquisitionco Limited	£272,132,000
Evonik Speciality Organics Limited	£270,403,136
CP Whinfell Village Limited	£268,400,000
Sims Group UK Limited	£268,308,000
Hartwell PLC	£267,796,992
Amey Hallam Highways Holdings Limited	£267,712,000
Amey Hallam Highways Limited	£267,712,000
Leicester City Football Club Limited	£266,288,992
Reach2 Academy Trust	£265,624,992
Experian International Unlimited	£264,841,680
Adient Properties UK Ltd	£264,452,992
Buzz Holdings Limited	£263,900,000
Filtrona Limited	£263,876,000
CP Elveden Village Limited	£263,800,000
Staffline Group PLC	£263,500,000
CEVA Logistics Limited	£263,416,992
Pendragon Management Services Limited	£263,284,000
Goodman Retail Limited	£261,764,992
Alere as Holdings Limited	£261,367,008
Pointtravel Co. Ltd	£260,576,992
Greencore UK Holdings Limited	£260,008,992
Nationwide Platforms Limited	£259,984,000
Marlborough Property Co Limited	£258,818,496
Halcyon Midco Limited	£257,718,000
Halcyon Financing Limited	£257,718,000
Marubeni Agrochemical Limited	£257,348,176
Etex (Exteriors) UK Limited	£257,300,000
Gregory Family Office Limited	£256,849,552
Boots Management Services Limited	£255,900,000
ML UK Holding Limited	£254,008,992
IRESS UK Holdings Limited	£253,960,000
White Capstan Limited	£253,486,640
Coveris Flexibles (Gainsborough) UK Limited	£252,456,992
Harworth Estates Property Group Limited	£251,047,008
Vaillant Netherlands Holdings Limited	£250,927,312
TI Group Automotive Systems (UK) Limited	£249,458,496
Carlsberg Supply Company UK Limited	£248,720,992
Acis Group Limited	£248,668,992
Carlsberg UK Holdings Limited	£248,622,000
Skiptex Limited	£247,730,000
Ingram Micro (UK) Limited	£247,646,000
TI Automotive German Holdings (UK) Limited	£247,134,656
TCCT Retail Limited	£247,055,008
SPL Logistics Holdings Acquisition Company (UK)	£246,895,648
TCCT Holdings UK Limited	£245,396,992
EIS UK Unlimited	£243,930,848
Jelson Limited	£243,792,432
Clowes Developments (UK) Limited	£243,769,712
MJ Gleeson PLC	£242,784,992
E M Holdings UK Limited	£241,863,008
Inspired Gaming (UK) Limited	£241,624,000
F. Perkins Limited	£241,420,992
PIB Group Limited	£240,946,000
EIS 2005 Limited	£240,893,968
Cromwell Tools Limited	£240,836,992
The Watches of Switzerland Group Limited	£240,542,800
EȮn Climate & Renewables UK Developments Ltd	£239,963,008
Sophos Treasury Limited	£239,916,752
Emerson Process Management Limited	£239,256,000
Impello Limited	£238,160,000
Tulip International (UK) Limited	£238,050,000
Argonaut Bidco Limited	£237,664,992
Aga-Rayburn Limited	£237,048,400
British Business Finance Ltd	£236,804,992
Four Seasons Health Care Holdings Limited	£236,339,008
Unipart Group Limited	£236,300,000
BBRG Finance (UK) Ltd.	£235,947,072
Wyndham Destination Network Europe Limited	£234,663,008
First Utility Limited	£234,584,992
DMWSL 632 Limited	£234,028,000
Stonewater Funding PLC	£233,543,008
Wabtec Rail Limited	£233,163,008
Longleat Property Limited	£233,000,000
Makita International Europe Limited	£232,562,000
Health & Diet Group Limited	£232,503,008
Versus Arthritis	£230,559,008
The West Retail Group Limited	£230,448,112
Pendragon Property Holdings Limited	£230,284,000
Buzz Group Limited	£230,083,008
Clinigen Healthcare Limited	£230,024,000
Andina PLC	£229,960,080
Allen Ford (UK) Limited	£227,707,008
Perrys Group Limited	£227,704,000
City Plumbing Supplies Holdings Limited	£227,700,000
Boketto Midco Limited	£227,534,000
UDG Healthcare UK (Holdco) Limited	£225,719,872
Yara UK Limited	£225,638,000
Makro Self Service Wholesalers Limited	£225,100,000
Avant Homes Holdings Limited	£224,984,000
Avant Homes Group No.2 Limited	£224,856,992
Antolin Interiors UK Limited	£224,808,000
Decidebloom Limited	£224,798,000
Noble Foods Limited	£224,698,000
Boots Opticians Professional Services Limited	£224,667,008
Guy Salmon Limited	£224,412,992
Cape Industrial Services Limited	£223,534,000
Breedon Cement Limited	£223,208,992
Greencore Foods Limited	£223,071,008
Paul Smith Limited	£222,534,000
RPC Asia Pacific Holdings Limited	£222,500,000
Oxford Instruments Nanotechnology Tools Holdings	£222,242,000
Enterprise Holding Company No 1 Limited	£222,176,992
East Coast Main Line Company Limited	£221,706,000
Suzuki GB PLC	£220,314,000
Wavin UK (Holdings) Limited	£220,024,000
Flogas Britain Limited	£219,307,008
Sealed Air Limited	£218,580,992
Grundon Waste Management Limited	£217,810,272
Circassia Limited	£217,764,000
Vaillant European Holdings Limited	£217,426,960
TI Automotive Korean Won Hedgeco Ltd	£217,416,176
Tunstall Holdings Limited	£216,888,000
3M Health Care Limited	£216,656,992
Evo Business Supplies Limited	£216,500,000
Adaptimmune Therapeutics PLC	£216,357,056
Harley-Davidson Europe Limited	£216,276,672
Multi-Tile Limited	£215,815,008
Zooom Holdings (UK) Limited	£215,624,992
Launchchange Finance Limited	£214,848,992
Kisimul School Holdings Limited	£214,306,368
Willoughby (35) Limited	£212,965,952
Salvesen Logistics Limited	£211,952,000
Pall UK Holdings Limited	£211,476,416
CPL Industries Limited	£210,672,000
Aurora Fashions Group Limited	£210,300,000
GL UK Holdings Limited	£209,686,000
Pendragon Premier Limited	£209,646,000
Corus Hotels Limited	£208,328,000
Stadco Limited	£208,258,000
GE Energy Power Conversion UK Limited	£207,780,992
Ricoh UK Limited	£207,564,000
Faero UK Holding Limited	£207,552,992
Futures Housing Group Limited	£207,435,008
WJH Limited	£207,152,000
DB Cargo (UK) Holdings Limited	£207,000,000
Waste Recycling Group (Central) Limited	£206,407,008
Tunstall Group Finance Limited	£205,084,992
Adaptimmune Limited	£204,950,000
BF Limited	£204,700,000
Saria Limited	£204,424,336
BPHA Finance PLC	£203,838,336
Mercedes-Benz Grand Prix Ltd	£203,688,000

Company	Value
Diamond Holdco 7 Limited	£203,200,000
Vow Europe Limited	£202,806,000
BSH Home Appliances Limited	£202,705,984
Insight Direct (UK) Ltd	£202,348,000
Deb Holdings Limited	£202,294,000
Pendragon Vehicle Management Limited	£202,274,000
EMH Treasury PLC	£201,902,000
Brady European Holdings Limited	£201,885,104
WA Capital Investments Limited	£201,000,880
P. D. Hook (Group) Limited	£200,842,000
Viking Direct (Holdings) Limited	£200,803,008
Norbrook Holdings Limited	£200,508,000
Home Retail Group (Finance) LLP	£200,362,000
Pertemps Limited	£200,260,000
Noble Foods Group Limited	£199,948,000
Greencore Prepared Meals Limited	£199,818,000
EResearchTechnology UK 1 Limited	£199,326,000
Rolls-Royce Total Care Services Limited	£199,004,992
FCC Buckinghamshire Limited	£198,706,000
BBRG Production (UK) Ltd.	£197,856,000
DH UK Finance Limited	£197,830,000
Warren James Holdings Limited	£197,324,672
Severn Trent Reservoirs Limited	£197,303,008
Diamond Holdco 2 Limited	£197,300,000
Audley Travel Group Limited	£196,992,000
E.On Climate & Renewables UK Robin Rigg West	£196,496,992
Pipe Holdings PLC	£196,124,992
Plastic Omnium Automotive Limited	£196,116,992
Elior UK Holdings Limited	£195,818,000
Immunocore Limited	£195,432,992
British Polythene Industries Limited	£194,800,000
Serasa Finance Limited	£194,519,664
Bodycote America Finance Limited	£193,121,872
Plusnet PLC	£192,660,992
Faccenda Foods Limited	£192,480,624
CEVA Supply Chain Solutions Limited	£192,280,000
Envigo CRS Limited	£192,271,008
Forgings International Limited	£192,144,000
Pertemps Recruitment Partnership Limited	£192,107,008
Experian Technology Limited	£192,073,904
Eaton Industries (U.K.) Limited	£191,852,992
Amey Services Limited	£191,682,000
Watch Bidco Limited	£191,430,000
Sensitlive Limited	£191,369,456
SIG European Holdings Limited	£190,487,008
Intervet UK Limited	£190,439,008
Paul Smith Group Holdings Limited	£190,391,008
Nisa Retail Limited	£190,331,008
Aurum Acquisitions Limited	£190,276,432
Crown Crest Group Limited	£188,994,976
Hillarys Blinds Limited	£188,800,000
Sheffield City Trust	£188,236,000
XPO Transport Solutions UK Limited	£187,542,000
Adient Holding UK Ltd	£187,503,008
Gilzoni Limited	£187,434,112
GE Energy Power Conversion UK Holdings Ltd	£186,824,000
Bellotto Finance Limited	£186,339,008
Bridon-Bekaert Ropes Group (UK) Ltd	£186,019,248
Davidsons Developments Limited	£185,924,000
Next Distribution Limited	£185,892,000
Saint-Gobain Glass (United Kingdom) Limited	£185,584,992
Ibstock Brick Holding Company Limited	£185,360,672
Infinity SDC Limited	£185,052,992
Rybrook Holdings Limited	£184,984,000
British Polythene Limited	£184,900,000
Mexichem Specialty Compounds Limited	£184,758,000
Amey Ventures Investments Limited	£184,158,000
Henry Boot Developments Limited	£184,080,672
Keadby Generation Limited	£183,900,000
Mercedes AMG High Performance Powertrains Ltd	£183,683,008
Wren Kitchens Limited	£183,475,712
Micromass UK Limited	£183,186,000
Vision Express (UK) Limited	£182,490,000
Bauer Consumer Media Limited	£182,107,008
Uniq Limited	£181,907,008
E.On Climate & Renewables UK Robin Rigg East	£181,874,000
Warren James (Jewellers) Limited	£181,514,000
SGBD Property Holdings Limited	£181,168,992
Marmon Group Limited (The)	£181,074,000
Umeco Limited	£180,368,992
Mintun 3 Limited	£180,032,992
Lincoln Diocesan Trust and Board of Finance Ltd	£179,920,000
Multi Packaging Solutions GB Limited	£179,894,016
B.I. (UK) Limited	£179,507,264
Atlas Hotels (Property and Trading) Limited	£179,232,720
DHL Services Limited	£179,232,000
David Wilson Homes Limited	£178,775,008
AMPY Holdings Limited	£178,723,760
Nine Elms LLP	£178,714,000
Cruickshank Motors Limited	£178,550,000
Resource Recovery Solutions (Derbyshire) Ltd	£177,975,008
T. C. Harrison Group Limited	£177,772,000
Pickering Developments Limited	£177,739,312
Bright Horizons Family Solutions Limited	£177,443,008
Aviagen International Holdings Ltd.	£176,738,400
Perrys Motor Sales Limited	£176,300,992
BBRG Operations (UK) Ltd.	£176,279,408
BBRG (Subsidiary) Ltd	£176,279,408
BBRG (Purchaser) Ltd	£176,279,408
ESNT Holdings (No.1) Limited	£175,962,000
East Worcester Water Limited	£175,799,008
CPRT LLP	£175,546,000
Foster Yeoman Limited	£175,499,008
Cromwell Group (Holdings) Limited	£175,218,000
Lighthouse UkCo 6 (Treasury) Limited	£175,070,000
Cognita Funding 1 Limited	£174,806,000
Buster Jimmy Limited	£174,358,256
Premdor U.K. Holdings Limited	£174,350,224
Pattonair (Derby) Limited	£174,239,008
Vaillant Group UK Limited	£174,224,992
Ross & Catherall Limited	£174,031,008
Tucker Fasteners Limited	£173,919,008
Tayto Group Limited	£173,737,056
Vision Express Limited	£173,711,360
Amey Community Limited	£173,544,000
Trafalgar Midco 1 Limited	£173,518,112
RCI Europe	£173,335,888
DMWSL 633 Limited	£173,098,000
DMWSL 631 Limited	£173,095,008
Premierfirst Vehicle Rental Holdings Limited	£172,844,992
Europcar UK Limited	£172,600,000
U-Pol Limited	£172,368,000
Brands Holdings Limited	£172,236,992
Cape UK Holdings Newco Limited	£171,998,000
Oclaro Technology Limited	£171,200,000
Morris Homes (Midlands) Limited	£171,006,000
Hudson Energy Supply UK Limited	£170,670,000
IG Design Group PLC	£170,628,000
Alere UK Holdings Limited	£170,150,000
Airwair International Limited	£169,150,000
Staffline Recruitment Limited	£168,884,992
Addo Food Group (Holdings) Ltd	£168,559,008
Jungheinrich Lift Truck Finance Limited	£168,527,008
Trafalgar Midco 2 Limited	£168,054,896
Maynard & Harris Plastics	£166,794,000
AGCO Manufacturing Limited	£166,626,000
Atlas Hotels (Borrowings 2) Limited	£166,511,232
Conquest Bidco Limited	£166,508,000
Gaming Acquisitions Limited	£166,144,000
BWSC North Lincs Limited	£166,052,992
Pegler Yorkshire Group Limited	£165,936,992
Chinook Sciences Holdings Limited	£165,451,232
The Two Counties Trust	£165,092,000
Eaton Industries (England) Limited	£164,844,000

Company	Value
Brighterkind (MW) Limited	£164,800,000
Snap-On U.K. Holdings Limited	£164,792,992
TNT Express ICS Limited	£164,754,000
BBRG Holding (UK) Ltd	£163,973,632
DTIL UK Limited	£163,836,992
BI Group Limited	£163,764,992
The Valspar (UK) Holding Corporation Limited	£163,723,424
Breedon Holdings Limited	£163,278,000
FSHC (UK) Limited	£163,179,008
Canaveral Holdco Limited	£162,996,992
CX Topco Limited	£162,892,992
Winvic Group Limited	£162,869,024
Apollo Support Services Group Limited	£162,647,008
Peveril Securities Limited	£162,151,904
Aviagen International Finance Four Limited	£161,996,992
Adient Financing International Ltd	£161,637,360
ESNT Holdings (No.2) Limited	£160,740,000
Severn Trent Overseas Holdings Limited	£159,324,000
Integrated Bradford Hold Co Two Limited	£158,996,992
Integrated Bradford SPV Two Limited	£158,996,992
Adidas (U.K.) Limited	£158,722,000
Wixams First Limited	£158,623,728
Aga Rangemaster Limited	£158,448,000
Emerson International Limited	£158,362,944
DSM Nutritional Products (UK) Limited	£158,362,000
Bayard Metering (UK)	£157,576,000
Pentagon Motor Holdings Limited	£157,456,992
Affinity Flying Training Services Limited	£157,351,008
Inspired Gaming Group Limited	£157,194,000
Winvic Construction Limited	£157,117,424
Achilles Subholdings Limited	£157,040,000
Pointeuro V Limited	£156,810,000
Woodland Trust (The)	£156,468,000
Amey Group Services Limited	£156,100,992
Kent Enviropower Limited	£155,992,000
Templeborough Biomass Power Plant Limited	£155,686,960
Premdor Crosby Limited	£155,546,000
Total Downstream UK PLC	£155,406,000
Brighterkind (CB) Limited	£155,172,992
Lloyds Pharmacy Clinical Homecare Limited	£155,136,992
Renewi Financial Management Limited	£154,980,992
Heygate & Sons Limited	£154,836,448
TEG Holdings Limited	£154,504,000
Amey Utility Services Limited	£154,235,008
William Davis Limited	£154,063,008
Lafarge Cauldon Limited	£153,439,008
Coveris Flexibles UK Limited	£153,338,000
Compare The Market Limited	£153,200,000
TI Automotive (China) Limited	£153,170,160
The Spencer Academies Trust	£153,132,992
Cognita Schools Limited	£152,970,000
Deritend International Limited	£152,631,008
Gands (U.K.)	£152,284,992
Monier (UK) Holdings Limited	£152,170,000
Close Brothers Vehicle Hire Limited	£152,168,352
Middleby UK Residential Holding Ltd	£151,674,960
Atlas Hotels (Trading) Limited	£151,550,512
Quicksilver Midco Limited	£151,415,008
Alliance Medical Limited	£150,962,000
Lavendon Holdings Limited	£150,900,992
Whitworths Holdings Limited	£150,598,000
Mytravel Pioneer Limited	£150,000,000
The David Ross Education Trust	£149,899,008
RR Donnelley UK Limited	£149,876,992
Brose Limited	£149,801,152
Futures Homescape Limited	£149,604,000
Booker Retail Partners (GB) Limited	£149,100,000
Regional & City Airports Holdings Limited	£149,008,992
SC Johnson Professional Group Limited	£148,983,008
EResearchTechnology Limited	£148,514,112
Briggs & Forrester Group Limited	£147,858,352
Pattonair Group Limited	£147,775,008
Makita (UK) Limited	£147,726,000
Motorpoint Limited	£147,600,000
General Domestic Appliances Holdings Limited	£146,974,000
Sports Information Services Limited	£146,928,992
Peterborough Diocesan Board of Finance (The)	£146,862,800
Kelta Limited	£146,109,968
Hyde Industrial Holdings Limited	£145,986,624
Amey Rail Limited	£145,967,008
Buckingham Group Contracting Limited	£145,475,792
Milton Keynes Parks Trust Limited	£145,340,992
Dransfield Properties Limited	£145,176,912
Dransfield Properties Investments Limited	£145,176,912
IB Group Ltd	£145,132,000
First Response Finance Limited	£144,949,504
MWUK Limited	£144,222,000
Jeld-Wen UK Limited	£144,108,992
London Vista Hotel Limited	£143,279,008
Kermotion UK Holdings Limited	£143,252,640
Red Bull Technology Limited	£143,099,008
Sports Information Services (Holdings) Limited	£142,440,000
Pickering Properties Limited	£142,215,360
Plaza on Hyde Park Limited	£141,871,712
Eaton Electrical Products Limited	£141,763,008
BASF U.K. Holdings Limited	£141,392,000
Community 1st Oldham Limited	£141,373,328
XPO Investment UK Limited	£141,300,992
Charles Wells,Limited	£141,250,000
The Derby County Football Club Limited	£141,195,248
The Brooke Weston Trust	£141,163,008
Copart UK Limited	£140,756,000
Fluidpower MIP Limited	£140,231,552
Grosvenor Contracts Leasing Limited	£140,178,608
Nova Education Trust	£140,140,000
Fisher Scientific U.K., Limited	£139,840,000
Dyon UK Limited	£139,712,000
FCC Waste Services (UK) Limited	£139,642,000
RTL Topco Limited	£139,618,000
RTL Cleanco Limited	£139,616,000
Chiron Midco Limited	£139,156,000
Hallam Land Management Limited	£139,087,056
East Midlands Trains Limited	£138,923,008
EResearchTechnology UK 2 Limited	£138,743,920
Kubota (U.K.) Limited	£138,674,464
Chiron Bidco Limited	£138,560,000
RTL Bidco Limited	£138,412,992
Motorpoint Group PLC	£138,400,000
Broadthorpe Limited	£138,382,000
Universal Salvage Limited	£138,166,000
Prime Life Limited	£138,126,000
Halcyon Acquisitions Limited	£138,008,000
Forterra Holdings Limited	£137,800,000
Sonepar UK Limited	£137,339,008
Consumer Champion Group Limited	£137,102,000
Lakeside Energy from Waste Limited	£136,944,528
Lakeside Energy from Waste Holdings Limited	£136,944,528
Daf Trucks Limited	£136,448,000
O & M-Movianto UK Holdings Ltd.	£136,410,000
A.E.S. Engineering Limited	£136,308,992
Chinook Sciences Limited	£136,166,624
Karen Millen Holdings Limited	£136,100,000
Stratstone Motor Holdings Limited	£136,032,992
Vesuvius UK Limited	£135,746,000
AmeyCespa (MK) Holding Co Limited	£135,712,000
AmeyCespa (MK) SPV Limited	£135,712,000
Bellotto Holdings Limited	£135,656,992
Fresenius Medical Care (Holdings) Limited	£134,811,008
RM PLC	£134,390,000
NIC Holdings (UK) Limited	£134,291,600
Agilent Technologies Lda UK Limited	£134,176,256
Oxfam	£134,100,000
Copart Europe Limited	£134,063,000
Hydro Extrusion UK Ltd	£133,599,000

Company	Value
Merkur Casino UK Ltd	£133,593,000
Atlas Hotels (Group 3 Property) Limited	£133,378,096
Briggs & Forrester (UK) Limited	£133,097,728
Redhill Academy Trust	£132,888,000
Toolstation Limited	£132,703,000
Funeral Partners Holdco Limited	£132,620,000
GE Energy Power Conversion Technology Limited	£132,434,808
Reg Vardy Limited	£132,349,000
Unipart Rail Limited	£132,317,000
Strata Homes Yorkshire Limited	£132,049,000
LTAG UK Limited	£132,048,000
Pendragon Motor Group Limited	£131,986,000
Primaflow Limited	£131,792,000
Sevco 5112 Limited	£131,623,352
E.On Climate & Renewables UK Biomass Limited	£131,411,000
Ametek Aerospace and Defense Group UK Limited	£131,210,000
Lincoln Corn Exchange and Markets (1991) Limited	£131,159,000
Eco-Bat Technologies GB	£131,111,000
NFT Distribution Holdings Limited	£131,028,000
Greenwood Academies Trust	£130,677,000
Acertec Engineering Limited	£130,610,000
Cognita Limited	£130,597,000
Amey OW Limited	£130,429,000
Hook 2 Sisters Limited	£130,400,000
Amey OWR Limited	£130,374,000
IRESS (UK) Limited	£130,352,000
Airbus Helicopters UK Limited	£130,161,000
Nationwide Crash Repair Centres Limited	£129,991,000
H. J. Enthoven Limited	£129,961,000
Oakhill Group Limited	£129,958,000
New Co (Satellite) 2 Limited	£129,710,000
Adient Seating UK Ltd	£129,651,000
Buzzard Leisure Limited	£129,000,000
Mick George Limited	£128,930,000
Cromwell Logistics Limited	£128,856,000
Westmoreland Properties Limited	£128,804,896
Amak Property Investments (London) Limited	£128,733,808
Consolidated Property Wilmslow Limited	£128,599,832
Druck Limited	£128,356,000
Ingram Micro Holdings Limited	£128,053,000
Tiles4less Limited	£128,010,000
Porvair PLC	£127,947,000
Gigaclear Limited	£127,430,000
Machine Mart Limited	£127,345,552
Magna International Holding (UK) Limited	£127,174,000
Scott Bader Commonwealth Limited (The)	£127,167,000
RMS Holdco Limited	£127,123,000
WD-40 Company Limited	£126,676,000
Scott Bader Company Limited	£126,529,000
Barclay Pharmaceuticals Limited	£126,254,000
Premierfirst Vehicle Rental EMEA Holdings Limited	£126,147,000
Cavan Investments Limited	£125,996,352
Forest Holidays Group Limited	£125,967,000
Forest Holidays Limited	£125,950,000
Chemetall Limited	£125,886,000
The Priory Federation of Academies	£125,785,000
Tata Technologies Europe Limited	£125,621,000
Porterbrook March Leasing (4) Limited	£125,617,000
Chartered Accountants' Benevolent Association	£125,537,000
Crown Crest (Leicester) PLC	£125,215,312
Asquith Court Holdings Limited	£125,189,000
Jaguar Land Rover (South Africa) Holdings Limited	£124,966,608
Intrexon UK Insect Holdings Limited	£124,861,232
Arconic Extruded Products (UK) Limited	£124,743,000
Williams Grand Prix Holdings PLC	£124,703,000
DMWSL 532 Limited	£124,646,000
Kent Power Corporation Limited	£124,543,984
Commify Topco Limited	£124,462,520
Falcon Equityco 2 Limited	£124,396,048
IRESS FS Limited	£124,159,000
Linx Printing Technologies Limited	£124,090,000
Gardner Aerospace Holdings Limited	£123,686,000
Radius Systems Limited	£123,585,000
Evonik Chemicals Limited	£123,518,000
Sodexo Motivation Solutions U.K. Limited	£123,465,000
Infineum UK Ltd.	£123,448,000
Sandicliffe Motor Holdings Limited	£123,430,000
Greencore Grocery Limited	£123,329,000
Avery Healthcare Holdings Limited	£123,312,000
Alloy Racing Equipment Limited	£123,228,000
Goldcrest Capital Investments Limited	£123,088,848
Guardian Industries U.K. Limited	£122,736,000
National Accident Helpline Limited	£122,673,000
Lynn Wind Farm Limited	£122,575,000
Santander Asset Finance (December) Limited	£122,558,512
GW 305 Limited	£122,457,920
Jungheinrich UK Limited	£122,148,000
Fugro Holdings Limited	£122,124,000
Flowtech Fluidpower PLC	£122,026,000
Sun Chemical Limited	£121,901,000
Giant Bidco Limited	£121,900,000
Avingtrans PLC	£121,749,000
Oxford Instruments Overseas Holdings Limited	£121,595,000
Manderley Food Group Limited	£121,420,080
Lubrizol Limited	£121,232,000
Tarras Park Properties Limited	£121,139,384
Strata Homes Limited	£121,086,000
Strata Homes Holdings Limited	£121,086,000
GRS Roadstone Group Limited	£121,054,608
Gallagher Estates Holdings Limited	£120,958,024
Tollbar Multi Academy Trust	£120,580,000
Saint-Gobain High Performance Materials UK Ltd	£120,475,000
Full Moon Holdco 4 Limited	£120,200,000
Co-operative Energy Limited	£120,199,000
VWR Holdco Limited	£120,099,000
St.Edward's School	£119,905,000
MWUK Holding Company Limited	£119,645,000
Jones Homes (North West) Limited	£119,170,312
CEVA Freight (UK) Limited	£119,163,000
Oxford Nanopore Technologies Limited	£119,123,000
Intervet UK Production Limited	£118,581,000
Williams Grand Prix Engineering Limited	£118,575,000
L.E.A.D. Trust	£118,396,000
Warwick International Holdings Limited	£118,097,000
H.W. Coates (Holdings) Limited	£117,945,904
Ferraris Piston Service Limited	£117,607,000
Nationwide Accident Repair Services Limited	£117,581,000
Minova International Limited	£117,443,000
Nominet UK	£117,283,000
H.W. Coates Limited	£117,224,128
United Rental Group Limited	£117,183,000
Oxford Instruments Nanotechnology Tools Limited	£116,811,000
Stepnell Holdings Limited	£116,734,560
LDH (La Doria) Limited	£116,552,000
CX Midco 2 Limited	£116,250,128
Games Workshop Group PLC	£116,229,000
Forbo Flooring UK Limited	£116,157,000
Perkins Group Limited	£116,042,000
E4D & G Project Co Limited	£116,035,000
E4D & G Holdco Limited	£116,035,000
RPS Group US Holdings Limited	£116,026,984
Oxford Immunotec Limited	£115,932,000
FSHC Properties (CH2) Limited	£115,918,000
Eaton Electrical Systems Limited	£115,648,000
C D Bramall Limited	£115,396,000
SDI (Oxford Street) Limited	£115,346,952
Jungheinrich Financial Services Limited	£114,947,000
Grand Union Group Funding PLC	£114,800,000
Produce Investments Limited	£114,788,000
CX Bidco Limited	£114,678,440
Eurocell PLC	£114,631,000
A.C. Nielsen Company Limited	£114,393,000
Doncasters Aerospace Limited	£114,212,000
Equity Solutions Lift Investments Limited	£114,051,320

Company	Turnover	Company	Turnover
Hutchinson Group Limited	£114,041,000	Atlas Hotels (Group 1) Limited	£104,491,328
Doncasters Blaenavon Limited	£113,937,872	NFU Mutual (Service Company) Limited	£104,461,504
Keystone Topco Limited	£113,879,000	Snap-On Finance UK Limited	£104,269,560
Stadium MK Group Limited	£113,836,768	EHI UK Unlimited	£103,789,776
Derbyshire Student Residences Limited	£113,616,000	TI Automotive Czech Holdings (UK) Limited	£103,670,432
Caledonia Venus Group Limited	£113,560,000	East Midlands Education Trust	£103,596,000
Airtanker Services Limited	£113,542,000	Greenyard Frozen UK Limited	£103,519,000
Amey LUL 2 Limited	£113,539,000	Oxcis Limited	£103,494,424
Servelec Limited	£113,405,000	Beechcroft Group Limited	£103,287,000
Seachill UK Limited	£113,339,000	AmeyCespa WM (East) Limited	£103,279,000
Lantmannen UK Holding Limited	£113,233,000	SPS Technologies Limited	£103,205,000
BCHK UK Limited	£113,075,976	BRS Limited	£103,186,000
Hartwell Automotive Group Limited	£113,020,000	Barbara Limited	£103,172,000
GCI Managed Services Group Limited	£112,308,688	Whitworth Bros.Limited	£103,154,000
Motorway Services Limited	£112,291,000	Keystone Bidco Limited	£102,818,000
Wakefield Waste PFI Limited	£112,236,000	FTD UK Holdings Limited	£102,686,912
Wakefield Waste Holdings Limited	£112,236,000	EHI 2005 Limited	£102,485,624
Orbit Homes (2020) Limited	£112,221,000	Farmland Reserve UK Limited	£102,399,000
CPL Industries Group Limited	£112,000,000	Keystone Financing PLC	£102,332,000
Mastercard Prepaid Management Services Limited	£111,878,000	YHA (England and Wales)	£102,297,000
RPS US Holdings Limited	£111,770,296	Dennis Eagle Limited	£102,292,000
ELWA Limited	£111,730,000	Jewel UK Topco Limited	£102,248,128
ELWA Holdings Limited	£111,730,000	Allied Textiles Limited	£102,188,000
Rockwell Automation Limited	£111,699,000	Cairnwell Estates Limited	£101,952,080
Vindis Group Limited	£111,467,584	Riverleen Finance Unlimited	£101,908,304
Everards Brewery Limited	£111,340,000	Oasis and Warehouse Holdco 2 Limited	£101,900,000
Ensco 645 Limited	£111,286,000	EESL Energypro Assets Limited	£101,814,504
HS 524 Limited	£110,800,000	Maneto (UK) 3 Limited	£101,781,000
Reeve (Derby) Limited	£110,577,000	The Education Fellowship Trust	£101,637,000
Severn Trent Green Power Limited	£110,560,000	SIG Hillsborough Limited	£101,552,032
Severn Trent LCP Limited	£110,454,000	Genzyme Therapeutics Limited	£101,503,000
Praesepe Holdings Limited	£110,447,000	Avdel UK Limited	£101,359,000
Elmsdale Estates Limited	£110,278,000	Rightmove Group Limited	£101,245,000
Fujifilm UK Limited	£110,252,000	SMC Pneumatics (U.K.) Limited	£100,994,928
L.E.A.D. Academy Trust	£110,028,000	Epyx Limited	£100,989,000
Lockheed Martin UK Ampthill Limited	£109,705,000	Oasis and Warehouse Limited	£100,800,000
Ibstock USA Limited	£109,383,800	Oasis and Warehouse Holdco 1 Limited	£100,800,000
Elior UK PLC	£109,246,848	Firth Rixson Forgings Limited	£100,564,000
Derwent Vehicles Limited	£108,958,000	Aviagen European Holdings Limited	£99,949,000
AFE Group Limited	£108,945,000	Kal Tire (UK) Limited	£99,773,000
Amey Belfast Schools Partnership PFI Co Limited	£108,656,000	Eaton MEDC Limited	£99,667,000
Amey Belfast Schools Partnership Hold Co Limited	£108,656,000	Acertec UK Limited	£99,666,616
Oxford Immunotec Global PLC	£108,605,648	Socotec UK Limited	£99,547,000
Travis Perkins Financing Company No.2 Limited	£108,600,000	Goosebrook Limited	£99,460,000
Project Grace	£108,466,000	Topps Tiles PLC	£99,372,000
Airline Investments Limited	£108,439,000	Polyco Healthline Limited	£99,279,000
Warwick International Intermediate Holdings Limited	£108,401,000	Quotient Sciences Holdings Limited	£99,154,000
A Shade Greener Debt (3) LLP	£108,393,344	Gallagher Developments Holdco Limited	£99,083,000
Alloy Technologies (UK) Limited	£108,349,000	Horiba Mira Limited	£99,073,000
SPS Aerostructures Limited	£108,337,000	Fulham Wharf LLP	£99,063,000
Openfield Agriculture Limited	£108,159,000	Enterprise (AOL) Limited	£98,943,000
Pets at Home Superstores Limited	£107,951,000	E.On Climate & Renewables UK Offshore Wind Ltd	£98,833,000
Heathcotes Group Limited	£107,904,800	Pipe Holdings 1 PLC	£98,832,000
Georgica Limited	£107,615,000	Makro Holding Limited	£98,656,000
LR (UK) Limited	£107,567,520	CP Longleat Village Limited	£98,600,000
The Amtico Company Limited	£107,334,000	Abaco UK Holdco Limited	£98,585,000
Southern View Finance UK Limited	£107,195,360	Amey Defence Services Limited	£98,574,280
The Manufacturing Technology Centre Limited	£106,949,000	Frederic Robinson Limited	£98,526,000
Bio-Techne Ltd	£106,905,000	Brighterkind Limited	£98,156,000
Agrivert Holdings Limited	£106,833,928	Companion Care (Services) Limited	£97,883,000
Chromalloy UK Holdings Ltd	£106,612,000	Owen Mumford Holdings Limited	£97,826,848
Stagecoach Services Limited	£106,608,000	H.L. Hutchinson Limited	£97,800,000
Full Moon Holdco 5 Limited	£106,600,000	Hyde Group Holdings Limited	£97,748,376
Alere Toxicology PLC	£106,227,000	Achilles Group Holdings Limited	£97,562,000
PAH Financial Services Limited	£106,206,000	P.E.Jones (Properties) Limited	£97,549,000
Ancon Limited	£105,859,000	Stagecoach South Western Trains Limited	£97,544,000
Uppingham School	£105,510,576	Carpenter Limited	£97,533,000
Mattioli Woods PLC	£105,426,000	Carpenter Holdings Limited	£97,470,000
Sitel Europe Limited	£105,102,560	Global Closure Systems UK Limited	£97,292,000
Diligenta Limited	£105,087,000	MacFarlane Group UK Limited	£97,151,000
Tingdene (MJ) Limited	£104,960,488	Calor Group Limited	£97,138,000
Pipe Holdings 2 Limited	£104,700,000	Anglian Venture Holdings Limited	£97,138,000

Company	Value
Beaver-Visitec International (UK) Limited	£97,121,000
Laver Regeneration Limited	£97,110,584
Arkle Finance Limited	£97,082,992
Belfield Group Limited	£97,055,000
Jacobs Douwe Egberts Ops GB Ltd	£96,983,000
RM Education Ltd	£96,976,000
PSV Claims Bureau Limited	£96,975,000
Global Derby (UK) Limited	£96,815,000
DFS Furniture Company Limited	£96,700,000
Gellaw 101 Limited	£95,955,000
Allied Textile Companies Limited	£95,901,000
HW Martin Holdings Limited	£95,822,304
Santander Estates Limited	£95,769,480
The Rugby Group Limited	£95,715,000
Synventive Acquisition UK Limited	£95,638,120
Funeral Partners Bidco Limited	£95,486,000
Graham Bell (Holdings) Limited	£95,327,000
API Group PLC	£95,276,000
Wickersley Partnership Trust	£95,214,560
Glenair UK Limited	£95,212,872
Firth Rixson Metals Limited	£95,092,000
Abbott Diabetes Care Limited	£94,911,000
Essentra Components Limited	£94,762,000
Symphony Holdings Limited	£94,677,000
The H D H Wills 1965 Charitable Trust	£94,618,984
Unipart Rail Holdings Limited	£94,480,000
Hancocks Acquisition Limited	£94,322,000
Glencore Agriculture UK Ltd.	£94,305,000
Achilles Holdco Limited	£94,300,000
The Symphony Group PLC	£94,256,000
J O Sims Holdings Limited	£94,023,232
AMG Superalloys UK Limited	£94,003,800
Eggborough Power Limited	£94,000,000
Beechcroft Developments Limited	£93,972,000
Yusen Logistics (UK) Limited	£93,909,000
CPL Aromas Limited	£93,899,000
Acushnet Europe Ltd	£93,835,000
Infineum International Limited	£93,823,000
Moyallen Woking Limited	£93,699,440
Sandicliffe Limited	£93,655,000
J O Sims Holdings (1896) Limited	£93,618,784
A.G. Parfett & Sons Limited	£93,546,384
Nirvana Holdings Limited	£93,461,592
Idis Group Limited	£92,804,000
Idis Group Holdings Limited	£92,804,000
Falcon Capital Investments Limited	£92,762,416
CTDI Repair Services Limited	£92,669,624
NFT Distribution Operations Limited	£92,601,000
Xylem Water Solutions UK Ltd	£92,568,000
Roquette UK Limited	£92,513,000
Movianto UK Limited	£92,244,000
Adare International Limited	£92,241,000
Blenheim Finance Limited	£91,981,384
Oakbrook Finance Limited	£91,867,000
Can-Pack UK Limited	£91,805,152
Fluidpower Group Limited	£91,745,104
Greater Manchester Buses South Limited	£91,745,000
Archway Learning Trust	£91,697,000
Clyde Union DB Limited	£91,607,000
Shoby Investments Limited	£91,371,040
Blythmore Limited	£91,203,000
Laver Regeneration Holdings Limited	£91,159,416
Loomis UK Limited	£91,055,000
NAHL Group PLC	£90,999,000
Joules Group PLC	£90,971,000
Owen Mumford Limited	£90,826,592
Diversey Limited	£90,623,000
A.C. Lloyd (Asset Management) Limited	£90,611,960
BCM Limited	£90,600,000
Vision Express Group Limited	£90,455,000
Taylor Lindsey Limited	£90,420,832
Countywide Developments Limited	£90,377,000
Gleeson Developments Limited	£90,362,000
Eaton Safety Limited	£90,359,000
Arconic Global Fasteners Limited	£90,291,000
Harrow View LLP	£90,027,000
Aurajoki Europe Limited	£90,018,000
EOS Inc. Ltd	£89,951,000
Rolls-Royce Submarines Limited	£89,896,000
ISDC Developments (No2) Limited	£89,764,000
Maxxia Finance Limited	£89,681,024
ALC (SPC) Limited	£89,635,000
Pets at Home Holdings Limited	£89,592,000
Boston Mayflower Finance PLC	£89,555,784
Pattonair Limited	£89,422,000
CI Brite (UK) Holdings Limited	£89,168,992
Aviagen International Finance Two Limited	£89,161,976
ALC (Superholdco) Limited	£89,138,000
Rybrook Limited	£89,038,128
Go Outdoors Limited	£89,033,000
Ensco 648 Limited	£89,030,000
Bell Rock Workplace Management Limited	£89,029,000
The Way Ahead Group Limited	£89,028,000
Punch Taverns (Services) Limited	£88,865,000
Ancala Water Services (Estates) Limited	£88,755,000
Accord Limited	£88,301,000
South East London & Kent Bus Company Limited	£88,215,000
DFDS Logistics Limited	£87,908,800
Resmed (UK) Limited	£87,751,696
Thoratec Europe Limited	£87,681,592
Renault Sport Racing Limited	£87,606,000
TDY Holdings Limited	£87,494,000
Roxhill Developments Group Limited	£87,487,160
Baxi Group Limited	£87,178,000
NMCN PLC	£87,105,000
Arena Coventry Limited	£86,580,000
Rybrook Cars Limited	£86,552,224
Lindum Group Limited	£86,492,992
Wasps Holdings Limited	£86,389,000
Bramall Quicks Dealerships Limited	£86,315,000
Clugston Group Limited	£86,212,000
QED Academy Trust	£86,195,264
Bosch Rexroth Limited	£86,185,000
Remy Cointreau UK Limited	£86,171,200
EPAL Holdings Limited	£86,069,008
Smith Brothers (Leicester) Limited	£85,993,968
Oxford Instruments Overseas Holdings 2008 Ltd	£85,992,344
Romo (Holdings) Limited	£85,977,000
Kinaxia Limited	£85,907,272
Addo Food Group Limited	£85,875,000
Blue Anchor Leisure Holdings Limited	£85,864,000
Blue Anchor Leisure Limited	£85,860,000
Dundee Pikco Limited	£85,790,000
Rigid Plastic Containers Packaging Limited	£85,500,000
Rushcliffe Care Holdings Limited	£85,287,888
Derby Diocesan Board of Finance Limited (The)	£85,183,112
Avon Insurance PLC	£85,100,000
Larkfleet Homes Limited	£85,049,576
Hankook Tyre U.K. Limited	£85,008,000
Westfield Contributory Health Scheme Limited	£84,999,000
Coventry Diocesan Board of Finance (The)	£84,892,000
Gardner Group Limited	£84,757,000
Warwick International Group Limited	£84,749,000
Indoor Bowling Equity Limited	£84,709,000
Sir John Port's Charity	£84,530,720
Drive Motor Retail Limited	£84,510,000
Nexperia UK Ltd.	£84,379,000
Leicester Diocesan Board of Finance (The)	£84,328,000
Rieke Packaging Systems Limited	£84,200,000
Harworth Estates (Waverley Prince) Ltd.	£83,992,000
Integrated Bradford Hold Co One Limited	£83,765,000
Integrated Bradford SPV One Limited	£83,765,000
Available Car Limited	£83,702,000
Guardian Industries UK Holding Limited	£83,650,000

Company	Turnover
H.I.G. Europe-Dart III, Ltd	£83,589,000
Aalberts Industries U.K. Ltd.	£83,396,000
Fluidpower Limited	£83,318,040
Gleeson Regeneration Limited	£83,243,000
Blancco Technology Group PLC	£83,201,000
Clientlogic Holding Limited	£83,188,000
Abaco Systems Limited	£83,175,000
B. Braun Medical Limited	£83,172,000
Greenvale AP Limited	£83,000,000
Rubicon Drinks Limited	£82,823,000
ELG Haniel Metals Ltd	£82,783,848
Shoosmiths LLP	£82,722,000
Avery Healthcare Group Limited	£82,681,968
Boutinot Limited	£82,608,976
Sheffield Forgemasters International Limited	£82,537,000
Wilson Bowden Developments Limited	£82,464,000
Harworth Estates (Agricultural Land) Limited	£82,423,000
AAH Limited	£82,404,000
Mahle Industries UK Limited	£82,402,000
Morphy Richards Limited	£82,365,000
Ideal Shopping Direct Limited	£82,227,000
Leica Biosystems Newcastle Limited	£82,198,000
Stampede Acquisition Limited	£81,993,000
Heyford Residential Limited	£81,983,264
Drive Holdings 2015 Limited	£81,981,000
Car Shops Limited	£81,721,000
Sytner Cars Limited	£81,719,000
Highcroft Investments PLC	£81,685,000
Idis Limited	£81,621,000
JFB Overseas Holdings Limited	£81,611,000
Portugal Finco Limited	£81,490,000
Sports and Leisure Management Ltd	£81,214,368
Alpro (UK) Limited	£81,150,000
Uniq (Holdings) Limited	£81,129,000
Waste Recycling Group (UK) Limited	£81,100,000
Environmental Scientifics Group Holdings Limited	£80,971,000
Oxford Instruments UK 2013 Limited	£80,291,624
Young's Seafood International Holdings Limited	£80,273,000
Bridgestone UK Limited	£80,055,000
Fraikin Limited	£79,994,048
Synventive Acquisition Unlimited	£79,989,104
Southwell & Nottingham Diocesan Board of Finance	£79,944,000
Field Boxmore II Limited	£79,822,016
Caesar Topco Limited	£79,753,000
Amtrust Lloyd's Holdings (UK) Limited	£79,752,976
Monier Redland Limited	£79,748,000
Landis + Gyr Limited	£79,693,000
U-Pol Finco Limited	£79,588,000
United Church Schools Trust	£79,497,000
Howmet Limited	£79,297,000
Dawsongroup Bus and Coach Limited	£79,261,000
Rodenhurst Estates Limited	£79,186,952
Ideagen PLC	£79,090,000
RTL Midco Limited	£79,073,000
Stockport Homes Limited	£78,991,000
A-Plan Holdings	£78,982,640
Country Court Care Homes 3 Propco Limited	£78,951,128
Church & Co Limited	£78,747,952
MPAC Group PLC	£78,500,000
Blanc Aero Industries UK Limited	£78,393,000
Sherwin-Williams UK Holding Limited	£78,390,672
Blue Chip Customer Engineering Limited	£78,379,000
Barry Callebaut Manufacturing (UK) Limited	£78,363,000
River Learning Trust	£78,234,512
Bell Rock Bidco Limited	£78,222,000
Fevore Limited	£78,099,904
Aston Community Education Trust	£78,059,000
Care Fertility Holdings Limited	£78,007,000
Solo Cup Finance Limited	£77,963,000
Stockshape Limited	£77,925,192
Dunelm Estates Limited	£77,881,000
William Cook Holdings Limited	£77,802,000
R Stratton & Co Ltd.	£77,799,000
Tingdene Parks Limited	£77,779,480
Amey Fleet Services Limited	£77,730,000
Software AG (UK) Limited	£77,714,000
Powerscreen International Limited	£77,711,000
Dyas Exploration UK Limited	£77,679,000
Van Elle Holdings PLC	£77,496,000
Blancco (Software) Services Limited	£77,475,976
Byrom Public Limited Company	£77,335,976
Aurajoki Romania Limited	£77,294,000
Harris Cars Limited	£77,278,864
SDL Property Services Group Limited	£77,266,000
Caesar Midco Limited	£76,895,928
Allegheny Technologies Limited	£76,828,000
Adare SEC Limited	£76,792,000
DCS Inc Limited	£76,723,000
Larkfleet Limited	£76,677,024
Barratt Metropolitan LLP	£76,644,416
Bridon International Ltd.	£76,623,000
J.H.& F.W.Green Limited	£76,484,688
Atlas Hotels (Group 2) Limited	£76,408,552
Homecrest Bidco Limited	£76,408,000
Novera Energy (Holdings 2) Limited	£76,390,000
Trucast Limited	£76,343,000
Sector Aircraft Leasing Limited	£76,198,000
Cimbria Holdings Limited	£76,175,592
UK Ticketing Ltd	£76,136,416
Vinters Engineering Limited	£76,100,000
Kinaxia Transport and Warehousing Limited	£76,024,496
Orbit Developments (Southern) Limited	£75,986,880
New Blue Chip Limited	£75,807,000
Charles Street Commercial Investments Limited	£75,588,368
Diverse Academies Trust	£75,510,000
Van Elle Limited	£75,390,000
Camping and Caravanning Club Limited (The)	£75,299,000
Tenpin Limited	£75,270,000
AC Nielsen Holdings UK Limited	£75,219,048
SPL Logistics UK Holdings Limited	£75,149,000
Advent Topco Limited	£75,144,608
Blue Cross	£75,100,000
Bodycote Heat Treatments Limited	£75,029,000
Graven Hill Village Development Company Limited	£75,001,128
Lenzing Fibers Grimsby Limited	£74,945,000
Boots International Limited	£74,912,000
Miele Company Limited	£74,872,000
Woodbury Residual Limited	£74,871,000
Asquith Nurseries Limited	£74,796,000
Gemsupa Limited	£74,767,688
Allerford Intermediate Newco Limited	£74,743,000
Warwick Independent Schools Foundation	£74,705,000
The Alumasc Group PLC	£74,704,000
Briggs & Forrester Living Limited	£74,703,144
MM (UK) Limited	£74,536,256
Sandicliffe Garage Limited	£74,399,000
In Vino Limited	£74,332,672
Victoria Square Woking Limited	£74,292,096
Coolsilk Property & Investment Limited	£74,251,992
Trimas Corporation Limited	£74,233,000
Welcome Financial Services Limited	£74,201,000
Coal Products Limited	£74,200,000
BDWZest LLP	£73,986,000
ZestBDW LLP	£73,986,000
Commify Limited	£73,771,536
J G Pears Power Limited	£73,620,192
Trapoc Limited	£73,593,000
Burghley House Preservation Trust Limited	£73,427,192
See Group Limited	£73,421,000
Severn Trent Services Defence Limited	£73,403,000
T.C. Harrison 1960 Limited	£73,381,000
Norton Finance Group Limited	£73,376,720
Diversey Holdings Limited	£73,196,000
Melbourne Holdings Limited	£73,193,600

Company	Value
Paccar Trucks U.K. Ltd	£73,155,000
Quotient Sciences Limited	£73,137,000
Codemasters Group Holdings PLC	£73,088,000
Swizzels Matlow Limited	£73,036,000
Neovia Logistics Services (U.K.) Limited	£72,810,000
Norton Home Loans Limited	£72,499,824
Jonas Computing (UK) Limited	£72,461,056
Arnold Laver Holdings Limited	£72,429,368
Arnold Laver & Company Limited	£72,428,368
Bell Rock Topco Limited	£72,373,000
KCI Holding UK Limited	£72,368,000
The Orders of St. John Care Trust	£72,343,000
Carmelite Finance Limited	£72,341,000
Stanley Works Limited (The)	£72,325,000
Niftylift Limited	£72,273,000
CPL Aromas (Holdings) Limited	£72,196,000
Loughborough Schools Foundation	£72,195,000
Noble Foods Holdings Limited	£72,170,000
Rain Dance Investments Limited	£72,054,144
Minerva Learning Trust	£72,026,800
The Deltic Group Holdings Limited	£72,011,000
Ten Entertainment Group PLC	£72,000,000
Strevens Vehicles Holdings Limited	£71,924,000
Dart Products Europe Ltd.	£71,869,000
Rightmove PLC	£71,813,000
NAH Holdings Limited	£71,759,040
Vale Academy Trust	£71,740,968
Omega PLC	£71,615,000
Good 'n' Natural Limited	£71,589,000
Butcher's Pet Care Limited	£71,421,000
Dawsongroup UK Limited	£71,413,000
Seth Topco Limited	£71,326,544
Sheffield Forgemasters Engineering Limited	£71,222,000
Colston Property Partners Limited	£71,205,368
Acorndrift Limited	£70,969,000
Dana UK Axle Limited	£70,951,000
Maneto (UK) 2 Limited	£70,938,000
Kuehne + Nagel Drinkflow Logistics Limited	£70,906,000
Kuehne + Nagel Drinkflow Logistics Holdings Limited	£70,906,000
3SE (Barnsley, Doncaster & Rotherham) Limited	£70,899,000
The Car People Limited	£70,560,000
GI Recruitment Limited	£70,540,000
Sidney Stringer Multi Academy Trust	£70,521,000
VWR International Ltd	£70,478,000
Alliance Medical Leasing Limited	£70,418,000
Sherwin-Williams Diversified Brands Limited	£70,249,040
The Deltic Group Limited	£70,244,000
MS International PLC	£70,141,000
Lanai Medical Ltd	£70,118,072
Crystal Martin International Limited	£70,101,504
Hanover Housing Developments Limited	£70,036,000
Green Biologics Limited	£69,993,720
Agrivert Biogas Limited	£69,765,568
Dyon E & P Limited	£69,762,000
Joules Limited	£69,734,000
Lionheart Academies Trust	£69,717,840
Perrys East Midlands Limited	£69,698,000
M.M.D. Mining Machinery Developments Limited	£69,656,352
Sistine Properties (Westbury) Limited	£69,596,000
Rushlift Limited	£69,578,000
SPL II Acquisition Company (UK) Limited	£69,358,280
Chess Limited	£69,288,000
Riviera Tours Limited	£69,235,000
RPS Consulting Services Limited	£69,223,000
SJC 15 Limited	£69,206,568
A Shade Greener Debt LLP	£69,177,224
Euro E-Land Company PLC	£69,175,704
Agrovista UK Limited	£69,007,000
Gleadell Agriculture Limited	£68,907,000
Faurecia Automotive Seating UK Limited	£68,854,160
Bright Tribe Trust	£68,817,000
Bridge Leisure Topco Limited	£68,786,960
Idverde UK Limited	£68,729,000
Sigma Components Holdings Limited	£68,678,000
Shoe Zone Retail Limited	£68,674,000
A Shade Greener (F17) LLP	£68,586,720
Bellrock Property & Facilities Management Limited	£68,586,000
Technolog Holdings Ltd	£68,348,000
Hall & Pickles 1812 Limited	£68,293,000
Tansor (Cornbow) Limited	£68,174,448
Framework Housing Association	£68,153,000
Steeple Topco Limited	£67,931,000
Cerealto UK Limited	£67,868,512
J & A Young Group Limited	£67,829,000
Pattonair Holdings Limited	£67,781,000
Pendragon Overseas Limited	£67,708,000
Harpmanor Limited	£67,700,000
Conchord Limited	£67,628,000
Brecknell, Willis & Co. Limited	£67,626,648
Hexadex Limited	£67,620,000
Refood UK Limited	£67,601,232
Karen Millen Holdco 1 Limited	£67,600,000
B & P Properties Limited	£67,579,656
Tove Learning Trust	£67,569,312
Shoe Zone PLC	£67,555,000
Taylor Hobson Limited	£67,472,000
Fossil (UK) Limited	£67,411,000
Jamie Lewis Residential Lettings Limited	£67,322,808
Aviagen International Finance One Limited	£67,295,664
Niscayah Holdings Limited	£67,170,256
Spear & Jackson Group Limited	£67,154,000
Oasis Fashions Holdings Limited	£67,000,000
Falcon Bidco Limited	£66,987,704
Cognita International Holdings Limited	£66,981,000
UCC Coffee UK Limited	£66,925,424
New York Bakery Company Limited	£66,859,000
Funeral Partners Limited	£66,808,000
Tapton School Academy Trust	£66,791,000
NAH Group Limited	£66,747,320
Fresenius Medical Care (UK) Limited	£66,627,000
Rolls-Royce Power Development Limited	£66,559,000
Ernest V. Waddington Limited	£66,493,952
Metsa Wood UK Limited	£66,394,000
Fresenius Medical Care Renal Services Limited	£66,362,000
XMA Limited	£66,361,000
Watermill-CT Holdings Limited	£66,332,000
S D C (Holdings) Limited	£66,188,496
Peopleplus Group Limited	£66,100,000
Wellglade Holdings Limited	£66,095,000
Renewi Cumbria Limited	£66,065,000
Sigma Components Limited	£66,051,704
Sitel UK Finance	£66,031,924
Bollington Wilson Group Limited	£66,028,000
A Shade Greener Debt (2) LLP	£65,964,724
QD Commercial Group Holdings Limited	£65,844,684
Eurocell Holdings Limited	£65,830,000
Balfour Beatty Plant & Fleet Services Limited	£65,790,000
GRT Nottingham Lift Project Company (No. 1) Ltd	£65,745,000
National Tyre Service Limited	£65,723,000
Nottingham Roman Catholic Diocesan Trustees	£65,718,000
Pulse Home Products (Holdings) Limited	£65,650,000
Oxford Biomedica (UK) Limited	£65,589,000
Caesar Bidco Limited	£65,567,220
Oxford Biomedica PLC	£65,402,000
Milton Keynes Development Partnership LLP	£65,392,000
Severn Trent Services International Overseas Hldgs	£65,367,000
J O Sims Limited	£65,364,976
Oxford Publishing Limited	£65,326,000
Staffline Holdings Limited	£65,210,100
Charles Wells Brewery Limited	£65,067,000
Mahle Powertrain Limited	£65,047,000
Stepnell Limited	£65,024,176
W. Cumber & Son (Theale) Limited	£65,017,084
Pork Farms Limited	£64,845,000

Company	Value
Clientlogic (UK) Holding Limited	£64,757,000
Falcon of Hull & Lincolnshire Limited	£64,739,000
CI Beatrice II Facility (BOWL) Limited	£64,433,192
Milton Keynes Community Foundation Limited	£64,318,392
Isotrak Midco Limited	£64,307,000
F.W. Baker Limited	£64,300,000
Foseco International Limited	£63,998,000
Trent Motor Traction Company Limited (The)	£63,894,000
Avanti Gas Limited	£63,887,000
CCN UK Unlimited	£63,854,176
Abingdon School	£63,765,000
Pressure Technologies PLC	£63,762,000
Millbrook Proving Ground Limited	£63,680,000
ACESO Healthcare Group Holdings Limited	£63,660,000
Renewi UK Services Limited	£63,642,000
The Diocese of Coventry Multi-Academy Trust	£63,641,000
Belron UK Limited	£63,566,000
WRG Acquisitions 2 Limited	£63,486,000
Purico Limited	£63,463,000
Guilbert UK Holdings Limited	£63,378,000
MAN Energy Solutions UK Limited	£63,367,000
Games Workshop Limited	£63,344,000
Massmould Limited	£63,340,000
Sensient Flavors Limited	£63,280,836
TNT Transport Limited	£63,234,140
Compass Holdco Limited	£63,214,060
Morgan Industrial Properties Limited	£63,117,560
CCN UK 2005 Limited	£63,061,412
Aaron Holdings Limited	£62,889,904
M.A.X. Funding Limited	£62,887,628
DCS Group (UK) Limited	£62,871,000
Desford Acquisition Company (UK) Limited	£62,834,000
Chatsworth Investments Limited	£62,832,000
Orchid Orthopedic Solutions Ltd	£62,814,000
Banner Group Limited	£62,802,000
CI Beatrice II Facility (CI II) Limited	£62,739,104
Stratford-upon-Avon Town Trust	£62,698,152
Barbon Holdings Limited	£62,664,256
Eastern Multi-Academy Trust	£62,657,000
Rushcliffe Care Limited	£62,654,056
Regenersis (Depot) Services Ltd	£62,627,000
TPH (UK) Limited	£62,613,000
Dawsongroup Vans Limited	£62,420,000
Progress Rail Services UK Limited	£62,417,000
SC Johnson Professional Limited	£62,328,000
Northcoast Seafoods Limited	£62,163,272
Maynard & Harris Plastics (UK) Limited	£62,098,000
Sanderson Group PLC	£62,000,000
Gefco U.K. Limited	£61,980,000
Dawsongroup Temperature Control Solutions Ltd	£61,924,000
Landau Forte Charitable Trust	£61,878,000
Ford & Slater Limited	£61,771,000
The Valspar (UK) Corporation, Limited	£61,608,072
Bridge Leisure Bidco Limited	£61,511,060
WFEL Limited	£61,485,000
A H Worth and Company Limited	£61,458,000
Frank Wright Limited	£61,443,000
The Ethical Property Company Limited	£61,361,504
Cosworth Group Holdings Limited	£61,305,000
Comet REFICO Limited	£61,100,000
Fugro Geoservices Limited	£61,064,000
Pektron Group Limited	£61,050,064
Stewart Milne Homes North West England Limited	£61,037,000
Magna Exteriors (Banbury) Limited	£61,034,000
Punch Partnerships (PGRP) Limited	£61,011,000
Smartway PW. Holdings Limited	£60,983,800
GRS (Roadstone) Limited	£60,919,592
A W James Limited	£60,900,548
Envigo RMS (UK) Limited	£60,876,000
Codemasters Holdings Limited	£60,871,000
Technolog Group Limited	£60,842,000
A Pearson Holdings Limited	£60,836,000

Company	Value
Matrix SCM Limited	£60,740,224
Frontline Limited	£60,731,000
Cristal Investments UK Limited	£60,621,300
T.C.L. Holdings (Midco) Limited	£60,493,312
Coloplast Limited	£60,367,000
Codemasters Software Company Limited (The)	£60,339,000
Fisher & Paykel Appliances Limited	£60,322,000
Wastenotts (Reclamation) Limited	£60,319,000
Gojo Industries - Europe Limited	£60,227,816
Mobica Holdings Limited	£60,203,652
Wanfeng MLTH Holdings Co., Ltd	£60,138,720
Mulberry Property Developments Ltd	£60,117,632
Schutz (U.K.) Limited	£60,117,000
Jotun Paints (Europe) Limited	£60,081,000
Nampak Plastics Europe Limited	£59,979,000
Reeves Wireline Technologies Limited	£59,962,000
Hafele U.K. Limited	£59,879,000
Synseal Extrusions Limited	£59,877,000
Flying High Trust	£59,743,008
J.Wharton (Shipping) Limited	£59,687,212
Steeple Bidco Limited	£59,676,000
Avdel Holding Limited	£59,666,000
RTI Europe Limited	£59,614,372
XPO Bulk UK Limited	£59,554,000
Uris Group Limited	£59,545,000
TI Group Automotive Systems Limited	£59,523,980
Redlawn Land Limited	£59,472,864
Briggs & Forrester Engineering Services Limited	£59,445,916
The Reflex Group Limited	£59,403,000
William Morgan Group Limited	£59,397,992
Essentra Packaging & Security Limited	£59,358,000
Calor Properties Limited	£59,285,000
Deb IP Limited	£59,278,000
Limes Developments Limited	£59,155,692
West Norfolk Academies Trust	£59,114,756
Romo Limited	£59,076,000
Sheffield Diocesan Board of Finance	£58,928,000
Deanbank Investments Limited	£58,912,012
GCI Network Solutions Limited	£58,881,056
Psioxus Therapeutics Limited	£58,869,872
Edina Acquisitions Limited	£58,848,416
Learndirect Limited	£58,800,000
Willowbrook Healthcare Debtco Limited	£58,756,492
QEGSMAT	£58,748,000
Technolog Limited	£58,735,000
Hyde Aero Products Limited	£58,527,352
Coolsilk Limited	£58,496,148
IG Design Group UK Limited	£58,422,000
Reflex Vehicle Hire Limited	£58,387,240
Sharnbrook Academy Federation	£58,341,944
McCann-Erickson Network Limited	£58,283,000
Heygates Limited	£58,237,828
Leicester Football Club PLC	£58,190,000
Ingeus UK Holdings Limited	£58,189,000
Noble Desserts Holdings Limited	£58,145,000
G.H.B. (Holding) Limited	£58,138,596
Supreme Concrete Limited	£58,081,888
Orbit Developments (Manchester) Limited	£58,045,664
Artex Limited	£58,028,000
Teletrac Navman (UK) Ltd	£58,012,000
Car Store Limited	£57,982,000
Branston Holdings Limited	£57,966,000
Fannin (UK) Limited	£57,940,000
English Electric Company,Limited (The)	£57,927,000
Belfield Furnishings Limited	£57,923,000
Eden Hotel Collection Limited	£57,861,968
Anatis UK Limited	£57,852,392
The Northworthy Trust	£57,777,296
Transform Trust	£57,772,828
Learning Without Limits Academy Trust	£57,645,172
HB Fuller UK Operations Limited	£57,599,000
John A.Wells Limited	£57,597,932

Company	Amount
Omex Agriculture Limited	£57,554,820
Benchmark Animal Health Group Limited	£57,462,508
CPL Industries Holdings Limited	£57,447,000
Oasis Fashions Limited	£57,400,000
Eurocell Profiles Limited	£57,300,000
Clugston Construction Limited	£57,284,892
Barwood Homes Limited	£57,280,088
Dean Property Group Limited	£57,174,888
Peterborough Keys Academies Trust	£57,105,000
Essentra Packaging Limited	£57,013,000
Cuttech Limited	£56,980,908
Wacoal EMEA Ltd	£56,953,000
Harworth Estates Limited	£56,918,000
Special Steel Co.,Limited	£56,908,880
Blue Skies Investments Limited	£56,818,044
OSI International Holdings Limited	£56,770,000
Northbridge Industrial Services PLC	£56,768,000
Cedar 2015 Limited	£56,676,000
Yourcash Limited	£56,644,000
Amey Ventures Asset Holdings Limited	£56,633,000
Mertex UK Limited	£56,626,848
Gallagher Longstanton Limited	£56,602,496
Veeva U.K. Holdings Limited	£56,580,776
Assemblies of God Property Trust	£56,562,000
Plymouth Grove Residential LLP	£56,539,280
Harrowden Farms Group Limited	£56,452,880
Scott Bader UK Limited	£56,425,000
Amey Defence Services (Housing) Limited	£56,414,452
Evobus (UK) Limited	£56,295,000
Kingdom Bank Limited	£56,250,000
RPS Energy Limited	£56,234,000
NCL Holdings Limited	£56,203,348
Hesley Holdings Limited	£56,175,568
Atlas Hotels (Greenwich) Limited	£56,144,288
Project Republica Bidco Limited	£56,127,780
Proseal UK Limited	£56,118,344
E.Surv Limited	£55,979,000
IMS Topco Limited	£55,909,000
Headcrown Group PLC	£55,900,000
Beatson Clark Limited	£55,796,000
The De Ferrers Trust	£55,783,000
Snap-On Equipment Limited	£55,747,728
Benoy Limited	£55,668,000
Benchmark Genetics Limited	£55,651,580
Idverde Holdings Limited	£55,633,000
Porterbrook Maintenance Limited	£55,504,000
Karen Millen Fashions Limited	£55,500,000
Phoenix Advance Limited	£55,333,000
The Avalon Trustee Company Limited	£55,281,008
U-Pol Bidco Limited	£55,250,000
Corby Land & Development Ltd	£55,244,364
McCann Manchester Limited	£55,203,000
F. Vindis & Sons (Bedford) Limited	£55,199,932
Acer Trust	£55,183,000
Northern Powerhouse Investments Limited	£55,161,000
Freudenberg Sealing Technologies Limited	£55,109,072
Leda Properties Limited	£55,097,852
DFDS Seaways PLC	£55,035,020
Equity Solutions Lift Investments Oldham Limited	£54,973,848
Essentra Filter Products International Limited	£54,970,000
Hancock Cash & Carry Limited	£54,948,000
Maxxia (UK) Limited	£54,919,792
APS Group Limited	£54,907,396
Wellspring Academy Trust	£54,849,528
J. and A. Young (Leicester) Limited	£54,839,000
Maximus HHS Holdings Limited	£54,803,996
Codemasters Group Limited	£54,784,000
Aghoco 1579 (Topco) Limited	£54,697,252
Recticel Limited	£54,681,000
The Challenger Multi Academy Trust	£54,674,760
MCE Insurance Limited	£54,674,540
Chromalloy United Kingdom Limited	£54,664,000
S.D.C. Builders Limited	£54,579,932
Nasmyth Group Limited	£54,570,000
Glenvale Transport Limited	£54,547,000
Nottingham City Transport Limited	£54,542,000
Naturex Limited	£54,492,000
Walter E. Sturgess & Sons Limited	£54,483,000
Amey Power Services Limited	£54,415,000
Stowe School,Limited	£54,321,720
Jaywing PLC	£54,287,000
Vaillant Industrial UK Limited	£54,248,000
Stanley Black & Decker Finance Limited	£54,236,536
WFEL Holdings Limited	£54,214,000
Fanuc UK Limited	£54,208,864
AmeyCespa Limited	£54,206,000
Armitage Pet Care Limited	£54,190,000
Coba International Limited	£54,055,000
Dudley Taylor Pharmacies Limited	£54,016,680
Summit Therapeutics PLC	£53,962,000
Trent Academies Group	£53,953,000
Colston Investment Properties LLP	£53,929,692
Nottingham Rehab Limited	£53,929,000
C.F.Booth Limited	£53,920,000
Henry Boot Construction Limited	£53,885,680
Montracon Limited	£53,875,076
Bournemouth Airport Property Investments (Industrial)	£53,864,000
E - Leather Limited	£53,823,740
Topps Tile Kingdom Limited	£53,822,000
Kautex Unipart Limited	£53,800,000
Lavendon Access Services (International) Limited	£53,709,000
CCW 600 Limited	£53,708,168
ACESO Healthcare Limited	£53,686,000
AmeyCespa (East) Limited	£53,630,000
Hotels4U.Com Limited	£53,600,000
Bifrangi UK Limited	£53,516,228
Sitel Solutions UK Limited	£53,476,700
Mid-UK Recycling Limited	£53,460,712
Vita Satellite 1 Limited	£53,357,000
New Co (Satellite) Limited	£53,356,000
Billing Finance Limited	£53,343,580
Element Six Technologies Limited	£53,281,000
Merloni Domestic Appliances Limited	£53,276,000
Sitel UK Limited	£53,260,000
Garner Holdings Limited	£53,201,252
Irth (15) Limited	£53,200,000
Mays Properties Limited	£53,178,188
Peak Gen Top Co Limited	£53,138,656
Brigantia Learning Trust Limited	£53,136,696
Eurocell Group Limited	£53,119,000
Sumo Group PLC	£53,101,000
Mobica Bidco Limited	£53,055,616
Pets at Home Vet Group Limited	£53,054,240
Aghoco 1566 (Bidco) Limited	£53,041,632
Mytravel North America Limited	£53,028,248
Totally PLC	£52,896,000
Nikon Metrology UK Limited	£52,877,000
Fred Sherwood Group Limited	£52,873,620
Branston Limited	£52,847,000
Uris Topco Limited	£52,830,000
Benchmarx Kitchens and Joinery Limited	£52,782,000
GI Group Recruitment Ltd	£52,732,296
Doosan Industrial Vehicle UK Ltd.	£52,678,000
Mulberry Commercial Developments Limited	£52,600,644
Carewatch Bidco Limited	£52,561,000
Euro Food Brands Limited	£52,531,304
Star Mayan Limited	£52,524,000
QD Commercial Group (Property) Limited	£52,467,952
Bodycote Finance UK Limited	£52,427,192
Singleton Birch Limited	£52,426,000
Ideal Industries Holdings Limited	£52,420,000
Freeths LLP	£52,379,000
Rigby Group Finance Limited	£52,321,000
Avery Homes (Nelson) Limited	£52,286,144

Louver-Lite Limited	£52,237,472	Stanley UK Services Limited	£49,019,000
Essentra Filter Products Limited	£52,233,000	Envigo International Limited	£48,956,000
Jones Homes (Southern) Limited	£52,111,448	Cashino Gaming Limited	£48,951,000
Ancala Water Services (Defence) Limited	£52,074,000	Prominent (Europe) Limited	£48,899,000
Wasp Management Software Limited	£51,981,000	Isotrak Holdings Limited	£48,887,000
Countrywide Principal Services Limited	£51,941,000	Rohm Electronics Europe Limited	£48,865,000
Harworth Services Limited	£51,908,000	EDL (UK) LFG Generation Limited	£48,837,960
Optimum Debtco Limited	£51,899,000	CVS Leasing Limited	£48,714,000
Harworth Estates Group Limited	£51,828,000	Idverde Limited	£48,700,000
UKLS Acquisitions Limited	£51,828,000	RM Property and Facilities Solutions Limited	£48,689,000
Finham Park Multi-Academy Trust	£51,751,000	Park Air Systems Limited	£48,685,000
GPP Langstone LLP	£51,733,540	Western Buses Limited	£48,620,000
Stepan UK Limited	£51,685,000	Betafence Limited	£48,609,000
New Testament Church of God	£51,564,572	CAE Aircrew Training Services PLC	£48,560,000
Markem-Imaje Industries Limited	£51,494,600	Napier Turbochargers Limited	£48,560,000
CX Midco Limited	£51,439,000	Learner Engagement and Achievement Partnership	£48,557,164
Chatfields Limited	£51,363,000	The Coalfields Regeneration Trust	£48,544,000
Optilan Group Limited	£51,285,000	Futures Homeway Limited	£48,433,000
A Shade Greener (F9) LLP	£51,281,936	Guilford Europe Limited	£48,429,000
TNT Express Worldwide Investments Limited	£51,239,308	Performance Health Global Limited	£48,379,000
A Shade Greener (F7) LLP	£51,170,952	Keelex 351 Limited	£48,340,644
Norcros Industry (International) Limited	£51,125,000	Swanton Care & Community Limited	£48,266,264
P.D.Hook (Hatcheries) Limited	£51,056,000	Donald Ward Limited	£48,229,512
Fullbrook Thorpe Investments LLP	£50,986,000	Redlawn Limited	£48,204,040
Citation Limited	£50,958,656	Konecranes Demag UK Limited	£48,192,000
DMG Mori UK Limited	£50,940,044	Cytec Industrial Materials (Derby) Limited	£48,132,000
Reflex Labels Limited	£50,931,000	Canal & River Trading CIC	£48,124,308
CPC Foods Limited	£50,807,104	RTI International Metals Limited	£48,113,352
BPW Limited	£50,800,936	Trackwork Limited	£48,096,000
First South Yorkshire Limited	£50,799,000	White Woods Primary Academy Trust	£47,991,000
Finance Yorkshire Limited	£50,730,180	The Abbey Group UK Limited	£47,965,696
Aviagen Turkeys Holdings Limited	£50,717,000	Bio Energy (UK) Limited	£47,917,588
BAJ 1 Limited	£50,682,432	The Hesley Group Limited	£47,874,436
Northampton Primary Academy Trust	£50,662,504	Cothill Trust	£47,861,000
The Oxford Asset Management Company Limited	£50,656,800	Community 1st Sheffield Limited	£47,838,428
Coventry University Enterprises Limited	£50,631,000	Aghoco 1578 (Midco) Limited	£47,802,924
Whistler Acquisitions Limited	£50,610,000	ITC Enterprises Limited	£47,797,640
Thomas Cook UK Travel Limited	£50,550,000	Kaye Aluminium (Holdings) Limited	£47,727,748
Usha Martin International Limited	£50,407,000	Staples Brothers Limited	£47,718,688
Holding JDR Limited	£50,391,784	PERI Limited	£47,621,504
Go Plant Fleet Services Ltd	£50,301,000	Sleekmade Property Co. Limited	£47,544,448
Baptist Union Corporation Limited (The)	£50,291,696	GL Events UK Limited	£47,543,180
Vine Mill Limited	£50,221,000	Sheffield Wednesday Football Club Limited	£47,511,000
Harlow Bros Holdings Limited	£50,181,472	Esendee Holdings Limited	£47,501,000
Jarden Consumer Solutions (Europe) Limited	£50,164,000	Scholastic Limited	£47,498,724
Cyden Homes Limited	£50,137,760	Orchard House Foods Limited	£47,484,000
Waterfall Elior Limited	£50,053,480	McCann Health Medical Communications Limited	£47,436,000
Graypaul Motors Limited	£49,990,000	Avalon (Europe) Limited	£47,358,072
Allied Publicity Services (Manchester) Limited	£49,978,984	Lawton Tube Company Limited (The)	£47,342,256
Pattonair UK Limited	£49,908,000	Kostal UK Limited	£47,309,000
Natl. Amusements (UK) Limited	£49,803,988	Country Court Care Homes 3 SB Limited	£47,278,724
Battery Energy Storage Solutions Limited	£49,787,864	Karcher (U.K.) Limited	£47,273,000
Homecrest Midco Limited	£49,713,000	CPL Distribution Limited	£47,141,000
Indoor Bowling Acquisitions Limited	£49,701,000	Insight Enterprises UK Limited	£47,110,592
Network Group Holdings Limited	£49,678,000	Walker & Son (Hauliers) Limited	£47,106,508
Huntercombe (SP) Limited	£49,660,000	MacDermid Autotype Limited	£47,015,000
A Shade Greener Limited	£49,625,400	Motherwell Bridge Limited	£46,987,000
Envigo Holdings Limited	£49,612,000	CCS Media Limited	£46,986,000
Personal Group Holdings PLC	£49,568,000	Kent Energy, Ltd.	£46,978,000
VJ Holdco UK Limited	£49,539,000	Mercia Learning Trust	£46,952,724
Brayford Hotels Holdings Ltd	£49,497,020	Amey Metering Limited	£46,923,000
Strawson Group Developments Limited	£49,445,000	Board24 Ltd	£46,822,800
Dragon School Trust Limited	£49,386,000	Arbor Forest Products Limited	£46,812,000
Alliance & Leicester Personal Finance Limited	£49,350,000	Xtratherm UK Limited	£46,791,264
Red Primrose Ltd	£49,325,288	Amscan International Limited	£46,771,000
Hexagon Leasing Limited	£49,305,688	Lillywhites Limited	£46,752,000
Wilson Bowden Limited	£49,290,000	County Milk Products Limited	£46,729,532
PV Crystalox Solar PLC	£49,198,812	Ametek Airtechnology Group Limited	£46,717,000
Bransby Horses	£49,104,004	Envigo Research Limited	£46,706,000
Network Ventures Limited	£49,075,000	Knowledgepoint360 UK Acquisitionco Limited	£46,650,000
Gripple Limited	£49,040,652	Sunshine Care Topco Limited	£46,642,936
Dawsongroup Material Handling Limited	£49,025,000	Beck Bidco Limited	£46,614,404

Company	Amount
Aintree Retail Park Limited	£46,612,888
Lands' End Europe Limited	£46,592,752
Beardow Adams Holdings Ltd	£46,559,456
College of Policing Limited	£46,522,000
Simons Group Limited	£46,462,000
Lincoln and London Holdings Limited	£46,462,000
H L Plastics Limited	£46,392,432
Tamar Energy Limited	£46,351,000
Optilan (UK) Limited	£46,330,000
Parkers of Leicester Limited	£46,278,668
Atlas Hotels (Property) Limited	£46,198,496
CDL Group Holdings Limited	£46,194,256
Asfordby Storage & Haulage Limited	£46,192,344
Oxford Gene Technology Limited	£46,143,844
Pirelli UK Limited	£46,054,000
HaskoningDHV UK Limited	£46,037,972
GL Industrial Services UK Ltd	£46,031,000
Argos Business Solutions Limited	£46,026,000
Dee Valley Water (Holdings) Limited	£46,000,000
Dunkley Family Investments Limited	£45,999,920
Go Inspire Group Limited	£45,994,000
Lousada PLC	£45,876,936
Kimbolton School	£45,850,828
James Durrans & Sons,Limited	£45,797,992
Mira Technology Park Limited	£45,775,000
FCC PFI Holdings Limited	£45,764,000
Thomas Deacon Education Trust	£45,750,000
MHR Global Holdings Limited	£45,741,248
IRESS FS Group Limited	£45,727,000
Crown Aerosols UK Ltd	£45,701,000
Canaveral Bidco Limited	£45,692,000
BPI Limited	£45,644,000
Source Bioscience Limited	£45,570,000
Dematic Limited	£45,564,000
Concha y Toro UK Limited	£45,458,360
BPI International (No 2) Limited	£45,409,172
The Waste and Resources Action Programme	£45,361,000
Aalberts Industries Limited	£45,360,000
Adams Challenge (UK) Limited	£45,328,288
Evotec (UK) Limited	£45,296,000
Southern Derbyshire Lift Project Company (No.1)	£45,288,000
Palletforce Holdings Limited	£45,211,000
Angel Cofund	£45,198,096
Farol Holdings Limited	£45,167,792
Hartwell Finance Limited	£45,120,000
Deichmann-Shoes UK Limited	£45,103,000
Wipac Limited	£45,089,432
Arena Event Services Group Limited	£45,085,000
Stagecoach (South) Limited	£45,054,000
BI Worldwide Limited	£45,043,664
New Era Development (UK) Limited	£45,021,072
Karen Millen Group Limited	£45,000,000
The Yorkshire Traction Company Limited	£44,991,000
IMS Bidco Limited	£44,980,000
Greenyard Fresh UK Ltd	£44,951,624
Compass Community Ltd	£44,944,664
Cooper Roller Bearings Company Limited	£44,938,000
Paralloy Limited	£44,903,000
Heyford Park Developments Limited	£44,884,496
KL Ventures Limited	£44,864,004
Peveril Securities Long Lane Limited	£44,825,144
Boughton Estates Limited (The)	£44,761,712
Leicester Lift Project Company (No. 1) Limited	£44,757,000
Perkins Small Engines Limited	£44,683,000
NMB-Minebea UK Ltd	£44,682,000
Equip Outdoor Technologies UK Limited	£44,646,000
Silkstone Finance Limited	£44,639,096
Trackwork Group Limited	£44,615,000
P.D. Hook (Breeders) Limited	£44,580,000
Sector Aviation Holdings Limited	£44,573,000
Brioche Pasquier U.K. Limited	£44,564,856
St. Clare's, Oxford.	£44,519,000

Company	Amount
Spark44 (JV) Limited	£44,516,328
Lomas Distribution Limited	£44,492,744
Aspireplus Educational Trust	£44,421,044
Nippon Gases UK Limited	£44,414,000
Rigid Containers Limited	£44,411,560
ITM Power PLC	£44,367,000
Dunlop Oil & Marine Limited	£44,321,000
Auto-Trail V.R. Limited	£44,286,888
North Nottinghamshire Lift Project Company (No.1)	£44,284,000
Carr's Flour Mills Limited	£44,238,000
Brady Corporation Limited	£44,200,000
Delifrance (UK) Limited	£44,190,000
Senad Limited	£44,169,000
Coveris Flexibles Holdings UK Limited	£44,130,000
Middleby Holding UK Ltd	£44,044,048
Orca Marine Leisure Limited	£44,011,976
Alumasc Limited	£44,007,000
Lincoln Electric UK Holdings Limited	£43,983,100
Sensient Holdings UK	£43,981,096
Abbey Forged Products Limited	£43,960,844
Exemplar Limited	£43,955,944
Country Court Care Homes 2 Limited	£43,948,052
Brentford Phase II LLP	£43,948,000
Community 1st Sheffield (Tranche 2) Limited	£43,925,960
UGI Midlands Limited	£43,916,000
Randall Parker Food Group Limited	£43,849,000
Acorndrive Limited	£43,825,000
Princess International Sales and Service Ltd	£43,817,912
Joules Investments Holdings Limited	£43,806,000
Steeple Midco Limited	£43,675,000
Steeple Holdco Limited	£43,675,000
U-Pol Mezzanine Limited	£43,669,000
Kuehne + Nagel Drinks Logistics Limited	£43,669,000
HR Wallingford Limited	£43,633,000
First Carton Group Ltd	£43,580,928
The Coaching Inn Group Ltd	£43,564,464
Raynsway Properties Limited	£43,558,304
W.R.Swann & Co.Limited	£43,492,824
Avon UK Holdings Limited	£43,487,420
Turbine Services Limited	£43,457,192
Wykes Engineering Co. (Rushden) Limited	£43,396,360
Darby Group Ltd	£43,390,568
L.J. Fairburn and Son Limited	£43,326,836
Vernon Holdings Limited	£43,320,692
Tanvic Group Holdings Limited	£43,307,736
Armitages Pet Products Limited	£43,296,000
Whitworths Limited	£43,284,000
Triumph Motorcycles (Overseas) Limited	£43,245,000
The Abbey Group Cambridgeshire Limited	£43,206,404
Terrace Hills Farm LLP	£43,204,452
Russell Burgess Limited	£43,137,000
Brooklands Milton Keynes LLP	£43,105,000
The A & S Leisure Group Limited	£43,101,272
William Lee Limited	£43,076,940
Faccenda Farms Limited	£43,051,948
Strawson Group Investments Limited	£43,045,000
Triumph Motorcycles Group Limited	£43,020,000
Pertemps Jobshop Limited	£43,017,080
Otter Controls Limited	£43,015,216
HR Wallingford Group Limited	£42,992,000
R Griggs & Co. Limited	£42,974,708
Bollin Group Limited	£42,958,000
Fellowes Ltd	£42,890,304
Promens Packaging Limited	£42,799,000
Marshalls Yard Limited	£42,795,640
Camden Ventures Limited	£42,794,000
ZF Services UK Limited	£42,787,000
Quartzinvest Limited	£42,785,000
Gallagher Elstow Limited	£42,762,696
Node 4 Holdings Limited	£42,762,000
A. Schulman Gainsborough Ltd	£42,659,000
Bakkavor Central Finance Limited	£42,641,000

Company	Value
Produce World Investments Ltd	£42,609,000
Avon Products Holding Limited	£42,586,644
Renewi PFI Investments Limited	£42,575,000
Rittal Holdings Limited	£42,555,000
Ballast Phoenix Limited	£42,484,000
ADA PD UK Limited	£42,404,728
Central Garage (Uppingham) Limited	£42,333,532
DHP Family Ltd.	£42,324,596
MSG Commercial Limited	£42,323,488
Vita First Street Limited	£42,261,000
L H Group Services Limited	£42,248,280
Griffith Foods Limited	£42,211,000
Ben Smith & Sons (Wantage) Limited	£42,205,732
LKAB Minerals Limited	£42,185,096
Cadent Services Limited	£42,170,000
Naylor Industries PLC	£42,131,664
Palma Bidco Limited	£42,128,000
Jones Homes (Lancashire) Limited	£42,023,128
One Call Insurance Services Limited	£41,951,292
ARG Corporate Services Limited	£41,931,072
East Kent Road Car Company,Limited	£41,929,000
Cemex UK Properties Limited	£41,906,092
Performance Health International Limited	£41,871,000
E.I.R.P Limited	£41,860,000
Inspire Trust	£41,844,496
Stagecoach Devon Limited	£41,835,000
Xeros Limited	£41,824,412
REALL Limited	£41,716,800
Trent College Limited	£41,712,000
Witham (Specialist Vehicles) Limited	£41,702,196
W & J Linney Limited	£41,696,000
Sheffield Forgemasters Steel Limited	£41,696,000
Solo Cup (UK) Limited	£41,692,000
The Duston Education Trust	£41,675,292
Slawston Limited	£41,656,812
Lafarge Ireland Limited	£41,607,000
Senad Investments Limited	£41,599,000
Tensator Limited	£41,491,000
Claydon Estate LLP	£41,473,832
C.J. Upton Holdings Ltd.	£41,464,304
Education Placement Group Limited	£41,430,000
MBS Lending Ltd	£41,396,184
SML Europe Limited	£41,386,000
Delaquest Limited	£41,333,924
Kite Packaging Group Holdings Limited	£41,280,000
Oakham School	£41,260,000
Browne Jacobson LLP	£41,244,708
The Mead Educational Trust	£41,237,152
Longcliffe Group Limited	£41,154,000
Coastfields Leisure Limited	£41,152,764
Carlsberg Chongqing Limited	£41,109,920
Aston Martin Works Limited	£41,091,000
Anglia Components Limited	£41,085,144
G.F.Tomlinson Group Limited	£41,067,588
Unipath Limited	£41,001,000
Wyboston Lakes Limited	£40,988,432
Salmon Harvester Properties Limited	£40,944,712
Ashfield Healthcare Limited	£40,897,088
Enviropower Investments Limited	£40,808,000
Precision Engineered Limited	£40,786,000
P A Wright & Sons Limited	£40,778,684
SDI Aviation Limited	£40,761,140
Anglia Components Investments Limited	£40,759,512
Oxbow Coal Limited	£40,720,300
Thwaites Limited	£40,656,000
Rockwell European Holdings Limited	£40,651,000
Leadec Limited	£40,641,000
Plastribution Limited	£40,640,132
Citation Holdings Limited	£40,582,072
Billington Holdings PLC	£40,564,000
The Coventry and Solihull Waste Disposal Co Ltd	£40,554,000
Oxford Metrics PLC	£40,553,000
Bridging Finance Limited	£40,507,000
Biocity Group Limited	£40,507,000
Paul Smith (Holdings) Ltd	£40,505,000
Milton Keynes Education Trust	£40,484,816
Luxury British Design Holdings Limited	£40,483,696
Fluidpower Shared Services Limited	£40,471,092
Anglian Water Facilities Management Hldgs UK Ltd	£40,454,000
Horiba UK Finance Limited	£40,435,788
Pioneer Foods (UK) Limited	£40,411,372
GUS 1998 Unlimited	£40,372,612
Kal Tire Southern African Holdings Limited	£40,369,548
B & K Building Services Limited	£40,357,416
Xeros Technology Group PLC	£40,356,000
Deeley Group Limited	£40,337,000
Mutual Clothing & Supply Company Limited	£40,296,000
Polydist Europe Holdings Limited	£40,269,000
CRT Property Investments Limited	£40,237,000
The Kingham Hill Trust	£40,230,660
Cambus Limited	£40,193,000
Gallagher Estates No. 2 Limited	£40,120,000
North West Portfolio Limited	£40,091,904
Klober Limited	£40,028,992
Knightwood Trust Farms Limited	£40,028,000
Lhoist UK Limited	£40,010,000
Rodericks Dental Limited	£39,917,208
Geberit Sales Limited	£39,873,000
Smith Brothers Stores Limited	£39,851,484
Shoby Properties Limited	£39,847,628
Isotrak Group Limited	£39,821,000
The Denby Pottery Company Limited	£39,799,000
TDY Limited	£39,768,832
Biogen (UK) Limited	£39,763,000
Maryland Securities Limited	£39,737,192
Grangefern Properties Limited	£39,736,972
The Freedom Travel Group Limited	£39,729,000
Adept Care Homes Limited	£39,712,232
Faccenda Property Limited	£39,708,724
Lipsy Limited	£39,669,000
G W Padley Holdings Limited	£39,665,000
Total Motion Limited	£39,616,488
Ossur UK Holding Limited	£39,583,300
The Barons Eden Group Limited	£39,580,232
British Racing Drivers Club Limited (The)	£39,565,000
Tawnywood Limited	£39,547,656
UKKI Limited	£39,547,428
Alkane Energy UK Limited	£39,513,000
Nene Park Trust	£39,504,000
Avro Energy Limited	£39,503,880
FMC Corporation United Kingdom Limited	£39,492,848
Biogen Holdings Limited	£39,454,000
Forticrete Limited	£39,450,000
Vita Student Southampton Portswood Limited	£39,417,000
E.F.B. Group Limited	£39,415,512
Turbine Surface Technologies Limited	£39,413,000
H.I.Weldrick Limited	£39,377,784
Nottingham City Homes Limited	£39,377,000
Smeg (UK) Limited	£39,357,496
Midland Red (South) Limited	£39,345,000
City Estates (UK) Limited	£39,344,000
Soufflet Malt UK Limited	£39,323,000
Evolution Homecare Services Limited	£39,302,000
Irth (19) Limited	£39,300,000
Collins Earthworks Limited	£39,295,376
Western Bridge (Shipping) Limited	£39,211,072
Oldrid & Co.,Limited	£39,196,568
Haas Formula UK Ltd	£39,166,000
Total Produce Limited	£39,150,000
Snowmountain Enterprises Limited	£39,137,432
Amtico Holdings Limited	£39,091,000
Prodrive Group Limited	£39,070,000
Hammond Grange Limited	£39,068,212
Routeco Limited	£39,037,000

Company	Value
Door-Stop International Limited	£38,991,000
Bodycote H.I.P. Limited	£38,990,000
Dee Valley Group Limited	£38,985,000
CNH Bidco Limited	£38,985,000
BPI International Limited	£38,944,144
MPS Care Group Limited	£38,940,096
Greencore Convenience Foods I LLP	£38,930,000
Tensator Holdings Ltd	£38,924,000
Ede Holdings Limited	£38,890,520
Laser Quantum Limited	£38,887,000
Bedfordia Group Limited	£38,883,044
Pukka Pies Limited	£38,881,576
Intercounty Truck and Van Limited	£38,879,708
Dow Chemical Services UK Limited	£38,865,000
Usha Martin UK Limited	£38,863,000
Thames Land Limited	£38,850,952
Rigby Capital Investments Ltd	£38,842,712
PIB Risk Services Limited	£38,819,148
UGC Properties Limited	£38,803,000
Equita Limited	£38,777,728
Ashfield Healthcare Communications Group Limited	£38,721,000
Parkway Derby Limited	£38,661,636
Grimsthorpe & Drummond Castle Trust Limited	£38,646,920
Jones Homes (Yorkshire) Limited	£38,639,136
Lazarus Properties Limited	£38,625,656
Bridon Limited	£38,618,000
Grupo Antolin Leamington Limited	£38,616,536
Funeral Partners Midco Limited	£38,597,000
Pendragon Sabre Limited	£38,590,000
Eurocell Building Plastics Limited	£38,584,000
Crossfleet Limited	£38,574,000
Cycene Limited	£38,569,000
FCC Environment Services (UK) Limited	£38,552,000
East London Bus Group Property Investments Limited	£38,537,000
Schoeller-Bleckmann Oilfield Equipment (UK) Limited	£38,530,556
Staples (Vegetables) Limited	£38,513,044
Hampton Academies Trust	£38,401,788
Sheepy Magna Limited	£38,377,512
Assured Group Investments Limited	£38,350,320
ZND (UK) Limited	£38,332,392
Bobby's Acquisition Limited	£38,279,000
Patrolmake Limited	£38,229,480
Fine Tubes Limited	£38,221,000
Cognita UK Brazil Holdings Limited	£38,215,000
Gibbs Croft Limited	£38,209,000
Allington Waste Company Limited	£38,161,000
Alpine Electronics of U.K. Limited	£38,128,000
Stowe Valley Multi Academy Trust	£38,118,504
Catesby Estates (Residential) Limited	£38,104,644
E.On Connecting Energies Limited	£38,100,000
Fine Lady Bakeries Limited	£38,071,288
Bakkavor Estates Limited	£38,042,000
AMT Fruit Limited	£38,018,400
Raleigh UK Ltd	£38,006,000
Produce World Group Ltd	£37,972,000
Clientlogic (UK) Limited	£37,931,000
Farol Limited	£37,922,220
Deb Group Holdings Limited	£37,913,000
Meadowhead School Academy Trust	£37,900,256
AESSEAL PLC	£37,884,000
Stocksbridge Regeneration Company Limited	£37,825,484
Warehouse Fashions Holdings Limited	£37,800,000
OM Properties Investment Company Limited	£37,761,572
1 Wintringham LLP	£37,756,480
UK Platforms Ltd	£37,753,000
Beaver-Visitec International Sales Limited	£37,746,000
Wheatcroft (Group) Limited	£37,742,000
RE3 Limited	£37,739,000
United Health Limited	£37,737,496
Dachser Limited	£37,730,296
Loxton Developments Limited	£37,719,608
Map Property Investments Limited	£37,697,388
Clegg Group Limited	£37,691,064
Red Bull Racing Limited	£37,651,000
Cytec Process Materials (Keighley) Limited	£37,644,000
Quartzelec Ltd	£37,627,000
BASF Pharma (Callanish) Limited	£37,618,000
Arconic Closure Systems International (UK) Limited	£37,559,000
Sysmex UK Limited	£37,554,648
Supported Living Care Property Limited	£37,538,520
Futaba Industrial U.K. Ltd.	£37,526,000
Papa John's (GB) Limited	£37,525,000
Toyoda Gosei UK Ltd.	£37,513,000
Levi Strauss (U.K.) Limited	£37,500,000
BI Worldwide Holdings Limited	£37,491,824
Special New Fruit Licensing Limited	£37,458,324
Bournemouth International Airport Limited	£37,404,000
Justrite Holdings Ltd	£37,352,620
Pork Farms Caspian Limited	£37,341,000
Caledonia Bidco Limited	£37,333,544
Oxford Gene Technology IP Limited	£37,289,304
Wanzl Limited	£37,270,076
Chatsworth House Trust	£37,254,000
Apec Limited	£37,209,000
Affinity Living Trinity Holdco Limited	£37,206,000
Anpario PLC	£37,201,000
Rolls-Royce International Limited	£37,193,000
FCC Environment (Berkshire) Limited	£37,188,000
Almadon Limited	£37,069,456
Lincolnshire Field Products Limited	£37,033,788
Corrpro Companies Engineering Limited	£37,020,040
Coast Holdco 2 Limited	£37,000,000
P R Marriott Drilling Limited	£36,986,408
Porvair Filtration Group Limited	£36,905,000
Schueco UK Limited	£36,897,000
The PCMS Group Limited	£36,889,776
MTC Operations Limited	£36,888,000
ACP Europe Limited	£36,865,424
T. C. Landscapes Limited	£36,846,728
Eyre & Elliston Holdings Limited	£36,812,000
Gardeden Topco Limited	£36,810,852
Bybox Holdings Limited	£36,809,848
Maynard & Harris Group Limited	£36,805,000
The Midland Academies Trust	£36,801,000
Smartway Pharmaceuticals Limited	£36,737,676
Dynex Semiconductor Limited	£36,715,000
Baker Perkins Holdings Limited	£36,686,000
National Fleet Solutions Limited	£36,683,000
Glinwell Public Limited Company	£36,657,000
RAL Limited	£36,601,640
Laver Leisure Limited	£36,588,088
HPC Healthline UK Limited	£36,579,000
Giant U.K. Limited	£36,572,792
J.F. Finnegan Limited	£36,542,448
Applied Composites Group Ltd	£36,541,000
Unicarriers Leasing UK Limited	£36,539,280
W.N. Developments Limited	£36,522,976
Hyperama PLC	£36,500,000
Cherry Valley Farms Limited	£36,448,360
H.B. Fuller Group Limited	£36,406,000
ELG Utica Alloys Limited	£36,393,140
Calverton Finance Limited	£36,386,992
EOTH Limited	£36,382,000
Aegion Rehabilitation Services Limited	£36,364,660
Maro Developments Limited	£36,362,832
Sharing in Growth UK Limited	£36,358,000
Wootton Academy Trust	£36,341,524
Robinson PLC	£36,336,000
Anchorage Capital Europe, LLP	£36,264,800
Patrick Dean Limited	£36,241,212
Care Fertility Group Limited	£36,240,000
Ruddy Joinery Limited	£36,239,128
A Shade Greener (F12) LLP	£36,236,920
Zinc Ahead Holdings Limited	£36,184,832

Company	Value
Robert Luff Foundation Limited	£36,151,768
Lincolnshire Road Car Company Limited	£36,145,000
Element Six (UK) Limited.	£36,104,112
Mortgage Advice Bureau (Holdings) PLC	£36,101,000
Micromass Limited	£36,079,000
Node 4 Limited	£36,064,000
Pinewood Technologies PLC	£36,029,000
3C Waste Limited	£36,024,000
East London Bus & Coach Company Limited	£36,020,000
Bramah Limited	£35,996,676
BV Holdings Limited	£35,990,700
Phoenix Parker Holdings Limited	£35,982,000
Igloo Books Limited	£35,934,872
Global Self Drive Limited	£35,909,784
B.M. Polyco Limited	£35,886,000
Caterpillar Logistics (UK) Limited	£35,869,000
A B Graphic International Limited	£35,804,784
Discovery Schools Academies Trust Ltd	£35,740,000
Jardines (U.K.) Limited	£35,723,272
Devonshire Green (Broomgrove Road) Limited	£35,699,000
Multipanel UK Limited	£35,696,800
Oxford Asset Management LLP	£35,671,376
Toy Brokers Holdings Limited	£35,664,852
R.H. Smith & Sons (Wigmakers) Limited	£35,659,572
Newton Europe Limited	£35,654,276
A.T.C. Manufacturing Limited	£35,650,000
T.C.L. Holdings (Parent) Limited	£35,599,568
East Midlands Property Developments Limited	£35,590,000
APS Produce Limited	£35,564,000
Newincco 1382 Limited	£35,547,360
Microlise Limited	£35,537,000
OISE Holdings Limited	£35,531,600
FCC Environment Developments Limited	£35,530,000
Alconbury Packing Solutions Limited	£35,466,480
Equals Trust	£35,429,000
Sigma Components Midco 2 Limited	£35,420,424
Sigma Components Midco 1 Limited	£35,420,424
Eyre & Elliston Limited	£35,406,592
Longcliffe Quarries Limited	£35,402,660
Steeple Group Limited	£35,401,000
Knowles (Transport) Limited	£35,372,984
Chandlers (Farm Equipment) Limited	£35,367,000
Total Worldfresh Limited	£35,346,000
Mullahead Property Company Limited	£35,313,256
Woodway Holdings Limited	£35,296,592
Ischebeck Titan Limited	£35,290,820
Buzz Entertainment Limited	£35,287,000
Lakeside 1 Limited	£35,286,000
Kaystan Holdings Limited	£35,285,840
Ebuyer (UK) Limited	£35,278,404
Rea Valley Tractors Limited	£35,261,100
Ten Albemarle Limited Liability Partnership	£35,244,564
Leicester Lettings Limited	£35,243,232
Leicester Grammar School Trust	£35,242,924
Syncreon UK Holdings Limited	£35,241,920
Derry Building Services Limited	£35,228,948
East Midlands Academy Trust	£35,208,172
AU79 Limited	£35,172,872
Martin Duckworth Limited	£35,161,448
Fred Sherwood & Sons (Transport) Limited	£35,150,764
I.G. Industries Holdings Limited	£35,140,952
Pets at Home Veterinary Specialist Group Limited	£35,132,000
Limagrain UK Limited	£35,130,804
M3 Medical Holdings Ltd	£35,121,668
MacIntyre Care	£35,098,000
Impala Bidco Limited	£35,078,200
Keller Limited	£35,071,000
Valpak Holdings Limited	£35,018,000
Global Brands (GBL) Holdings Limited	£34,925,000
Wasps Finance PLC	£34,908,000
Belvoir Lettings PLC	£34,902,000
Albert Browne Limited	£34,877,000
Belling (1992) Limited.	£34,870,000
Atlas Hotels (Bath) Limited	£34,833,492
Healthcare Software Solutions Ltd	£34,819,684
Quest Global Engineering Limited	£34,812,000
KCT Holdings Limited	£34,810,180
DK Group Investments Ltd.	£34,728,472
John Taylor MAT	£34,726,560
Unipart Logistics Limited	£34,718,000
Harrowden Farms Limited	£34,717,120
CPRT European Investments Limited	£34,716,916
Arlington Automotive Limited	£34,706,000
Amey Lighting (Norfolk) Holdings Limited	£34,704,000
Amey Lighting (Norfolk) Limited	£34,704,000
Brighterkind (PC) Limited	£34,691,000
I.G. Industries Public Limited Company	£34,680,196
Orbital Education Limited	£34,634,080
Ping Europe Limited	£34,633,984
Saint-Gobain Isover UK Limited	£34,632,000
Gemini Rail Services UK Ltd	£34,624,000
Dynamic Procurement Holdings Limited	£34,603,140
Booker Direct Limited	£34,600,000
Speedloan Finance Limited	£34,574,856
Opal Ventures Limited	£34,564,036
Multi Packaging Solutions Asia Holdings Limited	£34,553,404
Kingsway Financial Group Holdings Limited	£34,546,804
Baslow Holdings Developments Limited	£34,519,048
Cosworth Limited	£34,494,000
Kaefer Limited	£34,478,000
Atlas Hotels (Group 4 Property 2) Limited	£34,465,352
The Aire Valley Land LLP	£34,452,000
W.Westerman Limited	£34,427,560
Synectic Systems Group Limited	£34,342,000
Openshaw Regeneration Limited	£34,327,528
Daisy UK Holdco Limited	£34,300,000
Federal Estates Limited	£34,291,040
Revolve Group Limited	£34,271,000
Jigsaw Systems Limited	£34,200,000
Beckett's Foods Limited	£34,188,644
MoveWithUs Conveyancing Limited	£34,170,176
H (Lincs) Limited	£34,164,976
Anexhold Limited	£34,162,740
The Coal Industry Social Welfare Organisation 2014	£34,129,588
Pendragon Finance and Insurance Services Limited	£34,090,000
Victoria (Bavaria) Limited	£34,087,000
Swann-Morton Limited	£34,020,244
Crystal Martin Holdings Limited	£34,015,000
TMI Foods Limited	£34,009,152
Strata Products Limited	£33,964,000
Dunstall Holdings Limited	£33,954,956
Alltruck PLC	£33,926,028
The Oxford Science Park Limited	£33,921,848
Ousedale School	£33,919,824
Seth Finco Limited	£33,914,612
International Piping Products (Europe) Limited	£33,893,192
Guilford Mills Europe Limited	£33,866,792
ILI Limited	£33,845,880
Partners in Property (U.K.) Limited	£33,841,200
RTI Advanced Forming Limited	£33,835,772
Go Plant Limited	£33,832,000
Dodson & Horrell Group Limited	£33,823,728
ITM Power (Trading) Limited	£33,810,000
Cooke Optics Group Limited	£33,801,708
Genistics Holdings Limited	£33,790,896
Genistics Limited	£33,790,896
Datapath Limited	£33,767,120
Stream Topco Limited	£33,766,776
Church Army (The)	£33,760,000
Bell Euro Finance Limited	£33,745,324
Smith & Sons (Bletchington) Limited	£33,740,144
Lancer Property Holdings Limited	£33,733,008
Resonate Holdings Limited	£33,713,000
UOS LP Limited	£33,700,136

Company	Value
Blue Skies Holdings Limited	£33,666,788
Synergy Health Managed Services Limited	£33,663,000
Tingdene Marinas Limited	£33,652,272
HTC Wolffkran Limited	£33,645,000
Resonate Group Limited	£33,625,000
Smith & Brooks Limited	£33,615,704
E. P. B. Holdings Limited	£33,604,320
Megaclose Limited	£33,593,644
Peveril Homes Limited	£33,590,424
Fernwood Group Limited	£33,584,072
CPRT (Europe) Limited	£33,583,692
Alliance Medical Holdings Limited	£33,581,000
Symmetry Medical Sheffield Ltd.	£33,580,000
5 Dimensions Trust	£33,572,072
Luxury British Design 2 Limited	£33,530,308
Synventive Holding Limited	£33,511,908
Denby Holdings Limited	£33,474,000
Luxury British Design 1 Limited	£33,464,330
Stadco Holdings Ltd.	£33,450,000
PCMS International Holdings Limited	£33,447,740
C R Shield Holdings Limited	£33,426,190
Carewatch Holdings Limited	£33,405,000
ACM ULR Limited	£33,378,000
Brunel Healthcare Manufacturing Limited	£33,375,000
R.T. Consultants Limited	£33,365,464
Roxhill Developments Limited	£33,356,780
Tanglewood (Lincolnshire) Limited	£33,331,404
World Habitat	£33,282,272
V.I. Risk Capital LLP	£33,276,152
Caledonia Topco Limited	£33,254,164
T.C. Landscapes Group Limited	£33,204,140
The Hazeley Academy	£33,190,288
Eagle Hall Estates Limited	£33,189,990
Gapuma Group Limited	£33,175,924
The Fallibroome Trust	£33,159,614
Carewatch Care Services Limited	£33,150,000
Rail Express Systems Limited	£33,145,000
Total Produce Holdings (UK) Limited	£33,135,000
Busways Travel Services Limited	£33,127,000
Morrells Holdings Limited	£33,124,520
Wigley Contracts (Barby) Limited	£33,100,232
Microlise Holdings Limited	£33,097,000
GI Group Holdings Recruitment Limited	£33,078,628
Munster Joinery (U.K.) Limited	£33,069,872
Lockheed Martin UK Ampthill Group Limited	£33,037,000
Economy Energy Holdings Limited	£33,005,000
Green Sky Energy Limited	£33,004,604
OGF Bidco Limited	£32,987,248
Fox Lima Holdings Limited	£32,984,426
The Lockwood Group Limited	£32,953,374
Palletforce Limited	£32,949,000
Sunway Travel (Coaching) Holdings Limited	£32,882,400
Electronics for Imaging United Kingdom Limited	£32,857,000
PFM Group Limited	£32,853,454
Consortium for Purchasing and Distribution Limited	£32,853,000
FCC (E & M) Holdings Limited	£32,851,000
W S Yeates Limited	£32,846,200
Renault Truck Commercials Limited	£32,845,000
International Logging Technology Limited	£32,830,000
Paccor (Mansfield) UK Limited	£32,812,000
Inwido UK Limited	£32,799,442
Morpeth II Limited	£32,792,272
Corrboard UK Limited	£32,787,916
Fresh-Pak Chilled Foods Limited	£32,774,000
The Boston Witham Academies Federation	£32,713,000
Valassis Limited	£32,708,000
Regent Park Energy Limited	£32,708,000
Totemic (2014) Holdings Limited	£32,707,020
Caroline Chisholm Education Trust	£32,699,700
Abel Investments Limited	£32,694,672
Lagardere Sports UK Ltd	£32,690,780
Maintenance Management Limited	£32,688,378
Manthorpe Limited	£32,649,282
Sleaford Quality Foods Limited	£32,638,272
Equity Solutions Lift Investments Cornwall Limited	£32,629,044
WCS Care Group Limited	£32,599,000
ADP Gauselmann UK Limited	£32,579,384
E.On UK CHP Limited	£32,558,000
IRESS Portal Limited	£32,505,000
Community Schools Alliance Trust	£32,500,032
Gallagher Investments Holdco Limited	£32,490,482
Terberg Environmental UK Limited	£32,460,976
Potter's Leisure Ltd.	£32,456,296
Baker Perkins Limited	£32,418,000
Nasmyth Bulwell Limited	£32,411,000
Lawrence David Limited	£32,392,168
Padley & Venables Limited	£32,387,528
Cemex UK Services Limited	£32,376,000
Welspun UK Limited	£32,318,000
Penso Holdings Ltd	£32,314,338
Birds (Derby) Limited	£32,304,436
Zyox Limited	£32,231,810
British Aluminium Limited	£32,226,000
The Tolkien Trust	£32,220,090
Unipart International Holdings Limited	£32,207,000
E.P.Barrus Limited	£32,185,528
Mills CNC Limited	£32,183,518
Brisbane House Limited	£32,166,712
BCN Holdco Limited	£32,136,000
FTR Holdings Ltd	£32,104,168
Newincco 1386 Limited	£32,102,980
St Matthews Holdings Limited	£32,059,432
DFDS Pension Limited	£32,053,000
UYS Limited	£32,022,000
Nexeon Limited	£32,020,000
Natural Assets Investments Limited	£32,002,558
Nottingham High School	£31,977,000
Maltby Learning Trust	£31,977,000
Castle Square Developments Limited	£31,966,944
Hunt Group Limited	£31,947,550
United Health Group Limited	£31,933,370
Bridgstock Limited	£31,931,000
Esendex Bidco Limited	£31,868,736
George Pragnell Limited	£31,849,356
Mass Consultants Limited	£31,821,000
Beardow and Adams (Adhesives) Limited	£31,820,200
Warehouse Fashions Limited	£31,800,000
Muirhead Aerospace Limited	£31,775,000
Djanogly Learning Trust	£31,768,000
UK Steel Enterprise Limited	£31,765,700
Gapuma (UK) Limited	£31,741,526
Forcefield Bidco Limited	£31,739,000
Gallagher Developments Caerphilly Limited	£31,731,340
Tanglewood Care Homes Limited	£31,727,570
St George's Academy Trust	£31,681,502
TH Finance Limited	£31,681,000
Smart Currency Group Limited	£31,674,088
Glass Recycling (UK) Limited	£31,621,044
Roof-Maker Ltd	£31,602,158
Wellbeing Software Limited	£31,602,076
Co-op Group Travel 2 Holdings Limited	£31,587,000
Willowbrook Healthcare Limited	£31,573,242
Simoco Wireless Solutions Limited	£31,566,000
P. H. Properties Ltd	£31,553,584
Lousada Investments Limited	£31,533,344
Global Brands Limited	£31,514,000
Dodson & Horrell (Holdings) Limited	£31,473,468
MGA Entertainment (UK) Limited	£31,473,184
Amey Programme Management Limited	£31,470,000
Kingerlee Holdings Limited	£31,452,000
Welsh Slate Limited	£31,438,508
Energy Alloys UK Limited	£31,405,644
Barbon Insurance Group Limited	£31,403,360
ESCO EMEA Holdings (UK) Limited	£31,401,000

Company	Value
D Hales Limited	£31,339,000
H C Bourn (Holdings) Limited	£31,336,004
Secanim Limited	£31,335,372
Special Quality Alloys Limited	£31,311,974
Magdalen College School Oxford Limited	£31,304,888
The School of St. Helen and St. Katharine Trust	£31,304,708
Proact IT UK Limited	£31,299,148
Huntson Holdings Limited	£31,296,802
Edina UK Limited	£31,288,676
Regen Holdings Limited	£31,281,240
Crockett and Jones Limited	£31,254,000
Byzak Limited	£31,254,000
I M Kelly Holdings Limited	£31,244,322
Thames Transit Limited	£31,199,000
Alan Bartlett & Sons (Chatteris) Limited	£31,194,474
National Floorcoverings Group Limited	£31,161,980
Rutland and District Schools' Federation	£31,133,968
Norfolk Free Range Limited	£31,133,952
Cooke Optics Holdings Limited	£31,092,606
G.A.E. Smith (Holdings) Limited	£31,067,378
Element Six Limited	£31,062,224
J.T. Leavesley Limited	£31,022,758
Fulcrum Infrastructure Services Limited	£31,020,000
Brelade Estates Ltd	£30,987,112
Dare Warwick (Properties) Limited	£30,970,922
P. Hughes Construction Limited	£30,966,272
Wrengate Holdings Limited	£30,958,404
Promens Holding UK Limited	£30,927,000
Accelerated Digital Ventures Limited	£30,925,540
R.J. & A.E. Godfrey	£30,923,104
Steetley Dolomite Limited	£30,918,000
SYS8 Holding Limited	£30,913,722
Slawston Investments Ltd	£30,903,892
Affinity Capital Works Limited	£30,900,000
MRS Environmental Services Limited	£30,878,000
Ivygrove Developments Limited	£30,870,600
Engie Fabricom UK Limited	£30,868,000
Buttercup Topco Limited	£30,843,464
Rebellion Developments Limited	£30,837,036
Mill Garages North East Limited	£30,837,000
New Co (Beith Street) Limited	£30,827,000
J.E. Porter Limited	£30,817,196
Krohne Limited	£30,814,990
Severn Trent Services Holdings Limited	£30,814,000
Fluidone Holdings Limited	£30,813,000
Alumasc Exterior Building Products Limited	£30,800,000
Orchid Orthopedic Solutions Sheffield Ltd	£30,793,000
South Lincolnshire Academies Trust	£30,782,958
Leica Geosystems Limited	£30,730,000
Bridge Leisure Finco Limited	£30,725,428
Hancocks Holdings Limited	£30,703,000
Goldmore Asset Management Limited	£30,689,084
Cavendish Learning Trust	£30,687,880
Bridge Leisure Midco Limited	£30,684,620
Ridgeway Education Trust	£30,633,000
Allen Diesels Limited	£30,627,280
Carter Accommodation Group Limited	£30,601,708
United Cast Bar (UK) Limited	£30,568,852
Lister Wilder Group Limited	£30,568,458
Lister Wilder Limited	£30,567,844
Bybox Field Support Limited	£30,560,090
T & W Group Limited	£30,537,508
Keepstem Limited	£30,536,480
PKF Cooper Parry Group Limited	£30,533,884
MacIntyre Hudson LLP	£30,524,516
Achilles Group Limited	£30,522,000
Nova Bio-Pharma Holdings Limited	£30,521,822
Synchemicals Limited	£30,464,000
Echostar UK Holdings Limited	£30,446,216
M.P.B. Structures Ltd	£30,430,564
Ackroyd & Abbott Limited	£30,428,472
Naylor Drainage Ltd	£30,423,270
The Move Factory Holdings Limited	£30,421,000
E.Park & Sons Limited	£30,407,784
Coast Holdco 1 Limited	£30,400,000
EPC United Kingdom PLC	£30,353,000
Ingleby (1981) Limited	£30,351,000
Datac Adhesives Limited	£30,319,000
Horbury Group Limited	£30,313,430
Sherwood Holdings Limited	£30,310,000
Kisimul Group Limited	£30,288,564
Oxford Diocesan Schools Trust	£30,286,560
First Line Limited	£30,266,716
Buckingham Plant Hire Limited	£30,257,186
Cullingworth Commercials and Freight Services Ltd	£30,239,464
World Vision UK	£30,207,000
Simons Construction Limited	£30,203,836
Belle Engineering (Sheen) Limited	£30,200,648
Hammonds Furniture Limited	£30,197,076
J & A (International) Holdings Limited	£30,188,420
CEVA Freight (UK) Holding Company Limited	£30,172,160
CMS Cepcor (Holdings) Limited	£30,156,884
Weddel Swift Distribution Limited	£30,156,000
F & G Holdings Limited	£30,153,660
Pye Homes Limited	£30,113,102
Global Experience Specialists (GES) Limited	£30,104,000
Marshall Amplification PLC	£30,101,176
E.On Climate & Renewables UK Operations Limited	£30,064,000
Hyde Group Tooling Limited	£30,044,060
My Home Move Ltd	£30,032,000
Ellucian Global Limited	£30,010,564
Commify UK Limited	£30,009,248
KRNS Properties Ltd	£30,001,920
Genie UK Limited	£29,998,000
MHR International UK Limited	£29,987,460
Ratcliffe College	£29,943,412
Grantham Investments Limited	£29,935,004
Home Retail Group Insurance Services Limited	£29,932,000
Mortgage Advice Bureau Limited	£29,914,120
NSF International UK Limited	£29,905,000
Northampton Saints PLC	£29,896,332
Electro-Motive Diesel Limited	£29,892,000
EOF Holdings Limited	£29,886,888
Ridge and Partners LLP	£29,876,888
SJC 14 Limited	£29,847,156
Cespa UK Limited	£29,838,000
Wellbeing Software Group Ltd	£29,837,228
Broadgate Builders (Spalding) Limited	£29,816,798
Millennium EFW Limited	£29,799,300
Crabwall Claremont Limited	£29,788,000
Michael Pavis Limited	£29,785,108
Wacoal Europe Ltd	£29,762,000
Sycamore (Peterborough) Limited	£29,750,804
DP Group Developments Limited	£29,724,000
Southern Derbyshire Lift Project Company (No.2)	£29,718,000
Oxford Policy Management Limited	£29,716,650
North Oxford Garage Limited	£29,714,158
Red & White Services Limited	£29,690,000
Sumo Digital Ltd.	£29,675,900
Strawson Management Limited	£29,667,000
Stepnell Developments Limited	£29,656,914
Headington School Oxford Limited	£29,645,774
Lindab Limited	£29,606,000
GES Service Companies Limited	£29,580,000
Childbase Partnership Limited	£29,576,340
Manitowoc Crane Group (UK) Limited	£29,569,000
J.A.Pye (Oxford) Limited	£29,562,964
Devonshire Green Holdings Limited	£29,546,000
Camden Motors (Holdings) Limited	£29,539,000
Videojet Technologies Limited	£29,508,000
Comex 2000 (UK) Limited	£29,495,312
Silgan Closures UK Limited	£29,489,000
A C Lloyd Homes Limited	£29,455,862
J W D Holdings Limited	£29,450,662

Company	Turnover	Company	Turnover
Heptagon Limited	£29,387,000	RPS Environmental Management Limited	£28,347,000
Pendragon Automotive Services Limited	£29,385,000	Roger Bullivant Limited	£28,326,000
Avery Care (Cannock) Limited	£29,349,766	A.B. Hotels Limited	£28,312,584
Ensco 1066 Limited	£29,331,360	CarnaudMetalbox Overseas Ltd.	£28,311,000
Woodthorpe Hall Garden Centres Limited	£29,309,372	M.C.I. Developments Limited	£28,304,000
Bawtry Carbon International Limited	£29,300,920	Huntercombe (BIR) Limited	£28,292,000
R.H.Topham & Sons Limited	£29,288,316	Malco Holdings Limited	£28,285,800
Ball Horticultural Europe Limited	£29,276,000	Stockport Grammar School	£28,237,524
A Shade Greener (F15) LLP	£29,264,262	DP Realty Limited	£28,234,000
Newell and Wright (Holdings) Limited	£29,256,876	Raynsway Estates Limited	£28,222,928
Charles Street Buildings (U.K.) Limited	£29,242,836	Moorhen Holdings Limited	£28,197,070
Liberty Merchant Bar PLC	£29,232,000	SEK Holdings Limited	£28,191,242
Cooke Optics Limited	£29,227,452	DW3 Products Holdings Limited	£28,186,920
Hajco 199 Limited	£29,206,000	Bassi Group (Nottingham) Limited	£28,161,900
Paragon Interiors Group PLC	£29,201,000	B.T.E. Plant Sales Limited	£28,134,394
Church Mission Society	£29,197,000	Diamond Power Specialty Limited	£28,130,000
Q V Foods Limited	£29,194,000	Nell Gwynn Limited	£28,093,992
Freshlinc Group Limited	£29,158,818	Chevron Traffic Management Limited	£28,077,856
Warners (Midlands) Public Limited Company	£29,143,580	John Adams Leisure Limited	£28,062,388
Time Right Holdings Limited	£29,138,092	Frutarom (UK) Holdings Limited	£28,050,000
Koyo Bearings (Europe) Limited	£29,138,000	Principal Healthcare Finance (UK) No.2 Limited	£28,034,000
Elmwood Trading Limited	£29,078,036	James Neill Holdings Limited	£28,028,000
Ronald Hull Jnr. Limited	£29,074,124	The Aylesbury Vale Academy	£28,020,906
MCS Group Limited	£29,069,998	Infinis (Re-Gen) Limited	£28,011,000
WRG Environmental Limited	£29,065,000	ESKO Stonecube Limited	£27,972,644
The Together Trust	£29,063,000	Star Bidco Limited	£27,972,588
Skymark Packaging International Limited	£29,050,004	In Vino Bidco Limited	£27,959,740
Zahawi & Zahawi Ltd	£29,038,650	Datapath Group Limited	£27,891,466
S.Walsh & Son Limited	£29,036,976	Gibbons (Holdings) Limited	£27,881,952
Greenyard Flowers UK Ltd	£29,020,288	Wintringham Newco1 Limited	£27,856,380
Wellbeing Software Holdings Limited	£29,020,192	Waterfall Catering Group Limited	£27,854,048
Mansfield Sand Company Limited	£29,003,996	Syncimage Limited	£27,851,192
ACESO Healthcare Holdings Limited	£28,980,000	Purico Speciality Paper Company Limited	£27,840,850
The Denbigh Alliance	£28,977,100	Milton Keynes Academy Trust	£27,840,644
Polydist (UK) Limited	£28,948,000	Richardson Milling (UK) Limited	£27,817,562
Wollaston Motors Limited	£28,929,992	Rolls-Royce Controls and Data Services Limited	£27,800,000
Ocee International Ltd	£28,923,568	British Bakels Limited	£27,791,000
Knights of Old Group Limited	£28,909,016	Rumenco Limited	£27,780,518
AP Racing Limited	£28,905,000	S L G Charitable Trust Limited	£27,769,662
Branchwater Developments Limited	£28,857,242	Twycross Zoo - East Midland Zoological Society Ltd	£27,768,468
Stonebridge Homes Limited	£28,854,764	Community 1st Oldham (Werneth and Shaw) Limited	£27,751,590
MTU UK Limited	£28,852,860	Combisafe International Limited	£27,721,000
Motorhog Holdings Limited	£28,846,332	HFG Holdings Limited	£27,719,492
Linread Limited	£28,842,000	BHCF2 Limited	£27,696,260
Surfreset Limited	£28,840,904	Expert Tooling & Automation Limited	£27,669,168
Financial & Legal Insurance Company Ltd	£28,799,274	Moorcroft Group Public Limited Company	£27,668,094
Imtech Engineering Services Central Ltd	£28,789,000	Montsaye Community Learning Partnership	£27,664,000
AIAL Limited	£28,786,872	Northbridge Australia Limited	£27,658,412
Flamepro Limited	£28,763,098	Watling JCB Limited	£27,657,000
A.F. Switchgear (Holdings) Limited	£28,753,156	Auchencairn Forest LLP	£27,653,038
GRT Nottingham Lift Project Company (No.2) Limited	£28,721,000	Clean Estates Limited	£27,652,270
Burbage Capital Limited	£28,700,340	ASD Lighting PLC	£27,649,312
Wigston Academies Trust	£28,690,486	Reesink Turfcare UK Limited	£27,616,120
A Shade Greener (F11) LLP	£28,679,552	Abbey College, Ramsey	£27,607,926
Grass Valley Broadcast Solutions Limited	£28,666,000	Henry Boot Estates Limited	£27,578,454
Rigby Private Equity Limited	£28,642,000	Wood Green Animal Shelters	£27,560,376
Shield Engineering (Syston) Limited	£28,639,328	National Space Centre	£27,549,616
Yourcash Europe Limited	£28,639,000	The Sports & Leisure Group Ltd	£27,546,556
Hartwell Holdings Limited	£28,621,000	AK Retail Holdings Limited	£27,529,558
HAE Global Ltd	£28,606,052	E.On Control Solutions Limited	£27,509,344
Comau U.K. Limited	£28,567,000	New College Leicester Trust	£27,495,556
Hertford Heath Limited	£28,533,252	ASD Lighting Holdings Limited	£27,491,424
CEVA Container Logistics Limited	£28,520,000	ID Medical Group Limited	£27,489,010
Parkway Hellas Holdings Limited	£28,500,000	AEM Limited	£27,455,000
Stratford-upon-Avon School	£28,498,000	SWK (U.K.) Holding Limited	£27,441,972
DPFP LLP	£28,449,964	Groves of Thame (Holdings) Limited	£27,420,798
PX Manufacturing Ltd	£28,387,940	Roe Bros. & Co Ltd.	£27,416,088
Project Republica Topco Limited	£28,387,012	Evolution Power Tools Ltd	£27,397,624
Flow Energy Limited	£28,385,012	Wrengate Limited	£27,391,848
Freshlinc Limited	£28,383,608	Terex Pegson Limited	£27,317,000
Lincoln Electric (U.K.) Limited	£28,367,000	Sheffield United Limited	£27,309,348
The Samworth Church Academy	£28,362,210	Frasers Retail Limited	£27,271,532

Company	Value
Blueprint Operations Limited	£27,267,118
Limes Estates Limited	£27,259,252
Envisage Group Limited	£27,229,000
FSHC Properties (Manor) Limited	£27,208,000
Imagesound Limited	£27,190,000
Langley Aviation Limited	£27,159,438
Fengrain Limited	£27,137,816
Inception Point Systems Ltd	£27,105,288
Kite Packaging Limited	£27,098,000
O.T.R. Tyres Limited	£27,078,000
History & Heraldry Holdings Limited	£27,058,708
Penso Consulting Ltd	£27,053,340
Pet City Holdings Limited	£27,034,000
W T Parker Holdings Limited	£27,032,618
Northampton School for Boys	£27,008,058
Holdsworth Holdings Limited	£26,963,476
Jensten Group Limited	£26,954,544
Sunrise Eggs Holdings Limited	£26,953,262
Barry Callebaut Holding (UK) Limited	£26,944,000
Timico Limited	£26,941,000
Evo Group Services Limited	£26,935,000
Accelerating Growth Fund Ltd	£26,920,336
Icopal Limited	£26,900,000
Mathematical Market Research Limited	£26,861,352
The St Neots Learning Partnership	£26,849,380
HaskoningDHV UK Holdings Limited	£26,844,944
Assured Group Limited	£26,824,406
Yours Clothing Limited	£26,820,168
Frutarom UK Investments Limited	£26,820,000
Wm. Nelstrop & Co. Ltd	£26,796,592
Aster and Young Limited	£26,795,252
Mellors Group Fantasy Island Holdings Limited	£26,783,000
Clegg Holdings Limited	£26,779,640
The Dominic Barberi Multi Academy Company	£26,767,000
Vtech Electronics Europe PLC	£26,760,000
Trison Estates Limited	£26,725,196
Turbo-Union Limited	£26,709,416
Top Tubes Limited	£26,687,120
Leics & Rutland Organisation for Relief of Suffering	£26,678,724
Seth Midco Limited	£26,658,000
Seth Bidco Limited	£26,658,000
DB Cargo International Limited	£26,656,000
PJ Care Limited	£26,641,616
Solenis UK Limited	£26,638,408
Lincat Limited	£26,635,294
Horticultural Trades Association (The)	£26,633,132
GBA Group Limited	£26,581,736
Tubes Holdco Limited	£26,554,000
Bodypower Sports Holdings Limited	£26,549,612
Pelagia (UK) Limited	£26,545,000
T.C.L. Holdings Limited	£26,528,968
Triumph Designs Limited	£26,522,000
Charterhouse Holdings PLC	£26,511,000
Emerson Process Management Shared Services Ltd	£26,503,000
Nu-Oval Acquisitions 2 Limited	£26,500,000
SAI Global CIS UK Limited	£26,484,280
Whilton Marina Limited	£26,482,548
Avon Estates Limited	£26,481,574
Experian SURBS Investments Limited	£26,466,000
TGW Limited	£26,461,712
J.R. Clark Limited	£26,451,512
Carter Accommodation Holdings Limited	£26,450,444
Lamb-Weston/Meijer UK Limited	£26,444,370
Hughes Network Systems Limited	£26,437,000
Kidney Research UK	£26,428,000
Northampton Rugby Football Club Limited	£26,421,112
Interflora British Unit	£26,409,000
A Shade Greener (F14) LLP	£26,395,048
Habitat Retail Limited	£26,380,000
Friar 148 Limited	£26,374,042
HBB Relocation Services Limited	£26,372,456
Vacation Rental Group Holdings Limited	£26,361,000

Company	Value
TI Group Automotive Systems (Deeside) Limited	£26,348,396
Elsham Wold Estates Limited	£26,342,422
A1 Comms Limited	£26,334,614
Horiba UK Limited	£26,332,724
Smallpeice Trust (The)	£26,301,880
Hormann (U.K.) Limited	£26,285,496
URA Ventures Limited	£26,271,000
Horsforth Holdings Limited	£26,262,000
New Era Cap Company Limited	£26,233,362
Sharmans Agricultural Limited	£26,210,172
DW3 Products Group Limited	£26,209,480
Bowring Transport Limited	£26,204,456
Wade Group Limited	£26,197,000
U-Pol Bond Limited	£26,191,000
Stonepit Limited	£26,190,816
C. Walton Limited	£26,185,036
Knights of Old,Limited	£26,184,356
Nova Laboratories Limited	£26,162,616
T & W Civil Engineering Limited	£26,154,290
Kite Packaging Group Limited	£26,142,000
Wyndham Destination Network LLP	£26,125,000
Summit (Oxford) Limited	£26,124,170
Birchall Gardens LLP	£26,119,712
Blackrock Secured Finance Limited	£26,115,472
The Nuttall Group Limited	£26,112,000
The Alan Nuttall Partnership Limited	£26,110,000
Hyde Group Limited	£26,103,618
A.W.Lymn The Family Funeral Service Limited	£26,091,282
Total Fitness Health Clubs Limited	£26,087,000
Autins Group PLC	£26,078,000
Lymn Funeral Services Limited	£26,076,478
Cosma Casting UK R.E. Limited	£26,073,000
Sodick Europe Limited	£26,030,948
European Electronique Limited	£26,030,936
Atlas Hotels (Bristol North) Limited	£26,020,732
Wellingborough School	£26,010,012
Sheepy Magna Investments Ltd	£26,004,672
Bardsley Construction Limited	£26,004,510
Aspall Holdings Limited	£25,999,502
Aspall Cyder Limited	£25,999,500
Benchmark Vaccines Limited	£25,984,696
Citigen (London) Limited	£25,965,000
Durr Limited	£25,939,000
Apertio Limited	£25,936,000
Ritter-Courivaud Limited	£25,900,000
George Bateman & Son Limited	£25,884,940
Barron McCann Limited	£25,801,308
Catesby Strategic Land Limited	£25,790,838
Coverworld UK Limited	£25,785,004
Ark Capital Limited	£25,776,000
Cheltenham and Gloucester Omnibus Company Ltd	£25,770,000
Dry Mix Solutions UK Limited	£25,765,654
Russell Building Products Limited	£25,749,572
Tiny Tots Underwriting LLP	£25,736,480
Brita Water Filter Systems Limited	£25,718,566
Chivgate Limited	£25,710,050
Randall Parker Foods Limited	£25,683,000
Tyler Packaging Holdings Limited	£25,677,138
Riverside Motors Holdings Limited	£25,666,892
Suon Limited	£25,656,334
Star Midco 1 Limited	£25,648,046
Fusion Group Limited	£25,645,000
Ashfield Meetings & Events Limited	£25,639,212
Quadrant Security Group Limited	£25,632,000
M.P.K. Group Limited	£25,616,446
Tessella Limited	£25,563,326
Miller Wates (Southwater) Limited	£25,558,276
Cathelco Limited	£25,557,468
Beckhall Properties Ltd	£25,516,936
Mark H Poskitt Limited	£25,512,144
Plastek UK Ltd	£25,484,766
Motor Neurone Disease Association	£25,480,000

Company	Amount
Verder Holdings U.K. Limited	£25,466,856
Northern House School Academy Trust	£25,447,726
Bearward Engineering Limited	£25,432,938
Compu B Ltd	£25,404,456
Berville Limited	£25,402,116
Lifeplus Europe Limited	£25,389,920
Picsolve International Limited	£25,366,000
Kannegiesser UK Limited	£25,363,388
Everris Limited	£25,361,000
Hadleigh Holdings Limited	£25,341,416
Mowbray Education Trust Limited	£25,337,000
A.C.Flooring Ltd.	£25,319,304
Alliance Medical Radiopharmacy Limited	£25,311,000
Trek Bicycle Corporation Limited	£25,287,584
Bombardier Transportation (Rolling Stock) UK Ltd	£25,281,000
Basildon Chemical Co. Limited	£25,270,318
J W Grant Co	£25,227,008
Secure Holdings Limited	£25,227,000
GI Solutions Group Limited	£25,211,000
English Partnerships (LP) Limited	£25,174,480
The Barcode Warehouse Limited	£25,172,182
Toray Textiles Europe Limited	£25,162,740
ENVA England Limited	£25,143,000
County Estates (Bakewell) Limited	£25,135,136
Bridon Holdings Limited	£25,130,000
Carentan Holdings Limited	£25,097,604
Polyco (Group) Limited	£25,086,000
AG47 Limited	£25,080,460
Agreserves Limited	£25,076,988
Unicarriers UK Limited	£25,051,076
Winterhalter Ltd	£25,037,508
Century Health (Nottingham) Limited	£25,027,772
Ditchley Foundation (The)	£25,025,448
Myton School Trust	£25,020,000
PCMS Investments Holdings Limited	£25,000,000
Hagerty Holdings Limited	£25,000,000
Roxhill (Peterborough) Limited	£24,976,416
Sterling Safetywear Limited	£24,940,996
TFHC Investments Limited	£24,940,000
The Princethorpe Foundation	£24,928,256
Pyronix Limited	£24,870,000
Burrows Motor Company Limited	£24,860,000
Ice House Street (No.1) Limited	£24,846,380
Bibliotheca Limited	£24,843,000
Apex Stainless Fasteners Limited	£24,838,102
The Wilkins Group Limited	£24,835,600
Respond Group Limited	£24,835,428
Atlas Textiles Ltd.	£24,833,822
Worldwide Fruit Limited	£24,804,000
MPAC Overseas Holdings Limited	£24,787,580
Hatchback Ltd	£24,767,354
M & M (MK) Limited	£24,759,384
Ball Colegrave Limited	£24,740,000
Ultimate Packaging Limited	£24,737,268
Salvation Army Trading Company Limited	£24,733,172
Celanese Production UK Limited	£24,710,000
Fesa (UK) Limited	£24,704,206
Cook Defence Systems Limited	£24,685,644
Resmed EPN Ltd	£24,673,830
DHT Finance Limited	£24,662,340
Pen Hill LLP	£24,651,792
Thistle Insurance Services Limited	£24,635,000
Scholastic UK Ltd	£24,627,304
Anti-Waste (Restoration) Limited	£24,609,000
Games Workshop International Limited	£24,582,000
Stanhope Partnership Limited	£24,581,840
Sansbury Bailey Holdings Limited	£24,553,000
Cullum Detuners Investments Limited	£24,532,000
Lattice Trading Limited	£24,520,816
The Senad Group Limited	£24,502,000
Tensator Group Limited	£24,480,000
DNA (Holdings) Limited	£24,466,232
Caldic (UK) Ltd	£24,465,160
Devonshire Green (Residential Investments) Limited	£24,463,000
Distinction Doors Limited	£24,454,630
Elite Office Furniture (UK) Ltd.	£24,452,628
Mettler-Toledo Limited	£24,443,000
Agrivert Group Limited	£24,432,394
ADA Pacific Direct Limited	£24,411,416
Slack & Parr (Investments) Limited	£24,411,000
Ascend Global Intermediate Holdings, Ltd.	£24,409,136
Payzone UK Limited	£24,394,270
Land Instruments International Limited	£24,370,000
Wheatcroft Collections Limited	£24,349,758
Murray Bidco Limited	£24,348,976
TTS Group Limited	£24,346,000
Broadgate Homes Limited	£24,337,748
The Tolkien Estate Limited	£24,328,696
QMS International Limited	£24,323,732
UAV Tactical Systems Limited	£24,315,000
International Brand Management Limited	£24,309,540
The Bird Group of Companies Limited	£24,277,936
Chesterfield Poultry Limited	£24,273,272
Billington Structures Limited	£24,259,348
The Mill Academy	£24,253,402
Central Glass Europe Limited	£24,225,632
CMS Cepcor Limited	£24,201,578
Speeds Limited	£24,197,162
Esendex Topco Limited	£24,194,658
Esendex Midco Limited	£24,194,658
RH Development (Property) Limited	£24,188,000
Great Tew Properties Limited	£24,183,120
Derby Homes Limited	£24,182,000
Pilgrim Foodservice Limited	£24,178,890
Bravissimo Limited	£24,166,080
Barratt Wates (Lindfield) Limited	£24,153,000
PJ Care Group Limited	£24,134,532
Diverseylever Limited	£24,121,000
Urschel International Limited	£24,102,098
Beeson Wright Limited	£24,100,966
Weatherbys Thoroughbred Holdings Limited	£24,080,232
Rockwell Commercial Holdings Limited	£24,071,000
Axis Electronics Limited	£24,063,894
SCX Special Projects Holdings Limited	£24,059,160
Dubois Limited	£24,047,000
Punch Promotions Limited	£24,044,604
Eden Supported Living Limited	£24,027,328
Elsoms (Spalding) Limited	£24,026,982
Porvair Filtration Limited	£23,997,000
GUS 2004 Limited	£23,987,580
Walter Miles (Electrical Engineers) Limited	£23,971,230
Princebuild Holdings Limited	£23,969,410
Marubeni Agro Machinery Holding Limited	£23,948,000
Lamport Hall Preservation Trust Limited	£23,943,742
Roca Limited	£23,929,000
Ibstock Leasing Limited	£23,921,844
Loake Brothers Limited	£23,910,484
Sunrise Poultry Farms Limited	£23,902,944
Melett Limited	£23,894,000
Silgan Closures UK Holdings Limited	£23,894,000
The Trinley Estate Limited	£23,888,188
Workplace Systems International Limited	£23,886,000
Jazz Pharmaceuticals UK Limited	£23,883,872
Just A Bank Limited	£23,876,156
Whitworth Chemists Limited	£23,874,412
Pera International	£23,811,000
Matsuura Machinery Limited	£23,808,780
Agri-Epi Centre Limited	£23,790,000
N.F.U. Mutual Unit Managers Limited	£23,782,720
Apted Holdings Limited	£23,782,416
Community 1st Stockport Limited	£23,755,348
Nickle Holdings Limited	£23,754,636
Tamar Energy Operating Company (One) Limited	£23,734,000
Sheffield South East Trust	£23,725,000

Company	Value
Equity Solutions Lift Investments Sheffield Limited	£23,705,180
Rochmills (Holdings) Limited	£23,703,516
Buxton Consortium Limited	£23,679,408
Lucy Electric UK Limited	£23,641,248
Newton Industrial Consultants Holdings Limited	£23,640,816
Moorcroft Debt Recovery Limited	£23,637,828
Thornsett Properties Limited	£23,614,762
Kawneer U.K. Limited	£23,609,000
HAE Group Limited	£23,608,820
Atlas Hotels (Exeter) Limited	£23,599,980
Project Sinatra Topco Limited	£23,588,340
Bio-Rad AbD Serotec Ltd	£23,531,758
Humphris (Banbury) Limited	£23,529,512
West Atlantic UK Limited	£23,472,952
Gardner Aerospace - Derby Limited	£23,465,000
Freiberger (UK) Limited	£23,464,196
Linkage Community Trust	£23,459,206
Integral Powertrain Limited	£23,458,008
ULS Technology PLC	£23,455,000
Mondottica Limited	£23,438,000
Insituform Linings Limited	£23,435,142
Staircraft Group Limited	£23,431,634
OAT 2012 Limited	£23,404,640
Q.E.P. Co. U.K. Limited	£23,393,000
The White Hills Park Federation Trust	£23,393,000
Esendex Holdings Limited	£23,391,956
Huntercombe (No 12) Limited	£23,360,000
Farmington Trust Limited (The)	£23,347,052
HD Holdings II Limited	£23,338,382
FCC Wrexham PFI Limited	£23,328,000
The Tibbetts Group Limited	£23,296,296
SDI (Enfield) Limited	£23,285,102
Artform International Limited	£23,279,000
Focus100 Limited	£23,277,000
ASSA ABLOY Entrance Systems Ltd	£23,246,000
Crestchic Limited	£23,240,000
Crowcon Detection Instruments Limited	£23,237,412
M.F. Strawson Limited	£23,236,514
O.A.Taylor & Sons Bulbs Limited	£23,232,678
PMC Fluidpower Limited	£23,229,962
Parseq Limited	£23,217,000
ISN Europe Limited	£23,214,898
GRS (Bagging) Limited	£23,214,482
Blankney Estates Limited	£23,213,062
Monier (China) Holdings Limited	£23,212,000
Office Space in Town Limited	£23,204,936
SCI-MX Nutrition Limited	£23,201,000
Amtech Group Limited	£23,194,000
Kumho Tyre (U.K.) Limited	£23,179,000
BBHP Limited	£23,178,832
Essential Supply Products Limited	£23,164,076
Amey Group Information Services Limited	£23,156,000
Pricecheck Toiletries Limited	£23,155,352
Severn Trent Wind Power Limited	£23,152,000
Giorgio's Continental Ltd.	£23,144,680
A C PLC	£23,131,512
The Laurus Trust	£23,116,000
Brooklime Limited	£23,115,240
Yourcash Solutions Limited	£23,115,000
Catesby Estates PLC	£23,048,462
Davison & Co. (Barford) Limited	£23,040,450
Eamar Development (UK) Limited	£23,024,084
Karsten UK Limited	£23,012,368
Banc D'Arguin, and Coastal and Marine Biodiversity	£22,999,992
The St Lawrence Academy, Scunthorpe	£22,990,918
Amey Ventures Management Services Limited	£22,986,000
Nibgreen	£22,979,872
Aus-Bore Estates Limited	£22,971,240
TVS Europe Distribution Limited	£22,953,000
The Warriner Multi Academy Trust	£22,946,990
E-PPL Holdings Limited	£22,943,380
G.F. Tomlinson Building Limited	£22,930,102
Binney & Smith (Europe) Limited	£22,915,000
Ragdale Hall (1990) Limited	£22,908,896
PIMCO 2909 Limited	£22,901,000
Fairline Yachts Limited	£22,886,000
N.F.U. Mutual Management Company Limited	£22,875,150
The Sandwich Factory Holdings Limited	£22,874,000
Chestnutbay Acquisitionco Limited	£22,862,000
Welbeck Waste Management Limited	£22,857,000
Tile Giant Limited	£22,856,000
The Kelmarsh Trust	£22,848,880
Empowering Minds Academy Trust	£22,840,560
Sutton Park Holdings Limited	£22,837,256
The Ecclesbourne School	£22,829,980
Hatton Academies Trust	£22,826,000
Rycote Services Limited	£22,823,828
Clifton Packaging Group Limited	£22,816,976
Technicut Limited	£22,813,464
Monocon International Refractories Limited	£22,804,108
Bramheath Limited	£22,790,800
Keigar Homes Limited	£22,784,028
P H Property Holdings Limited	£22,769,468
Freeman Automotive (UK) Ltd	£22,769,274
Network Services (Nationwide) Limited	£22,756,448
The Alchemist Bar & Restaurant Limited	£22,744,144
Thomas Bell & Sons Limited	£22,737,012
Country Court Care Homes 3 MB Limited	£22,722,986
Apex Stainless Holdings Limited	£22,721,348
M.J.S. Holdings (March) Limited	£22,720,636
Foundation Technology Limited	£22,720,000
Christys By Design Limited	£22,693,000
Teconnex Limited	£22,644,000
ACES Academies Trust	£22,643,336
Country Court Care Homes 3 SB Holdco Limited	£22,641,746
Strawson Holdings Limited	£22,640,000
Bardsley Group Limited	£22,628,084
Johnsons Aggregates and Recycling Limited	£22,603,272
Carwood Holdings Limited	£22,602,718
Carwood Motor Units Limited	£22,602,580
MAM Software Limited	£22,598,000
Seymour Distribution Limited	£22,586,000
Metals & Materials Limited	£22,585,000
Personal Group Limited	£22,585,000
Michael I Holdsworth Limited	£22,577,952
Ability Matters Group Limited	£22,567,000
South Yorkshire Investment Fund Limited	£22,558,688
Kingscrown Properties Limited	£22,546,896
Sibson Mill Properties Limited	£22,530,868
Lunette Properties Limited	£22,493,000
Raleigh Learning Trust	£22,479,000
Nationwide Windows Holding Company Limited	£22,477,468
Northampton Acquisition Ltd	£22,457,206
Country Court Care Homes Limited	£22,454,608
Weidmuller Limited	£22,453,000
Monarch Knitting Machinery (U.K.) Limited	£22,452,356
Partnerships in Children's Services Limited	£22,451,042
Capital Refractories Limited	£22,431,048
Vicon Motion Systems Limited	£22,419,000
Somerset Equipment Finance (UK) Ltd	£22,412,556
Euramax Coated Products Limited	£22,412,000
Yardi Systems Limited	£22,411,498
SRC Transatlantic Limited	£22,400,000
Rigid Group Limited	£22,397,112
Winbro Group Technologies Limited	£22,369,476
Winbro Group UK Limited	£22,369,476
Satellite Applications Catapult Limited	£22,369,132
Kab Seating Limited	£22,367,000
Nene Education Trust	£22,339,000
Essentra Services Limited	£22,337,610
Stream Acquisitions Limited	£22,336,624
Eastgate Care Group Ltd	£22,335,386
Stanton Investments Limited	£22,321,092
Home Decor GB Limited	£22,320,224

Company	Amount
Boal U.K. Limited	£22,309,000
Flocklynn Limited	£22,303,452
Vow Retail Limited	£22,300,000
Transaction Network Services (UK) Limited	£22,297,696
Broomco (3019) Limited	£22,296,680
Tennant Metallurgical Group Holdings Limited	£22,280,682
Mahle Engine Systems UK Limited	£22,280,000
Alliance Asset Management Limited	£22,277,954
Tegama Limited	£22,271,920
Chorus Education Trust	£22,259,824
Westbourne Leisure Limited	£22,258,310
East of England Agricultural Society	£22,252,378
BW Integrated Systems UK Limited	£22,238,028
Matrix Polymers Limited	£22,237,000
Vulcan Engineering Limited	£22,233,164
SDI (Nottingham) Limited	£22,231,964
Slough Enterprise Limited	£22,229,000
Bassi Properties Limited	£22,223,894
Silverstone Circuits Limited	£22,212,000
Lehvoss UK Limited	£22,207,444
Tennant Metallurgical Group Limited	£22,205,244
World of Sweets Limited	£22,201,000
Westbridge Furniture Designs Limited	£22,186,000
Dhollandia U.K. Limited	£22,155,434
OISE Limited	£22,151,640
Vernon Finance Limited	£22,111,988
Firstan Limited	£22,094,060
North West Portfolio (No.3) Limited	£22,086,516
Skills Leisure Limited	£22,085,128
Picsolve Holdings Limited	£22,082,000
Alkane Energy Limited	£22,080,000
C Student Services Limited	£22,077,690
BCM Specials Limited	£22,076,000
MK Battery International Limited	£22,060,096
3 R Construction & Property Development Limited	£22,056,052
Manitowoc Crane Group (UK) Subco Limited	£22,040,852
Project Jupiter Limited	£22,036,000
AMG Aluminum UK Limited	£22,035,756
Clytha Holdings Limited	£22,035,164
Maurice Crouch (Growers) Limited	£22,013,528
NFU Mutual Select Investments Limited	£22,011,832
Life Multi-Academy Trust	£22,005,956
Bradbury & Son (Buxton) Limited	£22,004,224
Thyssenkrupp Elevator UK Limited	£21,992,000
Industrial Control Distributors (Holdings) Ltd	£21,976,760
Briggs of Burton PLC	£21,971,000
Phenomenex Limited	£21,925,454
Sami Property Co Ltd	£21,925,368
Holophane Europe Limited	£21,915,646
Interflora Holdings Limited	£21,908,000
Centres for Assisted Reproduction Limited	£21,905,000
Syncreon Technology (UK) Ltd	£21,904,072
Ashby School	£21,893,000
Bansols Beta Limited	£21,892,198
HBM United Kingdom Limited	£21,883,000
Willoughby (396) Limited	£21,873,136
Investhom Limited	£21,870,408
Princebuild Limited.	£21,868,492
Orion Media Limited	£21,853,000
Freefoam Plastics (U.K.) Limited	£21,851,000
I Holland Limited	£21,819,776
Burford Garden Centre Limited	£21,812,016
Burt Bros.(Hosiery) Limited	£21,805,960
Mogford Limited	£21,800,748
Bicester Learning Academy	£21,798,260
Knapp U.K. Limited	£21,792,000
Natco Foods Limited	£21,791,392
Amnack Limited	£21,782,600
Mirza (UK) Limited	£21,782,240
Barnack Estates UK Limited	£21,779,844
A Shade Greener (F5) LLP	£21,777,000
N.R. Evans and Son Limited	£21,739,000
John Nicholls (Holdings) Limited	£21,738,084
Harington Investments Limited	£21,737,536
The Stowe House Preservation Trust	£21,734,460
C & P Bird Bros. Limited	£21,734,368
Ken Wilkins Print Limited	£21,734,280
Poste Hotels Limited	£21,733,034
Perspective Financial Group Limited	£21,719,958
Stanton Bonna Concrete Limited	£21,693,000
Bio Dynamic (UK) Limited	£21,689,888
Bodypower Sports PLC	£21,681,590
Preci-Spark Limited	£21,671,686
Tanvic Group Limited	£21,664,816
L Jackson & Co Limited	£21,661,828
Interflora Group Limited	£21,657,000
Aptuit (Oxford) Limited	£21,646,620
Steris Solutions Limited	£21,630,576
F.H. Farms Limited	£21,621,972
Utopia Holdings (Chesterfield) Limited	£21,612,812
Stagecoach (North West) Limited	£21,601,000
Premonition Analytics Limited	£21,600,000
Nu Instruments Limited	£21,595,000
Thame Partnership Academy Trust	£21,591,224
Broadways Stampings Limited	£21,590,018
Cozart Limited	£21,577,000
Hancocks Group Holdings Limited	£21,572,000
Lawton Group Limited	£21,560,000
Derby Diocesan Academy Trust 2	£21,540,388
Woburn Enterprises Limited	£21,520,904
Brownhills Motorhomes Limited	£21,519,916
Hosting Developments Limited	£21,519,916
Kartell UK Limited	£21,500,352
Premium Restaurants Limited	£21,480,392
Cinch Connectors Limited	£21,478,824
Fusion Plastics Limited	£21,456,000
Utopia Tableware Limited	£21,450,968
Mil-Ver Metal Company Limited	£21,443,748
Northfleet Property LLP	£21,441,366
Whitemeadow Group Holdings Limited	£21,435,616
Wilson & Co. (Motor Sales) Limited	£21,434,108
Arena Coventry (2006) Limited	£21,433,000
Grimme (U.K.) Limited	£21,413,880
Oxford Economics Limited	£21,406,392
Salus Healthcare Limited	£21,404,000
T.J.D. Trade Limited	£21,399,280
Spaldings Limited	£21,397,000
R3 Polygon UK Ltd.	£21,393,000
Eastern Counties Properties Limited	£21,388,382
Westbrook Resources Limited	£21,379,606
Holding Holding Company Limited	£21,365,380
Saybest Limited	£21,355,000
Hawkes Limited	£21,351,756
Fashion Fabric Transprinters Limited	£21,344,470
Equilibrium Healthcare Limited	£21,327,060
P2I Ltd	£21,318,128
Micronclean Limited	£21,314,632
Oxford Products Limited	£21,311,456
J. Curtis & Sons Limited	£21,303,880
Draefern Limited	£21,296,308
Tudor Hall School	£21,283,540
Ametek (GB) Limited	£21,271,000
Aspire Learning Trust (Whittlesey)	£21,265,452
Thermasys CS UK Holding Limited	£21,252,936
Hyde Investments Limited	£21,241,024
Topps Europe Limited	£21,238,248
Eraih Limited	£21,236,962
Relta Limited	£21,222,828
Metalysis Limited	£21,208,000
SMA Estate Holdings Limited	£21,203,602
Tsubakimoto UK Limited	£21,192,000
Euramax Solutions Limited	£21,160,000
The Snaith School Academy Trust	£21,135,268
Haramead	£21,123,240

Company	Amount
Four CS MAT	£21,109,614
Lincoln College Academy Trust	£21,087,820
Mortons of Horncastle Limited	£21,081,548
Digital House Group Ltd	£21,071,540
Alumax U.K. Limited	£21,041,000
Bolsover Cruise Club Limited	£21,032,520
United Rental Group America Limited	£21,021,776
Quint Holdings Ltd	£21,016,622
I Go 4 Ltd.	£21,012,030
Uris Central Administration Limited	£21,001,000
ThruVision Group PLC	£20,999,000
API Foils Limited	£20,991,000
Berwin Rubber Company Limited	£20,986,660
Briggs & Forrester Limited	£20,986,168
Global Real Estate Portfolios Limited	£20,981,624
Manston Investments Limited	£20,979,076
Coed du Hall Limited	£20,970,992
Source Bioscience UK Limited	£20,967,000
Herts Insurance Consultants Limited	£20,964,260
Port of Boston Limited	£20,960,000
St. Ann's Hospice	£20,954,576
Omnitrade Limited	£20,951,888
Insituform Holdings (UK) Limited	£20,945,000
Tyler Packaging Limited	£20,931,750
Bedfordia Farms Limited	£20,928,480
Nottingham Citycare Partnership CIC	£20,925,394
The King's (The Cathedral) School, Peterborough	£20,919,308
Lochailort Fairfield Limited	£20,909,460
Barron McCann Holdings Limited	£20,899,306
API Laminates Limited	£20,886,000
Eminox Limited	£20,876,000
Clowes Developments (North West) Limited	£20,871,302
Seashell Trust	£20,846,000
Remedi Medical Holdings Limited	£20,844,708
Morningside Pharmaceuticals Limited	£20,841,896
Mira Land Limited	£20,838,000
Francis Jackson Homes Limited	£20,837,956
Pinstone Securities Limited	£20,835,808
Whirlow Developments Limited	£20,812,564
Blenheim Industrial Property Limited	£20,803,216
Anti-Waste Limited	£20,792,000
Cheadle Hulme School	£20,768,000
Phoenix Sports Limited	£20,757,000
Norbar Torque Tools Limited	£20,743,920
Cheshire Datasystems Limited	£20,741,484
Neal Brothers (Leicester) Limited	£20,732,320
McGowan Investments Limited	£20,725,456
FSP Acquisition Limited	£20,720,000
North Lincs Property Limited	£20,700,908
TTG Global Limited	£20,700,000
Hilton Garage Ltd	£20,696,034
Abbeymill Homes Limited	£20,683,028
Growth Partners Management Limited	£20,679,212
Andaray (Holdings) Limited	£20,676,000
Blue Boar Holdings Limited	£20,667,080
Energy Developments (UK) Limited	£20,661,088
Seaham Investments Limited	£20,660,704
The Evolve Trust	£20,656,000
Sleek International Limited	£20,647,000
J H & A J King Farms Limited	£20,645,944
Moulton Bulb Company Limited	£20,634,594
Belchim Crop Protection Limited	£20,629,048
Weatherbys Ltd	£20,621,860
GPS Estates Limited	£20,610,172
Exol Lubricants (Rotherham) Limited	£20,592,528
Evonik Goldschmidt UK Limited	£20,582,184
Severn Trent Services Operations UK Limited	£20,565,000
RMS Group Holdings Limited	£20,548,840
Interfuse Limited	£20,544,008
Gladstone Limited	£20,540,600
Ingleby (2016) Limited	£20,515,644
Tilbrook Enterprise Limited	£20,511,400
Sloane Helicopters Limited	£20,495,982
Midlands Land Portfolio Limited	£20,492,000
Medical Equipment Supplies and Management Ltd	£20,486,000
Brigam Limited	£20,485,224
Coundon Court	£20,470,000
ESNT Filter Products Limited	£20,452,492
Centurion Finance (Lincoln) Limited	£20,447,448
Passionate About People Limited	£20,447,100
Harrison SD Holdings Limited	£20,447,096
SCCS Survey Equipment Limited	£20,437,000
Simon Gibson Transport Limited	£20,426,252
EDL Holdings (UK) Limited	£20,424,804
Asgard Group Ltd	£20,424,232
Olam Food Ingredients UK Limited	£20,421,000
Eastgate Care Ltd	£20,418,850
Stoneleigh Abbey Limited	£20,390,164
Mobica Limited	£20,385,598
Stewart Milne Timber Systems Limited	£20,384,000
HLD Holdings Limited	£20,378,000
Fugro Properties Limited	£20,349,000
Keystone Developments (LG) Limited	£20,349,000
Hard 8 Limited	£20,344,496
Spear & Jackson Limited	£20,317,000
Seaside Leisure Parks Limited	£20,313,196
Bauer Golden Square Limited	£20,293,000
E.E.Blyth & Co Limited	£20,287,196
Washbrook Capital Limited	£20,285,024
Hill-Rom Limited	£20,284,000
Wickes Properties Limited	£20,283,000
HBB Bridging Loans Limited	£20,282,732
Community 1st Oldham (Chadderton) Limited	£20,278,692
Groves of Thame Limited	£20,275,936
A Shade Greener (F6) LLP	£20,263,986
Danieli UK Holding Limited	£20,255,316
Hendrickson United Kingdom Ltd	£20,241,540
Solidor Limited	£20,240,808
St Therese of Lisieux Catholic Multi Academy Trust	£20,240,432
J.C.M.Glassford Limited	£20,233,344
The Barcode Warehouse Group Limited	£20,232,734
T.H.Clements & Son Limited	£20,214,000
Practical Action	£20,201,000
Bauer AR Holdings Limited	£20,200,000
Autofil Holdings Limited	£20,192,060
Llamasoft Europe Holdings Limited	£20,188,632
Agritec Holdings Limited	£20,187,200
Kingston Equity & Finance Limited	£20,176,028
K L Technologies Limited	£20,173,406
Hesley Care & Education Limited	£20,159,432
Newlincs Development Limited	£20,158,892
Sigma Precision Components UK Limited	£20,150,360
Cullum Detuners Limited	£20,146,000
Germanischer Lloyd Industrial Services Holdings (UK)	£20,144,676
Hague Farming Limited	£20,132,472
Roberts Radio Limited	£20,128,000
Atlas Hotels (Liverpool) Limited	£20,125,844
Sarval (Hartshill) Limited	£20,119,218
Polar Technology Management Group Limited	£20,109,220
JR Motorsports Limited	£20,102,108
The Blue Coat Church of England Academy Limited	£20,075,000
Compass Acquisitions Limited	£20,070,004
Phoenix Oil & Marine Limited	£20,066,000
Autofil Yarns Limited	£20,062,062
Yu Group PLC	£20,061,000
The Chiltern Hills Academy	£20,046,388
Fengrain (Services) Limited	£20,043,212
Loades PLC	£20,039,950
Jennings of Garsington Limited	£20,036,320
Benteler Automotive UK Ltd	£20,035,144
Diam UK Ltd.	£20,027,164
British Journal of Anaesthesia	£20,020,528
Wheeldon Brothers Limited	£20,020,234
M.P.K. Garages Limited	£20,017,444

Company	Turnover
Accuma Plastics Limited	£20,001,046
Astrea Limited	£19,996,318
Redbridge Produce & Flowers Limited	£19,995,000
Vine Hotels Limited	£19,980,616
Bennie Holdings Limited	£19,970,332
Westbrook Holdings Limited	£19,969,358
The Sheffield UTC Academy Trust	£19,965,000
Bridgebank Limited	£19,964,268
European Support Services (UK) Limited	£19,954,100
Bruker UK Limited	£19,945,144
TGW (Holdings) Limited	£19,943,736
Banner Plant Limited	£19,941,128
Morrells Farming Limited	£19,940,550
Swanton Care & Community (Glenpath Holdings) Ltd	£19,931,918
Peak Multi Academy Trust	£19,909,604
Amey Highways Limited	£19,906,000
Frozen Value Limited	£19,904,000
Oxford Property Trading Ltd.	£19,904,000
Atlas Converting (UK Holdings) Limited	£19,901,000
Paramount Holdings (UK) Limited	£19,891,644
Orchid Cellmark Ltd	£19,885,000
Remploy Limited	£19,882,000
E.On IT UK Limited	£19,875,000
H.B. Fuller U.K. Limited	£19,873,486
Pall-Ex (U.K.) Limited	£19,873,000
SDL Bigwood Limited	£19,871,274
Bucyrus UK Limited	£19,857,000
Eynsham Partnership Academy	£19,848,518
OQEMA Limited	£19,841,708
HCH Property Limited	£19,840,476
The David Lewis Centre	£19,839,000
Autologic Diagnostics Limited	£19,837,912
Huntercombe Properties (Frenchay) Limited	£19,834,000
Syncreon Automotive (UK) Ltd.	£19,824,850
Valpak Limited	£19,820,000
Autins Limited	£19,807,000
Cavalier Marketing Holdings Limited	£19,803,596
Steel City Holdings Limited	£19,803,092
Luxus Limited	£19,796,036
MCS Build Limited	£19,795,916
O'Brien (Group) Limited	£19,778,684
John Bell & Croyden Limited	£19,767,000
George Fischer Sales Limited	£19,767,000
Alwalton Hill Peterborough LLP	£19,753,870
PH Alderley Park LLP	£19,739,724
Eden Care & Support Group Limited	£19,724,902
Encase Limited	£19,719,000
Brett Martin Daylight Systems Limited	£19,717,976
Project Sinatra Bidco Limited	£19,708,072
Squadron Medical Limited	£19,705,000
Entertainment Magpie Limited	£19,683,000
Peacock & Binnington	£19,682,708
Peacock & Binnington Holdings Limited	£19,677,984
A Shade Greener (Boilers) LLP	£19,672,570
E.D. & A.D. Cooke, Bourne (Farms) Limited	£19,668,346
F.P.Smith (Holdings) Limited	£19,659,640
MHH Contracting Limited	£19,657,400
K9 Midco Limited	£19,654,000
Henry Boot Land Holdings Limited	£19,649,078
Selective Marketplace Limited	£19,641,448
C.S. Ellis (Holdings) Limited	£19,635,062
Nationwide Fast Fit Plus Limited	£19,599,192
P3 Group Europe Limited	£19,593,440
Caunton Holdings Limited	£19,587,320
Caunton Engineering Limited	£19,587,220
Vindis Developments Limited	£19,585,020
Corby Power Limited	£19,582,000
Focus Solutions Group Limited	£19,571,984
Affinity Trust	£19,567,834
J.E.Piccaver & Co. (Gedney Marsh)	£19,566,324
Lincoln & York Limited	£19,566,230
Community 1st Sheffield (Holdco) Limited	£19,562,634
SAI Global Assurance Services Ltd	£19,560,904
Poste Holdings Limited	£19,559,456
Armitage Brothers Limited	£19,552,000
The Chimneys Investment Company Limited	£19,543,568
Thomas White Oxford Limited	£19,529,900
Interfood Technology Ltd.	£19,520,728
Meter Provida Holdco Limited	£19,519,000
Charles Pugh (Holdings) Limited	£19,505,664
Polynt Composites UK Limited	£19,497,000
Warwick Ward (Machinery) Limited	£19,477,660
John A. Stephens Holdings Limited	£19,476,816
Right Digital Limited	£19,473,000
Halliwell Jones (Wilmslow) Limited	£19,472,282
The CDA Group Limited	£19,460,396
Velocys PLC	£19,460,000
Warwick Ward (Holdings) Limited	£19,458,414
St Barnabas Hospice Trust (Lincolnshire)	£19,447,540
Jepco Limited	£19,430,632
Norbrook Laboratories (G.B.) Limited	£19,429,700
Company Shop Limited	£19,427,000
Eclipse Colour Print Limited	£19,426,000
Emmett UK Limited	£19,421,000
Everyone Active Administration Services Limited	£19,402,366
Ten Cate UK Limited	£19,402,068
Marshall Street Regeneration Limited	£19,401,520
Senior Architectural Systems Limited	£19,397,584
Streason Limited	£19,384,328
Ritrama (U.K.) Limited	£19,378,542
Synarbor Limited	£19,371,122
Patrick Ruddy Homes Limited	£19,358,160
Kenwood Hotel Property Limited	£19,351,262
Ritelite (Systems) Limited	£19,349,188
Hillco Investments (UK) Limited	£19,331,678
Sawatch Limited	£19,327,708
Pharos Group Limited	£19,317,840
W.T. Parker Ltd.	£19,301,972
Willoughby Farms Limited	£19,291,736
Pegler Holdings Limited	£19,285,000
Hazlewood (Blackditch) Limited	£19,281,000
Sharp Laboratories of Europe, Ltd.	£19,275,084
Chalcroft Limited	£19,274,662
The Company of Master Jewellers Limited	£19,260,942
Jabco Capital Limited	£19,246,940
General Conference of The New Church (The)	£19,244,564
Magnavale Limited	£19,239,278
Grammar School of King Edward VI at Stratford	£19,238,088
CHT Holdings Limited	£19,238,000
X-Cel Superturn Ltd	£19,232,348
C.A. Strawson Farming Limited	£19,231,838
N.M.T. Plant Hire Limited	£19,231,676
Grantham Industries Limited	£19,226,616
Mark Jarvis Limited	£19,226,224
FEL Group Limited	£19,218,502
Selden Research Limited	£19,214,784
Apex Credit Management Limited	£19,211,000
Atlas Hotels (Salford Quays) Limited	£19,190,272
SLM Fitness & Health Limited	£19,188,212
Sperry Rail (International) Limited	£19,176,000
GEA Mechanical Equipment UK Limited	£19,167,414
Rigby Real Estate Limited	£19,166,254
Harving Limited	£19,165,204
Adder Technology Limited	£19,150,376
GLW Feeds Limited	£19,148,656
SGP Holdings (UK) Limited	£19,143,714
Bradfield School	£19,143,634
W. T. Parker Group Services Limited	£19,119,028
Bells Motor Group Limited	£19,116,612
H.R Bourn & Sons (Linwood) Limited	£19,084,720
Set Copyrights Limited	£19,075,584
Evans Halshaw.Com Limited	£19,072,000
Integrated Waste Management Limited	£19,071,000
Prodrive (Holdings) Limited	£19,063,000

Company	Amount
Brokerbility Holdings Limited	£19,058,232
Newtco Limited	£19,039,560
Atlas Converting Equipment Limited	£19,025,000
Technical Absorbents Limited	£19,025,000
Sunshine Care Midco Limited	£19,000,000
Hillsborough Investments Limited	£18,988,876
The Collaborative Academies Trust	£18,988,000
Dr Martens Airwair Group Limited	£18,982,482
Wolstenholme Machine Knives Limited	£18,972,480
Arconic Fastening Systems & Rings Limited	£18,967,000
Simmerson Associates Ltd	£18,951,592
The Mellors Group Limited	£18,949,000
Lablogic Group Holdings Limited	£18,932,572
Suez Water Technologies & Solutions Services UK	£18,932,000
Symon Donovan Properties Limited	£18,927,936
Arthrex Limited	£18,927,242
Entertainment Magpie Group Limited	£18,913,000
Chartmoor Estates Limited	£18,912,928
The Ground Group Limited	£18,911,886
Street Crane Company Limited	£18,906,432
John W. Doubleday Limited	£18,903,896
Allen (Hanford) Limited	£18,898,178
Nottingham Industrial Group Limited	£18,889,000
House & Home (Lettings) Ltd	£18,888,938
Flowmax Limited	£18,880,820
Real Estate Income Trust Limited	£18,877,268
Grange Mill Developments Limited	£18,870,796
Industrial Scientific Holdings UK Ltd	£18,863,642
J.H. Moore & Son (Rickmansworth) Limited	£18,854,728
Moore Large & Co. Limited	£18,854,628
Business Control Solutions Group Limited	£18,851,000
W.E. Hewitt & Son Limited	£18,838,624
Mistras Group Limited	£18,807,000
T.L. Care Limited	£18,805,692
Hampton (Burlington Court) Ltd	£18,792,778
Deeley Construction Limited	£18,791,536
Pyvot Limited	£18,777,224
SCGH Limited	£18,764,000
The Dunamis Group Limited	£18,756,820
Rockwell International	£18,747,000
Bridgebank Holdings Limited	£18,738,084
CRH Fencing & Security Group (UK) Ltd	£18,732,000
Citynet Insurance Brokers Limited	£18,728,236
The Holy Spirit Catholic Multi Academy Company	£18,723,884
Beeston Site Services Limited	£18,712,000
FSHC Developments (Properties) Limited	£18,707,000
Standard Motor Products Europe Limited	£18,679,072
DGS Group PLC	£18,677,900
Anisa Consolidated Holdings Limited	£18,668,000
Fibrefab Limited	£18,664,952
Old Road Securities PLC	£18,652,532
HJE Limited	£18,651,000
Vesso Limited	£18,647,436
Satra	£18,646,000
Elmdene Group Limited	£18,636,912
Gamston Kennels & Farms Limited	£18,628,800
Oceala Limited	£18,624,612
Denby Potteries Limited	£18,623,000
Oxford Gene Technology (Operations) Ltd	£18,621,312
H.K. Wentworth Limited	£18,610,020
Skills Motor Coaches Limited	£18,607,370
Samuel Hodge Holdings Limited	£18,597,996
The Lettings Room Limited	£18,597,394
Jourdan PLC	£18,592,000
Salus Controls PLC	£18,588,322
Techrete (U.K.) Limited	£18,584,350
SPD Development Company Limited	£18,579,000
B.A.Bush & Son Limited	£18,578,744
Riverside Motors (Doncaster) Limited	£18,572,256
Graypen Limited	£18,572,252
Delano Birmingham 2009 Limited	£18,572,136
T. A. Savery & Co Limited	£18,546,000
Aylesford School and Sixth Form College	£18,546,000
Airbus Military UK Limited	£18,537,504
Kitchen Range Foods Limited	£18,533,000
CEMA Group Ltd	£18,527,126
Farmstar Limited	£18,509,448
Fold Hill Foods Limited	£18,500,264
Essenden Limited	£18,498,000
Encase Holdings Limited	£18,495,000
Lemac No.1 Limited	£18,493,000
Dunlin Limited	£18,490,996
Happy Days Farming Company Limited	£18,471,036
KHL Newco Limited	£18,463,552
Bassi Fashions Limited	£18,462,420
Reconnaissance Ventures Limited	£18,444,496
Yasa Limited	£18,436,236
Belgium Topco Limited	£18,426,710
Alan Howard (Stockport) Limited	£18,419,922
Gateway Plaza Limited	£18,419,902
Dawson-Wam Ltd	£18,410,196
Lexington Catering Limited	£18,409,752
Molson Compact Equipment Limited	£18,406,220
Transforming Lives Educational Trust	£18,403,410
The Elizabethan Academy Trust	£18,400,954
H & K Distribution Limited	£18,396,256
Nicholas Associates Group Limited	£18,387,540
Spalding Grammar School	£18,386,160
ARRK Europe Limited	£18,380,000
Nicholas Associates Holdings Limited	£18,378,070
Hive Topco Limited	£18,372,744
Church Growth Trust Limited	£18,361,312
Portwest Clothing Limited	£18,353,524
Edge Wear Properties Limited	£18,308,456
A F Switchgear Limited	£18,287,772
Penmarric Limited	£18,278,776
R U Estates Limited	£18,277,204
Agema Engineering Limited	£18,268,906
Unipart Powertrain Applications Limited	£18,260,000
Vocare Limited	£18,258,656
Alcaeus Holdings Limited	£18,258,394
Madecorn Leisure LLP	£18,242,442
Jardentome Limited	£18,237,644
Aven Tools Limited	£18,229,000
Portbond Limited	£18,228,068
Weddel Swift Limited	£18,214,000
Rittal Limited	£18,197,000
Business Control Solutions Public Limited Company	£18,195,678
U-Pull-It Limited	£18,189,000
Taylor Shaw Limited	£18,185,512
Friar's Pride Limited	£18,178,222
SDI (Manchester Cheetham Hill) Limited	£18,163,332
MMR Research Worldwide Limited	£18,160,790
Flo-Mech Holdings Limited	£18,153,820
Resmed European Holdings Limited	£18,137,366
TSYS Managed Services EMEA Limited	£18,133,000
Rotherwood Group Ltd	£18,132,932
The Fleet Auction Group Limited	£18,128,872
Cape Engineering Services Limited	£18,127,000
Bellcoin Holdings Limited	£18,123,984
National Examination Board in Occupational Safety	£18,118,000
Cromwell Community College	£18,111,240
Moulton School and Science College	£18,108,970
ASK4 LIMITED	£18,107,544
Consuma Paper Products Limited	£18,101,324
SDI (Jersey Holding) Limited	£18,100,100
Pattonair Europe Limited	£18,087,000
Kleemann Lifts UK Limited	£18,086,256
Vivarail Ltd	£18,085,264
Ikea Distribution Services Limited	£18,081,000
Brington North LLP	£18,038,368
Linecross Group Limited	£18,025,768
Easternrose Limited	£18,022,276
A.E. Lenton (Holdings) Limited	£18,018,910

Company	Turnover	Company	Turnover
Fox (Owmby) Limited	£18,016,820	Franke Sissons Limited	£17,589,000
Bedford School Trust	£18,014,488	Clegg Construction Limited	£17,576,952
Solartron Metrology Limited	£18,010,000	Astor Care Limited	£17,567,838
Welspun Home Textiles UK Limited	£18,003,000	Truelove Property & Construction Ltd	£17,554,214
AGD Holdings Limited	£18,000,228	Easey Pigs Limited	£17,540,858
AGD Equipment Limited	£18,000,116	Donvale Holdings Limited	£17,530,310
Helford Land Limited	£17,999,104	Nikken Kosakusho Europe Limited	£17,525,488
Christchurch Court Holdings Limited	£17,997,292	P.J. Duffy & Son (Farms) Limited	£17,515,656
Pedigree Wholesale Limited	£17,995,936	Breedon House Nurseries Limited	£17,497,492
ITP Engines UK Limited	£17,992,000	Ellucian SMS Ltd	£17,486,460
Beumer Group UK Limited	£17,970,872	Peartree Oxford Limited	£17,485,580
Battle,Hayward and Bower,Limited	£17,966,548	Sterling Press Limited	£17,482,326
Simply Cartons Limited	£17,963,000	Beechcroft UK Limited	£17,482,000
Charles Bentley Properties Limited	£17,958,958	OSI Food Solutions UK Limited	£17,471,000
Paragon Property Investments Limited	£17,940,832	ENSEK Holdings Limited	£17,438,534
Bicester Heritage Limited	£17,929,714	Randomlight Limited	£17,435,680
Vulcan SFM Limited	£17,926,000	Nationwide Healthcare Providers Limited	£17,414,986
Northamptonshire Association of Youth Clubs	£17,925,564	Dalepak Holdings Limited	£17,412,624
Wheatcroft Properties Limited	£17,918,960	Norton Financial Services Limited	£17,411,876
Sarval Limited	£17,894,198	Bushboard Limited	£17,407,000
Mark Lyndon Paper Enterprises (UK) Limited	£17,890,826	Berneslai Homes Limited	£17,405,000
Samsons Limited	£17,862,304	Arena Blinds Limited	£17,398,000
Avant Homes (Yorkshire) Limited	£17,853,000	Healing Multi Academy Trust	£17,398,000
YLH Limited	£17,850,864	Alpha Holdco 1 Limited	£17,394,000
Barton Petroleum (Holdings) Limited	£17,840,644	Bulk Freight (Midlands) Limited	£17,393,144
Olmar Investments Limited	£17,838,000	Four Seasons Homes No.4 Limited	£17,391,000
Comtec Group (International) Limited	£17,835,000	E S Management Services Limited	£17,390,608
The National Memorial Arboretum Company Limited	£17,834,000	Yokohama H.P.T. Limited	£17,388,252
The Robert Carre Trust	£17,832,712	Key Technologies Limited	£17,385,000
Fairchild Fasteners (UK) Limited	£17,828,000	Wolseley Utilities Limited	£17,374,000
Mike de Courcey Travel Limited	£17,826,296	Envisage Technologies Limited	£17,369,000
Stainless Metalcraft (Chatteris) Limited	£17,824,544	Santa Maria UK Limited	£17,363,000
Distinction Group Limited	£17,824,536	IVI UK Ltd	£17,359,520
C3 Construction Limited	£17,824,064	H.W. Martin (Traffic Management) Limited	£17,358,936
British Pregnancy Advisory Service	£17,824,000	J G Pears Machinery Limited	£17,354,020
Commercial Legal Limited	£17,823,404	Harlow Bros. Limited	£17,353,252
Fulcrum Pipelines Limited	£17,823,000	PEM 2000 Limited	£17,327,808
Concentia Capital Limited	£17,818,000	Simon Jersey Ltd	£17,321,092
Bell Rock Midco Limited	£17,807,000	V12 Sports & Classics Ltd	£17,318,790
SDI (Market Road) Limited	£17,806,204	Meter Provida Limited	£17,308,000
Kenyon Forge Limited	£17,799,604	UK Distributors (Footwear) Limited	£17,305,522
Christchurch Court (UK) Limited	£17,792,680	Intelligent Energy Limited	£17,300,000
BM Catalysts Limited	£17,788,374	John Saul Limited	£17,299,194
Engel U.K. Limited	£17,778,514	Project Sinatra Midco Limited	£17,295,372
Omega Red Holdings Limited	£17,762,000	Quadron Services Limited	£17,294,000
Luxury for Less Limited	£17,730,196	Gelder Group Holdings Limited	£17,261,842
Oxford Pharmagenesis Holdings Limited	£17,727,488	Amey Investments Limited	£17,240,000
Bridon-Bekaert Ropes Group Ltd	£17,723,000	Parker Plant Limited	£17,235,000
Spurgeons	£17,722,000	Newco (First Street) Limited	£17,235,000
CET Group Holdings Limited	£17,715,000	AMG Alpoco UK Limited	£17,215,672
Go Outdoors Topco Limited	£17,714,000	Toby Blackwell Limited	£17,202,380
Amey Finance Services Limited	£17,713,000	Povoas Packaging Limited	£17,198,000
Marden Limited	£17,711,796	Stauff UK Limited	£17,187,892
Smart Garden Products Ltd	£17,709,296	Avery Dennison Retail Information Services UK Ltd	£17,186,000
Delano Sutton 2007 Limited	£17,699,188	Caistor Seafoods Limited	£17,182,314
Continental Landscapes Limited	£17,696,814	OKA Direct Limited	£17,163,826
Alvedius Ltd	£17,691,094	Solpro Manufacturing Limited	£17,161,200
One51 ES Metals (UK) Limited	£17,687,000	Northwood Tissue (Disley) Limited	£17,158,760
Clegg Food Projects Limited	£17,671,088	G.H. Parker (North Cotes) Limited	£17,146,736
Heart of England School	£17,667,000	PPF Limited	£17,116,388
Urgo Limited	£17,661,302	Daleacre Healthcare Limited	£17,112,164
Bachmann Europe PLC	£17,658,000	Nottingham Forest Football Club Limited	£17,107,000
Breedon House Properties Limited	£17,657,660	Stockcroft Limited	£17,105,530
A Shade Greener (F4) LLP	£17,652,520	Gatecrasher Apartments Limited	£17,094,000
Barrough Hospitality Limited	£17,647,784	Hill Care 1 Limited	£17,084,456
System Q Limited	£17,646,988	RE Evans Farms Limited	£17,080,676
UBT (EU) Ltd	£17,639,492	Kendall Bros. (Portsmouth) Limited	£17,074,056
Yutaka Giken (UK) Limited	£17,631,000	T F Bowman & Son Limited	£17,070,040
K & S Buildings Limited	£17,612,800	Insight Networking Solutions Limited	£17,053,892
Aarsleff Ground Engineering Limited	£17,606,680	Cellar Trends Limited	£17,051,138
A Shade Greener (F13) LLP	£17,601,684	Atlas Hotels (Inverness) Limited	£17,045,570
Lakshmi & Son's Limited	£17,598,696	Gardner Aerospace - Basildon Limited	£17,031,000

Company	Value
Principal Healthcare Finance (UK) No.1 Limited	£17,022,000
Al-Ko Kober Limited	£17,006,000
Eden Care Solutions Limited	£17,003,308
IRESS Solutions Limited	£16,996,000
James Convenience Retail Limited	£16,984,000
Peppermint Technology Holdings Limited	£16,983,980
Proact IT (UK) Limited	£16,983,000
G.B. Terminals Limited	£16,957,776
Gallagher Llanwern Limited	£16,956,448
Tripod Crest Group Limited	£16,955,652
Hull Holdings Limited	£16,944,852
Owen Greenings & Mumford (Holdings) Limited	£16,931,750
Totally Local Company Limited	£16,927,000
T.P. Hopwell (Holdings) Limited	£16,926,856
Hopwells Ltd	£16,926,354
History & Heraldry Limited	£16,925,326
Agrivert Limited	£16,910,436
Social Justice and Human Rights Centre Limited	£16,909,168
Arpo Global Limited	£16,907,318
Barton Petroleum Limited	£16,906,184
Advanced Marketing (Europe) Limited	£16,904,000
Topps Tiles Distribution Limited	£16,904,000
Belgium Bidco Limited	£16,898,430
Keyclad Limited	£16,895,412
Robinson Healthcare Holdings Ltd	£16,895,000
Nexus Multi Academy Trust	£16,860,824
Waterline Limited	£16,854,604
Smith Construction Group Limited	£16,854,484
PTA Developments Limited	£16,852,348
William Kenyon & Sons Limited	£16,848,080
Clientlogic Limited	£16,843,000
Pelham Homes Limited	£16,838,000
Pitacs Limited	£16,835,538
The Flannels Group Limited	£16,827,000
Horbury Building Systems Limited	£16,810,012
JDP Furniture Group Limited	£16,794,000
Wake One Limited	£16,787,068
P.C. Howard Limited	£16,779,960
Bewick Holdings Ltd	£16,776,964
The Hayfield School	£16,761,000
R.A. Gibson (Colesden) Limited	£16,759,308
Bystronic UK Limited	£16,748,000
Hall Cross Academy Trust	£16,732,000
Ball. Roller & Transmission Bearings Limited	£16,730,120
Burford School	£16,711,000
Wood Hill Heights Limited	£16,709,396
Seymour International Limited	£16,707,000
A Shade Greener (F10) LLP	£16,703,374
Hungerhill Academy Trust	£16,691,005
Exlabesa Extrusions (Doncaster) Limited	£16,690,285
TRG Bonds IV Limited	£16,685,557
UK Biobank Limited	£16,678,800
Anderton Concrete Products Limited	£16,675,824
Haywood and Padgett Limited	£16,675,472
Quantum Clothing Group Limited	£16,673,129
Lincolnshire Wildlife Trust	£16,669,554
Kybotech Limited	£16,657,945
Atlas Copco Medical Limited	£16,656,000
Liberty Group Holdings Ltd	£16,645,598
Claypenny Property Services Limited	£16,639,423
Rotherwood Healthcare Limited	£16,633,693
Tessella Holdings Limited	£16,630,599
Kadima Holdings Limited	£16,630,000
BGB Engineering Limited	£16,622,086
Limestone Farming Company Limited	£16,622,000
Apac Group Limited	£16,617,467
Nortech Foods Limited	£16,607,925
Envigo Developments Limited	£16,606,000
Bury's Dryanstore Limited	£16,601,305
Agellus Holdings Limited	£16,594,000
Accuride International Limited	£16,590,000
CAME BPT UK Limited	£16,586,389
Lexitron Limited	£16,584,190
London Wiper Company Limited	£16,580,775
Bullimores Sand and Gravel Limited	£16,577,584
Abbotsley Farms Limited	£16,570,914
TII Technologies Limited	£16,569,326
Flo-Mech. Limited	£16,568,132
Dransfield Properties Finance Limited	£16,565,775
Rudridge Limited	£16,562,000
Grundon Sand & Gravel Limited	£16,561,905
J.H. Bacon Limited	£16,558,602
Emerson Management Services Limited	£16,553,057
Cape Environmental Services Onshore Limited	£16,553,000
Freightroute Limited	£16,552,893
Swanton Care & Community (Autism North) Limited	£16,547,625
Sywell Aerodrome,Limited	£16,546,482
Gallos Limited	£16,542,452
Saint-Gobain Performance Plastics Rencol Limited	£16,536,000
Four Seasons Health Care (Capital) Limited	£16,524,000
Sobell House Hospice Charity Limited	£16,519,417
Loadhog Limited	£16,518,220
Elisabeth The Chef Limited	£16,517,000
P.A. Estates Management Limited	£16,515,096
Choice Packaging Solutions Limited	£16,513,539
G.B.Turnbull Limited	£16,504,861
Praesepe Limited	£16,501,000
Satra Technology Centre Limited	£16,498,000
RTI Extrusions Europe Limited	£16,497,528
Solidus UK Solutions Ltd	£16,497,526
Canon Street Properties Limited	£16,492,414
Lowdham Leisureworld Ltd	£16,484,935
Stamford Property Company Limited	£16,482,476
CMI International Limited	£16,482,000
Woolley Bros. (Wholesale Meats) Limited	£16,480,908
Chalcroft Holdings Limited	£16,477,751
Forest Commercial Services Limited	£16,475,931
R C Tinsley 2012 Limited	£16,466,076
Campbell Scientific Limited	£16,464,374
The Freeman Company (UK) Limited	£16,461,000
T. Quality Limited	£16,453,471
Red Box Recorders Group Limited	£16,451,000
Keyence (UK) Limited	£16,449,613
Scotts Hire Limited	£16,444,590
H.W. Martin (Plant) Limited	£16,438,168
Wrendal Holdings Limited	£16,434,415
Storefield Group Limited	£16,427,610
Rowe Farming Limited	£16,421,000
PWP Building Services (Holdings) Limited	£16,418,966
Infinis Energy Services Limited	£16,413,000
Tamar (Selby) Limited	£16,411,788
RHS UK Holdings Limited	£16,398,000
Fandstan Electric Limited	£16,396,727
Oxford Pharmagenesis Limited	£16,395,210
The Pope Francis Catholic Multi Academy Company	£16,393,342
Dorothy Goodman School	£16,390,000
Fernbrook Investments (UK) Limited	£16,388,005
EGR Europe Limited	£16,387,822
D.H.Sanderson and Son Limited	£16,384,989
Paccar Parts U.K. Limited	£16,384,000
Lincat Group Limited	£16,383,962
Cygnia Logistics Limited	£16,381,903
J.G. Pears Limited	£16,369,623
Nationwide Windows Limited	£16,368,382
Ponsford Trading Limited	£16,366,892
Tullis Russell Coaters Limited	£16,359,000
Elsham Linc Limited	£16,355,370
Personal Assurance Public Limited Company	£16,352,000
Swanscombe Development LLP	£16,347,991
Charles Pugh (Glass) Limited	£16,338,299
Guilford Mills Limited	£16,328,470
Durham & Co Holdings Limited	£16,321,176
Scott's Developments Limited	£16,311,964
Pico Technology (Holdings) Limited	£16,307,159

Company	Amount
Boels Rental Limited	£16,303,964
Vehicle Credit Limited	£16,302,764
Denaro Partners LLP	£16,299,361
Encore Personnel Services Limited	£16,297,853
Berkshire, Buckinghamshire and Oxon Wildlife Trust	£16,296,000
ESNT Packaging & Securing Solutions Limited	£16,296,000
Redborne Upper School and Community College	£16,289,350
The Esland Group Limited	£16,285,993
Sun Healthcare Limited	£16,277,444
F.H.Rowse Limited	£16,274,960
Synergy Fund LLP	£16,264,006
Long Rake Spar Company Limited (The)	£16,263,875
Daimler Insurance Services UK Limited	£16,250,005
Magenta Storage Limited	£16,248,678
Wilkin Chapman LLP	£16,247,229
Wildgoose Construction Limited	£16,236,985
Diocese of Southwell and Nottingham Multi-Academy	£16,232,282
Forcefield Midco Limited	£16,226,000
Acorn Industrial Services Group Ltd	£16,222,389
Southport Golf Complex Limited	£16,220,996
Bantham Holdings Ltd	£16,209,586
Denaro (UK) Limited	£16,208,622
The Latvian Welfare Trust	£16,204,265
Ontex Healthcare UK Limited	£16,191,248
Buxton Press Limited	£16,188,802
The Clarendon Office Group Ltd.	£16,188,408
Strawson Limited	£16,180,023
Saw Property Company Limited	£16,162,275
Lincoln Science and Innovation Park Limited	£16,162,000
Swanton Care & Community (Maesteilo Care Homes)	£16,157,346
Mount St Mary's	£16,147,785
Albumedix Ltd	£16,125,000
Bell Equipment UK Limited	£16,119,246
Quicksilver Euro Loanco Limited	£16,119,000
British Waterways Marinas Limited	£16,114,944
Certikin International Limited	£16,114,825
Harrison Catering Services Limited	£16,113,552
Meter Provida Investments Limited	£16,111,000
Abney Trust	£16,106,212
Shield Properties Limited	£16,097,675
Hill-Rom UK (Holdings) Ltd	£16,093,000
Woodard Schools (Nottinghamshire) Limited	£16,091,216
Leen Gate Metals Limited	£16,085,271
Kaby Engineers Limited	£16,081,293
M.C.Mountain and Son Limited	£16,078,935
Boden & Davies Limited	£16,078,663
Semelab Limited	£16,075,000
Ulverscroft Group Limited	£16,066,000
Genie Topco Limited	£16,063,000
Total Computer Networks Limited	£16,062,277
BBB Services Limited	£16,060,391
St Ivo School	£16,058,093
FIM Solar Generation I LLP	£16,053,408
Tinsley Bridge Group Limited	£16,053,001
Quicksilver Dollar Loanco Limited	£16,053,000
Paul John Construction (Leicester) Limited	£16,047,551
Phoenix Transworld Limited	£16,046,000
Carbolite Holdings Limited	£16,040,409
Wellbeing Software Group Holdings Limited	£16,039,476
The Beechwood Estates Co.Limited	£16,030,155
Bericote Holdings Limited	£16,029,868
David Nieper Limited	£16,021,613
Trafalgar Court Northern Limited	£16,004,016
PWP Building Services Limited	£16,002,735
Tripleteam (Developments) Limited	£16,000,256
FCC Buckinghamshire Holdings Limited	£16,000,000
Saul Construction Limited	£15,985,385
Toymaster Limited	£15,969,000
1LIFE Management Solutions Limited	£15,968,000
RDG Midas Holdings (NI) Limited	£15,952,000
Hanborough Enterprises Limited	£15,951,372
Stonbury (Holdings) Limited	£15,947,746

Company	Amount
Langridge Homes Limited	£15,946,438
Huber + Suhner (UK) Limited	£15,944,000
Germany Farms Limited	£15,937,005
Scania Real Estate (UK) Limited	£15,934,618
The Academy @ Ridgewood Trust	£15,921,000
Regent Office Care Limited	£15,920,167
Champion Employment Limited	£15,915,368
Juniper Pharma Services Limited	£15,897,325
Castle Phoenix Trust	£15,897,025
Sunway Travel (Coaching) Limited	£15,894,209
Rannoch Food Group Limited	£15,890,600
Atlas Hotels (Glasgow) Limited	£15,884,934
The West Grantham Academies Trust	£15,876,771
Jepson & Co Limited	£15,876,416
GRI Libra Limited	£15,863,541
George Utz Limited	£15,862,000
Iceni Marine Services Limited	£15,861,246
Remy Cointreau UK Distribution Limited	£15,852,757
Manthorpe Building Products Limited	£15,847,099
Waterloo Quay Properties Limited	£15,846,381
Warwick Energy Limited	£15,839,028
Gardeden Midco Limited	£15,837,711
Universal Components UK Limited	£15,832,000
Carrier Refrigeration UK Limited	£15,830,000
M.Markovitz Limited	£15,829,443
Fir Vale School Academy Trust	£15,818,579
Gafoor Pure Halal Ltd	£15,816,910
Asteelflash (Bedford) Limited	£15,814,000
Aptean Limited	£15,811,436
Energy Technologies Institute LLP	£15,808,000
New Co (Newcastle) Limited	£15,793,000
Walter John Cook and Sons Limited	£15,791,169
Greene Tweed & Co Limited	£15,783,000
Forman Hardy Holdings Limited	£15,776,000
T N Capital Limited	£15,755,569
AWG Land Holdings Limited	£15,729,000
Independent Forgings & Alloys Limited	£15,719,572
Morningside Holdings Ltd	£15,713,345
Investfront (Oxon) Limited	£15,712,550
John A. Stephens Limited	£15,711,331
FCC Environment (Lincolnshire) Limited	£15,708,000
Bourne Grammar School	£15,707,177
Mallory Court Hotel Limited	£15,702,645
Aferry Ltd	£15,689,706
Michael Goodall Quality Homes Limited	£15,682,621
Elsoms Seeds Limited	£15,677,365
Brian James Trailers Limited	£15,675,592
Sundial Group Limited	£15,674,969
Recresco Limited	£15,671,505
SDI (Kingston) Limited	£15,669,615
Chestnut Homes Limited	£15,663,254
Bardsley Construction Holdings Limited	£15,660,832
North Bidco Limited	£15,655,510
C3 Construction Holdings Limited	£15,641,490
Congregational & General Charitable Trust (The)	£15,638,399
Talasey Ltd	£15,637,078
Broomgrove Properties Limited	£15,636,860
HBPO UK Limited	£15,635,246
H.W. Martin (Farms) LLP	£15,631,992
Lloyd Fraser Holdings Company Limited	£15,621,143
Sumo Digital Group Limited	£15,620,764
Robinson Healthcare Group Limited	£15,618,000
Archipelago Learning Holdings UK Limited	£15,615,130
PKF Cooper Parry LLP	£15,607,403
Whitecross@Stepnell Limited	£15,605,648
GEO Amey PECS Limited	£15,585,000
Nelsons Solicitors Limited	£15,576,820
F. Vindis & Sons (Sawston) Limited	£15,575,142
P.D. Hook (Rearing) Limited	£15,575,000
G.E. Porter & Sons Limited	£15,574,723
Kesteven and Grantham Girls' School Academy Trust	£15,574,587
A.C. Lloyd Holdings Limited	£15,567,460

Company	Value
T.D.P. Textiles Limited	£15,566,025
A J Mackaness Holdings Limited	£15,558,902
Bury Farm Sharpenhoe Limited	£15,556,298
A.J.Mackaness Limited	£15,551,749
GN Hearing UK Ltd	£15,548,342
P V H Holdings Limited	£15,532,225
Outdoor & Sports Company Limited	£15,532,123
Adam Equipment Co. Limited	£15,528,484
JTF Wholesale Limited	£15,527,000
Norbar Torque Tools Holdings Limited	£15,526,017
Firstan Holdings Limited	£15,523,632
Copley Scientific Limited	£15,517,443
Viewtone Limited	£15,516,000
The Lapwing Estate Limited	£15,510,614
Hicks (1) Limited	£15,508,969
CTDI Glenrothes Limited	£15,495,000
Philex Limited	£15,493,788
RTC Group PLC	£15,488,000
Autumnpark Limited	£15,470,725
C.John Norris (Cars & Caravans) Limited	£15,464,725
Technical Consumer Products Limited	£15,464,194
Britcon (UK) Limited	£15,462,231
Universal Flexible Packaging Limited	£15,459,610
Soncell International Limited	£15,450,418
Scantronic Holdings Limited	£15,449,000
Starkey Laboratories Limited	£15,446,542
Mahle Filter Systems UK Limited	£15,436,000
Vale Garden Houses Limited	£15,433,567
Hancocks Midco Limited	£15,432,000
Detrafford Sky Gardens Ltd	£15,431,956
Hotel MK Limited	£15,429,681
Complete Medical Group Worldwide Limited	£15,427,000
CMD Limited	£15,421,458
William Cook Cast Products Limited	£15,400,781
Kelkay Limited	£15,376,045
R Group Holdings Limited	£15,374,000
Granby Care Limited	£15,363,000
Proimmune Limited	£15,358,205
Gartree High School	£15,350,434
Bucks Investments Limited	£15,339,566
Buffaload Logistics Limited	£15,337,059
Amey Ventures Limited	£15,337,000
Westernrange Limited	£15,335,072
IFA Metals International Limited	£15,331,519
Sheffield Theatres Trust	£15,313,691
Tadano UK Ltd	£15,308,765
Group GTI Ltd	£15,302,493
TFHC 2015 Limited	£15,302,000
G F Tomlinson & Sons Ltd	£15,301,581
Accrofab Limited	£15,301,156
Hydrainer Pump Hire Limited	£15,295,568
Whizstock	£15,294,905
Static Control Components (Europe) Limited	£15,291,000
Hella Limited	£15,289,000
Atlas Hotels (Lincoln) Limited	£15,285,746
Ashmere Derbyshire Limited	£15,276,919
Catalent UK Supply Chain Limited	£15,276,553
Campion School & Language College	£15,269,586
R.A.Labone & Co Limited	£15,266,456
Whitemeadow Furniture Limited	£15,265,425
W.S.Chapman & Sons Limited	£15,258,661
Retail Merchant Finance Limited	£15,256,734
Wreake Valley Academy Trust	£15,255,000
The Lutterworth Academies Trust	£15,255,000
Braeside Group Limited	£15,245,118
MM Flowers Limited	£15,242,891
G. & R. Pykett Limited	£15,241,685
Nexans Logistics Limited	£15,240,179
Seckloe 297 Limited	£15,238,863
Thames Valley Cambac Limited	£15,238,503
First National Housing Trust Limited	£15,238,195
The Premier Group (Coventry) Limited	£15,230,954
Sovereign Crest Limited	£15,230,130
The Myers-Briggs Company (Europe) Limited	£15,226,960
OGF Topco Limited	£15,221,880
New City Hotels Limited	£15,220,027
H W Martin Waste Limited	£15,219,965
Asmet Limited	£15,219,460
Gee Bee Investments Limited	£15,208,432
Axis Intermodal Limited	£15,195,000
Novera Energy Generation No. 2 Limited	£15,191,000
ALS Environmental Limited	£15,190,000
Joseph Camm Farms Limited	£15,188,856
Alkane Energy CM Limited	£15,184,000
Cad Cam Holdings Limited	£15,166,791
Sterigenics UK Limited	£15,163,000
Pentagon Chrysler (Barnsley) Limited	£15,158,478
Inspire Education Trust	£15,156,705
Diversey UK Production Limited	£15,156,000
M.S.W (UK) Limited	£15,142,000
ESCO (UK) Holdings Limited	£15,135,000
Tolsa UK Limited	£15,134,000
Vinyl Compounds Holdings Limited	£15,127,357
Pyrotek Engineering Materials Limited	£15,122,706
VGI Holdings Limited	£15,121,763
Mitchell Diesel Limited	£15,119,251
Axis EMS Group Limited	£15,118,101
Watch Shop Ltd	£15,110,706
Meller Group Limited	£15,103,024
Icon Aerospace Technology Ltd	£15,102,000
Haughton Textiles Limited	£15,100,000
Collingwood Lighting Limited	£15,099,000
Hermitage Holdings (Wilmslow) Limited	£15,097,449
XPO Maintenance UK Limited	£15,094,000
VRES Holdings Limited	£15,088,000
Polypearl Management Ltd	£15,079,195
Bradgate Containers (Holdings) Limited	£15,070,836
Hichrom Limited	£15,070,568
Hook Norton Brewery Company,Limited (The)	£15,070,130
Technia Limited	£15,069,246
Sytner Vehicles Limited	£15,065,000
Leeson Chemicals Limited	£15,058,465
Summerfields School Trust,Limited	£15,052,345
Jaybeam Limited	£15,051,243
Hive Bidco Limited	£15,050,608
The Rolleston Hall Estates Limited	£15,045,641
Lucy Electric (EMS) Limited	£15,042,389
Techman Engineering Ltd.	£15,040,766
John Martin-Hoyes (Holdings) Limited	£15,038,335
LTI Metaltech Limited	£15,038,270
Gardner Aerospace-Broughton Limited	£15,036,000
Tytherington School	£15,030,000
Oxford Centre for Hebrew and Jewish Studies	£15,026,977
Education Solutions Speke Limited	£15,025,134
Thomas White Properties Limited	£15,020,046
HID Estates Limited	£15,017,495
Carno 2 LLP	£15,016,204
Manston Forests LLP	£15,008,161
Luxfab Limited	£15,002,966
Meynell Plant Hire Limited	£15,000,612
Auction Finance Limited	£15,000,000
Bourbon Automotive Plastics Northampton Limited	£14,992,073
Kingsway Leasing Limited	£14,981,897
Kent Pharmaceuticals Limited	£14,979,000
Lukegate Limited	£14,978,876
Wycliffe Hall	£14,977,116
Armstrong Brooks Limited	£14,975,103
Sunrisestar Limited	£14,974,522
Ballyclare Limited	£14,966,950
Atlas Hotels (Warwick) Limited	£14,966,200
Lockwood Estates Limited	£14,962,579
Willoughby 395 (EBK) Limited	£14,960,616
Jenoptik Holdings UK Ltd	£14,960,052
Cambridge Nutritional Foods Limited	£14,955,309

Company	Amount
Palm Recycling Limited	£14,946,428
Community 1st Oldham Tranche 2 Limited	£14,942,849
Bartec Auto ID Limited	£14,942,688
Searles (Camping Ground) Limited	£14,942,513
Bush & Company Rehabilitation Limited	£14,941,000
Frank Key Group Limited	£14,937,033
BASF Agricultural Specialities Limited	£14,914,000
Wade Spring Limited	£14,906,894
Raleigh Holdings Ltd	£14,894,000
J.J.Churchill Limited	£14,892,000
Allmakes Limited	£14,884,559
Abacus Hotels Limited	£14,878,855
Charles Thompson (UK) Limited	£14,860,894
Ashley King (Developments) Limited	£14,858,661
Inver UK Limited	£14,849,266
Silbury Marketing Limited	£14,845,283
Renco (Chesterfield) Limited	£14,842,150
Natures Menu Limited	£14,840,652
Hexagon Investment Holdings Limited	£14,830,570
FCL Organisation Ltd	£14,827,074
Interaction Recruitment PLC	£14,820,169
United Carpets Holdings Limited	£14,820,013
Ceylon Tea Growers Association,Limited	£14,818,926
Blackwell UK Limited	£14,810,000
Interlevin Holdings Limited	£14,809,999
Saint-Gobain Roofspace Limited	£14,792,000
Solutionhost Group Limited	£14,782,360
William Rowland Limited	£14,777,846
NJDR Group Ltd	£14,774,000
Autologic Diagnostics Holdings Limited	£14,772,500
Pauley Group Limited	£14,735,715
Grevayne Properties Limited	£14,733,888
Coversure Insurance Services Limited	£14,732,386
Loxam Access Limited	£14,727,816
Roy Hatfield (Holdings) Limited	£14,726,596
The Propeller Academy Trust	£14,725,481
Wolf Systems Limited	£14,717,805
Jepson Holdings Limited	£14,717,775
Murata Power Solutions (Milton Keynes) Limited	£14,715,815
Factory (M1) Limited	£14,712,183
Dar Lighting Limited	£14,710,000
Wade Furniture Group Limited	£14,709,265
DNC Holdings Limited	£14,708,122
Derbyshire Aggregates Limited	£14,705,983
M3 (EU) Limited	£14,705,050
E. Moss, Limited	£14,700,000
Alycidon Technologies Limited	£14,694,348
NHBC Building Control Services Limited	£14,692,550
Ruskin College	£14,691,934
Oxford University Innovation Limited	£14,687,000
Binks Developments Limited	£14,677,680
Gelder Limited	£14,677,074
D.B. Ramsden & Company Limited	£14,676,026
Aero Tec Laboratories Limited	£14,671,665
Normanby Estate Company Limited (The)	£14,659,411
Cooper and Turner Distribution Limited	£14,653,000
Scancell Holdings PLC	£14,637,040
The Giles Academy	£14,631,260
Advanex Europe Limited	£14,629,000
Jx2 Limited	£14,628,221
Viad Service Companies Limited	£14,624,000
Syita Properties Limited	£14,622,854
St. Paul's Developments PLC	£14,622,797
SPD Holdings Limited	£14,622,797
Pinelog Group Limited	£14,622,000
The Myton Hospices	£14,612,228
Walls and Floors Limited	£14,606,462
Fischer Future Heat UK Limited	£14,605,070
Pennine Property Partnership LLP	£14,603,667
Heavyweight Air Express Limited	£14,599,322
Festino (Finance) Limited	£14,596,897
Clarksteel Holdings Limited	£14,595,698

Company	Amount
Neill Tools Limited	£14,595,000
Financial Funding Limited	£14,594,277
St. Matthews Limited	£14,593,752
BRT (Wisbech) Limited	£14,590,516
Vaillant Home Products Limited	£14,586,199
A N Wallis & Company Limited	£14,582,818
Oxford Trust (The)	£14,580,424
Homag U.K. Ltd.	£14,580,000
Steel City Schools Partnership	£14,578,163
Caledonian Group Holdings Limited	£14,577,000
The Ely Cloisters Estate Limited	£14,572,743
Ravensburger Limited	£14,571,449
Acorn Industrial Services Limited	£14,566,906
Fugro Geos Limited	£14,557,000
Mercedes-Benz Brooklands Limited	£14,555,000
Oakbridge Financial Services Limited	£14,550,031
The Royal Latin School	£14,540,983
Bodycote Surface Technology Limited	£14,520,000
Beachampton Group Limited	£14,508,177
Marcol Limited	£14,506,218
A.B. Produce PLC	£14,504,000
A.B. Produce Trading Limited	£14,504,000
Kingerlee Limited	£14,500,000
Sensient Technologies Limited	£14,496,129
Celus Holdings Limited	£14,495,787
Weymead Holdings Limited	£14,480,580
Neonickel (Blackburn) Limited	£14,472,061
Bourns (UK) Acquisition Limited	£14,472,000
Frimstone Limited	£14,466,948
Horberg & Co Holdings Ltd	£14,461,032
Mosdorfer CCL Systems Limited	£14,459,424
Bristol Fruit Sales (Market) Limited	£14,458,000
Hill Care Limited	£14,451,284
Greater Nottingham Education Trust	£14,442,368
Larson-Juhl UK Limited	£14,439,753
Bloom Developments Limited	£14,439,591
Hadfield Properties Limited	£14,433,476
Belle Holdings Limited	£14,424,549
G W Padley Poultry Limited	£14,421,000
Read Motor Group Limited	£14,415,330
Oncimmune Holdings PLC	£14,411,000
Aircraft Research Association Limited	£14,410,782
Printing & Packaging Co. Limited	£14,410,308
Axon Public Safety UK Limited	£14,407,589
Freshtime UK Limited	£14,393,080
Protocol National Limited	£14,389,000
Beacon Bingo Limited	£14,388,000
A.M. Packaging Limited	£14,384,299
G.I. Hadfield & Son Limited	£14,379,448
Magdalen College School Brackley Academy Trust	£14,377,375
Homecome Limited	£14,372,641
Atlas Hotels (Stevenage) Limited	£14,361,879
Key Property Solutions Limited	£14,361,186
Panache Lingerie Limited	£14,359,000
Thetford Limited	£14,357,571
DCS 452 Limited	£14,340,399
Hella UK Holdings Limited	£14,334,734
The C. Alma Baker Trust	£14,331,364
IX Reach Ltd	£14,322,710
Canei International Limited	£14,321,534
Lincolnshire Agricultural Society	£14,316,083
JRI Orthopaedics Limited	£14,313,000
Johal Properties Leicester LLP	£14,302,626
SDI (Belfast) Limited	£14,298,857
Swanton Care & Community (Andrew Frederick)	£14,298,532
M N Holdings Limited	£14,294,102
Lawrence Sheriff School Academy Trust	£14,292,028
The Peach Pub Company (Holdings) Limited	£14,287,863
Qualter, Hall & Company Limited	£14,281,000
Springfield Park Properties Limited	£14,269,300
Dunster House Limited	£14,269,160
Devereux Capital LLP	£14,259,766

Company	Turnover
West Hill School	£14,258,000
Schering-Plough Limited	£14,245,000
Mayfourth Holdings Limited	£14,243,472
Court Properties (Portugal) Limited	£14,243,045
Dalziel & Pow Holdings Limited	£14,241,420
DCA Design International Limited	£14,239,717
Bushboard Holdings Limited	£14,234,000
Town and Country Petfoods Limited	£14,212,709
Leeson Polyurethanes Limited	£14,210,695
Stream Midco Limited	£14,210,268
Guilsborough Multi Academy Trust	£14,207,126
Robimatic Limited	£14,201,000
TAG Partnership LLP	£14,199,663
Inter M.K. Limited	£14,199,522
CFC 2001 Ltd	£14,198,847
Charles Bentley & Son Limited	£14,186,336
Stratford Girls' Grammar School	£14,184,000
Gill Marine Holdings Limited	£14,174,007
Croupier Underwriting Limited	£14,158,045
London Internet Exchange Limited	£14,157,472
Cambridge Weight Plan Limited	£14,148,885
Lima Orthopaedics UK Limited	£14,129,957
HC 1228 Limited	£14,125,977
Willowbrook Healthcare Group Limited	£14,117,978
Hazelton Homes (Midlands) Limited	£14,114,798
Cobra Beer Partnership Limited	£14,096,065
The Forest of Marston Vale Trust	£14,095,331
Ancillary Components Limited	£14,088,407
SKF. Lo (Chemists) Limited	£14,086,791
Robert Woodhead Holdings Limited	£14,078,079
Agellus Limited	£14,077,000
University of Warwick Science Park Limited	£14,060,089
P Investments Limited	£14,049,000
Rowlinson Constructions Limited	£14,042,626
HM Estates Limited	£14,041,498
Yotta Limited	£14,041,118
Harshl Limited	£14,039,460
Axis Fleet Management Limited	£14,038,308
Ghekko Holdings Limited	£14,026,472
Shrubhill Farms Limited	£14,022,251
Oxford West End Development Limited	£14,014,668
Murley Limited	£13,993,000
First for Wellbeing CIC	£13,992,000
Southgate Packaging Limited	£13,991,731
R.Caudwell (Produce) Limited	£13,978,393
Linbrooke Services Limited	£13,974,102
Wicksteed Leisure Limited	£13,964,784
Real Estate Income Trust (SC) Limited	£13,962,676
TNS Transxpress Holding Company (U.K.) Limited	£13,959,833
Harmor Limited	£13,954,000
Ariens Company Limited	£13,952,169
Trevor Parr Associates Limited	£13,951,406
Adara Group Limited	£13,948,076
Duo Processing Limited	£13,940,592
Cooper & Turner Limited	£13,940,000
Ascott Transport Limited	£13,934,461
Wellglade Limited	£13,933,000
Artisan (UK) PLC	£13,917,463
Chilled Foods (UK) Ltd	£13,904,000
Fichtner Consulting Engineers Limited	£13,900,118
Brian Currie (Milton Keynes) Limited	£13,893,238
Richard Lang & Son Limited	£13,885,326
Robinson (Overseas) Limited	£13,882,000
Rowden House School Limited	£13,881,000
Centro Place Investments Limited	£13,869,352
Vine Kenwood Limited	£13,863,118
Autocraft Drivetrain Solutions Limited	£13,860,000
Douglas Gill International Limited	£13,856,789
Graystacks Exeter Limited	£13,855,848
Bong UK Limited	£13,854,238
B. E. Webbe Removals (Derby) Limited	£13,850,542
Hill House School Limited	£13,849,135
Draper Commercial Limited	£13,848,695
Croner Group Limited	£13,843,029
Tillotts Pharma UK Limited	£13,840,558
Drayson Technologies Limited	£13,840,000
Trust Estates (Clarence Street) Limited	£13,832,904
F & A George Limited	£13,818,000
Moto Direct Holdings Limited	£13,817,671
Moto Direct Limited	£13,810,855
West Park School	£13,809,351
Destec Engineering Limited	£13,808,724
Plant Impact Limited	£13,787,000
Carbon International Limited	£13,782,652
Rushton Hall Limited	£13,777,817
A Tiny Hamlet Limited	£13,774,478
Cariole Limited	£13,771,000
CML Limited	£13,770,092
Jardines Finance Limited	£13,768,324
BDR Waste Disposal Limited	£13,767,000
A.E.Spink Limited	£13,764,359
Aroqua Power Services Ltd.	£13,759,360
Atlas Hotels (Bristol Property) Limited	£13,757,528
Thistledown Investments Limited	£13,755,406
On Line Group Limited	£13,753,600
Stillness 928 Limited	£13,753,404
Rick Bestwick Limited	£13,752,436
Parkers Motor Services (Syston) Limited	£13,748,349
K.J. Cherry & Sons Limited	£13,746,468
Vacu-Lug Traction Tyres Limited	£13,736,509
FPS Distribution Limited	£13,725,000
Belgrade Theatre Trust (Coventry) Limited	£13,724,719
Coba Automotive (UK) Limited	£13,722,188
Lifford Industrial Properties Ltd	£13,717,950
Aaroncare Limited	£13,717,181
Lakes Academies Trust	£13,715,497
Bradshaw Taylor Ltd.	£13,713,641
Taylor Bloxham Group Limited	£13,703,466
Estate Computer Systems (Holdings) Limited	£13,697,365
Siddall and Hilton,Limited	£13,692,284
Excel Parking Services Limited	£13,689,587
Broome Management Co. Limited	£13,685,268
Smiths Concrete Limited	£13,684,621
Bloxham School Limited	£13,684,093
Trueform Engineering Holdings Limited	£13,680,076
Comtec Cable Accessories Limited	£13,674,000
Milltarn Limited	£13,672,431
Anand International Limited	£13,670,408
The Palmer Family Trust PLC	£13,660,116
Investco Limited	£13,656,733
Drybrough Trading Limited	£13,644,000
Earlham Trading Company Limited	£13,644,000
Ad Meliora Academy Trust	£13,642,772
Eurofleet Rental Limited	£13,641,634
Zoo Digital Group PLC	£13,639,500
Carmac (Building & Civil Engineering) Limited	£13,637,166
Massarella Catering Group Limited	£13,628,210
Leicester Fancy Box Company Limited	£13,628,000
The Air Ambulance Service	£13,616,000
Kenilworth Multi Academy Trust	£13,599,000
RTFH Limited	£13,598,556
Nu-Oval Acquisitions 1 Limited	£13,598,000
Blitz Communications Limited	£13,595,000
Castlegate 624 Limited	£13,586,000
Quarrydale Academy	£13,575,880
Midland Communications Distribution Limited	£13,571,848
Beamglow Limited	£13,558,577
McLean Restaurants Limited	£13,547,698
John Smedley Limited	£13,545,000
Abbey Properties Cambridgeshire Limited	£13,544,637
Rushcliffe Specialist Schools (Mickleover) Limited	£13,542,334
Underwood Meat Company Limited	£13,539,622
Vita York 1 Limited	£13,538,000
Pury Hill Limited	£13,537,602

Company	Amount
Ryedale Estates Limited	£13,537,480
Blackwell Limited	£13,534,000
Ceravision Limited	£13,530,956
Rolec Services Limited	£13,523,962
Sonic Communications (International) Limited	£13,522,240
The Valspar (UK) Special Holding Corporation Ltd	£13,519,590
Waldersey Farms Limited	£13,519,531
Cad Cam Automotive Limited	£13,512,826
Millbrook European Holdings Limited	£13,488,061
Ducati U.K. Limited	£13,487,000
Building and Plumbing Supplies Limited	£13,478,421
Premium Plan Limited	£13,477,114
E.On Project Earth Limited	£13,472,000
EJ UK Fabrication & Access Solutions Holdings Ltd	£13,467,892
Equity Solutions Lift Investments Stockport Limited	£13,463,168
East Midlands Chamber (Derbys, Notts, Leics)	£13,461,595
York Ward & Rowlatt Limited	£13,454,056
HC1221 Limited	£13,441,330
Pickering Investments Limited	£13,439,710
CLS Finance Limited	£13,434,865
Omron Electronics Limited	£13,424,949
BPS Warwick Limited	£13,414,504
Blinds 2 Go Limited	£13,410,759
Quality Care (EM) Limited	£13,403,473
Center Parcs Limited	£13,400,000
Blue Support Services Limited	£13,399,942
Orano UK Limited	£13,393,509
Ducker Farming Limited	£13,392,216
Covrad Heat Transfer Limited	£13,391,333
L & R Medical UK Ltd.	£13,387,000
Willoughby 395 Limited	£13,384,609
Dodson & Horrell Limited	£13,381,204
Sanderson Multi-Channel Retail Solutions Limited	£13,378,000
The Christian Conference Trust	£13,375,401
Roko Health Clubs Limited	£13,367,562
S M C Design and Draughting Services Limited	£13,367,559
Barton Buses Limited	£13,362,000
Bonnington Plastics Limited	£13,360,291
Gladstone MRM Limited	£13,358,668
Brookfield School Academy Trust	£13,357,047
Pineapple Letting Ltd	£13,356,426
Biesse Group UK Limited	£13,351,993
Trigon Holdings Limited	£13,347,172
Fantasy Island Operations Limited	£13,332,000
Select Group International Limited	£13,330,788
Pinelodge Holidays Limited	£13,330,000
Nene Group PLC	£13,327,521
Nene Group Holdings PLC	£13,327,521
KNM Project Services Limited	£13,322,356
Minoli & Company Limited	£13,309,777
The Ferrers School	£13,308,671
J. Wharton (Agriculture) Limited	£13,303,142
Ellis Bros (Contractors) Limited	£13,295,898
T.W. Ward C.N.C. Machinery Limited	£13,290,806
Wathegar Wind Farm LLP	£13,279,476
H. Ponsford Limited	£13,278,010
Rapidrop Global Limited	£13,277,743
Mercer Farming Limited	£13,271,219
Classeq Limited	£13,263,026
The Print People Group Limited	£13,258,871
Richard Utley Limited	£13,258,401
Pinnacle International Freight Holdings Limited	£13,250,808
Burton McCall Limited	£13,249,940
Cranford House School Trust Limited	£13,249,350
Libra Speciality Chemicals Limited	£13,247,113
Mayflower Specialist School Academy Trust	£13,236,913
Pauley Properties Limited	£13,236,790
Caunton Investments Limited	£13,225,743
K.M. Packaging Services Limited	£13,225,403
S R S Rail System Limited	£13,223,888
Ascend Global Holdings, Ltd.	£13,216,702
UK Waste Solutions Limited	£13,206,633
Addington Fund	£13,204,020
Rylston Road Limited	£13,203,523
Anisa Group Holdings Limited	£13,199,000
Wood Boilers LLP	£13,193,122
Lincwaste Limited	£13,190,000
Harting UK Limited	£13,189,000
TVCO Limited	£13,182,188
Ibstock Community College	£13,179,000
Apteco Limited	£13,178,149
Whitley Academy	£13,163,103
Replimune Limited	£13,160,992
Games Workshop US Limited	£13,156,000
SRS Rail System (Holdings) Limited	£13,155,518
Sutton Park Motor Company Limited	£13,144,376
North Kesteven Academy	£13,141,000
Hi-Force Limited	£13,140,707
Nimogen Limited	£13,126,060
Quaker International Educational Trust	£13,123,526
Blackrow Corporation Limited	£13,119,816
Wallis Farms Limited	£13,107,936
Pentagon (Huddersfield) Limited	£13,101,049
Paragon Quality Foods Ltd	£13,099,159
John Nicholls (Trading) Limited	£13,091,394
Landmark Wholesale Limited	£13,090,641
Hopton Investment Holdings Limited	£13,080,000
Moran Commercials Ltd	£13,079,936
Rutland Plastics Limited	£13,076,959
Clyde Bergemann Materials Handling Limited	£13,071,000
Davane Holding Company Limited	£13,063,993
Avenue Lets Limited	£13,062,826
STS Defence Limited	£13,059,036
Duncan Investments Limited	£13,057,288
Barker Shoes Limited	£13,056,689
MSG Sandhurst Limited	£13,054,763
Lincoln Christ's Hospital School	£13,054,366
A.P.S. Salads Limited	£13,047,000
SJH-All Plant Group Limited	£13,044,290
Tappex Thread Inserts Limited	£13,036,052
Lenze U.K. Limited	£13,030,056
Festo Limited	£13,029,294
Sheffield International Venues Limited	£13,028,000
Four Seasons (DFK) Limited	£13,025,000
The Academy of Lincoln Trust	£13,023,938
The Heyfordian School Trust	£13,020,286
Ilmor Engineering Limited	£13,018,611
Argos SURBS Investments Limited	£13,015,000
Amega Sciences PLC	£12,999,733
Graham Holmes Astraseal Limited	£12,990,595
S Walsh Holdings Limited	£12,973,705
Encocam Limited	£12,972,333
Hofer Powertrain UK Limited	£12,971,522
Consuma Holdings Limited	£12,971,247
Crown Crest (Holdings) PLC	£12,965,969
South Yorkshire Community Foundation Limited	£12,951,421
Finbrook Limited	£12,946,667
Pengethley Potatoes Limited	£12,938,748
Brit de Vere Limited	£12,938,395
Conservation Education & Research Trust	£12,936,907
Pathfinders-Care (Ollerton) Limited	£12,934,941
Robert Pochin Limited	£12,932,083
R. H. Lamyman Limited	£12,924,962
Eclipse Magnetics Limited	£12,924,000
Robinson Healthcare Limited	£12,922,000
Lancer Properties Limited	£12,918,375
John Hargreaves,(Collyhurst and Stalybridge) Limited	£12,913,680
Taylors Service Garages (Boston) Limited	£12,896,352
Selectkey Limited	£12,889,762
The Yews Holding Company Limited	£12,885,003
Ross Ceramics Limited	£12,881,000
Georgia GC Holdings Limited	£12,875,683
Matthews Environmental Solutions Limited	£12,873,462
Going Plural Limited	£12,870,320

C.W.Fletcher & Sons,Limited £12,868,921
Silentpride Limited £12,868,090
Tenens Ede Limited £12,866,569
Bobby's Foods Limited £12,866,000
Methodist Guild Holidays Limited £12,865,749
Phytone Limited £12,865,109
Mark's Electrical Limited £12,862,496
Cambridge Display Technology Limited £12,851,000
De Trafford Property LLP £12,842,765
Full Moon Holdings Limited £12,839,397
Allmakes 4 X 4 Limited £12,834,927
GRI Group Limited £12,834,627
Generation Two Limited £12,834,540
Advancis Holdings Limited £12,834,396
Tickhill Engineering Company Limited £12,829,847
Eastmarket Grain LLP £12,828,413
Heraeus Electro-Nite (UK) Ltd £12,817,000
Prince Hotels Ltd £12,807,788
Cresta Court Hotel Holdings Limited £12,797,193
BTN Turbo Charger Service Limited £12,796,000
Progress Bedford Limited £12,791,645
Hyde Details Limited £12,789,330
Shipston High School £12,785,000
Yeovil Developments Limited £12,782,000
Weavers Close Limited £12,774,386
J.Jelley and Son Limited £12,767,714
British Drilling and Freezing Company Limited £12,765,735
Believe Academy Trust £12,759,905
Ambitions Personnel Limited £12,756,773
K.M. Packaging Holdings Limited £12,754,119
DV Ventures Limited £12,752,294
Vital Pet Group Limited £12,748,496
Oughtred & Harrison (Facilities) Ltd. £12,741,410
VM Fabrics Limited £12,739,089
Fisher German LLP £12,736,930
Banks & Lloyd (Shipping) Limited £12,732,897
B Taylor & Sons Transport Limited £12,731,083
The Hillarys Properties Partnership LLP £12,728,861
Woodford Investment Management Limited £12,727,758
Nenplas Limited £12,720,000
M.J.S. Construction (March) Limited £12,717,433
Ingenta PLC £12,717,000
Rawlins Academy £12,717,000
Oxera Consulting LLP £12,716,149
Johnson Bros (Tours) Limited £12,709,846
Reg Vardy (VMC) Limited £12,706,000
Union Papertech Limited £12,699,487
BPX Electro-Mechanical Company Limited £12,699,287
Leslie H. Trainer and Son Limited £12,699,000
Premier Sheet Metal (Coventry) Limited £12,697,002
Frosts Garden Centre Restructuring Limited £12,694,333
Abacus Lighting Holdings Limited £12,694,326
Warth Developments Ltd £12,694,023
Fswind Limited £12,692,700
Ashford Riverside Park Limited £12,673,818
Benchmark Animal Health Limited £12,672,501
A.W. Smith & Sons Limited £12,671,540
Ashwicken Sporting LLP £12,664,013
TRB Technology Group Limited £12,663,954
Simons Developments Limited £12,663,268
Whites Engineering Limited £12,663,090
Sheermans Limited £12,662,652
Expatriate Advisory Services PLC £12,659,995
Manor Crest Homes Limited £12,657,548
B. Braun Avitum UK Limited £12,657,000
Pfisterer Limited £12,644,010
Triumph Multi Academy Trust £12,632,082
Hikoki Power Tools (U.K.) Limited £12,627,777
Leicester Lift Project Company (No.2) Limited £12,618,000
I Holland Holdings Limited £12,611,013
Brayfour Limited £12,603,278
Brayford Plastics Limited £12,602,813
Maplebeck Holdings Limited £12,601,004
Glinwell Marketing Limited £12,596,000
Longshaw Developments Limited £12,586,313
Mahle Aftermarket Limited £12,586,000
B Braun Sterilog Limited £12,583,000
Sherwood Homes Limited £12,579,346
CDT Holdings Limited £12,570,000
Access Fertility Limited £12,568,077
Guidance Marine Limited £12,564,000
Mark Rutherford School Trust £12,563,608
Parex Ltd £12,562,067
Castel Froma Neuro Care Limited £12,558,864
Art Systems Limited £12,547,895
Hemswell Estates Limited £12,542,998
Carlton Street Trading Limited £12,538,582
Topps Europe Holdings Limited £12,536,490
Leicester Racecourse Holdings Limited £12,530,193
Global Experience Specialists (GES) Holdings Ltd £12,529,000
Oxford University Trading Limited £12,525,000
Belmont Press Limited £12,523,638
Pailton Engineering Limited £12,521,623
Howes Percival LLP £12,514,848
Topalpha (Warehouse) Limited £12,511,000
Guided Ultrasonics Limited £12,510,394
Manor Fresh Limited £12,508,413
Ponsford Investments Limited £12,502,140
Don Amott Parks Limited £12,499,099
King Edward VI Education Trust £12,491,977
Anisa Supply Chain Solutions Limited £12,488,000
Norton Motorcycles (UK) Limited £12,487,483
Granwood Holdings Limited £12,487,408
Hostombe Group Limited £12,486,340
Abraham Investments Limited £12,475,400
Moriah House Limited £12,473,141
Coster Aerosols Limited £12,473,066
R. Bratley (Quadring) Limited £12,471,111
Baker & Taylor (UK) Ltd £12,471,000
Myoderm Limited £12,466,631
Land and Estates Commercial Properties Limited £12,466,206
Pegler Limited £12,466,000
The Engineering Technology Group Limited £12,464,142
Fred Hartley (Estates) Limited £12,460,526
Atlas Hotels (Chingford) Limited £12,459,776
A.R. Craven Farms Limited £12,453,849
R.J.Brown & Sons Limited £12,453,486
Delgarth 2011 Limited £12,449,367
Coventry Chemicals Limited £12,446,000
All Assist Limited £12,444,519
Smith Bros.(Caerconan) Wholesale Limited £12,442,139
Varsity Design Limited £12,436,607
I M Kelly Automotive Limited £12,433,178
Alauna Renewable Energy Limited £12,432,000
T.S.B. (Developments) Limited £12,429,017
Myton Investments Ltd £12,426,853
Pacific Direct Finance Limited £12,424,259
Monarch Healthcare Limited £12,422,498
Kirona Holdings Limited £12,419,053
2morrow Group Limited £12,416,871
Avondale Property (Holdings) Limited £12,409,807
Jerry Green Dog Rescue £12,406,064
Cherwell Valley Silos Limited £12,403,760
Wales High School Academy Trust £12,402,351
Cenduit Limited £12,399,642
Versalift Distributors (U.K.) Limited £12,394,212
Wilcox Holdings Limited £12,389,194
Bosworth Independent College Limited £12,387,729
Edgetech (UK) Limited £12,377,002
Sheffcare Limited £12,373,644
Ragi Properties Limited £12,364,162
Buttercup Bidco Limited £12,358,554
Kadima Properties (UK) Limited £12,347,000
HRVS Group Limited £12,346,950

Tingdene Holdings Limited	£12,344,524
Clayson Country Homes Limited	£12,340,012
City Suites Manchester Limited	£12,336,000
Ebbsfleet Property Limited	£12,335,366
Hopton Retail Holdings Limited	£12,335,257
Stone House Investments Limited	£12,335,158
Eterna Lighting Limited	£12,333,316
Dyson Group PLC	£12,329,000
Slater Hogg Mortgages Limited	£12,327,000
Exel Computer Systems (Holdings) PLC	£12,326,835
Blenheim Agency Limited	£12,323,818
The Diocese of Sheffield Academies Trust	£12,323,000
Ruddington Homes Limited	£12,320,863
Doddington Farms LLP	£12,313,573
Abbeyfield V.E. Limited	£12,313,000
South Warwickshire Academy Trust	£12,312,000
Unique Window Systems Ltd	£12,308,379
Sourcecircle Holdings Limited	£12,295,135
Coverland UK Limited	£12,294,779
A.E. Lenton Limited	£12,291,994
Omex Agrifluids Limited	£12,278,895
H.I. Limited	£12,273,576
Mynydd Windfarm LLP	£12,265,063
Berwin Industrial Polymers Limited	£12,230,794
Unity Property Holdings Limited	£12,224,994
Coombe Abbey Park Limited	£12,220,523
Jack Loggin Limited	£12,216,867
Daloon Foods (U.K.) Limited	£12,210,241
IMCI (Services) Limited	£12,201,753
Maxim Logistics Group Limited	£12,196,617
SHH 101 LLP	£12,196,185
Darley Limited	£12,196,133
West Coventry Academy	£12,194,000
Landfill Management Limited	£12,191,000
MSW (Holdings) Limited	£12,186,000
Waterfall Services Limited	£12,179,623
Grafton Recruitment Limited	£12,170,531
Alco Estates Limited	£12,166,914
Forever Living Products (U.K.) Limited	£12,143,085
Creating Tomorrow Multi Academy Trust	£12,138,380
ABSL Power Solutions Ltd	£12,134,000
St. Matthews (North) Limited	£12,133,919
Wolf Safety Lamp Company Limited (The)	£12,127,347
Richard's Pharma Limited	£12,123,664
Society of The Sacred Mission (Europe)	£12,123,086
Omega Red Group Limited	£12,116,000
Welcome Break Services Limited	£12,116,000
Helen & Douglas House	£12,114,000
SHV Investments Limited	£12,103,281
Kyra Enterprises Limited	£12,097,675
SMS Electronics Limited	£12,094,000
Quartzinvest Properties Ltd	£12,092,000
TCL Tanker Rental Limited	£12,089,655
British Horse Society (The)	£12,089,000
Pharmacy Care Plus Limited	£12,084,689
DS John Holdings Limited	£12,079,970
TCI Renewables Limited	£12,076,373
Mondi Scunthorpe Limited	£12,075,195
Today's Wholesale Services Limited	£12,075,000
Stertil UK Ltd.	£12,071,584
Williams Jet Tenders (Holdings) Limited	£12,060,987
Zapp (GB) Limited	£12,060,669
Oxford Plastic Systems Limited	£12,059,123
Parallel Parents Ltd	£12,058,528
P.J. Thory Limited	£12,055,756
EMB-Group Ltd	£12,053,366
OCF PLC	£12,052,872
N K Motors Limited	£12,047,505
Bushmead Homes Ltd	£12,044,681
Kingsway Asset Finance Ltd	£12,043,525
Advance Tapes Group Limited	£12,038,837
Vectair Aviation (1995) Limited	£12,037,494
Allworks Properties Limited	£12,037,149
TTKW Limited	£12,036,129
Aspire Schools Trust	£12,029,376
BDB Design Build Holdings Limited	£12,024,925
Ransomwood Estates UK Limited	£12,023,390
Asmet (UK) Limited	£12,022,964
O'Brien Contractors Limited	£12,013,999
John Sinclair (Sheffield) Limited	£12,012,599
Hampton Steel Limited	£12,006,227
Dippy Ridge Limited	£12,001,912
API Overseas Holdings Limited	£12,000,000
Pyramid Posters Limited	£11,995,810
Earth Trust	£11,992,585
Potters-Ballotini Limited	£11,989,000
Jakto Group Limited	£11,986,100
Electrosteel Castings (UK) Limited	£11,985,000
Motspa Holdings Limited	£11,984,800
Roubaix Bidco Limited	£11,984,778
Larchsilver Properties Limited	£11,984,478
DFDS Seaways Newcastle Limited	£11,977,824
Select International Developments Limited	£11,977,001
RMA Investments Limited	£11,972,364
Hoban Limited	£11,955,814
WHC01 Limited	£11,949,275
Avery House Healthcare Limited	£11,945,000
J & E Importers & Distributors Green Jem Mfg	£11,941,527
SDI (Thurrock) Limited	£11,940,365
The Valve Partners Limited	£11,938,392
Knott-Avonride Limited	£11,934,429
Thorneycroft Solicitors Limited	£11,927,345
Brophy Grounds Maintenance Limited	£11,926,000
Trident 2020 Limited	£11,923,016
Premierfirst Vehicle Rental Franchising Limited	£11,923,000
St. Luke's Hospice	£11,921,917
Imago Holdings Limited	£11,907,902
L. & M. Investment Company Limited	£11,907,512
SDL Surveying Limited	£11,907,298
Birkdale School	£11,906,235
Memoria Limited	£11,905,482
Daifuku Europe Limited	£11,904,689
Wight Building Materials Ltd	£11,901,000
Munro Building Services Limited	£11,894,036
The Myers-Briggs Company Limited	£11,886,847
Damika Limited	£11,874,699
Haven Housing Limited	£11,873,607
Healix Property LLP	£11,869,227
Conrad Energy Group Limited	£11,867,000
Thomas Cook Aircraft Engineering Limited	£11,865,000
Perfectos Printing Inks Co Ltd.	£11,862,122
Oxford Instruments Industrial Products Limited	£11,860,000
Pinnacle International Freight Limited	£11,853,401
Yorkshire Repak Limited	£11,849,973
Dunn Motor Traction Ltd	£11,849,025
Oxhold Limited	£11,848,358
Blugilt Holdings Limited	£11,847,111
Future Travel Limited	£11,843,000
Wind Port of Liverpool Limited	£11,840,643
County Hotels Limited	£11,837,161
KSB Limited	£11,828,577
Webmart Limited	£11,824,170
Danaher & Walsh Group Limited	£11,823,120
Sheetfed Holdings Limited	£11,822,634
Oerlikon Balzers Coating UK Limited	£11,815,211
Maurice Mason Limited	£11,815,013
F G Alden Limited	£11,813,246
DSGPI 2015 Limited	£11,809,381
L C & M Holdings Limited	£11,803,283
Millgate Limited	£11,794,725
Pollard Boxes Limited	£11,792,000
Miswa Chemicals Limited	£11,790,007
William Farr Church of England Comprehensive School	£11,789,968
Winslow Court Ltd	£11,781,000

Company	Value
Melham Group Limited	£11,778,193
Servelec Healthcare Limited	£11,778,000
Howard & Hallam Limited	£11,777,446
Romax Technology Ltd.	£11,777,000
Bosch Packaging Technology Limited	£11,772,000
Thos.Winnard & Sons Limited	£11,770,005
Policyfast Limited	£11,766,191
T.H.Kingerlee & Sons Limited	£11,765,000
Tripod Crest Limited	£11,764,127
Bramptonia Limited	£11,762,337
Erapeutics PLC	£11,762,000
Manthorpe Engineering Limited	£11,756,208
Innovate Multi Academy Trust	£11,756,000
Henton & Chattell Limited	£11,749,660
Cannon Venture Finance Limited	£11,743,986
EMSC (UK) Limited	£11,739,226
Meller Design Solutions Limited	£11,733,302
Welland Park Community College Academy Trust	£11,725,000
WLP Holdings Limited	£11,724,866
Farmers Fresh Limited	£11,723,251
Kingston (City) Estates Trading Limited	£11,722,133
OSL Group Holdings Limited	£11,722,000
Hundred Percent Holdings Limited	£11,721,518
CPF Commercial Limited	£11,717,380
Stillness 930 Limited	£11,716,485
Crowland Cranes Limited	£11,713,837
Huttons Buildings Limited	£11,709,000
A Shade Greener Maintenance Limited	£11,708,343
Majestic Bingo Limited	£11,707,000
Bletchley Park Trust Limited	£11,706,900
Horncastle Education Trust	£11,700,372
Vista Engineering Limited	£11,700,160
Vita Student York Holding Company Limited	£11,699,000
Hoval Limited	£11,691,493
Chevron Traffic Management (Holdings) Limited	£11,686,187
Glanmoor Investments Limited	£11,684,111
Richard Sanders Limited	£11,682,366
Chesterfield Special Cylinders Limited	£11,679,000
Holly Farm Limited	£11,678,113
Advance Tapes International Limited	£11,673,251
Rushcliffe Specialist Schools Limited	£11,673,244
Blue Deer Limited	£11,669,975
North Midco Limited	£11,669,573
Ballylynch Capital Limited	£11,667,305
Magyar Farming Company Limited	£11,663,980
Golflane Limited	£11,663,503
Maggie Sottero Bridal (UK) Ltd.	£11,662,416
Ravent Limited	£11,661,564
Victim Support	£11,649,000
Chargill (Holdings) Ltd	£11,642,627
Sanderson Limited	£11,640,000
Meridian Lightweight Technologies UK Limited	£11,639,000
Orona Limited	£11,634,881
The T-Shirt Guy Holdings Limited	£11,632,537
Eaglebeam Limited	£11,631,677
Transit 2017 Limited	£11,631,073
Clayton (Lincoln) Limited	£11,628,661
Graham Bell Limited	£11,625,004
Absolute Radio Limited	£11,621,000
Eraglow Building Limited	£11,618,216
Merchant Taylors' Oxfordshire Academy Trust Ltd	£11,617,544
The Fernwood Academy Trust	£11,611,000
Church UK Retail Limited	£11,603,930
Mori Lee Europe Limited	£11,601,387
SDI (Liverpool) Limited	£11,595,828
2K Polymer Systems Limited	£11,588,000
Mulberry Waste Limited	£11,585,117
Premier Textiles Limited	£11,583,780
Stratton-Streles Estates Limited	£11,583,180
John Hebb (Motor Engineers) Limited	£11,582,605
Brookhead Estate Limited	£11,580,085
Cotswold Wild Life Park Limited	£11,578,170

Company	Value
Rowstock Limited	£11,577,484
Ranquin Underwriting Limited	£11,576,550
SDI (LSL Holdings) Limited	£11,574,303
Gurney Slade Lime & Stone Co.Limited	£11,557,376
Rotor Clip Limited	£11,556,244
ASG Group Associates Limited	£11,555,854
Burrough Court Estate Limited	£11,548,832
Welcomm Holdings Limited	£11,542,523
PMC Fluidpower Group Limited	£11,535,557
Rippleglen Limited	£11,535,000
Twitten Trustees Limited	£11,534,032
BESS Aylesford Limited	£11,518,742
Flair Flooring Supplies Limited	£11,517,975
HSH Cold Stores Limited	£11,514,369
Instill Education Limited	£11,508,038
Barker Ross Group Limited	£11,508,000
Cosworth Electronics Limited	£11,505,000
Ashberry Healthcare Limited	£11,502,204
Straightset Limited	£11,497,240
Profile Security Services Limited	£11,497,011
Grove Industries (Holdings) Ltd	£11,495,529
Geo.Akins (Holdings) Limited	£11,492,671
E.A.T. (Holdings) Limited	£11,492,570
Munks Agricultural Contractors Limited	£11,485,393
Windsor Vehicle Leasing Limited	£11,484,426
County Asset Finance Limited	£11,478,964
W.& S.(Long Eaton) Limited	£11,475,749
Mercian Limited	£11,474,907
The Mulberry Bush Organisation Limited	£11,460,324
Dynamic Cassette International Limited	£11,458,331
Miller Wates (Wallingford) Limited	£11,456,505
B.N.T. Properties Limited	£11,455,730
Myers-Briggs Company Holdings (Europe) Ltd	£11,454,362
Gallagher Bathgate Limited	£11,449,630
Dunns (Long Sutton) Limited	£11,449,457
Kindale Limited	£11,447,055
Flex-Seal Couplings Limited	£11,445,713
R.M.F. Properties Limited	£11,444,796
Bucyrus Europe Limited	£11,444,000
Bluebell Wood Children's Hospice	£11,442,000
Hi-Level Enterprises Limited	£11,438,746
Savoy Cinemas Limited	£11,437,876
Ney Limited	£11,434,374
Lebus Upholstery Limited	£11,432,992
Polytech International Limited	£11,421,716
William Cook Properties Limited	£11,418,241
Underwood Meat (Holdings) Limited	£11,413,887
Sash UK Limited	£11,410,639
Woodland Buildings Investment Company Limited	£11,407,371
Salter Bros,Limited	£11,399,065
Clark-Drain Limited	£11,395,618
Ryecroft Foods Limited	£11,395,000
CPG 2016 Limited	£11,393,989
De Trafford and Palatine Estates Limited	£11,388,384
Red Box Recorders Limited	£11,387,000
Funeral Services Partnership Limited	£11,385,000
Schades Limited	£11,384,000
Synthetic Resins Limited	£11,376,000
Tynemill Limited	£11,375,271
Netsupport Ltd.	£11,369,666
Thessco Limited	£11,367,347
Alumet Systems (UK) Limited	£11,364,865
Midcity Investments Limited	£11,358,064
Xanadu Investments Limited	£11,356,966
Condie Investments Limited	£11,348,234
Colortronic (U.K.) Limited	£11,348,179
J.B.Kind Limited	£11,340,749
Tom Hartley Cars Limited	£11,339,352
Loxwood Holdings Limited	£11,320,418
Barratt Evolution Limited	£11,320,000
Watts Industries UK Limited	£11,307,419
J.E. & V.M. Dalton Limited	£11,306,765

Roythornes Limited	£11,299,595	Zibrant Limited	£11,078,498
Aareon UK Limited	£11,290,871	Hillbridge Investments Limited	£11,078,000
Link Education Trust	£11,281,408	Yuill Family Properties Ltd	£11,074,581
Leaderflush + Shapland Holdings Limited	£11,280,000	Miller Wates (Didcot) Limited	£11,070,007
Leger Education Trust	£11,280,000	Breas Medical Limited	£11,067,163
Union Colours Limited	£11,279,744	BCQ (Holdings) Limited	£11,063,480
Sunshine Care Bidco Limited	£11,278,274	Prodrive Investments Limited	£11,057,000
Muslim Hands	£11,268,056	St Andrew's Hospice Limited	£11,055,795
BCM Employment & Management Services Limited	£11,264,000	Vencap International PLC	£11,054,859
Agriturf Holdings Limited	£11,263,723	LDC (Boston) Limited	£11,046,398
Manifesto Foods Ltd	£11,261,361	Laen Limited	£11,042,900
Agrihold Limited	£11,260,101	Elastomerics Limited	£11,042,438
Print-Rite Europe Ltd.	£11,254,724	Oriana Underwriting Limited	£11,042,431
Dering Properties Finance Limited	£11,253,871	Tioga Limited	£11,042,361
Christy Home Textiles Limited	£11,252,000	RRD GDS Limited	£11,042,000
Fidentia No 191 LLP	£11,249,996	Maranello Concessionaires Limited	£11,038,000
Jandu Developments Limited	£11,249,771	Tinsley Park Holdings Limited	£11,034,674
M.& N.Textiles Limited	£11,244,508	Georgetown Carr Limited	£11,031,204
Genie International Holdings Limited	£11,243,000	Bowers Metrology Limited	£11,031,000
Park Industrial and Agricultural Holdings Limited	£11,237,987	Insanely Great Limited	£11,029,000
Radford Holdings Limited	£11,237,923	Ben Bennett Jr Limited	£11,028,057
Country Attire Holdings Limited	£11,237,773	Morgana Systems Limited	£11,022,249
CLEB Holdings Limited	£11,237,000	Morgana Holdings Limited	£11,022,249
Halgram Limited	£11,230,573	Aspen Medical Europe Limited	£11,015,000
Darrington Quarries Limited	£11,229,000	Action for Care Limited	£11,013,143
Del Equipment (U.K.) Limited	£11,225,474	Potter Clarkson LLP	£11,006,000
Trina Solar (UK) Limited	£11,224,088	FKB Limited	£11,003,031
Gamston Aviation Limited	£11,219,322	UKMHPS Limited	£11,002,000
Grainsby Farms Limited	£11,215,108	Benchmark Leisure Limited	£10,994,773
K. & O. Peros (Oxford) Limited	£11,206,653	BDF Plant Limited	£10,991,122
Aspire Achieve Advance Group Limited	£11,205,631	Ivor Crowson Developments (Stamford) Limited	£10,990,456
BWB Holdings Limited	£11,203,379	Belsfield LLP	£10,982,332
The Ames Companies UK Ltd.	£11,202,576	Roxhill (Tilbury) Limited	£10,970,626
Sealord (Europe) Limited	£11,197,848	Hodge Clemco Limited	£10,965,684
Playfootball Ltd	£11,195,334	S.I.P.(Industrial Products) Limited	£10,959,528
Callington's Construction Limited	£11,192,120	HNB Care Limited	£10,959,301
R.H. Ward (Welton) Limited	£11,188,828	Boss Cabins Limited	£10,955,566
DSS Group Limited	£11,187,691	Florida Topco Limited	£10,954,186
Proctor Bros. (Long Sutton) Limited	£11,185,980	Cemex Seament Limited	£10,946,575
Ablehomes Limited	£11,184,825	Devonshire Green (Commercial Properties) Limited	£10,944,000
Advancis Limited	£11,180,922	Grandcross Limited	£10,940,000
Lets Connect It Solutions Limited	£11,175,000	Long Marsh Limited	£10,934,538
Amano Enzyme Europe Limited	£11,170,634	Mulberry Property Developments (HGP) Limited	£10,923,957
De Aston School Academy Trust	£11,170,087	B & K Thomas (Holdings) Limited	£10,920,678
Warners Group Publications PLC	£11,162,679	Gallagher Poole Limited	£10,919,548
Gosford Hill School	£11,161,550	Blue Planet Solar Park II Limited	£10,918,735
London Clapham Investments and Developments Ltd	£11,159,496	Intermed Limited	£10,914,762
Acentic Holdings Limited	£11,154,037	E-PPL Limited	£10,912,621
Estate Incomes Limited	£11,147,551	Triplex Lloyd Properties Limited	£10,909,000
Drennan International Limited	£11,145,589	Harewood Moor Estates Limited	£10,906,099
PCS Business Systems Limited	£11,144,562	E.On UK Cogeneration Limited	£10,896,000
Wisbech Grammar School	£11,139,702	Hadrian (Residential) Limited	£10,889,535
Spaldings Holdings Limited	£11,138,000	Florensis Flower Seeds UK Limited	£10,888,000
Renewi Cumbria Holdings Limited	£11,136,000	Cokethorpe Educational Trust Limited	£10,887,621
Motan Colortronic Limited	£11,133,702	Woolley GMC Engineering Holdings Limited	£10,882,082
Tradelink Direct Limited	£11,133,583	Tamar Renewable Power (Hoddesdon) Limited	£10,882,000
Warwick Care Limited	£11,132,863	SSCP Blink Bidco Limited	£10,881,720
Pattonair Properties Limited	£11,126,000	JJC Investments Limited	£10,878,177
Lesta Packaging PLC	£11,121,439	Human Appeal	£10,875,143
Acredula Group Limited	£11,111,967	Derbyshire Property Trust Limited (The)	£10,868,130
Brighton Marina Block F1 Ltd	£11,111,849	Pal International Limited	£10,865,394
South Coast Furnishing Company Limited	£11,110,070	Flint Holdings Limited	£10,852,433
LC Packaging UK Ltd	£11,107,196	Tours Abroad Group Limited	£10,849,663
Geoffrey Mason Limited	£11,099,426	MacIntyre Hudson Holdings Limited	£10,838,686
Dagless Limited	£11,098,141	Sheffield Business Park Limited	£10,834,924
E.M. Rogers Group Limited	£11,097,549	Touchgold Limited	£10,834,608
Sheffield Galleries & Museums Trust	£11,097,000	KJW Drylining Limited	£10,824,365
Stratus (Holdings) Limited	£11,088,684	Shire Foods Limited	£10,820,000
Four Seasons (Bamford) Limited	£11,087,000	Prahi Hotel Collection Limited	£10,819,000
C. Soar & Sons (UK) Limited	£11,085,835	Maltgrade Limited	£10,811,841
Mogford Hotels Limited	£11,084,442	Pennell's Holdings Limited	£10,808,333
Lifestyle Seeview Limited	£11,083,857	Forest Way School	£10,795,985

Company	Amount
Springfield Farm Limited	£10,782,044
Pirelli Motorsport Services Limited	£10,769,000
Abba Plant Hire Limited	£10,768,161
Trousdale Limited	£10,763,580
Sensient Colors UK Ltd	£10,762,310
Estates and Leisure Holdings Limited	£10,759,870
Alphyra Payment Services Limited	£10,758,164
BHIB Limited	£10,752,734
Russell Acott Limited	£10,749,327
Goodfellow Cambridge Limited	£10,748,000
PCS Business Systems Group Limited	£10,747,431
HB Healthcare Limited	£10,740,000
Chenderit School Academy Trust	£10,729,146
Hales Group Limited	£10,724,789
Sodick Europe Holdings Limited	£10,723,477
Hach Lange Ltd	£10,723,000
Boole's Tools & Pipe Fittings Limited	£10,717,000
Tuxford Exports Limited	£10,711,124
Rayfern Holdings Limited	£10,709,147
Jordan Developments (UK) Limited	£10,700,690
Vidal Group Holdings Ltd	£10,692,718
Measom (Dryline) Limited	£10,690,601
Chiltern Distribution Ltd	£10,685,822
Business Management Software Limited	£10,684,255
Bauer Digital Radio Limited	£10,683,000
Stephen Sanderson Transport Holdings Limited	£10,682,332
Alanod Limited	£10,678,000
Mortons Media Group Ltd	£10,676,518
Northamptonshire Arts Management Trust	£10,676,045
S & W Design & Build (Group) Limited	£10,672,160
Rilmac Holdings Limited	£10,668,831
Speeds (Burton) Limited	£10,664,374
Nesform Limited	£10,664,271
I & A Restaurants Ltd	£10,660,340
W.H.Munsey Limited	£10,656,905
NP Aerospace Limited	£10,652,000
Topalpha Limited	£10,638,000
B & S Hughes Limited	£10,637,752
Smithy Wood Business Parks Development LLP	£10,630,845
Peppermint Grove Ltd	£10,630,077
Custodian Real Estate (Leicester) Limited	£10,628,131
Fellside Estates Limited	£10,625,576
Fauxkin Limited	£10,619,485
Latimer Associates (U.K) Limited	£10,618,355
Brightwake Limited	£10,610,736
C.W.Parker (Wainfleet) Limited	£10,608,598
Ian Edgar (Liverpool) Limited	£10,604,746
Pergamon Finance Corporation Limited	£10,584,675
Nottingham Enterprise Zone Development Co Ltd	£10,580,000
Educationcity Limited	£10,574,993
Incat International PLC	£10,570,000
Davison Property Investments Ltd	£10,563,867
Averys (Radnage) Limited	£10,556,071
Chiltern Cold Storage Group Limited	£10,554,841
Pride Care Homes Peterborough Limited	£10,553,846
Palms Row Health Care Limited	£10,552,089
Danetre Holdings Limited	£10,549,632
Lord & Midgley Limited	£10,547,887
Fresh Approach (UK) Holdings Limited	£10,538,494
Monro Limited	£10,537,873
Liberty Guard (U.K.) Limited	£10,531,724
Adenwood Limited	£10,530,311
Eden Holdings Financing Limited	£10,530,101
Dagless Holdings Limited	£10,527,657
RVB Holding Company Limited	£10,520,611
RVB Investments	£10,520,507
Impero Developments Limited	£10,518,722
Midland Assured Finance Limited	£10,503,941
Designer Contracts Limited	£10,497,952
Bildurn (Properties) Limited	£10,492,870
Hall Contracts (Lakenheath) Limited	£10,485,211
R. C. Tinsley Limited	£10,482,164
Apollo Scientific Ltd	£10,479,916
Key Fund Investments Limited	£10,476,974
Cyprotex Discovery Limited	£10,472,861
Reabrook Ltd	£10,466,000
A.E.Hewison Limited	£10,463,817
People Potential Possibilities	£10,456,541
The Cardboard Box Company Limited	£10,455,473
Business By Technology (Holdings) Ltd	£10,454,444
Rainthorpe Farms Limited	£10,451,192
City Furniture Hire Limited	£10,445,167
Direct Leisure Supplies Limited	£10,442,968
Eurokey Recycling Limited	£10,441,729
Farnley Estates Limited	£10,438,859
AVK UK Limited	£10,436,884
Maccaferri Ltd	£10,431,969
Logistex Limited	£10,429,000
DSI Construction Holdings UK Ltd	£10,421,845
Diversey UK Services Limited	£10,418,000
Bishop Stopford School	£10,410,983
Frickley Holdings.Limited	£10,410,980
Logistex Europe Ltd	£10,402,000
A.M.S. Property Management Limited	£10,395,358
Lexden BH (Colchester) Limited	£10,394,363
Isle Education Trust	£10,389,000
Satake Europe Limited	£10,388,034
Thos. C. Wild Limited	£10,384,687
Tamar Renewable Power (Essex) Limited	£10,384,000
Branston Academy Trust	£10,378,458
Livwell Limited	£10,378,000
Enviroenergy Limited	£10,373,591
Abacus Lighting Limited	£10,372,725
107 Station Street Limited	£10,367,015
Willowbrook Healthcare Developments Limited	£10,361,659
Bodycote Treasury Services Limited	£10,360,914
Tresefir Limited	£10,351,061
Laurenglen Limited	£10,347,911
Filta Group Holdings PLC	£10,338,549
CASP	£10,329,564
Maplefields Academy	£10,328,000
Wingfield Academy	£10,326,888
Langley UK Limited	£10,319,585
Redx Pharma PLC	£10,319,000
Devol Kitchens Limited	£10,312,042
Specialised Fixings Limited	£10,310,000
TCS Biosciences Limited	£10,309,924
John Hurt Estates (UK) Limited	£10,308,607
Cedar House Investments Limited	£10,306,326
Berkeley Insurance Group Limited	£10,302,666
The Northampton Theatres Trust Limited	£10,300,841
Erlson Precision Holdings Limited	£10,299,348
Erlson Precision Components Limited	£10,299,347
Meridian Audio Limited	£10,298,243
Motors (Coalville) Limited	£10,294,739
Hague Plant Limited	£10,294,280
Williams Jet Tenders Limited	£10,292,524
Virani Food Products Limited	£10,288,916
Arden Dies Limited	£10,286,908
W. H. Strawson (Notts.) Limited	£10,272,617
Cogne U.K. Limited	£10,268,090
Yew Lodge Limited	£10,266,694
The I.S. Group Limited	£10,265,530
Fugro GB Marine Limited	£10,259,000
Fluorochem Limited	£10,257,235
Severn Trent Corporate Holdings Limited	£10,253,000
The Macclesfield Academy	£10,237,000
Ward Hi-Tech Limited	£10,236,854
Mumford's Mill Rentals Limited	£10,236,803
Omnico Plastics Limited	£10,236,000
GB Fleetcare Limited	£10,234,507
Axiom Group Limited	£10,225,742
RFE International (Group) Ltd	£10,224,672
Grant Farming Limited	£10,220,038

Kingsgate Community Church	£10,217,656
Origin Wine Limited	£10,213,517
Cope Children's Trust	£10,202,311
I.Grunwerg Limited	£10,201,053
Mission Resources Group Limited	£10,199,571
Robinsons Caravans Limited	£10,193,990
Robson Handling Technology Limited	£10,193,859
International Applications Limited	£10,187,534
In at the Side Limited	£10,186,398
M & J Group (Construction & Roofing) Ltd	£10,180,443
RMS Europe Group Limited	£10,177,256
Metflex Precision Mouldings Limited	£10,176,814
Chevin Homes Limited	£10,174,608
Wroxall Abbey Estate Limited	£10,155,555
Blenheim Land & Properties Ltd	£10,153,646
Trewhiddle Village Limited	£10,147,474
Nigel Skinner Financial Advisers Limited	£10,129,492
UK Egg Centre Limited	£10,126,671
Breas Technologies (UK) Limited	£10,118,530
Motorway Direct PLC	£10,118,439
J.O.Adams & Son Limited	£10,110,599
Carl F Groupco Limited	£10,107,000
Northern Endeavour Limited	£10,102,270
Special Piping Materials Limited	£10,101,811
Midcity Estates Limited	£10,095,962
Metlane Limited	£10,095,410
W. H. Strawson (Farms) Limited	£10,094,875
Cranbrook (Jewellers) Ltd	£10,092,124
Cambridge Realty Limited	£10,086,681
Hunter Estates Limited	£10,081,000
Impero Holdings Limited	£10,079,478
William Cook Stanhope Limited	£10,078,763
ALC (FMC) Limited	£10,069,000
Coolair Equipment Limited	£10,064,950
J. Curtis & Sons (Holdings) Limited	£10,064,585
McManus Pub Co. Limited	£10,064,473
TFS Holdings Limited	£10,062,000
Agrifac UK Ltd	£10,059,294
C & S Taylor LLP	£10,051,460
Scenic Land Developments Limited	£10,050,580
Carden Croft (2012) Limited	£10,050,000
Kalsi Properties (UK) Limited	£10,041,533
Amtico International Limited	£10,041,000
Arighi Bianchi Holdings Limited	£10,039,831
Questport Limited	£10,038,401
Midland Assured Holdings Limited	£10,029,386
Business Village Limited	£10,027,360
Harrowden Turf Limited	£10,018,512
Greenshoots Limited	£10,009,976
M.J. Worth Limited	£10,008,585
M.Baker Produce Limited	£10,007,478
Agrivert (West London) Limited	£10,006,628
Novo Community Ltd	£10,000,145
Software (Europe) Limited	£9,996,056
Magna Trust	£9,995,456
Bolsover Properties Limited	£9,995,433
Adam James Limited	£9,992,322
Celleron Therapeutics Limited	£9,989,254
Coleman Investments Limited	£9,986,199
Central Aggregates Ltd	£9,985,180
SCR Financial Interventions Holding Company Ltd	£9,982,754
Tanks and Vessels Industries Limited	£9,980,119
Hardys Farm Limited	£9,975,530
PPL PRS Limited	£9,972,214
M J Gleeson Group Limited	£9,958,000
Servelec Social Care Limited	£9,956,000
Richardson & Cock Limited	£9,954,495
Wispington Farms Limited	£9,954,001
Oakley Lorien Limited	£9,953,850
Stagecoach Supertram Maintenance Ltd.	£9,952,000
UK Vast Holdco Limited	£9,951,395
Car Electronics Limited	£9,949,485
Industrial Control Distributors Limited	£9,947,474
Samuel Hodge Limited	£9,941,724
Mutchmeats Limited	£9,936,108
Worksop Manor Estates,Limited	£9,932,204
Mintridge Investments (Wikowo) Limited	£9,932,111
Cleveland Transit Ltd.	£9,927,000
Caudwell Farms	£9,926,341
Premier Nursing Homes Limited	£9,924,491
North West Steel Limited	£9,922,967
Oncimmune Limited	£9,918,000
Tamar Energy (Holdings) Limited	£9,912,000
Saffron Apothecaries (Leicester) Limited	£9,908,729
Undercover Roofing Supplies Limited	£9,902,000
Undercover Holdings Limited	£9,902,000
Celixir PLC	£9,900,992
Wintringham Newco2 Limited	£9,900,001
J G Pears (Holdings) Limited	£9,899,906
R.J.Stokes & Co. Limited	£9,897,273
Total Integrated Solutions (Holdings) Limited	£9,897,131
NUS Services Limited	£9,893,195
Berkshire Hops Limited	£9,892,772
Exaclair Limited	£9,891,042
Yorkshire Repak Holdings Limited	£9,890,873
Gilo Investments Limited	£9,887,210
Roger Warnes Transport Limited	£9,884,686
Glazewing Limited	£9,882,679
Novoferm UK Holdings Limited	£9,870,990
Working Assets Limited	£9,870,008
Surfpipe Limited	£9,869,079
Glencalvie Estate	£9,863,303
AmeyCespa (MK) ODC Limited	£9,861,000
Tarka Controls Limited	£9,860,631
The National Church of England Academy Trust	£9,860,000
Glenco Limited	£9,859,501
NUS Holdings Limited	£9,856,502
Adient Holding Germany Ltd	£9,854,000
Rayburn Tours (Holdings) Limited	£9,853,639
Shima Seiki Europe Limited	£9,850,980
Acorn Partitions & Storage Systems Limited	£9,848,067
Central England Healthcare Limited	£9,847,547
Timico Technology Group Limited	£9,843,000
Blackburn Starling & Company Limited	£9,841,738
Society of The Salutation of Mary The Virgin Ltd	£9,840,483
Dana UK Driveshaft Limited	£9,840,000
V Installations Mechanical Handling Limited	£9,837,701
JFC Plastics Limited	£9,832,575
Thornhill Estates Limited	£9,829,936
Winter & Co. UK Limited	£9,825,453
S. & A. Drapers Limited	£9,820,608
Linford Properties (Leicester) Limited	£9,819,935
Clearmark Solutions (2019) LLP	£9,815,637
Barwood Strategic Land II LLP	£9,813,249
Supply Point Systems Limited	£9,808,176
Lucy Developments Limited	£9,807,830
Ceetak Holdings Limited	£9,781,113
Radical Sportscars Limited	£9,776,224
Prophet PLC	£9,775,140
Kennelpak Limited	£9,767,000
Potomac Capital Limited	£9,764,819
Colbert Wall Holdings Limited	£9,756,182
Wilcox Commercial Vehicles Limited	£9,755,909
Realpower Limited	£9,755,000
MCL Group of Companies Limited	£9,754,810
IRISNDT UK Holdings Limited	£9,754,032
HBB Homes Limited	£9,747,688
Linnell Brothers Limited	£9,747,243
Leaworks Limited	£9,737,703
Battles Limited	£9,735,624
Midland Sports Centre for The Disabled Trust Limited	£9,735,622
Umeco Composites Limited	£9,734,633
Tripal Group Limited	£9,734,422
Carlton Forest Group LLP	£9,724,436

JJS Manufacturing Limited	£9,717,731
Rye St. Antony School Limited	£9,715,829
D D Heating Limited	£9,708,957
Viewtone Trading Group Limited	£9,707,000
Rayburn Tours Limited	£9,697,573
Kingerlee Homes Limited	£9,694,000
Atlas Hotels (Derby) Limited	£9,692,667
Envirogen Water Technologies Limited	£9,690,000
Jaguar Estates Investments Limited	£9,689,521
Sureclean Holdco Limited	£9,686,074
J3 Business Park Doncaster LLP	£9,685,991
Mobius Motors Limited	£9,684,722
Yarborough Limited	£9,683,637
Warm A Home Limited	£9,682,973
M.J.C. Developments Limited	£9,680,337
Games Workshop US (Holdings) Limited	£9,679,000
Buccleuch Property (Shawfair) Limited	£9,670,884
Bristol Novelty Limited	£9,668,483
Apollo Partnership Trust	£9,663,000
Manor Crest Construction Limited	£9,659,841
Harley (Winchester) Limited	£9,655,092
Sir Robert Pattinson Academy	£9,650,669
Access Platform Sales Limited	£9,647,870
Gallagher Projects Limited	£9,645,564
Beechfield Estates Limited	£9,641,629
Imago @ Loughborough Limited	£9,641,477
BICL Limited	£9,637,162
Wright Hassall LLP	£9,636,983
TGH Finance Limited	£9,628,000
G2M Unilets Limited	£9,627,463
R.M. Cottingham Limited	£9,621,556
Charles Lawrence Surfaces Limited	£9,619,512
Cranford Asset Management Limited	£9,619,141
Detrafford No1 Castlefield Ltd	£9,615,195
Stephenson (MK) Trust	£9,613,879
Primesite UK Limited	£9,607,294
Agrivert (Wallingford) Limited	£9,606,135
Green Meadow Limited	£9,604,391
S.E.B. International Limited	£9,599,347
Oxford Said Business School Limited	£9,592,000
Meatsnacks Group Ltd.	£9,591,367
Ghekko Limited	£9,570,879
Moulsford Preparatory School Trust Limited	£9,565,906
Industrial Machinery Supplies Limited	£9,564,000
Evans Leicester Limited	£9,559,782
Mediline Home Care Limited	£9,557,678
Mowbray Indigo Limited	£9,554,123
TWS Property Limited	£9,550,827
Barry Wood Plant Hire Limited	£9,547,574
Stirling Management Group Limited	£9,547,495
Sparken Hill Academy Trust	£9,547,181
Belgium Midco Limited	£9,543,491
JSC EFarms LLP	£9,540,683
William F.Moore (Warplands) Limited	£9,540,275
Roc Oil (Europe) Limited	£9,536,238
The Juice Master Limited	£9,527,052
WJ South Limited	£9,525,391
Select Alloys & Materials Limited	£9,519,941
Cawrey Ltd	£9,495,730
Electronic Data Processing Limited	£9,486,000
Ivor Shaw Limited	£9,485,436
Afpro LLP	£9,475,689
Gibbs Technologies Limited	£9,473,443
Igloo Books Group Holdings Limited	£9,469,961
Slack & Parr Limited	£9,466,000
Ingka Energy Services UK Limited	£9,456,000
LGS Capital Limited	£9,445,694
Tripal International Limited	£9,442,573
Caljan Rite-Hite Limited	£9,441,462
Corran (Wakefield) Limited	£9,438,275
Imago Publishing Limited	£9,436,447
Dana Spicer Europe Limited	£9,435,000
Plaza Investments Limited	£9,433,733
Diamond Fuel Supplies Limited	£9,429,059
Zapf Creation (UK) Limited	£9,425,000
Jaddu Ltd	£9,421,109
J & A (International) Limited	£9,419,233
H.B. Pearce (Contractors) Limited	£9,406,729
Gardeden Bidco Limited	£9,397,929
Drishaun Holdings Limited	£9,396,106
Prahi (2017) Limited	£9,389,984
Avenuepoint Limited	£9,386,926
Great Tew Grain Processing Limited	£9,384,365
Cheaney Shoes Limited	£9,384,120
Verdon Holdings Limited	£9,383,555
East Coast Fittings Limited	£9,383,512
Grantham Bros. Limited	£9,363,603
Dri-Pak Limited	£9,362,620
Casterton College Rutland	£9,360,293
FFP Packaging Solutions Limited	£9,359,004
Youth Sport Trust	£9,339,981
Marlborough Property (Watermead) Limited	£9,333,959
J.W.Sivil Limited	£9,331,207
Munro Building Services Holdings Limited	£9,329,935
Dana UK Automotive Systems Limited	£9,328,000
Smith Cooper Audit Limited	£9,325,671
Radical Motorsport Limited	£9,324,192
Johnston Quarry Group Limited	£9,321,012
Tallington Holdings Limited	£9,320,761
Ten Cate Advanced Composites Limited	£9,319,386
Valens Resources Group PLC	£9,314,632
Navagator Limited	£9,311,000
Stamford Group Limited (The)	£9,308,000
Bolton Plastic Components Limited	£9,307,028
Oxford Renewable Fuel Ltd	£9,303,710
AEBI Schmidt UK Limited	£9,302,000
Hallamshire Developments Limited	£9,295,933
Reel Cinemas Limited	£9,295,855
BCTI Holdings Limited	£9,294,613
Sheffield Theatres Crucible Trust	£9,292,034
CNIM Clugston (Avonmouth) Limited	£9,290,450
Inclusion Care Holdings Limited	£9,278,432
Bowmer-Bond Narrow Fabrics Limited	£9,272,215
Sape Group Holdings UK Ltd	£9,251,404
Monoworld Recycling Ltd	£9,241,187
A4E Ltd	£9,241,000
Bradgate Containers Limited	£9,235,134
Curtis Instruments (U.K.) Limited	£9,233,203
Fired Earth Limited	£9,217,839
Cornshire Limited	£9,215,975
Alere Limited	£9,211,997
Inclusion Care Group Limited	£9,209,851
Turner Investments Ltd.	£9,208,461
James O'Flanagan Limited	£9,196,485
Spraycon Limited	£9,182,106
Bridgeway Consulting Limited	£9,180,867
Yourcash Holdings Limited	£9,176,000
ERF Electrical Wholesalers Ltd.	£9,162,934
Lo's Pharmacy Limited	£9,159,922
ScarsdaleVets LLP	£9,157,253
Milehouse Foods Limited	£9,156,419
C Butt Holdings Limited	£9,147,208
Fields Property Limited	£9,144,925
TI Automotive Canada Holdings Limited	£9,140,219
The Market Bosworth School	£9,128,000
Staton Young (Anglesey) Limited	£9,124,867
Mistral Capital Management Limited	£9,122,302
Reddil Properties Limited	£9,110,324
S.T.L. Trading Company Limited	£9,109,631
Huxlow Science College	£9,107,446
Sutton Carter Investments Limited	£9,105,911
Rotherham Sand and Gravel Company Limited (The)	£9,099,646
Belgrave Land (Wisbech) Limited	£9,096,071
Growth LED Innovation Driven Employee Company Ltd	£9,094,772

Arden Topco Limited	£9,087,467
Red Arrow Trading Limited	£9,073,917
Swiftbuild Properties Limited	£9,066,489
Ambury Developments Limited	£9,060,000
Gardner Aerospace - Hull Limited	£9,059,000
Fabrics & Yarns (Macclesfield) Ltd	£9,050,238
SDI (Edinburgh) Limited	£9,049,674
Burbidge Holdings Limited	£9,048,824
Fossil (UK) Holdings Limited	£9,021,268
Nottingham City Airport Limited	£9,020,083
E J Orr Limited	£9,016,520
Minorfern Limited	£9,013,893
Symm Group Limited	£9,013,413
Kidderminster Property Investments Limited	£9,012,595
Monocon Overseas Limited	£9,008,282
Effective Energy Solutions Ltd	£9,007,723
Higham Lane School	£9,005,000

This page is intentionally left blank

Age of Companies

1800s [28]
Armitage Brothers Limited
Baptist Union Corporation Limited
Boots Company PLC
Church Army
Derby County Football Club Limited
General Conference of The New Church
Samuel Hodge Limited
Ibstock Brick Limited
Leicester Racecourse Holdings Limited
Loake Brothers Limited
Lucy Group Ltd
Molson Coors Brewing Co (UK) Ltd
Molson Coors Holdings Limited
Next Holdings Limited
Quantum Clothing Group Limited
Robinson PLC
Schering-Plough Limited
Siddall and Hilton,Limited
Singleton Birch Limited
John Smedley Limited
Southwell and Nottingham Diocesan Board of Finance
Stadco Limited
Trent College Limited
Triplex Lloyd Properties Limited
United Cast Bar (UK) Limited
United Church Schools Foundation Ltd
Vesuvius UK Limited
Vinters Engineering Limited

1900-1909 [25]
Allied Textile Companies Limited
Albert Browne Limited
Carlsberg UK Limited
Thomas Cook Retail Limited
Dubois Limited
EPC United Kingdom PLC
Emhart International Limited
Evonik Chemicals Limited
C.W.Fletcher & Sons,Limited
Giant Booker Limited
Hartwell Finance Limited
Hook Norton Brewery Co Ltd
William Kenyon & Sons Limited
J.B.Kind Limited
Lincoln Diocesan Trust and Board of Finance Ltd
Raleigh Holdings Ltd
Reeves Wireline Technologies Limited
Ruskin College
Smith Brothers (Leicester) Limited
Source Bioscience Limited
Telent Limited
Tucker Fasteners Limited
Vaillant European Holdings Limited
Whirlpool UK Appliances Limited
Woodland Buildings Investment Co Ltd

1910-1919 [57]
AAH Pharmaceuticals Limited
BPB Limited
Barker Shoes Limited
E.P.Barrus Limited
Beatson Clark Limited
Binney & Smith (Europe) Limited
Henry Boot PLC
Breedon Southern Limited
British Polythene Industries Limited
Coleman Investments Limited
Diamond Power Specialty Limited
E.A.T. (Holdings) Limited
East Kent Road Car Co Ltd
Elliott Group Limited
English Electric Co Ltd
Exaclair Limited
Experian Finance PLC
Fanuc UK Limited
Firth Rixson Forgings Limited
Firth Rixson Metals Limited
J.H.& F.W.Green Limited
Hartwell Automotive Group Limited
Hartwell PLC
Headington School Oxford Limited
Infinis (Re-Gen) Limited
Jepson & Co Limited
W & J Linney Limited
MPAC Group PLC
W.H.Munsey Limited
National Farmers Union Mutual Insurance Society Ltd
James Neill Holdings Limited
Oxbow Coal Limited
Oxford Diocesan Board of Finance
PSA Retail UK Limited
Pendragon Vehicle Management Limited
Peugeot Motor Company PLC
Pirelli UK Limited
Pollard Boxes Limited
Qualter, Hall & Co Ltd
Raleigh UK Ltd
F.H.Rowse Limited
Russell Acott Limited
Salter Bros,Limited
Satra
Shoe Zone Retail Limited
Slack & Parr (Investments) Limited
St.Edward's School
Stagecoach (North West) Limited
Trent Motor Traction Co Ltd
Umeco Limited
Watches of Switzerland Co Ltd
Welcome Financial Services Limited
Charles Wells,Limited
Western Buses Limited
Wolf Safety Lamp Co Ltd
Frank Wright Limited
York Ward & Rowlatt Limited

1920-1929 [69]
A.T.C. Manufacturing Limited
AAH Limited
API Foils Limited
API Group PLC
API Laminates Limited
Admenta Holdings Limited
Aggregate Industries Holdings Limited
Ancon Limited
Avon Insurance PLC
George Bateman & Son Limited
Beechwood Estates Co.Limited
John Bell & Croyden Limited
Ben Bennett Jr Limited
Bodycote Surface Technology Limited
Booker Limited
Boots Properties Limited
Bridon Limited
Carpenter Limited
Ceylon Tea Growers Association,Limited
Church & Co Limited
Citroen U.K. Limited
Corus Hotels Limited
Cristal Pigment UK Limited
Croda Europe Limited
Croda International PLC
Crystal Martin Holdings Limited
Derby Diocesan Board of Finance Limited
James Durrans & Sons,Limited
Dyson Group PLC
Firth Rixson Limited
Forticrete Limited
Foster Yeoman Limited
John Hargreaves,(Collyhurst and Stalybridge) Ltd
Highcroft Investments PLC
Horticultural Trades Association
Jourdan PLC
KSB Limited
Lawton Tube Co Ltd
Leicester Diocesan Board of Finance
Lincolnshire Road Car Co Ltd
Linread Limited
MacDermid Autotype Limited
Methodist Guild Holidays Limited
Micronclean Limited
Morris Homes (Midlands) Limited
Mutual Clothing & Supply Co Ltd
Normanby Estate Co Ltd
Peterborough Diocesan Board of Finance
Robert Pochin Limited
Frederic Robinson Limited
Rodenhurst Estates Limited
Rodericks Dental Limited
Rugby Group Limited
SGBD Property Holdings Limited
Scott Bader Co Ltd
Sharmans Agricultural Limited
Sheffield Diocesan Board of Finance
Special Steel Co.,Limited
A.E.Spink Limited
Stanley Works Limited
R.J.Stokes & Co. Limited
Stowe School,Limited
Sycamore (Peterborough) Limited
Symm Group Limited
G.F.Tomlinson Group Limited
Total Downstream UK PLC
Wacoal EMEA Ltd
Warners (Midlands) PLC
Wildgoose Construction Limited

1930-1939 [108]
AMG Superalloys UK Limited
Accuride International Limited
Aga Rangemaster Group Limited
Aggregate Industries UK Limited
F G Alden Limited
Avdel Holding Limited
Avdel UK Limited
Averys (Radnage) Limited
Battle,Hayward and Bower,Limited
Berkshire Hops Limited
Betafence Limited
Birds (Derby) Limited
Blugilt Holdings Limited
Henry Boot Estates Limited
Boughton Estates Limited
Bradshaw Taylor Ltd.
Bramah Limited
Bramptonia Limited
Brecknell, Willis & Co. Limited
British Polythene Limited
British Racing Drivers Club Limited
Brookhead Estate Limited
R.J.Brown & Sons Limited

Building and Plumbing Supplies Limited
CEF Holdings Limited
Calor Gas Limited
Cemex Investments Limited
Chemetall Limited
J.J.Churchill Limited
City Electrical Factors Limited
Clugston Group Limited
Clyde Union DB Limited
Coventry Diocesan Board of Finance
Crown Aerosols UK Ltd
DHP Family Ltd.
Derbyshire Property Trust Limited
Dodson & Horrell (Holdings) Limited
Doncasters Limited
Essentra Filter Products Limited
Estate Incomes Limited
Evans Halshaw.Com Limited
Everards Brewery Limited
First National Housing Trust Limited
George Fischer Sales Limited
Forman Hardy Holdings Limited
Frontline Limited
GL UK Holdings Limited
Greencore Prepared Meals Limited
Hallamshire Developments Limited
Hostombe Group Limited
Hunter Estates Limited
Icon Aerospace Technology Ltd
Interflora British Unit
Jewson Limited
Laver Regeneration Limited
Lillywhites Limited
Limestone Farming Co Ltd
Logistex Limited
Longcliffe Quarries Limited
ML UK Holding Limited
E. Moss, Limited
Motors (Coalville) Limited
National House-Building Council
Naylor Drainage Ltd
Wm. Nelstrop & Co. Ltd
Norcros Industry (International) Limited
C.John Norris (Cars & Caravans) Limited
Oldrid & Co.,Limited
Paralloy Limited
Peacock & Binnington
F. Perkins Limited
Polynt Composites UK Limited
H. Ponsford Limited
Premierfirst Vehicle Rental Franchising Ltd
Charles Pugh (Glass) Limited
Pyrotek Engineering Materials Limited
Radford Holdings Limited
Renault Truck Commercials Limited
Rieke Packaging Systems Limited
Rigid Containers Limited
Rigid Group Limited
Rolls-Royce Leasing Limited
Rotherham Sand and Gravel Co Ltd
SPS Technologies Limited
Saint-Gobain High Performance Materials UK Ltd
Salvesen Logistics Limited
T. A. Savery & Co Limited
J.W.Sivil Limited
Smith Bros.(Caerconan) Wholesale Limited
Walter E. Sturgess & Sons Limited
Symmetry Medical Sheffield Ltd.
Synthetic Resins Limited
Sywell Aerodrome,Limited
Taylor Bloxham Group Limited
Telent Communications Holdings Limited
Terex Pegson Limited
Thistle Insurance Services Limited
Thornhill Estates Limited
Together Trust
Triplex Lloyd Limited
Vaillant Group UK Limited
WFEL Limited
Weetabix Limited
Westfield Contributory Health Scheme Ltd
J.Wharton (Shipping) Limited
Worksop Manor Estates,Limited
XPO Investment UK Limited
YHA (England and Wales)

1940-1949 [118]

A.E.S. Engineering Limited
Adient Seating UK Ltd
Alumasc Limited
Amey Fleet Services Limited
Aspen Medical Europe Limited
BI Group Limited
Barton Petroleum Limited
Blankney Estates Limited
Blue Cross
C.F.Booth Limited
Bradbury & Son (Buxton) Limited
C D Bramall Limited
Bridon International Ltd.
British Bakels Limited
British Horse Society
Burrough Court Estate Limited
Burt Bros.(Hosiery) Limited
Camping and Caravanning Club Limited
CarnaudMetalbox Overseas Ltd.
Carwood Motor Units Limited
Cemex UK Services Limited
Chatfields Limited
Church UK Retail Limited
William Cook Stanhope Limited
Crockett and Jones Limited
Maurice Crouch (Growers) Limited
W. Cumber & Son (Theale) Limited
Cummins Generator Technologies Limited
J. Curtis & Sons Limited
Dagless Limited
Dana Spicer Europe Limited
Darley Limited
William Davis Limited
Dawsongroup UK Limited
Deeley Construction Limited
Deritend International Limited
Derwent Vehicles Limited
Draper Commercial Limited
Elsoms (Spalding) Limited
Essentra Filter Products International Ltd
Eterna Lighting Limited
Eyre & Elliston Limited
Fine Lady Bakeries Limited
Fine Tubes Limited
J.F. Finnegan Limited
Foseco International Limited
GL Events UK Limited
F & A George Limited
R.A. Gibson (Colesden) Limited
Grundon Sand & Gravel Limited
Guilford Europe Limited
Halliwell Jones (Wilmslow) Limited
Fred Hartley (Estates) Limited
Hazlewood Foods Limited
H.L. Hutchinson Limited
Imtech Engineering Services Central Ltd
Jelson Holdings Limited
Kingham Hill Trust
Knowles (Transport) Limited
A.E. Lenton Limited
Lincolnshire Wildlife Trust
Linnell Brothers Limited
Lister Wilder Group Limited
A.C. Lloyd Holdings Limited
Loades PLC
MWUK Limited
A.J.Mackaness Limited
Maurice Mason Limited
Melham Group Limited
Mercedes-Benz Retail Group UK Limited
Monier Redland Limited
William F.Moore (Warplands) Limited
Morrells Holdings Limited
Mortons of Horncastle Limited
Motor Insurers' Bureau
M.C.Mountain and Son Limited
NMCN PLC
Nampak Plastics Europe Limited
Norbar Torque Tools Limited
North Oxford Garage Limited
James O'Flanagan Limited
Otter Controls Limited
H.B. Pearce (Contractors) Limited
Pegler Yorkshire Group Limited
Pera International
Potter's Leisure Ltd.
Proctor Bros. (Long Sutton) Limited
R3 Polygon UK Ltd.
Ritter-Courivaud Limited
Robson Handling Technology Limited
Romo Limited
SC Johnson Professional Limited
Samworth Brothers (Holdings) Limited
Sandicliffe Garage Limited
Secanim Limited
Sheffield United Limited
Smith & Sons (Bletchington) Limited
F.P.Smith (Holdings) Limited
Stepnell Limited
Stratton-Streles Estates Limited
W.R.Swann & Co.Limited
Synchemicals Limited
T. Quality Limited
Thwaites Limited
Travis Perkins (Properties) Limited
U-Pol Limited
Unipath Limited
VRES Holdings Limited
Ernest V. Waddington Limited
Waterline Limited
Wavin Limited
H.K. Wentworth Limited
W.Westerman Limited
Whitworth Bros.Limited
Wilko Retail Limited
Thos.Winnard & Sons Limited
A H Worth and Co Ltd
W S Yeates Limited

1950-1959 [191]

A B Graphic International Limited
AEBI Schmidt UK Limited
AEM Limited
AGCO Limited
AGCO Manufacturing Limited
AGCO Services Limited
ARG Corporate Services Limited
Acertec Engineering Limited

Ackroyd & Abbott Limited
J.O.Adams & Son Limited
Aircraft Research Association Limited
Al-Ko Kober Limited
Alanod Limited
Alco Estates Limited
Ametek Airtechnology Group Limited
Arbor Forest Products Limited
Arconic Closure Systems International (UK) Ltd
Arconic Manufacturing (GB) Limited
Ascott Transport Limited
Assemblies of God Property Trust
Avanti Gas Limited
Avon Cosmetics Limited
Banner Plant Limited
Barratt Developments P L C
Bedfordia Farms Limited
Bedfordia Group Limited
Belgrade Theatre Trust (Coventry) Ltd
Belmont Press Limited
Belron UK Limited
Berwin Industrial Polymers Limited
Berwin Rubber Co Ltd
Bodycote PLC
Bowmer-Bond Narrow Fabrics Limited
Buckingham Plant Hire Limited
Bullimores Sand and Gravel Limited
Russell Burgess Limited
Bury's Dryanstore Limited
CPL Distribution Limited
Carr's Flour Mills Limited
Caterpillar (U.K.) Limited
Cathelco Limited
Caudwell Farms
Central Garage (Uppingham) Limited
W.S.Chapman & Sons Limited
Cherry Valley Farms Limited
E.D. & A.D. Cooke, Bourne (Farms) Ltd
R.M. Cottingham Limited
Cullum Detuners Limited
DHL Supply Chain Limited
J.E. & V.M. Dalton Limited
Darrington Quarries Limited
Davison & Co. (Barford) Limited
Patrick Dean Limited
Ditchley Foundation
Diversey UK Services Limited
Donvale Holdings Limited
Dow Chemical Co Ltd
Dragon School Trust Limited
EJ UK Fabrication & Access Solutions Holdings Ltd
Eclipse Magnetics Limited
Ian Edgar (Liverpool) Limited
Envigo International Limited
Essentra Components Limited
Etex (Exteriors) UK Limited
Euramax Solutions Limited
GEA Mechanical Equipment UK Limited
GLW Feeds Limited
Gardner Aerospace - Hull Limited
General Domestic Appliances Holdings Ltd
Glanmoor Investments Limited
J.C.M.Glassford Limited
Gleadell Agriculture Limited
M J Gleeson Group Limited
R.J. & A.E. Godfrey
J W Grant Co
I.Grunwerg Limited
Gurney Slade Lime & Stone Co.Limited
Hawkes Limited
Hella Limited
Henton & Chattell Limited
Heygates Limited
Hodge Clemco Limited
Hoval Limited
Howard & Hallam Limited
P.C. Howard Limited
Jeld-Wen UK Limited
J.Jelley and Son Limited
Jelson Limited
Jennings of Garsington Limited
Jones Homes (North West) Limited
Keller Limited
Kendall Bros. (Portsmouth) Limited
Knights of Old,Limited
Langridge Homes Limited
J.T. Leavesley Limited
Lockheed Martin UK Ampthill Limited
Long Marsh Limited
Lord & Midgley Limited
M.& N.Textiles Limited
Maccaferri Ltd
M.Markovitz Limited
Geoffrey Mason Limited
Merloni Domestic Appliances Limited
Meynell Plant Hire Limited
Walter Miles (Electrical Engineers) Ltd
Morphy Richards Limited
Motorway Services Limited
Muirhead Aerospace Limited
Mulberry Bush Organisation Limited
Owen Mumford Holdings Limited
Nasmyth Bulwell Limited
Neal Brothers (Leicester) Limited
Neill Tools Limited
Norcros Group (Holdings) Limited
Olmar Investments Limited
Oxfam
G W Padley Holdings Limited
G.H. Parker (North Cotes) Limited
C.W.Parker (Wainfleet) Limited
W. T. Parker Group Services Limited
Perkins Holdings Limited
Peveril Securities Limited
J.E.Piccaver & Co. (Gedney Marsh)
Porterbrook Leasing Asset Co Ltd
Mark H Poskitt Limited
Potters-Ballotini Limited
Povoas Packaging Limited
George Pragnell Limited
J.A.Pye (Oxford) Limited
Richardson & Cock Limited
Rilmac Holdings Limited
Rockwell International
Rolls-Royce Submarines Limited
Rutland Plastics Limited
Rye St. Antony School Limited
D.H.Sanderson and Son Limited
Saria Limited
Sarval Limited
Scott Bader Commonwealth Limited
Seachill UK Limited
Searles (Camping Ground) Limited
Shield Engineering (Syston) Limited
Simons Developments Limited
J O Sims Holdings Limited
Skills Motor Coaches Limited
Ben Smith & Sons (Wantage) Limited
A.W. Smith & Sons Limited
Smiths Concrete Limited
Society of The Salutation of Mary The Virgin Ltd
South Coast Furnishing Co Ltd
Staples (Vegetables) Limited
Staples Brothers Limited
M.F. Strawson Limited
Street Crane Co Ltd
Summerfields School Trust,Limited
Swizzels Matlow Limited
TI Group Automotive Systems Limited
Tappex Thread Inserts Limited
Taylor Lindsey Limited
B & K Thomas (Holdings) Limited
R. C. Tinsley Limited
Total Lindsey Oil Refinery Limited
Tulip Limited
Tunstall Group Limited
G.B.Turnbull Limited
UK Steel Enterprise Limited
Unipart Group Limited
Unipart International Holdings Limited
Uniq (Holdings) Limited
Vacu-Lug Traction Tyres Limited
Vaillant Home Products Limited
Reg Vardy Limited
Versus Arthritis
Vinters International Limited
Volkswagen Group United Kingdom Limited
W.L. Shareholding Co Ltd
Walker & Son (Hauliers) Limited
C. Walton Limited
R.H. Ward (Welton) Limited
Dare Warwick (Properties) Limited
Weatherbys Ltd
Weidmuller Limited
H.I.Weldrick Limited
Wheatcroft Collections Limited
Wheatcroft Properties Limited
Wicksteed Leisure Limited
Willoughby Farms Limited
Windsor Vehicle Leasing Limited
Wolseley UK Limited
Wrendal Holdings Limited
Xylem Water Solutions UK Ltd

1960-1969 [270]

3M Health Care Limited
A & S Leisure Group Limited
A-Plan Holdings
AMG Alpoco UK Limited
ASSA ABLOY Entrance Systems Ltd
Advance Tapes Group Limited
Advance Tapes International Limited
Geo.Akins (Holdings) Limited
Aldermore Bank PLC
Allied Publicity Services (Manchester) Ltd
Alloy Racing Equipment Limited
Almadon Limited
AmeyCespa (East) Limited
Don Amott Parks Limited
Apec Limited
Arden Dies Limited
Armitages Pet Products Limited
Asfordby Storage & Haulage Limited
Autins Limited
BASF PLC
BHIB Limited
BPX Electro-Mechanical Co Ltd
F.W. Baker Limited
Ball Horticultural Europe Limited
Ball. Roller & Transmission Bearings Ltd
Bardsley Construction Limited
Beamglow Limited
Belle Engineering (Sheen) Limited

Berkshire, Buckinghamshire and Oxfordshire Wildlife Trust
Blackwell UK Limited
E.E.Blyth & Co Limited
Boden & Davies Limited
Bolsover Properties Limited
Boole's Tools & Pipe Fittings Limited
Boots UK Limited
Bosch Rexroth Limited
Wilson Bowden Developments Limited
Bowmer and Kirkland Limited
Bramall Quicks Dealerships Limited
R. Bratley (Quadring) Limited
Broadthorpe Limited
Brose Limited
Bruker UK Limited
Burghley House Preservation Trust Ltd
Buxton Press Limited
Buzz Entertainment Limited
Buzz Group Limited
CEVA Container Logistics Limited
Joseph Camm Farms Limited
Car Electronics Limited
Carlsberg UK Holdings Limited
Carrier Refrigeration UK Limited
R.Caudwell (Produce) Limited
Caunton Engineering Limited
Cawrey Ltd
Cemex UK Operations Limited
Cemex UK Properties Limited
Charles Street Buildings (Leicester) Ltd
K.J. Cherry & Sons Limited
Cherwell Valley Silos Limited
Clegg Construction Limited
T.H.Clements & Son Limited
Clowes Developments (UK) Limited
Clugston Construction Limited
Coba Automotive (UK) Limited
Cokethorpe Educational Trust Limited
Collingwood Lighting Limited
Copart UK Limited
Coster Aerosols Limited
Cothill Trust
Court Properties (Portugal) Limited
Covrad Heat Transfer Limited
Cranford Asset Management Limited
Crystal Martin International Limited
Cyden Homes Limited
DFDS Pension Limited
Dean Property Group Limited
Destec Engineering Limited
Doncasters Blaenavon Limited
Dri-Pak Limited
ERF Electrical Wholesalers Ltd.
Eclipse Colour Print Limited
Ede Holdings Limited
Electronic Data Processing Limited
Ellis Bros (Contractors) Limited
Elsoms Seeds Limited
Emerson Process Management Limited
Encase Limited
Engel U.K. Limited
Enterprise Managed Services Limited
Euramax Coated Products Limited
Eurofleet Rental Limited
Europcar UK Limited
Evolution Homecare Services Limited
Experian Limited
FFP Packaging Solutions Limited
Farmington Trust Limited
Fauxkin Limited
Fellowes Ltd
Festo Limited
Fox (Owmby) Limited
Gamston Kennels & Farms Limited
Gleeson Developments Limited
Glencore Agriculture UK Ltd.
Grainsby Farms Limited
Grantham Investments Limited
Graypen Limited
Greencore Food To Go Limited
Griffith Foods Limited
Hancock Cash & Carry Limited
Harlow Bros. Limited
T.C. Harrison 1960 Limited
Harrowden Farms Limited
Haven Housing Limited
Health & Diet Group Limited
Heygate & Sons Limited
Hill House School Limited
Holophane Europe Limited
P.D.Hook (Hatcheries) Limited
Huber + Suhner (UK) Limited
Humphris (Banbury) Limited
Hunter Douglas (UK) Limited
Hydro Extrusion UK Ltd
Ibstock Brick Holding Co Ltd
Ingenta PLC
Interfuse Limited
Intervet UK Limited
Irth (15) Limited
JFB Overseas Holdings Limited
Francis Jackson Homes Limited
Jarden Consumer Solutions (Europe) Ltd
Mark Jarvis Limited
P.E.Jones (Properties) Limited
Jotun Paints (Europe) Limited
Jungheinrich UK Limited
Kidney Research UK
T.H.Kingerlee & Sons Limited
L. & M. Investment Co Ltd
LDC (Boston) Limited
R.A.Labone & Co Limited
R. H. Lamyman Limited
Landmark Wholesale Limited
Lapwing Estate Limited
Charles Lawrence Surfaces Limited
Leica Geosystems Limited
A.E. Lenton (Holdings) Limited
Levi Strauss (U.K.) Limited
A C Lloyd Homes Limited
Lloyds Bank Commercial Finance Limited
Lloyds Pharmacy Limited
Long Rake Spar Co Ltd
Lousada PLC
Lubrizol Limited
Robert Luff Foundation Limited
Luxus Limited
MAN Energy Solutions UK Limited
MPAC Overseas Holdings Limited
MS International PLC
MacIntyre Care
Maranello Concessionaires Limited
Marshall Amplification PLC
Measom (Dryline) Limited
Megaflo Limited
Mercedes-Benz Grand Prix Ltd
Mercer Farming Limited
Mettler-Toledo Limited
Midland Assured Finance Limited
Miele Co Ltd
Milltarn Limited
Minoli & Co Ltd
Monarch Knitting Machinery (U.K.) Ltd
Montracon Limited
J.H. Moore & Son (Rickmansworth) Ltd
Morris Homes (North) Limited
Moulsford Preparatory School Trust Ltd
Moulton Bulb Co Ltd
Multi-Tile Limited
Mytravel Group Limited
Natco Foods Limited
Nationwide Accident Repair Services Ltd
Nationwide Crash Repair Centres Limited
Nationwide Fast Fit Plus Limited
New Testament Church of God
Nexans Logistics Limited
John Nicholls (Trading) Limited
David Nieper Limited
Oerlikon Balzers Coating UK Limited
Oxford Instruments Nanotechnology Tools Ltd
Oxford Instruments PLC
PMC Fluidpower Limited
G W Padley Poultry Limited
Palm Paper Limited
Palmer Family Trust PLC
Pektron Group Limited
Pendragon Finance and Insurance Services Ltd
Porvair Filtration Group Limited
Poste Hotels Limited
Practical Action
Preci-Spark Limited
Premierfirst Vehicle Rental Holdings Ltd
Princess International Sales and Service Ltd
D.B. Ramsden & Co Ltd
Ravensburger Limited
Reabrook Ltd
Recticel Limited
Robinsons Caravans Limited
Rockwell Automation Limited
Rolls-Royce International Limited
William Rowland Limited
S. & A. Drapers Limited
S.I.P.(Industrial Products) Limited
Saint-Gobain Construction Products UK Ltd
Sarval (Hartshill) Limited
Scania (Great Britain) Limited
Scholastic Limited
Sensient Colors UK Ltd
Set Copyrights Limited
Ivor Shaw Limited
Sheffield Theatres Trust
Sibson Mill Properties Limited
Sigma Precision Components UK Limited
Silverstone Circuits Limited
Simons Construction Limited
John Sinclair (Sheffield) Limited
Sleaford Quality Foods Limited
Smallpeice Trust
Smith Brothers Stores Limited
Snowmountain Enterprises Limited
Solpro Manufacturing Limited
St. Ann's Hospice
St. Luke's Hospice
Standard Motor Products Europe Limited
John A. Stephens Limited
W. H. Strawson (Farms) Limited
W. H. Strawson (Notts.) Limited
Streason Limited
Sutton Park Motor Co Ltd
Suzuki GB PLC
Swann-Morton Limited
Sytner Limited
TDY Limited

TI Group Automotive Systems (UK) Limited
Telent Technology Services Limited
Tennant Metallurgical Group Limited
Thyssenkrupp Elevator UK Limited
Tickhill Engineering Co Ltd
R.H.Topham & Sons Limited
Travelodge Hotels Limited
Travis Perkins PLC
Travis Perkins Trading Co Ltd
Truelove Property & Construction Ltd
Turbo-Union Limited
Turner Investments Ltd.
Unicarriers UK Limited
Richard Utley Limited
Vaillant Holdings Limited
W.& S.(Long Eaton) Limited
Weatherford U.K. Limited
Welbeck Estates Co Ltd
John A.Wells Limited
Westmoreland Investments Limited
Westmoreland Properties Limited
J. Wharton (Agriculture) Limited
Wigley Contracts (Barby) Limited
David Wilson Homes Limited
Wipac Limited
Woburn Enterprises Limited
Wollaston Motors Limited
Yarborough Limited
Yew Lodge Limited

1970-1979 [379]

A F Switchgear Limited
A.B. Hotels Limited
AGD Equipment Limited
AGD Holdings Limited
Accrofab Limited
Accuma Plastics Limited
Acushnet Europe Ltd
Adam Equipment Co. Limited
Adenwood Limited
Adidas (U.K.) Limited
Airbus Helicopters UK Limited
Albanwise Limited
Albumedix Ltd
Allmakes Limited
Amscan International Limited
Amtrust Europe Limited
Andaray (Holdings) Limited
Argos Limited
Artform International Limited
Aston Martin Lagonda Limited
Atlas Converting Equipment Limited
Avant Homes (England) Limited
Aven Tools Limited
Avondale Property (Holdings) Limited
Axiom Group Limited
B.L. Marketing Limited
B.M. Polyco Limited
BI Worldwide Limited
BTN Turbo Charger Service Limited
J.H. Bacon Limited
M.Baker Produce Limited
Barron McCann Limited
Basildon Chemical Co. Limited
Bauer Consumer Media Limited
Bauer Radio Limited
Beardow and Adams (Adhesives) Limited
Thomas Bell & Sons Limited
Charles Bentley & Son Limited
C & P Bird Bros. Limited
Blanc Aero Industries UK Limited
Blemain Finance Limited
Blue Anchor Leisure Limited
Bodycote H.I.P. Limited
Bodycote Heat Treatments Limited
Bodycote International Limited
Bonnington Plastics Limited
Henry Boot Developments Limited
Bowring Transport Limited
Bridgestone UK Limited
Briggs & Forrester Engineering Services Ltd
Brightwake Limited
Bristol Fruit Sales (Market) Limited
Broadgate Builders (Spalding) Limited
Broadways Stampings Limited
B.A.Bush & Son Limited
CEVA Freight (UK) Limited
CEVA Logistics Limited
CEVA Supply Chain Solutions Limited
CPL Aromas Limited
CTDI Glenrothes Limited
Barry Callebaut Manufacturing (UK) Ltd
Capital Refractories Limited
Cashino Gaming Limited
Ceetak Holdings Limited
Chalcroft Limited
Charles Street Buildings (U.K.) Limited
Charterhouse Holdings PLC
Chartmoor Estates Limited
Christys By Design Limited
Chromalloy United Kingdom Limited
Clark-Drain Limited
Clarksteel Holdings Limited
Clayton (Lincoln) Limited
Coal Products Limited
Coastfields Leisure Limited
Coloplast Limited
Colortronic (U.K.) Limited
Comtec Cable Accessories Limited
Thomas Cook UK Travel Limited
Walter John Cook and Sons Limited
Copley Scientific Limited
Cotswold Wild Life Park Limited
Coventry Chemicals Limited
Cromwell Logistics Limited
Cromwell Tools Limited
Crowcon Detection Instruments Limited
Ivor Crowson Developments (Stamford) Ltd
Curtis Instruments (U.K.) Limited
DFDS Seaways Newcastle Limited
DFS Furniture Co Ltd
DGS Group PLC
DMG Mori UK Limited
Dachser Limited
Daimler UK Limited
Dart Products Europe Ltd.
Lawrence David Limited
Deeley Group Limited
Direct Leisure Supplies Limited
Drennan International Limited
Durr Limited
Eaton Electrical Products Limited
Eaton MEDC Limited
Electronics for Imaging United Kingdom Ltd
Element Six (UK) Limited.
Elior UK PLC
Emerson Developments (Holdings) Limited
Emerson Management Services Limited
Eminox Limited
Engie Fabricom UK Limited
Envigo Developments Limited
Envigo RMS (UK) Limited
Equip Outdoor Technologies UK Limited
Eraglow Building Limited
Erlson Precision Components Limited
Essentra International Limited
Essentra Services Limited
Europcar Group UK Limited
Evonik Goldschmidt UK Limited
Expatriate Advisory Services PLC
Eyre & Elliston Holdings Limited
F.H. Farms Limited
FCC Waste Services (UK) Limited
L.J. Fairburn and Son Limited
Fairchild Fasteners (UK) Limited
Farmland Reserve UK Limited
Farol Holdings Limited
Fashion Fabric Transprinters Limited
Fengrain (Services) Limited
Fengrain Limited
Festino (Finance) Limited
Fevore Limited
Firstan Limited
Flo-Mech. Limited
Flogas Britain Limited
Fold Hill Foods Limited
Fraikin Limited
Freightroute Limited
Friar's Pride Limited
Frickley Holdings.Limited
Frimstone Limited
Frozen Value Limited
Fugro GB Marine Limited
Fugro Geoservices Limited
Fujifilm UK Limited
G.H.B. (Holding) Limited
Games Workshop Limited
Gamston Aviation Limited
Glass Recycling (UK) Limited
Glenair UK Limited
Glinwell PLC
Goodfellow Cambridge Limited
Grantham Bros. Limited
Grevayne Properties Limited
Grimsthorpe & Drummond Castle Trust Ltd
Groves of Thame Limited
H (Lincs) Limited
Hach Lange Ltd
Hague Plant Limited
Hammonds Furniture Limited
Haramead
HaskoningDHV UK Limited
Headcrown Group PLC
John Hebb (Motor Engineers) Limited
A.E.Hewison Limited
Hillarys Blinds Limited
Hilton Garage Ltd
Holdsworth Holdings Limited
Holly Farm Limited
Homag U.K. Ltd.
T.P. Hopwell (Holdings) Limited
Hopwells Ltd
Hormann (U.K.) Limited
Alan Howard (Stockport) Limited
Hyde Industrial Holdings Limited
I.S. Group Limited
IG Design Group PLC
Instill Education Limited
Inwido UK Limited
Ivygrove Developments Limited
JFC Plastics Limited
JRI Orthopaedics Limited
Warren James (Jewellers) Limited
Jaybeam Limited
Simon Jersey Ltd
Jones Homes (Lancashire) Limited

Kaby Engineers Limited
Kannegiesser UK Limited
Karcher (U.K.) Limited
Keigar Homes Limited
Kennelpak Limited
Key Property Solutions Limited
Kindale Limited
Kingerlee Holdings Limited
Kitchen Range Foods Limited
Konecranes Demag UK Limited
Krohne Limited
Kubota (U.K.) Limited
Kumho Tyre (U.K.) Limited
L H Group Services Limited
Lamport Hall Preservation Trust Limited
Landis + Gyr Limited
Langley Holdings PLC
Larson-Juhl UK Limited
Leda Properties Limited
Leicester Fancy Box Co Ltd
Leicestershire & Rutland Organisation for The Relief of Suffering Ltd
Lesta Packaging PLC
Lexitron Limited
Libra Speciality Chemicals Limited
Limagrain UK Limited
Limes Developments Limited
Lincat Group Limited
Lindum Group Limited
Linkage Community Trust
Listers Group Limited
Lockwood Estates Limited
Louver-Lite Limited
Lucy Electric UK Limited
Lukegate Limited
M & J Group (Construction & Roofing) Ltd
M.M.D. Mining Machinery Developments Ltd
M.P.K. Garages Limited
MCE Insurance Limited
Makita (UK) Limited
Makro Self Service Wholesalers Limited
Mallory Court Hotel Limited
Marmon Group Limited
Brett Martin Daylight Systems Limited
Massarella Catering Group Limited
Maynard & Harris Plastics
Melbourne Holdings Limited
Mills CNC Limited
Minorfern Limited
Mitchell Diesel Limited
Mondi Scunthorpe Limited
Monier (China) Holdings Limited
Monocon International Refractories Ltd
Moore Large & Co. Limited
Morgana Systems Limited
Motspa Holdings Limited
Movianto UK Limited
Owen Mumford Limited
N.M.T. Plant Hire Limited
NUS Holdings Limited
National Tyre Service Limited
Naturex Limited
Nene Group PLC
Nesform Limited
Ney Limited
Nicholas Associates Holdings Limited
Niftylift Limited
Nisa Retail Limited
The Alan Nuttall Partnership Limited
O.T.R. Tyres Limited
OISE Limited
OQEMA Limited
OSI Food Solutions UK Limited
Old Road Securities PLC
Omex Agriculture Limited
Orbit Developments (Manchester) Limited
Orchid Orthopedic Solutions Sheffield Ltd
Orona Limited
Outdoor & Sports Co Ltd
Oxford Centre for Hebrew and Jewish Studies
Oxford Instruments Industrial Products Ltd
P.A. Estates Management Limited
P3 Group Europe Limited
PCMS Group Limited
Pailton Engineering Limited
E.Park & Sons Limited
Park Industrial and Agricultural Holdings Ltd
W.T. Parker Ltd.
Parkers Motor Services (Syston) Limited
Trevor Parr Associates Limited
Pattonair Limited
Paul John Construction (Leicester) Ltd
Pedigree Wholesale Limited
Pegler Limited
Penmarric Limited
Perfectos Printing Inks Co Ltd.
Perrys Motor Sales Limited
Pickering Investments Limited
Ping Europe Limited
Pinnacle International Freight Limited
Plastribution Limited
Polypipe Limited
Powerscreen International Limited
Pricecheck Toiletries Limited
Princebuild Limited.
Pukka Pies Limited
RCI Europe
RM Education Ltd
RPS Consulting Services Limited
RPS Energy Limited
RS Components Limited
Randall Parker Foods Limited
Raynsway Properties Limited
Ricoh UK Limited
Rippleglen Limited
Rittal Limited
Rolls-Royce Power Engineering PLC
Ronald Hull Jnr. Limited
Routeco Limited
Ruddy Joinery Limited
S L G Charitable Trust Limited
S.D.C. Builders Limited
S.E.B. International Limited
SIG Trading Limited
SMC Pneumatics (U.K.) Limited
Saffron Apothecaries (Leicester) Limited
Saul Construction Limited
Seaside Leisure Parks Limited
Selden Research Limited
Senad Limited
Sensient Holdings UK
Servelec Healthcare Limited
Fred Sherwood & Sons (Transport) Ltd
Shire Foods Limited
R.H. Smith & Sons (Wigmakers) Limited
G.A.E. Smith (Holdings) Limited
Paul Smith Limited
Software AG (UK) Limited
Sonic Communications (International) Ltd
Speeds Limited
Stertil UK Ltd.
C.A. Strawson Farming Limited
Sunrise Poultry Farms Limited
Supreme Concrete Limited
Symphony Group PLC
TNT Transport Limited
Tanks and Vessels Industries Limited
Tanvic Group Limited
Tarka Controls Limited
O.A.Taylor & Sons Bulbs Limited
Taylors Service Garages (Boston) Limited
Technicut Limited
Teconnex Limited
Tessella Limited
Thames Valley Cambac Limited
Thetford Limited
P.J. Thory Limited
G F Tomlinson & Sons Ltd
Town and Country Petfoods Limited
Trackwork Limited
Leslie H. Trainer and Son Limited
Tresefir Limited
Tsubakimoto UK Limited
Tulip International (UK) Limited
Tullis Russell Coaters Limited
Tunstall Healthcare (UK) Limited
Twycross Zoo - East Midland Zoological Society Ltd
Tynemill Limited
Universal Salvage Limited
Urschel International Limited
Vaillant Industrial UK Limited
Viad Service Companies Limited
Virani Food Products Limited
Vista Engineering Limited
Vow Europe Limited
S.Walsh & Son Limited
Wanzl Limited
Donald Ward Limited
Warwick Ward (Machinery) Limited
Watling JCB Limited
Weavers Close Limited
B. E. Webbe Removals (Derby) Limited
Wickes Properties Limited
Williams Grand Prix Engineering Limited
Winter & Co. UK Limited
Winterhalter Ltd
Woodway Holdings Limited
Woolley Bros. (Wholesale Meats) Limited
World Habitat
M.J. Worth Limited
Wrengate Limited
Wyboston Lakes Limited
J. and A. Young (Leicester) Limited
ZF Services UK Limited
Mike de Courcey Travel Limited

1980-1989 [713]

3 R Construction & Property Development Ltd
A.B. Produce PLC
A.M. Packaging Limited
AESSEAL PLC
AGCO International Limited
ALS Environmental Limited
ASD Lighting PLC
AVK UK Limited
AWG Group Limited
Aaroncare Limited
Abaco Systems Limited
Abbey Forged Products Limited
Abbey Group Cambridgeshire Limited
Ablehomes Limited
Abraham Investments Limited
Access Platform Sales Limited

Acorn Industrial Services Limited
Acredula Group Limited
John Adams Leisure Limited
Adare International Limited
Adder Technology Limited
Adient Holding UK Ltd
Advanex Europe Limited
Agema Engineering Limited
Aldi Stores Limited
Alere Limited
Allegheny Technologies Limited
Alliance Medical Limited
Allworks Properties Limited
Alpine Electronics of U.K. Limited
Alumasc Group PLC
Amak Property Investments (London) Ltd
Amega Sciences PLC
Amey OW Limited
Amey PLC
Amtico Co Ltd
Amtico International Limited
Amtrust International Limited
Anand International Limited
Ancillary Components Limited
Anderton Concrete Products Limited
Anglian Water Services Limited
Anti-Waste Limited
Antolin Interiors UK Limited
Arconic Extruded Products (UK) Limited
Arconic Fastening Systems & Rings Ltd
Ariens Co Ltd
Armstrong Brooks Limited
Ashfield Healthcare Communications Group Ltd
Aspall Cyder Limited
Asteelflash (Bedford) Limited
Astor Care Limited
Autumnpark Limited
Avery Dennison Retail Information Services UK Ltd
Aviagen Limited
Avingtrans PLC
B & K Building Services Limited
B & P Properties Limited
BASF Agricultural Specialities Limited
BGB Engineering Limited
BM Catalysts Limited
BPI Limited
BPW Limited
BSH Home Appliances Limited
Bachmann Europe PLC
Baker & Taylor (UK) Ltd
Balfour Beatty Plant & Fleet Services Ltd
Ball Colegrave Limited
Barnack Estates UK Limited
Barton Buses Limited
Bauer Digital Radio Limited
Beacon Bingo Limited
Bearward Engineering Limited
Beckett's Foods Limited
Beechcroft Developments Limited
Bellcoin Holdings Limited
Bells Motor Group Limited
Rick Bestwick Limited
Big Food Group Limited
Bildurn (Properties) Limited
Billing Finance Limited
Billington Holdings PLC
Billington Structures Limited
Bio-Rad AbD Serotec Ltd
Blackburn Starling & Co Ltd
J.S.Bloor (Services) Limited
Bloor Holdings Limited
Bloor Homes Limited
Blue Chip Customer Engineering Limited
Boal U.K. Limited
Board24 Ltd
Bobby's Foods Limited
Bollin Group Limited
Bolton Plastic Components Limited
Bombardier Transportation (Holdings) UK Ltd
Bombardier Transportation UK Ltd
Bournemouth International Airport Ltd
Boutinot Limited
Wilson Bowden Limited
Bowers Metrology Limited
Bradgate Containers Limited
B. Braun Medical Limited
B Braun Sterilog Limited
Bridgebank Limited
Briggs & Forrester Living Limited
Briggs of Burton PLC
Bright Horizons Family Solutions Limited
Bristol Novelty Limited
British Drilling and Freezing Co Ltd
British Pregnancy Advisory Service
Brooke Weston Trust
Buckingham Group Contracting Limited
Bucyrus Europe Limited
Bulk Freight (Midlands) Limited
Burton McCall Limited
Business Control Solutions Group Limited
Busways Travel Services Limited
Butcher's Pet Care Limited
Bystronic UK Limited
Byzak Limited
CASP
CCF Limited
CMD Limited
CMS Cepcor Limited
Caldic (UK) Ltd
Calor Group Limited
Cambridge Weight Plan Limited
Cambus Limited
Campbell Scientific Limited
Car Store Limited
Carl F Groupco Limited
Carmac (Building & Civil Engineering) Ltd
CarnaudMetalbox Group UK Ltd.
Castle Square Developments Limited
Catalent UK Supply Chain Limited
Celus Holdings Limited
Cemex Seament Limited
Center Parcs Limited
Centurion Finance (Lincoln) Limited
Champion Employment Limited
Chandlers (Farm Equipment) Limited
Charles Street Commercial Investments Ltd
Chatsworth House Trust
Cheltenham and Gloucester Omnibus Co Ltd
Childbase Partnership Limited
Chivgate Limited
Cinch Connectors Limited
Citigen (London) Limited
J.R. Clark Limited
Classeq Limited
Clayson Country Homes Limited
Clientlogic Limited
Clowes Developments (North West) Limited
H.W. Coates Limited
Codemasters Software Co Ltd
Cognita Schools Limited
Comau U.K. Limited
Commatone Limited
Company Shop Limited
Company of Master Jewellers Limited
Congregational & General Charitable Trust
Consolidated Property Wilmslow Limited
Consuma Paper Products Limited
Continental Landscapes Limited
Thomas Cook Airlines Limited
Thomas Cook Group UK Limited
William Cook Properties Limited
Cooper Roller Bearings Co Ltd
Corby Power Limited
Cornshire Limited
Corrpro Companies Engineering Limited
Countrywide Principal Services Limited
Coventry University Enterprises Limited
Coversure Insurance Services Limited
Cranbrook (Jewellers) Ltd
Cranford House School Trust Limited
Crestchic Limited
Cromwell Group (Holdings) Limited
Cruickshank Motors Limited
Cullingworth Commercials and Freight Services Ltd
Brian Currie (Milton Keynes) Limited
Cuttech Limited
Cytec Industrial Materials (Derby) Ltd
Cytec Process Materials (Keighley) Ltd
DCA Design International Limited
DFDS Seaways PLC
DFS Trading Limited
DK Group Investments Ltd.
Dagless Holdings Limited
Daifuku Europe Limited
Daloon Foods (U.K.) Limited
Damika Limited
Danetre Holdings Limited
Datac Adhesives Limited
Datapath Limited
Dawson-Wam Ltd
Dawsongroup Bus and Coach Limited
Dawsongroup PLC
Dawsongroup Temperature Control Solutions Ltd
Deanbank Investments Limited
Del Equipment (U.K.) Limited
Delifrance (UK) Limited
Derbyshire Aggregates Limited
Derry Building Services Limited
Diamond Fuel Supplies Limited
Diversey UK Production Limited
Dodson & Horrell Limited
Draefern Limited
Druck Limited
Martin Duckworth Limited
P.J. Duffy & Son (Farms) Limited
Duncan Investments Limited
Dunelm (Soft Furnishings) Ltd
Dunlin Limited
Dynamic Cassette International Limited
E.Surv Limited
ELG Haniel Metals Ltd
ELG Utica Alloys Limited
EResearchTechnology Limited
ESNT International Limited
East Coast Fittings Limited
East London Bus & Coach Co Ltd
East Midlands Chamber (Derbyshire, Nottinghamshire, Leicestershire)
East Midlands International Airport Ltd
East Midlands Property Developments Ltd
East of England Agricultural Society
Eastern Counties Properties Limited

Eastgate Care Ltd
Eaton Safety Limited
Elastomerics Limited
Elior UK Holdings Limited
Elisabeth The Chef Limited
Elsevier Limited
Emerson International Limited
Emmett UK Limited
Encase Holdings Limited
Encocam Limited
Enterprise Holding Company No 1 Limited
Envigo CRS Limited
Eurocell Group Limited
European Electronique Limited
N.R. Evans and Son Limited
Extracare Charitable Trust
FCC Environment Services (UK) Limited
FSHC (UK) Limited
FSHC Properties (Manor) Limited
Fabrics & Yarns (Macclesfield) Ltd
Faccenda Farms Limited
Faccenda Foods Limited
Faccenda Investments Limited
Falcon of Hull & Lincolnshire Limited
Fandstan Electric Limited
Farmstar Limited
Farnley Estates Limited
Fesa (UK) Limited
Fired Earth Limited
First South Yorkshire Limited
Flair Flooring Supplies Limited
Flannels Group Limited
Flex-Seal Couplings Limited
Fluidpower Limited
Fluorochem Limited
Forever Living Products (U.K.) Limited
Foundation Technology Limited
Four Seasons (DFK) Limited
Franke Sissons Limited
Freeman Automotive (UK) Ltd
Freiberger (UK) Limited
Fresh-Pak Chilled Foods Limited
Full Moon Holdings Limited
GI Group Recruitment Ltd
Gallos Limited
Gefco U.K. Limited
Genie UK Limited
Mick George Limited
Germany Farms Limited
Giant U.K. Limited
Douglas Gill International Limited
Giorgio's Continental Ltd.
Gladstone MRM Limited
Glazewing Limited
Michael Goodall Quality Homes Limited
Grafton Recruitment Limited
Grass Valley Broadcast Solutions Limited
Greencore Grocery Limited
Greene Tweed & Co Limited
Greenyard Fresh UK Ltd
Gripple Limited
Grosvenor Contracts Leasing Limited
Guilford Mills Europe Limited
HBM United Kingdom Limited
HPC Healthline UK Limited
HR Wallingford Group Limited
G.I. Hadfield & Son Limited
Hafele U.K. Limited
Hague Farming Limited
Hallam Land Management Limited
Hammond Grange Limited
Harley-Davidson Europe Limited
Harpmanor Limited
Harris Cars Limited
T. C. Harrison Group Limited
Harting UK Limited
Harworth Estates Limited
Harworth Services Limited
Haywood and Padgett Limited
Hendrickson United Kingdom Ltd
Heraeus Electro-Nite (UK) Ltd
W.E. Hewitt & Son Limited
Hi-Level Enterprises Limited
Hichrom Limited
Hikoki Power Tools (U.K.) Limited
Hill-Rom Limited
Michael I Holdsworth Limited
Horiba UK Limited
P. Hughes Construction Limited
Hunt Group Limited
Huntson Holdings Limited
Hyde Group Limited
Hyde Investments Limited
Hydrainer Pump Hire Limited
I.G. Industries PLC
IG Design Group UK Limited
IMCI (Services) Limited
ITL Mortgages Limited
Ideal Shopping Direct Limited
Idis Limited
Ikea Limited
Imago @ Loughborough Limited
Imago Publishing Limited
Incat International PLC
Industrial Machinery Supplies Limited
Ingram Micro (UK) Limited
Ingram Micro Holdings Limited
Innspired (Cedar) Limited
Insituform Holdings (UK) Limited
Insituform Linings Limited
Integrated Waste Management Limited
Interaction Recruitment PLC
Interlevin Holdings Limited
Investco Limited
J & A (International) Limited
JJS Manufacturing Limited
Jaguar Land Rover Limited
Jardentome Limited
Jardines (U.K.) Limited
Jepson Holdings Limited
K.M. Packaging Services Limited
Kab Seating Limited
Keepmoat Homes Limited
Keepmoat Limited
Kelmarsh Trust
Keyclad Limited
Kingerlee Limited
Kingston Equity & Finance Limited
Klober Limited
Knott-Avonride Limited
LC Packaging UK Ltd
Lancer Properties Limited
Land Instruments International Limited
Landau Forte Charitable Trust
Landfill Management Limited
Richard Lang & Son Limited
Launchchange Instrumentation Limited
Laurenglen Limited
Leeson Polyurethanes Limited
Leica Biosystems Newcastle Limited
Leicester Grammar School Trust
Liberty Merchant Bar PLC
Lincat Limited
Lincoln Electric (U.K.) Limited
Lincolnshire Agricultural Society
Lincolnshire Field Products Limited
Lindab Limited
Linx Printing Technologies Limited
Lister Wilder Limited
Lloyd Fraser Holdings Co Ltd
London Wiper Co Ltd
Loxton Developments Limited
Lucy Electric (EMS) Limited
Luxfab Limited
A.W.Lymn The Family Funeral Service Ltd
M.P.B. Structures Ltd
M.S.W (UK) Limited
MAM Software Limited
MHH Contracting Limited
MHR International UK Limited
MRS Environmental Services Limited
MacFarlane Group UK Limited
Machine Mart Limited
Magdalen College School Oxford Limited
Mahle Filter Systems UK Limited
Manitowoc Crane Group (UK) Limited
Manthorpe Building Products Limited
Manthorpe Engineering Limited
Manthorpe Limited
Maplebeck Holdings Limited
Marcol Limited
Markem-Imaje Industries Limited
H.W. Martin (Plant) Limited
H.W. Martin (Traffic Management) Ltd
Maryland Securities Limited
Mass Consultants Limited
Massmould Limited
Mathematical Market Research Limited
Matrix SCM Limited
McCann Manchester Limited
McCann-Erickson Network Limited
Mercedes AMG High Performance Powertrains Ltd
Mercedes-Benz Cars UK Limited
Mexichem Specialty Compounds Limited
Midland Red (South) Limited
Midland Sports Centre for The Disabled Trust Ltd
Mil-Ver Metal Co Ltd
Millbrook Proving Ground Limited
Millennium Inorganic Chemicals Overseas Holdings
Milton Keynes Community Foundation Ltd
Mistras Group Limited
Miswa Chemicals Limited
Mogford Limited
Monro Limited
Moorcroft Debt Recovery Limited
Moorcroft Group PLC
Morgan Industrial Properties Limited
Mosdorfer CCL Systems Limited
Motor Neurone Disease Association
Murata Power Solutions (Milton Keynes) Ltd
Murley Limited
Mutchmeats Limited
Myers-Briggs Co Ltd
Myton Hospices
N.F.U. Mutual Management Co Ltd
N.F.U. Mutual Unit Managers Limited
NHBC Building Control Services Limited
NMB-Minebea UK Ltd
NUS Services Limited
Nationwide Platforms Limited
Nationwide Windows Limited
Natl. Amusements (UK) Limited
Natures Menu Limited

Nene Park Trust
Neovia Logistics Services (U.K.) Limited
Netsupport Ltd.
Nikken Kosakusho Europe Limited
Niscayah Holdings Limited
Norbrook Holdings Limited
Norbrook Laboratories (G.B.) Limited
Nortech Foods Limited
North West Steel Limited
Norton Financial Services Limited
Norton Home Loans Limited
Nottingham City Transport Limited
Nottingham Forest Football Club Limited
Nottingham Rehab Limited
Novera Energy Generation No. 2 Limited
Nuttall Group Limited
OM Properties Investment Co Ltd
Oceala Limited
Oclaro Technology Limited
Omega Red Group Limited
Omnitrade Limited
Ontex Healthcare UK Limited
Orbit Developments (Southern) Limited
Orbit Investments (Properties) Limited
Orchard House Foods Limited
E J Orr Limited
Oughtred & Harrison (Facilities) Ltd.
Oxford Economics Limited
Oxford Plastic Systems Limited
Oxford Products Limited
Oxford Publishing Limited
Oxford Science Park Limited
Oxford Trust
Oxford University Innovation Limited
PEM 2000 Limited
PERI Limited
PSV Claims Bureau Limited
PTS Group Limited
Panache Lingerie Limited
Paragon Interiors Group PLC
Parex Ltd
A.G. Parfett & Sons Limited
Park Air Systems Limited
Parkers of Leicester Limited
J.G. Pears Limited
Pendragon Management Services Limited
Pendragon Motor Group Limited
Pendragon Overseas Limited
Pendragon PLC
Pengethley Potatoes Limited
Perkins Engines Co Ltd
Perkins Group Limited
K. & O. Peros (Oxford) Limited
Perrys East Midlands Limited
Personal Assurance PLC
Pertemps Recruitment Partnership Limited
Pet City Holdings Limited
Pets at Home Ltd
Peveril Homes Limited
Phenomenex Limited
Philex Limited
Phytone Limited
Pickering Developments Limited
Pinelodge Holidays Limited
Port of Boston Limited
J.E. Porter Limited
Portwest Clothing Limited
Porvair PLC
Premier Nursing Homes Limited
Premier Textiles Limited
Primesite UK Limited
Princebuild Holdings Limited
Printing & Packaging Co. Limited
Prodrive Investments Limited
Profile Security Services Limited
Prophet PLC
Pyronix Limited
Q V Foods Limited
QD Commercial Group (Property) Limited
Quartzelec Ltd
R P S Group PLC
RAL Limited
RH Development (Property) Limited
RM PLC
RPS Environmental Management Limited
Radius Systems Limited
Ragdale Hall (1990) Limited
Randomlight Limited
Rayburn Tours Limited
Raynsway Estates Limited
Rea Valley Tractors Limited
Regent Office Care Limited
Renault Sport Racing Limited
Renco (Chesterfield) Limited
Renewi UK Services Limited
Richardson Milling (UK) Limited
Ritelite (Systems) Limited
Ritrama (U.K.) Limited
Rittal Holdings Limited
Riverside Motors (Doncaster) Limited
Riviera Tours Limited
Robimatic Limited
Rockwell European Holdings Limited
Roe Bros. & Co Ltd.
Rolec Services Limited
Rolls-Royce Total Care Services Limited
Romax Technology Ltd.
Roquette UK Limited
Ross Ceramics Limited
Rowden House School Limited
Rowstock Limited
Rubicon Drinks Limited
Ruddington Homes Limited
Rybrook Cars Limited
Ryecroft Foods Limited
S D C (Holdings) Limited
S R S Rail System Limited
SCR Financial Interventions Holding Co Ltd
SDL Surveying Limited
SHV Energy Holdings UK Limited
SIG European Investments Limited
SPS Aerostructures Limited
Saint-Gobain Building Distribution Ltd
Saint-Gobain Glass (United Kingdom) Ltd
Santa Maria UK Limited
Santander Asset Finance (December) Ltd
Santander Estates Limited
Sash UK Limited
Satake Europe Limited
John Saul Limited
Scantronic Holdings Limited
Schades Limited
School of St. Helen and St. Katharine Trust
Schutz (U.K.) Limited
Selective Marketplace Limited
Sensient Flavors Limited
Sensient Technologies Limited
Severn Trent Overseas Holdings Limited
Severn Trent PLC
Severn Trent Water Limited
Sheffield City Trust
Sheffield Forgemasters Steel Limited
Sheffield International Venues Limited
Shima Seiki Europe Limited
Silbury Marketing Limited
Simons Group Limited
J O Sims Limited
Skills Leisure Limited
Skiptex Limited
Skymark Packaging International Limited
Sleekmade Property Co. Limited
Sloane Helicopters Limited
Smeg (UK) Limited
Smith & Brooks Limited
Sofidel UK Limited
Sophos Limited
South East London & Kent Bus Co Ltd
Southport Golf Complex Limited
Spaldings Limited
Spear & Jackson Limited
Special Piping Materials Limited
Special Quality Alloys Limited
Sports Information Services (Holdings) Ltd
Sports and Leisure Management Ltd
Springfield Farm Limited
St. Clare's, Oxford.
St. Paul's Developments PLC
Stagecoach (South) Limited
Stagecoach Services Limited
Stagecoach Supertram Maintenance Ltd.
Stamford Group Limited
Stanton Bonna Concrete Limited
John A. Stephens Holdings Limited
Sterling Press Limited
Stirling Management Group Limited
Straightset Limited
Strata Homes Limited
Strata Homes Yorkshire Limited
Strata Products Limited
Strawson Holdings Limited
Sunway Travel (Coaching) Limited
Suon Limited
Syita Properties Limited
Syncreon Technology (UK) Ltd
T.D.P. Textiles Limited
TCS Biosciences Limited
TII Technologies Limited
TNT Express Worldwide Investments Ltd
TNT UK Limited
Tanglewood (Lincolnshire) Limited
Tata Technologies Europe Limited
B Taylor & Sons Transport Limited
Technolog Limited
Techrete (U.K.) Limited
Teletrac Navman (UK) Ltd
Ten Cate Advanced Composites Limited
Ten Cate UK Limited
Thames Land Limited
Thames Transit Limited
Thessco Limited
Tingdene Holdings Limited
Tinsley Bridge Group Limited
Together Commercial Finance Limited
G.F. Tomlinson Building Limited
Topps Europe Holdings Limited
Topps Tile Kingdom Limited
Toray Textiles Europe Limited
Total Worldfresh Limited
Toymaster Limited
Toyota Motor Manufacturing (UK) Limited
Trek Bicycle Corporation Limited
Tripod Crest Limited
Triumph Designs Limited
Triumph Motorcycles Group Limited
Triumph Motorcycles Limited
Turbine Services Limited

Tyler Packaging Limited
UCC Coffee UK Limited
UKMHPS Limited
Ultimate Packaging Limited
Ulverscroft Group Limited
Unipart Group of Companies Limited
University of Warwick Science Park Ltd
George Utz Limited
VWR International Ltd
Vacation Rental Group Holdings Limited
Vaillant Netherlands Holdings Limited
Varsity Design Limited
Vencap International PLC
Vicon Motion Systems Limited
Victim Support
Victoria (Bavaria) Limited
F. Vindis & Sons (Sawston) Limited
Vindis Developments Limited
Vindis Group Limited
Vision Express (UK) Limited
Volvo Group UK Limited
Vtech Electronics Europe PLC
Vulcan Engineering Limited
W.N. Developments Limited
WD-40 Co Ltd
WRG Environmental Limited
Wade Furniture Group Limited
Waldersey Farms Limited
Wallis Farms Limited
T.W. Ward C.N.C. Machinery Limited
Ward Hi-Tech Limited
Roger Warnes Transport Limited
Weatherford Eurasia Limited
Weddel Swift Distribution Limited
Welcome Break Limited
Wellglade Limited
Wheeldon Brothers Limited
Whilton Marina Limited
Wickes Building Supplies Limited
Ken Wilkins Print Limited
Witham (Specialist Vehicles) Limited
Wolf Systems Limited
Wood Green Animal Shelters
Robert Woodhead Holdings Limited
Woodland Trust
World Vision UK
P A Wright & Sons Limited
Wykes Engineering Co. (Rushden) Limited
X-Cel Superturn Ltd
XMA Limited
Yokohama H.P.T. Limited
Yorkshire Repak Limited
Yorkshire Traction Co Ltd
Yotta Limited
Zapp (GB) Limited
Zibrant Limited
Zyox Limited

1990-1994 [435]

1LIFE Management Solutions Limited
3C Waste Limited
A4E Ltd
ABSL Power Solutions Ltd
ADA Pacific Direct Limited
Aarsleff Ground Engineering Limited
Abbeymill Homes Limited
Abbott Diabetes Care Limited
Absolute Radio Limited
Adare SEC Limited
Agreserves Limited
Agrifac UK Ltd
Agrivert Limited
Aintree Retail Park Limited
Alkane Energy Limited
Alliance & Leicester Personal Finance Ltd
Alloy Technologies (UK) Limited
Alumasc Exterior Building Products Ltd
Alumet Systems (UK) Limited
Amano Enzyme Europe Limited
Ambitions Personnel Limited
Ametek (GB) Limited
Amey Community Limited
Amey Rail Limited
Amey Services Limited
Amey Utility Services Limited
Anti-Waste (Restoration) Limited
Apex Stainless Fasteners Limited
Apollo Scientific Ltd
Asmet (UK) Limited
Asquith Court Holdings Limited
Astrea Limited
Atlas Copco Medical Limited
Atlas Hotels (Group 3 Property) Limited
Autocraft Drivetrain Solutions Limited
Avalon Trustee Co Ltd
Axis Electronics Limited
B.T.E. Plant Sales Limited
BCM Limited
BDR Waste Disposal Limited
BFSL Limited
BGL Group Limited
BICL Limited
Bansols Beta Limited
Barclay Pharmaceuticals Limited
Bartec Auto ID Limited
Bassi Fashions Limited
Beechcroft UK Limited
Bell Rock Workplace Management Limited
Belling (1992) Limited.
Benchmarx Kitchens and Joinery Limited
Benoy Limited
Bibliotheca Limited
Biesse Group UK Limited
Bio-Techne Ltd
Bird Group of Companies Limited
Birkdale School
Blackwell Limited
Bletchley Park Trust Limited
Blitz Communications Limited
Blue Sea Overseas Investments Limited
Bombardier Transportation (Rolling Stock) UK Ltd
Henry Boot Construction Limited
Bosch Packaging Technology Limited
Branston Limited
Brita Water Filter Systems Limited
Britcon (UK) Limited
Brownhills Motorhomes Limited
Bucyrus UK Limited
Burford Garden Centre Limited
Business Management Software Limited
Byrom PLC
CDA Group Limited
CML Limited
CPL Industries Limited
CRH Fencing & Security Group (UK) Ltd
Barry Callebaut Holding (UK) Limited
Cambridge Display Technology Limited
Canei International Limited
Cape Engineering Services Limited
Carbon International Limited
Carewatch Care Services Limited
Caterpillar UK Holdings Limited
Chess Limited
Chestnut Homes Limited
City Plumbing Supplies Holdings Limited
Claypenny Property Services Limited
Cleveland Transit Ltd.
Clyde Bergemann Materials Handling Ltd
Clytha Holdings Limited
Coed du Hall Limited
Combisafe International Limited
Complete Medical Group Worldwide Limited
William Cook Cast Products Limited
Thomas Cook UK Limited
Coolair Equipment Limited
Coombe Abbey Park Limited
Cope Children's Trust
Corran (Wakefield) Limited
County Milk Products Limited
Countywide Developments Limited
Coventry and Solihull Waste Disposal Co Ltd
Coveris Flexibles UK Limited
Coverworld UK Limited
Crown Crest (Holdings) PLC
Cullum Detuners Investments Limited
DB Cargo (UK) Limited
DCS Group (UK) Limited
DP Realty Limited
Daf Trucks Limited
Danieli UK Holding Limited
Dawsongroup Material Handling Limited
Decidebloom Limited
Deichmann-Shoes UK Limited
Delaquest Limited
Diam UK Ltd.
Dippy Ridge Limited
Diverseylever Limited
John W. Doubleday Limited
Dr Martens Airwair Group Limited
Dransfield Properties Limited
Duki (2006) Finance Limited
Dunster House Limited
E.I.R.P Limited
E.On Climate & Renewables UK Operations Ltd
E.On UK CHP Limited
E.On UK Cogeneration Limited
EGR Europe Limited
ELWA Limited
East Worcester Water Limited
Eco-Bat Technologies Limited
Element Six Limited
Emerson Process Management Shared Services Ltd
H. J. Enthoven Limited
Estate Computer Systems (Holdings) Ltd
Estates and Leisure Holdings Limited
Ethical Property Co Ltd
Euro E-Land Company PLC
Euro Food Brands Limited
Eurocell Profiles Limited
Evobus (UK) Limited
Evonik Speciality Organics Limited
Evonik UK Holdings Limited
Evotec (UK) Limited
Excel Parking Services Limited
Exol Lubricants (Rotherham) Limited
FCC Environment (UK) Limited
FCC Recycling (UK) Limited
Fannin (UK) Limited
Faurecia Automotive Seating UK Limited
Federal Estates Limited
Fibrefab Limited
Fichtner Consulting Engineers Limited
Fisher Scientific U.K., Limited

Flocklynn Limited
Ford & Slater Limited
Fox Lima Holdings Limited
Fresenius Medical Care Renal Services Ltd
Frutarom (UK) Holdings Limited
Fugro Geos Limited
Fugro Holdings Limited
G.B. Terminals Limited
GI Recruitment Limited
GI Solutions Group Limited
GN Hearing UK Ltd
Gallagher Estates Holdings Limited
Games Workshop Group PLC
Games Workshop International Limited
Gands (U.K.)
Gelder Limited
Gemsupa Limited
Ghekko Limited
Glinwell Marketing Limited
Global Experience Specialists (GES) Holdings Ltd
Global Experience Specialists (GES) Ltd
Gojo Industries - Europe Limited
Granby Care Limited
Grangefern Properties Limited
Greater Manchester Buses South Limited
Greencore UK Holdings Limited
Grimme (U.K.) Limited
Guilbert UK Holdings Limited
H.I. Limited
HJE Limited
HR Wallingford Limited
Hampton Steel Limited
Hancocks Holdings Limited
Hankook Tyre U.K. Limited
Harrison Catering Services Limited
Hartwell Holdings Limited
Harving Limited
Harworth Estates (Agricultural Land) Ltd
Harworth Estates Group Limited
Harworth Group PLC
HaskoningDHV UK Holdings Limited
Healthcare at Home Ltd
Hesley Group Limited
Hexadex Limited
Holland & Barrett Retail Limited
Graham Holmes Astraseal Limited
P.D. Hook (Breeders) Limited
Horbury Building Systems Limited
Howmet Limited
Hyde Aero Products Limited
Hyde Details Limited
Hyperama PLC
IRESS FS Limited
IRESS Portal Limited
Icopal Limited
Ideagen PLC
Imago Holdings Limited
Insight Direct (UK) Ltd
International Logging Technology Limited
Ischebeck Titan Limited
J & E Importers & Distributors Green Jem Mfg Associates Co Ltd
Jandu Developments Limited
Jigsaw Systems Limited
Johnson Bros (Tours) Limited
Jordan Developments (UK) Limited
Joules Limited
KCI Holding UK Limited
KCT Holdings Limited
Kawneer U.K. Limited
Keadby Generation Limited
Kent Enviropower Limited
Keyence (UK) Limited
Kingston (City) Estates Trading Limited
Kostal UK Limited
Koyo Bearings (Europe) Limited
Lamb-Weston/Meijer UK Limited
Lands' End Europe Limited
Laser Quantum Limited
Launchchange Limited
Lavendon Group Limited
William Lee Limited
Lehvoss UK Limited
The David Lewis Centre
Leyland Trucks Limited
Limes Estates Limited
Lincoln & York Limited
Lincoln Corn Exchange and Markets (1991) Ltd
Lincwaste Limited
Lloyds Pharmacy Clinical Homecare Ltd
Jack Loggin Limited
Lomas Distribution Limited
Lunette Properties Limited
M.J.C. Developments Limited
MSG Commercial Limited
MSG Sandhurst Limited
Maltgrade Limited
Manston Investments Limited
P R Marriott Drilling Limited
HW Martin Holdings Limited
Usha Martin International Limited
Matrix Polymers Limited
Matsuura Machinery Limited
McCann Health Medical Communications Ltd
Mercedes-Benz Financial Services UK Ltd
Meridian Audio Limited
Metlane Limited
Milton Keynes Parks Trust Limited
Mirza (UK) Limited
Monarch Healthcare Limited
Morningside Pharmaceuticals Limited
Multi Packaging Solutions GB Limited
Multi Packaging Solutions UK Limited
Munro Building Services Limited
Nampak Holdings (UK) Limited
National Accident Helpline Limited
National Examination Board in Occupational Safety and Health
National Memorial Arboretum Co Ltd
Naylor Industries PLC
Neonickel (Blackburn) Limited
Network Services (Nationwide) Limited
New Terex Holdings UK Limited
Nimogen Limited
North West Portfolio Limited
Northamptonshire Association of Youth Clubs
Nova Laboratories Limited
Oakhill Group Limited
Office 1 Limited
Office Depot International (UK) Limited
Office Depot UK Limited
Olam Food Ingredients UK Limited
Omega PLC
Omex Agrifluids Limited
Omron Electronics Limited
Optilan (UK) Limited
Outokumpu Stainless Limited
Oxford Asset Management Co Ltd
Oxford Said Business School Limited
P V H Holdings Limited
PIB Risk Services Limited
PTA Developments Limited
PWP Building Services Limited
PX Manufacturing Ltd
Paccar Parts U.K. Limited
Padley & Venables Limited
Palms Row Health Care Limited
Papa John's (GB) Limited
Michael Pavis Limited
Peacock & Binnington Holdings Limited
J G Pears (Holdings) Limited
Pelagia (UK) Limited
Pendragon Stock Finance Limited
People Potential Possibilities
Perkins Small Engines Limited
Pertemps Jobshop Limited
Pickering Properties Limited
Picsolve International Limited
Pirelli UK Tyres Limited
Pitacs Limited
Polydist (UK) Limited
Porterbrook Leasing Co Ltd
Porterbrook March Leasing (4) Limited
Poste Holdings Limited
Premier Sheet Metal (Coventry) Limited
Primaflow Limited
Prime Life Limited
Prince Hotels Ltd
Prominent (Europe) Limited
Charles Pugh (Holdings) Limited
Pyramid Posters Limited
Quadron Services Limited
R.T. Consultants Limited
REALL Limited
RPC Containers Limited
RPC Group PLC
RPS US Holdings Limited
RTC Group PLC
RVB Investments
Rail Express Systems Limited
Rebellion Developments Limited
Red & White Services Limited
Redlawn Land Limited
Refresco Drinks UK Limited
Regenersis (Depot) Services Ltd
Resmed (UK) Limited
Roberts Radio Limited
Roc Oil (Europe) Limited
Roca Limited
E.M. Rogers Group Limited
Rolls-Royce Overseas Holdings Limited
Romo (Holdings) Limited
Rowlinson Constructions Limited
Rushcliffe Care Limited
S M C Design and Draughting Services Ltd
Saint-Gobain Performance Plastics Rencol Ltd
Salmon Harvester Properties Limited
Salvation Army Trading Co Ltd
Sealord (Europe) Limited
Severn Trent Utilities Finance PLC.
Seymour Distribution Limited
Seymour International Limited
Sharp Laboratories of Europe, Ltd.
Sheermans Limited
Sheffcare Limited
Sheffield Wednesday Football Club Ltd
Sherwin-Williams Diversified Brands Ltd
Silgan Closures UK Limited
Silkstone Finance Limited
Sims Group UK Holdings Limited
Sitel Europe Limited
Smith Construction Group Limited
Snap-On U.K. Holdings Limited

Socotec UK Limited
Sodexo Motivation Solutions U.K. Limited
Springfield Park Properties Limited
St Andrew's Hospice Limited
Stainless Metalcraft (Chatteris) Limited
Starkey Laboratories Limited
Static Control Components (Europe) Ltd
Stauff UK Limited
Sterigenics UK Limited
Steris Solutions Limited
R Stratton & Co Ltd.
Strevens Vehicles Holdings Limited
Sun Chemical Limited
Synseal Extrusions Limited
Sysmex UK Limited
System Q Limited
Sytner Cars Limited
Sytner Group Limited
T & W Civil Engineering Limited
T.L. Care Limited
TCL Tanker Rental Limited
Tawnywood Limited
Techman Engineering Ltd.
Technical Absorbents Limited
Together Financial Services Limited
Together Personal Finance Limited
Top Tubes Limited
Topps Europe Limited
Tradelink Direct Limited
Trafalgar Court Northern Limited
Transaction Network Services (UK) Ltd
Triumph Motorcycles (Overseas) Limited
Tudor Hall School
Twitten Trustees Limited
Umeco Composites Limited
Underwood Meat Co Ltd
United Carpets Holdings Limited
United Church Schools Trust
United Rental Group Limited
Uris Group Limited
Vale Garden Houses Limited
Van Elle Limited
Verder Holdings U.K. Limited
Versalift Distributors (U.K.) Limited
Viking Direct (Holdings) Limited
F. Vindis & Sons (Bedford) Limited
Vision Express Group Limited
Volkswagen Financial Services (UK) Ltd
WCS Care Group Limited
WJ South Limited
Wabtec Rail Limited
Wacoal Europe Ltd
Wade Spring Limited
Warners Group Publications PLC
Warwick International Group Limited
Waste Recycling Group (UK) Limited
Wastenotts (Reclamation) Limited
Waterloo Quay Properties Limited
Watts Industries UK Limited
Weatherbys Bank Limited
Welbeck Waste Management Limited
Willoughby (35) Limited
Winbro Group Technologies Limited
Winslow Court Ltd
Wolstenholme Machine Knives Limited
Barry Wood Plant Hire Limited
XPO Bulk UK Limited
XPO Holdings UK and Ireland Limited
Yours Clothing Limited
Yusen Logistics (UK) Limited

1995 [122]

A.C.Flooring Ltd.
Abacus Hotels Limited
Abbey Properties Cambridgeshire Limited
Abbeyfield V.E. Limited
Ability Matters Group Limited
Admenta UK Limited
Airwair International Limited
Alkane Energy UK Limited
Alliance Asset Management Limited
Alumax U.K. Limited
Amey Metering Limited
Amey OWR Limited
Amtico Holdings Limited
Art Systems Limited
Aus-Bore Estates Limited
BDW Trading Limited
Ballyvesey Holdings Limited
Banks & Lloyd (Shipping) Limited
Barbon Insurance Group Limited
Bellrock Property & Facilities Management Ltd
Benchmark Leisure Limited
Broadgate Homes Limited
CDT Holdings Limited
Carlsberg Chongqing Limited
Certikin International Limited
Chiltern Cold Storage Group Limited
Citation Limited
Comtec Group (International) Limited
Consortium for Purchasing and Distribution Ltd
County Asset Finance Limited
A.R. Craven Farms Limited
Crowland Cranes Limited
DB Cargo (UK) Holdings Limited
Dawsongroup Truck and Trailer Limited
Derbyshire Student Residences Limited
Dhollandia U.K. Limited
E - Leather Limited
Eaton Electrical Systems Limited
Envigo Holdings Limited
Envigo Research Limited
Essential Supply Products Limited
Eurocell Building Plastics Limited
Eurokey Recycling Limited
Financial & Legal Insurance Co Ltd
Fossil (UK) Limited
Gallagher Estates Limited
Global Self Drive Limited
Go Plant Limited
Goodman Retail Limited
Graypaul Motors Limited
Greenyard Flowers UK Ltd
Harington Investments Limited
Harworth Estates (Waverley Prince) Ltd.
Hella UK Holdings Limited
Heptagon Limited
Holland & Barrett Group Limited
Ikea Properties Investments Limited
Infineum UK Ltd.
Jones Homes (Southern) Limited
Kaefer Limited
Kingsway Asset Finance Ltd
London Internet Exchange Limited
M.J.S. Construction (March) Limited
Makita International Europe Limited
Marden Limited
Mattioli Woods PLC
McGowan Investments Limited
Mertex UK Limited
Metsa Wood UK Limited
Microlise Limited
Micromass Limited
Millennium Inorganic Chemicals UK Holdings Ltd
Mulberry Waste Limited
NIC Holdings (UK) Limited
New City Hotels Limited
Next Distribution Limited
Northampton Acquisition Ltd
Northampton Rugby Football Club Limited
Nu Instruments Limited
O'Brien Contractors Limited
Orders of St. John Care Trust
Oxford Biomedica (UK) Limited
Oxford Gene Technology Limited
Oxford Policy Management Limited
P. H. Properties Ltd
PCS Business Systems Limited
Payzone UK Limited
Pets at Home Superstores Limited
Porvair Filtration Limited
Produce World Group Ltd
Produce World Investments Ltd
Protocol National Limited
RPS Group US Holdings Limited
Randall Parker Food Group Limited
Red Bull Racing Limited
Redbridge Produce & Flowers Limited
Rolleston Hall Estates Limited
SRS Rail System (Holdings) Limited
Samworth Brothers Limited
Saybest Limited
Servelec Limited
Severn Trent Reservoirs Limited
Severn Trent Services International (Overseas Holdings) Ltd
Sheffield Business Park Limited
Sleek International Limited
Squadron Medical Limited
Stagecoach Devon Limited
Staircraft Group Limited
Stamford Property Co Ltd
Sunrisestar Limited
Syncreon Automotive (UK) Ltd.
TI Group Automotive Systems (Deeside) Ltd
Technolog Group Limited
Thoratec Europe Limited
Tripleteam (Developments) Limited
Unipart Rail Limited
Universal Flexible Packaging Limited
University of Derby
Valspar (UK) Corporation, Limited
Vectair Aviation (1995) Limited
Westernrange Limited
Wispington Farms Limited

1996 [132]

AMPY Holdings Limited
Alloga UK Limited
Amnack Limited
Argos Business Solutions Limited
Arthrex Limited
Ashfield Healthcare Limited
Assured Group Limited
Atlas Hotels (Bristol Property) Limited
Atlas Hotels Limited
Audley Travel Group Limited
Avant Homes Limited
BISL Limited
Ballast Phoenix Limited
Benteler Automotive UK Ltd
Breedon House Nurseries Limited

Bridging Finance Limited
Buzzard Leisure Limited
CAME BPT UK Limited
Caljan Rite-Hite Limited
Camden Motors (Holdings) Limited
Cape Environmental Services Onshore Ltd
Catesby Strategic Land Limited
Ceravision Limited
Christian Conference Trust
Coaching Inn Group Ltd
Codemasters Group Limited
Cogne U.K. Limited
William Cook Holdings Limited
Country Court Care Homes Limited
County Hotels Limited
Crown UK Holdings Limited
DB Cargo International Limited
Eco-Bat Technologies GB
Edge Wear Properties Limited
Energy Developments (UK) Limited
Envirogen Water Technologies Limited
Equilibrium Healthcare Limited
Equita Limited
Experian US Holdings Unlimited
Forest Commercial Services Limited
Fresenius Medical Care (Holdings) Ltd
Fresenius Medical Care (UK) Limited
Future Travel Limited
GL Industrial Services UK Ltd
GRS (Roadstone) Limited
Gibbons (Holdings) Limited
Greenvale AP Limited
Guilford Mills Limited
D Hales Limited
Halgram Limited
Hall & Pickles 1812 Limited
Hatchback Ltd
History & Heraldry Limited
Holland & Barrett Holdings Limited
Intervet UK Production Limited
JHC Finance Company
Warren James Holdings Limited
Jones Homes (Yorkshire) Limited
Kautex Unipart Limited
Kent Energy, Ltd.
Knightwood Trust Farms Limited
LDH (La Doria) Limited
Launchchange Holding Company
Lavendon Access Services (International) Ltd
Liberty Group Holdings Ltd
Lifeplus Europe Limited
Longcliffe Group Limited
Loomis UK Limited
Magna Exteriors (Banbury) Limited
Magna International Holding (UK) Limited
Micromass UK Limited
Millgate Limited
Monier (UK) Holdings Limited
William Morgan Group Limited
Motorway Direct PLC
Munster Joinery (U.K.) Limited
Newell and Wright (Holdings) Limited
A.C. Nielsen Co Ltd
Noble Foods Holdings Limited
Nominet UK
Nottingham Industrial Group Limited
OSI International Holdings Limited
Omnico Plastics Limited
Orbit Investments (Northern) Limited
Oxford Biomedica PLC
P H Property Holdings Limited

Pal International Limited
Pall-Ex (U.K.) Limited
Paragon Quality Foods Ltd
Paramount Holdings (UK) Limited
Patrolmake Limited
Personal Group Holdings PLC
Plastic Omnium Automotive Limited
Plusnet PLC
Polytech International Limited
G.E. Porter & Sons Limited
Premdor Crosby Limited
Premdor U.K. Holdings Limited
Print-Rite Europe Ltd.
Pury Hill Limited
RPC Packaging Holdings Limited
Renewi PFI Investments Limited
STS Defence Limited
Saint-Gobain Limited
Sandicliffe Limited
Sandwich Factory Holdings Limited
Schoeller-Bleckmann Oilfield Equipment (UK) Ltd
A. Schulman Gainsborough Ltd
Secure Holdings Limited
Sims Group UK Limited
Smith Cooper Audit Limited
St Barnabas Hospice Trust (Lincolnshire)
Stanton Investments Limited
Stepan UK Limited
Stoneleigh Abbey Limited
T.S.B. (Developments) Limited
TNT Holdings (UK) Limited
Taylor Hobson Limited
Tioga Limited
Tolsa UK Limited
Topalpha Limited
Topps Tiles PLC
Trimas Corporation Limited
UYS Limited
Unipart Rail Holdings Limited
Valspar (UK) Holding Corporation Limited
Viewtone Limited
Welcome Break Group Limited
Welcome Break Holdings Limited
White Capstan Limited
Working Assets Limited
Yutaka Giken (UK) Limited

1997 [138]

APS Produce Limited
ARRK Europe Limited
Abba Plant Hire Limited
Advanced Marketing (Europe) Limited
Agrihold Limited
Anpario PLC
Aptean Limited
Arena Blinds Limited
Arkle Finance Limited
Ashfield Meetings & Events Limited
Atlas Hotels (Derby) Limited
Atlas Hotels (Exeter) Limited
Atlas Hotels (Glasgow) Limited
Atlas Hotels (Group 4 Property 2) Ltd
Atlas Hotels (Salford Quays) Limited
Atlas Hotels (Warwick) Limited
Atlas Textiles Ltd.
BASF U.K. Holdings Limited
BPI International (No 2) Limited
BPI International Limited
Bauer AR Holdings Limited
Belle Holdings Limited
Bio Energy (UK) Limited

Blue Deer Limited
Bosworth Independent College Limited
Bourbon Automotive Plastics Northampton Ltd
Bravissimo Limited
Bridgeway Consulting Limited
CAE Aircrew Training Services PLC
CVS Leasing Limited
Canon Street Properties Limited
Cape Industrial Services Group Limited
Cape Industrial Services Limited
Caunton Investments Limited
Cedar House Investments Limited
Centres for Assisted Reproduction Ltd
Chatsworth Investments Limited
Chevron Traffic Management Limited
Choice Packaging Solutions Limited
Consuma Holdings Limited
Croda Overseas Holdings Limited
DHL Services Limited
DP Group Developments Limited
Dassault Systemes UK Limited
Diversey Limited
Dunlop Oil & Marine Limited
E. P. B. Holdings Limited
E.On Energy Solutions Limited
EDL Holdings (UK) Limited
ENVA England Limited
ESNT Holdings (No.1) Limited
ESNT Holdings (No.2) Limited
Eaton Holding (UK) II Limited
Educationcity Limited
Elite Office Furniture (UK) Ltd.
Elmwood Trading Limited
Evolution Power Tools Ltd
Experian Holdings Limited
Experian International Unlimited
FEL Group Limited
First Carton Group Ltd
Flowmax Limited
Forest of Marston Vale Trust
Framework Housing Association
H.B. Fuller U.K. Limited
GUS Catalogues Unlimited
Gallagher Estates No. 2 Limited
Gladstone Limited
Global Brands Limited
Go Plant Fleet Services Ltd
Grupo Antolin Leamington Limited
H L Plastics Limited
HRVS Group Limited
Hajco 199 Limited
Heavyweight Air Express Limited
Hillbridge Investments Limited
Hillsborough Investments Limited
Jepco Limited
Juniper Pharma Services Limited
Keepstem Limited
Kent Pharmaceuticals Limited
Kingscrown Properties Limited
Kingsway Financial Group Holdings Ltd
Kingsway Leasing Limited
Knapp U.K. Limited
Latimer Associates (U.K) Limited
Lazarus Properties Limited
Leadec Limited
Leicester Football Club PLC
Lexington Catering Limited
London Vista Hotel Limited
MHR Global Holdings Limited
Magyar Farming Co Ltd
Mid-UK Recycling Limited

Midland Communications Distribution Ltd
Monocon Overseas Limited
Mortgage Advice Bureau Limited
Motorpoint Limited
NP Aerospace Limited
National Space Centre
Oxford Instruments Overseas Holdings Ltd
PPF Limited
Partners in Property (U.K.) Limited
Pendragon Property Holdings Limited
Phoenix Sports Limited
Plaza on Hyde Park Limited
Principal Healthcare Finance (UK) No.1 Ltd
Principal Healthcare Finance (UK) No.2 Ltd
Punch Partnerships (PML) Limited
Radical Motorsport Limited
Ragi Properties Limited
Ravent Limited
Rigby Group (RG) PLC
Riverside Motors Holdings Limited
Robinson (Overseas) Limited
Rolls-Royce Power Development Limited
Patrick Ruddy Homes Limited
SJC 14 Limited
SJC 15 Limited
Sealed Air Limited
Sitel UK Limited
Slack & Parr Limited
Snap-On Finance UK Limited
Sportsdirect.Com Retail Limited
Stanley U.K. Holding Ltd.
Stowe House Preservation Trust
Strawson Management Limited
Sundial Group Limited
Swanton Care & Community (Glenpath Holdings) Ltd
TH Finance Limited
UDG Healthcare (UK) Holdings Limited
URA Ventures Limited
Unicarriers Leasing UK Limited
C.J. Upton Holdings Ltd.
VR Finance Company
Warm A Home Limited
Webmart Limited
ZND (UK) Limited

1998 [121]

AIAL Limited
API Overseas Holdings Limited
Aalberts Industries U.K. Ltd.
Abingdon School
Acis Group Limited
Aero Tec Laboratories Limited
Agrovista UK Limited
Amey LG Limited
Anisa Supply Chain Solutions Limited
Artisan (UK) PLC
Atlas Hotels (Bristol North) Limited
Atlas Hotels (Greenwich) Limited
Atlas Hotels (Inverness) Limited
Auto-Trail V.R. Limited
Autofil Holdings Limited
Autofil Yarns Limited
B.I. (UK) Limited
BPB Finance (No.2) Limited
BRS Limited
Bell Equipment UK Limited
Blue Boar Holdings Limited
Bodypower Sports PLC
Boels Rental Limited
Braeside Group Limited
C Student Services Limited
CEVA Freight (UK) Holding Co Ltd
Calverton Finance Limited
Carmelite Finance Limited
Catesby Estates PLC
Circassia Limited
Clegg Food Projects Limited
Clegg Group Limited
Clientlogic Holding Limited
Cooke Optics Limited
Crossfleet Limited
Daimler Insurance Services UK Limited
Dalepak Holdings Limited
E M Holdings UK Limited
E.On Climate & Renewables UK Robin Rigg East Ltd
Expert Tooling & Automation Limited
First Response Finance Limited
Flamepro Limited
Flint Holdings Limited
Fugro Properties Limited
HB Fuller UK Operations Limited
Fusion Group Limited
Fusion Plastics Limited
GUS 1998 Unlimited
GUS Holdings Unlimited
Gallagher Longstanton Limited
Gardner Aerospace - Derby Limited
Genie International Holdings Limited
Gibbs Technologies Limited
Go Outdoors Limited
Grandcross Limited
Green Meadow Limited
Guy Salmon Limited
Hall Contracts (Lakenheath) Limited
I Holland Limited
Idverde Limited
Ikea Distribution Services Limited
Industrial Control Distributors Limited
Infineum International Limited
Inspired Gaming (UK) Limited
Integral Powertrain Limited
Kisimul Group Limited
L & R Medical UK Ltd.
Lagardere Sports UK Ltd
Larkfleet Limited
A.C. Lloyd (Asset Management) Limited
Lo's Pharmacy Limited
M3 (EU) Limited
Magna Trust
Mahle Powertrain Limited
Usha Martin UK Limited
Megaclose Limited
Midcity Investments Limited
Mogford Hotels Limited
Morris Homes Limited
Mortons Media Group Ltd
Multi Packaging Solutions Acquisitions 2 Ltd
Nicholas Associates Group Limited
Nikon Metrology UK Limited
Noble Foods Limited
North Lincs Property Limited
Northampton Theatres Trust Limited
Openfield Agriculture Limited
Oxcis Limited
Oxford Pharmagenesis Limited
Paccar Trucks U.K. Ltd
Pinewood Technologies PLC
Plastek UK Ltd
Porterbrook Maintenance Limited
Powergen International Limited
Print People Group Limited
Promens Holding UK Limited
Proseal UK Limited
Purico Limited
Quaker International Educational Trust
RTI International Metals Limited
RVB Holding Co Ltd
Reel Cinemas Limited
SAI Global Assurance Services Ltd
SML Europe Limited
Sape Group Holdings UK Ltd
Sheffield Galleries & Museums Trust
Shield Properties Limited
Sterling Safetywear Limited
Supply Point Systems Limited
Swanton Care & Community (Andrew Frederick Care Homes) Ltd
TDY Holdings Limited
TNS Transxpress Holding Company (U.K.) Ltd
Tenens Ede Limited
Thistledown Investments Limited
Tinsley Park Holdings Limited
Trousdale Limited
Unipart Powertrain Applications Limited
Way Ahead Group Limited
Whites Engineering Limited
Wilson & Co. (Motor Sales) Limited
Young's Seafood International Holdings Ltd

1999 [142]

A.M.S. Property Management Limited
ACM ULR Limited
AFE Group Limited
AP Racing Limited
Accord Limited
Aga Rangemaster Limited
Agriturf Holdings Limited
Alpro (UK) Limited
Amey Group Services Limited
Atlas Hotels (Bath) Limited
Atlas Hotels (Chingford) Limited
Atlas Hotels (Group 2) Limited
Avalon (Europe) Limited
Axis Fleet Management Limited
Barcode Warehouse Limited
Barratt Evolution Limited
Baxi Global Limited
Baxi Heating UK Limited
Baxi Overseas Holdings Limited
Baxi Potterton Limited
Beckhall Properties Ltd
Graham Bell Limited
Bloxham School Limited
Bluebell Wood Children's Hospice
Blythmore Limited
Bong UK Limited
H.R Bourn & Sons (Linwood) Limited
Bransby Horses
Burrows Motor Co Ltd
Bybox Field Support Limited
CPL Aromas (Holdings) Limited
Cannon Venture Finance Limited
Capital One (Europe) PLC
Capital One Holdings Limited
Car People Limited
Carter Accommodation Holdings Limited
Cellar Trends Limited
Century Health (Nottingham) Limited
Cerealto UK Limited
Cheadle Hulme School
City Furniture Hire Limited
Clean Estates Limited
Coalfields Regeneration Trust

Comex 2000 (UK) Limited
Thomas Cook Tour Operations Limited
County Estates (Bakewell) Limited
Cygnia Logistics Limited
Deb IP Limited
Domino's Pizza Group PLC
Ducati U.K. Limited
Dynex Semiconductor Limited
E.On Climate & Renewables UK Developments Ltd
E.On Climate & Renewables UK Limited
Dennis Eagle Limited
Echostar UK Holdings Limited
Eggborough Power Limited
Experian Group Limited
Farmers Fresh Limited
Firstan Holdings Limited
Four Seasons Health Care Holdings Ltd
Freedom Travel Group Limited
Freefoam Plastics (U.K.) Limited
Freshtime UK Limited
Frutarom (UK) Limited
Gallagher Bathgate Limited
Gapuma (UK) Limited
Guided Ultrasonics Limited
HFG Holdings Limited
Hales Group Limited
Herts Insurance Consultants Limited
P.D. Hook (Rearing) Limited
ID Medical Group Limited
IRESS Solutions Limited
Inter M.K. Limited
Interfood Technology Ltd.
A W James Limited
Brian James Trailers Limited
Jeld-Wen Europe Ltd.
Kybotech Limited
Kyra Enterprises Limited
Lakeside Energy from Waste Limited
Leaderflush + Shapland Holdings Limited
Lenze U.K. Limited
MacIntyre Hudson Holdings Limited
Maggie Sottero Bridal (UK) Ltd.
Mansfield Sand Co Ltd
H W Martin Waste Limited
Midcity Estates Limited
Mori Lee Europe Limited
Multi Packaging Solutions Acquisitions 1 Ltd
My Home Move Ltd
Newlincs Development Limited
AC Nielsen Holdings UK Limited
Norbar Torque Tools Holdings Limited
Norcros PLC
OKA Direct Limited
Oxford Gene Technology (Operations) Ltd
Oxford Gene Technology IP Limited
Parkway Derby Limited
Pattonair (Derby) Limited
Pendragon Automotive Services Limited
Pendragon Premier Limited
Pendragon Sabre Limited
Penso Consulting Ltd
Pets at Home Holdings Limited
Pharos Group Limited
Pointeuro V Limited
Prodrive (Holdings) Limited
Proimmune Limited
Punch Taverns Limited
Ranquin Underwriting Limited
Reflex Labels Limited
Renewi Holdings Limited
Robinson Healthcare Limited
Rotor Clip Limited
SLM Fitness & Health Limited
Sanderson Limited
Satra Technology Centre Limited
Scoto Limited
Scusi Limited
Servelec Social Care Limited
Spraycon Limited
Stanley UK Services Limited
Stockshape Limited
Stratstone Motor Holdings Limited
Stripestar Limited
Surfpipe Limited
Surfreset Limited
Syncimage Limited
T-Mobile Holdings Limited
Thornsett Properties Limited
Totally PLC
Toyoda Gosei UK Ltd.
Tunstall Holdings Limited
Whitworth Chemists Limited
Whizstock
Winbro Group UK Limited
Worldwide Fruit Limited
Yara UK Limited
Young's Seafood Limited
Zapf Creation (UK) Limited
Zoo Digital Group PLC

2000 [195]

ASK4 LIMITED
AWG Parent Co Limited
Aareon UK Limited
Achilles Group Limited
Acorn Partitions & Storage Systems Ltd
Aferry Ltd
Allen (Hanford) Limited
Alliance Medical Holdings Limited
Allied Textiles Limited
Alltruck PLC
Amey Programme Management Limited
Anglian Water Facilities Management Holdings (UK) Ltd
Apac Group Limited
Apex Credit Management Limited
Apteco Limited
Arconic UK Finance
Arconic UK Holdings Limited
Arena Event Services Group Limited
Atlas Hotels (Property and Trading) Ltd
B & S Hughes Limited
BHFS One Limited
BHFS Two Limited
Bassi Properties Limited
Baxi Finance Limited
Baxi Group Limited
Benchmark Holdings PLC
Blinds 2 Go Limited
Bloom Developments Limited
Blue Skies Holdings Limited
Booker Direct Limited
Boots International Limited
Bourns (UK) Acquisition Limited
Bramheath Limited
Brands Holdings Limited
Brioche Pasquier U.K. Limited
British Aluminium Limited
Bushboard Limited
Bybox Holdings Limited
CDL Group Holdings Limited
Caistor Seafoods Limited
Cardboard Box Co Ltd
Cheshire Datasystems Limited
Christy Home Textiles Limited
Citation Holdings Limited
Citynet Insurance Brokers Limited
Clientlogic (UK) Limited
Collins Earthworks Limited
Concha y Toro UK Limited
Cooper & Turner Limited
Coverland UK Limited
DSM Nutritional Products (UK) Limited
Danaher & Walsh Group Limited
Deb Holdings Limited
Devonshire Green (Commercial Properties) Ltd
Devonshire Green Holdings Limited
Doncasters Aerospace Limited
Dunns (Long Sutton) Limited
Dyas UK Limited
E.On Climate & Renewables UK Offshore Wind Ltd
EOS Inc. Ltd
ESKO Stonecube Limited
Eaglebeam Limited
Easternrose Limited
Ebuyer (UK) Limited
Electrosteel Castings (UK) Limited
Elmsdale Estates Limited
Enviroenergy Limited
Epyx Limited
Experian Technology Limited
Fernwood Group Limited
Fifthgrange Limited
First Line Limited
Fisher & Paykel Appliances Limited
Fleet Auction Group Limited
Focus Solutions Group Limited
Focus100 Limited
Four Seasons Homes No.4 Limited
Freshlinc Limited
GB Fleetcare Limited
GCI Network Solutions Limited
GRS (Bagging) Limited
GUS 2000 Finance Unlimited
Gallagher Poole Limited
Gardner Aerospace - Basildon Limited
Georgica Limited
Gleeson Regeneration Limited
Glenvale Transport Limited
Going Plural Limited
Grange Mill Developments Limited
Hazlewood (Blackditch) Limited
Helen & Douglas House
Hertford Heath Limited
Home Retail Group Card Services Limited
Home Retail Group Insurance Services Ltd
Huntercombe Properties (Frenchay) Ltd
Hyde Group Holdings Limited
I & A Restaurants Ltd
I.G. Industries Holdings Limited
Imagesound Limited
Independent Forgings & Alloys Limited
Insight Enterprises UK Limited
Intelligent Energy Limited
J W D Holdings Limited
JDP Furniture Group Limited
Jaguar Land Rover Holdings Limited
I M Kelly Automotive Limited
Langley Aviation Limited
Lawton Group Limited
Learndirect Limited
Leen Gate Metals Limited
Lhoist UK Limited

Loughborough Schools Foundation
Loxam Access Limited
Meter Provida Limited
Methodist Homes
Micromass Holdings Limited
Moorhen Holdings Limited
Mortgage Advice Bureau (Holdings) PLC
Moto Direct Limited
N K Motors Limited
NCL Holdings Limited
Nationwide Windows Holding Co Ltd
Northampton Saints PLC
Northcoast Seafoods Limited
OCF PLC
Orchid Cellmark Ltd
Oxford Instruments Nanotechnology Tools Holdings Ltd
Oxford Metrics PLC
Oxford University Trading Limited
PJ Care Limited
Palletforce Limited
Perrys Group Limited
Phoenix Oil & Marine Limited
Phoenix Transworld Limited
Pioneer Foods (UK) Limited
Pirelli International PLC
Proact IT UK Limited
Punch Partnerships (PGRP) Limited
Punch Promotions Limited
Punch Taverns (PGE) Limited
RMA Investments Limited
RTI Europe Limited
Recresco Limited
Reeve (Derby) Limited
Revolve Group Limited
Rightmove Group Limited
Rohm Electronics Europe Limited
Rolls-Royce Overseas Investments Limited
Ross & Catherall Limited
Rudridge Limited
Rumenco Limited
Rylston Road Limited
Savoy Cinemas Limited
Select Alloys & Materials Limited
Senior Architectural Systems Limited
Severn Trent (W & S) Limited
Severn Trent Services Operations UK Ltd
Shoby Properties Limited
Sodick Europe Limited
Solo Cup (UK) Limited
Source Bioscience UK Limited
South Yorkshire Investment Fund Limited
Spire Homes (LG) Limited
Sports & Leisure Group Ltd
Spurgeons
Staffline Recruitment Limited
Steetley Dolomite Limited
Swanton Care & Community (Maesteilo Care Homes) Ltd
TI Automotive (China) Limited
TI Automotive Limited
Technolog Holdings Ltd
Tensator Limited
Tiles4less Limited
Tingdene Parks Limited
Trucast Limited
Turbine Surface Technologies Limited
UK Distributors (Footwear) Limited
UK Platforms Ltd
Uniq Limited
Utopia Tableware Limited
Vaillant Management Limited
Valassis Limited
A N Wallis & Co Ltd
Warwick Energy Limited
Waste Recycling Group (Central) Limited
Waste and Resources Action Programme
Weddel Swift Limited
Welcome Break Holdings (1) Limited
Welcome Break Services Limited
Welspun UK Limited
Westbrook Resources Limited
Wilcox Commercial Vehicles Limited
Workplace Systems International Limited
Wroxall Abbey Estate Limited
Yourcash Limited

2001 [142]

Acorndrift Limited
Acorndrive Limited
Alere UK Holdings Limited
Alphyra Payment Services Limited
Ambury Developments Limited
Amey Group Information Services Limited
Amey Ventures Limited
Anglia Components Limited
Anglian Water Services Financing PLC
Anglian Water Services Holdings Limited
Artex Limited
Available Car Limited
BF Limited
BI Worldwide Holdings Limited
Belgrave Land (Wisbech) Limited
Bifrangi UK Limited
Brady Corporation Limited
B. Braun Avitum UK Limited
Briggs & Forrester Group Limited
Brisbane House Limited
Brophy Grounds Maintenance Limited
CCN UK Unlimited
CCW 600 Limited
CFC 2001 Ltd
Capital One Investments Limited
Carpenter Holdings Limited
Catesby Estates (Residential) Limited
Cenduit Limited
Close Brothers Vehicle Hire Limited
Commify UK Limited
Companion Care (Services) Limited
Thomas Cook Aircraft Engineering Ltd
Croupier Underwriting Limited
Custodian Real Estate (Leicester) Ltd
Cyprotex Discovery Limited
Darby Group Ltd
Dee Valley Group Limited
Diversey Holdings Limited
Drive Motor Retail Limited
Drybrough Trading Limited
Dudley Taylor Pharmacies Limited
E-Therapeutics PLC
E.On Climate & Renewables UK Robin Rigg West Ltd
EHI UK Unlimited
EIS UK Unlimited
EMSC (UK) Limited
ESNT Packaging & Securing Solutions Ltd
Ebbsfleet Property Limited
Education Solutions Speke Limited
Encore Personnel Services Limited
English Partnerships (LP) Limited
European Support Services (UK) Limited
Exlabesa Extrusions (Doncaster) Limited
FPS Distribution Limited
Farol Limited
Ferraris Piston Service Limited
Fossil (UK) Holdings Limited
H.B. Fuller Group Limited
G2M Unilets Limited
GRI Group Limited
Gallagher Elstow Limited
Gallagher Projects Limited
Genistics Holdings Limited
Genistics Limited
Genzyme Therapeutics Limited
Glencalvie Estate
Golden Acquisition
Grantham Industries Limited
Green Planet Products Limited
Grundon Waste Management Limited
Guardian Industries U.K. Limited
Hexagon Leasing Limited
Hill Care Limited
Hotel MK Limited
Ingka Energy Services UK Limited
KL Ventures Limited
Kelkay Limited
Keystone Developments (LG) Limited
Ashley King (Developments) Limited
Kite Packaging Group Limited
Lighthouse UkCo 6 (Treasury) Limited
Lockheed Martin UK Ampthill Group Ltd
Lynn Wind Farm Limited
M & M (MK) Limited
MK Battery International Limited
MMR Research Worldwide Limited
Magenta Storage Limited
Maintenance Management Limited
Makro Holding Limited
Manor Crest Construction Limited
McLean Restaurants Limited
McManus Pub Co. Limited
Metalysis Limited
Mondottica Limited
Morrells Farming Limited
Moto Direct Holdings Limited
Motorhog Holdings Limited
MoveWithUs Conveyancing Limited
Mytravel North America Limited
Newton Europe Limited
PAG International Limited
Paccar Financial PLC
Paccor (Mansfield) UK Limited
Parallel Parents Ltd
Peach Pub Company (Holdings) Limited
Princethorpe Foundation
Punch Taverns (Services) Limited
RFE International (Group) Ltd
RM Property and Facilities Solutions Ltd
Red Box Recorders Limited
Reflex Group Limited
Sansbury Bailey Holdings Limited
Seashell Trust
Select Group International Limited
Slater Hogg Mortgages Limited
Snap-On Equipment Limited
Solartron Metrology Limited
Speedloan Finance Limited
Sports Information Services Limited
Stadco Holdings Ltd.
Stratford-upon-Avon Town Trust
Strawson Limited
Sun Healthcare Limited
TI Automotive Holdings Limited
Tadano UK Ltd
Tamar (Selby) Limited
Tansor (Cornbow) Limited

Technia Limited
Tensator Group Limited
Tile Giant Limited
Tuxford Exports Limited
Undercover Roofing Supplies Limited
Unipart Logistics Limited
Urgo Limited
WIC (1) Limited
Warwick Independent Schools Foundation
Wasps Holdings Limited
Wilcox Holdings Limited
Winvic Construction Limited
Wisbech Grammar School
Wyndham Holdings
Youth Sport Trust

2002 [153]

A1 Comms Limited
AWG Land Holdings Limited
Aalberts Industries Limited
Aaron Holdings Limited
Alliance Medical Radiopharmacy Limited
Amey LUL 2 Limited
Ancala Water Services (Defence) Limited
Ancala Water Services (Estates) Limited
Apertio Limited
Arena Coventry Limited
Aroqua Power Services Ltd.
Avant Homes (Yorkshire) Limited
B.N.T. Properties Limited
BCTI Holdings Limited
BPB Finance (No. 4) Limited
BPB Investments Overseas Limited
BV Holdings Limited
Beachampton Group Limited
Bedford School Trust
Belchim Crop Protection Limited
Belfield Furnishings Limited
Berneslai Homes Limited
Henry Boot Land Holdings Limited
Bradgate Containers (Holdings) Limited
Broomco (3019) Limited
Brunel Healthcare Manufacturing Limited
Business Village Limited
CCS Media Limited
CHT Holdings Limited
Center Parcs (Operating Company) Limited
Chesterfield Poultry Limited
Chevin Homes Limited
Clientlogic (UK) Holding Limited
Clifton Packaging Group Limited
Condie Investments Limited
Conservation Education & Research Trust
Crown Crest (Leicester) PLC
D D Heating Limited
Davidsons Developments Limited
Dee Valley Water (Holdings) Limited
Derby Homes Limited
Devonshire Green (Residential Investments) Ltd
Diamond Light Source Limited
Djanogly Learning Trust
EMA Holdings UK Limited
Eagle Hall Estates Limited
Earth Trust
Fernbrook Investments (UK) Limited
Forgings International Limited
Four Seasons Health Care (Capital) Ltd
Futures Homescape Limited
GPS Estates Limited
Gallagher Llanwern Limited
Games Workshop US (Holdings) Limited
Simon Gibson Transport Limited
Gilo Investments Limited
Granwood Holdings Limited
Green Biologics Limited
Greenyard Frozen UK Limited
Ground Group Limited
Holland & Barrett International Limited
Impello Limited
Indesit Company UK Holdings Limited
Insight Networking Solutions Limited
Intercounty Truck and Van Limited
Irth (19) Limited
JJC Investments Limited
Jazz Pharmaceuticals UK Limited
Johnsons Aggregates and Recycling Ltd
Just A Bank Limited
Key Fund Investments Limited
Kidderminster Property Investments Ltd
Kingdom Bank Limited
LKAB Minerals Limited
Laen Limited
Lakshmi & Son's Limited
Leeson Chemicals Limited
Leicester City Football Club Limited
Liberty Guard (U.K.) Limited
Linbrooke Services Limited
Longleat Property Limited
Lucy Developments Limited
MM (UK) Limited
MSW (Holdings) Limited
Mark's Electrical Limited
Maro Developments Limited
John Martin-Hoyes (Holdings) Limited
Mediline Home Care Limited
Melett Limited
Minova International Limited
Mytravel Pioneer Limited
National Fleet Solutions Limited
New Era Cap Co Ltd
New York Bakery Co Ltd
Next PLC
Next Retail Limited
Nottingham High School
OSL Group Holdings Limited
Oncimmune Limited
Oxford Immunotec Limited
PKF Cooper Parry LLP
Performance Health International Limited
Peugeot Citroen Automobiles UK Limited
Pinelog Group Limited
Pinstone Securities Limited
Plaza Investments Limited
Pointtravel Co. Ltd
Sir John Port's Charity
G. & R. Pykett Limited
R.M.F. Properties Limited
RHS UK Holdings Limited
Rannoch Food Group Limited
Regent Park Energy Limited
Relta Limited
Robinson Healthcare Holdings Ltd
Roko Health Clubs Limited
SJH-All Plant Group Limited
SKF. Lo (Chemists) Limited
SMS Electronics Limited
Richard Sanders Limited
Sandicliffe Motor Holdings Limited
Scholastic UK Ltd
Scott Bader UK Limited
Senad Group Limited
Severn Trent Corporate Holdings Limited
Severn Trent Green Power Limited
Severn Trent Services Holdings Limited
Simmerson Associates Ltd
Slough Enterprise Limited
Smart Garden Products Ltd
Paul Smith (Holdings) Ltd
Sodick Europe Holdings Limited
Sperry Rail (International) Limited
St. Matthews Limited
Stockport Homes Limited
Swanton Care & Community (Autism North) Ltd
TGW (Holdings) Limited
TMI Foods Limited
TTS Group Limited
Toolstation Limited
Topalpha (Warehouse) Limited
Underwood Meat (Holdings) Limited
United Learning Trust
V Installations Mechanical Handling Ltd
Reg Vardy (VMC) Limited
Wade Group Limited
Western Bridge (Shipping) Limited
Willoughby (396) Limited
Willoughby 395 Limited
Wixams First Limited
Woodthorpe Hall Garden Centres Limited
World of Sweets Limited
Xtratherm UK Limited

2003 [137]

2morrow Group Limited
Accelerating Growth Fund Ltd
Addington Fund
Air Ambulance Service
Allington Waste Co Ltd
Amey UK PLC
Amey Ventures Investments Limited
Ashberry Healthcare Limited
Atlas Hotels (Group 1) Limited
Atlas Hotels (Stevenage) Limited
Auction Finance Limited
Aviagen International Finance Four Ltd
Aviagen International Finance Limited
Aviagen International Finance One Ltd
Aviagen International Finance Two Ltd
Axis Intermodal Limited
BBB Services Limited
BBHP Limited
Barrough Hospitality Limited
Baxi Holdings Limited
Bayard Metering (UK)
Graham Bell (Holdings) Limited
Blenheim Land & Properties Ltd
Bodycote Finance UK Limited
Brigam Limited
British Waterways Marinas Limited
Browne Jacobson LLP
Business Control Solutions PLC
C3 Construction Limited
Castel Froma Neuro Care Limited
Central Glass Europe Limited
Chesterfield Special Cylinders Limited
Chinook Sciences Limited
Commercial Legal Limited
Coveris Flexibles (Gainsborough) UK Ltd
Dunelm Estates Limited
Dunelm Group PLC
E.On Climate & Renewables UK Humber Wind Ltd
E.On Control Solutions Limited
ESCO (UK) Holdings Limited
East Coast Main Line Co Ltd

Enterprise (AOL) Limited
Equity Solutions Lift Investments Ltd
Allen Ford (UK) Limited
Freeths LLP
GHP Midco Limited
GRT Nottingham Lift Project Company (No. 1) Ltd
GRT Nottingham Lift Project Company (No.2) Ltd
GW 305 Limited
Gardner Group Limited
Greenshoots Limited
HSH Cold Stores Limited
Hemswell Estates Limited
Hillarys Properties Partnership LLP
Hoban Limited
Hotels4U.Com Limited
Hutchinson Group Limited
IRISNDT UK Holdings Limited
Ideal Industries Holdings Limited
Igloo Books Limited
Jerrold Finco PLC
Juice Master Limited
Karsten UK Limited
Kimbolton School
Kite Packaging Limited
Leicester Lift Project Company (No. 1) Ltd
Linecross Group Limited
Loadhog Limited
MCS Build Limited
MTU UK Limited
Marshalls Yard Limited
Maynard & Harris Plastics (UK) Limited
Metflex Precision Mouldings Limited
Mintridge Investments (Wikowo) Limited
Mintun 3 Limited
Molson Compact Equipment Limited
Mulberry Commercial Developments Limited
Nasmyth Group Limited
Network Ventures Limited
John Nicholls (Holdings) Limited
Node 4 Limited
Norfolk Free Range Limited
North Nottinghamshire Lift Project Company (No.1) Ltd
Novoferm Europe Limited
One Call Insurance Services Limited
P Investments Limited
P2I Ltd
PAH Financial Services Limited
Parker Plant Limited
Pauley Group Limited
Pauley Properties Limited
Pegler Holdings Limited
Pertemps Limited
Premierfirst Vehicle Rental EMEA Holdings Ltd
Promens Packaging Limited
Q.E.P. Co. U.K. Limited
Quality Care (EM) Limited
Realpower Limited
SC Johnson Professional Group Limited
Samsons Limited
Sanderson Group PLC
Sheffield Forgemasters Engineering Ltd
Sheffield Forgemasters International Ltd
Silgan Closures UK Holdings Limited
C. Soar & Sons (UK) Limited
Society of The Sacred Mission (Europe)
Southern Derbyshire Lift Project Company (No. 1) Ltd
Spaldings Holdings Limited
Specialised Fixings Limited
Summit (Oxford) Limited
Sumo Digital Ltd.
Sutton Park Holdings Limited
Synventive Holding Limited
T. C. Landscapes Limited
T.J.D. Trade Limited
Tarras Park Properties Limited
Tegama Limited
Tenpin Limited
Thorneycroft Solicitors Limited
Timico Limited
Topps Tiles (UK) Limited
Total Computer Networks Limited
Total Motion Limited
Tripod Crest Group Limited
UBT (EU) Ltd
UGC Properties Limited
UK Biobank Limited
UK Waste Solutions Limited
Union Colours Limited
Van Elle Holdings PLC
Vulcan SFM Limited
Walls and Floors Limited
Wellingborough School
Whitworths Holdings Limited
Wilkins Group Limited
Yardi Systems Limited
Zooom Holdings (UK) Limited

2004 [143]

AK Retail Holdings Limited
Adept Care Homes Limited
Agellus Limited
Ark Capital Limited
Asquith Nurseries Limited
Aurum Acquisitions Limited
Avon UK Holdings Limited
BW Integrated Systems UK Limited
Barton Petroleum (Holdings) Limited
Bewick Holdings Ltd
Binks Developments Limited
Blancco Technology Group PLC
Booker Group Limited
Booker Wholesale Holdings Limited
Branchwater Developments Limited
Buccleuch Property (Shawfair) Limited
Bushboard Holdings Limited
CLEB Holdings Limited
CLS Finance Limited
Caterpillar Overseas Limited
Celleron Therapeutics Limited
Cemex UK
Centro Place Investments Limited
Coba International Limited
Cognita Holdings Limited
Cognita Limited
Community 1st Oldham Limited
Community 1st Sheffield Limited
Cosworth Electronics Limited
Cosworth Limited
Cozart Limited
DFDS Logistics Limited
Dar Lighting Limited
Davison Property Investments Ltd
Thomas Deacon Education Trust
Designer Contracts Limited
Distinction Doors Limited
Symon Donovan Properties Limited
E.On Climate & Renewables UK London Array Ltd
Energy Alloys UK Limited
Enviropower Investments Limited
Equity Solutions Lift Investments Cornwall Ltd
Equity Solutions Lift Investments Oldham Ltd
Equity Solutions Lift Investments Sheffield Ltd
Fellside Estates Limited
Field Boxmore II Limited
First Utility Limited
Fluidpower Shared Services Limited
Futaba Industrial U.K. Ltd.
GUS 2004 Limited
Giant Bidco Limited
Giant Midco Limited
Goosebrook Limited
Guidance Marine Limited
Heating Finance Limited
Hesley Care & Education Limited
Holcim Participations (UK) Limited
Home Decor GB Limited
Homecome Limited
P. D. Hook (Group) Limited
I Go 4 Ltd.
ITM Power PLC
IX Reach Ltd
Idis Group Limited
Interflora Holdings Limited
International Brand Management Limited
Adam James Limited
Jonas Computing (UK) Limited
Kaye Aluminium (Holdings) Limited
Kingsgate Community Church
LTI Metaltech Limited
Leaworks Limited
Linx Acquisition Limited
Lowdham Leisureworld Ltd
MCS Group Limited
Mays Properties Limited
Mercedes-Benz Brooklands Limited
Mercian Limited
Mobica Limited
Morris Group Limited
Multi-Tile Distribution Limited
Multipanel UK Limited
Muslim Hands
NFU Mutual (Service Company) Limited
Nirvana Holdings Limited
Nottingham City Airport Limited
Nottingham City Homes Limited
Novera Energy (Holdings 2) Limited
Oakbridge Financial Services Limited
Origin Wine Limited
PFM Group Limited
Parkway Hellas Holdings Limited
Pelham Homes Limited
Penso Holdings Ltd
Pico Technology (Holdings) Limited
Pinnacle International Freight Holdings Ltd
Pipe Holdings PLC
Precision Engineered Limited
Premier Group (Coventry) Limited
Questport Limited
Quotient Sciences Limited
RMS Europe Group Limited
Red Bull Technology Limited
Respond Group Limited
Ridge and Partners LLP
Rowe Farming Limited
S.T.L. Trading Co Ltd
SIG European Holdings Limited
SPD Holdings Limited
SWK (U.K.) Holding Limited

Salus Controls PLC
Severn Trent Services Defence Limited
Sovereign Crest Limited
Special New Fruit Licensing Limited
St Andrew's Healthcare
Staffline Group PLC
Suez Water Technologies & Solutions Services UK Ltd
Summit Therapeutics PLC
Swiftbuild Properties Limited
Synarbor Limited
TI Automotive Euro Holdings Limited
TI Automotive USA Holdings Limited
Talasey Ltd
Tallington Holdings Limited
Ten Albemarle Limited Liability Partnership
Topps Tiles Distribution Limited
Tripal International Limited
UAV Tactical Systems Limited
Unique Window Systems Ltd
Universal Components UK Limited
Valve Partners Limited
Vital Pet Group Limited
WRG Acquisitions 2 Limited
Watches of Switzerland Group Limited
West Atlantic UK Limited
West Retail Group Limited
Westbridge Furniture Designs Limited
Whitecross@Stepnell Limited
Whitworths Limited
Wienerberger Limited
Williams Jet Tenders Limited
Woodard Schools (Nottinghamshire) Ltd
Yeovil Developments Limited

2005 [158]

ACP Europe Limited
ALC (FMC) Limited
ALC (SPC) Limited
ALC (Superholdco) Limited
Acertec UK Limited
Acorn Industrial Services Group Ltd
Aga-Rayburn Limited
Aggregate Industries Limited
Alere Toxicology PLC
Amey Defence Services (Housing) Limited
Amey Defence Services Limited
Amey Holdings Limited
Amey Power Services Limited
Apollo Support Services Group Limited
Avenuepoint Limited
BASF Pharma (Callanish) Limited
BPB Group Finance Limited
BPB Group Operations Limited
Banner Group Limited
Biogen (UK) Limited
Toby Blackwell Limited
Brady European Holdings Limited
Brayford Plastics Limited
Brelade Estates Ltd
Buffaload Logistics Limited
Buxton Consortium Limited
CCN UK 2005 Limited
CET Group Holdings Limited
Cambridge Nutritional Foods Limited
Camden Ventures Limited
Car Shops Limited
Care Fertility Group Limited
Caterpillar Logistics (UK) Limited
Caterpillar UK Engines Co Ltd
Caterpillar UK Group Limited
Colston Property Partners Limited
Crabwall Claremont Limited
Diligenta Limited
Doncasters Group Limited
Dundee Holdco 2 Limited
Dundee Holdco 3 Limited
Dundee Holdco 4 Limited
Duo Processing Limited
Dyon E & P Limited
Dyon UK Limited
E.F.B. Group Limited
E.On IT UK Limited
EHI 2005 Limited
EIS 2005 Limited
East Midlands Trains Limited
Edina UK Limited
Elsham Linc Limited
Ely Cloisters Estate Limited
Environmental Scientifics Group Holdings Ltd
Envisage Technologies Limited
Esendex Holdings Limited
Essentra Finance Limited
Essentra PLC
Exemplar Limited
F & G Holdings Limited
FCC Environment (Berkshire) Limited
FCC PFI Holdings Limited
FCC Wrexham PFI Limited
FSHC Developments (Properties) Limited
FSHC Properties (CH2) Limited
GCI Managed Services Group Limited
GE Energy Power Conversion UK Limited
Gateway Plaza Limited
Global Closure Systems UK Limited
Global Real Estate Portfolios Limited
Golflane Limited
HBPO UK Limited
Hadleigh Holdings Limited
Hancocks Group Holdings Limited
Hexagon Investment Holdings Limited
Hughes Network Systems Limited
Huntercombe (BIR) Limited
Huntercombe (SP) Limited
John Hurt Estates (UK) Limited
ILI Limited
IRESS FS Group Limited
Ibstock Leasing Limited
Idis Group Holdings Limited
Ilmor Engineering Limited
Infinity SDC Limited
Interflora Group Limited
International Piping Products (Europe) Ltd
JTF Wholesale Limited
K & S Buildings Limited
Lakeside Energy from Waste Holdings Ltd
Lebus Upholstery Limited
M N Holdings Limited
MGA Entertainment (UK) Limited
MacIntyre Hudson LLP
A J Mackaness Holdings Limited
Madecorn Leisure LLP
Manor Fresh Limited
Marshall Street Regeneration Limited
Mastercard Prepaid Management Services Ltd
Midland Assured Holdings Limited
Moriah House Limited
Morpeth II Limited
Move Factory Holdings Limited
Mumford's Mill Rentals Limited
NAH Group Limited
Northbridge Industrial Services PLC
Ossur UK Holding Limited
Oxford Nanopore Technologies Limited
PMC Fluidpower Group Limited
Pfisterer Limited
Pilgrim Foodservice Limited
Pipe Holdings 1 PLC
Pipe Holdings 2 Limited
Plant Impact Limited
Playfootball Ltd
Policyfast Limited
Potomac Capital Limited
Potter Clarkson LLP
Produce Investments Limited
RE3 Limited
RRD GDS Limited
Rainthorpe Farms Limited
Rapidrop Global Limited
Renewi Financial Management Limited
Richard's Pharma Limited
Rushlift Limited
SCCS Survey Equipment Limited
Saint-Gobain Aldwych Limited
Select International Developments Ltd
Severn Trent Holdings Limited
Paul Smith Group Holdings Limited
Solidor Limited
Soncell International Limited
Stagecoach South Western Trains Limited
Stampede Acquisition Limited
Stanhope Partnership Limited
Stocksbridge Regeneration Co Ltd
Symphony Holdings Limited
Synventive Acquisition UK Limited
Synventive Acquisition Unlimited
TAG Partnership LLP
TCI Renewables Limited
TI Automotive Canada Holdings Limited
Tibbetts Group Limited
Tingdene (MJ) Limited
Tingdene Marinas Limited
Tunstall Group Acquisition Limited
Tunstall Group Finance Limited
Tunstall Group Holdings Limited
U-Pol Bond Limited
U-Pol Mezzanine Limited
Vow Retail Limited
WJH Limited
Wavin UK (Holdings) Limited
Weatherbys Bank Holdings Limited
Weatherbys Thoroughbred Holdings Limited
Thos. C. Wild Limited
Wright Hassall LLP

2006 [184]

A.B. Produce Trading Limited
A.P.S. Salads Limited
Abbey Group UK Limited
Adams Challenge (UK) Limited
Addo Food Group Limited
Allmakes 4 X 4 Limited
Amtech Group Limited
Arena Coventry (2006) Limited
Argos Holdings Limited
Argos SURBS Investments Limited
Asgard Group Ltd
Atlas Hotels (Lincoln) Limited
Atlas Hotels (Property) Limited
Atlas Hotels (Trading) Limited
Aviagen International Holdings Ltd.
BAJ 1 Limited
BCM Specials Limited
BDF Plant Limited
Baker Perkins Limited

The C. Alma Baker Trust
Barbara Limited
Barratt Metropolitan LLP
Battles Limited
Bawtry Carbon International Limited
Bodycote Investments
Bolsover Cruise Club Limited
Branston Holdings Limited
Briggs & Forrester Limited
Bucks Investments Limited
CEVA Limited
CPL Industries Holdings Limited
Celanese Production UK Limited
Chartered Accountants' Benevolent Association
Chiltern Distribution Ltd
Circassia Pharmaceuticals PLC
Colston Investment Properties Limited Liability Partnership
Comet REFICO Limited
Crown Crest Group Limited
DCS 452 Limited
DMWSL 532 Limited
DPG Holdings Limited
Dematic Limited
Drishaun Holdings Limited
EDL (UK) LFG Generation Limited
East London Bus Group Property Investments Ltd
Eaton Industries (U.K.) Limited
Electro-Motive Diesel Limited
Experian (UK) Holdings 2006 Limited
Experian Investment Holdings Limited
Experian SURBS Investments Limited
FTD UK Holdings Limited
Faccenda Property Limited
Fidentia No 191 LLP
Fischer Future Heat UK Limited
Fisher German LLP
Four Seasons (Bamford) Limited
Fulcrum Infrastructure Services Limited
Fulcrum Pipelines Limited
Full Moon Holdco 4 Limited
Full Moon Holdco 5 Limited
Full Moon Holdco 6 Limited
Futures Homeway Limited
GE Energy Power Conversion Technology Ltd
Gardner Aerospace-Broughton Limited
Gellaw 101 Limited
Godiva Mortgages Limited
Good 'n' Natural Limited
Group GTI Ltd
Nell Gwynn Limited
H & K Distribution Limited
HAE Group Limited
HM Estates Limited
Harrison SD Holdings Limited
Hi-Force Limited
Home Retail Group (UK) Limited
Home Retail Group Limited
Hook 2 Sisters Limited
Hopton Retail Holdings Limited
Howes Percival LLP
Huntercombe (No 12) Limited
Infinis Limited
Inspired Gaming Group Limited
Integrated Bradford Hold Co One Limited
Integrated Bradford SPV One Limited
International Applications Limited
Jaywing PLC
Jungheinrich Financial Services Limited
Jungheinrich Lift Truck Finance Limited
KJW Drylining Limited
Kadima Holdings Limited
Kadima Properties (UK) Limited
Kisimul School Holdings Limited
Kuehne + Nagel Drinkflow Logistics Holdings Ltd
Kuehne + Nagel Drinkflow Logistics Ltd
Kuehne + Nagel Drinks Logistics Limited
Lancer Property Holdings Limited
Latvian Welfare Trust
Launchchange Finance Limited
Lenzing Fibers Grimsby Limited
Lincoln Electric UK Holdings Limited
Lipsy Limited
MBS Lending Ltd
MM Flowers Limited
Malco Holdings Limited
Manor Crest Homes Limited
Maxim Logistics Group Limited
Meller Design Solutions Limited
Meller Group Limited
Mount St Mary's
Mullahead Property Co Ltd
NFT Distribution Operations Limited
Nenplas Limited
Nexeon Limited
Nexperia UK Ltd.
Noble Foods Group Limited
OISE Holdings Limited
Office Depot (Holdings) Limited
Office Depot Europe Holdings Limited
Osprey Acquisitions Limited
Osprey Holdco Limited
Oxford Asset Management LLP
PV Crystalox Solar PLC
Parseq Limited
Pathfinders-Care (Ollerton) Limited
Pattonair Properties Limited
Pen Hill LLP
Pennell's Holdings Limited
Pentagon Motor Holdings Limited
Peopleplus Group Limited
Pork Farms Limited
Praesepe Limited
Premium Plan Limited
Premium Restaurants Limited
Progress Bedford Limited
Project Grace
Psioxus Therapeutics Limited
Pye Homes Limited
Quadrant Security Group Limited
Quartzinvest Limited
R Group Holdings Limited
Ratcliffe College
Rayburn Tours (Holdings) Limited
Redlawn Limited
Resonate Group Limited
Resonate Holdings Limited
Right Digital Limited
Rybrook Holdings Limited
Rybrook Limited
SPD Development Co Ltd
Sanderson Multi-Channel Retail Solutions Ltd
Seckloe 297 Limited
Senad Investments Limited
Sheffield Theatres Crucible Trust
Shrubhill Farms Limited
Silentpride Limited
Simply Cartons Limited
Smithy Wood Business Parks Development LLP
Sobell House Hospice Charity Limited
Southern Derbyshire Lift Project Company (No.2) Ltd
Southgate Packaging Limited
Sports Direct International PLC
Swanton Care & Community Limited
Synectic Systems Group Limited
TGW Limited
TPH (UK) Limited
TSYS Managed Services EMEA Limited
TVCO Limited
Total Produce Holdings (UK) Limited
Total Produce Limited
Totally Local Co Ltd
Union Papertech Limited
United Health Group Limited
United Health Limited
V.I. Risk Capital LLP
V12 Sports & Classics Ltd
Velocys PLC
Videojet Technologies Limited
WFEL Holdings Limited
Waterfall Services Limited
Charles Wells Brewery Limited
Welspun Home Textiles UK Limited
The H D H Wills 1965 Charitable Trust
Winvic Group Limited
Xeros Limited

2007 [169]

2K Polymer Systems Limited
A.F. Switchgear (Holdings) Limited
Adaptimmune Limited
Aire Valley Land LLP
Airtanker Finance Limited
Airtanker Holdings Limited
Airtanker Limited
Airtanker Services Limited
Alliance Medical Acquisitionco Limited
Amey Lighting (Norfolk) Holdings Limited
Amey Lighting (Norfolk) Limited
AmeyCespa WM (East) Limited
Anglian Venture Holdings Limited
Argonaut Bidco Limited
Aston Martin Holdings (UK) Limited
Aston Martin Investments Limited
Atlas Hotels (Borrowings 2) Limited
Atlas Hotels (Liverpool) Limited
Avery House Healthcare Limited
BCQ (Holdings) Limited
BWSC North Lincs Limited
Beechfield Estates Limited
Bellotto Acquisition Limited
Bellotto Finance Limited
Bellotto Holdings Limited
Bodycote Finance Limited
Booker Retail Partners (GB) Limited
Breedon House Properties Limited
Bridgstock Limited
Brighterkind Limited
British Journal of Anaesthesia
Brooklime Limited
Can-Pack UK Limited
Carno 2 LLP
Carwood Holdings Limited
Castle 1 Limited
Central England Healthcare Limited
Chalcroft Holdings Limited
Chestnutbay Acquisitionco Limited
Chromalloy UK Holdings Ltd
Clegg Holdings Limited

Clinigen Healthcare Limited
Codemasters Group Holdings PLC
Codemasters Holdings Limited
Cognita International Holdings Limited
Community 1st Stockport Limited
Conquest Bidco Limited
Thomas Cook Finance PLC
Thomas Cook Investments (2) Limited
Copart Europe Limited
Cosworth Group Holdings Limited
Cristal Inorganic Chemicals UK Limited
Dana UK Automotive Systems Limited
Dana UK Axle Limited
Dana UK Driveshaft Limited
Delano Sutton 2007 Limited
Doddington Farms LLP
Dundee Pikco Limited
E4D & G Holdco Limited
E4D & G Project Co Limited
Elliott Group Holdings (UK) Limited
Elsham Wold Estates Limited
Energy Technologies Institute LLP
Enterprise PLC
Entertainment Magpie Limited
Equity Solutions Lift Investments Stockport Ltd
Evo Group Services Limited
FKB Limited
FR Acquisitions Corporation (Europe) Ltd
Funeral Partners Limited
Funeral Services Partnership Limited
Futures Housing Group Limited
GES Service Companies Limited
Geberit Sales Limited
Gee Bee Investments Limited
Germanischer Lloyd Industrial Services Holdings (UK) Ltd
Ghekko Holdings Limited
Global Derby (UK) Limited
Goldcrest Capital Investments Limited
Owen Greenings & Mumford (Holdings) Ltd
HLD Holdings Limited
Hadfield Properties Limited
Harley (Winchester) Limited
Hillco Investments (UK) Limited
Hilton Food Group PLC
Holding Holding Co Ltd
Horbury Group Limited
Hosting Developments Limited
ITM Power (Trading) Limited
Immunocore Limited
Intermed Limited
Investfront (Oxon) Limited
JR Motorsports Limited
Johnston Quarry Group Limited
K L Technologies Limited
K.M. Packaging Holdings Limited
Frank Key Group Limited
Knowledgepoint360 UK Acquisitionco Ltd
LR (UK) Limited
Lakeside 1 Limited
Lavendon Holdings Limited
Laver Regeneration Holdings Limited
Loxwood Holdings Limited
Mark Lyndon Paper Enterprises (UK) Ltd
Mahle Engine Systems UK Limited
Mahle Industries UK Limited
Maynard & Harris Group Limited
Meatsnacks Group Ltd.
Medical Equipment Supplies and Management Ltd
Mellors Group Limited
Milton Keynes Academy Trust
Mission Resources Group Limited
Molson Coors (UK) Holdings LLP
Monoworld Recycling Ltd
NAH Holdings Limited
NSF International UK Limited
Network Group Holdings Limited
Northern Endeavour Limited
Nu-Oval Acquisitions 1 Limited
Nu-Oval Acquisitions 2 Limited
Omega Red Holdings Limited
Optimum Debtco Limited
Orbit Treasury Limited
Orca Marine Leisure Limited
Perspective Financial Group Limited
Phoenix Parker Holdings Limited
Plymouth Grove Residential LLP
Polypipe Group PLC
Pressure Technologies PLC
Pulse Home Products (Holdings) Limited
RMS Group Holdings Limited
Reconnaissance Ventures Limited
Retail Merchant Finance Limited
Rightmove PLC
The David Ross Education Trust
Rushton Hall Limited
SDL Property Services Group Limited
Samworth Church Academy
Sandbrook Overseas Investments Limited
Scenic Land Developments Limited
Seaham Investments Limited
See Group Limited
Severn Trent Finance Holdings Limited
Severn Trent Finance Limited
Fred Sherwood Group Limited
Stadium MK Group Limited
Stockport Grammar School
Stonepit Limited
Storefield Group Limited
T.C. Landscapes Group Limited
T.C.L. Holdings Limited
TI Automotive Czech Holdings (UK) Ltd
TI Automotive German Holdings (UK) Ltd
TNT Express ICS Limited
TRB Technology Group Limited
Touchgold Limited
Tours Abroad Group Limited
Trapoc Limited
Trewhiddle Village Limited
UK Egg Centre Limited
UK Ticketing Ltd
Uris Central Administration Limited
Vine Mill Limited
Watch Shop Ltd
Welsh Slate Limited
Westbourne Leisure Limited
Westbrook Holdings Limited
Whitemeadow Furniture Limited
Wind Port of Liverpool Limited

2008 [140]

A C PLC
APS Group Limited
Abbotsley Farms Limited
Achilles Group Holdings Limited
Achilles Holdco Limited
Achilles Subholdings Limited
Action for Care Limited
Agrivert Biogas Limited
Amey Belfast Schools Partnership Hold Co Ltd
Amey Belfast Schools Partnership PFI Co Ltd
Amey Highways Limited
Appia Europe Limited
Avery Homes (Nelson) Limited
Aylesbury Vale Academy
Bakkavor Central Finance Limited
Bakkavor Estates Limited
Bakkavor Finance Limited
Bauer Golden Square Limited
Bennie Holdings Limited
Berkeley Insurance Group Limited
Berville Limited
Boots Opticians Professional Services Ltd
Breedon Holdings Limited
C Butt Holdings Limited
Carbolite Holdings Limited
Carewatch Bidco Limited
Carewatch Holdings Limited
Caunton Holdings Limited
Chilled Foods (UK) Ltd
Clinigen Group PLC
Cognita UK Holdings Limited
Community 1st Oldham (Chadderton) Ltd
Thomas Cook Continental Holdings Ltd
Thomas Cook Group Treasury Limited
Corby Land & Development Ltd
Coventry Building Society Covered Bonds LLP
Delano Birmingham 2009 Limited
Denby Holdings Limited
Devol Kitchens Limited
RR Donnelley UK Limited
Door-Stop International Limited
Easey Pigs Limited
Eden Hotel Collection Limited
Effective Energy Solutions Ltd
Ensco 645 Limited
Ensco 648 Limited
Experian Europe Unlimited
Freshlinc Group Limited
GE Energy Power Conversion UK Holdings Ltd
GPUK LLP
Gapuma Group Limited
Georgetown Carr Limited
Glid Wind Farms Topco Limited
Global Payments U.K. Ltd
Great Tew Grain Processing Limited
Hesley Holdings Limited
Hicks (1) Limited
ISDC Developments (No2) Limited
ITP Engines UK Limited
Idverde Holdings Limited
Idverde UK Limited
Inver UK Limited
Jaguar Land Rover Automotive PLC
Johal Properties Leicester LLP
KRNS Properties Ltd
Kartell UK Limited
Key Technologies Limited
Kingerlee Homes Limited
Kite Packaging Group Holdings Limited
Langley UK Limited
Livwell Limited
Mahle Aftermarket Limited
Manderley Food Group Limited
Maximus HHS Holdings Limited
Meridian Lightweight Technologies UK Ltd
Microlise Holdings Limited
Mill Garages North East Limited
Mistral Capital Management Limited
Motherwell Bridge Limited
Mowbray Indigo Limited

Moyallen Woking Limited
Munks Agricultural Contractors Limited
Napier Turbochargers Limited
Norton Motorcycles (UK) Limited
Nova Bio-Pharma Holdings Limited
Office Space in Town Limited
One51 ES Metals (UK) Limited
Optilan Group Limited
Orano UK Limited
Orbital Education Limited
Oxford Instruments Overseas Holdings 2008 Ltd
Pacific Direct Finance Limited
A Pearson Holdings Limited
Pharmacy Care Plus Limited
Picsolve Holdings Limited
Pineapple Letting Ltd
Priory Federation of Academies
Refood UK Limited
Rolls-Royce Controls and Data Services Ltd
Roythornes Limited
SYS8 Holding Limited
Scancell Holdings PLC
Scotts Hire Limited
Selectkey Limited
Semelab Limited
Sensitlive Limited
Sistine Properties (Westbury) Limited
St Lawrence Academy, Scunthorpe
Stepnell Developments Limited
Stepnell Holdings Limited
Strawson Group Developments Limited
Strawson Group Investments Limited
Sidney Stringer Multi Academy Trust
TGH Acquisitions Limited
TGH Finance Limited
TGH Investments Limited
TNT GRS 2008 Limited
Taylor Shaw Limited
Tayto Group Limited
Tensator Holdings Ltd
Tiny Tots Underwriting LLP
Trackwork Group Limited
Travis Perkins Finance Co Ltd
Travis Perkins Financing Company No.2 Ltd
Trigon Holdings Limited
Tunstall Healthcare Group Limited
U-Pull-It Limited
VWR Holdco Limited
Valens Resources Group PLC
WLP Holdings Limited
Warwick Care Limited
Warwick International Holdings Limited
Warwick International Intermediate Holdings Ltd
Wathegar Wind Farm LLP
Willowbrook Healthcare Debtco Limited
Willowbrook Healthcare Developments Ltd
Willowbrook Healthcare Limited
XPO Maintenance UK Limited
XPO Transport Solutions UK Limited
J & A Young Group Limited

2009 [150]

A Shade Greener Limited
AMT Fruit Limited
ASD Lighting Holdings Limited
ASG Group Associates Limited
Affinity Trust
Agrivert Group Limited
Alchemist Bar & Restaurant Limited
Allen Diesels Limited
Amey Birmingham Highways Limited
Amey Investments Limited
Amey Ventures Asset Holdings Limited
Amey Ventures Management Services Ltd
Anatis UK Limited
Anchorage Capital Europe, LLP
Asmet Limited
Aston Martin Works Limited
Aurora Fashions Finance Limited
Autologic Diagnostics Holdings Limited
Autologic Diagnostics Limited
Avant Homes (No.2) Limited
Avant Homes Group No.2 Limited
Aviagen European Holdings Limited
BCM Employment & Management Services Ltd
Banc D'Arguin, and Coastal and Marine Biodiversity Trust Fund Ltd
Bardsley Construction Holdings Limited
Alan Bartlett & Sons (Chatteris) Ltd
Barwood Homes Limited
Beeswax Dyson Farming Limited
Beumer Group UK Limited
Blackrock Secured Finance Limited
Blackrow Corporation Limited
Blue Support Services Limited
Bodycote America Finance Limited
Bodycote America Treasury Limited
Boots Management Services Limited
Boss Cabins Limited
Bournemouth Airport Property Investments (Industrial) Ltd
Brokerbility Holdings Limited
Burbage Capital Limited
Cairnwell Estates Limited
Cheaney Shoes Limited
Chevron Traffic Management (Holdings) Ltd
Christchurch Court (UK) Limited
Christchurch Court Holdings Limited
Church Mission Society
Co-operative Energy Limited
H.W. Coates (Holdings) Limited
Cobra Beer Partnership Limited
Cognita Funding 1 Limited
Community 1st Oldham (Werneth and Shaw) Ltd
Community 1st Oldham Tranche 2 Limited
Compu B Ltd
Conchord Limited
Consumer Champion Group Limited
Cook Defence Systems Limited
DH UK Finance Limited
De Trafford Property LLP
Denby Potteries Limited
Denby Pottery Co Ltd
Dunn Motor Traction Ltd
Dyas Exploration UK Limited
EMB-Group Ltd
ESNT Filter Products Limited
Elmdene Group Limited
Envisage Group Limited
Esland Group Limited
Essenden Limited
FSP Acquisition Limited
Finance Yorkshire Limited
Finbrook Limited
Florensis Flower Seeds UK Limited
Green Sky Energy Limited
Greenwood Academies Trust
HB Healthcare Limited
Hanover Housing Developments Limited
Tom Hartley Cars Limited
Healix Property LLP
IRESS (UK) Limited
Iceni Marine Services Limited
Integrated Bradford Hold Co Two Limited
Integrated Bradford SPV Two Limited
Irwin Mitchell LLP
Jaguar Estates Investments Limited
Jenoptik Holdings UK Ltd
Kal Tire (UK) Limited
Kenyon Forge Limited
L C & M Holdings Limited
Launchchange Holdings Limited
Launchchange Operations Limited
Leicester Lift Project Company (No.2) Ltd
Lemac No.1 Limited
Lets Connect It Solutions Limited
Lettings Room Limited
Jamie Lewis Residential Lettings Ltd
Lima Orthopaedics UK Limited
Maltby Learning Trust
Manufacturing Technology Centre Limited
Memoria Limited
Karen Millen Fashions Limited
Karen Millen Holdings Limited
Motan Colortronic Limited
Noble Desserts Holdings Limited
Northwood Tissue (Disley) Limited
Oakham School
Oasis Fashions Holdings Limited
Oasis Fashions Limited
Openshaw Regeneration Limited
Orbit Homes (2020) Limited
Oriana Underwriting Limited
Orion Media Limited
Paragon Property Investments Limited
Portbond Limited
Porterbrook Leasing Mid Co Ltd
Rain Dance Investments Limited
Read Motor Group Limited
Reddil Properties Limited
Renewi Cumbria Holdings Limited
Renewi Cumbria Limited
Resmed EPN Ltd
Resource Recovery Solutions (Derbyshire) Ltd
Rockwell Commercial Holdings Limited
Roxhill Developments Limited
Rushcliffe Specialist Schools (Mickleover) Ltd
Rushcliffe Specialist Schools Limited
Ryedale Estates Limited
SIG Hillsborough Limited
ScarsdaleVets LLP
Schueco UK Limited
Severn Trent Leasing Limited
Sherwin-Williams UK Holding Limited
Simoco Wireless Solutions Limited
Nigel Skinner Financial Advisers Ltd
St George's Academy Trust
St. Matthews (North) Limited
Stone House Investments Limited
Syncreon UK Holdings Limited
Synergy Fund LLP
Sytner Vehicles Limited
TIFS Holdings Limited
TTG Global Limited
Technical Consumer Products Limited
Toy Brokers Holdings Limited
Undercover Holdings Limited
Vernon Holdings Limited
Warehouse Fashions Holdings Limited
Warehouse Fashions Limited
Wilkin Chapman LLP

Wood Hill Heights Limited
Wren Kitchens Limited
Yasa Limited

January-June 2010 [68]

A Tiny Hamlet Limited
Archipelago Learning Holdings UK Limited
Aviagen Turkeys Holdings Limited
Avon Estates Limited
Avon Products Holding Limited
Beaver-Visitec International (UK) Ltd
Beaver-Visitec International Sales Ltd
Brayford Hotels Holdings Ltd
Breas Medical Limited
Burbidge Holdings Limited
Bush & Company Rehabilitation Limited
DFS Furniture Holdings PLC
DFS Furniture PLC
DMWSL 631 Limited
DMWSL 632 Limited
DMWSL 633 Limited
DV Ventures Limited
Deb Group Holdings Limited
Diamond Holdco 2 Limited
Diamond Holdco 7 Limited
Dow Chemical Services UK Limited
EResearchTechnology UK 1 Limited
EResearchTechnology UK 2 Limited
Eden Care & Support Group Limited
Eden Holdings Financing Limited
Eden Supported Living Limited
Erlson Precision Holdings Limited
Essentra Packaging & Security Limited
Gaming Acquisitions Limited
H.I.G. Europe-Dart III, Ltd
HD Holdings II Limited
Hanborough Enterprises Limited
Harmor Limited
Hazelton Homes (Midlands) Limited
Hill Care 1 Limited
Infinis Energy Services Limited
Jx2 Limited
Keelex 351 Limited
Lymn Funeral Services Limited
Midland Academies Trust
Mulberry Property Developments Ltd
Nelsons Solicitors Limited
New College Leicester Trust
Norton Finance Group Limited
Nottingham Roman Catholic Diocesan Trustees
Opal Ventures Limited
Oxhold Limited
Palm Recycling Limited
Pentagon Chrysler (Barnsley) Limited
Performance Health Global Limited
R U Estates Limited
Rampion Offshore Wind Limited
Red Arrow Trading Limited
Regional & City Airports Holdings Ltd
SRC Transatlantic Limited
Sophos Holdings Limited
Stonebridge Homes Limited
Tamar Renewable Power (Essex) Limited
Templeborough Biomass Power Plant Ltd
ThruVision Group PLC
Tilbrook Enterprise Limited
Tillotts Pharma UK Limited
VM Fabrics Limited
Wellglade Holdings Limited
Wyndham Destination Network Europe Ltd
Wyndham Destination Network LLP
Yourcash Holdings Limited
Zahawi & Zahawi Ltd

July-December 2010 [98]

Allerford Intermediate Newco Limited
Alwalton Hill Peterborough LLP
Ametek European Holdings Limited
AmeyCespa Limited
Anglian Water (Osprey) Financing PLC
Ashwicken Sporting LLP
Atlas Converting (UK Holdings) Limited
Aurora Fashions Group Limited
Axon Public Safety UK Limited
Ballyclare Limited
Barbon Holdings Limited
Beeston Site Services Limited
Benchmark Animal Health Group Limited
Blenheim Industrial Property Limited
Branston Academy Trust
Bridon Holdings Limited
Castlegate 624 Limited
Cespa UK Limited
Church Growth Trust Limited
Clearmark Solutions (2019) LLP
Co-op Group Travel 2 Holdings Limited
DCS Inc Limited
Davane Holding Co Ltd
Dawsongroup Vans Limited
De Ferrers Trust
Devereux Capital LLP
Dunstall Holdings Limited
ELWA Holdings Limited
Eastern Multi-Academy Trust
FCC Environment (Lincolnshire) Limited
Fallibroome Trust
William Farr Church of England Comprehensive School
Four CS MAT
Fswind Limited
Games Workshop US Limited
Gelder Group Holdings Limited
Gigaclear Limited
Giles Academy
Gilzoni Limited
Greencore Foods Limited
HBB Homes Limited
Habitat Retail Limited
Healing Multi Academy Trust
Samuel Hodge Holdings Limited
ITC Enterprises Limited
Igloo Books Group Holdings Limited
Kermotion UK Holdings Limited
Kinaxia Limited
King's (The Cathedral) School, Peterborough
Learner Engagement and Achievement Partnership Multi-Academy Trust
Lincoln and London Holdings Limited
Logistex Europe Ltd
MWUK Holding Co Ltd
Marubeni Agrochemical Limited
Karen Millen Group Limited
Mobius Motors Limited
Multi Packaging Solutions Asia Holdings Ltd
Myoderm Limited
Nationwide Healthcare Providers Limited
Newtco Limited
Northampton School for Boys
Northamptonshire Arts Management Trust
Northbridge Australia Limited
Oasis and Warehouse Limited
Peak Multi Academy Trust
Pirelli Motorsport Services Limited
Purico Speciality Paper Co Ltd
Redhill Academy Trust
Redx Pharma PLC
Rigid Plastic Containers Finance Limited
Rigid Plastic Containers Holdings Ltd
Rigid Plastic Containers Packaging Ltd
Roxhill (Peterborough) Limited
Roxhill Developments Group Limited
SAI Global CIS UK Limited
Sitel UK Finance
Solo Cup Finance Limited
Spencer Academies Trust
TCCT Retail Limited
C & S Taylor LLP
John Taylor MAT
Terrace Hills Farm LLP
Thermasys CS UK Holding Limited
Timico Technology Group Limited
Total Fitness Health Clubs Limited
Totemic (2014) Holdings Limited
Travis Perkins P & H Partner Limited
U-Pol Bidco Limited
U-Pol Finco Limited
ULS Technology PLC
Viewtone Trading Group Limited
WA Capital Limited
Wales High School Academy Trust
Whitemeadow Group Holdings Limited
Williams Grand Prix Holdings PLC
Woodbury Residual Limited
Wrengate Holdings Limited
Xanadu Investments Limited

January-June 2011 [133]

5 Dimensions Trust
Academy of Lincoln Trust
Agrivert (Wallingford) Limited
Alauna Renewable Energy Limited
Anisa Group Holdings Limited
Arconic Global Fasteners Limited
Aspire Achieve Advance Group Limited
Aston Community Education Trust
Beechcroft Group Limited
Beeson Wright Limited
Blue Coat Church of England Academy Ltd
Brookfield School Academy Trust
Roger Bullivant Limited
CP Elveden Village Limited
CP Longleat Village Limited
CP Sherwood Village Limited
CP Whinfell Village Limited
CP Woburn (Operating Company) Limited
CPC Foods Limited
Callington's Construction Limited
The Robert Carre Trust
Center Parcs (Holdings 1) Limited
Center Parcs (Holdings 3) Limited
Chargill (Holdings) Ltd
Caroline Chisholm Education Trust
Concentia Capital Limited
Cycene Limited
De Aston School Academy Trust
Denbigh Alliance
Diverse Academies Trust
Doosan Industrial Vehicle UK Ltd.
Dynamic Procurement Holdings Limited
E.On Climate & Renewables UK Biomass Ltd
E.On Connecting Energies Limited
EOTH Limited
East Midlands Education Trust
Ecclesbourne School
Esendee Holdings Limited

Everris Limited
Experian (UK) Finance Limited
Experian Latam Holdings Unlimited
Fernwood Academy Trust
Flow Energy Limited
Frasers Retail Limited
GEO Amey PECS Limited
GI Group Holdings Recruitment Limited
Go Outdoors Topco Limited
Greater Nottingham Education Trust
Growth LED Innovation Driven Employee Co Ltd
Guilsborough Multi Academy Trust
HID Estates Limited
HS 524 Limited
Halcyon Acquisitions Limited
Halcyon Financing Limited
Halcyon Midco Limited
Halcyon Topco Limited
Harlow Bros Holdings Limited
Harworth Estates Investments Limited
Hayfield School
Hazeley Academy
Heart of England School
Home Retail Group (Finance) LLP
Hudson Energy Supply UK Limited
Inclusion Care Group Limited
Inclusion Care Holdings Limited
L Jackson & Co Limited
KNM Project Services Limited
Kleemann Lifts UK Limited
Knights of Old Group Limited
Land and Estates Commercial Properties Ltd
Linford Properties (Leicester) Limited
M.C.I. Developments Limited
Macclesfield Academy
Middleby Holding UK Ltd
Midlands Land Portfolio Limited
Milton Keynes Education Trust
Mira Land Limited
Montsaye Community Learning Partnership
Morgana Holdings Limited
Mynydd Windfarm LLP
Myton School Trust
Natural Assets Investments Limited
North Kesteven Academy
Northworthy Trust
Nottingham Citycare Partnership CIC
Nova Education Trust
O'Brien (Group) Limited
Oakley Lorien Limited
Ousedale School
Oxford Property Trading Ltd.
Pattonair Europe Limited
Pattonair Group Limited
Pattonair Holdings Limited
Pattonair UK Limited
Pennine Property Partnership LLP
Pentagon (Huddersfield) Limited
Proact IT (UK) Limited
Progress Rail Services UK Limited
QED Academy Trust
Quest Global Engineering Limited
Quicksilver Midco Limited
Radical Sportscars Limited
Rawlins Academy
Redborne Upper School and Community College
Royal Latin School
Russell Building Products Limited
Rutland and District Schools' Federation
Scania Real Estate (UK) Limited
Severn Trent Carsington Limited
Severn Trent Draycote Limited
Severn Trent Investment Holdings Limited
Sharnbrook Academy Federation
Sheffield UTC Academy Trust
Sitel Solutions UK Limited
Social Justice and Human Rights Centre Ltd
South Lincolnshire Academies Trust
South Yorkshire Community Foundation Ltd
Spark44 (JV) Limited
Stratford Girls' Grammar School
Stratus (Holdings) Limited
Tove Learning Trust
Transforming Lives Educational Trust
Vale Academy Trust
Valpak Holdings Limited
Valpak Limited
Wabtec UK Holdings Limited
Welland Park Community College Academy Trust
West Coventry Academy
West Grantham Academies Trust
West Norfolk Academies Trust
West Park School
Whitley Academy
Zinc Ahead Holdings Limited

July-December 2011 [127]

3SE (Barnsley, Doncaster & Rotherham) Ltd
A Shade Greener (F4) LLP
A Shade Greener (F5) LLP
A Shade Greener (F6) LLP
A Shade Greener (F7) LLP
ACES Academies Trust
Abbey College, Ramsey
Academy @ Ridgewood Trust
Alere as Holdings Limited
Angel Cofund
Aptuit (Oxford) Limited
Archway Learning Trust
Aurajoki Europe Limited
Aylesford School and Sixth Form College
BRT (Wisbech) Limited
Ballylynch Capital Limited
Barwood Strategic Land II LLP
Bassi Group (Nottingham) Limited
Believe Academy Trust
Belvoir Lettings PLC
Bishop Stopford School
Bourne Grammar School
CNH Bidco Limited
CPL Industries Group Limited
Campion School & Language College
Canal & River Trust
Cape UK Holdings Newco Limited
Casterton College Rutland
Chiltern Hills Academy
Claydon Estate LLP
Community 1st Sheffield (Holdco) Limited
Community 1st Sheffield (Tranche 2) Ltd
Cristal Investments UK Limited
DNA (Holdings) Limited
Datapath Group Limited
Delgarth 2011 Limited
Deltic Group Holdings Limited
Deltic Group Limited
Denaro (UK) Limited
Devonshire Green (Broomgrove Road) Ltd
E-PPL Limited
Education Fellowship Trust
Ellucian Global Limited
Ellucian SMS Ltd
Evolve Trust
FCC Buckinghamshire Holdings Limited
FCC Buckinghamshire Limited
Falcon Capital Investments Limited
Finham Park Multi-Academy Trust
Gafoor Pure Halal Ltd
Grammar School of King Edward VI at Stratford-upon-Avon
Greencore Beechwood Limited
Greencore Northwood Limited
HBB Relocation Services Limited
HNB Care Limited
Higham Lane School
Horsforth Holdings Limited
IFA Metals International Limited
Ice House Street (No.1) Limited
Insanely Great Limited
Isle Education Trust
Jaguar Land Rover (South Africa) Holdings Ltd
Kal Tire Southern African Holdings Ltd
Kenilworth Multi Academy Trust
Kirona Holdings Limited
L.E.A.D. Trust
Lablogic Group Holdings Limited
Lantmannen UK Holding Limited
Larchsilver Properties Limited
Leger Education Trust
Lifford Industrial Properties Ltd
Lincoln Christ's Hospital School
Link Education Trust
Longshaw Developments Limited
Loomis Investments US Limited
Loomis UK Finance Co Ltd
Maneto (UK) 2 Limited
Maneto (UK) 3 Limited
Map Property Investments Limited
H.W. Martin (Farms) LLP
Matthews Environmental Solutions Limited
Merchant Taylors' Oxfordshire Academy Trust Ltd
Moulton School and Science College
Mowbray Education Trust Limited
National Church of England Academy Trust
National Floorcoverings Group Limited
Nene Education Trust
Newton Industrial Consultants Holdings Ltd
Oakbrook Finance Limited
PIMCO 2909 Limited
PKF Cooper Parry Group Limited
Passionate About People Limited
Sir Robert Pattinson Academy
Polar Technology Management Group Ltd
Praesepe Holdings Limited
QEGSMAT
Quarrydale Academy
Quartzinvest Properties Ltd
Quicksilver Dollar Loanco Limited
Quicksilver Euro Loanco Limited
RTI Advanced Forming Limited
Reflex Vehicle Hire Limited
Robinson Healthcare Group Limited
Severn Trent Wind Power Limited
Software (Europe) Limited
Somerset Equipment Finance (UK) Ltd
St Ivo School
St Matthews Holdings Limited
St Neots Learning Partnership
Stockcroft Limited
Stratford-upon-Avon School
TCCT Holdings UK Limited
TVS Europe Distribution Limited

Tamar Energy Limited
Tanglewood Care Homes Limited
Tapton School Academy Trust
Today's Wholesale Services Limited
Tolkien Estate Limited
Travis Perkins Plumbing & Heating LLP
Tripal Group Limited
Trueform Engineering Holdings Limited
UGI Midlands Limited
Wabtec UK Investments Limited
Wasp Management Software Limited
West Hill School
Whirlow Developments Limited
Wootton Academy Trust

January-March 2012 [56]

Anexhold Limited
Arighi Bianchi Holdings Limited
Aspire Learning Trust (Whittlesey)
Belsfield LLP
Cambridge & Counties Bank Limited
Cavendish Learning Trust
Chenderit School Academy Trust
Compass Acquisitions Limited
Compass Holdco Limited
Coundon Court
Cromwell Community College
EOF Holdings Limited
Eamar Development (UK) Limited
Elizabethan Academy Trust
Equity Solutions Asset Management Ltd
Eynsham Partnership Academy
Forest Way School
Gardner Aerospace Holdings Limited
Generation Two Limited
Goldmore Asset Management Limited
Hall Cross Academy Trust
Hatton Academies Trust
Heyford Residential Limited
Heyfordian School Trust
Hungerhill Academy Trust
Huxlow Science College
Industrial Control Distributors (Holdings) Ltd
K & A Merger Limited
Laurus Trust
Life Multi-Academy Trust
Lifestyle Seeview Limited
Luxury for Less Limited
Meadowhead School Academy Trust
Navagator Limited
Novoferm UK Holdings Limited
OAT 2012 Limited
Orchid Orthopedic Solutions Ltd
River Learning Trust
SMA Estate Holdings Limited
Satellite Applications Catapult Limited
Sector Aviation Holdings Limited
Severn Trent LCP Limited
Sheetfed Holdings Limited
St Therese of Lisieux Catholic Multi Academy Trust
Stephenson (MK) Trust
Charles Thompson (UK) Limited
R C Tinsley 2012 Limited
Trina Solar (UK) Limited
Two Counties Trust
Uppingham School
Vehicle Credit Limited
Victoria Square Woking Limited
Wellbeing Software Group Ltd
Thomas White Properties Limited
Wigston Academies Trust
Wreake Valley Academy Trust

April-June 2012 [56]

A Shade Greener (F9) LLP
Advancis Limited
Airbus Military UK Limited
Amey Hallam Highways Holdings Limited
Amey Hallam Highways Limited
Andina PLC
Anglia Components Investments Limited
Apollo Partnership Trust
Avant Homes Holdings Limited
Benchmark Vaccines Limited
Biogen Holdings Limited
Bloor Investments Limited
Broomgrove Properties Limited
Burford School
Calor Properties Limited
Canal & River Trading CIC
Care Fertility Holdings Limited
Cognita UK Brazil Holdings Limited
Compass Community Ltd
Thomas Cook Group Hedging Limited
DH Alpha Limited
DH Omega Limited
Denaro Partners LLP
Discovery Schools Academies Trust Ltd
E.On Project Earth Limited
Elli Finance (UK) PLC
Evans Leicester Limited
Everyone Active Administration Services Ltd
FMC Corporation United Kingdom Limited
Fir Vale School Academy Trust
Flying High Trust
Fulham Wharf LLP
Gartree High School
Global Brands (GBL) Holdings Limited
Dorothy Goodman School
Libra (Longhurst Group) Treasury PLC
Lutterworth Academies Trust
Maplefields Academy
Market Bosworth School
Marlborough Property Co Limited
Marubeni Agro Machinery Holding Limited
Mercia Learning Trust
Mill Academy
NFU Mutual Select Investments Limited
Rayfern Holdings Limited
Real Estate Income Trust Limited
Ridgeway Education Trust
Rycote Services Limited
SPL Logistics UK Holdings Limited
Sector Aircraft Leasing Limited
Shoosmiths LLP
Smart Currency Group Limited
Spear & Jackson Group Limited
Tollbar Multi Academy Trust
Tubes Holdco Limited
Wellspring Academy Trust

July-September 2012 [48]

A Shade Greener (Boilers) LLP
Airline Investments Limited
Ashby School
Aspire Schools Trust
Boston Witham Academies Federation
Bright Tribe Trust
CPRT (Europe) Limited
Cimbria Holdings Limited
Collaborative Academies Trust
Thomas Cook West Investments Limited
E S Management Services Limited
East Midlands Academy Trust
Element Six Technologies Limited
Essentra Packaging Limited
Forest Holidays Group Limited
Forest Holidays Limited
Grant Farming Limited
HAE Global Ltd
Happy Days Farming Co Ltd
Harworth Estates Property Group Limited
Hexpol Finance UK Limited
Horncastle Education Trust
Ibstock Community College
Inception Point Systems Ltd
Kesteven and Grantham Girls' School Academy Trust
Lincoln Science and Innovation Park Ltd
Manston Forests LLP
Merkur Casino UK Ltd
Murray Bidco Limited
Northampton Primary Academy Trust
Northern House School Academy Trust
O & M-Movianto UK Holdings Ltd.
Oxford Diocesan Schools Trust
Partnerships in Children's Services Ltd
Pergamon Finance Corporation Limited
Remy Cointreau UK Distribution Limited
Remy Cointreau UK Limited
Shipston High School
Stonewater Funding PLC
Tessella Holdings Limited
Thame Partnership Academy Trust
Thame and London Limited
Trent Academies Group
Uris Topco Limited
Wakefield Waste PFI Limited
Wheatcroft (Group) Limited
White Hills Park Federation Trust
Wolseley Utilities Limited

October-December 2012 [63]

AMG Aluminum UK Limited
Agrivert (West London) Limited
Ametek Aerospace and Defense Group UK Ltd
Apted Holdings Limited
Bardsley Group Limited
Bicester Heritage Limited
Blue Anchor Leisure Holdings Limited
Bradfield School
Breedon Cement Limited
Bushmead Homes Ltd
Buster Jimmy Limited
Caesar Bidco Limited
Caesar Midco Limited
Caesar Topco Limited
Carden Croft (2012) Limited
Castle Phoenix Trust
Chorus Education Trust
College of Policing Limited
Community Schools Alliance Trust
Coveris Flexibles Holdings UK Limited
Croda Investments Limited
Croda Investments No 2 Limited
J. Curtis & Sons (Holdings) Limited
Eastmarket Grain LLP
Eaton Industries (England) Limited
Experian Finance 2012 Limited
GPP Langstone LLP
Geely UK Limited
Gill Marine Holdings Limited
Gosford Hill School

Guardian Industries UK Holding Limited
Hancocks Acquisition Limited
Hancocks Midco Limited
History & Heraldry Holdings Limited
Jensten Group Limited
Jewel UK Bidco Limited
Jewel UK Midco Limited
Jewel UK Topco Limited
L.E.A.D. Academy Trust
Lincoln College Academy Trust
Magdalen College School Brackley Academy Trust
Marlborough Property (Watermead) Limited
Milton Keynes Development Partnership LLP
On Line Group Limited
Oxford Pharmagenesis Holdings Limited
Polyco (Group) Limited
Portugal Finco Limited
Propeller Academy Trust
Red Primrose Ltd
Roxhill (Tilbury) Limited
Mark Rutherford School Trust
Saw Property Co Ltd
Sharing in Growth UK Limited
J O Sims Holdings (1896) Limited
TWS Property Limited
Transform Trust
UKKI Limited
Vision Express Limited
Warth Developments Ltd
Welcome Break No. 1 Limited
Welcome Break No. 2 Limited
Wood Boilers LLP
Wyn Overseas Operations Limited

January-March 2013 [50]

Abel Investments Limited
Apex Stainless Holdings Limited
Arpo Global Limited
Aurajoki Romania Limited
The Dominic Barberi Multi Academy Company
Barker Ross Group Limited
Brighterkind (CB) Limited
Brighterkind (MW) Limited
Brighterkind (PC) Limited
CRT Property Investments Limited
Cooper and Turner Distribution Limited
Country Attire Holdings Limited
Diocese of Coventry Multi-Academy Trust
Doncasters UK Finance Limited
C.S. Ellis (Holdings) Limited
Filtrona Limited
Freeman Company (UK) Limited
Garner Holdings Limited
HBVB
Hard 8 Limited
Hill-Rom UK (Holdings) Ltd
Hofer Powertrain UK Limited
In Vino Bidco Limited
In Vino Limited
J3 Business Park Doncaster LLP
London EV Co Ltd
M.A.X. Funding Limited
Magnavale Limited
Maxxia (UK) Limited
Maxxia Finance Limited
Nottingham Enterprise Zone Development Co Ltd
Oxford Instruments UK 2013 Limited
Reach2 Academy Trust
Red Box Recorders Group Limited
SGP Holdings (UK) Limited
Salus Healthcare Limited
Scott's Developments Limited
Sherwood Homes Limited
Smartway PW. Holdings Limited
Southern View Finance UK Limited
Spalding Grammar School
Steel City Schools Partnership
Steeple Group Limited
Stillness 928 Limited
Synergy Health Managed Services Limited
Tolkien Trust
Vidal Group Holdings Ltd
Willowbrook Healthcare Group Limited
Yourcash Europe Limited
Yourcash Solutions Limited

April-June 2013 [44]

107 Station Street Limited
A Shade Greener (F10) LLP
A Shade Greener (F11) LLP
A Shade Greener (F12) LLP
A Shade Greener Debt LLP
A Shade Greener Maintenance Limited
A Shade Greener Tankersley LLP
Abacus Lighting Holdings Limited
Abacus Lighting Limited
AmeyCespa (MK) Holding Co Limited
AmeyCespa (MK) ODC Limited
AmeyCespa (MK) SPV Limited
Arlington Automotive Limited
Bell Rock Bidco Limited
Bio Dynamic (UK) Limited
Brigantia Learning Trust Limited
Eastgate Care Group Ltd
Eden Care Solutions Limited
Esendex Topco Limited
Greencore Convenience Foods I LLP
HBB Bridging Loans Limited
Human Appeal
Isotrak Group Limited
Isotrak Midco Limited
Lattice Trading Limited
Lionheart Academies Trust
Multi Packaging Solutions Global Holdings Ltd
Multi Packaging Solutions Limited
Nine Elms LLP
Node 4 Holdings Limited
Oxford Renewable Fuel Ltd
W T Parker Holdings Limited
Peak Gen Top Co Limited
J G Pears Machinery Limited
QD Commercial Group Holdings Limited
Quint Holdings Ltd
Rigby Real Estate Limited
Smartway Pharmaceuticals Limited
Sunway Travel (Coaching) Holdings Ltd
TCGH Holdings Limited
Vernon Finance Limited
White Woods Primary Academy Trust
Wight Building Materials Ltd
Wingfield Academy

July-September 2013 [50]

Adient Properties UK Ltd
Alliance Medical Group Limited
Avery Healthcare Group Limited
BDWZest Developments LLP
BDWZest LLP
BHCF2 Limited
BHL (UK) Holdings Ltd
BWSC Power Corporation Limited
Bell Rock Midco Limited
Bell Rock Topco Limited
Biocity Group Limited
British Business Bank PLC
Broome Management Co. Limited
Carlsberg Supply Company UK Limited
Carlton Forest Group LLP
Croner Group Limited
Doc Bidco Limited
Doc Debtco Limited
Doc Midco Limited
Doc Topco Limited
ESCO EMEA Holdings (UK) Limited
Edgetech (UK) Limited
Esendex Bidco Limited
Esendex Midco Limited
Eurocell Holdings Limited
Eurocell PLC
Ferrers School
Gemini Rail Services UK Ltd
Jerry Green Dog Rescue
Hyde Group Tooling Limited
IRESS UK Holdings Limited
Isotrak Holdings Limited
Jabco Capital Limited
MPS Care Group Limited
MTC Operations Limited
Metals & Materials Limited
Moran Commercials Ltd
Oxford Immunotec Global PLC
Pets at Home Vet Group Limited
RTI Extrusions Europe Limited
Resmed European Holdings Limited
Rigby Capital Investments Ltd
SHH 101 LLP
Stillness 930 Limited
Vivarail Ltd
Washbrook Capital Limited
Wellbeing Software Group Holdings Ltd
Wellbeing Software Limited
Xeros Technology Group PLC
ZestBDW LLP

October-December 2013 [47]

A Shade Greener (F13) LLP
A Shade Greener (F14) LLP
A Shade Greener (F15) LLP
Access Fertility Limited
Aegion Rehabilitation Services Limited
Agilent Technologies Lda UK Limited
AmeyCespa (AWRP) Holding Co Limited
AmeyCespa (AWRP) SPV Limited
Axis EMS Group Limited
Barratt Wates (Lindfield) Limited
Barron McCann Holdings Limited
Blue Skies Investments Limited
CPRT LLP
Cad Cam Automotive Limited
Carter Accommodation Group Limited
City Estates (UK) Limited
City Suites Manchester Limited
Coolsilk Limited
Coolsilk Property & Investment Limited
Corrboard UK Limited
DS John Holdings Limited
Daisy UK Holdco Limited
Diocese of Sheffield Academies Trust
Diocese of Southwell and Nottingham Multi-Academy Trust
EMH Treasury PLC

FCL Organisation Ltd
Gallagher Developments Caerphilly Ltd
Gallagher Developments Holdco Limited
Gallagher Investments Holdco Limited
Grand Union Group Funding PLC
R Griggs & Co. Limited
HC1221 Limited
Healthcare Software Solutions Ltd
Impero Holdings Limited
Inspire Trust
Joules Investments Holdings Limited
Kalsi Properties (UK) Limited
Majestic Bingo Limited
Meter Provida Holdco Limited
Meter Provida Investments Limited
New Era Development (UK) Limited
Remedi Medical Holdings Limited
Stephen Sanderson Transport Holdings Ltd
Sawatch Limited
S Walsh Holdings Limited
Wanfeng MLTH Holdings Co., Ltd
Wellbeing Software Holdings Limited

January-March 2014 [39]

AG47 Limited
AU79 Limited
Autins Group PLC
BPHA Finance PLC
Benchmark Animal Health Limited
Blancco (Software) Services Limited
Bodycote Treasury Services Limited
Brooklands Milton Keynes LLP
Buzz Holdings Limited
Carlton Street Trading Limited
Custodian REIT PLC
Durham & Co Holdings Limited
Exel Computer Systems (Holdings) PLC
Forterra Building Products Limited
Gibbs Croft Limited
Groves of Thame (Holdings) Limited
HCH Property Limited
Impero Developments Limited
Ingeus UK Holdings Limited
LGS Capital Limited
Lawrence Sheriff School Academy Trust
Mira Technology Park Limited
Pets at Home Group PLC
Pets at Home No.1 Limited
Sheepy Magna Limited
Shoe Zone PLC
Slawston Limited
Snaith School Academy Trust
Stream Acquisitions Limited
Sureclean Holdco Limited
Trident 2020 Limited
Trison Estates Limited
Trust Estates (Clarence Street) Limited
Tytherington School
WA Capital Investments Limited
Weymead Holdings Limited
Wickersley Partnership Trust
Wilkinson Hardware Stores, Limited
Willoughby 395 (EBK) Limited

April-June 2014 [71]

A Shade Greener Debt (2) LLP
A Shade Greener Debt (3) LLP
Alliance Medical Leasing Limited
Alycidon Technologies Limited
Arconic Limited
Ascend Global Holdings, Ltd.
Ascend Global Intermediate Holdings, Ltd.
BCA Marketplace PLC
Bantham Holdings Ltd
Bicester Learning Academy
Blenheim Finance Limited
Bodypower Sports Holdings Limited
Bridge Leisure Finco Limited
Bridge Leisure Midco Limited
Bridge Leisure Topco Limited
British Business Finance Ltd
British Business Investments Ltd
Business By Technology (Holdings) Ltd
Cavalier Marketing Holdings Limited
Country Court Care Homes 2 Limited
Dering Properties Finance Limited
Detrafford Sky Gardens Ltd
Dry Mix Solutions UK Limited
E-PPL Holdings Limited
Ensco 1066 Limited
Evo Business Supplies Limited
Flowtech Fluidpower PLC
Fluidpower MIP Limited
Fresh Approach (UK) Holdings Limited
GRS Roadstone Group Limited
Graven Hill Village Development Co Ltd
HC 1228 Limited
Hadrian (Residential) Limited
Homecrest Bidco Limited
Homecrest Midco Limited
In at the Side Limited
Innovate Multi Academy Trust
Keystone Bidco Limited
Keystone Financing PLC
Keystone JVCO Limited
Keystone Midco Limited
Keystone Topco Limited
Mead Educational Trust
NAHL Group PLC
NFT Distribution Holdings Limited
Nene Group Holdings PLC
Oxera Consulting LLP
Oxford Sciences Innovation PLC
PCS Business Systems Group Limited
Phoenix Advance Limited
Pork Farms Caspian Limited
RPC Asia Pacific Holdings Limited
Saint-Gobain Roofspace Limited
Sheepy Magna Investments Ltd
Slawston Investments Ltd
Solenis UK Limited
Staffline Holdings Limited
Staton Young (Anglesey) Limited
Stream Midco Limited
Stream Topco Limited
T N Capital Limited
T.C.L. Holdings (Midco) Limited
T.C.L. Holdings (Parent) Limited
Tamar Energy (Holdings) Limited
Tamar Energy Operating Company (One) Ltd
Tamar Renewable Power (Hoddesdon) Ltd
Time Right Holdings Limited
Utopia Holdings (Chesterfield) Limited
Vita York 1 Limited
Welcomm Holdings Limited
Wycliffe Hall

July-September 2014 [48]

Avery Care (Cannock) Limited
Avro Energy Limited
BCHK UK Limited
BCN Holdco Limited
Barons Eden Group Limited
Benchmark Genetics Limited
Boston Mayflower Finance PLC
Breas Technologies (UK) Limited
Bridge Leisure Bidco Limited
Brighton Marina Block F1 Ltd
Cariole Limited
Coal Industry Social Welfare Organisation 2014
Ducker Farming Limited
Experian Holdings (UK) Limited
Faero UK Holding Limited
Financial Funding Limited
Flo-Mech Holdings Limited
Forbo Flooring UK Limited
ADP Gauselmann UK Limited
Haas Formula UK Ltd
Hampton Academies Trust
Haughton Textiles Limited
Horberg & Co Holdings Ltd
I M Kelly Holdings Limited
Kelta Limited
LTAG UK Limited
Lockwood Group Limited
Lousada Investments Limited
MDS Estates Limited
Minerva Learning Trust
NBCMH Holdings Limited
NBH Holdco Limited
Nickle Holdings Limited
Pope Francis Catholic Multi Academy Company
Prahi Hotel Collection Limited
Punch Taverns Holdco (B) Limited
Real Estate Income Trust (SC) Limited
Renewi European Holdings Limited
SHV Investments Limited
Sami Property Co Ltd
Sonepar UK Limited
Strata Homes Holdings Limited
Sumo Digital Group Limited
T-Shirt Guy Holdings Limited
Trimas UK Aerospace Holdings Limited
Trinley Estate Limited
UKLS Acquisitions Limited
Waterfall Catering Group Limited

October-December 2014 [56]

A Shade Greener (F17) LLP
A-Plan Group Ltd
ACESO Healthcare Group Holdings Limited
ACESO Healthcare Holdings Limited
ACESO Healthcare Limited
Adaptimmune Therapeutics PLC
Avant Homes Group Limited
BBRG Finance (UK) Ltd.
BBRG Operations (UK) Ltd.
BBRG Production (UK) Ltd.
BPS Warwick Limited
Baslow Holdings Developments Limited
Blue Planet Solar Park II Limited
Bridon-Bekaert Ropes Group (UK) Ltd
Bridon-Bekaert Ropes Group Ltd
CPF Commercial Limited
Challenger Multi Academy Trust
DPFP LLP
DW3 Products Group Limited
DW3 Products Holdings Limited
Dematic (Services) Limited
Desford Acquisition Company (UK) Limited
Distinction Group Limited
Duston Education Trust
Eraih Limited

Friar 148 Limited
MJ Gleeson PLC
Harrowden Farms Group Limited
Harrowden Turf Limited
Huttons Buildings Limited
Ibstock Building Products Limited
Indoor Bowling Acquisitions Limited
KHL Newco Limited
Lafarge Cauldon Limited
Logistics Acquisition Company (UK) Ltd
London Clapham Investments and Developments Ltd
Novo Community Ltd
Peveril Securities Long Lane Limited
Porterbrook Holdings I Limited
Porterbrook Holdings II Limited
RPC Pisces Holdings Limited
RTL Bidco Limited
RTL Cleanco Limited
RTL Midco Limited
RTL Topco Limited
Regen Holdings Limited
Rigby Group Finance Limited
SPL II Acquisition Company (UK) Limited
SPL Logistics Holdings Acquisition Company (UK) Ltd
Sparken Hill Academy Trust
Speeds (Burton) Limited
Steris PLC
TFHC 2015 Limited
Trafalgar Bidco Limited
Trafalgar Midco 1 Limited
Trafalgar Midco 2 Limited

January 2015 [11]

Blueprint Operations Limited
CI Brite Limited
Cedar 2015 Limited
Creating Tomorrow Multi Academy Trust
FIM Solar Generation I LLP
Ibstock USA Limited
Jacobs Douwe Egberts Ops GB Ltd
Omega Acquisition Bidco Limited
Personal Group Limited
Soufflet Malt UK Limited
TI Fluid Systems PLC

February 2015 [24]

Arden Topco Limited
British Steel Limited
Buttercup Bidco Limited
Buttercup Topco Limited
Cavan Investments Limited
Cooke Optics Group Limited
Cooke Optics Holdings Limited
Derby Diocesan Academy Trust 2
Drayson Technologies Limited
Drive Holdings 2015 Limited
Fullbrook Thorpe Investments LLP
Holy Spirit Catholic Multi Academy Company
James Convenience Retail Limited
Kinaxia Transport and Warehousing Ltd
Munro Building Services Holdings Limited
Nielsen Holdings PLC
Premonition Analytics Limited
Remploy Limited
Rigby Private Equity Limited
Rushcliffe Care Holdings Limited
Solidus UK Solutions Ltd
Sutton Carter Investments Limited
TFHC Investments Limited
Wasps Finance PLC

March 2015 [19]

Alpha Holdco 1 Limited
Baker Perkins Holdings Limited
Beck Bidco Limited
Birchall Gardens LLP
Canaveral Bidco Limited
Canaveral Holdco Limited
Colbert Wall Holdings Limited
Economy Energy Holdings Limited
Engineering Technology Group Limited
Gregory Family Office Limited
HTC Wolffkran Limited
I Holland Holdings Limited
Myers-Briggs Company (Europe) Limited
Pets at Home Veterinary Specialist Group Ltd
QMS International Limited
Replimune Limited
Rotherwood Group Ltd
Shoby Investments Limited
Swanscombe Development LLP

April 2015 [8]

Barcode Warehouse Group Limited
Cambridge Realty Limited
Chimneys Investment Co Ltd
DTIL UK Limited
GBA Group Limited
Lafarge Ireland Limited
Rotherwood Healthcare Limited
SSCP Blink Bidco Limited

May 2015 [19]

Acer Trust
BWB Holdings Limited
CI Brite (UK) Holdings Limited
Dunkley Family Investments Limited
GRI Libra Limited
Gardeden Bidco Limited
Gardeden Midco Limited
Gardeden Topco Limited
Indoor Bowling Equity Limited
Larkfleet Homes Limited
Laver Leisure Limited
Mayflower Specialist School Academy Trust
Miller Wates (Didcot) Limited
Northfleet Property LLP
Sophos Group PLC
Sophos Treasury Limited
United Rental Group America Limited
Vine Hotels Limited
Thomas White Oxford Limited

June 2015 [18]

Agellus Holdings Limited
Auchencairn Forest LLP
Dematic Group Limited
Full Moon Holdco 7 Limited
Funeral Partners Bidco Limited
Funeral Partners Holdco Limited
Funeral Partners Midco Limited
Georgia GC Holdings Limited
Heyford Park Developments Limited
Horiba Mira Limited
Intrexon UK Insect Holdings Limited
King Edward VI Education Trust
J H & A J King Farms Limited
Millbrook European Holdings Limited
Peppermint Grove Ltd
SDI Aviation Limited
Vinyl Compounds Holdings Limited
Wake One Limited

July 2015 [27]

ADA PD UK Limited
Accelerated Digital Ventures Limited
Alconbury Packing Solutions Limited
Beardow Adams Holdings Ltd
Brayfour Limited
Cad Cam Holdings Limited
Clarendon Office Group Ltd.
Cognita BondCo Parent Limited
Cognita Financing PLC
Cognita Midco Limited
Education Placement Group Limited
Forcefield Bidco Limited
Forcefield Midco Limited
Graystacks Exeter Limited
Ingleby (1981) Limited
M.J.S. Holdings (March) Limited
Middleby UK Residential Holding Ltd
Palletforce Holdings Limited
Peartree Oxford Limited
Peppermint Technology Holdings Limited
SG International Holdings Limited
Star Bidco Limited
Star Midco 1 Limited
Supported Living Care Property Limited
UOS LP Limited
Warriner Multi Academy Trust
Warwick Ward (Holdings) Limited

August 2015 [12]

Agrivert Holdings Limited
Blenheim Agency Limited
DHT Finance Limited
Hardys Farm Limited
Inspire Education Trust
Investhom Limited
Jaddu Ltd
Lanai Medical Ltd
Sevco 5112 Limited
TTKW Limited
Vita Student York Holding Co Ltd
YLH Limited

September 2015 [20]

Charles Bentley Properties Limited
CMI International Limited
Coast Holdco 1 Limited
Coast Holdco 2 Limited
Dunamis Group Limited
Entertainment Magpie Group Limited
Fluidone Holdings Limited
Ibstock PLC
Karen Millen Holdco 1 Limited
Mobica Bidco Limited
Mobica Holdings Limited
Newincco 1382 Limited
Newincco 1386 Limited
Oasis and Warehouse Holdco 1 Limited
Oasis and Warehouse Holdco 2 Limited
Polypearl Management Ltd
SCI-MX Nutrition Limited
T & W Group Limited
Veeva U.K. Holdings Limited
Yorkshire Repak Holdings Limited

October 2015 [24]

Affinity Capital Works Limited
Affinity Flying Training Services Ltd
C3 Construction Holdings Limited
Caledonia Venus Acquisitions Limited
Caledonia Venus Group Limited
Caledonia Venus Holdings Limited
Country Court Care Homes 3 MB Limited
Country Court Care Homes 3 Propco Ltd
Country Court Care Homes 3 SB Holdco Ltd
Country Court Care Homes 3 SB Limited
Factory (M1) Limited
Hive Bidco Limited
Hive Topco Limited
IVI UK Ltd
Lubrizol Group, LLP
M.P.K. Group Limited
Manifesto Foods Ltd
Myton Investments Ltd
NJDR Group Ltd
Oncimmune Holdings PLC
SCGH Limited
Sunrise Eggs Holdings Limited
Vesso Limited
Vita First Street Limited

November 2015 [21]

Aspall Holdings Limited
BDB Design Build Holdings Limited
CEMA Group Ltd
Central Aggregates Ltd
DSGPI 2015 Limited
Ferrovial Services UK Ltd.
Fields Property Limited
First for Wellbeing CIC
Llamasoft Europe Holdings Limited
Milehouse Foods Limited
Miller Wates (Southwater) Limited
Northern Powerhouse Investments Limited
Pall UK Holdings Limited
Quotient Sciences Holdings Limited
Reesink Turfcare UK Limited
SDI (Belfast) Limited
SDI (Liverpool) Limited
TI Automotive Korean Won Hedgeco Ltd
TRG Bonds IV Limited
Wanfeng (UK) Aviation Co., Ltd
Watch Bidco Limited

December 2015 [28]

Abney Trust
Afpro LLP
Agri-Epi Centre Limited
Alvedius Ltd
Amey Finance Services Limited
BBRG (Subsidiary) Ltd
BBRG Holding (UK) Ltd
Boketto Bidco Limited
Boketto Holdco Limited
Boketto Midco Limited
Boketto Newco Limited
Croda Investments No 3 Limited
De Trafford and Palatine Estates Limited
Dransfield Properties Finance Limited
Dransfield Properties Investments Ltd
Go Inspire Group Limited
Hermitage Holdings (Wilmslow) Limited
M3 Medical Holdings Ltd
Morningside Holdings Ltd
PIB Group Limited
Polydist Europe Holdings Limited
RDG Midas Holdings (NI) Limited
SDL Bigwood Limited
TRRG Holding Limited
Vita Satellite 1 Limited
Vocare Limited
Wakefield Waste Holdings Limited
Yuill Family Properties Ltd

January 2016 [20]

Adara Group Limited
Adient Holding Germany Ltd
Arugani Limited
Avenue Lets Limited
H C Bourn (Holdings) Limited
Brington North LLP
CTDI Repair Services Limited
Daleacre Healthcare Limited
Fairline Yachts Limited
Forterra PLC
Leicester Lettings Limited
Nippon Gases UK Limited
North Bidco Limited
North Midco Limited
OGF Bidco Limited
OGF Topco Limited
Oxford West End Development Limited
Polyco Healthline Limited
Rochmills (Holdings) Limited
Steel City Holdings Limited

February 2016 [18]

Affinity Living Trinity Holdco Limited
Alkane Energy CM Limited
BBRG (Purchaser) Ltd
Carentan Holdings Limited
Earlham Trading Co Ltd
Fantasy Island Operations Limited
Forterra Holdings Limited
Genie Topco Limited
Glenco Limited
IB Group Ltd
ISN Europe Limited
MCL Group of Companies Limited
Mellors Group Fantasy Island Holdings Ltd
J G Pears Power Limited
Sigma Components Holdings Limited
Terberg Rosroca Group Limited
Total Integrated Solutions (Holdings) Ltd
Yu Group PLC

March 2016 [40]

Agritec Holdings Limited
Anisa Consolidated Holdings Limited
Belfield Group Limited
T F Bowman & Son Limited
CI Beatrice II Facility (BOWL) Limited
CI Beatrice II Facility (CI II) Limited
CPG 2016 Limited
Cadent Gas Limited
Cadent Services Limited
Caledonia Bidco Limited
Caledonia Topco Limited
DNC Holdings Limited
DSS Group Limited
Dodson & Horrell Group Limited
FTR Holdings Ltd
Filta Group Holdings PLC
Gatecrasher Apartments Limited
Harewood Moor Estates Limited
IMS Bidco Limited
IMS Topco Limited
Ingleby (2016) Limited
Lochailort Fairfield Limited
New Co (Beith Street) Limited
New Co (Newcastle) Limited
New Co (Satellite) 2 Limited
New Co (Satellite) Limited
Nexus Multi Academy Trust
North West Portfolio (No.3) Limited
Ocee International Ltd
Palma Bidco Limited
Pride Care Homes Peterborough Limited
Project Sinatra Bidco Limited
Project Sinatra Midco Limited
Project Sinatra Topco Limited
Riverleen Finance Unlimited
SDI (Enfield) Limited
SDI (Oxford Street) Limited
SDI (Thurrock) Limited
Stanley Black & Decker Finance Limited
Tyler Packaging Holdings Limited

April 2016 [20]

Bericote Holdings Limited
Brentford Phase II LLP
Briggs & Forrester (UK) Limited
Bury Farm Sharpenhoe Limited
Cintra Infrastructures SE
DSI Construction Holdings UK Ltd
Justrite Holdings Ltd
Motorpoint Group PLC
Mulberry Property Developments (HGP) Ltd
SDI (Edinburgh) Limited
SDI (Manchester Cheetham Hill) Limited
SDI (Nottingham) Limited
Sigma Components Limited
Sigma Components Midco 1 Limited
Sigma Components Midco 2 Limited
UDG Healthcare UK (Holdco) Limited
VJ Holdco UK Limited
Vita Student Southampton Portswood Ltd
Whistler Acquisitions Limited
Woodford Investment Management Limited

May 2016 [19]

Amtrust Lloyd's Holdings (UK) Limited
Applied Composites Group Ltd
Ashmere Derbyshire Limited
Bracken Midco2 Limited
British Steel Holdings Limited
Detrafford No1 Castlefield Ltd
Digital House Group Ltd
Fluidpower Group Limited
Joules Group PLC
Mayfourth Holdings Limited
Myers-Briggs Company Holdings (Europe) Ltd
PCMS International Holdings Limited
PCMS Investments Holdings Limited
Redhill Famco Limited
SDI (Jersey Holding) Limited
SDI (LSL Holdings) Limited
SEK Holdings Limited
Sourcecircle Holdings Limited
Waterfall Elior Limited

June 2016 [17]

Ashford Riverside Park Limited
BESS Aylesford Limited
Bracken Midco1 PLC
CX Bidco Limited
CX Midco 2 Limited
CX Midco Limited
CX Topco Limited
Harshl Limited
Kent Power Corporation Limited
Kenwood Hotel Property Limited
Lakes Academies Trust
PH Alderley Park LLP
PJ Care Group Limited
Roubaix Bidco Limited
SCX Special Projects Holdings Limited
Star Mayan Limited
Vine Kenwood Limited

July 2016 [17]

Ad Meliora Academy Trust
Advancis Holdings Limited
Alcaeus Holdings Limited
Belgium Bidco Limited
Belgium Midco Limited
Belgium Topco Limited
CPRT European Investments Limited
Cosma Casting UK R.E. Limited
Equals Trust
Learning Without Limits Academy Trust
New Blue Chip Limited
Newco (First Street) Limited
Pyvot Limited
Sherwood Holdings Limited
Stonbury (Holdings) Limited
UK Vast Holdco Limited
WHC01 Limited

August 2016 [14]

Bell Euro Finance Limited
Commify Topco Limited
FCC (E & M) Holdings Limited
FCC Environment Developments Limited
Freudenberg Sealing Technologies Limited
House & Home (Lettings) Ltd
Ponsford Investments Limited
Ponsford Trading Limited
Project Republica Bidco Limited
Project Republica Topco Limited
C R Shield Holdings Limited
Tanvic Group Holdings Limited
Woolley GMC Engineering Holdings Limited
Yews Holding Co Ltd

September 2016 [11]

Adient Financing International Ltd
Adient Financing Ltd
Brit de Vere Limited
Chiron Bidco Limited
Chiron Midco Limited
Commify Limited
Hull Holdings Limited
Stewart Milne Homes North West England Ltd
Stewart Milne Timber Systems Limited
PPL PRS Limited
Roof-Maker Ltd

October 2016 [16]

Adient UK Financing International Ltd
Adient UK Financing Ltd
Aster and Young Limited
BGL (Holdings) Limited
Battery Energy Storage Solutions Limited
Bobby's Acquisition Limited
Florida Topco Limited
Frosts Garden Centre Restructuring Ltd
Frutarom UK Investments Limited
Industrial Scientific Holdings UK Ltd
Infinis Energy Group Holdings Limited
Infinis Energy Management Limited
Miller Wates (Wallingford) Limited
Saint-Gobain Isover UK Limited
Stowe Valley Multi Academy Trust
Triumph Multi Academy Trust

November 2016 [12]

Abaco UK Holdco Limited
Assured Group Investments Limited
Bridgebank Holdings Limited
Caledonian Group Holdings Limited
RE Evans Farms Limited
Roy Hatfield (Holdings) Limited
Lexden BH (Colchester) Limited
Life UK Healthcare Limited
Ransomwood Estates UK Limited
Serasa Finance Limited
Sheffield South East Trust
Steeple Bidco Limited

December 2016 [12]

Avery Healthcare Holdings Limited
Celixir PLC
Chinook Sciences Holdings Limited
Elsevier Life Sciences IP Limited
Growth Partners Management Limited
Hagerty Holdings Limited
Horiba UK Finance Limited
Jardines Finance Limited
Kaystan Holdings Limited
Project Jupiter Limited
RTFH Limited
Valspar (UK) Special Holding Corporation Ltd

January 2017 [8]

EESL Energypro Assets Limited
Helford Land Limited
J & A (International) Holdings Limited
JSC EFarms LLP
Steeple Holdco Limited
Steeple Midco Limited
Steeple Topco Limited
Unity Property Holdings Limited

February 2017 [14]

All Assist Limited
Compare The Market Limited
Cresta Court Hotel Holdings Limited
Dalziel & Pow Holdings Limited
Harrow View LLP
Hopton Investment Holdings Limited
Arnold Laver & Co Ltd
PWP Building Services (Holdings) Limited
Quadgas Holdco Limited
Quadgas Midco Limited
RMS Holdco Limited
Raleigh Learning Trust
TEG Holdings Limited
Verdon Holdings Limited

March 2017 [11]

Addo Food Group (Holdings) Ltd
CMS Cepcor (Holdings) Limited
CNIM Clugston (Avonmouth) Limited
ENVA Topco Limited
Empowering Minds Academy Trust
Hundred Percent Holdings Limited
Arnold Laver Holdings Limited
Prodrive Group Limited
Severn Trent Trimpley Limited
Ten Entertainment Group PLC
VGI Holdings Limited

April 2017 [7]

1 Wintringham LLP
Holding JDR Limited
Nibgreen
S & W Design & Build (Group) Limited
TFS Holdings Limited
Wintringham Newco1 Limited
Wintringham Newco2 Limited

May 2017 [9]

Aspireplus Educational Trust
Falcon Bidco Limited
Falcon Equityco 2 Limited
Great Tew Properties Limited
Millennium EFW Limited
Prahi (2017) Limited
Tennant Metallurgical Group Holdings Ltd
Terberg Environmental UK Limited
Zonwering Holdings Limited

June 2017 [12]

Ames Companies UK Ltd.
Hampton (Burlington Court) Ltd
Manitowoc Crane Group (UK) Subco Limited
SDI (Market Road) Limited
Seth Bidco Limited
Seth Finco Limited
Seth Midco Limited
Seth Topco Limited
Solutionhost Group Limited
Sunshine Care Midco Limited
Sunshine Care Topco Limited
Transit 2017 Limited

July 2017 [12]

Acentic Holdings Limited
Aghoco 1566 (Bidco) Limited
Armitage Pet Care Limited
Bollington Wilson Group Limited
Conrad Energy Group Limited
Grove Industries (Holdings) Ltd
Impala Bidco Limited
K9 Midco Limited
Miller Homes Group Holdings PLC
RPC 2017 Holding Co Ltd
Sunshine Care Bidco Limited
Watermill-CT Holdings Limited

August 2017 [6]

Aghoco 1578 (Midco) Limited
Aghoco 1579 (Topco) Limited
ENSEK Holdings Limited
Heathcotes Group Limited
SDI (Kingston) Limited
Williams Jet Tenders (Holdings) Limited

November 2017

Advent Topco Limited
Jakto Group Limited
Sumo Group PLC

December 2017

Luxury British Design 1 Limited
Luxury British Design 2 Limited
Luxury British Design Holdings Limited
Peterborough Keys Academies Trust

January 2018

South Warwickshire Academy Trust

February 2018

EPAL Holdings Limited
Edina Acquisitions Limited

Company Profiles

1 Wintringham LLP
Incorporated: 5 April 2017
Net Worth: £36,566,768 *Total Assets:* £37,756,480
Registered Office: University Offices, University of Oxford, Wellington Square, Oxford, OX1 2JD
Officers: Anne Malcolm Cowell [1948] Member; Sir Andrew William Dilnot [1960] Member; Dr Catherine Anne Grocock [1947] Member; Ian Michael Laing [1946] Member

107 Station Street Limited
Incorporated: 23 May 2013 *Employees:* 1
Previous: Empyrean Burton Limited
Net Worth: £520,882 *Total Assets:* £10,367,015
Registered Office: 107 Station Street, Burton on Trent, Staffs, DE14 1SZ
Activities: Other letting and operating of own or leased real estate
Officers: Nicholas Philippos Charalambous [1973] Managing Director

1LIFE Management Solutions Limited
Incorporated: 7 December 1990 *Employees:* 313
Net Worth: £5,684,000 *Total Assets:* £15,968,000
Registered Office: LDH House, St Ives Business Park, Parsons Green, St Ives, Cambs, PE27 4AA
Activities: Operation of sports facilities
Officers: Ian Arthur Hendrie, Secretary; Mark Braithwaite [1978] Managing Director [British/South African]; Keith Hamill [1952] Director/Vice Chairman; Ian Arthur Hendrie [1970] Director; Julian Frederick Nicholls [1951] Director

2K Polymer Systems Limited
Incorporated: 6 February 2007 *Employees:* 68
Net Worth: £7,491,000 *Total Assets:* £11,588,000
Registered Office: Venture Crescent, Nixs Hill Industrial Estate, Alfreton, Derbys, DE55 7RA
Activities: Manufacture of other chemical products n.e.c.
Parent: Mitek Industries Limited
Officers: Nimesh Patel, Secretary/Director; Sydney James Griffiths [1947] Group Managing Director, Europe & Africa; Mark Hackett [1972] Finance Director; Nimesh Patel [1966] Director

2morrow Group Limited
Incorporated: 23 September 2003 *Employees:* 139
Net Worth: £2,931,966 *Total Assets:* £12,416,871
Registered Office: 2morrow Court, Appleford Road, Sutton Courtenay, Oxon, OX14 4FH
Activities: Activities of head offices
Parent: Howe-Davies Family Discretionary Trust
Officers: Robert Edward Green, Secretary; Christopher George Howe Davies [1946] Managing Director; James Alexander Howe Davies [1978] Director; Michael John Howe-Davies [1980] Director

3 R Construction & Property Development Limited
Incorporated: 10 March 1989 *Employees:* 8
Net Worth: £10,397,158 *Total Assets:* £22,056,052
Registered Office: Sital House, 3-6 Cattle Market, Loughborough, Leics, LE11 3DL
Activities: Construction of commercial buildings
Officers: Kailash Chander Suri, Secretary/Property Developer; Kailash Chander Suri [1955] Director/Property Developer; Naveen Suri [1985] Director; Rachna Suri [1983] Director; Suman Suri [1963] Director; Sunil Suri [1990] Director

3C Waste Limited
Incorporated: 25 July 1991 *Employees:* 54
Net Worth: £6,243,000 *Total Assets:* £36,024,000
Registered Office: Ground Floor West, 900 Pavilion Drive, Northampton Business Park, Northampton, NN4 7RG
Activities: Other business support service activities n.e.c.
Parent: 3C Holdings Limited
Officers: Carol Jayne Nunn, Secretary; Vicente Federico Orts-Llopis [1962] Director/Chief Financial Officer [Spanish]; Agustin Serrano Minchan [1959] Director/Technical Civil Engineer [Spanish]; Paul Taylor [1959] Director/Chief Executive Officer

3M Health Care Limited
Incorporated: 11 December 1969
Net Worth: £216,566,000 *Total Assets:* £216,656,992
Registered Office: 3M Health Care Limited, Derby Road, Loughborough, Leics, LE11 5SF
Activities: Non-trading company
Parent: 3M United Kingdom Public Limited Company
Officers: Ian Richard Brown, Secretary; David James Ashley [1968] Director/General Counsel; Mohammad Irfan Malik [1965] Director [Pakistani]; Simla Semerciyan [1973] Director/Finance Manager [Turkish]

3SE (Barnsley, Doncaster & Rotherham) Limited
Incorporated: 24 October 2011
Net Worth Deficit: £9,094,000 *Total Assets:* £70,899,000
Registered Office: Dunedin House, Auckland Park, Mount Farm, Milton Keynes, Bucks, MK1 1BU
Activities: Other service activities n.e.c.
Parent: 3SE (Barnsley, Doncaster & Rotherham) Holdings Limited
Officers: Philip Bernard Griffin-Smith, Secretary; Alistair Daniel Brookes [1976] Director; Ashley Comerford [1978] Director [Irish]; Adam Nathaniel Richford [1976] Director; Jonathan James Sime [1979] Director

5 Dimensions Trust
Incorporated: 7 April 2011 *Employees:* 206
Previous: Shenley Brook End School
Net Worth: £30,176,012 *Total Assets:* £33,572,072
Registered Office: Shenley Brook End School, Walbank Grove, Shenley Brook End, Milton Keynes, Bucks, MK5 7ZT
Activities: General secondary education
Officers: Ian Peter Clarkson [1954] Director/Chairman; Malcolm Hugh Dobell [1951] Director; Nicholas John Dredge [1959] Director; Peter John Gibson Horrocks [1959] Director/Consultant; Rebecca Jayne Howell [1974] Director/Senior Education Consultant; Dr Huw Christopher Humphreys [1959] Director/Educational Researcher; Roger Stuart Malpass [1960] Director/Training and Development; Glen David Martin [1961] Director/Principal; Jean Marion Nicholas [1944] Director/Retired Accountant; Dr John Graham Arthur Pembery [1958] Director; Darren Mark Thomas [1970] Director/Financial Analyst; Dr Margaret Elizabeth Wyke [1953] Director/Retired

The A & S Leisure Group Limited
Incorporated: 20 September 1968 *Employees:* 675
Net Worth: £37,844,348 *Total Assets:* £43,101,272
Registered Office: 15 Livesey Street, Sheffield, S6 2BL
Activities: Gambling and betting activities
Shareholders: David Easton Dey Allen; Mark Allen
Officers: Ashley Robert Miles, Secretary; David Easton Dey Allen [1942] Chairman/Director; Mark Allen [1970] Director; Linda Clark [1956] Director; Paul Barrie Coy [1970] Director

A B Graphic International Limited
Incorporated: 15 September 1954 *Employees:* 254
Net Worth: £16,667,203 *Total Assets:* £35,804,784
Registered Office: Celebration House, Stanley Street, Burton on Trent, Staffs, DE14 1DY
Activities: Manufacture of other general-purpose machinery n.e.c.
Parent: GHB Holding Ltd
Officers: Leslie John Lowde, Secretary; Tony William Harry Bell [1957] Director; Charles Nicholas Burton [1957] Director; Matthew Edward Burton [1985] Sales Director; Michael Peter Burton [1959] Director; David Lawson [1954] Director; Leslie John Lowde [1956] Finance Director

A C PLC
Incorporated: 6 March 2008 *Employees:* 75
Net Worth: £5,263,871 *Total Assets:* £23,131,512
Registered Office: Beancroft Farm, Beancroft Road, Marston Moretaine, Beds, MK43 0QE
Activities: Floor and wall covering
Officers: Angela Elizabeth Douty, Secretary; Angela Elizabeth Douty [1963] Financial Director; Jeremy James Kershaw [1963] Director; Andrew Colin Laing [1968] Director; Simon Charles Lousada [1963] Director

A F Switchgear Limited
Incorporated: 1 August 1974 *Employees:* 131
Net Worth: £7,540,098 *Total Assets:* £18,287,772
Registered Office: A F Switchgear Limited, Nunn Brook Road, Sutton in Ashfield, Notts, NG17 2HU
Activities: Manufacture of electronic components
Parent: A.F. Switchgear (Holdings) Limited
Officers: Mathew Stephen Slack, Secretary; Ian Henry Foster [1967] Managing Director; Michael George Harris [1953] Director/Engineering Manager; Mathew Stephen Slack [1969] Financial Director; Richard Thompson [1968] Sales Director

A Shade Greener (Boilers) LLP
Incorporated: 23 August 2012 *Employees:* 26
Net Worth: £1,264,386 *Total Assets:* £19,672,570
Registered Office: Sterling House, Maple Court, Tankersley, Barnsley, S Yorks, S75 3DP
Officers: Stewart James Davies [1951] Member

A Shade Greener (F10) LLP
Incorporated: 28 May 2013
Net Worth: £8,796,613 *Total Assets:* £16,703,374
Registered Office: Sterling House, Maple Court, Maple Road, Tankersley, S Yorks, S75 3DP

A Shade Greener (F11) LLP
Incorporated: 25 June 2013
Net Worth: £14,118,202 *Total Assets:* £28,679,552
Registered Office: Sterling House, Maple Court, Maple Road, Tankersley, S Yorks, S75 3DP

A Shade Greener (F12) LLP
Incorporated: 25 June 2013
Net Worth: £17,322,034 *Total Assets:* £36,236,920
Registered Office: Sterling House, Maple Court, Maple Road, Tankersley, S Yorks, S75 3DP

A Shade Greener (F13) LLP
Incorporated: 13 November 2013
Net Worth: £6,607,829 *Total Assets:* £17,601,684
Registered Office: Sterling House, Maple Court, Maple Road, Tankersley, S Yorks, S75 3DP

A Shade Greener (F14) LLP
Incorporated: 13 November 2013
Net Worth: £9,909,035 *Total Assets:* £26,395,048
Registered Office: Sterling House, Maple Court, Maple Road, Tankersley, S Yorks, S75 3DP

A Shade Greener (F15) LLP
Incorporated: 13 November 2013
Net Worth: £11,237,969 *Total Assets:* £29,264,262
Registered Office: Sterling House, Maple Court, Maple Road, Tankersley, S Yorks, S75 3DP

A Shade Greener (F17) LLP
Incorporated: 1 December 2014
Net Worth: £14,435,489 *Total Assets:* £68,586,720
Registered Office: Sterling House, Maple Court, Tankersley, Barnsley, S Yorks, S75 3DP

A Shade Greener (F4) LLP
Incorporated: 6 September 2011
Net Worth: £4,510,077 *Total Assets:* £17,652,520
Registered Office: Sterling House, Maple Court, Tankersley, Barnsley, S Yorks, S75 3DP

A Shade Greener (F5) LLP
Incorporated: 6 September 2011
Net Worth: £5,594,857 *Total Assets:* £21,777,000
Registered Office: Sterling House, Maple Court, Tankersley, Barnsley, S Yorks, S75 3DP

A Shade Greener (F6) LLP
Incorporated: 6 September 2011
Net Worth: £5,292,262 *Total Assets:* £20,263,986
Registered Office: Sterling House, Maple Court, Tankersley, Barnsley, S Yorks, S75 3DP

A Shade Greener (F7) LLP
Incorporated: 6 September 2011
Net Worth: £11,986,703 *Total Assets:* £51,170,952
Registered Office: Sterling House, Maple Court, Tankersley, Barnsley, S Yorks, S75 3DP

A Shade Greener (F9) LLP
Incorporated: 26 June 2012
Net Worth: £26,662,874 *Total Assets:* £51,281,936
Registered Office: Sterling House, Maple Court, Maple Road, Tankersley, S Yorks, S75 3DP

A Shade Greener Debt (2) LLP
Incorporated: 12 June 2014
Net Worth: £31,434,756 *Total Assets:* £65,964,724
Registered Office: Sterling House, Maple Court, Maple Road, Tankersley, S Yorks, S75 3DP

A Shade Greener Debt (3) LLP
Incorporated: 27 June 2014
Net Worth: £41,337,368 *Total Assets:* £108,393,344
Registered Office: Sterling House, Maple Court, Maple Road, Tankersley, S Yorks, S75 3DP

A Shade Greener Debt LLP
Incorporated: 25 June 2013
Net Worth: £35,634,932 *Total Assets:* £69,177,224
Registered Office: Sterling House, Maple Court, Maple Road, Tankersley, S Yorks, S75 3DP

A Shade Greener Limited
Incorporated: 2 June 2009 *Employees:* 14
Net Worth: £9,303,624 *Total Assets:* £49,625,400
Registered Office: Sterling House, Maple Court, Maple Road, Tankersley, S Yorks, S75 3DP
Activities: Production of electricity
Major Shareholder: Stewart James Davies
Officers: Anthony William Jude Cundall [1979] Managing Director; Stewart James Davies [1951] Director; Racheal May Parlett [1973] Director/Administration Manager

A Shade Greener Maintenance Limited
Incorporated: 25 June 2013 *Employees:* 34
Net Worth: £1,148,288 *Total Assets:* £11,708,343
Registered Office: Sterling House, Maple Court, Maple Road, Tankersley, S Yorks, S75 3DP
Activities: Repair of other equipment
Parent: SD2 Maintenance LLP
Officers: Stewart James Davies [1951] Director; Simon Robert Duncan [1961] Director

A Shade Greener Tankersley LLP
Incorporated: 25 June 2013
Net Worth: £141,249,504 *Total Assets:* £438,071,552
Registered Office: Sterling House, Maple Court, Maple Road, Tankersley, S Yorks, S75 3DP

A Tiny Hamlet Limited
Incorporated: 25 March 2010
Previous: Little Purlieu Limited
Net Worth: £5,654,200 *Total Assets:* £13,774,478
Registered Office: The Stables, Station Drive, Kirby Muxloe, Leicester, LE9 2ET
Activities: Buying and selling of own real estate
Shareholders: Simon Phillip Michaels; Elizabeth Michaels
Officers: Elizabeth Jane Michaels [1971] Director/Businesswoman; Simon Phillip Michaels [1972] Director/Businessman

A-Plan Group Ltd
Incorporated: 4 December 2014 *Employees:* 1,531
Previous: A-Plan Holdco Limited
Net Worth Deficit: £70,389,608 *Total Assets:* £340,239,104
Registered Office: 2 Des Roches Square, Witney, Oxon, OX28 4LE
Activities: Activities of other holding companies n.e.c.
Parent: HgCapital 7 Nominees Limited
Officers: Andrew James Galbraith, Secretary; Thomas Roger Attwood [1952] Director; James Maxwell Carruthers [1954] Director; Andrew James Galbraith [1970] Director/Accountant; Andrew Ronald Land [1972] Director/Investment Executive; Carl Anthony Shuker [1961] Director; Thorsten Toepfer [1978] Director

A-Plan Holdings
Incorporated: 18 February 1963 *Employees:* 1,313
Net Worth: £28,304,854 *Total Assets:* £78,982,640
Registered Office: 2 Des Roches Square, Witney, Oxon, OX28 4LE
Activities: Activities of insurance agents and brokers
Shareholders: Trafalgar Bidco Limited; Howardplace 5 Limited
Officers: Andrew James Galbraith, Secretary/Director; Jacqueline Marie Biddle [1973] People Director; James Maxwell Carruthers [1954] Director; Michael David Simon Edgeley [1966] Director; Andrew Galbraith [1970] Director; Kelly Anne Ogley [1970] Director; Carl Anthony Shuker [1961] Director

A.B. Hotels Limited
Incorporated: 19 December 1979 *Employees:* 281
Net Worth: £12,365,051 *Total Assets:* £28,312,584
Registered Office: West Walk Building, 110 Regent Road, Leicester, LE1 7LT
Activities: Hotels and similar accommodation
Major Shareholder: Abraham Bejerano
Officers: Alon Bejerano, Secretary; Abraham Bejerano [1947] Director/Hotelier; Alon Bejerano [1978] Director/Finance and Administration; Rafael Bejerano [1977] Director/Sales and Marketing; Sarah Adele Bejerano [1986] Director/Sales; Sharon Rose Bejerano [1982] Director; Vivien Judith Bejerano [1948] Director/Hotelier

A.B. Produce PLC
Incorporated: 6 April 1988 *Employees:* 158
Net Worth: £3,306,000 *Total Assets:* £14,504,000
Registered Office: Enterprise House, Westminster Industrial Estate, Repton Road, Measham, Swadlincote, Derbys, DE12 7DT
Activities: Post-harvest crop activities
Parent: A.B. Produce Trading Limited
Officers: Derek William Tomkinson, Secretary; Paul Julian Bridgen [1967] Director; Peter John Ellis [1954] Director; Neil Andrew Sharratt [1964] Finance Director; Derek William Tomkinson [1949] Director/Chartered Accountant

A.B. Produce Trading Limited
Incorporated: 4 December 2006 *Employees:* 158
Net Worth: £3,306,000 *Total Assets:* £14,504,000
Registered Office: Enterprise House, Westminster Industrial Estate, Repton Road, Measham, Swadlincote, Derbys, DE12 7DT
Activities: Activities of agricultural holding companies
Shareholders: Paul Julian Bridgen; Andrew Bridgen
Officers: Paul Julian Bridgen, Secretary; Paul Julian Bridgen [1967] Director; Peter John Ellis [1954] Director; Neil Andrew Sharratt [1964] Director; Derek William Tomkinson [1949] Director

A.C.Flooring Ltd.
Incorporated: 27 July 1995 *Employees:* 75
Net Worth: £6,532,808 *Total Assets:* £25,319,304
Registered Office: Beancroft Farm, Beancroft Road, Marston Moretaine, Beds, MK43 0QE
Activities: Floor and wall covering
Parent: AC PLC
Officers: Angela Elizabeth Douty, Secretary; Andrew Colin Laing [1968] Director/Flooring Specialist; Anthony John George Laing [1965] Contracts Director; Timothy Giles Pemberton [1973] Finance Director; Graham William Shannahan [1984] Pre-Construction Director; Richard James Woolston [1979] Commercial Director

A.E.S. Engineering Limited
Incorporated: 25 January 1945 *Employees:* 1,694
Net Worth: £96,749,000 *Total Assets:* £136,308,992
Registered Office: Global Technology Centre, Bradmarsh Business Park, Mill Close, Rotherham, S Yorks, S60 1BZ
Activities: Manufacture of other general-purpose machinery n.e.c.
Shareholders: Christopher John Rea; 3i Investments PLC; 3i Group PLC
Officers: Richard Edward Sullivan, Secretary; Simon Paul Blagden [1962] Director; James Neil Hamilton [1968] Director; Ian Matthew Lobley [1963] Director; Christopher John Rea [1954] Director; Stephen Martin Shaw [1958] Director; Richard Edward Sullivan [1985] Finance Director

A.F. Switchgear (Holdings) Limited
Incorporated: 16 July 2007 *Employees:* 165
Net Worth: £15,184,858 *Total Assets:* £28,753,156
Registered Office: Nunn Brook Road, Sutton in Ashfield, Notts, NG17 2HU
Activities: Activities of other holding companies n.e.c.
Major Shareholder: Ian Henry Foster
Officers: Mathew Stephen Slack, Secretary; Ian Henry Foster [1967] Managing Director

A.M. Packaging Limited
Incorporated: 30 October 1980 *Employees:* 154
Net Worth: £4,960,136 *Total Assets:* £14,384,299
Registered Office: Amp Rose, Somerby Way, Gainsborough, Lincs, DN21 1QT
Activities: Manufacture of machinery for food, beverage and tobacco processing
Major Shareholder: Alan Mann
Officers: Paul Vernon Mann, Secretary; Alan Mann [1946] Director/Chairman; Andrew Howard Mann [1969] Sales Director; David Alan Francis Mann [1977] Production Director; Paul Vernon Mann [1967] Managing Director

A.M.S. Property Management Limited
Incorporated: 16 April 1999
Net Worth: £1,627,567 *Total Assets:* £10,395,358
Registered Office: Lawmax House, 30-32 Nottingham Road, Stapleford, Nottingham, NG9 8AA
Activities: Other letting and operating of own or leased real estate
Major Shareholder: Andrew Martin Sykes
Officers: Paul Jon Minns, Secretary; Andrew Martin Sykes [1965] Director/Property Management

A.P.S. Salads Limited
Incorporated: 23 October 2006 *Employees:* 48
Net Worth Deficit: £362,000 *Total Assets:* £13,047,000
Registered Office: Enterprise House, 97 Alderley Road, Wilmslow, Cheshire, SK9 1PT
Activities: Wholesale of fruit and vegetables
Parent: A Pearson & Sons (1949) LLP
Officers: Ashley Robert Haworth, Secretary; Ashley Robert Haworth [1979] Financial Director; Mark Pearson [1973] Director/Tomato Grower; John Edward Phibbs [1950] Director/Accountant; Steve Sadler [1968] Finance Director

A.T.C. Manufacturing Limited
Incorporated: 29 August 1921
Net Worth: £30,044,000 *Total Assets:* £35,650,000
Registered Office: 1st Floor, 5 Morston Claycliffe Office Park, Whaley Road, Barnsley, S Yorks, S75 1HQ
Activities: Preparation and spinning of textile fibres
Shareholders: Allied Textile Companies Limited; Allied Textiles Companies Limited
Officers: Joanne Grace, Secretary; Joanne Grace [1971] Director/Chartered Accountant; Stewart Robert McGuffie [1968] Director/Chief Executive

A1 Comms Limited
Incorporated: 6 June 2002 *Employees:* 188
Net Worth: £4,857,624 *Total Assets:* £26,334,614
Registered Office: Contract House, Turnpike Business Park, Alfreton, Derbys, DE55 7AD
Activities: Retail sale of mobile telephones
Shareholders: Paul Sisson; Angela Rose Sisson
Officers: Angela Rose Sisson [1967] Director; Paul Sisson [1963] Director

A4E Ltd
Incorporated: 22 July 1991
Net Worth Deficit: £6,980,000 *Total Assets:* £9,241,000
Registered Office: 19-20 The Triangle, NG2 Business Park, Nottingham, NG2 1AE
Activities: Other service activities n.e.c.
Parent: Staffline Group PLC
Officers: Paul Simon Collins, Secretary; Christopher Mark Pullen [1970] Director/Chief Executive Officer; Michael Robert Watts [1974] Director/Chief Financial Officer

AAH Limited
Incorporated: 16 June 1923
Net Worth: £82,404,000 *Total Assets:* £82,404,000
Registered Office: Sapphire Court, Walsgrave Triangle, Coventry, Warwicks, CV2 2TX
Activities: Activities of head offices
Parent: Admenta UK Limited
Officers: Nichola Louise Legg, Secretary; Toby Matthew Anderson [1973] Director; Marcus Hilger [1977] Finance Director [German]; Catherine McDermott [1968] Operations Director; Nigel Swift [1966] Marketing & Sales Director

AAH Pharmaceuticals Limited
Incorporated: 27 July 1912 *Employees:* 2,989
Net Worth: £203,798,000 *Total Assets:* £999,052,032
Registered Office: Sapphire Court, Walsgrave Triangle, Coventry, Warwicks, CV2 2TX
Activities: Manufacture of basic pharmaceutical products
Parent: Admenta Holdings Limited
Officers: Nichola Louise Legg, Secretary; Toby Matthew Anderson [1973] Director; Marcus Hilger [1977] Finance Director [German]; Catherine McDermott [1968] Operations Director; Nigel Swift [1966] Marketing & Sales Director

Aalberts Industries Limited
Incorporated: 30 January 2002
Net Worth: £45,360,000 *Total Assets:* £45,360,000
Registered Office: Belmont Works, St Catherines Avenue, Doncaster, S Yorks, DN4 8DF
Activities: Activities of head offices
Parent: Aalberts Industries UK Limited
Officers: Kevin Michael Parker, Secretary; Craig Malloy [1970] Finance Director; Weibe Arnold Pelsma [1963] Director [Dutch]

Aalberts Industries U.K. Ltd.
Incorporated: 13 July 1998
Net Worth: £71,398,000 *Total Assets:* £83,396,000
Registered Office: Belmont Works, St Catherines Avenue, Doncaster, S Yorks, DN4 8DF
Activities: Activities of head offices
Parent: Aalberts Industries N.V.
Officers: Kevin Michael Parker, Secretary; John Eijgendaal [1964] Finance Director [Dutch]; Craig Malloy [1970] Finance Director; Wiebe Arnold Pelsma [1963] Director [Dutch]

Aareon UK Limited
Incorporated: 11 May 2000 *Employees:* 93
Net Worth: £4,384,136 *Total Assets:* £11,290,871
Registered Office: Building 500, Abbey Park, Stareton, Kenilworth, Warwicks, CV8 2LY
Activities: Business and domestic software development
Parent: 1st Touch Limited
Officers: Dr. Manfred Alflen [1961] Director/Chief Executive Officer [German]; Geraint Huw Griffiths [1972] Director; Amanda Sin Man Lee-Bennett [1976] Director/Accountant; Torsten Christian RAU [1971] Director [German]; Christian Mathias Schmahl [1964] Director/Chief Financial Officer [German]; Meriel Jane Sommers [1958] Director/Solicitor

Aaron Holdings Limited
Incorporated: 28 March 2002
Net Worth: £99,313 *Total Assets:* £62,889,904
Registered Office: Ferham House, Kimberworth Road, Masbrough, Rotherham, S Yorks, S61 1AJ
Activities: Residential nursing care facilities
Parent: Goldcrest Capital Investments Ltd
Officers: Elizabeth Jane Phipps, Secretary; Euan David Craig [1977] Director; John Henry Whitehead [1964] Director/Chief Finance Officer

Aaroncare Limited
Incorporated: 26 November 1986 *Employees:* 314
Net Worth: £11,163,038 *Total Assets:* £13,717,181
Registered Office: 91-97 Saltergate, Chesterfield, Derbys, S40 1LA
Activities: Residential care activities for the elderly and disabled
Parent: Hill Care Holdings Limited
Officers: Alexandra Hill, Secretary; Ian Mitchell, Secretary; John Andrew Hill [1965] Director; Wendy Jane Waddicor [1964] Director

Aarsleff Ground Engineering Limited
Incorporated: 25 June 1991 *Employees:* 164
Previous: Per Aarsleff (UK) Limited
Net Worth: £8,223,921 *Total Assets:* £17,606,680
Registered Office: Hawton Lane, Balderton, Newark, Notts, NG24 3BU
Activities: Other specialised construction activities n.e.c.
Parent: Per Aarsleff A/S
Officers: Lars Gottrup Christensen [1963] Director/Engineer [Danish]; Kevin Barry Hague [1978] Director/Engineer; Stig Gronbaek Weis [1961] Director/Civil Engineer [Danish]

Abaco Systems Limited
Incorporated: 30 July 1987 *Employees:* 259
Previous: GE Intelligent Platforms Holdings Limited
Net Worth: £53,803,000 *Total Assets:* £83,175,000
Registered Office: Tove Valley Business Park, Old Tiffield Road, Towcester, Northants, NN12 6PF
Activities: Manufacture of computers and peripheral equipment
Parent: Abaco UK Holdco Limited
Officers: John Vernon Tomlinson, Secretary; Andrew Neil MacCaig [1969] Director; William Read [1970] Finance Director [American]

Abaco UK Holdco Limited
Incorporated: 28 November 2016 *Employees:* 363
Net Worth Deficit: £68,532,000 *Total Assets:* £98,585,000
Registered Office: Abaco, Tove Valley Business Park, Old Tiffield Road, Towcester, Northants, NN12 6PF
Activities: Activities of head offices
Major Shareholder: Ramzi Musallam
Officers: John Vernon Tomlinson, Secretary; Andrew Neil MacCaig [1969] UK Managing Director & CIO; William Read [1970] Finance Director [American]

Abacus Hotels Limited
Incorporated: 13 September 1995 *Employees:* 295
Net Worth: £7,434,182 *Total Assets:* £14,878,855
Registered Office: White Lion House, 20 Station Street, Swaffham, Norfolk, PE37 7LH
Activities: Hotels and similar accommodation
Officers: Michael James Halls, Secretary/Director; Howard James Darking [1953] Director; Thomas Frederick Franke [1929] Director/Property Developer [American]; Michael James Halls [1947] Director

Abacus Lighting Holdings Limited
Incorporated: 18 April 2013 *Employees:* 164
Net Worth: £6,987,407 *Total Assets:* £12,694,326
Registered Office: Oddicroft Lane, Sutton in Ashfield, Notts, NG17 5FT
Activities: Activities of head offices
Parent: Intrinsic Equity Limited
Officers: Steven Paul Banks [1964] Director; James Bruce Grenfell [1965] Director; Peter Lindsey Jackson [1941] Director; Stephen Albert Lamb [1958] Director

Abacus Lighting Limited
Incorporated: 18 April 2013 *Employees:* 164
Net Worth: £6,942,396 *Total Assets:* £10,372,725
Registered Office: Oddicroft Lane, Sutton in Ashfield, Notts, NG17 5FT
Activities: Manufacture of other fabricated metal products n.e.c.
Parent: Abacus Lighting Holdings Limited
Officers: Christopher Ian Anderson [1980] Sales Director; Steven Paul Banks [1964] Director; James Bruce Grenfell [1965] Director; Peter Lindsey Jackson [1941] Director; Darren Wade Kokuciak [1970] Commercial Director; Stephen Albert Lamb [1958] Director; Camilla Louise Wigmore [1987] Operations Director

Abba Plant Hire Limited
Incorporated: 9 December 1997 *Employees:* 41
Net Worth: £4,775,387 *Total Assets:* £10,768,161
Registered Office: Martin House, Exchange Road, Doddington Road, Lincoln, LN6 3JZ
Activities: Renting and leasing of construction and civil engineering machinery and equipment
Major Shareholder: John Martin-Hoyes
Officers: Tracy Bourne, Secretary; Tracy Bourne [1981] Director/Account Supervisor; John Martin-Hoyes [1944] Director

Abbey College, Ramsey
Incorporated: 15 August 2011 *Employees:* 161
Net Worth: £26,613,448 *Total Assets:* £27,607,926
Registered Office: Abbey College, Abbey Road, Ramsey, Cambs, PE26 1DG
Activities: General secondary education
Officers: John Alexander Rodney Chrisp [1945] Director; Andrew Christoforou [1971] Director/Headmaster; Helen Clarke [1967] Director/Homemaker; Alan John Dods [1956] Director/IT Consultant; Esmond James Edwards [1949] Director/Chartered Accountant; Madeleine Ann Jackson [1950] Director/Retired; Gareth Idwal Jones [1952] Director/Design and Technology Technician; Neil Robinson [1961] Director/Teacher; Ian Rout [1970] Director/Support Worker - Adults with Disabilities; Stephen Roy Smith [1958] Director; John Francis Stevens [1959] Director/Surveyor; Lisa Jane Williamson [1969] Director/Administrator

Abbey Forged Products Limited
Incorporated: 18 June 1982 *Employees:* 194
Net Worth: £19,827,476 *Total Assets:* £43,960,844
Registered Office: Beeley Wood Works, Beeley Wood Lane, Sheffield, S6 1ND
Activities: Manufacture of basic iron and steel and of ferro-alloys
Parent: The Abbey Group UK Ltd
Officers: Jacqueline Margaret Neal, Secretary; Jacqueline Margaret Neal [1950] Director; Jason Stephen Neal [1970] Director; Roger Stephen Neal [1944] Director

The Abbey Group Cambridgeshire Limited
Incorporated: 24 November 1987 *Employees:* 20
Net Worth: £22,393,772 *Total Assets:* £43,206,404
Registered Office: Nene Lodge, Funthams Lane, Whittlesey, Peterborough, PE7 2PB
Activities: Activities of head offices
Major Shareholder: David Clifford Sutton
Officers: Tracey Jayne Salisbury, Secretary; Carl David Sutton [1975] Director; David Clifford Sutton [1950] Director; Nicholas Robert Sutton [1977] Director

The Abbey Group UK Limited
Incorporated: 31 July 2006 *Employees:* 197
Net Worth: £43,379,116 *Total Assets:* £47,965,696
Registered Office: Beeley Wood Works, Beeley Wood Lane, Sheffield, S6 1ND
Activities: Dormant company
Shareholders: Jacqueline Margaret Neal; Roger Stephen Neal
Officers: Roger Stephen Neal, Secretary; Jacqueline Margaret Neal [1950] Managing Director; Roger Stephen Neal [1944] Director

Abbey Properties Cambridgeshire Limited
Incorporated: 18 December 1995 *Employees:* 4
Net Worth: £11,274,060 *Total Assets:* £13,544,637
Registered Office: Nene Lodge, Funthams Lane, Whittlesey, Peterborough, Cambs, PE7 2PB
Activities: Development of building projects
Shareholders: Carl David Sutton; Nicholas Robert Sutton
Officers: Tracey Jayne Salisbury, Secretary; Carl David Sutton [1975] Director; David Clifford Sutton [1950] Director; Nicholas Robert Sutton [1977] Director

Abbeyfield V.E. Limited
Incorporated: 20 September 1995 *Employees:* 68
Net Worth: £1,901,000 *Total Assets:* £12,313,000
Registered Office: Mere Way, Ruddington Fields Business Park, Ruddington, Nottingham, NG11 6NZ
Activities: Activities of head offices
Parent: Vision Express (UK) Limited
Officers: Nicholas Dermott Vance Allen, Secretary; Nicholas Dermott Vance Allen [1968] Director/Chief Financial Officer; Michael Flint [1965] Director; Onur Koksal [1976] Director/Chief Executive [Turkish]

Abbeymill Homes Limited
Incorporated: 11 March 1991 *Employees:* 15
Net Worth: £718,054 *Total Assets:* £20,683,028
Registered Office: Market House, Silver End, Olney, Bucks, MK46 4AL
Activities: Other specialised construction activities n.e.c.
Shareholders: Peter John Pacifici; Lee Anthony Hagan
Officers: Lee Anthony Hagan, Secretary; Lee Anthony Hagan [1964] Director; James Pacifici [1987] Director/Project Manager; Peter John Pacifici [1957] Director

Abbotsley Farms Limited
Incorporated: 11 January 2008 *Employees:* 6
Net Worth: £8,412,428 *Total Assets:* £16,570,914
Registered Office: Suite C, Unex House, Bourges Boulevard, Peterborough, Cambs, PE1 1NG
Activities: Growing of cereals (except rice), leguminous crops and oil seeds
Shareholders: Michael Raymond Topham; Janice Mary Topham
Officers: Janice Topham, Secretary; Louise Margaret Santry [1986] Director; Janice Mary Topham [1955] Director; Michael Raymond Topham [1953] Director/Accountant; Samuel Peter Topham [1987] Director

Abbott Diabetes Care Limited
Incorporated: 12 October 1990 *Employees:* 627
Net Worth Deficit: £10,676,000 *Total Assets:* £94,911,000
Registered Office: Windrush Park, Range Road, Witney, Oxon, OX29 0YL
Activities: Manufacture of medical and dental instruments and supplies
Officers: Christopher Graham Bass, Secretary; Christopher Graham Bass [1982] Director; Shaun Julian Smith [1965] Director; Brian Yoor [1969] Director [American]

Abel Investments Limited
Incorporated: 21 February 2013
Net Worth: £18,680,842 *Total Assets:* £32,694,672
Registered Office: Moore Stephens, Oakley House, Headway Business Park, 3 Saxon Way West, Corby, Northants, NN17 1SE
Activities: Security dealing on own account
Shareholders: Claire Ann Spencer; John White
Officers: John White [1951] Director; Rosalind Mary White [1952] Director

Ability Matters Group Limited
Incorporated: 30 March 1995 *Employees:* 573
Net Worth: £10,564,000 *Total Assets:* £22,567,000
Registered Office: Ability House, 21 Nuffield Way, Abingdon, Oxon, OX14 1RL
Activities: Manufacture of lifting and handling equipment
Shareholder: Michael Anthony O'Byrne
Officers: Dominic Hannett [1977] Director; Neil Edward James [1973] Director; James Lawrence Lyons [1971] Director; John O'Byrne [1983] Director; Michael Thomas O'Byrne [1987] Director; Michael Anthony O'Byrne [1959] Director [Irish]; Paul David Robinson [1961] Director/Accountant

Abingdon School
Incorporated: 2 September 1998 *Employees:* 341
Net Worth: £56,222,000 *Total Assets:* £63,765,000
Registered Office: Abingdon School, Park Road, Abingdon, Oxon, OX14 1DE
Activities: Primary education
Officers: Justin Hodges, Secretary; Thomas Richard Ayling [1942] Director/Governor; Robert Nicholas Barr [1958] Director; Glynne Butt [1943] Director/Retired; Jonathan Aspull Carroll [1961] Director/Headteacher; Penny Chapman [1960] Director/Solicitor; Robert Andrew Jardine-Brown [1970] Director; Mark John Lascelles [1969] Director/Headmaster; Olga Florence Senior [1960] NHS Director; Steven John Sensecall [1960] Director; Professor Michael Stevens [1950] Director/Consultant Paediatric Oncologist; Matthew Tate [1976] Director/IT Consultant; Damian James Tracey [1965] Managing Director; Kenneth Bentley Welby [1966] Director; Harriet Margaret Corlett Woollard [1968] Director

Ablehomes Limited
Incorporated: 25 November 1982 *Employees:* 17
Net Worth: £9,666,927 *Total Assets:* £11,184,825
Registered Office: 4 Castle Gate, Newark, Notts, NG24 1AX
Activities: Construction of domestic buildings
Shareholders: Anthony Raymond Ablewhite; Carole Margaret Ablewhite
Officers: Carole Margaret Ablewhite, Secretary; Anthony Raymond Ablewhite [1957] Director; Carole Margaret Ablewhite [1957] Director

Abney Trust
Incorporated: 11 December 2015 *Employees:* 198
Net Worth: £12,742,815 *Total Assets:* £16,106,212
Registered Office: The Kingsway School, Foxland Road, Cheadle, Cheshire, SK8 4QX
Activities: General secondary education
Officers: Caroline Ann Booth [1963] Director/Editor; Gary Keown [1965] Director/Editor; Joanne Sarah Lowe [1967] Director/Headteacher; Anne Thompson [1946] Director/Retired

Abraham Investments Limited
Incorporated: 4 June 1982 *Employees:* 5
Net Worth: £10,275,758 *Total Assets:* £12,475,400
Registered Office: Equipoise House, Grove Place, Bedford, MK40 3LE
Activities: Development of building projects
Parent: Chartmoor Estates Limited
Officers: Gwendolyn Anne Marie Abraham, Secretary/Property Developer; Dean Abraham [1971] Managing Director; Edward John Abraham [1940] Director/Chairman; Gwendolyn Anne Marie Abraham [1944] Director/Property Developer

ABSL Power Solutions Ltd
Incorporated: 30 July 1993 *Employees:* 62
Net Worth: £5,345,000 *Total Assets:* £12,134,000
Registered Office: Building F4, Culham Science Centre, Culham, Abingdon, Oxon, OX14 3ED
Activities: Manufacture of batteries and accumulators
Parent: Enersys Holdings UK Ltd
Officers: Todd Michael Sechrist [1966] Director/President EMEA Enersys [American]; David Smart [1972] Senior Director, Sales and Marketing, Enersys; Henry Stratton-Brown [1965] Director/Vice President Finance, Americas

Absolute Radio Limited
Incorporated: 24 December 1991 *Employees:* 26
Net Worth: £8,454,000 *Total Assets:* £11,621,000
Registered Office: Media House, Peterborough Business Park, Lynch Wood, Peterborough, Cambs, PE2 6EA
Activities: Radio broadcasting
Parent: Bauer AR Holdings Limited
Officers: Deidre Ann Ford [1960] Managing Director; Paul Anthony Keenan [1963] Director/Publisher; Sarah Jane Vickery [1963] Finance Director

The Academy @ Ridgewood Trust
Incorporated: 3 October 2011 *Employees:* 152
Net Worth: £12,497,000 *Total Assets:* £15,921,000
Registered Office: Ridgewood School, Barnsley Road, Scawsby, Doncaster, S Yorks, DN5 7UB
Activities: General secondary education
Officers: Dominic Carlin [1989] Director/Teacher; Stuart Cameron Cousins [1955] Director/Educational Consultant; Margaret Helen Dunn [1965] Director/Headteacher; David Andrew Grace [1962] Director/Health and Safety Advisor; Adrian Hayes [1976] Director/Junior School Headteacher; Keith Arthur Mears [1940] Director/Specialist Teaching Assistant; Mandy Elizabeth Oxer [1958] Director; Galit Judith Sharpe [1973] Director/Retail Area Manager; Pamela Jane Ullyott [1964] Director/Solicitor

The Academy of Lincoln Trust
Incorporated: 9 March 2011 *Employees:* 228
Net Worth: £10,788,771 *Total Assets:* £13,023,938
Registered Office: Lincoln Castle Academy, Riseholme Road, Lincoln, LN1 3SP
Activities: General secondary education
Officers: Martin John Connor [1957] Director; Sonia Edith Feodosia Czabaniuk [1956] Director/Education & Training Consultant; Philip David Dubut [1966] Director/Legal Executive; Professor James Scott Fleming [1964] Director/University Senior Manager; Hannah Spencer [1947] Managing Director; Simon James Wilson [1969] Director/Financial Advisor

Accelerated Digital Ventures Limited
Incorporated: 20 July 2015 *Employees:* 10
Net Worth: £30,511,100 *Total Assets:* £30,925,540
Registered Office: Electric Works, Concourse Way, Sheffield, S1 2BJ
Activities: Activities of venture and development capital companies
Shareholders: Legal and General Capital Investments Limited; Woodford Investment Management Limited
Officers: Paul James Kenneth Miller [1976] Director; Lee Andrew Strafford [1972] Director; Keith William Teare [1954] Director

Accelerating Growth Fund Ltd
Incorporated: 14 March 2003
Net Worth: £6,387,140 *Total Assets:* £26,920,336
Registered Office: 2nd Floor, Blenheim Court, 19 George Street, Banbury, Oxon, OX16 5BH
Activities: Other professional, scientific and technical activities n.e.c.
Parent: Waste and Resources Action Programme
Officers: Philippa Foster, Secretary; Dr Marcus Paul Gover [1964] Director; Julie Elizabeth Hill [1961] Director/Environmental Consultant; Peter James Maddox [1962] Director

Access Fertility Limited
Incorporated: 29 October 2013 *Employees:* 8
Net Worth: £1,297,777 *Total Assets:* £12,568,077
Registered Office: Carlton House, High Street, Higham Ferrers, Northants, NN10 8BW
Activities: Specialists medical practice activities
Parent: Access Fertility Management Limited
Officers: Ashley Craig Carroll-Miller [1984] Director; Michael Levy [1959] Director [American]; Mark Segal [1964] Director [American]

Access Platform Sales Limited
Incorporated: 10 February 1987 *Employees:* 24
Net Worth: £325,979 *Total Assets:* £9,647,870
Registered Office: Leewood Business Park, Upton, Huntingdon, Cambs, PE28 5YQ
Activities: Other specialised construction activities n.e.c.
Parent: Access Platform Sales Holdings Limited
Officers: Kian Golestani, Secretary; Christopher William Banks [1967] Director/Technical Engineering Manager; Stephen Robert Couling [1957] Director; James Ian Daintith [1958] Director; Anthony David Jennings [1959] Director and Accountant; Lee Malcolm Louder [1962] Sales Director; Shane Paver [1968] Director/General Manager (Scotland); Kevin Brian John Shadbolt [1963] Director

Accord Limited
Incorporated: 11 January 1999
Net Worth: £1,413,000 *Total Assets:* £88,301,000
Registered Office: The Sherard Building, Edmund Halley Road, Oxford, OX4 4DQ
Activities: Other business support service activities n.e.c.
Parent: Enterprise PLC
Officers: Andrew Lee Milner [1969] Director/Chartered Engineer; Andrew Latham Nelson [1959] Finance Director

Accrofab Limited
Incorporated: 23 June 1977 *Employees:* 131
Net Worth: £13,629,920 *Total Assets:* £15,301,156
Registered Office: 81 Burton Road, Derby, DE1 1TJ
Activities: Machining
Major Shareholder: Paul David Wright
Officers: Sandra Hewitt, Secretary; Edward Julian Ashworth [1969] Operations Director; Nicholas Jonathan Godfrey [1969] Quality & Service Director; Sandra Hewitt [1961] Accounts & HR Director; Cyril Norman Wright [1931] Director/Chairman; Paul David Wright [1956] Director/General Manager

Accuma Plastics Limited
Incorporated: 27 April 1978 *Employees:* 74
Net Worth: £16,509,048 *Total Assets:* £20,001,046
Registered Office: 26 Princewood Road, Earlstrees Industrial Estate, Corby, Northants, NN17 4AP
Activities: Manufacture of other plastic products
Major Shareholder: Francesca Invernizzi
Officers: David Hector [1949] Director; Paolo Invernizzi [1969] Director [Italian]

Accuride International Limited
Incorporated: 9 May 1939 *Employees:* 32
Net Worth: £12,868,000 *Total Assets:* £16,590,000
Registered Office: Liliput Road, Brackmills Industrial Estate, Northampton, NN4 7AS
Activities: Non-specialised wholesale trade
Shareholders: Kent Alex Jordan; Scott Eric Jordan
Officers: Kay Valerie George, Secretary; James Armstrong [1958] Director; Peter Clive Baxter [1954] Director; Peter William Bayles [1957] Director; Scott Eric Jordan [1958] Director [American]

Acentic Holdings Limited
Incorporated: 21 July 2017 *Employees:* 102
Net Worth: £168,433 *Total Assets:* £11,154,037
Registered Office: The Limes, Dunstable Street, Ampthill, Bedford, MK45 2GJ
Activities: Activities of head offices
Shareholders: Walther Andreas Jacobs; Eric Ramon Recto
Officers: Richard Robinson, Secretary; Walther Andreas Jacobs [1963] Director [German]; Eric Ramon Recto [1963] Director/Business Executive [Filipino]; Richard Robinson [1969] Director

Acer Trust
Incorporated: 14 May 2015 *Employees:* 298
Net Worth: £50,199,000 *Total Assets:* £55,183,000
Registered Office: Matthew Arnold School, Arnolds Way, Oxford, OX2 9JE
Activities: General secondary education
Officers: Judith Anne Bennett [1947] Director/Independent Education Consultant; Jill Cottee [1964] Director/Business Consultant; Helen Joanne Curry [1980] Director/Self Employed; Paul Gravett [1976] Director/Tax Consultant; John William Green [1969] Director/Self Employed; Brendan Michael Kromer [1973] Senior Project Director; David Michael Marcou [1934] Director/Music & Education Consultant; Katherine Jane Ryan [1960] Director/Headteacher; Stanley Michael Linton Terry [1946] Director/Education Consultant

Acertec Engineering Limited
Incorporated: 5 October 1955
Net Worth: £122,021,000 *Total Assets:* £130,610,000
Registered Office: International House, Siskin Parkway East, Middlemarch Business Park, Coventry, Warwicks, CV3 4PE
Activities: Activities of head offices
Parent: Acertec (Edstone) Limited
Officers: Mark John Smith, Secretary; Christopher Paul Fisher [1962] Director; Mark John Smith [1968] Director

Acertec UK Limited
Incorporated: 18 March 2005
Net Worth: £30,725,526 *Total Assets:* £99,666,616
Registered Office: International House, Siskin Parkway East, Middlemarch Business Park, Coventry, Warwicks, CV3 4PE
Activities: Activities of head offices
Parent: Stadco Automotive Limited
Officers: Mark John Smith, Secretary; Christopher Paul Fisher [1962] Director; Mark John Smith [1968] Director

ACES Academies Trust
Incorporated: 8 August 2011 *Employees:* 239
Previous: Hinchingbrooke School
Net Worth: £20,510,594 *Total Assets:* £22,643,336
Registered Office: Hinchingbrooke School, Brampton Road, Huntingdon, Cambs, PE29 3BN
Activities: General secondary education
Officers: Beverley John Frederick Curtis [1945] Director/Retired; Paul Francis Fenney [1951] Director/Retired; Clifford Gary Fluet [1971] Director/Solicitor; Robin McGowan Gildersleeve [1949] Director/School Improvement Specialist; Andrew Ernest Goulding [1959] Director/Headmaster; Brian John Message [1965] Director/Business Owner; Gary James Weston [1973] Commercial Director

ACESO Healthcare Group Holdings Limited
Incorporated: 27 November 2014 *Employees:* 901
Net Worth Deficit: £13,198,000 *Total Assets:* £63,660,000
Registered Office: Sherwood House, Cartwright Way, Forest Business Park, Bardon Hill, Coalville, Leics, LE67 1UB
Activities: Non-specialised wholesale trade
Shareholder: Cooperatief H2 Equity Fund IV Holding W.A.
Officers: Jeremy Michael Benson [1963] Director; John Garner [1973] Director; Simon George Gilbert [1970] Director/Investment Professional; Patrick Henricus Lambertus Kalverboer [1972] Director/Investment Professional [Dutch]; Stephen Paul Kennedy [1960] Commercial Director; John Makin [1972] Finance Director

ACESO Healthcare Holdings Limited
Incorporated: 28 November 2014
Net Worth Deficit: £11,412,000 *Total Assets:* £28,980,000
Registered Office: Sherwood House, Cartwright Way, Forest Business Park, Bardon Hill, Coalville, Leics, LE67 1UB
Activities: Non-specialised wholesale trade
Parent: ACESO Healthcare Group Holdings Limited
Officers: Jeremy Michael Benson [1963] Director; John Garner [1973] Director; Simon George Gilbert [1970] Director/Investment Professional; Patrick Henricus Lambertus Kalverboer [1972] Director/Investment Professional [Dutch]; Stephen Paul Kennedy [1960] Commercial Director; John Makin [1972] Finance Director

ACESO Healthcare Limited
Incorporated: 28 November 2014
Net Worth Deficit: £4,099,000 *Total Assets:* £53,686,000
Registered Office: Sherwood House, Cartwright Way, Forest Business Park, Bardon Hill, Coalville, Leics, LE67 1UB
Activities: Non-specialised wholesale trade
Parent: ACESO Healthcare Holdings Limited
Officers: Jeremy Michael Benson [1963] Director; John Garner [1973] Director; Simon George Gilbert [1970] Director/Investment Professional; Patrick Henricus Lambertus Kalverboer [1972] Director/Investment Professional [Dutch]; Stephen Paul Kennedy [1960] Commercial Director; John Makin [1972] Finance Director

Achilles Group Holdings Limited
Incorporated: 1 April 2008 *Employees:* 805
Net Worth Deficit: £111,744,000 *Total Assets:* £97,562,000
Registered Office: 30 Western Avenue, Milton Park, Milton, Abingdon, Oxon, OX14 4SH
Activities: Activities of other holding companies n.e.c.
Shareholder: Pe1a LP
Officers: John O'Donnell, Secretary; Matthew Edward Brockman [1970] Director/Investment Manager; Jay Katzen [1966] Director/Chief Executive Officer [American]; Nicholas Charles Luckock [1972] Director/Investment Manager; John Robert Greville O'Donnell [1965] Director/Lawyer [Irish]

Achilles Group Limited
Incorporated: 5 April 2000
Net Worth: £8,136,000 *Total Assets:* £30,522,000
Registered Office: 30 Western Avenue, Milton Park, Milton, Abingdon, Oxon, OX14 4SH
Activities: Activities of other holding companies n.e.c.
Parent: Achilles Holdco Limited
Officers: Sally Suzanne Patrick, Secretary; Jay Katzen [1966] Director/Chief Executive Officer [American]; John Robert Greville O'Donnell [1965] Director/Lawyer [Irish]

Achilles Holdco Limited
Incorporated: 1 April 2008
Net Worth Deficit: £79,641,000 *Total Assets:* £94,300,000
Registered Office: 30 Western Avenue, Milton Park, Milton, Abingdon, Oxon, OX14 4SH
Activities: Activities of other holding companies n.e.c.
Parent: Achilles Subholdings Limited
Officers: John O'Donnell, Secretary; Matthew Edward Brockman [1970] Director/Investment Manager; Peter Daniel Facchino [1981] Finance Director; Jay Katzen [1966] Director/Chief Executive [American]; Nicholas Charles Luckock [1972] Director/Investment Manager; Donald Austin Robert [1959] Director

Achilles Subholdings Limited
Incorporated: 1 April 2008
Net Worth Deficit: £23,752,000 *Total Assets:* £157,040,000
Registered Office: 30 Western Avenue, Milton Park, Milton, Abingdon, Oxon, OX14 4SH
Activities: Activities of other holding companies n.e.c.
Parent: Achilles Group Holdings Limited
Officers: John O'Donnell, Secretary; Matthew Edward Brockman [1970] Director/Investment Manager; Jay Katzen [1966] Director/Chief Executive Officer [American]; Nicholas Charles Luckock [1972] Director/Investment Manager

Acis Group Limited
Incorporated: 6 July 1998 *Employees:* 209
Net Worth: £36,019,000 *Total Assets:* £248,668,992
Registered Office: ACIS House, Bridge Street, Gainsborough, Lincs, DN21 1GG
Activities: Renting and operating of Housing Association real estate
Officers: Catherine Alice Kelly, Secretary; Carole Anne Hodson [1960] Director/Project Manager; Michael Kay [1961] Group Director of Property; Bruce Kerr [1958] Director/Consultant; Denise Maguire [1962] Director/Retired Lawyer; Ronan O'Hara [1971] Director/Chartered Surveyor; Paul Satchwell [1979] Finance Director; Kathryn Lois Smart [1971] Director/Accountant; Graham Charles Ward [1960] Director of Own Consultancy Business; Nigel Robert Whitaker [1961] Director/Procurement Consultant

Ackroyd & Abbott Limited
Incorporated: 5 May 1952 *Employees:* 6
Net Worth: £20,333,680 *Total Assets:* £30,428,472
Registered Office: Ellin House, 42 Kingfield Road, Sheffield, S11 9DZ
Activities: Construction of domestic buildings
Major Shareholder: Johanna Margaret Rusling
Officers: Johanna Margaret Rusling, Secretary; Johanna Margaret Rusling [1960] Director/Company Secretary; Robert Matthew Rusling [1962] Director/Chairman; Thomas William Rusling [1989] Director

ACM ULR Limited
Incorporated: 27 August 1999
Net Worth: £14,149,000 *Total Assets:* £33,378,000
Registered Office: Pegasus House, Bakewell Road, Orton Southgate, Peterborough, Cambs, PE2 6YS
Activities: Other business support service activities n.e.c.
Parent: BISL Limited
Officers: Julian Charles Brown, Secretary; Matthew Oliver Donaldson [1973] Director; Duncan Alistair Finch [1965] Director/Chartered Accountant; Seamus Declan Keating [1963] Director [Irish]; Dominic James Platt [1969] Director/Chief Financial Officer; Peter Thompson [1970] Group Director

Acorn Industrial Services Group Ltd
Incorporated: 6 July 2005 *Employees:* 133
Net Worth: £9,513,445 *Total Assets:* £16,222,389
Registered Office: Unit A, Denby Way, Hellaby, Rotherham, S Yorks, S66 8HR
Activities: Wholesale of other machinery and equipment
Shareholders: Axel Johnson International AB; Axindustries AB
Officers: Martin Povey, Secretary; Bo Per-Olof Helgesson [1972] Director [Swedish]; Martin Povey [1971] Director; Ib Ola Lennart Sjolin [1966] Director [Swedish]; Paul Desmond Spillings [1970] Director

Acorn Industrial Services Limited
Incorporated: 23 June 1983 *Employees:* 109
Net Worth: £10,822,320 *Total Assets:* £14,566,906
Registered Office: Unit A, Denby Way, Hellaby, Rotherham, S Yorks, S66 8HR
Activities: Non-specialised wholesale trade
Parent: Acorn Industrial Services Group Ltd
Officers: Martin Povey, Secretary; Bo Per-Olof Helgesson [1972] Director [Swedish]; Martin Povey [1971] Director; Ib Ola Lennart Sjolin [1966] Director [Swedish]; Paul Desmond Spillings [1970] Director; Gavin Peter Stacey [1977] Sales Director; Svante Stenstrom [1969] Business Development & Supply Chain Director [Swedish]

Acorn Partitions & Storage Systems Limited
Incorporated: 4 April 2000 *Employees:* 49
Net Worth: £6,483,897 *Total Assets:* £9,848,067
Registered Office: Apss Ltd, Kingsley Road, Lincoln, LN6 3TA
Activities: Other specialised construction activities n.e.c.
Parent: 2097 Holdings Limited
Officers: Sarah Elizabeth Crookes, Secretary; Laurence Charles Barrass [1971] Operations Director; Darren Paul Crookes [1969] Director; Stuart Marsland [1976] Director/Sales Manager; Hannah Ruth Stockdale [1978] Finance Director; Adrian Miles Thomas [1971] Operations Director

Acorndrift Limited
Incorporated: 23 February 2001
Net Worth: £12,603,000 *Total Assets:* £70,969,000
Registered Office: 2 Crown Way, Rushden, Northants, NN10 6BS
Activities: Pre-primary education
Parent: Acorndrive Limited
Officers: Stephen Kramer, Secretary; Elizabeth Boland [1959] Director/Chief Financial Officer [American]; Stephen Dreier [1942] Director/Chief Admin Officer [American]; Dave Lissy [1965] Director/Chief Executive Officer [American]; James Walter Tugendhat [1971] Managing Director, International

Acorndrive Limited
Incorporated: 23 February 2001 *Employees:* 5
Net Worth Deficit: £41,095,000 *Total Assets:* £43,825,000
Registered Office: 2 Crown Way, Rushden, Northants, NN10 6BS
Activities: Pre-primary education
Parent: Chestnutbay Limited
Officers: Stephen Kramer, Secretary; Elizabeth Boland [1959] Director/Chief Financial Officer [American]; Stephen Dreier [1942] Director/Chief Admin Officer [American]; Dave Lissy [1965] Director/Chief Executive Officer [American]; James Walter Tugendhat [1971] Managing Director, International

ACP Europe Limited
Incorporated: 15 April 2005 *Employees:* 21
Net Worth: £8,895,905 *Total Assets:* £36,865,424
Registered Office: Mazars LLP, The Pinnacle, 160 Midsummer Boulevard, Milton Keynes, Bucks, MK9 1FF
Activities: Activities auxiliary to financial intermediation n.e.c.
Major Shareholder: Kevin Michael Ulrich
Officers: Thibault Gournay [1978] Director/Portfolio Manager [French]

Acredula Group Limited
Incorporated: 20 January 1982 *Employees:* 168
Net Worth: £9,037,132 *Total Assets:* £11,111,967
Registered Office: 47 Church Street, Barnsley, S Yorks, S70 2AS
Activities: Publishing of newspapers
Shareholders: Nicholas Charles Joseph Hewitt; Elizabeth Hewitt; Mary Josephine Hewitt
Officers: Kevin Bassinder [1959] Director; Charles Edward James Hewitt [1970] Director; Mary Josephine Hewitt [1951] Director; Michael Joseph Hewitt [1973] Director; Sir Nicholas Charles Joseph Hewitt [1947] Director/Publisher

Action for Care Limited
Incorporated: 21 August 2008 *Employees:* 148
Net Worth Deficit: £94,423 *Total Assets:* £11,013,143
Registered Office: 91-97 Saltergate, Chesterfield, Derbys, S40 1LA
Activities: Other human health activities
Major Shareholder: Robert Hadfield
Officers: Robert Hadfield, Secretary; Kirsty Elizabeth Jackson, Secretary; Robert Hadfield [1966] Director

Acushnet Europe Ltd
Incorporated: 29 January 1975 *Employees:* 296
Net Worth: £55,146,000 *Total Assets:* £93,835,000
Registered Office: Caxton Road, St Ives Industrial Estate, St Ives, Cambs, PE27 3LU
Activities: Manufacture of sports goods
Officers: Robin Maurice Newbery, Secretary; Matthew Christian Johnson [1973] Director/General Manager; Robin Maurice Newbery [1970] Financial Director; Thomas Pacheco [1968] Director/Executive VP CFO & Treasurer [American]; George Eugene Sine [1962] Director/Vice President Asia Pacific & EMEA [American]

Ad Meliora Academy Trust
Incorporated: 8 July 2016 *Employees:* 107
Net Worth: £12,343,274 *Total Assets:* £13,642,772
Registered Office: St Edmund's Academy, Kilhams Way, Kings Lynn, Norfolk, PE30 2HU
Activities: Other business support service activities n.e.c.
Officers: Barbara Jane Kimpton, Secretary; Lisa Cook [1972] Director/Headteacher; Karl Jermyn [1972] Director/Financial Consultant; William Brannan Mollison [1954] Director; Dorothy Ann Pulsford-Harris [1944] Director/Retired; Andrew James Walder [1959] Director/Retired

ADA Pacific Direct Limited
Incorporated: 6 September 1993 *Employees:* 26
Previous: Pacific Direct Limited
Net Worth: £21,139,192 *Total Assets:* £24,411,416
Registered Office: Trinity Gardens, 9-11 Bromham Road, Bedford, MK40 2BP
Activities: Non-specialised wholesale trade
Parent: ADA PD UK Limited
Officers: Karen Ruth Abel [1981] Director/Chartered Accountant; Sylvia Anne Jensch [1971] Director [German]; Wilhelm Bernhard Konning [1958] Director [German]

ADA PD UK Limited
Incorporated: 27 July 2015
Net Worth: £23,369,712 *Total Assets:* £42,404,728
Registered Office: Trinity Gardens, 9-11 Bromham Road, Bedford, MK40 2BP
Activities: Non-trading company
Officers: Karen Ruth Abel [1981] Director/Chartered Accountant; Sylvia Anne Jensch [1971] Director [German]; Wilhelm Konning [1958] Director [German]

Adam Equipment Co. Limited
Incorporated: 21 April 1977 *Employees:* 178
Net Worth: £14,212,811 *Total Assets:* £15,528,484
Registered Office: Adam Equipment Co Ltd, Maidstone Road, Kingston, Milton Keynes, Bucks, MK10 0BD
Activities: Manufacture of other general-purpose machinery n.e.c.
Shareholders: Alan Storey; June Elizabeth Storey
Officers: Tim David Storey, Secretary; Alan Storey [1946] Director; June Elizabeth Storey [1947] Director

J.O.Adams & Son Limited
Incorporated: 31 December 1955
Net Worth: £5,663,244 *Total Assets:* £10,110,599
Registered Office: Park House Farm, Kilsby Road, Watford, Northampton, NN6 7UT
Activities: Growing of cereals (except rice), leguminous crops and oil seeds
Officers: Joseph Oliver Adams [1954] Director/Farmer; Joshua Radburne Adams [1984] Director

Adams Challenge (UK) Limited
Incorporated: 28 March 2006 *Employees:* 2
Net Worth: £30,379,154 *Total Assets:* £45,328,288
Registered Office: Jubilee House, 32 Duncan Close, Moulton Park, Northampton, NN3 6WL
Activities: Support activities for petroleum and natural gas mining
Officers: Lee Cudmore, Secretary; Salah Khalifa Algosaibi [1949] Director [Saudi Arabian]

John Adams Leisure Limited
Incorporated: 13 October 1983 *Employees:* 36
Net Worth: £16,977,142 *Total Assets:* £28,062,388
Registered Office: Hercules House, Pierson Road, Alconbury Weald, Huntingdon, Cambs, PE28 4YA
Activities: Non-specialised wholesale trade
Officers: Anthony Carson Shepherd, Secretary/Director; Michael Richard Moody [1953] Director; Simon Richard Pilkington [1967] Managing Director; Anthony Carson Shepherd [1948] Director

Adaptimmune Limited
Incorporated: 19 December 2007 *Employees:* 221
Net Worth Deficit: £51,058,000 *Total Assets:* £204,950,000
Registered Office: 60 Jubilee Avenue, Milton Park, Milton, Abingdon, Oxon, OX14 4RX
Activities: Other research and experimental development on natural sciences and engineering
Parent: Adaptimmune Therapeutics PLC
Officers: Margaret Henry, Secretary; James Julian Noble [1959] Director; Adrian George Rawcliffe [1972] Director/Business Executive; Dr Helen Katrina Tayton-Martin [1967] Director/Business Executive

Adaptimmune Therapeutics PLC
Incorporated: 3 December 2014 *Employees:* 330
Net Worth: £157,477,216 *Total Assets:* £216,357,056
Registered Office: 60 Jubilee Avenue, Milton Park, Milton, Abingdon, Oxon, OX14 4RX
Activities: Research and experimental development on biotechnology
Officers: Margaret Henry, Secretary; Lawrence Michael Alleva [1949] Director [American]; Dr Ali Behbahani [1976] Director/Venture Capitalist [American]; Barbara Gayle Duncan [1964] Director [American]; John Paul Furey [1964] Director/Chief Operating Officer [Irish]; Giles Francis Bertram Kerr [1959] Director/Accountant; David Morrell Mott [1965] Director/Executive, General Partner [American]; James Julian Noble [1959] Director; Dr C Elliott Sigal [1952] Director, Executive [American]; Dr Tal Zvi Zaks [1965] Director/Medical Doctor [American]

Adara Group Limited
Incorporated: 21 January 2016 *Employees:* 105
Net Worth: £9,531,166 *Total Assets:* £13,948,076
Registered Office: 2 Seedfield Close, Northampton, NN3 3PA
Activities: Residential care activities for the elderly and disabled
Major Shareholder: Sutinder Kaur Hanspaul
Officers: Sutinder Kaur Hanspaul [1949] Director/Pharmacist; Donna Marie Holmes [1982] Director/Solicitor; John Howard Wearing [1963] Director/Solicitor

Adare International Limited
Incorporated: 3 February 1982 *Employees:* 549
Net Worth: £14,919,000 *Total Assets:* £92,241,000
Registered Office: Shakespeare Martineau, Two Colton Square, Leicester, LE1 1QH
Activities: Printing n.e.c.
Parent: Continuous Stationery Limited
Officers: Raymond Phillip Berry [1977] Finance Director; Andrew Mark Dutton [1971] Director/Chief Executive Officer; Tracy Ellison [1967] Divisional Managing Director; Mark Niall McDonnell [1969] Divisional Managing Director; Stephen Andrew Shaw [1964] Divisional Managing Director

Adare SEC Limited
Incorporated: 30 April 1993 *Employees:* 452
Previous: Adare Limited
Net Worth: £52,290,000 *Total Assets:* £76,792,000
Registered Office: 1 Meridian South, Meridian Business Park, Leicester, LE19 1WY
Activities: Manufacture of paper stationery
Shareholders: ACICS Limited; Adare Group Limited
Officers: John Iandolo [1965] Director/Chief Sales Officer; Rachael Rebecca Nevins [1967] Director/Chief Financial Officer; Tom Graham Prestwich [1983] Director/Chief Operating Officer; James Christopher Michael Woolley [1977] Director

Adder Technology Limited
Incorporated: 11 June 1984 *Employees:* 137
Net Worth: £15,875,333 *Total Assets:* £19,150,376
Registered Office: West Walk Building, 110 Regent Road, Leicester, LE1 7LT
Activities: Manufacture of computers and peripheral equipment
Major Shareholder: Adrain Christopher Dickens
Officers: Nigel Anthony Dickens, Secretary; Adrian Christopher Dickens [1961] Director; Nigel Anthony Dickens [1964] Technical Director

Addington Fund
Incorporated: 31 January 2003 *Employees:* 3
Net Worth: £12,181,779 *Total Assets:* £13,204,020
Registered Office: 9 Barford Exchange, Wellesbourne Road, Barford, Warwicks, CV35 8AQ
Activities: Support activities for animal production (other than farm animal boarding)
Officers: Peter Mark Snodgrass, Secretary; Alistair Michael Brooks [1972] Director/Farmer Grower; David Thomas Canty [1977] Director; Sheila Joy Cole [1941] Director; Louisa Jane Dibble [1963] Director/Community Learning Officer; Peter Charles Jinman [1951] Director/Veterinary Surgeon; Simon Gavin Mountjoy [1960] Director; Martin Robert Redfearn [1955] Director/Consultant; David Rowlands [1939] Director/Farmer; Councillor Christine Anne Ryder [1965] Director/Farmer; Peter Mark Snodgrass [1962] Director/Solicitor; Clair Victoria Stevens [1967] Director/Banker; Roger James Wyatt [1940] Director/Chartered Surveyor

Addo Food Group (Holdings) Ltd
Incorporated: 15 March 2017 *Employees:* 2,519
Net Worth Deficit: £7,404,000 *Total Assets:* £168,559,008
Registered Office: Queens Drive, Nottingham, NG2 1LU
Activities: Manufacture of other food products n.e.c.
Parent: LDC VI LP
Officers: Susan Deborah Benjamin [1960] Director; Andrew John Grove [1967] Director; Mark Anthony Hodson [1961] Director; Paul John Monk [1957] Director; Christopher Peters [1958] Director; Graham Paul Rutter [1954] Director; Martyn John Vitty [1975] Director

Addo Food Group Limited
Incorporated: 14 November 2006
Previous: Pork Farms Group Limited
Net Worth: £22,028,000 *Total Assets:* £85,875,000
Registered Office: c/o Pork Farms Limited, Queens Drive, Nottingham, NG2 1LU
Activities: Manufacture of other food products n.e.c.
Parent: Addo Food Group (Services) Ltd
Officers: Graham Rutter, Secretary; Mark Anthony Hodson [1961] Director; Christopher Peters [1958] Director; Graham Paul Rutter [1954] Company Secretary/Director

Adenwood Limited
Incorporated: 4 April 1972 *Employees:* 231
Net Worth: £6,892,956 *Total Assets:* £10,530,311
Registered Office: The Forge House, Church Lane, East Haddon, Northampton, NN6 8DB
Activities: Activities of head offices
Shareholder: David Hugh Barrow
Officers: Nicholas David Lantsbery, Secretary; David Hugh Barrow [1960] Production Director; Vanessa Julie Barrow [1965] Director; Fiona Margaret Turberville Smith [1962] Director; Virginia Claire Wallman [1972] Director

Adept Care Homes Limited
Incorporated: 23 December 2004 *Employees:* 499
Net Worth: £16,804,556 *Total Assets:* £39,712,232
Registered Office: The Standings, Fields Farm Business Centre, Hinckley Road, Sapcote, Leicester, LE9 4LH
Activities: Activities of head offices
Major Shareholder: David Nigel Lock
Officers: Barbara Mary Granger, Secretary; David Nigel Lock [1950] Residential Home Director; Emma Sara Philpott [1971] Operations Director; Peter Charles Savage [1958] Quality Director; Christopher John White [1962] Finance Director

Adidas (U.K.) Limited
Incorporated: 10 October 1972 *Employees:* 1,136
Net Worth: £30,332,000 *Total Assets:* £158,722,000
Registered Office: The Adidas Centre, Pepper Road, Hazel Grove, Stockport, Cheshire, SK7 5SA
Activities: Wholesale of textiles
Parent: Adidas AG
Officers: Bhupinder Singh Sandhu, Secretary; Andrew Richard Hackett [1972] Finance Director; Arthur Anton Hoeld [1969] Managing Director [German]; Andreas Johannes Richter [1973] Director/Head of Group Accounting [German]; Gavin Preston Thomson [1965] Managing Director

Adient Financing International Ltd
Incorporated: 30 September 2016
Net Worth: £161,637,360 *Total Assets:* £161,637,360
Registered Office: Building 2010, Meriden Business Park, Birmingham Road, Coventry, Warwicks, CV5 9RG
Activities: Financial intermediation not elsewhere classified
Parent: Adient Public Limited Company
Officers: Cathleen Ann Ebacher, Secretary; Cathleen Ann Ebacher [1962] Director/Business Executive [American]

Adient Financing Ltd
Incorporated: 30 September 2016
Net Worth: £643,744,320 *Total Assets:* £696,496,320
Registered Office: Building 2010, Meriden Business Park, Birmingham Road, Coventry, Warwicks, CV5 9RG
Activities: Financial intermediation not elsewhere classified
Parent: Adient Public Limited Company
Officers: Cathleen Ann Ebacher, Secretary; Cathleen Ann Ebacher [1962] Director/Business Executive [American]

Adient Holding Germany Ltd
Incorporated: 11 January 2016
Net Worth: £9,854,000 *Total Assets:* £9,854,000
Registered Office: Building 2010, Meriden Business Park, Birmingham Road, Coventry, Warwicks, CV5 9RG
Activities: Activities of head offices
Parent: Adient Public Limited Company
Officers: Cathleen Ann Ebacher [1962] Director/Business Executive [American]; Mark a Skonieczny Jr [1969] Director/Financial Controller [American]

Adient Holding UK Ltd
Incorporated: 29 January 1988
Previous: Johnson Controls (U.K.) Limited
Net Worth: £87,363,000 *Total Assets:* £187,503,008
Registered Office: Building 2010, Meriden Business Park, Birmingham Road, Coventry, Warwicks, CV5 9RG
Activities: Activities of head offices
Parent: Adient Public Limited Company
Officers: Cathleen Ann Ebacher [1962] Director/Business Executive [American]; Kevin Michael Flanagan [1965] Director/Business Executive; Mark a Skonieczny Jr [1969] Director/Business Executive [American]

Adient Properties UK Ltd
Incorporated: 24 July 2013
Previous: Johnson Controls Properties UK Ltd
Net Worth: £35,666,000 *Total Assets:* £264,452,992
Registered Office: Building 2010, Meriden Business Park, Birmingham Road, Coventry, Warwicks, CV5 9RG
Activities: Activities of head offices
Parent: Adient Public Limited Company
Officers: Cathleen Ann Ebacher [1962] Director/Business Executive [American]; Kevin Michael Flanagan [1965] Director/Business Executive; Mark a Skonieczny Jr [1969] Director/Business Executive [American]

Adient Seating UK Ltd
Incorporated: 15 October 1947 *Employees:* 1,792
Previous: Johnson Controls Automotive (UK) Ltd.
Net Worth: £31,555,000 *Total Assets:* £129,651,000
Registered Office: Building 2010, Meriden Business Park, Birmingham Road, Coventry, Warwicks, CV5 9RG
Activities: Manufacture of other parts and accessories for motor vehicles
Parent: Adient Public Limited Company
Officers: Cathleen Ann Ebacher [1962] Director/Business Executive [American]; Michael Flanagan [1965] Director/VP & General Manager [Irish]; David Patrick McMahon [1957] Director/VP and General Manager; Mark a Skonieczny Jr [1969] Director [American]; Ray Tate [1963] Operations Director

Adient UK Financing International Ltd
Incorporated: 24 October 2016
Net Worth: £166,083,520 *Total Assets:* £829,750,080
Registered Office: Building 2010, Meriden Business Park, Birmingham Road, Coventry, Warwicks, CV5 9RG
Activities: Other business support service activities n.e.c.
Parent: Adient Public Limited Company
Officers: Cathleen Ann Ebacher, Secretary; Cathleen Ann Ebacher [1962] Director/Business Executive [American]

Adient UK Financing Ltd
Incorporated: 24 October 2016
Total Assets: £725,251,008
Registered Office: Building 2010, Meriden Business Park, Birmingham Road, Coventry, Warwicks, CV5 9RG
Activities: Other business support service activities n.e.c.
Parent: Adient Public Limited Company
Officers: Cathleen Ann Ebacher, Secretary; Cathleen Ann Ebacher [1962] Director/Business Executive [American]

Admenta Holdings Limited
Incorporated: 12 December 1929
Net Worth Deficit: £286,824,000 *Total Assets:* £704,518,016
Registered Office: Sapphire Court, Walsgrave Triangle, Coventry, Warwicks, CV2 2TX
Activities: Activities of head offices
Parent: AAH Limited
Officers: Nichola Louise Legg, Secretary; Toby Matthew Anderson [1973] Director; Marcus Hilger [1977] Finance Director [German]; Catherine McDermott [1968] Operations Director; Nigel Swift [1966] Marketing & Sales Director

Admenta UK Limited
Incorporated: 19 January 1995 *Employees:* 8
Net Worth: £256,099,008 *Total Assets:* £1,821,915,008
Registered Office: Sapphire Court, Walsgrave Triangle, Coventry, Warwicks, CV2 2TX
Activities: Activities of head offices
Parent: Celesio AG
Officers: Nichola Louise Legg, Secretary; Toby Matthew Anderson [1973] Director; Marcus Hilger [1977] Finance Director [German]; Catherine McDermott [1968] Operations Director; Nigel Swift [1966] Marketing & Sales Director

Advance Tapes Group Limited
Incorporated: 15 June 1964 *Employees:* 148
Net Worth: £3,496,239 *Total Assets:* £12,038,837
Registered Office: 2 Westmoreland Avenue, Thurmaston, Leicester, LE4 8PH
Activities: Other manufacturing n.e.c.
Officers: Michael David Ayres [1963] Director; Kym Christopher Ellington [1969] Finance Director

Advance Tapes International Limited
Incorporated: 1 April 1968 *Employees:* 133
Net Worth: £6,216,879 *Total Assets:* £11,673,251
Registered Office: 2 Westmoreland Avenue, Thurmaston, Leicester, LE4 8PH
Activities: Other manufacturing n.e.c.
Officers: Michael David Ayres [1963] Director/Chief Executive; Sharon Mary Boyle [1971] Director; Kym Christopher Ellington [1969] Finance Director; Gillan James Woodward [1982] Operations Director

Advanced Marketing (Europe) Limited
Incorporated: 29 July 1997
Net Worth: £4,866,000 *Total Assets:* £16,904,000
Registered Office: Unit B, Bicester Park, Charbridge Way, Bicester, Oxon, OX26 4ST
Activities: Activities of other holding companies n.e.c.
Officers: Stuart James Biltcliffe, Secretary; Gareth David Powell [1965] Director/Accountant

Advancis Holdings Limited
Incorporated: 21 July 2016
Net Worth: £850 *Total Assets:* £12,834,396
Registered Office: Alexandra Court, Carrs Road, Cheadle, Cheshire, SK8 2JY
Activities: Activities of other holding companies n.e.c.
Officers: Melih Sakir Basar [1978] Director [American]; David Cecil John Knevitt [1959] Director [Australian]; Robert Ian Templeton [1941] Director/Chartered Accountant; Nicholas Adam Zapolski [1982] Director

Advancis Limited
Incorporated: 30 May 2012 *Employees:* 19
Net Worth Deficit: £3,985,290 *Total Assets:* £11,180,922
Registered Office: Alexandra Court, Carrs Road, Cheadle, Cheshire, SK8 2JY
Activities: Other credit granting n.e.c.
Parent: Advancis Holdings Limited
Officers: Nicholas Adam Zapolski [1982] Director/Chief Executive

Advanex Europe Limited
Incorporated: 30 September 1988 *Employees:* 155
Net Worth: £11,218,000 *Total Assets:* £14,629,000
Registered Office: Mill Park Way, off Station Road, Southwell, Notts, NG25 0ET
Activities: Manufacture of wire products, chain and springs
Parent: Advanex Group Inc
Officers: Marian Kessandrus Mullings, Secretary; Ian Beardsmore [1969] Managing Director; Adrian France [1962] Manufacturer & Engineering Director; Marian Kessandrus Mullings [1972] Finance Director; Toshiya Ohno [1959] Financial Director [Japanese]; Tsuneo Shibano [1960] Director [Japanese]

Advent Topco Limited
Incorporated: 8 November 2017 *Employees:* 339
Net Worth: £7,015,450 *Total Assets:* £75,144,608
Registered Office: Mountfields House, off Squirrel Way, Epinal Way, Loughborough, Leics, LE11 3GE
Activities: Activities of other holding companies n.e.c.
Shareholders: Bernadine Louise Gibson; Graphite Capital General Partner VIII LLP
Officers: Sandie Foxhall-Smith [1957] Director; Bernadine Louise Gibson [1971] Director; Jamie Alexander Wright [1983] Director

AEBI Schmidt UK Limited
Incorporated: 24 November 1955 *Employees:* 58
Net Worth: £2,939,000 *Total Assets:* £9,302,000
Registered Office: Southgate Way, Orton Southgate, Peterborough, Cambs, PE2 6GP
Activities: Sale of other motor vehicles
Parent: AEBI Schmidt Holding AG
Officers: Paul Martin Squires, Secretary; Richard John Bryant [1966] Director; Gerhard Neudorfer [1966] Commercial Director [Austrian]; Thomas Schenkirsch [1975] Director/Finance Controller [German]

Aegion Rehabilitation Services Limited
Incorporated: 6 December 2013 *Employees:* 1
Net Worth Deficit: £812,414 *Total Assets:* £36,364,660
Registered Office: 12-20 Brunel Close, Park Farm Industrial Estate, Wellingborough, Northants, NN8 6QX
Activities: Remediation activities and other waste management services
Officers: Sarah Bennison, Secretary; David Morris, Secretary; David Morris [1961] Director [American]; Kenneth Young [1951] Director/Senior VP - Treasurer [American]

AEM Limited
Incorporated: 3 February 1959 *Employees:* 206
Net Worth: £19,653,000 *Total Assets:* £27,455,000
Registered Office: P O Box 36, 2 New Star Road, Leicester, LE4 9JQ
Activities: Manufacture of air and spacecraft and related machinery
Parent: Ametek Aerospace and Defense Group UK Limited
Officers: Joy Atwell, Secretary; John Wesley Hardin [1965] Director/Senior Vice President - Aerospace [American]; Alan Adrian Harding [1958] Managing Director; Emanuela Speranza [1968] Director/Vice President/General Manager EMEA, India [Italian]; Thomas Girard Wilson [1954] Director/VP MRO Europe & Asia [American]; Pietro Luigi Enrico Zetti [1968] Finance Director [Italian]

Aero Tec Laboratories Limited
Incorporated: 9 January 1998 *Employees:* 100
Net Worth: £13,527,688 *Total Assets:* £14,671,665
Registered Office: ATL Technology Centre, Denbigh Road, Bletchley, Milton Keynes, Bucks, MK1 1DF
Activities: Manufacture of other rubber products
Major Shareholder: Peter James Regna
Officers: Peter James Regna, Secretary/Manager [American]; Giles Andrew Dawson [1984] Managing Director; Peter James Regna [1944] Director/Manager [American]

AESSEAL PLC
Incorporated: 19 February 1987 *Employees:* 438
Net Worth: £23,733,000 *Total Assets:* £37,884,000
Registered Office: Global Technology Centre, Bradmarsh Business Park, Mill Close, Rotherham, S Yorks, S60 1BZ
Activities: Other manufacturing n.e.c.
Parent: A.E.S. Engineering Limited
Officers: Stephen Martin Dodd, Secretary; Glyn Barry Bingham [1948] Director; Andrew Colverson [1975] Director; Claire Louise Dickinson [1984] Director/Financial Controller; Martin Janes Claude McKervey [1962] Director; Christopher John Rea [1954] Director; Rosalie Rea [1951] Director; Richard Jonathan Smith [1961] Director; James Stuart Welsh [1968] Director; Mark Owen Williams [1956] Director

AFE Group Limited
Incorporated: 8 November 1999 *Employees:* 1,233
Net Worth: £77,219,000 *Total Assets:* £108,945,000
Registered Office: 9 Bryggen Road, North Lynn Industrial Estate, King's Lynn, Norfolk, PE30 2HZ
Activities: Other manufacturing n.e.c.
Parent: ALI UK Limited
Officers: Timothy Simon Smith, Secretary/Director; Maurizio Anastasia [1970] Director/Chief Financial Officer [Italian]; Timothy Simon Smith [1966] Director

Aferry Ltd
Incorporated: 18 December 2000 *Employees:* 63
Previous: Thetravelgateway Limited
Net Worth: £2,581,834 *Total Assets:* £15,689,706
Registered Office: 2morrow Court, Appleford Road, Sutton Courtenay, Oxon, OX14 4FH
Activities: Travel agency activities
Parent: 2morrow Group Ltd
Officers: Robert Edward Green, Secretary; Christopher George Howe Davies [1946] Director; James Alexander Howe Davies [1978] Commercial Director; Michael John Howe-Davies [1980] Director/General Manager; Sarah Pitman [1965] Director/Head of Sales

Affinity Capital Works Limited
Incorporated: 2 October 2015
Net Worth: £18,947,000 *Total Assets:* £30,900,000
Registered Office: Hangar 29, RAF Cranwell, Sleaford, Lincs, NG34 8HB
Activities: Defence activities
Officers: Simon Jeffrey Usher, Secretary; Reuven Alon [1968] Director/Vice President [Israeli]; James Arthur Barrett [1965] Finance Director; Robert Paul Kerry [1956] Director/Commercial Manager; Peter John Meffan [1964] Director/Vice President Ventures; Adi Raviv [1976] Programme Director [Israeli]; Oren Reches [1970] Director/Vice President [Israeli]; Peter Smart [1951] Non-Executive Director

Affinity Flying Training Services Limited
Incorporated: 2 October 2015
Net Worth Deficit: £5,751,000 *Total Assets:* £157,351,008
Registered Office: Hangar 29, RAF Cranwell, Sleaford, Lincs, NG34 8HB
Activities: Defence activities
Officers: Simon Jeffrey Usher, Secretary; Reuven Alon [1968] Director/Vice President [Israeli]; Andrew Jonathan Barrie [1967] Director/Senior Vice President; Martin Clifford St John Fausset [1957] Director; Larry Jay Henry [1953] Director/Vice President Ventures [American]; Peter John Meffan [1964] Director/Vice President Ventures; Oren Reches [1970] Director/Vice President [Israeli]; Peter Smart [1951] Director

Affinity Living Trinity Holdco Limited
Incorporated: 24 February 2016
Net Worth Deficit: £8,000 *Total Assets:* £37,206,000
Registered Office: The Box, Horseshoe Lane, Alderley Edge, Cheshire, SK9 7QP
Activities: Development of building projects
Parent: Affinity Living Limited
Officers: Giles Beswick, Secretary; Giles Peter Beswick [1974] Director; Mark Christopher Dawson [1973] Director; Mark David Stott [1972] Director

Affinity Trust
Incorporated: 30 April 2009
Net Worth: £12,941,194 *Total Assets:* £19,567,834
Registered Office: 1 St Andrews Court, Wellington Street, Thame, Oxon, OX9 3WT
Activities: Other residential care activities n.e.c.
Officers: Leo Sowerby, Secretary; Anne Anketell [1962] Director/Consultant; Jennifer FitzGenerald Edwards [1954] Director/Consultant; John William Hawthorne [1932] Director/Clerk in The Holy Orders (Retired); Margaret Elizabeth Moody [1951] Director/Registered Nurse Management Consultant; Sian Alison Rees [1961] Director/Consultant; Dr Sue Ross [1952] Director/Consultant; Timothy Guy Tamblyn [1952] Director/Retired; Malcolm Thomas [1947] Director/Retired Banker; David Peter Walden [1954] Director

Afpro LLP
Incorporated: 17 December 2015
Net Worth: £2,012,567 *Total Assets:* £9,475,689
Registered Office: 114 Ecclesall Road, Sheffield, S11 8JB
Officers: Mahboob Ahmed Fazal [1959] Member; Masaud Ahmed Fazal [1971] Member

AG47 Limited
Incorporated: 3 February 2014
Net Worth: £23,053,034 *Total Assets:* £25,080,460
Registered Office: 164 Cowley Road, Cowley, Oxford, OX4 1UE
Activities: Activities of financial services holding companies
Officers: Kohei Ogawa [1956] Director [Japanese]

Aga Rangemaster Group Limited
Incorporated: 5 July 1939 *Employees:* 9
Previous: Aga Rangemaster Group PLC
Net Worth: £414,700,000 *Total Assets:* £531,000,000
Registered Office: c/o Aga Rangemaster, Meadow Lane, Long Eaton, Nottingham, NG10 2GD
Activities: Activities of head offices
Parent: Middleby UK Residential Holding Ltd
Officers: Timothy John FitzGenerald [1969] Director/Vice President and CFO [American]; Martin McKay Lindsay [1964] Director/Corporate Treasurer [American]; Agustin Zufia [1967] Director/Group Controller [Spanish]

Aga Rangemaster Limited
Incorporated: 8 November 1999 *Employees:* 1,077
Net Worth: £126,197,000 *Total Assets:* £158,448,000
Registered Office: c/o Aga Rangemaster, Meadow Lane, Long Eaton, Nottingham, NG10 2GD
Activities: Manufacture of ovens, furnaces and furnace burners
Parent: Aga-Rayburn Limited
Officers: Timothy John FitzGenerald [1969] Director/Vice President and CFO [American]; Martin McKay Lindsay [1964] Director/Corporate Treasurer [American]; Agustin Zufia [1967] Director/Group Controller [Spanish]

Aga-Rayburn Limited
Incorporated: 3 November 2005
Net Worth: £237,048,400 *Total Assets:* £237,048,400
Registered Office: c/o Aga Rangemaster, Meadow Lane, Long Eaton, Nottingham, NG10 2GD
Activities: Activities of other holding companies n.e.c.
Parent: Headland UK Limited
Officers: Timothy John FitzGenerald [1969] Director/Vice President and CFO [American]; Martin McKay Lindsay [1964] Director/Corporate Treasurer [American]; Agustin Zufia [1967] Director/Group Controller [Spanish]

AGCO International Limited
Incorporated: 24 May 1989
Net Worth: £450,608,000 *Total Assets:* £722,129,024
Registered Office: Abbey Park, Stoneleigh, Kenilworth, Warwicks, CV8 2TQ
Activities: Activities of head offices
Parent: AGCO Corporation
Officers: Roger Neil Batkin, Secretary; Roger Neil Batkin [1968] Director/Lawyer; Adam Charles Frost [1980] Director/Chartered Accountant

AGCO Limited
Incorporated: 24 June 1952 *Employees:* 500
Net Worth: £157,140,992 *Total Assets:* £340,856,992
Registered Office: Abbey Park, Stoneleigh, Kenilworth, Warwicks, CV8 2TQ
Activities: Manufacture of agricultural tractors
Parent: AGCO Manufacturing Limited
Officers: Claire Margaret McGeever-Cattell, Secretary; Adam Charles Frost [1980] Director/Chartered Accountant; Declan Francis Hayden [1953] Director/Marketing Professional [Irish]

AGCO Manufacturing Limited
Incorporated: 14 September 1956
Net Worth: £77,364,000 *Total Assets:* £166,626,000
Registered Office: Abbey Park, Stoneleigh, Kenilworth, Warwicks, CV8 2TQ
Activities: Activities of head offices
Parent: AGCO International Limited
Officers: Roger Neil Batkin, Secretary; Adam Charles Frost [1980] Director/Chartered Accountant; Declan Francis Hayden [1953] Director/Marketing Professional [Irish]

AGCO Services Limited
Incorporated: 24 June 1952
Net Worth: £45,901,120 *Total Assets:* £1,446,155,392
Registered Office: Abbey Park, Stoneleigh, Kenilworth, Warwicks, CV8 2TQ
Activities: Activities of head offices
Parent: AGCO International Limited
Officers: Roger Neil Batkin, Secretary; Adam Charles Frost [1980] Director/Chartered Accountant; Declan Francis Hayden [1953] Director/Marketing Professional [Irish]

AGD Equipment Limited
Incorporated: 3 September 1976 *Employees:* 68
Net Worth: £13,618,593 *Total Assets:* £18,000,116
Registered Office: Avonbrook House, 198 Masons Road, Stratford Enterprise Park, Stratford upon Avon, Warwicks, CV37 9LQ
Activities: Agents involved in the sale of machinery, industrial equipment, ships and aircraft
Officers: Anita Jill Law, Secretary; Elizabeth Ann Law [1968] Director/Communications; Robert William Law [1966] Director; William Housten Law [1937] Director

AGD Holdings Limited
Incorporated: 21 October 1970 *Employees:* 68
Net Worth: £13,626,213 *Total Assets:* £18,000,228
Registered Office: Avonbrook House, 198 Masons Road, Stratford Enterprise Park, Stratford upon Avon, Warwicks, CV37 9LQ
Activities: Non-trading company
Shareholder: William Housten Law
Officers: Anita Jill Law, Secretary; Elizabeth Ann Law [1968] Director; Robert William Law [1966] Director; William Housten Law [1937] Director

Agellus Holdings Limited
Incorporated: 24 June 2015 *Employees:* 213
Net Worth: £8,469,000 *Total Assets:* £16,594,000
Registered Office: Peterbridge House, 3 The Lakes, Northampton, NN4 7HB
Activities: Activities of head offices
Major Shareholder: Rachel Emmaline Harrod
Officers: Mark Anthony Harrod [1963] Director; Malcolm Frank Walton [1961] Director

Agellus Limited
Incorporated: 7 July 2004
Net Worth: £7,983,000 *Total Assets:* £14,077,000
Registered Office: Peterbridge House, 3 The Lakes, Northampton, NN4 7HB
Activities: Activities of head offices
Parent: Agellus Holdings Limited
Officers: Mark Anthony Harrod [1963] Managing Director; Malcolm Frank Walton [1961] Director

Agema Engineering Limited
Incorporated: 11 November 1986 *Employees:* 173
Net Worth: £11,476,765 *Total Assets:* £18,268,906
Registered Office: 21 Bayton Road, Bayton Road Industrial Estate, Exhall, Coventry, Warwicks, CV7 9EL
Activities: Manufacture of other plastic products
Major Shareholder: John Frank Edward Stringer
Officers: Julie Stringer, Secretary; John Frank Edward Stringer [1955] Director/Engineering; Jonathan Stringer [1983] Director

Aggregate Industries Holdings Limited
Incorporated: 12 June 1922
Net Worth: £642,899,968 *Total Assets:* £731,000,000
Registered Office: Bardon Hall, Copt Oak Road, Markfield, Leics, LE67 9PJ
Activities: Activities of construction holding companies
Parent: Holcim Participations (UK) Limited
Officers: Simon Gregory Crossley [1973] Director/Chartered Accountant; David Robert Forder [1965] Director/Manager, Financial Reporting & Planning; Laurent Eric Louis Jaques [1976] Director/CFO Corporate Holdings [Swiss]

Aggregate Industries Limited
Incorporated: 16 December 2005
Net Worth: £306,457,984 *Total Assets:* £376,136,000
Registered Office: Bardon Hall, Copt Oak Road, Markfield, Leics, LE67 9PJ
Activities: Activities of construction holding companies
Parent: Aggregate Industries Holdings Limited
Officers: James Atherton-Ham, Secretary; John Ferguson Bowater [1949] Director/Deputy Group Chief Executive; Guy Charles Edwards [1965] Director

Aggregate Industries UK Limited
Incorporated: 12 February 1930 *Employees:* 3,613
Net Worth: £149,438,000 *Total Assets:* £1,570,253,056
Registered Office: Bardon Hall, Copt Oak Road, Markfield, Leics, LE67 9PJ
Activities: Quarrying of ornamental and building stone, limestone, gypsum, chalk and slate
Parent: Aggregate Industries Limited
Officers: James West Atherton-Ham [1970] Director/Barrister; John Ferguson Bowater [1949] Director/Deputy Group Chief Executive Officer; Guy Charles Edwards [1965] Director; Pablo Libreros [1978] Managing Director, Aggregates [French]

Aghoco 1566 (Bidco) Limited
Incorporated: 27 July 2017 *Employees:* 6
Net Worth Deficit: £1,190,503 *Total Assets:* £53,041,632
Registered Office: The Discovery Building, Biocity, Pennyfoot Street, Nottingham, NG1 1GR
Activities: Research and experimental development on biotechnology
Parent: Aghoco 1578 (Midco) Limited
Officers: Dr Paul Jonathan Clewlow [1959] Director/Chemist; Simon Christopher Hirst [1964] Director; Kevin Jennings Keck [1974] Director [British/American]; Barry Robinson [1979] Director; Victoria Jane Tabiner [1971] Director/Chief Financial Officer; Dr Jonathan Gareth Williams [1963] Director/Chemist

Aghoco 1578 (Midco) Limited
Incorporated: 4 August 2017 *Employees:* 6
Net Worth Deficit: £729,576 *Total Assets:* £47,802,924
Registered Office: The Discovery Building, Biocity, Pennyfoot Street, Nottingham, NG1 1GR
Activities: Research and experimental development on biotechnology
Parent: Aghoco 1579 (Topco) Limited
Officers: Dr Paul Jonathan Clewlow [1959] Director/Chemist; Simon Christopher Hirst [1964] Director; Kevin Jennings Keck [1974] Director [British/American]; Barry Robinson [1979] Director; Victoria Jane Tabiner [1971] Director/Chief Financial Officer; Dr Jonathan Gareth Williams [1963] Director/Chemist

Aghoco 1579 (Topco) Limited
Incorporated: 4 August 2017 *Employees:* 216
Net Worth Deficit: £3,240,892 *Total Assets:* £54,697,252
Registered Office: The Discovery Building, Biocity, Pennyfoot Street, Nottingham, NG1 1GR
Activities: Research and experimental development on biotechnology
Shareholders: Simon Christopher Hirst; Phoenix Equity Partners 2016 Limited Partnership
Officers: Andy Black [1967] Director; Dr Paul Jonathan Clewlow [1959] Director/Chemist; Simon Christopher Hirst [1964] Director; Kevin Jennings Keck [1974] Director [British/American]; Barry Robinson [1979] Director; Victoria Jane Tabiner [1971] Director/Chief Financial Officer; Dr Jonathan Gareth Williams [1963] Director/Chemist

Agilent Technologies Lda UK Limited
Incorporated: 16 December 2013 *Employees:* 388
Net Worth: £82,652,896 *Total Assets:* £134,176,256
Registered Office: 5500 Lakeside, Cheadle Royal Business Park, Cheadle, Cheshire, SK8 3GR
Activities: Other professional, scientific and technical activities n.e.c.
Parent: Agilent Technologies Inc.
Officers: James Philip Wright, Secretary; Paul George Gourlay [1964] Director/Facilities Manager; Neil Watkin Rees [1966] Director/Business Executive; Karen Louise Waddell [1979] Director/HR Manager

Agreserves Limited
Incorporated: 8 July 1994 *Employees:* 15
Net Worth: £19,902,004 *Total Assets:* £25,076,988
Registered Office: Manor Farm, Church End, Woodwalton, Huntingdon, Cambs, PE28 5YU
Activities: Growing of cereals (except rice), leguminous crops and oil seeds
Parent: Farmland Reserve UK Limited
Officers: Paul Allen, Secretary; Benjamin Michael Conway [1980] Director/General Manager; Todd Nelson Jones [1962] Director/Vice President [American]; Don M Sleight [1955] Director/Vice President [American]

Agri-Epi Centre Limited
Incorporated: 18 December 2015 *Employees:* 9
Net Worth: £72,000 *Total Assets:* £23,790,000
Registered Office: Kent House, College Road, Wharley End, Cranfield, Bedford, MK43 0AL
Activities: Other research and experimental development on natural sciences and engineering
Officers: Uilleam Fraser Cameron, Secretary; Professor Richard James Dewhurst [1963] Director/Professor; Susan Elizabeth Furey [1965] Finance Director; Vincent Gillingham [1984] Director; Professor Leon Alexander Terry [1974] Director; William Anderson McColl Thomson [1963] Technical Director

Agrifac UK Ltd
Incorporated: 6 October 1994
Net Worth: £817,219 *Total Assets:* £10,059,294
Registered Office: 4 Thorby Avenue, March, Cambs, PE15 0AZ
Activities: Wholesale of other machinery and equipment
Parent: Agrifac Machinery BV
Officers: Andrew Carse [1986] Director

Agrihold Limited
Incorporated: 10 March 1997 *Employees:* 2
Net Worth: £10,987,069 *Total Assets:* £11,260,101
Registered Office: 64 St James's Street, Nottingham, NG1 6FJ
Activities: Non-trading company
Major Shareholder: Nicholas John Forman Hardy
Officers: Nicholas John Foreman Hardy [1948] Director; Thomas William Bailey Foreman Hardy [1983] Director

Agritec Holdings Limited
Incorporated: 3 March 2016
Net Worth: £15,163,213 *Total Assets:* £20,187,200
Registered Office: 91-97 Saltergate, Chesterfield, Derbys, S40 1LA
Activities: Activities of head offices
Shareholders: Robert Patrick Thornhill; Richard James Thornhill
Officers: Richard Barker [1968] Director; Marcus Nathan Bury [1959] Director; David Alexander Ross Horn [1968] Director; Richard James Thornhill [1954] Director; Robert Patrick Thornhill [1957] Director

Agriturf Holdings Limited
Incorporated: 27 October 1999 *Employees:* 71
Net Worth: £2,216,974 *Total Assets:* £11,263,723
Registered Office: Spalding Road, Sutterton, Boston, Lincs, PE20 2ET
Activities: Activities of head offices
Shareholders: Joseph Robert Ferris Lulham; Nigel Edward Wates
Officers: John Southern, Secretary; John Southern [1961] Finance Director; John William Wates [1957] Director/CS; Nigel Edward Wates [1956] Director

Agrivert (Wallingford) Limited
Incorporated: 16 June 2011 *Employees:* 3
Net Worth: £949,489 *Total Assets:* £9,606,135
Registered Office: The Stables, Radford, Chipping Norton, Oxon, OX7 4EB
Activities: Production of electricity
Parent: Agrivert Biogas Limited
Officers: Gemma Eagle, Secretary; Neil Corrigall [1976] Director; Robert Craig McPheely [1962] Director/Accountant; Andrew Patrick Smith [1960] Director

Agrivert (West London) Limited
Incorporated: 27 November 2012 *Employees:* 3
Net Worth Deficit: £1,916,333 *Total Assets:* £10,006,628
Registered Office: The Stables, Radford, Chipping Norton, Oxon, OX7 4EB
Activities: Production of electricity
Parent: Agrivert Biogas Limited
Officers: Gemma Eagle, Secretary; Neil Corrigall [1976] Director; Robert Craig McPheely [1962] Director/Accountant; Andrew Patrick Smith [1960] Director

Agrivert Biogas Limited
Incorporated: 28 July 2008 *Employees:* 2
Net Worth Deficit: £2,960,081 *Total Assets:* £69,765,568
Registered Office: The Stables, Radford, Chipping Norton, Oxon, OX7 4EB
Activities: Production of electricity
Parent: Agrivert Group Limited
Officers: Gemma Eagle, Secretary; Neil Corrigall [1976] Director; Robert Craig McPheely [1962] Director/Accountant; Andrew Patrick Smith [1960] Director

Agrivert Group Limited
Incorporated: 21 July 2009 *Employees:* 3
Net Worth: £11,138,844 *Total Assets:* £24,432,394
Registered Office: The Stables, Radford, Chipping Norton, Oxon, OX7 4EB
Activities: Activities of head offices
Parent: Agrivert Holdings Limited
Officers: Gemma Eagle, Secretary; Neil Corrigall [1976] Director; Robert Craig McPheely [1962] Director/Accountant; Andrew Patrick Smith [1960] Director

Agrivert Holdings Limited
Incorporated: 18 August 2015 *Employees:* 83
Net Worth: £26,686,456 *Total Assets:* £106,833,928
Registered Office: The Stables, Radford, Chipping Norton, Oxon, OX7 4EB
Activities: Activities of other holding companies n.e.c.
Parent: Severn Trent Green Power Limited
Officers: Gemma Eagle, Secretary; Neil Corrigall [1976] Director; Robert Craig McPheely [1962] Director/Accountant; Andrew Patrick Smith [1960] Director

Agrivert Limited
Incorporated: 6 January 1994 *Employees:* 53
Net Worth: £2,798,277 *Total Assets:* £16,910,436
Registered Office: The Stables, Radford, Chipping Norton, Oxon, OX7 4EB
Activities: Remediation activities and other waste management services
Parent: Agrivert Renewables Limited
Officers: Philip James Earl, Secretary; Philip James Earl [1972] Finance Director; Ralph Buchanan Alexander Maddan [1964] Director; Ronald James McIlwraith [1954] Director; Harry George Waters [1965] Director

Agrovista UK Limited
Incorporated: 11 March 1998 *Employees:* 316
Net Worth: £41,968,000 *Total Assets:* £69,007,000
Registered Office: Rutherford House, Nottingham Science & Technology Park, Nottingham, NG7 2PZ
Activities: Support activities for crop production
Officers: Duncan Leonard Thomas Brown, Secretary; Duncan Leonard Thomas Brown [1965] Director/Chartered Management Accountant; Christopher Clayton [1966] Director; Mutsumi Ishizuki [1958] Director [Japanese]; Yuha Kodaira [1968] Director/General Manager [Japanese]; Takaharu Oda [1968] Director/General Manager [Japanese]; Tsuyoshi Sekita [1977] Director/Businessman [Japanese]

AIAL Limited
Incorporated: 25 September 1998 *Employees:* 149
Previous: Alpha International Accommodation Limited
Net Worth: £686,916 *Total Assets:* £28,786,872
Registered Office: Plantation House, 261-263 Ecclesall Road, Sheffield, S11 8NX
Activities: Travel agency activities
Major Shareholder: Jason Bernard Fry
Officers: Jason Bernard Fry [1971] Director/Tour Operator

Aintree Retail Park Limited
Incorporated: 15 July 1994
Net Worth: £41,325,448 *Total Assets:* £46,612,888
Registered Office: Emerson House, Heyes Lane, Alderley Edge, Cheshire, SK9 7LF
Activities: Development of building projects
Parent: Orbit Investments (Properties) Limited
Officers: Varun Maharaj, Secretary; Anthony Emerson Jones [1967] Director; Mark Emerson Jones [1964] Director; Peter Emerson Jones [1935] Director

The Air Ambulance Service
Incorporated: 25 July 2003 *Employees:* 279
Net Worth: £9,959,000 *Total Assets:* £13,616,000
Registered Office: Blue Skies House, Butlers Leap, Rugby, Warwicks, CV21 3RQ
Activities: General medical practice activities
Officers: Neil John Grant Bandtock [1961] Managing Director; Michael Burgoyne [1949] Director/Retired; Christopher Maxwell Faircliffe [1944] Director/Retired; Philip Holdcroft [1968] Director; Dr Royston Delwyn Jones [1960] Director/Engineer; Peter Robin Whatmore [1973] Director/Strategic Advisor; John Leonard Williams [1947] Director/Accountant

Airbus Helicopters UK Limited
Incorporated: 22 March 1974 *Employees:* 258
Net Worth: £28,373,000 *Total Assets:* £130,161,000
Registered Office: Oxford Airport, Kidlington, Oxon, OX5 1QZ
Activities: Repair and maintenance of aircraft and spacecraft
Officers: Katherine Susan Bennett [1967] Director/Senior Vice President, Public Affairs, Airbus; Colin Arthur James [1968] Managing Director; Fernando Lombo [1969] Director/Head of Finance Europe Region & Spain [Spanish]; Olivier Michalon [1967] Director/Europe Key Regional Manager [French]

Airbus Military UK Limited
Incorporated: 16 April 2012
Net Worth: £1,463,191 *Total Assets:* £18,537,504
Registered Office: Britannia House, Unit 10 West Oxfordshire Business Park, Wavers Ground, Carterton, Oxon, OX18 3YJ
Activities: Manufacture of air and spacecraft and related machinery
Parent: Airbus SE
Officers: Julia Alexis Rose, Secretary; Ian Charles Burrett [1960] Director/Chief Executive Officer; John Michael Rawle [1966] Finance Director

Aircraft Research Association Limited
Incorporated: 22 January 1952 *Employees:* 144
Net Worth: £4,451,475 *Total Assets:* £14,410,782
Registered Office: Manton Lane, Bedford, MK41 7PF
Activities: Other research and experimental development on natural sciences and engineering
Officers: Robert Eric Shribbs, Secretary; Dr John David Dunn [1969] Director/Engineer; Steven Harding [1972] Finance Director; Christopher Stephen Job [1961] Director/Mechanical Engineer; Dr Carl Peter Loller [1958] Director - Advanced Projects; Andrew Terry [1963] Engineering Director IP&S Services; Kevin Young [1964] Engineering Director

The Aire Valley Land LLP
Incorporated: 3 July 2007
Net Worth: £27,296,000 *Total Assets:* £34,452,000
Registered Office: Advantage House, Poplar Way, Catcliffe, Rotherham, S Yorks, S60 5TR

Airline Investments Limited
Incorporated: 20 July 2012 *Employees:* 987
Net Worth: £14,890,000 *Total Assets:* £108,439,000
Registered Office: BMI Regional, Herald Way, East Midlands Airport, Castle Donington, Derbys, DE74 2TU
Activities: Activities of head offices
Shareholders: Stephen William Bond; Peter James Bond
Officers: Anne Fiona Bond [1960] Director; Peter James Bond [1961] Director; Stephen William Bond [1950] Director; Victoria Lee Bond [1964] Director; David Alexander Harrison [1960] Director/Accountant; Alan Adams Murray [1948] Director; Peter Anthony Simpson [1967] Director

Airtanker Finance Limited
Incorporated: 14 June 2007
Net Worth: £230,000 *Total Assets:* £2,482,470,912
Registered Office: Airtanker Hub, RAF Brize Norton, Carterton, Oxon, OX18 3LX
Activities: Other business support service activities n.e.c.
Parent: Airtanker Holdings Limited
Officers: Christopher Adam Brice, Secretary; John Blayney [1964] Director Services Business UK & International; Phillip Scott Blundell [1962] Director; Paul Anthony Craig [1964] Director/Executive Vice President - Defence Services; Rodrigo Caminero Garcia [1970] Director [Spanish]; Karen Veronica Hayzen-Smith [1970] Finance Director; Richard Henry Hine [1959] Commercial Director; Francisco de Borja Segovia Jaquete [1973] Director [Spanish]; Paul Andrew Jayne [1964] Finance Director; Paul Kimberley [1967] Managing Director; Dugald MacTaggart [1963] Director/VP Finance; Stephen Francis McCann [1968] Director Avionics, UK; Neal Gregory Misell [1967] Director; Kenneth John Morrison [1960] Chartered Accountant and Director; Gordon Francis de Courcy Page [1943] Director/Chairman; Didier Jean Luc Plantecoste [1965] Director/Head of MRTT & Airbus Derivatives Programmes [French]

Airtanker Holdings Limited
Incorporated: 14 June 2007
Net Worth Deficit: £287,804,992 *Total Assets:* £2,851,141,120
Registered Office: Airtanker Hub, RAF Brize Norton, Carterton, Oxon, OX18 3LX
Activities: Other business support service activities n.e.c.
Shareholder: Airbus Group SE
Officers: Christopher Adam Brice, Secretary; John Blayney [1964] Director Services Business UK & International; Phillip Scott Blundell [1962] Director; Paul Anthony Craig [1964] Director/Executive Vice President - Defence Services; Rodrigo Caminero Garcia [1970] Director [Spanish]; Karen Veronica Hayzen-Smith [1970] Finance Director; Richard Henry Hine [1959] Commercial Director; Francisco de Borja Segovia Jaquete [1973] Director [Spanish]; Paul Andrew Jayne [1964] Finance Director; Paul Kimberley [1967] Managing Director; Dugald MacTaggart [1963] Director/VP Finance; Stephen Francis McCann [1968] Director Avionics, UK; Neal Gregory Misell [1967] Director; Kenneth John Morrison [1960] Chartered Accountant and Director; Gordon Francis de Courcy Page [1943] Director/Chairman; Didier Jean Luc Plantecoste [1965] Director/Head of MRTT & Airbus Derivatives Programmes [French]

Airtanker Limited
Incorporated: 14 June 2007
Net Worth Deficit: £288,348,000 *Total Assets:* £2,850,868,992
Registered Office: Airtanker Hub, RAF Brize Norton, Carterton, Oxon, OX18 3LX
Activities: Other business support service activities n.e.c.
Parent: Airtanker Holdings Limited
Officers: Christopher Adam Brice, Secretary; John Blayney [1964] Director Services Business UK & International; Phillip Scott Blundell [1962] Director; Paul Anthony Craig [1964] Director/Executive Vice President - Defence Services; Rodrigo Caminero Garcia [1970] Director [Spanish]; Karen Veronica Hayzen-Smith [1970] Finance Director; Richard Henry Hine [1959] Commercial Director; Francisco de Borja Segovia Jaquete [1973] Director [Spanish]; Paul Andrew Jayne [1964] Finance Director; Paul Kimberley [1967] Managing Director; Dugald MacTaggart [1963] Director/VP Finance; Stephen Francis McCann [1968] Director Avionics, UK; Neal Gregory Misell [1967] Director; Kenneth John Morrison [1960] Chartered Accountant and Director; Gordon Francis de Courcy Page [1943] Director/Chairman; Didier Jean Luc Plantecoste [1965] Director/Head of MRTT & Airbus Derivatives Programmes [French]

Airtanker Services Limited
Incorporated: 14 June 2007 *Employees:* 658
Net Worth: £53,808,000 *Total Assets:* £113,542,000
Registered Office: Airtanker Hub, RAF Brize Norton, Carterton, Oxon, OX18 3LX
Activities: Non-scheduled passenger air transport
Shareholder: Airbus Group SE
Officers: Christopher Adam Brice, Secretary; John Blayney [1964] Director Services Business UK & International; Phillip Scott Blundell [1962] Director; Garrett Anthony Copeland [1959] Director of Engineering [Irish]; Paul Anthony Craig [1964] Director/Executive Vice President Defence Services; Javier Rivera Cuadros [1964] Director/Head of Transport and Mission AC Programs [Spanish]; Juan-Luis Corchon Gonzalez [1963] Director/Programme Manager [Spanish]; Karen Veronica Hayzen-Smith [1970] Finance Director; Richard Henry Hine [1959] Commercial Director; Francisco de Borja Segovia Jaquete [1973] Director [Spanish]; Paul Andrew Jayne [1964] Finance Director; Paul Kimberley [1967] Managing Director; Dugald MacTaggart [1963] Director/VP Finance; Stephen Francis McCann [1968] Director Avionics, UK; Neal Gregory Misell [1967] Director; Kenneth John Morrison [1960] Chartered Accountant and Director; Juan Sebastian Montero Yanez [1958] Director/Engineer [Spanish]

Airwair International Limited
Incorporated: 13 January 1995 *Employees:* 598
Net Worth: £130,299,000 *Total Assets:* £169,150,000
Registered Office: Cobbs Lane, Wollaston, Wellingborough, Northants, NN29 7SW
Activities: Wholesale of clothing and footwear
Parent: Martens Airwair Group Limited
Officers: Jon William Mortimore [1967] Director/Chief Financial Officer; Emily Clare Reichwald [1975] Director/General Counsel; Kenneth Charles Wilson [1966] Director

AK Retail Holdings Limited
Incorporated: 10 June 2004 *Employees:* 1,107
Net Worth: £10,133,386 *Total Assets:* £27,529,558
Registered Office: Unit B, Finmere Park, Southgate Road, Orton Southgate, Peterborough, Cambs, PE2 6YG
Activities: Retail sale of clothing in specialised stores
Major Shareholder: Andrew Robert Killingsworth
Officers: David James Preece, Secretary; Andrew Robert Killingsworth [1962] Director; David James Preece [1956] Director; Richard James Thurlow [1955] Director/Chartered Accountant

Geo.Akins (Holdings) Limited
Incorporated: 21 December 1964
Net Worth: £7,717,463 *Total Assets:* £11,492,671
Registered Office: 2 Lace Market Square, Nottingham, NG1 1PB
Activities: Activities of head offices
Officers: Sean Akins, Secretary/Director; George Henry Akins [1974] Director; Sean Akins [1973] Director; David Paul McDerment [1981] Finance Director

Al-Ko Kober Limited
Incorporated: 27 February 1951
Net Worth: £9,523,000 *Total Assets:* £17,006,000
Registered Office: South Warwickshire Business Park, Kineton Road, Southam, Warwicks, CV47 0AL
Activities: Manufacture of other transport equipment n.e.c.
Parent: Al-Ko Kober Holdings Limited
Officers: Peter John Eustace [1962] Director/Engineer; Herr Harald Hiller [1964] Director/Engineer [German]

Alanod Limited
Incorporated: 29 October 1957 *Employees:* 9
Net Worth: £9,192,000 *Total Assets:* £10,678,000
Registered Office: Chippenham Drive, Kingston, Milton Keynes, Bucks, MK10 0AN
Activities: Aluminium production
Officers: Stephen Charles Borrell [1961] Director; Oliver Storbeck [1971] Director [German]

Alauna Renewable Energy Limited
Incorporated: 31 March 2011
Net Worth: £2,797,000 *Total Assets:* £12,432,000
Registered Office: Milton Parc, Milton Ernest, Bedford, MK44 1YU
Activities: Production of electricity
Parent: Biogen EM Limited
Officers: Cathryn Lister [1982] Compliance Director; Simon Musther [1958] Commercial Director; Graeme Kenneth Charles Vincent [1965] Operations Director

Albanwise Limited
Incorporated: 22 March 1978 *Employees:* 91
Net Worth: £300,067,008 *Total Assets:* £821,648,000
Registered Office: Old School House, Fincham Road, Barton Bendish, King's Lynn, Norfolk, PE33 9DL
Activities: Growing of cereals (except rice), leguminous crops and oil seeds
Officers: Janine Grant, Secretary; Luca Rinaldo Contardo Padulli [1955] Director [Italian]

Albumedix Ltd
Incorporated: 29 October 1973 *Employees:* 96
Previous: Novozymes Biopharma UK Limited
Net Worth: £10,747,000 *Total Assets:* £16,125,000
Registered Office: Castle Court, 59 Castle Boulevard, Nottingham, NG7 1FD
Activities: Manufacture of basic pharmaceutical products
Major Shareholder: Peter Rosholm
Officers: Andrew Julian Thorpe, Secretary; Joseph Donald Debethizy [1950] Director/Biotechnology Manager [American]; Jonas Skjodt Moller [1986] Director/Chief Operating Officer [Danish]; Peter Rosholm [1965] Director/Chief Executive [Danish]; Andrew Julian Thorpe [1967] Director/Accountant

ALC (FMC) Limited
Incorporated: 14 April 2005 *Employees:* 96
Net Worth: £463,000 *Total Assets:* £10,069,000
Registered Office: The Sherard Building, Edmund Halley Road, Oxford, OX4 4DQ
Activities: Repair and maintenance of other transport equipment n.e.c.
Parent: ALC (Superholdco) Limited
Officers: Nicholas John Dawson [1961] Investment Director; James Mark Dixon [1962] Director/MD Defence Land; Amanda Lucia Fisher [1963] Managing Director; Asif Ghafoor [1970] Director; Mark David Lawton [1972] Finance Director; Jeremiah Joseph Moloney [1966] Business Director; Robert Hartley Pemberton [1967] Managing Director Equipment Support, Land; Richard Hewitt Taylor [1961] Director; Richard James Ward [1977] Director/Accountant

ALC (SPC) Limited
Incorporated: 14 April 2005
Net Worth: £29,063,000 *Total Assets:* £89,635,000
Registered Office: The Sherard Building, Edmund Halley Road, Oxford, OX4 4DQ
Activities: Other business support service activities n.e.c.
Parent: ALC (Holdco) Limited
Officers: Nicholas John Dawson [1961] Investment Director; James Mark Dixon [1962] Director/MD Defence Land; Louis Javier Falero [1977] Director/Fund Manager; Asif Ghafoor [1970] Director; Mark David Lawton [1972] Finance Director; Robert Hartley Pemberton [1967] Managing Director Equipment Support, Land; Richard Hewitt Taylor [1961] Director; Adam George Waddington [1974] Investment Director

ALC (Superholdco) Limited
Incorporated: 14 April 2005 *Employees:* 96
Net Worth: £26,333,000 *Total Assets:* £89,138,000
Registered Office: The Sherard Building, Edmund Halley Road, Oxford, OX4 4DQ
Activities: Activities of other holding companies n.e.c.
Shareholders: Amey Ventures Investments Limited; Babcock Defence and Security Investments Limited
Officers: Nicholas John Dawson [1961] Investment Director; James Mark Dixon [1962] Director/MD Defence Land; Louis Javier Falero [1977] Director/Fund Manager; Asif Ghafoor [1970] Director; Mark David Lawton [1972] Finance Director; Robert Hartley Pemberton [1967] Managing Director Equipment Support, Land; Richard Hewitt Taylor [1961] Director; Adam George Waddington [1974] Investment Director

Alcaeus Holdings Limited
Incorporated: 8 July 2016 *Employees:* 365
Previous: Project Alcaeus Topco Limited
Net Worth Deficit: £297,540 *Total Assets:* £18,258,394
Registered Office: Paragon House, Wolseley Road, Kempston, Bedford, MK42 7UP
Activities: Non-trading company
Major Shareholder: Christopher Michael Johnson
Officers: Simon Dabson, Secretary; Simon James Dabson [1960] Director; Stephen James Greaves [1964] Director; Christopher Michael Johnson [1956] Director

The Alchemist Bar & Restaurant Limited
Incorporated: 9 July 2009 *Employees:* 607
Net Worth: £5,455,486 *Total Assets:* £22,744,144
Registered Office: The Alchemist, Chadsworth House, Wilmslow Road, Handforth, Cheshire, SK9 3HP
Activities: Licenced restaurants
Parent: Buttercup Bidco Td
Officers: Mark Francis Burville [1976] Operations Director; Simon Potts [1980] Managing Director; Jeremy Kevin Roberts [1962] Director; Victoria Stewart [1980] Finance Director

Alco Estates Limited
Incorporated: 25 February 1950 *Employees:* 2
Net Worth: £11,270,330 *Total Assets:* £12,166,914
Registered Office: Boathouse, Sandhurst Road, Sandilands, Sutton on Sea, Lincs, LN12 2RH
Activities: Construction of domestic buildings
Shareholders: Alexander Graham Guy Henshaw; Judith Margaret Henshaw
Officers: Alexander Graham Guy Henshaw, Secretary; Alexander Graham Guy Henshaw [1943] Director; Judith Margaret Henshaw [1949] Director [Irish]

Alconbury Packing Solutions Limited
Incorporated: 24 July 2015 *Employees:* 3
Net Worth: £11,665 *Total Assets:* £35,466,480
Registered Office: Alconbury Packing Solutions Limited, Enterprise Campus, Alconbury Weald, Huntingdon, Cambs, PE28 4YA
Activities: Other letting and operating of own or leased real estate
Parent: MM Flowers Ltd
Officers: Amalio Fuster Fernandez-Delgado [1980] Director/Lawyer [Spanish]; Andrew James Kirkham [1968] Director; Philip Scott Whelan [1974] Managing Director

F G Alden Limited
Incorporated: 17 September 1937 *Employees:* 95
Net Worth: £6,832,564 *Total Assets:* £11,813,246
Registered Office: Langford Locks, Kidlington, Oxon, OX5 1LJ
Activities: Installation of industrial machinery and equipment
Officers: Michael David Pack, Secretary; Michael Cyril Connolly [1958] Director/Design Engineer; Christopher Jay Marsh [1937] Director/Heating Engineer; Michael Joseph Moore [1963] Director/Chart Engineer; Michael David Pack [1965] Finance Director; Martin James Young [1959] Director/Project Engineer

Aldermore Bank PLC
Incorporated: 10 February 1969 *Employees:* 936
Net Worth: £766,700,032 *Total Assets:* £10,467,399,680
Registered Office: 1st Floor, Block B, Western House, Lynch Wood, Peterborough, Cambs, PE2 6FZ
Activities: Banks
Parent: Aldermore Group PLC
Officers: Marius Van Niekerk, Secretary; Patrick Noel Butler [1960] Director [Irish]; Danuta Gray [1958] Director; John Charles Fortescue Hitchins [1955] Director; Hetash Surendrakumar Kellan [1971] Director [South African]; Christopher James Mack [1971] Director; Phillip Monks [1960] Director; Christine Joan Palmer [1966] Director/Chief Risk Officer; Alan Patrick Pullinger [1965] Director [South African]; Peter Anderson Shaw [1959] Director; Christopher Paul Stamper [1955] Director; Catherine Lucy Turner [1963] Director

Aldi Stores Limited
Incorporated: 25 November 1988 *Employees:* 33,123
Net Worth: £2,525,203,968 *Total Assets:* £4,331,130,880
Registered Office: Holly Lane, Atherstone, Warwicks, CV9 2SQ
Activities: Retail sale in non-specialised stores with food, beverages or tobacco predominating
Officers: Karl Peter Jansen, Secretary; Julie Anne Ashfield [1975] Managing Director - Corporate Buying; Giles Hurley [1975] Director/Chief Executive Officer - UK and Ireland [Irish]; James Hutcheson [1973] Managing Director Finance & Administration; Oliver James King [1978] Group Managing Director; Daniel Ronald [1976] Group Managing Director

Alere as Holdings Limited
Incorporated: 26 July 2011
Net Worth: £184,520,000 *Total Assets:* £261,367,008
Registered Office: Clearblue Innovation Centre, Priory Business Park, Stannard Way, Bedford, MK44 3UP
Activities: Activities of head offices
Parent: Alere International Limited
Officers: David Andrew Bond [1971] Director/Chartered Accountant; Benjamin Edward Oosterbaan [1963] Director/Assistant Treasurer [American]

Alere Limited
Incorporated: 20 April 1983 *Employees:* 43
Net Worth: £5,799,663 *Total Assets:* £9,211,997
Registered Office: Bio-Stat House, Pepper Road, Hazel Grove, Stockport, Cheshire, SK7 5BW
Activities: Manufacture of medical and dental instruments and supplies
Parent: Alere UK Holdings Limited
Officers: Trevor Fellows, Secretary; Tomas Blomquist [1970] Managing Director [Swedish]; Trevor Fellows [1969] Finance Director

Alere Toxicology PLC
Incorporated: 17 March 2005 *Employees:* 464
Net Worth: £20,201,000 *Total Assets:* £106,227,000
Registered Office: 21 Blacklands Way, Abingdon, Oxon, OX14 1DY
Activities: Other professional, scientific and technical activities n.e.c.
Parent: Alere UK Holdings Limited
Officers: Paolo Beato [1961] Director of Information Technology; Nicholas Anthony Breare [1972] Director/Accountant

Alere UK Holdings Limited
Incorporated: 9 August 2001
Net Worth Deficit: £28,013,000 *Total Assets:* £170,150,000
Registered Office: Clearblue Innovation Centre, Priory Business Park, Stannard Way, Bedford, MK44 3UP
Activities: Activities of head offices
Parent: Alere Switzerland GmbH
Officers: David Andrew Bond [1971] Director/Chartered Accountant; Benjamin Edward Oosterbaan [1963] Director/Assistant Treasurer [American]; Brian Gregory Shoup [1969] Director [American]

Alkane Energy CM Limited
Incorporated: 11 February 2016
Net Worth: £1,824,000 *Total Assets:* £15,184,000
Registered Office: First Floor, 500 Pavilion Drive, Northampton Business Park, Northampton, NN4 7YJ
Activities: Production of electricity
Parent: Alkane Energy CM Holdings Limited
Officers: Jacqueline Long, Secretary; Michael Damien Holton [1973] Finance Director; James Huxley Milne [1972] Director/Lawyer; Stephen Shane Pickering [1969] Managing Director

Alkane Energy Limited
Incorporated: 12 September 1994
Previous: Alkane Energy PLC
Net Worth: £20,061,000 *Total Assets:* £22,080,000
Registered Office: First Floor, 500 Pavilion Drive, Northampton Business Park, Northampton, NN4 7YJ
Activities: Production of electricity
Parent: Barbican Bidco Limited
Officers: Jacqueline Long, Secretary; Michael Damien Holton [1973] Finance Director; James Huxley Milne [1972] Director/Lawyer; Stephen Shane Pickering [1969] Managing Director

Alkane Energy UK Limited
Incorporated: 15 November 1995
Net Worth: £16,101,000 *Total Assets:* £39,513,000
Registered Office: First Floor, 500 Pavilion Drive, Northampton Business Park, Northampton, NN4 7YJ
Activities: Production of electricity
Parent: Alkane Energy Limited
Officers: Jacqueline Long, Secretary; Michael Damien Holton [1973] Finance Director; James Huxley Milne [1972] Director/Lawyer; Stephen Shane Pickering [1969] Managing Director

All Assist Limited
Incorporated: 23 February 2017 *Employees:* 215
Net Worth: £1,514,595 *Total Assets:* £12,444,519
Registered Office: 6th Floor, The Hub, 40 Friar Lane, Nottingham, NG1 6DQ
Activities: Activities of head offices
Shareholder: Foresight NFGP Limited as General Partner of Foresight Nottingham Fund LP
Officers: William Alexander Joss [1953] Director and Chairman; Renato Ettore Pastorino [1961] Director [Italian/South African]; Matthew Robert Proudlove [1971] Finance Director; Michael John Quinn [1978] Investor Director; Daniel Milton Smith [1962] Director

Allegheny Technologies Limited
Incorporated: 5 June 1985 *Employees:* 221
Previous: ATI Specialty Materials Limited
Net Worth: £34,298,000 *Total Assets:* £76,828,000
Registered Office: President Way Works, President Way, Sheffield, S4 7UR
Activities: Other business support service activities n.e.c.
Parent: TDY Limited
Officers: Elliot Staub Davis, Secretary; Pamela Margaret Broeker [1953] Director/Executive; Elliot Staub Davis [1961] Director/Company Secretary [American]; Patrick Decourcy [1962] Director/Chief Financial Officer [American]

Allen (Hanford) Limited
Incorporated: 21 June 2000 *Employees:* 42
Net Worth: £11,117,829 *Total Assets:* £18,898,178
Registered Office: North Stoke, Farm North Stoke, Wallingford, Oxon, OX10 6BL
Activities: Mixed farming
Shareholders: Charles Thomas Allen; Geoffery William Allen
Officers: Geoffrey William Allen, Secretary/Farmer; Charles Thomas Allen [1949] Director/Farmer; Edward William Allen [1987] Director/Farmer; Geoffrey William Allen [1956] Director/Farmer; Thomas Charles Allen [1981] Director/Farmer; Michael Montague Strainge [1981] Director/Farmer

Allen Diesels Limited
Incorporated: 18 August 2009 *Employees:* 28
Net Worth: £27,709,290 *Total Assets:* £30,627,280
Registered Office: Sandland Court, Pilgrim Centre, Brickhill Drive, Bedford, MK41 7PZ
Activities: Manufacture of engines and turbines, except aircraft, vehicle and cycle engines
Officers: Roger John Smyth, Secretary; Paul Martin Knight [1964] Director

Allerford Intermediate Newco Limited
Incorporated: 28 July 2010
Net Worth: £39,106,000 *Total Assets:* £74,743,000
Registered Office: Synseal Extrusions Limited, Common Road, Huthwaite, Notts, NG17 6AD
Activities: Activities of head offices
Parent: Allerford Holding Limited
Officers: Leigh Garner Daveran, Secretary; Leigh Garner Daveran [1979] Director; Rolf Peter Adrianus Nuijens [1969] Director/Investor & Advisor [Dutch]; Christian Reiner [1977] Investment Director [Swedish]

Alliance & Leicester Personal Finance Limited
Incorporated: 29 March 1990
Net Worth Deficit: £203,263,008 *Total Assets:* £49,350,000
Registered Office: Building 3, Floor 2, Carlton Park, Narborough, Leicester, LE19 0AL
Activities: Financial intermediation not elsewhere classified
Parent: Santander UK PLC
Officers: Reza Attar-Zadeh [1972] Director; Rachel Jane Morrison [1968] Director/Chartered Accountant; Gavin Raymond White [1977] Director/Chartered Secretary

Alliance Asset Management Limited
Incorporated: 28 September 1995 *Employees:* 44
Net Worth: £3,906,374 *Total Assets:* £22,277,954
Registered Office: 3 Eaton Court, Colmworth Business Park, Eaton Socon, Cambs, PE19 8ER
Activities: Other business support service activities n.e.c.
Major Shareholder: Jeremy Wayne Lavallin
Officers: Catherine Jane Werrett, Secretary; Kevin Joseph Finn [1960] Director; Jeremy Wayne Lavallin [1958] Director; Colin Mather [1963] Director; Catherine Jane Werrett [1972] Director/Accountant

Alliance Medical Acquisitionco Limited
Incorporated: 30 October 2007
Net Worth: £93,557,000 *Total Assets:* £272,132,000
Registered Office: ICENI Centre, Warwick Technology Park, Warwick, CV34 6DA
Activities: Activities of head offices
Parent: Alliance Medical Group Limited
Officers: Guy Edward Blomfield [1967] Director; Nicholas James Burley [1968] Director

Alliance Medical Group Limited
Incorporated: 8 July 2013 *Employees:* 1,779
Net Worth Deficit: £7,700,000 *Total Assets:* £324,400,000
Registered Office: ICENI Centre, Warwick Technology Park, Warwick, CV34 6DA
Activities: Other human health activities
Parent: Life UK Healthcare Limited
Officers: Guy Edward Blomfield [1967] Director; Nicholas James Burley [1968] Director; Adam Mills Pyle [1965] Director [South African]; Petrus Phillippus Van Der Westhuizen [1971] Director [South African]

Alliance Medical Holdings Limited
Incorporated: 23 November 2000 *Employees:* 13
Net Worth: £3,302,000 *Total Assets:* £33,581,000
Registered Office: ICENI Centre, Warwickshire Technology Park, Warwick, CV34 6DA
Activities: Activities of head offices
Parent: Alliance Medical Acquisitionco Limited
Officers: Nicholas James Burley [1968] Finance Director; Howard Alexander David Marsh [1974] Director/Accountant

Alliance Medical Leasing Limited
Incorporated: 30 May 2014
Net Worth Deficit: £1,364,000 *Total Assets:* £70,418,000
Registered Office: ICENI Centre, Warwick Technology Park, Gallows Hill, Warwick, CV34 6DA
Activities: Renting and leasing of other machinery, equipment and tangible goods n.e.c.
Parent: Alliance Medical Acquisitionco Limited
Officers: Mark David Chapman [1972] Managing Director; Edward Henry Lunt [1977] Finance Director; Petrus Phillippus Van Der Westhuizen [1971] Director/Chief Financial Officer [South African]

Alliance Medical Limited
Incorporated: 7 May 1987 *Employees:* 863
Net Worth: £13,579,000 *Total Assets:* £150,962,000
Registered Office: ICENI Centre, Warwick Technology Park, Warwick, CV34 6DA
Activities: Hospital activities
Parent: Alliance Medical Acquisitionco Limited
Officers: Guy Edward Blomfield [1967] Director/Group Chief Operating Officer; Nicholas James Burley [1968] Director/Group Chief Financial Officer; David Gerard James Cahill [1976] Commercial & Operations Director; Mark David Chapman [1972] Managing Director; Edward Henry Lunt [1977] Finance Director; Petrus Phillippus Van Der Westhuizen [1971] Director/Chief Financial Officer [South African]; Peter John Winchester [1971] Director

Alliance Medical Radiopharmacy Limited
Incorporated: 7 October 2002 *Employees:* 50
Net Worth: £18,145,000 *Total Assets:* £25,311,000
Registered Office: ICENI Centre, Warwick Technology Park, Gallows Hill, Warwick, CV34 6DA
Activities: Manufacture of pharmaceutical preparations
Parent: Alliance Medical Limited
Officers: Nicholas James Burley [1968] Director/Chairman; Howard Alexander David Marsh [1974] Director; Petrus Phillippus Van Der Westhuizen [1971] Director/Chief Financial Officer [South African]

Allied Publicity Services (Manchester) Limited
Incorporated: 25 January 1961 *Employees:* 595
Net Worth: £15,034,173 *Total Assets:* £49,978,984
Registered Office: Chetham House, Bird Hall Lane, Stockport, Cheshire, SK3 0ZP
Activities: Other business support service activities n.e.c.
Parent: APS Group Limited
Officers: Gillian Mary Snelson, Secretary; John Holmes [1966] Executive Director; Gillian Mary Snelson [1942] Director/Secretary; Malcolm Snelson [1939] Director/Publicity Contractor; Nicholas John Snelson [1965] Director/Publicity Contractor; Richard Humphrey Snelson [1967] Director/Publicity Contractor

Allied Textile Companies Limited
Incorporated: 23 June 1904 *Employees:* 2
Net Worth: £64,361,000 *Total Assets:* £95,901,000
Registered Office: 1st Floor, 5 Morston Claycliffe Office Park, Whaley Road, Barnsley, S Yorks, S75 1HQ
Activities: Activities of head offices
Parent: Allied Textiles Ltd
Officers: Joanne Grace, Secretary; Joanne Grace [1971] Director/Chartered Accountant; Stewart Robert McGuffie [1968] Director/Chief Executive

Allied Textiles Limited
Incorporated: 7 March 2000 *Employees:* 3
Net Worth: £5,284,000 *Total Assets:* £102,188,000
Registered Office: 1st Floor, 5 Morston Claycliffe Office Park, Whaley Road, Barnsley, S Yorks, S75 1HQ
Activities: Other business support service activities n.e.c.
Parent: Haughton Textiles Ltd
Officers: Joanne Grace, Secretary; Joanne Grace [1971] Director/Chartered Accountant; Stewart Robert McGuffie [1968] Director/Chief Executive

Allington Waste Company Limited
Incorporated: 9 June 2003
Net Worth: £37,837,000 *Total Assets:* £38,161,000
Registered Office: Ground Floor West, 900 Pavilion Drive, Northampton Business Park, Northampton, NN4 7RG
Activities: Other business support service activities n.e.c.
Parent: FCC Environment (UK) Limited
Officers: Carol Jayne Nunn, Secretary; Vicente Federico Orts-Llopis [1962] Director [Spanish]; Paul Taylor [1959] Director/Chief Executive Officer

Allmakes 4 X 4 Limited
Incorporated: 12 July 2006 *Employees:* 95
Net Worth: £2,717,480 *Total Assets:* £12,834,927
Registered Office: 18c Croft Drive, Milton Park, Milton, Abingdon, Oxon, OX14 4RP
Activities: Non-trading company
Major Shareholder: Richard Simon Howe
Officers: Jeremy David Chowns, Secretary; Jeremy David Chowns [1951] Director/Accountant; Richard Simon Howe [1963] Managing Director

Allmakes Limited
Incorporated: 18 May 1977 *Employees:* 95
Net Worth: £5,528,117 *Total Assets:* £14,884,559
Registered Office: 188 Park Drive, Milton Park, Milton, Abingdon, Oxon, OX14 4SR
Activities: Wholesale trade of motor vehicle parts and accessories
Parent: Allmakes 4x4 Limited
Officers: Jeremy David Chowns, Secretary; Jeremy David Chowns [1951] Director/Accountant; Richard Simon Howe [1963] Director/Manager

Alloga UK Limited
Incorporated: 7 March 1996
Previous: Unidrug Distribution Group Limited
Net Worth: £34,143,000 *Total Assets:* £442,500,992
Registered Office: Amber Park, Berristow Lane, South Normanton, Alfreton, Derbys, DE55 2FH
Activities: Wholesale of pharmaceutical goods
Parent: Alliance Boots Holdings Limited
Officers: Lucie Charlotte Massart, Secretary; John Kallend [1959] Director; Julian David Mount [1965] Director; Pablo Rivas Cortes [1972] Director [Spanish]

Alloy Racing Equipment Limited
Incorporated: 16 March 1967 *Employees:* 655
Net Worth: £15,784,000 *Total Assets:* £123,228,000
Registered Office: Loxley House, 2 Oakwood Court, Little Oak Drive, Annesley, Nottingham, NG15 0DR
Activities: Sale of new cars and light motor vehicles
Parent: Stratstone Motor Holdings Limited
Officers: Richard James Maloney, Secretary; Martin Shaun Casha [1960] Director; Trevor Garry Finn [1957] Director; Timothy Paul Holden [1964] Director/Chartered Accountant

Alloy Technologies (UK) Limited
Incorporated: 7 September 1994
Net Worth: £108,349,000 *Total Assets:* £108,349,000
Registered Office: 26a Atlas Way, Sheffield, S4 7QQ
Activities: Casting of other non-ferrous metals
Parent: Arconic Manufacturing (GB) Limited
Officers: Petra Papinniemi-Ainger, Secretary; Dr Kay Louise Dowdall [1969] Director/Accountant; Lluis Maria Fargas Mas [1966] Director/Lawyer [Spanish]

Alltruck PLC
Incorporated: 13 March 2000 *Employees:* 109
Net Worth: £3,363,371 *Total Assets:* £33,926,028
Registered Office: 7 St John Street, Mansfield, Notts, NG18 1QH
Activities: Maintenance and repair of motor vehicles
Shareholders: Paul Grosvenor Robinson; Judith Robinson
Officers: Debbie Ann Halliday, Secretary; Debbie Ann Halliday [1973] Director; Paul Grosvenor Robinson [1963] Director

Allworks Properties Limited
Incorporated: 9 September 1988 *Employees:* 45
Net Worth: £8,414,136 *Total Assets:* £12,037,149
Registered Office: Unit 4 Dene Valley Business Centre, Brookhampton Lane, Kineton, Warwick, CV35 0JD
Activities: Development of building projects
Officers: John Rivers, Secretary; John William Rivers [1951] Director/Builder; Josephine Julia Rivers [1952] Director/Secretary; Alan John Robbins [1953] Director/Quantity Surveyor

Almadon Limited
Incorporated: 30 January 1968 *Employees:* 30
Previous: Greenwoods Stock Boxes Ltd
Net Worth: £33,230,056 *Total Assets:* £37,069,456
Registered Office: Abbeyfield Road, Nottingham, NG7 2TH
Activities: Non-specialised wholesale trade
Shareholders: John Henry Greenwood; Christine Powers
Officers: Andrzej Marian Hausman, Secretary; John Henry Greenwood [1955] Director

Alpha Holdco 1 Limited
Incorporated: 18 March 2015
Net Worth Deficit: £4,432,000 *Total Assets:* £17,394,000
Registered Office: Jarvis House, 157 Sadler Road, Lincoln, LN6 3RS
Activities: Activities of head offices
Parent: Alpha Topco 1 Limited
Officers: Wendy Cope, Secretary; Andrew Iain Cope [1964] Director; Mark Robert Gallimore [1976] Director; Thomas Andrew Jack [1973] Director; Matthew Jubb [1985] Director; Paul Terence Langham [1955] Director; Colin Vaughan McLeod [1950] Director; Andrew James Bruce Young [1963] Finance Director

Alphyra Payment Services Limited
Incorporated: 6 September 2001
Net Worth: £1,417,639 *Total Assets:* £10,758,164
Registered Office: 4th Floor, Highbank House, Exchange Street, Stockport, Cheshire, SK3 0ET
Activities: Other information technology service activities
Officers: Mark Dann [1972] Director; Clive Ian Kahn [1957] Director; James Rupert Lowery [1965] Director; Andrew McCann [1981] Director

Alpine Electronics of U.K. Limited
Incorporated: 2 October 1985 *Employees:* 56
Net Worth: £16,369,000 *Total Assets:* £38,128,000
Registered Office: Alpine House, Fletchamstead Highway, Coventry, Warwicks, CV4 9TW
Activities: Wholesale trade of motor vehicle parts and accessories
Parent: Alpine Electronics Inc.
Officers: Jayesh Odedra, Secretary; Alberto Aramberri [1963] Director [Spanish]; Michael Antony Ford [1952] Director; Yasuhiro Ikeuchi [1957] Director [Japanese]; Shinji Inoue [1959] Director [Japanese]; Jun Wakebe [1968] Managing Director [Japanese]

Alpro (UK) Limited
Incorporated: 5 February 1999 *Employees:* 206
Net Worth: £48,926,000 *Total Assets:* £81,150,000
Registered Office: Latimer Business Park, Altendiez Way, Burton Latimer, Kettering, Northants, NN15 5YT
Activities: Manufacture of fruit and vegetable juice
Parent: Alpro European Holdings S.A.R.L.
Officers: Paul Denayer, Secretary; Paul Denayer [1969] Finance & Administration Director [Belgian]; Sven Lamote [1973] Director [Belgian]; Yves Pellegrino [1965] Director/EVP Finance [French]

ALS Environmental Limited
Incorporated: 21 July 1987 *Employees:* 488
Net Worth: £6,810,000 *Total Assets:* £15,190,000
Registered Office: ALS Environmental Limited, Torrington Avenue, Coventry, Warwicks, CV4 9GU
Activities: Technical testing and analysis
Officers: Neil Spencer Le Fondre, Secretary; Matthew Graham Masters [1973] Director/General Manager, Life Sciences, Western Europe; Rickard Olofsson [1974] Director [Swedish]

Alumasc Exterior Building Products Limited
Incorporated: 22 November 1994 *Employees:* 268
Net Worth: £3,036,000 *Total Assets:* £30,800,000
Registered Office: c/o The Alumasc Group PLC, Station Road, Burton Latimer, Kettering, Northants, NN15 5JP
Activities: Manufacture of metal structures and parts of structures
Parent: The Alumasc Group PLC
Officers: Andrew Magson, Secretary; Graham Paul Hooper [1956] Director/Chief Executive; Gilbert Jackson [1960] Director; Sarah Lee [1979] Director/Group Financial Controller; Andrew Magson [1966] Finance Director; Simon Poe [1975] Product Director; Paul Richard White [1969] Finance Director

The Alumasc Group PLC
Incorporated: 4 November 1983
Net Worth: £24,421,000 *Total Assets:* £74,704,000
Registered Office: Burton Latimer, Kettering, Northants, NN15 5JP
Activities: Activities of head offices
Officers: Helen Ashton, Secretary; David Christopher Armfield [1961] Director; Stephen James Beechey [1968] Director; Graham Paul Hooper [1956] Director/Chief Executive; Andrew Magson [1966] Director; John Stewart McCall [1945] Director/Chairman; Jon Peter Pither [1934] Director; Vijaykumar Champaklal Thakrar [1961] Director

Alumasc Limited
Incorporated: 3 May 1945 *Employees:* 127
Net Worth: £8,987,000 *Total Assets:* £44,007,000
Registered Office: c/o The Alumasc Group PLC, Station Road, Burton Latimer, Kettering, Northants, NN15 5JP
Activities: Manufacture of builders ware of plastic
Parent: The Alumasc Group PLC
Officers: Andrew Magson, Secretary; Peter Burnap [1955] Director; Darren Childs [1969] Finance Director; Simon Hipgrave [1967] Director; Graham Paul Hooper [1956] Director; Michael Leaf [1964] Director; Sarah Lee [1979] Director/Group Financial Controller; Andrew Magson [1966] Finance Director; John Stewart McCall [1945] Director/Chairman & Chief Executive

Alumax U.K. Limited
Incorporated: 11 December 1995
Net Worth: £21,036,000 *Total Assets:* £21,041,000
Registered Office: 26a Atlas Way, Sheffield, S4 7QQ
Activities: Activities of head offices
Parent: Arconic Closure Systems International (UK) Limited
Officers: Petra Papinniemi-Ainger, Secretary; Dr Kay Louise Dowdall [1969] Director/Accountant; Lluis Maria Fargas Mas [1966] Director [Spanish]

Alumet Systems (UK) Limited
Incorporated: 3 August 1992 *Employees:* 126
Net Worth: £3,486,380 *Total Assets:* £11,364,865
Registered Office: Senator House, Bourne End, Kineton Road Industrial Estate, Southam, Warwicks, CV47 0NA
Activities: Manufacture of metal structures and parts of structures
Major Shareholder: Gary Summers
Officers: Damien Bruce Hayward-Bradley, Secretary; Damien Bruce Hayward-Bradley [1976] Finance Director; Laurence McBeth [1958] Director; Steven James Smith [1969] Contracts Director; Blake Sebastian Summers [1986] Operations Director; Gary Summers [1960] Director; Lee Adam Summers [1981] Director

Alvedius Ltd
Incorporated: 15 December 2015 *Employees:* 64
Net Worth: £12,504,196 *Total Assets:* £17,691,094
Registered Office: The Oval, 57 New Walk, Leicester, LE1 7EA
Activities: Activities of other holding companies n.e.c.
Shareholder: Aitma Limited
Officers: Danesh Vinodkumar Gadhia, Secretary; Danesh Vinodkumar Gadhia [1965] Director; Mira Gadhia [1980] Director; Sanjay Kishan Gadhia [1978] Director; Sonal Danesh Gadhia [1969] Director

Alwalton Hill Peterborough LLP
Incorporated: 17 November 2010
Net Worth: £7,353,610 *Total Assets:* £19,753,870
Registered Office: Lumonics House, Valley Drive, Swift Valley Industrial Estate, Rugby, Warwicks, CV21 1TQ

Alycidon Technologies Limited
Incorporated: 15 April 2014 *Employees:* 158
Net Worth Deficit: £1,926,658 *Total Assets:* £14,694,348
Registered Office: 49 Main Road, Smalley, Ilkeston, Derbys, DE7 6EF
Activities: Activities of financial services holding companies
Major Shareholder: Darryl Charles Eales
Officers: Darryl Charles Eales [1960] Director

Amak Property Investments (London) Limited
Incorporated: 17 March 1982 *Employees:* 43
Net Worth: £79,360,656 *Total Assets:* £128,733,808
Registered Office: 20 Coxon Street, Spondon, Derby, DE21 7JG
Activities: Development of building projects
Shareholders: Maria Evangelou; Antonis Evangelou
Officers: Maria Evangelou, Secretary; Antonis Evangelou [1944] Director/Restaurateur; Maria Evangelou [1949] Director/Restaurateur

Amano Enzyme Europe Limited
Incorporated: 9 January 1992 *Employees:* 10
Net Worth: £4,351,070 *Total Assets:* £11,170,634
Registered Office: Roundway House, Cromwell Park, Chipping Norton, Oxon, OX7 5SR
Activities: Wholesale of pharmaceutical goods
Major Shareholder: Motoyuki Amano
Officers: Dr Mitsutaka Nishida, Secretary; Motoyuki Amano [1956] Director/Company Chairman [Japanese]; Kunio Hara [1959] Deputy Administration Director [Japanese]; Kazuhiko Horikawa [1972] Sales Director [Japanese]; Shigeki Kimura [1953] Marketing Director [Japanese]

Ambitions Personnel Limited
Incorporated: 6 February 1992 *Employees:* 89
Net Worth: £1,071,006 *Total Assets:* £12,756,773
Registered Office: 18 Northgate, Sleaford, Lincs, NG34 7BJ
Activities: Other activities of employment placement agencies
Officers: Amanda Ann Watson, Secretary/Recruitment Consultant; Claire Bishop [1968] Director/Recruitment Consultant; Paul Haggar [1956] Director; Amanda Ann Watson [1962] Director/Recruitment Consultant

Ambury Developments Limited
Incorporated: 6 March 2001
Net Worth: £6,105,000 *Total Assets:* £9,060,000
Registered Office: Lancaster House, Lancaster Way, Ermine Business Park, Huntingdon, Cambs, PE29 6XU
Activities: Development of building projects
Parent: AWG Property Limited
Officers: Elizabeth Ann Horlock Clarke, Secretary; John Francis Cormie [1958] Director; James Raymond Tilbrook [1973] Director/Surveyor

Amega Sciences PLC
Incorporated: 14 August 1984 *Employees:* 44
Net Worth: £9,580,225 *Total Assets:* £12,999,733
Registered Office: 17 Lanchester Way, Royal Oak Industrial Estate, Daventry, Northants, NN11 8PH
Activities: Manufacture of other chemical products n.e.c.
Parent: Amega Sciences Holdings Limited
Officers: Marco Rietveld [1975] Director [Dutch]; Stephen Squires [1966] Director

The Ames Companies UK Ltd.
Incorporated: 9 June 2017 *Employees:* 46
Net Worth Deficit: £454,432 *Total Assets:* £11,202,576
Registered Office: The Old Airfield, Heck and Pollington Lane, Pollington, E Yorks, DN14 0BA
Activities: Non-trading company
Parent: Griffon Corporation
Officers: Anthony Neil Harker [1969] Director; Brian Gerard Harris [1969] Director/SVP, CFO [American]; Simon Andrew Hupfeld [1976] Director/Chief Executive Officer [Australian]; Dale Elizabeth McGrath [1961] Director/Chief Financial Operator [Australian/American]; Robert Francis Mehmel [1962] Director/Business Executive [American]

Ametek (GB) Limited
Incorporated: 18 December 1990 *Employees:* 82
Previous: Lloyd Instruments Limited
Net Worth: £18,344,000 *Total Assets:* £21,271,000
Registered Office: P O Box 36, 2 New Star Road, Leicester, LE4 9JQ
Activities: Manufacture of electronic measuring, testing etc. equipment, not for industrial process control
Parent: Ametek Instruments Group UK Limited
Officers: Joy Atwell, Secretary; Alain Ponsot [1963] Managing Director [French]; Emanuela Speranza [1968] Director/Vice President/General Manager EMEA, India [Italian]; Bruce Peter Wilson [1956] Director; Pietro Luigi Enrico Zetti [1968] Finance Director [Italian]

Ametek Aerospace and Defense Group UK Limited
Incorporated: 13 December 2012 *Employees:* 1
Net Worth: £106,538,000 *Total Assets:* £131,210,000
Registered Office: P O Box 36, 2 New Star Road, Leicester, LE4 9JQ
Activities: Activities of head offices
Parent: EMA Holdings UK Limited
Officers: Joy Atwell, Secretary; Bruce Peter Wilson [1956] Director

Ametek Airtechnology Group Limited
Incorporated: 28 September 1951 *Employees:* 256
Net Worth: £37,202,000 *Total Assets:* £46,717,000
Registered Office: P O Box 36, 2 New Star Road, Leicester, LE4 9JQ
Activities: Machining
Parent: Ametek Aerospace and Defense Group UK Limited
Officers: Joy Atwell, Secretary; Sheraz Ahmed [1978] Managing Director; Pietro Luigi Enrico Zetti [1968] Finance Director [Italian]

Ametek European Holdings Limited
Incorporated: 5 October 2010 *Employees:* 2
Net Worth: £677,078,976 *Total Assets:* £1,102,743,040
Registered Office: P O Box 36, 2 New Star Road, Leicester, LE4 9JQ
Activities: Activities of head offices
Parent: Ametek Inc
Officers: Joy Atwell, Secretary; Emanuela Speranza [1968] Director/Vice President/General Manager EMEA, India [Italian]; Bruce Peter Wilson [1956] Director

Amey Belfast Schools Partnership Hold Co Limited
Incorporated: 31 January 2008
Net Worth Deficit: £17,725,000 *Total Assets:* £108,656,000
Registered Office: The Sherard Building, Edmund Halley Road, Oxford, OX4 4DQ
Activities: Activities of other holding companies n.e.c.
Parent: Amey Ventures Investments Limited
Officers: John Gerard Connelly [1960] Director/Head of Investment Management; Erwan Fouris [1972] Director [French]; Katherine Anne Louise Pearman [1961] Director/Chartered Accountant; Angela Louise Roshier [1975] Director

Amey Belfast Schools Partnership PFI Co Limited
Incorporated: 31 January 2008
Net Worth Deficit: £17,725,000 *Total Assets:* £108,656,000
Registered Office: The Sherard Building, Edmund Halley Road, Oxford, OX4 4DQ
Activities: Management of real estate on a fee or contract basis
Parent: Amey Belfast Schools Partnership Hold Co Limited
Officers: John Gerard Connelly [1960] Director/Head of Investment Management; Erwan Fouris [1972] Director [French]; Katherine Anne Louise Pearman [1961] Director/Chartered Accountant; Angela Louise Roshier [1975] Director

Amey Birmingham Highways Limited
Incorporated: 2 November 2009
Net Worth Deficit: £43,983,000 *Total Assets:* £280,692,000
Registered Office: The Sherard Building, Edmund Halley Road, Oxford, OX4 4DQ
Activities: Other transportation support activities
Parent: Amey Birmingham Highways Holdings Limited
Officers: Paul Ellis Gill [1975] Director/Investment Manager; Alan Graham Hugh Gullan [1960] Director; Sion Laurence Jones [1974] Director; Richard Daniel Knight [1974] Operations Director; Murdoch Lang McKillop [1947] Director

Amey Community Limited
Incorporated: 3 December 1990
Net Worth: £52,086,000 *Total Assets:* £173,544,000
Registered Office: The Sherard Building, Edmund Halley Road, Oxford, OX4 4DQ
Activities: General cleaning of buildings
Parent: Amey PLC
Officers: Amanda Lucia Fisher [1963] Director/MD Facilities Management, Defence and Justice; Andrew Lee Milner [1969] Director/Chartered Civil Engineer; Andrew Latham Nelson [1959] Director; Richard James Ward [1977] Director/Accountant

Amey Defence Services (Housing) Limited
Incorporated: 19 April 2005 *Employees:* 591
Previous: Carillionamey (Housing Prime) Limited
Net Worth: £14,085,401 *Total Assets:* £56,414,452
Registered Office: The Sherard Building, Edmund Halley Road, Oxford, OX4 4DQ
Activities: Other service activities n.e.c.
Parent: Enterprise Managed Services Limited
Officers: Amanda Lucia Fisher [1963] Managing Director; Nicholas David Maggs [1967] Director; Richard James Ward [1977] Finance Director

Amey Defence Services Limited
Incorporated: 19 April 2005 *Employees:* 950
Previous: Carillionamey Limited
Net Worth: £15,967,024 *Total Assets:* £98,574,280
Registered Office: The Sherard Building, Edmund Halley Road, Oxford, OX4 4DQ
Activities: Other service activities n.e.c.
Parent: Enterprise Managed Services Limited
Officers: Amanda Lucia Fisher [1963] Managing Director; Nicholas David Maggs [1967] Director; Richard James Ward [1977] Finance Director

Amey Finance Services Limited
Incorporated: 16 December 2015
Net Worth: £1,881,000 *Total Assets:* £17,713,000
Registered Office: The Sherard Building, Edmund Halley Road, Oxford, OX4 4DQ
Activities: Other activities auxiliary to insurance and pension funding
Parent: Amey PLC
Officers: Andrew Lee Milner [1969] Director/Chartered Engineer; Andrew Latham Nelson [1959] Director

Amey Fleet Services Limited
Incorporated: 21 December 1948
Net Worth: £48,265,000 *Total Assets:* £77,730,000
Registered Office: The Sherard Building, Edmund Halley Road, Oxford, OX4 4DQ
Activities: Renting and leasing of cars and light motor vehicles
Parent: Amey PLC
Officers: Nicola Ruth Hindle [1976] Finance Director; Andrew Lee Milner [1969] Director/Chartered Civil Engineer; Andrew Latham Nelson [1959] Director

Amey Group Information Services Limited
Incorporated: 10 January 2001
Net Worth: £5,866,000 *Total Assets:* £23,156,000
Registered Office: The Sherard Building, Edmund Halley Road, Oxford, OX4 4DQ
Activities: Other information technology service activities
Parent: Amey PLC
Officers: Andrew Lee Milner [1969] Director/Chartered Engineer; Andrew Latham Nelson [1959] Director

Amey Group Services Limited
Incorporated: 31 March 1999
Net Worth: £25,135,000 *Total Assets:* £156,100,992
Registered Office: The Sherard Building, Edmund Halley Road, Oxford, OX4 4DQ
Activities: Other business support service activities n.e.c.
Parent: Amey PLC
Officers: Andrew Lee Milner [1969] Director/Chartered Engineer; Andrew Latham Nelson [1959] Director

Amey Hallam Highways Holdings Limited
Incorporated: 27 June 2012
Net Worth Deficit: £46,690,000 *Total Assets:* £267,712,000
Registered Office: The Sherard Building, Edmund Halley Road, Oxford, OX4 4DQ
Activities: Activities of other holding companies n.e.c.
Shareholders: Amey Ventures Asset Holdings Limited; Aberdeen Infrastructure Investments (No 5) Limited; Equitix Highways 2 Limited
Officers: Philip Peter Ashbrook [1960] Director; John Gerard Connelly [1960] Director/Head of Investment Management; Asif Ghafoor [1970] Director; Paul Ellis Gill [1975] Director/Investment Manager; Sion Laurence Jones [1974] Director; Richard Daniel Knight [1974] Operations Director

Amey Hallam Highways Limited
Incorporated: 27 June 2012
Net Worth Deficit: £46,690,000 *Total Assets:* £267,712,000
Registered Office: The Sherard Building, Edmund Halley Road, Oxford, OX4 4DQ
Activities: Management of real estate on a fee or contract basis
Parent: Amey Hallam Highways Holdings Limited
Officers: Philip Peter Ashbrook [1960] Director; John Gerard Connelly [1960] Director/Head of Investment Management; Asif Ghafoor [1970] Director; Paul Ellis Gill [1975] Director/Investment Manager; Sion Laurence Jones [1974] Director; Richard Daniel Knight [1974] Operations Director

Amey Highways Limited
Incorporated: 22 May 2008
Net Worth Deficit: £18,657,000 *Total Assets:* £19,906,000
Registered Office: The Sherard Building, Edmund Halley Road, Oxford, OX4 4DQ
Activities: Other engineering activities
Parent: Amey PLC
Officers: James Stefan Haluch [1969] Highways Managing Director; Nicola Ruth Hindle [1976] Finance Director; Andrew Lee Milner [1969] Director/Chartered Civil Engineer; Andrew Latham Nelson [1959] Director

Amey Holdings Limited
Incorporated: 27 April 2005 *Employees:* 16,981
Previous: Enterprise-Peterborough Limited
Net Worth: £247,684,000 *Total Assets:* £1,869,203,968
Registered Office: Amey, The Sherard Building, Edmund Halley Road, Oxford, OX4 4DQ
Activities: Activities of other holding companies n.e.c.
Parent: Amey UK PLC
Officers: Andrew Lee Milner [1969] Director/Chartered Engineer; Andrew Latham Nelson [1959] Director

Amey Investments Limited
Incorporated: 5 November 2009
Net Worth: £5,244,000 *Total Assets:* £17,240,000
Registered Office: The Sherard Building, Edmund Halley Road, Oxford, OX4 4DQ
Activities: Other business support service activities n.e.c.
Parent: Amey PLC
Officers: John Gerard Connelly [1960] Director/Head of Investment Management; Asif Ghafoor [1970] Director; Andrew Lee Milner [1969] Director/Chartered Engineer; Andrew Latham Nelson [1959] Director

Amey LG Limited
Incorporated: 10 August 1998
Net Worth Deficit: £148,644,992 *Total Assets:* £320,791,008
Registered Office: The Sherard Building, Edmund Halley Road, Oxford, OX4 4DQ
Activities: Other business support service activities n.e.c.
Parent: Amey PLC
Officers: James Stefan Haluch [1969] Highways Managing Director; Nicola Ruth Hindle [1976] Finance Director; Andrew Lee Milner [1969] Director/Chartered Civil Engineer; Andrew Latham Nelson [1959] Director

Amey Lighting (Norfolk) Holdings Limited
Incorporated: 28 August 2007
Net Worth Deficit: £8,393,000 *Total Assets:* £34,704,000
Registered Office: The Sherard Building, Edmund Halley Road, Oxford, OX4 4DQ
Activities: Activities of other holding companies n.e.c.
Parent: Amey Ventures Investments Limited
Officers: Neeti Mukundrai Anand [1984] Director; Asif Ghafoor [1970] Director; Katherine Anne Louise Pearman [1961] Director/Chartered Accountant; Adam George Waddington [1974] Investment Director

Amey Lighting (Norfolk) Limited
Incorporated: 28 August 2007
Net Worth Deficit: £8,393,000 *Total Assets:* £34,704,000
Registered Office: The Sherard Building, Edmund Halley Road, Oxford, OX4 4DQ
Activities: Other business support service activities n.e.c.
Parent: Amey Lighting (Norfolk) Holdings Limited
Officers: Neeti Mukundrai Anand [1984] Director; Asif Ghafoor [1970] Director; Katherine Anne Louise Pearman [1961] Director/Chartered Accountant; Adam George Waddington [1974] Investment Director

Amey LUL 2 Limited
Incorporated: 27 November 2002
Net Worth: £94,693,000 *Total Assets:* £113,539,000
Registered Office: The Sherard Building, Edmund Halley Road, Oxford, OX4 4DQ
Activities: Urban and suburban passenger railway transportation by underground, metro and similar systems
Parent: Amey Tube Limited
Officers: Andrew Lee Milner [1969] Director/Chartered Civil Engineer; Andrew Latham Nelson [1959] Director

Amey Metering Limited
Incorporated: 27 November 1995
Net Worth: £7,385,000 *Total Assets:* £46,923,000
Registered Office: The Sherard Building, Edmund Halley Road, Oxford, OX4 4DQ
Activities: Other business support service activities n.e.c.
Parent: Enterprise Managed Services Limited
Officers: Darren Simon Jones [1973] Finance Director; David Michael McLoughlin [1962] Managing Director; Andrew Lee Milner [1969] Director/Chartered Engineer; Andrew Latham Nelson [1959] Finance Director

Amey OW Limited
Incorporated: 13 June 1985
Net Worth: £43,834,000 *Total Assets:* £130,429,000
Registered Office: The Sherard Building, Edmund Halley Road, Oxford, OX4 4DQ
Activities: Engineering related scientific and technical consulting activities
Parent: Amey OW Group Limited
Officers: James Stefan Haluch [1969] Highways Director; Nicola Ruth Hindle [1976] Finance Director; Andrew Lee Milner [1969] Director/Chartered Civil Engineer; Andrew Latham Nelson [1959] Director

Amey OWR Limited
Incorporated: 9 March 1995
Net Worth: £42,897,000 *Total Assets:* £130,374,000
Registered Office: The Sherard Building, Edmund Halley Road, Oxford, OX4 4DQ
Activities: Engineering related scientific and technical consulting activities
Parent: Amey OW Group Limited
Officers: Nicola Ruth Hindle [1976] Finance Director; Andrew Lee Milner [1969] Director/Chartered Civil Engineer; Andrew Latham Nelson [1959] Director

Amey PLC
Incorporated: 4 May 1989
Net Worth: £176,630,000 *Total Assets:* £1,308,209,024
Registered Office: The Sherard Building, Edmund Halley Road, Oxford, OX4 4DQ
Activities: Activities of head offices
Parent: Amey Holdings Limited
Officers: Jayne Satoshi Bowie, Secretary; Andres Camacho Donezar [1976] Director [Spanish]; Alfredo Garcia [1971] Director/Lawyer [Spanish]; Fernando Gonzalez de Canales Moyano [1965] Financial Director [Spanish]; Carol Hui [1956] Director/Lawyer; Fidel Lopez Soria [1967] Director [Spanish]; Andrew Lee Milner [1969] Director/Chartered Civil Engineer; Andrew Latham Nelson [1959] Director; Ian Paul Tyler [1960] Director

Amey Power Services Limited
Incorporated: 10 February 2005
Net Worth: £10,217,000 *Total Assets:* £54,415,000
Registered Office: The Sherard Building, Edmund Halley Road, Oxford, OX4 4DQ
Activities: Other specialised construction activities n.e.c.
Parent: Enterprise Managed Services Limited
Officers: Darren Simon Jones [1973] Finance Director; Nicholas David Maggs [1967] Operations Director; David Michael McLoughlin [1962] Managing Director; Andrew Lee Milner [1969] Director/Chartered Engineer; Andrew Latham Nelson [1959] Finance Director

Amey Programme Management Limited
Incorporated: 30 March 2000
Net Worth: £2,633,000 *Total Assets:* £31,470,000
Registered Office: The Sherard Building, Edmund Halley Road, Oxford, OX4 4DQ
Activities: Other business support service activities n.e.c.
Parent: Amey PLC
Officers: Andrew Lee Milner [1969] Director/Chartered Engineer; Andrew Latham Nelson [1959] Director

Amey Rail Limited
Incorporated: 28 November 1994
Net Worth: £34,185,000 *Total Assets:* £145,967,008
Registered Office: The Sherard Building, Edmund Halley Road, Oxford, OX4 4DQ
Activities: Construction of railways and underground railways
Parent: Amey PLC
Officers: Nicola Ruth Hindle [1976] Finance Director; Andrew Lee Milner [1969] Director/Chartered Civil Engineer; Andrew Latham Nelson [1959] Director

Amey Services Limited
Incorporated: 1 June 1990 *Employees:* 15,999
Net Worth: £116,971,000 *Total Assets:* £191,682,000
Registered Office: The Sherard Building, Edmund Halley Road, Oxford, OX4 4DQ
Activities: Human resources provision and management of human resources functions
Parent: Amey PLC
Officers: Andrew Lee Milner [1969] Director/Chartered Engineer; Andrew Latham Nelson [1959] Director

Amey UK PLC
Incorporated: 16 April 2003 *Employees:* 16,981
Net Worth: £250,452,000 *Total Assets:* £1,884,103,040
Registered Office: The Sherard Building, Edmund Halley Road, Oxford, OX4 4DQ
Activities: Activities of head offices
Officers: Jayne Satoshi Bowie, Secretary; Andres Camacho Donezar [1976] Director [Spanish]; Alfredo Garcia [1971] Director/Lawyer [Spanish]; Fernando Gonzalez de Canales Moyano [1965] Financial Director [Spanish]; Carol Hui [1956] Director/Lawyer; Fidel Lopez Soria [1967] Director [Spanish]; Andrew Lee Milner [1969] Director/Chartered Civil Engineer; Andrew Latham Nelson [1959] Director; Ian Paul Tyler [1960] Director

Amey Utility Services Limited
Incorporated: 30 January 1991
Net Worth: £2,818,000 *Total Assets:* £154,235,008
Registered Office: The Sherard Building, Edmund Halley Road, Oxford, OX4 4DQ
Activities: Other business support service activities n.e.c.
Parent: A.R.M Services Group Limited
Officers: Darren Simon Jones [1973] Finance Director; David Michael McLoughlin [1962] Managing Director; Andrew Lee Milner [1969] Director/Chartered Engineer; Andrew Latham Nelson [1959] Finance Director

Amey Ventures Asset Holdings Limited
Incorporated: 5 November 2009
Net Worth: £12,067,000 *Total Assets:* £56,633,000
Registered Office: The Sherard Building, Edmund Halley Road, Oxford, OX4 4DQ
Activities: Activities of other holding companies n.e.c.
Parent: Amey Investments Limited
Officers: John Gerard Connelly [1960] Director/Head of Investment Management; Asif Ghafoor [1970] Director; Andrew Lee Milner [1969] Director/Chartered Civil Engineer; Andrew Latham Nelson [1959] Director

Amey Ventures Investments Limited
Incorporated: 17 April 2003
Net Worth Deficit: £34,873,000 *Total Assets:* £184,158,000
Registered Office: The Sherard Building, Edmund Halley Road, Oxford, OX4 4DQ
Activities: Activities of other holding companies n.e.c.
Parent: DIF Infra JV UK Ltd
Officers: Neeti Mukundrai Anand [1984] Director; John Gerard Connelly [1960] Director/Head of Investment Management; Asif Ghafoor [1970] Director; Helen Mary Murphy [1981] Associate Director [Irish]

Amey Ventures Limited
Incorporated: 20 February 2001
Net Worth: £12,052,000 *Total Assets:* £15,337,000
Registered Office: The Sherard Building, Edmund Halley Road, Oxford, OX4 4DQ
Activities: Activities of other holding companies n.e.c.
Parent: Amey PLC
Officers: John Gerard Connelly [1960] Director/Head of Investment Management; Asif Ghafoor [1970] Director; Andrew Lee Milner [1969] Director/Chartered Engineer; Andrew Latham Nelson [1959] Director

Amey Ventures Management Services Limited
Incorporated: 5 November 2009
Net Worth: £1,143,000 *Total Assets:* £22,986,000
Registered Office: The Sherard Building, Edmund Halley Road, Oxford, OX4 4DQ
Activities: Activities of other holding companies n.e.c.
Parent: Amey Investments Limited
Officers: John Gerard Connelly [1960] Director/Head of Investment Management; Asif Ghafoor [1970] Director; Andrew Lee Milner [1969] Director/Chartered Engineer; Andrew Latham Nelson [1959] Director

AmeyCespa (AWRP) Holding Co Limited
Incorporated: 3 October 2013
Net Worth Deficit: £10,879,000 *Total Assets:* £335,423,008
Registered Office: The Sherard Building, Edmund Halley Road, Oxford, OX4 4DQ
Activities: Activities of other holding companies n.e.c.
Shareholders: Aberdeen Infrastructure Investments (No 5) Limited; Equitix Concessions 3 Ltd
Officers: Nicholas Tommy Cole [1978] Investment Director; John Gerard Connelly [1960] Director/Head of Investment Management; Fabio D'Alonzo [1976] Commercial Director [Italian]; Asif Ghafoor [1970] Director; Richard Daniel Knight [1974] Operations Director; Edward Arthur Wilson [1965] Director/Chief Investment Officer

AmeyCespa (AWRP) SPV Limited
Incorporated: 3 October 2013
Net Worth Deficit: £10,879,000 *Total Assets:* £335,423,008
Registered Office: The Sherard Building, Edmund Halley Road, Oxford, OX4 4DQ
Activities: Other business support service activities n.e.c.
Parent: AmeyCespa (AWRP) Holding Co Limited
Officers: Nicholas Tommy Cole [1978] Investment Director; John Gerard Connelly [1960] Director/Head of Investment Management; Fabio D'Alonzo [1976] Commercial Director [Italian]; Asif Ghafoor [1970] Director; Richard Daniel Knight [1974] Operations Director; Katherine Anne Louise Pearman [1961] Director/Chartered Accountant; Edward Arthur Wilson [1965] Director/Chief Investment Officer

AmeyCespa (East) Limited
Incorporated: 10 July 1969
Net Worth: £8,922,000 *Total Assets:* £53,630,000
Registered Office: The Sherard Building, Edmund Halley Road, Oxford, OX4 4DQ
Activities: Other business support service activities n.e.c.
Parent: AmeyCespa (East) Holdings Limited
Officers: John Gerard Connelly [1960] Director/Head of Investment Management; Asif Ghafoor [1970] Director; Francisco Hevia Gonzalez [1974] Director [Spanish]

AmeyCespa (MK) Holding Co Limited
Incorporated: 21 May 2013
Net Worth Deficit: £6,889,000 *Total Assets:* £135,712,000
Registered Office: The Sherard Building, Edmund Halley Road, Oxford, OX4 4DQ
Activities: Activities of other holding companies n.e.c.
Shareholders: Amey Ventures Asset Holdings Limited; Cespa Ventures Limited
Officers: John Gerard Connelly [1960] Director/Head of Investment Management; Asif Ghafoor [1970] Director; Francisco Hevia Gonzalez [1974] Director [Spanish]

AmeyCespa (MK) ODC Limited
Incorporated: 21 May 2013
Net Worth Deficit: £40,837,000 *Total Assets:* £9,861,000
Registered Office: The Sherard Building, Edmund Halley Road, Oxford, OX4 4DQ
Activities: Treatment and disposal of non-hazardous waste
Parent: AmeyCespa Limited
Officers: Francisco Hevia Gonzalez [1974] Director [Spanish]; Olga Redondo [1975] Finance Director [Spanish]

AmeyCespa (MK) SPV Limited
Incorporated: 21 May 2013
Net Worth Deficit: £6,889,000 *Total Assets:* £135,712,000
Registered Office: The Sherard Building, Edmund Halley Road, Oxford, OX4 4DQ
Activities: Other business support service activities n.e.c.
Parent: AmeyCespa (MK) Holding Co Limited
Officers: John Gerard Connelly [1960] Director/Head of Investment Management; Asif Ghafoor [1970] Director; Francisco Hevia Gonzalez [1974] Director [Spanish]

AmeyCespa Limited
Incorporated: 2 August 2010
Net Worth Deficit: £16,168,000 *Total Assets:* £54,206,000
Registered Office: The Sherard Building, Edmund Halley Road, Oxford, OX4 4DQ
Activities: Activities of head offices
Shareholders: Amey LG Limited; Cespa UK Limited
Officers: Asif Ghafoor [1970] Director; Francisco Hevia Gonzalez [1974] Director [Spanish]; Andrew Lee Milner [1969] Director/Chartered Engineer

AmeyCespa WM (East) Limited
Incorporated: 16 January 2007
Net Worth: £1,528,000 *Total Assets:* £103,279,000
Registered Office: The Sherard Building, Edmund Halley Road, Oxford, OX4 4DQ
Activities: Other business support service activities n.e.c.
Parent: AmeyCespa Services (East) Limited
Officers: John Gerard Connelly [1960] Director/Head of Investment Management; Asif Ghafoor [1970] Director; Francisco Hevia Gonzalez [1974] Director [Spanish]

AMG Alpoco UK Limited
Incorporated: 28 August 1969 *Employees:* 54
Net Worth: £6,300,494 *Total Assets:* £17,215,672
Registered Office: c/o AMG Superalloys UK Limited, Fullerton Road, Rotherham, S Yorks, S60 1DL
Activities: Aluminium production
Parent: AMG Superalloys UK Limited
Officers: Timothy Robyn Charles Palmer, Secretary; Kevin Lawson [1968] Managing Director; Leonora Maria Scaife [1971] Finance Director

AMG Aluminum UK Limited
Incorporated: 25 October 2012 *Employees:* 68
Net Worth: £8,720,426 *Total Assets:* £22,035,756
Registered Office: c/o AMG, Fullerton Road, Rotherham, S Yorks, S60 1DL
Activities: Aluminium production
Parent: AMG Advanced Metallurgical Group Investment B.V.
Officers: Timothy Robyn Charles Palmer, Secretary; Eric Emil Jackson [1952] Director/General Manager [American]; Kevin Lawson [1968] Director/General Manager; Leonora Maria Scaife [1971] Director/Chartered Accountant

AMG Superalloys UK Limited
Incorporated: 15 October 1938 *Employees:* 180
Net Worth: £61,810,576 *Total Assets:* £94,003,800
Registered Office: AMG Superalloys UK Limited, Fullerton Road, Rotherham, S Yorks, S60 1DL
Activities: Manufacture of other chemical products n.e.c.
Parent: AMG Advanced Metallurgical Group Invest BV
Officers: Timothy Robyn Charles Palmer, Secretary; Jackson Maddux Dunckel [1964] Director [American]; Eric Emil Jackson [1952] Director/Company President [American]; Kevin Lawson [1968] Managing Director; Leonora Maria Scaife [1971] Finance Director; Dennis Richard Shea [1963] Director [American]

Amnack Limited
Incorporated: 27 February 1996 *Employees:* 110
Net Worth: £1,221,980 *Total Assets:* £21,782,600
Registered Office: Millfield Industrial Estate, Arksey Lane, Bentley, Doncaster, S Yorks, DN5 0SJ
Activities: Manufacture of other electronic and electric wires and cables
Officers: Terence Guest [1957] Director; Christopher Cyril Mallinson [1947] Director/General Manager; Neil Mallinson [1971] Managing Director; Valentin Parisi [1964] Director/Accountant [French]

Don Amott Parks Limited
Incorporated: 22 July 1963 *Employees:* 79
Net Worth: £9,831,544 *Total Assets:* £12,499,099
Registered Office: Lakeside Park, North Somercotes, Louth, Lincs, LN11 7RB
Activities: Sale of new cars and light motor vehicles
Major Shareholder: Donald Keith Amott
Officers: Donald Keith Amott, Secretary; Donald Keith Amott [1949] Director/Manager; Richard James Bestwick [1978] Director; Samantha Claire Heap [1969] Director

AMPY Holdings Limited
Incorporated: 6 June 1996
Net Worth: £178,717,872 *Total Assets:* £178,723,760
Registered Office: 1 Lysander Drive, Northfields Industrial Estate, Market Deeping, Peterborough, PE6 8FB
Activities: Non-trading company
Parent: Landis + Gyr Holdco 2 LLC
Officers: Stephen George Cunningham [1966] Director/Chief Executive Officer; Charles Philip Walker [1972] Director/Chief Financial Officer

Amscan International Limited
Incorporated: 7 August 1973 *Employees:* 140
Net Worth: £13,494,000 *Total Assets:* £46,771,000
Registered Office: Brudenell Drive, Brinklow, Milton Keynes, Bucks, MK10 0DA
Activities: Non-specialised wholesale trade
Officers: Joseph Francis Hennigan [1983] Director/Chartered Accountant

AMT Fruit Limited
Incorporated: 3 March 2009
Net Worth: £7,873,851 *Total Assets:* £38,018,400
Registered Office: Frans House, Fenton Way, Chatteris, Cambs, PE16 6UP
Activities: Wholesale of fruit and vegetables
Parent: Munoz Group Ltd
Officers: Fernando Juan de Lucas Lopez [1973] Director [Spanish]; Jonathan Michael Hedge [1964] Director

Amtech Group Limited
Incorporated: 2 May 2006 *Employees:* 93
Net Worth: £17,670,000 *Total Assets:* £23,194,000
Registered Office: Bank House, 171 Midsummer Boulevard, Central Milton Keynes, Bucks, MK9 1EB
Activities: Other software publishing
Parent: Trimble Europe B.V.
Officers: James Anthony Kirkland, Secretary; John Henry Gale Heelas [1963] Director/Accountant; James Anthony Kirkland [1959] Director/VP Assistant Secretary and General Counsel [American]; Robbert Hendrik Herman Reeder [1970] European Director of Finance [Dutch]

The Amtico Company Limited
Incorporated: 11 October 1988 *Employees:* 499
Net Worth: £78,540,000 *Total Assets:* £107,334,000
Registered Office: Kingfield Road, Coventry, Warwicks, CV6 5AA
Activities: Manufacture of other plastic products
Officers: Trevor William Morrow, Secretary; Patrick Kevin Burke [1967] Director/Accountant [American]; Jonathan Matthew Duck [1961] Director; Andrew Edward Elsby Smith [1964] Finance Director; Russell Gary Grizzle [1956] Director/Chief Operating Officer [American]; Kevin Patrick Igo [1963] Director/Vice President of Corporate Finance [American]; Dr James Benjamin Naylor [1970] Director; Jason Paul Shelley [1968] Director; Philip Southall [1966] Sales Director

Amtico Holdings Limited
Incorporated: 9 November 1995 *Employees:* 3
Net Worth: £10,228,000 *Total Assets:* £39,091,000
Registered Office: Amtico International, Kingfield Road, Coventry, Warwicks, CV6 5AA
Activities: Manufacture of other plastic products
Parent: Maneto (UK) 2 Limited
Officers: Trevor William Morrow, Secretary; Patrick Kevin Burke [1967] Director/Accountant [American]; Jonathan Matthew Duck [1961] Director; Andrew Edward Elsby Smith [1964] Finance Director; Russell Gary Grizzle [1956] Director/Chief Operating Officer [American]; Kevin Patrick Igo [1963] Director/Vice President of Corporate Finance [American]

Amtico International Limited
Incorporated: 11 October 1988
Net Worth: £9,950,000 *Total Assets:* £10,041,000
Registered Office: Kingfield Road, Coventry, Warwicks, CV6 5AA
Activities: Manufacture of other plastic products
Parent: Amtico Holdings Limited
Officers: Trevor William Morrow, Secretary; Patrick Kevin Burke [1967] Director/Accountant [American]; Jonathan Matthew Duck [1961] Director; Andrew Edward Elsby Smith [1964] Finance Director; Russell Gary Grizzle [1956] Director/Chief Operating Officer [American]; Kevin Patrick Igo [1963] Director/Vice President of Corporate Finance [American]

Amtrust Europe Limited
Incorporated: 14 October 1975 *Employees:* 254
Net Worth: £382,436,992 *Total Assets:* £1,958,232,064
Registered Office: 10th Floor, Market Square House, St James's Street, Nottingham, NG1 6FG
Activities: Non-life insurance
Parent: Amtrust International Limited
Officers: Pauline Anne Cockburn, Secretary; Gordon Edward Bennett [1968] Director; Jeremy Edward Cadle [1965] Director/Lawyer; Peter Dewey [1976] Director; Joanne Patricia Fox [1964] Director; Mark Sutherland Johnson [1958] Director; Angel Guillermo Mas Murcia [1968] Director [Spanish]; Robert Irvin Stansbury [1954] Independent Director; Robin William Webster [1955] Director/Chief Risk Officer

Amtrust International Limited
Incorporated: 3 December 1982
Net Worth: £806,566,976 *Total Assets:* £952,264,000
Registered Office: 10th Floor, Market Square House, St James's Street, Nottingham, NG1 6FG
Activities: Activities of head offices
Officers: Pauline Anne Cockburn, Secretary; Jeremy Edward Cadle [1965] Director/Lawyer; Barry Zyskind [1971] Director/Insurance [American]

Amtrust Lloyd's Holdings (UK) Limited
Incorporated: 19 May 2016
Net Worth: £79,726,752 *Total Assets:* £79,752,976
Registered Office: 10th Floor, Market Square House, St James's Street, Nottingham, NG1 6FG
Activities: Life insurance
Parent: Amtrust International Limited
Officers: Jeremy Edward Cadle [1965] Director/Lawyer; Peter Dewey [1976] Director

Anand International Limited
Incorporated: 15 May 1981 *Employees:* 34
Net Worth: £10,300,649 *Total Assets:* £13,670,408
Registered Office: Meridian House, Centurion Way, Meridian Business Park, Leicester, LE19 1WH
Activities: Wholesale of audio tapes, records, CDs and video tapes and the equipment on which these are played
Shareholders: Harjot Singh Anand; Jaspreet Kaur Anand
Officers: Harjot Singh Anand, Secretary/Director; Harjot Singh Anand [1975] Director; Joginder Pal Singh Anand [1955] Director/General Trader

Anatis UK Limited
Incorporated: 13 April 2009
Net Worth: £32,267,118 *Total Assets:* £57,852,392
Registered Office: Cherry Valley House, Laceby Business Park, Grimsby Road, Laceby, N E Lincs, DN37 7DP
Activities: Activities of production holding companies
Officers: Katharine Mary Butler, Secretary; Peimin Liang [1974] Director/Businessman [Chinese]; Jiantong Liu [1968] Director/Businessman [Chinese]; Liang Shi [1983] Director/Businessman [Chinese]; Dr Xinjian Yan [1958] Managing Director [Chinese]

Ancala Water Services (Defence) Limited
Incorporated: 13 December 2002 *Employees:* 125
Previous: Kelda Water Services (Defence) Limited
Net Worth: £17,770,000 *Total Assets:* £52,074,000
Registered Office: 2nd Floor, One Capitol Court, Capitol Park, Dodworth, Barnsley, S Yorks, S75 3TZ
Activities: Sewerage
Parent: Ancala Water Services Bidco Limited
Officers: Spence Matthew Clunie [1972] Director/Investment Professional; David Godfrey [1966] Director/General Manager; Charles William Grant Herriott [1986] Director/Asset Manager; Rebecca Hicklin [1985] Director/Accountant

Ancala Water Services (Estates) Limited
Incorporated: 13 December 2002
Previous: Kelda Water Services (Estates) Limited
Net Worth: £5,722,000 *Total Assets:* £88,755,000
Registered Office: 2nd Floor, One Capitol Court, Capitol Park, Dodworth, Barnsley, S Yorks, S75 3TZ
Activities: Sewerage
Parent: Ancala Water Services Bidco Limited
Officers: Daniel Bacon [1990] Director/Investment Professional; David Godfrey [1966] Director/General Manager; Rebecca Hicklin [1985] Director/Accountant; David William Owens [1952] Director/Industry Partner

Anchorage Capital Europe, LLP
Incorporated: 17 February 2009 *Employees:* 21
Net Worth: £26,047,352 *Total Assets:* £36,264,800
Registered Office: Mazars LLP, The Pinnacle, 160 Midsummer Boulevard, Milton Keynes, Bucks, MK9 1FF
Officers: Thibault Gournay [1978] Member; James Frost [1977] LLP Member; Arun Nagwaney [1971] LLP Member

Ancillary Components Limited
Incorporated: 12 October 1983 *Employees:* 18
Net Worth: £11,033,286 *Total Assets:* £14,088,407
Registered Office: Goosey Lodge, Wymington, Rushden, Northants, NN10 9LU
Activities: Manufacture of other fabricated metal products n.e.c.
Major Shareholder: David John Wykes
Officers: David John Wykes [1958] Director/Engineer

Ancon Limited
Incorporated: 4 December 1925 *Employees:* 396
Net Worth: £83,934,000 *Total Assets:* £105,859,000
Registered Office: 9 President Way, President Park, Sheffield, S4 7UR
Activities: Manufacture of other fabricated metal products n.e.c.
Parent: CRH (UK) Limited
Officers: Josie Rebecca Welburn, Secretary; James Kehoe [1975] Director [Irish]; Peter Michael McDermott [1961] Operations Director; Mehmet Pekarun [1969] Director [Turkish]; Josie Rebecca Welburn [1972] Finance Director

Andaray (Holdings) Limited
Incorporated: 9 January 1974 *Employees:* 1
Net Worth: £15,835,000 *Total Assets:* £20,676,000
Registered Office: Templeborough Works, Sheffield Road, Sheffield, S9 1RS
Activities: Renting and leasing of other machinery, equipment and tangible goods n.e.c.
Parent: Watermill-CT Holdings Limited
Officers: Steven Edward Karol [1954] Director/Managing Partner [American]

Anderton Concrete Products Limited
Incorporated: 27 March 1985 *Employees:* 77
Net Worth: £13,148,889 *Total Assets:* £16,675,824
Registered Office: Leicester Road, Ibstock, Leics, LE67 6HS
Activities: Manufacture of other articles of concrete, plaster and cement
Parent: Ibstock PLC
Officers: Robert Douglas, Secretary; Michael David Fadden [1959] Director; Mark Whitfield Houghton [1961] Director; Kevin John Sims [1961] Director

Andina PLC
Incorporated: 6 June 2012 *Employees:* 755
Net Worth: £1,644,197 *Total Assets:* £229,960,080
Registered Office: 1 South Quay, Victoria Quays, Sheffield, S2 5SY
Activities: Production of electricity
Officers: Luis Enrique Alvarez Poli Petrungaro, Secretary; Carlos Manuel Bastos [1949] Director [Argentinian]; Neil Arthur Bleasdale [1956] Director; Marcelo Alberto Comba [1964] Director; Jorge Oscar Depresbiteris [1957] Director/Electrical Engineer [Argentinian]; Luis Enrique Alvarez Poli Petrungaro [1968] Director [Argentinian]

Anexhold Limited
Incorporated: 30 March 2012 *Employees:* 212
Net Worth: £10,576,574 *Total Assets:* £34,162,740
Registered Office: 22-26 King Street, King's Lynn, Norfolk, PE30 1HJ
Activities: Activities of production holding companies
Shareholders: Predict S.L.U.; Craig Richard Taylor
Officers: Gonzalo Raspall Coromina, Secretary; Gonzalo Raspall Coromina [1972] Director [Spanish]; Ramon Andreu Ferrando [1964] Director [Spanish]; Jeffrey John Halliwell [1954] Director; Craig Richard Taylor [1966] Director

Angel Cofund
Incorporated: 29 November 2011
Total Assets: £45,198,096
Registered Office: Cooper Buildings, Arundel Street, Sheffield, S1 2NS
Activities: Activities of venture and development capital companies
Officers: Christopher John Stanley Baker [1947] Director; Geoffrey Charles Byars Thomson [1958] Director; George Whitehead [1976] Director; Colin Willis [1967] Director

Anglia Components Investments Limited
Incorporated: 25 April 2012 *Employees:* 133
Net Worth: £7,058,268 *Total Assets:* £40,759,512
Registered Office: Old Linen Court, 83-85 Shambles Street, Barnsley, S Yorks, S70 2SB
Activities: Activities of other holding companies n.e.c.
Major Shareholder: Rawlins Stephen Gordon
Officers: Jill Bowie [1962] Director; John Bowman [1968] Director; Jaqui Fretwell [1970] Director; Keith Ronald Hover [1954] Director; Claire Joyce [1979] Director; David Pearson [1971] Director; Michaela Senior [1967] Director; Karen Suckling [1968] Director

Anglia Components Limited
Incorporated: 13 June 2001 *Employees:* 133
Net Worth: £11,497,853 *Total Assets:* £41,085,144
Registered Office: Anglia Components Limited, Sandall Road, Wisbech, Cambs, PE13 2PS
Activities: Wholesale of electronic and telecommunications equipment and parts
Parent: Anglia Components Investments Limited
Officers: Malcolm John Fry, Secretary; John Bowman [1968] Director

Anglian Venture Holdings Limited
Incorporated: 13 November 2007
Net Worth: £64,845,000 *Total Assets:* £97,138,000
Registered Office: Lancaster House, Lancaster Way, Ermine Business Park, Huntingdon, Cambs, PE29 6XU
Activities: Activities of head offices
Parent: Osprey Holdco Limited
Officers: Claire Tytherleigh Russell, Secretary; Anthony Donnelly [1964] Director; Scott Robert James Longhurst [1967] Finance Director; Claire Tytherleigh Russell [1964] Director/Lawyer; Peter John Simpson [1967] Director; Wayne Paul Young [1976] Director/Chartered Accountant

Anglian Water (Osprey) Financing PLC
Incorporated: 22 December 2010
Net Worth: £163,000 *Total Assets:* £455,227,008
Registered Office: Lancaster House, Lancaster Way, Ermine Business Park, Huntingdon, Cambs, PE29 6XU
Activities: Other business support service activities n.e.c.
Parent: Osprey Acqusitions Limited
Officers: Claire Tytherleigh Russell, Secretary; Dr Stephen Robert Billingham [1948] Director; Scott Robert James Longhurst [1967] Director; Peter John Simpson [1967] Director

Anglian Water Facilities Management Holdings (UK) Limited
Incorporated: 3 October 2000
Net Worth: £40,449,000 *Total Assets:* £40,454,000
Registered Office: Lancaster House, Lancaster Way, Ermine Business Park, Huntingdon, Cambs, PE29 6XU
Activities: Non-trading company
Parent: AWG Group Limited
Officers: Elizabeth Ann Horlock Clarke, Secretary; Alan Gladston [1970] Director/Accountant; Gerard Mackin Morgan [1957] Director/Head of Finance and Performance

Anglian Water Services Financing PLC
Incorporated: 28 November 2001
Net Worth: £48,000,000 *Total Assets:* £7,506,400,256
Registered Office: Lancaster House, Lancaster Way, Ermine Business Park, Huntingdon, Cambs, PE29 6XU
Activities: Other business support service activities n.e.c.
Parent: Anglian Water Services Limited
Officers: Claire Tytherleigh Russell, Secretary; Dr Stephen Robert Billingham [1948] Director; Natalie Ceeney [1971] Director; Dame Veronica Anne Courtice [1952] Director, University of Cambridge; John Raymond Hirst [1952] Director; Scott Robert James Longhurst [1967] Finance Director; Zarin Homi Patel [1961] Independent Director; Jane Elizabeth Pilcher [1962] Director; Alexander Charles Plant [1969] Director; Peter John Simpson [1967] Director; Paul Frederick Garry Whittaker [1960] Director

Anglian Water Services Holdings Limited
Incorporated: 28 November 2001
Net Worth: £1,609,092,992 *Total Assets:* £1,609,092,992
Registered Office: Lancaster House, Lancaster Way, Ermine Business Park, Huntingdon, Cambs, PE29 6XU
Activities: Activities of head offices
Parent: AWG Group Limited
Officers: Claire Tytherleigh Russell, Secretary; Dr Stephen Robert Billingham [1948] Director; Natalie Ceeney [1971] Director; Dame Veronica Anne Courtice [1952] Director, University of Cambridge; John Raymond Hirst [1952] Director; Scott Robert James Longhurst [1967] Finance Director; Zarin Homi Patel [1961] Independent Director; Jane Elizabeth Pilcher [1962] Director; Alexander Charles Plant [1969] Director; Peter John Simpson [1967] Director; Paul Frederick Garry Whittaker [1960] Director

Anglian Water Services Limited
Incorporated: 1 April 1989 *Employees:* 4,600
Net Worth: £1,217,400,064 *Total Assets:* £10,790,700,032
Registered Office: Lancaster House, Lancaster Way, Ermine Business Park, Huntingdon, Cambs, PE29 6XU
Activities: Water collection, treatment and supply
Parent: Anglian Water Services UK Parent Co Limited
Officers: Claire Tytherleigh Russell, Secretary; Dr Stephen Robert Billingham [1948] Director; James Alexander Bryce [1974] Director/Senior Principal; Natalie Ceeney [1971] Director; Dame Veronica Anne Courtice [1952] Director, University of Cambridge; John Raymond Hirst [1952] Director; Scott Robert James Longhurst [1967] Finance Director; Niall Patrick Mills [1968] Director/Chartered Engineer; Zarin Homi Patel [1961] Independent Director; Peter John Simpson [1967] Director/Chief Executive Officer; Duncan John Symonds [1973] Director/Civil Engineer; Paul Frederick Garry Whittaker [1960] Director

Anisa Consolidated Holdings Limited
Incorporated: 4 March 2016 *Employees:* 91
Net Worth: £5,799,000 *Total Assets:* £18,668,000
Registered Office: Sanderson House, Manor Road, Coventry, Warwicks, CV1 2GF
Activities: Activities of head offices
Parent: Sanderson Group PLC
Officers: Richard David Mogg [1976] Finance Director; Ian Newcombe [1955] Director; David Charles Renshaw [1958] Director; Ross Telford [1947] Director

Anisa Group Holdings Limited
Incorporated: 21 June 2011 *Employees:* 91
Net Worth Deficit: £1,108,000 *Total Assets:* £13,199,000
Registered Office: Sanderson House, Manor Road, Coventry, Warwicks, CV1 2GF
Activities: Activities of head offices
Parent: Anisa Consolidated Holdings Limited
Officers: Richard David Mogg [1976] Group Financial Director; Ian Newcombe [1955] Director; David Charles Renshaw [1958] Director; Ross Telford [1947] Director

Anisa Supply Chain Solutions Limited
Incorporated: 15 January 1998 *Employees:* 91
Previous: Anisa Group Limited
Net Worth: £1,934,000 *Total Assets:* £12,488,000
Registered Office: Sanderson House, Manor Road, Coventry, Warwicks, CV1 2GF
Activities: Activities of head offices
Parent: Anisa Group Holdings Limited
Officers: Richard David Mogg [1976] Finance Director; Ian Newcombe [1955] Director; David Charles Renshaw [1958] Director; Ross Telford [1947] Director/Business Executive

Anpario PLC
Incorporated: 7 April 1997 *Employees:* 111
Net Worth: £30,522,000 *Total Assets:* £37,201,000
Registered Office: Unit 5 Manton Wood Enterprise Park, Worksop, Notts, S80 2RS
Activities: Other manufacturing n.e.c.
Officers: Karen Lesley Prior, Secretary; Richard Peter Edwards [1965] Director; Peter Anthony Lawrence [1948] Director; Karen Lesley Prior [1960] Finance Director; Richard Kenneth Wood [1944] Director

Anti-Waste (Restoration) Limited
Incorporated: 23 November 1994
Net Worth: £24,000 *Total Assets:* £24,609,000
Registered Office: Ground Floor West, 900 Pavilion Drive, Northampton Business Park, Northampton, NN4 7RG
Activities: Other business support service activities n.e.c.
Parent: Anti-Waste Limited
Officers: Carol Jayne Nunn, Secretary; Vicente Federico Orts-Llopis [1962] Finance Director [Spanish]; Paul Taylor [1959] Director/Chief Executive Officer

Anti-Waste Limited
Incorporated: 22 June 1981 *Employees:* 48
Net Worth: £1,524,000 *Total Assets:* £20,792,000
Registered Office: Ground Floor West, 900 Pavilion Drive, Northampton Business Park, Northampton, NN4 7RG
Activities: Other business support service activities n.e.c.
Parent: FCC Environment (UK) Limited
Officers: Carol Jayne Nunn, Secretary; Vicente Federico Orts-Llopis [1962] Director/Chief Financial Officer [Spanish]; Agustin Serrano Minchan [1959] Director/Technical Civil Engineer [Spanish]; Paul Taylor [1959] Director/Chief Executive Officer

Antolin Interiors UK Limited
Incorporated: 9 November 1982 *Employees:* 2,312
Previous: Magna Interiors (UK) Limited
Net Worth: £70,398,000 *Total Assets:* £224,808,000
Registered Office: Apollo Way, Tachbrook Park, Warwick, CV34 6RW
Activities: Manufacture of other parts and accessories for motor vehicles
Officers: Pablo Martinez, Secretary; Jesus Pascual [1963] Director [Spanish]; Miguel Angel Prado [1968] Business Unit Industrial Director [Spanish]; Fernando Sanz [1966] Business Unit Industrial Director [Spanish]

AP Racing Limited
Incorporated: 24 June 1999 *Employees:* 137
Net Worth: £20,341,000 *Total Assets:* £28,905,000
Registered Office: Seven Stars Industrial Estate, Wheler Road, Coventry, Warwicks, CV3 4LB
Activities: Other manufacturing n.e.c.
Parent: Brembo S.P.A.
Officers: Dr Edward James Crust, Secretary; Mario Almondo [1964] Director [Italian]; Dr Edward James Crust [1977] Finance Director; Paolo Ferrari [1958] Director [Italian]; David Hamblin [1980] Managing Director; Dario Moretti [1970] Director [Italian]

Apac Group Limited
Incorporated: 22 June 2000 *Employees:* 138
Previous: Apac Packaging Limited
Net Worth: £8,576,712 *Total Assets:* £16,617,467
Registered Office: 6 Forest Road, Loughborough, Leics, LE11 3NP
Activities: Wholesale of household goods (other than musical instruments) n.e.c
Shareholder: Margaret Anne Carpenter
Officers: Kevin Dennis MacKay, Secretary; Margaret Anne Carpenter [1938] Director/Retired; Kevin Dennis MacKay [1984] Sales Director; Roger Dennis MacKay [1956] Director

Apec Limited
Incorporated: 8 June 1965 *Employees:* 111
Net Worth: £19,172,000 *Total Assets:* £37,209,000
Registered Office: Bridge House, 3 Timothy's Bridge Road, Stratford upon Avon, Warwicks, CV37 9NQ
Activities: Wholesale trade of motor vehicle parts and accessories
Parent: FPS Distribution Ltd
Officers: John Frederick Coombes, Secretary; Alistair Stuart Brown [1955] Director [New Zealander]; John Frederick Coombes [1965] Director; Steven Charles Fisher [1956] Director/Sales Executive; Jean-Jacques Mathieu Lafont [1959] Director [Belgian]; Terence Michael Wainwright [1947] Director

Apertio Limited
Incorporated: 10 May 2002
Net Worth: £25,062,000 *Total Assets:* £25,936,000
Registered Office: The Forum, Lancaster Way, Ermine Business Park, Huntingdon, Cambs, PE29 6XU
Activities: Other information technology service activities
Parent: Nokia UK Limited
Officers: Hans-Joerg Daub [1963] Director/Chief Financial Officer [German]; Trevor Dryden Foster [1970] Director/Accountant; Cormac Vincent Whelan [1964] Director [Irish]

Apex Credit Management Limited
Incorporated: 7 April 2000 *Employees:* 87
Net Worth Deficit: £2,960,000 *Total Assets:* £19,211,000
Registered Office: Buckingham Road, Brackley, Northants, NN13 7DN
Activities: Financial intermediation not elsewhere classified
Parent: Cabot Financial Debt Recovery Services Limited
Officers: Charlotte Taggart, Secretary; Craig Anthony Buick [1969] Finance Director [British/Australian]; Kenneth John Stannard [1966] Director/Chief Executive Officer

Apex Stainless Fasteners Limited
Incorporated: 22 July 1991 *Employees:* 116
Net Worth: £19,170,418 *Total Assets:* £24,838,102
Registered Office: 20 Somers Road, Rugby, Warwicks, CV22 7DH
Activities: Other specialised construction activities n.e.c.
Parent: Apex Stainless Holdings Limited
Officers: Tara Michelle Castle, Secretary; Willy Einungbrekke [1965] Director [Norwegian]; Paul Richard Lower [1948] Director; Jorgen Rosengren [1967] Director [Swedish]

Apex Stainless Holdings Limited
Incorporated: 14 February 2013
Net Worth: £19,221,332 *Total Assets:* £22,721,348
Registered Office: 20 Somers Road, Rugby, Warwicks, CV22 7DH
Activities: Activities of other holding companies n.e.c.
Parent: Bult Finnveden Aktiebolag
Officers: Tara Michelle Castle, Secretary; Willy Einungbrekke [1965] Director [Norwegian]; Paul Richard Lower [1948] Director; Jorgen Rosengren [1967] Director [Swedish]

API Foils Limited
Incorporated: 28 November 1924 *Employees:* 149
Net Worth Deficit: £1,503,000 *Total Assets:* £20,991,000
Registered Office: Second Avenue, Poynton Industrial Estate, Poynton, Stockport, Cheshire, SK12 1ND
Activities: Manufacture of other paper and paperboard containers
Parent: API Foils Holdings Limited
Officers: Claire Chadwick, Secretary; Peter Chapman [1960] Director; Robert Hall [1971] Director/Chief Financial Officer; Kostantinos Jim Kiriakopoulos [1970] Director [British/Canadian]; William George Oldham [1961] Director

API Group PLC
Incorporated: 24 July 1920 *Employees:* 630
Net Worth: £26,580,000 *Total Assets:* £95,276,000
Registered Office: Second Avenue, Poynton Industrial Estate, Poynton, Stockport, Cheshire, SK12 1ND
Activities: Packaging activities
Parent: Cedar 2015 Limited
Officers: Claire Chadwick, Secretary; Jack Lawrence Howard [1961] Director [American]

API Laminates Limited
Incorporated: 30 March 1921 *Employees:* 119
Net Worth: £6,935,000 *Total Assets:* £20,886,000
Registered Office: Second Avenue, Poynton Industrial Estate, Poynton, Stockport, Cheshire, SK12 1ND
Activities: Manufacture of plastic plates, sheets, tubes and profiles
Parent: API Group PLC
Officers: Claire Chadwick, Secretary; Peter Chapman [1960] Director; Robert Hall [1971] Director/Chief Financial Officer; Kostantinos Jim Kiriakopoulos [1970] Director [British/Canadian]

API Overseas Holdings Limited
Incorporated: 3 February 1998
Net Worth: £5,006,000 *Total Assets:* £12,000,000
Registered Office: Second Avenue, Poynton Industrial Estate, Poynton, Cheshire, SK12 1ND
Activities: Non-trading company
Shareholders: API Foils Holdings Limited; API Group PLC
Officers: Claire Chadwick, Secretary; Claire Marie Chadwick [1982] Director/Group Legal Counsel; Peter Chapman [1960] Director; Robert Hall [1971] Director/Chief Financial Officer; Kostantinos Jim Kiriakopoulos [1970] Director [British/Canadian]

Apollo Partnership Trust
Incorporated: 21 June 2012 *Employees:* 81
Previous: Castle Rock High School
Net Worth: £8,229,000 *Total Assets:* £9,663,000
Registered Office: Castle Rock High School, Meadow Lane, Coalville, Leics, LE67 4BR
Activities: General secondary education
Officers: Maxine Louise Adams, Secretary; Roger Cairns [1942] Director/Retired Teacher; Raymond Dennis [1939] Director; Joy Margaret Knifton [1976] Director/Accountant; Julia Elizabeth Patrick [1966] Director/Headteacher; Andrew William Presland [1957] Director/Retired; Andrew James Pritchard [1962] Director and Financial Consultant; Gill Stacey [1957] Personnel Director; Paul Fredrick Weston [1955] Director/Education Consultant; Michala Worrell [1973] Director/Project Manager

Apollo Scientific Ltd
Incorporated: 24 September 1993 *Employees:* 73
Net Worth: £8,634,848 *Total Assets:* £10,479,916
Registered Office: Whitefield Road, Bredbury, Stockport, Cheshire, SK6 2QR
Activities: Manufacture of other inorganic basic chemicals
Parent: Central Glass Europe Limited
Officers: Jennifer Anne Holland, Secretary; Mitsuru Tanuma [1961] Director [Japanese]; Nobuyuki Tokunaga [1961] Director/General Manager [Japanese]

Apollo Support Services Group Limited
Incorporated: 8 November 2005
Net Worth: £162,626,000 *Total Assets:* £162,647,008
Registered Office: The Waterfront, Lakeside Boulevard, Doncaster, S Yorks, DN4 5PL
Activities: Combined facilities support activities
Parent: Conquest Bidco Limited
Officers: Mark Richard Priest [1966] Director; James Michael Douglas Thomson [1966] Director

Appia Europe Limited
Incorporated: 31 January 2008
Net Worth: £72,311,000 *Total Assets:* £450,569,984
Registered Office: 2 Vantage Court, Tickford Street, Newport Pagnell, Bucks, MK16 9EZ
Activities: Activities of other holding companies n.e.c.
Officers: Joseph James Barrett [1966] Director [Irish]; John Diviney [1979] Director/Chief Executive Officer [Irish]; Niall Dolan [1973] Director/Financial Controller [Irish]; Charles John Gore Hazelwood [1963] Director/Accountant; Surinder Singh Toor [1972] Director/Accountant

Applied Composites Group Ltd
Incorporated: 20 May 2016 *Employees:* 577
Net Worth Deficit: £163,000 *Total Assets:* £36,541,000
Registered Office: Victoria Works, Thrumpton Lane, Retford, Notts, DN22 6HH
Activities: Activities of production holding companies
Shareholder: LDC (Managers) Limited
Officers: Robert John Jozef Apollo [1985] Director; Christopher Martin Coulton [1979] Director; Craig Andrew Harris [1969] Director/Chief Executive; David James Ring [1962] Director

APS Group Limited
Incorporated: 28 February 2008 *Employees:* 845
Net Worth: £15,191,612 *Total Assets:* £54,907,396
Registered Office: Chetham House, Bird Hall Lane, Stockport, Cheshire, SK3 0ZP
Activities: Activities of head offices
Major Shareholder: Nicholas John Snelson
Officers: John Holmes [1966] Director; Kim Melita Naylor [1962] Director; Erica Snelson [1965] Director; Nicholas John Snelson [1965] Director

APS Produce Limited
Incorporated: 27 June 1997 *Employees:* 270
Previous: Wight Salads Limited
Net Worth: £12,094,000 *Total Assets:* £35,564,000
Registered Office: Enterprise House, 97 Alderley Road, Wilmslow, Cheshire, SK9 1PT
Activities: Growing of other non-perennial crops
Parent: A Pearson Holdings Ltd
Officers: Ashley Robert Haworth, Secretary; Andrew Patrick Burke [1962] Trading Director; Emma Rachel Burke [1973] Director; Ashley Robert Haworth [1979] Financial Director; Mark Alan Pearson [1973] Director; Philip Pearson [1963] Director; John Edward Phibbs [1950] Director/Chartered Accountant; Paul Robert Thomas [1979] Managing Director

Aptean Limited
Incorporated: 7 July 1997 *Employees:* 64
Net Worth Deficit: £21,298,910 *Total Assets:* £15,811,436
Registered Office: 7 Rushmills, Northampton, NN4 7YB
Activities: Business and domestic software development
Officers: Sandra Ann Cummings [1964] Finance Director; Alan Gibson Somerville [1963] Managing Director; Hellen Maria Stein [1974] Director/Senior Legal Counsel

Apteco Limited
Incorporated: 28 April 2000 *Employees:* 37
Net Worth: £10,201,395 *Total Assets:* £13,178,149
Registered Office: Tink-A-Tank House, 21 Jury Street, Warwick, CV34 4EH
Activities: Business and domestic software development
Shareholders: James Christopher Myles Alty; Simon Edward Holderness; Robert Harry Downs
Officers: James Christopher Myles Alty, Secretary/Computer Consultant; James Christopher Myles Alty [1964] Director/Computer Consultant; Simon Edward Holderness [1969] Director/Computer Consultant

Apted Holdings Limited
Incorporated: 26 October 2012 *Employees:* 56
Net Worth: £6,063,063 *Total Assets:* £23,782,416
Registered Office: Unit G1, Holly Farm Business Park, Honiley, Kenilworth, Warwicks, CV8 1NP
Activities: Activities of other holding companies n.e.c.
Major Shareholder: Ian Worthington
Officers: Stephen Jackson, Secretary; Raymond William Apted [1948] Director

Aptuit (Oxford) Limited
Incorporated: 19 July 2011 *Employees:* 154
Net Worth: £8,822,988 *Total Assets:* £21,646,620
Registered Office: 111 Innovation Drive, Milton Park, Milton, Abingdon, Oxon, OX14 4RZ
Activities: Manufacture of pharmaceutical preparations
Parent: Evotec AG
Officers: Dr Christian Dargel, Secretary; Dr Petra Dieterich [1967] Director/Vice President and Head of Site [German]; Dr Christophe Muller [1971] Director [French]; Ralph Enno Spillner [1970] Director [German]

Arbor Forest Products Limited
Incorporated: 13 November 1951 *Employees:* 161
Net Worth: £27,845,000 *Total Assets:* £46,812,000
Registered Office: The Lincoln Castle, Lincoln Castle Way, New Holland, Barrow upon Humber, N Lincs, DN19 7RX
Activities: Sawmilling and planing of wood
Officers: Julie Ann Howarth, Secretary; Andrew Peter Howarth [1955] Director/Timber Merchant; Deborah Jane Howarth [1958] Director; Julie Ann Howarth [1960] Director; Nicholas David Howarth [1957] Director/Timber Merchant; Jason Ostler [1971] Managing Director; Philip Adam Yell [1959] Director/Operations Manager

Archipelago Learning Holdings UK Limited
Incorporated: 25 May 2010 *Employees:* 101
Net Worth: £772,260 *Total Assets:* £15,615,130
Registered Office: Unit 8 Saddlers Court, Barleythorpe, Oakham, Rutland, LE15 7GH
Activities: Other software publishing
Shareholder: Prospect Capital Corporation
Officers: Eric Doan, Secretary; Eric Doan [1979] Director/Chief Financial Officer [American]

Archway Learning Trust
Incorporated: 8 December 2011 *Employees:* 584
Previous: Bluecoat Academies Trust
Net Worth: £79,000,000 *Total Assets:* £91,697,000
Registered Office: Bluecoat Academy, Aspley Lane, Aspley, Nottingham, NG8 5GY
Activities: Primary education
Officers: Maria Lysenko, Secretary; Christopher John Archer [1948] Director/Educational Consultant; Sian Elizabeth Hampton [1966] Director/Teacher; Dr Jane Constance Moore [1966] Director/University Lecturer; Margaret Elizabeth Oldroyd [1948] Director/Retired; Tracy Ann Rees [1964] Director/Retired; Heidi Caroline Shewell-Cooper [1966] Director/Educational Project Manager; Nigel Spraggins [1959] Director/Diocesan Chief Executive; Paul Graham Sykes [1944] Director/Retired; Karen Lesley Wyer [1957] Director/Retired

Arconic Closure Systems International (UK) Limited
Incorporated: 2 November 1959
Previous: Alcoa Closure Systems International (UK) Limited
Net Worth: £37,530,000 *Total Assets:* £37,559,000
Registered Office: 26a Atlas Way, Sheffield, S4 7QQ
Activities: Other manufacturing n.e.c.
Parent: Arconic Manufacturing (GB) Limited
Officers: Petra Papinniemi-Ainger, Secretary; Dr Kay Louise Dowdall [1969] Director/Accountant; Lluis Maria Fargas Mas [1966] Director/Lawyer [Spanish]

Arconic Extruded Products (UK) Limited
Incorporated: 1 July 1985 *Employees:* 2
Previous: Alcoa Extruded Products (UK) Limited
Net Worth: £124,608,000 *Total Assets:* £124,743,000
Registered Office: 26a Atlas Way, Sheffield, S4 7QQ
Activities: Aluminium production
Parent: Alloy Technologies (UK) Limited
Officers: Petra Papinniemi-Ainger, Secretary; Dr Kay Louise Dowdall [1969] Director/Accountant; Lluis Maria Fargas Mas [1966] Director [Spanish]

Arconic Fastening Systems & Rings Limited
Incorporated: 1 July 1983 *Employees:* 130
Previous: Alcoa Fastening Systems Limited
Net Worth: £13,047,000 *Total Assets:* £18,967,000
Registered Office: 26a Atlas Way, Sheffield, S4 7QQ
Activities: Manufacture of fasteners and screw machine products
Parent: British Aluminium Limited
Officers: Petra Papinniemi-Ainger, Secretary; James Howard Arnold [1964] Director/Vice President and General Manager; Jonathan Quentin Craven [1971] Operations Director; Lluis Maria Fargas Mas [1966] Director/Lawyer [Spanish]; Dean Matthew Jones [1990] Director/Financial Controller

Arconic Global Fasteners Limited
Incorporated: 3 March 2011
Previous: Alcoa Global Fasteners Limited
Net Worth Deficit: £2,259,000 *Total Assets:* £90,291,000
Registered Office: 26a Atlas Way, Sheffield, S4 7QQ
Activities: Manufacture of wire products, chain and springs
Parent: Arconic Inc
Officers: Petra Papinniemi-Ainger, Secretary; Dr Kay Louise Dowdall [1969] Director/Accountant; Lluis Fargas [1966] Director [Spanish]

Arconic Limited
Incorporated: 18 June 2014
Previous: Arconic IH Limited
Net Worth: £278,710,528 *Total Assets:* £717,590,720
Registered Office: 26a Atlas Way, Sheffield, S4 7QQ
Activities: Other business support service activities n.e.c.
Parent: Arconic Inc.
Officers: Petra Papinniemi-Ainger, Secretary; Dr Kay Louise Dowdall [1969] Director/Chartered Accountant; Lluis Maria Fargas Mas [1966] Director/Lawyer [Spanish/Swiss]

Arconic Manufacturing (GB) Limited
Incorporated: 23 July 1959 *Employees:* 536
Previous: Alcoa Manufacturing (G.B.) Limited
Net Worth: £407,769,984 *Total Assets:* £589,929,984
Registered Office: 26a Atlas Way, Sheffield, S4 7QQ
Activities: Aluminium production
Parent: Arconic UK Holdings Limited
Officers: Kay Louise Dowdall, Secretary; Lluis Maria Fargas Mas [1966] Director [Spanish]; Mark Vrablec [1960] Director/Manager [American]; James Patrick Wallace [1962] Director/Plant Manager

Arconic UK Finance
Incorporated: 27 October 2000
Previous: Alcoa UK Finance
Net Worth: £209,327,008 *Total Assets:* £300,052,000
Registered Office: 26a Atlas Way, Sheffield, S4 7QQ
Activities: Activities of head offices
Parent: Arconic Manufacturing (GB) Limited
Officers: Petra Papinniemi-Ainger, Secretary; Dr Kay Louise Dowdall [1969] Director/Accountant; Lluis Maria Fargas Mas [1966] Director/Lawyer [Spanish]

Arconic UK Holdings Limited
Incorporated: 25 October 2000
Previous: Alcoa UK Holdings Limited
Net Worth Deficit: £39,268,000 *Total Assets:* £312,323,008
Registered Office: 26a Atlas Way, Sheffield, S4 7QQ
Activities: Activities of head offices
Parent: Alcoa Inc
Officers: Petra Papinniemi-Ainger, Secretary; Dr Kay Louise Dowdall [1969] Director/Accountant; Lluis Maria Fargas Mas [1966] Director/Lawyer [Spanish]

Arden Dies Limited
Incorporated: 26 February 1965 *Employees:* 166
Net Worth: £6,997,778 *Total Assets:* £10,286,908
Registered Office: Shepley Lane Industrial Estate, Hawk Green, Marple, Stockport, Cheshire, SK6 7JW
Activities: Manufacture of other fabricated metal products n.e.c.
Shareholders: Peter Marbach; Martin Philip Poynter
Officers: Andrew Reece Hall, Secretary; Andrew Reece Hall [1965] Director/Chartered Accountant; Simon David Lynch [1967] Director/General Manager; Peter Marbach [1960] Director [German]; Martin Philip Poynter [1957] Director

Arden Topco Limited
Incorporated: 12 February 2015 *Employees:* 39
Net Worth: £4,915,544 *Total Assets:* £9,087,467
Registered Office: 10 Banner Park, Wickmans Drive, Coventry, Warwicks, CV4 9XA
Activities: Activities of head offices
Shareholder: Gary Gordon Barr
Officers: Jonathan Mark Barlow [1966] Director; Richard Paul Bridges [1976] Director; Derek Robert Lowe [1961] Director; Stuart Jonathan Lowe [1958] Director; Sarah Ann Marsden [1965] Director; Andrew Richard Mewis [1975] Director; Timothy Charles Rayment [1962] Director; Helen Susanne Young [1971] Director

Arena Blinds Limited
Incorporated: 17 September 1997 *Employees:* 28
Previous: Arena Sun Control Systems Limited
Net Worth: £14,969,000 *Total Assets:* £17,398,000
Registered Office: Unit 2 Churchill Park, Private Road No 2, Colwick, Nottingham, NG4 2JR
Activities: Other business support service activities n.e.c.
Parent: Hillarys Blinds (Holdings) Limited
Officers: Ian Galpin [1974] Director; David Mathew Aubrey Lewis [1967] Director/Business Executive [Australian]; Darren Hansel Lock [1966] Director; John Risman [1965] Director; Andrew Richard Thomas [1972] Director/Business Executive

Arena Coventry (2006) Limited
Incorporated: 13 January 2006 *Employees:* 2
Net Worth: £10,028,000 *Total Assets:* £21,433,000
Registered Office: Ricoh Arena, Judds Lane, Longford, Coventry, Warwicks, CV6 6AQ
Activities: Letting and operating of conference and exhibition centres
Officers: Nicholas John Eastwood, Secretary; Nicholas John Eastwood [1959] Director/Chief Executive Officer; Jacquelyn Mary Isaac [1951] Director

Arena Coventry Limited
Incorporated: 16 May 2002 *Employees:* 57
Net Worth: £22,753,000 *Total Assets:* £86,580,000
Registered Office: Ricoh Arena, Judds Lane, Longford, Coventry, Warwicks, CV6 6AQ
Activities: Letting and operating of conference and exhibition centres
Major Shareholder: Derek Arthur Richardson
Officers: Nicholas John Eastwood, Secretary; Nicholas John Eastwood [1959] Director/Chief Executive Officer; Jacquelyn Mary Isaac [1951] Director

Arena Event Services Group Limited
Incorporated: 11 September 2000 *Employees:* 511
Net Worth: £16,151,000 *Total Assets:* £45,085,000
Registered Office: Needingworth Industrial Estate, Needingworth Road, St Ives, Cambs, PE27 4NB
Activities: Other sports activities
Parent: WB Co (1403) Limited
Officers: Gregory Malcolm Lawless [1960] Director [Irish]; Christopher James Piggott [1967] Director; Piers Leigh Stuart Wilson [1967] Director/Chartered Accountant; David John Withey [1957] Sales Director

ARG Corporate Services Limited
Incorporated: 2 April 1957
Net Worth Deficit: £235,687,520 *Total Assets:* £41,931,072
Registered Office: c/o Aga Rangemaster, Meadow Lane, Long Eaton, Nottingham, NG10 2GD
Activities: Other business support service activities n.e.c.
Parent: Aga Rangemaster Group Limited
Officers: Timothy John FitzGenerald [1969] Director/Vice President and CFO [American]; Martin McKay Lindsay [1964] Director/Corporate Treasurer [American]; Agustin Zufia [1967] Director/Group Controller [Spanish]

Argonaut Bidco Limited
Incorporated: 25 July 2007
Net Worth: £66,448,000 *Total Assets:* £237,664,992
Registered Office: 107 Station Street, Burton on Trent, Staffs, DE14 1SZ
Activities: Activities of head offices
Parent: Argonaut Midco Limited
Officers: John Bradshaw, Secretary; John Richard Bradshaw [1955] Director/Solicitor; Darryn Stanley Gibson [1965] Director [New Zealander]; John Spencer Sheridan [1973] Director

Argos Business Solutions Limited
Incorporated: 6 August 1996 *Employees:* 74
Net Worth: £32,841,000 *Total Assets:* £46,026,000
Registered Office: 489-499 Avebury Boulevard, Milton Keynes, Bucks, MK9 2NW
Activities: Activities of financial services holding companies
Parent: Argos Limited
Officers: Timothy Fallowfield, Secretary; Claire Louise Catlin [1980] Director

Argos Holdings Limited
Incorporated: 28 June 2006 *Employees:* 2
Net Worth: £1,262,541,056 *Total Assets:* £2,064,024,064
Registered Office: 489-499 Avebury Boulevard, Milton Keynes, Bucks, MK9 2NW
Activities: Activities of head offices
Parent: Home Retail Group (UK) Limited
Officers: Timothy Fallowfield, Secretary; Claire Louise Catlin [1980] Director

Argos Limited
Incorporated: 13 November 1972 *Employees:* 26,611
Net Worth: £571,054,976 *Total Assets:* £2,905,533,952
Registered Office: 489-499 Avebury Boulevard, Milton Keynes, Bucks, MK9 2NW
Activities: Other retail sale in non-specialised stores
Parent: Argos Holdings Limited
Officers: Timothy Fallowfield, Secretary; Claire Louise Catlin [1980] Director; Patrick Dunne [1968] Director; John Terence Rogers [1968] Director

Argos SURBS Investments Limited
Incorporated: 21 February 2006 *Employees:* 2
Net Worth: £4,561,000 *Total Assets:* £13,015,000
Registered Office: 489-499 Avebury Boulevard, Milton Keynes, Bucks, MK9 2NW
Activities: Non-trading company
Parent: Argos Limited
Officers: Timothy Fallowfield, Secretary; Claire Louise Catlin [1980] Director

Ariens Company Limited
Incorporated: 20 June 1983 *Employees:* 112
Previous: Countax Limited
Net Worth: £4,694,471 *Total Assets:* £13,952,169
Registered Office: Countax House, Great Haseley Trading Estate, Great Haseley, Oxon, OX44 7PF
Activities: Manufacture of other fabricated metal products n.e.c.
Parent: Ariens UK Limited
Officers: Daniel Timothy Ariens [1958] Director; Darren John Spencer [1973] Director/General Manager; Lawrence Joseph Weyers [1962] Director [American]

Arighi Bianchi Holdings Limited
Incorporated: 12 March 2012 *Employees:* 164
Net Worth: £3,165,174 *Total Assets:* £10,039,831
Registered Office: The Silk Road, Macclesfield, Cheshire, SK10 1LH
Activities: Other letting and operating of own or leased real estate
Officers: Sarah Bianchi, Secretary; John Bianchi [1964] Director; Paul Nicholas Ernesto Bianchi [1972] Director; Richard Enrico Bianchi [1961] Sales Director; Robert Anthony Bianchi [1970] Director; Robert Paul Bianchi [1937] Managing Director; Sarah Bianchi [1969] Director

Ark Capital Limited
Incorporated: 18 March 2004 *Employees:* 12
Net Worth: £24,438,000 *Total Assets:* £25,776,000
Registered Office: Unit 9 Riverside Court, Pride Park, Derby, DE24 8JN
Activities: Activities of head offices
Shareholder: Peter James Gadsby
Officers: Martyn John Cubbage, Secretary; Peter James Gadsby [1948] Director; Nicholas Hopkin [1955] Director/Chartered Accountant

Arkle Finance Limited
Incorporated: 3 July 1997 *Employees:* 38
Net Worth: £7,472,664 *Total Assets:* £97,082,992
Registered Office: Weatherbys, Sanders Road, Wellingborough, Northants, NN8 4BX
Activities: Financial leasing
Parent: Weatherbys Bank Limited
Officers: Adrian Stewart McGlynn, Secretary; Daniel Bailey [1983] Director; Paul Robert Matthew Bartley [1965] Director/Banking and Asset Finance Executive; Julian David Rose [1965] Director/Management Consultant; Andrew Turberville Smith [1966] Director/Banking Executive; Gareth James Wilding [1966] Director

Arlington Automotive Limited
Incorporated: 3 June 2013 *Employees:* 235
Previous: Rempower Ltd
Net Worth: £7,558,000 *Total Assets:* £34,706,000
Registered Office: 79 Torrington Avenue, Coventry, Warwicks, CV4 9AQ
Activities: Manufacture of other parts and accessories for motor vehicles
Parent: Arlington Automotive Holdings Limited
Officers: Peter William Coates [1971] Managing Director; Mark Bernard Franckel [1962] Director; Simon George Greenhalgh [1972] Director/Chief Financial Officer; Professor Kevin Thomas Morley [1950] Director

Armitage Brothers Limited
Incorporated: 1 April 1897 *Employees:* 3
Net Worth: £8,595,000 *Total Assets:* £19,552,000
Registered Office: Armitage House, Colwick, Nottingham, NG4 2BA
Activities: Manufacture of prepared pet foods
Parent: Focus 100 Limited
Officers: Mark John Andrews [1970] Director/Chief Executive; Alan Rae Dalziel Jamieson [1954] Director/Chairman; Sarah Louise Smith [1974] Finance Director

Armitage Pet Care Limited
Incorporated: 5 July 2017 *Employees:* 126
Net Worth Deficit: £984,000 *Total Assets:* £54,190,000
Registered Office: Armitage House, Colwick, Nottingham, NG4 2BA
Activities: Other business support service activities n.e.c.
Parent: K9 Midco Limited
Officers: Mark John Andrews [1970] Director/Chief Executive; Alan Rae Dalziel Jamieson [1954] Director; Kajen Mohanadas [1982] Director/Investment Management; Benjamin St Pierre Slatter [1973] Director/Investment Manager; Sarah Louise Smith [1974] Finance Director

Armitages Pet Products Limited
Incorporated: 9 May 1960 *Employees:* 126
Net Worth: £20,379,000 *Total Assets:* £43,296,000
Registered Office: Armitage House, Colwick, Nottingham, NG4 2BA
Activities: Manufacture of prepared pet foods
Parent: Armitage Brothers Limited
Officers: Mark John Andrews [1970] Director/Chief Executive; Alan Rae Dalziel Jamieson [1954] Director/Chairman; Sarah Louise Smith [1974] Finance Director

Armstrong Brooks Limited
Incorporated: 30 June 1988
Previous: Armstrong Brooks PLC
Net Worth: £7,746,527 *Total Assets:* £14,975,103
Registered Office: Riverside House, Kings Reach Business Park, Yew Street, Stockport, Cheshire, SK4 2HD
Activities: Activities of other holding companies n.e.c.
Officers: Robert Cory [1944] Director

Aroqua Power Services Ltd.
Incorporated: 14 June 2002 *Employees:* 12
Net Worth: £13,695,403 *Total Assets:* £13,759,360
Registered Office: Jubilee Place, Station Road, North Hykeham, Lincs, LN6 3QX
Activities: Installation of industrial machinery and equipment
Officers: Gary Curtis, Secretary/Business Development Manager; Gary Curtis [1960] Director/Business Development Manager; Barbara Allison Young [1965] Director/Business Manager

Arpo Global Limited
Incorporated: 27 February 2013 *Employees:* 45
Net Worth: £10,855,620 *Total Assets:* £16,907,318
Registered Office: Sterling House, Hamlin Way, Harwick Narrows Industrial Estate, Kings Lynn, Norfolk, PE30 4NG
Activities: Wholesale of other intermediate products
Officers: Charles David McIntyre [1974] Commercial Director; Clive Russell Turner [1977] Sales Director; Marcus James Turner [1970] Managing Director; Stephen Richard Turner [1972] Director/Merchant

ARRK Europe Limited
Incorporated: 13 August 1997 *Employees:* 273
Net Worth: £7,041,000 *Total Assets:* £18,380,000
Registered Office: Caldwell Road, Nuneaton, Warwicks, CV11 4NG
Activities: Other manufacturing n.e.c.
Parent: ARRK Product Development Group Limited
Officers: Simon Holmes, Secretary; Simon Holmes [1967] Finance Director; Kenichi Honna [1970] Director [Japanese]; Antony Stephen Hunter Lowe [1964] Director; Robin Craig Vickers [1959] Director

Art Systems Limited
Incorporated: 13 July 1995 *Employees:* 66
Net Worth: £2,843,442 *Total Assets:* £12,547,895
Registered Office: Unit 10, 11 & 12 Glaisdale Point, Glaisdale Parkway, Nottingham, NG8 4GP
Activities: Other information technology service activities
Shareholders: Art Systems (Holdings) Limited; Art Systems (Holdings) Limited
Officers: Stephen Francis Bliss [1967] Finance Director; Duncan Gavin Forsyth [1965] Director; Steven Hawker [1963] Sales Director; Leon Hemani [1971] Director; Sunil Jayantilal Madhani [1966] Director

Artex Limited
Incorporated: 12 January 2001 *Employees:* 94
Net Worth: £37,544,000 *Total Assets:* £58,028,000
Registered Office: Saint-Gobain House, Binley Business Park, Coventry, Warwicks, CV3 2TT
Activities: Manufacture of plaster products for construction purposes
Parent: Compagnie de Saint-Gobain
Officers: Alun Roy Oxenham, Secretary; Nicholas James Cammack [1972] Director; Michael Strickland Chaldecott [1960] Managing Director; Stephane Heraud [1965] Director [French]

Artform International Limited
Incorporated: 7 November 1973 *Employees:* 183
Net Worth: £13,378,000 *Total Assets:* £23,279,000
Registered Office: Bishop Meadow Road, Loughborough, Leics, LE11 5TH
Activities: Manufacture of other plastic products
Officers: Brian Diaz [1976] Director [American]; Lisa MacDonald [1970] Director

Arthrex Limited
Incorporated: 15 May 1996 *Employees:* 73
Net Worth: £14,385,418 *Total Assets:* £18,927,242
Registered Office: Unit 5 Smithy Wood Drive, Chapeltown, Sheffield, S35 1QN
Activities: Retail sale of medical and orthopaedic goods in specialised stores (not incl. hearing aids) n.e.c.
Officers: Stefan Krupp [1962] Managing Director [German]

Artisan (UK) PLC
Incorporated: 8 September 1998 *Employees:* 49
Net Worth: £6,187,662 *Total Assets:* £13,917,463
Registered Office: 2b Vantage Park, Washingley Road, Huntingdon, Cambs, PE29 6SR
Activities: Activities of head offices
Parent: Aspen Finance Limited
Officers: Philip Richard Speer, Secretary; Ian David Dyke [1959] Director; Michael John Eyres [1956] Director/Surveyor; Geoffrey James Lawler [1969] Director/Chartered Accountant; Geoffrey Hugh Melamet [1958] Director

Arugani Limited
Incorporated: 29 January 2016
Net Worth: £844,334,144 *Total Assets:* £850,376,448
Registered Office: Warren House, Bell Lane, Thame, Oxon, OX9 3AL
Activities: Activities of other holding companies n.e.c.
Shareholders: CPP Investment Board; Glencore PLC
Officers: John William Burton [1965] Director/Solicitor; Peter Mario Mouthaan [1970] Director/Chief Financial Officer [Dutch]; Timothy John Scott [1967] Director/Accountant

Ascend Global Holdings, Ltd.
Incorporated: 27 June 2014 *Employees:* 187
Net Worth Deficit: £23,291,388 *Total Assets:* £13,216,702
Registered Office: Dryden House, St Johns Street, Huntingdon, Cambs, PE29 3NU
Activities: Activities of other holding companies n.e.c.
Parent: Ascend Learning LLC
Officers: Tracey Gough, Secretary; Lawrence Adam Gold [1967] Director/Attorney [American]; Nicolas William Harding [1983] Director/Accountant; Mandeep Singh Johar [1971] Director/Chief Financial Officer [Indian]; Greg Sebasky [1958] Director [American]

Ascend Global Intermediate Holdings, Ltd.
Incorporated: 30 June 2014
Net Worth: £20,702,004 *Total Assets:* £24,409,136
Registered Office: Dryden House, St Johns Street, Huntingdon, Cambs, PE29 3NU
Activities: Activities of other holding companies n.e.c.
Parent: Ascend Global Holdings Ltd
Officers: Tracey Gough, Secretary; Lawrence Adam Gold [1967] Director/Attorney [American]; Nicolas William Harding [1983] Director/Accountant; Mandeep Singh Johar [1971] Director/Chief Financial Officer [Indian]; Greg Sebasky [1958] Director [American]

Ascott Transport Limited
Incorporated: 24 July 1959 *Employees:* 208
Net Worth: £3,966,846 *Total Assets:* £13,934,461
Registered Office: Hangar House, Woodyard Lane, Foston, Derby, DE65 5DJ
Activities: Freight transport by road
Parent: DNA (Holdings) Limited
Officers: Matthew Dean Ash, Secretary; Norma Rose Ascott [1942] Director; Peter Norman Ascott [1969] Director/Logistics; Stuart John Ascott [1971] Director/Logistics; Matthew Dean Ash [1985] Finance Director; Jonathan David Ward [1969] Managing Director

ASD Lighting Holdings Limited
Incorporated: 14 December 2009 *Employees:* 375
Net Worth: £19,893,712 *Total Assets:* £27,491,424
Registered Office: Mangham Road, Barbot Hall Industrial Estate, Rotherham, S Yorks, S61 4RJ
Activities: Non-trading company
Shareholders: Anthony Roy Stewart; Joan Margaret Stewart
Officers: Karen Thomas, Secretary; John Charles William Finelli [1956] Sales & Marketing Director; Julie Mary Hunt [1963] Director; Anthony Roy Stewart [1945] Managing Director; Karen Thomas [1970] Director/Accountant

ASD Lighting PLC
Incorporated: 12 November 1982 *Employees:* 205
Net Worth: £23,417,504 *Total Assets:* £27,649,312
Registered Office: Mangham Road, Barbot Hall Industrial Estate, Rotherham, S Yorks, S61 4RJ
Activities: Manufacture of electric lighting equipment
Parent: ASD Lighting Holdings Limited
Officers: Karen Thomas, Secretary; Darrell Clark [1966] Director; Jon Charles William Finelli [1956] Sales & Marketing Director; Julie Mary Hunt [1963] Director; Anthony Roy Stewart [1945] Managing Director; Richard Paul Stewart [1976] Director; Karen Thomas [1970] Director/Accountant

Asfordby Storage & Haulage Limited
Incorporated: 18 April 1961 *Employees:* 173
Net Worth: £44,027,440 *Total Assets:* £46,192,344
Registered Office: Saxby Road, Melton Mowbray, Leics, LE13 1BY
Activities: Operation of warehousing and storage facilities for land transport activities
Major Shareholder: Michael John Dolby
Officers: Anthony Edward Mason, Secretary; Briegeen Maria Dolby [1981] Director/Midwife; Michael John Dolby [1949] Director; Patrick James Dolby [1987] Director/Research Analyst; Maureen Patricia John [1948] Director; Anthony Edward Mason [1949] Director

ASG Group Associates Limited
Incorporated: 22 April 2009 *Employees:* 178
Net Worth: £9,594,724 *Total Assets:* £11,555,854
Registered Office: 997 London Road, Derby, DE24 8PX
Activities: Activities of head offices
Major Shareholder: Peter Neville Allman
Officers: Valerie Josephine Allman, Secretary; James Bruce Allman [1963] Director; Peter Neville Allman [1940] Director/Motor Engineer

Asgard Group Ltd
Incorporated: 13 October 2006 *Employees:* 116
Net Worth: £9,902,136 *Total Assets:* £20,424,232
Registered Office: Holiday Inn Royal Victoria, Victoria Station Road, Sheffield, S4 7YE
Activities: Activities of head offices
Shareholders: John Terence Conroy; Hermann Beck
Officers: Hermann Beck, Secretary [German]; Hermann Beck [1963] Director/Hotel Manager [German]; John Terence Conroy [1962] Director/Consultant

Ashberry Healthcare Limited
Incorporated: 3 September 2003 *Employees:* 433
Net Worth Deficit: £1,578,364 *Total Assets:* £11,502,204
Registered Office: 37 Market Square, Witney, Oxon, OX28 6RE
Activities: Medical nursing home activities
Officers: Virginia Deayton Groom, Secretary; Virginia Deayton-Groom [1958] Company Secretary/Director; Nigel John Denny [1959] Managing Director; Rosamund Jill Spalding [1952] Director

Ashby School
Incorporated: 2 July 2012 *Employees:* 230
Net Worth: £17,116,000 *Total Assets:* £21,893,000
Registered Office: Ashby School, Nottingham Road, Ashby-De-La-Zouch, Leics, LE65 1DT
Activities: General secondary education
Officers: Andrew James Burton, Secretary; Mathew Francis Anwyll [1980] Director/Teacher; Alison Margaret Bennett [1947] Director/Editorial Assistant; Elaine Anne Blunt [1962] Director and Company Secretary; Alan Davies [1952] Director/Retired; Kay Louise Davies [1973] Director/Town Planner; Dr Roy Percy Eady [1944] Director/Part Time Consultant; Judith Irene Hunt [1947] Director/Retired; Peter Leslie McBride [1943] Director/Consultant; Fiona Jacqueline McCafferty [1983] Director/Teacher; Peter Robin Page [1970] Director/IT Technician; Lawrence Arthur Robinson [1965] Director/Operations Manager; Geoffrey Peter Staniforth [1964] Director/Headteacher; Nicolas James Sutherland [1970] Sales Director; Charlotte Elizabeth Sutton [1977] Director/Teacher; Estelle Anita Vincent [1960] Director/Copywriter; Kirstie Wain [1974] Director/Trade Compliance Manager; Ralph Alexander Stephen Weir [1965] Director/Electrical Engineer

Ashfield Healthcare Communications Group Limited
Incorporated: 19 February 1985 *Employees:* 567
Previous: Knowledgepoint360 Group Limited
Net Worth: £19,601,000 *Total Assets:* £38,721,000
Registered Office: Ashfield House, Resolution Road, Ashby-De-La-Zouch, Leics, LE65 1HW
Activities: Other professional, scientific and technical activities n.e.c.
Parent: Knowledgepoint360 Group (Holdings) Limited
Officers: Richard Lawrence [1964] Director; Clifford Alexander McConkey [1970] Director

Ashfield Healthcare Limited
Incorporated: 2 December 1996 *Employees:* 1,025
Net Worth: £25,855,044 *Total Assets:* £40,897,088
Registered Office: Ashfield House, Resolution Road, Ashby De La Zouch, Leics, LE65 1HW
Activities: Other business support service activities n.e.c.
Parent: United Drug (UK) Holdings Limited
Officers: Stephen Martin Bainbridge, Secretary/Accountant; Stephen Martin Bainbridge [1961] Director/Accountant; Nicola Burns [1969] Director; Nigel John Mansford [1961] Director

Ashfield Meetings & Events Limited
Incorporated: 30 December 1997 *Employees:* 177
Net Worth: £3,098,557 *Total Assets:* £25,639,212
Registered Office: Ashfield House, Resolution Road, Ashby-De-La-Zouch, Leics, LE65 1HW
Activities: Other business support service activities n.e.c.
Parent: Ashfield Meetings & Events Group Limited
Officers: Stephen Bainbridge, Secretary; Stephen Martin Bainbridge [1961] Director/Accountant; Nicola Burns [1969] Operational Effectiveness Director; Penny Regina Callaghan [1965] European Operations Director

Ashford Riverside Park Limited
Incorporated: 21 June 2016
Net Worth Deficit: £3,077 *Total Assets:* £12,673,818
Registered Office: 37f Warpsgrove Lane, Chalgrove, Oxford, OX44 7RW
Activities: Construction of domestic buildings
Major Shareholder: Gabriel Michel El-Kassir
Officers: Gabriel Michel El-Kassir [1956] Director/Businessman

Ashmere Derbyshire Limited
Incorporated: 5 May 2016 *Employees:* 286
Net Worth: £9,865,408 *Total Assets:* £15,276,919
Registered Office: 90 Glass House, Hill, Codnor, Ripley, Derbys, DE5 9QT
Activities: Residential nursing care facilities
Shareholders: Michael Gerald Poxton; Gerald Poxton; David Andrew Poxton
Officers: Generald Poxton, Secretary; Michael Poxton, Secretary; David Andrew Poxton [1979] Director

Ashwicken Sporting LLP
Incorporated: 7 July 2010 *Employees:* 10
Net Worth: £8,737,820 *Total Assets:* £12,664,013
Registered Office: 22-26 King Street, King's Lynn, Norfolk, PE30 1HJ
Officers: David James Flux [1968] Member; Lisa Jane Flux [1972] Member; Oliver James Flux [1997] Member

ASK4 LIMITED
Incorporated: 26 April 2000 *Employees:* 115
Net Worth: £7,687,344 *Total Assets:* £18,107,544
Registered Office: Devonshire Green House, 14 Fitzwilliam Street, Sheffield, S1 4JL
Activities: Information technology consultancy activities
Parent: Stream Acquisitions Limited
Officers: Mark William Gerard Collins, Secretary; Jonathan James Burrows [1981] Director; Mark William Gerard Collins [1953] Finance Director; Michael Philip Cox [1974] Director; Robert Michael Crowther [1975] Group Sales Director; Simon John Day [1975] Director/Chief Operating Officer; Oliver Alexander George Riddle [1972] Sales Director; Jonathan Thornhill [1979] Director

Asmet (UK) Limited
Incorporated: 1 September 1993 *Employees:* 11
Net Worth: £8,600,588 *Total Assets:* £12,022,964
Registered Office: Jubilee House, Sheffield Road, Dronfield, Sheffield, S18 2HU
Activities: Wholesale of metals and metal ores
Parent: Asmet Limited
Officers: David Parker, Secretary; Ian Robert Copestake [1951] Director; David Parker [1946] Director

Asmet Limited
Incorporated: 11 September 2009 *Employees:* 11
Net Worth: £13,058,996 *Total Assets:* £15,219,460
Registered Office: Jubilee House, 61c Sheffield Road, Dronfield, Derbys, S18 2HU
Activities: Wholesale of metals and metal ores
Shareholders: David Parker; Ian Robert Copestake
Officers: Ian Robert Copestake [1951] Director; David Parker [1946] Director

Aspall Cyder Limited
Incorporated: 30 June 1986 *Employees:* 131
Net Worth: £950,877 *Total Assets:* £25,999,500
Registered Office: 137 High Street, Burton on Trent, Staffs, DE14 1JZ
Activities: Wholesale of wine, beer, spirits and other alcoholic beverages
Parent: Aspall Holdings Limited
Officers: Gemma Wisniewski, Secretary; Simon Kerry [1970] Director/Chief Finance Officer; James Christian Shearer [1980] Marketing Director; Philip Mark Whitehead [1977] Managing Director

Aspall Holdings Limited
Incorporated: 27 November 2015 *Employees:* 131
Net Worth: £1,190,862 *Total Assets:* £25,999,502
Registered Office: 137 High Street, Burton on Trent, Staffs, DE14 1JZ
Activities: Activities of other holding companies n.e.c.
Parent: Molson Coors Brewing Company (UK) Limited
Officers: Gemma Wisniewski, Secretary; Simon Kerry [1970] Director/Chief Finance Officer; James Christian Shearer [1980] Marketing Director; Philip Mark Whitehead [1977] Managing Director

Aspen Medical Europe Limited
Incorporated: 20 September 1947 *Employees:* 41
Net Worth: £9,022,000 *Total Assets:* £11,015,000
Registered Office: Clinitron House, Ashby Park, Ashby De La Zouch, Leics, LE65 1JG
Activities: Manufacture of basic pharmaceutical products
Parent: Hill-Rom UK (Holdings) Ltd
Officers: Stephen Sanders, Secretary; Carlos Alonso [1959] Director/President International [Spanish]; Duncan James Wilson [1969] Director

Aspire Achieve Advance Group Limited
Incorporated: 21 January 2011 *Employees:* 422
Net Worth: £5,085,844 *Total Assets:* £11,205,631
Registered Office: 2nd Floor, Sitwell House, Sitwell Street, Derby, DE1 2JT
Activities: Other education n.e.c.
Shareholders: Peter Marples; Diane McEvoy-Robinson
Officers: Richard Mark Gerver [1969] Director; Ian Grundy [1966] Finance Director; Richard Irons [1975] Director

Aspire Learning Trust (Whittlesey)
Incorporated: 26 March 2012 *Employees:* 258
Previous: Sir Harry Smith Academy Trust
Net Worth: £17,328,248 *Total Assets:* £21,265,452
Registered Office: Sir Harry Smith Academy, Eastrea Road, Whittlesey, Cambs, PE7 1XB
Activities: General secondary education
Officers: Susan Munns, Secretary; Stephen Ackerman [1964] Director/Operations Manager; Timothy John Beebe [1966] Director/Bank Manager; Jonathan Digby [1965] Director/College Principal; John Hall Donnachie [1945] Director/Retired; John King [1947] Director/Architect; John Michael Mullen [1950] Director/Retired; Joanna Phillips [1966] Director/Civil Servant; Jed Roberts [1955] Director/Retired

Aspire Schools Trust
Incorporated: 10 September 2012 *Employees:* 140
Previous: Aspire Schools Trust Ltd
Net Worth: £9,969,641 *Total Assets:* £12,029,376
Registered Office: Sir William Robertson Academy, Main Road, Welbourn, Lincoln, LN5 0PA
Activities: General secondary education
Officers: Sancha Georgette Maggs, Secretary; Mark Andrew Guest [1966] Director/Headteacher; Kerry Mary Stephanie Hamilton [1974] Director/Housewife; Timothy Sambrooke Kelway [1951] Director/Retired Lawyer; Brian Lucas [1940] Director/Archdeacon Emeritus of The Royal Air Force; Sylvia Mary Paddock [1962] Operations Director; Robert Jonathan William Sampson [1945] Director/Councillor; Simon Shaw [1969] Director/Accountant; Nicholas John Ashley Swindin [1968] Commercial Director

Aspireplus Educational Trust
Incorporated: 15 May 2017 *Employees:* 213
Net Worth: £41,853,348 *Total Assets:* £44,421,044
Registered Office: Longdendale High School, Spring Street, Hollingworth, Hyde, Cheshire, SK14 8LW
Activities: General secondary education
Officers: Louise Anne Hoyle, Secretary; Jane Barker [1971] Director; Matthew James Bowler [1971] Director; Barry John Harwood [1963] Director; Janet Anne Lambert [1965] Director; Dr Janet Nevin [1961] Director/College Principal; Jonathan Neil Reynolds [1980] Director; Kevin Taylor [1964] Director; Carol Thomas [1965] Director/School Improvement Consultant

Asquith Court Holdings Limited
Incorporated: 15 June 1990 *Employees:* 5
Net Worth: £116,790,000 *Total Assets:* £125,189,000
Registered Office: 2 Crown Way, Rushden, Northants, NN10 6BS
Activities: Non-trading company
Parent: Acorndrift Limited
Officers: Stephen Kramer, Secretary; Elizabeth Boland [1959] Director/Chief Financial Officer [American]; Stephen Dreier [1942] Director/Chief Admin Officer [American]; Dave Lissy [1965] Director/Chief Executive Officer [American]; James Walter Tugendhat [1971] Managing Director, International

Asquith Nurseries Limited
Incorporated: 20 May 2004 *Employees:* 1,938
Net Worth Deficit: £4,021,000 *Total Assets:* £74,796,000
Registered Office: 2 Crown Way, Rushden, Northants, NN10 6BS
Activities: Pre-primary education
Parent: Asquith Court Holdings Limited
Officers: Stephen Kramer, Secretary; Elizabeth Boland [1959] Director/Chief Financial Officer [American]; Stephen Dreier [1942] Director/Chief Admin Officer [American]; Dave Lissy [1965] Director/Chief Executive Officer [American]; James Walter Tugendhat [1971] Managing Director, International

ASSA ABLOY Entrance Systems Ltd
Incorporated: 17 July 1967 *Employees:* 204
Net Worth: £14,955,000 *Total Assets:* £23,246,000
Registered Office: 7 Churchill Way, Chapeltown, Sheffield, S35 2PY
Activities: Installation of industrial machinery and equipment
Parent: ASSA ABLOY AB
Officers: Nichola Jade Chapman, Secretary; John Steven Burton [1959] Managing Director; Biju Kochukunju Cherian [1974] Director/Business Controller; Per Olof Ingemar Hansson [1964] Director [Swedish]; Mogens Ahrens Jensen [1958] Director/Chief Executive [Danish]; Neil Joseph Mathews [1961] Managing Director

Assemblies of God Property Trust
Incorporated: 11 May 1954 *Employees:* 33
Net Worth: £6,091,000 *Total Assets:* £56,562,000
Registered Office: Ruddington Fields Business Park, Mere Way, Ruddington, Nottingham, NG11 6JS
Activities: Financial intermediation not elsewhere classified
Officers: Robert James Hyde, Secretary/Church Pastor; Remi Okechukwu Anekwe [1967] Director/Finance Broker; Rev Timothy William Bedward Jones [1969] Director/Church Pastor; Reverend Angela Butcher [1956] Director/Church Pastor; Robert James Hyde [1962] Director; Brian Campbell Niblock [1942] Director/Retired Pastor; David Ernest Shearman [1943] Director; Rev Kristian Paul Thorpe [1971] Director/Minister of Religion

Assured Group Investments Limited
Incorporated: 28 November 2016 *Employees:* 769
Net Worth: £15,463,715 *Total Assets:* £38,350,320
Registered Office: Heathcote Estate Works, Harriott Drive, Warwick, CV34 6TJ
Activities: Maintenance and repair of motor vehicles
Major Shareholder: Heath Simon Evans
Officers: Emanuel Crenstil Addae, Secretary; Emanuel Crenstil Addae [1962] Director; David John Evans [1976] Director; Heath Simon Evans [1968] Director; Martin Jon Rengger [1969] Director

Assured Group Limited
Incorporated: 2 May 1996 *Employees:* 344
Net Worth: £12,267,893 *Total Assets:* £26,824,406
Registered Office: Harriott Drive, Heathcote Industrial Estate, Warwick, CV34 6TJ
Activities: Maintenance and repair of motor vehicles
Shareholder: Heath Simon Evans
Officers: Emanuel Crenstil Addae, Secretary; Emanuel Crenstil Addae [1962] Director; David John Evans [1976] Director; Heath Simon Evans [1968] Director; Martin Jon Rengger [1969] Director

Asteelflash (Bedford) Limited
Incorporated: 6 May 1987 *Employees:* 107
Net Worth: £2,012,000 *Total Assets:* £15,814,000
Registered Office: Units 1 & 2, St Martins Business Centre, St Martins Way, Bedford, MK42 0LF
Activities: Manufacture of loaded electronic boards
Officers: Neil Stuart Mincher [1962] Director

Aster and Young Limited
Incorporated: 27 October 2016
Net Worth: £26,795,252 *Total Assets:* £26,795,252
Registered Office: Suite 5, Mansion House, Wellington Road South, Stockport, Cheshire, SK1 3UA
Activities: Trade of gas through mains
Major Shareholder: Mohammed Zain Chaudhry
Officers: Mohammed Zain Chaudhry [1992] Director

Aston Community Education Trust
Incorporated: 24 March 2011 *Employees:* 759
Net Worth: £64,802,000 *Total Assets:* £78,059,000
Registered Office: ACET House, 66 Holderness Drive, Aston, Sheffield, S26 2BH
Activities: Primary education
Officers: John Barton [1955] Director/Retired; Andrew Paul Brickles [1949] Director/Retired; Roy Dyson [1939] Director; Jenny Hudson [1945] Director/Retired; Catharine Kinsella [1948] Director/Retired; Miles Edward Parker [1971] Director/Lawyer; Iain Alexander Somerville [1965] Director/Reverend; John Francis Swift [1939] Director/Retired

Aston Martin Holdings (UK) Limited
Incorporated: 25 January 2007 *Employees:* 1,753
Net Worth: £140,196,000 *Total Assets:* £1,626,440,960
Registered Office: Aston Martin, Banbury Road, Gaydon, Warwick, CV35 0DB
Activities: Non-trading company
Parent: Aston Martin Lagonda Global Holdings PLC
Officers: Michael Marecki, Secretary; Dr Andrew Charles Palmer [1963] Director/Chief Executive

Aston Martin Investments Limited
Incorporated: 5 March 2007
Net Worth: £585,558,016 *Total Assets:* £585,558,016
Registered Office: Aston Martin, Banbury Road, Gaydon, Warwick, CV35 0DB
Activities: Non-trading company
Parent: Aston Martin Holdings (UK) Limited
Officers: Michael Marecki, Secretary; Dr Andrew Charles Palmer [1963] Director/Chief Executive

Aston Martin Lagonda Limited
Incorporated: 5 February 1975 *Employees:* 1,671
Net Worth: £269,708,992 *Total Assets:* £1,157,005,056
Registered Office: Banbury Road, Gaydon, Warwick, CV35 0DB
Activities: Manufacture of motor vehicles
Parent: Aston Martin Lagonda Group Limited
Officers: Michael Francis Marecki, Secretary; Dr Andrew Charles Palmer [1963] Director/Chief Executive Officer; Marek Paul Reichman [1966] Director; Mark Gerrard Wilson [1974] Director/Chief Financial Officer

Aston Martin Works Limited
Incorporated: 11 December 2009 *Employees:* 73
Net Worth: £15,191,000 *Total Assets:* £41,091,000
Registered Office: Banbury Road, Gaydon, Warwick, CV35 0DB
Activities: Maintenance and repair of motor vehicles
Shareholder: Aston Martin Lagonda Limited
Officers: Stephanie Yuen Yin Jackson, Secretary; Michael Francis Marecki, Secretary; Dawood Alhomoud [1952] Director [Kuwaiti]; Andrew Charles Palmer [1963] Director/Chief Executive; Christopher Mark Sheppard [1965] Director

Astor Care Limited
Incorporated: 17 August 1989 *Employees:* 20
Net Worth: £15,580,422 *Total Assets:* £17,567,838
Registered Office: 30 St Giles', Oxford, OX1 3LE
Activities: Residential nursing care facilities
Major Shareholder: Brian Cheung
Officers: Dr John Alastair James Chestnutt, Secretary; Dr Brian Cheung [1958] Director

Astrea Limited
Incorporated: 22 May 1990
Net Worth: £5,590,408 *Total Assets:* £19,996,318
Registered Office: 57-59 Saltergate, Chesterfield, Derbys, S40 1UL
Activities: Other letting and operating of own or leased real estate
Parent: Vertex Holdings Limited
Officers: Rupert John Henry Green, Secretary/Director; George Richard Green [1939] Director; Patrick William Green [1946] Director; Rupert John Henry Green [1959] Director; Sarah Edwina Green [1952] Director

Atlas Converting (UK Holdings) Limited
Incorporated: 30 September 2010 *Employees:* 139
Net Worth: £10,200,000 *Total Assets:* £19,901,000
Registered Office: c/o Atlas Converting Equipment Limited, Wolseley Road, Woburn Road Industrial Estate, Kempston, Bedford, MK42 7XT
Activities: Manufacture of plastics and rubber machinery
Officers: David Carson Reynolds, Secretary; Stanley Alan Braycotton [1958] Director; Alison Darlington [1960] Director; Stephen Jeffrey Darlington [1959] Director/Chairman; Barrie Kent Homewood [1963] Sales Director; Alan Ingram Johnson [1959] Director; David Carson Reynolds [1972] Finance Director; Thomas Riddell Walker [1953] Director

Atlas Converting Equipment Limited
Incorporated: 10 September 1976 *Employees:* 119
Net Worth: £9,004,000 *Total Assets:* £19,025,000
Registered Office: Wolseley Road, Kempston, Bedford, MK42 7XT
Activities: Manufacture of other general-purpose machinery n.e.c.
Parent: Atlas Converting (UK Holdings) Limited
Officers: David Carson Reynolds, Secretary; Stanley Alan Braycotton [1958] Sales Director; Stephen Jeffrey Darlington [1959] Director/Chairman; Barrie Kent Homewood [1963] Sales Director; Alan Ingram Johnson [1959] Managing Director; David Carson Reynolds [1972] Finance Director

Atlas Copco Medical Limited
Incorporated: 11 August 1994 *Employees:* 79
Net Worth: £11,725,000 *Total Assets:* £16,656,000
Registered Office: Telford Crescent, Speedwell Industrial Estate, Staveley, Chesterfield, Derbys, S43 3PF
Activities: Manufacture of medical and dental instruments and supplies
Parent: Atlas Copco UK Holding Ltd
Officers: Alex Christiaan Jan Bongaerts, Secretary; Susan Walker, Secretary; Alex Christiaan Jan Bongaerts [1960] Director/Holding Manager [Belgian]; Sanjay Safaya [1971] Director [Indian]; Ben Van Hove [1971] Director/Divisional President [Belgian]

Atlas Hotels (Bath) Limited
Incorporated: 18 November 1999 *Employees:* 25
Previous: Somerston Hotels (Bath) Limited
Net Worth: £31,310,732 *Total Assets:* £34,833,492
Registered Office: Bridgeway House, Bridgeway, Stratford upon Avon, Warwicks, CV37 6YX
Activities: Hotels and similar accommodation
Parent: Atlas Hotels Group Limited
Officers: Sean Joseph Lowe [1972] Director

Atlas Hotels (Borrowings 2) Limited
Incorporated: 25 May 2007 *Employees:* 1
Previous: Morethan Bidco Limited
Net Worth: £62,089,780 *Total Assets:* £166,511,232
Registered Office: Bridgeway House, Bridgeway, Stratford upon Avon, Warwicks, CV37 6YX
Activities: Activities of head offices
Parent: Atlas Hotels Group Limited
Officers: Sean Joseph Lowe [1972] Director

Atlas Hotels (Bristol North) Limited
Incorporated: 10 July 1998 *Employees:* 19
Previous: Somerston Hotels (Bristol North) Limited
Net Worth: £23,505,180 *Total Assets:* £26,020,732
Registered Office: Bridgeway House, Bridgeway, Stratford upon Avon, Warwicks, CV37 6YX
Activities: Hotels and similar accommodation
Parent: Atlas Hotels Group Limited
Officers: Sean Joseph Lowe [1972] Director

Atlas Hotels (Bristol Property) Limited
Incorporated: 11 October 1996
Previous: Morethanhotels (Bristol) Limited
Net Worth: £12,582,423 *Total Assets:* £13,757,528
Registered Office: Bridgeway House, Bridgeway, Stratford upon Avon, Warwicks, CV37 6YX
Activities: Hotels and similar accommodation
Parent: Atlas Hotels (Property) Limited
Officers: Sean Joseph Lowe [1972] Director

Atlas Hotels (Chingford) Limited
Incorporated: 24 November 1999 *Employees:* 21
Previous: Somerston Hotels (Chingford) Limited
Net Worth: £10,720,198 *Total Assets:* £12,459,776
Registered Office: Bridgeway House, Bridgeway, Stratford upon Avon, Warwicks, CV37 6YX
Activities: Hotels and similar accommodation
Parent: Atlas Hotels Group Limited
Officers: Sean Joseph Lowe [1972] Director

Atlas Hotels (Derby) Limited
Incorporated: 3 July 1997 *Employees:* 18
Previous: Somerston Hotels (Derby) Limited
Net Worth: £8,450,193 *Total Assets:* £9,692,667
Registered Office: Bridgeway House, Bridgeway, Stratford upon Avon, Warwicks, CV37 6YX
Activities: Hotels and similar accommodation
Parent: Atlas Hotels Group Limited
Officers: Sean Joseph Lowe [1972] Director

Atlas Hotels (Exeter) Limited
Incorporated: 30 May 1997 *Employees:* 20
Previous: Somerston Hotels (Exeter) Limited
Net Worth: £20,902,594 *Total Assets:* £23,599,980
Registered Office: Bridgeway House, Bridgeway, Stratford upon Avon, Warwicks, CV37 6YX
Activities: Hotels and similar accommodation
Parent: Atlas Hotels Limited
Officers: Sean Joseph Lowe [1972] Director

Atlas Hotels (Glasgow) Limited
Incorporated: 29 July 1997 *Employees:* 18
Previous: Somerston Hotels (Glasgow) Limited
Net Worth: £13,637,583 *Total Assets:* £15,884,934
Registered Office: Bridgeway House, Bridgeway, Stratford upon Avon, Warwicks, CV37 6YX
Activities: Hotels and similar accommodation
Parent: Atlas Hotels Group Limited
Officers: Christopher Richard Byrd, Secretary; Sean Joseph Lowe [1972] Director

Atlas Hotels (Greenwich) Limited
Incorporated: 17 April 1998 *Employees:* 26
Previous: Somerston Hotels (Greenwich) Limited
Net Worth: £49,271,864 *Total Assets:* £56,144,288
Registered Office: Bridgeway House, Bridgeway, Stratford upon Avon, Warwicks, CV37 6YX
Activities: Hotels and similar accommodation
Parent: Atlas Hotels Group Limited
Officers: Sean Joseph Lowe [1972] Director

Atlas Hotels (Group 1) Limited
Incorporated: 30 May 2003 *Employees:* 104
Previous: Somerston Hotels (Investments) Limited
Net Worth: £19,857,100 *Total Assets:* £104,491,328
Registered Office: Bridgeway House, Bridgeway, Stratford upon Avon, Warwicks, CV37 6YX
Activities: Hotels and similar accommodation
Parent: Atlas Hotels Group Limited
Officers: Sean Joseph Lowe [1972] Director

Atlas Hotels (Group 2) Limited
Incorporated: 28 April 1999 *Employees:* 61
Previous: Somerston Hotels (Properties) Limited
Net Worth: £55,933,280 *Total Assets:* £76,408,552
Registered Office: Bridgeway House, Bridgeway, Stratford upon Avon, Warwicks, CV37 6YX
Activities: Hotels and similar accommodation
Parent: Atlas Hotels Group Limited
Officers: Sean Joseph Lowe [1972] Director

Atlas Hotels (Group 3 Property) Limited
Incorporated: 12 December 1990 *Employees:* 1
Previous: Morethanhotels Limited
Net Worth: £98,385,848 *Total Assets:* £133,378,096
Registered Office: Bridgeway House, Bridgeway, Stratford upon Avon, Warwicks, CV37 6YX
Activities: Hotels and similar accommodation
Parent: Atlas Hotels (Property) Limited
Officers: Sean Joseph Lowe [1972] Director

Atlas Hotels (Group 4 Property 2) Limited
Incorporated: 6 March 1997
Previous: Morethanhotels FM Limited
Net Worth: £28,847,476 *Total Assets:* £34,465,352
Registered Office: Bridgeway House, Bridgeway, Stratford upon Avon, Warwicks, CV37 6YX
Activities: Hotels and similar accommodation
Parent: Atlas Hotels (Group 4 Property 1) Limited
Officers: Sean Joseph Lowe [1972] Director

Atlas Hotels (Inverness) Limited
Incorporated: 17 April 1998 *Employees:* 27
Previous: Somerston Hotels (Inverness) Limited
Net Worth: £15,209,329 *Total Assets:* £17,045,570
Registered Office: Bridgeway House, Bridgeway, Stratford upon Avon, Warwicks, CV37 6YX
Activities: Hotels and similar accommodation
Parent: Atlas Hotels Group Limited
Officers: Sean Joseph Lowe [1972] Director

Atlas Hotels (Lincoln) Limited
Incorporated: 6 December 2006 *Employees:* 33
Previous: Somerston Hotels (Lincoln) Limited
Net Worth: £9,752,902 *Total Assets:* £15,285,746
Registered Office: Bridgeway House, Bridgeway, Stratford upon Avon, Warwicks, CV37 6YX
Activities: Hotels and similar accommodation
Parent: Atlas Hotels Group Limited
Officers: Sean Joseph Lowe [1972] Director

Atlas Hotels (Liverpool) Limited
Incorporated: 9 November 2007 *Employees:* 24
Previous: Somerston Hotels (Liverpool) Limited
Net Worth: £4,483,355 *Total Assets:* £20,125,844
Registered Office: Bridgeway House, Bridgeway, Stratford upon Avon, Warwicks, CV37 6YX
Activities: Hotels and similar accommodation
Parent: Atlas Hotels Group Limited
Officers: Sean Joseph Lowe [1972] Director

Atlas Hotels (Property and Trading) Limited
Incorporated: 21 June 2000
Previous: Morethanhotels (No. 1) Limited
Net Worth: £30,014,380 *Total Assets:* £179,232,720
Registered Office: Bridgeway House, Bridgeway, Stratford upon Avon, Warwicks, CV37 6YX
Activities: Activities of head offices
Parent: Atlas Hotels (Borrowings 2) Limited
Officers: Sean Joseph Lowe [1972] Director

Atlas Hotels (Property) Limited
Incorporated: 21 June 2006
Previous: Morethanhotels Properties Limited
Net Worth: £46,198,496 *Total Assets:* £46,198,496
Registered Office: Bridgeway House, Bridgeway, Stratford upon Avon, Warwicks, CV37 6YX
Activities: Non-trading company
Parent: Atlas Hotels (Property and Trading) Limited
Officers: Sean Joseph Lowe [1972] Director

Atlas Hotels (Salford Quays) Limited
Incorporated: 13 February 1997 *Employees:* 17
Previous: Somerston Hotels (Salford Quays) Limited
Net Worth: £16,813,996 *Total Assets:* £19,190,272
Registered Office: Bridgeway House, Bridgeway, Stratford upon Avon, Warwicks, CV37 6YX
Activities: Hotels and similar accommodation
Parent: Atlas Hotels Group Limited
Officers: Christopher Richard Byrd, Secretary; Sean Joseph Lowe [1972] Director

Atlas Hotels (Stevenage) Limited
Incorporated: 11 February 2003 *Employees:* 20
Previous: Morethan Stevenage Limited
Net Worth: £1,758,824 *Total Assets:* £14,361,879
Registered Office: Bridgeway House, Bridgeway, Stratford upon Avon, Warwicks, CV37 6YX
Activities: Hotels and similar accommodation
Parent: Atlas Hotels Group Limited
Officers: Sean Joseph Lowe [1972] Director

Atlas Hotels (Trading) Limited
Incorporated: 21 June 2006 *Employees:* 218
Previous: Morethanhotels Trading Limited
Net Worth: £23,458,004 *Total Assets:* £151,550,512
Registered Office: Bridgeway House, Bridgeway, Stratford upon Avon, Warwicks, CV37 6YX
Activities: Hotels and similar accommodation
Parent: Atlas Hotels (Property and Trading) Limited
Officers: Sean Joseph Lowe [1972] Director

Atlas Hotels (Warwick) Limited
Incorporated: 13 February 1997 *Employees:* 17
Previous: Somerston Hotels (Warwick) Limited
Net Worth: £12,873,768 *Total Assets:* £14,966,200
Registered Office: Bridgeway House, Bridgeway, Stratford upon Avon, Warwicks, CV37 6YX
Activities: Hotels and similar accommodation
Parent: Atlas Hotels Group Limited
Officers: Sean Joseph Lowe [1972] Director

Atlas Hotels Limited
Incorporated: 1 July 1996 *Employees:* 54
Previous: Somerston Hotels Limited
Net Worth: £179,363,344 *Total Assets:* £655,684,864
Registered Office: Bridgeway House, Bridgeway, Stratford upon Avon, Warwicks, CV37 6YX
Activities: Hotels and similar accommodation
Parent: London & Regional Group Trading No.3 Limited
Officers: Sean Joseph Lowe [1972] Director; Desmond Louis Mildmay Taljaard [1961] Director

Atlas Textiles Ltd.
Incorporated: 26 March 1997 *Employees:* 9
Net Worth: £18,688,090 *Total Assets:* £24,833,822
Registered Office: 141 Barkby Road, Leicester, LE4 9LG
Activities: Wholesale of textiles
Major Shareholder: Shajid Razak Latif
Officers: Nazrana Shajid Latif, Secretary; Shajid Razak Latif [1972] Director

AU79 Limited
Incorporated: 3 February 2014 *Employees:* 391
Net Worth: £20,893,118 *Total Assets:* £35,172,872
Registered Office: 164 Cowley Road, Oxford, OX4 1UE
Activities: Activities of financial services holding companies
Officers: Kohei Ogawa [1956] Director [Japanese]

Auchencairn Forest LLP
Incorporated: 18 June 2015
Net Worth: £22,460,270 *Total Assets:* £27,653,038
Registered Office: Glebe Barn, Great Barrington, Burford, Oxon, OX18 4US
Officers: John Frederick Hartz [1963] Member; Catherine Jean Hartz [1958] LLP Member

Auction Finance Limited
Incorporated: 31 October 2003
Net Worth: £3,200,000 *Total Assets:* £15,000,000
Registered Office: Lake View, Lakeside, Cheadle, Cheshire, SK8 3GW
Activities: Activities of mortgage finance companies
Parent: Together Financial Services Limited
Officers: Sarah Elizabeth Batt, Secretary; Gary Derek Beckett [1969] Director; Wayne Bowser [1952] Director; Marc Richard Goldberg [1971] Director; Robert Michael McTighe [1953] Director; Henry Neville Moser [1949] Director

Audley Travel Group Limited
Incorporated: 25 April 1996 *Employees:* 463
Net Worth: £56,559,000 *Total Assets:* £196,992,000
Registered Office: New Mill, New Mill Lane, Witney, Oxon, OX29 9SX
Activities: Tour operator activities
Parent: Boketto Bidco Limited
Officers: Elizabeth Ann Ward, Secretary; Mark Christopher Hanson [1972] Director; Nicholas Winston Longman [1968] Director; Richard John Prosser [1957] Director/Chairman; Nils Olin Steinmeyer [1970] Director [German]

Aurajoki Europe Limited
Incorporated: 8 November 2011 *Employees:* 6
Previous: Dollar Financial Europe Limited
Net Worth: £88,526,000 *Total Assets:* £90,018,000
Registered Office: Unit 1 Castle Marina Road, Nottingham, NG7 1TN
Activities: Other credit granting n.e.c.
Parent: Aurajoki Holdings UK Limited
Officers: Jonathan Ashley [1966] Director [American]; Justin Staadecker [1968] Director

Aurajoki Romania Limited
Incorporated: 21 February 2013
Previous: DF Romania Holdings Limited
Net Worth: £77,294,000 *Total Assets:* £77,294,000
Registered Office: Unit 1 Castle Marina Road, Nottingham, NG7 1TN
Activities: Other credit granting n.e.c.
Parent: Aurajoki Europe Limited
Officers: Kevin Richard Kaye [1969] Finance Director

Aurora Fashions Finance Limited
Incorporated: 9 January 2009 *Employees:* 2
Net Worth: £13,500,000 *Total Assets:* £287,300,000
Registered Office: The Triangle, Stanton Harcourt Industrial Estate, Stanton Harcourt, Witney, Oxon, OX29 5UT
Activities: Activities of head offices
Parent: Aurora Fashions Holdings Limited
Officers: John Philip Madden III [1973] Director [American]; Johann Petur Reyndal [1962] Director [Icelander]

Aurora Fashions Group Limited
Incorporated: 18 October 2010 *Employees:* 6,513
Net Worth Deficit: £136,100,000 *Total Assets:* £210,300,000
Registered Office: The Triangle, Stanton Harcourt Industrial Estate, Stanton Harcourt, Witney, Oxon, OX29 5UT
Activities: Non-trading company
Parent: Aurora Guaranteeco Limited
Officers: John Philip Madden III [1973] Director [American]; Johann Petur Reyndal [1962] Director [Icelander]

Aurum Acquisitions Limited
Incorporated: 16 March 2004 *Employees:* 3
Net Worth: £190,091,808 *Total Assets:* £190,276,432
Registered Office: Aurum House, 2 Elland Road, Braunstone, Leicester, LE3 1TT
Activities: Retail sale of watches and jewellery in specialised stores
Parent: The Watches of Switzerland Group Limited
Officers: Gillian Oliff, Secretary; Anthony John Broderick [1958] Director/Chief Operating Officer; Hugh Brian Duffy [1954] Director/Chief Executive; Lars Anders Ragnar Romberg [1963] Director [Swedish]

Aus-Bore Estates Limited
Incorporated: 28 June 1995
Net Worth: £11,322,290 *Total Assets:* £22,971,240
Registered Office: Aus-Bore House, 19-25 Manchester Road, Wilmslow, Cheshire, SK9 1BQ
Activities: Development of building projects
Shareholders: Jonathon Scott Burgess; Elizabeth Jane Burgess
Officers: Elizabeth Jane Burgess, Secretary; Harriet Jane Burgess [1989] Director; James John Campbell Burgess [1987] Director; Jonathon Scott Burgess [1954] Managing Director

Autins Group PLC
Incorporated: 25 March 2014 *Employees:* 194
Previous: Autins Group Limited
Net Worth: £15,943,000 *Total Assets:* £26,078,000
Registered Office: Central Point One, Central Park Drive, Rugby, Warwicks, CV23 0WE
Activities: Activities of head offices
Officers: James Larner, Secretary; Adam Richard Attwood [1967] Director; Terence Garthwaite [1946] Director; Ian Roy Griffiths [1950] Director; Gareth Richard Norman Kaminski-Cook [1964] Director; James David Larner [1976] Director/Chartered Accountant

Autins Limited
Incorporated: 29 March 1966 *Employees:* 116
Previous: Automotive Insulations Limited
Net Worth: £3,898,000 *Total Assets:* £19,807,000
Registered Office: Central Point One, Central Park Drive, Rugby, Warwicks, CV23 0WE
Activities: Other manufacturing n.e.c.
Parent: Autins Group PLC
Officers: James Larner, Secretary; Gareth Richard Norman Kaminski-Cook [1964] Director; James David Larner [1976] Director/Chartered Accountant

Auto-Trail V.R. Limited
Incorporated: 24 March 1998 *Employees:* 213
Net Worth: £20,526,296 *Total Assets:* £44,286,888
Registered Office: Trigano House, Genesis Way, Europarc, Grimsby, N E Lincs, DN37 9TU
Activities: Manufacture of caravans
Shareholders: Francois Marie Feuillet; Trigano
Officers: Shane Guy Devoy, Secretary; Shane Guy Devoy [1964] Finance Director; Jean Paul Fassinotti [1957] Commercial Director [French]; Francois Marie Feuillet [1948] Director [French]; Marie Helene Simone Feuillet [1948] Director [French]; Michel Freiche [1960] Director/Chief Financial Officer [French]; David Gareth Thomas [1959] Joint Managing Director

Autocraft Drivetrain Solutions Limited
Incorporated: 24 August 1993 *Employees:* 188
Net Worth: £7,154,000 *Total Assets:* £13,860,000
Registered Office: Autocraft Drivetrain Solutions Limited, Main Road, Belton, Grantham, Lincs, NG32 2LY
Activities: Manufacture of other parts and accessories for motor vehicles
Parent: Harmor Ltd
Officers: Michael James Idwal Hague-Morgan [1974] Director; Steven Harris [1960] Director; John Neil Seaton [1967] Director/Accountant; Simon Derek Warburton [1968] Director/Engineering & Quality

Autofil Holdings Limited
Incorporated: 21 July 1998 *Employees:* 225
Net Worth: £7,679,092 *Total Assets:* £20,192,060
Registered Office: Unit 3 Orchard Court, Sutton in Ashfield, Notts, NG17 2HU
Activities: Non-trading company
Major Shareholder: Paolo Piana
Officers: Mark Stephen Llewellyn, Secretary; Jeff James Holder [1976] Director; Mark Stephen Llewellyn [1972] Director/Accountant

Autofil Yarns Limited
Incorporated: 21 July 1998 *Employees:* 225
Net Worth: £5,963,164 *Total Assets:* £20,062,062
Registered Office: Unit 3 Orchard Court, Nunn Brook Road, Sutton in Ashfield, Notts, NG17 2HU
Activities: Finishing of textiles
Shareholder: Paolo Piana
Officers: Mark Stephen Llewellyn, Secretary; Gianfranco Feldi [1968] Director/Engineer [Italian]; Jeff James Holder [1976] Director; Mark Stephen Llewellyn [1972] Director/Accountant

Autologic Diagnostics Holdings Limited
Incorporated: 18 November 2009
Net Worth: £5,171,977 *Total Assets:* £14,772,500
Registered Office: Autologic House, London Road, Wheatley, Oxon, OX33 1JH
Activities: Activities of other holding companies n.e.c.
Parent: Opus Group AB
Officers: Johan Linus Brandt [1966] Director [Swedish]; Lothar Geilen [1961] Director [German]; Brian Herron [1980] Director/President [American]

Autologic Diagnostics Limited
Incorporated: 9 February 2009 *Employees:* 77
Net Worth: £2,064,832 *Total Assets:* £19,837,912
Registered Office: Autologic House, London Road, Wheatley, Oxon, OX33 1JH
Activities: Manufacture of electronic measuring, testing etc. equipment, not for industrial process control
Parent: Autologic Diagnostics Holdings Limited
Officers: Johan Linus Brandt [1966] Director [Swedish]; Kevin Joseph Finn [1960] Managing Director [Irish]; Lothar Geilen [1961] Director [German]; Brian Herron [1980] Director/President [American]

Autumnpark Limited
Incorporated: 6 December 1984 *Employees:* 7
Net Worth: £11,273,712 *Total Assets:* £15,470,725
Registered Office: Cabourn House, Station Street, Bingham, Notts, NG13 8AQ
Activities: Other letting and operating of own or leased real estate
Shareholder: Autumnpark Holdings Limited
Officers: Emma Rebecca Eatch [1974] Director; Jonathan James Campbell Eatch [1970] Director/Builder; Andrew Peter Edwards [1967] Director/Building Contractor; Vanessa Carole Edwards [1968] Director

Available Car Limited
Incorporated: 7 November 2001 *Employees:* 720
Net Worth: £35,470,000 *Total Assets:* £83,702,000
Registered Office: Station Road, Castle Donington, Derbys, DE74 2NL
Activities: Sale of used cars and light motor vehicles
Parent: Graham Bell Holdings Limited
Officers: Alison Mary Bell, Secretary; Stephen Bryan Alcock [1958] Director; Paul Charles Arscott [1955] Director/General Manager; Alison Mary Bell [1960] Director; Clare Rachel Bell [1985] Director/Motor Trade; Graham Bell [1959] Director; Michael William Bell [1985] Director/Motor Trade; Elizabeth Mary Hitchen [1983] Director/Motor Trade

Avalon (Europe) Limited
Incorporated: 19 May 1999 *Employees:* 2
Net Worth Deficit: £645,288 *Total Assets:* £47,358,072
Registered Office: Unit A2, Brooke Court, Handforth Dean, Wilmslow, Cheshire, SK9 3ND
Activities: Funeral and related activities
Parent: Nirvana Holdings Limited
Officers: Mark Dugdale [1968] Director; Jason Peter Gardner [1973] Director; Peter Brian Leech [1983] Director

The Avalon Trustee Company Limited
Incorporated: 15 July 1993 *Employees:* 111
Net Worth Deficit: £8,653,524 *Total Assets:* £55,281,008
Registered Office: Unit A2, Brooke Court, Handforth Dean, Wilmslow, Cheshire, SK9 3ND
Activities: Funeral and related activities
Parent: Nirvana Holdings Limited
Officers: Ben Evans, Secretary; Mark Dugdale [1968] Director; Jason Peter Gardner [1973] Operations Director; Peter Brian Leech [1983] Director

Avant Homes (England) Limited
Incorporated: 23 February 1972 *Employees:* 450
Previous: Gladedale (South Yorkshire) Limited
Net Worth: £166,468,000 *Total Assets:* £521,600,992
Registered Office: Avant House, 6 and 9 Tallys End, Barlborough, Chesterfield, Derbys, S43 4WP
Activities: Construction of commercial buildings
Parent: Avant Homes Group Limited
Officers: Joanne Elizabeth Massey, Secretary; Stephen Jeremy Hirst [1965] Director; Colin Edward Lewis [1956] Director; Mark Stephen Mitchell [1980] Director; Aileen Payne [1969] Finance Director; Stuart Rowlands [1962] Director; Giles Henry Sharp [1970] Director/Chartered Accountant; Robert Anthony Slocombe [1966] Director; Jennifer Tupman [1976] Director/Accountant; Scott Varley [1980] Managing Director

Avant Homes (No.2) Limited
Incorporated: 11 August 2009
Previous: Avant Homes Limited
Net Worth: £29,236,000 *Total Assets:* £374,716,000
Registered Office: Avant House, 6 and 9 Tallys End, Barlborough, Chesterfield, Derbys, S43 4WP
Activities: Activities of head offices
Parent: Avant Homes Group Limited
Officers: Joanne Elizabeth Massey, Secretary; Colin Edward Lewis [1956] Director; Gerard Christopher Loftus [1960] Director; Mark Stephen Mitchell [1980] Director; Giles Henry Sharp [1970] Director/Chartered Accountant

Avant Homes (Yorkshire) Limited
Incorporated: 12 September 2002
Previous: High Royds Limited
Net Worth Deficit: £2,848,000 *Total Assets:* £17,853,000
Registered Office: Avant House, 6 and 9 Tallys End, Barlborough, Chesterfield, Derbys, S43 4WP
Activities: Development of building projects
Parent: Avant Homes (England) Limited
Officers: Joanne Elizabeth Massey, Secretary; Stephen Jeremy Hirst [1965] Director; Colin Edward Lewis [1956] Director; Mark Stephen Mitchell [1980] Director; Giles Henry Sharp [1970] Director/Chartered Accountant; Robert Anthony Slocombe [1966] Director

Avant Homes Group Limited
Incorporated: 10 November 2014 *Employees:* 676
Net Worth: £104,592,000 *Total Assets:* £518,963,008
Registered Office: Avant House, 6 and 9 Tallys End, Barlborough, Chesterfield, Derbys, S43 4WP
Activities: Activities of head offices
Officers: Joanne Elizabeth Massey, Secretary; Paul Malcolm Bridges [1958] Director/Chartered Accountant; Colin Edward Lewis [1956] Director; Gerard Christopher Loftus [1960] Director; Mark Stephen Mitchell [1980] Director; Giles Henry Sharp [1970] Director/Chartered Accountant; Michael Andrew James Smith [1962] Director

Avant Homes Group No.2 Limited
Incorporated: 10 August 2009
Previous: Avant Homes Group Limited
Net Worth Deficit: £12,096,000 *Total Assets:* £224,856,992
Registered Office: Avant House, 6 and 9 Tallys End, Barlborough, Chesterfield, Derbys, S43 4WP
Activities: Activities of head offices
Parent: Avant Homes Group Limited
Officers: Joanne Elizabeth Massey, Secretary; Colin Edward Lewis [1956] Director; Gerard Christopher Loftus [1960] Director; Mark Stephen Mitchell [1980] Director; Giles Henry Sharp [1970] Director/Chartered Accountant

Avant Homes Holdings Limited
Incorporated: 21 June 2012
Net Worth: £26,657,000 *Total Assets:* £224,984,000
Registered Office: Avant House, 6 and 9 Tallys End, Barlborough, Chesterfield, Derbys, S43 4WP
Activities: Activities of head offices
Parent: Avant Homes Group Limited
Officers: Joanne Elizabeth Massey, Secretary; Colin Edward Lewis [1956] Director; Gerard Christopher Loftus [1960] Director; Mark Stephen Mitchell [1980] Director; Giles Henry Sharp [1970] Director/Chartered Accountant

Avant Homes Limited
Incorporated: 21 June 1996 *Employees:* 81
Previous: Gladedale Holdings Limited
Net Worth Deficit: £11,224,000 *Total Assets:* £285,062,016
Registered Office: Avant House, 6 and 9 Tallys End, Barlborough, Chesterfield, Derbys, S43 4WP
Activities: Activities of head offices
Parent: Avant Homes (No.2) Limited
Officers: Joanne Elizabeth Massey, Secretary; Colin Edward Lewis [1956] Director; Mark Stephen Mitchell [1980] Director; Giles Henry Sharp [1970] Director/Chartered Accountant

Avanti Gas Limited
Incorporated: 18 April 1950 *Employees:* 233
Net Worth: £45,565,000 *Total Assets:* £63,887,000
Registered Office: UGI House, Gisborne Close, Staveley, Chesterfield, Derbys, S43 3JT
Activities: Wholesale of other fuels and related products
Parent: UGI Midlands Limited
Officers: Gabriel Gary Garcia [1966] Director/Treasurer [American]; Donald Groth [1966] Director/Vice President Finance [American]; Thaddeus J. Jastrzebski [1961] Director/Chief Financial Officer of UGI Corporation [American]; Neil Murphy [1961] Managing Director; Roger Perreault [1964] Director [Canadian]; Angela Margaret Widdup [1965] Finance Director

Avdel Holding Limited
Incorporated: 3 April 1936
Net Worth: £55,682,000 *Total Assets:* £59,666,000
Registered Office: 3 Europa Court, Sheffield Business Park, Sheffield, S9 1XE
Activities: Activities of head offices
Officers: Steven John Costello, Secretary; Amit Kumar Sood [1978] Finance Director

Avdel UK Limited
Incorporated: 11 June 1936 *Employees:* 307
Net Worth: £89,096,000 *Total Assets:* £101,359,000
Registered Office: 3 Europa Court, Sheffield Business Park, Sheffield, S9 1XE
Activities: Manufacture of fasteners and screw machine products
Parent: Avdel Holding Limited
Officers: Steven John Costello, Secretary; Amit Kumar Sood [1978] Finance Director

Aven Tools Limited
Incorporated: 23 September 1970
Net Worth: £18,229,000 *Total Assets:* £18,229,000
Registered Office: 3 Europa Court, Sheffield Airport Business Park, Sheffield, S9 1XE
Activities: Non-trading company
Parent: Black & Decker
Officers: Steven John Costello [1980] Director/Chartered Accountant; Mark Richard Smiley [1977] Director/General Manager UK & ROI; Amit Kumar Sood [1978] Director/Accountant

Avenue Lets Limited
Incorporated: 11 January 2016 *Employees:* 8
Net Worth Deficit: £35,297 *Total Assets:* £13,062,826
Registered Office: 16 Dudley Street, Grimsby, N E Lincs, DN31 2AB
Activities: Real estate agencies
Major Shareholder: Jonathan Christopher Lovelle
Officers: Jonathan Christopher Lovelle [1974] Director

Avenuepoint Limited
Incorporated: 8 September 2005 *Employees:* 1
Net Worth: £1,784,830 *Total Assets:* £9,386,926
Registered Office: 14 Clarendon Street, Nottingham, NG1 5HQ
Activities: Development of building projects
Shareholders: Clare Rachel Lago; Sarah Elizabeth Mehigan
Officers: Sarah Elizabeth Nudd [1962] Director/Property Consultants

Avery Care (Cannock) Limited
Incorporated: 11 September 2014
Net Worth Deficit: £1,776,591 *Total Assets:* £29,349,766
Registered Office: 3 Cygnet Drive, Swan Valley, Northampton, NN4 9BS
Activities: Activities of head offices
Parent: Avery Holdco Cannock Limited
Officers: Matthew Frederick Proctor, Secretary; Ian Matthews [1948] Director; Matthew Frederick Proctor [1967] Director; John Michael Barrie Strowbridge [1967] Director

Avery Dennison Retail Information Services UK Limited
Incorporated: 18 July 1984 *Employees:* 177
Net Worth: £4,003,000 *Total Assets:* £17,186,000
Registered Office: Unit 9-10 Castlebridge Office Village, Kirtley Drive, Nottingham, NG7 1LD
Activities: Preparation and spinning of textile fibres
Parent: Avery Dennison Corporation
Officers: Hulbert Nicolaas Van Gijn [1962] Finance Director [Dutch]; Christopher Russell Johnson [1975] Director [American]; Stephen Antony Mason [1966] Director

Avery Healthcare Group Limited
Incorporated: 5 July 2013 *Employees:* 4
Net Worth: £199,678 *Total Assets:* £82,681,968
Registered Office: 3 Cygnet Drive, Swan Valley, Northampton, NN4 9BS
Activities: Activities of head offices
Parent: Avery Healthcare Holdings Limited
Officers: Matthew Frederick Proctor, Secretary; Ian Matthews [1948] Director; Matthew Frederick Proctor [1967] Director; Justin Reynolds Skiver [1977] Director/Senior Vice President - International [American]; John Michael Barrie Strowbridge [1967] Director

Avery Healthcare Holdings Limited
Incorporated: 6 December 2016 *Employees:* 3,506
Net Worth Deficit: £36,973,000 *Total Assets:* £123,312,000
Registered Office: 3 Cygnet Drive, Swan Valley, Northampton, NN4 9BS
Activities: Activities of head offices
Parent: Xanadu Investments Limited
Officers: Matthew Frederick Proctor, Secretary; Ian Matthews [1948] Director; Matthew Frederick Proctor [1967] Director; John Michael Barrie Strowbridge [1967] Director

Avery Homes (Nelson) Limited
Incorporated: 24 July 2008 *Employees:* 1,456
Net Worth Deficit: £13,770,054 *Total Assets:* £52,286,144
Registered Office: 3 Cygnet Drive, Swan Valley, Northampton, NN4 9BS
Activities: Residential care activities for the elderly and disabled
Parent: Willowbrook Healthcare Debtco Limited
Officers: Matthew Fredrick Proctor, Secretary; Ian Matthews [1948] Director; Matthew Frederick Proctor [1967] Director; John Michael Barrie Strowbridge [1967] Director

Avery House Healthcare Limited
Incorporated: 20 August 2007 *Employees:* 84
Net Worth: £3,026,000 *Total Assets:* £11,945,000
Registered Office: Norcliffe House, Station Road, Wilmslow, Cheshire, SK9 1BU
Activities: Other human health activities
Parent: Optimum FS Care Developments Limited
Officers: Abigail Mattison, Secretary; Ryan Stuart MacAskill [1975] Director; Gregory Laurence Newman [1988] Director/Investment Professional; Jeremy Robert Arthur Richardson [1970] Director; Dr Maureen Claire Royston [1960] Director; Phillip Gary Thomas [1978] Director

Averys (Radnage) Limited
Incorporated: 25 March 1938 *Employees:* 3
Net Worth: £2,878,676 *Total Assets:* £10,556,071
Registered Office: Eastfield House, Eastfield Farm, Mavis Enderby, Spilsby, Lincs, PE23 4EJ
Activities: Mixed farming
Major Shareholder: Penelope Ruth Avery
Officers: Penelope Ruth Avery, Secretary; Penelope Ruth Avery [1950] Director/Farmer; Roderick James Avery [1977] Director/Farmer

Aviagen European Holdings Limited
Incorporated: 13 February 2009
Net Worth: £57,267,000 *Total Assets:* £99,949,000
Registered Office: Stratford Hatchery, Alscott Industrial Estate, Atherstone on Stour, Stratford upon Avon, Warwicks, CV37 8BH
Activities: Activities of agricultural holding companies
Parent: Aviagen International Finance Two Ltd
Officers: Blake Kenneth Williamson, Secretary; Wendrell Waller Dye [1967] Director [American]; Christopher Paul Hill [1964] Director; Blake Kenneth Williamson [1970] Director/Chartered Management Accountant

Aviagen International Finance Four Limited
Incorporated: 13 April 2003 *Employees:* 3
Net Worth: £120,536,000 *Total Assets:* £161,996,992
Registered Office: Stratford Hatchery, Alscott Industrial Estate, Atherstone on Stour, Stratford upon Avon, Warwicks, CV37 8BH
Activities: Activities of agricultural holding companies
Parent: Aviagen European Holdings Limited
Officers: Blake Kenneth Williamson, Secretary; Wendrell Waller Dye [1967] Director [American]; Christopher Paul Hill [1964] Director; Blake Kenneth Williamson [1970] Director/Chartered Management Accountant

Aviagen International Finance Limited
Incorporated: 18 May 2003 *Employees:* 2,914
Net Worth: £435,401,120 *Total Assets:* £559,744,640
Registered Office: Stratford Hatchery, Alscott Industrial Estate, Atherstone on Stour, Stratford upon Avon, Warwicks, CV37 8BH
Activities: Activities of agricultural holding companies
Shareholder: Erich Wesjohann
Officers: Christopher Paul Hill, Secretary; Wendrell Waller Dye [1967] Director [American]; Christopher Paul Hill [1964] Director

Aviagen International Finance One Limited
Incorporated: 12 March 2003 *Employees:* 2
Net Worth: £64,864,960 *Total Assets:* £67,295,664
Registered Office: Stratford Hatchery, Alscott Industrial Estate, Atherstone on Stour, Stratford upon Avon, Warwicks, CV37 8BH
Activities: Activities of agricultural holding companies
Parent: Aviagen International Finance Limited
Officers: Christopher Paul Hill, Secretary; Wendrell Waller Dye [1967] Director [American]; Christopher Paul Hill [1964] Director

Aviagen International Finance Two Limited
Incorporated: 12 March 2003 *Employees:* 3
Net Worth: £87,798,048 *Total Assets:* £89,161,976
Registered Office: Stratford Hatchery, Alscott Industrial Estate, Atherstone on Stour, Stratford upon Avon, Warwicks, CV37 8BH
Activities: Activities of agricultural holding companies
Parent: Aviagen International Finance One Limited
Officers: Blake Kenneth Williamson, Secretary; Wendrell Waller Dye [1967] Director [American]; Christopher Paul Hill [1964] Director; Blake Kenneth Williamson [1970] Director/Chartered Management Accountant

Aviagen International Holdings Ltd.
Incorporated: 20 November 2006 *Employees:* 5
Net Worth: £47,022,020 *Total Assets:* £176,738,400
Registered Office: Stratford Hatchery, Alscott Industrial Estate, Atherstone on Stour, Stratford upon Avon, Warwicks, CV37 8BH
Activities: Activities of agricultural holding companies
Parent: Aviagen Turkeys Limited
Officers: Blake Kenneth Williamson, Secretary; Robert William Dobbie [1956] Director/International President; Wendrell Waller Dye [1967] Director [American]; Christopher Paul Hill [1964] Director; Alphonsus Nicolaas Maria Koerhuis [1966] Director/Chief Technical Officer [Dutch]; Blake Kenneth Williamson [1970] Director/Chartered Management Accountant

Aviagen Limited
Incorporated: 3 February 1982 *Employees:* 297
Net Worth: £259,124,992 *Total Assets:* £338,387,008
Registered Office: Stratford Hatchery, Alscott Industrial Estate, Atherstone on Stour, Stratford upon Avon, Warwicks, CV37 8BH
Activities: Raising of poultry
Parent: Aviagen Turkeys Limited
Officers: Stephen Robert McPhillips, Secretary; Dr Santiago Avendano [1968] Director/Geneticist [Italian]; Wendrell Waller Dye [1967] Director/Accountant [American]; Christopher Paul Hill [1964] Finance Director; Stephen Robert McPhillips [1966] Director/Chartered Accountant; Lars Magnus Swalander [1972] Director/General Manager [Swedish]

Aviagen Turkeys Holdings Limited
Incorporated: 22 June 2010
Net Worth: £36,545,000 *Total Assets:* £50,717,000
Registered Office: Stratford Hatchery, Alscott Industrial Estate, Atherstone on Stour, Stratford upon Avon, Warwicks, CV37 8BH
Activities: Activities of agricultural holding companies
Parent: Aviagen International Finance Four Ltd
Officers: Blake Kenneth Williamson, Secretary; Wendrell Waller Dye [1967] Director [American]; Christopher Paul Hill [1964] Director; Blake Kenneth Williamsom [1970] Director/Chartered Management Accountant

Avingtrans PLC
Incorporated: 4 December 1985 *Employees:* 656
Net Worth: £69,076,000 *Total Assets:* £121,749,000
Registered Office: Chatteris Business Park, Honeysome Road, Chatteris, Cambs, PE16 6SA
Activities: Activities of head offices
Officers: Stephen Michael King, Secretary; John Simon Clarke [1959] Director; Stephen Michael King [1966] Director; Roger Steven McDowell [1955] Director; Stephen McQuillan [1961] Director; Leslie James Thomas [1957] Director; Dr Graham Kenneth Thornton [1948] Director

AVK UK Limited
Incorporated: 3 August 1984 *Employees:* 57
Net Worth: £2,930,517 *Total Assets:* £10,436,884
Registered Office: 8 Rushmills, Northampton, NN4 7YB
Activities: Manufacture of basic iron and steel and of ferro-alloys
Major Shareholder: Niels Aage Kjaer
Officers: Gayle Broadhurst, Secretary; Gayle Broadhurst [1978] Finance Director; John Paul Hubbard [1959] Director/Chairman; Paul Jennings [1962] Managing Director; Lars Kudsk [1960] Director [Danish]; Richard Charles Stone [1957] Director/Sales

Avon Cosmetics Limited
Incorporated: 21 October 1957 *Employees:* 1,426
Net Worth: £623,750,016 *Total Assets:* £1,282,434,304
Registered Office: Nunn Mills Road, Northampton, NN1 5PA
Activities: Retail sale of cosmetic and toilet articles in specialised stores
Parent: Avon Products, Inc.
Officers: Matthew Passingham, Secretary; Vikram Agarwal [1964] Director/Senior Vice President & Chief Supply Chain Officer [Indian]; Jonathan Charles Myers [1969] Director; James Simpson Wilson [1959] Director

Avon Estates Limited
Incorporated: 5 January 2010 *Employees:* 79
Net Worth: £18,750,938 *Total Assets:* £26,481,574
Registered Office: Avon Park, Warwick Road, Stratford upon Avon, Warwicks, CV37 0NS
Activities: Other holiday and other collective accommodation
Major Shareholder: Nicholas John Allen
Officers: Nicola Jane Powell, Secretary; Nicholas John Allen [1978] Director

Avon Insurance PLC
Incorporated: 11 November 1925 *Employees:* 16
Net Worth: £34,500,000 *Total Assets:* £85,100,000
Registered Office: Tiddington Road, Stratford upon Avon, Warwicks, CV37 7BJ
Activities: Non-life insurance
Parent: N.F.U. Mutual Management Company Limited
Officers: James Damian Creechan, Secretary; Joanne Cribb [1971] Director; Richard David Morley [1967] Director; Lindsay Neil Sinclair [1956] Director/Chief Executive

Avon Products Holding Limited
Incorporated: 15 March 2010
Net Worth: £42,097,404 *Total Assets:* £42,586,644
Registered Office: Nunn Mills Road, Northampton, NN1 5PA
Activities: Non-trading company
Officers: Matthew Passingham [1977] Director

Avon UK Holdings Limited
Incorporated: 9 September 2004
Net Worth: £157,802 *Total Assets:* £43,487,420
Registered Office: Nunn Mills Road, Northampton, NN1 5PA
Activities: Activities of head offices
Parent: Avon Cosmetics Limited
Officers: Lisa Lee Siders [1978] Executive Director, International Tax & Strategy [Chinese]; John Stephen Warwick [1961] Executive Director - Tax

Avondale Property (Holdings) Limited
Incorporated: 26 June 1970 *Employees:* 51
Net Worth: £5,617,992 *Total Assets:* £12,409,807
Registered Office: Witherley House, Carlyon Road, Atherstone, Warwicks, CV9 1JE
Activities: Recreational vehicle parks, trailer parks and camping grounds
Shareholders: Christopher Geoffrey Ball; Jennifer Susan Ball
Officers: Lee David Goodwin, Secretary; Carol Ball [1958] Director; Christopher Geoffrey Ball [1957] Director; Eileen May Ball [1928] Director; Graham Theodore Ball [1939] Director; Jennifer Susan Ball [1954] Director/Teacher; Fiona Mary Friswell [1967] Director/Clerical; Lee David Goodwin [1961] Director and Company Secretary; Robin Bryan Huckerby [1960] Parks Director

Avro Energy Limited
Incorporated: 14 August 2014 *Employees:* 39
Net Worth: £601,628 *Total Assets:* £39,503,880
Registered Office: Unit 8 The Courtyard, Goldsmith Way, Eliot Business Park, Nuneaton, Warwicks, CV10 7RJ
Activities: Wholesale of other fuels and related products
Shareholders: Philip Andrew Brown; Jake Andrew Brown
Officers: Jake Andrew Brown [1994] Director; Philip Andrew Brown [1963] Director

AWG Group Limited
Incorporated: 1 April 1989 *Employees:* 121
Net Worth: £2,326,373,888 *Total Assets:* £2,566,819,072
Registered Office: Lancaster House, Lancaster Way, Ermine Business Park, Huntingdon, Cambs, PE29 6XU
Activities: Activities of head offices
Parent: AWG (UK) Holdings Limited
Officers: Elizabeth Ann Horlock Clarke, Secretary; Claire Tytherleigh Russell, Secretary; Scott Robert James Longhurst [1967] Finance Director; Claire Tytherleigh Russell [1964] Director/Lawyer; Peter John Simpson [1967] Director

AWG Land Holdings Limited
Incorporated: 10 September 2002
Net Worth Deficit: £2,912,000 *Total Assets:* £15,729,000
Registered Office: Lancaster House, Lancaster Way, Ermine Business Park, Huntingdon, Cambs, PE29 6XU
Activities: Other letting and operating of own or leased real estate
Parent: AWG Property Limited
Officers: Elizabeth Ann Horlock Clarke, Secretary; John Francis Cormie [1958] Director; James Raymond Tilbrook [1973] Director/Surveyor

AWG Parent Co Limited
Incorporated: 29 February 2000
Net Worth: £3,471,886,080 *Total Assets:* £5,573,062,144
Registered Office: Lancaster House, Lancaster Way, Ermine Business Park, Huntingdon, Cambs, PE29 6XU
Activities: Activities of head offices
Parent: Osprey Acquisitions Limited
Officers: Claire Tytherleigh Russell, Secretary; Projesh Banerjea [1986] Director/Financier [Indian]; John Richard Barry [1968] Director/Investor; Dr Stephen Robert Billingham [1948] Director; James Alexander Bryce [1974] Director/Senior Principal; Mamoun Jamai [1981] Director/Senior Portfolio Manager [Moroccan]; Scott Robert James Longhurst [1967] Finance Director; Manoj Mehta [1970] Investment Director; Niall Patrick Mills [1968] Director/Chartered Engineer; Robert Stewart Napier [1947] Director/Chief Executive; Alexandros Nassuphis [1969] Director/Investment Professional [German]; Peter John Simpson [1967] Director; Duncan John Symonds [1973] Director/Civil Engineer

Axiom Group Limited
Incorporated: 19 June 1979 *Employees:* 46
Net Worth: £4,827,390 *Total Assets:* £10,225,742
Registered Office: Axiom House, Unit 3 Ampthill Business Park, Ampthill, Bedford, MK45 2QW
Activities: Floor and wall covering
Major Shareholder: Nicholas David Edwards
Officers: Martyn David Leonard, Finance Director; Nicholas David Edwards [1968] Director; Martyn David Leonard [1964] Finance Director; Julia Genevieve Valentine [1964] Director

Axis Electronics Limited
Incorporated: 26 October 1994 *Employees:* 177
Net Worth: £16,890,822 *Total Assets:* £24,063,894
Registered Office: Silbury Court, 420 Silbury Boulevard, Central Milton Keynes, Bucks, MK9 2AF
Activities: Manufacture of electronic components
Shareholders: Philip John Inness; Axis EMS Group Ltd
Officers: Paul Chaplin [1970] Purchasing Director; Sarah Clough [1966] Director; Philip John Inness [1961] Director; Paul Jackson [1968] Director; Christian William Jukes [1966] QA Director; Matthew James Turner [1968] Engineering Director

Axis EMS Group Limited
Incorporated: 20 November 2013 *Employees:* 177
Net Worth: £6,898,066 *Total Assets:* £15,118,101
Registered Office: Silbury Court, 420 Silbury Boulevard, Milton Keynes, Bucks, MK9 2AF
Activities: Manufacture of other electrical equipment
Shareholder: Philip John Inness
Officers: Paul Chaplin [1970] Purchasing Director; Philip John Inness [1961] Director; Paul Martin Jackson [1968] Director

Axis Fleet Management Limited
Incorporated: 27 August 1999 *Employees:* 40
Net Worth Deficit: £1,654,037 *Total Assets:* £14,038,308
Registered Office: 14 Fenlock Court, Lower Road, Long Hanborough, Oxon, OX29 8LN
Activities: Renting and leasing of trucks and other heavy vehicles
Parent: Axis Intermodal Limited
Officers: Stephen James Ball [1954] Finance Director; Leigh Goodland [1980] Sales Director; Robert Joel Montague [1948] Director

Axis Intermodal Limited
Incorporated: 1 December 2003 *Employees:* 40
Net Worth Deficit: £847,000 *Total Assets:* £15,195,000
Registered Office: 14 Fenlock Court, Lower Road, Long Hanborough, Oxon, OX29 8LN
Activities: Activities of head offices
Shareholder: Robert Joel Montague
Officers: Stephen James Ball [1954] Director; Robert Joel Montague [1948] Director

Axon Public Safety UK Limited
Incorporated: 28 September 2010 *Employees:* 19
Previous: Tactical Safety Responses Limited
Net Worth Deficit: £7,607,529 *Total Assets:* £14,407,589
Registered Office: Unit 2c Riley Close, Royal Oak Industrial Estate, Daventry, Northants, NN11 8QT
Activities: Agents involved in the sale of a variety of goods
Parent: Axon Public Safety B.V.
Officers: Jawad Ali Ashan [1979] Director/Chief Financial Officer [American]; Joshua Michael Isner [1985] Director/EVP, Global Sales [American]; Luke Samuel Larson [1981] Director/President [American]; Matthew John Spencer [1975] Managing Director

The Aylesbury Vale Academy
Incorporated: 10 November 2008 *Employees:* 180
Net Worth: £24,147,616 *Total Assets:* £28,020,906
Registered Office: Church House Oxford, Langford Locks, Kidlington, Oxon, OX5 1GF
Activities: Pre-primary education
Officers: Jacqueline Anne Bowers [1965] Director/HR Consultant; Roger David Ian Burman [1958] Director/Executive Principal; Graham Keith Dougall [1946] Director/Retired; Gavin Luke Angus Gibson [1975] Director/Teacher; Charlotte James [1979] Director/Special Educational Needs Adviser; Dr Kiran Jawaid [1984] Director/Clinical Research Associate; Rosalind Teresa Rochefort [1953] Director/Retired; Robin Anthony Scott [1955] Director/Senior Educational Psychologist; Sarah Jane Elliott Thomas [1962] Director/Principal School Adviser; David Robin Wallhouse [1942] Director/Accountant (Retired); Dr Sally Anne Waugh [1954] Director/University Teacher and Consultant

Aylesford School and Sixth Form College
Incorporated: 15 November 2011 *Employees:* 119
Net Worth: £17,286,000 *Total Assets:* £18,546,000
Registered Office: Tapping Way, Warwick, CV34 6XR
Activities: General secondary education
Officers: Susan Grinnell, Secretary; Peter Booty [1944] Director/Retired; Sue Clark [1972] Director/Teacher; David Clarke [1955] Director; Steven Hall [1957] Director/Headteacher; Timothy Hodgson [1963] Director/Deputy Headteacher; Stuart Kingsley Hood [1970] Director/Head of Business; Jacqueline Ann Levett [1952] Director; Richard Henry Lyttle [1950] Programme Director; Neil MacRae [1967] Director/Teacher; Bethan Claire Parsons [1970] Director; Donna-Marie Savage [1970] Director; Michael Swallow [1955] Director; Andrew Tonner [1970] Director/Bid/Business Management

B & K Building Services Limited
Incorporated: 27 May 1980 *Employees:* 62
Net Worth: £8,496,272 *Total Assets:* £40,357,416
Registered Office: High Edge Court, Heage, Belper, Derbys, DE56 2BW
Activities: Construction of commercial buildings
Parent: Bowmer & Kirkland Ltd.
Officers: Hilary Susan Leonard, Secretary; Adrian James Grocock [1966] Director/Surveyor; Michael John Kirkland [1979] Director; Hilary Susan Leonard [1960] Director/Accountant; Kevin John McGowan [1964] Director/Contracts Manager

B & P Properties Limited
Incorporated: 9 April 1986 *Employees:* 9
Net Worth: £36,166,648 *Total Assets:* £67,579,656
Registered Office: Sterling House, 19-23 High Street, Kidlington, Oxon, OX5 2DH
Activities: Buying and selling of own real estate
Major Shareholder: Michael Arthur Stanley Ponting
Officers: Cyril Brawn, Secretary; Andrew Simon Ponting [1984] Director/Property Manager; Michael Arthur Stanley Ponting [1951] Director; Patricia Ann Ponting [1953] Director

B & S Hughes Limited
Incorporated: 20 April 2000 *Employees:* 2
Net Worth: £7,650,950 *Total Assets:* £10,637,752
Registered Office: Oaktree, Tadmarton Road, Bloxham, Banbury, Oxon, OX15 4JA
Activities: Development of building projects
Officers: Carol Angela Davenport, Secretary; Laura Claire Davis [1977] Director; Bernard Hughes [1941] Director

B.I. (UK) Limited
Incorporated: 3 July 1998 *Employees:* 1
Net Worth: £163,145,040 *Total Assets:* £179,507,264
Registered Office: Wildmere Industrial Estate, Banbury, Oxon, OX16 3JU
Activities: Activities of distribution holding companies
Parent: Brady European Holdings Limited
Officers: Sally Felstead [1974] Director/General Manager; James Michael Nauman [1962] Director [American]; Aaron James Pearce [1970] Director [American]; Brett Wilms [1974] Managing Director [Belgian]

B.L. Marketing Limited
Incorporated: 29 January 1971 *Employees:* 7
Net Worth: £1,458,381,952 *Total Assets:* £1,462,039,040
Registered Office: Weetabix Mills, Burton Latimer, Kettering, Northants, NN15 5JR
Activities: Activities of head offices
Parent: Westminster Acquisition Limited
Officers: Richard William Thomas Martin, Secretary; Sally Jane Abbott [1967] Director; Richard William Thomas Martin [1962] Director

B.M. Polyco Limited
Incorporated: 12 May 1978 *Employees:* 96
Net Worth: £10,637,000 *Total Assets:* £35,886,000
Registered Office: Polyco Healthline, South Fen Road, Bourne, Lincs, PE10 0DN
Activities: Other manufacturing n.e.c.
Officers: David Greenwood [1955] Director; Jason Prichard [1969] Director/Company Secretary; Neil Antony Wilson [1976] Director

B.N.T. Properties Limited
Incorporated: 19 June 2002 *Employees:* 3
Net Worth: £1,027,365 *Total Assets:* £11,455,730
Registered Office: Sibson Mill, Wellsborough Road, Sibson, Nuneaton, Warwicks, CV13 6LR
Activities: Development of building projects
Officers: Jennifer Mary Theresa Smith, Secretary; Benjamin James Smith [1975] Director; Jennifer Mary Theresa Smith [1949] Director; Martin James Smith [1950] Director; Nicholas John Smith [1977] Director; Thomas Edward Smith [1978] Director

B.T.E. Plant Sales Limited
Incorporated: 19 October 1994 *Employees:* 59
Net Worth: £7,037,932 *Total Assets:* £28,134,394
Registered Office: 85 Ashby Road, Markfield, Leicester, LE67 9UA
Activities: Wholesale of mining, construction and civil engineering machinery
Major Shareholder: Ben Elliott
Officers: Rebecca Louise Bryson [1985] Commercial Director; Alan James Cribb [1984] Finance Director; Benedict Thomas Elliott [1965] Director; Judith Elaine Elliott [1966] Director; David Hawley [1971] Managing Director

Bachmann Europe PLC
Incorporated: 6 June 1989 *Employees:* 68
Net Worth: £10,050,000 *Total Assets:* £17,658,000
Registered Office: Moat Way, Barwell, Leicester, LE9 8EY
Activities: Manufacture of other games and toys, n.e.c.
Shareholders: Kenneth Ting; Kader Holdings Company Ltd
Officers: Samantha Louise Wright, Secretary; David Peter Haarhaus [1973] Director/Business Manager; Ivan Tien-Li Ting [1975] Director/Business Manager; Kenneth Ting [1942] Director

J.H. Bacon Limited
Incorporated: 11 March 1974 *Employees:* 9
Net Worth: £6,744,229 *Total Assets:* £16,558,602
Registered Office: Riby Grove, Riby, Grimsby, N E Lincs, DN37 8NP
Activities: Growing of cereals (except rice), leguminous crops and oil seeds
Shareholders: James Harold Bacon; Executors of James Harold Bacon
Officers: Edwin James Henry Bacon, Secretary; Edwin James Henry Bacon [1972] Director/Farmer; Lesley Mary Bacon [1942] Director

BAJ 1 Limited
Incorporated: 10 January 2006
Net Worth: £21,495,726 *Total Assets:* £50,682,432
Registered Office: 7 Merseyway, Stockport, Cheshire, SK1 1PN
Activities: Development of building projects
Shareholders: John Coulter; Ann Jones
Officers: Ann Jones, Secretary; John Coulter [1951] Director; Ann Jones [1954] Director; Uziel Zelig Katz [1960] Director

Baker & Taylor (UK) Ltd
Incorporated: 17 September 1986 *Employees:* 160
Net Worth: £8,404,000 *Total Assets:* £12,471,000
Registered Office: Unit B, Bicester Park, Charbridge Way, Bicester, Oxon, OX26 4ST
Activities: Non-specialised wholesale trade
Officers: Stuart James Biltcliffe, Secretary; Stuart James Biltcliffe [1972] Finance Director; Annette Burgess [1967] Director/Chief Operating Officer; Gareth David Powell [1965] Director/Accountant

F.W. Baker Limited
Incorporated: 6 August 1963 *Employees:* 293
Net Worth: £35,194,000 *Total Assets:* £64,300,000
Registered Office: Baker Group House, Dockham Way, Crick, Northants, NN6 7TZ
Activities: Other letting and operating of own or leased real estate
Major Shareholder: Graham William Baker
Officers: Francis Generald Powell, Secretary/Accountant; Elizabeth Anne Baker [1964] Director; Graham William Baker [1952] Director/Factory Management; Francis Generald Powell [1964] Director; Graham Robert Scott [1944] Director

Baker Perkins Holdings Limited
Incorporated: 10 March 2015 *Employees:* 378
Net Worth: £14,870,000 *Total Assets:* £36,686,000
Registered Office: Manor Drive, Paston Parkway, Peterborough, PE4 7AP
Activities: Activities of production holding companies
Major Shareholder: John Embleton Cowx
Officers: John Embleton Cowx [1946] Director

Baker Perkins Limited
Incorporated: 14 February 2006 *Employees:* 377
Net Worth: £10,640,000 *Total Assets:* £32,418,000
Registered Office: Manor Drive, Paston Parkway, Peterborough, PE4 7AP
Activities: Manufacture of machinery for food, beverage and tobacco processing
Officers: John Embleton Cowx [1946] Director

M.Baker Produce Limited
Incorporated: 1 March 1971 *Employees:* 16
Net Worth: £9,378,126 *Total Assets:* £10,007,478
Registered Office: Wyberton House, Main Road, Old Leake, Boston, Lincs, PE22 9HT
Activities: Growing of cereals (except rice), leguminous crops and oil seeds
Parent: The Trustees of M Baker Settlement
Officers: Edith Alice Baker, Secretary; Edith Alice Baker [1942] Director; Ian Michael Baker [1969] Director

The C. Alma Baker Trust
Incorporated: 16 March 2006 *Employees:* 11
Net Worth: £8,070,116 *Total Assets:* £14,331,364
Registered Office: Roythornes Solicitors, Enterprise Campus, Alconbury Weald, Huntingdon, Cambs, PE28 4XA
Activities: Mixed farming
Officers: Charles Robin Boyes [1939] Director/Retired Solicitor; Simon Fred Boyton Taylor [1945] Director/Farmer; Edward Francis Patrick Valletta [1962] Director/Bursar; David Heneage Wynne-Finch [1970] Director/Farmer

Bakkavor Central Finance Limited
Incorporated: 28 July 2008
Net Worth Deficit: £1,145,000 *Total Assets:* £42,641,000
Registered Office: Bakkavor, West Marsh Road, Spalding, Lincs, PE11 2BB
Activities: Accounting and auditing activities
Parent: Bakkavor Foods Limited
Officers: Simon Witham, Secretary; Marc Stephen Archer [1963] Director; Agust Gudmundsson [1964] Director [Icelander]

Bakkavor Estates Limited
Incorporated: 5 August 2008
Net Worth Deficit: £2,347,000 *Total Assets:* £38,042,000
Registered Office: Bakkavor, West Marsh Road, Spalding, Lincs, PE11 2BB
Activities: Activities of other holding companies n.e.c.
Parent: Bakkavor Foods Limited
Officers: Simon Witham, Secretary; Marc Stephen Archer [1963] Director; Agust Gudmundsson [1964] Director [Icelander]

Bakkavor Finance Limited
Incorporated: 28 July 2008
Net Worth: £456,792,000 *Total Assets:* £514,768,000
Registered Office: Bakkavor, West Marsh Road, Spalding, Lincs, PE11 2BB
Activities: Accounting and auditing activities
Parent: Bakkavor (London) Limited
Officers: Simon Witham, Secretary; Agust Gudmundsson [1964] Director [Icelander]

Balfour Beatty Plant & Fleet Services Limited
Incorporated: 6 December 1989
Net Worth: £65,790,000 *Total Assets:* £65,790,000
Registered Office: West Service Road, Raynesway, Derby, DE21 7BG
Activities: Repair and maintenance of other transport equipment n.e.c.
Shareholder: Balfour Beatty Group Limited
Officers: Philip Andrew Ormerod [1964] Director; Tracey Price [1972] Director; Ian Kenneth Rylatt [1965] Director/Engineer

Ball Colegrave Limited
Incorporated: 4 August 1981 *Employees:* 70
Net Worth: £11,186,000 *Total Assets:* £24,740,000
Registered Office: Milton Road, West Adderbury, Oxon, OX17 3EY
Activities: Wholesale of flowers and plants
Officers: Suzanne Broughton, Secretary; Anna Caroline Ball [1949] Director [American]; William Todd Billings [1962] Director/Chief Financial Officer [American]; Alexander James Shepherd [1963] Director; Colin Andrew Turvey [1961] Commercial Director

Ball Horticultural Europe Limited
Incorporated: 1 May 1962 *Employees:* 285
Net Worth: £20,470,000 *Total Assets:* £29,276,000
Registered Office: Milton Road, West Adderbury, Banbury, Oxon, OX17 3EY
Activities: Activities of head offices
Parent: Ball Horticultural Company
Officers: Suzanne Broughton, Secretary; Anna Caroline Ball [1949] Director [American]; William Todd Billings [1962] Director/Chief Financial Officer [American]; Alexander James Shepherd [1963] Director

Ball. Roller & Transmission Bearings Limited
Incorporated: 2 August 1967 *Employees:* 141
Net Worth: £7,662,792 *Total Assets:* £16,730,120
Registered Office: 21-24 Regal Road, Wisbech, Cambs, PE13 2RQ
Activities: Non-specialised wholesale trade
Parent: BRT (Wisbech) Ltd
Officers: Grahame Allen [1966] Director; Anthony George Clarke [1946] Director; Phillip David Clarke [1970] Director/Salesman; Simon David Clarke [1973] Director; Lindsey Jane Lowery [1961] Director

Ballast Phoenix Limited
Incorporated: 5 December 1996 *Employees:* 124
Net Worth: £15,017,000 *Total Assets:* £42,484,000
Registered Office: 1 Victoria Stables, Essex Way, Bourne, Lincs, PE10 9JZ
Activities: Manufacture of other non-metallic mineral products n.e.c.
Parent: Phoenix Advance Limited
Officers: Paul Christian Lee Knight [1971] Managing Director; Matthew Lloyd Turner [1966] Financial Director; David Michael York [1949] Director/Chairman

Ballyclare Limited
Incorporated: 8 December 2010 *Employees:* 86
Net Worth: £12,800,805 *Total Assets:* £14,966,950
Registered Office: The Forum, Hercules Business Park, Bird Hall Lane, Cheadle Hume, Stockport, Cheshire, SK3 0UX
Activities: Manufacture of workwear
Parent: Best Dressed Group Limited
Officers: Carlton Greener [1966] Director; Mirvet Russo [1968] Operations Director Group [Dutch]; Kieron Bartholemew Traynor [1960] Director

Ballylynch Capital Limited
Incorporated: 22 September 2011
Net Worth Deficit: £533,328 *Total Assets:* £11,667,305
Registered Office: 3 Castlegate, Grantham, Lincs, NG31 6SF
Activities: Activities of other holding companies n.e.c.
Major Shareholder: Carol Henry
Officers: Michael John Argyle [1961] Director/Chartered Accountant; Thomas Henley Henry [1940] Director [American]

Ballyvesey Holdings Limited
Incorporated: 12 June 1995 *Employees:* 2,521
Net Worth: £115,001,504 *Total Assets:* £413,624,768
Registered Office: c/o Montracon Limited, Carr Hill, Doncaster, S Yorks, DN4 8DE
Activities: Financial intermediation not elsewhere classified
Shareholders: The HH Montgomery A & M Trust; HH Montgomery Family Trust 2012
Officers: Harold Hugh Montgomery, Secretary; Nigel Moutray Anketell [1955] Director; David Nigel Birkmyre [1952] Director; James Alexander Darragh [1968] Director; Colin John Hugh Montgomery [1976] Director; Harold Mark Joseph Montgomery [1983] Director; Harold Hugh Montgomery [1948] Director/Haulage Contractor; Noreen P Montgomery [1949] Director

Banc D'Arguin, and Coastal and Marine Biodiversity Trust Fund Limited
Incorporated: 23 January 2009
Net Worth: £22,982,472 *Total Assets:* £22,999,992
Registered Office: 8 King Edward Street, Oxford, OX1 4HL
Activities: Botanical and zoological gardens and nature reserves activities
Officers: Ahmed Lefghih, Secretary; Sissako Abderrahmane [1961] Film Director [Mauritanian]; Oumoulkhairy BA [1963] Director/Certified Accountant [Mauritanian]; Guillaume Chiron [1967] Director/Chef Projet Biodiversite [French]; Moutha El Hadj [1967] Director/Advisor to The Prime Minister [Mauritanian]; Alexandre Manghi [1958] Director/Asset Manager [Swiss]; Jean-Paul Paddack [1966] Director WWF International [French]; Thorsten Schneider [1978] Director/Country Manager [German]; Abass Sylla [1963] Directeur General Cooperation Economique [Mauritanian]

Banks & Lloyd (Shipping) Limited
Incorporated: 4 August 1995 *Employees:* 36
Net Worth: £6,511,358 *Total Assets:* £12,732,897
Registered Office: Brook House, Church Street, Wilmslow, Cheshire, SK9 1AX
Activities: Other transportation support activities
Officers: Diane Elizabeth Verzijl, Secretary; Daria Mikhaylovna Banks [1987] Director; Philip Paul Lucas [1979] Director; Mark Edward Rahman [1967] Director; Diane Elizabeth Verzijl [1964] Director; Vincentius Verzijl [1966] Managing Director [Dutch]

Banner Group Limited
Incorporated: 18 July 2005 *Employees:* 243
Previous: Supplies Team Limited
Net Worth: £16,318,000 *Total Assets:* £62,802,000
Registered Office: K House, Sheffield Business Park, Europa Link, Sheffield, S9 1XU
Activities: Other business support service activities n.e.c.
Parent: Vasanta Group Limited
Officers: Lorna Kathleen Mendelsohn, Secretary; Andrew Peter Gale [1970] Finance Director; Stephen Haworth [1970] Director/Group CEO; Craig Anthony Varey [1974] Managing Director

Banner Plant Limited
Incorporated: 7 July 1958 *Employees:* 144
Net Worth: £10,739,252 *Total Assets:* £19,941,128
Registered Office: Banner Cross Hall, Ecclesall Road South, Sheffield, S11 9PD
Activities: Other specialised construction activities n.e.c.
Parent: Henry Boot PLC
Officers: Amy Louise Oakley, Secretary; David Giles Boot [1959] Director; Gary Crofts [1969] Director; Darren Louis Littlewood [1975] Finance Director; John Trevor Sutcliffe [1959] Finance Director

Bansols Beta Limited
Incorporated: 7 December 1993 *Employees:* 865
Net Worth: £15,038,004 *Total Assets:* £21,892,198
Registered Office: The Courtyard, Chapel Lane, Bodicote, Banbury, Oxon, OX15 4DB
Activities: Take-away food shops and mobile food stands
Major Shareholder: Moonpal Singh Grewal
Officers: Moonpal Singh Grewal [1969] Director

Bantham Holdings Ltd
Incorporated: 28 April 2014 *Employees:* 1
Net Worth: £2,591,721 *Total Assets:* £16,209,586
Registered Office: The Estate Office, Quarry Farm, Banbury Road, Great Tew, Chipping Norton, Oxon, OX7 4BT
Activities: Activities of other holding companies n.e.c.
Shareholders: Giantflow Limited; Flowgiant Limited
Officers: Rebecca Leah Iles, Secretary; Nicholas Matthew Middlemass Johnston [1972] Director

Baptist Union Corporation Limited (The)
Incorporated: 14 November 1890
Net Worth: £4,719,503 *Total Assets:* £50,291,696
Registered Office: Baptist House, Broadway, Didcot, Oxon, OX11 8XD
Activities: Activities of religious organisations
Shareholders: Paul Coleman; Revd Philip Lutterodt; Alastair Mitchell-Baker; Mark Spriggs; Revd Diane Watts; Revd Prof Philip McCormack MBE; Revd Philip Andrew Jump; Christina Carter; Andrew Cowley; Marion Downing Fiddes; Revd Lynn Margaret Green; John David Levick
Officers: Richard Ian Wilson, Secretary; Robert John English [1954] Director/Association Manager; Andrew William Hawksworth [1958] Director/Assistant Minister; Paul Lancaster [1955] Director/Administration Manager Local Authority; The Revd Joseph David Lennox [1944] Director/Retired; John David Levick [1954] Director; The Revd Christopher George Illytd Lewis [1954] Minister of Religion (Baptist) Director; Reverend Duncan Charles MacLean [1947] Director/Minister of Religion; Karen Averil Martindale [1962] Director/Administrator; Olusegun Oludipe Obidipe [1953] Director/Chartered Management Accountant; Jeremy Ponsford [1942] Director/Retired; Steven Michael Salmen [1954] Director Painting Company; Michael Arthur Southcombe [1952] Retired Construction Development Director; Graham Stewart Ward [1955] Director/IT Programme Manager; The Revd David Alfred Warrington [1955] Director/Minister of Religion; Stephen Peter Welch [1954] Director/Surveyor; Richard Ian Wilson [1977] Director/Team Leader Support Services

Barbara Limited
Incorporated: 24 January 2006
Net Worth Deficit: £32,951,000 *Total Assets:* £103,172,000
Registered Office: Unit 19 Redbrook Business Park, Wilthorpe Road, Barnsley, S Yorks, S75 1JN
Activities: Activities of head offices
Parent: Project Grace
Officers: Peter Assinder [1971] Strategic Sales & Technology Director; Michael Joseph Napoletano [1967] Director/Manager [American]

The Dominic Barberi Multi Academy Company
Incorporated: 20 March 2013 *Employees:* 386
Net Worth: £19,792,000 *Total Assets:* £26,767,000
Registered Office: c/o St Gregory The Great Catholic School, Cricket Road, Oxford, OX4 3DR
Activities: Other education n.e.c.
Officers: Kathleen Ann Horsfall, Secretary; Paul Joseph Concannon [1959] Director; Generald Anthony Crown [1977] Director/IT Consultant [Irish]; Edward Fraser Long [1969] Director, Executive Principal, Accounting Officer; Judith Schmidt [1944] Director/Retired; Canon Mervyn Tower [1950] Director/Parish Priest; Adrian Waters [1960] Director/Property Investment

Barbon Holdings Limited
Incorporated: 10 November 2010 *Employees:* 373
Net Worth: £51,512,388 *Total Assets:* £62,664,256
Registered Office: Hestia House, Edgewest Road, Lincoln, LN6 7EL
Activities: Activities of financial services holding companies
Parent: Beck Bidco Limited
Officers: Philp Screeton, Secretary; Brendan James McManus [1959] Director; Alexander Michael Pietruska [1959] Director [German]; Philip Screeton [1967] Director; Martin Richard Totty [1956] Director; Mark Stephen Witherspoon [1959] Director

Barbon Insurance Group Limited
Incorporated: 8 December 1995 *Employees:* 372
Net Worth: £24,268,682 *Total Assets:* £31,403,360
Registered Office: Hestia House, Edgewest Road, Lincoln, LN6 7EL
Activities: Non-life insurance
Parent: Barbon Holdings Limited
Officers: Philip Screeton, Secretary; Brendan James McManus [1959] Director; Alexander Michael Pietruska [1959] Director [German]; Philip Screeton [1967] Director; Martin Richard Totty [1956] Director; Mark Stephen Witherspoon [1959] Director

Barclay Pharmaceuticals Limited
Incorporated: 3 December 1992 *Employees:* 338
Net Worth: £95,268,000 *Total Assets:* £126,254,000
Registered Office: Sapphire Court, Walsgrave Triangle, Coventry, Warwicks, CV2 2TX
Activities: Wholesale of pharmaceutical goods
Parent: Admenta Holdings Limited
Officers: Nichola Louise Legg, Secretary; Toby Matthew Anderson [1973] Director; Marcus Hilger [1977] Finance Director [German]; Catherine McDermott [1968] Operations Director; Nigel Swift [1966] Marketing & Sales Director

The Barcode Warehouse Group Limited
Incorporated: 2 April 2015 *Employees:* 226
Net Worth: £3,730,085 *Total Assets:* £20,232,734
Registered Office: Telford Drive, Newark, Notts, NG24 2DX
Activities: Activities of head offices
Shareholders: Maureen Anne Lee; Ross Andrew Lee
Officers: Ross Andrew Lee [1948] Director; Kevan Ian Mutton [1966] Managing Director; Richard William Staniforth [1968] Director

The Barcode Warehouse Limited
Incorporated: 16 September 1999 *Employees:* 226
Net Worth: £12,247,966 *Total Assets:* £25,172,182
Registered Office: Telford Drive, Newark, Notts, NG24 2DX
Activities: Manufacture of printed labels
Officers: Sharon Ann Jury, Secretary; Lloyd John Jury [1971] Director; Sharon Ann Jury [1967] Director; Joanne Catherine Lee [1969] Director; Ross Joseph Lee [1984] Director; Ross Andrew Lee [1948] Director/Chairman; Kevan Ian Mutton [1966] Managing Director; Richard William Staniforth [1968] Director

Bardsley Construction Holdings Limited
Incorporated: 7 July 2009 *Employees:* 4
Net Worth: £4,787,015 *Total Assets:* £15,660,832
Registered Office: Globe Square, Dukinfield, Cheshire, SK16 4RG
Activities: Activities of construction holding companies
Parent: Project Gabriel Limited
Officers: Roland Bardsley [1964] Director; Robert Edmund Paul Bodnar-Horvath [1956] Director; Paul Strutt [1968] Director

Bardsley Construction Limited
Incorporated: 13 April 1964 *Employees:* 184
Net Worth: £10,041,690 *Total Assets:* £26,004,510
Registered Office: Globe Square, Dukinfield, Cheshire, SK16 4RG
Activities: Construction of commercial buildings
Parent: Bardsley Construction Holdings Limited
Officers: Emma Allsopp [1976] Director/Accountant; Jonathan Kingsley Cocker [1964] Director; Sean Andrew Kempley [1968] Director; Michael John Nevitt [1975] Director; Adrian Vincent Rooney [1973] Director; Gerard Rooney [1968] Director; Paul Strutt [1968] Director; Neil Taylor [1972] Director

Bardsley Group Limited
Incorporated: 1 November 2012 *Employees:* 184
Previous: Project Gabriel Limited
Net Worth: £5,845,864 *Total Assets:* £22,628,084
Registered Office: Globe Square, Globe Lane, Dukinfield, Cheshire, SK16 4RG
Activities: Activities of construction holding companies
Major Shareholder: Roland Bardsley
Officers: Roland Bardsley [1964] Director; Robert Edmund Paul Bodnar-Horvath [1956] Director; Paul Strutt [1968] Director

Barker Ross Group Limited
Incorporated: 18 February 2013 *Employees:* 141
Net Worth Deficit: £233,000 *Total Assets:* £11,508,000
Registered Office: Mercury Place, 11 St George Street, Leicester, LE1 1QG
Activities: Other activities of employment placement agencies
Major Shareholder: Paul Alexander Ross
Officers: Caroline Anne Bagguley, Secretary; Caroline Anne Bagguley [1968] Finance Director; Paul Alexander Ross [1961] Director; Tim Sutcliffe [1974] Director; Emma Caroline Tillotson [1967] Director

Barker Shoes Limited
Incorporated: 11 February 1914 *Employees:* 170
Net Worth: £6,908,005 *Total Assets:* £13,056,689
Registered Office: Station Road, Earls Barton, Northants, NN6 0NT
Activities: Manufacture of footwear
Major Shareholder: Anil Aggarwal
Officers: Kul Bhushan Sharma, Secretary; Anil Aggarwal [1961] Director [Indian]; Alan Bernard Pringle [1953] Director; Sandeep Kumar Rastogi [1972] Director/Executive

Barnack Estates UK Limited
Incorporated: 14 April 1987 *Employees:* 69
Previous: Barnack UK Limited
Net Worth: £8,745,932 *Total Assets:* £21,779,844
Registered Office: Barnack House, Southgate Way, Orton Southgate, Peterborough, Cambs, PE2 6GP
Activities: Non-specialised wholesale of food, beverages and tobacco
Shareholders: Robert Peter Turnbull Facer; Helen Margaret Facer
Officers: Helen Margaret Facer, Secretary; Helen Margaret Facer [1965] Director; Robert Peter Turnbull Facer [1962] Director

The Barons Eden Group Limited
Incorporated: 8 July 2014 *Employees:* 475
Net Worth: £13,571,698 *Total Assets:* £39,580,232
Registered Office: 8 The Shippon, Churchill Heath Farm, Kingham, Oxon, OX7 6UJ
Activities: Activities of head offices
Shareholders: Andre Max Elshout; Steven Earl Joynes
Officers: Steven John Clements [1959] Director; Andre Max Elshout [1958] Director; Steven Earl Joynes [1969] Director; Edward Henry Towry Law [1971] Director; Adrian John Pearson [1965] Director; Craig Winfield [1984] Finance Director

Barratt Developments P L C
Incorporated: 14 May 1958 *Employees:* 6,214
Net Worth: £4,590,199,808 *Total Assets:* £6,928,999,936
Registered Office: Barratt House, Cartwright Way, Forest Business Park, Bardon Hill, Coalville, Leics, LE67 1UF
Activities: Construction of commercial buildings
Officers: Kamalprit Kaur Bains, Secretary; Richard John Akers [1961] Director/Chartered Surveyor; John Murray Allan [1948] Director; Nina Stephanie Bibby [1965] Marketing and Consumer Director; Steven John Boyes [1960] Group Executive Director; John Fyfe Lennox [1956] Director; David Fraser Thomas [1963] Director; Jessica Elizabeth White [1978] Director/Chief Financial Officer; Sharon Michelle White [1967] Director/Chief Executive - Ofcom

Barratt Evolution Limited
Incorporated: 16 June 1999
Net Worth: £9,642,000 *Total Assets:* £11,320,000
Registered Office: Barratt House, Cartwright Way, Forest Business Park, Bardon Hill, Coalville, Leics, LE67 1UF
Activities: Construction of commercial buildings
Parent: BDW Trading Limited
Officers: Gary Martin Ennis [1969] Director [Irish]; Andrew Taylor [1973] Director/Accountant; David Fraser Thomas [1963] Director; Karly Adele Williams [1982] Regional Sales Director

Barratt Metropolitan LLP
Incorporated: 4 July 2006
Net Worth: £70,258,432 *Total Assets:* £76,644,416
Registered Office: Barratt House, Cartwright Way, Forest Business Park, Bardon Hill, Coalville, Leics, LE67 1UF

Barratt Wates (Lindfield) Limited
Incorporated: 16 December 2013
Net Worth: £2,055,000 *Total Assets:* £24,153,000
Registered Office: Barratt House, Cartwright Way, Forest Business Park, Bardon Hill, Coalville, Leics, LE67 1UF
Activities: Development of building projects
Shareholders: BDW Trading Limited; Wates Developments Limited
Officers: David Alexander Bowen [1967] Director/Chartered Accountant; David Michael Brocklebank [1970] Managing Director; Jeremy John Champion [1962] Divisional Development Director; Gary Martin Ennis [1969] Regional Managing Director [Irish]; Natalie Jane Flint [1969] Residential Investment Director; Julian Paul Hodder [1971] Director/Accountant; Martin Geoffrey Leach [1965] Operations Director; Andrew Colin Modle [1967] Finance Director; Colin Francis Quinn [1966] Finance Director; William Walsh [1985] Commercial Director

Barron McCann Holdings Limited
Incorporated: 10 October 2013 *Employees:* 264
Net Worth: £6,145,679 *Total Assets:* £20,899,306
Registered Office: Meteor Centre, Mansfield Road, Derby, DE21 4SY
Activities: Activities of other holding companies n.e.c.
Major Shareholder: Alan Robert Watson
Officers: Alan Watson [1956] Director

Barron McCann Limited
Incorporated: 12 September 1972 *Employees:* 264
Net Worth: £11,047,705 *Total Assets:* £25,801,308
Registered Office: Meteor Centre, Mansfield Road, Derby, DE21 4SY
Activities: Other information technology service activities
Parent: Barron McCann Holdings Limited
Officers: Alan Watson [1956] Director

Barrough Hospitality Limited
Incorporated: 30 October 2003
Net Worth: £3,417,117 *Total Assets:* £17,647,784
Registered Office: The Estate Office, Blenheim Palace, Woodstock, Oxon, OX20 1PP
Activities: Other letting and operating of own or leased real estate
Parent: Barrough Limited
Officers: Stephen James Spare, Secretary; Heather Rosemary Carter [1962] Operations Director; Roger Leslie File [1963] Director/Chartered Surveyor; Dominic Michael Hare [1969] Finance Director

E.P.Barrus Limited
Incorporated: 18 September 1917 *Employees:* 169
Net Worth: £14,607,454 *Total Assets:* £32,185,528
Registered Office: Glen Way, Launton Road, Bicester, Oxon, OX26 4UR
Activities: Operation of warehousing and storage facilities for land transport activities
Parent: E P B Holdings Ltd
Officers: Robert Richard Muir, Secretary; Jeffrey Carter Van Deuch [1966] Director/Chief Financial Officer [American]; Andrew James Feilden [1941] Managing Director; Robert Duncan Glen [1939] Director; Tara Louise Owen Glen [1971] Director/Accountant/Engineer; Dietrich Kaesgen [1936] Director [German]; Charles Merideth Moll [1971] Commercial Director [American]; Curtis Moll [1939] Director [American]; Robert Richard Muir [1956] Director

Bartec Auto ID Limited
Incorporated: 2 June 1992 *Employees:* 106
Net Worth: £11,756,794 *Total Assets:* £14,942,688
Registered Office: Unit 9 Redbrook Business Park, Wilthorpe Road, Barnsley, S Yorks, S75 1JN
Activities: Other business support service activities n.e.c.
Shareholders: Colin Paul Webb; Cheryl Denise Webb
Officers: Cheryl Denise Webb, Secretary; Charles Warren Beal [1956] Director/Electronic Design Engineer; Timothy Stephen Hobbs [1971] Director; David Gregory Patrickson [1972] Director; Cheryl Denise Webb [1959] Director; Colin Paul Webb [1954] Director; Philip James Wilson [1985] Director; Matthew James Woods [1970] Director

Alan Bartlett & Sons (Chatteris) Limited
Incorporated: 29 April 2009 *Employees:* 281
Net Worth: £12,529,731 *Total Assets:* £31,194,474
Registered Office: Great Acre Fen, Chatteris, Cambs, PE16 6EG
Activities: Growing of vegetables and melons, roots and tubers
Major Shareholder: Alan Bartlett
Officers: Pamela Jane Bartlett, Secretary; Alan Bartlett [1956] Director; Oliver Bartlett [1991] Director; Toby Bartlett [1991] Director; Terry Hawthorn [1964] Director

Barton Buses Limited
Incorporated: 14 February 1989 *Employees:* 274
Net Worth: £7,761,000 *Total Assets:* £13,362,000
Registered Office: Mansfield Road, Heanor, Derbys, DE75 7BG
Activities: Other urban, suburban or metropolitan passenger land transport (not underground, metro or similar)
Officers: Graham Sutton, Secretary/Financial Director; Jeffrey Counsell [1958] Managing Director; Brian Robert King [1944] Director/Chairman; Richard Ian Morgan [1951] Director/Deputy Chairman; Graham Sutton [1960] Financial Director

Barton Petroleum (Holdings) Limited
Incorporated: 15 March 2004 *Employees:* 88
Net Worth: £9,180,163 *Total Assets:* £17,840,644
Registered Office: Vaux Road, Finedon Road Industrial Estate, Wellingborough, Northants, NN8 4TG
Activities: Freight transport by road
Major Shareholder: Richard James Burton
Officers: Lily Marie Burton, Secretary; Richard James Burton [1959] Director

Barton Petroleum Limited
Incorporated: 8 May 1944 *Employees:* 71
Net Worth: £8,631,340 *Total Assets:* £16,906,184
Registered Office: Vaux Road, Finedon Road Industrial Estate, Wellingborough, Northants, NN8 4TG
Activities: Freight transport by road
Major Shareholder: Richard James Burton
Officers: Lily Marie Burton, Secretary; Richard James Burton [1959] Director

Barwood Homes Limited
Incorporated: 14 May 2009 *Employees:* 39
Net Worth: £1,689,065 *Total Assets:* £57,280,088
Registered Office: Grovelands Business Park, West Haddon Road, East Haddon, Northampton, NN6 8FB
Activities: Construction of domestic buildings
Parent: Barwood Homes Holdings Limited
Officers: Darren James Bland [1977] Finance Director; Bertram Richard Broadhead [1983] Director; Jamie Gibbins [1971] Director/Property Developer; Thomas Edward Lockyer Walsh [1977] Director/Fund Manager

Barwood Strategic Land II LLP
Incorporated: 17 October 2011
Net Worth: £5,882,706 *Total Assets:* £9,813,249
Registered Office: Grovelands Business Park, West Haddon Road, East Haddon, Northampton, NN6 8DT

BASF Agricultural Specialities Limited
Incorporated: 1 June 1982 *Employees:* 35
Net Worth: £12,471,000 *Total Assets:* £14,914,000
Registered Office: P O Box 4, Earl Road, Cheadle Hulme, Cheadle, Cheshire, SK8 6QG
Activities: Other manufacturing n.e.c.
Parent: Becker-Underwood (UK) Limited
Officers: Helen Victoria Koerner, Secretary; Richard John Carter [1962] Managing Director UK/Ireland; Karen Lois Harper [1964] Director/Head of HR UK & Ireland; Thomas Urwin [1966] Director/Finance Manager UK & Ireland

BASF Pharma (Callanish) Limited
Incorporated: 13 July 2005 *Employees:* 72
Net Worth Deficit: £22,432,000 *Total Assets:* £37,618,000
Registered Office: BASF, P O Box 4, Earl Road, Cheadle Hulme, Cheadle, Cheshire, SK8 6QG
Activities: Manufacture of oils and fats
Parent: BASF SE
Officers: Helen Victoria Koerner, Secretary; Richard John Carter [1962] Managing Director UK/Ireland; Karen Lois Harper [1964] Director/Head of HR UK & Ireland; Thomas Urwin [1966] Director/Finance Manager

BASF Public Limited Company
Incorporated: 18 August 1960 *Employees:* 1,128
Net Worth: £72,742,000 *Total Assets:* £411,519,008
Registered Office: Earl Road, Cheadle Hulme, Cheadle, Cheshire, SK8 6QG
Activities: Manufacture of other organic basic chemicals
Parent: BASF U.K. Holdings Limited
Officers: Helen Victoria Koerner, Secretary/Legal Counsel; Richard John Carter [1962] Managing Director UK/Ireland; Karen Lois Harper [1964] Director/Head of HR UK & Ireland; Geoffrey William Mackey [1965] Director/Head of Sustainable Development; Harald Pflanzl [1966] Director/Head of Subregion North West & Central Europe [Austrian]; Thomas Urwin [1966] Director/Finance Manager UK & Ireland

BASF U.K. Holdings Limited
Incorporated: 20 June 1997
Net Worth: £141,392,000 *Total Assets:* £141,392,000
Registered Office: P O Box 4, Earl Road, Cheadle Hulme, Cheadle, Stockport, Cheshire, SK8 6QG
Activities: Non-trading company
Parent: BASF SE
Officers: Helen Victoria Koerner, Secretary; Richard John Carter [1962] Managing Director UK/Ireland; Thomas Urwin [1966] Director/Accountant

Basildon Chemical Co. Limited
Incorporated: 29 June 1971 *Employees:* 58
Net Worth: £21,466,644 *Total Assets:* £25,270,318
Registered Office: Kimber Road, off Nuffield Way, Abingdon, Oxon, OX14 1RZ
Activities: Manufacture of other chemical products n.e.c.
Officers: Mong Ik Chung [1962] Director [South Korean]; Hyung UK Kim [1973] Director/Integration Manager [South Korean]; Ian Arthur Watling [1953] Managing Director

Baslow Holdings Developments Limited
Incorporated: 9 December 2014 *Employees:* 2
Net Worth: £29,031,578 *Total Assets:* £34,519,048
Registered Office: 213 Cromford Road, Langley Mill, Nottingham, NG16 4EU
Activities: Other letting and operating of own or leased real estate
Shareholders: Anthony James Barney; Donna Michelle Barney
Officers: Anthony James Barney [1965] Director; Donna Michelle Barney [1966] Director

Bassi Fashions Limited
Incorporated: 31 December 1991 *Employees:* 18
Net Worth: £17,905,220 *Total Assets:* £18,462,420
Registered Office: Duke House, Northern Court, Vernon Road, Basford, Nottingham, NG6 0BJ
Activities: Wholesale of clothing and footwear
Parent: Bassi Group (Nottingham) Limited
Officers: Avinash Bassi, Secretary; Avinash Bassi [1960] Director/Retailer & Wholesales; Subhash Kumar Bassi [1964] Sales Director

Bassi Group (Nottingham) Limited
Incorporated: 7 October 2011 *Employees:* 18
Net Worth: £24,109,048 *Total Assets:* £28,161,900
Registered Office: Duke House, Northern Court, Vernon Road, Basford, Nottingham, NG6 0BJ
Activities: Activities of head offices
Officers: Avinash Bassi [1960] Director; Subhash Kumar Bassi [1964] Director

Bassi Properties Limited
Incorporated: 11 August 2000 *Employees:* 2
Net Worth: £6,205,874 *Total Assets:* £22,223,894
Registered Office: Duke House, Northern Court, Vernon Road, Basford, Nottingham, NG6 0BJ
Activities: Renting and operating of Housing Association real estate
Parent: Bassi Group (Nottingham) Limited
Officers: Avinash Bassi [1960] Director; Subhash Kumar Bassi [1964] Director

George Bateman & Son Limited
Incorporated: 23 July 1928 *Employees:* 101
Net Worth: £18,917,072 *Total Assets:* £25,884,940
Registered Office: Salem Bridge Brewery, Mill Lane, Wainfleet, Lincs, PE24 4JE
Activities: Manufacture of beer
Officers: Jaclyn Carol Bateman [1957] Marketing Director; Stuart George Carson Bateman [1960] Managing Director (Trading); Haydn Biddle [1946] Director/Chairman; John Derek Else [1944] Director/Consultant; Ian William Furniss [1962] Finance Director; Jeffrey Philip Moore [1954] Director; Stephen John Oliver [1958] Director

Battery Energy Storage Solutions Limited
Incorporated: 19 October 2016 *Employees:* 6
Net Worth: £44,767,056 *Total Assets:* £49,787,864
Registered Office: Salcey Lawn House, Salcey Lawn, Hartwell, Northants, NN7 2HA
Activities: Production of electricity
Officers: Steven Gerard Christianne Meersman, Secretary; James Edward Stewart Basden [1967] Director; Hon. Nicholas Duncan Beatty [1961] Director/Land Owner; Alessandro Boninsegna [1969] Director/Investment Professional [Italian]; Emil William Henry [1960] Director/Investment Professional [American]; Steven John Holliday [1956] Director; Graham John Sharp [1960] Director

Battle,Hayward and Bower,Limited
Incorporated: 6 April 1933 *Employees:* 126
Net Worth: £11,230,759 *Total Assets:* £17,966,548
Registered Office: Crofton Drive, Allenby Road Industrial Estate, Lincoln, LN3 4NP
Activities: Non-specialised wholesale trade
Parent: Battles Limited
Officers: Richard Michael Dewey, Secretary; Anna Marie Clarke [1981] Director; Richard Michael Dewey [1971] Director

Battles Limited
Incorporated: 4 February 2006 *Employees:* 126
Net Worth: £2,944,834 *Total Assets:* £9,735,624
Registered Office: Battles Limited, Crofton Drive, Allenby Road Industrial Estate, Lincoln, LN3 4NP
Activities: Activities of head offices
Parent: DC Holdings (Lincoln) Limited
Officers: Richard Michael Dewey, Secretary; Anna Marie Clarke [1981] Director; Richard Michael Dewey [1971] Director/Accountant

Bauer AR Holdings Limited
Incorporated: 21 April 1997 *Employees:* 3
Net Worth: £20,200,000 *Total Assets:* £20,200,000
Registered Office: Media House, Peterborough Business Park, Lynch Wood, Peterborough, Cambs, PE2 6EA
Activities: Radio broadcasting
Parent: Bauer Golden Square Limited
Officers: Deidre Ann Ford [1960] Managing Director; Paul Anthony Keenan [1963] Director/Publisher; Sarah Jane Vickery [1963] Finance Director

Bauer Consumer Media Limited
Incorporated: 3 July 1974 *Employees:* 653
Net Worth: £165,030,000 *Total Assets:* £182,107,008
Registered Office: Media House, Peterborough Business Park, Lynch Wood, Peterborough, Cambs, PE2 6EA
Activities: Activities of head offices
Parent: HBVB
Officers: Paul Anthony Keenan [1963] Director/Publisher; Robert James Munro-Hall [1966] Group Managing Director; Sarah Jane Vickery [1963] Finance Director

Bauer Digital Radio Limited
Incorporated: 7 January 1985 *Employees:* 3
Net Worth: £7,828,000 *Total Assets:* £10,683,000
Registered Office: Media House, Peterborough Business Park, Lynch Wood, Peterborough, Cambs, PE2 6EA
Activities: Television programme production activities
Parent: Bauer Radio Limited
Officers: Graeme Maxwell Allan [1956] Director/Chartered Engineer; Richard Jackson [1969] Director/Head of Finance - Bauer Radio; Susan Ruth Tattum [1969] Director/Chartered Accountant

Bauer Golden Square Limited
Incorporated: 22 May 2008 *Employees:* 3
Net Worth: £20,293,000 *Total Assets:* £20,293,000
Registered Office: Media House, Peterborough Business Park, Lynch Wood, Peterborough, Cambs, PE2 6EA
Activities: Activities of head offices
Parent: Bauer Radio Limited
Officers: Deidre Ann Ford [1960] Managing Director; Paul Anthony Keenan [1963] Director/Publisher; Sarah Jane Vickery [1963] Finance Director

Bauer Radio Limited
Incorporated: 16 October 1978 *Employees:* 112
Net Worth: £311,529,984 *Total Assets:* £384,135,008
Registered Office: Media House, Peterborough Business Park, Lynch Wood, Peterborough, Cambs, PE2 6EA
Activities: Activities of head offices
Parent: HBVB
Officers: Deidre Ann Ford [1960] Managing Director; Paul Anthony Keenan [1963] Director/Publisher; Sarah Jane Vickery [1963] Finance Director

Bawtry Carbon International Limited
Incorporated: 4 January 2006 *Employees:* 69
Net Worth: £20,700,912 *Total Assets:* £29,300,920
Registered Office: High Street, Austerfield, Doncaster, S Yorks, DN10 6QT
Activities: Other manufacturing n.e.c.
Parent: Coretex Trading Limited
Officers: Carl Hammerton, Secretary; Yunjia Lu [1992] Director [Chinese]; Shuze Ren [1993] Director [Swiss]

Baxi Finance Limited
Incorporated: 8 June 2000
Net Worth Deficit: £107,686,000 *Total Assets:* £882,812,992
Registered Office: Brooks House, Coventry Road, Warwick, CV34 4LL
Activities: Activities of head offices
Officers: Karen Dawn Roberts, Secretary; Simon Charles Oliver [1968] Director; Jan-Feie Zwiers [1972] Director/Group Finance Controller [Dutch]

Baxi Global Limited
Incorporated: 12 November 1999
Net Worth: £705,094,016 *Total Assets:* £705,094,016
Registered Office: Brooks House, Coventry Road, Warwick, CV34 4LL
Activities: Other business support service activities n.e.c.
Officers: Karen Dawn Roberts, Secretary; Simon Charles Oliver [1968] Director; Jan-Feie Zwiers [1972] Director/Group Finance Controller [Dutch]

Baxi Group Limited
Incorporated: 30 August 2000
Net Worth: £85,688,000 *Total Assets:* £87,178,000
Registered Office: Brooks House, Coventry Road, Warwick, CV34 4LL
Activities: Activities of head offices
Officers: Karen Dawn Roberts, Secretary; Simon Charles Oliver [1968] Director; Jan-Feie Zwiers [1972] Director/Group Finance Controller [Dutch]

Baxi Heating UK Limited
Incorporated: 12 November 1999 *Employees:* 1,552
Net Worth: £326,892,992 *Total Assets:* £576,209,024
Registered Office: Brooks House, Coventry Road, Warwick, CV34 4LL
Activities: Manufacture of central heating radiators and boilers
Officers: Karen Dawn Roberts, Secretary; Simon Charles Oliver [1968] Director; David Stuart Pinder [1963] Director/Boiler Manufacturer; Jan Van Ooijen [1959] Director [Dutch]

Baxi Holdings Limited
Incorporated: 6 October 2003
Net Worth: £243,731,008 *Total Assets:* £924,073,984
Registered Office: Brooks House, Coventry Road, Warwick, CV34 4LL
Activities: Activities of head offices
Officers: Karen Dawn Roberts, Secretary; Simon Charles Oliver [1968] Director; Carolina Wielinga [1970] Director [Dutch]

Baxi Overseas Holdings Limited
Incorporated: 12 November 1999
Net Worth: £334,353,984 *Total Assets:* £410,859,008
Registered Office: Brooks House, Coventry Road, Warwick, CV34 4LL
Activities: Activities of head offices
Officers: Karen Dawn Roberts, Secretary; Simon Charles Oliver [1968] Director; Jan Van Ooijen [1959] Director/Chief Operating Officer [Dutch]; Jan-Feie Zwiers [1972] Director/Group Finance Controller [Dutch]

Baxi Potterton Limited
Incorporated: 12 November 1999
Net Worth: £699,126,976 *Total Assets:* £699,126,976
Registered Office: Brooks House, Coventry Road, Warwick, CV34 4LL
Activities: Activities of head offices
Officers: Karen Dawn Roberts, Secretary; Simon Charles Oliver [1968] Director; Jan-Feie Zwiers [1972] Director/Group Finance Controller [Dutch]

Bayard Metering (UK)
Incorporated: 5 August 2003
Net Worth: £52,814,000 *Total Assets:* £157,576,000
Registered Office: 1 Lysander Drive, Northfields Industrial Estate, Market Deeping, Peterborough, PE6 8FB
Activities: Activities of head offices
Parent: Landis + Gyr AG
Officers: Stephen George Cunningham [1966] Director/Chief Financial Officer; Charles Philip Walker [1972] Director/Chief Financial Officer

BBB Services Limited
Incorporated: 27 March 2003 *Employees:* 2
Net Worth Deficit: £886,323 *Total Assets:* £16,060,391
Registered Office: Unit 25 Bloom Lane, Scunthorpe, N Lincs, DN15 9AJ
Activities: Manufacture of other parts and accessories for motor vehicles
Shareholder: Egidio Brugola
Officers: Karl Erik Tommy Andersson [1963] Director/President [Swedish]; Carlo Rosario Arminio [1964] Director [Italian]; Elena Lidia Bestetti [1961] Director [Italian]; Egidio Stefano Brugola [1979] Director [Italian]; Steven David Gidney [1985] Director/Key Account Manager; Sukhvinder Gill [1966] Director/Project Manager; Sven Anders Karlsson [1949] Director [Swedish]; Neal Robert Thomas [1961] Director/Operations Manager; Anna Helena Christina Wennerstrom [1965] Director/Chief Financial Officer [Swedish]

BBHP Limited
Incorporated: 18 September 2003 *Employees:* 1
Net Worth: £7,983,189 *Total Assets:* £23,178,832
Registered Office: Magma House, 16 Davy Court, Castle Mound Way, Rugby, Warwicks, CV23 0UZ
Activities: Buying and selling of own real estate
Parent: No 71 Ltd
Officers: Timothy Edward Clark, Secretary/Accountant; James Bailey [1972] Director/Letting Agent; Timothy Edward Clark [1970] Director/Accountant; Nicholas John Humphreys [1970] Director/Estate Agent

BBRG (Purchaser) Ltd
Incorporated: 24 February 2016
Net Worth: £89,930,504 *Total Assets:* £176,279,408
Registered Office: Ground Floor, Icon Building, Balby Carr Bank, Doncaster, S Yorks, DN4 5JQ
Activities: Activities of head offices
Parent: BBRG (Subsidiary) Ltd
Officers: Claudia Maria Griffin [1967] Director/Chief Financial Officer [German]

BBRG (Subsidiary) Ltd
Incorporated: 3 December 2015
Net Worth: £78,351,744 *Total Assets:* £176,279,408
Registered Office: Ground Floor, Icon Building, Balby Carr Bank, Doncaster, S Yorks, DN4 5JQ
Activities: Activities of head offices
Parent: BBRG Holding (UK) Ltd
Officers: Claudia Maria Griffin [1967] Director/Chief Financial Officer [German]

BBRG Finance (UK) Ltd.
Incorporated: 3 October 2014 *Employees:* 22
Net Worth Deficit: £57,063,436 *Total Assets:* £235,947,072
Registered Office: Ground Floor, Icon Building, Balby Carr Bank, Doncaster, S Yorks, DN4 5JQ
Activities: Activities of head offices
Parent: BBRG Production (UK) Limited
Officers: Claudia Maria Griffin [1967] Director/Chief Financial Officer [German]; Brett Simpson [1964] Director/Chief Executive [Australian]

BBRG Holding (UK) Ltd
Incorporated: 3 December 2015
Net Worth: £20,342,124 *Total Assets:* £163,973,632
Registered Office: Ground Floor, Icon Building, Balby Carr Bank, Doncaster, S Yorks, DN4 5JQ
Activities: Activities of head offices
Parent: NV Bekaert
Officers: Matthew Taylor [1960] Director/Chief Executive Officer; Curd Vandekerckhove [1965] Director [Belgian]

BBRG Operations (UK) Ltd.
Incorporated: 5 November 2014 *Employees:* 4
Net Worth: £159,698,864 *Total Assets:* £176,279,408
Registered Office: Ground Floor, Icon Building, Balby Carr Bank, Doncaster, S Yorks, DN4 5JQ
Activities: Activities of head offices
Parent: Bridon-Bekaert Ropes Group (UK) Ltd
Officers: Claudia Maria Griffin [1967] Director/Chief Financial Officer [German]

BBRG Production (UK) Ltd.
Incorporated: 5 November 2014
Net Worth: £197,856,000 *Total Assets:* £197,856,000
Registered Office: Ground Floor, Icon Building, Balby Carr Bank, Doncaster, S Yorks, DN4 5JQ
Activities: Activities of head offices
Parent: BBRG Operations (UK) Ltd
Officers: Claudia Maria Griffin [1967] Director/Chief Financial Officer [German]

BCA Marketplace PLC
Incorporated: 30 April 2014 *Employees:* 7,205
Net Worth: £1,156,600,064 *Total Assets:* £2,256,100,096
Registered Office: Haversham House, Coronation Business Park, Kiln Road, Kempston, Hardwick, Bedford, MK43 9PR
Activities: Activities of head offices
Officers: Martin Richard Letza, Secretary; Petrus Antonius Johannes Coelewij [1960] Director; Stephen Gutteridge [1954] Director; Jonathan Damian Kamaluddin [1973] Director/Chartered Accountant; Timothy Giles Lampert [1970] Director; David George Lis [1950] Director; Avril Palmer-Baunack [1964] Director

BCHK UK Limited
Incorporated: 29 August 2014 *Employees:* 1
Net Worth: £96,196,552 *Total Assets:* £113,075,976
Registered Office: 19 Jessops Riverside, 800 Brightside Lane, Sheffield, S9 2RX
Activities: Activities of head offices
Parent: Danaher Corporation
Officers: Keith Graham Ward [1953] Director

BCM Employment & Management Services Limited
Incorporated: 12 November 2009 *Employees:* 961
Net Worth: £10,193,000 *Total Assets:* £11,264,000
Registered Office: D10 Building, 1 Thane Road, Nottingham, NG90 2PR
Activities: Other business support service activities n.e.c.
Parent: Fareva UK Limited
Officers: Andrew John Mortimer [1959] Director/Country Manager UK; Christophe Petras [1969] Director/Vice President Global Operations [French]; Richard David Whall [1962] Managing Director

BCM Limited
Incorporated: 20 August 1992
Net Worth: £61,600,000 *Total Assets:* £90,600,000
Registered Office: 1 Thane Road West, Nottingham, NG2 3AA
Activities: Manufacture of perfumes and toilet preparations
Parent: Fareva UK Limited
Officers: Andrew John Mortimer [1959] Director/Country Manager UK; Christophe Petras [1969] Director/Vice President Global Operations [French]; Benoit Pierre Portier [1966] Director/Engineer [French]; Richard David Whall [1962] Managing Director

BCM Specials Limited
Incorporated: 24 November 2006 *Employees:* 2
Net Worth: £20,849,000 *Total Assets:* £22,076,000
Registered Office: 1 Thane Road West, Nottingham, NG2 3AA
Activities: Manufacture of basic pharmaceutical products
Parent: Fareva UK Limited
Officers: Andrew John Mortimer [1959] Director/Country Manager UK; Christophe Petras [1969] Director/Vice President Global Operations [French]; Benoit Pierre Portier [1966] Director/Engineer [French]; Richard David Whall [1962] Managing Director

BCN Holdco Limited
Incorporated: 1 September 2014
Net Worth: £32,103,000 *Total Assets:* £32,136,000
Registered Office: 19 Jessops Riverside, 800 Brightside Lane, Sheffield, S9 2RX
Activities: Activities of head offices
Parent: Danaher Corporation
Officers: Keith Graham Ward [1953] Director

BCQ (Holdings) Limited
Incorporated: 2 January 2007 *Employees:* 121
Net Worth: £2,874,812 *Total Assets:* £11,063,480
Registered Office: 1 Osier Way, Swan Business Park, Buckingham, MK18 1TB
Activities: Non-trading company
Major Shareholder: Richard Durose Knowles
Officers: Hilary Knowles, Secretary; Richard Durose Knowles [1952] Director

BCTI Holdings Limited
Incorporated: 31 July 2002 *Employees:* 16
Previous: Black Country Traditional Inns Limited
Net Worth: £4,126,749 *Total Assets:* £9,294,613
Registered Office: Sovereign House, 12 Warwick Street, Coventry, Warwicks, CV5 6ET
Activities: Public houses and bars
Shareholders: Angus Gilchrist McMeeking; Pauline McMeeking
Officers: John Michael McMeeking, Secretary; Angus Gilchrist McMeeking [1962] Director/Pub Retailer; Pauline McMeeking [1954] Director

BDB Design Build Holdings Limited
Incorporated: 24 November 2015 *Employees:* 23
Net Worth: £1,376,219 *Total Assets:* £12,024,925
Registered Office: Unit 10 Churchill Way, Chapeltown, Sheffield, S35 2PY
Activities: Activities of head offices
Major Shareholder: Nicholas Edward Goodson
Officers: Andrea Claire Kelly, Secretary; Steven Mark Brown [1974] Director; Peter Richard Burdekin [1963] Executive Director; Nicholas Edward Goodson [1974] Director/Building Surveyor

BDF Plant Limited
Incorporated: 17 May 2006
Net Worth: £10,482,664 *Total Assets:* £10,991,122
Registered Office: Colwick Industrial Estate, Colwick, Nottingham, NG4 2BB
Activities: Renting and leasing of other machinery, equipment and tangible goods n.e.c.
Officers: David Miller, Secretary; Howard William Mew [1957] Director/Drilling Engineer; Peter James Wheelhouse [1957] Managing Director

BDR Waste Disposal Limited
Incorporated: 2 March 1992 *Employees:* 3
Net Worth: £3,941,000 *Total Assets:* £13,767,000
Registered Office: Ground Floor West, 900 Pavilion Drive, Northampton Business Park, Northampton, NN4 7RG
Activities: Other business support service activities n.e.c.
Parent: FCC Environment (UK) Limited
Officers: Carol Jayne Nunn, Secretary; Vicente Federico Orts-Llopis [1962] Director/Chief Financial Officer [Spanish]; Agustin Serrano Minchan [1959] Director/Technical Civil Engineer [Spanish]; Paul Taylor [1959] Director/Chief Executive Officer

BDW Trading Limited
Incorporated: 3 February 1995 *Employees:* 5,779
Net Worth: £3,113,240,064 *Total Assets:* £5,491,867,136
Registered Office: Barratt House, Cartwright Way, Forest Business Park, Bardon Hill, Coalville, Leics, LE67 1UF
Activities: Construction of commercial buildings
Parent: Barratt Developments P L C
Officers: Kamalprit Kaur Bains, Secretary; Steven John Boyes [1960] Director; Richard John Russell Brooke [1960] Director; Christopher Julian Burton [1962] Managing Director; Gary Martin Ennis [1969] Director [Irish]; Douglas McLeod [1953] Managing Director; Nicholas Hadden Richardson [1963] Director; Michael Roberts [1967] Managing Director; Bernard William Rooney [1957] Director; Robert Tansey [1961] Group HR Director; David Fraser Thomas [1963] Director; Jessica Elizabeth White [1978] Director/Chief Financial Officer

BDWZest Developments LLP
Incorporated: 24 July 2013
Net Worth: £171,686,000 *Total Assets:* £281,496,000
Registered Office: Barratt House, Cartwright Way, Forest Business Park, Bardon Hill, Coalville, Leics, LE67 1UF

BDWZest LLP
Incorporated: 22 July 2013 *Employees:* 2
Net Worth: £73,986,000 *Total Assets:* £73,986,000
Registered Office: Barratt House, Cartwright Way, Forest Business Park, Bardon Hill, Coalville, Leics, LE67 1UF

Beachampton Group Limited
Incorporated: 7 October 2002 *Employees:* 25
Net Worth: £8,389,765 *Total Assets:* £14,508,177
Registered Office: Station Yard, Station Road, Ridgmont, Beds, MK43 0XP
Activities: Activities of other holding companies n.e.c.
Major Shareholder: Andrew Dension Smith
Officers: Rosalind Ellen Hull, Secretary; Andrew Denison Smith [1968] Director; James George Smith [1934] Director; Sally Rowntree Smith [1971] Director/Manager

Beacon Bingo Limited
Incorporated: 30 January 1987 *Employees:* 237
Net Worth: £7,196,000 *Total Assets:* £14,388,000
Registered Office: Seebeck House, 1a Seebeck Place, Knowlhill, Milton Keynes, Bucks, MK5 8FR
Activities: Gambling and betting activities
Parent: Praesepe Holdings Limited
Officers: Stefan Bruns [1971] Director/Chief Executive Officer [German]; Borris Lungen [1962] Director/Chief Financial Officer [German]; Mark Stefan Schertle [1977] Director [German]

Beamglow Limited
Incorporated: 6 October 1966 *Employees:* 151
Net Worth: £5,657,228 *Total Assets:* £13,558,577
Registered Office: Somersham Road, St Ives, Huntingdon, Cambs, PE27 3LP
Activities: Other manufacturing n.e.c.
Shareholder: Moira Griffin
Officers: Adrian Philip Brown, Secretary; Wayne Bellchamber [1958] Technical Director; Adrian Philip Brown [1968] Finance Director; Brian Griffin [1947] Director; Moira Griffin [1947] Managing Director; Huw Roberts [1963] Sales Director

Beardow Adams Holdings Ltd
Incorporated: 13 July 2015 *Employees:* 245
Net Worth: £15,845,612 *Total Assets:* £46,559,456
Registered Office: 32 Blundells Road, Bradville, Milton Keynes, Bucks, MK13 7HF
Activities: Activities of production holding companies
Shareholders: Robert Edward Adams; Kim Neo Beardow; Nicholas James Beardow
Officers: Nicholas James Beardow, Secretary; Robert Edward Adams [1950] Director/Research Chemist; Nicolas James Beardow [1960] Sales Director; Adrian James Day [1977] Finance Director

Beardow and Adams (Adhesives) Limited
Incorporated: 16 July 1976 *Employees:* 106
Net Worth: £16,872,476 *Total Assets:* £31,820,200
Registered Office: 32 Blundells Road, Bradville, Milton Keynes, Bucks, MK13 7HF
Activities: Manufacture of glues
Parent: Beardow Adams Holdings Limited
Officers: Nicholas James Beardow, Secretary; Robert Edward Adams [1950] Director/Research Chemist; Nicholas James Beardow [1960] Sales Director; Adrian James Day [1977] Director/Accountant; Graeme Edward Nutting [1956] Director/UK Sales; Lesley Elizabeth Sheldon [1961] Product Development & Technical Services Director

Bearward Engineering Limited
Incorporated: 8 October 1981 *Employees:* 308
Net Worth: £19,771,496 *Total Assets:* £25,432,938
Registered Office: Main Road, Far Cotton, Northampton, NN4 8HJ
Activities: Manufacture of other special-purpose machinery n.e.c.
Officers: Mark Andrew Stafford, Secretary; Mark Andrew Stafford [1973] Finance Director; George William Wilson FitzGenerald [1968] Director

Beatson Clark Limited
Incorporated: 15 June 1910 *Employees:* 220
Net Worth: £24,279,000 *Total Assets:* £55,796,000
Registered Office: The Glassworks, Greasborough Road, Rotherham, S Yorks, S60 1TZ
Activities: Manufacture of hollow glass
Parent: Newship Limited
Officers: Andrew Paul Bale, Secretary; Andrew Paul Bale [1957] Director; Jeremy David Clarkson [1961] Director; Stephen Edwin John Compson [1954] Director; John Watson Newman [1945] Director; Richard John Newman [1979] Director; David Roberts [1967] Commercial Director; Lynn Sidebottom [1959] Sales Director

Beaver-Visitec International (UK) Limited
Incorporated: 18 June 2010 *Employees:* 530
Net Worth: £29,918,000 *Total Assets:* £97,121,000
Registered Office: 85b Centurion Court, Park Drive, Milton Park, Milton, Abingdon, Oxon, OX14 4RY
Activities: Other business support service activities n.e.c.
Officers: Denis Hinaut [1958] Director [French]; Shervin Joe Korangy [1974] Director/Chief Financial Officer [American]; Dana George Mead [1959] Director/President and CEO [American]

Beaver-Visitec International Sales Limited
Incorporated: 18 June 2010 *Employees:* 66
Net Worth: £25,763,000 *Total Assets:* £37,746,000
Registered Office: 85b Centurion Court, Park Drive, Milton Park, Milton, Abingdon, Oxon, OX14 4RY
Activities: Wholesale of other intermediate products
Officers: Denis Hinaut [1958] Director/Vice President, International Sales and Marketing [French]; Shervin Joe Korangy [1974] Director/Chief Financial Officer [American]; Dana George Mead [1959] Director/President and CEO [American]

Beck Bidco Limited
Incorporated: 6 March 2015
Net Worth: £46,614,404 *Total Assets:* £46,614,404
Registered Office: Hestia House, Edgewest Road, Lincoln, LN6 7EL
Activities: Activities of financial services holding companies
Officers: James Floyd Burr [1966] Director/Investor [American]; Philip Screeton [1967] Director; Martin Richard Totty [1956] Director

Beckett's Foods Limited
Incorporated: 12 May 1988 *Employees:* 330
Net Worth: £17,356,856 *Total Assets:* £34,188,644
Registered Office: Oak House, Heyford Close, Aldermans Green, Coventry, Warwicks, CV2 2QB
Activities: Retail sale of meat and meat products in specialised stores
Parent: CPC Foods Limited
Officers: Heike Roschkowski, Secretary; Carl Ernst Burger [1987] Director [German]; Jeremy Adam Cornes [1967] Director; Timothy William Cornes [1966] Director; Frank Duffe [1960] Director [German]; Carsten Svejgaard Jakobsen [1945] Director [Danish]

Beckhall Properties Ltd
Incorporated: 27 May 1999 *Employees:* 3
Net Worth: £9,855,646 *Total Assets:* £25,516,936
Registered Office: c/o DBS, 40 Lower Hillgate, Stockport, Cheshire, SK1 1JE
Activities: Buying and selling of own real estate
Major Shareholder: Karl Nolan
Officers: Karl Nolan [1970] Director/Consultant

Bedford School Trust
Incorporated: 8 July 2002
Net Worth: £17,215,070 *Total Assets:* £18,014,488
Registered Office: 10 Glebe Road, Bedford, MK40 2PL
Activities: Other education n.e.c.
Officers: Stuart Holliday, Secretary; Simon Culliford [1951] Director/Recruitment Consultant; Rex Michael Elliot [1950] Director/Chartered Surveyor; Mark David Hall [1973] Director; James Simon Hodgson [1969] Director/Headmaster; Nicholas Jones [1972] Director/Land Agent; Daniel Robert Koch [1981] Director/Vice Master, Bedford School; Philip John McDuell [1963] Director/Management Consultant; Rose-Marie Wellington [1966] Director/Lawyer

Bedfordia Farms Limited
Incorporated: 30 June 1958 *Employees:* 26
Net Worth: £15,809,013 *Total Assets:* £20,928,480
Registered Office: Milton House Farm, Milton Ernest, Beds, MK44 1YU
Activities: Growing of cereals (except rice), leguminous crops and oil seeds
Shareholders: John Charles Ibbett; Bedfordia Group Limited
Officers: Terry Wilding, Secretary; John Charles Ibbett [1962] Director; Ian Paul Smith [1969] Director; Charles Alan Whitaker [1962] Director/Agricultural Business Consultant

Bedfordia Group Limited
Incorporated: 11 September 1959 *Employees:* 42
Previous: Bedfordia Group PLC
Net Worth: £30,029,236 *Total Assets:* £38,883,044
Registered Office: Milton Parc, Milton Ernest, Beds, MK44 1YU
Activities: Activities of head offices
Officers: Terry Wilding, Secretary; David Alistair Gray [1955] Director/Chartered Accountant; John Charles Ibbett [1962] Director; Yolanda Alexandra Ibbett [1969] Director

Beechcroft Developments Limited
Incorporated: 9 March 1984 *Employees:* 47
Net Worth: £6,291,000 *Total Assets:* £93,972,000
Registered Office: 1 Church Lane, Wallingford, Oxon, OX10 0DX
Activities: Development of building projects
Parent: Beechcroft UK Limited
Officers: Brian Patrick Mills, Finance Director; Brian Patrick Mills [1969] Finance Director; Angela South [1962] Director; Christopher Richard Thompson [1964] Director

Beechcroft Group Limited
Incorporated: 21 June 2011 *Employees:* 47
Net Worth: £21,044,000 *Total Assets:* £103,287,000
Registered Office: 1 Church Lane, Wallingford, Oxon, OX10 0DX
Activities: Development of building projects
Parent: Alchemy Special Opportunities Fund II LP
Officers: Paul Malcolm Bridges [1958] Director/Chartered Accountant; Alexander Leicester [1979] Director/Investment Manager; Brian Patrick Mills [1969] Director/Management Accountant; Angela South [1962] Director; Christopher Richard Thompson [1964] Director

Beechcroft UK Limited
Incorporated: 11 May 1994 *Employees:* 1
Net Worth: £14,612,000 *Total Assets:* £17,482,000
Registered Office: 1 Church Lane, Wallingford, Oxon, OX10 0DX
Activities: Development of building projects
Parent: Beechcroft Group
Officers: Christopher Richard Thompson [1964] Director

Beechfield Estates Limited
Incorporated: 12 July 2007 *Employees:* 3
Net Worth: £5,355 *Total Assets:* £9,641,629
Registered Office: 19 King Street, King's Lynn, Norfolk, PE30 1HB
Activities: Development of building projects
Shareholders: Rui Pan; Qinqin Song; Chengrun He
Officers: Weipeng Gu, Secretary; Weipeng Gu [1989] Director [Chinese]; Andrew David Auldio Jamieson [1956] Director

The Beechwood Estates Co.Limited
Incorporated: 2 May 1922 *Employees:* 1
Net Worth: £15,321,392 *Total Assets:* £16,030,155
Registered Office: The Estate Office, Shirburn, Watlington, Oxon, OX49 5DL
Activities: Buying and selling of own real estate
Officers: Mary Joanna Isobel Boone [1951] Director/Administrator; Robert George Parker [1955] Director/Farmer

Beeson Wright Limited
Incorporated: 28 June 2011 *Employees:* 8
Net Worth: £8,713,585 *Total Assets:* £24,100,966
Registered Office: 4 Office Village, Forder Way, Hampton, Peterborough, Cambs, PE7 8GX
Activities: Construction of commercial buildings
Shareholders: Andrew Beeson; Neville David Wright; Joanne Beeson; Marilyn Jane Wright
Officers: Andrew Beeson [1976] Director; Joanne Beeson [1982] Director; Marilyn Jane Wright [1951] Director; Neville David Wright [1950] Director

Beeston Site Services Limited
Incorporated: 20 October 2010
Net Worth: £5,622,000 *Total Assets:* £18,712,000
Registered Office: 1 Thane Road West, Nottingham, NG2 3AA
Activities: Other business support service activities n.e.c.
Parent: Alliance Boots Holdings Limited
Officers: Andrew Richard Thompson, Secretary; Paul Jamie Dunne [1971] Supply Chain Director; Michael David Snape [1979] Director/Chief Financial Officer; Andrew Richard Thompson [1975] Director/Solicitor

Beeswax Dyson Farming Limited
Incorporated: 22 July 2009 *Employees:* 89
Previous: Beeswax Farming (Rainbow) Limited
Net Worth: £461,449,984 *Total Assets:* £473,896,000
Registered Office: The Estate Office, Cyclone Way, Nocton, Lincoln, LN4 2GR
Activities: Activities of agricultural holding companies
Parent: Weybourne Group Limited
Officers: Sir James Jeffrey Corfield Bucknall [1958] Director; Sir James Dyson [1947] Director; Edward David Fursdon [1952] Director; Caroline Jane Tucker [1980] Director/Chief Financial Officer; Richard John Williamson [1965] Director; Ben Wiseman [1969] Director/Chartered Accountant; Nicholas Hugh Worboys [1972] Director/Estate Manager; Philip Graham Wynn [1950] Director

Belchim Crop Protection Limited
Incorporated: 26 November 2002 *Employees:* 16
Net Worth: £12,570,761 *Total Assets:* £20,629,048
Registered Office: 1b Fenice Court, Eaton Socon, St Neots, Cambs, PE19 8EP
Activities: Wholesale of chemical products
Officers: Herbert Peumans [1968] Managing Director [Belgian]

Belfield Furnishings Limited
Incorporated: 15 April 2002 *Employees:* 2,181
Net Worth: £17,345,000 *Total Assets:* £57,923,000
Registered Office: Furnace Road, Ilkeston, Derbys, DE7 5EP
Activities: Manufacture of soft furnishings
Parent: Northedge Capital Fund II LP
Officers: Gary Lasham [1958] Director; Karl Ivor Stevens [1956] Finance Director

Belfield Group Limited
Incorporated: 14 March 2016 *Employees:* 2,181
Net Worth: £1,335,000 *Total Assets:* £97,055,000
Registered Office: Site 3 Furnace Road, Ilkeston, Derbys, DE7 5EP
Activities: Activities of head offices
Officers: John Breheny [1981] Director/Chartered Accountant; Gary Lasham [1958] Director; Alan James McWalter [1953] Director/Chairman; Keven David Parker [1969] Director/Private Equity Partner; Karl Ivor Stevens [1956] Finance Director

Belgium Bidco Limited
Incorporated: 13 July 2016 *Employees:* 4
Net Worth Deficit: £140,107 *Total Assets:* £16,898,430
Registered Office: Unit 25 Shortwood Court, Shortwood Business Park, Dearne Valley Parkway, Barnsley, S Yorks, S74 9LH
Activities: Activities of other holding companies n.e.c.
Parent: Belgium Midco Limited
Officers: Richard James Boston [1978] Director; Craig Burns [1975] Director

Belgium Midco Limited
Incorporated: 13 July 2016 *Employees:* 4
Net Worth Deficit: £895,575 *Total Assets:* £9,543,491
Registered Office: Unit 25 Shortwood Court, Shortwood Business Park, Dearne Valley Parkway, Barnsley, S Yorks, S74 9LH
Activities: Activities of other holding companies n.e.c.
Parent: Belgium Topco Limited
Officers: Richard James Boston [1978] Director; Craig Burns [1975] Director

Belgium Topco Limited
Incorporated: 12 July 2016 *Employees:* 42
Net Worth: £920,912 *Total Assets:* £18,426,710
Registered Office: Unit 25 Shortwood Court, Shortwood Business Park, Dearne Valley Parkway, Barnsley, S Yorks, S74 9LH
Activities: Activities of other holding companies n.e.c.
Parent: Blade Acquisition Limited
Officers: Richard James Boston [1978] Director; Craig Burns [1975] Director

Belgrade Theatre Trust (Coventry) Limited
Incorporated: 8 November 1957 *Employees:* 124
Net Worth: £11,845,503 *Total Assets:* £13,724,719
Registered Office: Belgrade Theatre, Belgrade Square, Coventry, Warwicks, CV1 1GS
Activities: Performing arts
Officers: Kathryn Joanna Reid, Secretary/Theatre Executive Director; Sheila Anne Bates [1965] Director/Children's Champion, City Council; Paul Carvell [1960] Managing Director; Nathaniel Dodzo [1973] Director/Lecturer/Consultant; Stewart Collis Fergusson [1950] Director/Retired; William Hamish Glen [1957] Theatre Director; Annette Hay [1966] Director/Senior Researcher; Tim John Mayer [1980] Director/Councillor; Alan Fraser Pollock [1962] Director/Writer; Kathryn Joanna Reid [1962] Theatre Executive Director; Councillor Anthony Charles Skipper [1946] Director/Councillor; Jonathan James Wilby [1966] Director/Solicitor

Belgrave Land (Wisbech) Limited
Incorporated: 12 June 2001 *Employees:* 3
Net Worth: £3,856,045 *Total Assets:* £9,096,071
Registered Office: Thomas House, Langford Locks, Kidlington, Oxon, OX5 1HR
Activities: Other letting and operating of own or leased real estate
Parent: BL (Wisbech) Limited
Officers: Roberta Caroline Miles, Secretary; Simon Timothy Gill [1956] Property Director; David Henry Kingerlee [1961] Director/Quantity Surveyor; Roberta Caroline Miles [1962] Finance Director

Believe Academy Trust
Incorporated: 2 August 2011 *Employees:* 195
Previous: Southwark Primary Academy Trust
Net Worth: £9,482,119 *Total Assets:* £12,759,905
Registered Office: Southwark Primary School, Park Lane, Old Basford, Nottingham, NG6 0DT
Activities: Primary education
Officers: Graham John Boyd [1977] Director/Chief Executive Officer; James Freeman [1989] Director/Senior Recruitment Consultant; Daniel James Harvey [1985] Director/Governor Support Officer Notts Local Authority; Anne Maria Christina Hurt [1952] Director/Retired; Russell Paul Lambert [1956] Director; Henrietta Robinson [1969] Director/Childminder; Alison Margaret Rogers [1963] Director/School Teacher; Kevin Sheppard [1980] Director/Commercial/Solutions Sales Manager Ergo IT

John Bell & Croyden Limited
Incorporated: 24 February 1928 *Employees:* 97
Net Worth: £4,387,000 *Total Assets:* £19,767,000
Registered Office: Sapphire Court, Walsgrave Triangle, Coventry, Warwicks, CV2 2TX
Activities: Dispensing chemist in specialised stores
Parent: Admenta Holdings Limited
Officers: Nichola Louise Legg, Secretary; Toby Matthew Anderson [1973] Director; Marcus Hilger [1977] Finance Director [German]; Catherine McDermott [1968] Operations Director; Nigel Swift [1966] Marketing & Sales Director

Thomas Bell & Sons Limited
Incorporated: 30 July 1976 *Employees:* 43
Net Worth: £10,489,621 *Total Assets:* £22,737,012
Registered Office: Bigby Road, Brigg, N Lincs, DN20 8RA
Activities: Agents selling agricultural raw materials, livestock, textile raw materials and semi-finished goods
Shareholders: Andrew Martin Major; Andrew Martin Major
Officers: Paula Major, Secretary; Matthew Peter Holden Dawson [1978] Director; Andrew Martin Major [1962] Managing Director

Graham Bell (Holdings) Limited
Incorporated: 8 December 2003 *Employees:* 730
Net Worth: £39,503,000 *Total Assets:* £95,327,000
Registered Office: Available Car, Station Road, Castle Donington, Derbys, DE74 2NL
Activities: Activities of other holding companies n.e.c.
Shareholders: Graham Bell; Alison Mary Bell
Officers: Alison Mary Bell, Secretary; Alison Mary Bell [1960] Director; Graham Bell [1959] Director

Bell Equipment UK Limited
Incorporated: 2 July 1998 *Employees:* 39
Net Worth: £9,030,944 *Total Assets:* £16,119,246
Registered Office: Unit 6c Graycar Business Park, Barton Turns, Barton Under Needwood, Burton on Trent, Staffs, DE13 8EN
Activities: Wholesale of mining, construction and civil engineering machinery
Officers: Victoria Sarah Riddell, Secretary; Nicolas Thomas Learoyd [1962] Director/General Manager; Douglas Morris [1974] Director [Zimbabwean]

Bell Euro Finance Limited
Incorporated: 10 August 2016
Net Worth: £25,448,032 *Total Assets:* £33,745,324
Registered Office: Unit 6c Graycar Business Park, Barton under Needwood, Burton on Trent, Staffs, DE13 8EN
Activities: Activities of other holding companies n.e.c.
Officers: Robert Cameron Crawford [1961] Director/Chartered Management Accountant [Irish]; Karen June Van Haght [1966] Director/Chartered Accountant [South African]

Graham Bell Limited
Incorporated: 22 April 1999 *Employees:* 10
Net Worth: £4,024,681 *Total Assets:* £11,625,004
Registered Office: Available Car, Station Road, Castle Donington, Derbys, DE74 2NL
Activities: Sale of used cars and light motor vehicles
Parent: Graham Bell Holdings Ltd
Officers: Graham Bell, Secretary/Director; Alison Mary Bell [1960] Director; Graham Bell [1959] Director

Bell Rock Bidco Limited
Incorporated: 26 April 2013
Net Worth: £8,258,000 *Total Assets:* £78,222,000
Registered Office: Peat House, 1 Waterloo Way, Leicester, LE1 6LP
Activities: Activities of venture and development capital companies
Parent: Bell Rock Midco Limited
Officers: Alexander Peter Marek Rudzinski, Secretary; Alexander Peter Marek Rudzinski [1975] Director; David John Smith [1964] Director

Bell Rock Midco Limited
Incorporated: 10 July 2013
Net Worth: £11,919,000 *Total Assets:* £17,807,000
Registered Office: Peat House, 1 Waterloo Way, Leicester, LE1 6LP
Activities: Activities of venture and development capital companies
Parent: Bell Rock Topco Ltd
Officers: Alexander Peter Marek Rudzinski, Secretary; Alexander Peter Marek Rudzinski [1975] Director; David John Smith [1964] Director

Bell Rock Topco Limited
Incorporated: 10 July 2013 *Employees:* 565
Net Worth: £4,401,000 *Total Assets:* £72,373,000
Registered Office: Peat House, 1 Waterloo Way, Leicester, LE1 6LP
Activities: Activities of venture and development capital companies
Parent: Lyceum Capital Partners LLP
Officers: Alexander Peter Marek Rudzinski, Secretary; Generald Andrew Higgins [1955] Director; Adam Stephen Lewis [1982] Director; Mark Rogerson [1964] Director/Business Executive; Alexander Peter Marek Rudzinski [1975] Director; David John Smith [1964] Director

Bell Rock Workplace Management Limited
Incorporated: 22 September 1994
Net Worth: £22,157,000 *Total Assets:* £89,029,000
Registered Office: Peat House, 1 Waterloo Way, Leicester, LE1 6LP
Activities: Activities of head offices
Parent: Bell Rock Bidco Limited
Officers: Alexander Peter Marek Rudzinski, Secretary; Alexander Peter Marek Rudzinski [1975] Director; David John Smith [1964] Director

Bellcoin Holdings Limited
Incorporated: 18 February 1985 *Employees:* 30
Net Worth: £10,089,830 *Total Assets:* £18,123,984
Registered Office: Plaza, off Edinburgh Avenue, Skegness, Lincs, PE25 2UG
Activities: Public houses and bars
Major Shareholder: Brian William Bell
Officers: Brian William Bell, Secretary; Brian William Bell [1940] Director/Amusement Caterer; Lyn Mary Bell [1952] Director/Amusement Caterer

Belle Engineering (Sheen) Limited
Incorporated: 9 February 1961 *Employees:* 169
Net Worth: £16,903,108 *Total Assets:* £30,200,648
Registered Office: Sheen, Buxton, Derbys, SK17 0EU
Activities: Manufacture of other special-purpose machinery n.e.c.
Parent: Belle Holdings Limited
Officers: Raymond Kennedy Neilson, Secretary; Raymond Kennedy Neilson [1966] Director

Belle Holdings Limited
Incorporated: 23 June 1997
Net Worth: £3,879,086 *Total Assets:* £14,424,549
Registered Office: Sheen, Buxton, Derbys, SK17 0EU
Activities: Other manufacturing n.e.c.
Major Shareholder: Mohamed Altrad
Officers: Raymond Kennedy Neilson, Secretary; Raymond Kennedy Neilson [1966] Director

Belling (1992) Limited.
Incorporated: 15 April 1992 *Employees:* 3
Net Worth: £32,642,000 *Total Assets:* £34,870,000
Registered Office: Adwick Park, Manvers, Rotherham, S Yorks, S63 5AB
Activities: Other business support service activities n.e.c.
Officers: Fergal Naughton, Secretary; Donal Francis Flynn [1973] Director/Chartered Accountant [Irish]; Fergal John Naughton [1975] Director [Irish]; Martin Lawrence Naughton [1939] Director [Irish]

Bellotto Acquisition Limited
Incorporated: 18 May 2007 *Employees:* 4
Net Worth: £32,338,000 *Total Assets:* £312,235,008
Registered Office: Unit 2 Churchill Park, Private Road No 2, Colwick, Nottingham, NG4 2JR
Activities: Activities of head offices
Parent: Bellotto Finance Limited
Officers: David Mathew Aubrey Lewis [1967] Director [Australian]; Darren Hansel Lock [1966] Director; John Risman [1965] Director; Andrew Richard Thomas [1972] Director/Business Executive

Bellotto Finance Limited
Incorporated: 18 May 2007 *Employees:* 4
Net Worth: £91,376,000 *Total Assets:* £186,339,008
Registered Office: Unit 2 Churchill Park, Private Road No 2, Colwick, Nottingham, NG4 2JR
Activities: Activities of head offices
Parent: Bellotto Holdings Limited
Officers: David Mathew Aubrey Lewis [1967] Director [Australian]; Darren Hansel Lock [1966] Director; John Risman [1965] Director; Andrew Richard Thomas [1972] Director/Business Executive

Bellotto Holdings Limited
Incorporated: 21 May 2007 *Employees:* 5
Net Worth: £82,562,000 *Total Assets:* £135,656,992
Registered Office: Unit 2 Churchill Park, Private Road No 2, Colwick, Nottingham, NG4 2JR
Activities: Activities of head offices
Parent: Zonwering Holdings Ltd
Officers: David Mathew Aubrey Lewis [1967] Director [Australian]; Darren Hansel Lock [1966] Director; John Risman [1965] Director; Andrew Richard Thomas [1972] Director/Business Executive

Bellrock Property & Facilities Management Limited
Incorporated: 4 July 1995 *Employees:* 450
Net Worth Deficit: £6,646,000 *Total Assets:* £68,586,000
Registered Office: Peat House, 1 Waterloo Way, Leicester, LE1 6LP
Activities: Management of real estate on a fee or contract basis
Shareholders: Bell Rock Workplace Managment Limited; Bell Rock Workplace Management Ltd
Officers: Alexander Peter Marek Rudzinski, Secretary; Alexander Peter Marek Rudzinski [1975] Director; David John Smith [1964] Director

Bells Motor Group Limited
Incorporated: 24 March 1988 *Employees:* 99
Net Worth: £9,910,325 *Total Assets:* £19,116,612
Registered Office: Norman-D-Gate, Bedford Road, Northampton, NN1 5NT
Activities: Sale of new cars and light motor vehicles
Officers: Clive Allen Bell, Secretary/Manager; Clive Allen Bell [1977] Managing Director; Katherine Victoria Bell [1982] Director; Keith Dennis Bell [1950] Director; Virginia Bell [1953] Director/Secretary; Emma Eales [1975] Director/Marketing Manager

Belmont Press Limited
Incorporated: 27 February 1952 *Employees:* 154
Net Worth: £9,193,493 *Total Assets:* £12,523,638
Registered Office: Sheaf Close, Lodge Farm Industrial Estate, Northampton, NN5 7UZ
Activities: Other publishing activities
Shareholders: Trevor James Thomas; Qwen James Thomas
Officers: Owen James Thomas, Secretary; Owen James Thomas [1975] Director; Trevor James Thomas [1943] Director/Printer

Belron UK Limited
Incorporated: 23 April 1951 *Employees:* 2,448
Net Worth: £8,231,000 *Total Assets:* £63,566,000
Registered Office: 1 Priory Business Park, Cardington, Bedford, MK44 3US
Activities: Maintenance and repair of motor vehicles
Parent: Belron International Limited
Officers: Neil Andrew Fraser Morgan, Secretary; Nigel Jeremy Doggett [1965] Managing Director; Taxiarchis Konstantopoulos [1970] Managing Director [Greek]; David Brian Meller [1966] Finance Director

Belsfield LLP
Incorporated: 14 March 2012 *Employees:* 59
Net Worth: £7,848,983 *Total Assets:* £10,982,332
Registered Office: Corus House, 1 Auckland Park, Milton Keynes, Bucks, MK1 1BU

Belvoir Lettings PLC
Incorporated: 15 November 2011 *Employees:* 96
Net Worth: £19,441,000 *Total Assets:* £34,902,000
Registered Office: The Old Courthouse, 60a London Road, Grantham, Lincs, NG31 6HR
Activities: Activities of other holding companies n.e.c.
Officers: Louise George, Secretary; Louise Joan George [1965] Company Secretary/Director; Paul George [1960] Director; Michael John Stephen Goddard [1949] Director; Dorian Gonsalves [1974] Director; Mark Newton [1955] Director; Michael Ian Stoop [1955] Director

Benchmark Animal Health Group Limited
Incorporated: 29 July 2010 *Employees:* 8
Net Worth: £4,763,310 *Total Assets:* £57,462,508
Registered Office: Benchmark House, 8 Smithy Wood Drive, Sheffield, S35 1QN
Activities: Veterinary activities
Parent: Benchmark Holdings PLC
Officers: Roland James Bonney [1964] Director; Christopher John Davy [1963] Operations Director; Stephen Wesley Andrew Knott [1969] Finance Director; Robert John Long [1954] Managing Director BVL; John William Marshall [1971] Director/Technical Development Officer; Mark James Plampin [1968] Director; Malcolm David Foster Pye [1957] Director; Marie-Clare Russell [1961] Managing Director; Lindsey Ann Toon [1974] Director/Regulatory Adviser; Robin Glevum Wardle [1961] Director; Fintan Alexander Weston [1968] Manufacturing Director

Benchmark Animal Health Limited
Incorporated: 31 January 2014 *Employees:* 27
Net Worth Deficit: £7,741,957 *Total Assets:* £12,672,501
Registered Office: Benchmark House, 8 Smithy Wood Drive, Sheffield, S35 1QN
Activities: Veterinary activities
Parent: Benchmark Animal Health Group Limited
Officers: Roland James Bonney [1964] Director; Christopher John Davy [1963] Operations Director; Stephen Wesley Andrew Knott [1969] Finance Director; John William Marshall [1971] Director/Technical Development Officer; Mark James Plampin [1968] Director/Accountant; Malcolm David Foster Pye [1957] Director; Robin Glevum Wardle [1961] Director

Benchmark Genetics Limited
Incorporated: 3 July 2014 *Employees:* 4
Net Worth: £15,318,617 *Total Assets:* £55,651,580
Registered Office: Benchmark House, 8 Smithy Wood Drive, Sheffield, S35 1QN
Activities: Freshwater aquaculture
Parent: Benchmark Holdings PLC
Officers: Jonathan Michael Crowther [1962] Director; Mark James Plampin [1968] Director; Malcolm David Foster Pye [1957] Director

Benchmark Holdings PLC
Incorporated: 28 November 2000 *Employees:* 881
Net Worth: £353,614,016 *Total Assets:* £507,848,992
Registered Office: Benchmark House, 8 Smithy Wood Drive, Sheffield, S35 1QN
Activities: Activities of head offices
Shareholder: Johan Henrik Andersen
Officers: Athene Eliana Georgina Blakeman, Secretary; Peter Lutz George [1961] Director; Yngve Myhre [1969] Director [Norwegian]; Mark James Plampin [1968] Director/Accountant; Malcolm David Foster Pye [1957] Director; Kevin Quinn [1960] Director/Chief Financial Officer; Dr Alexander Josef Raeber [1960] Director/Chief Scientific Officer [Swiss]; Susan Jane Searle [1963] Director; Hugo Joaquin Wahnish [1952] Director [American]

Benchmark Leisure Limited
Incorporated: 10 March 1995
Net Worth Deficit: £137,190 *Total Assets:* £10,994,773
Registered Office: Rock House, Scotgate, Stamford, Lincs, PE9 2YQ
Activities: Buying and selling of own real estate
Parent: BLL Investments Limited
Officers: Alex John Charles Duce [1980] Director; Roland John Bernard Duce [1948] Director; Brian Dryden Foord [1938] Director; Jonathan Dryden Foord [1967] Director

Benchmark Vaccines Limited
Incorporated: 4 May 2012 *Employees:* 61
Net Worth Deficit: £4,162,070 *Total Assets:* £25,984,696
Registered Office: Benchmark House, 8 Smithy Wood Drive, Sheffield, S35 1QN
Activities: Other manufacturing n.e.c.
Parent: Benchmark Animal Health Group Limited
Officers: Stephen Wesley Andrew Knott [1969] Finance Director; Robert John Long [1954] Managing Director BVL; John William Marshall [1971] Director; Mark James Plampin [1968] Director; Malcolm David Foster Pye [1957] Director; Robin Glevum Wardle [1961] Director; Fintan Alexander Weston [1968] Manufacturing Director

Benchmarx Kitchens and Joinery Limited
Incorporated: 15 January 1993 *Employees:* 1,129
Net Worth: £11,710,000 *Total Assets:* £52,782,000
Registered Office: Lodge Way House, Lodge Way, Harlestone Road, Northampton, NN5 7UG
Activities: Wholesale of household goods (other than musical instruments) n.e.c
Parent: BMSS Limited
Officers: John Peter Carter [1961] Director; Martin Richard Meech [1957] Director/Chartered Surveyor; Ivan James Trevor [1979] Director/Accountant; Alan Richard Williams [1969] Director/Accountant

Ben Bennett Jr Limited
Incorporated: 30 December 1925 *Employees:* 72
Net Worth: £8,906,822 *Total Assets:* £11,028,057
Registered Office: Danecourt, Lisle Road, Rotherham, S Yorks, S60 2RL
Activities: Quarrying of ornamental and building stone, limestone, gypsum, chalk and slate
Shareholders: Benjamin Bennett Jr; Jane Bennett
Officers: Philip Jonathan Udell, Finance Director; David Barks [1963] Director/Factory Management; Benjamin James Bennett [1990] Director/Production Management; Jane Bennett [1966] Director; Norma Bennett [1938] Director; Benjamin Bennett Jr [1941] Director; Andrew Stuart Rawson [1957] Director/Quarry Management; Philip Jonathan Udell [1960] Finance Director

Bennie Holdings Limited
Incorporated: 21 January 2008 *Employees:* 160
Net Worth: £8,517,648 *Total Assets:* £19,970,332
Registered Office: The Old Piggeries, Cranford Road, Burton Latimer, Kettering, Northants, NN15 5TB
Activities: Activities of head offices
Shareholders: Emma Ayres; Pamela Orr Toseland
Officers: Robin Chappell, Secretary; Emma Ayres [1962] Director; Pamela Orr Toseland [1936] Director/Housewife

Benoy Limited
Incorporated: 27 July 1992 *Employees:* 489
Net Worth: £34,063,000 *Total Assets:* £55,668,000
Registered Office: Handley House, Northgate, Newark, Notts, NG24 1EH
Activities: Architectural activities
Parent: Benoy Holdings Limited
Officers: Joan Mary Lord, Secretary; Graham Stanley Cartledge [1947] Director/Architect; Thomas Cartledge [1979] Director

Benteler Automotive UK Ltd
Incorporated: 23 July 1996 *Employees:* 302
Net Worth: £2,787,646 *Total Assets:* £20,035,144
Registered Office: Baird Road, Willowbrook North Industrial Estate, Corby, Northants, NN17 5BB
Activities: Manufacture of other parts and accessories for motor vehicles
Officers: Stewart George Abraham, Secretary; Uwe Henny [1967] Finance Director [German]; Darren Paul Jackson [1973] Director/Plant Manager

Charles Bentley & Son Limited
Incorporated: 16 January 1979 *Employees:* 130
Net Worth: £4,468,834 *Total Assets:* £14,186,336
Registered Office: 1 Monarch Way, Loughborough, Leics, LE11 5TP
Activities: Wholesale of household goods (other than musical instruments) n.e.c
Shareholders: Charles Bentley; Shirley Bentley
Officers: Shirley Jayne Bentley, Secretary; Charles William Bentley [1953] Director/Brush Manufacturer; James Ryan Bentley [1983] Director/General Manager; Shirley Jayne Bentley [1957] Director; Sadie Helen Pollard [1974] Finance Director; Andrew John Steel [1982] Ecommerce Director; Naomi Fleur Steel [1980] Director/General Manager

Charles Bentley Properties Limited
Incorporated: 2 September 2015 *Employees:* 130
Net Worth: £4,857,971 *Total Assets:* £17,958,958
Registered Office: 1 Monarch Way, Loughborough, Leics, LE11 5XG
Activities: Other letting and operating of own or leased real estate
Shareholders: Charles William Bentley; Shirley Bentley
Officers: Shirley Jayne Bentley, Secretary; Charles William Bentley [1953] Director; James Ryan Bentley [1983] Director; Shirley Jayne Bentley [1957] Director; Sadie Helen Pollard [1974] Finance Director

Bericote Holdings Limited
Incorporated: 11 April 2016 *Employees:* 8
Net Worth: £5,292,700 *Total Assets:* £16,029,868
Registered Office: Yotta House, 8 Hamilton Terrace, Leamington Spa, Warwicks, CV32 4LY
Activities: Non-trading company
Parent: Bericote Group Holdings Limited
Officers: Jonathan Nicholas Maher [1977] Director; Lee Pettit [1961] Director; Richard Carey Saint [1965] Director; Simon Rodney Spencer [1967] Director

Berkeley Insurance Group Limited
Incorporated: 6 February 2008 *Employees:* 77
Net Worth: £1,073,427 *Total Assets:* £10,302,666
Registered Office: 2 Colton Square, Leicester, LE1 1QH
Activities: Activities of insurance agents and brokers
Shareholders: Timothy Paul Maxted; Andrew Stephen Bedford
Officers: Jonathan Yeeles, Secretary; Andrew Stephen Bedford [1952] Director; Timothy Paul Maxted [1971] Director

Berkshire Hops Limited
Incorporated: 1 August 1935 *Employees:* 1
Net Worth: £9,665,565 *Total Assets:* £9,892,772
Registered Office: Sterling House, 19-23 High Street, Kidlington, Oxon, OX5 2DH
Activities: Mixed farming
Shareholders: Timothy James Blanchard; Trustees of The Golding Hop Accumulation and Maintenance Trust
Officers: Edward Mason Blanchard [1986] Director; James Henry Blanchard [1985] Director; Timothy James Blanchard [1954] Director/Farmer

Berkshire, Buckinghamshire and Oxfordshire Wildlife Trust
Incorporated: 9 January 1961 *Employees:* 101
Net Worth: £14,875,000 *Total Assets:* £16,296,000
Registered Office: The Lodge, 1 Armstrong Road, Littlemore, Oxford, OX4 4XT
Activities: Activities of other membership organisations n.e.c.
Officers: Frances Anne Maria Brindle [1964] Marketing Director; David Cairns [1946] Director/Chartered Accountant Retired; Jane Catherine Cotton [1959] Director/Retired; Dr Ian Arthur Davidson [1957] Director/Retired; James Gillies [1966] Director/Land Management Consultant; Sir Paul David Grenville Hayter [1942] Director/Retired; Timothy Walter John Lowth [1959] Director; Barbara Muston [1952] Director/Retired; Diana Nettleton [1953] Director/Retired; John Pulsinelli [1950] Director/Business Adviser; Joanna Simons [1959] Director/Consultant; Graeme Mark Thompson [1970] Director

Berneslai Homes Limited
Incorporated: 30 September 2002 *Employees:* 453
Net Worth Deficit: £11,041,000 *Total Assets:* £17,405,000
Registered Office: 10th Floor, Gateway Plaza, off Sackville Street, Barnsley, S Yorks, S70 2RD
Activities: Management of real estate on a fee or contract basis
Officers: Alison Rusdale, Secretary; Dorothy Coates [1965] Director/Councillor; Gary Edward Ellis [1958] Director/CEO of Coalfields Regeneration Trust; Paul Hayes [1957] Managing Director; Liana Khachatryan [1980] Director/Client Adviser [Armenian]; Councillor Caroline Makinson [1960] Director/Councillor; Roya Pourali [1973] Director/Councillor; Laura Eve Rawnsley [1954] Director/IT and Business Change Specialist; Simon Rogers [1957] Director/Board Member; Adriana Rrustemi [1982] Director/Business Support Officer; ASA Ronnie Steele [1973] Director/Volunteer Advisor

Berville Limited
Incorporated: 19 November 2008 *Employees:* 3
Net Worth: £4,661,358 *Total Assets:* £25,402,116
Registered Office: 264 Banbury Road, Oxford, OX2 7DY
Activities: Other business support service activities n.e.c.
Shareholders: Thomas John Duggan; David Maurice Saville
Officers: Thomas John Duggan, Secretary; Thomas John Duggan [1936] Director; David Maurice Saville [1932] Director

Berwin Industrial Polymers Limited
Incorporated: 29 October 1957 *Employees:* 93
Net Worth: £5,166,363 *Total Assets:* £12,230,794
Registered Office: Broadway, Globe Lane Industrial Estate, Dukinfield, Cheshire, SK16 4UJ
Activities: Manufacture of other rubber products
Parent: Berwin of Lydney
Officers: Andrew Thomas Bramwell, Secretary; Mikael Fryklund [1963] Director [Swedish]; Karin Elisabeth Bachmann Gunnarsson [1962] Director [Swedish]; Gareth Jefferson [1976] Director; Carsten Ruter [1971] Director/President Technology; Ralph Joseph Wolkener [1971] Director/Employee [Belgian]

Berwin Rubber Company Limited
Incorporated: 19 October 1953 *Employees:* 93
Net Worth: £11,687,709 *Total Assets:* £20,986,660
Registered Office: Broadway, Globe Lane Industrial Estate, Dukinfield, Cheshire, SK16 4UJ
Activities: Manufacture of other rubber products
Parent: Berwin Group
Officers: Andrew Thomas Bramwell, Secretary; Joseph Edmund Dowdall [1963] Director; Mikael Fryklund [1963] Director [Swedish]; Karin Elisabeth Bachmann Gunnarsson [1962] Director [Swedish]; Karin Elisabeth Bachmann Gunnarsson [1962] Director [Swedish]; Carsten Ruter [1971] Director/President Technology [German]; Ralph Joseph Wolkener [1971] Director/Employee [Belgian]

BESS Aylesford Limited
Incorporated: 6 June 2016 *Employees:* 3
Net Worth: £691,805 *Total Assets:* £11,518,742
Registered Office: Salcey Lawn House, Salcey Lawn, Hartwell, Northants, NN7 2HA
Activities: Production of electricity
Parent: Bess Holdco 3 Limited
Officers: James Edward Stewart Basden [1967] Director; Nicholas Duncan Beatty [1961] Director; Steven Gerrard Christianne Meersman [1986] Director [Belgian]

Rick Bestwick Limited
Incorporated: 17 April 1989 *Employees:* 103
Net Worth: £6,676,511 *Total Assets:* £13,752,436
Registered Office: Magnavale House, Park Road, Holmewood Industrial Park, Holmewood, Chesterfield, Derbys, S42 5UY
Activities: Processing and preserving of poultry meat
Parent: Magnavale Limited
Officers: Stuart Hancock [1972] Director; Andrew Campbell Lawrence [1989] Director/Operations Manager; Colin Taylor [1963] Director

Betafence Limited
Incorporated: 22 June 1933 *Employees:* 97
Net Worth: £11,690,000 *Total Assets:* £48,609,000
Registered Office: P O Box 119, Shepcote Lane, Sheffield, S9 1TY
Activities: Manufacture of wire products, chain and springs
Parent: ERPE Bidco Limited
Officers: Frankie Firmin Cyril Descamps [1961] Director/Group Control & Risk Manager [Belgian]; Paul Clifford Skertchly [1962] Director

Beumer Group UK Limited
Incorporated: 23 July 2009 *Employees:* 124
Net Worth Deficit: £2,832,196 *Total Assets:* £17,970,872
Registered Office: Beumer House, 9 Cartwright Court, Cartwright Way, Bardon Hill, Leics, LE67 1UE
Activities: Manufacture of other special-purpose machinery n.e.c.
Officers: David Raymond Critchley, Secretary; Ranjit Singh Bhabra [1964] Managing Director; Peter Gilks [1957] Director

Bewick Holdings Ltd
Incorporated: 13 January 2004
Net Worth: £16,775,176 *Total Assets:* £16,776,964
Registered Office: 40 Mill Street, Bedford, MK40 3HD
Activities: Construction of domestic buildings
Major Shareholder: Ivan Robert Twigden
Officers: David Robert Twigden, Secretary; David Robert Twigden [1964] Director/Accountant; Ivan Robert Twigden [1938] Director

BF Limited
Incorporated: 14 December 2001
Net Worth Deficit: £140,900,000 *Total Assets:* £204,700,000
Registered Office: Equity House, Irthlingborough Road, Wellingborough, Northants, NN8 1LT
Activities: Dormant company
Parent: The Big Food Group Limited
Officers: Veselin Bandev [1978] Finance Director [Bulgarian]; Charles Wilson [1965] Director

BFSL Limited
Incorporated: 13 April 1992
Net Worth: £21,837,000 *Total Assets:* £496,343,008
Registered Office: Pegasus House, Bakewell Road, Orton Southgate, Peterborough, Cambs, PE2 6YS
Activities: Activities of financial services holding companies
Parent: BISL Limited
Officers: Julian Charles Brown, Secretary; Matthew Oliver Donaldson [1973] Director; Duncan Alistair Finch [1965] Director/Chartered Accountant; Seamus Declan Keating [1963] Director [Irish]; Dominic James Platt [1969] Director/Chief Financial Officer; Peter Thompson [1970] Group Director

BGB Engineering Limited
Incorporated: 9 March 1987 *Employees:* 111
Previous: B.G.B Engineering Limited
Net Worth: £13,241,807 *Total Assets:* £16,622,086
Registered Office: Dysart Road, Grantham, Lincs, NG31 7NB
Activities: Manufacture of electronic components
Shareholders: David Richard Holt; David Trevor Holt
Officers: David Charles Gilbert [1965] Works Director; David Richard Holt [1974] Managing Director; Generaldine Ann Holt [1948] Director; Nicholas Hubbard [1972] HR Director; David Ian Jockel [1962] Director; Ian Joseph Waring [1963] Director and Company Secretary

BGL (Holdings) Limited
Incorporated: 18 October 2016 *Employees:* 2,684
Net Worth: £6,600,000 *Total Assets:* £648,499,968
Registered Office: Pegasus House, Southgate Park, Bakewell Road, Orton Southgate, Peterborough, Cambs, PE2 6YS
Activities: Activities of financial services holding companies
Parent: BHL (UK) Holdings Limited
Officers: Julian Charles Brown, Secretary; Katherine Hae-Eun Chung [1976] Director/Private Equity Investor [American]; Matthew Oliver Donaldson [1973] Director/Chief Executive Officer; Inaki Echave [1972] Director/Private Equity Investor [Spanish]; Lord Jitesh Kishorekumar Gadhia [1970] Director; Alison Deborah Hewitt [1963] Director; Patricia Doreen Jackson [1952] Director; Seamus Declan Keating [1963] Director [Irish]; Stephen Klinkert [1953] Director [British/Australian]; Dominic James Platt [1969] Director/Chief Financial Officer; Stephen John Van Rooyen [1973] Director/Chief Executive

BGL Group Limited
Incorporated: 21 March 1991 *Employees:* 2,608
Net Worth: £9,100,000 *Total Assets:* £439,000,000
Registered Office: Pegasus House, Bakewell Road, Orton Southgate, Peterborough, Cambs, PE2 6YS
Activities: Activities of financial services holding companies
Parent: BGL (Holdings) Limited
Officers: Julian Charles Brown, Secretary; Matthew Oliver Donaldson [1973] Director; Dominic James Platt [1969] Director/Chief Financial Officer

BHCF2 Limited
Incorporated: 11 September 2013 *Employees:* 639
Net Worth: £14,586,812 *Total Assets:* £27,696,260
Registered Office: 1 Nottingham Road, Long Eaton, Nottingham, NG10 1HQ
Activities: Pre-primary education
Major Shareholder: Margaret Mitchell Mason
Officers: Hugh Alan Mason [1941] Director

BHFS One Limited
Incorporated: 9 March 2000 *Employees:* 6,636
Net Worth Deficit: £32,895,000 *Total Assets:* £392,724,992
Registered Office: 2 Crown Court, Rushden, Northants, NN10 6BS
Activities: Pre-primary education
Parent: Bright Horizons Family Solutions LLC
Officers: Stephen Kramer, Secretary; Elizabeth Boland [1959] Director/Chief Financial Officer [American]; Stephen Dreier [1942] Director/Chief Administrative Officer [American]; Dave Lissy [1965] Director/Manager [American]; James Walter Tugendhat [1971] Managing Director, International

BHFS Two Limited
Incorporated: 9 March 2000
Net Worth: £335,102,016 *Total Assets:* £344,417,984
Registered Office: 2 Crown Court, Rushden, Northants, NN10 6BS
Activities: Pre-primary education
Parent: BHFS One Limited
Officers: Stephen Kramer, Secretary; Elizabeth Boland [1959] Director/Chief Financial Officer [American]; Stephen Dreier [1942] Director/Chief Administrative Officer [American]; Dave Lissy [1965] Director/Manager [American]; James Walter Tugendhat [1971] Managing Director, International

BHIB Limited
Incorporated: 2 December 1964 *Employees:* 104
Net Worth: £5,350,554 *Total Assets:* £10,752,734
Registered Office: AGM House, 3 Barton Close, Grove Park, Leicester, LE19 1SJ
Activities: Non-life insurance
Parent: Brokerbility Holdings Limited
Officers: Jitendra Patel, Secretary; Mark Anthony Bamkin [1958] Director/Insurance Broker; David Sidney McCallum [1953] Director; Ashwinkumar Govindbhai Mistry [1959] Director/Insurance Broker; Jitendra Patel [1965] Director and Company Secretary; Ian James Donaldson Stutz [1961] Director/Insurance Broker

BHL (UK) Holdings Ltd
Incorporated: 10 July 2013 *Employees:* 3,321
Net Worth: £55,700,000 *Total Assets:* £741,400,000
Registered Office: Bath House, 16 Bath Row, Stamford, Lincs, PE9 2QU
Activities: Activities of other holding companies n.e.c.
Officers: Lucy Sinfield, Secretary; Simon Andrew James [1970] Director; Stephen Klinkert [1953] Director [South African/British/Australian]; Ian Robert Leech [1960] Director/Chartered Accountant

BI Group Limited
Incorporated: 5 April 1948 *Employees:* 402
Previous: BI Group PLC
Net Worth: £128,844,000 *Total Assets:* £163,764,992
Registered Office: c/o United Cast Bar (UK) Limited, Spital Lane, Chesterfield, Derbys, S41 0EX
Activities: Activities of head offices
Parent: NIC Holdings (UK) Limited
Officers: Ahmad Mohammad Hasan Hussein [1946] Director [Jordanian]; Yaseen Mohamed Jaafar Mohamed Mohsen [1960] Director [Bahraini]; Mark Anderson Penman [1970] Director; Alessandro Bernardo Agostino Rottach [1963] Director [Italian]; Mubasher Hussain Sheikh [1970] Director [Pakistani]

BI Worldwide Holdings Limited
Incorporated: 6 June 2001 *Employees:* 246
Net Worth: £5,872,739 *Total Assets:* £37,491,824
Registered Office: 1 Vantage Court, Tickford Street, Newport Pagnell, Bucks, MK16 9EZ
Activities: Activities of head offices
Shareholder: Lawrence Guy Schoenecker
Officers: Jeffrey Brian Beegle [1951] Director/Vice President [American]; Michael Leslie Davies [1968] Director; Dale Patrick Kunz [1949] Director [American]; Lawrence Guy Schoenecker [1954] Director [American]; Nicola Urquhart [1970] Director/Chief Financial Officer

BI Worldwide Limited
Incorporated: 28 August 1979 *Employees:* 246
Net Worth: £13,452,707 *Total Assets:* £45,043,664
Registered Office: 1 Vantage Court, Tickford Street, Newport Pagnell, Bucks, MK16 9EZ
Activities: Travel agency activities
Shareholder: Lawrence Guy Schoenecker
Officers: Jeffrey Brian Beegle [1951] Director/Vice President [American]; Michael Leslie Davies [1968] Managing Director; Dale Patrick Kunz [1949] Director [American]; Lawrence Guy Schoenecker [1954] Director [American]; Nicola Urquhart [1970] Director/Chief Financial Officer

Bibliotheca Limited
Incorporated: 25 October 1994 *Employees:* 78
Net Worth: £9,359,000 *Total Assets:* £24,843,000
Registered Office: Landmark House, Station Road, Cheadle Hulme, Cheadle, Cheshire, SK8 7BS
Activities: Other information technology service activities
Parent: Bibliotheca Group GmbH
Officers: James Stephen Hopwood [1969] Managing Director & CTO; Phillip John Sykes [1974] Director Development

Bicester Heritage Limited
Incorporated: 30 October 2012 *Employees:* 11
Net Worth: £5,129,117 *Total Assets:* £17,929,714
Registered Office: Bicester Heritage, Buckingham Road, Bicester, Oxon, OX27 8AL
Activities: Letting and operating of conference and exhibition centres
Officers: Andrew Francis Robert Galashan [1963] Director; Daniel Jon Geoghegan [1973] Director/Investment; Bob Meijer [1945] Director [Dutch]; William Simon Paul [1973] Director; Michael Richard Parker Power [1953] Director/Chartered Accountant

Bicester Learning Academy
Incorporated: 23 May 2014 *Employees:* 218
Net Worth: £17,822,802 *Total Assets:* £21,798,260
Registered Office: The Cooper School, Churchill Road, Bicester, Oxon, OX26 4RS
Activities: Primary education
Officers: Benjamin James Baxter [1965] Director/Headteacher; Brian Brown [1962] Director/Research Consultant; Emma Brown [1967] Director; Beatrice Moreau-Gray Davies [1956] Director; Lucy Janet Katz [1966] Director; Stuart Redding [1966] Director/Police Officer; Carole Anne Thomson [1950] Director; Keith Charles Wadley [1952] Director; Councillor Michael Frederick Waine [1944] Director/Retired/Standing Councillor; Rebecca Wilson [1987] Director/Primary School Teacher

BICL Limited
Incorporated: 21 March 1991
Previous: Budget Insurance Company Limited
Net Worth: £9,579,563 *Total Assets:* £9,637,162
Registered Office: Bath House, 16 Bath Row, Stamford, Lincs, PE9 2QU
Activities: Non-life insurance
Parent: BHL (UK) Holdings Limited
Officers: Lucy Sinfield, Secretary; Stephen Klinkert [1953] Director [South African/British/Australian]; Ian Robert Leech [1960] Director

Biesse Group UK Limited
Incorporated: 10 November 1992 *Employees:* 91
Net Worth: £1,430,860 *Total Assets:* £13,351,993
Registered Office: Lamport Drive, Daventry, Northants, NN11 8YZ
Activities: Installation of industrial machinery and equipment
Parent: Biesse SpA
Officers: Paul Robert Carson, Secretary; Cristian Berardi [1974] Director/Chief Financial Officer [Italian]; Stephen Rowland Bulmer [1963] Sales Director; Paul Robert Carson [1970] Director/Certified Chartered Accountant

Bifrangi UK Limited
Incorporated: 31 August 2001 *Employees:* 212
Net Worth: £13,320,362 *Total Assets:* £53,516,228
Registered Office: Shardlow Works, Grange Mill Lane, Sheffield, S9 1HW
Activities: Forging, pressing, stamping and roll-forming of metal; powder metallurgy
Major Shareholder: Francesco Biasion
Officers: Francesca Biasion [1994] Director [Italian]; Francesco Biasion [1939] Director [Italian]; Paola Biasion [1966] Director [Italian]; Roberto Biasion [1970] Director/Engineer [Italian]

The Big Food Group Limited
Incorporated: 19 November 1980 *Employees:* 1
Net Worth: £165,000,000 *Total Assets:* £295,100,000
Registered Office: Equity House, Irthlingborough Road, Wellingborough, Northants, NN8 1LT
Activities: Non-specialised wholesale trade
Parent: Giant Bidco Limited
Officers: Veselin Bandev [1978] Finance Director [Bulgarian]; Charles Wilson [1965] Director

Bildurn (Properties) Limited
Incorporated: 7 June 1989
Net Worth Deficit: £404,148 *Total Assets:* £10,492,870
Registered Office: 2 Lace Market Square, Nottingham, NG1 1PB
Activities: Development of building projects
Officers: Sean Akins, Secretary/Director; George Henry Akins [1974] Director; George Henry Akins [1928] Director; Sean Akins [1973] Director; David Paul McDerment [1981] Finance Director

Billing Finance Limited
Incorporated: 21 January 1983 *Employees:* 65
Net Worth: £18,240,764 *Total Assets:* £53,343,580
Registered Office: Billing House, The Causeway, Great Billing, Northampton, NN3 9EX
Activities: Financial intermediation not elsewhere classified
Officers: Oliver James Mackaness, Secretary/Accountant; Gary Raymond Hill [1972] Sales Director; James Mackaness [1945] Director/Farmer; Oliver James Mackaness [1975] Director/Chartered Accountant

Billington Holdings PLC
Incorporated: 10 July 1989 *Employees:* 615
Net Worth: £21,976,000 *Total Assets:* £40,564,000
Registered Office: Barnsley Road, Wombwell, Barnsley, S Yorks, S73 8DS
Activities: Activities of head offices
Officers: Darren Paul Kemplay, Secretary; John Stuart Gordon [1966] Director; Ian Michael Lawson [1957] Director; Doctor Alexander Wolfgang Ospelt [1967] Director [Liechtensteiner]; Mark Smith [1966] Director; Trevor Michael Taylor [1981] Director; Stephen John Wardell [1963] Director

Billington Structures Limited
Incorporated: 12 June 1981 *Employees:* 155
Net Worth: £8,852,514 *Total Assets:* £24,259,348
Registered Office: Barnsley Road, Wombwell, Barnsley, S Yorks, S73 8DS
Activities: Manufacture of metal structures and parts of structures
Parent: Billington Holdings PLC
Officers: Darren Paul Kemplay, Secretary; Simon David Barnes [1976] Director; Martin Goddard [1966] Director; Mark Smith [1966] Director; Trevor Michael Taylor [1981] Director; Simon Thrift [1967] Director; Brian Turton [1970] Director

Binks Developments Limited
Incorporated: 16 June 2004 *Employees:* 15
Net Worth Deficit: £1,457,129 *Total Assets:* £14,677,680
Registered Office: Cawthorne House, 19 Tivy Dale, Cawthorne, Barnsley, S Yorks, S75 4EJ
Activities: Buying and selling of own real estate
Major Shareholder: Richard David Binks
Officers: Harriet Jane Hunter, Secretary; Hannah Rose-Emma Binks [1986] Director; Pauline Binks [1945] Director; Richard David Binks [1943] Director; Helen Louisa Davies [1975] Director/Solicitor; Harriet Hunter [1978] Director/Manager

Binney & Smith (Europe) Limited
Incorporated: 9 May 1916 *Employees:* 22
Net Worth: £11,572,000 *Total Assets:* £22,915,000
Registered Office: Bedford Heights, Manton Lane, Bedford, MK41 7PH
Activities: Other manufacturing n.e.c.
Parent: Binney & Smith, LLC
Officers: Dwight Calvin Arn, Secretary; John Wescott Yeaw [1967] Director/General Manager [American]

Bio Dynamic (UK) Limited
Incorporated: 18 June 2013 *Employees:* 16
Net Worth: £14,213,910 *Total Assets:* £21,689,888
Registered Office: c/o BDO LLP, Regent House, Clinton Avenue, Nottingham, NG5 1AZ
Activities: Production of electricity
Parent: Bagnall Group (Europe) Ltd
Officers: Billy Jay Bagnall [1976] Director; Maxwell Bagnall [1979] Director; William Keyes Bagnall [1945] Director

Bio Energy (UK) Limited
Incorporated: 25 March 1997
Net Worth: £4,148,361 *Total Assets:* £47,917,588
Registered Office: Chancery House, 199 Silbury Boulevard, Milton Keynes, Bucks, MK9 1JL
Activities: Activities of other holding companies n.e.c.
Parent: EDL Holdings (UK) Limited
Officers: James Christopher Harman [1968] Director [Australian]; David Truelove [1975] Director

Bio-Rad AbD Serotec Ltd
Incorporated: 16 December 1981 *Employees:* 81
Net Worth: £19,591,092 *Total Assets:* £23,531,758
Registered Office: Endeavour House, Langford Lane, Kidlington, Oxon, OX5 1GE
Activities: Manufacture of basic pharmaceutical products
Parent: Bio-Rad Laboratories, Inc.
Officers: Lee Keron Marles [1977] Director; Norman David Schwartz [1950] Director/C.E.O. & President [American]

Bio-Techne Ltd
Incorporated: 6 April 1990 *Employees:* 107
Previous: R & D Systems Europe Ltd.
Net Worth: £83,499,000 *Total Assets:* £106,905,000
Registered Office: 19 Barton Lane, Abingdon Science Park, Abingdon, Oxon, OX14 3NB
Activities: Non-specialised wholesale trade
Parent: Bio-Techne Corporation
Officers: Gina Sarah Watson, Secretary; Ruth Bright [1969] Director/Manager; Brenda Furlow [1958] Director/Manager [American]; Gary Michael Stapleton [1963] Director

Biocity Group Limited
Incorporated: 17 September 2013 *Employees:* 69
Net Worth: £8,925,000 *Total Assets:* £40,507,000
Registered Office: Biocity Nottingham, Pennyfoot Street, Nottingham, NG1 1GF
Activities: Other professional, scientific and technical activities n.e.c.
Officers: Jennifer Helen Anderson-Moore, Secretary; Daniel Abrams [1955] Director; Mark James Biggs [1966] Director/University Academic [Australian]; Dr John Robert Brown [1955] Director; Glenn Crocker [1964] Director; Stuart Jonathan Brodie Henderson [1959] Director; Paul Stephen Oliver [1978] Director/Chief Financial Officer; Toby James Brook Reid [1974] Director/Chief Executive; Prof Kevin Morris Shakesheff [1969] Director/Professor

Biogen (UK) Limited
Incorporated: 8 November 2005 *Employees:* 94
Net Worth Deficit: £5,872,000 *Total Assets:* £39,763,000
Registered Office: Milton Parc, Milton Ernest, Beds, MK44 1YU
Activities: Production of electricity
Parent: Biogen Holdings Limited
Officers: Adam Feneley [1980] Finance Director; Cathryn Lister [1982] Compliance Director; Simon Musther [1958] Commercial Director; Graeme Kenneth Charles Vincent [1965] Operations Director

Biogen Holdings Limited
Incorporated: 22 June 2012 *Employees:* 94
Net Worth: £21,873,000 *Total Assets:* £39,454,000
Registered Office: Milton Parc, Milton Ernest, Bedford, MK44 1YU
Activities: Activities of extraterritorial organisations and bodies
Parent: Ancala Bioenergy Limited
Officers: Adam Feneley [1980] Finance Director; Cathryn Lister [1982] Compliance Director; Simon Musther [1958] Commercial Director; Graeme Kenneth Charles Vincent [1965] Operations Director

Birchall Gardens LLP
Incorporated: 11 March 2015
Net Worth: £22,584,716 *Total Assets:* £26,119,712
Registered Office: Bardon Hall, Copt Oak Road, Markfield, Leics, LE67 9PJ

C & P Bird Bros. Limited
Incorporated: 13 October 1977 *Employees:* 61
Net Worth: £10,881,996 *Total Assets:* £21,734,368
Registered Office: Sunnyfarm, Swineshead, Beds, MK44 2SU
Activities: Wholesale of dairy products, eggs and edible oils and fats
Shareholders: Peter Bird; Carl Bird
Officers: Carl Bird, Secretary; Carl Bird [1948] Director/Poultry Farmer; Matthew Andrew Bird [1984] Director; Peter Bird [1948] Director/Poultry Farmer; Stuart Andrew Bird [1975] Director; Robin Charles Hele [1960] Director/Farm Manager; Aldo Mattei [1958] Director [Italian]

The Bird Group of Companies Limited
Incorporated: 16 November 1990 *Employees:* 15
Net Worth Deficit: £1,411,694 *Total Assets:* £24,277,936
Registered Office: The Hunting Lodge, Billesley Road, Upper Billesley, Stratford upon Avon, Warwicks, CV37 9RA
Activities: Buying and selling of own real estate
Shareholder: Anthony Patrick Michael Bird
Officers: John Henry Elliott, Secretary; Sonia Araceli Baker [1966] Managing Director; Anthony Nicholas Bird [1971] Director; Anthony Patrick Michael Bird [1935] Managing Director; Brian Francis Bird [1938] Director; John Henry Elliott [1946] Director/Company Secretary; Keith David Lawley [1954] Director/Chartered Accountant; Julian Michael Palmer [1966] Director; Rosemary Charlotte Alicia Palmer [1965] Director

Birds (Derby) Limited
Incorporated: 12 December 1930 *Employees:* 718
Net Worth: £29,724,442 *Total Assets:* £32,304,436
Registered Office: Ascot Drive, Derby, DE24 8GN
Activities: Manufacture of other food products n.e.c.
Shareholders: Nicholas James William Bird; Patrick Reginald Frank Bird
Officers: Nicholas James William Bird, Secretary; Nicholas James William Bird [1958] Joint Managing Director; Patrick Reginald Frank Bird [1952] Joint Managing Director

Birkdale School
Incorporated: 19 February 1993 *Employees:* 168
Net Worth: £10,437,775 *Total Assets:* £11,906,235
Registered Office: Oakholme Road, Sheffield, S10 3DH
Activities: General secondary education
Officers: David Herbert Taylor, Secretary; The Revd Canon Christopher Mark Burke [1965] Director/Clerk in Holy Orders; Professor Jeremy Francis Dawson [1976] Director/Professor of Health Management; Matthew Oliver Dennis [1988] Audio Engineer/Music Director; Graham Richard Dunn [1973] Director/Sole Trader; Elizabeth Ann Hetherington [1961] Director/Head of Therapy Services; Paul Richard Houghton [1970] Director/Chartered Accountant; Andrew McKenzie Smith [1962] Director/Solicitor; James Edward Oliver [1967] Director/Quantity Surveyor; Angela Mary Rees [1945] Director/Senior Academic Postholder; Dr Roger Clive Richardson [1946] Operations Director; Sarah Catherine Turner [1968] Director; James Adrian Viner [1965] Director/Self Employed; Kathryn Mary Walker [1959] Director/Housewife

Bishop Stopford School
Incorporated: 8 July 2011 *Employees:* 191
Net Worth: £8,729,945 *Total Assets:* £10,410,983
Registered Office: Headlands, Kettering, Northants, NN15 6BJ
Activities: General secondary education
Officers: Liana Blake, Secretary; James William Edward Balding [1975] Director/Health and Safety Consultant; Kate Elizabeth Beresford [1973] Director/Teacher; Stephen Brading [1965] Director/Head of Marketing; Maithri Vasantha Gunasekara [1961] Director/Garage Owner; Robert Hardcastle [1972] Director/Headteacher; John Charles Hill [1956] Director/Retired; Julian Ritson Lomas [1971] Director/Management Consultant; Diana Jean MacCarthy [1974] Director/Teacher; Stuart Mitchell [1974] Director/Chartered Civil Engineer; Dennis William Murray [1970] Director/Police Superintendent; Liz O'Leary [1967] Director/H R Specialist; Stuart Ian MacKenzie Ross [1970] Director/IT Consultant; Jill Silverthorne [1968] Director/Headteacher; Kevin John Slough [1978] Director/Facilities Team Manager; Michael Charles Stock [1963] Director/Accountant/Company Secretary; James Edward Turner [1978] Director/Deputy CEO; Matthew Turner [1966] Director; Dr Ronald Eric Whittaker [1945] Director; Brian James Withington [1954] Director/Rural Dean

BISL Limited
Incorporated: 30 July 1996
Net Worth: £183,900,000 *Total Assets:* £616,499,968
Registered Office: Pegasus House, Bakewell Road, Orton Southgate, Peterborough, Cambs, PE2 6YS
Activities: Other business support service activities n.e.c.
Parent: BGL Group Limited
Officers: Julian Charles Brown, Secretary; Matthew Oliver Donaldson [1973] Director; Duncan Alistair Finch [1965] Director/Chartered Accountant; Seamus Declan Keating [1963] Director [Irish]; Dominic James Platt [1969] Director/Chief Financial Officer; Peter Thompson [1970] Group Director

Blackburn Starling & Company Limited
Incorporated: 13 April 1987 *Employees:* 94
Net Worth: £6,279,779 *Total Assets:* £9,841,738
Registered Office: Queens Drive, Nottingham, NG2 3AY
Activities: Manufacture of electronic industrial process control equipment
Major Shareholder: Stephen Hooton
Officers: Garfield Marc Turner, Secretary; David Alan Gould [1964] Managing Director; Stephen Hooton [1955] Director & Chairman; Colin Sparham [1947] Director; Garfield Marc Turner [1973] Finance Director; David Martyn Whelan [1960] Technical Director; John Joseph Wilcock [1965] Automation Engineering Director

Blackrock Secured Finance Limited
Incorporated: 25 June 2009 *Employees:* 4
Previous: Alfandari Private Equities Ltd
Net Worth: £18,261,020 *Total Assets:* £26,115,472
Registered Office: 9 Osier Way, Olney Business Park, Olney, Bucks, MK46 5FP
Activities: Financial leasing
Parent: Goldmore Asset Management Limited
Officers: Matthew James Bass [1968] Director; Samuel Andrew England [1978] Commercial Director; Charles Pritchard [1993] Director; Kevin Anthony Robbins [1976] Director

Blackrow Corporation Limited
Incorporated: 13 October 2009 *Employees:* 145
Net Worth: £2,819,731 *Total Assets:* £13,119,816
Registered Office: Estate Road 7, South Humberside Industrial Estate, Grimsby, N E Lincs, DN31 2TP
Activities: Activities of head offices
Officers: Darren Broughton [1961] Director; Neil Ellis [1954] Director/Chartered Accountant; James Patrick Leahy [1955] Director; Christopher Marfleet [1955] Director; Glenn Andrew Ritchie [1961] Director

Blackwell Limited
Incorporated: 9 November 1992 *Employees:* 460
Net Worth Deficit: £4,329,000 *Total Assets:* £13,534,000
Registered Office: 50 Broad Street, Oxford, OX1 3BQ
Activities: Activities of head offices
Major Shareholder: Julian Blackwell
Officers: Timothy Eustace, Secretary; Dean Stephen Drew [1961] Sales & Marketing Director; Timothy Eustace [1945] Director/Chartered Secretary; Trevor Robert Ogilvie Goul-Wheeker [1953] Director; Emma Louise Hillyard [1970] Director/Accountant; David Julian Brian Prescott [1971] Business Development Director; Kieron James Smith [1972] Director/Bookseller; Kathryn Jayne Stilborn [1971] Director

Toby Blackwell Limited
Incorporated: 18 November 2005 *Employees:* 6
Net Worth: £14,235,090 *Total Assets:* £17,202,380
Registered Office: 7 Gardiner Close, Abingdon, Oxon, OX14 3YA
Activities: Management consultancy activities other than financial management
Major Shareholder: Julian Blackwell
Officers: Timothy Eustace, Secretary; Julian Blackwell [1929] Director/Bookseller Publisher; Derrick James Cook [1933] Director/Accountant

Blackwell UK Limited
Incorporated: 17 March 1964 *Employees:* 455
Net Worth Deficit: £4,831,000 *Total Assets:* £14,810,000
Registered Office: 50 Broad Street, Oxford, OX1 3BQ
Activities: Retail sale of books in specialised stores
Parent: Blackwell Limited
Officers: Timothy Eustace, Secretary; Dean Stephen Drew [1961] Sales & Marketing Director; Timothy Eustace [1945] Director/Chartered Secretary; Emma Louise Hillyard [1970] Director/Accountant; David Julian Brian Prescott [1971] Business Development Director; Kieron James Smith [1972] Director/Bookseller; Kathryn Jayne Stilborn [1971] Director

Blanc Aero Industries UK Limited
Incorporated: 15 October 1979 *Employees:* 402
Net Worth: £71,385,000 *Total Assets:* £78,393,000
Registered Office: 38 Butlers Leap, Rugby, Warwicks, CV21 3RQ
Activities: Manufacture of fasteners and screw machine products
Parent: Lisi S.A.
Officers: David Richard Suddens, Secretary; Jean Louis Colders [1960] Director CEO [French]; Cedric Dejean [1977] Director/Business Executive [French]; William Hill [1960] Director/General Manager; Emmanuel Viellard [1963] Director [French]

Blancco (Software) Services Limited
Incorporated: 5 March 2014
Previous: Blancco Technology Group Ltd
Net Worth: £11,350,195 *Total Assets:* £77,475,976
Registered Office: Unit 6b Vantage Park, Washingley Road, Huntingdon, Cambs, PE29 6SR
Activities: Activities of other holding companies n.e.c.
Parent: Blancco Technology Group PLC
Officers: Adam Paul Moloney [1969] Director

Blancco Technology Group PLC
Incorporated: 27 April 2004 *Employees:* 258
Previous: Regenersis PLC
Net Worth: £54,103,000 *Total Assets:* £83,201,000
Registered Office: Unit 6b Vantage Park, Washingley Road, Huntingdon, Cambs, PE29 6SR
Activities: Other telecommunications activities
Officers: Frank Blin [1954] Director; Matthew Craig Jones [1960] Director [American]; Adam Paul Moloney [1969] Director; Philip Graham Rogerson [1945] Director; Thomas Kevin Skelton [1960] Director/Chief Executive Officer [American]; Robert Stanley Lawrence Woodward [1959] Director/Chief Executive Officer

Blankney Estates Limited
Incorporated: 17 August 1940 *Employees:* 124
Net Worth: £12,658,261 *Total Assets:* £23,213,062
Registered Office: The Estate Office, Temple Grange, Navenby, Lincoln, LN5 0AX
Activities: Growing of cereals (except rice), leguminous crops and oil seeds
Shareholders: Richard William Parker; John Paul Michael Parker
Officers: John Paul Michael Parker, Secretary; Timothy Simon Banks [1961] Director/Farmer; Tim Harper [1964] Director; Graham John Page [1949] Director; John Paul Michael Parker [1947] Director; Richard William Parker [1942] Director; Ruth Margaret Parker [1943] Director; Julia Claire Vincent [1974] Director; Joseph John Wootton [1958] Director/Farm Business Consultant

Blemain Finance Limited
Incorporated: 24 September 1974 *Employees:* 663
Net Worth: £16,300,000 *Total Assets:* £476,400,000
Registered Office: Lake View, Lakeside, Cheadle, Cheshire, SK8 3GW
Activities: Credit granting by non-deposit taking finance houses and other specialist consumer credit grantors
Parent: Together Financial Services Limited
Officers: Sarah Elizabeth Batt, Secretary; Peter Simon Ball [1968] Director; Ronald Baxter [1951] Director; Gary Derek Beckett [1969] Director; Wayne Bowser [1952] Director; Richard John Gregory [1954] Director; Henry Neville Moser [1949] Director; Paul Antony Wilson [1971] Director

Blenheim Agency Limited
Incorporated: 5 August 2015
Net Worth: £1 *Total Assets:* £12,323,818
Registered Office: The Estate Office, Blenheim Palace, Woodstock, Oxon, OX20 1PP
Activities: Combined office administrative service activities
Shareholders: Edward Albert Charles Spencer-Churchill; Mark Aubrey Weinberg; Anthony John Thompson; Alexander Pepys Muir
Officers: Stephen James Spare, Secretary; Heather Rosemary Carter [1962] Operations Director; Roger Leslie File [1963] Director/Chartered Surveyor; Dominic Michael Hare [1969] Director/Chartered Accountant

Blenheim Finance Limited
Incorporated: 16 May 2014 *Employees:* 3
Net Worth Deficit: £80,890 *Total Assets:* £91,981,384
Registered Office: The Estate Office, Blenheim Palace, Woodstock, Oxon, OX20 1PP
Activities: Other letting and operating of own or leased real estate
Shareholders: Vanbrugh Trustees Limited; Vanbrugh Trustees No 2 Limited; Blenheim Trustee Company No 1 Limited; Vanbrugh Management Limited; Blenheim Trustee Company No 2 Limited
Officers: Stephen James Spare, Secretary; Heather Rosemary Carter [1962] Operations Director; Roger Leslie File [1963] Director/Chartered Surveyor; Dominic Michael Hare [1969] Director/Chartered Accountant

Blenheim Industrial Property Limited
Incorporated: 13 October 2010
Net Worth: £3,397,511 *Total Assets:* £20,803,216
Registered Office: The Estate Office, Blenheim Palace, Woodstock, Oxon, OX20 1PP
Activities: Other letting and operating of own or leased real estate
Parent: Barrough Limited
Officers: Stephen James Spare, Secretary; Heather Rosemary Carter [1962] Operations Director; Roger Leslie File [1963] Director; Dominic Michael Hare [1969] Director

Blenheim Land & Properties Ltd
Incorporated: 28 March 2003 *Employees:* 4
Previous: Blenheim Engineering Limited
Net Worth: £2,033,760 *Total Assets:* £10,153,646
Registered Office: Georges Court, Chestergate, Macclesfield, Cheshire, SK11 6DP
Activities: Buying and selling of own real estate
Shareholder: Christopher Jonathan Anderson
Officers: Christopher Jonathan Anderson [1984] Director/Commercial Letting Agent; Kevin Hatfield [1961] Director

Bletchley Park Trust Limited
Incorporated: 7 July 1992 *Employees:* 72
Net Worth: £11,051,168 *Total Assets:* £11,706,900
Registered Office: The Mansion, Bletchley Park, Sherwood Drive, Milton Keynes, Bucks, MK3 6EB
Activities: Museums activities
Officers: Jennifer Anne Milton, Secretary; Oliver Chitty Brookshaw [1956] Director/Solicitor; Sir David Martin Brown [1950] Director; Elizabeth Anne Bushell [1974] Finance Director; Jonathan Martin Card [1957] Director/Chartered Accountant; Sir Roger Carr [1946] Director/Chairman; Robert Hannigan [1965] Director/Consultant; Professor Elisabeth Alison Kabler [1963] Director/Academic; Charles William Iain MacDonald [1966] Director/Chief Executive; Professor Andrew Philip Martin [1968] Director/Professor; Hilary Anne McGowan [1955] Director/Museum Consultant; Duncan Ramon John Phillips [1972] Managing Director; Michael Sarna [1965] Director; Adam Nicholas Singer [1952] Director/Chair; Sir John Dermot Turing [1961] Director/Solicitor; Alan Francis Whelan [1961] Director

Blinds 2 Go Limited
Incorporated: 22 March 2000 *Employees:* 85
Net Worth: £4,002,447 *Total Assets:* £13,410,759
Registered Office: 1 Longwall Avenue, Queens Drive Industrial Estate, Nottingham, NG2 1NA
Activities: Retail sale via mail order houses or via Internet
Parent: Friar 148 Limited
Officers: Mark Bramley [1962] Director; Byron Alexander Crawford [1970] Director; Paul Clifford Hopkins [1958] Director

Blitz Communications Limited
Incorporated: 26 March 1991 *Employees:* 106
Net Worth: £9,355,000 *Total Assets:* £13,595,000
Registered Office: GES, Silverstone Drive, Gallagher Business Park, Coventry, Warwicks, CV6 6PA
Activities: Other service activities n.e.c.
Officers: Michael Stewart, Secretary; Ellen Marie Ingersoll [1964] Director [American]; Steven Moster [1970] Director/Chairman, President and CEO of Viad Corp [American]; Jason Popp [1970] Director/Vice President [American]

Bloom Developments Limited
Incorporated: 12 October 2000 *Employees:* 2
Net Worth: £6,417,963 *Total Assets:* £14,439,591
Registered Office: c/o Charnwood Accountants, Suite A, First Floor, The Point, Granite Way, Mountsorrel, Loughborough, Leics, LE12 7TZ
Activities: Other business support service activities n.e.c.
Major Shareholder: John Nigel Bloom
Officers: John Nigel Bloom, Secretary; John Nigel Bloom [1970] Director

J.S.Bloor (Services) Limited
Incorporated: 16 September 1987 *Employees:* 1,105
Net Worth: £38,871,000 *Total Assets:* £374,988,000
Registered Office: Ashby Road, Measham, Swadlincote, Derbys, DE12 7JP
Activities: Construction of domestic buildings
Shareholders: John Stuart Bloor; Bloor Holdings Limited
Officers: Dinesh Kumar Ishwerlal Khushalbhai Mehta, Secretary; Adrian John Bloor [1970] Director; John Stuart Bloor [1943] Director/Builder; John Lambert Eastham [1951] Director/Accountant; Dinesh Kumar Ishwerlal Khushalbhai Mehta [1951] Director/Chartered Accountant

Bloor Holdings Limited
Incorporated: 3 December 1986 *Employees:* 3,663
Net Worth: £960,841,024 *Total Assets:* £1,812,982,016
Registered Office: Ashby Road, Measham, Swadlincote, Derbys, DE12 7JP
Activities: Construction of domestic buildings
Shareholders: John Stuart Bloor; Bloor Investments Limited
Officers: Dinesh Kumar Ishwerlal Khushalbhai Mehta, Secretary; Adrian John Bloor [1970] Director; John Stuart Bloor [1943] Director/Builder; Nick Simon Bloor [1976] Director; John Lambert Eastham [1951] Director/Accountant; Dinesh Kumar Ishwerlal Khushalbhai Mehta [1951] Director/Chartered Accountant

Bloor Homes Limited
Incorporated: 9 September 1987 *Employees:* 4
Net Worth: £510,371,008 *Total Assets:* £1,495,132,032
Registered Office: Ashby Road, Measham, Swadlincote, Derbys, DE12 7JP
Activities: Construction of domestic buildings
Shareholders: John Stuart Bloor; Bloor Holdings Limited
Officers: Dinesh Kumar Ishwerlal Khushalbhai Mehta, Secretary; Adrian John Bloor [1970] Director; John Stuart Bloor [1943] Director/Builder; John Lambert Eastham [1951] Director/Accountant; Dinesh Kumar Ishwerlal Khushalbhai Mehta [1951] Director/Chartered Accountant

Bloor Investments Limited
Incorporated: 19 June 2012 *Employees:* 3,663
Net Worth: £964,083,968 *Total Assets:* £1,814,712,064
Registered Office: Ashby Road, Measham, Swadlincote, Derbys, DE12 7JP
Activities: Activities of head offices
Major Shareholder: John Stuart Bloor
Officers: Dineshkumar Ishwerlal Khushalbhai Mehta, Secretary; John Stuart Bloor [1943] Director; John Lambert Eastham [1951] Director; Dinesh Kumar Ishwerlal Khushalbhai Mehta [1951] Director

Bloxham School Limited
Incorporated: 28 May 1999 *Employees:* 243
Net Worth: £8,224,017 *Total Assets:* £13,684,093
Registered Office: Bloxham School, Banbury Road, Bloxham, Banbury, Oxon, OX15 4PE
Activities: General secondary education
Parent: The Woodard Corporation
Officers: Charlie Eric John Little, Secretary; Paul Roderick Clayson [1947] Director/Chartered Surveyor; Ian Richard Davenport [1960] Director/CEO of Springboard Bursary Foundation; Hermione Harper [1957] Director/Wedding Venue Manager; Miles Stuart Hedges [1956] Finance Director; Miranda Emily Hopkins [1967] Director; Professor Geraint Paul Jones [1976] Director/Dean of Education; Elisabeth Laura Lewis-Jones [1970] Director/PR Consultant; Robert Wilson Loades [1949] Managing Director; Charles Edward Lionel Mann [1948] Director/Management Consultant; Andrew Jonathan Peter Nott [1964] Director/Headmaster; Carol Ann Shaw [1961] Director/Solicitor; John Ernest Spratt [1947] Director/Lawyer; Fiona Margaret Turner [1958] Director/H R Consultancy; Martin Richard Ward [1966] Director; Simon Timothy Wood [1952] Director

Blue Anchor Leisure Holdings Limited
Incorporated: 6 December 2012 *Employees:* 201
Net Worth: £58,505,000 *Total Assets:* £85,864,000
Registered Office: Robin Hood Park, South Road, Chapel St Leonards, Skegness, Lincs, PE24 5TR
Activities: Buying and selling of own real estate
Officers: Peter Raymond Franciscus Holmes [1948] Director/Certified Accountant; Jonathan Scott Moses [1974] Director/Caravan Park Manager; Sally-Ann Woodward [1967] Director

Blue Anchor Leisure Limited
Incorporated: 22 January 1973 *Employees:* 201
Net Worth: £58,504,000 *Total Assets:* £85,860,000
Registered Office: Robin Hood Park, South Road, Chapel St Leonards, Skegness, Lincs, PE24 5TR
Activities: Recreational vehicle parks, trailer parks and camping grounds
Parent: Blue Anchor Leisure Holdings Limited
Officers: Peter Raymond Fransiscus Holmes [1948] Director/Certified Accountant; Jonathan Scott Moses [1974] Director/Caravan Park Manager; Sally-Ann Woodward [1967] Director

Blue Boar Holdings Limited
Incorporated: 25 August 1998 *Employees:* 211
Net Worth: £14,373,598 *Total Assets:* £20,667,080
Registered Office: 264 Banbury Road, Oxford, OX2 7DY
Activities: Management consultancy activities other than financial management
Shareholders: Thomas John Duggan; David Maurice Saville
Officers: Thomas John Duggan, Secretary/Director; Ian George Donald [1942] Economic Director; Thomas John Duggan [1936] Director; Scott Anthony Salter [1966] Director/Insurance; David Maurice Saville [1932] Director; Carl Anthony Shuker [1961] Director

Blue Chip Customer Engineering Limited
Incorporated: 13 July 1987 *Employees:* 242
Net Worth: £40,522,000 *Total Assets:* £78,379,000
Registered Office: Franklin Court, Priory Business Park, Bedford, MK44 3JZ
Activities: Other software publishing
Shareholder: Brian Meredith
Officers: Andy Rounding, Secretary; Lee John Bailey [1976] Director; Eddy Conway [1960] Director; Brian Meredith [1950] Director; Sadie Vanessa Nesbitt [1967] Director; Andrew James Rounding [1972] Director/Accountant; Tim Stringer [1976] Director; Derek Waterman [1972] Director

The Blue Coat Church of England Academy Limited
Incorporated: 6 April 2011 *Employees:* 189
Net Worth: £16,898,000 *Total Assets:* £20,075,000
Registered Office: Blue Coat Church of England School, Terry Road, Stoke, Coventry, Warwicks, CV1 2BA
Activities: General secondary education
Officers: Sarah Jane Durkin, Secretary; Rev Graeme Edgar Anderson [1959] Director/Vicar; Michael David Draper [1968] Director/Safety & Environment Manager; Oluremi Adetutu Etomi [1958] Director/Pastor [Nigerian]; Mark William Gore [1954] Director/Retired; Lyn Mary Johnson [1952] Director/Retired; David Edwin Kershaw [1942] Director/Consultant Headteacher & Elected Member (Coventry City Council); Peter Gavin Merrylees [1969] Director/Company Secretary; Janet Elizabeth Powell [1959] Director/Teacher; Victoria Elizabeth Shelley [1977] Director/Headteacher; Anna Louise Stacey [1976] Director/Teacher; Paul Tuffin [1968] Director/Headmaster; Lois Whitehouse [1967] Director/Certified Chartered Accountant

Blue Cross
Incorporated: 11 September 1940 *Employees:* 768
Net Worth: £65,604,000 *Total Assets:* £75,100,000
Registered Office: Shilton Road, Burford, Oxon, OX18 4PF
Activities: Other retail sale in non-specialised stores
Officers: Iain Sholto Heaton, Secretary; Zair David Berry [1954] Director/Chartered Accountant; Catherine Ann Brown [1966] Director [British/New Zealander]; Professor Stuart Carmichael [1955] Director/Veterinary Surgeon; Amy Clarke [1972] Director/Head of Private Clients, Philanthropy; Sue Ellis [1957] Director/Retired; Clive Everest [1963] Director/Retired; Caroline Sarah Gosling [1975] Director; Victoria Clare Hemming [1956] Charity Director; Dr Timothy Charles Hutton [1957] Director/Vet Surgeon; Nico Lutkins [1975] Marketing Director [Austrian]; Christopher Alwyn Martin [1964] IT Director; Timothy Henry Ralph Porter [1952] Director/Chartered Accountant; Hon. Henrietta Margaret Fleur Roper-Curzon [1955] Director; Jeremy Ross Stewart [1967] Director/Veterinary Surgeon; Stephen Paul Swift [1953] Director/Retired; Deirdre Walker [1962] Director/Solicitor

Blue Deer Limited
Incorporated: 12 May 1997 *Employees:* 2
Net Worth: £6,948,557 *Total Assets:* £11,669,975
Registered Office: 31 Great King Street, Macclesfield, Cheshire, SK11 6PL
Activities: Development of building projects
Parent: Good Eyed Deer Company Limited
Officers: Lynne Turner, Secretary; Timothy Peter Turner [1958] Director

Blue Planet Solar Park II Limited
Incorporated: 27 November 2014
Net Worth: £2,880,547 *Total Assets:* £10,918,735
Registered Office: 39-43 Bridge Street, Swinton, Mexborough, S Yorks, S64 8AP
Activities: Production of electricity
Parent: Aquila Capital Renewables Fund III S.A. SICAV-SIF
Officers: Bernhard Gierke [1983] Director/Investment Manager [German]; Ingmar Helmke [1979] Director/Investment Manager [German]

Blue Sea Overseas Investments Limited
Incorporated: 19 July 1994
Net Worth: £113,900,000 *Total Assets:* £1,090,800,000
Registered Office: Westpoint, Peterborough Business Park, Lynch Wood, Peterborough, Cambs, PE2 6FZ
Activities: Other business support service activities n.e.c.
Parent: Mytravel Group Limited
Officers: Shirley Bradley, Secretary; Alan Charles Donald [1963] Director

Blue Skies Holdings Limited
Incorporated: 8 August 2000 *Employees:* 4,405
Net Worth: £18,677,534 *Total Assets:* £33,666,788
Registered Office: Peterbridge House, The Lakes, Northampton, NN4 7HB
Activities: Other processing and preserving of fruit and vegetables
Shareholders: Anthony John Devereux Pile; Jenny Clare Pile
Officers: Jenny Clare Pile, Secretary; Dugald Komla Agble [1970] Director; Frank Nicolas Julia Braeken [1960] Director [Belgian]; John Johnovich Gadzi [1974] Director [American]; George Arthur Laugharne Hutton [1968] Managing Director; Guy Richard Seymour Murfitt [1968] Procurement Director; Bruce John Parsons [1946] Director; Anthony John Devereux Pile [1947] Director; Harriet Pile [1983] Director; Hugh James Devereux Pile [1980] Director/Marketing; Jenny Clare Pile [1951] Director/Office Manager; Helen Rumsey [1971] Director; Sarah Stevenson-McNeill [1972] Director/Civil Servant

Blue Skies Investments Limited
Incorporated: 29 October 2013 *Employees:* 2
Net Worth: £56,581,700 *Total Assets:* £56,818,044
Registered Office: Nene House, 4 Rushmills, Northampton, NN4 7YB
Activities: Activities of open-ended investment companies
Parent: Randal Holdings Limited
Officers: Monisha Nikesh Kotecha, Secretary; Monisha Nikesh Kotecha [1969] Director; Dr Nikesh Rasiklal Kotecha [1966] Director

Blue Support Services Limited
Incorporated: 4 November 2009 *Employees:* 79
Net Worth: £1,020,278 *Total Assets:* £13,399,942
Registered Office: Building 1000, Kings Reach, Yew Street, Stockport, Cheshire, SK4 2HG
Activities: Management of real estate on a fee or contract basis
Parent: E S Management Services Limited
Officers: Andrew Dwan [1965] Director; Michael Dwan [1959] Director

Bluebell Wood Children's Hospice
Incorporated: 19 July 1999 *Employees:* 139
Net Worth: £11,104,000 *Total Assets:* £11,442,000
Registered Office: Bluebell Wood Childrens Hospice, Cramfit Road, North Anston, Sheffield, S25 4AJ
Activities: Other human health activities
Officers: Steve Allen [1957] Director/Retired; Bethan Proctor Atkinson [1983] Director/Specialist Speech and Language Therapist; Anne Fowlie [1946] Director and Company Secretary; Scott Paul Green [1974] Director/Trustee; Jon David Lister [1973] Director; Keith Metcalf [1947] Director; Patricia Mary Seymour [1956] Director; James David Wenninger [1974] Finance & Commercial Director UK; Richard Christopher Worth [1948] Director/Trustee

Blueprint Operations Limited
Incorporated: 14 January 2015 *Employees:* 17
Net Worth: £6,292,121 *Total Assets:* £27,267,118
Registered Office: Fortune House, Northgate Terrace, Newark on Trent, Notts, NG24 2EU
Activities: Gambling and betting activities
Parent: ADP Gauselmann UK Limited
Officers: Simon Barff [1967] Director; Sophie Hannah Pope [1982] Director

Blugilt Holdings Limited
Incorporated: 2 December 1936 *Employees:* 259
Net Worth Deficit: £7,090,922 *Total Assets:* £11,847,111
Registered Office: Environment House, 6 Union Road, Nottingham, NG3 1FH
Activities: Activities of head offices
Officers: Roy Stewart Mochor [1950] Director; Anil Puri [1960] Director [Indian]

E.E.Blyth & Co Limited
Incorporated: 10 June 1964 *Employees:* 75
Net Worth: £16,646,664 *Total Assets:* £20,287,196
Registered Office: Carlton Industrial Estate, Carlton in Lindrick, Worksop, Notts, S81 9LB
Activities: Other letting and operating of own or leased real estate
Major Shareholder: Peter Eden Blyth
Officers: Patricia Ann Shepherd, Secretary; Dr Nicola Blyth [1956] Director/Economist; Peter Eden Blyth [1927] Director/Metal Alloy Merchant; Patricia Ann Shepherd [1959] Director/Management

Blythmore Limited
Incorporated: 31 March 1999 *Employees:* 1
Net Worth Deficit: £87,259,000 *Total Assets:* £91,203,000
Registered Office: Whitley Lodge, Whitley Bridge, Doncaster, S Yorks, DN14 0HR
Activities: Activities of head offices
Parent: Tunstall Holdings Limited
Officers: Jonathan Paul Furniss, Secretary; Craig Parsons [1970] Director; John Lee Robinson [1958] Director

BM Catalysts Limited
Incorporated: 22 October 1982 *Employees:* 190
Previous: Belton Massey Limited
Net Worth: £7,732,591 *Total Assets:* £17,788,374
Registered Office: Reed Mill, Sheepbridge Lane, Mansfield, Notts, NG18 5DL
Activities: Manufacture of other parts and accessories for motor vehicles
Parent: Belton Massey Limited
Officers: John Mark William Blinston [1979] Commercial Director; John Stephen Massey [1948] Director/Chairman; Susan Mary Massey [1949] Director; Toby Jonathan James Massey [1978] Managing Director

Boal U.K. Limited
Incorporated: 16 November 1987 *Employees:* 151
Net Worth: £6,839,000 *Total Assets:* £22,309,000
Registered Office: Ashby Road East, Shepshed, Loughborough, Leics, LE12 9BS
Activities: Aluminium production
Major Shareholder: Drs Pieter Ronald Boers
Officers: Drs Pieter Ronald Boers [1970] Director [Dutch]; Simon William Bradley [1960] Managing Director; Paulus Wilhelmus Andreas Donkers [1965] Managing Director [Dutch]

Board24 Ltd
Incorporated: 8 June 1987 *Employees:* 340
Net Worth: £15,244,651 *Total Assets:* £46,822,800
Registered Office: 2 Franks Road, Bardon Hill, Coalville, Leics, LE67 1TT
Activities: Packaging activities
Parent: Logson Investments (Midlands) Ltd
Officers: William Bingham Barnett [1976] Director; Alexander David Kelly [1967] Director; Richard Westwood McBride [1954] Director; Bernard Neillus McDonnell [1959] Director [Irish]

Bobby's Acquisition Limited
Incorporated: 6 October 2016 *Employees:* 4
Net Worth: £14,592,000 *Total Assets:* £38,279,000
Registered Office: 25 Jubilee Drive, Loughborough, Leics, LE11 5TX
Activities: Activities of head offices
Parent: Hancocks Holdings Limited
Officers: Wayne Beedle [1970] Director; Stephen Edward Foster [1976] Director

Bobby's Foods Limited
Incorporated: 24 September 1982 *Employees:* 27
Previous: Bobby's Foods PLC
Net Worth: £1,892,000 *Total Assets:* £12,866,000
Registered Office: 25 Jubilee Drive, Loughborough, Leics, LE11 5TX
Activities: Other food services
Parent: Bobby's Acquisition Limited
Officers: Wayne Beedle [1970] Director; Stephen Edward Foster [1976] Director; David Suckling [1972] Managing Director

Boden & Davies Limited
Incorporated: 21 July 1961 *Employees:* 85
Net Worth: £4,947,495 *Total Assets:* £16,078,663
Registered Office: Boden House, Mellor Hall, Mellor, Stockport, Cheshire, SK6 5LU
Activities: Raising of other animals
Major Shareholder: Joan Boden
Officers: Joan Boden, Secretary; Charles Boden [1963] Director/Farmer; George Boden [1955] Director/General Manager; Joan Boden [1936] Director/Administrator; Wayne Boden [1956] Director/Production Manager

Bodycote America Finance Limited
Incorporated: 14 August 2009
Net Worth: £193,121,872 *Total Assets:* £193,121,872
Registered Office: Springwood Court, Springwood Close, Tytherington Business Park, Macclesfield, Cheshire, SK10 2XF
Activities: Financial intermediation not elsewhere classified
Parent: Bodycote International Limited
Officers: Ute Suse Ball, Secretary; Ute Suse Ball [1961] Director/Company Secretary [German]; Michael John Harkcom [1975] Director/Solicitor; Dominique Yates [1967] Director/Accountant

Bodycote America Treasury Limited
Incorporated: 11 September 2009
Net Worth: £556,047,296 *Total Assets:* £565,867,264
Registered Office: Springwood Court, Springwood Close, Tytherington Business Park, Macclesfield, Cheshire, SK10 2XF
Activities: Banks
Parent: Bodycote International Limited
Officers: Ute Suse Ball, Secretary; Ute Suse Ball [1961] Director/Company Secretary [German]; Michael John Harkcom [1975] Director/Solicitor; Dominique Yates [1967] Director/Accountant

Bodycote Finance Limited
Incorporated: 10 July 2007 *Employees:* 2
Net Worth Deficit: £67,616,000 *Total Assets:* £775,449,024
Registered Office: Springwood Court, Springwood Close, Tytherington Business Park, Macclesfield, Cheshire, SK10 2XF
Activities: Other business support service activities n.e.c.
Parent: Bodycote PLC
Officers: Ute Suse Ball, Secretary; Michael John Harkcom [1975] Director/Solicitor; Dominique Yates [1967] Director/Accountant

Bodycote Finance UK Limited
Incorporated: 16 June 2003
Net Worth: £52,280,536 *Total Assets:* £52,427,192
Registered Office: Springwood Court, Springwood Close, Tytherington Business Park, Macclesfield, Cheshire, SK10 2XF
Activities: Activities of head offices
Officers: Ute Suse Ball, Secretary; Michael John Harkcom [1975] Director/Solicitor; Dominique Yates [1967] Director/Accountant

Bodycote H.I.P. Limited
Incorporated: 9 September 1976 *Employees:* 46
Net Worth: £6,979,000 *Total Assets:* £38,990,000
Registered Office: Springwood Court, Springwood Close, Tytherington Business Park, Macclesfield, Cheshire, SK10 2XF
Activities: Treatment and coating of metals
Parent: Bodycote PLC
Officers: Ute Suse Ball, Secretary; Ute Suse Ball [1961] Director/Company Secretary [German]; Michael John Harkcom [1975] Director/Solicitor; Dominique Yates [1967] Director/Accountant

Bodycote Heat Treatments Limited
Incorporated: 29 September 1971 *Employees:* 281
Net Worth: £21,017,000 *Total Assets:* £75,029,000
Registered Office: Springwood Court, Springwood Close, Tytherington Business Park, Macclesfield, Cheshire, SK10 2XF
Activities: Treatment and coating of metals
Parent: Bodycote PLC
Officers: Ute Suse Ball, Secretary; Ute Suse Ball [1961] Director/Company Secretary [German]; Michael John Harkcom [1975] Director/Solicitor; Dominique Yates [1967] Director/Accountant

Bodycote International Limited
Incorporated: 4 January 1972
Net Worth: £324,696,992 *Total Assets:* £1,188,212,992
Registered Office: Springwood Court, Springwood Close, Tytherington Business Park, Macclesfield, Cheshire, SK10 2XF
Activities: Other business support service activities n.e.c.
Parent: Bodycote PLC
Officers: Ute Suse Ball, Secretary; Michael John Harkcom [1975] Director/Solicitor; Dominique Yates [1967] Director/Accountant

Bodycote Investments
Incorporated: 13 December 2006
Net Worth: £316,989,440 *Total Assets:* £317,319,744
Registered Office: Springwood Court, Springwood Close, Tytherington Business Park, Macclesfield, Cheshire, SK10 2XF
Activities: Activities of head offices
Parent: Bodycote International Limited
Officers: Anthony Noonan, Secretary; Simon Paul Blantern [1961] Director/Sales and New Business Development; Anthony Noonan [1983] Director/Financial Controller

Bodycote PLC
Incorporated: 27 April 1953 *Employees:* 5,594
Net Worth: £697,000,000 *Total Assets:* £959,699,968
Registered Office: Springwood Court, Springwood Close, Tytherington Business Park, Macclesfield, Cheshire, SK10 2XF
Activities: Activities of head offices
Officers: Ute Suse Ball, Secretary; Lili Chahbazi [1966] Director/Consultant [Canadian]; Ian Barnet Duncan [1961] Non-Executive Director; Stephen Clive Harris [1958] Director; Patrick Lawrence Larmon [1952] Director [American]; Eva Lindqvist [1958] Director [Swedish]; Anne Cecille Quinn [1951] Director [New Zealander]; Dominique Yates [1967] Director/Accountant

Bodycote Surface Technology Limited
Incorporated: 20 February 1923 *Employees:* 100
Net Worth: £9,716,000 *Total Assets:* £14,520,000
Registered Office: Springwood Court, Springwood Close, Tytherington Business Park, Macclesfield, Cheshire, SK10 2XF
Activities: Treatment and coating of metals
Parent: Bodycote PLC
Officers: Ute Suse Ball, Secretary; Ute Suse Ball [1961] Director/Company Secretary [German]; Michael John Harkcom [1975] Director/Solicitor; Dominique Yates [1967] Director/Accountant

Bodycote Treasury Services Limited
Incorporated: 3 January 2014 *Employees:* 3
Net Worth Deficit: £32,365 *Total Assets:* £10,360,914
Registered Office: Springwood Court, Springwood Close, Tytherington Business Park, Macclesfield, Cheshire, SK10 2XF
Activities: Other business support service activities n.e.c.
Parent: Bodycote Finance Limited
Officers: Ute Suse Ball, Secretary; Ute Suse Ball [1961] Director/Company Secretary [German]; Michael John Harkcom [1975] Director/Solicitor; Dominique Yates [1967] Director/Accountant

Bodypower Sports Holdings Limited
Incorporated: 28 April 2014 *Employees:* 84
Net Worth: £20,625,212 *Total Assets:* £26,549,612
Registered Office: 13 Gate Lodge Close, Northampton, NN3 8RJ
Activities: Activities of head offices
Major Shareholder: Paul David Walker
Officers: Paul David Walker [1965] Director

Bodypower Sports PLC
Incorporated: 5 October 1998 *Employees:* 84
Net Worth: £13,694,613 *Total Assets:* £21,681,590
Registered Office: 13 Gate Lodge Close, Round Spinney Industrial Estate, Northampton, NN3 8RJ
Activities: Retail sale of electrical household appliances in specialised stores
Parent: Bodypower Sports Holdings Limited
Officers: Paul David Walker [1965] Director

Boels Rental Limited
Incorporated: 7 April 1998 *Employees:* 179
Previous: Supply UK Hire Shops Limited
Net Worth: £5,853,738 *Total Assets:* £16,303,964
Registered Office: Unit A8, Riverview, Embankment Business Park, Heaton Mersey, Stockport, Cheshire, SK4 3GN
Activities: Renting and leasing of construction and civil engineering machinery and equipment
Officers: Peter Bernard Marcel Boels [1962] Director [Dutch]; Elisabeth Petra Maria Boels-Van Kerkom [1967] Director [Dutch]; Piet Elisabeth Michiel Marie Donners [1962] Director [Dutch]

Boketto Bidco Limited
Incorporated: 9 December 2015 *Employees:* 9
Net Worth: £2,675,000 *Total Assets:* £369,238,016
Registered Office: New Mill, New Mill Lane, Witney, Oxon, OX29 9SX
Activities: Tour operator activities
Parent: Boketto Newco Limited
Officers: Elizabeth Ann Ward, Secretary; Nicholas Winston Longman [1968] Director; Richard John Prosser [1957] Director; Nils Olin Steinmeyer [1970] Director [German]

Boketto Holdco Limited
Incorporated: 9 December 2015 *Employees:* 645
Net Worth Deficit: £28,475,000 *Total Assets:* £468,905,984
Registered Office: New Mill, New Mill Lane, Witney, Oxon, OX29 9SX
Activities: Tour operator activities
Shareholder: 3i Group PLC
Officers: Elizabeth Ann Ward, Secretary; Alan Clifford Bence Giddins [1965] Director/Investment Manager; Rowena Gracey [1982] Director/Investment Manager; Mark Christopher Hanson [1972] Director; Jacqueline Anne Lewis [1966] Director [American]; Nicholas Winston Longman [1968] Director; Richard John Prosser [1957] Director; Ian David Simkins [1967] Director; Nils Olin Steinmeyer [1970] Director [German]

Boketto Midco Limited
Incorporated: 9 December 2015 *Employees:* 3
Net Worth: £875,000 *Total Assets:* £227,534,000
Registered Office: New Mill, New Mill Lane, Witney, Oxon, OX29 9SX
Activities: Tour operator activities
Parent: Boketto Holdco Limited
Officers: Elizabeth Ann Ward, Secretary; Nicholas Winston Longman [1968] Director; Richard John Prosser [1957] Director; Nils Olin Steinmeyer [1970] Director [German]

Boketto Newco Limited
Incorporated: 9 December 2015 *Employees:* 645
Net Worth Deficit: £26,557,000 *Total Assets:* £476,193,984
Registered Office: New Mill, New Mill Lane, Witney, Oxon, OX29 9SX
Activities: Tour operator activities
Parent: Boketto Midco Limited
Officers: Elizabeth Ann Ward, Secretary; Nicholas Winston Longman [1968] Director; Richard John Prosser [1957] Director; Nils Olin Steinmeyer [1970] Director [German]

Bollin Group Limited
Incorporated: 14 July 1989 *Employees:* 370
Net Worth: £19,954,000 *Total Assets:* £42,958,000
Registered Office: Bailey Court, Green Street, Macclesfield, Cheshire, SK10 1JQ
Activities: Activities of head offices
Shareholders: Alan David Walker; Herbert Anthony Cann; Carole Fahy; Hugh David Turner
Officers: Stephen James Cann, Secretary; Herbert Anthony Cann [1939] Director/Textile Technologist; Stephen James Cann [1965] Director

Bollington Wilson Group Limited
Incorporated: 28 July 2017 *Employees:* 380
Net Worth Deficit: £1,341,000 *Total Assets:* £66,028,000
Registered Office: Adlington Court, Adlington Business Park, Adlington, Macclesfield, Cheshire, SK10 4NL
Activities: Activities of other holding companies n.e.c.
Parent: Inflexion Buyout Fund IV (No.1) Limited Partnership
Officers: Leslie Thomas Richard Higgins [1953] Director/Chairman; Patrick Francis McDonnell [1965] Director [Irish]; Matthew Edward McKinlay [1988] Director; Paul Christopher Moors [1962] Director; Christopher Patterson [1971] Director; John Francis Wilson [1944] Director/Insurance Broker; Carl Edmund Wormald [1969] Investment Director

Bolsover Cruise Club Limited
Incorporated: 3 March 2006 *Employees:* 110
Net Worth: £15,552,737 *Total Assets:* £21,032,520
Registered Office: 35 Sherwood Street, Warsop, Mansfield, Notts, NG20 0JR
Activities: Travel agency activities
Major Shareholder: Michael Wilson
Officers: Julie Ann Straw, Secretary; Julie Ann Straw [1962] Director/Travel Agent; Michael Wilson [1959] Director/Travel Agent

Bolsover Properties Limited
Incorporated: 27 April 1966
Net Worth: £9,644,433 *Total Assets:* £9,995,433
Registered Office: Portland Estate Office, Cavendish House, Welbeck, Whitwell, Worksop, Notts, S80 3LL
Activities: Other letting and operating of own or leased real estate
Shareholders: Nigel Timothy Bentley; Denis Boucault; Ian Ledger; Carina Louise Robinson
Officers: Ian Goodwin, Secretary; Daisy Margharita Amelia Parente [1981] Director/Literary Agent; Henry Joseph Parente [1983] Director; William Henry Marcello Parente [1951] Director; Malcolm Peter Swan [1949] Director

Bolton Plastic Components Limited
Incorporated: 16 November 1983 *Employees:* 211
Net Worth: £5,860,239 *Total Assets:* £9,307,028
Registered Office: Environment House, 6 Union Road, Nottingham, NG3 1FH
Activities: Manufacture of other plastic products
Parent: Blugilt Holdings Limited
Officers: David George Butler [1952] Director; Nicholas James Holland [1962] Finance Director; John Middlehurst [1960] Director

Bombardier Transportation (Holdings) UK Ltd
Incorporated: 6 April 1983
Net Worth: £481,623,008 *Total Assets:* £631,014,976
Registered Office: Litchurch Lane, Derby, DE24 8AD
Activities: Manufacture of railway locomotives and rolling stock
Parent: Bombardier Transportation (Global Holdings) UK Limited
Officers: Lynn Suzanne West, Secretary; Garry John Mowbray [1970] Director, Controlling; Katherine Mari Parkes [1976] Director/Solicitor

Bombardier Transportation (Rolling Stock) UK Ltd
Incorporated: 9 November 1994 *Employees:* 259
Net Worth: £16,022,000 *Total Assets:* £25,281,000
Registered Office: Litchurch Lane, Derby, DE24 8AD
Activities: Manufacture of railway locomotives and rolling stock
Parent: Bombardier Transportation UK Limited
Officers: Lynn Suzanne West, Secretary; Garry John Mowbray [1970] Director Controlling; Katherine Mari Parkes [1976] Director/Solicitor

Bombardier Transportation UK Ltd
Incorporated: 25 March 1988 *Employees:* 3,686
Net Worth: £736,694,016 *Total Assets:* £2,189,654,016
Registered Office: Litchurch Lane, Derby, DE24 8AD
Activities: Manufacture of railway locomotives and rolling stock
Parent: Bombardier Transportation (Holdings) UK Limited
Officers: Lynn West, Secretary; Philip Hufton [1957] UK Managing Director; Allan Thomas Morgan [1965] Director RCS UK; Garry John Mowbray [1970] Director Controlling; Katherine Mari Parkes [1976] Director/Solicitor; Bernadette Westmoreland [1967] Country HR Director

Bong UK Limited
Incorporated: 17 December 1999 *Employees:* 110
Net Worth: £6,431,376 *Total Assets:* £13,854,238
Registered Office: The Envelope Building, Michigan Drive, Tongwell, Milton Keynes, Bucks, MK15 8HQ
Activities: Manufacture of paper stationery
Shareholder: Stephane Hamelin
Officers: Jeremy Parish, Secretary; Jeffrey Greenleaf [1962] Director; Jeremy Parish [1969] Finance Director; Kai Steigleder [1963] Director [German]

Bonnington Plastics Limited
Incorporated: 4 April 1977 *Employees:* 97
Net Worth: £3,754,954 *Total Assets:* £13,360,291
Registered Office: Kingfisher House, 9 Glaisdale Parkway, Bilborough, Nottingham, NG8 4GP
Activities: Non-specialised wholesale trade
Major Shareholder: Mark Grenville Fisher
Officers: Paul Andrew Cavanagh [1972] Director; Ian Charles Fisher [1978] Director; Sergio Pasquale Tartaglia [1967] Director [Italian]

Booker Direct Limited
Incorporated: 31 May 2000 *Employees:* 277
Net Worth: £33,600,000 *Total Assets:* £34,600,000
Registered Office: Equity House, Irthlingborough Road, Wellingborough, Northants, NN8 1LT
Activities: Non-specialised wholesale trade
Parent: Booker Wholesale Holdings Limited
Officers: Veselin Bandev [1978] Finance Director [Bulgarian]; Charles Wilson [1965] Director

Booker Group Limited
Incorporated: 4 June 2004 *Employees:* 13,208
Previous: Booker Group PLC
Net Worth: £584,400,000 *Total Assets:* £1,408,700,032
Registered Office: Equity House, Irthlingborough Road, Wellingborough, Northants, NN8 1LT
Activities: Non-specialised wholesale trade
Parent: Tesco Holdings Limited
Officers: Veselin Bandev [1978] Finance Director [Bulgarian]; Guy Charles Farrant [1961] Director; Charles Wilson [1965] Director

Booker Limited
Incorporated: 17 April 1924 *Employees:* 9,631
Net Worth: £805,200,000 *Total Assets:* £1,700,300,032
Registered Office: Equity House, Irthlingborough Road, Wellingborough, Northants, NN8 1LT
Activities: Non-specialised wholesale trade
Parent: Booker Wholesale Holdings Limited
Officers: Veselin Bandev [1978] Finance Director [Bulgarian]; Charles Wilson [1965] Director

Booker Retail Partners (GB) Limited
Incorporated: 28 December 2007 *Employees:* 1,233
Previous: Musgrave Retail Partners GB Limited
Net Worth: £118,900,000 *Total Assets:* £149,100,000
Registered Office: Equity House, Irthlingborough Road, Wellingborough, Northants, NN8 1LT
Activities: Non-specialised wholesale of food, beverages and tobacco
Parent: Booker Wholesale Holdings Limited
Officers: Veselin Bandev [1978] Finance Director [Bulgarian]; Charles Wilson [1965] Director

Booker Wholesale Holdings Limited
Incorporated: 26 May 2004 *Employees:* 2
Net Worth: £84,600,000 *Total Assets:* £1,168,700,032
Registered Office: Equity House, Irthlingborough Road, Wellingborough, Northants, NN8 1NZ
Activities: Non-trading company
Parent: Booker Group Limited
Officers: Veselin Bandev [1978] Finance Director [Bulgarian]; Charles Wilson [1965] Director

Boole's Tools & Pipe Fittings Limited
Incorporated: 17 February 1961 *Employees:* 53
Net Worth: £5,437,000 *Total Assets:* £10,717,000
Registered Office: Haigh Avenue, Whitehill Industrial Estate, Stockport, Cheshire, SK4 1NU
Activities: Non-specialised wholesale trade
Parent: Seville Holdings Ltd
Officers: Terence Seville [1962] Director; Tracy Anne Seville [1965] Director

Henry Boot Construction Limited
Incorporated: 14 December 1993 *Employees:* 173
Net Worth: £31,310,276 *Total Assets:* £53,885,680
Registered Office: Banner Cross Hall, Ecclesall Road South, Sheffield, S11 9PD
Activities: Construction of commercial buildings
Parent: Henry Boot PLC
Officers: Amy Louise Oakley, Secretary; Simon Alexander Carr [1958] Director/Chartered Surveyor; Darren Louis Littlewood [1975] Finance Director; David Pearson [1960] Director/Quantity Surveyor; Anthony David Shaw [1967] Director/Project Manager; John Trevor Sutcliffe [1959] Finance Director

Henry Boot Developments Limited
Incorporated: 21 September 1978 *Employees:* 37
Net Worth: £20,710,504 *Total Assets:* £184,080,672
Registered Office: Banner Cross Hall, Ecclesall Road South, Sheffield, S11 9PD
Activities: Development of building projects
Parent: Henry Boot PLC
Officers: Amy Louise Oakley, Secretary; Adam Robert Brady [1976] Director; Vivienne Clements [1967] Director; John Christopher Cullen [1959] Director; Nicholas Harris [1970] Director; Edward James Hutchinson [1977] Director/Chartered Surveyor; Darren Louis Littlewood [1975] Finance Director; Julian Lloyd Painter [1964] Director/Chartered Surveyor; Adrian Michael Schofield [1965] Director; John Trevor Sutcliffe [1959] Finance Director

Henry Boot Estates Limited
Incorporated: 6 June 1933 *Employees:* 6
Net Worth: £25,943,298 *Total Assets:* £27,578,454
Registered Office: Banner Cross Hall, Ecclesall Road South, Sheffield, S11 9PD
Activities: Buying and selling of own real estate
Parent: Henry Boot PLC
Officers: Amy Louise Oakley, Secretary; Edward James Hutchinson [1977] Director/Chartered Surveyor; Darren Louis Littlewood [1975] Finance Director; John Trevor Sutcliffe [1959] Finance Director

Henry Boot Land Holdings Limited
Incorporated: 23 October 2002
Net Worth: £1,136,543 *Total Assets:* £19,649,078
Registered Office: Banner Cross Hall, Ecclesall Road South, Sheffield, S11 9PD
Activities: Management of real estate on a fee or contract basis
Parent: Henry Boot PLC
Officers: Amy Louise Oakley, Secretary; Darren Louis Littlewood [1975] Finance Director; John Trevor Sutcliffe [1959] Director/Chartered Accountant

Henry Boot PLC
Incorporated: 26 November 1919 *Employees:* 486
Net Worth: £267,392,000 *Total Assets:* £428,059,008
Registered Office: Banner Cross Hall, Ecclesall Road South, Sheffield, S11 9PD
Activities: Activities of head offices
Officers: Amy Louise Oakley, Secretary; Edward James Boot [1951] Director; Generald Robert Jennings [1957] Director/Chartered Surveyor; Joanne Carolyn Lake [1963] Director; Darren Louis Littlewood [1975] Finance Director; Peter Mawson [1954] Director; John Trevor Sutcliffe [1959] Director/Chartered Accountant; Jonathan James Sykes [1964] Director/Chartered Accountant

C.F.Booth Limited
Incorporated: 27 August 1949 *Employees:* 305
Net Worth: £15,161,000 *Total Assets:* £53,920,000
Registered Office: Clarence Metal Works, Armer Street, Rotherham, S Yorks, S60 1AF
Activities: Treatment and disposal of non-hazardous waste
Shareholders: James Henry Booth; Clarence Kenneth Frederick Booth
Officers: James Henry Booth, Secretary; Clarence Kenneth Frederick Booth [1946] Director; James Henry Booth [1957] Director; Jason Kenneth Booth [1977] Director; Scott Federick Booth [1981] Director; Christopher Thomas Wilkinson [1949] Director

The Boots Company PLC
Incorporated: 7 November 1888
Previous: The Boots Company Limited
Net Worth: £706,000,000 *Total Assets:* £753,000,000
Registered Office: Nottingham, NG2 3AA
Activities: Activities of head offices
Parent: Alliance Boots Holdings Limited
Officers: Andrew Richard Thompson, Secretary; Rosemary Frances Counsell [1963] Director/Chief Financial Officer - Global Brands; Anne Louise Murphy [1967] Director; Andrew Richard Thompson [1975] Director/Solicitor

Boots International Limited
Incorporated: 11 July 2000
Net Worth: £43,343,000 *Total Assets:* £74,912,000
Registered Office: 1 Thane Road West, Nottingham, NG2 3AA
Activities: Wholesale of perfume and cosmetics
Parent: Alliance Boots Holdings Limited
Officers: Andrew Richard Thompson, Secretary; Rosemary Frances Counsell [1963] Director/Chief Financial Officer; Anne Louise Murphy [1967] Director

Boots Management Services Limited
Incorporated: 11 November 2009 *Employees:* 40,973
Net Worth: £141,400,000 *Total Assets:* £255,900,000
Registered Office: 1 Thane Road West, Nottingham, NG2 3AA
Activities: Other business support service activities n.e.c.
Parent: Alliance Boots Holdings Limited
Officers: Frank Standish, Secretary; Michael David Snape [1979] Director/Chief Financial Officer; Frank Standish [1963] Company Secretary/Director [Irish]; Andrew Richard Thompson [1975] Director/Solicitor

Boots Opticians Professional Services Limited
Incorporated: 23 December 2008 *Employees:* 4,760
Net Worth: £143,111,008 *Total Assets:* £224,667,008
Registered Office: 1 Thane Road West, Nottingham, NG2 3AA
Activities: Retail sale by opticians
Parent: Boots Optcial Investment Holdings Limited
Officers: Andrew Richard Thompson, Secretary; Kyla Anne Eunice Black [1973] Director/Optometrist; Jonathan James Gardner [1973] Managing Director, Boots Opticians; Emma Harris [1978] Finance Director; Mark David Harris [1971] Director/Head of Trading; Claire Louise Slade [1974] Director of Professional Services

Boots Properties Limited
Incorporated: 2 July 1928
Net Worth: £402,400,000 *Total Assets:* £420,800,000
Registered Office: Nottingham, NG2 3AA
Activities: Other letting and operating of own or leased real estate
Parent: Alliance Boots Holdings Limited
Officers: Andrew Richard Thompson, Secretary; Aidan Gerard Clare [1966] Director [Irish]; Michael David Snape [1979] Director/Chief Financial Officer; Frank Standish [1963] Director [Irish]

Boots UK Limited
Incorporated: 11 March 1968
Net Worth: £1,772,000,000 *Total Assets:* £3,464,999,936
Registered Office: Nottingham, NG2 3AA
Activities: Other retail sale in non-specialised stores
Parent: Alliance Boots Holdings Limited
Officers: Andrew Richard Thompson, Secretary; Richard Bradley [1976] Pharmacy Director; Elizabeth Fagan [1957] Managing Director - Boots UK & ROI; Sebastian Richard Edward Cuthbert James [1966] President & Managing Director; Michael David Snape [1979] Director/Chief Financial Officer

Bosch Packaging Technology Limited
Incorporated: 25 July 1991 *Employees:* 55
Net Worth Deficit: £1,394,000 *Total Assets:* £11,772,000
Registered Office: Unit 2a Meteor Business Park, Meteor Centre, Mansfield Road, Derby, DE21 4SU
Activities: Manufacture of other special-purpose machinery n.e.c.
Parent: Robert Bosch UK Holdings Limited
Officers: Jonathan Burton, Secretary; Marcus Behrens [1971] Director/General Manager [German]; Sarah Louise Gilleard [1980] Director/Regional Business Responsible Packaging Services; Uwe Michael Harbauer [1964] Director/Vice President [German]

Bosch Rexroth Limited
Incorporated: 22 July 1963 *Employees:* 688
Net Worth: £44,213,000 *Total Assets:* £86,185,000
Registered Office: 15 Cromwell Road, St Neots, Cambs, PE19 2ES
Activities: Manufacture of other special-purpose machinery n.e.c.
Parent: Robert Bosch Holdings Limited
Officers: Jonathan Burton, Secretary; Paul Anthony Bowden [1963] Director; Dr Steffen Tobias Hoffmann [1965] Director [German]; Alastair John Johnstone [1959] Manufacturing Director; Karl Frederik Nilner [1972] Director [Swedish]

Boss Cabins Limited
Incorporated: 1 December 2009 *Employees:* 96
Net Worth: £6,408,367 *Total Assets:* £10,955,566
Registered Office: BCS House, Pinfold Road, Bourne, Lincs, PE10 9HT
Activities: Manufacture of trailers and semi-trailers
Major Shareholder: Judith Wordsworth
Officers: Timothy Mark McBain Allan, Secretary; Timothy Mark McBain Allan [1963] Director; Graham Ian Stansfield [1969] Director; Harold Duncan Wordsworth [1940] Director; Judith Wordsworth [1962] Director; Matthew Jason Wordsworth [1973] Director; Niall Duncan Wordsworth [1968] Director

Boston Mayflower Finance PLC
Incorporated: 5 August 2014
Net Worth: £50,633 *Total Assets:* £89,555,784
Registered Office: Westgate Park, Charlton Street, Grimsby, N E Lincs, DN31 1SQ
Activities: Other accommodation
Parent: Lincolnshire Housing Partnership Limited
Officers: Michael James Walters, Secretary; Mark Jonathan Jones [1966] Director of Property; Bridget Elizabeth Lloyd [1962] Director of Customers; Murray Alexander MacDonald [1967] Director/CEO, Social Housing

The Boston Witham Academies Federation
Incorporated: 26 July 2012 *Employees:* 450
Net Worth: £26,633,000 *Total Assets:* £32,713,000
Registered Office: Marian Campus, Marian Road, Boston, Lincs, PE21 9HB
Activities: Pre-primary education
Officers: Daniel Mark Cowburn Elkington [1985] Director/Independent Financial Advisor; Tony Elmer [1939] Director/Retired Businessman; Jessica Gale [1950] Director/Retired; John Arthur McGarel [1945] Director; Christopher John Penney [1961] Director; Carole Shepheard [1947] Director/Retired Deputy Headteacher; Jodie Wrigglesworth [1988] Director/Lawyer

Bosworth Independent College Limited
Incorporated: 14 March 1997 *Employees:* 171
Net Worth: £4,659,613 *Total Assets:* £12,387,729
Registered Office: Nazareth House, The Old University Building, Barrack Road, Northampton, NN2 6AF
Activities: General secondary education
Shareholders: Joanne Marie Broadway; Mark Alexander Victor Broadway; Broadway Education (International) Limited
Officers: Paul Nathan Broadway, Secretary; Mark Alexander Victor Broadway [1961] Director

Boughton Estates Limited (The)
Incorporated: 28 December 1932
Net Worth: £40,507,852 *Total Assets:* £44,761,712
Registered Office: Estate Office, Weekley, Kettering, Northants, NN16 9UP
Activities: Buying and selling of own real estate
Parent: Buccleuch Holdings Ltd
Officers: Michael James McGrath, Secretary; John Ronald Kerr Glen [1959] Director; Damian Torquil Francis Charles Montagu Douglas Scott [1969] Director; Richard Walter John Montagu Douglas Scott [1954] Director; Elizabeth Marian Frances Scott [1954] Director

Bourbon Automotive Plastics Northampton Limited
Incorporated: 11 June 1997 *Employees:* 146
Net Worth Deficit: £1,889,771 *Total Assets:* £14,992,073
Registered Office: North Portway Close, Round Spinney Industrial Estate, Northampton, NN3 8RE
Activities: Manufacture of other parts and accessories for motor vehicles
Parent: Plastiques du Val de Loire
Officers: Vanessa Belinguier, Secretary; Patrick Jean-Louis Findeling [1947] Director [French]

H.R Bourn & Sons (Linwood) Limited
Incorporated: 1 April 1999
Net Worth: £11,277,616 *Total Assets:* £19,084,720
Registered Office: Navarino Louth Road, Wragby, Market Rasen, Lincs, LN8 5PH
Activities: Growing of cereals (except rice), leguminous crops and oil seeds
Major Shareholder: Kathleen Monica Bourn
Officers: Matthew James Cherry, Secretary; Hugh Christopher Bourn [1958] Director; Kathleen Monica Bourn [1934] Director

H C Bourn (Holdings) Limited
Incorporated: 28 January 2016
Net Worth: £2,640,994 *Total Assets:* £31,336,004
Registered Office: The Old Rectory, Louth Road, West Barkwith, Market Rasen, Lincs, LN8 5LF
Activities: Activities of other holding companies n.e.c.
Major Shareholder: Hugh Christopher Bourn
Officers: Matthew Cherry, Secretary; Hugh Christopher Bourn [1958] Director/Farmer; James George Christopher Bourn [1996] Director

Bourne Grammar School
Incorporated: 16 November 2011 *Employees:* 128
Net Worth: £12,941,521 *Total Assets:* £15,707,177
Registered Office: Bourne Grammar School, South Road, Bourne, Lincs, PE10 9JE
Activities: General secondary education
Officers: Fiona Hill, Secretary; Chris Atkinson [1957] Director; James Allen Barker [1992] Director/Systems Administrator; Stuart Brett [1971] Director; Robert Brown [1947] Director; Joyce Burrows [1944] Director; Clinton Delport [1978] Director/Teacher; Stephen Dharamraj [1967] Director; Ian Michael Fytche [1964] Director/Chief Executive; Geoffrey Richard Greatwood [1948] Director; Claire Fiona Hawkins [1972] Director/Chartered Accountant; Jonathan Mark Kendrew [1973] Director; Jonathan Paul Maddox [1965] Director/Headteacher; Ian John George Mears [1955] Director; Christopher Moon [1974] Director; Stephen Nightingale [1957] Director/Turf Accountant; Robert James Parker [1964] Director; Suneetha Venkata Vijaya Durga Siddabattuni [1978] Director/Doctor; Lincoln Scott Taylor [1969] Director; Sue Woolley [1958] Director/Councillor

Bournemouth Airport Property Investments (Industrial) Limited
Incorporated: 26 November 2009
Net Worth: £38,981,000 *Total Assets:* £53,864,000
Registered Office: Bridgeway House, Bridgeway, Stratford upon Avon, Warwicks, CV37 6YX
Activities: Buying and selling of own real estate
Parent: Bournemouth International Airport Limited
Officers: Katherine Georgina Cook, Secretary; Andrew Michael Bell [1979] Director; Steven Paul Rigby [1972] Director; Richard Seal [1958] Director/Chartered Surveyor

Bournemouth International Airport Limited
Incorporated: 27 November 1986 *Employees:* 141
Net Worth: £9,906,000 *Total Assets:* £37,404,000
Registered Office: Bridgeway House, Bridgeway, Stratford upon Avon, Warwicks, CV37 6YX
Activities: Scheduled passenger air transport
Parent: Regional & City Airports Holdings Limited
Officers: Katherine Georgina Cook, Secretary; Andrew Michael Bell [1979] Director; Stephen Leslie Gill [1964] Managing Director; Sir Peter Rigby [1943] Director; Richard Seal [1958] Director/Chartered Surveyor

Bourns (UK) Acquisition Limited
Incorporated: 10 March 2000 *Employees:* 143
Net Worth: £10,392,000 *Total Assets:* £14,472,000
Registered Office: Manton Lane, Bedford, MK41 7BJ
Activities: Activities of head offices
Officers: Ana Laura Rojo de La Vega Reyes, Secretary; Gordon Lee Bourns [1949] Director/Business Executive [American]; L. Erik Gunnar Meijer [1951] Director/President of Bourns, Inc [American]

Boutinot Limited
Incorporated: 25 November 1980 *Employees:* 140
Net Worth: £25,912,476 *Total Assets:* £82,608,976
Registered Office: Boundary House, Cheadle Point, Cheadle, Cheshire, SK8 2GG
Activities: Wholesale of wine, beer, spirits and other alcoholic beverages
Shareholders: Dennis Whiteley; Donna Whiteley; Araldica Castelvero SCA
Officers: Michael Joseph Moriarty, Secretary/Accountant; Antony Malcolm Brown [1957] Director; Iain Robert Davies [1970] Director; Claudio Manera [1963] Director [Italian]; Michael Joseph Moriarty [1965] Director/Accountant; Dennis Whiteley [1961] Deputy Managing Director

Wilson Bowden Developments Limited
Incorporated: 20 February 1969 *Employees:* 22
Net Worth: £43,785,000 *Total Assets:* £82,464,000
Registered Office: Barratt House, Cartwright Way, Forest Business Park, Bardon Hill, Coalville, Leics, LE67 1UF
Activities: Construction of commercial buildings
Parent: Wilson Bowden Limited
Officers: Steven John Boyes [1960] Group Executive Director; Nicholas William Davies [1961] Director; Nicholas Hadden Richardson [1963] Director; David Fraser Thomas [1963] Director; David John Ward [1959] Director; Jessica Elizabeth White [1978] Director/Chief Financial Officer

Wilson Bowden Limited
Incorporated: 26 September 1986
Net Worth: £48,231,000 *Total Assets:* £49,290,000
Registered Office: Barratt House, Cartwright Way, Forest Business Park, Bardon Hill, Coalville, Leics, LE67 1UF
Activities: Activities of head offices
Parent: Barratt Developments P L C
Officers: Steven John Boyes [1960] Group Executive Director; Nicholas William Davies [1961] Director; Nicholas Hadden Richardson [1963] Director; David Fraser Thomas [1963] Director; Jessica Elizabeth White [1978] Director/Chief Financial Officer

Bowers Metrology Limited
Incorporated: 30 October 1989 *Employees:* 88
Net Worth: £5,052,000 *Total Assets:* £11,031,000
Registered Office: c/o James Neill Holdings Ltd, Atlas Way, Atlas North Business Park, Sheffield, S4 7QQ
Activities: Manufacture of electronic measuring, testing etc. equipment, not for industrial process control
Parent: Bowers Group Limited
Officers: John Maurice Dallman, Company Secretary; Michael Paul Denton [1956] Director; Richard Douglas Grocott [1975] Director; Simon Nai Cheng Hsu [1960] Director/Businessman [Chinese]; Geoffrey David Jackson [1965] Director; Graham John Keefe [1958] Director/Engineer; Stuart David Millington [1958] Director; Alaina Shone [1962] Director/Chartered Accountant; Stephen Philip White [1966] Director/Sales/Marketing

T F Bowman & Son Limited
Incorporated: 11 March 2016 *Employees:* 2
Net Worth: £1,049,258 *Total Assets:* £17,070,040
Registered Office: 1-4 London Road, Spalding, Lincs, PE11 2TA
Activities: Other service activities n.e.c.
Officers: Peter Andrew Bowman [1954] Director; Rita Bowman [1953] Director

Bowmer and Kirkland Limited
Incorporated: 30 August 1961 *Employees:* 1,319
Net Worth: £400,713,056 *Total Assets:* £840,172,800
Registered Office: High Edge Court, Church Street, Heage, Belper, Derbys, DE56 2BW
Activities: Construction of commercial buildings
Officers: Michelle Ann Mucklestone, Secretary; Ralph Charles Jones [1950] Director/Manager; Christopher Robert Kirkland [1982] Director; John Alexander Charles Kirkland [1980] Director; John Nigel Kirkland [1938] Director; Michael John Kirkland [1979] Director/Surveyor; Robert Malcolm Kirkland [1946] Director/Builder; John Paul Lomas [1956] Director/Surveyor; Michelle Ann Mucklestone [1966] Director/Accountant

Bowmer-Bond Narrow Fabrics Limited
Incorporated: 15 January 1957 *Employees:* 92
Net Worth: £7,176,914 *Total Assets:* £9,272,215
Registered Office: Hanging Bridge Mills, Ashbourne, Derbys, DE6 2EA
Activities: Weaving of textiles
Parent: Bowmer Bond (Holdings) Limited
Officers: Mark Anthony Allender, Secretary; Mark Anthony Allender [1958] Director; Lindsey Langton Horsnall [1963] Director; Lydia Eleanor Horsnall [1993] Non-Executive Director; Philip Horsnall [1961] Director; Nigel Philip Ratcliffe [1962] Sales Director; Glyn David Sellers [1980] Operations Director

Bowring Transport Limited
Incorporated: 12 May 1975 *Employees:* 207
Net Worth: £13,707,072 *Total Assets:* £26,204,456
Registered Office: Windmill House Farm, Forest Road, Warsop, Notts, NG20 0EP
Activities: Freight transport by road
Major Shareholder: David Harold Bowring
Officers: Marie Bowring, Secretary; David Harold Bowring [1953] Director/Haulage Contractor; Gillian Christine Bowring [1955] Director/Secretary; James William Bowring [1988] Director/Farm Machinery Dealer Principal; Marie Bowring [1927] Director/Secretary; Victoria Annie Bowring [1991] Director/Farm Worker

BPB Finance (No. 4) Limited
Incorporated: 28 March 2002
Net Worth: £449,018,752 *Total Assets:* £449,071,040
Registered Office: Saint-Gobain House, Binley Business Park, Coventry, Warwicks, CV3 2TT
Activities: Activities of head offices
Parent: BPB Limited
Officers: Alun Roy Oxenham, Secretary; Nicholas James Cammack [1972] Director; Michael Strickland Chaldecott [1960] Managing Director

BPB Finance (No.2) Limited
Incorporated: 30 July 1998
Net Worth Deficit: £201,334,000 *Total Assets:* £328,143,008
Registered Office: Saint-Gobain House, Binley Business Park, Coventry, Warwicks, CV3 2TT
Activities: Activities of head offices
Parent: BPB Gypsum BV
Officers: Alun Roy Oxenham, Secretary; Nicholas James Cammack [1972] Director; Michael Strickland Chaldecott [1960] Managing Director

BPB Group Finance Limited
Incorporated: 31 May 2005
Net Worth: £2,239,023,104 *Total Assets:* £2,523,906,048
Registered Office: Saint-Gobain House, Binley Business Park, Coventry, Warwicks, CV3 2TT
Activities: Activities of head offices
Officers: Alun Roy Oxenham, Secretary; Nicholas James Cammack [1972] Director; Michael Strickland Chaldecott [1960] Managing Director

BPB Group Operations Limited
Incorporated: 10 May 2005
Net Worth: £1,273,667,968 *Total Assets:* £1,273,667,968
Registered Office: Saint-Gobain House, Binley Business Park, Coventry, Warwicks, CV3 2TT
Activities: Activities of head offices
Parent: BPB Group Finance Limited
Officers: Alun Roy Oxenham, Secretary; Nicholas James Cammack [1972] Director; Michael Strickland Chaldecott [1960] Managing Director

BPB Investments Overseas Limited
Incorporated: 25 February 2002
Net Worth: £126,036,000 *Total Assets:* £1,221,208,960
Registered Office: Saint-Gobain House, Binley Business Park, Coventry, Warwicks, CV3 2TT
Activities: Activities of head offices
Parent: BPB Group Operations Limited
Officers: Alun Roy Oxenham, Secretary; Nicholas James Cammack [1972] Director; Michael Strickland Chaldecott [1960] Managing Director; Stephane Heraud [1965] Director [French]

BPB Limited
Incorporated: 24 April 1917 *Employees:* 77
Net Worth: £847,851,008 *Total Assets:* £2,837,552,896
Registered Office: Saint-Gobain House, Binley Business Park, Coventry, Warwicks, CV3 2TT
Activities: Activities of head offices
Parent: Saint-Gobain Aldwych Limited
Officers: Alun Roy Oxenham, Secretary; Nicholas James Cammack [1972] Director; Michael Strickland Chaldecott [1960] Managing Director; Patrick Edouard Andre Dupin [1963] Finance Director [French]

BPHA Finance PLC
Incorporated: 6 March 2014
Net Worth: £12,500 *Total Assets:* £203,838,336
Registered Office: Bedford Heights, Manton Lane, Bedford, MK41 7BJ
Activities: Security dealing on own account
Officers: Philippa Spratley, Secretary; Kevin Ronald Bolt [1957] Director/Management Consultant; Paul Lawrence Gray [1961] Director/Chartered Accountant; Malgorzata Motler [1973] Director/Head of Corporate Finance

BPI International (No 2) Limited
Incorporated: 18 November 1997
Net Worth Deficit: £575,850 *Total Assets:* £45,409,172
Registered Office: Sapphire House, Crown Way, Rushden, Northants, NN10 6FB
Activities: Dormant company
Parent: British Polythene Industries Limited
Officers: Nicholas David Martin Giles, Secretary; Franciscus Lodewijk Paulus Doorenbosch [1964] Director [Dutch]; David George Duthie [1956] Finance Director; Andrew Samuel Green [1964] Director; Simon John Kesterton [1973] Director; Petrus Rudolf Maria Vervaat [1965] Director [Dutch]

BPI International Limited
Incorporated: 7 March 1997
Net Worth: £63,391 *Total Assets:* £38,944,144
Registered Office: Sapphire House, Crown Way, Rushden, Northants, NN10 6FB
Activities: Other business support service activities n.e.c.
Parent: British Polythene Industries Limited
Officers: Nicholas David Martin Giles, Secretary; Franciscus Lodewijk Paulus Doorenbosch [1964] Director [Dutch]; David George Duthie [1956] Director/Financial Controller; Andrew Samuel Green [1964] Director; Simon John Kesterton [1973] Director; Petrus Rudolf Maria Vervaat [1965] Director [Dutch]

BPI Limited
Incorporated: 24 June 1983
Previous: BPI PLC
Net Worth: £32,696,000 *Total Assets:* £45,644,000
Registered Office: Sapphire House, Crown Way, Rushden, Northants, NN10 6FB
Activities: Other letting and operating of own or leased real estate
Parent: British Polythene Industries Limited
Officers: Nicholas David Martin Giles, Secretary; Franciscus Lodewijk Paulus Doorenbosch [1964] Director [Dutch]; David George Duthie [1956] Finance Director; Andrew Samuel Green [1964] Director; Simon John Kesterton [1973] Director; Petrus Rudolf Maria Vervaat [1965] Director [Dutch]

BPS Warwick Limited
Incorporated: 7 November 2014 *Employees:* 163
Net Worth: £8,129,707 *Total Assets:* £13,414,504
Registered Office: Tachbrook Park Drive, Tachbrook Park, Leamington Spa, Warwick, CV34 6RH
Activities: Activities of head offices
Shareholder: Brian George Dibble
Officers: David Ian Battin, Secretary; Brian George Dibble [1927] Director; Emma Marjorie Dibble [1968] Training and Marketing Director; John Richard Dibble [1968] Managing Director

BPW Limited
Incorporated: 10 May 1984 *Employees:* 75
Net Worth: £13,451,863 *Total Assets:* £50,800,936
Registered Office: Legion Way, Meridian Business Park, Leicester, LE19 1UZ
Activities: Manufacture of other parts and accessories for motor vehicles
Officers: David John Smith, Secretary; Neill Groves [1970] Sales and Marketing Director; Achim Kotz [1975] Director/Managing Partner [German]; Friedrick Michael Pfeiffer [1959] Director/Managing Partner [German]; Stephen Brian Turton [1958] Managing Director

BPX Electro-Mechanical Company Limited
Incorporated: 8 November 1965 *Employees:* 144
Net Worth: £5,658,440 *Total Assets:* £12,699,287
Registered Office: Ross Walk, Leicester, LE4 5HA
Activities: Wholesale of electronic and telecommunications equipment and parts
Parent: BPX Group Limited
Officers: Roger William Collins, Secretary; Anthony Guy Collins [1959] Director; Roger William Collins [1959] Director; Sybil Marion Collins [1935] Director/Secretary

Bracken Midco1 PLC
Incorporated: 7 June 2016
Net Worth: £88,800,000 *Total Assets:* £383,700,000
Registered Office: Lake View, Lakeside, Cheadle, Cheshire, SK8 3GW
Activities: Activities of financial services holding companies
Parent: Bracken Topco Limited
Officers: Gary Derek Beckett, Secretary; Gary Derek Beckett [1969] Director; Henry Neville Moser [1949] Director

Bracken Midco2 Limited
Incorporated: 4 May 2016
Net Worth: £495,600,000 *Total Assets:* £731,699,968
Registered Office: Lake View, Lakeside, Cheadle, Cheshire, SK8 3GW
Activities: Activities of financial services holding companies
Parent: Bracken Midco1 PLC
Officers: Gary Derek Beckett, Secretary; Gary Derek Beckett [1969] Director; Henry Neville Moser [1949] Director

Bradbury & Son (Buxton) Limited
Incorporated: 13 September 1940 *Employees:* 235
Net Worth: £3,057,203 *Total Assets:* £22,004,224
Registered Office: Unit 2 Staden Lane, Buxton, Derbys, SK17 9RZ
Activities: Wholesale of dairy products, eggs and edible oils and fats
Parent: G. & M. Paul Limited
Officers: George Paul, Secretary; Christopher Chisnall [1976] Director/Sales & Marketing Manager; Stephen Dillon [1977] Finance Director; Michelle Jackson Hanstock [1968] Procurement and Supply Chain Director; Brian Leonard Murrell [1947] Director; George Paul [1949] Director/Cheese and Diary Produce; Richard John Paul [1970] Director/Sales Executive; Steven John Pritchard [1973] Sales Director

Bradfield School
Incorporated: 23 October 2012 *Employees:* 115
Net Worth: £17,957,478 *Total Assets:* £19,143,634
Registered Office: Bradfield School, Kirk Edge Road, Worrall, Sheffield, S35 0AE
Activities: General secondary education
Officers: Helen Louise Durdy, Secretary; Joanne Margeret Brook [1979] Director/Housewife; Jennifer Jane Callaghan [1986] Director/Teacher; Dr Ian Michael Gilbert [1968] Director/Headteacher; Susan Carol Gillott [1966] Director/Teaching Assistant; Hazel Mary Guy [1968] Director/Teacher; Dr Paul Stewart Husband [1970] Director/Research Fellow; Dr Anthony Lee Moody [1971] Director/Civil Servant; Peter Naldrett [1974] Director/Writer; Michelle Marie Nuttall [1983] Director/Civil Servant; Anita Padwagga [1974] Director/Senior IT Audit Manager; John David Austen Willington [1973] Director/Website Developer

Bradgate Containers (Holdings) Limited
Incorporated: 9 January 2002 *Employees:* 153
Net Worth: £5,298,716 *Total Assets:* £15,070,836
Registered Office: Leicester Road, Shepshed, Loughborough, Leics, LE12 9DF
Activities: Non-trading company
Officers: Danny Gallacher, Secretary; Danny Gallacher [1946] Director/Engineer; John Willis James [1934] Director/Engineer; William Alexander James [1938] Director/Engineer; Patrick Newell Stapleton [1950] Director/Engineer

Bradgate Containers Limited
Incorporated: 24 March 1982 *Employees:* 84
Net Worth: £2,611,881 *Total Assets:* £9,235,134
Registered Office: Leicester Road, Shepshed, Loughborough, Leics, LE12 9EG
Activities: Manufacture of other fabricated metal products n.e.c.
Parent: Bradgate Containers (Holdings) Limited
Officers: Danny Gallacher, Secretary; James Paul Bexon [1967] Sales Director; Adrian William Fox [1964] Technical Director; Danny Gallacher [1946] Director/Engineer; John Willis James [1934] Director/Engineer; William Alexander James [1938] Director/Engineer; Nicholas Charles Ryman [1953] Electrical Projects Director; Patrick Newell Stapleton [1950] Director/Engineer

Bradshaw Taylor Ltd.
Incorporated: 18 June 1935 *Employees:* 98
Net Worth: £9,845,792 *Total Assets:* £13,713,641
Registered Office: 16 Mill Street, Oakham, Rutland, LE15 6EA
Activities: Wholesale of clothing and footwear
Major Shareholder: Corry Edward Bradshaw Cavell-Taylor
Officers: Mercia Wakefield, Secretary; Corry Edward Bradshaw Cavell-Taylor [1961] Managing Director; Georgina Kirby [1979] Marketing Director; James Stewart McEuen [1969] Associate Director; Andrew Herbert Noel [1948] Director/Chartered Accountant; Sonia Prior [1971] Sales Director; Anne Mary Taylor [1934] Director; Mark Edward Taylor [1931] Director; Neil Jay Toothill [1974] Operations Director; Nicholas James Vance [1983] Director/Head of IT; Mercia Wakefield [1961] Director/Finance Controller

Brady Corporation Limited
Incorporated: 19 April 2001 *Employees:* 309
Net Worth: £37,424,000 *Total Assets:* £44,200,000
Registered Office: Wildmere Industrial Estate, Banbury, Oxon, OX16 3JU
Activities: Other service activities n.e.c.
Parent: B.I. (UK) Limited
Officers: Sally Felstead [1974] Director/General Manager; James Michael Nauman [1962] Director [American]; Aaron James Pearce [1970] Director [American]; Bart Henk Margriet Maria Vervinckt [1955] Director [Belgian]

Brady European Holdings Limited
Incorporated: 17 May 2005 *Employees:* 4
Net Worth: £63,182,780 *Total Assets:* £201,885,104
Registered Office: 14 Wildmere Industrial Estate, Banbury, Oxon, OX16 3JU
Activities: Activities of distribution holding companies
Officers: Sally Felstead [1974] Director/General Manager; James Michael Nauman [1962] Director [American]; Aaron James Pearce [1970] Director [American]; Bart Henk Margriet Maria Vervinckt [1955] Director [Belgian]; Brett Wilms [1974] Managing Director [Belgian]

Braeside Group Limited
Incorporated: 7 August 1998 *Employees:* 78
Previous: CBC Holdings UK Limited
Net Worth: £6,658,065 *Total Assets:* £15,245,118
Registered Office: 2 Franks Road, Bardon Hill, Coalville, Leics, LE67 1TT
Activities: Other business support service activities n.e.c.
Parent: Logson Holdings Limited
Officers: William Bingham Barnett [1976] Director; Alexander David Kelly [1967] Director; Bernard Neillus McDonnell [1959] Director [Irish]

Bramah Limited
Incorporated: 19 September 1930 *Employees:* 3
Net Worth: £34,710,632 *Total Assets:* £35,996,676
Registered Office: 274 Chesterfield Road, Dronfield, Derbys, S18 1XJ
Activities: Security dealing on own account
Officers: Michael Edward Jessop, Secretary; Jeremy Laurence Bramah [1959] Director; John Clive Bramah [1947] Director

C D Bramall Limited
Incorporated: 6 November 1947
Net Worth: £74,317,000 *Total Assets:* £115,396,000
Registered Office: Loxley House, 2 Oakwood Court, Little Oak Drive, Annesley, Nottingham, NG15 0DR
Activities: Sale of new cars and light motor vehicles
Officers: Richard James Maloney, Secretary; Martin Shaun Casha [1960] Director; Trevor Garry Finn [1957] Director; Timothy Paul Holden [1964] Director/Chartered Accountant

Bramall Quicks Dealerships Limited
Incorporated: 15 October 1965 *Employees:* 1,068
Net Worth: £4,367,000 *Total Assets:* £86,315,000
Registered Office: Loxley House, 2 Oakwood Court, Little Oak Drive, Annesley, Nottingham, NG15 0DR
Activities: Sale, maintenance and repair of motorcycles and related parts and accessories
Parent: Bramall Quicks Limited
Officers: Richard James Maloney, Secretary; Martin Shaun Casha [1960] Director; Trevor Garry Finn [1957] Director; Timothy Paul Holden [1964] Director/Chartered Accountant

Bramheath Limited
Incorporated: 7 November 2000 *Employees:* 2
Net Worth: £2,354,470 *Total Assets:* £22,790,800
Registered Office: Lime Tree House, Asthall, Burford, Oxon, OX18 4HW
Activities: Other letting and operating of own or leased real estate
Officers: Valerie MacKenzie, Secretary; Greg Graham MacKenzie [1956] Director/Property Investor [Australian]

Bramptonia Limited
Incorporated: 8 August 1939 *Employees:* 2
Net Worth Deficit: £6,229,274 *Total Assets:* £11,762,337
Registered Office: Studio F2/B, Witan Studios, 319 Upper Fourth Street, Milton Keynes, Bucks, MK9 1EH
Activities: Activities of head offices
Parent: Opal Ventures Ltd
Officers: Kanagaratnam Jeyakanthan, Secretary; Alan Henry English [1942] Director; Wendy Margaret English [1944] Director

Branchwater Developments Limited
Incorporated: 15 June 2004
Previous: Trewolla Limited
Net Worth Deficit: £392,161 *Total Assets:* £28,857,242
Registered Office: Cawthorne House, 19 Tivy Dale, Cawthorne, Barnsley, S Yorks, S75 4EJ
Activities: Other letting and operating of own or leased real estate
Parent: Blakeridge Holdings 2 Limited
Officers: Harriet Jane Hunter, Secretary/Director; Hannah Rose-Emma Binks [1986] Director; Pauline Binks [1945] Director; Richard David Binks [1943] Director; Helen Louisa Davies [1975] Director/Solicitor; Harriet Hunter [1978] Director/Manager

Brands Holdings Limited
Incorporated: 10 October 2000
Net Worth: £126,645,000 *Total Assets:* £172,236,992
Registered Office: Unit A, Brook Park East, Shirebrook, Derbys, NG20 8RY
Activities: Activities of other holding companies n.e.c.
Parent: Sports Direct International PLC
Officers: Cameron John Olsen, Secretary; Adedotun Ademola Adegoke [1973] Director/Senior Buyer; Rachel Isabel Lilian Stockton [1970] Director/Head of Customs and VAT

Bransby Horses
Incorporated: 11 February 1999 *Employees:* 106
Net Worth: £48,668,824 *Total Assets:* £49,104,004
Registered Office: Bransby House, Bransby, Lincoln, LN1 2PH
Activities: Non-trading company
Officers: Debbie Hall, Secretary; Elizabeth Anne Dawson [1963] Director/General Manager; Susan Jane Dolan [1959] Director/General Practitioner; Heather Carole Elston [1964] Director/Head of Animal & Equine Sciences; Carole Nora Fisher [1952] Director/Equestrian Farmer; Kathryn McFee [1975] Director/Learning and Development Advisor; Michael Steven Mitchell [1948] Director

Branston Academy Trust
Incorporated: 26 October 2010 *Employees:* 183
Net Worth: £9,191,439 *Total Assets:* £10,378,458
Registered Office: Branston Community Academy, Station Road, Branston, Lincoln, LN4 1LH
Activities: General secondary education
Officers: Marina Bell [1961] Director/Teacher; David Peter Boyd [1947] Director/Auditor; Pauline Louise Coombes [1969] Director/Childminder; David Peter Dearden [1966] Director/Bank Manager; Christopher Firth [1965] Director/Manager; Valerie Foottit [1954] Director/Charity Worker; Rebecca June Gilbert [1978] Director/Assistant Headteacher; Neil Harris [1952] Director; Robert Ledger [1961] Director/Retired; Malcolm John Norman [1957] Director/Operations Manager; Lisa Jane Sargeant [1970] Director/Student Support Officer; Dr Diana Thompson [1969] Director/Teacher; Joanne Turner [1970] Director/Principal of Secondary School; Mark Turner [1963] Director/Engineer; John Leslie Wilcox [1946] Director; Robert Arnold John Woollen [1934] Director

Branston Holdings Limited
Incorporated: 4 July 2006 *Employees:* 671
Net Worth: £38,998,000 *Total Assets:* £57,966,000
Registered Office: Mere Road, Branston, Lincoln, LN4 1NJ
Activities: Activities of head offices
Officers: James Windle, Secretary; Graeme Beattie [1955] Director; James Fitzroy Dean [1954] Director; John William Lockwood [1954] Director; Philip Guy McCracken [1948] Director; Brian Stein [1949] Director; Thomas James Truscott [1968] Director; Mark Willcox [1969] Director; James Windle [1979] Director

Branston Limited
Incorporated: 21 January 1994 *Employees:* 662
Net Worth: £34,778,000 *Total Assets:* £52,847,000
Registered Office: Mere Road, Branston, Lincoln, LN4 1NJ
Activities: Processing and preserving of potatoes
Parent: Branston Holdings Limited
Officers: James Windle, Secretary; John William Lockwood [1954] Director; Philip Guy McCracken [1948] Director; Thomas James Truscott [1968] Director; Mark Willcox [1969] Development Director; James Windle [1979] Director

R. Bratley (Quadring) Limited
Incorporated: 5 February 1962 *Employees:* 28
Net Worth: £4,568,046 *Total Assets:* £12,471,111
Registered Office: Quadring Eaudyke, Spalding, Lincs, PE11 4QB
Activities: Growing of cereals (except rice), leguminous crops and oil seeds
Shareholders: Carolyn Margaret Bratley; John Morris Bratley; Charlotte Emily Bratley
Officers: Carolyn Margaret Bratley, Secretary; Carolyn Margaret Bratley [1946] Director/Housewife; Charlotte Emily Bratley [1974] Director; John Morris Bratley [1943] Director/Farmer; Joseph Oliver Bratley [1973] Director/Farmer

B. Braun Avitum UK Limited
Incorporated: 5 February 2001 *Employees:* 259
Net Worth: £220,000 *Total Assets:* £12,657,000
Registered Office: B Braun Avitum UK Limited, Brookdale Road, Thorncliffe Park Estate, Chapeltown, Sheffield, S35 2PW
Activities: Other human health activities
Officers: Paul Henry Skelton, Secretary; Lisa Burns [1962] Director/Head of UK Group Human Resources; Christian Michael Clark [1964] Managing Director; Claire Louise Dawson-Hall [1980] Director/Financial Controller; Peter Stephen Griffiths [1963] Director/Financial Accountant; Hans Hux [1957] Director [German]; Michael Francis Parden [1975] Director; Paul Henry Skelton [1968] Director/Accountant

B. Braun Medical Limited
Incorporated: 14 September 1988 *Employees:* 557
Net Worth: £39,437,000 *Total Assets:* £83,172,000
Registered Office: Brookdale Road, Thorncliffe Park Estate, Chapeltown, Sheffield, S35 2PW
Activities: Other human health activities
Officers: Sir Andrew John Cash [1955] Director; Hans Hux [1957] Managing Director [German]; David Oates [1959] Director; Paul Henry Skelton [1968] Director; Paul Joseph Steel [1958] Director/Sales Manager

B Braun Sterilog Limited
Incorporated: 14 January 1980 *Employees:* 10
Net Worth Deficit: £12,423,000 *Total Assets:* £12,583,000
Registered Office: B Braun Sterilog Limited, Brookdale Road, Thorncliffe Park, Sheffield, S35 2PW
Activities: Other human health activities
Parent: B.Braun Medical Limited
Officers: Hans Hux [1957] Director [German]; Michael Francis Parden [1975] Operations Director; Paul Henry Skelton [1968] Director

Bravissimo Limited
Incorporated: 10 February 1997 *Employees:* 795
Net Worth: £14,460,692 *Total Assets:* £24,166,080
Registered Office: Imperial Court, Holly Walk, Leamington Spa, Warwicks, CV32 4YB
Activities: Retail sale of clothing in specialised stores
Shareholders: Sarah Jane Tremellen; Jonathan Michael Tremellen
Officers: Jonathan Michael Tremellen, Secretary; Jonathan Michael Tremellen [1965] Director; Sarah Jane Tremellen [1966] Director

Brayford Hotels Holdings Ltd
Incorporated: 7 April 2010 *Employees:* 139
Net Worth: £7,653,155 *Total Assets:* £49,497,020
Registered Office: 27-29 Lumley Avenue, Skegness, Lincs, PE25 2AT
Activities: Activities of head offices
Shareholders: Leigh Morris Hall; Dean Anthony Wann
Officers: Leigh Morris Hall, Secretary; Leigh Morris Hall [1969] Director; Dean Anthony Wann [1971] Director

Brayford Plastics Limited
Incorporated: 22 September 2005 *Employees:* 102
Net Worth: £3,342,253 *Total Assets:* £12,602,813
Registered Office: Horncastle Lane, Dunholme, Lincoln, LN2 3QF
Activities: Manufacture of plastic packing goods
Parent: Brayfour Limited
Officers: Jo Sztajnert, Secretary; Sean Michael Coxon [1968] Managing Director; John Andrew Lyon [1963] Director; Beverley Jayne Parr [1968] Director; Stephen James Woods [1974] Director

Brayfour Limited
Incorporated: 28 July 2015 *Employees:* 102
Net Worth: £3,342,719 *Total Assets:* £12,603,278
Registered Office: Horncastle Lane, Dunholme, Lincoln, LN2 3QF
Activities: Activities of production holding companies
Parent: I.G. Industries Holdings Limited
Officers: Jo Sztajnert, Secretary; Sean Michael Coxon [1968] Managing Director; John Andrew Lyon [1963] Director; Beverley Jayne Parr [1968] Director; Stephen James Woods [1974] Director

Breas Medical Limited
Incorporated: 16 March 2010
Previous: B & D Electromedical Limited
Net Worth: £9,204,898 *Total Assets:* £11,067,163
Registered Office: Barclays Bank Chambers, Bridge Street, Stratford upon Avon, Warwicks, CV37 6AH
Activities: Manufacture of medical and dental instruments and supplies
Parent: Breas Technologies (UK) Limited
Officers: Ola Jensell [1966] Director/SVP, CFO [Swedish]; Hongfei Jia [1967] Director/Business Executive [Canadian]

Breas Technologies (UK) Limited
Incorporated: 2 September 2014
Previous: PBM Technologies (UK) Limited
Net Worth: £10,117,330 *Total Assets:* £10,118,530
Registered Office: Barclays Bank Chambers, Bridge Street, Stratford upon Avon, Warwicks, CV37 6AH
Activities: Activities of other holding companies n.e.c.
Parent: Breas Technologies AB
Officers: Hongfei Jia [1967] Director/Business Executive [Canadian]

Brecknell, Willis & Co. Limited
Incorporated: 28 October 1935 *Employees:* 224
Net Worth: £20,321,684 *Total Assets:* £67,626,648
Registered Office: Howard House, Graycar Business Park, Barton Turn, Barton under Needwood, Burton on Trent, Staffs, DE13 8EN
Activities: Repair and maintenance of other transport equipment n.e.c.
Parent: Westinghouse Air Brake Technologies Corporation
Officers: Michael James Isaac, Secretary; Patrick David Dugan [1966] Director/Business Executive [American]; Johnathan Hugh Parker [1966] Director; David Michael Seitz [1965] Director/Business Executive [American]

Breedon Cement Limited
Incorporated: 7 November 2012 *Employees:* 384
Previous: Hope Cement Limited
Net Worth: £112,761,000 *Total Assets:* £223,208,992
Registered Office: Pinnacle House, Breedon Quarry, Breedon on the Hill, Derby, DE73 8AP
Activities: Quarrying of ornamental and building stone, limestone, gypsum, chalk and slate
Parent: Breedon Group PLC
Officers: Ross Edward McDonald, Secretary; Timothy John Billingham [1980] Director/Chartered Accountant; Ross Edward McDonald [1961] Director/Company Secretary; Patrick Robert Ward [1960] Director; Robert Wood [1966] Director/Chartered Accountant

Breedon Holdings Limited
Incorporated: 15 December 2008 *Employees:* 21
Net Worth Deficit: £41,108,000 *Total Assets:* £163,278,000
Registered Office: Pinnacle House, Breedon Quarry, Breedon on the Hill, Derby, DE73 8AP
Activities: Activities of head offices
Parent: Breedon Group PLC
Officers: Ross Edward McDonald, Company Secretary; Ross Edward McDonald [1961] Director/Company Secretary; Patrick Robert Ward [1960] Director/Chief Executive; Robert Wood [1966] Director/Chartered Accountant

Breedon House Nurseries Limited
Incorporated: 4 June 1996 *Employees:* 531
Net Worth: £7,160,851 *Total Assets:* £17,497,492
Registered Office: 1 Nottingham Road, Long Eaton, Nottingham, NG10 1HQ
Activities: Child day-care activities
Parent: Breedon House Group Limited
Officers: Catherine Griffin, Secretary; Adrian Leslie Mason, Secretary; Catherine Margaret Griffin [1957] Director/Day Nurseries; Adrian Leslie Mason [1970] Director; Julia Mason [1973] Director

Breedon House Properties Limited
Incorporated: 16 May 2007 *Employees:* 2
Net Worth: £6,253,155 *Total Assets:* £17,657,660
Registered Office: 1 Nottingham Road, Long Eaton, Nottingham, NG10 1HQ
Activities: Other letting and operating of own or leased real estate
Parent: Breedon House Group Limited
Officers: Catherine Griffin, Secretary; Adrian Leslie Mason [1970] Director; Hugh Mason [1941] Director

Breedon Southern Limited
Incorporated: 30 June 1919 *Employees:* 918
Previous: Breedon Aggregates England Limited
Net Worth: £138,988,000 *Total Assets:* £297,673,984
Registered Office: Pinnacle House, Breedon Quarry, Breedon on the Hill, Derby, DE73 8AP
Activities: Quarrying of ornamental and building stone, limestone, gypsum, chalk and slate
Parent: Breedon Group PLC
Officers: Ross Edward McDonald, Company Secretary; Elizabeth Helen Lyon [1983] Director/Chartered Accountant; Ross Edward McDonald [1961] Director/Company Secretary; Michael Paul Pearce [1964] Director/Chief Executive; Patrick Robert Ward [1960] Director; Robert Wood [1966] Director/Chartered Accountant

Brelade Estates Ltd
Incorporated: 4 May 2005 *Employees:* 3
Net Worth: £15,074,934 *Total Assets:* £30,987,112
Registered Office: 219 Burton Road, Derby, DE23 6AE
Activities: Financial intermediation not elsewhere classified
Shareholder: Nigel Stuart Straw
Officers: Nigel Stuart Straw, Secretary; Nigel Stuart Straw [1954] Director; Sharon Dawn Straw [1957] Director

Brentford Phase II LLP
Incorporated: 21 April 2016
Net Worth: £16,574,000 *Total Assets:* £43,948,000
Registered Office: First Floor, North Station House, 500 Elder Gate, Milton Keynes, Bucks, MK9 1BB

Bridge Leisure Bidco Limited
Incorporated: 3 July 2014 *Employees:* 3
Net Worth Deficit: £8,610,928 *Total Assets:* £61,511,060
Registered Office: 31 & 32 Shenley Pavilions, Chalkdell Drive, Shenley Wood, Milton Keynes, Bucks, MK5 6LB
Activities: Activities of head offices
Parent: Bridge Leisure Midco Ltd
Officers: Simon John Elliott [1969] Director/Investment Professional; Andrew Stephen Howe [1968] Director/Investment Professional; Simon Jamie Williams [1972] Director/Investment Professional

Bridge Leisure Finco Limited
Incorporated: 24 June 2014 *Employees:* 3
Net Worth Deficit: £9,412,108 *Total Assets:* £30,725,428
Registered Office: 31 & 32 Shenley Pavilions, Chalkdell Drive, Shenley Wood, Milton Keynes, Bucks, MK5 6LB
Activities: Activities of head offices
Parent: Bridge Leisure Topco Limited
Officers: Simon John Elliott [1969] Director/Investment Professional; Andrew Stephen Howe [1968] Director/Investment Professionals; Simon Williams [1972] Director

Bridge Leisure Midco Limited
Incorporated: 24 June 2014 *Employees:* 3
Net Worth: £75,465 *Total Assets:* £30,684,620
Registered Office: 31 & 32 Shenley Pavilions, Chalkdell Drive, Shenley Wood, Milton Keynes, Bucks, MK5 6LB
Activities: Activities of head offices
Parent: Bridge Leisure Finco Limited
Officers: Simon John Elliott [1969] Director/Investment Professional; Andrew Stephen Howe [1968] Director/Investment Professional; Simon Jamie Williams [1972] Director/Investment Professional

Bridge Leisure Topco Limited
Incorporated: 12 June 2014 *Employees:* 369
Net Worth Deficit: £13,813,769 *Total Assets:* £68,786,960
Registered Office: 31 & 32 Shenley Pavilions, Chalkdell Drive, Shenley Wood, Milton Keynes, Bucks, MK5 6LB
Activities: Activities of head offices
Officers: Simon John Elliott [1969] Director/Investment Professional; Andrew Stephen Howe [1968] Director/Investment Professional; Richard Andrew Hunt [1961] Director/Investment Professional; Alastair William Muirhead [1953] Director; William Skinner [1984] Director/Investment Professional; Simon Williams [1972] Director/Investment Professional

Bridgebank Holdings Limited
Incorporated: 10 November 2016 *Employees:* 40
Net Worth: £6,364,874 *Total Assets:* £18,738,084
Registered Office: Unit 3 Sherwood Oaks Close, Sherwood Oaks Business Park, Mansfield, Notts, NG18 4TB
Activities: Other business support service activities n.e.c.
Shareholders: Thomas Patrick Ryan; Andrew Philip Franklin
Officers: Andrew Philip Franklin, Secretary; Andrew Philip Franklin [1968] Director; Thomas Patrick Ryan [1969] Director

Bridgebank Limited
Incorporated: 7 October 1986 *Employees:* 40
Net Worth: £8,151,344 *Total Assets:* £19,964,268
Registered Office: Unit 3 Sherwood Oaks Close, Sherwood Oaks Business Park, Mansfield, Notts, NG18 4TB
Activities: Construction of other civil engineering projects n.e.c.
Shareholders: Thomas Ryan; Andrew Philip Franklin
Officers: Andrew Philip Franklin, Secretary; Andrew Philip Franklin [1968] Finance Director; Thomas Patrick Ryan [1969] Construction Director

Bridgestone UK Limited
Incorporated: 1 February 1972 *Employees:* 209
Net Worth: £38,153,000 *Total Assets:* £80,055,000
Registered Office: Athena Drive, Tachbrook Park, Warwick, CV34 6UX
Activities: Wholesale trade of motor vehicle parts and accessories
Parent: Bridgestone Corporation
Officers: Laurent Pascal Dartoux [1964] Director/Businessman [French]; Robin Shaw [1965] Regional Managing Director

Bridgeway Consulting Limited
Incorporated: 10 December 1997 *Employees:* 393
Net Worth: £3,727,985 *Total Assets:* £9,180,867
Registered Office: Bridgeway House, 2 Riverside Way, Nottingham, NG2 1DP
Activities: Construction of railways and underground railways
Major Shareholder: Pino De Rosa
Officers: Pino de Rosa, Secretary/Consulting Engineer; Pino de Rosa [1967] Director/Consulting Engineer

Bridging Finance Limited
Incorporated: 1 March 1996
Net Worth: £6,027,000 *Total Assets:* £40,507,000
Registered Office: Lake View, Lakeside, Cheadle, Cheshire, SK8 3GW
Activities: Credit granting by non-deposit taking finance houses and other specialist consumer credit grantors
Parent: Together Financial Services Limited
Officers: Sarah Elizabeth Batt, Secretary; Gary Derek Beckett [1969] Director; Wayne Bowser [1952] Director; Marc Richard Goldberg [1971] Director; Robert Michael McTighe [1953] Director; Henry Neville Moser [1949] Director

Bridgstock Limited
Incorporated: 6 December 2007 *Employees:* 92
Net Worth: £26,696,000 *Total Assets:* £31,931,000
Registered Office: Controlpoint House, Carrwood Road, Chesterfield, Derbys, S41 9QB
Activities: Other professional, scientific and technical activities n.e.c.
Officers: Maria Luise Warwick, Secretary; Helen Annabelle Boanas [1977] Director; Petronilla Monica Mary Bridgstock [1947] Company Secretary/Director; Stephen William Hamshaw [1970] Director; Nicholas Peter Mark [1974] Director

Bridon Holdings Limited
Incorporated: 23 August 2010 *Employees:* 2
Net Worth Deficit: £2,859,000 *Total Assets:* £25,130,000
Registered Office: Icon Building Firstpoint, Balby Carr Bank, Doncaster, S Yorks, DN4 5JQ
Activities: Activities of head offices
Parent: Bridon Limited
Officers: Claudia Maria Griffin [1967] Director/Chief Financial Officer [German]; Luc Vankemmelbeke [1971] Director/Executive Vice President [Belgian]

Bridon International Ltd.
Incorporated: 7 August 1946 *Employees:* 593
Net Worth Deficit: £34,904,000 *Total Assets:* £76,623,000
Registered Office: Icon Building, First Point, Balby Carr Bank, Doncaster, S Yorks, DN4 5JQ
Activities: Manufacture of wire products, chain and springs
Parent: Bridon Limited
Officers: Claudia Maria Griffin [1967] Director/Chief Financial Officer [German]; Luc Vankemmelbeke [1971] Director/Executive Vice President [Belgian]

Bridon Limited
Incorporated: 6 June 1924 *Employees:* 2
Net Worth: £38,266,000 *Total Assets:* £38,618,000
Registered Office: Icon Building, First Point, Balby Carr Bank, Doncaster, S Yorks, DN4 5JQ
Activities: Activities of head offices
Parent: Bridon-Bekaert Ropes Group
Officers: Claudia Maria Griffin [1967] Director/Chief Financial Officer [German]; Luc Vankemmelbeke [1971] Director/Executive Vice President [Belgian]

Bridon-Bekaert Ropes Group (UK) Ltd
Incorporated: 4 November 2014 *Employees:* 4
Previous: Bridge Holdco 1 Ltd.
Net Worth: £185,457,056 *Total Assets:* £186,019,248
Registered Office: Ground Floor, Icon Building, Balby Carr Bank, Doncaster, S Yorks, DN4 5JQ
Activities: Activities of head offices
Parent: BBRG (Purchaser) Ltd
Officers: Claudia Maria Griffin [1967] Director/Chief Financial Officer [German]

Bridon-Bekaert Ropes Group Ltd
Incorporated: 3 October 2014
Previous: Bridge Bidco Ltd.
Net Worth Deficit: £283,542,016 *Total Assets:* £17,723,000
Registered Office: Ground Floor, Icon Building, Balby Carr Bank, Doncaster, S Yorks, DN4 5JQ
Activities: Activities of head offices
Parent: BBRG Finance (UK) Limited
Officers: Claudia Maria Griffin [1967] Director/Chief Financial Officer [German]; Luc Vankemmelbeke [1971] Director/Executive Vice President [Belgian]

Brigam Limited
Incorporated: 21 May 2003 *Employees:* 265
Net Worth: £12,553,221 *Total Assets:* £20,485,224
Registered Office: Groveland House, Grovelands Industrial Estate, Longford Road, Exhall, Coventry, Warwicks, CV7 9NE
Activities: Activities of head offices
Major Shareholder: Sulakhan Sahota
Officers: Shashank Dhawan, Secretary; Shashank Dhawan [1970] Director and Company Secretary; Lynette Ann Sahota [1961] Director; Sulakhan Sahota [1960] Director

Brigantia Learning Trust Limited
Incorporated: 26 April 2013 *Employees:* 404
Previous: Hinde House Multi Academy Trust
Net Worth: £42,709,264 *Total Assets:* £53,136,696
Registered Office: Hinde House 3-16 School, Secondary Phase, Shiregreen Lane, Sheffield, S5 6AG
Activities: Pre-primary education
Officers: Jacqueline Simpson, Secretary; Kevin Leslie Clifford [1961] Director/Semi-Retired/Self-Employed Registered Nurse; David William Drayson [1950] Director/Pharmacist; Tracey Priestley [1964] Director/HR Officer; Nicola Rawlins [1972] Director/University Manager; Jane Louise Robinson [1971] Director/Business Consultant; Alison Jane Warner [1947] Director; Joshua Joseph Wilson [1996] Director/Customer Relations Advisor

Briggs & Forrester (UK) Limited
Incorporated: 6 April 2016 *Employees:* 780
Net Worth: £11,570,180 *Total Assets:* £133,097,728
Registered Office: Bembridge House, Bembridge Drive, Kingsthorpe, Northampton, NN2 6LZ
Activities: Activities of head offices
Shareholder: B & F Trustees Ltd, Trustee of The B & F EBT
Officers: John Charles Simson, Secretary; Duncan Nicholas Benedetti [1974] Director; Paul Burton [1963] Director; Ian Francis Lawrence [1962] Director; Michael Philip Stanton [1953] Director

Briggs & Forrester Engineering Services Limited
Incorporated: 5 April 1973 *Employees:* 323
Net Worth: £12,456,099 *Total Assets:* £59,445,916
Registered Office: Bembridge House, Bembridge Drive, Kingsthorpe, Northampton, NN2 6LZ
Activities: Electrical installation
Parent: Briggs & Forrester Group Ltd
Officers: John Charles Simson, Secretary; Paul Burton [1963] Director/Contracts Manager; Neil Franklin Greensill [1963] Director; Ian Francis Lawrence [1962] Director; Mark Payne [1964] Director/Contracts Manager; Alec George Sarjeant [1967] Director/Surveyor; Michael Philip Stanton [1953] Director

Briggs & Forrester Group Limited
Incorporated: 19 December 2001 *Employees:* 780
Net Worth: £26,331,748 *Total Assets:* £147,858,352
Registered Office: Bembridge House, Bembridge Drive, Kingsthorpe, Northampton, NN2 6LZ
Activities: Activities of head offices
Parent: Briggs & Forrester Limited
Officers: John Charles Simson, Secretary; Duncan Nicholas Benedetti [1974] Director; Paul Burton [1963] Director/Contract Manager; Ian Francis Lawrence [1962] Director; Graham John Longden Stanton [1957] Director; Michael Philip Stanton [1953] Director/Accountant

Briggs & Forrester Limited
Incorporated: 20 June 2006 *Employees:* 4
Net Worth: £1 *Total Assets:* £20,986,168
Registered Office: Bembridge House, Bembridge Drive, Kingsthorpe, Northampton, NN2 6LZ
Activities: Activities of head offices
Parent: Briggs & Forrester (UK) Ltd
Officers: John Charles Simson, Secretary; Paul Burton [1963] Director; Graham John Longden Stanton [1957] Director; Michael Philip Stanton [1953] Director

Briggs & Forrester Living Limited
Incorporated: 3 December 1984 *Employees:* 280
Previous: Briggs & Forrester (MEP) Limited
Net Worth: £10,816,978 *Total Assets:* £74,703,144
Registered Office: Bembridge House, Bembridge Drive, Kingsthorpe, Northampton, NN2 6LZ
Activities: Electrical installation
Parent: Briggs & Forrester Group Ltd
Officers: John Charles Simson, Secretary; Duncan Nicholas Benedetti [1974] Director; Paul Burton [1963] Director; Andrew Cooper [1964] Commercial Director; Ian Hardy [1968] Director/Building Services Manager; Michael Philip Stanton [1953] Director; Justin Van Walwyk [1971] Director

Briggs of Burton PLC
Incorporated: 27 November 1986 *Employees:* 134
Net Worth: £5,934,000 *Total Assets:* £21,971,000
Registered Office: Briggs of Burton PLC, Briggs House, Trent Works, Burton on Trent, Staffs, DE14 2LH
Activities: Manufacture of machinery for food, beverage and tobacco processing
Parent: Briggs Holdings Limited
Officers: Nathan Beddoe, Secretary; Nathan Beddoe [1970] Finance Director [Australian]; Robert John Buxton [1971] Engineering Director; George Matthew Crombie [1982] Director/Chartered Engineer; Anthony George Wagstaff [1960] Director/Chartered Engineer

Bright Horizons Family Solutions Limited
Incorporated: 15 December 1988 *Employees:* 5,333
Net Worth: £138,768,000 *Total Assets:* £177,443,008
Registered Office: 2 Crown Court, Rushden, Northants, NN10 6BS
Activities: Pre-primary education
Parent: BHFS Two Limited
Officers: Stephen Kramer, Secretary; Elizabeth Boland [1959] Director/Chief Financial Officer [American]; Stephen Dreier [1942] Director/Executive [American]; Dave Lissy [1965] Director/Chief Executive Officer [American]; James Walter Tugendhat [1971] Managing Director, International

Bright Tribe Trust
Incorporated: 16 July 2012 *Employees:* 564
Net Worth: £57,337,000 *Total Assets:* £68,817,000
Registered Office: Suite 9, 3rd Floor, Mansion House, 173-191 Wellington Road South, Stockport, Cheshire, SK1 3UA
Activities: Primary education
Officers: Angela Jean Barry [1962] Director/Executive Headteacher; Sarah Margaret Brown [1963] Director; Rupert Edinmore Gather [1962] Director; Stephen Christopher Gough [1979] Director; Nicolette King [1947] Director; Thomas James Maddison [1963] Director; Richard Eugene McDonnell [1958] Director

Brighterkind (CB) Limited
Incorporated: 8 March 2013 *Employees:* 1,950
Previous: Four Seasons (CB) Limited
Net Worth: £61,219,000 *Total Assets:* £155,172,992
Registered Office: Norcliffe House, Station Road, Wilmslow, Cheshire, SK9 1BU
Activities: Other human health activities
Parent: Brighterkind (PC) Limited
Officers: Abigail Mattison, Secretary; Stephen Mark Julius [1959] Director; Justin King [1961] Director; Ryan Stuart MacAskill [1975] Director; Gregory Laurence Newman [1988] Director/Investment Professional; Jeremy Robert Arthur Richardson [1970] Director; Dr Maureen Claire Royston [1960] Director; Phillip Gary Thomas [1978] Director

Brighterkind (MW) Limited
Incorporated: 8 March 2013
Previous: Four Seasons (MW) Limited
Net Worth: £34,123,000 *Total Assets:* £164,800,000
Registered Office: Norcliffe House, Station Road, Wilmslow, Cheshire, SK9 1BU
Activities: Other human health activities
Parent: Brighterkind (CB) Limited
Officers: Abigail Mattison, Secretary; Ryan Stuart MacAskill [1975] Director; Gregory Laurence Newman [1988] Director/Investment Professional; Jeremy Robert Arthur Richardson [1970] Director; Dr Maureen Claire Royston [1960] Director; Phillip Gary Thomas [1978] Director

Brighterkind (PC) Limited
Incorporated: 8 March 2013 *Employees:* 6
Previous: Four Seasons (PC) Limited
Net Worth: £34,691,000 *Total Assets:* £34,691,000
Registered Office: Norcliffe House, Station Road, Wilmslow, Cheshire, SK9 1BU
Activities: Other human health activities
Officers: Abigail Mattison, Secretary; Ryan Stuart MacAskill [1975] Director; Gregory Laurence Newman [1988] Director/Investment Professional; Dr Maureen Claire Royston [1960] Director; Benjamin Robert Taberner [1972] Director/Chartered Accountant

Brighterkind Limited
Incorporated: 7 February 2007 *Employees:* 20
Previous: Optimum Care Limited
Net Worth Deficit: £31,470,000 *Total Assets:* £98,156,000
Registered Office: Norcliffe House, Station Road, Wilmslow, Cheshire, SK9 1BU
Activities: Activities of head offices
Parent: Brighterkind (MW) Limited
Officers: Abigail Mattison, Secretary; Ryan Stuart MacAskill [1975] Director; Gregory Laurence Newman [1988] Director/Investment Professional; Jeremy Robert Arthur Richardson [1970] Director; Maureen Claire Royston [1960] Director; Phillip Gary Thomas [1978] Director

Brighton Marina Block F1 Ltd
Incorporated: 11 September 2014
Net Worth Deficit: £124,567 *Total Assets:* £11,111,849
Registered Office: 37f Monument Park, Chalgrove, Oxford, OX44 7RW
Activities: Buying and selling of own real estate
Major Shareholder: Gabriel Michel El-Kassir
Officers: Nicholas Vincent Walsh, Secretary; Gabriel Michel El-Kassir [1956] Director

Brightwake Limited
Incorporated: 7 March 1978 *Employees:* 203
Net Worth: £6,649,269 *Total Assets:* £10,610,736
Registered Office: Sidings Road, Lowmoor Industrial Estate, Kirkby in Ashfield, Notts, NG17 7JZ
Activities: Manufacture of medical and dental instruments and supplies
Major Shareholder: Kenneth Alfred Allen
Officers: Victoria Claire Allen, Secretary; Kenneth Alfred Allen [1948] Director; Stephen Cotton [1966] Director/Development Manager; Valerie England [1958] Director

Brington North LLP
Incorporated: 29 January 2016
Net Worth: £7,570,768 *Total Assets:* £18,038,368
Registered Office: James Hall, Parsons Green, St Ives, Cambs, PE27 4AA

Brioche Pasquier U.K. Limited
Incorporated: 24 July 2000 *Employees:* 101
Net Worth: £7,618,810 *Total Assets:* £44,564,856
Registered Office: 8 Garamonde Drive, Wymbush, Milton Keynes, Bucks, MK8 8DF
Activities: Manufacture of bread; manufacture of fresh pastry goods and cakes
Officers: Pascal Pasquier [1957] Director [French]; Fabrice Sciumbata [1968] Director [French]

Brisbane House Limited
Incorporated: 12 February 2001
Net Worth: £11,258,083 *Total Assets:* £32,166,712
Registered Office: Springfield House, Water Lane, Wilmslow, Cheshire, SK9 5BG
Activities: Other letting and operating of own or leased real estate
Parent: Dean Property Group Limited
Officers: Michael Edward O'Donnell, Secretary; Jonathan Charles Patrick Beever [1963] Director/Property Manager; Michael Edward O'Donnell [1969] Director/Property Investment; James Anthony Wild [1941] Director/Property Investment

Bristol Fruit Sales (Market) Limited
Incorporated: 30 June 1971 *Employees:* 339
Net Worth: £6,155,000 *Total Assets:* £14,458,000
Registered Office: Total Produce, Enterprise Way, Pinchbeck, Spalding, Lincs, PE11 3YR
Activities: Wholesale of fruit and vegetables
Parent: Total Produce Limited
Officers: Mark Christopher Owen, Secretary; Andrew Roger Allmond [1944] Director; Jacinta Frances Devine [1972] Director [Irish]; Nicholas George Matthews [1970] Managing Director; Francis Gerard McKernan [1962] Director; Mark Christopher Owen [1965] Director; Denis Leslie Punter [1953] Director

Bristol Novelty Limited
Incorporated: 6 April 1983 *Employees:* 39
Net Worth: £9,255,214 *Total Assets:* £9,668,483
Registered Office: Rubie's House, 3-4 Moses Winter Way, Wallingford, Oxon, OX10 9FE
Activities: Wholesale of clothing and footwear
Shareholders: Marc Beige; Howard Beige
Officers: Marc Beige, Secretary; Christopher Royston Bater [1962] Director/Novelty Wholesaler; Kevin James Bater [1966] Director/Novelty Wholesaler; Howard Beige [1958] Director/Retailer [American]; Marc Patrick Beige [1949] Director/Retailer [American]; Christopher John Shute Isitt [1956] Director

Brit de Vere Limited
Incorporated: 7 September 2016
Net Worth: £2,676,145 *Total Assets:* £12,938,395
Registered Office: Silbury Court, 420 Silbury Boulevard, Milton Keynes, Bucks, MK9 2AF
Activities: Development of building projects
Major Shareholder: Alan Stewart Kennedy
Officers: Dominic Augustine de Vere [1974] Director; Alan Stewart Kennedy [1958] Director

Brita Water Filter Systems Limited
Incorporated: 25 March 1992 *Employees:* 112
Net Worth: £13,284,677 *Total Assets:* £25,718,566
Registered Office: Brita House, 9 Granville Way, Bicester, Oxon, OX26 4JT
Activities: Wholesale of household goods (other than musical instruments) n.e.c
Officers: Hanns Jochen Siegrist, Secretary; Markus Hankammer [1968] Director [German]; Sarah Louise Taylor [1974] Managing Director; Neal Whitfield [1970] Managing Director of Operations

Britcon (UK) Limited
Incorporated: 26 January 1990 *Employees:* 90
Net Worth: £5,491,193 *Total Assets:* £15,462,231
Registered Office: 26-30 Midland Road, Scunthorpe, N Lincs, DN16 1DQ
Activities: Construction of commercial buildings
Shareholder: Derrick Thomas Hunt
Officers: Gloria Hunt, Secretary; Paul Clarkson [1966] Construction Director; Nicholas Irwin Evans [1959] Director/Engineering Manager; Derrick Thomas Hunt [1948] Director/Civil Engineer; Gloria Patricia Hunt [1949] Director/Secretary; Shaun Antony Hunt [1970] Director/Contracts Manager; John Whitmore [1961] Director/Senior Estimator

British Aluminium Limited
Incorporated: 27 April 2000
Net Worth: £32,192,000 *Total Assets:* £32,226,000
Registered Office: 26a Atlas Way, Sheffield, S4 7QQ
Activities: Aluminium production
Parent: Arconic Manufacturing (GB) Limited
Officers: Petra Papinniemi-Ainger, Secretary; Dr Kay Louise Dowdall [1969] Director/Accountant; Lluis Maria Fargas Mas [1966] Director/Lawyer [Spanish]

British Bakels Limited
Incorporated: 25 February 1947 *Employees:* 196
Net Worth: £16,283,000 *Total Assets:* £27,791,000
Registered Office: Granville Way, off Launton Road, Bicester, Oxon, OX26 4JT
Activities: Manufacture of other food products n.e.c.
Shareholders: Irene Siri Bakels-Noreen; Armin Ulrich; Christoph Ebersberg; Duncan Loney; Jurg Waeffler
Officers: Keith Houliston [1955] Director; David Kinney [1956] Director [Irish]; Paul Lawson Thomas Morrow [1955] Director; Armin Ulrich [1949] Director [Swiss]

British Business Bank PLC
Incorporated: 18 July 2013 *Employees:* 258
Net Worth: £1,354,162,048 *Total Assets:* £1,679,761,024
Registered Office: Steel City House, West Street, Sheffield, S1 2GQ
Activities: Activities of other holding companies n.e.c.
Parent: The Secretary of State for Business, Energy & Industrial Strategy
Officers: Shanika Amarasekara, Secretary; Neeta Avnash Kaur Atkar [1965] Director/Chief Risk Officer; Jonathan Britton [1954] Director/Chartered Accountant; Christopher Newton Fox [1970] Director/Chief Financial Officer; Jonathan Piers Daniel Linney [1971] Director/Investor; Patrick John Magee [1970] Director/Banker [Irish]; Christina Margaret McComb [1956] Director; Keith Charles William Morgan [1963] Director; Amanda Jane Rendle [1963] Director; Ceri Ivor Daniel Smith [1973] Director/Civil Servant; Lord Robert Haldane Smith [1944] Director

British Business Finance Ltd
Incorporated: 18 June 2014
Net Worth: £45,996,000 *Total Assets:* £236,804,992
Registered Office: Steel City House, West Street, Sheffield, S1 2GQ
Activities: Fund management activities
Parent: British Business Bank PLC
Officers: Neeta Avnash Kaur Atkar [1965] Director/Chief Risk Officer; Jonathan Britton [1954] Director; Christopher Newton Fox [1970] Director/Chief Financial Officer; Jonathan Piers Daniel Linney [1971] Director/Investor; Patrick John Magee [1970] Director/Banker [Irish]; Christina Margaret McComb [1956] Director; Keith Charles William Morgan [1963] Director; Amanda Jane Rendle [1963] Director; Ceri Ivor Daniel Smith [1973] Director/Civil Servant; Lord Robert Haldane Smith [1944] Director

British Business Investments Ltd
Incorporated: 18 June 2014 *Employees:* 14
Previous: British Business Bank Investments Ltd
Net Worth: £1,259,362,944 *Total Assets:* £1,277,634,944
Registered Office: Steel City House, West Street, Sheffield, S1 2GQ
Activities: Fund management activities
Parent: British Business Bank PLC
Officers: Shanika Amarasekara, Secretary; Sara Jane Halbard [1961] Director/Business Consultant; Catherine Elizabeth Lewis La Torre [1965] Director; Keith Charles William Morgan [1963] Director; Francis David Small [1958] Director/Chartered Accountant

British Drilling and Freezing Company Limited
Incorporated: 31 July 1989 *Employees:* 84
Net Worth: £11,531,150 *Total Assets:* £12,765,735
Registered Office: Colwick Industrial Estate, Colwick, Nottingham, NG4 2BB
Activities: Extraction of crude petroleum
Major Shareholder: Peter James Wheelhouse
Officers: David Miller, Secretary; Howard William Mew [1957] Director/Drilling Engineer; Graham Saunby [1961] Director/Drilling Manager; Peter James Wheelhouse [1957] Managing Director

British Horse Society (The)
Incorporated: 5 November 1947 *Employees:* 117
Net Worth: £8,689,000 *Total Assets:* £12,089,000
Registered Office: The British Horse Society, Abbey Park, Stareton, Kenilworth, Warwicks, CV8 2XZ
Activities: Sports and recreation education
Officers: Martin Clemmey [1960] Director/Management Consultant; Jane Amanda Domhill [1955] Director/Management Consultant; Kirsty Handel [1972] Director/Financial Controller; Kenneth Charles Law [1954] Director/Senior Safety Professional; David Barclay Sheerin [1977] Director/Chief Instructor of a BHS Approved Riding School; Sarah Garneta Simpson [1960] Director/Freelance Trainer; Diane Dorothy Tranter [1951] Director/Graphic Designer - PT & Riding Instructor - PT; Eva-Lotta Von Der Heyde [1959] Sales Director [Swedish]; Christine Mary Worthington [1954] Director/Equine Coach

British Journal of Anaesthesia
Incorporated: 26 October 2007 *Employees:* 11
Net Worth: £18,316,224 *Total Assets:* £20,020,528
Registered Office: Department CVS, Leicester Royal Infirmary, Infirmary Square, Leicester, LE1 5WW
Activities: Other education n.e.c.
Officers: Professor Helen Frances Galley, Secretary; Michael Brown [1972] Director/Publishing Consultancy; Professor Helen Frances Galley [1962] Director/Professor of Anaesthesia and Intensive Care; Dr Simon James Howell [1958] Director/Senior Lecturer in Anaesthesia; Professor David George Lambert [1963] Director/Professor of Anaesthetic Pharmacology; Professor David John Rowbotham [1955] Director/Professor of Anaesthesia; Professor Michel Maria Roger Fernand Struys [1966] Director/Professor of Anaesthesia [Belgian]

British Polythene Industries Limited
Incorporated: 16 March 1910 *Employees:* 8
Previous: British Polythene Industries PLC
Net Worth: £80,900,000 *Total Assets:* £194,800,000
Registered Office: Sapphire House, Crown Way, Rushden, Northants, NN10 6FB
Activities: Manufacture of other plastic products
Parent: RPC 2017 Holding Company Limited
Officers: Nicholas David Martin Giles, Secretary; Franciscus Lodewijk Paulus Doorenbosch [1964] Director [Dutch]; David George Duthie [1956] Finance Director; Andrew Samuel Green [1964] Director; Simon John Kesterton [1973] Director; Petrus Rudolf Maria Vervaat [1965] Director [Dutch]

British Polythene Limited
Incorporated: 17 March 1939 *Employees:* 1,321
Net Worth Deficit: £500,000 *Total Assets:* £184,900,000
Registered Office: Sapphire House, Crown Way, Rushden, Northants, NN10 6FB
Activities: Manufacture of other plastic products
Parent: British Polythene Industries Limited
Officers: Nicholas David Martin Giles, Secretary; Franciscus Lodewijk Paulus Doorenbosch [1964] Director [Dutch]; David George Duthie [1956] Director/Financial Controller; Dr Andrew Samuel Green [1964] Director; Simon John Kesterton [1973] Director; Petrus Rudolf Maria Vervaat [1965] Director [Dutch]

British Pregnancy Advisory Service
Incorporated: 26 March 1984 *Employees:* 705
Net Worth: £13,991,000 *Total Assets:* £17,824,000
Registered Office: 20 Timothys Bridge Road, Stratford Enterprise Park, Stratford upon Avon, Warwicks, CV37 9BF
Activities: Specialists medical practice activities
Officers: Ann Marie Furedi, Secretary; Amanda Callaghan [1964] Corporate Affairs Director; John Spencer Collier [1945] Director/Certified Chartered Accountant, Consultant; Dr David Munro Dickson [1954] Director/Consultant Anaesthetist; Professor Calliope Christina Samoulla Farsides [1959] Director/University Lecturer; Dr Clare Gerada [1959] Director/Doctor; Annabelle Frances Glasier [1950] Director/Research Professor; Dr Lucy Ann Moore [1960] Director; Sanjay Shah [1963] Director/Chief Financial Officer; Professor Sally Sheldon [1967] Director/Professor of Law; Anne Jane Shevas [1956] Director Head of Media Relations, HMRC; Professor Catherine Lilian Warwick [1952] Director/General Secretary Royal College of Midwives

British Racing Drivers Club Limited (The)
Incorporated: 23 July 1931 *Employees:* 158
Net Worth: £8,716,000 *Total Assets:* £39,565,000
Registered Office: Silverstone Circuit, Silverstone, Towcester, Northants, NN12 8TN
Activities: Operation of sports facilities
Officers: Generald Mark Couldrake, Secretary; Nick Adams [1948] Director/Insurance Loss Adjuster; Lord Maxwell William Beaverbrook [1951] Director; John Albert Martin Grant [1945] Director; Harry Martin Handkammer [1952] Development Director; Timothy Jason Plato [1967] Director; Gordon William Shedden [1979] Director; Philip Nigel Walker [1957] Director

British Steel Holdings Limited
Incorporated: 17 May 2016 *Employees:* 5,395
Net Worth: £79,249,000 *Total Assets:* £897,830,976
Registered Office: Administration Building, Brigg Road, Scunthorpe, N Lincs, DN16 1BP
Activities: Manufacture of basic iron and steel and of ferro-alloys
Shareholders: Marc Joseph Meyohas; Nathaniel Jerome Meyohas
Officers: Damian Paul Hargreaves, Secretary; Antonius Wilhelmus Marcus Jozef Deelen [1965] Director/Chief Marketing Officer [Dutch]; Daniel Moshe Goldstein [1978] Corporate Director; Samuel Peter Hancock [1980] Director; Roland Junck [1955] Director/Chairman [Luxembourger]; Marc Joseph Meyohas [1971] Director [French]; Generald Reichmann [1976] Director/Chief Financial Officer [Austrian]

British Steel Limited
Incorporated: 13 February 2015 *Employees:* 4,238
Net Worth: £18,892,000 *Total Assets:* £724,134,016
Registered Office: Administration Building, Brigg Road, Scunthorpe, N Lincs, DN16 1BP
Activities: Manufacture of basic iron and steel and of ferro-alloys
Parent: British Steel Holdings Limited
Officers: Damian Hargreaves, Secretary; Antonius Wilhelmus Marcus Jozef Deelen [1965] Director/Chief Marketing Officer [Dutch]; Roland Junck [1955] Director [Luxembourger]; Generald Reichmann [1976] Director/Chief Financial Officer [Austrian]

British Waterways Marinas Limited
Incorporated: 13 October 2003 *Employees:* 68
Net Worth: £11,475,890 *Total Assets:* £16,114,944
Registered Office: Sawley Marina, Long Eaton, Notts, NG10 3AE
Activities: Other amusement and recreation activities n.e.c.
Parent: Project Belize Limited
Officers: Stephen Bacon [1965] Finance Director; Darren Bramhall [1965] Operation Director; Alan Lloyd [1977] Finance Director; Jeffrey George Whyatt [1958] Director/Regional Manager

Broadgate Builders (Spalding) Limited
Incorporated: 2 February 1976 *Employees:* 80
Net Worth: £15,572,112 *Total Assets:* £29,816,798
Registered Office: Broadgate House, Broadgate, Weston Hills, Spalding, Lincs, PE12 6DB
Activities: Construction of domestic buildings
Major Shareholder: The Estate of the late David Deas Bissett-Clarke
Officers: Susan Jane Foreman, Secretary; Ian John Canham [1965] Director/Accountant

Broadgate Homes Limited
Incorporated: 3 January 1995 *Employees:* 57
Net Worth: £16,108,030 *Total Assets:* £24,337,748
Registered Office: Broadgate House, Broadgate, Weston Hills, Spalding, Lincs, PE12 6DB
Activities: Development of building projects
Shareholder: The Estate of the late David Deas Bissett-Clarke
Officers: Susan Jane Foreman, Secretary; Ian John Canham [1965] Director/Accountant

Broadthorpe Limited
Incorporated: 28 February 1962 *Employees:* 367
Net Worth: £116,656,000 *Total Assets:* £138,382,000
Registered Office: Forest Field, Forest Road, Loughborough, Leics, LE11 3NS
Activities: Development of building projects
Officers: Geoffrey Pearson, Secretary; Lucy Cooke [1974] Director; Edelin Davis [1935] Managing Director; George Henry Davis [1970] Director; William Benjamin Davis [1968] Director; Jane Eddershaw [1939] Director; Myles Halley [1956] Director; Harriet Katie Hellman [1962] Director; Guy Stuart Higgins [1962] Managing Director; Philippa Higgins [1966] Director; Terence Higgins [1926] Director; Georgina Newcombe [1960] Director; Rachel Pratt [1969] Director; Annabel Reeves [1970] Director

Broadways Stampings Limited
Incorporated: 29 April 1977 *Employees:* 210
Net Worth: £6,982,997 *Total Assets:* £21,590,018
Registered Office: Second Avenue, Denbigh West Industrial Estate, Bletchley, Milton Keynes, Bucks, MK1 1DT
Activities: Forging, pressing, stamping and roll-forming of metal; powder metallurgy
Shareholder: Enid Margaret Williams
Officers: Enid Margaret Williams, Secretary; Matthew Alan Abrahams [1970] Financial Director; Martyn Douglas Asque [1957] Director; Barrie John Ridgway [1949] Technical Director Broadways Stampings Ltd; Enid Margaret Williams [1947] Director; Grahame Michael Williams [1943] Director/Chairman Broadways Stampings Ltd; James Williams [1970] Director

Brokerbility Holdings Limited
Incorporated: 20 October 2009 *Employees:* 139
Net Worth: £7,491,095 *Total Assets:* £19,058,232
Registered Office: AGM House, 3 Barton Close, Grove Park, Enderby, Leicester, LE19 1SJ
Activities: Non-life insurance
Officers: Jitendra Patel, Secretary; Mark Anthony Bamkin [1958] Director/Insurance Broker; David Sidney McCallum [1953] Director; Ashwinkumar Govindbhai Mistry [1959] Director/Insurance Broker; Jitendra Patel [1965] Director; Ian James Donaldson Stutz [1961] Director/Insurance Broker

The Brooke Weston Trust
Incorporated: 4 July 1989 *Employees:* 1,112
Net Worth: £131,498,000 *Total Assets:* £141,163,008
Registered Office: Brooke Weston, Coomb Road, Great Oakley, Corby, Northants, NN18 8LA
Activities: Primary education
Officers: Debbie Tysoe, Secretary; Dr Andrew Roderick Campbell [1966] Director/Executive Principal; Alexander Edward de Capell Brooke [1968] Director; Philip Harris Bridge [1954] Director/Senior Executive; Robert John Lane [1949] Director; Richard Iain Morrison [1961] Business Performance Director; Sir Peter Austin Simpson [1950] Director/Retired; Heneage John Stevenson [1978] Director; Steve Taylor [1971] Director/Chief Executive; George Garfield Weston [1964] Director [Canadian]; Guy Howard Weston [1960] Director/Philanthropy [Canadian]

Brookfield School Academy Trust
Incorporated: 14 March 2011 *Employees:* 184
Net Worth: £10,221,398 *Total Assets:* £13,357,047
Registered Office: Brookfield Community School, Chatsworth Road, Chesterfield, Derbys, S40 3NS
Activities: General secondary education
Officers: Yvonne Myers, Secretary; Ben Paul Anderson [1976] Director/Teacher; James Thomas Bagley [1974] Director/Teacher; Audrey Broderick [1943] Director/Retired; Professor Douglas John Cleaver [1966] Director/University Professor; Sharon Davis [1968] Director/Carer; Martin Farr [1966] Director/Police Officer; Ashley Alexander Kirk [1967] Director of Electronics Company; Nicola Mainiero [1971] Director/Self Employed; Judy Needham [1946] Director/Retired; Harry Daniel Schofield Nixon [1984] Director/Teacher; Andrew Stead [1973] Director/Occupation Telecommunications Engineer and Manager; Dr. Justin Thacker [1969] Director/Doctor; Rosemary Joy Thompson [1949] Director/Retired; Marcia Woods [1960] Director/Examination Officer

Brookhead Estate Limited
Incorporated: 20 May 1937 *Employees:* 2
Net Worth: £5,373,870 *Total Assets:* £11,580,085
Registered Office: Clarke Nicklin House, Brooks Drive, Cheadle Royal Business Park, Cheadle, Cheshire, SK8 3TD
Activities: Buying and selling of own real estate
Parent: Broome Management Co. Limited
Officers: Rodney Ward, Secretary; David Karl McDonald [1966] Director/Property Management; Andrew John Robinson [1946] Director

Brooklands Milton Keynes LLP
Incorporated: 17 February 2014
Net Worth: £30,957,000 *Total Assets:* £43,105,000
Registered Office: Barratt House, Cartwright Way, Forest Business Park, Bardon Hill, Coalville, Leics, LE67 1UF

Brooklime Limited
Incorporated: 5 July 2007
Net Worth: £83,159 *Total Assets:* £23,115,240
Registered Office: Suite 576, 2nd Floor, Elder House, Elder Gate, Milton Keynes, Bucks, MK9 1LR
Activities: Financial intermediation not elsewhere classified
Officers: Lindsay Treasure, Secretary; Jonathan Paul Silver [1956] Director

Broomco (3019) Limited
Incorporated: 6 September 2002
Net Worth: £670,294 *Total Assets:* £22,296,680
Registered Office: Sunway House, Canklow Meadows, Rotherham, S Yorks, S60 2XR
Activities: Tour operator activities
Parent: Tours Abroad Group Limited
Officers: Andrew Oldfield, Secretary; Ian Duncan Henry [1963] Director; Kathleen Henry [1965] Director; Andrew Oldfield [1971] Finance Director

Broome Management Co. Limited
Incorporated: 10 September 2013
Net Worth: £13,685,268 *Total Assets:* £13,685,268
Registered Office: Clarke Nicklin House, Brooks Drive, Cheadle Royal Business Park, Cheadle, Cheshire, SK8 3TD
Activities: Other letting and operating of own or leased real estate
Officers: Rodney Ward, Secretary; David Karl McDonald [1966] Director; Andrew John Robinson [1946] Director

Broomgrove Properties Limited
Incorporated: 7 June 2012 *Employees:* 4
Net Worth: £5,404,748 *Total Assets:* £15,636,860
Registered Office: 5 Westbrook Court, Sharrowvale Road, Sheffield, S11 8YZ
Activities: Construction of domestic buildings
Officers: Satnam Singh Choker [1955] Director

Brophy Grounds Maintenance Limited
Incorporated: 26 March 2001
Net Worth: £7,961,000 *Total Assets:* £11,926,000
Registered Office: The Sherard Building, Edmund Halley Road, Oxford, OX4 4DQ
Activities: Other business support service activities n.e.c.
Parent: Enterprise Public Services Limited
Officers: James Stefan Haluch [1969] Highways Director; Andrew Lee Milner [1969] Director/Chartered Engineer; Andrew Latham Nelson [1959] Finance Director

Brose Limited
Incorporated: 18 May 1965 *Employees:* 758
Net Worth: £52,234,776 *Total Assets:* £149,801,152
Registered Office: Colliery Lane, Exhall, Coventry, Warwicks, CV7 9NW
Activities: Manufacture of other parts and accessories for motor vehicles
Officers: Peter Konrad Mahlenbrey, Secretary; Thomas Paul Wolfgang Spangler [1964] Director [German]; Steven David Wilkins [1972] Managing Director

R.J.Brown & Sons Limited
Incorporated: 15 February 1937
Net Worth: £10,972,692 *Total Assets:* £12,453,486
Registered Office: 12 Bridgford Road, West Bridgford, Nottingham, NG2 6AB
Activities: Management of real estate on a fee or contract basis
Officers: William Edward Curzon Cursham, Secretary; William Edward Curzon Cursham [1962] Director/Solicitor; Nigel William Turner [1956] Director

Browne Jacobson LLP
Incorporated: 31 December 2003 *Employees:* 861
Net Worth: £19,007,524 *Total Assets:* £41,244,708
Registered Office: Mowbray House, Castle Meadow Road, Nottingham, NG2 1BJ
Officers: Derek Ronald Bambury [1957] Member; Iain Peter Blatherwick [1967] Member; William Max Colacicchi [1954] Member; Gavin George Cummings [1970] Member; Dominic MacKenzie Swift [1965] Member; Mark Aldrich [1966] LLP Member; Peter Allen [1972] LLP Member; Michael Edward Anderson [1971] LLP Member; Tom Armstrong [1976] LLP Member; James Arrowsmith [1981] LLP Member; Jacqueline Suzanna Atkinson [1969] LLP Member; Clare Auty [1972] LLP Member; John Mark Barnett [1974] LLP Member; Roger David Birchall [1961] LLP Member; Nigel John Blackwell [1963] LLP Member; Mark Jonathan Blois [1970] LLP Member; Fiona Butler [1977] LLP Member; Amanda Jane Callaghan [1966] LLP Member; Martin John Canon [1964] LLP Member; Nikolas Neale Carle [1969] LLP Member; Timothy Daniel Claremont [1976] LLP Member; Richard Charles Cox [1970] LLP Member; Declan Cushley [1969] LLP Member; Kerren Ann Daly [1967] LLP Member; Mark Daniels [1974] LLP Member; James Christian Dingwall [1959] LLP Member; Paula Elsa Mary Dumbill [1967] LLP Member; David Steven Durbridge [1975] LLP Member; Jonathan David Laurence Edwards [1965] LLP Member; Craig Elder [1974] LLP Member; Sarah Louise Erwin [1969] LLP Member; Nichola Karen Evans [1968] LLP Member; James Fawcett [1976] LLP Member; Rebecca Fitzpatrick [1967] LLP Member; Rosalind Ann Foster [1971] LLP Member; Kathleen Fox-Murphy [1972] LLP Member; Jonathan Fuggle [1972] LLP Member; Mark Anthony John Gleeson [1967] LLP Member; Caroline Jane Green [1960] LLP Member; Julia Green [1962] LLP Member; Gerard Hanratty [1971] LLP Member; Lorna Hardman [1969] LLP Member; Jonathan Brian Hayden [1977] LLP Member; Emma Hinton [1981] LLP Member; Andrew John Hopkin [1967] LLP Member; Michael John Howard [1968] LLP Member; Laura Ann Hughes [1978] LLP Member; Mark Richard Hughes [1975] LLP Member; Jeremy Irving [1969] LLP Member; Mike Andrew Jackson [1981] LLP Member; Timothy Johnson [1981] LLP Member; Cerryg Jones [1962] LLP Member; Peter Melville Jones [1964] LLP Member; Kevin John Lawson [1972] LLP Member; Ian Michael Long [1967] LLP Member; Rachel Lyne [1973] LLP Member; Nigel Hugh Lyons [1964] LLP Member; Susan Joy Carol Mabbott [1963] LLP Member; Nicholas Edward MacKenzie [1978] LLP Member; Francis Otley Mackie [1952] LLP Member; David William Maggs [1962] LLP Member; Sarah Elizabeth Manning [1967] LLP Member; Stephen William Matthew [1957] LLP Member; Shaun Robert McCabe [1975] LLP Member; Richard James Medd [1977] LLP Member; Michael Mousedale [1962] LLP Member; Anthony John Nagle [1968] LLP Member; Jonathan Clifford Newbold [1978] LLP Member; Richard Paul Nicholas [1974] LLP Member; Charles Andrew Noble [1965] LLP Member; Gary Mark Oldroyd [1969] LLP Member; Sarah Parkinson [1969] LLP Member; Colin John Peck [1968] LLP Member; Andrew Joseph Peel [1963] LLP Member; Nicholas Keith Pontt [1977] LLP Member; Oliver Tim Pritchard [1968] LLP Member; Alan Joseph Henson Radford [1957] LLP Member; Paul William Wakelin Ray [1963] LLP Member; Lucy Jane Robinson [1971] LLP Member; Michael Sadler [1977] LLP Member; Adrian Shardlow [1964] LLP Member; Raymond Morris Silverstein [1964] LLP Member; Jonathan James Snade [1977] LLP Member; Michael John Stace [1971] LLP Member; Barry Sully [1969] LLP Member; James Tait [1973] LLP Member; Simon John William Tait [1964] LLP Member; Jonathan Christopher Tardif [1974] LLP Member; Bridget Anne Tatham [1966] LLP Member; Wenna Jerman Thompson [1961] LLP Member; Ben Troke [1973] LLP Member; Neil Stuart Ward [1970] LLP Member; Peter Timothy Ware [1975] LLP Member; Alexander Charles Johnstone Watt [1977] LLP Member; Sarah Jane White [1963] LLP Member; Matthew Roden Woodford [1972] LLP Member

Albert Browne Limited
Incorporated: 18 November 1908 *Employees:* 78
Net Worth: £27,396,344 *Total Assets:* £34,877,000
Registered Office: Chancery House, Rayns Way, Watermead Business Park, Syston, Leicester, LE7 1PF
Activities: Manufacture of other chemical products n.e.c.
Parent: Steris CH Limited
Officers: Ronald Snyder, Secretary; Julia Kipnis [1977] Director/Corporate Counsel [American]; Ronald E Snyder [1948] Director/Associate and Group General Counsel [American]; Michael Joseph Tokich [1968] Director/Chief Financial Officer [American]

Brownhills Motorhomes Limited
Incorporated: 8 December 1994 *Employees:* 148
Net Worth: £7,520,625 *Total Assets:* £21,519,916
Registered Office: A1-A46 Junction, Lincoln Road, Newark, Notts, NG24 2EA
Activities: Sale of other motor vehicles
Parent: Hosting Developments Limited
Officers: Stephen Bernard Cullen, Finance Director; Andrew Paul Craggs [1968] Sales Director; Stephen Bernard Cullen [1963] Director/Chief Operating Officer; Myles Halley [1956] Director

BRS Limited
Incorporated: 13 January 1998 *Employees:* 340
Net Worth: £49,312,000 *Total Assets:* £103,186,000
Registered Office: Wedgnock Industrial Estate, Wedgnock Lane, Warwick, CV34 5YA
Activities: Renting and leasing of trucks and other heavy vehicles
Parent: AB Volvo
Officers: Simon Derek Villanueva, Secretary; Olivier de Saint Meleuc [1978] Director/SVP Sales Area North Europe & Russia [French]; Arne Knaben [1958] Director [Norwegian]; Carlos Oliveira Rodrigues [1977] Director/Chief Financial Officer [Portuguese]; Simon Derek Villanueva [1973] Director

BRT (Wisbech) Limited
Incorporated: 8 July 2011 *Employees:* 141
Net Worth: £4,180,425 *Total Assets:* £14,590,516
Registered Office: 21-24 Regal Road, Wisbech, Cambs, PE13 2RQ
Activities: Non-specialised wholesale trade
Shareholders: Phillip David Clarke; Simon David Clarke
Officers: Grahame Allen [1966] Director; Anthony George Clarke [1946] Director; Phillip David Clarke [1970] Director; Simon David Clarke [1973] Director; Lindsey Jane Lowery [1961] Director

Bruker UK Limited
Incorporated: 30 November 1967 *Employees:* 135
Net Worth: £2,774,181 *Total Assets:* £19,945,144
Registered Office: Banner Lane, Coventry, Warwicks, CV4 9GH
Activities: Manufacture of electronic industrial process control equipment
Officers: Mark Clifton Holmes, Secretary; John Daniel Carr [1960] Senior Director, Tax, Bruker Corporation [American]; Generald Herman [1957] Director/VP and Controller, Bruker Corporation [Canadian]; Mark Clifton Holmes [1971] Director/Financial Controller

Brunel Healthcare Manufacturing Limited
Incorporated: 6 August 2002 *Employees:* 389
Net Worth: £5,113,000 *Total Assets:* £33,375,000
Registered Office: William Nadin Way, Swadlincote, Derbys, DE11 0BB
Activities: Manufacture of basic pharmaceutical products
Shareholder: Liang Chang
Officers: James David Amery, Secretary; James David Amery [1975] Finance Director; Richard Henry Fielding [1968] OTC Director; John Edward Hackett [1967] Director; Robert Andrew Jeremy Haytack [1978] Commercial Director; Matthew Robert Woodings [1970] Operations Director

BSH Home Appliances Limited
Incorporated: 28 August 1984 *Employees:* 1,196
Net Worth: £59,053,536 *Total Assets:* £202,705,984
Registered Office: Grand Union House, Old Wolverton Road, Wolverton, Milton Keynes, Bucks, MK12 5PT
Activities: Wholesale of radio, television goods & electrical household appliances (other than records, tapes, CDs)
Parent: BSH Finance & Holding GmbH
Officers: Kevin John Athow, Secretary; Thomas Baader [1965] Director [German]; Dr Andreas Meier [1968] Director/Chief Executive [German]; Ting Mensing [1972] Director/Chief Financial Officer [German]; Christian Gerhard Walter Prenzel [1967] Director/Head of Region Europe - Business Administration [German]

BTN Turbo Charger Service Limited
Incorporated: 7 June 1974
Net Worth: £9,566,000 *Total Assets:* £12,796,000
Registered Office: Bridge House, 3 Timothy's Bridge Road, Stratford upon Avon, Warwicks, CV37 9NQ
Activities: Wholesale trade of motor vehicle parts and accessories
Parent: FPS Distribution Limited
Officers: John Frederick Coombes, Secretary; Alistair Stuart Brown [1955] Director [New Zealander]; John Frederick Coombes [1965] Director; Mark John Dickinson [1965] Sales Marketing Director; Jean-Jacques Mathieu Lafont [1959] Director [Belgian]; Terence Michael Wainwright [1947] Director

Buccleuch Property (Shawfair) Limited
Incorporated: 17 March 2004
Net Worth: £9,615,428 *Total Assets:* £9,670,884
Registered Office: c/o Buccleuch Property Estate Office, Weekley, Kettering, Northants, NN16 9UP
Activities: Buying and selling of own real estate
Parent: Tarras Park Properties Limited
Officers: James Alexander Kenneth MacLeod, Secretary/Accountant; James Alexander Kenneth MacLeod [1975] Director/Chartered Accountant; David Howard Peck [1965] Director; Alexander Hay Laidlaw Smith [1972] Director; Nicholas Antony George Waugh [1960] Director

Buckingham Group Contracting Limited
Incorporated: 21 October 1987 *Employees:* 477
Net Worth: £31,725,242 *Total Assets:* £145,475,792
Registered Office: Blackpit Farm, Stowe, Buckingham, MK18 5LJ
Activities: Construction of commercial buildings
Officers: Patricia Jane Wheeler, Secretary; Timothy John Brown [1955] Commercial Director; Michael Thomas Kempley [1961] Director; Andrew Stuart Kerr [1965] Director; Ian McKinley McSeveney [1967] Civil Engineer and Director; Kevin Underwood [1955] Director; Simon David Walkley [1963] Civil Engineer and Director; Paul Watson Wheeler [1954] Director/Company Manager

Buckingham Plant Hire Limited
Incorporated: 1 January 1955 *Employees:* 148
Net Worth: £9,354,857 *Total Assets:* £30,257,186
Registered Office: Blackpit Farm, Silverstone Road, Stowe, Bucks, MK18 5LJ
Activities: Renting and leasing of construction and civil engineering machinery and equipment
Officers: Patricia Jane Wheeler, Secretary; Michael Tye [1956] Director; Patricia Jane Wheeler [1956] Director/Promotions Manager; Paul Watson Wheeler [1954] Director/Company Manager

Bucks Investments Limited
Incorporated: 7 November 2006 *Employees:* 2
Net Worth: £15,306,828 *Total Assets:* £15,339,566
Registered Office: Units 1 & 2 Bunny Trading Estate, Gotham Lane, Bunny, Nottingham, NG11 6QJ
Activities: Financial management
Officers: James Bysouth-Kemp, Secretary; James Bysouth-Kemp [1943] Director; Paul James Bysouth-Kemp [1968] Director

Bucyrus Europe Limited
Incorporated: 30 April 1985
Net Worth: £9,256,000 *Total Assets:* £11,444,000
Registered Office: Legal Services, Frank Perkins Way, Eastfield, Peterborough, Cambs, PE1 5FQ
Activities: Engineering design activities for industrial process and production
Parent: Bucyrus Europe Holdings Limited
Officers: Johanna Elizabeth Deason, Secretary; Nigel John Burroughs [1964] Director/Tax Accountant; Martin Daldrup [1964] Director [German]

Bucyrus UK Limited
Incorporated: 24 October 1994 *Employees:* 3
Net Worth: £19,802,000 *Total Assets:* £19,857,000
Registered Office: Legal Services, Frank Perkins Way, Eastfield, Peterborough, Cambs, PE1 5FQ
Activities: Engineering design activities for industrial process and production
Parent: Caterpillar Global Mining Europe GmbH
Officers: Johanna Elizabeth Deason, Secretary; Nigel John Burroughs [1964] Director/Tax Accountant; Martin Daldrup [1964] Managing Director [German]

Buffaload Logistics Limited
Incorporated: 3 March 2005 *Employees:* 218
Net Worth: £1,371,268 *Total Assets:* £15,337,059
Registered Office: Grove Parc, Grove Lane, Ellington, Huntingdon, Cambs, PE28 0AA
Activities: Non-specialised wholesale trade
Shareholders: Ranjit Singh Boparan; Bajinder Kaur Boparan; Ross John Taylor; Invest 1 Co Limited
Officers: Julie Feltwell, Secretary; Graham Mark Edwards [1970] Director; Julie Ann Feltwell [1968] Director/Transport Manager; Ian David Perks [1968] Business Development Director; Edward Samuel Power [1946] Director/Chairman [Irish]

Building and Plumbing Supplies Limited
Incorporated: 25 May 1934 *Employees:* 139
Net Worth: £8,458,393 *Total Assets:* £13,478,421
Registered Office: Tachbrook Park Drive, Tachbrook Park, Leamington Spa, Warwick, CV34 6RH
Activities: Agents involved in the sale of timber and building materials
Parent: BPS Warwick Limited
Officers: David Ian Battin, Secretary; David Ian Battin [1968] Director/Chartered Accountant; Brian George Dibble [1927] Director; Emma Marjorie Dibble [1968] Training & Marketing Director; John Richard Dibble [1968] Managing Director; Graham Nigel Stanley [1971] Director

Bulk Freight (Midlands) Limited
Incorporated: 13 February 1987 *Employees:* 148
Net Worth: £6,416,363 *Total Assets:* £17,393,144
Registered Office: 47 Ashby Road Central, Shepshed, Loughborough, Leics, LE12 9BS
Activities: Freight transport by road
Parent: Fred Sherwood & Sons (Transport) Ltd
Officers: Andrew John Disney, Secretary; Andrew John Disney [1972] Director/Accountant; Matthew Thomas Hibbert [1952] Director/Haulage Contractor; Ashley Paul Alan Sherwood [1969] Director/Haulage Contractor; Jayne Sherwood [1971] Director; Sheila Irene Sherwood [1944] Director

Bullimores Sand and Gravel Limited
Incorporated: 30 April 1959 *Employees:* 71
Net Worth: £13,402,656 *Total Assets:* £16,577,584
Registered Office: Thistleton Lane, South Witham, Grantham, Lincs, NG33 5QE
Activities: Quarrying of ornamental and building stone, limestone, gypsum, chalk and slate
Shareholders: Nicholas Simon James Quinton Bullimore; Christopher Nigel Pepper Bullimore
Officers: Elisabeth Hollingsworth, Secretary; Christopher Nigel Pepper Bullimore [1960] Director/Merchant; Nicholas Simon James Quinton Bullimore [1963] Director/Merchant

Roger Bullivant Limited
Incorporated: 24 June 2011 *Employees:* 510
Net Worth: £11,786,000 *Total Assets:* £28,326,000
Registered Office: RB Walton Park, Hearthcote Road, Swadlincote, Derbys, DE11 9DU
Activities: Other specialised construction activities n.e.c.
Parent: Soletanche Freyssinet SAS
Officers: Ian George Alcorn [1961] Commercial Director; Philip John Hines [1966] Director; Hugh Sloan [1957] Operations Director; Graham James Trafford [1972] Director/Accountant; Clifford John Wren [1960] Managing Director

Burbage Capital Limited
Incorporated: 3 June 2009
Net Worth: £17,937,548 *Total Assets:* £28,700,340
Registered Office: Conduit House, 65 St Giles Street, Northampton, NN1 1JF
Activities: Buying and selling of own real estate
Major Shareholder: John Edward Burbage
Officers: Lucinda Harrison Lamont Burbage, Secretary; John Edward Burbage [1956] Director/Chartered Surveyor

Burbidge Holdings Limited
Incorporated: 23 March 2010 *Employees:* 75
Net Worth: £7,118,192 *Total Assets:* £9,048,824
Registered Office: Burnsall Road, Canley, Coventry, Warwicks, CV5 6BS
Activities: Manufacture of kitchen furniture
Shareholders: David Lovell Burbidge; Sandra Elizabeth Burbidge
Officers: Emma Jane Burbidge, Secretary; Benedict James Burbidge [1967] Managing Director; Graham Heaven [1961] Financial Director

Burford Garden Centre Limited
Incorporated: 11 December 1992 *Employees:* 168
Net Worth: £13,623,901 *Total Assets:* £21,812,016
Registered Office: 8 King Edward Street, Oxford, OX1 4HL
Activities: Other retail sale of new goods in specialised stores (not commercial art galleries and opticians)
Major Shareholder: Nigel Johnson
Officers: Paul Gingell, Secretary; Meike Cassens [1969] Director/Retail Manager [German]; Elaine Day [1958] Director/Retail Manager; Paul Gingell [1968] Sales and Operations Director; Charlotte Louise Johnson [1961] Director/Retailer; Nigel Johnson [1956] Director/Retailer; Glen Sheldrake [1971] Director/Retail Manager

Burford School
Incorporated: 24 May 2012 *Employees:* 192
Net Worth: £12,461,000 *Total Assets:* £16,711,000
Registered Office: Burford School, Cheltenham Road, Burford, Oxon, OX18 4PL
Activities: General secondary education
Officers: Suzanne Reeve, Secretary; Andrea Bird [1963] Director/Finance Manager; Cheryl Bracey [1970] Director/Programme Manager; Clare Brown [1977] Director/Teacher, Head of Science; Steven Carroll [1971] Director/Senior Security Adviser; Christopher Cowley [1988] Director/Teacher; Philip Foster [1972] Managing Director; Derek Thomas Alfred Grimsley [1963] Director; Kathryn Marie Haig [1964] Director/Headteacher; Richard Martin [1952] Director/Self Employed; Sarah Matthews [1964] Director/Solicitor; Christopher Stuart Norridge [1950] Director/Teacher; Virginia Ann Renwick [1968] Director/Business Manager; Angela Michelle Sherwood [1969] Director/HR Executive; Julie Norreen Wall [1951] Director/Retired; John Jameson White [1938] Director/Retired Solicitor

Russell Burgess Limited
Incorporated: 17 November 1955 *Employees:* 613
Net Worth: £2,715,000 *Total Assets:* £43,137,000
Registered Office: Stanley's Farm, Great Drove, Yaxley, Peterborough, PE7 3TW
Activities: Activities of other holding companies n.e.c.
Shareholder: David William Ashley Burgess
Officers: David William Ashley Burgess, Secretary; Henry Zaccheus Brown [1957] Director; Andrew Stanley Burgess [1965] Director; David William Ashley Burgess [1968] Director; David Stanley Lambert Burgess [1939] Director; Jason Charles Burgess [1966] Director

Burghley House Preservation Trust Limited
Incorporated: 3 April 1969 *Employees:* 105
Net Worth: £68,039,648 *Total Assets:* £73,427,192
Registered Office: Burghley Estate Office, 61 St Martins, Stamford, Lincs, PE9 2LQ
Activities: Other letting and operating of own or leased real estate
Officers: Joshua Fitch, Secretary; Jonathan Charles Chenevix-Trench [1961] Director/Banker; Edward George Clive [1968] Director/Fine Art Auctioneer; Andrew James Feilden [1941] Director/Chartered Surveyor; Sir Giles Henry Charles Floyd [1932] Director/Farmer; Edward Mortimer Harley [1960] Director/Stockbroker; The Honorable Edward Douglas Leigh-Pemberton [1959] Director/Surveyor; Sir John Grenfell Nutting [1942] Director/Barrister; William Alexander Michael Oswald [1962] Director; William Henry Marcello Parente [1951] Director; Stuart John Richmond-Watson [1951] Director; Brian Turnbull Julius Stevens [1938] Director/Solicitor; Jane Tufnell [1964] Director/Investment Professional

Burrough Court Estate Limited
Incorporated: 12 January 1944 *Employees:* 7
Net Worth: £9,834,173 *Total Assets:* £11,548,832
Registered Office: 14 All Saints Street, Stamford, Lincs, PE9 2PA
Activities: Growing of cereals (except rice), leguminous crops and oil seeds
Shareholders: Dawn Elizabeth Wilson; Anthony Crawford Keene
Officers: Dawn Elizabeth Wilson, Secretary; Anthony Crawford Keene [1933] Director/Farmer; Dawn Elizabeth Wilson [1964] Director; Rebecca Alice Wilson [1992] Director; Richard Ian Wilson [1963] Director; Toby Richard Keene Wilson [1994] Director

Burrows Motor Company Limited
Incorporated: 1 June 1999 *Employees:* 355
Net Worth: £3,047,000 *Total Assets:* £24,860,000
Registered Office: Burrows Motor Company, Wheatley Hall Road, Doncaster, S Yorks, DN2 4LT
Activities: Sale of new cars and light motor vehicles
Shareholder: Steven Richard Burrows
Officers: Louise Holmes, Secretary; Steven Richard Burrows [1951] Director; Dean Cooper [1964] Operations Director

Burt Bros.(Hosiery) Limited
Incorporated: 18 March 1948 *Employees:* 32
Net Worth: £18,057,332 *Total Assets:* £21,805,960
Registered Office: Units A-D Willow Road, Lenton Industrial Estate, Nottingham, NG7 2TA
Activities: Wholesale of clothing and footwear
Major Shareholder: Kenneth Vaughan Burt
Officers: Hannah Burt [1978] Director; Wendy Burt [1955] Director

Burton McCall Limited
Incorporated: 24 September 1987 *Employees:* 77
Net Worth: £5,721,584 *Total Assets:* £13,249,940
Registered Office: 3 Bailey Court, Green Street, Macclesfield, Cheshire, SK10 1JQ
Activities: Non-specialised wholesale trade
Parent: Bollin Group Limited
Officers: Christopher Cooper, Secretary; Stephen James Cann [1965] Director/Accountant; Christopher Cooper [1972] Finance and Operations Director; Michelle Ann Dickinson [1964] Director

Bury Farm Sharpenhoe Limited
Incorporated: 1 April 2016
Net Worth: £70,606 *Total Assets:* £15,556,298
Registered Office: 1 Willow Road, Brackley, Northants, NN13 7EX
Activities: Growing of cereals (except rice), leguminous crops and oil seeds
Parent: Faccenda Farms Limited
Officers: Alison Gulliver, Secretary; Ian James Faccenda [1967] Director; Alison Jane Gulliver [1969] Director; John Charles Gulliver [1965] Director

Bury's Dryanstore Limited
Incorporated: 13 March 1956
Net Worth: £15,003,149 *Total Assets:* £16,601,305
Registered Office: 8 King Edward Street, Oxford, OX1 4HL
Activities: Other letting and operating of own or leased real estate
Shareholder: Mary Josephine Wilson
Officers: Mary Albertina Bury, Secretary; David Stewart Bury [1944] Director/Farmer; Mary Albertina Bury [1920] Director/Housewife; Mary Josephine Wilson [1953] Director/Clerical Assistant

Bush & Company Rehabilitation Limited
Incorporated: 5 March 2010 *Employees:* 47
Net Worth: £13,754,000 *Total Assets:* £14,941,000
Registered Office: 1430 Montagu Court, Kettering Parkway, Kettering, Northants, NN15 6XR
Activities: Other human health activities
Parent: Consumer Champion Group Limited
Officers: James David Saralis, Secretary; John Russell Atkinson [1965] Director; Rachel Ann Brodie [1967] Director; Helen Jackson [1977] Managing Director; James David Saralis [1978] Director

B.A.Bush & Son Limited
Incorporated: 7 April 1970 *Employees:* 226
Net Worth: £6,954,334 *Total Assets:* £18,578,744
Registered Office: Station Yard, Horncastle, Lincs, LN9 5AQ
Activities: Wholesale trade of motor vehicle parts and accessories
Shareholders: Nigel Arthur Bush; Simeon John Disley; Susan Elizabeth Bush; David John Dawson
Officers: Benjamin Clifford Bush, Secretary; Benjamin Clifford Bush [1983] Director; Nigel Arthur Bush [1956] Director; Thomas Arthur Bush [1986] Director

Bushboard Holdings Limited
Incorporated: 26 October 2004
Net Worth: £8,899,000 *Total Assets:* £14,234,000
Registered Office: 9-29 Rixon Road, Wellingborough, Northants, NN8 4BA
Activities: Manufacture of veneer sheets and wood-based panels
Parent: Wilsonart Limited
Officers: William Joseph Thesing, Secretary; Jeffrey Scott Lee [1969] Director/Business Executive [American]; Alan Timothy Pearson [1969] Director/Western Europe President; Jeffrey Hugh Robb [1967] Finance Director

Bushboard Limited
Incorporated: 9 March 2000 *Employees:* 101
Net Worth: £12,042,000 *Total Assets:* £17,407,000
Registered Office: 9-29 Rixon Road, Wellingborough, Northants, NN8 4BA
Activities: Manufacture of kitchen furniture
Parent: Wilsonart Limited
Officers: William Joseph Thesing, Secretary; Jeffrey Scott Lee [1969] Director/Business Executive [American]; Alan Timothy Pearson [1969] Director/Western Europe President; Jeffrey Hugh Robb [1967] Finance Director

Bushmead Homes Ltd
Incorporated: 29 November 2012
Net Worth: £11,168,606 *Total Assets:* £12,044,681
Registered Office: Bedford Heights, Manton Lane, Bedford, MK41 7BJ
Activities: Construction of domestic buildings
Officers: Philippa Spratley, Secretary; Ian Simon Ailles [1965] Director General of The House of Commons; Jeffrey Thomas Astle [1972] Director of Development and Sales; Kevin Ronald Bolt [1957] Director; Paul Lawrence Gray [1961] Director/Chartered Accountant; Paul Henry High [1959] Director

Business By Technology (Holdings) Ltd
Incorporated: 8 April 2014 *Employees:* 69
Net Worth: £3,144,023 *Total Assets:* £10,454,444
Registered Office: Orchard House, Binns Close, Torrington Avenue, Coventry, Warwicks, CV4 9TB
Activities: Non-trading company
Major Shareholder: Philip Runciman
Officers: Michael James Catterall [1959] Director; Philip Runciman [1967] Director

Business Control Solutions Group Limited
Incorporated: 14 January 1987 *Employees:* 191
Net Worth: £10,751,000 *Total Assets:* £18,851,000
Registered Office: Ground Floor, Churchgate, New Road, Peterborough, Cambs, PE1 1TT
Activities: Information technology consultancy activities
Parent: Business Control Solutions Group Trustees Ltd
Officers: Roger Alan Shepherd, Secretary; Alexander Campbell Anderson [1954] Director; Paul David Brock [1967] Director; Steve Russell [1945] Director; Roger Alan Shepherd [1966] Director/Accountant; Nigel David Walder [1963] Director

Business Control Solutions Public Limited Company
Incorporated: 28 July 2003 *Employees:* 178
Net Worth: £8,553,678 *Total Assets:* £18,195,678
Registered Office: Ground Floor, Churchgate, New Road, Peterborough, Cambs, PE1 1TT
Activities: Information technology consultancy activities
Parent: Business Control Solutions Group Limited
Officers: Roger Alan Shepherd, Secretary; Paul David Brock [1967] Director; Roger Alan Shepherd [1966] Finance Director

Business Management Software Limited
Incorporated: 31 October 1990 *Employees:* 65
Net Worth: £9,195,491 *Total Assets:* £10,684,255
Registered Office: 2 Peterborough Business Park, Lynch Wood, Peterborough, Cambs, PE2 6FZ
Activities: Information technology consultancy activities
Parent: Automatic Data Processing Inc.
Officers: Richard Anderson [1972] Director

Business Village Limited
Incorporated: 6 August 2002
Net Worth: £4,096,386 *Total Assets:* £10,027,360
Registered Office: Estates Office, Ladle Farm, Armscote, Stratford upon Avon, Warwicks, CV37 8DF
Activities: Other letting and operating of own or leased real estate
Shareholders: Anthony Julian Gaymond; Harry Alexander Acland
Officers: Anthony Julian Gaymond, Secretary/Civil Engineer; Harry Alexander Acland [1963] Director/Surveyor; Anthony Julian Gaymond [1956] Director/Civil Engineer

Buster Jimmy Limited
Incorporated: 4 December 2012
Net Worth: £166,060,464 *Total Assets:* £174,358,256
Registered Office: Castlefield, Mount Road, Bretby, Burton on Trent, Staffs, DE15 0RA
Activities: Financial management
Shareholders: Claire Ruth Wright; Michael Gordon Wright
Officers: Claire Ruth Wright [1962] Director/Marketing Consultant

Busways Travel Services Limited
Incorporated: 12 September 1988 *Employees:* 1,083
Net Worth: £14,457,000 *Total Assets:* £33,127,000
Registered Office: c/o Stagecoach Services Limited, One Stockport Exchange, 20 Railway Road, Stockport, Cheshire, SK1 3SW
Activities: Other urban, suburban or metropolitan passenger land transport (not underground, metro or similar)
Parent: Stagecoach Bus Holdings Limited
Officers: Michael John Vaux, Secretary; Colin Brown [1968] Director/Accountant; Arnold Mark Threapleton [1954] Managing Director; Steven Walker [1971] Director

Butcher's Pet Care Limited
Incorporated: 19 April 1983 *Employees:* 280
Net Worth: £31,629,000 *Total Assets:* £71,421,000
Registered Office: Baker Group House, Dockham Way, Crick, Northants, NN6 7TZ
Activities: Manufacture of prepared pet foods
Parent: F W Baker Limited
Officers: Jeffrey Richard Martins, Secretary; Graham William Baker [1952] Director/Factory Management; Geoffrey Dennis Eaton [1958] Director/Chairman; Jeffrey Richard Martins [1972] Director; Francis Generald Powell [1964] Finance Director; Graham Robert Scott [1944] Director; Timothy James Watsham [1975] Director; Steven John Wood [1969] Director

C Butt Holdings Limited
Incorporated: 20 May 2008 *Employees:* 115
Net Worth: £6,745,914 *Total Assets:* £9,147,208
Registered Office: Sheaf Close, Lodge Farm Industrial Estate, Northampton, NN5 7UL
Activities: Activities of head offices
Shareholders: Gerald William Butt; Jonathan Ian Butt; Brian Butt
Officers: Generald William Butt, Secretary; Brian John Butt [1936] Director; Generald William Butt [1935] Director/Chairman; Jonathan Ian Butt [1967] Director

Buttercup Bidco Limited
Incorporated: 13 February 2015
Net Worth Deficit: £4,185,695 *Total Assets:* £12,358,554
Registered Office: The Alchemist, Chadsworth House, Wilmslow Road, Handforth, Cheshire, SK9 3HP
Activities: Licenced restaurants
Parent: Buttercup Topco Ltd
Officers: Simon Potts [1980] Managing Director; Jeremy Kevin Roberts [1962] Director; Victoria Stewart [1980] Finance Director

Buttercup Topco Limited
Incorporated: 13 February 2015 *Employees:* 607
Net Worth Deficit: £1,958,789 *Total Assets:* £30,843,464
Registered Office: The Alchemist, Chadsworth House, Wilmslow Road, Handforth, Cheshire, SK9 3HP
Activities: Licenced restaurants
Parent: Palatine Private Equity LLP
Officers: Paul Adam Campbell [1964] Director; Kieran Anthony Lawton [1978] Investment Director; Simon Potts [1980] Managing Director; Jeremy Kevin Roberts [1962] Director; Victoria Stewart [1980] Finance Director; Gary William Tipper [1963] Director

Buxton Consortium Limited
Incorporated: 29 June 2005 *Employees:* 136
Net Worth: £18,474,532 *Total Assets:* £23,679,408
Registered Office: c/o Buxton Press Ltd, Palace Road, Buxton, Derbys, SK17 6AE
Activities: Activities of other holding companies n.e.c.
Major Shareholder: Bernard Galloway
Officers: Kirk Andrew Galloway, Secretary; Bernard Galloway [1936] Director

Buxton Press Limited
Incorporated: 20 June 1960 *Employees:* 136
Net Worth: £10,694,377 *Total Assets:* £16,188,802
Registered Office: Palace Road, Buxton, Derbys, SK17 6AE
Activities: Printing n.e.c.
Officers: Kirk Andrew Galloway, Secretary; Bernard Galloway [1936] Director; Kirk Andrew Galloway [1964] Director

Buzz Entertainment Limited
Incorporated: 20 April 1964
Previous: Gala Bingo Limited
Net Worth: £28,415,000 *Total Assets:* £35,287,000
Registered Office: New Castle House, Castle Boulevard, Nottingham, NG7 1FT
Activities: Activities of head offices
Parent: Buzz Holdings Limited
Officers: Chris John Matthews [1972] Director/Chief Executive Officer; Gary Payne [1969] Director

Buzz Group Limited
Incorporated: 6 March 1964 *Employees:* 3,775
Previous: Gala Leisure Limited
Net Worth: £162,331,008 *Total Assets:* £230,083,008
Registered Office: New Castle House, Castle Boulevard, Nottingham, NG7 1FT
Activities: Gambling and betting activities
Parent: Gala Bingo Limited
Officers: Chris John Matthews [1972] Director/Chief Executive Officer; Gary Payne [1969] Director

Buzz Holdings Limited
Incorporated: 18 February 2014
Previous: Gala Bingo Holdings Limited
Net Worth: £15,828,000 *Total Assets:* £263,900,000
Registered Office: New Castle House, Castle Boulevard, Nottingham, NG7 1FT
Activities: Activities of head offices
Parent: Caledonia Venus Acquisitions Limited
Officers: Chris John Matthews [1972] Director/Chief Executive Officer; Gary Payne [1969] Director

Buzzard Leisure Limited
Incorporated: 23 July 1996
Net Worth: £54,300,000 *Total Assets:* £129,000,000
Registered Office: Westpoint, Peterborough Business Park, Lynch Wood, Peterborough, Cambs, PE2 6FZ
Activities: Other business support service activities n.e.c.
Parent: Mytravel North America Limited
Officers: Shirley Bradley, Secretary; Paul Andrew Hemingway [1971] Director

BV Holdings Limited
Incorporated: 4 January 2002 *Employees:* 1,611
Net Worth: £2,751,479 *Total Assets:* £35,990,700
Registered Office: Clarke Nicklin House, Brooks Drive, Cheadle Royal Business Park, Cheadle, Cheshire, SK8 3TD
Activities: Other business support service activities n.e.c.
Major Shareholder: John Robert William Vernon
Officers: Lesley Jane Walker, Secretary; John Robert William Vernon [1947] Director; Richard Andrew Vernon [1976] Director; Lesley Jane Walker [1975] Director

BW Integrated Systems UK Limited
Incorporated: 4 August 2004 *Employees:* 107
Previous: Barry-Wehmiller Container Systems Limited
Net Worth: £3,124,645 *Total Assets:* £22,238,028
Registered Office: Plumtree Farm Industrial Estate, Bircotes, Doncaster, S Yorks, DN11 8EW
Activities: Manufacture of machinery for food, beverage and tobacco processing
Officers: Lee Mark Pinder, Secretary; Robert Hall Chapman [1945] Director [American]; Gregory Loran Coonrod [1956] Director [American]; Richard Martin Cranston [1969] Operations Director; Lee Mark Pinder [1967] Director/Accountant; Michael John Redwood [1970] Director

BWB Holdings Limited
Incorporated: 8 May 2015 *Employees:* 288
Net Worth: £2,231,937 *Total Assets:* £11,203,379
Registered Office: 5th Floor, Waterfront House, Station Street, Nottingham, NG2 3DQ
Activities: Other engineering activities
Parent: Construcciones y Auxiliar de Ferrocarriles, S.A
Officers: Urtzi Alzaga [1979] Director [Spanish]; Paul Michael Collins [1980] Director/Accountant; Martin Fuica [1969] Director [Spanish]; Dave Hollingsworth [1972] Director; Timothy David Loveridge [1968] Director; Greg Nicholson [1968] Director; Andy Passmore [1972] Director; John Pilkington [1949] Director; Stephen Wooler [1960] Director/Construction Engineer; Inigo Zabalondo [1968] Director [Spanish]; Stefan Zalega [1972] Director

BWSC North Lincs Limited
Incorporated: 8 August 2007 *Employees:* 3
Net Worth Deficit: £35,742,000 *Total Assets:* £166,052,992
Registered Office: c/o Templeborough Biomass Power Plant Ltd, River View, Sheffield Road, Rotherham, S Yorks, S60 1FA
Activities: Production of electricity
Parent: BWSC Power Corporation Limited
Officers: Christina Grumstrup Sorensen [1972] Director [Danish]; Christian Grundtvig [1959] Director [Danish]; Donald Paul Milligan [1967] Director/General Manager [Danish]

BWSC Power Corporation Limited
Incorporated: 30 July 2013 *Employees:* 3
Net Worth: £102,605,000 *Total Assets:* £356,623,008
Registered Office: c/o Templeborough Biomass Power Plant Ltd, River View, Sheffield Road, Rotherham, S Yorks, S60 1FA
Activities: Activities of other holding companies n.e.c.
Shareholder: Mitsui E & S Holdings Co., Ltd.
Officers: Christina Grumstrup Sorensen [1972] Director/Partner [Danish]; Christian Andreas Grundtvig [1959] Director [Danish]; Anna-Lena Jeppsson [1976] Director/Engineer [Swedish]; Donald Paul Milligan [1967] Director/General Manager [Danish]

Bybox Field Support Limited
Incorporated: 4 October 1999 *Employees:* 380
Net Worth: £19,752,468 *Total Assets:* £30,560,090
Registered Office: Winchester House, Oxford Science Park, Heatley Road, Oxford, OX4 4GE
Activities: Operation of warehousing and storage facilities for land transport activities
Parent: Bybox Holdings Limted
Officers: Peter David Rowse, Secretary; Stuart James Miller [1967] Director; Peter David Rowse [1968] Director

Bybox Holdings Limited
Incorporated: 27 December 2000 *Employees:* 469
Net Worth: £22,850,672 *Total Assets:* £36,809,848
Registered Office: Winchester House, Oxford Science Park, Heatley Road, Oxford, OX4 4GE
Activities: Renting and leasing of other machinery, equipment and tangible goods n.e.c.
Parent: Bybox Group Holdings Limited
Officers: Peter David Rowse, Secretary; Stuart James Miller [1967] Director; Peter David Rowse [1968] Director/Chief Financial Officer

Byrom Public Limited Company
Incorporated: 19 July 1991 *Employees:* 198
Net Worth: £20,300,316 *Total Assets:* £77,335,976
Registered Office: Seamos House, Brooks Drive, Cheadle, Cheshire, SK8 3SA
Activities: Activities of head offices
Officers: John Anthony Draper, Secretary; Enrique Byrom [1953] Director Economics Management [Mexican]; Jaime Byrom [1956] Director Management [Mexican]; Andrew David Jonathan Parker [1966] Marketing Director; Denis Anthony Robson [1934] Director

Bystronic UK Limited
Incorporated: 11 July 1988 *Employees:* 76
Net Worth: £8,076,000 *Total Assets:* £16,748,000
Registered Office: 6 Wayside Business Park, Wilsons Lane, Coventry, Warwicks, CV6 6NY
Activities: Installation of industrial machinery and equipment
Parent: Bystronic Group
Officers: Lee Paul Murrell, Secretary; Johan Elster [1964] Director [Norwegian]; Cornelia Gehrig [1966] Director [Swiss]; Lee Paul Murrell [1972] Financial Director; Daniel William Thombs [1973] Director

Byzak Limited
Incorporated: 17 April 1984
Net Worth: £4,494,000 *Total Assets:* £31,254,000
Registered Office: The Sherard Building, Edmund Halley Road, Oxford, OX4 4DQ
Activities: Other specialised construction activities n.e.c.
Parent: Globemile Limited
Officers: Darren Simon Jones [1973] Finance Director; David Michael McLoughlin [1962] Managing Director; Andrew Lee Milner [1969] Director/Chartered Engineer; Andrew Latham Nelson [1959] Finance Director

C Student Services Limited
Incorporated: 3 March 1998 *Employees:* 2
Previous: Clubeasy Student Services Ltd
Net Worth Deficit: £1,975,936 *Total Assets:* £22,077,690
Registered Office: 3 Ashby Square, Loughborough, Leics, LE11 5AA
Activities: Other letting and operating of own or leased real estate
Parent: Destinesia Limited
Officers: Raffaele Roberto Russo [1984] Director; Anna Louise Smale [1984] Director/Investment Analyst [New Zealander]

C3 Construction Holdings Limited
Incorporated: 30 October 2015 *Employees:* 76
Net Worth: £5,065,127 *Total Assets:* £15,641,490
Registered Office: 11 Merus Court, Meridian Business Park, Leicester, LE19 1RJ
Activities: Activities of other holding companies n.e.c.
Shareholders: C3 Holdings Limited; C3 Construction Group Limited
Officers: Samuel James Adams [1990] Director; Joel Denham [1982] Director/Quantity Surveyor; Mark James Johnson [1968] Director/Manager; Christopher Edward McCathie [1981] Director

C3 Construction Limited
Incorporated: 30 June 2003 *Employees:* 76
Net Worth: £7,247,701 *Total Assets:* £17,824,064
Registered Office: 11 Merus Court, Meridian Business Park, Leicester, LE19 1RJ
Activities: Construction of commercial buildings
Parent: C3 Construction Holdings Limited
Officers: Mark Adams [1969] Director; Samuel James Adams [1990] Director; Joel Denham [1982] Director/Quantity Surveyor; Darren James Humberstone [1970] Director/Site Engineer; Mark James Johnson [1968] Director/Manager; Christopher Edward McCathie [1981] Director; Matthew Christopher Weatherley [1983] Director

Cad Cam Automotive Limited
Incorporated: 25 October 2013 *Employees:* 133
Net Worth: £4,307,133 *Total Assets:* £13,512,826
Registered Office: Holbrook, Lane, Coventry, Warwicks, CV6 4AW
Activities: Manufacture of bodies (coachwork) for motor vehicles (except caravans)
Parent: Cad Cam Holdings Limited
Officers: Gregory Stephen Devine [1965] Director; Li Jian [1983] Director/General Manager [Chinese]; Adam Andrew James Roby [1970] Director; Yang Shouhai [1957] Director/Chairman [Chinese]; Martyn Noel Wheeler [1965] Director

Cad Cam Holdings Limited
Incorporated: 30 July 2015 *Employees:* 133
Net Worth: £6,593,795 *Total Assets:* £15,166,791
Registered Office: Holbrook Lane, Coventry, Warwicks, CV6 4AW
Activities: Activities of head offices
Officers: Gregory Stephen Devine [1965] Sales Director; Li Jian [1983] Director/General Manager [Chinese]; Adam Andrew James Roby [1970] Finance Director; Yang Shouhai [1957] Director/Chairman [Chinese]; Martyn Noel Wheeler [1965] Managing Director

Cadent Gas Limited
Incorporated: 23 March 2016 *Employees:* 4,102
Net Worth: £886,000,000 *Total Assets:* £9,879,000,064
Registered Office: Ashbrook Court, Prologis Park, Central Boulevard, Coventry, Warwicks, CV7 8PE
Activities: Distribution of gaseous fuels through mains
Parent: Quadgas Midco Limited
Officers: Mark Stuart Cooper, Secretary; David Andrew Howitt, Secretary; Abdulla Mohamed Al-Ansari [1988] Director/Investment Manager [Qatari]; Nicholas John Axam [1979] Director/Investment Manager [Australian]; Dr Catherine Elisabeth Dorcas Bell [1951] Director; Mark William Braithwaite [1965] Director; Iain Michael Coucher [1961] Director/Chief Executive; Eduard Benjamin Fidler [1977] Director [Canadian]; Richard Greenleaf [1981] Director/Asset Manager; Michael John Gregory [1968] Director; Howard Charles Higgins [1953] Director; Stephen Glynn Hurrell [1957] Director/Chief Financial Officer; Deven Karnik [1967] Director; Jaroslava Korpancova [1974] Director [Czech]; Mark William Mathieson [1966] Managing Director; Sir Adrian Alastair Montague [1948] Director/Chairman; Perry Denis Noble [1960] Director/Infrastructure Partner; Hua Su [1990] Director/Investment [Chinese]; Kevin Ian Whiteman [1956] Director; David Jinlin Xie [1978] Director/Investment Professional [American]

Cadent Services Limited
Incorporated: 23 March 2016
Net Worth: £5,659,000 *Total Assets:* £42,170,000
Registered Office: Ashbrook Court, Prologis Park, Central Boulevard, Coventry, Warwicks, CV7 8PE
Activities: Development of building projects
Parent: Quadgas Midco Limited
Officers: Mark Stuart Cooper, Secretary; David Andrew Howitt, Secretary; Mark William Braithwaite [1965] Managing Director; Stephen Glynn Hurrell [1957] Director; Jaroslava Korpancova [1974] Director [Czech]

CAE Aircrew Training Services PLC
Incorporated: 4 March 1997 *Employees:* 7
Net Worth: £20,682,000 *Total Assets:* £48,560,000
Registered Office: Medium Support Helicopter Aircrew Training Facility, RAF Benson, Wallingford, Oxon, OX10 6AA
Activities: Other professional, scientific and technical activities n.e.c.
Parent: CAE International Holdings Ltd
Officers: James Anthony Boyle, Secretary; James Anthony Boyle [1982] Finance Director; Pietro D'Ulisse [1960] Director/VP [Canadian]; James Christopher Heath [1975] Director; Andrew Naismith [1962] Managing Director; Mario Poirier [1965] Director/VP Finance [Canadian]; Scott Springett [1968] Director/Asset Manager

Caesar Bidco Limited
Incorporated: 5 December 2012 *Employees:* 3
Net Worth Deficit: £13,639,451 *Total Assets:* £65,567,220
Registered Office: Kings Court, Water Lane, Wilmslow, Cheshire, SK9 5AR
Activities: Activities of other holding companies n.e.c.
Parent: Caesar Midco Limited
Officers: Jenny Ingleby [1976] Sales & Marketing Director; Christopher Paul Morris [1972] Director; Eloise Wann [1977] Director/Chief Financial Officer

Caesar Midco Limited
Incorporated: 5 December 2012 *Employees:* 3
Net Worth Deficit: £2,392,516 *Total Assets:* £76,895,928
Registered Office: Kings Court, Water Lane, Wilmslow, Cheshire, SK9 5AR
Activities: Activities of other holding companies n.e.c.
Parent: Caesar Topco Limited
Officers: Jenny Ingleby [1976] Sales & Marketing Director; Christopher Paul Morris [1972] Director; Eloise Wann [1977] Director/Chief Financial Officer

Caesar Topco Limited
Incorporated: 5 December 2012
Net Worth: £853,000 *Total Assets:* £79,753,000
Registered Office: Kings Court, Water Lane, Wilmslow, Cheshire, SK9 5AR
Activities: Activities of other holding companies n.e.c.
Parent: HG Pooled Management Limited
Officers: Jenny Ingleby [1977] Sales and Marketing Director; Christopher Paul Morris [1972] Director; Eloise Wann [1977] Director/Chief Financial Officer

Cairnwell Estates Limited
Incorporated: 20 April 2009
Net Worth: £60,628,468 *Total Assets:* £101,952,080
Registered Office: Ferham House, Kimberworth Road, Masbrough, Rotherham, S Yorks, S61 1AJ
Activities: Residential nursing care facilities
Parent: Cairnwell Capital Limited
Officers: Elizabeth Jane Phipps, Secretary; Euan David Craig [1977] Director; John Henry Whitehead [1964] Director

Caistor Seafoods Limited
Incorporated: 28 April 2000 *Employees:* 203
Previous: Sealord Caistor Limited
Net Worth: £4,671,954 *Total Assets:* £17,182,314
Registered Office: Unit 7 Enterprise Road, Caistor, Lincs, LN7 6PX
Activities: Processing and preserving of fish, crustaceans and molluscs
Parent: Nippon Suisan (Europe) B.V.
Officers: Susan Andrea Prowse, Secretary; Daniel Gallou [1958] Director [French]; Terutaka Kuraishi [1967] Director [Japanese]; Hisami Sakai [1957] Director [Japanese]; Ken Yokoi [1964] Director [Japanese]

Caldic (UK) Ltd
Incorporated: 17 December 1986 *Employees:* 60
Net Worth: £1,926,815 *Total Assets:* £24,465,160
Registered Office: Stainsby Close, Holmewood Industrial Estate, Chesterfield, Derbys, S42 5UG
Activities: Wholesale of chemical products
Parent: Caldic B.V.
Officers: Danielle Francesca Auton, Secretary; John Philip Robinson [1963] Managing Director; Olav Casper Van Caldenborgh [1968] Director/C.E.O [Dutch]

Caledonia Bidco Limited
Incorporated: 30 March 2016 *Employees:* 3
Net Worth Deficit: £1,971,660 *Total Assets:* £37,333,544
Registered Office: DC139 Style Way, Pineham, Swan Valley, Northampton, NN4 9EX
Activities: Activities of head offices
Parent: Caledonia Topco Limited
Officers: Simon Clifford [1964] Sales Director; Glenn Jonathan Lindfield [1959] Director; Scott Christopher Merrick [1983] Director; Robert Jan Thompson [1977] Director/Chartered Accountant; Ian Winston Turner [1960] Director

Caledonia Topco Limited
Incorporated: 24 March 2016 *Employees:* 390
Net Worth Deficit: £15,931,268 *Total Assets:* £33,254,164
Registered Office: DC139 Style Way, Pineham, Swan Valley, Northampton, NN4 9EX
Activities: Activities of head offices
Parent: Sovereign Capital IV Limited Partnership
Officers: Simon Clifford [1964] Sales Director; Robert Keith Ellis [1951] Director/Management Consultant; Glenn Jonathan Lindfield [1959] Director; Scott Christopher Merrick [1983] Director; Robert Jan Thompson [1977] Director/Chartered Accountant; Ian Winston Turner [1960] Director

Caledonia Venus Acquisitions Limited
Incorporated: 19 October 2015
Net Worth: £6,180,000 *Total Assets:* £276,644,000
Registered Office: New Castle House, Castle Boulevard, Nottingham, NG7 1FT
Activities: Activities of head offices
Parent: Caledonia Venus Group Limited
Officers: Timothy Richard Gwynne Lewis [1978] Director; Chris John Matthews [1972] Director/Chief Executive Officer; Gary Payne [1969] Director

Caledonia Venus Group Limited
Incorporated: 19 October 2015
Net Worth: £645,000 *Total Assets:* £113,560,000
Registered Office: New Castle House, Castle Boulevard, Nottingham, NG7 1FT
Activities: Activities of head offices
Parent: Caledonia Venus Holdings Limited
Officers: Timothy Richard Gwynne Lewis [1978] Director; Chris John Matthews [1972] Director/Chief Executive Officer; Gary Payne [1969] Director

Caledonia Venus Holdings Limited
Incorporated: 19 October 2015 *Employees:* 3,895
Net Worth: £103,650,000 *Total Assets:* £284,654,016
Registered Office: New Castle House, Castle Boulevard, Nottingham, NG7 1FT
Activities: Activities of head offices
Shareholder: Caledonia Investments PLC
Officers: Sally Deborah Flanagan [1962] Director; John Michael Kelly [1947] Director; Timothy Richard Gwynne Lewis [1978] Director; Chris John Matthews [1972] Director/Chief Executive Officer; Gary Payne [1969] Director

Caledonian Group Holdings Limited
Incorporated: 14 November 2016 *Employees:* 226
Net Worth Deficit: £3,214,000 *Total Assets:* £14,577,000
Registered Office: Carlton Works, Ossington Road, Carlton on Trent, Newark, Notts, NG23 6NT
Activities: Non-trading company
Officers: Michael Kaufman [1972] Director/Investment Manager [American]; James Paul Lang [1967] Director

Caljan Rite-Hite Limited
Incorporated: 11 July 1996 *Employees:* 93
Net Worth: £1,544,473 *Total Assets:* £9,441,462
Registered Office: Clifford House, 37-39 Simpson Road, Fenny Stratford, Milton Keynes, Bucks, MK1 1BA
Activities: Manufacture of lifting and handling equipment
Major Shareholder: Michael Henry White
Officers: Craig Wolfe, Secretary; Henrik Olesen [1964] Director/General Manager [Danish]; Spencer Roberts [1968] Director

Barry Callebaut Holding (UK) Limited
Incorporated: 15 June 1990
Net Worth: £26,944,000 *Total Assets:* £26,944,000
Registered Office: Wildmere Road Industrial Estate, Banbury, Oxon, OX16 3UU
Activities: Manufacture of cocoa and chocolate confectionery
Parent: Barry Callebaut France SAS
Officers: Bart de Geyndt [1969] Director/CFO (Western Europe) [Belgian]; Andy Edward Fleming [1974] Director; Massimo Garavaglia [1966] Director/President Western Europe [Italian]

Barry Callebaut Manufacturing (UK) Limited
Incorporated: 14 January 1974 *Employees:* 177
Net Worth: £10,329,000 *Total Assets:* £78,363,000
Registered Office: Wildmere Industrial Estate, Banbury, Oxon, OX16 3UU
Activities: Manufacture of cocoa and chocolate confectionery
Parent: Barry Callebaut Holding (UK) Limited
Officers: Bart de Geyndt [1969] Director/CFO (Western Europe) [Belgian]; Andy Edward Fleming [1974] Sales Director; Massimo Garavaglia [1966] Director/President Western Europe [Italian]; Richard Martin Scott [1970] Operations Director; Robin Waters [1958] Director/Head of UK Sale

Callington's Construction Limited
Incorporated: 26 May 2011
Net Worth: £4,307,827 *Total Assets:* £11,192,120
Registered Office: Unit 5 Sheene Road, Gorse Hill Industrial Estate, Leicester, LE4 1BF
Activities: Development of building projects
Major Shareholder: Phillip Owen Callington
Officers: Phillip Owen Callington [1980] Director

Calor Gas Limited
Incorporated: 2 August 1935 *Employees:* 1,457
Net Worth: £113,100,000 *Total Assets:* £433,800,000
Registered Office: Athena House, Athena Drive, Tachbrook Park, Warwick, CV34 6RL
Activities: Wholesale of other fuels and related products
Parent: Calor Group Limited
Officers: Rowan Diane Marshall-Rowan, Secretary; Matthew Quentin Hickin [1967] Managing Director; Paul Alexander Instrell [1978] Sales and Marketing Director; Adam Euan Thompson [1974] Operations Director; Jonathan Mark Wood [1968] Finance Director

Calor Group Limited
Incorporated: 11 February 1987
Net Worth: £96,992,000 *Total Assets:* £97,138,000
Registered Office: Athena House, Athena Drive, Tachbrook Park, Warwick, CV34 6RL
Activities: Activities of head offices
Parent: SHV Energy Holdings UK Limited
Officers: Rowan Diane Marshall-Rowan, Secretary; Matthew Quentin Hickin [1967] Managing Director; Adam Euan Thompson [1974] Operations Director; Pieter Van Holten [1969] Director [Dutch]; Jonathan Mark Wood [1968] Finance Director

Calor Properties Limited
Incorporated: 4 April 2012
Total Assets: £59,285,000
Registered Office: Athena House, Athena Drive, Tachbrook Park, Warwick, CV34 6RL
Activities: Non-trading company
Parent: Calor Gas Limited
Officers: Rowan Diane Marshall-Rowan, Secretary; Matthew Quentin Hickin [1967] Managing Director; Adam Euan Thompson [1974] Operations Director; Jonathan Mark Wood [1968] Finance Director

Calverton Finance Limited
Incorporated: 10 August 1998 *Employees:* 45
Net Worth: £3,947,118 *Total Assets:* £36,386,992
Registered Office: Calverton House, 1 Keller Close, Kiln Farm, Milton Keynes, Bucks, MK11 3LL
Activities: Factoring
Parent: Calverton Group Limited
Officers: Samantha Etherington, Secretary; Mark Gerard Byrne [1960] Factoring Director; Carol Anne Cordrey [1951] Director; Peter Graham Cordrey [1947] Director/Banker; David Hogg [1949] Director; Gregory David Hussey [1971] Operations Director; Sharon Simpson [1973] Sales Director

Cambridge & Counties Bank Limited
Incorporated: 1 March 2012 *Employees:* 125
Net Worth: £76,243,000 *Total Assets:* £879,232,000
Registered Office: Charnwood Court, 5b New Walk, Leicester, LE1 6TE
Activities: Banks
Shareholders: Trinity Hall; Cambridgeshire County Council
Officers: Richard Edward Bryan, Secretary; Rachel Lisa Curtis-Bowen [1974] Director of Marketing and Customer Experience; Paul Ffolkes Davis [1954] Director/Bursar; Caroline Elizabeth Fawcett [1959] Director; Andrea Katherine Hodgson [1967] Director/Chartered Accountant; Michael James Kirsopp [1958] Director/Chief Operating Officer; Simon Richard Lindley [1966] Director/Banker; John Charles McGuire [1948] Director; Simon Alick Moore [1965] Director; Richard Anthony Perry [1957] Director/Civil Servant; Ian Sydney Smith [1958] Director

Cambridge Display Technology Limited
Incorporated: 2 January 1992 *Employees:* 106
Net Worth: £4,643,000 *Total Assets:* £12,851,000
Registered Office: Unit 12 Cardinal Park, Cardinal Way, Godmanchester, Cambs, PE29 2XG
Activities: Other research and experimental development on natural sciences and engineering
Parent: CDT Holdings Limited
Officers: Hilary Charles, Secretary; Yoshiaki Oda [1961] Director/Company Executive [Japanese]; Hiroshi Ueda [1956] Director/Company Executive [Japanese]; Jim Veninger [1962] Director/VP Technology Development [American]; Takeshi Yamada [1967] Director/Office Worker [Japanese]

Cambridge Nutritional Foods Limited
Incorporated: 8 August 2005 *Employees:* 229
Net Worth: £9,100,796 *Total Assets:* £14,955,309
Registered Office: Stafford House, Brakey Road, Weldon North Industrial Estate, Corby, Northants, NN17 5LU
Activities: Activities of head offices
Parent: Cambridge Employee Ownership Trust
Officers: Michael Francis Swinburne, Company Secretary; Gary Paul Davie [1967] Director/Solicitor; Kenneth John Lindsay [1966] Director; Christopher McDermott [1969] Director; Michael Francis Swinburne [1961] Finance Director

Cambridge Realty Limited
Incorporated: 14 April 2015
Net Worth: £310,684 *Total Assets:* £10,086,681
Registered Office: The Station House, 15 Station Road, St Ives, Cambs, PE27 5BH
Activities: Buying and selling of own real estate
Major Shareholder: John Edward Story
Officers: Simon Matthew Grice [1964] Director/Trader; John Edward Story [1951] Director; Regina Clara Wrench [1963] Director [American]; Spencer Frank Wrench [1961] Director

Cambridge Weight Plan Limited
Incorporated: 25 October 1982 *Employees:* 224
Net Worth: £10,217,734 *Total Assets:* £14,148,885
Registered Office: Stafford House, 10 Brakey Road, Weldon North Industrial Estate, Corby, Northants, NN17 5LU
Activities: Manufacture of other food products n.e.c.
Parent: Cambridge Nutritional Foods Ltd
Officers: Michael Francis Swinburne, Finance Director; Tyrone Douglas [1968] H R Director; Christine Ann James [1968] Marketing & Communications Director; Clifford Darren Jones [1979] UK Sales Director; Scott Law [1977] Operations Director; Christopher McDermott [1969] Managing Director; Michael Francis Swinburne [1961] Finance Director

Cambus Limited
Incorporated: 8 June 1984 *Employees:* 893
Net Worth: £25,711,000 *Total Assets:* £40,193,000
Registered Office: c/o Stagecoach Services Limited, One Stockport Exchange, 20 Railway Road, Stockport, Cheshire, SK1 3SW
Activities: Other urban, suburban or metropolitan passenger land transport (not underground, metro or similar)
Parent: Stagecoach Bus Holdings Limited
Officers: Michael John Vaux, Secretary; Colin Brown [1968] Director/Accountant; John Andrew Campbell [1953] Managing Director; Michelle Catherine Hargreaves [1963] Director; Arnold Mark Threapleton [1954] Managing Director

Camden Motors (Holdings) Limited
Incorporated: 18 September 1996 *Employees:* 2
Net Worth: £25,774,000 *Total Assets:* £29,539,000
Registered Office: 11 Osier Way, Olney Office Park, Olney, Bucks, MK46 5FP
Activities: Other letting and operating of own or leased real estate
Major Shareholder: Paul John Dunkley
Officers: David William Hammond, Secretary; Paul John Dunkley [1958] Director; David William Hammond [1963] Director

Camden Ventures Limited
Incorporated: 13 June 2005 *Employees:* 5
Net Worth: £34,455,000 *Total Assets:* £42,794,000
Registered Office: 11 Osier Way, Olney Office Park, Olney, Bucks, MK46 5FP
Activities: Other letting and operating of own or leased real estate
Major Shareholder: Paul John Dunkley
Officers: David William Hammond, Secretary; Paul John Dunkley [1958] Director; David William Hammond [1963] Director

CAME BPT UK Limited
Incorporated: 23 October 1996 *Employees:* 95
Net Worth: £10,416,312 *Total Assets:* £16,586,389
Registered Office: Unit 1b Sills Road, Castle Donington, Derbys, DE74 2US
Activities: Other business support service activities n.e.c.
Officers: Christopher John Robert Wilson, Secretary; James Benjamin Bostock [1978] Managing Director; Andrea Menuzzo [1975] Managing Director [Italian]; David Pagram [1967] Operations Director; Christopher John Robert Wilson [1979] Finance Director

Joseph Camm Farms Limited
Incorporated: 21 March 1962 *Employees:* 18
Net Worth: £14,311,667 *Total Assets:* £15,188,856
Registered Office: Upper Morton, Babworth, Retford, Notts, DN22 8HG
Activities: Growing of cereals (except rice), leguminous crops and oil seeds
Shareholders: Ruth Margaret Girdham; Beatrix Mary Easterbrook
Officers: Mark Pickard, Secretary; Beatrix Mary Easterbrook [1966] Director/Chartered Accountant; Mark Easterbrook [1966] Director/Brewer; Ruth Margaret Girdham [1959] Director; Margaret Emily Morrell [1931] Director/Farmer

Campbell Scientific Limited
Incorporated: 26 July 1985 *Employees:* 79
Net Worth: £14,714,937 *Total Assets:* £16,464,374
Registered Office: Campbell Park, 80 Hathern Road, Shepshed, Loughborough, Leics, LE12 9GX
Activities: Manufacture of electronic measuring, testing etc. equipment, not for industrial process control
Parent: Campbell,Scientific Inc.
Officers: Ann Margaret Greenwood, Secretary; Robert Hazelton Campbell [1973] Director/President of Parent Company [American]; Ann Margaret Greenwood [1954] Director/Chartered Accountant; Stephen Paul Severn [1958] Managing Director

Camping and Caravanning Club Limited (The)
Incorporated: 22 November 1947 *Employees:* 650
Net Worth: £50,189,000 *Total Assets:* £75,299,000
Registered Office: Greenfields House, Westwood Way, Westwood Business Park, Coventry, Warwicks, CV4 8JH
Activities: Recreational vehicle parks, trailer parks and camping grounds
Officers: Robert Christopher Louden, Secretary; Christine Archer [1947] Director; Stephen Alan Ashman [1955] Director/Retired; Gordon Robert Barlow [1947] Director/Retired; Paul John Bastin [1954] Director/Retired; Roy Kenneth Brown [1941] Director/Retired; Debra Carcary [1967] Director/Recruitment Officer; Stephen Wilfred Chandler [1957] Director/Teacher; Christopher Richard Chester [1958] Director/IT Support; Raymond Clarkson [1948] Director/Retired; Christine Cole [1952] Director/Station Administrator; Michael John Doody [1946] Director/Retired; Catherine Downie [1949] Director/Retired Civil Servant; Stephen William Harris [1949] Director/Logistics Manager; Norman Arther Hemsley [1948] Director/Retired; Philip John Henson [1951] Director/Retired; Melvin Hill [1949] Director/Contract Manager; Philip David Isbell [1956] Director; John Johnstone [1961] Financial Advisor/Director; Michael Alan Lawler [1958] Technical Director Printing; Stuart Alan Lawler [1985] Director/Technical Engineer; Elizabeth Masters [1962] Director/Pharmacy Dispenser; Phillip David Masters [1957] Director/Retired; Walter Nichols [1945] Director/Retired; Stephen Robert Parrett [1957] Director/Health & Safety Advisor; John Sydney Pennock [1957] Director; Mary Magdalena Poole [1949] Director/Retired; Christopher Robert Porter [1956] Director/Retired; Jane Elizabeth Read [1949] Director; Allen Russell [1948] Director/Surveyor; Robert Talbot [1960] Director/Sales Manager; Susan Taylor [1953] Director/Local Government Officer; Ross Leonard Walker [1947] Director/Retired; Myrna Wells [1947] Director/Retired; Robert White [1948] Director/Engineer

Campion School & Language College
Incorporated: 8 July 2011 *Employees:* 163
Net Worth: £13,380,446 *Total Assets:* £15,269,586
Registered Office: Campion School & Language College, Kislingbury Road, Bugbrooke, Northampton, NN7 3QG
Activities: General secondary education
Officers: Ruth Barry, Secretary; Jennifer Cheang [1976] Director/Financial Services Manager; Deborah Louise Clewes [1966] Director/Lecturer; Simone Rebecca Davies [1971] Director/Head of Planning and Resources; Mark Adrian Foster [1961] Director; Pamela Anne Hutchison [1948] Director/Retired; Jacquetta Elizabeth Manning [1977] Director/Accountant; Diana Jill McAfee [1965] Director/Engineering Manager; Simon Edward Potts [1968] Director/Househusband; Elizabeth Anne Waddingham [1960] Director/Retired; Claire Whitmore [1972] Director/Secondary School Headteacher; Sarah Louise Wicks [1983] Director/Teacher

Can-Pack UK Limited
Incorporated: 11 September 2007 *Employees:* 247
Net Worth: £54,659,472 *Total Assets:* £91,805,152
Registered Office: Plot 18 Skippingdale Industrial Estate, Holyrood Drive, Scunthorpe, N Lincs, DN15 8NN
Activities: Manufacture of light metal packaging
Parent: Can-Pack Spolka Akcyjna
Officers: Philip Fisher, Secretary; Gary Beard [1975] Director; Michael Brooke Burkinshaw [1957] Director; Philip Michael Fisher [1975] Director

Canal & River Trading CIC
Incorporated: 15 May 2012
Net Worth: £38,067,180 *Total Assets:* £48,124,308
Registered Office: First Floor, North Station House, 500 Elder Gate, Milton Keynes, Bucks, MK9 1BB
Activities: Development of building projects
Parent: Canal & River Trust
Officers: Yetunde Salami, Secretary; Thomas James Deards [1976] Director/Solicitor; Sandra Claire Kelly [1960] Director/Chartered Accountant; Stuart Christopher Mills [1967] Property Director; Quentin Patrick Pickford [1961] Director/Chartered Management Accountant; Steven Pullinger [1959] Director/Accountant

Canal & River Trust
Incorporated: 12 October 2011 *Employees:* 1,698
Net Worth: £791,200,000 *Total Assets:* £1,082,000,000
Registered Office: First Floor, North Station House, 500 Elder Gate, Milton Keynes, Bucks, MK9 1BB
Activities: Water collection, treatment and supply
Officers: Thomas James Deards, Secretary; Dame Jennifer Gita Abramsky [1946] Director; Nigel Charles Annett [1958] Director; Joseph Benjamin Gordon [1959] Director; Janet Hogben [1957] Director/Chief People Officer; Sir Christopher William Kelly [1946] Director; Allan Leslie Leighton [1953] Director/Trustees; Tim Reeve [1973] Director/Trustee; Susan Linda Wilkinson [1956] Director

Canaveral Bidco Limited
Incorporated: 26 March 2015 *Employees:* 3
Net Worth Deficit: £15,273,000 *Total Assets:* £45,692,000
Registered Office: 17a Thorney Leys Park, Witney, Oxon, OX28 4GE
Activities: Activities of other holding companies n.e.c.
Officers: Merrill Graham Goulding [1982] Director; Ian Barrie Jackson [1973] Director/Private Equity Executive; Christian Schmitz [1975] Director/Investment Professional [German]

Canaveral Holdco Limited
Incorporated: 26 March 2015 *Employees:* 3,812
Net Worth Deficit: £31,030,000 *Total Assets:* £162,996,992
Registered Office: 17a Thorney Leys Park, Witney, Oxon, OX28 4GE
Activities: Activities of other holding companies n.e.c.
Officers: Merrill Graham Goulding [1982] Director; Ian Barrie Jackson [1973] Director/Private Equity Executive; David Richard Pugh [1961] Finance Director; Christian Schmitz [1975] Director/Investment Professional [German]; Michael Alfred Wilmshurst [1960] Managing Director

Canei International Limited
Incorporated: 23 January 1991 *Employees:* 74
Net Worth: £8,056,854 *Total Assets:* £14,321,534
Registered Office: 4Brothers House, Wilsthorpe Road, Long Eaton, Nottingham, NG10 3LE
Activities: Sale of used cars and light motor vehicles
Officers: Bulbinder Bhardwaj, Secretary; Bulbinder Bhardwaj [1968] Director/Salesman; Kuldeep Kumar Bhardwaj [1965] Director; Roshan Lal Bhardwaj [1955] Director/Entrepreneur

Cannon Venture Finance Limited
Incorporated: 23 April 1999 *Employees:* 31
Previous: Ransomwood Estates Limited
Net Worth: £9,177,681 *Total Assets:* £11,743,986
Registered Office: Unit 50 Ransom Hall, Ransom Wood Business Park, Southwell Road West, Rainworth, Mansfield, Notts, NG21 0HJ
Activities: Other letting and operating of own or leased real estate
Major Shareholder: Michael Harry Wilson Cannon
Officers: Fiona Mary Canon, Secretary; Charles Michael George Canon [1971] Director/Manager; James Edward Thomas Canon [1975] Commercial Director; Michael Harry Wilson Canon [1943] Director/Asset Manager; Richard Thomas Kenning [1951] Director

Canon Street Properties Limited
Incorporated: 6 March 1997 *Employees:* 9
Net Worth: £16,415,189 *Total Assets:* £16,492,414
Registered Office: 5 Woodgate, Rothley, Leics, LE7 7LL
Activities: Activities of head offices
Officers: Janet Hutson [1938] Director; Jonathan Peter Hutson [1970] Director; Mark Andrew Hutson [1961] Director; Maurice Arthur Hutson [1934] Director; Helen Claire Wilkinson [1963] Director

Cape Engineering Services Limited
Incorporated: 12 January 1994 *Employees:* 660
Previous: Redhall Engineering Solutions Limited
Net Worth: £5,505,000 *Total Assets:* £18,127,000
Registered Office: Building 2, Fields End Business Park, Davey Road, Thurnscoe, Goldthorpe, Rotherham, S Yorks, S63 0JF
Activities: Manufacture of other fabricated metal products n.e.c.
Parent: Cape Industrial Services Group Limited
Officers: Simon Angus Hicks [1968] Director; Tony Jester [1968] Director; John Anthony Meade Walsh [1964] Finance Director

Cape Environmental Services Onshore Limited
Incorporated: 15 April 1996 *Employees:* 228
Net Worth: £11,803,000 *Total Assets:* £16,553,000
Registered Office: Building 2, Fields End Business Park, Davey Road, Thurnscoe, Goldthorpe, Rotherham, S Yorks, S63 0JF
Activities: General cleaning of buildings
Parent: Cape Intermediate Holdings Limited
Officers: Simon Angus Hicks [1968] Director; John Anthony Meade Walsh [1964] Finance Director

Cape Industrial Services Group Limited
Incorporated: 7 January 1997 *Employees:* 45
Net Worth: £86,763,000 *Total Assets:* £330,820,992
Registered Office: Building 2, Fields End Business Park, Davey Road, Thurnscoe, Goldthorpe, Rotherham, S Yorks, S63 0JF
Activities: Non-trading company
Parent: Cape UK Holdings Newco Limited
Officers: Richard Michael Alcock [1944] Director; Mohamed Altrad [1948] Director [French]; Louis Marie Maurice Roger Huetz [1970] Director [French]; Parminder Kaur Poonia [1974] Director/Solicitor

Cape Industrial Services Limited
Incorporated: 20 March 1997 *Employees:* 3,174
Net Worth Deficit: £14,522,000 *Total Assets:* £223,534,000
Registered Office: Building 2, Fields End Business Park, Davey Road, Thurnscoe, Goldthorpe, Rotherham, S Yorks, S63 0JF
Activities: Electrical installation
Parent: Cape Intermediate Holdings Limited
Officers: Simon Angus Hicks [1968] Director; John Anthony Meade Walsh [1964] Finance Director

Cape UK Holdings Newco Limited
Incorporated: 26 August 2011
Net Worth: £43,787,000 *Total Assets:* £171,998,000
Registered Office: Building 2, Fields End Business Park, Davey Road, Thurnscoe, Goldthorpe, Rotherham, S Yorks, S63 0JF
Activities: Activities of head offices
Parent: Cape PLC
Officers: Richard Michael Alcock [1944] Director; Mohamed Altrad [1948] Director [French]; Louis Marie Maurice Roger Huetz [1970] Director [French]

Capital One (Europe) PLC
Incorporated: 17 November 1999
Net Worth: £1,129,705,984 *Total Assets:* £2,533,635,072
Registered Office: Trent House, Station Street, Nottingham, NG2 3HX
Activities: Credit granting by non-deposit taking finance houses and other specialist consumer credit grantors
Shareholders: Capital One Holdings Limited; Capital One Investments Limited
Officers: Rupert John MacInnes, Secretary; Lucy Marie Hagues [1977] Director/Chief Marketing Officer; Robert Williiam Harding [1974] Director/Chief Information Officer; Amy Christine Lenander [1981] Director/Chief Marketing Officer [American]; Michael John Lynch [1970] Director [American]; Jeremy Robert Penzer [1971] Director/Chief Analytics Officer; Richard John Rolls [1968] Director/Business Chief Risk Officer

Capital One Holdings Limited
Incorporated: 19 October 1999
Net Worth: £325,215,008 *Total Assets:* £329,996,000
Registered Office: Trent House, Station Street, Nottingham, NG2 3HX
Activities: Activities of financial services holding companies
Officers: Rupert John MacInnes, Secretary; Robert Williiam Harding [1974] Director/Chief Operations and Technology Officer; Richard John Rolls [1968] Director/Business Chief Risk Officer

Capital One Investments Limited
Incorporated: 10 January 2001
Net Worth: £561,766,976 *Total Assets:* £567,590,976
Registered Office: Trent House, Station Street, Nottingham, NG2 3HX
Activities: Activities of financial services holding companies
Officers: Rupert John MacInnes, Secretary; Lucy Marie Hagues [1977] Director/Chief Marketing Officer; Richard John Rolls [1968] Director/Business Chief Risk Officer

Capital Refractories Limited
Incorporated: 13 March 1973 *Employees:* 257
Net Worth: £11,961,413 *Total Assets:* £22,431,048
Registered Office: Station Road, Clowne, Derbys, S43 4AB
Activities: Other manufacturing n.e.c.
Shareholder: Margot Lynne Stuart-Harris
Officers: Deirdre Helen Newsome, Secretary; James Philip Russell Newsome [1969] Director; Margot Lynne Stuart-Harris [1944] Director

Car Electronics Limited
Incorporated: 14 January 1964 *Employees:* 18
Net Worth: £8,852,418 *Total Assets:* £9,949,485
Registered Office: 9 Oakland Road, Leicester, LE2 6AN
Activities: Wholesale trade of motor vehicle parts and accessories
Parent: Celtrade Limited
Officers: Caroline Ann Ward, Secretary; Anthony John Green [1956] Director; Andrew James Marsden [1965] Director; Caroline Ann Ward [1958] Director

The Car People Limited
Incorporated: 30 March 1999 *Employees:* 474
Net Worth: £36,498,000 *Total Assets:* £70,560,000
Registered Office: 2 Penman Way, Grove Park, Leicester, LE19 1ST
Activities: Sale of used cars and light motor vehicles
Parent: Sytner Group Limited
Officers: Adam Collinson, Secretary; Adam Collinson [1972] Director; Darren Edwards [1968] Director

Car Shops Limited
Incorporated: 13 January 2005 *Employees:* 689
Net Worth: £21,386,000 *Total Assets:* £81,721,000
Registered Office: 2 Penman Way, Grove Park, Leicester, LE19 1ST
Activities: Sale of used cars and light motor vehicles
Parent: Sytner Group Limited
Officers: Adam Collinson, Secretary; Adam Collinson [1972] Director; James Dunkley [1986] Commercial Director; Jonathan Paul Dunkley [1984] Director; Darren Edwards [1968] Director; Brian John Scott [1973] Director

Car Store Limited
Incorporated: 29 February 1980 *Employees:* 549
Previous: Pendragon Used Cars Limited
Net Worth Deficit: £3,143,000 *Total Assets:* £57,982,000
Registered Office: Loxley House, 2 Oakwood Court, Annesley, Nottingham, NG15 0DR
Activities: Sale of new cars and light motor vehicles
Parent: Evans Halshaw Motor Holdings Limited
Officers: Richard James Maloney, Secretary; Martin Shaun Casha [1960] Director; Trevor Garry Finn [1957] Director; Timothy Paul Holden [1964] Director/Chartered Accountant

Carbolite Holdings Limited
Incorporated: 26 November 2008 *Employees:* 1
Net Worth: £11,073,348 *Total Assets:* £16,040,409
Registered Office: Parsons Lane, Hope Valley, Derbys, S33 6RB
Activities: Manufacture of ovens, furnaces and furnace burners
Parent: Verder Holdings UK Limited
Officers: Andrew James Beare, Secretary; Dr Jurgen Pankratz [1965] Director [German]

Carbon International Limited
Incorporated: 4 January 1991 *Employees:* 48
Net Worth: £11,025,904 *Total Assets:* £13,782,652
Registered Office: Phoenix Works, Thurlstone, Sheffield, S36 9QU
Activities: Manufacture of other non-metallic mineral products n.e.c.
Parent: James Durrans & Sons Limited
Officers: Graham Paul Hooper, Secretary; Christopher Foster Durrans [1960] Managing Director; Herr Andreas Jentsch [1965] Director [German]

The Cardboard Box Company Limited
Incorporated: 12 June 2000 *Employees:* 78
Net Worth: £3,725,193 *Total Assets:* £10,455,473
Registered Office: 2 Franks Road, Bardon Hill, Coalville, Leics, LE67 1TT
Activities: Manufacture of other paper and paperboard containers
Parent: Braeside Group Limited
Officers: William Bingham Barnett [1976] Director; Alexander David Kelly [1967] Director; Bernard Neillus McDonnell [1959] Director [Irish]; Ken Shackleton [1956] Director

Carden Croft (2012) Limited
Incorporated: 4 December 2012
Net Worth: £7,775,498 *Total Assets:* £10,050,000
Registered Office: c/o Allens Accountants, 123 Wellington Road South, Stockport, Cheshire, SK1 3TH
Activities: Activities of other holding companies n.e.c.
Shareholders: Simon Dennis Carden; David John Croft
Officers: David John Croft, Secretary; Simon Dennis Carden [1955] Director; David John Croft [1949] Director

Care Fertility Group Limited
Incorporated: 13 April 2005 *Employees:* 277
Net Worth: £23,972,000 *Total Assets:* £36,240,000
Registered Office: John Webster House, 6 Lawrence Drive, Nottingham Business Park, Nottingham, NG8 6PZ
Activities: Hospital activities
Parent: Care Fertility Holdings Limited
Officers: David Brian Burford [1980] Director; Alison Campbell [1970] Director; Dr Kenneth Dowell [1957] Director; Dr Simon Brian Fishel [1953] Director/Scientist; Michael Kevin Peter Grassby [1961] Investor Director; Nigel Mark Inches Robertson [1959] Director/Exec Chairman; David Torbet [1978] Investor Director

Care Fertility Holdings Limited
Incorporated: 12 June 2012 *Employees:* 277
Net Worth Deficit: £34,851,000 *Total Assets:* £78,007,000
Registered Office: John Webster House, 6 Lawrence Drive, Nottingham Business Park, Nottingham, NG8 6PZ
Activities: Specialists medical practice activities
Parent: Bowmark Capital (Holdings) Limited
Officers: David Brian Burford [1980] Director; Dr Kenneth Dowell [1957] Director; Dr Simon Brian Fishel [1953] Director; Michael Kevin Peter Grassby [1961] Director/Investment Manager; Nigel Mark Inches Robertson [1959] Non-Executive Director Chairman; David Torbet [1978] Director

Carentan Holdings Limited
Incorporated: 24 February 2016 *Employees:* 231
Net Worth Deficit: £450,077 *Total Assets:* £25,097,604
Registered Office: Ferrymoor Way, Park Springs, Grimethorpe, Barnsley, S Yorks, S72 7BN
Activities: Activities of head offices
Shareholders: Hamsard 3488 Limited; John Stewart Ross
Officers: John Stewart Ross [1965] Director

Carewatch Bidco Limited
Incorporated: 4 August 2008
Net Worth: £34,142,000 *Total Assets:* £52,561,000
Registered Office: Libra House, Sunrise Parkway, Linford Wood, Milton Keynes, Bucks, MK14 6PH
Activities: Activities of head offices
Parent: Carewatch Holdings Limited
Officers: Alistair McKenzie Miller [1969] Director/Chartered Accountant; Mark Rogerson [1964] Director/Chairman

Carewatch Care Services Limited
Incorporated: 18 July 1994 *Employees:* 4,705
Net Worth: £5,862,000 *Total Assets:* £33,150,000
Registered Office: Libra House, Sunrise Parkway, Linford Wood, Milton Keynes, Bucks, MK14 6PH
Activities: Social work activities without accommodation for the elderly and disabled
Parent: Carewatch Acquisitions Limited
Officers: Mark Rogerson [1964] Director/Chairman

Carewatch Holdings Limited
Incorporated: 13 August 2008 *Employees:* 4,705
Net Worth Deficit: £6,043,000 *Total Assets:* £33,405,000
Registered Office: Libra House, Sunrise Parkway, Linford Wood, Milton Keynes, Bucks, MK14 6PH
Activities: Activities of head offices
Parent: Lyceum Capital (GP2) Limited
Officers: Alistair McKenzie Miller [1969] Director/Chartered Accountant; Mark Rogerson [1964] Director/Chairman

Cariole Limited
Incorporated: 18 July 2014
Net Worth: £13,732,000 *Total Assets:* £13,771,000
Registered Office: Trent Barton Buses, Mansfield Road, Heanor, Derbys, DE75 7BG
Activities: Credit granting by non-deposit taking finance houses and other specialist consumer credit grantors
Shareholders: Helen King; Brian Robert King; Richard Ian Morgan
Officers: Brian Robert King [1944] Director; Richard Ian Morgan [1951] Director; Graham Sutton [1960] Finance Director

Carl F Groupco Limited
Incorporated: 14 July 1988 *Employees:* 40
Net Worth: £6,452,000 *Total Assets:* £10,107,000
Registered Office: Culley Court, Orton Southgate, Peterborough, Cambs, PE2 6WA
Activities: Wholesale of hardware, plumbing and heating equipment and supplies
Major Shareholder: Geoffrey David Gahan
Officers: David Peacefull Wakeley, Secretary; John Crittenden [1959] Managing Director; Geoffery David Gahan [1944] Director; John Martin King [1960] Sales Director; David Peacefull Wakeley [1955] Finance Director

Carlsberg Chongqing Limited
Incorporated: 12 June 1995 *Employees:* 3
Net Worth: £15,209,861 *Total Assets:* £41,109,920
Registered Office: c/o Carlsberg UK Limited, 140 Bridge Street, Northampton, NN1 1PZ
Activities: Non-trading company
Parent: Carlsberg A/S
Officers: Jeremy Robert Brown, Secretary; Ulrik Andersen [1963] Director/General Consul [Danish]; Jeremy Robert Brown [1972] Director/Legal Counsel; Julian Akhtar Karim Momen [1963] Director/Chief Financial Officer

Carlsberg Supply Company UK Limited
Incorporated: 26 July 2013 *Employees:* 899
Net Worth: £124,421,000 *Total Assets:* £248,720,992
Registered Office: Jacobsen House, 140 Bridge Street, Northampton, NN1 1PZ
Activities: Manufacture of beer
Parent: Carlsberg UK Limited
Officers: Jeremy Robert Brown, Secretary; Paul Benedict Armstrong [1957] Director [Irish]; Peter Clark Hammond [1979] Director/Vice President Production

Carlsberg UK Holdings Limited
Incorporated: 21 December 1965 *Employees:* 6
Net Worth: £40,910,000 *Total Assets:* £248,622,000
Registered Office: 140 Bridge Street, Northampton, NN1 1PZ
Activities: Non-trading company
Parent: Carlsberg A/S
Officers: Jeremy Robert Brown, Secretary; Paul Benedict Armstrong [1957] Director [Irish]; Anna Cecilia Gunnarsson Lundgren [1973] Director/CFO Western Europe [Swedish]; Peter Clark Hammond [1979] Director/Vice President Production; Andreas Bernhard Kirk [1974] Director [Danish]; Julian Akhtar Karim Momen [1963] Director/Chief Financial Officer; Stephen Stringer [1967] Director

Carlsberg UK Limited
Incorporated: 28 August 1903 *Employees:* 431
Net Worth: £151,572,992 *Total Assets:* £475,660,992
Registered Office: 140 Bridge Street, Northampton, NN1 1PZ
Activities: Manufacture of beer
Parent: Carlsberg UK Holdings Limited
Officers: Jeremy Robert Brown, Secretary; Anna Cecilia Gunnarsson Lundgren [1973] Director/CFO Western Europe [Swedish]; Andreas Bernhard Kirk [1974] Director [Danish]; Julian Akhtar Karim Momen [1963] Director/Chief Financial Officer; Stephen Stringer [1967] Director; Adam Stubbs [1972] Director

Carlton Forest Group LLP
Incorporated: 6 August 2013 *Employees:* 58
Net Worth: £4,670,095 *Total Assets:* £9,724,436
Registered Office: Carlton Forest Distribution Centre, Carlton Forest, Blyth Road, Worksop, Notts, S81 0TP
Officers: Andrew Mark Pepper [1970] Member; John Douglas Pepper [1940] Member; Diane Ward [1962] Member; Kerry Daniel Neath [1959] LLP Member; Lisa Pepper [1974] LLP Member

Carlton Street Trading Limited
Incorporated: 27 February 2014 *Employees:* 1
Net Worth: £2,530,960 *Total Assets:* £12,538,582
Registered Office: Units A-D Willow Road, Lenton Industrial Estate, Nottingham, NG7 2TA
Activities: Other letting and operating of own or leased real estate
Shareholders: Hannah Burt; Sammy Burt; Alice Burt
Officers: Hannah Burt [1978] Director

Carmac (Building & Civil Engineering) Limited
Incorporated: 18 May 1984 *Employees:* 52
Net Worth: £8,046,316 *Total Assets:* £13,637,166
Registered Office: Carmac, Burton Road, Finedon, Northants, NN9 5HX
Activities: Construction of other civil engineering projects n.e.c.
Shareholders: Thomas John McGowan; Roger McGowan
Officers: Ian George Finnie [1963] Director/Surveyor; Rodger Edward McGowan [1948] Director/Civil Engineer [Irish]; Thomas John McGowan [1950] Director/Groundworker [Irish]; Andrew Morris [1962] Director/Surveyor

Carmelite Finance Limited
Incorporated: 5 May 1998
Net Worth: £543,000 *Total Assets:* £72,341,000
Registered Office: Point 3 Haywood Road, Warwick, CV34 5AH
Activities: Activities of head offices
Parent: Carmelite Investments Limited
Officers: Mark Andrew Webberley [1964] Director/Chartered Accountant

CarnaudMetalbox Group UK Ltd.
Incorporated: 21 November 1988
Net Worth: £406,136,992 *Total Assets:* £521,129,984
Registered Office: Downsview Road, Wantage, Oxon, OX12 9BP
Activities: Activities of head offices
Parent: Crown UK Holdings Limited
Officers: Jennifer Patricia Simpson, Secretary; John Patrick Beardsley [1970] Director; Paul William Browett [1961] Director/Vice President/Treasurer; Timothy Joseph Donahue [1962] Director/President/Chief Operating Officer [American]; William Thomas Gallagher [1954] Director/General Counsel [American]; Thomas Anthony Kelly [1959] Director/SVP/CFO [American]; Sidonie Lecluse [1975] Director/VP Human Resources [French]

CarnaudMetalbox Overseas Ltd.
Incorporated: 21 June 1948
Net Worth: £28,295,000 *Total Assets:* £28,311,000
Registered Office: Downsview Road, Wantage, Oxon, OX12 9BP
Activities: Activities of head offices
Parent: Crown UK Holdings Limited
Officers: Jennifer Patricia Simpson, Secretary; John Patrick Beardsley [1970] Director; Paul William Browett [1961] Director/Vice President/Treasurer; Mehmet Ziya Ozay [1963] Director/SVP, Bevcan Europe & Middle East [Turkish]

Carno 2 LLP
Incorporated: 12 September 2007
Net Worth: £1,789,006 *Total Assets:* £15,016,204
Registered Office: Glebe Barn, Great Barrington, Burford, Oxon, OX18 4US
Officers: David Wynn Richards [1959] Member; David Wynn Richards [1959] Member; John Gwyndaf Thomas [1944] Member; Sion Eirian Thomas [1975] Member; Sion Eirian Thomas [1975] Member

Carpenter Holdings Limited
Incorporated: 22 August 2001 *Employees:* 331
Net Worth: £79,726,000 *Total Assets:* £97,470,000
Registered Office: Dinting Lodge Industrial Estate, Glossop, Derbys, SK13 6LE
Activities: Other business support service activities n.e.c.
Officers: Brian Messer, Secretary; David John Hulley [1962] Director; Brian Messer [1961] Director; Stanley Frank Pauley [1927] Director [American]

Carpenter Limited
Incorporated: 2 July 1926 *Employees:* 331
Net Worth: £79,753,000 *Total Assets:* £97,533,000
Registered Office: Dinting Lodge Industrial Estate, Glossop, Derbys, SK13 6LE
Activities: Manufacture of other plastic products
Officers: Brian Messer, Secretary; Jim Albert Hacker [1953] Director [American]; David John Hulley [1962] Managing Director; Brian Messer [1961] Director; Stanley Frank Pauley [1927] Director [American]

Carr's Flour Mills Limited
Incorporated: 31 March 1950 *Employees:* 166
Net Worth: £9,067,000 *Total Assets:* £44,238,000
Registered Office: Victoria Mills, London Road, Wellingborough, Northants, NN8 2DT
Activities: Grain milling
Parent: Whitworths Holdings Ltd
Officers: Simone Louise Large, Secretary; Allan William Burns [1959] Director; Roger William Butler [1960] Director/Flour Miller; Michael David George [1973] Director; Duncan Redfern Monroe [1957] Managing Director; George Wishart [1957] Director

The Robert Carre Trust
Incorporated: 15 June 2011 *Employees:* 216
Previous: Carre's Grammar School Academy Trust
Net Worth: £14,968,653 *Total Assets:* £17,832,712
Registered Office: Carre's Grammar School, Northgate, Sleaford, Lincs, NG34 7DD
Activities: General secondary education
Officers: Jeremy Paul Green, Secretary; Valerie Andrew [1962] Director/Semi-Retired Independent Consultant; Robin Baker [1938] Director/Retired; Karen Bradford [1966] Director/Deputy Chief Executive; David Hodgson [1968] Director/Headmaster; Mark Ian Housley [1963] Director/Public Servant; Nicholas Matthew Law [1970] Director; Malcolm Robertson [1941] Director; Garry David Titmus [1947] Director/Retired

Carrier Refrigeration UK Limited
Incorporated: 29 January 1968 *Employees:* 52
Net Worth: £898,000 *Total Assets:* £15,830,000
Registered Office: Ground Floor, Meridian House, East Point Business Park, Sandy Lane West, Oxford, OX4 6LB
Activities: Other service activities n.e.c.
Officers: Adrian Forastier [1966] Director/General Manager [Spanish]; Michael Mulhern [1968] Director [Irish]; Daniel Schmedding [1974] Legal Director [German]

Carter Accommodation Group Limited
Incorporated: 13 December 2013 *Employees:* 114
Previous: Ensco 1036 Limited
Net Worth: £439,043 *Total Assets:* £30,601,708
Registered Office: Garage Lane, Setchey, King's Lynn, Norfolk, PE33 0BE
Activities: Dormant company
Parent: Connection Capital LLP
Officers: Darren Anthony Arnold [1962] Director; Bernard John Dale [1964] Director; Carl Fisher [1968] Director; Jonathan Scott Smith [1970] Director

Carter Accommodation Holdings Limited
Incorporated: 13 December 1999
Previous: Carter (F.C.) Holdings Limited
Net Worth: £6,609,389 *Total Assets:* £26,450,444
Registered Office: Garage Lane, Setchey, King's Lynn, Norfolk, PE33 0BE
Activities: Activities of head offices
Parent: Carter Accommodation Group Limited
Officers: Darren Anthony Arnold [1962] Director; David Horkan [1967] Operations Director; Jonathan Scott Smith [1970] Director; Tzigane Abigail Woolner [1973] Finance Director

Carwood Holdings Limited
Incorporated: 9 October 2007 *Employees:* 252
Net Worth: £15,309,540 *Total Assets:* £22,602,718
Registered Office: Herald Way, Binley, Coventry, Warwicks, CV3 2RQ
Activities: Activities of head offices
Major Shareholder: Kevin Patrick Mulholland
Officers: Jane Mulholland, Secretary; Nigel Walter Pond, Secretary; Alan Campbell Baird [1957] Director of Quality; Gary Ronald Carter [1945] Director; David Nigel Hopkins [1959] Director; Kevin Patrick Mulholland [1956] Director; Nigel Walter Pond [1971] Finance Director

Carwood Motor Units Limited
Incorporated: 14 June 1949 *Employees:* 252
Net Worth: £15,292,504 *Total Assets:* £22,602,580
Registered Office: Herald Way, Binley, Coventry, Warwicks, CV3 2RQ
Activities: Manufacture of electrical and electronic equipment for motor vehicles and their engines
Parent: Carwood Limited
Officers: Nigel Walter Pond, Secretary; Alan Campbell Baird [1957] Director of Quality; Gary Ronald Carter [1945] Director; David Nigel Hopkins [1959] Technical Director; Kevin Patrick Mulholland [1956] Director; Nigel Walter Pond [1971] Finance Director

Cashino Gaming Limited
Incorporated: 14 January 1972 *Employees:* 904
Net Worth Deficit: £5,865,000 *Total Assets:* £48,951,000
Registered Office: Seebeck House, 1a Seebeck Place, Knowlhill, Milton Keynes, Bucks, MK5 8FR
Activities: Gambling and betting activities
Parent: Praesepe Holdings Limited
Officers: Stefan Bruns [1971] Director/Chief Executive Officer [German]; Borris Lungen [1962] Director/Chief Financial Officer [German]; Mark Stefan Schertle [1977] Director [German]

CASP
Incorporated: 13 January 1988 *Employees:* 23
Net Worth: £9,551,931 *Total Assets:* £10,329,564
Registered Office: Raleigh House, 14c Compass Point Business Park, Stocks Bridge Way, St Ives, Cambs, PE27 5JL
Activities: Other research and experimental development on natural sciences and engineering
Officers: Dr John Robert Parker, Secretary; Dr Andrew Buckley [1958] Director/Administrator; Dr Peter Friend [1934] Director/Retired; Sally Anne Gibson [1963] Director/Lecturer; Dr James Philip Parkinson Hirst [1958] Director/Geologist; David Murray Dennis James [1941] Director/Retired; Dr Stephanie Jane Kape [1971] Director/Chartered Geologist; Dr Bruce Levell [1954] Director/Professor; Professor John Edward Alan Marshall [1954] Director/Geologist; Dr Gary John Nichols [1957] Director/Technical Manager; Dr John Robert Parker [1942] Director/Retired; Clive Anthony Graham Pickton [1952] Director/Petroleum Consultant; Dr Martin John Whiteley [1955] Director/University Lecturer

Castel Froma Neuro Care Limited
Incorporated: 27 May 2003 *Employees:* 181
Previous: Castel Froma
Net Worth: £11,497,494 *Total Assets:* £12,558,864
Registered Office: Royal Midland Counties Home, 93 Lillington Road, Leamington Spa, Warwicks, CV32 6LL
Activities: Residential nursing care facilities
Officers: Alison Mary Stiles, Secretary; John Anthony Evison [1946] Director/Retired; Lesley Holiday [1949] Director; David Leigh-Hunt [1943] Director/Consultant Solicitor; Graham Arthur Murrell [1949] Director; Stephen John Nicklin [1950] Director/Retired

Casterton College Rutland
Incorporated: 26 July 2011 *Employees:* 120
Previous: Casterton Business and Enterprise College Academy Trust
Net Worth: £6,709,986 *Total Assets:* £9,360,293
Registered Office: Casterton Business and Enterprise College, Ryhall Road, Great Casterton, Stamford, Lincs, PE9 4AT
Activities: General secondary education
Officers: Helen Cook, Secretary; Susan Ball [1960] Director/Teacher; Victoria Isabella Brown [1976] Director/HR Manager; Bejamin George Foster Callaghan [1960] Director; David Chapman [1963] Director/Regional Safety Adviser; Stephen Henderson Craig [1953] Director/Retired Business Manager; Steve Cutler [1990] Director/Corporation Tax Assistant Manager; Sian Dwyer [1958] Director; Robin Jones [1976] Director/Retail Manager; Kevin John Norris [1958] Director/Self Employed; Matt Shough [1973] Director/Head of Higher Education; Robert Slack [1972] Director/Engineer; Carl Smith [1965] Director/Principal; Andrew Tindall [1962] Director/IT Manager; Mary Elizabeth Town [1964] Director/Business Manager; Alan Stewart Walters [1955] Director/Councillor

Castle 1 Limited
Incorporated: 9 August 2007
Net Worth: £437,824,000 *Total Assets:* £527,662,016
Registered Office: The Waterfront, Lakeside Boulevard, Doncaster, S Yorks, DN4 5PL
Activities: Activities of head offices
Parent: K & A Merger Limited
Officers: Timothy Mark Beale [1976] Director; Mark Richard Priest [1966] Director; James Michael Douglas Thomson [1966] Director

Castle Phoenix Trust
Incorporated: 14 December 2012 *Employees:* 439
Net Worth: £8,868,869 *Total Assets:* £15,897,025
Registered Office: Caludon Castle School, Axholme Road, Coventry, Warwicks, CV2 5BD
Activities: General secondary education
Officers: Helen Ada Harrison, Secretary; Neil Andrew Forrest [1974] Director/Sole Legal Counsel & Assistant Company Secretary; Mark Richard Friday [1967] Project Director; Lesley Hancock [1965] Director/Human Resources; Kate Ireland [1962] Director; Michele Anne Marr [1959] Director/Headteacher; Helen Mary Reilly [1966] Director/Registered Dietitian; Shafiq Ahmed Sharif [1966] Director; Paul Michael Simpson [1969] Director/National Sales Process & Compliance; Wieczyslaw Taylor-Dowson [1962] Sales Director

Castle Square Developments Limited
Incorporated: 8 December 1988 *Employees:* 10
Net Worth: £25,953,996 *Total Assets:* £31,966,944
Registered Office: Scampton House, Scampton, Lincoln, LN1 2SF
Activities: Buying and selling of own real estate
Major Shareholder: John William Lockwood
Officers: Matthew Charles Karran, Secretary; Matthew Charles Karran [1974] Finance Director; Arthur William Lockwood [1924] Director; George William Lockwood [1985] Director; John William Lockwood [1954] Director/Farmer; Judith Ann Lockwood [1956] Director; Sarah Helen May Lockwood [1987] Director

Castlegate 624 Limited
Incorporated: 28 July 2010 *Employees:* 198
Net Worth: £8,260,000 *Total Assets:* £13,586,000
Registered Office: c/o Dar Lighting Limited, Wildmere Road, Banbury, Oxon, OX16 3JZ
Activities: Activities of head offices
Major Shareholder: Nicola Jane McGuirk
Officers: Nicola Jane Cosgrove McGuirk, Secretary; Nicola Jane Cosgrove McGuirk [1961] Director

Catalent UK Supply Chain Limited
Incorporated: 25 September 1989
Previous: Juniper Pharmaceuticals UK Limited
Net Worth: £2,414,691 *Total Assets:* £15,276,553
Registered Office: 8 Orchard Place, Nottingham Business Park, Nottingham, NG8 6PX
Activities: Manufacture of basic pharmaceutical products
Parent: Juniper Pharmaceuticals, Inc.
Officers: Kirk Walsh, Secretary; Jonathan Arnold [1965] Director/President Oral Drug Delivery; Alessandro Maselli [1972] Director/SVP Operations [Italian]; Dr Nikin Patel [1972] Director/Chief Operating Officer; Kirk Walsh [1980] Director/VP Finance

Caterpillar (U.K.) Limited
Incorporated: 27 July 1950 *Employees:* 2,055
Net Worth: £659,652,992 *Total Assets:* £780,827,008
Registered Office: Peckleton Lane, Desford, Leicester, LE9 9JT
Activities: Manufacture of lifting and handling equipment
Parent: Caterpillar UK Holdings Limited
Officers: Johanna Elizabeth Deason, Secretary; Nigel John Burroughs [1964] Director/Tax Accountant; Stephen Canning [1971] Managing Director; Silvana Cecconello Godelaine [1958] Director/General Manager [Italian]; Steven David Wheeler [1968] Financial Director

Caterpillar Logistics (UK) Limited
Incorporated: 7 June 2005 *Employees:* 192
Net Worth Deficit: £1,286,000 *Total Assets:* £35,869,000
Registered Office: Eastfield, Frank Perkins Way, Peterborough, Cambs, PE1 5FQ
Activities: Wholesale trade of motor vehicle parts and accessories
Parent: Caterpillar (U.K.) Limited
Officers: Johanna Elizabeth Deason, Secretary; Nigel John Burroughs [1964] Director/Tax Accountant; Sandeep Virmani [1972] Director/Business Resource Manager

Caterpillar Overseas Limited
Incorporated: 27 July 2004
Net Worth: £307,575,008 *Total Assets:* £308,056,992
Registered Office: Eastfield, Frank Perkins Way, Peterborough, Cambs, PE1 5FQ
Activities: Other business support service activities n.e.c.
Parent: Caterpillar Overseas Credit Corporation SARL
Officers: Johanna Elizabeth Deason, Secretary; Nigel John Burroughs [1964] Director/Tax Accountant; Sandeep Virmani [1972] Director/Business Resource Manager

Caterpillar UK Engines Company Limited
Incorporated: 29 September 2005
Net Worth: £441,944,992 *Total Assets:* £441,944,992
Registered Office: Eastfield, Frank Perkins Way, Peterborough, Cambs, PE1 5FQ
Activities: Activities of head offices
Parent: Caterpillar Luxembourg S.A.R.L.
Officers: Johanna Elizabeth Deason, Secretary; Nigel John Burroughs [1964] Director/Taxation Accountant; David John Goldspink [1966] Director/General Manager; Paul David Thompson [1980] Director/Business Resource Manager [American]

Caterpillar UK Group Limited
Incorporated: 15 November 2005
Net Worth: £322,132,992 *Total Assets:* £322,132,992
Registered Office: Eastfield, Frank Perkins Way, Peterborough, Cambs, PE1 5FQ
Activities: Activities of head offices
Parent: Caterpillar UK Acquisition Partners LP
Officers: Nigel John Burroughs [1964] Director/Taxation Accountant; Sandeep Virmani [1972] Director/Business Resource Manager

Caterpillar UK Holdings Limited
Incorporated: 6 July 1992 *Employees:* 7
Net Worth: £325,852,000 *Total Assets:* £1,513,432,960
Registered Office: Peckleton Lane, Desford, Leicester, LE9 9JT
Activities: Other business support service activities n.e.c.
Parent: Caterpillar Investments
Officers: Johanna Elizabeth Deason, Secretary; Nigel John Burroughs [1964] Director/Taxation Accountant; Timothy Canning [1971] Director/Factory Manager; Mark Clinton Albert Dorsett [1962] HR Director; Silvana Cecconello Godelaine [1958] Director/General Manager [Italian]; Steven David Wheeler [1968] Director/Business Resource Manager

Catesby Estates (Residential) Limited
Incorporated: 5 March 2001 *Employees:* 4
Net Worth Deficit: £4,070,161 *Total Assets:* £38,104,644
Registered Office: Catesby House, 5b Tournament Court, Edgehill Drive, Warwick, CV34 6LG
Activities: Development of building projects
Parent: Catesby Estates (Newark) Limited
Officers: Robin Elliott Butler [1959] Director; Richard Andrew Coppell [1967] Director; David Lewis Wood [1971] Director

Catesby Estates PLC
Incorporated: 26 March 1998
Previous: Catesby Property Group PLC
Net Worth: £22,567,304 *Total Assets:* £23,048,462
Registered Office: Catesby House, 5b Tournament Court, Edgehill Drive, Warwick, CV34 6LG
Activities: Development of building projects
Parent: Urban & Civic PLC
Officers: David Morris, Secretary; Paul Brocklehurst [1965] Managing Director; Robin Elliott Butler [1959] Director; William Nigel Hugill [1958] Director; David Morris [1976] Planning Director; Myron Osborne [1980] Director

Catesby Strategic Land Limited
Incorporated: 30 July 1996 *Employees:* 16
Previous: Catesby Estates Limited
Net Worth: £6,225,964 *Total Assets:* £25,790,838
Registered Office: Catesby House, 5b Tournament Court, Edgehill Drive, Warwick, CV34 6LG
Activities: Development of building projects
Parent: Catesby Property Group PLC
Officers: Paul Brocklehurst [1965] Managing Director; David Morris [1976] Planning Director; Myron Osborne [1980] Director

Cathelco Limited
Incorporated: 15 March 1956 *Employees:* 138
Net Worth: £20,531,140 *Total Assets:* £25,557,468
Registered Office: Marine House, Dunston Road, Chesterfield, Derbys, S41 8NY
Activities: Building of ships and floating structures
Parent: Cathelco Holdings Limited
Officers: Justin William Joseph Salisbury, Secretary; Christian Richard Armstrong Bell [1974] Director/General Manager; Robert Douglas Reginald Field [1967] Technical Director; John Roger Hollis [1959] Director/Accountant; Justin William Joseph Salisbury [1956] Managing Director; James Talbot Sutherland [1960] Sales Director

R.Caudwell (Produce) Limited
Incorporated: 14 January 1964 *Employees:* 18
Net Worth: £12,479,800 *Total Assets:* £13,978,393
Registered Office: Estate Office, Ludborough, Grimsby, S Humbers, DN36 5SG
Activities: Growing of cereals (except rice), leguminous crops and oil seeds
Officers: Struan Thomas Caudwell Abbott, Secretary; Rosemary Anne Abbott [1944] Director/Farmer; Struan Thomas Caudwell Abbott [1970] Director/Farmer; Robert Lewis Hartley [1983] Director/Farm Manager; Ralph Michael Pinder [1949] Director/Farm Manager

Caudwell Farms
Incorporated: 15 May 1951 *Employees:* 10
Net Worth: £1,953,059 *Total Assets:* £9,926,341
Registered Office: The Estate Office, Hartley House, Holbeach St Matthews, Spalding, Lincs, PE12 8EW
Activities: Growing of cereals (except rice), leguminous crops and oil seeds
Parent: George Hay Company Limited
Officers: Leslie Nicola Hay, Secretary; Andrew George Hay [1964] Director

Caunton Engineering Limited
Incorporated: 19 December 1969 *Employees:* 245
Net Worth: £6,080,815 *Total Assets:* £19,587,220
Registered Office: National Workshops, Moorgreen Industrial Park, Moorgreen, Nottingham, NG16 3QU
Activities: Manufacture of metal structures and parts of structures
Parent: Caunton Holdings Limited
Officers: Helen Clare Bingham, Secretary; Jill Marilyn Bingham, Secretary; Robert John Berry [1956] Director; David Frederick Bingham [1942] Director/Engineer; Simon David Bingham [1970] Managing Director; Sara Jane Cundy [1969] Director; Grenville John Griffiths [1956] Director; Silviu Thomas Rudolph Klein [1949] Director; Joseph Locke [1937] Director/Engineer; Sir Charles David Naish [1940] Director; Matthew James Shimwell [1979] Director

Caunton Holdings Limited
Incorporated: 20 March 2008 *Employees:* 245
Net Worth: £6,080,915 *Total Assets:* £19,587,320
Registered Office: Caunton Engineering Limited, Engine Lane, Moorgreen Industrial Park, Newthorpe, Nottingham, NG16 3QU
Activities: Dormant company
Shareholders: David Frederick Bingham; Jill Marilyn Bingham; Sara Jane Cundy; Simon David Bingham
Officers: Sara Jane Cundy, Secretary/Director; Simon David Bingham [1970] Director; Sara Jane Cundy [1969] Director

Caunton Investments Limited
Incorporated: 24 October 1997 *Employees:* 3
Net Worth: £11,125,949 *Total Assets:* £13,225,743
Registered Office: Moorgreen Industrial Park, Moorgreen, Nottingham, NG16 3QU
Activities: Other letting and operating of own or leased real estate
Parent: Velocity Investments Limited
Officers: Sara Jane Cundy, Secretary; David Frederick Bingham [1942] Director; Simon David Bingham [1970] Director; Sara Jane Cundy [1969] Director

Cavalier Marketing Holdings Limited
Incorporated: 30 May 2014 *Employees:* 159
Net Worth: £3,291,170 *Total Assets:* £19,803,596
Registered Office: c/o GSSL, The Mill Lane, Glenfield, Leicester, LE3 8DX
Activities: Activities of other holding companies n.e.c.
Officers: John Frazer Harrison [1971] Director; Robert Hudson Harrison [1975] Director; Lindsay Kamal Khan [1962] Director; Demis Armen Ohandjanian [1978] Director

Cavan Investments Limited
Incorporated: 5 February 2015 *Employees:* 2
Net Worth: £78,634,728 *Total Assets:* £125,996,352
Registered Office: 14 Clarendon Street, Nottingham, NG1 5HQ
Activities: Other letting and operating of own or leased real estate
Major Shareholder: Clare Rachel Lago
Officers: Clare Rachel Lago [1963] Director

Cavendish Learning Trust
Incorporated: 3 February 2012 *Employees:* 299
Previous: Netherthorpe School
Net Worth: £26,711,272 *Total Assets:* £30,687,880
Registered Office: Staveley Hall, Staveley Hall Drive, Staveley, Chesterfield, Derbys, S43 3TN
Activities: General secondary education
Officers: Philip Brown [1953] Director/Retired; Lauren Jade Buxton [1987] Finance Director; Danielle Amanda Harris [1978] Director/Business Occupation & Transformation Consultant; Fiona Parsons [1977] Director/Accountant; Stephen Poole [1962] Director/Creative Design Publishing; Nigel Paul Sternberg [1954] Director/Retired; Anju Kaur Virdee [1977] Director/Strategic Manager; Barbara Ann Walsh [1955] Director/Retired; David Williams [1973] Director/Executive Headteacher

Cawrey Ltd
Incorporated: 17 November 1964 *Employees:* 16
Net Worth: £8,940,424 *Total Assets:* £9,495,730
Registered Office: Kirby Grange Farm, Taverner Drive, Ratby, Leics, LE6 0HQ
Activities: Development of building projects
Major Shareholder: John Arthur Cawrey
Officers: John Arthur Cawrey [1956] Director; Joanna Murphy-Cawrey [1960] Director; David Michael Walgate [1976] Director

CCF Limited
Incorporated: 30 April 1982 *Employees:* 988
Net Worth: £91,100,000 *Total Assets:* £767,400,000
Registered Office: Lodge Way House, Lodge Way, Harlestone Road, Northampton, NN5 7UG
Activities: Other building completion and finishing
Parent: Travis Perkins PLC
Officers: John Peter Carter [1961] Director; Francis Mark Elkins [1967] Director; Stephen Harris [1972] Director; Martin Richard Meech [1957] Director/Chartered Surveyor; Alan Richard Williams [1969] Director/Accountant

CCN UK 2005 Limited
Incorporated: 27 September 2005
Net Worth Deficit: £4,102,584 *Total Assets:* £63,061,412
Registered Office: The Sir John Peace Building, Experian Way, NG2 Business Park, Nottingham, NG80 1ZZ
Activities: Financial intermediation not elsewhere classified
Parent: Experian US Holdings Unlimited
Officers: Ronan Hanna, Secretary; Paul Alan Atkinson [1960] Director/Head of Group Tax; Antony Jonathan Ward Barnes [1964] Director of Tax and Treasury; Karen Julia Greenwood [1967] Director/Chartered Accountant; Daniel Tristan Lilley [1981] Director; Mark Edward Pepper [1963] Director/Financial Controller

CCN UK Unlimited
Incorporated: 23 October 2001
Net Worth: £63,854,176 *Total Assets:* £63,854,176
Registered Office: The Sir John Peace Building, Experian Way, NG2 Business Park, Nottingham, NG80 1ZZ
Activities: Financial intermediation not elsewhere classified
Parent: CCN UK 2005 Limited
Officers: Ronan Hanna, Secretary; Paul Alan Atkinson [1960] Director/Group Taxation Manager; Antony Jonathan Ward Barnes [1964] Director of Tax and Treasury; Karen Julia Greenwood [1967] Director/Chartered Accountant; Daniel Tristan Lilley [1981] Director; Mark Edward Pepper [1963] Director/Financial Controller

CCS Media Limited
Incorporated: 16 April 2002 *Employees:* 420
Previous: CCS Media Holdings Limited
Net Worth: £1,577,000 *Total Assets:* £46,986,000
Registered Office: Cumberland Court, 80 Mount Street, Nottingham, NG1 6HH
Activities: Other information technology service activities
Shareholder: Tomlinson FIC Limited
Officers: Alan Honarmand, Secretary/Director; Terence David Betts [1960] Director; James Edward Hardy [1982] Director; Alan Honarmand [1961] Director; Robert Tomlinson [1951] Director

CCW 600 Limited
Incorporated: 12 February 2001 *Employees:* 49
Net Worth: £8,897,553 *Total Assets:* £53,708,168
Registered Office: Global House, Saville Road, Peterborough, PE3 7PR
Activities: Renting and leasing of cars and light motor vehicles
Major Shareholder: Christopher Charles Webb
Officers: Fraser Alexander Winchester Morrison, Secretary; Christopher Charles Webb [1971] Director

The CDA Group Limited
Incorporated: 12 June 1991 *Employees:* 202
Net Worth: £3,221,487 *Total Assets:* £19,460,396
Registered Office: Warehouse Premises, Harby Road, Langar, Notts, NG13 9HY
Activities: Manufacture of electric domestic appliances
Parent: Amica SA
Officers: Mark Peter Gibbs, Secretary; Simon Douglas Roland James Emmons [1974] Sales Director; Mark Peter Gibbs [1964] Finance and IT Director; Wieslaw Tomasz Hagno [1969] Director [Polish]; Alina Maria Jankowska-Brzoska [1976] Director [Polish]; Ian Nigel Ratcliffe Kershaw [1968] Managing Director; Andrzej Ogrodowczyk [1982] Director [Polish]; Andrzej Marcin SAS [1975] Director [Polish]; Piotr Skubel [1974] Director/VP of The Board, Strategy and Controlling [Polish]

CDL Group Holdings Limited
Incorporated: 11 August 2000 *Employees:* 625
Net Worth: £37,146,620 *Total Assets:* £46,194,256
Registered Office: Strata House, Kings Reach Road, Stockport, Cheshire, SK4 2HD
Activities: Other information technology service activities
Officers: Melissa Fiona Johnson, Secretary; Thomas Harland Hogg [1935] Director; Gary Arthur Johnson [1966] Director; Melissa Fiona Johnson [1966] Director/HR Manager

CDT Holdings Limited
Incorporated: 20 June 1995 *Employees:* 106
Net Worth: £7,107,000 *Total Assets:* £12,570,000
Registered Office: Unit 12 Cardinal Park, Cardinal Way, Godmanchester, Cambs, PE29 2XG
Activities: Other professional, scientific and technical activities n.e.c.
Parent: Sumitomo Chemical Co., Limited
Officers: Hilary Charles, Secretary; Yoshiaki Oda [1961] Director/Company Executive [Japanese]; Hiroshi Ueda [1956] Director/Company Executive [Japanese]; Jim Veninger [1962] Director/VP Technology Development [American]; Takeshi Yamada [1967] Director/Office Worker [Japanese]

Cedar 2015 Limited
Incorporated: 9 January 2015 *Employees:* 2
Net Worth: £46,282,000 *Total Assets:* £56,676,000
Registered Office: Second Avenue, Poynton Industrial Estate, Poynton, Cheshire, SK12 1ND
Activities: Non-trading company
Parent: Steel Partners Holdings L.P.
Officers: Jack Howard [1961] Director/President of Steel Partners LP [American]

Cedar House Investments Limited
Incorporated: 5 June 1997 *Employees:* 1
Net Worth: £5,737,986 *Total Assets:* £10,306,326
Registered Office: 9 Riverside Court, Pride Park, Derby, DE24 8JN
Activities: Development of building projects
Parent: Ark Capital Limited
Officers: Martyn John Cubbage, Secretary; Martyn John Cubbage [1962] Director/Chartered Management Accountant; Peter James Gadsby [1948] Director

Ceetak Holdings Limited
Incorporated: 1 February 1971 *Employees:* 60
Net Worth: £7,604,307 *Total Assets:* £9,781,113
Registered Office: Fraser Road, Priory Business Park, Bedford, MK44 3WH
Activities: Activities of head offices
Shareholders: Thomas Raymond Baron; Thomas Raymond Baron
Officers: Suzanne Michelle Baron, Secretary; Priscilla Alison Mabel Baron [1945] Director; Suzanne Michelle Baron [1963] Director/Chartered Secretary; Thomas Raymond Baron [1935] Director/Engineer; David Frederick Lines [1949] Director/Engineer

CEF Holdings Limited
Incorporated: 4 July 1936 *Employees:* 2,806
Net Worth: £138,116,000 *Total Assets:* £370,702,016
Registered Office: Georgina Mackie House, 141 Farmer Ward Road, Kenilworth, Warwicks, CV8 2SU
Activities: Activities of head offices
Shareholder: Jacqueline Mackie
Officers: Mark Stephen Jacobs, Secretary; Kevin Alan David Barnett [1955] Director; Charles Henry Beddows [1957] Director/General Manager; Georgina Louise Hartland [1964] Director; Thomas Alan Hartland Mackie [1987] Director; Mark Stephen Jacobs [1959] Finance Director; Jacqueline Anne Mackie [1950] Director

Celanese Production UK Limited
Incorporated: 27 June 2006 *Employees:* 56
Previous: Celanese Acetate Limited
Net Worth Deficit: £16,639,000 *Total Assets:* £24,710,000
Registered Office: 1 Holme Lane, Spondon, Derby, DE21 7BS
Activities: Manufacture of other inorganic basic chemicals
Parent: Celanese Corporation
Officers: Mark John Lington [1961] Director/Operations Manager

Celixir PLC
Incorporated: 28 December 2016 *Employees:* 52
Net Worth Deficit: £3,160,967 *Total Assets:* £9,900,992
Registered Office: Celixir House, Stratford upon Avon Business & Technology Park, Innovation Way, Stratford upon Avon, Warwicks, CV37 7GZ
Activities: Activities of head offices
Officers: David Preston, Secretary; Dr Darrin Matthew Disley [1967] Director; Sir Martin John Evans [1941] Director/Professor; Chaim Hurvitz [1960] Director [Israeli]; Fiona Elizabeth Murray [1968] Director/Professor; Gary Paul Pisano [1961] Director/Professor [American]; Trevor Ajan Reginald [1972] Director

Cellar Trends Limited
Incorporated: 29 January 1999 *Employees:* 79
Net Worth: £7,201,901 *Total Assets:* £17,051,138
Registered Office: Rawdon House, Rawdon Terrace, Station Road, Ashby De La Zouch, Leics, LE65 2GN
Activities: Wholesale of wine, beer, spirits and other alcoholic beverages
Parent: Cellar Trends Holdings Limited
Officers: David Geoffrey Marriott, Secretary/Commission Agent; Seymour Paul Ferreira [1962] Director/Entrepreneur; David Geoffrey Marriott [1949] Director/Commission Agent; John Charles Marriott [1978] Director/National Accounts Manager; Hugues Michel Pietrini [1969] Director [French]; Geoffrey Fraser Watts [1977] Director/Manager; Martin Fraser Watts [1944] Director

Celleron Therapeutics Limited
Incorporated: 24 June 2004 *Employees:* 6
Net Worth: £9,881,840 *Total Assets:* £9,989,254
Registered Office: Magdalen Centre, Robert Robinson Avenue, Oxford Science Park, Oxford, OX4 4GA
Activities: Research and experimental development on biotechnology
Shareholder: Nicholas La Thangue
Officers: Douglas Fraser McDonald, Secretary; Ji Woong Chun [1982] Director/Bio Tech Investor & Pharmacist [South Korean]; Prof David James Kerr [1956] Director; Prof Nicholas Barrie La Thangue [1957] Director/Professor; Sangwoo Lee [1971] Executive Director [South Korean]; Doug Manion [1960] Director/CEO Kleo Pharmaceuticals [American/Canadian]

Celus Holdings Limited
Incorporated: 21 March 1984 *Employees:* 6
Net Worth: £12,996,178 *Total Assets:* £14,495,787
Registered Office: 4th Floor, Victoria House, 199 Avebury Boulevard, Milton Keynes, Bucks, MK9 1AU
Activities: Buying and selling of own real estate
Officers: Louisa Dent, Secretary; Caroline Sarah Dent [1960] Director; Cecil David Dent [1922] Director; Jonathan Paul Maurice Dent [1959] Director; Louisa Rachel Dent [1963] Director; Clifford Eric Shanbury [1945] Director

CEMA Group Ltd
Incorporated: 17 November 2015 *Employees:* 351
Net Worth: £9,252,823 *Total Assets:* £18,527,126
Registered Office: White House, Wollaton Street, Nottingham, NG1 5GF
Activities: Electrical installation
Major Shareholder: Franco Guido Ciaurro
Officers: Stephen Binns [1959] Director/Electrician; Franco Guido Ciaurro [1955] Director [Italian]; Michael Jakubiak [1962] Director/Electrician; Perry Littlehales [1963] Director/Electrician; Richard David Sharpe [1963] Director/Electrical Engineer

Cemex Investments Limited
Incorporated: 26 July 1930
Net Worth: £1,896,343,040 *Total Assets:* £2,672,257,024
Registered Office: Cemex House, Evreux Way, Rugby, Warwicks, CV21 2DT
Activities: Activities of head offices
Parent: Cemex UK
Officers: Rebecca Juliet Wright, Secretary; Laurence Burdett Dagley [1976] Director; Vishal Puri [1974] Director/Solicitor; Lex Hunter Russell [1965] Director/VP Aggregates and Asphalt; Larry Jose Zea Betancourt [1961] Business Service Organisation Director [Venezuelan]

Cemex Seament Limited
Incorporated: 5 March 1986
Net Worth: £10,946,575 *Total Assets:* £10,946,575
Registered Office: Cemex House, Evreux Way, Rugby, Warwicks, CV21 2DT
Activities: Dormant company
Parent: Cemex UK Operations Limited
Officers: Rebecca Juliet Wright, Secretary; Clare Pickering [1970] Director; Vishal Puri [1974] Director/Solicitor; Larry Jose Zea Betancourt [1961] Business Service Organisation Director [Venezuelan]

Cemex UK
Incorporated: 3 August 2004
Net Worth: £11,685,799,936 *Total Assets:* £14,785,547,264
Registered Office: Cemex House, Evreux Way, Rugby, Warwicks, CV21 2DT
Activities: Activities of other holding companies n.e.c.
Officers: Rebecca Juliet Wright, Secretary; Juan Pelegri Y Giron [1954] Director/Lawyer [Spanish]; Vishal Puri [1974] Director/Solicitor; Graham Nicholas George Russell [1972] Director; Larry Jose Zea Betancourt [1961] Business Service Organisation Director [Venezuelan]

Cemex UK Operations Limited
Incorporated: 6 May 1960 *Employees:* 2,814
Net Worth: £2,530,768,896 *Total Assets:* £3,840,877,056
Registered Office: Cemex House, Evreux Way, Rugby, Warwicks, CV21 2DT
Activities: Operation of gravel and sand pits; mining of clays and kaolin
Parent: Cemex Investments Limited
Officers: Rebecca Juliet Wright, Secretary; Philip John Simon Baynes-Clarke [1979] Director; Laurence Burdett Dagley [1976] Director; David Alec Hart [1973] Director; Carl Lindsay Platt [1973] Director; Vishal Puri [1974] Director/Solicitor; Lex Hunter Russell [1965] Director/VP Aggregates & Asphalt; Craig John Williamson [1969] Director; Larry Jose Zea Betancourt [1961] Business Service Organisation Director [Venezuelan]

Cemex UK Properties Limited
Incorporated: 15 February 1965 *Employees:* 1
Net Worth: £35,534,172 *Total Assets:* £41,906,092
Registered Office: Cemex House, Evreux Way, Rugby, Warwicks, CV21 2DT
Activities: Buying and selling of own real estate
Parent: Cemex Investments Limited
Officers: Rebecca Juliet Wright, Secretary; Vishal Puri [1974] Director/Solicitor; Stephen Redwood [1964] Director

Cemex UK Services Limited
Incorporated: 5 June 1946 *Employees:* 6
Net Worth: £12,200,000 *Total Assets:* £32,376,000
Registered Office: Cemex House, Evreux Way, Rugby, Warwicks, CV21 2DT
Activities: Other business support service activities n.e.c.
Parent: Cemex Investments Limited
Officers: Rebecca Juliet Wright, Secretary; Laurence Burdett Dagley [1976] Director; Vishal Puri [1974] Director/Solicitor; Larry Jose Zea Betancourt [1961] Business Service Organisation Director [Venezuelan]

Cenduit Limited
Incorporated: 12 January 2001 *Employees:* 8
Net Worth: £9,824,478 *Total Assets:* £12,399,642
Registered Office: The Apex, 2 Sheriffs Orchard, Coventry, Warwicks, CV1 3PP
Activities: Other professional, scientific and technical activities n.e.c.
Parent: Cenduit Holdings LLC
Officers: Paul Matthew Kelly, Secretary; Alexander James O'Toole [1974] Director/VP of Clinical Strategic Alliances [American]; John Brian Sabo [1970] Director [American]

Center Parcs (Holdings 1) Limited
Incorporated: 2 June 2011 *Employees:* 8,392
Net Worth Deficit: £187,600,000 *Total Assets:* £1,841,200,000
Registered Office: One Edison Rise, New Ollerton, Newark, Notts, NG22 9DP
Activities: Activities of other holding companies n.e.c.
Officers: Rajbinder Singh-Dehal, Secretary; Natalie Johanna Adomait [1989] Director [Canadian]; Martin Peter Dalby [1961] Director; Kevin O'Donnell McCrain [1979] Director [American]; Colin Grant McKinlay [1969] Director; Zachary Bryan Vaughan [1977] Director [Canadian]

Center Parcs (Holdings 3) Limited
Incorporated: 25 May 2011 *Employees:* 5
Net Worth: £550,200,000 *Total Assets:* £920,600,000
Registered Office: One Edison Rise, New Ollerton, Newark, Notts, NG22 9DP
Activities: Activities of other holding companies n.e.c.
Parent: Center Parcs (Holdings 2) Limited
Officers: Rajbinder Singh Dehal, Secretary; Natalie Johanna Adomait [1989] Director [Canadian]; Martin Peter Dalby [1961] Director; Kevin O'Donnell McCrain [1979] Director [American]; Colin Grant McKinlay [1969] Director; Zachary Bryan Vaughan [1977] Director [Canadian]

Center Parcs (Operating Company) Limited
Incorporated: 22 February 2002 *Employees:* 6,735
Net Worth: £5,500,000 *Total Assets:* £1,180,999,936
Registered Office: One Edison Rise, New Ollerton, Newark, Notts, NG22 9DP
Activities: Activities of head offices
Parent: Center Parcs (Holdings 3) Limited
Officers: Rajbinder Singh-Dehal, Secretary; Natalie Johanna Adomait [1989] Director [Canadian]; Martin Peter Dalby [1961] Director; Kevin O'Donnell McCrain [1979] Director [American]; Colin Grant McKinlay [1969] Director; Zachary Bryan Vaughan [1977] Director [Canadian]

Center Parcs Limited
Incorporated: 25 April 1985
Net Worth: £13,400,000 *Total Assets:* £13,400,000
Registered Office: One Edison Rise, New Ollerton, Newark, Notts, NG22 9DP
Activities: Activities of other holding companies n.e.c.
Parent: Center Parcs (Operating Company) Ltd
Officers: Rajbinder Singh-Dehal, Secretary; Natalie Johanna Adomait [1989] Director [Canadian]; Martin Peter Dalby [1961] Director; Paul Kent [1964] Director; Kevin O'Donnell McCrain [1979] Director [American]; Colin Grant McKinlay [1969] Director; Alan Stephen Park [1967] Director; Rajbinder Singh-Dehal [1977] Director/Solicitor; Zachary Bryan Vaughan [1977] Director [Canadian]; Colin Bernard Whaley [1961] Director

Central Aggregates Ltd
Incorporated: 12 November 2015 *Employees:* 75
Net Worth: £5,596,789 *Total Assets:* £9,985,180
Registered Office: Central House, Vulcan Way, Hermitage Industrial Estate, Coalville, Leics, LE67 3AP
Activities: Activities of head offices
Major Shareholder: Steven Charles Bennett
Officers: Pauline Neville Ball [1949] Director; Michael David Barham [1952] Director; Steven Charles Bennett [1971] Director; Karl Danes [1971] Director; Mark James Gee [1970] Director

Central England Healthcare Limited
Incorporated: 21 May 2007 *Employees:* 201
Net Worth: £1,810,431 *Total Assets:* £9,847,547
Registered Office: 8 Clarendon Place, Leamington Spa, Warwicks, CV32 5QN
Activities: Other business support service activities n.e.c.
Major Shareholder: Kulbir Kaur Kandola
Officers: Subaig Singh Kandola, Company Secretary; Suroop Singh Kandola, Secretary; Kulbir Kaur Kandola [1959] Director

Central Garage (Uppingham) Limited
Incorporated: 12 May 1952 *Employees:* 237
Net Worth: £12,589,624 *Total Assets:* £42,333,532
Registered Office: c/o Grant Thornton UK LLP, Regent House, 80 Regent Road, Leicester, LE1 7NH
Activities: Maintenance and repair of motor vehicles
Shareholders: Ilse-Charlotte Hamblin; Samantha Caroline Hamblin; Robert George Rowley
Officers: Ilse-Charlotte Hamblin [1940] Director [German]; Samantha Caroline Hamblin [1974] Director; Daniel Lee Stone [1968] Director/Chief Executive Officer

Central Glass Europe Limited
Incorporated: 30 July 2003 *Employees:* 4
Net Worth: £22,600,654 *Total Assets:* £24,225,632
Registered Office: Whitefield Road, Bredbury, Stockport, Cheshire, SK6 2QR
Activities: Agents specialised in the sale of other particular products
Major Shareholder: Shuichi Sarasawa
Officers: Andrew James Hiett, Secretary; Takao Onuma [1963] Director [Japanese]; Mitsuru Tanuma [1961] Director [Japanese]; Nobuyuki Tokunaga [1961] Director [Japanese]

Centres for Assisted Reproduction Limited
Incorporated: 5 March 1997 *Employees:* 131
Net Worth: £16,463,000 *Total Assets:* £21,905,000
Registered Office: John Webster House, 6 Lawrence Drive, Nottingham Business Park, Nottingham, NG8 6PZ
Activities: Hospital activities
Parent: Care Fertility Group Limited
Officers: David Brian Burford [1980] Director; Dr Kenneth Dowell [1957] Director/Medical Consultant; Dr Simon Brian Fishel [1953] Director/Scientist; Nigel Mark Inches Robertson [1959] Director/Exec Chairman

Centro Place Investments Limited
Incorporated: 28 September 2004
Net Worth: £9,857,079 *Total Assets:* £13,869,352
Registered Office: 1 Centro Place, Pride Park, Derby, DE24 8RF
Activities: Other business support service activities n.e.c.
Parent: Derwent Housing Association Ltd
Officers: Chris Martin, Secretary; Janice Boucher [1962] Managing Director and Accountant; Barbara Margaret Gildea [1954] Director; Richard Hopkin [1956] Director/Chartered Accountant

Centurion Finance (Lincoln) Limited
Incorporated: 27 March 1986 *Employees:* 2
Net Worth: £9,638,598 *Total Assets:* £20,447,448
Registered Office: 1st Floor, Centurion House, Unit J3 The Point, Weaver Road, Lincoln, LN6 3QN
Activities: Financial intermediation not elsewhere classified
Major Shareholder: Michael John Wroblewski
Officers: Timothy Stephen Parr, Secretary; Timothy Stephen Parr [1959] Director; Michael John Wroblewski [1946] Director

Century Health (Nottingham) Limited
Incorporated: 4 February 1999 *Employees:* 6
Net Worth: £10,112,849 *Total Assets:* £25,027,772
Registered Office: St Vincent House, Normanby Road, Scunthorpe, N Lincs, DN15 8QT
Activities: Other business support service activities n.e.c.
Shareholders: Clugston PF Limited; Aberdeen Infrastructure (No. 3) Limited
Officers: Ian Pattison, Secretary; Michael Andrew Donn [1972] Director; Karen Marie Hill [1977] Director/Investment Manager; Gavin Ingle [1976] Director/Accountant; Stephen John Radcliffe [1955] Director; Philip Robert Taylor [1958] Director/Microbiologist; Robert John Vickers [1956] Director/Chief Executive Officer

Ceravision Limited
Incorporated: 29 April 1996 *Employees:* 21
Net Worth: £3,226,392 *Total Assets:* £13,530,956
Registered Office: Sovereign Court, 230 Upper Fifth Street, Central Milton Keynes, Bucks, MK9 2HR
Activities: Other research and experimental development on natural sciences and engineering
Officers: Steven Leigh, Secretary; Abdulelah Abdu Mukred Ali [1958] Director [Yemeni]; Nigel Samuel Brooks [1949] Director; Daniel Martin Murphy [1963] Director/Solicitor [Irish]; Timothy John Reynolds [1964] Director; Adel Saudi [1962] Director/Banker [Libyan]

Cerealto UK Limited
Incorporated: 25 October 1999 *Employees:* 199
Previous: Siro (UK) Ltd
Net Worth: £7,172,389 *Total Assets:* £67,868,512
Registered Office: Cerealto Worksop, Claylands Avenue, Worksop, Notts, S81 7BQ
Activities: Agents specialised in the sale of other particular products
Parent: Siro Foods S.A.
Officers: Luis Angel Lopez [1964] Director/Consultant [Spanish]; Rut Aranda Carmona [1976] Director [Spanish]; Michael Harfleet [1949] Director/Salesman; Alfonso Arroyo Matia [1979] Director [Spanish]; Lorenza Bajo Tapia [1957] Director [Spanish]

Certikin International Limited
Incorporated: 19 April 1995 *Employees:* 114
Net Worth: £7,979,348 *Total Assets:* £16,114,825
Registered Office: Unit 9 Witan Park, Avenue 2, Station Lane Industrial Estate, Witney, Oxon, OX28 4FJ
Activities: Wholesale of hardware, plumbing and heating equipment and supplies
Parent: Fluidra Commercial SAU
Officers: Ian William Danne, Secretary; Enric Cabre Hernandez [1971] Director/General Manager [Spanish]; Ian William Danne [1966] Finance Director; Carlos Franquesa [1963] Director/General Manager [Spanish]; Neil Howard Murray [1958] Managing Director

Cespa UK Limited
Incorporated: 2 August 2010
Net Worth: £6,185,000 *Total Assets:* £29,838,000
Registered Office: The Sherard Building, Edmund Halley Road, Oxford, OX4 4DQ
Activities: Activities of head offices
Officers: Francisco Hevia Gonzalez [1974] Director [Spanish]; Olga Redondo [1975] Finance Director [Spanish]

CET Group Holdings Limited
Incorporated: 24 January 2005 *Employees:* 360
Net Worth Deficit: £8,061,000 *Total Assets:* £17,715,000
Registered Office: 3 Boundary Court, Warke Flatt, Willow Farm Business Park, Castle Donington, Derbys, DE74 2UD
Activities: Activities of head offices
Parent: Project C Bidco Limited
Officers: Stephen William Humphrey, Secretary; Anthony John Dickin [1970] Director; Peter Damian Eglinton [1969] Managing Director; Stephen William Humphrey [1966] Director/Chartered Accountant; Richard Charles Thomas [1981] Director

CEVA Container Logistics Limited
Incorporated: 20 March 1962
Net Worth: £3,600,000 *Total Assets:* £28,520,000
Registered Office: P O Box 8663, Ceva House, Excelsior Road, Ashby De La Zouch, Leics, LE65 9BA
Activities: Other transportation support activities
Parent: CEVA Network Logistics Limited
Officers: Dawn Amanda Wetherall, Secretary; Edward Aston [1968] Managing Director; Leigh Martin Pomlett [1956] Director/Executive Vice President

CEVA Freight (UK) Holding Company Limited
Incorporated: 5 August 1998
Net Worth: £24,179,448 *Total Assets:* £30,172,160
Registered Office: P O Box 8663, Ceva House, Excelsior Road, Ashby De La Zouch, Leics, LE65 9BA
Activities: Other service activities incidental to land transportation, n.e.c.
Parent: CEVA Freight Holdings Luxembourg SARL
Officers: Dawn Amanda Wetherall, Secretary; Edward Aston [1968] Managing Director; Leigh Martin Pomlett [1956] Director/Executive Vice President

CEVA Freight (UK) Limited
Incorporated: 19 November 1973 *Employees:* 274
Net Worth: £37,068,000 *Total Assets:* £119,163,000
Registered Office: P O Box 8663, Ceva House, Excelsior Road, Ashby De La Zouch, Leics, LE65 9BA
Activities: Cargo handling for water transport activities
Parent: CEVA Freight (UK) Holdings Limited
Officers: Dawn Amanda Wetherall, Secretary; Edward Aston [1968] Managing Director; Leigh Martin Pomlett [1956] Director/Executive Vice President

CEVA Limited
Incorporated: 9 August 2006
Net Worth: £1,557,216,896 *Total Assets:* £2,210,174,720
Registered Office: Ceva House, P O Box 8663, Excelsior Road, Ashby-De-La-Zouch, Leics, LE65 9BA
Activities: Activities of head offices
Officers: Michael O'Donoghue [1959] Director/Executive Vice President [Irish]; Leigh Martin Pomlett [1956] Director

CEVA Logistics Limited
Incorporated: 17 December 1976 *Employees:* 4,103
Net Worth: £56,451,000 *Total Assets:* £263,416,992
Registered Office: P O Box 8663, Ceva House, Excelsior Road, Ashby De La Zouch, Leics, LE65 9BA
Activities: Other transportation support activities
Shareholders: CEVA Container Logistics Limited; CEVA Supply Chain Solutions Limited
Officers: Dawn Amanda Wetherall, Secretary; Edward Aston [1968] Managing Director; Leigh Martin Pomlett [1956] Director/Executive Vice President

CEVA Supply Chain Solutions Limited
Incorporated: 14 November 1974 *Employees:* 2
Net Worth: £189,159,008 *Total Assets:* £192,280,000
Registered Office: P O Box 8663, Ceva House, Excelsior Road, Ashby De La Zouch, Leics, LE65 9BA
Activities: Other transportation support activities
Parent: CEVA Limited
Officers: Dawn Amanda Wetherall, Secretary; Edward Aston [1968] Managing Director; Leigh Martin Pomlett [1956] Director/Executive Vice President

Ceylon Tea Growers Association,Limited
Incorporated: 25 March 1929 *Employees:* 1
Net Worth: £13,205,048 *Total Assets:* £14,818,926
Registered Office: 12 Bridgford Road, West Bridgford, Nottingham, NG2 6AB
Activities: Management of real estate on a fee or contract basis
Officers: William Edward Curzon Cursham, Secretary; William Edward Curzon Cursham [1962] Director/Solicitor; Nigel William Turner [1956] Director

CFC 2001 Ltd
Incorporated: 20 August 2001 *Employees:* 237
Net Worth: £279,452 *Total Assets:* £14,198,847
Registered Office: The Proact Stadium, 1866 Sheffield Road, Chesterfield, Derbys, S41 8NZ
Activities: Activities of sport clubs
Major Shareholder: David Easton Dey Allen
Officers: Ashley Maxwell Carson, Secretary; John Croot [1964] Director; Michael Leslie Warner [1947] Director/Retired

Chalcroft Holdings Limited
Incorporated: 5 March 2007 *Employees:* 87
Net Worth: £474,660 *Total Assets:* £16,477,751
Registered Office: 2 Campbells Business Park, Campbells Meadow, King's Lynn, Norfolk, PE30 4YR
Activities: Activities of construction holding companies
Shareholders: Mark Andrew Reeve; David Reeve
Officers: Todd Clinton Hallam [1976] EHS Director [New Zealander]; Paul Morley [1969] Director; David Reeve [1970] Director; Mark Andrew Reeve [1966] Director

Chalcroft Limited
Incorporated: 9 July 1979
Net Worth: £3,554,910 *Total Assets:* £19,274,662
Registered Office: 4 Campbells Business Park, Campbells Meadow, King's Lynn, Norfolk, PE30 4YR
Activities: Construction of commercial buildings
Parent: Chalcroft Holdings Ltd
Officers: Todd Clinton Hallam [1976] Environmental, Health & Safety Director [New Zealander]; Paul Morley [1969] Construction Director; David Reeve [1970] Financial Director; Mark Andrew Reeve [1966] Director/Construction Engineer

The Challenger Multi Academy Trust
Incorporated: 17 October 2014 *Employees:* 548
Net Worth: £46,060,028 *Total Assets:* £54,674,760
Registered Office: Kempston Challenger Academy, Hill Rise, Kempston, Bedford, MK42 7EB
Activities: Other business support service activities n.e.c.
Officers: Stephen Martyn Chamberlain [1965] Director/Chief Executive Officer; Sally Ann Sheila Dicketts [1955] Director/Chief Executive; Alban Francis Xavier Green [1950] Director; Peter James Knell [1973] Business Director

Champion Employment Limited
Incorporated: 28 January 1985 *Employees:* 48
Net Worth: £13,425,272 *Total Assets:* £15,915,368
Registered Office: 55 Cornmarket Street, Oxford, OX1 3HB
Activities: Other activities of employment placement agencies
Officers: Quentin Michael Edwin Hoodless, Secretary; Quentin Michael Edwin Hoodless [1950] Director

Chandlers (Farm Equipment) Limited
Incorporated: 3 December 1982 *Employees:* 211
Net Worth: £14,915,000 *Total Assets:* £35,367,000
Registered Office: Belton, Grantham, Lincs, NG32 2LX
Activities: Sale of new cars and light motor vehicles
Major Shareholder: Joseph Howard Pell
Officers: David Allen Burrows, Secretary; Heather Jane Glenn [1967] Director/HR Manager; Felicity Hart [1980] Director/Equine Manager; Gavin Pell [1978] Director/Agricultural Sales Manager; Joseph Howard Pell [1950] Director; Rosemary Jill Pell [1953] Director; Geoffrey Michael Sharp [1947] Director; Rosemary Jane Sharp [1947] Director

W.S.Chapman & Sons Limited
Incorporated: 26 March 1957 *Employees:* 4
Net Worth: £12,278,359 *Total Assets:* £15,258,661
Registered Office: Burgess Hall, Burringham Road, Gunness, Scunthorpe, N Lincs, DN17 3LT
Activities: Growing of cereals (except rice), leguminous crops and oil seeds
Major Shareholder: James Stanewell Chapman
Officers: Josephine Chapman, Secretary; James Stanewell Chapman [1927] Director/Farmer; Josephine Chapman [1939] Director/Secretary; Tina Marie Ogg [1970] Director

Chargill (Holdings) Ltd
Incorporated: 9 June 2011 *Employees:* 72
Net Worth: £8,325,725 *Total Assets:* £11,642,627
Registered Office: Heathrow Building, Walton Road, Drakelow, Burton on Trent, Staffs, DE15 9UA
Activities: Activities of head offices
Parent: Chargill Properties (Holding) Limited
Officers: Charlotte Louise Brown, Secretary; Robert Alec Brown [1963] Director; Gillian Vanessa Pratt [1960] Director/Housewife; Martin Pratt [1960] Director

Charles Street Buildings (Leicester) Limited
Incorporated: 4 January 1961 *Employees:* 22
Net Worth: £676,519,232 *Total Assets:* £697,086,400
Registered Office: 1 Westmoreland Avenue, Thurmaston, Leicester, LE4 8PH
Activities: Buying and selling of own real estate
Officers: Robert Henry Smith, Secretary; Winifred Mary Linnett [1950] Director; Mary Agnes Middleton [1981] Director; Hugh Patrick Murphy [1948] Director; Joseph John Murphy [1978] Director/Solicitor; Margaret Ann Murphy [1951] Director; Patrick Hugh Murphy [1977] Director

Charles Street Buildings (U.K.) Limited
Incorporated: 17 November 1971 *Employees:* 6
Net Worth: £28,641,468 *Total Assets:* £29,242,836
Registered Office: 1 Westmoreland Avenue, Thurmaston, Leicester, LE4 8PH
Activities: Other letting and operating of own or leased real estate
Parent: Charles Street Buildings (Leicester) Limited
Officers: Robert Henry Smith, Secretary; Winifred Mary Linnett [1950] Director; Mary Agnes Middleton [1981] Director; Hugh Patrick Murphy [1948] Director; Joseph John Murphy [1978] Director/Solicitor; Margaret Ann Murphy [1951] Director; Patrick Hugh Murphy [1977] Director

Charles Street Commercial Investments Limited
Incorporated: 15 July 1983 *Employees:* 4
Net Worth: £24,488,148 *Total Assets:* £75,588,368
Registered Office: Lake View, Lakeside, Cheadle, Cheshire, SK8 3GW
Activities: Credit granting by non-deposit taking finance houses and other specialist consumer credit grantors
Major Shareholder: Henry Neville Moser
Officers: Gary Derek Beckett, Secretary; Gary Derek Beckett [1969] Director; Henry Neville Moser [1949] Director; Mark Mulgrew [1978] Finance Director

Chartered Accountants' Benevolent Association
Incorporated: 18 October 2006 *Employees:* 42
Net Worth: £124,640,000 *Total Assets:* £125,537,000
Registered Office: 8 Mitchell Court, Castle Mound Way, Rugby, Warwicks, CV23 0UY
Activities: Other social work activities without accommodation n.e.c.
Officers: Kathryn Joy Haines, Secretary; Kenneth Francis Coppock [1949] Director/Retired (Accountant); Susan Field [1947] Director/Chartered Accountant; Robin Paul Fieth [1963] Director/Chartered Accountant; Caitriona Flynn [1970] Director/Rewards Consultant; Michael Charles Grant [1956] Director/Retired Chartered Accountant; Mary Munro Hardy [1954] Director/Retired; Elizabeth Mildred Hazell [1961] Director/Chartered Accountant; Heather Robb Lamont [1962] Director; David Edward Leafe [1950] Director/Retired; Kaaeed Najmudin Adamjee Mamujee [1965] Director/Chartered Accountant; Helen Elizabeth Morris [1959] Director/Chartered Accountant; Colin James Nelson Williams [1943] Director/Retired Chartered Accountant

Charterhouse Holdings PLC
Incorporated: 12 June 1970 *Employees:* 89
Net Worth: £23,031,000 *Total Assets:* £26,511,000
Registered Office: Oakridge Park, Trent Lane, Castle Donington, Derbys, DE74 2PY
Activities: Wholesale of clothing and footwear
Shareholders: Kanha Clayton; Luke Ford Clayton; Jake Crispin Clayton; The Estate of Mr Maurice Ford Clayton
Officers: Stuart William Ellis, Secretary; Miles Graham Carter [1969] Director/Chief Executive Officer; Dr Jake Crispin Clayton [1989] Director; Kanha Clayton [1951] Director; Luke Ford Clayton [1981] Director; Stuart William Ellis [1963] Finance Director; Ryan Lee Hornbuckle [1972] Marketing Director

Chartmoor Estates Limited
Incorporated: 6 March 1978 *Employees:* 5
Net Worth: £15,110,204 *Total Assets:* £18,912,928
Registered Office: Equipoise House, Grove Place, Bedford, MK40 3LE
Activities: Development of building projects
Parent: Chartmoor Holdings Limited
Officers: Gwendolyn Anne Marie Abraham, Secretary/Property Developer; Dean Abraham [1971] Managing Director; Edward John Abraham [1940] Director/Chairman; Gwendolyn Anne Marie Abraham [1944] Director/Property Developer; Danielle Marie Jelfs [1969] Director/Therapist

Chatfields Limited
Incorporated: 16 March 1949 *Employees:* 285
Net Worth: £11,860,000 *Total Assets:* £51,363,000
Registered Office: Loxley House, 2 Oakwood Court, Little Oak Drive, Annesley, Nottingham, NG15 0DR
Activities: Sale of new cars and light motor vehicles
Officers: Richard James Maloney, Secretary; Martin Shaun Casha [1960] Director; Trevor Garry Finn [1957] Director; Timothy Paul Holden [1964] Director/Chartered Accountant

Chatsworth House Trust
Incorporated: 23 January 1981 *Employees:* 156
Net Worth: £23,824,000 *Total Assets:* £37,254,000
Registered Office: Estate Office, Edensor, Bakewell, Derbys, DE45 1PJ
Activities: Operation of historical sites and buildings and similar visitor attractions
Officers: Andrew Charles Lavery, Secretary; John David Sebastian Booth [1958] Director/Company Chairman; Amanda Carmen Cavendish [1944] Director; Peregrine Andrew Morny Cavendish [1944] Director; Mark William Fane [1958] Director; John Guy Elmhirst Monson [1962] Director/Managing Partner & Chief Investment Officer; Edward Roland Haslewood Perks [1958] Director/Solicitor; Lady Lucinda Victoria Shaw Stewart [1949] Director/Antique Dealer; Henry Mark Wyndham [1953] Director/Auctioneer

Chatsworth Investments Limited
Incorporated: 29 January 1997
Net Worth: £28,417,000 *Total Assets:* £62,832,000
Registered Office: The Sir John Peace Building, Experian Way, NG2 Business Park, Nottingham, NG80 1ZZ
Activities: Buying and selling of own real estate
Parent: Experian Finance PLC
Officers: Ronan Hanna, Secretary; Paul Alan Atkinson [1960] Director/Head of Group Tax; Antony Jonathan Ward Barnes [1964] Director of Tax and Treasury; Karen Julia Greenwood [1967] Director/Chartered Accountant; Daniel Tristan Lilley [1981] Director; Mark Edward Pepper [1963] Director/Financial Controller

Cheadle Hulme School
Incorporated: 10 August 1999 *Employees:* 277
Net Worth: £13,236,000 *Total Assets:* £20,768,000
Registered Office: Cheadle Hulme School, Claremont Road, Cheadle Hulme, Cheadle, Cheshire, SK8 6EF
Activities: Other education n.e.c.
Officers: Sue Kershaw, Secretary; Kamal Basran [1951] Director/Company Owner; Michael John Birchall [1967] Director/Solicitor; Joanne Elizabeth Birkett [1975] Director/Partner; Michael James Bolingbroke [1965] Director; Catherine Jane Boyd [1963] Director; Peter John Driver [1954] Director/Police Officer; Philip Robert Johnson [1946] Director/Chartered Accountant; Kay Marie Marshall [1959] Director/Head of Manchester Pharmacy School, University; Dr David Noel Riley [1958] Director/General Medical Practitioner; Christopher Andrew Roberts [1971] Director/Surveyor; Joanne Squire [1962] Director/HR Manager; Martin Gavin Tyley [1974] Director/Partner

Cheaney Shoes Limited
Incorporated: 14 May 2009 *Employees:* 164
Net Worth: £7,665,449 *Total Assets:* £9,384,120
Registered Office: 69 Rushton Road, Desborough, Northants, NN14 2RR
Activities: Manufacture of footwear
Shareholders: William John Church; Jonathan David Ian Church
Officers: Alexander James Bateman [1967] Production Director; Jonathan David Ian Church [1962] Joint Managing Director; William John Church [1967] Joint Managing Director

Cheltenham and Gloucester Omnibus Company Limited
Incorporated: 8 April 1983 *Employees:* 745
Net Worth: £13,469,000 *Total Assets:* £25,770,000
Registered Office: c/o Stagecoach Services Limited, One Stockport Exchange, 20 Railway Road, Stockport, Cheshire, SK1 3SW
Activities: Other urban, suburban or metropolitan passenger land transport (not underground, metro or similar)
Parent: Stagecoach Bus Holdings Limited
Officers: Michael John Vaux, Secretary; Colin Brown [1968] Director/Accountant; Rupert Miles Cox [1980] Managing Director; Arnold Mark Threapleton [1954] Managing Director

Chemetall Limited
Incorporated: 19 December 1930 *Employees:* 62
Net Worth: £108,570,000 *Total Assets:* £125,886,000
Registered Office: 65 Denbigh Road, Bletchley, Milton Keynes, Bucks, MK1 1PB
Activities: Wholesale of chemical products
Parent: Chemetall GmbH
Officers: Wayne Brown, Secretary; Wolfram Alfred Antonius Boegner [1965] Director/Lawyer [German]; Herr Giorgio Cortellaro [1964] Director/Vice President, General Manager [German]; Christopher Hans-Walter Hoffmann [1960] Managing Director [German]

Chenderit School Academy Trust
Incorporated: 6 January 2012 *Employees:* 124
Net Worth: £9,736,660 *Total Assets:* £10,729,146
Registered Office: Chenderit School Academy Trust, Archery Road, Middleton Cheney, Banbury, Oxon, OX17 2QR
Activities: General secondary education
Officers: Beverley Catherine Martin, Secretary; Roger John Hillcox Bell [1954] Director; Marian Patricia Carter [1969] Director/Teacher; Jane Cartwright [1964] Director/Headteacher; Dr Polly Miriam Davies [1967] Director/Doctor; Lisa Ann Davis [1968] Director/Chartered Accountant; Joanne Louise Mhairi Dowden [1982] Director/Senior Youth Worker; Claire Louise Marchand [1973] Director/Teacher; Phillip Simon Marchington [1960] Director/Teacher; Steven Meacham [1970] Director/Finance Manager; Anthony Thomas Pitchfork [1974] Director/Teacher; Alexandra Clare Pope [1975] Director/Nurse; Douglas Alan Scott [1953] Director/School Business Manager (Retired); Ian John Walker [1977] Director/Banker and Financial Consultant; Sophie Wilson [1963] Director

K.J. Cherry & Sons Limited
Incorporated: 8 July 1963 *Employees:* 118
Net Worth: £5,642,003 *Total Assets:* £13,746,468
Registered Office: Twyford, Banbury, Oxon, OX17 3AA
Activities: Growing of cereals (except rice), leguminous crops and oil seeds
Shareholder: Andrew Peter Cherry
Officers: Kevin John Matthews, Secretary; Richard Anthony Allen [1949] Director/Chartered Accountant; Andrew Peter Cherry [1963] Director; Caroline Ann Cherry [1964] Director/Housewife; Patrick John Cherry [1968] Director/Analyst; Kevin John Matthews [1958] Director/Accountant; Jo Whitaker [1966] Director/Housewife

Cherry Valley Farms Limited
Incorporated: 19 November 1959 *Employees:* 206
Net Worth: £33,085,916 *Total Assets:* £36,448,360
Registered Office: Cherry Valley House, Laceby Business Park, Grimsby Road, Laceby, N E Lincs, DN37 7DP
Activities: Raising of poultry
Parent: Anatis UK Limited
Officers: Katharine Mary Butler, Secretary; Katharine Mary Butler [1960] Director/Accountant; Yuqiang Cao [1965] Director/Businessman [Chinese]; Peimin Liang [1974] Director/Businessman [Chinese]; Jiantong Liu [1968] Director/Businessman [Chinese]; Liang Shi [1983] Director/Businessman [Chinese]; John Priestly Vernam [1956] Director; Dr Xinjian Yan [1958] Director/China Operations [Chinese]

Cherwell Valley Silos Limited
Incorporated: 20 June 1961 *Employees:* 115
Net Worth: £4,383,382 *Total Assets:* £12,403,760
Registered Office: Twyford, Banbury, Oxon, OX17 3AA
Activities: Manufacture of prepared feeds for farm animals
Parent: K J Cherry & Sons Limited
Officers: Kevin John Matthews, Secretary; Andrew Peter Cherry [1963] Director; Kevin John Matthews [1958] Director/Accountant; Bryan Robert Mills [1937] Sales Director; Grahame John Nicholls [1951] Freight Director

Cheshire Datasystems Limited
Incorporated: 11 May 2000 *Employees:* 625
Net Worth: £3,803,455 *Total Assets:* £20,741,484
Registered Office: Strata House, Kings Reach Road, Stockport, Cheshire, SK4 2HD
Activities: Other information technology service activities
Officers: Melissa Fiona Johnson, Secretary; Steven Aldred [1965] Finance Director; Stuart Bishop [1967] Director of Services; Thomas Harland Hogg [1935] Director; Gary Arthur Johnson [1966] Director; Melissa Fiona Johnson [1966] Director/HR Manager; Nigel Christopher Phillips [1969] Commercial Director; Frank Robinson [1958] Human Resources Director; Andrew Wormleighton [1972] Director of Software and Technology

Chess Limited
Incorporated: 10 March 1993 *Employees:* 562
Net Worth: £715,000 *Total Assets:* £69,288,000
Registered Office: Bridgford House, Heyes Lane, Alderley Edge, Cheshire, SK9 7JP
Activities: Other telecommunications activities
Major Shareholder: David Pollock
Officers: Tina Pollock, Secretary; John Richard Mark Btesh [1957] Finance Director; Stephen Dracup [1963] Director; Roger John William Hemming [1962] Director; Jessica Hughes [1988] Director; Mark Roy Lightfoot [1973] Financial Director; David Andrew Mason [1950] Director; Charles David Pollock [1960] Director; Charlie Pollock [1991] Director; Warren Andrew Pryer [1963] Director

Chesterfield Poultry Limited
Incorporated: 22 August 2002 *Employees:* 67
Net Worth: £8,560,189 *Total Assets:* £24,273,272
Registered Office: 5 Coulman Street, Thorne, Doncaster, S Yorks, DN8 5JT
Activities: Retail sale of meat and meat products in specialised stores
Shareholders: Mohamed Fayez Ahmed; Nadeem Iqbal
Officers: Mohamed Fayez Ahmed, Secretary; Mohammed Fayez Ahmed [1959] Director; Nadeem Iqbal [1972] Managing Director

Chesterfield Special Cylinders Limited
Incorporated: 18 August 2003 *Employees:* 67
Net Worth: £6,585,000 *Total Assets:* £11,679,000
Registered Office: Unit 6b, Newton Business Centre, Newton Chambers Road, Chapeltown, Sheffield, S35 2PH
Activities: Manufacture of other special-purpose machinery n.e.c.
Parent: Pressure Technologies PLC
Officers: Joanna Claire Allen [1976] Finance Director; Philip David Catton [1957] Director; Mick Pinder [1961] Director; Paul Michael Stanger [1978] Director; Christopher Lee Walters [1969] Director/Chief Executive

Chestnut Homes Limited
Incorporated: 21 October 1992 *Employees:* 54
Net Worth: £11,079,229 *Total Assets:* £15,663,254
Registered Office: The Old School, Wragby Road, Langworth, Lincs, LN3 5BJ
Activities: Construction of domestic buildings
Major Shareholder: David Sydney Newton
Officers: David Sydney Newton, Secretary; Neil Robert Kempster [1968] Director/Development Surveyor; David Sydney Newton [1958] Director/Housebuilder; Robert David Newton [1986] Director/Site Manager - Construction

Chestnutbay Acquisitionco Limited
Incorporated: 25 May 2007
Net Worth: £22,862,000 *Total Assets:* £22,862,000
Registered Office: 2 Crown Way, Rushden, Northants, NN10 6BS
Activities: Non-trading company
Parent: Conchord Limited
Officers: Stephen Kramer, Secretary; Elizabeth Boland [1959] Director/Chief Financial Officer [American]; Stephen Dreier [1942] Director/Chief Admin Officer [American]; Dave Lissy [1965] Director/Chief Executive Officer [American]; James Walter Tugendhat [1971] Managing Director, International

Chevin Homes Limited
Incorporated: 8 May 2002 *Employees:* 8
Net Worth: £1,748,032 *Total Assets:* £10,174,608
Registered Office: 44 Friar Gate, Derby, DE1 1DA
Activities: Buying and selling of own real estate
Shareholders: John David Fearnehough; James David Cokayne
Officers: John David Fearnehough, Secretary/Director; James David Cokayne [1974] Sales Director; John David Fearnehough [1972] Sales Director

Chevron Traffic Management (Holdings) Limited
Incorporated: 12 May 2009 *Employees:* 2
Net Worth: £6,206,787 *Total Assets:* £11,686,187
Registered Office: 3 Thame Park Business Centre, Wenman Road, Thame, Oxon, OX9 3XA
Activities: Activities of head offices
Parent: Chelsey Bidco Limited
Officers: Timothy Noel Cockayne [1978] Director/Construction Services; Anthony Livingstone [1971] Director/Accountant

Chevron Traffic Management Limited
Incorporated: 6 February 1997 *Employees:* 440
Net Worth: £14,776,970 *Total Assets:* £28,077,856
Registered Office: Unit 3 Thame Park Business Centre, Wenman Road, Thame, Oxon, OX9 3XA
Activities: Other transportation support activities
Parent: Chevron Traffic Management (Holdings) Limited
Officers: Timothy Noel Cockayne [1978] Director/Construction Services; Anthony Livingstone [1971] Director/Chartered Accountant; Matthew Noel Morphet [1971] Services Director

Childbase Partnership Limited
Incorporated: 31 August 1989 *Employees:* 1,691
Net Worth Deficit: £2,860,626 *Total Assets:* £29,576,340
Registered Office: Kingston House, Northampton Road, Newport Pagnell, Bucks, MK16 8NJ
Activities: Pre-primary education
Parent: Childbase Employee Ownership Trustee Limited
Officers: Michael Anthony Norcott Thompson, Secretary; Kate Broadhurst [1977] Director/Retail Specialist; Sarah Louise Hill [1973] Operations Director; Virginia Mead-Herbert [1960] Marketing Director; Emma Paula Rooney [1981] Director; Michael Anthony Norcott Thompson [1962] Director; Paul Simon Thompson [1969] Finance Director

Chilled Foods (UK) Ltd
Incorporated: 25 April 2008
Net Worth Deficit: £12,273,000 *Total Assets:* £13,904,000
Registered Office: Fresh-Pak Chilled Foods Ltd, Waterside Park, Valley Way, Wombwell, Barnsley, S Yorks, S73 0BB
Activities: Activities of production holding companies
Parent: Upsilon Bidco Limited
Officers: Stephen John Holding [1966] Director; Richard Mark Andrew Pattrick [1963] Director

Chiltern Cold Storage Group Limited
Incorporated: 3 February 1995 *Employees:* 242
Net Worth: £1,200,831 *Total Assets:* £10,554,841
Registered Office: Shrewsbury Avenue, Woodston Industrial Estate, Peterborough, Cambs, PE2 7LB
Activities: Operation of warehousing and storage facilities for land transport activities
Parent: Chiltern Storage Holdings Limited
Officers: John Selwyn Davidson [1970] Director/Cold Storage Manager; Thomas Edward Lewis [1989] Director

Chiltern Distribution Ltd
Incorporated: 5 April 2006 *Employees:* 243
Previous: Chiltern Cold Storage Group Holdings Limited
Net Worth: £1,660,534 *Total Assets:* £10,685,822
Registered Office: Building 3, Funthams Lane, Whittlesey, Peterborough, PE7 2PB
Activities: Activities of head offices
Major Shareholder: Paul Anthony Jackson
Officers: Paul Anthony Jackson [1962] Director

The Chiltern Hills Academy
Incorporated: 26 July 2011 *Employees:* 110
Net Worth: £18,015,876 *Total Assets:* £20,046,388
Registered Office: Church House Oxford, Langford Locks, Kidlington, Oxon, OX5 1GF
Activities: General secondary education
Officers: Chandra Jasmine Adams [1963] Director/Cover Supervisor; Steven Robert Adams [1980] Director/Policy and Public Affairs; Andrew Michael Brown [1956] Marketing Director; Stephen John Elkins-Jarrett [1961] Director; Giles William Michael Ellerton [1964] Director/Manager; Dr Philip Garner [1947] Director/Research Professor; Maryam Hasnain [1991] Director/Teacher; Graham John Hull [1961] Director/Management Consultant; Javad Malik [1965] Director/Freelance Project Manager; Caroline Lucy Mastrorilli [1968] Director/Learning Support Assistant; Kevin Patrick [1962] Director/Principal; Martin John Paxton [1961] Director/Ministry of Defense - Civilian Fee Earner; Rebecca Ghislaine Cote Rochon [1972] Director/Lecturer; Katharine Melissa Shaw [1972] HR Director; Peter Michael Andrew Stansbury [1964] Director/Consultant

The Chimneys Investment Company Limited
Incorporated: 13 April 2015
Net Worth: £904,875 *Total Assets:* £19,543,568
Registered Office: The Chimneys, 32 Ridgeway, Rothley, Leics, LE7 7LE
Activities: Financial intermediation not elsewhere classified
Shareholders: Lloyd John Charles Dunn; Fiona Louise Dunn
Officers: Fiona Louise Dunn [1973] Director; Lloyd John Charles Dunn [1958] Director

Chinook Sciences Holdings Limited
Incorporated: 28 December 2016 *Employees:* 35
Net Worth: £107,617,368 *Total Assets:* £165,451,232
Registered Office: No 1 Nottingham Science Park, Jesse Boot Avenue, University Boulevard, Nottingham, NG7 2RU
Activities: Manufacture of ovens, furnaces and furnace burners
Officers: Dr Fanli Meng, Secretary; Dr Rifat Al Chalabi [1963] Director [American]; Dr Fanli Meng [1964] Director/Vice President [American]

Chinook Sciences Limited
Incorporated: 22 July 2003 *Employees:* 29
Net Worth: £101,562,608 *Total Assets:* £136,166,624
Registered Office: No 1 Notttingham Science Park, Jesse Boot Avenue, University Boulevard, Nottingham, NG7 2RU
Activities: Manufacture of other special-purpose machinery n.e.c.
Shareholders: Chinook Sciences Holdings Limited; Rifat Al Chalabi
Officers: Dr Fanli Meng, Secretary; Rifat Al Chalabi [1963] Director; Dr Fanli Meng [1964] Director [American]

Chiron Bidco Limited
Incorporated: 27 September 2016 *Employees:* 4
Net Worth Deficit: £5,680,000 *Total Assets:* £138,560,000
Registered Office: Unit 1a-1b Millennium Way, Pride Park, Derby, DE24 8HZ
Activities: Other business support service activities n.e.c.
Parent: Chiron Midco Limited
Officers: Paul Bryce [1973] Business Development Director; Stephen Ross Delaney [1980] Director; Andrew Paul Gilbert [1980] Managing Director; Leon Benjamin Asher Keller [1980] Director/Chief Financial Officer

Chiron Midco Limited
Incorporated: 27 September 2016 *Employees:* 212
Net Worth: £27,603,000 *Total Assets:* £139,156,000
Registered Office: Unit 1a-1b Millennium Way, Pride Park, Derby, DE24 8HZ
Activities: Non-trading company
Officers: Paul Bryce [1973] Business Development Director; Stephen Ross Delaney [1980] Director; Andrew Paul Gilbert [1980] Managing Director; Leon Benjamin Asher Keller [1980] Director/Chief Financial Officer

Caroline Chisholm Education Trust
Incorporated: 18 May 2011 *Employees:* 241
Previous: Caroline Chisholm School
Net Worth: £30,862,640 *Total Assets:* £32,699,700
Registered Office: Caroline Chisholm School, Wooldale Centre for Learning, Wooldale Road, Wootton, Northants, NN4 6TP
Activities: Primary education
Officers: Sarah Ann Sweetland, Secretary; Jenny Blaize [1962] Director/Pastoral Manager; Stephanie Helen Boak [1974] Director/School Governor; Julie Croasdale [1963] Director/School Governor; Sue Duffy [1968] Director/Trustee; Simon Gregson [1979] Director/Teacher Governor; Graham Stuart Irons [1970] Director/Governor/Trustee; David James [1967] Director/School Principal; Tanya MacRae [1975] Director/School Governor [Ukrainian]; Susan Margaret Robson [1961] Director/School Governor; Louise Samways [1965] Director/Trustee; Andrew Sortwell [1951] Director/School Governor; Simon Jeremy Stringer [1974] Director/Governor

Chivgate Limited
Incorporated: 10 December 1986 *Employees:* 46
Net Worth: £6,643,029 *Total Assets:* £25,710,050
Registered Office: 40 Thorby Avenue, March, Cambs, PE15 0AZ
Activities: Activities of head offices
Officers: Rafal Tetnowski, Secretary; Elzbieta Tetnowska [1966] Director [Polish]; Dr Pawel Tomil Tetnowski [1970] Director; Rafal Tetnowski [1971] Director; Stanislaw Frank Tetnowski [1943] Director [Polish]

Choice Packaging Solutions Limited
Incorporated: 2 June 1997 *Employees:* 26
Net Worth: £13,925,543 *Total Assets:* £16,513,539
Registered Office: Denmark House, Brick Close, Kiln Farm, Milton Keynes, Bucks, MK11 3DP
Activities: Recovery of sorted materials
Officers: Raja Rizwan Iqbal [1966] Director

Chorus Education Trust
Incorporated: 12 November 2012 *Employees:* 147
Previous: Silverdale Multi Academy Trust
Net Worth: £19,839,792 *Total Assets:* £22,259,824
Registered Office: Silverdale School, Bents Crescent, Sheffield, S11 9QH
Activities: General secondary education
Officers: Ann Louise Glews Allen, Secretary; Dr Jennifer Carlring-Wright [1971] Director/Business Manager [Swedish]; Andrew Paul Heap [1970] Director; Kevin Charles James [1954] Director/Retired; Linda McAvan [1962] Director; Jonathan Watkin Mordecai [1951] Director/Local Government Officer; James Paul [1975] Director/Banking; Roisin Paul [1970] Director/Headteacher [Irish]; Howard Stephen Shaw [1958] Director/Chartered Accountant; Professor Samantha Twiselton [1964] Director of Sheffield Institute of Education

Christchurch Court (UK) Limited
Incorporated: 20 October 2009 *Employees:* 119
Net Worth: £2,622,091 *Total Assets:* £17,792,680
Registered Office: 2 Christchurch Road, Abington, Northampton, NN1 5LL
Activities: Other residential care activities n.e.c.
Parent: Christchurch Court Holdings Limited
Officers: Professor Michael Philip Barnes [1952] Director/Medical Practitioner; David Jackson [1959] Finance Director; Richard William James McKenzie [1965] Director/Chief Operating Officer

Christchurch Court Holdings Limited
Incorporated: 21 December 2009 *Employees:* 121
Net Worth Deficit: £18,587,072 *Total Assets:* £17,997,292
Registered Office: 2 Christchurch Road, Abington, Northampton, NN1 5LL
Activities: Other human health activities
Parent: SC Management III LP
Officers: David Jackson [1959] Finance Director; Richard William James McKenzie [1965] Director/Chief Executive

The Christian Conference Trust
Incorporated: 21 May 1996
Net Worth: £12,041,538 *Total Assets:* £13,375,401
Registered Office: The Hayes Conference Centre, Hayes Lane, Swanwick, Alfreton, Derbys, DE55 1AU
Activities: Hotels and similar accommodation
Officers: Dr Peter William Brierley [1938] Director/Retired; David John Evans [1950] Chartered Accountant/Director; Melanie Anne Finch [1950] Director/Retired; Dionne Priscilla Gravesande [1965] Director/Senior Manager; Michael James Kinton [1946] Director; Charles Richard Keith Lander [1947] Director/Charity Secretary; Rev Howard Michael Page [1950] Director/Minister of Religion, Prison Chaplain; Michael John Quantick [1947] Director/Retired

Christy Home Textiles Limited
Incorporated: 5 June 2000
Net Worth: £1,578,000 *Total Assets:* £11,252,000
Registered Office: Park Square, Bird Hall Lane, Stockport, Cheshire, SK3 0XF
Activities: Activities of head offices
Parent: CHT Holdings Ltd
Officers: Manish Bansal, Secretary; Manish Bansal [1972] Director/Accountant [Indian]; Dipali Balkrishan Goenka [1969] Director [Indian]

Christys By Design Limited
Incorporated: 14 June 1973 *Employees:* 32
Net Worth: £17,578,000 *Total Assets:* £22,693,000
Registered Office: The Christy Group, Capitol Close, Dodworth, Barnsley, S Yorks, S75 3UB
Activities: Manufacture of other wearing apparel and accessories n.e.c.
Officers: Andrew Gledhill, Secretary; Andrew Richard Gledhill [1966] Director/Accountant; Gary Charles Panons [1960] Director

Chromalloy UK Holdings Ltd
Incorporated: 29 November 2007 *Employees:* 3
Net Worth: £17,577,000 *Total Assets:* £106,612,000
Registered Office: 10 Clover Nook Road, Cotes Park Industrial Estate, Somercotes, Alfreton, Derbys, DE55 4RF
Activities: Activities of production holding companies
Parent: The Carlyle Group
Officers: David Kaplan, Secretary; Steven Robert Lowson, Secretary; Amanda Balog Sanders, Secretary; Dr Peter Howard [1959] Director/Engineer [American]; Paul Anthony Jerram [1964] Director/General Manager; Michael David Smith [1967] Director/Site Lead

Chromalloy United Kingdom Limited
Incorporated: 30 January 1970 *Employees:* 212
Net Worth: £18,170,000 *Total Assets:* £54,664,000
Registered Office: 10 Clover Nook Road, Cotes Park Industrial Estate, Somercotes, Alfreton, Derbys, DE55 4RF
Activities: Manufacture of other fabricated metal products n.e.c.
Parent: Chromalloy Metal Tectonics Limited
Officers: David Kaplan, Secretary; Steven Robert Lowson, Secretary; Amanda Balog Sanders, Secretary; Paul Anthony Jerram [1964] Director/General Manager; Michael David Smith [1967] Director/Site Lead

CHT Holdings Limited
Incorporated: 18 October 2002 *Employees:* 262
Net Worth: £2,367,000 *Total Assets:* £19,238,000
Registered Office: Park Square, Bird Hall Lane, Stockport, Cheshire, SK3 0XF
Activities: Retail sale of textiles in specialised stores
Parent: Welspun Home Textiles UK Ltd
Officers: Manish Bansal, Secretary; Manish Bansal [1972] Director/Accountant [Indian]; Dipali Balkrishan Goenka [1969] Director [Indian]

Church & Co Limited
Incorporated: 16 January 1926 *Employees:* 365
Net Worth: £61,154,496 *Total Assets:* £78,747,952
Registered Office: St James, Northampton, NN5 5JB
Activities: Manufacture of footwear
Officers: Hamun Shah, Secretary/Chartered Accountant; Patrizio Bertelli [1946] Director [Italian]; Carlo Mazzi [1946] Director/Manager [Italian]; Anthony Romano [1966] Director [New Zealander]

Church Army (The)
Incorporated: 14 September 1892 *Employees:* 158
Net Worth: £30,798,000 *Total Assets:* £33,760,000
Registered Office: Wilson Carlile Centre, 50 Cavendish Street, Sheffield, S3 7RZ
Activities: Other accommodation
Officers: Desmond Scott, Secretary; Bishop Alan Francis Abernethy [1957] Director/Bishop [Irish]; Doctor John Applegate [1956] Director/Principal of a Church Training Course; Christine Corteen [1956] Director/Retired; Stephen Geoffrey Cottrell [1958] Director/Bishop; Joanna Babington Cox [1948] Director/Advisor in Adult Education to Archbishops Council; Revd Judith Alison Davis [1988] Director/Vicar; Stephen George Eccleston [1964] Director/Solicitor; Robert Arthur Gillies [1951] Director/Retired; Kathleen Anne Green [1970] Director/Chaplain; Revd Canon Lusa Nsenga-Ngoy [1977] Director/Minister of Religion [Belgian]; Captain Graham Nunn [1955] Director/Minister of Religion; Joanna Susan Penberthy [1960] Director/Bishop; Mark Kenneth Russell [1974] Director/Charity Chief Executive [Irish]; Sister Karen Ruth Webb [1962] Director/Evangelist; John David Whitfield [1957] Director/Retired

Church Growth Trust Limited
Incorporated: 20 August 2010 *Employees:* 5
Net Worth: £17,938,684 *Total Assets:* £18,361,312
Registered Office: The Barn, Baines Lane, Seaton, Oakham, Rutland, LE15 9HP
Activities: Other letting and operating of own or leased real estate
Officers: Andrew Martyn Giles Arnold, Secretary; Nigel Eton Allen [1962] Director; Richard Edward Canham [1953] Director/Retired Finance Sales Manager; David Roger Foster [1948] Director/Retired; Trevor Ernest James [1948] Director/Chartered Accountant; Richard John Naylor [1944] Director; Neil James Walker [1958] Director/Teacher; Paul Withams [1959] Director

Church Mission Society
Incorporated: 8 August 2009 *Employees:* 187
Net Worth: £20,130,000 *Total Assets:* £29,197,000
Registered Office: Church Mission Society, Watlington Road, Cowley, Oxford, OX4 6BZ
Activities: Activities of religious organisations
Officers: Naomi Aidoo [1986] Director/Business Coach; Anthony Richard Bargioni [1944] Director/Retired; Andrew Mark Bowerman [1967] Director; Dr Ian Geoffrey Bromilow [1956] Director/Retired; Beauman Sing Tat Chong [1950] Director; Charles Clayton [1947] Director; Craig Hampton [1955] Director; Lonah Cheptoo Hebditch [1965] Director; Peter Robin Hyatt [1947] Director; Dr Kevin Robert McKemey [1946] Director/Consultant; Professor Salim Munayer [1955] Director of Musalaha - Reconciliation Ministry [Palestinian]; The Revd Jane Shaw [1947] Director/Retired; John Thoburn Stansfeld [1954] Director/Retired; The Revd Ian Malcolm Wallace [1957] Director

Church UK Retail Limited
Incorporated: 4 October 1946 *Employees:* 94
Net Worth: £6,082,498 *Total Assets:* £11,603,930
Registered Office: St James's, Northampton, NN5 5JB
Activities: Retail sale of footwear in specialised stores
Parent: Church & Co Ltd
Officers: Alessandra Cozzani [1963] Director/Manager [Italian]; Carlo Mazzi [1946] Director/Manager [Italian]; Anthony Romano [1966] Director [New Zealander]

J.J.Churchill Limited
Incorporated: 30 December 1937 *Employees:* 132
Net Worth: £5,199,000 *Total Assets:* £14,892,000
Registered Office: Station Road, Market Bosworth, Nuneaton, Warwicks, CV13 0PF
Activities: Other manufacturing n.e.c.
Shareholder: James Loveden Churchill
Officers: Michael Raymond Wallis, Secretary; Andrew James Churchill [1968] Managing Director; James Loveden Churchill [1937] Managing Director; John Wynne Churchill [1935] Director/Retired; Mark Cooper [1968] Sales & Marketing Director; Stuart Henry Goode [1969] Operations Director; Michael Raymond Wallis [1955] Director

CI Beatrice II Facility (BOWL) Limited
Incorporated: 8 March 2016 *Employees:* 2
Net Worth: £63,855,508 *Total Assets:* £64,433,192
Registered Office: c/o Templeborough Biomass, River View, Sheffield Road, Rotherham, S Yorks, S60 1FA
Activities: Activities of other holding companies n.e.c.
Parent: CI Beatrice II Facility (CI II) Limited
Officers: Christina Grumstrup Sorensen [1972] Director/Senior Partner [Danish]; Torsten Lodberg Smed [1970] Director/Senior Partner [Danish]

CI Beatrice II Facility (CI II) Limited
Incorporated: 7 March 2016 *Employees:* 3
Net Worth Deficit: £2,297,953 *Total Assets:* £62,739,104
Registered Office: c/o Templeborough Biomass Power Plant, River View, Sheffield Road, Rotherham, S Yorks, S60 1FA
Activities: Activities of other holding companies n.e.c.
Officers: Ronnie Bonnar [1963] Director; Christina Grumstrup Sorensen [1972] Director/Senior Partner [Danish]; Mark Newbery [1957] Director/Lawyer

CI Brite (UK) Holdings Limited
Incorporated: 6 May 2015 *Employees:* 3
Net Worth: £75,500,384 *Total Assets:* £89,168,992
Registered Office: c/o Templeborough Biomass Power Plant, River View, Sheffield Road, Rotherham, S Yorks, S60 1FA
Activities: Activities of other holding companies n.e.c.
Officers: Ronnie Bonnar [1963] Director; Mark Newbery [1957] Director/Lawyer; Christina Grumstrup Sorensen [1972] Director [Danish]

CI Brite Limited
Incorporated: 27 January 2015 *Employees:* 3
Net Worth: £83,855,448 *Total Assets:* £274,212,864
Registered Office: c/o Templeborough Biomass Power Plant, River View, Sheffield Road, Rotherham, S Yorks, S60 1FA
Activities: Activities of production holding companies
Parent: CI Brite (UK) Holdings Limited
Officers: Ronnie Bonnar [1963] Director; Mark Newbery [1957] Director/Lawyer; Christina Grumstrup Sorensen [1972] Director [Danish]

Cimbria Holdings Limited
Incorporated: 10 July 2012
Net Worth: £76,031,168 *Total Assets:* £76,175,592
Registered Office: Abbey Park, Stoneleigh, Kenilworth, Warwicks, CV8 2TQ
Activities: Manufacture of agricultural and forestry machinery other than tractors
Parent: AGCO International Limited
Officers: Roger Neil Batkin [1968] Director/Lawyer; Adam Charles Frost [1980] Director/Chartered Accountant

Cinch Connectors Limited
Incorporated: 15 October 1987 *Employees:* 74
Net Worth: £20,369,168 *Total Assets:* £21,478,824
Registered Office: Shireoaks Road, Worksop, Notts, S80 3HA
Activities: Manufacture of electronic components
Parent: Bel Fuse Inc
Officers: Andrew Deacon, Secretary; Scott Alan Martin, Secretary; Daniel Bernstein [1953] Director/Business Executive [American]; Pete Bittner [1970] Director/President of Bel Connectivity [American]; Craig Donald Brosious [1956] Director/Vice President of Finance [American]; Scott Alan Martin [1975] Director of Finance [American]

Cintra Infrastructures SE
Incorporated: 22 April 2016 *Employees:* 4
Net Worth: £759,270,976 *Total Assets:* £1,042,882,112
Registered Office: The Sherard Building, Edmund Halley Road, Oxford, OX4 4DQ
Activities: Development of building projects
Parent: Ferrovial International Ltd
Officers: Armstrong Agbor Ebot [1981] Member/Financial Controller [Cameroonian/Dutch]; Ana Del Rosario Castillo Molina - Van Der Laan [1973] Member/Financial Controller [Peruvian/Dutch]; Jose Angel Tamariz-Martel Goncer [1968] Member [Spanish]

Circassia Limited
Incorporated: 29 December 1998 *Employees:* 531
Net Worth Deficit: £202,148,992 *Total Assets:* £217,764,000
Registered Office: The Magdalen Centre, Robert Robinson Avenue, Science Park, Oxford, OX4 4GA
Activities: Research and experimental development on biotechnology
Parent: Circassia Pharmaceuticals PLC
Officers: Roderick Peter Hafner [1965] Director/R&D Biotechnology; David Richard Williams [1967] Director/General Counsel

Circassia Pharmaceuticals PLC
Incorporated: 19 May 2006 *Employees:* 366
Net Worth: £224,800,000 *Total Assets:* £402,400,000
Registered Office: The Magdalen Centre, Robert Robinson Avenue, Oxford Science Park, Oxford, OX4 4GA
Activities: Manufacture of pharmaceutical preparations
Officers: Julien Fabrice Cotta, Secretary; Julien Fabrice Cotta [1964] Director/Chief Financial Controller; Russell Cummings [1964] Director; Sharon Curran [1968] Director/Business Executive [Irish]; Dr Francesco Granata [1950] Director/Executive in Residence Warburg Pincus [Italian]; Roderick Peter Hafner [1965] Director/R&D Biotechnology; Steven Charles Andrew Harris [1966] Director; Jo Susan Le Couilliard [1963] Director/Business Executive; Dr Heribert Staudinger [1951] Director/Business Executive [German/American]; Lota Zoth [1959] Director [American]

Citation Holdings Limited
Incorporated: 9 November 2000 *Employees:* 3
Net Worth: £5,599,805 *Total Assets:* £40,582,072
Registered Office: Kings Court, Water Lane, Wilmslow, Cheshire, SK9 5AR
Activities: Non-trading company
Parent: Caesar Bidco Limited
Officers: Jenny Ingleby [1976] Sales & Marketing Director; Christopher Paul Morris [1972] Director; Eloise Wann [1977] Director/Chief Financial Officer

Citation Limited
Incorporated: 1 September 1995 *Employees:* 367
Net Worth: £33,939,212 *Total Assets:* £50,958,656
Registered Office: Kings Court, Water Lane, Wilmslow, Cheshire, SK9 5AR
Activities: Management consultancy activities other than financial management
Parent: Citation Holdings Limited
Officers: Jenny Ingleby [1976] Sales & Marketing Director; Christopher Paul Morris [1972] Director; Andrew Charles Pumphrey [1965] Managing Director; Eloise Wann [1977] Director/Chief Financial Officer

Citigen (London) Limited
Incorporated: 29 September 1989 *Employees:* 5
Net Worth: £1,746,000 *Total Assets:* £25,965,000
Registered Office: Westwood Way, Westwood Business Park, Coventry, Warwicks, CV4 8LG
Activities: Production of electricity
Parent: E.On UK CHP Limited
Officers: Michael Robert Day [1978] Director/Accountant; Michael Robert French [1968] Managing Director, Business & Community Solutions [German]; Michael Geoffrey Wake [1970] Director

Citroen U.K. Limited
Incorporated: 27 July 1923 *Employees:* 51
Net Worth: £70,886,000 *Total Assets:* £630,558,976
Registered Office: Pinley House, 2 Sunbeam Way, Coventry, Warwicks, CV3 1ND
Activities: Sale of new cars and light motor vehicles
Parent: Peugeot S.A.
Officers: Kinnary Vyas, Secretary; David James Connell [1972] Director of Human Resources GB & Ireland; Karl Howkins [1972] Managing Director; Linda Jackson [1958] Managing Director; Stephane Le Guevel [1967] Managing Director [French]; Nigel John Willetts [1972] Finance Director

City Electrical Factors Limited
Incorporated: 2 February 1938 *Employees:* 2,610
Net Worth: £161,747,120 *Total Assets:* £347,552,032
Registered Office: Georgina Mackie House, 141 Farmer Ward Road, Kenilworth, Warwicks, CV8 2SU
Activities: Wholesale of household goods (other than musical instruments) n.e.c
Shareholders: CEF Holdings Ltd; Jacqueline Mackie
Officers: Mark Stephen Jacobs, Secretary; Kevin Alan David Barnett [1955] Director; Charles Henry Beddows [1957] Director/General Manager; Georgina Louise Hartland [1964] Director; Thomas Alan Hartland Mackie [1987] Director; Mark Stephen Jacobs [1959] Finance Director; Jacqueline Anne Mackie [1950] Director

City Estates (UK) Limited
Incorporated: 22 November 2013 *Employees:* 28
Net Worth: £25,894,000 *Total Assets:* £39,344,000
Registered Office: 14 Fitzwilliam Street, Sheffield, S1 4JL
Activities: Other letting and operating of own or leased real estate
Major Shareholder: Brendan Elwood
Officers: Ewan Gairn Barclay Ross, Secretary; Brendan Elwood [1943] Director; Martin Patrick Elwood [1968] Director; Dale Lee Fixter [1967] Director

City Furniture Hire Limited
Incorporated: 24 March 1999
Net Worth: £6,385,005 *Total Assets:* £10,445,167
Registered Office: 20 Coxon Street, Spondon, Derby, DE21 7JG
Activities: Other business support service activities n.e.c.
Parent: Fredalou Holdings Limited
Officers: Veronica Negus, Secretary; Gary Mansfield [1967] Director; Lily Rose Mansfield [1992] Director/Processing Administrator

City Plumbing Supplies Holdings Limited
Incorporated: 5 April 1990 *Employees:* 1,923
Net Worth: £192,000,000 *Total Assets:* £227,700,000
Registered Office: Lodge Way House, Lodge Way, Harlestone Road, Northampton, NN5 7UG
Activities: Wholesale of hardware, plumbing and heating equipment and supplies
Parent: City Investments Limited
Officers: John Peter Carter [1961] Director/Chief Executive; David Michael Evans [1974] Director; Andrew Peter Harrison [1961] Director; Martin Richard Meech [1957] Director/Chartered Surveyor; Alan Richard Williams [1969] Director/Accountant

City Suites Manchester Limited
Incorporated: 7 November 2013
Net Worth: £764,000 *Total Assets:* £12,336,000
Registered Office: The Box, Horseshoe Lane, Alderley Edge, Cheshire, SK9 7QP
Activities: Development of building projects
Parent: City Suites Ltd
Officers: Giles Peter Beswick, Secretary; Giles Peter Beswick [1974] Director; Mark Christopher Dawson [1973] Director; Mark David Stott [1972] Director

Citynet Insurance Brokers Limited
Incorporated: 24 February 2000 *Employees:* 76
Net Worth: £3,451,307 *Total Assets:* £18,728,236
Registered Office: Rossington's Business Park, West Carr Road, Retford, Notts, DN22 7SW
Activities: Non-life insurance
Parent: Citynet London Holdings Limited
Officers: Ryan Christopher Brown [1973] Director; Adrian Colosso [1957] Director; Brendan James McManus [1959] Director; Richard John Scott [1968] Managing Director; David Walland [1968] Director/Chartered Management Accountant; Andrew Mark Walsh [1979] Motor Fleet Director

The Clarendon Office Group Ltd.
Incorporated: 29 July 2015 *Employees:* 49
Net Worth: £3,497,774 *Total Assets:* £16,188,408
Registered Office: Clarendon House, 52 Cornmarket Street, Oxford, OX1 3HJ
Activities: Activities of other holding companies n.e.c.
Shareholders: Julian Ashley Cooper; Kenneth Laurence Cooper
Officers: David Arthur Cooper [1940] Director; Julian Ashley Cooper [1974] Director; Kenneth Laurence Cooper [1944] Director; Candida Tania Maria Woodington [1970] Director

J.R. Clark Limited
Incorporated: 6 August 1981 *Employees:* 10
Net Worth: £19,249,406 *Total Assets:* £26,451,512
Registered Office: The Estate Office, Culverthorpe, Grantham, Lincs, NG32 3NQ
Activities: Growing of cereals (except rice), leguminous crops and oil seeds
Shareholders: Susan Louise Clark; Ashley-Marc Eric Arthur Clark
Officers: Susan Louise Clark, Secretary; Ashley-Marc Eric Arthur Clark [1984] Director; Susan Louise Clark [1960] Director/Secretary

Clark-Drain Limited
Incorporated: 2 November 1978 *Employees:* 199
Net Worth: £5,907,272 *Total Assets:* £11,395,618
Registered Office: Station Road, Yaxley, Peterborough, PE7 3EQ
Activities: Manufacture of other chemical products n.e.c.
Parent: Clarksteel Holdings Limited
Officers: Ronald Francis Clark [1949] Director/Engineer; Rebecca Louise Hardy [1982] Director; Darren John Hughes [1972] Director; Sarah Jayne Hughes [1973] Director; Pamela May Spencer [1960] Director; Rachel Ellen Stuffins [1976] Director

Clarksteel Holdings Limited
Incorporated: 20 May 1971 *Employees:* 199
Net Worth: £7,642,263 *Total Assets:* £14,595,698
Registered Office: Station Road, Yaxley, Peterborough, Cambs, PE7 3EQ
Activities: Manufacture of other fabricated metal products n.e.c.
Shareholders: Ronald Francis Clark; Graham Clive Holdich Smith; Pamela May Spencer
Officers: Ronald Francis Clark [1949] Director/Engineer; Pamela May Spencer [1960] Director

Classeq Limited
Incorporated: 10 October 1980 *Employees:* 58
Net Worth: £8,289,182 *Total Assets:* £13,263,026
Registered Office: Winterhalter House, Roebuck Way, Knowlhill, Milton Keynes, Bucks, MK5 8WH
Activities: Other manufacturing n.e.c.
Officers: David John Parsons, Secretary; Nick Burridge [1976] Director; Viktor Faller [1964] Director [German]; Peter Huber [1957] Director [German]; Gary Jones [1963] Director; David John Parsons [1961] Finance Director; Andrew Maurice Salter [1969] Director; David Smithson [1949] Director; Ludwig Weiss [1966] Director [German]

Claydon Estate LLP
Incorporated: 22 July 2011 *Employees:* 23
Net Worth: £39,862,464 *Total Assets:* £41,473,832
Registered Office: The Claydon Estate, Estate Office, Claydon Park, Middle Claydon, Bucks, MK18 2EX
Officers: Stuart John Richmond-Watson [1951] Member; Sir Edmund Ralph Verney [1950] Member; Nicholas Edmund Verney [1983] Member; Thomas Michael Wheelwright [1946] Member

Claypenny Property Services Limited
Incorporated: 22 November 1990 *Employees:* 4
Net Worth: £7,841,948 *Total Assets:* £16,639,423
Registered Office: 2 Rutland Park, Sheffield, S10 2PD
Activities: Other business support service activities n.e.c.
Shareholders: Guy Philip Alistair Ludlam; Fraser Ludlam
Officers: Fraser Ludlam, Secretary; Fraser Ludlam [1969] Director; Guy Philip Alistair Ludlam [1973] Director; Philip Graham Ludlam [1939] Director

Clayson Country Homes Limited
Incorporated: 9 January 1987 *Employees:* 16
Net Worth: £4,535,353 *Total Assets:* £12,340,012
Registered Office: 345 Wellingborough Road, Northampton, NN1 4ER
Activities: Development of building projects
Shareholder: Colin Clayson
Officers: Keith John Clayson, Secretary; Colin Geoffrey Clayson [1952] Director/House Builder

Clayton (Lincoln) Limited
Incorporated: 1 May 1975 *Employees:* 5
Net Worth: £11,364,089 *Total Assets:* £11,628,661
Registered Office: Harby Mill, Wigsley Road, Harby, Newark, Notts, NG23 7EF
Activities: Activities of property unit trusts
Shareholder: Derrick Raymond Clayton
Officers: Patricia Margaret Clayton, Secretary; Adele Clay [1979] Director/Social Worker; Derrick Raymond Clayton [1943] Director; Edward James Clayton [1976] Director/Social Worker; Patricia Margaret Clayton [1944] Director/Secretary; Maria Eileen Michael [1966] Director

Clean Estates Limited
Incorporated: 25 February 1999 *Employees:* 92
Net Worth: £2,528,577 *Total Assets:* £27,652,270
Registered Office: TCL House, 7 Outrams Wharf, Little Eaton, Derby, DE21 5EL
Activities: Other cleaning services
Parent: G. Burley & Sons Limited
Officers: Simon John Abley [1976] Director/Accountant; Simon John Cashmore [1970] Director/Accountant; Robert Chatwin [1984] Director

Clearmark Solutions (2019) LLP
Incorporated: 9 August 2010 *Employees:* 80
Previous: Clearmark Solutions LLP
Net Worth: £6,471,348 *Total Assets:* £9,815,637
Registered Office: Olympic House, Willow Drive, Annesley, Notts, NG15 0DP
Officers: Dave Bradbury [1960] Member; Christopher Gent [1959] Member; Christopher Philip Simpson [1961] Member

CLEB Holdings Limited
Incorporated: 18 May 2004
Net Worth: £3,471,000 *Total Assets:* £11,237,000
Registered Office: Southfield Lane, Whitwell, Worksop, Notts, S80 3LJ
Activities: Manufacture of other non-metallic mineral products n.e.c.
Parent: Lhoist UK Limited
Officers: Dirk Donck, Secretary; Axel Vincent Ampolini [1970] Vice President and Managing Director [American]; Cedric Joannes Rosa Georges de Vicq de Cumptich [1980] Director/Employee/Executive [Belgian]; Dirk Donck [1956] Director/General Counsel Europe [Belgian]

Clegg Construction Limited
Incorporated: 12 August 1960 *Employees:* 57
Net Worth: £8,161,622 *Total Assets:* £17,576,952
Registered Office: Bishops House, 42 High Pavement, The Lace Market, Nottingham, NG1 1HN
Activities: Construction of commercial buildings
Parent: Clegg Group Limited
Officers: Gary John Russell, Secretary; Michael Allsop [1979] Commercial Director; Keith Anderson [1962] Director; Simon John Blackburn [1960] Director; Timothy Brett Walker [1967] Director

Clegg Food Projects Limited
Incorporated: 17 December 1998 *Employees:* 30
Net Worth: £5,542,057 *Total Assets:* £17,671,088
Registered Office: Bishops House, 42 High Pavement, The Lace Market, Nottingham, NG1 1HN
Activities: Construction of commercial buildings
Parent: D E Clegg Holdings Limited
Officers: Gary John Russell, Secretary; Keith Anderson [1962] Commercial Director; Stephen Mark Giltrap [1960] Director/Chartered Builder; Ian King [1963] Director; John Richard Moxon [1961] Business Development Director; John Rogan [1965] Director

Clegg Group Limited
Incorporated: 17 December 1998 *Employees:* 100
Net Worth: £12,945,870 *Total Assets:* £37,691,064
Registered Office: Bishops House, 42 High Pavement, Nottingham, NG1 1HN
Activities: Activities of head offices
Parent: D E Clegg Holdings Limited
Officers: Gary John Russell, Secretary; Keith Anderson [1962] Director; Simon John Blackburn [1960] Director; Stephen Mark Giltrap [1960] Director

Clegg Holdings Limited
Incorporated: 3 July 2007 *Employees:* 100
Net Worth: £3,401,941 *Total Assets:* £26,779,640
Registered Office: 42 High Pavement, Nottingham, NG1 1HN
Activities: Activities of head offices
Officers: Gary John Russell, Secretary; Keith Anderson [1962] Director; Simon John Blackburn [1960] Director; Stephen Mark Giltrap [1960] Director; Timothy Stewart Richmond [1947] Director

T.H.Clements & Son Limited
Incorporated: 21 January 1966 *Employees:* 301
Net Worth: £7,532,000 *Total Assets:* £20,214,000
Registered Office: West End, Benington, Boston, Lincs, PE22 0EJ
Activities: Growing of vegetables and melons, roots and tubers
Parent: NG25 Limited
Officers: Simon John Lingard, Secretary; Christopher Ashley Clements [1981] Director/Business Manager; Christopher Terence Gedney [1959] Director; Richard James Mowbray [1974] Commercial Director

Cleveland Transit Ltd.
Incorporated: 8 October 1990 *Employees:* 284
Net Worth: £4,434,000 *Total Assets:* £9,927,000
Registered Office: c/o Stagecoach Services Limited, One Stockport Exchange, 20 Railway Road, Stockport, Cheshire, SK1 3SW
Activities: Other urban, suburban or metropolitan passenger land transport (not underground, metro or similar)
Parent: Stagecoach Bus Holdings Limited
Officers: Michael John Vaux, Secretary; Colin Brown [1968] Director/Accountant; Arnold Mark Threapleton [1954] Managing Director; Steven Walker [1971] Director

Clientlogic (UK) Holding Limited
Incorporated: 20 November 2002
Net Worth: £36,711,000 *Total Assets:* £64,757,000
Registered Office: Earlsdon Park, 53-55 Butts Road, Coventry, Warwicks, CV1 3BH
Activities: Activities of head offices
Officers: John William Hayward, Secretary/Solicitor; Karl Vernon Brough [1962] Director; Pedro Lozano de Castro [1963] Director [Spanish]

Clientlogic (UK) Limited
Incorporated: 1 December 2000
Net Worth: £20,626,000 *Total Assets:* £37,931,000
Registered Office: Earlsdon Park, 53-55 Butts Road, Coventry, Warwicks, CV1 3BH
Activities: Other business support service activities n.e.c.
Parent: Clientlogic Holding Limited
Officers: John William Hayward, Secretary/Solicitor; Karl Vernon Brough [1962] Director; Pedro Lozano de Castro [1963] Director [Spanish]

Clientlogic Holding Limited
Incorporated: 19 March 1998
Net Worth Deficit: £18,971,000 *Total Assets:* £83,188,000
Registered Office: Earlsdon Park, 53-55 Butts Road, Coventry, Warwicks, CV1 3BH
Activities: Activities of head offices
Parent: Clientlogic (UK) Holding Limited
Officers: John William Hayward, Secretary/Solicitor; Karl Vernon Brough [1962] Director; Pedro Lozano de Castro [1963] Director [Spanish]

Clientlogic Limited
Incorporated: 26 October 1984
Net Worth Deficit: £6,850,000 *Total Assets:* £16,843,000
Registered Office: Earlsdon Park, 53-55 Butts Road, Coventry, Warwicks, CV1 3BH
Activities: Activities of call centres
Officers: John William Hayward, Secretary/Solicitor; Karl Vernon Brough [1962] Director; Pedro Lozano de Castro [1963] Director [Spanish]

Clifton Packaging Group Limited
Incorporated: 20 December 2002 *Employees:* 100
Net Worth: £11,117,457 *Total Assets:* £22,816,976
Registered Office: Centurion Way, Meridian Business Park, Leicester, LE19 1WH
Activities: Other manufacturing n.e.c.
Shareholders: Shahid Rashid Sheikh; Tahir Javed Sheikh; Zahid Javed Sheikh
Officers: Shahid Rashid Sheikh, Secretary/Director; Shahid Rashid Sheikh [1968] Director; Tahir Javed Sheikh [1959] Director; Zahid Javed Sheikh [1961] Director

Clinigen Group PLC
Incorporated: 12 December 2008 *Employees:* 727
Net Worth: £311,386,304 *Total Assets:* £594,351,360
Registered Office: Pitcairn House, Crown Square, Centrum 100, Burton on Trent, Staffs, DE14 2WW
Activities: Manufacture of pharmaceutical preparations
Officers: Amanda Miller, Secretary; Martin James Abell [1974] Executive Director; Peter Vance Allen [1956] Director; Alan Keith Boyd [1954] Director; Shaun Edward Chilton [1967] Director/Chief Operating Officer; John Hartup [1951] Director; Anne Philomena Hyland [1960] Director; Ian James Nicholson [1960] Director

Clinigen Healthcare Limited
Incorporated: 18 May 2007 *Employees:* 32
Net Worth: £70,231,000 *Total Assets:* £230,024,000
Registered Office: Pitcairn House, Crown Square, Centrum 100, Burton on Trent, Staffs, DE14 2WW
Activities: Wholesale of pharmaceutical goods
Parent: Clinigen Holdings Limited
Officers: Amanda Miller, Secretary; Martin James Abell [1974] Director; Shaun Edward Chilton [1967] Director

Close Brothers Vehicle Hire Limited
Incorporated: 1 August 2001 *Employees:* 73
Previous: Commercial Vehicle Solutions Limited
Net Worth Deficit: £5,870,752 *Total Assets:* £152,168,352
Registered Office: Lows Lane, Stanton-by-Dale, Ilkeston, Derbys, DE7 4QU
Activities: Other service activities incidental to land transportation, n.e.c.
Parent: Close Brothers Limited
Officers: Sarah Louise Moss, Secretary; Luke Antony Bazzard [1965] Director/Chief Information Officer Banking Division; Theovinder Chatha [1980] Finance Director; Neil Geoffrey Davies [1957] Director; Richard Neil Gosling [1972] Sales Director; Sarah Louise Moss [1982] Director/Finance Manager; Terence Charles Ottey [1961] Finance Director; Adrian John Sainsbury [1968] Director/Banker; Charles Starr [1963] Commercial Director; David Peter Thomson [1963] Director

Clowes Developments (North West) Limited
Incorporated: 12 January 1988 *Employees:* 4
Net Worth: £4,264 *Total Assets:* £20,871,302
Registered Office: Ednaston Park, Painters Lane, Ednaston, Ashbourne, Derbys, DE6 3FA
Activities: Buying and selling of own real estate
Parent: Clowes Developments (UK) Limited
Officers: Andrew Michael Bock, Secretary; Andrew Michael Bock [1964] Property Director; David Charles Clowes [1969] Director/Pilot; Ian David Dickinson [1965] Director/Chartered Accountant; Marc Peter Freeman [1972] Director

Clowes Developments (UK) Limited
Incorporated: 17 September 1964 *Employees:* 40
Net Worth: £193,741,136 *Total Assets:* £243,769,712
Registered Office: Ednaston Park, Painters Lane, Ednaston, Ashbourne, Derbys, DE6 3FA
Activities: Buying and selling of own real estate
Parent: The Clowes Trust 2014
Officers: Andrew Michael Bock, Secretary/Chartered Surveyor; Gordon Robert Arthur [1958] Director; Andrew Michael Bock [1964] Director/Chartered Surveyor; David Charles Clowes [1969] Director/Airline Pilot; Ian David Dickinson [1965] Director/Accountant; Marc Peter Freeman [1972] Director/Property Developer; Robert Michael Hepwood [1965] Director/Chartered Surveyor; Ralph Charles Jones [1950] Director; James David Andrew Richards [1979] Director/Chartered Surveyor; Paul Shanley [1956] Director

CLS Finance Limited
Incorporated: 3 February 2004 *Employees:* 33
Net Worth: £1,635,569 *Total Assets:* £13,434,865
Registered Office: Unit 2 Alexandra Street, Hyde, Cheshire, SK14 1DX
Activities: Financial intermediation not elsewhere classified
Shareholders: Shaun Patrick Young; Charles Omar Holding
Officers: Shaun Patrick Young, Secretary; Charles Omar Holding [1969] Director; Shaun Patrick Young [1962] Director

Clugston Construction Limited
Incorporated: 25 January 1961 *Employees:* 441
Net Worth: £6,901,099 *Total Assets:* £57,284,892
Registered Office: St Vincent House, Normanby Road, Scunthorpe, N Lincs, DN15 8QT
Activities: Construction of commercial buildings
Parent: Clugston Group Limited
Officers: Ian Pattison, Secretary; Andrew Thomas Allingham [1961] Commercial Director; David Westland Antony Clugston [1972] Director; Roderick Malcolm Fry [1959] Director; Ian Pattison [1969] Finance Director; Stephen John Radcliffe [1955] Director; Robert John Vickers [1956] Director/Chief Executive Officer

Clugston Group Limited
Incorporated: 1 November 1937 *Employees:* 629
Net Worth: £14,317,000 *Total Assets:* £86,212,000
Registered Office: St Vincent House, Normanby Road, Scunthorpe, N Lincs, DN15 8QT
Activities: Activities of head offices
Shareholder: John Westland Antony Clugston
Officers: Ian Pattison, Secretary; David Westland Antony Clugston [1972] Director; John Westland Antony Clugston [1938] Director/Chairman; John Anthony Brian Kelly [1941] Director; Ian Pattison [1969] Finance Director; Stephen John Radcliffe [1955] Director; Robert John Vickers [1956] Director/Chief Executive Officer; Andrew William Walker [1944] Director/Lawyer

Clyde Bergemann Materials Handling Limited
Incorporated: 15 April 1994 *Employees:* 80
Net Worth Deficit: £5,696,000 *Total Assets:* £13,071,000
Registered Office: Lakeside Boulevard, Lakeside, Doncaster, S Yorks, DN4 5PL
Activities: Repair of machinery
Parent: Clyde Bergemann Investments Limited
Officers: Miles Brittain Ratcliffe, Finance Director; Stephen Michael Cragg [1959] Director; Ralph Alexander Ludwig [1963] Director [German]; Miles Brittain Ratcliffe [1965] Finance Director

Clyde Union DB Limited
Incorporated: 25 September 1937 *Employees:* 86
Net Worth: £85,053,000 *Total Assets:* £91,607,000
Registered Office: Green Road, Penistone, Sheffield, S36 6BJ
Activities: Manufacture of pumps
Parent: Clyde Union (Holdings) Limited
Officers: Paul Andrew Cahill [1974] Director/Accountant; Mark Edward Shanahan [1970] Director; Stephen Tsoris [1957] Director [American]

Clytha Holdings Limited
Incorporated: 26 September 1990 *Employees:* 176
Net Worth: £6,686,690 *Total Assets:* £22,035,164
Registered Office: Eland Road, Denaby Main, Doncaster, S Yorks, DN12 4HA
Activities: Wholesale of metals and metal ores
Parent: Endcliffe Holdings Limited
Officers: Robert George Anthony Barr [1956] Director [Irish]; Leslie Robert Buxton [1978] Director; James Richard Keeling-Heane [1980] Director; Mark Vincenzo Wadsworth [1973] Director/Systems General Manager; Mark Douglas Wheatley [1979] Director

CMD Limited
Incorporated: 26 August 1988
Net Worth: £11,535,415 *Total Assets:* £15,421,458
Registered Office: Sycamore Road, Eastwood Trading Estate, Rotherham, S Yorks, S65 1EN
Activities: Manufacture of other electrical equipment
Parent: Ideal Industries Holdings Ltd
Officers: Jeffrey Burkhardt [1966] Director [American]; Carmelle Marie Giblin [1967] Director [American]

CMI International Limited
Incorporated: 10 September 2015 *Employees:* 37
Net Worth: £4,048,000 *Total Assets:* £16,482,000
Registered Office: Viaduct Works, Canon Street, Leicester, LE4 6GH
Activities: Other manufacturing n.e.c.
Major Shareholder: Glenn Bryan Dalby
Officers: Glenn Bryan Dalby [1957] Director; Glyn John Wheeler [1957] Finance Director

CML Limited
Incorporated: 27 June 1990 *Employees:* 350
Net Worth: £823,186 *Total Assets:* £13,770,092
Registered Office: Vulcan Way, Magna Park, Lutterworth, Leics, LE17 4XR
Activities: Operation of warehousing and storage facilities for land transport activities
Shareholder: Graham John Copley
Officers: Kerry Delaney [1974] Commercial Director; Adrian Michael Goodman [1976] Finance Director; Rebecca Jenkins [1961] Freight Director; Richard Kennerley [1973] Director; Andreas Plikat [1966] Director [German]; Mark Webb [1969] Managing Director

CMS Cepcor (Holdings) Limited
Incorporated: 14 March 2017
Net Worth: £25,465,448 *Total Assets:* £30,156,884
Registered Office: 1 Vulcan Way, Coalville, Leics, LE67 3AP
Activities: Activities of other holding companies n.e.c.
Shareholders: David Ian Sydenham; Elizabeth Heather Sydenham
Officers: Christopher Iain Sydenham [1979] Director/Engineer; David Ian Sydenham [1942] Director/Engineer; Elizabeth Heather Sydenham [1946] Director/Bookkeeper; Matthew Thomas Weare [1970] Managing Director

CMS Cepcor Limited
Incorporated: 31 May 1989 *Employees:* 80
Previous: Crusher Manganese Steels Limited
Net Worth: £19,833,788 *Total Assets:* £24,201,578
Registered Office: 1 Vulcan Way, Coalville, Leics, LE67 3AP
Activities: Support activities for other mining and quarrying
Parent: CMS Cepcor (Holdings) Limited
Officers: Elizabeth Heather Sydenham, Secretary; Lee Robert Joseph Hodges [1976] Commercial Director; James Luke Shelley [1974] Sales Director; Christopher Iain Sydenham [1979] Director/Engineer; David Ian Sydenham [1942] Director/Engineer; Elizabeth Heather Sydenham [1946] Director/Bookkeeper; Matthew Thomas Weare [1970] Managing Director

CNH Bidco Limited
Incorporated: 3 October 2011 *Employees:* 1,801
Net Worth: £7,706,000 *Total Assets:* £38,985,000
Registered Office: CNH Bidco Limited, Lowton Way, Hellaby, Rotherham, S Yorks, S66 8RY
Activities: Activities of other holding companies n.e.c.
Officers: Rami Cassis [1968] Director [French]; Pieter Johannes Hooft [1963] Director/Investment Professional [Dutch]; James Lucien Alexander Szpiro [1973] Director/Investment Professional

CNIM Clugston (Avonmouth) Limited
Incorporated: 7 March 2017 *Employees:* 4
Net Worth Deficit: £1,141 *Total Assets:* £9,290,450
Registered Office: St Vincent House, Normanby Road, Scunthorpe, N Lincs, DN15 8QT
Activities: Other specialised construction activities n.e.c.
Shareholders: Soluni SA; CNIM SA; Clugston Construction Limited
Officers: Andrew Thomas Allingham [1961] Commercial Director; David Richard Alexandre Cinque [1981] Director of Projects [French]; Richard Greenwood [1968] Director/Business Unit Manager; Stephane Richard Scheirich [1969] Project Director [French]

Co-op Group Travel 2 Holdings Limited
Incorporated: 20 October 2010 *Employees:* 1
Net Worth: £1,609,000 *Total Assets:* £31,587,000
Registered Office: Westpoint, Peterborough Business Park, Lynch Wood, Peterborough, Cambs, PE2 6FZ
Activities: Other business support service activities n.e.c.
Parent: TCCT Holdings UK Limited
Officers: Shirley Bradley, Secretary; Alan Charles Donald [1963] Director

Co-operative Energy Limited
Incorporated: 18 August 2009
Net Worth Deficit: £4,065,000 *Total Assets:* £120,199,000
Registered Office: Co-operative House, Warwick Technology Park, Gallows Hill, Warwick, CV34 6DA
Activities: Data processing, hosting and related activities
Parent: The Midcounties Co-operative Limited
Officers: Edward Geoffrey Parker, Secretary; Stephen Raymond Allsopp [1952] Director/Personnel Section Manager; Olivia Birch [1967] Director; Leon Clive Booker [1944] Director/Retired; Martin Cook [1962] Director/Senior Manager; Judith Feeney [1946] Director; Eleanor Freeman [1989] Director; Patrick Hugo Gray [1947] Director/Economist; Gary William Hayes [1955] Director/Business Executive; Irene Louise Kirkman [1953] Director/Retired; Matthew David Nigel Lane [1985] Director; Donald Morrison [1947] Director/Probation Officer; Jean Elizabeth Nunn-Price [1943] Director/Semi-Retired/Trainee Solicitor; Kathryn Elizabeth Petersen [1962] Director/Chartered Accountant; Heather Adele Richardson [1976] Director/Senior Manager; Helen Rita Wiseman [1965] Director/HR Consultant; Vivian Stanley Woodell [1962] Director/Chief Executive The Phone Co-op

The Coaching Inn Group Ltd
Incorporated: 22 May 1996 *Employees:* 616
Previous: Bulldog Hotel Group Ltd.
Net Worth: £10,108,641 *Total Assets:* £43,564,464
Registered Office: Friars House, Quaker Lane, Boston, Lincs, PE21 6BZ
Activities: Other amusement and recreation activities n.e.c.
Shareholder: Business Growth Fund PLC
Officers: Mark William Porcher, Secretary; Kevin Charity [1965] Director; Lilian Margaret Charity [1958] Director; Mark Stephen Freer [1964] Director; Andrew Graham Guy [1948] Director/Chief Executive; Mark William Porcher [1964] Director; Edward Walsh [1986] Director

The Coal Industry Social Welfare Organisation 2014
Incorporated: 2 July 2014 *Employees:* 89
Net Worth: £32,879,476 *Total Assets:* £34,129,588
Registered Office: The Old Rectory, Rectory Drive, Whiston, Rotherham, S Yorks, S60 4JG
Activities: Other business support service activities n.e.c.
Officers: Nicola Marie Didlock, Secretary; Colin David Ambler [1947] Director; Patrick Matthew Carragher [1957] Director/Trade Union Official; Robert Gerard Cooper [1968] Director; Terence Leslie Fox [1960] Director; Jonathan Leslie Hatterlsey [1949] Director; John George Humble [1948] Director; Christine Kaye [1953] Director; Carole Langrick [1962] Director/NHS Manager; Gary Smith [1957] Director; Wayne Thomas [1960] Director; Jeffrey Wood [1961] Director

Coal Products Limited
Incorporated: 15 March 1973 *Employees:* 146
Net Worth: £23,100,000 *Total Assets:* £74,200,000
Registered Office: Westthorpe Fields Road, Killamarsh, Sheffield, S21 1TZ
Activities: Manufacture of other non-metallic mineral products n.e.c.
Shareholders: Julian Mash; SG Hambros Limited; CPL Industries Limited
Officers: Andrew Bishop [1960] Director; Stephen John Chisholm [1959] Director; Timothy William Minett [1960] Managing Director; Peter Scott [1953] Director; Jason David Sutton [1982] Director/Accountant

The Coalfields Regeneration Trust
Incorporated: 19 March 1999 *Employees:* 32
Net Worth: £39,087,000 *Total Assets:* £48,544,000
Registered Office: 1 Waterside Park, Valley Way, Wombwell, Barnsley, S Yorks, S73 0BB
Activities: Other service activities n.e.c.
Officers: Louise Dyson, Secretary; Michael Clapham [1943] Director; Dawn Davies [1963] Director/Chief Executive; Trudie McGuiness [1976] Director/Consultant; Peter McNestry [1942] Director/Retired; Terence Patrick O'Neill [1947] Director/Councillor; Nicky Stubbs [1991] Director/Researcher; Wayne Thomas [1960] Director/Trade Union Official; Sylvia Wileman [1941] Director/Retired; Nicholas Garson Wilson [1950] Director/Trade Union Official; Robert Young [1943] Director/Councillor

Coast Holdco 1 Limited
Incorporated: 21 September 2015 *Employees:* 1,034
Net Worth: £10,100,000 *Total Assets:* £30,400,000
Registered Office: The Triangle, Stanton Harcourt Industrial Estate, Stanton Harcourt, Witney, Oxon, OX29 5UT
Activities: Activities of head offices
Parent: Aurora Fashions Finance Limited
Officers: John Philip Madden III [1973] Director [American]; Johann Petur Reyndal [1962] Director [Icelander]

Coast Holdco 2 Limited
Incorporated: 21 September 2015
Net Worth: £37,000,000 *Total Assets:* £37,000,000
Registered Office: The Triangle, Stanton Harcourt Industrial Estate, Stanton Harcourt, Witney, Oxon, OX29 5UT
Activities: Activities of head offices
Parent: Coast Holdco 1 Limited
Officers: John Philip Madden III [1973] Director [American]; Johann Petur Reyndal [1962] Director [Icelander]

Coastfields Leisure Limited
Incorporated: 20 December 1972 *Employees:* 179
Net Worth: £12,102,961 *Total Assets:* £41,152,764
Registered Office: 4 Cyrus Way, Cygnet Park, Hampton, Peterborough, Cambs, PE7 8HP
Activities: Recreational vehicle parks, trailer parks and camping grounds
Shareholders: Lynda Joyce Silvester; Lloyd Bennet Silvester
Officers: Lloyd Bennet Silvester, Secretary; Lloyd Bennet Silvester [1972] Sales Director; Lynda Joyce Silvester [1947] Director/Caravan Site Proprietor

H.W. Coates (Holdings) Limited
Incorporated: 17 December 2009 *Employees:* 316
Net Worth: £101,594,592 *Total Assets:* £117,945,904
Registered Office: Ladywood House, Ladywood Works, Leicester Road, Lutterworth, Leics, LE17 4HD
Activities: Dormant company
Shareholders: Michael Henry Arnold Coates; Gerald George Coates
Officers: Rachael Morris, Secretary; George William Ball [1950] Director; Generald George Coates [1950] Director; Matthew Coates [1982] Director; Michael Henry Arnold Coates [1945] Director; Thomas Henry Coates [1970] Managing Director; Rachael Louise Morris [1976] Finance Director; Richard Perry [1972] Property Director

H.W. Coates Limited
Incorporated: 25 June 1981 *Employees:* 270
Net Worth: £101,956,968 *Total Assets:* £117,224,128
Registered Office: Ladywood House, Ladywood Works, Leicester Road, Lutterworth, Leics, LE17 4HD
Activities: Freight transport by road
Shareholders: Michael Henry Arnold Coates; Gerald George Coates
Officers: Rachael Morris, Secretary; George William Ball [1950] Director; Generald George Coates [1950] Director; Matthew Coates [1982] Director; Michael Henry Arnold Coates [1945] Director; Thomas Henry Coates [1970] Managing Director; Rachael Louise Morris [1976] Finance Director; Richard Perry [1972] Property Director

Coba Automotive (UK) Limited
Incorporated: 12 August 1966 *Employees:* 204
Previous: Coba Plastics Limited
Net Worth: £9,939,917 *Total Assets:* £13,722,188
Registered Office: Marlborough Drive, Fleckney, Leicester, LE8 8UR
Activities: Manufacture of plastic plates, sheets, tubes and profiles
Officers: Jonathan Clifford Atkinson [1972] Managing Director; Mark Anthony Cooke [1968] Director; Robert Nigel Peat [1969] Finance Director

Coba International Limited
Incorporated: 10 February 2004 *Employees:* 867
Net Worth: £39,706,000 *Total Assets:* £54,055,000
Registered Office: Marlborough Drive, Fleckney, Leicester, LE8 8UR
Activities: Activities of head offices
Major Shareholder: Mark Anthony Cooke
Officers: Jonathan Clifford Atkinson [1972] Managing Director; Joyce Cooke [1944] Director; Mark Anthony Cooke [1968] Director; Richard John Cooke [1969] Director; Robert Nigel Peat [1969] Finance Director

Cobra Beer Partnership Limited
Incorporated: 28 January 2009 *Employees:* 5
Net Worth: £12,104,656 *Total Assets:* £14,096,065
Registered Office: 137 High Street, Burton on Trent, Staffs, DE14 1JZ
Activities: Manufacture of beer
Shareholders: Karan Faridoon Bilimoria; Molson Coors Brewing Company (UK) Limited
Officers: Gemma Louise Wisniewski, Secretary; Lord Karan Faridoon Bilimoria [1961] Director; Simon John Cox [1967] Director; Dynshaw Fareed Italia [1970] Director; James Christian Shearer [1980] Marketing Director; Philip Mark Whitehead [1977] Director

Codemasters Group Holdings PLC
Incorporated: 21 February 2007 *Employees:* 465
Previous: Codemasters Group Holdings Limited
Net Worth Deficit: £90,138,000 *Total Assets:* £73,088,000
Registered Office: Codemasters Campus, Stoneythorpe, Southam, Warwicks, CV47 2DL
Activities: Other software publishing
Major Shareholder: Anil Dhirajlal Ambani
Officers: Gerhard Florin [1959] Director [German]; Ian Pierre Gomes [1957] Director; Frank Theodore Sagnier [1962] Director/Chief Executive Officer [French]; Shibasish Sarkar [1972] Director/Chief Financial Officer, Reliance Entertainment [Indian]; Rashid Ismail Varachia [1971] Director

Codemasters Group Limited
Incorporated: 14 February 1996
Net Worth: £424,000 *Total Assets:* £54,784,000
Registered Office: Codemasters Campus, Stoneythorpe, Southam, Warwicks, CV47 2DL
Activities: Other service activities n.e.c.
Parent: Codemasters Holdings Limited
Officers: Rashid Varachia, Secretary; Frank Theodore Sagnier [1962] Director/Chief Executive Officer [French]; Rashid Ismail Varachia [1971] Director

Codemasters Holdings Limited
Incorporated: 21 February 2007
Net Worth: £6,458,000 *Total Assets:* £60,871,000
Registered Office: Codemasters Campus, Stoneythorpe, Southam, Warwicks, CV47 2DL
Activities: Activities of other holding companies n.e.c.
Parent: Codemasters Group Holdings Limited
Officers: Rashid Varachia, Secretary; Frank Theodore Sagnier [1962] Director/Chief Executive Officer [French]; Rashid Ismail Varachia [1971] Director

Codemasters Software Company Limited (The)
Incorporated: 6 August 1986 *Employees:* 456
Net Worth Deficit: £63,456,000 *Total Assets:* £60,339,000
Registered Office: Codemasters Campus, Stoneythorpe, Southam, Warwicks, CV47 2DL
Activities: Information technology consultancy activities
Parent: Codemasters Group Holdings PLC
Officers: Rashid Varachia, Secretary; Frank Theodore Sagnier [1962] Director/Chief Executive Officer [French]; Shibasish Sarkar [1972] Director/CFO Reliance Entertainment [Indian]; Rashid Ismail Varachia [1971] Director/Chief Finance Officer

Coed du Hall Limited
Incorporated: 19 November 1993 *Employees:* 137
Net Worth: £9,145,091 *Total Assets:* £20,970,992
Registered Office: 6-8 Old Hall Road, Gatley, Cheadle, Cheshire, SK8 4BE
Activities: Residential care activities for learning difficulties, mental health and substance abuse
Parent: Shogun Limited
Officers: Michael Denis Hartey [1956] Director

Cogne U.K. Limited
Incorporated: 31 December 1996 *Employees:* 44
Net Worth: £2,894,081 *Total Assets:* £10,268,090
Registered Office: Uniformity Steel Works, Don Road, Newhall, Sheffield, S9 2UD
Activities: Wholesale of metals and metal ores
Parent: Cogne Acciai Speciali S.P.A.
Officers: David Michael Dalton, Secretary; Stephen Darren Hall [1962] Director; Eugenio Marzorati [1962] Director [Italian]; Monica Pirovano [1963] Director [Italian]

Cognita BondCo Parent Limited
Incorporated: 3 July 2015 *Employees:* 7,098
Net Worth Deficit: £5,505,000 *Total Assets:* £988,616,000
Registered Office: EMW, Seebeck House, 1 Seebeck Place, Knowlhill, Milton Keynes, Bucks, MK5 8FR
Activities: Activities of other holding companies n.e.c.
Parent: Cognita Midco Limited
Officers: Christopher Trevor Peter Jansen [1970] Director; Jayne Pinchbeck [1980] Legal Director; Michael Uzielli [1970] Finance Director

Cognita Financing PLC
Incorporated: 3 July 2015
Net Worth: £1,174,000 *Total Assets:* £433,271,008
Registered Office: EMW, Seebeck House, 1 Seebeck Place, Knowlhill, Milton Keynes, Bucks, MK5 8FR
Activities: Activities of other holding companies n.e.c.
Parent: Cognita BondCo Parent Limited
Officers: Christopher Trevor Peter Jansen [1970] Director; Jayne Pinchbeck [1980] Legal Director; Michael Uzielli [1970] Finance Director

Cognita Funding 1 Limited
Incorporated: 21 January 2009
Net Worth: £174,791,008 *Total Assets:* £174,806,000
Registered Office: Seebeck House, 1 Seebeck Place, Knowlhill, Milton Keynes, Bucks, MK5 8FR
Activities: Activities of other holding companies n.e.c.
Parent: Cognita Holdings Limited
Officers: Christopher Trevor Peter Jansen [1970] Director; Jayne Pinchbeck [1980] Legal Director; Michael Uzielli [1970] Finance Director

Cognita Holdings Limited
Incorporated: 9 November 2004 *Employees:* 6,475
Net Worth: £39,434,000 *Total Assets:* £907,203,008
Registered Office: Seebeck House, One Seebeck Place, Knowlhill, Milton Keynes, Bucks, MK5 8FR
Activities: Activities of other holding companies n.e.c.
Parent: Cognita BondCo Parent Limited
Officers: Christopher Trevor Peter Jansen [1970] Director; Jayne Pinchbeck [1980] Legal Director; Michael Uzielli [1970] Finance Director

Cognita International Holdings Limited
Incorporated: 10 May 2007
Net Worth: £35,597,000 *Total Assets:* £66,981,000
Registered Office: Seebeck House, One Seebeck Place, Knowlhill, Milton Keynes, Bucks, MK5 8FR
Activities: Activities of other holding companies n.e.c.
Parent: Cognita Limited
Officers: Christopher Trevor Peter Jansen [1970] Director; Jayne Pinchbeck [1980] Legal Director; Michael Uzielli [1970] Finance Director

Cognita Limited
Incorporated: 9 November 2004 *Employees:* 7
Net Worth Deficit: £88,138,000 *Total Assets:* £130,597,000
Registered Office: Seebeck House, One Seebeck Place, Knowlhill, Milton Keynes, Bucks, MK5 8FR
Activities: Activities of other holding companies n.e.c.
Parent: Cognita UK Holdings Limited
Officers: Christopher Trevor Peter Jansen [1970] Director; Jayne Pinchbeck [1980] Legal Director; Michael Uzielli [1970] Finance Director

Cognita Midco Limited
Incorporated: 3 July 2015
Net Worth: £507,576,992 *Total Assets:* £507,576,992
Registered Office: EMW, Seebeck House, 1 Seebeck Place, Knowlhill, Milton Keynes, Bucks, MK5 8FR
Activities: Activities of other holding companies n.e.c.
Officers: Christopher Trevor Peter Jansen [1970] Director; Jayne Pinchbeck [1980] Legal Director; Michael Uzielli [1970] Finance Director

Cognita Schools Limited
Incorporated: 4 November 1988 *Employees:* 2,424
Net Worth: £67,497,000 *Total Assets:* £152,970,000
Registered Office: Seebeck House, One Seebeck Place, Knowlhill, Milton Keynes, Bucks, MK5 8FR
Activities: Pre-primary education
Parent: Cognita Limited
Officers: Christopher Trevor Peter Jansen [1970] Director; Jayne Pinchbeck [1980] Legal Director; Stuart Stacy Rolland [1964] Director; Michael Uzielli [1970] Finance Director

Cognita UK Brazil Holdings Limited
Incorporated: 12 June 2012
Net Worth: £38,215,000 *Total Assets:* £38,215,000
Registered Office: Seebeck House, 1 Seebeck Place, Knowlhill, Milton Keynes, Bucks, MK5 8FR
Activities: Activities of other holding companies n.e.c.
Parent: Cognita Funding 1 Limited
Officers: Christopher Trevor Peter Jansen [1970] Director; Jayne Pinchbeck [1980] Legal Director; Michael Uzielli [1970] Finance Director

Cognita UK Holdings Limited
Incorporated: 23 September 2008 *Employees:* 6,475
Net Worth: £39,434,000 *Total Assets:* £907,203,008
Registered Office: Seebeck House, One Seebeck Place, Knowlhill, Milton Keynes, Bucks, MK5 8FR
Activities: Activities of other holding companies n.e.c.
Parent: Cognita Holdings Limited
Officers: Christopher Trevor Peter Jansen [1970] Director; Jayne Pinchbeck [1980] Legal Director; Michael Uzielli [1970] Finance Director

Cokethorpe Educational Trust Limited
Incorporated: 11 July 1963 *Employees:* 208
Net Worth: £5,903,987 *Total Assets:* £10,887,621
Registered Office: Cokethorpe School, Witney, Oxon, OX29 7PU
Activities: Primary education
Officers: Harriet Stapleton, Secretary; Alan James Bark [1964] Director/Banker; John Peter Bennett [1955] Director; Mark Robert Booty [1957] Director/Councillor; Bishop Colin William Fletcher [1950] Director/Bishop; Rita Gunn [1948] Director/Governor; Wendy Elizabeth Hart [1967] Director/Corporate Finance and Advisory Partner; Robert Francois Jonckheer [1948] Director/Consultant Solicitor; Dr Wai Wing Lau [1951] Director/Head Engineer Physics at Oxford University; Generaldine McAndrew [1951] Director/Chief Executive; Paul Arthur Tolley [1959] Director

Colbert Wall Holdings Limited
Incorporated: 20 March 2015
Net Worth: £9,597,144 *Total Assets:* £9,756,182
Registered Office: Downs Hollow, Burford Road, Chipping Norton, Oxon, OX7 5XB
Activities: Activities of head offices
Major Shareholder: Eileen Powell
Officers: Eileen Powell [1969] Director

Coleman Investments Limited
Incorporated: 12 February 1914 *Employees:* 2
Net Worth: £6,592,013 *Total Assets:* £9,986,199
Registered Office: Wells House, Stephensons Way, Wyvern Business Park, Chaddesden, Derby, DE21 6LY
Activities: Other letting and operating of own or leased real estate
Parent: Rother House Finance Limited
Officers: Susan Jane Arnott, Secretary; Susan Jane Arnott [1953] Director; Sir Anthony Nigel Russell Rudd [1946] Director/Chartered Accountant; Timothy Nigel Rudd [1971] Director/Businessman

The Collaborative Academies Trust
Incorporated: 3 August 2012 *Employees:* 532
Net Worth: £11,802,000 *Total Assets:* £18,988,000
Registered Office: c/o Kingsthorpe College, Boughton Green Road, Northampton, NN2 7HR
Activities: Other education n.e.c.
Officers: Andrew Roderick Campbell [1966] Director/Chief Executive; Philip Francis Harris-Bridge [1954] Non-Executive Director & Deputy Chair; Christoper John Hilliard [1957] Director/Education Consultant; Carly Waterman [1977] Director/Education Consultant

College of Policing Limited
Incorporated: 1 October 2012
Net Worth: £21,278,000 *Total Assets:* £46,522,000
Registered Office: Rugby Building, Leamington Road, Ryton on Dunsmore, Coventry, Warwicks, CV8 3EN
Activities: Activities of professional membership organisations
Officers: David Anthony Bamber [1968] Director/Police Federation England and Wales Representative; Millie Banerjee [1946] Director/Chair of Working Links [Indian]; Michael Bernard Cunningham [1961] Director/Chief Executive Officer; Christine Anne Elliott [1954] Director/Chief Executive; Ian John Hopkins [1967] Director/Chief Constable; Clare Minchington [1966] Director/Strategic Consultant; Stephen Graham Mold [1968] Director/Police and Crime Commissioner; Jacqueline Anne Smith [1962] Director; Gavin Douglas Thomas [1963] Director/Policeman; Robin Geoffrey Wilkinson [1968] HR Director, Metropolitan Police Service; Ian Martin Wylie [1955] Director

Collingwood Lighting Limited
Incorporated: 13 March 1967 *Employees:* 116
Net Worth: £9,633,000 *Total Assets:* £15,099,000
Registered Office: Brooklands House, Sywell Aerodrome, Wellingborough Road, Sywell, Northampton, NN6 0BT
Activities: Manufacture of electric lighting equipment
Parent: Collingwood Group Limited
Officers: Phillip Dennison Barker, Secretary; Philip Dennison Barker [1957] Director; Stephen Douglas Grao [1960] Director

Collins Earthworks Limited
Incorporated: 4 October 2000 *Employees:* 254
Net Worth: £16,873,920 *Total Assets:* £39,295,376
Registered Office: Unit 2b Park Lane, Kirkby in Ashfield, Notts, NG17 9LE
Activities: Demolition
Major Shareholder: David Greville Collins
Officers: Nicola Jane Collins, Secretary; Jack Gareth Cave [1992] Director; David Greville Collins [1968] Director; Padraig Joseph Gaffney [1971] Director/Engineer; Jill Marie Goodwin-Woodcock [1980] Director; Adam Simon Mark Procter [1979] Director

Coloplast Limited
Incorporated: 5 February 1973 *Employees:* 474
Net Worth: £28,085,000 *Total Assets:* £60,367,000
Registered Office: Nene Hall, Lynchwood Park, Peterborough Business Park, Peterborough, Cambs, PE2 6FX
Activities: Non-specialised wholesale trade
Parent: Coloplast A/S
Officers: Myles Davies [1972] Business Support Director; Henrik Deneke [1967] Director/Vice President [Danish]; Generaldine Anne Harkins [1961] Business Unit Director; Ashley Alexander Julian Knight [1969] Marketing Director; Alain Michel Herve Morvan [1962] Director [French]; Annemarie Van Neck [1975] Director/General Manager [Dutch]; Peter Volkers [1959] Director [Danish]

Colortronic (U.K.) Limited
Incorporated: 22 February 1974 *Employees:* 30
Net Worth: £6,990,754 *Total Assets:* £11,348,179
Registered Office: Matilda House, Carrwood Road, Chesterfield Trading Estate, Chesterfield, Derbys, S41 9QB
Activities: Agents involved in the sale of machinery, industrial equipment, ships and aircraft
Major Shareholder: Erwin Karl Miller
Officers: Karl Robert Miller, Secretary; Erwin Karl Miller [1944] Director/Engineer; Karl Robert Miller [1966] Director/Engineer

Colston Investment Properties Limited Liability Partnership
Incorporated: 18 September 2006
Net Worth: £53,854,980 *Total Assets:* £53,929,692
Registered Office: The Poplars, Lenton Lane, Nottingham, NG7 2PW
Officers: John Morley [1951] Member; Jason Denyer [1959] LLP Member; Pauline Hellenes Denyer Smith [1940] LLP Member; Sir Paul Brierley Smith [1946] LLP Member

Colston Property Partners Limited
Incorporated: 2 August 2005
Net Worth: £57,661,872 *Total Assets:* £71,205,368
Registered Office: The Poplars, Lenton Lane, Nottingham, NG7 2PW
Activities: Other letting and operating of own or leased real estate
Shareholder: Paul Brierley Smith
Officers: Ashley James Snowden Long, Secretary; John Morley [1951] Director; Sir Paul Brierley Smith [1946] Director; Pauline Hellenese Denyer Smith [1940] Director

Comau U.K. Limited
Incorporated: 8 September 1988 *Employees:* 107
Net Worth: £5,231,000 *Total Assets:* £28,567,000
Registered Office: Unit A2, Swift Park, Old Leicester Road, Rugby, Warwicks, CV21 1DZ
Activities: Other engineering activities
Parent: Fiat Chrysler Automobiles NV
Officers: John Irving, Secretary; Marica Cecilia Bernardi [1960] Director/Head of Banking Relations [Italian]; John Coombes [1969] Director; Stefano Curci [1981] Director/Manager [Italian]; Andrew Lloyd [1967] Director; Raffaella Papa [1969] Director/Chief Financial Officer [Italian]

Combisafe International Limited
Incorporated: 30 April 1993 *Employees:* 22
Net Worth: £5,652,000 *Total Assets:* £27,721,000
Registered Office: Safety Centre, Cheaney Drive, Grange Park, Northampton, NN4 5FB
Activities: Other specialised construction activities n.e.c.
Parent: Honeywell Safety Products International Ltd.
Officers: John Daniel Romano Jr [1972] Director [American]; Jonathan David Stephens [1969] Director; Daniel Vernuccio [1955] Director [Italian]

Comet REFICO Limited
Incorporated: 9 November 2006
Net Worth: £61,100,000 *Total Assets:* £61,100,000
Registered Office: One Edison Rise, New Ollerton, Newark, Notts, NG22 9DP
Activities: Activities of head offices
Parent: CP Comet Bidco Limimted
Officers: Rajbinder Singh-Dehal, Secretary; Natalie Johanna Adomait [1989] Director [Canadian]; Martin Peter Dalby [1961] Director; Kevin O'Donnell McCrain [1979] Director [American]; Colin Grant McKinlay [1969] Director; Zachary Bryan Vaughan [1977] Director [Canadian]

Comex 2000 (UK) Limited
Incorporated: 3 March 1999 *Employees:* 650
Net Worth: £21,227,344 *Total Assets:* £29,495,312
Registered Office: 3 Stadium Business Court, Millennium Way, Pride Park, Derby, DE24 8HP
Activities: Installation of industrial machinery and equipment
Shareholders: Neil Kenneth Smith; Neil Kenneth Smith
Officers: Mark Philby, Secretary; Mark Philby [1969] Managing Director; Neil Kenneth Smith [1968] Director/Chief Executive Officer

Commatone Limited
Incorporated: 30 May 1984
Net Worth: £1,504,935,936 *Total Assets:* £1,504,935,936
Registered Office: Saint-Gobain House, Binley Business Park, Coventry, Warwicks, CV3 2TT
Activities: Activities of head offices
Parent: BPB Investments Overseas Limited
Officers: Alun Roy Oxenham, Secretary; Nicholas James Cammack [1972] Director; Bertrand Pierre Antoine Clavel [1966] Director/CFO Gypsum Activity [French]; Alun Roy Oxenham [1956] Director/Company Secretary

Commercial Legal Limited
Incorporated: 14 March 2003 *Employees:* 32
Net Worth: £4,465,521 *Total Assets:* £17,823,404
Registered Office: Unit 1 Carolina Court, Doncaster, S Yorks, DN4 5RA
Activities: Other business support service activities n.e.c.
Major Shareholder: John Lawrence Radford
Officers: Alexandra Maria Sheriff, Secretary; Joshua Charles Barnsdale [1982] Director; Peter Graham Long [1986] Director; John Matthew Parker [1976] Claims Director; John Lawrence Radford [1965] Director/Chief Executive Officer

Commify Limited
Incorporated: 1 September 2016 *Employees:* 10
Net Worth Deficit: £62,101 *Total Assets:* £73,771,536
Registered Office: 20 Wollaton Street, Nottingham, NG1 5FW
Activities: Activities of other holding companies n.e.c.
Shareholders: Falcon Equityco 2 Limited; Esendex Group Topco Limited
Officers: Thomas Greer Boucher [1970] Director; Matthew Alexander Burnett [1976] Director/Chief Technology Officer; Paul Eric Jonathon Burton [1981] Director; Nicholas David Lloyd Jordan [1977] Director/Investment Manager; Geoffrey Adrian Love [1971] Director; Hayden David Robinson [1970] Director; David Andrew Smyth [1968] Director/Chief Commercial Officer

Commify Topco Limited
Incorporated: 5 August 2016 *Employees:* 217
Net Worth Deficit: £17,415,376 *Total Assets:* £124,462,520
Registered Office: 20 Wollaton Street, Nottingham, NG1 5FW
Activities: Activities of other holding companies n.e.c.
Parent: HgCapital Mercury Nominees Limited
Officers: James Francis Berry [1974] Director; Thomas Greer Boucher [1970] Director; Paul Eric Jonathon Burton [1981] Director; Carla Cico [1961] Director [Italian]; Nicholas David Lloyd Jordan [1977] Director/Investment Manager; Geoffrey Adrian Love [1971] Director; Mark Paraskeva [1961] Director; Hayden David Robinson [1970] Director

Commify UK Limited
Incorporated: 15 May 2001 *Employees:* 125
Previous: Esendex Limited
Net Worth: £11,909,029 *Total Assets:* £30,009,248
Registered Office: 20 Wollaton Street, Nottingham, NG1 5FW
Activities: Other telecommunications activities
Parent: Esendex Holdings Limited
Officers: Matthew Alexander Burnett [1976] Director/Chief Technology Officer; Paul Eric Jonathon Burton [1981] Director; Geoffrey Adrian Love [1971] Director/Chief Commercial Officer; Hayden David Robinson [1970] Director; David Andrew Smyth [1968] Director/Chief Commercial Officer

Community 1st Oldham (Chadderton) Limited
Incorporated: 29 March 2008
Net Worth: £6,836,762 *Total Assets:* £20,278,692
Registered Office: Building 1000, Kings Reach, Yew Street, Stockport, Cheshire, SK4 2HG
Activities: Other letting and operating of own or leased real estate
Parent: Community 1st Oldham Limited
Officers: Andrew Dwan [1965] Director; Michael Dwan [1959] Director; Edward Moores [1952] Director/Councillor

Community 1st Oldham (Werneth and Shaw) Limited
Incorporated: 28 October 2009
Net Worth: £12,492,350 *Total Assets:* £27,751,590
Registered Office: Building 1000, Kings Reach, Yew Street, Stockport, Cheshire, SK4 2HG
Activities: Other letting and operating of own or leased real estate
Parent: Community 1st Oldham Tranche 2 Limited
Officers: John Connolly [1961] Director; Andrew Dwan [1965] Director; Michael Dwan [1959] Director; Anthony Kane [1953] Director; Neil Geoffrey Ward [1959] Investment Director - CHP North

Community 1st Oldham Limited
Incorporated: 14 May 2004
Net Worth: £74,033,808 *Total Assets:* £141,373,328
Registered Office: Building 1000, Kings Reach, Yew Street, Stockport, Cheshire, SK4 2HG
Activities: Other letting and operating of own or leased real estate
Shareholders: Equity Solutions Lift Investments Oldham Limited; Community Health Partnerships Limited
Officers: John Connolly [1961] Director; Andrew Dwan [1965] Director; Michael Dwan [1959] Director; Anthony Kane [1953] Director; Neil Geoffrey Ward [1959] Investment Director - CHP North

Community 1st Oldham Tranche 2 Limited
Incorporated: 8 December 2009 *Employees:* 5
Net Worth: £14,942,849 *Total Assets:* £14,942,849
Registered Office: Building 1000, Kings Reach, Yew Street, Stockport, Cheshire, SK4 2HG
Activities: Other letting and operating of own or leased real estate
Parent: Community 1st Oldham Limited
Officers: John Connolly [1961] Director; Andrew Dwan [1965] Director; Michael Dwan [1959] Director; Anthony Kane [1953] Director; Neil Geoffrey Ward [1959] Investment Director - CHP North

Community 1st Sheffield (Holdco) Limited
Incorporated: 25 July 2011 *Employees:* 5
Net Worth: £19,562,634 *Total Assets:* £19,562,634
Registered Office: Building 1000, Kings Reach, Yew Street, Stockport, Cheshire, SK4 2HG
Activities: Other business support service activities n.e.c.
Parent: Community 1st Sheffield Limited
Officers: John Connolly [1961] Director; Andrew Dwan [1965] Director; Michael Dwan [1959] Director; Neil Geoffrey Ward [1959] Investment Director - CHP North

Community 1st Sheffield (Tranche 2) Limited
Incorporated: 26 July 2011
Net Worth: £16,341,199 *Total Assets:* £43,925,960
Registered Office: Building 1000, Kings Reach, Yew Street, Stockport, Cheshire, SK4 2HG
Activities: Other letting and operating of own or leased real estate
Parent: Community 1st Sheffield (Holdco) Limited
Officers: John Connolly [1961] Director; Andrew Dwan [1965] Director; Michael Dwan [1959] Director; Neil Geoffrey Ward [1959] Investment Director - CHP North

Community 1st Sheffield Limited
Incorporated: 14 May 2004
Net Worth: £33,205,260 *Total Assets:* £47,838,428
Registered Office: Building 1000, Kings Reach, Yew Street, Stockport, Cheshire, SK4 2HG
Activities: Other letting and operating of own or leased real estate
Shareholders: Equity Solutions Lift Investments Sheffield Limited; Community Health Partnerships Limited
Officers: John Connolly [1961] Director; Andrew Dwan [1965] Director; Michael Dwan [1959] Director; Neil Geoffrey Ward [1959] Investment Director - CHP North

Community 1st Stockport Limited
Incorporated: 16 February 2007
Net Worth: £9,970,319 *Total Assets:* £23,755,348
Registered Office: Building 1000, Kings Reach, Yew Street, Stockport, Cheshire, SK4 2HG
Activities: Other letting and operating of own or leased real estate
Parent: WGIF (Jersey) Trustee I Limited and WGIF (Jersey) Trustee II Limited
Officers: Christopher Guy Rogan Pratt [1961] Director/Chartered Surveyor; Patrick John Smith [1965] Director/Chartered Accountant

Community Schools Alliance Trust
Incorporated: 5 December 2012 *Employees:* 281
Previous: Cheney School Academy Trust
Net Worth: £28,222,216 *Total Assets:* £32,500,032
Registered Office: Cheney School, Cheney Lane, Headington, Oxford, OX3 7QH
Activities: Primary education
Officers: Gemma Jennings, Secretary; Ian Christopher Busby [1951] Director/Business Consultant; Dr Ann Childs [1957] Director/Associate Professor of Science Education; Dr. Bridget Durning [1965] Director/University Academic; Jolie Dorothea Kirby [1969] Director/Headteacher; Elizabeth Nuttall [1967] HR Director; Pat O'Shea [1948] Director/Retired; Elizabeth Tyler [1971] Director of Learning Services for UK Schools

Companion Care (Services) Limited
Incorporated: 15 January 2001 *Employees:* 359
Net Worth: £60,402,000 *Total Assets:* £97,883,000
Registered Office: Epsom Avenue, Stanley Green Trading Estate, Handforth, Cheshire, SK9 3RN
Activities: Other business support service activities n.e.c.
Parent: Pets at Home Vet Group Limited
Officers: Louise Ann Stonier, Secretary; Harvey Bertenshaw Ainley [1966] Director/Chief Financial Officer; Jane Balmain [1958] Director; Michael James Iddon [1965] Director; Louise Ann Stonier [1973] Director/Company Secretary

The Company of Master Jewellers Limited
Incorporated: 27 March 1980 *Employees:* 45
Net Worth: £2,275,340 *Total Assets:* £19,260,942
Registered Office: Somers House, 25 Somers Road, Rugby, Warwicks, CV22 7DG
Activities: Retail sale of antiques including antique books in stores
Officers: Russell Lewis, Secretary; Philip John Ainsworth [1966] Director/Retail Jeweller; Michael Aldridge [1959] Director; Jason Paul Allum [1970] Managing Director; Barrie Stephen Dobson [1954] Director; Christopher John Wesley Henn [1961] Director; Julie Elizabeth Langford [1963] Director/Retail Jeweller; Michele Karola Whittam [1964] Director

Company Shop Limited
Incorporated: 1 July 1985 *Employees:* 618
Net Worth: £11,424,000 *Total Assets:* £19,427,000
Registered Office: Company Shop Ltd, Wentworth Way, Tankersley, Barnsley, S Yorks, S75 3DH
Activities: Retail sale in non-specialised stores with food, beverages or tobacco predominating
Major Shareholder: John Michael Marren
Officers: John Kitson [1955] Finance Director; Jane Louise Marren [1966] Managing Director; John Michael Marren [1952] Director; Nathan John Mills [1972] Director; David John Salkeld [1956] Director

Compare The Market Limited
Incorporated: 23 February 2017
Net Worth: £104,500,000 *Total Assets:* £153,200,000
Registered Office: Pegasus House, Southgate Park, Bakewell Road, Orton Southgate, Peterborough, Cambs, PE2 6YS
Activities: Other business support service activities n.e.c.
Parent: BGL Group Limited
Officers: Julian Charles Brown, Secretary; Mark Andrew Allan [1981] Director/Chief Financial Officer; Jonathon Iain Carlton Brown [1971] Director/Chief Executive; Matthew Oliver Donaldson [1973] Director/Chief Executive Officer; Lord Jitesh Kishorekumar Gadhia [1970] Director/Banker; David John Osborne [1966] Global Director; Dominic James Platt [1969] Director/Chief Financial Officer

Compass Acquisitions Limited
Incorporated: 20 March 2012
Net Worth Deficit: £15,226,637 *Total Assets:* £20,070,004
Registered Office: Mountfields House, off Squirrel Way, Epinal Way, Loughborough, Leics, LE11 3GE
Activities: Activities of head offices
Parent: Compass Holdco Limited
Officers: Bernadine Louise Gibson [1971] Director; Jamie Alexander Wright [1983] Finance Director

Compass Community Ltd
Incorporated: 3 April 2012 *Employees:* 324
Net Worth: £9,483,555 *Total Assets:* £44,944,664
Registered Office: Mountfields House, off Squirrel Way, Epinal Way, Loughborough, Leics, LE11 3GE
Activities: Activities of head offices
Parent: Compass Acquisitions Limited
Officers: Bernadine Louise Gibson [1971] Director; Jamie Alexander Wright [1983] Finance Director

Compass Holdco Limited
Incorporated: 20 March 2012
Net Worth: £2,160,971 *Total Assets:* £63,214,060
Registered Office: Mountfields House, off Squirrel Way, Epinal Way, Loughborough, Leics, LE11 3GE
Activities: Activities of head offices
Parent: Advent Bidco Limited
Officers: Bernadine Louise Gibson [1971] Director; Jamie Alexander Wright [1983] Finance Director

Complete Medical Group Worldwide Limited
Incorporated: 27 April 1992
Net Worth: £601,000 *Total Assets:* £15,427,000
Registered Office: CMC House, 19 King Edward Street, Macclesfield, Cheshire, SK10 1AQ
Activities: Activities of head offices
Parent: IPG Holdings (UK) Limited
Officers: Louise Bean, Secretary; Charles Edward George Buckwell [1964] Director; Julie Ann James [1975] Director/Accountant; Phillip Sutcliffe [1968] Director/Chief Financial Officer

Compu B Ltd
Incorporated: 30 September 2009 *Employees:* 158
Previous: MacXchange Ltd
Net Worth: £4,152,593 *Total Assets:* £25,404,456
Registered Office: 23 Erica Road, Stacey Bushes, Milton Keynes, Bucks, MK12 6HS
Activities: Retail sale of computers, peripheral units and software in specialised stores
Parent: B Iconic Ltd
Officers: Russell Luke Timothy Cusack [1965] Director/Consultant; Ciaran Derek McCormack [1981] Director [Irish]

Comtec Cable Accessories Limited
Incorporated: 19 January 1978 *Employees:* 88
Net Worth: £3,229,000 *Total Assets:* £13,674,000
Registered Office: 2 Cardinal Distribution Park, Godmanchester, Huntingdon, Cambs, PE29 2XJ
Activities: Wired telecommunications activities
Major Shareholder: John Thomas Archer
Officers: John Thomas Archer [1955] Director; John Stuart Buck [1962] Director; Daniel Conway [1968] Director; Steven Paul Doddington [1972] Sales Director

Comtec Group (International) Limited
Incorporated: 2 June 1995 *Employees:* 159
Previous: Tayvin 40 Limited
Net Worth: £5,167,000 *Total Assets:* £17,835,000
Registered Office: Cardinal Way, Cardinal Distribution Park, Godmanchester, Huntingdon, Cambs, PE29 2XN
Activities: Wired telecommunications activities
Major Shareholder: John Thomas Archer
Officers: John Thomas Archer [1955] Director; John Stuart Buck [1962] Director; Daniel Conway [1968] Director

Concentia Capital Limited
Incorporated: 16 June 2011
Net Worth: £14,600,000 *Total Assets:* £17,818,000
Registered Office: Venture Way, Dunston Technology Park, Chesterfield, Derbys, S41 8NE
Activities: Reproduction of sound recording
Officers: Neil Robert Cook [1977] Finance Director; Derek Mapp [1950] Director; William John Truman [1974] Director

Concha y Toro UK Limited
Incorporated: 20 December 2000 *Employees:* 61
Net Worth: £9,835,044 *Total Assets:* £45,458,360
Registered Office: 9 Ashurst Court, London Road, Wheatley, Oxon, OX33 1ER
Activities: Wholesale of wine, beer, spirits and other alcoholic beverages
Officers: Enrique Ortuzar, Secretary; Thomas Domeyko [1967] Corporate Director Foreign Subsidiaries [Chilean]; Osvaldo Solar [1961] Director/Corporate C.F.O [Chilean]

Conchord Limited
Incorporated: 14 May 2009
Net Worth: £67,449,000 *Total Assets:* £67,628,000
Registered Office: 2 Crown Way, Rushden, Northants, NN10 6BS
Activities: Non-trading company
Parent: BFS Two Limited
Officers: Stephen Kramer, Secretary; Elizabeth Boland [1959] Director/Chief Financial Officer [American]; Stephen Dreier [1942] Director/Chief Admin Officer [American]; Dave Lissy [1965] Director/Chief Executive Officer [American]; James Walter Tugendhat [1971] Managing Director, International

Condie Investments Limited
Incorporated: 28 October 2002 *Employees:* 3
Net Worth: £3,991,628 *Total Assets:* £11,348,234
Registered Office: Fairhurst House, 7 Acorn Business Park, Heaton Lane, Stockport, Cheshire, SK4 1AS
Activities: Buying and selling of own real estate
Major Shareholder: John Charles Thornley
Officers: Nigel Robert Blyth [1969] Director; Stephen John Cox [1957] Director/Consultant; John Charles Thornley [1957] Director

Congregational & General Charitable Trust (The)
Incorporated: 24 March 1987
Net Worth: £15,354,586 *Total Assets:* £15,638,399
Registered Office: 15 Newland, Lincoln, LN1 1XG
Activities: Activities of religious organisations
Officers: William Raymond Pryde Adams [1949] Director/Minister of Religion; Margaret Elizabeth Atkinson [1947] Director; David George Coote [1949] Director/Minister of Religion; Alastair Charles Forsyth [1959] Director/Trustee; Jacqueline Haws [1948] Director/Trustee; John Francis Holmes [1958] Director/Retired; Reverend Eva Margaret Tait [1947] Director/Retired; Rev Richard Ian Turnbull [1946] Director/Trustee; Pamela Ward [1946] Director/Retired Minister

Conquest Bidco Limited
Incorporated: 28 June 2007
Net Worth: £11,426,000 *Total Assets:* £166,508,000
Registered Office: The Waterfront, Lakeside Boulevard, Doncaster, S Yorks, DN4 5PL
Activities: Other business support service activities n.e.c.
Parent: Keepmoat Limited
Officers: Mark Richard Priest [1966] Director; James Michael Douglas Thomson [1966] Director

Conrad Energy Group Limited
Incorporated: 14 July 2017 *Employees:* 14
Net Worth: £9,127,000 *Total Assets:* £11,867,000
Registered Office: Suites D & E, Windrush Court, Blacklands Way, Abingdon, Oxon, OX14 1SY
Activities: Activities of other holding companies n.e.c.
Shareholder: Michael Damian Darragh
Officers: Mark David New, Secretary; Gautam Bhandari [1969] Director [American]; Michael Damian Darragh [1971] Director/Investment Banker; Christopher John Stewart Dunley [1967] Finance Director; Mohamed Adel El Gazzar [1979] Director; Steven Neville Hardman [1968] Managing Director; Maxime Jean Pierre Jacqz [1979] Director [French]; Mark Evans Woodruff [1957] Director [American]

Conservation Education & Research Trust
Incorporated: 13 February 2002 *Employees:* 52
Net Worth: £12,160,691 *Total Assets:* £12,936,907
Registered Office: Mayfield House, 256 Banbury Road, Oxford, OX2 7DE
Activities: Other professional, scientific and technical activities n.e.c.
Officers: Peter Edward Stimpson, Secretary; Iain Michael Coucher [1961] Director; Dorothee D'Herde [1977] Director of Sustainability & Impact [Belgian]; Dr Edmund Peter Green [1965] Director/Charity CEO; Lucian John Hudson [1960] Director of Communications; Superna Khosla [1970] Director/Chartered Accountant; Lisa Jan King [1959] Director/Management Consultant; Geoffrey Lane [1963] Director/Partner, PWC; Dax Lovegrove [1971] Director/Sustainability; Dr Jack James Matthews [1988] Director/Geologist; Judith Mosely [1964] Director/Banker; Adam John Powell [1971] Director/PR Consultant

Consolidated Property Wilmslow Limited
Incorporated: 7 March 1986 *Employees:* 10
Net Worth: £88,486,096 *Total Assets:* £128,599,832
Registered Office: 56 London Road, Alderley Edge, Cheshire, SK9 7DZ
Activities: Development of building projects
Major Shareholder: Sally Jane Turner
Officers: William Marshall Smith, Secretary/Solicitor; Peter Stuart Dawson [1952] Director/Chartered Surveyor; William Marshall Smith [1955] Director/Company Solicitor; Martin Allan Ridgway [1968] Director/Chartered Surveyor; Sally Jane Turner [1984] Director/Chartered Surveyor

The Consortium for Purchasing and Distribution Limited
Incorporated: 8 September 1995 *Employees:* 283
Net Worth: £12,749,000 *Total Assets:* £32,853,000
Registered Office: 140 Eastern Avenue, Milton Park, Milton, Abingdon, Oxon, OX14 4SB
Activities: Non-specialised wholesale trade
Parent: Hammond Bridge Limited
Officers: Gregory Davidson-Shrine, Secretary; Gregory Davidson-Shrine [1974] Director; Neil Thomas George Martin [1972] Director; Andrew Wilson [1965] Director

Consuma Holdings Limited
Incorporated: 11 July 1997 *Employees:* 197
Previous: Staples Holdings Limited
Net Worth: £6,374,188 *Total Assets:* £12,971,247
Registered Office: Hurlingham Business Park, Fulbeck Heath, Grantham, Lincs, NG32 3HL
Activities: Manufacture of paper and paperboard
Parent: Ancelltek Holdings Limited
Officers: Oday Abbosh [1967] Director; Richard Haslam [1962] Production Director; Haydar Suham Shawkat [1966] Financial Director; Andrew Staples [1961] Director

Consuma Paper Products Limited
Incorporated: 23 July 1981 *Employees:* 193
Previous: Staples Disposables Limited
Net Worth: £11,543,652 *Total Assets:* £18,101,324
Registered Office: Hurlingham Business Park, Fulbeck Heath, Grantham, Lincs, NG32 3HL
Activities: Manufacture of paper and paperboard
Parent: Consuma Holdings Limited
Officers: Oday Abbosh [1967] Director; Richard Haslam [1962] Production Director; Haydar Suham Shawkat [1966] Financial Director; Andrew Staples [1961] Director

Consumer Champion Group Limited
Incorporated: 15 January 2009 *Employees:* 4
Net Worth Deficit: £5,496,000 *Total Assets:* £137,102,000
Registered Office: 1430 Montagu Court, Kettering Parkway, Kettering, Northants, NN15 6XR
Activities: Activities of head offices
Parent: NAHL Group PLC
Officers: James David Saralis, Secretary; John Russell Atkinson [1965] Director; James David Saralis [1978] Director

Continental Landscapes Limited
Incorporated: 24 August 1989 *Employees:* 702
Net Worth: £12,812,290 *Total Assets:* £17,696,814
Registered Office: Wychwood House, 4 Landscape, Close, Weston on the Green, Bicester, Oxon, OX25 3SX
Activities: Landscape service activities
Major Shareholder: Marinus Cornelis Johannes Marie Krinkels
Officers: William Trotman [1953] Managing Director

Thomas Cook Aircraft Engineering Limited
Incorporated: 12 December 2001 *Employees:* 468
Net Worth Deficit: £5,929,000 *Total Assets:* £11,865,000
Registered Office: Westpoint, Peterborough Business Park, Lynch Wood, Peterborough, Cambs, PE2 6FZ
Activities: Other business support service activities n.e.c.
Parent: Thomas Cook Airlines Limited
Officers: Emma Louise Langford, Secretary; John Mark Boler [1970] Director; Christoph Debus [1971] Director [German]; Paul William Hutchings [1966] Director

Thomas Cook Airlines Limited
Incorporated: 21 April 1986 *Employees:* 2,430
Net Worth: £405,780,000 *Total Assets:* £1,104,685,952
Registered Office: Westpoint, Peterborough Business Park, Lynch Wood, Peterborough, Cambs, PE2 6FZ
Activities: Scheduled passenger air transport
Parent: Thomas Cook Group Airlines Limited
Officers: Shirley Bradley, Secretary; John Mark Boler [1970] Director; Christoph Debus [1971] Director [German]; Paul William Hutchings [1966] Director

Walter John Cook and Sons Limited
Incorporated: 28 September 1976 *Employees:* 60
Net Worth: £10,620,473 *Total Assets:* £15,791,169
Registered Office: Richmond Holiday Centre, Richmond Drive, Skegness, Lincs, PE25 3TQ
Activities: Holiday centres and villages
Major Shareholder: Mark Robert Williams
Officers: Mark Robert Williams, Secretary; Andrew William Downing [1964] Managing Director; Stephen John Parish [1965] Financial Director; Mark Robert Williams [1968] Director/Caravan Park Manager

William Cook Cast Products Limited
Incorporated: 30 June 1992 *Employees:* 177
Net Worth: £7,109,352 *Total Assets:* £15,400,781
Registered Office: Parkway Avenue, Sheffield, S9 4UL
Activities: Casting of steel
Parent: William Cook Holdings Limited
Officers: Michael Keith Hodgson, Secretary/Chartered Accountant; Michael Keith Hodgson [1957] Director; Christopher David Seymour [1973] Group Financial Director

Thomas Cook Continental Holdings Limited
Incorporated: 9 June 2008
Net Worth: £597,218,560 *Total Assets:* £1,061,576,128
Registered Office: Westpoint, Peterborough Business Park, Lynch Wood, Peterborough, Cambs, PE2 6FZ
Activities: Other business support service activities n.e.c.
Parent: Thomas Cook Investments (2) Limited
Officers: Shirley Bradley, Secretary/Deputy Company Secretary; Alan Charles Donald [1963] Director

Cook Defence Systems Limited
Incorporated: 15 January 2009 *Employees:* 5
Net Worth: £13,218,126 *Total Assets:* £24,685,644
Registered Office: c/o William Cook Holdings Ltd, Parkway Avenue, Sheffield, S9 4UL
Activities: Agents involved in the sale of machinery, industrial equipment, ships and aircraft
Parent: William Cook Holdings Limited
Officers: Michael Keith Hodgson, Secretary; William James Cook [1988] Director; Christopher David Seymour [1973] Group Financial Director

Thomas Cook Finance PLC
Incorporated: 23 October 2007
Net Worth: £6,018,232 *Total Assets:* £361,270,912
Registered Office: Westpoint, Peterborough Business Park, Lynch Wood, Peterborough, Cambs, PE2 6FZ
Activities: Other business support service activities n.e.c.
Parent: Thomas Cook Group Tour Operations Limited
Officers: Rebecca Ann Symondson-Powell, Secretary; Christopher James Corner [1974] Director

Thomas Cook Group Hedging Limited
Incorporated: 10 April 2012
Net Worth: £990,998,016 *Total Assets:* £1,137,655,040
Registered Office: Westpoint, Peterborough Business Park, Lynch Wood, Peterborough, Cambs, PE2 6FZ
Activities: Other business support service activities n.e.c.
Parent: TCGH Holdings Limited
Officers: Shirley Bradley, Secretary; Christopher James Corner [1974] Director

Thomas Cook Group Treasury Limited
Incorporated: 24 April 2008
Net Worth Deficit: £84,319,000 *Total Assets:* £5,947,229,184
Registered Office: Westpoint, Peterborough Business Park, Lynch Wood, Peterborough, Cambs, PE2 6FZ
Activities: Other business support service activities n.e.c.
Parent: Thomas Cook Investments (2) Limited
Officers: Shirley Bradley, Company Secretary; Christopher James Corner [1974] Director

Thomas Cook Group UK Limited
Incorporated: 21 November 1988
Net Worth: £894,899,968 *Total Assets:* £962,800,000
Registered Office: Westpoint, Peterborough Business Park, Lynch Wood, Peterborough, Cambs, PE2 6FZ
Activities: Activities of head offices
Parent: Mytravel Group Limited
Officers: Shirley Bradley, Secretary; Alan Charles Donald [1963] Director

William Cook Holdings Limited
Incorporated: 25 November 1996 *Employees:* 494
Net Worth: £51,042,000 *Total Assets:* £77,802,000
Registered Office: Parkway Avenue, Sheffield, S9 4UL
Activities: Activities of production holding companies
Shareholders: Andrew John Cook; Froggatt Trustee Limited
Officers: Michael Keith Hodgson, Secretary; Sir Andrew John Cook [1949] Director/Chairman; William James Cook [1988] Commercial Director; Christopher David Seymour [1973] Group Financial Director

Thomas Cook Investments (2) Limited
Incorporated: 23 January 2007
Net Worth: £904,574,464 *Total Assets:* £3,789,469,184
Registered Office: Westpoint, Peterborough Business Park, Lynch Wood, Peterborough, Cambs, PE2 6FZ
Activities: Other business support service activities n.e.c.
Parent: Thomas Cook Group PLC
Officers: Shirley Bradley, Secretary; Alan Charles Donald [1963] Director

William Cook Properties Limited
Incorporated: 16 March 1989
Net Worth: £10,867,030 *Total Assets:* £11,418,241
Registered Office: Parkway Avenue, Sheffield, S9 4UL
Activities: Other letting and operating of own or leased real estate
Parent: William Cook Holdings Limited
Officers: Michael Keith Hodgson, Secretary/Chartered Accountant; Michael Keith Hodgson [1957] Director/Chartered Accountant; Christopher David Seymour [1973] Group Financial Director

Thomas Cook Retail Limited
Incorporated: 22 April 1909 *Employees:* 24
Net Worth: £158,612,992 *Total Assets:* £379,560,992
Registered Office: Westpoint, Peterborough Business Park, Lynch Wood, Peterborough, Cambs, PE2 6FZ
Activities: Travel agency activities
Parent: Thomas Cook Group UK Limited
Officers: Shirley Bradley, Company Secretary & Legal Adviser; Alan Charles Donald [1963] Director

William Cook Stanhope Limited
Incorporated: 29 February 1940 *Employees:* 90
Net Worth: £6,565,320 *Total Assets:* £10,078,763
Registered Office: c/o William Cook Holdings Limited, Parkway Avenue, Sheffield, S9 4UL
Activities: Casting of steel
Parent: William Cook Holdings Limited
Officers: Michael Keith Hodgson, Secretary; Michael Keith Hodgson [1957] Director; Christopher David Seymour [1973] Group Financial Director

Thomas Cook Tour Operations Limited
Incorporated: 18 May 1999 *Employees:* 270
Net Worth Deficit: £1,898,072,064 *Total Assets:* £546,156,992
Registered Office: Westpoint, Peterborough Business Park, Lynch Wood, Peterborough, Cambs, PE2 6FZ
Activities: Travel agency activities
Parent: Thomas Cook Group UK Limited
Officers: Shirley Bradley, Company Secretary & Legal Adviser; Alan Charles Donald [1963] Director

Thomas Cook UK Limited
Incorporated: 22 July 1991 *Employees:* 1,189
Net Worth Deficit: £58,580,000 *Total Assets:* £1,917,830,016
Registered Office: Westpoint, Peterborough Business Park, Lynch Wood, Peterborough, Cambs, PE2 6FZ
Activities: Other business support service activities n.e.c.
Parent: Sandbrook UK Investments Limited
Officers: Shirley Bradley, Secretary; Alan Charles Donald [1963] Director

Thomas Cook UK Travel Limited
Incorporated: 7 April 1978 *Employees:* 1,510
Net Worth: £50,546,000 *Total Assets:* £50,550,000
Registered Office: Westpoint, Peterborough Business Park, Lynch Wood, Peterborough, Cambs, PE2 6FZ
Activities: Other business support service activities n.e.c.
Parent: Thomas Cook UK Limited
Officers: Shirley Bradley, Secretary; Paul Andrew Hemingway [1971] Director

Thomas Cook West Investments Limited
Incorporated: 26 July 2012
Net Worth: £292,836,512 *Total Assets:* £327,123,232
Registered Office: Westpoint, Peterborough Business Park, Lynch Wood, Peterborough, Cambs, PE2 6FZ
Activities: Other business support service activities n.e.c.
Parent: Sandbrook Overseas Investments Limited
Officers: Shirley Bradley, Secretary; Alice Hannah Marsden [1983] Director

Cooke Optics Group Limited
Incorporated: 26 February 2015 *Employees:* 121
Net Worth: £2,961,763 *Total Assets:* £33,801,708
Registered Office: 1 Cooke Close, Thurmaston, Leicester, LE4 8PT
Activities: Manufacture of photographic and cinematographic equipment
Parent: Chaplin Bidco Limited
Officers: Robert Howard, Secretary; Robert Damian Howard [1957] Director; Lester Richard Zellan [1949] Director [American]

Cooke Optics Holdings Limited
Incorporated: 25 February 2015
Net Worth Deficit: £2,552,194 *Total Assets:* £31,092,606
Registered Office: 1 Cooke Close, Thurmaston, Leicester, LE4 8PT
Activities: Activities of production holding companies
Parent: Cooke Optics Group Limited
Officers: Robert Howard, Secretary; Robert Damian Howard [1957] Director; Lester Richard Zellan [1949] Director [American]

Cooke Optics Limited
Incorporated: 11 June 1998 *Employees:* 115
Net Worth: £19,926,396 *Total Assets:* £29,227,452
Registered Office: 1 Cooke Close, Thurmaston, Leicester, LE4 8PT
Activities: Manufacture of photographic and cinematographic equipment
Shareholders: Cooke Optics Holdings Limited; Cooke Optics Holdings Limited
Officers: Robert Damian Howard, Secretary/Director; Guy Noel Genin [1953] Director [French]; Robert Damian Howard [1957] Director; Barbara Lowry [1950] Director [American]; Lester Richard Zellan [1949] Director [American]

E.D. & A.D. Cooke, Bourne (Farms) Limited
Incorporated: 10 May 1951 *Employees:* 2
Net Worth: £16,440,375 *Total Assets:* £19,668,346
Registered Office: Larkfleet House, Falcon Way, Bourne, Lincs, PE10 0FF
Activities: Growing of cereals (except rice), leguminous crops and oil seeds
Shareholders: Adam George Andrew Cooke; Peter Edward Delanoix Cooke; Mark Thomas Hindmarch; Jarred Thomas Wright
Officers: Adam George Andrew Cooke, Secretary; Adam George Andrew Cooke [1962] Director/Farmer; Peter Edward Delanoix Cooke [1956] Director/Farmer

Coolair Equipment Limited
Incorporated: 22 December 1993 *Employees:* 87
Net Worth: £4,587,789 *Total Assets:* £10,064,950
Registered Office: Coolair House, Globe Lane, Broadway, Dukinfield, Cheshire, SK16 4UJ
Activities: Plumbing, heat and air-conditioning installation
Parent: Coolair Management Company Ltd
Officers: Helen Sharratt, Secretary; Adam Garstang [1968] Director/National General Manager; Jason Mark Garstang [1971] Director; Neil Simon Gibbard [1970] Sales Director; John James Otterson [1959] Director/Engineer; Helen Sharratt [1966] Director/Chartered Accountant; Steven Valentine [1972] Director

Coolsilk Limited
Incorporated: 10 December 2013 *Employees:* 295
Net Worth: £42,842,360 *Total Assets:* £58,496,148
Registered Office: Orchard Villa, Top Pasture Lane, North Wheatley, Retford, Notts, DN22 9BY
Activities: Non-trading company
Shareholders: Peter Dennis Swann; Karin Louise Swann; Christopher Swann; Barbara Ellison Wilkinson
Officers: Karin Louise Swann, Secretary; Karin Louise Swann [1964] Director; Peter Dennis Swann [1963] Director

Coolsilk Property & Investment Limited
Incorporated: 17 December 2013 *Employees:* 7
Net Worth: £60,482,504 *Total Assets:* £74,251,992
Registered Office: Orchard Villa, Top Pasture Lane, North Wheatley, Retford, Notts, DN22 9BY
Activities: Other professional, scientific and technical activities n.e.c.
Parent: Coolsilk Limited
Officers: Karin Louise Swann, Secretary; Karin Louise Swann [1964] Director; Peter Dennis Swann [1963] Director

Coombe Abbey Park Limited
Incorporated: 25 March 1992 *Employees:* 274
Net Worth: £5,499,137 *Total Assets:* £12,220,523
Registered Office: Coombe Abbey Hotel, Brinklow Road, Binley, Coventry, Warwicks, CV3 2AB
Activities: Hotels and similar accommodation
Shareholders: Coventry City Council; Coventry City Council
Officers: Anthony Mark Lightbound, Secretary; Gordon Frank Dunlop Bear [1942] Managing Director; Barry Hastie [1969] Director of Finance; Richard Edward Moon [1966] Director/Chartered Surveyor; Andrew Walster [1975] Local Authority Director

Cooper & Turner Limited
Incorporated: 26 June 2000 *Employees:* 165
Net Worth: £3,798,000 *Total Assets:* £13,940,000
Registered Office: Templeborough Works, Sheffield Road, Sheffield, S9 1RS
Activities: Manufacture of fasteners and screw machine products
Parent: Northern Endeavour Limited
Officers: Steven Edward Karol [1954] Director/Managing Partner [American]

Cooper and Turner Distribution Limited
Incorporated: 22 January 2013 *Employees:* 86
Net Worth: £3,900,000 *Total Assets:* £14,653,000
Registered Office: Unit 2 Canklow Meadows Industrial Estate, West Bawtry Road, Rotherham, S Yorks, S60 2XL
Activities: Manufacture of fasteners and screw machine products
Parent: Andaray (Holdings) Limited
Officers: Steven Edward Karol [1954] Director/Managing Partner [American]

Cooper Roller Bearings Company Limited
Incorporated: 16 June 1982 *Employees:* 176
Net Worth: £41,256,000 *Total Assets:* £44,938,000
Registered Office: Wisbech Road, Kings Lynn, Norfolk, PE30 5JX
Activities: Manufacture of bearings, gears, gearing and driving elements
Parent: Kaydon Europa BV
Officers: Paula Jane Owen, Secretary; Ian Lindsay Bloxham [1960] Director/General Manager; Sharon Linda Smith [1962] Managing Director; Bo Peter Torpman [1973] Director/Business Area Controller [Swedish]

Copart Europe Limited
Incorporated: 3 April 2007
Net Worth Deficit: £9,433,000 *Total Assets:* £134,063,000
Registered Office: Acrey Fields, Woburn Road, Wootton, Beds, MK43 9EJ
Activities: Activities of other holding companies n.e.c.
Parent: CPRT LLP
Officers: Aaron Jayson Adair [1969] Director/Chief Executive Officer [American]; Jonathan David Canning [1972] Director/General Counsel; Gregory Depasquale [1968] Director/SVP, General Counsel and Secretary of Copart, Inc [American]; William Easley Franklin [1956] Director/Chief Financial Officer [American]; Nigel James Paget [1966] Managing Director

Copart UK Limited
Incorporated: 28 March 1968 *Employees:* 765
Net Worth: £81,679,000 *Total Assets:* £140,756,000
Registered Office: Acrey Fields, Woburn Road, Wootton, Beds, MK43 9EJ
Activities: Sale of used cars and light motor vehicles
Parent: Universal Salvage Limited
Officers: Aaron Jayson Adair [1969] Director/Chief Executive Officer [American]; Jonathan David Canning [1972] Director/General Counsel; Gregory Depasquale [1968] Director/SVP, General Counsel and Secretary of Copart, Inc [American]; William Easley Franklin [1956] Director/Chief Financial Officer [American]; Nigel James Paget [1966] Managing Director; Simon Sheldon-Wilson [1969] Director; Paul Anthony Styer [1956] Director/General Counsel [American]

Cope Children's Trust
Incorporated: 27 August 1992 *Employees:* 189
Net Worth: £9,436,911 *Total Assets:* £10,202,311
Registered Office: Lark Rise, Fairmeadows Way, Loughborough, Leics, LE11 2HS
Activities: Other human health activities
Officers: Ronald Alexander Graham, Secretary; Richard Mark Bishop [1968] Director/Retired; Angela Jane Browning [1976] Director/Chartered Tax Advisor; Joanne Sarah Brunner [1956] Director/Business Consultant; Susan Elizabeth Dryden [1955] Director/Retired; Vipal Laxman Karavadra [1981] Director; Chandrakant Kataria [1961] Director/Chief Executive; Anne-Maria Newham [1964] Director/NHS Manager; Diane Sandra Postle [1957] Director/Trust Lead Nurse; Matthew William Rooney [1983] Director/Special Educational Needs and Disabilities (SEND); Vijay Sharma [1951] Director/Retired; Paul Robert Stothard [1958] Director/Partner of Pathways Management - Consultancy; Richard David Whall [1962] Operations Director; Dr Jane Williams [1959] Director/Doctor

Copley Scientific Limited
Incorporated: 20 September 1978 *Employees:* 23
Net Worth: £13,433,554 *Total Assets:* £15,517,443
Registered Office: Colwick Quays Business Park, Private Road No 2, Colwick, Nottingham, NG4 2JY
Activities: Manufacture of electronic measuring, testing etc. equipment, not for industrial process control
Shareholders: Anthony Robert Copley; Mark Andrew Copley
Officers: Anthony Robert Copley, Secretary; Anthony Robert Copley [1948] Director/Instrument Manufacturer; Mark Andrew Copley [1978] Director

Corby Land & Development Ltd
Incorporated: 19 February 2008
Previous: Paragon Flexible Storage Limited
Net Worth Deficit: £2,368,648 *Total Assets:* £55,244,364
Registered Office: Units 3-4 Twigden Barns, Grooms Lane, Creaton, Northampton, NN6 8NN
Activities: Other letting and operating of own or leased real estate
Shareholders: Mulberry Commercial Developments Limited; Frogmore Real Estate Partners GP3 LLP Acting in its Capacity as General Partner to Frogmore Real Estate Partners III LP
Officers: Jonathan Colin Tate, Secretary; Timothy Kennar Allibone [1972] Director/Chartered Surveyor; Josephine Clare Brand [1967] Director/Chartered Surveyor; Patrick Julian Hulme Smith [1968] Director/Chartered Surveyor; Jonathan Colin Tate [1969] Director and Company Secretary; Mark Ashby Wilkinson [1959] Director; Robert John Wilkinson [1962] Director/Property Developer

Corby Power Limited
Incorporated: 19 December 1988 *Employees:* 7
Net Worth: £8,292,000 *Total Assets:* £19,582,000
Registered Office: Mitchell Road, Phoenix Parkway, Corby, Northants, NN17 5QT
Activities: Production of electricity
Parent: ESBII UK Limited
Officers: John Healy, Secretary; Senan Colleran [1969] Director [Irish]; Mark Fogarty [1973] Director/Accountant [Irish]; John Healy [1959] Director/Risk Manager [Irish]; John Redmond [1955] Director/ESB Secretary [Irish]

Cornshire Limited
Incorporated: 19 January 1988
Net Worth: £7,576,556 *Total Assets:* £9,215,975
Registered Office: Studio 5, Rowditch Business Centre, 282 Uttoxeter New Road, Derby, DE22 3LN
Activities: Activities of head offices
Major Shareholder: Henry Charles Moreton
Officers: Henry Charles Moreton [1956] Director

Corran (Wakefield) Limited
Incorporated: 23 August 1994
Net Worth: £9,198,542 *Total Assets:* £9,438,275
Registered Office: The Estate Office, Wakefield Lodge Estate, Potterspury, Northants, NN12 7QX
Activities: Development of building projects
Parent: Dunlin Limited
Officers: Sarah Francis Richmond-Watson, Secretary; Daniel Thomas Richmond-Watson [1977] Director; Julian Howard Richmond-Watson [1947] Director/Farmer

Corrboard UK Limited
Incorporated: 23 October 2013 *Employees:* 88
Net Worth Deficit: £1,868,930 *Total Assets:* £32,787,916
Registered Office: Waldo Way, Normanby Enterprise Park, Scunthorpe, N Lincs, DN15 9GE
Activities: Manufacture of corrugated paper and paperboard, sacks and bags
Shareholder: VPK Packaging Group NV
Officers: John Charles Saynor, Secretary; Paul Barber [1979] Director; Ruth Cook [1968] Managing Director; Richard Coward [1960] Managing Director; Raffan West [1969] Director

Corrpro Companies Engineering Limited
Incorporated: 11 September 1984
Net Worth: £36,142,676 *Total Assets:* £37,020,040
Registered Office: 12-20 Brunel Close, Park Farm Industrial Estate, Wellingborough, Northants, NN8 6QX
Activities: Other service activities n.e.c.
Officers: Madame Sarah Bennison, Secretary; David Francis Morris, Secretary; Mark Thomas Russell Davies [1965] Managing Director; David Francis Morris [1961] Corporate Director and Officer [American]

Corus Hotels Limited
Incorporated: 4 November 1920 *Employees:* 605
Net Worth: £106,107,000 *Total Assets:* £208,328,000
Registered Office: Corus House, 1 Auckland Park, Milton Keynes, Bucks, MK1 1BU
Activities: Hotels and similar accommodation
Parent: Malayan United Industries
Officers: Khurram Mohmand, Secretary; Andrew Khoo [1972] Director [Australian]; Kay Peng Khoo [1938] Director [Malaysian]; Kim Li Kwa [1956] Director [Singaporean]; Yet King Loy [1946] Director [Canadian]; Nyen Faat Wong [1957] Director [Malaysian]

Cosma Casting UK R.E. Limited
Incorporated: 21 July 2016
Net Worth Deficit: £342,000 *Total Assets:* £26,073,000
Registered Office: International House, Siskin Parkway East, Middlemarch Business Park, Coventry, Warwicks, CV3 4PE
Activities: Buying and selling of own real estate
Parent: Magna International Holding (UK) Limited
Officers: Mark John Smith, Secretary; Mark John Smith [1968] Director/Manager

Coster Aerosols Limited
Incorporated: 7 February 1967 *Employees:* 33
Net Worth: £7,651,381 *Total Assets:* £12,473,066
Registered Office: 8 Lindrick Way, Barlborough, Chesterfield, Derbys, S43 4XE
Activities: Other manufacturing n.e.c.
Officers: Kevin Eric Holloway [1958] Director/UK Chief Executive; Damiano Marsilli [1986] Director [Italian]; Bernard Msellati [1963] Director [Italian]

Cosworth Electronics Limited
Incorporated: 3 November 2004 *Employees:* 73
Net Worth: £8,268,000 *Total Assets:* £11,505,000
Registered Office: The Octagon, St James Mill Road, Northampton, NN5 5RA
Activities: Other business support service activities n.e.c.
Parent: Cosworth Group Holdings Limited
Officers: Kevin Oscar Newton Kalkhoven [1944] Director/Investor; Hal Jon Reisiger [1960] Director/Chief Executive Officer [American]; Pierre Charles Wildman [1959] Director/Analyst [American]

Cosworth Group Holdings Limited
Incorporated: 30 November 2007 *Employees:* 394
Net Worth Deficit: £7,992,000 *Total Assets:* £61,305,000
Registered Office: The Octagon, St James Mill Road, Northampton, NN5 5RA
Activities: Activities of other holding companies n.e.c.
Shareholders: Gerald Forsythe; Quadrangle Trustee Company
Officers: Zakary Challen Brown [1971] Director/Chief Executive [American]; Alan John Donnelly [1957] Director/Executive Chairman; Carl-Peter Edmund Moriz Forster [1954] Director/Manager [German]; Kevin Oscar Newton Kalkhoven [1944] Director/Investor; Lawrence Allan Lagowski [1952] Director/President [American]; Hal Jon Reisiger [1960] Director/Chief Executive Officer [American]; Pierre Charles Wildman [1959] Director/Analyst [American]

Cosworth Limited
Incorporated: 13 July 2004 *Employees:* 268
Net Worth Deficit: £11,936,000 *Total Assets:* £34,494,000
Registered Office: The Octagon, St James Mill Road, Northampton, NN5 5RA
Activities: Other professional, scientific and technical activities n.e.c.
Parent: Cosworth Group Holdings Limited
Officers: Kevin Oscar Newton Kalkhoven [1944] Director/Investor; Hal Jon Reisiger [1960] Director/Chief Executive Officer [American]; Pierre Charles Wildman [1959] Director/Analyst [American]

Cothill Trust
Incorporated: 9 September 1969 *Employees:* 566
Previous: Cothill Educational Trust
Net Worth: £36,885,000 *Total Assets:* £47,861,000
Registered Office: 7 Cothill, Abingdon, Oxon, OX13 6JN
Activities: Primary education
Officers: Etienne David Bottari [1959] Director/Investment Banking [Italian]; Peter Morrison Cook [1953] Director; Countess Peta Martine Darnley [1968] Director/Farmer; Denise Marie-Reine Le Gal [1958] Director/County Councillor; Justin Marking [1958] Director; David John Miles [1954] Director/Lawyer; Katharine Mary Pryce [1961] Director/Homemaker; Dr Ralph Douglas Townsend [1951] Director/Headmaster

Cotswold Wild Life Park Limited
Incorporated: 17 March 1971 *Employees:* 140
Net Worth: £10,912,239 *Total Assets:* £11,578,170
Registered Office: Bradwell Grove, Burford, Oxon, OX18 4JP
Activities: Botanical and zoological gardens and nature reserves activities
Major Shareholder: Reginald Philip Heyworth
Officers: Susan Elizabeth Hamersley Heyworth, Secretary; Stuart John Fox [1949] Director/Accountant; Reginald Philip Heyworth [1961] Director/Farmer

R.M. Cottingham Limited
Incorporated: 24 February 1955 *Employees:* 9
Net Worth: £6,415,774 *Total Assets:* £9,621,556
Registered Office: The Office, Hoe Hill Farm, Swinhope, Binbrook, Lincoln, LN3 6HX
Activities: Growing of cereals (except rice), leguminous crops and oil seeds
Shareholders: David James Everatt; Lyn Hazel Cottingham; John Eastwood Cottingham; John Eastwood Cottingham
Officers: John Eastwood Cottingham, Secretary; John Eastwood Cottingham [1958] Director/Farmer; Lyn Hazel Cottingham [1954] Director

Coundon Court
Incorporated: 16 March 2012 *Employees:* 181
Net Worth: £16,606,000 *Total Assets:* £20,470,000
Registered Office: Coundon Court, Northbrook Road, Coundon, Coventry, Warwicks, CV6 2AJ
Activities: General secondary education
Officers: Linda Marie Phillips, Secretary; Antony Cash [1984] Director/Senior Officer Production - Ofqual; Andrew James Clay [1962] Director/Headteacher; Amanda Donnelly [1971] Director/Student Progress Manager; Joanne Doyle [1973] Director/Higher Level Teaching Assistant; Joanne Humphrey [1980] Director/Probation Officer; Bryn John Lewis [1971] Director/Local Government Officer; Mark Charles McNally [1968] Director/Solicitor; Christopher Millerclip [1959] Director/Mechanical & Electrical (M&E) Manager; Anthony Carl Mosley [1985] Director/Teacher; Mark Steven Payne [1966] Director/Vice-Principal, City College; Tom Roberts [1946] Director/Retired; Ravindranadh Vesta [1970] Engagement Director

Country Attire Holdings Limited
Incorporated: 26 February 2013
Net Worth: £10,351,476 *Total Assets:* £11,237,773
Registered Office: Fusion Way, Bolingbroke Road, Louth, Lincs, LN11 0WA
Activities: Activities of other holding companies n.e.c.
Parent: Internet Fusion Limited
Officers: Vinay Zaverilal Bhindi [1975] Director/Chartered Accountant; Martin Brailsford [1976] Director

Country Court Care Homes 2 Limited
Incorporated: 1 May 2014 *Employees:* 462
Net Worth: £20,322,836 *Total Assets:* £43,948,052
Registered Office: c/o Duncan & Toplis Limited, Enterprise Way, Pinchbeck, Spalding, Lincs, PE11 3YR
Activities: Residential nursing care facilities
Parent: Country Court Care Group Limited
Officers: Abdul Aziz Kachra [1952] Director; Al-Karim Kachra [1988] Finance Director; Alykhan Kachra [1986] Director

Country Court Care Homes 3 MB Limited
Incorporated: 7 October 2015
Net Worth: £1 *Total Assets:* £22,722,986
Registered Office: c/o Duncan & Toplis Limited, Enterprise Way, Pinchbeck, Spalding, Lincs, PE11 3YR
Activities: Activities of other holding companies n.e.c.
Parent: Country Court Care Homes 3 MB Holdco Limited
Officers: Abdul Aziz Kachra [1952] Director; Al-Karim Kachra [1988] Director; Alykhan Kachra [1986] Director/Operations

Country Court Care Homes 3 Propco Limited
Incorporated: 7 October 2015
Net Worth: £23,821,500 *Total Assets:* £78,951,128
Registered Office: c/o Duncan & Toplis Limited, Enterprise Way, Pinchbeck, Spalding, Lincs, PE11 3YR
Activities: Other letting and operating of own or leased real estate
Parent: Country Court Care Homes 3 SB Limited
Officers: Abdul Aziz Kachra [1952] Director; Al-Karim Kachra [1988] Director; Alykhan Kachra [1986] Director/Operations

Country Court Care Homes 3 SB Holdco Limited
Incorporated: 7 October 2015
Net Worth: £1 *Total Assets:* £22,641,746
Registered Office: c/o Duncan & Toplis Limited, Enterprise Way, Pinchbeck, Spalding, Lincs, PE11 3YR
Activities: Activities of other holding companies n.e.c.
Parent: Country Court Care Homes 3 MB Limited
Officers: Abdul Aziz Kachra [1952] Director; Al-Karim Kachra [1988] Director; Alykhan Kachra [1986] Director/Operations

Country Court Care Homes 3 SB Limited
Incorporated: 7 October 2015
Net Worth: £1 *Total Assets:* £47,278,724
Registered Office: c/o Duncan & Toplis Limited, Enterprise Way, Pinchbeck, Spalding, Lincs, PE11 3YR
Activities: Activities of other holding companies n.e.c.
Parent: Country Court Care Homes 3 SB Holdco Limited
Officers: Abdul Aziz Kachra [1952] Director; Al-Karim Kachra [1988] Director; Alykhan Kachra [1986] Director/Operations

Country Court Care Homes Limited
Incorporated: 23 September 1996 *Employees:* 477
Net Worth: £8,129,344 *Total Assets:* £22,454,608
Registered Office: c/o Duncan & Toplis Limited, Enterprise Way, Pinchbeck, Spalding, Lincs, PE11 3YR
Activities: Residential nursing care facilities
Parent: Country Court Care Group Limited
Officers: Al-Karim Kachra, Secretary; Abdulaziz Kachra [1952] Director; Al-Karim Kachra [1988] Financial Director; Alykhan Kachra [1986] Director/Operations

Countrywide Principal Services Limited
Incorporated: 17 March 1983 *Employees:* 755
Net Worth: £37,456,000 *Total Assets:* £51,941,000
Registered Office: Countrywide House, 6 Caldecotte Lake Business Park, Caldecotte Lake Drive, Caldecotte, Milton Keynes, Bucks, MK7 8JT
Activities: Financial intermediation not elsewhere classified
Parent: Balanus Limited
Officers: Gareth Rhys Williams, Secretary; Natalie Anna Ceeney [1971] Director; Paul Lewis Creffield [1954] Director; Peter Curran [1966] Director

County Asset Finance Limited
Incorporated: 14 June 1995 *Employees:* 7
Net Worth: £3,959,490 *Total Assets:* £11,478,964
Registered Office: Unit 11 Midland Court, Central Park, Lutterworth, Leics, LE17 4PN
Activities: Financial leasing
Shareholders: Christopher Laurie Malthouse; David Winton Harding
Officers: Dawn Belinda Tingay, Secretary; Juliana Marina Farha [1966] Director [Canadian]; Darren Andrew Shaw [1971] Director/Finance House; Dawn Belinda Tingay [1964] Director/Administration

County Estates (Bakewell) Limited
Incorporated: 6 September 1999 *Employees:* 1
Net Worth: £14,386,740 *Total Assets:* £25,135,136
Registered Office: Manor House, Stoke, Grindleford, Hope Valley, Derbys, S32 2HW
Activities: Development of building projects
Parent: County Developments (Bakewell) Limited
Officers: Helen Elizabeth Clapham, Secretary; Donald Alexander Clapham [1952] Director

County Hotels Limited
Incorporated: 6 December 1996 *Employees:* 64
Net Worth: £11,004,425 *Total Assets:* £11,837,161
Registered Office: Corus House, 1 Auckland Park, Milton Keynes, Bucks, MK1 1BU
Activities: Hotels and similar accommodation
Shareholders: Corus Hotels Limited; Jonadith UK Limited
Officers: Khurram Mohmand, Secretary; Andrew Khoo [1972] Director [Australian]; Yet King Loy [1946] Director [Canadian]; Khurram Mohmand [1972] Director/Accountant

County Milk Products Limited
Incorporated: 18 November 1993 *Employees:* 73
Net Worth: £11,622,186 *Total Assets:* £46,729,532
Registered Office: Dean Court, 85 Adlington Road, Wilmslow, Cheshire, SK9 2BT
Activities: Other retail sale of food in specialised stores
Major Shareholder: John Noel Langslow
Officers: Marie Elizabeth Langslow, Secretary; Steven James Howarth [1958] Director; John Noel Langslow [1941] Director; Mark David Langslow [1970] Director; Philip John Langslow [1967] Director; Timothy Daniel Lowth [1968] Director/Accountant; Peter David White [1966] Sales Director

Countywide Developments Limited
Incorporated: 25 October 1993 *Employees:* 11
Net Worth: £25,873,000 *Total Assets:* £90,377,000
Registered Office: Gallagher House, Gallagher Way, Gallagher Business Park, Heathcote, Warwick, CV34 6AF
Activities: Buying and selling of own real estate
Parent: Gallagher Developments Holdco Limited
Officers: Anthony Christopher Gallagher [1951] Director; Geoffrey Hugh Gosling [1947] Director/Chartered Accountant

Court Properties (Portugal) Limited
Incorporated: 15 November 1963 *Employees:* 11
Net Worth: £9,047,791 *Total Assets:* £14,243,045
Registered Office: Emerson House, Heyes Lane, Alderley Edge, Cheshire, SK9 7LF
Activities: Construction of domestic buildings
Shareholders: P.E. Jones (Properties) Limited; Deanbank Investments Limited
Officers: Varun Maharaj, Secretary; Anthony Emerson Jones [1967] Director; Audrey Jones [1936] Director; Mark Emerson Jones [1964] Director; Peter Emerson Jones [1935] Director; Maria Cidalia Serodio Rosa [1959] Director [Portuguese]

The Coventry and Solihull Waste Disposal Company Limited
Incorporated: 24 February 1992 *Employees:* 68
Net Worth: £22,818,000 *Total Assets:* £40,554,000
Registered Office: The Waste To Energy Plant, Bar Road, Coventry, Warwicks, CV3 4AN
Activities: Production of electricity
Parent: The Council of The City of Coventry
Officers: Christopher James Penson, Secretary; Richard Innes John Gray [1953] Director; Barry Hastie [1969] Director of Finance and Corporate Services; Paul Andrew Johnson [1965] Director of Resources, Solihull MBC; Christopher James Penson [1966] Finance Director; Karl Starkey [1971] Managing Director

Coventry Building Society Covered Bonds LLP
Incorporated: 4 June 2008
Net Worth: £3,974,000 *Total Assets:* £3,785,728,000
Registered Office: Oakfield House, Binley Business Park, Coventry, Warwicks, CV3 2TQ

Coventry Chemicals Limited
Incorporated: 3 April 1975 *Employees:* 135
Net Worth: £1,093,000 *Total Assets:* £12,446,000
Registered Office: Woodhams Road, Siskin Drive, Coventry, Warwicks, CV3 4FX
Activities: Manufacture of soap and detergents
Shareholder: Michael Scott Underdown
Officers: Stephen Quinlan, Secretary; Peter John Bridge [1955] Director; Darren Paul Langdon [1977] Operations Director; Paul Marsh [1967] Finance Director; Stephen Quinlan [1961] Managing Director; Michael Montgomery Scott-Underdown [1945] Director; Paul Starkey [1959] Operations Director

Coventry Diocesan Board of Finance (The)
Incorporated: 12 October 1936 *Employees:* 37
Net Worth: £80,830,000 *Total Assets:* £84,892,000
Registered Office: Diocesan Offices, 1 Hill Top, Coventry, Warwicks, CV1 5AB
Activities: Activities of religious organisations
Officers: Ruth Elizabeth Marlow, Secretary; Karen Mary Armbrister [1959] Director/Housewife; The Revd Stella Bailey [1976] Director/Clerk in Holy Orders; Christopher Henry Baker [1947] Director/Retired; Revd Canon Barbara Carol Clutton [1947] Director/Retired; Christopher John Cocksworth [1959] Director/Bishop; Timothy Hugh Day-Pollard [1986] Director/Transport Modeller; The Venerable Susan Elizabeth Field [1959] Director/Archdeacon; Canon Ian Ernest Francis [1938] Director/Retired; The Revd Charlotte Gale [1970] Director/Clerk in Holy Orders; Felicity Hawke [1955] Director/Charity Trustee; Revd Barry Jackson [1965] Director/Clerk in Holy Orders; Rev Nicholas William Michael Leggett [1962] Director/Clerk in Holy Orders; Revd Andrew March [1981] Director/Clerk in Holy Orders; Revd Kate Ishbel Massey [1977] Director/Clerk in Holy Orders; Helen Catherine Perryman [1986] Director/Veterinary Surgeon; The Venerable Morris Rodham [1959] Director/Archdeacon; Peter Charles Rogers [1947] Director/Retired; The Reverend Elaine Scrivens [1953] Director/Clerk in Holy Orders; Helen Simmonds [1951] Director/Retired; David Adrian Stone [1956] Director/Clerk in Holy Orders; The Rt Rev John Ronald Angus Stroyan [1955] Director/Bishop; Dr Jill Tucker [1947] Director/Clerk in Holy Orders; Dr Yvonne Warren [1938] Director/Psychotherapist; David George Wigman [1949] Director/Operations Manager; John Julian Witcombe [1959] Director/Clerk in Holy Orders

Coventry University Enterprises Limited
Incorporated: 31 July 1989 *Employees:* 67
Net Worth: £34,179,000 *Total Assets:* £50,631,000
Registered Office: Company Secretariat, Alan Berry Building, Coventry University, Priory Street, Coventry, Warwicks, CV1 5FB
Activities: Other professional, scientific and technical activities n.e.c.
Parent: Coventry University Higher Education Corporation
Officers: Gemma Louise Towns, Secretary; Nigel John Alcock [1965] Director/Deputy-Vice-Chancellor; Ravinder Singh Bagri [1965] Local Director; Margaret Anne Hoppitt [1962] HR Director; Andrew David Meehan [1955] Director; Frank Mills [1942] Director; Dr Richard Nicholas York Owen [1956] Director; Nicholas John Cameron Sale [1966] Director; Patrick Francis Wright [1962] Director; Nemone Louisa Wynn-Evans [1974] Director

Coveris Flexibles (Gainsborough) UK Limited
Incorporated: 4 June 2003 *Employees:* 1,075
Net Worth: £19,734,000 *Total Assets:* £252,456,992
Registered Office: Holland Place, Wardentree Park, Pinchbeck, Spalding, Lincs, PE11 3ZN
Activities: Manufacture of plastic packing goods
Officers: Trace Lee Norton [1963] Sales Director; Jonathan Pallas [1962] Director; Gary Edward Rehwinkel [1961] Director [American]

Coveris Flexibles Holdings UK Limited
Incorporated: 21 December 2012 *Employees:* 5
Previous: Portugal Topco Limited
Net Worth: £37,164,000 *Total Assets:* £44,130,000
Registered Office: Holland Place, Wardentree Park, Pinchbeck, Spalding, Lincs, PE11 3ZN
Activities: Activities of other holding companies n.e.c.
Officers: Sarah Gooding [1979] Director; Andreas Heigl [1977] Director/Group Treasurer [Austrian]; Jonathan Pallas [1962] Director; Gary Edward Rehwinkel [1961] Director [American]

Coveris Flexibles UK Limited
Incorporated: 4 May 1994 *Employees:* 1,303
Net Worth: £44,968,000 *Total Assets:* £153,338,000
Registered Office: Holland Place, Wardentree Park, Pinchbeck, Spalding, Lincs, PE11 3ZN
Activities: Printing n.e.c.
Officers: Trace Lee Norton [1963] Sales Director; Jonathan Pallas [1962] Director; Dennis Patterson [1959] Director/Operations Manager; Gary Edward Rehwinkel [1961] Director [American]

Coverland UK Limited
Incorporated: 18 January 2000 *Employees:* 3
Net Worth: £2,587,997 *Total Assets:* £12,294,779
Registered Office: Coverland UK Limited, Mansfield Road, Bramley Vale, Chesterfield, Derbys, S44 5GA
Activities: Other letting and operating of own or leased real estate
Major Shareholder: Peter Anderson Hunt
Officers: Angela Suzanne Hunt, Secretary; Peter Anderson Hunt [1960] Director

Coversure Insurance Services Limited
Incorporated: 10 May 1989 *Employees:* 83
Net Worth: £1,818,844 *Total Assets:* £14,732,386
Registered Office: Coversure House, Vantage Park, Washingley Road, Huntingdon, Cambs, PE29 6SR
Activities: Activities of insurance agents and brokers
Parent: C I S G Ltd
Officers: Georgina Elizabeth Bourner, Secretary; Carl Anthony Ashton [1980] Risk and Compliance Director; Cheryl Dawn Astley [1962] Director/Chief Technology Officer; Robert Michael Darling [1963] Finance Director; Sarah Darling [1969] Managing Director; Edward George FitzGenerald Hannan [1978] Director/Chief Financial Officer; Stephen Guy Parker [1965] Group Commercial Director; Christopher James Woosnam [1981] Mergers and Acquisitions Director

Coverworld UK Limited
Incorporated: 19 April 1990 *Employees:* 55
Net Worth: £20,787,740 *Total Assets:* £25,785,004
Registered Office: Mansfield Road, Bramley Vale, Chesterfield, Derbys, S44 5GA
Activities: Forging, pressing, stamping and roll-forming of metal; powder metallurgy
Major Shareholder: Peter Anderson Hunt
Officers: Angela Suzanne Hunt, Secretary; Peter Anderson Hunt [1960] Managing Director

Covrad Heat Transfer Limited
Incorporated: 1 February 1962 *Employees:* 112
Net Worth Deficit: £95,990 *Total Assets:* £13,391,333
Registered Office: Sir Henry Parkes Road, Canley, Coventry, Warwicks, CV5 6BN
Activities: Manufacture of engines and turbines, except aircraft, vehicle and cycle engines
Shareholders: Greg Feldman; William Dawson
Officers: Michael Wayne Bremmer, Secretary; James Michael Laisure [1952] Director [American]; Thomas Gerard Strauss [1957] Director/Chief Finance Officer [American]

Cozart Limited
Incorporated: 27 May 2004
Net Worth: £20,336,000 *Total Assets:* £21,577,000
Registered Office: 21 Blacklands Way, Abingdon, Oxon, OX14 1DY
Activities: Manufacture of medical and dental instruments and supplies
Parent: Alere Toxicology PLC
Officers: Paolo Beato [1961] Director of Information Technology; Nicholas Anthony Breare [1972] Director/Accountant

CP Elveden Village Limited
Incorporated: 2 June 2011 *Employees:* 5
Net Worth: £81,200,000 *Total Assets:* £263,800,000
Registered Office: One Edison Rise, New Ollerton, Newark, Notts, NG22 9DP
Activities: Other letting and operating of own or leased real estate
Parent: Center Parcs (Holdings 3) Limited
Officers: Rajbinder Singh Dehal, Secretary; Natalie Johanna Adomait [1989] Director [Canadian]; Martin Peter Dalby [1961] Director; Kevin O'Donnell McCrain [1979] Director [American]; Colin Grant McKinlay [1969] Director; Zachary Bryan Vaughan [1977] Director [Canadian]

CP Longleat Village Limited
Incorporated: 2 June 2011
Net Worth: £98,600,000 *Total Assets:* £98,600,000
Registered Office: One Edison Rise, New Ollerton, Newark, Notts, NG22 9DP
Activities: Other letting and operating of own or leased real estate
Parent: Center Parcs (Holdings 3) Limited
Officers: Rajbinder Singh Dehal, Secretary; Natalie Johanna Adomait [1989] Director [Canadian]; Martin Peter Dalby [1961] Director; Kevin O'Donnell McCrain [1979] Director [American]; Colin Grant McKinlay [1969] Director; Zachary Bryan Vaughan [1977] Director [Canadian]

CP Sherwood Village Limited
Incorporated: 25 May 2011
Net Worth: £80,700,000 *Total Assets:* £276,800,000
Registered Office: One Edison Rise, New Ollerton, Newark, Notts, NG22 9DP
Activities: Other letting and operating of own or leased real estate
Parent: Center Parcs (Holdings 3) Limited
Officers: Rajbinder Singh Dehal, Secretary; Natalie Johanna Adomait [1989] Director [Canadian]; Martin Peter Dalby [1961] Director; Kevin O'Donnell McCrain [1979] Director [American]; Colin Grant McKinlay [1969] Director; Zachary Bryan Vaughan [1977] Director [Canadian]

CP Whinfell Village Limited
Incorporated: 2 June 2011
Net Worth: £63,700,000 *Total Assets:* £268,400,000
Registered Office: One Edison Rise, New Ollerton, Newark, Notts, NG22 9DP
Activities: Other letting and operating of own or leased real estate
Parent: Center Parcs (Holdings 3) Limited
Officers: Rajbinder Singh Dehal, Secretary; Natalie Johanna Adomait [1989] Director [Canadian]; Martin Peter Dably [1961] Director; Kevin O'Donnell McCrain [1979] Director [American]; Colin Grant McKinlay [1969] Director; Zachary Bryan Vaughan [1977] Director [Canadian]

CP Woburn (Operating Company) Limited
Incorporated: 2 June 2011 *Employees:* 1,657
Net Worth: £22,400,000 *Total Assets:* £460,500,000
Registered Office: One Edison Rise, New Ollerton, Newark, Notts, NG22 9DP
Activities: Other accommodation
Parent: Center Parcs (Holdings 3) Limited
Officers: Rajbinder Singh-Dehal, Secretary; Natalie Johanna Adomait [1989] Director [Canadian]; Martin Peter Dalby [1961] Director; Kevin O'Donnell McCrain [1979] Director [American]; Colin Grant McKinlay [1969] Director; Zachary Bryan Vaughan [1977] Director [Canadian]

CPC Foods Limited
Incorporated: 5 April 2011 *Employees:* 397
Net Worth: £10,069,838 *Total Assets:* £50,807,104
Registered Office: Oak House, Heyford Close, Aldermans Green, Coventry, Warwicks, CV2 2QB
Activities: Processing and preserving of meat
Parent: Tonnies Holding GmbH & Co KG
Officers: Heike Roschkowski, Secretary; Carl Ernst Burger [1987] Director [German]; Frank Duffe [1960] Director [German]; Carsten Svejgaard Jakobsen [1945] Director [Danish]

CPF Commercial Limited
Incorporated: 28 November 2014 *Employees:* 112
Net Worth: £6,157,204 *Total Assets:* £11,717,380
Registered Office: Station Road, Stoney Stanton, Leicester, LE9 4LX
Activities: Activities of other holding companies n.e.c.
Major Shareholder: Christopher Paul Fox
Officers: Christopher Paul Fox [1968] Director

CPG 2016 Limited
Incorporated: 18 March 2016 *Employees:* 2
Net Worth: £1,281,372 *Total Assets:* £11,393,989
Registered Office: 56 London Road, Alderley Edge, Cheshire, SK9 7DZ
Activities: Other letting and operating of own or leased real estate
Major Shareholder: Peter Stuart Dawson
Officers: William Marshall Smith, Secretary; Peter Stuart Dawson [1952] Director/Chartered Surveyor; William Marshall Smith [1955] Director/Solicitor

CPL Aromas (Holdings) Limited
Incorporated: 13 September 1999 *Employees:* 485
Net Worth: £51,051,000 *Total Assets:* £72,196,000
Registered Office: CPL Aromas, Quarry Road, Brixworth, Northampton, NN6 9UB
Activities: Manufacture of perfumes and toilet preparations
Officers: Philip Jonathan Gardner, Secretary; Bruce Forbes [1956] IT Director; Philip Jonathan Gardner [1963] Finance Director; Peter Jonathan Jacobs [1955] Director; Anthony Ewart Lloyd [1973] Director; Christopher Pickthall [1968] Director; Francis Pickthall [1967] Director; Nicholas Pickthall [1976] Director; Terence Pickthall [1939] Director

CPL Aromas Limited
Incorporated: 16 November 1971 *Employees:* 535
Net Worth: £66,265,000 *Total Assets:* £93,899,000
Registered Office: CPL Aromas Limited, Quarry Road, Brixworth, Northampton, NN6 9UB
Activities: Manufacture of perfumes and toilet preparations
Parent: CPL Aromas Holdings Limited
Officers: Philip Jonathan Gardner, Secretary; Bruce Forbes [1956] IT Director; Philip Jonathan Gardner [1963] Finance Director; Peter Jonathan Jacobs [1955] Director; Anthony Ewart Lloyd [1973] Director; Christopher Pickthall [1968] Director; Francis Pickthall [1967] Director; Nicholas Pickthall [1976] Director; Terence Pickthall [1939] Director/Chairman

CPL Distribution Limited
Incorporated: 19 February 1955 *Employees:* 389
Net Worth: £24,641,000 *Total Assets:* £47,141,000
Registered Office: Westthorpe Fields Road, Killamarsh, Sheffield, S21 1TZ
Activities: Wholesale of other fuels and related products
Shareholders: SG Hambros Limited; Heptagon Limited; Julian Paul Vivian Mash
Officers: Richard John Barber [1961] Director; Julian David Martin [1971] Sales Director; Timothy William Minett [1960] Managing Director; Jason David Sutton [1982] Director/Accountant; Mark Noel Whiteley [1969] Director/Accountant

CPL Industries Group Limited
Incorporated: 25 July 2011 *Employees:* 663
Net Worth: £28,700,000 *Total Assets:* £112,000,000
Registered Office: Westthorpe Fields Road, Killamarsh, Sheffield, S21 1TZ
Activities: Activities of head offices
Shareholders: Julian Mash; SG Hambros Limited
Officers: Robert Bradley Kendall [1973] Director/Investment Manager; David John Lamb [1976] Director/Investor; Timothy William Minett [1960] Director; Jason David Sutton [1982] Director

CPL Industries Holdings Limited
Incorporated: 24 March 2006
Net Worth: £1,960,000 *Total Assets:* £57,447,000
Registered Office: Westthorpe Fields Road, Killamarsh, Sheffield, S21 1TZ
Activities: Activities of head offices
Shareholders: Julian Paul Vivian Mash; S G Hambros Limited; CPL Industries Group Limited
Officers: Robert Bradley Kendall [1973] Director; Timothy William Minett [1960] Director; Jason David Sutton [1982] Director/Accountant

CPL Industries Limited
Incorporated: 22 November 1994 *Employees:* 51
Net Worth: £184,914,000 *Total Assets:* £210,672,000
Registered Office: Westthorpe Fields Road, Killamarsh, Sheffield, S21 1TZ
Activities: Activities of head offices
Shareholders: SG Hambros Limited; CPL Industries Holdings Limited; Julian Paul Vivian Mash
Officers: Timothy William Minett [1960] Managing Director; David Steven Morgan [1976] Director/Solicitor; Peter Scott [1953] Director; Jason David Sutton [1982] Director/Chartered Accountant

CPRT (Europe) Limited
Incorporated: 19 September 2012
Net Worth: £32,841,488 *Total Assets:* £33,583,692
Registered Office: Acrey Fields, Woburn Road, Wootton, Beds, MK43 9EJ
Activities: Sale of other motor vehicles
Parent: Universal Salvage Limited
Officers: Aaron Jayson Adair [1969] Director/Chief Executive Officer [American]; Jonathan David Canning [1972] Director/General Counsel; Gregory Depasquale [1968] Director/SVP, General Counsel and Secretary of Copart, Inc [American]; William Easley Franklin [1956] Director/Chief Financial Officer [American]; Nigel James Paget [1966] Managing Director

CPRT European Investments Limited
Incorporated: 22 July 2016
Net Worth: £34,715,160 *Total Assets:* £34,716,916
Registered Office: Acrey Fields, Woburn Road, Wootton, Beds, MK43 9EJ
Activities: Financial management
Parent: Universal Salvage Limited
Officers: Aaron Jayson Adair [1969] Director/Chief Executive Officer [American]; Jonathan David Canning [1972] Director/General Counsel; Gregory Depasquale [1968] Director/SVP, General Counsel and Secretary of Copart, Inc [American]; William Easley Franklin [1956] Director/Executive Vice President of Copart, Inc [American]; Nigel James Paget [1966] Managing Director

CPRT LLP
Incorporated: 27 November 2013
Net Worth: £175,546,000 *Total Assets:* £175,546,000
Registered Office: Acrey Fields, Woburn Road, Wootton, Beds, MK43 9EJ

Crabwall Claremont Limited
Incorporated: 13 September 2005 *Employees:* 142
Net Worth Deficit: £1,773,000 *Total Assets:* £29,788,000
Registered Office: Norcliffe House, Station Road, Wilmslow, Cheshire, SK9 1BU
Activities: Other human health activities
Parent: Optimum Debtco Limited
Officers: Abigail Mattison, Secretary; Ryan Stuart MacAskill [1975] Director; Gregory Laurence Newman [1988] Director/Investment Professional; Jeremy Robert Arthur Richardson [1970] Director; Dr Maureen Claire Royston [1960] Director; Phillip Gary Thomas [1978] Director

Cranbrook (Jewellers) Ltd
Incorporated: 7 July 1989 *Employees:* 67
Net Worth: £9,323,598 *Total Assets:* £10,092,124
Registered Office: 8 Haymarket, Leicester, LE1 3GD
Activities: Retail sale of watches and jewellery in specialised stores
Major Shareholder: Richard Hunnisett
Officers: Richard Hunnisett [1957] Director/Jeweller/Pawnbroker

Cranford Asset Management Limited
Incorporated: 14 December 1962 *Employees:* 2
Net Worth: £8,830,644 *Total Assets:* £9,619,141
Registered Office: Artisans' House, 7 Queensbridge, Northampton, NN4 7BF
Activities: Mixed farming
Major Shareholder: Andrew Grant Robinson
Officers: Andrew Grant Robinson, Secretary/Sales Director; Andrew Grant Robinson [1971] Sales Director; Kenneth John Robinson [1933] Director; Margaret Christine Robinson [1935] Director

Cranford House School Trust Limited
Incorporated: 1 August 1980 *Employees:* 119
Net Worth: £6,196,449 *Total Assets:* £13,249,350
Registered Office: Cranford House School, Moulsford, Wallingford, Oxon, OX10 9HT
Activities: Pre-primary education
Officers: Jim Clarke [1970] Director/Chartered Accountant; Dr Robert Fisher [1960] Director/Senior Manager; Alison Gray [1946] Director; Lucy Franziska Kilroy [1971] Director/Senior Counsel; Amanda Page [1976] Director/Lawyer; Natalie Jane Scott-Ely [1967] Director; Peter Thomas [1973] Director/Deputy Head; Paul Tollet [1961] Director/Business Executive; Stuart Kenneth Wallis [1977] Executive Director

A.R. Craven Farms Limited
Incorporated: 19 October 1995 *Employees:* 14
Net Worth: £5,578,680 *Total Assets:* £12,453,849
Registered Office: Poplar Farm, Main Road, Stickford, Boston, Lincs, PE22 8EL
Activities: Mixed farming
Major Shareholder: Andrew Robert Craven
Officers: Judith Mary Craven, Secretary; Andrew Robert Craven [1961] Director/Farmer; Judith Mary Craven [1962] Director

Creating Tomorrow Multi Academy Trust
Incorporated: 16 January 2015 *Employees:* 95
Previous: Isebrook SEN Cognition & Learning College
Net Worth: £10,967,979 *Total Assets:* £12,138,380
Registered Office: Isebrook SEN College, Eastleigh Road, Kettering, Northants, NN15 6PT
Activities: Other education n.e.c.
Officers: Elinor Edwards, Secretary; Andrew John Bailey [1969] Assistant Director of Student Services; Ann Botterill [1941] Director/Retired; Jane Louise Boyt [1963] Director/Change Management Consultant; Kevin John Latham [1973] Director/Headteacher; Peter Fenwick Maddison [1954] Director/Retired; Jeannette Payne [1961] Director/Hospital Matron; Linda Saunders [1954] Finance Director

Cresta Court Hotel Holdings Limited
Incorporated: 13 February 2017 *Employees:* 84
Net Worth: £4,287,440 *Total Assets:* £12,797,193
Registered Office: c/o Director of Finance, Kenwood Hall Hotel, Kenwood Road, Sheffield, S7 1NQ
Activities: Other business support service activities n.e.c.
Shareholder: Gregory Dyke
Officers: Andrew Rouse, Secretary; Garin James Davies [1967] Director; Gregory Dyke [1947] Director; Andrew Gerard Rouse [1960] Director

Crestchic Limited
Incorporated: 24 November 1983 *Employees:* 82
Net Worth: £16,523,000 *Total Assets:* £23,240,000
Registered Office: Second Avenue, Centrum 100, Burton on Trent, Staffs, DE14 2WF
Activities: Manufacture of electric motors, generators and transformers
Parent: Northbridge Industrial Services PLC
Officers: Iwan Phillips, Secretary; Eric Ward Hook [1953] Director; Iwan Ceri Phillips [1984] Director/Chartered Accountant

CRH Fencing & Security Group (UK) Ltd
Incorporated: 29 July 1993 *Employees:* 305
Net Worth: £9,989,000 *Total Assets:* £18,732,000
Registered Office: Herons Way, Carr Hill, Balby, Doncaster, S Yorks, DN4 8WA
Activities: Other specialised construction activities n.e.c.
Parent: CRH (UK) Ltd
Officers: Darren Harrison [1975] Service Director; Andrew McMenzie [1967] Director/UK Country Manager; Gilles Rabot [1971] Director [French]; Hans Welting [1956] Managing Director [Dutch]; Michael Wightman [1961] Director

Cristal Inorganic Chemicals UK Limited
Incorporated: 19 March 2007 *Employees:* 3
Net Worth: £305,355,008 *Total Assets:* £305,355,008
Registered Office: Laporte Road, Stallingborough, Grimsby, N E Lincs, DN40 2PR
Activities: Activities of other holding companies n.e.c.
Parent: Cristal Inorganic Chemicals Netherlands B.V.
Officers: Maria Jegher, Secretary; Stephen Anthony Box [1959] Director/Financial Controller; Dr Robert McIntyre [1955] European Director of Technology and Innovation; Robert John Sarracini [1976] Site Director [British/Australian]

Cristal Investments UK Limited
Incorporated: 14 December 2011 *Employees:* 3
Net Worth: £60,621,304 *Total Assets:* £60,621,300
Registered Office: Laporte Road, Stallingborough, Grimsby, N E Lincs, DN40 2PR
Activities: Non-trading company
Parent: Millennium Inorganic Chemicals Overseas Holdings
Officers: Maria Jegher, Secretary; Stephen Anthony Box [1959] Director/Financial Controller; Dr Robert McIntyre [1955] European Director of Technology and Innovation; Robert John Sarracini [1976] Site Director [British/Australian]

Cristal Pigment UK Limited
Incorporated: 1 January 1920 *Employees:* 376
Net Worth: £311,062,016 *Total Assets:* £528,820,000
Registered Office: Laporte Road, Stallingborough, Grimsby, N E Lincs, DN40 2PR
Activities: Manufacture of other inorganic basic chemicals
Parent: Millennium Inorganic Chemicals Overseas Holdings
Officers: Maria Jegher, Secretary; Paul Andrew Hannington Barnett [1978] Director/Accountant; Stephen Anthony Box [1959] Director/Financial Controller; Koen Felix Lodewijk Docx [1974] Director/Finance Manager [Belgian]; Dr Robert McIntyre [1955] Commercial Research Director; Simon Morten [1957] Site Director; Robert John Sarracini [1976] Site Director [British/Australian]; Catherine Jane Simpson [1975] Director/Accountant

Crockett and Jones Limited
Incorporated: 7 April 1948 *Employees:* 413
Net Worth: £27,423,000 *Total Assets:* £31,254,000
Registered Office: 27 Perry Street, Northampton, NN1 4HN
Activities: Manufacture of footwear
Officers: Adam Coles, Secretary; Jonathan Philip Marshall Jones [1953] Director/Footwear Manufacturer; Nicholas Marshall Jones [1951] Director/Footwear Manufacturer; Mark Roland Wilson Jones [1956] Director/Academic

Croda Europe Limited
Incorporated: 7 May 1920 *Employees:* 918
Net Worth: £323,012,992 *Total Assets:* £513,164,992
Registered Office: Cowick Hall, Snaith, Goole, E Yorks, DN14 9AA
Activities: Manufacture of pesticides and other agrochemical products
Parent: Croda Investments No 3 Limited
Officers: Thomas Michael Brophy, Secretary; Stuart Arnott [1966] Director/President - Operations; Sandra Elaine Breene [1968] Managing Director; Thomas Michael Brophy [1973] Director/Group General Counsel and Company Secretary; Martin Conleth Campbell [1968] Finance Director; Anthony Damien Fitzpatrick [1968] Director/President Corporate Development; Stephen Edward Foots [1968] Director/Chief Executive; Maarten Willem Heijbroek [1965] Director/Sector President [Dutch]; Paul Anthony Newton [1967] Director/Management Accountant

Croda International Public Limited Company
Incorporated: 22 May 1925 *Employees:* 4,270
Net Worth: £822,300,032 *Total Assets:* £1,648,700,032
Registered Office: Cowick Hall, Snaith, Goole, E Yorks, DN14 9AA
Activities: Activities of head offices
Officers: Thomas Michael Brophy, Secretary; Roberto Cirillo [1971] Director/General Manager [Swiss]; Alan Murray Ferguson [1958] Director/Chartered Accountant; Jacqueline Patricia Christine Ferguson [1970] Director; Stephen Edward Foots [1968] Director/Chief Executive; Anita Margaret Frew [1957] Director; Doctor Helena Louise Ganczakowski [1962] Director; Dr Keith Layden [1959] Director/Chief Technology Officer; Jeremy Kim Maiden [1961] Director/Accountant; Stephen Geoffrey Williams [1948] Director

Croda Investments Limited
Incorporated: 27 November 2012 *Employees:* 2
Net Worth: £345,567,648 *Total Assets:* £366,340,000
Registered Office: Cowick Hall, Snaith, Goole, E Yorks, DN14 9AA
Activities: Non-trading company
Parent: Croda Overseas Holdings Limited
Officers: Jeremy Kim Maiden [1961] Director/Accountant; Graham Lloyd Myers [1963] Director/Group Financial Controller

Croda Investments No 2 Limited
Incorporated: 27 November 2012 *Employees:* 2
Net Worth: £104,165,944 *Total Assets:* £470,505,952
Registered Office: Cowick Hall, Snaith, Goole, E Yorks, DN14 9AA
Activities: Non-trading company
Parent: Croda Investments Inc
Officers: Jeremy Kim Maiden [1961] Director/Accountant; Graham Lloyd Myers [1963] Director/Group Financial Controller

Croda Investments No 3 Limited
Incorporated: 22 December 2015 *Employees:* 2
Net Worth: £232,650,000 *Total Assets:* £2,201,199,104
Registered Office: Cowick Hall, Snaith, Goole, E Yorks, DN14 9AA
Activities: Activities of head offices
Parent: Croda International PLC
Officers: Jeremy Kim Maiden [1961] Director; Graham Lloyd Myers [1963] Director

Croda Overseas Holdings Limited
Incorporated: 25 April 1997 *Employees:* 2
Net Worth: £373,454,656 *Total Assets:* £536,140,160
Registered Office: Cowick Hall, Snaith, Goole, E Yorks, DN14 9AA
Activities: Activities of head offices
Parent: Croda Investments No 3 Limited
Officers: Thomas Michael Brophy, Secretary; Stephen Edward Foots [1968] Director/Chief Executive; Graham Lloyd Myers [1963] Director/Group Financial Controller

Cromwell Community College
Incorporated: 16 March 2012 *Employees:* 167
Net Worth: £14,672,426 *Total Assets:* £18,111,240
Registered Office: Cromwell Community College, Wenny Road, Chatteris, Cambs, PE16 6UU
Activities: General secondary education
Officers: Karen Jarvis, Secretary; Lesley Patricia Adams [1955] Director/Retired; David John Bateson [1955] Director/Executive Principal; Jeremy Beswick [1958] Director/Consultant; Dr Adam David Boddison [1981] Director; Clive Robert James Bush [1951] Director/Retired; Jacqueline Cutchey [1950] Director/Retired; The Hon Richard Gregory Hely-Hutchinson [1980] Director and Company Secretary; Mark Andrew Kerr [1968] Director/Bank Manager; Marion Lloyd [1951] Director/Education Consultant; Gary Patrick Peile [1956] Director

Cromwell Group (Holdings) Limited
Incorporated: 27 September 1983 *Employees:* 1,654
Net Worth: £21,595,000 *Total Assets:* £175,218,000
Registered Office: P O Box 14, Chartwell Drive, Wigston, Leicester, LE18 1AT
Activities: Activities of distribution holding companies
Parent: GWW UK Holdings Limited
Officers: Horace Vincent Draa III, Secretary; Fred James Costello Jr [1960] Director/Business Executive [American]; Horace Vincent Draa III [1956] Director/Executive [American]; Neil Lawrence Jowsey [1964] Director/Business Executive; Richard Kevin Pott [1980] Director/Business Executive [American]

Cromwell Logistics Limited
Incorporated: 28 July 1975
Net Worth: £4,035,000 *Total Assets:* £128,856,000
Registered Office: P O Box 14, Chartwell Drive, Wigston, Leicester, LE18 1AT
Activities: Operation of warehousing and storage facilities for land transport activities
Parent: Cromwell Group (Holdings) Limited
Officers: Horace Vincent Draa III, Secretary; Fred James Costello Jr [1960] Director/Business Executive [American]; Horace Vincent Draa III [1956] Director/Business Executive [American]; Neil Lawrence Jowsey [1964] Director/Business Executive; Richard Kevin Pott [1980] Director/Business Executive [American]

Cromwell Tools Limited
Incorporated: 5 August 1970 *Employees:* 1,083
Net Worth: £75,252,000 *Total Assets:* £240,836,992
Registered Office: P O Box 14, Chartwell Drive, Wigston, Leicester, LE18 1AT
Activities: Non-specialised wholesale trade
Parent: Cronmwell Group (Holdings) Limited
Officers: Horace Vincent Draa III, Secretary; Fred James Costello Jr [1960] Director/Business Executive [American]; Horace Vincent Draa III [1956] Director/Business Executive [American]; Neil Lawrence Jowsey [1964] Director/Business Executive; Richard Kevin Pott [1980] Director/Business Executive [American]

Croner Group Limited
Incorporated: 16 August 2013 *Employees:* 260
Net Worth: £8,903,893 *Total Assets:* £13,843,029
Registered Office: Croner House, Wheatfield Way, Hinckley, Leics, LE10 1YG
Activities: Activities of patent and copyright agents; other legal activities n.e.c.
Parent: Peninsula Business Services Group Limited
Officers: Darren Stuart Chadwick [1970] Sales Training and Development Director; Peter Eric Done [1947] Director; Alan Price [1978] Director; David Price [1978] Sales & Marketing Director; Peter Nicholas Swift [1958] Director

Crossfleet Limited
Incorporated: 12 August 1998
Net Worth: £15,511,000 *Total Assets:* £38,574,000
Registered Office: Litchurch Lane, Derby, DE24 8AD
Activities: Manufacture of railway locomotives and rolling stock
Parent: Prorail Limited
Officers: Lynn Suzanne West, Secretary; Garry John Mowbray [1970] Director, Controlling; Katherine Mari Parkes [1976] Director/Solicitor

Maurice Crouch (Growers) Limited
Incorporated: 24 October 1944 *Employees:* 18
Net Worth: £17,717,880 *Total Assets:* £22,013,528
Registered Office: 12-13 The Crescent, Wisbech, Cambs, PE13 1EH
Activities: Growing of cereals (except rice), leguminous crops and oil seeds
Major Shareholder: Judith Anne Fairey
Officers: Peter Donald Cornwell, Secretary; Judith Anne Fairey [1944] Director; Michael David Richardson Fairey [1968] Director/Farmer; Nigel Verden Miller Walker [1947] Farm Director

Croupier Underwriting Limited
Incorporated: 28 August 2001
Net Worth: £2,572,796 *Total Assets:* £14,158,045
Registered Office: 3 Castlegate, Grantham, Lincs, NG31 6SF
Activities: Non-life insurance
Major Shareholder: Mark Ellwood Brockbank
Officers: Elizabeth Brockbank [1925] Director/Housewife; John Timothy Brockbank [1958] Director/Farmer; Stephen Routh Brockbank [1953] Director/Farmer

Crowcon Detection Instruments Limited
Incorporated: 6 May 1970 *Employees:* 184
Net Worth: £15,074,928 *Total Assets:* £23,237,412
Registered Office: 172 Brook Drive, Milton Park, Milton, Abingdon, Oxon, OX14 4SD
Activities: Manufacture of electronic measuring, testing etc. equipment, not for industrial process control
Parent: Halma PLC
Officers: Terence Michael McCarthy, Secretary; James Gravestock [1971] Managing Director; Frazer MacKay [1971] Operations Director; Terence Michael McCarthy [1965] Finance Director

Crowland Cranes Limited
Incorporated: 5 May 1995 *Employees:* 54
Net Worth: £7,402,271 *Total Assets:* £11,713,837
Registered Office: Crease Drove, Crowland, Peterborough, PE6 0BN
Activities: Other specialised construction activities n.e.c.
Parent: Crowland Cranes (Holdings) Limited
Officers: Jennifer Margaret Issitt, Secretary; Jennifer Margaret Issitt [1971] Director/Secretary; Peter James Issitt [1972] Director/Crane Engineer

Crown Aerosols UK Ltd
Incorporated: 14 May 1935 *Employees:* 369
Net Worth: £24,321,000 *Total Assets:* £45,701,000
Registered Office: Downsview Road, Wantage, Oxon, OX12 9BP
Activities: Manufacture of light metal packaging
Parent: Crown Packaging Manufacturing UK Limited
Officers: Jennifer Patricia Simpson, Secretary; Paul William Browett [1961] Director/VP/Treasurer; Jean-Francois Lelouch [1967] Director/Assistant General Counsel [French]; Laurent Watteaux [1972] Director/VP Aerosols & Promotional Packaging [French]

Crown Crest (Holdings) PLC
Incorporated: 28 September 1994 *Employees:* 3
Net Worth: £7,729,174 *Total Assets:* £12,965,969
Registered Office: 50 Woodgate, Leicester, LE3 5GF
Activities: Other letting and operating of own or leased real estate
Officers: Abdul Rashid Tayub, Secretary; Abdul Rashid Tayub [1948] Director; Sakil Rashid Tayub [1969] Director

Crown Crest (Leicester) PLC
Incorporated: 15 March 2002
Net Worth: £95,911,848 *Total Assets:* £125,215,312
Registered Office: Crown Crest, Desford Lane, Kirby Muxloe, Leics, LE9 2BJ
Activities: Non-specialised wholesale trade
Major Shareholder: Abdul Aziz Tayub
Officers: Hemant Patel, Secretary; Graham John Page [1949] Director; Hemant Patel [1961] Finance Director; Abdul Aziz Tayub [1955] Director; Shehzad Tayub [1985] Commercial Director

Crown Crest Group Limited
Incorporated: 7 February 2006 *Employees:* 5,725
Net Worth: £101,812,080 *Total Assets:* £188,994,976
Registered Office: Crown Crest, Desford Lane, Kirby Muxloe, Leics, LE9 2BJ
Activities: Activities of other holding companies n.e.c.
Major Shareholder: Abdul Aziz Tayub
Officers: Hemant Patel, Secretary; Graham John Page [1949] Director; Hemant Patel [1961] Finance Director; Abdul Aziz Tayub [1955] Managing Director; Shehzad Tayub [1985] Commercial Director

Crown UK Holdings Limited
Incorporated: 3 April 1996
Net Worth Deficit: £132,932,000 *Total Assets:* £427,123,008
Registered Office: Downsview Road, Wantage, Oxon, OX12 9BP
Activities: Activities of head offices
Parent: Crown Canadian Holdings ULC
Officers: Jennifer Patricia Simpson, Secretary; John Patrick Beardsley [1970] Director; Timothy Joseph Donahue [1962] Director/President/Chief Operating Officer [American]; Thomas Anthony Kelly [1959] Director/SVP/CFO [American]

Ivor Crowson Developments (Stamford) Limited
Incorporated: 10 January 1975 *Employees:* 4
Net Worth: £6,394,913 *Total Assets:* £10,990,456
Registered Office: Manor Stone House, Barnack, Stamford, Lincs, PE9 3DW
Activities: Development of building projects
Shareholders: Ivor Crowson; Marion Rose Crowson
Officers: Marion Rose Crowson, Secretary; Ivor Crowson [1946] Director; Julia Honey Crowson [1975] Director; Marion Rose Crowson [1946] Director; Nicholas Ivor Crowson [1972] Director

CRT Property Investments Limited
Incorporated: 29 January 2013 *Employees:* 2
Net Worth: £17,548,000 *Total Assets:* £40,237,000
Registered Office: 1 Waterside Park, Valley Way, Wombwell, Barnsley, S Yorks, S73 0BB
Activities: Other letting and operating of own or leased real estate
Parent: The Coalfields Regeneration Trust
Officers: Louise Dyson, Secretary; Louise Dyson [1978] Director/Accountant; Gary Edward Ellis [1958] Director/Accountant; Terence Patrick O'Neill [1947] Director/Councillor; Nicholas Garson Wilson [1950] Director/Trade Union Official

Cruickshank Motors Limited
Incorporated: 1 August 1984 *Employees:* 1,104
Net Worth: £34,141,000 *Total Assets:* £178,550,000
Registered Office: 2 Penman Way, Grove Park, Leicester, LE19 1ST
Activities: Sale of new cars and light motor vehicles
Parent: Sytner Group Limited
Officers: Adam Collinson, Secretary; Adam Collinson [1972] Finance Director; Darren Edwards [1968] Managing Director; Robert Harold Kurnick [1961] Director/Executive Vice President [American]; Jeremy Richard Mallett [1952] Director; Gerard Edward Nieuwenhuys [1960] Director; Laurence Edward William Vaughan [1963] Managing Director

Crystal Martin Holdings Limited
Incorporated: 28 December 1922 *Employees:* 3
Net Worth: £31,327,000 *Total Assets:* £34,015,000
Registered Office: Calladine Park, Orchard Way, Sutton in Ashfield, Notts, NG17 1GX
Activities: Manufacture of other women's outerwear
Parent: Crystal Martins Limited
Officers: Crispin John Hallam, Secretary; Christopher Ellis [1966] Finance Director; Anthony Nigel Clifton Griffiths [1943] Director; Ching Leung Andrew Lo [1965] Director [Canadian]; Lok Fung Kenneth Lo [1938] Director; Yuk Ching Yvonne Lo Choy [1945] Director; Darren James Shacklock [1968] Managing Director

Crystal Martin International Limited
Incorporated: 28 May 1964 *Employees:* 327
Net Worth: £26,152,722 *Total Assets:* £70,101,504
Registered Office: Calladine Park, Orchard Way, Sutton in Ashfield, Notts, NG17 1GX
Activities: Manufacture of other women's outerwear
Parent: Crystal Martin Holdings Limited
Officers: Crispin John Hallam, Secretary; Christopher Ellis [1966] Finance Director; Ching Leung Andrew Lo [1965] Director [Canadian]; Lok Fung Kenneth Lo [1938] Director; Yuk Ching Yvonne Lo Choy [1945] Director; Darren James Shacklock [1968] Managing Director

CTDI Glenrothes Limited
Incorporated: 4 July 1977 *Employees:* 397
Previous: Regenersis (Glenrothes) Ltd
Net Worth: £8,116,000 *Total Assets:* £15,495,000
Registered Office: CTDI Ltd, Featherstone Road, Wolverton Mill, Milton Keynes, Bucks, MK12 5TH
Activities: Manufacture of computers and peripheral equipment
Parent: Regenersis (Depot) Services Ltd
Officers: Richard Kieselstein [1977] Director [Hungarian]; Generald Joseph Parsons [1952] Director/Chairman & CEO [American]; Leo David Parsons [1960] Director/President & COO [American]; Scott Thomas Taylor [1976] Director

CTDI Repair Services Limited
Incorporated: 27 January 2016
Net Worth: £92,146,536 *Total Assets:* £92,669,624
Registered Office: CTDI Repair Services Limited, Featherstone Road, Wolverton Mill, Milton Keynes, Bucks, MK12 5TH
Activities: Repair of other equipment
Parent: CTDI Holdings Limited
Officers: Matthew James Bull [1975] Managing Director; Dieter Hollenbach [1964] Director [German]; Brian Christopher Parsons [1979] Director/Vice President [American]; Generald Joseph Parsons [1952] Director/Chairman [American]; Leo David Parsons [1960] Director/President [American]; Monika Rueth [1968] Director [German]

Cullingworth Commercials and Freight Services Limited
Incorporated: 11 July 1983 *Employees:* 53
Net Worth: £26,978,080 *Total Assets:* £30,239,464
Registered Office: 1 Pinnacle Way, Pride Park, Derby, DE24 8ZS
Activities: Freight transport by road
Major Shareholder: Roger David Feather
Officers: Roger David Feather, Secretary; Roger David Feather [1959] Director

Cullum Detuners Investments Limited
Incorporated: 1 March 1993 *Employees:* 179
Net Worth: £6,367,000 *Total Assets:* £24,532,000
Registered Office: Adams Close, Heanor Gate Industrial Park, Heanor, Derby, DE75 7SW
Activities: Financial intermediation not elsewhere classified
Parent: Cullum Trustees Limited
Officers: Ivor James Sellers Kirkman, Secretary; Michael George Gilbert [1951] Director; David John Leverton [1935] Director; Alan Leonard Walker [1947] Director/Chartered Tax Adviser

Cullum Detuners Limited
Incorporated: 26 May 1955 *Employees:* 173
Net Worth: £2,568,000 *Total Assets:* £20,146,000
Registered Office: Adams Close, Heanor Gate Industrial Park, Heanor, Derbys, DE75 7SW
Activities: Manufacture of metal structures and parts of structures
Parent: Cullum Detuners Investments Limited
Officers: Amanda Gent, Secretary; Amanda Gent [1972] Financial Director; Mark George [1968] Director/Sales Engineer; Mark Jansen [1979] Managing Director

W. Cumber & Son (Theale) Limited
Incorporated: 1 October 1949 *Employees:* 8
Net Worth: £49,178,868 *Total Assets:* £65,017,084
Registered Office: Manor Farm, Marcham, Abingdon, Oxon, OX13 6NZ
Activities: Mixed farming
Shareholder: W. Cumber & Son Limited
Officers: William John Cumber, Secretary; William John Cumber [1979] Director/Property Manager; Christopher Dolley [1963] Property Director

Cummins Generator Technologies Limited
Incorporated: 27 August 1947 *Employees:* 607
Net Worth: £2,401,757,952 *Total Assets:* £2,536,200,960
Registered Office: Fountain Court, Lynch Wood, Peterborough, Cambs, PE2 6FZ
Activities: Manufacture of electric motors, generators and transformers
Parent: Cummins EMEA Holdings Limited
Officers: Joseph Morgan Rigler, Secretary; John McCormack Barrowman [1952] Director/VP Operations; Rafael Villaneva Hernandez [1963] Director/Manager [Mexican]; Antonio Leitao [1964] Director [French]; Desmond Joseph McMenamin [1978] Director/General Manager; Joseph Morgan Rigler [1980] Director/Lawyer; Edward David Smith [1976] Director/Chartered Accountant; Alexey Ustinov [1970] Managing Director [Russian]

Brian Currie (Milton Keynes) Limited
Incorporated: 30 March 1982 *Employees:* 150
Net Worth: £2,391,078 *Total Assets:* £13,893,238
Registered Office: Chancery House, 199 Silbury Boulevard, Milton Keynes, Bucks, MK9 1JL
Activities: Sale of other motor vehicles
Shareholders: Patricia Currie; Brian Currie
Officers: Patricia Currie, Secretary; Desmond Patrick Conway [1959] Financial Director; Brian Currie [1953] Director; Patricia Currie [1946] Director; Thomas William Osborne [1979] Director

J. Curtis & Sons (Holdings) Limited
Incorporated: 11 October 2012 *Employees:* 2
Net Worth: £55,353 *Total Assets:* £10,064,585
Registered Office: Thrupp Lane, Radley, Abingdon, Oxon, OX14 3NQ
Activities: Activities of head offices
Major Shareholder: John Andrew Howard Curtis
Officers: John Andrew Howard Curtis [1942] Director; John Godfrey MacDonald [1931] Director

J. Curtis & Sons Limited
Incorporated: 3 December 1948 *Employees:* 4
Net Worth: £20,458,212 *Total Assets:* £21,303,880
Registered Office: Radley, Thrupp Lane, Abingdon, Oxon, OX14 3NG
Activities: Operation of gravel and sand pits; mining of clays and kaolin
Parent: J.Curtis & Sons (Holdings) Limited
Officers: John Godfrey MacDonald, Secretary; John Andrew Howard Curtis [1942] Director; John Godfrey MacDonald [1931] Director

Curtis Instruments (U.K.) Limited
Incorporated: 9 January 1974 *Employees:* 42
Net Worth: £5,155,733 *Total Assets:* £9,233,203
Registered Office: 5 Upper Priory Street, Northampton, NN1 2PT
Activities: Manufacture of electronic measuring, testing etc. equipment, not for industrial process control
Officers: Mark Ankers [1971] Director/VP of Product Management & European Sales Group; Nicholas Marwell [1980] Director/Vice President New Business Development [American]; Stuart Marwell [1948] Director/Accountant [American]; David Wilkes [1957] Managing Director

Custodian Real Estate (Leicester) Limited
Incorporated: 29 October 2001 *Employees:* 3
Previous: Belgrave Land (Leicester) Limited
Net Worth: £3,637,807 *Total Assets:* £10,628,131
Registered Office: 1 New Walk Place, Leicester, LE1 6RU
Activities: Development of building projects
Parent: BL (Leicester) Limited
Officers: Edward James Moore [1979] Director; Richard Shepherd-Cross [1971] Director/Property Consultant

Custodian REIT PLC
Incorporated: 27 January 2014
Net Worth: £415,201,984 *Total Assets:* £541,884,992
Registered Office: 1 New Walk Place, Leicester, LE1 6RU
Activities: Activities of real estate investment trusts
Officers: Nathan James McLean Imlach, Secretary; David Ian Hunter [1953] Director; Ian Thomas Mattioli [1962] Director; Matthew Wadman John Thorne [1952] Director

Cuttech Limited
Incorporated: 8 October 1980
Net Worth: £56,964,360 *Total Assets:* £56,980,908
Registered Office: President Way Works, President Way, Sheffield, S4 7UR
Activities: Activities of head offices
Parent: TDY Limited
Officers: Elliot Staub Davis, Secretary; Elliot Staub Davis [1961] Director/Company Secretary/Vice President [American]; Patrick Decoury [1962] Director/Chief Financial Officer [American]

CVS Leasing Limited
Incorporated: 5 February 1997
Net Worth Deficit: £8,320,000 *Total Assets:* £48,714,000
Registered Office: Medium Support Helicopter Aircrew Training Facility, RAF Benson, Wallingford, Oxon, OX10 6AA
Activities: Financial leasing
Parent: Infrastructure Investments General Partner Limited
Officers: James Anthony Boyle, Secretary; James Christopher Heath [1975] Director; Scott Springett [1968] Director/Asset Manager

CX Bidco Limited
Incorporated: 3 June 2016
Net Worth Deficit: £3,898,042 *Total Assets:* £114,678,440
Registered Office: Ferham House, Kimberworth Road, Rotherham, S Yorks, S61 1AJ
Activities: Residential nursing care facilities
Parent: CX Midco 2 Limited
Officers: Elizabeth Jane Phipps, Secretary; Euan David Craig [1977] Director; John Henry Whitehead [1964] Director/Chief Financial Officer

CX Midco 2 Limited
Incorporated: 2 June 2016
Net Worth Deficit: £10,656,463 *Total Assets:* £116,250,128
Registered Office: Ferham House, Kimberworth Road, Rotherham, S Yorks, S61 1AJ
Activities: Residential nursing care facilities
Parent: CX Midco Limited
Officers: Elizabeth Jane Phipps, Secretary; Euan David Craig [1977] Director; John Henry Whitehead [1964] Director/Chief Financial Officer

CX Midco Limited
Incorporated: 2 June 2016
Net Worth Deficit: £9,652,729 *Total Assets:* £51,439,000
Registered Office: Ferham House, Kimberworth Road, Rotherham, S Yorks, S61 1AJ
Activities: Residential nursing care facilities
Parent: CX Topco Limited
Officers: Elizabeth Jane Phipps, Secretary; Euan David Craig [1977] Director; John Henry Whitehead [1964] Director/Chief Financial Officer

CX Topco Limited
Incorporated: 2 June 2016 *Employees:* 2,094
Net Worth Deficit: £23,706,000 *Total Assets:* £162,892,992
Registered Office: Ferham House, Kimberworth Road, Rotherham, S Yorks, S61 1AJ
Activities: Residential nursing care facilities
Parent: CX Holdco Limited
Officers: Martin Nicholas Calderbank [1967] Director/Venture Capital; Euan David Craig [1977] Director; Liam Stuart Goddard [1982] Director/Venture Capital; Mark Bentley Jackson [1956] Director/Chairman; Panos Andreas Loizou [1964] Director/Venture Capital [Cypriot]

Cycene Limited
Incorporated: 18 March 2011 *Employees:* 341
Net Worth: £27,779,000 *Total Assets:* £38,569,000
Registered Office: Omega Boulevard, Capitol Park, Thorne, Doncaster, S Yorks, DN8 5TX
Activities: Manufacture of other furniture
Parent: Cycene Investments Limited
Officers: Richard Adam, Secretary; Simon Keith Barber [1967] Director; James John Robert Murray [1990] Director

Cyden Homes Limited
Incorporated: 27 August 1962 *Employees:* 35
Net Worth: £41,206,080 *Total Assets:* £50,137,760
Registered Office: Manor Farm Offices, Laceby, Grimsby, N E Lincs, DN37 7EA
Activities: Other letting and operating of own or leased real estate
Shareholders: Geoffrey Frederick Dyson; Jacqueline Diana Dyson
Officers: Sarah Powton, Secretary; Andrew Burling [1967] Director; Simon James Capps [1969] Director/Accountant; Geoffrey Frederick Dyson [1949] Director/Chartered Builder; Simon Geoffrey Dyson [1975] Director/Builder; Stuart Hockney [1966] Construction Director

Cygnia Logistics Limited
Incorporated: 8 April 1999 *Employees:* 390
Previous: Dalepak Limited
Net Worth: £7,413,989 *Total Assets:* £16,381,903
Registered Office: Style Way, Pineham, Swan Valley, Northampton, NN4 9EX
Activities: Operation of warehousing and storage facilities for water transport activities
Parent: Dalepak Holdings Limited
Officers: Simon Clifford [1964] Sales Director; Glenn Jonathan Lindfield [1959] Director; Scott Christopher Merrick [1983] Director; Robert Jan Thompson [1977] Director/Chartered Accountant; Ian Winston Turner [1960] Director

Cyprotex Discovery Limited
Incorporated: 21 March 2001 *Employees:* 120
Net Worth: £4,339,087 *Total Assets:* £10,472,861
Registered Office: 114 Innovation Drive, Milton Park, Milton, Abingdon, Oxon, OX14 4RZ
Activities: Other business support service activities n.e.c.
Parent: Cyprotex Limited
Officers: Kamran Bashir, Secretary; Dr Craig Johnstone [1970] Director; Dr Lloyd James Payne [1971] Director; Robert John Riley [1965] Director; Ralph Enno Spillner [1970] Director [German]

Cytec Industrial Materials (Derby) Limited
Incorporated: 6 June 1988 *Employees:* 210
Net Worth: £32,117,000 *Total Assets:* £48,132,000
Registered Office: Composites House, Sinclair Close, Heanor Gate Industrial Estate, Heanor, Derbys, DE75 7SP
Activities: Manufacture of other plastic products
Parent: Umeco Limited
Officers: Alison Murphy, Secretary; David Shaun Clears [1957] Sales Director; Stephen Matthew Glennon [1967] Director/Chartered Accountant; Jonathan David Norris [1963] Director

Cytec Process Materials (Keighley) Limited
Incorporated: 14 January 1980 *Employees:* 22
Net Worth: £36,340,000 *Total Assets:* £37,644,000
Registered Office: Composites House, Sinclair Close, Heanor Gate Industrial Estate, Heanor, Derbys, DE75 7SP
Activities: Manufacture of other plastic products
Parent: Umeco Limited
Officers: Alison Murphy, Secretary; David Shaun Clears [1957] Sales Director; Levi Edenbrow [1978] Finance Director

D D Heating Limited
Incorporated: 3 May 2002
Net Worth: £3,587,672 *Total Assets:* £9,708,957
Registered Office: Nottingham Road, Belper, Derbys, DE56 1JT
Activities: Manufacture of central heating radiators and boilers
Shareholders: Vaillant Management Ltd; Vaillant Netherlands Holdings Ltd
Officers: Alison Sarah Blincow, Secretary; Avdel Alper [1974] Director [Turkish]; Klaus Jesse [1959] Director [German]

Dachser Limited
Incorporated: 8 January 1975 *Employees:* 392
Net Worth: £12,824,844 *Total Assets:* £37,730,296
Registered Office: Northampton Logistics Centre, Thomas Dachser Way, Brackmills, Northampton, NN4 7HT
Activities: Freight transport by road
Parent: Dachser SE
Officers: Susan Lesley Rowley, Secretary; Thomas Krueger [1964] Director [German]; Wolfgang Helmut Reinel [1963] Director [German]; Mark Edward Michael Rollinson [1971] UK Managing Director

Daf Trucks Limited
Incorporated: 6 May 1993 *Employees:* 81
Net Worth: £44,899,000 *Total Assets:* £136,448,000
Registered Office: 9400 Garsington Road, Oxford Business Park, Cowley, Oxford, OX4 2HN
Activities: Sale of other motor vehicles
Parent: Paccar Inc
Officers: Alison Jones, Secretary; Robin Erik Easton [1966] Managing Director; Mark Evans [1975] Finance Director; Robert Preston Feight [1967] Director/President Daf Trucks N.V [American]; Richard Daniel Theodorus Zinc [1960] Director [Danish]

Dagless Holdings Limited
Incorporated: 8 February 1983 *Employees:* 213
Net Worth: £5,719,390 *Total Assets:* £10,527,657
Registered Office: Brigstock Road, Wisbech, Cambs, PE13 3JJ
Activities: Activities of head offices
Shareholders: Richard William Pennington; Simon Victor Smeeth
Officers: Carolyn Jane Smeeth, Secretary; Edmund Oliver Smeeth [1985] Director; Sam Peter Smeeth [1982] Director; Simon Victor Smeeth [1955] Director

Dagless Limited
Incorporated: 11 October 1945 *Employees:* 197
Net Worth: £5,533,326 *Total Assets:* £11,098,141
Registered Office: Brigstock Road, Wisbech, Cambs, PE13 3JJ
Activities: Manufacture of other products of wood; manufacture of articles of cork, straw and plaiting materials
Parent: Dagless Holdings Limited
Officers: Carolyn Jane Smeeth, Secretary; Carolyn Jane Smeeth [1958] Director/Secretary; Edmund Oliver Smeeth [1985] Director/Manager; Sam Peter Smeeth [1982] Director; Simon Victor Smeeth [1955] Director/Timber Importer

Daifuku Europe Limited
Incorporated: 20 September 1989 *Employees:* 71
Net Worth: £8,798,382 *Total Assets:* £11,904,689
Registered Office: Unit 5 Dunfermline Court, Kingston, Milton Keynes, Bucks, MK10 0BY
Activities: Repair and maintenance of other transport equipment n.e.c.
Parent: Daifuku Co.,Ltd
Officers: Satoshi Haruta [1961] Director/Department Manager, International Sales Department [Japanese]; Haruki Ishimoto [1964] Director/Employee [Japanese]

Daimler Insurance Services UK Limited
Incorporated: 13 February 1998 *Employees:* 58
Net Worth: £13,465,119 *Total Assets:* £16,250,005
Registered Office: Tongwell, Delaware Drive, Milton Keynes, Bucks, MK15 8BA
Activities: Financial intermediation not elsewhere classified
Parent: Daimler UK Limited
Officers: Jonathan Lipman, Secretary; Robert Scott Blyth [1964] Director/Senior Executive Insurance Services; Catherine Bruce [1962] Director; Brian Evon [1963] Finance Director [Canadian]; Alexander Douglas Matthews [1973] Director; Douglas Moody [1958] Managing Director; Christian Peters [1967] Director [German]

Daimler UK Limited
Incorporated: 22 October 1973
Net Worth: £723,057,984 *Total Assets:* £836,051,968
Registered Office: Mercedes-Benz Cars UK Limited, Delaware Drive, Tongwell, Milton Keynes, Bucks, MK15 8BA
Activities: Activities of head offices
Parent: Daimler AG (HRB 19360)
Officers: Jonathan Philip Rueben Lipman, Secretary; Harald Henn [1964] Director/Economist [German]; Gary Mark Savage [1961] Director

Daisy UK Holdco Limited
Incorporated: 16 October 2013 *Employees:* 2
Net Worth Deficit: £75,359,792 *Total Assets:* £34,300,000
Registered Office: 3-5 Commercial Gate, Mansfield, Notts, NG18 1EJ
Activities: Activities of production holding companies
Officers: Klaus Dieter Bergner [1961] Director [German]; Andrew Richard Hollyhead [1975] Director

Daleacre Healthcare Limited
Incorporated: 26 January 2016 *Employees:* 120
Net Worth: £13,656,276 *Total Assets:* £17,112,164
Registered Office: 11 Wilsthorpe Road, Breaston, Derby, DE72 3EA
Activities: Dispensing chemist in specialised stores
Parent: Daleacre Holdings Limited
Officers: David Richard Evans [1965] Director; Judith Ann Wendy Evans [1956] Director/Financial Controller; Jon Richard Such [1962] Director/Pharmacist

Dalepak Holdings Limited
Incorporated: 24 February 1998 *Employees:* 390
Net Worth: £8,492,827 *Total Assets:* £17,412,624
Registered Office: DC139 Style Way, Pineham, Swan Valley, Northampton, NN4 9EX
Activities: Activities of other holding companies n.e.c.
Parent: Caledonia Bidco Limited
Officers: Simon Clifford [1964] Sales Director; Glenn Jonathan Lindfield [1959] Director; Scott Christopher Merrick [1983] Director; Robert Jan Thompson [1977] Director/Chartered Accountant; Ian Winston Turner [1960] Director

Daloon Foods (U.K.) Limited
Incorporated: 24 August 1982 *Employees:* 106
Net Worth: £5,731,070 *Total Assets:* £12,210,241
Registered Office: Brunel Drive, Northern Road Industrial Estate, Newark, Notts, NG24 2EG
Activities: Manufacture of other food products n.e.c.
Parent: Daloon A/S
Officers: Johannes Franciscus Marie Kruijtzer [1967] Director [Dutch]; Kamiel Steendijk [1971] Director [Dutch]; Jeremy Michael Threadgold [1976] Director

J.E. & V.M. Dalton Limited
Incorporated: 22 April 1952 *Employees:* 44
Net Worth: £7,309,468 *Total Assets:* £11,306,765
Registered Office: Dalmark House, Eye, Peterborough, Cambs, PE6 7UD
Activities: Other manufacturing n.e.c.
Shareholders: Anthony John Dalton; Peter Duncan Fox
Officers: Matthew John Dalton, Secretary; Anthony John Dalton [1946] Director/Seed Representative; Linda Joyce Dalton [1950] Director/Secretary; Matthew John Dalton [1980] Director; Patrick Owen Dalton [1982] Director; Peter Duncan Fox [1962] Director/Production Manager; Ronald Francis Fox [1934] Director/Seed Representative; Emma Louise Windsor [1965] Director

Dalziel & Pow Holdings Limited
Incorporated: 3 February 2017 *Employees:* 121
Net Worth: £7,035,796 *Total Assets:* £14,241,420
Registered Office: 15 Newland, Lincoln, LN1 1XG
Activities: Artistic creation
Officers: Richard John Bennett [1975] Design Director; David John Dalziel [1957] Creative Director; Karen Lorraine Dalziel [1963] Director of Graphics; Sarah Louise Fairhurst [1978] Design Director; Timothy John Graveling [1972] Design Director; Alastair John Kean [1963] Development Director; Marcus King [1973] Design Director; Rosalyn Elizabeth Sarah Scott [1958] Managing Director; Keith Dennis Ware [1965] Director of Interiors; Paul John West [1979] Strategy Director; David Richard Wright [1973] Marketing Director

Damika Limited
Incorporated: 8 April 1988 *Employees:* 67
Net Worth: £10,424,173 *Total Assets:* £11,874,699
Registered Office: Oak House, Heyford Close, Aldermans Green, Coventry, Warwicks, CV2 2QB
Activities: Processing and preserving of meat
Parent: Becketts Foods Limited
Officers: Heike Roschkowski, Secretary; Carl Ernst Burger [1987] Director [German]; Jeremy Adam Cornes [1967] Director; Frank Duffe [1960] Director [German]; Carsten Svejgaard Jakobsen [1945] Director [Danish]

Dana Spicer Europe Limited
Incorporated: 20 April 1949 *Employees:* 11
Net Worth: £7,708,000 *Total Assets:* £9,435,000
Registered Office: Bridgeway House, Bridgeway, Stratford upon Avon, Warwicks, CV37 6YX
Activities: Machining
Parent: Dana Incorporated
Officers: John Thomas Coppage, Secretary; John Thomas Coppage [1980] Finance Director [American]; Juergen Wald [1969] Director/Head of Accounting Europe [German]

Dana UK Automotive Systems Limited
Incorporated: 7 February 2007
Net Worth: £9,328,000 *Total Assets:* £9,328,000
Registered Office: Bridgeway House, Bridgeway, Stratford upon Avon, Warwicks, CV37 6YX
Activities: Other business support service activities n.e.c.
Parent: Dana Incorporated
Officers: John Thomas Coppage, Secretary; John Thomas Coppage [1980] Finance Director [American]; Juergen Wald [1969] Director/Head of Accounting (Europe) [German]

Dana UK Axle Limited
Incorporated: 7 February 2007 *Employees:* 319
Net Worth: £34,768,000 *Total Assets:* £70,951,000
Registered Office: Bridgeway House, Bridgeway, Stratford upon Avon, Warwicks, CV37 6YX
Activities: Other business support service activities n.e.c.
Parent: Dana Incorporated
Officers: John Thomas Coppage, Secretary; John Thomas Coppage [1980] Director/Division Controller [American]; David Huw Davies [1964] Managing Director; Terence Feeney [1965] LV Operations Director

Dana UK Driveshaft Limited
Incorporated: 7 February 2007 *Employees:* 42
Net Worth: £6,281,000 *Total Assets:* £9,840,000
Registered Office: Bridgeway House, Bridgeway, Stratford upon Avon, Warwicks, CV37 6YX
Activities: Manufacture of other parts and accessories for motor vehicles
Parent: Dana Incorporated
Officers: Kerry Peacock, Secretary; Paul William John Burman [1961] Director; Gilles Yves Pladeau [1968] Director/General Manager [French]; Juergen Wald [1969] Director/Head of Accounting Europe [German]

Danaher & Walsh Group Limited
Incorporated: 20 March 2000 *Employees:* 91
Net Worth: £3,346,787 *Total Assets:* £11,823,120
Registered Office: 20 Granite Way, Mountsorrel, Loughborough, Leics, LE12 7TZ
Activities: Other specialised construction activities n.e.c.
Shareholders: Bridget Veronica Danaher; Daniel Henry Danaher
Officers: Sandra Danaher, Secretary; Paul Seymour Bonnett [1953] Director; Bridget Veronica Danaher [1936] Director [Irish]; Daniel Henry Danaher [1963] Director [Irish]; Sandra Danaher [1962] Director/Solicitor; Nicholas Alan Hill [1977] Finance Director

Danetre Holdings Limited
Incorporated: 2 May 1986 *Employees:* 109
Net Worth: £1,218,789 *Total Assets:* £10,549,632
Registered Office: The Robbins Building, Albert Street, Rugby, Warwicks, CV21 2SD
Activities: Management consultancy activities other than financial management
Major Shareholder: Richard Neil Johnson
Officers: Jill Margaret Sinclair, Secretary; Isobel Joan Johnson [2000] Director; Richard Neil Johnson [1965] Director/Motor Retailer; Jill Margaret Sinclair [1967] Director

Danieli UK Holding Limited
Incorporated: 1 December 1994 *Employees:* 51
Net Worth: £8,835,614 *Total Assets:* £20,255,316
Registered Office: 4 Ignite Magna Way, Rotherham, S Yorks, S60 1FD
Activities: Engineering design activities for industrial process and production
Parent: Industrielle Beteiligung SA
Officers: Philip John Jordan, Secretary/Solicitor; Andrew Philip Betts [1970] Director/Accountant; Georgios Ximeris [1960] Director [Italian]

Dar Lighting Limited
Incorporated: 27 October 2004 *Employees:* 196
Net Worth: £9,382,000 *Total Assets:* £14,710,000
Registered Office: c/o Dar Lighting, Wildmere Road, Banbury, Oxon, OX16 3JZ
Activities: Manufacture of electric lighting equipment
Officers: Nicola Jane Cosgrove-Mcguirk, Secretary; Nicola Jane Cosgrove McGuirk [1961] Director

Darby Group Ltd
Incorporated: 19 September 2001 *Employees:* 13
Previous: Darby Investments Limited
Net Worth: £27,173,780 *Total Assets:* £43,390,568
Registered Office: Eastgate House, 11 Cheyne Walk, Northampton, NN1 5PT
Activities: Other letting and operating of own or leased real estate
Shareholders: Andrew Jonathan Darby; Richard Alexander Darby; Paul Max Darby
Officers: Richard Alexander Darby, Secretary/Director; Andrew Jonathan Darby [1971] Director; Paul Max Darby [1965] Director; Richard Alexander Darby [1968] Director

Darley Limited
Incorporated: 6 March 1946 *Employees:* 89
Net Worth: £5,850,524 *Total Assets:* £12,196,133
Registered Office: Wellington Road, Burton on Trent, Staffs, DE14 2AD
Activities: Manufacture of other articles of paper and paperboard n.e.c.
Shareholders: Stewart Kelvin Hughes; John William Alton
Officers: Steven Richard Tawn, Secretary; John William Alton [1964] Director; Stephen Blake [1958] Director; Stewart Kelvin Hughes [1961] Director; Steven Richard Tawn [1983] Financial Director

Darrington Quarries Limited
Incorporated: 5 March 1957 *Employees:* 48
Net Worth Deficit: £843,000 *Total Assets:* £11,229,000
Registered Office: Ground Floor West, 900 Pavilion Drive, Northampton Business Park, Northampton, NN4 7RG
Activities: Other business support service activities n.e.c.
Parent: Finstop Limited
Officers: Carol Jayne Nunn, Secretary; Agustin Serrano Michan [1959] Director/Technical Civil Engineer [Spanish]; Vicente Federico Orts-Llopis [1962] Director/Chief Financial Officer [Spanish]; Paul Taylor [1959] Director/Chief Executive Officer

Dart Products Europe Ltd.
Incorporated: 12 May 1970 *Employees:* 496
Previous: Solo Cup Europe Limited
Net Worth: £56,706,000 *Total Assets:* £71,869,000
Registered Office: 3 Flaxley Road, Kingston Park, Peterborough, Cambs, PE2 9EN
Activities: Manufacture of other plastic products
Parent: Solo Cup (UK) Limited
Officers: Claire Theresa Dart [1929] Director/Businesswomen [American]; Robert Charles Dart [1958] Director/Businessman [Irish]; Thomas Lynn Jewell [1967] Director/Businessman [American]; James Donald Lammers [1959] Director/Businessman [American]

Dassault Systemes UK Limited
Incorporated: 11 December 1997 *Employees:* 317
Net Worth: £578,923,008 *Total Assets:* £620,798,976
Registered Office: 9 Riley Court, Milburn Hill Road, Coventry, Warwicks, CV4 7HP
Activities: Other software publishing
Parent: Dassault Systemes S.E.
Officers: Jean Hubert Philippe Gerard Balleidier [1969] Director [French]; John Howard Kitchingman [1966] Managing Director; Olivier Yvon Bernard Ribet [1967] Director/EVP EMEAR, Cross-Industry Initiatives [French]

Datac Adhesives Limited
Incorporated: 3 November 1980
Net Worth: £12,400,000 *Total Assets:* £30,319,000
Registered Office: Globe Lane Industrial Estate, Outram Road, Dukinfield, Cheshire, SK16 4XE
Activities: Manufacture of other chemical products n.e.c.
Parent: H. B. Fuller Company
Officers: Robert Joseph Martsching [1964] Director/Vice President and Corporate Controller [American]; Emilio Roque Vilas [1968] Business Director Hygiene [Spanish]; Heidi Ann Weiler [1966] Director/Vice President and Treasurer [American]

Datapath Group Limited
Incorporated: 28 November 2011 *Employees:* 115
Net Worth: £25,728,472 *Total Assets:* £27,891,466
Registered Office: Bemrose House, Bemrose Park, Wayzgoose Drive, Derby, DE21 6XQ
Activities: Activities of head offices
Shareholder: Tony Jones
Officers: Nigel Gregg Fasey, Secretary; Eugenia Clark [1958] Director [American]; Darin James Crosby [1968] Sales Director [Canadian]; Nigel Gregg Fasey [1968] Director/Chartered Accountant; Russell George Healey [1970] Director; Simon Anthony Hunt [1946] Director; Tony Jones [1952] Director; Bjorn Anders Gunnar Krylander [1963] Managing Director [Swedish]; Richard Smith [1965] Director/Engineer; John James Storey [1963] Director/Engineer

Datapath Limited
Incorporated: 25 January 1982 *Employees:* 101
Net Worth: £31,745,716 *Total Assets:* £33,767,120
Registered Office: Bemrose House, Bemrose Park, Wayzgoose Drive, Derby, DE21 6XQ
Activities: Manufacture of loaded electronic boards
Parent: Datapath Holdings Limited
Officers: Nigel Gregg Fasey, Secretary/Chartered Accountant; Darin James Crosby [1968] Sales Director [Canadian]; Nigel Gregg Fasey [1968] Director/Chartered Accountant; Simon Anthony Hunt [1946] Director; Tony Jones [1952] Director/Computer Analyst; Bjorn Anders Gunnar Krylander [1963] Managing Director [Swedish]; Richard Smith [1965] Director/Engineer; John James Storey [1963] Director/Engineer

Davane Holding Company Limited
Incorporated: 28 July 2010 *Employees:* 52
Net Worth: £5,561,983 *Total Assets:* £13,063,993
Registered Office: 36-38 Park Green, Macclesfield, Cheshire, SK11 7NE
Activities: Activities of head offices
Shareholders: Karl David Massey; Susan Massey
Officers: Karl David Massey [1964] Director

Lawrence David Limited
Incorporated: 26 April 1973 *Employees:* 258
Net Worth: £9,468,443 *Total Assets:* £32,392,168
Registered Office: Woodston Point, Shrewsbury Avenue, Peterborough, Cambs, PE2 7LB
Activities: Other engineering activities
Parent: Wielton S.A.
Officers: Paul Yallop, Secretary; Andrew Robert Dodge [1968] Director; Laurence David Marshall [1966] Managing Director; Jonathan Todd [1972] Director/Chief Financial Officer

Davidsons Developments Limited
Incorporated: 3 January 2002 *Employees:* 194
Net Worth: £112,001,000 *Total Assets:* £185,924,000
Registered Office: Fishers Solicitors, 4-8 Kilwardby Street, Ashby De La Zouch, Leics, LE65 2FU
Activities: Development of building projects
Shareholders: James David Wilson; Richard William Henry Wilson; Robert Edward Charles Wilson
Officers: Graham Marshall Brown, Secretary/Director; Graham Marshall Brown [1945] Director/Consultant; Gregson Horace Locke [1956] Director; Christian John O'Connell [1973] Director; David William Wilson [1941] Director/Company Chairman; James David Wilson [1972] Director

William Davis Limited
Incorporated: 12 May 1949 *Employees:* 311
Net Worth: £117,577,000 *Total Assets:* £154,063,008
Registered Office: Forest Field, Forest Road, Loughborough, Leics, LE11 3NS
Activities: Development of building projects
Parent: Broadthorpe Ltd
Officers: Geoffrey Pearson, Secretary; Edelin Davis [1935] Managing Director; Myles Halley [1956] Director; Guy Stuart Higgins [1962] Director; Terence Higgins [1926] Director

Davison & Co. (Barford) Limited
Incorporated: 7 July 1959 *Employees:* 29
Net Worth: £15,163,640 *Total Assets:* £23,040,450
Registered Office: College Farm, Great Barford, Beds, MK44 3JJ
Activities: Mixed farming
Shareholders: Duncan & Toplis Trustees Limited; Phillippa Brenda Davison; Edward Frank Davison
Officers: Gary Mark Davison, Secretary; Anthony Edward Davison [1961] Director; Charles Johnathan Davison [1961] Director/Farmer; Edward James Davison [1970] Director; Edward Frank Davison [1932] Director/Farmer; Gary Mark Davison [1960] Director/Farmer

Davison Property Investments Ltd
Incorporated: 27 January 2004 *Employees:* 2
Net Worth: £6,060,118 *Total Assets:* £10,563,867
Registered Office: 28 Bailey Street, Sheffield, S1 4EH
Activities: Other letting and operating of own or leased real estate
Major Shareholder: Matthew James Davison
Officers: Kerry Ann Davison, Company Secretary; Kerry Ann Davison [1970] Director; Matthew James Davison [1973] Director

Dawson-Wam Ltd
Incorporated: 3 December 1984 *Employees:* 108
Net Worth: £8,474,271 *Total Assets:* £18,410,196
Registered Office: The Moors, Westoning Road, Greenfield, Beds, MK45 5BJ
Activities: Construction of water projects
Major Shareholder: Dennis Edmund McGall
Officers: Wendy Sara Margaret Reid, Secretary; Nigel Philip Boullier [1954] Director/Civil Engineer; Paul Kelly [1980] Director/Civil Engineer; Dennis Edmund McGall [1947] Director/Civil Engineer; Jonathan Dennis McGall [1968] Director/Civil Engineer; Valerie McGall [1948] Director; Allen Robert McMullan [1957] Director/Civil Engineer; Rodney Moates [1966] Director/Civil Engineer; Wendy Sara Margaret Reid [1971] Director; Peter Graeme Robson [1959] Director/Civil Engineer; Colin Desmond James Russell [1960] Director/Engineer

Dawsongroup Bus and Coach Limited
Incorporated: 20 October 1989 *Employees:* 56
Previous: Dawsonrentals Bus and Coach Limited
Net Worth: £22,201,000 *Total Assets:* £79,261,000
Registered Office: c/o Dawsongroup PLC, Delaware Drive, Tongwell, Milton Keynes, Bucks, MK15 8JH
Activities: Renting and leasing of other machinery, equipment and tangible goods n.e.c.
Parent: Dawsongroup UK Limited
Officers: Lucinda Anne Kent, Secretary; Stephen David Callahan [1963] Director; Anthony Coleman [1973] Finance Director; Fraser John Innes [1966] Director/Sales Manager; Stephen James Miller [1965] Group Managing Director; Adrian Joseph Peter O'Reilly [1964] Director; Paul David Sainthouse [1967] Director

Dawsongroup Material Handling Limited
Incorporated: 8 October 1991 *Employees:* 103
Previous: Dawsonrentals Materials Handling Equipment Limited
Net Worth: £22,287,000 *Total Assets:* £49,025,000
Registered Office: Delaware Drive, Tongwell, Milton Keynes, Bucks, MK15 8JH
Activities: Renting and leasing of other machinery, equipment and tangible goods n.e.c.
Parent: Dawsongroup UK Limited
Officers: Lucinda Anne Kent, Secretary; Stephen David Callahan [1963] Director; Anthony Coleman [1973] Finance Director; Stephen James Miller [1965] Group Managing Director; Adrian Joseph Peter O'Reilly [1964] Director; Timothy Paul Shires [1960] Director

Dawsongroup PLC
Incorporated: 3 April 1985 *Employees:* 797
Net Worth: £245,322,000 *Total Assets:* £625,916,032
Registered Office: Delaware Drive, Tongwell, Milton Keynes, Bucks, MK15 8JH
Activities: Activities of head offices
Parent: Bryan Cave Leighton Paisner LLP
Officers: Lucinda Anne Kent, Secretary; Anthony Coleman [1973] Director; Freya Olivia Dawson [1987] Director; Peter Michael Dawson [1938] Director/Executive Chairman; Ian Jones [1954] Director; Stephen James Miller [1965] Director

Dawsongroup Temperature Control Solutions Limited
Incorporated: 18 February 1982 *Employees:* 111
Previous: Dawsonrentals Temperature Control Solutions Limited
Net Worth: £35,580,000 *Total Assets:* £61,924,000
Registered Office: Delaware Drive, Tongwell, Milton Keynes, Bucks, MK15 8JH
Activities: Renting and leasing of other machinery, equipment and tangible goods n.e.c.
Parent: Dawsongroup UK Limited
Officers: Lucinda Anne Kent, Secretary; Roderick Peter Benham [1958] Director; Stephen David Callahan [1963] Director; Anthony Coleman [1973] Finance Director; Jonathan David McKie [1978] Operations Director; Stephen James Miller [1965] Group Managing Director; Adrian Joseph Peter O'Reilly [1964] Director; David John Quinn [1961] Director; Gary Smith [1961] Director

Dawsongroup Truck and Trailer Limited
Incorporated: 17 July 1995 *Employees:* 198
Previous: Dawsonrentals Truck and Trailer Limited
Net Worth: £59,980,000 *Total Assets:* £302,532,992
Registered Office: Delaware Drive, Tongwell, Milton Keynes, Bucks, MK15 8JH
Activities: Renting and leasing of trucks and other heavy vehicles
Parent: Dawsongroup UK Limited
Officers: Lucinda Anne Kent, Secretary; Stephen David Calllahan [1963] Director; Anthony Coleman [1973] Finance Director; Peter Michael Dawson [1938] Director/Chairman; John Fletcher [1966] Director; Stephen James Miller [1965] Director; Adrian Joseph Peter O'Reilly [1964] Director; Peter Stuart Smith [1966] Sales Director; Peter Snowden [1963] Director

Dawsongroup UK Limited
Incorporated: 3 May 1948 *Employees:* 3
Previous: Dawsonrentals Limited
Net Worth: £71,413,000 *Total Assets:* £71,413,000
Registered Office: Delaware Drive, Tongwell, Milton Keynes, Bucks, MK15 8JH
Activities: Non-trading company
Parent: Dawsongroup PLC
Officers: Lucinda Anne Kent, Secretary; Anthony Coleman [1973] Finance Director; Peter Michael Dawson [1938] Director; Stephen James Miller [1965] Group Managing Director

Dawsongroup Vans Limited
Incorporated: 25 October 2010 *Employees:* 145
Previous: Dawsonrentals Vans Limited
Net Worth: £11,540,000 *Total Assets:* £62,420,000
Registered Office: Delaware Drive, Tongwell, Milton Keynes, Bucks, MK15 8JH
Activities: Renting and leasing of cars and light motor vehicles
Parent: Dawsongroup UK Limited
Officers: Lucinda Anne Kent, Secretary; Stephen David Callahan [1963] Director; Anthony Coleman [1973] Finance Director; Charles Piers Leighton Dawson [1990] Director; Stephen James Miller [1965] Managing Director; Adrian Joseph Peter O'Reilly [1964] Accounting Director; David Simon Ridley [1967] Director

DB Cargo (UK) Holdings Limited
Incorporated: 16 October 1995
Previous: DB Schenker Rail (UK) Holdings Limited
Net Worth: £180,000,000 *Total Assets:* £207,000,000
Registered Office: Lakeside Business Park, Carolina Way, Doncaster, S Yorks, DN4 5PN
Activities: Freight rail transport
Parent: DB (UK) Investments Limited
Officers: Helen Louise Young, Secretary; Andrea Rossi [1975] Director/Chief Financial Officer; Hans-Georg Werner [1959] Director/Business Administration [German]

DB Cargo (UK) Limited
Incorporated: 9 June 1994 *Employees:* 2,109
Previous: DB Schenker Rail (UK) Limited
Net Worth: £35,000,000 *Total Assets:* £437,000,000
Registered Office: Lakeside Business Park, Carolina Way, Doncaster, S Yorks, DN4 5PN
Activities: Freight rail transport
Parent: DB Cargo (UK) Holdings Limited
Officers: Helen Louise Young, Secretary; Andrea Rossi [1975] Director/Chief Financial Officer; Hans-Georg Werner [1959] Director/Business Administration [German]

DB Cargo International Limited
Incorporated: 26 July 1996 *Employees:* 113
Previous: DB Schenker Rail International Limited
Net Worth: £18,416,000 *Total Assets:* £26,656,000
Registered Office: Lakeside Business Park, Carolina Way, Doncaster, S Yorks, DN4 5PN
Activities: Freight rail transport
Parent: DB Cargo (UK) Holdings Limited
Officers: Helen Louise Young, Secretary; Andrea Rossi [1975] Director/Chief Financial Officer; Hans-Georg Werner [1959] Director/Business Administration [German]

DCA Design International Limited
Incorporated: 4 March 1986 *Employees:* 136
Net Worth: £10,412,927 *Total Assets:* £14,239,717
Registered Office: 19 Church Street, Warwick, CV34 4AB
Activities: Specialised design activities
Shareholders: Robert Woolston; Robert Bassil
Officers: Robert Bassil [1963] Director/Engineer; Nicholas James Mival [1970] Director/Designer; Robert Woolston [1964] Director/Designer

DCS 452 Limited
Incorporated: 12 October 2006 *Employees:* 2
Net Worth: £5,673,015 *Total Assets:* £14,340,399
Registered Office: c/o Grant Thornton UK LLP, Regent House, 80 Regent Road, Leicester, LE1 7NH
Activities: Construction of commercial buildings
Major Shareholder: James David Wilson
Officers: Keith McEwan, Secretary; Anna Marie Wilson [1973] Director; James David Wilson [1972] Director/Land Buyer

DCS Group (UK) Limited
Incorporated: 7 February 1991 *Employees:* 338
Net Worth: £17,348,000 *Total Assets:* £62,871,000
Registered Office: Oceans House, Noral Way, Banbury, Oxon, OX16 2AA
Activities: Other manufacturing n.e.c.
Major Shareholder: Denys Christopher Shortt
Officers: Johnathan Andrew Berry, Secretary; Johnathan Andrew Berry [1975] Director/Chartered Accountant; Michael John Lorimer [1963] Director; Julie Ann Price [1977] Financial Performance Director; Charles Patrick Shortt [1991] Director; Deborah Ann Shortt [1963] Commercial Director [American]; Denys Christopher Shortt [1964] Director/Chairman; Lydia Rosemary Shortt [1993] Director; Jorge Miguel Oliveira Silva [1972] IT Director [Portuguese]

DCS Inc Limited
Incorporated: 8 December 2010 *Employees:* 338
Net Worth: £20,406,000 *Total Assets:* £76,723,000
Registered Office: Oceans House, Noral Way, Banbury, Oxon, OX16 2AA
Activities: Activities of other holding companies n.e.c.
Major Shareholder: Denys Christopher Shortt
Officers: Johnathan Andrew Berry, Secretary; Michael John Lorimer [1963] Director; Charles Patrick Shortt [1991] Director; Deborah Ann Shortt [1963] Director [American]; Denys Christopher Shortt [1964] Director; Lydia Rosemary Shortt [1993] Director

De Aston School Academy Trust
Incorporated: 17 February 2011 *Employees:* 127
Net Worth: £9,242,598 *Total Assets:* £11,170,087
Registered Office: De Aston School, Willingham Road, Market Rasen, Lincs, LN8 3RF
Activities: General secondary education
Officers: Emma Kate Fairhall [1972] Director/School Business Manager; Andrew Thomas Hawes [1954] Director/Vicar; Grahame Killey [1961] Director/University Administrator; John Peter Garnet Matthews [1959] Director/Guest House Owner; Dr David Craig Naseby [1971] Director/Lecturer; Anthony Harry Neal [1945] Director/Retired; Simon Kevin Porter [1967] Director/Headmaster; Gary John Smith [1971] Managing Director; Frances Louise Varcoe [1978] Director/Teacher; Stella Maria Williams [1969] Director/Intervention Support Officer; Robert John Wilson [1962] Director/Builder

Mike de Courcey Travel Limited
Incorporated: 30 March 1978 *Employees:* 257
Net Worth: £5,789,774 *Total Assets:* £17,826,296
Registered Office: Rowley Drive, Stonebridge Highway, Industrial Estate, Coventry, Warwicks, CV3 4FG
Activities: Other passenger land transport
Parent: Inishbofin Holdings Limited
Officers: Adrian Michael Patrick de Courcey, Secretary/Director [Irish]; Adrian Michael Patrick de Courcey [1977] Director [Irish]; Mary Bernadette de Courcey [1944] Director [Irish]; Michael John Decourcey [1943] Director/Coach Hire Operator [Irish]

The De Ferrers Trust
Incorporated: 17 November 2010 *Employees:* 592
Previous: The De Ferrers Academy
Net Worth: £47,348,000 *Total Assets:* £55,783,000
Registered Office: c/o The De Ferrers Academy, St Mary's Drive, Burton on Trent, Staffs, DE13 0LL
Activities: Pre-primary education
Officers: Tamalyn Pyszky, Secretary; Andrew Burns [1970] Director/Chartered Surveyor; Elizabeth Ann Laughlin [1961] Director/Teacher; Sophie Ann Leadley [1980] Director; Dr Joseph Generald McSorley [1956] Director/Consultant; Claire Suzanne Shaw [1971] Diocesan Deputy Director of Education; Amy Smith [1992] Director/Civil Servant; Mark Richard Taylor [1961] Director/Accountant

De Trafford and Palatine Estates Limited
Incorporated: 18 December 2015
Net Worth: £308,243 *Total Assets:* £11,388,384
Registered Office: Suite 26g, Building 26, Alderley Park, Alderley Edge, Cheshire, SK10 4TG
Activities: Other business support service activities n.e.c.
Major Shareholder: Gary Thomas Jackson
Officers: Brian Lowndes, Secretary; Gary Thomas Jackson [1964] Director

De Trafford Property LLP
Incorporated: 17 December 2009
Net Worth: £2,335,853 *Total Assets:* £12,842,765
Registered Office: Suite 26g, Building 26, Alderley Park, Alderley Edge, Cheshire, SK10 4TG

Thomas Deacon Education Trust
Incorporated: 1 April 2004 *Employees:* 482
Previous: TDA Education Trust
Net Worth: £37,048,000 *Total Assets:* £45,750,000
Registered Office: The Thomas Deacon Academy, Queens Gardens, Peterborough, Cambs, PE1 2UW
Activities: Pre-primary education
Officers: Simon John Smith, Secretary; Dr Richard Barnes [1946] Director/Senior Tutor; Paul Antony Clegg [1959] Director/Manager; Mohamedraza Yusufali Mavani [1976] Director/Accountant; Kelly Peck [1976] Director/Solicitor; Mark James Potter [1974] Director/Headmaster; Saqib Rehman [1978] Director; Simon John Smith [1973] Director of Resources; Julie Ann Taylor [1961] Director/Principal; Eric William Winstone [1951] Director/Retired

Patrick Dean Limited
Incorporated: 13 March 1952 *Employees:* 28
Net Worth: £31,605,200 *Total Assets:* £36,241,212
Registered Office: The Estate Office, East Mere, Bracebridge Heath, Lincoln, LN4 2HU
Activities: Mixed farming
Officers: Alastair James Priestley, Secretary; James Fitzroy Dean [1954] Director/Chartered Surveyor; Alastair James Priestley [1981] Director/Farm Manager; Charles Andrew Wraith [1967] Director/Business Consultant

Dean Property Group Limited
Incorporated: 22 March 1963 *Employees:* 5
Net Worth: £41,624,896 *Total Assets:* £57,174,888
Registered Office: Springfield House, Water Lane, Wilmslow, Cheshire, SK9 5BG
Activities: Other letting and operating of own or leased real estate
Shareholders: Michael Edward O'Donnell; Ludo Ventures Limited; Otto Ventures Limited; TEOD (1963) Limited
Officers: Jonathan Charles Patrick Beever, Secretary; Jonathan Charles Patrick Beever [1963] Director; Michael Edward O'Donnell [1969] Director; James Anthony Wild [1941] Director/Chartered Accountant

Deanbank Investments Limited
Incorporated: 2 July 1981
Net Worth: £26,676,512 *Total Assets:* £58,912,012
Registered Office: Emerson House, Heyes Lane, Alderley Edge, Cheshire, SK9 7LF
Activities: Development of building projects
Parent: P E Jones (Properties) Limited
Officers: Varun Maharaj, Secretary; Anthony Emerson Jones [1967] Director; Audrey Jones [1936] Director; Mark Emerson Jones [1964] Director; Peter Emerson Jones [1935] Director

Deb Group Holdings Limited
Incorporated: 18 February 2010 *Employees:* 3
Net Worth: £30,611,000 *Total Assets:* £37,913,000
Registered Office: Denby Hall Way, Denby, Ripley, Derbys, DE5 8JZ
Activities: Activities of head offices
Parent: SCJ UK Finco Limited
Officers: Nicholas Noel Hardwick Matterson, Secretary; Gary Akavickas [1956] Director [American]; Mark Eckhardt [1958] Director [American]

Deb Holdings Limited
Incorporated: 23 November 2000 *Employees:* 2
Net Worth: £142,710,000 *Total Assets:* £202,294,000
Registered Office: Denby Hall Way, Denby, Ripley, Derbys, DE5 8JZ
Activities: Other business support service activities n.e.c.
Parent: Deb Group Limited
Officers: Nadia Patricia Estrada [1976] Director/Chief Financial Officer [American]; Nicholas Noel Hardwick Matterson [1963] Director/Lawyer

Deb IP Limited
Incorporated: 28 June 1999 *Employees:* 35
Net Worth: £45,109,000 *Total Assets:* £59,278,000
Registered Office: Denby Hall Way, Denby, Ripley, Derbys, DE5 8JZ
Activities: Other business support service activities n.e.c.
Parent: Deb Holdings Limited
Officers: Dr John David Hines [1970] Director; Nicholas Noel Hardwick Matterson [1963] Director/Lawyer

Decidebloom Limited
Incorporated: 21 December 1994 *Employees:* 2,369
Net Worth: £71,023,000 *Total Assets:* £224,798,000
Registered Office: Stoneacre, Omega Boulevard, Capitol Park, Thorne, Doncaster, S Yorks, DN8 5TX
Activities: Sale of new cars and light motor vehicles
Shareholders: Richard Stephen Teatum; Christine Patricia Teatum
Officers: Nigel Peter Wood, Secretary; Shaun Brookhouse [1967] Operations Director; Kenneth Craig [1950] Director/General Manager; Shaun Foweather [1963] Director/General Manager; Generald Peter George [1959] Operations Director; Richard Stephen Teatum [1957] Director; Paul Vozbutas [1979] Operations Director; Nigel Peter Wood [1964] Director/Accountant

Dee Valley Group Limited
Incorporated: 5 November 2001
Previous: Dee Valley Group PLC
Net Worth: £32,108,000 *Total Assets:* £38,985,000
Registered Office: Severn Trent Centre, St Johns Street, Coventry, Warwicks, CV1 2LZ
Activities: Activities of head offices
Parent: Severn Trent Water Limited
Officers: Gemma Louise Eagle, Secretary; John Anthony Jackson [1960] Director; Robert Craig McPheely [1962] Director; Adam Peter Stephens [1983] Director

Dee Valley Water (Holdings) Limited
Incorporated: 22 April 2002
Net Worth: £46,000,000 *Total Assets:* £46,000,000
Registered Office: Severn Trent Centre, St Johns Street, Coventry, Warwicks, CV1 2LZ
Activities: Activities of head offices
Parent: Chester Water Limited
Officers: Gemma Louise Eagle, Secretary; John Anthony Jackson [1960] Director; Robert Craig McPheely [1962] Director/Accountant

Deeley Construction Limited
Incorporated: 5 February 1948 *Employees:* 54
Net Worth: £11,329,111 *Total Assets:* £18,791,536
Registered Office: George House, Herald Avenue, Coventry, Warwicks, CV5 6UB
Activities: Construction of commercial buildings
Parent: Deeley Group Limited
Officers: Andrew Calvert Cann, Secretary; Peter Anthony William Deeley [1942] Director/Building Contractor; Martin John Gallagher [1970] Director/Surveyor; Stephen Carl Jones [1959] Director/Estimator; Steven Paul Turner [1972] Director/Surveyor

Deeley Group Limited
Incorporated: 6 January 1977 *Employees:* 63
Net Worth: £17,565,000 *Total Assets:* £40,337,000
Registered Office: George House, Herald Avenue, Coventry, Warwicks, CV5 6UB
Activities: Activities of head offices
Shareholders: Peter Anthony William Deeley; Trustees of The GW Deeley Settlement
Officers: Andrew Calvert Cann, Secretary; David Frank Austin [1938] Director/Quantity Surveyor; Andrew Calvert Cann [1963] Financial Director; Peter Anthony William Deeley [1942] Director/Building Contractor; Martin John Gallagher [1970] Managing Director; Peter James Norman Hartill [1949] Director/Business Consultant; Anthony James Holt [1970] Director; Patrick Moroney [1959] Director/Architect

Deichmann-Shoes UK Limited
Incorporated: 31 January 1994 *Employees:* 572
Net Worth: £18,324,000 *Total Assets:* £45,103,000
Registered Office: 16 Compass Point, Market Harborough, Leics, LE16 9HW
Activities: Retail sale of footwear in specialised stores
Officers: Christopher Martin Holden, Secretary/Financial Controller; Christopher Martin Holden [1971] Finance Director; Dr Olaf Bernd Ihde [1967] Director/Controller [German]; Andrew John Underwood [1962] Operations Director

Del Equipment (U.K.) Limited
Incorporated: 28 March 1984 *Employees:* 94
Net Worth: £8,090,196 *Total Assets:* £11,225,474
Registered Office: Building 1, Windrush Park Road, Windrush Industrial Park, Witney, Oxon, OX29 7HA
Activities: Manufacture of lifting and handling equipment
Parent: Cargotec Oyj
Officers: Manojkumar Prabhakar Abhyankar, Secretary; Simon Christopher Eskriett [1964] Sales Director; Philip Julian Pearson [1968] Sales Director; Ian Alan Street [1961] Manufacturing Director

Delano Birmingham 2009 Limited
Incorporated: 10 December 2008
Net Worth: £14,130,778 *Total Assets:* £18,572,136
Registered Office: Ferham House, Kimberworth Road, Masbrough, Rotherham, S Yorks, S61 1AJ
Activities: Residential nursing care facilities
Parent: Delano Investments Ltd
Officers: Elizabeth Jane Phipps, Secretary; Euan David Craig [1977] Director; John Henry Whitehead [1964] Director/Chief Financial Officer

Delano Sutton 2007 Limited
Incorporated: 20 March 2007
Net Worth: £16,235,030 *Total Assets:* £17,699,188
Registered Office: Ferham House, Kimberworth Road, Masbrough, Rotherham, S Yorks, S61 1AJ
Activities: Residential nursing care facilities
Parent: Cairnwell Estates Ltd
Officers: Elizabeth Jane Phipps, Secretary; Euan David Craig [1977] Director; John Henry Whitehead [1964] Director/Chief Financial Officer

Delaquest Limited
Incorporated: 29 November 1993 *Employees:* 215
Net Worth: £14,107,833 *Total Assets:* £41,333,924
Registered Office: Corus House, 1 Auckland Park, Milton Keynes, Bucks, MK1 1BU
Activities: Hotels and similar accommodation
Parent: Corus Hotels Limited
Officers: Khurram Mohmand, Secretary; Andrew Khoo [1972] Director [Australian]; Yet King Loy [1946] Director [Canadian]; Khurram Mohmand [1972] Director/Accountant

Delgarth 2011 Limited
Incorporated: 28 September 2011 *Employees:* 80
Net Worth: £3,541,357 *Total Assets:* £12,449,367
Registered Office: 300 Stratford Road, Wolverton, Milton Keynes, Bucks, MK12 5RS
Activities: Activities of other holding companies n.e.c.
Major Shareholder: David John Turney
Officers: David John Turney [1948] Director

Delifrance (UK) Limited
Incorporated: 2 November 1987 *Employees:* 352
Net Worth: £19,813,000 *Total Assets:* £44,190,000
Registered Office: 17 Chartwell Drive, Wigston, Leics, LE18 2FL
Activities: Manufacture of bread; manufacture of fresh pastry goods and cakes
Officers: Denis Rene Raymond Boutang [1964] Director [French]; Andrew Brian Cole [1966] Director; Arnold Girard [1974] Director/Chief Financial Officer [French]; Richard Mark Julian Turner [1964] Director/Finance and Administration Manager

The Deltic Group Holdings Limited
Incorporated: 5 December 2011 *Employees:* 1,345
Previous: Ranimul 1 Limited
Net Worth: £9,789,000 *Total Assets:* £72,011,000
Registered Office: Aurora House, Deltic Avenue, Rooksley, Milton Keynes, Bucks, MK13 8LW
Activities: Activities of other holding companies n.e.c.
Shareholder: Paul John Evans
Officers: Steven Lindsay Cloran [1964] Director/Company Executive; Paul John Evans [1947] Director; Alan James Fall [1965] Director/Company Executive; Peter Jack Marks [1960] Director/Chief Executive; Lawrence Edward McGreal [1960] Director/Accountant

The Deltic Group Limited
Incorporated: 5 December 2011 *Employees:* 1,345
Previous: The Luminar Group Limited
Net Worth: £9,656,000 *Total Assets:* £70,244,000
Registered Office: Aurora House, Deltic Avenue, Rooksley, Milton Keynes, Bucks, MK13 8LW
Activities: Licenced clubs
Parent: The Deltic Group Holdings Limited
Officers: Kelly Anne Young, Secretary; Robert Brannan [1956] Director; Steven Lindsay Cloran [1964] Director/Company Executive; Paul John Evans [1947] Director; Alan James Fall [1965] Director/Company Executive; Peter Jack Marks [1960] Director/Chief Executive; Lawrence Edward McGreal [1960] Director/Accountant; Alex Millington [1978] Finance Director

Dematic (Services) Limited
Incorporated: 19 December 2014
Net Worth: £1,028,689,664 *Total Assets:* £1,028,694,400
Registered Office: Banbury Business Park, Trinity Way, Adderbury, Banbury, Oxon, OX17 3SN
Activities: Activities of head offices
Parent: Kion Group AG
Officers: Thomas Schmelzer [1964] Director/Manager [German]; Dr Mahdi Daneshzadeh Tabrizi [1982] Director/Manager [German]

Dematic Group Limited
Incorporated: 23 June 2015 *Employees:* 4
Net Worth: £647,812,864 *Total Assets:* £665,142,656
Registered Office: Banbury Business Park, Trinity Way, Adderbury, Banbury, Oxon, OX17 3SN
Activities: Activities of head offices
Officers: Amy Elizabeth Busby, Secretary; Robyn Ann Sternberg Osborne, Secretary; Amy Elizabeth Busby [1980] Director; Matthew Carlson [1974] Director [American]; Robyn Ann Sternberg Osborne [1980] Director [British/South African]

Dematic Limited
Incorporated: 23 June 2006 *Employees:* 671
Net Worth: £13,823,000 *Total Assets:* £45,564,000
Registered Office: Banbury Business Park, Trinity Way, Adderbury, Banbury, Oxon, OX17 3SN
Activities: Manufacture of other special-purpose machinery n.e.c.
Parent: Dematic Group Limited
Officers: Robyn Ann Sternberg Osborne, Secretary; Amy Elizabeth Busby [1980] Finance Director; Robyn Ann Sternberg Osborne [1980] Legal Counsel and Director

Denaro (UK) Limited
Incorporated: 11 July 2011
Net Worth: £360 *Total Assets:* £16,208,622
Registered Office: 16 Dudley Street, Grimsby, N E Lincs, DN31 2AB
Activities: Other service activities n.e.c.
Officers: Anthony David Bracken [1961] Director; Colin George Hesketh [1962] Director

Denaro Partners LLP
Incorporated: 18 April 2012
Net Worth: £16,298,346 *Total Assets:* £16,299,361
Registered Office: 16 Dudley Street, Grimsby, N E Lincs, DN31 2AB

The Denbigh Alliance
Incorporated: 11 February 2011 *Employees:* 188
Previous: Denbigh School
Net Worth: £25,114,012 *Total Assets:* £28,977,100
Registered Office: Burchard Crescent, Shenley Church End, Milton Keynes, Bucks, MK5 6EX
Activities: General secondary education
Officers: William Gibson Butler [1953] Director/Management Consultant; John Robert Cove [1958] Director; Andrew Peter Dransfield [1947] Director; Bruce Hawthorne [1965] Director; Aleck Edward Hornshaw [1968] Director; John Stewart Howe [1950] Director/Retired; Roger Charles Lane-Nott [1945] Director/Retired; Sharon McGuire [1960] Director; Thornton George Naylor [1955] Director/Retired; Maureen O'Brien [1962] Director [Irish]; Deborah Plumb [1961] Director/Pharmacist; Colin Jonathan Solloway [1960] Director/School; Deborah Jane Sporn [1973] Director/PR Manager; Amdrew Squires [1970] Director/Headteacher

Denby Holdings Limited
Incorporated: 27 November 2008 *Employees:* 627
Net Worth: £1,702,000 *Total Assets:* £33,474,000
Registered Office: Denby Pottery, Denby, Derbys, DE5 8NX
Activities: Activities of production holding companies
Parent: Valco Capital Partner II Limited Partnership
Officers: Robert John Barton, Secretary/Director; Robert John Barton [1959] Director; Richard Paul Eaton [1963] Director; Christopher William Emmott [1977] Investment Director; Sebastian Lazell [1963] Director; Paul Patrick McGowan [1962] Director [Irish]

Denby Potteries Limited
Incorporated: 6 January 2009 *Employees:* 303
Net Worth: £1,730,000 *Total Assets:* £18,623,000
Registered Office: Denby Pottery, Denby, Derbys, DE5 8NX
Activities: Other manufacturing n.e.c.
Parent: Denby Holdings Limited
Officers: Robert John Barton, Secretary/Director; Robert John Barton [1959] Director; Richard Paul Eaton [1963] Director; Christopher William Emmott [1977] Investment Director; Sebastian Lazell [1963] Director; Paul Patrick McGowan [1962] Director [Irish]

The Denby Pottery Company Limited
Incorporated: 22 January 2009 *Employees:* 50
Net Worth: £4,515,000 *Total Assets:* £39,799,000
Registered Office: Denby Pottery, Denby, Derbys, DE5 8NX
Activities: Activities of head offices
Parent: Denby Holdings Limited
Officers: Robert John Barton, Secretary/Director; Robert John Barton [1959] Director; Richard Paul Eaton [1963] Director; Christopher William Emmott [1977] Investment Director; Sebastian Lazell [1963] Director; Paul Patrick McGowan [1962] Director [Irish]

The Derby County Football Club Limited
Incorporated: 14 August 1896 *Employees:* 152
Net Worth: £107,677,200 *Total Assets:* £141,195,248
Registered Office: Pride Park Stadium, Pride Park, Derby, DE24 8XL
Activities: Other sports activities
Officers: Stephen Anthony Pearce, Secretary; John Nigel Kirkland [1938] Director/Chairman of Bowmer & Kirkland Group of Companies; Roy Leslie McFarland [1948] Director/Retired; Melvyn Morris [1956] Director; Stephen Anthony Pearce [1980] Director/Chartered Accountant; David Henry Williams [1956] Director/Solicitor

Derby Diocesan Academy Trust 2
Incorporated: 16 February 2015 *Employees:* 298
Net Worth: £18,879,502 *Total Assets:* £21,540,388
Registered Office: Derby Diocese Board of Education, Full Street, Derby, DE1 3DR
Activities: Primary education
Officers: Jason Nicholas Hampton, Secretary; Lisa Jane Bloor [1968] Director/Financial Controller; Alison Mary Brown [1960] Deputy Director of Education and Schools' Adviser; Canon David John Channon [1968] Director; The Venerable Carol Ann Coslett [1963] Director/Archdeacon of Chesterfield; Michael John Ford [1982] Director; Mark Mallender [1975] Director; Declan McCauley [1962] Director/Interim Chief Executive Officer; Mark John Titterton [1965] Director/Group Chief Executive

Derby Diocesan Board of Finance Limited (The)
Incorporated: 16 April 1928 *Employees:* 48
Net Worth: £81,361,464 *Total Assets:* £85,183,112
Registered Office: Derby Church House, Full Street, Derby, DE1 3DR
Activities: Activities of religious organisations
Officers: Rachel Morris, Secretary; Duncan Charles John Ballard [1965] Director/Area Dean; Jack Cooper [1952] Director; The Venerable Carol Ann Coslett [1963] Director/Archdeacon; Christopher John Cunliffe [1955] Director/Archdeacon of Derby; The Reverend Peter James Davey [1959] Director; Frederick John Gascoyne [1945] Director/Retired; Stephen John Hance [1966] Director/Dean of Derby Cathedral; Christine Mary Holmes-Elener [1960] Director/Retired; Revd Alasdair Stewart Kay [1961] Director/Priest-in-Charge; The Right Reverend Janet Elizabeth McFarlane [1964] Director/Bishop; Christine Elizabeth McMullen [1943] Director/Retired; Brian Arthur Parker [1951] Director/Retired; Revd Colin Graham Pearson [1958] Director/Minister of Religion; Madalaine Thomas-Goddard [1944] Director; Mark John Titterton [1965] Managing Director; Peter Francis Vincent [1948] Director; Jason David Ward [1971] Director/Minister of Religion; William Edward Jonathan Whiten [1968] Director

Derby Homes Limited
Incorporated: 25 February 2002 *Employees:* 495
Net Worth Deficit: £3,069,000 *Total Assets:* £24,182,000
Registered Office: 839 London Road, Alvaston, Derby, DE24 8UZ
Activities: Management of real estate on a fee or contract basis
Parent: Derby City Council
Officers: David Enticott, Secretary; Michael Ainsley [1950] Director/Retired; Councillor Lucy Helen Care [1960] Director; Robert Astley Cooper [1984] Director; Sophia Gutsa [1975] Director/Relief Unit Assistant Manager; Fareed Hussain [1954] Director/Retired; Iain MacRae MacDonald [1943] Director; Robert George Hasty MacDonald [1946] Director; Dennis James Rees [1935] Director/Retired; Jsan Marie Shepherd [1965] Director/Self Employed

Derbyshire Aggregates Limited
Incorporated: 17 July 1984 *Employees:* 58
Net Worth: £11,532,497 *Total Assets:* £14,705,983
Registered Office: Arbor Low Works, Youlgreave, Bakewell, Derbys, DE45 1JS
Activities: Quarrying of ornamental and building stone, limestone, gypsum, chalk and slate
Shareholders: Adrian Paul Denny Fewings; Martin Poulter
Officers: Karen Belinda Poulter, Secretary; Kevan Brassington [1962] Operations Director; Samuel Brookes Buckley [1964] Commercial Director; Susan Kathleen Fewings [1961] Director; Karen Belinda Poulter [1965] Director; Martin Poulter [1958] Director

Derbyshire Property Trust Limited (The)
Incorporated: 14 February 1935 *Employees:* 4
Net Worth: £10,439,093 *Total Assets:* £10,868,130
Registered Office: Rose Cottage, Duffield Bank, Duffield, Belper, Derbys, DE56 4BG
Activities: Buying and selling of own real estate
Officers: Lorna Frances Edge, Secretary; Nicholas Francis Bohane [1962] Director/Internet; John Connell [1948] Director/Engineer; Lorna Frances Edge [1951] Director/Company Secretary

Derbyshire Student Residences Limited
Incorporated: 31 July 1995 *Employees:* 57
Net Worth: £78,486,000 *Total Assets:* £113,616,000
Registered Office: University of Derby, Kedleston Road, Derby, DE22 1GB
Activities: Other letting and operating of own or leased real estate
Officers: Susan Jane Ambler, Secretary; Professor Kathryn Mary Mitchell [1963] Director/Vice-Chancellor and CEO; Harindra Deepal Punchihewa [1961] Director of Finance; Mark John Travers [1960] Director/Operations Manager

Dering Properties Finance Limited
Incorporated: 2 May 2014
Net Worth: £1,331 *Total Assets:* £11,253,871
Registered Office: Newington House, Newington, Oxon, OX10 7AG
Activities: Buying and selling of own real estate
Major Shareholder: John James Dering Nettlet
Officers: John James Dering Nettleton, Secretary; John James Dering Nettleton [1982] Director/Accountant

Deritend International Limited
Incorporated: 13 March 1948 *Employees:* 596
Net Worth: £70,631,000 *Total Assets:* £152,631,008
Registered Office: Millennium Court, First Avenue, Burton on Trent, Staffs, DE14 2WH
Activities: Machining
Parent: Doncasters Limited
Officers: Ian Molyneux, Secretary; Duncan Andrew Hinks [1975] Director/Chief Financial Officer; Ian Molyneux [1964] Director/Solicitor; Lisa Marie Oxnard [1981] Director/Chief Financial Officer

Derry Building Services Limited
Incorporated: 22 February 1980 *Employees:* 239
Net Worth: £13,083,049 *Total Assets:* £35,228,948
Registered Office: The Old Hospital, London Road, Newark, Notts, NG24 1JP
Activities: Electrical installation
Parent: Bowmer & Kirkland Ltd.
Officers: Michelle Ann Mucklestone, Secretary; Stephen Gould Burley [1956] Construction Director; Richard Brian Hughes [1967] Director; Gregg Matthews [1968] Director; Mark Gary Townsend [1967] Managing Director

Derwent Vehicles Limited
Incorporated: 7 June 1943 *Employees:* 516
Net Worth: £23,182,000 *Total Assets:* £108,958,000
Registered Office: Loxley House, 2 Oakwood Court, Little Oak Drive, Annesley, Nottingham, NG15 0DR
Activities: Sale of new cars and light motor vehicles
Officers: Richard James Maloney, Secretary; Martin Shaun Casha [1960] Director; Trevor Garry Finn [1957] Director; Timothy Paul Holden [1964] Director/Chartered Accountant

Desford Acquisition Company (UK) Limited
Incorporated: 24 December 2014
Net Worth: £8,749,000 *Total Assets:* £62,834,000
Registered Office: Peckleton Lane, Desford, Leicester, LE9 9JT
Activities: Activities of other holding companies n.e.c.
Parent: Logistics Acquisition Company (UK) Limited
Officers: Zachary Green, Secretary; Zach Green [1960] Director/Attorney [American]; Nicholas Gerard Paterson [1966] Director, Operations

Designer Contracts Limited
Incorporated: 26 November 2004 *Employees:* 256
Net Worth: £2,594,012 *Total Assets:* £10,497,952
Registered Office: Unit 5 Freshwaters, Holmewood Industrial Estate, Park Road, Chesterfield, Derbys, S42 5UY
Activities: Floor and wall covering
Major Shareholder: Peter Anthony Kelsey
Officers: Susan Kelsey, Secretary; Peter Anthony Kelsey [1950] Director

Destec Engineering Limited
Incorporated: 23 January 1969 *Employees:* 86
Net Worth: £12,250,111 *Total Assets:* £13,808,724
Registered Office: M R Cowdrey & Co, 125 Nottingham Road, Stapleford, Nottingham, NG9 8AT
Activities: Manufacture of other fabricated metal products n.e.c.
Shareholders: John Alan Stewart MacLachlan; Barry Porter
Officers: M/S Karyn Louise Andrews, Secretary; Karyn Louise Andrews [1964] Financial Director; John Alan Stewart MacLachlan [1932] Director; Barry Porter [1938] Director

Detrafford No1 Castlefield Ltd
Incorporated: 13 May 2016
Previous: De Trafford Estates No.1 Castlefield Block A Ltd
Net Worth Deficit: £1,577 *Total Assets:* £9,615,195
Registered Office: Suite 26g, Building 26, Alderley Park, Alderley Edge, Cheshire, SK10 4TG
Activities: Other business support service activities n.e.c.
Major Shareholder: Gary Thomas Jackson
Officers: Brian Lowndes, Secretary; Gary Thomas Jackson [1964] Director

Detrafford Sky Gardens Ltd
Incorporated: 15 April 2014
Previous: De Trafford Estates Churchgate Limited
Net Worth Deficit: £1,891 *Total Assets:* £15,431,956
Registered Office: Suite 26g, Building 26, Alderley Park, Alderley Edge, Cheshire, SK10 4TG
Activities: Other business support service activities n.e.c.
Major Shareholder: Gary Thomas Jackson
Officers: Brian Lowndes, Secretary; Gary Thomas Jackson [1964] Director

Devereux Capital LLP
Incorporated: 12 August 2010
Net Worth: £256,380 *Total Assets:* £14,259,766
Registered Office: 3 Castlegate, Grantham, Lincs, NG31 6SF
Officers: John Richard Eric Devereux [1939] LLP Member; Wynnona Jane Devereux [1943] LLP Member

Devol Kitchens Limited
Incorporated: 25 September 2008 *Employees:* 135
Net Worth: £3,528,966 *Total Assets:* £10,312,042
Registered Office: Cotes Mill, Nottingham Road, Cotes, Loughborough, Leics, LE12 5TL
Activities: Manufacture of kitchen furniture
Major Shareholder: Paul John O'Leary
Officers: Robin McLellan [1985] Director; Paul John O'Leary [1963] Director/Designer

Devonshire Green (Broomgrove Road) Limited
Incorporated: 8 December 2011
Net Worth: £4,804,000 *Total Assets:* £35,699,000
Registered Office: Devonshire Green House, Fitzwilliam Street, Sheffield, S1 4JL
Activities: Other letting and operating of own or leased real estate
Parent: Devonshire Green Holdings Limited
Officers: Ewan Gairn Barclay Ross, Secretary; Brendan Elwood [1943] Director; Martin Patrick Elwood [1968] Director/Property Investment and Development; Dale Lee Fixter [1967] Director/Chartered Surveyor

Devonshire Green (Commercial Properties) Limited
Incorporated: 25 October 2000
Net Worth: £440,000 *Total Assets:* £10,944,000
Registered Office: Devonshire Green House, 14 Fitzwilliam Street, Sheffield, S1 4JL
Activities: Other letting and operating of own or leased real estate
Parent: Devonshire Green Holdings Limited
Officers: Ewan Gairn Barclay Ross, Secretary; Brendan Elwood [1943] Director/Property Investment and Development; Martin Patrick Elwood [1968] Director/Property Investment and Development; Dale Lee Fixter [1967] Director/Chartered Surveyor

Devonshire Green (Residential Investments) Limited
Incorporated: 10 April 2002
Net Worth: £12,824,000 *Total Assets:* £24,463,000
Registered Office: Devonshire Green House, 14 Fitzwilliam Street, Sheffield, S1 4JL
Activities: Other letting and operating of own or leased real estate
Parent: Devonshire Green Holdings Limited
Officers: Ewan Gairn Barclay Ross, Secretary; Brendan Elwood [1943] Director/Property Investment and Development; Martin Patrick Elwood [1968] Director/Property Investment and Development; Dale Lee Fixter [1967] Director/Chartered Surveyor

Devonshire Green Holdings Limited
Incorporated: 24 January 2000
Net Worth: £3,314,000 *Total Assets:* £29,546,000
Registered Office: Devonshire Green House, 14 Fitzwilliam Street, Sheffield, S1 4JL
Activities: Other letting and operating of own or leased real estate
Parent: Elmsdale Estates Limited
Officers: Ewan Gairn Barclay Ross, Secretary; Brendan Elwood [1943] Director/Property Investment & Development; Martin Patrick Elwood [1968] Director/Property Investment and Development; Dale Lee Fixter [1967] Director/Chartered Surveyor

DFDS Logistics Limited
Incorporated: 25 February 2004 *Employees:* 427
Previous: DFDS Logistics Partners Ltd
Net Worth: £11,875,085 *Total Assets:* £87,908,800
Registered Office: Nordic House, Western Access Road, Immingham Dock, Immingham, N E Lincs, DN40 2LZ
Activities: Freight transport by road
Officers: Per Lund Jensen, Secretary; Allan James MacIntyre Bell [1978] Director; Edward James Green [1957] Director; Sarah Holloway [1977] Director; Klaus Jonassen [1966] Director; Stephen William MacAulay [1960] Director

DFDS Pension Limited
Incorporated: 27 December 1963 *Employees:* 4
Previous: DFDS Logistics Limited
Net Worth: £23,545,000 *Total Assets:* £32,053,000
Registered Office: Nordic House, Western Access Road, Immingham Dock, Immingham, N E Lincs, DN40 2LZ
Activities: Pension funding
Officers: Per Lund Jensen, Secretary; Torben Carlsen [1965] Director/Chief Finance Officer [Danish]; Edward James Green [1957] Director/General Manager; Stephen William MacAulay [1960] Director/General Manager; Niels Smedergaard [1962] Director/Chief Executive Officer [Danish]

DFDS Seaways Newcastle Limited
Incorporated: 23 November 1970 *Employees:* 76
Net Worth: £8,041,481 *Total Assets:* £11,977,824
Registered Office: Nordic House, Western Access Road, Immingham Dock, Immingham, N E Lincs, DN40 2LZ
Activities: Sea and coastal passenger water transport
Officers: Per Lund Jensen, Secretary [Danish]; Niels Smedegaard [1962] Managing Director [Danish]

DFDS Seaways PLC
Incorporated: 2 April 1981 *Employees:* 582
Net Worth Deficit: £4,109,977 *Total Assets:* £55,035,020
Registered Office: Nordic House, Western Access Road, Immingham Dock, Immingham, N E Lincs, DN40 2LZ
Activities: Operation of warehousing and storage facilities for water transport activities
Officers: Per Lund Jensen, Secretary [Danish]; Andrew Geoffrey Byrne [1973] Director; Peder Gellert Pedersen [1958] Director [Danish]; Niels Smedegaard [1962] Managing Director [Danish]

DFS Furniture Company Limited
Incorporated: 11 February 1970 *Employees:* 7
Net Worth: £45,400,000 *Total Assets:* £96,700,000
Registered Office: 1 Rockingham Way, Redhouse Interchange, Adwick-le-Street, Doncaster, S Yorks, DN6 7NA
Activities: Activities of head offices
Parent: DFS Furniture Holdings PLC
Officers: Elizabeth McDonald, Secretary; Nicola Jayne Bancroft [1964] Director; Timothy Giles Stacey [1971] Director

DFS Furniture Holdings PLC
Incorporated: 9 April 2010
Net Worth: £97,900,000 *Total Assets:* £703,000,000
Registered Office: 1 Rockingham Way, Redhouse Interchange, Adwick-le-Street, Doncaster, S Yorks, DN6 7NA
Activities: Activities of head offices
Parent: Diamond Holdco 7 Limited
Officers: Elizabeth McDonald, Secretary; Nicola Jayne Bancroft [1964] Director; Ian Francis Filby [1959] Director

DFS Furniture PLC
Incorporated: 27 April 2010 *Employees:* 4,872
Previous: DFS Furniture Limited
Net Worth: £252,400,000 *Total Assets:* £774,200,000
Registered Office: 1 Rockingham Way, Redhouse Interchange, Adwick-le-Street, Doncaster, S Yorks, DN6 7NA
Activities: Activities of head offices
Officers: Elizabeth McDonald, Secretary; Nicola Jayne Bancroft [1964] Director; Joanna Boydell [1969] Director; Ian Charles Durant [1958] Director; Alison Elizabeth Hutchinson [1967] Director; Stephen Richard Johnson [1963] Director; Christopher Luke Mayhew [1953] Director; Julie Helen Southern [1959] Director; Timothy Giles Stacey [1971] Director

DFS Trading Limited
Incorporated: 1 July 1983 *Employees:* 3,801
Net Worth: £114,200,000 *Total Assets:* £326,100,000
Registered Office: 1 Rockingham Way, Redhouse Interchange, Adwick-le-Street, Doncaster, S Yorks, DN6 7NA
Activities: Retail of furniture, lighting, and similar (not musical instruments or scores) in specialised store
Parent: DFS Furniture Company Ltd
Officers: Elizabeth McDonald, Secretary; Nicola Jayne Bancroft [1964] Director of Commercial Finance; Harvey George Ellis [1956] Production Director; Scott Fishburn [1974] Director; Graham Mould [1966] Training Director; Timothy Giles Stacey [1971] Business Development Director; Andrew Stefan Trofimowicz [1962] Marketing Director; Andrew Henry Vaughan-Jones [1953] Buying Director; Toni Wood [1971] Director

DGS Group PLC
Incorporated: 21 November 1979 *Employees:* 187
Previous: Double Glazing Supplies Group PLC
Net Worth: £16,722,440 *Total Assets:* £18,677,900
Registered Office: 4 Bank Court, Weldon Road, Loughborough, Leics, LE11 5RF
Activities: Non-specialised wholesale trade
Shareholders: David Aucott; Derek Aucott
Officers: Elizabeth Slocombe, Secretary; Daniel Aucott [1988] Director; David Aucott [1958] Director; Derek Aucott [1931] Director; Helen Aucott [1985] Director; Margaret Rose Aucott [1932] Director; Elizabeth Slocombe [1960] Director

DH Alpha Limited
Incorporated: 13 April 2012 *Employees:* 1
Net Worth: £386,686,016 *Total Assets:* £1,826,075,008
Registered Office: 19 Jessops Riverside, 800 Brightside Lane, Sheffield, S9 2RX
Activities: Activities of head offices
Parent: Danaher Corporation
Officers: Keith Graham Ward [1953] Director/Finance and Accounting

DH Omega Limited
Incorporated: 13 April 2012 *Employees:* 1
Net Worth: £1,631,801,984 *Total Assets:* £1,656,760,960
Registered Office: 19 Jessops Riverside, 800 Brightside Lane, Sheffield, S9 2RX
Activities: Activities of head offices
Parent: DH Alpha Ltd
Officers: Keith Graham Ward [1953] Director/Finance and Accounting

DH UK Finance Limited
Incorporated: 7 December 2009 *Employees:* 1
Previous: DHR Finance Limited
Net Worth: £193,623,008 *Total Assets:* £197,830,000
Registered Office: 19 Jessops Riverside, 800 Brightside Lane, Sheffield, S9 2RX
Activities: Activities of head offices
Parent: Launchchange Holdings Limited
Officers: Keith Graham Ward [1953] Director

DHL Services Limited
Incorporated: 26 February 1997 *Employees:* 39,767
Net Worth Deficit: £213,874,000 *Total Assets:* £179,232,000
Registered Office: 251 Midsummer Boulevard, Milton Keynes, Bucks, MK9 1EQ
Activities: Other business support service activities n.e.c.
Parent: DHL Supply Chain Limited
Officers: Lindsay Elizabeth Bridges [1969] Director [Irish]; Karen Brown [1965] Director/Solicitor; Ian David Clough [1967] Director; Peter Gerrard Flanagan [1964] Director; James Andrew Hartshorne [1976] Director; Thorsten Kuhl [1974] Director [German]; Gavin John Murdoch [1967] Director; Jose Fernando Nava [1963] Director [American]; David Julian Pierpoint [1968] Director; Paul Robin Richardson [1963] Director; Philip William Roe [1966] Director; Timothy John Slater [1968] Managing Director; Martin James Willmor [1980] Managing Director; Marcus Wurker [1977] Director [German]

DHL Supply Chain Limited
Incorporated: 4 February 1954
Net Worth: £442,270,016 *Total Assets:* £1,214,093,056
Registered Office: 251 Midsummer Boulevard, Milton Keynes, Bucks, MK9 1EQ
Activities: Freight transport by road
Parent: Exel Investments Limited
Officers: Lindsay Elizabeth Bridges [1969] Director [Irish]; Ian David Clough [1967] Director; James Andrew Hartshorne [1976] Director; Thorsten Kuhl [1974] Director [German]; Jose Fernando Nava [1963] Director [American]; David Julian Pierpoint [1968] Director; Paul Robin Richardson [1963] Director; Philip William Roe [1966] Director/Transport Manager; Timothy John Slater [1968] Managing Director; Martin James Willmor [1980] Managing Director; Marcus Wurker [1977] Director [German]

Dhollandia U.K. Limited
Incorporated: 17 November 1995 *Employees:* 24
Net Worth: £13,235,641 *Total Assets:* £22,155,434
Registered Office: Dhollandia UK, Latham Road, Huntingdon, Cambs, PE29 6YG
Activities: Manufacture of other transport equipment n.e.c.
Major Shareholder: Nancy Alois Dhollander
Officers: Nancy Dhollander, Secretary; Nancy Dhollander [1968] Director [Belgian]; Christopher Mark Lay [1975] Director/Sales Manager

DHP Family Ltd.
Incorporated: 3 October 1931 *Employees:* 369
Net Worth: £8,729,735 *Total Assets:* £42,324,596
Registered Office: 2 Lace Market Square, Nottingham, NG1 1PB
Activities: Public houses and bars
Officers: Sean Akins, Secretary/Director; George Henry Akins [1974] Director; George Henry Akins [1928] Director; Sean Akins [1973] Director; David Paul McDerment [1981] Finance Director

DHT Finance Limited
Incorporated: 8 August 2015 *Employees:* 1
Net Worth: £17,708,964 *Total Assets:* £24,662,340
Registered Office: 11 Merus Court, Meridian Business Park, Leicester, LE19 1RJ
Activities: Other credit granting n.e.c.
Parent: Punch Promotions Limited
Officers: Richard John Hatton [1978] Director

Diam UK Ltd.
Incorporated: 12 November 1993 *Employees:* 220
Net Worth: £8,668,917 *Total Assets:* £20,027,164
Registered Office: 14-16 Jubilee Drive, Loughborough, Leics, LE11 5XS
Activities: Other manufacturing n.e.c.
Officers: Clive Simpson Bagley [1960] Director; David Simpson Bagley [1961] Director; Mark Simpson Bagley [1962] Tooling Director; Giles Easingwood [1965] Creative Director; Stuart Robert David Youngs [1964] Director/Production Manager

Diamond Fuel Supplies Limited
Incorporated: 30 January 1980 *Employees:* 4
Net Worth: £911,955 *Total Assets:* £9,429,059
Registered Office: The Freight Terminal, Bicester Road, Enstone, Chipping Norton, Oxon, OX7 4NP
Activities: Agents involved in the sale of fuels, ores, metals and industrial chemicals
Parent: Bagnalls Group (UK) Ltd
Officers: Douglas Charles Bagnall [1968] Sales Director; Jean Rosemary Ellen Bagnall [1938] Director/Secretary; Jonathan Phillip Bagnall [1961] Director; Paul Richard Bagnall [1963] Director

Diamond Holdco 2 Limited
Incorporated: 27 April 2010
Net Worth: £96,600,000 *Total Assets:* £197,300,000
Registered Office: 1 Rockingham Way, Redhouse Interchange, Adwick-le-Street, Doncaster, S Yorks, DN6 7NA
Activities: Activities of head offices
Parent: DFS Furniture PLC
Officers: Elizabeth McDonald, Secretary; Nicola Jayne Bancroft [1964] Director; Ian Francis Filby [1959] Director

Diamond Holdco 7 Limited
Incorporated: 27 April 2010
Net Worth: £200,900,000 *Total Assets:* £203,200,000
Registered Office: 1 Rockingham Way, Redhouse Interchange, Adwick-le-Street, Doncaster, S Yorks, DN6 7NA
Activities: Activities of head offices
Parent: Diamond Holdco 2 Limited
Officers: Elizabeth McDonald, Secretary; Nicola Jayne Bancroft [1964] Director; Ian Francis Filby [1959] Director

Diamond Light Source Limited
Incorporated: 18 February 2002 *Employees:* 639
Net Worth: £325,282,240 *Total Assets:* £404,731,616
Registered Office: Diamond House, Harwell Science and Innovation Campus, Didcot, Oxon, OX11 0DE
Activities: Other research and experimental development on natural sciences and engineering
Officers: Andrew Peter Richards, Secretary; Philip Leon Marshall Davies [1938] Director/Pharmacist; Professor Michael Edward Fitzpatrick [1970] Director/Executive Dean; Professor Andrew Harrison [1959] Director/Chief Executive; Professor Adrian Frederick Melhuish Smith [1946] Director/Vice-Chancellor; Professor Mark Andrew Thomson [1966] Director/Executive Chair; Professor Charles Michael Turner [1958] Director of Science; Professor Keith Sanderson Wilson [1949] Director/University Professor

Diamond Power Specialty Limited
Incorporated: 5 March 1913 *Employees:* 149
Net Worth: £23,305,000 *Total Assets:* £28,130,000
Registered Office: Unit 5b Heapham Road, Heapham Road Industrial Estate, Gainsborough, Lincs, DN21 1RZ
Activities: Machining
Parent: Diamond Power International Inc
Officers: Christopher James Paul, Secretary; Gary Campbell Cochrane [1977] Managing Director; Mika Jaakko Haikola [1969] Director [Finnish]; Michael Phillip Michael [1964] Director/Engineer [American]

Digital House Group Ltd
Incorporated: 13 May 2016
Net Worth: £21,003,152 *Total Assets:* £21,071,540
Registered Office: 4 Gransden Business Park, Potton Road, Abbotsley, St Neots, Cambs, PE19 6TY
Activities: Activities of financial services holding companies
Shareholder: Nelson Damian Duboscq
Officers: Eduardo Bruchou [1954] Director [Argentinian]; Nelson Damian Duboscq [1962] Director [Argentinian]; Hernan Jorge Kazah [1970] Director [Argentinian]; John Mark Rogers [1967] Director [American]; Luis Maria Julio Saguier [1966] Director [Argentinian]; Angel Jose Uribe [1975] Director/Investor [Argentinian]

Diligenta Limited
Incorporated: 12 August 2005 *Employees:* 2,686
Net Worth: £64,716,000 *Total Assets:* £105,087,000
Registered Office: Lynch Wood, Peterborough, Cambs, PE2 6FY
Activities: Financial intermediation not elsewhere classified
Officers: Alan Peter Jackson, Secretary; Sir Michael Anthony Arthur [1950] Director; Suresh Muthuswami [1963] Director/President & Global Head [Indian]; Ganapathy Subramaniam Natarajan [1959] Director/TCS Chief Operating Officer [Indian]; Sir Robert Paul Reid [1934] Director; Daniel Praveen Sundaradas [1972] Director/Chief Executive [Indian]

The Diocese of Coventry Multi-Academy Trust
Incorporated: 27 February 2013 *Employees:* 713
Net Worth: £51,391,000 *Total Assets:* £63,641,000
Registered Office: The Benn Education Centre, Craven Road, Rugby, Warwicks, CV21 3JZ
Activities: Primary education
Officers: Joanna Ruth Baker, Secretary; Andrew Rowland Armbrister [1962] Director/Retired; Ian Christopher Dewes [1980] Director/Headteacher; Peter Ewan Law [1949] Director/Retired; Ruth Elizabeth Marlow [1961] Director/Diocesan Secretary; Roger Terrence Arthur Medwell [1943] Director/Retired; Amanda Elizabeth Moreton [1972] Human Resources Director; Jason Slack [1971] Director/Headteacher; John Andrew Wade [1964] Managing Director

The Diocese of Sheffield Academies Trust
Incorporated: 23 October 2013 *Employees:* 396
Net Worth: £5,144,000 *Total Assets:* £12,323,000
Registered Office: Flanderwell Early Excellence Centre, Greenfield Court, Flanderwell, Rotherham, S Yorks, S66 2JF
Activities: Primary education
Officers: Heidi Jane Adcock [1969] Director/Diocesan Secretary; Lindsey-Jane Buxton [1981] Director/Communications Manager; James Robert Dugmore [1978] Director/Headteacher; Nicholas James Keightley [1970] Director/Environmental & Safety Manager; William Huw Thomas [1965] Diocesan Director of Education; Andrew Waldron [1968] Managing Director; Mark Wheeler [1960] Director/Headteacher

Diocese of Southwell and Nottingham Multi-Academy Trust
Incorporated: 18 October 2013 *Employees:* 403
Net Worth: £9,353,644 *Total Assets:* £16,232,282
Registered Office: Jubilee House, Westgate, Southwell, Notts, NG25 0JH
Activities: Other education n.e.c.
Officers: Joanne Saville, Secretary; Canon Philip John Blinston [1954] Director; Hilary Margaret Craik [1955] Director/Education Adviser H M Craik Education Consultancy; Ian David Griffiths [1952] IT Director; John William Hunter [1969] Director/Banker; Claire Jane Meese [1963] Diocesan Director of Education; Chris Moodie [1965] Director/CEO for Diocese of Southwell and Nottingham MAT; Angela Mary Pae [1958] Director/Education Consultant; Roger John Periam [1958] Director

Dippy Ridge Limited
Incorporated: 24 July 1992 *Employees:* 1
Net Worth: £2,319,347 *Total Assets:* £12,001,912
Registered Office: Pudding Lane, Pinchbeck, Spalding, Lincs, PE11 3TJ
Activities: Activities of head offices
Parent: J O Sims Holdings Limited
Officers: Andrew James Bell, Secretary; Christopher Oliver Sims [1959] Director

Direct Leisure Supplies Limited
Incorporated: 21 February 1973 *Employees:* 81
Net Worth: £8,126,819 *Total Assets:* £10,442,968
Registered Office: Occupation Lane, Gonerby Moor, Grantham, Lincs, NG32 2BP
Activities: Manufacture of other plastic products
Officers: George William Livingston Brewis, Secretary; George William Livingston Brewis [1964] Director; Ian Andrew Partridge [1973] Director

Discovery Schools Academies Trust Ltd
Incorporated: 13 June 2012 *Employees:* 694
Net Worth: £27,212,000 *Total Assets:* £35,740,000
Registered Office: Kibworth C of E Primary School, Hillcrest Avenue, Kibworth, Leicester, LE8 0NH
Activities: Primary education
Officers: Richard Guy Bettsworth [1965] Director/Head of Public Relations; Shane William Bray [1962] Managing Director; Dr Edmund Peter Green [1965] Director/Chief Executive; Jonathan Eaves Parsons [1974] HR Director; Gary David Sims [1965] Director; Margaret Spence [1954] Director/Specialist Traveller Education Teacher; Paul Sean Stone [1972] Director/Headteacher; Mihir Trivedi [1975] Programme Director; David Rowlands Williams [1953] Director/Retired

Distinction Doors Limited
Incorporated: 26 November 2004 *Employees:* 114
Net Worth: £10,341,438 *Total Assets:* £24,454,630
Registered Office: Wentworth 36, Wentworth Industrial Estate, Wentworth Way, Tankersley, Barnsley, S Yorks, S75 3DH
Activities: Agents involved in the sale of timber and building materials
Parent: Distinction Doors Holdings Limited
Officers: Victoria Mary Brown [1973] Finance Director; Andrew John Fowlds [1965] Director/Chief Executive; David Robert Gomersall [1969] Commercial Director; Helen Lovack [1958] HR Director; Chantel Nicola Roach [1974] Marketing Director; David Michael Walker [1967] Technical Director; Gareth Richard Edward Williams [1972] Director

Distinction Group Limited
Incorporated: 3 December 2014 *Employees:* 114
Net Worth: £2,711,345 *Total Assets:* £17,824,536
Registered Office: Wentworth 36, Wentworth Industrial Estate, Wentworth Way, Tankersley, Barnsley, S Yorks, S75 3DH
Activities: Activities of head offices
Shareholder: Andrew John Fowlds
Officers: David John Amos [1941] Director; Victoria Mary Brown [1973] Director; Andrew John Fowlds [1965] Director; David Robert Gomersall [1969] Director; Helen Lovack [1958] Director; Chantel Nicola Roach [1974] Director; David Michael Walker [1967] Director; Gareth Richard Edward Williams [1972] Director

Ditchley Foundation (The)
Incorporated: 24 February 1958 *Employees:* 25
Net Worth: £24,845,522 *Total Assets:* £25,025,448
Registered Office: Ditchley Park, Enstone, Chipping Norton, Oxon, OX7 4ER
Activities: Other education n.e.c.
Officers: Katie Rosemary Williams, Secretary; Lord Charles Harold Stuart Aldington [1948] Director/Advisor; Lord Karan Faridoon Bilimoria [1961] Director/Chairman & Crossbench Member of House of Lords; Lord Peter Selwyn Chadlington [1942] Director/Group Senior Advisor, Huntsworth PLC; Robert Michael James Gascoyne Cecil [1946] Director/Privy Counsellor; Charles Peter Grant Cmg [1958] Director; Dominic Charles Roberts Grieve [1956] Director; Peter John Hennessy [1947] Director/University Professor, Member of House of Lords; Jonathan Hopkin Hill [1960] Director/Consultant; Professor Sir David King [1939] Director/University Professor; Janis Rachel Lomax [1945] Director; Bronwen Maria Maddox [1963] Director/Editor and Chief Executive; Paul Newman [1956] Director/Chairman; Elizabeth Jane Padmore [1955] Director/Chairman, INED; Emma Reynolds MP [1977] Director/Member of Parliament; Sir Nigel Elton Sheinwald [1953] Director; Sir Martin Gregory Smith [1943] Director/Consultant; Philip Francis Stephens [1953] Director/Journalist; Dr Catherine Mary Hamilton Wills [1950] Director/Freelance Writer

Diverse Academies Trust
Incorporated: 9 June 2011 *Employees:* 1,129
Net Worth: £51,453,000 *Total Assets:* £75,510,000
Registered Office: Tuxford Academy, Marnham Road, Tuxford, Newark, Notts, NG22 0JH
Activities: General secondary education
Shareholders: Margaret Blore; Ingrid Wiggins
Officers: Alison Kathleen Elway, Secretary; Margaret Blore [1943] Director/Retired; Simon Paul Jones [1969] Director; Peter Kirk Mabbott [1980] Director/Banker; Michael William Quigley [1947] Director/Retired; John Richard Rolph [1949] Director/Chartered Accountant; Ian Richard Storey [1952] Director/Consultant; Cherie White [1992] Director/Consultant

Diversey Holdings Limited
Incorporated: 30 October 2001
Net Worth: £72,696,000 *Total Assets:* £73,196,000
Registered Office: Weston Favell Centre, Northampton, NN3 8PD
Activities: Manufacture of soap and detergents
Parent: BCPE Diamond UK Holdco Limited
Officers: Michael James Chapman, Secretary; Michael James Chapman [1961] Director/Solicitor; Colin Timothy Stubbs [1963] Director

Diversey Limited
Incorporated: 29 October 1997 *Employees:* 272
Net Worth: £43,086,000 *Total Assets:* £90,623,000
Registered Office: Weston Favell Centre, Northampton, NN3 8PD
Activities: Manufacture of soap and detergents
Parent: Diversey Holdings Limited
Officers: Raymond Keith Partridge [1966] Sales Director; Patrick Garfield Redman [1967] Sales Director; Colin Timothy Stubbs [1963] Sales Director; John-Paul Surdo [1984] Director/General Manager [American]

Diversey UK Production Limited
Incorporated: 14 September 1981 *Employees:* 91
Net Worth: £12,839,000 *Total Assets:* £15,156,000
Registered Office: Weston Favell Centre, Northampton, NN3 8PD
Activities: Manufacture of soap and detergents
Parent: Diversey Limited
Officers: Isobel Frances Cook [1971] Director/Quality Health and Safety and Environmental; David Charles White [1971] Director/Production Manager

Diversey UK Services Limited
Incorporated: 11 March 1954 *Employees:* 107
Net Worth: £1,184,000 *Total Assets:* £10,418,000
Registered Office: Mr M Chapman, Diversey Limited, Pyramid Close, Northampton, NN3 8PD
Activities: Manufacture of electronic industrial process control equipment
Parent: Diversey Limited
Officers: Michael James Chapman [1961] Director/Solicitor

Diverseylever Limited
Incorporated: 5 December 1990
Net Worth Deficit: £64,263,000 *Total Assets:* £24,121,000
Registered Office: Weston Favell Centre, Northampton, NN3 8PD
Activities: Non-trading company
Parent: Diversey Holdings Limited
Officers: Colin Timothy Stubbs [1963] Director

Djanogly Learning Trust
Incorporated: 25 September 2002 *Employees:* 360
Net Worth: £23,031,000 *Total Assets:* £31,768,000
Registered Office: Sherwood Rise, Nottingham Road, Nottingham, NG7 7AR
Activities: Other education n.e.c.
Officers: David Holdsworth, Secretary; Judith Elizabeth Anderson [1963] Director/Headteacher; Duncan Howard Bain [1961] Director/Chief Financial Officer; Professor Christopher Walter Day [1943] Director/Professor of Education; Paul Edward Feenan [1974] Director/Solicitor; Christine Goldstraw OBE JP DI [1946] Director/Semi Retired; David Holdsworth [1958] Director of Operations; Ronald Critchley Kenyon [1937] Director/Retired; Doctor Kenneth James Maxwell [1944] Director/Retired; Kris Naidu [1955] Director/Business Executive; Raphael Wisdom Richards [1953] Director/Chairman; Tim Slade [1958] Director/Consultant

DK Group Investments Ltd.
Incorporated: 14 February 1983 *Employees:* 517
Net Worth: £19,974,744 *Total Assets:* £34,728,472
Registered Office: Unit 5 Lawford Heath Industrial Estate, Rugby, Warwicks, CV23 9EU
Activities: Activities of head offices
Officers: Richard James Cookman [1977] Director; Frederick Nigel Griffiths [1948] Director [American]; Kevin Mark Higginson [1959] Managing Director; John Kinning [1939] Director; Heather Jean Pearson [1942] Director; Peter Jonathan Ward [1953] Director/Management Consultant

DMG Mori UK Limited
Incorporated: 5 November 1971 *Employees:* 94
Previous: DMG Mori Seiki UK Limited
Net Worth: £22,799,844 *Total Assets:* £50,940,044
Registered Office: 4030 Siskin Parkway East, Middlemarch Business Park, Coventry, Warwicks, CV3 4PE
Activities: Manufacture of other machine tools
Parent: DMG Mori Europe AG
Officers: Joanne Turner, Secretary; Steffen Rolf Burghoff [1968] Director [German]; Stephen Peter Finn [1958] Managing Director; Dr Ugo Ghilardi [1964] Director/Divisional Board Member Sales [Italian]; John Andrew Henderson [1963] Sales Director (North); Joanne Turner [1969] Finance Director

DMWSL 532 Limited
Incorporated: 13 November 2006 *Employees:* 1,894
Net Worth: £9,932,000 *Total Assets:* £124,646,000
Registered Office: Caenarvon House, 121 Knighton Church Road, Leicester, LE2 3JN
Activities: Other human health activities
Major Shareholder: Peter Alexander Van Herrewege
Officers: Janet Elizabeth Hairsine, Secretary; David Cheney [1971] Director of Estates; Benedicto Dawson [1958] Director of Adult Services; Jane Ginnelly [1962] Director of Adult Services; Ruth Hack [1967] Director of Elderly Services; Janet Elizabeth Hairsine [1977] Financial Development Director; Vicki Shaw [1970] Director; Diane Smith [1972] Operational Director; Peter Alexander Van Herrewege [1953] Director; Simon James Van Herrewege [1980] Director; James Wood [1969] Director

DMWSL 631 Limited
Incorporated: 3 March 2010 *Employees:* 805
Net Worth: £17,509,000 *Total Assets:* £173,095,008
Registered Office: 3 The Maltings, Wetmore Road, Burton on Trent, Staffs, DE14 1SE
Activities: Activities of other holding companies n.e.c.
Parent: DMWSL 632 Limited
Officers: Carys Damon, Secretary; Stewart Frank Bradley Baker [1983] Director/Chief Financial Officer; Carys Damon [1976] Director/Solicitor; Brooks Harrison Pierce [1961] Director/President [American]

DMWSL 632 Limited
Incorporated: 3 March 2010 *Employees:* 3
Net Worth: £232,664,992 *Total Assets:* £234,028,000
Registered Office: 3 The Maltings, Wetmore Road, Burton on Trent, Staffs, DE14 1SE
Activities: Activities of other holding companies n.e.c.
Parent: DMWSL 633 Limited
Officers: Carys Damon, Secretary; Stewart Frank Bradley Baker [1983] Director/Chief Financial Officer; Carys Damon [1976] Director/Solicitor; Brooks Harrison Pierce [1961] Director/President [American]

DMWSL 633 Limited
Incorporated: 3 March 2010 *Employees:* 805
Net Worth: £21,457,000 *Total Assets:* £173,098,000
Registered Office: 3 The Maltings, Wetmore Road, Burton on Trent, Staffs, DE14 1SE
Activities: Activities of other holding companies n.e.c.
Parent: Inspired Entertainment Inc.
Officers: Carys Damon, Secretary; Stewart Frank Bradley Baker [1983] Director/Chief Financial Officer; Carys Damon [1976] Director/Solicitor; Brooks Harrison Pierce [1961] Director/President [American]

DNA (Holdings) Limited
Incorporated: 9 December 2011 *Employees:* 208
Net Worth: £6,734,361 *Total Assets:* £24,466,232
Registered Office: The Mills, Canal Street, Derby, DE1 2RJ
Activities: Activities of distribution holding companies
Shareholders: Peter Norman Ascott; Stuart John Ascott
Officers: Hugh Ian Anthony Vint, Secretary; Norma Rose Ascott [1942] Director; Peter Norman Ascott [1969] Director; Stuart John Ascott [1971] Director; Matthew Dean Ash [1985] Finance Director; Hugh Ian Anthony Vint [1946] Director; Jonathan David Ward [1969] Managing Director

DNC Holdings Limited
Incorporated: 14 March 2016
Net Worth Deficit: £368,878 *Total Assets:* £14,708,122
Registered Office: Mill Lane Industrial Estate, The Mill Lane, Leicester, LE3 8DX
Activities: Activities of head offices
Major Shareholder: Lindsay Kamal Khan
Officers: Demis Armen Ohandjanian [1978] Director

Doc Bidco Limited
Incorporated: 7 August 2013 *Employees:* 1,174
Net Worth: £103,300,000 *Total Assets:* £446,500,000
Registered Office: Cobbs Lane, Wollaston, Northants, NN29 7SW
Activities: Activities of other holding companies n.e.c.
Parent: Doc Midco Limited
Officers: Cheryl Yvonne Hood [1969] Director; Jon William Mortimore [1967] Director/Chief Financial Officer; Emily Clare Reichwald [1975] Director/General Counsel; Kenneth Charles Wilson [1966] Director

Doc Debtco Limited
Incorporated: 8 August 2013 *Employees:* 3
Net Worth: £141,106,000 *Total Assets:* £353,089,984
Registered Office: Cobbs Lane, Wollaston, Northants, NN29 7SW
Activities: Activities of other holding companies n.e.c.
Parent: Doc Topco Limited
Officers: Cheryl Yvonne Hood [1969] Director; Jon William Mortimore [1967] Director/Chief Financial Officer; Kenneth Charles Wilson [1966] Director

Doc Midco Limited
Incorporated: 7 August 2013 *Employees:* 3
Net Worth: £141,700,000 *Total Assets:* £353,100,000
Registered Office: Cobbs Lane, Wollaston, Northants, NN29 7SW
Activities: Activities of other holding companies n.e.c.
Parent: Doc Debtco Limited
Officers: Cheryl Yvonne Hood [1969] Director; Jon William Mortimore [1967] Director/Chief Financial Officer; Kenneth Charles Wilson [1966] Director

Doc Topco Limited
Incorporated: 8 August 2013 *Employees:* 1,586
Net Worth Deficit: £29,400,000 *Total Assets:* £445,800,000
Registered Office: Cobbs Lane, Wollaston, Northants, NN29 7SW
Activities: Activities of other holding companies n.e.c.
Officers: Tara Alhadeff [1982] Director/Finance Professional; Cheryl Yvonne Hood [1969] Director; Paul Mason [1960] Director; Jon William Mortimore [1967] Director/Chief Financial Officer; Kenneth Charles Wilson [1966] Director

Doddington Farms LLP
Incorporated: 13 August 2007 *Employees:* 139
Net Worth: £10,655,561 *Total Assets:* £12,313,573
Registered Office: Doddington Hall, Lincoln, LN6 4RU
Officers: Claire Victoria Birch [1963] Member; George Christopher Birch [1990] Member; James Julius Christopher Birch [1962] Member

Dodson & Horrell (Holdings) Limited
Incorporated: 31 July 1939 *Employees:* 7
Net Worth: £16,657,044 *Total Assets:* £31,473,468
Registered Office: Kettering Road, Islip, Kettering, Northants, NN14 3JW
Activities: Other business support service activities n.e.c.
Parent: Dodson & Horrell Group Limited
Officers: Anna Mari Horrell [1971] Director/Solicitor; John Horrell [1944] Director; Richard Thomas Horrell [1941] Director; Samuel John Horrell [1985] Marketing Director; Richard Francis McCoy [1947] Director/Business Consultant

Dodson & Horrell Group Limited
Incorporated: 1 March 2016 *Employees:* 159
Net Worth: £19,814,968 *Total Assets:* £33,823,728
Registered Office: Dodson & Horrell, Kettering Road, Islip, Kettering, Northants, NN14 3JW
Activities: Activities of head offices
Shareholders: Neelam Maher; Richard Thomas Horrell; Anna Mari Horrell; Catherine Ruth Blackman; John Horrell; Anna Edwina Guest
Officers: Anna Mari Horrell [1971] Director; John Horrell [1944] Director; Richard Thomas Horrell [1941] Director; Samuel Horrell [1985] Director

Dodson & Horrell Limited
Incorporated: 11 February 1987 *Employees:* 156
Net Worth: £4,461,720 *Total Assets:* £13,381,204
Registered Office: Kettering Road, Islip, Kettering, Northants, NN14 3JW
Activities: Manufacture of prepared feeds for farm animals
Parent: Dodson & Horrell (Holdings) Limited
Officers: Anna Mari Horrell [1971] Director/Solicitor; Samuel John Horrell [1985] Marketing Director; Derek Michael Mackey [1971] Commercial Director [Irish]; Andrew John Hillhouse Reid [1965] Production Director; Verghese Elias Thanangadan [1957] Director/Accountant

Domino's Pizza Group PLC
Incorporated: 5 October 1999 *Employees:* 1,749
Net Worth: £43,800,000 *Total Assets:* £380,900,000
Registered Office: 1 Thornbury, West Ashland, Milton Keynes, Bucks, MK6 4BB
Activities: Licenced restaurants
Officers: Adrian John Bushnell, Secretary; Stephen David Barber [1952] Director; David Gregory Bauernfeind [1968] Director/Accountant; Colin Halpern [1937] Director [American]; Stephen Glen Hemsley [1957] Director/Chartered Accountant; Kevin Paul Higgins [1963] Director [Irish]; Ebbe Pelle Jacobsen [1949] Director [Danish]; Helen Margaret Keays [1964] Director; David James Wild [1955] Director

Doncasters Aerospace Limited
Incorporated: 24 October 2000 *Employees:* 397
Net Worth: £96,448,000 *Total Assets:* £114,212,000
Registered Office: Millennium Court, First Avenue, Burton on Trent, Staffs, DE14 2WH
Activities: Casting of other non-ferrous metals
Parent: Doncasters Limited
Officers: Ian Molyneux, Secretary; Duncan Andrew Hinks [1975] Director/Chief Financial Officer; Ian Molyneux [1964] Director/Solicitor; Lisa Marie Oxnard [1981] Director/Chief Financial Officer

Doncasters Blaenavon Limited
Incorporated: 23 October 1964 *Employees:* 2
Net Worth: £113,937,872 *Total Assets:* £113,937,872
Registered Office: Millennium Court, First Avenue, Burton on Trent, Staffs, DE14 2WH
Activities: Manufacture of other fabricated metal products n.e.c.
Parent: Doncasters Limited
Officers: Ian Molyneux, Secretary; Duncan Andrew Hinks [1975] Director/Chief Financial Officer; Ian Molyneux [1964] Director/Solicitor; Lisa Marie Oxnard [1981] Director/Chief Financial Officer

Doncasters Group Limited
Incorporated: 12 December 2005 *Employees:* 3,607
Net Worth Deficit: £461,000,000 *Total Assets:* £996,000,000
Registered Office: Millennium Court, First Avenue, Burton on Trent, Staffs, DE14 2WH
Activities: Other business support service activities n.e.c.
Major Shareholder: His Highness Sheikh Mohammed Bin Rashid Al Maktoum
Officers: Ian Molyneux, Secretary; Ian Dunkinson [1952] Director/Metallurgist; Duncan Andrew Hinks [1975] Director/Chief Financial Officer; David Madison Smoot [1969] Director/Investment Professional [American]

Doncasters Limited
Incorporated: 17 December 1936 *Employees:* 548
Net Worth: £187,647,008 *Total Assets:* £927,041,024
Registered Office: Millennium Court, First Avenue, Burton on Trent, Staffs, DE14 2WH
Activities: Manufacture of other fabricated metal products n.e.c.
Parent: Dundee Holdco 4 Limited
Officers: Ian Molyneux, Secretary; Paul John Clowes [1959] Director/Accountant; Duncan Andrew Hinks [1975] Director/Chief Financial Officer; Ian Molyneux [1964] Director/Solicitor; Lisa Marie Oxnard [1981] Director/Chief Financial Officer; David Madison Smoot [1969] Director/Investment Professional [American]

Doncasters UK Finance Limited
Incorporated: 12 March 2013
Net Worth: £114,522,120 *Total Assets:* £709,664,704
Registered Office: Millennium Court, First Avenue, Burton on Trent, Staffs, DE14 2WH
Activities: Other business support service activities n.e.c.
Parent: Dundee Holdco 4 Limited
Officers: Ian Molyneux, Secretary; Duncan Andrew Hinks [1975] Director/Chief Financial Officer; Ian Molyneux [1964] Director/General Counsel; Lisa Marie Oxnard [1981] Director/Chief Financial Officer

RR Donnelley UK Limited
Incorporated: 30 September 2008 *Employees:* 1,654
Previous: RR Donnelley Global Document Solutions Group Limited
Net Worth: £104,949,000 *Total Assets:* £149,876,992
Registered Office: Tower Close, Huntingdon, Cambs, PE29 7YD
Activities: Other business support service activities n.e.c.
Officers: Jonathan Simon Richard Dally, Secretary; John Samuel Farmer [1960] Director; Michael Stuart Gordon [1961] Director/Business Executive; Kevin Trevor Woor [1965] Director/Business Executive

Symon Donovan Properties Limited
Incorporated: 25 August 2004 *Employees:* 6
Net Worth: £8,875,929 *Total Assets:* £18,927,936
Registered Office: 117 St Mary's Road, Sheffield, S2 4BE
Activities: Other letting and operating of own or leased real estate
Shareholder: Symon Denis Donovan
Officers: Michelle Carmen Donovan, Secretary; James Generald Ashton [1982] Director; Symon Denis Donovan [1958] Director

Donvale Holdings Limited
Incorporated: 16 September 1950
Net Worth: £17,321,844 *Total Assets:* £17,530,310
Registered Office: c/o Bell & Buxton, Telegraph House, 11-15 High Street, Sheffield, S1 2GA
Activities: Activities of other holding companies n.e.c.
Parent: RH Trustees Limited
Officers: Brian Edward Bell, Secretary; Brian Edward Bell [1939] Director/Solicitor; Robert Michael Matthews [1946] Director/Accountant

Door-Stop International Limited
Incorporated: 11 February 2008 *Employees:* 199
Net Worth: £33,844,000 *Total Assets:* £38,991,000
Registered Office: Export Drive, Huthwaite, Sutton in Ashfield, Notts, NG17 6AF
Activities: Other manufacturing n.e.c.
Parent: Premdor Crosby Limited
Officers: Clare Doyle [1965] Managing Director [American]; Rose Murphy [1957] Director/Lawyer [American]

Doosan Industrial Vehicle UK Ltd.
Incorporated: 25 May 2011 *Employees:* 35
Net Worth: £1,053,000 *Total Assets:* £52,678,000
Registered Office: Unit 12 Kilvey Road, Brackmills Industrial Estate, Northampton, NN4 7BQ
Activities: Wholesale of other machinery and equipment
Parent: Doosan Corporation
Officers: David John Clarkson [1965] Director/Chief Executive Officer; Jongseon Kim [1966] Finance Director [South Korean]; Jae Hun Lee [1974] Director/Chief Financial Officer [South Korean]

John W. Doubleday Limited
Incorporated: 10 January 1992 *Employees:* 48
Net Worth: £9,668,622 *Total Assets:* £18,903,896
Registered Office: Holbeach St Johns, Spalding, Lincs, PE12 8SQ
Activities: Wholesale of agricultural machinery, equipment and supplies
Parent: J W D Holdings Limited
Officers: Graham Collishaw [1958] Director; Ian James Doubleday-Collishaw [1981] Director; Jayne Elizabeth Doubleday-Collishaw [1958] Director; Zoe Spencer [1985] Director

Dow Chemical Company Limited
Incorporated: 20 August 1954
Net Worth: £345,456,000 *Total Assets:* £464,392,000
Registered Office: Station Road, Birch Vale, High Peak, Derbys, SK22 1BR
Activities: Manufacture of other inorganic basic chemicals
Officers: Cathrine Anne Jenkins, Secretary; Eduardo Antonio Gadea [1961] Operations Director UK & Nordic [Spanish]; Andrew Michael Jones [1966] Commercial Director; Gino Eduardus Angela Van Poorten [1973] EMEAI Tax Director [Dutch]

Dow Chemical Services UK Limited
Incorporated: 25 March 2010 *Employees:* 277
Net Worth: £17,735,000 *Total Assets:* £38,865,000
Registered Office: Station Road, Birch Vale, High Peak, Derbys, SK22 1BR
Activities: Human resources provision and management of human resources functions
Parent: Dow Chemical Company Limited
Officers: Cathrine Anne Jenkins, Secretary; Luis Antuna [1963] Director/Corporate Counsel [Spanish]; Alejandro Jose Farre Pelaez [1967] Finance Director [Spanish]; Eduardo Antonio Gadea [1961] Operations Director, UK & Nordic [Spanish]; Andrew Michael Jones [1966] Director; Julie Emma Roberts [1970] Director/HR Leader/Nordic

DP Group Developments Limited
Incorporated: 13 August 1997
Net Worth Deficit: £2,056,000 *Total Assets:* £29,724,000
Registered Office: 1 Thornbury, West Ashland, Milton Keynes, Bucks, MK6 4BB
Activities: Development of building projects
Parent: Domino's Pizza Group PLC
Officers: Adrian John Bushnell, Secretary; David Gregory Bauernfeind [1968] Director/Accountant; Adrian John Bushnell [1964] Director/Chartered Secretary; Robin Keith Nigel Caley [1960] Director; David James Wild [1955] Director

DP Realty Limited
Incorporated: 15 December 1993 *Employees:* 4
Net Worth: £3,709,000 *Total Assets:* £28,234,000
Registered Office: 1 Thornbury, West Ashland, Milton Keynes, Bucks, MK6 4BB
Activities: Development of building projects
Parent: Domino's Pizza Group PLC
Officers: Adrian John Bushnell, Secretary; David Gregory Bauernfeind [1968] Director/Accountant; Adrian John Bushnell [1964] Director/Chartered Secretary; Robin Keith Nigel Caley [1960] Director; David James Wild [1955] Director

DPFP LLP
Incorporated: 3 December 2014
Net Worth: £27,576,556 *Total Assets:* £28,449,964
Registered Office: Headquarters, Butterley Hall, Ripley, Derbys, DE5 3RS

DPG Holdings Limited
Incorporated: 28 June 2006
Net Worth: £1,337,788,032 *Total Assets:* £1,423,794,944
Registered Office: 1 Thornbury, West Ashland, Milton Keynes, Bucks, MK6 4BB
Activities: Activities of head offices
Parent: Domino's Pizza Group PLC
Officers: Adrian John Bushnell, Secretary; David Gregory Bauernfeind [1968] Director/Accountant; Adrian John Bushnell [1964] Director/Chartered Secretary; Stephen Glen Hemsley [1957] Director; David James Wild [1955] Director

Dr Martens Airwair Group Limited
Incorporated: 17 January 1992 *Employees:* 5
Net Worth: £10,047,904 *Total Assets:* £18,982,482
Registered Office: Cobbs Lane, Wollaston, Wellingborough, Northants, NN29 7SW
Activities: Activities of head offices
Parent: Doc Bidco Limited
Officers: Tara Alhadeff [1982] Director/Finance Professional; Cheryl Yvonne Hood [1969] Director; Paul Mason [1960] Director; Jon William Mortimore [1967] Director/Chief Financial Officer; Geert Raymond Peeters [1966] Director [Belgian]; Emily Clare Reichwald [1975] Director/General Counsel; Kenneth Charles Wilson [1966] Director

Draefern Limited
Incorporated: 21 October 1986 *Employees:* 4,416
Net Worth: £3,709,990 *Total Assets:* £21,296,308
Registered Office: Draefern House, Dunston Court, Dunston Road, Chesterfield, Derbys, S41 8NL
Activities: Temporary employment agency activities
Parent: GI Recruitment Limited
Officers: Jane Elizabeth Brewin, Secretary; Jane Elizabeth Brewin [1970] Finance Director; Paul Anthony Smith [1969] Director; Beverley Marie White [1958] Director/Chief Executive

Dragon School Trust Limited
Incorporated: 6 October 1953 *Employees:* 354
Net Worth: £25,294,000 *Total Assets:* £49,386,000
Registered Office: Bardwell Road, Oxford, OX2 6SS
Activities: Pre-primary education
Officers: Martin Roy Johnson, Secretary; Mary Breen [1964] Director/Headmistress; Graham Paul Candy [1948] Director/Chartered Surveyor; Stephan Charles Chambers [1960] Director/Publisher; Ariane Chantal Genillard Cowley [1965] Director [Swiss]; Nigel Leslie Helliwell [1963] Director/Headmaster; Lucinda Jane Holmes [1961] Housewife Non-Executive Director; Christopher Ian Montague Jones [1955] Director; Sarah Jane Kerr-Dineen [1963] Director/Headteacher; Edmund Graham King [1975] Director/QC; Professor Angela Ruth McLean [1961] Director/Academic Research; Nathan Millard [1967] Director/Solicitor; Nigel David Portwood [1965] Director/CEO Oxford University Press; Lady Jennifer Avril Kinmond Stringer [1952] Director/Doctor; Sir William George Touche [1962] Director/Chartered Accountant; Caroline Jane Underwood [1963] Director; William Andrew Webb [1968] Director; Gillian Hazel Wilson [1947] Managing Director

Dransfield Properties Finance Limited
Incorporated: 18 December 2015 *Employees:* 25
Net Worth: £13,578,657 *Total Assets:* £16,565,775
Registered Office: Dransfield House, 2 Fox Valley Way, Fox Valley, Sheffield, S36 2AB
Activities: Activities of mortgage finance companies
Shareholders: Mark Dransfield; Deborah Holmes
Officers: Paula Marie Gregory, Secretary; Mark Dransfield [1962] Director; Deborah Holmes [1962] Director; Steven John Stead [1978] Director

Dransfield Properties Investments Limited
Incorporated: 18 December 2015 *Employees:* 21
Net Worth: £50,617,156 *Total Assets:* £145,176,912
Registered Office: Dransfield House, 2 Fox Valley Way, Fox Valley, Sheffield, S36 2AB
Activities: Activities of other holding companies n.e.c.
Major Shareholder: Deborah Holmes
Officers: Mark Dransfield [1962] Director; Deborah Holmes [1962] Director; Steven John Stead [1978] Director

Dransfield Properties Limited
Incorporated: 14 September 1992 *Employees:* 21
Net Worth: £50,617,156 *Total Assets:* £145,176,912
Registered Office: Dransfield House, 2 Fox Valley Way, Fox Valley, Sheffield, S36 2AB
Activities: Development of building projects
Parent: Dransfield Properties Investments Ltd
Officers: Steven Burgess [1966] Director/Accountant; Mark Dransfield [1962] Director; David Hale [1984] Director/Chartered Surveyor; Deborah Holmes [1962] Director; Andrew Christopher Malley [1965] Director/Commercial Property Consultant; James Edward Shepherd [1983] Director/Surveyor; Steven John Stead [1978] Finance Director; Amanda Jane Timms [1967] Director

Draper Commercial Limited
Incorporated: 29 May 1946 *Employees:* 4
Net Worth: £12,904,293 *Total Assets:* £13,848,695
Registered Office: The Guardhouse, Tigers Road, Wigston, Leicester, LE18 4WS
Activities: Other letting and operating of own or leased real estate
Parent: Guardhouse Holdings Limited
Officers: Sarah Christine Brown, Secretary; Christopher Edward Brown [1990] Property Director; Keith Anthony Brown [1952] Property Director; Sarah Christine Brown [1953] Director/Schoolteacher

Drayson Technologies Limited
Incorporated: 6 February 2015 *Employees:* 52
Net Worth: £12,215,000 *Total Assets:* £13,840,000
Registered Office: Schrodinger Building, Heatley Road, Oxford Science Park, Oxford, OX4 4GE
Activities: Manufacture of consumer electronics
Parent: Sensyne Health Limited
Officers: Lord Paul Rudd Drayson [1960] Director; Lorimer Headley [1978] Finance Director

Drennan International Limited
Incorporated: 16 May 1979 *Employees:* 80
Net Worth: £10,112,725 *Total Assets:* £11,145,589
Registered Office: Bocardo Court, Temple Road, Cowley, Oxford, OX4 2EX
Activities: Manufacture of sports goods
Shareholders: Frances Kathleen Drennan; Peter John Drennan
Officers: Frances Kathleen Drennan, Secretary; Frances Kathleen Drennan [1942] Director/Manufacturer; Peter John Drennan [1944] Director/Manufacturer; Sara Catherine Drennan [1970] Director; Jeffrey Michael Higgs [1972] Director/Commercial Management; Richard Mark Norris [1963] Director; Nicola Jayne White [1972] Director/Financial Management

Dri-Pak Limited
Incorporated: 11 October 1961 *Employees:* 155
Net Worth: £6,890,068 *Total Assets:* £9,362,620
Registered Office: Furnace Road, Ilkeston, Derbys, DE7 5EP
Activities: Manufacture of other food products n.e.c.
Officers: Lynn Elizabeth Brett, Secretary; Bruce James Peter Maxwell [1969] Director; Carolyn Mary Maxwell [1944] Director; Jillian Maxwell [1971] Director/Administrator; Peter Stuart Maxwell [1943] Managing Director

Drishaun Holdings Limited
Incorporated: 8 June 2006 *Employees:* 110
Net Worth: £6,632,347 *Total Assets:* £9,396,106
Registered Office: 199 & 201 Newhall Road, Sheffield, S9 2QJ
Activities: Activities of head offices
Shareholders: Michael Lancashire; Avril Margot Lancashire
Officers: Avril Margot Lancashire, Secretary; Michael Lancashire [1950] Director/Engineer

Drive Holdings 2015 Limited
Incorporated: 26 February 2015 *Employees:* 851
Net Worth: £10,089,000 *Total Assets:* £81,981,000
Registered Office: Freemens Common Road, Leicester, LE2 7SL
Activities: Sale of new cars and light motor vehicles
Officers: Stuart James Harrison, Secretary; Stephen Thomas Bessex [1957] Director; Richard Paul Manning [1954] Director

Drive Motor Retail Limited
Incorporated: 14 December 2001 *Employees:* 816
Net Worth: £17,961,000 *Total Assets:* £84,510,000
Registered Office: Freemens Common Road, Leicester, LE2 7SL
Activities: Sale of new cars and light motor vehicles
Parent: Drive Investments Limited
Officers: Stuart James Harrison, Secretary; Stephen Thomas Bessex [1957] Director; Stuart James Harrison [1978] Director/Accountant; Richard Paul Manning [1954] Director

Druck Limited
Incorporated: 9 October 1981 *Employees:* 97
Net Worth: £97,993,000 *Total Assets:* £128,356,000
Registered Office: Fir Tree Lane, Groby, Leics, LE6 0FH
Activities: Manufacture of electronic measuring, testing etc. equipment, not for industrial process control
Parent: GE Druck Holdings Limited
Officers: Rohan James Daniels [1977] Director/Global Finance Leader; Gordon Stewart Docherty [1976] Director/Engineering Manager; Guido Poggiali [1970] Director/Executive Product Manager [Italian]; Guillem Trullas Vila [1985] Director [Spanish]

Dry Mix Solutions UK Limited
Incorporated: 17 April 2014
Net Worth: £12,926,067 *Total Assets:* £25,765,654
Registered Office: Abeles Way, Holly Lane Industrial Estate, Atherstone, Warwicks, CV9 2QZ
Activities: Activities of head offices
Officers: Eric Charles Pierre Berge [1967] Director [French]; Mark Andrew Shorrock [1964] Director

Drybrough Trading Limited
Incorporated: 23 May 2001 *Employees:* 131
Net Worth: £8,006,000 *Total Assets:* £13,644,000
Registered Office: 4 Bayton Road, Exhall, Coventry, Warwicks, CV7 9DJ
Activities: Activities of head offices
Parent: Earlham Trading Company Ltd
Officers: Timothy John Burchell [1963] Director; Stephen James Payne [1970] Director; Patrick Joseph Anthony Sheehan [1941] Director

DS John Holdings Limited
Incorporated: 2 December 2013
Net Worth: £8,512,582 *Total Assets:* £12,079,970
Registered Office: Regents Pavilion, Summerhouse Road, Moulton Park Industrial Estate, Northampton, NN3 6BJ
Activities: Activities of head offices
Major Shareholder: David Paul Fitzjohn
Officers: David Paul Fitzjohn, Secretary; David Paul Fitzjohn [1979] Director/Accountant

DSGPI 2015 Limited
Incorporated: 12 November 2015 *Employees:* 74
Net Worth Deficit: £404,424 *Total Assets:* £11,809,381
Registered Office: Unity House, Hercules Office Park, Bird Hall Lane, Stockport, Cheshire, SK3 0UX
Activities: Financial intermediation not elsewhere classified
Shareholder: Promethean UK Opportunities Fund II LLP
Officers: Angus Moncrieff Burt [1984] Director/Entrepreneur; Mark Gow [1968] Director; Richard Matthew Hoggart [1971] Director; David Quate [1971] Director

DSI Construction Holdings UK Ltd
Incorporated: 1 April 2016
Net Worth Deficit: £1,053,456 *Total Assets:* £10,421,845
Registered Office: c/o DSI UK Construction Holdings Ltd, Northfield Road, Southam, Warwicks, CV47 0FG
Activities: Other business support service activities n.e.c.
Major Shareholder: Peder Erik Prahl
Officers: Tim Coton, Secretary; Torsten Engel [1967] Director [German]; Ian Michael Jarvis [1968] Director

DSM Nutritional Products (UK) Limited
Incorporated: 11 July 2000 *Employees:* 373
Net Worth: £24,648,000 *Total Assets:* £158,362,000
Registered Office: Delves Road, Heanor Gate, Heanor, Derbys, DE75 7SG
Activities: Manufacture of other chemical products n.e.c.
Parent: Koninklijke DSM NV
Officers: Colin Douglas Bratt, Secretary; Luca Rosetto [1963] Director [Italian]; Graeme Weir [1961] Director/Accountant

DSS Group Limited
Incorporated: 12 March 2016 *Employees:* 83
Net Worth: £3,247,190 *Total Assets:* £11,187,691
Registered Office: M & D House, Brooklands Road, Adwick-le-Street, Doncaster, S Yorks, DN6 7BA
Activities: Activities of other holding companies n.e.c.
Major Shareholder: Robert Ian Watson
Officers: Steven Roy Edgworth [1959] Director; David Drew Wylie [1963] Director

DTIL UK Limited
Incorporated: 30 April 2015 *Employees:* 1
Net Worth: £163,823,008 *Total Assets:* £163,836,992
Registered Office: 19 Jessops Riverside, 800 Brightside Lane, Sheffield, S9 2RX
Activities: Activities of head offices
Parent: Danaher Corporation
Officers: Keith Graham Ward [1953] Director

Dubois Limited
Incorporated: 12 July 1901 *Employees:* 114
Net Worth: £14,464,000 *Total Assets:* £24,047,000
Registered Office: Amaray House, Arkwright Road, Corby, Northants, NN17 5AE
Activities: Manufacture of other plastic products
Parent: Dubois Holdings Limited
Officers: Anthony Andrew Blades [1975] Director; Jamie Spencer Tinsley [1968] Director

Ducati U.K. Limited
Incorporated: 1 November 1999 *Employees:* 20
Net Worth: £3,750,000 *Total Assets:* £13,487,000
Registered Office: Unit 7 Technology Park, Silverstone Circuit, Silverstone, Towcester, Northants, NN12 8GX
Activities: Sale, maintenance and repair of motorcycles and related parts and accessories
Parent: Ducati Motor Holdings SpA
Officers: Christopher John Massey, Secretary; Timothy George MacCabee [1965] Managing Director; Francesco Milicia [1975] Sales Director [Italian]

Ducker Farming Limited
Incorporated: 29 August 2014
Net Worth: £13,383,546 *Total Assets:* £13,392,216
Registered Office: Littlestoke Manor, Little Stoke, Wallingford, Oxon, OX10 6AX
Activities: Mixed farming
Parent: Ducker Farming Holding Company Limited
Officers: Catherine Jayne Tustian [1973] Director

Martin Duckworth Limited
Incorporated: 15 May 1989 *Employees:* 141
Net Worth: £4,393,909 *Total Assets:* £35,161,448
Registered Office: Racecourse Garage, Willingham Road, Market Rasen, Lincs, LN8 3RE
Activities: Sale of new cars and light motor vehicles
Shareholders: Ben James Duckworth; Sally Jean Penelope Duckworth; Martin James Duckworth
Officers: Ben Duckworth [1977] Managing Director; Martin James Duckworth [1946] Director/Chairman; Sally Jean Penelope Duckworth [1949] Director; Darren Peter Wilson [1966] Finance Director

Dudley Taylor Pharmacies Limited
Incorporated: 10 October 2001 *Employees:* 665
Net Worth: £44,749,164 *Total Assets:* £54,016,680
Registered Office: Taylor Group House, Wedgnock Lane, Warwick, CV34 5YA
Activities: Dispensing chemist in specialised stores
Parent: Dudley Taylor Limited
Officers: Christopher John Taylor, Secretary; Michael James Taylor [1957] Director

P.J. Duffy & Son (Farms) Limited
Incorporated: 9 September 1986 *Employees:* 5
Net Worth: £14,046,387 *Total Assets:* £17,515,656
Registered Office: Lynway Nurseries, Stimpsons Cross, Algarkirk, Boston, Lincs, PE20 2BE
Activities: Growing of cereals (except rice), leguminous crops and oil seeds
Major Shareholder: Philip John Duffy
Officers: Philip John Duffy, Secretary; Karen Marina Duffy [1951] Director/Housewife; Philip John Duffy [1950] Director

Duki (2006) Finance Limited
Incorporated: 6 May 1993 *Employees:* 1
Previous: Danaher UK Industries (2006) Limited
Net Worth: £1,114,230,016 *Total Assets:* £1,269,117,952
Registered Office: 19 Jessops Riverside, 800 Brightside Lane, Sheffield, S9 2RX
Activities: Activities of head offices
Parent: JHC Finance Company
Officers: Keith Graham Ward [1953] Director/Finance

The Dunamis Group Limited
Incorporated: 4 September 2015 *Employees:* 46
Net Worth: £14,211,893 *Total Assets:* £18,756,820
Registered Office: 2 Europa View, Sheffield, S9 1XH
Activities: Activities of construction holding companies
Parent: Fulcrum Utility Services Limited
Officers: Daniel James Gray [1972] Director; Hazel Jayne Griffiths [1982] Director; Martin John Harrison [1969] Director; Richard Anthony Jupp [1963] Director/Electrical Engineer; Michael Anthony Long [1963] Director; Stephen Victor Macbeth [1957] Director

Duncan Investments Limited
Incorporated: 8 October 1986 *Employees:* 4
Net Worth: £7,752,199 *Total Assets:* £13,057,288
Registered Office: Low Farm, Clipston Road, Sibbertoft, Market Harborough, Leics, LE16 9UB
Activities: Buying and selling of own real estate
Major Shareholder: Alexander Edmund Duncan Robinson
Officers: Alexander Edmund Duncan Robinson [1955] Director; Carolyne de Courcy Robinson [1957] Director/Administrator

Dundee Holdco 2 Limited
Incorporated: 12 December 2005 *Employees:* 3
Net Worth: £81,532,000 *Total Assets:* £500,012,000
Registered Office: Millennium Court, First Avenue, Burton on Trent, Staffs, DE14 2WH
Activities: Other business support service activities n.e.c.
Parent: Doncasters Group Limited
Officers: Ian Molyneux, Secretary; Duncan Andrew Hinks [1975] Director/Chief Financial Officer; Ian Molyneux [1964] Director/Solicitor; Lisa Marie Oxnard [1981] Director/Chief Financial Officer; David Madison Smoot [1969] Director/Investment Professional [American]

Dundee Holdco 3 Limited
Incorporated: 12 December 2005 *Employees:* 3
Net Worth: £20,966,000 *Total Assets:* £848,078,016
Registered Office: Millennium Court, First Avenue, Burton on Trent, Staffs, DE14 2WH
Activities: Other business support service activities n.e.c.
Parent: Dundee Pikco Limited
Officers: Ian Molyneux, Secretary; Duncan Andrew Hinks [1975] Director/Chief Financial Officer; Ian Molyneux [1964] Director/Solicitor; Lisa Marie Oxnard [1981] Director/Chief Financial Officer; David Madison Smoot [1969] Director/Investment Professional [American]

Dundee Holdco 4 Limited
Incorporated: 12 December 2005 *Employees:* 3
Net Worth: £437,641,984 *Total Assets:* £1,069,793,024
Registered Office: Millennium Court, First Avenue, Burton on Trent, Staffs, DE14 2WH
Activities: Other business support service activities n.e.c.
Parent: Dundee Holdco 3 Limited
Officers: Ian Molyneux, Secretary; Duncan Andrew Hinks [1975] Director/Chief Financial Officer; Ian Molyneux [1964] Director/Solicitor; Lisa Marie Oxnard [1981] Director/Chief Financial Officer; David Madison Smoot [1969] Director/Investment Professional [American]

Dundee Pikco Limited
Incorporated: 22 February 2007
Net Worth Deficit: £440,852,000 *Total Assets:* £85,790,000
Registered Office: Millennium Court, First Avenue, Burton on Trent, Staffs, DE14 2WH
Activities: Other business support service activities n.e.c.
Parent: Dundee Holdco 2 Limited
Officers: Ian Molyneux, Secretary; Duncan Andrew Hinks [1975] Director/Chief Financial Officer; Ian Molyneux [1964] Director/Solicitor; Lisa Marie Oxnard [1981] Director/Chief Financial Officer

Dunelm (Soft Furnishings) Ltd
Incorporated: 8 May 1987 *Employees:* 6,543
Net Worth: £149,700,000 *Total Assets:* £440,900,000
Registered Office: Dunelm Store Support Centre, Watermead Business Park, Syston, Leicester, LE7 1AD
Activities: Retail sale of textiles in specialised stores
Shareholders: Dunelm Limited; William Lester Adderley; Dunelm Group PLC; W A Capital Limited
Officers: Dawn Elizabeth Durrant, Secretary; William Lester Adderley [1972] Director; Steven Barton [1965] Director/Chartered Surveyor; Laura Elizabeth Carr [1975] Director; James Rowell [1973] Director/Retail; Nicholas Guy Wilkinson [1966] Director

Dunelm Estates Limited
Incorporated: 23 March 2003
Net Worth: £10,649,000 *Total Assets:* £77,881,000
Registered Office: Dunelm Store Support Centre, Watermead Business Park, Syston, Leicester, LE7 1AD
Activities: Buying and selling of own real estate
Shareholders: William Lester Adderley; Dunelm Limited; Dunelm Group PLC; WA Capital Limited
Officers: Dawn Elizabeth Durrant, Secretary; William Lester Adderley [1972] Director/Chairman; Steven Barton [1965] Director/Chartered Surveyor; Laura Elizabeth Carr [1975] Director; Nicholas Guy Wilkinson [1966] Director

Dunelm Group PLC
Incorporated: 23 March 2003 *Employees:* 9,757
Net Worth: £134,700,000 *Total Assets:* £425,000,000
Registered Office: Dunelm Store Support Centre, Watermead Business Park, Syston, Leicester, LE7 1AD
Activities: Activities of head offices
Officers: Dawn Elizabeth Durrant, Secretary; William Lester Adderley [1972] Director; Laura Elizabeth Carr [1975] Director; Mary Elizabeth Doherty [1957] Independent Director; Andrew Harrison [1957] Director; William Frederick Reeve [1972] Director; Peter Timothy John Ruis [1967] Director/Chief Executive; Marion Jane Sears [1962] Director; Nicholas Guy Wilkinson [1966] Director

Dunkley Family Investments Limited
Incorporated: 12 May 2015 *Employees:* 4
Net Worth: £1,800,391 *Total Assets:* £45,999,920
Registered Office: 11 Osier Way, Olney Office Park, Olney, Bucks, MK46 5FP
Activities: Buying and selling of own real estate
Shareholders: Paul Dunkley; Denise Rachel Dunkley
Officers: Denise Dunkley [1959] Director; James Dunkley [1986] Director; Jonathan Paul Dunkley [1984] Director; Paul Dunkley [1958] Director

Dunlin Limited
Incorporated: 16 March 1987 *Employees:* 13
Net Worth: £18,102,020 *Total Assets:* £18,490,996
Registered Office: Estate Office, Wakefield Lodge Estate, Potterspury, Northants, NN12 7QX
Activities: Landscape service activities
Shareholder: Julian Howard Richmond-Watson
Officers: Sarah Francis Richmond-Watson, Secretary; Daniel Thomas Richmond-Watson [1977] Director; Julian Howard Richmond-Watson [1947] Director/Farmer; Sarah Francis Richmond-Watson [1951] Director

Dunlop Oil & Marine Limited
Incorporated: 26 November 1997 *Employees:* 304
Net Worth: £12,100,000 *Total Assets:* £44,321,000
Registered Office: Moody Lane, Pyewipe, Grimsby, N E Lincs, DN31 2SY
Activities: Manufacture of other rubber products
Parent: Phoenix Oil & Marine Limited
Officers: Dr Ali Reza Kambiez Zandiyeh [1960] Director/General Manager

Dunn Motor Traction Ltd
Incorporated: 30 January 2009 *Employees:* 129
Net Worth: £3,855,985 *Total Assets:* £11,849,025
Registered Office: Heanor Gate Industrial Estate, Heanor Gate Road, Heanor, Derbys, DE75 7RJ
Activities: Maintenance and repair of motor vehicles
Major Shareholder: Anthony Scott Dunn
Officers: Stephen Craig Ward, Secretary; Paul Ralph Major [1972] Operations Director; Stephen Craig Ward [1970] Director/Management Accountant

Dunns (Long Sutton) Limited
Incorporated: 11 August 2000 *Employees:* 41
Net Worth: £6,564,698 *Total Assets:* £11,449,457
Registered Office: Lindsey House, Hemswell Cliff, Gainsborough, Lincs, DN21 5TH
Activities: Seed processing for propagation
Officers: Michael John Thompson, Secretary; Christopher Michael Guest [1986] Director; Stuart James Shand [1962] Director/Agricultural Merchant; David Thomas Sheppard [1961] Director/Grain Trader; Michael John Thompson [1965] Director/Certified Accountant

Dunstall Holdings Limited
Incorporated: 9 November 2010 *Employees:* 111
Net Worth: £5,732,873 *Total Assets:* £33,954,956
Registered Office: Old Hall, Dunstall, Burton on Trent, Staffs, DE13 8BE
Activities: Activities of head offices
Major Shareholder: Simon William Clarke
Officers: Simon William Clarke [1965] Farmer and Director; Jane Louise Gerard-Pearse [1963] Director; Ian Edward Marshall [1963] Director; John Minshall [1940] Director; Steven Jon Petford [1979] Director/Chartered Accountant; Stephen Potter [1964] Director/Chartered Accountant

Dunster House Limited
Incorporated: 29 March 1994 *Employees:* 311
Net Worth: £5,985,577 *Total Assets:* £14,269,160
Registered Office: Dunster House, Caxton Road, Bedford, MK41 0LF
Activities: Manufacture of caravans
Shareholder: Christopher David Murphy
Officers: Michael Andrew Hart-King [1978] Director/Operations Manager; Malgorzata Kaczmarek [1982] Director/Financial Controller [Polish]; Christopher David Murphy [1947] Director

Duo Processing Limited
Incorporated: 26 April 2005 *Employees:* 50
Previous: Duo Mineral Processing Limited
Net Worth: £2,566,674 *Total Assets:* £13,940,592
Registered Office: 4 Rye Hill Office Park, Birmingham Road, Allesley, Coventry, Warwicks, CV5 9AB
Activities: Other mining and quarrying n.e.c.
Parent: DMP Assets Ltd
Officers: Simon John Hall, Secretary; Owen Stanley Bolt [1964] Director; Simon John Hall [1966] Director/Accountant; Martin Francis McWilliams [1976] Director; Alexander Franklin Moss [1949] Director; Trevor James Shaw [1955] Director; Donna Williams [1966] Director/Chief Finance Officer

Durham & Co Holdings Limited
Incorporated: 27 February 2014 *Employees:* 84
Net Worth: £10,240,435 *Total Assets:* £16,321,176
Registered Office: 15 High Street, Brackley, Northants, NN13 7DH
Activities: Activities of other holding companies n.e.c.
Shareholders: Karl Durham; Deborah Durham
Officers: Karl Durham [1970] Director

Durr Limited
Incorporated: 17 February 1971 *Employees:* 113
Net Worth: £6,299,000 *Total Assets:* £25,939,000
Registered Office: Durr Limited, Broxell Close, Warwick, CV34 5QF
Activities: Manufacture of other special-purpose machinery n.e.c.
Parent: Durr Systems AG
Officers: Keith Cheetham, Secretary; Darren Christopher Ashmore [1968] Managing Director; Keith Cheetham [1971] Finance Director

James Durrans & Sons,Limited
Incorporated: 15 December 1920 *Employees:* 196
Net Worth: £36,428,004 *Total Assets:* £45,797,992
Registered Office: Phoenix Works, Thurlstone, Sheffield, S36 9QU
Activities: Manufacture of other non-metallic mineral products n.e.c.
Shareholder: Nicholas Geoffrey Durrans
Officers: Graham Paul Hooper, Secretary; David John Armitage [1964] Operations Director; Christopher Foster Durrans [1960] Director; Nicholas Geoffrey Durrans [1967] Director; Graham Paul Hooper [1966] Director/Certified Chartered Accountant

The Duston Education Trust
Incorporated: 6 November 2014 *Employees:* 196
Net Worth: £38,768,088 *Total Assets:* £41,675,292
Registered Office: The Duston School, Berrywood Road, Duston, Northampton, NN5 6XA
Activities: Primary education
Officers: Fiona Cole [1977] Director; Glenn Stuart Daly [1975] Director/Mortgage Advisor; Maria Deacon-Viney [1966] Director/Head of Human Resources; Sarbjeet Gherra [1977] Director/Head of Business Development; Gabrielle Knowlton-Maile [1981] Director/Sales Manager; John Anthony Murray [1964] Director [Irish]; Samuel Philip Strickland [1978] Director/Principal

DV Ventures Limited
Incorporated: 29 June 2010 *Employees:* 3
Net Worth: £4,415,341 *Total Assets:* £12,752,294
Registered Office: Mount Farm, Shirley, Ashbourne, Derbys, DE6 3AR
Activities: Other letting and operating of own or leased real estate
Shareholders: Nigel Grenville Trafford; Philip Grenville Trafford; Jolyon Grenville Trafford
Officers: Philip Grenville Trafford, Secretary; Jolyon Grenville Trafford [1972] Director; Nigel Grenville Trafford [1967] Director; Philip Grenville Trafford [1969] Director/Accountant

DW3 Products Group Limited
Incorporated: 7 October 2014 *Employees:* 7
Net Worth: £97,345 *Total Assets:* £26,209,480
Registered Office: Birthwaite Business Park, Huddersfield Road, Darton, Barnsley, S Yorks, S75 5JS
Activities: Activities of head offices
Parent: DW3 Products Holdings Limited
Officers: Rose Murphy, Secretary; Clare Doyle [1965] Managing Director [American]; Joanne Freiberger [1964] Director/Vice President and Treasurer [American]; Rose Murphy [1957] Director/Lawyer [American]

DW3 Products Holdings Limited
Incorporated: 7 October 2014 *Employees:* 266
Net Worth: £960,747 *Total Assets:* £28,186,920
Registered Office: Birthwaite Business Park, Huddersfield Road, Darton, Barnsley, S Yorks, S75 5JS
Activities: Activities of head offices
Parent: Premdor Crosby Limited
Officers: Rose Murphy, Secretary; Clare Doyle [1965] Managing Director [American]; Joanne Freiberger [1964] Director/Vice President and Treasurer [American]; Rose Murphy [1957] Director/Lawyer [American]

Dyas Exploration UK Limited
Incorporated: 18 March 2009
Net Worth: £25,559,000 *Total Assets:* £77,679,000
Registered Office: Athena House, Athena Drive, Tachbrook Park, Warwick, CV34 6RL
Activities: Extraction of crude petroleum
Parent: Dyas UK Ltd
Officers: Robert Jan Baurdoux [1957] Director [Dutch]; Matthew Quentin Hickin [1967] Director; Adam Euan Thompson [1974] Director; Petrus Johannes Waaijer [1954] Director/Accountant/Chief Financial Officer [Dutch]

Dyas UK Limited
Incorporated: 27 June 2000
Net Worth: £406,224,992 *Total Assets:* £845,222,016
Registered Office: Athena House, Athena Drive, Tachbrook Park, Warwick, CV34 6RL
Activities: Extraction of crude petroleum
Officers: Geoffrey Picton-Turbervill, Secretary; Robert Jan Baurdoux [1957] Director [Dutch]; Matthew Quentin Hickin [1967] Director; Adam Euan Thompson [1974] Finance Director; Petrus Johannes Waaijer [1954] Director/Accountant/Chief Financial Officer [Dutch]

Dynamic Cassette International Limited
Incorporated: 29 September 1983 *Employees:* 183
Net Worth: £8,025,256 *Total Assets:* £11,458,331
Registered Office: Marsh Lane Industrial Estate, Boston, Lincs, PE21 7TX
Activities: Manufacture of plastics in primary forms
Major Shareholder: John William Studholme
Officers: John William Studholme [1943] Director/Engineer; Tammy Nicola Studholme [1968] Director/General Manager

Dynamic Procurement Holdings Limited
Incorporated: 15 June 2011 *Employees:* 57
Net Worth: £13,188,588 *Total Assets:* £34,603,140
Registered Office: 249 Midsummer Boulevard, Milton Keynes, Bucks, MK9 1EA
Activities: Activities of other holding companies n.e.c.
Shareholders: Julian John Lindsay Young; Ian Reiner Wolter
Officers: Graham John Anthony Dolan, Secretary; Paul Santo Martin [1971] Director; Ian Reiner Wolter [1966] Director; Julian John Lindsay Young [1966] Director

Dynex Semiconductor Limited
Incorporated: 13 August 1999 *Employees:* 357
Net Worth: £16,041,000 *Total Assets:* £36,715,000
Registered Office: Doddington Road, Lincoln, LN6 3LF
Activities: Manufacture of electronic components
Parent: Dynex Power Inc
Officers: Su Angela Bailey [1978] Director/Head of HR; Mark Andrew Kempton [1967] Director/Chief Operations Officer; Alan Gary Lyons [1971] Finance Director; Clive Graham Vacher [1970] Director

Dyon E & P Limited
Incorporated: 11 March 2005
Previous: Oranje-Nassau E & P Limited
Net Worth: £39,318,000 *Total Assets:* £69,762,000
Registered Office: Athena House, Athena Drive, Tachbrook Park, Warwick, CV34 6RL
Activities: Extraction of crude petroleum
Officers: Geoffrey Picton-Turbervill, Secretary; Robert Jan Baurdoux [1957] Director [Dutch]; Petrus Johannes Waaijer [1954] Director/Accountant Chief Financial Officer [Dutch]

Dyon UK Limited
Incorporated: 11 March 2005
Net Worth: £139,428,992 *Total Assets:* £139,712,000
Registered Office: Athena House, Athena Drive, Tachbrook Park, Warwick, CV34 6RL
Activities: Extraction of crude petroleum
Shareholders: Dyas UK; Dyon E & P Ltd
Officers: Geoffrey Picton-Turbervill, Secretary; Robert Jan Baurdoux [1957] Director [Dutch]; Petrus Johannes Waaijer [1954] Director/Accountant/Chief Financial Officer [Dutch]

Dyson Group PLC
Incorporated: 21 January 1920 *Employees:* 52
Net Worth: £12,077,000 *Total Assets:* £12,329,000
Registered Office: Totley Works, Baslow Road, Sheffield, S17 3BL
Activities: Activities of head offices
Shareholders: Svenska Handelsbanken AB; The Board of The Pension Protection Fund
Officers: Richard McQuinn, Secretary; Julian Edward Peregrine Cooper [1962] Managing Director, Corporate Advisory; Gavin Jon Rosson [1968] Finance Director; Magnus Goran Sternbrink [1977] Director/Investment Banker [Swedish]

E - Leather Limited
Incorporated: 31 January 1995 *Employees:* 169
Net Worth: £46,604,312 *Total Assets:* £53,823,740
Registered Office: Kingsbridge Centre, Sturrock Way, Peterborough, PE3 8TZ
Activities: Other manufacturing n.e.c.
Officers: John Kennedy, Secretary; Ian Duncan Boyce [1944] Director; Andrew Clifford Winawer Brandler [1956] Director; John Patrick Kennedy [1969] Director; Ilias Korosis [1979] Director/Partner [Greek]; James Lindsay Lewis [1975] Director [Australian]; Christopher James McBean [1958] Director; Arne Claudio Morteani [1974] Director/Principal, ETF Manager LLP [German]; Patrick Gerard Sheehan [1960] Director/Managing Partner

E M Holdings UK Limited
Incorporated: 27 October 1998
Net Worth: £45,606,000 *Total Assets:* £241,863,008
Registered Office: c/o Etex (Exteriors) UK Limited, Wellington Road, Burton on Trent, Staffs, DE14 2AP
Activities: Activities of head offices
Officers: Jayne Arkell [1974] Director/Country Manager UK; Xavier Georges Roger Janin [1969] Director/General Manager [French]

E S Management Services Limited
Incorporated: 27 July 2012 *Employees:* 118
Net Worth: £4,401,081 *Total Assets:* £17,390,608
Registered Office: Building 1000, Kings Reach, Yew Street, Stockport, Cheshire, SK4 2HG
Activities: Other business support service activities n.e.c.
Major Shareholder: Michael Dwan
Officers: Andrew Dwan [1965] Director; Michael Dwan [1959] Director; Marina Ann Guido [1985] Finance Director

E-PPL Holdings Limited
Incorporated: 28 May 2014 *Employees:* 300
Net Worth: £6,968,939 *Total Assets:* £22,943,380
Registered Office: Unit 2 Mallory Way, Gallagher Business Park, Coventry, Warwicks, CV6 6PB
Activities: Activities of other holding companies n.e.c.
Major Shareholder: Paul Adrian Simmerson
Officers: John Thomas Birch [1964] Director; Paul Adrian Simmerson [1977] Director/Holding Company; David Taylor [1965] Director

E-PPL Limited
Incorporated: 14 October 2011 *Employees:* 22
Net Worth: £4,324,738 *Total Assets:* £10,912,621
Registered Office: Unit 2 Mallory Way, Gallagher Business Park, Coventry, Warwicks, CV6 6PB
Activities: Other activities of employment placement agencies
Shareholders: Neil Christopher Simmerson; E-PPL Holdings Limited
Officers: John Thomas Birch [1964] Director; Neil Christopher Simmerson [1978] Director; Paul Adrian Simmerson [1977] Director; David Taylor [1965] Director

E-Therapeutics PLC
Incorporated: 15 October 2001 *Employees:* 20
Net Worth: £10,738,000 *Total Assets:* £11,762,000
Registered Office: 17 Blenheim Office Park, Long Hanborough, Oxon, OX29 8LN
Activities: Other research and experimental development on natural sciences and engineering
Shareholder: Invesco Ltd
Officers: Susan Margaret Steven, Secretary; Raymond John Barlow [1968] Director; Trevor Jones [1942] Director; Steven Medlicott [1965] Director; Iain Gladstone Ross [1954] Director; Christine Soden [1957] Chartered Accountant/Director

E. P. B. Holdings Limited
Incorporated: 30 June 1997 *Employees:* 169
Net Worth: £16,418,131 *Total Assets:* £33,604,320
Registered Office: E P Barrus Ltd, Glen Way, Launton Road, Bicester, Oxon, OX26 4UR
Activities: Dormant company
Officers: Robert Richard Muir, Secretary; Jeffery Carter Van Deuch [1966] Director/Chief Financial Officer [American]; Andrew James Feilden [1941] Managing Director; Robert Duncan Glen [1939] Director; Tara Louise Owen Glen [1971] Director/Accountant/Engineer; Dietrich Kaesgen [1936] Director [German]; Charles Merideth Moll [1971] Director [American]; Curtis Moll [1939] Director [American]; Robert Richard Muir [1956] Director

E.A.T. (Holdings) Limited
Incorporated: 3 December 1912 *Employees:* 5
Net Worth: £10,303,336 *Total Assets:* £11,492,570
Registered Office: 5 Ground Floor, Kings Court, Kettering Parkway, Kettering, Northants, NN15 6WJ
Activities: Activities of head offices
Shareholder: Elizabeth Jane Brown
Officers: Ian James Sharp, Secretary; Andrew Peter Brown [1974] Director/Architect; Christopher Rowan Brown [1980] Director/Financial Analyst; David Timson Brown [1972] Director/Groundsman/Engineer; Elizabeth Jane Brown [1944] Director; Ian James Sharp [1977] Director

E.F.B. Group Limited
Incorporated: 20 May 2005 *Employees:* 112
Net Worth: £13,711,032 *Total Assets:* £39,415,512
Registered Office: The Pinnacle, 170 Midsummer Boulevard, Milton Keynes, Bucks, MK9 1FE
Activities: Activities of head offices
Shareholders: E.F.B. Trustees Limited; Stephen Charles Barlow
Officers: Michael Adams [1956] Director; Stephen Charles Barlow [1956] Director/Chief Executive Officer; Peter John Butler [1966] Managing Director; Phil Gotch [1976] Financial Director; Brandon William Ransley [1965] Director/Solicitor

E.I.R.P Limited
Incorporated: 4 March 1994 *Employees:* 3
Net Worth: £37,785,000 *Total Assets:* £41,860,000
Registered Office: Unit 26 Maisies Way, South Normanton, Alfreton, Derbys, DE55 2DS
Activities: Other letting and operating of own or leased real estate
Major Shareholder: Gary Hugh Dutton
Officers: Jennifer Marie Hill, Secretary; Carol Ann Dutton [1948] Director; Gary Hugh Dutton [1949] Director/Chairman

E.On Climate & Renewables UK Biomass Limited
Incorporated: 22 February 2011 *Employees:* 25
Net Worth: £10,459,000 *Total Assets:* £131,411,000
Registered Office: Westwood Way, Westwood Business Park, Coventry, Warwicks, CV4 8LG
Activities: Production of electricity
Parent: E.On Climate & Renewables UK Limited
Officers: Michael Robert Day [1978] Director/Accountant; Michael Robert French [1968] Managing Director, Business & Community Solutions [German]; Michael Geoffrey Wake [1970] Director/Head of Business Heat & Power Solutions

E.On Climate & Renewables UK Developments Limited
Incorporated: 23 April 1999 *Employees:* 7
Net Worth: £33,037,000 *Total Assets:* £239,963,008
Registered Office: Westwood Way, Westwood Business Park, Coventry, Warwicks, CV4 8LG
Activities: Production of electricity
Parent: E.On Climate & Renewables UK Limited
Officers: Timothy James Bell [1973] Director/Head of Controlling Offshore and Onshore EU; Roland Sven Walter Flaig [1974] Director/Head of Operations Northern Europe [Swedish]; Adam Charles Greenslade [1981] Director/Onshore Wind Operations Manager UK & Nordic

E.On Climate & Renewables UK Humber Wind Limited
Incorporated: 15 September 2003 *Employees:* 1
Net Worth: £59,401,000 *Total Assets:* £645,260,992
Registered Office: Westwood Way, Westwood Business Park, Coventry, Warwicks, CV4 8LG
Activities: Production of electricity
Parent: E.On Climate & Renewables UK Limited
Officers: Timothy James Bell [1973] Director/Head of Controlling Offshore and Onshore EU; Adrian Joseph Chatterton [1963] Director/Head of Construction Offshore; Simon Prousch [1980] Director/Head of Operations, Offshore UK [German]

E.On Climate & Renewables UK Limited
Incorporated: 23 April 1999 *Employees:* 199
Net Worth: £40,798,000 *Total Assets:* £539,121,984
Registered Office: Westwood Way, Westwood Business Park, Coventry, Warwicks, CV4 8LG
Activities: Activities of other holding companies n.e.c.
Parent: E.On UK PLC
Officers: Timothy James Bell [1973] Director/Head of Controlling Offshore and Onshore EU; Adrian Joseph Chatterton [1963] Director/Head of Construction Offshore; Dr Thomas Michel [1978] Director Offshore Wind Operations [German]; Tim Stefan Moritz [1973] Director Accounting Business Partner ECR [German]; Matthew James Swanwick [1967] Project Director

E.On Climate & Renewables UK London Array Limited
Incorporated: 24 December 2004
Net Worth: £65,283,000 *Total Assets:* £547,182,976
Registered Office: Westwood Way, Westwood Business Park, Coventry, Warwicks, CV4 8LG
Activities: Production of electricity
Parent: E.On Climate & Renewables UK Limited
Officers: Timothy James Bell [1973] Director/Head of Controlling Offshore and Onshore EU; Adrian Joseph Chatterton [1963] Director/Head of Construction; Simon Prousch [1980] Director/Head of Operations, Offshore UK [German]

E.On Climate & Renewables UK Offshore Wind Limited
Incorporated: 19 December 2000 *Employees:* 14
Net Worth: £38,395,000 *Total Assets:* £98,833,000
Registered Office: Westwood Way, Westwood Business Park, Coventry, Warwicks, CV4 8LG
Activities: Production of electricity
Parent: E.On Climate & Renewables UK Limited
Officers: Timothy James Bell [1973] Director/Head of Controlling Offshore and Onshore EU; Adrian Joseph Chatterton [1963] Director/Head of Construction Offshore; Simon Prousch [1980] Director/Head of Operations, Offshore UK [German]

E.On Climate & Renewables UK Operations Limited
Incorporated: 2 March 1992
Net Worth: £22,863,000 *Total Assets:* £30,064,000
Registered Office: Westwood Way, Westwood Business Park, Coventry, Warwicks, CV4 8LG
Activities: Production of electricity
Parent: E.On Climate & Renewables UK Limited
Officers: Timothy James Bell [1973] Director/Head of Controlling Offshore and Onshore EU; Roland Sven Walter Flaig [1974] Director/Head of Operations Northern Europe [Swedish]; Adam Charles Greenslade [1981] Director/Onshore Wind Operations Manager UK & Nordic

E.On Climate & Renewables UK Robin Rigg East Limited
Incorporated: 21 May 1998 *Employees:* 22
Net Worth: £34,294,000 *Total Assets:* £181,874,000
Registered Office: Westwood Way, Westwood Business Park, Coventry, Warwicks, CV4 8LG
Activities: Production of electricity
Parent: E.On Climate & Renewables UK Limited
Officers: Timothy James Bell [1973] Director/Head of Controlling Offshore and Onshore EU; Adrian Joseph Chatterton [1963] Director/Head of Construction Offshore; Simon Prousch [1980] Director/Head of Operations, Offshore UK [German]

E.On Climate & Renewables UK Robin Rigg West Limited
Incorporated: 30 January 2001 *Employees:* 22
Net Worth: £42,807,000 *Total Assets:* £196,496,992
Registered Office: Westwood Way, Westwood Business Park, Coventry, Warwicks, CV4 8LG
Activities: Production of electricity
Parent: E.On Climate & Renewables UK Limited
Officers: Timothy James Bell [1973] Director/Head of Controlling Offshore and Onshore EU; Adrian Joseph Chatterton [1963] Director/Head of Construction Offshore; Simon Prousch [1980] Director/Head of Operations, Offshore UK [German]

E.On Connecting Energies Limited
Incorporated: 5 April 2011 *Employees:* 34
Net Worth Deficit: £15,605,000 *Total Assets:* £38,100,000
Registered Office: Westwood Way, Westwood Business Park, Coventry, Warwicks, CV4 8LG
Activities: Other business support service activities n.e.c.
Parent: E.On SE
Officers: Matthew Charles Brown [1972] Director/Chief Financial Officer; Gareth Elwyn Howells [1974] Director/Head of Legal

E.On Control Solutions Limited
Incorporated: 27 February 2003 *Employees:* 367
Previous: Matrix Control Solutions Limited
Net Worth: £14,625,298 *Total Assets:* £27,509,344
Registered Office: Westwood Way, Westwood Business Park, Coventry, Warwicks, CV4 8LG
Activities: Other professional, scientific and technical activities n.e.c.
Parent: Green Sky Energy Limited
Officers: Matthew Charles Brown [1972] Finance Director; David Peter Lewis [1968] Director; Michael William Ramsden [1973] Technology Director

E.On Energy Solutions Limited
Incorporated: 17 July 1997 *Employees:* 7,673
Net Worth: £1,036,000,000 *Total Assets:* £2,716,999,936
Registered Office: Westwood Way, Westwood Business Park, Coventry, Warwicks, CV4 8LG
Activities: Trade of electricity
Parent: E.On UK PLC
Officers: Deborah Gandley, Secretary; Christian Barr [1971] Director/Chief Financial Officer [German]; Michael Robert French [1968] Managing Director, Business & Community Solutions [German]; Michael David Lewis [1967] Director/Chief Executive Officer; Christopher James Lovatt [1969] Managing Director Residential; Sara Lyn Vaughan [1964] Political & Regulatory Affairs Director

E.On IT UK Limited
Incorporated: 9 November 2005 *Employees:* 442
Net Worth: £7,094,000 *Total Assets:* £19,875,000
Registered Office: Westwood Way, Westwood Business Park, Coventry, Warwicks, CV4 8LG
Activities: Other information technology service activities
Parent: E.On UK PLC
Officers: Deborah Gandley [1971] Director/Solicitor; Christoph Karl Wilhelm Hanewinkel [1971] Director/Head of Finance/Controlling, Digital & IT [German]; Michael David Lewis [1967] Director/Chief Executive Officer

E.On Project Earth Limited
Incorporated: 25 April 2012
Net Worth: £2,498,000 *Total Assets:* £13,472,000
Registered Office: Westwood Way, Westwood Business Park, Coventry, Warwicks, CV4 8LG
Activities: Other professional, scientific and technical activities n.e.c.
Parent: E.On Energy Solutions Limited
Officers: Michael Robert French [1968] Managing Director, Business & Community Solutions [German]; Michael Geoffrey Wake [1970] Director/Head of Business Heat & Power Solutions

E.On UK CHP Limited
Incorporated: 5 February 1992 *Employees:* 121
Net Worth: £8,219,000 *Total Assets:* £32,558,000
Registered Office: Westwood Way, Westwood Business Park, Coventry, Warwicks, CV4 8LG
Activities: Production of electricity
Parent: E.On UK PLC
Officers: Michael Robert Day [1978] Director/Accountant; Michael Robert French [1968] Managing Director, Business & Community Solutions [German]; Michael Geoffrey Wake [1970] Director/Head of Business Heat & Power Solutions

E.On UK Cogeneration Limited
Incorporated: 13 July 1992 *Employees:* 36
Net Worth Deficit: £1,026,000 *Total Assets:* £10,896,000
Registered Office: Westwood Way, Westwood Business Park, Coventry, Warwicks, CV4 8LG
Activities: Production of electricity
Parent: E.On UK CHP Limited
Officers: Michael Robert Day [1978] Director/Accountant; Michael Robert French [1968] Managing Director, Business & Community Solutions [German]; Michael Geoffrey Wake [1970] Director/Head of Business Heat & Power Solutions

E.Surv Limited
Incorporated: 2 June 1988 *Employees:* 606
Net Worth: £11,062,000 *Total Assets:* £55,979,000
Registered Office: Lahnstein House, Gold Street, Kettering, Northants, NN16 8AP
Activities: Activities of other holding companies n.e.c.
Parent: LSL Property Services PLC
Officers: Sapna Bedi FitzGenerald, Secretary/Solicitor; Adam Robert Castleton [1964] Director; Ronan Jennings [1964] Managing Director [Irish]; Paul Adam Marcus [1960] Director/Chartered Surveyor; Martin James Oliver [1967] Director; Charles Anthony Phayer [1958] Director; Timothy James Wood [1965] Director/Chartered Surveyor

E4D & G Holdco Limited
Incorporated: 5 October 2007
Net Worth Deficit: £15,423,000 *Total Assets:* £116,035,000
Registered Office: The Sherard Building, Edmund Halley Road, Oxford Science Park, Oxford, OX4 4DQ
Activities: Activities of other holding companies n.e.c.
Parent: Amey Ventures Investments Limited
Officers: Derek Orr Anderson [1964] Director; John Gerard Connelly [1960] Director/Head of Investment Management; Erwan Fouris [1972] Director [French]; Katherine Anne Louise Pearman [1961] Director/Chartered Accountant; Angela Louise Roshier [1975] Director

E4D & G Project Co Limited
Incorporated: 5 October 2007
Net Worth Deficit: £15,423,000 *Total Assets:* £116,035,000
Registered Office: The Sherard Building, Edmund Halley Road, Oxford Science Park, Oxford, OX4 4DQ
Activities: Management of real estate on a fee or contract basis
Parent: E4D & G Holdco Limited
Officers: Derek Orr Anderson [1964] Director; John Gerard Connelly [1960] Director/Head of Investment Management; Erwan Fouris [1972] Director [French]; Katherine Anne Louise Pearman [1961] Director/Chartered Accountant; Angela Louise Roshier [1975] Director

Eagle Hall Estates Limited
Incorporated: 17 April 2002
Net Worth: £27,417,512 *Total Assets:* £33,189,990
Registered Office: Clay Farm, North Scarle, Lincs, LN6 9ES
Activities: Activities of head offices
Officers: Carolyn Fiona Overton, Secretary; Andrew Curtis Chennells [1964] Director/Farmer; Gordon Harry Chennells [1928] Director/Farmer; Patrick Edward Chennells [1968] Director/Farmer; Julius John Joel [1961] Director

Dennis Eagle Limited
Incorporated: 23 June 1999 *Employees:* 804
Net Worth: £41,041,000 *Total Assets:* £102,292,000
Registered Office: Heathcote Way, Heathcote Industrial Estate, Warwick, CV34 6TE
Activities: Manufacture of bodies (coachwork) for motor vehicles (except caravans)
Parent: Terberg Rosroca Group Limited
Officers: Andrew Peter Uttley, Secretary; Timothy James Conlon [1966] Director; Keith Robert Day [1963] Purchasing Director; Kevin Else [1957] Director; Carl David Hughes [1969] Manufacturing Director; Richard Duncan Taylor [1971] Sales Director; Godefridus Terberg [1963] Director/Vice Chairman [Dutch]; Andrew Peter Uttley [1963] Director/Chartered Accountant

Eaglebeam Limited
Incorporated: 30 March 2000 *Employees:* 9
Net Worth: £8,257,503 *Total Assets:* £11,631,677
Registered Office: Stonebridge House, Kenilworth Road, Meriden, Coventry, Warwicks, CV7 7LJ
Activities: Public houses and bars
Officers: Mary Christina McLean, Secretary; Adrian John McLean [1969] Director [Irish]; Charles Noel McLean [1947] Director/Property Consultant [Irish]; Noel McLean [1975] Director

Eamar Development (UK) Limited
Incorporated: 23 March 2012 *Employees:* 1
Net Worth: £5,027,648 *Total Assets:* £23,024,084
Registered Office: 14 Green Pastures, Stockport, Cheshire, SK4 3RA
Activities: Other letting and operating of own or leased real estate
Parent: Eamar Al-Khaleej Saudi Real Estate Co Ltd
Officers: Saleh Abdullah Alnaeem [1964] Director/Chartered Accountant [Saudi Arabian]

Earlham Trading Company Limited
Incorporated: 12 February 2016 *Employees:* 131
Net Worth: £8,006,000 *Total Assets:* £13,644,000
Registered Office: 4 Bayton Road, Exhall, Coventry, Warwicks, CV7 9DJ
Activities: Activities of head offices
Major Shareholder: Stephen James Payne
Officers: Timothy John Burchell [1963] Director; Stephen James Payne [1970] Director; Patrick Joseph Anthony Sheehan [1941] Director

Earth Trust
Incorporated: 26 February 2002 *Employees:* 33
Net Worth: £11,574,715 *Total Assets:* £11,992,585
Registered Office: Earth Trust Centre, Little Wittenham, Abingdon, Oxon, OX14 4QZ
Activities: Growing of cereals (except rice), leguminous crops and oil seeds
Officers: Victoria Jayne Manley, Secretary; Lynda Susan Atkins [1961] Director/Councillor; Dr Mary Margaret Barkham [1961] Director/Forestry Commissioner; Dr Robin David Buxton [1950] Director/Retired; Dr Ian Arthur Davidson [1957] Director/Consultant; Christopher Charles Phillips [1950] Director/Retired; Timothy David Rossington [1958] Director/Consultant; Julian Anthony Sayers [1959] Director; Graham Ernest Shaw [1950] Director

Easey Pigs Limited
Incorporated: 16 January 2008 *Employees:* 16
Net Worth: £15,460,501 *Total Assets:* £17,540,858
Registered Office: Seton House, Warwick Technology Park, Gallows Hill, Warwick, CV34 6DA
Activities: Raising of swine and pigs
Parent: Easey Holdings Limited
Officers: Andrew Michael James Cracknell [1967] Director/CEO Senior Vice President; Andrew Keith Saunders [1957] Director

East Coast Fittings Limited
Incorporated: 4 March 1981 *Employees:* 133
Net Worth: £2,941,311 *Total Assets:* £9,383,512
Registered Office: Auster House, Rearsby Business Park, Gaddesby Lane, Rearsby, Leicester, LE7 4YH
Activities: Manufacture of kitchen furniture
Major Shareholder: Derek James Goodman
Officers: Victoria Mary Goodman, Secretary; Glen Coleman [1958] Director/Sales Manager; Christopher James Goodman [1974] Works Director; Derek James Goodman [1950] Director; Victoria Mary Goodman [1950] Director

East Coast Main Line Company Limited
Incorporated: 7 February 2003 *Employees:* 3,233
Net Worth Deficit: £169,528,000 *Total Assets:* £221,706,000
Registered Office: One Stockport Exchange, 20 Railway Road, Stockport, Cheshire, SK1 3SW
Activities: Passenger rail transport, interurban
Parent: Inter City Railways Limited
Officers: Timothy Kavanagh, Secretary; Martin Andrew Griffiths [1966] Director; Timothy Brendan Kavanagh [1968] Director; Patrick Charles Kingdon McCall [1964] Director/Senior Partner; Neil Micklethwaite [1973] Director/Transport; Ross John Paterson [1971] Finance Director; Timothy Colin Shoveller [1972] Director; James Richard Rowland Tipple [1971] Director

East Kent Road Car Company,Limited
Incorporated: 11 August 1916 *Employees:* 1,349
Net Worth: £15,742,000 *Total Assets:* £41,929,000
Registered Office: c/o Stagecoach Services Limited, One Stockport Exchange, 20 Railway Road, Stockport, Cheshire, SK1 3SW
Activities: Other urban, suburban or metropolitan passenger land transport (not underground, metro or similar)
Parent: Stagecoach Bus Holdings Limited
Officers: Michael John Vaux, Secretary; Colin Brown [1968] Director/Accountant; Arnold Mark Threapleton [1954] Managing Director; Michael Watson [1973] Director

East London Bus & Coach Company Limited
Incorporated: 14 December 1988 *Employees:* 2,169
Net Worth Deficit: £76,674,000 *Total Assets:* £36,020,000
Registered Office: c/o Stagecoach Services Limited, One Stockport Exchange, 20 Railway Road, Stockport, Cheshire, SK1 3SW
Activities: Other urban, suburban or metropolitan passenger land transport (not underground, metro or similar)
Parent: Stagecoach Bus Holdings Limited
Officers: Michael John Vaux, Secretary; Colin Brown [1968] Director/Accountant; Paul Graham Lynch [1962] Director; Arnold Mark Threapleton [1954] Managing Director

East London Bus Group Property Investments Limited
Incorporated: 9 May 2006
Net Worth: £30,081,000 *Total Assets:* £38,537,000
Registered Office: c/o Stagecoach Services Limited, One Stockport Exchange, 20 Railway Road, Stockport, Cheshire, SK1 3SW
Activities: Buying and selling of own real estate
Parent: Stagecoach Bus Holdings Limited
Officers: Michael John Vaux, Secretary; Colin Brown [1968] Director/Accountant; Paul Graham Lynch [1962] Director; Arnold Mark Threapleton [1954] Managing Director

East Midlands Academy Trust
Incorporated: 19 July 2012 *Employees:* 407
Previous: EMLC Academy Trust
Net Worth: £28,774,764 *Total Assets:* £35,208,172
Registered Office: Northampton International Academy, 55 Barrack Road, Northampton, NN1 1AA
Activities: Educational support services
Officers: Kevin George Crompton [1956] Director; Andrew Davis [1972] Director/Product and Technology Training Team Manager; Jonathan Henry Harris [1971] Director/Headteacher; Irfana Malik [1958] Director/Risk Officer; Stephen Paul Morales [1968] Director/CEO of ISBL; Ayo Salam [1979] Director/Governance Risk & Compliance Professional; Pauline Waterhouse [1953] Director/Principal and Chief Executive; Fiona Wheeler [1968] Director/Housewife

East Midlands Chamber (Derbyshire, Nottinghamshire, Leicestershire)
Incorporated: 24 January 1984 *Employees:* 156
Previous: East Midlands Chamber (Derbyshire, Nottinghamshire, Leicestershire) Limited
Net Worth: £10,052,295 *Total Assets:* £13,461,595
Registered Office: Commerce House, Millennium Way, Dunston Road, Chesterfield, Derbys, S41 8ND
Activities: Activities of other membership organisations n.e.c.
Officers: Lesley Finvola Dexter, Secretary; Dr Darren Alan Clark [1969] Director/Chief Executive Officer; Stuart Dawkins [1962] Director; Mark Deakin [1970] Director; Dawn Louise Edwards [1967] Director/Management Consultant; James Fry [1971] Director/Solicitor; Kevin Harris [1966] Director; Jafferhusein Kapasi [1950] Director/Businessman; Scott Knowles [1972] Director/Chief Executive; Robert Dennis Mayo [1965] Director; Stephen Howard Midgley [1956] Director; Richard Ian Morgan [1951] Director; Harindra Deepal Punchihewa [1961] Finance Director; Eileen Maria Richards [1970] Director; Martin John Rigley [1962] Director/Chartered Engineer; John Stuart Robinson [1942] Director/Semi-Retired; Lindsey Claire Williams [1964] Director/Group Chief Executive

East Midlands Education Trust
Incorporated: 15 February 2011 *Employees:* 1,041
Net Worth: £85,443,000 *Total Assets:* £103,596,000
Registered Office: The West Bridgford School, Loughborough Road, West Bridgford, Nottingham, NG2 7FA
Activities: General secondary education
Officers: Elaine Aldridge, Secretary; Councillor Christopher Paul Barnfather [1953] Director/Councillor; Patrick Terence Booth [1951] Director/Solicitor; Brian Andrew Carr [1964] Marketing Director; Neil Clifton [1955] Director/Retired; Dr John Frederick Collins [1954] Director/Business Coach and Consultant; Kathleen Margaret Foale [1954] Director/County Councillor; Susan Elizabeth Gubbins [1956] Director/Certified Chartered Accountant; Andrew Michael Hindmarsh [1959] Director/University Administrator; Robert McDonough [1963] Director/Secondary Headteacher; Elizabeth Celia Thomas [1948] Director/Retired; Paul John Winter [1968] Director/Police Chief Inspector

East Midlands International Airport Limited
Incorporated: 27 November 1986 *Employees:* 629
Net Worth: £94,056,000 *Total Assets:* £346,347,008
Registered Office: Building 34, East Midlands Airport, Castle Donnington, Derby, DE74 2SA
Activities: Scheduled passenger air transport
Parent: East Midlands Airport Nottingham Derby Leicester Ltd
Officers: Charles Thomas Cornish [1959] Director/Chief Executive; John Kenneth O'Toole [1974] Director [Irish]; Karen Smart [1966] Director; Neil Philip Thompson [1971] Director

East Midlands Property Developments Limited
Incorporated: 26 March 1984 *Employees:* 4
Net Worth: £17,937,000 *Total Assets:* £35,590,000
Registered Office: P O Box 14, Chartwell Drive, Wigston, Leicester, LE18 1AT
Activities: Development of building projects
Parent: Cromwell Group (Holdings) Limited
Officers: Horace Vincent Draa III, Secretary; Fred James Costello Jr [1960] Director/Business Executive [American]; Horace Vincent Draa III [1956] Director/Business Executive [American]; Neil Lawrence Jowsey [1964] Director/Business Executive; Richard Kevin Pott [1980] Director/Business Executive [American]

East Midlands Trains Limited
Incorporated: 24 January 2005 *Employees:* 2,304
Net Worth: £13,627,000 *Total Assets:* £138,923,008
Registered Office: Prospect House, No 1 Prospect Place, Millennium Way, Derby, DE24 8HG
Activities: Passenger rail transport, interurban
Parent: Stagecoach Rail Holdings Limited
Officers: Timothy Radcliffe Gledhill, Secretary; Lisa Janet Angus [1974] Director; Lawrence Matthew Bowman [1981] Director; Kirsty Derry [1968] Director; Timothy Radcliffe Gledhill [1966] Director/Accountant; Martin Andrew Griffiths [1966] Director; Jacob Henry Kelly [1974] Director; Adam John Piddington [1968] Director; Paul Rushton [1963] Director; Timothy Colin Shoveller [1972] Director; Darren James Ward [1969] Director; Christopher George Wright [1982] Director

East of England Agricultural Society
Incorporated: 7 October 1981 *Employees:* 31
Net Worth: £20,768,404 *Total Assets:* £22,252,378
Registered Office: East of England Showground, Alwalton, Peterborough, Cambs, PE2 6XE
Activities: Activities of other membership organisations n.e.c.
Officers: Hedley Richard Quentin Arnold, Secretary; Thomas Benjamin White Beazley [1963] Director/Farmer; Richard Cranmer Bramley [1958] Director/Retired; Robert William Dalgliesh [1954] Director/Chartered Surveyor; Geoffrey John Dodgson [1951] Director; Benjamin Mark John Harris [1978] Director/Farmer; James Robert Parrish [1968] Director/Farm Partner; John Stuart Greer Paton [1946] Director/Chartered Surveyor; Charles David Reynolds [1969] Director/Consultant; Andrew Henry Riddington [1965] Director; Nigel Peter Rome [1961] Director/Farmer

East Worcester Water Limited
Incorporated: 3 November 1992
Net Worth: £175,219,008 *Total Assets:* £175,799,008
Registered Office: Severn Trent Centre, 2 St John's Street, Coventry, Warwicks, CV1 2LZ
Activities: Other business support service activities n.e.c.
Parent: Severn Trent Water Limited
Officers: Aline Anne Campbell, Secretary; John Anthony Jackson [1960] Director; Bronagh Kennedy [1963] Director/General Counsel and Company Secretary; Robert Craig McPheely [1962] Director/Accountant

Eastern Counties Properties Limited
Incorporated: 21 March 1988
Net Worth: £3,649,206 *Total Assets:* £21,388,382
Registered Office: 370 Loughborough Road, Leicester, LE4 5PR
Activities: Other letting and operating of own or leased real estate
Parent: Jelson Holdings Limited
Officers: Julian Ian Bestwick [1967] Finance Director; Graham Stuart Jelley [1961] Director/Builder; Robert Stephen Jelley [1955] Director/Builder; Ronald Albert Jelley [1927] Director/Builder; Stuart Wilson [1970] Director

Eastern Multi-Academy Trust
Incorporated: 6 August 2010 *Employees:* 862
Previous: CWA Academy Trust
Net Worth: £53,622,000 *Total Assets:* £62,657,000
Registered Office: Trust Offices, Queen Mary Road, King's Lynn, Norfolk, PE30 4QG
Activities: Primary education
Officers: David Alan Evans, Secretary; Lady Karen Jean Fisher [1951] Director; Wendy Jayne Fisher [1965] Director/Freelance Consumer Researcher; Deborah Gates [1961] Local Authority Director; Jason William Hall [1972] Director/Chartered Accountant; Graham John Pearson [1958] Director/Account General Manager; Julie Perry [1972] Director/Global Risk Management; Dr Duncan Ramsey [1967] Director/Chief Executive; James Rowney [1967] Director; Derek Edward Stringer [1945] Director/Retired Management Consultant; Julie Ann Taylor [1961] Director/Chief Executive; David Malcolm Wilde [1966] Director

Easternrose Limited
Incorporated: 8 June 2000 *Employees:* 4
Net Worth: £4,884,616 *Total Assets:* £18,022,276
Registered Office: Margarethe House, Eismann Way, Phoenix Parkway, Corby, Northants, NN17 5ZB
Activities: Other letting and operating of own or leased real estate
Shareholders: Mary Agnes Fiona Canham; Roger Timothy Canham
Officers: Mary Agnes Fiona Canham, Secretary; Roger Timothy Canham [1964] Director; Mary Agnes Fiona Canham [1968] Director/Lawyer

Eastgate Care Group Ltd
Incorporated: 1 May 2013 *Employees:* 335
Previous: Newport 73 Ltd
Net Worth: £9,447,209 *Total Assets:* £22,335,386
Registered Office: 370-374 Nottingham Road, Newthorpe, Notts, NG16 2ED
Activities: Activities of head offices
Major Shareholder: James William Day
Officers: James William Day [1957] Director

Eastgate Care Ltd
Incorporated: 19 January 1988 *Employees:* 335
Net Worth: £6,360,609 *Total Assets:* £20,418,850
Registered Office: 370-374 Nottingham Road, Newthorpe, Nottingham, NG16 2ED
Activities: Residential nursing care facilities
Parent: Eastgate Care Group Ltd
Officers: James William Day, Secretary/Director; Janine Morgan, Secretary; James William Day [1957] Director/Developer

Eastmarket Grain LLP
Incorporated: 30 October 2012
Total Assets: £12,828,413
Registered Office: Office 11, 6-8 Dartford Road, March, Cambs, PE15 8AQ

Eaton Electrical Products Limited
Incorporated: 5 December 1977 *Employees:* 224
Previous: Cooper Fulleon Limited
Net Worth: £99,868,000 *Total Assets:* £141,763,008
Registered Office: Jephson Court, Tancred Close, Queensway, Royal Leamington Spa, Warwicks, CV31 3RZ
Activities: Manufacture of other electrical equipment
Parent: Eaton Corporation PLC
Officers: John William Michael Butters [1971] Director; Mike Carter [1963] Director; Richard Paul Howes [1971] Operations Director; Andrew Jackson [1973] Finance Director

Eaton Electrical Systems Limited
Incorporated: 23 January 1995 *Employees:* 703
Previous: Cooper Lighting and Safety Limited
Net Worth: £46,176,000 *Total Assets:* £115,648,000
Registered Office: Jephson Court, Tancred Close, Leamington Spa, Warwicks, CV31 3RZ
Activities: Manufacture of electric lighting equipment
Parent: Eaton Industries (U.K.) Limited
Officers: Stephen Currier [1969] Director; Robert John Davies [1967] Director/Business Executive; Martin Gerard Mullin [1966] Director/Business Executive; Simon Sparrow [1970] Director

Eaton Holding (UK) II Limited
Incorporated: 29 August 1997
Previous: Cooper Industries (U.K.) Limited
Net Worth: £243,518,000 *Total Assets:* £290,412,000
Registered Office: Jephson Court, Tancred Close, Queensway, Royal Leamington Spa, Warwicks, CV31 3RZ
Activities: Activities of other holding companies n.e.c.
Parent: Eaton Electric Holdings LLC
Officers: Richard Paul Howes [1971] Director; Andrew Jackson [1973] Finance Director

Eaton Industries (England) Limited
Incorporated: 29 October 2012
Previous: Cooper Industries (England) Limited
Net Worth: £144,438,000 *Total Assets:* £164,844,000
Registered Office: 6 Jephson Court, Tancred Close, Leamington Spa, Warwicks, CV31 3RZ
Activities: Activities of other holding companies n.e.c.
Parent: Cooper International Holdings S.A.R.L.
Officers: Paul Stephen Lewis [1963] Director/Business Executive; Martin Gerard Mullin [1966] Director/Vice President & GM

Eaton Industries (U.K.) Limited
Incorporated: 8 December 2006
Previous: Cooper Controls (U.K.) Limited
Net Worth Deficit: £37,762,000 *Total Assets:* £191,852,992
Registered Office: 6 Jephson Court, Tancred Close, Leamington Spa, Warwicks, CV31 3RZ
Activities: Activities of other holding companies n.e.c.
Parent: Eaton Holding IX S.A R.L.
Officers: Paul Stephen Lewis [1963] Director/Business Executive; Nicolas Papaioannou [1972] Director/Manager [Greek]

Eaton MEDC Limited
Incorporated: 3 March 1975 *Employees:* 223
Previous: Cooper MEDC Limited
Net Worth: £49,331,000 *Total Assets:* £99,667,000
Registered Office: Unit B, Sutton Parkway, Oddicroft Lane, Sutton in Ashfield, Notts, NG17 5FB
Activities: Manufacture of other electrical equipment
Parent: Eaton Industries (U.K.) Limited
Officers: Gavin Evans [1981] Director; Simon Forster [1964] Director; Simon James Matthieson [1977] Director

Eaton Safety Limited
Incorporated: 12 April 1985 *Employees:* 52
Previous: Cooper Safety Limited
Net Worth: £72,459,000 *Total Assets:* £90,359,000
Registered Office: Jephson Court, Tancred Close, Queeensway, Royal Leamington Spa, Warwicks, CV31 3RZ
Activities: Activities of other holding companies n.e.c.
Parent: Eaton Holding (UK) II Limited
Officers: Richard Paul Howes [1971] Operations Director; Andrew Jackson [1973] Finance Director

Ebbsfleet Property Limited
Incorporated: 23 May 2001
Previous: Blue Circle Ebbsfleet Limited
Net Worth: £12,264,664 *Total Assets:* £12,335,366
Registered Office: Bardon Hall, Copt Oak Road, Markfield, Leics, LE67 9PJ
Activities: Development of building projects
Shareholders: Anglo American International Holdings Limited; Lafarge Building Materials Limited
Officers: James West Atherton-Ham [1970] Director/General Counsel; John Ferguson Bowater [1949] Director/Chief Financial Officer; Elaine Christina Klonarides [1976] Director/Company Secretary and Solicitor; Terence Robert Last [1950] Director/Consultant

Ebuyer (UK) Limited
Incorporated: 7 March 2000 *Employees:* 228
Net Worth: £9,363,905 *Total Assets:* £35,278,404
Registered Office: The Nest, Falkland Way, Barton upon Humber, N Lincs, DN18 5RX
Activities: Retail sale via mail order houses or via Internet
Major Shareholder: Malcolm Stanley Healey
Officers: Jane Marie Oldfield, Secretary; Jane Marie Oldfield [1964] Director/Chartered Accountant; Mark Jonathan Pullan [1972] Director/Chartered Accountant; Andrew Allan Roberts [1973] E-Commerce Director; Amber Elizabeth Smith [1983] Sales Director; Lee Robert Weymouth [1981] Commercial Director

The Ecclesbourne School
Incorporated: 9 February 2011 *Employees:* 158
Net Worth: £21,076,532 *Total Assets:* £22,829,980
Registered Office: The Ecclesbourne School, Wirksworth Road, Duffield, Belper, Derbys, DE56 4GS
Activities: General secondary education
Officers: Generaldine Cawley, Secretary; Brenda Maria Mullen Goth [1962] Director/Education Consultant; Richard David Murray Lindop [1954] Director/Chartered Engineer; Brian Arthur Knox Wigram [1947] Director/Retired

Echostar UK Holdings Limited
Incorporated: 6 August 1999
Net Worth: £21,644,560 *Total Assets:* £30,446,216
Registered Office: Hughes House, Rockingham Drive, Linford Wood, Milton Keynes, Bucks, MK14 6PD
Activities: Activities of head offices
Parent: Echostar Corporation
Officers: Michael Talmon Dugan [1949] Director [American]; Charles William Ergen [1953] Director [American]; Dr Dean Alfred Manson [1967] Director/Lawyer [American]

Eclipse Colour Print Limited
Incorporated: 6 April 1960 *Employees:* 136
Net Worth: £9,773,000 *Total Assets:* £19,426,000
Registered Office: 147 Scudamore Road, Leicester, LE3 1UQ
Activities: Printing n.e.c.
Parent: Eclipse (Kettering) Limited
Officers: Sotos Constantinides [1966] Director; Patrick John Headley [1968] Director; Simon Ernest Moore [1965] Managing Director

Eclipse Magnetics Limited
Incorporated: 31 March 1954 *Employees:* 44
Net Worth: £8,042,000 *Total Assets:* £12,924,000
Registered Office: c/o James Neill Holdings Limited, Atlas Way, Atlas North Business Park, Sheffield, S4 7QQ
Activities: Manufacture of tools
Parent: Spear & Jackson Limited
Officers: John Maurice Dallman, Company Secretary; John Brown Dargavel [1956] Sales Director; Simon Nai Cheng Hsu [1960] Director/Businessman [Chinese]; Kevin Martin [1960] Director; Steven Boyde McAllorum [1974] Director; Alaina Shone [1962] Director/Chartered Accountant; Stephen Philip White [1966] Managing Director

Eco-Bat Technologies GB
Incorporated: 12 January 1996
Net Worth: £51,705,000 *Total Assets:* £131,111,000
Registered Office: Cowley Lodge, Warren Carr, Matlock, Derbys, DE4 2LE
Activities: Non-trading company
Parent: Eco-Bat Technologies Limited
Officers: Jimmy Herring, Secretary; Robert John Harris [1963] Managing Director - European Division; Jimmy R. Herring [1966] Director/Group Controller [American]

Eco-Bat Technologies Limited
Incorporated: 23 February 1994 *Employees:* 3,217
Net Worth: £808,788,992 *Total Assets:* £1,158,886,016
Registered Office: Cowley Lodge, Warren Carr, Matlock, Derbys, DE4 2LE
Activities: Activities of head offices
Parent: EB Holdings II, Inc.
Officers: Jimmy Herring, Secretary; Eran Shalom Ashany [1963] Director/Investment Banker [American]; Timothy Edward Brog [1964] Director [American]; Ian Christopher Davies [1959] Director; Graham Lawrence Footitt [1942] Director; Raymond Kubis [1954] Managing Director [American]; Mark Stuart Levy [1948] Director/Businessman [American]; Howard M Meyers [1942] Director [American]; Marschall I Smith [1944] Director [American]

Economy Energy Holdings Limited
Incorporated: 17 March 2015 *Employees:* 106
Net Worth: £6,125,000 *Total Assets:* £33,005,000
Registered Office: 3Mc Siskin Drive, Middlemarch Business Park, Coventry, Warwicks, CV3 4FJ
Activities: Activities of head offices
Shareholders: Lubna Khilji; Paul Cooke
Officers: Lubna Khilji [1985] Director

Ede Holdings Limited
Incorporated: 12 March 1964 *Employees:* 21
Net Worth: £35,885,264 *Total Assets:* £38,890,520
Registered Office: Eden House, Two Rivers, Station Lane, Witney, Oxon, OX28 4BL
Activities: Development of building projects
Shareholder: Daniel Robert Ede
Officers: Steven David Ingledew, Secretary; Daniel Robert Ede [1981] Director; Jonathan Ede [1949] Director; Sally Jane Catherine Ede [1959] Director/Legal Adviser; Steven David Ingledew [1959] Director

Eden Care & Support Group Limited
Incorporated: 7 June 2010 *Employees:* 608
Net Worth Deficit: £13,425,399 *Total Assets:* £19,724,902
Registered Office: Friary House, 17a Friary Road, Newark, Notts, NG24 1LE
Activities: Activities of head offices
Shareholders: Management Opportunities Limited; Sovereign Capital Partners LLP
Officers: Dawn Allyson Berry [1975] Director/Chief Operating Officer; Stephen John Collier [1957] Director; Andrew Paul Dean [1982] Director/Chief Financial Officer; Michael Nichol-Smith [1954] Director

Eden Care Solutions Limited
Incorporated: 20 May 2013 *Employees:* 529
Net Worth Deficit: £3,099,766 *Total Assets:* £17,003,308
Registered Office: Friary House, 17a Friary Road, Newark, Notts, NG24 1LE
Activities: Activities of head offices
Shareholders: Sovereign Capital Partners LLP; Management Opportunities Limited
Officers: Dawn Allyson Berry [1975] Director/Chief Operating Officer; Stephen John Collier [1957] Director; Andrew Paul Dean [1982] Director/Chief Financial Officer

Eden Holdings Financing Limited
Incorporated: 7 June 2010
Net Worth Deficit: £1,953,485 *Total Assets:* £10,530,101
Registered Office: Friary House, 17a Friary Road, Newark, Notts, NG24 1LE
Activities: Activities of other holding companies n.e.c.
Parent: Eden Care & Support Group Limited
Officers: Dawn Allyson Berry [1975] Director/Chief Operating Officer; Stephen John Collier [1957] Director; Andrew Paul Dean [1982] Director/Chief Financial Officer

Eden Hotel Collection Limited
Incorporated: 12 December 2008 *Employees:* 462
Net Worth: £34,579,500 *Total Assets:* £57,861,968
Registered Office: c/o Mallory Court Hotel, Harbury Lane, Bishops Tachbrook, Leamington Spa, Warwicks, CV33 9QB
Activities: Hotels and similar accommodation
Shareholders: Rigby Group (RG) PLC; Rigby Group (RG) PLC
Officers: Marian Cartter [1943] Director; Mark Edward Sydney Chambers [1970] Managing Director; Sir Peter Rigby [1943] Director

Eden Supported Living Limited
Incorporated: 7 June 2010 *Employees:* 556
Net Worth Deficit: £4,170,605 *Total Assets:* £24,027,328
Registered Office: Friary House, 17a Friary Road, Newark, Notts, NG24 1LE
Activities: Residential care activities for the elderly and disabled
Parent: Eden Holdings Financing Limited
Officers: Dawn Allyson Berry [1975] Director/Chief Operating Officer; Stephen John Collier [1957] Director; Andrew Paul Dean [1982] Director/Chief Financial Officer

Ian Edgar (Liverpool) Limited
Incorporated: 2 January 1957 *Employees:* 43
Net Worth: £3,135,177 *Total Assets:* £10,604,746
Registered Office: Units 2 & 3 Heather Close, Lyme Green Business Park, Macclesfield, Cheshire, SK11 0LR
Activities: Non-specialised wholesale trade
Shareholders: Allan Derek Edgar; Ian Edgar
Officers: Ian Edgar, Secretary; Ian Edgar [1939] Director; Ian Peter Gordon [1966] Director; Thea Susan Heapy [1984] Director; Thomas Jacob Timothy Heapy [1989] Director; Michael James Newman [1983] Director

Edge Wear Properties Limited
Incorporated: 26 March 1996
Net Worth: £14,292,812 *Total Assets:* £18,308,456
Registered Office: Emerson House, Heyes Lane, Alderley Edge, Cheshire, SK9 7LF
Activities: Other letting and operating of own or leased real estate
Shareholders: Milnes Investments Limited; P E Jones (Properties) Limited
Officers: Varun Maharaj, Secretary; Patricia Joyce Goddard [1944] Director; Mark Emerson Jones [1964] Director; Peter Emerson Jones [1935] Director; Amy Jade Kennedy [1990] Director/Business Executive

Edgetech (UK) Limited
Incorporated: 15 July 2013 *Employees:* 63
Net Worth: £9,818,118 *Total Assets:* £12,377,002
Registered Office: Stonebridge House, Rowley Drive, Stonebridge Trading Estate, Coventry, Warwicks, CV3 4FG
Activities: Manufacture of other rubber products
Parent: Quanex Building Products Corporation
Officers: Kevin Patrick Delaney, Secretary; Kevin Patrick Delaney [1961] Director/Vice President and General Counsel [American]; Brent Livingston Korb [1972] Director/Vice President and Chief Financial Officer [American]

Edina Acquisitions Limited
Incorporated: 21 February 2018
Net Worth Deficit: £220,661 *Total Assets:* £58,848,416
Registered Office: Edina, Unit 12 & 13 Rugby Park, Bletchley Road, Stockport, Cheshire, SK4 3EJ
Activities: Activities of other holding companies n.e.c.
Parent: EPAL Holdings Limited
Officers: Nitin Wadhwa, Secretary; Dr Steven Derrick Fawkes [1959] Director; Neelima Jain [1981] Director [Indian]; Saurabh Kumar [1967] Director [Indian]

Edina UK Limited
Incorporated: 21 December 2005 *Employees:* 133
Net Worth: £5,334,383 *Total Assets:* £31,288,676
Registered Office: 13 Rugby Park, Bletchley Road, Stockport, Cheshire, SK4 3EJ
Activities: Other manufacturing n.e.c.
Parent: Edina Acquisitions Limited
Officers: Ricardo Luis de Sousa Alves, Secretary; Neelima Jain [1981] Director [Indian]; Hugh Kerr Richmond [1962] Director/Head of Global Sales

EDL (UK) LFG Generation Limited
Incorporated: 25 August 2006
Net Worth: £15,578,526 *Total Assets:* £48,837,960
Registered Office: Chancery House, 199 Silbury Boulevard, Milton Keynes, Bucks, MK9 1JL
Activities: Production of electricity
Parent: Bio Energy (UK) Limited
Officers: James Christopher Harman [1968] Director [Australian]; David Truelove [1975] Director

EDL Holdings (UK) Limited
Incorporated: 25 March 1997
Net Worth: £7,500,373 *Total Assets:* £20,424,804
Registered Office: Chancery House, 199 Silbury Boulevard, Milton Keynes, Bucks, MK9 1JL
Activities: Activities of other holding companies n.e.c.
Parent: CK William UK Holdings Limited
Officers: James Christopher Harman [1968] Director [Australian]; David Truelove [1975] Director

The Education Fellowship Trust
Incorporated: 15 November 2011 *Employees:* 701
Net Worth: £88,343,000 *Total Assets:* £101,637,000
Registered Office: Montague House, 1 Chancery Lane, Thrapston, Kettering, Northants, NN14 4LN
Activities: Pre-primary education
Officers: Susan Maureen Robinson, Secretary; Irene Margaret Harris [1955] Director; Johnson Evan Kane [1954] Director; Rachel Elizabeth Mallows [1962] Director; Rev Dr David Wilkinson [1963] Director/Principal

Education Placement Group Limited
Incorporated: 17 July 2015 *Employees:* 189
Net Worth Deficit: £3,557,000 *Total Assets:* £41,430,000
Registered Office: 2nd Floor, Sir Wilfrid Newton House, Thorncliffe Park, Chapeltown, Sheffield, S35 2PH
Activities: Other activities of employment placement agencies
Parent: Sovereign Capital IV Limited Partnership
Officers: William John Etchell [1971] Director/Chief Financial Officer; Julian Edward Harley [1957] Director; Robyn Julieann Johnstone [1967] Director [British/Australian]; Robert Douglas King [1982] Director/Fund Manager

Education Solutions Speke Limited
Incorporated: 6 March 2001 *Employees:* 3
Net Worth Deficit: £2,334,927 *Total Assets:* £15,025,134
Registered Office: Building 1000, Kings Reach, Yew Street, Stockport, Cheshire, SK4 2HG
Activities: Management of real estate on a fee or contract basis
Parent: Equity Solutions Manchester Limited
Officers: Ian William Currie [1961] Director/Stockbroker; Alfred Michael Dwan [1959] Director; Richard Ian Hughes [1968] Director

Educationcity Limited
Incorporated: 2 April 1997 *Employees:* 100
Net Worth: £5,065,040 *Total Assets:* £10,574,993
Registered Office: 8 Saddlers Court, Barleythorpe, Oakham, Rutland, LE15 7GH
Activities: Other software publishing
Parent: Archipelago Learning Holdings (UK) Limited
Officers: Eric Doan, Secretary; Eric Doan [1979] Director/Chief Financial Officer [American]

EESL Energypro Assets Limited
Incorporated: 17 January 2017 *Employees:* 41
Net Worth: £26,873,064 *Total Assets:* £101,814,504
Registered Office: Edina, Unit 12 & 13 Rugby Park, Bletchley Road, Stockport, Cheshire, SK4 3EJ
Activities: Other business support service activities n.e.c.
Parent: Energy Efficiency Services Limited
Officers: Nitin Wadhwa, Secretary; Dr Steven Derrick Fawkes [1959] Director; Neelima Jain [1981] Director [Indian]; Saurabh Kumar [1967] Director [Indian]

Effective Energy Solutions Ltd
Incorporated: 6 November 2008 *Employees:* 47
Net Worth: £3,054,265 *Total Assets:* £9,007,723
Registered Office: 1 Boston Road, Leicester, LE4 1AA
Activities: Environmental consulting activities
Shareholders: Lee John Cottingham; Richard John Cox
Officers: Richard John Cox [1970] Director; Daniel George Graby [1981] Director/Operations Management

Eggborough Power Limited
Incorporated: 4 June 1999 *Employees:* 229
Net Worth Deficit: £17,000,000 *Total Assets:* £94,000,000
Registered Office: Eggborough Power Station, Eggborough, Goole, E Yorks, DN14 0BS
Activities: Production of electricity
Parent: EP UK Investments Ltd
Officers: Tarloke Singh Bains [1968] Director/Chartered Accountant; Adam Charles Booth [1976] Director/Chartered Accountant; Pavel Horsky [1973] Director [Czech]; Daniel Kretinsky [1975] Director [Czech]; Jan Springl [1978] Director [Czech]; Marek Spurny [1974] Director [Czech]

EGR Europe Limited
Incorporated: 10 April 1990 *Employees:* 28
Net Worth: £5,219,896 *Total Assets:* £16,387,822
Registered Office: Foxhunter Drive, Linford Wood, Milton Keynes, Bucks, MK14 6FE
Activities: Wholesale trade of motor vehicle parts and accessories
Shareholders: Gregory Miles Horwill; Rodney Edward Horwill
Officers: Rodney Edward Horwill, Secretary; Gregory Miles Horwill [1952] Director [Australian]; Rodney Edward Horwill [1948] Director

EHI 2005 Limited
Incorporated: 27 September 2005
Net Worth Deficit: £6,610,442 *Total Assets:* £102,485,624
Registered Office: The Sir John Peace Building, Experian Way, NG2 Business Park, Nottingham, NG80 1ZZ
Activities: Financial intermediation not elsewhere classified
Parent: Experian US Holdings Unlimited
Officers: Ronan Hanna, Secretary; Paul Alan Atkinson [1960] Director/Chartered Accountant; Antony Jonathan Ward Barnes [1964] Director of Tax and Treasury; Karen Julia Greenwood [1967] Director/Chartered Accountant; Daniel Tristan Lilley [1981] Director; Mark Edward Pepper [1963] Director/Financial Controller

EHI UK Unlimited
Incorporated: 23 October 2001
Net Worth: £103,789,776 *Total Assets:* £103,789,776
Registered Office: The Sir John Peace Building, Experian Way, NG2 Business Park, Nottingham, NG80 1ZZ
Activities: Financial intermediation not elsewhere classified
Parent: EHI 2005 Limited
Officers: Ronan Hanna, Secretary; Paul Alan Atkinson [1960] Director/Group Taxation Manager; Antony Jonathan Ward Barnes [1964] Director of Tax and Treasury; Karen Julia Greenwood [1967] Director/Chartered Accountant; Daniel Tristan Lilley [1981] Director; Mark Edward Pepper [1963] Director/Financial Controller

EIS 2005 Limited
Incorporated: 27 September 2005
Net Worth Deficit: £15,825,347 *Total Assets:* £240,893,968
Registered Office: The Sir John Peace Building, Experian Way, NG2 Business Park, Nottingham, NG80 1ZZ
Activities: Financial intermediation not elsewhere classified
Parent: Experian US Holdings Unlimited
Officers: Ronan Hanna, Secretary; Paul Alan Atkinson [1960] Director/Chartered Accountant; Antony Jonathan Ward Barnes [1964] Director of Tax and Treasury; Karen Julia Greenwood [1967] Director/Chartered Accountant; Daniel Tristan Lilley [1981] Director; Mark Edward Pepper [1963] Director/Financial Controller

EIS UK Unlimited
Incorporated: 23 October 2001
Net Worth: £243,930,848 *Total Assets:* £243,930,848
Registered Office: The Sir John Peace Building, Experian Way, NG2 Business Park, Nottingham, NG80 1ZZ
Activities: Financial intermediation not elsewhere classified
Parent: EIS 2005 Limited
Officers: Ronan Hanna, Secretary; Paul Alan Atkinson [1960] Director/Group Taxation Manager; Antony Jonathan Ward Barnes [1964] Director of Tax and Treasury; Karen Julia Greenwood [1967] Director/Chartered Accountant; Daniel Tristan Lilley [1981] Director; Mark Edward Pepper [1963] Director/Financial Controller

EJ UK Fabrication & Access Solutions Holdings Limited
Incorporated: 21 October 1959 *Employees:* 94
Previous: EJ UK Access Solutions Limited
Net Worth Deficit: £1,125,007 *Total Assets:* £13,467,892
Registered Office: Liberty House, Liberty Way, Attleborough Fields Industrial Estate, Nuneaton, Warwicks, CV11 6RZ
Activities: Non-trading company
Parent: EJ EMEA SAS
Officers: Philippe Alain Daniel Cavaille, Secretary; Philippe Alain Daniel Cavaille [1970] Director [French]; Andrew James Malpass [1973] Director/Executive [American]; Tracy Kevin Malpass [1955] Director/Executive [American]

Elastomerics Limited
Incorporated: 5 November 1981 *Employees:* 12
Net Worth: £8,212,487 *Total Assets:* £11,042,438
Registered Office: London Road, Adlington, Macclesfield, Cheshire, SK10 4DU
Activities: Wholesale of chemical products
Parent: Caldic (UK) Ltd
Officers: Danielle Francesca Auton, Secretary; John Philip Robinson [1963] Director; Olav Van Caldenborgh [1968] Director [Dutch]

Electro-Motive Diesel Limited
Incorporated: 18 August 2006 *Employees:* 158
Net Worth: £8,247,000 *Total Assets:* £29,892,000
Registered Office: c/o Perkins Engines Company Limited, Eastfield, Frank Perkins Way, Peterborough, Cambs, PE1 5FQ
Activities: Maintenance and repair of motor vehicles
Parent: Caterpillar International Holdings S.A.R.L
Officers: Johanna Elizabeth Deason, Secretary; Nigel John Burroughs [1961] Director/Tax Accountant; Jonathan Mark Caen [1967] Sales Director; Martin Albert Haycraft [1969] Director/Senior Vice President [American]; Colin Murphy [1962] Director/Chartered Accountant, Head of Finance

Electronic Data Processing Limited
Incorporated: 5 July 1965 *Employees:* 65
Previous: Electronic Data Processing Public Limited Company
Net Worth: £6,436,000 *Total Assets:* £9,486,000
Registered Office: 4th Floor, Fountain Precinct, Balm Green, Sheffield, S1 2JA
Activities: Business and domestic software development
Officers: Nigel Jonathan Bedford, Secretary; Nigel Jonathan Beford [1963] Director/Chartered Accountant; Ian Bendelow [1967] Director

Electronics for Imaging United Kingdom Limited
Incorporated: 7 October 1974 *Employees:* 174
Net Worth Deficit: £1,408,000 *Total Assets:* £32,857,000
Registered Office: Manor Farm, High Street, Dronfield, Derbys, S18 1PY
Activities: Information technology consultancy activities
Parent: Radius Solutions Limited
Officers: Alexis Konstantinovich Grab, Secretary; Gene Zamiska [1961] Director/Chief Accounting Officer [American]

Electrosteel Castings (UK) Limited
Incorporated: 22 August 2000 *Employees:* 40
Net Worth: £1,376,000 *Total Assets:* £11,985,000
Registered Office: Ambrose House, Broombank Road, Chesterfield, Derbys, S41 9QJ
Activities: Manufacture of other fabricated metal products n.e.c.
Parent: Electrosteel Castings Ltd
Officers: Shivendra Nath Agarwal [1976] Director/Service Employment [Indian]; Stewart Bailie [1966] Managing Director; Mahendra Kumar Jalan [1952] Director [Indian]; Piush Lohia [1970] Director [Indian]; Glenn Wheeler [1958] Director/Head of Sales

Element Six (UK) Limited.
Incorporated: 21 April 1972 *Employees:* 183
Net Worth Deficit: £43,019,004 *Total Assets:* £36,104,112
Registered Office: Global Innovation Centre, Fermi Avenue, Harwell, Didcot, Oxon, OX11 0QR
Activities: Other research and experimental development on natural sciences and engineering
Parent: Element Six Abrasives Holdings Limited
Officers: Yvonne Shave, Secretary; Siobhan Duffy [1966] Director [Irish]; Andrew Guthrie [1977] Director; Walter Friedrich Huhn [1962] Director [German]; Victoria Matthews [1970] Group HR Director

Element Six Limited
Incorporated: 8 July 1994
Net Worth: £4,507,782 *Total Assets:* £31,062,224
Registered Office: Global Innovation Centre, Fermi Avenue, Harwell, Didcot, Oxon, OX11 0QR
Activities: Non-trading company
Parent: Element Six Holdings Limited
Officers: Yvonne Shave, Secretary; Andrew Guthrie [1977] Director; Ciaran O'Donnell [1984] Director/Group Corporate Treasurer [Irish]

Element Six Technologies Limited
Incorporated: 7 September 2012 *Employees:* 81
Net Worth Deficit: £13,035,000 *Total Assets:* £53,281,000
Registered Office: Global Innovation Centre, Fermi Avenue, Harwell, Didcot, Oxon, OX11 0QR
Activities: Other manufacturing n.e.c.
Parent: Element Six Holdings Limited
Officers: Yvonne Shave, Secretary; Siobhan Duffy [1966] Executive Director - Innovation [Irish]; Andrew Guthrie [1977] Director; Walter Friedrich Huhn [1962] Director [German]; Victoria Matthews [1970] Group HR Director; Adam O'Grady [1980] Director/Head of Operations [Irish]; Dr Daniel Twitchen [1973] Director/Head of Technologies Business Development - CVD

ELG Haniel Metals Ltd
Incorporated: 18 September 1980 *Employees:* 124
Previous: E.L.G. Haniel Metals Limited
Net Worth: £19,632,560 *Total Assets:* £82,783,848
Registered Office: Templeborough Works, Sheffield Road, Tinsley, Sheffield, S9 1RT
Activities: Wholesale of metals and metal ores
Officers: Jon Paul Greenwood, Secretary; Jonathan Edward Bower [1970] Director/Commercial Trader; Detlef Drafz [1962] Director/Financial Controller [German]; Jon Paul Greenwood [1966] Director/Accountant; Dr Silke Landwehrmann [1971] Director [German]; Karsten Mueller [1972] Director [German]; Mark Andrew Vaughan [1967] Managing Director

ELG Utica Alloys Limited
Incorporated: 1 February 1980 *Employees:* 67
Previous: ABS Industrial Resources Limited
Net Worth: £17,306,966 *Total Assets:* £36,393,140
Registered Office: Unit 1 Adwick Park, Manvers, Rotherham, S Yorks, S63 5AB
Activities: Treatment and coating of metals
Officers: Andrew Jones [1966] Director

Elior UK Holdings Limited
Incorporated: 24 February 1989 *Employees:* 12,244
Net Worth: £33,398,484 *Total Assets:* £195,818,000
Registered Office: The Courtyard, Catherine Street, Macclesfield, Cheshire, SK11 6ET
Activities: Activities of head offices
Parent: Elior SA
Officers: Esther Gaide [1961] Director/Group Chief Financial Officer [French]; Catherine Margaret Roe [1960] Managing Director; Eleni Savva [1972] Finance Director

Elior UK PLC
Incorporated: 6 April 1973 *Employees:* 7,172
Net Worth: £47,065,168 *Total Assets:* £109,246,848
Registered Office: The Courtyard, Catherine Street, Macclesfield, Cheshire, SK11 6ET
Activities: Event catering activities
Parent: Elior UK Holdings Limited
Officers: Joanna Luke, Secretary; Esther Gaide [1961] Director/Group Chief Financial Officer [French]; Catherine Margaret Roe [1960] Managing Director; Eleni Savva [1972] Finance Director; Thierry Thonnier [1966] Director [French]

Elisabeth The Chef Limited
Incorporated: 13 May 1981 *Employees:* 777
Previous: Senoble UK Limited
Net Worth: £2,770,000 *Total Assets:* £16,517,000
Registered Office: 4 Berrington Road, Sydenham Industrial Estate, Leamington Spa, Warwicks, CV31 1NB
Activities: Manufacture of other food products n.e.c.
Parent: Elisabeth The Chef Holdings Limited
Officers: Charles Joseph Wood [1979] Director/Baker; Joseph Anthony Wood [1939] Director/Baker

Elite Office Furniture (UK) Ltd.
Incorporated: 6 May 1997 *Employees:* 136
Net Worth: £22,024,150 *Total Assets:* £24,452,628
Registered Office: Britannia Way, Goole, E Yorks, DN14 6ES
Activities: Manufacture of office and shop furniture
Major Shareholder: John Hull
Officers: Robert Clarke [1972] Production Director; Andrew Jason Hull [1972] Seating Director; John Hull [1950] Director; Julian Andrew Jowett [1976] Sales Director

The Elizabethan Academy Trust
Incorporated: 24 February 2012 *Employees:* 140
Net Worth: £15,505,561 *Total Assets:* £18,400,954
Registered Office: The Elizabethan Academy, Hallcroft Road, Retford, Notts, DN22 7PY
Activities: General secondary education
Officers: Christopher James Pedrozo D'Albuquerque, Secretary; Dr Derek Cheetham [1947] Director/Retired; Martin Meredith Evans [1965] Managing Director; Richard Colin Green [1955] Director/Retired; Christine Alice Horrocks [1965] Director/Academy Principal; Kathryn Lindsay Jones [1955] Director/Events & Conference Manager; Anthony Neil Leake [1965] Director; Matthew Lister [1990] Director/Teacher; Tony Mason [1966] Director/Teacher; Jacqueline McRory [1972] Director/Office Manager; Shaun Procter-Green [1967] Director/Teacher; Claire Turner [1972] Director/Office Manager; Stephen Walker [1956] Director/Businessman; Terry Robert Wright [1976] Director/Teacher

Elli Finance (UK) PLC
Incorporated: 6 June 2012
Net Worth: £222,096,000 *Total Assets:* £804,444,032
Registered Office: Norcliffe House, Station Road, Wilmslow, Cheshire, SK9 1BU
Activities: Activities of head offices
Parent: Elli Group (UK) Limited
Officers: Abigail Mattison, Secretary; Martin William Oliver Healy [1962] Director/Accountant [Irish]; Mark Samson Ordan [1959] Director [American]

Elliott Group Holdings (UK) Limited
Incorporated: 15 August 2007
Net Worth Deficit: £255,444,000 *Total Assets:* £311,284,000
Registered Office: Manor Drive, Peterborough, Cambs, PE4 7AP
Activities: Renting and leasing of other machinery, equipment and tangible goods n.e.c.
Parent: TDR Capital General Partner II Limited
Officers: James O'Malley, Secretary; James O'Malley [1977] Director/Lawyer [American]; Sundip Thakrar [1965] Director/Chief Financial Officer; Dr Andrew Oliver Tyler [1967] Director/Chief Executive; Lee Andrew Young [1972] Director

Elliott Group Limited
Incorporated: 21 April 1917 *Employees:* 1,028
Net Worth: £202,162,000 *Total Assets:* £383,399,008
Registered Office: Manor Drive, Peterborough, PE4 7AP
Activities: Other manufacturing n.e.c.
Parent: Elliott Group Holdings (UK) Limited
Officers: James O'Malley, Secretary; James O'Malley [1977] Director/Lawyer [American]; Sundip Thakrar [1965] Director/Chief Financial Officer; Dr Andrew Tyler [1976] Director/Chief Executive; Lee Andrew Young [1972] Director

C.S. Ellis (Holdings) Limited
Incorporated: 15 February 2013 *Employees:* 194
Net Worth: £10,560,679 *Total Assets:* £19,635,062
Registered Office: Wireless Hill, South Luffenham, Oakham, Rutland, LE15 8NF
Activities: Activities of head offices
Shareholder: Trevor Charles Ellis
Officers: Charles Steven Ellis, Secretary; Duncan James Clarke [1977] Finance Director; Hayley Elizabeth Cook [1983] HR Director; Charles Steven Ellis [1981] Director/Accountant; Trevor Charles Ellis [1956] Director/Road Haulier

Ellis Bros (Contractors) Limited
Incorporated: 10 January 1963 *Employees:* 96
Net Worth: £10,766,016 *Total Assets:* £13,295,898
Registered Office: 7 Lansdowne Road, Skegness, Lincs, PE25 2DJ
Activities: Growing of cereals (except rice), leguminous crops and oil seeds
Major Shareholder: Frederick William John Ellis
Officers: Frederick William John Ellis [1948] Director/Builder; Ian Frederick Ellis [1974] Director/Surveyor

Ellucian Global Limited
Incorporated: 18 November 2011 *Employees:* 37
Net Worth: £18,402,772 *Total Assets:* £30,010,564
Registered Office: Floors 2 & 3, Baird House, Seebeck Place, Knowlhill, Milton Keynes, Bucks, MK5 8FR
Activities: Information technology consultancy activities
Parent: Ellucian UK Limited
Officers: James Dever Bennett [1960] Director/Business Executive [American]; Harshan Bhangdia [1965] Director/Chief Financial Officer [Indian]; Richard James Forrest [1974] Director/VP Global Product Strategy; John Tom Georges [1971] Director/VP Tax and Treasury [American]

Ellucian SMS Ltd
Incorporated: 4 October 2011 *Employees:* 34
Net Worth: £328,205 *Total Assets:* £17,486,460
Registered Office: Floors 2 & 3, Baird House, Seebeck Place, Knowlhill, Milton Keynes, Bucks, MK5 8FR
Activities: Information technology consultancy activities
Parent: Ellucian Global Limited
Officers: James Dever Bennett [1960] Director/Business Executive [American]; Harshan Bhangdia [1965] Director/Chief Financial Officer [Indian]; Richard James Forrest [1974] Director/VP Global Product Strategy; John Tom Georges [1971] Director/VP Tax and Treasury [American]

Elmdene Group Limited
Incorporated: 28 April 2009 *Employees:* 137
Net Worth: £7,564,791 *Total Assets:* £18,636,912
Registered Office: Unit A, Castle Court, Bodmin Road, Coventry, Warwicks, CV2 5DB
Activities: Activities of head offices
Officers: Annette Rachel Douglass [1956] Director; Guy Douglass [1979] Director/Sales Consultant; Harvey James Douglass [1988] Director/Manufacturer; James Edward Douglass [1951] Director/Consultant; Jerry Douglass [1978] Director/Technical Engineer

Elmsdale Estates Limited
Incorporated: 24 January 2000 *Employees:* 26
Net Worth: £35,604,000 *Total Assets:* £110,278,000
Registered Office: Devonshire Green House, 14 Fitzwilliam Street, Sheffield, S1 4JL
Activities: Other letting and operating of own or leased real estate
Shareholders: Martin Patrick Elwood; Dale Lee Fixter; Brenden Elwood
Officers: Ewan Gairn Barclay Ross, Secretary; Brendan Elwood [1943] Director/Property Investment & Development; Martin Patrick Elwood [1968] Director/Property Investment and Development; Dale Lee Fixter [1967] Director/Chartered Surveyor

Elmwood Trading Limited
Incorporated: 29 July 1997
Net Worth: £387,227 *Total Assets:* £29,078,036
Registered Office: The Old Rectory, Louth Road, West Barkwith, Market Rasen, Lincs, LN8 5LF
Activities: Other business support service activities n.e.c.
Parent: H C Bourn (Holdings) Limited
Officers: Matthew James Cherry, Secretary; Hugh Christopher Bourn [1958] Director/Farmer; James George Christopher Bourn [1996] Director

Elsevier Life Sciences IP Limited
Incorporated: 21 December 2016
Net Worth Deficit: £18,426,638 *Total Assets:* £389,050,304
Registered Office: The Boulevard, Langford Lane, Kidlington, Oxon, OX5 1GB
Activities: Non-trading company
Shareholders: RELX Group PLC; RELX Group PLC
Officers: Il Thompson [1960] Director [American]; Henry Adam Udow [1957] Director/Chief Legal Officer; Alexander Philip Van Boetzelaer [1973] Director [Dutch]; Stuart Mark Whayman [1973] Finance Director

Elsevier Limited
Incorporated: 24 January 1986 *Employees:* 1,311
Net Worth: £429,687,008 *Total Assets:* £1,022,680,000
Registered Office: The Boulevard, Langford Lane, Kidlington, Oxon, OX5 1GB
Activities: Other information technology service activities
Shareholders: RELX (UK) Limited; RELX (UK) Limited
Officers: Kumsal Bayazit Besson [1974] Director [Turkish]; Laura Claire Crespi [1984] Director/Financial Controller; Ruth Anne Kitson [1962] Director/Publisher; Stuart Mark Whayman [1973] Director/Chief Financial Officer

Elsham Linc Limited
Incorporated: 2 August 2005 *Employees:* 75
Net Worth: £8,458,023 *Total Assets:* £16,355,370
Registered Office: Cadas House, Wootton Road, Elsham Top, Brigg, N Lincs, DN20 0NU
Activities: Raising of swine and pigs
Shareholders: Alexander Godfrey; Samuel Godfrey
Officers: Karin Elizabeth Lund, Secretary; Alexander Godfrey [1978] Director/Farmer; James Eric Godfrey [1953] Director; Sam Godfrey [1980] Director/Farmer

Elsham Wold Estates Limited
Incorporated: 12 June 2007 *Employees:* 106
Net Worth: £14,215,336 *Total Assets:* £26,342,422
Registered Office: Kahawa House, Elsham Wold Industrial Estate, Elsham, Brigg, N Lincs, DN20 0SP
Activities: Activities of other holding companies n.e.c.
Shareholders: Simon David Herring; James Timothy Sweeting
Officers: Nigel John Bean, Secretary; Simon David Herring [1964] Director; James Timothy Sweeting [1969] Director

Elsoms (Spalding) Limited
Incorporated: 4 December 1943 *Employees:* 98
Net Worth: £18,912,944 *Total Assets:* £24,026,982
Registered Office: Pinchbeck Road, Spalding, Lincs, PE11 1QG
Activities: Agents selling agricultural raw materials, livestock, textile raw materials and semi-finished goods
Shareholder: Roger Anthony Luke Keeling
Officers: Andrew Peter Davis, Secretary; John Michael Bloomer [1965] Director/Consultant; David James Sharples Coop [1970] Director; Andrew Peter Davis [1974] Finance Director; Andrew Piers Symons Keeling [1973] Director; Rachel Petronella Keeling [1972] Director; Roger Anthony Luke Keeling [1977] Director; Nicholas Waterman [1965] Director; Robin Laurie Wood [1961] Director/Seedsman

Elsoms Seeds Limited
Incorporated: 13 April 1960 *Employees:* 94
Net Worth: £9,459,536 *Total Assets:* £15,677,365
Registered Office: Pinchbeck Road, Spalding, Lincs, PE11 1QG
Activities: Agents selling agricultural raw materials, livestock, textile raw materials and semi-finished goods
Parent: Elsoms (Spalding) Limited
Officers: Andrew Peter Davis, Secretary; David James Sharples Coop [1970] Director; Andrew Peter Davis [1974] Finance Director; Roger Anthony Luke Keeling [1977] Director; Robin Laurie Wood [1961] Director/Seedsman

ELWA Holdings Limited
Incorporated: 28 September 2010
Net Worth: £15,159,000 *Total Assets:* £111,730,000
Registered Office: Dunedin House, Auckland Park, Mount Farm, Milton Keynes, Bucks, MK1 1BU
Activities: Non-trading company
Parent: John Laing Environmental Assets Group (UK) Limited
Officers: Philip Bernard Griffin-Smith, Secretary; Alistair Daniel Brookes [1976] Director; Johannes Petrus Heemelaar [1956] Director [Dutch]; Joseph Mark Linney [1958] Director; Adam Nathaniel Richford [1976] Director

ELWA Limited
Incorporated: 25 March 1992
Net Worth: £15,159,000 *Total Assets:* £111,730,000
Registered Office: Dunedin House, Auckland Park, Mount Farm, Milton Keynes, Bucks, MK1 1BU
Activities: Other service activities n.e.c.
Parent: ELWA Holdings Limited
Officers: Philip Bernard Griffin-Smith, Secretary; Dorothy Abena Akwaboah [1963] Director; Alistair Daniel Brookes [1976] Director; Johannes Petrus Heemelaar [1956] Asset Director [Dutch]; Joseph Mark Linney [1958] Director; Adam Nathaniel Richford [1976] Director

The Ely Cloisters Estate Limited
Incorporated: 17 November 2005
Net Worth: £6,075,848 *Total Assets:* £14,572,743
Registered Office: c/o Buccleuch Property Estate Office, Weekley, Kettering, Northants, NN16 9UP
Activities: Other letting and operating of own or leased real estate
Shareholders: Tarras Park Properties Ltd; H & K Enterprises Ltd
Officers: James Alexander Kenneth MacLeod, Secretary/Accountant; Alexander Douglas Douglas Hamilton Clydesdale [1978] Director; James Alexander Kenneth MacLeod [1975] Director/Accountant; David Howard Peck [1965] Managing Director

EMA Holdings UK Limited
Incorporated: 26 November 2002 *Employees:* 2
Net Worth: £739,144,000 *Total Assets:* £740,507,008
Registered Office: P O Box 36, 2 New Star Road, Leicester, LE4 9JQ
Activities: Activities of head offices
Parent: Ametek European Holdings Limited
Officers: Joy Atwell, Secretary; Emanuela Speranza [1968] Director/Vice President/General Manager EMEA, India [Italian]; Bruce Peter Wilson [1956] Director

EMB-Group Ltd
Incorporated: 26 November 2009 *Employees:* 103
Net Worth: £5,926,318 *Total Assets:* £12,053,366
Registered Office: 5 Merus Court, Meridian Business Park, Leicester, LE19 1RJ
Activities: Activities of head offices
Officers: Stuart Graham Dawkins [1962] Director; Phoebe Ann Edwards [1968] Director; Danielle Amanda Gillett [1968] Director; Paul Griffiths [1965] Director/Chief Executive; Kevin James Harris [1966] Director/Partner; Scott Knowles [1972] Director/Acting Chief Executive; Richard Mark Osborne [1974] Director; Eileen Maria Richards [1970] Managing Director; Kevin David Shapland [1956] Managing Director; Stephen David Smith [1958] Director; David Henry Williams [1956] Director/Solicitor

Emerson Developments (Holdings) Limited
Incorporated: 15 May 1974 *Employees:* 821
Net Worth: £894,854,976 *Total Assets:* £1,813,374,976
Registered Office: Emerson House, Heyes Lane, Alderley Edge, Cheshire, SK9 7LF
Activities: Buying and selling of own real estate
Officers: Varun Maharaj, Secretary; John Philip Allen [1953] Director; Jonathan Rodney Claber [1982] Director; Jonathan Haymer [1959] Director/Executive; Anthony Emerson Jones [1967] Director; Audrey Jones [1936] Director; Mark Emerson Jones [1964] Director; Peter Emerson Jones [1935] Director; Baron John Robert Louis Lee of Trafford [1942] Director; Mark Stephen Thomas Royle [1964] Director; Anne Catherine Weatherby [1954] Director/Solicitor; Simon Peter Wilson [1964] Director

Emerson International Limited
Incorporated: 6 April 1981
Net Worth: £24,360,600 *Total Assets:* £158,362,944
Registered Office: Emerson House, Heyes Lane, Alderley Edge, Cheshire, SK9 7LF
Activities: Activities of head offices
Parent: Emerson Developments (Holdings) Limited
Officers: Varun Marahaj, Secretary; Anthony Emerson Jones [1967] Director; Audrey Jones [1936] Director; Mark Emerson Jones [1964] Director; Peter Emerson Jones [1935] Director

Emerson Management Services Limited
Incorporated: 6 August 1971 *Employees:* 84
Net Worth: £3,458,368 *Total Assets:* £16,553,057
Registered Office: Emerson House, Heyes Lane, Alderley Edge, Cheshire, SK9 7LF
Activities: Other building completion and finishing
Parent: Emerson Developments (Holdings) Limited
Officers: Varun Maharaj, Secretary; Jonathan Clark [1968] Director/Business Executive; Michael James Drake [1971] Director/Business Executive; Anthony Emerson Jones [1967] Director; Audrey Jones [1936] Director; Mark Emerson Jones [1964] Director; Peter Emerson Jones [1935] Director; Peter John Shaw [1964] Director/Chartered Surveyor; Simon Peter Wilson [1964] Director; Carl Raymond Worthington [1967] Director/Chartered Surveyor

Emerson Process Management Limited
Incorporated: 5 October 1960 *Employees:* 589
Net Worth: £151,270,000 *Total Assets:* £239,256,000
Registered Office: Meridian Business Park, Meridian East, Leicester, LE19 1UX
Activities: Other manufacturing n.e.c.
Parent: Emerson Holding Company Limited
Officers: Stuart Brown [1969] Business Director; Steven Edward Clanfield [1966] Director Projects & Services UK & Ireland; Julian James Collis [1973] Business Director; Jeremy Rowley [1961] Director/Accountant

Emerson Process Management Shared Services Limited
Incorporated: 27 October 1993 *Employees:* 198
Net Worth: £11,107,000 *Total Assets:* £26,503,000
Registered Office: Meridian Business Park, Meridian East, Leicester, LE19 1UX
Activities: Accounting and auditing activities
Parent: Emerson Process Management Limited
Officers: Stuart Brown [1969] Director/Business Executive; Julian James Collis [1973] Director; Neale Preston Findley [1961] Finance Director; Jeremy Rowley [1961] Director/Accountant

EMH Treasury PLC
Incorporated: 10 October 2013
Net Worth: £97,000 *Total Assets:* £201,902,000
Registered Office: Memorial House, Stenson Road, Coalville, Leicester, LE67 4JP
Activities: Financial intermediation not elsewhere classified
Officers: Joanne Tilley, Secretary; Chandrakant Kataria [1961] Director/Chief Executive; Andrew David Kilby [1960] Finance Director; Professor David Martin Russell [1963] Director/Dean

Emhart International Limited
Incorporated: 21 August 1901
Net Worth: £498,116,992 *Total Assets:* £687,214,976
Registered Office: 3 Europa Court, Sheffield Airport Business Park, Sheffield, S9 1XE
Activities: Activities of head offices
Parent: Black & Decker Finance
Officers: Steven John Costello [1980] Director/Chartered Accountant; Mark Richard Smiley [1977] Director/General Manager UK & ROI; Amit Kumar Sood [1978] Director/Accountant

Eminox Limited
Incorporated: 20 January 1978 *Employees:* 230
Net Worth: £6,830,000 *Total Assets:* £20,876,000
Registered Office: The Old Court House, 24 Market Street, Gainsborough, Lincs, DN21 2BE
Activities: Manufacture of other fabricated metal products n.e.c.
Parent: Hexadex Limited
Officers: David John Hodgson, Secretary; Cyril Alexandre Emmanuel Journoux [1981] Sales Director [French]; Nicola Eileen Linsell [1977] Programmes Director; Irfan Harun Ayub Mahomed [1971] Finance Director; Andrew Joseph Meakin [1966] Director/Chartered Accountant; Mark Charles Runciman [1971] Director; Juan Carlos Vicente [1972] Sales Director

Emmett UK Limited
Incorporated: 22 November 1988 *Employees:* 241
Net Worth: £4,300,000 *Total Assets:* £19,421,000
Registered Office: Washway Road, Fosdyke, Spalding, Lincs, PE12 6LQ
Activities: Growing of vegetables and melons, roots and tubers
Parent: Sansbury Bailey Holdings Limited
Officers: Lisa Jayne Alcock, Secretary; Lisa Jayne Alcock [1984] Director; Colin Sansbury Bailey [1969] Director; Alexander Boughton [1987] Sales Director; David Alan Trumble [1980] Finance Director

Empowering Minds Academy Trust
Incorporated: 14 March 2017 *Employees:* 195
Net Worth: £18,900,056 *Total Assets:* £22,840,560
Registered Office: Southfield Primary School, Tranmoor Lane, Doncaster, S Yorks, DN3 3BN
Activities: Primary education
Officers: Sarah Cairns [1970] Director/Headteacher; Stephen Michael Coates [1975] Director; Alison England [1978] Director; Kate French [1950] Director; Emma Frost [1972] Director; Kim Kellett [1961] Director; Sarah Lindsay [1966] Director

EMSC (UK) Limited
Incorporated: 2 May 2001 *Employees:* 68
Net Worth: £7,589,628 *Total Assets:* £11,739,226
Registered Office: EMS House, Unit 2, 4 Cowley Way, Ecclesfield, Sheffield, S35 1QP
Activities: Manufacture of other electrical equipment
Shareholders: Alex Mardapittas; EMSC Global Ltd
Officers: Louise Mardapitta, Secretary; Stuart Clegg [1955] Commercial Director; Stephen David Hepplewhite [1953] Non-Executive Director Chairman; Lee Hudson [1974] Operations Director; Robert Macklin [1978] Finance Director; Dr Alex Mardapittas [1965] Director/Engineer [Cypriot]; Solon Savvas Mardapittas [1992] Director

Encase Holdings Limited
Incorporated: 15 January 1981 *Employees:* 236
Net Worth Deficit: £1,785,000 *Total Assets:* £18,495,000
Registered Office: Beaumont Road, Banbury, Oxon, OX16 1RE
Activities: Manufacture of corrugated paper and paperboard, sacks and bags
Shareholders: John Stephen Kalmanson; Susan Eva Rowett
Officers: Stephen Mark Maycock, Secretary; Anders Engel Christensen [1959] Director/Chief Executive Officer [Danish]; Niels Harald de Coninck-Smith [1956] Director; John Charles Wilks [1940] Director/Company Secretary

Encase Limited
Incorporated: 25 June 1965 *Employees:* 242
Net Worth Deficit: £157,000 *Total Assets:* £19,719,000
Registered Office: Encase Ltd, Beaumont Road, Banbury, Oxon, OX16 1RE
Activities: Manufacture of corrugated paper and paperboard, sacks and bags
Parent: Encase Holdings Limited
Officers: Stephen Mark Maycock, Secretary; Anders Engel Christensen [1959] Director [Danish]; Niels Coninck-Smith [1956] Independent Director [Danish]; John Arthur Lowe [1949] Director; Neal Gerard Mernock [1954] Director; Richard Anthony Walton [1964] Managing Director

Encocam Limited
Incorporated: 5 September 1985 *Employees:* 191
Net Worth: £8,726,336 *Total Assets:* £12,972,333
Registered Office: 5 Stukeley Business Centre, Blackstone Road, Huntingdon, Cambs, PE18 6EF
Activities: Other manufacturing n.e.c.
Major Shareholder: Mike Mehrdad Ashmead
Officers: Dr Mike Mehrdad Ashmead, Secretary; Dr Mike Mehrdad Ashmead [1949] Director/Founder & Chairman

Encore Personnel Services Limited
Incorporated: 17 July 2001 *Employees:* 192
Net Worth: £2,052,525 *Total Assets:* £16,297,853
Registered Office: First Floor, 32 Millstone Lane, Leicester, LE1 5JN
Activities: Temporary employment agency activities
Shareholders: Greg Latham; Chris Hockey
Officers: Tina Rachael Hercock, Secretary; Richard Mark Bishop [1968] Director; Ian Martin Briers [1972] Director/Recruitment Agent; Tina Rachael Hercock [1959] Finance Director; Christopher Hockey [1965] Director/Recruitment; Gregory Joseph Lawrence Latham [1964] Director/Recruitment Agent; Andrew Lewis [1976] Operations Director; Peter Charles Hirst Taylor [1970] Director

Energy Alloys UK Limited
Incorporated: 13 February 2004 *Employees:* 55
Net Worth: £12,148,338 *Total Assets:* £31,405,644
Registered Office: Suite 3, The Quadrant, 99 Parkway Avenue, Sheffield, S9 4WG
Activities: Support activities for petroleum and natural gas mining
Officers: John Charles Warren [1966] Director/Attorney [American]; Samuel Davis Warren [1957] Director/Company President [American]

Energy Developments (UK) Limited
Incorporated: 21 March 1996 *Employees:* 52
Net Worth: £7,646,070 *Total Assets:* £20,661,088
Registered Office: Chancery House, 199 Silbury Boulevard, Milton Keynes, Bucks, MK9 1JL
Activities: Production of electricity
Parent: EDL Holdings (UK) Limited
Officers: James Christopher Harman [1968] Director [Australian]; David Truelove [1975] Director

Energy Technologies Institute LLP
Incorporated: 12 December 2007 *Employees:* 58
Net Worth: £1,139,000 *Total Assets:* £15,808,000
Registered Office: Charnwood Building, Holywell Park, Loughborough, Leics, LE11 3AQ
Officers: Energy and Industrial Strategy Secretary of State for Business, Corporate-LLP Member

Engel U.K. Limited
Incorporated: 1 April 1964 *Employees:* 39
Net Worth: £3,273,691 *Total Assets:* £17,778,514
Registered Office: Apollo Way, Tachbrook Park, Warwick, CV34 6RW
Activities: Manufacture of plastics and rubber machinery
Shareholders: Birgitte Engleder; Helga Neumann
Officers: Emma Hastie, Secretary; Nigel John Baker [1963] Managing Director; Peter Anthony Borthwick [1964] Technical Director; Emma Judith Hastie [1976] Financial Director; Graeme Herlihy [1963] Director/Chairman; Dr Christoph Johannes Steger [1979] Director/Chairman [Austrian]

Engie Fabricom UK Limited
Incorporated: 1 November 1974 *Employees:* 274
Previous: Fabricom Oil, Gas and Power Limited
Net Worth: £3,736,000 *Total Assets:* £30,868,000
Registered Office: Origin 3, Origin Way, Europarc, Grimsby, S Humbers, DN37 9TZ
Activities: Other specialised construction activities n.e.c.
Parent: Engie UK Holding Services Limited
Officers: Claire Rachel Bateman, Secretary; Claire Rachel Bateman [1982] Finance Director; Eric de Ribaucourt [1972] Finance Director [Belgian]; Mark Dirckx [1965] Director [Belgian]; Philip Snoeck [1965] Director [Belgian]; Richard Mark Webster [1966] Director/Accountant

The Engineering Technology Group Limited
Incorporated: 5 March 2015 *Employees:* 111
Net Worth Deficit: £1,981,764 *Total Assets:* £12,464,142
Registered Office: Unit 16 Wellesbourne Distribution Park, Loxley Road, Wellesbourne, Warwicks, CV35 9JY
Activities: Activities of other holding companies n.e.c.
Shareholders: John Alan Temple; Martin James Doyle
Officers: Martin Doyle [1973] Director; Adam Antony Maher [1973] Director/Accountant; George Thomas Woodroofe Morrow [1952] Director/Accountant; John Alan Temple [1956] Director

English Electric Company,Limited (The)
Incorporated: 14 December 1918
Net Worth: £36,138,000 *Total Assets:* £57,927,000
Registered Office: Point 3 Haywood Road, Warwick, CV34 5AH
Activities: Activities of other holding companies n.e.c.
Parent: Telent Limited
Officers: Heather Marie Green [1971] Director/Chief Financial Officer; Mark Andrew Webberley [1964] Director/Chartered Accountant

English Partnerships (LP) Limited
Incorporated: 20 July 2001
Net Worth: £25,174,480 *Total Assets:* £25,174,480
Registered Office: c/o Homes England, Woodlands, Manton Lane, Manton Industrial Estate, Bedford, MK41 7LW
Activities: Other business support service activities n.e.c.
Parent: Department for Communities and Local Government
Officers: Malcolm Bruce Radley, Secretary; Ian David Piper [1961] Director/Chartered Surveyor

Ensco 1066 Limited
Incorporated: 3 April 2014 *Employees:* 92
Net Worth: £2,474,839 *Total Assets:* £29,331,360
Registered Office: Units 2 & 3 Tachbrook Link, Tachbrook Park Drive, Leamington Spa, Warwicks, CV34 6SN
Activities: Activities of head offices
Shareholders: Adam Richard Attwood; Tony Dale; Kevin Gilbert; Andrew John Knight; Nicholas White; Gateley Custodian and Nominee Services Limited
Officers: Adam Attwood [1967] Director; Tony Dale [1969] Technical Director; Kevin Lee Gilbert [1957] Operations Director; Andrew John Knight [1972] Director

Ensco 645 Limited
Incorporated: 14 January 2008
Net Worth: £109,754,000 *Total Assets:* £111,286,000
Registered Office: 3 Long Acres, Willow Farm Business Park, Castle Donington, Derbys, DE74 2UG
Activities: Activities of head offices
Parent: Ensco 648 Limited
Officers: Archibald Alexander Rhodes, Secretary; Jack Calandra [1967] Director [American]; Stuart William Graham [1954] Director; Archibald Alexander Rhodes [1959] Director [American]

Ensco 648 Limited
Incorporated: 16 January 2008
Net Worth: £89,030,000 *Total Assets:* £89,030,000
Registered Office: 3 Long Acres, Willow Farm Business Park, Castle Donington, Derbys, DE74 2UG
Activities: Activities of head offices
Parent: MWUK Holding Company Limited
Officers: Archibald Alexander Rhodes, Secretary; Jack Calandra [1967] Director [American]; Stuart William Graham [1954] Director; Archibald Alexander Rhodes [1959] Company Secretary/Director [American]

ENSEK Holdings Limited
Incorporated: 18 August 2017 *Employees:* 71
Net Worth: £4,572,134 *Total Assets:* £17,438,534
Registered Office: The Watercourt, 116-118 Canal Street, Nottingham, NG1 7HF
Activities: Information technology consultancy activities
Officers: David Bains [1982] Investor Director; Philip Edward Bennett [1979] Director; John Charles Green [1967] Investor Director; James Lee Kirk [1981] Director; Edward Peter Minshull [1958] Director; Ian Peters [1958] Director/Chairman; Jonathan Alexander Slade [1979] Director; Arran Jon Stevenson [1980] Director; Mark Wright [1970] Director

Enterprise (AOL) Limited
Incorporated: 15 October 2003
Net Worth: £69,927,000 *Total Assets:* £98,943,000
Registered Office: The Sherard Building, Edmund Halley Road, Oxford, OX4 4DQ
Activities: Other service activities n.e.c.
Parent: Accord Limited
Officers: James Stefan Haluch [1969] Highways Managing Director; Andrew Lee Milner [1969] Director/Chartered Engineer; Andrew Latham Nelson [1959] Finance Director

Enterprise Holding Company No 1 Limited
Incorporated: 5 July 1989
Net Worth: £63,600,000 *Total Assets:* £222,176,992
Registered Office: The Sherard Building, Edmund Halley Road, Oxford, OX4 4DQ
Activities: Activities of other holding companies n.e.c.
Parent: Enterprise PLC
Officers: Andrew Lee Milner [1969] Director/Chartered Engineer; Andrew Latham Nelson [1959] Finance Director

Enterprise Managed Services Limited
Incorporated: 13 October 1966
Net Worth: £63,223,000 *Total Assets:* £500,051,008
Registered Office: The Sherard Building, Edmund Halley Road, Oxford, OX4 4DQ
Activities: Other business support service activities n.e.c.
Parent: Amey Utility Services Limited
Officers: James Stefan Haluch [1969] Highways Director; Darren Simon Jones [1973] Finance Director; David Michael McLoughlin [1962] Managing Director; Andrew Lee Milner [1969] Director/Chartered Engineer; Andrew Latham Nelson [1959] Finance Director; Richard James Ward [1977] Director/Accountant

Enterprise PLC
Incorporated: 2 March 2007
Previous: Enterprise Limited
Net Worth Deficit: £3,788,000 *Total Assets:* £745,878,976
Registered Office: The Sherard Building, Edmund Halley Road, Oxford, OX4 4DQ
Activities: Activities of head offices
Parent: Amey PLC
Officers: Paul Birch, Secretary; Andrew Lee Milner [1969] Director/Chartered Engineer; Andrew Latham Nelson [1959] Finance Director

Entertainment Magpie Group Limited
Incorporated: 14 September 2015 *Employees:* 850
Net Worth: £490,000 *Total Assets:* £18,913,000
Registered Office: Stockport Exchange, Railway Road, Stockport, Cheshire, SK1 3SW
Activities: Activities of head offices
Officers: Andrew William Leach [1957] Director; Steven Oliver [1971] Director; Ian Matthew Storey [1976] Director

Entertainment Magpie Limited
Incorporated: 13 June 2007 *Employees:* 778
Net Worth Deficit: £3,755,000 *Total Assets:* £19,683,000
Registered Office: Stockport Exchange, Railway Road, Stockport, Cheshire, SK1 3SW
Activities: Retail sale via mail order houses or via Internet
Parent: Entertainment Magpie Holdings Limited
Officers: Walter Scott Gleeson [1966] IT Director; Steven Oliver [1971] Director; Ian Matthew Storey [1976] Director

H. J. Enthoven Limited
Incorporated: 26 May 1993 *Employees:* 408
Net Worth: £49,031,000 *Total Assets:* £129,961,000
Registered Office: Darley Dale Smelter, South Darley, Matlock, Derbys, DE4 2LP
Activities: Other non-ferrous metal production
Parent: Ecobat Technologies Limited
Officers: Jimmy Herring, Secretary; Peter Allbutt [1962] Operations Director; Jocelyn Donald Robin Campbell [1955] Director/Marketing Executive; Gregory Robert Clementson [1962] Director; Andrew Robert Hampson [1965] Director/Metals Processor; Robert John Harris [1963] Managing Director-European Division; Jimmy R. Herring [1966] Finance Director [American]

ENVA England Limited
Incorporated: 15 October 1997 *Employees:* 311
Previous: Wastecycle Limited
Net Worth: £16,089,000 *Total Assets:* £25,143,000
Registered Office: Enviro Building, Private Road No 4, Colwick Industrial Estate, Colwick, Nottingham, NG4 2JT
Activities: Collection of non-hazardous waste
Parent: Realpower Limited
Officers: Paul Alan Clements [1974] Commercial Director; Barry Coughlan [1971] Managing Director; Paul Richard Needham [1966] Director; Bill Joseph Power [1969] Director [Irish]; Thomas Walsh [1967] Director [Irish]; Simon Alasdair Woods [1969] Director/Chief Operating Officer

ENVA Topco Limited
Incorporated: 27 March 2017 *Employees:* 1,131
Net Worth Deficit: £12,639,000 *Total Assets:* £298,537,984
Registered Office: Brailwood Road, Bilsthorpe Industrial Estate, Bilsthorpe, Newark, Notts, NG22 8UA
Activities: Activities of other holding companies n.e.c.
Parent: Exponent Private Equity Partners GP III, LP
Officers: Timothy Edward Easingwood [1977] Director/Investment Professional; James Michael Gunton [1982] Director/Investment Professional; John Gerard Moore [1960] Director/Partner, Finance [Irish]; Michael Thomas Tracey [1961] Director; Niall James Wall [1962] Director [Irish]; Thomas Walsh [1967] Managing Director [Irish]; Simon Alasdair Woods [1969] Director/Chief Operating Officer

Envigo CRS Limited
Incorporated: 14 May 1984 *Employees:* 1,174
Previous: Huntingdon Life Sciences Limited
Net Worth Deficit: £27,962,000 *Total Assets:* £192,271,008
Registered Office: Woolley Road, Alconbury, Huntingdon, Cambs, PE28 4HS
Activities: Other research and experimental development on natural sciences and engineering
Parent: Envigo International Limited
Officers: Michael Gregory O'Reilly, Secretary; Michael Gregory O'Reilly [1966] Director/SVP Legal; Stephen Daniel Symonds [1974] Director/Financial Controller

Envigo Developments Limited
Incorporated: 20 July 1973
Previous: E.M. Developments Limited
Net Worth: £13,175,000 *Total Assets:* £16,606,000
Registered Office: Shardlow Business Park, London Road, Shardlow, Derbys, DE72 2GD
Activities: Activities of head offices
Parent: Envigo RMS (UK) Limited
Officers: Michael Gregory O'Reilly, Secretary; Michael Gregory O'Reilly [1966] Director; Stephen Daniel Symonds [1974] Director/Finance Controller

Envigo Holdings Limited
Incorporated: 6 January 1995
Previous: Harlan International Limited
Net Worth: £21,232,000 *Total Assets:* £49,612,000
Registered Office: Shaw's Farm, Station Road, Blackthorn, Bicester, Oxon, OX25 1TP
Activities: Combined office administrative service activities
Officers: Michael Gregory O'Reilly, Secretary; Michael Gregory O'Reilly [1966] Director/Legal Adviser; Stephen Daniel Symonds [1974] Director/Financial Controller

Envigo International Limited
Incorporated: 14 December 1951
Previous: Life Sciences Research Limited
Net Worth: £34,537,000 *Total Assets:* £48,956,000
Registered Office: Woolley Road, Alconbury, Huntingdon, Cambs, PE28 4HS
Activities: Other professional, scientific and technical activities n.e.c.
Major Shareholder: Andrew Baker
Officers: Michael Gregory O'Reilly, Secretary; Michael Gregory O'Reilly [1966] Director/SVP Legal; Stephen Daniel Symonds [1974] Director/Financial Controller

Envigo Research Limited
Incorporated: 12 January 1995 *Employees:* 262
Previous: Harlan Laboratories Ltd.
Net Worth: £31,926,000 *Total Assets:* £46,706,000
Registered Office: Shardlow Business Park, London Road, Shardlow, Derbys, DE72 2GD
Activities: Other professional, scientific and technical activities n.e.c.
Parent: Envigo Developments Limited
Officers: Michael Gregory O'Reilly, Secretary; Michael Gregory O'Reilly [1966] Director; Stephen Daniel Symonds [1974] Director/Financial Controller

Envigo RMS (UK) Limited
Incorporated: 30 September 1976 *Employees:* 190
Previous: Harlan Laboratories U.K. Ltd.
Net Worth: £48,683,000 *Total Assets:* £60,876,000
Registered Office: Shaw's Farm, Station Road, Blackthorn, Bicester, Oxon, OX25 1TP
Activities: Manufacture of basic pharmaceutical products
Shareholders: Envigo Holdings Limited; Envigo Holdings Limited
Officers: Michael Gregory O'Reilly, Secretary; Michael Gregory O'Reilly [1966] Director/Legal Adviser; Stephen Daniel Symonds [1974] Director/Financial Controller

Enviroenergy Limited
Incorporated: 27 December 2000 *Employees:* 4
Net Worth Deficit: £4,948,124 *Total Assets:* £10,373,591
Registered Office: London Road Heat Station, 12 London Road, Nottingham, NG2 3AB
Activities: Production of electricity
Parent: Nottingham City Council
Officers: Malcolm Robinson Townroe, Secretary; Councillor Leslie Ayoola [1971] Director/Management Consultant; Councillor Michael Mountford Edwards [1961] Director; Councillor John Alan Hartshorne [1944] Director/Postman; Councillor Sally Ann Longford [1954] Director/Councillor; Catherine Jean Woodward [1953] Director/Councillor

Envirogen Water Technologies Limited
Incorporated: 9 December 1996 *Employees:* 81
Net Worth Deficit: £7,283,000 *Total Assets:* £9,690,000
Registered Office: Unit 9 Wimsey Way, Somercotes, Alfreton, Derbys, DE55 4LS
Activities: Water collection, treatment and supply
Officers: Donald Scott Malvenan [1955] Director/Executive Chairman; Timothy Charles Metcalfe [1969] Finance Director

Environmental Scientifics Group Holdings Limited
Incorporated: 5 April 2005
Net Worth: £80,061,000 *Total Assets:* £80,971,000
Registered Office: Socotec House, Bretby Business Park, Bretby, Burton on Trent, Staffs, DE15 0YZ
Activities: Other business support service activities n.e.c.
Parent: Socotec UK Holding Limited
Officers: Andrew Christopher Bolter [1970] Finance Director; Ian Sparks [1961] Director

Enviropower Investments Limited
Incorporated: 23 January 2004
Total Assets: £40,808,000
Registered Office: Ground Floor West, 900 Pavilion Drive, Northampton Business Park, Northampton, NN4 7RG
Activities: Other business support service activities n.e.c.
Parent: Fomento de Construcciones y Contratas, S.A.
Officers: Carol Jayne Nunn, Secretary; Jose Liebana Alcantarilla [1965] Director [Spanish]; Tomas Nunez Vega [1954] Director/Industrial Engineer [Spanish]; Vicente Federico Orts-Llopis [1962] Director/Chief Financial Officer [Spanish]; Paul Taylor [1959] Director/Chief Executive Officer

Envisage Group Limited
Incorporated: 14 April 2009 *Employees:* 157
Net Worth: £1,523,000 *Total Assets:* £27,229,000
Registered Office: 12 Herald Way, Binley Industrial Estate, Coventry, Warwicks, CV3 2NY
Activities: Specialised design activities
Shareholders: Ruth Diana Claire Hudson; Envisage Investments Limited
Officers: Nigel Peter Howard, Secretary; James Andrew Aston [1971] Director; Bryan William Campbell [1944] Director; Alastair Kenneth Cattrell [1965] Director; Adrian Mark Coppin [1963] Operations Director; Dr Robert Simon Joyce [1958] Director

Envisage Technologies Limited
Incorporated: 9 August 2005 *Employees:* 87
Previous: Visioneering Limited
Net Worth Deficit: £360,000 *Total Assets:* £17,369,000
Registered Office: 12 Herald Way, Binley Industrial Estate, Coventry, Warwicks, CV3 2NY
Activities: Manufacture of other machine tools
Parent: Envisage Group Limited
Officers: Nigel Peter Howard, Secretary; Bryan William Campbell [1944] Director

EOF Holdings Limited
Incorporated: 7 March 2012 *Employees:* 136
Net Worth: £22,057,984 *Total Assets:* £29,886,888
Registered Office: Brittania Way, Goole, E Yorks, DN14 6ES
Activities: Non-trading company
Major Shareholder: John Hull
Officers: John Hull [1950] Director; Julian Andrew Jowett [1976] Sales Director

EOS Inc. Ltd
Incorporated: 2 June 2000
Net Worth: £15,265,000 *Total Assets:* £89,951,000
Registered Office: Advantage House, Poplar Way, Catcliffe, Rotherham, S Yorks, S60 5TR
Activities: Development of building projects
Parent: Harworth Estates Ltd
Officers: Andrew Michael David Kirkman [1972] Director/Chartered Accountant; Richard Owen Michaelson [1966] Director

EOTH Limited
Incorporated: 18 April 2011 *Employees:* 144
Net Worth: £17,082,000 *Total Assets:* £36,382,000
Registered Office: Equip, Wimsey Way, Somercotes, Alfreton, Derbys, DE55 4LS
Activities: Wholesale of clothing and footwear
Major Shareholder: Matthew Gowar
Officers: Andrew John Styan, Secretary; Frederick William Bacon [1988] Director; Timothy John Fish [1975] Director; Matthew Gowar [1971] Director; Jules Hydleman [1956] Director; Neil Robert McAdie [1963] Sales Director; Giles William Polito [1971] Director; Andrew John Styan [1973] Finance Director

EPAL Holdings Limited
Incorporated: 21 February 2018 *Employees:* 192
Net Worth: £57,521 *Total Assets:* £86,069,008
Registered Office: Edina, Unit 12 & 13 Rugby Park, Bletchley Road, Stockport, Cheshire, SK4 3EJ
Activities: Activities of other holding companies n.e.c.
Parent: EESL Energypro Assets Limited
Officers: Nitin Wadhwa, Secretary; Dr Steven Derrick Fawkes [1959] Director; Neelima Jain [1981] Director [Indian]; Saurabh Kumar [1967] Director [Indian]

EPC United Kingdom PLC
Incorporated: 6 April 1905 *Employees:* 256
Net Worth: £5,468,000 *Total Assets:* £30,353,000
Registered Office: Venture Crescent, Nix's Hill Industrial Estate, Alfreton, Derbys, DE55 7RA
Activities: Manufacture of other organic basic chemicals
Parent: Societe Anonyme D'Explosifs et de Produits Chimques
Officers: David Bloor, Secretary; Paul Gerard Francois Bertrand Chatel de Brancion [1951] Director/Company Chairman [French]; John French [1944] Director/Operations Manager; Raymond Roy Keen [1952] General Manager Director; Olivier Laurant Obst [1966] Director/General Manager [French]; Benjamin Charles Williams [1968] Director/Business Manager

Epyx Limited
Incorporated: 11 October 2000 *Employees:* 99
Net Worth: £87,560,000 *Total Assets:* £100,989,000
Registered Office: Heath Farm, Hampton Lane, Meriden, Coventry, Warwicks, CV7 7LL
Activities: Business and domestic software development
Parent: Quadrum Investment Group Limited
Officers: Eric Richard Dey [1959] Director [American]; Alan King [1976] Director; Anita Kravos-Medimorec [1974] Director/Chief Financial Officer; Steven Joseph Pisciotta [1964] Director [American]

Equals Trust
Incorporated: 14 July 2016 *Employees:* 217
Net Worth: £30,254,000 *Total Assets:* £35,429,000
Registered Office: Keyworth Primary and Nursery School, Nottingham Road, Keyworth, Nottingham, NG12 5FB
Activities: Primary education
Officers: Catherine Emma Cox, Secretary; Zubair Adam [1979] Finance Director; Peter John Foale [1954] Director/Education Consultant; Susan Mary Jaques [1966] Director; Christopher Keast [1967] Director/Senior Lecturer; Philip Duncan Victor Palmer [1963] Director/Chief Executive Officer; Jean Panagamuwa [1981] Director/Data Manager; Rashmi Morarbhai Patel [1970] Director/Head of Operations, HR; Bernard Ian Walker [1953] Director/Retired; Lyndon Wyn Williams [1969] Director/Management Consultant

Equilibrium Healthcare Limited
Incorporated: 15 February 1996 *Employees:* 96
Net Worth: £15,603,001 *Total Assets:* £21,327,060
Registered Office: Bollin House, Riverside Park, Bollin Link, Wilmslow, Cheshire, SK9 1DP
Activities: Hospital activities
Shareholders: Patrick John Keely; Harriet Jane Dudgeon
Officers: Patrick John Keely, Secretary/Manager; Harriet Jane Dudgeon [1959] Director; Patrick John Keely [1959] Director/Manager; David Phillip Madeley [1960] Director/Chartered Accountant

Equip Outdoor Technologies UK Limited
Incorporated: 29 April 1974 *Employees:* 117
Previous: Lowe Alpine UK Limited
Net Worth: £27,451,000 *Total Assets:* £44,646,000
Registered Office: Wimsey Way, Somercotes, Alfreton, Derbys, DE55 4LS
Activities: Wholesale of clothing and footwear
Parent: EOTH Limited
Officers: Andrew John Styan, Secretary; Timothy John Fish [1975] Director; Matthew Gowar [1971] Director; Neil Robert McAdie [1963] Director; Giles William Polito [1971] Director; Andrew John Styan [1973] Finance Director

Equita Limited
Incorporated: 29 February 1996 *Employees:* 209
Net Worth: £24,905,500 *Total Assets:* £38,777,728
Registered Office: 42-44 Henry Street, Northampton, NN1 4BZ
Activities: Activities of head offices
Parent: Capita Holdings Limited
Officers: Neil Forrester Smith [1965] Managing Director

Equity Solutions Asset Management Limited
Incorporated: 2 March 2012 *Employees:* 5
Net Worth: £99,288,648 *Total Assets:* £361,592,064
Registered Office: Building 1000, Kings Reach, Yew Street, Stockport, Cheshire, SK4 2HG
Activities: Other business support service activities n.e.c.
Major Shareholder: Michael Dwan
Officers: Amanda Jane Dwan [1969] Director; Michael Dwan [1959] Director; Marina Ann Guido [1985] Finance Director

Equity Solutions Lift Investments Cornwall Limited
Incorporated: 10 February 2004 *Employees:* 2
Net Worth: £30,159,986 *Total Assets:* £32,629,044
Registered Office: Building 1000, Kings Reach, Yew Street, Stockport, Cheshire, SK4 2HG
Activities: Other business support service activities n.e.c.
Parent: Equity Solutions Lift Investments Limited
Officers: Michael Dwan [1959] Director; Amanda Nottingham [1968] Director/Accountant

Equity Solutions Lift Investments Limited
Incorporated: 15 January 2003
Net Worth: £114,050,920 *Total Assets:* £114,051,320
Registered Office: Building 1000, Kings Reach, Yew Street, Stockport, Cheshire, SK4 2HG
Activities: Activities of other holding companies n.e.c.
Parent: Equity Solutions Asset Management Limited
Officers: Michael Dwan [1959] Director

Equity Solutions Lift Investments Oldham Limited
Incorporated: 14 May 2004
Net Worth: £49,959,904 *Total Assets:* £54,973,848
Registered Office: Building 1000, Kings Reach, Yew Street, Stockport, Cheshire, SK4 2HG
Activities: Other business support service activities n.e.c.
Parent: Equity Solutions Lift Investments Limited
Officers: Michael Dwan [1959] Director; Amanda Nottingham [1968] Director/Accountant

Equity Solutions Lift Investments Sheffield Limited
Incorporated: 14 May 2004
Net Worth: £21,383,264 *Total Assets:* £23,705,180
Registered Office: Building 1000, Kings Reach, Yew Street, Stockport, Cheshire, SK4 2HG
Activities: Other business support service activities n.e.c.
Parent: Equity Solutions Lift Investments Limited
Officers: Michael Dwan [1959] Director; Amanda Nottingham [1968] Director/Accountant

Equity Solutions Lift Investments Stockport Limited
Incorporated: 16 February 2007
Net Worth: £12,548,168 *Total Assets:* £13,463,168
Registered Office: Building 1000, Kings Reach, Yew Street, Stockport, Cheshire, SK4 2HG
Activities: Other service activities n.e.c.
Parent: Equity Solutions Lift Investments Limited
Officers: Michael Dwan [1959] Director

Eraglow Building Limited
Incorporated: 18 August 1977 *Employees:* 2
Net Worth: £8,385,892 *Total Assets:* £11,618,216
Registered Office: Units 4 & 5 Swinford Farm, Eynsham, Oxford, OX29 4BL
Activities: Other letting and operating of own or leased real estate
Shareholder: Rachael Millar
Officers: Rachael Millar, Secretary/Director; Michael Frere Clarke [1952] Director/Properties Manager; Rachael Millar [1981] Director; Tracey Ann Millar [1964] Director

Eraih Limited
Incorporated: 10 November 2014
Net Worth: £1,556,577 *Total Assets:* £21,236,962
Registered Office: The Home Close, 36 Edge Road, Matlock, Derbys, DE4 3NH
Activities: Buying and selling of own real estate
Major Shareholder: David Andrew Pass
Officers: David Andrew Pass [1966] Director

EResearchTechnology Limited
Incorporated: 28 April 1987 *Employees:* 122
Net Worth: £30,136,936 *Total Assets:* £148,514,112
Registered Office: Pearl House, Peterborough Business Park, Lynch Wood, Peterborough, Cambs, PE2 6FZ
Activities: Other professional, scientific and technical activities n.e.c.
Officers: Andrew Fitzgibbon, Secretary; James Corrigan [1963] Director [American]; Gary Mitcheltree [1963] Director/VP Finance [American]; Waqar Nasim [1966] Director [American]

EResearchTechnology UK 1 Limited
Incorporated: 17 May 2010 *Employees:* 611
Net Worth: £60,871,000 *Total Assets:* £199,326,000
Registered Office: Pearl House, Peterborough Business Park, Lynch Wood, Peterborough, Cambs, PE2 6FZ
Activities: Non-trading company
Officers: Andrew Fitzgibbon, Secretary; James Corrigan [1963] Director [American]; Gary Mitcheltree [1963] Director/VP Finance [American]; Waqar Nasim [1966] Director [American]

EResearchTechnology UK 2 Limited
Incorporated: 17 May 2010
Net Worth: £103,968,736 *Total Assets:* £138,743,920
Registered Office: Pearl House, Peterborough Business Park, Lynch Wood, Peterborough, Cambs, PE2 6FZ
Activities: Non-trading company
Officers: Andrew Fitzgibbon, Secretary; James Corrigan [1963] Director [American]; Gary Mitcheltree [1963] Director/VP Finance [American]; Waqar Nasim [1966] Director [American]

ERF Electrical Wholesalers Ltd.
Incorporated: 27 July 1967 *Employees:* 110
Net Worth: £2,076,242 *Total Assets:* £9,162,934
Registered Office: Salop Street, Daybrook, Nottingham, NG5 6HD
Activities: Wholesale of radio, television goods & electrical household appliances (other than records, tapes, CDs)
Shareholders: Robin Combellack; Timothy Combellack
Officers: Ashley Mark Smith, Secretary; Robin Combellack [1967] Director; Timothy Combellack [1971] Director; Simon Jones [1965] Director; Andrew John Laycock [1972] Director

Erlson Precision Components Limited
Incorporated: 6 June 1973 *Employees:* 254
Net Worth: £2,320,162 *Total Assets:* £10,299,347
Registered Office: 5 The Courtyard, Timothy's Bridge Road, Stratford Enterprise Park, Stratford upon Avon, Warwicks, CV37 9NP
Activities: Manufacture of other parts and accessories for motor vehicles
Parent: Erlson Precision Holdings Ltd
Officers: Leszek Richard Litwinowicz, Secretary; Peter Joseph Calderbank [1969] Director; Paul Andrew Clarkson [1975] Finance Director; Daniel Phillip Haigh [1976] Director; Leszek Richard Litwinowicz [1958] Director; Peter Francis Lombardi [1945] Director; Mark Geoffrey Sale [1964] Director

Erlson Precision Holdings Limited
Incorporated: 22 March 2010 *Employees:* 258
Net Worth: £1,315,789 *Total Assets:* £10,299,348
Registered Office: 5 The Courtyard, Timothys Bridge Road, Stratford upon Avon, Warwicks, CV37 9NP
Activities: Manufacture of other special-purpose machinery n.e.c.
Shareholders: Jonathan David Grove; Leszek Richard Litwinowicz; David Grove Discretionary Will Trust
Officers: Peter Joseph Calderbank [1969] Director; Paul Andrew Clarkson [1975] Finance Director; Daniel Phillip Haigh [1976] Director; Leszek Richard Litwinowicz [1958] Director; Peter Francis Lombardi [1945] Director; Mark Geoffrey Sale [1964] Director

ESCO (UK) Holdings Limited
Incorporated: 24 April 2003 *Employees:* 3
Net Worth Deficit: £377,000 *Total Assets:* £15,135,000
Registered Office: Esco (UK) Holdings Limited, Ings Road, Doncaster, S Yorks, DN5 9SN
Activities: Activities of head offices
Parent: ESCO EMEA Holdings (UK) Limited
Officers: Stephen Beresford Robinson, Secretary; Meredith Weisshaar, Secretary; Todd William Abel [1964] Director/VP - Finance & Accounting [American]; Philippe Kaskarian [1963] Director [French]; Jon Owens [1962] Director/Senior Vice President [American]

ESCO EMEA Holdings (UK) Limited
Incorporated: 13 September 2013 *Employees:* 144
Net Worth: £2,883,000 *Total Assets:* £31,401,000
Registered Office: Esco EMEA Holdings (UK) Limited, Ings Road, Doncaster, S Yorks, DN5 9SN
Activities: Activities of head offices
Officers: Stephen Beresford Robinson, Secretary; Meredith Weisshaar, Secretary; Todd William Abel [1964] Director/VP - Finance & Accounting [American]; Philippe Kaskarian [1963] Director [French]; Jon Owens [1962] Director/Senior Vice President [American]

Esendee Holdings Limited
Incorporated: 16 May 2011 *Employees:* 51
Net Worth: £6,796,000 *Total Assets:* £47,501,000
Registered Office: 4 Bank Court, Weldon Road, Loughborough, Leics, LE11 5RF
Activities: Activities of other holding companies n.e.c.
Shareholders: Steven John Tysoe; Sean Anthony Hoare
Officers: Sean Anthony Hoare [1977] Director [Irish]; Steven John Tysoe [1960] Director

Esendex Bidco Limited
Incorporated: 12 July 2013 *Employees:* 1
Net Worth: £9,699,561 *Total Assets:* £31,868,736
Registered Office: 20 Wollaton Street, Nottingham, NG1 5FW
Activities: Activities of head offices
Parent: Esendex Midco Limited
Officers: Paul Eric Jonathon Burton [1981] Director; Geoffrey Adrian Love [1971] Director; Hayden David Robinson [1970] Director

Esendex Holdings Limited
Incorporated: 19 May 2005 *Employees:* 1
Net Worth: £5,862,325 *Total Assets:* £23,391,956
Registered Office: 20 Wollaton Street, Nottingham, NG1 5FW
Activities: Activities of head offices
Shareholders: Esendex Bidco Limited; Esendex Bidco Limited
Officers: Paul Eric Jonathon Burton [1981] Director; Geoffrey Adrian Love [1971] Director/Chief Commercial Officer; Hayden David Robinson [1970] Director

Esendex Midco Limited
Incorporated: 12 July 2013 *Employees:* 138
Net Worth Deficit: £7,785,473 *Total Assets:* £24,194,658
Registered Office: 20 Wollaton Street, Nottingham, NG1 5FW
Activities: Activities of head offices
Shareholders: Esendex Topco Limited; Esendex Topco Limited
Officers: Paul Eric Jonathon Burton [1981] Director; Geoffrey Adrian Love [1971] Director; Hayden David Robinson [1970] Director

Esendex Topco Limited
Incorporated: 21 May 2013 *Employees:* 138
Net Worth Deficit: £7,714,983 *Total Assets:* £24,194,658
Registered Office: 20 Wollaton Street, Nottingham, NG1 5FW
Activities: Activities of head offices
Parent: Falcon Bidco Limited
Officers: Paul Eric Jonathon Burton [1981] Director; Geoffrey Adrian Love [1971] Director; Hayden David Robinson [1970] Director

ESKO Stonecube Limited
Incorporated: 27 December 2000 *Employees:* 7
Net Worth: £27,858,880 *Total Assets:* £27,972,644
Registered Office: 19 Jessops Riverside, 800 Brightside Lane, Sheffield, S9 2RX
Activities: Business and domestic software development
Parent: Danaher Corporation
Officers: Jeroen Minoodt [1976] Director [Belgian]; Keith Graham Ward [1953] Director; Bernard Albert Christiaan Zwaenepoel [1965] Director [Belgian]

The Esland Group Limited
Incorporated: 25 June 2009 *Employees:* 2
Net Worth: £5,537,170 *Total Assets:* £16,285,993
Registered Office: Suites 1 & 5 Riverside Business Centre, Foundry Lane, Milford, Belper, Derbys, DE56 0RN
Activities: Activities of other holding companies n.e.c.
Officers: Peter Neil Buller [1986] Managing Director; Lyndsey Sim [1984] Director/Chief Operating Officer

ESNT Filter Products Limited
Incorporated: 29 October 2009
Net Worth: £20,447,696 *Total Assets:* £20,452,492
Registered Office: Avebury House, 201-249 Avebury Boulevard, Milton Keynes, Bucks, MK9 1AU
Activities: Non-trading company
Parent: Essentra International Limited
Officers: Tay Swee Choon George, Secretary; Tay Swee Choon George [1975] Director [Singaporean]; Robert William Pye [1964] Director [Australian]

ESNT Holdings (No.1) Limited
Incorporated: 3 July 1997
Net Worth: £175,956,000 *Total Assets:* £175,962,000
Registered Office: Avebury House, 201-249 Avebury Boulevard, Milton Keynes, Bucks, MK9 1AU
Activities: Activities of head offices
Parent: Essentra International Limited
Officers: Patricia Kendall, Secretary; Jon Michael Green [1962] Director/Company Secretary & General Counsel; Lili Liu [1972] Director

ESNT Holdings (No.2) Limited
Incorporated: 3 July 1997
Net Worth: £160,688,992 *Total Assets:* £160,740,000
Registered Office: Avebury House, 201-249 Avebury Boulevard, Milton Keynes, Bucks, MK9 1AU
Activities: Activities of head offices
Shareholders: ESNT Holdings (No.1) Limited; ESNT Holdings (No.1) Limited
Officers: Jon Michael Green, Secretary; Jon Michael Green [1962] Director/Company Secretary & General Counsel; Lili Liu [1972] Director

ESNT International Limited
Incorporated: 1 August 1985
Net Worth Deficit: £10,809,000 *Total Assets:* £304,440,000
Registered Office: Avebury House, 201-249 Avebury Boulevard, Milton Keynes, Bucks, MK9 1AU
Activities: Non-trading company
Parent: Essentra International Limited
Officers: Patricia Kendall, Secretary; Jon Michael Green [1962] Director/Company Secretary & General Counsel; Lili Liu [1972] Director

ESNT Packaging & Securing Solutions Limited
Incorporated: 27 April 2001
Net Worth: £6,339,000 *Total Assets:* £16,296,000
Registered Office: Avebury House, 201-249 Avebury Boulevard, Milton Keynes, Bucks, MK9 1AU
Activities: Non-trading company
Parent: Essentra International Limited
Officers: Patricia Kendall, Secretary; Jon Michael Green [1962] Director/Company Secretary & General Counsel; Lili Liu [1972] Director

Essenden Limited
Incorporated: 5 March 2009
Previous: Essenden Public Limited Company
Net Worth: £16,537,000 *Total Assets:* £18,498,000
Registered Office: Aragon House, Cranfield Technology Park, Cranfield, Bedford, MK43 0EQ
Activities: Activities of head offices
Parent: Indoor Bowling Acquisitions Limited
Officers: Mark Willis, Secretary; Nicholas Andrew Basing [1962] Director; Graham Edwin Blackwell [1969] Director; Dr Duncan Steven Garrood [1958] Director; Mark Simon Willis [1976] Director

Essential Supply Products Limited
Incorporated: 8 November 1995 *Employees:* 74
Net Worth: £3,359,395 *Total Assets:* £23,164,076
Registered Office: Magma House, 16 Davy Court, Castle Mound Way, Rugby, Warwicks, CV23 0UZ
Activities: Other business support service activities n.e.c.
Major Shareholder: Carl Jonathan Theakston
Officers: Carl Jonathan Theakston, Secretary/Director; Riccardo Fortini [1969] Production Director [Italian]; Carl Jonathan Theakston [1963] Director; Amanda Jayne Waterman [1970] Director/Financial; Craig James Williams [1972] Sales Director

Essentra Components Limited
Incorporated: 6 April 1955 *Employees:* 350
Net Worth: £74,999,000 *Total Assets:* £94,762,000
Registered Office: Avebury House, 201-249 Avebury Boulevard, Milton Keynes, Bucks, MK9 1AU
Activities: Manufacture of other plastic products
Parent: Essentra International Limited
Officers: Jon Michael Green, Secretary; Scott Morgan Taylor Fawcett [1971] Director; Aamir Mohiuddin [1980] Director

Essentra Filter Products International Limited
Incorporated: 17 February 1945
Net Worth: £26,564,000 *Total Assets:* £54,970,000
Registered Office: Avebury House, 201-249 Avebury Boulevard, Milton Keynes, Bucks, MK9 1AU
Activities: Activities of head offices
Parent: ESNT Filter Products Limited
Officers: Tay Swee Choon George, Secretary; Tay Swee Choon George [1975] Director [Singaporean]; Robert William Pye [1964] Director [Australian]

Essentra Filter Products Limited
Incorporated: 1 October 1931 *Employees:* 23
Net Worth: £50,860,000 *Total Assets:* £52,233,000
Registered Office: Avebury House, 201-249 Avebury Boulevard, Milton Keynes, Bucks, MK9 1AU
Activities: Dormant company
Parent: Essentra Filter Products International Limited
Officers: Tay Swee Choon George, Secretary; Tay Swee Choon George [1975] Director [Singaporean]; Robert William Pye [1964] Director [Australian]

Essentra Finance Limited
Incorporated: 27 January 2005
Net Worth: £193,628,992 *Total Assets:* £1,269,492,992
Registered Office: Avebury House, 201-249 Avebury Boulevard, Milton Keynes, Bucks, MK9 1AU
Activities: Other business support service activities n.e.c.
Parent: Essentra International Limited
Officers: Patricia Kendall, Secretary; Jon Michael Green [1962] Director/Company Secretary & General Counsel; Lili Liu [1972] Director

Essentra International Limited
Incorporated: 5 June 1974 *Employees:* 72
Net Worth: £294,852,992 *Total Assets:* £478,504,000
Registered Office: Avebury House, 201-249 Avebury Boulevard, Milton Keynes, Bucks, MK9 1AU
Activities: Activities of head offices
Parent: Essentra PLC
Officers: Patricia Kendall, Secretary; Jon Michael Green [1962] Director/Solicitor; Lili Liu [1972] Director

Essentra Packaging & Security Limited
Incorporated: 2 June 2010 *Employees:* 462
Net Worth Deficit: £38,674,000 *Total Assets:* £59,358,000
Registered Office: Avebury House, 201-249 Avebury Boulevard, Milton Keynes, Bucks, MK9 1AU
Activities: Manufacture of plastic packing goods
Parent: ESNT Packaging & Securing Solutions Limited
Officers: Jon Michael Green, Secretary; Bradley Aaron Schechtman [1981] Director [American]; Robert Sykes [1970] Director; Timothy Kenneth Wilson [1960] Director [American]

Essentra Packaging Limited
Incorporated: 24 September 2012 *Employees:* 413
Net Worth: £48,198,000 *Total Assets:* £57,013,000
Registered Office: Avebury House, 201-249 Avebury Boulevard, Milton Keynes, Bucks, MK9 1AU
Activities: Manufacture of other plastic products
Parent: ESNT International Limited
Officers: Jon Michael Green, Secretary; Iain Philip Percival [1967] Director; Andrew Colin Riley [1967] Director

Essentra PLC
Incorporated: 5 May 2005 *Employees:* 8
Net Worth: £612,300,032 *Total Assets:* £1,239,699,968
Registered Office: Avebury House, 201-249 Avebury Boulevard, Milton Keynes, Bucks, MK9 1AU
Activities: Activities of head offices
Officers: Jon Michael Green, Secretary; Thomas Benedict Breen [1959] Director [Irish]; Paul Anthony Foreman [1965] Director/Chief Executive Officer; Paul John Lester [1949] Director; Lili Liu [1972] Director; Mary Reilly [1953] Director; Margaret Lorraine Trainer [1952] Director; Ralf Klaus Wunderlich [1966] Director/Senior Adviser [German]

Essentra Services Limited
Incorporated: 1 December 1976
Net Worth Deficit: £91,627,552 *Total Assets:* £22,337,610
Registered Office: Avebury House, 201-249 Avebury Boulevard, Milton Keynes, Bucks, MK9 1AU
Activities: Non-trading company
Parent: Essentra International Limited
Officers: Patricia Kendall, Secretary; Jon Michael Green [1962] Director/Company Secretary & General Counsel; Lili Liu [1972] Director

Estate Computer Systems (Holdings) Limited
Incorporated: 30 August 1991
Net Worth Deficit: £854,667 *Total Assets:* £13,697,365
Registered Office: Westgate House, Westgate, Sleaford, Lincs, NG34 7RJ
Activities: Business and domestic software development
Parent: MRI Software Limited
Officers: John Adler Ensign, Secretary; John Adler Ensign [1972] Director/Lawyer [American]; Patrick Joseph Ghilani [1971] Director/Chief Executive Officer [American]; Roman Telerman [1986] Director/Accountant [American]

Estate Incomes Limited
Incorporated: 29 October 1932 *Employees:* 5
Net Worth: £10,511,180 *Total Assets:* £11,147,551
Registered Office: Bobsons Cottage, 56 Main Street, Whissendine, Oakham, Rutland, LE15 7ET
Activities: Other letting and operating of own or leased real estate
Officers: Clare Francis Thomas, Secretary; Robin Andrew Harford [1972] Director/Chief Operating Officer; David William Horton [1942] Director; John Rawson Maxey [1959] Director/Chartered Surveyor; Timothy Goodwin Shaw [1948] Director/Chartered Accountant; Clare Francis Thomas [1963] Director/Administrator

Estates and Leisure Holdings Limited
Incorporated: 16 February 1990 *Employees:* 2
Net Worth: £5,508,934 *Total Assets:* £10,759,870
Registered Office: 19 Chestergate, Macclesfield, Cheshire, SK11 6BX
Activities: Other letting and operating of own or leased real estate
Shareholders: Nicholas Brian Lewis; Brian Edward Lewis
Officers: Nicholas Brian Lewis, Secretary; Brian Edward Lewis [1942] Director; Nicholas Brian Lewis [1967] Director

Eterna Lighting Limited
Incorporated: 16 May 1946 *Employees:* 39
Net Worth: £10,383,116 *Total Assets:* £12,333,316
Registered Office: Eterna Lighting, Huxley Close, Park Farm South, Wellingborough, Northants, NN8 6AB
Activities: Wholesale of furniture, carpets and lighting equipment
Major Shareholder: Arnold Geoffrey Denman
Officers: Andrew Jameson Freeman, Secretary; Neil Howard Clydesdale [1972] Managing Director; Arnold Geoffrey Denman [1936] Director; Michael Dennis Denman [1970] Director; Andrew Jameson Freeman [1962] Finance Director; George MacDonald Ratcliffe Smith [1966] Sales Director; Martin John Stone [1963] Managing Director; Lucy Ellen Wade [1977] Commercial Director

Etex (Exteriors) UK Limited
Incorporated: 6 September 1950 *Employees:* 861
Previous: Marley Eternit Limited
Net Worth: £196,700,000 *Total Assets:* £257,300,000
Registered Office: Etex (Exteriors) UK Limited, Wellington Road, Burton on Trent, Staffs, DE14 2AP
Activities: Sawmilling and planing of wood
Parent: Etex (U.K.) Limited
Officers: Jayne Arkell [1974] Director/Country Manager UK; Morten Steen Hansen [1963] Director [Danish]; Xavier Georges Roger Janin [1969] Director/General Manager [French]

The Ethical Property Company Limited
Incorporated: 23 August 1994 *Employees:* 65
Net Worth: £43,986,792 *Total Assets:* £61,361,504
Registered Office: The Old Music Hall, 106-108 Cowley Road, Oxford, OX4 1JE
Activities: Other letting and operating of own or leased real estate
Officers: Penelope Jane Gardner, Secretary; Paul Neil Bellack [1955] Director of Commercial Property Company; Samuel Patrick Charles Clarke [1948] Director; James Graham Hartzell [1958] Director; David Loggia [1975] Director/Investor [Australian/Italian]; Mark Alan Luntley [1960] Director/Local Government Accountant

Euramax Coated Products Limited
Incorporated: 18 May 1965 *Employees:* 78
Net Worth: £754,000 *Total Assets:* £22,412,000
Registered Office: Brunel Road, Earlstrees Industrial Estate, Corby, Northants, NN17 4JW
Activities: Treatment and coating of metals
Parent: Euramax UK Ltd
Officers: Pedro Baptista, Secretary; Mary Cullin [1965] Director/Chief Financial Officer [American]; Christoph Jacob [1962] Director/President [German]

Euramax Solutions Limited
Incorporated: 12 August 1950 *Employees:* 221
Net Worth: £9,457,000 *Total Assets:* £21,160,000
Registered Office: Euramax House, Ashroyd Business Park, Ashroyd's Way, Platts Common, Barnsley, S Yorks, S74 9SB
Activities: Other manufacturing n.e.c.
Officers: Nick Cowley [1972] Managing Director; Mary Cullin [1965] Director [American]; Christoph Jacob [1962] Director [German]; Benjamin Thomas Watson [1987] Director

Euro E-Land Company PLC
Incorporated: 16 November 1994
Net Worth Deficit: £16,686,823 *Total Assets:* £69,175,704
Registered Office: Baron Avenue, Earls Barton, Northampton, NN6 0JE
Activities: Activities of head offices
Shareholder: Song Soo Park
Officers: Craig Murray, Secretary; Chunsoo Chon [1963] Director [South Korean]; Sung Ho Kim [1965] Director/Accountant [South Korean]

Euro Food Brands Limited
Incorporated: 11 January 1991 *Employees:* 113
Net Worth: £18,186,880 *Total Assets:* £52,531,304
Registered Office: The Pinnacle, 170 Midsummer Boulevard, Milton Keynes, Bucks, MK9 1FE
Activities: Non-specialised wholesale of food, beverages and tobacco
Parent: E.F.B. Group Limited
Officers: Michael Adams [1956] Director; Stephen Charles Barlow [1956] Director/Chief Executive Officer; Peter John Butler [1966] Managing Director; Phil Gotch [1976] Financial Director; Brandon William Ransley [1965] Director/Solicitor

Eurocell Building Plastics Limited
Incorporated: 22 June 1995 *Employees:* 678
Net Worth: £9,847,000 *Total Assets:* £38,584,000
Registered Office: Fairbrook House, Clover Nook Road, Alfreton, Derbys, DE55 4RF
Activities: Non-specialised wholesale trade
Parent: Eurocell Group Limited
Officers: Generald Copley, Secretary; Mark Jonathan Warwick Kelly [1960] Director; Michael Iain Scott [1966] Finance Director

Eurocell Group Limited
Incorporated: 8 February 1988 *Employees:* 143
Previous: Eurocell Group PLC
Net Worth: £10,865,000 *Total Assets:* £53,119,000
Registered Office: Fairbrook House, Clover Nook Road, Alfreton, Derby, DE55 4RF
Activities: Activities of head offices
Parent: Eurocell Holdings Limited
Officers: Generald Copley, Secretary; Mark Jonathan Warwick Kelly [1960] Director; Ian Joseph Kemp [1966] Director; Michael Iain Scott [1966] Finance Director; Anthony John Smith [1956] Director

Eurocell Holdings Limited
Incorporated: 16 August 2013
Net Worth: £18,326,000 *Total Assets:* £65,830,000
Registered Office: Fairbrook House, Clovernook Road, Alfreton, Derbys, DE55 4RF
Activities: Activities of head offices
Parent: Eurocell PLC
Officers: Generald Copley, Secretary; Mark Jonathan Warwick Kelly [1960] Director; Michael Iain Scott [1966] Finance Director

Eurocell PLC
Incorporated: 16 August 2013 *Employees:* 1,496
Net Worth: £49,374,000 *Total Assets:* £114,631,000
Registered Office: Fairbrook House, Clovernook Road, Alfreton, Derbys, DE55 4RF
Activities: Activities of head offices
Officers: Generald Copley, Secretary; Martyn Coffey [1962] Director; Sucheta Govil [1963] Director; Patrick Henricus Lambertus Kalverboer [1972] Director/Managing Partner [Dutch]; Mark Jonathan Warwick Kelly [1960] Director; Robert Arthur Lawson [1944] Director; Francis Eamon Nelson [1951] Director; Michael Iain Scott [1966] Director/Chief Financial Officer

Eurocell Profiles Limited
Incorporated: 30 September 1991 *Employees:* 456
Net Worth: £25,594,000 *Total Assets:* £57,300,000
Registered Office: Fairbrook House, Clovernook Road, Alfreton, Derby, DE55 4RF
Activities: Manufacture of other plastic products
Parent: Eurocell Group Limited
Officers: Generald Copley, Secretary; Mark Jonathan Warwick Kelly [1960] Director; Michael Iain Scott [1966] Finance Director

Eurofleet Rental Limited
Incorporated: 1 December 1964 *Employees:* 4
Net Worth: £919,322 *Total Assets:* £13,641,634
Registered Office: Little Wigston, Swadlincote, Derbys, DE12 7BJ
Activities: Renting and leasing of trucks and other heavy vehicles
Parent: Ballyvesey Holdings Limited
Officers: Harold Hugh Montgomery, Secretary; Harold Hugh Montgomery [1948] Director/Haulier

Eurokey Recycling Limited
Incorporated: 10 August 1995 *Employees:* 52
Net Worth: £3,204,448 *Total Assets:* £10,441,729
Registered Office: 9 Merus Court, Meridian Business Park, Leicester, LE19 1RJ
Activities: Recovery of sorted materials
Shareholders: Harinder Singh Dhillon; Belinder Kaur Dhillon
Officers: Harinder Singh Dhillon, Secretary; Belinder Kaur Dhillon [1968] Director; Harinder Singh Dhillon [1970] Director

Europcar Group UK Limited
Incorporated: 1 January 1973 *Employees:* 2,387
Net Worth: £34,944,000 *Total Assets:* £536,308,000
Registered Office: James House, 55 Welford Road, Leicester, LE2 7AR
Activities: Renting and leasing of cars and light motor vehicles
Parent: Premierfirst Vehicle Rental Holdings Limited
Officers: Luc Etienne Peligry [1964] Director/Chief Financial Officer [French]; Gary Neil Smith [1970] Director

Europcar UK Limited
Incorporated: 30 March 1966
Net Worth: £172,598,000 *Total Assets:* £172,600,000
Registered Office: James House, 55 Welford Road, Leicester, LE2 7AR
Activities: Renting and leasing of cars and light motor vehicles
Parent: Europcar Groupe SA
Officers: Olivier Pierre Baldassari [1964] Director [French]; Luc Etienne Peligry [1964] Director/Chief Financial Officer [French]; Gary Neil Smith [1970] Director

European Electronique Limited
Incorporated: 7 March 1983 *Employees:* 139
Net Worth: £3,575,562 *Total Assets:* £26,030,936
Registered Office: Forward House, Oakwood, Oakfields Industrial Estate, Eynsham, Oxon, OX29 4TT
Activities: Information technology consultancy activities
Officers: Stephen John Mason, Secretary; Michael Joseph Gill [1960] Director; Yolanta Anastazja Gill [1963] Director; Garry Street [1973] Technical Director

European Support Services (UK) Limited
Incorporated: 25 January 2001 *Employees:* 36
Net Worth: £4,981,568 *Total Assets:* £19,954,100
Registered Office: 15 Newland, Lincoln, LN1 1XG
Activities: Other business support service activities n.e.c.
Shareholders: Burton Cedar Investments Ltd; European Soft Touch Ltd
Officers: Robert John Dye [1954] Director/Engineer; Roy Kjellerup [1971] Director/Manager [Danish]

N.R. Evans and Son Limited
Incorporated: 2 August 1985 *Employees:* 468
Net Worth: £6,067,000 *Total Assets:* £21,739,000
Registered Office: Azalea Close, Clover Nook Industrial Park, Somercotes, Alfreton, Derbys, DE55 4QX
Activities: Freight transport by road
Parent: N R Evans Holdings Ltd
Officers: Mark Davis, Secretary; Mark Davis [1972] Director; Jay Lee Edwards [1978] Director; Ross David Eggleton [1977] Director; Simon Richard Pearson [1967] Director; Heath Brian Zarin [1975] Director [Kittitian]

RE Evans Farms Limited
Incorporated: 14 November 2016 *Employees:* 14
Net Worth: £1,848,130 *Total Assets:* £17,080,676
Registered Office: Peterbridge House, MacIntyre Hudson, The Lakes, Northampton, NN4 7HB
Activities: Mixed farming
Shareholders: Rachel Emmaline Harrod; Mark Anthony Harrod
Officers: Mark Anthony Harrod [1963] Director; Rachel Emmaline Harrod [1976] Director

Evans Halshaw.Com Limited
Incorporated: 20 April 1937 *Employees:* 3
Net Worth: £19,067,000 *Total Assets:* £19,072,000
Registered Office: Loxley House, 2 Oakwood Court, Little Oak Drive, Annesley, Nottingham, NG15 0DR
Activities: Activities of head offices
Parent: Reg Vardy Limited
Officers: Richard James Maloney, Secretary; Martin Shaun Casha [1960] Director; Trevor Garry Finn [1957] Director; Timothy Paul Holden [1964] Director/Chartered Accountant

Evans Leicester Limited
Incorporated: 1 June 2012 *Employees:* 33
Net Worth: £3,049,933 *Total Assets:* £9,559,782
Registered Office: 8 Cloverpark, Cloverfield, Hinckley, Leics, LE10 1YD
Activities: Activities of construction holding companies
Officers: Rhys David Evans [1986] Director/Entrepreneur; Thomas Lister Evans [1985] Director

Everards Brewery Limited
Incorporated: 7 October 1936 *Employees:* 75
Net Worth: £81,160,000 *Total Assets:* £111,340,000
Registered Office: Devana Avenue, Optimus Point, Glenfield, Leicester, LE3 8JS
Activities: Mixed farming
Major Shareholder: Richard Anthony Spencer Everard
Officers: Nigel Geoffrey Allen, Secretary; Nigel Geoffrey Allen [1975] Finance Director; Julian William Spencer Everard [1988] Director; Richard Anthony Spencer Everard [1954] Director; Stephen Gould [1968] Director; John Nicholas Lloyd [1948] Director; Serena Anne Richards [1952] Director; Charlotte Ione Vowles [1985] Director; Adrian Robert Weston [1935] Director

Everris Limited
Incorporated: 1 February 2011 *Employees:* 55
Net Worth: £5,278,000 *Total Assets:* £25,361,000
Registered Office: 17 Lanchester Way, Royal Oak Industrial Estate, Daventry, Northants, NN11 8PH
Activities: Other manufacturing n.e.c.
Parent: Cleveland Potash Limited
Officers: Cornelis Petrus Langeveld [1952] Managing Director [Dutch]; Stephen Squires [1966] Business Director

Everyone Active Administration Services Limited
Incorporated: 13 April 2012
Net Worth: £10 *Total Assets:* £19,402,366
Registered Office: 2 Watling Drive, Sketchley Meadows, Hinckley, Leics, LE10 3EY
Activities: Operation of sports facilities
Officers: Jane Ellen Jebb, Secretary; Martin Bell [1961] Director; David John Bibby [1961] Director; Joseph Mark Drysdale [1963] Finance Director

Evo Business Supplies Limited
Incorporated: 28 May 2014 *Employees:* 1,790
Net Worth: £11,900,000 *Total Assets:* £216,500,000
Registered Office: K House, Sheffield Business Park, Europa Link, Sheffield, S9 1XU
Activities: Wholesale of other office machinery and equipment
Shareholders: Endless II GP LLP; Endless III General Partner LLP; Endless LLP
Officers: Lorna Kathleen Mendelsohn, Secretary; Mathew William Deering [1977] Director; Andrew Peter Gale [1970] Director; Stephen Haworth [1970] Director/Group CEO; Andrew Ross [1977] Director; Stephen Thomson [1959] Director/Chairman; Kenneth Andrew Williamson [1962] Director

Evo Group Services Limited
Incorporated: 23 May 2007
Previous: Vasanta Group Limited
Net Worth Deficit: £8,961,000 *Total Assets:* £26,935,000
Registered Office: K House, Sheffield Business Park, Europa Link, Sheffield, S9 1XU
Activities: Activities of head offices
Parent: Evo Business Supplies Limited
Officers: Lorna Kathleen Mendelsohn, Secretary; Andrew Peter Gale [1970] Finance Director; Stephen Haworth [1970] Director/Group CEO

Evobus (UK) Limited
Incorporated: 21 December 1993 *Employees:* 81
Net Worth: £8,127,000 *Total Assets:* £56,295,000
Registered Office: Ashcroft Way, Cross Point Business Park, Coventry, Warwicks, CV2 2TU
Activities: Sale of other motor vehicles
Parent: Daimler UK Limited
Officers: Michal Pawel Chylinski, Secretary; Roman Guido Willy Biondi [1968] Director/Market Management and Subsidiaries [German]; Michael Franz-Josef Thielmann [1961] Director [German]

Evolution Homecare Services Limited
Incorporated: 24 March 1966 *Employees:* 74
Net Worth Deficit: £19,228,000 *Total Assets:* £39,302,000
Registered Office: Sapphire Court, Walsgrave Triangle, Coventry, Warwicks, CV2 2TX
Activities: Medical nursing home activities
Parent: Admenta Holdings Limited
Officers: Nichola Louise Legg, Secretary; Toby Matthew Anderson [1973] Director; Marcus Hilger [1977] Finance Director [German]; Catherine McDermott [1968] Operations Director; Nigel Swift [1966] Marketing & Sales Director

Evolution Power Tools Ltd
Incorporated: 30 September 1997 *Employees:* 98
Net Worth: £10,047,378 *Total Assets:* £27,397,624
Registered Office: Venture One, Longacre Close, Holbrook Industrial Estate, Sheffield, S20 3FR
Activities: Wholesale of machine tools
Major Shareholder: Matthew Gavins
Officers: Danny Peter Taylor, Secretary; James Ashley Bamber [1981] Director; Barry Bloomer [1962] Supply Chain and Procurement Director; David Arthur Bygraves [1965] Managing Director; Rod Howard Dorman [1957] Director [American]; Matthew James Gavins [1975] Director

The Evolve Trust
Incorporated: 28 October 2011 *Employees:* 287
Net Worth: £14,167,000 *Total Assets:* £20,656,000
Registered Office: c/o The Beech Academy, Fairholme Drive, Mansfield, Notts, NG19 6DX
Activities: General secondary education
Officers: Barbara Alice Sims, Secretary; John Dryden [1951] Director/Educational Consultant; Maureen Fowler [1954] Director; Julie Mary Horton [1958] Director; Ian Jephson [1962] Director; Fiona Stagg [1966] Director/National Leader of Governance; Dominic MacKenzie Swift [1965] Director/Solicitor; Peter Wright [1953] Director

Evonik Chemicals Limited
Incorporated: 13 February 1907 *Employees:* 64
Previous: Air Products (Chemicals) Limited
Net Worth: £90,934,000 *Total Assets:* £123,518,000
Registered Office: Tego House, Chippenham Drive, Kingston, Milton Keynes, Bucks, MK10 0AF
Activities: Manufacture of other organic basic chemicals
Parent: Evonik UK Holdings Limited
Officers: Geneva Angela Stapleton, Secretary; Anh TU Luu [1979] Director/Solicitor; Howard James Lynn [1968] Director/European Operations Manager; Dr Martina Pfirmann [1962] Director/Chemist [German]; Dr Dirk Reichel [1965] Director/Chemist [German]

Evonik Goldschmidt UK Limited
Incorporated: 5 October 1972 *Employees:* 14
Net Worth: £19,500,316 *Total Assets:* £20,582,184
Registered Office: Tego House, Chippenham Drive, Kingston, Milton Keynes, Bucks, MK10 0AF
Activities: Manufacture of soap and detergents
Parent: Evonik UK Holdings Limited
Officers: Geneva Angela Stapleton, Secretary; Clive Martin Gould [1956] Director/General Manager; Anh Luu [1979] Director/Legal Counsel

Evonik Speciality Organics Limited
Incorporated: 24 April 1992 *Employees:* 1
Net Worth: £270,348,288 *Total Assets:* £270,403,136
Registered Office: Tego House, Chippenham Drive, Kingston, Milton Keynes, Bucks, MK10 0AF
Activities: Activities of head offices
Parent: Evonik UK Holdings Limited
Officers: Geneva Angela Stapleton, Secretary; Matthias Kittler [1971] Director/Legal Counsel [German]; Anh TU Luu [1979] Director/Solicitor; Vera Iris Wruck [1969] Director/HR Partner [German]

Evonik UK Holdings Limited
Incorporated: 3 March 1992 *Employees:* 7
Previous: Evonik Degussa UK Holdings Limited
Net Worth: £665,363,712 *Total Assets:* £674,511,296
Registered Office: Tego House, Chippenham Drive, Kingston, Milton Keynes, Bucks, MK10 0AF
Activities: Activities of head offices
Parent: Evonik Industries AG
Officers: Geneva Angela Stapleton, Secretary; Julio Diniz Pereira de Almeida [1968] Director/Accountant [Brazilian]; Matthias Josef Peter Hau [1963] Director [German]; Anh TU Luu [1979] Director/Solicitor

Evotec (UK) Limited
Incorporated: 19 December 1991 *Employees:* 291
Net Worth: £38,406,000 *Total Assets:* £45,296,000
Registered Office: 114 Innovation Drive, Milton Park, Milton, Abingdon, Oxon, OX14 4RZ
Activities: Research and experimental development on biotechnology
Parent: Evotec AG
Officers: Kamran Bashir, Secretary; Dr Werner Lanthaler [1968] Director [Austrian]; Dr Christophe Muller [1971] Director [French]; Ralph Enno Spillner [1970] Director [German]

Exaclair Limited
Incorporated: 18 October 1911 *Employees:* 78
Net Worth: £4,129,577 *Total Assets:* £9,891,042
Registered Office: Guildhall House, Old Medow Road, Hardwick Industrial Estate, Kings Lynn, Norfolk, PE30 4LW
Activities: Other manufacturing n.e.c.
Parent: Exaclair Holdings Ltd
Officers: Mark Anthony Daisley [1965] Managing Director; Charles Nusse [1972] Director/Chairman [French]; Francois Nusse [1935] Director [French]

Excel Parking Services Limited
Incorporated: 6 December 1993 *Employees:* 334
Net Worth: £8,553,332 *Total Assets:* £13,689,587
Registered Office: 2 Europa Court, Sheffield Business Park, Sheffield, S9 1XE
Activities: Other service activities incidental to land transportation, n.e.c.
Major Shareholder: Simon Robert Renshaw-Smith
Officers: Karen Gillott, Secretary; Alun Cockcroft [1967] Commercial Director; Simon Robert Renshaw-Smith [1966] Director

Exel Computer Systems (Holdings) PLC
Incorporated: 17 January 2014 *Employees:* 87
Net Worth: £8,374,721 *Total Assets:* £12,326,835
Registered Office: Bothe Hall Sawley, Long Eaton, Nottingham, NG10 3XL
Activities: Activities of other holding companies n.e.c.
Shareholder: John Merfyn Ellis
Officers: Dr John Merfyn Ellis, Secretary; Rue Dilhe [1969] Director; Dr John Merfyn Ellis [1941] Director

Exemplar Limited
Incorporated: 23 March 2005
Net Worth: £490,230 *Total Assets:* £43,955,944
Registered Office: Ferham House, Kimberworth Road, Rotherham, S Yorks, S61 1AJ
Activities: Residential nursing care facilities
Parent: Aaron Holdings Ltd
Officers: Elizabeth Jane Phipps, Secretary; Euan David Craig [1977] Director; David Pancott [1975] Director; Elizabeth Jane Phipps [1977] Director/Solicitor; James Robson [1978] Director/Chief Transformation Officer; David Sturrock [1970] Development Director; John Henry Whitehead [1964] Director/Chief Financial Officer

Exlabesa Extrusions (Doncaster) Limited
Incorporated: 20 February 2001 *Employees:* 52
Previous: Kaye Aluminium Limited
Net Worth: £12,280,915 *Total Assets:* £16,690,285
Registered Office: Ogden Road, Wheatley Hills, Doncaster, S Yorks, DN2 4SG
Activities: Manufacture of metal structures and parts of structures
Officers: Belen Arias Rubiales, Secretary; Felipe Quinta Marino [1979] Director [Spanish]; Fernando Quinta Marino [1970] Director [Spanish]

Exol Lubricants (Rotherham) Limited
Incorporated: 13 April 1993 *Employees:* 32
Net Worth: £5,343,673 *Total Assets:* £20,592,528
Registered Office: Northfield Road, Rotherham, S Yorks, S60 1RR
Activities: Other treatment of petroleum products (excluding petrochemicals manufacture)
Major Shareholder: Darren Barber Frogson
Officers: Steven David Everitt, Secretary; Scott William Donaldson [1970] Finance Director; Stephen Lang Dunn [1969] Sales Director; Steven David Everitt [1967] Managing Director; Darren Barber Frogson [1966] Director

Expatriate Advisory Services PLC
Incorporated: 13 February 1978 *Employees:* 14
Net Worth: £11,894,188 *Total Assets:* £12,659,995
Registered Office: 16 High Street, Kegworth, Derbys, DE74 2DA
Activities: Financial intermediation not elsewhere classified
Officers: Mark Betts [1973] Director/Financial Advisor; Hardev Singh [1962] Director/Businessman [Indian]

Experian (UK) Finance Limited
Incorporated: 7 March 2011
Net Worth: £5,108,015,616 *Total Assets:* £10,532,550,656
Registered Office: The Sir John Peace Building, Experian Way, NG2 Business Park, Nottingham, NG80 1ZZ
Activities: Other information service activities n.e.c.
Parent: Experian Investment Holdings Limited
Officers: Ronan Hanna, Secretary; Paul Alan Atkinson [1960] Director; Antony Jonathan Ward Barnes [1964] Director; Charles Bennett Brown [1966] Director [Irish]; Karen Julia Greenwood [1967] Director/Chartered Accountant; Daniel Tristan Lilley [1981] Director; Mark Edward Pepper [1963] Director; Lloyd Mark Pitchford [1971] Director

Experian (UK) Holdings 2006 Limited
Incorporated: 28 June 2006
Previous: Experian (UK) Holdings Limited
Net Worth: £2,056,951,680 *Total Assets:* £6,428,568,064
Registered Office: The Sir John Peace Building, Experian Way, NG2 Business Park, Nottingham, NG80 1ZZ
Activities: Financial intermediation not elsewhere classified
Parent: GUS 2000 Finance Limited
Officers: Ronan Hanna, Secretary; Paul Alan Atkinson [1960] Director/Chartered Accountant; Antony Jonathan Ward Barnes [1964] Director/Treasurer; Karen Julia Greenwood [1967] Director/Chartered Accountant; Daniel Tristan Lilley [1981] Director; Mark Edward Pepper [1963] Director

Experian Europe Unlimited
Incorporated: 7 May 2008
Net Worth: £594,088,000 *Total Assets:* £594,088,000
Registered Office: The Sir John Peace Building, Experian Way, NG2 Business Park, Nottingham, NG80 1ZZ
Activities: Activities auxiliary to financial intermediation n.e.c.
Parent: GUS Holdings Unlimited
Officers: Ronan Hanna, Secretary; Paul Alan Atkinson [1960] Director; Antony Jonathan Ward Barnes [1964] Director of Tax and Treasury; Karen Julia Greenwood [1967] Director/Chartered Accountant; Daniel Tristan Lilley [1981] Director; Mark Edward Pepper [1963] Director

Experian Finance 2012 Limited
Incorporated: 24 October 2012
Net Worth: £475,063,264 *Total Assets:* £475,067,072
Registered Office: The Sir John Peace Building, Experian Way, NG2 Business Park, Nottingham, NG80 1ZZ
Activities: Activities of financial services holding companies
Parent: GUS Holdings Unlimited
Officers: Ronan Peter Hanna, Secretary; Paul Alan Atkinson [1960] Director; Antony Jonathan Ward Barnes [1964] Director; Karen Julia Greenwood [1967] Director/Chartered Accountant; Daniel Tristan Lilley [1981] Director; Mark Edward Pepper [1963] Director

Experian Finance PLC
Incorporated: 17 March 1917 *Employees:* 204
Net Worth: £6,099,057,152 *Total Assets:* £25,103,120,384
Registered Office: The Sir John Peace Building, Experian Way, NG2 Business Park, Nottingham, NG80 1ZZ
Activities: Activities of financial services holding companies
Parent: Experian (UK) Finance Limited
Officers: Ronan Hanna, Secretary; Paul Alan Atkinson [1960] Director; Antony Jonathan Ward Barnes [1964] Director; Charles Bennett Brown [1966] Director/Company Secretary [Irish]; Brian Jude Cassin [1967] Director/Chief Financial Officer [Irish]; Durk Reinder de Vries [1970] Director/Group Treasurer [Dutch]; Mark Edward Pepper [1963] Director; Lloyd Mark Pitchford [1971] Director; Donald Austin Robert [1959] Director; Mark Wells [1963] Group HR Director

Experian Group Limited
Incorporated: 25 February 1999
Net Worth: £290,928,480 *Total Assets:* £390,820,352
Registered Office: The Sir John Peace Building, Experian Way, NG2 Business Park, Nottingham, NG80 1ZZ
Activities: Activities of other holding companies n.e.c.
Parent: Experian Holdings Limited
Officers: Ronan Hanna, Secretary; Julia Mary Cattanach [1971] Director [British/New Zealander]; Mark Edward Pepper [1963] Director

Experian Holdings (UK) Limited
Incorporated: 29 July 2014
Net Worth: £116,220,960 *Total Assets:* £10,856,400,896
Registered Office: The Sir John Peace Building, Experian Way, NG2 Business Park, Nottingham, NG80 1ZZ
Activities: Other information service activities n.e.c.
Parent: Experian PLC
Officers: Ronan Peter Hanna, Secretary; Paul Alan Atkinson [1960] Director; Antony Jonathan Ward Barnes [1964] Director; Karen Julia Greenwood [1967] Director/Chartered Accountant; Daniel Tristan Lilley [1981] Director; Mark Edward Pepper [1963] Director

Experian Holdings Limited
Incorporated: 10 December 1997
Net Worth: £4,743,191,552 *Total Assets:* £5,077,927,936
Registered Office: The Sir John Peace Building, Experian Way, NG2 Business Park, Nottingham, NG80 1ZZ
Activities: Activities of other holding companies n.e.c.
Parent: GUS Holdings Unlimited
Officers: Charles Bennett Brown, Secretary; Antony Jonathan Ward Barnes [1964] Director; Charles Langhorne Butterworth [1970] Director; Brian Jude Cassin [1967] Director/Chief Financial Officer [Irish]; Malcolm John Pape [1979] Director; Mark Edward Pepper [1963] Director; Lloyd Mark Pitchford [1971] Director; Donald Robert [1959] Director [American]; Jose Luiz Teixeira Rossi [1958] Director [Brazilian]; Kerry Lee Williams [1962] Director/Business Executive [American]

Experian International Unlimited
Incorporated: 2 May 1997
Net Worth: £264,841,680 *Total Assets:* £264,841,680
Registered Office: The Sir John Peace Building, Experian Way, NG2 Business Park, Nottingham, NG80 1ZZ
Activities: Other information technology service activities
Parent: Experian Limited
Officers: Ronan Hanna, Secretary; Paul Alan Atkinson [1960] Director; Antony Jonathan Ward Barnes [1964] Director of Tax and Treasury; Karen Julia Greenwood [1967] Director/Chartered Accountant; Daniel Tristan Lilley [1981] Director; Mark Edward Pepper [1963] Director

Experian Investment Holdings Limited
Incorporated: 22 September 2006
Net Worth: £9,514,292,224 *Total Assets:* £12,533,737,472
Registered Office: The Sir John Peace Building, Experian Way, NG2 Business Park, Nottingham, NG80 1ZZ
Activities: Financial intermediation not elsewhere classified
Parent: Experian Holdings (UK) Limited
Officers: Ronan Hanna, Secretary; Paul Alan Atkinson [1960] Director/Group Tax Manager; Antony Jonathan Ward Barnes [1964] Director/Treasurer; Karen Julia Greenwood [1967] Director/Chartered Accountant; Daniel Tristan Lilley [1981] Director; Mark Edward Pepper [1963] Director/Financial Controller; Lloyd Mark Pitchford [1971] Director

Experian Latam Holdings Unlimited
Incorporated: 25 March 2011
Net Worth: £420,489,152 *Total Assets:* £420,489,152
Registered Office: The Sir John Peace Building, Experian Way, NG2 Business Park, Nottingham, NG80 1ZZ
Activities: Activities of other holding companies n.e.c.
Parent: Experian Holdings Limited
Officers: Ronan Hanna, Secretary; Paul Alan Atkinson [1960] Director; Antony Jonathan Ward Barnes [1964] Director; Karen Julia Greenwood [1967] Director/Chartered Accountant; Daniel Tristan Lilley [1981] Director; Mark Edward Pepper [1963] Director

Experian Limited
Incorporated: 22 March 1960 *Employees:* 3,338
Net Worth: £185,000,000 *Total Assets:* £970,000,000
Registered Office: The Sir John Peace Building, Experian Way, NG2 Business Park, Nottingham, NG80 1ZZ
Activities: Information technology consultancy activities
Parent: Experian Group Limited
Officers: Ronan Hanna, Secretary; Charles Langhorne Butterworth [1970] Director; Julia Mary Cattanach [1971] Director [British/New Zealander]; Roger William John Davis [1956] Director; Stuart John Deane [1965] Director; Malcolm John Pape [1979] Director

Experian SURBS Investments Limited
Incorporated: 21 February 2006
Net Worth: £13,697,000 *Total Assets:* £26,466,000
Registered Office: The Sir John Peace Building, Experian Way, NG2 Business Park, Nottingham, NG80 1ZZ
Activities: Other information technology service activities
Parent: Experian Limited
Officers: Ronan Hanna, Secretary; Paul Alan Atkinson [1960] Director; Antony Jonathan Ward Barnes [1964] Director of Tax and Treasury; Karen Julia Greenwood [1967] Director/Chartered Accountant; Daniel Tristan Lilley [1981] Director; Mark Edward Pepper [1963] Director; Mark Wells [1963] Director

Experian Technology Limited
Incorporated: 20 April 2000
Net Worth: £156,066,848 *Total Assets:* £192,073,904
Registered Office: The Sir John Peace Building, Experian Way, NG2 Business Park, Nottingham, NG80 1ZZ
Activities: Other software publishing
Parent: GUS Holdings Unlimited
Officers: Ronan Hanna, Secretary; Paul Alan Atkinson [1960] Director; Antony Jonathan Ward Barnes [1964] Director of Treasury and Tax; Karen Julia Greenwood [1967] Director/Chartered Accountant; Mervyn Gerard Lally [1976] Director [Irish]; Daniel Tristan Lilley [1981] Director; Andrew John Mills [1966] Director/Solicitor; Mark Edward Pepper [1963] Director; Nadia Ridout-Jamieson [1968] Director

Experian US Holdings Unlimited
Incorporated: 26 July 1996
Net Worth: £3,338,498,048 *Total Assets:* £3,338,498,048
Registered Office: The Sir John Peace Building, Experian Way, NG2 Business Park, Nottingham, NG80 1ZZ
Activities: Activities of construction holding companies
Parent: Experian Holdings Limited
Officers: Ronan Hanna, Secretary; Paul Alan Atkinson [1960] Director; Antony Jonathan Ward Barnes [1964] Director of Tax and Treasury; Karen Julia Greenwood [1967] Director/Chartered Accountant; Daniel Tristan Lilley [1981] Director; Mark Edward Pepper [1963] Director

Expert Tooling & Automation Limited
Incorporated: 6 January 1998 *Employees:* 196
Net Worth: £4,522,463 *Total Assets:* £27,669,168
Registered Office: Technology Centre, 30 Sayer Drive, Coventry, Warwicks, CV5 9PF
Activities: Manufacture of other machine tools
Officers: Angelo Edwardo Luciano, Secretary/Director; Angelo Edwardo Luciano [1964] Director; Susan Gillian Luciano [1964] Director

The Extracare Charitable Trust
Incorporated: 11 December 1987 *Employees:* 1,592
Net Worth: £60,445,000 *Total Assets:* £278,743,008
Registered Office: 7 Harry Weston Road, Binley Business Park, Binley, Coventry, Warwicks, CV3 2SN
Activities: Renting and operating of Housing Association real estate
Officers: Matthew Challoner, Secretary; Rebekah Eden [1969] Director/Civil Servant; Michael Ruston Higgs [1953] Director; Ruth Jennifer Hyndman [1949] Director; Paul Warwick Jennings [1955] Director/NHS Chief Executive; Martin Neal Leppard [1957] Director; David Walmsley Martin [1954] Director/Trustee; Mary Julia Martin [1952] Director; David Stuart Mell [1947] Director/Retired; Judith Anne Mortimer Sykes [1957] Director & Trustee; Martin William Shreeve [1943] Director/Management Consultant

Eynsham Partnership Academy
Incorporated: 7 February 2012 *Employees:* 304
Net Worth: £15,614,763 *Total Assets:* £19,848,518
Registered Office: Bartholomew School, Witney Road, Eynsham, Witney, Oxon, OX29 4AP
Activities: General secondary education
Officers: Rosslyn Dawn Avery, Secretary; Frances Mary Bartlett [1970] Director/School Advisor, Oxford DBE; James Christian Bird [1970] Director/Lecturer and Teacher; Anne Mary Carter [1960] Director/Local Government Officer; Hilary Frances Emery [1955] Director/Education Consultant; Dr Jennifer Faulkner [1970] Director/Lecturer; Michael Adrian Foster [1961] Director/Senior Nurse Manager; Sarah Kerswell [1965] Director/Headteacher; Rain Newton Newton-Smith [1975] Director/Economist [British/Canadian]; Janet Susan Osborne [1947] Director/Retired; Peter John Reynolds [1972] Curriculum Director; Michael Ryan [1942] Director/Retired; Craig Thomas [1972] Director/Headteacher

Eyre & Elliston Holdings Limited
Incorporated: 29 March 1974 *Employees:* 456
Net Worth: £23,900,000 *Total Assets:* £36,812,000
Registered Office: 191 Chatsworth Road, Chesterfield, Derbys, S40 2BD
Activities: Other business support service activities n.e.c.
Officers: William Newton Canon [1968] Director; Jeremy Christopher Michael Eyre [1976] Regional Director; John Rees Eyre [1948] Director; Geoffrey Douglas Shawcross [1932] Director and Chairman

Eyre & Elliston Limited
Incorporated: 3 October 1940 *Employees:* 406
Net Worth: £19,622,646 *Total Assets:* £35,406,592
Registered Office: 191 Chatsworth Road, Chesterfield, Derbys, S40 2BD
Activities: Wholesale of other machinery and equipment
Parent: Eyre & Elliston Holdings Limited
Officers: Richard Patrick Cosgrove, Secretary; Tracy Canon [1967] Director; William Newton Canon [1968] Director; Richard Patrick Cosgrove [1957] Director; Jeremy Christopher Michael Eyre [1976] Director; John Rees Eyre [1948] Director; Nicholas John Garratt [1969] Director; Robert William White [1974] Director

F & G Holdings Limited
Incorporated: 13 May 2005 *Employees:* 144
Net Worth: £3,518,842 *Total Assets:* £30,153,660
Registered Office: Shawfield Road, Carlton Industrial Estate, Carlton, Barnsley, S Yorks, S71 3HS
Activities: Activities of other holding companies n.e.c.
Shareholders: Frank Woodhead; Glenn Andrew Stevenson
Officers: Cheryl Woodhead, Secretary; Glenn Andrew Stevenson [1969] Director; Frank Woodhead [1965] Director

F.H. Farms Limited
Incorporated: 3 November 1972
Net Worth: £19,376,848 *Total Assets:* £21,621,972
Registered Office: 64 St James's Street, Nottingham, NG1 6FJ
Activities: Growing of cereals (except rice), leguminous crops and oil seeds
Parent: Agrihold Limited
Officers: Jane Maude Foreman Hardy [1951] Director; Nicholas John Foreman Hardy [1948] Director; Thomas William Bailey Foreman Hardy [1983] Director

Fabrics & Yarns (Macclesfield) Ltd
Incorporated: 29 October 1987 *Employees:* 10
Net Worth: £7,968,866 *Total Assets:* £9,050,238
Registered Office: Charter Way, Hurdsfield Industrial Estate, Macclesfield, Cheshire, SK10 2NG
Activities: Wholesale of textiles
Shareholder: Kaldoun Hussamy
Officers: Margaret Irene Comer, Secretary; David Jonathan Crowther [1958] Director; Mohamed Khaled Nashar [1975] Director

Faccenda Farms Limited
Incorporated: 3 February 1982 *Employees:* 5
Net Worth: £36,504,040 *Total Assets:* £43,051,948
Registered Office: Willow Road, Brackley, Northants, NN13 7EX
Activities: Mixed farming
Parent: Faccenda Investments Limited
Officers: Susan Faccenda, Secretary; Helen Faccenda [1972] Director; Ian James Faccenda [1967] Director; Robin Michael Faccenda [1937] Director; Susan Faccenda [1941] Director; Alison Jane Gulliver [1969] Director

Faccenda Foods Limited
Incorporated: 3 February 1982 *Employees:* 3,277
Net Worth: £142,242,464 *Total Assets:* £192,480,624
Registered Office: Willow Road, Brackley, Northants, NN13 7EX
Activities: Processing and preserving of poultry meat
Parent: Avara Foods Limited
Officers: Andrew James Brodie [1971] People & Communications Director; Philip Murray Alexander Davidson [1970] Operations Director; Andrew Dawkins [1961] Director/Chief Executive Officer; Deborah Jane Foster [1967] Finance and I.S. Director; Christopher James Hall [1966] Director/Chief Commercial Officer; David Keeble [1959] Transformation Director; Philip Edmund Proud [1957] Technical Director; John William Reed [1956] Agricultural Director

Faccenda Investments Limited
Incorporated: 7 June 1984 *Employees:* 3,867
Net Worth: £293,123,840 *Total Assets:* £398,034,688
Registered Office: Willow Road, Brackley, Northants, NN13 7EX
Activities: Activities of head offices
Parent: Faccenda Holdings Limited
Officers: Susan Faccenda, Secretary; Benjamin Faccenda [1998] Director; Helen Faccenda [1972] Director; Ian James Faccenda [1967] Director; Robin Michael Faccenda [1937] Director; Susan Faccenda [1941] Director; Alison Jane Gulliver [1969] Director

Faccenda Property Limited
Incorporated: 23 November 2006 *Employees:* 11
Net Worth: £2,513,940 *Total Assets:* £39,708,724
Registered Office: Willow Road, Brackley, Northants, NN13 7EX
Activities: Development of building projects
Parent: Faccenda Investments Limited
Officers: Susan Faccenda, Secretary; Helen Faccenda [1972] Director; Ian James Faccenda [1967] Director; Robin Michael Faccenda [1937] Director; Susan Faccenda [1941] Director; Alison Jane Gulliver [1969] Director

Factory (M1) Limited
Incorporated: 19 October 2015
Net Worth: £1,390 *Total Assets:* £14,712,183
Registered Office: 5 The Quadrant, Coventry, Warwicks, CV1 2EL
Activities: Development of building projects
Shareholder: Salboy Limited
Officers: Chris Bowman [1980] Director; John Haynes [1969] Director; Naushad Islam [1970] Director; Simon Anthony Ismail [1976] Director

Faero UK Holding Limited
Incorporated: 29 September 2014
Net Worth: £201,002,000 *Total Assets:* £207,552,992
Registered Office: The Sherard Building, Edmund Halley Road, Oxford, OX4 4DQ
Activities: Activities of other holding companies n.e.c.
Parent: Ferrovial S.A
Officers: Ignacio Aitor Garcia Bilbao [1970] Director/Financier [Spanish]; Carlos Joaquin Enrech Frances [1969] Tax Director [Spanish/British]; Juan Gonzalez de Torres [1980] Director/Financial Controller [Spanish]

L.J. Fairburn and Son Limited
Incorporated: 3 September 1974 *Employees:* 212
Net Worth: £12,890,182 *Total Assets:* £43,326,836
Registered Office: Ivy House Farm Office, Farlesthorpe Road, Bilsby, Alford, Lincs, LN13 9PL
Activities: Raising of poultry
Major Shareholder: Stuart Henry Fairburn
Officers: Stuart Henry Fairburn, Secretary; Daniel James Fairburn [1977] Director; Sarah Louise Fairburn [1984] Brand Director; Stuart Henry Fairburn [1951] Director/Poultry Farmer; Caroline Mary Fairburn-Wright [1973] Director; Sarah Jayne Hall [1971] Director

Fairchild Fasteners (UK) Limited
Incorporated: 15 June 1973
Net Worth: £17,704,000 *Total Assets:* £17,828,000
Registered Office: 26a Atlas Way, Sheffield, S4 7QQ
Activities: Non-specialised wholesale trade
Parent: Alumax U.K. Limited
Officers: Petra Papinniemi-Ainger, Secretary; Dr Kay Louise Dowdall [1969] Director/Accountant; Lluis Maria Fargas Mas [1966] Director/Lawyer [Spanish]

Fairline Yachts Limited
Incorporated: 6 January 2016 *Employees:* 302
Net Worth Deficit: £8,344,000 *Total Assets:* £22,886,000
Registered Office: Nene Valley Business Park, Oundle, Peterborough, Cambs, PE8 4HN
Activities: Building of pleasure and sporting boats
Shareholders: Igor Glyanenko; Alexander Volov
Officers: Larisa Bondareva [1964] Finance Director; Karl Tristan Gilding [1959] Director; Igor Glyanenko [1972] Director [Russian]; Martyn John Hicks [1976] Director; Andrey Lomakin [1968] Director [Russian]; David Rolfe Tydeman [1955] Director; Alexander Volov [1972] Director [Russian]

Falcon Bidco Limited
Incorporated: 18 May 2017 *Employees:* 5
Net Worth Deficit: £2,225,588 *Total Assets:* £66,987,704
Registered Office: 20 Wollaton Street, Nottingham, NG1 5FW
Activities: Activities of other holding companies n.e.c.
Parent: Falcon Holdco Limited
Officers: Thomas Greer Boucher [1970] Director; Paul Eric Jonathon Burton [1981] Director; Nicholas David Lloyd Jordan [1977] Director/Investment Manager; Geoffrey Adrian Love [1971] Director; Hayden David Robinson [1970] Director

Falcon Capital Investments Limited
Incorporated: 3 August 2011
Net Worth Deficit: £35,348 *Total Assets:* £92,762,416
Registered Office: Ferham House, Kimberworth Road, Masbrough, Rotherham, S Yorks, S61 1AJ
Activities: Residential nursing care facilities
Parent: CX Bidco Ltd
Officers: Elizabeth Jane Phipps, Secretary; Euan David Craig [1977] Director; John Henry Whitehead [1964] Director/Chief Financial Officer

Falcon Equityco 2 Limited
Incorporated: 18 May 2017 *Employees:* 217
Net Worth Deficit: £7,211,581 *Total Assets:* £124,396,048
Registered Office: 20 Wollaton Street, Nottingham, NG1 5FW
Activities: Activities of other holding companies n.e.c.
Parent: Falcon Equityco 1 Limited
Officers: Thomas Greer Boucher [1970] Director; Paul Eric Jonathon Burton [1981] Director; Nicholas David Lloyd Jordan [1977] Director/Investment Manager; Geoffrey Adrian Love [1971] Director; Hayden David Robinson [1970] Director

Falcon of Hull & Lincolnshire Limited
Incorporated: 4 July 1989 *Employees:* 308
Net Worth: £10,277,000 *Total Assets:* £64,739,000
Registered Office: Othello House, Stratford Business & Technology Park, Banbury Road, Stratford upon Avon, Warwicks, CV37 7GY
Activities: Sale of new cars and light motor vehicles
Parent: Listers Group Ltd
Officers: Martin James Vessey, Secretary; Keith George Bradshaw [1943] Director; Timothy Charles Bradshaw [1973] Director; Geoffrey James Lister [1971] Director/Chief Executive; Terence Lister [1943] Managing Director

The Fallibroome Trust
Incorporated: 16 August 2010 *Employees:* 456
Net Worth: £26,513,300 *Total Assets:* £33,159,614
Registered Office: The Fallibroome Academy, Priory Lane, Macclesfield, Cheshire, SK10 4AF
Activities: Pre-primary education
Officers: Alison Elizabeth Nuttall, Secretary; John Brooks [1956] Director/Businessman; Peter Cresswell [1947] Director/Retired; Geoffrey Michael Gorton [1956] Director/Farmer; Richard David Hipperson [1947] Director; Vivienne Meredith [1968] Director/Human Resources; Andrew Gary Naylor [1967] Director/Finance; Peter William Rubery [1957] Director/Academy Principal; Paul Thornber [1964] Bid Director for Infrastructure Investment Company; Joanne Watkins [1970] Director/Transformation Manager

Fandstan Electric Limited
Incorporated: 9 January 1980
Net Worth: £16,367,334 *Total Assets:* £16,396,727
Registered Office: Howard House, Graycar Business Park, Barton Turn, Barton under Needwood, Burton on Trent, Staffs, DE13 8EN
Activities: Activities of head offices
Parent: Westinghouse Air Brake Technologies Corporation
Officers: Michael James Isaac, Secretary; Patrick David Dugan [1966] Director/Business Executive [American]; Michael James Isaac [1963] Director; David Michael Seitz [1965] Director/Business Executive [American]

Fannin (UK) Limited
Incorporated: 18 November 1991 *Employees:* 74
Net Worth Deficit: £1,081,000 *Total Assets:* £57,940,000
Registered Office: DCC Vital, Westminster Industrial Estate, Repton Road, Measham, Swadlincote, Derbys, DE12 7DT
Activities: Retail sale of medical and orthopaedic goods in specialised stores (not incl. hearing aids) n.e.c.
Parent: B.M.Browne (UK Holdings) Limited
Officers: Anthony O'Connor, Secretary; Conor Francis Costigan [1971] Director/Accountant [Irish]; Leslie Deacon [1963] Director/Chartered Accountant [Irish]; Harry Keenan [1959] Managing Director [Irish]; Redmond McEvoy [1964] Director [Irish]; Patrick Tracey [1958] Director [Irish]

Fantasy Island Operations Limited
Incorporated: 4 February 2016 *Employees:* 93
Net Worth Deficit: £1,990,000 *Total Assets:* £13,332,000
Registered Office: 57 Front Street, Arnold, Nottingham, NG5 7EA
Activities: Activities of amusement parks and theme parks
Parent: Mellors Group Fantasy Island Holdings Ltd
Officers: Brian Rowland Cobb [1951] Director; Edward James Mellors [1979] Director/Showman; James Frederick Mellors [1977] Director/Showman; James Henry Mellors [1945] Director/Amusement Caterer

Fanuc UK Limited
Incorporated: 18 February 1919 *Employees:* 109
Net Worth: £32,012,852 *Total Assets:* £54,208,864
Registered Office: Sapphire Way, Ansty Business Park, Coventry, Warwicks, CV7 9DR
Activities: Manufacture of other special-purpose machinery n.e.c.
Parent: Fanuc Europe Corporation SA
Officers: Alastair John Lumb, Secretary/Chartered Accountant; Thomas Michael Bouchier [1962] Director [Irish]

Farmers Fresh Limited
Incorporated: 30 September 1999 *Employees:* 56
Net Worth: £5,275,350 *Total Assets:* £11,723,251
Registered Office: The Abattoir, Rouncil Lane, Kenilworth, Warwicks, CV8 1NN
Activities: Wholesale of meat and meat products
Parent: Farmers First Limited
Officers: Wayne Anthony Lammas [1963] Director/Abattoir Manager; David Trevor Owen [1948] Director; Dean Powell [1981] Finance Director; Terence Ian Simpson [1962] Director/Livestock Dealer

Farmington Trust Limited (The)
Incorporated: 15 September 1964 *Employees:* 1
Net Worth: £22,793,240 *Total Assets:* £23,347,052
Registered Office: Harris Manchester College, Mansfield Road, Oxford, OX1 3TD
Activities: Activities of religious organisations
Officers: Peter Noel Houldsworth Gibbs [1948] Director/Farmer; Henry Merton Henderson [1952] Director/Stockbroker; Robert David Charles Henderson [1948] Director/Banker; Sir John Kemp-Welch [1936] Director; Imogen Larissa Hamilton Ormerod [1976] Director/Trainee Solicitor; Dr Catherine Mary Hamilton Wills [1950] Director; Peter John Hamilton Wills [1941] Director/Farmer; Richard Henry Wills [1974] Director/Farmer; Robert Ian Hamilton Wills [1948] Director/Farmer

Farmland Reserve UK Limited
Incorporated: 4 October 1977 *Employees:* 15
Net Worth: £101,516,000 *Total Assets:* £102,399,000
Registered Office: Manor Farm, Church End, Woodwalton, Huntingdon, Cambs, PE28 5YU
Activities: Buying and selling of own real estate
Parent: Farmland Reserve, Inc.
Officers: Brent J Garlic, Secretary; Benjamin Michael Conway [1980] Director/Financial Controller; Don M Sleight [1955] Director/Company President [American]

Farmstar Limited
Incorporated: 26 May 1988 *Employees:* 76
Net Worth: £3,963,482 *Total Assets:* £18,509,448
Registered Office: Grove Farm, Church Lane, Marr, Doncaster, S Yorks, DN5 7AU
Activities: Wholesale of agricultural machinery, equipment and supplies
Shareholders: Charles Rupert Brown; Daphne Rebecca Moxon
Officers: Laura Thomas, Secretary; Brian Maurice Bannister [1960] Branch Director; Charles Rupert Brown [1957] Director/Farmer; Shaun Nigel Husler [1961] Group Service Director; Richard Anthony Lister [1973] Branch Sales Director; Andrew Thomas Waddington [1971] Managing Director

Farnley Estates Limited
Incorporated: 26 September 1986 *Employees:* 2
Net Worth: £8,612,446 *Total Assets:* £10,438,859
Registered Office: Marland House, 13 Huddersfield Road, Barnsley, S Yorks, S70 2LW
Activities: Mixed farming
Shareholders: John David Sykes; Sprillers Limited
Officers: Timothy Paul Sykes, Secretary; Prudence Louise Sykes [1989] Director; Timothy Paul Sykes [1959] Director

Farol Holdings Limited
Incorporated: 2 November 1973 *Employees:* 201
Net Worth: £12,437,635 *Total Assets:* £45,167,792
Registered Office: Rycote Lane Farm, Milton Common, Oxon, OX9 2NZ
Activities: Activities of head offices
Shareholders: Benjamin Thomas Vellacott; Matthew Edward Vellacott
Officers: Benjamin Thomas Vellacott, Secretary; Benjamin Thomas Vellacott [1976] Director; Matthew Edward Vellacott [1972] Director

Farol Limited
Incorporated: 9 February 2001 *Employees:* 201
Net Worth: £11,341,997 *Total Assets:* £37,922,220
Registered Office: Rycote Lane Farm, Milton Common, Thame, Oxon, OX9 2NZ
Activities: Wholesale of agricultural machinery, equipment and supplies
Officers: Benjamin Thomas Vellacott, Secretary; Matthew Jack Balch [1981] Director/Management Accountant; Peter Arthur Bennett [1952] Director of Tyre; Guy Roger Strutte Champion [1984] Director/Sales Marketing; Martin Hayland Jones [1961] Finance Director; James Ronald Charles Moore [1979] Director of Golf & Grass Machinery; Benjamin Thomas Vellacott [1976] After Sales Director; Matthew Edward Vellacott [1972] Managing Director

William Farr Church of England Comprehensive School
Incorporated: 14 December 2010 *Employees:* 161
Net Worth: £9,056,391 *Total Assets:* £11,789,968
Registered Office: Lincoln Road, Welton, Lincoln, LN2 3JB
Activities: General secondary education
Officers: Sally Patricia Coulter, Secretary; Helen Brittain [1958] Director/Teacher; Marcus Wallace Flindall Brittain [1972] Director/Teacher; Edward Mark Garthwaite [1966] Director/Police Inspector; David Grant [1961] Director; Benjamin Simon Hazzledine [1964] Director; The Revd Canon Dr Jeffrey George Heskins [1955] Director/Clerk in Holy Orders; Simon Hinton [1966] Director/Site Manager; Paul David Merrell [1973] Director/Tax Adviser; Dr Abigail Louise Parrish [1982] Director/Senior Lecturer; Tim Smith [1966] Academy Director; Shaun Alan Stevenson [1964] Director/Facilities Manager; Andrew Clifford Stones [1963] Director/Headteacher; David William Subden [1964] Director; Reverend Adam Stewart Watson [1975] Director/Minister of Religion (C of E); Angela May White [1944] Director/Retired; Daryl Anthony Wicks-Randy [1976] Director/Royal Air Force

Fashion Fabric Transprinters Limited
Incorporated: 20 November 1975 *Employees:* 235
Net Worth: £8,709,493 *Total Assets:* £21,344,470
Registered Office: 333 Humberstone Lane, Thurmaston, Leicester, LE4 9JR
Activities: Manufacture of knitted and crocheted fabrics
Officers: Yusuf Ahmed, Secretary; Ibrahim Ahmed [1943] Director; Yunus Yusuf Ahmed [1967] Director; Yusuf Ahmed [1941] Director; Daud Ahmed Ismail [1960] Director; Hussein Ismail [1983] Director

Faurecia Automotive Seating UK Limited
Incorporated: 7 November 1990 *Employees:* 189
Net Worth: £39,206,588 *Total Assets:* £68,854,160
Registered Office: Cherwell III, Middleton Close, Banbury, Oxon, OX16 4RS
Activities: Manufacture of other parts and accessories for motor vehicles
Parent: Faurecia SA
Officers: Christophe Piponnier [1967] Director/Economist [French]

Fauxkin Limited
Incorporated: 24 February 1967 *Employees:* 2
Net Worth: £5,368,711 *Total Assets:* £10,619,485
Registered Office: 65 Mulehouse Road, Sheffield, S10 1TA
Activities: Other letting and operating of own or leased real estate
Shareholders: Hannah White; Dominic John Charles White
Officers: Hannah White, Secretary; Hannah White [1969] Director/Property Manager

FCC (E & M) Holdings Limited
Incorporated: 11 August 2016
Total Assets: £32,851,000
Registered Office: Ground Floor West, 900 Pavilion Drive, Northampton Business Park, Northampton, NN4 7RG
Activities: Other business support service activities n.e.c.
Parent: FCC Environment Developments Limited
Officers: Carol Jayne Nunn, Secretary; Carlos Afonso Ferrer [1972] Director [Spanish]; Vicente Federico Orts-Llopis [1962] Director [Spanish]; Paul Taylor [1959] Director

FCC Buckinghamshire Holdings Limited
Incorporated: 15 September 2011
Net Worth: £1,000,000 *Total Assets:* £16,000,000
Registered Office: Ground Floor West, 900 Pavilion Drive, Northampton, NN4 7RG
Activities: Other business support service activities n.e.c.
Parent: FCC PFI Holdings Limited
Officers: Carol Jayne Nunn, Secretary; Vicente Federico Orts-Llopis [1962] Director [Spanish]; Paul Taylor [1959] Director

FCC Buckinghamshire Limited
Incorporated: 16 September 2011 *Employees:* 4
Net Worth: £5,012,000 *Total Assets:* £198,706,000
Registered Office: Ground Floor West, 900 Pavilion Drive, Northampton, NN4 7RG
Activities: Other business support service activities n.e.c.
Parent: FCC Buckinghamnshire Holdings Limited
Officers: Carol Jayne Nunn, Secretary; Vicente Federico Orts-Llopis [1962] Director [Spanish]; Paul Taylor [1959] Director

FCC Environment (Berkshire) Limited
Incorporated: 29 December 2005 *Employees:* 59
Net Worth: £33,280,000 *Total Assets:* £37,188,000
Registered Office: Ground Floor West, 900 Pavilion Drive, Northampton Business Park, Northampton, NN4 7RG
Activities: Other business support service activities n.e.c.
Parent: FCC Environment (UK) Limited
Officers: Carol Jayne Nunn, Secretary; Vicente Federico Orts-Llopis [1962] Director [Spanish]; Paul Taylor [1959] Director/Chief Executive Officer

FCC Environment (Lincolnshire) Limited
Incorporated: 25 October 2010 *Employees:* 5
Net Worth: £12,777,000 *Total Assets:* £15,708,000
Registered Office: Ground Floor West, 900 Pavilion Drive, Northampton Business Park, Northampton, NN4 7RG
Activities: Other business support service activities n.e.c.
Parent: FCC Environment (UK) Limited
Officers: Carol Jayne Nunn, Secretary; Vicente Federico Orts-Llopis [1962] Director [Spanish]; Paul Taylor [1959] Director/Chief Executive Officer

FCC Environment (UK) Limited
Incorporated: 21 February 1994 *Employees:* 1,696
Net Worth: £100,805,000 *Total Assets:* £631,352,000
Registered Office: Ground Floor West, 900 Pavilion Drive, Northampton Business Park, Northampton, NN4 7RG
Activities: Other business support service activities n.e.c.
Parent: Azincourt Investment S.L. Unipersonal
Officers: Carol Jayne Nunn, Secretary; Pablo Colio Abril [1968] Director [Spanish]; Miguel Angel Martinez Parra [1972] Director/Chief Financial Officer [Spanish]; Tomas Nunez Vega [1954] Director/Industrial Engineer [Spanish]; Vicente Federico Orts-Llopis [1962] Finance Director [Spanish]; Paul Taylor [1959] Director/Chief Executive Officer

FCC Environment Developments Limited
Incorporated: 11 August 2016
Net Worth Deficit: £1,272,000 *Total Assets:* £35,530,000
Registered Office: Ground Floor West, 900 Pavilion Drive, Northampton Business Park, Northampton, NN4 7RG
Activities: Other business support service activities n.e.c.
Parent: Fomento de Construcciones y Contratas, S.A.
Officers: Carol Jayne Nunn, Secretary; Carlos Afonso Ferrer [1972] Director [Spanish]; Vicente Federico Orts-Llopis [1962] Director [Spanish]; Paul Taylor [1959] Director

FCC Environment Services (UK) Limited
Incorporated: 25 April 1989 *Employees:* 562
Net Worth: £29,113,000 *Total Assets:* £38,552,000
Registered Office: Ground Floor West, 900 Pavilion Drive, Northampton Business Park, Northampton, NN4 7RG
Activities: Other business support service activities n.e.c.
Parent: FCC Medio Ambiente, S.A
Officers: Carol Jayne Nunn, Secretary; Tomas Nunez [1954] Director [Spanish]; Vicente Federico Orts-Llopis [1962] Director/Chief Financial Officer [Spanish]; Agustin Serrano Minchan [1959] Director/Technical Civil Engineer [Spanish]; Paul Taylor [1959] Director/Chief Executive Officer

FCC PFI Holdings Limited
Incorporated: 19 September 2005
Net Worth Deficit: £29,888,000 *Total Assets:* £45,764,000
Registered Office: Ground Floor West, 900 Pavilion Drive, Northampton Business Park, Northampton, NN4 7RG
Activities: Other business support service activities n.e.c.
Parent: Fomento de Construcciones y Contratas, S.A.
Officers: Carol Jayne Nunn, Secretary; Jose Liebana Alcantarilla [1965] Director [Spanish]; Tomas Nunez Vega [1954] Director/Industrial Engineer [Spanish]; Vicente Federico Orts-Llopis [1962] Director/Chief Finance Officer [Spanish]; Paul Taylor [1959] Director/Chief Executive Officer

FCC Recycling (UK) Limited
Incorporated: 24 December 1991 *Employees:* 579
Net Worth: £46,199,000 *Total Assets:* £644,808,000
Registered Office: Ground Floor West, 900 Pavilion Drive, Northampton Business Park, Northampton, NN4 7RG
Activities: Other business support service activities n.e.c.
Parent: FCC Environment (UK) Limited
Officers: Carol Jayne Nunn, Secretary; Vicente Federico Orts-Llopis [1962] Finance Director [Spanish]; Agustin Serrano Minchan [1959] Director/Technical Civil Engineer [Spanish]; Paul Taylor [1959] Director/Chief Executive Officer

FCC Waste Services (UK) Limited
Incorporated: 8 September 1970 *Employees:* 474
Net Worth: £24,364,000 *Total Assets:* £139,642,000
Registered Office: Ground Floor West, 900 Pavilion Drive, Northampton Business Park, Northampton, NN4 7RG
Activities: Other business support service activities n.e.c.
Parent: Waste Recycling Group (UK) Limited
Officers: Carol Jayne Nunn, Secretary; Vicente Federico Orts-Llopis [1962] Director/Chief Financial Officer [Spanish]; Agustin Serrano Minchan [1959] Director/Technical Civil Engineer [Spanish]; Paul Taylor [1959] Director/Chief Executive Officer

FCC Wrexham PFI Limited
Incorporated: 23 September 2005 *Employees:* 2
Net Worth Deficit: £4,933,000 *Total Assets:* £23,328,000
Registered Office: Ground Floor West, 900 Pavilion Drive, Northampton Business Park, Northampton, NN4 7RG
Activities: Other business support service activities n.e.c.
Parent: FCC Wrexham PFI Holdings Limited
Officers: Carol Jayne Nunn, Secretary; Vicente Federico Orts-Llopis [1962] Director [Spanish]; Paul Taylor [1959] Director/Chief Executive Officer

FCL Organisation Ltd
Incorporated: 3 December 2013 *Employees:* 105
Net Worth: £166,978 *Total Assets:* £14,827,074
Registered Office: Unit B & C Longman Court, 8 Sketty Close, Brackmills, Northampton, NN4 7PL
Activities: Activities of head offices
Shareholder: Stacy Trewin
Officers: Michael Byrne [1988] Director; James Hudson [1983] Director; Philip Henry Charles Hudson [1962] Director; Adam Hughes [1979] Director; Darran Ashley Johnson [1965] Director; Martin Philip Jones [1959] Director; Deryck Norville [1952] Director; Stacy Norville [1979] Director; James Pearman [1978] Director

Federal Estates Limited
Incorporated: 10 June 1994 *Employees:* 1
Net Worth: £9,441,358 *Total Assets:* £34,291,040
Registered Office: Goosey Lodge, Wymington, Rushden, Northants, NN10 9LU
Activities: Production of electricity
Major Shareholder: David John Wykes
Officers: David John Wykes, Secretary; Elizabeth Joy Wykes [1959] Director/Secretary

FEL Group Limited
Incorporated: 27 March 1997 *Employees:* 61
Previous: Foster Environmental Limited
Net Worth: £2,222,011 *Total Assets:* £19,218,502
Registered Office: Normanby Gateway, Lysaghts Way, Normanby Road, Scunthorpe, N Lincs, DN15 9YG
Activities: Plumbing, heat and air-conditioning installation
Parent: Nickle Holdings Limited
Officers: Darren Crawford [1972] Director/Service Manager; Gerard Doolan [1962] Director/Chief Executive Officer; John Nigel Higginbottom [1975] Director/Chief Financial Officer; Michelle Wainwright [1973] Operations Director

Fellowes Ltd
Incorporated: 30 November 1965 *Employees:* 131
Net Worth: £16,476,719 *Total Assets:* £42,890,304
Registered Office: Unit 2 Ontario Drive, New Rossington, Doncaster, S Yorks, DN11 0BF
Activities: Wholesale of other office machinery and equipment
Parent: Fellowes Inc
Officers: Andrew John Toon, Secretary; Steven Leroy Carson [1963] Director/VP and General Counsel [American]; James Fellowes [1946] Director [American]; John Everett Fellowes [1978] Director [American]; Andrew John Toon [1958] Director of Finance

Fellside Estates Limited
Incorporated: 10 August 2004 *Employees:* 8
Net Worth: £6,264,772 *Total Assets:* £10,625,576
Registered Office: 3 Castlegate, Grantham, Lincs, NG31 6SF
Activities: Buying and selling of own real estate
Major Shareholder: Neil Arthur Mason
Officers: Paula Vince Mason, Secretary; Neil Arthur Mason [1949] Director; Rebecca Mason [1981] Director; Thomas Neil Mason [1978] Director; Laura Ellen Seago [1976] Director

Fengrain (Services) Limited
Incorporated: 1 August 1972
Net Worth: £582,561 *Total Assets:* £20,043,212
Registered Office: Fengrain, Hook Lane, Wimblington, March, Cambs, PE15 0QN
Activities: Wholesale of grain, unmanufactured tobacco, seeds and animal feeds
Parent: Fengrain Ltd
Officers: Kevin Peter Cooper, Secretary/Company Accountant; Kevin Peter Cooper [1962] Director/Accountant; Sarah Elizabeth Easton [1966] Director/Farmer & Chartered Accountant; Donald James McGowan [1963] Director/Farmer; Richard Means [1977] Director/Chartered Surveyor; Michael James Mottram [1958] Director/Farmer; Robert Hugh Munro [1966] Marketing Director; Nigel Raymond Russell [1952] Director/Farmer; Michael Harold Speed Sly [1968] Director/Farmer; John Robert Wall [1949] Director/Accountant; Harold Miles Warnick [1956] Director/Chartered Engineer; Paul Nigel Wilkinson [1945] Director

Fengrain Limited
Incorporated: 1 September 1972 *Employees:* 47
Net Worth: £1,648,013 *Total Assets:* £27,137,816
Registered Office: Hook Lane, Wimblington, Cambs, PE15 0QN
Activities: Agents selling agricultural raw materials, livestock, textile raw materials and semi-finished goods
Officers: Kevin Peter Cooper, Secretary/Company Accountant; Kevin Peter Cooper [1962] Director/Accountant; Sarah Elizabeth Easton [1966] Director/Farmer & Chartered Accountant; Donald James McGowan [1963] Director/Farmer; Richard Means [1977] Director/Chartered Surveyor; Michael James Mottram [1958] Director/Farmer; Robert Hugh Munro [1966] Marketing Director; Nigel Raymond Russell [1952] Director/Farmer; Michael Harold Speed Sly [1968] Director/Farmer; John Robert Wall [1949] Director/Accountant; Harold Miles Warnick [1956] Director/Chartered Engineer; Paul Nigel Wilkinson [1945] Director

Fernbrook Investments (UK) Limited
Incorporated: 21 November 2002 *Employees:* 3
Net Worth: £7,261,704 *Total Assets:* £16,388,005
Registered Office: 158 Washbrook Road, Rushden, Northants, NN10 6AA
Activities: Leasing of intellectual property and similar products, except copyright works
Major Shareholder: Patricia Cherry
Officers: Susan Jane Simpson, Secretary; Shaun Alan Cherry [1972] Director; Philip Freeman [1951] Director

The Fernwood Academy Trust
Incorporated: 8 April 2011 *Employees:* 144
Net Worth: £9,358,000 *Total Assets:* £11,611,000
Registered Office: The Fernwood School, Goodwood Road, Wollaton, Nottingham, NG8 2FT
Activities: General secondary education
Officers: Paul John Robinson, Secretary; Umbrin Afzal [1978] Director/Teacher; Dr Shamim Iqbal Ahmad [1945] Director/Retired Lecturer; Stephen Peter Battlemuch [1962] Director/Trade Union Official; Ruth Margaret Bennett [1974] Director/Optometrist; Kevin John Beswick [1955] Director/Retired; Alan Mark Blatchly [1963] Director/Retired; Paul Anthony Burke [1968] Director/Headteacher; Richard John Stacey Burnet [1969] Director; Stephen Deadman-Corsie [1972] Director/Teaching/Health Professional; Christopher Ian Gregory [1968] Director; Rosemarie Hudlin [1970] Director/Personal Assistant; Andrew David Hunt [1963] Director/Commercial Finance Consultant; Paul Anthony Irons [1947] Director/Retired; Assim Ishaque [1974] Director; Alasdair Neil Jackson [1964] Director/Teacher; Edwina Jane Jackson [1969] Director/Psychotherapist; Leighton John Mead [1974] Director/Teacher; Karen Shale [1968] Director/Business Analyst; Amanda Jane Smart Gosrani [1966] Director/Teacher Christian Ministry; Alex Young [1985] Director/Teacher

Fernwood Group Limited
Incorporated: 31 March 2000 *Employees:* 51
Net Worth: £31,201,752 *Total Assets:* £33,584,072
Registered Office: Fernwood House, Fernwood Drive, Watnall, Nottingham, NG16 1LA
Activities: Activities of head offices
Shareholders: Charles Edward Hallam Holehouse; Kate Elizabeth Cressey; Roger Paul Holehouse; Rosemary Holehouse
Officers: Andrew Michael Brailsford, Secretary; Katie Elizabeth Cressey [1973] Director; Charles Edward Hallam Holehouse [1971] Director; Roger Paul Holehouse [1941] Director

Ferraris Piston Service Limited
Incorporated: 26 January 2001 *Employees:* 1,013
Net Worth: £69,429,000 *Total Assets:* £117,607,000
Registered Office: Bridge House, 3 Timothy's Bridge Road, Stratford upon Avon, Warwicks, CV37 9NQ
Activities: Wholesale trade of motor vehicle parts and accessories
Parent: FPS Distribution Ltd
Officers: John Frederick Coombes, Secretary; Alistair Stuart Brown [1955] Director [New Zealander]; John Frederick Coombes [1965] Director; Jonathan Clive Eden [1958] Director; Jean-Jacques Mathieu Lafont [1959] Director [Belgian]; Terence Michael Wainwright [1947] Managing Director

The Ferrers School
Incorporated: 23 July 2013 *Employees:* 122
Net Worth: £11,461,724 *Total Assets:* £13,308,671
Registered Office: The Ferrers School, Queensway, Higham Ferrers, Rushden, Northants, NN10 8LF
Activities: General secondary education
Officers: Tracy Watson, Secretary; Vivienne Joy Barnard [1960] Director/Administrator; Andrew John Briggs [1959] Director/Business Manager; Tania Marie Clarke [1971] Director; Richard Jackson Downs [1990] Director/Teacher; Mark Anthony Foster [1974] Director/Manager; Deborah Michelle Haldane [1973] Director/Clerical Officer; Anthony Edward Hopkins [1982] Director/Police Officer; Melvyn George Kay [1944] Director/Chartered Engineer; Maria Jane King [1975] Director/Clerical Officer; James Adam Nicholson [1970] Director/Chartered Accountant; Angela Claire Smith [1972] Director/Headteacher

Ferrovial Services UK Ltd.
Incorporated: 23 November 2015
Net Worth: £439,240,928 *Total Assets:* £439,264,480
Registered Office: The Sherard Building, Edmund Halley Road, Oxford, OX4 4DQ
Activities: Activities of other holding companies n.e.c.
Parent: Ferrovial Services International SE
Officers: Alfredo Javier Garcia Lopez [1971] Director/Lawyer [Spanish]; Fernando Juan Gonzalez de Canales Moyano [1965] Director [Spanish]; Fidel Lopez Soria [1967] Director [Spanish]

Fesa (UK) Limited
Incorporated: 18 October 1984 *Employees:* 104
Net Worth: £7,753,724 *Total Assets:* £24,704,206
Registered Office: Claylake, Spalding, Lincs, PE12 6BL
Activities: Wholesale of fruit and vegetables
Shareholders: James Frank Rogers; Jose Ortiz-Carrillo; Anecoop
Officers: Hakim Elmouaffaq, Secretary; Hakim El Mouaffaq [1967] Deputy Managing Director [French]; Joan Mir Piqueras [1958] Director [Spanish]; Maria Del Carmen Morales Abad [1967] Director [Spanish]; Jose Ortiz Carrillo [1926] Director/Chairman [Spanish]; Jose Ortiz Pintor [1957] Director [Spanish]; James Frank Rogers [1947] Director/Vice-Chairman; Justin Szymborski [1970] Managing Director; Francisco Tello-Espinosa [1975] Commercial Director [Spanish]

Festino (Finance) Limited
Incorporated: 28 March 1973 *Employees:* 2
Net Worth: £8,832,411 *Total Assets:* £14,596,897
Registered Office: The Poplars, Bridge Street, Brigg, S Humbers, DN20 8NQ
Activities: Other business support service activities n.e.c.
Major Shareholder: David John Hebb
Officers: David John Hebb, Secretary; Christopher John Hebb [1984] Director; David John Hebb [1954] Director/Motor Engineer

Festo Limited
Incorporated: 2 February 1968 *Employees:* 133
Net Worth: £7,098,269 *Total Assets:* £13,029,294
Registered Office: Applied Automation Centre, Caswell Road, Brackmills Industrial Estate, Northampton, NN4 7PY
Activities: Manufacture of fluid power equipment
Parent: Festo AG
Officers: Andrea Dawn Brown, Secretary; Giampiero Bighiani [1965] Director/Head of Sales Management Region Europe [Italian]; Jorg Naumburger [1965] Director [German]; Eliza Hoi Sie Rawlings [1966] Director/General Manager

Fevore Limited
Incorporated: 12 January 1977 *Employees:* 190
Net Worth: £15,848,670 *Total Assets:* £78,099,904
Registered Office: Denbigh House, Denbigh Road, Bletchley, Milton Keynes, Bucks, MK1 1DF
Activities: Activities of head offices
Shareholders: George Roger Oscroft; Anne Lesley Oscroft
Officers: Clive Gear, Secretary; Andrew Francis Dick [1954] Finance Director; Richard John Foreman [1955] Director; Clive Gear [1950] Director/Financial Consultant; Anne Lesley Oscroft [1945] Director; George Roger Oscroft [1947] Director; Jennifer Vivienne Mary Oscroft [1981] Director/Barrister

FFP Packaging Solutions Limited
Incorporated: 2 December 1966 *Employees:* 137
Net Worth: £4,295,402 *Total Assets:* £9,359,004
Registered Office: 1-7 Tenter Road, Moulton Park Industrial Estate, Northampton, NN3 6PZ
Activities: Printing n.e.c.
Shareholder: Robin William Chudley
Officers: Robin William Chudley [1954] Managing Director; Helen Clements [1975] Commercial Director; David William Cooper [1979] Managing Director; Ian Hedges [1968] Director

Fibrefab Limited
Incorporated: 28 July 1992 *Employees:* 151
Net Worth: £9,983,882 *Total Assets:* £18,664,952
Registered Office: Davy Avenue, Knowlhill, Central Milton Keynes, Bucks, MK5 8HJ
Activities: Wholesale of electronic and telecommunications equipment and parts
Parent: Optronics Limited
Officers: Stephen Wesley Althoff [1961] Director/Telecommunications [American]; Paul Adrian Hussein [1969] Director of Marketing; Kheng Seng [1971] Director/General Manager [Singaporean]; Helene Simone Catherine Waterhouse [1967] Director of Operations [French]

Fichtner Consulting Engineers Limited
Incorporated: 25 April 1991 *Employees:* 119
Net Worth: £8,979,998 *Total Assets:* £13,900,118
Registered Office: Kingsgate, Wellington Road North, Stockport, Cheshire, SK4 1LW
Activities: Other engineering activities
Parent: Fichtner GmbH & Co KG
Officers: Elizabeth Edgley, Secretary; Duncan Stuart Abernethy [1977] Director/Business Development Manager; Phineas Mark Eddy [1960] Director/Consulting Engineer; Elizabeth Louise Edgley [1965] Finance Director; Nicholas Searle Gamble [1946] Director/Consulting Engineer; Robert John Hawcutt [1974] Director/Consultant Engineer; Tilman Herzig [1971] Director [German]; Stephen Mark Othen [1972] Director/Consultant; Dr Edmund John Weatherby [1959] Director/Consultant; Michael Wilfer [1956] Director IT Fichtner GmbH & Co KG [German]; Stuart Andrew Wilson [1970] Director/Senior Consultant [Australian]

Fidentia No 191 LLP
Incorporated: 20 September 2006
Net Worth Deficit: £94,569 *Total Assets:* £11,249,996
Registered Office: 3 Castlegate, Grantham, Lincs, NG31 6SF

Field Boxmore II Limited
Incorporated: 18 November 2004 *Employees:* 2
Net Worth: £79,822,016 *Total Assets:* £79,822,016
Registered Office: Millennium Way West, Phoenix Centre, Nottingham, NG8 6AW
Activities: Non-trading company
Parent: Field Boxmore Limited
Officers: Mark Richard Priestley, Secretary; Andrew Darrington [1977] Director/Assistant Financial Controller; Mark Richard Priestley [1964] Director/Accountant

Fields Property Limited
Incorporated: 26 November 2015 *Employees:* 1
Net Worth: £6,211,296 *Total Assets:* £9,144,925
Registered Office: 183 Trowell Road, Wollaton, Nottingham, NG8 2EN
Activities: Other letting and operating of own or leased real estate
Major Shareholder: Simon Fields
Officers: Simon Fields [1974] Director/Property Manager

Fifthgrange Limited
Incorporated: 14 September 2000 *Employees:* 2
Net Worth: £342,580,992 *Total Assets:* £342,580,992
Registered Office: Witan Gate House, 500-600 Witan Gate, Milton Keynes, Bucks, MK9 1BA
Activities: Activities of head offices
Parent: Homebase Group Limited
Officers: Simone Tudor, Secretary; Andrew Charles Coleman [1974] Director/General Manager, Finance & IT; Damian Garry McGloughlin [1969] Acting Managing Director

Filta Group Holdings PLC
Incorporated: 31 March 2016 *Employees:* 67
Net Worth: £4,057,155 *Total Assets:* £10,338,549
Registered Office: The Locks, Hillmorton, Rugby, Warwicks, CV21 4PP
Activities: Other business support service activities n.e.c.
Shareholders: Roy Charles Sayers; Dawn Caroline Sayers
Officers: Brian Joseph Hogan, Secretary; Victor Clewes [1957] Director; Brian Joseph Hogan [1964] Director/Chief Financial Officer [American]; Lloyd Martin [1954] Director; Jason Charles Sayers [1970] Director; Roy Charles Sayers [1942] Director; Jlubomir Urosevic [1952] Director; Graham Jeffrey Woolfman [1956] Director; Timothy John Worlledge [1952] Director/Corporate Finance Adviser

Filtrona Limited
Incorporated: 5 March 2013
Net Worth: £21,320,000 *Total Assets:* £263,876,000
Registered Office: Avebury House, 201-249 Avebury Boulevard, Milton Keynes, Bucks, MK9 1AU
Activities: Dormant company
Parent: Essentra Finance Limited
Officers: Patricia Kendall, Secretary; Jon Michael Green [1962] Director; Lili Liu [1972] Director

FIM Solar Generation I LLP
Incorporated: 29 January 2015
Net Worth: £7,338,973 *Total Assets:* £16,053,408
Registered Office: Glebe Barn, Great Barrington, Burford, Oxon, OX18 4US

Finance Yorkshire Limited
Incorporated: 13 November 2009 *Employees:* 5
Net Worth: £4,881,750 *Total Assets:* £50,730,180
Registered Office: Capitol Business Park, 1 Capitol Court, Dodworth, Barnsley, S Yorks, S75 3TZ
Activities: Activities of venture and development capital companies
Officers: Trevor Walters, Secretary; Jennifer Mary Adams [1963] Director/Investment Analyst; David John Bagley [1956] Director/Chartered Accountant; Alexander James McWhirter [1958] Business Development Director; Peter Edward Myers [1963] Director/Chief Executive; James Henry Newman [1950] Director/Chairman/Non-Executive Director; Challans Anthony Parsons [1949] Director/Retired Bank Manager

Financial & Legal Insurance Company Ltd
Incorporated: 17 March 1995 *Employees:* 25
Net Worth: £3,333,455 *Total Assets:* £28,799,274
Registered Office: 1 Lakeside, Cheadle Royal Business Park, Cheadle, Cheshire, SK8 3GW
Activities: Non-life insurance
Major Shareholder: Nicholas David Garner
Officers: Serena Angela Garner, Secretary; Susan Margaret Baldwin [1964] Director; Nicholas David Garner [1978] Director; Anthony Scott Hughes [1967] Director; Michael Francis Timmons [1956] Director

Financial Funding Limited
Incorporated: 28 July 2014
Net Worth: £3,644,448 *Total Assets:* £14,594,277
Registered Office: 13-15 Netherhall Road, Doncaster, S Yorks, DN1 2PH
Activities: Financial intermediation not elsewhere classified
Shareholders: Neville Christopher Brown; Diane Glenys Brown
Officers: Neville Christopher Brown [1959] Director

Finbrook Limited
Incorporated: 22 July 2009 *Employees:* 145
Net Worth: £6,312,877 *Total Assets:* £12,946,667
Registered Office: 28 Anglesey Drive, Poynton, Stockport, Cheshire, SK12 1BU
Activities: Residential care activities for the elderly and disabled
Officers: John Arthur Odell, Secretary; John Arthur Odell [1947] Director/Chartered Accountant; Kathryn Joan Odell [1946] Director/Care Home Proprietor

Fine Lady Bakeries Limited
Incorporated: 18 June 1948 *Employees:* 618
Net Worth: £5,543,082 *Total Assets:* £38,071,288
Registered Office: Bugbrooke Mills, Bugbrooke, Northampton, NN7 3QH
Activities: Manufacture of bread; manufacture of fresh pastry goods and cakes
Parent: Heygate & Sons Limited
Officers: Stephen Chia, Secretary; Stephen Cook [1962] Director/Engineer; Arthur Robert Heygate [1974] Director; Arthur Robert Heygate [1945] Director/Farmer and Flour Miller; Paul Michael Heygate [1943] Director/Miller and Farmer; David Anthony Robert Howlett [1966] Sales Director; Sarah Elizabeth Kreckler [1977] Director; Christopher Dathan Roberts [1969] Finance Director; Joseph Stanley Street [1947] Director/Bakery Manager

Fine Tubes Limited
Incorporated: 16 June 1943 *Employees:* 235
Net Worth: £21,387,000 *Total Assets:* £38,221,000
Registered Office: 2 New Star Road, Leicester, LE4 9JQ
Activities: Manufacture of tubes, pipes, hollow profiles and related fittings, of steel
Parent: Tubes Holdco Limited
Officers: Joy Atwell, Secretary; David Alan Cawse [1964] Operations Director; Emanuela Speranza [1968] Director [Italian]

Finham Park Multi-Academy Trust
Incorporated: 11 July 2011 *Employees:* 422
Previous: Finham Park School
Net Worth: £43,440,000 *Total Assets:* £51,751,000
Registered Office: Finham Park Multi-Academy Trust, Green Lane, Coventry, Warwicks, CV3 6EA
Activities: General secondary education
Officers: Amanda Therese Gilmore, Secretary; Fanny Anderson [1971] Director/Finance Manager; Mark William Bailie [1968] Director/Headteacher; John Anthony Blundell [1951] Director/Property Manager; Peter Burns [1946] Director/Retired; Pauline Elizabeth Parkes [1958] Director/Retired Teacher

J.F. Finnegan Limited
Incorporated: 10 February 1945 *Employees:* 51
Net Worth: £24,497,756 *Total Assets:* £36,542,448
Registered Office: Wards Exchange, 199 Ecclesall Road, Sheffield, S11 8HW
Activities: Development of building projects
Parent: Amon Limited
Officers: John Patrick Diggins [1967] Finance Director; Nicholas John Gillott [1972] Director; Gary Alexander Smith [1964] Director

Fir Vale School Academy Trust
Incorporated: 31 May 2012 *Employees:* 135
Net Worth: £13,790,716 *Total Assets:* £15,818,579
Registered Office: Fir Vale School, Owler Lane, Sheffield, S4 8GB
Activities: General secondary education
Officers: Darryl Smedley, Secretary; Enos Osoo Akunda [1968] Director; Shaista Asad [1977] Director; Nazma Begum [1956] Director/Physiotherapist; John Richard Edwards [1963] Director; Nicola Fear [1970] Director/Attendance Manager; Paul Highfield [1952] Director/Teacher; Tania Mary Hussey-Yeo [1959] Director/School Governor; Usma Saeed [1976] Director/Shop Owner; Rachel Smith [1969] Director/Headteacher/Accounting Officer

Fired Earth Limited
Incorporated: 22 June 1983 *Employees:* 296
Net Worth Deficit: £5,128,233 *Total Assets:* £9,217,839
Registered Office: c/o Aga Rangemaster, Meadow Lane, Long Eaton, Nottingham, NG10 2GD
Activities: Retail sale of carpets, rugs, wall and floor coverings in specialised stores
Parent: Aga Rangemaster Group Limited
Officers: Timothy John FitzGenerald [1969] Director/Vice President and CFO [American]; Martin McKay Lindsay [1964] Director/Corporate Treasurer [American]; Agustin Zufia [1967] Director/Group Controller [Spanish]

First Carton Group Ltd
Incorporated: 22 December 1997 *Employees:* 2
Net Worth: £43,580,928 *Total Assets:* £43,580,928
Registered Office: Millennium Way West, Phoenix Centre, Nottingham, NG8 6AW
Activities: Activities of other holding companies n.e.c.
Parent: Multi Packaging Solutions UK Limited
Officers: Mark Richard Priestley, Secretary; Andrew Darrington [1977] Director/Financial Controller; Mark Richard Priestley [1964] Director/Accountant

First for Wellbeing CIC
Incorporated: 4 November 2015 *Employees:* 300
Total Assets: £13,992,000
Registered Office: One Angel Square, Angel Street, Northampton, NN1 1ED
Activities: Regulation of health care, education, cultural and other social services, not incl. social security
Officers: Allis Miah Karim, Secretary; Lucy Ann Dadge [1964] NHS Director; Anna Catherine Earnshaw [1968] Managing Director (NASS); Sandra Jane Mellors [1961] Director/Physiotherapist; Dr. Stephen Martin O'Brien [1959] Director/Dean of Faculty of Health and Society

First Line Limited
Incorporated: 13 April 2000 *Employees:* 148
Net Worth: £9,759,239 *Total Assets:* £30,266,716
Registered Office: Chalker Way, Banbury, Oxon, OX16 4XD
Activities: Wholesale trade of motor vehicle parts and accessories
Shareholders: Peter Gordon Joyner; John Roger Madden
Officers: Keith Schofield, Secretary; Daniel Charles Joyner [1974] Managing Director; Joanne Mary Joyner [1977] Director; John Roger Madden [1949] Director/Vice Chairman; Keith Schofield [1960] Finance Director

First National Housing Trust Limited
Incorporated: 26 May 1933 *Employees:* 4
Net Worth: £15,068,055 *Total Assets:* £15,238,195
Registered Office: Banner Cross Hall, Ecclesall Road South, Sheffield, S11 9PD
Activities: Management of real estate on a fee or contract basis
Parent: Henry Boot PLC
Officers: Amy Louise Oakley, Secretary; Edward James Hutchinson [1977] Director/Chartered Surveyor; Darren Louis Littlewood [1975] Finance Director; John Trevor Sutcliffe [1959] Finance Director

First Response Finance Limited
Incorporated: 8 May 1998 *Employees:* 270
Net Worth: £35,629,184 *Total Assets:* £144,949,504
Registered Office: 5 Regan Way, Chetwynd Business Park, Chilwell, Nottingham, NG9 6RZ
Activities: Credit granting by non-deposit taking finance houses and other specialist consumer credit grantors
Parent: Itochu Europe PLC
Officers: John Stewart Fellows, Secretary/Head of Training & Compliance; Jason Kevin Britton [1971] Finance Director; Donald James Brough [1962] Director/Business Manager; Micky Ishida [1968] Director/Business Manager [Japanese]; Tetsuji Kawakami [1964] Director/Business Manager [Japanese]; Tsunehiko Murai [1967] Director/Business Manager [Japanese]; Jonathan Pollard [1972] Business Director; Caerie Sanders [1979] Director/Business Manager [South African/British]

First South Yorkshire Limited
Incorporated: 3 January 1989 *Employees:* 1,369
Net Worth Deficit: £20,098,000 *Total Assets:* £50,799,000
Registered Office: Olive Grove, Sheffield, S2 3GA
Activities: Other urban, suburban or metropolitan passenger land transport (not underground, metro or similar)
Parent: Mainline Partnership Limited
Officers: Michael Hampson, Secretary; David Brian Alexander [1965] Regional Managing Director; Garry Birmingham [1974] Director; John Christopher Gent [1968] Engineering Director; Mohammed Imran [1957] Employee Director; Allan David Riggall [1983] Director; Andrew John Simpson [1964] Operations Director

First Utility Limited
Incorporated: 11 March 2004 *Employees:* 1,070
Net Worth: £38,972,000 *Total Assets:* £234,584,992
Registered Office: Columbus House, Westwood Business Park, Coventry, Warwicks, CV4 8HS
Activities: Trade of electricity
Parent: Impello Limited
Officers: Malcolm Victor Henchley, Secretary; Susannah Dallison Collier [1972] Director/Lawyer [Trinidadian]; Colin Andrew Crooks [1966] Director; Brian Charles Davis [1966] Director/Vice President; Louise Mary Mooney [1976] Director/Finance Executive

Firstan Holdings Limited
Incorporated: 28 October 1999 *Employees:* 152
Net Worth: £7,874,565 *Total Assets:* £15,523,632
Registered Office: The Packaging Centre, Cardinal Way, Godmanchester, Huntingdon, Cambs, PE29 2XN
Activities: Manufacture of other paper and paperboard containers
Major Shareholder: Andrew Thomas Hartwig
Officers: Dawn Mutter, Secretary; Andrew Thomas Hartwig [1954] Director; Lynn Hartwig [1964] Director; Paul Terence Hartwig [1965] Production Director; Sally Hartwig [1962] Director

Firstan Limited
Incorporated: 27 April 1976 *Employees:* 152
Net Worth: £14,444,992 *Total Assets:* £22,094,060
Registered Office: The Packaging Centre, Cardinal Way, Godmanchester, Huntingdon, Cambs, PE29 2XN
Activities: Manufacture of paper and paperboard
Parent: Firstan Holding Ltd
Officers: Dawn Mutter, Secretary; Andrew Thomas Hartwig [1954] Director; Paul Terence Hartwig [1965] Director; Sally Hartwig [1962] Director; Simon Lacey [1969] Commercial Director; Dawn Mutter [1965] Finance Director

Firth Rixson Forgings Limited
Incorporated: 10 September 1919 *Employees:* 461
Net Worth: £46,660,000 *Total Assets:* £100,564,000
Registered Office: 26a Atlas Way, Sheffield, S4 7QQ
Activities: Forging, pressing, stamping and roll-forming of metal; powder metallurgy
Parent: Firth Rixson Limited
Officers: Petra Papinniemi-Ainger, Secretary; Lluis Maria Fargas Mas [1966] Director [Swiss]; Timothy Lloyd Gibbons [1963] Director/Plant Manager; Benjamin Steven Timothy McIvor [1974] Director of Operations; Boyd Mueller [1959] Director/Vice President Technology and Alloy [American]; Tamas Papp [1986] Director/Plant Manager [Hungarian]

Firth Rixson Limited
Incorporated: 24 May 1928 *Employees:* 6
Net Worth: £616,537,984 *Total Assets:* £739,376,000
Registered Office: 26a Atlas Way, Sheffield, S4 7QQ
Activities: Activities of head offices
Parent: Forgings International Limited
Officers: Petra Papinniemi-Ainger, Secretary; Dr Kay Louise Dowdall [1969] Director/Chartered Accountant; Lluis Maria Fargas Mas [1966] Director [Swiss]

Firth Rixson Metals Limited
Incorporated: 19 December 1914 *Employees:* 273
Net Worth: £59,835,000 *Total Assets:* £95,092,000
Registered Office: 26a Atlas Way, Sheffield, S4 7QQ
Activities: Forging, pressing, stamping and roll-forming of metal; powder metallurgy
Parent: Firth Rixson Limited
Officers: Petra Papinniemi-Ainger, Secretary; Lluis Maria Fargas Mas [1966] Director [Swiss]; Benjamin Steven Timothy McIvor [1974] Director; Boyd Mueller [1959] Director/Vice President of Technology & Alloy [American]; Graham Francis Read [1984] Director/Plant Manager; Nicholas Charles Smith [1957] Director; Andrew Michael Torn [1970] Director/Plant Manager; Stephen Matthew Woods [1972] Director/Chartered Accountant

Fischer Future Heat UK Limited
Incorporated: 7 December 2006 *Employees:* 96
Net Worth: £4,028,820 *Total Assets:* £14,605,070
Registered Office: The Waterfront, 19-20 North Mills, Frog Island, Leicester, LE3 5DH
Activities: Other retail sale not in stores, stalls or markets
Parent: Bastian PLC
Officers: Maria Angeles Bastian, Secretary; Keith Cornelius Bastian [1965] Director; Maria Angeles Bastian [1965] Director [Spanish]

George Fischer Sales Limited
Incorporated: 3 March 1933 *Employees:* 87
Net Worth: £5,758,000 *Total Assets:* £19,767,000
Registered Office: Paradise Way, Coventry, Warwicks, CV2 2ST
Activities: Wholesale of hardware, plumbing and heating equipment and supplies
Officers: Narinder Kaur Bains, Secretary; Mads Joergensen [1969] Director/Chief Financial Officer [Danish]; Mark Darren Loader [1969] Sales Director - South East/South West; Sarah Louise Matthews [1975] Commercial Director; David Michael Outhwaite [1966] Finance Director; Benjamin James Pinder [1979] Sales Director - Midlands/North/Scotland/Ireland; Ian Ross [1958] IT Director; Richard Trevaskis [1960] Director; Dominique Andre Van Ackere [1962] Director/Senior Vice President-Head of Business Unit Europe [Belgian]

Fisher & Paykel Appliances Limited
Incorporated: 28 March 2000 *Employees:* 49
Net Worth: £55,439,000 *Total Assets:* £60,322,000
Registered Office: Turing House, Ortensia Drive, Milton Keynes, Bucks, MK17 8LX
Activities: Wholesale of radio, television goods & electrical household appliances (other than records, tapes, CDs)
Officers: Alan Kenneth Frost, Secretary/Chartered Accountant; Stuart Broadhurst [1966] Director/Chief Executive Officer [New Zealander]; Graham Raymond Judge [1951] Director/Accountant [New Zealander]; Laurence Andrew Mawhinney [1969] Director/VP Sales and Customer Experience [New Zealander]

Fisher German LLP
Incorporated: 31 January 2006 *Employees:* 437
Net Worth: £8,163,659 *Total Assets:* £12,736,930
Registered Office: The Head Office, Ivanhoe Office Park, Ivanhoe Park Way, Ashby-De-La-Zouch, Leics, LE65 2AB
Officers: Andrew John Bridge [1972] Member; Andrew Robert Jackson [1959] Member; Timothy Edward Shuldham [1958] Member; Matthew Edward Allen [1981] LLP Member; Richard George Franklin Baker [1973] LLP Member; Daniel Howard Ballard [1975] LLP Member; Matthew John Russell Barker [1973] LLP Member; Duncan Peter Bedhall [1964] LLP Member; Richard Christopher Benson [1963] LLP Member; Richard William Broome [1983] LLP Member; Paul Stephen Brown [1968] LLP Member; Anthony Nimrod Champion [1953] LLP Member; Robert Philip Nimrod Champion [1981] LLP Member; Edward Rawson Clark [1964] LLP Member; Jeremy John Clayson [1953] LLP Member; Jason Peter Clines [1966] LLP Member; Rupert William Neild Collis [1971] LLP Member; Kay Louise Davies [1973] LLP Member; Alasdair John Dunne [1973] LLP Member; Darren Martyn Edwards [1984] LLP Member; Robin Nicholas James Eyles [1969] LLP Member; Stuart David Flint [1969] LLP Member; William Gagie [1969] LLP Member; Christopher Yan Hardy Gittins [1971] LLP Member; James Goodson [1971] LLP Member; Michael John Harris [1969] LLP Member; Guy Langley Hemus [1985] LLP Member; Christopher George Stephen Hicks [1973] LLP Member; Matthew James Hodgetts [1977] LLP Member; Neil Ewan Hogbin [1977] LLP Member; Robert James Hurst [1955] LLP Member; John Ikin [1977] LLP Member; Sebastian Kingsley [1980] LLP Member; Giles Anthony Bramham Lister [1966] LLP Member; Benjamin Andrew Marshalsay [1978] LLP Member; Hugh John Farquhar Maxfield [1977] LLP Member; Anthony Nigel Mayell [1955] LLP Member; Julian Atherley Mellis [1958] LLP Member; David Henry Merton [1967] LLP Member; Charles Philip Meynell [1956] LLP Member; Nigel Peter Nattress [1968] LLP Member; John Reginald David Palmer [1957] LLP Member; Holly Parry [1986] LLP Member; Gillian Clare Phillipson [1966] LLP Member; Michael William Price [1970] LLP Member; Rebecca Joan Ruck Keene [1982] LLP Member; John Robert Russell [1953] LLP Member; Stephen Cornelius Rutledge [1975] LLP Member; Christian John Sanders [1964] LLP Member; Richard Edward Thomas Sanders [1961] LLP Member; Richard John Scriven [1972] LLP Member; George William Simpson [1976] LLP Member; Liberty Alexandra Stones [1983] LLP Member; Richard George Tomlinson [1971] LLP Member; Matthew James Trewartha [1979] LLP Member; Adrian Nicholas Webb [1964] LLP Member

Fisher Scientific U.K., Limited
Incorporated: 24 December 1993
Net Worth: £91,193,000 *Total Assets:* £139,840,000
Registered Office: Bishop Meadow Road, Loughborough, Leics, LE11 5RG
Activities: Other business support service activities n.e.c.
Parent: Fisher Scientific Holding U.K., Limited
Officers: Rhona Gregg, Secretary; Euan Daney Ross Cameron [1976] Director; Lucie Mary Katja Grant [1976] Director/Solicitor; Monica Del Carmen Manotas Urueta [1973] Director/President RDS Europe [American]; Thomas Arthur Nicholson [1972] Director; David John Norman [1960] Director/Chartered Accountant; Anthony Hugh Smith [1962] Director/Vice President, Tax and Treasury [American]

FKB Limited
Incorporated: 4 September 2007 *Employees:* 1
Net Worth Deficit: £1,068,047 *Total Assets:* £11,003,031
Registered Office: 14 London Road, Newark, Notts, NG24 1TW
Activities: Support activities for crop production
Major Shareholder: Robert Helge Beck
Officers: Tove Beck, Secretary; Robert Helge Beck [1977] Director/Advisor & Economist [Danish]

Flair Flooring Supplies Limited
Incorporated: 10 September 1982 *Employees:* 99
Net Worth: £4,005,357 *Total Assets:* £11,517,975
Registered Office: Etherow Works, Etherow Industrial Estate, Woolley Bridge Road, Hadfield, Glossop, Derbys, SK13 2NS
Activities: Manufacture of woven or tufted carpets and rugs
Officers: Helen Shah, Secretary; Tina Ruth Carswell [1972] Director/Accountant; Dineshkumar Premchand Shah [1950] Director; Neel Shah [1982] Director; Rekha Shah [1952] Director

Flamepro Limited
Incorporated: 14 December 1998 *Employees:* 47
Net Worth: £10,891,353 *Total Assets:* £28,763,098
Registered Office: Corus House, 1 Auckland Park, Milton Keynes, Bucks, MK1 1BU
Activities: Hotels and similar accommodation
Parent: Corus Hotels Limited
Officers: Khurram Mohmand, Secretary; Andrew Khoo [1972] Director [Australian]; Yet King Loy [1946] Director [Canadian]; Khurram Mohmand [1972] Director/Accountant

The Flannels Group Limited
Incorporated: 17 November 1988 *Employees:* 224
Net Worth: £5,318,000 *Total Assets:* £16,827,000
Registered Office: Unit A, Brook Park East, Shirebrook, Derbys, NG20 8RY
Activities: Retail sale of clothing in specialised stores
Parent: Sportsdirect.Com Retail Limited
Officers: Cameron John Olsen, Secretary; Adedotun Ademola Adegoke [1973] Director/Senior Buyer; Rachel Isabel Lilian Stockton [1970] Director/Head of Customs and VAT

The Fleet Auction Group Limited
Incorporated: 15 August 2000 *Employees:* 78
Net Worth: £9,507,070 *Total Assets:* £18,128,872
Registered Office: The Fleet Auction Group Limited, Brindley Road, Stephenson Industrial Estate, Coalville, Leics, LE67 3HG
Activities: Sale of used cars and light motor vehicles
Officers: Faisal Al-Sabah [1984] Director [Kuwaiti]; Ali Mubarak Aldabbous [1958] Director [Kuwaiti]; Khalid Mahmoud Hamad Almahdi [1979] Director [Kuwaiti]; Martin Stuart Betts [1961] Director; Samuel Kevin Leigh Clarke [1967] Director; Michael Gray [1959] Director; Guy Christopher Pearce [1962] Sales Director; Andrew William John Timmis [1964] Director; Andrew Richard Walker [1966] Director; Charles Peter Wright [1970] Director

C.W.Fletcher & Sons,Limited
Incorporated: 11 May 1908 *Employees:* 190
Net Worth: £9,283,804 *Total Assets:* £12,868,921
Registered Office: Sterling Works, Mansfield Road, Wales Bar, Kiveton Park, Sheffield, S26 5PQ
Activities: Other manufacturing n.e.c.
Officers: Rebecca Willis, Secretary; David John Fletcher [1960] Director; Stephen Kirk [1964] Director/Engineer; Rebecca Willis [1976] Director/Chartered Accountant

Flex-Seal Couplings Limited
Incorporated: 11 December 1989 *Employees:* 94
Net Worth: £6,175,243 *Total Assets:* £11,445,713
Registered Office: Endeavour Works, Newlands Way, Valley Park, Wombwell, Barnsley, S Yorks, S73 0UW
Activities: Other manufacturing n.e.c.
Parent: Fernco Inc
Officers: Andrew John Williams, Company Secretary/Accountant; Christopher Cooper [1965] Director [American]; Scott Alexander McMurray [1967] Sales Director; Lee Andrew Pashley [1971] Director/Sales; Andrew John Williams [1961] Director/Accountant

Flint Holdings Limited
Incorporated: 1 July 1998 *Employees:* 121
Net Worth: £8,822,658 *Total Assets:* £10,852,433
Registered Office: Colliers House, Dunsil Road, Moorgreen Industrial Estate, Moorgreen, Newthorpe, Nottingham, NG16 3TN
Activities: Activities of head offices
Shareholders: Elizabeth Dawn Flint; Mark John Flint
Officers: Elizabeth Dawn Flint, Secretary/Admin/Accounts; Elizabeth Dawn Flint [1964] Director/Admin/Accounts; Mark John Flint [1962] Director/Engineer

Flo-Mech Holdings Limited
Incorporated: 29 September 2014 *Employees:* 44
Net Worth: £5,375,959 *Total Assets:* £18,153,820
Registered Office: 1 The Forum, Minerva Business Park, Lynch Wood, Peterborough, Cambs, PE2 6FT
Activities: Other business support service activities n.e.c.
Major Shareholder: Alan John Elderkin
Officers: Alan John Elderkin [1945] Director/Engineer; Patricia Mary Elderkin [1948] Director

Flo-Mech. Limited
Incorporated: 11 November 1974 *Employees:* 44
Net Worth: £5,833,334 *Total Assets:* £16,568,132
Registered Office: Flo-Mech House, Paxton Road, Orton Goldhay, Peterborough, Cambs, PE2 5YA
Activities: Manufacture of machinery for food, beverage and tobacco processing
Parent: Flo-Mech Holdings Ltd
Officers: Colin William Hill, Secretary; Robin Alec Cattermole [1976] Director; Simon Andrew Richard Dealtrey [1972] Director; Alan John Elderkin [1945] Director; Andrew James Elderkin [1978] Director; Patricia Mary Elderkin [1948] Director; Stuart John Elderkin [1972] Director; Christopher Graham Ellis [1968] Director/Systems and Controls Specialist; Colin William Hill [1957] Director

Flocklynn Limited
Incorporated: 4 June 1991 *Employees:* 166
Net Worth: £12,408,475 *Total Assets:* £22,303,452
Registered Office: Marley Road, St Ives, Huntingdon, Cambs, PE27 3EX
Activities: Activities of head offices
Officers: Michael Andrew Smith, Secretary; Michael Andrew Smith [1962] Director; Stephen James Smith [1960] Director

Flogas Britain Limited
Incorporated: 5 November 1970 *Employees:* 955
Net Worth: £53,339,000 *Total Assets:* £219,307,008
Registered Office: 81 Rayns Way, Syston, Leicester, LE7 1PF
Activities: Wholesale of petroleum and petroleum products
Shareholders: Flogas Limited; DCC Energy UK Limited
Officers: Oliver Joseph Hall, Secretary; James Henry Cubbon [1960] Managing Director; William Francis Gannon [1957] Sales and Marketing Director; Stephen Valentine Johnston [1970] Director [Irish]; Alan Charles Robinson Kirk [1968] Operations Director; Mark Edward Plyte [1961] Finance Director; James William Rudman [1964] Technical Director

Florensis Flower Seeds UK Limited
Incorporated: 30 June 2009 *Employees:* 5
Net Worth: £7,491,000 *Total Assets:* £10,888,000
Registered Office: Florensis, Milton Road, West Adderbury, Banbury, Oxon, OX17 3EY
Activities: Growing of other non-perennial crops
Parent: Ball Horticultural Company
Officers: William Todd Billings [1962] Director/Chief Financial Officer [American]; Alexander James Shepherd [1963] Director

Florida Topco Limited
Incorporated: 7 October 2016 *Employees:* 74
Net Worth: £3,007,766 *Total Assets:* £10,954,186
Registered Office: 3 Electric Avenue, Witham St Hughs, Lincoln, LN6 9BJ
Activities: Non-trading company
Shareholders: Pacific Shelf 1851 Limited; Core GP II LLP
Officers: Stephen Peter Edwards [1964] Director/Investment Manager; Walid Khalil Fakhry [1968] Director/Investment Manager; Trevor James Swales [1963] Director/Chairman; Christopher John Turner [1968] Director/Chief Executive Officer; William James Willows-Chamberlin [1989] Finance Director

Flow Energy Limited
Incorporated: 11 January 2011 *Employees:* 255
Net Worth Deficit: £38,305,024 *Total Assets:* £28,385,012
Registered Office: Co-operative House, Warwick Technology Park, Gallows Hill, Warwick, CV34 6DA
Activities: Trade of electricity
Parent: Flowgroup PLC
Officers: Edward Geoffrey Parker, Secretary; Stephen Raymond Allsopp [1952] Director; Olivia Birch [1967] Director; Clive Leon Booker [1944] Director/Retired; Eleanor Boyle [1989] Director; Judith Feeney [1946] Director; Patrick Hugo Gray [1947] Director; Gary William Hayes [1955] Director; Irene Louise Kirkman [1953] Director; Matthew David Nigel Lane [1985] Director; Donald Morrison [1947] Director; Jean Elizabeth Nunn-Price [1943] Director; Kathryn Elizabeth Petersen [1962] Director; Heather Adele Richardson [1976] Director/Manager; Helen Rita Wiseman [1965] Director/HR Consultant; Vivian Stanley Woodell [1962] Director/Senior Manager

Flowmax Limited
Incorporated: 24 October 1997 *Employees:* 149
Net Worth: £13,745,973 *Total Assets:* £18,880,820
Registered Office: 2 Chawley Park, Cumnor Hill, Oxford, OX2 9GG
Activities: Wholesale of other machinery and equipment
Officers: Carl Philip Coutts-Trotter [1975] Director/Deputy Executive Chairman [South African]; Philip Coutts-Trotter [1946] Director [South African]; Graham Joseph Morrell [1964] Director; Sam Michael Sweeney [1981] Director

Flowtech Fluidpower PLC
Incorporated: 24 April 2014 *Employees:* 414
Net Worth: £74,864,000 *Total Assets:* £122,026,000
Registered Office: Bollin House, Riverside Business Park, Wilmslow, Cheshire, SK9 1DP
Activities: Activities of head offices
Officers: Bryce Brooks, Secretary; Bryce Rowan Brooks [1965] Finance Director; Russell Cash [1966] Director; Malcolm McDonald Diamond [1948] Director; Nigel Richens [1955] Director; Bill Wilson [1955] Director

Fluidone Holdings Limited
Incorporated: 21 September 2015
Previous: Rigby Technology Investments Limited
Net Worth Deficit: £1,706,000 *Total Assets:* £30,813,000
Registered Office: Bridgeway House, Bridgeway, Stratford upon Avon, Warwicks, CV37 6YX
Activities: Other business support service activities n.e.c.
Parent: Rigby Group Finance Limited
Officers: James Peter Rigby [1971] Director; Steven Paul Rigby [1972] Director; John Paul Taylor [1970] Managing Director

Fluidpower Group Limited
Incorporated: 16 May 2016
Net Worth: £100 *Total Assets:* £91,745,104
Registered Office: Bollin House, Riverside Business Park, Wilmslow, Cheshire, SK9 1DP
Activities: Activities of distribution holding companies
Parent: Fluidpower MIP Limited
Officers: Bryce Rowan Brooks [1965] Director; Russell Cash [1966] Director

Fluidpower Limited
Incorporated: 15 October 1982 *Employees:* 141
Previous: Flowtech Limited
Net Worth: £48,241,176 *Total Assets:* £83,318,040
Registered Office: Bollin House, Riverside Business Park, Wilmslow, Cheshire, SK9 1DP
Activities: Wholesale of hardware, plumbing and heating equipment and supplies
Parent: Fluidpower Group Limited
Officers: Bryce Rowan Brooks [1965] Finance Director; Russell Cash [1966] Director; Alan Keith Dickinson [1957] Sales Director; John Farmer [1964] Director

Fluidpower MIP Limited
Incorporated: 6 May 2014 *Employees:* 2
Previous: Flowtech MIP Limited
Net Worth: £32,384,768 *Total Assets:* £140,231,552
Registered Office: Bollin House, Riverside Business Park, Wilmslow, Cheshire, SK9 1DP
Activities: Activities of head offices
Parent: Flowtech Fluidpower PLC
Officers: Bryce Rowan Brooks [1965] Director; Russell Cash [1966] Director

Fluidpower Shared Services Limited
Incorporated: 17 August 2004 *Employees:* 15
Previous: Flowtech Holdings Limited
Net Worth: £30,998,488 *Total Assets:* £40,471,092
Registered Office: Bollin House, Riverside Business Park, Wilmslow, Cheshire, SK9 1DP
Activities: Activities of distribution holding companies
Parent: Fluidpower MIP Limited
Officers: Bryce Rowan Brooks [1965] Director/Accountant; Russell Cash [1966] Director

Fluorochem Limited
Incorporated: 22 August 1986 *Employees:* 43
Net Worth: £8,501,910 *Total Assets:* £10,257,235
Registered Office: Unit 14 Graphite Way, Hadfield, Glossop, Derbys, SK13 1QH
Activities: Wholesale of chemical products
Parent: Synthetic Technologies Ltd
Officers: Douglas Birch, Secretary; Douglas Birch [1957] Director/Chartered Accountant; Lee David Jones [1980] Director; Dr Martin Fraser Woolley [1967] Director/Sales

Flying High Trust
Incorporated: 21 May 2012 *Employees:* 949
Net Worth: £43,887,248 *Total Assets:* £59,743,008
Registered Office: Flying High Trust, Candleby Lane, Cotgrave, Nottingham, NG12 3LG
Activities: Primary education
Officers: Nick Layfield, Secretary; Jason Beaumont [1970] Director; Paul Henry Bennett [1950] Director/Education Consultant; Sioned Lucy Littlefair [1974] Director/Shared Services Manager; Kate McKenna [1962] Director/Head of School; Neil Duncan Robinson [1961] Director/Local Government Officer; Christopher Wheatley [1971] Director/Chief Executive Head

FMC Corporation United Kingdom Limited
Incorporated: 7 June 2012 *Employees:* 40
Net Worth: £36,327,760 *Total Assets:* £39,492,848
Registered Office: Third Avenue, Centrum One Hundred, Burton on Trent, Staffs, DE14 2WD
Activities: Non-trading company
Parent: N & H International Holding 2
Officers: Janette de Gennaro, Secretary; James Decleene [1961] Director/H and N Controller [American]

Focus Solutions Group Limited
Incorporated: 18 January 2000 *Employees:* 6
Net Worth Deficit: £2,161,304 *Total Assets:* £19,571,984
Registered Office: Cranford House, Kenilworth Road, Blackdown, Leamington Spa, Warwicks, CV32 6RQ
Activities: Activities of head offices
Parent: Standard Life Aberdeen PLC
Officers: Paul McKenna, Secretary; Jonathan Michael Kennedy [1968] Director; Edward Reynolds [1970] Director; David Stephen Upton [1970] Managing Director; Andrew Simon Warner [1967] Director

Focus100 Limited
Incorporated: 27 December 2000 *Employees:* 4
Net Worth: £1,331,000 *Total Assets:* £23,277,000
Registered Office: Armitage House, Colwick, Nottingham, NG4 2BA
Activities: Other professional, scientific and technical activities n.e.c.
Parent: Armitage Pet Care Limited
Officers: Mark John Andrews [1970] Director/Chief Executive; Sarah Louise Smith [1974] Finance Director

Fold Hill Foods Limited
Incorporated: 6 June 1979 *Employees:* 165
Net Worth: £13,206,181 *Total Assets:* £18,500,264
Registered Office: Fold Hill, Old Leake, Boston, Lincs, PE22 9PJ
Activities: Manufacture of prepared pet foods
Parent: J. W. Grant
Officers: James Edward Grant, Secretary; Andrew John Grant [1955] Director/Farmer; James Edward Grant [1953] Director/Farmer

Forbo Flooring UK Limited
Incorporated: 2 September 2014 *Employees:* 556
Net Worth: £7,352,000 *Total Assets:* £116,157,000
Registered Office: High Holborn Road, Ripley, Derbys, DE5 3NT
Activities: Other manufacturing n.e.c.
Parent: Forbo Holding AG
Officers: Eric Speed, Secretary; Angus Baikie Fotheringhame [1971] Director/General Manager; Douglas Greenway [1962] Operations Director; Urs Uehlinger [1966] Director/Forbo Group Chief Financial Officer [Swiss]; Jean-Michel Wins [1967] Director/Executive Vice President Forbo Flooring Systems [Belgian]

Forcefield Bidco Limited
Incorporated: 16 July 2015
Net Worth Deficit: £2,673,000 *Total Assets:* £31,739,000
Registered Office: Callister Way, Centrum West, Burton on Trent, Staffs, DE14 2SY
Activities: Activities of distribution holding companies
Parent: Forcefield Midco Limited
Officers: Neil Andrew Carpenter [1963] Director; Michael Conroy [1968] Director; David Holland [1971] Director; Dean John Hughes [1974] Director; Chuang Hue Moh [1975] Director/Merchant [Singaporean]; Simon Richard Pearson [1967] Director/Management Consultant; Heath Brian Zarin [1975] Director/Finance [Kittitian]

Forcefield Midco Limited
Incorporated: 15 July 2015
Net Worth Deficit: £392,000 *Total Assets:* £16,226,000
Registered Office: Callister Way, Centrum West, Burton on Trent, Staffs, DE14 2SY
Activities: Activities of distribution holding companies
Parent: Palletforce Holdings Limited
Officers: Neil Andrew Carpenter [1963] Director; Michael Conroy [1968] Director; David Holland [1971] Director; Dean John Hughes [1974] Director; Chuang Hue Moh [1975] Director/Merchant [Singaporean]; Simon Richard Pearson [1967] Director/Management Consultant; Heath Brian Zarin [1975] Director/Finance [Kittitian]

Ford & Slater Limited
Incorporated: 23 April 1990 *Employees:* 742
Net Worth: £10,232,000 *Total Assets:* £61,771,000
Registered Office: Hazel Drive, Narborough Road South, Leicester, LE3 2JG
Activities: Sale of other motor vehicles
Parent: Strevens Vehicles Holdings Limited
Officers: Nigel Jeremy Strevens, Secretary; Phillip John Clayton [1952] Director/Dealer Principal; Christopher James Hutt [1951] Fleet Sales Director; Haroon Yakub Patel [1972] Director/Chartered Management Accountant; Keith Robin Spurway [1965] Director/Dealer Principal; Janet Hyde Strevens [1944] Director; Nigel Jeremy Strevens [1971] Director/Chartered Accountant; Peter Alan Dawson Strevens [1938] Director/Chairman; Timothy Maxwell Strevens [1974] Joint Managing Director

Allen Ford (UK) Limited
Incorporated: 1 June 2003 *Employees:* 1,355
Net Worth: £37,968,000 *Total Assets:* £227,707,008
Registered Office: Allen Ford- Warwick, Tachbrook Park Drive, Warwick, CV34 6SY
Activities: Sale of new cars and light motor vehicles
Parent: SG International Holdings Limited
Officers: Colin Alexander Brown [1969] Director/Accountant [South African]; Peter William Mountford [1957] Director/Chief Executive Officer; Michael William Phillips [1956] Director; Graeme Bryan Watson [1967] Director/Motor Dealer [South African]; Paula Wood [1969] Director

Forest Commercial Services Limited
Incorporated: 18 March 1996 *Employees:* 3
Net Worth: £8,867,916 *Total Assets:* £16,475,931
Registered Office: Holwell, St Paul's Street, Stamford, Lincs, PE9 2BG
Activities: Other professional, scientific and technical activities n.e.c.
Major Shareholder: Simon Robert Smith
Officers: Simon Robert Smith [1964] Director/Road Haulage Manager

Forest Holidays Group Limited
Incorporated: 27 July 2012 *Employees:* 621
Net Worth: £12,791,000 *Total Assets:* £125,967,000
Registered Office: Bath Yard, Bath Lane, Moira, Swadlincote, Derbys, DE12 6BA
Activities: Other reservation service activities n.e.c.
Parent: Canopy Bidco Limited
Officers: Jonathan Luke Ellis [1978] Director; Bruce McKendrick [1962] Director

Forest Holidays Limited
Incorporated: 27 July 2012 *Employees:* 612
Net Worth: £6,507,000 *Total Assets:* £125,950,000
Registered Office: Bath Yard, Bath Lane, Moira, Swadlincote, Derbys, DE12 6BA
Activities: Other reservation service activities n.e.c.
Parent: Forest Holidays Group Limited
Officers: Jonathan Luke Ellis [1978] Director; Bruce McKendrick [1962] Director

The Forest of Marston Vale Trust
Incorporated: 7 November 1997 *Employees:* 48
Net Worth: £13,825,211 *Total Assets:* £14,095,331
Registered Office: The Forest Centre, Station Road, Marston Moretaine, Beds, MK43 0PR
Activities: Silviculture and other forestry activities
Officers: Nicholas John Webb, Secretary; Craig Spencer Austin [1966] Director; Rodney John Calvert [1943] Director/Retired; Cllr Norman Bryan Costin [1945] Director/Accountant; Richard Gareth Ellis [1959] Director/Energy & Environment Manager; Peter John Faulkner [1951] Director; Debra Jayne Hassall [1963] Director/Property; John Christopher Thelwall [1950] Director/Retired; Robert Wallace [1944] Director/Retired; Sally Anne Williams [1956] Director/Retired

Forest Way School
Incorporated: 1 February 2012 *Employees:* 146
Net Worth: £8,212,613 *Total Assets:* £10,795,985
Registered Office: Forest Way School, Warren Hills Road, Coalville, Leics, LE67 4UU
Activities: Pre-primary education
Officers: Ian Mark Wood, Secretary; Kim Booth [1965] Director/Teacher; Jason Brooks [1968] Director/Headteacher; Laura Browne [1984] Director; Roy Cafferty [1952] Director/Retired; Rebecca Hayes [1965] Director/Senior Teaching Assistant; Patricia Adena Marney [1950] Director/Secretary; Gail Seaton [1966] Director/Headteacher; Jame Shanley [1960] Director/Retired; Mark Ronald Snow [1960] Director/Manager/Business Consultant; Julie Watkinson [1961] Director/Foster Carer

Forever Living Products (U.K.) Limited
Incorporated: 22 June 1988 *Employees:* 121
Net Worth: £7,665,114 *Total Assets:* £12,143,085
Registered Office: Longbridge Manor, Longbridge, Warwick, CV34 6RB
Activities: Non-specialised wholesale trade
Major Shareholder: Rex Maughan
Officers: Gregg Elliott Maughan, Secretary; Gregg Elliott Maughan [1968] Director [American]; Rex G Maughan [1936] Director/Company Chairman [American]

Forgings International Limited
Incorporated: 22 November 2002
Net Worth: £139,156,000 *Total Assets:* £192,144,000
Registered Office: 26a Atlas Way, Sheffield, S4 7QQ
Activities: Non-trading company
Parent: Forgings International Holdings 3 Limited
Officers: Petra Papinniemi-Ainger, Secretary; Dr Kay Louise Dowdall [1969] Director/Chartered Accountant; Lluis Maria Fargas Mas [1966] Director [Swiss]

Forman Hardy Holdings Limited
Incorporated: 10 August 1939 *Employees:* 4
Net Worth: £12,878,000 *Total Assets:* £15,776,000
Registered Office: 64 St James's Street, Nottingham, NG1 6FJ
Activities: Security and commodity contracts dealing activities
Parent: Nottingham Industrial Group Limited
Officers: Nicholas John Foreman Hardy [1948] Director; Thomas William Bailey Foreman Hardy [1983] Director; Peter Anthony Letley [1945] Director

Forterra Building Products Limited
Incorporated: 26 March 2014 *Employees:* 1,663
Net Worth: £98,300,000 *Total Assets:* £273,300,000
Registered Office: 5 Grange Park Court, Roman Way, Northampton, NN4 5EA
Activities: Manufacture of bricks, tiles and construction products, in baked clay
Parent: Forterra Holdings Limited
Officers: Ashley George Thompson, Secretary; Shatish Damodar Dasani [1962] Director; Matthew Edward Day [1972] Director; Benjamin John Guyatt [1975] Director/Chartered Accountant; Stephen Richard Harrison [1968] Director; Edward Thomas Haslam [1979] Director of Human Resources; Darren Peter Rix [1983] Director; Adam Julian Smith [1967] Commercial Director; George Walter Arthur Stewart [1964] Director; Peter Spencer Varnsverry [1964] Director

Forterra Holdings Limited
Incorporated: 2 February 2016
Net Worth: £120,000,000 *Total Assets:* £137,800,000
Registered Office: 5 Grange Park Court, Roman Way, Northampton, NN4 5EA
Activities: Activities of other holding companies n.e.c.
Parent: Forterra PLC
Officers: Ashley George Thompson, Secretary; Shatish Damodar Dasani [1962] Director; Stephen Richard Harrison [1968] Managing Director

Forterra PLC
Incorporated: 21 January 2016
Net Worth: £104,700,000 *Total Assets:* £279,300,000
Registered Office: 5 Grange Park Court, Roman Way, Northampton, NN4 5EA
Activities: Activities of other holding companies n.e.c.
Officers: Benjamin Guyatt, Secretary; Justin Richard Atkinson [1960] Director; Shatish Damodar Dasani [1962] Director; Stephen Richard Harrison [1968] Managing Director; Katherine Christina Mary Innes Ker [1960] Director; Paul John Lester [1949] Director; James Vincent Niblett [1958] Director; Divya Seshamani [1978] Director [Singaporean]; Martin Conrad Sutherland [1968] Director

Forticrete Limited
Incorporated: 13 April 1927 *Employees:* 355
Net Worth: £18,661,000 *Total Assets:* £39,450,000
Registered Office: Leicester Road, Ibstock, Leics, LE67 6HS
Activities: Manufacture of concrete products for construction purposes
Parent: Ibstock PLC
Officers: Robert Douglas, Secretary; Mark Derek Brind [1968] Director; Mark Whitfield Houghton [1961] Director; Joseph Henry Hudson [1969] Director; Mark Richmond [1967] Director/Accountant; Kevin John Sims [1961] Director; Ian Alan Tichias [1969] Finance Director

Foseco International Limited
Incorporated: 6 May 1949 *Employees:* 19
Net Worth: £45,463,000 *Total Assets:* £63,998,000
Registered Office: 1 Midland Way, Central Park, Barlborough Links, Chesterfield, Derbys, S43 4XA
Activities: Manufacture of other chemical products n.e.c.
Parent: Vesuvius Overseas Limited
Officers: Michael Satterthwaite, Secretary; Henry James Knowles [1969] Director/Company Secretary; Ian James Lawson [1968] Director/Accountant; Michael Satterthwaite [1967] Finance Director; Garry Smith [1959] Director/Technology and IP Manager; Sunderrajan Venkatraman [1960] Director/Vice President Finance - Advanced Refractories [Indian]

Fossil (UK) Holdings Limited
Incorporated: 3 April 2001 *Employees:* 1
Net Worth: £9,021,268 *Total Assets:* £9,021,268
Registered Office: Featherstone House, Featherstone Road, Wolverton Mill, Milton Keynes, Bucks, MK12 5TH
Activities: Activities of other holding companies n.e.c.
Parent: Fossil (Europe) BV
Officers: Daniel Charles McAllister, Secretary; Richard Collins [1973] Managing Director; Martin Frey [1955] Director/Senior VP Regional Operations [Swiss]; Florian Stalder [1969] Sr Director, General Counsel EMEA [Swiss]

Fossil (UK) Limited
Incorporated: 30 May 1995 *Employees:* 463
Net Worth: £18,053,000 *Total Assets:* £67,411,000
Registered Office: Featherstone House, Featherstone Road, Wolverton Mill, Milton Keynes, Bucks, MK12 5TH
Activities: Wholesale of watches and jewellery
Parent: Fossil (UK) Holdings Ltd
Officers: Daniel Charles McAllister, Secretary; Richard Collins [1973] Managing Director; Antonio Nigro [1978] Director/VP Europe North [Italian]

Foster Yeoman Limited
Incorporated: 10 October 1923
Net Worth: £174,983,008 *Total Assets:* £175,499,008
Registered Office: Bardon Hall, Copt Oak Road, Markfield, Leics, LE67 9PJ
Activities: Activities of construction holding companies
Parent: Aggregate Industries UK Limited
Officers: James West Atherton-Ham [1970] Director/Barrister; John Ferguson Bowater [1949] Director; Guy Charles Edwards [1965] Director

Foundation Technology Limited
Incorporated: 11 December 1989 *Employees:* 81
Net Worth: £12,650,000 *Total Assets:* £22,720,000
Registered Office: Tove Valley Business Park, Old Tiffield Road, Towcester, Northants, NN12 6PF
Activities: Manufacture of loaded electronic boards
Parent: Abaco Systems Limited
Officers: John Vernon Tomlinson, Secretary; Andrew Neil MacCaig [1969] Director; William Read [1970] Director [American]

Four CS MAT
Incorporated: 2 August 2010 *Employees:* 350
Previous: Arthur Mellows Village College
Net Worth: £17,003,708 *Total Assets:* £21,109,614
Registered Office: Company Secretary Office, Arthur Mellows Village College, Helpston Road, Glinton, Peterborough, PE6 7JX
Activities: Regulation of health care, education, cultural and other social services, not incl. social security
Officers: Dr Emma Louise Black [1987] Managing Director of Cascade Cash Management; Gary Edward James Dawkins [1955] Director/Retired; Iain Erskine [1954] Director/Co-Principal of The Fulbridge Academy; Dr Mary Kiernan [1960] Director/Academic; David Gilmour McLaren [1944] Director/Retired; Jonathan Stephen Theobalds [1964] Managing Director; David Alan Whiles [1958] Director/Chartered Engineer

Four Seasons (Bamford) Limited
Incorporated: 7 June 2006 *Employees:* 2,093
Net Worth Deficit: £14,548,000 *Total Assets:* £11,087,000
Registered Office: Norcliffe House, Station Road, Wilmslow, Cheshire, SK9 1BU
Activities: Other human health activities
Parent: Four Seasons Health Care Group Limited
Officers: Abigail Mattison, Secretary; Timothy Richard William Hammond [1959] Director; Dr Maureen Claire Royston [1960] Director; Benjamin Robert Taberner [1972] Director/Chartered Accountant

Four Seasons (DFK) Limited
Incorporated: 13 August 1985 *Employees:* 257
Net Worth: £11,670,000 *Total Assets:* £13,025,000
Registered Office: Norcliffe House, Station Road, Wilmslow, Cheshire, SK9 1BU
Activities: Other human health activities
Parent: Four Seasons Health Care Group Limited
Officers: Abigail Mattison, Secretary; Timothy Richard William Hammond [1959] Director; Dr Maureen Claire Royston [1960] Director; Benjamin Robert Taberner [1972] Director/Chartered Accountant

Four Seasons Health Care (Capital) Limited
Incorporated: 26 June 2002
Net Worth: £16,524,000 *Total Assets:* £16,524,000
Registered Office: Norcliffe House, Station Road, Wilmslow, Cheshire, SK9 1BU
Activities: Activities of head offices
Parent: Four Seasons Health Care Limited
Officers: Abigail Mattison, Secretary; Timothy Richard William Hammond [1959] Director; Dr Maureen Claire Royston [1960] Director; Benjamin Robert Taberner [1972] Director/Chartered Accountant

Four Seasons Health Care Holdings Limited
Incorporated: 8 July 1999
Net Worth: £236,339,008 *Total Assets:* £236,339,008
Registered Office: Norcliffe House, Station Road, Wilmslow, Cheshire, SK9 1BU
Activities: Other human health activities
Parent: Mericourt Limited
Officers: Abigail Mattison, Secretary; Dr Maureen Claire Royston [1960] Director; Benjamin Robert Taberner [1972] Director/Chartered Accountant

Four Seasons Homes No.4 Limited
Incorporated: 21 June 2000 *Employees:* 813
Net Worth: £14,799,000 *Total Assets:* £17,391,000
Registered Office: Norcliffe House, Station Road, Wilmslow, Cheshire, SK9 1BU
Activities: Other human health activities
Parent: Four Seasons Group Holdings Limited
Officers: Abigail Mattison, Secretary; Timothy Richard William Hammond [1959] Director; Dr Maureen Claire Royston [1960] Director; Benjamin Robert Taberner [1972] Director/Chartered Accountant

Fox (Owmby) Limited
Incorporated: 11 May 1964 *Employees:* 129
Net Worth: £7,605,899 *Total Assets:* £18,016,820
Registered Office: Caenby Hall, Caenby Corner, Market Rasen, Lincs, LN8 2BU
Activities: Construction of other civil engineering projects n.e.c.
Major Shareholder: Stephen Harold Fox
Officers: Wendy Lorraine Bean, Secretary; Claire Fox [1962] Director; Stephen Harold Fox [1956] Director; Richard Gudgin [1953] Commercial Director

Fox Lima Holdings Limited
Incorporated: 5 January 1993 *Employees:* 113
Net Worth: £28,978,144 *Total Assets:* £32,984,426
Registered Office: Whitefurze, Burnsall Road, Coventry, Warwicks, CV5 6BT
Activities: Activities of head offices
Major Shareholder: Philip Alexander Lanni
Officers: Claire Laraine Smith, Secretary; Philip Alexander Lanni [1960] Director/Business Executive

FPS Distribution Limited
Incorporated: 28 February 2001
Net Worth: £723,000 *Total Assets:* £13,725,000
Registered Office: Bridge House, 3 Timothy's Bridge Road, Stratford upon Avon, Warwicks, CV37 9NQ
Activities: Wholesale trade of motor vehicle parts and accessories
Parent: Alliance Automotive Holding Ltd
Officers: John Frederick Coombes, Secretary; Alistair Stuart Brown [1955] Director [New Zealander]; John Frederick Coombes [1965] Director; Jonathan Clive Eden [1958] Director; Jean-Jacques Mathieu Lafont [1959] Director [Belgian]; Terence Michael Wainwright [1947] Managing Director

FR Acquisitions Corporation (Europe) Limited
Incorporated: 18 October 2007
Net Worth: £109,628,000 *Total Assets:* £628,000,000
Registered Office: 26a Atlas Way, Sheffield, S4 7QQ
Activities: Activities of head offices
Parent: Arconic IH Limited
Officers: Petra Papinniemi-Ainger, Secretary; Dr Kay Louise Dowdall [1969] Director/Chartered Accountant; Lluis Maria Fargas Mas [1966] Director/Lawyer [Spanish/Swiss]

Fraikin Limited
Incorporated: 31 January 1978 *Employees:* 315
Net Worth: £51,797,220 *Total Assets:* £79,994,048
Registered Office: First Floor, 2M, Middlemarch Business Park, Siskin Drive, Coventry, Warwicks, CV3 4FJ
Activities: Renting and leasing of trucks and other heavy vehicles
Parent: Financiere Truck (Investissement) SAS
Officers: Pierre Louis Colin [1963] Director/Chief Executive [French]; Edward William John Cowell [1970] Director/Chief Executive

Framework Housing Association
Incorporated: 14 February 1997 *Employees:* 3
Net Worth: £56,313,000 *Total Assets:* £68,153,000
Registered Office: Val Roberts House, 25 Gregory Boulevard, Nottingham, NG7 6NX
Activities: Renting and operating of Housing Association real estate
Officers: Naomi Anna Dobraszczyc, Secretary; Andrew Redfern, Secretary; Diane Diacon [1954] Director; Jane Margaret Geraghty [1951] Director/Chair of Durham Adult & Children's Board; Caris Aran Henry [1984] Director/Strategy and Transformation Consultant; Deborah Maitland [1967] HR Director; Patrick Michael Mitchell [1964] Director - NHS; Diana Mary Parrish [1942] Director/Retired; Christopher John Prentice [1963] Director; Rebecca Jane Rance [1965] Director/Chief Executive; Dr Vinay Shankar [1986] Director/GP

Franke Sissons Limited
Incorporated: 28 November 1986 *Employees:* 60
Net Worth: £4,641,000 *Total Assets:* £17,589,000
Registered Office: 14 Napier Court, Gander Lane, Barlborough, Chesterfield, Derbys, S43 4PZ
Activities: Wholesale of other intermediate products
Major Shareholder: Michael Pieper
Officers: Daniel Orwin, Secretary; Roger Basler [1965] Director/Chief Executive Officer [Swiss]; Patrick Truttmann [1975] Director/Chief Financial Officer [Swiss]

Frasers Retail Limited
Incorporated: 13 May 2011 *Employees:* 211
Net Worth: £18,778,120 *Total Assets:* £27,271,532
Registered Office: Georgetown House, 6 Foxhall Road, Didcot, Oxon, OX11 7AA
Activities: Other retail sale in non-specialised stores
Officers: Diana Elizabeth Fraser [1953] Director; Elizabeth Elena Fraser [1947] Director; Hugh Everard Duncan Fraser [1951] Director; Jonathan Hugh Sarel Fraser [1982] Director; Nicholas Robertson Fraser [1978] Director; Robert Warden Fraser [1949] Director

The Freedom Travel Group Limited
Incorporated: 30 July 1999 *Employees:* 7
Net Worth: £2,387,000 *Total Assets:* £39,729,000
Registered Office: Westpoint, Peterborough Business Park, Lynch Wood, Peterborough, Cambs, PE2 6FZ
Activities: Travel agency activities
Parent: Future Travel Limited
Officers: Shirley Bradley, Secretary; Alan Charles Donald [1963] Director

Freefoam Plastics (U.K.) Limited
Incorporated: 26 April 1999 *Employees:* 136
Net Worth: £6,918,000 *Total Assets:* £21,851,000
Registered Office: Freefoam Plastice (UK) Limited, 77-83 St James Mill Road, Northampton, NN5 5JP
Activities: Manufacture of builders ware of plastic
Officers: Daniel Aidan Harte, Secretary; Daniel Aidan Harte [1965] Director [Irish]; Anthony Walsh [1945] Director [Irish]

Freeman Automotive (UK) Ltd
Incorporated: 13 January 1983 *Employees:* 109
Net Worth: £17,353,640 *Total Assets:* £22,769,274
Registered Office: EBC Brakes World Headquarters, Upton Valley Way East, Pineham, Northampton, NN4 9EF
Activities: Wholesale trade of motor vehicle parts and accessories
Parent: EBC Holdings Limited
Officers: James Hallett [1974] Managing Director

The Freeman Company (UK) Limited
Incorporated: 4 March 2013 *Employees:* 272
Net Worth Deficit: £7,777,000 *Total Assets:* £16,461,000
Registered Office: Unit DC5 Prologis Park, Imperial Road, Coventry, Warwicks, CV8 3EA
Activities: Activities of exhibition and fair organisers
Officers: Dawnn Marie Repp, Secretary; Jr Popolo [1967] Director/Chairman of Face to Face Marketing Company [American]; Christopher John Preston [1964] Managing Director

Freeths LLP
Incorporated: 16 May 2003 *Employees:* 405
Net Worth: £24,403,000 *Total Assets:* £52,379,000
Registered Office: 80 Mount Street, Nottingham, NG1 6HH
Officers: Charles Nigel Cullen [1944] Member; Karl Peter Jansen [1967] Member; Julian Matthew Middleton [1963] Member; Charles Robert Stephen Powell [1958] Member; Paul Derek Thorogood [1958] Member; Simon Michael Abbott [1959] LLP Member; Ateeq Ahmed [1977] LLP Member; Christopher Mark Ainsworth [1975] LLP Member; Perveen Akhter [1978] LLP Member; Leon Francis Arnold [1973] LLP Member; Philip David Baigent [1973] LLP Member; Simon Charles Baigent [1968] LLP Member; Peter Baker [1958] LLP Member; Elizabeth Mary Banks [1978] LLP Member; Simon David Barker [1971] LLP Member; James Berry [1981] LLP Member; Richard Anthony Beverley [1961] LLP Member; Nigel Bolton [1966] LLP Member; James Thomas Boulton [1976] LLP Member; Tom Henry Bradford [1979] LLP Member; Paul John Brailsford [1975] LLP Member; Andrew MacDonald Bretherton [1973] LLP Member; Emma Brooksbank [1976] LLP Member; Mark James Brown [1979] LLP Member; Thomas William Brown [1978] LLP Member; Robert John Bruce [1974] LLP Member; Paul Anthony Burnley [1955] LLP Member; Joseph Oliver Gerard Byrne [1969] LLP Member; Paul Chadder [1971] LLP Member; Shashi Chambers [1973] LLP Member; James Stephen Clamp [1985] LLP Member; Lindsey Dawn Clegg [1980] LLP Member; Lee David Clifford [1973] LLP Member; Richard Keith Coates [1979] LLP Member; Claire Louise Colbert [1977] LLP Member; Jenny Cooper [1978] LLP Member; Diana Rosemary Copestake [1954] LLP Member; Peter James Crawford [1981] LLP Member; Duncan Christopher Crine [1963] LLP Member; Charles Jerome Darby [1961] LLP Member; Heather Ruth Davies [1959] LLP Member; Iain Robert Davis [1968] LLP Member; Philippa Andrea Sinclare Dempster [1965] LLP Member; Sarah Duffy [1980] LLP Member; James Michael Dyson [1981] LLP Member; Mark Crispin Emery [1964] LLP Member; Colin Stewart Flanagan [1951] LLP Member; Sarah Foster [1968] LLP Member; Andrew James Francey [1974] LLP Member; Christopher Freeston [1976] LLP Member; Nigel Bryce Gardner [1965] LLP Member; Peter Gavin [1962] LLP Member; Keith John Gilbert [1972] LLP Member; Lisa Joanne Gilligan [1971] LLP Member; Michael David Gilmour [1971] LLP Member; Thomas Martyn Golding [1982] LLP Member; Jane Goulding [1960] LLP Member; Mark Kellerd Gradwell [1968] LLP Member; Valerie Christine Green [1963] LLP Member; Graham Mark Greenfield [1963] LLP Member; Sarah Griggs [1979] LLP Member; Matthew David Grocock [1968] LLP Member; Adrian Paul Hackett [1963] LLP Member; Stephen William Hadley [1963] LLP Member; Joseph Hale [1977] LLP Member; Jonathan Lee Hambleton [1964] LLP Member; James Robert Hart [1978] LLP Member; James Lawrence Hartley [1966] LLP Member; John Michael Heaphy [1966] LLP Member; Peter Douglas Hill [1956] LLP Member; Simon Quincey Hobbs [1972] LLP Member; Nathan Holden [1969] LLP Member; Christopher Alexander Holwell [1965] LLP Member; Luke James Andrew Hopkins [1982] LLP Member; Deryck Martin Houghton [1957] LLP Member; Rebecca Howlett [1979] LLP Member; Robert Anthony Hughes [1947] LLP Member; Oliver Jackson [1980] LLP Member; Balvinder Singh Jaj [1970] LLP Member; Jonathan David Frank Jefferies [1963] LLP Member; Mark Arthur Keeley [1970] LLP Member; Atiyya Khaliq [1970] LLP Member; Katherine Clare King [1979] LLP Member; Martyn Andrew Kolankiewicz [1981] LLP Member; David James Lane [1986] LLP Member; James Larmour [1975] LLP Member; Parminder Kaur Latimer [1969] LLP Member; Samantha Louise Leigh [1968] LLP Member; Stephen Gareth Lewis [1974] LLP Member; Carolyn Lowe [1970] LLP Member; Rena Magdani [1972] LLP Member; Jane Mary Maitland [1954] LLP Member; Max Marrison [1975] LLP Member; David Ian Marsden [1974] LLP Member; Andrew Maxwell [1971] LLP Member; John Paul May [1966] LLP Member; Matthew McBride [1976] LLP Member; Amy Kate Morley [1970] LLP Member; Philip Simon Myers [1977] LLP Member

Freiberger (UK) Limited
Incorporated: 4 July 1989 *Employees:* 14
Net Worth: £2,968,656 *Total Assets:* £23,464,196
Registered Office: Broadgate House, Westlode Street, Spalding, Lincs, PE11 2AF
Activities: Wholesale of other food, including fish, crustaceans and molluscs
Parent: Suedzucker AG
Officers: Andrew John Thorne, Secretary; Herr Hans Detlev Schulz [1953] Director [German]; Andrew John Thorne [1965] Director/Salesman

Freightroute Limited
Incorporated: 15 December 1972 *Employees:* 419
Net Worth: £10,175,189 *Total Assets:* £16,552,893
Registered Office: Station Road, Irthlingborough, Northants, NN9 5QQ
Activities: Freight transport by road
Major Shareholder: Gavin Peter Grant
Officers: Bryan Mounch, Secretary; Alison Bird [1965] Director/Bookkeeper; Nigel Cardwell [1963] Director/Transport Manager; Gavin Peter Grant [1968] Director; Karl James Grant [1963] Director; Christopher Meadowcroft [1955] Sales Director; Bryan Mounch [1968] Director/Certified Chartered Accountant

Fresenius Medical Care (Holdings) Limited
Incorporated: 28 June 1996 *Employees:* 851
Net Worth: £60,147,000 *Total Assets:* £134,811,008
Registered Office: Nunn Brook Road, Huthwaite, Sutton in Ashfield, Notts, NG17 2HU
Activities: Other human health activities
Parent: Fresenius Medical Care AG & Co. KGaA
Officers: Laura Bell [1982] Director; Helena Lambertina Edmunda Maria Gijsbers [1967] Managing Director [Dutch]; Marco Greco [1968] Director/CFO & Head of Commercial Services Western Europe [Italian]; Armin Karch [1968] Director/Head of Southern Western Europe [German]; Frank Michael Wagner [1959] Director/Executive Vice President Western Europe [German]; Timothy Scott Wheeldon [1970] Director

Fresenius Medical Care (UK) Limited
Incorporated: 24 May 1996 *Employees:* 214
Net Worth: £40,262,000 *Total Assets:* £66,627,000
Registered Office: Nunn Brook Road, Huthwaite, Sutton in Ashfield, Notts, NG17 2HU
Activities: Other human health activities
Parent: Fresenius Medical Care (Holdings) Limited
Officers: Laura Bell [1982] Director; Thierry Alain Eyrard [1965] Director/President and General Manager [French]; Timothy Scott Wheeldon [1970] Director

Fresenius Medical Care Renal Services Limited
Incorporated: 26 November 1992 *Employees:* 80
Net Worth: £20,219,000 *Total Assets:* £66,362,000
Registered Office: Nunn Brook Road, Huthwaite, Sutton in Ashfield, Notts, NG17 2HU
Activities: Other human health activities
Parent: Fresenius Medical Care (Holdings) Ltd
Officers: Laura Bell [1982] Director; Helena Lambertina Edmunda Maria Gijsbers [1967] Managing Director [Dutch]; Timothy Scott Wheeldon [1970] Director

Fresh Approach (UK) Holdings Limited
Incorporated: 22 April 2014 *Employees:* 78
Net Worth Deficit: £3,844,510 *Total Assets:* £10,538,494
Registered Office: Fin House, 1 Oakwater Avenue, Cheadle Royal, Cheadle, Cheshire, SK8 3SR
Activities: Management consultancy activities other than financial management
Officers: Karl Nicholas Cockwill [1965] Director; Lee Harris [1975] Director; Patrick Mathias Rhys Howells [1978] Director; Antony Peter Wilson [1976] Director

Fresh-Pak Chilled Foods Limited
Incorporated: 23 February 1982 *Employees:* 462
Net Worth: £20,125,000 *Total Assets:* £32,774,000
Registered Office: 1 Waterside Park, Valley Way, Wombwell, Barnsley, S Yorks, S73 0BB
Activities: Manufacture of other food products n.e.c.
Parent: Chilled Foods (UK) Ltd
Officers: Richard Mark Andrew Pattrick, Secretary; Stephen John Holding [1966] Director; James Christopher L'estrange [1976] Commercial Director; Paul James MacNish [1965] Operations Director; Richard Mark Andrew Pattrick [1963] Finance Director

Freshlinc Group Limited
Incorporated: 24 January 2008 *Employees:* 359
Previous: Freshlinc (Spalding) Limited
Net Worth: £4,485,797 *Total Assets:* £29,158,818
Registered Office: Wool Hall Farm, Cross Gate, Wykeham, Spalding, Lincs, PE12 6HW
Activities: Freight transport by road
Shareholder: Robin Hancox
Officers: Aubrey Edward Day, Secretary/Chartered Management Accountant; Aubrey Edward Day [1958] Director/Chartered Management Accountant; Robin Hancox [1956] Director; Martin John Tate [1966] Director

Freshlinc Limited
Incorporated: 2 November 2000 *Employees:* 330
Net Worth: £3,795,428 *Total Assets:* £28,383,608
Registered Office: Wool Hall Farm, Cross Gate, Wykeham, Spalding, Lincs, PE12 6HW
Activities: Freight transport by road
Parent: Freshlinc Group Limited
Officers: Aubrey Edward Day, Secretary/Chartered Management Accountant; Aubrey Edward Day [1958] Director/Chartered Management Accountant; Robin Hancox [1956] Director; Lee Scott Juniper [1972] Operations Director; Stephen John King [1972] Director/Management Accountant; Martin John Tate [1966] Director

Freshtime UK Limited
Incorporated: 16 November 1999 *Employees:* 324
Net Worth: £1,659,736 *Total Assets:* £14,393,080
Registered Office: Riverside Industrial Estate, Marsh Lane, Boston, Lincs, PE21 7RJ
Activities: Manufacture of other food products n.e.c.
Parent: The Bay Group Limited
Officers: Ian Ripley, Secretary; Richard Ian Andrews [1955] Director/Sales Manager; Stephen John Evans [1967] Managing Director; John Curran Mills Richmond [1953] Director; Kathryn Louise Richmond [1986] Director/Barrister; Ian Ripley [1962] Director; Jane Diane Speakman [1966] Director

Freudenberg Sealing Technologies Limited
Incorporated: 25 August 2016 *Employees:* 282
Net Worth: £32,415,754 *Total Assets:* £55,109,072
Registered Office: c/o Spearing Waite LLP, 34 Pocklingtons Walk, Leicester, LE1 6BU
Activities: Manufacture of plastics and rubber machinery
Officers: Michael Raymond Lawson, Secretary; Patricia MacDougall, Secretary; Peter Ronald Charles Johnson [1968] Director; Ludger Neuwinger-Heimes [1958] Director/Chief Financial Officer [German]; Dieter Schaefer [1956] Director [German]

Friar 148 Limited
Incorporated: 25 November 2014
Net Worth: £16,001,271 *Total Assets:* £26,374,042
Registered Office: 1 Longwall Avenue, Queens Drive Industrial Estate, Nottingham, NG2 1NA
Activities: Activities of other holding companies n.e.c.
Parent: Hunter Douglas NV
Officers: Mark Bramley [1962] Director; Byron Alexander Crawford [1970] Director; Paul Clifford Hopkins [1958] Director

Friar's Pride Limited
Incorporated: 19 May 1975 *Employees:* 177
Net Worth: £13,383,481 *Total Assets:* £18,178,222
Registered Office: Oxney Road West Industrial Estate, Oxney Road, Peterborough, Cambs, PE1 5YW
Activities: Non-specialised wholesale of food, beverages and tobacco
Shareholder: Rebecca Jane Lord
Officers: Rebecca Jane Lord, Secretary/Managing Director; David Bryn Major Briggs [1946] Director; Josephine Briggs [1944] Director; Rebecca Jane Lord [1973] Managing Director; Louise Marshall [1976] Director; Nigel Swepson [1975] Director; Vincent Willows [1958] Director

Frickley Holdings.Limited
Incorporated: 10 February 1971
Net Worth: £9,911,699 *Total Assets:* £10,410,980
Registered Office: Woodfield House, New Close Lane, Skelbrooke, Doncaster, S Yorks, DN6 8NA
Activities: Growing of cereals (except rice), leguminous crops and oil seeds
Officers: Anthony Michael Massarella, Secretary; Charles Michael Scholey [1955] Director/Farmer; Margaret Barbara Scholey [1931] Director/Farmer

Frimstone Limited
Incorporated: 3 November 1975 *Employees:* 100
Net Worth: £7,076,191 *Total Assets:* £14,466,948
Registered Office: 6 Lancaster Way, Ermine Business Park, Huntingdon, Cambs, PE29 6XU
Activities: Operation of gravel and sand pits; mining of clays and kaolin
Parent: Mick George Limited
Officers: Karen Farrell, Secretary; Mark Edward Davenport [1967] Director; Michael Alexander George [1984] Managing Director; Michael Eric George [1956] Managing Director; Sharon Colette Spain [1972] Director; Jonathan Paul Stump [1964] Finance Director; Mark Andrew Swan [1967] Commercial Director

Frontline Limited
Incorporated: 8 July 1937 *Employees:* 274
Net Worth Deficit: £279,000 *Total Assets:* £60,731,000
Registered Office: Media House, Peterborough Business Park, Lynch Wood, Peterborough, Cambs, PE2 6EA
Activities: Retail sale of newspapers and stationery in specialised stores
Parent: Bauer Consumer Media Limited
Officers: Thomas Pierre Bureau [1968] Director; Kevin Costello [1964] Director; Brian John Freeman [1964] Director/Accountant; Nicholas Paul Howitt [1967] Director; Paul Anthony Keenan [1963] Director/Publisher; Kevin Donald Langford [1964] Director; Robert James Munro-Hall [1966] Group Managing Director; Frank Carl Straetmans [1971] Managing Director [Belgian]

Frosts Garden Centre Restructuring Limited
Incorporated: 11 October 2016
Net Worth: £6,391,339 *Total Assets:* £12,694,333
Registered Office: Frosts Garden Centre, Woburn Sands, Milton Keynes, Bucks, MK17 8UE
Activities: Other retail sale of new goods in specialised stores (not commercial art galleries and opticians)
Parent: FGC Holdings Ltd
Officers: James Antony Frost [1964] Director; Jeremy Charles Frost [1961] Director

Frozen Value Limited
Incorporated: 24 February 1971 *Employees:* 921
Net Worth: £11,681,000 *Total Assets:* £19,904,000
Registered Office: Unit 6 Bretton Point, Dearne Mills, Darton, Barnsley, S Yorks, S75 5NH
Activities: Other retail sale of food in specialised stores
Parent: Viewtone Limited
Officers: Karen Mona Gunter, Secretary; Nicholas James Gore [1985] Finance Director; Karen Mona Gunter [1963] Finance Director; Kevin Gunter [1961] Managing Director; Adam Joel Todd [1969] Director

Frutarom (UK) Holdings Limited
Incorporated: 12 July 1991
Net Worth: £28,050,000 *Total Assets:* £28,050,000
Registered Office: Frutarom (UK) Ltd, Turnells Mill Lane, Denington Industrial Estate, Wellingborough, Northants, NN8 2RN
Activities: Manufacture of other food products n.e.c.
Parent: Frutarom Ltd
Officers: Karen Jane Russell, Secretary; Amos Anatot [1953] Director [Israeli]; Robert Gerard Anderson [1965] Director/Business Management [American]; Richard Allen O'Leary [1960] Director/Business Management [American]

Frutarom (UK) Limited
Incorporated: 28 May 1999 *Employees:* 326
Net Worth: £86,405,000 *Total Assets:* £280,056,992
Registered Office: Frutarom (UK) Ltd, Turnells Mill Lane, Denington Industrial Estate, Wellingborough, Northants, NN8 2RN
Activities: Manufacture of other food products n.e.c.
Parent: Frutarom (UK) Holdings Ltd
Officers: Karen Jane Russell, Secretary; Amos Anatot [1953] Director [Israeli]; Robert Gerard Anderson [1965] Director/Business Management [American]; Richard Allen O'Leary [1960] Director/Business Management [American]

Frutarom UK Investments Limited
Incorporated: 21 October 2016
Net Worth: £618,000 *Total Assets:* £26,820,000
Registered Office: Karen Russell, Frutarom (UK) Ltd, Turnells Mill Lane, Denington Industrial Estate, Wellingborough, Northants, NN8 2RN
Activities: Financial management
Parent: Frutarom (UK) Ltd
Officers: Karen Russell, Secretary; Amos Anatot [1953] Director [Israeli]; Robert Gerard Anderson [1965] Director/Business Management [American]; John Taylor [1967] Director/Business Management [American]

FSHC (UK) Limited
Incorporated: 30 June 1986
Net Worth: £163,179,008 *Total Assets:* £163,179,008
Registered Office: Norcliffe House, Station Road, Wilmslow, Cheshire, SK9 1BU
Activities: Activities of head offices
Parent: Four Seasons Group Holdings Limited
Officers: Abigail Mattison, Secretary; Timothy Richard William Hammond [1959] Director; Dr Maureen Claire Royston [1960] Director; Benjamin Robert Taberner [1972] Director/Chartered Accountant

FSHC Developments (Properties) Limited
Incorporated: 18 July 2005 *Employees:* 6
Net Worth Deficit: £14,991,000 *Total Assets:* £18,707,000
Registered Office: Norcliffe House, Station Road, Wilmslow, Cheshire, SK9 1BU
Activities: Other human health activities
Officers: Abigail Mattison, Secretary; Timothy Richard William Hammond [1959] Director; Benjamin Robert Taberner [1972] Director/Chartered Accountant

FSHC Properties (CH2) Limited
Incorporated: 20 May 2005 *Employees:* 5
Net Worth Deficit: £266,226,000 *Total Assets:* £115,918,000
Registered Office: Norcliffe House, Station Road, Wilmslow, Cheshire, SK9 1BU
Activities: Other human health activities
Officers: Abigail Mattison, Secretary; Timothy Richard William Hammond [1959] Director; Benjamin Robert Taberner [1972] Director/Chartered Accountant

FSHC Properties (Manor) Limited
Incorporated: 5 August 1987 *Employees:* 3
Previous: Huntercombe Manor Limited
Net Worth: £24,258,000 *Total Assets:* £27,208,000
Registered Office: Norcliffe House, Station Road, Wilmslow, Cheshire, SK9 1BU
Activities: Other human health activities
Officers: Abigail Mattison, Secretary; Timothy Richard William Hammond [1959] Director; Dr Maureen Claire Royston [1960] Director; Benjamin Robert Taberner [1972] Director/Chartered Accountant

FSP Acquisition Limited
Incorporated: 15 June 2009
Net Worth Deficit: £30,577,000 *Total Assets:* £20,720,000
Registered Office: 80 Mount Street, Nottingham, NG1 6HH
Activities: Activities of other holding companies n.e.c.
Parent: FSP Holdco Limited
Officers: Andrew Hector Fraser, Secretary; Andrew Hector Fraser [1971] Director; Samuel Patrick Donald Kershaw [1963] Funeral Director

Fswind Limited
Incorporated: 20 July 2010
Net Worth: £1,838,978 *Total Assets:* £12,692,700
Registered Office: Glebe Barn, Great Barrington, Burford, Oxon, OX18 4US
Activities: Production of electricity
Parent: Torrance Windfarm LLP
Officers: Stephen James Beck [1973] Director/Chartered Accountant; Dr Wayne Robert Ian Cranstone [1969] Director/Chief Operating Officer; Carole Ann Harris [1971] Director/Asset Manager

FTD UK Holdings Limited
Incorporated: 4 July 2006
Net Worth: £67,908,896 *Total Assets:* £102,686,912
Registered Office: Interflora House, Watergate, Sleaford, Lincs, NG34 7TB
Activities: Activities of head offices
Parent: FTD Inc.
Officers: John Curzon Dunstan, Secretary; John Curzon Dunstan [1967] Finance Director; Rhys John Hughes [1969] Director/Company Executive

FTR Holdings Ltd
Incorporated: 18 March 2016
Net Worth: £99,674 *Total Assets:* £32,104,168
Registered Office: 2nd Floor, Partis House, Knowlhill, Milton Keynes, Bucks, MK5 8HJ
Activities: Activities of other holding companies n.e.c.
Shareholders: Barry Andrew Moseley; Mark Anthony Pepper; Barry Andrew Moseley; Mark Anthony Pepper
Officers: Barry Andrew Moseley [1965] Managing Director; Mark Anthony Pepper [1972] Director

Fugro GB Marine Limited
Incorporated: 21 September 1973 *Employees:* 143
Previous: Fugro Geoconsulting Limited
Net Worth: £8,130,000 *Total Assets:* £10,259,000
Registered Office: Fugro House, Hithercroft Road, Wallingford, Oxon, OX10 9RB
Activities: Other professional, scientific and technical activities n.e.c.
Parent: Fugro Holdings Limited
Officers: Gordon John Duncan, Secretary; Anthony Thomas Gaffney [1966] Service Line Director, Metocean; Brian MacKenzie [1970] Director/Head of Consultancy; Andrew John Wood [1967] Managing Director

Fugro Geos Limited
Incorporated: 1 November 1994 *Employees:* 132
Net Worth: £11,175,000 *Total Assets:* £14,557,000
Registered Office: Fugro House, Hithercroft Road, Wallingford, Oxon, OX10 9RB
Activities: Other professional, scientific and technical activities n.e.c.
Parent: Fugro Holdings Limited
Officers: Gordon John Duncan, Secretary; Anthony Thomas Gaffney [1966] Director; Philip Gerard Meaden [1962] Director

Fugro Geoservices Limited
Incorporated: 1 November 1976 *Employees:* 440
Previous: Fugro Seacore Limited
Net Worth: £24,508,000 *Total Assets:* £61,064,000
Registered Office: Fugro House, Hithercroft Road, Wallingford, Oxon, OX10 9RB
Activities: Other professional, scientific and technical activities n.e.c.
Parent: Fugro Holdings Limited
Officers: Linda Pasmore, Secretary; Mark Adams [1971] Director; Leslie Llewellyn Lugg [1975] Director; Ross Allen Stevens [1973] Director

Fugro Holdings Limited
Incorporated: 26 March 1993
Net Worth: £23,567,000 *Total Assets:* £122,124,000
Registered Office: Fugro House, Hithercroft Road, Wallingford, Oxon, OX10 9RB
Activities: Financial management
Parent: Fugro International Holding AG
Officers: Gordon John Duncan, Secretary; Philip Gerard Meaden [1962] Managing Director

Fugro Properties Limited
Incorporated: 14 January 1998
Net Worth: £15,336,000 *Total Assets:* £20,349,000
Registered Office: Fugro House, Hithercroft Road, Wallingford, Oxon, OX10 9RB
Activities: Other letting and operating of own or leased real estate
Parent: Fugro Holdings Limited
Officers: Emma Louise Herlihy, Secretary; Gordon John Duncan [1963] Director/Regional Controller UK & Ireland; Philip Gerard Meaden [1962] Managing Director

Fujifilm UK Limited
Incorporated: 22 June 1976 *Employees:* 324
Net Worth: £75,588,000 *Total Assets:* £110,252,000
Registered Office: St Martins Business Centre, St Martins Way, Bedford, MK42 0LF
Activities: Wholesale of radio, television goods & electrical household appliances (other than records, tapes, CDs)
Parent: Fujifilm Holdings Corporation
Officers: Neil Llewellyn Denham, Secretary; Yoshitaka Nakamura [1967] Director [Japanese]; Masato Yamamoto [1963] Director [Japanese]

Fulcrum Infrastructure Services Limited
Incorporated: 22 November 2006
Net Worth Deficit: £2,296,000 *Total Assets:* £31,020,000
Registered Office: 2 Europa View, Sheffield Business Park, Sheffield, S9 1XH
Activities: Other business support service activities n.e.c.
Parent: Fulcrum Utility Services Limited
Officers: Ian Foster [1966] Director; Martin John Harrison [1969] Director

Fulcrum Pipelines Limited
Incorporated: 22 November 2006
Net Worth: £4,981,000 *Total Assets:* £17,823,000
Registered Office: 2 Europa View, Sheffield Business Park, Sheffield, S9 1XH
Activities: Other business support service activities n.e.c.
Parent: Fulcrum Utility Services Limited
Officers: Ian Foster [1966] Director; Martin John Harrison [1969] Director

Fulham Wharf LLP
Incorporated: 18 June 2012
Net Worth: £97,089,000 *Total Assets:* £99,063,000
Registered Office: Barratt House, Cartwright Way, Forest Business Park, Bardon Hill, Coalville, Leics, LE67 1UF

Full Moon Holdco 4 Limited
Incorporated: 2 August 2006
Net Worth: £2,800,000 *Total Assets:* £120,200,000
Registered Office: Sleepy Hollow, Aylesbury Road, Thame, Oxon, OX9 3AT
Activities: Other business support service activities n.e.c.
Parent: Thame and London Limited
Officers: Joanna Boydell, Secretary; Katherine Anna Ashford Thomas, Secretary; Joanna Boydell [1969] Director/Chief Financial Officer; Peter Darren Gowers [1972] Director/Chief Executive Officer; Paul Victor Harvey [1961] Director; Brian Godman Wallace [1954] Director

Full Moon Holdco 5 Limited
Incorporated: 2 August 2006
Net Worth Deficit: £76,200,000 *Total Assets:* £106,600,000
Registered Office: Sleepy Hollow, Aylesbury Road, Thame, Oxon, OX9 3AT
Activities: Other business support service activities n.e.c.
Parent: Full Moon Holdco 4 Limited
Officers: Joanna Boydell, Secretary; Katherine Anna Ashford Thomas, Secretary; Joanna Boydell [1969] Director/Chief Financial Officer; Peter Darren Gowers [1972] Director/Chief Executive Officer; Paul Victor Harvey [1961] Director

Full Moon Holdco 6 Limited
Incorporated: 2 August 2006
Net Worth: £522,200,000 *Total Assets:* £954,200,000
Registered Office: Sleepy Hollow, Aylesbury Road, Thame, Oxon, OX9 3AT
Activities: Other business support service activities n.e.c.
Parent: Full Moon Holdco 5 Limited
Officers: Joanna Boydell, Secretary; Katherine Anna Ashford Thomas, Secretary; Joanna Boydell [1969] Director/Chief Financial Officer; Peter Darren Gowers [1972] Director/Chief Executive Officer; Paul Victor Harvey [1961] Director

Full Moon Holdco 7 Limited
Incorporated: 25 June 2015
Net Worth: £306,600,000 *Total Assets:* £810,099,968
Registered Office: Sleepy Hollow, Aylesbury Road, Thame, Oxon, OX9 3AT
Activities: Other business support service activities n.e.c.
Parent: Full Moon Holdco 6 Limited
Officers: Joanna Boydell, Secretary; Katherine Anna Ashford Thomas, Secretary; Joanna Boydell [1969] Director/Chief Financial Officer; Peter Darren Gowers [1972] Director; Paul Victor Harvey [1961] Director

Full Moon Holdings Limited
Incorporated: 22 March 1985
Net Worth: £3,089,337 *Total Assets:* £12,839,397
Registered Office: Station Works, Station Road, Long Buckby, Northampton, NN6 7PF
Activities: Activities of head offices
Parent: Sina Holdco Limited
Officers: Khosrow Jahanshad [1953] Director/Mining Engineer [Iranian]; Gogol Kafi [1950] Director

Fullbrook Thorpe Investments LLP
Incorporated: 4 February 2015 *Employees:* 1
Net Worth: £50,897,000 *Total Assets:* £50,986,000
Registered Office: The Boardwalk, Mercia Marina, Findern Lane, Willington, Derbys, DE65 6DW
Officers: Andrew Thomas Borkowski [1962] Member; Thomas Andrew Leaver [1992] Member; Andrew Derrick Leaver [1962] LLP Member

H.B. Fuller Group Limited
Incorporated: 7 September 2001
Net Worth: £26,218,000 *Total Assets:* £36,406,000
Registered Office: Globe Lane Industrial Estate, Outram Road, Dukinfield, Cheshire, SK16 4XE
Activities: Activities of head offices
Parent: Datac Adhesives Limited
Officers: Robert Joseph Martsching [1964] Director/Vice President and Corporate Controller [American]; Emilio Roque Vilas [1968] Business Director Hygiene [Spanish]; Heidi Ann Weiler [1966] Director/Vice President and Treasurer [American]

H.B. Fuller U.K. Limited
Incorporated: 20 November 1997 *Employees:* 28
Net Worth: £18,651,996 *Total Assets:* £19,873,486
Registered Office: Globe Lane Industrial Estate, Outram Road, Dukinfield, Cheshire, SK16 4XE
Activities: Other business support service activities n.e.c.
Parent: H.B. Fuller U.K. Operations Limited
Officers: Robert Joseph Martsching [1964] Director/Vice President and Corporate Controller [American]; Emilio Roque Vilas [1968] Business Director Hygiene [Spanish]

HB Fuller UK Operations Limited
Incorporated: 27 March 1998
Net Worth: £36,084,000 *Total Assets:* £57,599,000
Registered Office: Globe Lane Industrial Estate, Dukinfield, Cheshire, SK16 4XE
Activities: Manufacture of other chemical products n.e.c.
Parent: H.B. Fuller Group Limited
Officers: Robert Joseph Martsching [1964] Director/Vice President and Corporate Controller [American]; Emilio Roque Vilas [1968] Business Director Hygiene [Spanish]; Heidi Ann Weiler [1966] Director/Vice President and Treasurer [American]

Funeral Partners Bidco Limited
Incorporated: 3 June 2015 *Employees:* 15
Net Worth Deficit: £18,713,000 *Total Assets:* £95,486,000
Registered Office: 80 Mount Street, Nottingham, NG1 6HH
Activities: Activities of other holding companies n.e.c.
Parent: Funeral Partners Holdco Limited
Officers: Andrew Hector Fraser, Secretary; Andrew Hector Fraser [1971] Director; Neil Robert Graham [1966] Investment Director; Paul Christopher Hawkes [1975] Director; Samuel Patrick Donald Kershaw [1963] Funeral Director

Funeral Partners Holdco Limited
Incorporated: 3 June 2015 *Employees:* 561
Net Worth Deficit: £9,304,000 *Total Assets:* £132,620,000
Registered Office: 80 Mount Street, Nottingham, NG1 6HH
Activities: Activities of other holding companies n.e.c.
Parent: Funeral Partners Midco Limited
Officers: Andrew Hector Fraser, Secretary; Andrew Hector Fraser [1971] Director; Samuel Patrick Donald Kershaw [1963] Funeral Director

Funeral Partners Limited
Incorporated: 12 June 2007 *Employees:* 547
Net Worth: £25,148,000 *Total Assets:* £66,808,000
Registered Office: Cumberland Court, 80 Mount Street, Nottingham, NG1 6HH
Activities: Funeral and related activities
Parent: Funeral Services Partnership Limited
Officers: Andrew Hector Fraser, Secretary; Andrew Hector Fraser [1971] Director; Paul Christopher Hawkes [1975] Director; Samuel Patrick Donald Kershaw [1963] Funeral Director

Funeral Partners Midco Limited
Incorporated: 3 June 2015
Net Worth Deficit: £7,389,000 *Total Assets:* £38,597,000
Registered Office: 80 Mount Street, Nottingham, NG1 6HH
Activities: Activities of other holding companies n.e.c.
Parent: Funeral Partners Topco Limited
Officers: Andrew Hector Fraser, Secretary; Andrew Hector Fraser [1971] Director; Samuel Patrick Donald Kershaw [1963] Funeral Director

Funeral Services Partnership Limited
Incorporated: 19 January 2007
Net Worth Deficit: £2,980,000 *Total Assets:* £11,385,000
Registered Office: 80 Mount Street, Nottingham, NG1 6HH
Activities: Activities of other holding companies n.e.c.
Parent: FSP Acquisition Limited
Officers: Andrew Hector Fraser, Secretary; Andrew Hector Fraser [1971] Director; Samuel Patrick Donald Kershaw [1963] Funeral Director

Fusion Group Limited
Incorporated: 14 May 1998 *Employees:* 23
Net Worth: £10,719,000 *Total Assets:* £25,645,000
Registered Office: Smeckley Wood Close, Chesterfield Trading Estate, Chesterfield, Derbys, S41 9PZ
Activities: Other professional, scientific and technical activities n.e.c.
Parent: Fusion Investco Ltd
Officers: Gayle Broadhurst, Secretary; Neil Anthony Green [1965] Finance Director; Paul John Hubbard [1959] Director; Joergen Bo Johansen [1969] Technical Director [Danish]; Lars Kudsk [1960] Director [Danish]

Fusion Plastics Limited
Incorporated: 14 May 1998 *Employees:* 135
Net Worth: £3,174,000 *Total Assets:* £21,456,000
Registered Office: Smeckley Wood Close, Chesterfield Trading Estate, Chesterfield, Derbys, S41 9PZ
Activities: Manufacture of plastics in primary forms
Parent: Fusion Group Ltd
Officers: Gayle Broadhurst, Secretary; Neil Anthony Green [1965] Finance Director; Paul John Hubbard [1959] Director; Joergen Bo Johansen [1969] Technical Director [Danish]; Lars Kudsk [1960] Director [Danish]

Futaba Industrial U.K. Ltd.
Incorporated: 26 November 2004 *Employees:* 228
Net Worth: £5,397,000 *Total Assets:* £37,526,000
Registered Office: Park Avenue, Dove Valley Park, Foston, Derbys, DE65 5BT
Activities: Manufacture of other fabricated metal products n.e.c.
Parent: Futaba Industrial Co Ltd
Officers: Masami Fukui, Secretary; Masami Fukui [1962] Director [Japanese]; Uichi Maeda [1961] Director [Japanese]; Tetsunori Matsuo [1961] Director [Japanese]; Kevin Schofield [1958] Director; Kenji Tsuyuguchi [1959] Director [Japanese]

Future Travel Limited
Incorporated: 25 November 1996 *Employees:* 7
Net Worth: £716,000 *Total Assets:* £11,843,000
Registered Office: Westpoint, Peterborough Business Park, Lynch Wood, Peterborough, Cambs, PE2 6FZ
Activities: Travel agency activities
Parent: Co-op Group Travel 2 Holdings Limited
Officers: Shirley Bradley, Secretary; Alan Charles Donald [1963] Director; David John Elstob [1944] Director; Paul Russell [1962] Director

Futures Homescape Limited
Incorporated: 25 February 2002 *Employees:* 60
Net Worth: £16,909,000 *Total Assets:* £149,604,000
Registered Office: Asher House, Asher Lane Business Park, Ripley, Derbys, DE5 3SW
Activities: Renting and operating of Housing Association real estate
Officers: Ian Skipp, Secretary; David Gary Brooks [1967] Director; Mary Theresa Daunt [1963] Trustee & Non-Executive Director; Stephen Matthew Hale [1962] Director of Property Services; Raymond Harding [1950] Director; Sheila Ann Hyde [1956] Director; David James Leathley [1947] Director/Accountant; Ciara Clare McMillan [1980] Industry Director; Timothy Ian Slater [1964] Director/IT Manager; Michael William Stevenson [1963] Retired Commercial Banking Director; Howard Anthony Maldwyn Taylor [1945] Director/Retired; Philip John Tooley [1960] Director/Bursar and Company Secretary; Lindsey Claire Williams [1964] Director/Group Chief Executive

Futures Homeway Limited
Incorporated: 10 April 2006 *Employees:* 17
Previous: Daventry & District Housing Limited
Net Worth Deficit: £3,343,000 *Total Assets:* £48,433,000
Registered Office: Asher House, Asher Lane Business Park, Ripley, Derbys, DE5 3SW
Activities: Renting and operating of Housing Association real estate
Officers: Ian Skipp, Secretary; David Gary Brooks [1967] Director; Mary Theresa Daunt [1963] Trustee & Non-Executive Director; Stephen Matthew Hale [1962] Director of Property Services; Raymond Harding [1950] Director; Sheila Ann Hyde [1956] Director/Retired; David James Leathley [1947] Director/Accountant; Ciara Clare McMillan [1980] Industry Director; Timothy Ian Slater [1964] Director/IT Manager; Michael William Stevenson [1963] Retired Commercial Banking Director; Howard Anthony Maldwyn Taylor [1945] Director/Retired; Philip John Tooley [1960] Company Secretary/Director; Lindsey Claire Williams [1964] Director/Group Chief Executive

Futures Housing Group Limited
Incorporated: 26 June 2007 *Employees:* 282
Net Worth: £20,024,000 *Total Assets:* £207,435,008
Registered Office: Asher House, Asher Lane Business Park, Ripley, Derbys, DE5 3SW
Activities: Activities of head offices
Officers: Ian Skipp, Secretary; David Gary Brooks [1967] Director; Mary Theresa Daunt [1963] Trustee & Non-Executive Director; Stephen Matthew Hale [1962] Director of Property Services; Raymond Harding [1950] Director; Sheila Ann Hyde [1956] Director; David James Leathley [1947] Director/Accountant; Ciara Clare McMillan [1980] Industry Director; Timothy Ian Slater [1964] Director/IT Manager; Michael William Stevenson [1963] Retired Commercial Banking Director; Howard Anthony Maldwyn Taylor [1945] Director/Retired; Philip John Tooley [1960] Director/Company Secretary; Lindsey Claire Williams [1964] Director/Group Chief Executive

G.B. Terminals Limited
Incorporated: 24 June 1991 *Employees:* 291
Net Worth: £5,985,986 *Total Assets:* £16,957,776
Registered Office: Meridian House, Alexandra Dock North, Grimsby, N E Lincs, DN31 3UA
Activities: Operation of warehousing and storage facilities for water transport activities
Parent: GBA (Holdings) Limited
Officers: John Charles Gunn, Secretary; Maureen Judah [1953] Director; Samson Sassoon Samuel Judah [1953] Director

G.H.B. (Holding) Limited
Incorporated: 5 January 1977 *Employees:* 357
Net Worth: £31,814,534 *Total Assets:* £58,138,596
Registered Office: Celebration House, Stanley Street, Burton on Trent, Staffs, DE14 1DY
Activities: Manufacture of other general-purpose machinery n.e.c.
Shareholders: Michael Peter Burton; Charles Nicholas Burton
Officers: Michael Peter Burton, Secretary; Tony William Harry Bell [1957] Sales Director; Charles Nicholas Burton [1957] Director; Jo Ann Burton [1958] Director; Michael Peter Burton [1959] Director; Stephen Ingram [1949] Director/Corporate Finance Advisor; Leslie John Lowde [1956] Director/Chartered Accountant

G2M Unilets Limited
Incorporated: 31 July 2001 *Employees:* 2
Net Worth: £6,652,235 *Total Assets:* £9,627,463
Registered Office: 25 Jetstream Drive, Aukley, Doncaster, S Yorks, DN9 3QS
Activities: Other letting and operating of own or leased real estate
Shareholders: Paul Darren Morton; Victoria Louise Winchester Morton
Officers: Victoria Morton, Secretary; Paul Darren Morton [1971] Director/Accountant

Gafoor Pure Halal Ltd
Incorporated: 9 December 2011 *Employees:* 274
Net Worth: £7,547,235 *Total Assets:* £15,816,910
Registered Office: 109 Coleman Road, Leicester, LE5 4LE
Activities: Production of meat and poultry meat products
Major Shareholder: Ozayr Patel
Officers: Ozayr Patel [1986] Director

Gallagher Bathgate Limited
Incorporated: 29 September 1999
Net Worth: £9,523,890 *Total Assets:* £11,449,630
Registered Office: Gallagher House, Gallagher Business Park, Heathcote, Warwick, CV34 6AF
Activities: Development of building projects
Shareholders: Taylor Wimpey UK Limited; J J Gallagher Ltd
Officers: Katherine Elizabeth Hindmarsh, Secretary; William Rae Burns [1964] Director; Anthony Christopher Gallagher [1951] Director; Geoffrey Hugh Gosling [1947] Director/Chartered Accountant; Graeme Smith [1969] Finance Director

Gallagher Developments Caerphilly Limited
Incorporated: 11 December 2013
Net Worth: £666,857 *Total Assets:* £31,731,340
Registered Office: Gallagher House, Gallagher Way, Gallagher Business Park, Heathcote, Warwick, CV34 6AF
Activities: Other letting and operating of own or leased real estate
Parent: Gallagher Developments Holdco Limited
Officers: Anthony Christopher Gallagher [1951] Chairman/Director; Geoffrey Hugh Gosling [1947] Director

Gallagher Developments Holdco Limited
Incorporated: 11 December 2013 *Employees:* 2
Net Worth: £77,335,000 *Total Assets:* £99,083,000
Registered Office: Gallagher House, Gallagher Way, Gallagher Business Park, Heathcote, Warwick, CV34 6AF
Activities: Buying and selling of own real estate
Major Shareholder: Anthony Christopher Gallagher
Officers: Anthony Christopher Gallagher [1951] Chairman/Director; Geoffrey Hugh Gosling [1947] Director

Gallagher Elstow Limited
Incorporated: 30 November 2001 *Employees:* 4
Net Worth Deficit: £6,325,251 *Total Assets:* £42,762,696
Registered Office: Gallagher House, Gallagher Way, Gallagher Business Park, Heathcote, Warwick, CV34 6AF
Activities: Buying and selling of own real estate
Parent: Wixams First Limited
Officers: Edward Paul Farnsworth [1982] Director of Business Planning; Craig David Luttman [1975] Development Director; Martin Rowland Richmond [1953] Group Legal Director; Gregg Spencer Wilkinson [1973] Managing Director

Gallagher Estates Holdings Limited
Incorporated: 19 November 1993
Previous: Gallagher Estates No. 1 Limited
Net Worth: £120,926,280 *Total Assets:* £120,958,024
Registered Office: Gallagher House, Gallagher Way, Gallagher Business Park, Heathcote, Warwick, CV34 6AF
Activities: Buying and selling of own real estate
Officers: Edward Paul Farnsworth [1982] Director of Business Planning; Craig David Luttman [1975] Development Director; Martin Rowland Richmond [1953] Group Legal Director; Gregg Spencer Wilkinson [1973] Managing Director

Gallagher Estates Limited
Incorporated: 21 March 1995 *Employees:* 37
Previous: J.J.Gallagher Limited
Net Worth: £204,456,048 *Total Assets:* £383,724,096
Registered Office: Gallagher House, Gallagher Way, Gallagher Business Park, Heathcote, Warwick, CV34 6AF
Activities: Buying and selling of own real estate
Parent: Gallagher Estates No. 2 Limited
Officers: Edward Paul Farnsworth [1982] Director of Business Planning; Craig David Luttman [1975] Development Director; Martin Rowland Richmond [1953] Group Legal Director; Gregg Spencer Wilkinson [1973] Managing Director

Gallagher Estates No. 2 Limited
Incorporated: 21 February 1997 *Employees:* 4
Previous: A C Gallagher Holdings Limited
Net Worth: £24,661,664 *Total Assets:* £40,120,000
Registered Office: Gallagher House, Gallagher Way, Gallagher Business Park, Heathcote, Warwick, CV34 6AF
Activities: Buying and selling of own real estate
Parent: GW 305 Limited
Officers: Edward Paul Farnsworth [1982] Director of Business Planning; Craig David Luttman [1975] Development Director; Martin Rowland Richmond [1953] Group Legal Director; Gregg Spencer Wilkinson [1973] Managing Director

Gallagher Investments Holdco Limited
Incorporated: 11 December 2013 *Employees:* 2
Net Worth: £32,152,348 *Total Assets:* £32,490,482
Registered Office: Gallagher House, Gallagher Way, Gallagher Business Park, Heathcote, Warwick, CV34 6AF
Activities: Buying and selling of own real estate
Parent: Gallagher Developments Holdco Limited
Officers: Anthony Christopher Gallagher [1951] Chairman/Director; Geoffrey Hugh Gosling [1947] Director

Gallagher Llanwern Limited
Incorporated: 25 June 2002 *Employees:* 4
Net Worth: £4,055,753 *Total Assets:* £16,956,448
Registered Office: Gallagher House, Gallagher Way, Gallagher Business Park, Heathcote, Warwick, CV34 6AF
Activities: Buying and selling of own real estate
Officers: Edward Paul Farnsworth [1982] Director of Business Planning; Craig David Luttman [1975] Development Director; Martin Rowland Richmond [1953] Group Legal Director; Gregg Spencer Wilkinson [1973] Managing Director

Gallagher Longstanton Limited
Incorporated: 26 March 1998 *Employees:* 5
Net Worth: £13,475,150 *Total Assets:* £56,602,496
Registered Office: Gallagher House, Gallagher Way, Gallagher Business Park, Heathcote, Warwick, CV34 6AF
Activities: Buying and selling of own real estate
Officers: Edward Paul Farnsworth [1982] Director of Business Planning; Craig David Luttman [1975] Development Director; Martin Rowland Richmond [1953] Group Legal Director; Gregg Spencer Wilkinson [1973] Managing Director

Gallagher Poole Limited
Incorporated: 24 May 2000 *Employees:* 4
Net Worth Deficit: £4,169,340 *Total Assets:* £10,919,548
Registered Office: Gallagher House, Gallagher Way, Gallagher Business Park, Heathcote, Warwick, CV34 6AF
Activities: Buying and selling of own real estate
Officers: Edward Paul Farnsworth [1982] Director of Business Planning; Craig David Luttman [1975] Development Director; Martin Rowland Richmond [1953] Group Legal Director; Gregg Spencer Wilkinson [1973] Managing Director

Gallagher Projects Limited
Incorporated: 30 November 2001
Net Worth: £8,981,136 *Total Assets:* £9,645,564
Registered Office: Gallagher House, Gallagher Way, Gallagher Business Park, Heathcote, Warwick, CV34 6AF
Activities: Management of real estate on a fee or contract basis
Officers: Edward Paul Farnsworth [1982] Director of Business Planning; Craig David Luttman [1975] Development Director; Martin Rowland Richmond [1953] Group Legal Director; Gregg Spencer Wilkinson [1973] Managing Director

Gallos Limited
Incorporated: 9 December 1988
Net Worth Deficit: £7,214,591 *Total Assets:* £16,542,452
Registered Office: Ashby Road, Measham, Swadlincote, Derbys, DE12 7JP
Activities: Financial intermediation not elsewhere classified
Shareholders: John Stuart Bloor; Bloor Holdings Limited
Officers: Dinesh Kumar Ishwerlal Khushalbhai Mehta, Secretary; John Stuart Bloor [1943] Director; John Lambert Eastham [1951] Director/Accountant; Dinesh Kumar Ishwerlal Khushalbhai Mehta [1951] Director/Chartered Accountant

Games Workshop Group PLC
Incorporated: 9 December 1991 *Employees:* 1,907
Net Worth: £84,478,000 *Total Assets:* £116,229,000
Registered Office: Willow Road, Lenton, Nottingham, NG7 2WS
Activities: Activities of other holding companies n.e.c.
Officers: Rachel Tongue, Secretary; John Richard Alistair Brewis [1966] Managing Director; Nicholas John Donaldson [1953] Director; Christopher John Myatt [1943] Director; Elaine O'Donnell [1970] Non-Executive Director/Chartered Accountant [Irish]; Kevin Derek Rountree [1969] Director/Accountant; Rachel Frances Tongue [1971] Director/Accountant

Games Workshop International Limited
Incorporated: 29 April 1994 *Employees:* 2
Net Worth: £24,580,000 *Total Assets:* £24,582,000
Registered Office: Willow Road, Lenton, Nottingham, NG7 2WS
Activities: Manufacture of other games and toys, n.e.c.
Officers: Rachel Tongue, Secretary; Kevin Derek Rountree [1969] Director/Accountant; Rachel Frances Tongue [1971] Director/Accountant

Games Workshop Limited
Incorporated: 17 December 1979 *Employees:* 1,163
Net Worth: £36,359,000 *Total Assets:* £63,344,000
Registered Office: Willow Road, Lenton, Nottingham, NG7 2WS
Activities: Manufacture of other games and toys, n.e.c.
Parent: Games Workshop Group PLC
Officers: Rachel Tongue, Secretary; Kevin Derek Rountree [1969] Director/Accountant; Rachel Frances Tongue [1971] Director/Accountant

Games Workshop US (Holdings) Limited
Incorporated: 1 May 2002 *Employees:* 2
Net Worth: £9,679,000 *Total Assets:* £9,679,000
Registered Office: Willow Road, Lenton, Nottingham, NG7 2WS
Activities: Manufacture of other games and toys, n.e.c.
Parent: Games Workshop International
Officers: Rachel Tongue, Secretary; Kevin Derek Rountree [1969] Director/Accountant; Rachel Frances Tongue [1971] Director/Accountant

Games Workshop US Limited
Incorporated: 7 December 2010 *Employees:* 2
Net Worth: £13,156,000 *Total Assets:* £13,156,000
Registered Office: Willow Road, Lenton, Nottingham, NG7 2WS
Activities: Manufacture of other games and toys, n.e.c.
Parent: Games Workshop US (Holdings) Limited
Officers: Rachel Tongue, Secretary; Kevin Derek Rountree [1969] Director/Accountant; Rachel Tongue [1971] Director/Accountant

Gaming Acquisitions Limited
Incorporated: 9 January 2010 *Employees:* 3
Net Worth: £48,149,000 *Total Assets:* £166,144,000
Registered Office: 3 The Maltings, Wetmore Road, Burton on Trent, Staffs, DE14 1SE
Activities: Activities of other holding companies n.e.c.
Parent: DMWSL 631 Limited
Officers: Carys Damon, Secretary; Stewart Frank Bradley Baker [1983] Director/Chief Financial Officer; Carys Damon [1976] Director/Solicitor; Brooks Harrison Pierce [1961] Director/President [American]

Gamston Aviation Limited
Incorporated: 27 October 1977 *Employees:* 20
Net Worth: £10,303,195 *Total Assets:* £11,219,322
Registered Office: Retford (Gamston) Airport, Gamston Airfield, Gamston, Retford, Notts, DN22 0QL
Activities: Service activities incidental to air transportation
Major Shareholder: Kevin McDonald
Officers: Donna Brigitte McDonald, Secretary; Amie McDonald [1993] Director; Donna Brigitte McDonald [1962] Director; Kevin McDonald [1933] Managing Director

Gamston Kennels & Farms Limited
Incorporated: 1 January 1964 *Employees:* 210
Net Worth: £11,155,514 *Total Assets:* £18,628,800
Registered Office: Pedigree House, Ambleside, Gamston, Nottingham, NG2 6NQ
Activities: Activities of head offices
Shareholders: Stephen Andrew Brown; Terence William Brown
Officers: Christopher James Laud, Secretary; Michelle Brown [1969] Director; Stephen Andrew Brown [1971] Managing Director; Terence William Brown [1943] Director; Wendy Lynn Brown [1948] Director; Christopher James Laud [1964] Director/Chartered Accountant

Gands (U.K.)
Incorporated: 4 February 1993 *Employees:* 540
Net Worth: £71,576,000 *Total Assets:* £152,284,992
Registered Office: c/o OSI Food Solutions UK Ltd, Luneburg Way, Scunthorpe, N Lincs, DN15 8LP
Activities: Activities of head offices
Shareholders: Sheldon Lavin; Gerald Arthur Kolschowsky
Officers: Martin Howard Back, Secretary; Sherry Anne de Meulenaere, Secretary; Sherry Anne Demeulenaere [1958] Director and Company Secretary [American]; Sheldon Lavin [1932] Director/President OSI Industries Inc [American]; David Gerard McDonald [1964] Director [American]

Gapuma (UK) Limited
Incorporated: 8 April 1999 *Employees:* 24
Net Worth: £15,998,793 *Total Assets:* £31,741,526
Registered Office: Mazars LLP, The Pinnacle, 160 Midsummer Boulevard, Milton Keynes, Bucks, MK9 1FF
Activities: Other business support service activities n.e.c.
Parent: Gapuma Group Limited
Officers: Jack Bardakjian, Secretary/Director; Jack Bardakjian [1970] Director; Puzant Hagop Bardakjian [1937] Director

Gapuma Group Limited
Incorporated: 1 April 2008 *Employees:* 56
Net Worth: £15,638,542 *Total Assets:* £33,175,924
Registered Office: Mazars LLP, The Pinnacle, 160 Midsummer Boulevard, Milton Keynes, Bucks, MK9 1FF
Activities: Activities of head offices
Parent: Gapuma Holdings Limited
Officers: Jack Bardakjian, Secretary; Jack Bardakjian [1970] Director; Amit Mahesh Parekh [1966] Director

Gardeden Bidco Limited
Incorporated: 18 May 2015
Net Worth Deficit: £159,071 *Total Assets:* £9,397,929
Registered Office: 1st Floor, Broadoak, Southgate Park, Bakewell Road, Orton Southgate, Peterborough, Cambs, PE2 6YS
Activities: Activities of other holding companies n.e.c.
Parent: Rutland III GP LLP
Officers: Paul Ian Cartwright [1961] Director/Chartered Accountant; Jonathan Halford [1968] Director; Benjamin St Pierre Slatter [1973] Director/Investment Manager; Robert Jan Thompson [1977] Director; Peter Andrew Utting [1967] Director/Chief Executive

Gardeden Midco Limited
Incorporated: 18 May 2015
Net Worth Deficit: £3,951,564 *Total Assets:* £15,837,711
Registered Office: 1st Floor, Broadoak, Southgate Park, Bakewell Road, Orton Southgate, Peterborough, Cambs, PE2 6YS
Activities: Activities of other holding companies n.e.c.
Parent: Rutland III GP LLP
Officers: Paul Ian Cartwright [1961] Director/Chartered Accountant; Jonathan Halford [1968] Director; Benjamin St Pierre Slatter [1973] Director/Investment Manager; Robert Jan Thompson [1977] Director; Peter Andrew Utting [1967] Director/Chief Executive

Gardeden Topco Limited
Incorporated: 18 May 2015
Net Worth Deficit: £5,629,787 *Total Assets:* £36,810,852
Registered Office: 1st Floor, Broadoak, Southgate Park, Bakewell Road, Orton Southgate, Peterborough, Cambs, PE2 6YS
Activities: Activities of other holding companies n.e.c.
Parent: Rutland III GP LLP
Officers: Paul Ian Cartwright [1961] Director/Chartered Accountant; Jonathan Halford [1968] Director; Benjamin St Pierre Slatter [1973] Director/Investment Manager; Robert Jan Thompson [1977] Director; Peter Andrew Utting [1967] Director/Chief Executive

Gardner Aerospace - Basildon Limited
Incorporated: 8 February 2000 *Employees:* 176
Net Worth: £6,139,000 *Total Assets:* £17,031,000
Registered Office: Unit 9 Victory Park, Victory Road, Derby, DE24 8ZF
Activities: Machining
Parent: Gardner Group Limited
Officers: Jackie Anne Storer, Secretary; Dominic Owen Cartwright [1976] Director/Vice President, Business Development; Nicholas Ian Burgess Sanders [1961] Director; Antony John Upton [1975] Director; Kenneth Ian Worth [1967] Director

Gardner Aerospace - Derby Limited
Incorporated: 8 May 1998 *Employees:* 217
Net Worth: £6,741,000 *Total Assets:* £23,465,000
Registered Office: Unit 9 Victory Park, Victory Road, Derby, DE24 8ZF
Activities: Manufacture of air and spacecraft and related machinery
Parent: Gardner Group Limited
Officers: Jackie Anne Storer, Secretary; Dominic Owen Cartwright [1976] Director/Vice President, Business Development; Nicholas Ian Burgess Sanders [1961] Director; Antony John Upton [1975] Director; Kenneth Ian Worth [1967] Director

Gardner Aerospace - Hull Limited
Incorporated: 10 December 1959 *Employees:* 82
Net Worth: £2,898,000 *Total Assets:* £9,059,000
Registered Office: Unit 9 Victory Park, Victory Road, Derby, DE24 8ZF
Activities: Manufacture of air and spacecraft and related machinery
Parent: Gardner Group Limited
Officers: Jackie Anne Storer, Secretary; Dominic Owen Cartwright [1976] Director/Vice President, Business Development; Nicholas Ian Burgess Sanders [1961] Director; Antony John Upton [1975] Director; Kenneth Ian Worth [1967] Director

Gardner Aerospace Holdings Limited
Incorporated: 6 March 2012 *Employees:* 1,483
Net Worth: £54,648,000 *Total Assets:* £123,686,000
Registered Office: Unit 9 Victory Park, Victory Road, Derby, DE24 8ZF
Activities: Activities of production holding companies
Shareholder: Zheng Zhang
Officers: Jackie Anne Storer, Secretary; Dominic Owen Cartwright [1976] Director/Vice President, Business Development; Nicholas James Guttridge [1959] Director; Nicholas Ian Burgess Sanders [1961] Director; Antony John Upton [1975] Director; Lizhi Wang [1949] Director [Taiwanese]; Kenneth Ian Worth [1967] Director

Gardner Aerospace-Broughton Limited
Incorporated: 21 September 2006 *Employees:* 89
Net Worth: £6,139,000 *Total Assets:* £15,036,000
Registered Office: Unit 9 Victory Park, Victory Road, Derby, DE24 8ZF
Activities: Manufacture of metal structures and parts of structures
Parent: Gardner Group Limited
Officers: Jackie Anne Storer, Secretary; Dominic Owen Cartwright [1976] Director/Vice President, Business Development; Nicholas Ian Burgess Sanders [1961] Director; Antony John Upton [1975] Director; Kenneth Ian Worth [1967] Director

Gardner Group Limited
Incorporated: 20 February 2003 *Employees:* 62
Net Worth: £24,820,000 *Total Assets:* £84,757,000
Registered Office: Unit 9 Victory Park, Victory Road, Derby, DE24 8ZF
Activities: Manufacture of air and spacecraft and related machinery
Parent: Gardner Aerospace Holdings Limited
Officers: Jackie Anne Storer, Secretary; Dominic Owen Cartwright [1976] Director/Vice President, Business Development; Nicholas James Guttridge [1959] Director; Nicholas Ian Burgess Sanders [1961] Director/Partner; Antony John Upton [1975] Director; Kenneth Ian Worth [1967] Director

Garner Holdings Limited
Incorporated: 14 February 2013 *Employees:* 112
Previous: Garner Properties Limited
Net Worth: £30,887,508 *Total Assets:* £53,201,252
Registered Office: Garner House, Ormonde Drive, Denby Hall Business Park, Denby, Derbys, DE5 8LE
Activities: Other letting and operating of own or leased real estate
Shareholders: Janet Ann Hartshorn; Roger Laurence Hartshorn
Officers: Emma Arrell, Secretary; Janet Ann Hartshorn [1965] Director; Roger Laurence Hartshorn [1960] Director; Ross Hartshorn [1993] Director

Gartree High School
Incorporated: 10 April 2012 *Employees:* 106
Net Worth: £13,971,638 *Total Assets:* £15,350,434
Registered Office: Gartree High School, Ridge Way, Oadby, Leicester, LE2 5TQ
Activities: General secondary education
Officers: Eleanor Johnston Delday, Secretary; Paul Edward Bannister [1961] Director/Teacher; Dr Donald Brian Candlin [1932] Director/Retired; Jyotika Hammonds [1969] Director/Floristry Business Owner; Sally Kay Hawksworth [1968] Director/Teacher; Pankaj Pancholi [1955] Managing Director; Donna Parmar [1966] Director/Registered Nurse; Adrian Peryer [1954] Director/Consultant; Reverend John Cooksley Rackley [1949] Director/Retired Minister; Professor James Mark Saker [1952] Associate Dean & Director of Marketing; Sonia Louise Singleton [1968] Director/Headteacher; Philip Storey [1966] Director/Land Registry Officer; Shantilal Mathuradas Thanki [1949] Director/Retired

Gatecrasher Apartments Limited
Incorporated: 4 March 2016
Net Worth: £2,459,000 *Total Assets:* £17,094,000
Registered Office: Devonshire Green House, 14 Fitzwilliam Street, Sheffield, S1 4JL
Activities: Other letting and operating of own or leased real estate
Parent: Devonshire Green (Broomgrove Road) Limited
Officers: Ewan Gairn Barclay Ross, Secretary; Brendan Elwood [1943] Director; Martin Patrick Elwood [1968] Director/Property Investment and Development; Dale Lee Fixter [1967] Director/Chartered Surveyor

Gateway Plaza Limited
Incorporated: 31 May 2005
Net Worth: £3,559,733 *Total Assets:* £18,419,902
Registered Office: Lower Plaza 1, Gateway Plaza, Fitzwilliam Street, Barnsley, S Yorks, S70 2RF
Activities: Development of building projects
Parent: Quest Property Limited
Officers: Matthew Bell, Secretary; Jason Lee Brook [1972] Executive Director; John Martin Brook [1948] Director/Chairman

ADP Gauselmann UK Limited
Incorporated: 9 July 2014 *Employees:* 12
Net Worth: £8,203,323 *Total Assets:* £32,579,384
Registered Office: Fortune House, Northgate Terrace, Newark on Trent, Notts, NG24 2EU
Activities: Activities of other holding companies n.e.c.
Officers: Sascha Blodau [1969] Director [German]; Jochen Clemens [1986] Managing Director [German]; Sophie Hannah Pope [1982] Director

GB Fleetcare Limited
Incorporated: 11 September 2000 *Employees:* 86
Net Worth: £8,008,776 *Total Assets:* £10,234,507
Registered Office: 10 Thorpe Way, Banbury, Oxon, OX16 4SP
Activities: Maintenance and repair of motor vehicles
Officers: Paul Peter Grimes, Secretary; Peter Denis Banwell [1951] Director; Paul Peter Grimes [1967] Director; Joanna Marguerite Patel-Banwell [1973] Director

GBA Group Limited
Incorporated: 13 April 2015 *Employees:* 467
Net Worth: £10,515,215 *Total Assets:* £26,581,736
Registered Office: Meridian House, Alexandra Dock North, Grimsby, N E Lincs, DN31 3UA
Activities: Activities of other holding companies n.e.c.
Shareholder: Maureen Judah
Officers: John Charles Gunn, Secretary; Maureen Judah [1953] Director; Samson Sassoon Samuel Judah [1953] Managing Director

GCI Managed Services Group Limited
Incorporated: 17 March 2005 *Employees:* 398
Previous: GCI Telecom Group Limited
Net Worth: £23,834,344 *Total Assets:* £112,308,688
Registered Office: Global House, 2 Crofton Close, Lincoln, LN3 4NT
Activities: Other telecommunications activities
Shareholders: JTC Trustees Limited; Wayne Jason Martin
Officers: Mark David Allen, Secretary; Mark David Allen [1975] Director; Adrian Albert Thirkill [1963] Director/Chief Executive

GCI Network Solutions Limited
Incorporated: 3 October 2000 *Employees:* 237
Previous: Wan Services Limited
Net Worth: £46,612,728 *Total Assets:* £58,881,056
Registered Office: Global House, Crofton Close, Lincoln, LN3 4NT
Activities: Other telecommunications activities
Parent: GCI Managed Services Group Limited
Officers: Mark David Allen, Secretary; Mark David Allen [1975] Director; Adrian Albert Thirkill [1963] Director/Chief Executive

GE Energy Power Conversion Technology Limited
Incorporated: 1 September 2006
Net Worth: £104,913,072 *Total Assets:* £132,434,808
Registered Office: Boughton Road, Rugby, Warwicks, CV21 1BU
Activities: Other research and experimental development on natural sciences and engineering
Parent: GE Energy Power Conversion UK Holdings Limited
Officers: David John Allcock [1965] Director [British/Canadian]; Andrew James Bullock [1972] Director; Andrew Mark Cooper [1967] Director; Derek William Grieve [1957] Director; Iain Graham Ross MacDonald [1966] Director/Solicitor; Peter Oram [1970] Commercial Director; Nicholas Alexander Shelbourne [1975] Director/Accountant; Nicholas Simon Smith [1969] Technical Solutions Director

GE Energy Power Conversion UK Holdings Limited
Incorporated: 18 September 2008
Net Worth: £11,428,000 *Total Assets:* £186,824,000
Registered Office: Boughton Road, Rugby, Warwicks, CV21 1BU
Activities: Repair of electrical equipment
Parent: GE UK Holdings
Officers: Stuart James Bage [1971] Director/Human Resources Manager; Andrew James Bullock [1972] Director; Andrew Mark Cooper [1967] Director; Paul Mark English [1968] Director; Derek William Grieve [1957] Director; Syreeta Odette Jeffs [1975] Commercial and Risk Director; Iain Graham Ross MacDonald [1966] Director/Solicitor; Peter Oram [1970] Commercial Director; Nicholas Alexander Shelbourne [1975] Director/Accountant

GE Energy Power Conversion UK Limited
Incorporated: 22 September 2005 *Employees:* 902
Net Worth Deficit: £96,920,000 *Total Assets:* £207,780,992
Registered Office: Boughton Road, Rugby, Warwicks, CV21 1BU
Activities: Repair of electrical equipment
Parent: GE Energy Power Conversion UK Holdings Limited
Officers: Stuart James Bage [1971] Director/Human Resources Manager; Andrew James Bullock [1972] Director; Andrew Mark Cooper [1967] Director; Paul Mark English [1968] Director; Derek William Grieve [1957] Director; Syreeta Odette Jeffs [1975] Commercial and Risk Director; Iain Graham Ross MacDonald [1966] Director/Solicitor; Peter Oram [1970] Commercial Director; Nicholas Alexander Shelbourne [1975] Director/Accountant

GEA Mechanical Equipment UK Limited
Incorporated: 22 September 1958 *Employees:* 49
Net Worth: £5,174,624 *Total Assets:* £19,167,414
Registered Office: Westfalia House, Old Wolverton Road, Old Wolverton, Milton Keynes, Bucks, MK12 5PY
Activities: Wholesale of other machinery and equipment
Officers: Nicolas Richard Preston, Secretary; Ilija Aprcovic [1966] Managing Director; Timothy John Donbavand [1967] Finance Director; Tracey Ann Oneill [1968] Director/Human Resources

Geberit Sales Limited
Incorporated: 7 March 2007 *Employees:* 154
Net Worth: £22,644,000 *Total Assets:* £39,873,000
Registered Office: Geberit House, Edgehill Drive, Warwick, CV34 6NH
Activities: Wholesale of hardware, plumbing and heating equipment and supplies
Officers: Christine Susan Morris, Secretary; Christian Dominik Buhl [1973] Director [Swiss]; Mark David Larden [1965] Managing Director; Christine Susan Morris [1982] Finance Director; Dr Karl Spachmann [1958] European Sales Director [German]

Gee Bee Investments Limited
Incorporated: 5 April 2007 *Employees:* 2
Net Worth: £2,590,648 *Total Assets:* £15,208,432
Registered Office: Highdown House, 11 Highdown Road, Sydenham, Leamington Spa, Warwicks, CV31 1XT
Activities: Development of building projects
Officers: Dr Gurmit Singh, Secretary/Director; Burinder Kaur Singh [1969] Director; Dr Gurmit Singh [1961] Director

Geely UK Limited
Incorporated: 19 December 2012 *Employees:* 532
Net Worth: £119,481,000 *Total Assets:* £549,401,024
Registered Office: Li Close, Ansty Park, Ansty, Coventry, Warwicks, CV7 9RF
Activities: Other manufacturing n.e.c.
Major Shareholder: Li Shufu
Officers: Conghui [1970] Director/President & CEO, Geely Holding Group [Chinese]; Carl-Peter Edmund Moriz Forster [1954] Director/Manager [German]; Donghui Li [1970] Director [Chinese]; Jianqun Zhou [1965] Director [Chinese]

Gefco U.K. Limited
Incorporated: 10 February 1981 *Employees:* 498
Net Worth: £16,995,000 *Total Assets:* £61,980,000
Registered Office: Central Boulevard, Prologis Park, Coventry, Warwicks, CV6 4BX
Activities: Maintenance and repair of motor vehicles
Parent: JSC Russian Railways
Officers: Thomas Marie Carre [1966] Director [French]; Pierre Jean Marie Lorrain [1961] Director [French]; Olivier Andre Claude Tissier [1967] Director/Head of Legal Services Department [French]

Gelder Group Holdings Limited
Incorporated: 2 December 2010 *Employees:* 285
Net Worth: £4,072,363 *Total Assets:* £17,261,842
Registered Office: Tillbridge Lane, Sturton by Stow, Lincoln, LN1 2DS
Activities: Activities of head offices
Major Shareholder: Stephen Paul Gelder
Officers: Wendy Diane Gelder, Secretary; Stephen Paul Gelder [1966] Director; David Anthony Jeffery Gladwin [1967] Director

Gelder Limited
Incorporated: 29 April 1993 *Employees:* 263
Net Worth: £3,266,268 *Total Assets:* £14,677,074
Registered Office: Tillbridge Lane, Sturton by Stow, Lincoln, LN1 2DS
Activities: Construction of commercial buildings
Major Shareholder: Stephen Paul Gelder
Officers: Arran James Michael Fullwood, Secretary; Arran James Michael Fullwood [1982] Director; Stephen Paul Gelder [1966] Director/Builder; David Anthony Jeffery Gladwin [1967] Director/Builder

Gellaw 101 Limited
Incorporated: 15 February 2006
Net Worth: £1,000 *Total Assets:* £95,955,000
Registered Office: Pride Park Stadium, Pride Park, Derby, DE24 8XL
Activities: Activities of head offices
Parent: Global Derby (UK) Limited
Officers: Stephen Anthony Pearce, Secretary; Melvyn Morris [1956] Director; Stephen Anthony Pearce [1980] Director/Chartered Accountant

Gemini Rail Services UK Ltd
Incorporated: 19 August 2013 *Employees:* 375
Previous: Knorr-Bremse Railservices (UK) Limited
Net Worth Deficit: £30,693,000 *Total Assets:* £34,624,000
Registered Office: Wolverton Works, Stratford Road, Wolverton, Milton Keynes, Bucks, MK12 5NT
Activities: Repair and maintenance of other transport equipment n.e.c.
Parent: Mutares Holding-25 AG
Officers: Lee Watkins, Secretary; Nicholas Fitzwater [1970] Managing Director; Christian Klingler [1975] Director [Austrian]; Lee Watkins [1967] Finance Director

Gemsupa Limited
Incorporated: 21 June 1994
Net Worth: £72,449,312 *Total Assets:* £74,767,688
Registered Office: 56 London Road, Alderley Edge, Cheshire, SK9 7DZ
Activities: Activities of other holding companies n.e.c.
Major Shareholder: Jennifer Louise Dawson
Officers: William Marshall Smith, Secretary/Solicitor; Jennifer Louise Dawson [1984] Director; Peter Stuart Dawson [1952] Director/Chartered Surveyor; William Marshall Smith [1955] Director/Company Solicitor; Martin Allan Ridgway [1968] Director/Chartered Surveyor

General Conference of The New Church (The)
Incorporated: 16 February 1872 *Employees:* 23
Net Worth: £18,747,064 *Total Assets:* £19,244,564
Registered Office: Purley Chase Centre, Purley Chase Lane, Mancetter, Atherstone, Warwicks, CV9 2RQ
Activities: Activities of religious organisations
Officers: Jennifer Zoe Brooks, Secretary; Jennifer Zoe Brooks [1944] Director/Retired Public Servant; Richard Harold Cunningham [1957] Director/Assessor; Maurice David Haseler [1943] Director/Retired; Lara Kay Nicholls [1969] Director/Pre-School Practitioner; Judith Margaret Wilson [1942] Director/Retired

General Domestic Appliances Holdings Limited
Incorporated: 2 September 1958
Net Worth: £114,043,000 *Total Assets:* £146,974,000
Registered Office: Morley Way, Peterborough, Cambs, PE2 9JB
Activities: Activities of head offices
Parent: Indesit Company UK Holdings Limited
Officers: Tetiana Pidhaina, Secretary; Lucianna Raffaini Carvalho [1973] Director [Italian]; Andrzej Tuleja [1973] Director [Polish]

Generation Two Limited
Incorporated: 27 March 2012 *Employees:* 87
Net Worth: £7,357,379 *Total Assets:* £12,834,540
Registered Office: Coolair House, Globe Lane, Dukinfield, Cheshire, SK16 4UJ
Activities: Activities of head offices
Shareholder: John James Otterson
Officers: Adam Anthony Garstang [1968] Director; Mark Garstang [1971] Director; Neil Simon Gibbard [1970] Director; John James Otterson [1959] Director; Helen Sharratt [1966] Director/Chartered Accountant; Steven Valentine [1972] Director

Genie International Holdings Limited
Incorporated: 15 June 1998
Net Worth: £6,523,000 *Total Assets:* £11,243,000
Registered Office: The Maltings, Wharf Road, Grantham, Lincs, NG31 6BH
Activities: Activities of other holding companies n.e.c.
Parent: Terex Corporation
Officers: Eric Cohen, Secretary/Business Executive [American]; Eric I Cohen [1958] Director/Business Executive [American]; Matthew Sean Fearon [1961] Director/President, Terex Aerial Work Platforms [American]; Joseph M. George [1956] Director/Vice President, Operations, Aerial Work Platforms [American]; John Daniel Sheehan [1960] Director/Chief Financial Officer [American]

Genie Topco Limited
Incorporated: 10 February 2016 *Employees:* 43
Net Worth Deficit: £3,424,000 *Total Assets:* £16,063,000
Registered Office: Suite 1, Clare Hall, St Ives Business Park, Parsons Green, St Ives, Cambs, PE27 4WY
Activities: Activities of other holding companies n.e.c.
Shareholders: Livingbridge Enterprise LLP; Livingbridge Enterprise GP Limited
Officers: Lee Andrew Cowles [1969] Director; Simone Ceri Girardeau [1989] Director; Simon Angus Guild [1964] Director; David John Kirby [1985] Director; Robert James Maynard [1974] Finance Director; Paul James Ward [1968] Director

Genie UK Limited
Incorporated: 13 December 1989 *Employees:* 72
Net Worth: £10,655,000 *Total Assets:* £29,998,000
Registered Office: The Maltings, Wharf Road, Grantham, Lincs, NG31 6BH
Activities: Other specialised construction activities n.e.c.
Parent: Terex Corporation
Officers: Eric I Cohen, Secretary/Business Executive [American]; Eric I Cohen [1958] Director/Business Executive [American]; Matthew Sean Fearon [1961] Director/President, Terex Aerial Work Platforms [American]; Joseph M. George [1956] Director/Vice President, Operations, Aerial Work Platforms [American]; Matthias Jung [1967] Director [German]; John Daniel Sheehan [1960] Director/Chief Financial Officer [American]

Genistics Holdings Limited
Incorporated: 30 July 2001
Net Worth Deficit: £5,342,150 *Total Assets:* £33,790,896
Registered Office: Rolls Royce PLC, P O Box 31, Moor Lane, Derby, DE24 8BJ
Activities: Activities of head offices
Shareholders: Investment Holdings (Genistics) Limited; Rolls-Royce PLC
Officers: Carolyn Marie Sharpe, Secretary; Andrew Biggs [1966] Managing Director; John Cavill [1972] Director/Partner; Avinash Misra [1977] Finance Director [Indian]; Peter John Sheldrake [1959] Director

Genistics Limited
Incorporated: 30 July 2001
Net Worth Deficit: £5,342,150 *Total Assets:* £33,790,896
Registered Office: Rolls Royce PLC, P O Box 31, Moor Lane, Derby, DE24 8BJ
Activities: Repair of electrical equipment
Parent: Genistics Holdings Limited
Officers: Carolyn Marie Sharpe, Secretary; Andrew Biggs [1966] Managing Director; John Cavill [1972] Director/Partner; Avinash Misra [1977] Finance Director [Indian]; Peter John Sheldrake [1959] Director

Genzyme Therapeutics Limited
Incorporated: 5 November 2001 *Employees:* 100
Net Worth: £42,235,000 *Total Assets:* £101,503,000
Registered Office: 4620 Kingsgate, Cascade Way, Oxford Business Park South, Oxford, OX4 2SU
Activities: Wholesale of pharmaceutical goods
Parent: Sanofi-Aventis UK Holdings Limited
Officers: Francois-Xavier Duhalde [1965] Director/Chief Finance Office UK [French]; Peter Sjoerd Kuiper [1960] Director/General Manager [Dutch]

GEO Amey PECS Limited
Incorporated: 8 March 2011 *Employees:* 2,347
Net Worth: £4,300,000 *Total Assets:* £15,585,000
Registered Office: The Sherard Building, Edmund Halley Road, Oxford, OX4 4DQ
Activities: Other passenger land transport
Shareholders: Amey Community Limited; The Geo Group Limited
Officers: David Donahue [1959] Director/Vice President US Corrections & Detention [American]; Brian Robert Evans [1967] Director/Chief Financial Officer [American]; Amanda Lucia Fisher [1963] Managing Director; Asif Ghafoor [1970] Director; Amber Dawn Martin [1962] Director/Corrections [American]; Kyle Peter Schiller [1965] Director/Vice President, Operations/Administration [American]; Richard James Ward [1977] Finance Director; George C Zoley [1950] Director/Chairman & CEO [American]

Mick George Limited
Incorporated: 29 August 1989 *Employees:* 921
Net Worth: £32,593,000 *Total Assets:* £128,930,000
Registered Office: 6 Lancaster Way, Ermine Business Park, Huntingdon, Cambs, PE29 6XU
Activities: Quarrying of ornamental and building stone, limestone, gypsum, chalk and slate
Major Shareholder: Michael Eric George
Officers: Karen Ann Farrell, Secretary; Geoffrey Craven [1964] Logistics Director; Michael Alexander George [1984] Contracts Director; Michael Eric George [1956] Director/Haulage Contractor; Neil Graham Johnson [1971] Technical Waste Director; Peter David Newman [1957] Engineering Director; Jonathan Paul Stump [1964] Finance Director

F & A George Limited
Incorporated: 11 August 1941 *Employees:* 8
Net Worth: £4,563,000 *Total Assets:* £13,818,000
Registered Office: Victoria Mills, Wellingborough, Northants, NN8 2DT
Activities: Growing of cereals (except rice), leguminous crops and oil seeds
Major Shareholder: Martin Francis George
Officers: Simone Louise Large, Secretary; Martin Francis George [1942] Director; Michael David George [1973] Director; Angus Charles Gunning [1946] Director; Simone Louise Large [1979] Director/Chartered Accountant

Georgetown Carr Limited
Incorporated: 18 August 2008 *Employees:* 2
Net Worth: £92,441 *Total Assets:* £11,031,204
Registered Office: Britannic House, Regent Street, Barnsley, S Yorks, S70 2EQ
Activities: Buying and selling of own real estate
Officers: Michael John Milnes Walker, Secretary/Solicitor; Michael John Milnes Walker [1938] Director/Solicitor; Robert Michael Walker [1972] Director/Chartered Surveyor

Georgia GC Holdings Limited
Incorporated: 12 June 2015
Net Worth: £5,821,498 *Total Assets:* £12,875,683
Registered Office: Fremantle House, 2 Oakwater Avenue, Cheadle Royal Business Park, Cheadle, Cheshire, SK8 3SR
Activities: Activities of head offices
Shareholders: Stephen James Mort; Tracy Lynn Mort; Business Growth Fund PLC BGF Investments LP
Officers: Steven James Mort, Secretary; Richard Cotter [1961] Director/Chairman; Tracy Lynn Mort [1974] Managing Director; Paul Leslie Oldham [1964] Director; John Alan Thompson [1969] Director/Chief Operations Officer

Georgica Limited
Incorporated: 24 July 2000
Net Worth: £106,605,000 *Total Assets:* £107,615,000
Registered Office: Aragon House, Cranfield Technology Park, Cranfield, Bedford, MK43 0EQ
Activities: Other amusement and recreation activities n.e.c.
Parent: Essenden Limited
Officers: George Jason Sheppard, Secretary; Nicholas Andrew Basing [1962] Director; Graham Edwin Blackwell [1969] Commercial Director; Alan Michael Hand [1968] Operations Director [Irish]; George Jason Sheppard [1981] Director/Chartered Accountant; Mark Simon Willis [1976] Director

Germanischer Lloyd Industrial Services Holdings (UK) Limited
Incorporated: 3 July 2007
Net Worth: £20,144,676 *Total Assets:* £20,144,676
Registered Office: Holywell Park, Ashby Road, Loughborough, Leics, LE11 3GR
Activities: Activities of head offices
Officers: Mervyn Cajetan Fernandez [1956] Finance Director; James Lee [1972] Director/Chartered Accountant; Dr Michael John Pritchard [1955] Director/VP Process and Integrity

Germany Farms Limited
Incorporated: 27 April 1989 *Employees:* 15
Net Worth: £3,616,433 *Total Assets:* £15,937,005
Registered Office: Lodge Farm, Norwell, Newark, Notts, NG23 6LA
Activities: Raising of poultry
Shareholders: Christopher James Germany; John Robert Germany; Robert Germany
Officers: Suzanne Marie Germany, Secretary; Christopher James Germany [1967] Director/Farmer; John Robert Germany [1960] Director/Farmer; Robert Germany [1939] Director/Farmer

GES Service Companies Limited
Incorporated: 25 January 2007
Net Worth: £26,498,000 *Total Assets:* £29,580,000
Registered Office: GES, Silverstone Drive, Gallagher Business Park, Coventry, Warwicks, CV6 6PA
Activities: Non-trading company
Officers: Michael Stewart, Secretary; Ellen Marie Ingersoll [1964] Director [American]; Steven Moster [1970] Director/Chairman, President and CEO of Viad Corp [American]; Jason Popp [1970] Director/Vice President [American]

Ghekko Holdings Limited
Incorporated: 4 December 2007 *Employees:* 61
Net Worth: £9,892,582 *Total Assets:* £14,026,472
Registered Office: Primary House, Spring Gardens, Macclesfield, Cheshire, SK10 2AP
Activities: Activities of head offices
Major Shareholder: Nigel Robin Skinner
Officers: Michael Andrew Taylor, Secretary; Nigel Robin Skinner [1967] Director

Ghekko Limited
Incorporated: 6 November 1991 *Employees:* 34
Net Worth: £307,760 *Total Assets:* £9,570,879
Registered Office: Amtri House, Hulley Road, Macclesfield, Cheshire, SK10 2NE
Activities: Wholesale of electronic and telecommunications equipment and parts
Major Shareholder: Nigel Robin Skinner
Officers: Michael Andrew Taylor, Secretary; Michael William Neillans [1980] Director; Nigel Robin Skinner [1967] Director/Secretary

GHP Midco Limited
Incorporated: 6 October 2003
Net Worth: £713,638,016 *Total Assets:* £713,638,016
Registered Office: Brooks House, Coventry Road, Warwick, CV34 4LL
Activities: Activities of head offices
Officers: Karen Dawn Roberts, Secretary; Simon Charles Oliver [1968] Director; Jan-Feie Zwiers [1972] Director/Group Finance Controller [Dutch]

GI Group Holdings Recruitment Limited
Incorporated: 24 March 2011
Net Worth Deficit: £790,080 *Total Assets:* £33,078,628
Registered Office: Draefern House, Dunston Court, Dunston Road, Chesterfield, Derbys, S41 8NL
Activities: Other activities of employment placement agencies
Parent: GI International S.R.L.
Officers: Jane Elizabeth Brewin, Secretary; Jane Elizabeth Brewin [1970] Finance Director; Stefano Luciano Oreste Colli-Lanzi [1964] Director/Chief Executive Officer [Italian]; Maurizio Uboldi [1963] Director [Italian]; Beverley Marie White [1958] Director/Chief Executive

GI Group Recruitment Ltd
Incorporated: 23 September 1985 *Employees:* 9,696
Net Worth: £12,254,796 *Total Assets:* £52,732,296
Registered Office: Draefern House, Dunston Court, Dunston Road, Chesterfield, Derbys, S41 8NL
Activities: Temporary employment agency activities
Parent: GI Recruitment
Officers: Jane Elizabeth Brewin, Secretary; Jane Elizabeth Brewin [1970] Finance Director; Paul Anthony Smith [1969] Director; Beverley Marie White [1958] Director/Chief Executive

GI Recruitment Limited
Incorporated: 14 July 1993 *Employees:* 14,112
Net Worth: £15,593,000 *Total Assets:* £70,540,000
Registered Office: Draefern House, Dunston Court, Dunston Road, Chesterfield, Derbys, S41 8NL
Activities: Temporary employment agency activities
Parent: GI Group Holdings Recruitment
Officers: Jane Elizabeth Brewin, Secretary; Jane Elizabeth Brewin [1970] Finance Director; Stefano Luciano Oreste Colli-Lanzi [1964] Director/Chief Financial Officer [Italian]; Pietro Ghizzoni [1962] Director/Chief Financial Officer [Italian]; Maurizio Uboldi [1963] Director [Italian]; Bev Marie White [1958] Director/Chief Executive; Beverley Marie White [1958] Director/Chief Executive

GI Solutions Group Limited
Incorporated: 28 July 1992 *Employees:* 286
Net Worth: £11,545,000 *Total Assets:* £25,211,000
Registered Office: 147 Scudamore Road, Leicester, LE3 1UQ
Activities: Other manufacturing n.e.c.
Parent: GI Solutions Holdings Limited
Officers: Sotos Constantinides [1966] Director; Patrick John Headley [1968] Director

Giant Bidco Limited
Incorporated: 10 December 2004
Net Worth Deficit: £408,600,000 *Total Assets:* £121,900,000
Registered Office: Equity House, Irthlingborough Road, Wellingborough, Northants, NN8 1LT
Activities: Dormant company
Parent: Giant Midco Limited
Officers: Veselin Bandev [1978] Finance Director [Bulgarian]; Charles Wilson [1965] Director

Giant Booker Limited
Incorporated: 29 March 1900
Net Worth: £238,600,000 *Total Assets:* £524,000,000
Registered Office: Equity House, Irthlingborough Road, Wellingborough, Northants, NN8 1LT
Activities: Dormant company
Parent: BF Limited
Officers: Veselin Bandev [1978] Finance Director [Bulgarian]; Charles Wilson [1965] Director

Giant Midco Limited
Incorporated: 10 December 2004
Net Worth Deficit: £16,300,000 *Total Assets:* £286,200,000
Registered Office: Equity House, Irthlingborough Road, Wellingborough, Northants, NN8 1LT
Activities: Dormant company
Parent: Booker Wholesale Holdings Limited
Officers: Veselin Bandev [1978] Finance Director [Bulgarian]; Charles Wilson [1965] Director

Giant U.K. Limited
Incorporated: 21 September 1987 *Employees:* 24
Net Worth: £10,421,486 *Total Assets:* £36,572,792
Registered Office: Charnwood Edge, Syston Road, Cossington, Leicester, LE7 4UZ
Activities: Non-specialised wholesale trade
Officers: Aaron Bargewell, Secretary/Finance Manager; Ian Jeffery Beasant [1968] Managing Director; John Kam Hoi Koo [1961] Director/Corporate President [Malaysian]; Pi-Yu Wang [1965] Director/Finance [Taiwanese]

Gibbons (Holdings) Limited
Incorporated: 4 January 1996 *Employees:* 6
Net Worth: £26,415,372 *Total Assets:* £27,881,952
Registered Office: Manor Farm, Baston, Peterborough, Cambs, PE6 9PB
Activities: Growing of cereals (except rice), leguminous crops and oil seeds
Major Shareholder: David John Gibbons
Officers: Andrew Colin Eason, Secretary; David John Gibbons [1951] Managing Director

Gibbs Croft Limited
Incorporated: 8 January 2014 *Employees:* 138
Net Worth Deficit: £18,873,000 *Total Assets:* £38,209,000
Registered Office: Chetwode House, 1 Samworth Way, Melton Mowbray, Leics, LE13 1GA
Activities: Manufacture of rusks and biscuits; manufacture of preserved pastry goods and cakes
Parent: Samworth Brothers (Holdings) Limited
Officers: Timothy James Barker, Secretary; Steven Clive Bailey [1961] Director; Flor Aiden Healy [1962] Director [Irish]; Richard Alexis Robertson Marris [1968] Director; Mark Charles Chetwode Samworth [1970] Director

Gibbs Technologies Limited
Incorporated: 21 December 1998
Net Worth: £3,699,930 *Total Assets:* £9,473,443
Registered Office: Avenue Road, Nuneaton, Warwicks, CV11 4LY
Activities: Manufacture of other transport equipment n.e.c.
Officers: Alan Timothy Gibbs [1939] Director [New Zealander]; Neil Graham Jenkins [1954] Director; Noel Alfred Lane [1955] Director [New Zealander]

R.A. Gibson (Colesden) Limited
Incorporated: 12 October 1945 *Employees:* 10
Net Worth: £14,475,672 *Total Assets:* £16,759,308
Registered Office: Bell Farm, Colesden, Beds, MK44 3DB
Activities: Growing of cereals (except rice), leguminous crops and oil seeds
Officers: Matthew Broadhurst, Secretary; Ivor Allen Gibson [1957] Director/Surveyor; Jill Diana Gibson [1927] Director; Laura Gibson [1987] Director/Teacher; Nigel Roy Gibson [1951] Director/Journalist; Ross Alexander Gibson [1992] Director/Student; Emily Rose Reynolds [1985] Director/Meteorologist

Simon Gibson Transport Limited
Incorporated: 24 September 2002 *Employees:* 186
Net Worth: £4,297,844 *Total Assets:* £20,426,252
Registered Office: Unit 1, A W Nielsen Road, Goole, E Yorks, DN14 6UE
Activities: Freight transport by road
Shareholders: Simon Gibson; GCA Europe S.A.
Officers: Delphine Andre [1966] Director [French]; Jacques Duvauchelle [1974] Director [French]; Simon Gibson [1974] Director/Haulage Contractor; Jean-Emmanuel Mongnot [1967] Director [French]

Gigaclear Limited
Incorporated: 22 December 2010 *Employees:* 178
Previous: Gigaclear PLC
Net Worth: £99,077,000 *Total Assets:* £127,430,000
Registered Office: Building One, Wyndyke Furlong, Abingdon, Oxon, OX14 1UQ
Activities: Other telecommunications activities
Parent: Infracapital (GC) GP Limited
Officers: Michele Armanini [1979] Director/Investment Manager [Italian]; Charles Stuart McGregor [1957] Director; Edward Peter Minshull [1958] Director; Stephen Keith James Nelson [1963] Asset Management Director; Gareth John Williams [1966] Director/Chief Executive Officer

The Giles Academy
Incorporated: 20 August 2010 *Employees:* 165
Net Worth: £12,988,601 *Total Assets:* £14,631,260
Registered Office: The Giles Academy, Church End, Old Leake, Boston, Lincs, PE22 9LD
Activities: General secondary education
Officers: Diane Patricia Burrell, Secretary; Helen Theresa Banham [1967] Director; Albert Guy Bull [1953] Director; Alan Castley [1959] Director/Teacher; Roy Timothy Cowern [1953] Director/Retired; Sophie Curtis [1996] Director/Sales & Marketing Executive; Maxine Hill [1957] Director/Florist; Geoffrey Martin Prior [1951] Director/Business Manager; David Relton [1957] Director/Teacher of Design Technology; Sarah Anwen Whelbourn [1961] Director; Ian Charles Widdows [1968] Director/Headteacher

Douglas Gill International Limited
Incorporated: 2 December 1985 *Employees:* 47
Net Worth: £12,331,519 *Total Assets:* £13,856,789
Registered Office: Manor House Road, Long Eaton, Nottingham, NG10 1LR
Activities: Manufacture of other wearing apparel and accessories n.e.c.
Parent: Gill Marine Holdings Limited
Officers: Matthew Francis Clark [1973] Director; Dominic Charles McCarthy [1980] Director; Ian Graydon Poore [1967] Director; Jamie Thomas Tunnicliffe [1971] Director

Gill Marine Holdings Limited
Incorporated: 1 November 2012 *Employees:* 47
Net Worth: £349,317 *Total Assets:* £14,174,007
Registered Office: Manor House Road, Long Eaton, Nottingham, NG10 1LR
Activities: Activities of head offices
Shareholders: Jessica Blair Kimmel; Laura Davies; Thomas Campbell Kenneth Myers
Officers: Neil Crowe [1983] Director; Elijah Duckworth-Schachter [1969] Director [American]; Richard Dennis Jones [1965] Director; Shaun Nesbitt [1985] Director; Ian Graydon Poore [1967] Director; Peter Thomas [1950] Director/Consultant [New Zealander]; Jamie Thomas Tunnicliffe [1971] Director

Gilo Investments Limited
Incorporated: 19 April 2002 *Employees:* 4
Net Worth: £9,830,156 *Total Assets:* £9,887,210
Registered Office: Sovereign Court, 230 Upper Fifth Street, Central Milton Keynes, Bucks, MK9 2HR
Activities: Financial intermediation not elsewhere classified
Shareholders: Philip Matthews and Martin Maguire as Trustees of Charles Coward 1967 Settlement & Trustees of CR Coward 1986 Settlement & Charles Coward 1967 Settlement; Philip Matthews and Martin Maguire as Trustees of Charles Coward 1967 Settlement & Trustees of CR Coward 1986 Settlement & Charles Coward 1967 Settlement
Officers: Martin Patrick Maguire, Secretary/Chartered Accountant; Anna Coward [1978] Director/Solicitor; Giles Alexander Coward [1974] Director/Surveyor; Martin Patrick Maguire [1955] Director/Chartered Accountant; Philip Matthews [1954] Director/Solicitor

Gilzoni Limited
Incorporated: 2 November 2010 *Employees:* 1
Net Worth: £187,426,032 *Total Assets:* £187,434,112
Registered Office: 19 Jessops Riverside, 800 Brightside Lane, Sheffield, S9 2RX
Activities: Activities of head offices
Parent: Danaher Corporation
Officers: Keith Graham Ward [1953] Director/Finance and Accounting

Giorgio's Continental Ltd.
Incorporated: 1 June 1987 *Employees:* 88
Net Worth: £10,100,531 *Total Assets:* £23,144,680
Registered Office: Moorgreen Industrial Park, Dunsil Road, Engine Lane, Newthorpe, Nottingham, NG16 3PX
Activities: Processing and preserving of meat
Officers: Salvatore Devivo [1966] Managing Director

GL Events UK Limited
Incorporated: 4 January 1945 *Employees:* 196
Previous: Owen Brown Limited
Net Worth: £28,591,942 *Total Assets:* £47,543,180
Registered Office: Station Road, Castle Donington, Derbys, DE74 2NL
Activities: Other specialised construction activities n.e.c.
Parent: GL Events SA
Officers: Dan Black, Secretary; Francois Appy [1960] Director [French]; Keith Bishop [1965] Director; Dan Black [1966] Finance Director; Olivier Ginon [1958] Director [French]; Scott William Jameson [1977] Managing Director; Eric Rostagnat [1952] Director [French]

GL Industrial Services UK Ltd
Incorporated: 18 December 1996 *Employees:* 333
Net Worth: £22,389,000 *Total Assets:* £46,031,000
Registered Office: Holywell Park, Ashby Road, Loughborough, Leics, LE11 3GR
Activities: Engineering related scientific and technical consulting activities
Officers: Mervyn Cajetan Fernandez [1956] Director; Dr Michael John Pritchard [1955] Director; Pradeep Vamadevan [1967] Director/Regional Manager

GL UK Holdings Limited
Incorporated: 31 December 1930 *Employees:* 1
Previous: Gilbarco Limited
Net Worth: £209,682,000 *Total Assets:* £209,686,000
Registered Office: 19 Jessops Riverside, 800 Brightside Lane, Sheffield, S9 2RX
Activities: Activities of head offices
Shareholder: DH Omega Limited
Officers: Keith Graham Ward [1953] Finance Director

Gladstone Limited
Incorporated: 4 March 1997 *Employees:* 3
Net Worth: £16,389,699 *Total Assets:* £20,540,600
Registered Office: c/o Gladstone MRM, Hithercroft Road, Wallingford, Oxon, OX10 9BT
Activities: Activities of head offices
Parent: Constellation Software UK Holdco Ltd
Officers: Jemma Belghoul, Secretary; Darrell Peter Boxall [1970] Director/Portfolio Manager; Richard Clancy [1973] Director/Portfolio Manager; Jeffrey Raymond MacKinnon [1969] Director [Canadian]; Scott Ryan Saklad [1972] Director [American]; Barry Symons [1970] Director [Canadian]

Gladstone MRM Limited
Incorporated: 4 March 1981 *Employees:* 141
Net Worth: £869,578 *Total Assets:* £13,358,668
Registered Office: Hithercroft Road, Wallingford, Oxon, OX10 9BT
Activities: Business and domestic software development
Parent: Gladstone Limited
Officers: Jemma Belghoul, Secretary; Darrell Peter Boxall [1970] Director/Portfolio Manager; Scott Ryan Saklad [1972] Director [American]; Thomas Withers [1975] Director/MD

Glanmoor Investments Limited
Incorporated: 16 October 1953 *Employees:* 5
Net Worth: £11,536,976 *Total Assets:* £11,684,111
Registered Office: The Chapel, High Street, Pytchley, Kettering, Northants, NN14 1EN
Activities: Development of building projects
Officers: William James Herbert Spooner, Secretary/Director; Georgina Ann Glover [1945] Director/Photographer; Max George Lousada [1973] Director/Record Label Manager; Tomas Julian Lousada [1977] Director/Executive Designer; Professor Geoffrey Charles Philip Rayner [1950] Director/Health Policy Analyst; Jessica Rayner [1985] Director/Artist; Adrian Generald John Spooner [1960] Director/Insurance Broker; Sir James Douglas Spooner [1932] Director; Tania Mary Spooner [1964] Director/Writer; William James Herbert Spooner [1965] Director/Surveyor

Glass Recycling (UK) Limited
Incorporated: 8 May 1974 *Employees:* 55
Net Worth: £29,752,776 *Total Assets:* £31,621,044
Registered Office: 418 Carlton Road, Carlton, Barnsley, S Yorks, S71 3HX
Activities: Treatment and disposal of non-hazardous waste
Major Shareholder: Trevor Sykes
Officers: Trevor Sykes, Secretary/Director; Michael Joseph Durr [1963] Director/Works Manager; Trevor Sykes [1944] Director

J.C.M.Glassford Limited
Incorporated: 25 June 1959 *Employees:* 12
Net Worth: £13,456,997 *Total Assets:* £20,233,344
Registered Office: Apley Head Farm, Clumber, Notts, S80 3NU
Activities: Growing of cereals (except rice), leguminous crops and oil seeds
Parent: J.C.M Glassford (Holdings) Limited
Officers: Lesley Bradshaw, Secretary; Timothy Charles Bradshaw [1959] Director/Farmer

Glazewing Limited
Incorporated: 15 April 1986 *Employees:* 82
Net Worth: £181,901 *Total Assets:* £9,882,679
Registered Office: Glazewing House, Station Road, West Dereham, Kings Lynn, Norfolk, PE33 9RR
Activities: Wholesale of waste and scrap
Parent: Valens Resources Group PLC
Officers: Simon David Miles, Secretary/Chartered Accountant; Jonathan Miles [1963] Director; Simon David Miles [1960] Director/Chartered Accountant; Jason Minns [1976] Director/Accountant

Gleadell Agriculture Limited
Incorporated: 3 June 1954 *Employees:* 163
Net Worth: £16,326,000 *Total Assets:* £68,907,000
Registered Office: Lindsey House, Hemswell Cliff, Gainsborough, Lincs, DN21 5TH
Activities: Wholesale of grain, unmanufactured tobacco, seeds and animal feeds
Shareholders: ADM Arkady Limited; Invivo Grains
Officers: Michael John Thompson, Secretary; Stephane Bernhard [1970] Director [French]; Timothy John Cahalin [1964] Director; Jonathan Edward Lane [1976] Director; Gary Thomas McGuigan [1971] Director [Irish]; Stuart James Shand [1962] Director/Agricultural Merchant; David Thomas Sheppard [1961] Director/Grain Trader; Michael John Thompson [1965] Director/Certified Accountant

Gleeson Developments Limited
Incorporated: 13 May 1965 *Employees:* 463
Net Worth: £74,074,000 *Total Assets:* £90,362,000
Registered Office: 6 Europa Court, Sheffield Business Park, Sheffield, S9 1XE
Activities: Construction of domestic buildings
Parent: MJ Gleeson PLC
Officers: Stefan Peter Allanson [1965] Director/Accountant; Dermot James Gleeson [1949] Director; Jolyon Leonard Harrison [1948] Director

M J Gleeson Group Limited
Incorporated: 15 March 1950 *Employees:* 2
Net Worth: £5,815,000 *Total Assets:* £9,958,000
Registered Office: 6 Europa Court, Sheffield Business Park, Sheffield, S9 1XE
Activities: Construction of commercial buildings
Parent: MJ Gleeson PLC
Officers: Stefan Peter Allanson [1965] Director/Accountant; Dermot James Gleeson [1949] Director; Jolyon Leonard Harrison [1948] Director

MJ Gleeson PLC
Incorporated: 16 October 2014 *Employees:* 480
Net Worth: £188,099,008 *Total Assets:* £242,784,992
Registered Office: 6 Europa Court, Sheffield Business Park, Sheffield, S9 1XE
Activities: Construction of commercial buildings
Officers: Stefan Peter Allanson, Secretary; Stefan Peter Allanson [1965] Director/Accountant; James Ross Ancell [1953] Director [British/New Zealander]; Colin Albert Dearlove [1951] Director; Dermot James Gleeson [1949] Director; Jolyon Leonard Harrison [1948] Director; Christopher Harwood Bernard Mills [1952] Director

Gleeson Regeneration Limited
Incorporated: 4 February 2000
Net Worth: £34,415,000 *Total Assets:* £83,243,000
Registered Office: 6 Europa Court, Sheffield Business Park, Sheffield, S9 1XE
Activities: Construction of domestic buildings
Parent: MJ Gleeson PLC
Officers: Stefan Peter Allanson [1965] Director/Accountant; Jolyon Leonard Harrison [1948] Director

Glenair UK Limited
Incorporated: 28 January 1975 *Employees:* 820
Net Worth: £65,773,040 *Total Assets:* £95,212,872
Registered Office: 40 Lower Oakham Way, Oakham Business Park, Mansfield, Notts, NG18 5BY
Activities: Manufacture of electronic components
Shareholder: James Docheray Jameson
Officers: Teresa Jean Sheward, Secretary; Anthony John Birks [1958] Managing Director; Andrew John Coulson [1959] Sales Director; Timothy Joseph Gaffney [1956] Director [American]; James Docheray Jameson [1949] Director [American]; Patrick Louis McGee [1956] Director/Accountant [American]

Glencalvie Estate
Incorporated: 26 July 2001
Net Worth: £7,533,213 *Total Assets:* £9,863,303
Registered Office: 64 St James's Street, Nottingham, NG1 6FJ
Activities: Other amusement and recreation activities n.e.c.
Parent: Harbour Investments
Officers: Charles Richard Bennion [1948] Director/Solicitor; Nicholas John Foreman Hardy [1948] Director

Glenco Limited
Incorporated: 24 February 2016
Net Worth: £5,897,033 *Total Assets:* £9,859,501
Registered Office: 39 Broadway, Bramhall, Stockport, Cheshire, SK7 3BU
Activities: Other accommodation
Shareholders: Navin Patel; Rita Patel
Officers: Navin Kumar Patel [1953] Director/Dentist; Rita Patel [1955] Director/Pharmacist

Glencore Agriculture UK Ltd.
Incorporated: 15 September 1969 *Employees:* 44
Previous: Glencore Grain UK Ltd.
Net Worth: £8,520,000 *Total Assets:* £94,305,000
Registered Office: Warren House, Bell Lane, Thame, Oxon, OX9 3AL
Activities: Wholesale of grain, unmanufactured tobacco, seeds and animal feeds
Shareholders: Plavax Limited; Belfurt Limited
Officers: Shailesh Prataprai Pujara, Secretary; James Daniel Maw [1963] Managing Director; Peter Mario Mouthaan [1970] Director/Chief Financial Officer [Dutch]

Glenvale Transport Limited
Incorporated: 11 May 2000 *Employees:* 1,231
Net Worth: £26,834,000 *Total Assets:* £54,547,000
Registered Office: c/o Stagecoach Services Limited, One Stockport Exchange, 20 Railway Road, Stockport, Cheshire, SK1 3SW
Activities: Other urban, suburban or metropolitan passenger land transport (not underground, metro or similar)
Parent: Stagecoach Bus Holdings Limited
Officers: Michael John Vaux, Secretary; Colin Brown [1968] Director/Accountant; Robert Jones [1974] Managing Director; Arnold Mark Threapleton [1954] Managing Director

Glid Wind Farms Topco Limited
Incorporated: 25 September 2008
Net Worth Deficit: £99,034,000 *Total Assets:* £309,873,984
Registered Office: Grimsby Renewables, Operations Base, North Quay, Grimsby, N E Lincs, DN31 3SY
Activities: Activities of head offices
Shareholders: RI Income UK Holdings Limited; UK Green Investment LID Limited
Officers: Keith Mangan [1973] Director/Investment Manager [Irish]; Peter George Raftery [1968] Director/Engineer; Karl Ben Smith [1977] Director/Banker; Alexis Eduardo Ulens [1967] Fund Director [Belgian]

Glinwell Marketing Limited
Incorporated: 6 October 1994 *Employees:* 203
Net Worth Deficit: £182,000 *Total Assets:* £12,596,000
Registered Office: c/o Mazars LLP, The Pinnacle, 160 Midsummer Boulevard, Milton Keynes, Bucks, MK9 1FF
Activities: Wholesale of fruit and vegetables
Parent: Glinwell Public Limited Company
Officers: Salvatore Cannatella [1974] Director; Giuseppe Colletti [1975] Director/Horticulture

Glinwell Public Limited Company
Incorporated: 18 March 1977 *Employees:* 287
Net Worth: £19,269,000 *Total Assets:* £36,657,000
Registered Office: c/o Mazars LLP, The Pinnacle, 160 Midsummer Boulevard, Milton Keynes, Bucks, MK9 1FF
Activities: Growing of vegetables and melons, roots and tubers
Shareholder: Felicia Cannatella
Officers: Giuseppe Colletti, Secretary; Salvatore Cannatella [1974] Director; Giuseppe Colletti [1975] Packhouse Director

Global Brands (GBL) Holdings Limited
Incorporated: 24 May 2012 *Employees:* 228
Net Worth: £11,389,000 *Total Assets:* £34,925,000
Registered Office: 5th Floor, Casa, Lockoford Lane, Chesterfield, Derbys, S41 7JB
Activities: Other business support service activities n.e.c.
Major Shareholder: Steven James Garcia Perez
Officers: Shaun Bacon [1965] Finance Director; Steven James Garcia Perez [1956] Director; Mark Peter James [1971] Director

Global Brands Limited
Incorporated: 7 May 1997 *Employees:* 124
Net Worth: £15,690,000 *Total Assets:* £31,514,000
Registered Office: 5th Floor, Casa, Lockoford Lane, Chesterfield, Derbys, S41 7JB
Activities: Other professional, scientific and technical activities n.e.c.
Officers: Dawn Walton, Secretary; Shaun Bacon [1965] Director/Accountant; Steven James Garcia Perez [1956] Director; Mark Peter James [1971] Sales Director

Global Closure Systems UK Limited
Incorporated: 26 September 2005
Net Worth Deficit: £16,095,000 *Total Assets:* £97,292,000
Registered Office: Sapphire House, Crown Way, Rushden, Northants, NN10 6FB
Activities: Manufacture of other plastic products
Parent: GCS Holdco Finance II SARL
Officers: Nicholas David Martin Giles, Secretary; Franciscus Lodewijk Paulus Doorenbosch [1964] Director/CEO of GCS [Dutch]; Simon John Kesterton [1973] Director; Petrus Rudolf Maria Vervaat [1965] Director [Dutch]

Global Derby (UK) Limited
Incorporated: 30 November 2007
Net Worth: £329,000 *Total Assets:* £96,815,000
Registered Office: Number One Pride Place, Pride Park, Derby, DE24 8QR
Activities: Activities of head offices
Parent: Sevco 5112 Limited
Officers: Stephen Anthony Pearce, Secretary; Melvyn Morris [1956] Director

Global Experience Specialists (GES) Holdings Ltd
Incorporated: 25 April 1994
Net Worth: £2,462,000 *Total Assets:* £12,529,000
Registered Office: GES, Silverstone Drive, Gallagher Business Park, Coventry, Warwicks, CV6 6PA
Activities: Other business support service activities n.e.c.
Officers: Michael Stewart, Secretary; Ellen Marie Ingersoll [1964] Director [American]; Steven Moster [1970] Director/Chairman, CEO and President of Viad Corp [American]; Jason Popp [1970] Director/Vice President [American]

Global Experience Specialists (GES) Limited
Incorporated: 19 May 1994 *Employees:* 375
Net Worth: £12,590,000 *Total Assets:* £30,104,000
Registered Office: Gallager Business Park, Silverstone Drive, Coventry, Warwicks, CV6 6PA
Activities: Other business support service activities n.e.c.
Officers: Michael Stewart, Secretary; Ellen Marie Ingersoll [1964] Director [American]; Steven Moster [1970] Director/Chairman, President and CEO of Viad Corp [American]; Jason Popp [1970] Director/Vice President [American]

Global Payments U.K. Ltd
Incorporated: 9 May 2008 *Employees:* 323
Net Worth: £296,577,984 *Total Assets:* £1,358,274,944
Registered Office: 51 De Montfort Street, Leicester, LE1 7BB
Activities: Other business support service activities n.e.c.
Parent: Global Payments Inc.
Officers: Christopher Kevin Davies [1955] Managing Director; David Lawrence Green [1967] Director/Attorney [American]

Global Real Estate Portfolios Limited
Incorporated: 4 January 2005 *Employees:* 4
Net Worth: £56,635 *Total Assets:* £20,981,624
Registered Office: 37f Warpsgrove Lane, Chalgrove, Oxford, OX44 7RW
Activities: Buying and selling of own real estate
Major Shareholder: Gabriel Michel El-Kassir
Officers: Rachel Elizabeth El Kassir, Secretary; Michael Gabriel El-Kassir, Secretary/Real Estate Development Executive; Nicholas Vincent Walsh, Secretary; Gabriel Michel El-Kassir [1956] Director

Global Self Drive Limited
Incorporated: 5 December 1995 *Employees:* 44
Net Worth: £2,890,433 *Total Assets:* £35,909,784
Registered Office: Global House, Saville Road, Peterborough, PE3 7PR
Activities: Renting and leasing of cars and light motor vehicles
Parent: CCW 600 Limited
Officers: Fraser Alexander Winchester Morrison, Secretary/Accountant; Christopher Charles Webb [1971] Director/Manager

GLW Feeds Limited
Incorporated: 29 March 1952 *Employees:* 135
Net Worth: £8,323,707 *Total Assets:* £19,148,656
Registered Office: Lindum Mill, Shepshed, Loughborough, Leics, LE12 9BS
Activities: Manufacture of prepared feeds for farm animals
Shareholders: George Llewellyn White; Susan Mary White
Officers: Susan Mary White, Secretary; Graham Marcus Palmer [1961] Director; George Llewellyn White [1982] Sales Director; George Llewellyn White [1955] Director/Corn Merchant; Susan Mary White [1952] Director/Corn Merchant

GN Hearing UK Ltd
Incorporated: 31 October 1994 *Employees:* 42
Previous: GN Resound Ltd
Net Worth: £8,997,595 *Total Assets:* £15,548,342
Registered Office: Building A, Kirtlington Business Centre, Slade Farm, Portway, Kirtlington, Kidlington, Oxon, OX5 3JA
Activities: Manufacture of medical and dental instruments and supplies
Parent: GN Hearing A/S
Officers: Lisa Roxan Waithe, Secretary; Paul Gilbert Daft [1979] Managing Director; Johann Van Huyssteen [1959] Director/Chief Financial Officer

Go Inspire Group Limited
Incorporated: 4 December 2015 *Employees:* 566
Net Worth Deficit: £2,761,000 *Total Assets:* £45,994,000
Registered Office: 147 Scudamore Road, Leicester, LE3 1UQ
Activities: Activities of other holding companies n.e.c.
Officers: Sotos Constantinides, Secretary; Sotos Constantinides [1966] Director; Darren John Crawford [1968] Director; Stephen Dolton [1962] Director; Patrick John Headley [1968] Director; Leszek Richard Lkitwinowicz [1958] Director; Simon Ernest Moore [1965] Director; Andrew Wood [1967] Director

Go Outdoors Limited
Incorporated: 19 February 1998 *Employees:* 2,370
Net Worth: £15,216,000 *Total Assets:* £89,033,000
Registered Office: Cuthbert House, Arley Street, Sheffield, S2 4QP
Activities: Other retail sale of new goods in specialised stores (not commercial art galleries and opticians)
Parent: Go Outdoors Topco Limited
Officers: Louise Ayling, Secretary; Lee Paul Bagnall [1969] Managing Director; Peter Alan Cowgill [1953] Director; Neil James Greenhalgh [1971] Director

Go Outdoors Topco Limited
Incorporated: 23 March 2011
Net Worth: £17,714,000 *Total Assets:* £17,714,000
Registered Office: Cuthbert House, Arley Street, Sheffield, S2 4QP
Activities: Other retail sale of new goods in specialised stores (not commercial art galleries and opticians)
Parent: JD Sports Fashion PLC
Officers: Louise Ayling, Secretary; Lee Paul Bagnall [1969] Managing Director; Peter Alan Cowgill [1953] Director; Neil James Greenhalgh [1971] Director

Go Plant Fleet Services Ltd
Incorporated: 18 March 1997 *Employees:* 157
Previous: Essential Fleet Services Limited
Net Worth: £10,017,000 *Total Assets:* £50,301,000
Registered Office: Jarvis House, 157 Sadler Road, Lincoln, LN6 3RS
Activities: Other urban, suburban or metropolitan passenger land transport (not underground, metro or similar)
Parent: Alpha Holdco 1 Limited
Officers: Andrew Iain Cope [1964] Director; Mark Robert Gallimore [1976] Director; Paul Terence Langham [1955] Director; Colin Vaughan McLeod [1950] Director; Andrew James Bruce Young [1963] Finance Director

Go Plant Limited
Incorporated: 3 November 1995 *Employees:* 407
Net Worth: £18,164,000 *Total Assets:* £33,832,000
Registered Office: Jarvis House, 157 Sadler Road, Lincoln, LN6 3RS
Activities: Renting and leasing of trucks and other heavy vehicles
Parent: Alpha Holdco 1 Limited
Officers: Mark Robert Gallimore [1976] Director; Paul Langham [1955] Director; Colin Vaughan McLeod [1950] Director; Andrew James Bruce Young [1963] Finance Director

R.J. & A.E. Godfrey
Incorporated: 13 July 1950 *Employees:* 39
Net Worth: £19,740,864 *Total Assets:* £30,923,104
Registered Office: Cadas House, Wootton Road, Elsham Top, Brigg, N Lincs, DN20 0NU
Activities: Mixed farming
Shareholders: Alexander Godfrey; Samuel Godfrey
Officers: Karin Elizabeth Lund, Secretary; Alexander Godfrey [1978] Director/Farmer; James Eric Godfrey [1953] Director/Farmer; Sam Godfrey [1980] Director/Farmer

Godiva Mortgages Limited
Incorporated: 26 May 2006
Net Worth: £325,424,000 *Total Assets:* £12,311,784,448
Registered Office: Oakfield House, Binley Business Park, Harry Weston Road, Coventry, Warwicks, CV3 2TQ
Activities: Activities of mortgage finance companies
Parent: Coventry Building Society
Officers: Thomas Jonathan Crane, Secretary; Michele Jean Faull [1960] Director/Chief Financial Officer; Mark Alistair Parsons [1961] Director

Going Plural Limited
Incorporated: 11 August 2000
Net Worth Deficit: £1,077,730 *Total Assets:* £12,870,320
Registered Office: 20 Coxon Street, Spondon, Derby, DE21 7JG
Activities: Management consultancy activities other than financial management
Major Shareholder: Allan Leslie Leighton
Officers: Christine Staveley, Secretary; Allan Leslie Leighton [1953] Director

Gojo Industries - Europe Limited
Incorporated: 22 February 1990 *Employees:* 385
Net Worth: £8,726,525 *Total Assets:* £60,227,816
Registered Office: Unit 5 & 6 Stratus Park, Brinklow, Milton Keynes, Bucks, MK10 0DA
Activities: Wholesale of perfume and cosmetics
Officers: Mark Steven Lerner, Secretary [American]; Timothy Dye [1965] Commercial Director [American]; Joseph Samuel Kanfer [1947] Director/President [American]; Mark Steven Lerner [1949] Director/Secretary & Treasurer [American]; Scott Levin [1952] Director [American]

Goldcrest Capital Investments Limited
Incorporated: 25 October 2007
Net Worth: £75,113,256 *Total Assets:* £123,088,848
Registered Office: Ferham House, Kimberworth Road, Masbrough, Rotherham, S Yorks, S61 1AJ
Activities: Residential nursing care facilities
Parent: Falcon Capital Investments Limited
Officers: Elizabeth Jane Phipps, Secretary; Euan David Craig [1977] Director; John Henry Whitehead [1964] Director/Chief Financial Officer

Golden Acquisition
Incorporated: 12 November 2001
Net Worth: £286,539,008 *Total Assets:* £906,520,000
Registered Office: 137 High Street, Burton on Trent, Staffs, DE14 1JZ
Activities: Non-trading company
Parent: Molson Coors (UK) Holdings LLP
Officers: David Alexander Heede [1961] Director; Simon Kerry [1970] Director; Philip Mark Whitehead [1977] Director

Goldmore Asset Management Limited
Incorporated: 30 January 2012 *Employees:* 24
Net Worth: £25,061,276 *Total Assets:* £30,689,084
Registered Office: 9 Osier Way, Olney Business Park, Olney, Bucks, MK46 5FP
Activities: Activities of financial services holding companies
Major Shareholder: Martin John Robbins
Officers: Matthew James Bass [1968] Director; Kevin Anthony Robbins [1976] Director

Golflane Limited
Incorporated: 25 October 2005 *Employees:* 1
Net Worth: £10,344,137 *Total Assets:* £11,663,503
Registered Office: Manor Farm, High Street, Dronfield, Derbys, S18 1PY
Activities: Information technology consultancy activities
Parent: Electronics for Imaging Inc
Officers: Alexis Konstantinovich Grab, Secretary; Gene Zamiska [1961] Director/Chief Accounting Officer [American]

Good 'n' Natural Limited
Incorporated: 16 August 2006
Net Worth: £69,023,000 *Total Assets:* £71,589,000
Registered Office: Samuel Ryder House, Barling Way, Eliot Park, Nuneaton, Warwicks, CV10 7RH
Activities: Activities of head offices
Parent: Holland and Barrett Group Limited
Officers: Lisa Mary Garley-Evans, Secretary; Lisa Mary Garley-Evans [1968] Director/Solicitor; Christian Keen [1964] Director/Chief Financial Officer

Michael Goodall Quality Homes Limited
Incorporated: 30 March 1987 *Employees:* 16
Net Worth: £13,674,079 *Total Assets:* £15,682,621
Registered Office: Brunel Drive, Stretton, Burton on Trent, Staffs, DE13 0BY
Activities: Construction of domestic buildings
Major Shareholder: Michael Stuart Goodall
Officers: Andrew Eric Kay, Secretary; Michael Stuart Goodall [1945] Director/Property Builder/Developer

Goodfellow Cambridge Limited
Incorporated: 23 October 1974 *Employees:* 72
Net Worth: £8,410,000 *Total Assets:* £10,748,000
Registered Office: Units C1 and C2, Spitfire Close, Ermine Business Park, Huntingdon, Cambs, PE29 6WR
Activities: Manufacture of other plastic products
Parent: Metals & Materials Limited
Officers: Andrew Watson, Secretary; Stephen Charles Aldersley [1957] Director; Jane Elizabeth Stoner [1961] Director

Goodman Retail Limited
Incorporated: 1 September 1995 *Employees:* 1,785
Net Worth: £41,780,000 *Total Assets:* £261,764,992
Registered Office: 2 Penman Way, Grove Park, Leicester, LE19 1ST
Activities: Sale of new cars and light motor vehicles
Parent: Sytner Group Limited
Officers: Adam Collinson, Secretary; Adam Collinson [1972] Finance Director; Darren Edwards [1968] Managing Director; Robert Harold Kurnick [1961] Director/Executive Vice President [American]; Jeremy Richard Mallett [1952] Director; Gerard Edward Nieuwenhuys [1960] Director; Laurence Edward William Vaughan [1963] Managing Director

Dorothy Goodman School
Incorporated: 16 May 2012 *Employees:* 196
Net Worth: £12,873,000 *Total Assets:* £16,390,000
Registered Office: Dorothy Goodman School, Stoke Road, Hinckley, Leics, LE10 0EA
Activities: Primary education
Officers: Caroline Louise Lakin, Secretary; Anthony Matthew Carr [1966] Director/Engineer; Ian Douglas Coe [1965] Director/Senior Teaching Assistant; Caroline Louise Henton [1973] Director/Local Government Officer; Danielle Holder [1988] Director/Teacher; Simon Richard Love [1973] Director/Regulation Manager; Sharron Louise Richards [1969] Director; Claire Elizabeth Shardlow [1982] Director/Parent/Career; Janet Claire Thompson [1964] Director/Headteacher; Christopher White [1958] Director/Chief Executive

Goosebrook Limited
Incorporated: 22 April 2004 *Employees:* 4
Net Worth: £69,822,000 *Total Assets:* £99,460,000
Registered Office: 2 Crown Way, Rushden, Northants, NN10 6BS
Activities: Other letting and operating of own or leased real estate
Parent: Asquith Court Holdings Limited
Officers: Stephen Kramer, Secretary; Elizabeth Boland [1959] Director/Chief Financial Officer [American]; Stephen Dreier [1942] Director/Chief Admin Officer [American]; Dave Lissy [1965] Director/Chief Executive Officer [American]; James Walter Tugendhat [1971] Managing Director, International

Gosford Hill School
Incorporated: 2 October 2012 *Employees:* 108
Net Worth: £8,855,658 *Total Assets:* £11,161,550
Registered Office: Gosford Hill School, Oxford Road, Kidlington, Oxon, OX5 2NT
Activities: General secondary education
Officers: Adrian Mark Ross Corness [1967] Director; Hayley Curtis [1984] Director/Teacher; Andrew John Gauld [1974] Director; Elaine Millard [1972] Director/Human Resources Manager; Brian John Moss [1942] Director; Nigel John Sellars [1977] Director/Headteacher; Generaldine Diane Shepherd [1947] Director/Human Resources Manager; Adrian Hiorns Thomas [1974] Director/Police Officer; David John Thompson [1946] Director/Retired; Kay Usher [1969] Director; Clive Arthur Walsh [1958] Director/BT Patch Manager; Stephanie Caroline Woodley [1972] Director/Financial Services Manager

GPP Langstone LLP
Incorporated: 8 November 2012
Net Worth: £50,997,724 *Total Assets:* £51,733,540
Registered Office: 2a Chequers Court, Huntingdon, Cambs, PE29 3LJ

GPS Estates Limited
Incorporated: 14 October 2002 *Employees:* 8
Net Worth: £12,614,922 *Total Assets:* £20,610,172
Registered Office: Room 212, Endeavour House, Building 50, Wrest Park, Silsoe, Bedford, MK45 4HS
Activities: Development of building projects
Shareholders: John Joseph Gill; Darren Gill
Officers: Darren Gill, Secretary; Darren Gill [1969] Director/Builder; John Joseph Gill [1949] Director/Builder

GPUK LLP
Incorporated: 8 May 2008
Net Worth: £319,945,984 *Total Assets:* £1,203,758,976
Registered Office: De Montfort House, 51 De Montfort Street, Leicester, LE1 7BB

Grafton Recruitment Limited
Incorporated: 19 December 1984 *Employees:* 103
Net Worth: £2,272,312 *Total Assets:* £12,170,531
Registered Office: 19-20 The Triangle, Nottingham, NG2 1AE
Activities: Other activities of employment placement agencies
Parent: Staffline Recruitment Limited
Officers: Paul Simon Collins, Secretary; Martina Elizabeth McKenzie [1973] Director; Christopher Mark Pullen [1970] Director; Michael Robert Watts [1974] Director

Grainsby Farms Limited
Incorporated: 18 October 1963 *Employees:* 10
Net Worth: £9,978,211 *Total Assets:* £11,215,108
Registered Office: The Estate Office, Grainsby, Grimsby, N E Lincs, DN36 5PU
Activities: Growing of cereals (except rice), leguminous crops and oil seeds
Shareholder: Richard Holland Caton Haigh
Officers: Fanny Elizabeth Mary Muldoon, Secretary; Daniel Lewis Caton Haigh [1980] Director/Musician; Hannah Elizabeth Haigh [1981] Director; Richard Holland Caton Haigh [1951] Director/Farmer; Matthew Philip Spence [1978] Director/Farm Manager

The Grammar School of King Edward VI at Stratford-upon-Avon
Incorporated: 7 July 2011 *Employees:* 96
Net Worth: £17,989,796 *Total Assets:* £19,238,088
Registered Office: Church Street, Stratford upon Avon, Warwicks, CV37 6HB
Activities: General secondary education
Officers: Michael David Hawley, Secretary; Andrew Blann [1973] Director/Medical Sales; Bennet Carr [1970] Director/Headmaster; Dr David Robert Derbyshire [1952] Director; Michael David Evans [1983] Director; Alison Fiona Fairbairn [1962] Director; Kirsty Hayward [1973] Director/Laboratory Technician; James Anthony Jones [1963] Director; Victor Geoffrey Flavell Matts [1955] Director; Philip Andrew Maundrill [1958] Director; Shane McCrink [1983] Director; Marie Therese Rendell [1959] Director; Councillor Juliet Dorothy Short [1948] Director; Christopher John Smith [1950] Director; Emma Jane Speechley [1963] Director; Neil Treble [1982] Director/Teacher

Granby Care Limited
Incorporated: 29 October 1991 *Employees:* 5
Net Worth: £15,363,000 *Total Assets:* £15,363,000
Registered Office: Norcliffe House, Station Road, Wilmslow, Cheshire, SK9 1BU
Activities: Other human health activities
Parent: Brighterkind Health Care Group Limited
Officers: Abigail Mattison, Secretary; Jeremy Robert Arthur Richardson [1970] Director; Phillip Gary Thomas [1978] Director

Grand Union Group Funding PLC
Incorporated: 1 November 2013
Net Worth: £50,000 *Total Assets:* £114,800,000
Registered Office: Derwent House, University Way, Cranfield Technology Park, Cranfield, Bedford, MK43 0AZ
Activities: Financial intermediation not elsewhere classified
Officers: Chris Bellamy, Secretary; Philip John Edwards [1955] Director/Semi Retired Consultant; Aileen Christine Evans [1960] Director/Chief Executive; Nicola Ewen [1974] Director/Accountant; Peter Anthony Fielder [1952] Director/Retired Banker; Mona Shah [1968] Finance Director

Grandcross Limited
Incorporated: 6 January 1998 *Employees:* 265
Net Worth: £9,394,000 *Total Assets:* £10,940,000
Registered Office: Norcliffe House, Station Road, Wilmslow, Cheshire, SK9 1BU
Activities: Other human health activities
Parent: Four Seasons Health Care Group Limited
Officers: Abigail Mattison, Secretary; Timothy Richard William Hammond [1959] Director; Dr Maureen Claire Royston [1960] Director; Benjamin Robert Taberner [1972] Director/Chartered Accountant

Grange Mill Developments Limited
Incorporated: 17 February 2000
Net Worth: £5,316,100 *Total Assets:* £18,870,796
Registered Office: West Dene, Abingdon Road, Tubney, Abingdon, Oxon, OX13 5QQ
Activities: Development of building projects
Parent: Grange Mill Holdings Ltd
Officers: Robert John Rendell [1952] Director

Grangefern Properties Limited
Incorporated: 21 October 1991
Net Worth: £30,833,128 *Total Assets:* £39,736,972
Registered Office: Emerson House, Heyes Lane, Alderley Edge, Cheshire, SK9 7LF
Activities: Other letting and operating of own or leased real estate
Parent: Orbit Investments (Properties) Limited
Officers: Varun Maharaj, Secretary; Anthony Emerson Jones [1967] Director; Mark Emerson Jones [1964] Director; Peter Emerson Jones [1935] Director

J W Grant Co
Incorporated: 8 October 1954 *Employees:* 188
Previous: J.W.Grant
Net Worth: £17,440,776 *Total Assets:* £25,227,008
Registered Office: Fold Hill, Old Leake, Boston, Lincs, PE22 9PJ
Activities: Growing of cereals (except rice), leguminous crops and oil seeds
Shareholders: James Edward Grant Trustee of WE Grant Settlement 1982; James Edward Grant Trustee of WE Grant Settlement 1989
Officers: James Edward Grant, Secretary; Andrew John Grant [1955] Director/Farmer; James Edward Grant [1953] Director/Farmer; John James Grant [1930] Director/Farmer; June Grant [1927] Director/Married Woman

Grant Farming Limited
Incorporated: 7 September 2012 *Employees:* 7
Net Worth: £5,133,944 *Total Assets:* £10,220,038
Registered Office: Laburnum House, Main Road, Langrick, Boston, Lincs, PE22 7AN
Activities: Activities of agricultural holding companies
Major Shareholder: Linda May Whatton
Officers: Mark Richard Grant [1967] Director/Farmer; Nicola Jayne Grant [1972] Director; Paul John Grant [1969] Director/Farmer

Grantham Bros. Limited
Incorporated: 6 June 1978 *Employees:* 10
Net Worth: £8,389,524 *Total Assets:* £9,363,603
Registered Office: Warwick Road, Fairfield Industrial Estate, Louth, Lincs, LN11 0YB
Activities: Growing of cereals (except rice), leguminous crops and oil seeds
Shareholders: Peter Charles Grantham; David Harold Grantham
Officers: Peter Charles Grantham, Secretary; David Harold Grantham [1947] Director/Builder; Peter Charles Grantham [1945] Director/Builder; Simon Harvey Grantham [1973] Director/Site Manager

Grantham Industries Limited
Incorporated: 3 May 2001 *Employees:* 80
Net Worth: £10,096,492 *Total Assets:* £19,226,616
Registered Office: Warwick Road, Fairfield Industrial Estate, Louth, Lincs, LN11 0YB
Activities: Treatment and disposal of non-hazardous waste
Major Shareholder: Simon Harvey Grantham
Officers: Peter Charles Grantham, Secretary; Adrian Martin Corrigan [1971] Director/Chartered Surveyor/Demolition Engineer; Andrew Charles Grantham [1976] Director/Site Manager; David Harold Grantham [1947] Director; Peter Charles Grantham [1945] Director; Simon Harvey Grantham [1973] Director

Grantham Investments Limited
Incorporated: 8 May 1964 *Employees:* 16
Net Worth: £19,158,870 *Total Assets:* £29,935,004
Registered Office: 3 Castlegate, Grantham, Lincs, NG31 6SF
Activities: Buying and selling of own real estate
Shareholder: Hindmarch Properties Limited
Officers: Kevin Glyn Williams, Secretary; Hugh Munro Bater Caseley [1960] Director/Chartered Surveyor; Geoffrey Ellwood Fearn [1937] Director; David John Hindmarch [1965] Director; Mark Thomas Hindmarch [1963] Director/Accountant

Granwood Holdings Limited
Incorporated: 30 October 2002 *Employees:* 33
Net Worth: £11,141,745 *Total Assets:* £12,487,408
Registered Office: 10 Imperial Road, Matlock, Derbys, DE4 3NL
Activities: Activities of head offices
Shareholders: Simon Arthur Pass; Mark Anthony Pass; David Andrew Pass
Officers: Richard Charles Taylor, Secretary/Director; David Andrew Pass [1966] Director; Mark Anthony Pass [1964] Director; Simon Arthur Pass [1963] Director; Richard Charles Taylor [1949] Director

Grass Valley Broadcast Solutions Limited
Incorporated: 6 May 1986 *Employees:* 110
Previous: Miranda Technologies Limited
Net Worth Deficit: £1,179,000 *Total Assets:* £28,666,000
Registered Office: Pembroke House, Pegasus Business Park, Beverley Road, Castle Donnington, Derbys, DE74 2HN
Activities: Wholesale of electronic and telecommunications equipment and parts
Parent: Belden UK Holdings Limited
Officers: Brian Edward Anderson, Secretary; Brian Edward Anderson [1974] Director [American]; Alec Thomas Lappe [1981] Director/Business Executive [American]; Anne La Belle Malyszko [1980] Director/Vice President [American]

Graven Hill Village Development Company Limited
Incorporated: 25 June 2014 *Employees:* 14
Net Worth: £18,814,880 *Total Assets:* £75,001,128
Registered Office: The Plot Shop, Pioneer Square, Bicester, Oxon, OX26 6JU
Activities: Other business support service activities n.e.c.
Officers: Ian Corkin [1963] Director/Partner; Karen Curtin [1974] Director; Peter John Alexander Arthur Muir [1947] Director; Daniel Edward Sames [1972] Director/Councillor; Susan Smith [1957] Director/Local Government Officer; Adrian David Unitt [1963] Operations Director; Maldwyn Hedd Vaughan-Evans [1984] Director/Project Manager

Graypaul Motors Limited
Incorporated: 12 July 1995 *Employees:* 185
Net Worth: £16,057,000 *Total Assets:* £49,990,000
Registered Office: 2 Penman Way, Grove Park, Leicester, LE19 1ST
Activities: Sale of new cars and light motor vehicles
Parent: Sytner Group Limited
Officers: Adam Collinson, Secretary; Adam Collinson [1972] Finance Director; Darren Edwards [1968] Managing Director; Robert Harold Kurnick [1961] Director/Executive Vice President [American]; Jeremy Richard Mallett [1952] Director; Gerard Edward Nieuwenhuys [1960] Director; Laurence Edward William Vaughan [1963] Managing Director

Graypen Limited
Incorporated: 23 October 1969
Net Worth: £2,552,811 *Total Assets:* £18,572,252
Registered Office: The Bridge, One Graypen Way, Queens Road, Immingham, N E Lincs, DN40 1QN
Activities: Sea and coastal freight water transport
Parent: Graypen Cymru Limited
Officers: Lee Hutchinson, Secretary; Simon John Coghlan [1969] Group Managing Director; Philip Daniel Johnson [1978] Group Director; Daniel Gavin Payne [1973] Director

Graystacks Exeter Limited
Incorporated: 13 July 2015
Net Worth Deficit: £1,488,516 *Total Assets:* £13,855,848
Registered Office: 14 Clarendon Street, Nottingham, NG1 5HQ
Activities: Development of building projects
Parent: Broadwood Developments Limited
Officers: Yuk Shan Leung [1972] Director [Chinese]; Andrew Keith Roberts [1972] Director

Great Tew Grain Processing Limited
Incorporated: 30 September 2008 *Employees:* 5
Net Worth: £5,879,608 *Total Assets:* £9,384,365
Registered Office: The Estate Office, Quarry Farm, Banbury Road, Great Tew, Chipping Norton, Oxon, OX7 4BT
Activities: Post-harvest crop activities
Parent: GTBH Limited
Officers: Rebecca Leah Iles, Secretary; Nicholas Matthew Middlemass Johnston [1972] Director/Farmer

Great Tew Properties Limited
Incorporated: 13 May 2017 *Employees:* 1
Net Worth: £18,257,674 *Total Assets:* £24,183,120
Registered Office: The Estate Office, Quarry Farm, Banbury Road, Great Tew, Chipping Norton, Oxon, OX7 4BT
Activities: Other letting and operating of own or leased real estate
Shareholders: Flowgiant Limited; Giantflow Limited
Officers: Rebecca Leah Iles, Secretary; Nicholas Matthew Middlemass Johnston [1972] Director

Greater Manchester Buses South Limited
Incorporated: 12 May 1993 *Employees:* 2,319
Net Worth: £21,890,000 *Total Assets:* £91,745,000
Registered Office: c/o Stagecoach Services Limited, One Stockport Exchange, 20 Railway Road, Stockport, Cheshire, SK1 3SW
Activities: Other urban, suburban or metropolitan passenger land transport (not underground, metro or similar)
Parent: Stagecoach Bus Holdings Limited
Officers: Michael John Vaux, Secretary; Colin Brown [1968] Director/Accountant; Elisabeth Ann Tasker [1967] Director; Arnold Mark Threapleton [1954] Managing Director

Greater Nottingham Education Trust
Incorporated: 22 February 2011 *Employees:* 224
Previous: Carlton Le Willows Academy
Net Worth: £10,510,529 *Total Assets:* £14,442,368
Registered Office: Carlton-le-Willows Academy, Wood Lane, Gedling, Nottingham, NG4 4AA
Activities: General secondary education
Officers: Michael Stephen Davies, Secretary; Amanda Dawson [1964] Director/Headteacher; Jonathan Mark Garibaldi [1963] Director/University Lecturer; Paulo Whitfield Karat [1973] Director/Solicitor and Business MD; Wayne Alan Smith [1967] Director/Solicitor; Jonathan Craig Weaver [1964] Director

Green Biologics Limited
Incorporated: 23 January 2002 *Employees:* 98
Net Worth: £9,372,694 *Total Assets:* £69,993,720
Registered Office: 154AH Brook Drive, Milton Park, Milton, Abingdon, Oxon, OX14 4SD
Activities: Research and experimental development on biotechnology
Shareholder: Cell Energy Limited
Officers: Martin Incledon Blair [1958] Director; Martin Cubbon [1957] Director; Paul Robert Henson [1961] Director/Chartered Accountant; James Joseph Hohman [1948] Director/Retired Chemical Industry Executive [American]; Brad Pritchard [1967] Managing Director [American]; John Bruce Rae-Smith [1963] Director; Keon Alexander Reed [1989] Director [American]; Sean George Cronin Sutcliffe [1963] Director

Jerry Green Dog Rescue
Incorporated: 16 July 2013 *Employees:* 64
Net Worth: £12,304,891 *Total Assets:* £12,406,064
Registered Office: Jerry Green Dog Rescue, Broughton, Brigg, N Lincs, DN20 0BJ
Activities: Other service activities n.e.c.
Officers: Ian Arthur Cawsey [1960] Charity Director; Jayne Marie Chudley [1967] Director/Trustee; Lynn Frances Hewison [1984] Director/Trustee; Paul McCartan [1979] Director/Human Resources Manager; Kevin Lawrence Peart [1966] Director/Trustee; Andrew Paul Robinson [1964] Director/Chartered Accountant

J.H.& F.W.Green Limited
Incorporated: 30 August 1917 *Employees:* 467
Net Worth: £46,760,384 *Total Assets:* £76,484,688
Registered Office: 57 Saltergate, Chesterfield, Derbys, S40 1UL
Activities: Mixed farming
Officers: Rupert John Henry Green, Secretary/Director; Edward Richard Green [1988] Director/Chartered Surveyor; George Richard Green [1939] Director; Henry Charles Edward Green [1971] Director; Jane Green [1947] Director; Patrick William Green [1946] Director; Robert Henry Green [1941] Director; Rupert John Henry Green [1959] Director; Susan Daphne Green [1954] Director

Green Meadow Limited
Incorporated: 8 September 1998 *Employees:* 6
Net Worth: £7,822,530 *Total Assets:* £9,604,391
Registered Office: Unit 61 Wymeswold Industrial Estate, Burton on the Wolds, Loughborough, Leics, LE12 5TY
Activities: Recovery of sorted materials
Major Shareholder: Geoffrey James Harvey
Officers: Geoffrey James Harvey [1955] Director

Green Planet Products Limited
Incorporated: 23 March 2001 *Employees:* 416
Net Worth: £27,927,271,424 *Total Assets:* £72,075,780,096
Registered Office: Home Farm, 38 Town Road, Quarrington, Sleaford, Lincs, NG34 8RS
Activities: Activities of other holding companies n.e.c.
Officers: Mowbray Christopher Mountain, Secretary/Director; Mowbray Edmund Stephens Mountain [1948] Director; Mowbray Christopher Mountain [1973] Director; Darren Thompson [1967] Finance Director

Green Sky Energy Limited
Incorporated: 18 September 2009
Net Worth: £3,010,368 *Total Assets:* £33,004,604
Registered Office: Westwood Way, Westwood Business Park, Coventry, Warwicks, CV4 8LG
Activities: Activities of head offices
Parent: E.On SE
Officers: Matthew Charles Brown [1972] Finance Director; Franz Hubertus Cavin Pietzsch [1975] Director/Vice President Energy Efficiency [German]

Greencore Beechwood Limited
Incorporated: 7 July 2011
Net Worth: £102,249,000 *Total Assets:* £599,827,968
Registered Office: Greencore Group UK Centre, Midland Way, Barlborough Links Business Park, Barlborough, Chesterfield, Derbys, S43 4XA
Activities: Activities of extraterritorial organisations and bodies
Parent: Talroff Limited
Officers: Michael Evans, Secretary; Catherine Bradshaw [1975] Finance Director; Michael Evans [1967] Director; Eoin Philip Tonge [1972] Director [Irish]

Greencore Convenience Foods I LLP
Incorporated: 30 April 2013
Net Worth: £6,752,000 *Total Assets:* £38,930,000
Registered Office: Greencore Group UK Centre, Midland Way, Barlborough, Chesterfield, Derbys, S43 4XA

Greencore Food To Go Limited
Incorporated: 12 April 1962 *Employees:* 7,161
Net Worth: £164,830,000 *Total Assets:* £411,808,992
Registered Office: Greencore Group UK Centre, Midland Way, Barlborough Links Business Park, Barlborough, Chesterfield, Derbys, S43 4XA
Activities: Manufacture of prepared meals and dishes
Parent: Uniq Limited
Officers: Michael Evans, Secretary; Catherine Bradshaw [1975] Finance Director; Michael Evans [1967] Director/Group Communications Officer; Kevin Raymond George Moore [1970] Director; Eoin Philip Tonge [1972] Director [Irish]

Greencore Foods Limited
Incorporated: 16 November 2010 *Employees:* 235
Net Worth: £59,208,000 *Total Assets:* £223,071,008
Registered Office: Midland Way, Barlborough Links Business Park, Barlborough, Chesterfield, Derbys, S43 4XA
Activities: Manufacture of prepared meals and dishes
Parent: Greencore Beechwood Limited
Officers: Michael Evans, Secretary; Catherine Bradshaw [1975] Finance Director; Michael Evans [1967] Director/Communications Officer; Eoin Philip Tonge [1972] Director [Irish]

Greencore Grocery Limited
Incorporated: 20 September 1983 *Employees:* 1,496
Net Worth: £33,088,000 *Total Assets:* £123,329,000
Registered Office: Greencore Group UK Centre, Midland Way, Barlborough Links Business Park, Barlborough, Chesterfield, Derbys, S43 4XA
Activities: Manufacture of prepared meals and dishes
Parent: Greencore Foods Limited
Officers: Michael Evans, Secretary; David William Boyes [1966] Finance Director; Michael Evans [1967] Director/Communications Manager; Clare Rees [1974] Managing Director; Eoin Philip Tonge [1972] Managing Director [Irish]

Greencore Northwood Limited
Incorporated: 8 July 2011
Net Worth: £15,952,000 *Total Assets:* £300,446,016
Registered Office: Greencore Group UK Centre, Midland Way, Barlborough Links Business Park, Barlborough, Chesterfield, Derbys, S43 4XA
Activities: Activities of extraterritorial organisations and bodies
Parent: Greencore UK Holdings Limited
Officers: Michael Evans, Secretary; Michael Evans [1967] Director; Eoin Philip Tonge [1972] Director [Irish]

Greencore Prepared Meals Limited
Incorporated: 15 March 1935 *Employees:* 2,537
Net Worth: £67,518,000 *Total Assets:* £199,818,000
Registered Office: Greencore Group UK Centre, Links Business Park, Midland Way, Barlborough, Chesterfield, Derbys, S43 4XA
Activities: Manufacture of other food products n.e.c.
Parent: Greencore Foods Limited
Officers: Michael Evans, Secretary; David William Boyes [1966] Finance Director; Michael Evans [1967] Director; Clare Rees [1974] Director; Eoin Philip Tonge [1972] Director [Irish]

Greencore UK Holdings Limited
Incorporated: 24 May 1991
Net Worth Deficit: £284,859,008 *Total Assets:* £260,008,992
Registered Office: Greencore Group UK Centre, Midland Way, Barlborough Links Business Park, Barlborough, Chesterfield, Derbys, S43 4XA
Activities: Activities of extraterritorial organisations and bodies
Parent: Greencore Beechwood Limited
Officers: Michael Evans, Secretary; Catherine Bradshaw [1975] Finance Director; Michael Evans [1967] Director; Eoin Philip Tonge [1972] Director [Irish]

Greene Tweed & Co Limited
Incorporated: 15 June 1982 *Employees:* 134
Net Worth: £7,783,000 *Total Assets:* £15,783,000
Registered Office: Mere Way, Ruddington Fields, Ruddington, Nottingham, NG11 6JS
Activities: Manufacture of other plastic products
Officers: Paul O'Brien, Secretary; Laurie James Bentley [1982] Director/European Financial Controller; Michael Delfiner [1955] Director/Chairman [American]; Kevin Lukiewski [1958] Director/Chief Financial Officer [American]; Kenneth Stanley [1949] Director [American]

Owen Greenings & Mumford (Holdings) Limited
Incorporated: 25 May 2007 *Employees:* 182
Net Worth: £11,175,280 *Total Assets:* £16,931,750
Registered Office: Unit 1 Mead Road, Oxford Industrial Park, Yarnton, Kidlington, Oxon, OX5 1QU
Activities: Manufacture of other plastic products
Officers: Paul Wightman, Secretary; Adam John Mumford [1968] Director; Mark Ivan Owen [1960] Director; Dr Jane Ellen Elizabeth Shepherd [1955] Director/Medical Practitioner; Paul Wightman [1968] Director; Vivienne June Wightman [1937] Director

Greenshoots Limited
Incorporated: 30 May 2003 *Employees:* 28
Net Worth: £848,419 *Total Assets:* £10,009,976
Registered Office: Hollyhouse Farm, Horseway, Chatteris, Cambs, PE16 6XQ
Activities: Growing of vegetables and melons, roots and tubers
Officers: Ian David Hall, Secretary; Patrick William Allpress [1964] Director/Farmer; Ian David Hall [1967] Director/General Manager; Christopher Fred Hartley [1950] Director/Farmer; James Harry Hawes [1988] Director/Farmer; Marc Edwin Heading [1965] Director/Farmer; James Frederick Martin [1961] Director/Farmer

Greenvale AP Limited
Incorporated: 23 February 1996 *Employees:* 718
Net Worth: £21,214,000 *Total Assets:* £83,000,000
Registered Office: Greenvale AP, Floods Ferry Road, Doddington, March, Cambs, PE15 0UW
Activities: Growing of vegetables and melons, roots and tubers
Parent: Produce Investments PLC
Officers: Angus Stuart Walton Armstrong [1964] Director; Andrew Clarkson [1977] Retail Commercial Director; Paul Michael Coleman [1965] Director/Technical Manager; Nicholas John Douglas [1974] Director; Andrew Ferguson [1967] HR Director; Leon Mundey [1975] Director; David Campbell Rankin [1972] Director

Greenwood Academies Trust
Incorporated: 31 March 2009 *Employees:* 1,956
Net Worth: £82,883,000 *Total Assets:* £130,677,000
Registered Office: Greenwood House, Colwick Quays Business Park, Private Road No 2, Colwick, Nottingham, NG4 2JY
Activities: General secondary education
Officers: David Maxwell Anstead [1956] Director/Educational Consultant; Graham Leslie Feek [1970] Director/Accountant; Professor Kenneth Francis Gill [1956] Director/Chief Executive Officer; Timothy Guyler [1975] Director of Improvement and Integration; Professor Christine Joy Hall [1951] Director/Professor of Education; Michael Hamlin [1949] Director/Retired; Shahbaz Haque [1975] Director/Management Consultant; Simon Peter Anthony Massarella [1960] Director/Retired; Suzanne Millership-Liddle [1973] Business Performance Director; Wayne Norrie [1972] Director/Chief Executive; Lesley Janet Odell [1949] Director/Retired; Mark James Rutherford [1966] Director/Solicitor; Joanne Smart [1970] Director/Head of HR Business Partnering; Andrew David Walker [1977] Director/Certified Chartered Accountant

Greenyard Flowers UK Ltd
Incorporated: 9 January 1995 *Employees:* 124
Previous: Winchester Growers Limited
Net Worth: £22,736,456 *Total Assets:* £29,020,288
Registered Office: c/o Duncan & Toplis Limited, Enterprise Way, Pinchbeck, Spalding, Lincs, PE11 3YR
Activities: Growing of other non-perennial crops
Shareholder: Hein Valere Maria Deprez
Officers: Giles Anthony Armstrong, Secretary; Giles Anthony Armstrong [1970] Financial Director; Alan Alexander Forrester [1957] Director; Stella Willcox [1959] Human Resources Director

Greenyard Fresh UK Ltd
Incorporated: 8 August 1989 *Employees:* 546
Previous: Univeg Katope UK Ltd
Net Worth: £21,837,072 *Total Assets:* £44,951,624
Registered Office: c/o Duncan & Toplis Limited, Enterprise Way, Pinchbeck, Spalding, Lincs, PE11 3YR
Activities: Wholesale of fruit and vegetables
Shareholder: Hein Valere Maria Deprez
Officers: Giles Anthony Armstrong, Secretary; Giles Anthony Armstrong [1970] Financial Director; Hein Valere Maria Deprez [1961] Director [Belgian]; Veerle Maria Deprez [1960] Director [Belgian]; Alan Alexander Forrester [1957] Director; Karl Jozef Peeters [1957] Director [Belgian]; Stella Willcox [1959] Director

Greenyard Frozen UK Limited
Incorporated: 24 April 2002 *Employees:* 291
Previous: Pinguin Foods UK Limited
Net Worth: £13,599,000 *Total Assets:* £103,519,000
Registered Office: Greenyard Frozen UK Limited, Greenyard Way, Hardwick Industrial Estate, King's Lynn, Norfolk, PE30 4WS
Activities: Other processing and preserving of fruit and vegetables
Shareholder: Hein Valere Maria Deprez
Officers: Arjan Buschman, Secretary; Nigel Stuart Terry [1951] Non-Executive Director Chairman

Gregory Family Office Limited
Incorporated: 5 March 2015 *Employees:* 1
Net Worth: £256,573,328 *Total Assets:* £256,849,552
Registered Office: Offices of Mayfield & Co, 2 Merus Court, Meridian Business Park, Leicester, LE19 1RJ
Activities: Financial management
Parent: The Alps Settlement
Officers: James William Sibley, Secretary; Sarah Jane Gregory [1967] Director

Grevayne Properties Limited
Incorporated: 20 January 1972 *Employees:* 5
Net Worth: £12,457,104 *Total Assets:* £14,733,888
Registered Office: Office Suite 7, Shrieves Walk, 39 Sheep Street, Stratford upon Avon, Warwicks, CV37 6GJ
Activities: Development of building projects
Officers: Jonathan Peter Collis, Secretary; Jonathan Peter Collis [1956] Director/Property Developer; Anthony Michael Vincent Coombs [1952] Director/Property Developer; Graham Derek Clifford Coombs [1952] Director/Property Developer; Lee Martin Edwards [1983] Director/Land Purchaser

GRI Group Limited
Incorporated: 20 February 2001 *Employees:* 6
Net Worth: £12,568,899 *Total Assets:* £12,834,627
Registered Office: 5 Acorn Business Park, Woodseats Close, Sheffield, S8 0TB
Activities: Activities of head offices
Major Shareholder: Graham Royle
Officers: David Thomas Kearns, Secretary; David Thomas Kearns [1968] Finance Director; Graham Royle [1959] Director/Chief Executive Officer

GRI Libra Limited
Incorporated: 14 May 2015 *Employees:* 57
Net Worth: £6,494,596 *Total Assets:* £15,863,541
Registered Office: Unit 5 Acorn Business Park, Woodseats Close, Sheffield, S8 0TB
Activities: Activities of head offices
Officers: David Thomas Kearns [1968] Director; Daniel James Royle [1992] Director; Graham Royle [1959] Director/Chairman & CEO; Nicola Rachel Royle [1990] Director; Susan Royle [1961] Director

Griffith Foods Limited
Incorporated: 22 May 1969 *Employees:* 292
Previous: Griffith Laboratories Limited
Net Worth: £10,919,000 *Total Assets:* £42,211,000
Registered Office: Cotes Park Industrial Estate, Somercotes, Alfreton, Derbys, DE55 4NN
Activities: Manufacture of other food products n.e.c.
Officers: Wim Van Roekel, Secretary; William Charles Frost [1953] Director [American]; Fernando Gomez Ortis [1970] Director/Vice President Finance Europe [Mexican]; Joseph Maslick [1948] Director/Chief Financial Officer [American]; Wim Van Roekel [1970] Director/European President [Dutch]

R Griggs & Co. Limited
Incorporated: 17 December 2013
Net Worth: £6,703,582 *Total Assets:* £42,974,708
Registered Office: Studio 2, Diamonds Business Centre, Nene Park, Attley Way, Irthlingborough, Northants, NN9 5GF
Activities: Security dealing on own account
Officers: Howard Mills Johnstone, Secretary; Benjamin Roy Griggs [1992] Director; Samuel William Griggs [1991] Director; Stephen Wm Griggs [1961] Director; William Maximillian Griggs [1938] Director; Howard Mills Johnstone [1946] Director

Grimme (U.K.) Limited
Incorporated: 20 August 1993 *Employees:* 85
Net Worth: £10,572,309 *Total Assets:* £21,413,880
Registered Office: Station Road, Swineshead, Boston, Lincs, PE20 3PS
Activities: Manufacture of agricultural and forestry machinery other than tractors
Shareholders: Christoph Grimme; Philipp Grimme; Franz Josef Bernard Grimme
Officers: Donna Hall, Secretary; Patrick Albert Franz Graf Grote [1990] Managing Director [German]; Donna Hall [1980] Finance Director; Jens Walter [1963] Director/Administrative Manager [German]; Barry Vernon White [1959] Director

Grimsthorpe & Drummond Castle Trust Limited
Incorporated: 9 March 1978 *Employees:* 105
Net Worth: £38,195,548 *Total Assets:* £38,646,920
Registered Office: Grimsthorpe Estate Office, Grimsthorpe, Bourne, Lincs, PE10 0LY
Activities: Silviculture and other forestry activities
Officers: Francis John Fane Marmion Dymoke, Secretary; Richard Edward Ion Calvocoressi [1951] National Museum Director NDPB; Francis John Fane Marmion Dymoke [1955] Director/Land Owner; Sir Mark Ellis Powell Jones [1951] Director/College Warden; David Logan Laird [1937] Director/Retired; Sir John Lucas-Tooth [1932] Director/Banker; Hugh Patrick Matheson [1949] Director/Farmer; Sebastian Miller [1965] Director/Army Officer; Lady Jane Willoughby de Eresby [1934] Director

Gripple Limited
Incorporated: 25 November 1983 *Employees:* 637
Net Worth: £18,745,210 *Total Assets:* £49,040,652
Registered Office: The Old West Gun Works, 201 Savile St East, Sheffield, S4 7UQ
Activities: Manufacture of other fabricated metal products n.e.c.
Shareholder: Hugh David Facey
Officers: Katherine Bernadette Cullen, Secretary; Robert Andrew Davies [1954] Director; Hugh David Facey [1945] Executive Chairman and Director; Roger Hall [1946] Director/Accountant; David Arthur Routledge [1958] Director/Business Consultant; James David Sallows [1979] Director/Project Manager; Edward John Peter Stubbs [1983] Director; Paul Taylor [1961] Director

Grosvenor Contracts Leasing Limited
Incorporated: 2 June 1981 *Employees:* 267
Net Worth: £29,031,092 *Total Assets:* £140,178,608
Registered Office: Balmoral House, Kettering Venture Park, Kettering, Northants, NN15 6XU
Activities: Sale of other motor vehicles
Major Shareholder: Brian Johnson
Officers: James Fleming Clark, Secretary; Shaun William Barritt [1957] Director; Joanne Brown [1963] Director; James Fleming Clark [1956] Director; Mary Cecilia Dopson Taylor [1968] Customer Service Director; Clive Nicholas Hughes [1966] Director/Retail Operator; Brian Johnson [1945] Director; Nicola Margaret Johnson [1965] Director; Nicholas William Murphy [1972] Director; Andrew Paul Reed [1965] Director/Contract Hire

The Ground Group Limited
Incorporated: 8 February 2002 *Employees:* 7
Net Worth: £2,675,000 *Total Assets:* £18,911,886
Registered Office: Unit 12 Merchant Way, Doncaster, S Yorks, DN2 4QR
Activities: Buying and selling of own real estate
Shareholders: Nigel Stephen Griffiths; Darren Wayne Griffiths
Officers: Nigel Stephen Griffiths, Secretary/Director; Darren Wayne Griffiths [1967] Director; Nigel Stephen Griffiths [1966] Director

Group GTI Ltd
Incorporated: 4 April 2006 *Employees:* 189
Net Worth Deficit: £118,222,560 *Total Assets:* £15,302,493
Registered Office: The Fountain Building, Howbery Park, Benson Lane, Wallingford, Oxon, OX10 8BA
Activities: Activities of head offices
Parent: Exponent Private Equity Partners LP
Officers: Martin John Halliday, Secretary/Director; Mark Rupert Blythe [1967] Director; Richard Loxton Campin [1961] Director; Timothy Edward Easingwood [1977] Director/Investment Professional; James Michael Gunton [1982] Director/Investment Professional; Martin John Halliday [1960] Director; John Gerard Moore [1960] Director [Irish]; Graham Neil Storey [1963] Director; Mark Tims [1956] Director; Adrian Steven Wood [1967] Director

Grove Industries (Holdings) Ltd
Incorporated: 21 July 2017
Net Worth: £11,495,529 *Total Assets:* £11,495,529
Registered Office: The Old Bank, 14 Bank Street, Lutterworth, Leics, LE17 4AJ
Activities: Activities of head offices
Shareholders: Jonathan David Grove; Simon Leslie Grove
Officers: Jonathan David Grove [1981] Director; Simon Leslie Grove [1983] Director

Groves of Thame (Holdings) Limited
Incorporated: 3 February 2014 *Employees:* 95
Net Worth: £24,729,068 *Total Assets:* £27,420,798
Registered Office: 73 Southern Road, Thame, Oxon, OX9 2ED
Activities: Activities of distribution holding companies
Officers: Martin Groves, Secretary; Andrew Simon Groves [1964] Director; Marlene Miriam Groves [1937] Director; Martin John Groves [1965] Director; Nicholas Peter Groves [1971] Director; Rodney Groves [1935] Director

Groves of Thame Limited
Incorporated: 24 March 1975 *Employees:* 95
Net Worth: £17,635,596 *Total Assets:* £20,275,936
Registered Office: Groves, Eastern Bypass, Thame, Oxon, OX9 3FU
Activities: Wholesale of household goods (other than musical instruments) n.e.c
Parent: Groves of Thame (Holdings) Ltd
Officers: Martin Groves, Secretary; Andrew Simon Groves [1964] Managing Director; Marlene Miriam Groves [1937] Director; Martin John Groves [1965] Finance Director; Nicholas Peter Groves [1971] Director/Manager; Rodney Groves [1935] Director/Chairman Importer & Distributor; Gareth Trevor Pope [1969] Sales Director

Growth LED Innovation Driven Employee Company Ltd
Incorporated: 18 March 2011
Net Worth: £8,674,218 *Total Assets:* £9,094,772
Registered Office: The Old West Gun Works, 201 Savile Street East, Sheffield, S4 7UQ
Activities: Non-trading company
Officers: Katherine Cullen, Secretary; Martin Leslie Baker [1984] Director/Loadhog - Design Engineer; Joel Barrera [1993] Director/Packing and Shipping [American]; Florence Beaudic [1979] Director/Europe [French]; Boris Berghmans [1988] Director/Sales Manager [Belgian]; Toby James Bradley [1992] Director/PMS Design Engineer; James Curry [1989] Director/Production Team Leader; Robert Andrew Davies [1954] Business Development Director; Jeremy Martin Dennis [1981] Director/Gripple Management - Graphic Designer; Daniel Andre Desler [1986] Director/Product Manager; Carolyn Ekins [1966] Director; Dr Caroline Facey [1982] Director/Doctor; Hugh David Facey [1945] Director; Juliet Elizabeth Facey [1988] Director/National Account Manager; Florence Fiedler [1970] Director/Sales Management Coordinator [French]; Timothy Fletcher [1968] Director/Production Operative; Joseph Goldthorpe [1996] Director/Engineering Apprentice; Katie Haldenby-Brown [1981] Director/Product Coordinator; Roger Hall [1946] Finance Director; Jake Hallatt [1999] Director/Gripple Factory Moulding Setter/Technician; Dennis Edward Hand [1965] Director; Michael Hodgson [1989] Director/Digital Content & Communications Manager; Abhinav Jain [1988] Director/National Technical Manager [Indian]; Chloe Joho [1993] Director/Europe [French]; Naomi Jones [1986] Director/Sales & Marketing Coordinator; Nicholas Phillip Jones [1993] Director/Design Engineer; Kimberley Danielle Jowett [1981] Director/Accounts and HR Assistant PMS; Siddhesh Narayan Kanvinde [1981] Director/Area Technical Manager India [Indian]; Ewa Lakoma [1988] Director/Assistant Accountant [Polish]; Dan Modjeski [1991] Director/Marketing Coordinator [American]; David Christopher Palmer [1981] Director/Gripple Management - Manager; Kyle Raffo [1990] Director/Moulding Team Leader; Anna Reibel-Kubiak [1979] Director/Gripple Europe - Internal Sales Manager [Polish]; David Arthur Routledge [1958] Director; Kirstie Royston [1972] Director/Sales Administrator; Natalie Rusling [1974] Director/Team Leader; James David Sallows [1979] Director/Team Leader Production; Claire Tunnard [1973] Director/Team Leader; Aston James Wagstaff [1999] Director/Production Operative; Kane Wasnidge [1999] Director/Apprentice Tool Maker; Ross Wegman [1987] Director/Financial Controller [American]

Growth Partners Management Limited
Incorporated: 12 December 2016
Net Worth: £19,999,584 *Total Assets:* £20,679,212
Registered Office: 2 Colton Square, Leicester, LE1 1QH
Activities: Information technology consultancy activities
Major Shareholder: Paul Bresnhan
Officers: Paul Anthony Bresnihan [1976] Director

GRS (Bagging) Limited
Incorporated: 28 January 2000
Net Worth: £8,046,469 *Total Assets:* £23,214,482
Registered Office: 10 Goldsmith Way, Eliot Business Park, Nuneaton, Warwicks, CV10 7RJ
Activities: Wholesale of wood, construction materials and sanitary equipment
Parent: GRS Roadstone Group Limited
Officers: Jonathan Gareth Fisher [1977] Managing Director; Martin Victor Hill [1954] Director; Lee Hudson [1974] Director; Jordan Paul Webb [1988] Director

GRS (Roadstone) Limited
Incorporated: 9 October 1996 *Employees:* 189
Net Worth: £18,706,056 *Total Assets:* £60,919,592
Registered Office: 10 Goldsmith Way, Eliot Business Park, Nuneaton, Warwicks, CV10 7RJ
Activities: Other mining and quarrying n.e.c.
Parent: GRS Roadstone Group Ltd
Officers: Yvette Bailey [1974] Director; Antony Charles Beamish [1978] Regional Director; Philip Martin Cox [1959] Director; Jonathan Gareth Fisher [1977] Sales Director; Adam Hancock [1980] Director/General Manager; Craig Martin Hill [1985] Director; Martin Victor Hill [1954] Director/Marketing Executive; Lee Hudson [1974] Sales Director; Dyfrig Morgan James [1954] Director and Consultant; Ilija Radomilovic [1965] Sales Director; Andrew John Regan [1983] Director/General Manager; Martin Paul Reid [1967] Director; Martin Kenneth Riley [1967] Managing Director Lafarge Tarmac Aggregates; Andrew Rogerson [1970] Director; Christopher James Woodward [1988] Director/General Manager

GRS Roadstone Group Limited
Incorporated: 29 April 2014 *Employees:* 763
Net Worth: £14,939,337 *Total Assets:* £121,054,608
Registered Office: Unit 10 Goldsmith Way, Eliot Business Park, Nuneaton, Warwicks, CV10 7RJ
Activities: Support activities for other mining and quarrying
Officers: Antony Charles Beamish [1978] Director; Liam Colm Charalambou [1983] Director/Solicitor; Jonathan Gareth Fisher [1977] Director; Martin Victor Hill [1954] Director; Lee Hudson [1974] Director; Dyfrig Morgan James [1954] Director; Ilija Radomilovic [1965] Director; Martin Paul Reid [1967] Director; Martin Kenneth Riley [1967] Director

GRT Nottingham Lift Project Company (No. 1) Limited
Incorporated: 8 October 2003
Net Worth Deficit: £7,748,000 *Total Assets:* £65,745,000
Registered Office: Unit G1, Ash Tree Court, Nottingham Business Park, Nottingham, NG8 6PY
Activities: Other business support service activities n.e.c.
Parent: GRT Nottingham Lift Midco (No.1) Limited
Officers: Michael George Duggan, Secretary; Richard John Coates [1966] CHP Investment Director; Lucy Ann Dadge [1964] NHS Director; Charlotte Sophie Ellen Douglass [1978] Director/Chartered Surveyor; Gavin William MacKinlay [1957] Associate Director; Kirsty O'Brien [1982] Director/Operations Manager; Paddy Tipping [1949] Director/Member of Parliament

GRT Nottingham Lift Project Company (No.2) Limited
Incorporated: 10 October 2003
Net Worth Deficit: £6,841,000 *Total Assets:* £28,721,000
Registered Office: Unit G1, Ash Tree Court, Nottingham Business Park, Nottingham, NG8 6PY
Activities: Non-trading company
Parent: GRT Nottingham Lift Midco (No.2) Limited
Officers: Michael George Duggan, Secretary; Richard John Coates [1966] CHP Investment Director; Lucy Ann Dadge [1964] NHS Director; Charlotte Sophie Ellen Douglass [1978] Director/Chartered Surveyor; Gavin William MacKinlay [1957] Associate Director; Kirsty O'Brien [1982] Director/Operations Manager; Paddy Tipping [1949] Director/Member of Parliament

Grundon Sand & Gravel Limited
Incorporated: 3 October 1947 *Employees:* 22
Net Worth: £12,762,504 *Total Assets:* £16,561,905
Registered Office: Thames House, Oxford Road, Benson, Wallingford, Oxon, OX10 6LX
Activities: Operation of gravel and sand pits; mining of clays and kaolin
Major Shareholder: Norman Stephen Grundon
Officers: Simon Arnold, Secretary; Philip John Atkinson [1977] Director; Neil Norman Grundon [1969] Development Director; Norman Stephen Grundon [1941] Director/Chairman; Stephen Brian Roscoe [1959] Technical Director; Bradley James Smith [1977] Sales and Marketing Director; Clayton Sinclair Sullivan-Webb [1973] Managing Director

Grundon Waste Management Limited
Incorporated: 4 July 2001 *Employees:* 817
Net Worth: £111,236,216 *Total Assets:* £217,810,272
Registered Office: Thames House, Oxford Road, Benson, Wallingford, Oxon, OX10 6LX
Activities: Collection of non-hazardous waste
Shareholders: Norman Stephen Grundon; Neil Norman Grundon
Officers: Simon Arnold, Secretary; Philip John Atkinson [1977] Director; Neil Norman Grundon [1969] Director; Norman Stephen Grundon [1941] Director; Stephen Brian Roscoe [1959] Technical Director; Bradley James Smith [1977] Sales and Marketing Director; Clayton Sinclair Sullivan-Webb [1973] Managing Director

I.Grunwerg Limited
Incorporated: 29 November 1954 *Employees:* 51
Net Worth: £5,598,976 *Total Assets:* £10,201,053
Registered Office: Silversteel House, 29-49 Rockingham Street, Sheffield, S1 4EA
Activities: Wholesale of household goods (other than musical instruments) n.e.c
Shareholder: David Anthony Grunwerg
Officers: David Anthony Grunwerg, Secretary; David Anthony Grunwerg [1950] Director

Grupo Antolin Leamington Limited
Incorporated: 3 December 1997
Net Worth: £6,359,507 *Total Assets:* £38,616,536
Registered Office: Tachbrook Park Drive, Leamington Spa, Warwick, CV34 6RH
Activities: Manufacture of other parts and accessories for motor vehicles
Officers: Pablo Martinez, Secretary; Jesus Pascual [1963] Director [Spanish]; Pedro Santesteban [1967] Director [Spanish]

Guardian Industries U.K. Limited
Incorporated: 11 January 2001 *Employees:* 251
Net Worth: £113,111,000 *Total Assets:* £122,736,000
Registered Office: Tom Pudding Way, Goole, E Yorks, DN14 8GA
Activities: Manufacture of flat glass
Parent: Guardian Industries UK Holding Limited
Officers: Vincent Pringiers, Secretary; Gustav Boekhoudt [1963] Vice President & Managing Director [Dutch]; Gabor Harakaly [1968] Director/Chief Financial Officer [Hungarian]

Guardian Industries UK Holding Limited
Incorporated: 9 November 2012
Net Worth: £12,093,000 *Total Assets:* £83,650,000
Registered Office: Tom Pudding Way, Goole, E Yorks, DN14 8GA
Activities: Activities of production holding companies
Officers: Ana Martinez de Lecea Noain, Secretary; Gabor Harakaly [1968] Director/Chief Financial Officer [Hungarian]; Vincent Pringiers [1964] Director/Secretary [Belgian]

Guidance Marine Limited
Incorporated: 15 September 2004 *Employees:* 45
Previous: Guidance Navigation Limited
Net Worth: £9,907,000 *Total Assets:* £12,564,000
Registered Office: 5 Tiber Way, Meridian Business Park, Leicester, LE19 1QP
Activities: Manufacture of other electrical equipment
Parent: Guidance Navigation Holdings Limited
Officers: Jan Grothusen [1972] Managing Director [British/German]; Maik Stoevhase [1967] Managing Director [German]; Mika Tapio Verronen [1972] Commercial Director [Finnish]

Guided Ultrasonics Limited
Incorporated: 20 July 1999 *Employees:* 34
Net Worth: £11,547,358 *Total Assets:* £12,510,394
Registered Office: 7 St John Street, Mansfield, Notts, NG18 1QH
Activities: Manufacture of other electrical equipment
Officers: Malcolm Russell, Secretary/Consultant; David Alleyne [1959] Director/Engineer; Prof Peter Cawley [1953] Director/University Professor; Professor Michael John Stuart Lowe [1957] Director/University Professor; Dr Brian Nicholas Pavlakovic [1971] Director/Software Designer [American]; Malcolm Russell [1954] Director/Engineer

Guilbert UK Holdings Limited
Incorporated: 16 February 1994 *Employees:* 2
Net Worth: £60,850,000 *Total Assets:* £63,378,000
Registered Office: 501 Beaumont Leys Lane, Leicester, LE4 2BN
Activities: Activities of head offices
Parent: Office Depot International (UK) Limited
Officers: Jacqueline Susan Hills, Secretary; Neil David Maslen [1972] Director/SVP Contract Europe; Michael William Walby [1973] Managing Director [Irish]

Guilford Europe Limited
Incorporated: 16 February 1944 *Employees:* 452
Net Worth: £31,758,000 *Total Assets:* £48,429,000
Registered Office: Cotes Park, Somercotes, Derbys, DE55 4NJ
Activities: Manufacture of other technical and industrial textiles
Parent: Guilford Mills Europe Limited
Officers: Martin Henningsen [1967] Director/Associate General Counsel [German]; Robert Chalders Hooper [1953] Director/Chartered Accountant

Guilford Mills Europe Limited
Incorporated: 13 February 1981
Net Worth: £33,855,200 *Total Assets:* £33,866,792
Registered Office: Cotes Park, Somercotes, Derbys, DE55 4NJ
Activities: Activities of head offices
Parent: Guilford Mills Limited
Officers: Martin Henningsen [1967] Director/Associate General Counsel [German]; Robert Chalders Hooper [1953] Director/Chartered Accountant

Guilford Mills Limited
Incorporated: 17 May 1996
Net Worth: £12,322,985 *Total Assets:* £16,328,470
Registered Office: Cotes Park, Somercotes, Derbys, DE55 4NJ
Activities: Activities of head offices
Officers: Martin Henningsen [1967] Director/Associate General Counsel [German]; Robert Chalders Hooper [1953] Director/Chartered Accountant

Guilsborough Multi Academy Trust
Incorporated: 18 February 2011 *Employees:* 161
Net Worth: £13,161,928 *Total Assets:* £14,207,126
Registered Office: Guilsborough Academy, West Haddon Road, Guilsborough, Northampton, NN6 8QE
Activities: General secondary education
Officers: Angela Carter [1955] Director/Accountant; Timothy Michael Heydon [1958] Director; Wayne Jones [1977] Director/Headteacher; Julie Swales [1966] Director/Principal; Nicholas Richard Wilson [1968] Director/Project Manager

Gurney Slade Lime & Stone Co.Limited
Incorporated: 30 January 1953 *Employees:* 66
Net Worth: £6,484,566 *Total Assets:* £11,557,376
Registered Office: c/o LKAB Minerals Limited, Raynesway, Derby, DE21 7BE
Activities: Other mining and quarrying n.e.c.
Parent: LKAB Minerals Limited
Officers: Richard Mark Wheatley, Secretary; David Thomas Balch [1981] Director; Darren Anthony Wilson [1969] Managing Director

GUS 1998 Unlimited
Incorporated: 3 February 1998
Net Worth: £30,320,478 *Total Assets:* £40,372,612
Registered Office: The Sir John Peace Building, Experian Way, NG2 Business Park, Nottingham, NG80 1ZZ
Activities: Financial intermediation not elsewhere classified
Shareholders: Experian Finance PLC; Experian Nominees Limited
Officers: Ronan Hanna, Secretary; Paul Alan Atkinson [1960] Director; Antony Jonathan Ward Barnes [1964] Director of Tax and Treasury; Karen Julia Greenwood [1967] Director/Chartered Accountant; Daniel Tristan Lilley [1981] Director; Mark Edward Pepper [1963] Director

GUS 2000 Finance Unlimited
Incorporated: 13 October 2000
Previous: GUS 2000 Finance Limited
Net Worth: £17,996,853,248 *Total Assets:* £17,997,971,456
Registered Office: The Sir John Peace Building, Experian Way, NG2 Business Park, Nottingham, NG80 1ZZ
Activities: Financial intermediation not elsewhere classified
Parent: Experian Finance PLC
Officers: Ronan Hanna, Secretary; Paul Alan Atkinson [1960] Director/Group Taxation Manager; Antony Jonathan Ward Barnes [1964] Director of Tax and Treasury; Karen Julia Greenwood [1967] Director/Chartered Accountant; Daniel Tristan Lilley [1981] Director; Mark Edward Pepper [1963] Director/Financial Controller

GUS 2004 Limited
Incorporated: 23 January 2004
Net Worth: £23,965,344 *Total Assets:* £23,987,580
Registered Office: The Sir John Peace Building, Experian Way, NG2 Business Park, Nottingham, NG80 1ZZ
Activities: Financial intermediation not elsewhere classified
Parent: GUS Holdings Unlimited
Officers: Ronan Hanna, Secretary; Paul Alan Atkinson [1960] Director; Antony Jonathan Ward Barnes [1964] Director of Tax and Treasury; Karen Julia Greenwood [1967] Director/Chartered Accountant; Daniel Tristan Lilley [1981] Director; Mark Edward Pepper [1963] Director

GUS Catalogues Unlimited
Incorporated: 11 December 1997
Previous: GUS Catalogues Limited
Net Worth: £4,974,806,528 *Total Assets:* £4,974,806,528
Registered Office: The Sir John Peace Building, Experian Way, NG2 Business Park, Nottingham, NG80 1ZZ
Activities: Activities of other holding companies n.e.c.
Parent: Experian Finance PLC
Officers: Ronan Hanna, Secretary; Paul Alan Atkinson [1960] Director; Antony Jonathan Ward Barnes [1964] Director of Tax and Treasury; Karen Julia Greenwood [1967] Director/Chartered Accountant; Daniel Tristan Lilley [1981] Director; Mark Edward Pepper [1963] Director

GUS Holdings Unlimited
Incorporated: 16 January 1998
Net Worth: £758,927,424 *Total Assets:* £7,850,981,888
Registered Office: The Sir John Peace Building, Experian Way, NG2 Business Park, Nottingham, NG80 1ZZ
Activities: Activities of other holding companies n.e.c.
Parent: Experian (UK) Holdings 2006 Limited
Officers: Ronan Hanna, Secretary; Paul Alan Atkinson [1960] Director; Antony Jonathan Ward Barnes [1964] Director of Tax and Treasury; Karen Julia Greenwood [1967] Director/Chartered Accountant; Daniel Tristan Lilley [1981] Director; Mark Edward Pepper [1963] Director

Guy Salmon Limited
Incorporated: 3 June 1998 *Employees:* 1,226
Net Worth: £53,129,000 *Total Assets:* £224,412,992
Registered Office: 2 Penman Way, Grove Park, Leicester, LE19 1ST
Activities: Sale of new cars and light motor vehicles
Parent: Sytner Group Limited
Officers: Adam Collinson, Secretary; Adam Collinson [1972] Finance Director; Darren Edwards [1968] Managing Director; Robert Harold Kurnick [1961] Director/Executive Vice President [American]; Jeremy Richard Mallett [1952] Director; Gerard Edward Nieuwenhuys [1960] Director; Laurence Edward William Vaughan [1963] Managing Director

GW 305 Limited
Incorporated: 17 March 2003 *Employees:* 4
Net Worth: £39,465,656 *Total Assets:* £122,457,920
Registered Office: Gallagher House, Gallagher Way, Gallagher Business Park, Heathcote, Warwick, CV34 6AF
Activities: Buying and selling of own real estate
Parent: Gallagher Estates Holdings Limited
Officers: Edward Paul Farnsworth [1982] Director of Business Planning; Craig David Luttman [1975] Development Director; Martin Rowland Richmond [1953] Group Legal Director; Gregg Spencer Wilkinson [1973] Managing Director

Nell Gwynn Limited
Incorporated: 7 November 2006
Net Worth Deficit: £149,550 *Total Assets:* £28,093,992
Registered Office: 1a Needlers End Lane, Balsall Common, Coventry, Warwicks, CV7 7AF
Activities: Management of real estate on a fee or contract basis
Major Shareholder: Frank Howard Hunter
Officers: Kim Beresford [1962] Director/Accountant; Frank Howard Hunter [1945] Director/Surveyor

H & K Distribution Limited
Incorporated: 17 February 2006
Net Worth: £13,002,339 *Total Assets:* £18,396,256
Registered Office: 1 Cosford Lane, Swift Valley, Rugby, Warwicks, CV21 1QN
Activities: Other manufacturing n.e.c.
Major Shareholder: David Charles Bobbett
Officers: Nick Scallan, Secretary; Keith Cassidy [1966] Managing Director [Irish]; David Spain [1969] Director [Irish]

H (Lincs) Limited
Incorporated: 20 October 1978 *Employees:* 44
Net Worth: £19,164,148 *Total Assets:* £34,164,976
Registered Office: Sausthorpe Hall, Sausthorpe, Spilsby, Lincs, PE23 4JN
Activities: Activities of head offices
Officers: Roger William Hawkes, Secretary; Roger William Hawkes [1942] Director/Farmer

H L Plastics Limited
Incorporated: 28 April 1997 *Employees:* 481
Net Worth: £32,620,016 *Total Assets:* £46,392,432
Registered Office: Flamstead House, Denby Hall Business Park, Denby, Derbys, DE5 8JX
Activities: Manufacture of other plastic products
Parent: Quanex Building Products Corporation
Officers: Monika Bailey, Secretary; Monika Bailey [1978] Finance Director; Kevin Patrick Delaney [1961] Director [American]; Brent Livingston Korb [1972] Director [American]; Martin Thurley [1969] Managing Director

H.I. Limited
Incorporated: 4 February 1992 *Employees:* 2
Net Worth: £5,327,441 *Total Assets:* £12,273,576
Registered Office: Estate Office, Rushton Hall, Rushton, Northants, NN14 1RR
Activities: Buying and selling of own real estate
Shareholders: Simon Richard Hazelton; Thomas Robert Hazelton
Officers: Simon Richard Hazelton, Secretary; Simon Richard Hazelton [1969] Director; Thomas Robert Hazelton [1966] Managing Director; Valerie Danielle Hazelton [1969] Director

H.I.G. Europe-Dart III, Ltd
Incorporated: 3 February 2010 *Employees:* 1,159
Net Worth Deficit: £32,259,000 *Total Assets:* £83,589,000
Registered Office: Synseal Extrusions Limited, Common Road, Huthwaite, Notts, NG17 6AD
Activities: Non-trading company
Shareholders: Sami Mnaymneh; Anthony Tamer
Officers: Leigh Garner Daveran [1979] Director; Alastair Mills [1975] Director

Haas Formula UK Ltd
Incorporated: 29 July 2014 *Employees:* 78
Net Worth: £8,638,000 *Total Assets:* £39,166,000
Registered Office: Haas Racing, Overthorpe Road, Banbury, Oxon, OX16 4PN
Activities: Other sports activities
Major Shareholder: Gene Francis Haas
Officers: Gene Francis Haas [1952] Director/Corporate Executive [American]; Scott Richard Roggenbauer [1968] Director/Finance [American]

Habitat Retail Limited
Incorporated: 19 November 2010 *Employees:* 244
Net Worth: £5,591,000 *Total Assets:* £26,380,000
Registered Office: 489-499 Avebury Boulevard, Milton Keynes, Bucks, MK9 2NW
Activities: Other retail sale in non-specialised stores
Parent: Home Retail Group (UK) Limited
Officers: Timothy Fallowfield, Secretary; Clare Victoria Askem [1969] Director; Claire Louise Catlin [1980] Director

Hach Lange Ltd
Incorporated: 1 November 1971 *Employees:* 110
Net Worth: £2,802,000 *Total Assets:* £10,723,000
Registered Office: 19 Jessops Riverside, 800 Brightside Lane, Sheffield, S9 2RX
Activities: Manufacture of electronic measuring, testing etc. equipment, not for industrial process control
Parent: Launchchange Operations Ltd
Officers: Graeme Francis Cullinan [1963] Director; Darin Stell [1965] Director; Keith Graham Ward [1953] Financial Director

G.I. Hadfield & Son Limited
Incorporated: 4 November 1980 *Employees:* 163
Net Worth: £8,800,923 *Total Assets:* £14,379,448
Registered Office: Brailwood Road, Bilsthorpe Industrial Estate, Newark, Notts, NG22 8UA
Activities: Recovery of sorted materials
Parent: GI Hadfield Holdings Limited
Officers: Bill Joseph Power, Secretary; Bill Joseph Power [1969] Finance Director [Irish]; Tom Walsh [1967] Director/Chief Executive Officer [Irish]; Simon Alasdair Woods [1969] Director/Chief Operating Officer

Hadfield Properties Limited
Incorporated: 7 February 2007 *Employees:* 132
Net Worth: £13,342,238 *Total Assets:* £14,433,476
Registered Office: 2 Chawley Park, Cumnor Hill, Oxford, OX2 9GG
Activities: Activities of head offices
Major Shareholder: Simon Denis Michael Porritt
Officers: Simon Denis Michael Porritt [1967] Director/Nursing Home Manager

Hadleigh Holdings Limited
Incorporated: 15 February 2005 *Employees:* 235
Net Worth: £17,241,192 *Total Assets:* £25,341,416
Registered Office: 22-26 King Street, King's Lynn, Norfolk, PE30 1HJ
Activities: Non-life insurance
Shareholders: David James Flux; Yvonne Flux
Officers: David James Flux, Secretary; David James Flux [1968] Director/Insurance Broker; Yvonne Flux [1948] Director/Insurance Broker

Hadrian (Residential) Limited
Incorporated: 8 May 2014
Net Worth Deficit: £3,383,712 *Total Assets:* £10,889,535
Registered Office: c/o White Rose Accountants, 15a Hallgate, Doncaster, S Yorks, DN1 3NA
Activities: Buying and selling of own real estate
Officers: Michael Patrick Murray [1969] Director/Property Developer; Glyn Dale Smith [1964] Director/Property Developer

HAE Global Ltd
Incorporated: 9 July 2012 *Employees:* 194
Net Worth: £14,678,770 *Total Assets:* £28,606,052
Registered Office: 3 Cygnus Court, Beverley Road, East Midlands Airport, Derby, DE74 2SA
Activities: Freight air transport
Parent: World Freight Company Investment UK Ltd
Officers: Pierre Jacques Gerard Brunet [1960] Director [French]; Colin Richard White [1963] Director/Chartered Accountant

HAE Group Limited
Incorporated: 10 October 2006
Net Worth: £631,187 *Total Assets:* £23,608,820
Registered Office: 3 Cygnus Court, Beverley Road, East Midlands Airport, Derby, DE74 2SA
Activities: Freight air transport
Parent: HAE Global Ltd
Officers: Colin Richard White, Secretary/Chartered Accountant; Neville Karai [1966] Director; Richard Thackeray [1968] Director/Business Development Manager; Colin Richard White [1963] Director

Hafele U.K. Limited
Incorporated: 18 March 1980 *Employees:* 409
Net Worth: £36,792,000 *Total Assets:* £59,879,000
Registered Office: Swift Valley Industrial Estate, Rugby, Warwicks, CV21 1RD
Activities: Non-specialised wholesale trade
Parent: Hafele Holding GmbH
Officers: Craig Stephen Chambers [1962] Managing Director; Nathan Brynley Cole [1975] Finance Director; Sibylle Annemarie Thierer [1960] Director [German]

Hagerty Holdings Limited
Incorporated: 1 December 2016
Net Worth: £25,000,000 *Total Assets:* £25,000,000
Registered Office: The Arch Barn, Pury Hill Farm, Towcester, Northants, NN12 7TB
Activities: Activities of financial services holding companies
Shareholders: Kim Hagerty; McKeel O'Hagerty; Tammy J Hagerty
Officers: James Angus Forsyth [1963] Director/Insurance Broker; McKeel O Hagerty [1967] Director [American]; Thomas Chester Jones [1946] Director/Insurance Executive [American]

Hague Farming Limited
Incorporated: 13 May 1988 *Employees:* 11
Net Worth: £14,556,877 *Total Assets:* £20,132,472
Registered Office: Jubilee House, Claywheels Lane, Sheffield, S6 1LZ
Activities: Growing of cereals (except rice), leguminous crops and oil seeds
Shareholders: David William Hague; Dianne Hague; Martin Hartley Hague
Officers: David William Hague [1951] Director; Dianne Hague [1954] Director; William Philip Hague [1974] Director/Manager

Hague Plant Limited
Incorporated: 12 August 1975 *Employees:* 48
Net Worth: £8,825,715 *Total Assets:* £10,294,280
Registered Office: Jubilee House, Claywheels Lane, Sheffield, S6 1LZ
Activities: Other specialised construction activities n.e.c.
Shareholders: David William Hague; Dianne Hague; Martin Hartley Hague
Officers: David William Hague [1951] Director/Farmer and Contractor; Dianne Hague [1954] Director/Secretary; William Philip Hague [1974] Managing Director

Hajco 199 Limited
Incorporated: 28 November 1997 *Employees:* 187
Net Worth: £16,407,000 *Total Assets:* £29,206,000
Registered Office: c/o Watling JCB Ltd, Dog and Gun Lane, Whetstone, Leicester, LE8 6LJ
Activities: Wholesale of mining, construction and civil engineering machinery
Major Shareholder: Richard Edmund Telfer
Officers: Rachel Telfer, Secretary; Richard Edmund Telfer [1969] Director

Halcyon Acquisitions Limited
Incorporated: 16 June 2011
Net Worth Deficit: £121,399,000 *Total Assets:* £138,008,000
Registered Office: 107 Station Street, Burton on Trent, Staffs, DE14 1SZ
Activities: Activities of other holding companies n.e.c.
Parent: Halcyon Financing Limited
Officers: John Bradshaw, Secretary; John Richard Bradshaw [1955] Director/Solicitor; Darryn Stanley Gibson [1965] Director [New Zealander]; John Spencer Sheridan [1973] Director

Halcyon Financing Limited
Incorporated: 16 June 2011
Net Worth: £2,016,000 *Total Assets:* £257,718,000
Registered Office: 107 Station Street, Burton on Trent, Staffs, DE14 1SZ
Activities: Activities of other holding companies n.e.c.
Parent: Halcyon Midco Limited
Officers: John Bradshaw, Secretary; John Richard Bradshaw [1955] Director/Solicitor; Darryn Stanley Gibson [1965] Director [New Zealander]; John Spencer Sheridan [1973] Director

Halcyon Midco Limited
Incorporated: 16 June 2011
Net Worth: £7,173,000 *Total Assets:* £257,718,000
Registered Office: 107 Station Street, Burton on Trent, Staffs, DE14 1SZ
Activities: Activities of other holding companies n.e.c.
Parent: Halcyon Topco Limited
Officers: John Bradshaw, Secretary; John Richard Bradshaw [1955] Director/Solicitor; Darryn Stanley Gibson [1965] Director [New Zealander]; John Spencer Sheridan [1973] Director

Halcyon Topco Limited
Incorporated: 16 June 2011 *Employees:* 1,706
Net Worth Deficit: £217,582,000 *Total Assets:* £467,729,984
Registered Office: 107 Station Street, Burton on Trent, Staffs, DE14 1SZ
Activities: Activities of other holding companies n.e.c.
Parent: Vitruvian Partners LLP
Officers: John Bradshaw, Secretary; Darryn Stanley Gibson [1965] Director [New Zealander]; Peter Nicklin [1963] Director; Douglas Oppenheim [1976] Director; John Spencer Sheridan [1973] Director

Hales Group Limited
Incorporated: 21 April 1999 *Employees:* 1,747
Net Worth: £2,982,122 *Total Assets:* £10,724,789
Registered Office: Unit 3b, Flag Business Exchange, Vicarage Farm Road, Peterborough, Cambs, PE1 5TX
Activities: Temporary employment agency activities
Shareholders: Nicola Amanda Fowler; Nigel William Wray
Officers: Jeffrey Fowler [1954] Director; Nicola Jane Mewse [1970] Group Managing Director; Kamal Somchand Shah [1959] Director

D Hales Limited
Incorporated: 18 October 1996 *Employees:* 59
Net Worth: £14,125,000 *Total Assets:* £31,339,000
Registered Office: Acrey Fields, Woburn Road, Wootton, Beds, MK43 9EJ
Activities: Sale of used cars and light motor vehicles
Parent: Copart UK Limited
Officers: Aaron Jayson Adair [1969] Director/Chief Executive Officer [American]; Jonathan David Canning [1972] Director/General Counsel; Gregory Depasquale [1968] Director/SVP, General Counsel and Secretary of Copart, Inc [American]; William Easley Franklin [1956] Director/Chief Financial Officer [American]; Nigel James Paget [1966] Managing Director; Simon Sheldon-Wilson [1969] Director; Paul Anthony Styer [1956] Director/General Counsel [American]

Halgram Limited
Incorporated: 12 March 1996 *Employees:* 3
Net Worth: £6,517,678 *Total Assets:* £11,230,573
Registered Office: 10 Oxford Street, Nottingham, NG1 5BG
Activities: Other letting and operating of own or leased real estate
Shareholders: John Martin Proctor; David Gordon Hargreaves
Officers: John Martin Proctor, Secretary/Chartered Surveyor; John Martin Proctor [1962] Director/Chartered Surveyor

Hall & Pickles 1812 Limited
Incorporated: 21 February 1996 *Employees:* 263
Net Worth: £24,484,000 *Total Assets:* £68,293,000
Registered Office: Poynton Industrial Estate, London Road, Poynton, Stockport, Cheshire, SK12 1NB
Activities: Wholesale of metals and metal ores
Shareholder: Matthew Kindersley Hall
Officers: Arnold Hillier, Secretary/Chartered Accountant; Alexander Richard Congreve Hall [1966] Director; Matthew Kindersley Hall [1967] Director; Arnold Hillier [1930] Director/Chartered Accountant

Hall Contracts (Lakenheath) Limited
Incorporated: 10 July 1998 *Employees:* 11
Net Worth: £8,017,037 *Total Assets:* £10,485,211
Registered Office: 27-29 Old Market, Wisbech, Cambs, PE13 1NE
Activities: Real estate agencies
Major Shareholder: Jeffrey Hall
Officers: Timothy William Stevenson, Secretary; Jeffrey Hall [1964] Director/Builder; Nicola Fiona Hall [1967] Director

Hall Cross Academy Trust
Incorporated: 9 January 2012 *Employees:* 296
Net Worth: £11,813,000 *Total Assets:* £16,732,000
Registered Office: Hall Cross Academy, Thorne Road, Doncaster, S Yorks, DN1 2HY
Activities: General secondary education
Officers: Kimberley Ann Sritharan, Secretary; Tausif Abdul [1979] Director/Regional Manager; David Charles Cox [1966] Director/Head of Security; Pippa Dodgshon [1964] Director/Headteacher; Tracy Drabble [1965] Director/Public Sector for The Care Quality Commission; Josephine Foxton [1948] Director/Retired; Thomas Edward Hince [1979] Director/Commercial Manager; Antony King [1973] Director/Year Manager; Beverley John Marshall [1951] Director/Retired; Shaun Masterman [1965] Director/Carer; Lee Parish [1974] Director/Manager; Tony Thorpe [1949] Director/Retired; Andrew Townsend [1978] Director/Certified Chartered Accountant; Ian Trevillion [1975] Director/Primary Teacher; David Antony Westwood [1967] Director/Police Officer; Roger Menai Williams [1945] Director/Solicitor

Hallam Land Management Limited
Incorporated: 29 December 1989 *Employees:* 37
Net Worth: £82,422,680 *Total Assets:* £139,087,056
Registered Office: Banner Cross Hall, Ecclesall Road South, Sheffield, S11 9PD
Activities: Development of building projects
Parent: Henry Boot PLC
Officers: Amy Louise Oakley, Secretary; Andrew Birch [1979] Director; Paul Stuart Burton [1971] Director/Land Buyer; Nicholas Joseph Duckworth [1967] Director/Chartered Town Planner; Peter Glazebrook [1968] Director/Planner; Darren Louis Littlewood [1975] Finance Director; Ruth Helen McKeown [1968] Director/Town Planner; Gary Edward Smith [1973] Director; John Trevor Sutcliffe [1959] Finance Director; Rebecca Jane Wasse [1974] Director

Hallamshire Developments Limited
Incorporated: 3 May 1937
Net Worth: £5,438,365 *Total Assets:* £9,295,933
Registered Office: Capstone House, Prospect Park, Dunston Way, Dunston Road, Chesterfield, Derbys, S41 9RD
Activities: Non-trading company
Major Shareholder: John Lindley Wilson
Officers: Angela Suzanne Hunt, Secretary; Robert Arnold Veerman [1959] Director/Accountant [Dutch]; John Lindley Wilson [1943] Director/Civil Engineer

Halliwell Jones (Wilmslow) Limited
Incorporated: 25 September 1945 *Employees:* 110
Net Worth: £2,834,832 *Total Assets:* £19,472,282
Registered Office: Manchester Road, Wilmslow, Cheshire, SK9 2LE
Activities: Sale of new cars and light motor vehicles
Parent: Roundel Limited
Officers: Margaret Louise Clough, Secretary; James Mark Charles Houghton [1960] Sales Director; Glyn Anthony Howes [1962] Director; Phillip Jones [1950] Director

Hammond Grange Limited
Incorporated: 15 May 1984 *Employees:* 6
Net Worth: £37,575,000 *Total Assets:* £39,068,212
Registered Office: 139 Gloucester Crescent, Wigston, Leics, LE18 4YL
Activities: Other letting and operating of own or leased real estate
Major Shareholder: William Terrence Lander
Officers: Brenda June Lander, Secretary; Brenda June Lander [1949] Director/Property Owner; William Terrence Lander [1945] Director/Property Owner

Hammonds Furniture Limited
Incorporated: 7 July 1977 *Employees:* 873
Net Worth: £16,556,881 *Total Assets:* £30,197,076
Registered Office: Manor Court Chambers, Townsend Drive, Nuneaton, Warwicks, CV11 6RU
Activities: Manufacture of other furniture
Parent: HFG Holdings Limited
Officers: Glenn Anthony Hammonds [1967] Production Director; Mark John Hammonds [1961] Joint Managing Director; Richard John Hammonds [1963] Director/Chairman; Jill Richardson [1942] Director

Hampton (Burlington Court) Ltd
Incorporated: 1 June 2017
Net Worth: £1,867,129 *Total Assets:* £18,792,778
Registered Office: 369 Wellingborough Road, Northampton, NN1 4EU
Activities: Other letting and operating of own or leased real estate
Shareholder: Rochmills (Holdings) Limited
Officers: Jatinder Singh Sehmi [1948] Managing Director

Hampton Academies Trust
Incorporated: 14 July 2014 *Employees:* 227
Net Worth: £36,159,132 *Total Assets:* £38,401,788
Registered Office: Hampton College, Eagle Way, Hampton Vale, Peterborough, Cambs, PE7 8BF
Activities: Primary education
Officers: Caroline Angela Behan, Secretary; Laura Rhiannon Cross [1965] Director/Civil Servant; Samantha Olivia East [1973] Director/Solicitor; Arturo Kim Garcia [1952] Director; John Grant [1947] Director/Retired; Alastair John Kingsley [1969] Managing Director; Matthew James Patchett [1979] Director/Office Supervisor; Deborah Pope [1980] Director/Business Development Manager; Helen Elizabeth Price [1966] Director/Headteacher; Tessa Jane Wilson [1969] Director/Office Manager

Hampton Steel Limited
Incorporated: 8 July 1991 *Employees:* 72
Net Worth: £4,612,091 *Total Assets:* £12,006,227
Registered Office: 34-42 Sanders Road, Finedon Road Industrial Estate, Wellingborough, Northants, NN8 4NL
Activities: Manufacture of wire products, chain and springs
Officers: Brian Edmund Jury, Secretary; Ian Michael Bates [1972] Production Director; Christopher John Walter Durham [1942] Director; Mark Andrew Johnson [1956] Director/Chartered Accountant; Peter Nigel Matten [1965] Sales Director; Patrick Westwood [1973] Technical Director

Hanborough Enterprises Limited
Incorporated: 8 April 2010 *Employees:* 21
Net Worth: £9,407,381 *Total Assets:* £15,951,372
Registered Office: Jamesons House, Compton Way, Witney, Oxon, OX28 3AB
Activities: Renting and leasing of cars and light motor vehicles
Major Shareholder: Stewart James Donald
Officers: Alan Carreras [1970] Director/Vehicle Leasing Broker; Stewart James Donald [1974] Director/Insurance Broker; Duncan FitzGenerald [1981] Director/Insurance Broker

Hancock Cash & Carry Limited
Incorporated: 4 January 1966 *Employees:* 282
Net Worth: £18,292,000 *Total Assets:* £54,948,000
Registered Office: 25 Jubilee Drive, Loughborough, Leics, LE11 5TX
Activities: Non-specialised wholesale of food, beverages and tobacco
Parent: Hancocks Holdings Limited
Officers: Wayne Beedle [1970] Director; Stephen Edward Foster [1976] Director

Hancocks Acquisition Limited
Incorporated: 24 October 2012 *Employees:* 5
Net Worth: £18,262,000 *Total Assets:* £94,322,000
Registered Office: 25 Jubilee Drive, Loughborough, Leics, LE11 5TX
Activities: Activities of head offices
Parent: Hancocks Midco Limited
Officers: Wayne Beedle [1970] Director; Stephen Edward Foster [1976] Director

Hancocks Group Holdings Limited
Incorporated: 12 December 2005 *Employees:* 5
Net Worth: £1,421,000 *Total Assets:* £21,572,000
Registered Office: 25 Jubilee Drive, Loughborough, Leics, LE11 5TX
Activities: Activities of head offices
Parent: Hancocks Acquisition Limited
Officers: Wayne Beedle [1970] Director; Stephen Edward Foster [1976] Director

Hancocks Holdings Limited
Incorporated: 4 January 1994 *Employees:* 3
Net Worth: £10,865,000 *Total Assets:* £30,703,000
Registered Office: 25 Jubilee Drive, Loughborough, Leics, LE11 5TX
Activities: Activities of head offices
Parent: Hancocks Group Holdings Limited
Officers: Wayne Beedle [1970] Director; Stephen Edward Foster [1976] Director

Hancocks Midco Limited
Incorporated: 24 October 2012 *Employees:* 5
Net Worth Deficit: £8,742,000 *Total Assets:* £15,432,000
Registered Office: 25 Jubilee Drive, Loughborough, Leics, LE11 5TX
Activities: Activities of head offices
Parent: Hancocks Topco Limited
Officers: Wayne Beedle [1970] Director; Stephen Edward Foster [1976] Director

Hankook Tyre U.K. Limited
Incorporated: 27 April 1993 *Employees:* 51
Net Worth: £11,925,000 *Total Assets:* £85,008,000
Registered Office: Fawsley Drive, Heartlands Business Park, Daventry, Northants, NN11 8UG
Activities: Manufacture of rubber tyres and tubes; retreading and rebuilding of rubber tyres
Officers: Patrica Julie Beere, Secretary; Brett Emerson [1966] Managing Director

Hanover Housing Developments Limited
Incorporated: 24 March 2009
Net Worth: £68,982,000 *Total Assets:* £70,036,000
Registered Office: Nelson House, Alington Road, Little Barford, St Neots, Cambs, PE19 6RE
Activities: Development of building projects
Parent: Hanover Housing Association
Officers: Michael Douglas Fuller, Secretary; Mary Keane, Secretary; Jane Rachel Ashcroft [1966] Director/Chief Executive; Mark Curran [1959] Director of Development; Mark Charles Greaves [1966] Managing Director of Care Services; Sarah Elizabeth Jones [1968] Director/Chief Financial Officer; Christopher David Munday [1959] Managing Director Housing Operations; Rona Nicholson [1957] Director of Governance and Compliance

Happy Days Farming Company Limited
Incorporated: 5 September 2012 *Employees:* 5
Net Worth: £3,786,905 *Total Assets:* £18,471,036
Registered Office: 4a Eastgate, Lincoln, LN2 1QA
Activities: Growing of cereals (except rice), leguminous crops and oil seeds
Officers: Barrie Michael Claude Kendal Truelove [1965] Director/Farmer; Jacqueline Patricia Truelove [1961] Director/Secretary; Paul Anthony John Truelove [1958] Director/Farmer

Haramead
Incorporated: 9 August 1972 *Employees:* 6
Net Worth: £15,840,588 *Total Assets:* £21,123,240
Registered Office: 1 Westmoreland Avenue, Thurmaston, Leicester, LE4 8PH
Activities: Other letting and operating of own or leased real estate
Parent: Charles Street Buildings (UK) Limited
Officers: Robert Henry Smith, Secretary; Winifred Mary Linnett [1950] Director; Mary Agnes Middleton [1981] Director; Hugh Patrick Murphy [1948] Director; Joseph John Murphy [1978] Director/Solicitor; Margaret Ann Murphy [1951] Director; Patrick Hugh Murphy [1977] Director

Hard 8 Limited
Incorporated: 13 February 2013 *Employees:* 5
Net Worth: £22,005 *Total Assets:* £20,344,496
Registered Office: The Shed, Charbridge Lane, Bicester, Oxon, OX26 4SS
Activities: Activities of other holding companies n.e.c.
Major Shareholder: Nigel John Harris
Officers: David John Burns [1962] Director; Nigel John Harris [1970] Director; Thomas Toland [1959] Director/Accountant Hospitality & Retail

Hardys Farm Limited
Incorporated: 11 August 2015 *Employees:* 11
Net Worth: £8,107,515 *Total Assets:* £9,975,530
Registered Office: Grays Farm, Anchor Lane, Ingoldmells, Skegness, Lincs, PE25 1LZ
Activities: Growing of cereals (except rice), leguminous crops and oil seeds
Parent: Hardys Farm Group Limited
Officers: Geoffrey David Hardy [1960] Director/Farmer; John George Hardy [1956] Director/Farmer; Stuart Dean Hardy [1981] Director/Farmer

Harewood Moor Estates Limited
Incorporated: 7 March 2016
Net Worth: £9,746,363 *Total Assets:* £10,906,099
Registered Office: Brookfield Hall, Manchester Road, Buxton, Derbys, SK17 6SU
Activities: Other letting and operating of own or leased real estate
Parent: The Harewood Moor Estates Limited Succession Trust
Officers: Stephen Matthew Richard Lamb [1975] Director

John Hargreaves,(Collyhurst and Stalybridge) Limited
Incorporated: 22 April 1924 *Employees:* 50
Net Worth: £952,436 *Total Assets:* £12,913,680
Registered Office: Tameside Paper Mills, Stalybridge, Cheshire, SK15 3AJ
Activities: Manufacture of paper and paperboard
Major Shareholder: John Michael Peter Hargreaves
Officers: Andrew Michael Robins, Secretary; Alistair Nicholas Hargreaves [1960] Director; John Michael Peter Hargreaves [1966] Director

Harington Investments Limited
Incorporated: 22 May 1995 *Employees:* 1
Net Worth: £11,056,912 *Total Assets:* £21,737,536
Registered Office: Nixon Mee Ltd, Unit 9 Whitwick Business Centre, Stenson Road, Coalville, Leics, LE67 4JP
Activities: Other letting and operating of own or leased real estate
Major Shareholder: Simon Neville Chamberlain
Officers: Simon Neville Chamberlain, Secretary; Desmond John Chamberlain [1971] Director; Simon Neville Chamberlain [1967] Director

Harley (Winchester) Limited
Incorporated: 17 December 2007
Net Worth: £4,740,630 *Total Assets:* £9,655,092
Registered Office: Gallagher House, Gallagher Way, Gallagher Business Park, Heathcote, Warwick, CV34 6AF
Activities: Buying and selling of own real estate
Parent: Gallagher Estates Limited
Officers: Richard Lindsey Brake [1959] Director/Property Developer; Martin Rowland Richmond [1953] Group Legal Director; Gregg Spencer Wilkinson [1973] Managing Director

Harley-Davidson Europe Limited
Incorporated: 10 March 1989 *Employees:* 105
Net Worth: £100,989,776 *Total Assets:* £216,276,672
Registered Office: Oxford Business Park, 6000 Garsington Road, Cowley, Oxford, OX4 2DQ
Activities: Sale, maintenance and repair of motorcycles and related parts and accessories
Parent: Harley-Davidson Holding Co., Inc.
Officers: Andrew Benka [1970] Director/General Manager [American]; Christian Thieme [1974] Finance Director [German]

Harlow Bros Holdings Limited
Incorporated: 29 March 2011 *Employees:* 455
Net Worth: £33,996,772 *Total Assets:* £50,181,472
Registered Office: c/o Harlow Bros Limited, Hathern Road, Long Whatton, Loughborough, Leics, LE12 5DE
Activities: Agents involved in the sale of timber and building materials
Shareholder: John Robinson Harlow
Officers: David Alan Poli, Secretary; John Robinson Harlow [1960] Director; Paul Vincent John Harlow [1966] Director; Robert Vernon Harlow [1959] Director; David Alan Poli [1959] Director/Accountant

Harlow Bros. Limited
Incorporated: 1 June 1967 *Employees:* 265
Net Worth: £12,560,838 *Total Assets:* £17,353,252
Registered Office: Hathern Road, Long Whatton, Loughborough, Leics, LE12 5DE
Activities: Sawmilling and planing of wood
Parent: Harlow Bros Holdings Ltd
Officers: David Alan Poli, Secretary; Lee William Christie [1976] Director; John Robinson Harlow [1960] Director; Paul Vincent John Harlow [1966] Director; Robert Vernon Harlow [1959] Director; Neil Sabey [1971] Director; James Sharkey [1974] Director

Harmor Limited
Incorporated: 12 April 2010 *Employees:* 197
Net Worth: £7,987,000 *Total Assets:* £13,954,000
Registered Office: Main Road, Belton, Grantham, Lincs, NG32 2LY
Activities: Manufacture of other parts and accessories for motor vehicles
Shareholders: Steven Harris; Michael James Idwal Hague-Morgan
Officers: Brian Barr [1963] Director; Michael James Idwal Hague-Morgan [1974] Commercial Director; Steven Harris [1960] Managing Director

Harpmanor Limited
Incorporated: 4 November 1985
Net Worth: £5,300,000 *Total Assets:* £67,700,000
Registered Office: Lake View, Lakeside, Cheadle, Cheshire, SK8 3GW
Activities: Credit granting by non-deposit taking finance houses and other specialist consumer credit grantors
Parent: Together Financial Services Limited
Officers: Sarah Elizabeth Batt, Secretary; Gary Derek Beckett [1969] Director; Wayne Bowser [1952] Director; Marc Richard Goldberg [1971] Director; Robert Michael McTighe [1953] Director; Henry Neville Moser [1949] Director

Harris Cars Limited
Incorporated: 23 September 1981 *Employees:* 359
Previous: Harris Cars PLC
Net Worth: £13,824,538 *Total Assets:* £77,278,864
Registered Office: 154 Ulverscroft Lane, Newtown Linford, Leicester, LE6 0AJ
Activities: Sale of used cars and light motor vehicles
Shareholders: Peter Michael Harris; Vanessa Jayne Harris
Officers: Vanessa Jayne Harris, Secretary; Peter Michael Harris [1953] Director; Vanessa Jayne Harris [1955] Director

T.C. Harrison 1960 Limited
Incorporated: 5 February 1960 *Employees:* 45
Net Worth: £2,510,000 *Total Assets:* £73,381,000
Registered Office: Milford House, Mill Street, Bakewell, Derbys, DE45 1HH
Activities: Renting and leasing of cars and light motor vehicles
Parent: T. C. Harrison Group Limited
Officers: Timothy Simon Simcox, Secretary; Anthony Coar [1958] Director/Chartered Accountant; Mark Raymond Hammond [1960] Director/Chartered Accountant; James Robert Harrison [1961] Director; Jonathan Edward Harrison [1963] Director; Thomas William Edward Harrison [1968] Director

Harrison Catering Services Limited
Incorporated: 23 September 1993 *Employees:* 2,155
Net Worth: £5,563,607 *Total Assets:* £16,113,552
Registered Office: Oxford House, Oxford Road, Thame, Oxon, OX9 2AH
Activities: Other food services
Parent: Harrison SD Holdings Limited
Officers: Richard David Harrison, Secretary; Claire Jeanette Aylward [1969] Director; Gareth Geoffrey Harrison [1973] Director; Geoffrey Charles Harrison [1946] Director/Caterer; Richard David Harrison [1968] Finance Director; Jonathan Chafer Shinner [1953] Director/Plant Contractor; Mark Stephen Stower [1966] Director

T. C. Harrison Group Limited
Incorporated: 13 November 1984 *Employees:* 577
Net Worth: £45,842,000 *Total Assets:* £177,772,000
Registered Office: Milford House, Mill Street, Bakewell, Derbys, DE45 1HH
Activities: Sale of new cars and light motor vehicles
Shareholder: Irelrop Investments Limited
Officers: Timothy Simon Simcox, Secretary; Anthony Coar [1958] Director/Chartered Accountant; James Robert Harrison [1961] Director; Jonathan Edward Harrison [1963] Director; Thomas William Edward Harrison [1968] Director

Harrison SD Holdings Limited
Incorporated: 13 April 2006 *Employees:* 2,159
Net Worth: £9,505,541 *Total Assets:* £20,447,096
Registered Office: Oxford House, Oxford Road, Thame, Oxon, OX9 2AH
Activities: Activities of other holding companies n.e.c.
Major Shareholder: Geoffrey Charles Harrison
Officers: Richard David Harrison, Finance Director; Claire Jeanette Aylward [1969] Director; Donald Andrew Davenport [1943] Director; Gareth Geoffrey Harrison [1973] Director; Geoffrey Charles Harrison [1946] Director; Richard David Harrison [1968] Finance Director; Jonathan Chafer Shinner [1953] Director/Plant Contractor

Harrow View LLP
Incorporated: 13 February 2017
Net Worth: £51,643,000 *Total Assets:* £90,027,000
Registered Office: Barratt House, Cartwright Way, Forest Business Park, Bardon Hill, Coalville, Leics, LE67 1UF

Harrowden Farms Group Limited
Incorporated: 24 November 2014 *Employees:* 101
Net Worth: £28,964,040 *Total Assets:* £56,452,880
Registered Office: Colpmans Farm, Islip, Kettering, Northants, NN14 3LT
Activities: Growing of cereals (except rice), leguminous crops and oil seeds
Shareholders: Frederick George Hilsdon; Chantall Sylvette Florence Ridd-Jones
Officers: Amy Hilsdon [1981] Director; Frederick George Hilsdon [1978] Farmer/Director; John Frederick Hilsdon [1944] Director/Farmer; Tryntje Hilsdon [1946] Director/Farmer [Dutch]; Chantall Sylvette Florence Ridd-Jones [1974] Director/Accountant; Stuart Benjamin Ridd-Jones [1972] Director

Harrowden Farms Limited
Incorporated: 5 March 1964 *Employees:* 4
Net Worth: £25,440,932 *Total Assets:* £34,717,120
Registered Office: Manor Farm, 3 Orlingbury Road, Great Harrowden, Wellingborough, Northants, NN9 5AF
Activities: Growing of cereals (except rice), leguminous crops and oil seeds
Parent: Harrowden Farms Group Limited
Officers: Amy Hilsdon, Secretary; Amy Hilsdon [1981] Director; Frederick George Hilsdon [1978] Managing Director; John Frederick Hilsdon [1944] Director/Farmer; Tryntje Hilsdon [1946] Director/Farmer [Dutch]; Chantall Sylvette Florence Ridd-Jones [1974] Director/Chartered Accountant; Stuart Benjamin Ridd-Jones [1972] Finance Director

Harrowden Turf Limited
Incorporated: 5 November 2014 *Employees:* 52
Net Worth Deficit: £355,704 *Total Assets:* £10,018,512
Registered Office: Colpmans Farm, Islip, Kettering, Northants, NN14 3LT
Activities: Growing of other perennial crops
Parent: Harrowden Farms Limited
Officers: Chantall Sylvette Florence Ridd-Jones [1974] Director/Accountant; Stuart Benjamin Ridd-Jones [1972] Director

Harshl Limited
Incorporated: 24 June 2016
Net Worth: £1,241,352 *Total Assets:* £14,039,460
Registered Office: Marland House, 13 Huddersfield Road, Barnsley, S Yorks, S70 2LW
Activities: Other service activities n.e.c.
Major Shareholder: Andrew John Siddall
Officers: Andrew John Siddall [1959] Director

Harting UK Limited
Incorporated: 16 April 1980 *Employees:* 106
Net Worth: £7,530,000 *Total Assets:* £13,189,000
Registered Office: Jubilee House, 32 Duncan Close, Moulton Park, Northampton, NN3 6WL
Activities: Activities of head offices
Major Shareholder: Dietmar Harting
Officers: Peter Jack Hannon, Secretary; Peter Jack Hannon [1959] Managing Director; Maresa Wally Marie Harting-Hertz [1977] Director/Master of Science, Board Finance & Global Purchasing [German]

Fred Hartley (Estates) Limited
Incorporated: 15 July 1947 *Employees:* 15
Net Worth: £6,511,300 *Total Assets:* £12,460,526
Registered Office: The Offices, Town Street, Upwell, Wisbech, Cambs, PE14 9DQ
Activities: Growing of cereals (except rice), leguminous crops and oil seeds
Major Shareholder: Christopher Fred Hartley
Officers: Christopher Fred Hartley, Secretary; Christopher Fred Hartley [1950] Director/Farmer

Tom Hartley Cars Limited
Incorporated: 29 October 2009 *Employees:* 10
Net Worth: £8,587,863 *Total Assets:* £11,339,352
Registered Office: 159 Moira Road, Overseal, Swadlincote, Derbys, DE12 6JD
Activities: Sale of new cars and light motor vehicles
Major Shareholder: Thomas Hartley
Officers: Carl William Hartley [1987] Director/Car Dealer; Thomas Hartley [1961] Director/Car Dealer

Hartwell Automotive Group Limited
Incorporated: 2 September 1919
Net Worth: £59,319,000 *Total Assets:* £113,020,000
Registered Office: Wootton Business Park, Besselsleigh Road, Wootton, Oxon, OX13 6FD
Activities: Sale of new cars and light motor vehicles
Parent: Hartwell PLC
Officers: Georgina Suzanne Forbes, Secretary; Kevin Paul Godfrey [1961] Managing Director; Andrew Mark Lemon [1966] Director/Chartered Accountant; Atiq Rehman [1978] Director/Chartered Accountant; Nicholas John Tucker [1959] Director

Hartwell Finance Limited
Incorporated: 19 November 1900 *Employees:* 9
Net Worth: £44,502,000 *Total Assets:* £45,120,000
Registered Office: Wootton Business Park, Besselsleigh Road, Wootton, Oxon, OX13 6FD
Activities: Credit granting by non-deposit taking finance houses and other specialist consumer credit grantors
Parent: Hartwell PLC
Officers: Georgina Suzanne Forbes, Secretary; Andrew Mark Lemon [1966] Director/Chartered Accountant; Atiq Rehman [1978] Director/Certified Chartered Accountant; Nicholas John Tucker [1959] Director

Hartwell Holdings Limited
Incorporated: 21 June 1990
Net Worth: £28,621,000 *Total Assets:* £28,621,000
Registered Office: Wootton Business Park, Besselsleigh Road, Wootton, Oxon, OX13 6FD
Activities: Activities of head offices
Parent: Oakhill Group Limited
Officers: Georgina Suzanne Forbes, Secretary; Manyadath Balachandran [1952] Director [Indian]; Atiq Rehman [1978] Director/Chartered Accountant

Hartwell PLC
Incorporated: 20 May 1919 *Employees:* 550
Net Worth: £154,840,992 *Total Assets:* £267,796,992
Registered Office: Wootton Business Park, Besselsleigh Road, Wootton, Oxon, OX13 6FD
Activities: Activities of head offices
Parent: Hartwell Holdings Limited
Officers: Georgina Suzanne Forbes, Secretary; Mayadath Balachandran [1952] Director [Indian]; Craig Robert Gibbin [1971] Director; Kevin Paul Godfrey [1961] Director; Andrew Mark Lemon [1966] Director/Accountant; Robert Mark Pilkington [1972] Director; Atiq Rehman [1978] Director/Certified Chartered Accountant

Harving Limited
Incorporated: 17 April 1990 *Employees:* 2
Net Worth: £10,463,717 *Total Assets:* £19,165,204
Registered Office: 3 Castlegate, Grantham, Lincs, NG31 6SF
Activities: Other letting and operating of own or leased real estate
Shareholders: Richard Hugh Parry; James Hugo Parry; Caroline Serena Parry
Officers: James Hugo Parry [1981] Director/Surveyor; Richard Hugh Parry [1949] Director/Farmer

Harworth Estates (Agricultural Land) Limited
Incorporated: 13 July 1993
Net Worth: £77,091,000 *Total Assets:* £82,423,000
Registered Office: Advantage House, Poplar Way, Catcliffe, Rotherham, S Yorks, S60 5TR
Activities: Development of building projects
Parent: Harworth Estates Ltd
Officers: Andrew Michael David Kirkman [1972] Director/Chartered Accountant; Richard Owen Michaelson [1966] Director

Harworth Estates (Waverley Prince) Ltd.
Incorporated: 10 February 1995
Net Worth: £16,595,000 *Total Assets:* £83,992,000
Registered Office: Advantage House, Poplar Way, Catcliffe, Rotherham, S Yorks, S60 5TR
Activities: Development of building projects
Parent: Harworth Estates Limited
Officers: Andrew Michael David Kirkman [1972] Director/Chartered Accountant; Richard Owen Michaelson [1966] Director

Harworth Estates Group Limited
Incorporated: 13 July 1993
Previous: Harworth Mining Services Limited
Net Worth: £51,715,000 *Total Assets:* £51,828,000
Registered Office: Advantage House, Poplar Way, Catcliffe, Rotherham, S Yorks, S60 5TR
Activities: Open cast coal working
Parent: Harworth Estates Property Group Ltd
Officers: Andrew Michael David Kirkman [1972] Director/Chartered Accountant; Richard Owen Michaelson [1966] Director

Harworth Estates Investments Limited
Incorporated: 16 February 2011
Net Worth: £110,113,000 *Total Assets:* £272,420,992
Registered Office: Advantage House, Poplar Way, Catcliffe, Rotherham, S Yorks, S60 5TR
Activities: Development of building projects
Parent: Harworth Estates Ltd
Officers: Andrew Michael David Kirkman [1972] Director/Chartered Accountant; Richard Owen Michaelson [1966] Director

Harworth Estates Limited
Incorporated: 5 October 1987 *Employees:* 49
Net Worth: £20,400,000 *Total Assets:* £56,918,000
Registered Office: Advantage House, Poplar Way, Catcliffe, Rotherham, S Yorks, S60 5TR
Activities: Non-trading company
Parent: Harworth Services Limited
Officers: Andrew Michael David Kirkman [1972] Director/Chartered Accountant; Richard Owen Michaelson [1966] Director

Harworth Estates Property Group Limited
Incorporated: 28 September 2012
Net Worth: £224,427,008 *Total Assets:* £251,047,008
Registered Office: Advantage House, Poplar Way, Catcliffe, Rotherham, S Yorks, S60 5TR
Activities: Buying and selling of own real estate
Parent: Harworth Group PLC
Officers: Andrew Michael David Kirkman [1972] Director/Chartered Accountant; Richard Owen Michaelson [1966] Director/Chartered Surveyor

Harworth Group PLC
Incorporated: 27 September 1991 *Employees:* 53
Previous: Coalfield Resources PLC
Net Worth: £409,311,008 *Total Assets:* £496,958,016
Registered Office: Advantage House, Poplar Way, Catcliffe, Rotherham, S Yorks, S60 5TR
Activities: Activities of head offices
Officers: Christopher Michael Birch, Secretary; Paul Martyn Bowes [1964] Director; Lisa Jane Clement [1967] Director; Andrew Rolland Cunningham [1956] Director/Chartered Accountant; Anthony Donnelly [1964] Director; Andrew Michael David Kirkman [1972] Director/Chartered Accountant; Alastair David Lyons [1953] Director/Chairman; Richard Owen Michaelson [1966] Director; Steven Keith Underwood [1974] Director

Harworth Services Limited
Incorporated: 3 January 1989
Net Worth: £50,724,000 *Total Assets:* £51,908,000
Registered Office: Advantage House, Poplar Way, Catcliffe, Rotherham, S Yorks, S60 5TR
Activities: Open cast coal working
Parent: Harworth Estates Group Limited
Officers: Andrew Michael David Kirkman [1972] Director/Chartered Accountant; Richard Owen Michaelson [1966] Director

HaskoningDHV UK Holdings Limited
Incorporated: 23 June 1994
Net Worth: £20,746,128 *Total Assets:* £26,844,944
Registered Office: Rightwell House, Bretton Centre, Peterborough, PE3 8DW
Activities: Activities of head offices
Officers: Jonathan Simon Bull [1974] Director/Chartered Structural Engineer; Craig John Huntbatch [1961] Director/Chartered Civil and Structural Engineer; Mazhar Hussain [1964] Director/Accountant; Johan Theodorus Van Manen [1953] Director/Financial Controller [Dutch]

HaskoningDHV UK Limited
Incorporated: 1 November 1977 *Employees:* 490
Net Worth: £12,385,852 *Total Assets:* £46,037,972
Registered Office: Rightwell House, Bretton Centre, Peterborough, PE3 8DW
Activities: Activities of head offices
Parent: HaskoningDHV UK Holdings Limited
Officers: Jonathan Simon Bull [1974] Director/Chartered Structural Engineer; Craig John Huntbatch [1961] Director; Mazhar Hussain [1964] Director/Accountant; Johan Theodorus Van Manen [1953] Director/Financial Controller [Dutch]

Hatchback Ltd
Incorporated: 17 September 1996 *Employees:* 4
Net Worth: £13,175,689 *Total Assets:* £24,767,354
Registered Office: 31 High View Close, Leicester, LE4 9LJ
Activities: Development of building projects
Major Shareholder: Hardeep Singh Malle
Officers: Jagdish Kaur Malle, Secretary; Hardeep Singh Malle [1982] Managing Director; Shalbinder Singh Malle [1951] Director

Roy Hatfield (Holdings) Limited
Incorporated: 1 November 2016 *Employees:* 35
Net Worth: £8,327,026 *Total Assets:* £14,726,596
Registered Office: Roy Hatfield Ltd, Fullerton Road, Rotherham, S Yorks, S60 1DH
Activities: Activities of other holding companies n.e.c.
Shareholders: Roy Hatfield; Margaret Hatfield
Officers: Grant Edward Hatfield [1983] Director; Margaret Hatfield [1956] Director; Mark Roy Hatfield [1981] Director; Roy Hatfield [1936] Director/Chairman

Hatton Academies Trust
Incorporated: 14 February 2012 *Employees:* 309
Net Worth: £19,178,000 *Total Assets:* £22,826,000
Registered Office: Sir Christopher Hatton Academy, The Pyghtle, Wellingborough, Northants, NN8 4RP
Activities: Primary education
Officers: Colin George Hinds, Secretary; Susan Victoria Bishop [1954] Director/Headteacher; Simon Paul Dawson [1974] Director/Manager; Susan FitzGenerald [1971] Director/Managing Partner for GP Surgery; Colin George Hinds [1971] Director; Rashesh Babu Joshi [1970] Director/Chartered Accountant; Graham Michael Lawman [1953] Director/Councillor; David John Morris [1967] Director; William Arnold Thallon [1962] Director/Education Consultant

Haughton Textiles Limited
Incorporated: 30 August 2014 *Employees:* 234
Net Worth: £5,400,000 *Total Assets:* £15,100,000
Registered Office: 1st Floor, 5 Morston Claycliffe Office Park, Whaley Road, Barnsley, S Yorks, S75 1HQ
Activities: Other business support service activities n.e.c.
Shareholder: James Peter Smith
Officers: Joanne Grace [1971] Finance Director; Stewart Robert McGuffie [1968] Director; David John Smith [1972] Director/Investment Professional; James Peter Smith [1952] Director

Haven Housing Limited
Incorporated: 24 May 1962 *Employees:* 5
Net Worth: £11,647,800 *Total Assets:* £11,873,607
Registered Office: Bridgeway House, Bridgeway, Stratford upon Avon, Warwicks, CV37 6YY
Activities: Other letting and operating of own or leased real estate
Officers: Benjamin Nicholson, Secretary; Lucy Rebecca Bunger [1979] Director/Civil Servant; Paul Robert Chapman [1962] Director/Chartered Accountant; Benjamin Nicholson [1977] Director/Chartered Surveyor; Harry Martell Parker [1983] Director/Sales Manager; Ross Scott Parker [1985] Director/Building Foreman

Hawkes Limited
Incorporated: 18 March 1959 *Employees:* 25
Net Worth: £5,821,461 *Total Assets:* £21,351,756
Registered Office: Sausthorpe Hall, Sausthorpe, Spilsby, Lincs, PE23 4JN
Activities: Raising of swine and pigs
Officers: Roger William Hawkes, Secretary; Roger William Hawkes [1942] Director/Farmer; Simon Roger Hawkes [1967] Director/Farmer

The Hayfield School
Incorporated: 1 March 2011 *Employees:* 130
Net Worth: £15,702,000 *Total Assets:* £16,761,000
Registered Office: The Hayfield School, Hurst Lane, Auckley, Doncaster, S Yorks, DN9 3HG
Activities: General secondary education
Officers: Heather Jane Rose, Secretary; Uzma Ahmed [1965] Director/Consultant; Annamarie Alton [1976] Director/Teaching Assistant; Steven Leslie Cross [1964] Director/Market Strategist; Debbie Dickerson [1969] Director/Local Government Officer; Stephen Featherstone [1957] Director/Manager; Nikki Ford [1962] Director/Charity Worker; Lisa Fox [1968] Director/Headteacher; Lesley Esther Gilfedder [1962] Director/Administrator; Graham Hartshorn [1948] Director; Mark Bradley Huby [1978] Director/Financial Adviser; Helen Jackson [1976] Director/Assistant Principal; David Langford [1948] Director/Retired; Lucinda Claire Oldfield [1978] Director/Teacher; Georgina Diane Parkes [1957] Director/Attendance Officer; Angela Scott [1948] Director/Retired; Scott Wilson [1972] Director/Teacher

Haywood and Padgett Limited
Incorporated: 13 November 1987 *Employees:* 150
Net Worth: £13,836,127 *Total Assets:* £16,675,472
Registered Office: The Bakery, Shawfield Road, Carlton Industrial Estate, Barnsley, S Yorks, S71 3HS
Activities: Manufacture of bread; manufacture of fresh pastry goods and cakes
Major Shareholder: Wayne Padgett
Officers: Wayne Padgett, Secretary/Managing Director; Michelle Padgett [1966] Director; Rebecca Maria Padgett [1990] Director; Wayne Padgett [1961] Director/Secretary

The Hazeley Academy
Incorporated: 20 April 2011 *Employees:* 178
Net Worth: £29,981,228 *Total Assets:* £33,190,288
Registered Office: The Hazeley Academy, Emperor Drive, Milton Keynes, Bucks, MK8 0PT
Activities: General secondary education
Officers: Jasmine Marie Ampaw-Farr [1970] Director; Matthew James Bonnett [1989] Director/Teacher; Mohammed Shaffiq Bostan [1968] Director/Computer Engineer; Ian Peter Clarkson [1954] Director; Malcolm Hugh Dobell [1951] Director; Rebecca Jayne Howell [1974] Director/Education Consultant; Taskeen Naqvi [1977] Director/Teacher; Anthony Richard Nelson [1971] Director/Headmaster; Jane Chinedu Osayimwen [1973] Director/Project Manager; Sarah Thompson [1976] Director/Apprenticeship Manager; Dr Margaret Elizabeth Wyke [1953] Director/Retired

Hazelton Homes (Midlands) Limited
Incorporated: 25 February 2010 *Employees:* 28
Net Worth: £2,558,715 *Total Assets:* £14,114,798
Registered Office: Estate Office, Rushton Hall, Rushton, Northants, NN14 1RR
Activities: Construction of domestic buildings
Major Shareholder: Thomas Robert Hazelton
Officers: Thomas Robert Hazelton [1966] Director; Valerie Danielle Hazelton [1969] Director

Hazlewood (Blackditch) Limited
Incorporated: 13 December 2000
Net Worth: £19,281,000 *Total Assets:* £19,281,000
Registered Office: Greencore Group UK Centre, Midland Way, Barlborough Links Business Park, Barlborough, Chesterfield, Derbys, S43 4XA
Activities: Dormant company
Parent: Hazlewood Foods Limited
Officers: Michael Evans, Secretary; Catherine Bradshaw [1975] Finance Director; Michael Evans [1967] Director; Eoin Philip Tonge [1972] Director [Irish]

Hazlewood Foods Limited
Incorporated: 17 February 1942
Net Worth: £88,919,000 *Total Assets:* £466,135,008
Registered Office: Greencore Group UK Centre, Midland Way, Barlborough Links Business Park, Barlborough, Chesterfield, Derbys, S43 4XA
Activities: Activities of extraterritorial organisations and bodies
Parent: Greencore Beechwood Limited
Officers: Michael Evans, Secretary; Catherine Bradshaw [1975] Finance Director; Michael Evans [1967] Director; Eoin Philip Tonge [1972] Director [Irish]

HB Healthcare Limited
Incorporated: 5 December 2009 *Employees:* 114
Net Worth: £5,969,000 *Total Assets:* £10,740,000
Registered Office: Partis House, Davy Avenue, Milton Keynes, Bucks, MK5 8HJ
Activities: Activities of head offices
Officers: Graham John Anthony Dolan, Secretary; James Caan [1961] Director; Deepak Jalan [1974] Director; Jason Alexander Robert Norman Stewart [1968] Director; Luke Alexander Williams [1974] Director

HBB Bridging Loans Limited
Incorporated: 30 May 2013
Net Worth: £520,744 *Total Assets:* £20,282,732
Registered Office: 7 Faraday Court, Centrum One Hundred, Burton on Trent, Staffs, DE14 2WX
Activities: Credit granting by non-deposit taking finance houses and other specialist consumer credit grantors
Shareholders: HBB Homes Limited; Middleton Enterprises Limited
Officers: Simon Charles Blunt [1966] Director; Michael David Elliot [1982] Director/Chartered Accountant; Christopher John Hodgkinson [1971] Director; M David Robert Preece [1960] Director; Sonia Lorraine Shortland [1981] Director

HBB Homes Limited
Incorporated: 8 December 2010
Net Worth: £7,606,949 *Total Assets:* £9,747,688
Registered Office: 7 Faraday Court, Centrum One Hundred, Burton on Trent, Staffs, DE14 2WX
Activities: Buying and selling of own real estate
Major Shareholder: Simon Charles Blunt
Officers: Christabel Blunt, Secretary; Christabel Blunt [1979] Director; Simon Charles Blunt [1966] Director

HBB Relocation Services Limited
Incorporated: 23 November 2011 *Employees:* 13
Net Worth: £1,024,942 *Total Assets:* £26,372,456
Registered Office: 2 The Cornerstone, Market Place, Kegworth, Derby, DE74 2EE
Activities: Buying and selling of own real estate
Shareholders: HBB Homes Limited; Middleton Enterprises Limited
Officers: Simon Charles Blunt [1966] Director; Michael David Elliot [1982] Director/Chartered Accountant; Christopher John Hodgkinson [1971] Director

HBM United Kingdom Limited
Incorporated: 7 October 1981 *Employees:* 77
Net Worth: £15,154,000 *Total Assets:* £21,883,000
Registered Office: Technology Centre, Advanced Manufacturing Park, Brunel Way, Catcliffe, Rotherham, S Yorks, S60 5WG
Activities: Other software publishing
Parent: Spectris Group Holdings Limited
Officers: Stephen Fleet, Secretary; Paul Beardsworth [1964] Director/Sales Engineer; Andreas Huellhorst [1957] Director [German]

HBPO UK Limited
Incorporated: 8 September 2005 *Employees:* 64
Net Worth: £2,540,093 *Total Assets:* £15,635,246
Registered Office: HBPO UK Limited, Wildmere Road, Banbury, Oxon, OX16 3EY
Activities: Manufacture of other parts and accessories for motor vehicles
Officers: John William Downes, Secretary; Robert William Fairclough [1963] Managing Director; Martin Erdmann Schuler [1967] Director [German]

HBVB
Incorporated: 20 March 2013 *Employees:* 472
Net Worth Deficit: £147,328,992 *Total Assets:* £810,892,032
Registered Office: Media House, Peterborough Business Park, Lynch Wood, Peterborough, Cambs, PE2 6EA
Activities: Activities of other holding companies n.e.c.
Major Shareholder: Yvonne Saskia Bauer
Officers: Paul Anthony Keenan [1963] Director/Publisher; Sarah Jane Vickery [1963] Finance Director

HC 1228 Limited
Incorporated: 22 May 2014 *Employees:* 110
Net Worth Deficit: £1,752,617 *Total Assets:* £14,125,977
Registered Office: 5 The Courtyard, Timothys Bridge Road, Stratford Enterprise Park, Stratford upon Avon, Warwicks, CV37 9NP
Activities: Other business support service activities n.e.c.
Officers: Thomas Engelen [1958] Director [Dutch]; Robert Anthony Hankinson [1972] Director/Accountant; Leszek Richard Litwinowicz [1958] Director; Paulus Rohof [1957] Director [Dutch]; Paul Keith Styles [1950] Director

HC1221 Limited
Incorporated: 17 December 2013
Net Worth Deficit: £2,165 *Total Assets:* £13,441,330
Registered Office: 5 The Courtyard, Timothys Bridge Road, Stratford Enterprise Park, Stratford upon Avon, Warwicks, CV37 9NP
Activities: Other business support service activities n.e.c.
Parent: HC 1228 Limited
Officers: Thomas Engelen [1958] Director [Dutch]; Robert Anthony Hankinson [1972] Director/Accountant; Leszek Richard Litwinowicz [1958] Director; Paulus Rohof [1957] Director [Dutch]; Paul Keith Styles [1950] Director

HCH Property Limited
Incorporated: 7 February 2014
Net Worth: £13,250,641 *Total Assets:* £19,840,476
Registered Office: 8 The Shippon, Kingham, Chipping Norton, Oxon, OX7 6UJ
Activities: Other letting and operating of own or leased real estate
Officers: Steven Earl Joynes, Secretary; Steven John Clements [1959] Director; Andre Max Elshout [1958] Director; Steven Earl Joynes [1969] Director; Edward Henry Towry Law [1971] Director; Adrian John Pearson [1985] Director/Group MD; Craig Winfield [1984] Finance Director

HD Holdings II Limited
Incorporated: 25 May 2010 *Employees:* 335
Net Worth Deficit: £7,924,091 *Total Assets:* £23,338,382
Registered Office: Innovation Way, Woodhouse Mill, Sheffield, S13 9AD
Activities: Activities of other holding companies n.e.c.
Officers: Travis Daniel Kelly [1976] Director/CFO & Senior Operating Executive [American]; Ken Juan Carlos Kohrs [1975] Director/Banking/Finance; Francisco Roman Lamas Mendez-Villamil [1966] Director/Consultant [Spanish]; Paul Lusardi [1976] Director/Banker [American]; Joseph Anthony Naccarato [1971] Director/Banking/Finance

Headcrown Group PLC
Incorporated: 19 October 1979 *Employees:* 315
Net Worth: £20,047,000 *Total Assets:* £55,900,000
Registered Office: Wards Exchange, 199 Ecclesall Road, Sheffield, S11 8HW
Activities: Other service activities n.e.c.
Shareholders: Carl Adrian Brian; Sonia Adrienne Brian
Officers: Sonia Adrienne Brian, Secretary; Carl Adrian Brian [1965] Director/Chartered Accountant; Sonia Adrienne Brian [1962] Director; Simon Andrew Camamile [1955] Director/Chartered Surveyor

Headington School Oxford Limited
Incorporated: 23 July 1915 *Employees:* 395
Net Worth: £22,937,188 *Total Assets:* £29,645,774
Registered Office: The Bursary, Headington School, Headington Road, Oxford, OX3 0BL
Activities: Pre-primary education
Shareholders: Carol Oster Warriner; Father Darren William McFarland; Sallie Christina Salvidant; Sue Burge; Professor Constance Catherine Drummond; Steven Charles Andrew Harris; Lady Nancy Caroline Kenny; Penelope Anne Lenon; Bryony Crawford Moore; Sandra Claire Phipkin; Catherine Mary Ringham; Margaret Florence Rudland; Reginald Stephen Shipperley
Officers: Richard Charles Couzens, Secretary; Dr Susan Burge [1951] Director/Retired Consultant Dermatologist; Professor Constance Catherine Drummond [1955] Director/University Fellow; Steven Charles Andrew Harris [1966] Director; Lady Nancy Caroline Kenny [1943] Director/University Administrator; Penelope Anne Lenon [1956] Director/Retired; Father Darren William McFarland [1971] Director/Vicar [Irish]; Bryony Crawford Moore [1953] Director/Management Consultant; Carol Oster Warriner [1963] Director/Retired; Sandra Claire Phipkin [1960] Finance Director; Dr Catherine Mary Ringham [1965] Director/Lecturer; Margaret Florence Rudland [1945] Director/Retired; Sallie Christina Salvidant [1950] Director/Retired; Reginald Stephen Shipperley [1958] Director

Healing Multi Academy Trust
Incorporated: 13 August 2010 *Employees:* 298
Net Worth: £14,140,000 *Total Assets:* £17,398,000
Registered Office: Low Road, Healing, Grimsby, N E Lincs, DN41 7QD
Activities: Primary education
Officers: Hayley Carlberg, Secretary; Karina Marianne Ellis [1973] Director; Jonathan Thornes Goolden [1965] Director/Solicitor; Peter Kipling [1949] Director; Leonora Yvonne Rew Kitchin [1971] Director; Mark Robert Knapton [1973] Director; Debra Peers [1964] Director/Civil Servant; Graham John McRae Walker [1963] Director

Healix Property LLP
Incorporated: 2 July 2009
Net Worth: £11,829,397 *Total Assets:* £11,869,227
Registered Office: 30 Upper High Street, Thame, Oxon, OX9 3EZ
Officers: Dr Paul Geoffrey Hassan Beven [1959] Member; Peter Adrian Richard Mason [1958] Member; Belinda Louise Butcher [1967] LLP Member; Richard Mason [1990] LLP Member; William Mason [1993] LLP Member; Dr Myles Finnegan Morgan [1970] LLP Member; John David Pugh [1952] LLP Member; Michael David Webb [1960] LLP Member

Health & Diet Group Limited
Incorporated: 29 December 1969
Net Worth: £63,259,000 *Total Assets:* £232,503,008
Registered Office: Samuel Ryder House, Barling Way, Eliot Park, Nuneaton, Warwicks, CV10 7RH
Activities: Activities of head offices
Parent: Holland & Barrett Group Limited
Officers: Lisa Mary Garley-Evans, Secretary; Lisa Mary Garley-Evans [1968] Director/Solicitor

Healthcare at Home Ltd
Incorporated: 28 October 1992 *Employees:* 1,550
Net Worth: £124,418,000 *Total Assets:* £553,518,976
Registered Office: 107 Station Street, Burton on Trent, Staffs, DE14 1SZ
Activities: Medical nursing home activities
Parent: EGX Group Limited
Officers: John Bradshaw, Secretary; Jonathan Elliott Asbridge [1959] Clinical Director; John Richard Bradshaw [1955] Director/Solicitor; Darryn Stanley Gibson [1965] Director [New Zealander]; John Spencer Sheridan [1973] Director; Gareth Simon Williams [1980] Group Commercial Director

Healthcare Software Solutions Ltd
Incorporated: 24 October 2013 *Employees:* 89
Net Worth Deficit: £9,251,982 *Total Assets:* £34,819,684
Registered Office: Office Suite 0.1, l2 Mansfield, Hamilton Way, Oakham Business Park, Mansfield, Notts, NG18 5FB
Activities: Other information technology service activities
Officers: Claire Christina White, Secretary; Graham Paul Ridgway [1960] Director; Claire Christina White [1967] Director; Christopher Paul Yeowart [1976] Director

Heart of England School
Incorporated: 1 June 2011 *Employees:* 142
Net Worth: £14,915,000 *Total Assets:* £17,667,000
Registered Office: Heart of England School, Gipsy Lane, Balsall Common, Coventry, Warwicks, CV7 7FW
Activities: General secondary education
Officers: Dr Neil James Cooke [1971] Director/Lecturer; Malcolm Peter Halliday [1954] Director/Retired; Jonathan Haston [1988] Director/Teacher; Jacqueline Hughes-Williams [1965] Director/Teacher; Anne Lycett [1959] Director/Company Secretary; Lesley Markham [1945] Director/Retired; Graham Philip Parry [1963] Director; Tim Perry-Ogden [1967] Director/Programme Manager; Charlotte Shadbolt [1970] Director; Linda Williams [1964] Director/Exams Officer; Anthony Sandever Richard Worth [1972] Director/Audit Manager

Heathcotes Group Limited
Incorporated: 15 August 2017
Net Worth: £34,448,160 *Total Assets:* £107,904,800
Registered Office: 91-97 Saltergate, Chesterfield, Derbys, S40 1LA
Activities: Non-trading company
Shareholders: Simon John Maxwell Cobb; John Hill
Officers: Simon John Maxwell Cobb [1958] Director; David Astill Harrison [1961] Director; John Hill [1964] Director; Angela Jayne Sydenham [1974] Director

Heating Finance Limited
Incorporated: 14 January 2004
Net Worth: £9,638,000 *Total Assets:* £1,727,757,056
Registered Office: Brooks House, Coventry Road, Warwick, CV34 4LL
Activities: Activities of head offices
Officers: Karen Dawn Roberts, Secretary; Simon Charles Oliver [1968] Director; Carolina Wielinga [1970] Director [Dutch]

Heavyweight Air Express Limited
Incorporated: 28 July 1997 *Employees:* 68
Net Worth: £10,572,391 *Total Assets:* £14,599,322
Registered Office: 3 Cygnus Court, Beverley Road, East Midlands Airport, Derby, DE74 2SA
Activities: Freight air transport
Parent: HAE Group Ltd
Officers: Colin Richard White, Secretary; Neville Karai [1966] Director; Richard Thackeray [1968] Director/Business Development Manager; Colin Richard White [1963] Director/Chartered Accountant

John Hebb (Motor Engineers) Limited
Incorporated: 11 October 1972 *Employees:* 2
Net Worth: £11,573,510 *Total Assets:* £11,582,605
Registered Office: 40 Cherry Lane, Wootton, Ulceby, N Lincs, DN39 6RL
Activities: Sale of other motor vehicles
Major Shareholder: David John Hebb
Officers: Catherine Ann Hebb, Secretary; Catherine Ann Hebb [1957] Director/Secretary; Christopher John Hebb [1984] Director; David John Hebb [1954] Director/Motor Engineer; Matthew Richard Hebb [1991] Director

Helen & Douglas House
Incorporated: 6 December 2000 *Employees:* 229
Net Worth: £11,073,000 *Total Assets:* £12,114,000
Registered Office: 14a Magdalen Road, Oxford, OX4 1RW
Activities: Other human health activities
Officers: Andrew Michael Cooper, Secretary; Ian Warwick Blair [1953] Director/Parliamentarian; Katherine Boyce [1961] Director; Sir Stephen John Bubb [1952] Director/Charity Chief Executive; Catherine Bridget Chumbley [1978] Director/Head of Communications; Elizabeth Ann Drew [1949] Director; David Hugh Gye [1947] Director/Retired Investment Banker; Jean Raphael Heritage [1934] Director; Colin Andrew Love [1950] Director; Dr Andrew Robert Wilkinson [1943] Director/Paediatrician; Nicholas Wilkinson [1972] Director

Helford Land Limited
Incorporated: 25 January 2017
Net Worth: £8,598,012 *Total Assets:* £17,999,104
Registered Office: 17 Dormer Place, Leamington Spa, Warwicks, CV32 5AA
Activities: Non-trading company
Officers: Jodi Dawn Ferris [1965] Director; Steven Antony Ferris [1964] Director

Hella Limited
Incorporated: 26 January 1959 *Employees:* 70
Net Worth: £6,600,000 *Total Assets:* £15,289,000
Registered Office: Unit 6 EPS Industrial Estate, Appletree Road, Chipping Warden, Banbury, Oxon, OX17 1LL
Activities: Wholesale trade of motor vehicle parts and accessories
Officers: Ismael Leon Carmena [1972] IAM Regional Director Western Europe [Spanish]; Neil Grant [1981] Finance Director; Spencer Grinham [1968] SOE Sales Director; Matthew Say [1978] Managing Director

Hella UK Holdings Limited
Incorporated: 19 April 1995
Net Worth: £14,322,049 *Total Assets:* £14,334,734
Registered Office: Unit 6 EPS Industrial Estate, Appletree Road, Chipping Warden, Banbury, Oxon, OX17 1LL
Activities: Activities of head offices
Officers: Neil Grant [1981] Finance Director; Matthew Say [1978] Managing Director; Karsten Voss [1971] Director/Head of Corporate Accounting [German]

Hemswell Estates Limited
Incorporated: 3 November 2003 *Employees:* 6
Net Worth: £3,143,897 *Total Assets:* £12,542,998
Registered Office: Norton Place, Bishop Norton, Market Rasen, Lincs, LN8 2AX
Activities: Other letting and operating of own or leased real estate
Shareholders: Adam Matthew Duguid; Ronald Matthew Duguid
Officers: Adam Matthew Duguid, Secretary/Solicitor; Adam Matthew Duguid [1972] Director/Solicitor; Ronald Matthew Duguid [1941] Director/Farmer

Hendrickson United Kingdom Ltd
Incorporated: 15 April 1985 *Employees:* 45
Previous: Hendrickson Europe Limited
Net Worth: £12,568,251 *Total Assets:* £20,241,540
Registered Office: 1-9 Booth Drive, Park Farm Industrial Estate, Wellingborough, Northants, NN8 6GR
Activities: Manufacture of other parts and accessories for motor vehicles
Shareholders: Hendrickson Holdings NL Cooperatief UA; Hendrickson Investments Europe Ltd; H Holdings Netherlands CV; Hendrickson Ventures Corporation Europe; Hendrickson Holdings LLC; The Boler Company
Officers: Tamara Anne Pateman, Secretary/Financial Director; Gary Gerstenslager [1955] Director/President American Owned Companies [American]; Helfried Jelinek [1973] General Managing Director [Austrian]; Richardo Andrew Martin [1966] Director/VP of International Operations [Australian]; Mark Philip Geoffrey Page [1969] Director

Henton & Chattell Limited
Incorporated: 18 November 1959 *Employees:* 69
Net Worth: £4,505,701 *Total Assets:* £11,749,660
Registered Office: London Road, Nottingham, NG2 3HW
Activities: Agents involved in the sale of machinery, industrial equipment, ships and aircraft
Major Shareholder: Anne Margaret Chaloner
Officers: Elizabeth Bronya Chaloner, Secretary; Anne Margaret Chaloner [1938] Director; Peter John Chaloner [1968] Director; James McGlinchey [1952] Director

Heptagon Limited
Incorporated: 16 March 1995
Net Worth: £10,006,000 *Total Assets:* £29,387,000
Registered Office: Westthorpe Fields Road, Killamarsh, Sheffield, S21 1TZ
Activities: Dormant company
Shareholders: SG Hambros Limited; CPL Industries Limited; Julian Paul Vivian Mash
Officers: Timothy William Minett [1960] Managing Director; Jason David Sutton [1982] Director/Accountant

Heraeus Electro-Nite (UK) Ltd
Incorporated: 9 February 1989 *Employees:* 56
Net Worth: £9,655,000 *Total Assets:* £12,817,000
Registered Office: Carlisle Close, Chesterfield, Derbys, S41 9ED
Activities: Manufacture of other special-purpose machinery n.e.c.
Officers: Mark Lee, Secretary/Manager; Veerle Rita Hendrickx [1968] Director/Head of Finance [Belgian]; Mark Lee [1970] Director/Manager

Hermitage Holdings (Wilmslow) Limited
Incorporated: 9 December 2015
Net Worth: £14,814,463 *Total Assets:* £15,097,449
Registered Office: Paradigm House, Brooke Court, Wilmslow, Cheshire, SK9 3ND
Activities: Management consultancy activities other than financial management
Shareholder: Paul Henry Hogarth
Officers: Judith Anne Hogarth [1966] Director; Paul Henry Hogarth [1959] Director

Hertford Heath Limited
Incorporated: 15 March 2000 *Employees:* 565
Net Worth: £3,963,720 *Total Assets:* £28,533,252
Registered Office: The Courtyard, Chapel Lane, Bodicote, Banbury, Oxon, OX15 4DB
Activities: Take-away food shops and mobile food stands
Parent: Palico Limited
Officers: Harpal Singh Grewal [1979] Director

Herts Insurance Consultants Limited
Incorporated: 15 March 1999 *Employees:* 201
Net Worth: £11,858,359 *Total Assets:* £20,964,260
Registered Office: 22-26 King Street, King's Lynn, Norfolk, PE30 1HJ
Activities: Non-life insurance
Parent: Hadleigh Holdings Ltd
Officers: David James Flux, Secretary/Insurance Broker; David James Flux [1968] Director/Insurance Broker; Yvonne Flux [1948] Director/Insurance Broker

Hesley Care & Education Limited
Incorporated: 10 June 2004
Net Worth: £5,544,034 *Total Assets:* £20,159,432
Registered Office: Central Services, Hesley Hall, Tickhill, Doncaster, S Yorks, DN11 9HH
Activities: Other residential care activities n.e.c.
Parent: Hesley Holdings Limited
Officers: David Bryan Maynard [1973] Sales Director; Susan McLean [1966] Operations Director; Christopher McSharry [1959] Director; Graham Smith [1960] Director/Chairman

The Hesley Group Limited
Incorporated: 22 November 1991 *Employees:* 1,520
Net Worth: £7,894,933 *Total Assets:* £47,874,436
Registered Office: Central Services, Hesley Hall, Tickhill, Doncaster, S Yorks, DN11 9HH
Activities: Other residential care activities n.e.c.
Parent: Hesley Care & Education Limited
Officers: David Bryan Maynard [1973] Sales Director; Susan McLean [1966] Operations Director; Christopher McSharry [1959] Director; Graham Smith [1950] Director/Chairman

Hesley Holdings Limited
Incorporated: 20 March 2008 *Employees:* 1,520
Net Worth: £15,764,222 *Total Assets:* £56,175,568
Registered Office: Central Services, Hesley Hall, Tickhill, Doncaster, S Yorks, DN11 9HH
Activities: Other residential care activities n.e.c.
Parent: Honour Project Bidco Limited
Officers: David Bryan Maynard [1973] Sales Director; Susan McLean [1966] Operations Director; Christopher McSharry [1959] Director; Graham Smith [1950] Director/Chairman

A.E.Hewison Limited
Incorporated: 24 December 1971 *Employees:* 2
Net Worth: £2,729,699 *Total Assets:* £10,463,817
Registered Office: Ashtree Farm House, Mill Lane, Addlethorpe, Skegness, Lincs, PE25 1HW
Activities: Retail sale in non-specialised stores with food, beverages or tobacco predominating
Major Shareholder: David MacDonald Hewison
Officers: David MacDonald Hewison [1962] Director/Store Manager; Janet Christine Hewison [1956] Director

W.E. Hewitt & Son Limited
Incorporated: 24 June 1985 *Employees:* 48
Net Worth: £10,844,764 *Total Assets:* £18,838,624
Registered Office: 45 Cambridge Road, Cosby, Leicester, LE9 1SJ
Activities: Other manufacturing n.e.c.
Major Shareholder: John William Hewitt
Officers: Patricia Barbara Hewitt, Secretary; John William Hewitt [1956] Director/Sports Ground Contractor; Patricia Barbara Hewitt [1956] Director/Secretary; Ryan William Hewitt [1978] Director/Sports Ground Contractor

Hexadex Limited
Incorporated: 31 December 1991 *Employees:* 726
Net Worth: £49,858,000 *Total Assets:* £67,620,000
Registered Office: The Old Court House, 24 Market Street, Gainsborough, Lincs, DN21 2BE
Activities: Activities of head offices
Officers: David John Hodgson, Secretary; William James Buchan [1959] Director; Dr Pelham Nigel Hawker [1953] Director; Andrew Joseph Meakin [1966] Director/Chartered Accountant; Barnaby Arthur Jennings Milles [1975] Director [British/Australian]; David Herbert Milles [1942] Director; William David Milles [1970] Director; Dr Robert Joseph Rule [1964] Director

Hexagon Investment Holdings Limited
Incorporated: 11 May 2005 *Employees:* 3,200
Net Worth: £994,190 *Total Assets:* £14,830,570
Registered Office: Interaction House, 43 High Street, Huntingdon, Cambs, PE29 3AQ
Activities: Temporary employment agency activities
Major Shareholder: Andrew Iain Gilchrist
Officers: Geoff Holder, Secretary; David Mark Dickson [1962] Sales Director; Andrew Iain Gilchrist [1962] Director/Chartered Accountant

Hexagon Leasing Limited
Incorporated: 22 February 2001 *Employees:* 18
Net Worth: £4,719,528 *Total Assets:* £49,305,688
Registered Office: c/o Imperial Commercials DAF, Ashbourne Road, Mackworth, Derby, DE22 4NB
Activities: Sale of other motor vehicles
Shareholders: Susan Penny Granger; Michelle Louise Peterson
Officers: Kevin Paul Pearson, Secretary; Martin John Cook [1964] Finance Director; Mark Andrew Fletcher [1970] Commercial Director; Anthony John Granger [1955] Director/Consultant

Hexpol Finance UK Limited
Incorporated: 9 August 2012
Net Worth: £332,912,672 *Total Assets:* £334,771,904
Registered Office: c/o Berwin Polymers, Broadway, Globe Lane Industrial Estate, Dukinfield, Cheshire, SK16 4UJ
Activities: Activities of production holding companies
Parent: Hexpol AB
Officers: Joseph Edmund Dowdall [1963] Director; Tracy Alan Garrison [1967] Director/Rubber Compounding-President & CEO [American]; Karin Elisabeth Bachmann Gunnarsson [1962] Director/Group Chief Financial Officer [Swedish]; David Andrew Hayes [1968] Director/Financial Controller

Heyford Park Developments Limited
Incorporated: 9 June 2015
Net Worth Deficit: £2,366,016 *Total Assets:* £44,884,496
Registered Office: Heyford Park House, Heyford Park, Upper Heyford, Bicester, Oxon, OX25 5HD
Activities: Buying and selling of own real estate
Parent: Dorchester Settlements Limited
Officers: Ian Michael Amdur [1963] Director; Gary Alexander Silver [1970] Director; Paul Anthony Silver [1972] Director

Heyford Residential Limited
Incorporated: 2 March 2012
Net Worth Deficit: £11,711,419 *Total Assets:* £81,983,264
Registered Office: Heyford Park House, Heyford Park, Upper Heyford, Bicester, Oxon, OX25 5HD
Activities: Other letting and operating of own or leased real estate
Parent: Heyford Park Holdings Limited
Officers: Ian Michael Amdur [1963] Director; Dr Gary Alexander Silver [1970] Director/Physician; Paul Anthony Silver [1972] Director/Accountant

The Heyfordian School Trust
Incorporated: 27 January 2012 *Employees:* 53
Net Worth: £12,519,599 *Total Assets:* £13,020,286
Registered Office: 74 Camp Road, Upper Heyford, Bicester, Oxon, OX25 5HD
Activities: Other education n.e.c.
Officers: Emily Boswell [1975] Director of High Education; Debra Cotton [1981] Director/Administrator; Steve Gee [1971] Managing Director; Gale Patricia Law [1961] Director/Housewife; Adrian William Henry Lockwood [1956] Director; Stephen Charles Maltby [1943] Director; Jan Maulden [1946] Director; Sarah Bianca McCready [1990] Director/Head of Social Infrastructure; Charles Morgan-Harris [1975] Director/IT; Simon Morrell [1985] Director/Chartered Accountant; Elaine Jane Robinson [1947] Director; Paul Anthony Silver [1972] Director/Chartered Accountant

Heygate & Sons Limited
Incorporated: 28 March 1962 *Employees:* 1,059
Net Worth: £66,816,348 *Total Assets:* £154,836,448
Registered Office: Bugbrooke Mills, Bugbrooke, Northampton, NN7 3QH
Activities: Manufacture of prepared feeds for farm animals
Shareholders: Paul Michael Heygate; Arthur Robert Heygate
Officers: Stephen Chia, Secretary; Arthur Robert Heygate [1945] Director/Farmer and Flour Miller; Paul Michael Heygate [1943] Director/Miller and Farmer

Heygates Limited
Incorporated: 22 April 1958 *Employees:* 276
Net Worth: £21,725,848 *Total Assets:* £58,237,828
Registered Office: Bugbrooke Mills, Bugbrooke, Northampton, NN7 3QH
Activities: Grain milling
Parent: Heygate & Sons Limited
Officers: Stephen Chia, Secretary; Stephen Kha Yin Chia [1957] Director; Arthur Robert Heygate [1974] Director; Arthur Robert Heygate [1945] Director/Farmer and Flour Miller; Paul Michael Heygate [1943] Director/Miller and Farmer; Sarah Elizabeth Kreckler [1977] Director

HFG Holdings Limited
Incorporated: 11 November 1999 *Employees:* 873
Net Worth: £12,362,930 *Total Assets:* £27,719,492
Registered Office: Manor Court Chambers, Townsend Drive, Nuneaton, Warwicks, CV11 6RU
Activities: Manufacture of other furniture
Shareholder: Jill Richardson
Officers: Mark John Hammonds [1961] Joint Managing Director; Richard John Hammonds [1963] Chairman & Joint Managing Director; Jill Richardson [1942] Director

Hi-Force Limited
Incorporated: 2 June 2006 *Employees:* 81
Net Worth: £9,220,627 *Total Assets:* £13,140,707
Registered Office: Prospect Way, Royal Oak Industrial Estate, Daventry, Northants, NN11 8PL
Activities: Manufacture of lifting and handling equipment
Officers: Kevin Peter Brown, Secretary; Christine Jane Betts [1970] HR Director; David James Brookes [1981] Technical Director; Craig Peter Brown [1978] Sales Director; Kevin Peter Brown [1958] Director; Christopher Brian Dickinson [1960] Director; Marieanne May Meek [1979] Director

Hi-Level Enterprises Limited
Incorporated: 4 August 1988 *Employees:* 26
Net Worth: £10,921,512 *Total Assets:* £11,438,746
Registered Office: Millennium Warehouse, Sandall Lane, Kirk Sandall Industrial Estate, Doncaster, S Yorks, DN3 1QL
Activities: Sale, maintenance and repair of motorcycles and related parts and accessories
Officers: James Beukelman [1963] Finance Director [American]; Bradley J Roberts [1981] Director [American]; Steve Stubitz [1957] Director [American]; James Wisnoski [1961] Director [American]

Hichrom Limited
Incorporated: 21 December 1984 *Employees:* 91
Net Worth: £13,010,257 *Total Assets:* £15,070,568
Registered Office: Hichrom Limited, Hunter Boulevard, Magna Park, Lutterworth, Leics, LE17 4XN
Activities: Manufacture of basic pharmaceutical products
Parent: VWR Holdco Limited
Officers: Karen Jane Pulford, Secretary; William Patrick Hogan [1959] Managing Director [Irish]; Karen Jane Pulford [1968] Director/Accountant; Andrew Smith [1972] Operations Director

Hicks (1) Limited
Incorporated: 17 July 2008 *Employees:* 100
Net Worth: £3,998,212 *Total Assets:* £15,508,969
Registered Office: Unit 2 Bruntingthorpe Industrial Estate, Lutterworth, Leics, LE17 5QZ
Activities: Activities of head offices
Major Shareholder: Stephen Robert Sverdloff
Officers: Keith Graham Persin [1963] Director/Engineer

HID Estates Limited
Incorporated: 28 June 2011 *Employees:* 7
Net Worth: £3,036,567 *Total Assets:* £15,017,495
Registered Office: 20 Kent Road, Northampton, NN5 4DR
Activities: Construction of commercial buildings
Parent: Swan Barrett LLP
Officers: John Burns Barrett [1963] Director; Peter James Hubbard [1958] Director; Matthew David Swan [1963] Director

Higham Lane School
Incorporated: 16 November 2011 *Employees:* 182
Net Worth: £5,348,000 *Total Assets:* £9,005,000
Registered Office: Higham Lane School, Shanklin Drive, Nuneaton, Warwicks, CV10 0BJ
Activities: General secondary education
Officers: Benjamin David Elliott, Secretary; Ian Aley [1968] Director/Police Officer; Carl Bentley [1974] Director/Division Manager; Stephen Bibby [1969] Director/Bakery Manager; Karen Bowers [1966] Director/HLTA [South African]; Jackie Brooks [1963] Director/Teacher; Roger John Campbell Brown [1953] Director; David Buckle [1959] Director/College Vice Principal; Romayne Charles [1985] Director/Teacher; David Cleaver [1966] Director/Police Officer; Jeffrey Davenport [1958] Director/Civil Servant; Hayley Doyne-Ditmas [1981] Director/Teacher; Professor Michael Duncan [1977] Director/Professor of Sport and Exercise Science [Irish]; John Murray Garner [1944] Director; Nicole Hemmings [1993] Director/Teacher; Keith Hobbs [1983] Director/Deputy Headteacher; Claire Holland-Turner [1968] Director/Early Years Practitioner; Philip Kelly [1964] Director [Irish]; Nafees Qamar Khan [1965] Director/Homemaker; James Littlehales [1978] Director/Police Officer; Beccie Lloyd [1981] Director/Self Employed; Gabrielle Middleton [1975] Director/Civil Servant; Joel Nason [1974] Director/Chartered Engineer; Dawn Shaw [1969] Director/Quality Administrator

Highcroft Investments PLC
Incorporated: 7 September 1927 *Employees:* 6
Net Worth: £59,977,000 *Total Assets:* £81,685,000
Registered Office: Thomas House, Langford Locks, Kidlington, Oxon, OX5 1HR
Activities: Other letting and operating of own or leased real estate
Officers: Roberta Caroline Miles, Secretary; Charles Alistair Neilson Butler [1972] Director; Charles Simon Arthur Costa [1963] Director/Bursar; Simon Timothy Gill [1956] Property Director; David Henry Kingerlee [1961] Director/Quantity Surveyor; Roberta Caroline Miles [1962] Finance Director

Hikoki Power Tools (U.K.) Limited
Incorporated: 12 February 1981 *Employees:* 35
Previous: Hitachi Power Tools (U.K.) Limited
Net Worth: £7,206,532 *Total Assets:* £12,627,777
Registered Office: Precedent Drive, Rooksley, Milton Keynes, Bucks, MK13 8PJ
Activities: Wholesale of mining, construction and civil engineering machinery
Parent: KKR & Co. Inc.
Officers: Shuichi Shiina, Secretary; Yoshio Komei [1973] Director [Japanese]; Shuichi Shiina [1965] Director [Japanese]; Hiroyuki Usuku [1966] Director [Japanese]

Hill Care 1 Limited
Incorporated: 5 March 2010 *Employees:* 243
Net Worth: £5,584,783 *Total Assets:* £17,084,456
Registered Office: 91-97 Saltergate, Chesterfield, Derbys, S40 1LA
Activities: Residential nursing care facilities
Parent: Hill Care Holdings Ltd
Officers: Alexandra Josephine Hill, Secretary; Ian Philip Mitchell, Secretary; John Andrew Hill [1965] Director; Wendy Jane Waddicor [1964] Operations Director

Hill Care Limited
Incorporated: 27 February 2001 *Employees:* 347
Net Worth Deficit: £1,650,211 *Total Assets:* £14,451,284
Registered Office: 93-97 Saltergate, Chesterfield, Derbys, S40 1LA
Activities: Other human health activities
Parent: Hill Care Holdings Limited
Officers: Alexandra Josephine Hill, Secretary; Ian Philip Mitchell, Secretary; John Andrew Hill [1965] Director/Care Home Proprietor; Wendy Jane Waddicor [1964] Operations Director

Hill House School Limited
Incorporated: 14 June 1967 *Employees:* 130
Net Worth: £6,186,090 *Total Assets:* £13,849,135
Registered Office: Sixth Avenue, Auckley, Doncaster, S Yorks, DN9 3GG
Activities: Primary education
Officers: Robert Scott Colbear [1966] Director/Marketing Executive; Dr Antonia Helen Cooper [1970] Director/Clinical Psychologist; Valerie Cusworth [1949] Director/Retired; Richard Anthony de Mulder [1966] Director; Neil Royston Ebden [1973] Director/Banker; Dr Dean Justin Eggitt [1980] Director/GP; Joan Wickes Fearns [1956] Director/Retired; Dr Madeline Jane Fraser [1956] Director/Retired; Maura Jaqueline Jameson [1960] Director/Consultant; Robert Paul Leggott [1970] Director; Jason Antony Lee Sprenger [1973] Director; Michael John Wilson-Maccormack [1970] Director/Architect

Hill-Rom Limited
Incorporated: 3 May 1988 *Employees:* 162
Net Worth: £14,303,000 *Total Assets:* £20,284,000
Registered Office: Clinitron House, Ashby Park, Ashby De La Zouch, Leics, LE65 1JG
Activities: Other human health activities
Parent: Hill-Rom UK (Holdings) Ltd
Officers: Stephen Sanders, Secretary; Carlos Alonso [1959] Director/President International [Spanish]; David Michael Gittings [1962] Director/Business Manager; Peter McLauchlan Simpson Moss [1973] Director/General Manager; Duncan James Wilson [1969] Director

Hill-Rom UK (Holdings) Ltd
Incorporated: 7 February 2013
Net Worth Deficit: £14,935,000 *Total Assets:* £16,093,000
Registered Office: Clinitron House, Excelsior Road, Ashby De La Zouch, Leics, LE65 1JG
Activities: Activities of other holding companies n.e.c.
Officers: Stephen Sanders, Secretary; Sebastien Evain [1968] Director/European Regional Controller [French]; Duncan James Wilson [1969] Director; Subramaniam Yogendran [1957] Director/Business Executive [American]

Hillarys Blinds Limited
Incorporated: 14 January 1975 *Employees:* 1,470
Net Worth: £130,448,000 *Total Assets:* £188,800,000
Registered Office: Unit 2 Churchill Park, Private Road No 2, Colwick, Nottingham, NG4 2JR
Activities: Other manufacturing n.e.c.
Parent: Hillarys Blinds (Holdings) Limited
Officers: Craig Edwards [1974] Director; David Mathew Aubrey Lewis [1967] Director/Business Executive [Australian]; Darren Hansel Lock [1966] Director; John Risman [1965] Director; Andrew Richard Thomas [1972] Director/Business Executive; Susan Ann White [1976] Director

The Hillarys Properties Partnership LLP
Incorporated: 21 February 2003
Net Worth Deficit: £720,766 *Total Assets:* £12,728,861
Registered Office: Rolleston Manor, Station Road, Rolleston, Newark, Notts, NG23 5SE
Officers: Anthony Hungerford Hillary [1943] Member; Michelle Irene Hillary [1956] Member

Hillbridge Investments Limited
Incorporated: 4 November 1997 *Employees:* 72
Net Worth: £6,321,000 *Total Assets:* £11,078,000
Registered Office: Castle Environmental, Crompton Road, Ilkeston, Derbys, DE7 4BG
Activities: Activities of head offices
Major Shareholder: Michael Roger Hewitt
Officers: Andrew Marc Smith, Secretary; Thomas Charles Andrew Diggle [1961] Commercial Director; Andrew Mark Elliott [1966] Director; David Robert Ellison [1942] Director; Michael Roger Hewitt [1942] Director/Consultant; Helen Mary Robinson [1960] Director/Personal Assistant; Andrew Marc Smith [1975] Director/Certified Chartered Accountant

Hillco Investments (UK) Limited
Incorporated: 21 December 2007 *Employees:* 3
Net Worth: £17,188,092 *Total Assets:* £19,331,678
Registered Office: 49 Mill Street, Bedford, MK40 3EU
Activities: Other business support service activities n.e.c.
Officers: Sandra Daly, Secretary; David Matthew Rustin Howell [1960] Director/Commercial Property Consultant

Hillsborough Investments Limited
Incorporated: 27 June 1997
Net Worth: £18,988,876 *Total Assets:* £18,988,876
Registered Office: Adsetts House, 16 Europa View, Sheffield Business Park, Sheffield, S9 1XH
Activities: Dormant company
Parent: SIG PLC
Officers: Richard Charles Monro, Secretary; Ian Jackson [1979] Director/Accountant; Richard Charles Monro [1958] Director/Chartered Secretary

Hilton Food Group PLC
Incorporated: 16 March 2007 *Employees:* 3,545
Net Worth: £158,650,000 *Total Assets:* £433,360,000
Registered Office: 2-8 Interchange, Latham Road, Huntingdon, Cambs, PE29 6YE
Activities: Activities of head offices
Officers: Neil Michael George, Secretary; Christine Cross [1951] Director; Philip John Heffer [1966] Director; Nigel Richard Majewski [1960] Finance Director; Dr Angus James Porter [1957] Director; Robert Andrew Watson [1958] Director/Chief Executive Officer; John Graham Worby [1950] Director

Hilton Garage Ltd
Incorporated: 17 August 1978 *Employees:* 74
Net Worth: £9,209,682 *Total Assets:* £20,696,034
Registered Office: 10 Stadium Business Court, Millennium Way, Pride Park, Derby, DE24 8HP
Activities: Sale of used cars and light motor vehicles
Major Shareholder: David Manning
Officers: Linda Jane Manning, Secretary; David Manning [1947] Director/Motor Vehicle Sales Executive; George Manning [1996] Director/Motor Dealer; Linda Jane Manning [1947] Director/Motor Car Salesman; Richard Wayne Manning [1968] Director/Motor Dealer

History & Heraldry Holdings Limited
Incorporated: 25 October 2012 *Employees:* 225
Net Worth: £23,217,316 *Total Assets:* £27,058,708
Registered Office: 2 Denby Way, Hellaby Industrial Estate, Rotherham, S Yorks, S66 8HR
Activities: Activities of head offices
Shareholders: Malcolm Charles Ogg; Dianne Clothier
Officers: Amanda Dawn Hill, Secretary; Dianne Clothier [1965] Director; Malcolm Charles Ogg [1960] Director

History & Heraldry Limited
Incorporated: 26 July 1996 *Employees:* 93
Net Worth: £2,276,330 *Total Assets:* £16,925,326
Registered Office: 2 Denby Way, Hellaby Industrial Estate, Rotherham, S Yorks, S66 8HR
Activities: Non-specialised wholesale trade
Parent: History & Heraldry Holdings Limited
Officers: Amanda Dawn Hill, Secretary; Malcolm Charles Ogg [1960] Director/Company Partner

Hive Bidco Limited
Incorporated: 9 October 2015
Net Worth Deficit: £4,656,304 *Total Assets:* £15,050,608
Registered Office: Grafton House, Grafton Street, Hyde, Cheshire, SK14 2AX
Activities: Activities of other holding companies n.e.c.
Parent: Hive Topco Limited
Officers: Jonathan Kay, Secretary; Daniel Charles Ball [1969] Director; Paul Anthony Ellis [1970] Director; Jonathan Walton Kay [1969] Director; Christopher Smith [1971] Director

Hive Topco Limited
Incorporated: 9 October 2015 *Employees:* 84
Net Worth Deficit: £4,927,933 *Total Assets:* £18,372,744
Registered Office: Grafton House, Grafton Street, Hyde, Cheshire, SK14 2AX
Activities: Activities of other holding companies n.e.c.
Parent: August Equity Partners III GP Limited
Officers: Jonathan Kay, Secretary; Daniel Charles Ball [1969] Director; Mike Biddulph [1974] Director; Paul Anthony Ellis [1970] Director; Jonathan Walton Kay [1969] Director; John Robert Edward Thompson [1971] Non-Executive Director Chairman

HJE Limited
Incorporated: 26 July 1993
Net Worth: £13,860,000 *Total Assets:* £18,651,000
Registered Office: Cowley Lodge, Warren Carr, Matlock, Derbys, DE4 2LE
Activities: Activities of head offices
Parent: Eco-Bat Technologies Limited
Officers: Jimmy Herring, Secretary; Robert John Harris [1963] Managing Director - European Division; Jimmy R. Herring [1966] Finance Director [American]

HLD Holdings Limited
Incorporated: 12 January 2007 *Employees:* 328
Previous: Pall-Ex Group Limited
Net Worth: £3,442,000 *Total Assets:* £20,378,000
Registered Office: Pall Ex House, Victoria Road, Ellistown, Leics, LE67 1FH
Activities: Activities of head offices
Major Shareholder: Hilary Lorraine Devey
Officers: Robert James Benoist [1948] Director/Lawyer; Hilary Lorraine Devey [1957] Director

HM Estates Limited
Incorporated: 10 February 2006 *Employees:* 1
Net Worth: £5,373,421 *Total Assets:* £14,041,498
Registered Office: 154 Cowley Road, Oxford, OX4 1UE
Activities: Development of building projects
Officers: Abdul Khuja, Secretary; Tariq Qume Khuja [1977] Director/Letting Agent

HNB Care Limited
Incorporated: 8 July 2011
Net Worth: £96,922 *Total Assets:* £10,959,301
Registered Office: The Finches, Southam Road, Radford Semele, Leamington Spa, Warwicks, CV31 1TZ
Activities: Residential nursing care facilities
Shareholders: Balbir Singh Bains; Kulvinder Kaur Bains
Officers: Balbir Singh Bains, Secretary; Balbir Singh Bains [1963] Director; Kulvinder Kaur Bains [1968] Director

Hoban Limited
Incorporated: 7 August 2003 *Employees:* 42
Net Worth: £4,011,519 *Total Assets:* £11,955,814
Registered Office: Hoban House, Chesney Wold, Bleak Hall, Milton Keynes, Bucks, MK6 1NE
Activities: Freight transport by road
Major Shareholder: Michael Hoban
Officers: Claire Rachel Hoban, Secretary; Claire Hoban [1974] Director; Michael Hoban [1973] Director/Road Haulier

Hodge Clemco Limited
Incorporated: 20 April 1959 *Employees:* 86
Net Worth: £6,807,573 *Total Assets:* £10,965,684
Registered Office: 36 Orgreave Drive, Sheffield, S13 9NR
Activities: Manufacture of other fabricated metal products n.e.c.
Parent: Samuel Hodge Holdings Ltd
Officers: Hamish Bowick Kinmond, Secretary/Accountant; Neal David Crisford [1961] Director/Company Executive; Paul Michael Grattan [1963] Director/Executive; Hamish Bowick Kinmond [1952] Director/Accountant

Samuel Hodge Holdings Limited
Incorporated: 29 October 2010 *Employees:* 217
Net Worth: £6,679,296 *Total Assets:* £18,597,996
Registered Office: 36 Orgreave Drive, Sheffield, S13 9NR
Activities: Activities of other holding companies n.e.c.
Shareholders: Hamish Bowick Kinmond; Neal David Crisford
Officers: Hamish Bowick Kinmond, Secretary; Neal David Crisford [1961] Director/Executive; Hamish Bowick Kinmond [1952] Director

Samuel Hodge Limited
Incorporated: 17 May 1897 *Employees:* 7
Net Worth Deficit: £857,680 *Total Assets:* £9,941,724
Registered Office: 36 Orgreave Drive, Sheffield, S13 9NR
Activities: Activities of head offices
Parent: Samuel Hodge Holdings Ltd
Officers: Hamish Bowick Kinmond, Secretary/Accountant; Neal David Crisford [1961] Director; Hamish Bowick Kinmond [1952] Director/Accountant

Hofer Powertrain UK Limited
Incorporated: 19 March 2013 *Employees:* 29
Net Worth: £1,007,976 *Total Assets:* £12,971,522
Registered Office: 2 Titan Business Centre, Spartan Close, Warwick, CV34 6RR
Activities: Other engineering activities
Parent: Hofer Mechatronik GmbH
Officers: William Mellodew Hartley [1979] Director/Engineer; Martin Maier [1972] Director/Engineer [German]

Holcim Participations (UK) Limited
Incorporated: 13 December 2004
Net Worth: £873,958,976 *Total Assets:* £1,916,173,952
Registered Office: Bardon Hall, Copt Oak Road, Markfield, Leics, LE67 9PJ
Activities: Activities of other holding companies n.e.c.
Parent: Holderfin B.V.
Officers: Simon Gregory Crossley [1973] Director/Chartered Accountant; David Robert Forder [1965] Director/Manager, Financial Reporting & Planning; Laurent Eric Louis Jaques [1976] Director/CFO Corporate Holdings [Swiss]

Holding Holding Company Limited
Incorporated: 11 December 2007 *Employees:* 63
Net Worth: £11,468,990 *Total Assets:* £21,365,380
Registered Office: St Andrews Court, Lees Lane, Mottram St Andrew, Macclesfield, Cheshire, SK10 4LJ
Activities: Other letting and operating of own or leased real estate
Shareholders: Joanne Marinda Holding; Simon Timothy Holding; Timothy Ronald Lovett
Officers: Simon Timothy Holding, Secretary/Director; Simon Timothy Holding [1972] Director

Holding JDR Limited
Incorporated: 20 April 2017 *Employees:* 5
Net Worth Deficit: £1,040,166 *Total Assets:* £50,391,784
Registered Office: Innovation Centre, Gallows Hill, Warwick, CV34 6UW
Activities: Management consultancy activities other than financial management
Parent: Tele-Fonika Holdings Limited
Officers: Pawel Michal Bak [1976] Director [Polish]; Monika Cupial-Zgryzek [1977] Director [Polish]; Michal Pawel Hassa [1978] Director [Polish]

Holdsworth Holdings Limited
Incorporated: 7 October 1976 *Employees:* 423
Net Worth: £16,203,076 *Total Assets:* £26,963,476
Registered Office: Manchester Road, Tideswell, Buxton, Derbys, SK17 8LN
Activities: Other business support service activities n.e.c.
Major Shareholder: Michael Ian Holdsworth
Officers: Esther Victoria Trevethick, Secretary; Rupert Michael Ellis Holdsworth [1978] Director/Depot Manager; John Andrew Marriott [1950] Director; Esther Victoria Trevethick [1974] Director/Marketing Manager

Michael I Holdsworth Limited
Incorporated: 12 June 1986 *Employees:* 417
Net Worth: £12,652,102 *Total Assets:* £22,577,952
Registered Office: Manchester Road, Tideswell, Buxton, Derbys, SK17 8LN
Activities: Operation of warehousing and storage facilities for land transport activities
Shareholder: Michael Ian Holdsworth
Officers: Esther Victoria Trevethick, Secretary; Rupert Michael Ellis Holdsworth [1978] Director/Depot Manager; John Andrew Marriott [1950] Managing Director; Esther Victoria Trevethick [1974] Director/Marketing Manager; Rebecca Jane Christine Warhurst [1961] Director/Finance

Holland & Barrett Group Limited
Incorporated: 1 August 1995 *Employees:* 97
Previous: Vitamin World Limited
Net Worth: £283,366,016 *Total Assets:* £1,427,422,976
Registered Office: Samuel Ryder House, Barling Way, Eliot Park, Nuneaton, Warwicks, CV10 7RH
Activities: Retail sale via mail order houses or via Internet
Parent: Holland & Barrett International Limited
Officers: Lisa Mary Garley-Evans, Secretary; Lisa Mary Garley-Evans [1968] Director/Solicitor; Christian Keen [1964] Director/Chief Financial Officer

Holland & Barrett Holdings Limited
Incorporated: 11 October 1996
Net Worth: £109,155,000 *Total Assets:* £738,716,992
Registered Office: Samuel Ryder House, Barling Way, Eliot Park, Nuneaton, Warwicks, CV10 7RH
Activities: Activities of head offices
Parent: Holland & Barrett Group Limited
Officers: Lisa Mary Garley-Evans, Secretary; Lisa Mary Garley-Evans [1968] Director/Solicitor; Christian Keen [1964] Director/Chief Financial Officer

Holland & Barrett International Limited
Incorporated: 20 August 2002 *Employees:* 7,166
Previous: NBTY Europe Limited
Net Worth: £277,879,008 *Total Assets:* £713,566,976
Registered Office: Samuel Ryder House, Barling Way, Eliot Park, Nuneaton, Warwicks, CV10 7RH
Activities: Activities of head offices
Officers: Lisa Mary Garley-Evans, Secretary; Peter Howard Aldis [1964] Director/Chief Executive Officer [Irish]; Steve Trevor Carson [1967] Managing Director; Mark Robert Fabes [1962] Group IT Director; Lisa Mary Garley-Evans [1968] Director/Solicitor; Lena Marie Caroline Hipperson [1974] Group Brand Marketing Director [Swedish]; John Anthony Houghton [1972] Group Retail & Property Director; Christian Keen [1964] Director/Chief Financial Officer; Hilary Margaret Leam [1971] Group Trading Director; Hongyan Lu [1974] Managing Director International [Chinese]; Emma Jane Mead [1967] Group Digital Director

Holland & Barrett Retail Limited
Incorporated: 26 October 1992 *Employees:* 5,155
Net Worth: £279,508,000 *Total Assets:* £1,213,031,936
Registered Office: Samuel Ryder House, Barling Way, Eliot Park, Nuneaton, Warwicks, CV10 7RH
Activities: Retail sale of beverages in specialised stores
Parent: Holland & Barrett Holdings Limited
Officers: Lisa Mary Garley-Evans, Secretary; Steve Trevor Carson [1967] Managing Director; Lisa Mary Garley-Evans [1968] Director/Solicitor; Christian Keen [1964] Director/Chief Financial Officer; Hilary Margaret Leam [1971] Group Trading Director

I Holland Holdings Limited
Incorporated: 27 March 2015 *Employees:* 157
Net Worth: £2,097,324 *Total Assets:* £12,611,013
Registered Office: Meadow Lane, Long Eaton, Nottingham, NG10 2GD
Activities: Activities of head offices
Shareholders: David Gary Hinds; John Michael Woloszczak
Officers: David Gary Hinds [1966] Director; John Michael Woloszczak [1961] Director

I Holland Limited
Incorporated: 3 February 1998 *Employees:* 154
Net Worth: £12,046,944 *Total Assets:* £21,819,776
Registered Office: Meadow Lane, Long Eaton, Nottingham, NG10 2GD
Activities: Manufacture of tools
Parent: Cognoisette Limited
Officers: David Gary Hinds, Secretary; Stephen Ivan Deakin [1961] Director; David Gary Hinds [1966] Finance Director; Christopher Clive Prideaux [1955] Managing Director; Javier Raposo Acebedo [1976] Director [Spanish]; John Michael Woloszczak [1961] Director/Engineer

Holly Farm Limited
Incorporated: 29 November 1976 *Employees:* 2
Net Worth: £9,473,965 *Total Assets:* £11,678,113
Registered Office: Holly Farm, Honiley, Kenilworth, Warwicks, CV8 1NP
Activities: Development of building projects
Shareholders: John Robert Taylor; Richards Family Investments LLP
Officers: Margaret Taylor, Secretary; Graham Anthony Richards [1937] Director; John Robert Taylor [1943] Director

Graham Holmes Astraseal Limited
Incorporated: 21 March 1991 *Employees:* 197
Net Worth: £8,098,340 *Total Assets:* £12,990,595
Registered Office: Astraseal House, Paterson Road, Finedon Road Industrial Estate, Wellingborough, Northants, NN8 4EX
Activities: Manufacture of doors and windows of metal
Parent: Astraseal (Holdings) Limited
Officers: Malcolm Alfred Naylor, Secretary; Richard John Matthew Essam [1968] Commercial Director; Andrew McKeown [1949] Director; Mark McMullan [1967] Building Director; Malcolm Alfred Naylor [1957] Director/Accountant; Colin John Stanley [1978] Operations Director

Holophane Europe Limited
Incorporated: 29 March 1965 *Employees:* 103
Net Worth: £4,434,934 *Total Assets:* £21,915,646
Registered Office: Bond Avenue, Bletchley, Milton Keynes, Bucks, MK1 1JG
Activities: Manufacture of electric lighting equipment
Officers: Alasdair Roderick McRury [1956] Managing Director; Richard Kent Reece [1956] Director/Executive Vice President [American]

The Holy Spirit Catholic Multi Academy Company
Incorporated: 10 February 2015 *Employees:* 323
Net Worth: £14,878,202 *Total Assets:* £18,723,884
Registered Office: Our Lady and St Joseph Catholic Academy, Riversely Park, Coton Road, Nuneaton, Warwicks, CV11 5TY
Activities: Pre-primary education
Officers: Leo Burton [1968] Director/Teacher; Kevin Joseph Dunnion [1965] Director/Regional Sales Manager; James Daniel Foley [1952] Director/Retired; Father Simon Hall [1977] Director/Parish Priest; Richard Pitt [1959] Director/Retired; Darren Riddell [1972] Director/MCR Manager; Julie Sewell [1967] Director/Practice Manager; Sinead Catherine Mary Smith [1979] Director/Headteacher; Avril Margaret Staley [1975] Director/HR & Business Manager; Thomas Temple [1943] Director/Retired Headteacher; Claire Louise Wright [1973] Director/Deputy Headmistress

Homag U.K. Ltd.
Incorporated: 7 December 1973 *Employees:* 70
Net Worth: £4,356,000 *Total Assets:* £14,580,000
Registered Office: 10c Sills Road, Willow Farm Business Park, Castle Donington, Derbys, DE74 2US
Activities: Agents involved in the sale of machinery, industrial equipment, ships and aircraft
Parent: Homag Finance GmbH
Officers: David Boyd Hammond, Secretary; Simon Mark Steven Brooks [1968] Sales and Marketing Director; Frederik Meyer [1980] Director [German]; Paul Newman [1959] After Sales Director

Home Decor GB Limited
Incorporated: 25 October 2004 *Employees:* 180
Net Worth: £9,538,604 *Total Assets:* £22,320,224
Registered Office: Innovation Way, Woodhouse Mill, Sheffield, S13 9AD
Activities: Manufacture of other furniture
Parent: HD Holdings II Limited
Officers: Jason Paul Limbert [1970] Director

Home Retail Group (Finance) LLP
Incorporated: 21 January 2011
Net Worth: £200,362,000 *Total Assets:* £200,362,000
Registered Office: 489-499 Avebury Boulevard, Milton Keynes, Bucks, MK9 2NW

Home Retail Group (UK) Limited
Incorporated: 13 June 2006 *Employees:* 2
Net Worth: £2,005,330,944 *Total Assets:* £2,790,338,048
Registered Office: 489-499 Avebury Boulevard, Milton Keynes, Bucks, MK9 2NW
Activities: Other business support service activities n.e.c.
Parent: Home Retail Group Limited
Officers: Timothy Fallowfield, Secretary; Claire Louise Catlin [1980] Director; John Terence Rogers [1968] Director

Home Retail Group Card Services Limited
Incorporated: 2 June 2000 *Employees:* 654
Net Worth Deficit: £14,264,000 *Total Assets:* £788,092,992
Registered Office: 489-499 Avebury Boulevard, Milton Keynes, Bucks, MK9 2NW
Activities: Credit granting by non-deposit taking finance houses and other specialist consumer credit grantors
Parent: Sainsbury's Bank PLC
Officers: Donald Hamish MacLeod McNaughton, Secretary; Katherine Carlson [1973] Commercial Director; Mark Christopher Hemus [1976] Finance and Credit Risk Director

Home Retail Group Insurance Services Limited
Incorporated: 16 November 2000
Net Worth: £21,000 *Total Assets:* £29,932,000
Registered Office: 489-499 Avebury Boulevard, Milton Keynes, Bucks, MK9 2NW
Activities: Financial intermediation not elsewhere classified
Parent: Sainsbury's Bank PLC
Officers: Donald Hamish MacLeod McNaughton, Secretary; Katherine Carlson [1973] Commercial Director; Mark Christopher Hemus [1976] Finance and Credit Risk Director

Home Retail Group Limited
Incorporated: 30 June 2006
Previous: Home Retail Group PLC
Net Worth: £748,099,968 *Total Assets:* £2,453,499,904
Registered Office: 489-499 Avebury Boulevard, Milton Keynes, Bucks, MK9 2NW
Activities: Activities of head offices
Parent: Sainsbury's Intermediate Holdings Limited
Officers: Timothy Fallowfield, Secretary; Claire Louise Catlin [1980] Director; John Terence Rogers [1968] Director

Homecome Limited
Incorporated: 31 March 2004 *Employees:* 6
Net Worth: £10,415,352 *Total Assets:* £14,372,641
Registered Office: 57 Blackbird Road, Leicester, LE4 0AR
Activities: Other letting and operating of own or leased real estate
Officers: Michael John Forrester, Secretary; Lisa Jacqueline Barker [1962] Director/MD of Housing Consultancy; David John Brazier [1953] Director; Councillor Andrew Ian Connelly [1960] Director/Postman; Jafferhusein Akberali Kapasi [1950] Director/Businessman; Patricia McCabe [1956] Managing Director; Richard Edwin Moore [1945] Director/Retired

Homecrest Bidco Limited
Incorporated: 4 April 2014 *Employees:* 4
Net Worth: £12,156,000 *Total Assets:* £76,408,000
Registered Office: Azalea Close, Clover Nook Industrial Park, Somercotes, Derbys, DE55 4QX
Activities: Activities of distribution holding companies
Parent: Homecrest Midco Limited
Officers: Mark Davis [1972] Legal Director; Jay Lee Edwards [1978] Director; Heath Brian Zarin [1975] Director/Finance [American]

Homecrest Midco Limited
Incorporated: 4 April 2014 *Employees:* 4
Net Worth: £15,971,000 *Total Assets:* £49,713,000
Registered Office: Azalea Close, Clover Nook Industrial Park, Somercotes, Derbys, DE55 4QX
Activities: Activities of distribution holding companies
Parent: NFT Distribution Holdings Limited
Officers: Mark Davis [1972] Legal Director; Jay Lee Edwards [1978] Director; Heath Brian Zarin [1975] Director/Finance [American]

P.D. Hook (Breeders) Limited
Incorporated: 20 September 1993 *Employees:* 446
Net Worth: £10,057,000 *Total Assets:* £44,580,000
Registered Office: PD Hook (Breeders) Ltd, Cote, Bampton, Oxon, OX18 2EG
Activities: Raising of poultry
Officers: Nigel Leslie Boyle, Secretary/Director; Claire Joanna Beavis [1987] Director; Nigel Leslie Boyle [1956] Director/Accountant; Fiona Anne Hook [1960] Director; James William Hook [1956] Director/Farmer; Patrick Mark Hook [1986] Director; Adrian Rushby [1968] Director; Mark Roy Wannell [1965] Director/Accountant

P. D. Hook (Group) Limited
Incorporated: 3 August 2004 *Employees:* 1,130
Net Worth: £111,363,000 *Total Assets:* £200,842,000
Registered Office: Cote, Bampton, Oxon, OX18 2EG
Activities: Activities of head offices
Major Shareholder: James William Hook
Officers: Mark Roy Wannell, Secretary; Fiona Anne Hook [1960] Director; James William Hook [1956] Director/Farmer; Patrick Mark Hook [1986] Director/Production Manager; Mark Roy Wannell [1965] Director/Accountant

P.D.Hook (Hatcheries) Limited
Incorporated: 21 October 1963 *Employees:* 337
Net Worth: £21,504,000 *Total Assets:* £51,056,000
Registered Office: PD Hook (Hatcheries) Ltd, Cote, Bampton, Oxon, OX18 2EG
Activities: Raising of poultry
Officers: Nigel Leslie Boyle, Secretary/Director; Claire Joanna Beavis [1987] Director; Nigel Leslie Boyle [1956] Director/Accountant; Fiona Anne Hook [1960] Director; James William Hook [1956] Director/Farmer; Patrick Mark Hook [1986] Director; Adrian Rushby [1968] Director; Mark Roy Wannell [1965] Director/Accountant

P.D. Hook (Rearing) Limited
Incorporated: 22 October 1999 *Employees:* 83
Net Worth: £9,076,000 *Total Assets:* £15,575,000
Registered Office: P D Hook (Hatcheries) Ltd, Cote, Bampton, Oxon, OX18 2EG
Activities: Raising of poultry
Officers: Nigel Leslie Boyle, Secretary; Claire Joanna Beavis [1987] Director; Nigel Leslie Boyle [1956] Director/Accountant; Fiona Anne Hook [1960] Director; James William Hook [1956] Director/Farmer; Patrick Mark Hook [1986] Director; Adrian Rushby [1968] Director; Mark Roy Wannell [1965] Director/Accountant

Hook 2 Sisters Limited
Incorporated: 17 October 2006 *Employees:* 998
Net Worth: £4,754,000 *Total Assets:* £130,400,000
Registered Office: Cote, Bampton, Oxon, OX18 2EG
Activities: Raising of poultry
Officers: Mark Roy Wannell, Secretary; Ranjit Singh Boparan [1966] Director; James William Hook [1956] Director/Farmer; Craig Ashley Tomkinson [1982] Director; Mark Roy Wannell [1965] Director/Accountant

Hook Norton Brewery Company,Limited (The)
Incorporated: 12 July 1900 *Employees:* 60
Net Worth: £11,771,134 *Total Assets:* £15,070,130
Registered Office: The Brewery, Hook Norton, Banbury, Oxon, OX15 5NY
Activities: Manufacture of beer
Shareholder: Fiona Elisabeth Williams
Officers: David Nigel Vardon Churton, Secretary; David Nigel Vardon Churton [1949] Director; James William Clarke [1971] Managing Director; Dr Jonathan David Paveley [1963] Director; Charles Henry Williams [1957] Director/Estate Owner; Fiona Elisabeth Williams [1954] Director/Housewife

Hopton Investment Holdings Limited
Incorporated: 1 February 2017
Net Worth: £13,079,987 *Total Assets:* £13,080,000
Registered Office: The Mills, Canal Street, Derby, DE1 2RJ
Activities: Retail sale of mobile telephones
Shareholders: Mark Timothy Hopton; Debra Jane Hopton
Officers: Debra Jane Hopton, Secretary; Mark Timothy Hopton [1977] Director

Hopton Retail Holdings Limited
Incorporated: 15 February 2006
Net Worth: £11,276,032 *Total Assets:* £12,335,257
Registered Office: The Mills, Canal Street, Derby, DE1 2RJ
Activities: Retail sale of mobile telephones
Parent: Hopton Trading Holdings Limited
Officers: Debra Jane Hopton, Secretary; Mark Timothy Hopton [1977] Director/Sales Person

T.P. Hopwell (Holdings) Limited
Incorporated: 10 November 1976 *Employees:* 283
Net Worth: £6,721,582 *Total Assets:* £16,926,856
Registered Office: Glaisdale Drive, Bilborough, Nottingham, NG8 4LU
Activities: Other service activities n.e.c.
Major Shareholder: Lilian Hopwell
Officers: Martin Patrick Field, Secretary; Martin Patrick Field [1964] Director/Chartered Accountant; Lilian Hopwell [1942] Director/Secretary; Tristan Curtis Hopwell [1970] Director/Executive

Hopwells Ltd
Incorporated: 8 December 1978 *Employees:* 283
Net Worth: £11,805,034 *Total Assets:* £16,926,354
Registered Office: Glaisdale Drive, Bilborough, Nottingham, NG8 4LU
Activities: Other food services
Officers: Martin Patrick Field, Secretary; Martin Patrick Field [1964] Director/Chartered Accountant; Ashley Travis Hopwell [1977] Commercial Director; Lilian Hopwell [1942] Director/Secretary; Tristan Curtis Hopwell [1970] Managing Director; Ian Fraser Merrilees [1970] Technical Director; Kevin Peck [1962] Operations Director

Horberg & Co Holdings Ltd
Incorporated: 21 August 2014 *Employees:* 49
Net Worth Deficit: £386,620 *Total Assets:* £14,461,032
Registered Office: c/o Navigator MSL Limited, Mill Road, Sharnbrook, Beds, MK44 1NP
Activities: Activities of head offices
Shareholders: Bengt Horberg; Cecelia Horberg
Officers: Andrew Smith, Secretary; Bengt Horberg [1952] Director [Swedish]; Cecilia Horberg [1954] Director [Swedish]

Horbury Building Systems Limited
Incorporated: 14 December 1992 *Employees:* 141
Net Worth: £2,256,830 *Total Assets:* £16,810,012
Registered Office: South Grove House, South Grove, Rotherham, S Yorks, S60 2AF
Activities: Development of building projects
Parent: Horbury Group Limited
Officers: Gavin Louis Leverett, Secretary; Gavin Louis Leverett [1970] Finance Director; Ian Syddall [1963] Contracts Director; David Lee Taylor [1974] Director; David Williams [1950] Director/Consultant; Trevor John Wragg [1965] Managing Director

Horbury Group Limited
Incorporated: 18 April 2007 *Employees:* 299
Net Worth: £4,326,286 *Total Assets:* £30,313,430
Registered Office: South Grove House, South Grove, Rotherham, S Yorks, S60 2AF
Activities: Activities of head offices
Major Shareholder: Trevor John Wragg
Officers: Gavin Louis Leverett, Secretary; Gavin Louis Leverett [1970] Finance Director; Mark Thomas Rigby [1963] Director/Chartered Accountant; David Williams [1950] Director/Chairman; Trevor John Wragg [1965] Managing Director

Horiba Mira Limited
Incorporated: 5 June 2015 *Employees:* 443
Net Worth: £21,116,000 *Total Assets:* £99,073,000
Registered Office: Watling Street, Nuneaton, Warwicks, CV10 0TU
Activities: Other research and experimental development on natural sciences and engineering
Parent: Horiba, Ltd
Officers: Timothy Paul Nathan, Secretary; Declan Joseph Allen [1966] Director/Business Executive; Miller Deane Crockart [1969] Director/Chief Commercial Officer; Geoffrey Maxwell Davis [1976] Director/Business Executive; Richard Charles Drake [1949] Director/Business Executive; Takeshi Fukushima [1966] Director [Japanese]; Dr George Thompson Gillespie [1963] Director/Business Executive; Takashi Nagano [1962] Director/Senior Corporate Officer [Japanese]; Timothy Paul Nathan [1969] Director/Business Executive; Masao Okawa [1966] Director [Japanese]; Juichi Saito [1958] Director/Executive Vice President [Japanese]; Robert Graeme Stewart [1975] Director/Chief Technical Officer [Irish]

Horiba UK Finance Limited
Incorporated: 9 December 2016
Net Worth: £40,340,288 *Total Assets:* £40,435,788
Registered Office: Horiba UK Ltd, Kyoto Close, Moulton Park Industrial Estate, Northampton, NN3 6FL
Activities: Financial intermediation not elsewhere classified
Parent: Horiba, Ltd
Officers: Richard Charles Drake [1949] Director/Business Executive; Takeshi Fukushima [1966] Director/Corporate Control Dept Manager [Japanese]; Takashi Nagano [1962] Director [Japanese]; Junichi Tajika [1973] Director/Deputy General Manager, Finance & Control Division [Japanese]

Horiba UK Limited
Incorporated: 11 April 1988 *Employees:* 184
Net Worth: £9,305,565 *Total Assets:* £26,332,724
Registered Office: Kyoto Close, Moulton Park Industrial Estate, Northampton, NN3 6FL
Activities: Manufacture of electronic measuring, testing etc. equipment, not for industrial process control
Officers: David John Heskins, Secretary; Richard George Carter [1977] Director; Richard Charles Drake [1949] Director; David Drewry [1958] Director; Takeshi Fukushima [1966] Director [Japanese]; Stuart Alan Knight [1968] Director; Masao Okawa [1966] Director [Japanese]; Cleveland George Wright [1958] Director

Hormann (U.K.) Limited
Incorporated: 30 July 1979 *Employees:* 137
Previous: Hormann (U.K.) Limited
Net Worth: £12,158,403 *Total Assets:* £26,285,496
Registered Office: Gee Road, Coalville, Leics, LE67 4JW
Activities: Other manufacturing n.e.c.
Officers: Paul Anthony Eadie, Secretary; Wolfgang George Vincent Gorner [1966] Director; Christoph Hormann [1967] Director [German]; Thomas Jobst Hormann [1938] Director/Engineer [German]

Horncastle Education Trust
Incorporated: 10 August 2012 *Employees:* 123
Previous: Queen Elizabeth's Grammar School Horncastle
Net Worth: £9,992,737 *Total Assets:* £11,700,372
Registered Office: Queen Elizabeth's Grammar School, West Street, Horncastle, Lincs, LN9 5AD
Activities: General secondary education
Officers: David Richard Mason Bennett [1943] Director; Ian James Birchall [1977] Director/RAF Pilot; Susan Jane Brackenbury [1947] Director/Retired; Paul Brewster [1964] Director/Client Services Manager; Joanne Casey [1977] Director/Head of Service - Children's Services; Wendy Theresa Ireland [1964] Director/Self Employed Business Consultant; Nicola Dawn Kelsey [1974] Director/Accounts & Systems Manager; Heather Payne [1962] Director/Headteacher; Andrew David Turner [1971] Director/Senior Manager; Chris James Waters [1971] Director/Operations Manager

Horsforth Holdings Limited
Incorporated: 21 November 2011 *Employees:* 356
Net Worth: £3,246,000 *Total Assets:* £26,262,000
Registered Office: LDH House, St Ives Business Park, Parsons Green, St Ives, Cambs, PE27 4AA
Activities: Other business support service activities n.e.c.
Officers: Mark Braithwaite [1978] Managing Director [British/South African]; Jonathan Philip Dyson [1964] Director; Keith Hamill [1952] Director; Ian Arthur Hendrie [1970] Director; Julian Frederick Nicholls [1951] Director

Horticultural Trades Association (The)
Incorporated: 12 August 1920 *Employees:* 47
Net Worth: £922,096 *Total Assets:* £26,633,132
Registered Office: Horticulture House, Chilton, Didcot, Oxon, OX11 0RN
Activities: Activities of business and employers membership organisations
Officers: Matthew Bent [1974] Managing Director; Boyd John Douglas-Davies [1968] Director/Chief Executive; Brian Donald Fraser [1965] Director/General Manager; Simon John Fraser [1972] Managing Director; Robert John Hewitt [1956] Director/CEO Klondyke Garden Centre; Richard Michael Pyrah [1970] Sales Director; Alexander James Shepherd [1963] Director; Hon Adam Edwin John Taylor [1975] Director; Alexandria Christine Vick [1971] Finance Director; Adam William Wigglesworth [1965] Director

Hosting Developments Limited
Incorporated: 9 August 2007 *Employees:* 148
Net Worth: £7,719,181 *Total Assets:* £21,519,916
Registered Office: A1-A46 Junction, Lincoln Road, Newark, Notts, NG24 2EA
Activities: Activities of head offices
Shareholders: Andrew Paul Craggs; Stephen Bernard Cullen
Officers: Stephen Bernard Cullen, Company Secretary; Andrew Paul Craggs [1968] Sales Director; Stephen Bernard Cullen [1963] Director/Chief Executive Officer; Myles Halley [1956] Director

Hostombe Group Limited
Incorporated: 4 January 1939 *Employees:* 80
Net Worth: £6,240,833 *Total Assets:* £12,486,340
Registered Office: Fullwood Hall, Harrison Lane, Sheffield, S10 4PA
Activities: Activities of head offices
Shareholder: Roger Eric Hostombe
Officers: Roger Eric Hostombe [1942] Director/Chairman

Hotel MK Limited
Incorporated: 30 May 2001 *Employees:* 247
Net Worth: £3,657,819 *Total Assets:* £15,429,681
Registered Office: Stadium MK, Stadium Way, Milton Keynes, Bucks, MK1 1ST
Activities: Hotels and similar accommodation
Parent: Inter MK Group Limited
Officers: Anthony Neil Richens, Secretary; Anthony Neil Richens [1989] Finance Director; Nielsen Stead [1973] Hotel Director; Mark Turner [1968] Director; Peter John Winkelman [1957] Director; Bernadette Winkleman [1958] Director

Hotels4U.Com Limited
Incorporated: 28 January 2003
Net Worth: £26,947,000 *Total Assets:* £53,600,000
Registered Office: Westpoint, Peterborough Business Park, Lynch Wood, Peterborough, Cambs, PE2 6FZ
Activities: Travel agency activities
Parent: Thomas Cook Retail Limited
Officers: Shirley Bradley, Secretary; Alan Charles Donald [1963] Director

House & Home (Lettings) Ltd
Incorporated: 4 August 2016 *Employees:* 4
Net Worth: £5,148,233 *Total Assets:* £18,888,938
Registered Office: 26 Greek Street, Stockport, Cheshire, SK3 8AB
Activities: Other letting and operating of own or leased real estate
Shareholders: Alasdair MacDonald; Amanda MacDonald
Officers: Alasdair MacDonald [1967] Director; Amanda MacDonald [1972] Director

Hoval Limited
Incorporated: 31 October 1957 *Employees:* 92
Net Worth: £1,241,925 *Total Assets:* £11,691,493
Registered Office: Northgate, Newark, Notts, NG24 1JN
Activities: Manufacture of central heating radiators and boilers
Officers: Ian David Dagley [1960] Director/Sales Marketing; Fabian Frick [1969] Director/Management [Liechtensteiner]; Peter Frick [1941] Engineer/Director [Liechtensteiner]; Peter Gerner [1967] Financial Director [Liechtensteiner]; Kenneth Ross Halley [1971] Director; Keith Hibberd [1955] Operations Director; Roy David Martin [1941] Engineer/Director; Anthony James Roche [1953] Director/Production Manager [Irish]; Dr Richard Martin Senti [1964] Director [Liechtensteiner]; Kevin Stones [1959] Director/Technical Manager

Howard & Hallam Limited
Incorporated: 17 February 1954 *Employees:* 2
Net Worth: £11,700,899 *Total Assets:* £11,777,446
Registered Office: Redgate, 3 London Road, Uppingham, Rutland, LE15 9TJ
Activities: Fund management activities
Major Shareholder: Richard Hallam
Officers: Elisabet Feldmann, Secretary; Elisabet Feldmann [1967] Director; Richard Hallam [1962] Director

Alan Howard (Stockport) Limited
Incorporated: 21 September 1973 *Employees:* 305
Net Worth: £8,943,895 *Total Assets:* £18,419,922
Registered Office: Section 12, Woodbank Industrial Estate, Turncroft Lane, Stockport, Cheshire, SK1 4AR
Activities: Non-specialised wholesale trade
Major Shareholder: Howard Littler
Officers: Anthony James Littler [1976] Director; Howard Littler [1944] Director/Chairman; Jonathan Mark Littler [1973] Director/Sales Manager

P.C. Howard Limited
Incorporated: 1 June 1951 *Employees:* 199
Net Worth: £7,187,709 *Total Assets:* £16,779,960
Registered Office: West Hay, Stamford Road, King's Cliffe, Peterborough, PE8 6XX
Activities: Freight transport by road
Officers: Percival William Howard, Secretary; Andrew Percival Howard [1960] Director/Chartered Accountant; Anthony Frederick Howard [1948] Director/Haulage Contractor & Farmer; Percival William Howard [1943] Director/Haulage Contractor & Farmer; Peter Charles Howard [1960] Director

Howes Percival LLP
Incorporated: 28 September 2006 *Employees:* 221
Net Worth: £7,660,330 *Total Assets:* £12,514,848
Registered Office: Nene House, 4 Rushmills, Northampton, NN4 7YB
Officers: Paula Kim Bailey [1974] Member; Geraint Keith Davies [1967] Member; Jonathan Ayton Greenhalgh [1971] Member; Tessa Jane Haskey [1972] Member; Jahid Ahmed Ali [1978] LLP Member; Daniel William Banton [1982] LLP Member; Steven William Beach [1960] LLP Member; Oliver Chitty Brookshaw [1956] LLP Member; Stuart Hugh Burns [1980] LLP Member; Satnam Kaur Chayra [1978] LLP Member; Robert Peter Colman [1976] LLP Member; Morris Patrick Corker-Peacock [1970] LLP Member; Generald Mark Couldrake [1960] LLP Member; Mark Phillip Davies [1972] LLP Member; Simon David de Maid [1976] LLP Member; Justine Samantha Flack [1968] LLP Member; Michael Anthony Green [1973] LLP Member; Michaela Jane Henson [1970] LLP Member; Nathan Jon Horton [1970] LLP Member; James Edward Howarth [1975] LLP Member; Tracey Caroline Hughes [1963] LLP Member; Paul David Hunt [1963] LLP Member; Graham Stuart Irons [1970] LLP Member; Nicholas Graham James [1969] LLP Member; Jamie Paul Kidd [1974] LLP Member; Alison Marie Kirby [1973] LLP Member; Thomas Lawrence [1981] LLP Member; Edward Paul Lee [1962] LLP Member; Lucy Ellen Lord [1976] LLP Member; Stuart Peter Maggs [1972] LLP Member; Lisa Marie Mantle [1971] LLP Member; Christopher Andrew May [1981] LLP Member; Carl Mifflin [1979] LLP Member; Alan Millband [1958] LLP Member; Simon James Murphy [1972] LLP Member; Joanna Louise Nicholls [1972] LLP Member; Deborah Androulla Nigh [1963] LLP Member; Matthew Bryan Potter [1970] LLP Member; Catherine Susanne Judith Scott [1971] LLP Member; William Brian Shirley [1969] LLP Member; Haydon Anthony Charles Simmonds [1981] LLP Member; Katharine Claire Summers [1967] LLP Member; Matthew Richard Talbot [1968] LLP Member; Amy Jane Walpole [1979] LLP Member; Paul James Wootton [1968] LLP Member; Roger Jonathan Francis Wortley [1954] LLP Member

Howmet Limited
Incorporated: 4 November 1991 *Employees:* 534
Net Worth: £43,994,000 *Total Assets:* £79,297,000
Registered Office: 26a Atlas Way, Sheffield, S4 7QQ
Activities: Casting of other non-ferrous metals
Parent: Arconic Extruded Products (UK) Limited
Officers: Petra Papinniemi-Ainger, Secretary; Lluis Maria Fargas Mas [1966] Director/Lawyer [Spanish]; Boyd Mueller [1959] Director/Vice President Technology & Alloy [American]; Patrick Michael Talbot [1975] Director/Plant Manager; Stephen Matthew Woods [1972] Director/Chartered Accountant

HPC Healthline UK Limited
Incorporated: 14 March 1986 *Employees:* 132
Net Worth: £11,392,000 *Total Assets:* £36,579,000
Registered Office: Polyco Healthline, South Fen Road, Bourne, Lincs, PE10 0DN
Activities: Wholesale of clothing and footwear
Parent: Polyco Healthline Limited
Officers: Jason Matthew Prichard, Secretary; Neil Antony Wilson, Secretary; David Greenwood [1955] Director; Jason Matthew Prichard [1969] Director; Neil Antony Wilson [1976] Director

HR Wallingford Group Limited
Incorporated: 15 March 1982 *Employees:* 265
Net Worth: £30,328,000 *Total Assets:* £42,992,000
Registered Office: Howbery Park, Wallingford, Oxon, OX10 8BA
Activities: Other research and experimental development on natural sciences and engineering
Officers: Nicole Ann Jane Norris, Secretary; Andrew James Brown [1964] Director; Geoffrey Howard French [1947] Director/Chartered Civil Engineer; Graham David Leeming [1968] Finance Director; Keith Andrew Powell [1958] Director/Civil Engineer; David William Rooke [1955] Director/Chartered Engineer; Dr Susan Margaret Sharland [1961] Director/Chief Executive; Dr Bruce Nicholas Tomlinson [1965] Director/Chief Executive; Peter Richard Worrall [1961] Director/Civil Servant

HR Wallingford Limited
Incorporated: 26 November 1990 *Employees:* 243
Net Worth: £31,231,000 *Total Assets:* £43,633,000
Registered Office: Howbery Park, Wallingford, Oxon, OX10 8BA
Activities: Other research and experimental development on natural sciences and engineering
Parent: HR Wallingford Group Ltd
Officers: Nicole Ann Jane Norris, Secretary; Andrew James Brown [1964] Director; Graham David Leeming [1968] Finance Director; Dr Keith Andrew Powell [1958] Director; Dr Bruce Nicholas Tomlinson [1965] Director/Chief Executive

HRVS Group Limited
Incorporated: 6 August 1997 *Employees:* 187
Previous: Heage Road Vehicle Services Limited
Net Worth: £2,729,528 *Total Assets:* £12,346,950
Registered Office: Ripley Road, Sawmills, Belper, Derbys, DE56 2JR
Activities: Maintenance and repair of motor vehicles
Parent: The Lockwood Group Limited
Officers: Deborah Louise King [1966] Director; Robert Ian Lockwood [1968] Managing Director; Keith Leslie Sims [1961] Group Service Director

HS 524 Limited
Incorporated: 10 January 2011 *Employees:* 2
Net Worth: £76,200,000 *Total Assets:* £110,800,000
Registered Office: The Triangle, Stanton Harcourt Industrial Estate, Stanton Harcourt, Witney, Oxon, OX29 5UT
Activities: Non-trading company
Parent: Karen Millen Group Limited
Officers: Beth Janet Butterwick [1965] Director; Emily Sarah Tate [1974] Director

HSH Cold Stores Limited
Incorporated: 21 August 2003 *Employees:* 87
Net Worth: £2,913,980 *Total Assets:* £11,514,369
Registered Office: Birchin Way, Grimsby, N E Lincs, DN31 2SG
Activities: Operation of warehousing and storage facilities for land transport activities
Officers: Christine Anita Howard, Secretary; Anthony John Howard [1972] Director/Cold Store Manager; Christine Anita Howard [1942] Director; Lewis Howard [2000] Director

HTC Wolffkran Limited
Incorporated: 5 March 2015 *Employees:* 373
Net Worth: £12,982,000 *Total Assets:* £33,645,000
Registered Office: HTC Wolffkran Limited, Grange Mill Lane, Kimberworth, Sheffield, S9 1HW
Activities: Other specialised construction activities n.e.c.
Parent: Wolffkran Holdings AG
Officers: Laurent Baechler [1974] Director/Group CFO [Swiss]; Richard John Coughtrey [1975] Financial Director; Julian Charles Dyer [1966] Sales Director; David John Holder [1965] Director General Manager; Duncan Salt [1965] Director/Chief Operating Officer; Peter Schiefer [1967] Director/Engineer [German]

Huber + Suhner (UK) Limited
Incorporated: 30 March 1967 *Employees:* 129
Net Worth: £5,832,000 *Total Assets:* £15,944,000
Registered Office: Telford Road, Bicester, Oxon, OX26 4LA
Activities: Manufacture of electronic components
Parent: Huber & Suhner AG
Officers: Lars Kolbjerg, Secretary; Drew Nixon [1965] Director/COO Global Sales [American]; Urs Ryffel [1967] Director/C.E.O [Swiss]; Dr Ivo Wechsler [1969] Director/Chief Financial Officer [Swiss]

Hudson Energy Supply UK Limited
Incorporated: 11 January 2011 *Employees:* 124
Net Worth: £14,186,000 *Total Assets:* £170,670,000
Registered Office: Third Floor, Elder House, 586-592 Elder Gate, Milton Keynes, Bucks, MK9 1LR
Activities: Trade of electricity
Parent: Hudson Energy Holdings UK Limited
Officers: Claudia Mason, Secretary; James Brown [1963] Director [American]; Patrick McCullough [1972] Director [American]; James Pickren [1966] Director [American]

P. Hughes Construction Limited
Incorporated: 11 November 1987 *Employees:* 167
Net Worth: £26,823,172 *Total Assets:* £30,966,272
Registered Office: 21 Main Road, Underwood, Notts, NG16 5GP
Activities: Construction of other civil engineering projects n.e.c.
Shareholders: Philip Hughes; John Patrick Hughes
Officers: Philip Hughes, Secretary; Philip Hughes [1961] Director

Hughes Network Systems Limited
Incorporated: 4 January 2005 *Employees:* 60
Net Worth: £6,700,000 *Total Assets:* £26,437,000
Registered Office: Hughes House, Rockingham Drive, Linford Wood, Milton Keynes, Bucks, MK14 6PD
Activities: Satellite telecommunications activities
Parent: Echostar Corporation
Officers: Dr Dean Alfred Manson, Secretary/Vice President & General Counsel [American]; Christopher David Britton [1958] Director/Company President; Dr Dean Alfred Manson [1967] Director/Vice President & General Counsel [American]

Hull Holdings Limited
Incorporated: 8 September 2016
Net Worth: £1,763 *Total Assets:* £16,944,852
Registered Office: 27-29 Lumley Avenue, Skegness, Lincs, PE25 2AT
Activities: Dormant company
Parent: Brayford Hotels Holdings Limited
Officers: Leigh Morris Hall [1969] Director; Dean Anthony Wann [1971] Director

Human Appeal
Incorporated: 3 June 2013 *Employees:* 104
Previous: Human Appeal International
Net Worth: £6,421,506 *Total Assets:* £10,875,143
Registered Office: 1 Cheadle Point, Carrs Road, Cheadle, Cheshire, SK8 2BL
Activities: Other human health activities
Officers: Omar Mashjari [1992] Director/Lecturer; Dr Hussein Mostafa Nagi [1958] Director [Irish]; Kamil Zakariyya Omoteso [1970] Director/Head of The School of Economics; Kasim Iqbal Hussain Randeree [1971] Director/Lecturer; Ihab Mohammad Hamdi Saad [1962] Director/Professor [American]; Mohamad Hamed Yousef [1958] Director; Imad Zahidah [1959] Director

Humphris (Banbury) Limited
Incorporated: 25 October 1961 *Employees:* 2
Net Worth: £21,230,014 *Total Assets:* £23,529,512
Registered Office: 30 Albert Street, Banbury, Oxon, OX16 5DG
Activities: Other letting and operating of own or leased real estate
Officers: Christopher Jonathan Humphris [1956] Funeral Director; Martin Alan Humphris [1957] Funeral Director; Maurice Jason Humphris [1935] Director/Retired

Hundred Percent Holdings Limited
Incorporated: 24 March 2017 *Employees:* 78
Net Worth: £4,346,472 *Total Assets:* £11,721,518
Registered Office: Prodrive Headquarters, Chalker Way, Banbury, Oxon, OX16 4XD
Activities: Hotels and similar accommodation
Shareholders: Richards Family Holdings Limited; David Pender Richards
Officers: Robert Eden, Secretary; Mr David Pender Richards [1952] Director/Motorsport Consultant; Karen Richards [1953] Director

Hungerhill Academy Trust
Incorporated: 7 February 2012 *Employees:* 178
Net Worth: £13,663,979 *Total Assets:* £16,691,005
Registered Office: Hungerhill School, Hungerhill Lane, Edenthorpe, Doncaster, S Yorks, DN3 2JY
Activities: General secondary education
Officers: Rachel Wilcox, Secretary; Nicholas Burne [1949] Director/Retired; Nicola Crowder [1983] Director/Teacher; Hannah Maria D'Rozario [1989] Director/Teacher; Daniel Thomas Fell [1981] Director/Chief Executive Officer; Kelvin Fitton [1968] Director/Chartered Accountant; Stephen Andrew France [1975] Director/Self Employed; Teresa Kathleen Ladley [1967] Director/School Business Manager; Oliver Marriott [1994] Director/Assistant ICT Technician; David Campbell Munro [1979] Director/Systems and Technology Manager; Dr Stephen John Newman [1956] Director/Lecturer; George William Peacock [1953] Director/Retired; Neil Purvis [1976] Director/Audit Manager; Helen Jean Redford-Hernandez [1964] Director/Headteacher; Andrea Robinson [1961] Director/Local Authority Officer; Paul Martin Senior [1956] Director; Philip Wedell [1956] Director/Kennels Proprietor

Hunt Group Limited
Incorporated: 15 October 1982 *Employees:* 154
Net Worth: £18,475,352 *Total Assets:* £31,947,550
Registered Office: 26-30 Midland Road, Scunthorpe, N Lincs, DN16 1DQ
Activities: Activities of head offices
Major Shareholder: Derrick Thomas Hunt
Officers: Gloria Patricia Hunt, Secretary; Brian David Hostad [1967] Finance Director; Darren Robert Hunt [1967] Surfacing Director; Derrick Thomas Hunt [1948] Director/Chairman; Gloria Patricia Hunt [1949] Director/Company Secretary; Shaun Antony Hunt [1970] Director/Vice Chairman

Hunter Douglas (UK) Limited
Incorporated: 30 May 1969 *Employees:* 417
Net Worth: £24,022,000 *Total Assets:* £445,752,000
Registered Office: c/o Hunter Douglas Limited, Mersey Industrial Estate, Battersea Road, Heaton Mersey, Stockport, Cheshire, SK4 3EQ
Activities: Other manufacturing n.e.c.
Officers: Robert Henry George Durston, Secretary; Harold Clement Fuller [1933] Director/Accountant; Adrianus Kuiper [1960] Director [Dutch]; Russell Mark Malley [1960] Managing Director; Leendert Reijtenbagh [1942] Financial Director [Dutch]

Hunter Estates Limited
Incorporated: 8 June 1932
Net Worth: £7,037,000 *Total Assets:* £10,081,000
Registered Office: Lodge Way House, Lodge Way, Harlestone Road, Northampton, NN5 7UG
Activities: Management of real estate on a fee or contract basis
Parent: Wickes Limited
Officers: John Peter Carter [1961] Director; Alan Richard Williams [1969] Director/Accountant

Huntercombe (BIR) Limited
Incorporated: 20 May 2005 *Employees:* 4
Previous: FSHC Properties (BIR) Limited
Net Worth: £8,174,000 *Total Assets:* £28,292,000
Registered Office: Norcliffe House, Station Road, Wilmslow, Cheshire, SK9 1BU
Activities: Other human health activities
Parent: Huntercombe (SP) Limited
Officers: Abigail Mattison, Secretary; Valerie Louise Michie [1975] Director; Mark James Williamson [1973] Director

Huntercombe (No 12) Limited
Incorporated: 7 June 2006 *Employees:* 288
Previous: Four Seasons (No 12) Limited
Net Worth: £22,141,000 *Total Assets:* £23,360,000
Registered Office: Norcliffe House, Station Road, Wilmslow, Cheshire, SK9 1BU
Activities: Other human health activities
Parent: The Huntercombe Group Limited
Officers: Abigail Mattison, Secretary; Valerie Louise Michie [1975] Director; Mark James Williamson [1973] Director

Huntercombe (SP) Limited
Incorporated: 20 May 2005 *Employees:* 5
Previous: FSHC (SP) Limited
Net Worth Deficit: £37,752,000 *Total Assets:* £49,660,000
Registered Office: Norcliffe House, Station Road, Wilmslow, Cheshire, SK9 1BU
Activities: Other human health activities
Parent: The Huntercombe Group Limited
Officers: Abigail Mattison, Secretary; Valerie Louise Michie [1975] Director; Mark James Williamson [1973] Director

Huntercombe Properties (Frenchay) Limited
Incorporated: 12 January 2000 *Employees:* 512
Previous: Four Seasons Health Care Properties (Frenchay) Limited
Net Worth: £17,891,000 *Total Assets:* £19,834,000
Registered Office: Norcliffe House, Station Road, Wilmslow, Cheshire, SK9 1BU
Activities: Other human health activities
Parent: Huntercombe (No 12) Limited
Officers: Abigail Mattison, Secretary; Valerie Louise Michie [1975] Director; Mark James Williamson [1973] Director

Huntson Holdings Limited
Incorporated: 13 February 1989 *Employees:* 245
Previous: Huntson Holdings PLC
Net Worth: £9,791,342 *Total Assets:* £31,296,802
Registered Office: Brimington Road North, Chesterfield, Derbys, S41 9AJ
Activities: Sale of new cars and light motor vehicles
Parent: BRMCO (213) Limited
Officers: Shaun Foweather [1963] Director; Richard Stephen Teatum [1957] Director; Nigel Peter Wood [1964] Director/Company Accountant

John Hurt Estates (UK) Limited
Incorporated: 6 May 2005
Previous: Bulroc Holdings Limited
Net Worth: £9,637,425 *Total Assets:* £10,308,607
Registered Office: 760a Chatsworth Road, Chesterfield, Derbys, S40 3PN
Activities: Other letting and operating of own or leased real estate
Major Shareholder: John Arthur Hurt
Officers: John Arthur Hurt, Secretary/Director; John Arthur Hurt [1936] Director; Susan Hurt [1954] Director

Hutchinson Group Limited
Incorporated: 3 February 2003 *Employees:* 442
Net Worth: £80,591,000 *Total Assets:* £114,041,000
Registered Office: Hutchinson Group Limited, Weasenham Lane, Wisbech, Cambs, PE13 2RN
Activities: Support activities for crop production
Shareholders: David Anthony Hutchinson; Michael Leslie Hutchinson
Officers: David Anthony Hutchinson, Secretary/Director; David Anthony Hutchinson [1962] Director; Jean Mary Hutchinson [1924] Director; Melanie Jane Hutchinson [1961] Director; Michael Leslie Hutchinson [1964] Director

H.L. Hutchinson Limited
Incorporated: 15 December 1947 *Employees:* 395
Net Worth: £60,818,000 *Total Assets:* £97,800,000
Registered Office: Hutchinsons, Weasenham Lane, Wisbech, Cambs, PE13 2RN
Activities: Support activities for crop production
Parent: Hutchinson Group Limited
Officers: Richard Keith Johnson, Secretary; David Howell Crossman [1962] Director; John Robert Cawdron Harris [1947] Director; David Anthony Hutchinson [1962] Director/Chartered Accountant; Michael Leslie Hutchinson [1964] Director; Richard Keith Johnson [1966] Finance Director; Andrew McShane [1963] Managing Director; Andrew Richard Orme [1963] Director

Huttons Buildings Limited
Incorporated: 2 December 2014
Net Worth: £6,099,000 *Total Assets:* £11,709,000
Registered Office: 14 Fitzwilliam Street, Sheffield, S1 4JL
Activities: Other letting and operating of own or leased real estate
Parent: Devonshire Green (Broomgrove Road) Limited
Officers: Ewan Gairn Barclay Ross, Secretary; Brendan Elwood [1943] Director; Martin Patrick Elwood [1968] Director/Property Investment and Developer; Dale Lee Fixter [1967] Director/Chartered Surveyor

Huxlow Science College
Incorporated: 8 March 2012 *Employees:* 121
Net Worth: £7,577,876 *Total Assets:* £9,107,446
Registered Office: Huxlow Science College, Finedon Road, Irthlingborough, Wellingborough, Northants, NN9 5TY
Activities: General secondary education
Officers: Heather Louise Avey, Secretary; Robert John Barron [1942] Director; Emma Davies [1993] Director/Teacher; Andrew Dickerson [1982] Director/Sainsbury's Manager; Michael Fargher [1967] Director/Civil Servant; Stephen William Gordon [1965] Director/Headteacher; Peter John Kelby [1954] Director/Management Consultancy; David John McVean [1965] Director/Civil Servant; Gordon Michael Perkins [1970] Director/IT; Tracey Louise Walton [1966] Director/Self Employed; Stephen Ward [1945] Director/Electrical Engineer

Hyde Aero Products Limited
Incorporated: 16 December 1991 *Employees:* 356
Net Worth: £34,766,696 *Total Assets:* £58,527,352
Registered Office: Stamford House, 185 Stamford Street, Stalybridge, Cheshire, SK15 1QZ
Activities: Other engineering activities
Officers: Mark Vernon Haslam, Secretary; David Vincent Cooper [1950] Director; Michael Ford [1945] Director/Accountant; Darrin John Grant [1966] Director; Anthony Brendan Hammond [1970] Director/Engineer; Mark Vernon Haslam [1968] Director; Paul Mellor [1973] Director/Engineer; Malcolm O'Connor [1965] Director/Accountant; Matthew Smallman [1971] Director/Accountant; Steve Turner [1966] Director/Engineer

Hyde Details Limited
Incorporated: 8 October 1991 *Employees:* 59
Net Worth: £9,309,322 *Total Assets:* £12,789,330
Registered Office: Stamford House, 185 Stamford Street, Stalybridge, Cheshire, SK15 1QZ
Activities: Other engineering activities
Officers: Mark Vernon Haslam, Secretary; Steven James Brown [1987] Director; David Vincent Cooper [1950] Director; Michael Ford [1945] Director/Accountant; Andrew Harding [1971] Director; Mark Vernon Haslam [1968] Director; Malcolm Oconnor [1965] Director

Hyde Group Holdings Limited
Incorporated: 13 March 2000 *Employees:* 730
Net Worth: £83,950,024 *Total Assets:* £97,748,376
Registered Office: Stamford House, 185 Stamford Street, Stalybridge, Cheshire, SK15 1QZ
Activities: Accounting and auditing activities
Officers: Mark Vernon Haslam, Secretary; David Vincent Cooper [1950] Director/Engineer; Michael Ford [1945] Director/Accountant; Darrin John Grant [1966] Director; Malcolm O'Connor [1965] Director/Engineer

Hyde Group Limited
Incorporated: 21 October 1981 *Employees:* 26
Net Worth: £13,367,793 *Total Assets:* £26,103,618
Registered Office: Stamford House, 185 Stamford Street, Stalybridge, Cheshire, SK15 1QZ
Activities: Other engineering activities
Officers: Mark Vernon Haslam, Secretary; Graham Atkinson [1965] Director; Philip Beard [1965] Director; David Vincent Cooper [1950] Director; Paul Cox [1978] Director/Engineer; Michael Ford [1945] Director/Accountant; Mark Vernon Haslam [1968] Director; Michael Lynch [1966] Director; Malcolm Oconnor [1965] Director

Hyde Group Tooling Limited
Incorporated: 14 August 2013 *Employees:* 31
Net Worth: £14,796,509 *Total Assets:* £30,044,060
Registered Office: Stamford House, 185 Stamford Street, Stalybridge, Cheshire, SK15 1QZ
Activities: Machining
Officers: Mark Vernon Haslam, Secretary; Michael Ford [1945] Director; Mark Vernon Haslam [1968] Director; Malcolm O'Connor [1965] Director

Hyde Industrial Holdings Limited
Incorporated: 3 April 1974 *Employees:* 785
Net Worth: £121,153,944 *Total Assets:* £145,986,624
Registered Office: Stamford House, 185 Stamford Street, Stalybridge, Cheshire, SK15 1QZ
Activities: Activities of financial services holding companies
Officers: Mark Vernon Haslam, Secretary; Michael Ford [1945] Director/Accountant; Gary John Grant [1945] Director

Hyde Investments Limited
Incorporated: 18 September 1984 *Employees:* 1
Net Worth: £19,866,840 *Total Assets:* £21,241,024
Registered Office: Stamford House, 185 Stamford Street, Stalybridge, Cheshire, SK15 1QZ
Activities: Buying and selling of own real estate
Officers: Mark Vernon Haslam, Secretary; Michael Ford [1945] Director/Accountant

Hydrainer Pump Hire Limited
Incorporated: 14 October 1980 *Employees:* 80
Net Worth: £5,675,122 *Total Assets:* £15,295,568
Registered Office: Norwood Industrial Estate, Rotherham Close, Killamarsh, Sheffield, S21 2JU
Activities: Renting and leasing of other machinery, equipment and tangible goods n.e.c.
Parent: Hydrainer Holdings Limited
Officers: Louise Marion Patricia MacDonald, Secretary; Jeffrey Allan Barden [1944] Director/Chairman; Angus Donald Mackintosh Macdonald [1939] Director/Banker

Hydro Extrusion UK Ltd
Incorporated: 11 September 1969 *Employees:* 555
Previous: Sapa Profiles UK Limited
Net Worth: £104,906,000 *Total Assets:* £133,599,000
Registered Office: Unit 1 Sawpit Lane, Tibshelf, Alfreton, Derbys, DE55 5NH
Activities: Aluminium production
Parent: Sapa Aluminium Holdings UK Limited
Officers: Roger Colin Ablett, Secretary; Roger Colin Ablett [1970] Finance Director; Paulo Miguel Cardoso Generaldes Paiagua [1970] Managing Director [Portuguese]; David James Williams [1978] Director/Regional Controller East

Hyperama PLC
Incorporated: 26 November 1991 *Employees:* 337
Net Worth: £12,792,000 *Total Assets:* £36,500,000
Registered Office: Hyperama Buildings, Bull Close Road, Nottingham, NG7 2UT
Activities: Non-specialised wholesale of food, beverages and tobacco
Major Shareholder: Markham Singh Johal
Officers: Sharan Kaur, Secretary; Peter Robert Fairley [1968] Finance Director; Markhan Singh Johal [1951] Director/Wholesaler; Marcus Singh [1979] Director

I & A Restaurants Ltd
Incorporated: 1 February 2000 *Employees:* 862
Net Worth: £704,799 *Total Assets:* £10,660,340
Registered Office: 34 The Parade, Leamington Spa, Warwicks, CV32 4DN
Activities: Unlicenced restaurants and cafes
Major Shareholder: Ismail Anilmis
Officers: Ann-Marie Anilmis, Secretary; Ann-Marie Anilmis [1959] Director; Ismail Anilmis [1958] Director

I Go 4 Ltd.
Incorporated: 5 April 2004 *Employees:* 252
Net Worth Deficit: £5,226,103 *Total Assets:* £21,012,030
Registered Office: IGO4 House, Staniland Way, Peterborough, Cambs, PE4 6JT
Activities: Activities of insurance agents and brokers
Officers: Geoffrey Cornelis Baars [1965] Director [Australian]; Mark Edwin Holmes Bennett [1975] Director; David Nicholas Burns [1960] Director; Christopher Felix Boyce Mays [1962] Director; Matthew Paul Munro [1973] Managing Director; Christian Charles Plumer [1966] Director/Chief Financial Officer; Philip Douglas Burgoyne Zeidler [1968] Director/Chairman

I.G. Industries Holdings Limited
Incorporated: 15 November 2000 *Employees:* 115
Net Worth: £20,655,764 *Total Assets:* £35,140,952
Registered Office: The Flarepath, Elsham Wold, Brigg, N Lincs, DN20 0SP
Activities: Activities of head offices
Officers: Kevan Lari, Secretary; Ahmad Lari [1960] Director [German]; Hossein Lari [1931] Director [British/Iranian]; Kevan Lari [1960] Director; Parvaneh Lari [1940] Director; Mahnaz Larizadeh [1942] Director

I.G. Industries Public Limited Company
Incorporated: 8 March 1988 *Employees:* 115
Net Worth: £20,201,544 *Total Assets:* £34,680,196
Registered Office: The Flarepath, Elsham Wold, Brigg, N Lincs, DN20 0SP
Activities: Manufacture of other plastic products
Parent: I.G. Industries Holdings Limited
Officers: Kevan Lari, Secretary; Ahmad Lari [1960] Director [German]; Hossein Lari [1931] Director [British/Iranian]; Kevan Lari [1960] Director; Parvaneh Lari [1940] Director; Mahnaz Larizadeh [1942] Director

The I.S. Group Limited
Incorporated: 14 May 1979 *Employees:* 73
Net Worth: £6,502,455 *Total Assets:* £10,265,530
Registered Office: Stirling House, Stirling Way, Bretton, Peterborough, Cambs, PE3 8YD
Activities: Agents involved in the sale of a variety of goods
Officers: Sandip Rajbhandari, Secretary; Nigel Richard Douthwaite [1954] Director/Consultant; Peter Vincent Lansdale [1952] Director/Florist; Mario Doroteo Larreta [1953] Managing Director; Neil Anthony Warwick [1963] Director

IB Group Ltd
Incorporated: 5 February 2016 *Employees:* 528
Net Worth: £2,180,000 *Total Assets:* £145,132,000
Registered Office: 25 Jubilee Drive, Loughborough, Leics, LE11 5TX
Activities: Other business support service activities n.e.c.
Parent: IB Topco Limited
Officers: Wayne Beedle [1970] Director; Ian Bishop [1970] Director; Stephen Edward Foster [1976] Director; Richard Sidney Rose [1956] Director/Chairman; Kevin Richard Widdrington [1979] Director

Ibstock Brick Holding Company Limited
Incorporated: 12 December 1963 *Employees:* 2
Previous: Ibstock Building Products Limited
Net Worth: £63,720,264 *Total Assets:* £185,360,672
Registered Office: Ibstock Brick Holding Company Limited, Leicester Road, Ibstock, Leics, LE67 6HS
Activities: Activities of head offices
Parent: Ibstock PLC
Officers: Robert Douglas, Secretary; Joseph Henry Hudson [1969] Director; Kevin John Sims [1961] Director/Accountant

Ibstock Brick Limited
Incorporated: 4 August 1899 *Employees:* 1,485
Net Worth: £286,918,016 *Total Assets:* £585,729,024
Registered Office: Leicester Road, Ibstock, Leics, LE67 6HS
Activities: Manufacture of bricks, tiles and construction products, in baked clay
Parent: Ibstock PLC
Officers: Robert Douglas, Secretary; Darren Bowkett [1968] Director; Andrew Nicholas Craddock [1970] Production Director; Antony Gerard France [1960] Sales Director; Joseph Henry Hudson [1969] Director; Julie Vanessa Miller [1958] HR Director; Mark Richmond [1967] Director; Kevin John Sims [1961] Director/Accountant; Ian Alan Tichias [1969] Finance Director

Ibstock Building Products Limited
Incorporated: 26 November 2014
Net Worth: £186,452,992 *Total Assets:* £413,817,984
Registered Office: Ibstock Building Products Limited, Leicester Road, Ibstock, Leics, LE67 6HS
Activities: Activities of head offices
Parent: Ibstock PLC
Officers: Robert Douglas, Secretary; Joseph Henry Hudson [1969] Director; Kevin John Sims [1961] Director

Ibstock Community College
Incorporated: 9 July 2012 *Employees:* 128
Net Worth: £11,557,000 *Total Assets:* £13,179,000
Registered Office: Ibstock Community College, Central Avenue, Ibstock, Leics, LE67 6NE
Activities: General secondary education
Officers: Caroline Patricia Smithers, Secretary; Anne-Marie Blewitt [1962] Director/Exec Headteacher; Lee William Donaghy [1982] Director/Participant Development Lead-Teach First; Joanne Marie Fairbrother [1971] Director/Community Leisure Manager; Gary Michael Grey [1962] Director/Engineer; Michael Brian Griffiths [1954] Director/Retired; Edward George Hines [1948] Director/Retired; Dawn-Marie Horne [1971] Director/Manager; Haseeb Ilyas [1982] Director/Legal Executive (Graduate); John Turnbull Kailofer [1948] Director; Katharine Anne Meadows [1972] Director/Estates Planner; Polly Michelle Todd [1965] Director/Inspector

Ibstock Leasing Limited
Incorporated: 28 February 2005 *Employees:* 2
Net Worth: £23,921,844 *Total Assets:* £23,921,844
Registered Office: Leicester Road, Ibstock, Leics, LE67 6HS
Activities: Renting and leasing of construction and civil engineering machinery and equipment
Parent: Ibstock PLC
Officers: Robert Douglas, Secretary; Angus William Bennion [1967] Director; Kevin John Sims [1961] Director

Ibstock PLC
Incorporated: 3 September 2015 *Employees:* 2,627
Net Worth: £420,828,000 *Total Assets:* £744,843,008
Registered Office: Ibstock PLC, Leicester Road, Ibstock, Leics, LE67 6HS
Activities: Manufacture of bricks, tiles and construction products, in baked clay
Officers: Robert Douglas, Secretary; Louis Leslie Alexander Eperjesi [1962] Director [British/Canadian]; Tracey Graham [1965] Director; Claire Louise Hawkings [1969] Director; Joseph Henry Hudson [1969] Director; Jonathan Clive Nicholls [1957] Director; Justin Richard Read [1961] Director; Kevin John Sims [1961] Executive Director

Ibstock USA Limited
Incorporated: 30 January 2015 *Employees:* 2
Previous: Figgs Bidco 2 Limited
Net Worth: £109,383,792 *Total Assets:* £109,383,800
Registered Office: Leicester Road, Ibstock, Leics, LE67 6HS
Activities: Activities of head offices
Parent: Ibstock PLC
Officers: Robert Douglas, Secretary; Joseph Henry Hudson [1969] Director; Kevin John Sims [1961] Director

Ice House Street (No.1) Limited
Incorporated: 5 September 2011
Net Worth Deficit: £9,091,202 *Total Assets:* £24,846,380
Registered Office: 3 Castlegate, Grantham, Lincs, NG31 6SF
Activities: Non-life insurance
Parent: Ice House Street UK Limited
Officers: Michael John Argyle [1961] Director/Chartered Accountant; Christopher John Walker [1959] Director/Solicitor

Iceni Marine Services Limited
Incorporated: 24 February 2009 *Employees:* 19
Net Worth: £3,004,815 *Total Assets:* £15,861,246
Registered Office: Fulwood Road South, Sutton in Ashfield, Notts, NG17 2JZ
Activities: Other business support service activities n.e.c.
Parent: Turner & Co (Glasgow) Ltd
Officers: Graham Bruce Knox [1967] Director; Ian Parrack [1961] Director; Richard Thurlow [1982] Director; Alan Gerard Turner [1965] Director

Icon Aerospace Technology Ltd
Incorporated: 14 December 1933 *Employees:* 270
Previous: Icon Polymer Limited
Net Worth: £6,249,000 *Total Assets:* £15,102,000
Registered Office: Victoria Works, Thrumpton Lane, Retford, Notts, DN22 6HH
Activities: Manufacture of air and spacecraft and related machinery
Parent: Crosslink Technology Holdings Ltd
Officers: Craig Andrew Harris [1969] Director/Chief Executive; James Robert Hill [1978] Director/Chief Financial Officer; David James Ring [1962] Director

Icopal Limited
Incorporated: 21 February 1990 *Employees:* 136
Net Worth: £9,772,000 *Total Assets:* £26,900,000
Registered Office: BMI House, 2 Pitfield, Kiln Farm, Milton Keynes, Bucks, MK11 3LW
Activities: Production of abrasive products
Parent: BMI Group Holdings UK Limited
Officers: Andrew John Dennis [1965] Managing Director; Klaus Sonne Ravn [1966] Finance Director [Danish]; Dr Johannes Georg Schmidt-Schultes [1966] Director/Chief Financial Officer [German]

ID Medical Group Limited
Incorporated: 23 August 1999 *Employees:* 543
Net Worth: £4,140,931 *Total Assets:* £27,489,010
Registered Office: ID House, 1 Mill Square, Featherstone Road, Wolverton Mill South, Milton Keynes, Bucks, MK12 5ZD
Activities: Temporary employment agency activities
Parent: ID Medical Group Holdings Limited
Officers: Lynne Alden, Secretary; Gus Haydn Brimson [1974] Director; Ranjit Singh Nandha [1978] Director; David Simbarashe Newton [1981] Director; Deenu Rajesh Patel [1979] Director; Dr Mahomed Hanif Allimahomed Sacoor [1939] Director; Michael Sacoor [1970] Director; Stefan Thygesen [1979] Director

Ideagen PLC
Incorporated: 30 March 1993 *Employees:* 375
Net Worth: £50,484,000 *Total Assets:* £79,090,000
Registered Office: Ergo House, Mere Way, Ruddington Fields Business Park, Ruddington, Notts, NG11 6JS
Activities: Business and domestic software development
Officers: Graeme Peter Spenceley, Secretary; Alan Michael Carroll [1951] Director; Benjamin Charles Dorks [1974] Director; David Robert Knight Hornsby [1967] Director/Executive; Barnaby Luke Kent [1976] Director; Tony Rodriguez [1969] Director; Graeme Peter Spenceley [1965] Director/Chartered Accountant; Jonathan Peter Wearing [1952] Director/Consultant

Ideal Industries Holdings Limited
Incorporated: 18 December 2003 *Employees:* 283
Net Worth: £41,831,000 *Total Assets:* £52,420,000
Registered Office: c/o CMD Limited, Sycamore Road, Eastwood Trading Estate, Rotherham, S Yorks, S65 1EN
Activities: Activities of head offices
Officers: Carmelle Marie Giblin [1967] Director [American]; Kevin James Lamb [1959] Director [American]

Ideal Shopping Direct Limited
Incorporated: 15 December 1980 *Employees:* 799
Net Worth: £28,518,000 *Total Assets:* £82,227,000
Registered Office: Ideal Home House, Newark Road, Peterborough, Cambs, PE1 5WG
Activities: Retail sale via mail order houses or via Internet
Parent: Aurelius Alpha Limited
Officers: Jamie Brian Morris Martin [1972] Director; Martin Shaun Purcell [1955] Director; Dr Caspaar Friedrich Trautwein [1964] Director [German]

Idis Group Holdings Limited
Incorporated: 11 March 2005
Net Worth: £36,613,000 *Total Assets:* £92,804,000
Registered Office: Pitcairn House, Crown Square, First Avenue, Burton on Trent, Staffs, DE14 2WW
Activities: Wholesale of pharmaceutical goods
Parent: Clinigen Holdings Limited
Officers: Amanda Miller, Secretary; Martin James Abell [1974] Director; Shaun Edward Chilton [1967] Director

Idis Group Limited
Incorporated: 25 October 2004
Net Worth: £36,322,000 *Total Assets:* £92,804,000
Registered Office: Pitcairn House, Crown Square, First Avenue, Burton on Trent, Staffs, DE14 2WW
Activities: Non-trading company
Parent: Idis Group Holdings Limited
Officers: Amanda Miller, Secretary; Martin James Abell [1974] Director; Shaun Edward Chilton [1967] Director

Idis Limited
Incorporated: 29 June 1987 *Employees:* 167
Net Worth: £17,865,000 *Total Assets:* £81,621,000
Registered Office: Pitcairn House, Crown Square, First Avenue, Burton on Trent, Staffs, DE14 2WW
Activities: Wholesale of pharmaceutical goods
Parent: Idis Group Limited
Officers: Amanda Miller, Secretary; Martin James Abell [1974] Director; Shaun Edward Chilton [1967] Director

Idverde Holdings Limited
Incorporated: 19 March 2008
Previous: Hare Bidco Limited
Net Worth: £13,653,000 *Total Assets:* £55,633,000
Registered Office: Landscapes House, 3 Rye Hill Office Park, Birmingham Road, Allesley, Coventry, Warwicks, CV5 9AB
Activities: Activities of head offices
Parent: Idverde UK
Officers: Jonathan Edward Rhodes, Secretary; Eric Faivre D'Arcier [1968] Director/Engineer [French/British]; Douglas John Graham [1969] Finance Director; Herve Lancon [1958] Director [French]; Jonathan Edward Rhodes [1977] Director/Chartered Accountant; Nicholas Temple-Heald [1961] Director

Idverde Limited
Incorporated: 8 April 1998 *Employees:* 1,508
Previous: The Landscape Group Limited
Net Worth: £20,964,000 *Total Assets:* £48,700,000
Registered Office: Landscapes House, 3 Rye Hill Office Park, Birmingham Road, Allesley, Coventry, Warwicks, CV5 9AB
Activities: Landscape service activities
Officers: Jonathan Edward Rhodes, Secretary; Douglas John Graham [1969] Finance Director; Sarah Anne Hughes-Clarke [1959] Director; Saul Huxley [1972] Director; Jonathan Edward Rhodes [1977] Director/Chartered Accountant; Nicholas Temple-Heald [1961] Director

Idverde UK Limited
Incorporated: 19 March 2008 *Employees:* 2,068
Previous: Idverde Limited
Net Worth: £15,724,000 *Total Assets:* £68,729,000
Registered Office: Landscapes House, 3 Rye Hill Office Park, Birmingham Road, Allesley, Coventry, Warwicks, CV5 9AB
Activities: Activities of head offices
Parent: Idverde SAS
Officers: Jonathan Edward Rhodes, Secretary; Eric Timothy Faivre D'Arcier [1968] Director/Engineer [French]; Andrea Kate Gomm [1977] Director; Douglas John Graham [1969] Finance Director; Sarah Anne Hughes-Clarke [1959] Director; Saul Huxley [1972] Director; Herve Lancon [1958] Director [French]; Jonathan Edward Rhodes [1977] Director/Chartered Accountant; Nicholas Temple-Heald [1961] Director

IFA Metals International Limited
Incorporated: 4 August 2011 *Employees:* 155
Net Worth: £6,602,561 *Total Assets:* £15,331,519
Registered Office: Victoria Forge, Livesey Street, Sheffield, S6 2BL
Activities: Activities of head offices
Parent: IFA Group Limited
Officers: Craig Syson, Secretary; Gareth Davies [1970] Director; Andrew McGuinness [1966] Director; Craig Syson [1971] Director

IG Design Group PLC
Incorporated: 22 November 1978 *Employees:* 1,954
Previous: International Greetings PLC
Net Worth: £96,855,000 *Total Assets:* £170,628,000
Registered Office: No 7 Water End Barns, Water End, Eversholt, Beds, MK17 9EA
Activities: Activities of head offices
Officers: Joy Laws, Secretary; Dr Elaine Amanda Bond [1972] Director; Lance Andrew Burn [1964] Director; John Stuart Northcliffe Charlton [1946] Director; Paul Elliot Fineman [1959] Director; Stig Anders Hedlund [1957] Director [Swedish]; Mark Ian Tentori [1963] Finance Director; Giles Kirkley Willits [1966] Finance Director

IG Design Group UK Limited
Incorporated: 8 June 1988 *Employees:* 483
Previous: International Greetings UK Limited
Net Worth: £8,514,000 *Total Assets:* £58,422,000
Registered Office: No 7 Water End Barns, Water End, Eversholt, Beds, MK17 9EA
Activities: Manufacture of other articles of paper and paperboard n.e.c.
Shareholders: IG Design Group PLC; Belgraave Graphics Limited
Officers: Robert Geoffrey Alstead [1967] Finance Director; Lance Andrew Burn [1964] Managing Director; Paul Elliot Fineman [1959] Director; Giles Kirkley Willits [1966] Finance Director

Igloo Books Group Holdings Limited
Incorporated: 10 November 2010 *Employees:* 2
Net Worth: £3,612,626 *Total Assets:* £9,469,961
Registered Office: Cottage Farm, Mears Ashby Farm, Sywell, Northants, NN6 0BJ
Activities: Book publishing
Parent: Bonnier Publishing Limited
Officers: Paul Timothy Gregory [1965] Director; Jonathan Talbot Perdoni [1982] Director/Chartered Accountant; Hakan Rudels [1974] Director [Swedish]; Jim Rickard Zetterlund [1984] Director [Swedish]

Igloo Books Limited
Incorporated: 25 July 2003 *Employees:* 145
Net Worth Deficit: £1,287,076 *Total Assets:* £35,934,872
Registered Office: Cottage Farm, Mears Ashby Road, Sywell, Northants, NN6 0BJ
Activities: Book publishing
Parent: Igloo Holdings Limited
Officers: Paul Timothy Gregory [1965] Director; Jonathan Talbot Perdoni [1982] Director/Chartered Accountant; Hakan Rudels [1974] Director [Swedish]; Jim Rickard Zetterlund [1984] Director [Swedish]

Ikea Distribution Services Limited
Incorporated: 21 May 1998 *Employees:* 839
Net Worth: £9,104,000 *Total Assets:* £18,081,000
Registered Office: Witan Gate House, 500-600 Witan Gate West, Milton Keynes, Bucks, MK9 1SH
Activities: Wholesale of furniture, carpets and lighting equipment
Parent: Ikea Limited
Officers: Aaron Edward Musca [1977] Director/Chief Financial Officer [Australian]; Jay Sellwood-Brown [1973] Director; Sajal Shah [1976] Director

Ikea Limited
Incorporated: 5 February 1986
Net Worth: £253,328,992 *Total Assets:* £589,835,008
Registered Office: Witan Gate House, 500-600 Witan Gate West, Milton Keynes, Bucks, MK9 1SH
Activities: Retail of furniture, lighting, and similar (not musical instruments or scores) in specialised store
Officers: Javier Quinones Cespedes [1977] Director [Spanish]; Marzanna Deblinska-Hajdas [1969] Director/Business Navigation, Operations & Finance Business [Polish]; Henrik Olshov [1966] Director/Legal Counsel [Swedish]; Sajal Shah [1976] Director; Belen Frau Uriarte [1974] Director [Spanish]

Ikea Properties Investments Limited
Incorporated: 24 February 1995 *Employees:* 19
Net Worth: £681,772,032 *Total Assets:* £1,384,669,056
Registered Office: Witan Gate House, 500-600 Witan Gate West, Milton Keynes, Bucks, MK9 1SH
Activities: Other letting and operating of own or leased real estate
Parent: Ikea Limited
Officers: Javier Quinones Cespedes [1977] Director [Spanish]; Simon Maynard [1959] Director/Deputy Group Property Manager; Richard Rands [1967] Director/Property Manager UK & Ireland; Sajal Shah [1976] Director

ILI Limited
Incorporated: 28 October 2005 *Employees:* 21
Net Worth: £27,663,614 *Total Assets:* £33,845,880
Registered Office: Partis House, Davy Avenue, Knowlhill, Milton Keynes, Bucks, MK5 8HJ
Activities: Other information service activities n.e.c.
Parent: SAI Global CIS UK Limited
Officers: Hean Siew, Secretary; Kim Jenkins [1966] Director [Australian]; Tracy Elaine Roskell [1966] Finance Director

Ilmor Engineering Limited
Incorporated: 8 June 2005 *Employees:* 87
Net Worth: £388,503 *Total Assets:* £13,018,611
Registered Office: Quarry Road, Brixworth, Northants, NN6 9UB
Activities: Manufacture of engines and turbines, except aircraft, vehicle and cycle engines
Shareholders: Mario Illien; Penske Racing of Delaware
Officers: Philip John Rogers, Secretary; Stephen John O'Connor [1971] Director/Engineer; Roger Searle Penske [1937] Director/Executive [American]

Imagesound Limited
Incorporated: 20 October 2000 *Employees:* 100
Net Worth: £11,432,000 *Total Assets:* £27,190,000
Registered Office: Venture Way, Dunston Technology Park, Chesterfield, Derbys, S41 8NE
Activities: Reproduction of sound recording
Officers: William John Truman, Secretary; Philip John Burroughes [1970] Director; Neil Robert Cook [1977] Finance Director; Derek Mapp [1950] Director; Simon John Pearson [1978] IT Director; William John Truman [1974] Finance Director

Imago @ Loughborough Limited
Incorporated: 6 March 1989 *Employees:* 142
Net Worth: £6,754,428 *Total Assets:* £9,641,477
Registered Office: Finance Office, Loughborough University, Loughborough, Leics, LE11 3TU
Activities: Hotels and similar accommodation
Parent: Loughborough University
Officers: Andrew Paul Stephens, Secretary; Kay Elizabeth England [1964] Director/Chief Executive; Laurence Joseph McCarthy [1964] Director/Catering Consultancy; Frances Mary Stone [1959] Director; Jane Tabor [1961] Director; Richard Stewart Taylor [1973] Director/Chief Operating Officer

Imago Holdings Limited
Incorporated: 16 September 1992 *Employees:* 101
Net Worth Deficit: £4,131,710 *Total Assets:* £11,907,902
Registered Office: Albury Court, Albury, Thame, Oxon, OX9 2LP
Activities: Other publishing activities
Officers: David Michael Whiting, Secretary; How Dig Kendrick Cheung [1959] Managing Director; Howard Musk [1963] Director/Print Consultant; Kee Chuan NG [1963] Managing Director [Singaporean]; Simon Alexei Rosenheim [1965] Director/Publishing Consultant

Imago Publishing Limited
Incorporated: 27 August 1980 *Employees:* 40
Net Worth Deficit: £2,129,161 *Total Assets:* £9,436,447
Registered Office: Albury Court, Albury, Thame, Oxon, OX9 2LP
Activities: Book publishing
Parent: IMAGP Holdings Limited
Officers: David Courbois [1982] Sales Director [French]; Deborah Jane Knight [1964] Director/Publishing Consultant; Amanda Louise Lugg [1970] Director of Client Services; Simon Alexei Rosenheim [1965] Director/Publishing Consultant; Dietlinde Martina Scheible [1963] Director/Publishing Consultant [German]; David Michael Whiting [1975] Director/Chartered Accountant

IMCI (Services) Limited
Incorporated: 13 April 1987 *Employees:* 11
Net Worth: £8,289,836 *Total Assets:* £12,201,753
Registered Office: Progress House, Newby Road, Hazel Grove, Stockport, Cheshire, SK7 5DA
Activities: Other business support service activities n.e.c.
Shareholders: Charbel Youssef Faddoul; Avril Mairead O'Hanlon
Officers: Charbel Youssef Faddoul, Secretary; Avril Mairead O'Hanlon [1958] Director [Irish]

Immunocore Limited
Incorporated: 18 December 2007 *Employees:* 368
Net Worth: £135,738,000 *Total Assets:* £195,432,992
Registered Office: 101 Park Drive, Milton Park, Milton, Abingdon, Oxon, OX14 4RY
Activities: Other research and experimental development on natural sciences and engineering
Officers: Sir John Irving Bell [1952] Director/Physician [British/Canadian]; Jean-Michel Yves Sylvain Cossery [1959] Director [French]; Nicholas John Cross [1947] Director; Shah Abbas Hussain [1965] Director/President GSK; Dr Bent Karsten Jakobsen [1959] Director/Senior Vice President Research [Danish]; Bahija Jallal [1961] Director/Chief Executive Officer [American/Moroccan]; Dr Jonathan Kenneth Charles Knowles [1947] Director/Scientist; Ian Michael Laing [1946] Director; Kristine Peterson [1959] Director/Business Executive [American]; George Edward Silvanus Robinson [1956] Director; Laura Wade-Gery [1965] Director

Impala Bidco Limited
Incorporated: 21 July 2017 *Employees:* 87
Net Worth: £21,641,148 *Total Assets:* £35,078,200
Registered Office: Oak House, Mere Way, Ruddington Fields Business Park, Ruddington, Nottingham, NG11 6JS
Activities: Activities of other holding companies n.e.c.
Officers: Julian Charles Lucas Bennet [1982] Director/Investment Manager; Gilbert Benjamin Kamieniecky [1981] Director/Investment Manager [German]

Impello Limited
Incorporated: 9 October 2002 *Employees:* 1,137
Previous: Impello PLC
Net Worth: £25,079,000 *Total Assets:* £238,160,000
Registered Office: Columbus House, Westwood Business Park, Coventry, Warwicks, CV4 8HS
Activities: Trade of electricity
Parent: Shell Petroleum Company Limited
Officers: Malcolm Victor Henchley, Secretary; Susannah Dallison Collier [1972] Director/Lawyer [Trinidadian]; Brian Charles Davis [1966] Director/Vice President; Bianca Swanston [1984] Director/Finance Manager [Austrian]

Impero Developments Limited
Incorporated: 14 March 2014 *Employees:* 6
Net Worth: £2,241,899 *Total Assets:* £10,518,722
Registered Office: Oak House, Mere Way, Ruddington Fields Business Park, Ruddington, Nottingham, NG11 6JS
Activities: Management consultancy activities other than financial management
Parent: Impero Holdings Limited
Officers: Richard Fuller [1962] Director; Andrew William Parr [1974] Director

Impero Holdings Limited
Incorporated: 9 December 2013 *Employees:* 6
Net Worth: £7,060,089 *Total Assets:* £10,079,478
Registered Office: Oak House, Mere Way, Ruddington Fields Business Park, Ruddington, Nottingham, NG11 6JS
Activities: Management consultancy activities other than financial management
Parent: Impala Bidco Limited
Officers: Julian Charles Lucas Bennet [1982] Director/Investment Manager; Richard Fuller [1962] Director; Gilbert Benjamin Kamieniecky [1981] Director/Investment Manager [German]; Andrew William Parr [1974] Director; Joe Ross [1969] Director [American]; Philip John Kedgerley Walters [1954] Director

IMS Bidco Limited
Incorporated: 17 March 2016
Net Worth Deficit: £1,870,000 *Total Assets:* £44,980,000
Registered Office: Venture Way, Dunston Technology Park, Chesterfield, Derbys, S41 8NE
Activities: Other professional, scientific and technical activities n.e.c.
Officers: Neil Robert Cook [1977] Finance Director; John Andrew Hayhurst [1970] Director/Venture Capitalist; Derek Mapp [1950] Director; William John Truman [1974] Director

IMS Topco Limited
Incorporated: 17 March 2016 *Employees:* 100
Net Worth Deficit: £7,049,000 *Total Assets:* £55,909,000
Registered Office: Venture Way, Dunston Technology Park, Chesterfield, Derbys, S41 8NE
Activities: Other professional, scientific and technical activities n.e.c.
Officers: Philip Burroughes [1970] Director; Neil Robert Cook [1977] Finance Director; John Andrew Hayhurst [1970] Director/Venture Capitalist; Axel Jennewein [1973] Director [German]; Derek Mapp [1950] Director; Simon John Pearson [1978] Director; William John Truman [1974] Director

Imtech Engineering Services Central Ltd
Incorporated: 11 October 1947 *Employees:* 326
Net Worth Deficit: £564,000 *Total Assets:* £28,789,000
Registered Office: G & H House, Hooton Street, Carlton Road, Nottingham, NG3 5GL
Activities: Electrical installation
Parent: ESSCI Engineering Services Limited
Officers: Neil Geoffrey Evans, Secretary; Michael Booth [1974] Director/Chief Financial Officer; Colin Robert Brunton [1973] Director/Electrical Engineer; Neil Geoffrey Evans [1972] Finance Director; Darron Johnathan Littlehales [1966] Director/Electrical Engineer

In at the Side Limited
Incorporated: 10 April 2014
Net Worth: £10,120,148 *Total Assets:* £10,186,398
Registered Office: Unit 3 Rugby Park, Battersea Road, Heaton Mersey, Stockport, Cheshire, SK4 3EB
Activities: Other professional, scientific and technical activities n.e.c.
Shareholders: Philip James Chong; Katharine Rachel Chong
Officers: Philip James Chong, Secretary; Joey Chong [2002] Director; Philip James Chong [1962] Director; Samuel James Chong [2000] Director/Administrator

In Vino Bidco Limited
Incorporated: 7 February 2013
Net Worth: £6,392,794 *Total Assets:* £27,959,740
Registered Office: Boundary House, Cheadle Point, Cheadle, Cheshire, SK8 2GG
Activities: Wholesale of wine, beer, spirits and other alcoholic beverages
Parent: In Vino Limited
Officers: Michael Joseph Moriarty, Secretary; Claudio Manera [1963] Director [Italian]; Michael Joseph Moriarty [1965] Director; Dennis Whiteley [1961] Director

In Vino Limited
Incorporated: 7 February 2013 *Employees:* 147
Net Worth: £14,220,430 *Total Assets:* £74,332,672
Registered Office: Boundary House, Cheadle Point, Cheadle, Cheshire, SK8 2GG
Activities: Wholesale of wine, beer, spirits and other alcoholic beverages
Shareholders: Dennis Whiteley; Donna Whiteley; Araldica Castelvero S.C.A.
Officers: Michael Joseph Moriarty, Secretary; Claudio Manera [1963] Director [Italian]; Michael Joseph Moriarty [1965] Director; Dennis Whiteley [1961] Director

Incat International PLC
Incorporated: 28 April 1989
Net Worth: £5,974,000 *Total Assets:* £10,570,000
Registered Office: European Innovation and Development Centre (EIDC), Olympus Avenue, Tachbrook Park, Warwick, CV34 6RJ
Activities: Activities of head offices
Officers: Warren Kevin Harris [1963] Director; Praveen Purushottam Kadle [1957] Director [Indian]; Arun Krishnamurthi [1969] Director [Indian]

Inception Point Systems Ltd
Incorporated: 25 July 2012
Net Worth: £27,104,302 *Total Assets:* £27,105,288
Registered Office: Emerson Business Centre, Regent House, Heaton Lane, Stockport, Cheshire, SK4 1BS
Activities: Other professional, scientific and technical activities n.e.c.
Officers: Tzung Liang Lin [1964] Director/Chairman of VTC [Taiwanese]; Michael James Sheehan [1968] Director/CEO of VTC [American]

Inclusion Care Group Limited
Incorporated: 14 April 2011 *Employees:* 200
Net Worth Deficit: £5,160,064 *Total Assets:* £9,209,851
Registered Office: 1110 Elliott Court, Coventry Business Park, Coventry, Warwicks, CV5 6UB
Activities: Activities of head offices
Parent: Rehability UK Community Ltd
Officers: Sujahan Begum Jalil [1974] Director; Rehana Kousar [1975] Director

Inclusion Care Holdings Limited
Incorporated: 18 April 2011 *Employees:* 2
Net Worth Deficit: £3,001,152 *Total Assets:* £9,278,432
Registered Office: 1110 Elliott Court, Coventry Business Park, Coventry, Warwicks, CV5 6UB
Activities: Activities of other holding companies n.e.c.
Parent: Inclusion Care Group Limited
Officers: Sujahan Begum Jalil [1974] Director; Rehana Kousar [1975] Director

Independent Forgings & Alloys Limited
Incorporated: 11 December 2000 *Employees:* 155
Net Worth: £8,622,550 *Total Assets:* £15,719,572
Registered Office: Victoria Forge, Livesey Street, Sheffield, S6 2BL
Activities: Forging, pressing, stamping and roll-forming of metal; powder metallurgy
Parent: IFA Metals International Limited
Officers: Craig Syson, Secretary; Martin Edward Burnham [1956] Managing Director; Gareth Davies [1970] Director; Andrew McGuinness [1966] Director; Eunice May Metcalfe [1955] Quality Director; Martin Naylor [1972] Director; Anthony David Savile [1962] Sales Director; Craig Syson [1971] Finance Director; Andrew Paul Wade [1972] Director

Indesit Company UK Holdings Limited
Incorporated: 13 February 2002
Net Worth Deficit: £72,993,784 *Total Assets:* £291,823,264
Registered Office: Morley Way, Peterborough, Cambs, PE2 9JB
Activities: Activities of other holding companies n.e.c.
Parent: Whirlpool Corporation
Officers: Tetiana Pidhaina, Secretary; Lucianna Raffaini Carvalho [1973] Director [Italian]; Andrzej Tuleja [1973] Director [Polish]

Indoor Bowling Acquisitions Limited
Incorporated: 28 November 2014
Net Worth: £5,081,000 *Total Assets:* £49,701,000
Registered Office: Aragon House, Cranfield Technology Park, Cranfield, Bedford, MK43 0EQ
Activities: Activities of head offices
Parent: Indoor Bowling Equity Limited
Officers: Mark Simon Willis, Secretary; Nicolas Andrew Basing [1962] Director; Graham Edwin Blackwell [1969] Director; Dr Duncan Steven Garrood [1958] Director; Mark Simon Willis [1976] Director

Indoor Bowling Equity Limited
Incorporated: 29 May 2015 *Employees:* 2
Net Worth: £39,469,000 *Total Assets:* £84,709,000
Registered Office: Aragon House, Cranfield Technology Park, Cranfield, Bedford, MK43 0EQ
Activities: Activities of head offices
Parent: TEG Holdings Limited
Officers: Mark Willis, Secretary; Nicolas Andrew Basing [1962] Director; Graham Edwin Blackwell [1969] Director; Dr Duncan Steven Garrood [1958] Director; Mark Simon Willis [1976] Director

Industrial Control Distributors (Holdings) Ltd
Incorporated: 28 March 2012 *Employees:* 35
Net Worth: £7,145,492 *Total Assets:* £21,976,760
Registered Office: 30 Harborough Road, Northampton, NN2 7AZ
Activities: Activities of other holding companies n.e.c.
Major Shareholder: Jeffrey Frank Smith
Officers: Jeffrey Frank Smith [1966] Director

Industrial Control Distributors Limited
Incorporated: 4 August 1998 *Employees:* 34
Net Worth: £3,563,370 *Total Assets:* £9,947,474
Registered Office: Units 8-9 Bridle Close, Finedon Road Industrial Estate, Wellingborough, Northants, NN8 4RN
Activities: Manufacture of communication equipment other than telegraph, and telephone apparatus and equipment
Parent: Industrial Control Distributors (Holdings) Ltd
Officers: Jeffrey Frank Smith, Secretary/Industrial Control Distributor; Ian James Beaumont [1962] Director/Production Manager; Helen Marden [1967] Director; Mark Edward Parker [1968] Director; Jeffrey Frank Smith [1966] Director/Industrial Control Distributor

Industrial Machinery Supplies Limited
Incorporated: 4 October 1982 *Employees:* 33
Net Worth: £2,346,000 *Total Assets:* £9,564,000
Registered Office: Trans Tech House, Gelders Hall Road, Shepshed, Loughborough, Leics, LE12 9NH
Activities: Operation of warehousing and storage facilities for land transport activities
Officers: Michael Leonard Walker, Secretary; Jannes Bouman [1969] Director [Dutch]; Andrew Trevor Dyer [1967] Managing Director

Industrial Scientific Holdings UK Ltd
Incorporated: 18 October 2016
Net Worth: £18,853,742 *Total Assets:* £18,863,642
Registered Office: Suite 1, Bollin House, Bollin Walk, Wilmslow, Cheshire, SK9 1DP
Activities: Activities of other holding companies n.e.c.
Officers: Todd Richard Lindemuth [1964] Director/Vice President, Finance & Chief Financial Officer [American]; Justin Kent McElhattan [1972] Director/President and Chief Executive Officer [American]

Infineum International Limited
Incorporated: 28 August 1998
Net Worth: £68,931,000 *Total Assets:* £93,823,000
Registered Office: Corporate Centre, P O Box 1, Milton Hill, Abingdon, Oxon, OX13 6BB
Activities: Manufacture of other organic basic chemicals
Shareholders: ExxonMobil Corporation; Royal Dutch Shell PLC
Officers: Carl David Howard, Secretary; Brian Paul Eggleston [1976] Director/Finance [American]; Johann Maria Alexander Farina [1963] Director/Engineer [German]; Leonard Martin Fox [1963] Director/Vice President, Business Services & Treasurer [American]; Karen Trimby Frankland [1966] Director/Chemical Engineer/Senior VP of Basic Chemicals [American]; Juhan Robberts [1963] Director/Manager Planning and Business Development [Dutch]; Cheong Leong Seng [1958] Director/VP Chemicals APME, Global Ventures & NBD [Singaporean]

Infineum UK Ltd.
Incorporated: 7 December 1995
Net Worth: £61,276,000 *Total Assets:* £123,448,000
Registered Office: P O Box 1, Milton Hill, Abingdon, Oxon, OX13 6BB
Activities: Manufacture of other organic basic chemicals
Parent: Infineum International Limited
Officers: Jane Ann Palmer, Secretary; Peter George Blackman [1960] Director/Manager; Rebecca Clare Oldfield [1975] HR Director; Michelle Pye [1975] Director/Global Controls and Risk Manager

Infinis (Re-Gen) Limited
Incorporated: 14 October 1918
Net Worth: £19,985,000 *Total Assets:* £28,011,000
Registered Office: First Floor, 500 Pavilion Drive, Northampton Business Park, Northampton, NN4 7YJ
Activities: Production of electricity
Parent: Infinis Limited
Officers: Jacqueline Long, Secretary; Michael Damien Holton [1973] Finance Director; James Huxley Milne [1972] Director/Lawyer; Stephen Shane Pickering [1969] Director of Operations

Infinis Energy Group Holdings Limited
Incorporated: 17 October 2016 *Employees:* 276
Net Worth: £45,072,000 *Total Assets:* £642,665,024
Registered Office: First Floor, 500 Pavilion Drive, Northampton Business Park, Northampton, NN4 7YJ
Activities: Activities of other holding companies n.e.c.
Parent: 3i Infrastructure PLC
Officers: Michael Damien Holton [1973] Director; James Huxley Milne [1972] Director; Stephen Shane Pickering [1969] Director; Tim Short [1981] Director, 3i Infrastructure

Infinis Energy Management Limited
Incorporated: 18 October 2016 *Employees:* 276
Net Worth: £45,129,000 *Total Assets:* £517,940,000
Registered Office: First Floor, 500 Pavilion Drive, Northampton Business Park, Northampton, NN4 7YJ
Activities: Activities of other holding companies n.e.c.
Parent: Infinis Energy Group Holdings Limited
Officers: Anthony David Cocker [1959] Director; Michael Damien Holton [1973] Director; Scott Robert James Longhurst [1967] Finance Director; James Huxley Milne [1972] Director; Stephen Shane Pickering [1969] Director; Daniel Schulenburg [1981] Director [German]; Tim Short [1981] Director, 3i Infrastructure; Lars Oscar Tylegard [1985] Director [Swedish]

Infinis Energy Services Limited
Incorporated: 23 February 2010 *Employees:* 276
Net Worth: £3,563,000 *Total Assets:* £16,413,000
Registered Office: First Floor, 500 Pavillion Drive, Northampton Business Park, Northampton, NN4 7YJ
Activities: Other service activities n.e.c.
Parent: Infinis Energy Management Limited
Officers: Jacqueline Long, Secretary; Michael Damien Holton [1973] Finance Director; James Huxley Milne [1972] Director/Lawyer; Stephen Shane Pickering [1969] Director of Operations

Infinis Limited
Incorporated: 23 February 2006
Previous: Infinis PLC
Net Worth: £212,790,000 *Total Assets:* £486,323,008
Registered Office: First Floor, 500 Pavilion Drive, Northampton Business Park, Northampton, NN4 7YJ
Activities: Production of electricity
Parent: Infinis Energy Management Limited
Officers: Jacqueline Long, Secretary; Michael Damien Holton [1973] Finance Director; James Huxley Milne [1972] Director/Lawyer; Stephen Shane Pickering [1969] Director of Operations

Infinity SDC Limited
Incorporated: 6 October 2005 *Employees:* 30
Net Worth: £44,965,000 *Total Assets:* £185,052,992
Registered Office: Witan Gate House, 500-600 Witan Gate West, Milton Keynes, Bucks, MK9 1SH
Activities: Other business support service activities n.e.c.
Officers: David Mark Ben-Ur [1971] Director/Chief Investment Officer [American]; Clive Martin Dolman [1960] Director/Investor; Simon David Pitcher [1972] Director/Investment Manager; Matthew Cye Sandoval [1966] Director/Financial Management; Stuart Sutton [1968] Director; John Thompson [1961] Financial Director; Stephen Anthony Zimmerman [1949] Director/Investor

Ingenta PLC
Incorporated: 10 February 1965 *Employees:* 141
Previous: Publishing Technology PLC
Net Worth: £6,300,000 *Total Assets:* £12,717,000
Registered Office: 8100 Alec Issigonis Way, Oxford Business Park North, Oxford, OX4 2HU
Activities: Business and domestic software development
Shareholders: Kestrel Partners LLP; Martyn Rose
Officers: Jonathan Richard Sheffield, Secretary; Bo Henrik Holmstrom [1965] Director [Swedish]; Neil William Kirton [1963] Director; Martyn Craig Rose [1948] Director; Mark Alexander Rowse [1960] Director; Matthew Max Edward Royde [1972] Director; Jonathan Richard Sheffield [1976] Director/Chartered Accountant; Scott Winner [1967] Director [American]

Ingeus UK Holdings Limited
Incorporated: 26 March 2014
Previous: Pinnacle UK Bidco Limited
Net Worth Deficit: £1,957,000 *Total Assets:* £58,189,000
Registered Office: Magma House, 16 Davy Court, Castle Mound Way, Rugby, Warwicks, CV23 0UZ
Activities: Activities of head offices
Parent: Providence Service Corporation
Officers: Kevin Dotts, Secretary; Kevin Dotts [1963] Director [American]

Ingka Energy Services UK Limited
Incorporated: 15 August 2001
Previous: Ikea Energy Services UK Limited
Net Worth: £3,415,000 *Total Assets:* £9,456,000
Registered Office: Witan Gate House, 500-600 Witan Gate West, Milton Keynes, Bucks, MK9 1SH
Activities: Other business support service activities n.e.c.
Parent: Ikea Limited
Officers: Javier Quinones Cespedes [1977] Director [Spanish]; Sajal Shah [1976] Director

Ingleby (1981) Limited
Incorporated: 1 July 2015
Net Worth Deficit: £5,302,000 *Total Assets:* £30,351,000
Registered Office: Bridgeway House, Bridgeway, Stratford upon Avon, Warwicks, CV37 6YX
Activities: Other business support service activities n.e.c.
Parent: Rigby Private Equity Limited
Officers: Julian Hodge [1970] Director; James Peter Rigby [1971] Director; Steven Paul Rigby [1972] Director

Ingleby (2016) Limited
Incorporated: 15 March 2016 *Employees:* 534
Net Worth Deficit: £3,007,453 *Total Assets:* £20,515,644
Registered Office: Unit 22 Lodge Way, Lodge Farm Industrial Estate, Northampton, NN5 7US
Activities: Activities of head offices
Shareholders: Colin McCarthy; LDC Nominees Ltd
Officers: Gregor Frank Ball [1963] Director; Victoria Marcer [1975] Director; Colin McCarthy [1962] Director; Robert Anthony Schofield [1971] Director

Ingram Micro (UK) Limited
Incorporated: 29 January 1982 *Employees:* 499
Net Worth: £32,090,000 *Total Assets:* £247,646,000
Registered Office: CBXII, 406-432 Midsummer Boulevard, Milton Keynes, Bucks, MK9 2EA
Activities: Wholesale of computers, computer peripheral equipment and software
Parent: Ingram Micro Holdings Ltd
Officers: Karel Everaet, Secretary; Benjamin Gamble, Secretary; Karel Everaet [1965] Director/Lawyer [Belgian]; Kris Emile Paul Mees [1972] Director [Belgian]; Matthew Sanderson [1971] Managing Director

Ingram Micro Holdings Limited
Incorporated: 14 May 1985 *Employees:* 4
Net Worth Deficit: £7,370,000 *Total Assets:* £128,053,000
Registered Office: 2nd Floor, CBX II Building West, 406-432 Midsummer Boulevard, Milton Keynes, Bucks, MK9 2EA
Activities: Activities of head offices
Officers: Karel Everaet, Secretary; Karel Everaet [1965] Director/Lawyer [Belgian]; Kris Emile Paul Mees [1972] Commercial Director [Belgian]; Matthew Sanderson [1971] Managing Director

Innovate Multi Academy Trust
Incorporated: 4 June 2014 *Employees:* 140
Net Worth: £10,249,000 *Total Assets:* £11,756,000
Registered Office: Weedon BEC Primary School, West Street, Weedon, Northants, NN7 4QU
Activities: Primary education
Officers: Lucy Marie Flavell, Secretary; Peter Banks [1947] Director; Anna Patricia Barnett [1967] People Director; Ian Crossland Brown [1945] Director/Retired; Lindsey Evans [1977] Director/Headteacher; Karen Margaret Falvey [1967] Director/Company Secretary; Andrew Laurence Howden [1981] Director/Education Technology Consultant; Andrew Simon David Kerr [1964] Director/Solicitor; Terry Lifford [1945] Director/University Tutor; Lucy Elizabeth Stawt [1982] Director; Antony Glyn Witheyman [1978] Director/Headteacher

Innspired (Cedar) Limited
Incorporated: 29 May 1981
Net Worth Deficit: £172,000 *Total Assets:* £379,367,008
Registered Office: Jubilee House, Second Avenue, Burton on Trent, Staffs, DE14 2WF
Activities: Non-trading company
Parent: Punch Taverns (RH) Limited
Officers: Francesca Appleby, Secretary; Edward Michael Bashforth [1973] Director; Stephen Peter Dando [1972] Director/Chartered Accountant

Insanely Great Limited
Incorporated: 19 September 2011
Net Worth Deficit: £3,591,000 *Total Assets:* £11,029,000
Registered Office: c/o Jigsaw24, The Old Mill, High Church Street, New Basford, Nottingham, NG7 7JA
Activities: Non-trading company
Parent: Insanely Great Holdings Limited
Officers: John Richard Hal Hughes [1964] Director; Roger Keith Whittle [1964] Director

Insight Direct (UK) Ltd
Incorporated: 5 February 1991 *Employees:* 816
Net Worth: £74,694,000 *Total Assets:* £202,348,000
Registered Office: Technology Building, Insight Campus, Terry Street, Sheffield, S9 2BU
Activities: Other information technology service activities
Parent: Insight Enterprises UK Limited
Officers: Jetinder Golia, Secretary; Glynis Ann Bryan [1958] Director/Chief Financial Officer [American]; Russell Eric Leighton [1971] Director/Chartered Accountant

Insight Enterprises UK Limited
Incorporated: 8 August 2000
Net Worth: £44,824,184 *Total Assets:* £47,110,592
Registered Office: Technology Building, Insight Campus, Terry Street, Sheffield, S9 2BU
Activities: Other information technology service activities
Parent: Insight Enterprises Inc
Officers: Jetinder Golia, Secretary; Glynis Ann Bryan [1958] Director/Chief Financial Officer [American]; Russell Eric Leighton [1971] Director/Chartered Accountant

Insight Networking Solutions Limited
Incorporated: 11 July 2002 *Employees:* 22
Net Worth: £11,225,386 *Total Assets:* £17,053,892
Registered Office: Technology Building, Insight Campus, Terry Street, Sheffield, S9 2BU
Activities: Other information technology service activities
Parent: Insight Direct (UK) Limited
Officers: Jetinder Golia, Secretary; Russell Eric Leighton [1971] Director/Chartered Accountant

Insituform Holdings (UK) Limited
Incorporated: 3 June 1988
Net Worth: £8,024,000 *Total Assets:* £20,945,000
Registered Office: 12-20 Brunel Close, Park Farm Industrial Estate, Wellingborough, Northants, NN8 6QX
Activities: Other specialised construction activities n.e.c.
Officers: Sarah Bennison, Secretary; David Francis Morris, Secretary/General Counsel [American]; Mark Bates [1964] Director; David Francis Morris [1961] Director/General Counsel [American]

Insituform Linings Limited
Incorporated: 2 June 1983 *Employees:* 36
Net Worth: £19,375,584 *Total Assets:* £23,435,142
Registered Office: 12-20 Brunel Close, Park Farm Industrial Estate, Wellingborough, Northants, NN8 6QX
Activities: Other manufacturing n.e.c.
Officers: Sarah Bennison, Secretary; David Morris, Secretary; Mark Bates [1964] Business Director-Financial Officer; David Francis Morris [1961] Director/Business Executive [American]

Inspire Education Trust
Incorporated: 12 August 2015 *Employees:* 217
Net Worth: £11,611,968 *Total Assets:* £15,156,705
Registered Office: c/o Walsgrave CE Academy School, House Lane, Walsgrave, Coventry, Warwicks, CV2 2BA
Activities: Primary education
Officers: Antoinette Heffernan, Secretary; Gillian Bowser [1972] Director/Headteacher; Kim Docking [1956] Director/Executive Headteacher; Sybil Hanson [1940] Director/Teacher (Retired); Lisa Hayes [1969] Director/HR Officer; David Edwin Kershaw [1942] Director/Cabinet Lead for Education; Reverend Malcolm Tyler [1956] Director/Vicar; Graham Wise [1963] Director/Personal Banking Manager

Inspire Trust
Incorporated: 14 November 2013 *Employees:* 342
Previous: Oakwood Learning Community Trust
Net Worth: £36,524,724 *Total Assets:* £41,844,496
Registered Office: Oakwood High School, Moorgate Road, Rotherham, S Yorks, S60 2UH
Activities: Primary education
Officers: Paula Elizabeth Brockwell [1979] Director/Occupational Psychologist; Tracey Hayley Gammons [1972] Director; John Peter Gorman [1956] Director/National Account Manager; Paul Jagger [1946] Director/Retired; Tracey Leeson [1965] Director/Health & Safety Consultant; Timothy Mulroy [1960] Director/Principal Lecturer; David Michael Naisbitt [1967] Director/Headteacher; Adrian Robinson [1965] Director; David John Roche [1948] Director/Local Government Counsellor; Misba Shabir [1987] Director/Solicitor; Peter Sheldon [1965] Director/Learning and Development Manager

Inspired Gaming (UK) Limited
Incorporated: 18 May 1998 *Employees:* 776
Net Worth: £79,044,000 *Total Assets:* £241,624,000
Registered Office: 3 The Maltings, Wetmore Road, Burton on Trent, Staffs, DE14 1SE
Activities: Other manufacturing n.e.c.
Parent: Inspired Gaming (Holdings) Limited
Officers: Carys Damon, Secretary; Stewart Frank Bradley Baker [1983] Director/Chief Financial Officer; Carys Damon [1976] Director/Solicitor; Brooks Harrison Pierce [1961] Director/President [American]

Inspired Gaming Group Limited
Incorporated: 3 May 2006 *Employees:* 805
Net Worth: £46,965,000 *Total Assets:* £157,194,000
Registered Office: 3 The Maltings, Wetmore Road, Burton on Trent, Staffs, DE14 1SE
Activities: Activities of head offices
Parent: Gaming Acquisitions Limited
Officers: Carys Damon, Secretary; Stewart Frank Bradley Baker [1983] Director/Chief Financial Officer; Carys Damon [1976] Director/Solicitor; Brooks Harrison Pierce [1961] Director/President [American]

Instill Education Limited
Incorporated: 5 January 1977 *Employees:* 366
Net Worth: £9,269,682 *Total Assets:* £11,508,038
Registered Office: 38 Binsey Lane, Oxford, OX2 0EY
Activities: General secondary education
Major Shareholder: Till Gins
Officers: Till Gins [1950] Director [French]

Integral Powertrain Limited
Incorporated: 18 December 1998 *Employees:* 116
Net Worth: £17,408,974 *Total Assets:* £23,458,008
Registered Office: Denbigh Road, Bletchley, Milton Keynes, Bucks, MK1 1DB
Activities: Engineering related scientific and technical consulting activities
Officers: Roger Frank Duckworth, Secretary/Engineer; David Luke Barker [1963] Director/Engineer; Darren Christopher Cairns [1962] Director/Engineer; Roger Frank Duckworth [1965] Director/Engineer; John Forlow McLean [1962] Director/Engineer

Integrated Bradford Hold Co One Limited
Incorporated: 27 April 2006
Net Worth Deficit: £18,173,000 *Total Assets:* £83,765,000
Registered Office: The Sherard Building, Edmund Halley Road, Oxford, OX4 4DQ
Activities: Activities of other holding companies n.e.c.
Shareholders: Dolphin One Limited; Infrastructure Investments Holdings Limited; Amey Ventures Investments Limited
Officers: John Gerard Connelly [1960] Director/Head of Investment Management; Anthony Robert Faulkner [1973] Director/Chartered Accountant; Stewart Chalmers Grant [1951] Director/Asset Manager; Michael John Gregory [1968] Director/Chartered Builder; Nicholas James MacKee [1976] Director/Solicitor; Gary William Mills [1956] Director/Project Manager; Katherine Anne Louise Pearman [1961] Director/Chartered Accountant; Mark Christopher Wayment [1958] Director/Asset Manager

Integrated Bradford Hold Co Two Limited
Incorporated: 19 June 2009
Net Worth Deficit: £8,517,000 *Total Assets:* £158,996,992
Registered Office: The Sherard Building, Edmund Halley Road, Oxford, OX4 4DQ
Activities: Activities of other holding companies n.e.c.
Shareholders: Dolphin 2 Limited; Infrastructure Investments Holdings Limited
Officers: John Gerard Connelly [1960] Director/Head of Investment Management; Anthony Robert Faulkner [1973] Director/Chartered Accountant; Michael John Gregory [1968] Director/Chartered Builder; Nicholas James MacKee [1976] Director/Solicitor; Gary William Mills [1956] Director/Project Manager; Katherine Anne Louise Pearman [1961] Director/Chartered Accountant; Mark Christopher Wayment [1958] Director/Asset Manager

Integrated Bradford SPV One Limited
Incorporated: 27 April 2006
Net Worth Deficit: £18,173,000 *Total Assets:* £83,765,000
Registered Office: The Sherard Building, Edmund Halley Road, Oxford, OX4 4DQ
Activities: Management of real estate on a fee or contract basis
Parent: Integrated Bradford Hold Co One Limited
Officers: John Gerard Connelly [1960] Director/Head of Investment Management; Anthony Robert Faulkner [1973] Director/Chartered Accountant; Stewart Chalmers Grant [1951] Director/Asset Manager; Michael John Gregory [1968] Director/Chartered Builder; Nicholas James MacKee [1976] Director/Solicitor; Gary William Mills [1956] Director/Project Manager; Katherine Anne Louise Pearman [1961] Director/Chartered Accountant; Mark Christopher Wayment [1958] Director/Asset Manager

Integrated Bradford SPV Two Limited
Incorporated: 19 June 2009
Net Worth Deficit: £8,517,000 *Total Assets:* £158,996,992
Registered Office: The Sherard Building, Edmund Halley Road, Oxford, OX4 4DQ
Activities: Management of real estate on a fee or contract basis
Parent: Integrated Bradford Hold Co Two Limited
Officers: John Gerard Connelly [1960] Director/Head of Investment Management; Anthony Robert Faulkner [1973] Director/Chartered Accountant; Michael John Gregory [1968] Director/Chartered Builder; Nicholas James MacKee [1976] Director/Solicitor; Gary William Mills [1956] Director/Project Manager; Katherine Anne Louise Pearman [1961] Director/Chartered Accountant; Mark Christopher Wayment [1958] Director/Asset Manager

Integrated Waste Management Limited
Incorporated: 18 October 1989 *Employees:* 11
Net Worth: £3,440,000 *Total Assets:* £19,071,000
Registered Office: Ground Floor West, 900 Pavilion Drive, Northampton Business Park, Northampton, NN4 7RG
Activities: Other business support service activities n.e.c.
Parent: FCC Environment (UK) Limited
Officers: Carol Jayne Nunn, Secretary; Vicente Federico Orts-Llopis [1962] Director/Chief Financial Officer [Spanish]; Agustin Serrano Minchan [1959] Director/Technical Civil Engineer [Spanish]; Paul Taylor [1959] Director/Chief Executive Officer

Intelligent Energy Limited
Incorporated: 28 March 2000 *Employees:* 137
Net Worth Deficit: £229,200,000 *Total Assets:* £17,300,000
Registered Office: Charnwood Building, Holywell Park, Ashby Road, Loughborough, Leics, LE11 3GB
Activities: Other research and experimental development on natural sciences and engineering
Officers: Jasbir Uppal, Secretary; Alistair Henry Ian Ball [1976] Director/Interim CEO; David Ian Woolhouse [1966] Director/Chief Executive

Inter M.K. Limited
Incorporated: 24 June 1999 *Employees:* 11
Net Worth: £4,293,419 *Total Assets:* £14,199,522
Registered Office: Stadium MK, Stadium Way, Milton Keynes, Bucks, MK1 1ST
Activities: Construction of commercial buildings
Major Shareholder: Peter John Winkelman
Officers: Anthony Neil Richens, Secretary; Mark Turner [1968] Director; Peter John Winkelman [1957] Director; Bernadette Winkleman [1958] Director

Interaction Recruitment PLC
Incorporated: 26 July 1989 *Employees:* 3,200
Net Worth: £5,241,129 *Total Assets:* £14,820,169
Registered Office: Interaction House, 43 High Street, Huntingdon, Cambs, PE29 3AQ
Activities: Temporary employment agency activities
Parent: Hexagon Investment Holdings
Officers: Geoff Holder, Secretary; Benjamin Ambler [1981] Corporate Portfolio Director; Mark Dickson [1962] Sales Director; Andrew Iain Gilchrist [1962] Director/Accountant; Geoffrey George Holder [1972] Finance Director; Jean Lenton [1961] Operations Director; John Vazquez [1982] Director

Intercounty Truck and Van Limited
Incorporated: 25 October 2002 *Employees:* 247
Net Worth: £3,726,135 *Total Assets:* £38,879,708
Registered Office: c/o Ballyvesey Holdings Limited, Stewarts Road, Finedon Road Industrial Estate, Wellingborough, Northants, NN8 4TR
Activities: Sale of other motor vehicles
Parent: Ballyvesey Holdings Ltd
Officers: Stephen John Kidney, Secretary; David Nigel Birkmyre [1952] Director; Steven Hunt [1960] Director; Stephen John Kidney [1959] Financial Director; Harold Hugh Montgomery [1948] Director

Interflora British Unit
Incorporated: 11 February 1935 *Employees:* 248
Net Worth: £2,685,000 *Total Assets:* £26,409,000
Registered Office: Interflora House, Watergate, Sleaford, Lincs, NG34 7TB
Activities: Retail sale via mail order houses or via Internet
Shareholder: Interflora Group Limited
Officers: John Curzon Dunstan, Secretary; John Curzon Dunstan [1967] Finance Director; Rhys John Hughes [1969] Director/Company Executive

Interflora Group Limited
Incorporated: 4 February 2005
Net Worth: £21,657,000 *Total Assets:* £21,657,000
Registered Office: Interflora House, Watergate, Sleaford, Lincs, NG34 7TB
Activities: Activities of head offices
Parent: Interflora Holdings Limited
Officers: John Curzon Dunstan, Secretary; John Curzon Dunstan [1967] Finance Director; Rhys John Hughes [1969] Director/Company Executive

Interflora Holdings Limited
Incorporated: 15 November 2004
Net Worth: £13,698,000 *Total Assets:* £21,908,000
Registered Office: Interflora House, Watergate, Sleaford, Lincs, NG34 7TB
Activities: Activities of head offices
Parent: FTD UK Holdings Limited
Officers: John Curzon Dunstan, Secretary; John Curzon Dunstan [1967] Finance Director; Rhys John Hughes [1969] Director/Company Executive

Interfood Technology Ltd.
Incorporated: 2 July 1999 *Employees:* 63
Net Worth: £8,597,206 *Total Assets:* £19,520,728
Registered Office: 30 Upper High Street, Thame, Oxon, OX9 3EZ
Activities: Wholesale of agricultural machinery, equipment and supplies
Major Shareholder: Frank Niedecker
Officers: Jennifer Lynn Houston Costello, Secretary; Mark Guy Bishop [1964] Director/Selling of Industrial Food Machinery; Joachim Meyrahn [1957] Director/President CEO [German]; James Ian Sydenham [1967] Director/Selling of Industrial Food Machinery; Robert Malcolm Unwin [1973] Director

Interfuse Limited
Incorporated: 26 May 1965 *Employees:* 41
Net Worth: £17,380,104 *Total Assets:* £20,544,008
Registered Office: 370 Loughborough Road, Leicester, LE4 5PR
Activities: Other manufacturing n.e.c.
Parent: Jelson Holdings Limited
Officers: Julian Ian Bestwick [1967] Finance Director; Graham Stuart Jelley [1961] Director/Builder; Robert Stephen Jelley [1955] Director/Builder; Ronald Albert Jelley [1927] Director/Builder; Russell John Dickinson Pytches [1958] Managing Director

Interlevin Holdings Limited
Incorporated: 17 February 1984 *Employees:* 41
Net Worth: £9,170,070 *Total Assets:* £14,809,999
Registered Office: West Meadow Rise, Castle Donington, Derbys, DE74 2HL
Activities: Activities of head offices
Shareholder: Torben Lindblad Christensen
Officers: Torben Lindblad Christensen [1967] Director [Danish]; Jesper Kirkeby Hansen [1966] Director/Chief Executive [Danish]

Intermed Limited
Incorporated: 16 May 2007 *Employees:* 148
Net Worth: £5,557,871 *Total Assets:* £10,914,762
Registered Office: 1-5 Barton Lane, Abingdon Science Park, Abingdon, Oxon, OX14 3NB
Activities: Manufacture of medical and dental instruments and supplies
Officers: Stuart Kenneth Franklin, Secretary; Stuart Kenneth Franklin [1976] Finance Director; Aditya Gupta [1969] Director/Business Development [Indian]; Ajay Jindal [1984] Director [Indian]; Sunil Kumar Khurana [1961] Director/Service [Indian]; Harsh Nanda [1979] Director/Service [Indian]; Peter Anthony Worrallo [1962] Director

International Applications Limited
Incorporated: 14 February 2006 *Employees:* 44
Net Worth: £6,182,033 *Total Assets:* £10,187,534
Registered Office: 15 High Street, Brackley, Northants, NN13 7DH
Activities: Non-specialised wholesale trade
Parent: Durham & Co Holdings Limited
Officers: Deborah Durham [1973] Director/Consultant; Karl Durham [1970] Director/Chairman; Llewelyn Mulder [1959] Managing Director [South African]

International Brand Management Limited
Incorporated: 1 June 2004
Net Worth Deficit: £3,265,797 *Total Assets:* £24,309,540
Registered Office: Unit A, Brook Park East, Shirebrook, Derbys, NG20 8RY
Activities: Other service activities n.e.c.
Parent: Sports Direct International PLC
Officers: Cameron John Olsen, Secretary; Adedotun Ademola Adegoke [1973] Director/Senior Buyer; Rachel Isabel Lilian Stockton [1970] Director/Head of Customs and VAT

International Logging Technology Limited
Incorporated: 8 March 1990 *Employees:* 136
Net Worth: £21,433,000 *Total Assets:* £32,830,000
Registered Office: Weatherford, Gotham Road, East Leake, Loughborough, Leics, LE12 6JX
Activities: Extraction of crude petroleum
Parent: Weatherford International Public Limited Company
Officers: Richard Khalil Strachan, Secretary; Neil Alexander MacLeod [1966] Director/Region Tax Manager - Europe; Richard Khalil Strachan [1985] Director/Lawyer

International Piping Products (Europe) Limited
Incorporated: 1 November 2005 *Employees:* 70
Net Worth: £15,329,331 *Total Assets:* £33,893,192
Registered Office: Unit C, Barton Business Park, Barton under Needwood, Staffs, DE13 8BX
Activities: Wholesale of other intermediate products
Parent: IPP International Piping Products (Cyprus) Limited
Officers: Mark Winnard, Secretary; Jared Ayres [1967] Managing Director; Sarah Laura Ayres [1970] Director; Helen Julia Simcox [1966] Director

Intervet UK Limited
Incorporated: 29 January 1969 *Employees:* 202
Net Worth: £102,744,000 *Total Assets:* £190,439,008
Registered Office: Walton Manor, Walton, Milton Keynes, Bucks, MK7 7AJ
Activities: Other research and experimental development on natural sciences and engineering
Parent: Merck & Co., Inc.
Officers: Ebru Can Temucin [1972] Director [Turkish]; Allen Harberg Jr [1971] Director [American]; Jan Moehlenbrock [1970] Managing Director [German]

Intervet UK Production Limited
Incorporated: 13 May 1996 *Employees:* 192
Net Worth: £61,146,000 *Total Assets:* £118,581,000
Registered Office: Walton Manor, Walton, Milton Keynes, Bucks, MK7 7AJ
Activities: Manufacture of pharmaceutical preparations
Parent: Intervet UK Limited
Officers: Ebru Can Temucin [1972] Director [Turkish]; Allen Harberg Jr [1971] Director [American]; Jan Moehlenbrock [1970] Managing Director [German]

Intrexon UK Insect Holdings Limited
Incorporated: 1 June 2015
Net Worth: £124,861,232 *Total Assets:* £124,861,232
Registered Office: 71 Innovation Drive, Milton Park, Milton, Abingdon, Oxon, OX14 4RQ
Activities: Activities of head offices
Parent: Intrexon UK Holdings Inc.
Officers: Ricky Sterling [1964] Director/Chief Financial Officer [American]; Christian Ulrich [1973] Director/Attorney, Chief M&A [American]

Inver UK Limited
Incorporated: 25 September 2008
Net Worth: £14,844,166 *Total Assets:* £14,849,266
Registered Office: The Valspar UK Corporation, Avenue One, Witney, Oxon, OX28 4XR
Activities: Manufacture of paints, varnishes and similar coatings, mastics and sealants
Parent: Inver S.P.A
Officers: Ezio Nicola Giacomo Braggio [1956] Director/Business Executive [Italian]; Jeffrey James Miklich [1974] Director/Business Executive [American]; Allen Joseph Mistysyn [1968] Director/Business Executive [American]

Investco Limited
Incorporated: 5 June 1989 *Employees:* 1
Net Worth: £6,487,700 *Total Assets:* £13,656,733
Registered Office: 1 The Yews, Oadby, Leicester, LE2 5EF
Activities: Other letting and operating of own or leased real estate
Shareholders: Ramnik Ramji Patel; Vasant Patel
Officers: Kanta Ramnik Patel, Secretary; Ramnik Ramji Patel [1952] Director/Chartered Accountant

Investfront (Oxon) Limited
Incorporated: 23 February 2007 *Employees:* 129
Net Worth Deficit: £1,963,859 *Total Assets:* £15,712,550
Registered Office: Bicester Hotel, Chesterton, Bicester, Oxon, OX26 1TE
Activities: Construction of commercial buildings
Major Shareholder: Graham John Payne
Officers: Benjamin John Payne [1978] Director/Farmer; Emma Louise Payne [1987] Director/Artist; Graham James Payne [1947] Director; Margaret Payne [1947] Director; Matthew Oliver Payne [1980] Director/Farmer

Investhom Limited
Incorporated: 27 August 2015
Net Worth: £21,686,372 *Total Assets:* £21,870,408
Registered Office: Number Ten Elm Court, Arden Street, Stratford upon Avon, Warwicks, CV37 6PA
Activities: Fund management activities
Shareholders: Martin Peter Green; William Francis Thomas
Officers: William Francis Thomas [1950] Director

Inwido UK Limited
Incorporated: 26 April 1973 *Employees:* 2
Net Worth: £2,751,856 *Total Assets:* £32,799,442
Registered Office: 28 Nuffield Way, Nuffield Centrum, Abingdon, Oxon, OX14 1RL
Activities: Glazing
Parent: Inwido AB
Officers: Mattias Sven Bertil Andersson [1975] Director [Swedish]; Asger Drewes Joergensen [1975] Director [Danish]

IRESS (UK) Limited
Incorporated: 4 March 2009
Net Worth: £87,925,000 *Total Assets:* £130,352,000
Registered Office: 1 Kingmaker Court, Warwick Technology Park, Gallows Hill, Warwick, CV34 6DY
Activities: Business and domestic software development
Parent: IRESS UK Holdings Limited
Officers: Rebecca Kelly, Secretary; Simon Andrew Badley [1967] Commercial Director; Peter George Ferguson [1963] Director/General Counsel [Australian]; John Andrew Harris [1970] Director/Chief Financial Officer [Australian]; Andrew Leslie Walsh [1974] Director [Australian]

IRESS FS Group Limited
Incorporated: 18 May 2005
Net Worth: £13,012,000 *Total Assets:* £45,727,000
Registered Office: 1 Kingmaker Court, Warwick Technology Park, Gallows Hill, Warwick, CV34 6DY
Activities: Information technology consultancy activities
Parent: IRESS (UK) Limited
Officers: Rebecca Kelly, Secretary; Simon Andrew Badley [1967] Commercial Director; Peter George Ferguson [1963] Director/General Counsel [Australian]; John Andrew Harris [1970] Director/Chief Financial Officer [Australian]; Andrew Leslie Walsh [1974] Director [Australian]

IRESS FS Limited
Incorporated: 12 August 1994 *Employees:* 297
Net Worth Deficit: £7,985,000 *Total Assets:* £124,159,000
Registered Office: 1 Kingmaker Court, Warwick Technology Park, Gallows Hill, Warwick, CV34 6DY
Activities: Other software publishing
Parent: IRESS FS Group Limited
Officers: Rebecca Kelly, Secretary; Simon Andrew Badley [1967] Commercial Director; Peter George Ferguson [1963] Director/General Counsel [Australian]; John Andrew Harris [1970] Director/Chief Financial Officer [Australian]; Andrew Leslie Walsh [1974] Director [Australian]

IRESS Portal Limited
Incorporated: 28 March 1991
Net Worth: £18,687,000 *Total Assets:* £32,505,000
Registered Office: 1 Kingmaker Court, Warwick Technology Park, Gallows Hill, Warwick, CV34 6DY
Activities: Information technology consultancy activities
Parent: IRESS FS Limited
Officers: Rebecca Kelly, Secretary; Simon Andrew Badley [1967] Commercial Director; Peter George Ferguson [1963] Director/General Counsel [Australian]; John Andrew Harris [1970] Director/Chief Financial Officer [Australian]; Andrew Leslie Walsh [1974] Director [Australian]

IRESS Solutions Limited
Incorporated: 17 December 1999
Net Worth: £14,414,000 *Total Assets:* £16,996,000
Registered Office: 1 Kingmaker Court, Warwick Technology Park, Gallows Hill, Warwick, CV34 6DY
Activities: Other software publishing
Parent: IRESS FS Limited
Officers: Rebecca Kelly, Secretary; Simon Andrew Badley [1967] Commercial Director; Peter George Ferguson [1963] Director/General Counsel [Australian]; John Andrew Harris [1970] Director/Chief Financial Officer [Australian]; Andrew Leslie Walsh [1974] Director [Australian]

IRESS UK Holdings Limited
Incorporated: 16 July 2013 *Employees:* 691
Net Worth: £135,963,008 *Total Assets:* £253,960,000
Registered Office: 1 Kingmaker Court, Warwick Technology Park, Warwick, CV34 6DY
Activities: Dormant company
Parent: Apollo III Holdings Limited
Officers: Rebecca Kelly, Secretary; Simon Andrew Badley [1967] Director/Chief Executive Officer; Peter George Ferguson [1963] Director/General Counsel [Australian]; John Andrew Harris [1970] Director/Chief Financial Officer [Australian]; Andrew Leslie Walsh [1974] Director/Chief Executive Officer [Australian]

IRISNDT UK Holdings Limited
Incorporated: 1 May 2003 *Employees:* 160
Net Worth: £1,962,408 *Total Assets:* £9,754,032
Registered Office: Middleplatt Road, Immingham, N E Lincs, DN40 1AH
Activities: Activities of other holding companies n.e.c.
Officers: Roman Kyrnyckyj, Secretary; Janice May Barbour [1978] Director [Canadian]; Mike Bazzi [1959] Director [American]; Marcel Ronald Blinde [1969] Director [Dutch]; Roman Michael Kyrnyckyj [1961] Director/Inspection Engineer; James Richard Sheard [1946] Director

Irth (15) Limited
Incorporated: 9 March 1960 *Employees:* 1
Previous: Booker Overseas Trading Limited
Net Worth Deficit: £4,300,000 *Total Assets:* £53,200,000
Registered Office: Equity House, Irthlingborough Road, Wellingborough, Northants, NN8 1LT
Activities: Other business support service activities n.e.c.
Parent: Giant Booker Limited
Officers: Veselin Bandev [1978] Finance Director [Bulgarian]; Charles Wilson [1965] Director

Irth (19) Limited
Incorporated: 18 December 2002 *Employees:* 2
Previous: Booker US Limited
Net Worth: £39,300,000 *Total Assets:* £39,300,000
Registered Office: Equity House, Irthlingborough Road, Wellingborough, Northants, NN8 1LT
Activities: Activities of head offices
Parent: Giant Booker Limited
Officers: Veselin Bandev [1978] Finance Director [Bulgarian]; Charles Wilson [1965] Director

Irwin Mitchell LLP
Incorporated: 10 March 2009 *Employees:* 2,254
Net Worth: £93,331,000 *Total Assets:* £290,464,992
Registered Office: Riverside East, 2 Millsands, Sheffield, S3 8DT
Officers: Sarah Tracey Anne Ball [1970] Member; Victoria Carole Brackett [1970] Member; Garry Gene Dowdle [1959] Member; Stuart Austin Henderson [1958] Member; Bruce Islay Macmillan [1971] Member; Craig Alexander Marshall [1967] Member; Andrew David Merrick [1961] Member; Andrea Jayne Preston [1973] Member; Andrew Tucker [1960] Member; David Martin Ward [1970] Member; Benjamin David Acheson [1977] LLP Member; Mark Leslie Allen [1972] LLP Member; Yogendra Amin [1973] LLP Member; Gordon Wilson Anderson [1977] LLP Member; Catherine May Angel [1964] LLP Member; Timothy Christopher Annett [1973] LLP Member; Rachael Aram [1975] LLP Member; Jennifer Margaret Arrowsmith [1976] LLP Member; Kirsty Ayre [1968] LLP Member; Ian Henry Bailey [1966] LLP Member; Satinder Kaur Bains [1968] LLP Member; Christopher Robert Baker [1959] LLP Member; Niall David Baker [1966] LLP Member; Sarah Balfour [1983] LLP Member; Philip John Banks [1963] LLP Member; Faye Kirstie Bargery [1979] LLP Member; Thomas Alexander Barker [1978] LLP Member; Adrian Peter Barlow [1963] LLP Member; Philip Nigel Barth [1956] LLP Member; Daniel John Bastide [1972] LLP Member; Steven John Beahan [1971] LLP Member; Michelle Beat [1974] LLP Member; Heather Michelle Beaumont [1976] LLP Member; Roy George Beckett [1958] LLP Member; Jonathan David Betts [1974] LLP Member; Rosalyn Bever [1971] LLP Member; Jonathan Simon Robert Bew [1969] LLP Member; David Iain Bird [1965] LLP Member; Sarah Catherine Birkbeck [1974] LLP Member; Bryan Edward Bletso [1965] LLP Member; Anthony Bogle [1985] LLP Member; Joanne Bone [1967] LLP Member; Sallie Booth [1962] LLP Member; Ruth Imogen Booy [1968] LLP Member; Matthew Richard Harry Brown [1974] LLP Member; Andrew Paul Buckham [1972] LLP Member; Adrian Partick Boyce Budgen [1963] LLP Member; Emma Louise Callow [1976] LLP Member; Sarah Katherine Cardew [1973] LLP Member; Jennifer Anne Cawthorne [1976] LLP Member; Virginia Caroline Chalmers [1961] LLP Member; Sukhdev Singh Chhokar [1973] LLP Member; Ian Mark Daniel Christian [1975] LLP Member; Helen Clarke [1975] LLP Member; Mark Clinton [1959] LLP Member; Hannah Charlotte Clipston [1977] LLP Member; Alida Coates [1969] LLP Member; Karen Lesley Codling [1963] LLP Member; Penelope Susan Meredith Cogher [1967] LLP Member; Emilie Claire Cole [1980] LLP Member; Sarah Victoria Coles [1972] LLP Member; Sara Collett [1970] LLP Member; Georgina Alexandra Laurel Collins [1974] LLP Member; Claire-Marie Elizabeth Cornford [1980] LLP Member; Gillian Coverley [1971] LLP Member; Martin Nicholas Cross [1953] LLP Member; Matthew James Currie [1969] LLP Member; Demetrius Danas [1969] LLP Member; Luke William Daniels [1978] LLP Member; Guy William Edward Darlaston [1969] LLP Member; James Peter Davies [1971] LLP Member; Nicholas Sam Dawson [1978] LLP Member; Charankamal Dhaliwal [1982] LLP Member; Amandeep Singh Dhillon [1980] LLP Member; Fergal Nicholas Dowling [1968] LLP Member; Dean Patrick Drew [1961] LLP Member; Carl Donald Dyer [1959] LLP Member; Alison Eddy [1954] LLP Member; Glen Kendall Edney [1968] LLP Member; Gavin Mark Faber [1972] LLP Member; David Paul Fanchi [1977] LLP Member; Darran Robert Fawcett [1973] LLP Member; Alison Fernandes [1969] LLP Member; John Michael Flathers [1962] LLP Member; Guy William Forster [1978] LLP Member; Kevin Richard Fox [1981] LLP Member; Joanne Fraser [1981] LLP Member; Clive Anthony Winston Garner [1966] LLP Member; Laurence Michael Gavin [1967] LLP Member; Stephen Peter George [1968] LLP Member; Richard Mark Geraghty [1969] LLP Member; Neil Robin Gilbert [1973] LLP Member; Rosemary Giles [1957] LLP Member; Dean Brian Gormley [1974] LLP Member; Philip Hamilton Gray [1976] LLP Member; Steven Andrew Green [1968] LLP Member; Winston Ernest Green [1974] LLP Member; Kelly Naomi Greig [1983] LLP Member; Joanna Louise Grewer [1979] LLP Member; Auriana Yolanda Griffiths [1974] LLP Member

Ischebeck Titan Limited
Incorporated: 3 July 1990 *Employees:* 128
Net Worth: £20,918,364 *Total Assets:* £35,290,820
Registered Office: John Dean House, Wellington Road, Burton on Trent, Staffs, DE14 2TG
Activities: Other specialised construction activities n.e.c.
Parent: Ischebeck Doepp and Co KG
Officers: Shirley Anne Hutchinson, Secretary; Stuart William Bamford [1969] Engineering Director; Shirley Anne Hutchinson [1966] Director/Chartered Accountant; Bjorn Ernst Ischebeck [1976] Managing Director [German]; Lars Kristian Ischebeck [1979] Director/Lawyer/Business Manager [German]; Philip Waldron [1954] Sales & Marketing Director

ISDC Developments (No2) Limited
Incorporated: 12 February 2008
Net Worth Deficit: £23,451,000 *Total Assets:* £89,764,000
Registered Office: Witan Gate House, 500-600 Witan Gate West, Milton Keynes, Bucks, MK9 1SH
Activities: Other business support service activities n.e.c.
Parent: Infinity SDC Limited
Officers: Stuart Sutton [1968] Director; John Thompson [1961] Director

Isle Education Trust
Incorporated: 18 October 2011 *Employees:* 184
Net Worth: £8,924,000 *Total Assets:* £10,389,000
Registered Office: South Axholme Academy, Burnham Road, Epworth, Doncaster, S Yorks, DN9 1BY
Activities: Primary education
Officers: Karen Amanda Wild, Secretary; Paul Barratt [1951] Director/Bookmaker; Trevor Bean [1954] Director/Educationalist; Stuart Carrington [1980] Director/Chief Financial Officer; Aleksandra Flack [1988] Director/Solicitor [Polish]; Steven John Holt [1978] Assistant Managing Director; Sarah Jane Sprack [1972] Director/Principal; James Richard Stables [1978] Director/Senior Audit Manager; Karolina Whilde [1984] Director/Group Property Business Partner, Civil Rolls Royce [Polish]

ISN Europe Limited
Incorporated: 18 February 2016 *Employees:* 126
Net Worth: £2,863,672 *Total Assets:* £23,214,898
Registered Office: Unit 5 Lotus Court, Harvard Industrial Estate, Harvard Way, Kimbolton, Huntingdon, Cambs, PE28 0NJ
Activities: Other business support service activities n.e.c.
Officers: James Colin Boon [1972] Director; John Anthony Snowden [1966] Director [American]; Peter Charles Spraggs [1960] Director; David Bruce Weber [1963] Director [American]

Isotrak Group Limited
Incorporated: 26 April 2013 *Employees:* 150
Previous: Finn Topco Limited
Net Worth: £203,000 *Total Assets:* £39,821,000
Registered Office: 36 Queensbridge, Northampton, NN4 7BF
Activities: Non-trading company
Shareholders: Lyceum Capital (GP3) Limited; Lyceum Capital Partners LLP
Officers: Andrew William Overton [1965] Director; Mark Rogerson [1964] Director/Business Executive; Martin Squier [1982] Director; Jim Sumner [1966] Director

Isotrak Holdings Limited
Incorporated: 5 July 2013 *Employees:* 6
Previous: Finn Bidco Limited
Net Worth Deficit: £23,697,000 *Total Assets:* £48,887,000
Registered Office: 36 Queensbridge, Northampton, NN4 7BF
Activities: Non-trading company
Parent: Isotrak Midco Ltd
Officers: Andrew William Overton [1965] Director; Mark Rogerson [1964] Director; Jim Sumner [1966] Director

Isotrak Midco Limited
Incorporated: 26 April 2013
Previous: Finn Midco Limited
Net Worth Deficit: £2,560,000 *Total Assets:* £64,307,000
Registered Office: 36 Queensbridge, Northampton, NN4 7BF
Activities: Non-trading company
Parent: Isotrak Group Ltd
Officers: Andrew William Overton [1965] Director; Mark Rogerson [1964] Director; Jim Sumner [1966] Director

ITC Enterprises Limited
Incorporated: 20 September 2010
Net Worth Deficit: £51,373,904 *Total Assets:* £47,797,640
Registered Office: Westpoint, Peterborough Business Park, Lynch Wood, Peterborough, Cambs, PE2 6FZ
Activities: Other business support service activities n.e.c.
Parent: Thomas Cook Continental Holdings Limited
Officers: Litsa Constantinou [1955] Director; Thomas Fridolin Hohn [1965] Director [German]; Marcus Rohricht [1974] Director [German]

ITL Mortgages Limited
Incorporated: 25 November 1988
Net Worth: £71,625,000 *Total Assets:* £561,296,000
Registered Office: P O Box 600, Oakfield House, Binley Business Park, Coventry, Warwicks, CV3 9YR
Activities: Activities of mortgage finance companies
Parent: Coventry Building Society
Officers: Thomas Jonathan Crane, Secretary; Michele Jean Faull [1960] Director/Chief Financial Officer; Mark Alistair Parsons [1961] Director

ITM Power (Trading) Limited
Incorporated: 13 March 2007 *Employees:* 88
Net Worth Deficit: £18,969,000 *Total Assets:* £33,810,000
Registered Office: 22 Atlas Way, Sheffield, S4 7QQ
Activities: Manufacture of other electrical equipment
Parent: ITM Power PLC
Officers: Andrew Charles Allen, Secretary; Dr Simon Bourne [1975] Director; Dr Graham Edward Cooley [1964] Director; Professor Roger George Putnam [1945] Director; Dr Rachel Smith [1974] Executive Director

ITM Power PLC
Incorporated: 1 March 2004 *Employees:* 92
Net Worth: £35,591,000 *Total Assets:* £44,367,000
Registered Office: 22 Atlas Way, Sheffield, S4 7QQ
Activities: Manufacture of other electrical equipment
Officers: Andrew Charles Allen, Secretary; Andrew Charles Allen [1981] Director/Chartered Accountant; Sir Roger Bridgland Bone [1944] Director/Businessman; Dr Simon Bourne [1975] Director; Dr Graham Edward Cooley [1964] Director; Roger Norman Freeman [1942] Director; Robert Michael Pendlebury [1941] Director/Engineering Consultant; Professor Roger George Putnam [1945] Director; Dr Rachel Smith [1974] Director/Scientist

ITP Engines UK Limited
Incorporated: 29 February 2008 *Employees:* 170
Net Worth: £10,849,000 *Total Assets:* £17,992,000
Registered Office: The Whittle Estate, Cambridge Road, Whetstone, Leicester, LE8 6LH
Activities: Manufacture of air and spacecraft and related machinery
Parent: Industria de Turbo Propulsores, S.A
Officers: Robert Steven Beighton, Secretary; Alvaro Santodomingo Martell [1974] Executive Director [Spanish]

IVI UK Ltd
Incorporated: 23 October 2015 *Employees:* 11
Net Worth Deficit: £5,288,575 *Total Assets:* £17,359,520
Registered Office: 30 St Giles', Oxford, OX1 3LE
Activities: Specialists medical practice activities
Shareholder: Jose Alejandro Remohi
Officers: Saber Baccouche [1963] Director/Senior Management [Tunisian]; Maria Isabel Ferrer [1967] Director/Chief Financial Officer [Spanish]; Luis Saurat Marin [1962] Director/Economist & Lawyer - IVI CEO [Spanish]; Dr Richard Thomas SCOTT Jr [1958] Director/Physician [American]

Ivygrove Developments Limited
Incorporated: 29 September 1976 *Employees:* 27
Net Worth: £12,632,640 *Total Assets:* £30,870,600
Registered Office: Racecourse Industrial Park, Mansfield Road, Derby, DE21 4SX
Activities: Construction of commercial buildings
Officers: Andrew Mark Foulke, Secretary; David John Ball [1954] Director; John Samuel Blount [1944] Director; Nicholas John Blount [1971] Director; Richard Anthony Blount [1971] Director/General Manager; Andrew Mark Foulke [1963] Director/Company Accountant

IX Reach Ltd
Incorporated: 7 July 2004 *Employees:* 23
Previous: Console Network Solutions Limited
Net Worth Deficit: £3,574,541 *Total Assets:* £14,322,710
Registered Office: Southgate 2, 321 Wilmslow Road, Heald Green, Cheadle, Cheshire, SK8 3PW
Activities: Wired telecommunications activities
Shareholders: Stephen James Wilcox; Allegro Technology Investments Limited
Officers: Clare Tattersall [1979] Finance Director; Stephen James Wilcox [1978] Director

J & A (International) Holdings Limited
Incorporated: 31 January 2017
Net Worth: £28,684,488 *Total Assets:* £30,188,420
Registered Office: Insignia House, Vale Road, Spilsby, Lincs, PE23 5HE
Activities: Activities of production holding companies
Shareholders: Peter Leslie Cropley; Simon James Fry; Charles Jeremy Fry
Officers: Peter Jeffery Law, Secretary; Randy Carr [1972] Director; Charles Jeremy Fry [1967] Director

J & A (International) Limited
Incorporated: 11 June 1981 *Employees:* 138
Net Worth: £8,041,417 *Total Assets:* £9,419,233
Registered Office: Insignia House, Vale Road, Spilsby, Lincs, PE23 5HE
Activities: Other manufacturing n.e.c.
Parent: J & A (International) Holdings Limited
Officers: Peter Jeffery Law, Secretary; Adrian Peter Apletree [1964] International Sales & Marketing Director; Jamie Carr [1970] Director [American]; Randy Carr [1972] Director [American]; Charles Jeremy Fry [1967] Director/Chief Executive Officer; Simon Dominic Holderness [1966] UK Sales & Service Director; Martin David Kemp [1968] Managing Director

J & E Importers & Distributors Green Jem Mfg Associates Co Ltd
Incorporated: 2 July 1992 *Employees:* 17
Net Worth: £11,471,883 *Total Assets:* £11,941,527
Registered Office: Unit 18 Longwood Road, Corringham Road Industrial Estate, Corringham Road, Gainsborough, Lincs, DN21 1QB
Activities: Non-specialised wholesale trade
Shareholders: Jeremy Hemsley Levick; Ernest Hensley Levick
Officers: Janis Palmer Levick, Secretary; Ernest Hemsley Levick [1932] Director; Jeremy Hemsley Levick [1962] Director

J W D Holdings Limited
Incorporated: 14 August 2000 *Employees:* 55
Net Worth: £17,079,732 *Total Assets:* £29,450,662
Registered Office: Holbeach St Johns, Spalding, Lincs, PE12 8SQ
Activities: Activities of head offices
Officers: Graham Collishaw [1958] Director; Charles Graham Doubleday-Collishaw [1987] Director; Ian James Doubleday-Collishaw [1981] Director; Jayne Elizabeth Doubleday-Collishaw [1958] Director; Zoe Spencer [1985] Director

J3 Business Park Doncaster LLP
Incorporated: 22 February 2013 *Employees:* 1
Net Worth: £6,140,661 *Total Assets:* £9,685,991
Registered Office: A E Morris Limited, Bankwood Lane, New Rossington, Doncaster, S Yorks, DN11 0PS
Officers: Nichola May Foster [1983] Member; Robert David Patrick Lowe [1971] Member; Alan Edwin Morris [1951] Member; Barbara Ann Morris [1959] Member; Samuel Alan Morris [1980] Member; Thomas Edwin Morris [1982] Member; James Albert Sean Ian Lowe [1982] LLP Member

Jabco Capital Limited
Incorporated: 3 September 2013 *Employees:* 162
Net Worth: £13,732,246 *Total Assets:* £19,246,940
Registered Office: Herald Way, Binley Industrial Estate, Coventry, Warwicks, CV3 2RQ
Activities: Activities of head offices
Officers: Ian Greaves, Secretary; Edward Allen Boucher [1955] Director/Vice-Chairman of The Board [American]; James Boucher [1953] Director/Chairman of The Board [American]; Ian Greaves [1967] Director; Robert Lelio [1956] Director/Chief Financial Officer [American]; Eric William Mertz [1969] Director/Chief Executive Officer [American]; Mag Saba [1954] Director [Canadian]; Ken Stein Wilson [1971] Finance Director

L Jackson & Co Limited
Incorporated: 17 February 2011 *Employees:* 9
Net Worth: £19,947,116 *Total Assets:* £21,661,828
Registered Office: Rocket Site Misson, Bawtry, Doncaster, S Yorks, DN10 6ET
Activities: Sale of other motor vehicles
Shareholders: Andrew Jackson; Matthew David Jackson
Officers: Matthew David Jackson [1988] Director/Plant and Machinery Sales Manager

Francis Jackson Homes Limited
Incorporated: 7 February 1966 *Employees:* 30
Net Worth: £11,946,863 *Total Assets:* £20,837,956
Registered Office: 6 High Street, Olney, Bucks, MK46 4BB
Activities: Construction of domestic buildings
Major Shareholder: Nicholas Robert Jackson
Officers: Katrina Martine Watkiss, Secretary; Nicholas Robert Jackson [1970] Director/Chartered Surveyor; Kevin David Johnson [1979] Commercial Director; Paul Christopher Johnson [1979] Land and Planning Director

Jacobs Douwe Egberts Ops GB Ltd
Incorporated: 22 January 2015 *Employees:* 378
Net Worth: £83,157,000 *Total Assets:* £96,983,000
Registered Office: Ruscote Avenue, Banbury, Oxon, OX16 2QU
Activities: Production of coffee and coffee substitutes
Officers: Sophy Pashley, Secretary; Nurain Mohamed [1985] Director; Robert Donald Williams [1976] Director

Jaddu Ltd
Incorporated: 25 August 2015
Previous: D & A Property Management Ltd
Net Worth: £2,750,571 *Total Assets:* £9,421,109
Registered Office: 74 Hampden Road, Leicester, LE4 9EQ
Activities: Other letting and operating of own or leased real estate
Shareholders: Dhiraj Morjaria; Aruna Morjaria
Officers: Arunaben Morjaria, Secretary; Arunaben Morjaria [1966] Director/Manager; Dhirajlal Morjaria [1960] Director/Manager

Jaguar Estates Investments Limited
Incorporated: 16 March 2009
Net Worth: £8,343,224 *Total Assets:* £9,689,521
Registered Office: 201 High Street, Ecclesfield, Sheffield, S35 9XB
Activities: Buying and selling of own real estate
Shareholder: Punchbell Investments
Officers: Roderick Geoffrey Wadsworth [1951] Director; Timothy James Wadsworth [1979] Director

Jaguar Land Rover (South Africa) Holdings Limited
Incorporated: 9 September 2011 *Employees:* 2
Net Worth: £122,085,992 *Total Assets:* £124,966,608
Registered Office: Abbey Road, Whitley, Coventry, Warwicks, CV3 4LF
Activities: Sale of new cars and light motor vehicles
Parent: Jaguar Land Rover Limited
Officers: Susan Lesley Pearson, Secretary; Richard Gouverneur [1973] Managing Director [South African]; Liaan Etienne Kretzschmar [1982] Finance Director [South African]

Jaguar Land Rover Automotive PLC
Incorporated: 18 January 2008 *Employees:* 34,533
Net Worth: £9,980,000,256 *Total Assets:* £26,780,000,256
Registered Office: Abbey Road, Whitley, Coventry, Warwicks, CV3 4LF
Activities: Activities of head offices
Parent: Tata Sons Limited
Officers: Keith John Benjamin, Secretary; Pathamadam Balaji [1969] Director [Indian]; Natarajan Chandrasekaran [1963] Director [Indian]; Nassereddin Mukhtar Munjee [1952] Director/Banker and Consultant [Indian]; Andrew MacKenzie Robb [1942] Director; Hanne Birgitte Breinbjerg Sorensen [1965] Director [Danish]; Dr Ralf Dieter Speth [1955] Director/Chairman and CEO [German]

Jaguar Land Rover Holdings Limited
Incorporated: 16 June 2000
Net Worth: £4,558,000,128 *Total Assets:* £5,514,299,904
Registered Office: Abbey Road, Whitley, Coventry, Warwicks, CV3 4LF
Activities: Manufacture of motor vehicles
Officers: Amanda Jane Beaton, Secretary; Keith John Benjamin, Secretary; Susan Lesley Pearson, Secretary; Abbie Louisa Rees-Browne, Secretary; Felix Brautigam [1967] Managing Director [German]; Kenneth David Matheson Gregor [1967] Director/Chief Financial Officer; Ian Jeffrey Harnett [1961] Purchasing Director; Hanno Kirner [1970] Director [German]; Grant Alexander McPherson [1966] Director; Nicholas Martin Rogers [1967] Director; Dr Ralf Dieter Speth [1955] Director/Chairman and CEO [German]

Jaguar Land Rover Limited
Incorporated: 15 October 1982 *Employees:* 38,333
Net Worth: £9,064,999,936 *Total Assets:* £24,846,000,128
Registered Office: Abbey Road, Whitley, Coventry, Warwicks, CV3 4LF
Activities: Manufacture of motor vehicles
Parent: Jaguar Land Rover Holdings Limited
Officers: Amanda Jane Beaton, Secretary; Keith John Benjamin, Secretary; Susan Lesley Pearson, Secretary; Abbie Louisa Rees-Browne, Secretary; Felix Brautigam [1967] Managing Director [German]; Kenneth David Matheson Gregor [1967] Director/Chief Financial Officer; Ian Jeffrey Harnett [1961] Purchasing Director; Hanno Kirner [1970] Director [German]; Grant Alexander McPherson [1966] Director; Nicholas Martin Rogers [1967] Director; Dr Ralf Dieter Speth [1955] Director/Chairman and CEO [German]

Jakto Group Limited
Incorporated: 8 November 2017 *Employees:* 61
Net Worth: £5,423,926 *Total Assets:* £11,986,100
Registered Office: Oaks Lane, Stairfoot, Barnsley, S Yorks, S71 1HT
Activities: Activities of other holding companies n.e.c.
Shareholders: Adrian Hellewell; Neil Anthony Hellewell
Officers: Adrian Hellewell [1971] Director; Neil Anthony Hellewell [1965] Director

Warren James (Jewellers) Limited
Incorporated: 21 June 1979 *Employees:* 1,451
Net Worth: £93,036,000 *Total Assets:* £181,514,000
Registered Office: 7 Merseyway, Stockport, Cheshire, SK1 1PN
Activities: Other retail sale of new goods in specialised stores (not commercial art galleries and opticians)
Parent: WJH Limited
Officers: Ann Jones, Secretary; John Coulter [1951] Director/Jeweller; Ann Jones [1954] Director/Jeweller

James Convenience Retail Limited
Incorporated: 11 February 2015 *Employees:* 638
Net Worth Deficit: £1,058,000 *Total Assets:* £16,984,000
Registered Office: Hazel Court, Midland Way, Barlborough, Chesterfield, Derbys, S43 4FD
Activities: Retail sale in non-specialised stores with food, beverages or tobacco predominating
Major Shareholder: Jonathan Martin James
Officers: Jonathan Martin James [1968] Director; Mark John Titterton [1965] Director/Group Chief Executive

Warren James Holdings Limited
Incorporated: 27 November 1996
Net Worth: £93,058,048 *Total Assets:* £197,324,672
Registered Office: 7 Merseyway, Stockport, Cheshire, SK1 1PN
Activities: Activities of head offices
Parent: WJA Limited
Officers: Ann Jones, Secretary; John Coulter [1951] Director/Jeweller; Ann Jones [1954] Director/Jeweller

A W James Limited
Incorporated: 20 October 1999 *Employees:* 4
Net Worth: £24,795,940 *Total Assets:* £60,900,548
Registered Office: Linford Hall, Church Lane, Little Linford, Milton Keynes, Bucks, MK19 7EB
Activities: Other letting and operating of own or leased real estate
Shareholders: Peter John Wilson; Jane Elizabeth Wilson; Andrew James Wilson
Officers: Sebastian Mark Tubb, Secretary; Paul George Mace [1969] Estates Director; Colin Richard Spring [1952] Director; Sebastian Mark Tubb [1967] Director/Chartered Accountant; Andrew James Wilson [1976] Director; David Andrew Wilson [1947] Director; Jane Elizabeth Wilson [1950] Director; Peter John Wilson [1944] Director

Adam James Limited
Incorporated: 10 August 2004 *Employees:* 6
Net Worth: £4,461,300 *Total Assets:* £9,992,322
Registered Office: James Shipstone House, Radford Road, Nottingham, NG7 7EA
Activities: Other letting and operating of own or leased real estate
Shareholders: John Joseph Pye; Margaret Ann Pye
Officers: Margaret Ann Pye, Secretary; Adam John William Pye [1972] Director/Auctioneer and Valuer; John Joseph Pye [1930] Director/Auctioneer and Valuer; Margaret Ann Pye [1940] Accounts Director

Brian James Trailers Limited
Incorporated: 20 September 1999 *Employees:* 143
Net Worth: £10,945,040 *Total Assets:* £15,675,592
Registered Office: Central Chambers, 45-47 Albert Street, Rugby, Warwicks, CV21 2SG
Activities: Manufacture of trailers and semi-trailers
Parent: Brian James Trailers Holdings Limited
Officers: Brandon Earl James, Secretary; Brandon Earl James [1966] Director

Jandu Developments Limited
Incorporated: 4 April 1990 *Employees:* 20
Net Worth: £6,920,394 *Total Assets:* £11,249,771
Registered Office: Unit 7a Wheler Road, Seven Stars Industrial Estate, Coventry, Warwicks, CV3 4LJ
Activities: Finishing of textiles
Officers: Rabinder Kaur Jandu, Secretary; Jagtar Singh Jandu [1976] Director/Administrator; Naginder Singh Jandu [1939] Director; Satwinder Singh Jandu [1969] Director

Jarden Consumer Solutions (Europe) Limited
Incorporated: 25 January 1962 *Employees:* 115
Net Worth: £25,937,000 *Total Assets:* £50,164,000
Registered Office: 5400 Lakeside, Cheadle Royal Business Park, Cheadle, Cheshire, SK8 3GQ
Activities: Manufacture of electric domestic appliances
Parent: Vine Mill Limited
Officers: Ben Hartley [1976] Director/Attorney; Benjamin James Sturgell [1981] Director/Attorney [American]

Jardentome Limited
Incorporated: 1 March 1989 *Employees:* 153
Net Worth: £12,476,851 *Total Assets:* £18,237,644
Registered Office: Wicksteed Leisure Ltd, Digby Street, Kettering, Northants, NN16 8YJ
Activities: Activities of head offices
Shareholders: Harry Donald MacDonald Teacher; William Berry
Officers: Charles Edward John Howard [1986] Director; The Lord Howard of Rising [1941] Director/Landowner

Jardines (U.K.) Limited
Incorporated: 26 June 1984 *Employees:* 170
Net Worth: £19,833,716 *Total Assets:* £35,723,272
Registered Office: Lakeside, Shirwell Crescent, Furzton, Milton Keynes, Bucks, MK4 1GA
Activities: Dispensing chemist in specialised stores
Major Shareholder: Hasmukh Modi
Officers: Prity Modi, Secretary; David John Howton [1954] Director/Estates Manager; Hasmukh Modi [1950] Director/Pharmacist; Prity Modi [1959] Director/Marketing

Jardines Finance Limited
Incorporated: 22 December 2016 *Employees:* 2
Net Worth: £9,173,711 *Total Assets:* £13,768,324
Registered Office: Jardines, Lakeside, Shirwell Crescent, Furzton, Milton Keynes, Bucks, MK4 1GA
Activities: Fund management activities
Major Shareholder: Hasmukh Modi
Officers: Prity Modi, Secretary; Hasmukh Modi [1950] Director; Prity Modi [1959] Director

Mark Jarvis Limited
Incorporated: 19 March 1964 *Employees:* 264
Net Worth: £16,408,042 *Total Assets:* £19,226,224
Registered Office: Ascot House, 104 High Street, Leicester, LE1 5YP
Activities: Gambling and betting activities
Major Shareholder: Ronald Keith Hallam
Officers: Andrew Graham, Secretary; David Arnold Cox [1949] Director/Manager; Andrew Graham [1947] Director/Accountant; Paul Graham [1973] Director; Ronald Keith Hallam [1935] Director/Bookmaker

Jaybeam Limited
Incorporated: 22 April 1971 *Employees:* 72
Net Worth: £10,623,092 *Total Assets:* £15,051,243
Registered Office: Rutherford Drive, Park Farm South, Wellingborough, Northants, NN8 6AX
Activities: Manufacture of electronic components
Parent: Amphenol Limited
Officers: Lance Edward D'Amico, Secretary; Craig Anthony Lampo [1969] Director/Business Executive [American]; Richard Adam Norwitt [1969] Director/Business Executive [American]; Zachary Winner Raley [1969] Director/Business Executive [American]

Jaywing PLC
Incorporated: 14 September 2006 *Employees:* 639
Net Worth: £32,123,000 *Total Assets:* £54,287,000
Registered Office: Albert Works, Sidney Street, Sheffield, S1 4RG
Activities: Activities of head offices
Officers: Michael Sprot, Secretary; Martin Boddy [1964] Director; Mark Robert Carrington [1983] Director; Philip David Hanson [1957] Director; Adrian Lingard [1971] Director; Ian George Robinson [1947] Director; Robert Bernard Shaw [1970] Director; Michael Sprot [1979] Director

Jazz Pharmaceuticals UK Limited
Incorporated: 7 October 2002 *Employees:* 78
Previous: EUSA Pharma (Europe) Limited
Net Worth: £17,424,544 *Total Assets:* £23,883,872
Registered Office: Wing B, Building 5700, Spires House, John Smith Drive, Oxford Business Park South, Oxford, OX4 2RW
Activities: Other professional, scientific and technical activities n.e.c.
Parent: Jazz Pharmaceuticals Lux SARL
Officers: Aislinn Jane Doody, Secretary; Hugh Kiely [1973] Tax Director [Irish]; Iain Robert McGill [1972] Director/Chief Commercial Officer; Bridget Mary O'Brien [1971] Director/Accountant [Irish]

JDP Furniture Group Limited
Incorporated: 18 April 2000 *Employees:* 662
Net Worth: £10,046,000 *Total Assets:* £16,794,000
Registered Office: JDP Group Showroom, Wellington Street, Long Eaton, Nottingham, NG10 4HS
Activities: Manufacture of other furniture
Officers: Steven Turnbull, Secretary; John Derek Payne [1945] Director; Judith Anne Payne [1944] Director; Steven Turnbull [1968] Director

Jeld-Wen Europe Ltd.
Incorporated: 6 July 1999
Previous: RJAC Limited
Net Worth: £391,470,016 *Total Assets:* £604,894,016
Registered Office: Retford Road, Woodhouse Mill, Sheffield, S13 9WH
Activities: Activities of head offices
Parent: Jeld-Wen ApS
Officers: Keith Charles Dodd, Secretary; Keith Charles Dodd [1965] Managing Director; Peter Willis Maxwell [1962] Director/Executive Vice President, European Operations; Simon David Whittaker [1968] Director/Chief Financial Officer - Europe

Jeld-Wen UK Limited
Incorporated: 21 September 1951 *Employees:* 951
Net Worth: £117,641,000 *Total Assets:* £144,108,992
Registered Office: Retford Road, Woodhouse Mill, Sheffield, S13 9WH
Activities: Sawmilling and planing of wood
Parent: RJAC Limited
Officers: Keith Charles Dodd, Secretary; Keith Charles Dodd [1965] Managing Director; Peter Willis Maxwell [1962] Director/Executive Vice President, European Operations; Simon David Whittaker [1968] Director/Chief Financial Officer - Europe

J.Jelley and Son Limited
Incorporated: 30 August 1956
Net Worth: £10,500,492 *Total Assets:* £12,767,714
Registered Office: 370 Loughborough Road, Leicester, LE4 5PR
Activities: Other letting and operating of own or leased real estate
Shareholders: Robert Stephen Jelley; Graham Stuart Jelley; Patricia Christine Pytches
Officers: Brian John Doherty, Secretary/Accountant; Graham Stuart Jelley [1961] Director/Builder; Robert Stephen Jelley [1955] Director/Builder; Ronald Albert Jelley [1927] Director/Builder; Patricia Christine Pytches [1957] Director

Jelson Holdings Limited
Incorporated: 16 September 1946 *Employees:* 735
Net Worth: £166,557,152 *Total Assets:* £291,072,416
Registered Office: 370 Loughborough Road, Leicester, LE4 5PR
Activities: Activities of head offices
Officers: Julian Ian Bestwick [1967] Finance Director; Graham Stuart Jelley [1961] Director/Builder; Robert Stephen Jelley [1955] Director/Builder; Ronald Albert Jelley [1927] Director/Builder; Patricia Christine Pytches [1957] Director; Russell John Pytches [1958] Director; Scott Tallis [1980] Health & Safety Director

Jelson Limited
Incorporated: 18 September 1956 *Employees:* 329
Net Worth: £125,574,552 *Total Assets:* £243,792,432
Registered Office: 370 Loughborough Road, Leicester, LE4 5PR
Activities: Construction of domestic buildings
Parent: Jelson Holdings Limited
Officers: Julian Ian Bestwick [1967] Finance Director; Graham Stuart Jelley [1961] Director/Builder; James Jelley [1985] Operations Director; Robert Stephen Jelley [1955] Director/Builder; Ronald Albert Jelley [1927] Director/Builder; Mark Powell [1960] Construction Director; Michael Leigh Spencer [1958] Director; Scott Tallis [1980] Health & Safety Director; Robert Mark Thorley [1974] Land Director; Stuart Wilson [1970] Director

Jennings of Garsington Limited
Incorporated: 23 January 1953 *Employees:* 24
Net Worth: £13,173,304 *Total Assets:* £20,036,320
Registered Office: Hampden House, Monument Business Park, Chalgrove, Oxford, OX44 7RW
Activities: Other letting and operating of own or leased real estate
Parent: J.W.Jennings Ltd
Officers: Michael David Jennings, Secretary; Andrew Keith Maxwell Ashton [1950] Director/Solicitor; James Bartholemew Clements [1984] Director/IT Consultant; Richard Gibbs [1960] Director; Keith John Jennings [1956] Director; Michael David Jennings [1956] Director/Accountant; Paul Brian Mabbutt [1964] Director/Property Manager

Jenoptik Holdings UK Ltd
Incorporated: 20 October 2009 *Employees:* 78
Previous: Vysionics Limited
Net Worth Deficit: £12,226,090 *Total Assets:* £14,960,052
Registered Office: Witan Gate House, 500-600 Witan Gate West, Milton Keynes, Bucks, MK9 1SH
Activities: Activities of head offices
Parent: Jenoptik AG
Officers: Kevin Chevis [1960] Director; Richard Gorringe [1984] Financial Director; Henrik Leps [1977] Director [German]

Jensten Group Limited
Incorporated: 22 November 2012 *Employees:* 179
Previous: CISG Limited
Net Worth: £3,556,652 *Total Assets:* £26,954,544
Registered Office: Coversure House, Vantage Park, Washingley Road, Huntingdon, Cambs, PE29 6SR
Activities: Activities of financial services holding companies
Parent: Cambridge Bidco Limited
Officers: Georgina Elizabeth Bourner, Secretary; Carl Anthony Ashton [1980] Director; Cheryl Dawn Astley [1962] Director; Robert Michael Darling [1963] Director; Sarah Darling [1969] Director; Edward George FitzGenerald Hannan [1978] Director/Chief Financial Officer; Stephen Guy Parker [1965] Director

Jepco Limited
Incorporated: 24 December 1997 *Employees:* 127
Net Worth: £9,459,250 *Total Assets:* £19,430,632
Registered Office: Norfolk House Farm, Gedney Marsh, Spalding, Lincs, PE12 9PB
Activities: Activities of agricultural holding companies
Shareholder: Stuart William Piccaver
Officers: Simon Goddard, Secretary; Simon Goddard [1959] Director/Accountant; Phillip Paul Hubbert [1955] Director/Farm Manager; Stuart William Piccaver [1971] Sales & Marketing Director

Jepson & Co Limited
Incorporated: 1 December 1910 *Employees:* 65
Net Worth: £9,413,000 *Total Assets:* £15,876,416
Registered Office: 44 East Bank Road, Sheffield, S2 3QN
Activities: Other manufacturing n.e.c.
Parent: Jepson Holdings Limited
Officers: Jonathan Hartley [1966] Director/Sales and Marketing; Peter Geoffrey Jepson [1964] Managing Director

Jepson Holdings Limited
Incorporated: 8 February 1988 *Employees:* 80
Net Worth: £12,095,119 *Total Assets:* £14,717,775
Registered Office: 2 Broomgrove Road, Sheffield, S10 2LR
Activities: Other manufacturing n.e.c.
Parent: GE Jepson Discretionary Settlement
Officers: Beverley Ann Jepson [1964] Director/University Hospital Secretary; Peter Geoffrey Jepson [1964] Director; Susan Elaine Jepson [1942] Director/Administrator

Jerrold Finco PLC
Incorporated: 31 October 2003
Net Worth: £1,480,900 *Total Assets:* £739,092,672
Registered Office: Lake View, Lakeside, Cheadle, Cheshire, SK8 3GW
Activities: Activities of financial services holding companies
Parent: Together Financial Services Limited
Officers: Gary Derek Beckett, Secretary; Gary Derek Beckett [1969] Director; Marc Richard Goldberg [1971] Director; John Lowe [1972] Director; Henry Neville Moser [1949] Director

Simon Jersey Ltd
Incorporated: 26 March 1971 *Employees:* 141
Net Worth Deficit: £5,017,219 *Total Assets:* £17,321,092
Registered Office: The Forum, Hercules Business Park, Bird Hall Lane, Cheadle Hulme, Stockport, Cheshire, SK3 0UX
Activities: Wholesale of clothing and footwear
Parent: Simon Jersey Group Limited
Officers: Mirvet Russo [1968] Operations Director Group [Dutch]; Kieron Bartholemew Traynor [1960] Director

Jewel UK Bidco Limited
Incorporated: 23 November 2012 *Employees:* 6
Net Worth: £239,252,576 *Total Assets:* £350,400,512
Registered Office: Aurum House, 2 Elland Road, Braunstone, Leicester, LE3 1TT
Activities: Retail sale of watches and jewellery in specialised stores
Parent: Jewel UK Midco Limited
Officers: Anthony John Broderick [1958] Director/Chief Operating Officer; Hugh Brian Duffy [1954] Director/Chief Executive; Fabrice Nottin [1978] Director/Investment Professional [French]; Michele Raba [1984] Director/Investment Professional [Italian]; Lars Anders Ragnar Romberg [1963] Director [Swedish]

Jewel UK Midco Limited
Incorporated: 23 November 2012 *Employees:* 2,015
Net Worth: £85,057,000 *Total Assets:* £527,827,008
Registered Office: Aurum House, 2 Elland Road, Braunstone, Leicester, LE3 1TT
Activities: Retail sale of watches and jewellery in specialised stores
Parent: Jewel UK Topco Limited
Officers: Fabrice Nottin [1978] Director/Investment Professional [French]; Michele Raba [1984] Director/Investment Professional [Italian]

Jewel UK Topco Limited
Incorporated: 23 November 2012 *Employees:* 3
Net Worth: £102,248,128 *Total Assets:* £102,248,128
Registered Office: Aurum House, 2 Elland Road, Braunstone, Leicester, LE3 1TT
Activities: Retail sale of watches and jewellery in specialised stores
Officers: Charles Galinier-Warrain [1988] Director/Investment Professional [French]; Fabrice Nottin [1978] Director/Investment Professional [French]; Michele Raba [1984] Director/Investment Professional [Italian]

Jewson Limited
Incorporated: 13 January 1939 *Employees:* 9,229
Net Worth: £29,800,000 *Total Assets:* £1,212,049,024
Registered Office: Saint-Gobain House, Binley Business Park, Coventry, Warwicks, CV3 2TT
Activities: Wholesale of wood, construction materials and sanitary equipment
Parent: Compagnie de Saint-Gobain
Officers: Alun Roy Oxenham, Secretary; Nicholas James Cammack [1972] Director; Michael Strickland Chaldecott [1960] Managing Director; Michael David Newnham [1966] Director

JFB Overseas Holdings Limited
Incorporated: 18 March 1966
Net Worth: £4,400,000 *Total Assets:* £81,611,000
Registered Office: 26a Atlas Way, Sheffield, S4 7QQ
Activities: Activities of head offices
Parent: Firth Rixson Limited
Officers: Petra Papinniemi-Ainger, Secretary; Dr Kay Louise Dowdall [1969] Director/Chartered Accountant; Lluis Maria Fargas Mas [1966] Director [Swiss]

JFC Plastics Limited
Incorporated: 18 January 1972 *Employees:* 35
Net Worth: £1,062,890 *Total Assets:* £9,832,575
Registered Office: Unit 6 Goldicote Business Park, Ettington, Stratford upon Avon, Warwicks, CV37 7NB
Activities: Manufacture of plastic plates, sheets, tubes and profiles
Parent: JFC Manufacturing Co Ltd
Officers: Patricia Concannon, Secretary; John Francis Concannon [1953] Director [Irish]; Patricia Concannon [1955] Director/Administration [Irish]; Dclan Patrick Reidy [1961] Director/Accountant [Irish]

JHC Finance Company
Incorporated: 19 June 1996 *Employees:* 1
Previous: Jacobs Holding Company
Net Worth: £615,028,992 *Total Assets:* £649,312,000
Registered Office: 19 Jessops Riverside, 800 Brightside Lane, Sheffield, S9 2RX
Activities: Activities of head offices
Parent: Launchchange Limited
Officers: Keith Graham Ward [1953] Director

Jigsaw Systems Limited
Incorporated: 30 January 1992 *Employees:* 229
Net Worth: £10,659,000 *Total Assets:* £34,200,000
Registered Office: c/o Jigsaw24, The Old Mill, High Church Street, New Basford, Nottingham, NG7 7JA
Activities: Wholesale of computers, computer peripheral equipment and software
Parent: Jigsaw Holdings Limited
Officers: John Richard Hal Hughes, Secretary/Accountant; John Richard Hal Hughes [1964] Director/Accountant; Roger Keith Whittle [1964] Director

JJC Investments Limited
Incorporated: 15 April 2002 *Employees:* 3
Net Worth: £10,534,218 *Total Assets:* £10,878,177
Registered Office: Sovereign Court, 230 Upper Fifth Street, Central Milton Keynes, Bucks, MK9 2HR
Activities: Financial intermediation not elsewhere classified
Shareholders: Philip Matthews and Martin Maguire as Trusttes of CR Coward 1986 Settlement & Charles Coward 1967 Settlement; Philip Matthews and Martin Maguire as Trustees of CR Coward 1986 Settlement & Charles Coward 1967 Settlement
Officers: Martin Patrick Maguire, Secretary; James Justin Coward [1971] Director/Researcher; Martin Patrick Maguire [1955] Director/Chartered Accountant; Philip Matthews [1954] Director/Solicitor

JJS Manufacturing Limited
Incorporated: 22 December 1983 *Employees:* 117
Previous: JJS Electronics Limited
Net Worth: £2,033,131 *Total Assets:* £9,717,731
Registered Office: Paragon House, Wolseley Road, Kempston, Bedford, MK42 7UP
Activities: Manufacture of loaded electronic boards
Parent: Paragon Electronics Limited
Officers: Simon James Dabson, Secretary/Director; Simon James Dabson [1960] Director/Chartered Accountant; Stephen James Greaves [1964] Director; Christopher Michael Johnson [1956] Chairman and Director

Johal Properties Leicester LLP
Incorporated: 20 November 2008
Net Worth Deficit: £201,126 *Total Assets:* £14,302,626
Registered Office: Unit D, Forest Business Park, Walker Road, Bardon, Coalville, Leicester, LE67 1TU
Officers: Inderjit Singh Johal [1961] LLP Member

Johnson Bros (Tours) Limited
Incorporated: 20 April 1994 *Employees:* 141
Net Worth: £10,089,185 *Total Assets:* £12,709,846
Registered Office: Green Acres, Green Lane, Hodthorpe, Worksop, Notts, S80 4XR
Activities: Repair and maintenance of other transport equipment n.e.c.
Shareholders: Christopher Anthony Johnson; Sheila Johnson
Officers: Sheila Johnson, Company Secretary; Antony Darren Johnson [1965] Director/Chief Engineer; Christopher Anthony Johnson [1943] Director; Coleen Johnson [1971] Director/Secretary; Lee Phillip Johnson [1967] Director/Transport Manager; Scott Paul Johnson [1978] Director/Chief Engineer; Sheila Johnson [1943] Director

Johnsons Aggregates and Recycling Limited
Incorporated: 5 February 2002 *Employees:* 85
Net Worth: £3,244,168 *Total Assets:* £22,603,272
Registered Office: Johnsons Recycling Centre, Crompton Road, off Merlin Way, Ilkeston, Derbys, DE7 4BG
Activities: Collection of non-hazardous waste
Shareholders: BGF Nominees Limited; Steven David Johnson
Officers: Helen Maria Johnson, Secretary/Director; Paul Warwick Capell [1957] Director; Jonathan Gareth Earl [1976] Director; Steven David Johnson [1963] Director; Phil David Wood [1977] Director

Johnston Quarry Group Limited
Incorporated: 4 October 2007
Previous: Oathill Quarry Limited
Net Worth: £1,499,525 *Total Assets:* £9,321,012
Registered Office: The Estate Office, Quarry Farm, Banbury Road, Great Tew, Chipping Norton, Oxon, OX7 4BT
Activities: Quarrying of ornamental and building stone, limestone, gypsum, chalk and slate
Major Shareholder: Nicholas Matthew Middlemass Johnston
Officers: Nicholas Matthew Middlemass Johnston [1972] Director

Jonas Computing (UK) Limited
Incorporated: 1 December 2004 *Employees:* 11
Net Worth: £23,313,786 *Total Assets:* £72,461,056
Registered Office: Gladstone House, Hithercroft Road, Wallingford, Oxon, OX10 9BT
Activities: Business and domestic software development
Parent: Constellation Software UK Holdco Ltd
Officers: Thomas Baptie, Secretary; Darrell Peter Boxall [1970] Director/Portfolio Manager; Richard Clancy [1973] Director/Portfolio Manager; Jeffrey Raymond MacKinnon [1969] Director [Canadian]; Scott Ryan Saklad [1972] Director [American]; Barry Symons [1970] Director [Canadian]

P.E.Jones (Properties) Limited
Incorporated: 10 August 1960 *Employees:* 18
Net Worth: £61,284,000 *Total Assets:* £97,549,000
Registered Office: Emerson House, Heyes Lane, Alderley Edge, Cheshire, SK9 7LF
Activities: Other letting and operating of own or leased real estate
Officers: Varun Maharaj, Secretary; Anthony Emerson Jones [1967] Director; Audrey Jones [1936] Director; Mark Emerson Jones [1964] Director; Peter Emerson Jones [1935] Director

Jones Homes (Lancashire) Limited
Incorporated: 17 May 1976 *Employees:* 44
Previous: Newfield Construction Limited
Net Worth: £23,370,200 *Total Assets:* £42,023,128
Registered Office: Emerson House, Heyes Lane, Alderley Edge, Cheshire, SK9 7LF
Activities: Construction of domestic buildings
Parent: Emerson Developments (Holdings) Ltd
Officers: Varun Maharaj, Secretary; Ralph Bacon [1960] Director/Company Executive; Jonathan Rodney Claber [1982] Director; Gary John Hardy [1959] Director; Mark Emerson Jones [1964] Director/Business Executive; Peter Emerson Jones [1935] Director

Jones Homes (North West) Limited
Incorporated: 24 April 1959 *Employees:* 81
Previous: P.E.Jones (Contractors) Limited
Net Worth: £78,861,904 *Total Assets:* £119,170,312
Registered Office: Emerson House, Heyes Lane, Alderley Edge, Cheshire, SK9 7LF
Activities: Construction of domestic buildings
Parent: Emerson Developments (Holdings) Limited
Officers: Varun Maharaj, Secretary; Jonathan Rodney Claber [1982] Director; Nigel John Galleymore [1955] Director; Gary John Hardy [1959] Director; Anthony Emerson Jones [1967] Director; Audrey Jones [1936] Director; Mark Emerson Jones [1964] Director; Peter Emerson Jones [1935] Director; Lee Sale [1973] Director/Business Executive

Jones Homes (Southern) Limited
Incorporated: 20 October 1995 *Employees:* 28
Net Worth: £23,048,092 *Total Assets:* £52,111,448
Registered Office: Emerson House, Heyes Lane, Alderley Edge, Cheshire, SK9 7LF
Activities: Construction of domestic buildings
Parent: Jones Homes (North West) Limited
Officers: Varun Maharaj, Secretary; Jeremy Paul Attwater [1969] Director/Business Executive; Terence Stephen Charles Brown [1961] Director/Business Executive; Jonathan Rodney Claber [1982] Director; Anthony Emerson Jones [1967] Director; Mark Emerson Jones [1964] Director; Peter Emerson Jones [1935] Director; Sara Jane Stanhope [1967] Director

Jones Homes (Yorkshire) Limited
Incorporated: 16 April 1996 *Employees:* 50
Previous: Jones Homes (Northern) Limited
Net Worth: £25,894,036 *Total Assets:* £38,639,136
Registered Office: Emerson House, Heyes Lane, Alderley Edge, Cheshire, SK9 7LF
Activities: Construction of domestic buildings
Parent: Jones Homes (North West) Limited
Officers: Varun Maharaj, Secretary; Jonathan Rodney Claber [1982] Director; Allan Glenn Cooke [1971] Technical Director; Gary John Hardy [1959] Director; Anthony Emerson Jones [1967] Director; Mark Emerson Jones [1964] Director; Peter Emerson Jones [1935] Director; David William Ruffley [1962] Director/Business Executive; Jayne Angela Swift [1973] Sales & Marketing Director

Jordan Developments (UK) Limited
Incorporated: 31 January 1992 *Employees:* 5
Net Worth: £5,767,540 *Total Assets:* £10,700,690
Registered Office: 110 Regent Road, Leicester, LE1 7LT
Activities: Other letting and operating of own or leased real estate
Major Shareholder: Robert Anthony Jordan
Officers: Jane Elizabeth Jordan, Secretary; Jane Elizabeth Jordan [1965] Director; Robert Anthony Jordan [1964] Director/Property Developer; Thomas Robert Jordan [1993] Director

Jotun Paints (Europe) Limited
Incorporated: 22 December 1967 *Employees:* 220
Net Worth: £22,350,000 *Total Assets:* £60,081,000
Registered Office: Jotun Paints (Europe) Ltd, Stather Road, Flixborough, Scunthorpe, N Lincs, DN15 8RR
Activities: Manufacture of paints, varnishes and similar coatings, mastics and sealants
Parent: Jotun A/S
Officers: John William West, Secretary; Stian Fjeldskar [1974] Director/Vice President Business Support [Norwegian]; Harald Hvalvik [1956] Director/Regional Vice President [Norwegian]; Michael John Young [1961] Director/General Manager

Joules Group PLC
Incorporated: 5 May 2016 *Employees:* 1,765
Net Worth: £38,366,000 *Total Assets:* £90,971,000
Registered Office: Joules Building, The Point, Rockingham Road, Market Harborough, Leics, LE16 7QU
Activities: Wholesale of clothing and footwear
Shareholder: Tom Simon Lee Joule
Officers: Jonathan William Dargie, Secretary; Marcus Simon Dench [1970] Director; Ian Francis Filby [1959] Director and Chairman; Tom Simon Lee Joule [1968] Director; Jill Caroline Little [1953] Director; Colin Nigel Porter [1961] Director; David Anthony Stead [1958] Director

Joules Investments Holdings Limited
Incorporated: 29 October 2013
Net Worth: £43,696,000 *Total Assets:* £43,806,000
Registered Office: Joules Building, The Point, Rockingham Road, Market Harborough, Leics, LE16 7QU
Activities: Activities of head offices
Parent: Joules Group PLC
Officers: Jon Dargie, Secretary; Marcus Simon Dench [1970] Director/Finance; Tom Simon Lee Joule [1968] Director; Colin Nigel Porter [1961] Director

Joules Limited
Incorporated: 31 May 1994 *Employees:* 1,546
Net Worth: £26,568,000 *Total Assets:* £69,734,000
Registered Office: Joules Building, The Point, Rockingham Road, Market Harborough, Leics, LE16 7QU
Activities: Wholesale of clothing and footwear
Parent: Joules Investments Holdings Limited
Officers: Jonathan William Dargie, Secretary; Marcus Simon Dench [1970] Director/Finance; Andrea Michelle Gray [1969] Director; Tom Simon Lee Joule [1968] Director/Retailer of Hats and Clothing; Penny Jane Parry [1979] European Wholesale Director; Colin Nigel Porter [1961] Managing Director; Chloe Ward [1980] Director/Designer

Jourdan PLC
Incorporated: 16 August 1926
Net Worth: £16,509,000 *Total Assets:* £18,592,000
Registered Office: Elm House, Elmer Street North, Grantham, Lincs, NG31 6RE
Activities: Activities of head offices
Major Shareholder: John David Abell
Officers: Martha Blanche Waymark Bruce, Secretary; John David Abell [1942] Director; Robert Ridley Morris [1942] Director; Jon Peter Pither [1934] Director

JR Motorsports Limited
Incorporated: 21 March 2007 *Employees:* 49
Previous: J.R. Motorsports Limited
Net Worth Deficit: £23,788,984 *Total Assets:* £20,102,108
Registered Office: Units 3-4 Rutherford Way, Drayton Fields Industrial Estate, Daventry, Northants, NN11 8XW
Activities: Sale of other motor vehicles
Parent: JRM Group Limited
Officers: Jason James King [1971] Managing Director; James Alexander Rumsey [1979] Director/Farm Manager; Stephen John Raymond Rumsey [1950] Director/Investment Manager

JRI Orthopaedics Limited
Incorporated: 6 April 1970 *Employees:* 105
Net Worth: £11,875,000 *Total Assets:* £14,313,000
Registered Office: 18 Churchill Way, 35a Business Park, Chapeltown, Sheffield, S35 2PY
Activities: Manufacture of medical and dental instruments and supplies
Major Shareholder: Zhijiang Li
Officers: Jeremy Edward Agass [1959] Operations Director; Stephen George Ayres [1969] Director; Wang David Guowei [1961] Director [American]; Zhao Xiaohong [1977] Director [Chinese]; Li Zhijiang [1968] Director [Chinese]

JSC EFarms LLP
Incorporated: 31 January 2017
Net Worth: £9,493,332 *Total Assets:* £9,540,683
Registered Office: Glebe Farm, London Road, Shardlow, Derbys, DE72 2GW
Officers: Charles Edwick Chamberlain [1961] Member; James Edwick Chamberlain [1959] Member; Susan Hunter-Pease [1959] Member; Louise Ann Chamberlain [1967] LLP Member; Sally Chamberlain [1962] LLP Member; Charles Hunter-Pease [1946] LLP Member

JTF Wholesale Limited
Incorporated: 21 December 2005 *Employees:* 483
Net Worth: £2,772,000 *Total Assets:* £15,527,000
Registered Office: Walker Industrial Estate, Ollerton Road, Tuxford, Newark, Notts, NG22 0PQ
Activities: Non-specialised wholesale trade
Major Shareholder: Timothy James Whitworth
Officers: Guy Spence Daltry [1968] Director/Chief Executive; Liam James Gill [1985] Retail Director; John Charles Hepworth [1964] Finance Director; Timothy James Whitworth [1971] Director/Chairman

The Juice Master Limited
Incorporated: 10 January 2003 *Employees:* 10
Net Worth: £8,382,817 *Total Assets:* £9,527,052
Registered Office: The Juice Factory, 8-12 Stanley Road, Wellingborough, Northants, NN8 1DY
Activities: Other human health activities
Major Shareholder: Jason Bean Vale
Officers: Jason Vale, Secretary; Jason Bean Vale [1969] Director

Jungheinrich Financial Services Limited
Incorporated: 5 June 2006 *Employees:* 7
Net Worth: £11,223,000 *Total Assets:* £114,947,000
Registered Office: Sherbourne House, Sherbourne Drive, Tilbrook, Milton Keynes, Bucks, MK7 8HX
Activities: Financial leasing
Parent: Jungheinrich UK Holdings Limited
Officers: Christian Hanke [1974] Director/Head of Financial Services [German]; Arne Christian Rosenkranz [1983] Finance Director [German]

Jungheinrich Lift Truck Finance Limited
Incorporated: 5 June 2006
Net Worth: £4,912,000 *Total Assets:* £168,527,008
Registered Office: Sherbourne House, Sherbourne Drive, Tilbrook, Milton Keynes, Bucks, MK7 8HX
Activities: Financial leasing
Parent: Jungheinrich UK Holdings Limited
Officers: Christian Hanke [1974] Director/Head of Financial Services [German]; Arne Christian Rosenkranz [1983] Finance Director [German]

Jungheinrich UK Limited
Incorporated: 10 April 1963 *Employees:* 781
Net Worth: £40,940,000 *Total Assets:* £122,148,000
Registered Office: Sherbourne House, Sherbourne Drive, Tilbrook, Milton Keynes, Bucks, MK7 8HX
Activities: Manufacture of lifting and handling equipment
Parent: Jungheinrich UK Holdings Ltd
Officers: Arne Christian Rosenkranz [1983] Finance Director [German]; Luuk Theodorus Antonius Snijders [1982] Managing Director [Dutch]

Juniper Pharma Services Limited
Incorporated: 3 July 1997 *Employees:* 128
Previous: Molecular Profiles Ltd
Net Worth: £7,423,823 *Total Assets:* £15,897,325
Registered Office: 8 Orchard Place, Nottingham Business Park, Nottingham, NG8 6PX
Activities: Other research and experimental development on natural sciences and engineering
Parent: Juniper Pharmaceuticals UK Limited
Officers: Kirk Walsh, Secretary; Jonathan Arnold [1965] Director/President Oral Drug Delivery; Dr Claire Elizabeth Madden Smith [1973] Commercial Director; Alessandro Maselli [1972] Director/SVP Operations [Italian]; Dr Nikin Patel [1972] Director; Kirk Walsh [1980] Director/VP Finance

Just A Bank Limited
Incorporated: 16 July 2002
Net Worth Deficit: £8,820,047 *Total Assets:* £23,876,156
Registered Office: P O Box 9562, Kempton House, Kempton Way, Grantham, Lincs, NG31 0EA
Activities: Other business support service activities n.e.c.
Parent: Totemic (2014) Holdings Limited
Officers: Halina Briggs, Secretary; Lianne Estelle Firth [1966] Finance Director; Gordon Philip Dale Rann [1950] General Director

Justrite Holdings Ltd
Incorporated: 12 April 2016 *Employees:* 184
Net Worth: £18,344,602 *Total Assets:* £37,352,620
Registered Office: Arden Works, Whitefield Road, Bredbury, Stockport, Cheshire, SK6 2SS
Activities: Activities of other holding companies n.e.c.
Officers: Paul Darlington [1962] Director; Mark David McElhinny [1967] Director/President, CEO Justrite Mfg [American]

Jx2 Limited
Incorporated: 2 February 2010 *Employees:* 40
Net Worth: £5,712,539 *Total Assets:* £14,628,221
Registered Office: Unit 6a, 1 West Meadow Rise, Castle Donington, Derbys, DE74 2HL
Activities: Other letting and operating of own or leased real estate
Shareholders: Jacob Magill; Joseph Magill
Officers: Jacob Magill [1976] Director; Joseph Magill [1979] Director

K & A Merger Limited
Incorporated: 11 January 2012
Net Worth: £77,418,000 *Total Assets:* £297,492,992
Registered Office: The Waterfront, Lakeside Boulevard, Doncaster, S Yorks, DN4 5PL
Activities: Activities of head offices
Parent: Lakeside 1 Limited
Officers: Timothy Mark Beale [1976] Director; Mark Richard Priest [1966] Director; James Michael Douglas Thomson [1966] Director

K & S Buildings Limited
Incorporated: 5 April 2005 *Employees:* 2
Net Worth: £6,321,819 *Total Assets:* £17,612,800
Registered Office: Kashgroup House, 897 Silbury Boulevard, Milton Keynes, Bucks, MK9 3XJ
Activities: Retail sale in non-specialised stores with food, beverages or tobacco predominating
Shareholder: Kashif Nadeem Jaffar
Officers: Kashif Nadeem Jaffar, Secretary/Food Store Owner; Kashif Nadeem Jaffar [1968] Director/Food Store Owner; Sarwat Jaffar [1979] Director/Food Store Owner

K L Technologies Limited
Incorporated: 4 June 2007 *Employees:* 316
Net Worth: £7,949,446 *Total Assets:* £20,173,406
Registered Office: Riverside Industrial Estate, Estuary Road, Kings Lynn, Norfolk, PE30 2HS
Activities: Activities of production holding companies
Parent: KL Technologies Holdings Limited
Officers: Mark William Hamilton, Secretary; Geoffrey Paul Davies [1959] Director; Mark William Hamilton [1969] Director; Mark Littlewood [1962] Director

K.M. Packaging Holdings Limited
Incorporated: 5 October 2007 *Employees:* 20
Net Worth: £9,411,593 *Total Assets:* £12,754,119
Registered Office: 44 West Street, Oundle, Northants, PE8 4EF
Activities: Activities of head offices
Shareholder: Charles Smithson
Officers: James Edwin Bruce Close, Secretary; James Edwin Bruce Close [1951] Director; Graham Holding [1960] Commercial Director; Charles Smithson [1964] Director

K.M. Packaging Services Limited
Incorporated: 2 August 1984 *Employees:* 20
Net Worth: £9,882,877 *Total Assets:* £13,225,403
Registered Office: 44 West Street, Oundle, Northants, PE8 4EF
Activities: Manufacture of plastic packing goods
Shareholder: Charles Smithson
Officers: James Edwin Bruce Close, Secretary; James Edwin Bruce Close [1951] Director; Graham Holding [1960] Commercial Director; Charles Smithson [1964] Director

K9 Midco Limited
Incorporated: 5 July 2017
Net Worth Deficit: £1,154,000 *Total Assets:* £19,654,000
Registered Office: Armitage House, Colwick, Nottingham, NG4 2BA
Activities: Other business support service activities n.e.c.
Parent: K9 Topco Limited
Officers: Mark John Andrews [1970] Director/Chief Executive; Alan Rae Dalziel Jamieson [1954] Director; Kajen Mohanadas [1982] Director/Investment Management; Benjamin St Pierre Slatter [1973] Director/Investment Manager; Sarah Louise Smith [1974] Finance Director

Kab Seating Limited
Incorporated: 2 March 1987 *Employees:* 376
Net Worth Deficit: £1,017,000 *Total Assets:* £22,367,000
Registered Office: Stone Circle Road, Round Spinney, Northampton, NN3 8RS
Activities: Manufacture of other parts and accessories for motor vehicles
Parent: CVS Holdings Limited
Officers: Kirk Feiler [1971] Director/Vice President Financial Reporting [American]; Terry Hammett [1964] Director/Treasurer & Vice President of Investor Relations [American]; Michael Pritchard [1956] Director/Vice President of EMEA Supply Chain & Logistics

Kaby Engineers Limited
Incorporated: 6 May 1975 *Employees:* 265
Net Worth: £6,201,809 *Total Assets:* £16,081,293
Registered Office: 14-16 Upper Charnwood Street, Leicester, LE2 0AU
Activities: Manufacture of metal structures and parts of structures
Shareholders: Gurbakhash Singh Sanghera; Gurdeep Kaur Sanghera; Charles Victor Bagshaw
Officers: Kulwinder Kaur Sanghera, Secretary; Baljinder Singh Sanghera [1965] Managing Director; Kulwinder Kaur Sanghera [1971] Director

Kadima Holdings Limited
Incorporated: 19 April 2006 *Employees:* 20
Net Worth Deficit: £34,981,000 *Total Assets:* £16,630,000
Registered Office: The Courtaulds Building, 292 Haydn Road, Nottingham, NG5 1EB
Activities: Activities of head offices
Major Shareholder: Hwee Khim Neo
Officers: Roger Ian Harry Broadberry, Secretary; Wai Wah Chang [1957] Director/Merchant [Malaysian]

Kadima Properties (UK) Limited
Incorporated: 19 April 2006
Net Worth: £3,561,000 *Total Assets:* £12,347,000
Registered Office: The Courtaulds Building, 292 Haydn Road, Nottingham, NG5 1EB
Activities: Other letting and operating of own or leased real estate
Parent: Kadima Holdings Limited
Officers: Roger Ian Harry Broadberry, Secretary; Wai Wah Chang [1957] Director/Merchant [Malaysian]

Kaefer Limited
Incorporated: 1 December 1995 *Employees:* 1,135
Previous: Kaefer C & D Limited
Net Worth: £6,208,000 *Total Assets:* £34,478,000
Registered Office: 63 Portland Street, Mansfield Woodhouse, Mansfield, Notts, NG19 8BE
Activities: Other specialised construction activities n.e.c.
Parent: Kaefer Isoliertechnik GmbH & Co. KG
Officers: William Russell Cook, Secretary; William Russell Cook [1963] Director/Accountant; Kevin Heilbron [1960] Director/Manager; Paul George Hoyle [1960] Director; Ian Tattersall [1964] Director; Trevor James Woodward [1974] Director

Kal Tire (UK) Limited
Incorporated: 9 September 2009 *Employees:* 1,966
Net Worth Deficit: £17,714,000 *Total Assets:* £99,773,000
Registered Office: 8 Bluebell Close, Clover Nook Industrial Park, Alfreton, Derbys, DE55 4RD
Activities: Support activities for other mining and quarrying
Officers: Daniel Martin Allan [1963] Director/Senior Vice President Kal Tire - Mining Tire Group [Canadian]; Iain David Butler [1970] Director/Vice President Finance; Douglas Glenn Lemiski [1958] Director/Senior Vice President Business Services [Canadian]

Kal Tire Southern African Holdings Limited
Incorporated: 28 December 2011 *Employees:* 3
Net Worth Deficit: £16,123,591 *Total Assets:* £40,369,548
Registered Office: 8 Bluebell Close, Clover Nook Industrial Park, Somercotes, Alfreton, Derbys, DE55 4RD
Activities: Activities of head offices
Parent: OTR Holdings Limited
Officers: Daniel Martin Allan [1963] Director/Senior Vice President Kal Tire - Mining Tire Group [Canadian]; Iain David Butler [1970] Director/Vice President Finance

Kalsi Properties (UK) Limited
Incorporated: 13 December 2013
Net Worth: £1,922,763 *Total Assets:* £10,041,533
Registered Office: 1110 Elliott Court, Coventry Business Park, Herald Avenue, Coventry, Warwicks, CV5 6UB
Activities: Development of building projects
Officers: Harbans Singh Kalsi, Secretary; Harbans Singh Kalsi [1971] Director; Sohan Singh Kalsi [1961] Director

Kannegiesser UK Limited
Incorporated: 9 March 1978 *Employees:* 174
Net Worth: £5,977,097 *Total Assets:* £25,363,388
Registered Office: Kannegiesser UK, Beaumont Road, Banbury, Oxon, OX16 1QZ
Activities: Manufacture of other fabricated metal products n.e.c.
Officers: Katherina Paulina Hartley, Secretary; Andrew David Cartwright [1963] Director; Katherina Paulina Hartley [1967] Director; Dr Paul Nicholas Morley [1972] Director; Uwe Kurt Priester [1963] Director [German]

Karcher (U.K.) Limited
Incorporated: 26 January 1978 *Employees:* 324
Net Worth: £17,751,000 *Total Assets:* £47,273,000
Registered Office: Karcher House, Brookhill Way, Banbury, Oxon, OX16 3ED
Activities: Agents involved in the sale of machinery, industrial equipment, ships and aircraft
Parent: Karcher Beteiligungs-GmbH
Officers: Mark Richard Venner, Secretary; Markus Jakob Asch [1971] Director [German]; Hartmut Otto Jenner [1965] Director [German]; Simon Charles Keeping [1960] Director; Christian May [1972] Director [German]; Mark Richard Venner [1969] Director/Accountant

Karsten UK Limited
Incorporated: 5 December 2003
Net Worth: £10,361,438 *Total Assets:* £23,012,368
Registered Office: Karsten UK Ltd, Camel Gate, Spalding, Lincs, PE12 6ES
Activities: Support activities for crop production
Officers: Hermanus Gideon Engelbrecht, Secretary [South African]; Hermanus Gideon Engelbrecht [1968] Director/Chartered Accountant [South African]; Belia Hendrika Karsten [1978] Director/Chartered Accountant [South African]; Petrus Abraham Karsten Jr [1975] Director/Fruit Producer Exporter [South African]; Petrus Abraham Karsten [1948] Director/Farmer [South African]

Kartell UK Limited
Incorporated: 27 August 2008 *Employees:* 178
Net Worth: £1,327,289 *Total Assets:* £21,500,352
Registered Office: Thistle Down Barn, Holcot Lane, Sywell, Northampton, NN6 0BG
Activities: Other retail sale not in stores, stalls or markets
Shareholders: Alexander Darryl Norford; Erol Usten
Officers: Alexander Darryl Norford [1978] Director; Erol Usten [1957] Director

Kautex Unipart Limited
Incorporated: 23 May 1996 *Employees:* 289
Net Worth: £21,600,000 *Total Assets:* £53,800,000
Registered Office: Unipart House, Garsington Road, Cowley, Oxford, OX4 2PG
Activities: Manufacture of other parts and accessories for motor vehicles
Shareholders: Unipart Manufacturing Limited; Kautex Textron (UK) Limited
Officers: Robert Paul David O'Brien, Secretary; Richard William Stuart Brooks [1963] Director; Carol Burke [1967] Managing Director; Eric Gregory Cardinali [1965] Director [American]; Jonathan Chitty [1976] Director/Accountant; Joerg Rautenstrauch [1967] Director [German]

Kawneer U.K. Limited
Incorporated: 11 April 1994 *Employees:* 179
Net Worth: £15,618,000 *Total Assets:* £23,609,000
Registered Office: 26a Atlas Way, Sheffield, S4 7QQ
Activities: Aluminium production
Parent: Fairchild Fasteners (UK) Limited
Officers: Petra Papinniemi-Ainger, Secretary; Lluis Maria Fargas Mas [1966] Director/Lawyer [Spanish]; Robert Edward Hughes [1975] Director/Chartered Accountant; Philip Randles [1970] Finance Director

Kaye Aluminium (Holdings) Limited
Incorporated: 12 May 2004 *Employees:* 234
Net Worth: £26,103,040 *Total Assets:* £47,727,748
Registered Office: Ogden Road, Wheatley Hills, Doncaster, S Yorks, DN2 4SG
Activities: Manufacture of other fabricated metal products n.e.c.
Officers: Belen Arias Rubiales, Secretary; Felipe Quinta Marino [1979] Director [Spanish]; Fernando Quinta Marino [1970] Director [Spanish]

Kaystan Holdings Limited
Incorporated: 21 December 2016 *Employees:* 113
Net Worth: £30,181,336 *Total Assets:* £35,285,840
Registered Office: c/o Sims Group UK Limited, Long Marston, Stratford upon Avon, Warwicks, CV37 8AQ
Activities: Activities of other holding companies n.e.c.
Parent: Sims Group UK Limited
Officers: David Michael Williams, Secretary; Mark Ian Saunders [1968] Director; David Michael Williams [1964] Director; Paul Michael Wright [1969] Director

KCI Holding UK Limited
Incorporated: 23 March 1994
Net Worth: £20,281,000 *Total Assets:* £72,368,000
Registered Office: Unit 1 Charter Point Way, Coalfield Way, Ashby Business Park, Ashby De La Zouch, Leics, LE65 1NF
Activities: Activities of head offices
Parent: Konecranes Finance Oy
Officers: Andrew Timothy Spencer, Secretary; Mark Bennett [1962] Managing Director; Tomas Myntti [1963] Regional Director [Finnish]; Teo Juhani Ottola [1968] Director/Chief Financial Officer [Finnish]; Sirpa Talvikki Poitsalo [1963] Director General Counsel [Finnish]

KCT Holdings Limited
Incorporated: 31 March 1994 *Employees:* 218
Net Worth: £16,585,615 *Total Assets:* £34,810,180
Registered Office: Unit 22 Hayhill Industrial Estate, Barrow upon Soar, Loughborough, Leics, LE12 8LD
Activities: Activities of head offices
Major Shareholder: Robert Derrick John Fothergill
Officers: Christopher John Hart Hill, Secretary; Clare Marie Fothergill [1952] Director; David John Fothergill [1980] Managing Director; Robert Daniel Fothergill [1984] Director/Business Manager; Robert Derrick John Fothergill [1949] Director; Christopher John Hart Hill [1954] Director/Chartered Accountant; Sarah Anne Wyatt [1982] Director/Marketing Assistant

Keadby Generation Limited
Incorporated: 8 July 1992 *Employees:* 181
Net Worth Deficit: £273,500,000 *Total Assets:* £183,900,000
Registered Office: Keadby Power Station, Trentside, Keadby, Scunthorpe, N Lincs, DN17 3EF
Activities: Production of electricity
Parent: SSE Generation Limited
Officers: Sally Fairbairn, Secretary; Mark Richard Hayward [1963] Director/Manager; James Isaac Smith [1962] Director/Engineer

Keelex 351 Limited
Incorporated: 30 March 2010 *Employees:* 380
Net Worth: £38,851,088 *Total Assets:* £48,340,644
Registered Office: Howard House, Graycar Business Park, Barton Turn, Barton under Needwood, Burton on Trent, Staffs, DE13 8EN
Activities: Dormant company
Parent: Wabtec Air Brake Technologies
Officers: Michael James Isaac, Secretary; Michael James Isaac [1963] Director/Chartered Accountant; Christopher John Weatherall [1961] Managing Director

Keepmoat Homes Limited
Incorporated: 22 December 1987 *Employees:* 968
Net Worth: £109,364,000 *Total Assets:* £452,708,000
Registered Office: Keepmoat, The Waterfront, Lakeside Boulevard, Doncaster, S Yorks, DN4 5PL
Activities: Construction of domestic buildings
Parent: Keepmoat Limited
Officers: Lyn Michelle Charters, Secretary; Timothy Mark Beale [1976] Director; Mark Richard Priest [1966] Director; James Michael Douglas Thomson [1966] Director

Keepmoat Limited
Incorporated: 12 March 1986 *Employees:* 1,098
Net Worth: £181,755,008 *Total Assets:* £538,776,000
Registered Office: Keepmoat, The Waterfront, Lakeside Boulevard, Doncaster, S Yorks, DN4 5PL
Activities: Activities of head offices
Parent: Castle 1 Limited
Officers: Lyn Michelle Charters, Secretary; Timothy Mark Beale [1976] Director; Mark Richard Priest [1966] Director; James Michael Douglas Thomson [1966] Director

Keepstem Limited
Incorporated: 14 November 1997 *Employees:* 161
Net Worth: £3,629,446 *Total Assets:* £30,536,480
Registered Office: Wool Hall Farm, Cross Gate, Wykeham, Spalding, Lincs, PE12 6HW
Activities: Growing of vegetables and melons, roots and tubers
Shareholder: Robin Hancox
Officers: Aubrey Edward Day, Secretary/Chartered Management Accountant; Aubrey Edward Day [1958] Director/Chartered Management Accountant; Robin Hancox [1956] Director; Martin John Tate [1966] Director

Keigar Homes Limited
Incorporated: 18 January 1979 *Employees:* 56
Net Worth: £18,885,592 *Total Assets:* £22,784,028
Registered Office: Keigar Lodge, Canberra View, Barton upon Humber, N Lincs, DN18 5GR
Activities: Construction of domestic buildings
Shareholders: Garry William Whall; Patricia Wendy Whall
Officers: Garry William Whall, Secretary; Bradley Warren Whall [1987] Operations Director; Garry William Whall [1960] Director; Nathan William Whall [1984] Sales Director; Patricia Wendy Whall [1960] Director Bookkeeper

Kelkay Limited
Incorporated: 18 May 2001 *Employees:* 93
Net Worth: £10,872,375 *Total Assets:* £15,376,045
Registered Office: The Old Airfield, Heck and Pollington Lane, Pollington, E Yorks, DN14 0BA
Activities: Non-specialised wholesale trade
Parent: Altia Holdings Limited
Officers: Anthony Neil Harker [1969] Managing Director; Brian Gerard Harris [1969] Director/SVP, CFO [American]; Robert John Hewitt [1956] Director; Simon Andrew Hupfeld [1976] Director [Australian]; Robert Francis Mehmel [1962] Director/Business Executive [American]; Richard Pyrah [1970] Director/Sales Manager; Jonathan Wilson [1963] Operations Director

Keller Limited
Incorporated: 25 August 1950 *Employees:* 390
Net Worth: £9,230,000 *Total Assets:* £35,071,000
Registered Office: Keller Limited, Oxford Road, Ryton on Dunsmore, Coventry, Warwicks, CV8 3EG
Activities: Other specialised construction activities n.e.c.
Parent: Keller Group PLC
Officers: Roger Bryan Barratt, Secretary; Roger Bryan Barratt [1960] Director; James Emile de Waele [1967] Director/Civil Engineer; Julian Jon Fletcher [1969] Director/Civil Engineer; Joseph Christopher Hubback [1976] Business Unit Managing Director; Kerry Anne Abigail Porritt [1970] Director/Company Secretary; Robert Malcolm Thompson [1959] Director/Civil Engineer

I M Kelly Automotive Limited
Incorporated: 24 February 2000 *Employees:* 283
Net Worth: £7,728,958 *Total Assets:* £12,433,178
Registered Office: Orion Way, Kettering Business Park, Kettering, Northants, NN15 6NL
Activities: Manufacture of other parts and accessories for motor vehicles
Shareholders: Luc Christiaen; Martine Christiaen
Officers: Luc Christiaen [1949] Managing Director [Belgian]; Martine Christiaen [1951] Director [Belgian]; Nicky Christiaen [1979] Director [Belgian]; John Antony Matthews [1966] Director/Accountant; Geoff Louis Simmonds [1961] Director

I M Kelly Holdings Limited
Incorporated: 15 July 2014 *Employees:* 359
Net Worth: £22,066,994 *Total Assets:* £31,244,322
Registered Office: Orion Way, Kettering Business Park, Kettering, Northants, NN15 6NL
Activities: Activities of head offices
Shareholders: Martine Christiaen; Luc Christiaen
Officers: Luc Christiaen [1949] Managing Director [Belgian]; Martine Christiaen [1951] Director [Belgian]; Nicky Christiaen [1979] Director [Belgian]; John Antony Matthews [1966] Director/Accountant

The Kelmarsh Trust
Incorporated: 15 October 1982 *Employees:* 16
Net Worth: £22,149,312 *Total Assets:* £22,848,880
Registered Office: Kelmarsh Hall, Kelmarsh, Northampton, NN6 9LY
Activities: Other letting and operating of own or leased real estate
Officers: Lesley Ann Denton, Secretary; Bruno Philip Robert Bargery [1966] Director/Trustee; Caroline Cordelia Ridley Brocklehurst [1959] Director/Trustee; Richard George Flenley [1946] Director/Landscape Designer; Charles Lovett Greville-Heygate [1950] Director/Land Agent; James David Lancaster [1954] Director/Trustee; Lady Diane Nutting [1941] Director/Private Means; Lady Anne Constance Parsons [1951] Director

Kelta Limited
Incorporated: 23 September 2014 *Employees:* 1,212
Net Worth: £138,703,984 *Total Assets:* £146,109,968
Registered Office: Eagle House, 28 Billing Road, Northampton, NN1 5AJ
Activities: Activities of other holding companies n.e.c.
Major Shareholder: Parag Mehta
Officers: Parag Mehta [1968] Director [American]

Kendall Bros. (Portsmouth) Limited
Incorporated: 9 February 1950 *Employees:* 76
Net Worth: £12,560,429 *Total Assets:* £17,074,056
Registered Office: Bardon Hall, Copt Oak Road, Markfield, Leics, LE67 9PJ
Activities: Other specialised construction activities n.e.c.
Parent: Aggregate Industries UK Limited
Officers: James West Atherton-Ham [1970] Director/Barrister; John Ferguson Bowater [1949] Director/Deputy Group CEO

Kenilworth Multi Academy Trust
Incorporated: 11 July 2011 *Employees:* 99
Previous: The Westwood Academy (Coventry)
Net Worth: £11,467,000 *Total Assets:* £13,599,000
Registered Office: Leyes Lane, Kenilworth, Warwicks, CV8 2DA
Activities: General secondary education
Officers: Elizabeth Louise Shaw, Secretary; Hayden Abbott [1959] Director/Headteacher; Susan Mary Casey [1966] Director/Manager; Stuart John Croft [1963] Director/University Vice Chancellor; Paul Harris [1968] Director/Regional Pre Construction Manager; Stephen Paul Morales [1968] Director/Chief Executive [Spanish]

Kennelpak Limited
Incorporated: 16 August 1973 *Employees:* 269
Net Worth: £5,358,000 *Total Assets:* £9,767,000
Registered Office: Palmer Drive, Bessell Lane, Stapleford, Notts, NG9 7BW
Activities: Wholesale of grain, unmanufactured tobacco, seeds and animal feeds
Parent: Enact Newco 8 Limited
Officers: Daniel James Constance [1970] Production Director; Andrew Jones [1979] Director/Chief Transformation Officer; Simon Paul Tutt [1972] Director/Chief Financial Officer

Kent Energy, Ltd.
Incorporated: 16 January 1996
Net Worth: £3,549,000 *Total Assets:* £46,978,000
Registered Office: Ground Floor West, 900 Pavilion Drive, Northampton Business Park, Northampton, NN4 7RG
Activities: Other business support service activities n.e.c.
Shareholders: FCC Energy Limited; FCC Energy Limited
Officers: Carol Jayne Nunn, Secretary; Vicente Federico Orts-Llopis [1962] Director [Spanish]; Agustin Serrano Minchan [1959] Director/Technical Civil Engineer [Spanish]; Paul Taylor [1959] Director/Chief Executive Officer

Kent Enviropower Limited
Incorporated: 3 February 1994
Net Worth Deficit: £3,669,000 *Total Assets:* £155,992,000
Registered Office: Ground Floor West, 900 Pavilion Drive, Northampton Business Park, Northampton, NN4 7RG
Activities: Other business support service activities n.e.c.
Parent: Kent Energy Limited
Officers: Carol Jayne Nunn, Secretary; Vicente Federico Orts-Llopis [1962] Director [Spanish]; Agustin Serrano Minchan [1959] Director/Technical Civil Engineer [Spanish]; Paul Taylor [1959] Director/Chief Executive Officer

Kent Pharmaceuticals Limited
Incorporated: 15 May 1997 *Employees:* 43
Net Worth Deficit: £1,369,000 *Total Assets:* £14,979,000
Registered Office: DCC Vital, Westminster Industrial Estate, Repton Road, Measham, Swadlincote, Derbys, DE12 7DT
Activities: Manufacture of basic pharmaceutical products
Parent: DCC Vital UK Limited
Officers: Conor Francis Costigan [1971] Director/Chartered Accountant [Irish]; Leslie Deacon [1963] Director/Chartered Accountant [Irish]; Harry Keenan [1959] Managing Director [Irish]; Redmond McEvoy [1964] Director [Irish]

Kent Power Corporation Limited
Incorporated: 17 June 2016 *Employees:* 3
Net Worth: £30,857,122 *Total Assets:* £124,543,984
Registered Office: River View, Sheffield Road, Rotherham, S Yorks, S60 1FA
Activities: Activities of other holding companies n.e.c.
Parent: Mitsui E & S Holdings Co., Ltd.
Officers: Ronnie Bonnar [1963] Director; Christian Grundtvig [1959] Director [Danish]; Mark Newbery [1957] Director/Lawyer

Kenwood Hotel Property Limited
Incorporated: 14 June 2016
Net Worth: £4,722,572 *Total Assets:* £19,351,262
Registered Office: c/o Director of Finance, Kenwood Hall Hotel, Kenwood Road, Sheffield, S7 1NQ
Activities: Hotels and similar accommodation
Parent: Vine Kenwood Ltd
Officers: Garin James Davies [1967] Director; Gregory Dyke [1947] Director; Susan Howes [1949] Director; Andrew Gerard Rouse [1960] Director

William Kenyon & Sons Limited
Incorporated: 27 July 1907 *Employees:* 105
Net Worth: £15,028,100 *Total Assets:* £16,848,080
Registered Office: P O Box 33, Chapel Field Works, Dukinfield, Cheshire, SK14 4RP
Activities: Activities of head offices
Officers: Piers Kenyon, Secretary/Managing Director; Christopher George Kenyon [1939] Director/Chairman; Helen Mary Kenyon [1966] Director; Margaret Kenyon [1940] Director; Piers Kenyon [1968] Managing Director; Sarah Ann Kenyon [1968] Director; William Kenyon [1965] Director/Chartered Accountant

Kenyon Forge Limited
Incorporated: 4 September 2009
Net Worth: £4,525,732 *Total Assets:* £17,799,604
Registered Office: Swallow House, Shilton Industrial Estate, Shilton, Coventry, Warwicks, CV7 9JY
Activities: Buying and selling of own real estate
Parent: Birmingham Swallow Investments Limited
Officers: David Nicholas Jopling [1960] Director; Neil Edward Smith [1957] Director; Steve Westhorpe [1958] Director

Kermotion UK Holdings Limited
Incorporated: 1 November 2010 *Employees:* 1
Net Worth: £143,248,160 *Total Assets:* £143,252,640
Registered Office: 19 Jessops Riverside, 800 Brightside Lane, Sheffield, S9 2RX
Activities: Activities of head offices
Parent: Danaher Corporation
Officers: Keith Graham Ward [1953] Director/Finance and Accounting

Kesteven and Grantham Girls' School Academy Trust
Incorporated: 6 July 2012 *Employees:* 171
Net Worth: £13,614,478 *Total Assets:* £15,574,587
Registered Office: Kesteven and Grantham Girls' School, Sandon Road, Grantham, Lincs, NG31 9AU
Activities: General secondary education
Officers: Alison Bryony Evershed, Secretary; Jayne Ballaam [1965] Director/Arts Practitioner; Heidi Elizabeth Blyth [1967] Director/Teacher (HHE); Nicholas James Boddington [1974] Director/Bank Manager; Darren David Bungay [1974] Director; Estelle Conron [1970] Director/Partner Solicitors Practice; Amanda Dorkes [1974] Executive Director; David Robert Dunbar [1970] Director/Architect; Nicholas Anthony Flanagan [1975] Director/Bank Manager; Joanne Lorraine Green [1979] Director/Personal Assistant; Joanne Harcombe [1965] Director/Senior Manager, Public Health England; Kay Helen Hardiman [1973] Director/Arts Education, Arts Council England; Ian Stephen McBain [1974] Director/Garden Designer; Lucy Anne Moncur [1969] Director/Teacher; David Scott [1960] Director/Headteacher; Mark Edward Shardlow [1961] Director/Journalist/TV Presenter; Carine Soudanne [1977] Director/Teacher [French]; Sean Michael Tarver [1965] Director/Teacher; Dr Diane Heather Watson [1949] Director; Melanie Jane Watson [1972] Director/Finance Assistant

Key Fund Investments Limited
Incorporated: 2 August 2002 *Employees:* 13
Net Worth: £5,479,899 *Total Assets:* £10,476,974
Registered Office: Unit 9-12 Jessops Riverside, Brightside Lane, Sheffield, S9 2RX
Activities: Financial intermediation not elsewhere classified
Officers: Giles Bloomer [1943] Director/Retired; Ian Francis Drayton [1955] Director/Entrepreneur; Stephen Ingram [1949] Director/Financial Consultant; Deborah Lamb [1957] Director/Business Advisor; Isobel Mills [1956] Director/Civil Servant; James Henry Newman [1950] Director/Retired; Melanie Jane Perkins [1955] Director/Investment Manager; Jennifer Margaret Pupius [1950] Director/Business Consultant; Hugh Max Rolo [1954] Director/Charity Manager; Andrew Ian Tupholme [1969] Director/Chief Executive

Frank Key Group Limited
Incorporated: 14 September 2007 *Employees:* 209
Net Worth: £7,791,362 *Total Assets:* £14,937,033
Registered Office: 22a Portland Street, Daybrook, Nottingham, NG5 6BL
Activities: Agents involved in the sale of timber and building materials
Shareholders: Robert Michael Sansom; Susan Erica Sansom
Officers: James Victor Norton, Secretary; James Victor Norton [1980] Group Managing Director; Robert Michael Sansom [1946] Director; Susan Erica Sansom [1958] Director

Key Property Solutions Limited
Incorporated: 7 June 1976 *Employees:* 64
Net Worth: £4,115,294 *Total Assets:* £14,361,186
Registered Office: High Edge Court, Church Street, Heage, Belper, Derbys, DE56 2BW
Activities: Other construction installation
Parent: Bowmer & Kirkland Ltd.
Officers: Michelle Ann Mucklestone, Secretary; Gavin Common [1973] Operations Director; Donald James Johansen [1962] Director/Contracts Manager; Ralph Charles Jones [1950] Director/Manager

Key Technologies Limited
Incorporated: 27 February 2008 *Employees:* 238
Net Worth: £5,679,000 *Total Assets:* £17,385,000
Registered Office: 5 The Courtyard, Timothys Bridge Road, Stratford upon Avon, Warwicks, CV37 9NP
Activities: Activities of head offices
Officers: Kevin Hilton, Secretary; Jonathon David Grove [1981] Director; Simon Leslie Grove [1983] Director; Kevin Hilton [1958] Director; Leszek Richard Litwinowicz [1958] Director; Trevor Middleton [1957] Director

Keyclad Limited
Incorporated: 29 September 1989 *Employees:* 42
Net Worth: £2,343,454 *Total Assets:* £16,895,412
Registered Office: High Edge Court, Heage, Belper, Derbys, DE56 2BW
Activities: Roofing activities
Parent: Bowmer & Kirkland Ltd.
Officers: Michelle Ann Mucklestone, Secretary; James Anthony Evans [1974] Director/Quantity Surveyor; Jonathan Mark Lazell [1962] Director/Sales Executive

Keyence (UK) Limited
Incorporated: 14 May 1993 *Employees:* 77
Net Worth: £12,647,301 *Total Assets:* £16,449,613
Registered Office: Avebury House, 219-225 Avebury Boulevard, Milton Keynes, Bucks, MK9 1AU
Activities: Wholesale of other machinery and equipment
Parent: Keyence Corporation
Officers: Kengo Owa, Secretary; Keiichi Kimura [1968] Director [Japanese]; Akinori Yamamoto [1965] Managing Director of Keyence Corporation Japan [Japanese]

Keystone Bidco Limited
Incorporated: 3 June 2014
Net Worth: £97,621,000 *Total Assets:* £102,818,000
Registered Office: The Waterfront, Lakeside Boulevard, Doncaster, S Yorks, DN4 5PL
Activities: Activities of head offices
Parent: Keystone Midco Limited
Officers: Timothy Mark Beale [1976] Director; Mark Andrew Budd [1975] Director/Investment Professional; Edward Jonathan Cameron Hawkes [1977] Director; Mark Richard Priest [1966] Director; Stephen James Robertson [1960] Director/Investment Manager; James Michael Douglas Thomson [1966] Director

Keystone Developments (LG) Limited
Incorporated: 11 September 2001
Net Worth: £2,725,000 *Total Assets:* £20,349,000
Registered Office: Leverett House, Gilbert Drive, Endeavour Park, Boston, Lincs, PE21 7TQ
Activities: Construction of domestic buildings
Officers: Robert Ian Griffiths, Secretary; Patricia Elizabeth Brandum [1955] Director/Consultant; Robert Ian Griffiths [1976] Finance Director; William Alan James Patman [1956] Director/Retired; Robert Gerrard Wilson [1950] Director/Retired

Keystone Financing PLC
Incorporated: 3 June 2014
Net Worth Deficit: £2,832,000 *Total Assets:* £102,332,000
Registered Office: The Waterfront, Lakeside Boulevard, Doncaster, S Yorks, DN4 5PL
Activities: Activities of head offices
Parent: Keystone Bidco Limited
Officers: Lyn Charters, Secretary; Timothy Mark Beale [1976] Director; Mark Richard Priest [1966] Director; James Michael Douglas Thomson [1966] Director

Keystone JVCO Limited
Incorporated: 8 April 2014 *Employees:* 1,098
Net Worth: £60,360,000 *Total Assets:* £503,755,008
Registered Office: Keepmoat, Lakeside Boulevard, Doncaster, S Yorks, DN4 5PL
Activities: Activities of head offices
Officers: Mark Andrew Budd [1975] Director/Investment Professional; Edward Jonathan Cameron Hawkes [1977] Director; Stephen James Robertson [1960] Director/Investment Manager

Keystone Midco Limited
Incorporated: 21 May 2014 *Employees:* 1,098
Net Worth: £64,057,000 *Total Assets:* £504,443,008
Registered Office: The Waterfront, Lakeside Boulevard, Doncaster, S Yorks, DN4 5PL
Activities: Activities of head offices
Parent: Keystonetopco Limited
Officers: Timothy Mark Beale [1976] Director; Mark Andrew Budd [1975] Director/Investment Professional; Edward Jonathan Cameron Hawkes [1977] Director; Mark Richard Priest [1966] Director; Stephen James Robertson [1960] Director/Investment Manager; James Michael Douglas Thomson [1966] Director

Keystone Topco Limited
Incorporated: 21 May 2014
Net Worth: £113,142,000 *Total Assets:* £113,879,000
Registered Office: The Waterfront, Lakeside Boulevard, Doncaster, S Yorks, DN4 5PL
Activities: Activities of head offices
Parent: Keystone JVCO Limited
Officers: Timothy Mark Beale [1976] Director; Mark Andrew Budd [1975] Director/Investment Professional; Edward Jonathan Cameron Hawkes [1977] Director; Stephen James Robertson [1960] Director/Investment Manager; David Anthony Sheridan [1962] Director; James Michael Douglas Thomson [1966] Director

KHL Newco Limited
Incorporated: 9 October 2014 *Employees:* 85
Net Worth Deficit: £3,528,228 *Total Assets:* £18,463,552
Registered Office: Barrington House, Heyes Lane, Alderley Edge, Cheshire, SK9 7LA
Activities: Business and domestic software development
Shareholder: Livingbridge VC LLP
Officers: Peter Clarke [1967] Director; Graham Mark Gilbert [1963] Director; Neil Harvey [1972] Director; Michael Anthony Marrison [1962] Director/Chartered Accountant; David John Murray [1970] Director

Kidderminster Property Investments Limited
Incorporated: 22 October 2002 *Employees:* 3
Net Worth: £2,566,608 *Total Assets:* £9,012,595
Registered Office: Estate Office, Oakley House, Oakley, Beds, MK43 7ST
Activities: Other letting and operating of own or leased real estate
Shareholders: Euroway Homes Limited; Lousada Investments Limited
Officers: Sharon Anne Hunt, Secretary; Alan Geoffrey Fernback [1947] Director/Property Investment; Paul Simon Fernback [1976] Director/Property Developer; Simon Charles Lousada [1963] Director

Kidney Research UK
Incorporated: 12 May 1967 *Employees:* 54
Net Worth: £10,105,000 *Total Assets:* £26,428,000
Registered Office: Nene Hall, Lynch Wood Park, Peterborough, Cambs, PE2 6FZ
Activities: Other human health activities
Officers: Anne Marie McCarthy, Secretary; Adrian Christopher Akers [1952] Director/Retired; Professor Sunil Bhandari [1966] Director/NHS Medical Consultant; Doctor David Hughes [1956] Director/Consultant Paediatric Nephrologist; Professor Jeremy Hughes [1961] Director/Doctor; Dr Deirdre Ellen Jennings [1969] Director [Irish]; Brian Thomas Kelly [1979] Director/Financial Services; Professor Elizabeth Beatrice Lightstone [1959] Director/Medical Practitioner; Julia Dorothy Moross [1962] Director; Dr Jill Tessa Norman [1955] Director/University Faculty; Iain Charles Pearson [1954] Director/Retired; Federica Pizzasegola [1978] Director/Financial Services [Italian]; David Prosser [1959] Director/Retired; Dr Adnan Sharif [1979] Director/Doctor; Dr Charles Richard Vernon Tomson [1956] Director/Doctor

Kimbolton School
Incorporated: 8 April 2003 *Employees:* 300
Net Worth: £38,528,408 *Total Assets:* £45,850,828
Registered Office: Kimbolton School, Kimbolton, Huntingdon, Cambs, PE28 0EA
Activities: Primary education
Officers: Edward Francis Patrick Valletta, Secretary; Peter Richard Frank Dobson Aylott [1965] Director/Chief Operating Officer; Sarah Marion Brereton [1973] Director/Marketing Consultant; John William Bridge [1950] Director; Professor Fiona Broughton Pipkin [1946] Director/University Professor; Joanna Louise Doyle [1965] Director; Sarah Elizabeth Duberly [1945] Director/Married Woman; Peter John Farrar [1952] Director/Retired Headmaster; Jonathan Alexander Gray [1970] Director/Insurance Sales; Debra Ann Hellett [1962] Director/Housewife; Dr Thomas Paul Hynes [1952] Director/University Lecturer; Katherine Lancaster [1968] Director/Solicitor; Bron Ellen Madson [1965] Director/Public Relations/Reputation Management; Simon Frederick Jonathan Page [1964] Director/Sales Manager; Graham Rex Kenworthy Peace [1945] Director/Retired; Joanna Louise Rice [1967] Director; Derek John Suckling [1972] Director/Airline Pilot; George Robb Yeandle [1957] Director/Accountant (Retired)

Kinaxia Limited
Incorporated: 10 December 2010 *Employees:* 1,085
Net Worth: £9,719,482 *Total Assets:* £85,907,272
Registered Office: Kinaxia, Adlington Business Park, Adlington, Macclesfield, Cheshire, SK10 4NL
Activities: Activities of head offices
Shareholders: Peter Richard Fields; Graham Richard Norfolk
Officers: Peter Richard Fields [1960] Director; Graham Richard Norfolk [1961] Director

Kinaxia Transport and Warehousing Limited
Incorporated: 19 February 2015 *Employees:* 9
Net Worth: £9,042,050 *Total Assets:* £76,024,496
Registered Office: Kinaxia, Adlington Business Park, Adlington, Macclesfield, Cheshire, SK10 4NL
Activities: Activities of head offices
Parent: Kinaxia Logistics
Officers: Peter Richard Fields [1960] Director; Kevin Norman Johnson [1964] Managing Director; Graham Richard Norfolk [1961] Director; Benjamin James Warrillow [1974] Finance Director

J.B.Kind Limited
Incorporated: 12 October 1906 *Employees:* 57
Net Worth: £5,710,937 *Total Assets:* £11,340,749
Registered Office: Portal Place, Astron Business Park, Hearthcote Road, Swadlincote, Derbys, DE11 9DW
Activities: Agents involved in the sale of timber and building materials
Parent: Jamanisi Holdings Limited
Officers: Nicky Sreevalsan, Secretary; James Patrick David Cadman [1964] Managing Director; Martin John Hile [1962] Commercial Director; Simon Miles Johnson [1972] Sales Director; Andrew Pearce [1964] Director; Nicky Sreevalsan [1972] Finance Director

Kindale Limited
Incorporated: 27 April 1976 *Employees:* 11
Net Worth: £5,489,896 *Total Assets:* £11,447,055
Registered Office: 11 Bedford Road, Barton-le-Clay, Beds, MK45 4JU
Activities: Buying and selling of own real estate
Major Shareholder: Clewin Charles George Hughes
Officers: Peter Aikman, Secretary; Peter Aikman [1946] Director; Clewin Charles George Hughes [1940] Director; Jean Hughes [1949] Director; Peter Michael Hughes [1975] Director; Kevin Michael Wharton [1963] Director

Ashley King (Developments) Limited
Incorporated: 27 June 2001 *Employees:* 23
Net Worth: £5,978,256 *Total Assets:* £14,858,661
Registered Office: 1 Goodison Road, Lincs Gateway Business Park, Spalding, Lincs, PE12 6FY
Activities: Development of building projects
Parent: Ashley King Group Limited
Officers: Ashley John King [1967] Director/Property Developer; Jane King [1964] Director/Property Developer

King Edward VI Education Trust
Incorporated: 11 June 2015 *Employees:* 104
Net Worth: £9,780,547 *Total Assets:* £12,491,977
Registered Office: King Edward VI Grammar School, Edward Street, Louth, Lincs, LN11 9LL
Activities: Primary education
Officers: Reverend Nicholas James Watson Brown [1976] Director/Priest; Sean Chesman [1970] Director/Engineering Manager; Dale Robert Crombleholme [1968] Director/Solicitor; Andrew Brian Harrison [1960] Director/Works Engineer; Allison Jayne Jay [1974] Director/Head of Awarding Body and Compliance; James Alexander Lascelles [1970] Director/Headteacher; Philip Norton [1951] Director/Professor

J H & A J King Farms Limited
Incorporated: 2 June 2015 *Employees:* 2
Net Worth: £6,524,265 *Total Assets:* £20,645,944
Registered Office: 1 Goodison Road, Lincs Gateway Business Park, Spalding, Lincs, PE12 6FY
Activities: Growing of cereals (except rice), leguminous crops and oil seeds
Parent: Ashley King Group Limited
Officers: Ashley John King [1967] Director/Farmer; Jane King [1964] Director/Farmer

The King's (The Cathedral) School, Peterborough
Incorporated: 8 December 2010 *Employees:* 152
Net Worth: £19,403,846 *Total Assets:* £20,919,308
Registered Office: The King's (The Cathedral) School, Park Road, Peterborough, Cambs, PE1 2UE
Activities: General secondary education
Officers: Martin Robert Blee, Secretary; Sharon Jerusha Abbott [1975] Director/Businesswoman; Tina Jane Allen [1976] Director/Teacher; Hedley Richard Quentin Arnold [1963] Finance Director; Darren Ayling [1965] Director/Headteacher; Martin Derek Bloom [1956] Director; Andrew Peter Boulton [1969] Director; Canon Sarah Romilly Denner Brown [1965] Director/Minister of Religion; Susan Mary Burgess [1972] Director/Chiropodist; Tansy Castledine [1978] Director of Music; Stephen John Crane [1951] Director/Education Adviser; Christopher Charles Dalliston [1956] Director/Dean of The Church of England; Elizabeth Jane Dunmore [1977] Director/Teacher; Reverend Mandy Carol Flaherty [1963] Director/Parish Priest & School Chaplain; Timothy John Hitch [1952] Director; Barbara Susan John [1959] Director/Psychotherapist; Susan Elizabeth Lowe-Lauri [1958] Director; Kevin Stephan Palmer [1957] Director; Christopher Frank Trotman [1945] Director

Kingdom Bank Limited
Incorporated: 3 January 2002 *Employees:* 28
Net Worth: £5,778,000 *Total Assets:* £56,250,000
Registered Office: Ruddington Fields Business Park, Mere Way, Ruddington, Nottingham, NG11 6JS
Activities: Banks
Parent: Assemblies of God Property Trust
Officers: Matthew James Slack, Secretary; Miles Richard Buttrick [1952] Director; Malcolm Norman Hayes [1946] Director; Sarah Rosina Pierce [1987] Director; Christopher John Sheldon [1960] Director/Chief Executive; Matthew James Slack [1977] Finance Director; William David Reid Swanney [1945] Director

T.H.Kingerlee & Sons Limited
Incorporated: 22 December 1961
Net Worth: £5,156,000 *Total Assets:* £11,765,000
Registered Office: Thomas House, Langford Locks, Kidlington, Oxon, OX5 1HR
Activities: Buying and selling of own real estate
Parent: Kingerlee Holdings Ltd
Officers: David Henry Kingerlee, Secretary/Surveyor; Darren Leslie Arekion [1967] Director; David Henry Kingerlee [1961] Director/Surveyor; David John Warlow [1969] Director/Accountant; Richard John Wilsdon [1952] Director/Buyer

Kingerlee Holdings Limited
Incorporated: 14 July 1970 *Employees:* 100
Net Worth: £21,567,000 *Total Assets:* £31,452,000
Registered Office: Thomas House, Langford Locks, Kidlington, Oxon, OX5 1HR
Activities: Buying and selling of own real estate
Officers: David Henry Kingerlee, Secretary/Surveyor; David Henry Kingerlee [1961] Director/Surveyor; Sharon Jane Marsh [1970] Director/Engineer; David John Warlow [1969] Director/Accountant; Richard John Wilsdon [1952] Director/Buyer; Anthony Robert Woodward [1950] Development Director

Kingerlee Homes Limited
Incorporated: 12 March 2008
Net Worth: £2,273,000 *Total Assets:* £9,694,000
Registered Office: Thomas House, Langford Locks, Kidlington, Oxon, OX5 1HR
Activities: Buying and selling of own real estate
Parent: Kingerlee Holdings Ltd
Officers: David Henry Kingerlee, Secretary/Surveyor; Darren Leslie Arekion [1967] Director; David Emmerson Coates [1951] Director; David Henry Kingerlee [1961] Director/Surveyor; David John Warlow [1969] Director/Accountant; Clive Philip Wiggins [1957] Director/Quantity Surveyor; Richard John Wilsdon [1952] Director/Buyer

Kingerlee Limited
Incorporated: 22 February 1980 *Employees:* 100
Net Worth: £6,103,000 *Total Assets:* £14,500,000
Registered Office: Thomas House, Langford Locks, Kidlington, Oxon, OX5 1HR
Activities: Construction of commercial buildings
Parent: Kingerlee Holdings Ltd
Officers: David Henry Kingerlee, Secretary; Darren Leslie Arekion [1967] Director; Glynn David Biggins [1961] Construction Director; Colin Leslie Botton [1959] Commercial Director; Robin Hambidge [1980] Director; Paul Hardy [1968] Construction Director; David Henry Kingerlee [1961] Director/Surveyor; James Richard Smith [1979] Director; David John Warlow [1969] Director/Accountant; Clive Wiggins [1957] Director/Quantity Surveyor

The Kingham Hill Trust
Incorporated: 10 March 1941 *Employees:* 213
Net Worth: £37,770,120 *Total Assets:* £40,230,660
Registered Office: Kingham Hill School, Kingham, Chipping Norton, Oxon, OX7 6TH
Activities: General secondary education
Officers: Neil Jackson Pearson, Secretary; Jeremy David Bruce Anderson [1958] Director/Financial Consultant; Kenji Michael Bachelor [1983] Director/Solicitor; Nicholas Cecil John Bewes [1967] Director; John William Lewis [1957] Director/Army Officer; Rev Robert Marsden [1959] Director/Clerk in Holy Orders; Rev Gregory Justin Mote [1960] Director/Clergyman; Caroline Margaret Pellereau [1958] Director/Retired; Simon Humphrey Westland Pilcher [1966] Director

Kingscrown Properties Limited
Incorporated: 8 January 1997 *Employees:* 6
Net Worth: £7,532,105 *Total Assets:* £22,546,896
Registered Office: Suites 7-10, Prudential Buildings, 61 St Petersgate, Stockport, Cheshire, SK1 1DH
Activities: Development of building projects
Shareholders: Barrie Stephen Pollock; Paula Pollock
Officers: Laurie Sharples, Secretary; Barrie Stephen Pollock [1951] Director; Daniel Stefan Pollock [1984] Director

Kingsgate Community Church
Incorporated: 11 May 2004 *Employees:* 90
Net Worth: £7,013,242 *Total Assets:* £10,217,656
Registered Office: 2 Staplee Way, Parnwell, Peterborough, Cambs, PE1 4YT
Activities: Activities of religious organisations
Officers: Sally Ann Duffy, Secretary; Albert Barry Featherstone [1946] Director; Richard Keith Johnson [1966] Director; Matthew Graham Negus [1982] Director; Norman Paskin [1949] Director; David Andrew Smith [1963] Director/Senior Pastor; Simon Duncan Wilson [1963] Director/Solicitor

Kingston (City) Estates Trading Limited
Incorporated: 20 May 1993 *Employees:* 2
Net Worth: £11,546,505 *Total Assets:* £11,722,133
Registered Office: King Charles House, Park End Street, Oxford, OX1 1JD
Activities: Other business support service activities n.e.c.
Officers: Robert Guy Godfrey [1971] Director

Kingston Equity & Finance Limited
Incorporated: 2 December 1985 *Employees:* 14
Net Worth: £5,223,693 *Total Assets:* £20,176,028
Registered Office: Concord House, Bessemer Way, Scunthorpe, N Lincs, DN15 8XE
Activities: Financial intermediation not elsewhere classified
Shareholder: John Ralph Williams
Officers: Heather Frances Mary Williams, Secretary/Director; Gareth John Williams [1980] Director/Finance Broker; Heather Frances Mary Williams [1954] Director; John Ralph Williams [1952] Director; Stuart Daniel Williams [1983] Director/Finance Broker

Kingsway Asset Finance Ltd
Incorporated: 27 June 1995 *Employees:* 14
Net Worth: £3,064,811 *Total Assets:* £12,043,525
Registered Office: Barons Court, Manchester Road, Wilmslow, Cheshire, SK9 1BQ
Activities: Financial leasing
Parent: Kingsway Financial Group Holdings Limited
Officers: Michael Walling, Secretary; Adrian James Anthon [1954] Director/Financier; Paul Nicholas Bradbury [1962] Director; Martin David Harrison [1951] Director; Peadar James O'Reilly [1976] Director [Irish]; Martin Basil Richards [1952] Director/Accountant; Jack Daniel Summers [1984] Director

Kingsway Financial Group Holdings Limited
Incorporated: 1 October 1997 *Employees:* 14
Net Worth: £2,085,973 *Total Assets:* £34,546,804
Registered Office: Barons Court, Manchester Road, Wilmslow, Cheshire, SK9 1BQ
Activities: Financial leasing
Parent: PAF Group Limited
Officers: Michael Walling, Secretary; Adrian James Anthon [1954] Director/Financier; Paul Nicholas Bradbury [1962] Director; Martin David Harrison [1951] Director/Financier; Peadar James O'Reilly [1976] Director [Irish]; Martin Basil Richards [1952] Finance Director; Jack Daniel Summers [1984] Director

Kingsway Leasing Limited
Incorporated: 30 July 1997
Net Worth: £774,358 *Total Assets:* £14,981,897
Registered Office: Barons Court, Manchester Road, Wilmslow, Cheshire, SK9 1BQ
Activities: Financial leasing
Parent: Kingsway Financial Group Holdings Limited
Officers: Michael Walling, Secretary; Adrian James Anthon [1954] Director/Financier; Paul Nicholas Bradbury [1962] Director; Martin David Harrison [1951] Director/Financier; Peadar James O'Reilly [1976] Director [Irish]; Martin Basil Richards [1952] Finance Director; Jack Daniel Summers [1984] Director

Kirona Holdings Limited
Incorporated: 7 November 2011 *Employees:* 1
Net Worth Deficit: £115,063 *Total Assets:* £12,419,053
Registered Office: Barrington House, Heyes Lane, Alderley Edge, Cheshire, SK9 7LA
Activities: Business and domestic software development
Parent: KHL Newco Limited
Officers: Michael Anthony Marrison, Secretary; Neil Harvey [1972] Director; Michael Anthony Marrison [1962] Director/Chartered Accountant; David John Murray [1970] Director

Kisimul Group Limited
Incorporated: 11 September 1998 *Employees:* 1,039
Net Worth: £15,528,688 *Total Assets:* £30,288,564
Registered Office: The Old Vicarage, High Street, Swinderby, Lincoln, LN6 9LU
Activities: Other education n.e.c.
Parent: Kisimul School Holdings Limited
Officers: Andrew John Murrell, Secretary; Margaret Hill [1956] Director/Chief Executive Officer; Andrew John Murrell [1969] Director/Accountant; Jayne Starkie [1966] Director; Andrew Stevens [1965] Director; Donna Varley-Turner [1972] Director

Kisimul School Holdings Limited
Incorporated: 21 March 2006
Net Worth: £187,757,760 *Total Assets:* £214,306,368
Registered Office: The Old Vicarage, High Street, Swinderby, Lincs, LN6 9LU
Activities: Other education n.e.c.
Shareholders: Cedar Project Bidco Limited; Educo Three Limited
Officers: Andrew John Murrell, Secretary; Margaret Hill [1956] Director/Chief Executive Officer; Andrew John Murrell [1969] Director/Accountant; Andrew Stevens [1965] Director

Kitchen Range Foods Limited
Incorporated: 12 March 1971 *Employees:* 193
Net Worth: £12,511,000 *Total Assets:* £18,533,000
Registered Office: Kingfisher Way, Hinching Brooke Business Park, Huntingdon, Cambs, PE29 6FJ
Activities: Manufacture of rusks and biscuits; manufacture of preserved pastry goods and cakes
Parent: Moy Park (Newco) Limited
Officers: Raymond Gerard McGinley, Secretary; Christopher John Kirke [1970] Director/Company President; Flavio Gomes Malnarcic [1964] Director [Portuguese]; Fabio Sandri [1971] Director [Brazilian]

Kite Packaging Group Holdings Limited
Incorporated: 20 February 2008 *Employees:* 245
Previous: KPG Holdings Limited
Net Worth: £21,667,000 *Total Assets:* £41,280,000
Registered Office: 186 Torrington Avenue, Tile Hill, Coventry, Warwicks, CV4 9AJ
Activities: Activities of other holding companies n.e.c.
Officers: Marie Bernadette Franziska Lydia Ashe, Secretary; Leonard William Durham [1950] Director

Kite Packaging Group Limited
Incorporated: 15 January 2001 *Employees:* 245
Net Worth: £11,862,000 *Total Assets:* £26,142,000
Registered Office: 186 Torrington Avenue, Tile Hill, Coventry, Warwicks, CV4 9AJ
Activities: Activities of other holding companies n.e.c.
Officers: Marie Bernadette Franziska Lydia Ashe, Secretary; Marie-Bernadette Franziska Ashe [1969] Director/Accountant

Kite Packaging Limited
Incorporated: 27 February 2003 *Employees:* 236
Net Worth: £9,855,000 *Total Assets:* £27,098,000
Registered Office: 186 Torrington Avenue, Tile Hill, Coventry, Warwicks, CV4 9AJ
Activities: Packaging activities
Officers: Marie Bernadette Franziska Lydia Ashe, Secretary; Marie-Bernadette Franziska Ashe [1969] Director/Accountant

KJW Drylining Limited
Incorporated: 2 March 2006 *Employees:* 19
Net Worth: £5,917,566 *Total Assets:* £10,824,365
Registered Office: 42 High Street, Flitwick, Bedford, MK45 1DU
Activities: Plastering
Shareholders: Kevin James Wright; Helene Evelyn Wright
Officers: Helene Wright, Secretary; Helene Evelyn Wright [1971] Director/Secretary; Kevin Wright [1970] Director

KL Ventures Limited
Incorporated: 26 September 2001 *Employees:* 1,261
Net Worth: £16,147,961 *Total Assets:* £44,864,004
Registered Office: The Courtyard, Chapel Lane, Bodicote, Banbury, Oxon, OX15 4DB
Activities: Take-away food shops and mobile food stands
Major Shareholder: Satnam Singh Grewal
Officers: Satnam Singh Grewal [1971] Director

Kleemann Lifts UK Limited
Incorporated: 22 March 2011 *Employees:* 4
Net Worth: £15,272,870 *Total Assets:* £18,086,256
Registered Office: Unit 8 Arena 14, Charbridge Lane, Bicester, Oxon, OX26 4ST
Activities: Manufacture of lifting and handling equipment
Parent: Kleemann Hellas SA
Officers: Panagiotis Chadoudis [1974] Director/Manager [Greek]; Konstantinos Koukountzos [1973] Director [Greek]; Nikolaos Koukountzos [1977] Director [Greek]

Klober Limited
Incorporated: 4 September 1985 *Employees:* 27
Net Worth: £36,152,576 *Total Assets:* £40,028,992
Registered Office: BMI House, 2 Pitfield, Kiln Farm, Milton Keynes, Bucks, MK11 3LW
Activities: Agents involved in the sale of timber and building materials
Parent: Klober GmbH
Officers: Jason John Bradley [1963] Director/Accountant; Andrew John Dennis [1965] Managing Director; Adrian Gregory Fishley [1960] Director/Sales Manager; Alfons Horn [1970] Managing Director [German]; Klaus Sonne Ravn [1966] Finance Director [Danish]

Knapp U.K. Limited
Incorporated: 29 August 1997 *Employees:* 199
Net Worth: £2,658,372 *Total Assets:* £21,792,000
Registered Office: Unit 60 Monument Business Park, Warpsgrove Lane, Chalgrove, Oxon, OX44 7RW
Activities: Repair of machinery
Officers: Tracey Margaret Sanderson, Secretary/Office Manager; Nathan Spencer Billing [1971] Customer Service Director; Tyrone Anthony Driscoll [1969] Projects Director; Philip Houghton [1964] Business Development Director; Craig Peter Rollason [1970] Sales & Marketing Director

Knights of Old Group Limited
Incorporated: 16 June 2011 *Employees:* 576
Net Worth: £4,565,475 *Total Assets:* £28,909,016
Registered Office: Kettering Venture Park, Kettering Parkway, Kettering, Northants, NN15 6XU
Activities: Activities of other holding companies n.e.c.
Shareholders: Alexander Paul Abbott; William Ian Pentland Beattie
Officers: Alexander Paul Abbott [1966] Director; William Ian Pentland Beattie [1966] Director; Simon Nelson [1966] Director

Knights of Old,Limited
Incorporated: 3 May 1957 *Employees:* 395
Net Worth: £9,843,571 *Total Assets:* £26,184,356
Registered Office: Kettering Parkway, Kettering Venture Park, Kettering, Northants, NN15 6XU
Activities: Freight transport by road
Parent: Knights of Old Group Limited
Officers: William Ian Pentland Beattie, Secretary/Director; Alexander Paul Abbott [1966] Director; William Ian Pentland Beattie [1966] Director; Simon Nelson [1966] Director

Knightwood Trust Farms Limited
Incorporated: 13 May 1996 *Employees:* 3
Net Worth: £25,924,000 *Total Assets:* £40,028,000
Registered Office: Rowland Hall Farm, Newsholme, Howden, Goole, E Yorks, DN14 7JW
Activities: Growing of cereals (except rice), leguminous crops and oil seeds
Parent: Knightwood Holdings (2011) Limited
Officers: James Watson Eyre Wild, Secretary; Elizabeth Anne Bisson [1963] Director/Land Agent; Colin Garfoot [1952] Director/Farm Manager

KNM Project Services Limited
Incorporated: 7 February 2011
Net Worth: £153,767 *Total Assets:* £13,322,356
Registered Office: Ruthlyn House, 90 Lincoln Road, Peterborough, Cambs, PE1 2SP
Activities: Other specialised construction activities n.e.c.
Parent: KNM Europa BV
Officers: Filippo Molinari [1975] Director/General Manager [Italian]; Flavio Porro [1970] Director [Italian]

Knott-Avonride Limited
Incorporated: 14 January 1983 *Employees:* 118
Net Worth: £2,765,866 *Total Assets:* £11,934,429
Registered Office: Europa House, Second Avenue, Centrum 100, Burton on Trent, Staffs, DE14 2WF
Activities: Manufacture of other transport equipment n.e.c.
Parent: Knott Holding GmbH
Officers: Neil Patrick Collins, Secretary; Philip Anthony Brown [1957] Joint Managing Director Technical; Neil Patrick Collins [1967] Director; Valentin Knott [1942] Director [German]; Mark Graham Nugent [1963] Director

Knowledgepoint360 UK Acquisitionco Limited
Incorporated: 14 March 2007
Net Worth: £21,372,000 *Total Assets:* £46,650,000
Registered Office: Ashfield House, Resolution Road, Ashby-De-La-Zouch, Leics, LE65 1HW
Activities: Non-trading company
Parent: UDG Healthcare (UK) Holdings Limited
Officers: Clifford Alexander McConkey [1970] Director; Alison Richardson [1962] Director

Knowles (Transport) Limited
Incorporated: 10 December 1947 *Employees:* 234
Net Worth: £24,465,176 *Total Assets:* £35,372,984
Registered Office: New Road, Wimblington, March, Cambs, PE15 0RG
Activities: Freight transport by road
Shareholders: Pamela Ann Knowles; Anthony Roy Knowles
Officers: Marcus Allebone, Secretary; Alexander Anthony Knowles [1990] Director; Anthony Roy Knowles [1945] Director/Haulage Contractor; Pamela Ann Knowles [1958] Director

Konecranes Demag UK Limited
Incorporated: 8 January 1970 *Employees:* 441
Previous: Konecranes UK Limited
Net Worth: £8,427,000 *Total Assets:* £48,192,000
Registered Office: Unit 1 Charter Point, Coalfield Way, Ashby Business Park, Ashby De La Zouch, Leics, LE65 1NF
Activities: Manufacture of lifting and handling equipment
Officers: Andrew Timothy Spencer, Secretary; Mark Bennett [1962] Managing Director; Wayne David Branton [1976] Service Director; Andrew Timothy Spencer [1984] Finance Director; Marko Tapani Tulokas [1972] Director [Finnish]

Kostal UK Limited
Incorporated: 14 March 1990 *Employees:* 500
Net Worth: £26,747,000 *Total Assets:* £47,309,000
Registered Office: Unit 16 Goldthorpe Industrial Estate, Goldthorpe, Rotherham, S Yorks, S63 9BL
Activities: Manufacture of electrical and electronic equipment for motor vehicles and their engines
Parent: Leopold Kostal GmbH & Co KG
Officers: Daniel Tristan Finger, Secretary; Martin Clay [1975] Managing Director; Andreas Kostal [1979] Director/Chairman & CEO [German]; Christopher Nigel Sanders [1957] Director/Manager; Ulrich Zimmermann [1958] Director [German]

Koyo Bearings (Europe) Limited
Incorporated: 12 February 1990 *Employees:* 257
Net Worth Deficit: £3,934,000 *Total Assets:* £29,138,000
Registered Office: P O Box 101, Elmhirst Lane, Dodworth, Barnsley, S Yorks, S75 3TA
Activities: Manufacture of bearings, gears, gearing and driving elements
Parent: JTEKT Corporation
Officers: James Richard Thomson, Secretary; Kousaku Asamoto [1965] Director/President [Japanese]; David Betney [1972] Director; Francis Szabo Bush [1963] Director [American]; John Christopher Lenihan [1954] Director

KRNS Properties Ltd
Incorporated: 30 December 2008 *Employees:* 12
Net Worth: £5,749,391 *Total Assets:* £30,001,920
Registered Office: Sital House, 3-6 Cattle Market, Loughborough, Leics, LE11 3DL
Activities: Hotels and similar accommodation
Shareholders: Sunil Suri; Naveen Suri; Rachna Suri
Officers: Kailash Chander Suri, Secretary/Managing Director; Kailash Chander Suri [1955] Managing Director; Naveen Suri [1985] Director; Rachna Suri [1983] Producer Director; Suman Suri [1963] Director/Teacher; Sunil Suri [1990] Director

Krohne Limited
Incorporated: 14 April 1976 *Employees:* 219
Net Worth: £18,834,588 *Total Assets:* £30,814,990
Registered Office: 34-38 Rutherford Drive, Park Farm Industrial Estate, Wellingborough, Northants, NN8 6AE
Activities: Manufacture of electronic industrial process control equipment
Officers: Julian Charles Millar, Secretary; William Robert Aitchison [1969] Operations Director; Edward Peter Jukes [1973] General Manager & Technical Director; Julian Charles Millar [1961] Director/Accountant; Andrew Barrie Muschamp [1962] Sales Director

KSB Limited
Incorporated: 8 March 1923 *Employees:* 113
Net Worth: £4,093,981 *Total Assets:* £11,828,577
Registered Office: 2 Cotton Way, Loughborough, Leics, LE11 5TF
Activities: Wholesale of other machinery and equipment
Parent: KSB Finanz
Officers: James Walsh, Secretary; Dale Geoffrey Croker [1964] Managing Director; Helmut Lammers [1961] Sales Director [German]; Dieter Woller [1969] Director/Regional Finance Officer Europe/MEA [German]

Kubota (U.K.) Limited
Incorporated: 21 February 1977 *Employees:* 121
Net Worth: £90,352,456 *Total Assets:* £138,674,464
Registered Office: Dormer Road, Thame, Oxon, OX9 3UN
Activities: Wholesale of agricultural machinery, equipment and supplies
Parent: Kubota Holdings Europe B.V.
Officers: Kyota Toyoki, Secretary; David James Hart [1965] Managing Director; Takehiro Ueda [1970] Director [Japanese]

Kuehne + Nagel Drinkflow Logistics Holdings Limited
Incorporated: 19 April 2006
Net Worth Deficit: £153,000 *Total Assets:* £70,906,000
Registered Office: Kuehne + Nagel House, Sunrise Parkway, Linford Wood, Milton Keynes, Bucks, MK14 6BW
Activities: Activities of head offices
Shareholder: Kuehne + Nagel Limited
Officers: Tristan Richard Michael Stokes, Secretary; Allison Michelle Best [1969] Finance Director; Brian Cox [1969] Managing Director

Kuehne + Nagel Drinkflow Logistics Limited
Incorporated: 19 April 2006 *Employees:* 3
Net Worth: £2,344,000 *Total Assets:* £70,906,000
Registered Office: Kuehne + Nagel House, Sunrise Parkway, Linford Wood, Milton Keynes, Bucks, MK14 6BW
Activities: Operation of warehousing and storage facilities for land transport activities
Parent: Kuehne + Nagel Drinkflow Logistics Holdings Limited
Officers: Tristan Richard Michael Stokes, Secretary; Allison Michelle Best [1969] Finance Director; Brian Cox [1969] Managing Director

Kuehne + Nagel Drinks Logistics Limited
Incorporated: 29 March 2006 *Employees:* 2,399
Net Worth Deficit: £16,226,000 *Total Assets:* £43,669,000
Registered Office: Kuehne + Nagel House, Sunrise Parkway, Linford Wood, Milton Keynes, Bucks, MK14 6BW
Activities: Operation of warehousing and storage facilities for land transport activities
Parent: Kuehne + Nagel Limited
Officers: Tristan Richard Michael Stokes, Secretary; Allison Michelle Best [1969] Finance Director; Brian Cox [1969] Managing Director

Kumho Tyre (U.K.) Limited
Incorporated: 28 September 1977 *Employees:* 29
Net Worth Deficit: £1,980,000 *Total Assets:* £23,179,000
Registered Office: Unit 3310 Hunter Boulevard, Magna Park, Lutterworth, Leics, LE17 4XN
Activities: Non-specialised wholesale trade
Officers: Myong Joong Choi [1975] Managing Director [South Korean]; Ja Woong Koo [1981] Finance Director [South Korean]

Kybotech Limited
Incorporated: 8 April 1999 *Employees:* 95
Net Worth: £7,189,662 *Total Assets:* £16,657,945
Registered Office: Dukeries Industrial Estate, Claylands Avenue, Worksop, Notts, S81 7BQ
Activities: Other retail sale not in stores, stalls or markets
Major Shareholder: Edward Charles Walton
Officers: Edward Charles Walton [1977] Director

Kyra Enterprises Limited
Incorporated: 20 September 1999 *Employees:* 649
Net Worth: £3,522,901 *Total Assets:* £12,097,675
Registered Office: The Manor House, Lower End, Bubbenhall, Coventry, Warwicks, CV8 3BW
Activities: Unlicenced restaurants and cafes
Major Shareholder: Glyn Pashley
Officers: Evelyne Pashley, Secretary; Glyn Pashley [1962] Director

L & R Medical UK Ltd.
Incorporated: 9 September 1998 *Employees:* 119
Previous: Activa Healthcare Limited
Net Worth: £10,248,000 *Total Assets:* £13,387,000
Registered Office: 1 Wellington Court, Newborough Road, Needwood, Burton on Trent, Staffs, DE13 9PS
Activities: Wholesale of pharmaceutical goods
Parent: Lohmann and Rauscher GmbH
Officers: Jane Elizabeth Doades [1974] Marketing Director; Simon Mangan [1971] Managing Director; Martin Johannes Ortwin Pohl [1976] Director [German]; Doctor Klemens Walter Schulz [1965] Director [German]; Wolfgang Suessle [1966] Director/Healthcare [German]

L C & M Holdings Limited
Incorporated: 27 October 2009 *Employees:* 49
Net Worth: £11,016,908 *Total Assets:* £11,803,283
Registered Office: Bay 18 Beevor Street, Lincoln, LN6 7DN
Activities: Renting and leasing of other machinery, equipment and tangible goods n.e.c.
Shareholders: Michael Geoffery Harwood; Charles Edenfield
Officers: Stephen William Price, Secretary; Charles Edenfield [1944] Director [American]; Colin Graves [1949] Director/Technical Manager; Michael Geoffery Harwood [1950] Managing Director; Richard John Lewis [1968] Director/Self Employed; Robert Nicholas Lewis [1966] Director/Self Employed; Anna Marie Lonsdale [1973] Director/Nurse; Ian Frederick Ramm [1963] Director/Self Employed

L H Group Services Limited
Incorporated: 13 October 1978 *Employees:* 380
Net Worth: £25,512,584 *Total Assets:* £42,248,280
Registered Office: Howard House, Graycar Business Park, Barton Turn, Barton under Needwood, Burton on Trent, Staffs, DE13 8EN
Activities: Machining
Parent: Westinghouse Air Brake Technologies Corporation
Officers: Michael James Isaac, Secretary; Michael James Isaac [1963] Director/Chartered Accountant; Christopher John Weatherall [1961] Managing Director

L. & M. Investment Company Limited
Incorporated: 3 November 1960 *Employees:* 3
Net Worth: £8,622,970 *Total Assets:* £11,907,512
Registered Office: West Walk Building, 110 Regent Road, Leicester, LE1 7LT
Activities: Other letting and operating of own or leased real estate
Parent: L & M Investment Holdings Limited
Officers: Ashley Marc Stevenson [1981] Director; Nigel Lee Stevenson [1944] Director

L.E.A.D. Academy Trust
Incorporated: 16 November 2012 *Employees:* 1,541
Previous: L.E.A.D. Multi-Academy Trust
Net Worth: £80,795,000 *Total Assets:* £110,028,000
Registered Office: The Old Pumphouse, 5 The Ropewalk, Nottingham, NG1 5DU
Activities: Primary education
Shareholder: Deryn Harvey
Officers: Louise Victoria Bird, Secretary; Mark Jonathan Blois [1970] Director/Solicitor; Paul Graham [1971] Director; Ian Hancocks [1975] Director of a Training Company; Melvin Thomas Kenyon [1957] Non-Executive Director and IT Consultant; Diana Owen [1964] Director/Chief Executive; David Vaughan Williams [1957] Director/Retired; Nicholas Abdo Rodney Ydlibi [1966] Director/Chartered Accountant

L.E.A.D. Trust
Incorporated: 8 September 2011 *Employees:* 1,088
Previous: L.E.A.D Academy Trust
Net Worth: £89,059,000 *Total Assets:* £118,396,000
Registered Office: 5a The Ropewalk, Nottingham, NG1 5DU
Activities: Primary education
Shareholders: Mark Blois; Diana Owen; Deryn Harvey
Officers: Peter John Berry [1953] Director/Consultant; Mark Jonathan Blois [1970] Director/Lawyer; Howard William Dowell [1951] Director/Chartered Surveyor; Deryn Harvey [1949] Director/Education Consultant; Diana Owen [1964] Director/Chief Executive

Lablogic Group Holdings Limited
Incorporated: 5 September 2011 *Employees:* 70
Previous: Lablogic (2011) Limited
Net Worth: £12,782,905 *Total Assets:* £18,932,572
Registered Office: Paradigm House, 3 Melbourne Avenue, Broomhill, Sheffield, S10 2QJ
Activities: Business and domestic software development
Major Shareholder: John Kenneth Clapham
Officers: Michelle Brown, Secretary; Richard Anthony Brown [1965] Director; John Kenneth Clapham [1946] Director; Peter Kenneth Clapham [1972] Director

R.A.Labone & Co Limited
Incorporated: 8 January 1965 *Employees:* 281
Net Worth: £10,259,361 *Total Assets:* £15,266,456
Registered Office: R A Labone & Co Ltd, Lower Middleton Street, Ilkeston, Derbys, DE7 5TN
Activities: Manufacture of other plastic products
Shareholders: Ann Blanche Stiegler; The Labone Charitable Trust
Officers: Ruth Frances Young, Secretary; Richard Byron Goldthorpe [1970] Engineering Director; Ashley Kenneth Roe [1968] Quality Assurance Director; Lindsay John Roe [1963] Production Director; Alfred Anthony Stiegler [1938] Director/Chairman; Ann Blanche Stiegler [1940] Director; Christopher John Young [1964] Managing Director; Ruth Frances Young [1964] Finance Director

Laen Limited
Incorporated: 17 December 2002
Net Worth: £10,864,139 *Total Assets:* £11,042,900
Registered Office: c/o Gaswise Services Limited, Horsleys Fields, Hardwick Road, Kings Lynn, Norfolk, PE30 5DD
Activities: Other letting and operating of own or leased real estate
Officers: Susan Barbara Neal, Secretary; Frank Anthony Neal [1949] Director/Engineer; Mark James Neal [1972] Director/Manager; Paul Anthony Neal [1969] Director/Manager; Susan Barbara Neal [1950] Director/Manager

Lafarge Cauldon Limited
Incorporated: 25 November 2014 *Employees:* 146
Net Worth: £16,612,000 *Total Assets:* £153,439,008
Registered Office: Bardon Hall, Copt Oak Road, Markfield, Leics, LE67 9PJ
Activities: Quarrying of ornamental and building stone, limestone, gypsum, chalk and slate
Parent: Aggregate Industries UK Limited
Officers: John Ferguson Bowater [1949] Director/Deputy Group CEO; Guy Charles Edwards [1965] Director; Barry Paul Hope [1968] Director

Lafarge Ireland Limited
Incorporated: 24 April 2015 *Employees:* 50
Net Worth Deficit: £6,275,000 *Total Assets:* £41,607,000
Registered Office: Bardon Hall, Copt Oak Road, Markfield, Leics, LE67 9PJ
Activities: Other mining and quarrying n.e.c.
Parent: Aggregate Industries UK Limited
Officers: John Ferguson Bowater [1949] Director/Deputy Group CEO; Barry Paul Hope [1968] Director

Lagardere Sports UK Ltd
Incorporated: 17 July 1998 *Employees:* 48
Previous: Sportfive Limited
Net Worth: £14,898,887 *Total Assets:* £32,690,780
Registered Office: 2nd Floor, 40 Water Lane, Wilmslow, Cheshire, SK9 5AP
Activities: Advertising agencies
Parent: Lagardere Sports Germany GmbH
Officers: Tim Birt, Secretary; Tim Birt [1975] Director/Chartered Accountant; Andrew Georgiou [1974] Director/Chief Operating Officer [Greek]; Paul Michael O'Dowd [1972] Director/General Counsel; Ugo Valensi [1981] Director [French]; Carl Woodman [1979] Director

Lakes Academies Trust
Incorporated: 10 June 2016 *Employees:* 112
Net Worth: £11,674,150 *Total Assets:* £13,715,497
Registered Office: c/o Water Hall Primary School, Fern Grove, Bletchley, Milton Keynes, Bucks, MK2 3QF
Activities: Primary education
Officers: Lucy Abbott [1974] Director/Head of Service Delivery and Management; Marta Brzezinska [1975] Director/Architect [Polish]; Anthony Charles Draper [1962] Director/Headteacher; Kay Emms [1968] Director/Banking Manager; Sean FitzGenerald [1967] Director/Solicitor; Roy Malcolm Leighton [1961] Director; Karen Lesley Roberts [1960] Director/Deputy Headteacher

Lakeside 1 Limited
Incorporated: 9 August 2007
Net Worth: £21,836,000 *Total Assets:* £35,286,000
Registered Office: The Waterfront, Lakeside Boulevard, Doncaster, S Yorks, DN4 5PL
Activities: Activities of head offices
Parent: Keystone Bidco Limited
Officers: Timothy Mark Beale [1976] Director; Mark Andrew Budd [1975] Director/Investment Professional; Edward Jonathan Cameron Hawkes [1977] Director; Mark Richard Priest [1966] Director; Stephen James Robertson [1960] Director/Investment Manager; James Michael Douglas Thomson [1966] Director

Lakeside Energy from Waste Holdings Limited
Incorporated: 31 October 2005 *Employees:* 58
Net Worth: £21,817,500 *Total Assets:* £136,944,528
Registered Office: Thames House, Oxford Road, Benson, Wallingford, Oxon, OX10 6LX
Activities: Activities of head offices
Shareholders: Viridor Waste Management Ltd; Grundon Waste Management Ltd
Officers: Clayton Sinclair Sullivan-Webb, Secretary; Douglas William Benjafield [1944] Director/Chairman; Neil Norman Grundon [1969] Director; Norman Stephen Grundon [1941] Director; Richard James Pennells [1964] Managing Director; Simon Anthony Follet Pugsley [1968] Director; Paul Michael Ringham [1969] Director; Richard MacAndrew Skehens [1950] Director

Lakeside Energy from Waste Limited
Incorporated: 19 October 1999 *Employees:* 58
Net Worth: £21,817,500 *Total Assets:* £136,944,528
Registered Office: Thames House, Oxford Road, Benson, Wallingford, Oxon, OX10 6LX
Activities: Production of electricity
Parent: Lakeside Energy from Waste Holdings Ltd
Officers: Clayton Sinclair Sullivan-Webb, Secretary; Douglas William Benjafield [1944] Director/Chairman; Neil Norman Grundon [1969] Director; Norman Stephen Grundon [1941] Director; Richard Pennells [1964] Managing Director; Simon Anthony Follet Pugsley [1968] Director; Paul Michael Ringham [1969] Director; Richard MacAndrew Skehens [1950] Managing Director

Lakshmi & Son's Limited
Incorporated: 21 March 2002 *Employees:* 131
Net Worth: £12,627,887 *Total Assets:* £17,598,696
Registered Office: Hamilton Office Park, 31 High View Close, Leicester, LE4 9LJ
Activities: Manufacture of other food products n.e.c.
Parent: Narottam Holdings Limited
Officers: Priyesh Dineshbhai Patel, Secretary/Food Manufacturer; Kevin Raymond George Moore [1970] Director; Arun Patel [1960] Director/Food Manufacturer; Dhirajlal Patel [1951] Director/Food Manufacturer; Dineshbhai Patel [1941] Director/Food Manufacturer; Minesh Dineshbhai Patel [1973] Director/Food Manufacturer; Priyesh Dineshbhai Patel [1972] Director/Food Manufacturer

Lamb-Weston/Meijer UK Limited
Incorporated: 14 February 1991 *Employees:* 141
Net Worth: £20,780,262 *Total Assets:* £26,444,370
Registered Office: Wesenham Lane, Wisbech, Cambs, PE13 2RN
Activities: Other business support service activities n.e.c.
Parent: Smith & Holbourne (Holdings) Limited
Officers: Simon Hendrik Peter Van Wouwe, Secretary; Bas Albas [1960] Managing Director [Dutch]; Simon Hendrik Pieter Van Wouwe [1967] Director [Dutch]; Johannes Adriaan Willem Wiskerke [1971] Director [Dutch]

Lamport Hall Preservation Trust Limited
Incorporated: 18 June 1974 *Employees:* 8
Net Worth: £23,832,784 *Total Assets:* £23,943,742
Registered Office: Lamport Hall, Northampton, NN6 9HD
Activities: Other social work activities without accommodation n.e.c.
Officers: George Drye, Secretary; Elizabeth Angela Brayshaw [1957] Director/Consultant; Charlotte Louisa Brudenell [1959] Director/Chatelaine; Willum Robin Butterfield [1942] Director/Farmer; Anthony Benedict Xavier Fenwick [1934] Director/Company Chairman; John Thomas George Harris [1959] Director/Accountant; Crispin David Jermyn Holborow [1963] Director/Chartered Surveyor; Richard Leonard Vere Isham [1958] Director/Solicitor; Rosemary Winifred Newman [1948] Art Director & Curator; Lady Kathryn Gayle Elizabeth Robinson [1942] Director

R. H. Lamyman Limited
Incorporated: 20 July 1965 *Employees:* 9
Net Worth: £6,633,206 *Total Assets:* £12,924,962
Registered Office: Wilsford Heath Farm, Ancaster, Grantham, Lincs, NG32 3QD
Activities: Growing of cereals (except rice), leguminous crops and oil seeds
Shareholders: Michael Henry Lamyman; Robert Hugh Fell; Mark John Hewlett
Officers: Michael Henry Lamyman, Secretary; Michael Henry Lamyman [1968] Director/Chartered Surveyor

Lanai Medical Ltd
Incorporated: 12 August 2015
Net Worth: £33,177,950 *Total Assets:* £70,118,072
Registered Office: c/o Performance Health Limited, Nunn Brook Road, Huthwaite, Sutton in Ashfield, Notts, NG17 2HU
Activities: Activities of other holding companies n.e.c.
Parent: Lanai Holdings III, Inc.
Officers: Andrew Michael Booker [1967] Finance Director; Isabel Maria Pereira Mota Afonso [1973] Managing Director [Portuguese]

Lancer Properties Limited
Incorporated: 16 January 1987 *Employees:* 1
Net Worth: £8,545,433 *Total Assets:* £12,918,375
Registered Office: Beech Lawn, Green Lane, Belper, Derbys, DE5 1BY
Activities: Development of building projects
Parent: Bowmer & Kirkland Ltd.
Officers: Michelle Ann Mucklestone, Secretary; Ralph Charles Jones [1950] Managing Director

Lancer Property Holdings Limited
Incorporated: 7 February 2006 *Employees:* 14
Net Worth: £30,107,060 *Total Assets:* £33,733,008
Registered Office: c/o Freeths LLP, Routeco Office Park, Davy Avenue, Knowlhill, Milton Keynes, Bucks, MK5 8HJ
Activities: Management of real estate on a fee or contract basis
Parent: ABDJ Holdings Limited
Officers: Duncan Robert Ferguson, Secretary/Chartered Surveyor; Duncan Robert Ferguson [1960] Director/Chartered Surveyor; John Townley Kevill [1962] Director; Andrew John Windle Lax [1949] Director; Byron Howard Pull [1947] Director

Land and Estates Commercial Properties Limited
Incorporated: 23 March 2011
Net Worth: £5,937,706 *Total Assets:* £12,466,206
Registered Office: 398 Ecclesall Road, Sheffield, S11 8PJ
Activities: Other letting and operating of own or leased real estate
Shareholders: Paul Caplan; John Llewelyn Graham
Officers: Paul Caplan [1955] Director/Retailer; John Llewelyn Graham [1962] Director/Retail Manager; Peter Turkington [1954] Director/Property Letting Manager

Land Instruments International Limited
Incorporated: 19 August 1982 *Employees:* 103
Net Worth: £20,830,000 *Total Assets:* £24,370,000
Registered Office: P O Box 36, 2 New Star Road, Leicester, LE4 9JQ
Activities: Manufacture of electronic measuring, testing etc. equipment, not for industrial process control
Parent: EMA Holdings UK Limited
Officers: Joy Atwell, Secretary; Justin Smith [1972] Managing Director; Emanuela Speranza [1968] Director/Vice President/General Manager EMEA, India [Italian]; Pietro Luigi Enrico Zetti [1968] Finance Director [Italian]

Landau Forte Charitable Trust
Incorporated: 23 May 1989 *Employees:* 441
Net Worth: £53,882,000 *Total Assets:* £61,878,000
Registered Office: Landau Forte College, Fox Street, Derby, DE1 2LF
Activities: Primary education
Officers: Christopher Manning, Secretary; Teresa Margaret Bell [1947] Director; Michael Thomas Davies [1947] Director; Keith Roy Doble [1944] Director/Engineering Consultant; Sarah Findlay-Cobb [1964] Director/Chief Executive; Rocco Forte [1945] Director/Chief Executive; John Nigel Kirkland [1938] Director; Martin Richard Landau [1937] Director; David Malcolm McAlpine [1946] Director; Rosemary Jane Morgan [1954] Director/Investment Management; Terence Raymond Ousley [1946] Director; The Hon Olga Marie Louise Anna Polizzi di Sorrentini [1946] Director; Alessandra Maria Luigia Anna Polizzi di Sorrentino [1971] Director/TV Presenter; Simon John Shooter [1964] Director/Solicitor; David Alan Shore [1959] Director

Landfill Management Limited
Incorporated: 3 November 1986 *Employees:* 1
Net Worth: £11,338,000 *Total Assets:* £12,191,000
Registered Office: Ground Floor West, 900 Pavilion Drive, Northampton Business Park, Northampton, NN4 7RG
Activities: Other business support service activities n.e.c.
Parent: 3C Waste Limited
Officers: Carol Jayne Nunn, Secretary; Vicente Federico Orts-Llopis [1962] Director/Chief Financial Officer [Spanish]; Agustin Serrano Minchan [1959] Director/Technical Civil Engineer [Spanish]; Paul Taylor [1959] Director/Chief Executive Officer

Landis + Gyr Limited
Incorporated: 4 March 1975 *Employees:* 778
Net Worth Deficit: £47,075,000 *Total Assets:* £79,693,000
Registered Office: 1 Lysander Drive, Northfields Industrial Estate, Market Deeping, Peterborough, PE6 8FB
Activities: Manufacture of electronic components
Parent: Bayard Metering (UK)
Officers: Stephen George Cunningham [1966] Director/Chief Executive Officer UK and Ireland; Adrian Theiler [1972] Director [Swiss]; Charles Philip Walker [1972] Director/Chief Financial Officer

Landmark Wholesale Limited
Incorporated: 17 May 1960 *Employees:* 39
Net Worth: £2,834,511 *Total Assets:* £13,090,641
Registered Office: 3 Carolina Court, Wisconsin Drive, Doncaster, S Yorks, DN4 5RA
Activities: Agents involved in the sale of food, beverages and tobacco
Officers: Andrew Mark Thewlis, Secretary/Director; Shamir Bihal [1974] Director; David Grimes [1965] Director; George Garland Hepburn [1948] Director; Sharmmila Jeganmogan [1979] Director; Manmohan Khurana [1957] Director; Geoffrey Norman John Mills [1958] Managing Director; Amaan Ramzan [1987] Director; James William Oxley Russell [1977] Director; Marcus Singh [1979] Director; Jehangir Suterwalla [1970] Director; Andrew Mark Thewlis [1964] Director; William Christopher Wilcox [1955] Director; Gurdashan Singh Wouhra [1960] Managing Director

Lands' End Europe Limited
Incorporated: 19 February 1991 *Employees:* 323
Net Worth: £36,415,632 *Total Assets:* £46,592,752
Registered Office: Lands End Way, Oakham, Rutland, LE15 6US
Activities: Retail sale via mail order houses or via Internet
Parent: Lands End Inc
Officers: Justin James McLarney, Secretary; James Frederick Gooch [1967] Director/COO/CFO [American]; Peter Lloyd Gray [1968] Director/Chief Admin Officer [American]; Monique Louis [1967] Managing Director

Richard Lang & Son Limited
Incorporated: 10 February 1988 *Employees:* 23
Net Worth: £13,661,639 *Total Assets:* £13,885,326
Registered Office: 1 Little Chester Park, Alfreton Road, Derby, DE21 4AA
Activities: Wholesale of household goods (other than musical instruments) n.e.c
Major Shareholder: Rolf David Lang
Officers: Florence Betty Roberts, Secretary; Teresa Gorecka [1952] Director/Sales Coordinator; Rolf David Lang [1955] Director

Langley Aviation Limited
Incorporated: 7 January 2000 *Employees:* 3
Net Worth Deficit: £9,951,051 *Total Assets:* £27,159,438
Registered Office: Enterprise Way, Retford, Notts, DN22 7HH
Activities: Non-trading company
Parent: Langley Holdings PLC
Officers: Anthony John Langley [1954] Director; Bernard James Langley [1993] Director

Langley Holdings PLC
Incorporated: 15 July 1977 *Employees:* 4,229
Net Worth: £567,751,296 *Total Assets:* £791,284,864
Registered Office: Enterprise Way, Retford, Notts, DN22 7HH
Activities: Activities of head offices
Major Shareholder: Anthony John Langley
Officers: Bernard Anthony Watson, Secretary; Anthony John Langley [1954] Director; Bernard James Langley [1993] Director; Bernard Anthony Watson [1956] Commercial Director

Langley UK Limited
Incorporated: 18 July 2008 *Employees:* 70
Net Worth: £3,888,800 *Total Assets:* £10,319,585
Registered Office: Langley House, Lamport Drive, Heartlands Business Park, Daventry, Northants, NN11 8YH
Activities: Roofing activities
Major Shareholder: Antonio Silvestri
Officers: Ella Maureen Churchman, Secretary; Antonio Silvestri [1969] Director; Roger Neil Williams [1961] Finance Director

Langridge Homes Limited
Incorporated: 14 August 1957 *Employees:* 31
Net Worth: £10,302,868 *Total Assets:* £15,946,438
Registered Office: 17-21 Clumber Avenue, Sherwood Rise, Nottingham, NG5 1AG
Activities: Construction of domestic buildings
Major Shareholder: John Wilfred Fletcher
Officers: Michael John Fletcher, Secretary; Hazel Fletcher [1935] Director; John Wilfred Fletcher [1934] Director; Michael John Fletcher [1961] Director; Roger Lee Foxall [1946] Director/Surveyor; Jane Deborah Walsh [1973] Director

Lantmannen UK Holding Limited
Incorporated: 22 September 2011 *Employees:* 4
Net Worth: £16,105,000 *Total Assets:* £113,233,000
Registered Office: Maidstone Road, Kingston, Milton Keynes, Bucks, MK10 0BD
Activities: Manufacture of bread; manufacture of fresh pastry goods and cakes
Officers: Morten Leth [1967] Finance Director [Danish]; Erik Flemming Nielsen [1951] Director [Danish]; Nils Olov Nyberg [1958] Director [Swedish]; Tim Robinson [1974] Managing Director

The Lapwing Estate Limited
Incorporated: 30 December 1966 *Employees:* 3
Previous: Loveden Estates Limited
Net Worth: £15,324,456 *Total Assets:* £15,510,614
Registered Office: Everton Carr Farm, Claybank Lane, Everton, Doncaster, S Yorks, DN10 5BZ
Activities: Growing of cereals (except rice), leguminous crops and oil seeds
Parent: Loveden Estates Limited
Officers: James Frederick Spence Brown, Secretary; James Frederick Spence Brown [1982] Director/Accountant; Nigel Denis Spence Brown [1946] Director

Larchsilver Properties Limited
Incorporated: 11 November 2011
Net Worth: £1,067,806 *Total Assets:* £11,984,478
Registered Office: The Firs, Willington, Shipston on Stour, Warwicks, CV36 5AS
Activities: Other letting and operating of own or leased real estate
Shareholders: Daniel Jellinek; Patricia Stryker
Officers: Raymond Antony Hugh O'Malley, Secretary; Daniel Jellinek [1976] Director/Chief Executive [Hungarian]

Larkfleet Homes Limited
Incorporated: 27 May 2015 *Employees:* 86
Net Worth: £23,762,122 *Total Assets:* £85,049,576
Registered Office: Larkfleet House, Falcon Way, Southfields Business Park, Bourne, Lincs, PE10 0FF
Activities: Activities of head offices
Shareholders: Karl Stephen Hick; Kingfisher Ventures Limited
Officers: Deborah Brown, Secretary; Helen Hick [1959] Director; Karl Stephen Hick [1959] Director

Larkfleet Limited
Incorporated: 2 March 1998 *Employees:* 79
Net Worth: £23,784,376 *Total Assets:* £76,677,024
Registered Office: Larkfleet House, Falcon Way, Southfields Business Park, Bourne, Lincs, PE10 0FF
Activities: Construction of domestic buildings
Parent: Larkfleet Holdings Limited
Officers: Deborah Brown, Secretary; Daniel Michael Endersby [1986] Director; Helen Hick [1956] Director; Karl Stephen Hick [1959] Director; Daryl Kirkland [1967] Director; Mark Mann [1960] Director; Terry Rene Roydon [1946] Director

Larson-Juhl UK Limited
Incorporated: 17 January 1975 *Employees:* 75
Previous: Arqadia Limited
Net Worth: £6,208,441 *Total Assets:* £14,439,753
Registered Office: Arqadia House, 2 Wolseley Road, Kempston, Bedford, MK42 7AD
Activities: Wholesale of other intermediate products
Officers: Deborah Marion Fraser, Company Secretary; Arie Cornelis Bijsterveld [1968] Finance Director [Dutch]; Michael John Brown [1958] Managing Director; Jonathan Leslie Burrage [1972] Managing Director

Laser Quantum Limited
Incorporated: 27 September 1994 *Employees:* 133
Net Worth: £34,215,000 *Total Assets:* £38,887,000
Registered Office: Emery Court, Vale Road, Stockport, Cheshire, SK4 3GL
Activities: Manufacture of optical precision instruments
Parent: Novanta Technologies UK Ltd
Officers: Doctor Steve Haydn Lane, Secretary; Robert John Buckley [1974] Director [American]; Doctor Alan Michael Cox [1972] Technical Director; Matthijs Glastra [1969] Director [Dutch]; Lawrence Anthony William Gloster [1969] Director/Chief Executive; Doctor Steve Haydn Lane [1971] Business Director; Philip Martin [1963] Director [American]; Brian Samuel Young [1969] Director [American]

Latimer Associates (U.K) Limited
Incorporated: 19 August 1997
Net Worth Deficit: £12,995,214 *Total Assets:* £10,618,355
Registered Office: 1st Floor, 181 Queensway, Bletchley, Milton Keynes, Bucks, MK2 2DZ
Activities: Other business support service activities n.e.c.
Parent: Pedralbes Limited
Officers: Craig William Keech [1960] Director; Dennis Keech [1931] Director; Matthew David Keech [1967] Director

Lattice Trading Limited
Incorporated: 1 May 2013 *Employees:* 6
Net Worth: £20,782,896 *Total Assets:* £24,520,816
Registered Office: Totemic House, Caunt Road, Grantham, Lincs, NG31 7FZ
Activities: Activities of financial services holding companies
Shareholders: Gordon Philip Dale Rann; Lesley Elizabeth Rann; Lianne Estelle Tapson
Officers: Halina Briggs, Secretary; Rachel Elizabeth Duffey [1978] Director; Lianne Estelle Firth [1966] HR Director; Andrew John Kirk [1981] Finance Director; Lesley Elizabeth Rann [1959] Sales Director

The Latvian Welfare Trust
Incorporated: 21 June 2006 *Employees:* 116
Net Worth: £13,914,815 *Total Assets:* £16,204,265
Registered Office: Catthorpe Manor, Lilbourne Road, Catthorpe, Leics, LE17 6DF
Activities: Activities of other membership organisations n.e.c.
Officers: Uldis Janis Revelins, Secretary; Edite Brauele [1973] Director/Corporate Client Advisor [Latvian]; Ilze Grickus [1947] Director/Retired [British/Latvian]; Marcis Jansons [1985] Director/Kitchen Fitter [Latvian]; Kriss Ligers [1936] Director/Retired [British/Latvian]; Maris Pulkstenis [1956] Director/Postman [British/Latvian]; Uldis Janis Revelins [1943] Director/Retired [British/Latvian]; Ivar Aivars Juris Sinka [1960] Director/Business Consultant [British/Latvian]; Miks Vizbulis [1990] Director/Recruitment Consultant [Latvian]; Karoline Isabella Zobens East [1987] Director/Legal and Business Affairs Coordinator [British/Latvian]

Launchchange Finance Limited
Incorporated: 13 December 2006 *Employees:* 1
Net Worth: £171,294,000 *Total Assets:* £214,848,992
Registered Office: 19 Jessops Riverside, 800 Brightside Lane, Sheffield, S9 2RX
Activities: Activities of head offices
Parent: Launchchange Holdings Limited
Officers: Keith Graham Ward [1953] Financial Director

Launchchange Holding Company
Incorporated: 4 October 1996 *Employees:* 3
Net Worth: £3,103,300,096 *Total Assets:* £3,902,550,016
Registered Office: 19 Jessops Riverside, 800 Brightside Lane, Sheffield, S9 2RX
Activities: Activities of other holding companies n.e.c.
Parent: Danaher Corporation
Officers: Frank Talbot McFaden [1961] Director/Treasurer [American]; Keith Graham Ward [1953] Director/Finance and Accounting; Philip Bernard Whitehead [1951] Director

Launchchange Holdings Limited
Incorporated: 16 December 2009 *Employees:* 1
Net Worth: £378,664,000 *Total Assets:* £397,692,992
Registered Office: 19 Jessops Riverside, 800 Brightside Lane, Sheffield, S9 2RX
Activities: Activities of head offices
Parent: Launchchange Operations Ltd
Officers: Keith Graham Ward [1953] Financial Director

Launchchange Instrumentation Limited
Incorporated: 23 December 1988 *Employees:* 1
Net Worth: £2,235,901,952 *Total Assets:* £2,891,536,896
Registered Office: 19 Jessops Riverside, 800 Brightside Lane, Sheffield, S9 2RX
Activities: Activities of head offices
Parent: VR Finance Company
Officers: Keith Graham Ward [1953] Director/Accountant

Launchchange Limited
Incorporated: 22 August 1991 *Employees:* 1
Net Worth: £1,068,153,984 *Total Assets:* £1,552,833,024
Registered Office: 19 Jessops Riverside, 800 Brightside Lane, Sheffield, S9 2RX
Activities: Activities of head offices
Parent: Launchchange Instrumentation Limited
Officers: Keith Graham Ward [1953] Director/Finance & Accounting

Launchchange Operations Limited
Incorporated: 15 December 2009 *Employees:* 14
Net Worth: £734,723,008 *Total Assets:* £1,332,269,056
Registered Office: 19 Jessops Riverside, 800 Brightside Lane, Sheffield, S9 2RX
Activities: Activities of head offices
Parent: Duki (2006) Finance Limited
Officers: Frank Talbot McFaden [1961] Director/Treasurer [American]; Keith Graham Ward [1953] Financial Director; Philip Bernard Whitehead [1951] Director

Laurenglen Limited
Incorporated: 23 September 1986 *Employees:* 1
Net Worth: £2,720,246 *Total Assets:* £10,347,911
Registered Office: 16 Binley Road, Gosford Green, Coventry, Warwicks, CV3 1HZ
Activities: Activities of head offices
Shareholders: Kirpal Singh Donsanjh; Hardeep Kaur Dosanjh
Officers: Hardip Kaur Dosanjh, Secretary; Kirpal Singh Dosanjh [1951] Director [Indian]

The Laurus Trust
Incorporated: 12 January 2012 *Employees:* 326
Previous: Cheadle Hulme Education Trust
Net Worth: £19,757,000 *Total Assets:* £23,116,000
Registered Office: Cheadle Hulme High School, Woods Lane, Cheadle Hulme, Cheadle, Cheshire, SK8 7JY
Activities: General secondary education
Officers: Nicola Burgess, Secretary; Pauline Elizabeth Benton [1940] Director/Retired Teacher; David Brown [1967] Director/Teacher; Leonard James Elias [1950] Director/Retired; Catherine Dorothy Fisher [1949] Director/Retired; Dagmar Kent Kershaw [1968] Director/Chief Executive; Anthony Richard Morrell Little [1954] Director/Group Chief Education Officer; Linda Mary Magrath [1960] Director; Wendy Mason [1975] Director/Chief Financial Officer; Rev Charles John Nevin [1945] Director/Retired Methodist Minister; Kalkivayi Seshagiri Ravi Kumar [1968] Director; Jenny Louise Singleton [1969] Director/Principal and CEO; Lisa Woolley [1977] Director/Headteacher

Lavendon Access Services (International) Limited
Incorporated: 28 August 1996
Net Worth: £2,165,000 *Total Assets:* £53,709,000
Registered Office: 15 Midland Court, Central Park, Lutterworth, Leics, LE17 4PN
Activities: Activities of head offices
Officers: Jerome Sarragozi, Secretary; Thomas Donald Kenny [1954] Director/Group CEO [Irish]; Thomas Anthony Murray [1967] Director/Chartered Accountant

Lavendon Group Limited
Incorporated: 2 December 1992 *Employees:* 83
Previous: Lavendon Group PLC
Net Worth: £185,015,008 *Total Assets:* £386,055,008
Registered Office: 15 Midland Court, Central Park, Lutterworth, Leics, LE17 4PN
Activities: Renting and leasing of other machinery, equipment and tangible goods n.e.c.
Major Shareholder: Gerard Deprez
Officers: Jerome Sarragozi, Secretary; Patrick Bourmaud [1969] Director/Chief Financial Officer of Loxam SAS [French]; Gerard Deprez [1954] Director/President and CEO of Loxam SAS [French]; Stephane Henon [1968] Director/General Manager of Loxam SAS [French]; Thomas Donald Kenny [1954] Director/Chief Executive [Irish]; Thomas Anthony Murray [1967] Director/Chartered Accountant

Lavendon Holdings Limited
Incorporated: 14 June 2007
Net Worth: £81,146,000 *Total Assets:* £150,900,992
Registered Office: 15 Midland Court, Central Park, Lutterworth, Leics, LE17 4PN
Activities: Activities of head offices
Parent: Lavendon Group PLC
Officers: Jerome Sarragozi, Secretary; Thomas Donald Kenny [1954] Director/Group CEO [Irish]; Thomas Anthony Murray [1967] Director/Chartered Accountant

Arnold Laver & Company Limited
Incorporated: 8 February 2017 *Employees:* 723
Net Worth: £37,237,124 *Total Assets:* £72,428,368
Registered Office: Bramall Lane, Sheffield, S2 4RJ
Activities: Agents involved in the sale of timber and building materials
Parent: Arnold Laver Holdings Ltd
Officers: Robert Todd Barclay [1969] Director; Mark Richard Bower [1959] Director/Accountant; John Alexander George Douglas [1964] Director; Patrick James Guest [1968] Commercial Director; Andrew James Laver [1966] Director/Accountant; Neil Andrew McGill [1977] Director; Stuart Whiteford [1990] Director

Arnold Laver Holdings Limited
Incorporated: 28 March 2017 *Employees:* 723
Net Worth: £37,238,124 *Total Assets:* £72,429,368
Registered Office: Bramall Lane, Sheffield, S2 4RJ
Activities: Non-trading company
Parent: National Timber Group Midco Limited
Officers: Mark Richard Bower, Secretary; Robert Todd Barclay [1969] Director; Mark Richard Bower [1959] Director/Accountant; John Alexander George Douglas [1964] Director; Andrew James Laver [1966] Director/Accountant; Neil Andrew McGill [1977] Director; Stuart Whiteford [1990] Director

Laver Leisure Limited
Incorporated: 7 May 2015
Net Worth: £10,927,622 *Total Assets:* £36,588,088
Registered Office: Bramall Lane, Sheffield, S2 4RJ
Activities: Other holiday and other collective accommodation
Parent: Laver Regeneration Group Limited
Officers: Mark Richard Bower, Secretary; Mark Richard Bower [1959] Director/Accountant; Andrew James Laver [1966] Director/Timber Merchant; Nigel Fredrick Thomas Hugh Petrie [1946] Director

Laver Regeneration Holdings Limited
Incorporated: 15 June 2007 *Employees:* 542
Previous: Arnold Laver Holdings Limited
Net Worth: £31,852,598 *Total Assets:* £91,159,416
Registered Office: c/o Arnold Laver & Company Limited, Bramall Lane, Sheffield, S2 4RJ
Activities: Activities of head offices
Major Shareholder: Andrew James Laver
Officers: Mark Richard Bower, Secretary; Mark Richard Bower [1959] Director/Accountant; Andrew James Laver [1966] Director/Accountant; Nigel Fredrick Thomas Hugh Petrie [1946] Director and Consultant

Laver Regeneration Limited
Incorporated: 20 August 1932 *Employees:* 542
Previous: Arnold Laver & Company Limited
Net Worth: £62,076,128 *Total Assets:* £97,110,584
Registered Office: Bramall Lane, Sheffield, S2 4RJ
Activities: Development of building projects
Parent: Laver Regeneration Group Limited
Officers: Mark Richard Bower, Secretary; Mark Richard Bower [1959] Director/Accountant; Andrew James Laver [1966] Director/Timber Merchant

Lawrence Sheriff School Academy Trust
Incorporated: 27 March 2014 *Employees:* 97
Net Worth: £9,430,395 *Total Assets:* £14,292,028
Registered Office: Lawrence Sheriff School, Clifton Road, Rugby, Warwicks, CV21 3AG
Activities: General secondary education
Officers: Dennis Christopher Barnett [1950] Director/Retired Teacher; Matthew Canale-Parola [1980] Director; Janet Lynne Eastwood [1968] Director/Marketing Consultant; Jeffrey Richard Glenn [1949] Director/Solicitor; David Michael Howe [1940] Director/Retired; Peter Kent [1961] Director/Headmaster; Kevin Paul Mahon [1943] Director/Retired; Carol Anne Moor [1964] Director/Personnel; Justin Muston [1967] Director/Teacher; Ian James Nichol [1954] Director/Financial Consultant; Susan Christine Peach [1950] Director/Retired; Rebecca Jane Rees [1974] Director/Solicitor; Gwendoline Temple [1964] Director/Senior Deputy Headteacher; Paula Jayne Whitfield [1967] Director/Chartered Accountant

Charles Lawrence Surfaces Limited
Incorporated: 17 May 1968 *Employees:* 47
Net Worth: £1,791,536 *Total Assets:* £9,619,512
Registered Office: Brunel House, Jessop Way, Northern Road Industrial Estate, Newark, Notts, NG24 2ER
Activities: Manufacture of other rubber products
Officers: Charles Roderick Stewart, Secretary; Martin Kiely [1963] Director/Civil Engineer; Andrew Buchanan Malcolm [1962] Director/Haulage Contractor; Walter Hattrick Malcolm [1960] Director/Haulage Contractor

Lawton Group Limited
Incorporated: 7 March 2000 *Employees:* 169
Net Worth: £6,469,000 *Total Assets:* £21,560,000
Registered Office: Norcliffe House, Station Road, Wilmslow, Cheshire, SK9 1BU
Activities: Other human health activities
Parent: Lawton Group Holdings Limited
Officers: Abigail Mattison, Secretary; Ryan Stuart MacAskill [1975] Director; Gregory Laurence Newman [1988] Director/Investment Professional; Jeremy Robert Arthur Richardson [1970] Director; Maureen Claire Royston [1960] Director; Phillip Gary Thomas [1978] Director

Lawton Tube Company Limited (The)
Incorporated: 11 March 1920 *Employees:* 100
Net Worth: £29,714,012 *Total Assets:* £47,342,256
Registered Office: Torrington Avenue, Coventry, Warwicks, CV4 9AB
Activities: Copper production
Officers: Simon John Waldron, Secretary; Rudolf Herold [1950] Director [German]; Giles Frederick Lawton [1969] Director; Oliver Vernon Lawton [1970] Director; Robert Alistair Lawton [1974] Director; Simon John Waldron [1969] Director

Lazarus Properties Limited
Incorporated: 3 June 1997 *Employees:* 5
Net Worth: £23,413,472 *Total Assets:* £38,625,656
Registered Office: 3 Bradford Row, Doncaster, S Yorks, DN1 3NF
Activities: Other letting and operating of own or leased real estate
Shareholders: John Edgar Lloyd Nicholson; Michael Patrick Murray
Officers: Michael Patrick Murray [1969] Director; John Edgar Lloyd Nicholson [1962] Director/Farmer

LC Packaging UK Ltd
Incorporated: 24 April 1981 *Employees:* 54
Net Worth: £3,227,389 *Total Assets:* £11,107,196
Registered Office: Bridge Road, Long Sutton, Spalding, Lincs, PE12 9EF
Activities: Non-specialised wholesale trade
Parent: LC Packaging International BV
Officers: Lucas Lammers [1966] Director [Dutch]; Martijn Schrooder [1969] Director [Dutch]

LDC (Boston) Limited
Incorporated: 13 October 1964
Net Worth: £10,716,034 *Total Assets:* £11,046,398
Registered Office: 14a South Parade, Boston, Lincs, PE21 7PL
Activities: Growing of cereals (except rice), leguminous crops and oil seeds
Major Shareholder: Willem Adrianus Den-Hartog
Officers: Adrian Den Hartog, Secretary; Adrian Den Hartog [1969] Director/Manager; Willem Adrianus Den-Hartog [1939] Director [Dutch]; Karen Louise Kirkendall [1968] Director

LDH (La Doria) Limited
Incorporated: 12 December 1996 *Employees:* 73
Net Worth: £58,814,000 *Total Assets:* £116,552,000
Registered Office: LDH House, Parsons Green, St Ives, Cambs, PE27 4AA
Activities: Wholesale of fruit and vegetables
Parent: La Doria S.P.A.
Officers: Enzo Diodato Lamberti, Secretary; Giuseppe di Martino [1970] Director [Italian]; Andrea Ferraioli [1957] Director [Italian]; Antonio Ferraioli [1954] Director [Italian]; Rosa Ferraioli [1951] Director/Manager [Italian]; Alberto Festa [1960] Director of Finance [Italian]; Barry Ivor Fine [1958] Director; David Elias Fine [1952] Director; Sergio Persico [1938] Director/Tax Consultant [Italian]; Paul Gerrard Reenan [1967] Managing Director John West UK Ltd [Irish]; David Sankowicz [1968] Director/Lawyer [French]

Leadec Limited
Incorporated: 29 September 1997 *Employees:* 2,616
Previous: Voith Industrial Services Limited
Net Worth: £7,672,000 *Total Assets:* £40,641,000
Registered Office: Leadec House, 2 Academy Drive, Warwick, CV34 6QZ
Activities: Other manufacturing n.e.c.
Officers: Paul Steven Griffiths, Secretary; Maralyn Kitchingman [1968] Human Resources Director; Paulina Irene Lujan [1969] Finance Director [Argentinian]; Philip Richard McClennon [1971] Managing Director; Lee Simon Smith [1968] Operations Director

Leaderflush + Shapland Holdings Limited
Incorporated: 5 August 1999 *Employees:* 2
Net Worth: £5,675,000 *Total Assets:* £11,280,000
Registered Office: Adsetts House, 16 Europa View, Sheffield Business Park, Sheffield, S9 1XH
Activities: Activities of head offices
Parent: SIG Dormant Company Number Ten Limited
Officers: Richard Charles Monro, Secretary; Ian Jackson [1979] Director/Accountant; Richard Charles Monro [1958] Director/Chartered Secretary

Learndirect Limited
Incorporated: 19 April 2000 *Employees:* 1,992
Net Worth Deficit: £19,754,000 *Total Assets:* £58,800,000
Registered Office: Dearing House, 1 Young Street, Sheffield, S1 4UP
Activities: Post-secondary non-tertiary education
Parent: PIMCO 2909 Limited
Officers: Wayne Janse Van Rensburg [1981] Director; Andrew Richard Alexander Palmer [1976] Director/Group Chief Executive

Learner Engagement and Achievement Partnership Multi-Academy Trust
Incorporated: 31 August 2010 *Employees:* 497
Previous: Brinsworth Comprehensive School Academy Trust
Net Worth: £41,858,776 *Total Assets:* £48,557,164
Registered Office: Brinsworth Academy, Brinsworth Road, Brinsworth, Rotherham, S Yorks, S60 5EJ
Activities: General secondary education
Officers: Richard William Wheatcroft, Secretary; Wayne Barsby [1966] Director/Headteacher; Kimberley Jane Bottomley [1971] Director/Operations Manager; Gregory Paul Burke [1962] Director/Civil Servant; Mark Andrew Garrison [1964] Director/Chartered Accountant; Andrew James Riches [1966] Director/Headteacher; Brian Bernard Rossiter [1955] Director/Education Consultant; William Mark Slocombe [1967] Director/Management Consultant

Learning Without Limits Academy Trust
Incorporated: 8 July 2016 *Employees:* 455
Net Worth: £51,910,112 *Total Assets:* £57,645,172
Registered Office: 150 Strasbourg Drive, Leicester, LE4 0SZ
Activities: General secondary education
Officers: Kevin Allen-Khimani, Secretary; Miranda Carleton Canon [1975] Local Government Director; Margaret Mary Galliers [1952] Director; Bernadette Green [1956] Director/Retired; Andrew Gerard Hubert Lane [1956] Director/Accountant; Julie Diane Rawle [1979] Director/Headteacher; Eleanor Barbara Shaw [1953] Director/Retired; Paul Andrew Wilson [1970] Director/Headmaster; Glynis Wright [1963] Director/Solicitor

J.T. Leavesley Limited
Incorporated: 28 April 1950 *Employees:* 67
Net Worth: £18,645,586 *Total Assets:* £31,022,758
Registered Office: Ryknield House, Alrewas, Burton on Trent, Staffs, DE13 7AB
Activities: Activities of head offices
Shareholders: James Thomas Leavesley; John William Leavesley
Officers: John William Leavesley, Secretary; Alistair John D'Aubney [1967] Director/Chartered Accountant; James Thomas Leavesley [1962] Director/Surveyor; John William Leavesley [1969] Director/Solicitor; Naomi Sarah Light [1978] Director/Town Planner

Leaworks Limited
Incorporated: 8 November 2004
Net Worth: £1,094,135 *Total Assets:* £9,737,703
Registered Office: Leaworks House, 10 Ronald Street, Nottingham, NG7 3GY
Activities: Manufacture of printed labels
Major Shareholder: Lin Fang
Officers: Lin Fang [1970] Director [Chinese]; Wei Li [1982] Director/Business Executive [Chinese]

Lebus Upholstery Limited
Incorporated: 14 September 2005 *Employees:* 489
Net Worth: £3,181,479 *Total Assets:* £11,432,992
Registered Office: Queensway Industrial Estate, Dunlop Way, Scunthorpe, N Lincs, DN16 3RN
Activities: Manufacture of other furniture
Parent: Tornado Meubelen BV
Officers: Darrell Peter Thomas Bettany, Secretary/Financial Director; Darrell Peter Thomas Bettany [1962] Director Finance Accountant; John Brewster [1960] Director; Henk Van Der Veen [1959] Director [Dutch]; Karl Frederick Walker [1958] Director

Leda Properties Limited
Incorporated: 6 May 1976 *Employees:* 24
Net Worth: £26,944,778 *Total Assets:* £55,097,852
Registered Office: Tyre Sales Abingdon, Marcham Road, Abingdon, Oxon, OX14 1TZ
Activities: Growing of cereals (except rice), leguminous crops and oil seeds
Shareholders: Andrew Leslie Basson; Mark Basson
Officers: Leslie William Basson, Secretary; Andrew Leslie Basson [1954] Director/Farmer Garage Retailer; Leslie William Basson [1931] Director/Farmer Garage Retailer; Mark Basson [1960] Director/Farmer and Garage Retailer; Nicholas John Hardcastle [1973] Director; David Jennings [1957] Director

William Lee Limited
Incorporated: 23 January 1991 *Employees:* 402
Net Worth: £31,959,536 *Total Assets:* £43,076,940
Registered Office: Callywhite Lane, Dronfield, Derbys, S18 2XU
Activities: Casting of iron
Parent: Castings PLC
Officers: Steven James Mant, Secretary; Simon John Alexander [1968] Director; Toni Carannante [1960] Director/Engineering; Brian John Cooke [1939] Director/Chairman; Shaun Crofts [1968] Technical Director; David Nikolas Dobbs [1963] Director; Christopher Hall Hodson [1966] Sales Director; Adrian Mark Lacey [1968] Operations Director; Steven James Mant [1975] Director/Chartered Accountant; Tracy McLoughlin [1973] Finance Director; Adam Vicary [1968] Director

Leen Gate Metals Limited
Incorporated: 1 June 2000 *Employees:* 43
Net Worth: £678,724 *Total Assets:* £16,085,271
Registered Office: Redfield Road, Lenton, Nottingham, NG7 2UJ
Activities: Wholesale of metals and metal ores
Parent: Leen Gate Metal Holdings Limited
Officers: Anthony Richard Simmons, Secretary/Director; Anthony John Gill [1969] Director/Warehouse Manager; Kevin Simeon Henson [1973] Director/Sales Manager; Gary Richard Peters [1980] Director; Anthony Richard Simmons [1968] Director; Robert Gerrard Smith [1962] Director

Leeson Chemicals Limited
Incorporated: 10 December 2002 *Employees:* 39
Net Worth: £10,144,674 *Total Assets:* £15,058,465
Registered Office: Hermes Close, Tachbrook Park, Warwick, CV34 6RP
Activities: Manufacture of other chemical products n.e.c.
Shareholders: Leeson Investments Limited; David Leeson
Officers: Kathleen Sheila Bain Leeson, Secretary/Commercial Director; David Leeson [1946] Director/Chairman; Kathleen Sheila Bain Leeson [1948] Commercial Director

Leeson Polyurethanes Limited
Incorporated: 8 April 1986 *Employees:* 39
Net Worth: £9,689,193 *Total Assets:* £14,210,695
Registered Office: Hermes Close, Tachbrook Park, Warwick, CV34 6RP
Activities: Manufacture of other chemical products n.e.c.
Parent: Leeson Chemicals Limited
Officers: David Leeson, Secretary; David Leeson [1946] Director/Chairman; Joel David Rattray Leeson [1977] Managing Director; Kathleen Sheila Bain Leeson [1948] Commercial Director

Leger Education Trust
Incorporated: 10 August 2011 *Employees:* 143
Previous: Campsmount Community Academy Trust
Net Worth: £10,188,000 *Total Assets:* £11,280,000
Registered Office: Campsmount Academy, Ryecroft Road, Norton, Doncaster, S Yorks, DN6 9AS
Activities: General secondary education
Officers: Kirstie Anne Lee, Secretary; Claire Elizabeth Allen [1958] Director/Teacher; Helen Brookes [1976] Director/Teaching Assistant; Melanie Campbell [1966] Director/Housewife; Adam Christopher Dale [1973] Director/Headteacher; Martin Edward Drake [1975] Director/Farmer; Bridget Mary Gill [1958] Director/Administrator; Geoffrey Hall [1941] Director/Retired; Christopher Knight [1953] Director/Accountant; Berbet Esmilda Lynds [1968] Financial Director; David McEwan [1949] Director/Firearms Enquiry Officer/Explosive Liaison Officer; Tracy Julie Millard [1972] Director/Headteacher; Jenny Parkinson [1967] Director/Senior Student Advisor; Lesley Ann Sullivan [1972] Director/Administrative Assistant; Sarah Marie Thompson [1979] Director/Housewife; Rev Mark Wigglesworth [1960] Director/Vicar

Lehvoss UK Limited
Incorporated: 27 February 1992 *Employees:* 48
Net Worth: £8,003,543 *Total Assets:* £22,207,444
Registered Office: Westminster House, 10 Westminster Road, Macclesfield, Cheshire, SK10 1BX
Activities: Wholesale of chemical products
Officers: Ivan Pennington, Secretary; Ivan Pennington [1972] Director

Leica Biosystems Newcastle Limited
Incorporated: 10 September 1987 *Employees:* 225
Net Worth: £26,049,000 *Total Assets:* £82,198,000
Registered Office: 19 Jessops Riverside, 800 Brightside Lane, Sheffield, S9 2RX
Activities: Other professional, scientific and technical activities n.e.c.
Parent: Launchchange Operations Ltd
Officers: Sarah Garrett [1971] Director; Vicky Reid [1973] Director; Matthew William West [1968] Director

Leica Geosystems Limited
Incorporated: 31 August 1964 *Employees:* 106
Net Worth: £15,714,000 *Total Assets:* £30,730,000
Registered Office: Hexagon House, Michigan Drive, Tongwell, Milton Keynes, Bucks, MK15 8HT
Activities: Wholesale of mining, construction and civil engineering machinery
Parent: Hexagon AB
Officers: Andrew Paul Young, Secretary; John Edward Fraser [1972] Regional Director

Leicester City Football Club Limited
Incorporated: 18 November 2002 *Employees:* 252
Net Worth: £143,062,000 *Total Assets:* £266,288,992
Registered Office: King Power Stadium, Filbert Way, Leicester, LE2 7FL
Activities: Other sports activities
Parent: King Power International Company Limited
Officers: Simon Capper, Secretary; Shilai Liu [1972] Director [Chinese]; Aiyawatt Srivaddhanaprabha [1985] Director [Thai]; Apichet Srivaddhanaprabha [1982] Director [Thai]; Susan Valerie Whelan [1963] Executive Director [Irish]

Leicester Diocesan Board of Finance (The)
Incorporated: 4 January 1928 *Employees:* 65
Net Worth: £80,061,000 *Total Assets:* £84,328,000
Registered Office: St Martins House, 7 Peacock Lane, Leicester, LE1 5PZ
Activities: Activities of religious organisations
Officers: Jonathan William Kerry, Secretary; Stephen George Barney [1950] Director/Retired; Bernard David Beeson [1937] Director/Farmer; Gary Brown [1966] Director; The Revd Cynthia Margaret Hebden [1947] Director/Transition Priest; Revd Anthony Robert Leighton [1956] Director/Clerk in Holy Orders; Guy William Newbury [1947] Director/Chartered Accountant; Sheila Anne Lane Newbury [1948] Director/Personal Tax Manager; Canon David John Palmer [1946] Director/Retired; John Charles Frank Roberson [1948] Director/Retired; Christopher John Sheldon [1960] Director/Chief Executive; Bishop Martyn James Snow [1968] Director/Bishop of Leicester; Madeleine Valerie Wang [1955] Director/Patient Advocate; Revd John Whittaker [1969] Director/Minister of Religion; Claire Wood [1963] Director/Archdeacon; Richard Vernon Worsfold [1964] Director/Archdeacon of Leicester

Leicester Fancy Box Company Limited
Incorporated: 5 May 1970 *Employees:* 313
Net Worth: £6,748,000 *Total Assets:* £13,628,000
Registered Office: Feldspar Close, Enderby, Leicester, LE19 4SD
Activities: Activities of head offices
Shareholders: Mark William Pollard; Julie Ann Jarvis
Officers: Catherine Mary Pollard, Secretary; Peter Charles Conner [1956] Director; Julie Ann Jarvis [1968] Director; Catherine Mary Pollard [1943] Director; Mark William Pollard [1965] Director

Leicester Football Club PLC
Incorporated: 28 October 1997 *Employees:* 167
Net Worth: £35,633,000 *Total Assets:* £58,190,000
Registered Office: The Club House, Aylestone Road, Leicester, LE2 7TR
Activities: Activities of sport clubs
Shareholder: Thomas Richard Scott
Officers: Mary Ford, Secretary; John David Abell [1942] Director; Peter Howard Aldis [1964] Director/Chief Executive Officer [Irish]; Simon Joshua Cohen [1956] Director/Chief Executive Officer; Terence Michael Gateley [1953] Director; Lord Digby Marritt Jones [1955] Director; Benedict James Kay [1975] Director; Andrea Claire Pinchen [1967] Commercial Director; Thomas Richard Scott [1975] Director/Chartered Accountant; Peter William Gregory Tom [1940] Director; Rory Underwood [1963] Director; Francis Ian Walker [1957] Director/Accountant

Leicester Grammar School Trust
Incorporated: 13 October 1980 *Employees:* 237
Net Worth: £12,120,492 *Total Assets:* £35,242,924
Registered Office: Leicester Grammar School, London Road, Great Glen, Leicester, LE8 9FL
Activities: Primary education
Officers: Nicholas John Edwards, Secretary; Alison Jean Shakespeare, Secretary; Elisabeth Michelle Bailey [1971] IT Director; Julia Burns [1953] Director/Retired Headmistress/Independent Education Consultant; Dr Sarah Margaret Dauncey [1957] Director/Retired; Steven Gasztowicz [1959] Director/Barrister; Duncan Comrie Green [1960] Director/Consulting Engineer & Architect; Dr Susan Elizabeth Hadley [1961] Director/General Practitioner; Michael John Holley [1955] Finance Director; Nathan James McLean Imlach [1969] Director/Chartered Accountant; Keith John Julian [1946] Director/Higher Education; Dr Deenesh Ishver Khoosal [1952] Director/Medical Practitioner; Dr Laura Mongan-Cockcroft [1970] Director/University Senior Lecturer; David Robert Malvern Monteith [1968] Director/Priest; Amanda Georgina O'Donovan [1976] Director/Solicitor; Professor James Mark Saker [1952] Director/University Professor

Leicester Lettings Limited
Incorporated: 22 January 2016 *Employees:* 7
Net Worth: £22,227,678 *Total Assets:* £35,243,232
Registered Office: 42 Western Road, Leicester, LE3 0GH
Activities: Other letting and operating of own or leased real estate
Major Shareholder: Jamieson Alessandro Lewis
Officers: Jamieson Alessandro Lewis [1971] Director

Leicester Lift Project Company (No. 1) Limited
Incorporated: 8 October 2003
Net Worth Deficit: £4,339,000 *Total Assets:* £44,757,000
Registered Office: G1 Ash Tree Court, Nottingham Business Park, Nottingham, NG8 6PY
Activities: Other business support service activities n.e.c.
Parent: Leicester Lift (Midco) Limited
Officers: Michael George Duggan, Secretary; Richard John Coates [1966] Director; Charlotte Sophie Ellen Douglass [1978] Director/Chartered Surveyor; Gavin William MacKinlay [1957] Associate Director; Kirsty O'Brien [1982] Director/Operations Manager; Sarah Jayne Prema [1965] Director Strategy and Implementation; Simon Patrick Tipping [1949] Director

Leicester Lift Project Company (No.2) Limited
Incorporated: 6 November 2009
Net Worth Deficit: £2,211,000 *Total Assets:* £12,618,000
Registered Office: G1 Ash Tree Court, Nottingham Business Park, Nottingham, NG8 6PY
Activities: Other letting and operating of own or leased real estate
Parent: Leicester Lift Midco (No.2) Limited
Officers: Michael George Duggan, Secretary; Richard John Coates [1966] Director; Charlotte Sophie Ellen Douglass [1978] Director/Chartered Surveyor; Gavin William MacKinlay [1957] Associate Director; Kirsty O'Brien [1982] Director/Operations Manager; Sarah Jayne Prema [1965] Director Strategy and Implementation; Simon Patrick Tipping [1949] Director

Leicester Racecourse Holdings Limited
Incorporated: 14 October 1884 *Employees:* 142
Net Worth: £11,191,212 *Total Assets:* £12,530,193
Registered Office: The Racecourse, London Road, Leicester, LE2 4AL
Activities: Other sports activities
Officers: Philip Andrew Booth [1967] Director/Solicitor; Clive Richard Buckle [1943] Director/Property Owner; Captain Nicholas Ernest Samuel Lees [1939] Director/Licensed Racing Official; Marc William Nelson [1960] Director/Accountant

Leicestershire & Rutland Organisation for The Relief of Suffering Limited
Incorporated: 14 February 1977 *Employees:* 355
Net Worth: £25,055,468 *Total Assets:* £26,678,724
Registered Office: The Leicestershire & Rutland Hospice, Groby Road, Leicester, LE3 9QE
Activities: Other human health activities
Officers: John Robert Knight, Secretary; Richard Louis Brucciani [1945] Director/Company Chairman; Dr Sian Gwynne Cheverton [1954] Director/Doctor; Professor Robin Alan Charles Graham-Brown [1949] Director/Consultant Dermatologist; Chris Ranald Greenwell [1960] Director/Solicitor; Elizabeth Anne Kitchen [1953] Director/Events Coordinator; Doctor Nik Kotecha [1966] Director/Business Owner; David John Lindley [1952] Director; Ajmer Kaur Mahal [1962] Director; Timothy Paul Maxted [1971] Director; Dr Kathryn Jane Oliver [1967] Director/General Practitioner; Priyesh Dineshbhai Patel [1972] Director; Hugh Michael Pearson [1942] Director; Andrew Warren Stant [1956] Director/Chartered Accountant; Pauline Tagg [1956] Director

Lemac No.1 Limited
Incorporated: 12 October 2009 *Employees:* 409
Net Worth: £9,042,000 *Total Assets:* £18,493,000
Registered Office: 35-37 Cotton End Road, Wilstead, Beds, MK45 3BX
Activities: Activities of head offices
Parent: McGavigan Corporate Limited
Officers: Caroline Rena Smith, Secretary; Francis Paul Duffin [1957] Director; Stephen John Mathers [1962] Director; David Francis Taylor [1963] Director

A.E. Lenton (Holdings) Limited
Incorporated: 8 May 1961 *Employees:* 31
Net Worth: £10,580,934 *Total Assets:* £18,018,910
Registered Office: Church End, Friskney, Boston, Lincs, PE22 8NE
Activities: Activities of agricultural holding companies
Shareholders: Markham Timothy Lenton Burnett; Graham John Shooter
Officers: Markham Timothy Lenton Burnett, Secretary; Markham Timothy Lenton Burnett [1967] Sales Director; Alan Edward Lenton Shooter [1978] Director; Graham John Shooter [1947] Director; Oliver John Lenton Shooter [1980] Farm Director

A.E. Lenton Limited
Incorporated: 6 October 1949 *Employees:* 16
Net Worth: £5,702,028 *Total Assets:* £12,291,994
Registered Office: Church End, Friskney, Lincs, PE22 8NE
Activities: Wholesale of fruit and vegetables
Parent: A.E. Lenton (Holdings) Limited
Officers: Marlene Shooter, Secretary; Markham Timothy Lenton Burnett [1967] Sales Director; Graham John Shooter [1947] Director; Oliver John Lenton Shooter [1980] Farm Director

Lenze U.K. Limited
Incorporated: 19 January 1999
Net Worth: £8,504,970 *Total Assets:* £13,030,056
Registered Office: Lenze Limited, Fraser Road, Priory Business Park, Bedford, MK44 3WH
Activities: Activities of other holding companies n.e.c.
Parent: Lenze BV
Officers: Simon John Cherry, Secretary; Hendricus Damianus Wilhelmus Maria Van Den Broek [1965] Director [Dutch]; Christian Albert Wendler [1962] Director [German]

Lenzing Fibers Grimsby Limited
Incorporated: 14 February 2006 *Employees:* 174
Net Worth: £61,890,000 *Total Assets:* £74,945,000
Registered Office: Energy Park Way, Grimsby, N E Lincs, DN31 2TT
Activities: Manufacture of man-made fibres
Parent: Lenzing Aktiengesellschaft
Officers: Jemma Louise Turrell, Secretary; Adrian Charles Francis Dodds [1965] Director/Regional HR Manager UK; Philip Munson [1964] Director/Site Manager; Jemma Louise Turrell [1973] Director/Financial Controller

Lesta Packaging PLC
Incorporated: 23 October 1978 *Employees:* 35
Net Worth: £4,718,930 *Total Assets:* £11,121,439
Registered Office: 21 Nedham Street, Leicester, LE2 0HD
Activities: Non-specialised wholesale trade
Shareholders: Mahomed Farouk Alimahomed; Osman Farouk Alimahomed
Officers: Khairoonisha Farouk Alimahomed, Secretary; Mahomed Farouk Alimahomed [1949] Director/Developer; Osman Farouk Alimahomed [1985] Director/Consultant

Lets Connect It Solutions Limited
Incorporated: 7 April 2009 *Employees:* 28
Net Worth: £2,779,000 *Total Assets:* £11,175,000
Registered Office: John Ormond House, 899 Silbury Boulevard, Milton Keynes, Bucks, MK9 3XL
Activities: Information technology consultancy activities
Parent: Personal Group Limited
Officers: Sarah Anne Mace, Secretary; Mike Dugdale [1962] Director; Mark William Scanlon [1968] Director [Irish]

The Lettings Room Limited
Incorporated: 27 January 2009 *Employees:* 31
Net Worth: £5,481,762 *Total Assets:* £18,597,394
Registered Office: The Hart Shaw Building, Europa Link, Sheffield Business Park, Sheffield, S9 1XU
Activities: Renting and operating of Housing Association real estate
Parent: Tirtlr Holdings Limited
Officers: Julie Jones, Secretary; Julie Jones [1981] Director/Property Manager; Lee Daniel Jones [1978] Director/Property Trader

Levi Strauss (U.K.) Limited
Incorporated: 22 November 1966 *Employees:* 876
Net Worth: £19,689,000 *Total Assets:* £37,500,000
Registered Office: Swan Valley, Northampton, NN4 9BA
Activities: Other business support service activities n.e.c.
Officers: Richard Michael John Hurren [1972] Director/General Manager; Hiren Sawjani [1973] Retail, Franchise and Expansion Director

The David Lewis Centre
Incorporated: 6 September 1990 *Employees:* 762
Net Worth: £11,852,000 *Total Assets:* £19,839,000
Registered Office: Mill Lane, Warford, Alderley Edge, Cheshire, SK9 7UD
Activities: Other education n.e.c.
Officers: Neil Alan Edwards, Secretary; Roisin Beressi [1965] Director/Solicitor; Darren Karl Cornwall [1969] Director/Group CFO; George Devlin [1952] Director/Retired; Stephen Devlin [1957] Director/Solicitor; Linda Feerick [1963] Director/Professional Coach; Alistair Vincent Hollows [1959] Director; Alastair Milne Imrie [1947] Director/Retired; Geoff Loughlin [1953] Director/Retired; Marie Elizabeth McLaughlin [1959] Director/Civil Servant; Susan Jane Tebby-Lees [1961] Director/Consultant Radiologist

Jamie Lewis Residential Lettings Limited
Incorporated: 28 October 2009 *Employees:* 21
Net Worth: £60,462,168 *Total Assets:* £67,322,808
Registered Office: 42 Western Road, Leicester, LE3 0GH
Activities: Buying and selling of own real estate
Parent: JL Residential Holdings Limited
Officers: Jamieson Alessandro Lewis [1971] Director

Lexden BH (Colchester) Limited
Incorporated: 9 November 2016
Net Worth: £1 *Total Assets:* £10,394,363
Registered Office: Witan Gate House, 500-600 Witan Gate, Milton Keynes, Bucks, MK9 1BA
Activities: Other retail sale in non-specialised stores
Parent: Homebase Limited
Officers: Simone Tudor, Secretary; Andrew Charles Coleman [1974] Director/General Manager, Finance & IT; Damian Garry McGloughlin [1969] Acting Managing Director

Lexington Catering Limited
Incorporated: 3 September 1997 *Employees:* 851
Net Worth: £7,862,705 *Total Assets:* £18,409,752
Registered Office: The Courtyard, Catherine Street, Macclesfield, Cheshire, SK11 6ET
Activities: Other business support service activities n.e.c.
Parent: Elior UK Holdings Limited
Officers: Joanna Luke, Secretary; Julia Caroline Edmonds [1968] Managing Director; Pascal Lefebvre [1960] Director [French]; Catherine Margaret Roe [1960] Managing Director; Eleni Savva [1972] Finance Director; Michael Andrew Sunley [1959] Director/Contract Catering

Lexitron Limited
Incorporated: 6 March 1975 *Employees:* 2
Net Worth: £10,037,229 *Total Assets:* £16,584,190
Registered Office: Marley Road, St Ives, Huntingdon, Cambs, PE27 3EX
Activities: Other letting and operating of own or leased real estate
Officers: Michael Andrew Smith, Secretary; Michael Andrew Smith [1962] Director; Stephen James Smith [1960] Director

Leyland Trucks Limited
Incorporated: 29 April 1993 *Employees:* 791
Net Worth: £195,190,000 *Total Assets:* £275,276,000
Registered Office: 9400 Garsington Road, Oxford Business Park, Cowley, Oxford, OX4 2HN
Activities: Manufacture of motor vehicles
Parent: Paccar Parts U.K. Limited
Officers: Alison Jones, Secretary; Ronald Eugene Armstrong [1955] Director/CEO of Paccar Inc [American]; Mark Charles Pigott [1954] Director/Chairman [American]; Bryan Michael Sitko [1976] Managing Director [American]

LGS Capital Limited
Incorporated: 4 March 2014
Net Worth: £594,883 *Total Assets:* £9,445,694
Registered Office: The Lodge, Station Road, Melton Mowbray, Leics, LE14 3BQ
Activities: Activities of financial services holding companies
Major Shareholder: Jonathan William Sturmey
Officers: Jonathan Sturmey, Secretary; Jonathan Sturmey [1972] Director/Banker

Lhoist UK Limited
Incorporated: 21 August 2000 *Employees:* 79
Net Worth: £13,786,000 *Total Assets:* £40,010,000
Registered Office: Lhoist UK Limited, Buxton Road, Hindlow, Buxton, Derbys, SK17 0EL
Activities: Manufacture of lime and plaster
Officers: Dirk Donck, Secretary; Axel Vincent Ampolini [1970] Vice President and Managing Director [American]; Cedric Joannes Rosa Georges de Vicq de Cumptich [1980] Director [Belgian]; Dirk Donck [1956] Director/Legal Advisor [Belgian]

Liberty Group Holdings Ltd
Incorporated: 28 August 1996 *Employees:* 78
Previous: Pasuda Group Holdings Limited
Net Worth: £10,968,934 *Total Assets:* £16,645,598
Registered Office: 68 Queen Street, Sheffield, S1 1WR
Activities: Activities of other holding companies n.e.c.
Shareholders: Gordon Jones; Susan Jones
Officers: Susan Jones, Secretary; John Bamford [1956] Director

Liberty Guard (U.K.) Limited
Incorporated: 3 October 2002 *Employees:* 43
Net Worth: £4,914,204 *Total Assets:* £10,531,724
Registered Office: The Old Airfield, Belton Road, Sandtoft, Doncaster, S Yorks, DN8 5SX
Activities: Other specialised construction activities n.e.c.
Major Shareholder: Gordon Jones
Officers: John Bamford, Secretary; Emma Louise Jones Mackie [1977] Director/Manager; Darren Wasilewski [1976] Sales Director

Liberty Merchant Bar PLC
Incorporated: 1 November 1984 *Employees:* 151
Previous: Liberty Merchant Bar Limited
Net Worth: £5,585,000 *Total Assets:* £29,232,000
Registered Office: Liberty House, Scunthorpe Steel Works, Brigg Road, Scunthorpe, N Lincs, DN16 1XJ
Activities: Manufacture of basic iron and steel and of ferro-alloys
Major Shareholder: Sanjeev Gupta
Officers: Sanjay Tohani, Secretary; Virinder Bahadur Garg [1965] Director; Sanjay Tohani [1971] Director

Libra (Longhurst Group) Treasury PLC
Incorporated: 21 May 2012
Net Worth Deficit: £26,534,000 *Total Assets:* £411,956,992
Registered Office: Leverett House, Gilbert Drive, Endeavour Park, Boston, Lincs, PE21 7TQ
Activities: Renting and operating of Housing Association real estate
Parent: Longhurst Group Limited
Officers: Robert Ian Griffiths, Secretary; Clive Barnett [1957] Director/Business Executive; Daniel James Elkins [1971] Director; Robert Ian Griffiths [1976] Finance Director; Hilary Frances Lindsay [1948] Director/Retired; Angela Morris [1960] Director/Self Employed Health Consultant

Libra Speciality Chemicals Limited
Incorporated: 27 April 1971 *Employees:* 57
Net Worth: £8,203,749 *Total Assets:* £13,247,113
Registered Office: 5 Acorn Business Park, Woodseats Close, Sheffield, S8 0TB
Activities: Manufacture of soap and detergents
Officers: David Thomas Kearns, Secretary; Philip Mathew Carson [1981] Supply Chain Director; Dr Graham Cox [1960] Operations Director; Lorraine Forshaw [1963] Finance Director; David Thomas Kearns [1968] Director; Richard Antony David Lock [1982] Sales & Marketing Director; Graham Royle [1959] Director

Life Multi-Academy Trust
Incorporated: 15 March 2012 *Employees:* 10
Previous: Bosworth Academy
Net Worth: £17,117,922 *Total Assets:* £22,005,956
Registered Office: Bosworth Academy, Leicester Lane, Desford, Leicester, LE9 9JL
Activities: General secondary education
Officers: Sarah Jayne Fortune Mayes, Secretary; Maria Everley [1957] Director/Education Consultant [Irish]; Christopher Willian Garnett [1957] Director/Retired Teacher; Jennifer Anne Hobden [1975] Director/Learning Support Assistant; Geoffrey Charles Hurst [1968] Director/Chief Information Officer; Iain Duncan Kinnis [1966] Director/Change Manager; David Noble [1982] Director/Assistant Headteacher; Christoper Parkinson [1970] Director/Headteacher; Andrew Robert Smith [1966] Finance Director

Life UK Healthcare Limited
Incorporated: 8 November 2016 *Employees:* 6
Net Worth: £531,195,008 *Total Assets:* £783,152,000
Registered Office: ICENI Centre, Warwick Technology Park, Warwick, CV34 6DA
Activities: Hospital activities
Parent: Life UK Holdco Limited
Officers: Guy Edward Blomfield [1967] Director; Nicholas James Burley [1968] Director; Adam Mills Pyle [1965] Director/Group Marketing Executive [South African]; Petrus Phillippus Van Der Westhuizen [1971] Director/Chief Financial Officer [South African]; Shrey Balaguru Viranna [1975] Director/Chief Executive Officer [South African]

Lifeplus Europe Limited
Incorporated: 31 July 1996 *Employees:* 334
Net Worth: £12,297,067 *Total Assets:* £25,389,920
Registered Office: Lifeplus House, Little End Road, Eaton Socon, St Neots, Cambs, PE19 8JH
Activities: Retail sale via mail order houses or via Internet
Officers: Robert E Christian, Secretary/Executive [American]; Richard Joseph Cesarski [1964] Director [American]; Robert E Christian [1961] Director/Executive [American]; William J Evans [1969] Director/Executive [American]; Frank Newton III [1940] Director/Executive [American]; Malcolm Vincent [1965] Director

Lifestyle Seeview Limited
Incorporated: 24 January 2012 *Employees:* 4
Net Worth: £6,834,445 *Total Assets:* £11,083,857
Registered Office: 213 Cromford Road, Langley Mill, Nottingham, NG16 4EU
Activities: Recreational vehicle parks, trailer parks and camping grounds
Parent: Lifestyle Homes N.Ireland Ltd
Officers: Anthony James Barney [1965] Director; Donna Michelle Barney [1966] Director; Dannielle Ann Harvey [1987] Commercial Director; Jonathan Robert Harvey [1982] Director/Chartered Surveyor

Lifford Industrial Properties Ltd
Incorporated: 15 July 2011
Net Worth: £2,106,862 *Total Assets:* £13,717,950
Registered Office: Unit 5 Lawford Heath Industrial Estate, Lawford Heath Lane, Lawford Heath, Rugby, Warwicks, CV23 9EU
Activities: Other letting and operating of own or leased real estate
Officers: Richard James Cookman [1977] Director; Kevin Mark Higginson [1959] Managing Director

Lighthouse UkCo 6 (Treasury) Limited
Incorporated: 28 December 2001
Previous: Findus Treasury Limited
Net Worth Deficit: £417,641,984 *Total Assets:* £175,070,000
Registered Office: Ross House, Wickham Road, Grimsby, N E Lincs, DN31 3SW
Activities: Manufacture of other food products n.e.c.
Parent: Lighthouse UKCo 5 (Holdings) Limited
Officers: William John Showalter [1963] Director/Chief Financial Officer [American]

Lillywhites Limited
Incorporated: 4 August 1934 *Employees:* 167
Net Worth: £46,038,000 *Total Assets:* £46,752,000
Registered Office: Unit A, Brook Park East, Shirebrook, Derbys, NG20 8RY
Activities: Retail sale of sports goods, fishing gear, camping goods, boats and bicycles
Parent: Sportsdirect.Com Retail Limited
Officers: Cameron John Olsen, Secretary; Adedotun Ademola Adegoke [1973] Director/Senior Buyer; Rachel Isabel Lilian Stockton [1970] Director/Head of Customs and VAT

Lima Orthopaedics UK Limited
Incorporated: 23 December 2009 *Employees:* 35
Net Worth: £4,672,742 *Total Assets:* £14,129,957
Registered Office: 2a Chequers Court, Huntingdon, Cambs, PE29 3LJ
Activities: General medical practice activities
Parent: Limacorporate S.P.A
Officers: Luigi Ferrari [1968] Director [Italian]

Limagrain UK Limited
Incorporated: 30 March 1977 *Employees:* 185
Net Worth: £16,437,760 *Total Assets:* £35,130,804
Registered Office: Joseph Nickerson Research Centre, Rothwell, Market Rasen, Lincs, LN7 6DT
Activities: Agents selling agricultural raw materials, livestock, textile raw materials and semi-finished goods
Parent: Limagrain Verneuil Holding SA
Officers: Robert John Cowling, Secretary; Alain Albert Joseph Barbier [1957] Finance Director [French]; Bruno Jean Carette [1955] Director [French]

Limes Developments Limited
Incorporated: 25 March 1976 *Employees:* 10
Net Worth: £53,021,312 *Total Assets:* £59,155,692
Registered Office: Limes House, Burton Park, Lincoln, LN1 2RB
Activities: Activities of other holding companies n.e.c.
Shareholders: Marcus James Miles Jolly; Fiona Claire Curtis
Officers: Stephen Paul Diver, Secretary; James Charles Ross Curtis [1966] Director/Screen Writer; Gillian Mary Jolly [1940] Director; Marcus James Miles Jolly [1967] Director/Chartered Surveyor; Robert Miles Jolly [1937] Director

Limes Estates Limited
Incorporated: 24 September 1990
Net Worth: £17,753,638 *Total Assets:* £27,259,252
Registered Office: Limes House, Burton Park, Lincoln, LN1 2RB
Activities: Other letting and operating of own or leased real estate
Shareholders: Marcus James Miles Jolly; Fiona Claire Curtis
Officers: Stephen Paul Diver, Secretary; James Charles Ross Curtis [1966] Director/Screen Writer; Marcus James Miles Jolly [1967] Director/Chartered Surveyor; Robert Miles Jolly [1937] Director

Limestone Farming Company Limited
Incorporated: 25 July 1936 *Employees:* 57
Net Worth: £6,373,466 *Total Assets:* £16,622,000
Registered Office: The Estate Office, Willoughton Manor, Willoughton, Gainsborough, Lincs, DN21 5SH
Activities: Growing of cereals (except rice), leguminous crops and oil seeds
Shareholders: Clifford Graham Rowles Nicholson; John William Rowles
Officers: Richard Arthur Giles, Secretary; Bruce Henry Rowles [1960] Farmer & Director; John William Rowles [1929] Farmer & Director; Clifford Graham Rowles Nicholson [1955] Farmer & Director

Linbrooke Services Limited
Incorporated: 16 July 2002 *Employees:* 285
Net Worth: £984,354 *Total Assets:* £13,974,102
Registered Office: Unit 3 Sheffield Business Park, Churchill Way, Sheffield, S35 2PY
Activities: Construction of railways and underground railways
Shareholders: Lee Hallam; Andrew Brian Wilson; Paul Bailey
Officers: Lee Hallam, Secretary; Paul Martin Bailey [1965] Director; Lee Hallam [1972] Director/Telecoms; Andrew Brian Wilson [1961] Director/Telecoms

Lincat Group Limited
Incorporated: 23 July 1971 *Employees:* 5
Net Worth: £16,260,616 *Total Assets:* £16,383,962
Registered Office: Whisby Road, Lincoln, LN6 3QZ
Activities: Activities of head offices
Parent: Middleby Holding UK Limited
Officers: Jonathan Dove, Secretary; Selim Antoine Bassoul [1957] Director/Chief Executive Officer [American]; Jonathan Mark Dove [1963] Director; Timothy John FitzGenerald [1969] Director/Chief Financial Officer [American]; Martin McKay Lindsay [1964] Director/Corporate Treasurer [American]; Oussama Ahmad Sidani [1957] Director/Vice President [American]

Lincat Limited
Incorporated: 8 October 1987 *Employees:* 249
Net Worth: £17,213,300 *Total Assets:* £26,635,294
Registered Office: Whisby Road, Lincoln, LN6 3QZ
Activities: Other manufacturing n.e.c.
Parent: Lincat Group Limited
Officers: Jonathan Mark Dove, Secretary; Jonathan Mark Dove [1963] Director; Andrew William Mark Elsigood [1961] Director; Christian Jones [1975] Director; Jonathan Michael White [1974] Director

Lincoln & York Limited
Incorporated: 28 January 1994 *Employees:* 66
Net Worth: £12,089,237 *Total Assets:* £19,566,230
Registered Office: Kahawa House, Elsham Wold Industrial Estate, Elsham, Brigg, N Lincs, DN20 0SP
Activities: Production of coffee and coffee substitutes
Parent: Elsham Wold Estates Limited
Officers: Nigel John Bean, Secretary; Simon David Herring [1964] Director; James Timothy Sweeting [1969] Director

Lincoln and London Holdings Limited
Incorporated: 21 September 2010 *Employees:* 182
Net Worth: £3,604,000 *Total Assets:* £46,462,000
Registered Office: 991 Doddington Road, Lincoln, LN6 3AA
Activities: Construction of commercial buildings
Officers: Michael Harrison Kasher, Secretary; Paul Richard Hodgkinson [1956] Director/Architect; Philip David Hodgkinson [1958] Director/Property Surveyor; Michael Harrison Kasher [1965] Director; Philip James Kendall [1965] Director; Thomas Daniel Edwin Robinson [1970] Director

Lincoln Christ's Hospital School
Incorporated: 8 August 2011 *Employees:* 188
Net Worth: £10,687,363 *Total Assets:* £13,054,366
Registered Office: Lincoln Christ's Hospital School, Wragby Road, Lincoln, LN2 4PN
Activities: General secondary education
Officers: Hayley Marie Allison-Warby [1978] Director; Anna Sophie Godley Edlin [1980] Director; David Gibbons [1965] Director/Headmaster; Richard Greenfield [1968] Director; James Hanrahan [1956] Director/Chartered Town Planner; Rachel Louise Knowles [1982] Director/Teacher; Rebecca Malam [1969] Director/Headmistress; John Males [1941] Director/Retired; Martin Ernest McKeown [1976] Director/Headmaster; Alan Mills [1957] Director/Forensic Vehicle Investigator; John Andrew Patrick [1962] Director/Subdean; Dr Steven Thomas Puttick [1982] Director; Dr Stacy Rowland [1966] Director/Teacher [American]; Michael William Savage [1948] Director/Retired; Diana Scammell [1952] Director/Teacher; Paul Frederick Watson [1956] Director/Retired; Sharon Wilkinson [1964] Director/Catering Manager; Catherine Wilson [1963] Director

Lincoln College Academy Trust
Incorporated: 3 October 2012 *Employees:* 148
Net Worth: £18,964,660 *Total Assets:* £21,087,820
Registered Office: Lincoln College, Monks Road, Lincoln, LN2 5HQ
Activities: General secondary education
Officers: Keith James Batty [1958] Director of Education Services; Tracey Anne Boyd [1969] Director/Talent Agent; Shaun Michael Flynn [1968] Director/Management; Anna Louise Leng [1980] Director/Acting Principal; Helen Sarah Molloy [1979] Director/Solicitor; Andrew John Morgan [1963] Director/Chief Executive; Valerie Ann Waby [1968] Director/Chief Executive

Lincoln Corn Exchange and Markets (1991) Limited
Incorporated: 25 October 1990 *Employees:* 1
Net Worth: £62,054,000 *Total Assets:* £131,159,000
Registered Office: Stanley Bett House, 15-23 Tentercroft Street, Lincoln, LN5 7DB
Activities: Buying and selling of own real estate
Parent: LCS Property Ltd
Officers: Jane Powell, Group Secretary; Stephen Robert Hughes [1961] Director/Pharmacist; Reverend Barbara Anne Hutchinson [1955] Director/Reverend; David Frank Maltby [1956] Director/Retired; Jane Moate [1957] Director/Retired Bank Manager; Susan Neal [1951] Director/Manager; Claudia Nel [1966] Director/Solicitor & Data Protection Officer; Stuart William Parker [1958] Director/Engineer; Julia Anne Romney [1956] Director/Post Office Clerk; Margaret Williamson Tranter [1947] Director/Retired

Lincoln Diocesan Trust and Board of Finance Limited
Incorporated: 17 March 1908 *Employees:* 65
Net Worth: £174,618,000 *Total Assets:* £179,920,000
Registered Office: Edward King House, Minster Yard, Lincoln, LN2 1PU
Activities: Buying and selling of own real estate
Officers: The Revd David Ian Dadswell, Secretary; Justine Penelope Heathcote Allain Chapman [1967] Director/Minister of Religion; Paul James Arnold [1945] Director; Nigel Bacon [1955] Director/Engineering Manager; The Revd Sonia Patricia Barron [1955] Director/Priest; John Henry Boddy [1945] Director/Retired; Reverend Nicholas James Watson Brown [1976] Director/Clerk in Holy Orders; The Revd Alyson Christina Buxton [1965] Director/Clerk in Holy Orders; Nicholas Alan Chamberlain [1963] Director/Bishop; Christopher James Clarke [1951] Director/Retired; Richard Hilton Clegg [1949] Director/Business Consultant; Russell Coulter [1951] Director/Retired; David Eric Court [1958] Director/Bishop; David Cyril Cowell [1956] Director/Semi-Retired Consultant; The Revd Canon Andrew Patrick Dodd [1968] Director/Clerk in Holy Orders; The Ven Gavin John Kirk [1961] Director/Clerk in Holy Orders; Christopher Lowson [1953] Director/Clerk in Holy Orders; Jane Powell [1962] Director/Company Secretary; Muriel Anita Robinson [1954] Director/Retired; Susan Gay Slater [1944] Director/Retired; The Ven Mark John Steadman [1974] Director/Priest; Christine Louise Wilson [1958] Director/Dean of Lincoln; David Thomas Wright [1960] Director/Consultant

Lincoln Electric (U.K.) Limited
Incorporated: 27 January 1986 *Employees:* 66
Net Worth: £16,048,000 *Total Assets:* £28,367,000
Registered Office: Mansfield Road, Aston, Sheffield, S26 2BS
Activities: Cold drawing of wire
Parent: Lincoln Electric UK Holdings Limited
Officers: Amanda Jayne Cresswell, Secretary; Michael Alexander Chalmers [1956] Managing Director; Daniel John Marascalchi [1957] Director/Vice President of Operations Lincoln Electric EMEA [American]

Lincoln Electric UK Holdings Limited
Incorporated: 10 October 2006 *Employees:* 2
Net Worth: £12,503,333 *Total Assets:* £43,983,100
Registered Office: c/o Lincoln Electric UK Limited, Mansfield Road, Aston, Sheffield, S26 2BS
Activities: Activities of other holding companies n.e.c.
Parent: Lincoln Electric Holdings, Inc
Officers: Amanda Jayne Cresswell, Secretary; Michael Alexander Chalmers [1956] Commercial Director; Daniel John Marascalchi [1957] Director/Vice President of Operations Lincoln Electric EMEA [American]

Lincoln Science and Innovation Park Limited
Incorporated: 10 July 2012
Net Worth: £103,000 *Total Assets:* £16,162,000
Registered Office: Stanley Bett House, 15-23 Tentercroft Street, Lincoln, LN5 7DB
Activities: Research and experimental development on social sciences and humanities
Parent: Lincolnshire Co-operative Ltd
Officers: Jane Powell, Secretary; Haydn Biddle [1946] Director/Chairman (Non-Executive) George Bateman & Son Ltd; Stephen Mark Galjaard [1972] Director/Chief Financial Officer; Stephen Robert Hughes [1961] Director/Pharmacist; John Christopher Latham [1960] Director of DVC Projects; Ursula Frances Rosamond Lidbetter [1962] Director/Chief Executive; David Frank Maltby [1956] Director/Retired; Julia Anne Romney [1956] Director/Security Controller; Professor Mary Stewart Stuart [1957] Director/Vice Chancellor [Irish]

Lincolnshire Agricultural Society
Incorporated: 4 September 1984 *Employees:* 21
Net Worth: £13,851,966 *Total Assets:* £14,316,083
Registered Office: Lincolnshire Showground, Grange-De-Lings, Lincoln, LN2 2NA
Activities: Activities of other membership organisations n.e.c.
Officers: Jayne Southall, Secretary; Graeme Beattie [1955] Director; Nigel Robert Bottom [1975] Managing Director; Andrew Laurance Buckley [1964] Director/Farmer; Jane Hiles [1953] Director/Retired; Robert Howard [1966] Director/Farmer; Andrew Harding Price [1961] Director/Farmer; Andrew Charles Read [1962] Director/Farmer; Christopher Charles Rothery [1946] Director/Retired; David John Wallis [1961] Director/Farmer; Andrew William Ward [1960] Director/Farmer; Steve Ward [1959] Director/Farmer

Lincolnshire Field Products Limited
Incorporated: 10 December 1984 *Employees:* 139
Net Worth: £14,126,545 *Total Assets:* £37,033,788
Registered Office: Wool Hall Farm, Cross Gate, Wykeham, Spalding, Lincs, PE12 6HW
Activities: Growing of vegetables and melons, roots and tubers
Parent: Keepstem Limited
Officers: Aubrey Edward Day, Secretary; Aubrey Edward Day [1958] Director/Chartered Management Accountant; Robin Hancox [1956] Director; Martin John Tate [1966] Director

Lincolnshire Road Car Company Limited
Incorporated: 20 August 1928 *Employees:* 1,299
Net Worth: £24,163,000 *Total Assets:* £36,145,000
Registered Office: c/o Stagecoach Services Limited, One Stockport Exchange, 20 Railway Road, Stockport, Cheshire, SK1 3SW
Activities: Other urban, suburban or metropolitan passenger land transport (not underground, metro or similar)
Parent: The Yorkshire Traction Company Limited
Officers: Michael John Vaux, Secretary; Colin Brown [1968] Director/Accountant; Matthew James Cranwell [1981] Managing Director; Arnold Mark Threapleton [1954] Managing Director

Lincolnshire Wildlife Trust
Incorporated: 2 December 1948 *Employees:* 76
Net Worth: £15,463,736 *Total Assets:* £16,669,554
Registered Office: Banovallum House, Manor House Street, Horncastle, Lincs, LN9 5HF
Activities: Other professional, scientific and technical activities n.e.c.
Officers: Paul Voce Learoyd, Secretary; Matthew James Capper [1974] Director/Senior Site Manager; David Alan Cohen [1949] Director; Clare Elizabeth Harrison [1955] Director/Farmers Wife; Patricia Janet Mellor [1946] Director; Clifford Raymond Morrison [1945] Director/Retired; Robert Oates [1952] Director/Conservation Management; Julian Connor Purvis [1959] Director/Chartered Accountant; Anita Claire Quigley [1957] Director; Stephanie Jane Round [1957] Director/Retired; Timothy Stephen Sands [1945] Director/Retired Conservationist; Dr David Alan Sheppard [1952] Director/Scientist (Public Services); Mark Smith [1966] Director/Health and Safety Manager; Peter Stapleton [1947] Director/Chartered Accountant; Beth Tyrrel [1972] Director/Management Consultant

Lincwaste Limited
Incorporated: 6 December 1991 *Employees:* 18
Net Worth Deficit: £5,583,000 *Total Assets:* £13,190,000
Registered Office: Ground Floor West, 900 Pavilion Drive, Northampton Business Park, Northampton, NN4 7RG
Activities: Other business support service activities n.e.c.
Parent: FCC Environment Limited
Officers: Carol Jayne Nunn, Secretary; Vicente Federico Orts-Llopis [1962] Director/Chief Financial Officer [Spanish]; Agustin Serrano Minchan [1959] Director/Technical Civil Engineer [Spanish]; Paul Taylor [1959] Director/Chief Executive Officer

Lindab Limited
Incorporated: 4 June 1982 *Employees:* 302
Net Worth: £19,204,000 *Total Assets:* £29,606,000
Registered Office: Units 9-10 Carousel Way, Riverside Business Park, Northampton, NN3 9HG
Activities: Manufacture of tubes, pipes, hollow profiles and related fittings, of steel
Parent: Lindab International AB
Officers: Robert Henry Evans, Secretary; Fredrik Lidholm [1964] Director [Swedish]; Iain Thomas Robertson [1966] Joint Managing Director; Inga Malin Samuelsson [1972] Director [Swedish]

Lindum Group Limited
Incorporated: 4 December 1975 *Employees:* 629
Net Worth: £40,583,592 *Total Assets:* £86,492,992
Registered Office: Lindum Business Park, Station Road, North Hykeham, Lincs, LN6 3QX
Activities: Construction of commercial buildings
Major Shareholder: David Christopher Chambers
Officers: Herman Frans Frederik Kok, Secretary; David Christopher Chambers [1956] Director/Chairman; Edward Christopher Paul Chambers [1984] Director; Frederick Edward Chambers [1982] Director; Kevin Edward Damarell [1962] Director; Simon John Gregory [1960] Construction Director; Robbie Alexander Jan Kok [1978] Finance Director; Stuart David Mitchell [1976] Director

Linecross Group Limited
Incorporated: 24 February 2003 *Employees:* 251
Net Worth: £7,271,799 *Total Assets:* £18,025,768
Registered Office: Station Road, South Luffenham, Oakham, Rutland, LE15 8NG
Activities: Activities of head offices
Shareholders: David Trevor Austin; Stuart David Fry
Officers: David Trevor Austin, Secretary; David Trevor Austin [1969] Finance Director; Stuart David Fry [1970] Managing Director

Linford Properties (Leicester) Limited
Incorporated: 7 June 2011 *Employees:* 2
Net Worth: £4,864,946 *Total Assets:* £9,819,935
Registered Office: Leofric House, Binley Road, Coventry, Warwicks, CV3 1JN
Activities: Management of real estate on a fee or contract basis
Officers: Christopher Gerard Reid [1945] Director; Sean Reid [1970] Director

Link Education Trust
Incorporated: 10 November 2011 *Employees:* 137
Previous: New Dawn Trust
Net Worth: £8,337,942 *Total Assets:* £11,281,408
Registered Office: Hartsholme Academy, Carrington Drive, Lincoln, LN6 0DE
Activities: Primary education
Officers: Donna Louise Wakefield, Secretary; James Edward Barron [1985] Director/Solicitor; Carrie Anne Greenfield [1977] Director/Bookkeeper; Aimee Elizabeth Horton [1982] Director/Writer/Consultant

Linkage Community Trust
Incorporated: 14 January 1976 *Employees:* 619
Previous: Linkage Community Trust Limited (The)
Net Worth: £17,905,428 *Total Assets:* £23,459,206
Registered Office: Toynton Hall, Main Road, Toynton All Saints, Spilsby, Lincs, PE23 5AE
Activities: Other education n.e.c.
Officers: Anthony Terence Bake [1955] Director/Retired; Michael Bell [1952] Director/Self Employed; Professor Stephen Frederick Brown [1939] Director/Retired; Reginald Roger Harfoot [1945] Director/Retired; Simon James Hatchman [1972] Finance Director; Clare Jervis [1973] Director/Full Time Mother; Azad Shamcaddin Najmaldin [1950] Director/Paediatrician [Iraqi]; Michael John Oliver [1949] Director/Retired; Stephanie May Simpson [1972] Director/Management Consultant; Samantha Jane Stewart [1966] Director/Schools Effectiveness Adviser

Linnell Brothers Limited
Incorporated: 29 June 1940 *Employees:* 37
Net Worth: £5,074,574 *Total Assets:* £9,747,243
Registered Office: Silverstone Fields Farm, Towcester Road, Silverstone, Towcester, Northants, NN12 8FS
Activities: Sawmilling and planing of wood
Officers: Edmund John Sidney Linnell [1971] Director; James Victor Linnell [1971] Director; Roger Linnell [1968] Director/Business Manager

W & J Linney Limited
Incorporated: 31 August 1914 *Employees:* 858
Previous: W.& J.Linney,Limited
Net Worth: £8,006,000 *Total Assets:* £41,696,000
Registered Office: Adamsway, Mansfield, Notts, NG18 4FW
Activities: Printing n.e.c.
Parent: WJL Group Limited
Officers: Shaun Finn, Secretary; Charles Harwood Cash Linney [1979] Director; Miles Jonathan Hilton Linney [1967] Director; Nicholas Steven Linney [1952] Director

Linread Limited
Incorporated: 1 August 1925 *Employees:* 322
Net Worth: £17,249,000 *Total Assets:* £28,842,000
Registered Office: 26a Atlas Way, Sheffield, S4 7QQ
Activities: Manufacture of wire products, chain and springs
Parent: Arconic Global Fasteners Limited
Officers: Petra Papinniemi-Ainger, Secretary; Craig Brown [1961] Director/Engineer [American]; Paul Christopher Brown [1963] Managing Director; Todd Andrew Emerick [1968] Director/Plant Manager; Lluis Maria Fargas Mas [1966] Director/Lawyer [Spanish]; Vitaliy Rusakov [1970] Director/President, Alcoa Fastening Systems [American]; Martin Noel Ryan [1953] Director/Senior Vice President, Technology [American]; Graham David Swan [1958] Director/Financial Controller

Linx Acquisition Limited
Incorporated: 7 October 2004 *Employees:* 1
Net Worth: £271,399,008 *Total Assets:* £292,431,008
Registered Office: 19 Jessops Riverside, 800 Brightside Lane, Sheffield, S9 2RX
Activities: Activities of head offices
Parent: Duki (2006) Finance Ltd
Officers: Keith Graham Ward [1953] Director

Linx Printing Technologies Limited
Incorporated: 22 October 1986 *Employees:* 218
Net Worth: £107,983,000 *Total Assets:* £124,090,000
Registered Office: Linx House, 8 Stocks Bridge Way, Compass Point Business Park, St Ives, Cambs, PE27 5JL
Activities: Manufacture of other special-purpose machinery n.e.c.
Parent: Launchchange Operations Ltd
Officers: Mark James Cooper [1973] Commercial Director; Harinder Singh Sandhu [1980] Finance Director; Keith Graham Ward [1953] Director

Lionheart Academies Trust
Incorporated: 4 April 2013 *Employees:* 592
Net Worth: £58,121,724 *Total Assets:* £69,717,840
Registered Office: Beauchamp College, Ridge Way, Oadby, Leicester, LE2 5TP
Activities: Other education n.e.c.
Officers: Mark David Grant [1964] Director/Charity Chief Executive; Stephen Ian Harris [1950] Director; Dilip Kumar Kadodwala [1955] Director/Education Consultant; Anne Elizabeth Peacocke Lamb [1974] Deputy HR Director; Alan Love [1959] Director/Facilities Management; Robert Mason [1962] Director/Chartered Accountant; Shreekant Thakoral Raivadera [1971] Director; Christine Jane Swan [1962] Director; Dushyant Natwarlal Tanna [1961] Director/Solicitor

Lipsy Limited
Incorporated: 2 March 2006 *Employees:* 204
Net Worth: £7,992,000 *Total Assets:* £39,669,000
Registered Office: Desford Road, Enderby, Leicester, LE19 4AT
Activities: Wholesale of clothing and footwear
Parent: Next Holdings Limited
Officers: Seonna Anderson, Secretary; Seonna Anderson [1966] Director/Company Secretary [Irish]; Amanda James [1971] Director; Simon Adam Lord Wolfson of Aspley Guise [1967] Director/Chief Executive

Lister Wilder Group Limited
Incorporated: 7 November 1946 *Employees:* 211
Previous: Lister Wilder Group PLC
Net Worth: £4,328,154 *Total Assets:* £30,568,458
Registered Office: The Park, Port Way, Crowmarsh, Wallingford, Oxon, OX10 8FG
Activities: Activities of head offices
Officers: Denis John King, Secretary; Charles Edward King [1981] Commercial Director; Denis John King [1941] Director; James Bruce Scott [1940] Director; Jason David Scott [1970] Director

Lister Wilder Limited
Incorporated: 28 November 1985 *Employees:* 211
Net Worth: £3,958,840 *Total Assets:* £30,567,844
Registered Office: The Park, Port Way, Crowmarsh, Wallingford, Oxon, OX10 8FG
Activities: Other retail sale not in stores, stalls or markets
Parent: Lister Wilder Group Limited
Officers: Denis John King, Secretary; Gary Hayden [1960] Service Director; Phillip George Hughes [1975] Director; Charles Edward King [1981] Commercial Director; Denis John King [1941] Director; William John King [1978] Director; Ian Harold Nutt [1957] Managing Director; Keith John Osborne [1959] Parts Director; James Bruce Scott [1940] Director; Jason David Scott [1970] Director/Depot Manager

Listers Group Limited
Incorporated: 20 November 1978 *Employees:* 2,355
Net Worth: £77,798,000 *Total Assets:* £385,247,008
Registered Office: Othello House, Stratford Business & Technology Park, Banbury Road, Stratford upon Avon, Warwicks, CV37 7GY
Activities: Sale of new cars and light motor vehicles
Shareholder: Terence Lister
Officers: Martin James Vessey, Secretary; David George Bradshaw [1968] Director; Keith George Bradshaw [1943] Director; Pamela Bradshaw [1943] Director; Timothy Charles Bradshaw [1973] Director; Geoffrey James Lister [1971] Director/Chief Executive; Katherine Jane Lister [1974] Director; Margaret Susan Lister [1945] Director; Terence Lister [1943] Managing Director; Kenneth William Round [1942] Finance Director

Livwell Limited
Incorporated: 12 March 2008 *Employees:* 110
Net Worth: £1,083,000 *Total Assets:* £10,378,000
Registered Office: South Park Suite, Unit 1 & 2 North Farm Road, South Park Industrial Estate, Bottesford, Lincs, DN17 2AY
Activities: Manufacture of bread; manufacture of fresh pastry goods and cakes
Parent: Genius Foods Limited
Officers: Jeremy Peter Bradley [1961] Director/Chief Executive Officer; Lucinda Emma Kate Bruce-Gardyne [1971] Director

LKAB Minerals Limited
Incorporated: 19 December 2002 *Employees:* 148
Net Worth: £22,301,012 *Total Assets:* £42,185,096
Registered Office: Mica Works, Raynesway, Derby, DE21 7BE
Activities: Manufacture of other non-metallic mineral products n.e.c.
Parent: LKAB Minerals AB
Officers: Richard Mark Wheatley, Secretary; Paul Boustead [1979] Operations Director; Magnus Forsberg [1971] Director [Swedish]; Gary Ronald Mansfield [1961] Director; Richard Mark Wheatley [1962] Finance Director; Darren Anthony Wilson [1969] Managing Director

Llamasoft Europe Holdings Limited
Incorporated: 10 November 2015 *Employees:* 99
Net Worth: £5,392,223 *Total Assets:* £20,188,632
Registered Office: Ground Floor, Dovecote, Pury Hill Business Park, Alderton Road, Paulerspury, Towcester, Northants, NN12 7LS
Activities: Information technology consultancy activities
Officers: Alex Frith, Secretary; Martin Fitzpatrick [1969] Director [American]; Alex Frith [1979] Director; Razat Gaurav [1973] Director [Indian]

A.C. Lloyd (Asset Management) Limited
Incorporated: 20 February 1998 *Employees:* 36
Net Worth: £78,433,440 *Total Assets:* £90,611,960
Registered Office: Nicholls House, Homer Close, Tachbrook Park, Warwick, CV34 6TT
Activities: Development of building projects
Shareholders: Ann Cecelia Richardson; Janet Elizabeth Stallard
Officers: Hans Peter Skeat, Secretary; Peter Charles Beddoes [1954] Director/Solicitor; Robert Alistair Clark [1961] Director; Mark Royston Edwards [1968] Director; Ann Cecelia Richardson [1955] Director; Hans Peter Skeat [1963] Director/Chartered Accountant; Janet Elizabeth Stallard [1948] Director; Michael John Stallard [1968] Director/Builder/Carpenter; Michael John Stallard [1944] Director; Desmond Patrick Wynne [1957] Director/Surveyor

Lloyd Fraser Holdings Company Limited
Incorporated: 5 October 1987 *Employees:* 512
Net Worth: £9,095,483 *Total Assets:* £15,621,143
Registered Office: Regent House, Clinton Avenue, Nottingham, NG5 1AZ
Activities: Activities of head offices
Officers: Francis James Allan [1942] Director/Retired; Neil Fraser McConchie [1953] Director; Keith Edwin Spencer [1965] Logistics Director

A.C. Lloyd Holdings Limited
Incorporated: 30 September 1948 *Employees:* 4
Net Worth: £7,382,077 *Total Assets:* £15,567,460
Registered Office: Nicholls House, Homer Close, Tachbrook Park, Warwick, CV34 6TT
Activities: Construction of commercial buildings
Parent: AC Lloyd (Asset Management) Limited
Officers: Hans Peter Skeat, Secretary; Peter Charles Beddoes [1954] Director/Solicitor; Robert Alistair Clark [1961] Director; Mark Royston Edwards [1968] Director; Hans Peter Skeat [1963] Director/Chartered Accountant; Desmond Patrick Wynne [1957] Director/Surveyor

A C Lloyd Homes Limited
Incorporated: 16 December 1963 *Employees:* 4
Net Worth: £4,125,921 *Total Assets:* £29,455,862
Registered Office: Nicholls House, Homer Close, Tachbrook Park, Warwick, CV34 6TT
Activities: Construction of domestic buildings
Parent: AC Lloyd (Asset Management) Limited
Officers: Hans Peter Skeat, Secretary; Darren Avern [1973] Director/Civil Engineer; Peter Charles Beddoes [1954] Director/Solicitor; Robert Alistair Clark [1961] Director; David Philip Henley [1959] Contracts Director; Darrenn Malcolm Meredith [1964] Director/Chartered Surveyor; Hans Peter Skeat [1963] Director/Chartered Accountant; Desmond Patrick Wynne [1957] Director/Surveyor

Lloyds Bank Commercial Finance Limited
Incorporated: 21 August 1962 *Employees:* 412
Net Worth: £24,315,000 *Total Assets:* £495,780,992
Registered Office: No 1 Brookhill Way, Banbury, Oxon, OX16 3EL
Activities: Financial leasing
Parent: Lloyds Bank PLC
Officers: Paul Gittins, Secretary; Danielle Kara Reed [1972] Director; Ben Stephenson [1981] Director

Lloyds Pharmacy Clinical Homecare Limited
Incorporated: 10 November 1992 *Employees:* 998
Previous: Bupa Home Healthcare Limited
Net Worth: £14,703,000 *Total Assets:* £155,136,992
Registered Office: Sapphire Court, Walsgrave Triangle, Coventry, Warwicks, CV2 2TX
Activities: Wholesale of pharmaceutical goods
Officers: Nichola Legg, Secretary; Toby Matthew Anderson [1973] Director; Marcus Hilger [1977] Finance Director [German]; Catherine McDermott [1968] Operations Director; Nigel Swift [1966] Director

Lloyds Pharmacy Limited
Incorporated: 19 April 1963 *Employees:* 19,086
Net Worth Deficit: £53,467,000 *Total Assets:* £805,225,024
Registered Office: Sapphire Court, Walsgrave Triangle, Coventry, Warwicks, CV2 2TX
Activities: Dispensing chemist in specialised stores
Parent: Admenta Holdings Limited
Officers: Nichola Louise Legg, Secretary; Toby Matthew Anderson [1973] Director; Marcus Hilger [1977] Finance Director [German]; Catherine McDermott [1968] Operations Director; Nigel Swift [1966] Marketing & Sales Director

Lo's Pharmacy Limited
Incorporated: 19 June 1998 *Employees:* 70
Net Worth: £5,852,777 *Total Assets:* £9,159,922
Registered Office: Unit 5 Farfield Park, Manvers, Rotherham, S Yorks, S63 5DB
Activities: Dispensing chemist in specialised stores
Shareholders: Steven Kwok Fu Lo; Kevin Kwok Kei Lo
Officers: Kevin Kwok Kei Lo, Secretary/Shop Manager; Iris Tung Wa Lo [1963] Director; Kevin Kwok Kei Lo [1962] Director/Shop Manager; Steven Kwok Fu Lo [1965] Director/Pharmacist

Loades PLC
Incorporated: 13 June 1942 *Employees:* 6
Net Worth: £18,940,736 *Total Assets:* £20,039,950
Registered Office: The Hub, 54 Bayton Road, Exhall, Coventry, Warwicks, CV7 9TH
Activities: Renting and operating of Housing Association real estate
Shareholder: Santsbury Limited
Officers: Stewart Paton Weavers, Secretary; Anthony Edward Loades [1942] Director; Robert Wilson Loades [1949] Director; Stewart Paton Weavers [1959] Director and Company Secretary

Loadhog Limited
Incorporated: 2 January 2003 *Employees:* 76
Net Worth: £6,003,226 *Total Assets:* £16,518,220
Registered Office: The Hog Works, Hawke Street, Sheffield, S9 2SU
Activities: Manufacture of other plastic products
Shareholder: Hugh David Facey
Officers: Richard Greenup Fry, Secretary; Hugh David Facey [1945] Director; Roger Hall [1946] Director/Accountant; Shah Nawaz Khan [1975] Managing Director; Edward John Peter Stubbs [1983] Director

Loake Brothers Limited
Incorporated: 21 January 1895 *Employees:* 155
Net Worth: £20,718,236 *Total Assets:* £23,910,484
Registered Office: Unique Works, Wood Street, Kettering, Northants, NN16 9SN
Activities: Manufacture of footwear
Officers: Robert William Kent, Secretary; Peter Nigel Davis [1962] Director/Footwear Manufacturer; Graham Charles Dutton [1958] Director/Designer; Robert William Kent [1964] Finance Director; Andrew Ernest Loake [1958] Director/Shoe Manufacturer; Jonathan Andrew Campbell Perkins Cory [1970] Director/Salesman

Lochailort Fairfield Limited
Incorporated: 11 March 2016
Net Worth Deficit: £6,914 *Total Assets:* £20,909,460
Registered Office: James Hall, Parsons Green, St Ives, Cambs, PE27 4AA
Activities: Development of building projects
Parent: JCAM Commercial Real Estate Property XVII Ltd
Officers: Hugo Peter Haig [1962] Director; Toby John Markham [1966] Director

Lockheed Martin UK Ampthill Group Limited
Incorporated: 15 January 2001
Net Worth: £6,045,000 *Total Assets:* £33,037,000
Registered Office: Reddings Wood, Ampthill, Bedford, MK45 2HD
Activities: Activities of head offices
Parent: Lockheed Martin UK Holdings Limited
Officers: David Arms Heywood, Secretary; James Joseph Glaub [1963] Director/Business Executive [American]; Neil Martin Hebron [1962] Director/Engineer; Alan Edward Lines [1958] Managing Director; Peter William David Ruddock [1954] Director/Business Executive; Michael Eric Williamson [1960] Director/Business Executive [American]

Lockheed Martin UK Ampthill Limited
Incorporated: 20 June 1957 *Employees:* 791
Net Worth Deficit: £59,863,000 *Total Assets:* £109,705,000
Registered Office: Reddings Wood, Ampthill, Beds, MK45 2HD
Activities: Manufacture of military fighting vehicles
Parent: Lockheed Martin UK Ampthill Group
Officers: David Arms Heywood, Secretary; James Joseph Glaub [1963] Director/Business Executive [American]; Neil Martin Hebron [1962] Director/Engineer; Alan Edward Lines [1958] Managing Director; Peter William David Ruddock [1954] Director/Business Executive; Michael Eric Williamson [1960] Director/Business Executive [American]

Lockwood Estates Limited
Incorporated: 4 September 1974 *Employees:* 20
Net Worth: £9,176,335 *Total Assets:* £14,962,579
Registered Office: Scampton House, Scampton, Lincoln, LN1 2SF
Activities: Growing of cereals (except rice), leguminous crops and oil seeds
Major Shareholder: John William Lockwood
Officers: Matthew Charles Karran, Secretary; Andrew Buckley [1964] Farm Director; Arthur William Lockwood [1924] Director; James Patrick Alexander Lockwood [1991] Director; John William Lockwood [1954] Director/Farmer; Judith Ann Lockwood [1956] Company Secretary/Director

The Lockwood Group Limited
Incorporated: 11 August 2014 *Employees:* 388
Net Worth: £7,376,545 *Total Assets:* £32,953,374
Registered Office: Lockwood Group, Ripley Road Sawmills, Ambergate, Derbys, DE56 2JR
Activities: Activities of head offices
Shareholders: Deborah Louise King; Robert Ian Lockwood
Officers: Deborah Louise King [1966] Director; Robert Ian Lockwood [1968] Managing Director

Jack Loggin Limited
Incorporated: 8 February 1990 *Employees:* 3
Net Worth: £6,585,379 *Total Assets:* £12,216,867
Registered Office: Donisthorpe Hall, Hall Lane, Donisthorpe, Leics, DE12 7PZ
Activities: Retail sale of automotive fuel in specialised stores
Shareholders: Peter Alan Jacques; David William Jacques
Officers: Peter Alan Jacques, Secretary; David William Jacques [1961] Director; Peter Alan Jacques [1962] Director

Logistex Europe Ltd
Incorporated: 2 July 2010 *Employees:* 254
Net Worth: £4,873,000 *Total Assets:* £10,402,000
Registered Office: 2700 Kettering Parkway, Kettering, Northants, NN15 6XR
Activities: Installation of industrial machinery and equipment
Parent: Logistex Trustees Limited
Officers: Mark Andrew Nicholson, Secretary; Andrew David Branch [1965] Engineering Director; Derek Charles Kay [1965] Business Development Director; Mark Andrew Nicholson [1961] Director; Kevin Anthony Joseph Sheridan [1955] Operations Director; Simon Milton Webber [1962] Director; Jeremy William Woodhouse [1958] Director

Logistex Limited
Incorporated: 30 November 1937 *Employees:* 254
Net Worth: £4,850,000 *Total Assets:* £10,429,000
Registered Office: 2700 Kettering Parkway, Kettering, Northants, NN15 6XR
Activities: Other service activities incidental to land transportation, n.e.c.
Parent: Logistex Europe Ltd
Officers: Mark Andrew Nicholson, Secretary; Andrew David Branch [1965] Engineering Director; Derek Charles Kay [1965] Business Development Director; Mark Andrew Nicholson [1961] Director; Kevin Anthony Joseph Sheridan [1944] Operations Director; Simon Milton Webber [1962] Director; Jeremy William Woodhouse [1958] Director

Logistics Acquisition Company (UK) Limited
Incorporated: 2 October 2014
Net Worth: £372,693,408 *Total Assets:* £375,031,040
Registered Office: Peckleton Lane, Desford, Leicester, LE9 9JT
Activities: Activities of other holding companies n.e.c.
Officers: Zach Green, Secretary; Robert Agostinelli [1953] Director/Private Equity Investment [American]; Franz-Ferdinand Buerstedde [1975] Managing Director [German]; Ferdinando Falco Beccalli [1949] Director [Italian]; Charles Gailliot [1978] Director/Investor [American]; Bradley James Gross [1972] Director/Investment Banker [American]; Steve Larson [1956] Director [American]; Patrick Olney [1968] Director/Chief Executive Officer [Canadian]; Steven Wunning [1951] Director [American]

Lomas Distribution Limited
Incorporated: 28 January 1994 *Employees:* 256
Net Worth: £8,397,610 *Total Assets:* £44,492,744
Registered Office: 1 Waterswallows Industrial Park, Waterswallows Road, Buxton, Derbys, SK17 7JB
Activities: Freight transport by road
Shareholders: Lynne Beverley Lomas; Richard Anthony Lomas; Richard Lomas
Officers: Lynne Beverley Lomas, Company Secretary; Lynne Beverley Lomas [1961] Director/Company Secretary; Richard Lomas [1939] Director/Service Manager; Richard Anthony Lomas [1967] Managing Director

London Clapham Investments and Developments Limited
Incorporated: 16 October 2014 *Employees:* 5
Net Worth: £358,777 *Total Assets:* £11,159,496
Registered Office: Suite 4, 164-170 Queens Road, Sheffield, S2 4DH
Activities: Other letting and operating of own or leased real estate
Major Shareholder: Michael Neville Bullas
Officers: Michael Neville Bullas [1965] Director

London EV Company Limited
Incorporated: 11 January 2013 *Employees:* 418
Previous: The London Taxi Corporation Limited
Net Worth: £112,147,000 *Total Assets:* £533,179,008
Registered Office: Li Close, Ansty Park, Ansty, Coventry, Warwicks, CV7 9RF
Activities: Manufacture of motor vehicles
Parent: Geely UK Limited
Officers: Haochun Dong [1961] Finance Director [Chinese]; Xiaolu Duanmu [1969] Director [Chinese]; Carl-Peter Edmund Moriz Forster [1954] Director/Manager [German]; Christopher Patrick Marston Gubbey [1956] Director/Automotive Executive; James Lin [1962] Director [Chinese]; Mingshi Lin [1969] Director [Chinese]; Jianqun Zhou [1965] Director [Chinese]

London Internet Exchange Limited
Incorporated: 14 December 1995 *Employees:* 68
Net Worth: £11,834,525 *Total Assets:* £14,157,472
Registered Office: Trinity Court, Trinity Street, Priestgate, Peterborough, Cambs, PE1 1DA
Activities: Other telecommunications activities
Officers: Howard John Fisher, Secretary; Michael Andrew Blanche [1976] Director/Program Manager; Lee Mark Hetherington [1982] Director/Interconnection Manager; Malcolm Samuel Agar Hutty [1973] Director/Head of Public Affairs; Thomas Sebastien Antero Lahtinen [1979] Director; Kurt Erik Johannes Lindqvist [1974] Director/Chief Marketing Officer [Finnish]; Richard Petrie [1971] Director/Chief Technical Officer; John Bernard Souter [1952] Director/Chief Executive Officer; Simon Paul Woodhead [1974] Director; Steven Wright [1986] Director/Internet Service Provider

London Vista Hotel Limited
Incorporated: 9 September 1997 *Employees:* 605
Net Worth: £14,480,000 *Total Assets:* £143,279,008
Registered Office: Corus House, 1 Auckland Park, Milton Keynes, Bucks, MK1 1BU
Activities: Hotels and similar accommodation
Parent: Malayan United Industries
Officers: Khurram Mohmand, Secretary; Andrew Khoo [1972] Director [Australian]; Yet King Loy [1946] Director [Canadian]; Khurram Mohmand [1972] Director/Accountant

London Wiper Company Limited
Incorporated: 30 September 1987 *Employees:* 52
Net Worth: £2,209,134 *Total Assets:* £16,580,775
Registered Office: Sidings House, Sidings Court, Lakeside, Doncaster, S Yorks, DN4 5NU
Activities: Recovery of sorted materials
Officers: Charles Arthur Hughes, Secretary/Director; Charles Arthur Hughes [1929] Director; James Charles Hughes [1988] Director; John Robert Hughes [1958] Production Director

Long Marsh Limited
Incorporated: 27 August 1956 *Employees:* 38
Net Worth: £4,878,651 *Total Assets:* £10,934,538
Registered Office: Heron House, The Embankment, Wellingborough, Northants, NN8 1LD
Activities: Renting and leasing of cars and light motor vehicles
Major Shareholder: Scott Ian Groome
Officers: Frank David George Cattley, Secretary; Sallyann Groome [1974] Director; Scott Ian Groome [1963] Managing Director

Long Rake Spar Company Limited (The)
Incorporated: 5 August 1960 *Employees:* 80
Net Worth: £9,777,638 *Total Assets:* £16,263,875
Registered Office: Long Rake, Middleton-by-Youlgrave, Bakewell, Derbys, DE45 1LW
Activities: Other mining and quarrying n.e.c.
Major Shareholder: Trevor Broadhurst
Officers: Jean Broadhurst, Secretary; Christopher William Bourne [1979] Director; Trevor Broadhurst [1955] Director/Mineral Merchant; Sarah Hill [1973] Marketing Director; Richard Maughan [1963] Director/Salesman; Daniel Travis [1981] Director

Longcliffe Group Limited
Incorporated: 13 December 1996 *Employees:* 183
Net Worth: £7,510,000 *Total Assets:* £41,154,000
Registered Office: Longcliffe, Brassington, Matlock, Derbys, DE4 4BZ
Activities: Activities of head offices
Officers: Ian Gorbould, Secretary; Lavender Jane Anne Edwards [1958] Director; Ian Gorbould [1962] Director; Andrew Littler [1954] Director; Vivian Geoffrey Russell [1961] Director; Alice Mary Louise Shields [1957] Director; John Francis Gillies Shields [1980] Director; Robert John Gillies Shields [1954] Director/Manager; Rosemary Joy Shields [1930] Director/Manager

Longcliffe Quarries Limited
Incorporated: 25 February 1933 *Employees:* 159
Net Worth: £9,345,231 *Total Assets:* £35,402,660
Registered Office: Head Office, Longcliffe Quarries Ltd, Longcliffe, Brassington, Matlock, Derbys, DE4 4HN
Activities: Quarrying of ornamental and building stone, limestone, gypsum, chalk and slate
Parent: Longcliffe Group Limited
Officers: Ian Gorbould, Secretary; Michael Barkley [1958] Sales Director; Ian Gorbould [1962] Director; Andrew Littler [1954] Director; Vivian Geoffrey Russell [1961] Director; John Francis Gillies Shields [1980] Director; Robert John Gillies Shields [1954] Director/Manager; Chris Wainwright [1964] Director

Longleat Property Limited
Incorporated: 22 February 2002
Net Worth: £62,300,000 *Total Assets:* £233,000,000
Registered Office: One Edison Rise, New Ollerton, Newark, Notts, NG22 9DP
Activities: Renting and operating of Housing Association real estate
Parent: CP Longleat Village Limited
Officers: Rajbinder Singh-Dehal, Secretary; Natalie Johanna Adomait [1989] Director [Canadian]; Martin Peter Dalby [1961] Director; Kevin O'Donnell McCrain [1979] Director [American]; Colin Grant McKinlay [1969] Director; Zachary Bryan Vaughan [1977] Director [Canadian]

Longshaw Developments Limited
Incorporated: 20 July 2011
Net Worth: £6,135,443 *Total Assets:* £12,586,313
Registered Office: 91-97 Saltergate, Chesterfield, Derbys, S40 1LA
Activities: Activities of other holding companies n.e.c.
Parent: Heathcotes Group Limited
Officers: Simon John Maxwell Cobb [1958] Director; David Astill Harrison [1961] Director; John Andrew Hill [1965] Director

Loomis Investments US Limited
Incorporated: 3 November 2011
Net Worth: £82,908,328 *Total Assets:* £426,816,288
Registered Office: Unit 1 Alder Court, Rennie Hogg Road, Nottingham, NG2 1RX
Activities: Activities of other holding companies n.e.c.
Parent: Loomis AB
Officers: Timothy David Gibbs [1976] Director/Head of Finance & Administration; Johan Anders Martin Haker [1961] Director/Chief Financial Officer [Swedish]; Nils Sven Patrik Hogberg [1968] Managing Director [Swedish]

Loomis UK Finance Company Limited
Incorporated: 3 November 2011 *Employees:* 3
Net Worth: £344,448,064 *Total Assets:* £347,518,464
Registered Office: Unit 1 Alder Court, Rennie Hogg Road, Nottingham, NG2 1RX
Activities: Activities of other holding companies n.e.c.
Parent: Loomis AB
Officers: Timothy David Gibbs [1976] Director/Head of Finance & Administration; Johan Anders Martin Haker [1961] Director/Chief Financial Officer [Swedish]; Nils Sven Patrik Hogberg [1968] Managing Director [Swedish]

Loomis UK Limited
Incorporated: 17 May 1996 *Employees:* 2,013
Net Worth: £53,268,000 *Total Assets:* £91,055,000
Registered Office: 1 Alder Court, Rennie Hogg Road, Nottingham, NG2 1RX
Activities: Private security activities
Parent: Loomis Holding UK Limited
Officers: Timothy David Gibbs [1976] Director/Head of Finance & Administration; Nils Sven Patrik Hogberg [1968] Managing Director [Swedish]; Stefan Olov Gustav Wikman [1966] Operations Director [Swedish]

Lord & Midgley Limited
Incorporated: 26 June 1957 *Employees:* 50
Net Worth: £6,913,702 *Total Assets:* £10,547,887
Registered Office: c/o Sims Group UK Limited, Long Marston, Stratford upon Avon, Warwicks, CV37 8AQ
Activities: Wholesale of waste and scrap
Parent: Kaystan Holdings Limited
Officers: David Michael Williams, Secretary; Mark Ian Saunders [1968] Director; David Michael Williams [1964] Director; Paul Michael Wright [1969] Director

Loughborough Schools Foundation
Incorporated: 20 July 2000 *Employees:* 269
Previous: Loughborough Endowed Schools
Net Worth: £68,658,000 *Total Assets:* £72,195,000
Registered Office: 3 Burton Walks, Loughborough, Leics, LE11 2DU
Activities: Pre-primary education
Officers: James William Doherty, Secretary; Paul Simon Alexander [1972] Director/Data Management/Marketing; Professor Robert John Allison [1961] Director/Vice-Chancellor of Loughborough University; Elizabeth Kirwin Critchley [1952] Director/University Lecturer; Professor Alan Henry Dodson [1951] Director/University Professor; Professor John Pliny Feather [1947] Director/Professor; Geoffrey Peter Fothergill [1945] Director; Mary Gershlick [1949] Director; Roger Harrison [1973] Director/Architect; Peter Maitland Jackson [1949] Director; Anthony David Jones [1959] Director/Business Consultant; Professor Julian Mark Ketley [1960] Director/University Professor; Jennifer Lady Gretton [1943] Director/Estate Owner; Sister Celine Mary Leydon [1946] Director/Retired [Irish]; Rowena Jane Elizabeth Limb [1967] Director/Civil Servant; Peter Middleton [1968] Director/Education - Headteacher; Anna Murphy [1978] Director/Senior Parliamentary Official; Phillippa Helen Mary O'Neill [1972] Director/Solicitor; Gillian Richards [1951] Director/School Headmistress; Paul Joseph Snelling [1957] Director/Engineer (Retired); Sir Trevor Alan Soar [1957] Director; John Arthur Stone [1948] Director/Retired; Louise Catherine Webb [1974] Director

Lousada Investments Limited
Incorporated: 16 September 2014 *Employees:* 2
Net Worth: £923,069 *Total Assets:* £31,533,344
Registered Office: Estate Office, Oakley House, The Drive, Church Lane, Oakley, Bedford, MK43 7ST
Activities: Buying and selling of own real estate
Parent: Lousada Investments Holdings Limited
Officers: Sharon Anne Hunt, Secretary; Simon Charles Lousada [1963] Director; Susan Jane Lousada [1960] Director

Lousada PLC
Incorporated: 27 June 1969 *Employees:* 9
Net Worth: £43,058,400 *Total Assets:* £45,876,936
Registered Office: Estate Office, Oakley House, Oakley, Beds, MK43 7ST
Activities: Buying and selling of own real estate
Parent: Lousada Holdings Limited
Officers: Sharon Anne Hunt, Secretary; Simon Charles Lousada [1963] Director; Susan Jane Lousada [1960] Director

Louver-Lite Limited
Incorporated: 17 May 1971 *Employees:* 345
Net Worth: £48,565,424 *Total Assets:* £52,237,472
Registered Office: Ashton Road, Hyde, Cheshire, SK14 4BG
Activities: Other manufacturing n.e.c.
Major Shareholder: Reginald Charles Allsopp
Officers: Simon Jon Monk, Secretary; Antony Barnes [1964] Director; Stephen William Birtles [1955] Director; Simon Jon Monk [1966] Finance Director; David Peter Robinson [1958] Sales and Marketing Director

Lowdham Leisureworld Ltd
Incorporated: 7 September 2004 *Employees:* 133
Net Worth: £3,883,636 *Total Assets:* £16,484,935
Registered Office: Lowdham Leisure, Lowdham Road, Gunthorpe, Nottingham, NG14 7ES
Activities: Sale of other motor vehicles
Shareholders: Wilfred Roger Crafts; Judith Anne Crafts; Emma Louise Sharpe
Officers: Judith Anne Crafts, Secretary; Emma Sharpe, Secretary; Ian Edward Brown [1966] Group After Sales Director; Judith Anne Crafts [1947] Director; Wilfred Roger Crafts [1944] Director; Emma Louise Sharpe [1967] Director; Stephen Richard Sharpe [1963] Group Managing Director

Loxam Access Limited
Incorporated: 9 May 2000 *Employees:* 90
Net Worth: £14,727,816 *Total Assets:* £14,727,816
Registered Office: 15 Midland Court, Central Park, Lutterworth, Leics, LE17 4PN
Activities: Renting and leasing of construction and civil engineering machinery and equipment
Parent: Loxam SAS
Officers: Patrick Bourmaud, Secretary; Gerard Deprez [1954] Director [French]; Stephane Henon [1968] Director [French]

Loxton Developments Limited
Incorporated: 30 September 1987 *Employees:* 7
Net Worth: £21,197,184 *Total Assets:* £37,719,608
Registered Office: Longbourn Farm, Pittern Hill, Kineton, Warwick, CV35 0JF
Activities: Other letting and operating of own or leased real estate
Shareholders: Mark John Brining Roberts; Belinda Louise Roberts
Officers: Belinda Louise Roberts, Secretary; Belinda Louise Roberts [1961] Director; Mark John Brining Roberts [1960] Managing Director

Loxwood Holdings Limited
Incorporated: 17 May 2007 *Employees:* 6
Net Worth: £5,162,889 *Total Assets:* £11,320,418
Registered Office: 2 Begbroke Manor, Spring Hill Road, Begbroke, Kidlington, Oxon, OX5 1SH
Activities: Development of building projects
Shareholders: Christopher John Holland; Elizabeth Anne Holland
Officers: Elizabeth Anne Holland, Secretary; Christopher John Holland [1954] Director; Elizabeth Anne Holland [1961] Director

LR (UK) Limited
Incorporated: 7 February 2007 *Employees:* 3
Net Worth Deficit: £79,546,624 *Total Assets:* £107,567,520
Registered Office: BMI House, 2 Pitfield, Kiln Farm, Milton Keynes, Bucks, MK11 3LW
Activities: Roofing activities
Parent: BMI Group Holdings UK Limited
Officers: Andrew John Dennis [1965] Managing Director; Klaus Sonne Ravn [1966] Finance Director [Danish]; Dr Johannes Georg Schmidt-Schultes [1966] Director/Chief Financial Officer [German]

LTAG UK Limited
Incorporated: 1 September 2014
Net Worth: £132,041,000 *Total Assets:* £132,048,000
Registered Office: 19 Jessops Riverside, 800 Brightside Lane, Sheffield, S9 2RX
Activities: Activities of head offices
Parent: Danaher Corporation
Officers: Keith Graham Ward [1953] Director

LTI Metaltech Limited
Incorporated: 30 November 2004 *Employees:* 96
Net Worth: £10,712,731 *Total Assets:* £15,038,270
Registered Office: 163 Brook Drive, Milton Park, Milton, Abingdon, Oxon, OX14 4SD
Activities: Manufacture of other fabricated metal products n.e.c.
Officers: Klaus Isaak [1942] Director [German]; Markus Kaiser [1968] Director [German]; Philippe Lacey [1960] Operations Director; Edgar Rayner [1966] Director/Chartered Engineer

Lubrizol Group, LLP
Incorporated: 29 October 2015
Net Worth: £2,421,921,280 *Total Assets:* £2,421,948,928
Registered Office: The Knowle, Nether Lane, Hazelwood, Derby, DE56 4AN

Lubrizol Limited
Incorporated: 26 September 1963 *Employees:* 505
Net Worth: £67,746,000 *Total Assets:* £121,232,000
Registered Office: The Knowle, Nether Lane, Hazelwood, Derby, DE56 4AN
Activities: Manufacture of other chemical products n.e.c.
Parent: Lubrizol Group LLP
Officers: Marc Martha Joseph Verthongen, Secretary; Simon John Griffiths [1962] Director/General Manager; Anthony Michael Smits [1972] Director/Attorney [American]

Lucy Developments Limited
Incorporated: 18 December 2002
Net Worth: £5,170,894 *Total Assets:* £9,807,830
Registered Office: W Lucy & Co, Eagle Works, Walton Well Road, Oxford, OX2 6EE
Activities: Development of building projects
Parent: W.Lucy & Co.Limited
Officers: Madeline Laxton, Secretary; Ian Alexander Ashcroft [1968] Director/Property Manager; Gary David Ashton [1961] Finance Director; Charles Richard Dick [1950] Managing Director and Chairman; Jonathan Charles Finch-Dick [1980] Director/Chartered Surveyor; Mark Frederick Hilton [1976] Director/Building Manager

Lucy Electric (EMS) Limited
Incorporated: 2 December 1981 *Employees:* 115
Previous: Lucy Switchgear (EMS) Limited
Net Worth: £6,747,500 *Total Assets:* £15,042,389
Registered Office: Eagle Works, Walton Well Road, Oxford, OX2 6EE
Activities: Other research and experimental development on natural sciences and engineering
Parent: Lucy Group Ltd
Officers: Madeline Laxton, Secretary; Gary David Ashton [1961] Finance Director; Charles Richard Dick [1950] Director; Jonathan Charles Finch-Dick [1980] Executive Director; John Griffiths [1962] Director

Lucy Electric UK Limited
Incorporated: 1 August 1974 *Employees:* 133
Previous: Lucy Switchgear Limited
Net Worth: £12,274,869 *Total Assets:* £23,641,248
Registered Office: Eagle Works, Walton Well Road, Oxford, OX2 6EE
Activities: Manufacture of other electrical equipment
Parent: W.Lucy & Co.Limited
Officers: Madeline Laxton, Secretary; Gary David Ashton [1961] Director; Charles Richard Dick [1950] Director; Jonathan Charles Finch-Dick [1980] Executive Director; John Griffiths [1962] Director

Lucy Group Ltd
Incorporated: 1 April 1897 *Employees:* 1,353
Previous: W.Lucy & Co.Limited
Net Worth: £190,682,000 *Total Assets:* £275,097,984
Registered Office: Eagle Works, Walton Well Road, Oxford, OX2 6EE
Activities: Manufacture of electricity distribution and control apparatus
Parent: W.L. Shareholding Company Limited
Officers: Madeline Laxton, Secretary/Solicitor; Gary David Ashton [1961] Finance Director; Charles Richard Dick [1950] Director; Robert Ian Dick [1939] Director; Jonathan Charles Finch-Dick [1980] Director/Chartered Surveyor; Philippa Latham [1960] Director; Madeline Laxton [1965] Director/Secretary

Robert Luff Foundation Limited
Incorporated: 11 November 1966
Net Worth: £36,128,140 *Total Assets:* £36,151,768
Registered Office: Waters Edge, Ferry Lane, Moulsford, Wallingford, Oxon, OX10 9JF
Activities: Other social work activities without accommodation n.e.c.
Officers: Richard Peter Jeremy Price, Secretary; Lady Margaret Ruth Bodey [1947] Director/Retired Nurse; Sir Paul James Duke Coleridge [1949] Director/Retired High Court Judge; Melanie Clare Lydiate Condon [1961] Director/Travel Agent; Dr Helen Elizabeth Hughes [1958] Director/General Practitioner; Brian David Nicholson [1944] Director/Accountant; Richard Peter Jeremy Price [1948] Director/Solicitor; Jean Tomlinson [1935] Director/Housewife; Reverend Matthew Tomlinson [1961] Director/Vicar

Lukegate Limited
Incorporated: 21 June 1979 *Employees:* 5
Net Worth: £12,185,296 *Total Assets:* £14,978,876
Registered Office: Unit F, Whiteacres, Cambridge Road, Whetstone, Leics, LE8 6ZG
Activities: Other letting and operating of own or leased real estate
Shareholders: Shyam Dass Chawla; Chander Chawla
Officers: Chander Chawla, Secretary; Sonia Chawla Barnes [1973] Director; Chander Chawla [1950] Director & Secretary; Shyam Dass Chawla [1940] Director

Lunette Properties Limited
Incorporated: 26 September 1990
Net Worth: £12,045,000 *Total Assets:* £22,493,000
Registered Office: 15 Saxon Way East, Oakley Hay Industrial Estate, Corby, Northants, NN18 9EY
Activities: Other business support service activities n.e.c.
Officers: Anona Jane Young, Secretary; Anona Jane Young [1951] Director/Plastics Merchant; Dominic Peter Robert Young [1975] Director; Jason James Graham Young [1970] Director; Jeremy Robert Andrew Young [1949] Director/Plastics Merchant

The Lutterworth Academies Trust
Incorporated: 19 April 2012 *Employees:* 202
Net Worth: £9,964,000 *Total Assets:* £15,255,000
Registered Office: Lutterworth College, Bitteswell Road, Lutterworth, Leics, LE17 4EW
Activities: General secondary education
Officers: Helen Caple [1974] Director/Nurse; Helen Kerrison Christie [1964] Director/Teacher; Maureen Elizabeth Daley [1956] Director/Social Care Consultant; Russell Edward Grant [1965] Director/Business Consultant; Vivianne Laura Lawson [1967] Director/Teacher; Russell Ivan Murch [1977] Managing Director; Chris Skelton [1961] Finance Director; Rev Charlie Adam Mark Styles [1981] Director/Minister of Religion; Nick Summers [1964] Director/Headteacher; John Grant Peter Warren [1951] Director

Luxfab Limited
Incorporated: 28 February 1989
Net Worth: £11,212,582 *Total Assets:* £15,002,966
Registered Office: Head Office, Bond Avenue, Bletchley, Milton Keynes, Bucks, MK1 1JG
Activities: Activities of head offices
Officers: Alasdair Roderick McRury [1956] Managing Director; Richard Kent Reece [1956] Director/Executive Vice President [American]

Luxury British Design 1 Limited
Incorporated: 11 December 2017
Net Worth: £192,229 *Total Assets:* £33,464,330
Registered Office: 170 Brook Drive, Milton Park, Milton, Abingdon, Oxon, OX14 4SD
Activities: Non-trading company
Parent: Luxury British Design Holdings Limited
Officers: Emilio Giuseppe Foa [1963] Director; Mark John James Little [1965] Director/Accountant

Luxury British Design 2 Limited
Incorporated: 11 December 2017 *Employees:* 2
Net Worth Deficit: £41,793 *Total Assets:* £33,530,308
Registered Office: 170 Brook Drive, Milton Park, Milton, Abingdon, Oxon, OX14 4SD
Activities: Non-trading company
Parent: Luxury British Design 1 Limited
Officers: Emilio Giuseppe Foa [1963] Director; Mark John James Little [1965] Director/Accountant

Luxury British Design Holdings Limited
Incorporated: 11 December 2017 *Employees:* 238
Net Worth: £79,613 *Total Assets:* £40,483,696
Registered Office: 170 Brook Drive, Milton Park, Milton, Abingdon, Oxon, OX14 4SD
Activities: Non-trading company
Officers: Roberto Ardagna [1980] Director/Investment Advisor [Italian]; Annabel Lucy Veronica Astor [1948] Director; Emilio Giuseppe Foa [1963] Director; Michael Karangelen [1968] Director [American]; Joerg Bernhard Klasmeyer [1982] Director/Investment Professional [German]; Mark John James Little [1965] Director/Accountant; Alessandro Tome [1963] Director/Strategic Advisor [Swiss]

Luxury for Less Limited
Incorporated: 30 March 2012 *Employees:* 200
Net Worth Deficit: £6,533,086 *Total Assets:* £17,730,196
Registered Office: Attleborough House, Townsend Drive, Attleborough Fields Industrial Estate, Nuneaton, Warwicks, CV11 6RU
Activities: Other business support service activities n.e.c.
Parent: Wolseley Limited
Officers: Matthew Neville, Secretary; Christopher Bale [1963] Director; Zhuo Li [1983] Director [Chinese]; Matthew James Neville [1968] Finance Director; Simon Nicholas Oakland [1969] Director/Businessman

Luxus Limited
Incorporated: 15 January 1965 *Employees:* 206
Net Worth: £4,717,592 *Total Assets:* £19,796,036
Registered Office: Belvoir Way, Fairfield Industrial Estate, Louth, Lincs, LN11 0LQ
Activities: Manufacture of plastics in primary forms
Shareholders: Peter Nigel Atterby; Barry John Clift
Officers: Barry John Clift, Secretary; Peter Nigel Atterby [1953] Director; Barry John Clift [1942] Director

Lymn Funeral Services Limited
Incorporated: 3 March 2010 *Employees:* 106
Net Worth: £22,399,336 *Total Assets:* £26,076,478
Registered Office: Robin Hood House, Robin Hood Street, Nottingham, NG3 1GF
Activities: Funeral and related activities
Major Shareholder: Nigel Lymn Rose
Officers: Shaun Michael Caine, Secretary; Jacqueline Lymn Rose [1956] Director; Matthew Alexander Lymn Rose [1982] Funeral Director; Nigel Lymn Rose [1954] Funeral Director; Penelope Jane Lymn Rose [1956] Director; Sheila Margaret Rose [1928] Funeral Director

A.W.Lymn The Family Funeral Service Limited
Incorporated: 30 March 1984 *Employees:* 106
Net Worth: £22,399,336 *Total Assets:* £26,091,282
Registered Office: Robin Hood House, Robin Hood Street, Nottingham, NG3 1GF
Activities: Funeral and related activities
Major Shareholder: Nigel Lymn Rose
Officers: Shaun Michael Caine, Secretary/Accountant; Jacqueline Lymn Rose [1956] Funeral Director; Matthew Alexander Lymn Rose [1982] Funeral Director; Nigel Lymn Rose [1954] Funeral Director; Penelope Jane Lymn Rose [1956] Director; Sheila Margaret Rose [1928] Funeral Director

Mark Lyndon Paper Enterprises (UK) Limited
Incorporated: 20 June 2007 *Employees:* 22
Net Worth: £3,493,569 *Total Assets:* £17,890,826
Registered Office: 12 The Triangle, NG2 Business Park, Nottingham, NG2 1AE
Activities: Wholesale of waste and scrap
Major Shareholder: Albert Tung Choi Chiu
Officers: Albert Tung Choi Chiu, Secretary; Albert Tung Choi Chiu [1948] Director/Sales [Canadian]

Lynn Wind Farm Limited
Incorporated: 7 February 2001
Net Worth: £3,466,000 *Total Assets:* £122,575,000
Registered Office: Grimsby Renewables, Operations Base, North Quay, Grimsby, N E Lincs, DN31 3SY
Activities: Production of electricity
Parent: Glid Wind Farms Topco Limited
Officers: Keith Mangan [1973] Director/Investment Manager [Irish]; Peter George Raftery [1968] Director/Engineer; Karl Ben Smith [1977] Director/Banker; Alexis Eduardo Ulens [1967] Fund Director [Belgian]

M & J Group (Construction & Roofing) Ltd
Incorporated: 31 May 1978 *Employees:* 44
Net Worth: £5,531,132 *Total Assets:* £10,180,443
Registered Office: M & J Group Hammond Road, Elms Farm Industrial Estate, Bedford, MK41 0UD
Activities: Roofing activities
Officers: Clare Marie Henrickson, Secretary; Dean Henrickson [1971] Finance Director; Jack William Henrickson [1989] Director; Peter Henrickson [1961] Contracts Director

M & M (MK) Limited
Incorporated: 6 April 2001 *Employees:* 45
Net Worth: £18,802,840 *Total Assets:* £24,759,384
Registered Office: Sovereign Court, 230 Upper Fifth Street, Central Milton Keynes, Bucks, MK9 2HR
Activities: Activities of other holding companies n.e.c.
Shareholders: Julie Storey; Mark Peter Storey; Matthew Roger Storey; Mark Peter Storey; Matthew Roger Storey; Mark Peter Storey; Matthew Roger Storey
Officers: Mark Peter Storey, Secretary/Joint CEO; Mark Peter Storey [1968] Director/Joint CEO; Matthew Roger Storey [1973] Director/Joint CEO

M N Holdings Limited
Incorporated: 23 February 2005 *Employees:* 126
Net Worth: £9,894,816 *Total Assets:* £14,294,102
Registered Office: Cromer Street, Newbridge Lane, Stockport, Cheshire, SK1 2NP
Activities: Activities of other holding companies n.e.c.
Shareholders: Gary Edwin Rhodes; Edwin Rhodes
Officers: Andrea Carole Rhodes, Secretary; Edwin Rhodes [1927] Director/Engineer; Gary Edwin Rhodes [1961] Director

M.& N.Textiles Limited
Incorporated: 23 July 1959 *Employees:* 18
Net Worth: £10,472,612 *Total Assets:* £11,244,508
Registered Office: 10 Riverview, The Embankment, Vale Road, Heaton Mersey, Stockport, Cheshire, SK4 3GN
Activities: Wholesale of textiles
Parent: Wrengate Limited
Officers: Souad Musry, Secretary; Alan Philip David Musry [1963] Director/Accountant; Ronald Musry [1935] Director; Souad Musry [1936] Director/Company Secretary

M.A.X. Funding Limited
Incorporated: 15 January 2013 *Employees:* 5
Net Worth: £59,338,384 *Total Assets:* £62,887,628
Registered Office: Greylands, Macclesfield Road, Alderley Edge, Cheshire, SK9 7BS
Activities: Other credit granting n.e.c.
Shareholder: Myrna Madeleine Essayan
Officers: Beryl Essayan [1934] Director; Max Lucas Essayan [1933] Director; Myrna Madeleine Essayan [1937] Director; Jacqueline Clare Wortley [1961] Director

M.C.I. Developments Limited
Incorporated: 25 February 2011
Net Worth: £19,033,000 *Total Assets:* £28,304,000
Registered Office: The Waterfront, Lakeside Boulevard, Doncaster, S Yorks, DN4 5PL
Activities: Construction of domestic buildings
Parent: Beecham Developments Limited
Officers: Timothy Mark Beale [1976] Director; James Andrew Garnett [1983] Director; James Michael Douglas Thomson [1966] Director

M.J.C. Developments Limited
Incorporated: 11 July 1991 *Employees:* 2
Net Worth: £8,004,465 *Total Assets:* £9,680,337
Registered Office: 15a School Street Trading Estate, Hazel Grove, Stockport, Cheshire, SK7 4RA
Activities: Development of building projects
Officers: Madalane Cundiff, Secretary; Keilly Jane Barnes [1976] Director; Richard James Cundiff [1979] Director

M.J.S. Construction (March) Limited
Incorporated: 23 November 1995 *Employees:* 48
Net Worth: £5,890,212 *Total Assets:* £12,717,433
Registered Office: MJS House, Wisbech Road, Westry, March, Cambs, PE15 0BA
Activities: Construction of commercial buildings
Officers: Judith Anne Saxby, Secretary; Jamie Burton [1981] Director; Ben John Saxby [1988] Director/Construction Manager; Michael John Saxby [1954] Director; Sean Michael Saxby [1992] Construction Director

M.J.S. Holdings (March) Limited
Incorporated: 14 July 2015 *Employees:* 48
Net Worth: £15,889,415 *Total Assets:* £22,720,636
Registered Office: MJS House, Wisbech Road, Westry, March, Cambs, PE15 0BA
Activities: Other specialised construction activities n.e.c.
Shareholders: Ben John Saxby; Sean Michael Saxby
Officers: Ben John Saxby [1988] Director; Sean Michael Saxby [1992] Director

M.M.D. Mining Machinery Developments Limited
Incorporated: 7 August 1978 *Employees:* 174
Net Worth: £53,727,656 *Total Assets:* £69,656,352
Registered Office: MMD Group, Cotes Park Lane, Somercotes, Alfreton, Derbys, DE55 4NJ
Activities: Manufacture of machinery for mining
Major Shareholder: Alan Potts
Officers: Judy Debra Cusimano [1960] Personnel Director; Graham Tony Griffiths [1973] Manufacturing Director; Christine Martin [1963] Finance Director

M.P.B. Structures Ltd
Incorporated: 20 March 1986 *Employees:* 65
Net Worth: £10,376,180 *Total Assets:* £30,430,564
Registered Office: 14 Crucible Road, Corby, Northants, NN17 5TS
Activities: Construction of other civil engineering projects n.e.c.
Shareholders: Michael John Boyle; Eileen Boyle
Officers: Michael John Boyle, Secretary; Eileen Boyle [1940] Director; Michael John Boyle [1936] Director/Civil Engineer; Patrick John Joseph Boyle [1963] Director; Sean Gerard Boyle [1975] Director

M.P.K. Garages Limited
Incorporated: 1 August 1979 *Employees:* 171
Net Worth: £3,649,677 *Total Assets:* £20,017,444
Registered Office: MPK House, 318 Melton Road, Leicester, LE4 7SL
Activities: Retail sale of automotive fuel in specialised stores
Parent: MPK Group Limited
Officers: Nerissa Haskic [1988] Director [Australian]; Paul Anthony Kershaw [1962] Director/General Manager; John Telford Stewart [1970] Director/Merchant Banker [Australian]

M.P.K. Group Limited
Incorporated: 15 October 2015 *Employees:* 171
Net Worth: £3,670,167 *Total Assets:* £25,616,446
Registered Office: MPK House, 318 Melton Road, Leicester, LE4 7SL
Activities: Activities of head offices
Parent: Stratford Retail Group Limited
Officers: Nerissa Haskic [1988] Director/Management Consultant [Australian]; Paul Anthony Kershaw [1962] Director/Petrol Retailing; John Telford Stewart [1970] Director/Merchant Banker [Australian]

M.S.W (UK) Limited
Incorporated: 10 October 1989 *Employees:* 29
Net Worth: £12,916,000 *Total Assets:* £15,142,000
Registered Office: Acton Grove, Long Eaton, Notts, NG10 1FY
Activities: Other specialised construction activities n.e.c.
Parent: MSW Holdings Limited
Officers: Sara Louise Barley [1979] Sales Director; Daniel Thomas Gorman [1974] Director; Anton Otto Grodon [1957] Director; Derek Johnston [1962] Managing Director; Alan Stokoe [1968] Director; Sebastian John Wilkinson [1985] Director

M3 (EU) Limited
Incorporated: 13 March 1998 *Employees:* 184
Net Worth: £4,011,114 *Total Assets:* £14,705,050
Registered Office: 20 Western Avenue, Milton Park, Milton, Abingdon, Oxon, OX14 4SH
Activities: Other information service activities n.e.c.
Parent: M3 USA Corporation
Officers: Anton Richter [1975] Director; Itaru Tanimura [1965] Director/Chief Executive Officer [Japanese]; Akihiko Tomaru [1972] Director/Business Manager [Japanese]

M3 Medical Holdings Ltd
Incorporated: 10 December 2015
Previous: Axio Medical Holdings Limited
Net Worth: £31,460,036 *Total Assets:* £35,121,668
Registered Office: 2nd Floor, 20 Western Avenue, Milton Park, Milton, Abingdon, Oxon, OX14 4SH
Activities: Activities of head offices
Parent: M3 Inc
Officers: Chris Thiele, Secretary; Anton Richter [1975] Director; Itaru Tanimura [1965] Director [Japanese]; Akihiko Tomaru [1972] Director [Japanese]

Maccaferri Ltd
Incorporated: 14 March 1956 *Employees:* 39
Net Worth: £1,988,577 *Total Assets:* £10,431,969
Registered Office: Building 168, Maxwell Avenue, Harwell, Didcot, Oxon, OX11 0QT
Activities: Wholesale of wood, construction materials and sanitary equipment
Parent: Officine Maccaferri SpA
Officers: Anthony William Rutter, Secretary; Timothy John Balderson [1970] Director; Stephen James Miller [1968] Managing Director; Matthew Andrew Stephen Showan [1971] Director/International Sales & Marketing Manager

The Macclesfield Academy
Incorporated: 8 April 2011 *Employees:* 70
Net Worth: £8,297,000 *Total Assets:* £10,237,000
Registered Office: Macclesfield College, Park Lane, Macclesfield, Cheshire, SK11 8LF
Activities: General secondary education
Officers: Jeremy John Green [1958] Director; Professor Alistair Gordon Sutcliffe [1951] Director/Retired; Anne Merle Thomson [1953] Director

MacDermid Autotype Limited
Incorporated: 1 October 1923 *Employees:* 217
Net Worth: £40,426,000 *Total Assets:* £47,015,000
Registered Office: Grove Road, Wantage, Oxon, OX12 7BZ
Activities: Manufacture of other plastic products
Parent: Surface Treatments Limited
Officers: Jeffrey William Braham [1964] Sales & Marketing Director; John Patrick Connolly [1966] Director/Chief Financial Officer [American]; Joe Headon [1978] Manufacturing Director; Stefano Rosati [1972] Director/Legal Counsel [Italian]

MacFarlane Group UK Limited
Incorporated: 20 April 1982 *Employees:* 699
Net Worth: £6,735,000 *Total Assets:* £97,151,000
Registered Office: Siskin Parkway East, Middlemarch Business Park, Coventry, Warwicks, CV3 4PE
Activities: Packaging activities
Parent: MacFarlane Group PLC
Officers: John Love, Secretary; Peter Duncan Atkinson [1956] Director; Ivor Gray [1969] Director; John Love [1960] Director/Chartered Accountant

Machine Mart Limited
Incorporated: 13 April 1981 *Employees:* 425
Net Worth: £112,832,528 *Total Assets:* £127,345,552
Registered Office: 211 Lower Parliament Street, Nottingham, NG1 1GN
Activities: Other retail sale in non-specialised stores
Parent: Clarke Group International Limited
Officers: Jacqueline Williams, Secretary; John Alan Clarke [1943] Director; Sandra Elaine Clarke [1943] Director; Tracey Clarke [1964] Director; Jacqueline Williams [1965] Director/Company Secretary

MacIntyre Care
Incorporated: 15 December 1966 *Employees:* 2,198
Net Worth: £30,400,000 *Total Assets:* £35,098,000
Registered Office: 602 South Seventh Street, Central Milton Keynes, Bucks, MK9 2JA
Activities: Residential care activities for the elderly and disabled
Officers: Claire Toombs, Secretary; John Robert Lloyd Berriman [1956] Director/Chartered Accountant; Rajdeep Kaur Gahir [1989] Director/Consultant; Adam Farley Goldstein [1978] Director/Chief Operating Officer; Rosemary Diane Hart [1954] Director/Solicitor; Dragana Josifova [1958] Director/Consultant Clinical Geneticist [Macedonian]; Neil Stephen Macmillan [1962] Director/Insurance; Pamela Katharine Meek [1971] Director/Deputy Principal; Ruth Elizabeth Smyth [1976] Director/HR Consultant; Duncan Anthony Strachan [1954] Director/Solicitor; Rachel Mary Taylor [1976] Director/Professional Services Consultant; Nikki Williams-Ellis [1956] Director; Martin Zahra [1959] Director [Maltese]

MacIntyre Hudson Holdings Limited
Incorporated: 22 February 1999 *Employees:* 23
Net Worth: £5,743,614 *Total Assets:* £10,838,686
Registered Office: Moorgate House, 201 Silbury Boulevard, Milton Keynes, Bucks, MK9 1LZ
Activities: Activities of head offices
Parent: MacIntyre Hudson LLP
Officers: Atul Kariya [1972] Director/Accountant; Steven Moore [1963] Director/Chartered Accountant; Rachel Nutt [1975] Director/Accountant; Rakesh Shaunak [1956] Director/Chartered Accountant

MacIntyre Hudson LLP
Incorporated: 19 March 2005 *Employees:* 683
Net Worth: £11,142,451 *Total Assets:* £30,524,516
Registered Office: Moorgate House, 201 Silbury Boulevard, Milton Keynes, Bucks, MK9 1LZ
Officers: Atul Kariya [1972] Member; Steven Moore [1963] Member; Rachel Nutt [1975] Member; Rakesh Shaunak [1956] Member; Stephen James Thomas Askew [1954] LLP Member; Michael Jonathan Ball [1975] LLP Member; Christopher Stephen Barlow [1971] LLP Member; Dennis Neil Berry [1976] LLP Member; Tasneem Bharmal [1974] LLP Member; Christopher John Blundell [1962] LLP Member; Jay Boyce [1958] LLP Member; Anthony David Brand [1957] LLP Member; Michael James Brown [1949] LLP Member; John Charles Burwood [1951] LLP Member; Patrick Joseph Byrne [1949] LLP Member; Francis Peter Cheney [1950] LLP Member; Duncan George Cochrane-Dyet [1966] LLP Member; Alison Jayne Conley [1964] LLP Member; Andrew Cameron Cook [1954] LLP Member; David John Coppard [1954] LLP Member; John Edwin Coverdale [1965] LLP Member; Matthew Alexander Coward [1966] LLP Member; Alan Peter Craddock [1964] LLP Member; Georgette Alicia Crisp [1985] LLP Member; Candice Terri-Anne Czeremuszkin [1986] LLP Member; Gavin Clifford Davis [1961] LLP Member; Paul Michael Davis [1960] LLP Member; Christian Stephen Denning [1966] LLP Member; Sarah Jane Dodds [1975] LLP Member; Georgina Marie Eason [1978] LLP Member; Nigel Antony Eastaway [1943] LLP Member; Stephen Kenneth Freeman [1968] LLP Member; David Mark Gallagher [1970] LLP Member; Harminther Singh Gill [1960] LLP Member; Grant Courtney Gleghorn [1956] LLP Member; James Gransby [1979] LLP Member; Marcel Samuel Grech-Marguerat [1950] LLP Member; Christopher Alexander Harris [1963] LLP Member; Alan Peter Herbert [1963] LLP Member; Martin Steve Herron [1968] LLP Member; Alison Clare Horner [1964] LLP Member; Alyson Marina Howard [1962] LLP Member; Rebecca Jane Hughes [1977] LLP Member; Frances Catherine James [1963] LLP Member; Michael John Kay [1969] LLP Member; Robert John Kidson [1956] LLP Member; Patrick George King [1962] LLP Member; James Robert Kipping [1983] LLP Member; Simon Andrew Vivian Knibbs [1980] LLP Member; Howard Keith Lewis [1951] LLP Member; Stuart John Manning [1959] LLP Member; Nigel Campbell May [1965] LLP Member; John Baptist Avelino Mendes [1956] LLP Member; Cara Colleen Miller [1981] LLP Member; Colin George Mills [1954] LLP Member; Mark Ernest James Minus [1963] LLP Member; Jason Michel Mitchell [1964] LLP Member; Justin Stephen Moss [1980] LLP Member; Andrew Jamie Moyser [1982] LLP Member; Robert Anthony Nelson [1963] LLP Member; Elaine Susan Olson-Williams [1962] LLP Member; Yogan Adabhai Patel [1959] LLP Member; Martin David Payne [1952] LLP Member; Gareth David Peters [1981] LLP Member; Stephen John Poleykett [1973] LLP Member; Richard John Powell [1971] LLP Member; David Keith Purser [1954] LLP Member; Martin Ramsey [1968] LLP Member; Brian Neil Richens [1952] LLP Member; Michael Colin John Sanders [1966] LLP Member; Brendan Michael Sharkey [1955] LLP Member; Rajeev Shaunak [1968] LLP Member; Elaine Rosemary Shoesmith [1951] LLP Member; Bianca Kamala Silva [1960] LLP Member; Katharine Jane Simon [1977] LLP Member; Sudhir Singh [1963] LLP Member; Tobias Robert Stephenson [1966] LLP Member; Neil Richard Stern [1981] LLP Member; Christopher Frederick Stratton [1949] LLP Member; Christopher Nigel Sutton [1956] LLP Member; Gregory Luke Taylor [1978] LLP Member; Glen David Thomas [1967] LLP Member; Robert William Trunchion [1956] LLP Member; David James Walker [1977] LLP Member; Jane Walker-Smith [1977] LLP Member; Deborah Weston [1959] LLP Member; Laurence Whitehead [1966] LLP Member; David Wignall [1965] LLP Member; Adam John Young [1969] LLP Member; Graeme Lindsay Young [1956] LLP Member

A J Mackaness Holdings Limited
Incorporated: 8 August 2005 *Employees:* 2
Net Worth: £15,558,902 *Total Assets:* £15,558,902
Registered Office: Billing House, The Causeway, Great Billing, Northampton, NN3 9EX
Activities: Activities of head offices
Parent: A J Mackaness Group Limited
Officers: Oliver James Mackaness, Secretary/Chartered Accountant; James Mackaness [1945] Director; Oliver James Mackaness [1975] Director/Chartered Accountant

A.J.Mackaness Limited
Incorporated: 4 May 1946 *Employees:* 7
Net Worth: £9,863,345 *Total Assets:* £15,551,749
Registered Office: Billing House, The Causeway, Great Billing, Northampton, NN3 9EX
Activities: Other letting and operating of own or leased real estate
Officers: Oliver James Mackaness, Secretary/Accountant; Louise Docker [1973] Director/Food Stylist; Frank Hodson [1949] Director/Group Financial Manager; James Mackaness [1945] Director; Oliver James Mackaness [1975] Director/Chartered Accountant

Madecorn Leisure LLP
Incorporated: 23 September 2005 *Employees:* 14
Net Worth: £8,699,670 *Total Assets:* £18,242,442
Registered Office: Mercia Marina, Findern Lane, Willington, Derbys, DE65 6DW

Magdalen College School Brackley Academy Trust
Incorporated: 3 December 2012 *Employees:* 159
Net Worth: £11,685,408 *Total Assets:* £14,377,375
Registered Office: Magdalen College School, Waynflete Avenue, Brackley, Northants, NN13 6FB
Activities: General secondary education
Officers: Neil Arnold [1960] Director; Jonathan Michael Andrew Bilson [1967] Director/Management Accountant; Louise Bowe [1968] Director/Senior Manager (Environment Sector); Christopher Edward Clapham [1941] Director; Ian Hugh Colling [1966] Director/Headteacher; Hugh Francis Esau Cooper [1943] Director; Dr Nicholas Michael Dixon [1976] Director; Graham Henry George Ellis [1945] Director/Chairman; Daniel Jeremy Peter Garratt [1965] Director; Colm Harte [1965] Director; Sheila Jane King [1959] Director; Dr James Benjamin Naylor [1970] Manufacturing Director; Ana Teresa Peres Da Silva Gomes Dos Santos [1974] Director/EHS Regulatory Consultant [Portuguese]; Dr Mark Philip Pobjoy [1967] Director; Dr Jane Powell [1957] Director/National Talent Manager English Lacrosse; Thomas Keith Redman [1987] Director/Solicitor; Michael John Roberts [1963] Director/Teacher; John Barnaby Thorne [1969] Director

Magdalen College School Oxford Limited
Incorporated: 5 March 1987 *Employees:* 261
Net Worth: £23,391,512 *Total Assets:* £31,304,888
Registered Office: Magdalen College School, Cowley Place, Oxford, OX4 1DZ
Activities: Primary education
Officers: Toby Matthew George John Beaumont, Secretary; Dr Catharine Alice Benson [1962] Director/Doctor; Penelope Ann Cameron Watt [1959] Managing Director; Professor Constantin Coussios [1977] Director/University Professor [Greek]; Timothy Peter Warren Edwards [1956] Director/Company Chief Executive; Adrian Dennis James [1962] Director/Architect; Professor Daniel Heinrich Friedrich Kroening [1975] Director/University Professor [German]; Judith Anne Lennox Longworth [1951] Development Director; Dr Stuart Robert MacKenzie [1971] Director/University Fellow; Jan Ann Phillips [1962] Director/Lawyer; Neil Peter Record [1953] Director/Chairman, Investment Management; Dr Nigel Peter Vincent Richardson [1948] Director/Retired Headmaster; Dr Richard Andrew Saldanha [1966] Director/Management Consultant; Benjamin Alastair Martin Vessey [1967] Director/Headmaster; Paul Nigel Withers [1956] Director; Charles Gerard Young [1947] Director/Bursar

Magenta Storage Limited
Incorporated: 17 August 2001
Previous: Magenta Nottingham Limited
Net Worth: £8,684,924 *Total Assets:* £16,248,678
Registered Office: The Lodge, High Street, Odell, Beds, MK43 7BB
Activities: Other retail sale in non-specialised stores
Major Shareholder: Mark Glenn Bridgman Shaw
Officers: Lesley Shaw, Secretary; Christopher Wright, Secretary; Rebecca-Jane Harland Fairweather [1972] Director; Lara-Kate Bridgman Jones [1983] Director; Jason Mark Bridgman Shaw [1970] Director; Marietta Louise Shaw [1981] Director; Mark Glenn Bridgman Shaw [1947] Director

Maggie Sottero Bridal (UK) Ltd.
Incorporated: 3 June 1999
Net Worth: £10,971,569 *Total Assets:* £11,662,416
Registered Office: The Old Mill, Blisworth Hill Farm, Stoke Road, Blisworth, Northampton, NN7 3DB
Activities: Wholesale of clothing and footwear
Shareholders: Lesley Margaret Webster; Wayne Porter Webster Jr
Officers: Thomas Manning, Secretary; Thomas Clair Manning [1965] Director/President Maggie Sottero Designs [American]; Clyde Lorrin Redford [1953] Director/EVP & CFO Maggie Sottero Designs [American]; Lesley Margaret Webster [1949] Director [Australian]; Wayne Porter Webster [1942] Director/Executive [Australian]

Magna Exteriors (Banbury) Limited
Incorporated: 23 September 1996 *Employees:* 698
Previous: Decoma Exterior Systems U.K. Limited
Net Worth: £30,470,000 *Total Assets:* £61,034,000
Registered Office: Unit C, Beaumont Road Industrial Estate, Banbury, Oxon, OX16 1TR
Activities: Manufacture of bodies (coachwork) for motor vehicles (except caravans)
Parent: Magna International Inc
Officers: Grahame Keith Burrow [1963] Director [Canadian]; Anthony Robert Charles William Park [1972] Director; Mark John Smith [1968] Director

Magna International Holding (UK) Limited
Incorporated: 28 February 1996 *Employees:* 90
Previous: Magna Interiors Holding (UK) Limited
Net Worth: £27,561,000 *Total Assets:* £127,174,000
Registered Office: International House, Siskin Parkway East, Middlemarch Business Park, Coventry, Warwicks, CV3 4PE
Activities: Manufacture of other parts and accessories for motor vehicles
Parent: Magna International Inc
Officers: Mark John Smith, Secretary/Director of Finance; Ralf Paul Hupe [1962] Director/Lawyer [German]; Mark John Smith [1968] Director

Magna Trust
Incorporated: 23 February 1998 *Employees:* 73
Net Worth: £9,181,303 *Total Assets:* £9,995,456
Registered Office: Magna Templeborough Offices, Sheffield Road, Rotherham, S Yorks, S60 1DX
Activities: Other amusement and recreation activities n.e.c.
Officers: Brian Chapple [1948] Director/Retired; Michael John Smith [1957] Director/Transport Manager; Kevin Tomlinson [1953] Director/Business Executive; Michael Stewart Yarlett [1954] Director/Retired

Magnavale Limited
Incorporated: 20 February 2013 *Employees:* 229
Net Worth: £759,183 *Total Assets:* £19,239,278
Registered Office: Magnavale House, Park Road, Holmewood Industrial Park, Holmewood, Chesterfield, Derbys, S42 5UY
Activities: Processing and preserving of poultry meat
Parent: Beta (International) Limited
Officers: Stuart Hancock [1972] Director; Andrew Campbell Lawrence [1989] Director/Operations Manager; Colin Taylor [1963] Director

Magyar Farming Company Limited
Incorporated: 5 September 1997 *Employees:* 45
Net Worth: £9,122,792 *Total Assets:* £11,663,980
Registered Office: 7 Abbey Court, Fraser Road, Priory Business Park, Bedford, MK44 3WH
Activities: Mixed farming
Officers: William Robert Nicholas Tapp, Secretary; Christopher George Combe [1962] Director/Farmer; David Bosworth Gunner [1952] Director; William Robert Nicholas Tapp [1957] Director/Farmer; Simon Lewis Weaver [1960] Director/Farmer

Mahle Aftermarket Limited
Incorporated: 3 November 2008 *Employees:* 40
Net Worth: £6,942,000 *Total Assets:* £12,586,000
Registered Office: 2 Central Park Drive, Rugby, Warwicks, CV23 0WE
Activities: Wholesale trade of motor vehicle parts and accessories
Officers: Heiko Pott [1969] Director/Vice President Accounting and Finance Europe [German]; Jonathan Charles Walker [1969] Director

Mahle Engine Systems UK Limited
Incorporated: 2 February 2007 *Employees:* 272
Net Worth: £4,013,000 *Total Assets:* £22,280,000
Registered Office: 2 Central Park Drive, Central Park, Rugby, Warwicks, CV23 0WE
Activities: Manufacture of bearings, gears, gearing and driving elements
Officers: Scott Henry Ferguson [1955] Director/Business Manager; Heiko Pott [1969] Director/Vice President Finance and Accounting Europe [German]

Mahle Filter Systems UK Limited
Incorporated: 12 March 1981 *Employees:* 187
Net Worth: £1,396,000 *Total Assets:* £15,436,000
Registered Office: 2 Central Park Drive, Rugby, Warwicks, CV23 0WE
Activities: Manufacture of other parts and accessories for motor vehicles
Officers: Scott Henry Ferguson [1955] Director/Engineer; Heiko Pott [1969] Director/Vice President Finance and Accounting Europe [German]; Juergen Heinz Schwertner [1961] Director/Executive Vice President [German]

Mahle Industries UK Limited
Incorporated: 21 November 2007 *Employees:* 57
Net Worth: £47,054,000 *Total Assets:* £82,402,000
Registered Office: 2 Central Park Drive, Central Park, Rugby, Warwicks, CV23 0WE
Activities: Other business support service activities n.e.c.
Officers: Scott Henry Ferguson [1955] Director/Business Manager; Michael Glowatzki [1960] Director/Attorney at Law [German]; Heiko Pott [1969] Director/Vice President Finance and Accounting Europe [German]

Mahle Powertrain Limited
Incorporated: 15 May 1998 *Employees:* 400
Net Worth: £48,627,000 *Total Assets:* £65,047,000
Registered Office: Costin House, St James Mill Road, Northampton, NN5 5TZ
Activities: Manufacture of other parts and accessories for motor vehicles
Officers: Dr Martin Berger [1974] Director/Engineer [German]; Scott Henry Ferguson [1955] Director/Business Manager; Dr. Joerg Bernd Theodor Stratmann [1969] Director/Chief Executive Officer [German]; Fred Tuerk [1961] Director/Vice President Profit Center Motorsport

Maintenance Management Limited
Incorporated: 21 August 2001 *Employees:* 98
Net Worth: £1,552,670 *Total Assets:* £32,688,378
Registered Office: Apollo House, 6 Bramley Road, Mount Farm, Milton Keynes, Bucks, MK1 1PT
Activities: Other business support service activities n.e.c.
Parent: Seckloe 280 Limited
Officers: Charles Hawkins, Secretary; Michael Hughes [1964] Director; Colin John Seggie [1973] Director; Alan John Tough [1959] Finance Director

Majestic Bingo Limited
Incorporated: 10 October 2013 *Employees:* 338
Net Worth: £2,452,000 *Total Assets:* £11,707,000
Registered Office: Regent Bingo Club, Westlode Street, Spalding, Lincs, PE11 2AE
Activities: Gambling and betting activities
Major Shareholder: Luke Oliver Johnson
Officers: Gary Roger Bennett [1973] Director/Chartered Accountant; Mark Edward Jepp [1967] Director/Gaming Consultant; Luke Oliver Johnson [1962] Director/Businessman; Paul Lewis Viner [1970] Director

Makita (UK) Limited
Incorporated: 13 December 1972 *Employees:* 171
Net Worth: £96,723,000 *Total Assets:* £147,726,000
Registered Office: Michigan Drive, Tongwell, Milton Keynes, Bucks, MK15 8JD
Activities: Wholesale of other machinery and equipment
Parent: Makita International Europe Ltd
Officers: Ryuichi Hashizume, Secretary; Yasushi Fukaya [1959] Director/Manager [Japanese]; Kenichi Ohara [1968] Director/Chief Executive [Japanese]; Takashi Omote [1959] Director/General Manager of International Sales HQ [Japanese]; Barry Forbes Smart [1958] Sales and Marketing Director

Makita International Europe Limited
Incorporated: 9 March 1995 *Employees:* 5
Net Worth: £232,355,008 *Total Assets:* £232,562,000
Registered Office: Michigan Drive, Tongwell, Milton Keynes, Bucks, MK15 8JD
Activities: Management consultancy activities other than financial management
Parent: Makita Corporation
Officers: Hiromu Ishikawa, Secretary; Yasushi Fukaya [1959] Director [Japanese]; Takashi Omote [1959] Director [Japanese]

Makro Holding Limited
Incorporated: 24 October 2001
Net Worth Deficit: £12,000 *Total Assets:* £98,656,000
Registered Office: Equity House, Irthlingborough Road, Wellingborough, Northants, NN8 1LT
Activities: Other business support service activities n.e.c.
Parent: Booker Wholesale Holdings Limited
Officers: Veselin Bandev [1978] Finance Director [Bulgarian]; Charles Wilson [1965] Director

Makro Self Service Wholesalers Limited
Incorporated: 25 February 1970 *Employees:* 1,707
Net Worth: £150,000,000 *Total Assets:* £225,100,000
Registered Office: Equity House, Irthlingborough Road, Wellingborough, Northants, NN8 1LT
Activities: Non-specialised wholesale trade
Parent: Makro Holding Limited
Officers: Veselin Bandev [1978] Finance Director [Bulgarian]; Charles Wilson [1965] Director

Malco Holdings Limited
Incorporated: 3 October 2006 *Employees:* 4
Net Worth: £20,032,404 *Total Assets:* £28,285,800
Registered Office: 26 Chaseview Road, Alrewas, Burton on Trent, Staffs, DE13 7EL
Activities: Buying and selling of own real estate
Shareholders: Malcolm Richard Paul; Hannah Eleanor Paul
Officers: Gary Joseph Summers, Secretary/Chartered Accountant; Anita Jeanne Paul [1953] Director; Malcolm Richard Paul [1949] Director

Mallory Court Hotel Limited
Incorporated: 23 August 1976 *Employees:* 98
Net Worth: £7,537,218 *Total Assets:* £15,702,645
Registered Office: Harbury Lane, Bishops Tachbrook, Leamington Spa, Warwicks, CV33 9QB
Activities: Hotels and similar accommodation
Shareholders: Eden Hotel Collection Limited; Eden Hotel Collection Limited
Officers: Marian Cartter [1943] Director/Retired; Sir Peter Rigby [1943] Director & Hotel Proprietor

Maltby Learning Trust
Incorporated: 29 September 2009 *Employees:* 416
Net Worth: £25,249,000 *Total Assets:* £31,977,000
Registered Office: Braithwell Road, Maltby, Rotherham, S Yorks, S66 8AB
Activities: Pre-primary education
Officers: Marcus Beck [1959] Director/Senior Lecturer; Richard Alan Belcher [1970] Director/Chartered Accountant; Jerry Percival Jarvis [1946] Director; Julie Ann Kenny [1957] Managing Director; Paul Martin [1957] Director/Management Consultant/Investigator; Peter James Sorsby [1968] Director; Glyn Staves [1985] Director; Richard Stubbs [1976] Director/Chief Executive Officer; David Lee Sutton [1965] Director/Headteacher

Maltgrade Limited
Incorporated: 23 July 1993
Net Worth: £4,625,711 *Total Assets:* £10,811,841
Registered Office: Wootton Grange, Wold Road, Wootton, Ulceby, N Lincs, DN39 6RG
Activities: Development of building projects
Shareholder: Angela Jane Graves
Officers: Mark Arthur Graves, Secretary/Director; Mark Arthur Graves [1957] Director; Jonathan Frank Jackson [1955] Director

MAM Software Limited
Incorporated: 5 March 1984 *Employees:* 167
Net Worth: £18,518,000 *Total Assets:* £22,598,000
Registered Office: Units 5 6 & 7 Maple Park, Maple Court, Tankersley, Barnsley, S Yorks, S75 3DP
Activities: Computer facilities management activities
Parent: MAM Software Group Inc
Officers: John Toland, Secretary; Brian Harold Callahan [1971] Director/Accounting/Finance [American]; Michael Grant Jamieson [1967] Director

MAN Energy Solutions UK Limited
Incorporated: 1 May 1963 *Employees:* 230
Previous: MAN Diesel & Turbo UK Ltd
Net Worth: £31,412,000 *Total Assets:* £63,367,000
Registered Office: 1 Mirrlees Drive, Hazel Grove, Stockport, Cheshire, SK7 5BP
Activities: Repair of machinery
Parent: MAN Energy Solutions SE
Officers: Ann Louise Durose, Secretary/Solicitor; Robin Wilhelm Sebastian Freiherr Von Plettenberg [1976] Sales Director [German]; Richard Colin Guest [1963] Managing Director; Wayne Jones [1966] Director; Per Rud Jorgensen [1965] Sales Director [Danish]; Michael Pfluger [1964] Finance Director [German]

Manderley Food Group Limited
Incorporated: 28 February 2008 *Employees:* 1,384
Net Worth: £57,612,152 *Total Assets:* £121,420,080
Registered Office: c/o Tayto Group Limited, Princewood Road, Earlstrees Industrial Estate, Corby, Northants, NN17 4AP
Activities: Manufacture of other food products n.e.c.
Officers: Stephen Thomas Alexander Hutchinson, Secretary; Paul Martin Allen [1968] Director/Accountant; Raymond Latimer Hutchinson [1949] Director; Stephen Thomas Alexander Hutchinson [1958] Director; Anne Alexandra Hutchinson Kane [1949] Director

Maneto (UK) 2 Limited
Incorporated: 21 December 2011
Net Worth: £14,404,000 *Total Assets:* £70,938,000
Registered Office: Kingfield Road, Coventry, Warwicks, CV6 5AA
Activities: Manufacture of other plastic products
Parent: Maneto (UK) 3 Limited
Officers: Tervor Morrow, Secretary; Patrick Kevin Burke [1967] Director/Accountant [American]; Andrew Elsby-Smith [1964] Finance Director; Russell Gary Grizzle [1956] Director/Chief Operating Officer [American]; Kevin Patrick Igo [1963] Director/Vice President of Corporate Finance Assistant Secretary [American]

Maneto (UK) 3 Limited
Incorporated: 20 December 2011 *Employees:* 568
Net Worth: £13,012,000 *Total Assets:* £101,781,000
Registered Office: Kingfield Road, Coventry, Warwicks, CV6 5AA
Activities: Manufacture of other plastic products
Officers: Trevor Morrow, Secretary; Patrick Kevin Burke [1967] Director/Accountant [American]; Andrew Elsby-Smith [1964] Finance Director; Russell Gary Grizzle [1956] Director/Chief Operating Officer [American]; Kevin Patrick Igo [1963] Director/Vice President of Corporate Finance Assistant Secretary [American]

Manifesto Foods Ltd
Incorporated: 12 October 2015 *Employees:* 229
Net Worth: £120,827 *Total Assets:* £11,261,361
Registered Office: Number One Pride Place, Pride Park, Derby, DE24 8QR
Activities: Processing and preserving of meat
Shareholder: Colin Vincent Wright
Officers: Anthony Martin Christiaanse [1962] Director [Dutch]; Julie Fancourt [1975] Director; Grant Ronald Moir [1965] Director; Colin Vincent Wright [1962] Director

Manitowoc Crane Group (UK) Limited
Incorporated: 3 September 1984 *Employees:* 40
Net Worth: £20,609,000 *Total Assets:* £29,569,000
Registered Office: Manitowoc House, Network 421, Radclive Road, Gawcott, Buckingham, MK18 4FD
Activities: Agents involved in the sale of machinery, industrial equipment, ships and aircraft
Parent: The Manitowoc Company Inc
Officers: Kim Dandridge [1959] Director; Corinne Nathalie Pouyet [1970] Director [French]

Manitowoc Crane Group (UK) Subco Limited
Incorporated: 28 June 2017
Net Worth: £22,040,852 *Total Assets:* £22,040,852
Registered Office: Manitowoc House, Network 421, Radclive Road, Gawcott, Bucks, MK18 4FD
Activities: Non-trading company
Parent: Manitowoc Crane Group (UK) Limited
Officers: David Antoniuk [1957] Director [American]; Uwe Woywode [1964] Director/Tax Manager [German]

Manor Crest Construction Limited
Incorporated: 30 May 2001 *Employees:* 7
Previous: Manor Crest (Carline) Ltd
Net Worth: £338,350 *Total Assets:* £9,659,841
Registered Office: 27-29 Lumley Avenue, Skegness, Lincs, PE25 2AT
Activities: Construction of domestic buildings
Parent: Manor Crest Homes Limited
Officers: Leigh Morris Hall, Secretary/Director; Leigh Morris Hall [1969] Director; Dean Anthony Wann [1971] Director

Manor Crest Homes Limited
Incorporated: 24 February 2006 *Employees:* 29
Net Worth: £7,745,280 *Total Assets:* £12,657,548
Registered Office: 27-29 Lumley Avenue, Skegness, Lincs, PE25 2AT
Activities: Construction of domestic buildings
Shareholders: Leigh Morris Hall; Dean Anthony Wann
Officers: Leigh Morris Hall, Secretary; Leigh Morris Hall [1969] Director; Deborah Ledbrook [1964] Director/Operations Manager; Dean Anthony Wann [1971] Director

Manor Fresh Limited
Incorporated: 18 November 2005 *Employees:* 172
Net Worth: £5,578,542 *Total Assets:* £12,508,413
Registered Office: Manor Farm, Holbeach Hurn, Spalding, Lincs, PE12 8LR
Activities: Wholesale of fruit and vegetables
Shareholders: Fresca Group Limited; A H Worth & Company Limited
Officers: Nigel Roland Baker, Secretary; Nigel Roland Baker [1962] Director; Ian Alexander Craig [1957] Director; Michael David Scott [1966] Director; Brett Geoffrey Sumner [1973] Finance Director; Martin John Taylor [1971] Director; Duncan Richard Worth [1965] Director

Mansfield Sand Company Limited
Incorporated: 19 April 1999 *Employees:* 73
Net Worth: £15,828,989 *Total Assets:* £29,003,996
Registered Office: Sandhurst Avenue, Mansfield, Notts, NG18 4BE
Activities: Operation of gravel and sand pits; mining of clays and kaolin
Major Shareholder: David Roderick Abraham
Officers: Nicholas Charles Dove, Secretary; David Roderick Abraham [1948] Director; Rachel Abraham [1982] Director/Midwife; Richard John Abraham [1978] Quarry Manager Director; Dominic Adrian Delich [1965] Director/General Manager [New Zealander]; Nicholas Charles Dove [1963] Finance Director

Manston Forests LLP
Incorporated: 16 August 2012
Net Worth: £15,000,751 *Total Assets:* £15,008,161
Registered Office: 1 St Helen's Court, North Street, Ashby-De-La-Zouch, Leics, LE65 1HS
Officers: Julian Anthony William Boardman-Weston [1954] Member; Simon Nicholas Harold Boardman-Weston [1958] Member

Manston Investments Limited
Incorporated: 14 September 1994 *Employees:* 8
Net Worth: £13,358,487 *Total Assets:* £20,979,076
Registered Office: 1 St Helen's Court, North Street, Ashby De La Zouch, Leics, LE65 1HS
Activities: Development of building projects
Shareholders: Simon Nicholas Harold Boardman-Weston; Amanda Elizabeth Boardman-Weston; Pamela Susan Boardman-Weston; Julian Anthony William Boardman-Weston
Officers: Lynne Archer [1962] Operations Director; Julian Anthony William Boardman-Weston [1954] Director; Simon Nicholas Harold Boardman-Weston [1958] Director; Thomas Kenneth Cecil Boardman-Weston [1987] Director; Dorothy Louann Hotson [1953] Director/Chartered Accountant

Manthorpe Building Products Limited
Incorporated: 17 December 1985 *Employees:* 96
Net Worth: £9,554,876 *Total Assets:* £15,847,099
Registered Office: Broomhouse Lane, Edlington, Doncaster, S Yorks, DN12 1ES
Activities: Manufacture of other plastic products
Parent: Manthorpe Building Products Holdings Limited
Officers: Emma Gayle Versluys, Secretary; Paul Anthony James [1965] Director; Martin Keith Payne [1965] Director

Manthorpe Engineering Limited
Incorporated: 24 April 1984 *Employees:* 103
Net Worth: £3,590,617 *Total Assets:* £11,756,208
Registered Office: Manthorpe House, Brittain Drive, Codnor Gate Industrial Estate, Ripley, Derbys, DE5 3ND
Activities: Machining
Parent: Manthorpe Limited
Officers: Carol Susan Pochciol, Secretary; Mark Elliott [1967] Director/Engineer; Carol Susan Pochciol [1950] Director; Thomas Fraser Pochciol [1984] Director/Business Development

Manthorpe Limited
Incorporated: 2 July 1987 *Employees:* 213
Net Worth: £21,641,916 *Total Assets:* £32,649,282
Registered Office: Manthorpe House, Brittain Drive, Codnor Gate Industrial Estate, Ripley, Derbys, DE5 3ND
Activities: Activities of head offices
Shareholder: Paul Gordon Pochciol
Officers: Carol Susan Pochciol, Secretary; Carol Susan Pochciol [1950] Director; Thomas Fraser Pochciol [1984] Director/Business Development

The Manufacturing Technology Centre Limited
Incorporated: 10 February 2009 *Employees:* 599
Net Worth: £6,194,000 *Total Assets:* £106,949,000
Registered Office: Pilot Way, Ansty Business Park, Ansty, Coventry, Warwicks, CV7 9JU
Activities: Other research and experimental development on natural sciences and engineering
Officers: Adrian James Cooper, Secretary; Adrian James Cooper [1968] Finance Director; Melvyn Ewell [1958] Director; Dr Clive Hickman [1954] Director/Chief Executive; Svetan Marin Ratchev [1959] Director/Academic; Professor Steven Joseph Rothberg [1965] Director/University Professor; Victoria Jane Sanderson [1966] Human Resources Director; Professor Andrew John Schofield [1966] Professor/Director; Andrew Paul Stephens [1970] Director; James Alexander Stephenson [1945] Director/Engineer

Map Property Investments Limited
Incorporated: 22 December 2011 *Employees:* 1
Net Worth: £17,163,928 *Total Assets:* £37,697,388
Registered Office: 141 Barkby Road, Leicester, LE4 9LG
Activities: Renting and operating of Housing Association real estate
Shareholders: Nazrana Shajid Latif; Bilal Shajid Latif
Officers: Shajid Razak Latif [1972] Director

Maplebeck Holdings Limited
Incorporated: 15 December 1982 *Employees:* 1
Net Worth: £10,847,050 *Total Assets:* £12,601,004
Registered Office: National Workshops, Moorgreen Industrial Park, Moorgreen, Nottingham, NG16 3QU
Activities: Other letting and operating of own or leased real estate
Parent: Maplebeck Investments Limited
Officers: Sara Jane Cundy, Secretary; David Frederick Bingham [1942] Director/Engineer; Simon David Bingham [1970] Director; Sara Jane Cundy [1969] Director/Accountant

Maplefields Academy
Incorporated: 14 May 2012 *Employees:* 72
Net Worth: £9,196,000 *Total Assets:* £10,328,000
Registered Office: Maplefields Academy, Tower Hill Road, Corby, Northants, NN18 0TH
Activities: General secondary education
Officers: Stephen James Sercombe, Secretary; Susan Bernard [1976] Director/Teacher; Carina Emma Bradshaw [1975] Director; James Briggs [1982] Director; Paul Matthews [1989] Director/Teacher; Susan Patricia McKim [1946] Director/Retired; Howard Frederick Reid [1954] Director/Teacher; Jessie Walker [1977] Director/Headteacher

Maranello Concessionaires Limited
Incorporated: 1 April 1960 *Employees:* 26
Net Worth: £5,409,000 *Total Assets:* £11,038,000
Registered Office: 2 Penman Way, Grove Park, Leicester, LE19 1ST
Activities: Sale of new cars and light motor vehicles
Parent: Maranello Holdings Limited
Officers: Adam Collinson, Secretary; Adam Collinson [1972] Finance Director; Darren Edwards [1968] Managing Director; Jeremy Richard Mallett [1952] Director; Gerard Edward Nieuwenhuys [1960] Director; Laurence Edward William Vaughan [1963] Managing Director

Marcol Limited
Incorporated: 9 December 1980 *Employees:* 20
Net Worth: £2,344,466 *Total Assets:* £14,506,218
Registered Office: Wolds Garage, Melton Road, Burton on the Wolds, Loughborough, Leics, LE12 5AG
Activities: Renting and leasing of trucks and other heavy vehicles
Officers: Simon Robert Bannister [1974] Sales Director; Keith Alan Bellwood [1962] Director/Engineering Consultant; Martin Stuart Betts [1961] Director; Anthony John O'Dowd [1954] Director/Contracts Manager; Nathan Rowell [1969] Director/Operations Manager; Mark Ward [1961] Director/Motor Trade

Marden Limited
Incorporated: 12 December 1995 *Employees:* 8
Net Worth: £12,785,446 *Total Assets:* £17,711,796
Registered Office: Chipping Court, Alveston Hill, Stratford upon Avon, Warwicks, CV37 7RR
Activities: Buying and selling of own real estate
Parent: Beaufield Investments Limited
Officers: Jane Moore, Secretary; Jane Moore [1942] Director/Housewife; Jolyon Moore [1971] Director/Investment Manager; Charles William Moyle [1965] Director; William Dennis Moyle [1938] Director/Solicitor; Timothy John Prosser [1965] Director

Mark's Electrical Limited
Incorporated: 18 June 2002 *Employees:* 93
Net Worth: £3,626,763 *Total Assets:* £12,862,496
Registered Office: 4 Boston Road, Leicester, LE4 1AQ
Activities: Retail sale of electrical household appliances in specialised stores
Major Shareholder: Mark Adrian Smithson
Officers: Mark Adrian Smithson [1965] Director/Retailer

Markem-Imaje Industries Limited
Incorporated: 21 August 1985 *Employees:* 87
Net Worth: £30,993,372 *Total Assets:* £51,494,600
Registered Office: Alexander Fleming Building, Nottingham Science Park, University Boulevard, Nottingham, NG7 2QN
Activities: Repair of other equipment
Officers: Anne-Sophie Alric [1975] Director/Financial Controller [French]; Timothy Arthur James Riley [1961] Director; Simon Wakeford [1971] Director/Management Accountant

The Market Bosworth School
Incorporated: 12 April 2012 *Employees:* 109
Net Worth: £7,816,000 *Total Assets:* £9,128,000
Registered Office: Market Bosworth High School, Station Road, Market Bosworth, Nuneaton, Warwicks, CV13 0JT
Activities: General secondary education
Officers: Bianca Leigh Farrell, Secretary; Rachel Kate de Fraja [1962] Director; Mark Hazell [1968] Director/Premises Manager; Eugenie Anne Herd [1944] Director/Retired; Madeleine Elizabeth Kennedy [1965] Director/Governor; Charlotte Anne Ward Lewis [1971] Director/Head of School Effectiveness; Steven John Malcherczyk [1952] Director/Substance Misuse Treatment Specialist; NEER Modha [1987] Director; Natalie Joan Moreland [1990] Director/Teacher; Jeanette Perry [1950] Director/University Administrator; Elizabeth Waterlow [1954] Director/Retired; Fiona Wilson [1969] Director/Teacher; Stuart Cain Wilson [1974] Director/Headteacher; Denis Winterbottom [1956] Director/Local Authority Town Planner

M.Markovitz Limited
Incorporated: 6 May 1959 *Employees:* 180
Net Worth: £6,424,390 *Total Assets:* £15,829,443
Registered Office: Town End Yard, Richard Lane, Tideswell, Buxton, Derbys, SK17 8PZ
Activities: Agents involved in the sale of timber and building materials
Officers: Robert William Hopkins, Secretary; Audrey Hopkins [1934] Director/Manager; David John Brian Hopkins [1966] Director; Robert William Hopkins [1972] Director

Marlborough Property (Watermead) Limited
Incorporated: 16 October 2012
Net Worth: £1,244,560 *Total Assets:* £9,333,959
Registered Office: Two Marlborough Court, Watermead Business Park, Syston, Leicester, LE7 1AD
Activities: Other letting and operating of own or leased real estate
Parent: Marlborough Property Co Limited
Officers: William Lester Adderley [1972] Director; Darren Lee Wright [1977] Director/Chartered Accountant

Marlborough Property Co Limited
Incorporated: 4 April 2012
Net Worth: £28,385,242 *Total Assets:* £258,818,496
Registered Office: Two Marlborough Court, Watermead Business Park, Syston, Leics, LE7 1AD
Activities: Management of real estate on a fee or contract basis
Parent: WA Capital Limited
Officers: William Lester Adderley [1972] Director; Darren Lee Wright [1977] Director/Chartered Accountant

Marmon Group Limited (The)
Incorporated: 30 June 1978 *Employees:* 414
Net Worth: £33,779,000 *Total Assets:* £181,074,000
Registered Office: 2-20 Booth Drive, Park Farm Industrial Estate, Wellingborough, Northants, NN8 6GR
Activities: Other service activities n.e.c.
Parent: Berkshire Hathaway Inc
Officers: Gary Vernon Phillips, Secretary; Daniel Ignatius Hanrahan [1974] Director/Lawyer [American]; Gary Vernon Phillips [1967] Director; Wesley Andrew Sothen [1979] Director/VP of Finance [American]

Maro Developments Limited
Incorporated: 13 June 2002 *Employees:* 4
Net Worth Deficit: £23,795,224 *Total Assets:* £36,362,832
Registered Office: Metropolitan House, Station Road, Cheadle Hulme, Cheadle, Cheshire, SK8 7AZ
Activities: Buying and selling of own real estate
Major Shareholder: John Hargreaves
Officers: Christopher O'Brien, Secretary; John Nicholas Mills [1955] Director; Christopher O'Brien [1963] Director/Accountant

P R Marriott Drilling Limited
Incorporated: 18 March 1991 *Employees:* 56
Net Worth: £14,150,394 *Total Assets:* £36,986,408
Registered Office: Spring Water House, Old Pit Lane, Danesmoor, Chesterfield, Derbys, S45 9BQ
Activities: Test drilling and boring
Shareholder: Jonathan William Hobday
Officers: David Ivor Jones, Secretary; Andrew John Beswick [1941] Director/Chartered Engineer; Jonathan William Hobday [1972] Director

Marshall Amplification PLC
Incorporated: 19 May 1964 *Employees:* 426
Net Worth: £24,074,732 *Total Assets:* £30,101,176
Registered Office: Denbigh Road, Denbigh Industrial Estate, Bletchley, Milton Keynes, Bucks, MK1 1DQ
Activities: Manufacture of other electrical equipment
Officers: Andrew Robert Charles, Secretary; Andrew Robert Charles [1966] Director; Jonathan Martin Ellery [1957] Managing Director; Barry Moon [1955] Director

Marshall Street Regeneration Limited
Incorporated: 8 August 2005
Net Worth Deficit: £3,284,713 *Total Assets:* £19,401,520
Registered Office: 15 Newland, Lincoln, LN1 1XG
Activities: Development of building projects
Parent: The Vinyl Factory Limited
Officers: Mark Wadhwa, Secretary/Director; Tim Joicey Robinson [1964] Director

Marshalls Yard Limited
Incorporated: 23 June 2003
Net Worth: £16,901,456 *Total Assets:* £42,795,640
Registered Office: Dransfield House, 2 Fox Valley Way, Fox Valley, Sheffield, S36 2AB
Activities: Other letting and operating of own or leased real estate
Shareholders: Dransfield Properties Ltd; Prospect Estates Ltd
Officers: Mark Dransfield [1962] Director; John Ellison Lund [1954] Director; Terri Louise Lund [1957] Director; James Edward Shepherd [1983] Estates Director

H.W. Martin (Farms) LLP
Incorporated: 26 October 2011 *Employees:* 2
Net Worth: £15,562,388 *Total Assets:* £15,631,992
Registered Office: Fordbridge Lane, Blackwell, Alfreton, Derbys, DE55 5JY
Officers: Harold William Martin [1935] Member; Iris Martin [1939] Member

H.W. Martin (Plant) Limited
Incorporated: 28 July 1980 *Employees:* 43
Net Worth: £2,259,891 *Total Assets:* £16,438,168
Registered Office: Fordbridge Lane, Blackwell, Alfreton, Derbys, DE55 5JY
Activities: Repair and maintenance of other transport equipment n.e.c.
Parent: H W Martin Holdings Limited
Officers: Mark James Faulconbridge [1964] Director/General Manager; Nigel Charles Faulconbridge [1966] Financial Director; Harold William Martin [1935] Managing Director; Kevin Martin [1960] Director/Manager

H.W. Martin (Traffic Management) Limited
Incorporated: 15 February 1988 *Employees:* 343
Net Worth: £10,210,225 *Total Assets:* £17,358,936
Registered Office: Fordbridge Lane, Blackwell, Alfreton, Derbys, DE55 5JY
Activities: Other specialised construction activities n.e.c.
Parent: H W Martin Holdings Limited
Officers: Grahame Roger Beswick [1956] Director/General Manager; Nigel Charles Faulconbridge [1966] Director; Harold William Martin [1935] Managing Director; Kevin Martin [1960] Director/Manager

Brett Martin Daylight Systems Limited
Incorporated: 10 September 1975 *Employees:* 159
Net Worth: £14,372,742 *Total Assets:* £19,717,976
Registered Office: Sandford Close, Aldermans Green Industrial Estate, Coventry, Warwicks, CV2 2QU
Activities: Manufacture of plastic plates, sheets, tubes and profiles
Parent: Brett Martin Holdings Ltd
Officers: Stephen Lewis, Secretary; Brian James Martin [1961] Director; William Laurence Martin [1957] Director

HW Martin Holdings Limited
Incorporated: 23 June 1994 *Employees:* 823
Net Worth: £71,799,256 *Total Assets:* £95,822,304
Registered Office: Fordbridge Lane, Blackwell, Alfreton, Derbys, DE55 5JY
Activities: Activities of head offices
Major Shareholder: Harold William Martin
Officers: Nigel Charles Faulconbridge [1966] Director/Company Secretary; Harold William Martin [1935] Director/Fencing Contractor; Kevin Martin [1960] Director/Manager

Usha Martin International Limited
Incorporated: 12 May 1994 *Employees:* 188
Net Worth: £34,688,000 *Total Assets:* £50,407,000
Registered Office: Sandy Lane, Worksop, Notts, S80 3ES
Activities: Other manufacturing n.e.c.
Parent: Usha Martin Limited
Officers: Simon Hood, Secretary; Pravin Kumar Jain [1954] Director [Indian]; Prashant Jhawar [1963] Director/Industrialist; Rajeev Jhawar [1964] Director/Industrialist [Indian]; Shyam Jodhawat [1948] Director/Co Executive

Usha Martin UK Limited
Incorporated: 8 July 1998 *Employees:* 152
Net Worth: £27,215,000 *Total Assets:* £38,863,000
Registered Office: Sandy Lane, Worksop, Notts, S80 3ES
Activities: Other manufacturing n.e.c.
Parent: Usha Martin International Limited
Officers: Simon Hood, Secretary; Pravin Kumar Jain [1954] Director [Indian]; Rajeev Jhawar [1964] Director/Businessman [Indian]; Shyam Jodhawat [1948] Director/Company Executive

H W Martin Waste Limited
Incorporated: 17 September 1999 *Employees:* 167
Net Worth: £11,782,994 *Total Assets:* £15,219,965
Registered Office: Fordbridge Lane, Blackwell, Alfreton, Derbys, DE55 5JY
Activities: Treatment and disposal of non-hazardous waste
Parent: H W Martin Holdings Limited
Officers: Mark James Faulconbridge [1964] Director/General Manager; Nigel Charles Faulconbridge [1966] Director; Harold William Martin [1935] Director; Kevin Martin [1960] Director/Manager

John Martin-Hoyes (Holdings) Limited
Incorporated: 14 November 2002 *Employees:* 82
Net Worth: £8,364,778 *Total Assets:* £15,038,335
Registered Office: Martin House, Exchange Road, Doddington Road, Lincoln, LN6 3JZ
Activities: Development of building projects
Major Shareholder: John Martin-Hoyes
Officers: Tracy Bourne, Secretary; Tracy Bourne [1981] Director/Accounts Supervisor; John Martin-Hoyes [1944] Director

Marubeni Agro Machinery Holding Limited
Incorporated: 5 April 2012 *Employees:* 161
Net Worth: £8,059,000 *Total Assets:* £23,948,000
Registered Office: 25-35 Sadler Road, Lincoln, LN6 3XJ
Activities: Support activities for crop production
Parent: Marubeni Corporation
Officers: Shuichi Kamizono [1965] Director [Japanese]; Susumu Wakamori [1967] Director [Japanese]; Noboru Yamamoto [1970] Director/Chairman [Japanese]

Marubeni Agrochemical Limited
Incorporated: 2 December 2010
Net Worth: £257,162,544 *Total Assets:* £257,348,176
Registered Office: Rutherford House, Nottingham Science and Technology Park, University Boulevard, Nottingham, NG7 2PZ
Activities: Activities of agricultural holding companies
Parent: Marubeni Corporation
Officers: Michael Hammill, Secretary; Yuha Kodaira [1968] Director [Japanese]

Maryland Securities Limited
Incorporated: 23 April 1986 *Employees:* 12
Net Worth: £18,352,604 *Total Assets:* £39,737,192
Registered Office: Ashfield House, Ashfield Road, Cheadle, Cheshire, SK8 1BB
Activities: Other letting and operating of own or leased real estate
Officers: Paul Nigel Manifold, Secretary; David Jebreel [1951] Director/Property Dealer; Ebrahim Jebreel [1954] Director; Jacob Jebreel [1962] Director

Maurice Mason Limited
Incorporated: 9 October 1947 *Employees:* 19
Net Worth: £5,929,332 *Total Assets:* £11,815,013
Registered Office: Hall Farm, Fincham, Kings Lynn, Norfolk, PE33 9DQ
Activities: Growing of cereals (except rice), leguminous crops and oil seeds
Major Shareholder: Hugh Mason
Officers: Hugh Mason [1964] Director/Farmer

Geoffrey Mason Limited
Incorporated: 20 October 1954 *Employees:* 16
Net Worth: £6,146,493 *Total Assets:* £11,099,426
Registered Office: Great Palgrave Farm, Sporle, King's Lynn, Norfolk, PE32 2EL
Activities: Growing of cereals (except rice), leguminous crops and oil seeds
Shareholders: Jeremy Geoffrey George Mason; Gillian Mason
Officers: Jeremy Geoffrey George Mason, Secretary; Gillian Mason [1963] Director/Housewife; Jeremy Geoffrey George Mason [1960] Director/Farmer

Mass Consultants Limited
Incorporated: 11 March 1983 *Employees:* 301
Net Worth: £24,341,000 *Total Assets:* £31,821,000
Registered Office: Enterprise House, Great North Road, Little Paxton, St Neots, Cambs, PE19 6BN
Activities: Information technology consultancy activities
Parent: Mass Limited
Officers: Sarita Bilkhu, Secretary; Christopher Andrew Stanley [1964] Director; Andrew Stephen Thomis [1964] Director; Simon Robert Walther [1967] Director

Massarella Catering Group Limited
Incorporated: 25 May 1978 *Employees:* 1,307
Net Worth: £5,550,473 *Total Assets:* £13,628,210
Registered Office: Thurcroft Hall, Brookhouse, Laughton, Sheffield, S25 1XZ
Activities: Activities of head offices
Officers: Jeremy Peter Massarella, Secretary; Mark Stephen Massarella [1951] Director; Michael John Massarella [1948] Director; Stephen Richard Massarella [1955] Director

Massmould Limited
Incorporated: 11 November 1981 *Employees:* 183
Net Worth: £26,331,000 *Total Assets:* £63,340,000
Registered Office: Sapphire House, Crown Way, Rushden, Northants, NN10 6FB
Activities: Manufacture of plastic packing goods
Officers: Nicholas David Martin Giles, Secretary; Franciscus Lodewijk Paulus Doorenbosch [1964] Director [Dutch]; Matthew Harrison [1972] Director; Simon John Kesterton [1973] Director; Paul Alan Lister [1965] Director; Louis Meyerowitz [1955] Director; Petrus Rudolf Maria Vervaat [1965] Director [Dutch]; Neil John Rolt Webb [1966] Managing Director

Mastercard Prepaid Management Services Limited
Incorporated: 20 April 2005 *Employees:* 166
Previous: Access Prepaid Worldwide Ltd.
Net Worth: £70,805,000 *Total Assets:* £111,878,000
Registered Office: Access House, Cygnet Road, Cygnet Park, Hampton, Peterborough, PE7 8FJ
Activities: Other business support service activities n.e.c.
Parent: Mastercard Incorporated
Officers: Daniel Kim, Secretary; Fabrizio Burlando [1974] Director [Italian]; Joseph Rickard Halprin [1964] Director/Group Head, Lead Global Core Products Counsel [American]; Andrea Scerch [1964] Director [Italian]; Robert Scott Williams [1958] Director [American]

Mathematical Market Research Limited
Incorporated: 11 October 1988 *Employees:* 352
Net Worth: £12,607,834 *Total Assets:* £26,861,352
Registered Office: Wallingford House, 46 High Street, Wallingford, Oxon, OX10 0DB
Activities: Market research and public opinion polling
Major Shareholder: David Marshall Hall Thomson
Officers: Christopher Rogers, Secretary; Teresa Carol Church [1959] Director; Christopher Rogers [1966] Director; Seshagiri Sondur [1982] Finance Director; Prof David Marshall Hall Thomson [1954] Director

Matrix Polymers Limited
Incorporated: 5 July 1991 *Employees:* 125
Net Worth: £3,073,000 *Total Assets:* £22,237,000
Registered Office: The Priory, Orchard Hill, Little Billing, Northampton, NN3 9AG
Activities: Manufacture of other plastic products
Major Shareholder: Martin Langley Coles
Officers: Simon Joseph Wallington, Secretary; Martin Langley Coles [1964] Director; Mark Morgan [1971] Operations Director; Aldo Quaratino [1970] Operations & Technical Director [Italian]; Simon Joseph Wallington [1975] Finance Director

Matrix SCM Limited
Incorporated: 7 March 1988 *Employees:* 52
Net Worth: £2,865,740 *Total Assets:* £60,740,224
Registered Office: 2nd Floor, Partis House, Knowlhill, Milton Keynes, Bucks, MK5 8HJ
Activities: Other business support service activities n.e.c.
Shareholders: FTR Holdings Limited; FTR Holdings Limited
Officers: Barry Andrew Moseley [1965] Director; Mark Anthony Pepper [1972] Director

Matsuura Machinery Limited
Incorporated: 15 March 1991 *Employees:* 68
Net Worth: £11,315,422 *Total Assets:* £23,808,780
Registered Office: Gee Road, Whitwick Business Park, Coalville, Leics, LE67 4NH
Activities: Wholesale of machine tools
Parent: Matsuura Europe GmbH
Officers: David Alan Chapman, Secretary; David Alan Chapman [1966] Finance Director; Roger Paul Howkins [1959] Director/Sales

Matthews Environmental Solutions Limited
Incorporated: 27 October 2011 *Employees:* 22
Previous: Todaysure Matthews Limited
Net Worth: £1,759,651 *Total Assets:* £12,873,462
Registered Office: Unit 3 Dunkirk Lane, Hyde, Cheshire, SK14 4NL
Activities: Manufacture of other special-purpose machinery n.e.c.
Parent: Matthews Corporation Holding Company (UK) Limited
Officers: Joseph Carlo Bartolacci [1960] Director [American]; Paul Rahill [1956] Director [American]; Pier Luigi Romanelli [1964] Director [Italian]

Mattioli Woods PLC
Incorporated: 21 December 1995 *Employees:* 618
Net Worth: £78,950,000 *Total Assets:* £105,426,000
Registered Office: 1 New Walk Place, Leicester, LE1 6RU
Activities: Other business support service activities n.e.c.
Officers: Nathan James McLean Imlach, Secretary/Chartered Accountant; Carol Avis Duncumb [1962] Director; Anne Margaret Gunther [1955] Director; Nathan James McLean Imlach [1969] Director; Joanne Carolyn Lake [1963] Director; Ian Thomas Mattioli [1962] Director; Murray Beveridge Smith [1969] Director

Maxim Logistics Group Limited
Incorporated: 3 January 2006 *Employees:* 103
Net Worth: £6,485,633 *Total Assets:* £12,196,617
Registered Office: 2 Darwin Road, Willowbrook East Industrial Estate, Corby, Northants, NN17 5XZ
Activities: Freight transport by road
Major Shareholder: Andrew Simpson Lawrence
Officers: Andrew Simpson Lawrence [1970] Director

Maximus HHS Holdings Limited
Incorporated: 8 May 2008
Net Worth: £49,671,432 *Total Assets:* £54,803,996
Registered Office: 18c Meridian East, Meridian Business Park, Leicester, LE19 1WZ
Activities: Activities of head offices
Parent: Maximus Companies Limited
Officers: Michael Batty [1972] Finance Director; Dr Paul Anthony Williams [1963] Director

Maxxia (UK) Limited
Incorporated: 24 January 2013
Net Worth: £40,668,120 *Total Assets:* £54,919,792
Registered Office: Corporate House, Jenna Way, Interchange Park, Newport Pagnell, Bucks, MK16 9QB
Activities: Activities of financial services holding companies
Parent: McMillan Shakespeare Limited
Officers: Lisa Joanne Edwards, Secretary; Mark Sutherland Blackburn [1957] Director [Australian]; Geoffrey Robert Kruyt [1968] Director/Business Executive [Australian]; Michael Neil Salisbury [1965] Director [Australian]; Gareth Shaw [1971] Director/Chartered Accountant

Maxxia Finance Limited
Incorporated: 24 January 2013 *Employees:* 4
Net Worth: £26,971,140 *Total Assets:* £89,681,024
Registered Office: Corporate House, Jenna Way, Interchange Park, Newport Pagnell, Bucks, MK16 9QB
Activities: Financial leasing
Parent: McMillan Shakespeare Limited
Officers: Lisa Joanne Edwards, Secretary; Mark Sutherland Blackburn [1957] Director [Australian]; Geoffrey Robert Kruyt [1968] Director/Business Executive [Australian]; Michael Neil Salisbury [1965] Director [Australian]; Gareth Shaw [1971] Director/Chartered Accountant

Mayflower Specialist School Academy Trust
Incorporated: 27 May 2015 *Employees:* 112
Net Worth: £10,596,618 *Total Assets:* £13,236,913
Registered Office: Warren Wood - A Specialist Academy, Middlefield Lane, Gainsborough, Lincs, DN21 1PU
Activities: Primary education
Officers: Anne Collishaw, Secretary; Anne Collishaw [1960] Director/Business Manager; Claire Cumberlidge [1965] Director/Head of School; Jonathan Peter Downes [1965] Director/Operations Manager; Dee Lloyd Freeman [1954] Director/Priest; Penny Holmes [1971] Director/Working Mother and Scientist; Peter Stephen Krick [1960] Director/Solicitor; Michele Lamb [1959] Director/Head of School; Gary Nixon [1965] Director/Executive Principal; Michael John Page [1951] Director/Retired

Mayfourth Holdings Limited
Incorporated: 28 May 2016 *Employees:* 96
Net Worth: £303,511 *Total Assets:* £14,243,472
Registered Office: Electus House, 900 Pavilion Drive, Northampton, NN4 7RG
Activities: Trade of electricity
Major Shareholder: Gary Richard Styles
Officers: Pankaj Jethwa, Secretary; David Andrew Coombs [1962] Director; Peter Marirosans [1977] Director; Ron Pearson [1963] Director; Thomas Doane Perry [1975] Director [American]; Gary Richard Styles [1974] Director

Maynard & Harris Group Limited
Incorporated: 31 August 2007 *Employees:* 5
Net Worth: £36,785,000 *Total Assets:* £36,805,000
Registered Office: Sapphire House, Crown Way, Rushden, Northants, NN10 6FB
Activities: Activities of production holding companies
Parent: RPC Packaging Holdings Ltd
Officers: Nicholas David Martin Giles, Secretary; Simon Chidgey [1960] Director; David Duffield [1964] Director; Simon John Kesterton [1973] Finance Director; Doug Mark Muttitt [1976] Finance Director; Petrus Rudolf Maria Vervaat [1965] Director/Chief Executive [Dutch]

Maynard & Harris Plastics
Incorporated: 2 January 1975 *Employees:* 971
Net Worth: £92,611,000 *Total Assets:* £166,794,000
Registered Office: Sapphire House, Crown Way, Rushden, Northants, NN10 6FB
Activities: Manufacture of plastic packing goods
Parent: Maynard & Harris Plastics (UK) Ltd
Officers: Nicholas David Martin Giles, Secretary; Simon Chidgey [1960] Director; David Duffield [1964] Managing Director; Simon John Kesterton [1973] Finance Director; Doug Mark Muttitt [1976] Director; Petrus Rudolf Maria Vervaat [1965] Director/Chief Executive [Dutch]

Maynard & Harris Plastics (UK) Limited
Incorporated: 18 February 2003 *Employees:* 6
Net Worth Deficit: £63,297,000 *Total Assets:* £62,098,000
Registered Office: Sapphire House, Crown Way, Rushden, Northants, NN10 6FB
Activities: Activities of production holding companies
Parent: Maynard & Harris Group Ltd
Officers: Nicholas David Martin Giles, Secretary; Simon Chidgey [1960] Director; David Duffield [1964] Director; Simon John Kesterton [1973] Finance Director; Doug Mark Muttitt [1976] Director; Petrus Rudolf Maria Vervaat [1965] Director/Chief Executive [Dutch]

Mays Properties Limited
Incorporated: 13 January 2004 *Employees:* 5
Net Worth: £45,757,600 *Total Assets:* £53,178,188
Registered Office: The Tower, Unit A5 Fairacres Retail Park, Marcham Road, Abingdon, Oxon, OX14 1TP
Activities: Other letting and operating of own or leased real estate
Officers: Mark Bayliss, Secretary; David John May [1963] Director/Manager; John Robert May [1938] Director/Manager; Richard Edward May [1965] Director/Manager

MBS Lending Ltd
Incorporated: 23 November 2006
Net Worth: £856,840 *Total Assets:* £41,396,184
Registered Office: Mutual House, Leicester Road, Melton Mowbray, Leics, LE13 0DB
Activities: Activities of mortgage finance companies
Parent: Melton Mowbray Building Society
Officers: Karen Nicola Mabbott, Secretary; John Philip Mulvey [1975] Finance Director; Martin John Reason [1960] Director/Chief Executive

McCann Health Medical Communications Limited
Incorporated: 17 May 1990 *Employees:* 339
Previous: McCann Complete Medical Limited
Net Worth: £24,396,000 *Total Assets:* £47,436,000
Registered Office: CMC House, 19 King Edward Street, Macclesfield, Cheshire, SK10 1AQ
Activities: Activities of head offices
Parent: McCann-Erickson UK Group Limited
Officers: Louise Bean, Secretary; Charles Edward George Buckwell [1964] Director; Julie Ann James [1975] Director/Accountant; Phillip Sutcliffe [1968] Director/Accountant

McCann Manchester Limited
Incorporated: 28 February 1986 *Employees:* 347
Net Worth: £26,577,000 *Total Assets:* £55,203,000
Registered Office: Bonis Hall, Prestbury, Macclesfield, Cheshire, SK10 4EF
Activities: Advertising agencies
Parent: McCann-Erickson Network Limited
Officers: Louise Bean, Secretary; Jane Ann Cottrill [1977] Director/Accountant; Martin James Jackson [1968] Director/Chartered Accountant; Susan Ann Little [1955] Director/Advertising Executive; Helen Denise Sullivan [1979] Director/Chartered Accountant

McCann-Erickson Network Limited
Incorporated: 14 January 1986
Net Worth: £58,263,000 *Total Assets:* £58,283,000
Registered Office: Bonis Hall, Prestbury, Macclesfield, Cheshire, SK10 4EF
Activities: Advertising agencies
Parent: McCann-Erickson UK Group Limited
Officers: Louise Bean, Secretary; Jane Ann Cottrill [1977] Director/Accountant; Martin James Jackson [1968] Director/Chartered Accountant; Helen Denise Sullivan [1979] Director/Chartered Accountant

MCE Insurance Limited
Incorporated: 7 November 1975 *Employees:* 307
Net Worth: £16,263,594 *Total Assets:* £54,674,540
Registered Office: Sapphire House, Crown Way, Rushden, Northants, NN10 6FB
Activities: Non-life insurance
Shareholders: Michael Charles Edwards; Julian Thomas Edwards
Officers: Christopher Deacon, Secretary; Matthew Garth Duck [1978] Director; Julian Thomas Edwards [1976] Director/Insurance Broker; Michael Charles Edwards [1949] Director/Insurance Broker; Simon Peter French [1974] Director

McGowan Investments Limited
Incorporated: 25 April 1995 *Employees:* 8
Net Worth: £7,365,800 *Total Assets:* £20,725,456
Registered Office: Catherine House, Harborough Road, Brixworth, Northants, NN6 9BX
Activities: Other letting and operating of own or leased real estate
Shareholder: Deborah Lousie Hill
Officers: Malcolm Robert Longley, Secretary; Malcolm Robert Longley [1946] Director/Engineer; Valerie Mary Longley [1947] Director/Teacher; George Muir [1968] Director/Engineer; Karen Mary Muir [1969] Director/Teacher

MCL Group of Companies Limited
Incorporated: 8 February 2016
Previous: MCL Holdco C Limited
Net Worth: £9,754,810 *Total Assets:* £9,754,810
Registered Office: 50 Woodgate, Leicester, LE3 5GF
Activities: Other service activities n.e.c.
Major Shareholder: Nitin Chouhan
Officers: Nitin Chouhan [1963] Director; Terry Grubb [1953] Director

McLean Restaurants Limited
Incorporated: 29 November 2001 *Employees:* 686
Net Worth: £2,551,920 *Total Assets:* £13,547,698
Registered Office: 20 Queens Road, Nuneaton, Warwicks, CV11 5JW
Activities: Unlicenced restaurants and cafes
Major Shareholder: Sarah McLean
Officers: Nigel McLean, Secretary; Sarah Jane McLean [1961] Director

McManus Pub Co. Limited
Incorporated: 23 April 2001 *Employees:* 46
Net Worth: £2,963,010 *Total Assets:* £10,064,473
Registered Office: Barratts Club, Kingsthorpe Road, Northampton, NN2 6HT
Activities: Public houses and bars
Shareholders: Gary Michael McManus; Paul Martin McManus
Officers: Christopher Neil Wright, Secretary; Gary Michael McManus [1961] Director; Paul Martin McManus [1969] Director; Ian Morris [1961] Director/Solicitor; Christopher Neil Wright [1969] Director

MCS Build Limited
Incorporated: 1 August 2003 *Employees:* 44
Net Worth: £1,706,382 *Total Assets:* £19,795,916
Registered Office: Station Works, Station Road, Claverdon, Warwick, CV35 8PE
Activities: Construction of commercial buildings
Parent: MCS Group Limited
Officers: Susan Jane Edmonds, Secretary; Keir Simon Edmonds [1973] Director; Timothy Mark David Perkins [1974] Director; Alan Shadbolt [1980] Commercial Director

MCS Group Limited
Incorporated: 31 August 2004 *Employees:* 55
Net Worth: £4,763,212 *Total Assets:* £29,069,998
Registered Office: Station Works, Station Road, Claverdon, Warwick, CV35 8PE
Activities: Construction of commercial buildings
Shareholder: Keir Simon Edmonds
Officers: Keir Simon Edmonds, Secretary; Keir Simon Edmonds [1973] Director; Timothy Mark David Perkins [1974] Director; Alan Shadbolt [1980] Commercial Director

The MDS Estates Limited
Incorporated: 16 September 2014 *Employees:* 436
Net Worth: £143,684,000 *Total Assets:* £298,008,000
Registered Office: Buccleuch Property Estate Office, Weekley, Kettering, Northants, NN16 9UP
Activities: Activities of agricultural holding companies
Parent: MDS Trustees Limited
Officers: Michael James McGrath, Secretary; John Ronald Kerr Glen [1959] Director/Chief Executive; Bernard Higgins [1960] Director; Damian Torquil Francis Charles Montagu Douglas Scott [1969] Director; Elizabeth Marian Frances Montagu Douglas Scott [1954] Director; Richard Walter John Montagu Douglas Scott [1954] Director; Walter John Francis Montagu Douglas Scott [1984] Director; Lord William Henry John Montagu Douglas Scott [1957] Director; Pauline Mary Walsh [1967] Director [Irish]

The Mead Educational Trust
Incorporated: 10 June 2014 *Employees:* 650
Previous: The Mead Educational Trust Ltd.
Net Worth: £31,690,704 *Total Assets:* £41,237,152
Registered Office: The Mead Centre, 343 Gipsy Lane, Leicester, LE4 9DD
Activities: Primary education
Officers: Cathy Brown, Secretary; Gemma Bhagalia [1986] Director/Projects Manager; Rachael Clarke [1984] Director/Contract Manager; Colin Forknall [1945] Director/Retired; Anthony Joseph Glover [1950] Director/Consultant; Deepak Karia [1963] Director/IT Controller; Hetal Parmar [1979] Director/Head of Banking; Carolyn Patricia Robson [1953] Director/Chief Executive; Margaret Elaine Taylor [1949] Director/National Lead for Modern Languages

Meadowhead School Academy Trust
Incorporated: 2 February 2012 *Employees:* 198
Net Worth: £34,887,392 *Total Assets:* £37,900,256
Registered Office: Meadowhead School, Dyche Lane, Sheffield, S8 8BR
Activities: General secondary education
Officers: Janet Elizabeth Ledger, Secretary; David Kevin Blagden [1967] Director/Chartered Quantify Surveyor; Kenneth Arthur Cook [1940] Director/Retired; Kam Grewal-Joy [1968] Director/Headteacher; Anja Kelly [1977] Director/Teacher [German]; Richard David Law [1962] Commercial Director; Elaine Middleton [1963] Director/Parent Governor; Maureen Alicia Neill [1932] Director; Lisa Margaret Read [1975] Director/Parent Governor; Elizabeth Smith [1977] Director/School Business Manager; Lynda Taylor [1944] Director; Peter Wilson [1958] Director/Retired University Lecturer

Measom (Dryline) Limited
Incorporated: 13 March 1969 *Employees:* 65
Net Worth: £5,417,219 *Total Assets:* £10,690,601
Registered Office: 2 Merus Court, Meridian Business Park, Leicester, LE19 1RJ
Activities: Other specialised construction activities n.e.c.
Shareholders: Andrew Richard Measom; Kelbenton Limited
Officers: Vaughan Cooper, Secretary; Andrew Richard Measom [1962] Director; Judith Ann Measom [1937] Director

Meatsnacks Group Ltd.
Incorporated: 10 May 2007 *Employees:* 125
Previous: The Meat Snacks Group Limited
Net Worth: £1,259,470 *Total Assets:* £9,591,367
Registered Office: 2 Tilers Road, Kiln Farm, Milton Keynes, Bucks, MK11 3LH
Activities: Processing and preserving of meat
Officers: Alan Charles Craig [1962] Director; Richard Alun Davies [1971] Director; Dennis Woodgate Low [1936] Director/Food Production; Thomas Cameron Morrison [1960] Director; James Peter Newitt [1967] Director/Consultant; Matthew Townsend [1967] Director/General Manager

Medical Equipment Supplies and Management Ltd
Incorporated: 18 July 2007 *Employees:* 73
Net Worth: £7,515,000 *Total Assets:* £20,486,000
Registered Office: VWR International Limited, Hunter Boulevard, Magna Park, Lutterworth, Leics, LE17 4XN
Activities: Retail sale of medical and orthopaedic goods in specialised stores (not incl. hearing aids) n.e.c.
Officers: Karen Pulford, Secretary; Bernd Goell [1969] Director/VP Finance-Treasury [German]; David Parry [1968] Director; Karen Jane Pulford [1968] Director

Mediline Home Care Limited
Incorporated: 3 December 2002 *Employees:* 619
Previous: Mediline Nurses & Carers Limited
Net Worth: £2,009,240 *Total Assets:* £9,557,678
Registered Office: 3rd Floor, Butt Dyke House, 33 Park Row, Nottingham, NG1 6EE
Activities: Other human health activities
Parent: Peter Cook Limited
Officers: Sylvia Denise Cook, Secretary; Michael William Baines [1961] Managing Director; Peter Cyril Cook [1943] Director; Sylvia Denise Cook [1947] Director

Megaclose Limited
Incorporated: 20 January 1998 *Employees:* 19
Net Worth: £11,352,539 *Total Assets:* £33,593,644
Registered Office: 120 North Sherwood Street, Nottingham, NG1 4EF
Activities: Other letting and operating of own or leased real estate
Major Shareholder: Sharar Aharon Lipinski
Officers: Paul Thrower, Secretary; Shahar Aharon Lipinski [1970] Managing Director [Israeli]

Megaflo Limited
Incorporated: 22 December 1965
Net Worth: £358,404,992 *Total Assets:* £358,404,992
Registered Office: Brooks House, Coventry Road, Warwick, CV34 4LL
Activities: Activities of head offices
Officers: Karen Dawn Roberts, Secretary; Simon Charles Oliver [1968] Director; David Stuart Pinder [1963] Director/Boiler Manufacturer; Jan-Feie Zwiers [1972] Director/Group Finance Controller [Dutch]

Melbourne Holdings Limited
Incorporated: 16 July 1979 *Employees:* 125
Net Worth: £55,740,688 *Total Assets:* £73,193,600
Registered Office: Station Road, Heckington, Sleaford, Lincs, NG34 9NF
Activities: Development of building projects
Major Shareholder: John Priestley
Officers: Lucy Bryant [1980] Director; James Langstaff Priestley [1983] Director; John Langstaff Priestley [1946] Director; Lynne Priestley [1949] Director; Kathrine Jane Thomas [1964] Commercial Director

Melett Limited
Incorporated: 20 May 2002 *Employees:* 205
Net Worth: £19,176,000 *Total Assets:* £23,894,000
Registered Office: Unit N, Zenith Park, Whaley Road, Barnsley, S Yorks, S75 1HT
Activities: Manufacture of other parts and accessories for motor vehicles
Parent: Wabtec UK Holdings Limited
Officers: David Michael Seitz, Secretary; John Anthony Mastalerz [1966] Director/Senior VP Finance [American]; Jason David Moore [1971] Director; David Michael Seitz [1965] Director/VP and Senior Counsel [American]; James Edward Stones [1972] Director

Melham Group Limited
Incorporated: 24 May 1949 *Employees:* 9
Net Worth: £9,930,842 *Total Assets:* £11,778,193
Registered Office: Environment House, 6 Union Road, Nottingham, NG3 1FH
Activities: Activities of head offices
Major Shareholder: Nathu Ram Puri
Officers: Roy Stewart Mochor [1950] Director; Anil Puri [1960] Director [Indian]

Meller Design Solutions Limited
Incorporated: 28 March 2006 *Employees:* 36
Net Worth: £4,879,533 *Total Assets:* £11,733,302
Registered Office: Unit H, Bedford Business Centre, Mile Road, Bedford, MK42 9TW
Activities: Wholesale of perfume and cosmetics
Shareholders: David Robert Meller; Michael Joseph Meller
Officers: Jeremy Curtis, Secretary; John Christopher McGrath [1969] Director/Accountant

Meller Group Limited
Incorporated: 16 February 2006 *Employees:* 119
Net Worth: £10,469,384 *Total Assets:* £15,103,024
Registered Office: Unit H, Bedford Business Centre, Mile Road, Bedford, MK42 9TW
Activities: Activities of head offices
Shareholders: Michael Joseph Meller; David Robert Meller
Officers: Jeremy Curtis, Secretary; John Christopher McGrath [1969] Director/Accountant

Mellors Group Fantasy Island Holdings Limited
Incorporated: 4 February 2016 *Employees:* 135
Net Worth: £2,303,000 *Total Assets:* £26,783,000
Registered Office: 57 Front Street, Arnold, Nottingham, NG5 7EA
Activities: Other letting and operating of own or leased real estate
Shareholders: James Frederick Mellors; Edward James Mellors
Officers: Brian Rowland Cobb [1951] Director; Edward James Mellors [1979] Director/Showman; James Frederick Mellors [1977] Director/Showman; James Henry Mellors [1945] Director/Amusement Caterer

The Mellors Group Limited
Incorporated: 10 July 2007 *Employees:* 91
Net Worth: £11,496,000 *Total Assets:* £18,949,000
Registered Office: 57 Front Street, Arnold, Nottingham, NG5 7EA
Activities: Activities of head offices
Officers: Susan Mellors, Secretary; Brian Rowland Cobb [1951] Director; Edward James Mellors [1979] Director/Showman; James Frederick Mellors [1977] Director/Showman; James Henry Mellors [1945] Director/Amusement Caterer; Susan Mellors [1947] Director/Amusement Caterer

Memoria Limited
Incorporated: 27 January 2009 *Employees:* 7
Net Worth: £548,083 *Total Assets:* £11,905,482
Registered Office: The Pool House, Bicester Road, Stratton Audley, Bicester, Oxon, OX27 9BS
Activities: Development of building projects
Shareholders: Howard Osman Paul Hodgson; Michael Anthony Hackney
Officers: Michael Anthony Hackney, Secretary; Michael Anthony Hackney [1950] Director; Howard Osmond Paul Hodgson [1950] Director; Jamieson Charles Alexandre Howard Hodgson [1983] Director/Consultant

Mercedes AMG High Performance Powertrains Limited
Incorporated: 11 October 1983 *Employees:* 637
Net Worth: £77,960,000 *Total Assets:* £183,683,008
Registered Office: Mercedes-Benz Technology Centre, Morgan Drive, Brixworth, Northants, NN6 9GZ
Activities: Other research and experimental development on natural sciences and engineering
Parent: Daimler UK Limited
Officers: Dr Alexander Riess, Secretary; Andy Cowell [1969] Managing Director; Dr Torsten Eder [1971] Director [German]; Ola Kaellenius [1969] Director [Swedish]; Andreas Nikolaus Lauda [1949] Director/Entrepreneur [Austrian]

Mercedes-Benz Brooklands Limited
Incorporated: 11 May 2004
Net Worth Deficit: £72,045 *Total Assets:* £14,555,000
Registered Office: Delaware Drive, Tongwell, Milton Keynes, Bucks, MK15 8BA
Activities: Buying and selling of own real estate
Parent: Mercedes-Benz Cars UK Limited
Officers: Jonathan Philip Reuben Lipman, Secretary; Marcus Werner Breitschwerdt [1961] Director [German]; Harald Henn [1964] Director/Economist [German]; Gary Mark Savage [1961] Director

Mercedes-Benz Cars UK Limited
Incorporated: 1 December 1989 *Employees:* 507
Previous: Mercedes-Benz UK Limited
Net Worth: £235,114,000 *Total Assets:* £1,414,178,048
Registered Office: Mercedes-Benz UK Limited, Delaware Drive, Tongwell, Milton Keynes, Bucks, MK15 8BA
Activities: Sale of new cars and light motor vehicles
Parent: Daimler UK Limited
Officers: Jonathan Philip Reuben Lipman, Secretary; Marcus Werner Breitschwerdt [1961] Director/President & CEO [German]; Harald Henn [1964] Director/Economist [German]; Gary Mark Savage [1961] CEO/Managing Director

Mercedes-Benz Financial Services UK Limited
Incorporated: 21 February 1990 *Employees:* 506
Net Worth: £473,240,992 *Total Assets:* £7,566,894,080
Registered Office: Delaware Drive, Tongwell, Milton Keynes, Bucks, MK15 8BA
Activities: Financial intermediation not elsewhere classified
Parent: Daimler UK Limited
Officers: Jonathan Lipman, Secretary; Brian Evon [1963] Finance Director [Canadian]; Ilka Fuerstenberger [1969] Managing Director Financial Services Industry [German]; Richard Andrew Howard [1965] Director/President & CEO; Christian Peters [1967] Managing Director [German]; Franz-Josef Reiner [1967] Director [American]; Oliver Christian Winkler [1970] Finance Director [Austrian]

Mercedes-Benz Grand Prix Ltd
Incorporated: 9 January 1964 *Employees:* 912
Net Worth: £30,183,000 *Total Assets:* £203,688,000
Registered Office: Operations Centre, Brackley, Northants, NN13 7BD
Activities: Other sports activities
Shareholders: Toto Wolff; Daimler UK Limited
Officers: Oliver James Rumsey, Secretary; Rene Berger [1972] Director/Business Executive [Austrian]; Sten Ola Kallenius [1969] Director/Member of The Divisional Board Mercedes-Benz Cars [Swedish]; Andreas Nikolaus Lauda [1949] Director/Entrepreneur [Austrian]; Britta Seeger [1969] Director/Member of The Board of Management Daimler AG [German]; Bodo Knut Uebber [1959] Director/Member of Board of Management [German]; Toto Wolff [1972] Director/Business Executive [Austrian]

Mercedes-Benz Retail Group UK Limited
Incorporated: 10 September 1946 *Employees:* 1,612
Net Worth: £82,581,000 *Total Assets:* £519,217,984
Registered Office: Mercedes-Benz UK Limited, Tongwell, Milton Keynes, Bucks, MK15 8BA
Activities: Sale of new cars and light motor vehicles
Parent: Daimler UK Limited
Officers: Jonathan Philip Reuben Lipman, Secretary; Vittorio Braguglia [1970] Director After Sales and Retail Operations [Swiss]; Marcus Werner Breitschwerdt [1961] Director [German]; Marcell Ruoff [1980] Director/CFO Own Retail Group Europe [German]

Mercer Farming Limited
Incorporated: 13 November 1964
Net Worth: £7,609,337 *Total Assets:* £13,271,219
Registered Office: Blakenhall Park, Barton under Needwood, Burton on Trent, Staffs, DE13 8AJ
Activities: Mixed farming
Parent: A R Mercer Holdings Ltd
Officers: Alec Roger Mercer [1983] Director/Farming; Roger Mallaber Mercer [1953] Director

The Merchant Taylors' Oxfordshire Academy Trust Ltd
Incorporated: 3 August 2011 *Employees:* 125
Previous: Wallingford Schools Academy Trust
Net Worth: £8,263,488 *Total Assets:* £11,617,544
Registered Office: Wallingford School, St George's Road, Wallingford, Oxon, OX10 8HH
Activities: General secondary education
Officers: Lynne Jane Harrison, Secretary; Hugh Buchanan Carter [1960] Director/Investment Banker; Janice Chilton [1943] Director/Minister of Religion CofE; Ian Domville [1964] Director/Telecom Consultant; Jonathan Pebworth [1950] Director/Chartered Management Accountant (Retired); Gordon Bryant Stewart [1966] Director/Registrar & Secretary, University of Plymouth; Alastair Scott Wilcox [1966] Director; Nigel John Willis [1959] Director/Headteacher

Mercia Learning Trust
Incorporated: 26 June 2012 *Employees:* 425
Net Worth: £37,829,380 *Total Assets:* £46,952,724
Registered Office: 79 Glen Road, Sheffield, S7 1RB
Activities: Primary education
Officers: Charlotte Frances Chance, Secretary; John Francis Deal [1953] Director/Project Manager; Rhona Anne Dodds [1964] Director/Housewife; James Paul Hope-Gill [1969] Director; Joanne Nicola Millward [1985] Director/Civil Servant; Sarah Charlotte Generaldine Pearson [1967] Director/University Researcher; Philip David Smith [1967] Director/Independent Financial Advisor

Mercian Limited
Incorporated: 22 September 2004 *Employees:* 8
Net Worth: £5,329,094 *Total Assets:* £11,474,907
Registered Office: Units 3 & 4 The Barns, Highfield Farm, Mill Lane, Snelson, Macclesfield, Cheshire, SK11 9BN
Activities: Wholesale of fruit and vegetables
Shareholder: WHK Partnership Limited
Officers: Anthony Crawford Heal, Secretary; John Lee Carter [1970] Director; Anthony Crawford Heal [1963] Director; Phillip James Kemp [1966] Director; Martyn James Frank Read [1967] Director; Gary Thomas Stanier [1967] Director

Meridian Audio Limited
Incorporated: 29 April 1992 *Employees:* 75
Net Worth Deficit: £613,868 *Total Assets:* £10,298,243
Registered Office: Latham Road, Huntingdon, Cambs, PE29 6YE
Activities: Manufacture of consumer electronics
Major Shareholder: Donald John Buchanan
Officers: Neil Robson, Secretary; Allen John Boothroyd [1943] Director/Product Design Consultant; Donald John Buchanan [1973] Director; Sean David Jagoe [1951] Director/Investment Banker [Irish]; Sang Woo Park [1965] Director [South Korean]; Neil Robson [1969] Finance Director

Meridian Lightweight Technologies UK Limited
Incorporated: 9 June 2008 *Employees:* 97
Net Worth Deficit: £23,367,000 *Total Assets:* £11,639,000
Registered Office: Meridian, Orchard Way, Callidine Park, Sutton in Ashfield, Notts, NG17 1JU
Activities: Casting of light metals
Parent: Zhejiang Wanfeng Auto Wheel Co., Ltd
Officers: Rong Chen, Secretary; Bin Chen [1979] Director [Chinese]; Jian Luo [1971] Director [Chinese]

Merkur Casino UK Ltd
Incorporated: 14 August 2012 *Employees:* 1,408
Net Worth: £55,035,000 *Total Assets:* £133,593,000
Registered Office: Seebeck House, 1a Seebeck Place, Knowlhill, Milton Keynes, Bucks, MK5 8FR
Activities: Activities of other holding companies n.e.c.
Officers: Stefan Bruns [1971] Director/Chief Executive Officer [German]; Borris Lungen [1962] Director/Chief Financial Officer [German]; Meik Sellenriek [1968] Director [German]

Merloni Domestic Appliances Limited
Incorporated: 2 March 1959
Net Worth: £44,445,000 *Total Assets:* £53,276,000
Registered Office: Morley Way, Peterborough, Cambs, PE2 9JB
Activities: Wholesale of radio, television goods & electrical household appliances (other than records, tapes, CDs)
Parent: Indesit Company UK Holdings Limited
Officers: Tetiana Pidhaina, Secretary; Lucianna Raffaini Carvalho [1973] Director [Italian]; Andrzej Tuleja [1973] Director [Polish]

Mertex UK Limited
Incorporated: 23 June 1995 *Employees:* 10
Net Worth: £15,949,080 *Total Assets:* £56,626,848
Registered Office: Highdown House, 11 Highdown Road, Leamington Spa, Warwicks, CV31 1XT
Activities: Other service activities n.e.c.
Major Shareholder: Jaswinder Singh Kohli
Officers: Pritpal Kaur Kohli, Secretary; Jaswinder Singh Kohli [1969] Director/Import & Export Merchant

Metals & Materials Limited
Incorporated: 27 September 2013
Net Worth: £17,391,000 *Total Assets:* £22,585,000
Registered Office: Units C1 and C2 Spitfire Close, Ermine Business Park, Huntingdon, Cambs, PE29 6WR
Activities: Activities of head offices
Major Shareholder: Stephen Charles Aldersley
Officers: Andrew Watson, Secretary; Stephen Charles Aldersley [1957] Director; Stephen Marcel Grenier [1961] Director; Simon John Kenney [1967] Sales Director; Jane Elizabeth Stoner [1961] Director; Andrew Watson [1986] Finance Director

Metalysis Limited
Incorporated: 15 October 2001 *Employees:* 68
Net Worth: £9,746,000 *Total Assets:* £21,208,000
Registered Office: Unit 4 R-Evolution@TheAMP, Brindley Way, Catcliffe, Rotherham, S Yorks, S60 5FS
Activities: Other research and experimental development on natural sciences and engineering
Shareholder: Illuka (UK) Limited
Officers: Douglas Caster [1953] Director; John Daryl Kelly Collett [1958] Director/Portfolio Manager [Italian]; Ian Page [1948] Business Development Director; Anthony Paul Pedder [1949] Director; Anthony James Ratcliffe [1964] Director/Chartered Accountant; Patrick Gerard Sheehan [1960] Director/Venture Capital; Dion Andrew Jones Vaughan [1960] Director

Meter Provida Holdco Limited
Incorporated: 7 October 2013 *Employees:* 58
Net Worth: £1,143,000 *Total Assets:* £19,519,000
Registered Office: Meter House, Enterprise Way, Duckmanton, Chesterfield, Derbys, S44 5FD
Activities: Activities of other holding companies n.e.c.
Parent: Total Capital Partners Manhattan Investments LP
Officers: Thierry Georges Bouzac [1961] Director [French]; Stephen Mark Burr [1964] Director; Natalie Jane Eastham [1973] Director; Dipesh Pradip Lathigra [1983] Financial Director

Meter Provida Investments Limited
Incorporated: 7 October 2013 *Employees:* 2
Net Worth: £907,000 *Total Assets:* £16,111,000
Registered Office: Meter House, Enterprise Way, Duckmanton, Chesterfield, Derbys, S44 5FD
Activities: Activities of head offices
Shareholders: Total Capital Partners Manhattan LP; Meter Provida Holdco Limited
Officers: Thierry Georges Bouzac [1961] Director [French]; Stephen Mark Burr [1964] Director; Dipesh Pradip Lathigra [1983] Finance Director

Meter Provida Limited
Incorporated: 22 August 2000 *Employees:* 56
Net Worth: £6,275,000 *Total Assets:* £17,308,000
Registered Office: Meter House, Enterprise Way, Duckmanton, Chesterfield, Derbys, S44 5FD
Activities: Operation of warehousing and storage facilities for land transport activities
Parent: Meter Provida Investements Ltd
Officers: Thierry Georges Bouzac [1961] Director [French]; Stephen Mark Burr [1964] Director; Dipesh Pradip Lathigra [1983] Finance Director; David Pye [1964] Director/Sales Director

Metflex Precision Mouldings Limited
Incorporated: 25 April 2003 *Employees:* 76
Net Worth: £8,795,732 *Total Assets:* £10,176,814
Registered Office: c/o Spearing Waite LLP, 34 Pocklingtons Walk, Leicester, LE1 6BU
Activities: Manufacture of other rubber products
Parent: Freudenberg Sealing Technologies Limited
Officers: Peter Ronald Charles Johnson [1968] Director; Michael Raymond Lawson [1974] Director/Accountant; Tim Smith [1970] Director/General Manager [American]

Methodist Guild Holidays Limited
Incorporated: 12 August 1927 *Employees:* 186
Net Worth: £10,357,453 *Total Assets:* £12,865,749
Registered Office: 2nd Floor, Building 10, Cromford Mill Mill Road, Cromford, Matlock, Derbys, DE4 3RQ
Activities: Hotels and similar accommodation
Officers: Peter Anthony Mills, Secretary; Rev Keith Richard Albans [1956] Director/Ordained Presbyter of The Methodist Church; Canon Ann Margaret Barwood [1941] Director/Canon Librarian; Michael George Bateman [1950] Director/Self Employed Business Consultant; Peter Ronald Binks [1942] Director/Retired; Peter Anthony Mills [1949] Finance Director; John Evan Moffoot [1949] Director/Retired Local Government Officer; Martin John Wrench [1945] Director/Retired

Methodist Homes
Incorporated: 28 July 2000 *Employees:* 5,803
Net Worth: £276,992,000 *Total Assets:* £503,104,000
Registered Office: Epworth House, Stuart Street, Derby, DE1 2EQ
Activities: Residential nursing care facilities
Officers: Mandy Joanne Mottram, Secretary; Ian Simon Ailles [1965] Director; Deborah Ann Aplin [1963] Director; Hilary Margaret Cocker [1956] Director/Board Member; Andrew Geoffrey Cozens CBE [1955] Director; Balachandren Muthuvaloe Gnanapragasam [1944] Director; Dr David Hall [1941] Director/Retired; Vanella Jackson [1961] Director; Norman John Mann [1942] Director/Board Member; James Anthony Reilly [1958] Director; John Harris Robinson [1940] Director/Retired

Metlane Limited
Incorporated: 9 August 1994
Net Worth: £3,649,641 *Total Assets:* £10,095,410
Registered Office: 19 Blackwell Road, Huthwaite, Notts, NG17 2QS
Activities: Other letting and operating of own or leased real estate
Major Shareholder: Jonathan Rye
Officers: Jonathan Rye, Secretary; Jonathan Rye [1966] Director/Builder; Rattanaporn Rye [1980] Director [Thai]

Metsa Wood UK Limited
Incorporated: 21 June 1995 *Employees:* 446
Net Worth: £37,490,000 *Total Assets:* £66,394,000
Registered Office: Old Golf Course, Fishtoft Road, Boston, Lincs, PE21 0BJ
Activities: Sawmilling and planing of wood
Parent: Metsaliitto Oy
Officers: Alice Olsson, Secretary; Alice Olsson [1978] Finance Director; Henrik Soderstrom [1979] Director/Senior Vice President Timber & Upgrades [Finnish]

Mettler-Toledo Limited
Incorporated: 11 August 1969 *Employees:* 246
Net Worth: £11,321,000 *Total Assets:* £24,443,000
Registered Office: 64 Boston Road, Beaumont Leys, Leicester, LE4 1AW
Activities: Manufacture of electronic measuring, testing etc. equipment, not for industrial process control
Officers: Nigel Mason, Secretary; James Thomas Bellerjeau [1968] Director/Lawyer [American]; Nigel Mason [1959] Director/Chartered Accountant; Mark Ronald Purle [1965] Director/Business Manager

Mexichem Specialty Compounds Limited
Incorporated: 6 July 1981 *Employees:* 218
Previous: Alphagary Limited
Net Worth: £145,648,992 *Total Assets:* £184,758,000
Registered Office: c/o Mexichem, 8 Beler Way, Leicester Road Industrial Estate, Melton Mowbray, Leics, LE13 0DG
Activities: Manufacture of other plastic products
Officers: Daniel Jean Delisle [1965] Director/General Manager [American]; Michael Ray Funderburg [1958] Director [American]; Gautam Nivarthy [1973] Director/Businessman [American]

Meynell Plant Hire Limited
Incorporated: 18 September 1956 *Employees:* 121
Net Worth: £4,436,892 *Total Assets:* £15,000,612
Registered Office: 370 Loughborough Road, Leicester, LE4 5PR
Activities: Renting and leasing of cars and light motor vehicles
Parent: Jelson Holdings Limited
Officers: Julian Ian Bestwick [1967] Finance Director; Troy Harrison [1967] Director; Graham Stuart Jelley [1961] Director/Builder; Robert Stephen Jelley [1955] Director/Builder; Ronald Albert Jelley [1927] Director/Builder; Stephen Jelley [1982] Director

MGA Entertainment (UK) Limited
Incorporated: 13 December 2005 *Employees:* 40
Net Worth Deficit: £8,563,553 *Total Assets:* £31,473,184
Registered Office: Regent Business Park, 50 Presley Way, Crownhill, Milton Keynes, Bucks, MK8 0ES
Activities: Non-specialised wholesale trade
Parent: MGA Entertainment Inc
Officers: Isaac Larian [1954] Director/Chief Executive Officer [American]

MHH Contracting Limited
Incorporated: 12 June 1985 *Employees:* 48
Net Worth: £15,312,763 *Total Assets:* £19,657,400
Registered Office: 559 Carlisle Street East, Sheffield, S4 8DT
Activities: Non-specialised wholesale trade
Shareholders: Jean Angela Hague; Martin Hartley Hague
Officers: Jean Angela Hague, Secretary; Jean Angela Hague [1957] Director/Secretary; Martin Hartley Hague [1957] Director/Plant Manager

MHR Global Holdings Limited
Incorporated: 14 November 1997 *Employees:* 622
Previous: Midland Software Holdings Limited
Net Worth: £23,783,128 *Total Assets:* £45,741,248
Registered Office: The Old Hall, Ashwell, Oakham, Rutland, LE15 7LJ
Activities: Activities of head offices
Officers: Andrew Peet, Secretary; Elizabeth Anne Mills [1945] Director [New Zealander]; Jessica Margaret Mills [1982] Director; John Roger Mills [1938] Director

MHR International UK Limited
Incorporated: 3 October 1984 *Employees:* 622
Previous: Midland Software Limited
Net Worth: £8,118,372 *Total Assets:* £29,987,460
Registered Office: Peterbridge House, The Lakes, Northampton, NN4 7HB
Activities: Other information technology service activities
Parent: Midland Software Holdings Limited
Officers: Peter Ward, Secretary; Jessica Margaret Mills [1982] Director; John Roger Mills [1938] Director/Computer Consultant; Andrew Peet [1970] Director/Chief Financial Officer; Anton Roe [1972] Director/Chief Technical Officer

Microlise Holdings Limited
Incorporated: 21 January 2008 *Employees:* 420
Previous: Microlise Group Holdings Limited
Net Worth: £10,164,000 *Total Assets:* £33,097,000
Registered Office: Microlise, Farrington Way, Eastwood, Nottingham, NG16 3AG
Activities: Business and domestic software development
Parent: Microlise Group Holdings Limited
Officers: Nicholas James Wightman, Secretary; Roy Allum [1960] Director; Robert David Harbey [1965] Director; Nadeem Raza [1967] Director; William Wynn [1963] Director

Microlise Limited
Incorporated: 21 March 1995 *Employees:* 300
Net Worth: £5,453,000 *Total Assets:* £35,537,000
Registered Office: Farrington Way, Eastwood, Nottingham, NG16 3AG
Activities: Manufacture of computers and peripheral equipment
Parent: Microlise Group Limited
Officers: Nicholas James Wightman, Secretary; Robert David Harbey [1965] Director; Nadeem Raza [1967] Director; William Wynn [1963] Director

Micromass Holdings Limited
Incorporated: 10 March 2000
Net Worth: £197,422,000 *Total Assets:* £465,121,984
Registered Office: Waters Wilmslow, Stamford Avenue, Altrincham Road, Wilmslow, Cheshire, SK9 4AX
Activities: Activities of head offices
Parent: Waters Corporation
Officers: Mark Tyrell Beaudouin, Secretary; Mark T Beaudouin [1955] Director/Attorney [American]; Andrew Aitchison Schoon [1970] Finance Director; Brian William Smith [1961] Director

Micromass Limited
Incorporated: 20 December 1995
Net Worth: £35,948,000 *Total Assets:* £36,079,000
Registered Office: Waters Wilmslow, Stamford Avenue, Altrincham Road, Wilmslow, Cheshire, SK9 4AX
Activities: Activities of head offices
Parent: Micromass Holdings Limited
Officers: Mark Tyrell Beaudouin, Secretary; Mark T Beaudouin [1955] Director/Attorney [American]; Andrew Aitchison Schoon [1970] Finance Director; Brian William Smith [1961] Director

Micromass UK Limited
Incorporated: 22 February 1996 *Employees:* 622
Net Worth: £137,456,000 *Total Assets:* £183,186,000
Registered Office: Waters Wilmslow, Stamford Avenue, Altrincham Road, Wilmslow, Cheshire, SK9 4AX
Activities: Manufacture of electronic measuring, testing etc. equipment, not for industrial process control
Parent: Micromass Limited
Officers: Mark Tyrell Beaudouin, Secretary; Susan Joy Robinson, Secretary; Mark T Beaudouin [1955] Director/Attorney [American]; Stephen Gary Curbishley [1963] Operations Director; Andrew Aitchison Schoon [1970] Finance Director; Brian William Smith [1961] Director; Stephen Mark Smith [1967] Senior Director Informatics

Micronclean Limited
Incorporated: 31 August 1921 *Employees:* 455
Previous: Fenland Laundries Limited
Net Worth: £14,661,862 *Total Assets:* £21,314,632
Registered Office: Roman Bank, Skegness, Lincs, PE25 1SQ
Activities: Washing and (dry-)cleaning of textile and fur products
Major Shareholder: Simon James Fry
Officers: Michelle Sharon Simpson, Secretary; Philip Cresswell [1963] Sales Director; Clare Margaret Fry [1964] Director; Simon James Fry [1963] Director; Andrew John Kettle [1967] Director; Robert James Parker [1964] Director/Accountant

Mid-UK Recycling Limited
Incorporated: 22 December 1997 *Employees:* 416
Net Worth: £20,360,860 *Total Assets:* £53,460,712
Registered Office: Summit House, Quarrington, Sleaford, Lincs, NG34 8RS
Activities: Collection of non-hazardous waste
Parent: Green Planet Products Limited
Officers: Darren Thompson, Secretary; Susan Armstrong [1953] Director; Mowbray Christopher Mountain [1973] Director; Mowbray Edmund Stephens Mountain [1948] Director; Simon Leslie Mountain [1978] Director; Thomas Nicholas Mountain [1975] Director; Simon Derek Pattison [1960] Director; Darren Thompson [1967] Finance Director

Midcity Estates Limited
Incorporated: 2 June 1999 *Employees:* 4
Net Worth: £3,129,777 *Total Assets:* £10,095,962
Registered Office: The Arches, 220 West Street, Sheffield, S1 4EU
Activities: Other letting and operating of own or leased real estate
Officers: John Michael Gareth Whitaker, Secretary/Property Developer; William Vaughan Rodgers [1947] Director/Property Developer; John Michael Gareth Whitaker [1936] Director/Property Developer

Midcity Investments Limited
Incorporated: 16 February 1998
Net Worth: £7,398,832 *Total Assets:* £11,358,064
Registered Office: 1a Needlers End Lane, Balsall Common, Coventry, Warwicks, CV7 7AF
Activities: Other letting and operating of own or leased real estate
Parent: Rentfield Limited
Officers: Frank Howard Hunter [1945] Director/Surveyor; Michael Harold Hunter [1943] Director/Solicitor

Middleby Holding UK Ltd
Incorporated: 17 March 2011 *Employees:* 3
Net Worth: £26,899,204 *Total Assets:* £44,044,048
Registered Office: Whisby Road, Lincoln, LN6 3QZ
Activities: Activities of head offices
Officers: Timothy John FitzGenerald [1969] Director/VP and CFO [American]; Martin McKay Lindsay [1964] Director/Corporate Treasurer [American]; Agustin Zufia [1967] Director/Group Controller [Spanish]

Middleby UK Residential Holding Ltd
Incorporated: 9 July 2015
Net Worth: £51,388,248 *Total Assets:* £151,674,960
Registered Office: c/o Aga Rangemaster, Meadow Lane, Long Eaton, Nottingham, NG10 2GD
Activities: Activities of head offices
Parent: The Middleby Corporation
Officers: Timothy John FitzGenerald [1969] Director/Vice President and CFO [American]; Martin McKay Lindsay [1964] Director/Corporate Treasurer [American]; Agustin Zufia [1967] Director/Group Controller [Spanish]

The Midland Academies Trust
Incorporated: 16 March 2010 *Employees:* 305
Net Worth: £28,860,000 *Total Assets:* £36,801,000
Registered Office: North Warwickshire & Hinckley College, Hinckley Road, Nuneaton, Warwicks, CV11 6BH
Activities: General secondary education
Officers: Rachel Alexandra Marshall, Secretary; Michael John Coult [1953] Director/Retired; Ian Keith Dunn [1968] Director/Pro Vice Chancellor; Jeremy Hutchinson [1955] Director/Solicitor; Wendy Elizabeth Martin [1948] Director/Consultant; Ann Elizabeth Melville [1946] Director; Marion Grace Plant [1961] Director/Principal Chief Executive NWHC; John James Ramsay [1966] Director/Relationship Manager - Banking; Timothy Ennis Render [1953] Director/Accountant; Dr Joseph Anthony Walsh [1956] Senior Manager/Director

Midland Assured Finance Limited
Incorporated: 13 February 1963
Net Worth: £7,860,117 *Total Assets:* £10,503,941
Registered Office: 5 Olympus Court, Olympus Avenue, Tachbrook Park, Warwick, CV34 6RZ
Activities: Financial intermediation not elsewhere classified
Major Shareholder: Peter John Davis
Officers: Dr Linda Ann Davis, Secretary; Dr Linda Ann Davis [1946] Director; Peter John Davis [1935] Director/Solicitor

Midland Assured Holdings Limited
Incorporated: 8 December 2005
Net Worth: £2,329,592 *Total Assets:* £10,029,386
Registered Office: Unit 5 Olympus Court, Olympus Avenue, Tachbrook Park, Warwick, CV34 6RZ
Activities: Activities of head offices
Shareholders: Sarah Louise Shannon; Simon James Davis; Paul Martin Davis
Officers: Sarah Louise Shannon [1975] Director

Midland Communications Distribution Limited
Incorporated: 4 August 1997 *Employees:* 32
Net Worth: £2,427,221 *Total Assets:* £13,571,848
Registered Office: Unit 1 Colwick Quays, Business Park, Colwick, Nottingham, NG4 2JY
Activities: Wireless telecommunications activities
Shareholder: EE Limited
Officers: Gail Elizabeth Liley, Secretary; Mark Jonathan Hendricks [1974] Director/Accountant; Tanaquil Louise Jeffrey [1970] Managing Director; Gail Elizabeth Liley [1959] Director; Mark Liley [1955] Director; Jason Ormonde [1986] Director/Accountant [Irish]; Mike Tomlinson [1967] Marketing Director

Midland Red (South) Limited
Incorporated: 15 April 1981 *Employees:* 1,196
Net Worth Deficit: £1,622,000 *Total Assets:* £39,345,000
Registered Office: c/o Stagecoach Services Limited, One Stockport Exchange, 20 Railway Road, Stockport, Cheshire, SK1 3SW
Activities: Other urban, suburban or metropolitan passenger land transport (not underground, metro or similar)
Parent: Stagecoach Bus Holdings Limited
Officers: Michael John Vaux, Secretary; Colin Brown [1968] Director/Accountant; Philip Howard Medlicott [1962] Director; Arnold Mark Threapleton [1954] Managing Director; Mark Venables [1975] Director

Midland Sports Centre for The Disabled Trust Limited
Incorporated: 22 September 1983
Net Worth: £9,731,829 *Total Assets:* £9,735,622
Registered Office: Xcel Leisure Centre, Mitchell Avenue, Cranley, Coventry, Warwicks, CV4 8DY
Activities: Operation of sports facilities
Officers: Paul Breed, Secretary [New Zealander]; Professor Robert James Grieve [1951] Director/Medical Practitioner; Alan John McCarry [1947] Director/Chairman of Industrial Tribute; John Alistair Reid McIntosh [1936] Director/Clinical Scientist (Retired)

Midlands Land Portfolio Limited
Incorporated: 10 March 2011
Net Worth: £2,503,000 *Total Assets:* £20,492,000
Registered Office: Severn Trent Centre, 2 St John's Street, Coventry, Warwicks, CV1 2LZ
Activities: Buying and selling of own real estate
Parent: Severn Trent Holdings Limited
Officers: Gemma Eagle, Secretary; Robert Craig McPheely [1962] Director/Accountant; Julie Fiona Rossiter [1969] Director/Chartered Surveyor; Andrew Patrick Smith [1960] Director

Miele Company Limited
Incorporated: 26 July 1963 *Employees:* 429
Net Worth: £20,282,000 *Total Assets:* £74,872,000
Registered Office: Fairacres, Marcham Road, Abingdon, Oxon, OX14 1TW
Activities: Agents involved in the sale of furniture, household goods, hardware and ironmongery
Officers: John Robert Pickering, Secretary; Rolf Kihm [1967] Director [Swiss]; John Robert Pickering [1968] Director; Nicolas Zbinden [1977] Director [Swiss]

Mil-Ver Metal Company Limited
Incorporated: 11 May 1982 *Employees:* 97
Net Worth: £1,189,162 *Total Assets:* £21,443,748
Registered Office: Coronel Avenue, Rowleys Green Industrial Estate, Coventry, Warwicks, CV6 6AP
Activities: Aluminium production
Parent: Amalgamated Metal Investment Holdings Limited
Officers: Hamish Terence Kinnear Brown [1957] Director/Management Accountant; David Stephen Sher [1983] Managing Director

Milehouse Foods Limited
Incorporated: 16 November 2015 *Employees:* 135
Net Worth: £1,163,664 *Total Assets:* £9,156,419
Registered Office: 45-49 Greek Street, Stockport, Cheshire, SK3 8AX
Activities: Activities of other holding companies n.e.c.
Shareholders: Paul Andrew Burkitt; Mark Jones
Officers: Paul Andrew Burkitt [1962] Director; Mark Jones [1965] Director

Walter Miles (Electrical Engineers) Limited
Incorporated: 6 April 1954 *Employees:* 21
Net Worth: £20,544,718 *Total Assets:* £23,971,230
Registered Office: Christopher House, 94b London Road, Leicester, LE2 0QS
Activities: Electrical installation
Parent: Walter Miles Holdings Limited
Officers: David Grenville Miles, Secretary; Michael Richard Harrison [1976] Director; David Grenville Miles [1967] Managing Director

The Mill Academy
Incorporated: 8 May 2012 *Employees:* 214
Previous: The Henry Box School
Net Worth: £20,615,724 *Total Assets:* £24,253,402
Registered Office: Church Green, Witney, Oxon, OX28 4AX
Activities: General secondary education
Officers: Tracy Marie Hodges, Secretary; Wendy Hemmingsley [1970] Director/Headteacher; Gordon George Joyner [1965] Deputy Director of Education for ODBE; Claire King [1978] Director/Learning Consultant; Colin Keith Mitchell [1947] Director/Corporate Finance Consultant; Nigel Keith Moore [1962] Marketing Director; John Haydn West-Burnham [1946] Director/Leadership Development Consultant,Writer,Teacher

Mill Garages North East Limited
Incorporated: 18 March 2008 *Employees:* 188
Net Worth: £4,363,000 *Total Assets:* £30,837,000
Registered Office: Stoneacre, Omega Boulevard, Capitol Park, Thorne, Doncaster, S Yorks, DN8 5TX
Activities: Sale of new cars and light motor vehicles
Parent: Decidebloom Limited
Officers: Shaun Foweather [1963] Director; Richard Stephen Teatum [1957] Director; Nigel Peter Wood [1964] Director

Millbrook European Holdings Limited
Incorporated: 25 June 2015
Net Worth: £7,834,105 *Total Assets:* £13,488,061
Registered Office: Millbrook, Bedford, MK45 2JQ
Activities: Non-trading company
Parent: Spectris Group Holdings Limited
Officers: Alexander Mark Burns [1963] Director/Engineer; Martin Owen Hughes [1964] Director; Andrew Edward Bass Nelson [1976] Director/Chief Finance Officer; Eoghan Pol O'Lionaird [1966] Business Group Director [Irish]

Millbrook Proving Ground Limited
Incorporated: 14 March 1988 *Employees:* 527
Net Worth: £25,244,000 *Total Assets:* £63,680,000
Registered Office: Millbrook, Bedford, MK45 2JQ
Activities: Technical testing and analysis
Parent: Spectris Group Holdings Limited
Officers: Alexander Mark Burns [1963] Director/Engineer; Jonathan Andrew Eaton [1959] Director; Martin Owen Hughes [1964] Director; Andrew Edward Bass Nelson [1976] Director/Chief Finance Officer; Eoghan Pol O'Lionaird [1966] Business Group Director

Karen Millen Fashions Limited
Incorporated: 17 February 2009 *Employees:* 868
Net Worth: £1,700,000 *Total Assets:* £55,500,000
Registered Office: The Triangle, Stanton Harcourt Industrial Estate, Stanton Harcourt, Witney, Oxon, OX29 5UT
Activities: Retail sale of clothing in specialised stores
Parent: Karen Millen Holdings Limited
Officers: Beth Janet Butterwick [1965] Director; Neil William McCausland [1960] Director; Emily Sarah Tate [1974] Director

Karen Millen Group Limited
Incorporated: 18 October 2010
Net Worth Deficit: £65,800,000 *Total Assets:* £45,000,000
Registered Office: The Triangle, Stanton Harcourt Industrial Estate, Stanton Harcourt, Witney, Oxon, OX29 5UT
Activities: Non-trading company
Parent: Karen Millen Holdco 1 Limited
Officers: Beth Janet Butterwick [1965] Director; John Philip Madden III [1973] Director [American]; Neil William McCausland [1960] Director; Johann Petur Reyndal [1962] Director [Icelander]; Emily Sarah Tate [1974] Director

Karen Millen Holdco 1 Limited
Incorporated: 21 September 2015 *Employees:* 1,460
Net Worth Deficit: £12,700,000 *Total Assets:* £67,600,000
Registered Office: The Triangle, Stanton Harcourt Industrial Estate, Stanton Harcourt, Witney, Oxon, OX29 5UT
Activities: Activities of head offices
Parent: Aurora Fashions Finance Limited
Officers: Beth Janet Butterwick [1965] Director; John Philip Madden III [1973] Director [American]; Neil William McCausland [1960] Director; Johann Petur Reyndal [1962] Director [Icelander]; Emily Sarah Tate [1974] Director; Robin Terrell [1970] Director

Karen Millen Holdings Limited
Incorporated: 13 February 2009
Net Worth: £59,300,000 *Total Assets:* £136,100,000
Registered Office: The Triangle, Stanton Harcourt Industrial Estate, Stanton Harcourt, Witney, Oxon, OX29 5UT
Activities: Activities of head offices
Parent: Karen Millen Group Limited
Officers: Beth Janet Butterwick [1965] Director; Neil William McCausland [1960] Director; Emily Sarah Tate [1974] Director

Millennium EFW Limited
Incorporated: 16 May 2017
Net Worth Deficit: £68,191 *Total Assets:* £29,799,300
Registered Office: No 1 Notttingham Science Park, Jesse Boot Avenue, University Boulevard, Nottingham, NG7 2RU
Activities: Treatment and disposal of non-hazardous waste
Shareholders: Chinook Engineering Limited; Alfanar Energy Company LLC
Officers: Dr Rifat Al Chalabi [1963] Director [American]; Mohammed Akbar Alam [1971] Director/Development Manager-Alfanar Energy [Indian]; William St John Temple [1978] Director; Jamal Wadi [1961] Director [Canadian]

Millennium Inorganic Chemicals Overseas Holdings
Incorporated: 16 March 1989 *Employees:* 4
Net Worth: £555,143,808 *Total Assets:* £698,991,872
Registered Office: Laporte Road, Stallingborough, Grimsby, N E Lincs, DN40 2PR
Activities: Activities of other holding companies n.e.c.
Parent: Cristal Inorganic Chemicals Netherlands B.V.
Officers: Maria Jegher, Secretary; Stephen Anthony Box [1959] Director/Financial Controller; Koen Felix Lodewijk Docx [1974] Director/Finance Manager [Belgian]; Dr Robert McIntyre [1955] Commercial Research Director; Robert John Sarracini [1976] Site Director [British/Australian]

Millennium Inorganic Chemicals UK Holdings Limited
Incorporated: 25 August 1995 *Employees:* 4
Net Worth: £432,966,016 *Total Assets:* £432,994,464
Registered Office: Laporte Road, Stallingborough, Grimsby, N E Lincs, DN40 2PR
Activities: Activities of other holding companies n.e.c.
Parent: Millennium Inorganic Chemicals Overseas Holdings
Officers: Maria Jegher, Secretary; Stephen Anthony Box [1959] Director/Financial Controller; Koen Felix Lodewijk Docx [1974] Director/Finance Manager [Belgian]; Dr Robert McIntyre [1955] Commercial Research Director; Robert John Sarracini [1976] Site Director [British/Australian]

Miller Homes Group Holdings PLC
Incorporated: 6 July 2017 *Employees:* 850
Net Worth: £157,800,000 *Total Assets:* £978,000,000
Registered Office: 2 Centro Place, Pride Park, Derby, DE24 8RF
Activities: Activities of construction holding companies
Officers: Julie Mansfield Jackson, Secretary; Scott Chamberlin [1967] Divisional Managing Director; Christopher John Endsor [1961] Director/Chief Executive; Julie Mansfield Jackson [1965] Director/General Counsel; Darren Robert Jones [1969] Divisional Managing Director; Stewart Alan Lynes [1978] Divisional Managing Director; Ian Murdoch [1970] Finance Director

Miller Wates (Didcot) Limited
Incorporated: 23 May 2015
Net Worth: £4,077,886 *Total Assets:* £11,070,007
Registered Office: 2 Centro Place, Pride Park, Derby, DE24 8RF
Activities: Construction of domestic buildings
Shareholders: Miller Homes Holdings Limited; Wates Group Limited
Officers: David Alexander Bowen [1967] Director; Michael Howard Brayshaw [1964] Director; David Michael Brocklebank [1970] Managing Director; Natalie Jane Flint [1969] Director; Tracey Lorraine Forbes-Taylor [1970] Director; Julie Mansfield Jackson [1965] Director/Solicitor; Darren Robert Jones [1969] Director; Martin Geoffrey Leach [1965] Operations Director; Andrew Colin Modle [1967] Finance Director; John Ian Murdoch [1970] Finance Director

Miller Wates (Southwater) Limited
Incorporated: 11 November 2015
Net Worth Deficit: £1,670,397 *Total Assets:* £25,558,276
Registered Office: 2 Centro Place, Pride Park, Derby, DE24 8RF
Activities: Construction of domestic buildings
Shareholders: Miller Homes Holdings Limited; Wates Group Limited
Officers: David Alexander Bowen [1967] Finance Director; Michael Brayshaw [1967] Director; David Michael Brocklebank [1970] Managing Director; Natalie Jane Flint [1969] Residential Investments Director; Tracey Lorraine Forbes-Taylor [1970] Operations Director; Julie Mansfield Jackson [1965] Legal Director; Darren Robert Jones [1969] Managing Director; Martin Geoffrey Leach [1965] Operations Director; Andrew Colin Modle [1967] Finance Director; Ian Murdoch [1970] Finance Director

Miller Wates (Wallingford) Limited
Incorporated: 17 October 2016
Net Worth Deficit: £441,197 *Total Assets:* £11,456,505
Registered Office: 2 Centro Park, Pride Park, Derby, DE24 8RF
Activities: Construction of domestic buildings
Shareholders: Wates Group Limited; Miller Homes Holdings Limited
Officers: David Alexander Bowen [1967] Finance Director; Michael Howard Brayshaw [1964] Director; David Michael Brocklebank [1970] Business Unit Managing Director; Natalie Jane Flint [1969] Sales Marketing Director; Tracey Lorraine Forbes-Taylor [1970] Operations Director; Julie Mansfield Jackson [1965] Solicitor and Legal Director; Darren Robert Jones [1969] Director; Martin Geoffrey Leach [1965] Operations Director; Andrew Colin Modle [1967] Finance Director; Ian Murdoch [1970] Finance Director

Millgate Limited
Incorporated: 25 July 1996 *Employees:* 108
Previous: Millgate Computer Systems Limited
Net Worth: £1,302,760 *Total Assets:* £11,794,725
Registered Office: 7 Vantage Drive, Tinsley, Sheffield, S9 1RG
Activities: Wholesale of computers, computer peripheral equipment and software
Major Shareholder: Christopher David Calvert
Officers: Jacquelyn Ann Brown, Secretary; Jacquelyn Ann Brown [1962] Director; Christopher David Calvert [1964] Director

Mills CNC Limited
Incorporated: 11 January 1974 *Employees:* 91
Net Worth: £11,640,404 *Total Assets:* £32,183,518
Registered Office: Units 2 & 3 Tachbrook Link, Tachbrook Park Drive, Leamington Spa, Warwicks, CV34 6SN
Activities: Manufacture of other fabricated metal products n.e.c.
Parent: Ensco 1066 Limited
Officers: Adam Richard Attwood [1967] Director; Tony Dale [1969] Director; Kevin Lee Gilbert [1957] Director; Andrew John Knight [1972] Director

Milltarn Limited
Incorporated: 1 January 1968
Net Worth: £5,518,244 *Total Assets:* £13,672,431
Registered Office: 398 Ecclesall Road, Sheffield, S11 8PJ
Activities: Management of real estate on a fee or contract basis
Parent: Caplan & Co Limited
Officers: Peter Turkington, Secretary; Paul Caplan [1955] Director

Stewart Milne Homes North West England Limited
Incorporated: 14 September 2016
Net Worth: £7,195,000 *Total Assets:* £61,037,000
Registered Office: Falcon House, Curbridge Business Park, Downs Road, Witney, Oxon, OX29 7WJ
Activities: Other business support service activities n.e.c.
Parent: HSDL Nominees Limited
Officers: Michael Sinclair Medine, Secretary; Glenn Fraser Whyte Allison [1956] Director; Alex Goodfellow [1967] Director; Stuart Alastair MacGregor [1971] Finance Director; Stewart Milne [1950] Director

Stewart Milne Timber Systems Limited
Incorporated: 14 September 2016
Net Worth: £852,000 *Total Assets:* £20,384,000
Registered Office: Falcon House, Curbridge Business Park, Downs Road, Witney, Oxon, OX29 7WJ
Activities: Other business support service activities n.e.c.
Parent: HSDL Nominees Limited
Officers: Michael Sinclair Medine, Secretary; Glenn Fraser Whyte Allison [1956] Director; Alex Goodfellow [1967] Director; Stuart Alastair MacGregor [1971] Finance Director; Stewart Milne [1950] Director

Milton Keynes Academy Trust
Incorporated: 29 March 2007 *Employees:* 166
Net Worth: £22,977,298 *Total Assets:* £27,840,644
Registered Office: The Milton Keynes Academy, Fulwoods Drive, Leadenhall, Milton Keynes, Bucks, MK6 5LA
Activities: General secondary education
Officers: Mark Andrew Blyton, Secretary; Adrian Mark Bowater [1958] Director of Finance; Nicolas John Heslop [1966] Director/Public Affairs Manager; Vic Maher [1952] Director/Consultant; Barry John Neale [1969] Director/Fast Food; Brian Rabe [1966] Director/Company Secretary; Fiona Seddon [1978] Director/Principal; Dr Philip Henry Smith [1946] Director; Diane Taylor [1964] Director/Data Manager Education

Milton Keynes Community Foundation Limited
Incorporated: 30 June 1986 *Employees:* 19
Net Worth: £62,117,640 *Total Assets:* £64,318,392
Registered Office: Acorn House, 381 Midsummer Boulevard, Central Milton Keynes, Bucks, MK9 3HP
Activities: Other social work activities without accommodation n.e.c.
Officers: Carole Diane Baume [1949] Director/Retired; Kate Elizabeth Chadwick [1980] Director/Gallery Manager; Steve Harris [1957] Director/Retired; Jill Eileen Heaton [1962] Director/Solicitor; Shirley Jones [1958] Director/Businesswoman; Folashade Oluyemisi Komolafe [1967] Director; Shaun Lee [1956] Director/Retired; Dr Alice Mary Maynard [1957] Director; Kurshida Mirza [1958] Director/Retired Civil Servant; Lawrence Louis Revill [1956] Director/Town Planner; Keith Silverthorne [1949] Director/Retired

Milton Keynes Development Partnership LLP
Incorporated: 7 December 2012 *Employees:* 10
Net Worth: £30,340,000 *Total Assets:* £65,392,000
Registered Office: Civic Offices, 1 Saxon Gate East, Milton Keynes, Bucks, MK9 3HG
Officers: Peter Marland [1980] Member

Milton Keynes Education Trust
Incorporated: 9 June 2011 *Employees:* 409
Net Worth: £34,562,656 *Total Assets:* £40,484,816
Registered Office: Walton High, Fyfield Barrow, Walnut Tree, Milton Keynes, Bucks, MK7 7WH
Activities: General secondary education
Officers: Sheila Mary Bushnell, Secretary; Lisa Jane Alexander [1966] Director [British/New Zealander]; Michelle Elizabeth Currie [1961] Director/Principal; Jane Trudy Edwards [1966] Director/Headteacher; Kevin John Gowans [1959] Director; Simon Paul Haddy [1979] Managing Director - Construction; Reynold Philip James Lee [1965] HR Director; Dr Ann Generaldine Limb [1953] Non-Executive Director Chairman; Robert John George Rymarz [1949] Director/Retired; Richard Clive Smith [1964] Director/Chartered Accountant

Milton Keynes Parks Trust Limited
Incorporated: 6 July 1990 *Employees:* 58
Net Worth: £109,754,000 *Total Assets:* £145,340,992
Registered Office: Campbell Park Pavillion, 1300 Silbury Boulevard, Campbell Park, Milton Keynes, Bucks, MK9 4AD
Activities: Landscape service activities
Officers: David Richard Foster, Secretary/Chief Executive; Alexander David Chapman [1989] Director/Postgraduate Researcher; Samuel Bennett Crooks [1946] Director/Retired; John Bertram Eaton [1951] Director; Junita Fernandez [1966] Director, Finance & Corporate Operations; Richard John Foreman [1955] Director; Daniel Gilbert [1986] Director/Public Relations; Ian William Jackson [1967] Director/Chartered Surveyor; Andrew David Lawes [1963] Director/Chartered Accountant; Nicholas Geoffrey Lloyd [1971] Director/Solicitor; James Armour Macmillan [1965] Director/Charity Executive; Jennifer McCelvie Marklew [1985] Director/Insight Analyst; Jean Marion Nicholas [1944] Director/Retired Accountant; Richard Pearce [1973] Director/Woodland Officer; Zoe Anne Raven [1962] Director; Ian John Russell [1980] Director/Environment Manager; Clare Meg Stacey [1988] Director/Athlete Liaison Officer; Dr Philip Wheeler [1978] Director/University Lecturer; Gamiel Ahmed Yafai [1962] Director/Management Consultant

Minerva Learning Trust
Incorporated: 2 September 2014 *Employees:* 559
Net Worth: £61,695,676 *Total Assets:* £72,026,800
Registered Office: Handsworth Grange Community Sports College, Handsworth Grange Road, Sheffield, S13 9HJ
Activities: General secondary education
Officers: Kabier Aslam [1971] Director of Property Development Company; Genny Bradley [1951] Director/Retired; David Alan Burkinshaw [1957] Director/HR Consultant; Stephen Peter Chew [1950] Director; Jonathan Crossley-Holland [1947] Director; James Bernard McDonnell [1980] Director/Solicitor; Irvin Alan Robinson [1950] Director/Retired Financial Consultant; Edward Alan Wydenbach [1948] Director/Retired Headteacher & National Leader of Governance

Minoli & Company Limited
Incorporated: 29 July 1960 *Employees:* 41
Net Worth: £11,306,253 *Total Assets:* £13,309,777
Registered Office: Minoli Buildings, Transport Way, Watlington Road, Cowley, Oxford, OX4 6LX
Activities: Retail sale of carpets, rugs, wall and floor coverings in specialised stores
Major Shareholder: Jonathon David Minoli
Officers: David John Wright, Secretary; Jonathon David Minoli [1968] Sales & Marketing Director

Minorfern Limited
Incorporated: 18 April 1978 *Employees:* 243
Net Worth: £4,208,154 *Total Assets:* £9,013,893
Registered Office: Holland House, Furnace Hill Road, Clay Cross, Chesterfield, Derbys, S45 9NF
Activities: Other retail sale in non-specialised stores
Shareholders: Nicholas James Holland; Peter Holland; Heather Holland
Officers: Heather Holland, Secretary; Heather Holland [1954] Director; Nicholas James Holland [1982] Sales Director; Peter Holland [1946] Managing Director; Darren Steven Murray [1974] Director; Nigel Ronald Ratcliffe [1961] Director

Minova International Limited
Incorporated: 13 February 2002 *Employees:* 7
Net Worth: £71,499,000 *Total Assets:* £117,443,000
Registered Office: Unit 19 Redbrook Business Park, Wilthorpe Road, Barnsley, S Yorks, S75 1JN
Activities: Activities of head offices
Parent: Mintun 4 Limited
Officers: Peter Assinder [1971] Strategic Sales & Technology Director; Michael Joseph Napoletano [1967] Director/Manager [American]; Hugh Marcus Pelham [1967] Director/Manager

Mintridge Investments (Wikowo) Limited
Incorporated: 1 September 2003
Net Worth Deficit: £678,472 *Total Assets:* £9,932,111
Registered Office: The Coach House, Wentworth Farm, Great Harrowden, Wellingborough, Northants, NN9 5AD
Activities: Activities of head offices
Shareholders: Harrowden Farms Limited; Mintridge Holdings Limited
Officers: Stuart Benjamin Ridd-Jones, Secretary/Director; John Frederick Hilsdon [1944] Director; Joanna Mary Paske [1965] Director; Norman Charles Paske [1962] Director; Chantall Sylvette Florence Ridd-Jones [1974] Director; Stuart Benjamin Ridd-Jones [1972] Director

Mintun 3 Limited
Incorporated: 9 January 2003
Net Worth: £153,975,008 *Total Assets:* £180,032,992
Registered Office: Unit 19 Redbrook Business Park, Wilthorpe Road, Barnsley, S Yorks, S75 1JN
Activities: Activities of head offices
Parent: Mintun 2 Limited
Officers: Peter Assinder [1971] Strategic Sales & Technology Director; Michael Joseph Napoletano [1967] Director/Manager [American]

Mira Land Limited
Incorporated: 18 May 2011
Net Worth: £3,989,000 *Total Assets:* £20,838,000
Registered Office: Mira Land Limited, Watling Street, Nuneaton, Warwicks, CV10 0TU
Activities: Other letting and operating of own or leased real estate
Parent: Horiba Mira Certification Limited
Officers: Timothy Nathan, Secretary; George Thompson Gillespie [1963] Director/Chief Executive Officer; Timothy Paul Nathan [1969] Finance Director

Mira Technology Park Limited
Incorporated: 14 January 2014
Previous: Mira 2014 Limited
Net Worth: £16,750,000 *Total Assets:* £45,775,000
Registered Office: Mira, Watling Street, Nuneaton, Warwicks, CV10 0TU
Activities: Other letting and operating of own or leased real estate
Officers: Timothy Nathan, Secretary; George Thompson Gillespie [1963] Director; Andrew Edward Douglas MacDonald [1966] Director; Timothy Nathan [1969] Director; Terry Spall [1962] Director

Mirza (UK) Limited
Incorporated: 23 March 1993 *Employees:* 19
Net Worth: £8,155,668 *Total Assets:* £21,782,240
Registered Office: Mirza House, Sherbourne Drive, Tilbrook, Milton Keynes, Bucks, MK7 8HY
Activities: Wholesale of clothing and footwear
Parent: Tilbrook Enterprise Limited
Officers: Anwarul Habib, Secretary; Anwarul Habib [1977] Director; Sabiha Hussain [1960] Director/Bookkeeper; Rashid Ahmed Mirza [1957] Director [Indian]; Tauseef Mirza [1969] Director [Indian]; Paul Jason Mugglestone [1968] Sales & Marketing Director

Mission Resources Group Limited
Incorporated: 22 June 2007
Previous: Mission Recycling Limited
Net Worth: £8,129,517 *Total Assets:* £10,199,571
Registered Office: Barclays Bank Chambers, Bridge Street, Stratford upon Avon, Warwicks, CV37 6AH
Activities: Activities of head offices
Major Shareholder: Nicholas Clark Spencer
Officers: Jodie Spencer, Secretary; Nicholas Clark Spencer [1970] Director

Mistral Capital Management Limited
Incorporated: 2 September 2008
Net Worth: £55,120 *Total Assets:* £9,122,302
Registered Office: Office 2-02, 1st Floor, The Business Resource Network, 53 Whateleys Drive, Kenilworth, Warwicks, CV8 2GY
Activities: Non-specialised wholesale trade
Officers: Leyya Djoma [1979] Director

Mistras Group Limited
Incorporated: 17 October 1983 *Employees:* 216
Net Worth: £14,256,000 *Total Assets:* £18,807,000
Registered Office: 1 Dillington, Great Staughton, St Neots, Cambs, PE19 5DH
Activities: Other professional, scientific and technical activities n.e.c.
Parent: Mistras Group Inc.
Officers: Mark Timothy Wilkins, Secretary; Mehdi Batel [1977] Director [French]; Timothy Peter Bradshaw [1976] Director; Kenneth Barclay Bruce [1962] Delivery Director; Nicola Diane McGlynn [1969] Director; Sotirios Vahaviolos [1946] Director/President Physical Acoustics Corporation [American]; Timothy Martin Walsh [1962] Director; Jonathon Richard Watson [1975] Director; Mark Timothy Wilkins [1962] Director/Chartered Accountant

Miswa Chemicals Limited
Incorporated: 13 August 1981 *Employees:* 69
Net Worth: £6,175,435 *Total Assets:* £11,790,007
Registered Office: Caswell Road, Brackmills, Northampton, NN4 7PW
Activities: Manufacture of other chemical products n.e.c.
Major Shareholder: Swati Patel-Champion
Officers: Swati Patel Champion, Secretary; Ratilal Rambhai Patel [1927] Director/Financial Consultant; Swati Patel Champion [1958] Director/Pharmacy Technician

Mitchell Diesel Limited
Incorporated: 2 August 1974 *Employees:* 170
Net Worth: £9,379,675 *Total Assets:* £15,119,251
Registered Office: Fulwood Road South, Sutton in Ashfield, Notts, NG17 2JZ
Activities: Repair of other equipment
Parent: Turner & Co (Glasgow) Ltd
Officers: Darren David Hill [1970] Aftermarket Sales Director; Graham Bruce Knox [1967] Director/Engineer; Dean Paul Mansell [1975] Director; Alan Gerard Turner [1965] Director/Engineer

MK Battery International Limited
Incorporated: 28 November 2001 *Employees:* 24
Net Worth: £20,612,884 *Total Assets:* £22,060,096
Registered Office: 93 Headlands, Kettering, Northants, NN15 6BL
Activities: Manufacture of batteries and accumulators
Officers: Heather Jan Scanlon, Secretary; Bruce Cole [1962] Director [American]; Christopher Edward Pruitt [1962] Director/President [American]; Heather Jan Scanlon [1955] Director/VP Finance [American]; Mark Gregory Wels [1953] Director/Business Manager [American]

ML UK Holding Limited
Incorporated: 1 August 1934
Previous: Marley Limited
Net Worth: £84,514,000 *Total Assets:* £254,008,992
Registered Office: c/o Etex (Exteriors) UK Limited, Wellington Road, Burton on Trent, Staffs, DE14 2AP
Activities: Activities of head offices
Parent: E M Holdings UK Limited
Officers: Jayne Arkell [1974] Director/Country Manager UK; Xavier Georges Roger Janin [1969] Director/General Manager [French]

MM (UK) Limited
Incorporated: 4 September 2002 *Employees:* 313
Net Worth: £21,561,596 *Total Assets:* £74,536,256
Registered Office: Frans House, Fenton Way, Chatteris, Cambs, PE16 6UP
Activities: Wholesale of fruit and vegetables
Parent: Munoz Group Ltd
Officers: Fernando Juan de Lucas Lopez [1973] Director [Spanish]; David John Haresign [1963] Director; Jonathan Michael Hedge [1964] Director; Ian Duncan MacIntyre [1954] Director; Alvaro Munoz Beraza [1966] Director [Spanish]; Philip Scott Whelan [1974] Director

MM Flowers Limited
Incorporated: 4 February 2006 *Employees:* 146
Net Worth: £917,341 *Total Assets:* £15,242,891
Registered Office: APS Enterprise Campus, Alconbury Weald, Huntingdon, Cambs, PE28 4YA
Activities: Wholesale of flowers and plants
Shareholders: Munoz-Elite Flowers Ltd; Millhouse Limited
Officers: David Michael Johnson [1968] Director; Andrew James Kirkham [1968] Director; Juan Carlos Madrinan [1969] Director [Colombian]; Alonso Paredes [1958] Director/Lawyer [Colombian]; Philip Scott Whelan [1974] Managing Director; Colin Malcolm Williamson [1972] Director

MMR Research Worldwide Limited
Incorporated: 19 March 2001 *Employees:* 142
Net Worth: £9,790,085 *Total Assets:* £18,160,790
Registered Office: Wallingford House, 46 High Street, Wallingford, Oxon, OX10 0DB
Activities: Market research and public opinion polling
Major Shareholder: David Marshall Hall Thomson
Officers: Christopher Rogers, Secretary; Dr Louisa Kathryn Griffiths [1973] Director/Research Developer; Matthew Lintern [1973] Director Market Research; Christopher Rogers [1966] Director; Seshagiri Sondur [1982] Finance Director; Prof David Marshall Hall Thomson [1954] Director

Mobica Bidco Limited
Incorporated: 23 September 2015 *Employees:* 6
Net Worth Deficit: £458,272 *Total Assets:* £53,055,616
Registered Office: Crown House, Manchester Road, Wilmslow, Cheshire, SK9 1BH
Activities: Other service activities n.e.c.
Parent: Mobica Holdings Limited
Officers: Jonathan Braddock Clayton [1958] Director; Andrew Neil Collis [1980] Director/Chief Financial Officer; Catherine Allingham Richards [1973] Director/Investment Professional; Nicholas Leet Stammers [1963] Director; James Wigglesworth [1986] Director; Simon John Wilkinson [1965] Director

Mobica Holdings Limited
Incorporated: 21 September 2015 *Employees:* 1,102
Net Worth: £2,710,197 *Total Assets:* £60,203,652
Registered Office: Crown House, Manchester Road, Wilmslow, Cheshire, SK9 1BH
Activities: Other service activities n.e.c.
Shareholder: Nicholas Leet Stammers
Officers: Jonathan Braddock Clayton [1958] Director; Andrew Neil Collis [1980] Director/Chief Financial Officer; Catherine Allingham Richards [1973] Director/Investment Professional; Nicholas Leet Stammers [1963] Director; James Wigglesworth [1986] Director; Simon John Wilkinson [1965] Director

Mobica Limited
Incorporated: 2 July 2004 *Employees:* 1,096
Net Worth: £15,500,413 *Total Assets:* £20,385,598
Registered Office: Crown House, Manchester Road, Wilmslow, Cheshire, SK9 1BH
Activities: Ready-made interactive leisure and entertainment software development
Parent: Mobica Bidco Limited
Officers: Nicholas Leet Stammers, Secretary; James Alexander Carroll [1971] Director; Jonathan Braddock Clayton [1958] Director; Andrew Neil Collis [1980] Director/Chief Financial Officer; Nicholas Leet Stammers [1963] Director; Simon John Wilkinson [1965] Director

Mobius Motors Limited
Incorporated: 2 September 2010
Net Worth: £9,684,722 *Total Assets:* £9,684,722
Registered Office: Cliffe Barn, Church Lane, Tideswell, Derbys, SK17 8PD
Activities: Manufacture of motor vehicles
Shareholders: Ronald Lauder; Richard Parsons
Officers: Joel Alexander Jackson [1985] Director

Mogford Hotels Limited
Incorporated: 18 May 1998 *Employees:* 101
Net Worth: £4,713,715 *Total Assets:* £11,084,442
Registered Office: 36 St Giles, Oxford, OX1 3LD
Activities: Hotels and similar accommodation
Officers: Elaine Rosalie Shelver, Secretary; Hilary Jane Mogford [1948] Director; Jeremy Lewis Mogford [1947] Director/Restaurateur & Hotelier

Mogford Limited
Incorporated: 29 January 1987 *Employees:* 202
Net Worth: £9,464,530 *Total Assets:* £21,800,748
Registered Office: 36 St Giles, Oxford, OX1 3LD
Activities: Hotels and similar accommodation
Shareholders: Hilary Jane Mogford; Jeremy Lewis Mogford
Officers: Elaine Rosalie Shelver, Secretary; Hilary Jane Mogford [1948] Director; Jeremy Lewis Mogford [1947] Director

Molson Compact Equipment Limited
Incorporated: 19 September 2003 *Employees:* 20
Previous: A & Y Equipment Limited
Net Worth: £9,562,251 *Total Assets:* £18,406,220
Registered Office: Bearley, Stratford upon Avon, Warwicks, CV37 0TY
Activities: Wholesale of mining, construction and civil engineering machinery
Parent: A & Y Equipment Group Ltd
Officers: Robert Stephen Brown [1960] Managing Director; Robin Nicholas Powell [1969] Director; Jonathan Mark Wilson [1966] Director

Molson Coors (UK) Holdings LLP
Incorporated: 20 March 2007 *Employees:* 2
Net Worth: £1,409,360,000 *Total Assets:* £1,409,360,000
Registered Office: 137 High Street, Burton on Trent, Staffs, DE14 1JZ

Molson Coors Brewing Company (UK) Limited
Incorporated: 3 March 1888 *Employees:* 1,993
Net Worth: £332,433,984 *Total Assets:* £878,267,008
Registered Office: 137 High Street, Burton on Trent, Staffs, DE14 1JZ
Activities: Manufacture of beer
Parent: Molson Coors Holdings Limited
Officers: Kristin Wolfe, Secretary; Simon Kerry [1970] Director; James Christian Shearer [1980] Marketing Director; Philip Mark Whitehead [1977] Director

Molson Coors Holdings Limited
Incorporated: 13 January 1888
Net Worth: £535,775,008 *Total Assets:* £602,753,984
Registered Office: 137 High Street, Burton on Trent, Staffs, DE14 1JZ
Activities: Other business support service activities n.e.c.
Parent: Golden Acquisition
Officers: Susan Albion [1972] Director/Lawyer; David Alexander Heede [1961] Director; Simon Kerry [1970] Director; Philip Mark Whitehead [1977] Director

Monarch Healthcare Limited
Incorporated: 6 July 1992 *Employees:* 235
Net Worth: £5,519,777 *Total Assets:* £12,422,498
Registered Office: Clifton Manor Care Home, Rivergreen, Clifton, Nottingham, NG11 8AW
Activities: Other human health activities
Parent: Macbeth 49 Limited
Officers: Angela Bir, Secretary/Director; Angela Bir [1962] Director; Hiten Shanghavi [1966] Director/Self Employed

Monarch Knitting Machinery (U.K.) Limited
Incorporated: 4 April 1968 *Employees:* 46
Net Worth: £12,741,181 *Total Assets:* £22,452,356
Registered Office: 47 Friar Lane, Leicester, LE1 5QX
Activities: Wholesale of machinery for the textile industry and of sewing and knitting machines
Officers: David John Brunton [1961] Managing Director; Craig Daniel Pernick [1986] Director [American]

Mondi Scunthorpe Limited
Incorporated: 5 September 1979 *Employees:* 141
Net Worth Deficit: £8,482,391 *Total Assets:* £12,075,195
Registered Office: Roxburgh House, Clayfield Road, Foxhills Industrial Estate, Scunthorpe, N Lincs, DN15 8QJ
Activities: Manufacture of plastic packing goods
Parent: Mondi Investments Limited
Officers: Alyson Jayne Wiltshire, Secretary; Sandor Kardos [1970] Director [German]; Allan Martin Lock [1970] Director

Mondottica Limited
Incorporated: 31 July 2001 *Employees:* 114
Net Worth: £484,000 *Total Assets:* £23,438,000
Registered Office: Michael House, Riverside Business Park, Rennie Hogg Road, Nottingham, NG2 1RX
Activities: Non-specialised wholesale trade
Major Shareholder: Michael Roy Jardine
Officers: Keith Wragg, Secretary; Michael Roy Jardine [1953] Director/Trader [Canadian]; David James Ravencroft [1973] Director

Monier (China) Holdings Limited
Incorporated: 31 December 1976
Net Worth: £22,673,000 *Total Assets:* £23,212,000
Registered Office: BMI House, 2 Pitfield, Kiln Farm, Milton Keynes, Bucks, MK11 3LW
Activities: Activities of head offices
Parent: Braas Monier Building Group Holding SA
Officers: Jason John Bradley, Secretary; Thomas Joseph Anderson [1956] Director/Chief Operating Officer [American]; Jason John Bradley [1963] Director/Accountant; Dr Johannes Georg Schmidt-Schultes [1966] Director/Chief Financial Officer [German]

Monier (UK) Holdings Limited
Incorporated: 7 March 1996 *Employees:* 3
Net Worth: £77,004,000 *Total Assets:* £152,170,000
Registered Office: BMI House, 2 Pitfield, Kiln Farm, Milton Keynes, Bucks, MK11 3LW
Activities: Activities of head offices
Officers: Jason John Bradley [1963] Director/Accountant; Andrew John Dennis [1965] Managing Director; Alfons Horn [1970] Managing Director [German]; Klaus Sonne Ravn [1966] Finance Director [Danish]

Monier Redland Limited
Incorporated: 2 April 1946 *Employees:* 480
Net Worth: £65,581,000 *Total Assets:* £79,748,000
Registered Office: BMI House, 2 Pitfield, Kiln Farm, Milton Keynes, Bucks, MK11 3LW
Activities: Manufacture of concrete products for construction purposes
Parent: Braas Monier Building Group Holding SA
Officers: Graham Roy Barlow [1981] HR Director; Jason John Bradley [1963] Director/Accountant; Andrew John Dennis [1965] Sales Director; Alfons Horn [1970] Managing Director [German]; Klaus Sonne Ravn [1966] Finance Director [Danish]

Monocon International Refractories Limited
Incorporated: 23 October 1973 *Employees:* 68
Net Worth: £12,569,152 *Total Assets:* £22,804,108
Registered Office: Denaby Main Industrial Estate, Denaby Lane, Old Denaby, Doncaster, S Yorks, DN12 4LQ
Activities: Manufacture of refractory products
Parent: IFGL Monocon Holding Limited
Officers: Dheeraj Parakh, Secretary; Mihir Prakash Bajoria [1985] Director [Indian]; David Andrew Harris [1955] Director; Dr Paul Myers [1973] Technical Director; Dheeraj Parakh [1978] Director/Accountant; Mark Allan Payne [1961] Sales Director; Manoj Rakhecha [1977] Commercial Director [Indian]

Monocon Overseas Limited
Incorporated: 15 May 1997 *Employees:* 3
Net Worth: £7,008,282 *Total Assets:* £9,008,282
Registered Office: Monocon Office, Davy Road, Old Denaby, Doncaster, S Yorks, DN12 4LQ
Activities: Non-trading company
Parent: Monocon International Refractories Limited
Officers: Dheeraj Parakh, Secretary; Mihir Prakash Bajoria [1985] Director [Indian]; Dheeraj Parakh [1978] Director/Chartered Accountant; Manoj Rakhecha [1977] Director [Indian]

Monoworld Recycling Ltd
Incorporated: 23 July 2007 *Employees:* 37
Net Worth: £2,638,203 *Total Assets:* £9,241,187
Registered Office: 180 Irchester Road, Rushden, Northants, NN10 9QU
Activities: Treatment and disposal of non-hazardous waste
Parent: Monoworld Group PLC
Officers: Christopher O'Farrell [1971] Director; Michael Wykes [1954] Director

Monro Limited
Incorporated: 13 July 1984 *Employees:* 45
Net Worth: £6,414,234 *Total Assets:* £10,537,873
Registered Office: Interlink Way South, Interlink Park, Bardon, Coalville, Leicester, LE67 1PG
Activities: Wholesale of other intermediate products
Major Shareholder: Melvyn Coupland
Officers: Sharon Theresa Hurst, Secretary; Melvyn Coupland [1949] Managing Director; Matthew Sibson [1973] Sales Development Director

Montracon Limited
Incorporated: 21 March 1963 *Employees:* 526
Net Worth: £4,439,247 *Total Assets:* £53,875,076
Registered Office: Carr Hill, Doncaster, S Yorks, DN4 8DE
Activities: Manufacture of trailers and semi-trailers
Parent: Ballyvesey Holding Limited
Officers: Mark David Kidney, Secretary; Philip Ashton [1968] Sales Director; Mark David Kidney [1975] Director/Chartered Management Accountant; Colin John Hugh Montgomery [1976] Director; Harold Hugh Montgomery [1948] Director/Haulier

Montsaye Community Learning Partnership
Incorporated: 15 June 2011 *Employees:* 522
Net Worth: £23,508,000 *Total Assets:* £27,664,000
Registered Office: Montsaye Community Learning Partnership, Greening Road, Rothwell, Kettering, Northants, NN14 6BB
Activities: Primary education
Officers: Peter Charles Leaver, Secretary; Alan Bindley [1962] Director/Bank Manager; Craig Martin Charteris [1975] Director/Headteacher; Adrian Clifford Cummings [1953] Director; Ann Davey [1961] Director/Headteacher; Jill Anne Moore [1947] Director/Retired; Lisa Ellen Pruden [1979] Director/Self Employed; Dawn Simpson Lane [1969] HR Director

Moorcroft Debt Recovery Limited
Incorporated: 2 March 1983
Net Worth: £13,788,733 *Total Assets:* £23,637,828
Registered Office: Moorcroft House, No 2 Spring Gardens, Stockport, Cheshire, SK1 4AA
Activities: Financial intermediation not elsewhere classified
Parent: Moorcroft Group PLC
Officers: Andrew James McRoberts, Secretary; Amanda Martin McRoberts [1970] Director; Andrew James McRoberts [1965] Director; Neil George McRoberts [1943] Director; Rodney Neil McRoberts [1967] Director

Moorcroft Group Public Limited Company
Incorporated: 3 March 1983 *Employees:* 469
Net Worth: £14,427,895 *Total Assets:* £27,668,094
Registered Office: Moorcroft House, No 2 Spring Gardens, Stockport, Cheshire, SK1 4AA
Activities: Financial intermediation not elsewhere classified
Major Shareholder: Neil George McRoberts
Officers: Andrew James McRoberts, Secretary; Amanda Martin-McRoberts [1970] Director; Andrew James McRoberts [1965] Director; Neil George McRoberts [1943] Director; Rodney Neil McRoberts [1967] Director

J.H. Moore & Son (Rickmansworth) Limited
Incorporated: 22 March 1960 *Employees:* 105
Net Worth: £15,576,829 *Total Assets:* £18,854,728
Registered Office: Moore Large & Co Ltd, Sinfin Industrial Estate, Sinfin Lane, Derby, DE24 9GL
Activities: Activities of head offices
Parent: Christine Moore and Nigel Moore as Trustees of The Trustees of The Moore Family Settlement 1997
Officers: Zillah Caunt, Secretary; Stephen John Caunt [1959] Finance Director; Christine Moore [1935] Director; Nigel Robert Moore [1961] Director; Timothy John Moore [1960] Director

William F.Moore (Warplands) Limited
Incorporated: 30 March 1948 *Employees:* 9
Net Worth: £6,865,268 *Total Assets:* £9,540,275
Registered Office: Fleet House Farm, West Butterwick, Scunthorpe, N Lincs, DN17 3JZ
Activities: Growing of cereals (except rice), leguminous crops and oil seeds
Shareholders: David James Moore; Christopher William Moore
Officers: Christina Mary Moore, Secretary; Christopher William Moore [1960] Director/Farmer; David James Moore [1962] Director/Farmer

Moore Large & Co. Limited
Incorporated: 14 March 1974 *Employees:* 105
Net Worth: £14,984,550 *Total Assets:* £18,854,628
Registered Office: Grampian Buildings, Sinfin Lane Industrial Estate, Sinfin Lane, Derby, DE24 9GL
Activities: Operation of warehousing and storage facilities for land transport activities
Officers: Cathy Moore, Secretary; Adam Biggs [1987] Sales Director; Stephen John Caunt [1959] Finance Director; Adam Garner [1987] Brand Director; Nigel Robert Moore [1961] Director; Timothy Moore [1960] Director; Paul Stewart [1964] Director Cycle Sales; Dale Harrison Vanderplank [1973] Director

Moorhen Holdings Limited
Incorporated: 18 April 2000 *Employees:* 57
Net Worth: £22,651,286 *Total Assets:* £28,197,070
Registered Office: Moorhen Holdings Limited, Mansfied Road, Bramley Vale, Chesterfield, Derbys, S44 5GA
Activities: Non-trading company
Officers: Angela Suzanne Hunt, Secretary; Peter Anderson Hunt [1960] Director

Moran Commercials Ltd
Incorporated: 2 July 2013
Net Worth: £2,231,827 *Total Assets:* £13,079,936
Registered Office: Moran House, Arundel Avenue, Castle Donington, Derbys, DE74 2HJ
Activities: Renting and leasing of trucks and other heavy vehicles
Major Shareholder: Harry Peter Moran
Officers: Harry Peter Moran [1964] Director

William Morgan Group Limited
Incorporated: 18 October 1996 *Employees:* 319
Net Worth: £3,848,350 *Total Assets:* £59,397,992
Registered Office: Bedford Road, Northampton, NN1 5SZ
Activities: Sale of new cars and light motor vehicles
Shareholders: Christian William Le Fevre; Martin Huw Morgan Allard
Officers: Martin Huw Morgan Allard [1967] Director; Terence George Bramall [1942] Director; Christian William Le Fevre [1967] Director

Morgan Industrial Properties Limited
Incorporated: 5 November 1986 *Employees:* 5
Net Worth: £56,364,880 *Total Assets:* £63,117,560
Registered Office: Alfreton Road, Derby, DE2 4AP
Activities: Development of building projects
Shareholders: Neil John Morgan; Philip David Morgan; Robert Frederick Morgan
Officers: Philip David Morgan, Secretary; George Morgan [1931] Director/Electronics Production Engineer; Julie Morgan [1960] Director; Neil John Morgan [1958] Director/Electronics Engineer; Philip David Morgan [1961] Director/Electronics Engineer; Robert Frederick Morgan [1968] Director/Electronics Production Engineer

Morgana Holdings Limited
Incorporated: 26 April 2011 *Employees:* 78
Net Worth: £6,858,683 *Total Assets:* £11,022,249
Registered Office: Morgana House, Davy Avenue, Knowlhill, Milton Keynes, Bucks, MK5 8HJ
Activities: Activities of head offices
Major Shareholder: Salvatore Grimaldi
Officers: Salvatore Grimaldi [1945] Director [Swedish]; Jan Marstorp [1963] Director [Swedish]; Ola Lars Erik Nilsson [1975] Director/VP Finance [Swedish]

Morgana Systems Limited
Incorporated: 25 October 1977 *Employees:* 78
Net Worth: £6,858,683 *Total Assets:* £11,022,249
Registered Office: Morgana House, Davy Avenue, Knowlhill, Milton Keynes, Bucks, MK5 8HJ
Activities: Manufacture of other special-purpose machinery n.e.c.
Officers: Salvatore Grimaldi [1945] Director [Swedish]; Jan Marstorp [1963] Director [Swedish]; Ola Lars Erik Nilsson [1975] Director/VP Finance [Swedish]

Mori Lee Europe Limited
Incorporated: 4 March 1999 *Employees:* 17
Net Worth: £6,601,616 *Total Assets:* £11,601,387
Registered Office: Unit 5 Northgate Terrace, Northern Road, Newark, Notts, NG24 2EU
Activities: Wholesale of clothing and footwear
Parent: Mori Lee LLC
Officers: Graham Paul Connell, Secretary

Moriah House Limited
Incorporated: 13 January 2005 *Employees:* 161
Net Worth: £5,057,320 *Total Assets:* £12,473,141
Registered Office: The Tax Partnership, 2 Cheapside, Derby, DE1 1BR
Activities: Residential care activities for the elderly and disabled
Major Shareholder: Paul Hearn
Officers: Paul Hearn [1962] Director/Care Home Owner [Irish]

Morningside Holdings Ltd
Incorporated: 15 December 2015 *Employees:* 4
Net Worth: £15,686,100 *Total Assets:* £15,713,345
Registered Office: The Oval, 57 New Walk, Leicester, LE1 7EA
Activities: Activities of other holding companies n.e.c.
Officers: Danesh Vinodkumar Gadhia [1965] Director; Mira Gadhia [1980] Director; Sanjay Kishan Gadhia [1978] Director; Sonal Danesh Gadhia [1969] Director

Morningside Pharmaceuticals Limited
Incorporated: 18 December 1991 *Employees:* 50
Net Worth: £6,005,035 *Total Assets:* £20,841,896
Registered Office: Nene House, 4 Rushmills, Northampton, NN4 7YB
Activities: Manufacture of pharmaceutical preparations
Parent: Remedi Medical Holdings Limited
Officers: Monisha Nikesh Kotecha, Secretary; Monisha Nikesh Kotecha [1969] Director; Dr Nikesh Rasiklal Kotecha [1966] Director

Morpeth II Limited
Incorporated: 31 October 2005
Net Worth: £10,142,101 *Total Assets:* £32,792,272
Registered Office: Dransfield House, 2 Fox Valley Way, Fox Valley, Sheffield, S36 2AB
Activities: Other letting and operating of own or leased real estate
Parent: Austin Dransfield Morpeth Ltd
Officers: Steven Burgess, Secretary; Mark Dransfield [1962] Director; Steven John Stead [1978] Director

Morphy Richards Limited
Incorporated: 16 December 1959 *Employees:* 219
Net Worth: £42,110,000 *Total Assets:* £82,365,000
Registered Office: Mexborough, S Yorks, S64 8AJ
Activities: Wholesale of radio, television goods & electrical household appliances (other than records, tapes, CDs)
Officers: Fergal Naughton, Secretary; Donal Francis Flynn [1973] Director/Chartered Accountant [Irish]; Fergal John Naughton [1975] Director [Irish]; Martin Lawrence Naughton [1939] Director [Irish]; Victoria Louise Philemon [1972] Managing Director

Morrells Farming Limited
Incorporated: 21 August 2001 *Employees:* 6
Net Worth: £4,679,476 *Total Assets:* £19,940,550
Registered Office: Sandford Common, Sandford St Martin, Chipping Norton, Oxon, OX7 7AE
Activities: Growing of cereals (except rice), leguminous crops and oil seeds
Parent: Morrells Holdings Limited
Officers: Jonathan Rupert Blakiston Lovegrove Fielden, Secretary; Anne Catherine Ballard [1949] Director/Office Manager; Jonathan Rupert Blakiston Lovegrove Fielden [1949] Director/Chartered Surveyor; Dr David George James Morrell [1959] Director/Farmer

Morrells Holdings Limited
Incorporated: 8 April 1943 *Employees:* 7
Net Worth: £26,826,024 *Total Assets:* £33,124,520
Registered Office: Sandford Common Farm, Sandford Common, Sandford St Martin, Chipping Norton, Oxon, OX7 7AE
Activities: Activities of head offices
Officers: Jonathan Rupert Blakiston Lovegrove-Fielden, Secretary; Jonathan Rupert Blakiston Lovegrove-Fielden [1949] Director/Chartered Surveyor; Dr David George James Morrell [1959] Director/Researcher; Richard Harry Wells [1953] Director

Morris Group Limited
Incorporated: 27 January 2004 *Employees:* 256
Net Worth: £128,005,000 *Total Assets:* £421,991,008
Registered Office: Morland House, Altrincham Road, Wilmslow, Cheshire, SK9 5NW
Activities: Activities of head offices
Officers: Joanne Iddon, Secretary; Michael Norman Carruthers [1980] Director; Arthur Derrey [1989] Director [French]; Martin Paul Edmunds [1961] Director; Michael John Gaskell [1962] Director/Chartered Accountant; David Peter Hesson [1972] Director; Joanne Iddon [1969] Director/Accountant; Bernard Robert Norman [1941] Director; Andrew Marmaduke Lane Tuckey [1943] Director

Morris Homes (Midlands) Limited
Incorporated: 28 September 1922 *Employees:* 70
Net Worth: £16,700,000 *Total Assets:* £171,006,000
Registered Office: Morland House, Altrincham Road, Wilmslow, Cheshire, SK9 5NW
Activities: Construction of domestic buildings
Officers: Joanne Iddon, Secretary; Martin Paul Edmunds [1961] Director; Michael John Gaskell [1962] Director/Chartered Accountant; David Peter Hesson [1972] Director; Joanne Iddon [1969] Director/Accountant

Morris Homes (North) Limited
Incorporated: 25 March 1964 *Employees:* 108
Net Worth: £110,824,000 *Total Assets:* £325,529,984
Registered Office: Morland House, Altrincham Road, Wilmslow, Cheshire, SK9 5NW
Activities: Construction of domestic buildings
Officers: Joanne Iddon, Secretary; Martin Paul Edmunds [1961] Land Director; Michael John Gaskell [1962] Director/Chartered Accountant; David Peter Hesson [1972] Director; Joanne Iddon [1969] Director/Accountant

Morris Homes Limited
Incorporated: 7 July 1998 *Employees:* 256
Net Worth: £175,852,000 *Total Assets:* £513,183,008
Registered Office: Morland House, Altrincham Road, Wilmslow, Cheshire, SK9 5NW
Activities: Construction of domestic buildings
Officers: Joanne Iddon, Secretary; Martin Paul Edmunds [1961] Land Director; Michael John Gaskell [1962] Director/Chartered Accountant; David Peter Hesson [1972] Director; Joanne Iddon [1969] Director/Accountant

Mortgage Advice Bureau (Holdings) PLC
Incorporated: 28 December 2000 *Employees:* 157
Net Worth: £18,166,000 *Total Assets:* £36,101,000
Registered Office: Capital House, Pride Place, Pride Park, Derby, DE24 8QR
Activities: Activities of head offices
Shareholder: Peter Steven Christopher Brodnicki
Officers: Lucy Claire Tilley, Secretary; Peter Christopher Steven Brodnicki [1962] Director/Chief Executive; Nathan James McLean Imlach [1969] Director; Katherine Christina Mary Innes Ker [1960] Director; M David Robert Preece [1960] Director; Stephen Charles Addison Smith [1957] Director; Benjamin David Thompson [1969] Managing Director; Lucy Claire Tilley [1971] Finance Director

Mortgage Advice Bureau Limited
Incorporated: 9 May 1997 *Employees:* 157
Net Worth: £5,263,923 *Total Assets:* £29,914,120
Registered Office: Capital House, Pride Place, Pride Park, Derby, DE24 8QR
Activities: Financial intermediation not elsewhere classified
Parent: Mortgage Advice Bureau (Holdings) PLC
Officers: Lucy Claire Tilley, Secretary; Peter Christopher Steven Brodnicki [1962] Director/Chief Executive; M David Robert Preece [1960] Director; Benjamin David Thompson [1969] Managing Director; Lucy Claire Tilley [1971] Finance Director

Mortons Media Group Ltd
Incorporated: 30 November 1998 *Employees:* 217
Net Worth: £5,771,002 *Total Assets:* £10,676,518
Registered Office: Media Centre, Morton Way, Horncastle, Lincs, LN9 6JR
Activities: Publishing of consumer and business journals and periodicals
Officers: Kathryn Alexandra Pinder, Secretary; Ian David Fisher [1966] Director; Nigel Hole [1977] Director; Kathryn Alexandra Pinder [1966] Director/Chartered Accountant; Andrew Paul Savage [1966] Director; Angela Mary Spencer [1965] Director; Steven Michael Wickwar [1968] Director

Mortons of Horncastle Limited
Incorporated: 7 August 1947 *Employees:* 217
Net Worth: £16,630,840 *Total Assets:* £21,081,548
Registered Office: Newspaper House, Morton Way, Horncastle, Lincs, LN9 6JR
Activities: Publishing of consumer and business journals and periodicals
Officers: Kathryn Alexandra Pinder, Secretary; Ian David Fisher [1966] Director; Helen Elizabeth Harness [1968] Director; Kathryn Alexandra Pinder [1966] Director/Chartered Accountant; Jean Mary Sharpe [1942] Director/Printer; Philip Howard Sharpe [1944] Director/Journalist; Angela Mary Spencer [1965] Director

Mosdorfer CCL Systems Limited
Incorporated: 5 September 1988 *Employees:* 39
Net Worth: £9,313,342 *Total Assets:* £14,459,424
Registered Office: Industrial Estate, Market Overton, Oakham, Rutland, LE15 7PP
Activities: Manufacture of metal structures and parts of structures
Parent: Knill Energy Holdings GmbH
Officers: John Leslie Morris, Secretary; Christian Knill [1970] Director [Austrian]; John Leslie Morris [1958] Managing Director

E. Moss, Limited
Incorporated: 27 March 1934
Net Worth: £14,423,000 *Total Assets:* £14,700,000
Registered Office: 1 Thane Road West, Nottingham, NG2 3AA
Activities: Other business support service activities n.e.c.
Parent: Alliance Boots Holdings Limited
Officers: Andrew Richard Thompson, Secretary; Michael David Snape [1979] Director/Chief Financial Officer; Andrew Richard Thompson [1975] Director/Solicitor

Motan Colortronic Limited
Incorporated: 28 October 2009 *Employees:* 30
Net Worth: £6,776,284 *Total Assets:* £11,133,702
Registered Office: Matilda House, Carrwood Road, Chesterfield, Derbys, S41 9QB
Activities: Installation of industrial machinery and equipment
Parent: Colortronic (UK) Limited
Officers: Ulrich Eberhardt [1954] Director [German]; Erwin Karl Miller [1944] Director; Karl Robert Miller [1966] Director

Motherwell Bridge Limited
Incorporated: 13 May 2008 *Employees:* 243
Net Worth: £24,915,000 *Total Assets:* £46,987,000
Registered Office: Building 2, Fields End Business Park, Davey Road, Thurnscoe, Goldthorpe, Rotherham, S Yorks, S63 0JF
Activities: Other specialised construction activities n.e.c.
Parent: Cape Industrial Services Group Limited
Officers: Jane Victoria Atkinson [1971] Director; Simon Angus Hicks [1968] Director; John Anthony Meade Walsh [1964] Finance Director

Moto Direct Holdings Limited
Incorporated: 22 October 2001 *Employees:* 83
Net Worth: £7,830,309 *Total Assets:* £13,817,671
Registered Office: Euro House, The Nursery, 1 Wincobank Way, South Normanton, Derbys, DE55 2FX
Activities: Dormant company
Shareholder: Deborah Margaret Bullock
Officers: Roland Bullock, Secretary; Terry Birtles [1972] Director; Deborah Margaret Bullock [1960] Managing Director; Stuart Edward Davis [1974] Director; John Robert Swinbank [1962] Supply Chain Director; Johnathan Paul Towers [1965] Director

Moto Direct Limited
Incorporated: 16 March 2000 *Employees:* 83
Net Worth: £7,826,936 *Total Assets:* £13,810,855
Registered Office: Euro House, The Nursery, 1 Wincobank Way, South Normanton, Derbys, DE55 2FX
Activities: Wholesale of clothing and footwear
Shareholder: Deborah Margaret Bullock
Officers: Roland Bullock, Secretary; Terry Birtles [1972] Director; Deborah Margaret Bullock [1960] Managing Director; Stuart Edward Davis [1974] Financial Director; John Robert Swinbank [1962] Supply Chain Director; Jonathan Paul Towers [1966] Sales Director

Motor Insurers' Bureau
Incorporated: 14 June 1946 *Employees:* 519
Total Assets: £2,400,355,072
Registered Office: Linford Wood House, 6-12 Capital Drive, Linford Wood, Milton Keynes, Bucks, MK14 6XT
Activities: Other business support service activities n.e.c.
Officers: Wendy Budd, Secretary; Dr Jacob Abboud [1960] Director/Chief Information Officer; Simon Paul Baker [1960] Director/Insurance Manager; Timothy Bishop [1966] Director/Chief Risk Officer; Rhodri Prys Charles [1975] Director/Insurance Executive; Adam James Clarke [1972] Underwriting Director; Dominic John Clayden [1966] Director of Claims; Michael Paul Crane [1968] Managing Director; Karl Helgesen [1972] Director/Chief Claims Officer, UK & International; Steven Maddock [1968] Managing Director; Gareth David McChesney [1969] Director Underwriting & Pricing

Motor Neurone Disease Association
Incorporated: 4 April 1986 *Employees:* 190
Net Worth: £10,201,000 *Total Assets:* £25,480,000
Registered Office: David Niven House, 10-15 Notre Dame Mews, Northampton, NN1 2BG
Activities: Other human health activities
Officers: Joanna Mary Darby, Secretary; Emma Adams [1967] Sales Director; Wendy Balmain [1962] Director/Civil Servant; Richard John Coleman [1943] Director; Susan Edwards [1951] Director; Alan Philip Graham [1947] Director/Retired; Timothy Charles Kidd [1965] Director/Accountant; Charlotte Jane Layton [1979] Director; Janis Ruth Parks [1951] Director/Retired; Steven Charles Parry-Hearn [1968] Director; Siobhan Rooney [1955] Director/Retired; Dr Peter Scott-Morgan [1958] Director/Retired; Dr Nikhil Sharma [1974] Director/Doctor; Dr Heather Jacqueline Louise Smith [1973] Director/Accessibility Specialist; Katharine Alexandra Styles [1967] Director/Volunteer; Janet Warren [1954] Director

Motorhog Holdings Limited
Incorporated: 7 September 2001 *Employees:* 238
Net Worth: £13,224,599 *Total Assets:* £28,846,332
Registered Office: Bentley Moor Lane, Adwick-le-Street, Doncaster, S Yorks, DN6 7BD
Activities: Activities of head offices
Parent: Hog Properties Limited
Officers: David Martin, Secretary; David Martin [1961] Director; Richard Martin [1965] Director

Motorpoint Group PLC
Incorporated: 12 April 2016 *Employees:* 755
Net Worth: £26,400,000 *Total Assets:* £138,400,000
Registered Office: Motorpoint, Chartwell Drive, West Meadows Industrial Estate, Derby, DE21 6BZ
Activities: Sale of used cars and light motor vehicles
Officers: Manjit Kaur Virk, Secretary; Mark Gwilym Carpenter [1972] Director; James Gilmour [1976] Director; Gordon Mark Hurst [1962] Director; Mary Jane McNamara [1960] Director; Mark Christopher Morris [1960] Director; David Edward Shelton [1953] Director; Stephen Andrew Weller [1972] Director

Motorpoint Limited
Incorporated: 17 December 1997 *Employees:* 755
Net Worth: £35,700,000 *Total Assets:* £147,600,000
Registered Office: Motorpoint, Chartwell Drive, West Meadows, Derby, DE21 6BZ
Activities: Other retail sale not in stores, stalls or markets
Parent: Motorpoint Group PLC
Officers: Manjit Kaur Virk, Secretary; Jonathan Baird [1977] Commercial Director; Mark Gwilym Carpenter [1972] Director; James Gilmour [1976] Finance Director

Motors (Coalville) Limited
Incorporated: 3 September 1937 *Employees:* 36
Net Worth: £5,902,288 *Total Assets:* £10,294,739
Registered Office: Park House, 37 Clarence Street, Leicester, LE1 3RW
Activities: Sale of new cars and light motor vehicles
Major Shareholder: Richard Mark Dalby
Officers: Eileen Molly Dalby, Secretary; Eileen Molly Dalby [1932] Director; Richard Mark Dalby [1961] Director/Sales Manager

Motorway Direct PLC
Incorporated: 4 July 1996 *Employees:* 141
Net Worth: £2,423,329 *Total Assets:* £10,118,439
Registered Office: Warranty House, Savile Street East, Sheffield, S4 7UQ
Activities: Activities of insurance agents and brokers
Officers: Helen Robinson, Secretary; David Antcliff [1949] Director; George Edward Higginson [1945] Director/Insurance Consultant; David Lee Pinkney [1952] Director; Frederick Donald Pinkney [1950] Director; Paul Nigel Pinkney [1956] Director/Salesman

Motorway Services Limited
Incorporated: 14 September 1959 *Employees:* 678
Net Worth: £89,656,000 *Total Assets:* £112,291,000
Registered Office: 2 Vantage Court, Tickford Street, Newport Pagnell, Bucks, MK16 9EZ
Activities: Retail sale in non-specialised stores with food, beverages or tobacco predominating
Parent: Welcome Break Limited
Officers: Joseph James Barrett [1966] Director [Irish]; Timothy Edward Lightfoot [1974] Director/Group Financial Controller

Motspa Holdings Limited
Incorporated: 10 August 1970
Net Worth: £9,558,515 *Total Assets:* £11,984,800
Registered Office: 2 Rutland Park, Sheffield, S10 2PD
Activities: Development of building projects
Officers: Abigail Kay Hartley, Secretary; Abigail Kay Hartley [1967] Director; Andrew Russell Hartley [1935] Director; Ashby Russell Hartley [1961] Director; Pamela Hartley [1936] Director

Moulsford Preparatory School Trust Limited
Incorporated: 19 December 1966 *Employees:* 84
Net Worth: £6,131,245 *Total Assets:* £9,565,906
Registered Office: Moulsford Preparatory School, Moulsford, Wallingford, Oxon, OX10 9HR
Activities: Primary education
Officers: John Robert Wyndham Wilder, Secretary; Edward Louis Agnew Boddington [1965] Director; Alexandra Elizabeth Bonney [1972] Director/Lawyer; Richard John Bussell [1966] Director/Solicitor; Gwyneth Mary Crane [1948] Director/Retired; Timothy Robert Davis [1961] Director/Accountant; Catherine Elaine Lakofski Dreyer [1967] Director/Self Employed; Justin Barron Friend [1970] Director/Marketing Manager; Thomas Julian Cadbury Garnier [1968] Director/Headmaster; Charlotte Ann Miles-Kingston [1976] Director/IT Consultant; Susan Alice Morley [1972] Director/Teacher; John Stuart Moule [1971] Director/Headmaster; Hugh Edward Mark Osmond [1962] Director; Toby William James Phelps [1973] Director; Richard Alexander Buchan Smith [1969] Director

Moulton Bulb Company Limited
Incorporated: 24 February 1964 *Employees:* 242
Net Worth: £12,595,600 *Total Assets:* £20,634,594
Registered Office: Long Lane, Moulton, Spalding, Lincs, PE12 6PP
Activities: Other processing and preserving of fruit and vegetables
Shareholders: Denis John Grimwood; Robert Henry Oldershaw Snr
Officers: Jane Roberta Ashby Cooke, Secretary; Jane Roberta Ashby Cooke [1949] Director; Alfred Richard Greetham [1962] Director/Packhouse Manager; Denis John Grimwood [1945] Director/Farmers Onion Grower; David William Hodgson [1946] Managing Director; Robert Henry Oldershaw Jnr [1979] Director/Account Manager; Robert Henry Oldershaw Snr [1952] Director/Farmer & Onion Grower; Bridgett Lucy Posey [1958] Director; Christopher Jamie Woodrow [1977] Director

Moulton School and Science College
Incorporated: 12 October 2011 *Employees:* 162
Net Worth: £16,809,012 *Total Assets:* £18,108,970
Registered Office: Moulton School and Science College, Pound Lane, Moulton, Northampton, NN3 7SD
Activities: General secondary education
Shareholders: Anne Elizabeth Jeffrey; Simon Philip Barrick; Trevor Andrew Jones
Officers: Mandy Dane, Secretary; Eric Anakwwa [1971] Director/Teacher; Frank Ashby [1960] Director/Retired; Simon Philip Barrick [1966] Director/Gas Engineer; Carol Elizabeth Coulson [1961] Director/Exams Manager; Michelle Fiona Devine [1967] Director/Money Market Dealer; Fiona Fox [1967] Director/Teacher; Karen Godfrey [1974] Director; Anne Elizabeth Jeffrey [1955] Director/PA/Audit Assistant; Trevor Andrew Jones [1965] Director/Headteacher; Emily Lile [1975] Director; Rosemary Carol Lucas [1963] Director/Chartered Accountant; Katharine Mary Mason [1976] Director; Harry Christoper Portrey [1968] Director/Headmaster; Stephen John Robinson [1966] Director/Accountant; David John Sherwood [1963] Director/Police Officer

Mount St Mary's
Incorporated: 21 July 2006 *Employees:* 191
Net Worth: £10,694,241 *Total Assets:* £16,147,785
Registered Office: Mount St Marys College, Spinkhill, Sheffield, S21 3YL
Activities: Pre-primary education
Officers: Ian Garnet Ford, Secretary; Michael Beattie [1936] Director/RC Priest; Joan Marian Bolton [1951] Director/Retired; Reverend Simon David Ellis [1968] Director/Clergy; Dr Richard David Field [1945] Director/Company Chairman; Ian Murphy [1970] Director/Headmaster; Dr Helen Mary Phillips [1966] Director/Doctor [Irish]; James Alexander Phinn [1972] Director/Commercial Lawyer; Adrian Porter [1959] Director/Jesuit Priest; William George Armstrong Shaw [1966] Director/Solicitor; Professor Martial Jean-Marie Staub [1964] Director/Professor of Medieval History [French/German]; John Dominic Twist [1939] Director/Jesuit Priest

M.C.Mountain and Son Limited
Incorporated: 26 August 1940 *Employees:* 5
Net Worth: £8,745,485 *Total Assets:* £16,078,935
Registered Office: Home Farm, 38 Town Road, Quarrington, Sleaford, Lincs, NG34 8RS
Activities: Growing of cereals (except rice), leguminous crops and oil seeds
Parent: Green Planet Products Limited
Officers: Mowbray Christopher Mountain, Secretary/Director; Mowbray Christopher Mountain [1973] Director; Mowbray Edmund Stephens Mountain [1948] Director; Simon Leslie Mountain [1978] Director; Thomas Nicholas Mountain [1975] Director; Darren Thompson [1967] Finance Director

The Move Factory Holdings Limited
Incorporated: 23 November 2005 *Employees:* 691
Net Worth: £14,728,000 *Total Assets:* £30,421,000
Registered Office: 1 Frances Way, Grove Park, Enderby, Leicester, LE19 1SH
Activities: Activities of head offices
Parent: Smedvig Capital AS
Officers: Julia Waite, Secretary; Douglas John Crawford [1961] Director/Chief Executive Officer; Ian Geoffrey Floyed [1953] Director; John Clinton Hewett [1963] Director; Jordan Mayo [1981] Director/Investment Manager; Robert Peter Toms [1962] Director

MoveWithUs Conveyancing Limited
Incorporated: 10 July 2001 *Employees:* 60
Net Worth: £23,314,574 *Total Assets:* £34,170,176
Registered Office: Grant Hall, St Ives Business Park, Parsons Green, St Ives, Cambs, PE27 4AA
Activities: Other service activities n.e.c.
Parent: Move with Us Limited
Officers: Robert Matson, Secretary; Benjamin Paul Greco [1979] Director; David Jeremy Grossman [1970] Director; Robert Matson [1970] Director/Chartered Accountant

Movianto UK Limited
Incorporated: 11 February 1976 *Employees:* 670
Net Worth Deficit: £510,000 *Total Assets:* £92,244,000
Registered Office: 1 Progress Park, Elstow, Bedford, MK42 9XE
Activities: Wholesale of pharmaceutical goods
Parent: Healthcare Services Group Limited
Officers: Kamaljit Singh Hunjan [1967] Director/Senior VP Movianto; Julia M. Munzinger [1968] Director/Accountant [American]; Nicholas Joseph Pace [1970] Director [American]; David John Tinsley [1977] Director

Mowbray Education Trust Limited
Incorporated: 4 October 2011 *Employees:* 391
Net Worth: £20,739,000 *Total Assets:* £25,337,000
Registered Office: John Ferneley College, Scalford Road, Melton Mowbray, Leics, LE13 1LH
Activities: Primary education
Officers: Rachel Elizabeth Middleton, Secretary; Adam Craig Brewster [1964] Director/Teacher; Siobhan Connolly [1968] Director/Licenced Conveyancer; Gurpal Darar [1983] Director/Finance Management; Bart MacCarthy [1955] Director/Professor [Irish]; Drew Richardson-Walsh [1986] Director/Recruitment Consultant; Rachel Jane Scott Roberts [1963] Director/Chartered Accountant; Phil Mark Smith [1976] Commercial Director; Nicholas Merrick Watchorn [1978] HR Director; Elaine Welsh [1962] Director/Sales Representative; Glenys Willars [1951] Director/Retired

Mowbray Indigo Limited
Incorporated: 13 February 2008 *Employees:* 2
Net Worth: £4,124,142 *Total Assets:* £9,554,123
Registered Office: 36 Phillips Court, Water Street, Stamford, Lincs, PE9 2EE
Activities: Dental practice activities
Major Shareholder: Christopher George Sprinz
Officers: Christopher George Sprinz [1959] Director

Moyallen Woking Limited
Incorporated: 20 May 2008 *Employees:* 8
Net Worth Deficit: £45,855,088 *Total Assets:* £93,699,440
Registered Office: 5 Olympus Court, Olympus Avenue, Leamington Spa, Warwicks, CV34 6RJ
Activities: Buying and selling of own real estate
Parent: Moyallen Holdings Limited
Officers: Paul Leonard Hearn, Secretary; John Thomas Alexander Robinson [1964] Director; Peter Arthur Hayes Robinson [1961] Director

MPAC Group PLC
Incorporated: 18 October 1912 *Employees:* 518
Previous: Molins Public Limited Company
Net Worth: £42,800,000 *Total Assets:* £78,500,000
Registered Office: 13 Westwood Way, Westwood Business Park, Coventry, Warwicks, CV4 8HS
Activities: Installation of industrial machinery and equipment
Officers: Duncan Edward Tyler, Secretary; John Lewis Davies [1949] Director/Retired Business Executive; Andrew James Kitchingman [1964] Director; Douglas Grant Robertson [1953] Director; Antony Steels [1965] Director; William Christopher Wilkins [1972] Director/Accountant

MPAC Overseas Holdings Limited
Incorporated: 30 October 1969
Previous: Molins Overseas Holdings Limited
Net Worth: £24,787,580 *Total Assets:* £24,787,580
Registered Office: 13 Westwood Way, Westwood Business Park, Coventry, Warwicks, CV4 8HS
Activities: Non-trading company
Parent: Molins PLC
Officers: Duncan Edward Tyler, Secretary; William Christopher Wilkins [1972] Director/Accountant

MPS Care Group Limited
Incorporated: 15 July 2013 *Employees:* 696
Net Worth: £12,802,676 *Total Assets:* £38,940,096
Registered Office: MPS Administration, Office No 6 & 7, Key Point Office Village, Nix's Hill, Alfreton, Derbys, DE55 7FQ
Activities: Activities of head offices
Major Shareholder: Paul Warren-Gray
Officers: Paul Warren-Gray [1954] Director

MRS Environmental Services Limited
Incorporated: 8 October 1987
Net Worth: £19,783,000 *Total Assets:* £30,878,000
Registered Office: The Sherard Building, Edmund Halley Road, Oxford, OX4 4DQ
Activities: Other business support service activities n.e.c.
Parent: Enterprise Holding Company No1 Limited
Officers: James Stefan Haluch [1969] Highways Director; Andrew Lee Milner [1969] Director/Chartered Engineer; Andrew Latham Nelson [1959] Finance Director

MS International PLC
Incorporated: 24 March 1960 *Employees:* 431
Net Worth: £33,400,000 *Total Assets:* £70,141,000
Registered Office: Balby Carr Bank, Balby, Doncaster, S Yorks, DN4 8DH
Activities: Activities of head offices
Shareholder: Michael James Bell
Officers: David Kirkup, Secretary; Michael James Bell [1946] Director/Chairman & Chief Executive; Nicholas Michael Arthur James Bell [1974] Managing Director; David George Hansell [1945] Director; Roger Lane Smith [1945] Director/Solicitor; Michael Patrick Andrew O'Connell [1949] Director; David Pyle [1946] Director

MSG Commercial Limited
Incorporated: 22 June 1993 *Employees:* 42
Net Worth: £13,952,286 *Total Assets:* £42,323,488
Registered Office: The Courtyard, Chapel Lane, Bodicote, Banbury, Oxon, OX15 4DB
Activities: Take-away food shops and mobile food stands
Major Shareholder: Moonpal Singh Grewal
Officers: Moonpal Singh Grewal [1969] Director

MSG Sandhurst Limited
Incorporated: 19 January 1994 *Employees:* 361
Net Worth: £10,553,450 *Total Assets:* £13,054,763
Registered Office: The Courtyard, Chapel Lane, Bodicote, Banbury, Oxon, OX15 4DB
Activities: Take-away food shops and mobile food stands
Parent: Bansols Beta Limited
Officers: Moonpal Singh Grewal [1969] Director

MSW (Holdings) Limited
Incorporated: 18 October 2002
Net Worth: £12,186,000 *Total Assets:* £12,186,000
Registered Office: Acton Grove, Long Eaton, Nottingham, NG10 1FY
Activities: Non-trading company
Parent: MSW Limited
Officers: Derek Johnston [1962] Managing Director; Sebastian John Wilkinson [1985] Director

MTC Operations Limited
Incorporated: 26 September 2013 *Employees:* 412
Previous: The Manufacturing Technology Centre Services Limited
Net Worth: £5,186,000 *Total Assets:* £36,888,000
Registered Office: Ansty Park, Pilot Way, Ansty, Coventry, Warwicks, CV7 9JU
Activities: Other research and experimental development on natural sciences and engineering
Parent: The Manufacturing Technology Centre Limited
Officers: Robert O'Sullivan, Secretary; Adrian James Cooper [1968] Finance Director; Dr Clive Hickman [1954] Director/Chief Executive; Paul Victor William Markwick [1957] Director

MTU UK Limited
Incorporated: 10 March 2003 *Employees:* 78
Net Worth: £9,043,774 *Total Assets:* £28,852,860
Registered Office: Rolls-Royce PLC, Moor Lane, Derby, DE24 8BJ
Activities: Other business support service activities n.e.c.
Parent: Vinters International Limited
Officers: Andreas Goertz [1965] Director [German]; Bruce James Phillips [1973] Director/Professional Engineer; Thomas Schuler [1977] Director [German]

Muirhead Aerospace Limited
Incorporated: 13 January 1956 *Employees:* 62
Net Worth: £24,521,000 *Total Assets:* £31,775,000
Registered Office: P O Box 36, 2 New Star Road, Leicester, LE4 9JQ
Activities: Repair of electrical equipment
Parent: Ametek Aerospace and Defense Group UK Limited
Officers: Joy Atwell, Secretary; John Wesley Hardin [1965] Director/President - Electronic Instruments [American]; Stephen Keith Wells [1956] Managing Director Avionics; Thomas Girard Wilson [1954] Director/VP MRO Europe & Asia [American]; Pietro Luigi Enrico Zetti [1968] Finance Director [Italian]

The Mulberry Bush Organisation Limited
Incorporated: 2 October 1954 *Employees:* 117
Net Worth: £10,907,139 *Total Assets:* £11,460,324
Registered Office: c/o Critchleys LLP, Beaver House, 23-38 Hythe Bridge Street, Oxford, OX1 2EP
Activities: Primary education
Officers: Barry Alexander Armstrong [1961] Director/Head of Safeguarding; Margaret Dawn Eynon [1946] Director; Simon Peacock [1961] Director/Social Worker; Hugh Randall Pidgeon [1944] Director/Organisational Consultant; Richard Robert Rollinson [1949] Director/Consultant-Care, Education and Treatment of Children [American]; Michael John Paul Sarrington [1968] Director/Independent Consultant; Satvinder Kaur Sondhi [1977] Director; Mark Thomas [1960] Director/Team Manager

Mulberry Commercial Developments Limited
Incorporated: 20 May 2003 *Employees:* 5
Previous: Greatline Developments Ltd
Net Worth: £29,260,724 *Total Assets:* £52,600,644
Registered Office: Units 3-4 Twigden Barns, Grooms Lane, Creaton, Northampton, NN6 8NN
Activities: Development of building projects
Shareholders: Robert John Wilkinson; Mark Ashby Wilkinson
Officers: Jonathan Colin Tate, Secretary; Jonathan Colin Tate [1969] Director; Mark Ashby Wilkinson [1959] Director; Robert John Wilkinson [1962] Director

Mulberry Property Developments (HGP) Limited
Incorporated: 25 April 2016
Net Worth: £337,210 *Total Assets:* £10,923,957
Registered Office: Units 3-4 Twigden Barns, Grooms Lane, Creaton, Northampton, NN6 8NN
Activities: Buying and selling of own real estate
Parent: Mulberry Property Developments Limited
Officers: Jonathan Colin Tate, Secretary; Steven Jason Mitchell [1970] Director; Jonathan Colin Tate [1969] Director; Mark Ashby Wilkinson [1959] Director; Robert John Wilkinson [1962] Director

Mulberry Property Developments Ltd
Incorporated: 13 May 2010 *Employees:* 61
Net Worth Deficit: £1,541,598 *Total Assets:* £60,117,632
Registered Office: Units 3-4 Twigden Barns, Grooms Lane, Creaton, Northampton, NN6 8LU
Activities: Construction of commercial buildings
Major Shareholder: Robert John Wilkinson
Officers: Jon Tate, Secretary; Tony Barry Flatters [1973] Finance Director; Steven Jason Mitchell [1970] Director; Ian Sadler [1966] Managing Director; Jonathan Colin Tate [1969] Director; Mark Ashby Wilkinson [1959] Director; Robert John Wilkinson [1962] Director

Mulberry Waste Limited
Incorporated: 28 April 1995 *Employees:* 52
Net Worth: £3,490,085 *Total Assets:* £11,585,117
Registered Office: 8 Vernon Street, Derby, DE1 1FR
Activities: Collection of non-hazardous waste
Parent: Mulberry Waste Holdings Limited
Officers: Shenaz Isaji, Company Secretary; Paul John Evans [1973] Director; Hassanali Isaji [1969] Director; Shenaz Isaji [1974] Director/Company Secretary; Abrar Hussain Khan [1967] Director; Zac Alan Sansom [1973] Director

Mullahead Property Company Limited
Incorporated: 2 February 2006
Net Worth: £8,494,712 *Total Assets:* £35,313,256
Registered Office: c/o Tayto Group Limited, Princewood Road, Earlstrees Industrial Estate, Corby, Northants, NN17 4AP
Activities: Other business support service activities n.e.c.
Parent: Tayto Group Limited
Officers: Stephen Thomas Alexander Hutchinson, Secretary; Paul Martin Allen [1968] Director/Accountant; Raymond Latimer Hutchinson [1949] Director; Stephen Thomas Alexander Hutchinson [1958] Director; Anne Alexandra Hutchinson-Kane [1947] Director

Multi Packaging Solutions Acquisitions 1 Limited
Incorporated: 18 January 1999
Net Worth: £775,889,536 *Total Assets:* £821,265,216
Registered Office: Millennium Way West, Phoenix Centre, Nottingham, NG8 6AW
Activities: Activities of head offices
Parent: Multi Packaging Solutions Acquisitions 2 Limited
Officers: Mark Richard Priestley, Secretary; Christina Marie Able [1973] Director/SVP Tax [American]; Andrew Darrington [1977] Director/Financial Controller; Kevin Alden Maxwell [1975] Director/Attorney [American]; Mark Richard Priestley [1964] Tax Director

Multi Packaging Solutions Acquisitions 2 Limited
Incorporated: 17 December 1998 *Employees:* 4
Net Worth: £55,066,176 *Total Assets:* £1,067,397,696
Registered Office: Millennium Way West, Phoenix Centre, Nottingham, NG8 6AW
Activities: Activities of other holding companies n.e.c.
Parent: Multi Packaging Solutions Limited
Officers: Mark Richard Priestley, Secretary; Deborah Black [1959] Director/Group Treasurer; Andrew Darrington [1977] Director/Financial Controller; Mark Richard Priestley [1964] Director-Tax and Insurance

Multi Packaging Solutions Asia Holdings Limited
Incorporated: 28 September 2010
Previous: AGI Media UK Limited
Net Worth: £34,552,656 *Total Assets:* £34,553,404
Registered Office: Phoenix Centre, Millennium Way West, Nottingham, NG8 6AW
Activities: Activities of other holding companies n.e.c.
Parent: Multi Packaging Solutions Acquisitions 2 Limited
Officers: Mark Priestley, Secretary; Deborah Black [1959] Director/Group Treasurer; Neil Wilkinson [1964] Finance Director

Multi Packaging Solutions GB Limited
Incorporated: 24 April 1991
Net Worth: £66,009,120 *Total Assets:* £179,894,016
Registered Office: Millennium Way West, Phoenix Centre, Nottingham, NG8 6AW
Activities: Activities of other holding companies n.e.c.
Parent: Multi Packaging Solutions UK Limited
Officers: Mark Richard Priestley, Secretary; Christina Marie Able [1973] Director/SVP Tax [American]; Andrew Darrington [1977] Director/Financial Controller; Kevin Alden Maxwell [1975] Director/Attorney [American]; Mark Richard Priestley [1964] Director/Accountant

Multi Packaging Solutions Global Holdings Limited
Incorporated: 13 June 2013
Net Worth: £455,382,880 *Total Assets:* £455,382,880
Registered Office: Multi Packaging Solutions, Millennium Way West, Phoenix Centre, Nottingham, NG8 6AW
Activities: Activities of other holding companies n.e.c.
Parent: Westrock Company
Officers: Andrew Darrington [1977] Director/Financial Controller; Mark John Wenham [1965] Director/Executive Vice President

Multi Packaging Solutions Limited
Incorporated: 13 June 2013 *Employees:* 19
Net Worth: £585,260,992 *Total Assets:* £791,438,976
Registered Office: Multi Packaging Solutions, Millennium Way West, Phoenix Centre, Nottingham, NG8 6AW
Activities: Manufacture of other paper and paperboard containers
Parent: Multi Packaging Solutions Global Holdings Limited
Officers: Christina Marie Able [1973] Director/SVP Tax [American]; Andrew Darrington [1977] Director/Financial Controller; Kevin Alden Maxwell [1975] Director/Attorney [American]; Mark John Wenham [1965] Director; Neil Wilkinson [1964] Director, Finance

Multi Packaging Solutions UK Limited
Incorporated: 1 March 1991 *Employees:* 1,811
Net Worth: £822,819,008 *Total Assets:* £1,162,897,024
Registered Office: Millennium Way West, Phoenix Centre, Nottingham, NG8 6AW
Activities: Manufacture of other paper and paperboard containers
Parent: Multi Packaging Solutions Acquisitions 1 Limited
Officers: Mark Richard Priestley, Secretary; Christina Marie Able [1973] Director/SVP Tax [American]; Deborah Black [1959] Director/Group Treasurer; Andrew Darrington [1977] Director/Assistant Financial Controller - Europe; Malcolm Raymond Farnan [1958] Marketing Director; Kevin Alden Maxwell [1975] Director/Lawyer [American]; Mark Richard Priestley [1964] Director/Accountant; Mark John Wenham [1965] Managing Director; Neil Wilkinson [1964] Director/Accountant

Multi-Tile Distribution Limited
Incorporated: 7 January 2004 *Employees:* 2
Net Worth: £282,120,000 *Total Assets:* £283,544,000
Registered Office: Topps Tiles, Thorpe Way, Grove Park, Enderby, Leics, LE19 1SU
Activities: Activities of distribution holding companies
Parent: Topps Tiles Kingdom Limited
Officers: Alistair Robert Hodder, Secretary; Robert Parker [1972] Director/Accountant; Matthew Thomas Mathieson Williams [1974] Director

Multi-Tile Limited
Incorporated: 8 June 1964 *Employees:* 193
Net Worth: £179,124,000 *Total Assets:* £215,815,008
Registered Office: Topps Tiles, Thorpe Way, Grove Park, Enderby, Leics, LE19 1SU
Activities: Retail sale of hardware, paints and glass in specialised stores
Parent: Topps Tile Kingdom Limited
Officers: Alistair Robert Hodder, Secretary; Robert Parker [1972] Director/Accountant; Matthew Thomas Mathieson Williams [1974] Director

Multipanel UK Limited
Incorporated: 23 January 2004 *Employees:* 98
Net Worth: £10,974,361 *Total Assets:* £35,696,800
Registered Office: The Old Mill, Blisworth Hill Farm, Stoke Road, Blisworth, Northampton, NN7 3DB
Activities: Manufacture of other fabricated metal products n.e.c.
Major Shareholder: Andrew Charles Cock
Officers: George Edward Hollands, Secretary; Andrew Charles Cock [1961] Director; Nicola May [1973] Director

Owen Mumford Holdings Limited
Incorporated: 29 September 1955 *Employees:* 720
Net Worth: £80,387,280 *Total Assets:* £97,826,848
Registered Office: Brook Hill, Woodstock, Oxford, OX20 1TU
Activities: Activities of production holding companies
Shareholder: Adam John Mumford
Officers: Mark Ivan Owen, Secretary; Adam John Mumford [1968] Director; Ivan Thomas Owen [1930] Director/Medical Instrument Maker; Mark Ivan Owen [1960] Technical Director

Owen Mumford Limited
Incorporated: 10 May 1976 *Employees:* 720
Net Worth: £71,980,512 *Total Assets:* £90,826,592
Registered Office: Owen Mumford Limited, Brook Hill, Woodstock, Oxon, OX20 1TU
Activities: Manufacture of medical and dental instruments and supplies
Parent: Owen Mumford Holdings Limited
Officers: Gavin Mark Jones, Secretary; Gavin Mark Jones [1967] Director/Accountant; Adam John Mumford [1968] Sales and Marketing Director; Ivan Thomas Owen [1930] Director/Medical Instrument Maker; Mark Ivan Owen [1960] Director/Chairman; Jarl Michael Severn [1964] Managing Director; Andrew John Varde [1965] Director

Mumford's Mill Rentals Limited
Incorporated: 10 March 2005
Net Worth: £1,971,170 *Total Assets:* £10,236,803
Registered Office: Unex House, Bourges Boulevard, Peterborough, Cambs, PE1 1NG
Activities: Other letting and operating of own or leased real estate
Shareholder: Charles John Yarborough
Officers: Lord Charles John Yarborough [1963] Director/Landowner

Munks Agricultural Contractors Limited
Incorporated: 6 March 2008 *Employees:* 15
Net Worth: £6,332,499 *Total Assets:* £11,485,393
Registered Office: The Grange, Wood Lane, South Kyme, Lincs, LN4 4AB
Activities: Support activities for crop production
Shareholders: Damien Wesley Munks; Stefan Munks
Officers: Stefan Munks, Secretary; Damian Wesley Munks [1968] Director; Stefan Munks [1972] Director

Munro Building Services Holdings Limited
Incorporated: 9 February 2015 *Employees:* 159
Net Worth: £2,994,934 *Total Assets:* £9,329,935
Registered Office: High Edge Court, Church Street, Heage, Belper, Derbys, DE56 2BW
Activities: Activities of head offices
Parent: Bowmer and Kirkland Limited
Officers: Michelle Ann Mucklestone, Secretary; Stephen Michael Barry [1963] Managing Director; John Alexander Charles Kirkland [1980] Director; Mark Gary Townsend [1967] Director

Munro Building Services Limited
Incorporated: 1 November 1990 *Employees:* 159
Net Worth: £5,095,090 *Total Assets:* £11,894,036
Registered Office: High Edge Court, Church Street, Heage, Belper, Derbys, DE56 2BW
Activities: Electrical installation
Parent: Munro Building Services Holdings Limited
Officers: Michelle Ann Mucklestone, Secretary; Stephen Michael Barry [1963] Director/Projects Manager; John Alexander Charles Kirkland [1980] Director; Mark Gary Townsend [1967] Director

W.H.Munsey Limited
Incorporated: 10 April 1913 *Employees:* 3
Net Worth: £7,379,592 *Total Assets:* £10,656,905
Registered Office: Osney Mill, Mill Street, Oxford, OX2 0AN
Activities: Repair and maintenance of ships and boats
Shareholders: William Paul Munsey; Antony Hugh Munsey
Officers: William Paul Munsey, Secretary; Anthony Hugh Munsey [1960] Director/Chartered Surveyor; William Paul Munsey [1956] Director/Flour Miller; William Keith Munsey [1933] Director/Flour Miller

Munster Joinery (U.K.) Limited
Incorporated: 19 January 1996
Net Worth: £8,264,225 *Total Assets:* £33,069,872
Registered Office: Dene Park, Stratford Road, Wellesbourne, Warwicks, CV35 9RY
Activities: Joinery installation
Officers: Fergal Walsh, Secretary; Antoinette Lucia Mulcahy [1967] Director/Accountant [Irish]; Fergal Walsh [1972] Director/Accountant [Irish]

Murata Power Solutions (Milton Keynes) Limited
Incorporated: 10 March 1982 *Employees:* 76
Net Worth: £12,741,834 *Total Assets:* £14,715,815
Registered Office: Power Solutions House, Presley Way, Crownhill, Milton Keynes, Bucks, MK8 0ES
Activities: Manufacture of electronic components
Parent: NCL Holdings Limited
Officers: Jane Ridley, Secretary; Tatsuo Bizen [1961] Director [Japanese]; Matthew Scott Cooper [1974] Director; Norio Nakajima [1961] Director [Japanese]; Stephen Jerome Pimpis [1962] Director [American]

Murley Limited
Incorporated: 5 December 1986 *Employees:* 97
Net Worth: £3,251,000 *Total Assets:* £13,993,000
Registered Office: Nelson Lane, Warwick, CV34 5JB
Activities: Activities of other holding companies n.e.c.
Shareholders: William Gerald Crawford; Royal Bank of Canada
Officers: Simon John Willmott, Secretary; Andrew David Chatham [1962] Commercial Director; William Generald Crawford [1942] Director [Irish]; Justin Timothy Hamilton [1979] Commercial Director; Simon John Willmott [1961] Finance Director; John Edward Woodrow [1948] Director/Accountant

Murray Bidco Limited
Incorporated: 23 July 2012
Net Worth Deficit: £1,885,794 *Total Assets:* £24,348,976
Registered Office: Wavendon Tower, Ortensia Drive, Wavendon, Milton Keynes, Bucks, MK17 8LX
Activities: Activities of head offices
Parent: Partnerships in Children's Services Limited
Officers: Jo August [1971] Director; Jonathan David Clark [1977] Director; Venetia Cooper [1974] Director/Chief Financial Officer

Muslim Hands
Incorporated: 22 March 2004 *Employees:* 91
Net Worth: £10,770,197 *Total Assets:* £11,268,056
Registered Office: 148-164 Gregory Boulevard, Nottingham, NG7 5JE
Activities: Non-trading company
Officers: Dr Musharraf Hussain, Secretary/Imam & Teacher; Syed Lakhte Hassanain [1961] Director/Teacher; Mohammad Arshad Jamil [1956] Director/Charity Worker; Sahibzada Ghulam Jeelani [1958] Director/Minister of Religion; Mohammed Amin-Ul Hasanat Shah [1952] Director/Teacher [Pakistani]; Saffi Ullah [1968] Director/Minister of Religion

Mutchmeats Limited
Incorporated: 29 December 1981 *Employees:* 66
Net Worth: £4,310,610 *Total Assets:* £9,936,108
Registered Office: Newclose Lane, Witney, Oxon, OX29 7GX
Activities: Wholesale of meat and meat products
Major Shareholder: John Edward Mutch
Officers: Maree Craig Westwood, Secretary; Andrew John Mutch [1961] Director; Iain Mutch [1962] Director; John Edward Mutch [1936] Director; Maree Craig Westwood [1967] Accounts Director

Mutual Clothing & Supply Company Limited
Incorporated: 11 May 1922 *Employees:* 361
Net Worth: £38,983,000 *Total Assets:* £40,296,000
Registered Office: 39-43 Bedford Street South, Leicester, LE1 3JN
Activities: Credit granting by non-deposit taking finance houses and other specialist consumer credit grantors
Shareholder: Adrian Charles Keene
Officers: Adrian Charles Keene, Secretary; Adrian Charles Keene [1952] Director; Duncan Paul Keene [1982] Director/Retail Manager; Stuart Peter Keene [1988] Director/General Manager; Victor Walter Keene [1935] Director; Geoffrey Charles Schwarz [1978] Director/Credit Manager

MWUK Holding Company Limited
Incorporated: 30 July 2010 *Employees:* 1
Net Worth: £54,028,000 *Total Assets:* £119,645,000
Registered Office: 3 Long Acre, Willow Farm, Castle Donington, Derbys, DE74 2UG
Activities: Activities of head offices
Officers: Archibald Alexander Rhodes, Secretary; Jack Calandra [1967] Director [American]; Stuart William Graham [1958] Director; Archibald Alexander Rhodes [1959] Director [American]

MWUK Limited
Incorporated: 19 May 1948 *Employees:* 643
Net Worth: £103,100,000 *Total Assets:* £144,222,000
Registered Office: 3 Long Acres, Willow Farm, Castle Donington, Derbys, DE74 2UG
Activities: Manufacture of workwear
Parent: Ensco 645 Limited
Officers: Archibald Alexander Rhodes, Secretary; Jack Calandra [1997] Director [American]; Stuart William Graham [1954] Director; Archibald Alexander Rhodes [1959] Director [American]

My Home Move Ltd
Incorporated: 10 November 1999 *Employees:* 588
Net Worth: £15,664,000 *Total Assets:* £30,032,000
Registered Office: 1 Frances Way, Grove Park, Enderby, Leicester, LE19 1SH
Activities: Activities of head offices
Parent: The Move Factory Holdings Limited
Officers: Julia Waite, Secretary; Douglas John Crawford [1961] Director/Chief Executive Officer; John William Duke [1964] Director; Anthony Luke Killeen [1965] Operations Director; Sukhdev Malle [1968] Group Sales Director; Mark Montgomery [1971] Customer Strategy and Marketing Director; Karen Linda Pay [1968] HR Director; Neal Geoffrey Preece [1964] Consumer Online Director; Paul Jonathan Tennant [1971] IT Director

The Myers-Briggs Company (Europe) Limited
Incorporated: 6 March 2015
Previous: OPP Holdings Limited
Net Worth: £7,083,892 *Total Assets:* £15,226,960
Registered Office: Elsfield Hall, 15-17 Elsfield Way, Oxford, OX2 8EP
Activities: Other publishing activities
Parent: CPP Oriel Limited
Officers: Sian Samantha Bishop, Secretary; Calvin Finch [1960] Director/Accountant [American]; Jeffrey Hayes [1961] Director [American]; William Christopher Matthew O'Connor [1966] Director; Thaddeus Stephens [1969] Director/Attorney [American]

The Myers-Briggs Company Holdings (Europe) Limited
Incorporated: 20 May 2016 *Employees:* 116
Previous: CPP Oriel Limited
Net Worth Deficit: £165,911 *Total Assets:* £11,454,362
Registered Office: Elsfield Hall, 15-17 Elsfield Way, Oxford, OX2 8EP
Activities: Other publishing activities
Parent: CPP, Inc.
Officers: Sian Samantha Bishop, Secretary; Calvin Finch [1960] Director/Accountant [American]; Jeffrey Hayes [1961] Director [American]; William Christopher Matthew O'Connor [1966] Director/Chartered Accountant; Thaddeus Stephens [1969] Director/Attorney [American]

The Myers-Briggs Company Limited
Incorporated: 5 February 1988 *Employees:* 116
Previous: OPP Limited
Net Worth: £8,247,550 *Total Assets:* £11,886,847
Registered Office: Elsfield Hall, 15-17 Elsfield Way, Oxford, OX2 8EP
Activities: Other publishing activities
Parent: The Myers-Briggs Company (Europe) Limited
Officers: Sian Samantha Bishop, Secretary; Calvin Finch [1960] Director/Accountant [American]; Jeffrey Hayes [1961] Director [American]; Elizabeth Kendall [1961] Director/Psychologist; William Christopher Matthew O'Connor [1966] Director/Chartered Accountant; Thaddeus Stephens [1969] Director/Attorney [American]

Mynydd Windfarm LLP
Incorporated: 10 May 2011
Net Worth: £4,077,823 *Total Assets:* £12,265,063
Registered Office: Glebe Barn, Great Barrington, Burford, Oxon, OX18 4US
Officers: Edward John Daniels [1973] Member

Myoderm Limited
Incorporated: 30 September 2010 *Employees:* 13
Net Worth: £6,239,064 *Total Assets:* £12,466,631
Registered Office: 1 Meer End, Birstall, Leicester, LE4 3EH
Activities: Other business support service activities n.e.c.
Major Shareholder: Michael Allen Cohen
Officers: Michael Allen Cohen [1970] Director [American]

The Myton Hospices
Incorporated: 13 April 1982 *Employees:* 269
Net Worth: £13,360,598 *Total Assets:* £14,612,228
Registered Office: Myton Hamlet Hospice, Myton Lane, Myton Road, Warwick, CV34 6PX
Activities: Other human health activities
Officers: Gemma Marie Morgan, Secretary; Kelvin George Beer-Jones [1953] Director/Retired; Karl Wasyl Demian [1959] Charity Director; Noel Campbell Hunter [1946] Director/Retired; Dr David Morgan [1949] Director/Retired; Margaret Elsie Morris [1943] Director/Retired; Graham Scott Nicoll [1977] Director/Banker; Suzanna Patchett [1977] Director/Solicitor; Dr Valerie Anne Robson [1952] Director/Doctor; Paul David Taylor [1956] Director/Management Consultant; Nadiya Virani-Bland [1981] Director/Solicitor

Myton Investments Ltd
Incorporated: 8 October 2015
Net Worth: £10,946,460 *Total Assets:* £12,426,853
Registered Office: Highdown House, 11 Highdown Road, Leamington Spa, Warwicks, CV31 1XT
Activities: Other letting and operating of own or leased real estate
Shareholders: Christopher Michael Bosworth; Vivienne Majory Bosworth
Officers: Christopher Michael Bosworth [1972] Director; Joan Patricia Bosworth [1943] Director/Retired; Michael Bosworth [1945] Director/Retired; Vivienne Majory Bosworth [1971] Director

Myton School Trust
Incorporated: 14 June 2011 *Employees:* 196
Net Worth: £22,353,000 *Total Assets:* £25,020,000
Registered Office: Myton School, Myton Road, Warwick, CV34 6PJ
Activities: General secondary education
Officers: Elizabeth Jane Burrows, Secretary; Garjinder Singh Basi [1962] Director; Joanna Kate Bessant [1967] Director; Diane Marie Burley [1964] Director; Judith Ann Fell [1959] Director; Paul David Morley [1977] Director; Andrew Richard Perry [1975] Director; Ekta Punj [1989] Director; Prof James Cooper Robinson [1969] Director; Wayne Barry Charles Tooze [1964] Director; Sarah Jane Windrum [1980] Director

Mytravel Group Limited
Incorporated: 3 December 1962
Net Worth: £420,700,000 *Total Assets:* £2,188,100,096
Registered Office: Westpoint, Peterborough Business Park, Lynch Wood, Peterborough, Cambs, PE2 6FZ
Activities: Other business support service activities n.e.c.
Parent: Thomas Cook Investments (2) Limited
Officers: Shirley Bradley, Secretary; Alan Charles Donald [1963] Director

Mytravel North America Limited
Incorporated: 21 March 2001
Net Worth Deficit: £299,224,864 *Total Assets:* £53,028,248
Registered Office: Westpoint, Peterborough Business Park, Lynch Wood, Peterborough, Cambs, PE2 6FZ
Activities: Other business support service activities n.e.c.
Parent: Thomas Cook Group UK Limited
Officers: Shirley Bradley, Secretary; Paul Andrew Hemingway [1971] Director

Mytravel Pioneer Limited
Incorporated: 25 April 2002
Net Worth Deficit: £20,700,000 *Total Assets:* £150,000,000
Registered Office: Westpoint, Peterborough Business Park, Lynch Wood, Peterborough, Cambs, PE2 6FZ
Activities: Non-trading company
Parent: Mytravel Group Limited
Officers: Shirley Bradley, Secretary; Shirley Bradley [1960] Director

N K Motors Limited
Incorporated: 13 June 2000 *Employees:* 81
Net Worth: £3,898,927 *Total Assets:* £12,047,505
Registered Office: 2 Orient Way, Pride Park, Derby, DE24 8BY
Activities: Sale of new cars and light motor vehicles
Officers: Ravi Kumari, Secretary; Narinder Kumar [1955] Director; Sanjeev Kumar [1982] Director/Motor Dealer; Ravi Kumari [1959] Director

N.F.U. Mutual Management Company Limited
Incorporated: 30 July 1982
Net Worth: £22,835,392 *Total Assets:* £22,875,150
Registered Office: Tiddington Road, Stratford upon Avon, Warwicks, CV37 7BJ
Activities: Activities of financial services holding companies
Parent: The National Farmers Union Mutual Insurance Society Limited
Officers: James Damian Creechan, Secretary; Charles Richard Percy [1953] Director/Farmer Agricultural Consultant; Lindsay Neil Sinclair [1956] Director/Chief Executive

N.F.U. Mutual Unit Managers Limited
Incorporated: 31 July 1984
Net Worth: £17,023,328 *Total Assets:* £23,782,720
Registered Office: Tiddington Road, Stratford upon Avon, Warwicks, CV37 7BJ
Activities: Fund management activities
Parent: The National Farmers Union Mutual Insurance Society Limited
Officers: James Damian Creechan, Secretary; Nigel David Bryan [1974] Director/Finance Manager; Paul Andrew Glover [1965] Director; Charlotte Judd [1983] Director/Head of Operations (Financial Services); Jonathan Priestley [1971] Director/Head of Life Actuarial & Chief Actuary (Life)

N.M.T. Plant Hire Limited
Incorporated: 22 November 1978 *Employees:* 103
Net Worth: £6,949,749 *Total Assets:* £19,231,676
Registered Office: 2 Postley Road, Woburn Road Industrial Estate, Kempston, Beds, MK42 7BU
Activities: Renting and leasing of construction and civil engineering machinery and equipment
Shareholders: Mark Richard Ambridge; Timothy Lawrence Ambridge; Nicholas Paul Ambridge
Officers: Mark Richard Ambridge [1960] Director/Plant Hire Contractor; Nicholas Paul James Ambridge [1957] Director/Plant Hire Contractor; Timothy Lawrence Ambridge [1963] Director

NAH Group Limited
Incorporated: 31 October 2005
Net Worth: £411,037 *Total Assets:* £66,747,320
Registered Office: 1430 Montagu Court, Kettering Parkway, Kettering, Northants, NN15 6XR
Activities: Activities of head offices
Parent: NAH Holdings Limited
Officers: James David Saralis, Secretary; John Russell Atkinson [1965] Director; James David Saralis [1978] Director

NAH Holdings Limited
Incorporated: 28 August 2007
Net Worth: £1,756,629 *Total Assets:* £71,759,040
Registered Office: 1430 Montagu Court, Kettering Parkway, Kettering, Northants, NN15 6XR
Activities: Activities of head offices
Parent: Consumer Champion Group Limited
Officers: James David Saralis, Secretary; John Russell Atkinson [1965] Director; James David Saralis [1978] Director

NAHL Group PLC
Incorporated: 14 April 2014 *Employees:* 206
Net Worth: £61,708,000 *Total Assets:* £90,999,000
Registered Office: 1430 Montagu Court, Kettering Parkway, Kettering, Northants, NN15 6XR
Activities: Activities of other holding companies n.e.c.
Officers: James David Saralis, Secretary; Timothy John Mellor Aspinall [1956] Director; John Russell Atkinson [1965] Director; Dr Caroline Anne Brown [1962] Director; Robert Stephen Halbert [1958] Director; Gillian Dawn Celia Kent [1963] Director; James David Saralis [1978] Director

Nampak Holdings (UK) Limited
Incorporated: 19 September 1994
Net Worth: £200,582,960 *Total Assets:* £333,298,176
Registered Office: Interchange Park, Jenna Way, Newport Pagnell, Bucks, MK16 9QJ
Activities: Activities of head offices
Parent: Nampak International Limited
Officers: Andre Marinus de Ruyter [1968] Director [Dutch]; Glenn Ramsay Fullerton [1967] Director/Chartered Accountant [South African]; Luke Domonic Mark Haggett [1981] Director; Arnold Mitterer [1964] Director [Austrian]; David John Tocher [1961] Director

Nampak Plastics Europe Limited
Incorporated: 2 November 1945 *Employees:* 488
Net Worth: £19,878,000 *Total Assets:* £59,979,000
Registered Office: Jenna Way, Interchange Park, Newport Pagnell, Bucks, MK16 9QJ
Activities: Manufacture of plastic packing goods
Parent: Nampak Holdings UK Limited
Officers: Andre Marinus de Ruyter [1968] Director [Dutch]; Glenn Ramsay Fullerton [1967] Director/Chartered Accountant [South African]; Luke Domonic Mark Haggett [1981] Director; Arnold Mitterer [1964] Director [Austrian]

Napier Turbochargers Limited
Incorporated: 25 February 2008 *Employees:* 126
Net Worth: £42,093,000 *Total Assets:* £48,560,000
Registered Office: Howard House, Graycar Business Park, Barton Turn, Barton under Needwood, Burton on Trent, Staffs, DE13 8EN
Activities: Manufacture of other special-purpose machinery n.e.c.
Parent: Westinghouse Air Brake Technologies
Officers: Michael James Isaac, Secretary; Michael Edward Fetsko III [1965] Director [American]; John Anthony Mastalerz Jr [1966] Director/Accountant [American]; David Michael Seitz [1965] Director/Vice President [American]; Jaidip SEN [1963] Director

Nasmyth Bulwell Limited
Incorporated: 12 July 1956 *Employees:* 308
Previous: Bulwell Precision Engineers Limited
Net Worth: £14,687,000 *Total Assets:* £32,411,000
Registered Office: Nasmyth Building, Coventry Road, Exhall, Coventry, Warwicks, CV7 9FT
Activities: Manufacture of air and spacecraft and related machinery
Parent: Nasmyth Group Limited
Officers: Paul Robert Jones, Secretary; Simon William Beech [1961] Director; Paul Robert Jones [1973] Director/Chartered Accountant; Peter John Smith [1949] Director

Nasmyth Group Limited
Incorporated: 15 October 2003 *Employees:* 734
Net Worth: £19,757,000 *Total Assets:* £54,570,000
Registered Office: Nasmyth House, Coventry Road, Exhall, Coventry, Warwicks, CV7 9FT
Activities: Activities of head offices
Major Shareholder: Peter John Smith
Officers: Paul Robert Jones, Secretary; Simon William Beech [1961] Director; Paul Robert Jones [1973] Director/Chartered Accountant; Peter John Smith [1949] Director

Natco Foods Limited
Incorporated: 28 November 1963 *Employees:* 156
Net Worth: £6,388,966 *Total Assets:* £21,791,392
Registered Office: Unit 2 Swan Business Park, Osier Way, Buckingham, MK18 1TB
Activities: Non-specialised wholesale of food, beverages and tobacco
Parent: T Choithram & Sons (London) Ltd
Officers: Ramesh Pohumal Thanwani, Secretary; Lekhraj Thakurdas Pagarani [1954] Director/Merchant; Luke Pagarani [1983] Director/Merchant; Ramchand Dharamdas Rajwani [1930] Director/Merchant [Indian]; Ramesh Pohumal Thanwani [1946] Director/Merchant [Indian]

National Accident Helpline Limited
Incorporated: 28 September 1993 *Employees:* 116
Net Worth: £58,845,000 *Total Assets:* £122,673,000
Registered Office: 1430 Montagu Court, Kettering Parkway, Kettering, Northants, NN15 6XR
Activities: Advertising agencies
Parent: NAH Group Limited
Officers: James David Saralis, Secretary; John Russell Atkinson [1965] Director; Debra Jayne Britton [1965] Director; Thomas Edward FitzGenerald [1984] Director; Matthew Adam Nabozny [1975] Director; James David Saralis [1978] Director; Simon Trott [1969] Director; Jonathan William White [1972] Director

The National Church of England Academy Trust
Incorporated: 18 July 2011 *Employees:* 139
Net Worth: £6,569,000 *Total Assets:* £9,860,000
Registered Office: The National C of E Academy, Annesley Road, Hucknall, Nottingham, NG15 7DB
Activities: General secondary education
Officers: Alison Elway, Secretary; Lisa Marie Allen [1972] Director/Procurement Manager; Constance Mary Ball [1945] Director/Retired; Kirsty Catriona Taylor Cowley [1970] Director/Deanery Administrator; Craig William Dean [1976] Director; Joanna Kristine Eastwood [1970] Director; Amy Victoria Harmston-Hall [1984] Director; Emma Jayne Hopkin [1988] Director/Teacher; Hayley Marie James [1986] Director/Performance Consultant; Gemma Johnson [1987] Director/Teacher; Simon William Jones [1970] Director/Education; Benjamin Robert Marshall [1984] Director; Andrew Stephen McKibbin [1987] Director/Academy Chaplain; Kathryn Ann Mitford [1967] Director/Hairdressing; John Oldfield [1974] Director/Deputy Headteacher; Martin Edward Paine [1973] Director/Businessman; Reverend Joanna Louise Stephens [1969] Director/Vicar; Steven Michael Yardley [1967] Director/Business Executive

The National Examination Board in Occupational Safety and Health
Incorporated: 18 March 1992 *Employees:* 107
Net Worth: £16,439,000 *Total Assets:* £18,118,000
Registered Office: 5 Dominus Way, Meridian Business Park, Leicester, LE19 1QW
Activities: Technical and vocational secondary education
Officers: Peter Paul Ryan, Secretary; Professor Mariane Cavalli [1958] Director/Consultant; Richard Brenig Moore [1966] Director; David John Morgan [1957] Director; Dr William Nixon [1952] Director/Retired; Leslie Philpott [1958] Director/Retired; Joy Smith [1965] Director/Service Liaison Lead - HMICFRS; Antonina Sulkhova [1972] Director/Health and Safety Consultant [Canadian]

National Farmers Union Mutual Insurance Society Limited (The)
Incorporated: 30 September 1910 *Employees:* 3,707
Net Worth: £7,489,999,872 *Total Assets:* £19,342,000,128
Registered Office: Tiddington Road, Stratford upon Avon, Warwicks, CV37 7BJ
Activities: Life insurance
Officers: James Damian Creechan, Secretary; Jonathan Robert Bailie [1963] Director; Steven Mark Bower [1962] Director; Alison Mary Capper [1968] Director; Brian James Duffin [1955] Director/Actuary; Dr Harriet Christine Kennedy [1955] Director; Eileen Elizabeth McCusker [1953] Director; James Crawford McLaren [1967] Director/Farmer; Richard David Morley [1967] Director; Charles Richard Percy [1953] Director/Farmer/Agricultural Consultant; Lindsay Neil Sinclair [1956] Director/Chief Executive; Christopher MacDonald Stooke [1957] Director; Nicholas James Turner [1967] Director

National Fleet Solutions Limited
Incorporated: 24 December 2002 *Employees:* 17
Net Worth: £5,688,000 *Total Assets:* £36,683,000
Registered Office: Loxley House, 2 Oakwood Court, Little Oak Drive, Annesley, Nottingham, NG15 0DR
Activities: Sale of new cars and light motor vehicles
Parent: Reg Vardy Limited
Officers: Richard James Maloney, Secretary; Martin Shaun Casha [1960] Director; Trevor Garry Finn [1957] Director; Timothy Paul Holden [1964] Director/Chartered Accountant

National Floorcoverings Group Limited
Incorporated: 28 October 2011 *Employees:* 123
Net Worth: £28,372,592 *Total Assets:* £31,161,980
Registered Office: 10 Imperial Road, Matlock, Derbys, DE4 3NL
Activities: Activities of head offices
Officers: David Andrew Pass [1966] Director; Mark Anthony Pass [1964] Director; Simon Arthur Pass [1963] Director; Richard Charles Taylor [1949] Director

National House-Building Council
Incorporated: 17 November 1936 *Employees:* 1,252
Net Worth: £462,449,984 *Total Assets:* £1,674,989,952
Registered Office: NHBC House, Davy Avenue, Knowlhill, Milton Keynes, Bucks, MK5 8FP
Activities: Non-life insurance
Officers: Anne Carol Durkin, Secretary; Paul Bishop [1954] Director; Ian Adam Craston [1966] Investment Director; Katherine Davies [1956] Director/Chief Executive; Paul John Hosking [1967] Director/Chief Financial Officer; Isabel Frances Hudson [1959] Director; Neil Jefferson [1971] Director; Jean Craig Park [1954] Director/Chief Risk Officer; Sir Alistair Muir Russell [1949] Director; Stephen Stone [1954] Director/Architect; Steven Archibald Wood [1960] Director/Chief Executive

The National Memorial Arboretum Company Limited
Incorporated: 10 May 1994 *Employees:* 44
Net Worth: £17,109,000 *Total Assets:* £17,834,000
Registered Office: Croxall Road, Alrewas, Staffs, DE13 7AR
Activities: Museums activities
Officers: Luke Joannou, Secretary; Jason Coward [1967] Director/Marketing Consultant; Kate Rebecca Davies [1980] Director; Andrew Peter Farquhar [1953] Managing Director - GW Consulting (UK) Limited; Paul Harris [1955] Director; Gary John Ryan [1971] Marketing Director; David Whimpenny [1960] Director/Manager

National Space Centre
Incorporated: 18 December 1997 *Employees:* 120
Net Worth: £24,410,208 *Total Assets:* £27,549,616
Registered Office: National Space Centre, Exploration Drive, Leicester, LE4 5NS
Activities: Educational support services
Shareholders: University of Leicester; Leicestershire Chamber of Commerce; Leicester City Council
Officers: Jennifer Anne Barnacle, Secretary; Charles St Hill Bishop [1967] Director/Chief Executive; Edward Cassidy Mbe [1946] Director/Part-time Manager; Rebecca Anne Evernden [1976] Director/Civil Servant; James Edward Fry [1971] Director/Solicitor; William Haley [1950] Director/Designer; Verity Anne Hancock [1967] Director/Principal; Arvind Michael Kapur [1962] Director/Accountant; Gary Alan Moss [1962] Director/Brand Consultant; Professor Surinder Mohan Sharma [1953] Diversity Director; Nigel Paul Siesage [1952] Director/University Administrator; Professor David John Southwood [1945] Director of Scientific Program; Sir Martin Nicholas Sweeting [1951] Director/Professor; Karen Jayne Thomas [1961] Director/Head of HR; Joanne Elizabeth Wheeler [1971] Director/Lawyer; Professor Emma Yeoman [1975] Director/Professor

National Tyre Service Limited
Incorporated: 12 August 1970 *Employees:* 1,209
Net Worth: £13,093,000 *Total Assets:* £65,723,000
Registered Office: c/o National Tyres, Regent House, Heaton Lane, Stockport, Cheshire, SK4 1BS
Activities: Maintenance and repair of motor vehicles
Parent: Axle Group Limited
Officers: John Alexander Taylor, Secretary/Accountant; John Irvine Caldwell [1956] Director/Sales & Marketing; Alan Livingstone Revie [1959] Director; John Alexander Taylor [1964] Director/Accountant

Nationwide Accident Repair Services Limited
Incorporated: 24 November 1969 *Employees:* 3,812
Previous: Nationwide Accident Repair Services PLC
Net Worth Deficit: £16,715,000 *Total Assets:* £117,581,000
Registered Office: 17a Thorney Leys Park, Witney, Oxon, OX28 4GE
Activities: Maintenance and repair of motor vehicles
Officers: David Richard Pugh [1961] Finance Director; Michael Alfred Wilmshurst [1960] Director/Chief Executive

Nationwide Crash Repair Centres Limited
Incorporated: 25 February 1960 *Employees:* 3,457
Net Worth Deficit: £58,217,000 *Total Assets:* £129,991,000
Registered Office: 17a Thorney Leys Park, Witney, Oxon, OX28 4GE
Activities: Maintenance and repair of motor vehicles
Officers: David Richard Pugh [1961] Finance Director; Michael Alfred Wilmshurst [1960] Managing Director

Nationwide Fast Fit Plus Limited
Incorporated: 31 December 1966
Net Worth: £19,537,642 *Total Assets:* £19,599,192
Registered Office: 17a Thorney Leys Park, Witney, Oxon, OX28 4GE
Activities: Non-trading company
Officers: David Richard Pugh [1961] Finance Director; Michael Alfred Wilmshurst [1960] Managing Director

Nationwide Healthcare Providers Limited
Incorporated: 20 December 2010 *Employees:* 185
Net Worth: £12,023,769 *Total Assets:* £17,414,986
Registered Office: 2nd Floor, New Brook House, 385 Alfreton Road, Nottingham, NG7 5LR
Activities: Dental practice activities
Major Shareholder: Jamil Ahmad
Officers: Jamil Ahmad, Secretary; Dr Jamil Ahmad [1959] Director; Doctor Marie Christina Hallen [1973] Director [Swedish]; Majvi Anette Neimi Persson [1954] Director [Swedish]

Nationwide Platforms Limited
Incorporated: 17 June 1988 *Employees:* 871
Net Worth: £128,510,000 *Total Assets:* £259,984,000
Registered Office: 15 Midland Court, Central Park, Lutterworth, Leics, LE17 4PN
Activities: Renting and leasing of other machinery, equipment and tangible goods n.e.c.
Parent: Zooom Holdings (UK) Limited
Officers: Jerome Sarragozi, Secretary; Thomas Donald Kenny [1954] Director/Group CEO [Irish]; Thomas Anthony Murray [1967] Director/Chartered Accountant

Nationwide Windows Holding Company Limited
Incorporated: 12 December 2000 *Employees:* 216
Net Worth: £11,461,382 *Total Assets:* £22,477,468
Registered Office: Nationwide House, 74-88 Somers Road, Rugby, Warwicks, CV22 7DH
Activities: Activities of head offices
Shareholders: Daryl Cashmore; John Whalley
Officers: John Whalley, Secretary; Daryl Cashmore [1964] Operations Director; Adrian Pavey [1959] Director; John Whalley [1967] Director

Nationwide Windows Limited
Incorporated: 5 June 1986 *Employees:* 216
Net Worth: £6,235,348 *Total Assets:* £16,368,382
Registered Office: Nationwide House, 74-88 Somers Road, Rugby, Warwicks, CV22 7DH
Activities: Other manufacturing n.e.c.
Shareholders: John Whalley; Daryl Cashmore
Officers: John Whalley, Secretary/Director; Daryl Cashmore [1964] Operations Director; Adrian Pavey [1959] Director; John Whalley [1967] Director

Natl. Amusements (UK) Limited
Incorporated: 18 June 1987 *Employees:* 1,317
Net Worth Deficit: £9,466,007 *Total Assets:* £49,803,988
Registered Office: Redfield Way, Lenton, Nottingham, NG7 2UW
Activities: Motion picture projection activities
Officers: Lisa Marie Martignetti, Secretary; Thaddeus Peter Jankowski [1950] Director/Attorney at Law [American]; Paula Jean Keough [1960] Director/Vice President & Associate General Counsel [American]; Shari Ellen Redstone [1954] Director/Business Executive [American]; Sumner Michael Redstone [1923] Director/Business Executive [American]

Natural Assets Investments Limited
Incorporated: 24 February 2011 *Employees:* 142
Net Worth Deficit: £32,283,324 *Total Assets:* £32,002,558
Registered Office: 1st Floor, Whitecroft House, 51 Water Lane, Wilmslow, Cheshire, SK9 5BQ
Activities: Other accommodation
Officers: Umar Mark Aziz [1979] Director/Solicitor; Timothy Dennis [1975] Director; Fraser MacDonald Douglas [1950] Director/Retired; David Michael Gorton [1963] Director/Fund Manager; Ewan James Kearney [1971] Director; Matthew Dawson Spence [1963] Director; Anthony Wild [1974] Director

Natures Menu Limited
Incorporated: 2 March 1981 *Employees:* 208
Net Worth: £2,973,791 *Total Assets:* £14,840,652
Registered Office: 22-26 King Street, King's Lynn, Norfolk, PE30 1HJ
Activities: Manufacture of prepared feeds for farm animals
Parent: Anexhold Limited
Officers: Gonzalo Raspall Coromina, Secretary; Paula Michelle Clatworthy [1970] Director; Gonzalo Raspall Coromina [1972] Director [Spanish]; Ramon Andreu Ferrando [1964] Director [Spanish]; Peter Coventry Roy [1971] Director; Craig Richard Taylor [1966] Director; Francisco Javier Serra Torres [1957] Director/Businessman [Spanish]

Naturex Limited
Incorporated: 24 November 1971 *Employees:* 99
Net Worth: £48,005,000 *Total Assets:* £54,492,000
Registered Office: Park Road, Overseal, Swadlincote, Derbys, DE12 6JX
Activities: Manufacture of other food products n.e.c.
Parent: Naturex, Societe Anonyme
Officers: Sean Cumiskey [1967] Director/Vice President Sales Benelux Germany Poland; Pradeep Parmar [1958] Finance Director

Navagator Limited
Incorporated: 27 January 2012 *Employees:* 175
Net Worth: £7,773,000 *Total Assets:* £9,311,000
Registered Office: Stamford Works, Bayley Street, Stalybridge, Cheshire, SK15 1QQ
Activities: Non-trading company
Officers: Katie Jane Ferris [1971] Director; Stephen Keith Picot [1950] Director; Alan Reay [1938] Director

Naylor Drainage Ltd
Incorporated: 1 July 1938 *Employees:* 290
Net Worth: £6,770,565 *Total Assets:* £30,423,270
Registered Office: Clough Green, Cawthorne, Barnsley, S Yorks, S75 4AD
Activities: Other manufacturing n.e.c.
Officers: Ruth Moran, Secretary; Ruth Moran [1961] Director and Company Secretary; Edward George Naylor [1963] Director; Bridget Clare Warner-Adsetts [1967] Director

Naylor Industries PLC
Incorporated: 15 March 1994 *Employees:* 335
Net Worth: £14,843,586 *Total Assets:* £42,131,664
Registered Office: Clough Green, Cawthorne, Barnsley, S Yorks, S75 4AD
Activities: Other manufacturing n.e.c.
Officers: Ruth Moran, Secretary; David Fletcher [1945] Director; Ruth Moran [1961] Finance Director; Edward George Naylor [1963] Director/Chartered Accountant; Bridget Warner-Adsetts [1967] Director/Chief Operating Officer

NBCMH Holdings Limited
Incorporated: 28 August 2014 *Employees:* 1
Net Worth: £1,289,338,752 *Total Assets:* £1,297,876,736
Registered Office: 19 Jessops Riverside, 800 Brightside Lane, Sheffield, S9 2RX
Activities: Activities of head offices
Parent: NBH Holdco Limited
Officers: Keith Graham Ward [1953] Finance Director

NBH Holdco Limited
Incorporated: 29 August 2014 *Employees:* 1
Net Worth: £1,274,993,024 *Total Assets:* £1,301,528,704
Registered Office: 19 Jessops Riverside, 800 Brightside Lane, Sheffield, S9 2RX
Activities: Activities of head offices
Parent: Danaher Corporation
Officers: Keith Graham Ward [1953] Finance Director

NCL Holdings Limited
Incorporated: 17 July 2000
Net Worth: £55,848,544 *Total Assets:* £56,203,348
Registered Office: Power Solutions House, Presley Way, Crown Hill, Milton Keynes, Bucks, MK8 0ES
Activities: Activities of head offices
Officers: Jane Ridley, Secretary; Tatsuo Bizen [1961] Director [Japanese]; Norio Nakajima [1961] Director [Japanese]

Neal Brothers (Leicester) Limited
Incorporated: 20 December 1956 *Employees:* 237
Net Worth: £7,443,181 *Total Assets:* £20,732,320
Registered Office: 110 Regent Road, Leicester, LE1 7LT
Activities: Manufacture of wooden containers
Major Shareholder: David Kenneth Neal
Officers: Christopher Mark Williams, Secretary; David Kenneth Neal [1948] Director/Removals Manager

James Neill Holdings Limited
Incorporated: 30 September 1916 *Employees:* 13
Net Worth Deficit: £32,998,000 *Total Assets:* £28,028,000
Registered Office: Atlas Way, Atlas North, Sheffield, S4 7QQ
Activities: Activities of other holding companies n.e.c.
Parent: Spear & Jackson Limited
Officers: John Maurice Dallman, Company Secretary; Simon Nai Cheng Hsu [1960] Director/Businessman [Chinese]; Alaina Shone [1962] Director/Chartered Accountant

Neill Tools Limited
Incorporated: 8 August 1958 *Employees:* 51
Net Worth Deficit: £1,705,000 *Total Assets:* £14,595,000
Registered Office: c/o James Neill Holdings Limited, Atlas Way, Atlas North Business Park, Sheffield, S4 7QQ
Activities: Manufacture of tools
Parent: James Neill Holdings Limited
Officers: John Maurice Dallman, Company Secretary; Ian Robert Archer [1968] Director; Simon Nai Cheng Hsu [1960] Director/Businessman [Chinese]; Alaina Shone [1962] Director/Chartered Accountant

Nelsons Solicitors Limited
Incorporated: 9 April 2010 *Employees:* 159
Net Worth: £5,197,085 *Total Assets:* £15,576,820
Registered Office: Pennine House, 8 Stanford Street, Nottingham, NG1 7BQ
Activities: Solicitors
Officers: James Edward Russell Coningsby [1964] Director/Solicitor; Stephen James Fern [1979] Finance Director; Timothy Michael Hastings [1956] Director/Chief Executive; Cathryn Rachel Selby [1971] Director; Stewart Neil Vandermark [1970] Director/Solicitor; Bruce Howard Leighton Williams [1959] Director/Solicitor

Wm. Nelstrop & Co. Ltd
Incorporated: 2 November 1931 *Employees:* 46
Net Worth: £21,818,028 *Total Assets:* £26,796,592
Registered Office: Albion Flour Mills, Stockport, Cheshire, SK4 1TZ
Activities: Grain milling
Shareholder: Conrad Jarlath Nelstrop
Officers: Alexander Paul Fraser Nelstrop [1975] Director/Flour Miller; Conrad Jarlath Nelstrop [1939] Director/Chairman; Dr George Anthony Nelstrop [1938] Director; Matthew Benjamin Nelstrop [1974] Director/Flour Miller; Paul Alan Roberts [1956] Director; Simon John Morley Roberts [1960] Director; Conrad Huw Syers [1961] Director

Nene Education Trust
Incorporated: 19 October 2011 *Employees:* 212
Previous: Nene Education Trust Ltd
Net Worth: £19,931,000 *Total Assets:* £22,339,000
Registered Office: Nene Education Trust, Mountbatten Way, Raunds, Wellingborough, Northants, NN9 6PA
Activities: General secondary education
Officers: David Keith Phillips, Secretary; Stephen John Atkins [1961] Director; Nathanael Bonser-Ward [1986] Director/Bank Staff; Michael Busby [1944] Director; Russell John Hargrave [1964] Director/Management Consultant; Anne Tansi Harper [1951] Director; Christopher Hill [1975] Director/Headteacher; Dudley Charles Hughes [1946] Director; Anthony John Laughton [1983] Director/Chartered Accountant; Amanda Ling [1975] Director [French]; Stuart Richardson [1979] Programme Director - Financial Services; Reverend Douglas Spenceley [1949] Director/Church of England Minister; Melanie Spinks-Wilson [1972] Director/Programme Manager; Christopher Edwin Ward [1975] Director/Civil Servant; Nina Kerr Wilson [1973] Director/Solicitor

Nene Group Holdings PLC
Incorporated: 15 May 2014 *Employees:* 12
Net Worth: £7,053,049 *Total Assets:* £13,327,521
Registered Office: Nene House, Station Road, Watford Village, Northampton, NN6 7XN
Activities: Activities of head offices
Shareholders: Thomas Anthony Pearson; Linda Maria Steele
Officers: Louise Jane Sharif, Secretary; Paul Darrell Fagan [1959] Director; Thomas William Pearson [1999] Director/Contract Manager; Thomas Anthony Pearson [1961] Director; Louise Jane Sharif [1965] Finance Director; Linda Maria Steele [1958] Director

Nene Group PLC
Incorporated: 21 December 1973 *Employees:* 12
Net Worth: £6,897,579 *Total Assets:* £13,327,521
Registered Office: Nene House, Station Road, Watford Village, Northampton, NN6 7XN
Activities: Other letting and operating of own or leased real estate
Officers: Louise Jane Sharif, Secretary; Paul Darrell Fagan [1959] Director; Thomas William Pearson [1999] Director/Contract Manager; Thomas Anthony Pearson [1961] Director; Louise Jane Sharif [1965] Finance Director; Linda Maria Steele [1958] Director

Nene Park Trust
Incorporated: 23 August 1988 *Employees:* 51
Net Worth: £38,654,000 *Total Assets:* £39,504,000
Registered Office: Ham Farm House, Ham Lane, Peterborough, Cambs, PE2 5UU
Activities: Other amusement and recreation activities n.e.c.
Officers: Philip Hugh Rolfe, Secretary; Simon Frederick Barkham [1983] Director/Salesman; Matthew Anthony Wilson Bradbury [1964] Director/Chief Executive; Councillor Graham Peter Casey [1963] Director/Musician; Martin Brian Chillcott [1956] Director/Marketing Consultant; Thomas Hornby Graham Cooper [1950] Director/Chartered Surveyor; Christine Anne de Ferrars Green [1964] Director/Solicitor; Professor Ian David Hodge [1952] Director/University Professor; Jonathan Clifford Marsden [1959] Director/Local Government Officer; Colin Duncan Prosser [1963] Director/Geologist; Paul Thomas Simmons [1955] Director/Business Coach; Allan Simpson [1984] Director/Town Planner, Utilities; Councillor June Elizabeth Stokes [1942] Director/Councillor

Nenplas Limited
Incorporated: 15 March 2006 *Employees:* 113
Net Worth: £6,892,000 *Total Assets:* £12,720,000
Registered Office: Airfield Industrial Estate, Blenheim Road, Ashbourne, Derbys, DE6 1HA
Activities: Manufacture of other plastic products
Parent: Nenplas Holdings Limited
Officers: Richard Anthony Lumb, Secretary; Robert James Butcher [1966] Managing Director; Gary Horrobin [1968] Operations Director; Stephen Jones [1968] Director; Richard Anthony Lumb [1967] Finance Director

Neonickel (Blackburn) Limited
Incorporated: 3 June 1993 *Employees:* 69
Net Worth: £8,265,598 *Total Assets:* £14,472,061
Registered Office: Unit 1 Java Park, Bradbourne Drive, Tilbrook, Milton Keynes, Bucks, MK7 8AT
Activities: Wholesale of metals and metal ores
Officers: David Anthony O'Keeffe, Secretary/Financial Controller; Johannes Petrus Arnoldus Buijnsters [1953] Director/Vice President [Dutch]; David Anthony O'Keeffe [1956] Director/Financial Controller

Neovia Logistics Services (U.K.) Limited
Incorporated: 2 June 1987 *Employees:* 899
Net Worth: £28,774,000 *Total Assets:* £72,810,000
Registered Office: Peckleton Lane, Desford, Leicester, LE9 9JU
Activities: Operation of warehousing and storage facilities for land transport activities
Parent: SPL Logistics UK Holdings Limited
Officers: Zach Green [1960] Director/Attorney [American]; Terrance Glenn Sandlin [1968] Director/Executive Vice President and CFO [American]

Nesform Limited
Incorporated: 28 March 1977 *Employees:* 6
Net Worth: £9,931,144 *Total Assets:* £10,664,271
Registered Office: Sky View, Argosy Road, East Midlands Airport, Castle Donington, Derbys, DE74 2SA
Activities: Sale of other motor vehicles
Major Shareholder: Michael James Lawrence
Officers: Michael James Lawrence [1951] Director/Motor Engineer

Netsupport Ltd.
Incorporated: 18 May 1989 *Employees:* 92
Net Worth: £10,353,678 *Total Assets:* £11,369,666
Registered Office: Netsupport House, Towngate East, Market Deeping, Peterborough, Cambs, PE6 8NE
Activities: Business and domestic software development
Parent: 4a Investment (Jersey) Ltd
Officers: Helen Hankinson, Secretary; Andrew John Gibbons [1968] Technical Director; Robert David Hawkins [1968] Development Director; Matthew Jones [1971] Director/Business Development; Alastair John Kingsley [1969] Managing Director; Marcus Rex Kingsley [1973] Marketing Director

Network Group Holdings Limited
Incorporated: 15 June 2007 *Employees:* 667
Net Worth: £14,053,000 *Total Assets:* £49,678,000
Registered Office: Meriden Hall, Main Road, Meriden, Coventry, Warwicks, CV7 7PT
Activities: Activities of head offices
Officers: Nigel John Dudley, Secretary; Glyn Davies [1959] Director; Paul Thomas Davis [1973] Director; Matthew David Ellis [1972] Director; Martin Michael Gunn [1970] Director; Paul Ronald Hanke [1955] Director; Spencer Raymond Arthur Jones [1972] Director; Jonathon David Smith [1955] Director

Network Services (Nationwide) Limited
Incorporated: 13 May 1991 *Employees:* 149
Net Worth: £9,698,536 *Total Assets:* £22,756,448
Registered Office: 17a Thorney Leys Park, Witney, Oxon, OX28 4GE
Activities: Renting and leasing of cars and light motor vehicles
Officers: David Richard Pugh [1961] Finance Director; Michael Alfred Wilmshurst [1960] Managing Director

Network Ventures Limited
Incorporated: 29 August 2003 *Employees:* 15
Net Worth: £11,799,000 *Total Assets:* £49,075,000
Registered Office: Meriden Hall, Main Road, Meriden, Coventry, Warwicks, CV7 7PT
Activities: Other activities of employment placement agencies
Officers: Nigel John Dudley, Secretary; Paul Thomas Davis [1973] Director; Spencer Raymond Arthur Jones [1972] Director; Jonathon David Smith [1955] Director

New Blue Chip Limited
Incorporated: 15 July 2016 *Employees:* 242
Net Worth: £10,734,000 *Total Assets:* £75,807,000
Registered Office: Unit 1 Franklin Court, Stannard Way, Priory Business Park, Bedford, MK44 3JZ
Activities: Other software publishing
Officers: Andrew Rounding, Secretary; Lee John Bailey [1976] Director; Eddy Conway [1960] Director; Brian Meredith [1950] Director; Sadie Vanessa Nesbitt [1967] Director; Andrew James Rounding [1972] Director; Tim Stringer [1976] Director; Derek Waterman [1972] Director

New City Hotels Limited
Incorporated: 27 February 1995 *Employees:* 3
Net Worth: £13,375,391 *Total Assets:* £15,220,027
Registered Office: 70 Clarkehouse Road, Sheffield, S10 2LJ
Activities: Other letting and operating of own or leased real estate
Officers: Andrew Dean Womack, Secretary; Trevor John Day [1948] Director/Chartered Accountant; Sarah Louise Hawksworth [1962] Director/Housewife; Andrew Dean Womack [1961] Director

New Co (Beith Street) Limited
Incorporated: 18 March 2016
Net Worth Deficit: £7,000 *Total Assets:* £30,827,000
Registered Office: The Box, Horseshoe Lane, Alderley Edge, Cheshire, SK9 7QP
Activities: Development of building projects
Parent: Vita Glasgow 1 Limited
Officers: Giles Beswick, Secretary; Giles Peter Beswick [1974] Director; Mark Christopher Dawson [1973] Director; Michael Keith Slater [1974] Director; Mark David Stott [1972] Director

New Co (Newcastle) Limited
Incorporated: 18 March 2016
Net Worth Deficit: £7,000 *Total Assets:* £15,793,000
Registered Office: The Box, Horseshoe Lane, Alderley Edge, Cheshire, SK9 7QP
Activities: Development of building projects
Parent: Vita Ventures Limited
Officers: Giles Beswick, Secretary; Giles Peter Beswick [1974] Director; Mark Christopher Dawson [1973] Director; Michael Keith Slater [1974] Director; Mark David Stott [1972] Director

New Co (Satellite) 2 Limited
Incorporated: 18 March 2016
Net Worth: £20,348,000 *Total Assets:* £129,710,000
Registered Office: The Box, Horseshoe Lane, Alderley Edge, Cheshire, SK9 7QP
Activities: Development of building projects
Parent: New Co (Satellite) Limited
Officers: Giles Beswick, Secretary; Giles Peter Beswick [1974] Director; Mark Christopher Dawson [1973] Director; Michael Keith Slater [1974] Director; Mark David Stott [1972] Director

New Co (Satellite) Limited
Incorporated: 18 March 2016
Net Worth Deficit: £7,000 *Total Assets:* £53,356,000
Registered Office: The Box, Horseshoe Lane, Alderley Edge, Cheshire, SK9 7QP
Activities: Development of building projects
Parent: Vita Satellite 1 Limited
Officers: Giles Beswick, Secretary; Giles Peter Beswick [1974] Director; Mark Christopher Dawson [1973] Director; Michael Keith Slater [1974] Director; Mark David Stott [1972] Director

New College Leicester Trust
Incorporated: 27 May 2010
Net Worth: £27,495,556 *Total Assets:* £27,495,556
Registered Office: New College Leicester, Greencoat Road, Leicester, LE3 6RN
Activities: General secondary education
Officers: Anthony Richard Barradell, Secretary; Anthony Richard Barradell [1963] Director/Management Trainer; Susan Billington [1954] Director; Jane Brown [1967] Director/Teacher; Ian Christopher Chakravorty [1964] Director/Management Consultant; Angus Robin Fraser [1973] Director/Business Owner; Dipak Patel [1972] Director/Management Consultant

New Era Cap Company Limited
Incorporated: 25 November 2002 *Employees:* 165
Net Worth: £14,190,970 *Total Assets:* £26,233,362
Registered Office: 1st Floor, CBX II East, Midsummer Boulevard, Milton Keynes, Bucks, MK9 2EA
Activities: Wholesale of clothing and footwear
Major Shareholder: Christopher Koch
Officers: Alan Jones, Secretary; Paul Gils [1960] Director [Belgian]; Alan Jones [1960] Director/Chartered Accountant; Christopher Koch [1960] Director [American]; Kevin Robert Wilson [1964] Director [Canadian]

New Era Development (UK) Limited
Incorporated: 11 October 2013
Net Worth Deficit: £1,264,082 *Total Assets:* £45,021,072
Registered Office: Office 1, 10 New Era Square, Sheffield, S2 4BF
Activities: Development of building projects
Shareholders: Zhen Qin; Rongmin Qin
Officers: Wan Loi Cheung [1961] Director; Yin Gao [1972] Director [Chinese]; Rongmin Qin [1986] Executive Director; Ruiya Qin [1962] Director

New Terex Holdings UK Limited
Incorporated: 26 August 1994 *Employees:* 2
Net Worth: £117,543,000 *Total Assets:* £296,780,000
Registered Office: The Pinnacle, 170 Midsummer Boulevard, Milton Keynes, Bucks, MK9 1FE
Activities: Activities of other holding companies n.e.c.
Parent: Terex Corporation
Officers: Eric I Cohen, Secretary/Lawyer [American]; Eric I Cohen [1958] Director/Lawyer [American]; Brian Henry [1958] Director/Executive; John Daniel Sheehan [1960] Director/Chief Financial Officer [American]

New Testament Church of God
Incorporated: 4 October 1967 *Employees:* 120
Net Worth: £37,756,832 *Total Assets:* £51,564,572
Registered Office: 3 Cheyne Walk, Northampton, NN1 5PT
Activities: Activities of head offices
Officers: Bishop Donald Bolt, Secretary; Reverend Donnovan Alexander Allen [1963]; Reverend Spencer Anderson [1954] Director/Pastor [Jamaican]; Rev Andrew Bailey [1965]; Rev Patricia Bailey [1949]; Clyde Leon Baker [1944] Director/Minister; Daniel Leeburne Barnett [1974]; Rev George Beason [1950]; Edward Johnson Benjamin [1943] Director; Rev Donald Bolt [1951]; Bishop Eric Arthur Brown [1949]; Reverend Renford Benjamin Brown [1946]; Revd Barrington Burrell [1947]; Rev Leon Cameron [1959]; Rev Prince Wade Chambers [1966]; Keith Delano Clarke [1965]; Rev Vincent Cox [1965]; Rev Malcolm Llewellyn Cummins [1969]; Bishop Lincoln Hugh Davis [1962] Director; Reverend Deverton Douglas [1963] Director/Minister of Religion [Jamaican]; Reverend Derrick John Eccleston [1940]; Ellis David Edwards [1981]; Helen Edwards [1952]; Rev Adrian Hopeton Foster [1963]; Reverend Owen Dacosta Francis [1960]; Lester Anthony Freckleton [1959]; Headley Raymond Gayle [1939]; Lindford Franklyn George [1953]; Paul Darrly Gidharry [1970]; Norman Gooden [1944] Director/Minister; Paul Nathan Gordon [1966]; Rev Claion Banjamin Grandison [1966] Director/Pastor; Rev Paul Ronald Grey [1970] Director/Minister; Rev Donovan Haslam [1978]; Joel Haye [1957] Director/Social Worker; Allan Rupert Hayles [1953] Director/Owner Manager; Lloyd George Henry [1955] Director/Pastor; Reverend Vincent Howell [1930]; Rev Rowland Sunday Ijoma [1956]; John Wade Oral Jackson [1968]; Jonathan Jackson [1969] Director; Revd Hermilyn James [1951]; Rev Davey Johnson [1960]; Revd Jancie Johnson [1964]; Rev Richard Jones [1964]; Rev Erinle Kikelomo [1959]; Rev Ruben Samuel King [1966]; Reginald Kumar [1950]; Reverend Palamuttathu Chacko Joe Kurian [1956] Director/Minister; Reverend Francis Letford [1934]; Sheryl Denise Lindo-Mason [1967]; Rev Sandra Marie Litchmore [1969]; Rev Saji Mathew [1965]; Revd Paulette Matthews [1956]; Roger George Maynard [1966]; Rev Herbert McKenzie [1954]; Bishop Louis Richard McLeod [1957] Director/Minister; Barrington Augustus Mullings [1964]; Benham Ray Nelson [1961] Director/Minister; Jacqueline Marie Newsome [1968] Director/Pastor; Reverend Iyeli Mabs Nkumu [1964] Director/Minister of Gospel; Stanford Natal Notice [1958] Director/Pastor; Revd Graham John Owen [1958] Director/Business Development Manager; Revd Ceceile Angela Palmer [1960]; Revd Gregory Anthony Parry [1960] Director/Service Manager; Wayne Antonio Perkins [1966]; Revd Patrick Pryce [1965]; Revd Hadassah Radway [1956]; Rev Elaire Ellonia Reid [1969]; Rev Priolin Reynolds [1966]; Joseph Roberts [1942]; Revd Brian Robinson [1948]; Revd Pearl Roper [1936]; Rev Wesely Sealy [1965]; Revd Sharon Smith [1964]; Bishop Trevor Anthony Smith [1957]; Rev Vaz Emanuel Smith [1957]; Rev Ranjan Das Sri [1962]; Edward Sterling [1958]; Reverend Terence Taylor [1966] Director/Minister; Winston Anthony Taylor [1961]; Reverend Carla Patricia Thomas [1971] Director/Pastor [Bahamian]; Reverend Paul Anthony Thomas [1961] Director/Careers Service Manager; Reverend Samuel Augustus Thomas [1968] Director/Accounts Manager; Revd Pamela Thompson [1966]; Samuel George Thompson [1963]; Reverend Albert Nathaniel Watson [1956]; Derek Anthony Webley [1961]; David Anthony Williams [1965]; Revd Marlene Williams [1953]; Nettie May Williams [1950]; Steve Williams [1952]; Wilfred Clairmonte Willins [1939]; Revd Laurel Woodstock [1960] Director/Minister of Religion

New York Bakery Company Limited
Incorporated: 23 October 2002 *Employees:* 536
Net Worth: £46,190,000 *Total Assets:* £66,859,000
Registered Office: Swinton Meadows Industrial Estate, Swinton, Rotherham, S Yorks, S64 8AB
Activities: Manufacture of bread; manufacture of fresh pastry goods and cakes
Officers: Clifford Edward Irwin [1962] Director; Darrel Miller [1968] Director [American]; John Stratton [1977] Finance Director

Newco (First Street) Limited
Incorporated: 28 July 2016
Net Worth Deficit: £3,000 *Total Assets:* £17,235,000
Registered Office: The Box, Horseshoe Lane, Alderley Edge, Cheshire, SK9 7QP
Activities: Buying and selling of own real estate
Parent: Vita Ventures Limited
Officers: Giles Peter Beswick [1974] Director; Mark Christopher Dawson [1973] Director; Michael Keith Slater [1974] Director; Mark David Stott [1972] Director

Newell and Wright (Holdings) Limited
Incorporated: 24 July 1996 *Employees:* 470
Net Worth: £6,368,989 *Total Assets:* £29,256,876
Registered Office: Templeborough Depot, Sheffield Road, Tinsley, Sheffield, S9 1RT
Activities: Activities of head offices
Shareholders: Francis Ronald Newell; Hilary Jane Wright
Officers: Simon James Lawtey [1962] Finance Director; Francis Ronald Newell [1952] Director; Stephen James Newell [1978] Director

Newincco 1382 Limited
Incorporated: 3 September 2015 *Employees:* 956
Net Worth Deficit: £7,145,519 *Total Assets:* £35,547,360
Registered Office: Milton Chambers, 19 Milton Street, Nottingham, NG1 3EU
Activities: Activities of head offices
Shareholders: Robert Michael Beacham; Livingbridge Enterprise GP Limited; John Henry Thomas Whitehead
Officers: Robert Michael Beacham [1967] Director/Restaurateur; John Derkach [1956] Director; Adam Benjamin Griggs [1974] Director/Accountant; Louise Kingston [1981] Director; Nicholas James White [1968] Director; John Henry Thomas Whitehead [1968] Director/Restaurateur

Newincco 1386 Limited
Incorporated: 2 September 2015
Net Worth Deficit: £6,082,266 *Total Assets:* £32,102,980
Registered Office: Milton Chambers, 19 Milton Street, Nottingham, NG1 3EU
Activities: Activities of head offices
Parent: Newincco 1382 Limited
Officers: Robert Michael Beacham [1967] Director/Restaurateur; Adam Benjamin Griggs [1974] Director/Accountant; Louise Kingston [1981] Director; Nicholas James White [1968] Director; John Henry Thomas Whitehead [1968] Director/Restaurateur

Newlincs Development Limited
Incorporated: 4 May 1999 *Employees:* 2
Net Worth: £4,304,601 *Total Assets:* £20,158,892
Registered Office: Integrated Waste Management Facility, South Marsh Road, Stallingborough, N E Lincs, DN41 8BZ
Activities: Other business support service activities n.e.c.
Officers: George Richard Guthrie, Secretary; Anne Cecile Eleonore Loussouarn [1971] Director of Finance and Performance [French]; Laurent Magnin [1973] Director [French]

Newtco Limited
Incorporated: 10 September 2010
Net Worth: £6,085,003 *Total Assets:* £19,039,560
Registered Office: National House, 80-82 Wellington Road North, Stockport, Cheshire, SK4 1HW
Activities: Activities of head offices
Major Shareholder: Michael David Noblett
Officers: Michael David Noblett [1972] Director

Newton Europe Limited
Incorporated: 30 August 2001 *Employees:* 252
Net Worth: £23,116,124 *Total Assets:* £35,654,276
Registered Office: 2 Kingston Business Park, Kingston Bagpuize, Abingdon, Oxon, OX13 5FE
Activities: Management consultancy activities other than financial management
Parent: Newton Industrial Consultants Holdings Limited
Officers: Stephen David Dyde, Secretary; Andrew James Clarke [1964] Director; Andrew Marcus Hawes [1974] Director/Management Consultants; Kevin Anthony Jones [1974] Director/Management Consultants; Steven John Phillips [1976] Director; Thomas Dudley Wedgwood [1971] Director/Management Consultant

Newton Industrial Consultants Holdings Limited
Incorporated: 29 September 2011 *Employees:* 252
Net Worth: £2,669,140 *Total Assets:* £23,640,816
Registered Office: 2 Kingston Business Park, Kingston Bagpuize, Abingdon, Oxon, OX13 5FE
Activities: Management consultancy activities other than financial management
Shareholders: Andrew Marcus Hawes; Thomas Dudley Wedgwood; Kevin Anthony Jones
Officers: Andrew Marcus Hawes [1974] Director/Management Consultant; Kevin Anthony Jones [1974] Director/Management Consultant; Thomas Dudley Wedgwood [1971] Director

Nexans Logistics Limited
Incorporated: 30 March 1962 *Employees:* 31
Net Worth: £7,498,623 *Total Assets:* £15,240,179
Registered Office: Nexans House, Chesney Wold, Bleak Hall, Milton Keynes, Bucks, MK6 1LA
Activities: Agents specialised in the sale of other particular products
Parent: Nexans Participations
Officers: Jamie Edward Steele, Secretary; Anne-Lise Aukner [1956] Director [Norwegian]; Pierre Emmanuel Buret [1958] Director [French]; Kieron Lee Hall [1976] Director; Jamie Edward Steele [1982] Director/Finance Manager

Nexeon Limited
Incorporated: 22 February 2006
Net Worth: £29,386,000 *Total Assets:* £32,020,000
Registered Office: 136 Eastern Avenue, Milton Park, Milton, Abingdon, Oxon, OX14 4SB
Activities: Manufacture of other chemical products n.e.c.
Shareholders: Invesco Ltd; Imperial Innovations Businesses LLP
Officers: Michael Peter Black, Secretary; Michael Peter Black [1965] Director/Accountant; Dr Scott Selby Durrand Brown [1963] Director; Russell Cummings [1964] Director; Ian Tudor Jenks [1954] Director; Christina Margaret McComb [1956] Investment Director; Anthony Leo Posawatz [1960] Director [American]

Nexperia UK Ltd.
Incorporated: 11 May 2006 *Employees:* 587
Previous: NXP Semiconductors UK Limited
Net Worth: £46,839,000 *Total Assets:* £84,379,000
Registered Office: Bramhall Moor Lane, Hazel Grove, Stockport, Cheshire, SK7 5BJ
Activities: Manufacture of electronic components
Parent: China Jianyin Investment Ltd
Officers: Rachel Whittaker, Secretary; Michael Julian Humphreys [1962] Director/Vice-President & General Manager; Ruben Everard Gerard Lichtenberg [1967] Director/Senior Legal Counsel [Dutch]; Rachel Whittaker [1975] Financial Director

Next Distribution Limited
Incorporated: 12 April 1995 *Employees:* 6,253
Net Worth: £126,151,000 *Total Assets:* £185,892,000
Registered Office: Next PLC, Desford Road, Enderby, Leicester, LE19 4AT
Activities: Operation of warehousing and storage facilities for land transport activities
Parent: Next Holdings Limited
Officers: Seonna Anderson, Secretary; Amanda James [1971] Director; Simon Adam Lord Wolfson of Aspley Guise [1967] Director; Richard Simon Vaughan Papp [1967] Director; Jane Margaret Shields [1963] Director

Next Holdings Limited
Incorporated: 11 November 1891 *Employees:* 49
Previous: Next Holdings PLC
Net Worth: £781,299,968 *Total Assets:* £1,523,399,936
Registered Office: Desford Road, Enderby, Leicester, LE19 4AT
Activities: Activities of head offices
Parent: Next Group PLC
Officers: Seonna Anderson, Secretary; Amanda James [1971] Director; Simon Adam Lord Wolfson of Aspley Guise [1967] Director; Richard Simon Vaughan Papp [1967] Director; Jane Margaret Shields [1963] Director

Next PLC
Incorporated: 9 April 2002 *Employees:* 43,970
Net Worth: £482,600,000 *Total Assets:* £2,561,499,904
Registered Office: Desford Road, Enderby, Leicester, LE19 4AT
Activities: Activities of head offices
Officers: Seonna Anderson, Secretary; Jonathan Michael Arundell Bewes [1965] Director/Investment Banker; Tristia Adele Harrison [1973] Director; Amanda James [1971] Director; Simon Adam Lord Wolfson of Aspley Guise [1967] Director; Richard Simon Vaughan Papp [1967] Director; Michael Roney [1954] Director [American/British]; Francis William Salway [1957] Director; Jane Margaret Shields [1963] Director; Dianne Thompson [1950] Director

Next Retail Limited
Incorporated: 29 August 2002 *Employees:* 33,554
Net Worth: £2,955,148,032 *Total Assets:* £4,591,239,168
Registered Office: Desford Road, Enderby, Leicester, LE19 4AT
Activities: Retail sale of clothing in specialised stores
Parent: Next Holdings Limited
Officers: Seonna Anderson, Secretary; Amanda James [1971] Director; Simon Adam Lord Wolfson of Aspley Guise [1967] Director

Nexus Multi Academy Trust
Incorporated: 21 March 2016 *Employees:* 362
Net Worth: £9,782,029 *Total Assets:* £16,860,824
Registered Office: Hilltop School, Larch Road, Maltby, Rotherham, S Yorks, S66 8AZ
Activities: Other education n.e.c.
Officers: Steven Richard Booth [1950] Director; Peter John Castleton [1947] Director/Retired; Andrew Child [1955] Director/Education Governance Consultant; John Coleman [1955] Director/Retired [Irish]; Professor Nick Hodge [1962] Director/Professor; Raymond Palmer [1968] Director/Health and Safety Consultant; Rachel Elizabeth Potts [1963] Director/Retired; Susan Jane Shelley [1957] Director

Ney Limited
Incorporated: 21 April 1976 *Employees:* 70
Net Worth: £4,755,384 *Total Assets:* £11,434,374
Registered Office: Ney, Sibree Road, Stonebridge Trading Estate, Coventry, Warwicks, CV3 4FD
Activities: Agents involved in the sale of machinery, industrial equipment, ships and aircraft
Officers: Heinrich Cotting [1944] Director [Swiss]; Shahana Kishver [1956] Managing Director; Gerd Christoph Ney [1940] Director

NFT Distribution Holdings Limited
Incorporated: 4 April 2014 *Employees:* 2,561
Net Worth: £20,563,000 *Total Assets:* £131,028,000
Registered Office: Azalea Close, Clover Nook Industrial Park, Somercotes, Derbys, DE55 4QX
Activities: Activities of distribution holding companies
Major Shareholder: Heath Brian Zarin
Officers: Mark Davis [1972] Legal Director; Jay Lee Edwards [1978] Director; Ross David Eggleton [1977] Director; David Frankish [1954] Director/Chief Executive Officer; Chuang Hue Moh [1975] Director [Singaporean]; Simon Richard Pearson [1967] Managing Director; Heath Brian Zarin [1975] Director/Finance [American]

NFT Distribution Operations Limited
Incorporated: 18 May 2006 *Employees:* 2,092
Net Worth: £15,184,000 *Total Assets:* £92,601,000
Registered Office: 1 Azalea Close, Clover Nook Industrial Park, Somercotes, Alfreton, Derbys, DE55 4QX
Activities: Freight transport by road
Parent: Homecrest Bidco Limited
Officers: Mark Davis, Secretary; Mark Davis [1972] Director and Company Secretary; Jay Lee Edwards [1978] Director; Ross David Eggleton [1977] Director; Simon Richard Pearson [1967] Director; Heath Zarin [1975] Director [American]

NFU Mutual (Service Company) Limited
Incorporated: 13 December 2004 *Employees:* 3,707
Net Worth: £51,965,544 *Total Assets:* £104,461,504
Registered Office: Tiddington Road, Stratford upon Avon, Warwicks, CV37 7BJ
Activities: Other business support service activities n.e.c.
Parent: N.F.U. Mutual Management Company Limited
Officers: James Damian Creechan, Secretary; Maureen Patricia Jones [1958] HR Director [Irish]; Lindsay Neil Sinclair [1956] Director/Chief Executive

NFU Mutual Select Investments Limited
Incorporated: 27 April 2012
Net Worth: £13,727,595 *Total Assets:* £22,011,832
Registered Office: Tiddington Road, Stratford upon Avon, Warwicks, CV37 7BJ
Activities: Financial intermediation not elsewhere classified
Parent: The National Farmers Union Mutual Insurance Society Limited
Officers: Sian Elizabeth Johns, Secretary; Gina Fusco [1962] Director; Graham Harvey [1958] Director/Head of Financial Services; David Charles Moran [1967] Director/Chartered Accountant; Richard David Morley [1967] Director; Nicholas James Turner [1967] Director

NHBC Building Control Services Limited
Incorporated: 4 October 1985
Net Worth: £4,194,071 *Total Assets:* £14,692,550
Registered Office: NHBC House, Davy Avenue, Knowlhill, Milton Keynes, Bucks, MK5 8FP
Activities: Other business support service activities n.e.c.
Parent: National House-Building Council
Officers: Sarah Jane Mapplebeck, Secretary; Paul John Hosking [1967] Director/Chief Financial Officer; Diane Paula Marshall [1965] Director/Manager; Andrew Rothrie [1956] Director/Senior Head of Inspection; Steven Archibald Wood [1960] Director/Chief Executive

Nibgreen
Incorporated: 3 April 2017
Net Worth: £430,365 *Total Assets:* £22,979,872
Registered Office: Suite 100, Regus-Atterbury Lakes, Fairbourne Drive, Atterbury, Milton Keynes, Bucks, MK10 9RG
Activities: Security dealing on own account
Shareholders: Andrew Robinson; Julie Elizabeth Robinson
Officers: Andrew Robinson [1968] Director; Julie Elizabeth Robinson [1972] Director

NIC Holdings (UK) Limited
Incorporated: 1 November 1995
Previous: NIC Holdings (UK) PLC
Net Worth: £133,391,592 *Total Assets:* £134,291,600
Registered Office: c/o United Cast Bar (UK) Limited, Spital Lane, Chesterfield, Derbys, S41 0EX
Activities: Activities of head offices
Officers: Dr Adel Khalid Al Subaih [1954] Director [Kuwaiti]; Ahmad Mohammad Hasan Hussein [1946] Director [Jordanian]; Yaseen Mohamed Jaafar Mohamed Mohsen [1960] Director [Bahraini]; Mark Anderson Penman [1970] Director

Nicholas Associates Group Limited
Incorporated: 29 July 1998 *Employees:* 5,653
Previous: Stafforce Personnel Limited
Net Worth: £2,101,787 *Total Assets:* £18,387,540
Registered Office: Reginald Arthur House, Percy Street, Rotherham, S Yorks, S65 1ED
Activities: Management consultancy activities other than financial management
Parent: Nicholas Associates Holdings Limited
Officers: Marie Cragg, Secretary; Bruce John Allen [1966] Director/Chartered Accountant; Anthony Newton Boorman [1972] Director of Strategic Partnerships; Paul Michael Brammer [1973] Director of Services; Nicholas George William Cragg [1949] Director; Lisa Helen Gainsford [1964] Director

Nicholas Associates Holdings Limited
Incorporated: 2 February 1977 *Employees:* 3,664
Previous: Nicholas Associates Limited
Net Worth: £1,243,076 *Total Assets:* £18,378,070
Registered Office: Reginald Arthur House, 4 Percy Street, Rotherham, S Yorks, S65 1ED
Activities: Activities of head offices
Major Shareholder: Nicholas George William Cragg
Officers: Bruce John Allen [1966] Director/Chartered Accountant; Nicholas George William Cragg [1949] Director/Engineer; Lisa Helen Gainsford [1964] Director

John Nicholls (Holdings) Limited
Incorporated: 8 January 2003 *Employees:* 215
Net Worth: £7,442,738 *Total Assets:* £21,738,084
Registered Office: c/o John Nicholls Limited, Overthorpe Road, Banbury, Oxon, OX16 4TB
Activities: Activities of head offices
Shareholders: John Andrew Milton Nicholls; Philip Edward Gary Nicholls
Officers: David James Hebdon [1962] Director; John Andrew Milton Nicholls [1948] Director/Manager; Philip Edward Gary Nicholls [1951] Director/Sales Manager; Mark James Walton [1973] Finance Director

John Nicholls (Trading) Limited
Incorporated: 8 March 1965 *Employees:* 169
Net Worth: £2,718,517 *Total Assets:* £13,091,394
Registered Office: Overthorpe Industrial Estate, Overthorpe Road, Banbury, Oxon, OX16 4TB
Activities: Agents involved in the sale of timber and building materials
Shareholder: John Andrew Milton Nicholls
Officers: Adam England [1980] Director; David James Hebdon [1962] Managing Director; John Andrew Milton Nicholls [1948] Director/Chief Executive; Philip Edward Gary Nicholls [1951] Group Director; Mark James Walton [1973] Director/Accountant

Nickle Holdings Limited
Incorporated: 15 July 2014 *Employees:* 61
Net Worth: £6,422,375 *Total Assets:* £23,754,636
Registered Office: Crosby Grange, Ferry Road West, Scunthorpe, N Lincs, DN15 8UH
Activities: Activities of head offices
Major Shareholder: Carl Richard Foster
Officers: Carl Richard Foster [1966] Director/Engineer; Michelle Wainwright [1973] Director

A.C. Nielsen Company Limited
Incorporated: 9 October 1996 *Employees:* 725
Net Worth: £52,866,000 *Total Assets:* £114,393,000
Registered Office: Nielsen House, John Smith Drive, Oxford, OX4 2WB
Activities: Market research and public opinion polling
Parent: AC Nielsen Holdings UK Limited
Officers: Catherine Mollie Earle [1963] Director; James Martin Oates [1972] Analytic Director UK and Ireland; Luigi Sacchetti [1978] Finance Director [Italian]; Paul Walker [1973] Director

Nielsen Holdings PLC
Incorporated: 4 February 2015 *Employees:* 44
Net Worth: £3,316,468,224 *Total Assets:* £12,345,899,008
Registered Office: Nielsen House, John Smith Drive, Oxford, OX4 2WB
Activities: Market research and public opinion polling
Officers: Emily Epstein, Secretary; Attwood Jr James Albert [1958] Director [American]; Guerrino de Luca [1952] Director [Italian]; Karen Miesel Hoguet [1956] Director/Chief Financial Officer [American]; David Wayne Kenny [1961] Director [American]; Harish Manwani [1953] Director [Singaporean]; Robert Charles Pozen [1946] Director/Senior Lecturer; David Rawlinson [1976] Director [American]; Javier Garcia Teruel [1950] Director [Mexican]; Lauren Jane Zalaznick [1963] Director [American]

AC Nielsen Holdings UK Limited
Incorporated: 22 October 1999 *Employees:* 2
Net Worth: £70,452,328 *Total Assets:* £75,219,048
Registered Office: Nielson House, John Smith Drive, Oxford, OX4 2WB
Activities: Other business support service activities n.e.c.
Parent: Nielsen Holdings PLC
Officers: Luigi Sacchetti [1978] Finance Director [Italian]; Paul Walker [1973] Director

David Nieper Limited
Incorporated: 23 March 1961 *Employees:* 269
Net Worth: £13,464,674 *Total Assets:* £16,021,613
Registered Office: Woodend, Cromford, Matlock, Derbys, DE4 5JJ
Activities: Manufacture of other women's outerwear
Shareholders: David Harry Nieper; Rosemary Diana Nieper
Officers: Hazel Elizabeth Dickinson, Secretary; Andre Roger Alexandre Delbecq [1929] Director/Consultant [French]; Raymond Alan Mellor [1947] Director/Business Consultant; David Christopher Nieper [1964] Director; David Harry Nieper [1931] Director; Rosemary Diana Nieper [1936] Director; Rev Paul Martin Pritchard [1946] Director/Clerk in Holy Orders

Niftylift Limited
Incorporated: 21 June 1976 *Employees:* 481
Net Worth: £42,972,000 *Total Assets:* £72,273,000
Registered Office: Niftylift Limited, Chalkdell Drive, Shenley Wood, Milton Keynes, Bucks, MK5 6GF
Activities: Manufacture of other special-purpose machinery n.e.c.
Major Shareholder: Frank Roger Bowden
Officers: Simon Mark Beadle, Secretary; Simon Mark Beadle [1963] Finance Director; Steven Douglas Beckwith [1968] Operations Director; Frank Roger Bowden [1947] Director and Engineer; John Phillip Keely [1960] Managing Director; Steven Alan Redding [1969] Development Director

Nikken Kosakusho Europe Limited
Incorporated: 2 November 1988 *Employees:* 95
Net Worth: £9,198,347 *Total Assets:* £17,525,488
Registered Office: Precision House, Mangham Way, Barbot Hall Industrial Estate, Rotherham, S Yorks, S61 4RL
Activities: Wholesale of machine tools
Parent: Nikken Kosakusho Works Ltd
Officers: Paul Robert Allison, Secretary; Angela Helen Bowkett [1963] Executive Director; Anthony David Bowkett [1963] Director/President & CEO; Stephen Eckersall [1970] Technical Sales & Marketing Director; Carl Vincent Hughey [1966] Export Sales Director; Akiharu Nagahama [1958] Executive Director [Japanese]; Gary Williamson [1965] UK Sales Director

Nikon Metrology UK Limited
Incorporated: 23 November 1998 *Employees:* 137
Net Worth Deficit: £483,000 *Total Assets:* £52,877,000
Registered Office: Argosy Road, East Midlands Airport, Castle Donington, Derbys, DE74 2SA
Activities: Manufacture of other special-purpose machinery n.e.c.
Parent: Nikon Metrology NV
Officers: Koenraad Van Der Elst, Secretary; Berend Van Iterson [1970] Director/Manager [Dutch]

Nimogen Limited
Incorporated: 16 October 1991 *Employees:* 52
Net Worth: £5,644,955 *Total Assets:* £13,126,060
Registered Office: 36-38 Park Green, Macclesfield, Cheshire, SK11 7NE
Activities: Retail sale of watches and jewellery in specialised stores
Parent: Roller Pen Limited
Officers: Karl David Massey [1964] Director/Jeweller; Natasha Jane Massey [1988] Director/Jeweller

Nine Elms LLP
Incorporated: 25 April 2013
Net Worth: £133,555,000 *Total Assets:* £178,714,000
Registered Office: Barratt House, Cartwright Way, Forest Business Park, Bardon Hill, Coalville, Leics, LE67 1UF

Nippon Gases UK Limited
Incorporated: 6 January 2016 *Employees:* 52
Previous: Praxair Gases UK Ltd
Net Worth: £32,288,000 *Total Assets:* £44,414,000
Registered Office: Gresley Way, Immingham Docks, Immingham, N E Lincs, DN40 2NT
Activities: Manufacture of other inorganic basic chemicals
Officers: Mathieu Amar [1975] Managing Director France, UK, Ireland [French]; Pedro Mazarrasa Llosa [1983] Director [Spanish]

Nirvana Holdings Limited
Incorporated: 26 May 2004 *Employees:* 205
Net Worth Deficit: £20,081,892 *Total Assets:* £93,461,592
Registered Office: Unit A2, Brooke Court, Handforth Dean, Wilmslow, Cheshire, SK9 3ND
Activities: Activities of financial services holding companies
Officers: Sheila Finegan, Secretary; Mark Dugdale [1968] Director; Jason Peter Gardner [1973] Director; David Gasparro [1965] Director; Peter Brian Leech [1983] Director

Nisa Retail Limited
Incorporated: 29 May 1970 *Employees:* 327
Net Worth: £20,003,000 *Total Assets:* £190,331,008
Registered Office: Member Support Centre, Waldo Way, Normanby Enterprise Park, Scunthorpe, N Lincs, DN15 9GE
Activities: Activities of business and employers membership organisations
Officers: Caroline Jane Sellers, Secretary; James Antony Corbett Clark [1968] Director/Accountant; Steven Nuttall [1976] Finance Director; Kenneth Ian Towle [1964] Director/Retail CEO

Niscayah Holdings Limited
Incorporated: 12 November 1986 *Employees:* 3
Net Worth Deficit: £24,476,256 *Total Assets:* £67,170,256
Registered Office: 3 Europa Court, Sheffield Business Park, Sheffield, S9 1XE
Activities: Activities of other holding companies n.e.c.
Officers: Steven John Costello, Secretary; Andrew Stephen Lord [1972] Director/Accountant; Matthew Giles Thomas Marriott [1971] Director/Regional General Manager; Stephanie Irene Merrifield [1978] HR Director

NJDR Group Ltd
Incorporated: 13 October 2015 *Employees:* 249
Net Worth: £2,795,000 *Total Assets:* £14,774,000
Registered Office: 25 Morris Road, Clarendon Industrial Estate, Leicester, LE2 6AL
Activities: Activities of head offices
Shareholder: Maven Co-Invest GP Limited
Officers: Neil Simpson, Secretary; Neil Bottrill [1972] Commercial Director; Daniel Mark Cashmore [1983] Director/Senior Contracts Manager; Michael Christopher Collis [1965] Director; Richard Leonard Hollingsworth [1979] Director/Senior Quantity Surveyor; Daniel John Richardson [1970] Production Director; Neil Simpson [1979] Director/Chartered Accountant; Keith Alexander Cairns Swinley [1961] Director/Chairman

NMB-Minebea UK Ltd
Incorporated: 17 November 1987 *Employees:* 292
Net Worth: £13,350,000 *Total Assets:* £44,682,000
Registered Office: Doddington Road, Lincoln, LN6 3RA
Activities: Manufacture of other fabricated metal products n.e.c.
Parent: Minebea Mitsumi Inc
Officers: Alison Jayne Robinson, Secretary; Shigeru None [1959] Director [Japanese]; Yugen Ota [1959] Director [Japanese]; Mark Stansfield [1965] Director

NMCN PLC
Incorporated: 6 December 1946 *Employees:* 1,422
Previous: North Midland Construction Public Limited Company
Net Worth: £12,833,000 *Total Assets:* £87,105,000
Registered Office: Nunn Close, The County Estate, Huthwaite, Sutton in Ashfield, Notts, NG17 2HW
Activities: Construction of domestic buildings
Officers: Daniel Adam Taylor, Secretary; Ian Elliott [1947] Director/Retired; Michael Holt [1960] Director; John William Homer [1961] Director/Chief Executive; Andrew David Langman [1965] Director; Robert Moyle [1952] Director/Civil Engineer; Donald Stuart Proud [1954] Director/Civil Engineer; David Peter Rogers [1954] Director/Solicitor; Daniel Adam Taylor [1982] Director/Chartered Accountant

Noble Desserts Holdings Limited
Incorporated: 14 December 2009 *Employees:* 210
Net Worth: £22,569,000 *Total Assets:* £58,145,000
Registered Office: Cotswold Farm, Standlake, Witney, Oxon, OX29 7RB
Activities: Manufacture of other food products n.e.c.
Shareholder: Michael Richard John Kent
Officers: John Charles Patey, Secretary; Dale Burnett [1961] Managing Director; John Gildersleeve [1944] Director

Noble Foods Group Limited
Incorporated: 23 May 2006 *Employees:* 706
Net Worth: £40,059,000 *Total Assets:* £199,948,000
Registered Office: Cotswold Farm, Standlake, Witney, Oxon, OX29 7RB
Activities: Activities of other holding companies n.e.c.
Shareholder: Michael Richard John Kent
Officers: John Charles Patey, Secretary; Dale Burnett [1961] Director; John Gildersleeve [1944] Director

Noble Foods Holdings Limited
Incorporated: 11 November 1996
Net Worth: £2,449,000 *Total Assets:* £72,170,000
Registered Office: Cotswold Farm, Standlake, Witney, Oxon, OX29 7RB
Activities: Activities of other holding companies n.e.c.
Parent: Noble Foods Group Limited
Officers: John Charles Patey, Secretary; Dale Burnett [1961] Director

Noble Foods Limited
Incorporated: 22 September 1998 *Employees:* 694
Net Worth: £66,840,000 *Total Assets:* £224,698,000
Registered Office: Cotswold Farm, Standlake, Witney, Oxon, OX29 7RB
Activities: Manufacture of other food products n.e.c.
Parent: Noble Foods Holdings Limited
Officers: John Charles Patey, Secretary; Dale Burnett [1961] Director; John Gildersleeve [1944] Director

Node 4 Holdings Limited
Incorporated: 8 May 2013 *Employees:* 3
Net Worth Deficit: £15,340,000 *Total Assets:* £42,762,000
Registered Office: Unit 1a-1b Millennium Way, Pride Park, Derby, DE24 8HZ
Activities: Activities of head offices
Parent: Chiron Bidco Limited
Officers: Paul Bryce [1973] Business Development Director; Andrew Paul Gilbert [1980] Managing Director; Leon Benjamin Asher Keller [1980] Director/Chief Financial Officer

Node 4 Limited
Incorporated: 12 May 2003 *Employees:* 204
Net Worth: £26,697,000 *Total Assets:* £36,064,000
Registered Office: Unit 1a-1b Millennium Way, Pride Park, Derby, DE24 8HZ
Activities: Other information technology service activities
Parent: Node 4 Holdings Limited
Officers: Paul Bryce [1973] Business Development Director; Andrew Paul Gilbert [1980] Managing Director; Leon Benjamin Asher Keller [1980] Director/Chief Financial Officer

Nominet UK
Incorporated: 24 May 1996 *Employees:* 166
Net Worth: £74,335,000 *Total Assets:* £117,283,000
Registered Office: Minerva House, Edmund Halley Road, Oxford Science Park, Oxford, OX4 4DQ
Activities: Data processing, hosting and related activities
Officers: Rory Brendan Kelly, Secretary; Robert Hugh Binns [1968] Director; James Michael Bladel [1970] Director [American]; Eleanor Hester Bradley [1973] Director/Chief Operating Officer; Volker Alexander Greimann [1974] Director/General Counsel [German]; Russell Adam Haworth [1971] Director/Chief Executive; Benjamin Edwin Hill [1969] Director/Chief Financial Officer; Dr Stephen Dowland Page [1961] Director [Australian]; Kelly Louise Salter [1974] Director; David Edward Thornton [1979] Director; Jane Elizabeth Tozer [1947] Director; Mark William Wood [1952] Director/Chairman

Norbar Torque Tools Holdings Limited
Incorporated: 30 November 1999
Net Worth: £11,684,585 *Total Assets:* £15,526,017
Registered Office: Norbar Torque Tools Holdings Limited, Wildmere Road, Banbury, Oxon, OX16 3JU
Activities: Activities of head offices
Parent: Snap-On Investment Limited
Officers: Catherine Louise Rohll, Secretary; Neill Ashley Brodey [1959] Director/Engineer; Philip Anthony Brodey [1963] Sales Director; Timothy Lee Chambers [1964] Director [American]; Mark Gapinski [1975] Director [American]; Jeffrey Kostrzewa [1964] Director/Treasurer [American]; Richard Miller [1970] Director/Associate General Counsel [American]; Catherine Louise Rohll [1965] Director/Solicitor

Norbar Torque Tools Limited
Incorporated: 8 May 1943 *Employees:* 298
Net Worth: £16,884,788 *Total Assets:* £20,743,920
Registered Office: Norbar Torque Tools Limited, Wildmere Road, Banbury, Oxon, OX16 3JU
Activities: Manufacture of tools
Parent: Snap-On U.K. Holdings Limited
Officers: Catherine Louise Rohll, Secretary; Neill Ashley Brodey [1959] Director/Chartered Engineer; Philip Anthony Brodey [1963] Director/Sales Engineer; Timothy Lee Chambers [1964] Director [American]; Mark Gapinski [1975] Director [American]; Jeffrey Kostrzewa [1964] Director [American]; Richard Miller [1970] Director/Associate General Counsel [American]; Catherine Louise Rohll [1965] Director

Norbrook Holdings Limited
Incorporated: 16 May 1988 *Employees:* 2,068
Net Worth: £128,167,000 *Total Assets:* £200,508,000
Registered Office: 1 Saxon Way East, Corby, Northants, NN18 9EY
Activities: Activities of head offices
Shareholders: Robert William Roy McNulty; Philip Charles Cornwallis Trousdell; Lady Ballyedmond
Officers: Martin Patrick Murdock, Secretary; Lady Mary Gordon Ballyedmond [1947] Director; Sir Ian Gibson [1947] Director; The Honourable Edward Gordon Shannon Haughey [1979] Director; James Quinton Stewart Haughey [1981] Director/Medical Doctor; John Paul McGrath [1972] Director [Irish]; Liam Nagle [1962] Director [Irish]

Norbrook Laboratories (G.B.) Limited
Incorporated: 16 December 1983 *Employees:* 51
Net Worth: £10,635,163 *Total Assets:* £19,429,700
Registered Office: 1 Saxon Way East, Corby, Northants, NN18 9EY
Activities: Wholesale of pharmaceutical goods
Shareholders: Lady Ballyedmond; Robert William Roy McNulty; Philip Charles Cornwallis Trousdell
Officers: Martin Patrick Murdock, Secretary; John Paul McGrath [1972] Finance Director [Irish]; Martin Patrick Murdock [1962] Director/Accountant [Irish]; Liam Nagle [1962] Director [Irish]

Norcros Group (Holdings) Limited
Incorporated: 29 May 1956 *Employees:* 1,000
Net Worth: £172,856,000 *Total Assets:* £384,046,016
Registered Office: Ladyfield House, Station Road, Wilmslow, Cheshire, SK9 1BU
Activities: Activities of head offices
Officers: Richard Hawke Collins, Secretary; Richard Hawke Collins [1962] Director/Company Secretary and Group Counsel; Nicholas Paul Kelsall [1956] Director; Robert James Sidell [1976] Director/Financial Controller; Shaun Michael Smith [1961] Finance Director

Norcros Industry (International) Limited
Incorporated: 6 January 1936
Net Worth: £43,672,000 *Total Assets:* £51,125,000
Registered Office: Ladyfield House, Station Road, Wilmslow, Cheshire, SK9 1BU
Activities: Non-trading company
Officers: Richard Hawke Collins, Secretary; Richard Hawke Collins [1962] Director/Company Secretary & Group Counsel; Nicholas Paul Kelsall [1956] Director; Shaun Michael Smith [1961] Finance Director

Norcros PLC
Incorporated: 5 January 1999
Net Worth: £104,600,000 *Total Assets:* £313,000,000
Registered Office: Ladyfield House, Station Road, Wilmslow, Cheshire, SK9 1BU
Activities: Activities of head offices
Officers: Richard Hawke Collins, Secretary; Joanna Christine Hallas [1970] Director; Nicholas Paul Kelsall [1956] Director; David William McKeith [1951] Director; Shaun Michael Smith [1961] Finance Director; Martin George Towers [1952] Director

Norfolk Free Range Limited
Incorporated: 19 December 2003 *Employees:* 106
Net Worth: £11,630,317 *Total Assets:* £31,133,952
Registered Office: Snowre Hall, Main Road, Fordham, Downham Market, Norfolk, PE38 0LN
Activities: Raising of swine and pigs
Shareholders: Steven Hart; Sally Ann Hart
Officers: Sally Ann Hart, Secretary/Farmer; Sally Ann Hart [1969] Director/Farmer; Steven Hart [1960] Director/Farmer

Normanby Estate Company Limited (The)
Incorporated: 22 July 1920 *Employees:* 7
Net Worth: £11,973,076 *Total Assets:* £14,659,411
Registered Office: Estate Office, Main Street, Normanby, Scunthorpe, N Lincs, DN15 9HS
Activities: Other service activities n.e.c.
Major Shareholder: Reginald Adrian Berkeley Sheffield
Officers: Sir Reginald Adrian Berkeley Sheffield, Secretary; Sir Reginald Adrian Berkeley Sheffield [1946] Director; Robert Charles Berkeley Sheffield [1984] Director; Lady Victoria Penelope Sheffield [1949] Director

C.John Norris (Cars & Caravans) Limited
Incorporated: 11 January 1939 *Employees:* 43
Net Worth: £10,893,977 *Total Assets:* £15,464,725
Registered Office: Thorney Road, Eye, Peterborough, PE6 7UB
Activities: Sale of new cars and light motor vehicles
Shareholders: Executors of Jonathan Norris; Sally Norris
Officers: Sally Norris, Secretary; Sally Norris [1963] Director/Company Secretary; Anna Spriggs [1963] Director/Solicitor

Nortech Foods Limited
Incorporated: 9 December 1982 *Employees:* 75
Net Worth: £5,202,345 *Total Assets:* £16,607,925
Registered Office: Ings Road, Doncaster, S Yorks, DN5 9TL
Activities: Manufacture of oils and fats
Parent: Saria Limited
Officers: Andrew Richard Smith [1962] Director

North Bidco Limited
Incorporated: 8 January 2016 *Employees:* 4
Net Worth Deficit: £2,136,811 *Total Assets:* £15,655,510
Registered Office: 2nd Floor, Sir Wilfrid Newton House, Thorncliffe Park Estate, Newton Chambers Road, Chapeltown, Sheffield, S35 2PH
Activities: Activities of head offices
Parent: North Midco Limited
Officers: Caroline Marie Cafferty [1981] Operations Director [Irish]; William John Etchell [1971] Director/Chief Financial Officer; Julian Edward Harley [1957] Director/Chairman; Robyn Julieann Johnstone [1967] Director/Group CEO [British/Australian]; David Mark Jones [1965] Director; Robert Douglas King [1982] Director/Fund Manager

North Kesteven Academy
Incorporated: 3 June 2011 *Employees:* 153
Previous: North Kesteven School
Net Worth: £9,241,000 *Total Assets:* £13,141,000
Registered Office: North Kesteven School, Moor Lane, North Hykeham, Lincoln, LN6 9AG
Activities: General secondary education
Officers: Romina Goldsworthy, Secretary; Rachel Elizabeth Barrett [1972] Director/Accountant; Judith Anne Burnett [1941] Director; Nicholas Geoffrey Cooper [1987] Director/Project Leader; Michael Charles Gallimore [1963] Director/Cover Manager; Andrew Greenwood [1965] Director; Antonia Lloyd [1975] Director/Teacher; Darren Salisbury [1965] Director; Jonathan Peter Sloan [1974] Director/Manager; Martyn Andrew Taylor [1955] Director/Retired; Joanne Faye Tunnicliffe [1975] Director/Headteacher; Susan Lesley Van Zyl [1953] Director/Retired

North Lincs Property Limited
Incorporated: 25 August 1998 *Employees:* 4
Net Worth: £11,620,133 *Total Assets:* £20,700,908
Registered Office: Sandtoft Industrial Estate, Belton, Doncaster, S Yorks, DN9 1PN
Activities: Operation of gravel and sand pits; mining of clays and kaolin
Shareholder: Richard John Mills
Officers: Karen Mills, Secretary; Richard John Mills [1965] Director

North Midco Limited
Incorporated: 8 January 2016 *Employees:* 4
Net Worth Deficit: £38,301 *Total Assets:* £11,669,573
Registered Office: 2nd Floor, Sir Wilfrid Newton House, Thorncliffe Park Estate, Newton Chambers Road, Chapeltown, Sheffield, S35 2PH
Activities: Activities of head offices
Parent: Education Placement Group Limited
Officers: Caroline Marie Cafferty [1981] Operations Director [Irish]; William John Etchell [1971] Director/Chief Financial Officer; Julian Edward Harley [1957] Director/Chairman; Robyn Julieann Johnstone [1967] Director/Group CEO [British/Australian]; David Mark Jones [1965] Director; Robert Douglas King [1982] Director/Fund Manager

North Nottinghamshire Lift Project Company (No.1) Limited
Incorporated: 10 October 2003
Net Worth Deficit: £7,094,000 *Total Assets:* £44,284,000
Registered Office: Unit G1, Ash Tree Court, Nottingham Business Park, Nottingham, NG8 6PY
Activities: Construction of commercial buildings
Parent: North Nottinghamshire Lift (Midco) Limited
Officers: Michael George Duggan, Secretary; Richard John Coates [1966] CHP Investment Director; Lucy Ann Dadge [1964] NHS Director; Charlotte Sophie Ellen Douglass [1978] Director/Chartered Surveyor; Gavin William MacKinlay [1957] Associate Director; Kirsty O'Brien [1982] Director/Operations Manager; Paddy Tipping [1949] Director/Member of Parliament

North Oxford Garage Limited
Incorporated: 15 October 1945 *Employees:* 164
Net Worth: £4,173,983 *Total Assets:* £29,714,158
Registered Office: Wollaston Motors, Bedford Road, Northampton, NN1 5SZ
Activities: Sale of other motor vehicles
Parent: William Morgan Group Ltd
Officers: Martin Huw Morgan Allard [1967] Director; Christian William Le Fevre [1967] Director

North West Portfolio (No.3) Limited
Incorporated: 23 March 2016
Net Worth: £780,584 *Total Assets:* £22,086,516
Registered Office: Emerson House, Heyes Lane, Alderley Edge, Cheshire, SK9 7LF
Activities: Development of building projects
Parent: Emerson Developments (Holdings) Limited
Officers: Varun Maharaj, Secretary; Paul James Hubball [1973] Director/Business Executive; Anthony Emerson Jones [1967] Director; Mark Emerson Jones [1964] Director; Peter Emerson Jones [1935] Director

North West Portfolio Limited
Incorporated: 12 August 1992
Net Worth: £15,957,115 *Total Assets:* £40,091,904
Registered Office: Emerson House, Heyes Lane, Alderley Edge, Cheshire, SK9 7LF
Activities: Development of building projects
Parent: Emerson Developments (Holdings) Limited
Officers: Varun Maharaj, Secretary; Paul James Hubball [1973] Director; Anthony Emerson Jones [1967] Director; Mark Emerson Jones [1964] Director; Peter Emerson Jones [1935] Director

North West Steel Limited
Incorporated: 22 June 1988 *Employees:* 26
Net Worth: £7,383,586 *Total Assets:* £9,922,967
Registered Office: 1 Fenlake Business Centre, Fengate, Peterborough, Cambs, PE1 5BQ
Activities: Other specialised construction activities n.e.c.
Major Shareholder: John Patrick William Roe
Officers: Jean Robertson [1964] Director; John Patrick William Roe [1958] Director; Clinton John Taylor [1961] Director

Northampton Acquisition Ltd
Incorporated: 25 May 1995
Net Worth: £19,032,336 *Total Assets:* £22,457,206
Registered Office: 2 Wolseley Road, Woburn Road Industrial Estate, Kempston, Beds, MK42 7AD
Activities: Non-trading company
Officers: Deborah Marion Fraser, Secretary; Arie Cornelis Bijsterveld [1968] European Director of IT and Finance [Dutch]; Michael John Brown [1958] Managing Director

Northampton Primary Academy Trust
Incorporated: 8 August 2012 *Employees:* 640
Net Worth: £43,441,880 *Total Assets:* £50,662,504
Registered Office: Headlands Primary School, Bushland Road, Northampton, NN3 2NS
Activities: Primary education
Officers: Annie Mary Booth, Secretary; Julie Clarke [1960] Director/Business Consultant; John Charles Fazackerley [1953] Director/Retired; Julia Kedwards [1967] Director/Headteacher; Stuart Lee Lock [1977] Director/Chief Executive; Thomas David Rees [1977] Director/Headteacher; Graham Neil Smith [1971] Director/Business Change Consultant; Julie Verena Stapleton [1963] Director/Independent HR Consultant; Adrian White [1968] Director; Nicholas Wilson [1968] Director/Project Manager

Northampton Rugby Football Club Limited
Incorporated: 19 December 1995 *Employees:* 278
Net Worth: £12,508,123 *Total Assets:* £26,421,112
Registered Office: Franklins Gardens, Weedon Road, Northampton, NN5 5BG
Activities: Operation of sports facilities
Parent: Northampton Saints PLC
Officers: Julia Anne Chapman, Secretary; Keith Leslie Barwell [1944] Director; Nicholas David Beal [1970] Director/Financial Advisor; Ella Bevan [1972] Director/Business Consultant; Julia Anne Chapman [1972] Director/Chartered Accountant; Mark Darbon [1979] Director/Chief Executive Officer; Jonathan James William Drown [1965] Financial Director; Anthony Clive Hewitt [1949] Director; Colin Povey [1960] Director; Matthew George Smith [1971] Director/Chief Finance Officer; John White [1951] Director/Business Consultant

Northampton Saints PLC
Incorporated: 4 September 2000 *Employees:* 278
Net Worth: £16,983,444 *Total Assets:* £29,896,332
Registered Office: Franklins Gardens, Weedon Road, Northampton, NN5 5BG
Activities: Activities of sport clubs
Officers: Julia Anne Chapman, Secretary; Keith Leslie Barwell [1944] Director; Nicholas David Beal [1970] Director/Financial Advisor; Ella Bevan [1972] Director/Business Consultant; Julia Anne Chapman [1972] Director/Chartered Accountant; Mark Darbon [1979] Director/Chief Executive Officer; Jonathan James William Drown [1965] Financial Director; Anthony Clive Hewitt [1949] Director; Colin Povey [1960] Director; Matthew George Smith [1971] Director/Chief Finance Officer; John White [1951] Director/Business Consultant

Northampton School for Boys
Incorporated: 3 August 2010 *Employees:* 222
Net Worth: £25,139,488 *Total Assets:* £27,008,058
Registered Office: Northampton School for Boys, Billing Road, Northampton, NN1 5RT
Activities: General secondary education
Officers: Richard Bernard, Secretary; Peter John Bason [1956] Director/Dental Surgeon; John Alfred Beswick [1938] Director/Scientist; Matthew John Ebsworth [1961] Director; Yvonne Edwards [1934] Director; Alan William Hakes [1962] Director; Oliver Harris [1957] Director/Retired; Maureen Patricia Jamieson [1959] Director; Mary Elizabeth Kay [1943] Director; Neil Martin [1957] Director/Dentist; Lucienne Jessica Shakir [1984] Director/Teacher; Angela Shaw [1963] Director/Finance Assistant; Dr Fiona Jane Thompson [1964] Director/Consultant Paediatrician; Alastair Stuart Thomson [1958] Director/Education Officer; Morcea Antoinette Walker [1949] Director; Jonathan Peter Webb [1958] Director/Chartered Surveyor

The Northampton Theatres Trust Limited
Incorporated: 30 September 1998 *Employees:* 177
Net Worth: £4,794,683 *Total Assets:* £10,300,841
Registered Office: Northampton Theatres Trust, 19-21 Guildhall Road, Northampton, NN1 1DP
Activities: Performing arts
Parent: Northamptonshire Arts Management Trust Ltd
Officers: Joanna Rose Gordon, Secretary; Jane Catherine Bloomer [1976] Director/Solicitor; Stephen Robert Edmonds [1952] Director/Consultant; Brandon Eldred [1972] Director/Civil Servant; Frances Eleanor Holloway [1983] Director/Accountant; Bernadette Angela Lally [1983] Director/Civil Servant; Roger Martin [1967] Director; Victoria Jane Miles [1966] Director/Chief Executive; Hannah Fay Miller [1976] Director/Head of Casting; Kay Elizabeth Roberts [1957] Director; Clare Siobhan Slater [1983] Director/Literary Manager and Dramaturg; Cllr Danielle Veronica Stone [1950] Director/Councillor

Northamptonshire Arts Management Trust
Incorporated: 9 August 2010 *Employees:* 219
Net Worth: £4,856,583 *Total Assets:* £10,676,045
Registered Office: 19-21 Guildhall Road, Northampton, NN1 1DP
Activities: Combined office administrative service activities
Officers: Joanna Rose Gordon, Secretary; Gail Elizabeth Arnott [1951] Director; Stephen Robert Edmonds [1952] Director/Consultant; Victoria Jane Miles [1966] Director/Chief Executive Officer; Gary Robert Tait [1963] Director/Solicitor

Northamptonshire Association of Youth Clubs
Incorporated: 23 March 1990 *Employees:* 236
Net Worth: £14,853,883 *Total Assets:* £17,925,564
Registered Office: Kings Park, Kings Park Road, Northampton, NN3 6LL
Activities: Other sports activities
Officers: John Mark Whittaker, Secretary; David Edward Darby [1942] Director/Builder; John Purdie Gilmour [1935] Director/Farmer Retired; Sylvia Susan Gilmour [1942] Director/Administrator; Peter John Hales [1943] Director/Chief Surveyor; David Eric Laing [1945] Director/Architect; Timothy Mountford Leese [1937] Director; Rachel Elizabeth Mallows [1962] Director/Manager; Rev David Shearer [1939] Director/Minister of Religion; Joan Mary Tice [1933] Director

Northbridge Australia Limited
Incorporated: 5 July 2010
Net Worth: £27,130,884 *Total Assets:* £27,658,412
Registered Office: Second Avenue, Centrum 100, Burton on Trent, Staffs, DE14 2WF
Activities: Activities of head offices
Parent: Northbridge Industrial Services PLC
Officers: Iwan Phillips, Secretary; Eric Ward Hook [1953] Director; Iwan Ceri Phillips [1984] Director/Chartered Accountant

Northbridge Industrial Services PLC
Incorporated: 7 January 2005
Net Worth: £35,685,000 *Total Assets:* £56,768,000
Registered Office: Second Avenue, Centrum 100, Burton on Trent, Staffs, DE14 2WF
Activities: Manufacture of electric motors, generators and transformers
Officers: Iwan Phillips, Secretary; Judith Aldersey-Williams [1963] Director/Lawyer; Ian James Gardner [1966] Managing Director; Peter Robert Harris [1951] Director; Eric Ward Hook [1953] Director; Nitin Kaul [1974] Director; David Courtnall Marshall [1944] Director; Ashoni Kumar Mehta [1965] Director; Iwan Ceri Phillips [1984] Finance Director

Northcoast Seafoods Limited
Incorporated: 25 September 2000 *Employees:* 27
Net Worth: £13,198,969 *Total Assets:* £62,163,272
Registered Office: Plot 12, Estate Road No 1, South Humberside Industrial Estate, Grimsby, N E Lincs, DN31 2TB
Activities: Wholesale of other food, including fish, crustaceans and molluscs
Shareholders: Nim Limited; Kangamiut Holding A/S; Fridrik Mar Thorsteinsson
Officers: Fridrik Mar Thorsteinsson, Secretary; Ulrik Bjerre Rasmussen [1964] Financial Director [Danish]; Fridrik Mar Thorsteinsson [1971] Director [Icelander]

Northern Endeavour Limited
Incorporated: 5 March 2007
Net Worth: £100,000 *Total Assets:* £10,102,270
Registered Office: Templeborough Works, Sheffield Road, Sheffield, S9 1RS
Activities: Dormant company
Parent: Andaray (Holdings) Limited
Officers: Steven Edward Karol [1954] Director/Managing Partner [American]

Northern House School Academy Trust
Incorporated: 12 July 2012 *Employees:* 189
Net Worth: £19,846,568 *Total Assets:* £25,447,726
Registered Office: Northern House School, South Parade, Summer Town, Oxford, OX2 7JN
Activities: Primary education
Officers: David Ian Barker [1952] Director/Headteacher; Jean Carr [1944] Director/Psychotherapist; Seonaid Susan Danziger [1941] Director/Retired; Philip Hanford Leivers [1966] Director/Schools' Officer; Jon Davis Emanuel Rayman [1938] Director/Solicitor; William Hubert Powlett Smith [1950] Director/Retired Accountant; Kevin Thompson [1965] Director/General Manager; Dr Marshall David Young [1947] Director/Retired University Professor

Northern Powerhouse Investments Limited
Incorporated: 26 November 2015
Total Assets: £55,161,000
Registered Office: Steel City House, West Street, Sheffield, S1 2GQ
Activities: Activities of venture and development capital companies
Officers: Shanika Amarasekara, Secretary; Kenneth Duncan Cooper [1963] Managing Director; Patrick John Magee [1970] Director/Banker [Irish]; Keith Charles William Morgan [1963] Director

Northfleet Property LLP
Incorporated: 1 May 2015
Net Worth: £21,089,160 *Total Assets:* £21,441,366
Registered Office: Bardon Hall, Copt Oak Road, Markfield, Leics, LE67 9PJ

Northwood Tissue (Disley) Limited
Incorporated: 17 September 2009 *Employees:* 62
Net Worth: £7,337,198 *Total Assets:* £17,158,760
Registered Office: Waterside, Disley, Stockport, Cheshire, SK12 2HW
Activities: Manufacture of household and sanitary goods and of toilet requisites
Major Shareholder: Paul Fecher
Officers: Paul Edward King, Secretary; Christopher John Davies [1965] Director; Adam Scott Fecher [1974] Director; Marc Darren Fecher [1971] Director; Paul Fecher [1946] Director/Paper Agent; David Bryn Harries [1978] Director; Paul Edward King [1974] Director/Accountant

The Northworthy Trust
Incorporated: 16 February 2011 *Employees:* 421
Previous: The Long Eaton School Academy Trust
Net Worth: £48,640,312 *Total Assets:* £57,777,296
Registered Office: Thoresby Road, Long Eaton, Nottingham, NG10 3NP
Activities: General secondary education
Officers: Mike Ainsley [1950] Director/Retired; Neil Robert Champness [1968] Director/Professor; Mark Timothy Gallimore [1959] Director/Learning Training and Development; Jon Robert Hemsley [1970] Director/Engineering Consultant; Claire Louise Jackson [1973] Director/HR Administrator; Stephen Anthony Pearce [1980] Director/Chief Financial Officer; Beth Phillips [1981] Director/Accountant; Professor Malcolm Joseph Todd [1965] Director/Pro Vice-Chancellor, Student Experience

Norton Finance Group Limited
Incorporated: 4 May 2010 *Employees:* 164
Net Worth: £26,754,116 *Total Assets:* £73,376,720
Registered Office: Norton House, Mansfield Road, Rotherham, S Yorks, S60 2DR
Activities: Financial intermediation not elsewhere classified
Shareholder: Keith Stringer
Officers: Keith Stringer [1941] Director; Mark Stringer [1967] Director; Paul Stringer [1970] Director

Norton Financial Services Limited
Incorporated: 2 March 1983 *Employees:* 115
Net Worth: £15,356,224 *Total Assets:* £17,411,876
Registered Office: Norton House, Mansfield Road, Rotherham, S Yorks, S60 2DR
Activities: Financial intermediation not elsewhere classified
Parent: Norton Finance Group Limited
Officers: Jennifer Susan Stringer, Secretary; Keith Stringer [1941] Director/Insurance and Finance Broker; Mark Stringer [1967] Director; Paul Stringer [1970] Director

Norton Home Loans Limited
Incorporated: 8 March 1985
Net Worth: £10,079,160 *Total Assets:* £72,499,824
Registered Office: Norton House, Mansfield Road, Rotherham, S Yorks, S60 2DR
Activities: Financial intermediation not elsewhere classified
Parent: Norton Finance Group Limited
Officers: Keith Stringer, Secretary; Keith Stringer [1941] Director/Insurance and Finance Broker; Mark Stringer [1967] Director; Paul Stringer [1970] Director

Norton Motorcycles (UK) Limited
Incorporated: 8 October 2008 *Employees:* 71
Net Worth: £2,191,429 *Total Assets:* £12,487,483
Registered Office: Donington Hall, Castle Donington, Derby, DE74 2SG
Activities: Manufacture of motorcycles
Major Shareholder: Stuart James Garner
Officers: Stuart James Garner [1968] Director; Simon Peter Skinner [1973] Director

Nottingham City Airport Limited
Incorporated: 5 April 2004 *Employees:* 12
Net Worth: £622,832 *Total Assets:* £9,020,083
Registered Office: Granary House, Melton Road, Edwalton, Nottingham, NG12 4DA
Activities: Other letting and operating of own or leased real estate
Shareholders: John A Wells Limited; Truman Contractors (East Midlands) Ltd
Officers: Roy Thomas Hill, Secretary/Accountant; Roy Thomas Hill [1935] Director/Accountant; Victor William Truman [1944] Director; John Brian Wells [1939] Director

Nottingham City Homes Limited
Incorporated: 22 November 2004 *Employees:* 961
Net Worth Deficit: £87,427,000 *Total Assets:* £39,377,000
Registered Office: Loxley House, Station Street, Nottingham, NG2 3NJ
Activities: Other business support service activities n.e.c.
Parent: Nottingham City Council
Officers: George Walker Pashley, Secretary; William Frederick Blincoe [1954] Director; Michael Anthony Khouri-Bent [1964] Director; Jackie Morris [1945] Director/City Councillor; Sarita-Marie Rehman-Wall [1974] Director/Homemaker; Michael David Savage [1963] Director/Shop Manager; M Malcolm Sharp [1949] Director/Self Employed; Geoffrey Twining Walker [1961] Director/Retired; Samuel Edward Webster [1979] Director/Councillor; Councillor Stephen Young [1956] Director/Retired

Nottingham City Transport Limited
Incorporated: 27 March 1986 *Employees:* 1,080
Net Worth: £17,157,000 *Total Assets:* £54,542,000
Registered Office: Lower Parliament Street, Nottingham, NG1 1GG
Activities: Other urban, suburban or metropolitan passenger land transport (not underground, metro or similar)
Shareholders: Nottingham City Council; Transdev PLC
Officers: Robert James Hicklin, Secretary/Director; David Astill [1964] Director; Councillor Jonathan Neil Collins [1960] Director/Councillor; Mark James Fowles [1956] Director; Robert James Hicklin [1968] Director; Alex Lloyd Hornby [1981] Director; Barry Hutton [1972] Director/Bus Driver; Corrall Jenkins [1960] Director/Councillor; John Lumbis [1954] Director/Engineer; Gary Mason [1956] Director; Brian Parbutt [1965] Director/Printer; Nicola Tidy [1957] Director; Councillor Linda Woodings [1965] Director/Councillor

Nottingham Citycare Partnership CIC
Incorporated: 2 March 2011 *Employees:* 1,468
Net Worth: £4,603,526 *Total Assets:* £20,925,394
Registered Office: 1 Standard Court, Park Row, Nottingham, NG1 6GN
Activities: Other human health activities
Officers: Kathryn Isobel Gillatt, Secretary; Lyn McDerment Bacon [1961] Director (CEO); Anne Jacqueline Dray [1960] Director/Accountant; Kathryn Isobel Gillatt [1961] Director; Tracy Ann Tyrrell [1967] Director; Michael Williams [1948] Director; Lynn Jane Woods [1959] Director

Nottingham Enterprise Zone Development Company Limited
Incorporated: 20 March 2013
Net Worth: £10,000,000 *Total Assets:* £10,580,000
Registered Office: 1 Thane Road West, Nottingham, NG2 3AA
Activities: Other professional, scientific and technical activities n.e.c.
Shareholders: Alliance Boots Holdings Limited; Department for Communities & Local Government
Officers: Andrew Richard Thompson, Secretary; Lucy Ann Blasdale [1976] Director/Chartered Surveyor; Jonathan Mark Chivers [1968] Director/Surveyor; Elizabeth Fagan [1957] Managing Director

Nottingham Forest Football Club Limited
Incorporated: 20 April 1982 *Employees:* 197
Net Worth Deficit: £38,759,000 *Total Assets:* £17,107,000
Registered Office: The City Ground, Pavilion Road, West Bridgford, Nottingham, NG2 5FJ
Activities: Activities of sport clubs
Parent: NF Football Investments Ltd
Officers: Samantha Gordon [1971] Director; Johannes Anthonius Bernardus Metgod [1958] Director [Dutch]; Jonathan Tudor Owen [1971] Director; Nicholas Randall [1966] Director/Barrister Queen's Counsel; Ioannis Vrentzos [1977] Director/Chief Executive Officer [Greek]

Nottingham High School
Incorporated: 29 August 2002 *Employees:* 249
Net Worth: £22,867,000 *Total Assets:* £31,977,000
Registered Office: Waverley Mount, Nottingham, NG7 4ED
Activities: Primary education
Officers: Stuart Ian Robert Ramsey, Secretary; Timothy Peter Allen [1955] Director; Stephen Banks [1963] Director; Christopher Francis Doleman [1964] Finance Director; Mark Flanagan [1977] Director/Chartered Accountant; Stephen Michael Green [1956] Director/Retired Police Officer; Dr Basheera Hanslo [1969] Director/Dentist; John Stephen Jackson [1953] Director; Nehgat Nawaz Khan [1981] Director/Councillor; Dr Sharmini Krishanand [1974] Director/Doctor; Philippa Kate McNamara [1965] Director/Manager; Syed Aftad Mohyuddin [1964] Director/Lecturer; Peter Nicholas Munro [1947] Director/Retired; Sir John Peace [1949] Director; Christopher James Robinson [1949] Director/Retired; Navdeep Sethi [1979] Director/Business Consultant; Dr Gail Margaret Walton [1960] Director/Doctor; David William Wild [1956] Director/Solicitor

Nottingham Industrial Group Limited
Incorporated: 16 September 1996 *Employees:* 42
Net Worth: £15,229,000 *Total Assets:* £18,889,000
Registered Office: 64 St James's Street, Nottingham, NG1 6FJ
Activities: Non-trading company
Shareholders: Charles Richard Bennion; Nicholas John Forman Hardy
Officers: Nicholas John Foreman Hardy [1948] Director; Thomas William Bailey Foreman Hardy [1983] Director; Peter Anthony Letley [1945] Director

Nottingham Rehab Limited
Incorporated: 18 September 1985 *Employees:* 901
Net Worth: £37,376,000 *Total Assets:* £53,929,000
Registered Office: Sherwood House, Cartwright Way, Forest Business Park, Bardon Hill, Coalville, Leics, LE67 1UB
Activities: Non-specialised wholesale trade
Parent: Salus Healthcare Limited
Officers: John Makin, Secretary; Jeremy Michael Benson [1963] Director; Stephen Paul Kennedy [1960] Occupation Purchasing Director; John Makin [1972] Director/Chartered Accountant

Nottingham Roman Catholic Diocesan Trustees
Incorporated: 9 February 2010 *Employees:* 78
Net Worth: £63,734,000 *Total Assets:* £65,718,000
Registered Office: Willson House, 25 Derby Road, Nottingham, NG1 5AW
Activities: Activities of extraterritorial organisations and bodies
Officers: Edward Stephen Poyser, Secretary; Michael Thomas Abbott [1936] Director/Retired Chartered Surveyor; Reverend Paul Chipchase [1953] Director/Priest; Katherine Mary Cohoon [1942] Director/Solicitor; Martin John Hardy [1966] Director/Priest; Reverend Edward Stanislaw Jarosz [1964] Director/Priest; Rev Patrick Joseph McKinney [1954] Director [Irish]; Rev Thomas Michael Moore [1950] Director/Priest [Irish]; Christopher Stephen Sowman [1954] Director/Chartered Accountant; Reverend Joseph Thomas Wheat [1975] Director/Priest; Edmund John Whittaker [1962] Director; David Alan Wilson [1949] Director/Retired

Nova Bio-Pharma Holdings Limited
Incorporated: 22 May 2008 *Employees:* 221
Net Worth: £23,014,768 *Total Assets:* £30,521,822
Registered Office: Martin House, Gloucester Crescent, Wigston, Leics, LE18 4YL
Activities: Activities of head offices
Shareholders: Peter John Pitt White; Regina Teresa White
Officers: Clement Roger Staniforth, Secretary; Dr Peter John Pitt White [1948] Director/Pharmacist

Nova Education Trust
Incorporated: 16 May 2011 *Employees:* 956
Previous: Torch Academy Gateway Trust
Net Worth: £121,258,000 *Total Assets:* £140,140,000
Registered Office: Nova Education Trust Office (C19), The Sir Colin Campbell Building, The University of Nottingham, Triumph Road, Nottingham, NG7 2TU
Activities: General secondary education
Officers: Alison Jayne Ingram, Secretary; Michael Roy Auty [1963] Director/Barrister-at-Law Queen's Counsel; Lucy Mary Burrow [1978] IT Director; Richard Charles Flewitt [1961] Director; Melanie Lawson [1970] Director/Headteacher; Sylvia MacDougall [1943] Director/Financial Administrator; John Nicholas Mills [1955] Director/Company Chairman; John Saunders [1948] Director/Retired; Brian Stein [1949] Director/Retired; John Tomasevic [1955] Director/Headteacher; Janice White [1943] Director/Retired; Albert John Woods [1949] Director/Retired Heating Engineer

Nova Laboratories Limited
Incorporated: 25 November 1993 *Employees:* 217
Net Worth: £14,533,310 *Total Assets:* £26,162,616
Registered Office: Martin House, Gloucester Crescent, Wigston, Leics, LE18 4YL
Activities: Manufacture of basic pharmaceutical products
Parent: Nova Bio-Pharma Holdings Limited
Officers: Clement Roger Staniforth, Secretary; Dr Peter John Pitt White [1948] Director/Pharmacist

Novera Energy (Holdings 2) Limited
Incorporated: 28 October 2004
Net Worth Deficit: £5,010,000 *Total Assets:* £76,390,000
Registered Office: First Floor, 500 Pavilion Drive, Northampton Business Park, Northampton, NN4 7YJ
Activities: Production of electricity
Parent: Infinis Limited
Officers: Jacqueline Long, Secretary; Michael Damien Holton [1973] Finance Director; James Huxley Milne [1972] Director/Lawyer; Stephen Shane Pickering [1969] Director of Operations

Novera Energy Generation No. 2 Limited
Incorporated: 1 April 1989
Net Worth: £9,092,000 *Total Assets:* £15,191,000
Registered Office: First Floor, 500 Pavilion Drive, Northampton Business Park, Northampton, NN4 7YJ
Activities: Production of electricity
Parent: Novera Energy (Holdings 2) Limited
Officers: Jacqueline Long, Secretary; Michael Damien Holton [1973] Finance Director; James Huxley Milne [1972] Director/Lawyer; Stephen Shane Pickering [1969] Director of Operations

Novo Community Ltd
Incorporated: 28 October 2014
Net Worth: £95 *Total Assets:* £10,000,145
Registered Office: The Sherard Building, Edmund Halley Road, Oxford, OX4 4DQ
Activities: Justice and judicial activities
Parent: Amey Community Limited
Officers: Ian Harry Deninson [1964] Group HR Director; Amanda Lucia Fisher [1963] Director/MD Facilities Management, Defence and Justice; Asif Ghafoor [1970] Director; Andrew Lee Milner [1969] Director/Chartered Civil Engineer

Novoferm Europe Limited
Incorporated: 23 September 2003 *Employees:* 2,506
Net Worth: £189,888,640 *Total Assets:* £421,993,952
Registered Office: 125 Matilda Street, Sheffield, S1 4QG
Activities: Wholesale of wood, construction materials and sanitary equipment
Parent: Sanwa Holdings Corporation
Officers: Peter Kruse, Secretary; Hiroatsu Fujisawa [1953] Director [Japanese]; Masahiro Fukuda [1955] Director [Japanese]; Thomas Hage [1958] Director [German]; Takenobu Hoizumi [1959] Director [Japanese]; Rainer Schackmann [1965] Managing Director [German]; Toshitaka Takayama [1939] Director/President of Sanwa Shutter Corp [Japanese]; Yasushi Takayama [1971] Director [Japanese]

Novoferm UK Holdings Limited
Incorporated: 20 January 2012 *Employees:* 5
Net Worth: £646,242 *Total Assets:* £9,870,990
Registered Office: 125 Matilda Street, Sheffield, S1 4QG
Activities: Other service activities n.e.c.
Shareholder: Novoferm Europe Limited
Officers: Amber Louise Baker [1974] Director; Jeremy Patrick Scott Baker [1960] Director; Dirk Goessling [1970] Director [German]; Thomas Hage [1958] Director [German]; Rainer Schackmann [1965] Director [German]

NP Aerospace Limited
Incorporated: 27 November 1997 *Employees:* 144
Net Worth: £5,519,000 *Total Assets:* £10,652,000
Registered Office: 473 Foleshill Road, Coventry, Warwicks, CV6 5AQ
Activities: Manufacture of other plastic products
Parent: TCG Guardian 2 Limited
Officers: James Kempston [1982] Director [Canadian]; David Adam Petheram [1974] Director; Adrian Paul Smith [1975] Director

NSF International UK Limited
Incorporated: 16 July 2007
Net Worth: £26,206,000 *Total Assets:* £29,905,000
Registered Office: Hanborough Business Park, Long Hanborough, Oxford, OX29 8SJ
Activities: Activities of other holding companies n.e.c.
Officers: Lesley Chipper, Secretary; Lesley Ann Chipper [1965] Finance Director; Kevan Paul Lawlor [1957] Director/President and Chief Executive [American]; Michael Patrick Walsh [1964] Director/Vice President CFO [American]

Nu Instruments Limited
Incorporated: 13 April 1995 *Employees:* 112
Net Worth: £17,932,000 *Total Assets:* £21,595,000
Registered Office: P O Box 36, 2 New Star Road, Leicester, LE4 9JQ
Activities: Manufacture of electronic measuring, testing etc. equipment, not for industrial process control
Parent: EMA Holdings UK Limited
Officers: Joy Atwell, Secretary; Emanuela Speranza [1968] Director [Italian]; Russell Webster [1964] Managing Director

Nu-Oval Acquisitions 1 Limited
Incorporated: 10 April 2007
Net Worth: £11,157,000 *Total Assets:* £13,598,000
Registered Office: Polypipe Ltd, Broomhouse Lane, Edlington, Doncaster, S Yorks, DN12 1ES
Activities: Activities of other holding companies n.e.c.
Parent: Polypipe Limited
Officers: Emma Gayle Versluys, Secretary; Paul Anthony James [1967] Director/Chief Financial Officer; Martin Keith Payne [1965] Director

Nu-Oval Acquisitions 2 Limited
Incorporated: 10 April 2007
Net Worth Deficit: £51,110,000 *Total Assets:* £26,500,000
Registered Office: Polypipe Ltd, Broomhouse Lane, Edlington, Doncaster, S Yorks, DN12 1ES
Activities: Activities of other holding companies n.e.c.
Parent: Nu-Oval Acquisitions 1 Limited
Officers: Emma Gayle Versluys, Secretary; Paul Anthony James [1967] Director/Chief Financial Officer; Martin Keith Payne [1965] Director

NUS Holdings Limited
Incorporated: 1 February 1974 *Employees:* 33
Net Worth: £4,816,672 *Total Assets:* £9,856,502
Registered Office: Ian King House, Snape Road, Macclesfield, Cheshire, SK10 2NZ
Activities: Management consultancy activities other than financial management
Parent: National Union of Students (United Kingdom)
Officers: Shakira Cotcheta Martin [1988] Director/NUS National President; Ali Reza Milani [1994] Director/NUS Officer; Peter Jerome Robertson [1963] Managing Director; Douglas Taylor [1954] Director/General Manager NUS

NUS Services Limited
Incorporated: 1 June 1982 *Employees:* 56
Net Worth Deficit: £403,442 *Total Assets:* £9,893,195
Registered Office: Snape Road, Macclesfield, Cheshire, SK10 2NZ
Activities: Non-specialised wholesale trade
Parent: NUS Holdings Limited
Officers: Audrey Clare Burns [1966] Director/Chief Executive; Melanie Kee [1995] Director/SU Elected Officer; Ahmed Muntaqim Mahbub [1995] Director/President of Students' Union; Ahtesham Mahmood [1993] Director/Volunteer; Ali Reza Milani [1994] Director/NUS Officer; Patricia Anne O'Neill [1972] Director/Chief Executive; Daryl John Ormerod [1981] Director; Chisomo Phiri [1996] Director/Womens Officer; David Gavin Redpath [1978] IT Director; Graeme Wood [1970] Commercial Director

The Nuttall Group Limited
Incorporated: 1 March 1988 *Employees:* 546
Net Worth: £12,360,000 *Total Assets:* £26,112,000
Registered Office: Orchard House, Dodwells Bridge Industrial Estate, Hinckley, Leics, LE10 3BZ
Activities: Activities of head offices
Officers: Alan David Nuttall [1942] Director; Neil Alec Westwick [1970] Director

The Alan Nuttall Partnership Limited
Incorporated: 20 November 1974 *Employees:* 546
Previous: Alan Nuttall Limited
Net Worth: £8,761,000 *Total Assets:* £26,110,000
Registered Office: Orchard House, Dodwells Road, Hinckley, Leics, LE10 3BZ
Activities: Manufacture of other fabricated metal products n.e.c.
Officers: Darren Martyn Emms, Secretary; Darren Martyn Emms [1974] Financial Director; Matthew Brian Hornblower [1972] Operations Director; Jamie Joyce [1979] Operations Director; Alan David Nuttall [1942] Director; Michael James Steele [1961] Director; Neil Alec Westwick [1970] Director

O & M-Movianto UK Holdings Ltd.
Incorporated: 14 August 2012 *Employees:* 27
Net Worth: £36,373,000 *Total Assets:* £136,410,000
Registered Office: 1 Progress Park, Elstow, Bedford, MK42 9XE
Activities: Activities of head offices
Officers: Kamaljit Singh Hunjan [1967] Director/Senior VP Movianto; Julia M. Munzinger [1968] Director/Accountant [American]; Barbara O'Neill [1969] Director/Lawyer [American]; Nicholas Joseph Pace [1970] Director [American]

O'Brien (Group) Limited
Incorporated: 30 March 2011 *Employees:* 44
Net Worth: £11,831,914 *Total Assets:* £19,778,684
Registered Office: 15 Warwick Road, Stratford upon Avon, Warwicks, CV37 6YW
Activities: Activities of construction holding companies
Shareholders: Peter Nicholas O'Brien; Michael Patrick O'Brien
Officers: Michael Patrick O'Brien [1960] Director; Peter Nicholas O'Brien [1956] Director

O'Brien Contractors Limited
Incorporated: 13 February 1995 *Employees:* 44
Net Worth: £6,270,510 *Total Assets:* £12,013,999
Registered Office: Manor Cottage, Church Lane, Cubbington, Leamington Spa, Warwicks, CV32 7JT
Activities: Site preparation
Shareholders: Peter Nicholas O'Brien; Michael Patrick O'Brien; O'Brien (Group) Limited
Officers: Michael Patrick O'Brien, Secretary/Building Contractor; Stuart Chamberlain [1963] Director; Michael Patrick O'Brien [1960] Director/Building Contractor; Peter Nicholas O'Brien [1956] Director/Building Contractor

James O'Flanagan Limited
Incorporated: 7 June 1949 *Employees:* 10
Net Worth: £8,514,599 *Total Assets:* £9,196,485
Registered Office: The Jetty, 108 Broad Street, Coventry, Warwicks, CV6 5AZ
Activities: Construction of commercial buildings
Major Shareholder: Martin Thomas O Flanagan
Officers: Martin Thomas O'Flanagan, Secretary; Kathleen Cecilia O'Flanagan [1953] Director/Rent Manager; Martin Thomas O'Flanagan [1947] Director; Daniel Joseph O'Flanagan [1979] Director

O.T.R. Tyres Limited
Incorporated: 13 May 1977 *Employees:* 116
Net Worth: £4,072,000 *Total Assets:* £27,078,000
Registered Office: 8 Bluebell Close, Clover Nook Industrial Park, Somercotes, Alfreton, Derbys, DE55 4RD
Activities: Support activities for other mining and quarrying
Parent: OTR Holdings Limited
Officers: Angela Durham, Secretary; Daniel Martin Allan [1963] Director/Senior Vice President Kal Tire - Mining Tire Group [Canadian]; Iain David Butler [1970] Director/Vice President Finance; Darren Andrew Flint [1964] Director

Oakbridge Financial Services Limited
Incorporated: 1 November 2004 *Employees:* 6
Net Worth: £4,526,205 *Total Assets:* £14,550,031
Registered Office: 10 Riverview, The Embankment, Vale Road, Heaton Mersey, Stockport, Cheshire, SK4 3GN
Activities: Financial intermediation not elsewhere classified
Parent: Wrengate Holdings Limited
Officers: Andrew Michael Grimshaw [1957] Director/Chartered Accountant; Wyn Morrell [1953] Director; Alan Philip David Musry [1963] Director/Chartered Accountant; Ronald Musry [1935] Director

Oakbrook Finance Limited
Incorporated: 2 November 2011 *Employees:* 85
Net Worth Deficit: £39,774,000 *Total Assets:* £91,867,000
Registered Office: The Poynt North, 45 Wollaton Street, Nottingham, NG1 5FW
Activities: Financial management
Officers: Paul Aylieff [1964] Director; Manoj Kumar Badale [1967] Director; Martin Hagerty [1957] Director/Contractor; Charles Stuart Mindenhall [1971] Director/Business Partner; Mark James Onyett [1971] Director; Mark David Sanders [1969] Director; Michael Charles Woodburn [1970] Director

Oakham School
Incorporated: 4 June 2009 *Employees:* 556
Net Worth: £28,156,000 *Total Assets:* £41,260,000
Registered Office: Chapel Close, Market Place, Oakham, Rutland, LE15 6DT
Activities: General secondary education
Officers: Simon Christopher Piggott, Secretary; The Right Reverend Donald Spargo Allister [1952] Director/Bishop; Professor Philip Baker [1962] Director/University Professor; John Edward Czarnota [1965] Director; Mark Clinton Albert Dorsett [1962] Director/HR Manager; Philip Simon Douty [1962] Director/Manager; Richard Foulkes [1945] Director/Retired; Dr Sarah Haddon Furness [1956] Director/The Lord-Lieutenant of Rutland; Joan Gibson [1958] Director/Headmistress; Professor Neil Thomson Gorman [1950] Director; Julia Helen Grundy [1963] Director; Hansjorg Haefeli [1958] Director [Swiss]; Nicholas Jones [1972] Director; Anthony Richard Morrell Little [1954] Director/Headmaster; Jane Lucas [1961] Director/Investment Management; Josephine Mary Osborne [1957] Director/Lawyer; Rashmi Morarbhai Patel [1970] Director/HR Manager; Professor Stewart Alan Petersen [1951] Professor Medical Education & Director of Medical Education; Martin George Wilson [1957] Director/Architect; Stephen Howard Woolfe [1949] Director/Solicitor

Oakhill Group Limited
Incorporated: 5 March 1990 *Employees:* 550
Net Worth: £16,729,000 *Total Assets:* £129,958,000
Registered Office: Wootton Business Park, Besselsleigh Road, Wootton, Oxon, OX13 6FD
Activities: Development of building projects
Officers: Georgina Suzanne Forbes, Secretary; Manyadath Balachandran [1952] Director [Indian]; Andrew Mark Lemon [1966] Director/Certified Chartered Accountant; Atiq Rehman [1978] Director/Certified Chartered Accountant

Oakley Lorien Limited
Incorporated: 16 May 2011 *Employees:* 2
Net Worth: £3,892,339 *Total Assets:* £9,953,850
Registered Office: 45 Green Farm Road, Newport Pagnell, Milton Keynes, Bucks, MK16 0JY
Activities: Other letting and operating of own or leased real estate
Officers: Derek O'Neill [1963] Director/Accountant; Karen O'Neill [1966] Director/Certified Chartered Accountant

Oasis and Warehouse Holdco 1 Limited
Incorporated: 21 September 2015 *Employees:* 3,589
Net Worth: £17,500,000 *Total Assets:* £100,800,000
Registered Office: The Triangle, Stanton Harcourt Industrial Estate, Stanton Harcourt, Witney, Oxon, OX29 5UT
Activities: Activities of head offices
Parent: Aurora Fashions Finance Limited
Officers: Hashim Ladha [1974] Director; John Philip Madden III [1973] Director [American]; Johann Petur Reyndal [1962] Director [Icelander]

Oasis and Warehouse Holdco 2 Limited
Incorporated: 21 September 2015
Net Worth: £101,900,000 *Total Assets:* £101,900,000
Registered Office: The Triangle, Stanton Harcourt Industrial Estate, Stanton Harcourt, Witney, Oxon, OX29 5UT
Activities: Activities of head offices
Parent: Oasis and Warehouse Holdco 1 Limited
Officers: John Philip Madden III [1973] Director [American]; Johann Petur Reyndal [1962] Director [Icelander]

Oasis and Warehouse Limited
Incorporated: 18 October 2010 *Employees:* 3,589
Net Worth: £15,600,000 *Total Assets:* £100,800,000
Registered Office: The Triangle, Stanton Harcourt Industrial Estate, Stanton Harcourt, Witney, Oxon, OX29 5UT
Activities: Non-trading company
Parent: Oasis and Warehouse Holdco 2 Limited
Officers: Hashim Ladha [1974] Director; Sanam Soufipour [1972] Director

Oasis Fashions Holdings Limited
Incorporated: 13 February 2009 *Employees:* 2,010
Net Worth: £24,300,000 *Total Assets:* £67,000,000
Registered Office: The Triangle, Stanton Harcourt Industrial Estate, Stanton Harcourt, Witney, Oxon, OX29 5UT
Activities: Activities of head offices
Parent: Oasis and Warehouse Limited
Officers: Hashim Ladha [1974] Director; Sanam Soufipour [1972] Director

Oasis Fashions Limited
Incorporated: 17 February 2009 *Employees:* 1,780
Net Worth: £18,700,000 *Total Assets:* £57,400,000
Registered Office: The Triangle, Stanton Harcourt Industrial Estate, Stanton Harcourt, Witney, Oxon, OX29 5UT
Activities: Retail sale of clothing in specialised stores
Parent: Oasis Fashions Holdings Limited
Officers: Hashim Ladha [1974] Director; Sanam Soufipour [1972] Director; Sarah Welsh [1971] Director

OAT 2012 Limited
Incorporated: 2 February 2012 *Employees:* 105
Net Worth: £20,223,028 *Total Assets:* £23,404,640
Registered Office: Washway House Farm, Washway Road, Holbeach, Spalding, Lincs, PE12 7PP
Activities: Growing of cereals (except rice), leguminous crops and oil seeds
Shareholders: John Derek Taylor of Holbeach; Roger David Taylor; Sam Roger Taylor; Sarah Ann Taylor; Lady Julia Aileen Taylor; Brian Dennis Taylor; Hon Adam Edwin John Taylor
Officers: Sam Roger Taylor, Secretary; Hon Adam Edwin John Taylor [1975] Marketing Director; Roger David Taylor [1945] Director/Bulb Wholesaler; Sam Roger Taylor [1977] Agricultural and Horticultural Director

Oceala Limited
Incorporated: 5 October 1982 *Employees:* 15
Net Worth: £15,339,716 *Total Assets:* £18,624,612
Registered Office: Oceala, Feldspar Close, Warren Industrial Park, Enderby, Leicester, LE19 4SD
Activities: Collection of non-hazardous waste
Officers: Maxine Woolley, Secretary; Corinne Corser [1957] Director/Sales Executive; Georgina Cullen [1980] Director/Purchasing Executive; Tracy Scoular [1967] Director/Finance Manager; Mark Smith [1963] Director/Manager; Martin Smith [1964] Director/Commercial Representative; Maxine Woolley [1956] Director/Office Manager

Ocee International Ltd
Incorporated: 8 March 2016 *Employees:* 173
Net Worth: £6,443,781 *Total Assets:* £28,923,568
Registered Office: Design House, Caswell Road, Brackmills Industrial Estate, Northampton, NN4 7PW
Activities: Manufacture of office and shop furniture
Shareholders: BGF GP Limited; Alistair Storrar Gough
Officers: Stephen Alan Thomas, Secretary; Neil Clark [1968] Sales Director; Mark Stephen Freer [1964] Director; Alistair Storrar Gough [1963] Managing Director; Ervin Keldorff [1952] Director [Danish]; Christian Julin Markenfeldt [1966] Director [Danish]; Stephen Alan Thomas [1970] Finance Director; Anders Juhl Thomsen [1966] Director [Danish]

OCF PLC
Incorporated: 29 December 2000 *Employees:* 43
Net Worth: £3,917,224 *Total Assets:* £12,052,872
Registered Office: Unit 5 Rotunda Business Centre, Thorncliffe Park, Chapeltown, Sheffield, S35 2PG
Activities: Other information technology service activities
Shareholders: Julian Scott Fielden; Steve Reynolds
Officers: Julian Scott Fielden, Secretary/Director; Arif Ali [1980] Technical Director; Julian Scott Fielden [1955] Director; Stephen Alan Reynolds [1962] Director/Manager; Russell Graham Slack [1976] Operations Director

Oclaro Technology Limited
Incorporated: 22 September 1988 *Employees:* 348
Net Worth: £21,274,000 *Total Assets:* £171,200,000
Registered Office: Caswell, Towcester, Northants, NN12 8EQ
Activities: Manufacture of telegraph and telephone apparatus and equipment
Parent: Oclaro Innovations LLP
Officers: Keith Geoffrey Border, Secretary; Keith Geoffrey Border [1964] Director/Vice President of Finance

Oerlikon Balzers Coating UK Limited
Incorporated: 16 August 1960 *Employees:* 49
Net Worth: £5,547,203 *Total Assets:* £11,815,211
Registered Office: Oerlikon, Bradbourne Drive, Tilbrook, Milton Keynes, Bucks, MK7 8AT
Activities: Treatment and coating of metals
Officers: Dr Mike Dietrich [1979] Director/Head of Controlling [German]; Dr Wolfgang Josef Schmitz [1965] Director/Regional Executive [German]

Office 1 Limited
Incorporated: 19 August 1993 *Employees:* 2
Net Worth: £772,288,000 *Total Assets:* £783,990,976
Registered Office: 501 Beaumont Leys Lane, Leicester, LE4 2BN
Activities: Activities of head offices
Parent: Office Depot (Holdings) Limited
Officers: Jacqueline Susan Hills, Secretary; Neil David Maslen [1972] Director/SVP Contract Europe; Michael William Walby [1973] Managing Director [Irish]

Office Depot (Holdings) Limited
Incorporated: 28 September 2006
Net Worth: £768,809,728 *Total Assets:* £768,821,184
Registered Office: 501 Beaumont Leys Lane, Leicester, LE4 2BN
Activities: Activities of head offices
Parent: Office Depot Europe Holdings Limited
Officers: Jacqueline Susan Hills, Secretary; Neil David Maslen [1972] Director/SVP Contract Europe; Michael William Walby [1973] Managing Director [Irish]

Office Depot Europe Holdings Limited
Incorporated: 28 September 2006
Net Worth Deficit: £217,851,008 *Total Assets:* £759,043,968
Registered Office: 501 Beaumont Leys Lane, Leicester, LE4 2BN
Activities: Activities of head offices
Parent: Aurelius Equity Opportunities SE & Co KGaA
Officers: Jacqueline Susan Hills, Company Secretary; Neil David Maslen [1972] Director/SVP Contract Europe; Michael William Walby [1973] Managing Director [Irish]

Office Depot International (UK) Limited
Incorporated: 21 February 1990 *Employees:* 880
Net Worth: £363,739,008 *Total Assets:* £510,411,008
Registered Office: 501 Beaumont Leys Lane, Leicester, LE4 2BN
Activities: Retail sale via mail order houses or via Internet
Shareholders: Viking Direct (Holdings) Limited; Viking Finance (Ireland) Limited
Officers: Jacqueline Susan Hills, Secretary; Michael Jon McCreesh [1976] Procurement and Supply Chain Director; Michael William Walby [1973] Director/Vice President Sales [Irish]

Office Depot UK Limited
Incorporated: 16 October 1991 *Employees:* 404
Net Worth: £64,246,000 *Total Assets:* £347,735,008
Registered Office: 501 Beaumont Leys Lane, Leicester, LE4 2BN
Activities: Non-specialised wholesale trade
Parent: Guilbert UK Holdings Limited
Officers: Jacqueline Susan Hills, Secretary; Neil David Maslen [1972] Director/SVP Contract Europe; Michael Jon McCreesh [1976] Procurement and Supply Chain Director; Michael William Walby [1973] Director/Vice President Sales [Irish]

Office Space in Town Limited
Incorporated: 3 March 2008 *Employees:* 7
Net Worth: £21,606,860 *Total Assets:* £23,204,936
Registered Office: 10 Canberra House, Corbygate Business Park, Corby, Northants, NN17 5JG
Activities: Other business support service activities n.e.c.
Shareholders: Giles Michael Gummer Fuchs; Nicola Claire Gummer Fuchs
Officers: Simon Eastlake [1978] Director/General Manager; Giles Michael Gummer Fuchs [1964] Director; Nicola Clare Gummer Fuchs [1968] Director/Manager; Tracey Catherine Holloway [1962] Director/Centre Manager; Sarah Singlehurst [1966] Director/Centre Manager; Julie Anne Ward [1958] Director/Accountant

OGF Bidco Limited
Incorporated: 18 January 2016
Net Worth: £2,373,291 *Total Assets:* £32,987,248
Registered Office: Wavendon Tower, Ortensia Drive, Wavendon, Milton Keynes, Bucks, MK17 8LX
Activities: Activities of head offices
Parent: OGF Midco Limited
Officers: Jo August [1971] Director; Jonathan David Clark [1977] Director; Venetia Cooper [1974] Director/Chartered Accountant

OGF Topco Limited
Incorporated: 18 January 2016
Net Worth: £3,094,648 *Total Assets:* £15,221,880
Registered Office: Wavendon Tower, Ortensia Drive, Wavendon, Milton Keynes, Bucks, MK17 8LX
Activities: Activities of head offices
Parent: Boston Holdco B Limited
Officers: Jo August [1971] Director; Jonathan David Clark [1977] Director; Venetia Cooper [1974] Director/Chief Financial Officer

OISE Holdings Limited
Incorporated: 3 July 2006 *Employees:* 545
Net Worth: £28,378,232 *Total Assets:* £35,531,600
Registered Office: OISE House, Binsey Lane, Oxford, OX2 0EY
Activities: Activities of head offices
Major Shareholder: Till Gins
Officers: Bonnie Phillips Dean [1957] Director; Till Gins [1950] Managing Director [French]; Edward John Lincoln [1961] Director/Head of Sales [Irish]

OISE Limited
Incorporated: 19 July 1977 *Employees:* 24
Net Worth: £8,590,782 *Total Assets:* £22,151,640
Registered Office: OISE House, Binsey Lane, Oxford, OX2 0EY
Activities: Other education n.e.c.
Major Shareholder: Till Gins
Officers: Till Gins [1950] Managing Director [French]

OKA Direct Limited
Incorporated: 1 March 1999 *Employees:* 238
Net Worth: £12,417,122 *Total Assets:* £17,163,826
Registered Office: 170 Brook Drive, Milton Park, Milton, Abingdon, Oxon, OX14 4SD
Activities: Retail sale via mail order houses or via Internet
Parent: Luxury British Design 2 Limited
Officers: Mark John James Little, Secretary; Annabel Lucy Veronica Astor [1948] Director; Miranda Christie [1974] Director; Emilio Giuseppe Foa [1963] Director; Susan Caroline Jones [1957] Director; Mark John James Little [1965] Director; Lucinda Ileene Waterhouse [1955] Director

Olam Food Ingredients UK Limited
Incorporated: 26 January 1994 *Employees:* 43
Net Worth: £19,136,000 *Total Assets:* £20,421,000
Registered Office: Britannia Way, Goole, E Yorks, DN14 6ES
Activities: Manufacture of oils and fats
Parent: Olam Europe Limited
Officers: Andrew Richard Samuel, Secretary; Gerard Anthony Manley [1958] Director

Old Road Securities PLC
Incorporated: 9 February 1973 *Employees:* 9
Net Worth: £17,516,062 *Total Assets:* £18,652,532
Registered Office: The Gables, Westfield Road, Oakley, Bedford, MK43 7SU
Activities: Raising of horses and other equines
Major Shareholder: Christopher Richard Kilroy
Officers: Marcus John Bates [1953] Director/Chartered Surveyor; Ian Charles Codrington [1938] Director/Solicitor; Carol Irene Kilroy [1944] Director; Christopher Richard Kilroy [1944] Director; Catherine Sylvester Kilroy [1969] Director/Planner

Oldrid & Co.,Limited
Incorporated: 1 February 1934 *Employees:* 715
Net Worth: £29,004,424 *Total Assets:* £39,196,568
Registered Office: 11 Strait Bargate, Boston, Lincs, PE21 6UF
Activities: Other retail sale in non-specialised stores
Officers: Peter Isaac, Secretary; Richard Keith Broadhead [1969] Managing Director; Steven David Goulder [1960] Director; Kathryn Ann Ingleton [1963] Staff Director; Dawn Marie Isaac [1972] Director/Garden Designer; Martin James Isaac [1961] Director/Retail Manager; Peter Edward Isaac [1977] Director/Chartered Accountant; Marcus Anthony Meadows [1971] Retail Operations Director; Natalie Skins [1979] Staff Director; Ruth Elizabeth Stephenson [1959] Director

Olmar Investments Limited
Incorporated: 25 February 1957 *Employees:* 173
Net Worth: £7,606,000 *Total Assets:* £17,838,000
Registered Office: Eagle House, 28 Billing Road, Northampton, NN1 5AJ
Activities: Agents selling agricultural raw materials, livestock, textile raw materials and semi-finished goods
Officers: Luis Fernando Dato [1968] Director/Commercial Manager [Argentinian]; Robert William Hall [1951] Director

OM Properties Investment Company Limited
Incorporated: 13 November 1985 *Employees:* 2
Net Worth: £29,677,354 *Total Assets:* £37,761,572
Registered Office: The Pantiles, Gartree Road, Oadby, Leicester, LE2 2FB
Activities: Other letting and operating of own or leased real estate
Officers: Arjun Mirchumal Chugani [1942] Director/Semi Retired

Omega Acquisition Bidco Limited
Incorporated: 22 January 2015
Net Worth: £714,900,480 *Total Assets:* £1,283,037,440
Registered Office: 4650 Kingsgate, Cascade Way, Oxford Business Park South, Oxford, OX4 2SU
Activities: Activities of head offices
Parent: TI Fluid Systems PLC
Officers: Matthew Keats Paroly, Secretary; Robert Michael Allen [1964] Director/Accountant; Timothy James Knutson [1967] Director [American]; William Lawrence Kozyra [1957] Director [American]

Omega PLC
Incorporated: 24 March 1992 *Employees:* 341
Net Worth: £62,785,000 *Total Assets:* £71,615,000
Registered Office: Omega Boulevard, Capitol Park, Thorne, Doncaster, S Yorks, DN8 5TX
Activities: Manufacture of other furniture
Parent: Cycene Limited
Officers: Richard Adam, Secretary; Richard David Adam [1971] Finance Director; Simon Keith Barber [1967] Director; John Cahill [1963] Director; Alastair Strang England [1969] Director; Tracey Anne Labbett [1967] Director; James John Robert Murray [1990] Director; Sir Robert Sydney Murray [1946] Director; Richard Harvey Tattersall [1961] Director

Omega Red Group Limited
Incorporated: 24 November 1987 *Employees:* 226
Net Worth: £8,981,000 *Total Assets:* £12,116,000
Registered Office: Dabell Avenue, Blenheim Industrial Estate, Bulwell, Nottingham, NG6 8WA
Activities: Technical testing and analysis
Parent: Omega Red Holdings Limited
Officers: Ranbir Kumar Bhalla, Secretary; Adrian Peter Page [1965] Director/Chartered Accountant; Neil Richard Shailer [1969] Director; David Taylor [1975] Director

Omega Red Holdings Limited
Incorporated: 16 October 2007
Net Worth: £981,000 *Total Assets:* £17,762,000
Registered Office: Dabell Avenue, Blenheim Industrial Estate, Bulwell, Nottingham, NG6 8WA
Activities: Activities of head offices
Parent: Hydriades Limited
Officers: Ranbir Kumar Bhalla, Secretary; Adrian Peter Page [1965] Director/Chartered Accountant; Neil Richard Shailer [1969] Director; David Taylor [1975] Director

Omex Agriculture Limited
Incorporated: 27 February 1976 *Employees:* 73
Net Worth: £33,635,004 *Total Assets:* £57,554,820
Registered Office: Bardney Airfield, Bardney, Lincs, LN3 5TP
Activities: Manufacture of fertilizers and nitrogen compounds
Parent: Omex Agricultural Holdings Ltd
Officers: David O'Donnell, Secretary; Robert Burton [1969] Sales Director; Andrew David Butler [1964] Sales Director; John Andrew Eccles [1959] Director/Agronomist; Andrew Mark Tootal [1961] Director; Maximilian Olof Winkler Von Stiernhielm [1987] Director; Olof Joachim Winkler Von Stiernhielm [1949] Director [German]

Omex Agrifluids Limited
Incorporated: 28 January 1991 *Employees:* 34
Net Worth: £8,279,193 *Total Assets:* £12,278,895
Registered Office: OMEX Agrifluids Ltd, Saddlebow Road, Kings Lynn, Norfolk, PE34 3JA
Activities: Manufacture of fertilizers and nitrogen compounds
Officers: David O'Donnell, Secretary; Manuela Bowyer [1963] Director; Christopher James Gipp [1961] Production Director; David Alan Lowes [1953] Export Director; Marcelo Luiz Marino Santos [1967] Director [Brazilian]; David O'Donnell [1958] Finance Director; Peter Charles Elvy Prentis [1958] Export Director; Nils Alexander Winkler Von Stiernhielm [1985] Director; Olof Joachim Winkler Von Stiernhielm [1949] Director [German]

Omnico Plastics Limited
Incorporated: 26 January 1996
Net Worth: £500,000 *Total Assets:* £10,236,000
Registered Office: Adsetts House, 16 Europa View, Sheffield Business Park, Sheffield, S9 1XH
Activities: Dormant company
Parent: Specialised Fixings Limited
Officers: Richard Charles Monro, Secretary; Ian Jackson [1979] Director/Accountant; Richard Charles Monro [1958] Director/Chartered Secretary

Omnitrade Limited
Incorporated: 28 November 1980
Net Worth: £13,374,344 *Total Assets:* £20,951,888
Registered Office: Telford House, Outrams Wharf, Little Eaton, Derby, DE21 5EL
Activities: Other letting and operating of own or leased real estate
Major Shareholder: Robert Marc Graham
Officers: Hanne Graham, Secretary; Hanne Graham [1944] Director/Fashion Designer; Paul David Graham [1946] Director/Fashion Designer

Omron Electronics Limited
Incorporated: 18 April 1991 *Employees:* 119
Net Worth: £5,376,943 *Total Assets:* £13,424,949
Registered Office: Opal Drive, Fox Milne, Milton Keynes, Bucks, MK15 0DG
Activities: Wholesale of electronic and telecommunications equipment and parts
Officers: Clare Jane Thomson, Secretary; Gary Banks [1958] Director/Manager, General Affairs, EMEA; Heath Mark Davis [1974] Director/Business Controller [Australian]

On Line Group Limited
Incorporated: 4 October 2012 *Employees:* 463
Previous: On Line Design & Engineering Group Limited
Net Worth: £8,655,277 *Total Assets:* £13,753,600
Registered Office: On Line House, Pelham Road, Immingham, N E Lincs, DN40 1AB
Activities: Activities of head offices
Major Shareholder: Susan Laird
Officers: Louise Jacqueline Arnett [1974] Director/HR Professional; Melanie Jane Dent [1975] Director/Graphic Designer; Jeffrey Laird [1946] Director/Chartered Engineer; Stephen Anthoney Laird [1974] Director/Accountant; Susan Laird [1951] Group Director

Oncimmune Holdings PLC
Incorporated: 9 October 2015 *Employees:* 52
Net Worth: £13,562,000 *Total Assets:* £14,411,000
Registered Office: Clinical Sciences Building, City Hospital, Hucknall Road, Nottingham, NG5 1PB
Activities: Activities of head offices
Officers: Andrew Neil Stewart, Secretary; Timothy Brian Bunting [1963] Director; Geoffrey Neil Hamilton-Fairley [1961] Director; Dr Adam Mark Hill [1980] Director; Julian Clement Hirst [1958] Director; Dr Anna Lisa Marie Jenkins [1965] Director; Meinhard Folkert Schmidt [1960] Director [German]; Carsten Schroeder [1965] Director [German]; Richard Sharp [1956] Director; Dr Cheung To [1963] Director [Chinese]; Andrew Vaughan Unitt [1957] Director

Oncimmune Limited
Incorporated: 3 December 2002 *Employees:* 29
Net Worth Deficit: £14,154,000 *Total Assets:* £9,918,000
Registered Office: Clinical Sciences Building, City Hospital, Hucknall Road, Nottingham, NG5 1PB
Activities: Research and experimental development on social sciences and humanities
Parent: Oncimmune Holdings PLC
Officers: Andrew Neil Stewart, Secretary; Dr Adam Mark Hill [1980] Director; Dr Andrea Murray [1968] Director

One Call Insurance Services Limited
Incorporated: 11 March 2003 *Employees:* 448
Net Worth: £17,577,676 *Total Assets:* £41,951,292
Registered Office: Saturn Building, First Point, Balby Carr Bank, Doncaster, S Yorks, DN4 5JQ
Activities: Activities of insurance agents and brokers
Major Shareholder: John Lawrence Radford
Officers: Alexandra Maria Sheriff, Secretary; Joshua Charles Barnsdale [1982] Director; William Laurence Broughton [1975] Director/Solicitor; Sarah Louise Chadburn [1978] Compliance Director; John David Goacher [1964] Finance Director; Peter Graham Long [1986] Operations Director; John Matthew Parker [1976] Claims Director; Carolyn Marie Radford [1982] PR Director; John Lawrence Radford [1965] Director/Chief Executive Officer; Oliver Paul Rose [1986] Director; Nicholas Graham Springthorpe [1971] Managing Director; John Steele [1953] Director/Head of Compliance, Risk and Internal Audit

One51 ES Metals (UK) Limited
Incorporated: 15 July 2008
Net Worth Deficit: £21,553,000 *Total Assets:* £17,687,000
Registered Office: Ampthill Metal Company Limited, Station Road Industrial Estate, Ampthill, Bedford, MK45 2QY
Activities: Recovery of sorted materials
Officers: Christian Marcoux, Secretary; Patrick Dalton [1965] Director/Company Executive [Irish]; Alan Walsh [1976] Director/Company Executive [Irish]

Ontex Healthcare UK Limited
Incorporated: 5 July 1988 *Employees:* 71
Net Worth: £8,385,249 *Total Assets:* £16,191,248
Registered Office: 300 Pavilion Drive, Northampton, NN4 7YE
Activities: Combined office administrative service activities
Officers: Steven Paul Jules Vandenbogaerde, Secretary; Pascal Jose Nizette [1972] Finance Director [Belgian]

Opal Ventures Limited
Incorporated: 22 June 2010 *Employees:* 130
Net Worth: £7,893,014 *Total Assets:* £34,564,036
Registered Office: Studio F2/B, Witan Studios, 319 Upper Fourth Street, Milton Keynes, Bucks, MK9 1EH
Activities: Management consultancy activities other than financial management
Shareholders: Alice Jane English; Alan Henry English
Officers: Kanagaratnam Jeyakanthan, Secretary; Alan Henry English [1942] Director; Peter William Grose [1958] Director/Chartered Accountant

Openfield Agriculture Limited
Incorporated: 17 April 1998 *Employees:* 245
Net Worth: £15,986,000 *Total Assets:* £108,159,000
Registered Office: Honey Pot Lane, Colsterworth, Grantham, Lincs, NG33 5LY
Activities: Post-harvest crop activities
Parent: Openfield Group Limited
Officers: Alan James Murray, Secretary; David Russell Hamilton Anderson [1969] Director/Chief Financial Officer; James Dallas [1965] Managing Director; Richard John Jenner [1968] Director; Mark John Worrell [1965] Director

Openshaw Regeneration Limited
Incorporated: 12 June 2009
Net Worth: £11,308,905 *Total Assets:* £34,327,528
Registered Office: Dransfield House, 2 Fox Valley Way, Fox Valley, Sheffield, S36 2AB
Activities: Other letting and operating of own or leased real estate
Parent: Dransfield Properties Ltd
Officers: Steven Burgess, Secretary; Mark Dransfield [1962] Director; Steven John Stead [1978] Director

Optilan (UK) Limited
Incorporated: 19 May 1992 *Employees:* 151
Net Worth: £19,754,000 *Total Assets:* £46,330,000
Registered Office: Stonebridge Trading Estate, Sibree Road, Coventry, Warwicks, CV3 4FD
Activities: Other telecommunications activities
Parent: Optilan Group Limited
Officers: Timothy John Gray, Secretary/Director; Richard Buckland [1965] Director; Timothy John Gray [1963] Director; Balvinder Kler [1961] Sales Director; Christopher Yarwood [1968] Technical Director

Optilan Group Limited
Incorporated: 20 February 2008 *Employees:* 197
Net Worth: £7,046,000 *Total Assets:* £51,285,000
Registered Office: Stonebridge Trading Estate, Sibree Road, Coventry, Warwicks, CV3 4FD
Activities: Activities of head offices
Shareholder: Richard Buckland
Officers: Timothy John Gray, Secretary/Director; Richard Buckland [1965] Director; Timothy John Gray [1963] Director; Balvinder Kler [1961] Director; Christopher Yarwood [1968] Director

Optimum Debtco Limited
Incorporated: 24 January 2007
Net Worth Deficit: £22,606,000 *Total Assets:* £51,899,000
Registered Office: Norcliffe House, Station Road, Wilmslow, Cheshire, SK9 1BU
Activities: Activities of other holding companies n.e.c.
Parent: Brighterkind Limited
Officers: Abigail Mattison, Secretary; Ryan Stuart MacAskill [1975] Director; Gregory Laurence Newman [1988] Director/Investment Professional; Jeremy Robert Arthur Richardson [1970] Director; Dr Maureen Claire Royston [1960] Director; Phillip Gary Thomas [1978] Director

OQEMA Limited
Incorporated: 13 October 1975 *Employees:* 40
Previous: OQEMA Public Limited Company
Net Worth: £9,749,807 *Total Assets:* £19,841,708
Registered Office: Winstons House, Carterton, Oxford, OX18 3EZ
Activities: Manufacture of other inorganic basic chemicals
Officers: Andrew Ian Cheesman, Secretary; Stuart Alexander [1977] Director; Andrew Ian Cheesman [1965] Director/Accountant; Herr Heinrich Eickmann [1957] Director [German]; Robert Moss [1968] Director; Herr Peter Overlack [1957] Director [German]

Orano UK Limited
Incorporated: 10 October 2008 *Employees:* 12
Previous: Areva UK Limited
Net Worth Deficit: £255,202 *Total Assets:* £13,393,509
Registered Office: Suite 7, Hitching Court, Abingdon Business Park, Abingdon, Oxon, OX14 1RA
Activities: Other business support service activities n.e.c.
Parent: Orano SA
Officers: Sylvain Douglas Andre Esperou Du Tremblay [1962] Director/CEO Areva UK [French]; Patrick Jacq [1958] Director [French]

Orbit Developments (Manchester) Limited
Incorporated: 4 May 1971
Net Worth: £52,676,112 *Total Assets:* £58,045,664
Registered Office: Emerson House, Heyes Lane, Alderley Edge, Cheshire, SK9 7LF
Activities: Development of building projects
Parent: Emerson Developments (Holdings) Limited
Officers: Varun Maharaj, Secretary; Simon Gavin Clarke-Williams [1951] Marketing Director; Giles Ivan Hardern [1967] Director/Chartered Surveyor; Anthony Emerson Jones [1967] Director; Audrey Jones [1936] Director; Mark Emerson Jones [1964] Director; Peter Emerson Jones [1935] Director; Paul Robert McLeman [1963] Director/Chartered Surveyor; Mark Stephen Thomas Royle [1964] Director/Architect; Simon Peter Wilson [1964] Director

Orbit Developments (Southern) Limited
Incorporated: 10 March 1987 *Employees:* 5
Net Worth: £18,642,984 *Total Assets:* £75,986,880
Registered Office: Emerson House, Heyes Lane, Alderley Edge, Cheshire, SK9 7LF
Activities: Development of building projects
Parent: Emerson Developments (Holdings) Limited
Officers: Varun Maharaj, Secretary; Anthony Emerson Jones [1967] Director; Audrey Jones [1936] Director; Mark Emerson Jones [1964] Director; Peter Emerson Jones [1935] Director; Simon Peter Wilson [1964] Director

Orbit Homes (2020) Limited
Incorporated: 2 July 2009
Net Worth: £123,000 *Total Assets:* £112,221,000
Registered Office: Garden Court, Harry Weston Road, Binley Business Park, Coventry, Warwicks, CV3 2SU
Activities: Buying and selling of own real estate
Officers: Richard Wright, Secretary; Richard Patrick Berrett [1954] Director/Consultant; Wendy Elizabeth Colgrave [1965] Director/Accountant; Christopher Peter Crook [1958] Managing Director; Shirley Watson [1954] Director/Civil Engineer

Orbit Investments (Northern) Limited
Incorporated: 31 May 1996
Net Worth: £228,684,944 *Total Assets:* £407,171,232
Registered Office: Emerson House, Heyes Lane, Alderley Edge, Cheshire, SK9 7LF
Activities: Development of building projects
Parent: Emerson Developments (Holdings) Limited
Officers: Varun Maharaj, Secretary; Robert Anthony Hallworth [1968] Director/Business Executive; Giles Ivan Hardern [1967] Director/Chartered Surveyor; Anthony Emerson Jones [1967] Director; Mark Emerson Jones [1964] Director; Peter Emerson Jones [1935] Director; Mark Stephen Thomas Royle [1964] Director/Architect

Orbit Investments (Properties) Limited
Incorporated: 6 July 1988
Net Worth: £152,579,728 *Total Assets:* £503,718,944
Registered Office: Emerson House, Heyes Lane, Alderley Edge, Cheshire, SK9 7LF
Activities: Development of building projects
Parent: Emerson Developments (Holdings) Limited
Officers: Varun Maharaj, Secretary; Giles Ivan Hardern [1967] Director/Chartered Surveyor; Anthony Emerson Jones [1967] Director; Audrey Jones [1936] Director; Mark Emerson Jones [1964] Director; Peter Emerson Jones [1935] Director; Mark Stephen Thomas Royle [1964] Director/Architect; Simon Peter Wilson [1964] Director

Orbit Treasury Limited
Incorporated: 31 May 2007
Net Worth Deficit: £109,381,000 *Total Assets:* £817,558,016
Registered Office: Garden Court, Harry Weston Road, Binley Business Park, Coventry, Warwicks, CV3 2SU
Activities: Financial intermediation not elsewhere classified
Officers: Richard Wright, Secretary; Joy Elizabeth Baggaley [1958] Finance Director; Stuart John Fisher [1979] Finance Director; Mark Hoyland [1970] Director/Chief Executive; David Weaver [1959] Director/Consultant; Lorne Charles Robert Williams [1961] Director/Building Society Treasurer; David Ernest Young [1942] Finance Director

Orbital Education Limited
Incorporated: 25 January 2008 *Employees:* 446
Net Worth: £5,644,157 *Total Assets:* £34,634,080
Registered Office: Landmark House, Station Road, Cheadle Hulme, Cheadle, Cheshire, SK8 7BS
Activities: Activities of head offices
Major Shareholder: Kevin Joseph McNeany
Officers: James William Stewart, Secretary; Kevin Joseph McNeany [1943] Director; Myles Antony McNeany [1986] Director/Group Head of IT; David Irvine Pottinger [1960] Director; James William Stewart [1965] Director

Orca Marine Leisure Limited
Incorporated: 8 November 2007 *Employees:* 116
Previous: Princess Motor Yacht Sales Holdings Limited
Net Worth: £6,917,047 *Total Assets:* £44,011,976
Registered Office: 6 Athena Court, Athena Drive, Tachbrook Park, Warwick, CV34 6RT
Activities: Activities of head offices
Major Shareholder: Peter William Whale
Officers: Jatinder Pal Singh Nurpuri, Secretary; Jatinder Pal Singh Nurpuri [1963] Director/Chartered Accountant; Henry William Whale [1973] Director; Max Howard Whale [1976] Director; Peter William Whale [1949] Director/Manager

Orchard House Foods Limited
Incorporated: 21 March 1985 *Employees:* 1,205
Net Worth: £7,621,000 *Total Assets:* £47,484,000
Registered Office: 79 Manton Road, Earlstrees Industrial Estate, Corby, Northants, NN17 4JL
Activities: Manufacture of fruit and vegetable juice
Parent: Hain Frozen Foods UK Limited
Officers: Nick Keen, Secretary; Denise Menikheim Faltischek [1973] Director/Attorney [American]; James Michael Langrock [1965] Director [American]; Mark Lawrence Schiller [1961] Director/CEO Hain Celestial [American]; Robin James Skidmore [1968] Director

Orchid Cellmark Ltd
Incorporated: 28 July 2000 *Employees:* 524
Net Worth: £17,178,000 *Total Assets:* £19,885,000
Registered Office: Abingdon Business Park, 16 Blacklands Way, Abingdon, Oxon, OX14 1DY
Activities: Technical testing and analysis
Officers: David John Hartshorne [1964] Commercial Director

Orchid Orthopedic Solutions Ltd
Incorporated: 13 February 2012 *Employees:* 281
Net Worth Deficit: £364,000 *Total Assets:* £62,814,000
Registered Office: Parkway Close, Parkway Industrial Estate, Sheffield, S9 4WH
Activities: Activities of head offices
Parent: Orchid MPS Holdings LLC
Officers: Jacqueline Payne, Secretary; David Patrick Beighton [1963] Director/General Manager; Matthew Burba [1972] Director/Executive Vice President Orchid [American]; Jerome Jurkiewicz [1963] Director [American]

Orchid Orthopedic Solutions Sheffield Ltd
Incorporated: 12 January 1973 *Employees:* 192
Net Worth: £14,440,000 *Total Assets:* £30,793,000
Registered Office: Parkway Close, Parkway Industrial Estate, Sheffield, S9 4WH
Activities: Manufacture of medical and dental instruments and supplies
Parent: Orchid Orthopedic Solutions Ltd (UK)
Officers: Jacqueline Payne, Secretary; David Patrick Beighton [1963] Director/General Manager; Jerome Jurkiewicz [1963] Director [American]

The Orders of St. John Care Trust
Incorporated: 27 June 1995 *Employees:* 3,330
Net Worth: £48,346,000 *Total Assets:* £72,343,000
Registered Office: 1 Des Roches Square, Witney, Oxon, OX28 4BE
Activities: Residential nursing care facilities
Officers: Joanna Carole Downing, Secretary; Timothy Edward Church [1955] Director; Dr Anne Mary de Bono [1947] Director/Consultant Occupational Physician; Professor Claire Goodman [1958] Director/Academic; Richard Andrew Fitzalan Howard [1953] Director; Jill Gabriel Anne Hughes [1950] Director/Literary Agent; Graham Stuart Hutton [1958] Director/Partner; Professor Gillian Teresa Manthorpe [1955] Director/University Professor; Robert William Saswalo Shirley [1952] Director; Dr Ralph Harry Stephenson [1944] Director/Retired; Mildred Maria Elisabeth Wentworth-Stanley [1965] Director/Solicitor [Dutch]; Donald Wood [1945] Director/Chief Executive; Judith Kathleen Wright [1944] Director/Retired

Oriana Underwriting Limited
Incorporated: 25 September 2009
Net Worth Deficit: £398,909 *Total Assets:* £11,042,431
Registered Office: 3 Castlegate, Grantham, Lincs, NG31 6SF
Activities: Non-life insurance
Major Shareholder: John Carl Cotton
Officers: John Carl Cotton [1938] Director/Investor [American]; Jennifer May Jones [1955] Director/Business Consultant/Portfolio Manager [Canadian]

Origin Wine Limited
Incorporated: 20 May 2004 *Employees:* 13
Net Worth: £2,665,196 *Total Assets:* £10,213,517
Registered Office: Rivermead House, 7 Lewis Court, Grove Park, Enderby, Leicester, LE19 1SD
Activities: Wholesale of wine, beer, spirits and other alcoholic beverages
Officers: Yves Bernard Adrien Fontannaz [1967] Director [Swiss]

Orion Media Limited
Incorporated: 7 May 2009
Net Worth Deficit: £10,185,000 *Total Assets:* £21,853,000
Registered Office: Media House, Peterborough Business Park, Lynch Wood, Peterborough, Cambs, PE2 6EA
Activities: Television programme production activities
Parent: Orion Media Holdings Limited
Officers: Deidre Ann Ford [1960] Managing Director; Paul Anthony Keenan [1963] Director/Publisher; Sarah Jane Vickery [1963] Finance Director

Orona Limited
Incorporated: 17 June 1977 *Employees:* 228
Net Worth: £2,241,961 *Total Assets:* £11,634,881
Registered Office: 9 Europa View, Sheffield Business Park, Sheffield, S9 1XH
Activities: Repair of machinery
Parent: Ace Elevators (Southern) Limited
Officers: Garikoitz Ameztoy Garcia, Secretary; Garikoitz Ameztoy Garcia [1981] Finance Director [Spanish]; Javier Mutuberria Echeverria [1958] Director [Spanish]; Igor Etxabe [1972] Director [Spanish]; Joao Ribeiro [1977] Managing Director [Portuguese]

E J Orr Limited
Incorporated: 20 May 1983 *Employees:* 29
Net Worth: £7,490,606 *Total Assets:* £9,016,520
Registered Office: 17 Notts South & Wilford Industrial Estate, Ruddington Lane, Nottingham, NG11 7EP
Activities: Wholesale of textiles
Shareholders: William Tweedie Orr (Jnr); Victoria Rebecca Jane Orr
Officers: Victoria Rebecca Jane Orr, Secretary; Victoria Rebecca Jane Orr [1969] Director/Marketing Executive; William Tweedie Orr Jnr [1969] Director

OSI Food Solutions UK Limited
Incorporated: 6 June 1978 *Employees:* 172
Net Worth: £3,734,000 *Total Assets:* £17,471,000
Registered Office: Luneberg Way, Skippingdale, Scunthorpe, N Lincs, DN15 8LP
Activities: Production of meat and poultry meat products
Parent: Gands (UK)
Officers: Martin Howard Back, Secretary; Martin Howard Back [1952] Director/Accountant; Sherry Anne de Meulenaere [1958] Director [American]; David Gerard McDonald [1964] Director [American]

OSI International Holdings Limited
Incorporated: 18 April 1996
Net Worth: £56,687,000 *Total Assets:* £56,770,000
Registered Office: Luneburg Way, Scunthorpe, N Lincs, DN15 8LP
Activities: Activities of head offices
Parent: Gands (UK)
Officers: Martin Howard Back, Secretary; Sherry Anne de Meulenaere, Secretary; Sherry Anne Demeulenaere [1958] Director and Company Secretary [American]; Sheldon Lavin [1932] Director/President [American]; David Gerard McDonald [1964] Director/VP OSI [American]

OSL Group Holdings Limited
Incorporated: 9 August 2002 *Employees:* 189
Net Worth: £6,868,000 *Total Assets:* £11,722,000
Registered Office: c/o OSL Cutting Technologies Ltd, Burgess Road, Attercliffe, Sheffield, S9 3WD
Activities: Manufacture of other rubber products
Major Shareholder: David Grey
Officers: Victoria Richardson, Secretary; Philip Gregory Benjamin [1961] Director; David Grey [1956] Director; Mathew James Grey [1985] Director; Christopher Charles Standring Heaton [1958] Director

Osprey Acquisitions Limited
Incorporated: 24 August 2006 *Employees:* 4,727
Net Worth: £630,600,000 *Total Assets:* £11,306,300,416
Registered Office: Lancaster House, Lancaster Way, Ermine Business Park, Huntingdon, Cambs, PE29 6XU
Activities: Other business support service activities n.e.c.
Parent: Osprey Holdco Limited
Officers: Claire Tytherleigh Russell, Secretary; Projesh Banerjea [1986] Director/Financier [Indian]; John Richard Barry [1968] Director/Investor; Dr Stephen Robert Billingham [1948] Director; James Alexander Bryce [1974] Director/Senior Principal; Mamoun Jamai [1981] Director/Senior Portfolio Manager [Moroccan]; Scott Robert James Longhurst [1967] Finance Director; Manoj Mehta [1970] Investment Director; Niall Patrick Mills [1968] Director/Chartered Engineer; Robert Stewart Napier [1947] Director/Chief Executive; Alexandros Nassuphis [1969] Director/Investment Professional [German]; Peter John Simpson [1967] Director; Duncan John Symonds [1973] Director/Civil Engineer

Osprey Holdco Limited
Incorporated: 24 August 2006 *Employees:* 4,939
Net Worth: £436,900,000 *Total Assets:* £11,413,799,936
Registered Office: Lancaster House, Lancaster Way, Ermine Business Park, Huntingdon, Cambs, PE29 6XU
Activities: Activities of head offices
Officers: Claire Tytherleigh Russell, Secretary; Projesh Banerjea [1986] Director/Financier [Indian]; John Richard Barry [1968] Director/Investor; Dr Stephen Robert Billingham [1948] Director; James Alexander Bryce [1974] Director/Senior Principal; Mamoun Jamai [1981] Director/Senior Portfolio Manager [Moroccan]; Scott Robert James Longhurst [1967] Finance Director; Manoj Mehta [1970] Investment Director; Niall Patrick Mills [1968] Director/Chartered Engineer; Robert Stewart Napier [1947] Director/Chief Executive; Alexandros Nassuphis [1969] Director/Investment Professional [German]; Peter John Simpson [1967] Director; Duncan John Symonds [1973] Director/Civil Engineer

Ossur UK Holding Limited
Incorporated: 28 November 2005
Net Worth: £1,368,158 *Total Assets:* £39,583,300
Registered Office: Unit No 1 S:Park, Hamilton Road, Stockport, Cheshire, SK1 2AE
Activities: Activities of head offices
Parent: Ossur Europe B.V.
Officers: Emlyn Lewis, Secretary; Jos Van Poorten [1964] Finance Director [Dutch]

Otter Controls Limited
Incorporated: 26 March 1946 *Employees:* 1,181
Net Worth: £28,613,392 *Total Assets:* £43,015,216
Registered Office: Tongue Lane Industrial Estate, Dew Pond Lane, Fairfield, Buxton, Derbys, SK17 7LF
Activities: Manufacture of electronic measuring, testing etc. equipment, not for industrial process control
Officers: Graeme Thomas Brown, Secretary; Paul Boundy [1960] Director/Mechanical Engineer; Michael Leonard Colling [1962] Director/Chartered Accountant; Johannes Joesphus Berendinus Maria Derksen [1960] Director [Dutch]; William Ross Jolliffe [1965] Director; Brian Smith [1952] Director; Dr David Andrew Smith [1964] Director/Chartered Certified Accountant; Simon Mark Whiteley [1960] Director/Mechanical Engineer

Oughtred & Harrison (Facilities) Ltd.
Incorporated: 9 June 1988 *Employees:* 178
Net Worth: £2,945,107 *Total Assets:* £12,741,410
Registered Office: 5 Larsen Road, Goole, E Yorks, DN14 6XG
Activities: Other manufacturing n.e.c.
Shareholders: Endless LLP; Endless IV (GP) LLP
Officers: David Grey [1956] Director; Wesley David Beattie Linton [1977] Director; Kevin Stevens [1967] Operations Director

Ousedale School
Incorporated: 25 May 2011 *Employees:* 203
Net Worth: £29,748,180 *Total Assets:* £33,919,824
Registered Office: Ousedale School, Newport Pagnell Campus, The Grove, Newport Pagnell, Bucks, MK16 0BJ
Activities: General secondary education
Officers: Imogen Mary Allen [1964] Director/Home Maker; David Beaney [1971] Director/Certified Chartered Accountant; Vicki Beynon [1977] Director/Senior Manager; Susan Margaret Carbert [1961] Director/Headteacher; Paul Robert Collins [1950] Director; Susan Rita Garner [1969] Managing Director, Training Company; Dr Yolande Frances Elizabeth Herbath [1966] Director/Solicitor; Clair Ann King [1972] Director/Solicitor; Andrew Peter Lawson [1974] Director/Head of Finance; Hazel Leighfield [1965] Director/Service Delivery Manager; Faye McClenahan [1974] Managing Director; Andrew Charles Millburn [1953] Director/Retired Civil Servant; David Trevor Malcolm Moulson [1950] Director/Programme Manager; Urvashi Parashar [1974] Director/Civil Servant/Economist; Jennifer Ann Frances Parker [1958] Director/Risk and Control Manager; Karen Spriddle [1981] Director/Head of S&V Finance; John James Stevenson [1960] Director/Workshop Manager; Claire Tierney [1980] Director/6th Form Study Centre Co-ordinator

Outdoor & Sports Company Limited
Incorporated: 9 September 1970 *Employees:* 125
Net Worth: £4,877,067 *Total Assets:* £15,532,123
Registered Office: 3 Bailey Court, Green Street, Macclesfield, Cheshire, SK10 1JQ
Activities: Manufacture of other wearing apparel and accessories n.e.c.
Parent: Outdoor & Sports Company (Holdings) Limited
Officers: Stephen James Cann, Secretary/Director; Paul Anthony Allison [1961] Director/Certified Chartered Accountant; Stephen James Cann [1965] Director/Chartered Accountant

Outokumpu Stainless Limited
Incorporated: 26 February 1993 *Employees:* 534
Net Worth: £156,400,000 *Total Assets:* £298,100,000
Registered Office: P O Box 161, Main Administration Building, Europa Link, Sheffield, S9 1TZ
Activities: Manufacture of basic iron and steel and of ferro-alloys
Parent: Outokumpu Oyj
Officers: Richard Waugh, Secretary; Ian Holdsworth [1969] Director/General Manager UK/Ireland; Jonathan Charles Homewood [1969] Director/General Manager, SMACC; Alison Jayne Taylor [1975] Director/General Manager ASR & SSB; Kari Juhani Tuutti [1970] Director/President Long Products [Finnish]

Oxbow Coal Limited
Incorporated: 25 September 1913 *Employees:* 19
Net Worth: £16,261,788 *Total Assets:* £40,720,300
Registered Office: Southern Way, Immingham Dock, Immingham, N E Lincs, DN40 2NX
Activities: Wholesale of other fuels and related products
Officers: Matthew Evelyn Goodwin, Secretary; Patrick Sjoerd Bruning [1966] Managing Director [Dutch]; David William Clark [1954] Director/Legal Adviser [American]; Michael John Cusick [1962] Commercial Director; William Douglas Parmelee [1957] Director/Accountant [American]

Oxcis Limited
Incorporated: 1 April 1998
Net Worth Deficit: £481,398 *Total Assets:* £103,494,424
Registered Office: Oxford Centre for Islamic Studies, Marston Road, Marston, Oxford, OX3 0EE
Activities: Real estate agencies
Officers: Gordon William Brown [1954] Director/Administrator; Dr Basil Abdul-Jabbar Mustafa [1954] Director

Oxera Consulting LLP
Incorporated: 3 April 2014 *Employees:* 125
Net Worth: £9,075,700 *Total Assets:* £12,716,149
Registered Office: Park Central, 40-41 Park End Street, Oxford, OX1 1JD
Officers: Paul Stephen Breakwell [1961] Member; Dr Luis Miguel Correia Da Silva Domingos [1968] Member; Professor Julian Ralph Franks [1946] Member; Helen Elizabeth Jenkins [1966] Member; Professor Timothy John Jenkinson [1961] Member; Andrew Thomas Judt [1967] Member; Dr Gunnar Niels [1970] Member; Dr. Avantika Chowdhury [1979] LLP Member; Maurice Bernardus Antonius Gerardus Maria de Valois Turk [1973] LLP Member; Pascale Dechamps [1980] LLP Member; Catherine Renee Dominian [1964] LLP Member; Enno Habbo Eilts [1978] LLP Member; Felipe Alfonso Florez Duncan [1978] LLP Member; Peter William Hope [1981] LLP Member; Alan Paul Horncastle [1969] LLP Member; David Jevons [1978] LLP Member; Matthew Johnson [1975] LLP Member; James Kavanagh [1979] LLP Member; Jostein Kristensen [1977] LLP Member; Dr Leonardo Mautino [1968] LLP Member; Andrew Paul Meaney [1976] LLP Member; Robin Philip Noble [1979] LLP Member; Nicole Robins [1980] LLP Member; Dr Min Shi [1973] LLP Member; Deborah Stump [1975] LLP Member; Reinder Menno Van Dijk [1973] LLP Member

Oxfam
Incorporated: 1 October 1958 *Employees:* 4,747
Net Worth: £84,200,000 *Total Assets:* £134,100,000
Registered Office: Oxfam House, John Smith Drive, Oxford, OX4 2JY
Activities: Water collection, treatment and supply
Officers: Jonathan Stirling Saunders, Secretary; Kenneth Mathieson Caldwell [1955] Director/Consultant; Nicholas Drew Cheeseman [1979] Director/Academic; Angela Cluff [1962] Director/Fundraising Consultant; Lois Alyson Jacobs [1954] Director/CEO Lander; Mohammed Wakkas Khan [1979] Director/Dentist; Lydinyda Bunyi Nacpil [1960] Director/Coordinator Asian Peoples Movement on Debt [Filipino]; Babatunde Taiwo Olanrewaju [1979] Director/Management Consultant; Katy Mary Steward [1964] Director/Senior Fellow King's Fund; Gavin MacNeill Stewart [1959] Director/Business Consultant; Caroline Agnes Morgan Thomson [1954] Director/Chair Digital UK; Stephen Mark Walton [1954] Director/Auditor

The Oxford Asset Management Company Limited
Incorporated: 13 April 1993 *Employees:* 84
Net Worth: £5,768,322 *Total Assets:* £50,656,800
Registered Office: Oxam House, 6 George Street, Oxford, OX1 2BW
Activities: Activities of open-ended investment companies
Shareholders: Andre Stern; Stephen Neil Mobbs
Officers: Dr. Steven Michael Kurlander [1967] Director/Research [American]; Stephen Neil Mobbs [1957] Director/Investment; Dr Andre Stern [1964] Director/Investment [German]

Oxford Asset Management LLP
Incorporated: 11 January 2006
Net Worth: £32,709,844 *Total Assets:* £35,671,376
Registered Office: Oxam House, 6 George Street, Oxford, OX1 2BW
Officers: Dr. Steven Michael Kurlander [1967] Member; Stephen Neil Mobbs [1957] Member; Dr Andre Stern [1964] Member; David Lamper [1977] LLP Member; Dr Thomas Newcomb [1977] LLP Member; Dr David Andrew Turner [1975] LLP Member

Oxford Biomedica (UK) Limited
Incorporated: 3 March 1995 *Employees:* 295
Net Worth Deficit: £184,606,000 *Total Assets:* £65,589,000
Registered Office: Windrush Court, Transport Way, Oxford, OX4 6LT
Activities: Research and experimental development on biotechnology
Parent: Oxford Biomedica PLC
Officers: Stuart Paynter, Secretary; John Andrew Dawson [1959] Director; Stuart Paynter [1974] Director/Chief Financial Officer

Oxford Biomedica PLC
Incorporated: 20 September 1996 *Employees:* 295
Net Worth: £6,146,000 *Total Assets:* £65,402,000
Registered Office: Windrush Court, Transport Way, Oxford, OX4 6LT
Activities: Research and experimental development on biotechnology
Officers: Stuart Paynter, Secretary; John Andrew Dawson [1959] Director; Martin Henry Diggle [1962] Director [South African]; Dr Andrew John William Heath [1948] Director; Stuart Jonathon Brodie Henderson [1959] Director; Stuart Paynter [1974] Director/Chief Financial Officer; Doctor Heather Elizabeth Preston [1966] Managing Director; Doctor Lorenzo Tallarigo [1951] Director [Italian]

Oxford Centre for Hebrew and Jewish Studies
Incorporated: 18 April 1973 *Employees:* 4
Net Worth: £14,568,435 *Total Assets:* £15,026,977
Registered Office: Clarendon Institute Building, Walton Street, Oxford, OX1 2HG
Activities: Post-graduate level higher education
Officers: Martin David Paisner, Secretary/Solicitor; Lord Stanley Fink [1957] Director/Chief Executive Public Company; Professor Martin David Goodman [1953] Director/University Professor; Charles Ronald Llewelyn Guthrie [1938] Director; Dr Sondra Leslie Hausner [1969] Director/Associate Professor; Professor Edmund Martin Herzig [1958] Director/University Professor; David Philip Joseph [1961] Director/Barrister; David John Lewis [1939] Director/Chartered Surveyor; Dr Laurent Jean Nicolas Mignon [1971] Director/University Lecturer in Turkish [Luxembourger]; Professor Judith Olszowy Schlanger [1967] Director/Academic [French]; Martin David Paisner [1943] Director/Solicitor; Daniel Patterson [1960] Director/TV Producer; Daniel Peltz [1961] Director; Marc Andre Lorin Polonsky [1960] Director/Lawyer; Sir Bernard Anthony Rix [1944] Director/Judge; Stuart Grant Roden [1963] Director/Hedge Fund Manager; Professor Anna Brechta Sapir Abulafia [1952] Director/University Professor [Dutch]; Charles Adam Laurie Sebag-Montefiore [1949] Director; Anne Rachel Webber [1951] Charity Director; Professor Hugh Godfrey Maturin Williamson [1947] Director/University Professor

Oxford Diocesan Board of Finance (The)
Incorporated: 10 February 1916 *Employees:* 75
Net Worth: £443,952,992 *Total Assets:* £456,952,000
Registered Office: Church House, Oxford Langford Locks, Kidlington, Oxon, OX5 1GF
Activities: Activities of religious organisations
Officers: Canon Rosemary Anne Pearce, Secretary; Dr Andrew Robert Bell [1957] Director/Retired Academic; Susan Elizabeth Booys [1956] Director/Minister of Religion; Reverend Verena Breed [1969] Director/Clerk in Holy Orders [German]; Mark Nicholas Burton [1957] Director/Retired; The Right Reverend Steven John Lindsey Croft [1957] Director/Bishop of Oxford; Reverend Elizabeth Kate Denno [1979] Director/Clerk in Holy Orders; Julie Patricia Dziegiel [1963] Director/Accountant; The Venerable Guy Charles Elsmore [1966] Director/Archdeacon of Buckingham; Bishop Colin William Fletcher [1950] Director/Bishop of Dorchester; The Venerable Judith Karen French [1960] Director/Archdeacon of Dorchester; Henry Gibbon [1962] Director; The Venerable Martin Charles Gorick [1962] Director/Archdeacon of Oxford; The Ven Olivia Josephine Graham [1956] Director/Archdeacon of Berkshire; Reverend Richard John Lamey [1977] Director/Clerk in Holy Orders; James Justin MacNamara [1956] Director; Reverend David John Meakin [1961] Director/Clerk in Holy Orders; Revd Cassa Messervy [1975] Director/Clerk in Holy Orders; Professor John Frederick Missenden [1949] Director/Retired University Lecturer; Jayne Margaret Ozanne [1968] Director Radcliffe Hospital Charitable Fund; Martyn Percy [1962] Director/Clerk in Holy Orders; Michael Brian Powell [1938] Director/Retired; Andrew Proud [1954] Director/Church of England Bishop; Simon Anthony Richards [1956] Director/Chartered Accountant; Susan Elizabeth Scane [1956] Director/Retired; John Pescott Smith [1953] Director; Reverend Michael Keith John Smith [1966] Director/Clerk in Holy Orders; John Neil Sykes [1949] Director/Consultant; The Revd John Hartley Tattersall [1952] Director; Dr Anna Thomas-Betts [1941] Director; Michael Hugh Waring [1931] Director/Retired; Allan Forbes Whittow [1944] Director/Management Accountant; Alan Thomas Lawrence Wilson [1955] Director/Bishop of Buckingham

Oxford Diocesan Schools Trust
Incorporated: 13 July 2012 *Employees:* 921
Net Worth: £16,943,492 *Total Assets:* £30,286,560
Registered Office: Church House, Langford Locks, Kidlington, Oxon, OX5 1GF
Activities: Educational support services
Officers: Stephen James Barber [1946] Director; Sir Clive Booth [1943] Director/Retired; Dr Priscilla Chadwick [1947] Director; Revd Canon Brendan David Clover [1958] Director/Senior Provost Woodard Schools; Jacqueline Anne Davey [1966] Director of Education; Josephine Fageant [1960] Director/Independent SIAMS Inspector; Bishop Colin William Fletcher [1950] Director/Anglican Bishop; Joanna Moriarty [1961] Director; Christopher Wheaton [1973] Director/Energy Sector Analyst; Tony Wilson [1968] Diocesan Director of Education; Kathryn Mary Winrow [1950] Director

Oxford Economics Limited
Incorporated: 23 April 1981 *Employees:* 244
Net Worth: £3,280,827 *Total Assets:* £21,406,392
Registered Office: Abbey House, 121 St Aldates, Oxford, OX1 1HB
Activities: Other professional, scientific and technical activities n.e.c.
Major Shareholder: John Walker
Officers: Charles Philip Henry Burton, Secretary; Christopher John Allsopp [1941] Director/Economist; Andrea George Boltho [1939] Director/University Don [German]; Charles Philip Henry Burton [1952] Director/Economists; Adrian John Cooper [1964] Director/Economist; Bruno Daniel Geoffrey Delacave [1961] Director [Belgian]; John Walker [1949] Director/Economist

Oxford Gene Technology (Operations) Ltd
Incorporated: 21 September 1999 *Employees:* 47
Net Worth Deficit: £31,588,164 *Total Assets:* £18,621,312
Registered Office: Begbroke Science Park, Begbroke Hill, Woodstock Road, Begbroke, Oxon, OX5 1PF
Activities: Research and experimental development on biotechnology
Parent: Oxford Gene Technology IP Limited
Officers: Anthony John Lenhardt, Secretary/Accountant; Dr John George Anson [1960] Director; Dr Michael Robert Evans [1958] Director and CEO; Dr David Andrew Arlwydd Owen [1944] Director; David Aufrere Oxlade [1949] Director; Kenji Tsujimoto [1971] Director/Business Executive [Japanese]; Gregory Alun Williams [1980] Director

Oxford Gene Technology IP Limited
Incorporated: 21 September 1999 *Employees:* 13
Net Worth: £96,695 *Total Assets:* £37,289,304
Registered Office: Begbroke Science Park, Begbroke Hill, Woodstock Road, Begbroke, Oxon, OX5 1PF
Activities: Research and experimental development on biotechnology
Parent: Sysmex Corporation
Officers: Anthony John Lenhardt, Secretary/Accountant; Dr John George Anson [1960] Director; Dr Michael Robert Evans [1958] Director; Dr David Andrew Arlwydd Owen [1944] Director; David Aufrere Oxlade [1949] Director; Kenji Tsujimoto [1971] Director/Business Executive [Japanese]; Gregory Alun Williams [1980] Director

Oxford Gene Technology Limited
Incorporated: 10 April 1995
Net Worth: £14,747,368 *Total Assets:* £46,143,844
Registered Office: Begbroke Science Park, Begbroke Hill, Woodstock Road, Begbroke, Oxon, OX5 1PF
Activities: Other research and experimental development on natural sciences and engineering
Parent: Oxford Gene Technology IP Limited
Officers: Anthony John Lenhardt, Secretary; Dr John George Anson [1960] Director; Dr Michael Robert Evans [1958] Director; Dr David Andrew Arlwydd Owen [1944] Director; David Aufrere Oxlade [1949] Director; Kenji Tsujimoto [1971] Director/Business Executive [Japanese]; Gregory Alun Williams [1980] Director

Oxford Immunotec Global PLC
Incorporated: 16 August 2013 *Employees:* 454
Net Worth: £64,888,136 *Total Assets:* £108,605,648
Registered Office: 94c Innovation Drive, Milton Park, Milton, Abingdon, Oxon, OX14 4RZ
Activities: Manufacture of pharmaceutical preparations
Officers: Elizabeth Keiley, Secretary; Ronald Andrews [1959] Director/Consultant [American]; Patrick Balthrop Snr [1956] Director/Retired CEO, Principal of Apalachee Ventures [American]; Mark Klausner [1965] Director/Investor Relations [American]; Patricia Randall [1950] Director/Attorney [American]; Herman Rosenman [1947] Director/Senior Executive [American]; Richard Alvin Sandberg [1942] Director/Entrepreneur [American]; James Tobin [1944] Director/Consultant [American]; Andrew Scott Walton [1967] Director/Business Executive [American]; Dr Peter James Wrighton-Smith [1974] Director

Oxford Immunotec Limited
Incorporated: 21 August 2002 *Employees:* 86
Net Worth: £97,352,000 *Total Assets:* £115,932,000
Registered Office: 94c Innovation Drive, Milton Park, Milton, Abingdon, Oxon, OX14 4RZ
Activities: Manufacture of pharmaceutical preparations
Parent: Oxford Immunotec Global PLC
Officers: Elizabeth Keiley, Secretary; Richard Alvin Sandberg [1942] Director/Entrepreneur [American]; Dr Peter James Wrighton-Smith [1974] Director

Oxford Instruments Industrial Products Limited
Incorporated: 28 February 1972 *Employees:* 42
Net Worth: £4,891,000 *Total Assets:* £11,860,000
Registered Office: Tubney Woods, Abingdon, Oxon, OX13 5QX
Activities: Manufacture of electronic measuring, testing etc. equipment, not for industrial process control
Parent: Oxford Instruments Industrial Products Holdings Ltd
Officers: Susan Karen Johnson-Brett, Secretary; Gavin Fenton Hill [1968] Finance Director; Simon David Holden [1962] Director; Jonathan Paul Turner [1978] Finance Director

Oxford Instruments Nanotechnology Tools Holdings Limited
Incorporated: 8 September 2000
Net Worth: £222,242,000 *Total Assets:* £222,242,000
Registered Office: Tubney Woods, Abingdon, Oxon, OX13 5QX
Activities: Activities of head offices
Parent: Oxford Instruments PLC
Officers: Susan Karen Johnson-Brett, Secretary; Dr Ian Richard Barkshire [1965] Director/Chief Operating Officer; Thomas Curtis [1970] Director/Chartered Accountant; Gavin Fenton Hill [1968] Finance Director

Oxford Instruments Nanotechnology Tools Limited
Incorporated: 28 September 1961 *Employees:* 598
Net Worth: £33,304,000 *Total Assets:* £116,811,000
Registered Office: Tubney Woods, Abingdon, Oxon, OX13 5QX
Activities: Manufacture of electronic measuring, testing etc. equipment, not for industrial process control
Parent: Oxford Instruments Nanotechnology Tools Holdings Ltd
Officers: Susan Karen Johnson-Brett, Secretary; Dr Ian Richard Barkshire [1965] Director/Physicist; Gavin Fenton Hill [1968] Finance Director; Simon David Holden [1962] Director; Beverley Jane Hutchings [1966] Director/Accountant; Adam Surriff Jaufurally [1978] Director/Chartered Accountant; Jonathan Paul Turner [1978] Finance Director; Ian Christopher Wilcock [1967] Managing Director

Oxford Instruments Overseas Holdings 2008 Limited
Incorporated: 14 March 2008 *Employees:* 3
Net Worth: £85,838,424 *Total Assets:* £85,992,344
Registered Office: Tubney Woods, Abingdon, Oxon, OX13 5QX
Activities: Activities of head offices
Parent: Oxford Instruments Overseas Holdings Ltd
Officers: Susan Karen Johnson-Brett, Secretary; Dr Ian Richard Barkshire [1965] Director/Chief Operating Officer; Thomas Curtis [1970] Director/Chartered Accountant; Gavin Fenton Hill [1968] Finance Director

Oxford Instruments Overseas Holdings Limited
Incorporated: 14 January 1997
Net Worth: £121,540,000 *Total Assets:* £121,595,000
Registered Office: Tubney Woods, Abingdon, Oxon, OX13 5QX
Activities: Activities of head offices
Parent: Oxford Instruments PLC
Officers: Susan Karen Johnson-Brett, Secretary; Dr Ian Richard Barkshire [1965] Director/Chief Operating Officer; Thomas Curtis [1970] Director/Chartered Accountant; Gavin Fenton Hill [1968] Finance Director

Oxford Instruments PLC
Incorporated: 30 September 1963 *Employees:* 1,642
Net Worth: £179,600,000 *Total Assets:* £345,200,000
Registered Office: Tubney Woods, Abingdon, Oxon, OX13 5QX
Activities: Activities of head offices
Officers: Susan Karen Johnson-Brett, Secretary; Dr Ian Richard Barkshire [1965] Director/Chief Operating Officer; Stephen Blair [1959] Director; Neil Andrew Patrick Carson [1957] Director; Richard Henry Friend [1953] Director/University Professor; Thomas Otto Geitner [1955] Director [German]; Gavin Fenton Hill [1968] Finance Director; Mary Elizabeth Waldner [1969] Director

Oxford Instruments UK 2013 Limited
Incorporated: 1 February 2013
Net Worth: £77,200,088 *Total Assets:* £80,291,624
Registered Office: Oxford Instruments, Tubney Woods, Abingdon, Oxon, OX13 5QX
Activities: Activities of other holding companies n.e.c.
Parent: Oxford Instruments Overseas Holdings 2008 Limited
Officers: Susan Karen Johnson-Brett, Secretary; Dr Ian Richard Barkshire [1965] Director/Chief Operating Officer; Thomas Curtis [1970] Director/Chartered Accountant; Gavin Fenton Hill [1968] Finance Director

Oxford Metrics PLC
Incorporated: 22 May 2000 *Employees:* 234
Previous: OMG PLC
Net Worth: £29,970,000 *Total Assets:* £40,553,000
Registered Office: 6 Oxford Industrial Park, Yarnton, Oxon, OX5 1QU
Activities: Activities of head offices
Officers: Catherine Lindsay Robertson, Secretary/Director; Nicholas Paul Bolton [1969] Director; Adrian Courtney Carey [1957] Director; David Anthony Deacon [1960] Director; Roger George Parry [1953] Director; Jonathon Reeve [1949] Director/Consultant Engineer; Catherine Lindsay Robertson [1958] Director

Oxford Nanopore Technologies Limited
Incorporated: 9 March 2005 *Employees:* 343
Net Worth: £93,584,000 *Total Assets:* £119,123,000
Registered Office: Gosling Building, Edmund Halley Road, Oxford Science Park, Oxford, OX4 4DQ
Activities: Other research and experimental development on natural sciences and engineering
Officers: Peter Vance Allen [1956] Director; Alan John Aubrey [1961] Director/Chief Executive Officer; Timothy Cowper [1965] Director; Sarah Lucinda Gordon Wild [1959] Director; Dr Gurdial Singh Sanghera [1961] Director; Dr James Peter Willcocks [1976] Director

Oxford Pharmagenesis Holdings Limited
Incorporated: 5 October 2012 *Employees:* 184
Net Worth: £11,929,791 *Total Assets:* £17,727,488
Registered Office: Tubney Warren Barn, Tubney, Abingdon, Oxon, OX13 5QJ
Activities: Other publishing activities
Officers: Jeanette Mary Costigan [1957] Director; Alison Hillman [1956] Director; Graham Anthony Brian Shelton [1950] Director/Chairman; Andrew Sheridan [1968] Director; Dr Richard White [1975] Director; Dr Christopher Charles Winchester [1971] Director

Oxford Pharmagenesis Limited
Incorporated: 6 January 1998 *Employees:* 155
Net Worth: £11,881,557 *Total Assets:* £16,395,210
Registered Office: Tubney Warren Barn, Tubney, Oxford, OX13 5QJ
Activities: Other publishing activities
Parent: Oxford Pharmagenesis Holdings Limited
Officers: Graham Anthony Brian Shelton [1950] Director/Chairman; Dr Richard White [1975] Director; Dr Christopher Charles Winchester [1971] Director

Oxford Plastic Systems Limited
Incorporated: 11 November 1985 *Employees:* 89
Net Worth: £7,795,168 *Total Assets:* £12,059,123
Registered Office: Unit T2, Enstone Airfield, Enstone, Chipping Norton, Oxon, OX7 4NP
Activities: Manufacture of other plastic products
Parent: Oxford Plastic Systems (Holdings) Limited
Officers: Robin Gilman Arculus, Secretary; Alice Jane Belinda Whiteley, Secretary/Manager; Helen Mary Claire Anderson [1965] Director; Alice Jane Belinda Whiteley [1966] Director; Christopher James Whiteley [1958] Director

Oxford Policy Management Limited
Incorporated: 6 November 1995 *Employees:* 392
Net Worth: £7,175,533 *Total Assets:* £29,716,650
Registered Office: Level 3, Clarendon House, Cornmarket Street, Oxford, OX1 3HJ
Activities: Management consultancy activities other than financial management
Shareholder: Oxford Policy Management EBT Ltd
Officers: Raquel Ann McGrath, Secretary; Professor Christopher Scott Adam [1963] Director/Professor of Economics; Anna Da Silva [1972] Director/Consultant; Sourovi De [1988] Director/Economist Consultant [Indian]; Dr Samuel Richard Piers Franzen [1984] Director/Senior Consultant; Dougal Adam Freeman [1970] Finance Director; Simon Paul Crisp Hunt [1956] Managing Director; Carolyn Miller [1951] Director/Consultant; Philippe Antoinne Vincent Naert [1943] Director [Belgian]; Micheline Ntiru [1975] Director/Business Facilitator [Ugandan]; Tania Louise Songini [1969] Director [British/Italian]; Professor Katherine Jane Willis [1964] Director of Science

Oxford Products Limited
Incorporated: 29 March 1983 *Employees:* 126
Net Worth: £8,684,172 *Total Assets:* £21,311,456
Registered Office: 5 South Parade, Summertown, Oxford, OX2 7JL
Activities: Other manufacturing n.e.c.
Parent: OP Holdings Limited (Bare Legal Title)
Officers: Mark Bernard Wallbutton, Secretary/Finance Controller; Andrew Robert Alan Hammond [1971] Managing Director; Arthur Charles Hammond [1945] Director/Chairman; David Kinnaird [1967] Sales Director; Henry Rivers Fletcher [1975] Marketing Director; Christopher Shearer [1959] Export Director; Mark Bernard Wallbutton [1965] Finance Director

Oxford Property Trading Ltd.
Incorporated: 28 March 2011 *Employees:* 3
Net Worth: £4,360,000 *Total Assets:* £19,904,000
Registered Office: The Box, Horseshoe Lane, Alderley Edge, Cheshire, SK9 7QP
Activities: Development of building projects
Parent: Select Charles Street Residential (Holdings) Limited
Officers: Mark Christopher Dawson [1973] Director; Kenneth John Knott [1959] Director; Michael Keith Slater [1974] Director

Oxford Publishing Limited
Incorporated: 25 August 1983
Net Worth: £56,270,000 *Total Assets:* £65,326,000
Registered Office: Oxford University Press, Great Clarendon Street, Oxford, OX2 6DP
Activities: Book publishing
Officers: John Patrick Walsh, Secretary; Kevin James Brown [1962] Director/Chartered Accountant; Nigel David Portwood [1965] Director/Chief Executive; Giles Richard Lovell Spackman [1964] Finance Director

Oxford Renewable Fuel Ltd
Incorporated: 10 June 2013
Net Worth: £4,995,429 *Total Assets:* £9,303,710
Registered Office: Magdalen Centre, The Oxford Science Park, Oxford, OX4 4GA
Activities: Other research and experimental development on natural sciences and engineering
Shareholder: Adrian John Eyre
Officers: Adrian John Eyre [1954] Director

Oxford Said Business School Limited
Incorporated: 3 March 1994 *Employees:* 100
Net Worth: £2,317,000 *Total Assets:* £9,592,000
Registered Office: University Offices, Wellington Square, Oxford, OX1 2JD
Activities: General secondary education
Officers: Sophia Pryor, Secretary; Jolyon Leo Harris [1974] Director/Accountant; Lindsay Ronald Pearson [1974] Deputy Director of Finance; Professor Peter Tufano [1957] Director/Dean [American]; Andrew White [1974] Director/Academic

The Oxford Science Park Limited
Incorporated: 16 August 1988 *Employees:* 25
Previous: Magdalen Development Company Limited
Net Worth: £21,096,126 *Total Assets:* £33,921,848
Registered Office: Magdalen College, High Street, Oxford, OX1 4AU
Activities: Development of building projects
Parent: President and Scholars of The College of St Mary Magdalen in the University of Oxford
Officers: Margaret Helen Anne Knight, Secretary; Dr Byron Walter Byrne [1972] Director/Academic [Australian]; Prof David Charles Clary [1953] Director/Academic; Kay Patrick Despard [1958] Director/Chartered Surveyor; Prof Alison Mary Etheridge [1964] Director/Academic; Oliver Thomas Willoughby Hawkins [1976] Director/Investor; John Rory Hamilton Maw [1964] Director/Bursar; Prof Rahul Santhanam [1977] Director/University Lecturer [Indian]; Piers Jason Alexander Scrimshaw-Wright [1971] Managing Director

Oxford Sciences Innovation PLC
Incorporated: 19 June 2014 *Employees:* 294
Net Worth: £666,009,024 *Total Assets:* £668,587,008
Registered Office: King Charles House, Park End Street, Oxford, OX1 1JD
Activities: Activities of venture and development capital companies
Officers: Alan John Aubrey [1961] Director; John Irving Bell [1952] Director/Physician Scientist [British/Canadian]; Christopher Michael Chambers [1961] Director; Peter Graham Davies [1972] Director/Finance; Giles Kerr [1959] Finance Director; Bernard John Taylor [1956] Director; James Henry Wilkinson [1966] Director/Chief Financial Officer

Oxford Trust (The)
Incorporated: 22 March 1985 *Employees:* 22
Net Worth: £14,352,218 *Total Assets:* £14,580,424
Registered Office: Oxford Centre for Innovation, New Road, Oxford, OX1 1BY
Activities: Other research and experimental development on natural sciences and engineering
Officers: Stephen Rhys Burgess, Secretary; Dr Jean-Marc Boyle [1962] IT Director; Dr Paul Robert Brankin [1943] Director; Paul David Dean [1961] Director; Mary Georgina Ferry [1955] Director/Writer; Professor Alistair David Fitt [1957] Director/University Pro Vice-Chancellor; David Jonathan Flint [1961] Director; Professor William Siward James [1960] Director/Research Scientist and Academic; Megan Mai Morys-Carter [1983] Deputy Director; Professor Julia Alison Noble [1965] Director/University Professor; Ceris Lynne Pebworth [1957] Director/Retired; Jonathan William Welfare [1944] Director/Retired

Oxford University Innovation Limited
Incorporated: 27 November 1987 *Employees:* 75
Previous: Isis Innovation Limited
Net Worth: £7,568,000 *Total Assets:* £14,687,000
Registered Office: University Offices, Wellington Square, Oxford, OX1 2JD
Activities: Other business support service activities n.e.c.
Officers: Sophia Pryor, Secretary; Prof Charanjit Bountra [1960] Director/Professor; Professor Stephen Graham Davies [1950] Director/Professor of Chemistry; David Jonathan Flint [1961] Director; Professor Patrick Spencer Grant [1966] Director/University Professor; Nigel John Keen [1947] Director; Professor Helen McShane [1967] Director/University Professor; Dr Matthew Perkins [1962] Director/Chief Executive; Professor Lionel Tarassenko [1957] Director/University Professor; Prof Matthew John Andrew Wood [1963] Director/Professor of Neuroscience [Irish]

Oxford University Trading Limited
Incorporated: 13 September 2000
Net Worth: £847,000 *Total Assets:* £12,525,000
Registered Office: University Offices, Wellington Square, Oxford, OX1 2JD
Activities: Other service activities n.e.c.
Officers: Sophia Elizabeth Sarah Pryor, Secretary; Nigel Sean Anderson [1964] Director/Treasurer; Nicholas Benjamin Heath [1962] Director/Accountant; Stephen Leslie Purbrick [1969] Director/Accountant

Oxford West End Development Limited
Incorporated: 18 January 2016
Net Worth Deficit: £1,883,875 *Total Assets:* £14,014,668
Registered Office: St Aldates Chambers, 109-113 St Aldates, Oxford, OX1 1DS
Activities: Development of building projects
Shareholders: Nuffield College, Oxford; Oxford City Council
Officers: Lindsay David Cane, Secretary; Ian Justin Gray [1968] Director/Council Officer; Kevin Andrew Minns [1967] Director/Property Developer; Gordon Scotland Mitchell [1956] Director/Local Government Officer; Thomas Moore [1977] Director/College Bursar

Oxhold Limited
Incorporated: 29 June 2010 *Employees:* 3
Net Worth: £2,086,507 *Total Assets:* £11,848,358
Registered Office: Prama House, 267 Banbury Road, Oxford, OX2 7HT
Activities: Other letting and operating of own or leased real estate
Officers: Christopher Bright [1959] Director/Solicitor; Professor Susan Bright [1960] Director/Professor of Law; Thomas Christopher Bright [1989] Director/Property Investment

P H Property Holdings Limited
Incorporated: 16 February 1996 *Employees:* 36
Net Worth: £6,984,208 *Total Assets:* £22,769,468
Registered Office: Bollin House, Oakfield Road, Cheadle Royal Business Park, Cheadle, Cheshire, SK8 3GX
Activities: Development of building projects
Major Shareholder: Paul Henry Hogarth
Officers: Philip Nigel Hughes, Secretary; Daniel Richard Gale [1965] Director/Chartered Surveyor; James Randle Heyworth [1968] Director/Chartered Surveyor; Paul Henry Hogarth [1959] Director; Philip Nigel Hughes [1965] Director/Self Employed; John McKelvey [1964] Construction Director; Lee Francis Wood [1972] Technical Director

P Investments Limited
Incorporated: 29 August 2003 *Employees:* 25
Net Worth Deficit: £852,000 *Total Assets:* £14,049,000
Registered Office: Meriden Hall, Main Road, Meriden, Coventry, Warwicks, CV7 7PT
Activities: Other activities of employment placement agencies
Officers: Nigel John Dudley, Secretary; John Edward Smith [1948] Director; Timothy Watts [1949] Director; Susan Ann Wilcox [1960] Director

P V H Holdings Limited
Incorporated: 23 March 1990 *Employees:* 29
Net Worth: £9,944,454 *Total Assets:* £15,532,225
Registered Office: Howdenshire Way, Knedlington Road, Howden, Goole, E Yorks, DN14 7HZ
Activities: Activities of construction holding companies
Shareholders: Arnold Bernard Gerardus Van Huet; Simon David Pearson
Officers: Frank Langstraat [1952] Director [Dutch]; Simon David Pearson [1962] Director; Alan Jonathan Simpson [1966] Director; Arnold Bernard Gerardus Van Huet [1953] Director [Dutch]; Alan William Virgo [1958] Director

P. H. Properties Ltd
Incorporated: 22 September 1995 *Employees:* 266
Net Worth: £8,762,631 *Total Assets:* £31,553,584
Registered Office: Dunns Close, Nuneaton, Warwicks, CV11 4NF
Activities: Activities of head offices
Shareholders: Anna Margaret Hamilton; Andrew Melville Hamilton
Officers: Dean Lucas, Secretary; Francis Mark Elkins [1967] Director; Andrew Melville Hamilton [1965] Director; Dean Lucas [1968] Director

P.A. Estates Management Limited
Incorporated: 19 September 1978
Net Worth: £5,649,229 *Total Assets:* £16,515,096
Registered Office: 23 Commonside, Walkley, Sheffield, S10 1GD
Activities: Other letting and operating of own or leased real estate
Major Shareholder: Pamela Susan Marsh
Officers: Alan Geoffrey Waller, Secretary; Pamela Susan Marsh [1951] Director/Married Woman; Susan Constance Marsh [1981] Managing Director; Alan Geoffrey Waller [1948] Director/Accountant

P2I Ltd
Incorporated: 30 June 2003 *Employees:* 155
Net Worth: £13,548,605 *Total Assets:* £21,318,128
Registered Office: 127 North Milton Park, Milton, Abingdon, Oxon, OX14 4SA
Activities: Other manufacturing n.e.c.
Officers: Adrian Paul Moores, Secretary; Stephen Henry Ralph Brooke [1973] Director; Dr Stephen Coulson [1974] Director; Prasoon Dayal [1970] Director [Chinese]; Bradley Dean Landes [1959] Director/Private Equity [American]; Andrew Lane [1962] Director; Panayotis John Malliris [1970] Director/Finance [American]; Adrian Paul Moores [1972] Director/Chartered Accountant; Nigel Robert Young [1953] Director/Chartered Accountant

P3 Group Europe Limited
Incorporated: 3 March 1970 *Employees:* 416
Net Worth: £5,769,404 *Total Assets:* £19,593,440
Registered Office: Nimlok House, Booth Drive, Park Farm, Wellingborough, Northants, NN8 6NL
Activities: Activities of head offices
Shareholders: Timothy Paul George Perutz; Nimlok Company
Officers: Jeremy Dean Roberts, Secretary; Simon Generald Alexander Perutz [1958] Director/Business Executive; Timothy Paul George Perutz [1965] Managing Director

Paccar Financial PLC
Incorporated: 15 February 2001 *Employees:* 53
Net Worth: £111,031,000 *Total Assets:* £679,089,984
Registered Office: 9400 Garsington Road, Oxford Business Park, Cowley, Oxford, OX4 2HN
Activities: Financial intermediation not elsewhere classified
Parent: Paccar Inc
Officers: Alison Jones, Secretary; Stephen Barfoot [1961] Director; Gerrit Jan Bas [1969] Director [Dutch]; Todd Hubbard [1962] Director/Vice President (Paccar Financial) [American]

Paccar Parts U.K. Limited
Incorporated: 15 March 1993 *Employees:* 127
Net Worth: £13,926,000 *Total Assets:* £16,384,000
Registered Office: 9400 Garsington Road, Oxford Business Park, Cowley, Oxford, OX4 2HN
Activities: Manufacture of motor vehicles
Parent: Paccar Trucks UK Limited
Officers: Alison Jones, Secretary; Ronald Armstrong [1956] Director [American]; Dick Leek [1963] Director/General Manager Paccar Parts Europe [Dutch]; Henricus Christianus Adrianus Maria Schippers [1962] Director/President Daf Trucks NV [Dutch]

Paccar Trucks U.K. Ltd
Incorporated: 5 March 1998
Net Worth: £73,155,000 *Total Assets:* £73,155,000
Registered Office: 9400 Garsington Road, Oxford Business Park, Cowley, Oxford, OX4 2HN
Activities: Manufacture of motor vehicles
Parent: Paccar Inc
Officers: Alison Jones, Secretary; Ronald Eugene Armstrong [1955] Director/CEO of Paccar Inc [American]; Bryan Michael Sitko [1976] Managing Director [American]

Paccor (Mansfield) UK Limited
Incorporated: 1 November 2001 *Employees:* 130
Previous: Coveris Rigid (Mansfield) UK Limited
Net Worth: £24,694,000 *Total Assets:* £32,812,000
Registered Office: 3-5 Commercial Gate, Mansfield, Notts, NG18 1EJ
Activities: Manufacture of other plastic products
Parent: Daisy UK Holdco Limited
Officers: Andrew Richard Hollyhead [1975] Director; Keith Ashley Jones [1960] Director; Stephen Naylor [1974] Director

Pacific Direct Finance Limited
Incorporated: 17 March 2008
Net Worth Deficit: £18,327,950 *Total Assets:* £12,424,259
Registered Office: Trinity Gardens, 9-11 Bromham Road, Bedford, MK40 2BP
Activities: Non-trading company
Parent: ADA PD UK Ltd
Officers: Karen Ruth Abel [1981] Director/Chartered Accountant; Sylvia Anne Jensch [1971] Director [German]; Wilhelm Bernhard Konning [1958] Director [German]

Padley & Venables Limited
Incorporated: 8 January 1993 *Employees:* 193
Net Worth: £30,094,732 *Total Assets:* £32,387,528
Registered Office: Callywhite Lane, Dronfield, Sheffield, S18 2XT
Activities: Other manufacturing n.e.c.
Major Shareholder: Fred Michael Brunner
Officers: Darren David Bradwell, Secretary; Fred Michael Brunner [1962] Director/Manufacturing Executive [American]

G W Padley Holdings Limited
Incorporated: 31 July 1959 *Employees:* 53
Net Worth: £37,429,000 *Total Assets:* £39,665,000
Registered Office: Cumberland Court, 80 Mount Street, Nottingham, NG1 6HH
Activities: Activities of head offices
Officers: David George Padley [1954] Director/Chairman; Doris Padley [1927] Director

G W Padley Poultry Limited
Incorporated: 19 August 1960 *Employees:* 2
Net Worth: £12,533,000 *Total Assets:* £14,421,000
Registered Office: Cumberland Court, 80 Mount Street, Nottingham, NG1 6HH
Activities: Production of meat and poultry meat products
Parent: G W Padley Holdings Limited
Officers: David George Padley [1954] Director/Chairman; Doris Padley [1927] Director

PAG International Limited
Incorporated: 5 December 2001
Previous: UAG UK Holdings Limited
Net Worth: £350,011,008 *Total Assets:* £363,934,016
Registered Office: 2 Penman Way, Grove Park, Leicester, LE19 1ST
Activities: Activities of head offices
Shareholder: Roger Searle Penske
Officers: Adam Collinson, Secretary; Maggie Feher, Secretary; Aaron Michael, Secretary; John Dennis Carlson [1969] Director/Accountant [American]; Adam Collinson [1972] Finance Director; Darren Edwards [1968] Managing Director; Robert Harold Kurnick [1961] Director/Executive Vice President [American]

PAH Financial Services Limited
Incorporated: 13 January 2003
Net Worth Deficit: £1,140,000 *Total Assets:* £106,206,000
Registered Office: Epsom Avenue, Stanley Green Trading Estate, Handforth, Cheshire, SK9 3RN
Activities: Other business support service activities n.e.c.
Parent: Pet at Home Ltd
Officers: Louise Ann Stonier, Secretary; Michael James Iddon [1965] Director; Peter Pritchard [1970] Director; Louise Ann Stonier [1973] Director/Company Secretary

Pailton Engineering Limited
Incorporated: 5 July 1978 *Employees:* 168
Net Worth: £10,286,118 *Total Assets:* £12,521,623
Registered Office: Phoenix House, Holbrook Lane, Coventry, Warwicks, CV6 4AD
Activities: Manufacture of other parts and accessories for motor vehicles
Officers: Christopher John Chapman, Secretary; John Ralph Nollett [1969] Director; Veronica Nollett [1946] Director

Pal International Limited
Incorporated: 31 October 1996 *Employees:* 71
Net Worth: £5,964,912 *Total Assets:* £10,865,394
Registered Office: Bilton Way, Lutterworth, Leics, LE17 4JA
Activities: Other manufacturing n.e.c.
Officers: Richard Louis Brucciani [1945] Director; Sheila Margaret Brucciani [1949] Director/Solicitor; Anthea Louise Nelson [1974] Director/Legal Consultant; Perminder Singh Rupra [1977] Director

Pall UK Holdings Limited
Incorporated: 10 November 2015
Net Worth: £211,475,584 *Total Assets:* £211,476,416
Registered Office: 19 Jessops Riverside, 800 Brightside Lane, Sheffield, S9 2RX
Activities: Activities of head offices
Parent: Danaher Corporation
Officers: Deen William Harman [1964] Manufacturing Director; Antony Paul Mason [1966] Managing Director; Christina Ellen Munslow [1959] Director/Solicitor

Pall-Ex (U.K.) Limited
Incorporated: 6 February 1996 *Employees:* 152
Net Worth: £3,871,000 *Total Assets:* £19,873,000
Registered Office: Pall-Ex House, Victoria Road, Ellistown, Leics, LE67 1FH
Activities: Freight transport by road
Major Shareholder: Hilary Lorraine Devey
Officers: Kevin Buchanan [1965] Managing Director; Hilary Lorraine Devey [1954] Managing Director; Ruth Elizabeth Moor [1965] Director/Chartered Accountant; Peter Paxton [1964] Director/Accountant

Palletforce Holdings Limited
Incorporated: 14 July 2015 *Employees:* 328
Net Worth: £5,638,000 *Total Assets:* £45,211,000
Registered Office: Callister Way, Centrum West, Burton on Trent, Staffs, DE14 2SY
Activities: Activities of distribution holding companies
Major Shareholder: Heath Brian Zarin
Officers: Neil Andrew Carpenter [1963] Director; Michael Conroy [1968] Director; David Holland [1971] Director; Dean John Hughes [1974] Director; Chuang Hue Moh [1975] Director/Merchant [Singaporean]; Simon Richard Pearson [1967] Director/Management Consultant; Mark William Tapper [1965] Director; Heath Brian Zarin [1975] Director/Finance [Kittitian]

Palletforce Limited
Incorporated: 11 October 2000 *Employees:* 172
Previous: Palletforce PLC
Net Worth: £13,900,000 *Total Assets:* £32,949,000
Registered Office: Callister Way, Centrum West, Burton on Trent, Staffs, DE14 2SY
Activities: Freight transport by road
Parent: Forcefield Bidco Limited
Officers: Neil Andrew Carpenter, Secretary; Steve Back [1960] Director; David Ian Breeze [1963] Director; Neil Andrew Carpenter [1963] Director; Michael Conroy [1968] Director/Chief Executive; David Holland [1971] Director; Dean John Hughes [1974] Director; Chuang Hue Moh [1975] Director/Merchant [Singaporean]; Simon Richard Pearson [1967] Director/Management Consultant; Mark Jeremy Tabor [1963] Director; Mark William Tapper [1965] Director; Heath Brian Zarin [1975] Director/Finance [Kittitian]

Palm Paper Limited
Incorporated: 23 July 1964 *Employees:* 187
Net Worth: £349,697,280 *Total Assets:* £380,070,784
Registered Office: Saddlebow Industrial Estate, Poplar Avenue, Kings Lynn, Norfolk, PE34 3AL
Activities: Manufacture of paper and paperboard
Parent: Hera GmbH
Officers: Jose Antonio Villatoro, Secretary; Wolfgang Palm [1953] Director/Businessman [German]

Palm Recycling Limited
Incorporated: 5 February 2010 *Employees:* 14
Net Worth: £5,198,240 *Total Assets:* £14,946,428
Registered Office: Saddlebow Industrial Estate, Poplar Avenue, Kings Lynn, Norfolk, PE34 3AL
Activities: Recovery of sorted materials
Parent: Palm Paper Limited
Officers: Jose Antonio Villatoro, Secretary; Gero Hempel [1966] Managing Director [German]; Wolfgang Palm [1953] Director/Businessman [German]

Palma Bidco Limited
Incorporated: 14 March 2016 *Employees:* 5
Net Worth: £3,264,000 *Total Assets:* £42,128,000
Registered Office: Site 3 Furnace Road, Ilkeston, Derbys, DE7 5EP
Activities: Activities of head offices
Officers: John Breheny [1981] Director/Chartered Accountant; Gary Lasham [1958] Director; Alan James McWalter [1953] Director/Chairman; Keven David Parker [1969] Director/Private Equity Partner; Karl Ivor Stevens [1956] Finance Director

The Palmer Family Trust PLC
Incorporated: 6 November 1962 *Employees:* 5
Net Worth: £10,253,525 *Total Assets:* £13,660,116
Registered Office: Hassett Chambers, Hassett Street, Bedford, MK40 1HA
Activities: Development of building projects
Major Shareholder: Marian Palmer
Officers: Jill Palmer, Secretary; Michael Nicholson Lord [1938] Director/Member of The House of Lords; David Palmer [1961] Managing Director; Jill Palmer [1958] Director/Solicitor; Marian Palmer [1933] Director/Housewife; Mark Palmer [1956] Director/Computer Manager; Roy Mervin Palmer [1929] Director/Solicitor; Sara Palmer [1964] Director/Solicitor

Palms Row Health Care Limited
Incorporated: 8 May 1992 *Employees:* 209
Net Worth: £4,442,247 *Total Assets:* £10,552,089
Registered Office: 379 Earl Marshall Road, Sheffield, S4 8FA
Activities: Medical nursing home activities
Parent: Palms Row Heatlhcare Holdings Ltd
Officers: Nicola Jane Richards, Secretary/Accountant; Nicola Jane Richards [1973] Managing Director

Panache Lingerie Limited
Incorporated: 22 October 1980 *Employees:* 117
Net Worth: £9,124,000 *Total Assets:* £14,359,000
Registered Office: 7 Drake House Crescent, Waterthorpe, Sheffield, S20 7HT
Activities: Wholesale of clothing and footwear
Officers: William Edward Henry Montague, Secretary; Siobhan Marie Grantham [1962] Director; Daniel Thomas Power [1975] Director; John Anthony Power [1965] Managing Director; Louise Ellen Power [1964] Director

Papa John's (GB) Limited
Incorporated: 20 December 1990 *Employees:* 105
Net Worth: £26,182,000 *Total Assets:* £37,525,000
Registered Office: Papa John's UK & European Campus, 11 Northfield Drive, Northfield, Milton Keynes, Bucks, MK15 0DQ
Activities: Retail sale in non-specialised stores with food, beverages or tobacco predominating
Officers: Joseph Hale Smith [1963] Director/Global Franchisee Sales [American]; Jack Harold Swaysland [1964] Managing Director; Elizabeth Williams [1975] Managing Director

Paragon Interiors Group PLC
Incorporated: 24 January 1986 *Employees:* 113
Net Worth: £8,084,000 *Total Assets:* £29,201,000
Registered Office: Paragon House, Orchard Place, Nottingham Business Park, Nottingham, NG8 6PX
Activities: Other specialised construction activities n.e.c.
Major Shareholder: Alan Hardy
Officers: Alan Hardy, Secretary/Director; Guy Mark Dibley [1957] Director/Commercial Manager; Alan Hardy [1964] Director

Paragon Property Investments Limited
Incorporated: 11 February 2009 *Employees:* 120
Net Worth: £11,976,695 *Total Assets:* £17,940,832
Registered Office: Quadrant 3, Yorkshire Way, Armthorpe, Doncaster, S Yorks, DN3 3FB
Activities: Other letting and operating of own or leased real estate
Major Shareholder: Metin Pekin
Officers: Metin Pekin [1976] Managing Director

Paragon Quality Foods Ltd
Incorporated: 5 February 1996 *Employees:* 120
Net Worth: £7,459,938 *Total Assets:* £13,099,159
Registered Office: Paragon Quality Foods Limited, Yorkshire Way, Armthorpe, Doncaster, S Yorks, DN3 3FB
Activities: Production of meat and poultry meat products
Major Shareholder: Metin Pekin
Officers: Metin Pekin [1969] Director

Parallel Parents Ltd
Incorporated: 26 October 2001
Net Worth: £10,828,034 *Total Assets:* £12,058,528
Registered Office: 2nd Floor, Lansdowne House, 85 Buxton Road, Heaviley, Stockport, Cheshire, SK3 8LZ
Activities: Other social work activities without accommodation n.e.c.
Shareholders: Sean Anthony Fitzpatrick; Ellen Fitzpatrick
Officers: Ellen Fitzpatrick, Secretary; Dr Sean Anthony Fitzpatrick [1948] Director/Residential Childcare

Paralloy Limited
Incorporated: 1 December 1931 *Employees:* 211
Net Worth: £17,583,000 *Total Assets:* £44,903,000
Registered Office: Millennium Court, First Avenue, Burton on Trent, Staffs, DE14 2WH
Activities: Casting of other non-ferrous metals
Parent: Doncasters Limited
Officers: Ian Molyneux, Secretary; Duncan Andrew Hinks [1975] Director/Chief Financial Officer; Ian Molyneux [1964] Director/Solicitor; Lisa Marie Oxnard [1981] Director/Chief Financial Officer

Paramount Holdings (UK) Limited
Incorporated: 9 April 1996 *Employees:* 4
Net Worth: £17,737,256 *Total Assets:* £19,891,644
Registered Office: 22a Centurion Way, Meridian Business Park, Leicester, LE19 1WH
Activities: Activities of head offices
Shareholders: Asraf Abdul Sattar Omar; Aniz Abdul Sattar Omar
Officers: Aniz Abdul Sattar Omar, Secretary; Abdul Sattar Omar [1939] Director; Aniz Abdul Sattar Omar [1966] Director; Asraf Abdul Sattar Omar [1960] Director; Kulsum Abdul Sattar Omar [1940] Director

Parex Ltd
Incorporated: 8 December 1989 *Employees:* 74
Net Worth: £8,173,476 *Total Assets:* £12,562,067
Registered Office: Abeles Way, Holly Lane Industrial Estate, Atherstone, Warwicks, CV9 2QZ
Activities: Other manufacturing n.e.c.
Parent: Dry Mix Solution Ltd
Officers: Anne Cogbill, Secretary; Eric Charles Pierre Berge [1967] Director [French]; Mark Andrew Shorrock [1964] Managing Director

A.G. Parfett & Sons Limited
Incorporated: 15 January 1980 *Employees:* 560
Net Worth: £25,968,006 *Total Assets:* £93,546,384
Registered Office: Didsbury Road, Stockport, Cheshire, SK4 2JP
Activities: Non-specialised wholesale of food, beverages and tobacco
Parent: Parfetts Employee Trust Limited
Officers: David Grimes, Secretary; David Grimes [1965] Director/Chartered Accountant; Gregory Suszczenia [1966] Director; Guy Swindell [1981] Retail Director; Andrew Whitworth [1971] Director

E.Park & Sons Limited
Incorporated: 24 February 1972 *Employees:* 170
Net Worth: £25,328,264 *Total Assets:* £30,407,784
Registered Office: Bentworth, Lees Lane, Newton Adlington, Macclesfield, Cheshire, SK10 4LL
Activities: Processing and preserving of potatoes
Parent: Bentworth Holdings Limited
Officers: Lynne Patricia Arnot, Secretary; Richard Park [1954] Director; Stephen Richard Park [1972] Operations Director

Park Air Systems Limited
Incorporated: 1 October 1985 *Employees:* 136
Net Worth: £31,591,000 *Total Assets:* £48,685,000
Registered Office: Northfields, Market Deeping, Peterborough, Cambs, PE6 8UE
Activities: Wireless telecommunications activities
Parent: NGC UK Limited
Officers: Susie Lee Choung, Secretary; Roger Campbell Wiltshire, Secretary; Peter Beange [1958] Director Commercial Operations Europe; Daniel Milligan [1956] Managing Director; Jeffrey Quentin Palombo [1960] Director/VP Business Development, Mission Systems [American]; Steven David Spiegel [1964] Director [American]; Roger Campbell Wiltshire [1967] Deputy European Legal Director

Park Industrial and Agricultural Holdings Limited
Incorporated: 23 March 1978 *Employees:* 37
Net Worth: £5,820,113 *Total Assets:* £11,237,987
Registered Office: Private Road No 4, Colwick Industrial Estate, Nottingham, NG4 2JT
Activities: Freight transport by road
Shareholders: Midos GC Limited; WF Estates Ltd
Officers: Stephen Ralph Gibson [1951] Director; Moses Schreiber [1986] Director

G.H. Parker (North Cotes) Limited
Incorporated: 26 February 1953 *Employees:* 10
Net Worth: £4,711,509 *Total Assets:* £17,146,736
Registered Office: The Farm Office, Pinchbeck Farm, Sea Lane, Wainfleet St Mary, Skegness, Lincs, PE24 4BA
Activities: Growing of cereals (except rice), leguminous crops and oil seeds
Parent: Anne's Settlement
Officers: Anne Elizabeth Hickling, Secretary; Anne Elizabeth Hickling [1955] Director; William Henry Wrisdale [1985] Director/Farm Manager

C.W.Parker (Wainfleet) Limited
Incorporated: 5 April 1951 *Employees:* 10
Net Worth: £4,732,407 *Total Assets:* £10,608,598
Registered Office: The Farm Office, Pinchbeck Farm, Sea Lane, Wainfleet St Mary, Skegness, Lincs, PE24 4BA
Activities: Growing of cereals (except rice), leguminous crops and oil seeds
Shareholders: Anne Elizabeth Hickling; A E Hickling Accum. and Maint.
Officers: Emma Jane Cook, Secretary; Anne Elizabeth Hickling [1955] Director; Craig Jonathan Norwood [1961] Director/Manager

W. T. Parker Group Services Limited
Incorporated: 25 March 1950 *Employees:* 24
Previous: W.T. Parker Group Ltd.
Net Worth: £11,837,186 *Total Assets:* £19,119,028
Registered Office: 24-28 Moor Street, Burton on Trent, Staffs, DE14 3SX
Activities: Activities of head offices
Parent: Aliter Capital LLP
Officers: John Keith Beeston [1974] Director/Chartered Accountant; Stuart James Driscoll [1971] Director; Sean Tracy Smyth [1955] Director

W T Parker Holdings Limited
Incorporated: 25 June 2013 *Employees:* 459
Net Worth: £13,627,124 *Total Assets:* £27,032,618
Registered Office: 24-28 Moor Street, Burton on Trent, Staffs, DE14 3SX
Activities: Activities of head offices
Parent: Edwin James Holdings Ltd
Officers: John Keith Beeston [1974] Director/Chartered Accountant; Sean Tracy Smyth [1955] Director

W.T. Parker Ltd.
Incorporated: 27 July 1976 *Employees:* 251
Net Worth: £10,678,434 *Total Assets:* £19,301,972
Registered Office: 24-28 Moor Street, Burton on Trent, Staffs, DE14 3SX
Activities: Electrical installation
Parent: Aliter Capital LLP
Officers: John Keith Beeston [1974] Director/Chartered Accountant; Nigel Bonner [1961] Director Estimating Department; Stuart James Driscoll [1971] Director; Sean Tracy Smyth [1955] Managing Director

Parker Plant Limited
Incorporated: 23 September 2003 *Employees:* 122
Net Worth: £4,627,000 *Total Assets:* £17,235,000
Registered Office: Viaduct Works, Canon Street, Leicester, LE4 6GH
Activities: Manufacture of equipment for concrete crushing and screening and roadworks
Parent: Phoenix Parker Holdings Limited
Officers: Simon Paul Wilkinson, Secretary; Anthony Kenneth Butler [1956] Director; Glenn Bryan Dalby [1957] Director; Russell Dart Sciville [1955] Director; Glyn John Wheeler [1957] Director

Parkers Motor Services (Syston) Limited
Incorporated: 10 June 1975 *Employees:* 352
Net Worth: £4,571,929 *Total Assets:* £13,748,349
Registered Office: 6 Foundry Square, Belgrave Gate, Leicester, LE1 3WW
Activities: Activities of head offices
Officers: James Malcolm Parker, Secretary; Heather Parker [1945] Director/Secretary; James Malcolm Parker [1940] Director/Company Secretary; John Watson Parker [1947] Director; Pamela Anne Parker [1940] Director; Robin David Parker [1972] Director; Sheila Parker [1946] Director; William George Parker [1944] Director

Parkers of Leicester Limited
Incorporated: 8 June 1987 *Employees:* 6
Net Worth: £37,713,448 *Total Assets:* £46,278,668
Registered Office: 3-5 North Lane, Foxton, Market Harborough, Leics, LE16 7RF
Activities: Activities of head offices
Officers: Paul Scott Marriage, Secretary; Adrian Charles Parker Lott [1973] Director; Stephen Lawrence Parker Lott [1976] Director; Katherine Playfair [1974] Director; Lady Hilary Susan Ripley [1941] Director

Parkway Derby Limited
Incorporated: 8 June 1999 *Employees:* 273
Net Worth: £7,220,640 *Total Assets:* £38,661,636
Registered Office: Parkway Volkswagen, Locomotive Way, Pride Park, Derby, DE24 8PU
Activities: Sale of other motor vehicles
Major Shareholder: Sean Robert Booth
Officers: Alison Patricia Booth, Secretary; Alison Booth [1965] Director/PA; Sean Robert Booth [1964] Director/Brand Manager

Parkway Hellas Holdings Limited
Incorporated: 29 October 2004
Net Worth: £27,500,000 *Total Assets:* £28,500,000
Registered Office: Westpoint, Peterborough Business Park, Lynch Wood, Peterborough, Cambs, PE2 6FZ
Activities: Other business support service activities n.e.c.
Parent: Thomas Cook Group Hedging Limited
Officers: Shirley Bradley, Secretary; Alan Charles Donald [1963] Director

Trevor Parr Associates Limited
Incorporated: 16 March 1971 *Employees:* 5
Net Worth: £5,623,383 *Total Assets:* £13,951,406
Registered Office: 10 Stadium Business Court, Millennium Way, Pride Park, Derby, DE24 8HP
Activities: Other letting and operating of own or leased real estate
Major Shareholder: Dominic Harold Forsyth Parr
Officers: Annabel Kirsty Mary Parr, Secretary; Annabel Kirsty Mary Parr [1974] Director; Dominic Harold Forsyth Parr [1973] Director

Parseq Limited
Incorporated: 12 May 2006 *Employees:* 1,681
Net Worth: £2,514,000 *Total Assets:* £23,217,000
Registered Office: Parseq, Lowton Way, Hellaby, Rotherham, S Yorks, S66 8RY
Activities: Data processing, hosting and related activities
Parent: Light Second Limited
Officers: Alan Ka Wai Chan, Secretary; Rami Cassis [1968] Director [French]; Alan Chan [1981] Director and Company Secretary; Robert Littlewood [1982] Director; Craig Naylor-Smith [1977] Director

Partners in Property (U.K.) Limited
Incorporated: 13 March 1997 *Employees:* 156
Net Worth: £2,210,775 *Total Assets:* £33,841,200
Registered Office: Grant Hall, Parsons Green, St Ives, Cambs, PE27 4AA
Activities: Buying and selling of own real estate
Parent: Move with Us Ltd
Officers: Robert Matson, Secretary; Benjamin Paul Greco [1979] Director; David Jeremy Grossman [1970] Director; Robert Matson [1970] Director/Chartered Accountant

Partnerships in Children's Services Limited
Incorporated: 23 July 2012 *Employees:* 311
Net Worth Deficit: £599,936 *Total Assets:* £22,451,042
Registered Office: Wavendon Tower, Ortensia Drive, Wavendon, Milton Keynes, Bucks, MK17 8LX
Activities: Activities of head offices
Parent: Nutrius UK Bidco Limited
Officers: Jo August [1971] Director; Jonathan David Clark [1977] Director; Venetia Cooper [1974] Director/Chief Financial Officer

Passionate About People Limited
Incorporated: 16 August 2011 *Employees:* 156
Net Worth: £4,381,761 *Total Assets:* £20,447,100
Registered Office: 19-20 The Triangle, NG2 Business Park, Nottingham, NG2 1AE
Activities: Activities of head offices
Parent: Staffline Recruitment Limited
Officers: Paul Collins, Secretary; Mark Keegan [1979] Director; Christopher Mark Pullen [1970] Director; Mark William Underwood [1977] Director; Michael Robert Watts [1974] Director

Pathfinders-Care (Ollerton) Limited
Incorporated: 2 August 2006 *Employees:* 208
Net Worth: £6,467,537 *Total Assets:* £12,934,941
Registered Office: Cabourn House, Station Street, Bingham, Notts, NG13 8AQ
Activities: Other human health activities
Shareholders: Somerville Paterson; Angela Joan Nall; Andrea Stephanida Bikow
Officers: Dr Angela Joan Nall [1962] Director; Somerville Paterson [1950] Director

Patrolmake Limited
Incorporated: 29 February 1996 *Employees:* 2
Net Worth: £13,164,908 *Total Assets:* £38,229,480
Registered Office: Corus House, 1 Auckland Park, Milton Keynes, Bucks, MK1 1BU
Activities: Hotels and similar accommodation
Parent: Corus Hotels Limited
Officers: Khurram Mohmand, Secretary; Andrew Khoo [1972] Director [Australian]; Yet King Loy [1946] Director [Canadian]; Khurram Mohmand [1972] Director/Accountant

Sir Robert Pattinson Academy
Incorporated: 1 July 2011 *Employees:* 158
Net Worth: £8,107,719 *Total Assets:* £9,650,669
Registered Office: Robert Pattinson School, Moor Lane, North Hykeham, Lincs, LN6 9AF
Activities: General secondary education
Officers: Alicia Jane Goffe, Secretary; Dr Neil Thomas Appleby [1967] Director/Dentist Management; Alison Braithwaite [1965] Director/Careers Adviser; Nicholas Jon Chambers [1968] Director/Chief Executive LACE Housing; Paul Mark Fenton [1971] Director/University Lecturer; Tracey Gibson [1965] Director; Dale Hardy [1974] Director/Headteacher; Heather Dawn Lee [1969] Director/Head of Human Resources; Karen Rita Merchant [1964] Director; Toni O'Brien [1970] Director/Business Adviser; Paula Jane Robinson [1974] Director/Community Life Champion; Alan John Robson [1960] Director; Peter Andrew Ward [1977] Director/Teacher

Pattonair (Derby) Limited
Incorporated: 5 November 1999 *Employees:* 393
Net Worth: £26,087,000 *Total Assets:* £174,239,008
Registered Office: Ascot Business Park, 50 Longbridge Lane, Derby, DE24 8UJ
Activities: Wholesale of other machinery and equipment
Parent: Pattonair UK Limited
Officers: Zoe Robertson, Secretary; Wayne Richard Hollinshead [1966] Director/Distribution; Christopher Andrew Humphreys [1965] Director/Chief Financial Officer

Pattonair Europe Limited
Incorporated: 4 May 2011
Net Worth: £1,516,000 *Total Assets:* £18,087,000
Registered Office: Ascot Business Park, 50 Longbridge Lane, Derby, DE24 8UJ
Activities: Wholesale of other machinery and equipment
Parent: Pattonair Group Limited
Officers: Zoe Robertson, Secretary; Wayne Richard Hollinshead [1966] Director; Christopher Andrew Humphreys [1965] Director/Chief Financial Officer

Pattonair Group Limited
Incorporated: 10 February 2011 *Employees:* 2
Net Worth: £118,293,000 *Total Assets:* £147,775,008
Registered Office: Ascot Business Park, 50 Longbridge Lane, Derby, DE24 8UJ
Activities: Activities of distribution holding companies
Parent: Quicksilver Midco Limited
Officers: Zoe Robertson, Secretary; Wayne Richard Hollinshead [1966] Director; Christopher Andrew Humphreys [1965] Director/Chief Financial Officer

Pattonair Holdings Limited
Incorporated: 10 February 2011 *Employees:* 2
Net Worth: £2,424,000 *Total Assets:* £67,781,000
Registered Office: Ascot Business Park, 50 Longbridge Lane, Derby, DE24 8UJ
Activities: Activities of distribution holding companies
Parent: Pioneer IV Limited
Officers: Zoe Robertson, Secretary; Wayne Richard Hollinshead [1966] Director; Christopher Andrew Humphreys [1965] Director/Chief Financial Officer

Pattonair Limited
Incorporated: 18 March 1970 *Employees:* 187
Net Worth: £44,224,000 *Total Assets:* £89,422,000
Registered Office: Ascot Business Park, 50 Longbridge Lane, Derby, DE24 8UJ
Activities: Wholesale of other intermediate products
Parent: Orchard House Limited
Officers: Zoe Robertson, Secretary; Wayne Richard Hollinshead [1966] Director; Christopher Andrew Humphreys [1965] Director/Chief Financial Officer

Pattonair Properties Limited
Incorporated: 9 August 2006
Net Worth: £622,000 *Total Assets:* £11,126,000
Registered Office: Ascot Business Park, 50 Longbridge Lane, Derby, DE24 8UJ
Activities: Buying and selling of own real estate
Parent: Pattonair UK Limited
Officers: Zoe Robertson, Secretary; Wayne Richard Hollinshead [1966] Managing Director; Christopher Andrew Humphreys [1965] Director/Chief Financial Officer

Pattonair UK Limited
Incorporated: 13 April 2011 *Employees:* 2
Net Worth: £21,586,000 *Total Assets:* £49,908,000
Registered Office: Ascot Business Park, 50 Longbridge Lane, Derby, DE24 8UJ
Activities: Wholesale of other machinery and equipment
Parent: Pattonair Group Limited
Officers: Zoe Robertson, Secretary; Wayne Richard Hollinshead [1966] Director; Christopher Andrew Humphreys [1965] Director/Chief Financial Officer

Paul John Construction (Leicester) Limited
Incorporated: 16 June 1976 *Employees:* 73
Net Worth: £2,715,515 *Total Assets:* £16,047,551
Registered Office: Telford Way, Stephenson Industrial Estate, Coalville, Leics, LE67 3HE
Activities: Construction of domestic buildings
Shareholders: Beverley Henry; John Timothy Henry
Officers: James Francis, Secretary; Beverley Henry [1957] Director; James Patrick Henry [1954] Director/Surveyor; John Timothy Henry [1955] Director; Kieran Henry [1984] Director; Jeff James Holder [1976] Director

Pauley Group Limited
Incorporated: 11 February 2003 *Employees:* 253
Net Worth: £5,393,889 *Total Assets:* £14,735,715
Registered Office: School House, Tattenhoe Lane, Bletchley, Milton Keynes, Bucks, MK3 7EG
Activities: Activities of head offices
Officers: Philip Michael Frederick Pauley, Secretary; Andrew Pauley [1970] Director/Civil Servant; Hilary Ann Pauley [1946] Director/Headmistress; Nicholas James George Pauley [1972] Art Director; Philip Michael Frederick Pauley [1975] Director/Administrator

Pauley Properties Limited
Incorporated: 12 February 2003
Net Worth: £2,269,846 *Total Assets:* £13,236,790
Registered Office: School House, Tattenhoe Lane, Bletchley, Milton Keynes, Bucks, MK3 7EG
Activities: Other letting and operating of own or leased real estate
Parent: Pauley Group Limited
Officers: Philip Michael Frederick Pauley, Secretary; Hilary Ann Pauley [1946] Director/Headmistress

Michael Pavis Limited
Incorporated: 22 November 1990 *Employees:* 55
Net Worth: £21,529,828 *Total Assets:* £29,785,108
Registered Office: 29 Arboretum Street, Nottingham, NG1 4JA
Activities: Wholesale of hardware, plumbing and heating equipment and supplies
Major Shareholder: Jean Pavis as Trustee
Officers: Jean Pavis, Secretary; James Pavis [1972] Commercial Director; Jean Pavis [1947] Director/Businesswoman

Payzone UK Limited
Incorporated: 14 September 1995 *Employees:* 341
Net Worth Deficit: £12,410,735 *Total Assets:* £24,394,270
Registered Office: 4th Floor, Highbank House, Exchange Street, Stockport, Cheshire, SK3 0ET
Activities: Other information technology service activities
Officers: Mark Dann [1972] Director; Clive Ian Kahn [1957] Director; James Rupert Lowery [1965] Director; Andrew McCann [1981] Director

The PCMS Group Limited
Incorporated: 6 November 1979 *Employees:* 314
Previous: The PCMS Group PLC
Net Worth: £21,119,418 *Total Assets:* £36,889,776
Registered Office: PCMS House, Torwood Close, Westwood Business Park, Coventry, Warwicks, CV4 8HX
Activities: Information technology consultancy activities
Parent: PCMS Holdings Limited
Officers: David William Burke [1966] Director [Australian]; Anthony Houldsworth [1962] Business Development Director; Garry Craig McLauchlan [1963] Director; Martyn Harvey Osborne [1972] Director

PCMS International Holdings Limited
Incorporated: 5 May 2016 *Employees:* 484
Net Worth: £16,565,718 *Total Assets:* £33,447,740
Registered Office: PCMS House, Torwood Close, Westwood Business Park, Coventry, Warwicks, CV4 8HX
Activities: Activities of head offices
Parent: Torwood Bidco Limited
Officers: David William Burke [1966] Director [Australian]; Anthony Houldsworth [1962] Director; Garry Craig McLauchlan [1963] Director; Martyn Harvey Osborne [1972] Director

PCMS Investments Holdings Limited
Incorporated: 25 May 2016
Net Worth: £25,000,000 *Total Assets:* £25,000,000
Registered Office: 88 Meeting House Lane, Balsall Common, Coventry, Warwicks, CV7 7GE
Activities: Activities of other holding companies n.e.c.
Shareholders: Brenda Mary Smith; Richard Anthony Smith
Officers: Brenda Mary Smith [1947] Director; Richard Anthony Smith [1948] Director

PCS Business Systems Group Limited
Incorporated: 17 June 2014 *Employees:* 60
Net Worth: £3,658,192 *Total Assets:* £10,747,431
Registered Office: 2 Northfield Point, Cunliffe Drive, Kettering, Northants, NN16 9QJ
Activities: Activities of other holding companies n.e.c.
Officers: Lynda Marie Morrissey, Secretary; Steven John Cream [1961] Director; Stuart Anthony Knott [1977] Director; Lynda Marie Morrissey [1966] Finance Director

PCS Business Systems Limited
Incorporated: 20 July 1995 *Employees:* 60
Net Worth: £4,694,496 *Total Assets:* £11,144,562
Registered Office: 2-4 Northfield Point, Cunliffe Drive, Kettering, Northants, NN16 9QJ
Activities: Other information technology service activities
Parent: PCS Business Systems Holdings Limited
Officers: Lynda Marie Morrissey, Secretary/Secretary/PA; Stuart Anthony Knott [1977] Managing Director; Lynda Marie Morrissey [1966] Finance Director

The Peach Pub Company (Holdings) Limited
Incorporated: 10 August 2001 *Employees:* 454
Net Worth: £1,790,381 *Total Assets:* £14,287,863
Registered Office: Peach Barns, Somerton Road, North Aston, Oxon, OX25 6HX
Activities: Activities of other holding companies n.e.c.
Shareholder: Lee Roger Cash
Officers: Lee Roger Cash [1974] Director; Joanne Eames [1965] Director; Barbara May Laing [1952] Director; Christopher Norman Stagg [1963] Operations Director; Wilfrid Hamish Stoddart [1964] Director

Peacock & Binnington
Incorporated: 18 June 1937 *Employees:* 117
Net Worth: £5,728,634 *Total Assets:* £19,682,708
Registered Office: Old Foundry, Bridge Street, Brigg, N Lincs, DN20 8NR
Activities: Agents involved in the sale of machinery, industrial equipment, ships and aircraft
Parent: Peacock & Binnington Holdings Limited
Officers: Mark Peter Farleigh, Secretary; Les Bacon [1957] Challenger Sales Director; Marcus James Bourne [1970] Director; Richard Cross [1972] Director; Mark Peter Farleigh [1981] Finance Director; Graham William Main [1970] Managing Director; Michael Allen Peacock [1933] Director/Chairman; Nicholas Allen Peacock [1969] Director/Barrister; Andrew James Walker [1976] Louth Sales Director

Peacock & Binnington Holdings Limited
Incorporated: 6 July 1990 *Employees:* 117
Net Worth: £5,717,220 *Total Assets:* £19,677,984
Registered Office: Old Foundry, Bridge Street, Brigg, N Lincs, DN20 8NR
Activities: Activities of head offices
Shareholder: Michael Allen Peacock
Officers: Mark Peter Farleigh, Secretary; Les Bacon [1957] Director/Salesman; Marcus James Bourne [1970] Director; Richard Cross [1972] Director; Mark Peter Farleigh [1981] Finance Director; Graham William Main [1970] Director; Michael Allen Peacock [1933] Director/Agricultural Engineer; Nicholas Allen Peacock [1969] Director/Barrister; Andrew James Walker [1976] Louth Sales Director

Peak Gen Top Co Limited
Incorporated: 24 May 2013 *Employees:* 14
Net Worth: £15,189,951 *Total Assets:* £53,138,656
Registered Office: Gables Lodge, 62 Kenilworth Road, Leamington Spa, Warwicks, CV32 6JX
Activities: Activities of head offices
Officers: Jonathan Fairchild, Secretary; Jose-Ignacio Alvarez Landaluce [1976] Director; Jose-Miguel Alvarez Landaluce [1977] Director; Mark Robert Draper [1963] Director

Peak Multi Academy Trust
Incorporated: 4 November 2010 *Employees:* 205
Previous: Chellaston Academy
Net Worth: £17,361,314 *Total Assets:* £19,909,604
Registered Office: Chellaston Academy, Swarkestone Road, Chellaston, Derby, DE73 5UB
Activities: General secondary education
Officers: Kevin John Gaiderman [1964] Director/Headteacher; Nicholas Brian Hollis [1965] Director/Project Manager; Alistair James Roe [1966] Director/Police Officer

H.B. Pearce (Contractors) Limited
Incorporated: 9 July 1945 *Employees:* 4
Net Worth: £1,787,403 *Total Assets:* £9,406,729
Registered Office: Thorpe House, 93 Headlands, Kettering, Northants, NN15 6BL
Activities: Development of building projects
Officers: Elizabeth Ruth Pearce, Secretary; Elizabeth Ruth Pearce [1937] Director/Company Secretary; Louise Elizabeth Pearce [1962] Director/Marketing Communications Consultant; Rosalind Louise Pearce [1966] Director; Timothy Benjamin Pearce [1965] Director/Manager

J G Pears (Holdings) Limited
Incorporated: 28 January 1994
Net Worth: £551,370 *Total Assets:* £9,899,906
Registered Office: Bella Vista Farm, Hartcliffe Road, Penistone, Sheffield, S36 9FN
Activities: Activities of other holding companies n.e.c.
Parent: J G Pears Holdings (Jersey) Limited
Officers: Heather Morag Pears, Secretary/Housewife; Paul Spencer Beaumont [1971] Finance Director; Alistair Craig Collins [1975] Operations Director; Lisa Ann Hunt [1979] Director; Graham Mark Pears [1985] Director; Heather Morag Pears [1959] Director/Housewife

J.G. Pears Limited
Incorporated: 19 March 1987 *Employees:* 6
Net Worth: £2,323,281 *Total Assets:* £16,369,623
Registered Office: Abbots Birks Farm, Hillside, Thurlstone, Sheffield, S36 9QJ
Activities: Raising of other cattle and buffaloes
Shareholders: Jeffery Gordon Pears; Heather Morag Pears
Officers: Heather Morag Pears, Secretary; Lisa Ann Hunt [1979] Director; Graham Mark Pears [1985] Director; Heather Morag Pears [1959] Director/Secretary

J G Pears Machinery Limited
Incorporated: 18 June 2013
Net Worth: £1,505,245 *Total Assets:* £17,354,020
Registered Office: Bell Vista Farm, Hartcliffe Road, Penistone, Sheffield, S36 9FN
Activities: Renting and leasing of cars and light motor vehicles
Parent: J G Pears (Holdings) Limited
Officers: Paul Spencer Beaumont [1971] Finance Director; Alistair Craig Collins [1975] Director; Lisa Ann Hunt [1979] Director; Graham Mark Pears [1985] Director; Heather Morag Pears [1959] Director

J G Pears Power Limited
Incorporated: 10 February 2016
Net Worth: £1,877,652 *Total Assets:* £73,620,192
Registered Office: Bella Vista Farm, Hartcliffe Road, Penistone, Sheffield, S36 9FN
Activities: Production of electricity
Parent: J G Pears (Holdings) Limited
Officers: Paul Spencer Beaumont [1971] Finance Director; Alistair Craig Collins [1975] Director; Lisa Ann Hunt [1979] Director; Graham Mark Pears [1985] Director; Heather Morag Pears [1959] Director

A Pearson Holdings Limited
Incorporated: 12 March 2008 *Employees:* 652
Net Worth: £5,868,000 *Total Assets:* £60,836,000
Registered Office: Enterprise House, 97 Alderley Road, Wilmslow, Cheshire, SK9 1PT
Activities: Activities of head offices
Officers: John Edward Phibbs, Secretary; Paul Raymond Mitchell [1951] Director; Mark Pearson [1973] Director; John Edward Phibbs [1950] Director/Accountant; Matthew Joseph Widdall [1972] Director/Investor

Peartree Oxford Limited
Incorporated: 25 July 2015 *Employees:* 2
Net Worth: £17,413,712 *Total Assets:* £17,485,580
Registered Office: 8 King Edward Street, Oxford, OX1 4HL
Activities: Development of building projects
Parent: St John Baptist College in the University of Oxford
Officers: William Alan Donger [1953] Director/Chartered Surveyor; Mark Taylor [1955] Director/Solicitor

Pedigree Wholesale Limited
Incorporated: 28 March 1972 *Employees:* 158
Net Worth: £11,080,782 *Total Assets:* £17,995,936
Registered Office: Pedigree House, Ambleside, Gamston, Nottingham, NG2 6NQ
Activities: Manufacture of other food products n.e.c.
Parent: Gamston Kennels & Farms Ltd
Officers: Christopher James Laud, Secretary; Stephen Andrew Brown [1971] Director/Manager; Terence William Brown [1943] Director; Christopher James Laud [1964] Director/Chartered Accountant

Pegler Holdings Limited
Incorporated: 10 October 2003
Net Worth: £2,444,000 *Total Assets:* £19,285,000
Registered Office: St Catherines Avenue, Doncaster, S Yorks, DN4 8DF
Activities: Forging, pressing, stamping and roll-forming of metal; powder metallurgy
Parent: Aalberts Industries UK Limited
Officers: Kevin Michael Parker, Secretary; Craig Malloy [1970] Finance Director

Pegler Limited
Incorporated: 20 December 1974 *Employees:* 299
Net Worth: £11,527,000 *Total Assets:* £12,466,000
Registered Office: Belmont Works, St Catherines Avenue, Doncaster, S Yorks, DN4 8DF
Activities: Forging, pressing, stamping and roll-forming of metal; powder metallurgy
Parent: Pegler Holdings Limited
Officers: Kevin Michael Parker, Secretary; Craig Malloy [1970] Finance Director

Pegler Yorkshire Group Limited
Incorporated: 5 December 1945 *Employees:* 107
Net Worth: £70,696,000 *Total Assets:* £165,936,992
Registered Office: Belmont Works, St Catherines Avenue, Doncaster, S Yorks, DN4 8DF
Activities: Manufacture of other fabricated metal products n.e.c.
Parent: Aalberts Industries France SNC
Officers: Kevin Michael Parker, Secretary; Graham Fawcett [1963] Manufacturing Director; Andre in Het Veld [1966] Director [Dutch]; Bryan Liddle [1961] Commercial Director; Craig Malloy [1970] Finance Director; Wiebe Arnold Pelsma [1963] Director [Dutch]

Pektron Group Limited
Incorporated: 15 October 1964 *Employees:* 345
Net Worth: £50,077,240 *Total Assets:* £61,050,064
Registered Office: Pektron, Alfreton Road, Derby, DE21 4AP
Activities: Manufacture of electronic components
Shareholder: George Morgan
Officers: Barbara Anne Morgan, Secretary; Ian Stewart Harpham [1963] Manufacturing Director; Jayson Mark Hatton [1971] Group Supply Chain Director; George Morgan [1931] Director/Electronics Production Engineer; John Robert Potts [1968] Sales Director

Pelagia (UK) Limited
Incorporated: 11 September 1992 *Employees:* 60
Previous: United Fish Industries (UK) Limited
Net Worth: £16,886,000 *Total Assets:* £26,545,000
Registered Office: Gilbey Road, Pyewipe, Grimsby, N E Lincs, DN31 2SL
Activities: Manufacture of prepared feeds for farm animals
Officers: Michael McEllone, Secretary; Arnt-Ove Hoddevik [1965] Director [Norwegian]; Michael McEllone [1974] Director/Company Secretary [Irish]

Pelham Homes Limited
Incorporated: 20 July 2004
Previous: Lets Select Limited
Net Worth: £7,994,000 *Total Assets:* £16,838,000
Registered Office: 14 Pelham Road, Sherwood Rise, Nottingham, NG5 1AP
Activities: Development of building projects
Officers: Brian Sweeney, Secretary; Michael Anthony Bent [1964] Director/Business Consultant; Paul Vincent Casey [1960] Director/Consultant; Lucy Ann Dadge [1964] Director/NHS Manager; Allan Fisher [1971] Assistant Director of Development & New Business; Paul Moat [1967] Director/Chief Executive

PEM 2000 Limited
Incorporated: 23 October 1987
Previous: G K 2000 Limited
Net Worth Deficit: £2,374,375 *Total Assets:* £17,327,808
Registered Office: Suite 1, 500 Pavilion Drive, Northampton, NN4 7YJ
Activities: Other letting and operating of own or leased real estate
Parent: Perrys East Midlands Limited
Officers: Neil Howard Taylor, Secretary; Darren Ardron [1967] Director; Richard George Ingram [1957] Director/Lawyer; Denise Millard [1958] Director; Ken Francis Savage [1962] Director; Neil Howard Taylor [1960] Director/Chartered Accountant

Pen Hill LLP
Incorporated: 17 August 2006 *Employees:* 3
Net Worth: £531,550 *Total Assets:* £24,651,792
Registered Office: 3 Castlegate, Grantham, Lincs, NG31 6SF

Pendragon Automotive Services Limited
Incorporated: 3 September 1999
Net Worth: £23,819,000 *Total Assets:* £29,385,000
Registered Office: Loxely House, 2 Oakwood Court, Little Oak Drive, Annesley, Nottingham, NG15 0DR
Activities: Other professional, scientific and technical activities n.e.c.
Parent: Pendragon PLC
Officers: Richard James Maloney, Secretary; Martin Shaun Casha [1960] Director; Trevor Garry Finn [1957] Director; Timothy Paul Holden [1964] Director/Chartered Accountant

Pendragon Finance and Insurance Services Limited
Incorporated: 29 March 1966 *Employees:* 2
Net Worth: £32,123,000 *Total Assets:* £34,090,000
Registered Office: Loxley House, 2 Oakwood Court, Little Oak Drive, Annesley, Nottingham, NG15 0DR
Activities: Non-trading company
Parent: Pendragon PLC
Officers: Richard James Maloney, Secretary; Martin Shaun Casha [1960] Director; Trevor Garry Finn [1957] Director; Timothy Paul Holden [1964] Director/Chartered Accountant; Jeremy Stuart King [1957] Director

Pendragon Management Services Limited
Incorporated: 4 November 1987 *Employees:* 676
Net Worth: £10,762,000 *Total Assets:* £263,284,000
Registered Office: Loxley House, 2 Oakwood Court, Little Oak Drive, Annesley, Nottingham, NG15 0DR
Activities: Activities of head offices
Officers: Richard James Maloney, Secretary; Martin Shaun Casha [1960] Director; Trevor Garry Finn [1957] Director; Timothy Paul Holden [1964] Director/Chartered Accountant

Pendragon Motor Group Limited
Incorporated: 14 September 1987 *Employees:* 1,354
Net Worth: £18,791,000 *Total Assets:* £131,986,000
Registered Office: Loxley House, 2 Oakwood Court, Little Oak Drive, Annesley, Nottingham, NG15 0DR
Activities: Sale of new cars and light motor vehicles
Parent: Stratstone Motor Holdings Limited
Officers: Richard James Maloney, Secretary; Martin Shaun Casha [1960] Director; Trevor Garry Finn [1957] Director; Timothy Paul Holden [1964] Director/Chartered Accountant

Pendragon Overseas Limited
Incorporated: 5 December 1989
Net Worth: £5,855,000 *Total Assets:* £67,708,000
Registered Office: Loxley House, 2 Oakwood Court, Little Oak Drive, Annesley, Nottingham, NG15 0DR
Activities: Activities of head offices
Parent: Pendragon PLC
Officers: Richard James Maloney, Secretary; Martin Shaun Casha [1960] Director; Trevor Garry Finn [1957] Director; Timothy Paul Holden [1964] Director/Chartered Accountant

Pendragon PLC
Incorporated: 12 October 1988 *Employees:* 9,989
Net Worth: £425,400,000 *Total Assets:* £2,060,600,064
Registered Office: Loxley House, 2 Oakwood Court, Little Oak Drive, Annesley, Nottingham, NG15 0DR
Activities: Sale of new cars and light motor vehicles
Officers: Richard James Maloney, Secretary; Martin Shaun Casha [1960] Director; Christopher Michael Chambers [1961] Director; Trevor Garry Finn [1957] Director; Timothy Paul Holden [1964] Director/Chartered Accountant; Gillian Dawn Celia Kent [1963] Director; Richard Alan Laxer [1961] Director [British/American]; Michael Wright [1953] Director

Pendragon Premier Limited
Incorporated: 3 September 1999 *Employees:* 1,065
Net Worth: £26,379,000 *Total Assets:* £209,646,000
Registered Office: Loxley House, 2 Oakwood Court, Little Oak Drive, Annesley, Nottingham, NG15 0DR
Activities: Sale of new cars and light motor vehicles
Officers: Richard James Maloney, Secretary; Martin Shaun Casha [1960] Director; Trevor Garry Finn [1957] Director; Timothy Paul Holden [1964] Director/Chartered Accountant

Pendragon Property Holdings Limited
Incorporated: 19 September 1997
Net Worth: £2,087,000 *Total Assets:* £230,284,000
Registered Office: Loxley House, 2 Oakwood Court, Little Oak Drive, Annesley, Nottingham, NG15 0DR
Activities: Buying and selling of own real estate
Officers: Richard James Maloney, Secretary; Martin Shaun Casha [1960] Director; Trevor Garry Finn [1957] Director; Timothy Paul Holden [1964] Director/Chartered Accountant

Pendragon Sabre Limited
Incorporated: 3 September 1999 *Employees:* 204
Net Worth: £6,104,000 *Total Assets:* £38,590,000
Registered Office: Loxely House, 2 Oakwood Court, Little Oak Drive, Annesley, Nottingham, NG15 0DR
Activities: Sale of new cars and light motor vehicles
Parent: Pendragon Motor Holdings Limited
Officers: Richard James Maloney, Secretary; Martin Shaun Casha [1960] Director; Trevor Garry Finn [1957] Director; Timothy Paul Holden [1964] Director/Chartered Accountant

Pendragon Stock Finance Limited
Incorporated: 17 February 1994
Net Worth Deficit: £3,556,000 *Total Assets:* £306,244,992
Registered Office: Loxley House, 2 Oakwood Court, Little Oak Drive, Annesley, Notts, NG15 0DR
Activities: Non-trading company
Parent: Pendragon Group Services Limited
Officers: Richard James Maloney, Secretary; Martin Shaun Casha [1960] Director; Trevor Garry Finn [1957] Director; Timothy Paul Holden [1964] Director/Chartered Accountant

Pendragon Vehicle Management Limited
Incorporated: 26 August 1915 *Employees:* 75
Previous: Pendragon Contracts Limited
Net Worth: £20,296,000 *Total Assets:* £202,274,000
Registered Office: Loxley House, 2 Oakwood Court, Little Oak Drive, Annesley, Nottingham, NG15 0DR
Activities: Sale of new cars and light motor vehicles
Parent: Pendragon Automotive Services Limited
Officers: Richard James Maloney, Secretary; Martin Shaun Casha [1960] Director; Trevor Garry Finn [1957] Director; Timothy Paul Holden [1964] Director/Chartered Accountant

Pengethley Potatoes Limited
Incorporated: 17 January 1989 *Employees:* 2
Net Worth: £7,637,191 *Total Assets:* £12,938,748
Registered Office: 5 Resolution Close, Endeavour Park, Boston, Lincs, PE21 7TT
Activities: Growing of cereals (except rice), leguminous crops and oil seeds
Shareholders: Stephen James Pugh; Shirley Ann Pugh
Officers: Shirley Ann Pugh, Secretary; Shirley Ann Pugh [1943] Director; Stephen James Pugh [1965] Director

Penmarric Limited
Incorporated: 27 September 1979
Net Worth Deficit: £3,239,723 *Total Assets:* £18,278,776
Registered Office: Suite One, Courthill House, 66 Water Lane, Wilmslow, Cheshire, SK9 5AP
Activities: Other business support service activities n.e.c.
Shareholder: Joseph Claude Dwek
Officers: Joseph Claude Dwek [1940] Managing Director; Linda Rosalind Dwek [1945] Director

Pennell's Holdings Limited
Incorporated: 23 November 2006 *Employees:* 162
Net Worth: £8,246,080 *Total Assets:* £10,808,333
Registered Office: Newark Road, South Hykeham, Lincoln, LN6 9NT
Activities: Retail sale of flowers, plants, seeds, fertilizers, pet animals and pet food in specialised stores
Major Shareholder: Richard Nicholas Pennell
Officers: Julie Ann Pennell, Secretary; Julie Ann Pennell [1959] Director/Secretary; Richard Nicholas Pennell [1953] Director; William Edward Pennell [1983] Director/Garden Centre Retailer

Pennine Property Partnership LLP
Incorporated: 22 March 2011
Net Worth: £7,774,483 *Total Assets:* £14,603,667
Registered Office: Banner Cross Hall, Ecclesall Road South, Sheffield, S11 9PD

Penso Consulting Ltd
Incorporated: 11 June 1999 *Employees:* 185
Net Worth: £3,477,360 *Total Assets:* £27,053,340
Registered Office: 2 Woodhams Road, Coventry, Warwicks, CV3 4FX
Activities: Specialised design activities
Shareholders: Daniel Hurcombe; David Roche
Officers: Lord Geoffrey Robert James Borwick [1955] Director; Andrew Davies [1966] Finance Director; Daniel Hurcombe [1972] Managing Director; Sarah Kate Morton [1973] Director; David Roche [1974] Technical Director; Jenny Linda Roche [1979] Director; Jevon Thurston-Thorpe [1959] Director

Penso Holdings Ltd
Incorporated: 10 June 2004 *Employees:* 228
Net Worth: £6,189,838 *Total Assets:* £32,314,338
Registered Office: 2 Woodhams Road, Coventry, Warwicks, CV3 4FX
Activities: Activities of head offices
Shareholders: Bicester Lane Limited; Daniel Hurcombe; David Roche
Officers: Lord Geoffrey Robert James Borwick [1955] Director/Chairman; Andrew Davies [1966] Finance Director; Daniel Hurcombe [1972] Managing Director; Fabrizio Ponte [1970] Strategy & Business Development Director [Italian]; David Roche [1974] Technical Director; Jevon Thurston-Thorpe [1959] Director

Pentagon (Huddersfield) Limited
Incorporated: 10 January 2011 *Employees:* 66
Net Worth Deficit: £76,396 *Total Assets:* £13,101,049
Registered Office: Pentagon Island, Nottingham Road, Derby, DE21 6HB
Activities: Sale of other motor vehicles
Parent: Pentagon Motor Holdings Limited
Officers: David Lewis [1962] Director; Andrew Barrie Welch [1965] Director

Pentagon Chrysler (Barnsley) Limited
Incorporated: 5 January 2010 *Employees:* 79
Net Worth Deficit: £219,380 *Total Assets:* £15,158,478
Registered Office: Pentagon Island, Nottingham Road, Derby, DE21 6HB
Activities: Sale of new cars and light motor vehicles
Parent: Pentagon Motor Holdings Limited
Officers: David Lewis [1962] Director; Andrew Barrie Welch [1965] Director

Pentagon Motor Holdings Limited
Incorporated: 13 April 2006 *Employees:* 1,173
Net Worth: £20,061,000 *Total Assets:* £157,456,992
Registered Office: Pentagon Island, Nottingham Road, Derby, DE21 6HB
Activities: Sale of new cars and light motor vehicles
Parent: IH Mobility Holdings (UK) Limited
Officers: David Lewis [1962] Director; Andrew Barrie Welch [1965] Director

People Potential Possibilities
Incorporated: 24 April 1990 *Employees:* 590
Net Worth: £5,392,820 *Total Assets:* £10,456,541
Registered Office: Eagle House, Cotmanhay Road, Ilkeston, Derbys, DE7 8HU
Activities: Other service activities n.e.c.
Officers: Kathryn Kozlowski, Secretary; Carol Ann Carter [1960] Director/Chief Executive; Bobbie Rebecca Graham [1965] Director/Consultant; Adam Jonathan Patrick Hackett [1950] Director; Dorothy Lane [1945] Director/Retired; Dale Inez Simon [1964] Director/Management Consultant; John Frederick Spriggs Taylor [1963] Director; Mark Terry [1963] Director of Finance

Peopleplus Group Limited
Incorporated: 27 February 2006 *Employees:* 1,180
Previous: Avanta Enterprise Limited
Net Worth: £42,700,000 *Total Assets:* £66,100,000
Registered Office: 19-20 The Triangle, NG2 Business Park, Nottingham, NG2 1AE
Activities: Other education n.e.c.
Parent: Staffline Group PLC
Officers: Paul Simon Collins, Secretary; Jonathan Bowler [1969] Finance Director; Christopher Mark Pullen [1970] Director/Chief Executive Officer; Simon Paul Rouse [1974] Managing Director; Michael Robert Watts [1974] Director/Chief Financial Officer

Peppermint Grove Ltd
Incorporated: 16 June 2015 *Employees:* 6
Net Worth: £4,330,685 *Total Assets:* £10,630,077
Registered Office: 57-59 Saltergate, Chesterfield, Derbys, S40 1UL
Activities: Other letting and operating of own or leased real estate
Shareholders: Simon Richard Priestnall; Stephen David Priestnall
Officers: Anthony Frederick Cordin [1963] Director; Simon Richard Priestnall [1975] Director; Stephen David Priestnall [1973] Director; Susan Elizabeth Priestnall [1946] Director/Motor Dealer

Peppermint Technology Holdings Limited
Incorporated: 9 July 2015 *Employees:* 72
Net Worth: £8,305,191 *Total Assets:* £16,983,980
Registered Office: Oaktree House, 2 Phoenix Place, Phoenix Court, Nottingham, NG8 6BA
Activities: Other business support service activities n.e.c.
Parent: Sep IV LP
Officers: Arlene Adams, Secretary; Arlene Adams [1973] Director; Neville Davis [1955] Director; Nicola Helen Grundy [1966] Director; Fraser McLatchie [1979] Director/Investment Professional; David John Sneddon [1962] Director/Investment Professional; Gary Stuart Young [1965] Director [Canadian]

Pera International
Incorporated: 13 June 1946 *Employees:* 12
Net Worth: £21,611,000 *Total Assets:* £23,811,000
Registered Office: Pera Business Park, Nottingham Road, Melton Mowbray, Leics, LE13 0PB
Activities: Other research and experimental development on natural sciences and engineering
Officers: Lorraine Ann Badjie, Secretary; Alan John Baxter [1950] Director; Peter Robert Hughes [1948] Director; Roger James Whysall [1945] Managing Director

Perfectos Printing Inks Co Ltd.
Incorporated: 12 September 1974 *Employees:* 56
Net Worth: £5,779,989 *Total Assets:* £11,862,122
Registered Office: 3rd Floor, Butt Dyke House, 33 Park Row, Nottingham, NG1 6EE
Activities: Manufacture of printing ink
Parent: Perfectos Printing Inks Group Ltd
Officers: Jacqueline Louise Price, Secretary/Director; Edward James Henry Price [1977] Director; Jacqueline Louise Price [1971] Director; Dr John Henry Price [1943] Director; Steven John Henry Price [1968] Director

Performance Health Global Limited
Incorporated: 10 June 2010
Previous: Patterson Global Limited
Net Worth: £38,303,000 *Total Assets:* £48,379,000
Registered Office: Patterson Medical Limited, Nunn Brook Road, Huthwaite, Sutton in Ashfield, Notts, NG17 2HU
Activities: Activities of other holding companies n.e.c.
Parent: Lanai Medical Ltd
Officers: Andrew Booker, Secretary; Isabel Maria Pereira Mota Afonso [1973] Managing Director & Head of International [Portuguese]

Performance Health International Limited
Incorporated: 15 February 2002 *Employees:* 177
Previous: Patterson Medical Limited
Net Worth: £35,322,000 *Total Assets:* £41,871,000
Registered Office: Nunn Brook Road, Huthwaite, Sutton in Ashfield, Notts, NG17 2HU
Activities: Wholesale of other machinery and equipment
Shareholder: Performance Health Global Ltd
Officers: Andrew Booker, Secretary; Andrew Michael Booker [1967] Finance Director; Isabel Maria Pereira Mota Afonso [1973] Managing Director & Head of International [Portuguese]

Pergamon Finance Corporation Limited
Incorporated: 10 July 2012 *Employees:* 1
Net Worth: £1,943,261 *Total Assets:* £10,584,675
Registered Office: 5 South Parade, Summertown, Oxford, OX2 7JL
Activities: Activities of open-ended investment companies
Officers: Richard Vivian Vanbergen [1949] Director

PERI Limited
Incorporated: 12 July 1989 *Employees:* 248
Net Worth: £41,715,252 *Total Assets:* £47,621,504
Registered Office: Market Harborough Road, Clifton upon Dunsmore, Rugby, Warwicks, CV23 0AN
Activities: Renting and leasing of construction and civil engineering machinery and equipment
Parent: PERI GmbH
Officers: Trudie Louise Swift, Secretary; Carl Frederick Heathcote [1964] Managing Director; Alasdair Llewellyn Stables [1972] Managing Director

Perkins Engines Company Limited
Incorporated: 14 January 1987 *Employees:* 2,306
Net Worth: £356,225,984 *Total Assets:* £748,249,984
Registered Office: Eastfield, Frank Perkins Way, Peterborough, Cambs, PE1 5FQ
Activities: Manufacture of engines and turbines, except aircraft, vehicle and cycle engines
Parent: Caterpillar UK Engines Company Limited
Officers: Johanna Elizabeth Deason, Secretary; Nigel John Burroughs [1964] Director/Tax Accountant; Mark Clinton Albert Dorsett [1962] HR Director; Steven Ferguson [1968] Director/Vice President [American]; Jasbir Singh Gill [1965] Director/General Manager; David John Goldspink [1966] Director/General Manager; Paul David Thompson [1980] Director/Business Resource Manager [American]

Perkins Group Limited
Incorporated: 24 May 1989 *Employees:* 3
Net Worth: £35,440,000 *Total Assets:* £116,042,000
Registered Office: Eastfield, Frank Perkins Way, Peterborough, Cambs, PE1 5FQ
Activities: Manufacture of engines and turbines, except aircraft, vehicle and cycle engines
Parent: Caterpillar International Holding S.A.R.L
Officers: Johanna Elizabeth Deason, Secretary; Nigel John Burroughs [1964] Director/Tax Accountant; David John Goldspink [1966] Director/General Manager; Paul David Thompson [1980] Director/Business Resource Manager [American]

Perkins Holdings Limited
Incorporated: 1 February 1952 *Employees:* 1
Net Worth: £489,863,008 *Total Assets:* £490,375,008
Registered Office: Eastfield, Frank Perkins Way, Peterborough, Cambs, PE1 5FQ
Activities: Activities of head offices
Parent: Perkins International Inc
Officers: Johanna Elizabeth Deason, Secretary; Nigel John Burroughs [1964] Director/Tax Accountant; Steven Ferguson [1968] Director/Vice President [American]; David John Goldspink [1966] Director/General Manager; Paul David Thompson [1980] Director/Business Resource Manager [American]

F. Perkins Limited
Incorporated: 7 June 1932 *Employees:* 3
Net Worth: £178,160,992 *Total Assets:* £241,420,992
Registered Office: Eastfield, Frank Perkins Way, Peterborough, Cambs, PE1 5FQ
Activities: Other letting and operating of own or leased real estate
Parent: Caterpillar International Holding S.A.R.L
Officers: Johanna Elizabeth Deason, Secretary; Nigel John Burroughs [1964] Director/Tax Accountant; David John Goldspink [1966] Director/General Manager; Paul David Thompson [1980] Director/Business Resource Manager [American]

Perkins Small Engines Limited
Incorporated: 12 October 1994 *Employees:* 174
Previous: Perkins Shibaura Engines Limited
Net Worth: £21,288,000 *Total Assets:* £44,683,000
Registered Office: Eastfield, Frank Perkins Way, Peterborough, Cambs, PE1 5FQ
Activities: Manufacture of engines and turbines, except aircraft, vehicle and cycle engines
Officers: Johanna Elizabeth Deason, Secretary; Michael John Casey [1974] Director/Senior Business Resource Manager [American]; Steven Ferguson [1968] Director/Vice President [American]; David John Goldspink [1966] Director/General Manager; Paul David Thompson [1980] Director/Business Resource Manager [American]

K. & O. Peros (Oxford) Limited
Incorporated: 28 February 1986 *Employees:* 2
Net Worth: £10,194,141 *Total Assets:* £11,206,653
Registered Office: Cotswold Lodge Hotel, 66a Banbury Road, Oxford, OX2 6JP
Activities: Other letting and operating of own or leased real estate
Shareholders: Kyriacos Peros; Olga Peros
Officers: Olga Peros, Secretary/Hotel Proprietor; Kyriacos Peros [1934] Director/Hotel Proprietor; Olga Peros [1943] Director/Hotel Proprietor

Perrys East Midlands Limited
Incorporated: 2 January 1987 *Employees:* 402
Previous: G K Group Limited
Net Worth: £13,093,000 *Total Assets:* £69,698,000
Registered Office: Suite 1, 500 Pavilion Drive, Brackmills, Northampton, NN4 7YJ
Activities: Sale of new cars and light motor vehicles
Parent: Perrys Group Limited
Officers: Neil Howard Taylor, Secretary; Darren Ardron [1967] Director; Richard George Ingram [1957] Director/Lawyer; Denise Millard [1958] Director; Ken Francis Savage [1962] Director; Neil Howard Taylor [1960] Director/Chartered Accountant

Perrys Group Limited
Incorporated: 11 October 2000 *Employees:* 1,918
Net Worth: £60,544,000 *Total Assets:* £227,704,000
Registered Office: Suite 1, 500 Pavilion Drive, Northampton Business Park, Brackmills, Northampton, NN4 7YJ
Activities: Sale of new cars and light motor vehicles
Major Shareholder: Denise Millard
Officers: Neil Taylor, Secretary; Darren Ardron [1967] Managing Director; Richard George Ingram [1957] Director/Solicitor; Denise Millard [1958] Director; Ken Francis Savage [1962] Director/Chairman; Neil Howard Taylor [1960] Director/Chartered Accountant

Perrys Motor Sales Limited
Incorporated: 12 February 1970 *Employees:* 1,516
Net Worth: £67,916,000 *Total Assets:* £176,300,992
Registered Office: Suite 1, 500 Pavilion Drive, Northampton Business Park, Brackmills, Northampton, NN4 7YJ
Activities: Sale of new cars and light motor vehicles
Parent: Perrys Group Limited
Officers: Neil Taylor, Secretary; Darren Ardron [1967] Managing Director; Richard George Ingram [1957] Director/Solicitor; Denise Millard [1958] Director; Ken Francis Savage [1962] Director/Chairman; Neil Howard Taylor [1960] Director/Chartered Accountant

Personal Assurance Public Limited Company
Incorporated: 11 July 1984 *Employees:* 5
Net Worth: £12,453,000 *Total Assets:* £16,352,000
Registered Office: John Ormond House, 899 Silbury Boulevard, Milton Keynes, Bucks, MK9 3XL
Activities: Non-life insurance
Parent: Personal Group Limited
Officers: Sarah Anne Mace, Secretary; Michael Ian Dugdale [1962] Director/Chief Financial Officer; Robert Michael Head [1958] Director; Andrew George Lothian [1971] Director/Sales Manager; Deborah Karen Rees-Frost [1966] Director; Kenneth William Rooney [1950] Director/Financial Advisor; Mark William Scanlon [1968] Director [Irish]; Mark Winlow [1962] Director

Personal Group Holdings PLC
Incorporated: 7 May 1996 *Employees:* 215
Net Worth: £33,756,000 *Total Assets:* £49,568,000
Registered Office: John Ormond House, 899 Silbury Boulevard, Milton Keynes, Bucks, MK9 3XL
Activities: Activities of head offices
Officers: Sarah Anne Mace, Secretary; Michael Ian Dugdale [1962] Director/Chief Financial Officer; Robert Michael Head [1958] Director; Andrew George Lothian [1971] Director/Sales Manager; Deborah Karen Rees-Frost [1966] Director; Kenneth William Rooney [1950] Director; Mark William Scanlon [1968] Director [Irish]; Mark Winlow [1962] Director

Personal Group Limited
Incorporated: 30 January 2015
Net Worth: £22,375,000 *Total Assets:* £22,585,000
Registered Office: John Ormond House, 899 Silbury Boulevard, Milton Keynes, Bucks, MK9 3XL
Activities: Activities of head offices
Parent: Personal Group Holdings PLC
Officers: Sarah Anne Mace, Secretary; Michael Ian Dugdale [1962] Director/Chief Financial Officer; Robert Michael Head [1958] Director; Andrew George Lothian [1971] Director/Sales Manager; Deborah Karen Rees-Frost [1966] Director; Kenneth William Rooney [1950] Director; Mark William Scanlon [1968] Director [Irish]; Mark Winlow [1962] Director

Perspective Financial Group Limited
Incorporated: 18 December 2007 *Employees:* 171
Net Worth Deficit: £5,448,664 *Total Assets:* £21,719,958
Registered Office: Paradigm House, Lower Meadow Road, Handforth, Wilmslow, Cheshire, SK9 3ND
Activities: Financial intermediation not elsewhere classified
Shareholder: Paul Henry Hogarth
Officers: David John Philip Hesketh, Secretary; Julie Suzanne Hepworth [1974] Compliance Director; David John Philip Hesketh [1981] Director/Accountant; Paul Henry Hogarth [1959] Director; Paul Michael Newton [1964] Director/Accountant; Michael Peter Rogan [1968] Director; Ian Mitcheal Wilkinson [1970] Financial Adviser Director

Pertemps Jobshop Limited
Incorporated: 16 June 1993
Net Worth: £17,941,724 *Total Assets:* £43,017,080
Registered Office: Meriden Hall, Main Road, Meriden, Coventry, Warwicks, CV7 7PT
Activities: Other activities of employment placement agencies
Officers: Nigel John Dudley, Secretary; Stephen Carlo Mogano [1959] Director; Kent Thompson [1964] Director/Manager; Carmen Anne Watson [1956] Director; Timothy Watts [1949] Director; Stephen William West [1964] Director

Pertemps Limited
Incorporated: 29 August 2003 *Employees:* 1,036
Net Worth: £49,231,000 *Total Assets:* £200,260,000
Registered Office: Meriden Hall, Main Road, Meriden, Coventry, Warwicks, CV7 7PT
Activities: Temporary employment agency activities
Officers: Nigel John Dudley, Secretary; Tracy Michelle Evans [1964] HR Director; Martin Michael Gunn [1970] Director; Stephen Carlo Mogano [1959] Director/Accountant; Celia Perry [1969] Director; Kent Thompson [1964] Director; Carmen Anne Watson [1956] Director; Tim Watts [1949] Director; Stephen William West [1964] Director

Pertemps Recruitment Partnership Limited
Incorporated: 17 June 1982 *Employees:* 844
Net Worth: £54,360,000 *Total Assets:* £192,107,008
Registered Office: Meriden Hall, Main Road, Meriden, Coventry, Warwicks, CV7 7PT
Activities: Temporary employment agency activities
Officers: Nigel John Dudley, Secretary; Nicola Jane Barr [1973] Director; Catherine Anne Brown [1977] Director; Wayne Michael Clarkson [1969] Director; Lisa Duncan [1972] Accounts Director; Tracy Michelle Evans [1964] Director; Abigail Farnham [1971] Director; Helen Louise Hibbert [1969] Director; William Robert Hodson [1968] Director/Company Executive; Stephen Carlo Mogano [1959] Director; Barry Moorman [1956] Director/Company Executive; Louise Owen [1965] Director; Celia Perry [1969] Director; John Poliquin [1966] Director/Company Executive [Canadian]; Kent Thompson [1964] Director/Manager; Lisa Alice Thurkettle [1977] Director; Carmen Anne Watson [1956] Director; Stephen William West [1964] Director/Manager; Christopher Wyres [1962] Director

Pet City Holdings Limited
Incorporated: 1 February 1989
Net Worth: £27,034,000 *Total Assets:* £27,034,000
Registered Office: Epsom Avenue, Stanley Green Trading Estate, Handsforth, Wilmslow, Cheshire, SK9 3RN
Activities: Non-trading company
Parent: Pets at Home Holdings Limited
Officers: Louise Ann Stonier, Secretary; Michael James Iddon [1965] Director; Peter Pritchard [1970] Director; Louise Ann Stonier [1973] Director/Company Secretary

Peterborough Diocesan Board of Finance (The)
Incorporated: 4 December 1922 *Employees:* 191
Net Worth: £142,791,952 *Total Assets:* £146,862,800
Registered Office: Diocesan Office, The Palace, Minster Precincts, Peterborough, Cambs, PE1 1YB
Activities: Other business support service activities n.e.c.
Officers: Andrew Roberts, Secretary; The Right Reverend Donald Spargo Allister [1952] Director/Lord Bishop of Peterborough; Robert Frederick Baker [1950] Director; The Revd Jane Elizabeth Baxter [1951] Director/Clerk in Holy Orders; Neil John Bradley [1970] Director/Retired; Dr Paul Vinton Buckingham [1948] Director/Medical Practitioner; Isobel Jane Burbidge [1950] Director/Retired; Dr Hilary Creek [1947] Director/Retired University Administrator; Norman James Critchlow [1948] Director/Retired; Hilary Jane Daniels [1954] Director; Christine Hall [1962] Director; Mr Andrew Clive Hawkins [1958] Director/Retail Assistant Manager; John Hindle [1950] Director/Self Employed; Gerard John Hoare [1942] Director/Farm Consultant; The Right Reverend John Holbrook [1962] Director/Bishop; The Reverend Katrina Hutchins [1962] Director/Clerk in Holy Orders; The Reverend Mark Wesley Lucas [1962] Director/Clerk in Holy Orders; Peter Holtby McKay [1943] Director/Retired; Jeremy Orme [1943] Director/Accountant; Richard Jeremy Ormston [1961] Director/Archdeacon of Northampton; Andrew Kenneth Owst [1956] Finance Director; Robert Purser [1950] Director; Neil Andrew Elsom Robertson [1942] Director; Reverend George Huchinson Rogers [1951] Director/Vicar [Canadian/British]; The Venerable Gordon John Steele [1955] Director/Minster of Religion; Michael John Truman [1942] Director/Certified Accountant Retired

Peterborough Keys Academies Trust
Incorporated: 12 December 2017 *Employees:* 807
Net Worth: £49,097,000 *Total Assets:* £57,105,000
Registered Office: Jack Hunt School, Bradwell Road, Peterborough, PE3 9PY
Activities: Primary education
Officers: Bernard Martin Champness [1950] Director/Clerk to Parish Council; Colin Graham Hammond [1965] Director/Business Development Manager; Tracey Elizabeth Hedges [1981] Director/Accountant; Claire Patricia Higgins [1963] Director/Chief Executive; William Peter Kerry [1985] Director/Accountant; Lisa Dawn Lloyd [1981] Director/Education, Head of House; Adriano Pacitti [1978] Director/Chartered Engineer; Alan Ralph Sadler [1958] Director/Self Employed

Pets at Home Group PLC
Incorporated: 10 February 2014 *Employees:* 6,701
Net Worth: £906,352,000 *Total Assets:* £1,339,376,000
Registered Office: Epsom Avenue, Stanley Green Trading Estate, Handforth, Cheshire, SK9 3RN
Activities: Activities of head offices
Officers: Louise Ann Stonier, Secretary; Dr Susan Dawson [1961] Director; Antonio Denunzio [1960] Non-Executive Director/Consultant; Sharon Emma Flood [1965] Director; Michael James Iddon [1965] Director; Stanislas Marie Laurent [1968] Director [French]; Dennis Henry Millard [1949] Director; Paul Stephen Moody [1957] Director; Peter Pritchard [1970] Director

Pets at Home Holdings Limited
Incorporated: 25 October 1999
Net Worth: £18,712,000 *Total Assets:* £89,592,000
Registered Office: Pets at Home Ltd, Epsom Avenue, Stanley Green Trading Estate, Handforth, Cheshire, SK9 3RN
Activities: Non-trading company
Parent: Pets at Home No.1 Limited
Officers: Louise Ann Stonier, Secretary; Michael James Iddon [1965] Director; Peter Pritchard [1970] Director; Louise Ann Stonier [1973] Director/Company Secretary

Pets at Home Ltd
Incorporated: 7 June 1984 *Employees:* 5,878
Net Worth: £729,417,984 *Total Assets:* £1,030,350,976
Registered Office: Epsom Avenue, Stanley Green Trading Estate, Handforth, Cheshire, SK9 3RN
Activities: Other retail sale of new goods in specialised stores (not commercial art galleries and opticians)
Parent: Pets at Home Superstores Limited
Officers: Louise Ann Stonier, Secretary; Michael James Iddon [1965] Director; Peter Pritchard [1970] Director; Louise Ann Stonier [1973] Director/Company Secretary

Pets at Home No.1 Limited
Incorporated: 11 February 2014
Net Worth: £670,284,032 *Total Assets:* £1,595,992,960
Registered Office: Epsom Avenue, Stanley Green Trading Estate, Handforth, Cheshire, SK9 3RN
Activities: Non-trading company
Parent: Pets at Home Group PLC
Officers: Louise Ann Stonier, Secretary; Michael James Iddon [1965] Director; Peter Pritchard [1970] Director; Louise Ann Stonier [1973] Director/Company Secretary

Pets at Home Superstores Limited
Incorporated: 30 October 1995
Net Worth: £5,940,000 *Total Assets:* £107,951,000
Registered Office: Epsom Avenue, Stanley Green Trading Estate, Handforth, Cheshire, SK9 3RN
Activities: Non-trading company
Parent: Pets at Home Holdings Limited
Officers: Louise Ann Stonier, Secretary; Michael James Iddon [1965] Director; Peter Pritchard [1970] Director; Louise Ann Stonier [1973] Director/Company Secretary

Pets at Home Vet Group Limited
Incorporated: 3 July 2013
Net Worth: £53,054,240 *Total Assets:* £53,054,240
Registered Office: Epsom Avenue, Stanley Green Trading Estate, Handforth, Cheshire, SK9 3RN
Activities: Non-trading company
Parent: Pets at Home Holdings Limited
Officers: Louise Stonier, Secretary; Harvey Bertenshaw Ainley [1966] Director/Chief Financial Officer; Jane Balmain [1958] Director; Michael James Iddon [1965] Director; Peter Pritchard [1970] Director; Louise Ann Stonier [1973] Director/Company Secretary

Pets at Home Veterinary Specialist Group Limited
Incorporated: 25 March 2015
Net Worth Deficit: £4,205,000 *Total Assets:* £35,132,000
Registered Office: Pets at Home Limited, Epsom Avenue, Stanley Green Trading Estate, Handforth, Wilmslow, Cheshire, SK9 3RN
Activities: Non-trading company
Parent: Pets at Home Holdings Limited
Officers: Louise Stonier, Secretary; Michael James Iddon [1965] Director; Peter Pritchard [1970] Director; Matthew William Grange Stead [1970] Business Development Director; Louise Ann Stonier [1973] Director/Company Secretary; Dr Richard Andrew Stanley White [1952] Director/Veterinary Surgeon

Peugeot Citroen Automobiles UK Limited
Incorporated: 25 January 2002 *Employees:* 387
Net Worth: £153,056,000 *Total Assets:* £663,350,976
Registered Office: Pinley House, 2 Sunbeam Way, Coventry, Warwicks, CV3 1ND
Activities: Activities of head offices
Parent: Peugeot S.A.
Officers: Kinnary Vyas, Secretary; David James Connell [1972] Director - Group Operations; Linda Jackson [1958] Managing Director; Stephane Le Guevel [1967] Managing Director [French]; Kevin Michael O'Kelly [1966] Director Parts Logistics; Nigel John Willetts [1972] Director/Chartered Accountant

Peugeot Motor Company PLC
Incorporated: 26 September 1917 *Employees:* 162
Net Worth: £186,396,992 *Total Assets:* £893,265,024
Registered Office: Pinley House, 2 Sunbeam Way, Coventry, Warwicks, CV3 1ND
Activities: Sale of new cars and light motor vehicles
Parent: Peugeot S.A.
Officers: Kinnary Vyas, Secretary; David James Connell [1972] Director; Jean-Philippe Georges Imparato [1966] Director [French]; Stephane Le Guevel [1967] Managing Director [French]; Kevin Michael O'Kelly [1966] Director Parts Logistics; David Peel [1965] Director; Nigel John Willetts [1972] Director/Chartered Accountant

Peveril Homes Limited
Incorporated: 21 February 1985 *Employees:* 46
Net Worth: £17,366,568 *Total Assets:* £33,590,424
Registered Office: High Edge Court, Church Street, Heage, Belper, Derbys, DE56 2BW
Activities: Construction of domestic buildings
Parent: Bowmer & Kirkland Ltd.
Officers: Michelle Ann Mucklestone, Secretary; Alison Jane Cocks [1964] Sales and Marketing Director; Ralph Charles Jones [1950] Director/Quantity Surveyor; Christopher Robert Kirkland [1982] Director; James Adrian Smith [1973] Director; Colin George Wright [1958] Director/Quantity Surveyor

Peveril Securities Limited
Incorporated: 4 March 1953 *Employees:* 3
Net Worth: £37,104,212 *Total Assets:* £162,151,904
Registered Office: High Edge Court, Heage, Belper, Derbys, DE56 2BW
Activities: Development of building projects
Parent: Bowmer & Kirkland Ltd.
Officers: Michelle Ann Mucklestone, Secretary/Accountant; Ralph Charles Jones [1950] Director/Quantity Surveyor; Christopher Robert Kirkland [1982] Director; John Alexander Charles Kirkland [1980] Director

Peveril Securities Long Lane Limited
Incorporated: 10 December 2014 *Employees:* 6
Net Worth Deficit: £229,303 *Total Assets:* £44,825,144
Registered Office: High Edge Court, Heage, Belper, Derbys, DE56 2BW
Activities: Development of building projects
Shareholders: Joanna Brooks; Peveril Securities Limited
Officers: Joanna Claire Brooks [1972] Director; Sean Patrick Dempsey [1968] Director; Simon Hosking [1964] Director; Ralph Charles Jones [1950] Director; Michelle Ann Mucklestone [1966] Group Financial Director; James Adrian Smith [1973] Director

Pfisterer Limited
Incorporated: 27 September 2005 *Employees:* 39
Net Worth: £8,793,141 *Total Assets:* £12,644,010
Registered Office: 2-4 Orgreave Place, Dore House, Industrial Estate, Sheffield, S13 9LU
Activities: Manufacture of electricity distribution and control apparatus
Officers: David Paul Reed, Secretary/Managing Director; Martin Billhardt [1962] Director/Chairman [German]; Richard Ian Lockwood [1973] Director; Gregg Alan Marshall [1982] Director; David Paul Reed [1967] Director

PFM Group Limited
Incorporated: 2 April 2004 *Employees:* 3
Net Worth Deficit: £589,669 *Total Assets:* £32,853,454
Registered Office: Paradigm House, Brooke Court, Wilmslow, Cheshire, SK9 3ND
Activities: Other business support service activities n.e.c.
Parent: Perspective Financial Group Ltd
Officers: David John Philip Hesketh, Secretary; Julie Suzanne Hepworth [1974] Director; David John Philip Hesketh [1981] Director; Ian Mitcheal Wilkinson [1970] Director

PH Alderley Park LLP
Incorporated: 17 June 2016
Net Worth: £11,166,222 *Total Assets:* £19,739,724
Registered Office: Bollin House, Oakfield Road, Cheadle Royal Business Park, Cheadle, Cheshire, SK8 3GX

Pharmacy Care Plus Limited
Incorporated: 3 March 2008 *Employees:* 127
Net Worth: £4,818,116 *Total Assets:* £12,084,689
Registered Office: Suite M, No 2 The Courtyard, Earl Road, Stanley Green, Cheadle Hulme, Cheadle, Cheshire, SK8 6GN
Activities: Other human health activities
Officers: Michael Niblock, Secretary; Dr Robert George Andrew [1961] Director; Michael Niblock [1981] Director; Dr Devendra Shah [1967] Director

Pharos Group Limited
Incorporated: 25 June 1999 *Employees:* 56
Net Worth: £10,684,386 *Total Assets:* £19,317,840
Registered Office: Unit 1 Holly Farm Business Park, Honiley, Kenilworth, Warwicks, CV8 1NP
Activities: Activities of head offices
Parent: Apted Holdings Limited
Officers: Stephen Jackson, Secretary; Raymond William Apted [1948] Director

Phenomenex Limited
Incorporated: 12 May 1987 *Employees:* 81
Net Worth: £19,252,464 *Total Assets:* £21,925,454
Registered Office: Melville House, Queens Avenue, Hurdsfield Industrial Estate, Macclesfield, Cheshire, SK10 2BN
Activities: Wholesale of chemical products
Parent: AB Sciex UK Limited
Officers: Michelle Elizabeth Caron [1967] Director [American]; Dennis Shane Lyons [1957] Director [American]; Keith Graham Ward [1953] Director

Philex Limited
Incorporated: 16 April 1982 *Employees:* 90
Net Worth: £5,101,486 *Total Assets:* £15,493,788
Registered Office: Philex House, Kingfisher Wharf, London Road, Bedford, MK42 0NX
Activities: Activities of head offices
Parent: Philex Holdings Limited
Officers: Hilary Price, Secretary/Admin HR; Andrew Nicholas Hewson [1958] Director/Chartered Accountant; Weng Mun Kok [1972] Finance Director; Keith Pacey [1949] Director; Massoud Sabourian [1950] Director/Importer; Karl Martyn Thomas [1981] Managing Director

Phoenix Advance Limited
Incorporated: 5 June 2014 *Employees:* 127
Net Worth: £611,000 *Total Assets:* £55,333,000
Registered Office: 1 Victoria Stables, Essex Way, Bourne, Lincs, PE10 9JZ
Activities: Activities of other holding companies n.e.c.
Officers: Paul Christian Lee Knight [1971] Managing Director; Matthew Lloyd Turner [1966] Financial Director; David Michael York [1949] Director/Chairman

Phoenix Oil & Marine Limited
Incorporated: 12 June 2000 *Employees:* 1
Net Worth: £14,509,000 *Total Assets:* £20,066,000
Registered Office: Moody Lane, Pyewipe, Grimsby, N E Lincs, DN31 2SY
Activities: Activities of head offices
Parent: Phoenix Fluid Handling Industry GmbH
Officers: Dr Ali Reza Kambiez Zandiyeh [1960] Director/General Manager

Phoenix Parker Holdings Limited
Incorporated: 11 December 2007 *Employees:* 159
Net Worth: £23,789,000 *Total Assets:* £35,982,000
Registered Office: Viaduct Works, Canon Street, Leicester, LE4 6GH
Activities: Activities of production holding companies
Shareholders: Patricia Lorraine Dalby; Glenn Bryan Dalby
Officers: Glyn John Wheeler, Secretary; Brett Lee Dalby [1980] Director; Glenn Bryan Dalby [1957] Director; Glyn John Wheeler [1957] Director

Phoenix Sports Limited
Incorporated: 24 December 1997
Net Worth Deficit: £139,000 *Total Assets:* £20,757,000
Registered Office: 23 Carbrook Hall Road, Sheffield, S9 2EH
Activities: Operation of sports facilities
Officers: Andrew Edward Snelling [1963] Finance Director

Phoenix Transworld Limited
Incorporated: 31 July 2000 *Employees:* 42
Net Worth: £13,028,000 *Total Assets:* £16,046,000
Registered Office: Viaduct Works, Canon Street, Leicester, LE4 6GH
Activities: Dormant company
Parent: Phoenix Parker Holdings Limited
Officers: Glyn John Wheeler, Secretary; Glyn John Wheeler [1957] Director

Phytone Limited
Incorporated: 10 February 1989 *Employees:* 40
Net Worth: £9,700,020 *Total Assets:* £12,865,109
Registered Office: Third Avenue, Centrum 100, Burton on Trent, Staffs, DE14 2WD
Activities: Other processing and preserving of fruit and vegetables
Parent: FMC Corporation United Kingdom Limited
Officers: Janette de Gennaro, Secretary; James Decleene [1961] Director/H and N Controller [American]

PIB Group Limited
Incorporated: 3 December 2015 *Employees:* 710
Net Worth: £125,827,000 *Total Assets:* £240,946,000
Registered Office: Rossington's Business Park, West Carr Road, Retford, Notts, DN22 7SW
Activities: Activities of insurance agents and brokers
Officers: Ryan Christopher Brown [1973] Director; James Floyd Burr [1966] Director/Investor [American]; Christopher Michael Giles [1964] Director; Brendan James McManus [1959] Director

PIB Risk Services Limited
Incorporated: 30 January 1992 *Employees:* 209
Previous: PIB Risk Services PLC
Net Worth: £4,442,755 *Total Assets:* £38,819,148
Registered Office: Rossington's Business Park, West Carr Road, Retford, Notts, DN22 7SW
Activities: Non-life insurance
Parent: PIB Group Limited
Officers: Timothy Tracy Brooke [1960] Director; Ryan Christopher Brown [1973] Director; Adrian Colosso [1957] Director; Elisa Marie Griffin [1978] Director/Insurance Brokers; Brendan James McManus [1959] Director/Insurance Broker; Nigel Peter Geoffrey Salisbury [1958] Director/Insurance Broker; Jonathan Paul Stanley [1965] Director/Chief Risk Officer

J.E.Piccaver & Co. (Gedney Marsh)
Incorporated: 28 June 1950 *Employees:* 127
Net Worth: £9,399,683 *Total Assets:* £19,566,324
Registered Office: Norfolk House Farm, Gedney Marsh, Spalding, Lincs, PE12 9PB
Activities: Growing of vegetables and melons, roots and tubers
Parent: Jepco Ltd
Officers: Simon Goddard, Secretary; Simon Goddard [1959] Director/Accountant; Phillip Paul Hubbert [1955] Director/Farm Manager; Anthony Padoan [1964] Managing Director; Stuart William Piccaver [1971] Sales & Marketing Director

Pickering Developments Limited
Incorporated: 16 December 1985 *Employees:* 10
Net Worth: £68,801,120 *Total Assets:* £177,739,312
Registered Office: Cabourn House, Station Street, Bingham, Notts, NG13 8AQ
Activities: Other letting and operating of own or leased real estate
Parent: Pickering Investments Limited
Officers: Jill Brand [1953] Director/Secretary; Alan Philip Morris [1951] Director; Sue Morris [1955] Director/Hotelier

Pickering Investments Limited
Incorporated: 6 October 1971
Net Worth: £13,439,710 *Total Assets:* £13,439,710
Registered Office: Cabourn House, Station Street, Bingham, Notts, NG13 8AQ
Activities: Activities of other holding companies n.e.c.
Parent: Willoughby 35 Limited
Officers: Jill Brand [1953] Director/Secretary; Alan Philip Morris [1951] Director; Sue Morris [1955] Director/Hotelier

Pickering Properties Limited
Incorporated: 12 September 1994 *Employees:* 2
Net Worth: £85,613,408 *Total Assets:* £142,215,360
Registered Office: 14 Clarendon Street, Nottingham, NG1 5HQ
Activities: Other letting and operating of own or leased real estate
Parent: Highfield House Investment Properties Limited
Officers: Sarah Elizabeth Pickering, Secretary; Sarah Elizabeth Pickering [1966] Director

Pico Technology (Holdings) Limited
Incorporated: 15 November 2004 *Employees:* 127
Net Worth: £13,593,981 *Total Assets:* £16,307,159
Registered Office: James House, Colmworth Business Park, Eaton Socon, St Neots, Cambs, PE19 8YP
Activities: Manufacture of electronic measuring, testing etc. equipment, not for industrial process control
Major Shareholder: Alan David Tong
Officers: Jane Ellen Ann Percy, Secretary; Guy Allen Roderick [1939] Director; Alan David Tong [1970] Director; Caroline Tong [1973] Director

Picsolve Holdings Limited
Incorporated: 16 May 2008 *Employees:* 1,407
Previous: Scream 4 Limited
Net Worth: £11,255,000 *Total Assets:* £22,082,000
Registered Office: Picsolve International Limited, Victoria Way, Pride Park, Derby, DE24 8AN
Activities: Non-trading company
Officers: John Bernard Behrendt [1961] Director/Consultant; Melanie Louise Halsey [1974] Director/Head of HR; David Hockley [1965] Director/Chartered Accountant; Colin John Tenwick [1960] Director

Picsolve International Limited
Incorporated: 18 January 1994 *Employees:* 77
Net Worth: £6,952,000 *Total Assets:* £25,366,000
Registered Office: 9 Victoria Way, Pride Park, Derby, DE24 8AN
Activities: Photographic activities not elsewhere classified
Parent: Right Digital Limited
Officers: John Bernard Behrendt [1961] Director/Senior Management; David Hockley [1965] Director/Chartered Accountant; Colin John Tenwick [1960] Director

Pilgrim Foodservice Limited
Incorporated: 3 August 2005 *Employees:* 259
Net Worth: £12,999,264 *Total Assets:* £24,178,890
Registered Office: Marsh Lane, Boston, Lincs, PE21 7SJ
Activities: Non-specialised wholesale of food, beverages and tobacco
Major Shareholder: Peter John Bateman
Officers: Charles John Bateman, Secretary; Charles John Bateman [1987] Director; Peter John Bateman [1959] Director; Philip Parker [1953] Procurement Director

PIMCO 2909 Limited
Incorporated: 7 September 2011
Net Worth: £22,893,000 *Total Assets:* £22,901,000
Registered Office: Dearing House, 1 Young Street, Sheffield, S1 4UP
Activities: Post-secondary non-tertiary education
Officers: Wayne Janse Van Rensburg [1981] Director; Andrew Richard Alexander Palmer [1976] Director

Pineapple Letting Ltd
Incorporated: 22 December 2008 *Employees:* 3
Net Worth: £3,916,105 *Total Assets:* £13,356,426
Registered Office: 24 Manchester Road, Wilmslow, Cheshire, SK9 1BG
Activities: Other letting and operating of own or leased real estate
Officers: Arthur John Abercromby [1943] Director; Judith Abercromby [1941] Director/Company Secretary; Marie-Louise Abercromby [1978] Director; Mark Lhind Abercromby [1975] Director

Pinelodge Holidays Limited
Incorporated: 28 November 1985 *Employees:* 199
Net Worth: £3,530,000 *Total Assets:* £13,330,000
Registered Office: Darwin Forest Country Park, Darley Moor, Two Dales, Matlock, Derbys, DE4 5LN
Activities: Holiday centres and villages
Parent: Pinelog Group Limited
Officers: Judith Goldacre, Secretary; Paul St John Daly [1951] Director; Judith Goldacre [1969] Director/Chartered Accountant; Beverley Anne Grayson [1947] Director; John Hugh Grayson [1944] Director/Chartered Accountant; Lyndsey Fiona Grayson [1973] Director; Nicholas Mark Hugh Grayson [1972] Director

Pinelog Group Limited
Incorporated: 18 April 2002 *Employees:* 269
Net Worth: £8,847,000 *Total Assets:* £14,622,000
Registered Office: Darwin Forest Country Park, Darley Moor, Two Dales, Matlock, Derbys, DE4 5LN
Activities: Activities of head offices
Shareholder: Beverley Anne Grayson
Officers: Judith Goldacre, Secretary; James Whistler Berresford [1956] Director; Paul St John Daly [1951] Director; Beverley Anne Grayson [1947] Director; John Hugh Grayson [1944] Director/Chartered Accountant; Lyndsey Fiona Grayson [1973] Director; Nicholas Mark Hugh Grayson [1972] Director; Nigel Byron Wimpenny [1955] Director

Pinewood Technologies PLC
Incorporated: 8 April 1998 *Employees:* 182
Net Worth: £28,618,000 *Total Assets:* £36,029,000
Registered Office: Loxley House, 2 Oakwood Court, Little Oak Drive, Annesley, Nottingham, NG15 0DR
Activities: Business and domestic software development
Parent: Pendragon PLC
Officers: Richard James Maloney, Secretary; Martin Shaun Casha [1960] Director; Trevor Garry Finn [1957] Director; Timothy Paul Holden [1964] Director/Chartered Accountant

Ping Europe Limited
Incorporated: 16 August 1973 *Employees:* 252
Net Worth: £22,944,544 *Total Assets:* £34,633,984
Registered Office: Corringham Road Industrial Estate, Gainsborough, Lincs, DN21 1XZ
Activities: Manufacture of sports goods
Shareholders: John Andrew Solheim; Allan Dale Solheim
Officers: Ian Hamilton Smith, Secretary; John James Clark [1956] Managing Director; Allan Dale Solheim [1940] Director/Manager [American]; John Andrew Solheim [1945] Director/Chairman & Manager [American]; Karsten Louis Solheim [1937] Director [American]

Pinnacle International Freight Holdings Limited
Incorporated: 12 January 2004 *Employees:* 68
Net Worth: £5,706,122 *Total Assets:* £13,250,808
Registered Office: Unit 1 Swannington Road, Broughton Astley, Leicester, LE9 6TU
Activities: Activities of head offices
Shareholders: Nathan James Burrell; Paul Stuart Burrell
Officers: Nathan James Burrell, Secretary; Nathan James Burrell [1974] Director; Paul Stuart Burrell [1975] Director/Freight

Pinnacle International Freight Limited
Incorporated: 26 June 1972 *Employees:* 61
Net Worth: £6,614,173 *Total Assets:* £11,853,401
Registered Office: Unit 1 Swannington Road, Broughton Astley, Leicester, LE9 6TU
Activities: Freight transport by road
Shareholders: Nathan James Burrell; Paul Stuart Burrell
Officers: Nathan James Burrell [1974] Director/Freight; Paul Stuart Burrell [1975] Director/Freight; Kym Christopher Ellington [1969] Director; Gavin Newman [1976] Director

Pinstone Securities Limited
Incorporated: 13 May 2002 *Employees:* 5
Net Worth: £18,360,532 *Total Assets:* £20,835,808
Registered Office: Watlington Business Centre, 1 High Street, Watlington, Oxon, OX49 5PH
Activities: Other letting and operating of own or leased real estate
Parent: STM Fidecs Trust Company Limited
Officers: Chandrakant Khimji Bagga, Secretary; Chandrakant Khimji Bagga [1966] Director; Adam Roger Jerome Sturdy [1976] Director; Roger Beresford Sturdy [1940] Director; Joanna Woods [1966] Director

Pioneer Foods (UK) Limited
Incorporated: 25 September 2000 *Employees:* 280
Previous: Bokomo Foods (UK) Ltd
Net Worth: £20,153,860 *Total Assets:* £40,411,372
Registered Office: 40 Bradfield Road, Finedon Road Industrial, Wellingborough, Northants, NN8 4HB
Activities: Grain milling
Officers: Steven Daniel Goodes, Secretary; Steven Daniel Goodes [1984] Director/Finance Manager; Thushen Agambaram Govender [1976] Director/Business Executive [South African]; Douglas Paul Howard [1969] Commercial Director; Andrew Richard Jones [1963] Operations Director; Felix Lombard [1969] Director/Businessman [South African]; Jonathon Wilhelm Thorn [1985] Director/General Manager

Pipe Holdings 1 PLC
Incorporated: 6 June 2005 *Employees:* 2
Net Worth: £10,520,000 *Total Assets:* £98,832,000
Registered Office: Broomhouse Lane, Edlington, Doncaster, S Yorks, DN12 1ES
Activities: Activities of production holding companies
Officers: Emma Gayle Versluys, Secretary; Paul Anthony James [1967] Director/Chief Financial Officer; Martin Keith Payne [1965] Director

Pipe Holdings 2 Limited
Incorporated: 27 June 2005 *Employees:* 2
Net Worth: £98,300,000 *Total Assets:* £104,700,000
Registered Office: Broomhouse Lane, Edlington, Doncaster, S Yorks, DN12 1ES
Activities: Activities of production holding companies
Parent: Pipe Holdings 1 PLC
Officers: Emma Gayle Versluys, Secretary; Paul Anthony James [1967] Director/Chief Financial Officer; Martin Keith Payne [1965] Director

Pipe Holdings PLC
Incorporated: 15 June 2004 *Employees:* 2
Net Worth: £7,818,000 *Total Assets:* £196,124,992
Registered Office: Broomhouse Lane, Edlington, Doncaster, S Yorks, DN12 1ES
Activities: Activities of production holding companies
Parent: Pipe Holdings 2 Limited
Officers: Emma Gayle Versluys, Secretary; Paul Anthony James [1967] Director/Chief Financial Officer; Martin Keith Payne [1965] Director

Pirelli International PLC
Incorporated: 10 November 2000 *Employees:* 6
Net Worth: £216,150,624 *Total Assets:* £2,200,726,016
Registered Office: Pirelli, Derby Road, Burton on Trent, Staffs, DE13 0BH
Activities: Financial intermediation not elsewhere classified
Parent: Pirelli & C. S.P.A
Officers: Charanjit Singh Sagoo, Secretary; Glen Andrews [1958] Director/Business Executive; William David James Ballan [1956] Director/Executive; Vincenzo de Cesaris [1975] Director/Business Executive [Italian]; Dominic Antonio Sandivasci [1955] Director/Executive [Italian]; Robert Julian Stone [1958] Director/Executive; Francesco Tanzi [1964] Director/Executive [Italian]

Pirelli Motorsport Services Limited
Incorporated: 21 October 2010 *Employees:* 44
Net Worth: £3,728,000 *Total Assets:* £10,769,000
Registered Office: Derby Road, Burton on Trent, Staffs, DE13 0BH
Activities: Wholesale trade of motor vehicle parts and accessories
Parent: Pirelli & C. S.P.A
Officers: Charanjit Singh Sagoo, Secretary; Glen Andrews [1958] Director/Executive; Mario Isola [1969] Director/Business Executive [Italian]; Dominic Antonio Sandivasci [1955] Director/Executive [Italian]

Pirelli UK Limited
Incorporated: 20 January 1914 *Employees:* 4
Net Worth: £18,510,000 *Total Assets:* £46,054,000
Registered Office: Pirelli, Derby Road, Stretton, Burton on Trent, Staffs, DE13 0BH
Activities: Activities of head offices
Parent: Pirelli & C. S.P.A
Officers: Charanjit Singh Sagoo, Secretary; Glen Andrews [1958] Director/Business Executive; William David James Ballan [1956] Director/Executive; Vincenzo de Cesaris [1975] Director/Business Executive [Italian]; Dominic Antonio Sandivasci [1955] Director/Executive [Italian]

Pirelli UK Tyres Limited
Incorporated: 19 June 1991 *Employees:* 1,253
Net Worth: £100,403,000 *Total Assets:* £337,968,992
Registered Office: Derby Road, Burton on Trent, Staffs, DE13 0BH
Activities: Manufacture of rubber tyres and tubes; retreading and rebuilding of rubber tyres
Parent: Pirelli & C. S.P.A
Officers: Charanjit Singh Sagoo, Secretary; Glen Andrews [1958] Director/Executive; Livio Magni [1976] Director/Business Executive [Italian]; Lorenzo Panizzari [1964] Director/Business Executive [Italian]; Dominic Antonio Sandivasci [1955] Director/Executive [Italian]; Piero Giorgio Sierra [1934] Director/Executive [Italian]

Pitacs Limited
Incorporated: 24 May 1990 *Employees:* 64
Net Worth: £7,168,496 *Total Assets:* £16,835,538
Registered Office: Bradbourne Point, Bradbourne Drive, Tilbrook, Milton Keynes, Bucks, MK7 8AT
Activities: Non-specialised wholesale trade
Shareholders: Saffet Kalender; Levent Aci
Officers: Levent Aci, Secretary; Levent Aci [1961] Director; Saffet Kalender [1960] Director

PJ Care Group Limited
Incorporated: 1 June 2016 *Employees:* 451
Net Worth: £7,322,901 *Total Assets:* £24,134,532
Registered Office: 153 Sherwood Drive, Bletchley, Milton Keynes, Bucks, MK3 6RT
Activities: Other residential care activities n.e.c.
Major Shareholder: Janice Flawn
Officers: Janice Evelyn Flawn [1947] Director; Neil Russell [1969] Director

PJ Care Limited
Incorporated: 29 February 2000 *Employees:* 451
Net Worth: £11,434,948 *Total Assets:* £26,641,616
Registered Office: 153 Sherwood Drive, Bletchley, Milton Keynes, Bucks, MK3 6RT
Activities: Other residential care activities n.e.c.
Parent: P J Care Holdings Limited
Officers: Mark Peter Butler [1957] Director; Janice Evelyn Flawn [1947] Director/Registered Nurse; Allan David Perry [1968] Director of Clinical Services; Neil Russell [1969] Director

PKF Cooper Parry Group Limited
Incorporated: 3 October 2011 *Employees:* 341
Net Worth: £7,967,578 *Total Assets:* £30,533,884
Registered Office: Sky View, Argosy Road, East Midlands Airport, Castle Donington, Derbys, DE74 2SA
Activities: Information technology consultancy activities
Parent: PKF Cooper Parry LLP
Officers: Simon Atkins [1975] Director/Accountant; Adrian Paul Cheatham [1971] Director/Chartered Accountant; James David Parnell [1978] Director/Chief Financial Officer

PKF Cooper Parry LLP
Incorporated: 18 March 2002 *Employees:* 372
Net Worth: £2,998,643 *Total Assets:* £15,607,403
Registered Office: Sky View, Argosy Road, East Midlands Airport, Castle Donington, Derbys, DE74 2SA
Officers: Simon Atkins [1975] Member; Jeremy James Bowler [1952] Member; Abigail Bown [1978] Member; Adrian Paul Cheatham [1971] Member; Andrew Madjid Mehrabizadeh Honarmand [1967] Member; Ricahrd Jones [1966] Member; April Oconnell [1982] Member; James David Parnell [1978] Member; Peter Robert Sterling [1959] Member; Sarah Axe [1973] LLP Member; Simon Mark Baines [1967] LLP Member; Stephen Robert Bryan [1961] LLP Member; Andrew Charles Chandler [1968] LLP Member; Robin Clegg [1977] LLP Member; Brett Critchley [1974] LLP Member; Victoria Critchley [1975] LLP Member; Jonathan Michael Elsigood [1966] LLP Member; Alison Elizabeth Fovargue [1981] LLP Member; Krista Margaret Fox [1972] LLP Member; Paul Michael Hayes [1978] LLP Member; Philip Hinson [1973] LLP Member; Stephen Lewis Jones [1970] LLP Member; Sukhjit Kaur [1975] LLP Member; Christopher Robert Knott [1974] LLP Member; Andrew Parker [1966] LLP Member; Daniel Parker [1973] LLP Member; Sally Pickersgill [1979] LLP Member; Scott Riley [1976] LLP Member; Philip Andrew Rogers [1963] LLP Member; Ben Rookes [1980] LLP Member; Paul David Rowley [1972] LLP Member; Colin Richard Shaw [1962] LLP Member; Katharine Warrington [1972] LLP Member; Ivan Wilcox [1976] LLP Member

Plant Impact Limited
Incorporated: 4 May 2005 *Employees:* 56
Previous: Plant Impact PLC
Net Worth: £10,243,000 *Total Assets:* £13,787,000
Registered Office: Cowick Hall, Snaith, Goole, E Yorks, DN14 9AA
Activities: Research and experimental development on biotechnology
Parent: Croda Europe Limited
Officers: Thomas Michael Brophy, Secretary; Nicholas Ian Challoner [1968] Director/President, Life Sciences; David Timothy Cherry [1969] Managing Director Crop Care and Health Care; Graham Lloyd Myers [1963] Director/Group Financial Controller

Plastek UK Ltd
Incorporated: 20 May 1998 *Employees:* 139
Net Worth: £19,955,626 *Total Assets:* £25,484,766
Registered Office: Crown Farm Way, Forest Town, Mansfield, Notts, NG19 0FT
Activities: Manufacture of other plastic products
Parent: Plastek Industries Inc.
Officers: Michael Dzurik, Secretary; Daniel John Prischak [1961] Director [American]; Dennis John Prischak [1960] Director [American]; Joseph John Prischak [1931] Director [American]

Plastic Omnium Automotive Limited
Incorporated: 8 November 1996 *Employees:* 1,034
Net Worth: £22,588,000 *Total Assets:* £196,116,992
Registered Office: Westminster Industrial Estate, Huntingdon Way, Measham, Swadlincote, Derbys, DE12 7DS
Activities: Manufacture of other plastic products
Officers: Brian O'Sullivan, Secretary; Patrick Le Garrec [1963] Director [French]; Jean Michel Szczerba [1960] Director [French]

Plastribution Limited
Incorporated: 14 November 1979 *Employees:* 71
Net Worth: £8,400,895 *Total Assets:* £40,640,132
Registered Office: Clinitron House, Ashby Park, Ashby-De-La-Zouch, Leics, LE65 1JG
Activities: Wholesale of chemical products
Parent: Itochu Europe PLC
Officers: Simon Thompson, Secretary; Michael David Boswell [1964] Managing Director; Philippe Lequertier [1961] Director [French]; Alan Cameron Moules [1964] Commercial Director; Masutaka Onishi [1967] Director [Japanese]; Caerie Sanders [1979] Director [South African/British]; Nobuyuki Tabata [1968] Director [Japanese]; Katherine White [1973] Director

Playfootball Ltd
Incorporated: 25 January 2005 *Employees:* 149
Net Worth Deficit: £14,351,931 *Total Assets:* £11,195,334
Registered Office: Roko Health Club, Wilford Lane, West Bridgford, Nottingham, NG2 7RN
Activities: Operation of sports facilities
Parent: The Sports & Leisure Group Ltd
Officers: Nigel Raymond Maglione, Secretary; Barry Roy Hunter [1962] Director; Nigel Raymond Maglione [1956] Finance Director

Plaza Investments Limited
Incorporated: 12 March 2002 *Employees:* 11
Net Worth: £2,280,817 *Total Assets:* £9,433,733
Registered Office: Bells Amusements, Vickers Point, Anchor Lane, Ingoldmells, Skegness, Lincs, PE25 1LX
Activities: Other amusement and recreation activities n.e.c.
Major Shareholder: Frazer William Bell
Officers: Rachel Scarborough, Secretary; Frazer William Bell [1967] Director; Rachel Elizabeth Scarborough [1987] Director

Plaza on Hyde Park Limited
Incorporated: 3 October 1997 *Employees:* 114
Net Worth: £55,433,648 *Total Assets:* £141,871,712
Registered Office: Corus House, 1 Auckland Park, Milton Keynes, Bucks, MK1 1BU
Activities: Hotels and similar accommodation
Parent: Corus Hotels Limited
Officers: Khurram Mohmand, Secretary; Andrew Khoo [1972] Director [Australian]; Yet King Loy [1946] Director [Canadian]; Khurram Mohmand [1972] Director/Accountant

Plusnet PLC
Incorporated: 15 November 1996 *Employees:* 1,615
Net Worth: £107,346,000 *Total Assets:* £192,660,992
Registered Office: The Balance, 2 Pinfold Street, Sheffield, S1 2GU
Activities: Other information technology service activities
Parent: British Telecommunications PLC
Officers: Marc David Allera [1972] Director/BT Executive; Andrew John Baker [1972] Director; Stephen Christopher Harris [1970] Director/Accountant; Paula Smith [1973] Director/Chartered Accountant

Plymouth Grove Residential LLP
Incorporated: 1 October 2007
Net Worth Deficit: £23,586,664 *Total Assets:* £56,539,280
Registered Office: Landmark House, Station Road, Cheadle Hulme, Cheadle, Cheshire, SK8 7BS
Officers: Julie Anne Everton [1968] Member; Richard Albert Everton [1952] Member; Charles Everton [1988] LLP Member

PMC Fluidpower Group Limited
Incorporated: 19 April 2005 *Employees:* 9
Previous: PMC Fluidpower Limited
Net Worth: £1,482,560 *Total Assets:* £11,535,557
Registered Office: Bollin House, Riverside Business Park, Wilmslow, Cheshire, SK9 1DP
Activities: Activities of other holding companies n.e.c.
Parent: Fluidpower MIP Limited
Officers: Jon Burke, Secretary/Financial Manager; Bryce Rowan Brooks [1965] Director; Russell Cash [1966] Director

PMC Fluidpower Limited
Incorporated: 1 February 1968 *Employees:* 70
Previous: Primary Fluid Power Limited
Net Worth: £7,778,978 *Total Assets:* £23,229,962
Registered Office: Bollin House, Riverside Business Park, Wilmslow, Cheshire, SK9 1DP
Activities: Manufacture of fluid power equipment
Parent: PMC Fluidpower Limited
Officers: Jon Burke, Secretary/Financial Manager; Bryce Rowan Brooks [1965] Director; Anthony Browne [1958] Director; Jon Burke [1972] Director; Russell Cash [1966] Director; Paul Andrew McGrady [1970] Director

Robert Pochin Limited
Incorporated: 6 February 1922 *Employees:* 110
Net Worth: £5,799,164 *Total Assets:* £12,932,083
Registered Office: Pochin House, 2 Murrayfield Road, Leicester, LE3 1UW
Activities: Wholesale of hardware, plumbing and heating equipment and supplies
Major Shareholder: David Roy Pochin
Officers: Glynn Barrington, Secretary; Glynn Barrington [1959] Finance Director; Simon Froggatt [1965] Director; David Roy Pochin [1958] Director; Stuart Press [1963] Director

Pointeuro V Limited
Incorporated: 24 November 1999
Net Worth: £7,285,000 *Total Assets:* £156,810,000
Registered Office: Haylock House, Kettering Parkway, Kettering, Northants, NN15 6EY
Activities: Non-trading company
Parent: Wyndham Holdings
Officers: Andrew Clarke [1976] Senior Director Finance; Andrew Liggins [1962] Director/Accountant

Pointtravel Co. Ltd
Incorporated: 10 April 2002
Net Worth: £1,872,000 *Total Assets:* £260,576,992
Registered Office: Haylock House, Kettering Parkway, Kettering, Northants, NN15 6EY
Activities: Non-trading company
Parent: Wyndham Holdings
Officers: Andrew Clarke [1976] Senior Director Finance

Polar Technology Management Group Limited
Incorporated: 25 November 2011 *Employees:* 190
Net Worth: £1,314,958 *Total Assets:* £20,109,220
Registered Office: Penrose House, 67 Hightown Road, Banbury, Oxon, OX16 9BE
Activities: Activities of other holding companies n.e.c.
Shareholders: Scott Silas John Roberts; Michael James Dewhirst
Officers: Michael James Dewhirst [1972] Director; Scott Silas John Roberts [1966] Director

Policyfast Limited
Incorporated: 30 September 2005 *Employees:* 67
Net Worth: £2,012,283 *Total Assets:* £11,766,191
Registered Office: Unit 5 Vantage Park, Washingley Road, Huntingdon, Cambs, PE29 6SR
Activities: Activities of insurance agents and brokers
Parent: C I S G Ltd
Officers: Georgina Elizabeth Bourner, Secretary; Carl Anthony Ashton [1980] Risk and Compliance Director; Cheryl Dawn Astley [1962] Director/Chief Technology Officer; Robert Michael Darling [1963] Managing Director; Sarah Darling [1969] Group Sales and Marketing Director; Edward George FitzGenerald Hannan [1978] Director/Chief Financial Officer; Stephen Guy Parker [1965] Managing Director

Pollard Boxes Limited
Incorporated: 19 September 1919 *Employees:* 313
Net Worth: £5,843,000 *Total Assets:* £11,792,000
Registered Office: Feldspar Close, Enderby, Leicester, LE19 4SD
Activities: Other manufacturing n.e.c.
Parent: Leicester Fancy Box Company Limited
Officers: Catherine Mary Pollard, Secretary; Peter Charles Conner [1956] Director; Julie Ann Jarvis [1968] Director; Catherine Mary Pollard [1943] Director; Mark William Pollard [1965] Director; Michael Richard Stacey [1982] Director/Accountant

Polyco (Group) Limited
Incorporated: 5 October 2012
Net Worth: £14,609,000 *Total Assets:* £25,086,000
Registered Office: Polyco Healthline, South Fen Road, Bourne, Lincs, PE10 0DN
Activities: Other manufacturing n.e.c.
Officers: Neil Antony Wilson, Secretary; David Greenwood [1955] Director; Jason Prichard [1969] Director; Neil Antony Wilson [1976] Director/Chief Financial Officer

Polyco Healthline Limited
Incorporated: 8 January 2016 *Employees:* 274
Net Worth Deficit: £12,209,000 *Total Assets:* £99,279,000
Registered Office: Polyco Healthline, South Fen Road, Bourne, Lincs, PE10 0DN
Activities: Other manufacturing n.e.c.
Officers: Neil Wilson, Secretary; Leslie Miles Blustin [1951] Director; David Greenwood [1955] Director; Lesley Jayne Lindberg [1966] Director; Gregory James Murray [1949] Director; Barry Peter Prichard [1943] Director; Jason Prichard [1969] Director; Scott Michael Prichard [1971] Director; Neil Antony Wilson [1976] Director

Polydist (UK) Limited
Incorporated: 19 November 1992 *Employees:* 23
Previous: Resin Trade Limited
Net Worth: £5,383,000 *Total Assets:* £28,948,000
Registered Office: 7 Granary Wharf, The Old Granary, Wetmore Road, Burton on Trent, Staffs, DE14 1DU
Activities: Wholesale of chemical products
Parent: Polydist Europe Holdings Limited
Officers: Maria Michelle Smith, Secretary; Said Al Naqeeb [1955] Director/Businessman [Kuwaiti]; Tareq Al Naqeeb [1985] Director/Business Development [Kuwaiti]; Richard Francis George Bradwell [1951] Director/Materials Distribution; Henry Roth [1952] Director [Swiss]; Germene Gerges Yamine [1964] Director [Lebanese]

Polydist Europe Holdings Limited
Incorporated: 2 December 2015 *Employees:* 52
Net Worth: £6,938,000 *Total Assets:* £40,269,000
Registered Office: 7 Granary Wharf Business Park, Wetmore Road, Burton on Trent, Staffs, DE14 1DU
Activities: Wholesale of chemical products
Major Shareholder: Said Al Naqeeb
Officers: Maria Smith, Secretary; Said Al Naqeeb [1955] Director [Kuwaiti]; Tareq Al Naqeeb [1985] Director [Kuwaiti]; Richard Francis George Bradwell [1951] Director; Henry Frederick Roth [1952] Director [Swiss]; Germene Gerges Yamine [1964] Director [Lebanese]

Polynt Composites UK Limited
Incorporated: 25 July 1938 *Employees:* 27
Net Worth: £8,073,000 *Total Assets:* £19,497,000
Registered Office: Laporte Road, Stallingborough, Grimsby, N E Lincs, DN41 8DR
Activities: Manufacture of plastics in primary forms
Officers: David Peter Betti [1958] Director/Chief Financial Officer [American]; Jeffrey Humberstone [1965] Director/General Manager

Polypearl Management Ltd
Incorporated: 4 September 2015
Net Worth: £5,052,995 *Total Assets:* £15,079,195
Registered Office: 54 Oswald Road, Scunthorpe, N Lincs, DN15 7PQ
Activities: Activities of head offices
Shareholder: Ian Rodney Tebb
Officers: Hilary Margaret Tebb, Secretary; Marie Louise Robinson [1973] Director/Finance Manager; Andrew Graham Tebb [1975] Operations Director; Ian Rodney Tebb [1947] Director; Michelle Claire Lorraine Wilson [1981] Director/Office Manager

Polypipe Group PLC
Incorporated: 19 January 2007
Net Worth: £302,000,000 *Total Assets:* £602,800,000
Registered Office: Broomhouse Lane, Edlington, Doncaster, S Yorks, DN12 1ES
Activities: Activities of production holding companies
Officers: Emma Versluys, Secretary; Paul David Dean [1961] Director; Mark William Hammond [1968] Director/Fund Manager; Louise Jane Hardy [1966] Director; Paul Anthony James [1967] Director/Chief Financial Officer; Sheikh Mansurah Tal-At Mannings [1963] Director/Lawyer; Ronald John Edward Marsh [1950] Director; Martin Keith Payne [1965] Director/Chief Executive Officer; Glen Brian Sabin [1958] Director/Chief Operating Officer

Polypipe Limited
Incorporated: 28 February 1973 *Employees:* 2,747
Net Worth: £257,400,000 *Total Assets:* £537,100,032
Registered Office: Broomhouse Lane, Edlington, Doncaster, S Yorks, DN12 1ES
Activities: Manufacture of plastics in primary forms
Parent: Pipe Holdings PLC
Officers: Emma Gayle Versluys, Secretary; Paul Anthony James [1967] Director/Chief Financial Officer; Martin Keith Payne [1965] Director; Glen Brian Sabin [1958] Director/Chief Operating Officer

Polytech International Limited
Incorporated: 26 February 1996 *Employees:* 22
Net Worth: £6,047,853 *Total Assets:* £11,421,716
Registered Office: 7 St Petersgate, Stockport, Cheshire, SK1 1EB
Activities: Manufacture of synthetic rubber in primary forms
Officers: David Alan Bell [1977] Director/Commercial; Paul Alexander Crellin [1971] Operations Director; Christopher Simon Nicholls [1955] Director; Karen Wells [1973] Director/Sales

Ponsford Investments Limited
Incorporated: 1 August 2016
Net Worth: £10,070,939 *Total Assets:* £12,502,140
Registered Office: 577-609 London Road, Sheffield, S2 4HS
Activities: Other letting and operating of own or leased real estate
Major Shareholder: Adrian William Ponsford
Officers: Adrian William Ponsford [1939] Director; Alan Ponsford [1943] Director; Robert Angus Ponsford [1971] Director

H. Ponsford Limited
Incorporated: 30 September 1936
Net Worth: £9,986,646 *Total Assets:* £13,278,010
Registered Office: 581 London Road, Sheffield, S2 4HS
Activities: Other letting and operating of own or leased real estate
Parent: Ponsford Trading Limited
Officers: Adrian William Ponsford, Secretary; Adrian William Ponsford [1939] Director/Manager; Alan Ponsford [1943] Director; Robert Angus Ponsford [1971] Director of Ponsford Ltd

Ponsford Trading Limited
Incorporated: 1 August 2016 *Employees:* 88
Net Worth: £13,784,084 *Total Assets:* £16,366,892
Registered Office: 577-609 London Road, Sheffield, S2 4HS
Activities: Activities of head offices
Major Shareholder: Adrian William Ponsford
Officers: Adrian William Ponsford [1939] Director; Alan Ponsford [1943] Director; Robert Angus Ponsford [1971] Director

The Pope Francis Catholic Multi Academy Company
Incorporated: 2 July 2014 *Employees:* 198
Net Worth: £12,948,451 *Total Assets:* £16,393,342
Registered Office: Blessed George Napier Catholic School and Sixth Form, Addison Road, Banbury, Oxon, OX16 9DG
Activities: Pre-primary education
Officers: Lorna Buchanan [1968] Director; Paul Joseph Concannon [1959] Director; Edward Fraser Long [1969] Director; Tony O'Donnell [1964] Director; Michael Robarts [1944] Director/Retired; Father Richard Walker [1960] Director/Priest; Rob Walsh [1970] Director; Adrian Waters [1960] Director

Pork Farms Caspian Limited
Incorporated: 26 June 2014 *Employees:* 1,083
Net Worth Deficit: £16,978,000 *Total Assets:* £37,341,000
Registered Office: c/o Pork Farms Limited, Queens Drive, Nottingham, NG2 1LU
Activities: Manufacture of other food products n.e.c.
Parent: Addo Food Group Limited
Officers: Graham Paul Rutter, Secretary; Mark Anthony Hodson [1961] Director; Christopher Peters [1958] Director; Graham Paul Rutter [1954] Director

Pork Farms Limited
Incorporated: 14 November 2006 *Employees:* 1,432
Net Worth Deficit: £29,694,000 *Total Assets:* £64,845,000
Registered Office: Tottle Bakery, Queens Drive, Nottingham, NG2 1LU
Activities: Manufacture of other food products n.e.c.
Parent: Addo Food Group Limited
Officers: Graham Paul Rutter, Secretary; Mark Anthony Hodson [1961] Director; Christopher Peters [1958] Director; Graham Paul Rutter [1954] Director

Port of Boston Limited
Incorporated: 25 November 1987 *Employees:* 69
Net Worth: £12,664,000 *Total Assets:* £20,960,000
Registered Office: The Dock, Boston, Lincs, PE21 6BN
Activities: Cargo handling for water transport activities
Major Shareholder: Mark Alexander Vernon Gatehouse
Officers: David Sydney Martin, Secretary; Mark Alexander Vernon Gatehouse [1949] Director; Andrew Duncan Lawrence [1964] Port Director; David Sydney Martin [1955] Director

Sir John Port's Charity
Incorporated: 20 March 2002 *Employees:* 601
Net Worth: £75,143,536 *Total Assets:* £84,530,720
Registered Office: Bursar's Office, Repton School, Repton, Derby, DE65 6FH
Activities: Pre-primary education
Officers: Carl Peter Bilson, Secretary; Andrew Michael Bock [1964] Director/Chartered Surveyor; Professor Alastair Mitchell Buchan [1955] Director/Physician; Andrew James Churchill [1968] Managing Director; David Nigel Vardon Churton [1949] Director; Ian Richard Davenport [1960] Director/Chief Executive; Dr Katharine Julia Dell [1961] Director/Lecturer; Sir Henry John Michael Every [1947] Director/Chartered Accountant; Timothy James Hannam [1973] Director/Barrister; Anne Elisabeth Hill [1950] Director/Housewife; Roger Anthony Litchfield [1946] Director; Matthew James Charles Needham [1967] Director/Solicitor; Robert John Richard Owen [1940] Director/Banker; Edward Mark Shires [1955] Director/Chartered Accountant; Kathryn Elizabeth Stone [1963] Director/Civil Servant; William Tucker [1945] Director/Retired; Dawn Patricia Ward [1961] Director/Chief Executive; Martin Richard Hugh Wimbush [1943] Director/Retired

Portbond Limited
Incorporated: 9 March 2009 *Employees:* 52
Net Worth: £7,383,547 *Total Assets:* £18,228,068
Registered Office: Sidings House, Sidings Court, Doncaster, S Yorks, DN4 5NU
Activities: Activities of other holding companies n.e.c.
Shareholders: Lisa Mary Pickering; John Robert Hughes
Officers: Charles Arthur Hughes, Secretary; Charles Arthur Hughes [1929] Director; James Charles Hughes [1988] Director; John Robert Hughes [1958] Director

G.E. Porter & Sons Limited
Incorporated: 24 September 1996 *Employees:* 12
Net Worth: £6,375,046 *Total Assets:* £15,574,723
Registered Office: Barn Farm, Lowfields, Navenby, Lincoln, LN5 0LN
Activities: Raising of poultry
Shareholders: Roythornes Trustees Limited; Graham Edward Porter
Officers: Graham Edward Porter, Secretary/Farmer; Graham Edward Porter [1953] Director/Farmer; Kathryn Mary Porter [1959] Director

J.E. Porter Limited
Incorporated: 22 February 1985 *Employees:* 45
Net Worth: £24,632,036 *Total Assets:* £30,817,196
Registered Office: Barn Farm, Lowfields, Navenby, Lincoln, LN5 0LN
Activities: Manufacture of prepared feeds for farm animals
Shareholders: Roythornes Trustees Limited; Graham Edward Porter
Officers: Graham Edward Porter, Secretary; Graham Edward Porter [1953] Director/Farmer; Kathryn Mary Porter [1959] Director

Porterbrook Holdings I Limited
Incorporated: 6 October 2014 *Employees:* 108
Net Worth: £1,119,298,944 *Total Assets:* £3,921,875,968
Registered Office: Ivatt House, 7 The Point, Pinnacle Way, Pride Park, Derby, DE24 8ZS
Activities: Activities of financial services holding companies
Shareholders: Allianz SE; RBS Pension Trustee Limited; HM Government of Alberta
Officers: Chris McClure, Secretary; Andrew Julian Frederick Cox [1967] Director; Pierre Benoist D'Anthenay [1975] Director [French]; Rachel Drew [1976] Director [Irish]; Tim Richard Dugher [1959] Director; Adam James Harbora [1984] Director [Canadian]; Christoph Holzer [1979] Director/Investment Manager [Austrian]; Valeria Rosati [1975] Director/Fund Manager [Italian]; Kevin Benjamin Roseke [1982] Director, Investments [Canadian]; Marissa Ann Szczepaniak [1980] Director/Fund Manager

Porterbrook Holdings II Limited
Incorporated: 6 October 2014
Net Worth: £1,261,911,040 *Total Assets:* £1,262,193,024
Registered Office: Ivatt House, 7 The Point, Pinnacle Way, Pride Park, Derby, DE24 8ZS
Activities: Activities of financial services holding companies
Officers: Christopher Bonnar McClure, Secretary; Peter Timothy Coates [1963] Director; Andrew Julian Frederick Cox [1967] Director; Pierre Benoist D'Anthenay [1975] Director [French]; Rachel Drew [1976] Director [Irish]; Tim Richard Dugher [1959] Director; Mary Alexander Grant [1969] Director; Adam James Harbora [1984] Director [Canadian]; Christoph Holzer [1979] Director/Investment Manager [Austrian]; Christopher Bonnar McClure [1963] Director/General Counsel; Stephen James McGurk [1973] Director/Solicitor; Valeria Rosati [1975] Director/Fund Manager [Italian]; Kevin Benjamin Roseke [1982] Director, Investments [Canadian]; Marissa Ann Szczepaniak [1980] Director/Fund Manager; Philip Michael White [1949] Director

Porterbrook Leasing Asset Company Limited
Incorporated: 14 August 1959
Net Worth: £1,951,216,000 *Total Assets:* £1,951,216,000
Registered Office: Ivatt House, 7 The Point, Pinnacle Way, Pride Park, Derby, DE24 8ZS
Activities: Financial leasing
Parent: Porterbrook Leasing Company Limited
Officers: Christopher Bonnar McClure, Secretary; Peter Timothy Coates [1963] Director; Mary Alexander Grant [1969] Director; Christopher Bonnar McClure [1963] Director/General Counsel; Stephen James McGurk [1973] Director/Solicitor

Porterbrook Leasing Company Limited
Incorporated: 21 March 1994 *Employees:* 37
Net Worth: £279,791,008 *Total Assets:* £3,403,115,008
Registered Office: Ivatt House, 7 The Point, Pinnacle Way, Pride Park, Derby, DE24 8ZS
Activities: Financial intermediation not elsewhere classified
Parent: Porterbrook Leasing Mid Company Limited
Officers: Christopher Bonnar McClure, Secretary; Haydn Turner Abbott [1949] Director; Peter Timothy Coates [1963] Director; Andrew Julian Frederick Cox [1967] Director; Pierre Benoist D'Anthenay [1975] Director [French]; Rachel Drew [1976] Director [Irish]; Tim Richard Dugher [1959] Director; Mary Alexander Grant [1969] Director; Adam James Harbora [1984] Director [Canadian]; Christoph Holzer [1979] Director/Investment Manager [Austrian]; Christopher Bonnar McClure [1963] Director/General Counsel; Stephen James McGurk [1973] Director/Solicitor; Andrew Christopher Pitt [1959] Director; Valeria Rosati [1975] Director/Fund Manager [Italian]; Kevin Benjamin Roseke [1982] Director, Investments [Canadian]; Marissa Ann Szczepaniak [1980] Director/Fund Manager; Philip Michael White [1949] Director

Porterbrook Leasing Mid Company Limited
Incorporated: 3 September 2009
Net Worth: £231,456,992 *Total Assets:* £1,010,468,992
Registered Office: Ivatt House, 7 The Point, Pinnacle Way, Pride Park, Derby, DE24 8ZS
Activities: Financial leasing
Parent: Porterbrook Holdings II Limited
Officers: Christopher Bonnar McClure, Secretary; Peter Timothy Coates [1963] Director; Andrew Julian Frederick Cox [1967] Director; Pierre Benoist D'Anthenay [1975] Director [French]; Rachel Drew [1976] Director [Irish]; Tim Richard Dugher [1959] Director; Mary Alexander Grant [1969] Director; Adam James Harbora [1984] Director [Canadian]; Christoph Holzer [1979] Director/Investment Manager [Austrian]; Christopher Bonnar McClure [1963] Director/General Counsel; Stephen James McGurk [1973] Director/Solicitor; Valeria Rosati [1975] Director/Fund Manager [Italian]; Kevin Benjamin Roseke [1982] Director, Investments [Canadian]; Marissa Ann Szczepaniak [1980] Director/Fund Manager; Philip Michael White [1949] Director

Porterbrook Maintenance Limited
Incorporated: 28 October 1998 *Employees:* 71
Net Worth: £45,823,000 *Total Assets:* £55,504,000
Registered Office: Ivatt House, 7 The Point, Pinnacle Way, Pride Park, Derby, DE24 8ZS
Activities: Passenger rail transport, interurban
Parent: Porterbrook Leasing Company Limited
Officers: Christopher Bonnar McClure, Secretary; Peter Timothy Coates [1963] Director; Mary Alexander Grant [1969] Director; Christopher Bonnar McClure [1963] Director/General Counsel; Stephen James McGurk [1973] Director/Solicitor

Porterbrook March Leasing (4) Limited
Incorporated: 30 January 1992
Net Worth Deficit: £10,891,000 *Total Assets:* £125,617,000
Registered Office: Ivatt House, 7 The Point, Pinnacle Way, Pride Park, Derby, DE24 8ZS
Activities: Financial leasing
Parent: Porterbrook Leasing Company Limited
Officers: Christopher Bonnar McClure, Secretary; Peter Timothy Coates [1963] Director; Mary Alexander Grant [1969] Director; Christopher Bonnar McClure [1963] Director/General Counsel; Stephen James McGurk [1973] Director/Solicitor

Portugal Finco Limited
Incorporated: 21 December 2012
Net Worth: £33,403,000 *Total Assets:* £81,490,000
Registered Office: Holland Place, Wardentree Park, Pinchbeck, Spalding, Lincs, PE11 3ZN
Activities: Activities of other holding companies n.e.c.
Officers: Jonathan Pallas [1962] Director; Gary Edward Rehwinkel [1961] Director [American]

Portwest Clothing Limited
Incorporated: 11 April 1988 *Employees:* 211
Net Worth: £11,979,834 *Total Assets:* £18,353,524
Registered Office: Unit 5 Fields End Business Park, Thurnscoe, Rotherham, S Yorks, S63 0JF
Activities: Agents involved in the sale of textiles, clothing, fur, footwear and leather goods
Officers: Helen Maria Noud, Secretary; Cathal Hughes [1951] Textile Director [Irish]; Harry Hughes [1953] Director [Irish]; Owen Jarlath Hughes [1955] Director [Irish]; Richard Jones [1980] Sales Director

Porvair Filtration Group Limited
Incorporated: 28 September 1966 *Employees:* 315
Net Worth: £23,126,000 *Total Assets:* £36,905,000
Registered Office: 7 Regis Place, Bergen Way, King's Lynn, Norfolk, PE30 2JN
Activities: Manufacture of other plastic products
Parent: Porvair Filtration Limited
Officers: Dr Simon Jon Rodgers, Secretary; Ian Stuart Boxall [1963] Technical Director; Thomas Mark Liddell [1975] Sales Director; David Malcolm Mellor [1979] Finance Director; Ian Stirling [1953] Director; Benjamin Denys William Stocks [1962] Director; Christopher Patric Tyler [1962] Finance Director; Stuart Wells [1950] Operations Director

Porvair Filtration Limited
Incorporated: 18 October 1995
Net Worth: £5,291,000 *Total Assets:* £23,997,000
Registered Office: 7 Regis Place, Bergen Way, King's Lynn, Norfolk, PE30 2JN
Activities: Non-trading company
Parent: Porvair PLC
Officers: Dr Simon Jon Rodgers, Secretary; Benjamin Denys William Stocks [1962] Director; Christopher Patric Tyler [1962] Finance Director

Porvair PLC
Incorporated: 3 September 1982 *Employees:* 819
Net Worth: £74,869,000 *Total Assets:* £127,947,000
Registered Office: 7 Regis Place, Bergen Way, Kings Lynn, Norfolk, PE30 2JN
Activities: Manufacture of basic pharmaceutical products
Officers: Christopher Patric Tyler, Finance Director; Paul David Dean [1961] Director; Sarah Jean Martin [1965] Director [Irish]; John Edward Nicholas [1956] Director; Benjamin Denys William Stocks [1962] Director; Christopher Patric Tyler [1962] Finance Director

Mark H Poskitt Limited
Incorporated: 30 August 1956 *Employees:* 321
Net Worth: £17,478,374 *Total Assets:* £25,512,144
Registered Office: The Firs, Kellington, Goole, York, DN14 0SB
Activities: Mixed farming
Shareholders: Stephen Guy Poskitt; Sonia Romayne Poskitt
Officers: Stephen Guy Poskitt, Secretary; Judith Clare Poskitt [1963] Director/Account Manager; Sonia Romayne Poskitt [1933] Director/Farmer; Stephen Guy Poskitt [1963] Director/Farmer

Poste Holdings Limited
Incorporated: 15 July 1994 *Employees:* 174
Net Worth: £7,949,329 *Total Assets:* £19,559,456
Registered Office: The George Hotel, Stamford, Lincs, PE9 2LB
Activities: Hotels and similar accommodation
Shareholders: Lawrence Oliver Hoskins; I.P.M. Trustees Limited
Officers: David Stephen Landry, Finance Director; Lawrence Oliver Hoskins [1940] Director/Hotelier

Poste Hotels Limited
Incorporated: 7 November 1968 *Employees:* 174
Net Worth: £17,002,508 *Total Assets:* £21,733,034
Registered Office: The George Hotel, Stamford, Lincs, PE9 2LB
Activities: Hotels and similar accommodation
Shareholders: Lawrence Oliver Hoskins; Poste Holdings Limited
Officers: David Stephen Landry, Secretary; Emily Jane Casey [1972] Director/Teacher; Andrea Aline Nelia Hoskins [1952] Director/Hotelier; Andrew Martin Hoskins [1972] Director/Hotelier; Lawrence Oliver Hoskins [1940] Director/Hotelier; Mark Oliver Hoskins [1972] Director/Hotelier; David Stephen Landry [1949] Director/Finance; Ivo Vannocci [1938] Director/Hotelier [Italian]

Potomac Capital Limited
Incorporated: 4 February 2005 *Employees:* 1
Net Worth: £9,701,799 *Total Assets:* £9,764,819
Registered Office: c/o Booth Ainsworth LLP, Alpha House, 4 Greek Street, Stockport, Cheshire, SK3 8AB
Activities: Development of building projects
Parent: New Potomac Limited
Officers: Steven Alfred Hurrell, Secretary; Warren Hill McInteer [1959] Director

Potter Clarkson LLP
Incorporated: 15 September 2005 *Employees:* 151
Net Worth: £6,508,000 *Total Assets:* £11,006,000
Registered Office: The Belgrave Centre, Talbot Street, Nottingham, NG1 5GG
Officers: Colin John Baker [1963] Member; Richard Simon Bassett [1957] Member; Mohammed Saiful Khan [1971] Member; Doctor Stephanie Joan Pilkington [1966] Member; Stephen Edward Smith [1968] Member; Raymond Julian Charig [1963] LLP Member; David Julian Clark [1979] LLP Member; Dr Charlotte Waveney Crowhurst [1970] LLP Member; Ian Mark Dee [1963] LLP Member; Dr Mark Paul Didmon [1975] LLP Member; Sanjay Kapur [1966] LLP Member; Ben James Lincoln [1979] LLP Member; Caroline Marshall [1976] LLP Member; Nicholas McDonald [1977] LLP Member; Stephen Phillip McNeeney [1965] LLP Member; Darren Andrew Mitchell [1972] LLP Member; John Brendan Peacock [1963] LLP Member; Timothy John Powell [1963] LLP Member; Doctor Robert Ian Pugh [1975] LLP Member; Richard Andrew Roberts [1979] LLP Member; Ian Edward Stevens [1964] LLP Member; Philip John Duval Thomas [1968] LLP Member; Jane Helen Wainwright [1978] LLP Member; Dr Andrew John Wright [1973] LLP Member

Potter's Leisure Ltd.
Incorporated: 3 May 1948 *Employees:* 558
Net Worth: £17,067,396 *Total Assets:* £32,456,296
Registered Office: Heblethwaites, 2 Westbrook Court, Sharrow Vale Road, Sheffield, S11 8YZ
Activities: Other amusement and recreation activities n.e.c.
Officers: John Hector Potter [1969] Director; Judith Mary Potter [1944] Holiday Centre Director; Sarah Jane Potter [1966] Director/Manager

Potters-Ballotini Limited
Incorporated: 14 October 1957 *Employees:* 45
Net Worth Deficit: £5,034,000 *Total Assets:* £11,989,000
Registered Office: Borough Flint Glassworks, Pontefract Road, Barnsley, S Yorks, S71 1HJ
Activities: Shaping and processing of flat glass
Parent: Potters International Holdings S.A.R.L
Officers: Joseph Steven Koscinski [1965] Director/General Counsel [American]; Kelly Michael O'Brien [1969] Director/Business Executive [American]

Povoas Packaging Limited
Incorporated: 1 March 1954 *Employees:* 120
Net Worth: £11,906,000 *Total Assets:* £17,198,000
Registered Office: Stoke Albany Road, Desborough, Kettering, Northants, NN14 2SR
Activities: Manufacture of plastic packing goods
Shareholder: Simon John Povoas
Officers: Jonathan Mark Kendall, Secretary; Margaret Roberta Brewin [1946] Director/Retired Schoolteacher; Adam James Kendall [1971] Director/Solicitor; Jonathan Mark Kendall [1970] Director/Accountant; Simon John Povoas [1966] Managing Director

Powergen International Limited
Incorporated: 17 April 1998
Net Worth: £796,187,008 *Total Assets:* £805,467,008
Registered Office: Westwood Way, Westwood Business Park, Coventry, Warwicks, CV4 8LG
Activities: Activities of other holding companies n.e.c.
Parent: E.On UK PLC
Officers: David Charles Adrian Baumber [1974] Director/Head of Accounting Business Partner Team; Deborah Gandley [1971] Director/Solicitor

Powerscreen International Limited
Incorporated: 7 August 1970
Net Worth: £51,771,000 *Total Assets:* £77,711,000
Registered Office: The Pinnacle, 170 Midsummer Boulevard, Milton Keynes, Bucks, MK9 1FE
Activities: Activities of other holding companies n.e.c.
Parent: New Terex Holdings UK Limited
Officers: Eric I Cohen, Secretary [American]; Eric I Cohen [1958] Director/Lawyer [American]; John Daniel Sheehan [1960] Director/Chief Financial Officer [American]

PPF Limited
Incorporated: 14 April 1997 *Employees:* 757
Net Worth: £4,748,034 *Total Assets:* £17,116,388
Registered Office: Meriden Hall, Main Road, Meriden, Coventry, Warwicks, CV7 7PT
Activities: Temporary employment agency activities
Officers: Nigel John Dudley, Secretary; Steve Davis [1969] Finance Director; George Mark Howitt [1975] Development Director; Peter James Howitt [1979] Southern Operations Director; Stephen Carlo Mogano [1959] Director; Stephen Andrew Risbridger [1963] IT Director; Andrew John Rodgers [1975] Operations Director; Kent Steven Thompson [1964] Director; Andrew Waldron [1968] Managing Director; Stephen William West [1964] Director

PPL PRS Limited
Incorporated: 14 September 2016 *Employees:* 25
Net Worth: £16,686 *Total Assets:* £9,972,214
Registered Office: Mercury Place, St George Street, Leicester, LE1 1QG
Activities: Other business support service activities n.e.c.
Shareholders: Phonographic Performance Limited; PRS for Music Limited
Officers: Joanne Winfield, Secretary; Robert John Ashcroft [1956] Director; Christian Barton [1977] Finance Director; Paul Charles Clements [1971] Commercial Director; Antje Christine Geissmar [1960] Operations Director [German]; Peter John Leathem [1965] Director; Roberto Bruno Neri [1973] Managing Director

Practical Action
Incorporated: 21 February 1966 *Employees:* 558
Net Worth: £11,578,000 *Total Assets:* £20,201,000
Registered Office: The Robbins Building, 25 Albert Street, Rugby, Warwicks, CV21 2SD
Activities: Other social work activities without accommodation n.e.c.
Officers: John Duncan Lockett, Secretary; Roger Clarke [1948] Director; Elwaleed Mohamed Elbashir Elobeid [1962] Director/Development and Humanitarian Assistance Advisor [Sudanese]; Valerie Celia Jolliffe [1954] Director/Retired; Brenda Ann Lipson [1954] Director/Freelance Consultant; Helena Molyneux [1948] Director/Retired; Richard Nigel Saxby-Soffe [1949] Director/Retired; Professor James Rob Smith [1973] Director/Academic; Joanne Smith [1964] Director/Fundraising Consultant; Ian Andrew Thornton [1985] Director/Strategy Consultant; Helena Wayth [1970] Managing Director Marketing Consultancy [Australian]; Graham David Young [1952] Director/Management Consultant

Praesepe Holdings Limited
Incorporated: 3 November 2011 *Employees:* 58
Net Worth: £38,586,000 *Total Assets:* £110,447,000
Registered Office: Seebeck House, 1a Seebeck Place, Knowlhill, Milton Keynes, Bucks, MK5 8FR
Activities: Activities of other holding companies n.e.c.
Parent: Merkur Casino UK Limited
Officers: Stefan Bruns [1971] Director/Chief Executive Officer [German]; Borris Lungen [1962] Director/Chief Financial Officer [German]

Praesepe Limited
Incorporated: 16 March 2006 *Employees:* 3
Net Worth: £16,501,000 *Total Assets:* £16,501,000
Registered Office: Seebeck House, 1a Seebeck Place, Knowhill, Milton Keynes, Bucks, MK5 8FR
Activities: Financial intermediation not elsewhere classified
Parent: Praesepe Holdings Limited
Officers: Stefan Bruns [1971] Director/Chief Executive Officer [German]; Borris Lungen [1962] Director/Chief Financial Officer [German]

George Pragnell Limited
Incorporated: 6 June 1956 *Employees:* 89
Net Worth: £23,528,214 *Total Assets:* £31,849,356
Registered Office: 5 & 6 Wood Street, Stratford upon Avon, Warwicks, CV37 6JA
Activities: Retail sale of watches and jewellery in specialised stores
Shareholders: Charles Edward Pragnell; Jeremy Martin Pragnell
Officers: Charles Edward Pragnell, Secretary; Sarah Anne Georgina Margaret Crookenden [1956] Director/Solicitor; Charles Edward Pragnell [1978] Director; Jeremy Martin Pragnell [1949] Director; Michael Patrick Pragnell [1946] Director

Prahi (2017) Limited
Incorporated: 25 May 2017
Net Worth: £197,502 *Total Assets:* £9,389,984
Registered Office: 75-129 Carlisle Street, Sheffield, S4 7LJ
Activities: Activities of other holding companies n.e.c.
Officers: Ashfaq Ahmed [1973] Director

Prahi Hotel Collection Limited
Incorporated: 13 August 2014 *Employees:* 187
Previous: Hotel Collection Hotel No. 7 Limited
Net Worth: £1,168,000 *Total Assets:* £10,819,000
Registered Office: 75-129 Carlisle Street, Sheffield, S4 7LJ
Activities: Hotels and similar accommodation
Officers: Ashfaq Ahmed [1973] Director

Preci-Spark Limited
Incorporated: 8 June 1960 *Employees:* 461
Net Worth: £14,732,090 *Total Assets:* £21,671,686
Registered Office: Engineering Factory, Chapel Street, Syston, Leicester, LE7 1HN
Activities: Other service activities n.e.c.
Shareholder: Dorothy Lilian Jones
Officers: Dorothy Lilian Jones, Secretary; David William Jones [1953] Director/Engineer; Dorothy Lilian Jones [1926] Director/Secretary; Godfrey Denton Jones [1953] Director/Engineer; Matthew Henry Jones [1977] Director; Vincent Heath Jones [1948] Director/Engineer; William Heath Jones [1974] Director

Precision Engineered Limited
Incorporated: 1 March 2004
Net Worth: £40,786,000 *Total Assets:* £40,786,000
Registered Office: Samuel Ryder House, Barling Way, Eliot Park, Nuneaton, Warwicks, CV10 7RH
Activities: Non-trading company
Parent: Holland & Barrett BV
Officers: Lisa Mary Garley-Evans, Secretary; Lisa Mary Garley-Evans [1968] Director/Solicitor; Christian Keen [1964] Director/Chief Financial Officer

Premdor Crosby Limited
Incorporated: 19 July 1996 *Employees:* 524
Net Worth: £97,534,000 *Total Assets:* £155,546,000
Registered Office: Birthwaite Business Park, Darton, Barnsley, S Yorks, S75 5JS
Activities: Manufacture of other products of wood; manufacture of articles of cork, straw and plaiting materials
Parent: Premdor U.K. Holdings Limited
Officers: Rose Murphy, Secretary/Lawyer [American]; Clare Doyle [1965] Managing Director [American]; Rose Murphy [1957] Director/Lawyer [American]

Premdor U.K. Holdings Limited
Incorporated: 17 July 1996
Net Worth: £20,593,422 *Total Assets:* £174,350,224
Registered Office: Premdor Crosby Limited, Birthwaite Business Park, Darton, Barnsley, S Yorks, S75 5JS
Activities: Activities of head offices
Parent: Masonite International Corporation
Officers: Rose Murphy, Secretary/Lawyer [American]; Clare Doyle [1965] Managing Director [American]; Rose Murphy [1957] Director/Lawyer [American]

The Premier Group (Coventry) Limited
Incorporated: 11 May 2004 *Employees:* 190
Net Worth: £7,704,517 *Total Assets:* £15,230,954
Registered Office: Brindley Road North, Bayton Road Industrial Estate, Exhall, Coventry, Warwicks, CV7 9EP
Activities: Activities of production holding companies
Major Shareholder: Denis Patrick Meagher
Officers: John Derek Jackson, Secretary; Adam Meagher [1983] Director; Denis Patrick Meagher [1958] Director/Engineer; Nichola Meagher [1985] Director

Premier Nursing Homes Limited
Incorporated: 4 December 1989 *Employees:* 287
Net Worth: £8,609,920 *Total Assets:* £9,924,491
Registered Office: 91-97 Saltergate, Chesterfield, Derbys, S40 1LA
Activities: Residential care activities for the elderly and disabled
Parent: Hill Care Holdings Limited
Officers: Alexandra Hill, Secretary; John Andrew Hill [1965] Director; Wendy Jane Waddicor [1964] Director

Premier Sheet Metal (Coventry) Limited
Incorporated: 19 April 1994 *Employees:* 151
Net Worth: £6,517,990 *Total Assets:* £12,697,002
Registered Office: Brindley Road North, Bayton Road Industrial Estate, Exhall, Coventry, Warwicks, CV7 9EP
Activities: Manufacture of bodies (coachwork) for motor vehicles (except caravans)
Parent: The Premier Group (Coventry) Limited
Officers: John Derek Jackson, Secretary/Accountant; Gerard William Halton [1961] Director; Adam Meagher [1983] Director; Denis Patrick Meagher [1958] Director/Engineer; Nichola Meagher [1985] Director

Premier Textiles Limited
Incorporated: 14 December 1981 *Employees:* 28
Net Worth: £10,343,323 *Total Assets:* £11,583,780
Registered Office: Green Lane Industrial Estate, Green Lane, Stockport, Cheshire, SK4 2JR
Activities: Wholesale of textiles
Major Shareholder: Ashok Abraham Kallumpram
Officers: Anna Eapen Kallumpram, Secretary; Anna Eapen Kallumpram [1961] Director/Lawyer; Ashok Abraham Kallumpram [1958] Director/Businessman; Nicholas Peter Smith [1971] Director

Premierfirst Vehicle Rental EMEA Holdings Limited
Incorporated: 2 October 2003
Net Worth: £124,644,000 *Total Assets:* £126,147,000
Registered Office: James House, 55 Welford Road, Leicester, LE2 7AR
Activities: Activities of head offices
Parent: Europcar UK Limited
Officers: Luc Etienne Peligry [1964] Director/Chief Financial Officer [French]; Gary Neil Smith [1970] Director

Premierfirst Vehicle Rental Franchising Limited
Incorporated: 8 September 1938 *Employees:* 2
Net Worth: £11,192,000 *Total Assets:* £11,923,000
Registered Office: James House, 55 Welford Road, Leicester, LE2 7AR
Activities: Renting and leasing of cars and light motor vehicles
Parent: Premierfirst Vehicle Rental Holdings Limited
Officers: Luc Etienne Peligry [1964] Director/Chief Financial Officer [French]; Gary Neil Smith [1970] Director

Premierfirst Vehicle Rental Holdings Limited
Incorporated: 8 September 1967
Net Worth: £146,160,000 *Total Assets:* £172,844,992
Registered Office: James House, 55 Welford Road, Leicester, LE2 7AR
Activities: Activities of head offices
Parent: Premierfirst Vehicle Rental EMEA Holdings Limited
Officers: Luc Etienne Peligry [1964] Director/Chief Financial Officer [French]; Gary Neil Smith [1970] Director

Premium Plan Limited
Incorporated: 24 October 2006 *Employees:* 30
Net Worth: £880,756 *Total Assets:* £13,477,114
Registered Office: P O Box 9562, Kempton House, Kempton Way, Grantham, Lincs, NG31 0EA
Activities: Credit granting by non-deposit taking finance houses and other specialist consumer credit grantors
Parent: Totemic (2014) Holdings Limited
Officers: Halina Briggs, Secretary; Ryan Anthony Clarke [1984] Finance Director; Simon Oliver Greiner [1961] Director; Jill Sparks [1980] Director; Dale Stringer [1972] Director

Premium Restaurants Limited
Incorporated: 10 May 2006 *Employees:* 2,138
Net Worth: £6,565,351 *Total Assets:* £21,480,392
Registered Office: 6 Carlisle Street, Goole, E Yorks, DN14 5BX
Activities: Unlicenced restaurants and cafes
Shareholders: Premium Foods Limited; McDonald's Restaurants Limited
Officers: Christiane Singh, Secretary [Belgian]; Harriet Jane Kathleen Hounsell [1970] Director/Chief People Officer; John Park [1976] Director/Chartered Accountant; Christiane Singh [1962] Director [Belgian]; Pritpal Grewal Singh [1961] Director

Premonition Analytics Limited
Incorporated: 24 February 2015
Net Worth: £21,600,000 *Total Assets:* £21,600,000
Registered Office: 2 Low Road, Congham, King's Lynn, Norfolk, PE32 1AE
Activities: Other information service activities n.e.c.
Shareholders: Stratagem Ops Limited; Setasi Holdings Limited
Officers: Guy Kurlandski [1968] Director; Roberto Marco Francesco Pola [1955] Director/Chartered Accountant; Toby William Unwin [1973] Director

Pressure Technologies PLC
Incorporated: 2 March 2007 *Employees:* 239
Net Worth: £33,803,000 *Total Assets:* £63,762,000
Registered Office: Unit 6b Newton Business Centre, Newton Chambers Road, Chapeltown, Sheffield, S35 2PH
Activities: Activities of head offices
Officers: Joanna Claire Allen, Secretary; Joanna Claire Allen [1976] Director/Chartered Accountant; Neil Andrew MacDonald [1956] Director; Brian Morley Newman [1947] Director; Christopher Lee Walters [1969] Director/Chief Executive; Alan James Stark Wilson [1957] Director

Pricecheck Toiletries Limited
Incorporated: 22 March 1978 *Employees:* 123
Net Worth: £12,630,976 *Total Assets:* £23,155,352
Registered Office: Pricecheck Toiletries Ltd, Old Colliery Way, Beighton, Sheffield, S20 1DJ
Activities: Wholesale of perfume and cosmetics
Shareholders: Mark Andrew Lythe; Deborah Harrison
Officers: Mark Andrew Lythe, Secretary; Barry John Corker [1972] Director; Deborah Harrison [1970] Sales Director; Jonathan Edward Harrison [1963] Director; Amanda Jane Lythe [1965] Director; Mark Andrew Lythe [1967] Director; Lee Philip Walker [1975] Finance Director

Pride Care Homes Peterborough Limited
Incorporated: 2 March 2016 *Employees:* 49
Net Worth: £4,063,726 *Total Assets:* £10,553,846
Registered Office: 236 Eastfield Road, Peterborough, PE1 4BD
Activities: Residential care activities for the elderly and disabled
Officers: Ajay Majara [1979] Director; Amar Majara [1977] Director; Baldev Singh Majara [1947] Director; Shamshad Bano Majara [1945] Director

Primaflow Limited
Incorporated: 12 November 1991 *Employees:* 92
Net Worth: £20,504,000 *Total Assets:* £131,792,000
Registered Office: Lodge Way House, Lodge Way, Harlestone Road, Northampton, NN5 7UG
Activities: Wholesale of hardware, plumbing and heating equipment and supplies
Parent: Travis Perkins PLC
Officers: David Michael Evans [1974] Director; Jed Kenrick [1965] Director [Nigerian]; Alan Richard Williams [1969] Director/Accountant

Prime Life Limited
Incorporated: 14 January 1993 *Employees:* 1,894
Net Worth: £62,703,000 *Total Assets:* £138,126,000
Registered Office: Caenarvon House, 121 Knighton Church Road, Leicester, LE2 3JN
Activities: Other human health activities
Parent: DMWSL 532 Ltd
Officers: Janet Elizabeth Hairsine, Secretary; Benedicto Dawson [1958] Director of Adult Services; Ruth Hack [1967] Director of Elderly Services; Janet Elizabeth Hairsine [1977] Director of Finance Development; Peter Alexander Van Herrewege [1953] Director/Chairman; Simon James Van Herrewege [1980] Director; James Wood [1969] Managing Director

Primesite UK Limited
Incorporated: 30 October 1987 *Employees:* 4
Net Worth: £2,675,901 *Total Assets:* £9,607,294
Registered Office: Omega Court, 360 Cemetery Road, Sheffield, S11 8FT
Activities: Development of building projects
Parent: Hinchliffe Group Limited
Officers: Michael John Nelson, Secretary/Legal Advisor; David Scott Hinchliffe [1975] Director; David Ernest Hinchliffe [1947] Director

Prince Hotels Ltd
Incorporated: 28 November 1994 *Employees:* 174
Net Worth: £9,374,603 *Total Assets:* £12,807,788
Registered Office: Birmingham Road, Allesley, Coventry, Warwicks, CV5 9BA
Activities: Hotels and similar accommodation
Major Shareholder: Prince Minaz Nasser
Officers: Prince Minaz Nasser [1959] Director/Hotel Owner

Princebuild Holdings Limited
Incorporated: 27 November 1985 *Employees:* 201
Net Worth: £12,185,303 *Total Assets:* £23,969,410
Registered Office: Empson Road, Peterborough, Cambs, PE1 5UP
Activities: Development of building projects
Officers: Stuart Stanley Pudney, Secretary; Dale John Asplin [1970] Director/Contracts Manager; Derek John Asplin [1947] Director; Mark Derek Asplin [1966] Director/Contracts Manager; Jonathan Mark Pudney [1969] Director/Contracts Manager; Matthew James Pudney [1972] Director/Contracts Manager; Stuart Stanley Pudney [1944] Director

Princebuild Limited.
Incorporated: 7 October 1971 *Employees:* 196
Net Worth: £7,126,583 *Total Assets:* £21,868,492
Registered Office: Empson Road, Peterborough, Cambs, PE1 5UP
Activities: Development of building projects
Parent: Princebuild Holdings Ltd
Officers: Stuart Stanley Pudney, Secretary; Dale John Asplin [1970] Director; Derek John Asplin [1947] Director; Mark Derek Asplin [1966] Director; Paul Baker [1979] Construction Director; James Manning [1972] Director; Jonathan Mark Pudney [1969] Director; Matthew James Pudney [1972] Director; Stuart Stanley Pudney [1944] Director

Princess International Sales and Service Ltd
Incorporated: 2 December 1964 *Employees:* 74
Net Worth: £7,849,111 *Total Assets:* £43,817,912
Registered Office: 6 Athena Court, Athena Drive, Tachbrook Park, Warwick, CV34 6RT
Activities: Sea and coastal freight water transport
Parent: Orca Marine Leisure Limited
Officers: Jatinder Pal Singh Nurpuri, Secretary; Colin John Capewell [1966] Director; Roger Philip Lipman [1963] Director; Jatinder Pal Singh Nurpuri [1963] Director/Chartered Accountant; Henry William Whale [1973] Director; Max Howard Whale [1976] Director; Peter William Whale [1949] Director

The Princethorpe Foundation
Incorporated: 12 March 2001 *Employees:* 288
Net Worth: £18,231,740 *Total Assets:* £24,928,256
Registered Office: Princethorpe College, Princethorpe, Rugby, Warwicks, CV23 9PX
Activities: Pre-primary education
Officers: Edward James Kenneth Tolcher, Secretary; Athelstane Quintin David Cornforth [1958] Director; Michael William Fletcher [1964] Director/Retired; Elizabeth Mary Frances Griffin [1956] Director/Retired Teacher; David George Jackson [1949] Director/Vice Principal; Charles Henry Jenkinson [1962] Director/Supply Chain & Compliance Consultant; Elizabeth Clare Kenward [1958] Director/Retired Deputy Headteacher; Cecilia Mary Lane [1966] Director; Patricia Mary Lines [1949] Director/Retired Primary School Teacher; Caroline Maria McGrory [1972] Director/General Counsel; Teresa Mary McNamara [1950] Director/Headteacher; Colin James Russell [1965] Director/Sales Management; Kieron Dermot Shaw [1947] Director/Retired Bursar & Senior Military Officer; Bernard John Warner [1948] Director/Retired Master Mariner

Principal Healthcare Finance (UK) No.1 Limited
Incorporated: 10 October 1997
Net Worth Deficit: £63,059,000 *Total Assets:* £17,022,000
Registered Office: Norcliffe House, Station Road, Wilmslow, Cheshire, SK9 1BU
Activities: Renting and operating of Housing Association real estate
Parent: Principal Healthcare Finance (UK) No 2 Limited
Officers: Abigail Mattison, Secretary; Timothy Richard William Hammond [1959] Director; Benjamin Robert Taberner [1972] Director/Chartered Accountant

Principal Healthcare Finance (UK) No.2 Limited
Incorporated: 10 October 1997 *Employees:* 5
Net Worth: £28,034,000 *Total Assets:* £28,034,000
Registered Office: Norcliffe House, Station Road, Wilmslow, Cheshire, SK9 1BU
Activities: Renting and operating of Housing Association real estate
Parent: Principal Healthcare Ltd
Officers: Abigail Mattison, Secretary; Timothy Richard William Hammond [1959] Director; Benjamin Robert Taberner [1972] Director/Chartered Accountant

The Print People Group Limited
Incorporated: 23 October 1998 *Employees:* 188
Net Worth: £886,799 *Total Assets:* £13,258,871
Registered Office: Tollwell Road, Bursom Industrial Estate, Beaumont Leys, Leicester, LE4 1BR
Activities: Printing n.e.c.
Officers: Robert Charles Lockwood [1958] Finance Director; April Jacqueline Sharpless [1975] Director

Print-Rite Europe Ltd.
Incorporated: 17 May 1996 *Employees:* 28
Net Worth: £2,694,374 *Total Assets:* £11,254,724
Registered Office: Unit A2, Bailey Brook Industrial Estate, Nottingham, NG16 4BE
Activities: Other manufacturing n.e.c.
Shareholders: Leung Mui Ho; Yuk Chun Gayle Fung
Officers: Martin Crinks, Secretary; Yuk Chun Gayle Fung [1957] Director [Chinese]; Leung Mui Ho [1959] Director [Chinese]; Sau Yin Vivian Tsui [1977] Director/Business Executive

Printing & Packaging Co. Limited
Incorporated: 13 May 1986 *Employees:* 37
Net Worth: £13,167,961 *Total Assets:* £14,410,308
Registered Office: Jacknell Road, Dodwells Bridge Industrial Estate, Hinckley, Leics, LE10 3BS
Activities: Manufacture of other paper and paperboard containers
Shareholder: Joginder Singh Sall
Officers: Amarjit Kaur Sall, Secretary; Amarjit Kaur Sall [1945] Director/Secretary; Hardeep Sall [1973] Director/Office Administrator; Joginder Singh Sall [1944] Director; Manjit Singh Sall [1972] Director; Perminder Sall [1969] Director/Office Administrator; Satpal Singh Sall [1968] Director

The Priory Federation of Academies
Incorporated: 3 January 2008 *Employees:* 999
Net Worth: £115,383,000 *Total Assets:* £125,785,000
Registered Office: 23 Cross O'Cliff Hill, Lincoln, LN5 8PW
Activities: Pre-primary education
Officers: Domenico Carchedi, Secretary; Howard David Gee [1957] Director/Demand Manager; Peter Charles Houten [1956] Director/Retired; Ian Jones [1964] Director/Headmaster; Francis Lionel Knowles [1944] Director/Education Consultant; Jonathan David MacKinder [1993] Director/Solicitor; Richard John Partington [1969] Director/Senior University Teacher; Simon Richardson [1975] Director

Proact IT (UK) Limited
Incorporated: 14 January 2011
Net Worth Deficit: £653,000 *Total Assets:* £16,983,000
Registered Office: Grayson House, Venture Way, Chesterfield, Derbys, S41 8NE
Activities: Other information technology service activities
Parent: Proact IT Group AB
Officers: Jonas Johan Fredrik Hasselberg [1967] Director/Group CEO [Swedish]; Jakob Hoholdt [1969] Director/Vice President at Proact IT Group AB [Danish]; Jan Anders Jonas Persson [1972] Director/CFO at Proact IT Group AB [Swedish]

Proact IT UK Limited
Incorporated: 10 April 2000 *Employees:* 230
Net Worth: £8,165,187 *Total Assets:* £31,299,148
Registered Office: Grayson House, Venture Way, Chesterfield, Derbys, S41 8NE
Activities: Other information technology service activities
Officers: Jonas Johan Fredrik Hasselberg [1967] Director/Group CEO [Swedish]; Jakob Hoholdt [1969] Director [Danish]; Jan Anders Jonas Persson [1972] Director [Swedish]

Proctor Bros. (Long Sutton) Limited
Incorporated: 14 March 1949 *Employees:* 35
Net Worth: £4,855,801 *Total Assets:* £11,185,980
Registered Office: c/o Duncan & Toplis Limited, Enterprise Way, Pinchbeck, Spalding, Lincs, PE11 3YR
Activities: Growing of cereals (except rice), leguminous crops and oil seeds
Major Shareholder: Stafford Julian Allin Proctor
Officers: Stafford Julian Allin Proctor, Secretary; Julian Hickman Proctor [1938] Director/Farmer; Rosalind Diana May Proctor [1939] Director; Stafford Julian Allin Proctor [1968] Director/Farm Manager; Sue Emma Proctor [1967] Director/Freelance Journalist

Prodrive (Holdings) Limited
Incorporated: 8 October 1999 *Employees:* 28
Net Worth Deficit: £19,191,000 *Total Assets:* £19,063,000
Registered Office: Prodrive Headquarters, Chalker Way, Banbury, Oxon, OX16 4XD
Activities: Activities of head offices
Parent: Prodrive Investments Limited
Officers: Roupen Avsharian [1962] Director/General Counsel [American]; Tim Mark Colchester [1971] Finance Director; David Pender Richards [1952] Director/Chief Executive; Karen Richards [1953] Director; Susan Margaret Scarf [1963] Director

Prodrive Group Limited
Incorporated: 24 March 2017 *Employees:* 29
Net Worth: £1,142,000 *Total Assets:* £39,070,000
Registered Office: Prodrive Headquarters, Chalker Way, Banbury, Oxon, OX16 4XD
Activities: Manufacture of motor vehicles
Shareholders: Richards Family Holdings Limited; David Pender Richards
Officers: Tim Mark Colchester [1971] Finance Director; Mr David Pender Richards [1952] Director/Motorsport Consultant

Prodrive Investments Limited
Incorporated: 21 September 1988 *Employees:* 3
Previous: Hundred Percent Properties Limited
Net Worth: £11,057,000 *Total Assets:* £11,057,000
Registered Office: Prodrive Headquarters, Chalker Way, Banbury, Oxon, OX16 4XD
Activities: Activities of head offices
Parent: Prodrive Group Limited
Officers: Tim Mark Colchester [1971] Finance Director; David Pender Richards [1952] Director/Motorsport Consultant; Karen Richards [1953] Director

Produce Investments Limited
Incorporated: 16 November 2005 *Employees:* 1,233
Previous: Produce Investments PLC
Net Worth: £44,146,000 *Total Assets:* £114,788,000
Registered Office: Greenvale AP, Floods Ferry Road, Doddington, March, Cambs, PE15 0UW
Activities: Activities of head offices
Officers: John Clegg, Secretary; Angus Stuart Walton Armstrong [1964] Director; Angus Burt [1984] Director; Michael Burt [1975] Director; Mark Raymond Clarke [1964] Director; John Clegg [1979] Director

Produce World Group Ltd
Incorporated: 23 October 1995 *Employees:* 606
Net Worth: £4,392,000 *Total Assets:* £37,972,000
Registered Office: Stanley's Farm, Great Drove, Yaxley, Peterborough, PE7 3TW
Activities: Wholesale of fruit and vegetables
Parent: Produce World Investments Ltd
Officers: Ian Alexander Anderson [1968] Director; James Edward Barker [1977] Director; David William Ashley Burgess [1968] Director; Geoff Calder [1953] Director

Produce World Investments Ltd
Incorporated: 27 September 1995 *Employees:* 612
Net Worth: £3,618,000 *Total Assets:* £42,609,000
Registered Office: Stanley's Farm, Great Drove, Yaxley, Peterborough, PE7 3TW
Activities: Activities of head offices
Parent: Russell Burgess Ltd
Officers: James Edward Barker [1977] Director; Andrew Stanley Burgess [1965] Director; David William Ashley Burgess [1968] Director; Jason Charles Burgess [1966] Director; David Michael Higgins [1956] Director; Robert Giles Russell Smith [1951] Director/Farming

Profile Security Services Limited
Incorporated: 13 April 1989 *Employees:* 1,890
Net Worth: £1,454,589 *Total Assets:* £11,497,011
Registered Office: Stable Yard, Walk House Farm, Barrow upon Humber, N Lincs, DN19 7DZ
Activities: Other service activities n.e.c.
Parent: Profile Security Group Ltd
Officers: Dharmesh Parekh, Secretary/Accountant; Hon Jonathan Andrew Forbes [1947] Director; Martin McGowan Scanlon [1958] Managing Director; Dharmesh Parekh [1970] Director/Accountant; Brigadier Andrew Parker Bowles [1939] Director; Andrew Prendergast [1952] Director; Alistair Anthony James Lionel Troughton [1954] Director/Consultant

Progress Bedford Limited
Incorporated: 26 June 2006 *Employees:* 104
Net Worth: £1,264,485 *Total Assets:* £12,791,645
Registered Office: Liberty Works, Shuttleworth Road, Bedford, MK41 0EN
Activities: Sale of new cars and light motor vehicles
Parent: Progress Bedford (Holdings) Limited
Officers: Emma Byrne [1972] Director/Secretary; Terence Patrick Byrne [1971] Director

Progress Rail Services UK Limited
Incorporated: 28 February 2011 *Employees:* 400
Net Worth: £43,466,000 *Total Assets:* £62,417,000
Registered Office: Eastfield, Frank Perkins Way, Peterborough, Cambs, PE1 5FQ
Activities: Construction of railways and underground railways
Parent: Caterpillar Luxembourg S.A.R.L.
Officers: Johanna Elizabeth Deason, Secretary; Nigel John Burroughs [1964] Director/Tax Account; Colin Murphy [1962] Managing Director; Jonathan George Newman [1974] Director/Senior Vice President Corporate Services [American]

Proimmune Limited
Incorporated: 8 November 1999 *Employees:* 23
Net Worth: £14,221,814 *Total Assets:* £15,358,205
Registered Office: Magdalen Centre, Oxford Science Park, Oxford, OX4 4GA
Activities: Other human health activities
Officers: Dr Linda Cheng Choo Tan, Secretary; Doctor Nikolai Franz Schwabe [1970] Managing Director [German]; Dr Linda Cheng Choo Tan [1972] Director/Manager [Singaporean]

Project Grace
Incorporated: 12 October 2006
Net Worth Deficit: £109,900,000 *Total Assets:* £108,466,000
Registered Office: Unit 19 Redbrook Business Park, Wilthorpe Road, Barnsley, S Yorks, S75 1JN
Activities: Other business support service activities n.e.c.
Parent: Project Grace Holdings
Officers: Peter Assinder [1971] Strategic Sales & Technology Director; Michael Joseph Napoletano [1967] Director/Manager [American]

Project Jupiter Limited
Incorporated: 15 December 2016
Net Worth: £17,850,000 *Total Assets:* £22,036,000
Registered Office: 1430 Montagu Court, Kettering Parkway, Kettering, Northants, NN15 6XR
Activities: Other business support service activities n.e.c.
Parent: Consumer Champion Group Limited
Officers: James David Saralis, Secretary; John Russell Atkinson [1965] Director; James David Saralis [1978] Director

Project Republica Bidco Limited
Incorporated: 26 August 2016 *Employees:* 7
Net Worth: £2,472,242 *Total Assets:* £56,127,780
Registered Office: 32 Jessops Riverside, Brightside Lane, Sheffield, S9 2RX
Activities: Ready-made interactive leisure and entertainment software development
Parent: Project Republica Topco Limited
Officers: Steven John Webb, Secretary; Carl Cavers [1967] Director; David Charles Wilton [1962] Director

Project Republica Topco Limited
Incorporated: 26 August 2016 *Employees:* 7
Net Worth: £28,086,922 *Total Assets:* £28,387,012
Registered Office: 32 Jessops Riverside, Brightside Lane, Sheffield, S9 2RX
Activities: Ready-made interactive leisure and entertainment software development
Parent: Sumo Group PLC
Officers: Steven John Webb, Secretary; Carl Cavers [1967] Director; Darren Richard Mills [1970] Director; Paul Reginald Porter [1971] Director; David Charles Wilton [1962] Director

Project Sinatra Bidco Limited
Incorporated: 10 March 2016 *Employees:* 2
Net Worth Deficit: £546,648 *Total Assets:* £19,708,072
Registered Office: Babington House, Mallard Way, Pride Park, Derby, DE24 8GX
Activities: Educational support services
Officers: Richard Charles Austin Caston [1967] Director; Adrian Russell Fantham [1972] Director; David Marsh [1980] Director/Chief Executive

Project Sinatra Midco Limited
Incorporated: 10 March 2016
Net Worth Deficit: £2,195,170 *Total Assets:* £17,295,372
Registered Office: Babington House, Mallard Way, Pride Park, Derby, DE24 8GX
Activities: Other education n.e.c.
Officers: Adrian Russell Fantham [1972] Director; David Marsh [1980] Director/Chief Executive

Project Sinatra Topco Limited
Incorporated: 10 March 2016 *Employees:* 394
Net Worth Deficit: £4,249,075 *Total Assets:* £23,588,340
Registered Office: Babington House, Mallard Way, Pride Park, Derby, DE24 8GX
Activities: Other education n.e.c.
Officers: Richard Charles Austin Caston [1967] Director; Adrian Russell Fantham [1972] Director; Andrew Hall [1956] Director; David Marsh [1980] Director/Chief Executive

Promens Holding UK Limited
Incorporated: 23 November 1998
Net Worth: £164,000 *Total Assets:* £30,927,000
Registered Office: Sapphire House, Crown Way, Rushden, Northants, NN10 6FB
Activities: Activities of production holding companies
Parent: Promens Group BV
Officers: Nicholas David Martin Giles, Secretary; Simon John Kesterton [1973] Director; Petrus Rudolf Maria Vervaat [1965] Director [Dutch]

Promens Packaging Limited
Incorporated: 25 July 2003 *Employees:* 152
Net Worth: £19,491,000 *Total Assets:* £42,799,000
Registered Office: Sapphire House, Crown Way, Rushden, Northants, NN10 6FB
Activities: Manufacture of plastic packing goods
Parent: Promens Holding UK Ltd
Officers: Nicholas David Martin Giles, Secretary; Nicholas David Martin Giles [1971] Director/Company Secretary; Simon John Kesterton [1973] Director; Petrus Rudolf Maria Vervaat [1965] Director [Dutch]

Prominent (Europe) Limited
Incorporated: 20 January 1993 *Employees:* 210
Net Worth: £10,966,000 *Total Assets:* £48,899,000
Registered Office: Unit 8 Wheatcroft Business Park, Landmere Lane, Edwalton, Nottingham, NG12 4DG
Activities: Wholesale of clothing and footwear
Parent: Itochu Europe Limited
Officers: Dominic Walsh, Secretary; Hiroyuki Akahori [1968] Director [Japanese]; Ryoichi Ichihara [1966] Director [Japanese]; Mitsutaka Ishida [1968] Director [Japanese]; Nigel John Lugg [1956] Director; Mitsuru Umino [1966] Director [Japanese]; Dominic Walsh [1967] Director/Accountant

The Propeller Academy Trust
Incorporated: 21 December 2012 *Employees:* 126
Net Worth: £11,951,603 *Total Assets:* £14,725,481
Registered Office: Fitzwaryn School, Denchworth Road, Wantage, Oxon, OX12 9ET
Activities: Other education n.e.c.
Officers: Tracey Stratton, Secretary; Gay Campbell [1966] Director/Risk Manager Banking; Christine Doubleday [1955] Director/Retired; Barbara Harker [1950] Director/Retired; Dr Samuel Wolfe [1990] Director/Educationalist

Prophet PLC
Incorporated: 16 October 1989 *Employees:* 92
Net Worth: £6,796,132 *Total Assets:* £9,775,140
Registered Office: Unit 1 Villiers Court, Meriden Business Park, Copse Drive, Meriden, W Midlands, CV5 9RG
Activities: Business and domestic software development
Shareholders: Terence Brian Peachey; Mark Robert Peachey
Officers: Mark Robert Peachey, Secretary; Antony Stuart Farley [1976] Director of Design; David John Houlihan [1961] Human Resources Director; Mark Robert Peachey [1962] Director; Terence Brian Peachey [1938] Director; Paul Andrew Seekins [1970] Director; Stephen Paul Wade [1966] Director/Software Developer; Paul Walker [1958] Director

Proseal UK Limited
Incorporated: 15 January 1998 *Employees:* 368
Net Worth: £41,910,964 *Total Assets:* £56,118,344
Registered Office: Unit B, Adlington Industrial Estate, Adlington, Cheshire, SK10 4NL
Activities: Manufacture of other special-purpose machinery n.e.c.
Officers: Stephen Mark Malone, Secretary/Engineer; Robert Julian Hargreaves [1963] Director/Engineer; Stephen Mark Malone [1960] Director/Engineer

Protocol National Limited
Incorporated: 9 January 1995 *Employees:* 90
Net Worth: £7,373,000 *Total Assets:* £14,389,000
Registered Office: The Point, Welbeck Road, West Bridgford, Nottingham, NG2 7QW
Activities: Educational support services
Officers: Michael John Kelly, Secretary/Accountant; Michael John Kelly [1959] Director/Accountant; Ian Michael Sackree [1969] Director/Accountant

PSA Retail UK Limited
Incorporated: 27 June 1913 *Employees:* 1,316
Previous: Peugeot Citroen Retail UK Limited
Net Worth: £41,284,000 *Total Assets:* £285,931,008
Registered Office: Pinley House, 2 Sunbeam Way, Coventry, Warwicks, CV3 1ND
Activities: Sale of new cars and light motor vehicles
Parent: Peugeot Motor Company PLC
Officers: Kinnary Vyas, Secretary; David James Connell [1972] Director; Jean-Philippe Georges Imparato [1966] Director [French]; Simon David Lawrence [1962] Director/Chartered Accountant; Stephane Le Guevel [1967] Managing Director [French]; James Daniel Weston [1976] Director/Chief Executive; Nigel John Willetts [1972] Director/Chartered Accountant

Psioxus Therapeutics Limited
Incorporated: 17 November 2006 *Employees:* 54
Net Worth: £45,917,016 *Total Assets:* £58,869,872
Registered Office: Psioxus House, 4-10 The Quadrant, Abingdon Science Park, Abingdon, Oxon, OX14 3YS
Activities: Research and experimental development on biotechnology
Officers: Priya Mande, Secretary; Mette Kristine Agger [1964] Director/Managing Partner at Lundbeckfond [Danish]; Dr John William Beadle [1964] Director; Matthew Foy [1980] Director/Venture Capitalist; J. Duncan Higgons [1955] Director [American]; Priya Mande [1971] Director; Dr Paolo Paoletti [1950] Director/President GSK Oncology [American]; Charles Rowland Jr [1958] Director [American]

PSV Claims Bureau Limited
Incorporated: 26 July 1988 *Employees:* 38
Net Worth: £5,627,000 *Total Assets:* £96,975,000
Registered Office: c/o Stagecoach Services Limited, One Stockport Exchange, 20 Railway Road, Stockport, Cheshire, SK1 3SW
Activities: Other activities auxiliary to insurance and pension funding
Parent: Stagecoach Bus Holdings Limited
Officers: Michael John Vaux, Secretary; Robert Gervase Andrew [1963] Director; Colin Brown [1968] Director/Accountant; Samuel Derek Greer [1968] Director; Malcolm Marwick [1971] Managing Director; Michael John Vaux [1971] Director/Solicitor

PTA Developments Limited
Incorporated: 18 October 1990 *Employees:* 3
Net Worth Deficit: £1,067,604 *Total Assets:* £16,852,348
Registered Office: Abbeydale Hall, Abbeydale Road South, Sheffield, S17 3LJ
Activities: Development of building projects
Officers: Paul Gareth Cunningham [1958] Director

PTS Group Limited
Incorporated: 9 February 1988 *Employees:* 3,388
Net Worth: £439,700,000 *Total Assets:* £1,065,400,000
Registered Office: Lodge Way House, Lodge Way, Harlestone Road, Northampton, NN5 7UG
Activities: Agents involved in the sale of timber and building materials
Parent: The BSS Group Limited
Officers: John Peter Carter [1961] Director; David Michael Evans [1974] Director; Andrew Peter Harrison [1961] Director; Alan Richard Williams [1969] Director/Accountant

Charles Pugh (Glass) Limited
Incorporated: 29 May 1935 *Employees:* 109
Net Worth: £7,640,299 *Total Assets:* £16,338,299
Registered Office: Longwood Road, Brookhill Industrial Estate, Pinxton, Nottingham, NG16 6NT
Activities: Wholesale trade of motor vehicle parts and accessories
Parent: Charles Pugh (Holdings) Ltd
Officers: Adrian Paul Miller, Secretary; Evelyn Eisenbraun [1928] Director; Adrian Paul Miller [1958] Director/Accountant; Charles Tudor Pugh [1935] Director; David Tudor Pugh [1964] Director; Edward Tudor Pugh [1965] Director; Valerie Amy Pugh [1936] Director

Charles Pugh (Holdings) Limited
Incorporated: 19 July 1991 *Employees:* 333
Net Worth: £11,083,297 *Total Assets:* £19,505,664
Registered Office: Longwood Road, Brookhill Industrial Estate, Pinxton, Derbys, NG16 6NT
Activities: Activities of head offices
Major Shareholder: Charles Tudor Pugh
Officers: Adrian Paul Miller, Secretary; Evelyn Eisenbraun [1928] Director; Adrian Paul Miller [1958] Director/Accountant; Charles Tudor Pugh [1935] Director; David Tudor Pugh [1964] Director; Edward Tudor Pugh [1965] Director; Valerie Amy Pugh [1936] Director

Pukka Pies Limited
Incorporated: 22 April 1971 *Employees:* 334
Net Worth: £35,506,400 *Total Assets:* £38,881,576
Registered Office: The Halfcroft, Syston, Leicester, LE7 1LD
Activities: Production of meat and poultry meat products
Shareholders: Valerie Clayton Storer; Timothy David Storer; Andrew Jonathan Storer
Officers: Andrew Jonathan Storer, Secretary; Andrew Jonathan Storer [1960] Director; Timothy David Storer [1963] Director; Valerie Clayton Storer [1935] Director

Pulse Home Products (Holdings) Limited
Incorporated: 24 July 2007
Net Worth: £65,650,000 *Total Assets:* £65,650,000
Registered Office: 5400 Lakeside, Cheadle Royal Business Park, Cheadle, Cheshire, SK8 3GQ
Activities: Agents involved in the sale of furniture, household goods, hardware and ironmongery
Parent: Holmes Products (Europe) Limited
Officers: Raj Bhalchandra Dave [1974] Director/Attorney [American]; Ben Hartley [1976] Director/Attorney

Punch Partnerships (PGRP) Limited
Incorporated: 9 May 2000
Net Worth: £48,557,000 *Total Assets:* £61,011,000
Registered Office: Jubilee House, Second Avenue, Burton on Trent, Staffs, DE14 2WF
Activities: Public houses and bars
Parent: Punch Taverns (PGE) Limited
Officers: Francesca Appleby, Secretary; Edward Michael Bashforth [1973] Director; Stephen Peter Dando [1972] Director/Chartered Accountant

Punch Partnerships (PML) Limited
Incorporated: 14 February 1997
Net Worth: £219,087,008 *Total Assets:* £1,022,707,968
Registered Office: Jubilee House, Second Avenue, Burton on Trent, Staffs, DE14 2WF
Activities: Retail sale of beverages in specialised stores
Parent: Punch Taverns (PMH) Limited
Officers: Francesca Appleby, Secretary; Stephen James Allen [1973] Director; Edward Michael Bashforth [1973] Director; Stephen Peter Dando [1972] Director/Chartered Accountant

Punch Promotions Limited
Incorporated: 14 December 2000 *Employees:* 5
Net Worth: £20,045,304 *Total Assets:* £24,044,604
Registered Office: 11 Merus Court, Meridian Business Park, Leicester, LE19 1RJ
Activities: Other sports activities
Shareholders: Mark Harrison; Paul Martin Dodds
Officers: Richard John Hatton [1978] Director/Boxer

Punch Taverns (PGE) Limited
Incorporated: 28 April 2000
Net Worth: £700,104,000 *Total Assets:* £2,376,764,928
Registered Office: Jubilee House, Second Avenue, Burton on Trent, Staffs, DE14 2WF
Activities: Activities of head offices
Parent: Punch Taverns Limited
Officers: Francesca Appleby, Secretary; Edward Michael Bashforth [1973] Director; Stephen Peter Dando [1972] Director/Chartered Accountant

Punch Taverns (Services) Limited
Incorporated: 23 May 2001 *Employees:* 517
Net Worth: £587,000 *Total Assets:* £88,865,000
Registered Office: Jubilee House, Second Avenue, Burton on Trent, Staffs, DE14 2WF
Activities: Other service activities n.e.c.
Parent: Punch Taverns (PGE) Limited
Officers: Francesca Appleby, Secretary; Edward Michael Bashforth [1973] Director; Stephen Peter Dando [1972] Director/Chartered Accountant

Punch Taverns Holdco (B) Limited
Incorporated: 24 September 2014
Net Worth: £255,452,992 *Total Assets:* £838,428,032
Registered Office: Jubilee House, Second Avenue, Burton on Trent, Staffs, DE14 2WF
Activities: Non-trading company
Parent: Punch Taverns (PMG) Limited
Officers: Francesca Ann Appleby, Secretary; Edward Michael Bashforth [1973] Director; Stephen Peter Dando [1972] Director

Punch Taverns Limited
Incorporated: 15 April 1999 *Employees:* 517
Previous: Punch Taverns PLC
Net Worth: £617,500,032 *Total Assets:* £2,190,899,968
Registered Office: Jubilee House, Second Avenue, Burton on Trent, Staffs, DE14 2WF
Activities: Activities of head offices
Parent: Vine Acquisitions Limited
Officers: Edward Michael Bashforth, Secretary; Noah Aaron Bulkin [1977] Director; Stephen Peter Dando [1972] Director/Chartered Accountant; Stephen Edward Timothy Green [1967] Director; Shane Edward Law [1972] Director

Purico Limited
Incorporated: 30 July 1998 *Employees:* 201
Net Worth: £42,641,000 *Total Assets:* £63,463,000
Registered Office: Environment House, 6 Union Road, Nottingham, NG3 1FH
Activities: Activities of head offices
Officers: Roy Stewart Mochor [1950] Director; Anil Puri [1960] Director [Indian]

Purico Speciality Paper Company Limited
Incorporated: 23 December 2010 *Employees:* 113
Previous: UPT (Holdings) Limited
Net Worth: £7,088,247 *Total Assets:* £27,840,850
Registered Office: Environment House, 6 Union Road, Nottingham, NG3 1FH
Activities: Activities of head offices
Parent: Purico Limited
Officers: Anil Puri [1960] Director [Indian]

Pury Hill Limited
Incorporated: 26 September 1996
Net Worth: £5,534,421 *Total Assets:* £13,537,602
Registered Office: Pury Hill Farm, Alderton Road, Towcester, Northants, NN12 7LS
Activities: Other letting and operating of own or leased real estate
Shareholders: Neill Donald Taylor; Julie Elizabeth Taylor
Officers: Julie Elizabeth Taylor, Secretary/Property Development & Management; Julie Elizabeth Taylor [1961] Director/Property Development & Management; Neill Donald Taylor [1963] Director/Property Development and Management

PV Crystalox Solar PLC
Incorporated: 5 December 2006 *Employees:* 126
Net Worth: £45,281,204 *Total Assets:* £49,198,812
Registered Office: 11b(ii) Park House, Milton Park, Milton, Abingdon, Oxon, OX14 4RS
Activities: Activities of head offices
Officers: Matthew John Julius Wethey, Company Secretary; Iain Anthony Dorrity [1952] Director/Chief Executive Officer; Michael David Parker [1946] Director; John Keith Sleeman [1949] Director/Investment Banker

PWP Building Services (Holdings) Limited
Incorporated: 25 February 2017 *Employees:* 163
Net Worth: £2,973,869 *Total Assets:* £16,418,966
Registered Office: Alexandra House, 43 Alexandra Street, Nottingham, NG5 1AY
Activities: Electrical installation
Officers: David Brian England [1963] Director; Timothy Paul Holt [1962] Director; Ian Jarvis [1966] Director; Nigel William Richardson [1960] Director; Robert John Sowter [1957] Director; Richard Sweet [1960] Director; Ian Wardman [1962] Director

PWP Building Services Limited
Incorporated: 16 June 1993 *Employees:* 163
Net Worth: £12,176,671 *Total Assets:* £16,002,735
Registered Office: Alexandra House, 43 Alexandra Street, Nottingham, NG5 1AY
Activities: Electrical installation
Parent: PWP Building Services (Holdings) Ltd
Officers: Nigel William Richardson, Secretary/Director; David Brian England [1963] Electrical Contracts Director; Timothy Paul Holt [1962] Mechanical Contracts Director; Ian Jarvis [1966] Specialist Services Director; Nigel William Richardson [1960] Director; Robert John Sowter [1957] Director; Richard Sweet [1960] Director; Ian Wardman [1962] Electrical Contracts Director

PX Manufacturing Ltd
Incorporated: 19 October 1994 *Employees:* 46
Previous: P X Manufacturing & Distribution Company Limited
Net Worth: £9,952,654 *Total Assets:* £28,387,940
Registered Office: 40 Thorby Avenue, March, Cambs, PE15 0AZ
Activities: Manufacture of electricity distribution and control apparatus
Officers: Elzbieta Tetnowska, Secretary; Dr Pawel Tomil Tetnowski [1970] Director; Rafal Tetnowski [1971] Director; Stanislaw Frank Tetnowski [1943] Director [Polish]

J.A.Pye (Oxford) Limited
Incorporated: 15 October 1957 *Employees:* 31
Net Worth: £17,651,560 *Total Assets:* £29,562,964
Registered Office: Langford Locks, Kidlington, Oxford, OX5 1HZ
Activities: Construction of domestic buildings
Parent: Vanbrugh Trustees Ltd
Officers: Alan David Price, Secretary; Graham Anthony Flint [1969] Director; Rachel Wendy Lewis [1963] Sales Director; Alan David Price [1964] Director; Andrew Peter Turnbull Smith [1958] Director/Quantity Surveyor; Stuart Andrew Wright [1957] Technical Director

Pye Homes Limited
Incorporated: 10 November 2006 *Employees:* 32
Net Worth: £23,865,308 *Total Assets:* £30,113,102
Registered Office: Langford Locks, Kidlington, Oxford, OX5 1HZ
Activities: Construction of domestic buildings
Parent: Vanbrugh Trustees Ltd
Officers: Alan David Price, Secretary; Graham Anthony Flint [1969] Director; Alan David Price [1964] Director and Company Secretary; Paul Edward Rivers [1954] Director

G. & R. Pykett Limited
Incorporated: 9 August 2002 *Employees:* 10
Net Worth: £14,090,465 *Total Assets:* £15,241,685
Registered Office: Poplar Farm, Skeavingtons Lane, Cotmanhay, Ilkeston, Derbys, DE7 8SU
Activities: Wholesale of agricultural machinery, equipment and supplies
Shareholders: Richard Clive Pykett; George Winston Pykett
Officers: Marilyn Ann Pykett, Secretary; George Winston Pykett [1965] Director/Farmer; Richard Clive Pykett [1967] Director/Farmer

Pyramid Posters Limited
Incorporated: 27 August 1992 *Employees:* 137
Net Worth: £4,222,566 *Total Assets:* £11,995,810
Registered Office: Unit A, Bruce Way, Whetstone, Leicester, LE8 6HP
Activities: Non-specialised wholesale trade
Major Shareholder: Allistair William Thomson Mayer
Officers: Ian Pridmore, Secretary/Financial Controller; Mordecai Benaiah [1965] Licensing Director; Allistair William Thomson Mayer [1961] Director; Ian Pridmore [1971] Financial Director

Pyronix Limited
Incorporated: 6 March 1986 *Employees:* 261
Net Worth: £1,741,000 *Total Assets:* £24,870,000
Registered Office: Secure House, Braithwell Way, Hellaby, Rotherham, S Yorks, S66 8QY
Activities: Manufacture of electronic components
Parent: Secure Holdings Limited
Officers: Guy Dodd [1968] Sales Director; Valeri Filianov [1965] Sales Director [Italian]; Carol Sheila Herdman [1970] Finance Director; Juan Sebastian Herrera [1964] Director/Electronics Engineer; Jiangfeng Zhi [1983] Director [Chinese]

Pyrotek Engineering Materials Limited
Incorporated: 19 October 1932 *Employees:* 101
Net Worth: £11,072,533 *Total Assets:* £15,122,706
Registered Office: Garamonde Drive, Wymbush, Milton Keynes, Bucks, MK8 8LN
Activities: Other manufacturing n.e.c.
Parent: Pyrotek Inc
Officers: Anita Susan Hollis, Secretary; Anita Susan Hollis [1964] Director/Accountant; Steven Frank Ray [1970] Director/General Manager; Allan George Roy [1936] Director [American]; Mark Brian Vincent [1963] Director/Manufacturing

Pyvot Limited
Incorporated: 14 July 2016
Net Worth Deficit: £2,523,257 *Total Assets:* £18,777,224
Registered Office: 2 Des Roches Square, Witney, Oxon, OX28 4LE
Activities: Other business support service activities n.e.c.
Shareholders: Philip Andrew Wilding; UK Vast Holdco Limited
Officers: Geoffrey Frank Harold Bibby [1965] Director; James Maxwell Carruthers [1954] Director; Christopher Kindt [1984] Director/Investments Professional; Jonathan Michael Morrell [1961] Director; Carl Anthony Shuker [1961] Director; Philip Andrew Wilding [1975] Director; John David Worthington [1981] Director/Accountant

Q V Foods Limited
Incorporated: 14 June 1988 *Employees:* 379
Net Worth: £10,826,000 *Total Assets:* £29,194,000
Registered Office: Fleet Estate Office, Manor Farm, Holbeach Hurn, Holbeach, Spalding, Lincs, PE12 8LR
Activities: Other processing and preserving of fruit and vegetables
Parent: AHW (Operating) Co Limited
Officers: Mark Richard Henson, Secretary; Martin John Taylor [1971] Group Managing Director; Duncan Richard Worth [1965] Director/Farmer

Q.E.P. Co. U.K. Limited
Incorporated: 8 December 2003 *Employees:* 85
Net Worth: £2,123,000 *Total Assets:* £23,393,000
Registered Office: The Maltsters, Wetmore Road, Burton on Trent, Staffs, DE14 1LS
Activities: Wholesale of hardware, plumbing and heating equipment and supplies
Parent: QEP Co Inc
Officers: Paul Boyce, Secretary/Director; Paul Anthony Boyce [1967] Director; Lewis Gould [1942] Director/Executive [American]

QD Commercial Group (Property) Limited
Incorporated: 22 September 1988
Net Worth: £2,788,127 *Total Assets:* £52,467,952
Registered Office: Westbridge House, Holland Street, Hyson Green, Nottingham, NG7 5DS
Activities: Buying and selling of own real estate
Parent: QD Commercial Group Holdings Limited
Officers: Graham Ernest Moxon, Secretary; Graham Ernest Moxon [1954] Financial Director; Danny Rubins [1930] Managing Director; Nicholas David Rubins [1967] Director

QD Commercial Group Holdings Limited
Incorporated: 26 April 2013 *Employees:* 1,099
Net Worth: £36,731,028 *Total Assets:* £65,844,684
Registered Office: Westbridge House, Holland Street, Hyson Green, Nottingham, NG7 5DS
Activities: Retail sale via mail order houses or via Internet
Shareholders: Nicholas David Rubins; Danny Rubins
Officers: Graham Ernest Moxon [1954] Financial Director; Danny Rubins [1930] Chairman and Director; Nicholas David Rubins [1967] CEO and Director; Samantha Jayne Rubins Thomas [1969] Director; Nicola Waterman [1970] Human Resources Director

QED Academy Trust
Incorporated: 14 January 2011 *Employees:* 343
Net Worth: £82,952,640 *Total Assets:* £86,195,264
Registered Office: Penrose House, 67 Hightown Road, Banbury, Oxon, OX16 9BE
Activities: General secondary education
Officers: Paul Michael Holliday, Secretary; Philip Eric Carter [1945] Director/Retired; Geoff Terence Cooper [1953] Director/Retired; Joan Hazel Greening [1947] Director/Writer; Yaa Akyiama Larbi [1969] Director; Allan Walker [1958] Director; Andrew Wallis [1970] Director/Care Worker

QEGSMAT
Incorporated: 8 July 2011 *Employees:* 351
Previous: Queen Elizabeth's Grammar School Ashbourne Academy
Net Worth: £52,335,000 *Total Assets:* £58,748,000
Registered Office: Queen Elizabeth's Grammar School, Ashbourne Academy, The Green Road, Ashbourne, Derbys, DE6 1EP
Activities: General secondary education
Officers: Lisa Key, Secretary; Michael Jeremy Betteridge [1950] Director/Retired; Max Edward Jeffery [1973] Director/Programme Manager; Mark Mallender [1975] Director; Anne Martin [1969] Director/Headteacher; Ryan McCombs [1983] Director/Strategic Purchasing Executive [American]; Rose Schofield [1959] Director/Commercial Lead for Educational Leadership; Jane Shepherd [1971] Director; Simon John Smith [1974] Director/HR; Hereward Tolmie Tresidder [1954] Director/Accountant; Keith Wesley [1950] Director/Retired; Alex Wolvers [1970] Director/Christian Distinctiveness Advisor

QMS International Limited
Incorporated: 26 March 2015 *Employees:* 69
Net Worth: £2,710,589 *Total Assets:* £24,323,732
Registered Office: Kings Court, Water Lane, Wilmslow, Cheshire, SK9 5AR
Activities: Other business support service activities n.e.c.
Parent: Citation Holdings Limited
Officers: Christopher Paul Morris [1972] Director; Matthew Brian Stacey [1977] Finance Director; Eloise Wann [1977] Director/Chief Financial Officer

Quadgas Holdco Limited
Incorporated: 10 February 2017 *Employees:* 4,012
Net Worth: £5,401,999,872 *Total Assets:* £17,127,000,064
Registered Office: Ashbrook Court, Prologis Park, Central Boulevard, Coventry, Warwicks, CV7 8PE
Activities: Activities of head offices
Shareholders: National Grid Holdings One PLC; Quadgas Investments Bidco Limited
Officers: Mark Stuart Cooper, Secretary; David Andrew Howitt, Secretary; Abdulla Mohamed Al-Ansari [1988] Director/Investment Manager [Qatari]; Nicholas John Axam [1979] Director/Investment Manager [Australian]; Mark William Braithwaite [1965] Director; Iain Michael Coucher [1961] Director/Chief Executive; Eduard Benjamin Fidler [1977] Director [Canadian]; Richard Greenleaf [1981] Director/Asset Manager; Michael John Gregory [1968] Director; Howard Charles Higgins [1953] Director; Deven Karnik [1967] Director; Jaroslava Korpancova [1974] Director [Czech]; Mark William Mathieson [1966] Managing Director; Perry Denis Noble [1960] Director/Infrastructure Partner; Hua Su [1990] Director/Investment [Chinese]; David Jinlin Xie [1978] Director/Investment Professional [American]

Quadgas Midco Limited
Incorporated: 13 February 2017 *Employees:* 4,012
Net Worth: £5,401,999,872 *Total Assets:* £17,127,000,064
Registered Office: Ashbrook Court, Prologis Park, Central Boulevard, Coventry, Warwicks, CV7 8PE
Activities: Other business support service activities n.e.c.
Parent: Quadgas Pledgeco Limited
Officers: Mark Stuart Cooper, Secretary; David Andrew Howitt, Secretary; Abdulla Mohamed Al-Ansari [1988] Director/Investment Manager [Qatari]; Nicholas John Axam [1979] Director/Investment Manager [Australian]; Mark William Braithwaite [1965] Director; Iain Michael Coucher [1961] Director/Chief Executive; Eduard Benjamin Fidler [1977] Director [Canadian]; Richard Greenleaf [1981] Director/Asset Manager; Michael John Gregory [1968] Director; Howard Charles Higgins [1953] Director; Deven Karnik [1967] Director; Jaroslava Korpancova [1974] Director [Czech]; Mark William Mathieson [1966] Managing Director; Perry Denis Noble [1960] Director/Infrastructure Partner; Hua Su [1990] Director/Investment [Chinese]; David Jinlin Xie [1978] Director/Investment Professional [American]

Quadrant Security Group Limited
Incorporated: 30 May 2006 *Employees:* 182
Net Worth: £2,413,000 *Total Assets:* £25,632,000
Registered Office: 3 Attenborough Lane, Chilwell, Nottingham, NG9 5JN
Activities: Security systems service activities
Parent: Synectics PLC
Officers: Simon Beswick, Secretary; Stacey Louise Anderson [1980] Operations Director; Simon Beswick [1964] Finance Director; Michael Graham Brocklesby [1968] Director; Mark Pennington [1965] Managing Director; Julie Town [1965] Director/Accountant; Paul Anthony Webb [1965] Director

Quadron Services Limited
Incorporated: 19 April 1993 *Employees:* 534
Net Worth: £7,789,000 *Total Assets:* £17,294,000
Registered Office: Landscapes House, Rye Hill Office Park, Birmingham Road, Allesley, Coventry, Warwicks, CV5 9AB
Activities: Landscape service activities
Officers: Jonathan Edward Rhodes, Secretary; Josephine Daughtry [1962] Director; Douglas John Graham [1969] Finance Director; Clive Nigel Ivil [1958] Director; Jonathan Edward Rhodes [1977] Director/Chartered Accountant; Nicholas Temple-Heald [1961] Director

Quaker International Educational Trust
Incorporated: 15 October 1998 *Employees:* 200
Net Worth: £10,231,455 *Total Assets:* £13,123,526
Registered Office: c/o Critchleys LLP, Beaver House, 23-38 Hythe Bridge Street, Oxford, OX1 2EP
Activities: Pre-primary education
Officers: Juhaina Albert Abu Khalil [1963] Director/Teacher [Lebanese]; Averil Armstrong [1950] Director/Retired; John Edward Crosfield [1953] Director/Civil Engineer; William David Adams Haire [1956] Director/Retired Civil Servant; David Fleming Hickok [1959] Director/Retired Banker [American]; Paul Bernard High [1942] Director/Retired Educationalist; Hani Aboul Jabine [1943] Director/Retired [Lebanese]; Philippa Neave [1960] Director/United Nations Advisor; Digby Geoffrey Swift [1945] Director/Retired Civil Servant; Antoine Wakim [1945] Director/Retired [Lebanese]

Quality Care (EM) Limited
Incorporated: 29 January 2003 *Employees:* 311
Net Worth: £6,245,468 *Total Assets:* £13,403,473
Registered Office: 5 Prospect Place, Millennium Way, Pride Park, Derby, DE24 8HG
Activities: Residential care activities for learning difficulties, mental health and substance abuse
Parent: QCH (Holdings) Limited
Officers: Sarah Hall, Secretary; Teresa Clare Nathudkhan [1961] Director; Jamie John Rankin [1981] Director

Qualter, Hall & Company Limited
Incorporated: 9 November 1910 *Employees:* 130
Previous: Qualter,Hall & Co.,Limited
Net Worth: £5,379,000 *Total Assets:* £14,281,000
Registered Office: 16 Johnson Street, Barnsley, S Yorks, S75 2BY
Activities: Manufacture of metal structures and parts of structures
Parent: Waagner Biro AG
Officers: George Wild, Secretary; Graham Carr [1964] Technical Director; George Orton [1953] Managing Director; Keith Martin Richardson [1958] Production Director

Quantum Clothing Group Limited
Incorporated: 11 January 1865 *Employees:* 80
Net Worth Deficit: £436,177 *Total Assets:* £16,673,129
Registered Office: Unit 12 Wheatcroft Business Park, Landmere Lane, Edwalton, Nottingham, NG12 4DG
Activities: Manufacture of other men's outerwear
Officers: Anishke Dilan Christopher Gooneratne [1973] Director [Sri Lankan]; Trevine Lalith Francis Waas Jayasekara [1953] Director [Sri Lankan]; Mohamed Ashroff Omar [1955] Director [Sri Lankan]

Quarrydale Academy
Incorporated: 23 December 2011 *Employees:* 156
Net Worth: £9,885,106 *Total Assets:* £13,575,880
Registered Office: Quarrydale Academy, Stoneyford Road, Sutton in Ashfield, Notts, NG17 2DU
Activities: General secondary education
Shareholders: John Anthony Heald; Philip Graham Marshall
Officers: Amanda Louise Adamson, Secretary; Peter John Gregory [1951] Director/Pharmacist; John Anthony Heald [1938] Director/Retired; Adam Douglas Heathcote [1986] Director/Teacher; Paul Thomas Hodson [1983] Director/Teacher; Emma Kate Leaver [1984] Director/Marketing Coordinator; Nicholas William Luke [1960] Director/Teacher; Julie Marsh [1959] Director/Finance Manager; Philip Graham Marshall [1954] Director/Retired; Timothy James Paling [1973] Director/Headteacher; Jonathan Smart [1973] Director/Marketing & Communications Manager; Neil Walton [1962] Director/Engineer; Louise Ward [1985] Director/Healthcare Professional; Jill Wildsmith [1958] Director

Quartzelec Ltd
Incorporated: 22 March 1989 *Employees:* 566
Net Worth: £16,187,000 *Total Assets:* £37,627,000
Registered Office: Quartzelec Ltd, Castle Mound Way, Central Park, Rugby, Warwicks, CV23 0WB
Activities: Manufacture of other fabricated metal products n.e.c.
Parent: Quartzinvest Limited
Officers: Kenneth Edward Wanless, Secretary/Accountant; Daniel Robert Pierre Laval [1956] Director [French]; Kenneth Edward Wanless [1967] Director/Accountant

Quartzinvest Limited
Incorporated: 6 December 2006 *Employees:* 599
Net Worth: £14,437,000 *Total Assets:* £42,785,000
Registered Office: Quartzelec Ltd, Castle Mound Way, Central Park, Rugby, Warwicks, CV23 0WB
Activities: Activities of other holding companies n.e.c.
Officers: Kenneth Edward Wanless, Secretary/Accountant; Raymond John Annable [1955] Director/Business Manager; Dominic Charles Buse [1965] Director/Business Manager; David Ronald Graham [1956] Director/Business Manager; Timothy John Langhorn [1955] Director/Business Consultant; Daniel Robert Pierre Laval [1956] Director [French]; Bryn Morris [1959] Director/Business Manager; Peter Morgan Owen [1946] Director/Business Manager; Roger Henry Regan [1948] Director/Business Manager; Kenneth Edward Wanless [1967] Director/Accountant; David Morrison Whyte [1951] Director/Human Resources

Quartzinvest Properties Ltd
Incorporated: 13 July 2011 *Employees:* 2
Net Worth: £3,388,000 *Total Assets:* £12,092,000
Registered Office: Quartzelec Ltd, Castle Mound Way, Central Park, Rugby, Warwicks, CV23 0WB
Activities: Other letting and operating of own or leased real estate
Parent: Quartzinvest Limited
Officers: Daniel Robert Pierre Laval [1956] Director [French]; Kenneth Edward Wanless [1967] Director/Accountant

Quest Global Engineering Limited
Incorporated: 7 June 2011 *Employees:* 187
Net Worth: £23,346,000 *Total Assets:* £34,812,000
Registered Office: Derwent House, RTC Business Park, London Road, Derby, DE24 8UP
Activities: Specialised design activities
Officers: Rajendra Kumar Shreemal [1970] Director [Indian]

Questport Limited
Incorporated: 16 July 2004
Net Worth Deficit: £1,524,928 *Total Assets:* £10,038,401
Registered Office: 10 Riverview, The Embankment, Vale Road, Heaton Mersey, Stockport, Cheshire, SK4 3GN
Activities: Financial intermediation not elsewhere classified
Shareholders: Ronald Musry; Alan Philip David Musry
Officers: Alan Philip David Musry, Secretary/Director; Alan Philip David Musry [1963] Director/Chartered Accountant; Ronald Musry [1935] Director

Quicksilver Dollar Loanco Limited
Incorporated: 13 July 2011 *Employees:* 2
Net Worth: £13,823,000 *Total Assets:* £16,053,000
Registered Office: Ascot Business Park, 50 Longbridge Lane, Derby, DE24 8UJ
Activities: Activities of distribution holding companies
Parent: Pattonair Group Limited
Officers: Zoe Robertson, Secretary; Wayne Richard Hollinshead [1966] Director; Christopher Andrew Humphreys [1965] Director/Chief Financial Officer

Quicksilver Euro Loanco Limited
Incorporated: 13 July 2011 *Employees:* 2
Net Worth: £8,694,000 *Total Assets:* £16,119,000
Registered Office: Ascot Business Park, 50 Longbridge Lane, Derby, DE24 8UJ
Activities: Activities of distribution holding companies
Parent: Pattonair Group Limited
Officers: Zoe Robertson, Secretary; Wayne Richard Hollinshead [1966] Director; Christopher Andrew Humphreys [1965] Director/Chief Financial Officer

Quicksilver Midco Limited
Incorporated: 10 February 2011 *Employees:* 2
Net Worth Deficit: £55,183,000 *Total Assets:* £151,415,008
Registered Office: Ascot Business Park, 50 Longbridge Lane, Derby, DE24 8UJ
Activities: Activities of distribution holding companies
Parent: Pattonair Holdings Limited
Officers: Zoe Robertson, Secretary; Wayne Richard Hollinshead [1966] Director; Christopher Andrew Humphreys [1965] Director/Chief Financial Officer

Quint Holdings Ltd
Incorporated: 11 April 2013 *Employees:* 110
Previous: Quintessential Hdgs Limited
Net Worth: £2,790,748 *Total Assets:* £21,016,622
Registered Office: Cottage Street Mill, Cottage Street, Macclesfield, Cheshire, SK11 8DZ
Activities: Activities of financial services holding companies
Major Shareholder: Gregory Charles Cox
Officers: Gregory Charles Cox [1981] Director; Kate Jowitt [1978] Director/Personal Assistant

Quotient Sciences Holdings Limited
Incorporated: 19 November 2015
Net Worth: £66,657,000 *Total Assets:* £99,154,000
Registered Office: Quotient Clinical Limited, Mere Way, Ruddington, Nottingham, NG11 6JS
Activities: Research and experimental development on biotechnology
Parent: Watch Midco 1 Limited
Officers: Gordon Biggart Cameron [1966] Director; Dr Mark Egerton [1963] Director; Alan Browning MacKay [1962] Director/Private Equity Executive; Michael Irvine Mortimer [1960] Director/Private Equity Executive

Quotient Sciences Limited
Incorporated: 3 September 2004 *Employees:* 330
Previous: Quotient Clinical Limited
Net Worth: £44,304,000 *Total Assets:* £73,137,000
Registered Office: Trent House, Mere Way, Ruddington Fields Business Park, Ruddington, Nottingham, NG11 6JS
Activities: Research and experimental development on biotechnology
Parent: Watch Bidco Limited
Officers: Gordon Biggart Cameron, Secretary; Gordon Biggart Cameron [1966] Director; Dr Mark Egerton [1953] Director/Chief Executive Officer

R Group Holdings Limited
Incorporated: 21 November 2006
Net Worth Deficit: £506,000 *Total Assets:* £15,374,000
Registered Office: Total Produce, Enterprise Way, Pinchbeck, Spalding, Lincs, PE11 3YR
Activities: Activities of head offices
Parent: TPH (UK) Ltd
Officers: Mark Christopher Owen, Secretary; Jacinta Frances Devine [1972] Director [Irish]; Francis Gerard McKernan [1962] Director [Irish]; Mark Christopher Owen [1965] Director; Denis Leslie Punter [1953] Director

R P S Group PLC
Incorporated: 8 January 1987 *Employees:* 5,340
Net Worth: £369,784,000 *Total Assets:* £612,729,024
Registered Office: 20 Western Avenue, Milton Park, Milton, Abingdon, Oxon, OX14 4SH
Activities: Other business support service activities n.e.c.
Officers: Davie Joseph Gormley, Secretary; Allison Margaret Bainbridge [1960] Director; John Matheson Douglas [1962] Director [Australian]; Catherine Janet Glickman [1957] Director; Kenneth Lever [1953] Director; Michael McKelvy [1959] Director [American]; Robert Lewis Miller-Bakewell [1953] Director/Consultant; Elizabeth Ann Peace [1952] Director; Gary Richard Young [1960] Finance Director

R U Estates Limited
Incorporated: 17 March 2010
Net Worth: £2,118,619 *Total Assets:* £18,277,204
Registered Office: ASD Lighting, Mangham Road, Greasbrough, Rotherham, S Yorks, S61 4RJ
Activities: Other specialised construction activities n.e.c.
Officers: Anthony Roy Stewart [1945] Managing Director; Richard Paul Stewart [1976] Director

R.M.F. Properties Limited
Incorporated: 16 January 2002 *Employees:* 6
Net Worth: £11,085,825 *Total Assets:* £11,444,796
Registered Office: 11 Highdown Road, Leamington Spa, Warwicks, CV31 1XT
Activities: Renting and operating of Housing Association real estate
Officers: Ronald Joseph Foskett, Secretary; Janet Elaine Foskett [1946] Director; Mark Adrian Foskett [1969] Director; Ronald Joseph Foskett [1944] Director of Motor Dealership; Lisa Jane Foskett-Plumb [1966] Director; Joanne Louise Ward [1976] Director

R.T. Consultants Limited
Incorporated: 13 March 1991
Net Worth: £22,360,996 *Total Assets:* £33,365,464
Registered Office: Stoneacre, Omega Boulevard, Capitol Park, Thorne, S Yorks, DN8 5TX
Activities: Other letting and operating of own or leased real estate
Shareholders: Richard Stephen Teatum; Christine Patricia Teatum
Officers: Nigel Peter Wood, Secretary; Christine Patricia Teatum [1951] Director; Richard Stephen Teatum [1957] Director; Nigel Peter Wood [1964] Director

R3 Polygon UK Ltd.
Incorporated: 3 January 1946 *Employees:* 350
Net Worth: £12,266,000 *Total Assets:* £21,393,000
Registered Office: Blackstone Road, Stukeley Meadows Industrial Estate, Huntingdon, Cambs, PE29 6EE
Activities: Other specialised construction activities n.e.c.
Parent: Polygon International AB
Officers: Purmpal Singh Taggar, Secretary; Axel Jorg Granitz [1968] Director [German]; Mats Sixten Norberg [1959] Director [Swedish]; Jeremy Anthony Langrove Sykes [1961] Managing Director

Radford Holdings Limited
Incorporated: 16 March 1934 *Employees:* 25
Net Worth: £9,187,978 *Total Assets:* £11,237,923
Registered Office: Park House, Mile End Road, Colwick, Nottingham, NG4 2DW
Activities: Development of building projects
Shareholder: Veronica Christine Alice Radford
Officers: Veronica Christine Alice Radford, Secretary; Adam William Radford [1976] Director; Veronica Christine Alice Radford [1941] Director

Radical Motorsport Limited
Incorporated: 28 January 1997 *Employees:* 92
Net Worth Deficit: £4,641,265 *Total Assets:* £9,324,192
Registered Office: 24 Ivatt Way, Peterborough, Cambs, PE3 7PG
Activities: Manufacture of motor vehicles
Parent: Radical Sportscars Limited
Officers: Hitesh Katechia, Secretary; Joseph Anwyll [1956] Director; Hitesh Katechia [1966] Director/Chartered Accountant; Jan Martin Osterloh [1971] Director [German]

Radical Sportscars Limited
Incorporated: 14 March 2011 *Employees:* 118
Net Worth: £1,731,436 *Total Assets:* £9,776,224
Registered Office: 24 Ivatt Way, Peterborough, PE3 7PG
Activities: Activities of production holding companies
Shareholders: Andreas Ernst Zielke; Jan Martin Osterloh
Officers: Hitesh Katechia, Secretary; Joseph Anwyll [1956] Director; Hitesh Katechia [1966] Director/Chartered Accountant; Dr Jan Martin Osterloh [1971] Director [German]; Andreas Ernst Zielke [1960] Director/Entrepreneur [German]

Radius Systems Limited
Incorporated: 14 September 1981 *Employees:* 265
Net Worth: £97,955,000 *Total Assets:* £123,585,000
Registered Office: Radius House, Berristow Lane, South Normanton, Alfreton, Derbys, DE55 2JJ
Activities: Manufacture of other plastic products
Officers: David Walsh, Secretary; Valentin Buyanovsky [1964] Director in Polyplastic Group Ltd; Miron Gorilovskiy [1960] Director/Chairman of The Board [Russian]; Mark Thomas Stanway [1971] Director/Accountant; Andrew Rankine Taylor [1955] Director; David Walsh [1966] Finance Director

Ragdale Hall (1990) Limited
Incorporated: 28 October 1987 *Employees:* 513
Net Worth: £15,655,980 *Total Assets:* £22,908,896
Registered Office: Magma House, 16 Davy Court, Castle Mound Way, Rugby, Warwicks, CV23 0UZ
Activities: Hotels and similar accommodation
Shareholders: Michael Irving Simon Henry Isaacs; Penelope Freda Nesbitt
Officers: Clare Brandish [1959] Director; Allison Garner [1966] Director; David Hamdorff [1964] Director; Michael Irving Simon Henry Isaacs [1951] Director; Penelope Freda Nesbitt [1948] Director; Tristan Nesbitt [1974] Hotel Sales Director; Hugh St.John Wilson [1960] Director

Ragi Properties Limited
Incorporated: 19 March 1997 *Employees:* 4
Net Worth: £8,238,358 *Total Assets:* £12,364,162
Registered Office: Prebend House, 72 London Road, Leicester, LE2 0QR
Activities: Buying and selling of own real estate
Shareholders: Sarbjit Singh Ragi; Bhajan Singh Ragi
Officers: Sarbjit Singh Ragi, Secretary/Director; Joginder Kaur [1951] Director; Davinder Singh Ragi [1990] Director; Sarbjit Singh Ragi [1973] Director; Bhajan Singh [1952] Director

Rail Express Systems Limited
Incorporated: 9 June 1994
Net Worth: £33,046,000 *Total Assets:* £33,145,000
Registered Office: Lakeside Business Park, Carolina Way, Doncaster, S Yorks, DN4 5PN
Activities: Freight rail transport
Parent: DB Cargo (UK) Holdings Limited
Officers: Helen Louise Young, Secretary; Andrea Rossi [1975] Director/Chief Financial Officer; Hans-Georg Werner [1959] Director/Business Administration [German]

Rain Dance Investments Limited
Incorporated: 14 August 2009 *Employees:* 2
Net Worth: £58,801,596 *Total Assets:* £72,054,144
Registered Office: St Lawrence, 28 Station Road, Bardney, Lincoln, LN3 5UD
Activities: Activities of head offices
Major Shareholder: Donald Francis Irwin-Houston
Officers: Harry Ernest Jeffery, Secretary; Donald Francis Irwin Houston [1960] Director/Chartered Engineer; William Robert Kelly [1959] Director

Rainthorpe Farms Limited
Incorporated: 15 July 2005 *Employees:* 12
Net Worth: £5,926,895 *Total Assets:* £10,451,192
Registered Office: Reasby Hall, Stainton by Langworth, Lincoln, LN3 5BW
Activities: Growing of cereals (except rice), leguminous crops and oil seeds
Officers: Diane Marshall, Secretary; Helen Joanne Clarke [1971] Director/Teacher; Ben Joshua Rainthorpe [1991] Director/Student; Robert Rainthorpe [1969] Director/Programmer; Susan Kathleen Rainthorpe [1947] Director

RAL Limited
Incorporated: 16 August 1985 *Employees:* 1,026
Net Worth: £22,067,596 *Total Assets:* £36,601,640
Registered Office: Birch House, Woodlands Business Park, Linford Wood, Milton Keynes, Bucks, MK14 6EW
Activities: Gambling and betting activities
Parent: Talarius Limited
Officers: Neil Paramore, Secretary; Tom Allison [1963] Director; Paul David Hyman [1969] Director; Zane Cedomir Mersich [1972] Director; Neil Paramore [1962] Director

Raleigh Holdings Ltd
Incorporated: 26 January 1903
Net Worth: £4,780,000 *Total Assets:* £14,894,000
Registered Office: Church Street, Eastwood, Nottingham, NG16 3HT
Activities: Wholesale of household goods (other than musical instruments) n.e.c
Parent: Swissbike Vertriebs GmbH
Officers: Stuart Atkins, Secretary; Anthonie Hilbert Anbeek [1962] Director [Dutch]; Philippa Wibberley [1972] Director

Raleigh Learning Trust
Incorporated: 9 February 2017 *Employees:* 253
Net Worth: £16,114,000 *Total Assets:* £22,479,000
Registered Office: Woodlands School, Beechdale Road, Nottingham, NG8 3EZ
Activities: Primary education
Officers: Claire Alexandra McAlonan, Secretary; David Alexander Burnett [1979] Director/Programme Manager; Thomas Shaw [1976] Director/Carer; Gloria Spencer [1948] Director/Retired; Mario Vignali [1964] Franchise & Managing Director; Professor Bernadette Nancy Youens [1961] Director/University Professor

Raleigh UK Ltd
Incorporated: 21 January 1915 *Employees:* 135
Net Worth: £10,070,000 *Total Assets:* £38,006,000
Registered Office: Church Street, Eastwood, Nottingham, NG16 3HT
Activities: Wholesale of household goods (other than musical instruments) n.e.c
Parent: Raleigh Holdings Ltd
Officers: Stuart Atkins, Secretary; Anthonie Hilbert Anbeek [1962] Director [Dutch]; Philippa Wibberley [1972] Director

Rampion Offshore Wind Limited
Incorporated: 23 March 2010
Previous: E.On Climate & Renewables UK Rampion Offshore Wind Limited
Net Worth: £992,558,976 *Total Assets:* £1,145,164,032
Registered Office: Westwood Way, Westwood Business Park, Coventry, Warwicks, CV4 8LG
Activities: Production of electricity
Parent: E.On Climate & Renewables UK Limited
Officers: Jerrid Andrew Anderson [1967] Director, European Power, Major Projects [American]; Timothy James Bell [1973] Director/Head of Controlling Offshore and Onshore EU; Adrian Joseph Chatterton [1963] Director/Head of Construction Offshore; Matthew Porter [1977] Director/Banker; Lawrence Troy Rilea [1961] Director/Head of Commercial Development [Canadian]; Christian Richard Kurt Schrimpf [1978] Director Partnering [German]; Matthew James Swanwick [1967] Project Director; David Paul Tilstone [1969] Managing Director; Sven Utermohlen [1968] Director Construction & Engineering [German]

D.B. Ramsden & Company Limited
Incorporated: 31 May 1961 *Employees:* 121
Net Worth: £5,891,253 *Total Assets:* £14,676,026
Registered Office: Adam Smith Street, Grimsby, S Humbers, DN31 1SJ
Activities: Non-specialised wholesale of food, beverages and tobacco
Parent: Ramsden Holdings Limited
Officers: Louisa Jane Metcalf, Secretary; Dudley Burton Ramsden [1943] Director; Nicholas Ronald Ramsden [1978] Director

Randall Parker Food Group Limited
Incorporated: 30 June 1995 *Employees:* 488
Net Worth: £15,047,000 *Total Assets:* £43,849,000
Registered Office: The Old Rectory, Cold Higham, Towcester, Northants, NN12 8LR
Activities: Other service activities n.e.c.
Shareholders: Ronald Leslie Randall; W & J Parker Limited
Officers: David Richard Brady, Secretary; David Richard Brady [1950] Director/Chartered Accountant; Andrew William Parker [1971] Director; Pragnesh Patel [1975] Director; Gary Randall [1978] Director; Ronald Leslie Randall [1947] Director/Master Butcher; Stuart Graham Randall [1987] CEO & Director; Tony Randall [1975] Director

Randall Parker Foods Limited
Incorporated: 6 May 1971 *Employees:* 340
Net Worth: £11,305,000 *Total Assets:* £25,683,000
Registered Office: The Old Rectory, Banbury Lane, Cold Higham, Towcester, Northants, NN12 8LR
Activities: Wholesale of meat and meat products
Shareholders: W & J Parker Limited; Ronald Leslie Randall
Officers: David Richard Brady, Secretary; David Richard Brady [1950] Director/Chartered Accountant; James Mario Gaffney [1956] Managing Director; Andrew William Parker [1971] Director; Pragnesh Patel [1975] Director; Gary Randall [1978] Director; Ronald Leslie Randall [1947] Director/Master Butcher; Stuart Graham Randall [1987] CEO and Director; Tony Randall [1975] Director

Randomlight Limited
Incorporated: 10 March 1989 *Employees:* 97
Net Worth: £4,191,969 *Total Assets:* £17,435,680
Registered Office: 6-8 Old Hall Road, Gatley, Cheadle, Cheshire, SK8 4BE
Activities: Hospital activities
Parent: Ovalseal Limited
Officers: Michael Denis Hartey [1956] Director

Rannoch Food Group Limited
Incorporated: 3 April 2002 *Employees:* 1
Net Worth: £7,164,345 *Total Assets:* £15,890,600
Registered Office: Albion House, 32 Pinchbeck Road, Spalding, Lincs, PE11 1QD
Activities: Other business support service activities n.e.c.
Officers: John Edward Dutton [1954] Director; Robert John Williams [1942] Director

Ranquin Underwriting Limited
Incorporated: 24 September 1999
Net Worth: £1,348,142 *Total Assets:* £11,576,550
Registered Office: 3 Castlegate, Grantham, Lincs, NG31 6SF
Activities: Non-life insurance
Officers: Ronald Leonard McCarthy [1933] Director [Irish]

Ransomwood Estates UK Limited
Incorporated: 11 November 2016 *Employees:* 31
Net Worth: £86,506 *Total Assets:* £12,023,390
Registered Office: Unit 50 Ransom Hall, Ransom Wood Business Park, Southwell Road West, Rainworth, Mansfield, Notts, NG21 0HJ
Activities: Other letting and operating of own or leased real estate
Parent: Ransomwood Estates Holdings Limited
Officers: Fiona Mary Canon, Secretary; Charles Michael George Canon [1971] Director/Manager; James Edward Thomas Canon [1975] Commercial Director; Michael Harry Wilson Canon [1943] Director/Asset Manager; Richard Thomas Kenning [1951] Director

Rapidrop Global Limited
Incorporated: 8 July 2005 *Employees:* 93
Net Worth: £5,092,387 *Total Assets:* £13,277,743
Registered Office: Unit 1-3 Rutland Business Park, Newark Road, Peterborough, Cambs, PE1 5WA
Activities: Other specialised construction activities n.e.c.
Major Shareholder: Daniel Percy James Gill
Officers: Martyn Alan Curran [1977] Sales Director; Dominic Lawrence Ellicott [1973] Finance Director; Keith Stephen Plater [1964] Director; Mark Smith [1968] Commercial Director; Martyn Peter Willimer [1975] Sales Director

Ratcliffe College
Incorporated: 9 August 2006 *Employees:* 257
Net Worth: £23,986,170 *Total Assets:* £29,943,412
Registered Office: Ratcliffe College, Fosse Way, Ratcliffe on the Wreake, Leicester, LE7 4SG
Activities: Pre-primary education
Officers: Dr Sheelagh Brigid Bolt [1943] Director/Doctor; Father Brian Eric Cuddihy [1943] Director/R.C. Priest; Father Anthony Joseph Furlong [1956] Director/Priest; Richard William Gamble [1946] Director; Mary Dianne Goldstraw [1946] Director; Louis Paul Massarella [1973] Director; Father Anthony Desmond Meredith [1940] Director/Priest; Father David John Myers [1941] Director/Priest [Irish]; Father Joseph O'Reilly [1960] Director/Priest [Irish]; Paul Raymond Francis Rudd [1941] Director; Father Philip Anthony Sainter [1952] Director/Catholic Priest; Joan Margaret Smidowicz [1943] Director; Father Tom Thomas [1972] Director/Priest [Indian]

Ravensburger Limited
Incorporated: 26 August 1964 *Employees:* 20
Net Worth: £3,326,215 *Total Assets:* £14,571,449
Registered Office: Unit 1 Avonbury Business Park, Howes Lane, Bicester, Oxon, OX26 2UB
Activities: Manufacture of other games and toys, n.e.c.
Officers: John Howard Wilkinson, Secretary; Timothy Hall [1962] Managing Director; Martin Stowahse [1972] Managing Director [German]

Ravent Limited
Incorporated: 31 July 1997
Net Worth: £5,004,889 *Total Assets:* £11,661,564
Registered Office: 2 Whiteley Wood Road, Sheffield, S11 7FE
Activities: Other letting and operating of own or leased real estate
Parent: Great Central Developments Ltd
Officers: Frederick James Gould, Secretary; Frederick James Gould [1957] Director; Joanna Margaret Gould [1967] Director/Chartered Accountant

Rawlins Academy
Incorporated: 31 May 2011 *Employees:* 211
Net Worth: £7,920,000 *Total Assets:* £12,717,000
Registered Office: Rawlins Community College, Loughborough Road, Quorn, Loughborough, Leics, LE12 8DY
Activities: General secondary education
Officers: Louise Marie Daykin, Secretary; Helen Carolyn Beaton [1963] Director/Retired; Megan Anna Bezzano-Griffiths [1969] Director/Community Centre Manager; Reverend David Henderson Bowler [1954] Director/Clerk in Holy Order; Sarah Madeline Cook [1978] Director/Teacher; Clare Patricia Darby [1968] Director/Principal; Lee Dobinson [1963] Director/Manager Automotive; Sarah Elizabeth Hammond [1972] Director/Teacher; Ruth Elizabeth Lewin [1975] Director/HR Advisor; Ian Gerard Marron [1963] Director/Consultant [Irish]; Elizabeth Walling [1956] Director/Retired; Emma Weston [1971] Director/University Teacher; Ann-Marie Willett [1968] Director/School Business Management

Rayburn Tours (Holdings) Limited
Incorporated: 13 July 2006 *Employees:* 87
Net Worth: £1,429,900 *Total Assets:* £9,853,639
Registered Office: c/o Rayburn Tours Ltd, Rayburn House, 37 Brunel Parkway, Pride Park, Derby, DE24 8HR
Activities: Tour operator activities
Shareholders: John Boyden; Brenda Boyden
Officers: Katie Boyden, Secretary; Brenda Boyden [1947] Director; James Thomas Boyden [1981] Director; John Boyden [1947] Director; Katie Boyden [1975] Director

Rayburn Tours Limited
Incorporated: 9 October 1984 *Employees:* 87
Net Worth: £913,040 *Total Assets:* £9,697,573
Registered Office: Rayburn House, 37 Brunel Parkway, Pride Park, Derby, DE24 8HR
Activities: Tour operator activities
Shareholders: John Boyden; Brenda Boyden
Officers: Brenda Boyden, Secretary; Brenda Boyden [1947] Director/Secretary; James Thomas Boyden [1981] Director/Tour Operator; John Boyden [1947] Director/Manager; Katie Boyden [1975] Director/General Manager; Lucy Gwendoline James [1975] Finance Director

Rayfern Holdings Limited
Incorporated: 14 June 2012 *Employees:* 153
Net Worth: £6,050,135 *Total Assets:* £10,709,147
Registered Office: Treerange House, Minerva Business Park, Lynch Wood, Peterborough, Cambs, PE2 6QR
Activities: Activities of head offices
Parent: Edwin James Holdings Limited
Officers: John Keith Beeston [1974] Director/Chartered Accountant; Ashley James Maile [1970] Director; Darren John Martin [1970] Director; Ian Roy Morris [1963] Director; Derek Smith [1966] Director/Chief Executive

Raynsway Estates Limited
Incorporated: 9 February 1988
Net Worth: £9,035,804 *Total Assets:* £28,222,928
Registered Office: Rayns House, Rayns Way, Watermead Business Park, Syston, Leics, LE7 1PF
Activities: Other letting and operating of own or leased real estate
Parent: Rayns of Leicester Holdings Limited
Officers: Amey Maria Perry, Secretary; Giannina Gabriella Rayns, Secretary; Giannina Gabriella Rayns [1959] Director

Raynsway Properties Limited
Incorporated: 7 June 1976 *Employees:* 11
Net Worth: £23,006,310 *Total Assets:* £43,558,304
Registered Office: Rayns House, Rayns Way, Watermead Business Park, Syston, Leics, LE7 1PF
Activities: Other letting and operating of own or leased real estate
Major Shareholder: Giannina Gabriella Rayns
Officers: Amey Maria Perry, Secretary; Giannina Gabriella Rayns, Secretary; Giannina Gabriella Rayns [1959] Director/Secretary

RCI Europe
Incorporated: 29 November 1973 *Employees:* 215
Net Worth: £66,798,040 *Total Assets:* £173,335,888
Registered Office: Haylock House, Kettering Parkway, Kettering Venture Park, Kettering, Northants, NN15 6EY
Activities: Other service activities n.e.c.
Parent: PointTravel Co. Ltd
Officers: Andrew Clarke [1976] Director; Andrew Liggins [1962] Director/Accountant

RDG Midas Holdings (NI) Limited
Incorporated: 15 December 2015
Net Worth Deficit: £1,623,000 *Total Assets:* £15,952,000
Registered Office: Quay Point, Lakeside Boulevard, Doncaster, S Yorks, DN4 5PL
Activities: Activities of financial services holding companies
Parent: Direct Group Limited
Officers: Scott William Hough [1971] Finance Director

RE3 Limited
Incorporated: 29 December 2005 *Employees:* 7
Net Worth: £1,117,000 *Total Assets:* £37,739,000
Registered Office: Ground Floor West, 900 Pavilion Drive, Northampton Business Park, Northampton, NN4 7RG
Activities: Other business support service activities n.e.c.
Parent: RE3 Holding Limited
Officers: Carol Jayne Nunn, Secretary; Vicente Federico Orts-Llopis [1962] Director [Spanish]; Paul Taylor [1959] Director/Chief Executive Officer

Rea Valley Tractors Limited
Incorporated: 4 May 1984 *Employees:* 77
Net Worth: £9,506,322 *Total Assets:* £35,261,100
Registered Office: Old Hall, Dunstall, Burton on Trent, Staffs, DE13 8BE
Activities: Installation of industrial machinery and equipment
Parent: Dunstall Holdings Limited
Officers: Stephen Potter, Secretary; Simon William Clarke [1965] Farmer and Director; Glenn Anthony Logan [1965] After Sales Director; Steven Jon Petford [1979] Director/Accountant; Stephen Potter [1964] Director/Chartered Accountant; Nigel John Worthington [1975] Sales Director

Reabrook Ltd
Incorporated: 11 May 1964 *Employees:* 220
Net Worth: £3,680,000 *Total Assets:* £10,466,000
Registered Office: Reabrook Building, Rawdon Road, Moira, Swadlincote, Derbys, DE12 6DA
Activities: Manufacture of other chemical products n.e.c.
Parent: TGOM Limited
Officers: Malcolm Peter Watkins, Secretary; Anthony William Brealey [1957] Commercial Director; Malcolm Peter Watkins [1954] Director/Accountant

Reach2 Academy Trust
Incorporated: 19 March 2013 *Employees:* 2,869
Previous: Reach2essex Academy Trust
Net Worth: £225,403,008 *Total Assets:* £265,624,992
Registered Office: c/o Henhurst Ridge Primary Academy, Henhurst Ridge, Branston, Burton on Trent, Staffs, DE13 9SZ
Activities: Primary education
Officers: Dr Louise Askew [1964] Director/Interpreter and Translator; Teresa Dawn Beach [1971] Managing Director; Walter Anthony Gilbey [1966] Director/Banker; Jeremy Bennett Biddle King [1981] Director; Ralph David Kugler [1956] Director; Sir Steve Lyndon Lancashire [1963] Director/Chief Executive; Jonathan Lewis [1978] Director of Education; Wade Rames Newmark [1960] Director; Michael Claude Peters [1955] Management Consultant and Project Director; Victoria Sarah Pigott [1978] Director/Lawyer; Colin George Powell [1963] Director of Education; Gavin Robert [1967] Director/Solicitor; Clive Nigel Rockingham [1965] Health and Safety Director

Read Motor Group Limited
Incorporated: 21 December 2009 *Employees:* 100
Net Worth: £2,626,936 *Total Assets:* £14,415,330
Registered Office: Altyre Way, Hewitts Avenue Business Park, Humberston, Grimsby, S Humbers, DN36 4RJ
Activities: Sale of new cars and light motor vehicles
Major Shareholder: Michael Read
Officers: Nicola Jane Read, Secretary; Michael David Read [1964] Director/Motor Dealer; Nicola Jane Read [1963] Director/Marketing Manager

Real Estate Income Trust (SC) Limited
Incorporated: 4 July 2014 *Employees:* 1
Net Worth Deficit: £1,738,677 *Total Assets:* £13,962,676
Registered Office: Suite S04, The Atkins Building, Lower Bond Street, Hinckley, Leics, LE10 1QU
Activities: Other letting and operating of own or leased real estate
Officers: Anthony John Hanson [1936] Director

Real Estate Income Trust Limited
Incorporated: 4 April 2012 *Employees:* 1
Net Worth: £139,373 *Total Assets:* £18,877,268
Registered Office: Suite S04, The Atkins Building, Lower Bond Street, Hinckley, Leics, LE10 1QU
Activities: Other letting and operating of own or leased real estate
Officers: Anthony John Hanson [1936] Director

REALL Limited
Incorporated: 12 May 1992 *Employees:* 21
Previous: Homeless International
Net Worth: £40,108,584 *Total Assets:* £41,716,800
Registered Office: 8-14 Harnall Row, Coventry, Warwicks, CV1 5DR
Activities: Development of building projects
Officers: Shantanu Bhagwat [1966] Director/Venture Partner [Indian]; Professor Alison Margaret Braithwaite Brown [1950] Director/Professor of Urban Planning, Cardiff University; Suzanne Marie Forster [1968] Finance Director; David Campbell Orr [1955] Director/Chief Executive; Steven Geoffrey Troop [1956] Director/Retired; Kate Wareing [1973] Director

Realpower Limited
Incorporated: 9 April 2003 *Employees:* 1
Net Worth: £6,063,000 *Total Assets:* £9,755,000
Registered Office: Enviro Building, Private Road No 4, Colwick Industrial Estate, Colwick, Nottingham, NG4 2JT
Activities: Activities of head offices
Parent: ENVA UK Bidco Limited
Officers: Paul Richard Needham [1966] Director; Bill Joseph Power [1969] Director [Irish]; Thomas Walsh [1967] Director [Irish]; Simon Alasdair Woods [1969] Director/Chief Operating Officer

Rebellion Developments Limited
Incorporated: 4 December 1992 *Employees:* 175
Net Worth: £25,046,210 *Total Assets:* £30,837,036
Registered Office: Riverside House, Osney Mead, Oxford, OX2 0ES
Activities: Publishing of computer games
Parent: Rebellion Games Holdings Ltd
Officers: Christopher Ross Kingsley, Secretary; Christopher Ross Kingsley [1966] Director; Jonathon Jason Kingsley [1964] Director

Reconnaissance Ventures Limited
Incorporated: 4 January 2007 *Employees:* 64
Net Worth: £2,965,078 *Total Assets:* £18,444,496
Registered Office: RVL House, Building 21, Anson Road, East Midlands Airport, Castle Donington, Derbys, DE74 2SA
Activities: Activities of head offices
Shareholders: Stephen Guynan; Business Growth Fund PLC
Officers: Stephen Guynan, Secretary/Director; Graham Nigel Cole [1948] Director; Stephen Guynan [1962] Director; Steven David Smith [1960] Director; James Michael Syrotiuk [1985] Director

Recresco Limited
Incorporated: 6 September 2000 *Employees:* 161
Net Worth: £5,513,966 *Total Assets:* £15,671,505
Registered Office: 37 Urban Road, Kirkby in Ashfield, Nottingham, NG17 8AP
Activities: Recovery of sorted materials
Officers: Graham Gent, Secretary; Eric Gent [1982] Director; Graham Gent [1961] Director/Administration Manager; Steven Gent [1963] Technical Director; Timothy Gent [1967] Director/Contracts Manager

Recticel Limited
Incorporated: 18 July 1960 *Employees:* 481
Net Worth: £15,923,000 *Total Assets:* £54,681,000
Registered Office: Bluebell Close, Clover Nook Industrial Park, Alfreton, Derbys, DE55 4RD
Activities: Manufacture of plastics in primary forms
Parent: Recticel S.A./N.V.
Officers: Paul Moss, Secretary; Ralf Becker [1960] Director/Group General Manager Insulation [Belgian]; Eric Bray [1966] Global Manufacturing Director [French]

Red & White Services Limited
Incorporated: 6 November 1990 *Employees:* 898
Net Worth: £17,449,000 *Total Assets:* £29,690,000
Registered Office: c/o Stagecoach Services Limited, One Stockport Exchange, 20 Railway Road, Stockport, Cheshire, SK1 3SW
Activities: Other urban, suburban or metropolitan passenger land transport (not underground, metro or similar)
Parent: Stagecoach Bus Holdings Limited
Officers: Michael John Vaux, Secretary; Colin Brown [1968] Director/Accountant; Arnold Mark Threapleton [1954] Managing Director; Nigel Winter [1963] Director

Red Arrow Trading Limited
Incorporated: 30 January 2010 *Employees:* 33
Net Worth: £28,370 *Total Assets:* £9,073,917
Registered Office: 39-43 Bridge Street, Swinton, Mexborough, S Yorks, S64 8AP
Activities: Agents involved in the sale of timber and building materials
Shareholders: Red Arrow Holdings Limited; Cranstoun Bruce Arnot; Marcelle Gerda Arnot; Aiden Morren; Kim Morren
Officers: Cranstoun Bruce Arnot [1948] Director; Marcelle Gerda Arnot [1952] Director; Stephen Charles Bricknell [1973] Director [Irish]; Aiden Morren [1973] Director; Kim Morren [1971] Director

Red Box Recorders Group Limited
Incorporated: 18 March 2013 *Employees:* 96
Net Worth Deficit: £3,094,000 *Total Assets:* £16,451,000
Registered Office: Bradmore Business Park, Loughborough Road, Bradmore, Nottingham, NG11 6QA
Activities: Business and domestic software development
Shareholders: Livingbridge GP LP; Livingbridge EP LLP
Officers: Martin Clements [1963] Director; Eleri Davies [1975] Director; Peter Charles Ellis [1967] Director/Chief Operating Officer; Adam Stuart Holloway [1967] Director; Ian Michael McKay [1955] Director; Richard James Stevenson [1966] Director; Martyn Thomas Ward [1965] Director/Chief Revenue Officer; Alison Lynne Young [1967] Director/Chief Operating Officer

Red Box Recorders Limited
Incorporated: 23 March 2001 *Employees:* 93
Net Worth: £4,417,000 *Total Assets:* £11,387,000
Registered Office: Bradmore Business Park, Loughborough Road, Bradmore, Nottingham, NG11 6QA
Activities: Other telecommunications activities
Parent: Red Box Recorders Group Limited
Officers: Martin Clements [1963] Director; John Richard Nicholas Corker [1965] Director; Lee Michael Jones [1966] Director/Chief Executive; Richard James Stevenson [1966] Director/Chief Executive

Red Bull Racing Limited
Incorporated: 1 November 1995 *Employees:* 58
Net Worth: £4,959,000 *Total Assets:* £37,651,000
Registered Office: Building 2, Bradbourne Drive, Tilbrook, Milton Keynes, Bucks, MK7 8AT
Activities: Other sports activities
Parent: Red Bull Technology Limited
Officers: Christian Horner [1973] Director/Team Principal; Dr Helmut Marko [1943] Director/Hotelier [Austrian]; Dietrich Mateschitz [1944] Director Soft Drinks Manufacturer [Austrian]

Red Bull Technology Limited
Incorporated: 11 August 2004 *Employees:* 793
Net Worth: £33,425,000 *Total Assets:* £143,099,008
Registered Office: Building 1, Bradbourne Drive, Tilbrook, Milton Keynes, Bucks, MK7 8BJ
Activities: Other manufacturing n.e.c.
Shareholder: Dietrich Mateschitz
Officers: Christian Horner [1973] Director - Motor Racing; Alistair David Rew [1963] Finance Director

Red Primrose Ltd
Incorporated: 5 December 2012 *Employees:* 2
Net Worth: £22,287,954 *Total Assets:* £49,325,288
Registered Office: 20 Coxon Street, Spondon, Derby, DE21 7JG
Activities: Management of real estate on a fee or contract basis
Shareholders: Angela Pishiris; Koulla Phylactou
Officers: Koulla Phylactou [1978] Director; Angela Pishiris [1975] Director

Redborne Upper School and Community College
Incorporated: 16 March 2011 *Employees:* 191
Net Worth: £13,697,859 *Total Assets:* £16,289,350
Registered Office: Redborne Upper School and Community College, Flitwick Road, Ampthill, Bedford, MK45 2NU
Activities: General secondary education
Officers: Dr Richard A'court [1958] Director; Charles Birtwisle [1968] Director/University Lecturer; Tim Corkett [1959] Director/Journalist; Claire Crowther [1963] Director/Teacher; Alexander Day [1969] Director/Teacher; Barry Farbon [1951] Director/Retired; David Farbon [1954] Director; Jane Elizabeth Galvin [1969] Managing Director; Stephen John Gray [1955] Director/Headteacher; Richard Mark Last [1964] Director/Chartered Surveyor; Richard Christopher Mintern [1961] Director; Professor Joe Morris [1948] Director/University Lecturer; Donna Nunn [1968] Director/Examinations Officer; Gerry Pereira [1960] Director/Driving Instructor; Elaine Dawn Tebbutt [1965] Director; Christopher Paul Templeman [1963] Director/Chartered Accountant; Jennifer Tucker [1944] Director/Retired; Elizabeth Jane Woodward [1967] Director/Solicitor

Redbridge Produce & Flowers Limited
Incorporated: 17 March 1995 *Employees:* 340
Net Worth: £7,212,000 *Total Assets:* £19,995,000
Registered Office: Total Produce, Enterprise Way, Pinchbeck, Spalding, Lincs, PE11 3YR
Activities: Wholesale of fruit and vegetables
Parent: Saybest Limited
Officers: Mark Christopher Owen, Secretary; Andrew Roger Allmond [1944] Director/Certified Accountant; Jacinta Frances Devine [1972] Director [Irish]; Francis Gerard McKernan [1962] Director [Irish]; Mark Christopher Owen [1965] Director; Denis Leslie Punter [1953] Managing Director

Reddil Properties Limited
Incorporated: 13 October 2009 *Employees:* 2
Net Worth: £5,372,636 *Total Assets:* £9,110,324
Registered Office: First Floor, Woburn Court, 2 Railton Road, Woburn Road Industrial Estate, Kempston, Bedford, MK42 7PN
Activities: Buying and selling of own real estate
Shareholders: Bhupinder Singh Lidder; Kaulwant Kaur Lidder
Officers: Bhupinder Singh Lidder [1966] Director; Kaulwant Kaur Lidder [1971] Director

Redhill Academy Trust
Incorporated: 4 November 2010 *Employees:* 1,146
Net Worth: £110,939,000 *Total Assets:* £132,888,000
Registered Office: Redhill Academy Trust, Redhill Road, Arnold, Nottingham, NG5 8GX
Activities: Pre-primary education
Officers: Jonathan French, Secretary; Barry John Bexton [1948] Director; Julian Mark Bond [1964] Director/Chartered Engineer; Mike Booth [1968] Director; Barry Michael Daley [1944] Director/Retired; Kevin Paul Edwards [1953] Director/Retired; David Hallam [1951] Director/Retired; Deborah Jane Haynes [1962] Director; Simon Healy [1974] Director; Sally Hopkin [1970] Director/Administration; Stephen William Hopkins [1955] Director/Independent Financial Advisor; Graham Maurice Mansfield [1943] Director/Retired; Stephen Peter Mathers [1952] Director/Student Support Manager; Cllr Michael Richard Payne [1987] Director/Councillor; Stephen Keith Shaw [1947] Director/Retired; Michelle Sills [1973] Director

Redhill Famco Limited
Incorporated: 4 May 2016 *Employees:* 514
Net Worth: £316,900,000 *Total Assets:* £2,278,099,968
Registered Office: Lake View, Lakeside, Cheadle, Cheshire, SK8 3GW
Activities: Activities of financial services holding companies
Shareholders: Dorah Leah Moser; Henry Neville Moser
Officers: Gary Derek Beckett, Secretary; Gary Derek Beckett [1969] Director; Henry Neville Moser [1949] Director

Redlawn Land Limited
Incorporated: 2 July 1992 *Employees:* 4
Net Worth: £48,303,576 *Total Assets:* £59,472,864
Registered Office: Gallagher House, Gallagher Way, Gallagher Business Park, Heathcote, Warwick, CV34 6AF
Activities: Buying and selling of own real estate
Parent: Gallagher Estates Limited
Officers: Edward Paul Farnsworth [1982] Director of Business Planning; Craig David Luttman [1975] Development Director; Martin Rowland Richmond [1953] Group Legal Director; Gregg Spencer Wilkinson [1973] Managing Director

Redlawn Limited
Incorporated: 14 December 2006 *Employees:* 5
Net Worth: £1,553,781 *Total Assets:* £48,204,040
Registered Office: Gallagher House, Gallagher Way, Gallagher Business Park, Heathcote, Warwick, CV34 6AF
Activities: Buying and selling of own real estate
Officers: Edward Paul Farnsworth [1982] Director of Business Planning; Craig David Luttman [1975] Development Director; Martin Rowland Richmond [1953] Group Legal Director; Gregg Spencer Wilkinson [1973] Managing Director

Redx Pharma PLC
Incorporated: 7 September 2010 *Employees:* 52
Previous: Redx Pharma Limited
Net Worth: £5,764,000 *Total Assets:* £10,319,000
Registered Office: Block 33 Mereside, Alderley Park, Macclesfield, Cheshire, SK10 4TG
Activities: Research and experimental development on biotechnology
Officers: Andrew William Booth, Secretary; Lisa Mary Whewell Anson [1968] Director/Pharmaceuticals Executive; Dr Bernhard Jurgen Kirschbaum [1958] Director [German]; James Robert Mead [1977] Finance Director; Peter Eric Presland [1950] Director/Chartered Accountant; Iain Gladstone Ross [1954] Director

Reel Cinemas Limited
Incorporated: 11 May 1998 *Employees:* 183
Net Worth: £6,158,793 *Total Assets:* £9,295,855
Registered Office: Sital House, 3-6 Cattle Market, Loughborough, Leics, LE11 3DL
Activities: Motion picture projection activities
Parent: Reel Cinemas (Europe) Limited
Officers: Kailash Chander Suri, Secretary/Property Developer; Kailash Chander Suri [1955] Director/Property Developer; Naveen Suri [1985] Director; Rachna Suri [1983] Producer Director; Suman Suri [1963] Director; Sunil Suri [1990] Director

Reesink Turfcare UK Limited
Incorporated: 27 November 2015 *Employees:* 139
Net Worth: £8,718,239 *Total Assets:* £27,616,120
Registered Office: 1 Station Road, St Neots, Huntingdon, Cambs, PE19 1QH
Activities: Agents involved in the sale of machinery, industrial equipment, ships and aircraft
Officers: David Jonathan Cole [1962] Director; Hieronymus Menzo Hylkema [1954] Director/The Netherlands [Dutch]; Gerrit Van Der Scheer [1960] Director [Dutch]

Reeve (Derby) Limited
Incorporated: 6 December 2000 *Employees:* 725
Net Worth: £14,107,000 *Total Assets:* £110,577,000
Registered Office: Pentagon Island, Nottingham Road, Derby, DE21 6HB
Activities: Sale of new cars and light motor vehicles
Parent: Pentagon Motor Holdings Limited
Officers: David Lewis [1962] Director; Andrew Barrie Welch [1965] Director

Reeves Wireline Technologies Limited
Incorporated: 7 January 1908 *Employees:* 87
Net Worth: £45,548,000 *Total Assets:* £59,962,000
Registered Office: Gotham Road, East Leake, Loughborough, Leics, LE12 6JX
Activities: Other manufacturing n.e.c.
Parent: Weatherford Eurasia Limited
Officers: Richard Khalil Strachan, Secretary; Martin John Adams [1959] Director/General Manager; Richard Khalil Strachan [1985] Director/Lawyer

The Reflex Group Limited
Incorporated: 17 December 2001 *Employees:* 520
Net Worth: £18,341,000 *Total Assets:* £59,403,000
Registered Office: Vision House, Hamilton Way, Mansfield, Notts, NG18 5BU
Activities: Manufacture of printed labels
Shareholders: Ian George Kendall; John Michael Turner
Officers: Michael Turner, Secretary; Catherine Kendall [1966] Director/Business Manager; Ian George Kendall [1965] Director; Michael Turner [1956] Financial Director

Reflex Labels Limited
Incorporated: 1 February 1999 *Employees:* 327
Net Worth: £14,478,000 *Total Assets:* £50,931,000
Registered Office: Vision House, Hamilton Way, Oakham Business Park, Mansfield, Notts, NG18 5BU
Activities: Manufacture of printed labels
Parent: The Reflex Group Ltd
Officers: John Michael Turner, Secretary/Director; Ian George Kendall [1965] Director; John Michael Turner [1956] Director

Reflex Vehicle Hire Limited
Incorporated: 17 October 2011 *Employees:* 73
Previous: LCV Hire Solutions Limited
Net Worth: £15,203,383 *Total Assets:* £58,387,240
Registered Office: 22 Belton Road West, Loughborough, Leics, LE11 5TR
Activities: Renting and leasing of cars and light motor vehicles
Shareholder: BGF GP Limited
Officers: Ian Downing [1969] Director/Investment Manager; Mark Patrick Gerard Lewis [1964] Director/Solicitor; Ian Fraser Mackie [1962] Finance Director; Stewart Oades [1953] Independent Director; Lisa Marie Spong [1978] Sales Director; Anthony John Trahar [1949] Director; Oliver Frank Howard Waring [1972] Director

Refood UK Limited
Incorporated: 10 April 2008 *Employees:* 171
Net Worth: £5,395,874 *Total Assets:* £67,601,232
Registered Office: Ings Road, Bentley, Doncaster, S Yorks, DN5 9TL
Activities: Production of electricity
Parent: Saria Limited
Officers: Phillip Antony Simpson [1966] Director; Andrew Richard Smith [1962] Director/Commercial Manager; Franz-Bernhard Thier [1965] Director [German]

Refresco Drinks UK Limited
Incorporated: 14 July 1993 *Employees:* 1,121
Previous: Cott Beverages Limited
Net Worth: £583,336,000 *Total Assets:* £751,484,992
Registered Office: Citrus Grove, Sideley, Kegworth, Derby, DE74 2FJ
Activities: Manufacture of soft drinks; production of mineral waters and other bottled waters
Parent: Pride Foods Limited
Officers: Aart Duijzer [1963] Director [Dutch]; Hans Roelofs [1963] Director [Dutch]; David John Saint [1964] Managing Director

Regen Holdings Limited
Incorporated: 12 December 2014 *Employees:* 160
Net Worth: £19,191,170 *Total Assets:* £31,281,240
Registered Office: The Mine Site, Mill Lane, South Witham, Grantham, Lincs, NG33 5QN
Activities: Collection of non-hazardous waste
Shareholders: TPG Art-Aiv, LP; TPG Art-Aiv, LP
Officers: Christopher John O'Donoghue, Secretary; James Alexander Waldorf Astor [1965] Director; Roel Win Collier [1973] Director [Belgian]; Lewis MacRae Dodds [1965] Director; Geoffrey Mark Duyk [1959] Managing Director & Partner [American]; Clive Desmond Tyler [1957] Director

Regenersis (Depot) Services Ltd
Incorporated: 8 September 1994 *Employees:* 5
Previous: Regenersis (Group) Ltd
Net Worth: £46,673,000 *Total Assets:* £62,627,000
Registered Office: Featherstone Road, Wolverton Mill, Milton Keynes, Bucks, MK12 5TH
Activities: Activities of head offices
Parent: CTDI Repair Services Limited
Officers: Matthew Bull [1975] Managing Director; Dieter Hollenbach [1964] Director [German]; Generald Joseph Parsons [1952] Director/Chairman & CEO [American]; Leo David Parsons [1960] Director/President & COO [American]; Monika Ruth [1968] Director [German]

Regent Office Care Limited
Incorporated: 18 February 1986 *Employees:* 3,490
Net Worth: £2,943,102 *Total Assets:* £15,920,167
Registered Office: Unit 2 Oak Court Pilgrims Walk, Prologis Park, Coventry, Warwicks, CV6 4QH
Activities: General cleaning of buildings
Officers: Baldip Kaur Brreach [1983] Director/Accountant; John Critchell [1958] Director/Sales Manager; Jonathan King [1963] Director/Cleaning Manager; Olivier Noel Ange Alfred Payen [1966] Director [French]; Christian Andre Marie Joseph Roulleau [1951] Director [French]

Regent Park Energy Limited
Incorporated: 9 October 2002
Net Worth: £23,086,000 *Total Assets:* £32,708,000
Registered Office: First Floor, 500 Pavilion Drive, Northampton Business Park, Northampton, NN4 7YJ
Activities: Extraction of crude petroleum
Parent: Alkane Energy Limited
Officers: Jacqueline Long, Secretary; Michael Damien Holton [1973] Finance Director; James Huxley Milne [1972] Director/Lawyer; Stephen Shane Pickering [1969] Managing Director

Regional & City Airports Holdings Limited
Incorporated: 16 March 2010 *Employees:* 771
Net Worth: £34,642,000 *Total Assets:* £149,008,992
Registered Office: Bridgeway House, Bridgeway, Stratford upon Avon, Warwicks, CV37 6YX
Activities: Activities of other holding companies n.e.c.
Parent: Rigby Group (RG) PLC
Officers: Katherine Georgina Cook, Secretary; Andrew Michael Bell [1979] Director; Sir Peter Rigby [1943] Director

Relta Limited
Incorporated: 15 May 2002 *Employees:* 2
Net Worth: £19,636,688 *Total Assets:* £21,222,828
Registered Office: Estate Office, Oakley House, Oakley, Beds, MK43 7ST
Activities: Buying and selling of own real estate
Shareholders: Iain Catleugh Hutchinson; Lousada Investments Limited
Officers: Sharon Anne Hunt, Secretary; Iain Catleugh Hutchinson [1965] Director; Simon Charles Lousada [1963] Director

Remedi Medical Holdings Limited
Incorporated: 16 October 2013 *Employees:* 50
Net Worth: £6,007,621 *Total Assets:* £20,844,708
Registered Office: Nene House, 4 Rushmills, Northampton, NN4 7YB
Activities: Manufacture of pharmaceutical preparations
Shareholders: Monisha Nikesh Kotecha; Nikesh Rasiklal Kotecha; Blue Skies Investments Limited
Officers: Monisha Nikesh Kotecha, Secretary; Monisha Nikesh Kotecha [1969] Director; Dr Nikesh Rasiklal Kotecha [1966] Director

Remploy Limited
Incorporated: 24 February 2015 *Employees:* 873
Net Worth: £6,676,000 *Total Assets:* £19,882,000
Registered Office: 18c Meridian East, Meridian Business Park, Leicester, LE19 1WZ
Activities: Other activities of employment placement agencies
Parent: Maximus Companies Limited
Officers: Susan Bramley, Secretary; Michael Batty [1972] Director; Susan Bramley [1966] Director/Head of Contracts; Elizabeth Muir Carruthers [1966] Director; Kathryn Anne Irons [1984] Director; Gareth Parry [1967] Director; Akbar Piloti [1957] Director [American]

Remy Cointreau UK Distribution Limited
Incorporated: 4 July 2012 *Employees:* 57
Net Worth Deficit: £323,968 *Total Assets:* £15,852,757
Registered Office: Mazars LLP, The Pinnacle, 160 Midsummer Boulevard, Milton Keynes, Bucks, MK9 1FF
Activities: Wholesale of wine, beer, spirits and other alcoholic beverages
Parent: Remy Cointreau UK Limited
Officers: Madame Valerie Marie Anne Chapoulaud-Floquet [1962] Managing Director [French]; Spyridon Ghikas [1959] Director [Greek]; Peter John Sant [1960] Managing Director

Remy Cointreau UK Limited
Incorporated: 4 July 2012 *Employees:* 2
Net Worth: £58,708,336 *Total Assets:* £86,171,200
Registered Office: Mazars LLP, The Pinnacle, 160 Midsummer Boulevard, Milton Keynes, Bucks, MK9 1FF
Activities: Non-trading company
Parent: Remy Cointreau S.A.
Officers: Madame Valerie Marie Anne Chapoulaud-Floquet [1962] Managing Director [French]; Luca Calogero Pietro Marotta [1965] Director/Chief Financial Officer [Italian]

Renault Sport Racing Limited
Incorporated: 5 April 1984 *Employees:* 606
Previous: Lotus F1 Team Limited
Net Worth Deficit: £33,564,000 *Total Assets:* £87,606,000
Registered Office: Whiteways Technical Centre, Enstone, Chipping Norton, Oxon, OX7 4EE
Activities: Operation of sports facilities
Parent: Grigny (UK) Limited
Officers: Benedicte Mercer, Secretary; Cyril Francois Roger Abiteboul [1977] Managing Director [French]; Thierry Yves Henri Bollore [1963] Director/Chief Competitive Office [French]; Thierry Antoine Joseph Cognet [1955] Finance Director [French]; Gerard Lopez [1971] Director [Spanish]; Jerome Xavier Stoll [1954] Director/Chief Performance Office [French]

Renault Truck Commercials Limited
Incorporated: 27 July 1934 *Employees:* 238
Net Worth: £20,249,000 *Total Assets:* £32,845,000
Registered Office: Wedgnock Industrial Estate, Wedgnock Lane, Warwick, CV34 5YA
Activities: Sale of new cars and light motor vehicles
Parent: Volvo Group UK Limited
Officers: Simon Derek Villanueva, Secretary; Olivier de Saint Meleuc [1978] Director/SVP Sales Area North Europe & Russia [French]; Arne Knaben [1958] Director [Norwegian]; Carlos Oliveira Rodrigues [1977] Director/Chief Financial Officer [Portuguese]; Simon Derek Villanueva [1973] Director

Renco (Chesterfield) Limited
Incorporated: 9 November 1987 *Employees:* 1
Net Worth: £14,121,437 *Total Assets:* £14,842,150
Registered Office: The Rutland Arms Hotel, The Square, Bakewell, Derbys, DE45 1BT
Activities: Development of building projects
Major Shareholder: Christopher Renshaw
Officers: Hazel Joyce Renshaw, Secretary; Christopher John Renshaw [1945] Director

Renewi Cumbria Holdings Limited
Incorporated: 23 January 2009
Previous: Shanks Cumbria Holdings Limited
Net Worth: £100,000 *Total Assets:* £11,136,000
Registered Office: Dunedin House, Auckland Park, Mount Farm, Milton Keynes, Bucks, MK1 1BU
Activities: Activities of head offices
Parent: Renewi PFI Investments Limited
Officers: Philip Bernard Griffin-Smith, Secretary; Alistair Daniel Brookes [1976] Director; Mark Alfred Cowan [1970] Director; Mark Andrew Rawling [1979] Director/Financial Controller

Renewi Cumbria Limited
Incorporated: 23 January 2009
Previous: Shanks Cumbria Limited
Net Worth Deficit: £11,947,000 *Total Assets:* £66,065,000
Registered Office: Dunedin House, Auckland Park, Mount Farm, Milton Keynes, Bucks, MK1 1BU
Activities: Other service activities n.e.c.
Parent: Renewi Cumbria Holdings Limited
Officers: Philip Bernard Griffin-Smith, Secretary; Alistair Daniel Brookes [1976] Director; Mark Alfred Cowan [1970] Director; Mark Andrew Rawling [1979] Director/Financial Controller

Renewi European Holdings Limited
Incorporated: 22 July 2014
Previous: Shanks European Holdings Limited
Net Worth: £561,234,880 *Total Assets:* £567,320,000
Registered Office: Dunedin House, Auckland Park, Mount Farm, Milton Keynes, Bucks, MK1 1BU
Activities: Other service activities n.e.c.
Parent: Renewi Holdings Limited
Officers: Philip Bernard Griffin-Smith, Secretary; Peter George Dilnot [1969] Director; Toby Richard Woolrych [1966] Director/Accountant

Renewi Financial Management Limited
Incorporated: 16 February 2005
Previous: Shanks Financial Management Limited
Net Worth: £154,336,000 *Total Assets:* £154,980,992
Registered Office: Dunedin House, Auckland Park, Mount Farm, Milton Keynes, Bucks, MK1 1BU
Activities: Non-trading company
Parent: Renewi European Holdings Limited
Officers: Philip Bernard Griffin-Smith, Secretary; Peter George Dilnot [1969] Director; Toby Richard Woolrych [1966] Director

Renewi Holdings Limited
Incorporated: 30 November 1999
Previous: Shanks Holdings Limited
Net Worth: £213,676,000 *Total Assets:* £497,993,984
Registered Office: Dunedin House, Auckland Park, Mount Farm, Milton Keynes, Bucks, MK1 1BU
Activities: Other service activities n.e.c.
Parent: Renewi PLC
Officers: Philip Bernard Griffin-Smith, Secretary; Peter George Dilnot [1969] Director; Toby Richard Woolrych [1966] Director

Renewi PFI Investments Limited
Incorporated: 8 February 1996
Previous: Shanks PFI Investments Limited
Net Worth Deficit: £1,325,000 *Total Assets:* £42,575,000
Registered Office: Dunedin House, Auckland Park, Mount Farm, Bletchley, Milton Keynes, Bucks, MK1 1BU
Activities: Non-trading company
Parent: Renewi PLC
Officers: Philip Bernard Griffin-Smith, Secretary; Alistair Daniel Brookes [1976] Director; Toby Richard Woolrych [1966] Director

Renewi UK Services Limited
Incorporated: 8 June 1989 *Employees:* 654
Previous: Shanks Waste Management Limited
Net Worth Deficit: £95,630,000 *Total Assets:* £63,642,000
Registered Office: Dunedin House, Auckland Park, Milton Keynes, Bucks, MK1 1BU
Activities: Collection of non-hazardous waste
Parent: Renewi PLC
Officers: Philip Bernard Griffin-Smith, Secretary; Neil Rowland Miles [1970] Director; James Austin Priestley [1963] Managing Director; Toby Richard Woolrych [1966] Director

Replimune Limited
Incorporated: 18 March 2015 *Employees:* 26
Net Worth: £11,547,827 *Total Assets:* £13,160,992
Registered Office: 69 Innovation Drive, Milton Park, Milton, Abingdon, Oxon, OX14 4RQ
Activities: Research and experimental development on biotechnology
Officers: Philip Astley-Sparke [1971] Director; Colin Love [1958] Director/Development Scientist

Resmed (UK) Limited
Incorporated: 19 October 1993 *Employees:* 92
Net Worth: £18,123,138 *Total Assets:* £87,751,696
Registered Office: First Floor, Quad 1, Becquerel Avenue, Harwell Campus, Didcot, Oxon, OX11 0RA
Activities: Non-specialised wholesale trade
Parent: Resmed Inc.
Officers: Nigel Wayne Robinson, Secretary; Andrew Huxter [1969] Director; David Brian Pendarvis [1959] Director/General Counsel [American]

Resmed EPN Ltd
Incorporated: 30 March 2009 *Employees:* 23
Net Worth: £14,669,361 *Total Assets:* £24,673,830
Registered Office: First Floor, Quad 1, Becquerel Avenue, Harwell Campus, Didcot, Oxon, OX11 0RA
Activities: Non-specialised wholesale trade
Parent: Resmed (UK) Limited
Officers: Nigel Wayne Robinson, Secretary; Andrew Huxter [1969] Director/General Manager; David Brian Pendarvis [1959] Director/General Counsel and Corporate Secretary [American]

Resmed European Holdings Limited
Incorporated: 15 August 2013
Net Worth: £18,137,366 *Total Assets:* £18,137,366
Registered Office: First Floor, Quad 1, Becquerel Avenue, Harwell Campus, Didcot, Oxon, OX11 0RA
Activities: Activities of other holding companies n.e.c.
Parent: Resmed Inc.
Officers: Nigel Wayne Robinson, Secretary; Andrew Huxter [1969] Finance Director; David Brian Pendarvis [1959] Director/Legal Counsel [American]

Resonate Group Limited
Incorporated: 7 June 2006 *Employees:* 156
Previous: Deltarail Group Limited
Net Worth Deficit: £8,013,000 *Total Assets:* £33,625,000
Registered Office: Hudson House, 2 Hudson Way, Pride Park, Derby, DE24 8HS
Activities: Business and domestic software development
Parent: Resonate Holdings Limited
Officers: Peter Terence Millican, Secretary; Adrian Lee Barwell [1973] Director; Anna Christina Ince [1963] Director; Adam Perry [1964] Director

Resonate Holdings Limited
Incorporated: 7 June 2006 *Employees:* 166
Previous: Deltarail Holdings Limited
Net Worth Deficit: £8,021,000 *Total Assets:* £33,713,000
Registered Office: Hudson House, 2 Hudson Way, Pride Park, Derby, DE24 8HS
Activities: Activities of head offices
Shareholder: Anna Christina Ince
Officers: Peter Terence Millican, Secretary; Adrian Lee Barwell [1973] Director; Anna Christina Ince [1963] Director; Adam Perry [1964] Director

Resource Recovery Solutions (Derbyshire) Limited
Incorporated: 3 March 2009
Net Worth Deficit: £18,973,000 *Total Assets:* £177,975,008
Registered Office: Dunedin House, Auckland Park, Mount Farm, Milton Keynes, Bucks, MK1 1BU
Activities: Collection of non-hazardous waste
Parent: Resource Recovery Solutions (Derbyshire) Holdings Limited
Officers: Philip Bernard Griffin-Smith, Secretary; Nicholas John Bliss [1959] Director/Solicitor, Consultant; Alistair Daniel Brookes [1976] Director; Rajan Goyal [1966] Director/Accountant; Neil Rowland Miles [1970] Director; Andrew John Sutton [1956] Director

Respond Group Limited
Incorporated: 24 September 2004 *Employees:* 20
Net Worth: £16,498,621 *Total Assets:* £24,835,428
Registered Office: 7 Rushmills, Northampton, NN4 7YB
Activities: Business and domestic software development
Officers: Sandra Ann Cummings [1964] Finance Director; Alan Gibson Somerville [1963] Managing Director; Hellen Maria Stein [1974] Director/Senior Legal Counsel

Retail Merchant Finance Limited
Incorporated: 2 February 2007 *Employees:* 84
Net Worth: £13,799,895 *Total Assets:* £15,256,734
Registered Office: Matrix House, North Fourth Street, Milton Keynes, Bucks, MK9 1NJ
Activities: Other service activities n.e.c.
Officers: Jeremy Jolyon Nicholls, Secretary; Jeremy Jolyon Nicholls [1977] Director/Chief Financial Officer; Kevin Patrick O'Keefe [1973] Director/Commercial & Sales Strategy Officer [American]

Revolve Group Limited
Incorporated: 26 April 2000 *Employees:* 185
Net Worth: £2,302,000 *Total Assets:* £34,271,000
Registered Office: The Priory, Orchard Hill, Little Billing, Northampton, NN3 9AG
Activities: Activities of head offices
Major Shareholder: Martin Langley Coles
Officers: Simon Joseph Wallington, Secretary; Martin Langley Coles [1964] Director/Business Manager

RFE International (Group) Ltd
Incorporated: 8 February 2001 *Employees:* 40
Net Worth Deficit: £1,245,046 *Total Assets:* £10,224,672
Registered Office: 8 Clarendon Drive, Wymbush, Milton Keynes, Bucks, MK8 8ED
Activities: Wholesale of household goods (other than musical instruments) n.e.c
Major Shareholder: Anthony James Patrick Hooper
Officers: Cristy Paige Vincent, Secretary; Daniel John Allinson [1982] Marketing Director; James Gurney Bettle [1975] Director; Anthony James Patrick Hooper [1962] Director/Accountant; Judith Margaret Hooper [1962] Director/Accountant; Isobel Sophie Tuckett [1988] Technical Director

RH Development (Property) Limited
Incorporated: 11 July 1988 *Employees:* 87
Net Worth: £3,263,000 *Total Assets:* £24,188,000
Registered Office: Unit 7A, Colwick Quays Business Park, Colwick, Nottingham, NG4 2JY
Activities: Development of building projects
Shareholder: Nigel Andrew Baxter
Officers: Nigel Andrew Baxter, Secretary; Neville Alfred Baxter [1939] Director; Nigel Andrew Baxter [1963] Director; Peter James Baxter [1973] Director

RHS UK Holdings Limited
Incorporated: 1 October 2002
Net Worth: £9,768,000 *Total Assets:* £16,398,000
Registered Office: First Floor, Lynchgate House, Cannon Park Shopping, Canley, Coventry, Warwicks, CV4 7EH
Activities: Activities of head offices
Parent: Regis International Holdings SARL
Officers: Eric Allen Bakken, Secretary/Lawyer [American]; Eric Allen Bakken [1967] Director/Lawyer [American]

Richard's Pharma Limited
Incorporated: 14 March 2005 *Employees:* 24
Net Worth: £7,278,274 *Total Assets:* £12,123,664
Registered Office: Taylor Group House, Wedgnock Lane, Warwick, CV34 5YA
Activities: Activities of other holding companies n.e.c.
Officers: Laurence Dudley Taylor, Secretary; Malcolm Clive Ramsay [1964] Director; Simone Elizabeth Taylor [1958] Director

Richardson & Cock Limited
Incorporated: 26 March 1955 *Employees:* 12
Net Worth: £9,032,700 *Total Assets:* £9,954,495
Registered Office: Cedar Lodge, Postland, Crowland, Peterborough, Cambs, PE6 0JX
Activities: Growing of cereals (except rice), leguminous crops and oil seeds
Officers: Simon Jonathan James Blake, Secretary; Simon Jonathan James Blake [1981] Director/Farmer; Michael John Cock [1949] Director/Farmer; Robert Harry Richardson [1954] Director/Farmer

Richardson Milling (UK) Limited
Incorporated: 6 February 1984 *Employees:* 144
Previous: European Oat Millers Limited
Net Worth: £16,382,679 *Total Assets:* £27,817,562
Registered Office: Mile Road, Bedford, MK42 9TB
Activities: Grain milling
Officers: Carl Martin Smith, Secretary; Albertus Brand [1965] Managing Director; Richard David Jordan [1950] Director; Darwin Glen Sobkow [1969] Businessman/Director [Canadian]; Curtis Russel Vossen [1953] Businessman/Director [Canadian]

Ricoh UK Limited
Incorporated: 29 July 1976 *Employees:* 2,326
Net Worth: £60,273,000 *Total Assets:* £207,564,000
Registered Office: Ricoh House, 800 Pavilion Drive, Northampton, NN4 7YL
Activities: Information technology consultancy activities
Parent: Ricoh Europe Holdings PLC
Officers: Nicola Clare Downing, Secretary; Nicola Clare Downing [1974] Director/Lawyer; Richard Martin Hewitt [1961] Finance Director; Philip Joseph Keoghan [1955] Director; David Mills [1958] Director

Ridge and Partners LLP
Incorporated: 28 September 2004 *Employees:* 536
Net Worth: £14,849,532 *Total Assets:* £29,876,888
Registered Office: The Cowyards, Blenheim Park, Oxford Road, Woodstock, Oxon, OX20 1QR
Officers: Philip Andrew Baker [1974] Member; Graham James Blackburn [1966] Member; Stephen Cooper [1970] Member; John Murray Farrant [1964] Member; Paul Jonathan Fong [1965] Member; Matthew Graham Francis [1966] Member; Richard David Hand [1967] Member; Jason Alexander Howard [1968] Member; Adrian William O'Hickey [1966] Member; Lucy Mary Osborne [1971] Member; Jolyon Robert Mark Price [1976] Member; Mark Richards [1971] Member; Richard Thorpe [1970] Member; David John Walker [1960] Member; Adrian Westbury [1967] Member; Christopher Alan Bradburn [1966] LLP Member; Adrian Goulding [1973] LLP Member; Christopher John Haworth [1968] LLP Member; David James Johnson [1972] LLP Member; Roger Sandell [1972] LLP Member

Ridgeway Education Trust
Incorporated: 13 June 2012 *Employees:* 322
Previous: Didcot Academy of Schools
Net Worth: £25,630,000 *Total Assets:* £30,633,000
Registered Office: Didcot Girls' School, Manor Crescent, Didcot, Oxon, OX11 7AJ
Activities: General secondary education
Officers: Sophy Jane Parkin-Haig, Secretary; Paul Robert Allen [1970] Director/Chartered Surveyor; Christopher Charles Campbell [1959] Director/Project Management; Ruth Elizabeth Elliot [1977] Director/Chartered Accountant; Dr Marcus Paul Gover [1964] Director; Richard John Hadland [1975] Director/Business Development Manager; Dr Andrew Harrison [1959] Director; Kathryn Jill Judson [1950] Director/Education Consultant; Dr Andrew David Kaye [1959] Director/Scientific Manager; Rachael Warwick [1969] Director/Headteacher; Stephen Henry White [1950] Director

Rieke Packaging Systems Limited
Incorporated: 6 September 1934 *Employees:* 100
Net Worth: £29,082,000 *Total Assets:* £84,200,000
Registered Office: 44 Scudamore Road, Leicester, LE3 1UG
Activities: Manufacture of other plastic products
Parent: Trimas Corporation Limited
Officers: Mark Edward Box [1962] Managing Director; David John Pritchett [1966] Director; Joshua Alan Sherbin [1963] Director/Attorney [American]; Robert Joseph Zalupski [1959] Director [American]

Rigby Capital Investments Ltd
Incorporated: 25 July 2013 *Employees:* 3
Net Worth: £38,549,440 *Total Assets:* £38,842,712
Registered Office: Bridgeway House, Bridgeway, Stratford upon Avon, Warwicks, CV37 6YX
Activities: Other business support service activities n.e.c.
Major Shareholder: Peter Rigby
Officers: James Peter Rigby [1971] Director; Sir Peter Rigby [1943] Director; Steven Paul Rigby [1972] Director

Rigby Group (RG) PLC
Incorporated: 19 September 1997 *Employees:* 7,509
Net Worth: £285,327,008 *Total Assets:* £1,243,282,944
Registered Office: Bridgeway House, Bridgeway, Stratford upon Avon, Warwicks, CV37 6YX
Activities: Non-trading company
Shareholders: Peter Rigby; Rigby Capital Investments Ltd
Officers: Steven Paul Rigby, Secretary; Herbert Walter Campion [1953] Director; James Peter Rigby [1971] Director; Patricia Ann Rigby [1942] Director; Sir Peter Rigby [1943] Director; Steven Paul Rigby [1972] Director

Rigby Group Finance Limited
Incorporated: 9 December 2014
Net Worth: £4,976,000 *Total Assets:* £52,321,000
Registered Office: Bridgeway House, Bridgeway, Stratford upon Avon, Warwicks, CV37 6YX
Activities: Activities of other holding companies n.e.c.
Parent: Rigby Group (RG) PLC
Officers: Sir Peter Rigby [1943] Director; Steven Paul Rigby [1972] Director

Rigby Private Equity Limited
Incorporated: 4 February 2015
Net Worth Deficit: £55,000 *Total Assets:* £28,642,000
Registered Office: Bridgeway House, Bridgeway, Stratford upon Avon, Warwicks, CV37 6YX
Activities: Activities of other holding companies n.e.c.
Parent: Rigby Group Finance Limited
Officers: Julian Hodge [1970] Director/Chief Financial Officer; Sir Peter Rigby [1943] Director; Steven Paul Rigby [1972] Director

Rigby Real Estate Limited
Incorporated: 12 June 2013
Previous: Rigby Group Property Holdings Limited
Net Worth: £11,244,869 *Total Assets:* £19,166,254
Registered Office: Bridgeway House, Bridgeway, Stratford upon Avon, Warwicks, CV37 6YX
Activities: Other business support service activities n.e.c.
Parent: Rigby Group (RG) PLC
Officers: James Peter Rigby [1971] Director; Sir Peter Rigby [1943] Director; Steven Paul Rigby [1972] Director

Right Digital Limited
Incorporated: 15 March 2006
Net Worth Deficit: £107,000 *Total Assets:* £19,473,000
Registered Office: Picsolve International Limited, Victoria Way, Pride Park, Derby, DE24 8AN
Activities: Non-trading company
Parent: Picsolve Holdings Limited
Officers: John Bernard Behrendt [1961] Director/Senior Management; Colin John Tenwick [1960] Director

Rightmove Group Limited
Incorporated: 16 May 2000 *Employees:* 477
Net Worth: £45,322,000 *Total Assets:* £101,245,000
Registered Office: 2 Caldecotte Lake Business Park, Caldecotte Lake Drive, Caldecotte, Milton Keynes, Bucks, MK7 8LE
Activities: Other information technology service activities
Parent: Rightmove PLC
Officers: Sandra Judith Odell, Secretary; Peter Brooks-Johnson [1972] Director; Robyn Perriss [1973] Finance Director

Rightmove PLC
Incorporated: 14 November 2007 *Employees:* 479
Net Worth: £17,183,000 *Total Assets:* £71,813,000
Registered Office: 2 Caldecotte Lake Business Park, Caldecotte Lake Drive, Caldecotte, Milton Keynes, Bucks, MK7 8LE
Activities: Other information technology service activities
Officers: Sandra Judith Odell, Secretary; Peter Brooks Johnson [1972] Director; Jacqueline de Rojas CBE [1962] Director; Andrew Robert Findlay [1969] Finance Director; Scott Edward Forbes [1957] Director [American/British]; Rakhi Parekh [1974] Director [American]; Robyn Perriss [1973] Finance Director; Lorna Mona Tilbian [1957] Director; Peter Wodehouse Williams [1953] Director

Rigid Containers Limited
Incorporated: 2 August 1934 *Employees:* 586
Net Worth: £16,029,110 *Total Assets:* £44,411,560
Registered Office: Stoke Albany Road, Desborough, Kettering, Northants, NN14 2SR
Activities: Manufacture of corrugated paper and paperboard, sacks and bags
Officers: Lars Olaf Maynard, Secretary; Richard John Walker Coward [1960] Managing Director; Geert de Meyer [1963] Director [Belgian]; Jean Paul Wilfrid Macharis [1955] Director [Belgian]; Pierre Ivan Rene Macharis [1962] Director [Belgian]; Lars Olaf Maynard [1959] Director/Chartered Accountant; Erik Peeters [1969] Director [Belgian]

Rigid Group Limited
Incorporated: 12 October 1932 *Employees:* 3
Net Worth: £18,667,512 *Total Assets:* £22,397,112
Registered Office: Stoke Albany Road, Desborough, Kettering, Northants, NN14 2SR
Activities: Manufacture of paper and paperboard
Parent: VPK Packaging Group NV
Officers: Lars Olaf Maynard, Secretary; Richard John Walker Coward [1960] Managing Director; Jean Paul Wilfrid Macharis [1955] Director [Belgian]; Pierre Ivan Rene Macharis [1962] Director [Belgian]; Lars Olaf Maynard [1959] Director/Chartered Accountant; Erik Peeters [1969] Director [Belgian]

Rigid Plastic Containers Finance Limited
Incorporated: 9 August 2010 *Employees:* 2
Net Worth: £175,093,136 *Total Assets:* £321,447,584
Registered Office: Sapphire House, Crown Way, Rushden, Northants, NN10 6FB
Activities: Non-trading company
Parent: RPC Packaging Holdings Ltd
Officers: Nicholas David Martin Giles, Secretary; Simon John Kesterton [1973] Director; Petrus Rudolf Maria Vervaat [1965] Director/Accountant [Dutch]

Rigid Plastic Containers Holdings Limited
Incorporated: 9 August 2010 *Employees:* 2
Net Worth: £1,398,899,968 *Total Assets:* £1,898,800,000
Registered Office: Sapphire House, Crown Way, Rushden, Northants, NN10 6FB
Activities: Non-trading company
Parent: RPC 2017 Holding Company Limited
Officers: Nicholas David Martin Giles, Secretary; Simon John Kesterton [1973] Director; Petrus Rudolf Maria Vervaat [1965] Director/Accountant [Dutch]

Rigid Plastic Containers Packaging Limited
Incorporated: 9 August 2010
Net Worth: £85,200,000 *Total Assets:* £85,500,000
Registered Office: Sapphire House, Crown Way, Rushden, Northants, NN10 6FB
Activities: Non-trading company
Parent: RPC Packaging Holdings Ltd
Officers: Nicholas David Martin Giles, Secretary; Simon John Kesterton [1973] Director; Petrus Rudolf Maria Vervaat [1965] Director/Accountant [Dutch]

Rilmac Holdings Limited
Incorporated: 24 July 1957 *Employees:* 291
Net Worth: £2,889,205 *Total Assets:* £10,668,831
Registered Office: Crofton Drive, Allenby Road Industrial Estate, Lincoln, LN3 4NJ
Activities: Activities of head offices
Shareholder: Paul Keith Walker
Officers: Nicola Walker, Secretary; Steven Andrew Baxter [1962] Managing Director; Paul Keith Walker [1952] Director/Chairman

Rippleglen Limited
Incorporated: 20 February 1979 *Employees:* 146
Net Worth: £835,000 *Total Assets:* £11,535,000
Registered Office: Hazel Court, Midland Way, Barlborough, Chesterfield, Derbys, S43 4FD
Activities: Retail sale in non-specialised stores with food, beverages or tobacco predominating
Parent: First Stop News Limited
Officers: Jonathan Martin James, Secretary; Jonathan Martin James [1968] Director; Mark John Titterton [1965] Director/Group Chief Executive

Ritelite (Systems) Limited
Incorporated: 29 February 1988 *Employees:* 46
Net Worth: £17,752,740 *Total Assets:* £19,349,188
Registered Office: Meadow Park, Bourne Road, Essendine, Stamford, Lincs, PE9 4LT
Activities: Manufacture of electric lighting equipment
Major Shareholder: Marcus John Batty
Officers: Sarah Batty, Secretary; Marcus John Batty [1964] Director

Ritrama (U.K.) Limited
Incorporated: 27 February 1981 *Employees:* 67
Net Worth: £7,348,233 *Total Assets:* £19,378,542
Registered Office: Unit 2 Fifth Avenue, Dukinfield, Cheshire, SK16 4PP
Activities: Other manufacturing n.e.c.
Officers: Peter Burton, Secretary; Dr Martin David Attwood [1963] Technical Director; Peter Lawrence Burton [1966] Finance Director; Mark Leonard Evans [1969] Managing Director; Ricardo Rink [1968] Director [Italian]; Ronald Rink [1971] Director [Italian]; Tomas Fredrico Rink [1944] Director [Venezuelan]; Lee Peter Ward [1969] Sales Director

Rittal Holdings Limited
Incorporated: 5 November 1980 *Employees:* 464
Net Worth: £22,394,000 *Total Assets:* £42,555,000
Registered Office: Roy's Barn, North Street, Burnham Market, King's Lynn, Norfolk, PE31 8HG
Activities: Non-trading company
Officers: Dr Stephen Hobbs, Secretary; Christopher Shelley Barker [1932] Director/Retired Solicitor; Dr Stephen Hobbs [1956] Managing Director; Herr Friedhelm Loh [1946] Director [German]

Rittal Limited
Incorporated: 14 September 1978 *Employees:* 104
Net Worth: £9,885,000 *Total Assets:* £18,197,000
Registered Office: Braithwell Way, Hellaby Industrial Estate, Hellaby, Rotherham, S Yorks, S66 8QY
Activities: Other service activities n.e.c.
Parent: Rittal Holdings
Officers: Martin Glyndwr Hurst Williams, Secretary; Dr Stephen Hobbs [1956] Managing Director

Ritter-Courivaud Limited
Incorporated: 1 October 1940 *Employees:* 248
Net Worth: £21,800,000 *Total Assets:* £25,900,000
Registered Office: Equity House, Irthlingborough Road, Wellingborough, Northants, NN8 1LT
Activities: Wholesale of other food, including fish, crustaceans and molluscs
Parent: Booker Wholesale Holdings Limited
Officers: Veselin Bandev [1978] Finance Director [Bulgarian]; Charles Wilson [1965] Director

River Learning Trust
Incorporated: 27 February 2012 *Employees:* 732
Previous: The Cherwell School Academy Trust
Net Worth: £64,676,168 *Total Assets:* £78,234,512
Registered Office: The Cherwell School, Marston Ferry Road, Oxford, OX2 7EE
Activities: Pre-primary education
Officers: Ruth Bennie [1966] Director/School Teacher; Moira Joyce Dorey [1962] Director/Environmental Consultant; Prof Deborah Mary Eyre [1954] Director; Paul Alexander James [1973] Director/Headteacher; Julie Clare McCulloch [1973] Director/Education Policy Specialist; Giles Orr [1967] Director/Manager; Adam Stephen de Voghelaere Parr [1965] Director/Businessman [British/French]; Adrian Jeremy Price [1951] Director/Architectural Designer; Kirsten Robinson [1964] Finance Director; Deborah Stanbury [1967] Director

Riverleen Finance Unlimited
Incorporated: 2 March 2016
Net Worth: £101,908,304 *Total Assets:* £101,908,304
Registered Office: Sir John Peace Building, Experian Way, NG2 Business Park, Nottingham, NG80 1ZZ
Activities: Fund management activities
Parent: Experian Group Limited
Officers: Ronan Peter Hanna, Secretary; Paul Alan Atkinson [1960] Director; Antony Jonathan Ward Barnes [1964] Director; Karen Julia Greenwood [1967] Director/Chartered Accountant; Daniel Tristan Lilley [1981] Director; Mark Edward Pepper [1963] Director

Riverside Motors (Doncaster) Limited
Incorporated: 2 July 1982 *Employees:* 70
Net Worth: £6,722,390 *Total Assets:* £18,572,256
Registered Office: Riverside House, Wheatley Hall Road, Doncaster, S Yorks, DN2 4NL
Activities: Sale of new cars and light motor vehicles
Parent: Riverside Motors Holdings Limited
Officers: Denise Wright, Secretary; Mark Duane Denton [1963] Sales Director; Stephen Wright [1954] Operations Director

Riverside Motors Holdings Limited
Incorporated: 7 October 1997 *Employees:* 141
Net Worth: £9,684,826 *Total Assets:* £25,666,892
Registered Office: 13 Huddersfield Road, Barnsley, S Yorks, S70 2LW
Activities: Activities of head offices
Shareholders: Mark Duane Denton; Stephen Wright
Officers: Christine Vasey, Secretary; Mark Duane Denton [1963] Director; Stephen Wright [1954] Director

Riviera Tours Limited
Incorporated: 6 December 1984 *Employees:* 142
Net Worth: £47,509,000 *Total Assets:* £69,235,000
Registered Office: New Manor, 328 Wetmore Road, Burton on Trent, Staffs, DE14 1SP
Activities: Tour operator activities
Parent: RTL Bidco Limited
Officers: David Clemson [1966] Director; Ben Hitchcock [1976] Director; Ewan Moore [1974] Director; Kieron John Pollock [1967] Director

RM Education Ltd
Incorporated: 30 November 1973
Net Worth: £24,155,000 *Total Assets:* £96,976,000
Registered Office: 140 Eastern Avenue, Milton Park, Milton, Abingdon, Oxon, OX14 4SB
Activities: Other information technology service activities
Parent: RM PLC
Officers: Gregory Davidson-Shrine, Secretary; John Anthony Baskerville [1973] Managing Director; David John Brooks [1969] Director; Gregory Davidson-Shrine [1974] Director/Lawyer; Neil Thomas George Martin [1972] Director; Angela Michelle Sherwood [1969] HR Director

RM PLC
Incorporated: 2 September 1983 *Employees:* 1,734
Net Worth: £29,875,000 *Total Assets:* £134,390,000
Registered Office: 140 Eastern Avenue, Milton Park, Milton, Abingdon, Oxon, OX14 4SB
Activities: Activities of head offices
Officers: Gregory Davidson-Shrine, Secretary; Andrew Martin Blundell [1960] Director; David John Brooks [1969] Director; Patrick Neil Martell [1963] Director; Neil Thomas George Martin [1972] Director; Deena Mattar [1965] Director; John William Poulter [1942] Director

RM Property and Facilities Solutions Limited
Incorporated: 15 June 2001 *Employees:* 2,884
Previous: Romec Limited
Net Worth: £16,585,000 *Total Assets:* £48,689,000
Registered Office: Highbank House, Exchange Street, Stockport, Cheshire, SK3 0ET
Activities: Other engineering activities
Parent: Royal Mail Group Limited
Officers: Kulbinder Kaur Dosanjh, Secretary; Dr Shaun Paul Davis [1974] Director; Martin David Gafsen [1961] Director; Jayesh Patel [1974] Director

RMA Investments Limited
Incorporated: 15 August 2000
Net Worth: £6,709,320 *Total Assets:* £11,972,364
Registered Office: Claremont House, 1 Market Square, Bicester, Oxon, OX26 6AA
Activities: Management of real estate on a fee or contract basis
Shareholders: Taj Begum; Mohammed Arshad
Officers: Mohammed Arshad [1965] Director

RMS Europe Group Limited
Incorporated: 23 January 2004
Net Worth: £4,198,516 *Total Assets:* £10,177,256
Registered Office: Boothferry Terminal, Bridge Street, Goole, E Yorks, DN14 5SS
Activities: Activities of head offices
Parent: RMS Group Holdings Limited
Officers: Jonathan James Hunter [1972] Director/Chartered Accountant; Ian Dominic Parsons [1949] Director

RMS Group Holdings Limited
Incorporated: 4 May 2007 *Employees:* 224
Net Worth: £4,630,409 *Total Assets:* £20,548,840
Registered Office: Boothferry Terminal, Bridge Street, Goole, N Humbers, DN14 5SS
Activities: Activities of head offices
Officers: Andrew Jonathan Dixon [1968] Managing Director; Stephen Peter Harrison [1977] Director/Investment Professional; Gavin Michael Hindley [1977] Director; Craig Robert Hodgson [1986] Group Commercial Director; Jonathan James Hunter [1972] Finance Director; Ian Dominic Parsons [1949] Director; Jeremy Stuart Saunt [1961] Director/Seed Merchant

RMS Holdco Limited
Incorporated: 2 February 2017 *Employees:* 264
Net Worth Deficit: £84,000 *Total Assets:* £127,123,000
Registered Office: Matrix House, North Fourth Street, Milton Keynes, Bucks, MK9 1NJ
Activities: Activities of other holding companies n.e.c.
Officers: Muzammal Ashraf [1986] Director/Investment Manager [Pakistani]; James Michael Aviles [1960] Director/Business Owner/Investor [American]; Paul Generald Bentham [1960] Director; Christopher Phelan Marshall [1968] Director/Investment Manager [American]; Kevin Patrick O'Keefe [1973] Director/Chief Executive Officer [American]

Roberts Radio Limited
Incorporated: 13 October 1994 *Employees:* 35
Net Worth: £15,125,000 *Total Assets:* £20,128,000
Registered Office: Talbot Road, Swinton, Mexborough, S Yorks, S64 8AJ
Activities: Wholesale of radio, television goods & electrical household appliances (other than records, tapes, CDs)
Parent: Glen Electric Ltd
Officers: Nicholas Anthony Shaw, Secretary; Donal Francis Flynn [1973] Director/Chartered Accountant [Irish]; Fergal John Naughton [1975] Director [Irish]; Martin Lawrence Naughton [1939] Director [Irish]; Neil Naughton [1969] Director [Irish]; Nicholas Anthony Shaw [1974] Finance Director; Owen John Watters [1968] Director/Chief Executive

Robimatic Limited
Incorporated: 16 July 1980 *Employees:* 71
Net Worth: £12,607,000 *Total Assets:* £14,201,000
Registered Office: Broomhouse Lane, Edlington, Doncaster, S Yorks, DN12 1ES
Activities: Manufacture of plastics in primary forms
Parent: Polypipe Limited
Officers: Emma Gayle Versluys, Secretary; Paul Anthony James [1967] Director/Chief Financial Officer; Martin Keith Payne [1965] Director

Robinson (Overseas) Limited
Incorporated: 24 October 1997
Net Worth: £1,704,000 *Total Assets:* £13,882,000
Registered Office: Field House, Wheatbridge, Chesterfield, Derbys, S40 2AB
Activities: Activities of head offices
Parent: Robinson PLC
Officers: Michael Peter Cusick, Secretary; Martin Paul McGee [1955] Director/Chief Executive; Charles William Guy Robinson [1956] Director/Chartered Accountant

Robinson Healthcare Group Limited
Incorporated: 21 July 2011 *Employees:* 171
Net Worth: £12,587,000 *Total Assets:* £15,618,000
Registered Office: Unit 3 Lawn Road Industrial Estate, Carlton in Lindrick, Worksop, Notts, S81 9LB
Activities: Manufacture of medical and dental instruments and supplies
Major Shareholder: Leigh Thomasson
Officers: Richard Andrew Hall [1976] Operations Director; Mark Richardson [1964] Sales Director; Gavin David Smith [1964] Director; Leigh Thomasson [1959] Managing Director

Robinson Healthcare Holdings Ltd
Incorporated: 15 April 2002 *Employees:* 171
Net Worth: £13,189,000 *Total Assets:* £16,895,000
Registered Office: Unit 3 Lawn Road Industrial Estate, Carlton in Lindrick, Worksop, Notts, S81 9LB
Activities: Manufacture of medical and dental instruments and supplies
Major Shareholder: Leigh Thomasson
Officers: Richard Andrew Hall [1976] Operations Director; Mark Richardson [1964] Sales Director; Gavin David Smith [1964] Finance Director; Leigh Thomasson [1959] Managing Director

Robinson Healthcare Limited
Incorporated: 19 May 1999 *Employees:* 171
Net Worth: £9,064,000 *Total Assets:* £12,922,000
Registered Office: Unit 3 Lawn Road Industrial Estate, Carlton in Lindrick, Worksop, Notts, S81 9LB
Activities: Manufacture of medical and dental instruments and supplies
Major Shareholder: Leigh Thomasson
Officers: Richard Andrew Hall [1976] Operations Director; Mark Richardson [1964] Sales Director; Gavin David Smith [1964] Finance Director; Leigh Thomasson [1959] Managing Director

Frederic Robinson Limited
Incorporated: 7 October 1920 *Employees:* 517
Net Worth: £83,431,000 *Total Assets:* £98,526,000
Registered Office: Unicorn Brewery, Lower Hillgate, Stockport, Cheshire, SK1 1JJ
Activities: Manufacture of beer
Shareholders: Dennis William Robinson; Peter Bryan Robinson; David John Robinson
Officers: Sara Xanthe Robinson, Secretary; John Edwards [1957] Director; Stephen John Oliver [1958] Director; David John Robinson [1937] Director; Dennis William Robinson [1933] Director; Oliver John Robinson [1971] Director; Paul Andrew Robinson [1969] Director; Peter Bryan Robinson [1931] Director; Veronica Helen Robinson [1969] Director; William Joseph Robinson [1971] Director; Neil Robinson-Stanier [1966] Director

Robinson PLC
Incorporated: 25 October 1893 *Employees:* 312
Net Worth: £23,056,000 *Total Assets:* £36,336,000
Registered Office: Field House, Wheatbridge, Chesterfield, Derbys, S40 2AB
Activities: Activities of head offices
Officers: Charles William Guy Robinson, Secretary; Michael Peter Cusick [1985] Commercial Director; Charles Compton Anthony Glossop [1941] Director/Solicitor; Sara Frances Halton [1963] Director/Chartered Accountant; Martin Paul McGee [1955] Director/Chief Executive; Alan McLean Raleigh [1959] Director/Supply Chain Executive; Charles William Guy Robinson [1956] Director/Chartered Accountant

Robinsons Caravans Limited
Incorporated: 9 May 1963 *Employees:* 83
Net Worth: £6,200,633 *Total Assets:* £10,193,990
Registered Office: Ringwood Road, Brimington, Chesterfield, Derbys, S43 1DG
Activities: Other retail sale not in stores, stalls or markets
Shareholders: John Ernest Robinson; Margaret Anne Robinson
Officers: Rachael Jane Lee, Secretary; Carol Anne Kirkwood [1965] Director/Stock Administrator; Rachael Jane Lee [1961] Director/Shop & Purchasing Manager; David John Robinson [1959] Director/Caravan Salesman; John Ernest Robinson [1936] Director; Margaret Ann Robinson [1939] Director

Robson Handling Technology Limited
Incorporated: 26 March 1943 *Employees:* 167
Previous: Geo. Robson & Co. (Conveyors) Limited
Net Worth: £5,045,161 *Total Assets:* £10,193,859
Registered Office: Coleford Road, Darnall, Sheffield, S9 5PA
Activities: Manufacture of lifting and handling equipment
Shareholder: Christine Robson
Officers: Abigail Young, Secretary; Colin Max Beresford [1959] Director/Chief Executive; James Neil Gardiner [1970] Operations Director; Julie Ann Kenny [1957] Director/Business Consultant; Christine Robson [1947] Director/Housewife; Stuart Westley [1968] Sales Director; Carolyn Wright [1975] Director/Management Accountant

Roc Oil (Europe) Limited
Incorporated: 12 February 1993 *Employees:* 2
Net Worth: £9,523,859 *Total Assets:* £9,536,238
Registered Office: Nicholsons Chartered Accountants, Newland House, The Point, Weaver Road, Lincoln, LN6 3QN
Activities: Extraction of crude petroleum
Parent: Roc Oil Company Limited
Officers: Neil Butler, Secretary/Financial Manager; Anne Thi Anh Tuyet Vu, Secretary; Neil Butler [1946] Finance Director; Lorne Harry Krafchik [1971] Director/Chief Financial Officer [South African]

Roca Limited
Incorporated: 25 November 1992 *Employees:* 107
Net Worth: £9,062,000 *Total Assets:* £23,929,000
Registered Office: Interlink 145, Interlink Way West, Bardon Hill, Coalville, Leics, LE67 1LD
Activities: Wholesale of hardware, plumbing and heating equipment and supplies
Officers: Miguel Angel Munar Saura, Secretary; Juan Albos Barbarrosa [1963] Director/Lawyer; Alan Thomas Grieve Dodds [1957] Director/Business Executive; Miguel Angel Munar Saura [1962] Director/Lawyer [Spanish]; Rashpal Sidhu [1972] Finance Director

Rochmills (Holdings) Limited
Incorporated: 21 January 2016 *Employees:* 193
Net Worth: £11,213,410 *Total Assets:* £23,703,516
Registered Office: Burlington House, 369 Wellingborough Road, Northampton, NN1 4EU
Activities: Activities of other holding companies n.e.c.
Shareholders: Jatinder Singh Sehmi; Donna Marie Holmes; John Howard Wearing
Officers: Jatinder Singh Sehmi [1948] Director/Pharmacist

Rockwell Automation Limited
Incorporated: 23 February 1966 *Employees:* 688
Net Worth: £79,940,000 *Total Assets:* £111,699,000
Registered Office: Pitfield, Kiln Farm, Milton Keynes, Bucks, MK11 3DR
Activities: Manufacture of electronic industrial process control equipment
Parent: Rockwell Automation, Inc
Officers: Mark Christopher Bottomley [1976] Director; Kawal Maharaj [1967] Director/EMEA Regional Controller [Dutch]; William Joseph Quinn [1955] Director/Chartered Engineer; Alan Kenneth Suttle [1948] Director/Electrical Engineer

Rockwell Commercial Holdings Limited
Incorporated: 24 September 2009
Net Worth: £24,048,000 *Total Assets:* £24,071,000
Registered Office: Pitfield, Kiln Farm, Milton Keynes, Bucks, MK11 3DR
Activities: Activities of head offices
Parent: Rockwell European Holdings Limited
Officers: Kawal Maharaj [1967] Director/EMEA Regional Controller [Dutch]

Rockwell European Holdings Limited
Incorporated: 28 May 1980
Net Worth: £40,098,000 *Total Assets:* £40,651,000
Registered Office: Pitfield, Kiln Farm, Milton Keynes, Bucks, MK11 3DR
Activities: Other business support service activities n.e.c.
Parent: Rockwell Automation, Inc
Officers: Erik Julien Jozef Casselman [1967] Director/General Counsel EMEA Region [Belgian]; Kawal Maharaj [1967] Director/EMEA Regional Controller [Dutch]

Rockwell International
Incorporated: 20 October 1950
Net Worth: £18,196,000 *Total Assets:* £18,747,000
Registered Office: Pitfield, Kiln Farm, Milton Keynes, Bucks, MK11 3DR
Activities: Other business support service activities n.e.c.
Parent: Rockwell European Holdings Limited
Officers: Kawal Maharaj [1967] Director/EMEA Regional Controller [Dutch]

Rodenhurst Estates Limited
Incorporated: 2 May 1924 *Employees:* 3
Net Worth: £55,240,332 *Total Assets:* £79,186,952
Registered Office: Thomas House, Langford Locks, Kidlington, Oxon, OX5 1HR
Activities: Other letting and operating of own or leased real estate
Parent: Highcroft Investments PLC
Officers: Simon Timothy Gill [1956] Property Director; David Henry Kingerlee [1961] Director/Quantity Surveyor; Roberta Caroline Miles [1962] Finance Director

Rodericks Dental Limited
Incorporated: 26 May 1923 *Employees:* 730
Previous: Rodericks Limited
Net Worth: £5,669,853 *Total Assets:* £39,917,208
Registered Office: 15 Basset Court, Loake Close, Grange Park, Northampton, NN4 5EZ
Activities: Dental practice activities
Parent: Rodericks Dental Holdings Limited
Officers: Shalin Mehra, Secretary/Dentist; Carlos Clark [1969] Director; Dawn Farrell [1970] Director; Alpesh Khetia [1976] Director/Dentist; Shalin Mehra [1961] Director/Dentist; Richard Charles Smith [1957] Director/Consultant

Roe Bros. & Co Ltd.
Incorporated: 1 June 1981 *Employees:* 149
Net Worth: £13,288,519 *Total Assets:* £27,416,088
Registered Office: 1 Fenlake Business Centre, Fengate, Peterborough, Cambs, PE1 5BQ
Activities: Manufacture of other fabricated metal products n.e.c.
Shareholders: Frank William Randle Roe; John Patrick William Roe; Richard John Clark; Paul Roe
Officers: Jean Robertson [1964] Director; John Patrick William Roe [1958] Director/Chartered Accountant; Clinton John Taylor [1961] Director

E.M. Rogers Group Limited
Incorporated: 6 August 1990 *Employees:* 97
Net Worth: £6,285,096 *Total Assets:* £11,097,549
Registered Office: The Offices, Ryehill Close, Lodge Farm Industrial Estate, Northampton, NN5 7UA
Activities: Activities of head offices
Shareholders: John Edward Rogers; David Morse Rogers
Officers: John Edward Rogers, Secretary; David Morse Rogers [1951] Director/Haulage Contractor; John Edward Rogers [1954] Director/Haulage Contractor

Rohm Electronics Europe Limited
Incorporated: 18 October 2000
Net Worth: £48,843,000 *Total Assets:* £48,865,000
Registered Office: 41 Caldecotte Lake Drive, Caldecotte Lake Business Park, Milton Keynes, Bucks, MK7 8LF
Activities: Activities of head offices
Parent: Rohm Co. Ltd
Officers: Robert Christian Andre [1961] Director [French]; Kunio Uehara [1960] Director/General Manager of Accounting & Finance Division [Japanese]; Shinichi Yoshimi [1966] Director/General Manager of Human Resources Division [Japanese]

Roko Health Clubs Limited
Incorporated: 9 April 2002 *Employees:* 155
Net Worth Deficit: £2,179,521 *Total Assets:* £13,367,562
Registered Office: Roko Health Club, Wilford Lane, West Bridgford, Nottingham, NG2 7RN
Activities: Fitness facilities
Parent: The Sports & Lesiure Group Ltd
Officers: Nigel Raymond Maglione, Secretary; Raymond John Peter Haskell [1960] Director/Estate Manager; Barry Roy Hunter [1962] Director

Rolec Services Limited
Incorporated: 9 September 1988 *Employees:* 95
Net Worth: £11,860,578 *Total Assets:* £13,523,962
Registered Office: Ralphs Lane, Frampton West, Boston, Lincs, PE20 1QU
Activities: Electrical installation
Major Shareholder: Kieron Jeffery Alsop
Officers: Kieron Jeffery Alsop [1961] Managing Director; Holly Toni Brown [1975] Operations Director; Martin Georgeson [1973] Sales Director; Lee Orrey [1978] Director

The Rolleston Hall Estates Limited
Incorporated: 18 September 1995 *Employees:* 3
Net Worth: £3,276,247 *Total Assets:* £15,045,641
Registered Office: Rolleston Hall, Rolleston, Leics, LE7 9EN
Activities: Growing of cereals (except rice), leguminous crops and oil seeds
Major Shareholder: Robert John Wilkinson
Officers: Susan Ann Wilkinson, Secretary; Robert John Wilkinson [1962] Director; Susan Ann Wilkinson [1961] Director

Rolls-Royce Controls and Data Services Limited
Incorporated: 2 September 2008 *Employees:* 398
Net Worth: £27,800,000 *Total Assets:* £27,800,000
Registered Office: P O Box 31, Moor Lane, Derby, DE24 8BJ
Activities: Other manufacturing n.e.c.
Parent: Rolls-Royce Engine Controls Holdings Limited
Officers: Jacqueline Marie Gentles, Secretary; Andrew Gary Bowden [1968] Director; Andrew Hutson-Smith [1967] Director

Rolls-Royce International Limited
Incorporated: 1 August 1963 *Employees:* 41
Net Worth: £23,119,000 *Total Assets:* £37,193,000
Registered Office: Moor Lane, Derby, DE24 8BJ
Activities: Activities of head offices
Parent: Rolls-Royce PLC
Officers: Jacqueline Marie Gentles, Secretary; Andrew Gary Bowden [1968] Director; Peter Alan Knight [1968] Director

Rolls-Royce Leasing Limited
Incorporated: 2 July 1937
Net Worth: £15,438,000 *Total Assets:* £535,630,016
Registered Office: Moor Lane, Derby, DE24 8BJ
Activities: Renting and leasing of air passenger transport equipment
Parent: Rolls-Royce PLC
Officers: Jonathan Noel Burgess [1971] Director/Vice President - Engine Leasing

Rolls-Royce Overseas Holdings Limited
Incorporated: 30 October 1991
Net Worth: £845,070,976 *Total Assets:* £1,363,266,944
Registered Office: Moor Lane, Derby, DE24 8BJ
Activities: Financial intermediation not elsewhere classified
Parent: Rolls-Royce PLC
Officers: Jacqueline Marie Gentles, Secretary; Jason Howard Luke [1972] Director; William Scott Mansfield [1964] Director/Group Chief Accountant

Rolls-Royce Overseas Investments Limited
Incorporated: 29 August 2000
Net Worth: £2,311,311,104 *Total Assets:* £2,318,479,616
Registered Office: Moor Lane, Derby, DE24 8BJ
Activities: Other business support service activities n.e.c.
Parent: Rolls-Royce Overseas Holdings Limited
Officers: Jason Howard Luke [1972] Director; William Scott Mansfield [1964] Director/Group Chief Accountant; Daniel Szczyrba [1960] Director/Chartered Accountant [Canadian]

Rolls-Royce Power Development Limited
Incorporated: 8 December 1997
Net Worth: £36,153,000 *Total Assets:* £66,559,000
Registered Office: Moor Lane, Derby, DE24 8BJ
Activities: Buying and selling of own real estate
Parent: Rolls-Royce PLC
Officers: Alistair David Katsuhiko MacKenzie [1970] Director/EVP Commercial - Marine

Rolls-Royce Power Engineering PLC
Incorporated: 25 March 1977 *Employees:* 2,614
Net Worth: £534,600,000 *Total Assets:* £988,800,000
Registered Office: Moor Lane, Derby, DE24 8BJ
Activities: Machining
Parent: Rolls-Royce PLC
Officers: Georgios Chatzopoulos, Secretary; Richard Philip Curtis [1954] Director; William Scott Mansfield [1964] Director/Group Chief Accountant

Rolls-Royce Submarines Limited
Incorporated: 6 February 1959 *Employees:* 508
Previous: Rolls-Royce Marine Power Operations Limited
Net Worth: £33,149,000 *Total Assets:* £89,896,000
Registered Office: Atlantic House, Raynesway, Derby, DE21 7BE
Activities: Manufacture of steam generators, except central heating hot water boilers
Parent: Rolls-Royce PLC
Officers: Steven Carlier [1971] Director; Steven Roy Dearden [1960] Director; Christopher John Goulty [1966] Director; Harry Arthur Blair Holt [1968] Director/President, Rolls Royce Controls & Data Services; David Leon Orr [1960] Director; Rosalind Ellen MacAulay Owens [1966] Director

Rolls-Royce Total Care Services Limited
Incorporated: 9 January 1986
Net Worth: £162,438,000 *Total Assets:* £199,004,992
Registered Office: Moor Lane, Derby, DE24 8BJ
Activities: Cargo handling for air transport activities
Parent: Rolls-Royce PLC
Officers: Gareth James Hopkinson [1976] Director

Romax Technology Ltd.
Incorporated: 9 February 1989 *Employees:* 220
Net Worth: £3,721,000 *Total Assets:* £11,777,000
Registered Office: Romax Technology Centre, University of Nottingham Innovation Park, Triumph Road, Nottingham, NG7 2TU
Activities: Other engineering activities
Shareholder: Siu Yun (Peter) Poon
Officers: John Bernard Behrendt [1961] Director; Dr Xiaobing Hu [1979] Director/Chief Commercial Officer; James Farnsworth Lowther [1968] Director; Andrew Poon [1969] Director; Daniel Poon [1967] Director; Rupert Poon [1966] Director/Chief Software Architect; Dr Siu Yun Poon [1934] Director; Mark Benjamin Wells [1955] Director

Romo (Holdings) Limited
Incorporated: 18 February 1991 *Employees:* 377
Net Worth: £74,442,000 *Total Assets:* £85,977,000
Registered Office: Lowmoor Road, Kirkby in Ashfield, Notts, NG17 7DE
Activities: Wholesale of textiles
Shareholders: Robert Mould; Jonathan Frank Mould
Officers: Neil Benjamin Sexton, Secretary; Lindsay Phillippa Biddulph [1976] Director/Sales; Emily Dawn Mould [1979] Director/Design; Felicity May Mould [1977] Director/Manager; Jonathan Frank Mould [1953] Director; Jordan Alexander Mould [1985] Creative Director; Robert Anthony Mould [1948] Director

Romo Limited
Incorporated: 21 February 1944 *Employees:* 286
Net Worth: £51,785,000 *Total Assets:* £59,076,000
Registered Office: Lowmoor Road, Kirkby in Ashfield, Nottingham, NG17 7DE
Activities: Wholesale of textiles
Parent: Romo (Holdings) Limited
Officers: Neil Benjamin Sexton, Secretary; Lindsay Phillippa Biddulph [1976] Director/Sales; David Canovan [1956] Sales Director; Emily Dawn Mould [1979] Director/Design; Felicity May Mould [1977] Director/Manager; Jonathan Frank Mould [1953] Director/Chief Executive; Jordan Alexander Edward Mould [1985] Director; Robert Anthony Mould [1948] Managing Director; Neil Benjamin Sexton [1978] Director/Chartered Accountant

Ronald Hull Jnr. Limited
Incorporated: 23 September 1976 *Employees:* 145
Net Worth: £22,336,364 *Total Assets:* £29,074,124
Registered Office: Mangham Works, Mangham Road, Parkgate, Rotherham, S Yorks, S62 6EF
Activities: Treatment and disposal of non-hazardous waste
Major Shareholder: Ronald Hull
Officers: Vivien Joan Hull, Secretary; David James Hull [1973] Director; Mark Ronald Hull [1980] Director; Nigel Phillip Hull [1976] Director; Ronald Hull [1949] Director; Vivien Joan Hull [1950] Director/Secretary

Roof-Maker Ltd
Incorporated: 22 September 2016 *Employees:* 81
Net Worth: £29,163,576 *Total Assets:* £31,602,158
Registered Office: 1 Pinfold Road, Thurmaston, Leicester, LE4 8AS
Activities: Manufacture of doors and windows of metal
Shareholders: Rachel Ann Owen; Scott Edward Nicholas
Officers: John Julian Browett [1963] Director; Scott Edward Nicholas [1972] Director; Neil Edwin Smith [1971] Director

Roquette UK Limited
Incorporated: 19 March 1980 *Employees:* 142
Net Worth: £40,156,000 *Total Assets:* £92,513,000
Registered Office: 22 Sallow Road, Weldon North Industrial Estate, Corby, Northants, NN17 5JX
Activities: Manufacture of starches and starch products
Parent: Roquette Freres
Officers: Mr Matthew James Flawn [1977] Finance Director; Gianfranco Patrucco [1959] Director [Italian]; Nigel Brian Streatfield [1964] Director/Head of Supply Chain; Christophe Jean Philippe Vanpoulle [1958] Director [French]

Ross & Catherall Limited
Incorporated: 20 November 2000 *Employees:* 211
Net Worth: £157,866,000 *Total Assets:* £174,031,008
Registered Office: Millennium Court, First Avenue, Burton on Trent, Staffs, DE14 2WH
Activities: Other non-ferrous metal production
Parent: Doncasters Limited
Officers: Ian Molyneux, Secretary; Duncan Andrew Hinks [1975] Director/Chief Financial Officer; Ian Molyneux [1964] Director/Solicitor; Lisa Marie Oxnard [1981] Director/Chief Financial Officer

Ross Ceramics Limited
Incorporated: 10 February 1988 *Employees:* 218
Net Worth: £9,765,000 *Total Assets:* £12,881,000
Registered Office: Moor Lane, Derby, DE24 8BJ
Activities: Manufacture of other ceramic products n.e.c.
Parent: Vinters Engineering Limited
Officers: Simon Brailey [1973] Director/Financial Controller Turbines; Dan Parrott [1975] Director

The David Ross Education Trust
Incorporated: 26 March 2007 *Employees:* 1,991
Net Worth: £113,043,000 *Total Assets:* £149,899,008
Registered Office: Charnwood College, Thorpe Hill, Loughborough, Leics, LE11 4SQ
Activities: Primary education
Officers: Maria Maltby, Secretary; Ben Simon Brown [1979] Director; Richard Paul Emerton [1960] Director/Management Consultant; Sir Andrew William Foster [1944] Director; David Hall [1963] Director; Joanne Clair Hoareau [1965] Director/Manager of The David Ross Foundation; John Edward Holbrook [1962] Director/The Bishop of Brixworth; Nigel Jeremy Langstaff [1968] Director; Tracey Maloney [1972] Director/Educational Consultant; David Peter John Ross [1965] Director

Rotherham Sand and Gravel Company Limited (The)
Incorporated: 6 November 1930 *Employees:* 15
Net Worth: £8,480,449 *Total Assets:* £9,099,646
Registered Office: Scrooby Top Quarries, Scrooby, Doncaster, S Yorks, DN10 6AY
Activities: Operation of gravel and sand pits; mining of clays and kaolin
Major Shareholder: Stephen Paul Scholey
Officers: Susan Elizabeth Scholey, Secretary; George Scholey [1987] Director; Nicholas Paul Scholey [1984] Director; Stephen Paul Scholey [1944] Director

Rotherwood Group Ltd
Incorporated: 31 March 2015 *Employees:* 337
Net Worth: £1,180,571 *Total Assets:* £18,132,932
Registered Office: c/o MHA MacIntyre Hudson, 11 Merus Court, Leicester, LE19 1RJ
Activities: Activities of other holding companies n.e.c.
Shareholder: Richard Charles Claridge
Officers: Richard Claridge [1960] Director; John Peter Frederick Fennell [1980] Director

Rotherwood Healthcare Limited
Incorporated: 1 April 2015 *Employees:* 3
Net Worth: £494,171 *Total Assets:* £16,633,693
Registered Office: MHA MacIntyre Hudson, 11 Merus Court, Leicester, LE19 1RJ
Activities: Management of real estate on a fee or contract basis
Parent: Rotherwood Group Limited
Officers: Richard Claridge [1960] Director; John Peter Frederick Fennell [1980] Director

Rotor Clip Limited
Incorporated: 7 September 1999 *Employees:* 144
Net Worth: £2,449,419 *Total Assets:* £11,556,244
Registered Office: 2 Rutland Park, Sheffield, S10 2PD
Activities: Manufacture of other fabricated metal products n.e.c.
Shareholders: Jonathan Slass; Craig Slass
Officers: Craig Slass [1967] Director/Vice President Sales [American]; Jonathan Slass [1966] Director/General Manager [American]

Roubaix Bidco Limited
Incorporated: 29 June 2016 *Employees:* 175
Net Worth Deficit: £473,938 *Total Assets:* £11,984,778
Registered Office: 5 Larsen Road, Goole, E Yorks, DN14 6XG
Activities: Manufacture of other transport equipment n.e.c.
Shareholders: Endless IV (GP) LP; Endless LLP
Officers: David Grey [1956] Director

Routeco Limited
Incorporated: 15 July 1976 *Employees:* 256
Net Worth: £16,211,000 *Total Assets:* £39,037,000
Registered Office: Davy Avenue, Knowlhill, Milton Keynes, Bucks, MK5 8HJ
Activities: Wholesale of other machinery and equipment
Officers: Sean Thomas Evans, Secretary; David Amps [1975] Director; Sean Thomas Evans [1968] Finance Director; Ian Stewart [1960] Director

Rowden House School Limited
Incorporated: 7 November 1985 *Employees:* 126
Net Worth: £12,416,000 *Total Assets:* £13,881,000
Registered Office: 1 St George's Vernon Gate, Derby, DE1 1UQ
Activities: Other education n.e.c.
Parent: Qatar Investment Authority
Officers: James Richard Atkinson, Finance Director; James Richard Atkinson [1968] Finance Director; Brian James Jones [1950] Director/Chief Executive

Rowe Farming Limited
Incorporated: 19 November 2004 *Employees:* 205
Net Worth: £6,650,000 *Total Assets:* £16,421,000
Registered Office: Greenvale AP Limited, Floods Ferry Road, Doddington, March, Cambs, PE15 0UW
Activities: Growing of vegetables and melons, roots and tubers
Parent: Produce Investments PLC
Officers: Angus Stuart Walton Armstrong [1964] Director; Daniel Collins [1980] Director; Caroline Davies [1974] Director; Robert James Keverne Stacey [1974] Director

William Rowland Limited
Incorporated: 6 July 1965 *Employees:* 29
Net Worth: £2,994,454 *Total Assets:* £14,777,846
Registered Office: 9 Meadow Street, Sheffield, S3 7BL
Activities: Wholesale of metals and metal ores
Parent: Amalgamated Metal Investment Holdings Limited
Officers: Hamish Terence Kinnear Brown, Secretary; Hamish Terence Kinnear Brown [1957] Director/Accountant; Richard Mark Lowe [1976] Director/Industrial Sales & Strategic Marketer; David Stephen Sher [1983] Managing Director; Karen Louise Tazzyman [1966] Director/Metal Trader

Rowlinson Constructions Limited
Incorporated: 31 March 1991 *Employees:* 59
Net Worth: £8,410,039 *Total Assets:* £14,042,626
Registered Office: London House, London Road South, Poynton, Stockport, Cheshire, SK12 1YP
Activities: Development of building projects
Officers: Adrian Charles Simpson, Secretary; David Simon Chilton [1969] Director; Adrian Charles Simpson [1959] Director; Stephen Joseph Weir [1972] Director

F.H.Rowse Limited
Incorporated: 26 August 1919 *Employees:* 2
Net Worth: £7,171,534 *Total Assets:* £16,274,960
Registered Office: 4 St Mary's Arcade, Wallingford, Oxon, OX10 0EY
Activities: Activities of head offices
Officers: Richard Montague Rowse [1948] Director/Retailer

Rowstock Limited
Incorporated: 16 July 1986 *Employees:* 15
Net Worth: £11,040,089 *Total Assets:* £11,577,484
Registered Office: Rowstock House, Rowstock, Didcot, Oxon, OX11 0JN
Activities: Sale of new cars and light motor vehicles
Officers: Luke Ryan Davis, Secretary; Georgina Davis [1957] Director/Secretary; Joseph Little John Davis [1958] Director/Car Dealer

Roxhill (Peterborough) Limited
Incorporated: 23 September 2010 *Employees:* 4
Net Worth Deficit: £2,614,856 *Total Assets:* £24,976,416
Registered Office: Lumonics House, Valley Drive, Swift Valley, Rugby, Warwicks, CV21 1TQ
Activities: Buying and selling of own real estate
Officers: Josh Furniss, Secretary; Ashley John Hollinshead [1977] Finance Director; David Christopher Lindsay Kier [1962] Director; Graham Nicholas Pardoe [1973] Director

Roxhill (Tilbury) Limited
Incorporated: 12 November 2012 *Employees:* 4
Net Worth: £593,615 *Total Assets:* £10,970,626
Registered Office: Lumonics House, Valley Drive, Swift Valley, Rugby, Warwicks, CV21 1TQ
Activities: Buying and selling of own real estate
Officers: Josh Furniss, Secretary; Charles James Blake [1978] Director/Chartered Surveyor; Jason Andrew Denholm Dalby [1967] Director/Chartered Surveyor; Ashley John Hollinshead [1977] Finance Director; David Christopher Lindsay Kier [1962] Director/Executive Chairman

Roxhill Developments Group Limited
Incorporated: 11 November 2010
Net Worth: £37,537,708 *Total Assets:* £87,487,160
Registered Office: Lumonics House, Valley Drive, Swift Valley, Rugby, Warwicks, CV21 1TQ
Activities: Development of building projects
Shareholder: Frxl Co-Investment GP 1 Limited
Officers: Ashley John Hollinshead, Secretary; Alexander Robert Bignell [1972] Director; Mark Lewis Glatman [1956] Director; Ashley John Hollinshead [1977] Finance Director; David Christopher Lindsay Keir [1962] Director; Stephanie Miles [1972] Finance Director; Jeremy James Plummer [1959] Director/Fund Manager; Andrew Nicholas Walker [1962] Director

Roxhill Developments Limited
Incorporated: 9 November 2009 *Employees:* 4
Net Worth: £431,530 *Total Assets:* £33,356,780
Registered Office: Lumonics House, Valley Drive, Swift Valley, Rugby, Warwicks, CV21 1TQ
Activities: Construction of commercial buildings
Officers: Josh Furniss, Secretary; Ashley John Hollinshead [1977] Finance Director; David Christopher Lindsay Kier [1962] Director; Graham Nicholas Pardoe [1973] Director/Developer

The Royal Latin School
Incorporated: 28 June 2011 *Employees:* 110
Net Worth: £12,062,787 *Total Assets:* £14,540,983
Registered Office: The Royal Latin School, Chandos Road, Buckingham, MK18 1AX
Activities: General secondary education
Officers: Rebecca Lucy Wilson, Secretary; Katrine Brown [1964] Director/Bookkeeper; Virginia Jane Brown [1967] Director/Finance Manager; Dr Alan Grenville Clamp [1966] Director/Chief Executive; Glenn Collins [1968] Director of Finance Operations; Philip John Dart [1968] Service Director, Bucks County Council; Kenneth Mark Davis [1971] Director; Graham Ernest Paul French [1954] Director/Caretaker; Christine Hickey [1969] Director/Solicitor; David William Hudson [1962] Director/Headteacher; Andrew Trevor Jarvis [1972] Director; David Edward Allan Jenkins [1987] Director/Teacher; Rashesh Babu Joshi [1970] Director/Chartered Accountant; Alice Louise Morgan [1963] Director/Market Research Consultant; Rajinder Sharma [1969] Director/Commercial Manager for Business Engagement; Naveed Razak Sheikh [1964] Director/Manager; The Revd Canon Dr Peter Williams [1941] Director/Retired; Baron Wayne Wilson [1954] Director/Chartered Accountant

Roythornes Limited
Incorporated: 4 June 2008 *Employees:* 188
Net Worth: £7,756,359 *Total Assets:* £11,299,595
Registered Office: Roythornes Limited, Enterprise Way, Pinchbeck, Spalding, Lincs, PE11 3YR
Activities: Other business support service activities n.e.c.
Officers: Ann Elizabeth Barrasso, Secretary; Peter William Wels Cusick [1965] Director/Solicitor; Thomas Guy Foottit [1961] Director/Solicitor; Nicholas Guy Ingrey [1957] Director/Lawyer; Vember Mortlock [1966] Director/Solicitor; Jarred Thomas Wright [1973] Director/Solicitor

RPC 2017 Holding Company Limited
Incorporated: 21 July 2017
Net Worth: £1,791,699,968 *Total Assets:* £2,271,000,064
Registered Office: Sapphire House, Crown Way, Rushden, Northants, NN10 6FB
Activities: Activities of production holding companies
Parent: RPC Group PLC
Officers: Nicholas David Martin Giles, Secretary; Nicholas David Martin Giles [1971] Director/Company Secretary; Simon John Kesterton [1973] Director; Petrus Rudolf Maria Vervaat [1965] Director [Dutch]

RPC Asia Pacific Holdings Limited
Incorporated: 14 April 2014 *Employees:* 2
Net Worth: £64,800,000 *Total Assets:* £222,500,000
Registered Office: Sapphire House, Crown Way, Rushden, Northants, NN10 6FB
Activities: Activities of production holding companies
Parent: RPC Packaging Holdings Ltd
Officers: Nicholas David Martin Giles, Secretary; Simon John Kesterton [1973] Director; Petrus Rudolf Maria Vervaat [1965] Director/Accountant [Dutch]

RPC Containers Limited
Incorporated: 3 February 1993 *Employees:* 1,531
Net Worth: £268,300,000 *Total Assets:* £455,600,000
Registered Office: Sapphire House, Crown Way, Rushden, Northants, NN10 6FB
Activities: Manufacture of plastic packing goods
Parent: Rigid Plastic Containers Holdings Ltd
Officers: Nicholas David Martin Giles, Secretary; David James Baker [1960] Director/General Manager; Nicholas David Martin Giles [1971] Director; Simon John Kesterton [1973] Director

RPC Group PLC
Incorporated: 31 January 1991 *Employees:* 24,295
Net Worth: £1,917,100,032 *Total Assets:* £4,783,399,936
Registered Office: Sapphire House, Crown Way, Rushden, Northants, NN10 6FB
Activities: Activities of head offices
Officers: Nicholas David Martin Giles, Secretary; Dr Lynn Drummond [1959] Director; Simon John Kesterton [1973] Director; James Robert Provan Pike [1955] Director; Dr Rosalind Catherine Rivaz [1955] Director; Kevin John Thompson [1959] Director; Petrus Rudolf Maria Vervaat [1965] Director/Accountant [Dutch]; Godwin Shek-Ho Wong [1949] Director/Adjunct Professor [American/Hong Kong]

RPC Packaging Holdings Limited
Incorporated: 26 November 1996 *Employees:* 2
Net Worth: £1,094,200,064 *Total Assets:* £2,108,800,000
Registered Office: Sapphire House, Crown Way, Rushden, Northants, NN10 6FB
Activities: Activities of production holding companies
Parent: Rigid Plastic Containers Holdings Ltd
Officers: Nicholas David Martin Giles, Secretary; Simon John Kesterton [1973] Director; Petrus Rudolf Maria Vervaat [1965] Director/Accountant [Dutch]

RPC Pisces Holdings Limited
Incorporated: 11 November 2014 *Employees:* 2
Net Worth: £949,884,672 *Total Assets:* £1,390,544,640
Registered Office: Sapphire House, Crown Way, Rushden, Northants, NN10 6FB
Activities: Activities of head offices
Parent: RPC Packaging Holdings Ltd
Officers: Nicholas David Martin Giles, Secretary; Nicholas David Martin Giles [1971] Director/Company Secretary; Simon John Kesterton [1973] Director; Petrus Rudolf Maria Vervaat [1965] Director [Dutch]

RPS Consulting Services Limited
Incorporated: 31 December 1979 *Employees:* 1,157
Previous: The Environmental Consultancy Limited
Net Worth: £32,146,000 *Total Assets:* £69,223,000
Registered Office: 20 Western Avenue, Milton Park, Milton, Abingdon, Oxon, OX14 4SH
Activities: Other engineering activities
Parent: RPS Group PLC
Officers: David Joseph Gormley, Secretary; John James Chubb [1965] Director; Siobhan Claire Martin [1979] Director; Gary Richard Young [1960] Finance Director

RPS Energy Limited
Incorporated: 7 December 1979 *Employees:* 184
Net Worth: £25,642,000 *Total Assets:* £56,234,000
Registered Office: 20 Western Avenue, Milton Park, Milton, Abingdon, Oxon, OX14 4SH
Activities: Support activities for petroleum and natural gas mining
Parent: RPS Group PLC
Officers: David Joseph Gormley, Secretary; Edward Jankowski [1956] Director; Gary Richard Young [1960] Director

RPS Environmental Management Limited
Incorporated: 26 September 1983 *Employees:* 1,064
Net Worth: £16,958,000 *Total Assets:* £28,347,000
Registered Office: 20 Western Avenue, Milton Park, Milton, Abingdon, Oxon, OX14 4SH
Activities: Other engineering activities
Parent: RPS Group PLC
Officers: David Joseph Gormley, Secretary; William Paul Aitken [1966] Director; Robert Owen [1965] Director; Gary Richard Young [1960] Finance Director

RPS Group US Holdings Limited
Incorporated: 7 March 1995
Net Worth: £115,207,392 *Total Assets:* £116,026,984
Registered Office: 20 Western Avenue, Milton Park, Milton, Abingdon, Oxon, OX14 4SH
Activities: Other engineering activities
Parent: RPS Group PLC
Officers: David Joseph Gormley, Secretary; Peter Charles Fearn [1953] Director; David Joseph Gormley [1963] Director; Gary Richard Young [1960] Director

RPS US Holdings Limited
Incorporated: 15 February 1990
Net Worth: £2,899,640 *Total Assets:* £111,770,296
Registered Office: 20 Western Avenue, Milton Park, Milton, Abingdon, Oxon, OX14 4SH
Activities: Other engineering activities
Parent: RPS America Group Inc
Officers: David Joseph Gormley, Secretary; Peter Charles Fearn [1953] Director; David Joseph Gormley [1963] Director; Gary Richard Young [1960] Finance Director

RRD GDS Limited
Incorporated: 14 April 2005
Net Worth: £11,042,000 *Total Assets:* £11,042,000
Registered Office: Tower Close, Huntingdon, Cambs, PE29 7YD
Activities: Other business support service activities n.e.c.
Parent: RR Donnelley Global Document Solutions Group Limited
Officers: Jonathan Simon Richard Dally, Secretary; John Samuel Farmer [1960] Director; Kevin Trevor Woor [1965] Director/Financial Controller

RS Components Limited
Incorporated: 9 February 1971 *Employees:* 2,944
Net Worth: £217,300,000 *Total Assets:* £534,700,000
Registered Office: Birchington Road, Weldon, Corby, Northants, NN17 9RS
Activities: Wholesale of electronic and telecommunications equipment and parts
Parent: Electrocomponents PLC
Officers: Ian Peter Haslegrave, Secretary; David John Egan [1967] Finance Director [British/Australian]; Michael John England [1974] Director/Country Manager UK and Head of Region, Northern Europe; Elaine Jane Pointon [1975] Director/Accountant; Lindsley Ruth [1970] Director [American]

RTC Group PLC
Incorporated: 15 November 1990 *Employees:* 199
Net Worth: £4,189,000 *Total Assets:* £15,488,000
Registered Office: The Derby Conference Centre, London Road, Derby, DE24 8UX
Activities: Activities of head offices
Officers: Sarah Louise Dye, Secretary; William James Charles Douie [1939] Director; Sarah Louise Dye [1966] Finance Director; Brian Ward May [1951] Director; Andrew Mark Pendlebury [1960] Director

RTFH Limited
Incorporated: 17 December 2016 *Employees:* 87
Net Worth: £2,728,072 *Total Assets:* £13,598,556
Registered Office: Rayburn House, Brunel Parkway, Pride Park, Derby, DE24 8HR
Activities: Activities of other holding companies n.e.c.
Shareholders: John Boyden; Brenda Boyden; Katie Boyden; James Thomas Boyden
Officers: Jenny Squires, Secretary; Brenda Boyden [1947] Director; James Thomas Boyden [1981] Director; John Boyden [1947] Director; Katherine Boyden [1975] Director

RTI Advanced Forming Limited
Incorporated: 26 August 2011 *Employees:* 139
Net Worth: £10,589,588 *Total Assets:* £33,835,772
Registered Office: 26a Atlas Way, Sheffield, S4 7QQ
Activities: Other non-ferrous metal production
Parent: RTI Europe Limited
Officers: Petra Papinniemi-Ainger, Secretary; Lluis Maria Fargas Mas [1966] Director/Lawyer [Swiss]; Harald Martin Klein [1959] Director/VP Sales Europe AES; Graham Dennis Vickers [1967] Director/General Manager; Simon James Wareham [1979] Director/Segment Controller

RTI Europe Limited
Incorporated: 11 January 2000
Net Worth: £57,015,892 *Total Assets:* £59,614,372
Registered Office: Alcoa House, 26a Atlas Way, Sheffield, S4 7QQ
Activities: Manufacture of other fabricated metal products n.e.c.
Parent: Arconic Inc.
Officers: Petra Papinniemi-Ainger, Secretary; Dr Kay Louise Dowdall [1969] Director/Chartered Accountant; Lluis Maria Fargas Mas [1966] Director/Lawyer [Swiss]

RTI Extrusions Europe Limited
Incorporated: 11 July 2013 *Employees:* 70
Net Worth: £12,195,512 *Total Assets:* £16,497,528
Registered Office: 26a Atlas Way, Sheffield, S4 7QQ
Activities: Manufacture of other fabricated metal products n.e.c.
Parent: RTI Extrusions Europe (Holdings) Limited
Officers: Petra Papinniemi-Ainger, Secretary; Lluis Maria Fargas Mas [1966] Director/Lawyer [Swiss]; Harald Martin Klein [1959] Director; Graham Dennis Vickers [1967] Director/General Manager; Simon James Wareham [1979] Director/Segment Controller

RTI International Metals Limited
Incorporated: 23 June 1998 *Employees:* 56
Net Worth: £18,759,984 *Total Assets:* £48,113,352
Registered Office: 26a Atlas Way, Sheffield, S4 7QQ
Activities: Other manufacturing n.e.c.
Parent: RTI Europe Limited
Officers: Petra Papinniemi-Ainger, Secretary; Peter John Eccles [1972] Director/Accountant; Lluis Maria Fargas Mas [1966] Director/Lawyer [Swiss]; Harald Martin Klein [1959] Director/VP Sales Europe AES; Anthony Malcolm Roberts [1963] Director/Plant Manager [British/American]

RTL Bidco Limited
Incorporated: 27 November 2014
Net Worth Deficit: £11,377,000 *Total Assets:* £138,412,992
Registered Office: New Manor, 328 Wetmore Road, Burton on Trent, Staffs, DE14 1SP
Activities: Activities of other holding companies n.e.c.
Parent: RTL Cleanco Limited
Officers: David Clemson [1966] Director; Kieron John Pollock [1967] Director

RTL Cleanco Limited
Incorporated: 27 November 2014 *Employees:* 142
Net Worth Deficit: £20,485,000 *Total Assets:* £139,616,000
Registered Office: New Manor, 328 Wetmore Road, Burton on Trent, Staffs, DE14 1SP
Activities: Activities of other holding companies n.e.c.
Parent: RTL Midco Limited
Officers: David Clemson [1966] Director; Kieron John Pollock [1967] Director

RTL Midco Limited
Incorporated: 27 November 2014
Net Worth Deficit: £23,979,000 *Total Assets:* £79,073,000
Registered Office: New Manor, 328 Wetmore Road, Burton on Trent, Staffs, DE14 1SP
Activities: Activities of other holding companies n.e.c.
Parent: RTL Topco Limited
Officers: David Clemson [1966] Director; Kieron John Pollock [1967] Director

RTL Topco Limited
Incorporated: 27 November 2014 *Employees:* 142
Net Worth Deficit: £45,133,000 *Total Assets:* £139,618,000
Registered Office: New Manor, 328 Wetmore Road, Burton on Trent, Staffs, DE14 1SP
Activities: Activities of other holding companies n.e.c.
Parent: Maverick Bidco Limited
Officers: David Clemson [1966] Director; Kieron John Pollock [1967] Director

Rubicon Drinks Limited
Incorporated: 14 September 1981
Net Worth: £80,284,000 *Total Assets:* £82,823,000
Registered Office: Crossley Drive, Magna Park, Milton Keynes, Bucks, MK17 8FL
Activities: Manufacture of soft drinks; production of mineral waters and other bottled waters
Parent: A.G. Barr P.L.C.
Officers: Julie Anne Barr, Secretary; Stuart Lorimer [1966] Finance Director; Roger Alexander White [1965] Director

Ruddington Homes Limited
Incorporated: 10 April 1985 *Employees:* 119
Net Worth: £9,025,593 *Total Assets:* £12,320,863
Registered Office: 2 Cheapside, Derby, DE1 1BR
Activities: Residential care activities for the elderly and disabled
Major Shareholder: Paul Hearn
Officers: Paul Hearn [1962] Director [Irish]

Patrick Ruddy Homes Limited
Incorporated: 9 October 1997
Net Worth: £12,818,623 *Total Assets:* £19,358,160
Registered Office: Enterprise Way, Flitwick, Bedford, MK45 5BS
Activities: Other business support service activities n.e.c.
Major Shareholder: Patrick Joseph Ruddy
Officers: Lee Myles Ruddy, Secretary/Chartered Management Accountant; Alan Joseph Ruddy [1974] Director/Chartered Surveyor; Eileen Catherine Ruddy [1939] Director/Company Secretary [Irish]; Lee Myles Ruddy [1976] Director/Chartered Management Accountant; Patrick Joseph Ruddy [1938] Director [Irish]

Ruddy Joinery Limited
Incorporated: 13 February 1978 *Employees:* 170
Net Worth: £18,865,300 *Total Assets:* £36,239,128
Registered Office: Enterprise Way, Flitwick, Beds, MK45 5BS
Activities: Other construction installation
Major Shareholder: Patrick Joseph Ruddy
Officers: Michael McGilloway [1963] Director/Commercial Manager [Irish]; Alan Joseph Ruddy [1974] Director/Surveyor; Eileen Catherine Ruddy [1939] Director/Secretary [Irish]; Lee Myles Ruddy [1976] Director/Chartered Management Accountant; Patrick Joseph Ruddy [1938] Director [Irish]

Rudridge Limited
Incorporated: 11 February 2000 *Employees:* 75
Net Worth: £7,515,000 *Total Assets:* £16,562,000
Registered Office: Lodge Way House, Lodge Way, Harlestone Road, Northampton, NN5 7UG
Activities: Agents involved in the sale of timber and building materials
Parent: Travis Perkins PLC
Officers: Francis Mark Elkins [1967] Director; Stephen Harris [1972] Director; Alan Richard Williams [1969] Director/Accountant

The Rugby Group Limited
Incorporated: 30 June 1925
Net Worth: £90,092,000 *Total Assets:* £95,715,000
Registered Office: Cemex House, Evreux Way, Rugby, Warwicks, CV21 2DT
Activities: Non-trading company
Parent: Cemex UK Operations Limited
Officers: Rebecca Juliet Wright, Secretary; Vishal Puri [1974] Director/Solicitor; Larry Jose Zea Betancourt [1961] Business Service Organisation Director [Venezuelan]

Rumenco Limited
Incorporated: 16 June 2000 *Employees:* 179
Net Worth: £16,682,370 *Total Assets:* £27,780,518
Registered Office: Stretton House, Derby Road, Stretton, Burton on Trent, Staffs, DE13 0DW
Activities: Manufacture of prepared feeds for farm animals
Officers: Nicholas John Duncalf, Secretary; Nicholas John Duncalf [1956] Director/Accountant; Dr Frank Cedric Heap [1939] Director; Nigel Richard Lyon [1968] Managing Director

Rushcliffe Care Holdings Limited
Incorporated: 24 February 2015 *Employees:* 1,038
Net Worth: £31,413,728 *Total Assets:* £85,287,888
Registered Office: 3rd Floor, Butt Dyke House, 33 Park Row, Nottingham, NG1 6EE
Activities: Activities of other holding companies n.e.c.
Major Shareholder: Surjit Singh Rai
Officers: David Kaplan, Secretary; Surjit Singh Rai [1958] Director/Chief Executive [Indian]

Rushcliffe Care Limited
Incorporated: 7 October 1992 *Employees:* 794
Net Worth: £16,360,568 *Total Assets:* £62,654,056
Registered Office: 3rd Floor, Butt Dyke House, 33 Park Row, Nottingham, NG1 6EE
Activities: Residential nursing care facilities
Officers: David Kaplan, Secretary; Karen Anne Noon, Secretary; Sue Lesley Wilkinson, Secretary; Surjit Singh Rai [1958] Director/Nursing Home Proprietor [Indian]

Rushcliffe Specialist Schools (Mickleover) Limited
Incorporated: 20 May 2009 *Employees:* 116
Net Worth: £899,934 *Total Assets:* £13,542,334
Registered Office: 3rd Floor, Butt Dyke House, 33 Park Row, Nottingham, NG1 6EE
Activities: Activities of other holding companies n.e.c.
Officers: David Kaplan, Secretary; Karen Ann Noon, Secretary; Sue Lesley Wilkinson, Secretary; Surjit Singh Rai [1958] Director/Nursing Home Proprietor [Indian]

Rushcliffe Specialist Schools Limited
Incorporated: 1 September 2009
Net Worth Deficit: £139,676 *Total Assets:* £11,673,244
Registered Office: 3rd Floor, Butt Dyke House, 33 Park Row, Nottingham, NG1 6EE
Activities: Activities of other holding companies n.e.c.
Officers: David Kaplan, Secretary; Karen Ann Noon, Secretary; Sue Lesley Wilkinson, Secretary; Surjit Singh Rai [1958] Director/Nursing Home Proprietor [Indian]

Rushlift Limited
Incorporated: 28 June 2005 *Employees:* 245
Net Worth: £10,216,000 *Total Assets:* £69,578,000
Registered Office: Unit 12 Kilvey Road, Brackmills Industrial Estate, Northampton, NN4 7BQ
Activities: Renting and leasing of trucks and other heavy vehicles
Parent: Doosan Materials Handling UK Ltd
Officers: David John Clarkson [1965] Director/Chief Executive Officer; Se Yun Hwang [1980] Human Resources Director [South Korean]; Jae Hun Lee [1974] Director/Chief Financial Officer [South Korean]; Carl Anthony Whyment [1977] Operations Director; Timothy James Willett [1963] Operations Director G.S.E

Rushton Hall Limited
Incorporated: 24 September 2007 *Employees:* 100
Net Worth: £3,716,874 *Total Assets:* £13,777,817
Registered Office: Estate Office, Rushton Hall, Rushton, Northants, NN14 1RR
Activities: Hotels and similar accommodation
Major Shareholder: Thomas Robert Hazelton
Officers: Thomas Robert Hazelton [1966] Director; Valerie Danielle Hazelton [1969] Director

Ruskin College
Incorporated: 11 June 1900 *Employees:* 65
Net Worth: £10,224,683 *Total Assets:* £14,691,934
Registered Office: Ruskin College, Dunstan Road, Headington, Oxford, OX3 9BZ
Activities: Other education n.e.c.
Officers: Heather Cross, Secretary; Neil Richard Crew [1961] Director/Trade Union Official; Paul di Felice [1963] Director/Acting Principal; Dr Peter Gerard Dwyer [1965] Director/Tutor; Kevin William Flanagan [1954] Director; Ed Hart [1961] Director/Audio Visual Technician; Elizabeth Anne Hock [1952] Managing Director; Theresa Hoenig [1956] Director/Retired; Paul Inman [1959] Director/University Senior Manager; Doug James Nicholls [1956] Director/TV Secretary; Michael John Parker [1948] Director/Retired; Pearl Georgette Ryall [1958] Director/Education Manager

Russell Acott Limited
Incorporated: 23 November 1912 *Employees:* 4
Net Worth: £9,003,784 *Total Assets:* £10,749,327
Registered Office: 30 St Giles, Oxford, OX1 3LE
Activities: Other letting and operating of own or leased real estate
Shareholders: Russell Derek Ansell; Graham Richard Ansell
Officers: Graham Richard Ansell, Secretary; Graham Richard Ansell [1944] Director; Russell Derek Ansell [1942] Director

Russell Building Products Limited
Incorporated: 28 June 2011 *Employees:* 181
Net Worth: £7,132,523 *Total Assets:* £25,749,572
Registered Office: Nicolson Way, off Wellington Road, Burton on Trent, Staffs, DE14 2AW
Activities: Other manufacturing n.e.c.
Shareholders: Beks S.A. de C.V.; Bernardo Garza de la Fuente; Banco Invex S.A. IBM Invex Grupo Financerio Trust No 3206; Crown Global Equity S.A.P.I. de CV; Grupo Japresor S.A.P.I. de C.V.
Officers: Araminta Constance Chesters [1977] Finance Director; Andrew Hayward [1964] Managing Director; Juan Prestamo [1966] Director [Mexican]

Mark Rutherford School Trust
Incorporated: 3 December 2012 *Employees:* 215
Net Worth: £11,190,044 *Total Assets:* £12,563,608
Registered Office: Mark Rutherford School, Wentworth Drive, Bedford, MK41 8PX
Activities: General secondary education
Officers: Michelle Nicole Bye-Gannon, Secretary; Robert Francis Barker [1978] Director/Raising Achievement Manager; Christine Helen Bertram [1949] Director/Retired; Warwick Edward Lloyd Browning [1957] Director; Joseph Emmanuel Campbell [1986] Director/Accountant; Stephanie Jane Field [1970] Director/PA Administrator; Katrina Grant [1975] Director/Restaurant Manager; Daniel Robert Koch [1981] Director/Teacher; Sarah Lapidge [1972] Director/Personal Assistant; Alasdair MacLennan [1979] Director/Teacher; John Marsh [1942] Director/Retired; Richard Alan Millard [1962] Director/Headteacher; Paula Anne Page [1972] Director/Project Manager; Dr Arlene Rust [1968] Director/Product Manager; Ian Peter Simpson [1971] Director/Chartered Accountant; Nicola Stephanie Southgate [1968] Director/Learning Area Manager; Nicole Stout [1976] Director/Civil Servant

Rutland and District Schools' Federation
Incorporated: 4 March 2011 *Employees:* 211
Previous: Catmose Federation
Net Worth: £28,582,846 *Total Assets:* £31,133,968
Registered Office: Catmose College, Huntsmans Drive, Oakham, Rutland, LE15 6RP
Activities: General secondary education
Officers: Nicola Tyers, Secretary; Ian James Dodd [1947] Director/Self-Employed Business Consultant; Emma Chloe Gautrey [1967] Director/Full Time Mother; Judith Elizabeth Gilboy [1951] Director; Doctor Neil Thomson Gorman [1950] Director/Retired; Dr Robert Bruce Guthrie [1949] Director/Retired; Samantha Jane Hearth [1975] Director/Childminder; Andrew Holt [1962] Director; Sarah Elizabeth Kirkby [1975] Director; Alexandra Mould [1971] Director; Robert Edward Mulvey [1963] Director/Packaging Design Technologist; Mark Gerard McLaren Nicoll [1965] Director/Senior Sound Supervisor; Martyn Rhowbotham [1956] Director/Retired HMI; Nicholas Mark Wainwright [1960] Director; Stuart Paul Williams [1971] Director/Executive Principal

Rutland Plastics Limited
Incorporated: 17 January 1956 *Employees:* 146
Net Worth: £9,898,189 *Total Assets:* £13,076,959
Registered Office: Cold Overton Road, Oakham, Rutland, LE15 6NU
Activities: Manufacture of other plastic products
Shareholder: Stephen Richard Ayre
Officers: Mark William Dolby, Secretary; Michael Edward Ayre [1948] Managing Director; Sarah Emily Louise Ayre [1974] Director; Stephen Richard Ayre [1975] Director/IT Analyst; Caroline Rachel Johnston [1977] Director/Marketing Consultant; Stuart Adam Johnston [1976] Director/General Manager

RVB Holding Company Limited
Incorporated: 19 October 1998 *Employees:* 1
Net Worth: £3,344,980 *Total Assets:* £10,520,611
Registered Office: 5 South Parade, Summertown, Oxford, OX2 7JL
Activities: Activities of head offices
Major Shareholder: Richard Vivian Vanbergen
Officers: Richard Vivian Vanbergen [1949] Director

RVB Investments
Incorporated: 6 November 1992 *Employees:* 1
Net Worth: £5,974,029 *Total Assets:* £10,520,507
Registered Office: 5 South Parade, Summertown, Oxford, OX2 7JL
Activities: Fund management activities
Parent: RVB Holding Company Limited
Officers: Richard Vivian Vanbergen [1949] Director

Rybrook Cars Limited
Incorporated: 16 June 1988 *Employees:* 359
Net Worth: £11,408,610 *Total Assets:* £86,552,224
Registered Office: 6 Athena Court, Athena Drive, Tachbrook Park, Warwick, CV34 6RT
Activities: Sale of new cars and light motor vehicles
Parent: Rybrook Holdings Limited
Officers: Jatinder Pal Singh Nurpuri, Secretary; Jatinder Pal Singh Nurpuri [1963] Director/Chartered Accountant; Henry William Whale [1973] Director; Peter William Whale [1949] Director

Rybrook Holdings Limited
Incorporated: 16 May 2006 *Employees:* 923
Net Worth: £33,372,000 *Total Assets:* £184,984,000
Registered Office: 6 Athena Court, Athena Drive, Tachbrook Park, Warwick, CV34 6RT
Activities: Activities of head offices
Shareholders: Peter William Whale; Kyffin David Simpson
Officers: Jatinder Pal Singh Nurpuri, Secretary; Jatinder Pal Singh Nurpuri [1963] Director/Chartered Accountant; Kyffin David Simpson [1973] Director [Barbadian]; Kyffin Donald Simpson [1942] Director [Barbadian]; Henry William Whale [1973] Director; Max Howard Whale [1976] Director; Peter William Whale [1949] Director

Rybrook Limited
Incorporated: 16 May 2006 *Employees:* 455
Net Worth: £17,294,614 *Total Assets:* £89,038,128
Registered Office: 6 Athena Court, Athena Drive, Tachbrook Park, Warwick, CV34 6RT
Activities: Sale of new cars and light motor vehicles
Parent: Rybrook Holdings Limited
Officers: Jatinder Pal Singh Nurpuri, Secretary; Jatinder Pal Singh Nurpuri [1963] Director/Chartered Accountant; Henry William Whale [1973] Director; Peter William Whale [1949] Director

Rycote Services Limited
Incorporated: 28 June 2012 *Employees:* 4
Net Worth: £19,716,476 *Total Assets:* £22,823,828
Registered Office: The Estate Office, Rycote Park, Thame, Oxon, OX9 2PE
Activities: Support activities for animal production (other than farm animal boarding)
Shareholders: Sarah Jane Taylor; Bernard John Taylor; Henry Bernard Charles Taylor
Officers: Bernard John Taylor, Secretary; Sarah Jane Flavell [1986] Director/Accountant; Henry Bernard Charles Taylor [1992] Director/Farmer; Sarah Jane Taylor [1957] Director/Farmer

Rye St. Antony School Limited
Incorporated: 6 October 1958 *Employees:* 118
Net Worth: £8,754,716 *Total Assets:* £9,715,829
Registered Office: Pullens Lane, Headington Hill, Oxford, OX3 0BY
Activities: Pre-primary education
Officers: Teresa Mary Hudson, Secretary; Ian David Callaghan [1947] Director/Retired Banker; Sean Kevin Calnan [1948] Director/Meat Trade; Dr Tomasz Marian Maksymilian Czepiel [1963] Director/Lecturer; Simon Jacques Hugh Detre [1977] Director/Headmaster; Susan Hampshire [1961] Director/Resuscitation Officer; John Jackson [1952] Director/Chaplain [American]; Dr Eleanor Elizabeth Lowe [1978] Director/Senior Lecturer in Drama; Shuna Helen McGregor [1960] Director/Senior Probation Officer; Timothy John Morton [1948] Director/Solicitor; David John Parke [1948] Director/Project Manager; Raymond David Potts [1951] Director/Chartered Accountant; Andrew Robert Rattue [1960] Director/Principal (Education); Sean Patrick Skehan [1964] Director/Teacher; Hilary Jane Carless Stafford Northcote [1945] Director/Headmistress

Ryecroft Foods Limited
Incorporated: 15 November 1983 *Employees:* 36
Net Worth: £8,384,000 *Total Assets:* £11,395,000
Registered Office: Weetabix Mills, Burton Latimer, Kettering, Northants, NN15 5JR
Activities: Manufacture of other food products n.e.c.
Parent: Weetabix Limited
Officers: Richard William Thomas Martin, Secretary; Sally Jane Abbott [1967] Director; Richard William Thomas Martin [1962] Director

Ryedale Estates Limited
Incorporated: 16 December 2009 *Employees:* 4
Net Worth: £6,528,932 *Total Assets:* £13,537,480
Registered Office: 13-17 Paradise Square, Sheffield, S1 2DE
Activities: Other letting and operating of own or leased real estate
Shareholder: David Rhodes
Officers: David Rhodes [1951] Director; Laura Rhodes [1985] Director; Stephen David Rhodes [1985] Director

Rylston Road Limited
Incorporated: 15 March 2000
Net Worth: £10,977,922 *Total Assets:* £13,203,523
Registered Office: Jubilee House, Jubilee Court, Dersingham, Kings Lynn, Norfolk, PE31 6HH
Activities: Buying and selling of own real estate
Shareholders: Nigel Anthony Knighton; Suzanne Knighton
Officers: Nigel Anthony Knighton [1959] Director/Surveyor; Suzanne Knighton [1960] Director/Investment Manager

S & W Design & Build (Group) Limited
Incorporated: 3 April 2017
Net Worth: £10,670,398 *Total Assets:* £10,672,160
Registered Office: S & W House, Longhill Road, March, Cambs, PE15 0BL
Activities: Activities of other holding companies n.e.c.
Major Shareholder: Richard Whyles
Officers: Diane Lynn Nunn [1961] Director; Brett Whyles [1982] Director; Richard Whyles [1980] Director

S D C (Holdings) Limited
Incorporated: 26 September 1983 *Employees:* 376
Net Worth: £10,437,292 *Total Assets:* £66,188,496
Registered Office: Limegrove House, Caxton Road, Elms Farm Industrial Estate, Bedford, MK41 0QQ
Activities: Activities of construction holding companies
Parent: The SDC EBT Limited
Officers: Andrew Ronald Mitchell, Secretary; Martin Alan Lowndes [1950] Director/Accountant; Craig William Millar [1968] Director/Mechanical Engineer; Francis Peter Shiner [1959] Director/Quantity Surveyor; Gary Lloyd Wykes [1963] Director/Quantity Surveyor

S L G Charitable Trust Limited
Incorporated: 24 September 1970 *Employees:* 15
Net Worth: £27,654,456 *Total Assets:* £27,769,662
Registered Office: Convent of The Incarnation, Fairacres, Parker Street, Oxford, OX4 1TB
Activities: Activities of religious organisations
Officers: Jennifer Gayle Foster [1963] Director/Sister in Religion; Avis Mary Grainger [1952] Director/Sister in Religion; Clare Louise Marriott [1962] Director/Sister in Religion; Sister Susan Shannon [1942] Director/Sister in Religion; Sister Christine Jane South [1946] Director/Sister in Religion [British/Canadian]

S M C Design and Draughting Services Limited
Incorporated: 4 November 1994
Net Worth: £10,720,980 *Total Assets:* £13,367,559
Registered Office: Unit 6 Colwick Quays Business Park, Road No 2, Colwick, Nottingham, NG4 2JY
Activities: Engineering design activities for industrial process and production
Shareholders: Diane Joy McBallantine; Steven McBallantine
Officers: Diane Joy McBallantine, Secretary; Diane Joy McBallantine [1967] Financial Director; Steven McBallantine [1968] Managing Director

S R S Rail System Limited
Incorporated: 15 December 1986 *Employees:* 101
Net Worth: £11,039,546 *Total Assets:* £13,223,888
Registered Office: Unit 3 Riverside Way, Gateway Business Park, Bolsover, Derbys, S44 6GA
Activities: Construction of railways and underground railways
Parent: SRS Rail System (Holdings) Limited
Officers: John Denis Norie Rooke [1933] Director; Richard Mark Whatley [1968] Director; Simon John Whatley [1970] Director

S. & A. Drapers Limited
Incorporated: 30 May 1969 *Employees:* 14
Net Worth: £7,128,312 *Total Assets:* £9,820,608
Registered Office: Westwood House, 78 Loughborough Road, Quorn, Leics, LE12 8DX
Activities: Retail sale of clothing in specialised stores
Shareholder: Suraj Bhan Khandelwal
Officers: Anil Khandelwal [1966] Director; Shanta Khandelwal [1939] Director; Suraj Bhan Khandelwal [1936] Director

S.D.C. Builders Limited
Incorporated: 26 March 1976 *Employees:* 369
Net Worth: £8,153,387 *Total Assets:* £54,579,932
Registered Office: Lime Grove House, Caxton Road, Bedford, MK41 0QQ
Activities: Construction of commercial buildings
Parent: SDC (Holdings) Limited
Officers: Andrew Ronald Mitchell, Secretary; Adam Ratliffe Knaggs [1977] Director/Construction Engineer; Martin Alan Lowndes [1950] Director/Accountant; Craig William Millar [1968] Director/Building Services; Francis Peter Shiner [1959] Director/Quantity Surveyor; Gary Lloyd Wykes [1963] Director/Quantity Surveyor

S.E.B. International Limited
Incorporated: 31 August 1971 *Employees:* 25
Net Worth: £7,541,347 *Total Assets:* £9,599,347
Registered Office: Unity Road, Lowmoor Business Park, Kirkby in Ashfield, Nottingham, NG17 7LE
Activities: Other engineering activities
Major Shareholder: Barrie Raymond Storey
Officers: Valerie Ann Storey, Secretary; Barrie Raymond Storey [1939] Director; Valerie Ann Storey [1943] Director

S.I.P.(Industrial Products) Limited
Incorporated: 13 November 1968 *Employees:* 70
Net Worth: £5,728,595 *Total Assets:* £10,959,528
Registered Office: Gelders Hall Road, Shepshed, Loughborough, Leics, LE12 9NH
Activities: Wholesale of other machinery and equipment
Parent: Trident 2020 Limited
Officers: Paul Ippaso, Secretary; Adriana Edy Ippaso [1938] Director; Paul Ippaso [1967] Director; Roger Clive Povoas [1945] Director/Solicitor

S.T.L. Trading Company Limited
Incorporated: 14 September 2004 *Employees:* 30
Previous: S.T.L. Trading Company
Net Worth: £7,250,486 *Total Assets:* £9,109,631
Registered Office: Blue Diamond House, Sandall Stones Road, Kirk Sandall Industrial Estate, Doncaster, S Yorks, DN3 1QR
Activities: Wholesale of other intermediate products
Shareholder: John West
Officers: Rachel West, Secretary; John West [1957] Managing Director; Lee West [1982] Director/Sales; Shaun West [1978] Director/Sales; Trevor West [1980] Director/Sales

Saffron Apothecaries (Leicester) Limited
Incorporated: 16 December 1976 *Employees:* 47
Net Worth: £249,674 *Total Assets:* £9,908,729
Registered Office: 16 Central Street, Countesthorpe, Leics, LE8 5QJ
Activities: Dispensing chemist in specialised stores
Parent: Chase Pharmacy Limited
Officers: Baljinder Kaur Johal, Secretary; Amarbir Singh Johal [1961] Director/Pharmacist; Aranvir Singh Johal [1992] Director

SAI Global Assurance Services Ltd
Incorporated: 23 December 1998 *Employees:* 276
Net Worth Deficit: £10,687,825 *Total Assets:* £19,560,904
Registered Office: Partis House, Davy Avenue, Knowlhill, Milton Keynes, Bucks, MK5 8HJ
Activities: Other professional, scientific and technical activities n.e.c.
Parent: SAI Global UK Holdings Limited
Officers: Hean Siew, Secretary; Adam James Christensen [1982] Director [Australian]; Paul Phyall [1965] Director

SAI Global CIS UK Limited
Incorporated: 3 November 2010 *Employees:* 3
Net Worth Deficit: £3,761,697 *Total Assets:* £26,484,280
Registered Office: Partis House, Davy Avenue, Knowlhill, Milton Keynes, Bucks, MK5 8HJ
Activities: Activities of head offices
Officers: Hean Siew, Secretary; Kim Jenkins [1966] Commercial Director [Australian]; Tracy Elaine Roskell [1966] Finance Director

Saint-Gobain Aldwych Limited
Incorporated: 29 March 2005
Net Worth: £3,853,840,896 *Total Assets:* £3,853,967,872
Registered Office: Saint-Gobain House, Binley Business Park, Coventry, Warwicks, CV3 2TT
Activities: Non-trading company
Officers: Alun Roy Oxenham, Secretary; Nicholas James Cammack [1972] Director; Michael Strickland Chaldecott [1960] Managing Director; Jean-Dominique Gregoire [1964] Director [Belgian]

Saint-Gobain Building Distribution Limited
Incorporated: 29 June 1982 *Employees:* 3,277
Net Worth: £320,908,992 *Total Assets:* £868,233,024
Registered Office: Saint-Gobain House, Binley Business Park, Coventry, Warwicks, CV3 2TT
Activities: Wholesale of wood, construction materials and sanitary equipment
Parent: Saint-Gobain Limited
Officers: Alun Roy Oxenham, Secretary; Nicholas James Cammack [1972] Director; Michael Strickland Chaldecott [1960] Managing Director; Patrick Edouard Andre Dupin [1963] Finance Director [French]; Michael David Newnham [1966] Director

Saint-Gobain Construction Products UK Limited
Incorporated: 4 September 1962 *Employees:* 2,450
Previous: BPB United Kingdom Limited
Net Worth: £197,832,000 *Total Assets:* £858,835,968
Registered Office: Saint-Gobain House, Binley Business Park, Coventry, Warwicks, CV3 2TT
Activities: Activities of head offices
Parent: BPB Group Operations Limited
Officers: Alun Roy Oxenham, Secretary; Nicholas James Cammack [1972] Director; Michael Strickland Chaldecott [1960] Managing Director; Patrick Edouard Andre Dupin [1963] Finance Director [French]

Saint-Gobain Glass (United Kingdom) Limited
Incorporated: 13 November 1989 *Employees:* 1,269
Net Worth: £25,511,000 *Total Assets:* £185,584,992
Registered Office: Saint-Gobain House, Binley Business Park, Coventry, Warwicks, CV3 2TT
Activities: Shaping and processing of flat glass
Parent: Saint-Gobain Limited
Officers: Alun Roy Oxenham, Secretary; Michael Strickland Chaldecott [1960] Managing Director; David Leslie Kilby [1967] Director; Amarjit Singh Sandhu [1976] Director; Stephen Richard Severs [1963] Managing Director

Saint-Gobain High Performance Materials UK Limited
Incorporated: 12 February 1930 *Employees:* 238
Previous: Saint-Gobain Ceramics & Plastics Limited
Net Worth: £56,018,000 *Total Assets:* £120,475,000
Registered Office: Saint-Gobain House, Binley Business Park, Coventry, Warwicks, CV3 2TT
Activities: Activities of head offices
Parent: Compagnie de Saint-Gobain
Officers: Alun Roy Oxenham, Secretary; Nicholas James Cammack [1972] Director; Michael Strickland Chaldecott [1960] Managing Director; Marie-Armelle Chupin [1957] Legal Relations Director [French]; Laurent Guillot [1969] Director [French]

Saint-Gobain Isover UK Limited
Incorporated: 24 October 2016 *Employees:* 128
Net Worth: £3,241,000 *Total Assets:* £34,632,000
Registered Office: Saint-Gobain House, Binley Business Park, Coventry, Warwicks, CV3 2TT
Activities: Activities of head offices
Parent: Saint-Gobain Construction Products UK Limited
Officers: Alun Roy Oxenham, Secretary; Nicholas James Cammack [1972] Director; Michael Strickland Chaldecott [1960] Managing Director

Saint-Gobain Limited
Incorporated: 13 December 1996 *Employees:* 294
Net Worth: £1,370,759,936 *Total Assets:* £2,026,028,032
Registered Office: Saint-Gobain House, Binley Business Park, Coventry, Warwicks, CV3 2TT
Activities: Activities of head offices
Parent: Compagnie de Saint-Gobain
Officers: Alun Roy Oxenham, Secretary; Richard John Batley [1963] UK Human Resources Director; Nicholas James Cammack [1972] Director; Michael Strickland Chaldecott [1960] Managing Director

Saint-Gobain Performance Plastics Rencol Limited
Incorporated: 14 October 1992 *Employees:* 147
Net Worth: £12,003,000 *Total Assets:* £16,536,000
Registered Office: Saint-Gobain House, Binley Business Park, Coventry, Warwicks, CV3 2TT
Activities: Activities of head offices
Officers: Alun Roy Oxenham, Secretary; Michael Strickland Chaldecott [1960] Managing Director; Vincent Monziols [1973] Director [French]

Saint-Gobain Roofspace Limited
Incorporated: 16 June 2014 *Employees:* 3
Previous: SIG Roofspace Limited
Net Worth Deficit: £217,000 *Total Assets:* £14,792,000
Registered Office: Saint-Gobain House, Binley Business Park, Coventry, Warwicks, CV3 2TT
Activities: Roofing activities
Parent: Saint-Gobain Building Distribution Limited
Officers: Alun Roy Oxenham, Secretary; Nicholas James Cammack [1972] Finance Director; Michael David Newnham [1966] Director; Michael Strickland Chaldecott [1960] Managing Director

Salmon Harvester Properties Limited
Incorporated: 21 April 1994 *Employees:* 8
Net Worth: £5,195,618 *Total Assets:* £40,944,712
Registered Office: Tiddington Road, Stratford upon Avon, Warwicks, CV37 7BJ
Activities: Development of building projects
Shareholders: The National Farmers Union Mutual Insurance Society Limited; Salmon Developments Limited
Officers: Sian Elizabeth Johns, Secretary; Abigail Samantha Louise Beasley [1977] Director/Property Accountant; Rorie Graham Farquharson Henderson [1959] Director/Chartered Surveyor; Richard David Morley [1967] Director; Douglas James Stewart [1958] Director/Chartered Surveyor; Richard Mark Topps [1967] Director/Group Head of Properties

Salter Bros,Limited
Incorporated: 5 March 1915 *Employees:* 4
Net Worth: £8,795,951 *Total Assets:* £11,399,065
Registered Office: Folly Bridge, Oxford, OX1 4LA
Activities: Inland passenger water transport
Major Shareholder: John Stephen Edward Salter
Officers: John Stephen Edward Salter [1953] Director; Paul John Salter [1988] Director

Salus Controls PLC
Incorporated: 26 February 2004 *Employees:* 39
Net Worth: £3,552,347 *Total Assets:* £18,588,322
Registered Office: Unit 1 Dodworth Business Park South, Whinby Road, Dodworth, Barnsley, S Yorks, S75 3SP
Activities: Wholesale of electronic and telecommunications equipment and parts
Officers: Fiona Louise Pembery, Secretary; Yuen Lam Una Auyang [1963] Director [Hong Kong]; Wai Leung Ha [1958] Director/Vice President [Portuguese]; Dean Richard Jepson [1972] Managing Director; King Owyang [1945] Director [American]

Salus Healthcare Limited
Incorporated: 22 February 2013
Net Worth: £14,831,000 *Total Assets:* £21,404,000
Registered Office: NRS Healthcare, Sherwood House, Cartwright Way, Forest Business Park, Bardon Hill, Coalville, Leics, LE67 1UB
Activities: Non-specialised wholesale trade
Parent: ACESO Healthcare Limited
Officers: John Makin, Secretary; Jeremy Michael Benson [1963] Director; Stephen Paul Kennedy [1960] Commercial Director; John Makin [1972] Finance Director

Salvation Army Trading Company Limited
Incorporated: 29 April 1991 *Employees:* 796
Net Worth: £15,923,422 *Total Assets:* £24,733,172
Registered Office: 66-78 Denington Road, Dennington Industrial Estate, Wellingborough, Northants, NN8 2QH
Activities: Retail sale of other second-hand goods in stores (not incl. antiques)
Officers: Beverley Phillips, Secretary; Trevor Paul Caffull [1960] Director; Dr Stephen Roland Cobb [1953] Director; Judith Anne Hilditch [1961] Director; Anthony Alistair Mark Hosking [1956] Director/Head of Clothing Collection Division; Jonathan Peacock [1961] Director/Head of Property; Beverley Phillips [1958] Finance Director; Alan Read [1958] Director/Secretary for Business Administration; John Barrie Stubbings [1942] Director/Management Consultant

Salvesen Logistics Limited
Incorporated: 16 November 1938 *Employees:* 1
Net Worth: £210,526,000 *Total Assets:* £211,952,000
Registered Office: XPO House, Lodge Way, New Duston, Northampton, NN5 7SL
Activities: Non-trading company
Parent: XPO Holdings UK and Ireland Limited
Officers: Georgina Garratt, Secretary; Georgina Garratt [1981] Director/Head of Legal; Daniel Stephen Myers [1976] Managing Director

Sami Property Co Ltd
Incorporated: 23 September 2014 *Employees:* 4
Net Worth: £4,252,554 *Total Assets:* £21,925,368
Registered Office: Park House, 37 Clarence Street, Leicester, LE1 3RW
Activities: Buying and selling of own real estate
Officers: Sonera Sabir Tayub, Secretary; Shakera Sabir Tayub [1971] Director; Sonera Sabir Tayub [1993] Director

Samsons Limited
Incorporated: 28 February 2003 *Employees:* 1
Net Worth: £9,817,707 *Total Assets:* £17,862,304
Registered Office: First Floor, Woburn Court, 2 Railton Road, Woburn Road Industrial Estate, Kempston, Bedford, MK42 7PN
Activities: Other letting and operating of own or leased real estate
Shareholders: Safir Akhter; Mohammed Saleem
Officers: Safir Akhter, Secretary; Mohammed Saleem [1958] Director

Samworth Brothers (Holdings) Limited
Incorporated: 3 May 1946 *Employees:* 9,273
Net Worth: £244,688,000 *Total Assets:* £501,324,000
Registered Office: Chetwode House, 1 Samworth Way, Melton Mowbray, Leics, LE13 1GA
Activities: Activities of head offices
Officers: Timothy James Barker, Secretary/Chairman; Flor Aiden Healy [1962] Director [Irish]; William Bruce Kendall [1961] Director; Nicholas Steven Linney [1952] Director; Aileen Verity Richards [1959] Director; Hannu Ragnvald Ryopponen [1952] Director [Finnish]; Mark Charles Chetwode Samworth [1970] Director; Jeffrey Peter Van Der Eems [1962] Director

Samworth Brothers Limited
Incorporated: 20 October 1995 *Employees:* 8,803
Net Worth: £221,899,008 *Total Assets:* £478,072,000
Registered Office: Chetwode House, 1 Samworth Way, Melton Mowbray, Leics, LE13 1GA
Activities: Manufacture of other food products n.e.c.
Parent: Samworth Brothers (Holdings) Limited
Officers: Timothy James Barker, Secretary/Chairman; Steven Clive Bailey [1962] Finance Director; Paul John Davey [1964] Director; Flor Aiden Healy [1962] Director [Irish]; Mary-Ann Lake [1970] Director; Mark Charles Chetwode Samworth [1970] Director; Simon James Penny Wookey [1966] Director

The Samworth Church Academy
Incorporated: 8 February 2007 *Employees:* 133
Net Worth: £24,692,052 *Total Assets:* £28,362,210
Registered Office: The Samworth Church Academy, Sherwood Hall Road, Mansfield, Notts, NG18 2DY
Activities: General secondary education
Officers: Ellie Rose Slack, Secretary; Edward Michael Astley-Arlington [1953] Director/Farmer; Stephen Neil Garner [1956] Director/Councillor; Valerie Jane Leivers [1946] Director/Retired; Nicholas Steven Linney [1952] Director/Company Chairman; Michael Longdon [1947] Director/Retired; Lisa McVeigh [1978] Director/Academy Principal; Tyrone Reiss Robinson [1991] Director/School Teacher; Nigel Spraggins [1959] Director/Chief Executive; Samantha Isobel Sykes [1972] Director/Service Lead for CAMHS-NHS; Caroline Anne Whitty [1958] Director/Consultant

Sandbrook Overseas Investments Limited
Incorporated: 10 October 2007
Net Worth: £1,459,459,456 *Total Assets:* £1,577,538,688
Registered Office: Westpoint, Peterborough Business Park, Lynch Wood, Peterborough, Cambs, PE2 6FZ
Activities: Activities of head offices
Parent: Thomas Cook Group PLC
Officers: Shirley Bradley, Secretary; Alice Hannah Marsden [1983] Director

Richard Sanders Limited
Incorporated: 6 June 2002 *Employees:* 92
Net Worth: £4,468,940 *Total Assets:* £11,682,366
Registered Office: Brunel Close, Northfield Avenue, Kettering, Northants, NN16 9HU
Activities: Sale of new cars and light motor vehicles
Shareholder: Richard Owen Compton Sanders
Officers: Jennifer Dawn Sanders [1947] Director; Mark Richard Sanders [1973] Director; Nicholas Owen Sanders [1976] Director; Richard Owen Compton Sanders [1947] Managing Director

D.H.Sanderson and Son Limited
Incorporated: 29 November 1957 *Employees:* 9
Net Worth: £13,980,676 *Total Assets:* £16,384,989
Registered Office: St John's Farm, Beachamwell, King's Lynn, Norfolk, PE37 8BE
Activities: Growing of cereals (except rice), leguminous crops and oil seeds
Shareholders: John Stanley Hamilton Sanderson; Gillian Sanderson
Officers: Gillian Sanderson, Secretary; Caroline Lindsay Sanderson [1967] Director; Gillian Sanderson [1937] Director/Secretary; Hugh Howard Hamilton Sanderson [1966] Director/Purchasing Manager; John Stanley Hamilton Sanderson [1934] Director/Farmer; Thomas Charles Hamilton Sanderson [1964] Director

Sanderson Group PLC
Incorporated: 18 November 2003 *Employees:* 318
Net Worth: £35,000,000 *Total Assets:* £62,000,000
Registered Office: Sanderson House, Manor Road, Coventry, Warwicks, CV1 2GF
Activities: Business and domestic software development
Officers: Richard Mogg, Secretary; David James Gutteridge [1951] Director; Richard David Mogg [1976] Finance Director; Ian Newcombe [1955] Managing Director; John Clement MacKenzie Paterson [1946] Director; Christopher Winn [1950] Director

Sanderson Limited
Incorporated: 30 March 1999 *Employees:* 64
Net Worth: £1,402,000 *Total Assets:* £11,640,000
Registered Office: Sanderson House, Manor Road, Coventry, Warwicks, CV1 2GF
Activities: Other information technology service activities
Parent: Sanderson Group PLC
Officers: Richard Mogg, Secretary; Mark Andrew Adamson [1962] Director and Company Secretary; Richard David Mogg [1976] Finance Director; Ian Newcombe [1955] Director

Sanderson Multi-Channel Retail Solutions Limited
Incorporated: 23 January 2006 *Employees:* 35
Previous: Sanderson Multi-Channel Solutions Limited
Net Worth: £5,830,000 *Total Assets:* £13,378,000
Registered Office: Sanderson House, Manor Road, Coventry, Warwicks, CV1 2GF
Activities: Other information technology service activities
Parent: Sanderson Group PLC
Officers: Richard Mogg, Secretary; Mark Andrew Adamson [1962] Commercial Director; Richard David Mogg [1976] Finance Director; Ian Newcombe [1955] Director

Stephen Sanderson Transport Holdings Limited
Incorporated: 3 October 2013 *Employees:* 92
Net Worth: £6,939,833 *Total Assets:* £10,682,332
Registered Office: Bowden House, 36 Northampton Road, Market Harborough, Leics, LE16 9HE
Activities: Activities of distribution holding companies
Major Shareholder: Stephen Sanderson
Officers: Janice Angela Sanderson [1961] Director/Secretary; Stephen Sanderson [1953] Director/Haulage Contractor

Sandicliffe Garage Limited
Incorporated: 20 April 1948 *Employees:* 45
Net Worth: £13,279,000 *Total Assets:* £74,399,000
Registered Office: Nottingham Road, Stapleford, Notts, NG9 8AU
Activities: Sale of new cars and light motor vehicles
Parent: Sandicliffe Motor Holdings Limited
Officers: Nicholas William Thomas Woodhouse, Secretary; Thomas Henry Barton [1925] Director/Farmer; Thomas Henry Alystair Barton [1963] Director/Farmer; Darren James Beddard [1977] Finance Director; Ian Middleton [1950] Director Contract Hire; Nicholas William Thomas Woodhouse [1952] Director/Garage Proprietor; Paul Richard George Woodhouse [1977] Director; Richard Andrew Joseph Barton Woodhouse [1945] Director/Motor Engineer

Sandicliffe Limited
Incorporated: 2 May 1996 *Employees:* 667
Net Worth: £17,787,000 *Total Assets:* £93,655,000
Registered Office: 155-185 Derby Road, Loughborough, Leics, LE11 5HN
Activities: Sale of new cars and light motor vehicles
Parent: Sandicliffe Garage Limited
Officers: Nicholas William Thomas Woodhouse, Secretary/Director; Thomas Henry Alystair Barton [1963] Director/Farmer; Thomas Henry Barton [1925] Director/Farmer; Darren James Beddard [1977] Finance Director; Nicholas William Thomas Woodhouse [1952] Director/Garage Proprietor; Paul Richard George Woodhouse [1977] Director; Richard Andrew Joseph Barton Woodhouse [1945] Director/Motor Engineer

Sandicliffe Motor Holdings Limited
Incorporated: 5 December 2002 *Employees:* 712
Net Worth: £17,869,000 *Total Assets:* £123,430,000
Registered Office: 152 Nottingham Road, Stapleford, Nottingham, NG9 8AU
Activities: Sale of new cars and light motor vehicles
Shareholder: Thomas Henry Alystair Barton
Officers: Nicholas William Thomas Woodhouse, Secretary; Thomas Henry Alystair Barton [1963] Director/Motor Dealer; Thomas Henry Barton [1925] Director/Motor Dealer; Darren James Beddard [1977] Finance Director; Penelope Elizabeth May Hills [1949] Director; Elizabeth Angela Murfitt [1957] Director/Administrator; Nicholas William Thomas Woodhouse [1952] Director/Motor Dealer; Paul Richard George Woodhouse [1977] Director; Richard Andrew Joseph Barton Woodhouse [1945] Director/Motor Dealer

The Sandwich Factory Holdings Limited
Incorporated: 3 May 1996 *Employees:* 603
Net Worth: £5,949,000 *Total Assets:* £22,874,000
Registered Office: Midland Way, Barlborough Links Business Park, Barlborough, Chesterfield, Derbys, S43 4XA
Activities: Manufacture of other food products n.e.c.
Parent: Greencore Foods Limited
Officers: Michael Evans, Secretary; Catherine Bradshaw [1975] Finance Director; Michael Evans [1967] Director/Communications Officer; Kevin Raymond George Moore [1970] Director; Eoin Philip Tonge [1972] Director [Irish]

Sansbury Bailey Holdings Limited
Incorporated: 30 March 2001 *Employees:* 358
Net Worth: £4,725,000 *Total Assets:* £24,553,000
Registered Office: Washway Road, Fosdyke, Spalding, Lincs, PE12 6LQ
Activities: Other service activities n.e.c.
Major Shareholder: Colin Sansbury Bailey
Officers: Lisa Jayne Alcock, Secretary; Lisa Jayne Alcock [1984] Director; Colin Sansbury Bailey [1969] Director; Sarah Bailey [1976] Director; Alexander Boughton [1987] Sales Director; Tim James Fitzsimmons [1976] Operations Director; David Alan Trumble [1980] Finance Director

Santa Maria UK Limited
Incorporated: 24 February 1989 *Employees:* 132
Net Worth Deficit: £4,736,000 *Total Assets:* £17,363,000
Registered Office: Nimbus House, Maidstone Road, Milton Keynes, Bucks, MK10 0BD
Activities: Manufacture of bread; manufacture of fresh pastry goods and cakes
Officers: Nicholas Antony John Hayman, Secretary; Jens Olaf Andreas Malmus [1966] Director/General Management [German]; Diane McKenna [1966] Director/H R Manager; Bruno Noppe [1971] Operations Director [Belgian]; Henrik Per Samuelson [1971] Director/General Management [Swedish]

Santander Asset Finance (December) Limited
Incorporated: 20 May 1981
Net Worth: £48,961,792 *Total Assets:* £122,558,512
Registered Office: Carlton Park, Narborough, Leicester, LE19 0AL
Activities: Financial leasing
Parent: Santander Asset Finance PLC
Officers: Stephen David Affleck [1979] Finance Director; Mr George Smith-Salmond Ashworth [1956] Managing Director; Anna Maria Konter [1967] Director [Dutch]

Santander Estates Limited
Incorporated: 12 October 1988
Net Worth: £3,645,547 *Total Assets:* £95,769,480
Registered Office: Building 3, Floor 2, Carlton Park, Narborough, Leicester, LE19 0AL
Activities: Management of real estate on a fee or contract basis
Parent: Santander UK PLC
Officers: Rachel Jane Morrison [1968] Director/Chartered Accountant; Nicholas Guy Roberts [1968] Director/Chartered Surveyor

Sape Group Holdings UK Ltd
Incorporated: 27 October 1998 *Employees:* 1
Net Worth: £3,841,681 *Total Assets:* £9,251,404
Registered Office: The Stable Yard, Vicarage Road, Stony Stratford, Milton Keynes, Bucks, MK11 1BN
Activities: Activities of other holding companies n.e.c.
Major Shareholder: Per Troen
Officers: Per Troen [1955] Director/Solicitor [Danish]

Saria Limited
Incorporated: 7 April 1955 *Employees:* 114
Net Worth: £134,111,176 *Total Assets:* £204,424,336
Registered Office: Ings Road, Bentley, Doncaster, S Yorks, DN5 9TL
Activities: Activities of head offices
Officers: Richard Anthony de Mulder [1966] Director/Sales Executive; Robert Vincent Ratcliffe [1958] Director/Senior Operations Manager; Phillip Antony Simpson [1966] Director/Commercial Services Manager; Andrew Richard Smith [1962] Director/Senior Commercial Services Manager; Franz Bernhard Thier [1965] Director [German]

Sarval (Hartshill) Limited
Incorporated: 21 April 1960 *Employees:* 80
Net Worth Deficit: £6,818,701 *Total Assets:* £20,119,218
Registered Office: Ings Road, Doncaster, S Yorks, DN5 9TL
Activities: Manufacture of oils and fats
Parent: Saria Limited
Officers: Robert Vincent Ratcliffe [1958] Director; Andrew Richard Smith [1962] Director

Sarval Limited
Incorporated: 6 April 1954 *Employees:* 110
Net Worth Deficit: £10,570,195 *Total Assets:* £17,894,198
Registered Office: Ings Road, Doncaster, S Yorks, DN5 9TL
Activities: Manufacture of oils and fats
Parent: Saria Limited
Officers: Robert Vincent Ratcliffe [1958] Director; Phillip Antony Simpson [1966] Director; Andrew Richard Smith [1962] Director/Group Commercial Manager

Sash UK Limited
Incorporated: 4 March 1981 *Employees:* 185
Net Worth: £3,609,184 *Total Assets:* £11,410,639
Registered Office: Ferrymoor Way, Park Springs, Grimethorpe, Barnsley, S Yorks, S72 7BN
Activities: Manufacture of builders ware of plastic
Officers: John Stewart Ross [1965] Director

Satake Europe Limited
Incorporated: 6 March 1984 *Employees:* 40
Net Worth: £8,533,266 *Total Assets:* £10,388,034
Registered Office: Satake Europe Ltd, Horsfield Way, Bredbury Park Industrial Estate, Bredbury, Stockport, Cheshire, SK6 2SU
Activities: Installation of industrial machinery and equipment
Major Shareholder: Toshiko Satake
Officers: Yoshihiro Kunimitsu, Secretary; Hajime Harada [1954] Director/Manager [Japanese]; Kazuyuki Kihara [1949] Director [Japanese]; Yoshihiro Kunimitsu [1960] Director/General Manager [Japanese]

Satellite Applications Catapult Limited
Incorporated: 24 February 2012 *Employees:* 131
Net Worth: £12,057,966 *Total Assets:* £22,369,132
Registered Office: Electron Building, Fermi Avenue, Harwell, Didcot, Oxon, OX11 0QR
Activities: Other professional, scientific and technical activities n.e.c.
Officers: Richard James Tuffill, Secretary; Simon Hugh Verdon Acland [1958] Director/Venture Capitalist; Chad Clark Anderson [1980] Managing Director [American]; Lucy Kathryne Edge [1975] Director; Susan Margaret Hunt [1964] Director/Public Servant; William Nicholas Hutton [1950] Director/Principal of Oxford College; Dr Vanessa Vivienne Lawrence [1962] Director/Geographer; Stuart David Martin [1968] Director/Chief Executive; Lynne Marie Patmore [1962] Director/Financial Consultant; Ruy Jose Carvalho Pinto [1959] Director/Chief Technology Officer; Timothy Robin Sherwood [1954] Director; Richard James Tuffill [1971] Director

Satra
Incorporated: 4 March 1919 *Employees:* 202
Net Worth: £3,855,000 *Total Assets:* £18,646,000
Registered Office: Wyndham Way, Telford Way, Kettering, Northants, NN16 8SD
Activities: Other research and experimental development on natural sciences and engineering
Officers: Timothy John Blades [1957] Director/Chartered Accountant; Simon David Botterill [1957] Finance Director; Roger John Denton [1967] Managing Director; Stephen Etheridge [1959] Director; John Gilbert Hooker [1967] Director; Antony Jonathan Perillo [1971] Director [New Zealander]; Austin Colin Simmons [1958] Director/Chief Executive; Dr Ronald Eric Whittaker [1945] Director

Satra Technology Centre Limited
Incorporated: 11 October 1999 *Employees:* 188
Net Worth: £4,620,000 *Total Assets:* £16,498,000
Registered Office: Wyndham Way, Telford Way, Kettering, Northants, NN16 8SD
Activities: Other research and experimental development on natural sciences and engineering
Parent: Satra
Officers: Timothy John Blades [1957] Director/Chartered Accountant; Simon David Botterill [1957] Finance Director; Roger John Denton [1967] Managing Director; Stephen Etheridge [1959] Director; John Gilbert Hooker [1967] Director; Antony Jonathan Perillo [1971] Director [New Zealander]; Austin Colin Simmons [1958] Director/Chief Executive; Dr Ronald Eric Whittaker [1945] Director

Saul Construction Limited
Incorporated: 5 April 1973 *Employees:* 69
Net Worth: £9,456,865 *Total Assets:* £15,985,385
Registered Office: Burntwood Office Park, Brierley Common, Barnsley, S Yorks, S72 9ET
Activities: Development of building projects
Major Shareholder: John Robert Saul
Officers: Florrie Saul, Secretary; Florrie Saul [1933] Director/Catering Business Proprietor; Jack Saul [1931] Director/Building Contractor; John Robert Saul [1967] Director

John Saul Limited
Incorporated: 6 April 1989 *Employees:* 26
Net Worth: £8,468,932 *Total Assets:* £17,299,194
Registered Office: The Hall, Outgate, Leverton, Boston, Lincs, PE22 0AA
Activities: Growing of cereals (except rice), leguminous crops and oil seeds
Shareholders: Arthur Saul; Graham Clive Holdich Smith; Brian Thomas Borrill; John Saul (Holdings) Limited
Officers: Paul Richard Freeman [1953] Director/Farm Management; Arthur Saul [1955] Director/Farmer; Michele Mary Saul [1955] Director/Farmer; Oliver Saul [1987] Director/Farmer

T. A. Savery & Co Limited
Incorporated: 14 January 1933 *Employees:* 263
Net Worth: £10,899,914 *Total Assets:* £18,546,000
Registered Office: Grovelands, Longford Road, Exhall, Coventry, Warwicks, CV7 9NE
Activities: Manufacture of pumps
Parent: Thomas Savery Pumps Limited
Officers: Shashank Dhawan, Secretary; Shashank Dhawan [1970] Director and Company Secretary; Lynette Ann Sahota [1961] Director/Dinner Lady; Sulakhan Sahota [1960] Director

Savoy Cinemas Limited
Incorporated: 12 October 2000 *Employees:* 65
Net Worth: £9,436,173 *Total Assets:* £11,437,876
Registered Office: Savoy Cinemas, 233 Derby Road, Nottingham, NG7 1QN
Activities: Motion picture projection activities
Major Shareholder: James Robert Collington
Officers: James Robert Collington [1971] Director; Mark Andrew Welberry [1978] Operations Director

Saw Property Company Limited
Incorporated: 6 December 2012 *Employees:* 3
Net Worth: £12,798,640 *Total Assets:* £16,162,275
Registered Office: Robin Hood Park, South Road, Chapel St Leonards, Skegness, Lincs, PE24 5TR
Activities: Buying and selling of own real estate
Parent: SAW Property Company Holdings Limited
Officers: Peter Raymond Franciscus Holmes [1948] Director/Certified Accountant; Jonathan Scott Moses [1974] Director/Caravan Park Manager; Sally-Ann Woodward [1967] Director

Sawatch Limited
Incorporated: 12 December 2013
Net Worth Deficit: £16,268,206 *Total Assets:* £19,327,708
Registered Office: Hughes House, Rockingham Drive, Linford Wood, Milton Keynes, Bucks, MK14 6PD
Activities: Other telecommunications activities
Parent: Echostar Corporation
Officers: Dean Alfred Manson, Secretary; Michael Talmon Dugan [1949] Director [American]; Charles William Ergen [1953] Director [American]; Dean Alfred Manson [1967] Director [American]

Saybest Limited
Incorporated: 21 February 1995
Net Worth: £12,136,000 *Total Assets:* £21,355,000
Registered Office: Total Produce, Enterprise Way, Pinchbeck, Spalding, Lincs, PE11 3YR
Activities: Activities of head offices
Parent: Redbridge Holdings Limited
Officers: Mark Christopher Owen, Secretary; Andrew Roger Allmond [1944] Director/Certified Accountant; Jacinta Frances Devine [1972] Director [Irish]; Francis Gerard McKernan [1962] Director [Irish]; Mark Christopher Owen [1965] Director; Denis Leslie Punter [1953] Director/Chief Executive

SC Johnson Professional Group Limited
Incorporated: 16 October 2003 *Employees:* 36
Previous: Deb Group Limited
Net Worth Deficit: £98,562,000 *Total Assets:* £148,983,008
Registered Office: Denby Hall Way, Denby, Ripley, Derbys, DE5 8JZ
Activities: Other business support service activities n.e.c.
Parent: SCJ UK Finco Ltd
Officers: Nadia Patricia Estrada [1976] Director/Chief Financial Officer [American]; Nicholas Noel Hardwick Matterson [1963] Director/Lawyer

SC Johnson Professional Limited
Incorporated: 2 January 1941 *Employees:* 197
Previous: Deb Limited
Net Worth: £33,252,000 *Total Assets:* £62,328,000
Registered Office: Denby Hall Way, Denby, Ripley, Derbys, DE5 8JZ
Activities: Manufacture of soap and detergents
Parent: Deb Holdings Limited
Officers: Nadia Patricia Estrada [1976] Director/Chief Financial Officer [American]; Nicholas Noel Hardwick Matterson [1963] Director/Lawyer

Scancell Holdings PLC
Incorporated: 14 April 2008 *Employees:* 19
Net Worth: £13,940,950 *Total Assets:* £14,637,040
Registered Office: John Eccles House, Robert Robinson Avenue, Oxford Science Park, Oxford, OX4 4GP
Activities: Other research and experimental development on natural sciences and engineering
Officers: Dr Sally Elizabeth Adams [1960] Director/Development Scientist; Dr John Chiplin [1958] Director; Prof Linda Gillian Durrant [1957] Director/Scientist; Dr Matthew Gerard Winston Frohn [1967] Director/Venture Capital; Doctor Richard Morley Goodfellow [1950] Director; Dr Cliff Holloway [1960] Director; Dr Alan James Lewis [1945] Director

Scania (Great Britain) Limited
Incorporated: 14 December 1964 *Employees:* 1,687
Net Worth: £48,784,000 *Total Assets:* £692,945,984
Registered Office: Delaware Drive, Tongwell, Milton Keynes, Bucks, MK15 8HB
Activities: Sale of other motor vehicles
Parent: Volkswagen Aktiengesellschaft
Officers: Richard Kevin Gray, Secretary; Urban Birger Erdtman [1945] Director [Swedish]; Martin Hay [1965] Managing Director; Roger McCarthy [1951] Director; Carl Johan Martin Stahlberg [1964] Director [Swedish]; Per Anders Williamsson [1969] Director [Swedish]

Scania Real Estate (UK) Limited
Incorporated: 26 May 2011
Net Worth: £6,420,045 *Total Assets:* £15,934,618
Registered Office: Delaware Drive, Tongwell, Milton Keynes, Bucks, MK15 8HB
Activities: Other letting and operating of own or leased real estate
Parent: Volkswagen Aktiengesellschaft
Officers: Richard Kevin Gray, Secretary; Martin Hay [1965] Director; Tommy Per-Ola Lindeberg [1966] Director [Swedish]; Kjell Borje Ortengren [1958] Managing Director [Swedish]

Scantronic Holdings Limited
Incorporated: 22 November 1983
Net Worth: £15,449,000 *Total Assets:* £15,449,000
Registered Office: Jephson Court, Tancred Close, Queensway, Royal Leamington Spa, Warwicks, CV31 3RZ
Activities: Activities of other holding companies n.e.c.
Parent: Eaton Safety Limited
Officers: Richard Paul Howes [1971] Director; Andrew Jackson [1973] Finance Director

ScarsdaleVets LLP
Incorporated: 17 December 2009
Net Worth: £5,400,517 *Total Assets:* £9,157,253
Registered Office: Pride Veterinary Centre, Riverside Road, Pride Park, Derby, DE24 8HX
Officers: Frances Gillian Bird [1978] Member; Francis Patrick Joseph Boyer [1973] Member; Anna Katherine Cockle [1972] Member; Karen Jean Davis [1966] Member; Wendy Anne Furness [1973] Member; Jeffrey James Gascoyne [1976] Member; Rose Astarte Jackson [1980] Member; Alexander Morgan Jamieson [1963] Member; Christopher Stephen Parker [1959] Member; Paul Harvey Revell [1976] Member; Paul Damian Sands [1967] Member; Julie Alison Todd [1964] Member; John David Turkington [1967] Member

SCCS Survey Equipment Limited
Incorporated: 18 August 2005 *Employees:* 97
Previous: Paul MacArthur Limited
Net Worth: £14,313,000 *Total Assets:* £20,437,000
Registered Office: Alpha House, Alpha Drive, Eaton Socon, St Neots, Cambs, PE19 8JJ
Activities: Other specialised construction activities n.e.c.
Parent: Hexagon AB
Officers: Andrew Paul Young, Secretary; Paul Walker Peter MacArthur [1955] Director

Scenic Land Developments Limited
Incorporated: 9 May 2007
Net Worth Deficit: £315,975 *Total Assets:* £10,050,580
Registered Office: Oddington Grange, Weston on the Green, Bicester, Oxon, OX25 3QW
Activities: Buying and selling of own real estate
Shareholders: Deana Janette Barbour; Robert Thomas Alexander Browne; Sapphire Browne
Officers: Deana Janette Barbour, Secretary/Property Developer; Deana Janette Barbour [1961] Director/Property Developer; Robert James Barbour [1958] Director/Farmer; Robert Thomas Alexander Browne [1970] Director/Farmer

SCGH Limited
Incorporated: 30 October 2015 *Employees:* 126
Net Worth: £6,946,000 *Total Assets:* £18,764,000
Registered Office: c/o Simply Cartons Ltd, Perry Road, Nottingham, NG5 1GQ
Activities: Activities of other holding companies n.e.c.
Major Shareholder: Craig Mather
Officers: Craig Mather [1971] Director

Schades Limited
Incorporated: 26 January 1988 *Employees:* 51
Net Worth: £306,000 *Total Assets:* £11,384,000
Registered Office: Brittain Drive, Codnor Gate Industrial Estate, Ripley, Derbys, DE5 3RZ
Activities: Manufacture of paper and paperboard
Officers: Sally Aldridge, Secretary; Marcel Bergmann [1979] Director/Chairman [German]; Jack Martin Hugill [1966] Managing Director; Byung Gab Yang [1971] Director [South Korean]

Schering-Plough Limited
Incorporated: 31 December 1884
Net Worth: £10,558,000 *Total Assets:* £14,245,000
Registered Office: Walton Manor, Walton, Milton Keynes, Bucks, MK7 7AJ
Activities: Manufacture of basic pharmaceutical products
Parent: Merck & Co., Inc.
Officers: Richard Robinski, Secretary; Ebru Can Temucin [1972] Director [Turkish]; Martin Ian Rogers [1968] Director

Schoeller-Bleckmann Oilfield Equipment (UK) Limited
Incorporated: 22 August 1996
Net Worth: £32,521,276 *Total Assets:* £38,530,556
Registered Office: Techman House, Broombank Park, Chesterfield Trading Estate, Chesterfield, Derbys, S41 9RT
Activities: Mining of other non-ferrous metal ores
Parent: Schoeller-Bleckmann Oilfield Equipment AG
Officers: Tracey Walters, Secretary; Generald Grohmann [1953] Director [Austrian]; Campbell Mckay Macpherson [1974] Director; Klaus Hermann Mader [1970] Director/Chief Financial Officer [Austrian]

Scholastic Limited
Incorporated: 22 August 1961 *Employees:* 291
Net Worth: £26,405,900 *Total Assets:* £47,498,724
Registered Office: Westfield Road, Southam, Leamington Spa, Warwick, CV47 0RA
Activities: Book publishing
Parent: Scholastic UK Limited
Officers: Nicola Frances Dixon, Finance Director; Nicola Frances Dixon [1969] Finance Director; Catherine Jane Moreton [1969] Group Co-Managing Director; Maurice Richard Robinson [1937] Director/Publisher [American]; Steven Keith Thompson [1972] Director/Accountant

Scholastic UK Ltd
Incorporated: 30 May 2002
Net Worth: £21,825,292 *Total Assets:* £24,627,304
Registered Office: Westfield Road, Southam, Warwicks, CV47 0RA
Activities: Book publishing
Parent: Scholastic Corporation
Officers: Nicola Frances Dixon, Finance Director; Nicola Frances Dixon [1969] Finance Director; Catherine Jane Moreton [1969] Group Co-Managing Director; Richard Robinson [1937] Director/Publisher [American]; Steven Keith Thompson [1972] Director/Accountant

The School of St. Helen and St. Katharine Trust
Incorporated: 29 March 1983
Net Worth: £23,049,540 *Total Assets:* £31,304,708
Registered Office: Faringdon Road, Abingdon, Oxon, OX14 1BE
Activities: General secondary education
Officers: David Richard Eley, Secretary; Pauline Elizabeth Cakebread [1958] Director/Accountant; Giles Robert Crowe [1962] Director/Banker; Sally Ann Sheila Dicketts [1955] Director/Education; Adrian Dray [1964] Director/Finance; Piers Heyworth [1953] Director/Retired Headmaster; Rebecca Mary Kashti [1966] Director/Solicitor; Hazel Knott [1953] Retired NHS Director of Clinical Services; David John LEA [1953] Director/Chemical Engineer; Kevan Paul Leggett [1964] Director; Joanne Loveridge [1978] Director/Solicitor; Jennifer Mitchell [1967] Director/Advanced Nurse Practitioner; Stephen Suresh Ramkaran [1975] Director/Pilot; Olivia Susannah Rathbone [1975] Director/Student

Schueco UK Limited
Incorporated: 19 October 2009 *Employees:* 142
Net Worth: £28,952,000 *Total Assets:* £36,897,000
Registered Office: Whitehall Avenue, Kingston, Milton Keynes, Bucks, MK10 0AL
Activities: Wholesale of other machinery and equipment
Officers: David Dees, Secretary; Andreas Engelhardt [1960] Director [German]; Thomas Stefan Humpf [1965] Director [German]; Herr Philipp Caspar Alfred Hubertus Neuhaus [1965] Director [German]; Michael John Simpson Lane [1968] Managing Director

A. Schulman Gainsborough Ltd
Incorporated: 9 October 1996 *Employees:* 75
Previous: ICO (UK) Limited
Net Worth: £7,013,000 *Total Assets:* £42,659,000
Registered Office: Sandars Road, Heapham Road Industrial Estate, Gainsborough, Lincs, DN21 1RZ
Activities: Manufacture of other plastic products
Officers: Christopher Anthony Bridle, Secretary/Financial Controller; Christopher Anthony Bridle [1964] Director/Management Accountant; Heinrich Benedikt Lingnau-Schneider [1962] Director/Business Executive [German]

Schutz (U.K.) Limited
Incorporated: 14 February 1989 *Employees:* 121
Net Worth: £52,841,000 *Total Assets:* £60,117,000
Registered Office: Claylands Avenue, Dukeries Industrial Estate, Worksop, Notts, S81 7BE
Activities: Manufacture of plastic packing goods
Parent: Schutz GmbH and Co KGaA
Officers: Martin Gerard Colley, Secretary; Veit Enders [1972] Director/Merchant [German]; Dr Johann Christian Meier [1960] Director/Merchant [German]; Roland Strassburger [1964] Director/Merchant [German]

SCI-MX Nutrition Limited
Incorporated: 4 September 2015 *Employees:* 28
Net Worth Deficit: £2,603,000 *Total Assets:* £23,201,000
Registered Office: Chetwode House, 1 Samworth Way, Melton Mowbray, Leics, LE13 1GA
Activities: Non-specialised wholesale of food, beverages and tobacco
Parent: Samworth Brothers (Holdings) Limited
Officers: Tim James Barker, Secretary; Steven Clive Bailey [1962] Director; Flor Aiden Healy [1962] Director [Irish]; Richard Alexis Robertson Marris [1968] Director; Mark Charles Chetwode Samworth [1970] Director

Scoto Limited
Incorporated: 24 June 1999
Net Worth: £1,013,542,016 *Total Assets:* £1,568,481,024
Registered Office: c/o Stagecoach Services Limited, One Stockport Exchange, 20 Railway Road, Stockport, Cheshire, SK1 3SW
Activities: Activities of head offices
Parent: Stagecoach Transport Holdings Limited
Officers: Michael John Vaux, Secretary; Colin Brown [1968] Director/Accountant; John Connor Hamilton [1967] Director/Tax Accountant

Scott Bader Commonwealth Limited (The)
Incorporated: 1 June 1951
Net Worth: £82,733,000 *Total Assets:* £127,167,000
Registered Office: Wollaston Hall, Wollaston, Wellingborough, Northants, NN29 7RL
Activities: Activities of head offices
Officers: Hayley Louise Sutherland, Secretary; Christine Thomas, Secretary; Gary Francis Coldwell [1965] Director/Sales Development Manager; Karl Heinz Funke [1960] Director [German]; Robert Martin Gibson [1948] Director/Retired; David William Harris [1985] Director/Chemist; Hansi Gabrielle Scott Manning [1960] Director/Assistant Dental Technician; Angela Louise Miller [1978] Director/Chemist; John Pike [1969] Director/Process Operator; Adrian Howard Pryce [1958] Director/University Lecturer; Zelda Malak Yanovich [1976] Director/Senior Initiatives Manager

Scott Bader Company Limited
Incorporated: 10 April 1923 *Employees:* 685
Net Worth: £81,391,000 *Total Assets:* £126,529,000
Registered Office: Wollaston Hall, Wollaston, Wellingborough, Northants, NN29 7RL
Activities: Manufacture of plastics in primary forms
Officers: Matthew Ian Collins, Secretary; Steven Lochiel Brown [1977] Director/Polymer Development Manager; Matthew Ian Collins [1972] Director; Malcolm William Forsyth [1962] Director; Karl-Heinz Funke [1960] Director [German]; Ruzica Geceg [1960] Finance Director [Croatian]; Calvin James John O'Connor [1952] Director; Jean-Claude Pierre [1964] Director/Group Chief Executive [French]; David Rossouw [1969] Finance Director [South African]; Dianne Gillian Davies Walker [1965] Director

Scott Bader UK Limited
Incorporated: 15 October 2002 *Employees:* 225
Net Worth: £36,429,000 *Total Assets:* £56,425,000
Registered Office: Wollaston Hall, Wollaston, Wellingborough, Northants, NN29 7RL
Activities: Manufacture of plastics in primary forms
Officers: Andrew Bibby [1973] Director/Material Testing Technician; David Black [1973] Director/Quality Manager; James Boyle [1970] Director/HR Manager; Robert John Knight [1970] Director/Financial Controller; James McTaggart [1968] Director/Operations Manager

Scott's Developments Limited
Incorporated: 21 January 2013 *Employees:* 8
Net Worth Deficit: £1,607,717 *Total Assets:* £16,311,964
Registered Office: Steel City House, West Street, Sheffield, S1 2GQ
Activities: Development of building projects
Major Shareholder: Garry Scotting
Officers: Garry Scotting [1956] Director; John Robert Briers Scotting [1980] Director; Peter David Williams [1971] Director [Australian]

Scotts Hire Limited
Incorporated: 1 July 2008 *Employees:* 32
Net Worth: £4,477,790 *Total Assets:* £16,444,590
Registered Office: Alpha House, 4 Greek Street, Stockport, Cheshire, SK3 8AB
Activities: Renting and leasing of construction and civil engineering machinery and equipment
Shareholders: Martin Robert Smithson; Jane Elizabeth Smithson
Officers: Wayne Roberts [1975] Director; Martin Robert Smithson [1963] Director

SCR Financial Interventions Holding Company Ltd
Incorporated: 25 November 1985
Previous: Sheffield Supertram Limited
Net Worth: £2 *Total Assets:* £9,982,754
Registered Office: Sheffield City Region SCR Finance, Floor 1, 11 Broad Street West, Sheffield, S1 2BQ
Activities: Financial management
Parent: Sheffield City Region Combined Authority
Officers: Claire James, Secretary; Ruth Clare Adams [1967] Director; Mike Thomas [1975] Director/Senior Finance Manager

Scusi Limited
Incorporated: 11 June 1999
Net Worth: £631,070,976 *Total Assets:* £769,230,016
Registered Office: c/o Stagecoach Services Limited, One Stockport Exchange, 20 Railway Road, Stockport, Cheshire, SK1 3SW
Activities: Activities of head offices
Parent: Scoto Limited
Officers: Michael John Vaux, Secretary; Colin Brown [1968] Director/Accountant; Bruce Dingwall [1983] Director/Accountant; John Connor Hamilton [1967] Director/Tax Manager; Andrew Jacques Levy [1963] Legal Director

SCX Special Projects Holdings Limited
Incorporated: 21 June 2016 *Employees:* 69
Net Worth: £13,155,638 *Total Assets:* £24,059,160
Registered Office: 30 Roman Ridge Road, Sheffield, S9 1GA
Activities: Activities of head offices
Shareholder: Simon James Eastwood
Officers: Jocelyn Sarah Street, Secretary; Simon James Eastwood [1963] Director; Martin Street [1955] Director; Sarah Ann Vickers [1961] Director

SDI (Belfast) Limited
Incorporated: 16 November 2015
Net Worth Deficit: £333,818 *Total Assets:* £14,298,857
Registered Office: Unit A, Brook Park East, Shirebrook, Derbys, NG20 8RY
Activities: Other letting and operating of own or leased real estate
Parent: SDI Property Limited
Officers: Cameron John Olsen, Secretary; Adedotun Ademola Adegoke [1973] Director/Senior Buyer; Rachel Isabel Lilian Stockton [1970] Director/Head of Customs and VAT

SDI (Edinburgh) Limited
Incorporated: 4 April 2016
Net Worth Deficit: £73,477 *Total Assets:* £9,049,674
Registered Office: Unit A, Brook Park East, Shirebrook, Derbys, NG20 8RY
Activities: Other letting and operating of own or leased real estate
Parent: SDI Property Limited
Officers: Cameron John Olsen, Secretary; Adedotun Ademola Adegoke [1973] Director/Senior Buyer; Rachel Isabel Lilian Stockton [1970] Director/Head of Customs and VAT

SDI (Enfield) Limited
Incorporated: 29 March 2016
Net Worth Deficit: £167,097 *Total Assets:* £23,285,102
Registered Office: Unit A, Brook Park East, Shirebrook, Derbys, NG20 8RY
Activities: Other letting and operating of own or leased real estate
Parent: SDI Property Limited
Officers: Cameron John Olsen, Secretary; Adedotun Ademola Adegoke [1973] Director/Senior Buyer; Rachel Isabel Lilian Stockton [1970] Director/Head of Customs and VAT

SDI (Jersey Holding) Limited
Incorporated: 12 May 2016
Net Worth: £100 *Total Assets:* £18,100,100
Registered Office: Unit A, Brook Park East, Shirebrook, Derbys, NG20 8RY
Activities: Other letting and operating of own or leased real estate
Parent: SDI Property Limited
Officers: Cameron John Olsen, Secretary; Adedotun Ademola Adegoke [1973] Director/Senior Buyer; Rachel Isabel Lilian Stockton [1970] Director/Head of Customs and VAT

SDI (Kingston) Limited
Incorporated: 14 August 2017
Net Worth Deficit: £584,767 *Total Assets:* £15,669,615
Registered Office: Unit A, Brook Park East, Shirebrook, Derbys, NG20 8RY
Activities: Non-trading company
Parent: SDI Property Limited
Officers: Cameron John Olsen, Secretary; Adedotun Ademola Adegoke [1973] Director/Senior Buyer; Rachel Isabel Lilian Stockton [1970] Director/Head of Customs and VAT

SDI (Liverpool) Limited
Incorporated: 25 November 2015
Net Worth: £1,271,464 *Total Assets:* £11,595,828
Registered Office: Unit A, Brook Park East, Shirebrook, Derbys, NG20 8RY
Activities: Other letting and operating of own or leased real estate
Parent: SDI Property Limited
Officers: Cameron John Olsen, Secretary; Adedotun Ademola Adegoke [1973] Director/Senior Buyer; Rachel Isabel Lilian Stockton [1970] Director/Head of Customs and VAT

SDI (LSL Holdings) Limited
Incorporated: 4 May 2016
Net Worth: £100 *Total Assets:* £11,574,303
Registered Office: Unit A, Brook Park East, Shirebrook, Derbys, NG20 8RY
Activities: Activities of other holding companies n.e.c.
Parent: Sportsdirect.Com Retail Limited
Officers: Cameron John Olsen, Secretary; Adedotun Ademola Adegoke [1973] Director/Senior Buyer; Rachel Isabel Lilian Stockton [1970] Director/Head of Customs and VAT

SDI (Manchester Cheetham Hill) Limited
Incorporated: 4 April 2016
Net Worth: £782,465 *Total Assets:* £18,163,332
Registered Office: Unit A, Brook Park East, Shirebrook, Derbys, NG20 8RY
Activities: Other letting and operating of own or leased real estate
Parent: SDI Property Limited
Officers: Cameron John Olsen, Secretary; Adedotun Ademola Adegoke [1973] Director/Senior Buyer; Rachel Isabel Lilian Stockton [1970] Director/Head of Customs and VAT

SDI (Market Road) Limited
Incorporated: 1 June 2017
Net Worth Deficit: £1,252,010 *Total Assets:* £17,806,204
Registered Office: Unit A, Brook Park East, Shirebrook, Derbys, NG20 8RY
Activities: Non-trading company
Officers: Cameron John Olsen, Secretary; Adedotun Ademola Adegoke [1973] Director/Senior Buyer; Rachel Isabel Lilian Stockton [1970] Director/Head of Customs and VAT

SDI (Nottingham) Limited
Incorporated: 4 April 2016
Net Worth: £645,782 *Total Assets:* £22,231,964
Registered Office: Unit A, Brook Park East, Shirebrook, Derbys, NG20 8RY
Activities: Other letting and operating of own or leased real estate
Parent: SDI Property Limited
Officers: Cameron John Olsen, Secretary; Adedotun Ademola Adegoke [1973] Director/Senior Buyer; Rachel Isabel Lilian Stockton [1970] Director/Head of Customs and VAT

SDI (Oxford Street) Limited
Incorporated: 7 March 2016
Net Worth Deficit: £15,571,427 *Total Assets:* £115,346,952
Registered Office: Unit A, Brook Park East, Shirebrook, Derbys, NG20 8RY
Activities: Other letting and operating of own or leased real estate
Parent: SDI Property Limited
Officers: Cameron John Olsen, Secretary; Adedotun Ademola Adegoke [1973] Director/Senior Buyer; Rachel Isabel Lilian Stockton [1970] Director/Head of Customs & VAT

SDI (Thurrock) Limited
Incorporated: 30 March 2016
Net Worth Deficit: £3,415,304 *Total Assets:* £11,940,365
Registered Office: Unit A, Brook Park East, Shirebrook, Derbys, NG20 8RY
Activities: Other letting and operating of own or leased real estate
Parent: SDI Property Limited
Officers: Cameron John Olsen, Secretary; Adedotun Ademola Adegoke [1973] Director/Senior Buyer; Rachel Isabel Lilian Stockton [1970] Director/Head of Customs and VAT

SDI Aviation Limited
Incorporated: 10 June 2015
Net Worth Deficit: £2,879,548 *Total Assets:* £40,761,140
Registered Office: Unit A, Brook Park East, Shirebrook, Derbys, NG20 8RY
Activities: Renting and leasing of air passenger transport equipment
Parent: Sports Direct International PLC
Officers: Cameron John Olsen, Secretary; Adedotun Ademola Adegoke [1973] Director/Senior Buyer; Rachel Isabel Lilian Stockton [1970] Director/Head of Customs and VAT

SDL Bigwood Limited
Incorporated: 9 December 2015 *Employees:* 4
Net Worth: £17,517,156 *Total Assets:* £19,871,274
Registered Office: 3-4 Regan Way, Chetwynd Business Park, Chilwell, Beeston, Nottingham, NG9 6RZ
Activities: Activities of head offices
Parent: SDL Property Services Group Limited
Officers: Sarah Kate Tuck, Secretary; Colin James Anderton [1977] Finance Director; Paul Robert Gratton [1959] Director

SDL Property Services Group Limited
Incorporated: 17 January 2007 *Employees:* 607
Previous: Shepherd Direct Limited
Net Worth: £20,020,000 *Total Assets:* £77,266,000
Registered Office: 3-4 Regan Way, Chetwynd Business Park, Chilwell, Nottingham, NG9 6RZ
Activities: Activities of head offices
Shareholder: BGF GP Limited
Officers: Sarah Kate Tuck, Secretary; Jonathan William Bloomer [1954] Director; George Pattullo Brewster [1960] Director/Surveyor; Robert Martin Clifford [1968] Group Commercial Director; Ian Downing [1969] Investor Director; Ian James Fergusson [1965] Director/Chartered Surveyor; Paul Robert Gratton [1959] Director; Christopher Charles Hickling [1961] Director; Nigel Vernon Tamplin [1951] Director

SDL Surveying Limited
Incorporated: 8 August 1989 *Employees:* 191
Previous: Direct Valuations Limited
Net Worth: £7,487,378 *Total Assets:* £11,907,298
Registered Office: 3 and 4 Regan Way, Chetwynd Business Park, Chilwell, Nottingham, NG9 6RZ
Activities: Other professional, scientific and technical activities n.e.c.
Parent: SDL Property Services Group Limited
Officers: Sarah Kate Tuck, Secretary; Colin James Anderton [1977] Director; George Pattullo Brewster [1960] Director; Ian James Fergusson [1965] Director; Paul Robert Gratton [1959] Director; Simon Paul Jackson [1968] Director

Seachill UK Limited
Incorporated: 20 April 1950 *Employees:* 772
Previous: Icelandic Group UK Limited
Net Worth: £56,612,000 *Total Assets:* £113,339,000
Registered Office: Hilton Food Group PLC, 2-8 The Interchange, Latham Road, Huntingdon, Cambs, PE29 6YE
Activities: Manufacture of prepared meals and dishes
Parent: Hilton Foods Limited
Officers: Neil Michael George, Secretary; Philip John Heffer [1966] Director; Nigel Richard Majewski [1960] Director; Frank McMyler [1969] Director [Irish]; Andrew John Harding Rutherford [1969] Finance Director; Simon John Smith [1962] Director

Seaham Investments Limited
Incorporated: 9 May 2007 *Employees:* 4
Net Worth: £1 *Total Assets:* £20,660,704
Registered Office: Crown Crest, Desford Lane, Kirby Muxloe, Leics, LE9 2BJ
Activities: Dormant company
Major Shareholder: Abdul Aziz Tayub
Officers: Hemant Patel, Secretary; Graham John Page [1949] Director; Hemant Patel [1961] Finance Director; Abdul Aziz Tayub [1955] Director; Shehzad Tayub [1985] Commercial Director

Sealed Air Limited
Incorporated: 2 October 1997 *Employees:* 431
Net Worth: £122,594,000 *Total Assets:* £218,580,992
Registered Office: Clifton House, 1 Marston Road, St Neots, Huntingdon, Cambs, PE19 2HN
Activities: Manufacture of plastic packing goods
Parent: Sealed Air B.V.
Officers: Karenjit Kaur Kalirai, Secretary; Karenjit Kaur Kalirai [1975] Director/Global Business Services [British/Canadian]; Chad Louis Keller [1969] Director/Treasurer [American]; William Gregory Stiehl [1961] Director/Controller [American]; Michael Peter Thurland [1956] Director/Global Process Management Partner

Sealord (Europe) Limited
Incorporated: 4 January 1993
Net Worth: £11,197,638 *Total Assets:* £11,197,848
Registered Office: Cartergate House, 26 Chantry Lane, Grimsby, N E Lincs, DN31 2LJ
Activities: Activities of other holding companies n.e.c.
Officers: Gary Andrew Neill [1967] Director [New Zealander]; Steven Arnold Yung [1961] Director [Canadian]

Searles (Camping Ground) Limited
Incorporated: 14 January 1954 *Employees:* 197
Net Worth: £6,977,921 *Total Assets:* £14,942,513
Registered Office: 3 South Beach Road, Hunstanton, Norfolk, PE36 5BB
Activities: Hotels and similar accommodation
Officers: Victoria Rebecca Searle, Company Secretary; Andrew John Geoffrey Searle [1972] Leisure Resort Director; Paul Richard Searle [1970] Managing Director; William John Searle [1951] Sea Tours Director; Joanna Alice Elizabeth Symonds [1978] Financial Director

Seashell Trust
Incorporated: 15 May 2001 *Employees:* 526
Net Worth: £19,761,000 *Total Assets:* £20,846,000
Registered Office: Stanley Road, Cheadle Hulme, Stockport, Cheshire, SK8 6RQ
Activities: Other education n.e.c.
Officers: Mark John Ascroft, Secretary; Edward Baines [1951] Director/Solicitor; Julie Vanessa Besbrode [1971] Director; Nicola Jane Bottley [1968] Director/Accountant; Gwen Carr [1955] Deputy Director Research Group University; Stephen Paul Gillingham [1969] Director of Property and Consultancy Group; Nicholas John Gower [1959] Director/Chartered Accountant; Doctor Afshan Naseem Khawaja [1970] Director/Doctor; Jane Teresa Raca [1963] Director/Writer, Speaker and Campaigner on Disability Issue; Dr David Sanders [1949] Director/Local Government; David Charles Shipley [1943] Director; Christopher Luke Smale [1954] Director/Retired

Seaside Leisure Parks Limited
Incorporated: 7 August 1978 *Employees:* 16
Net Worth: £12,918,141 *Total Assets:* £20,313,196
Registered Office: 27-29 Lumley Avenue, Skegness, Lincs, PE25 2AT
Activities: Recreational vehicle parks, trailer parks and camping grounds
Shareholders: Reginald Roy Pritchard; Pamela Joan Pritchard
Officers: Pamela Joan Pritchard, Secretary; Andrew Robin Charles Pritchard [1966] Director; Pamela Joan Pritchard [1930] Director; Reginald Roy Pritchard [1928] Director

Secanim Limited
Incorporated: 4 August 1948 *Employees:* 157
Net Worth: £18,218,908 *Total Assets:* £31,335,372
Registered Office: Ings Road, Doncaster, S Yorks, DN5 9TL
Activities: Manufacture of oils and fats
Parent: Saria Limited
Officers: Robert Vincent Ratcliffe [1958] Director; Andrew Richard Smith [1962] Director

Seckloe 297 Limited
Incorporated: 13 January 2006 *Employees:* 211
Net Worth: £1,089,475 *Total Assets:* £15,238,863
Registered Office: c/o Sterling Press Ltd, Kettering Venture Park, Kettering, Northants, NN15 6XU
Activities: Activities of head offices
Major Shareholder: Steven David Pizzey
Officers: Steven David Pizzey, Secretary/Printer; John Frederick Pizzey [1957] Director/Printer; Steven David Pizzey [1962] Director/Printer

Sector Aircraft Leasing Limited
Incorporated: 2 May 2012
Net Worth: £28,771,000 *Total Assets:* £76,198,000
Registered Office: BMI Regional, Herald Way, East Midlands Airport, Castle Donington, Derbys, DE74 2TU
Activities: Renting and leasing of air passenger transport equipment
Parent: Sector Aviation Holdings Limited
Officers: Alan Adams Murray [1948] Director

Sector Aviation Holdings Limited
Incorporated: 31 January 2012 *Employees:* 5
Net Worth Deficit: £1,008,000 *Total Assets:* £44,573,000
Registered Office: Pegasus Business Park, Herald Way, East Midlands Airport, Castle Donington, Derbys, DE74 2TU
Activities: Activities of head offices
Parent: Airline Investments Limited
Officers: Peter James Bond [1961] Director; Stephen William Bond [1950] Director; David Alexander Harrison [1960] Director; Alan Adams Murray [1948] Director; Peter Anthony Simpson [1967] Director

Secure Holdings Limited
Incorporated: 28 June 1996 *Employees:* 266
Net Worth: £3,213,000 *Total Assets:* £25,227,000
Registered Office: Secure House, Braithwell Way, Hellaby, Rotherham, S Yorks, S66 8QY
Activities: Non-trading company
Officers: Weiqi Wu [1964] Director/Vice President [Chinese]; Bo Yang [1984] Director/Regional Manager [Chinese]; Jiangfeng Zhi [1983] Director [Chinese]

See Group Limited
Incorporated: 21 August 2007 *Employees:* 56
Net Worth: £67,932,000 *Total Assets:* £73,421,000
Registered Office: Norfolk House, 47 Upper Parliment Street, Nottingham, NG1 2AB
Activities: Other amusement and recreation activities n.e.c.
Officers: Leanne Lipscombe, Secretary; Simon John Gillham [1956] Director/Senior Executive VP Comms Vivendi; Robert Ian Wilmshurst [1969] Director

SEK Holdings Limited
Incorporated: 10 May 2016 *Employees:* 434
Net Worth Deficit: £1,764,130 *Total Assets:* £28,191,242
Registered Office: 8 Shipton Way, Express Business Park, Rushden, Northants, NN10 6GL
Activities: Other manufacturing n.e.c.
Officers: Mark Christison, Secretary; Stephen Arnett [1965] Director; Mark Andrew Christison [1972] Director/Chartered Accountant; Debbie Joanne Foulke [1973] Director/Chartered FCIPD; Silvano Geranio [1969] Director [Italian]; Keith Andrew Hanger [1961] Director; Eric Jones [1952] Director; Jonathan Wake [1969] Sales Director; Andrew Westwood [1970] Sales Director

Selden Research Limited
Incorporated: 10 July 1970 *Employees:* 203
Net Worth: £12,177,326 *Total Assets:* £19,214,784
Registered Office: Staden Business Park, Staden Lane, Buxton, Derbys, SK17 9RZ
Activities: Manufacture of soap and detergents
Shareholders: Sandra Buchanan Woodhead; Denis Edwin Woodhead
Officers: Sandra Buchanan Woodhead, Secretary; David Alexander Woodhead [1967] Works Director; Denis Edwin Woodhead [1937] Director Industrial Chemist; Mark Andrew Woodhead [1963] Sales Director; Peter Philip Woodhead [1975] Technical Director; Sandra Buchanan Woodhead [1942] Director Secretary

Select Alloys & Materials Limited
Incorporated: 18 December 2000
Net Worth: £6,076,023 *Total Assets:* £9,519,941
Registered Office: Rimswell House, Sandbeck Lane, Tickhill, Doncaster, S Yorks, DN11 9PJ
Activities: Precious metals production
Shareholders: Terrence Moore; Tracey Moore
Officers: Tracey June Moore, Secretary; David Fairchild [1973] Director; Terrence Moore [1958] Director/Broker of Semi Precious Metals; Tracey June Moore [1968] Director

Select Group International Limited
Incorporated: 3 October 2001
Net Worth: £5,970,483 *Total Assets:* £13,330,788
Registered Office: The Box, Horseshoe Lane, Alderley Edge, Cheshire, SK9 7QP
Activities: Activities of head offices
Parent: Select Group International (Holdings) Limited
Officers: Giles Peter Beswick, Secretary/Director; Giles Peter Beswick [1974] Director; Mark Stephen Littlewood [1977] Director; Mark David Stott [1972] Director

Select International Developments Limited
Incorporated: 10 June 2005
Net Worth: £11,025 *Total Assets:* £11,977,001
Registered Office: The Box, Horseshoe Lane, Alderley Edge, Cheshire, SK9 7QP
Activities: Development of building projects
Parent: Select International Developments (Holdings) Limited
Officers: Giles Peter Beswick, Secretary; Giles Peter Beswick [1974] Director; Mark Stephen Littlewood [1977] Director; Mark David Stott [1972] Managing Director

Selective Marketplace Limited
Incorporated: 8 June 1981 *Employees:* 115
Net Worth: £14,561,432 *Total Assets:* £19,641,448
Registered Office: Belton Road West, Loughborough, Leics, LE11 5XL
Activities: Retail sale of clothing in specialised stores
Shareholders: John Colin Dashper; Jane Elizabeth Dashper; Luke Dashper
Officers: John Colin Dashper, Secretary/Managing Director; Jane Elizabeth Dashper [1944] Director/Secretary; John Colin Dashper [1941] Managing Director; Luke Dashper [1968] Director

Selectkey Limited
Incorporated: 20 May 2008
Net Worth: £4,487,882 *Total Assets:* £12,889,762
Registered Office: 12 Bridgford Road, West Bridgford, Nottingham, NG2 6AB
Activities: Other letting and operating of own or leased real estate
Officers: Donna Louise Tully, Secretary; Nicola Clare Feast [1972] Director; Caroline Sarah Howes [1978] Director/PA; Donna Louise Tully [1976] Director/Financial Analyst

Semelab Limited
Incorporated: 17 July 2008 *Employees:* 134
Net Worth: £12,862,000 *Total Assets:* £16,075,000
Registered Office: Coventry Road, Lutterworth, Leics, LE17 4JB
Activities: Manufacture of electronic components
Parent: TT Electronics Group Holdings Limited
Officers: Lynton David Boardman, Secretary; Simon Peter Carberry Evans [1974] Director; Thomas Brendan Garvey [1968] Director; Mark Hoad [1970] Director

The Senad Group Limited
Incorporated: 10 December 2002 *Employees:* 2
Net Worth Deficit: £12,370,000 *Total Assets:* £24,502,000
Registered Office: 1 St George's Vernon Gate, Derby, DE1 1UQ
Activities: Other education n.e.c.
Parent: Qatar Investment Authority
Officers: James Richard Atkinson, Finance Director; James Richard Atkinson [1968] Finance Director; Brian James Jones [1950] Director/Education

Senad Investments Limited
Incorporated: 12 June 2006 *Employees:* 30
Net Worth Deficit: £9,039,000 *Total Assets:* £41,599,000
Registered Office: 1 St George's Vernon Gate, Derby, DE1 1UQ
Activities: Other business support service activities n.e.c.
Parent: Qatar Investment Authority
Officers: James Richard Atkinson, Finance Director; James Richard Atkinson [1968] Finance Director; Abdul Rahim Bin Mohammed Ali [1977] Associate Director [Malaysian]; Navid Chamdia [1973] Director; Dr Mark Flynn [1965] Director/Chief Operations Officer; Brian James Jones [1950] Director/Chief Operations Officer

Senad Limited
Incorporated: 8 July 1974 *Employees:* 522
Net Worth: £34,656,000 *Total Assets:* £44,169,000
Registered Office: 1 St Georges Vernon Gate, Derby, DE1 1UQ
Activities: Other education n.e.c.
Parent: Qatar Investment Authority
Officers: James Richard Atkinson, Finance Director; James Richard Atkinson [1968] Finance Director; Brian James Jones [1950] Director/Chief Executive

Senior Architectural Systems Limited
Incorporated: 18 January 2000 *Employees:* 147
Net Worth: £4,590,825 *Total Assets:* £19,397,584
Registered Office: Eland Road, Denaby Main, Doncaster, S Yorks, DN12 4HA
Activities: Wholesale of metals and metal ores
Parent: Clytha Holdings Limited
Officers: Leslie Robert Buxton [1978] Director; James Richard Keeling-Heane [1980] Sales Director; Mark Vincenzo Wadsworth [1973] Director/Systems General Manager; Mark Douglas Wheatley [1979] Technical Director

Sensient Colors UK Ltd
Incorporated: 15 November 1962 *Employees:* 68
Net Worth: £4,413,664 *Total Assets:* £10,762,310
Registered Office: Oldmedow Road, Hardwick Industrial Estate, Kings Lynn, Norfolk, PE30 4LA
Activities: Manufacture of dyes and pigments
Parent: Sensient Holdings UK Limited
Officers: Bradley Michael Conners [1977] Director/Senior Attorney [American]; Nicola Claire Laroiya [1974] Director/General Manager; Jeffrey Thomas Makal [1963] Director [American]

Sensient Flavors Limited
Incorporated: 29 August 1980 *Employees:* 222
Net Worth: £4,328,703 *Total Assets:* £63,280,836
Registered Office: Bilton Road, Bletchley, Milton Keynes, Bucks, MK1 1HP
Activities: Other processing and preserving of fruit and vegetables
Parent: Sensient Holdings UK
Officers: Michael Francois de Meyer [1959] Director/General Manager; Jeffrey Thomas Makal [1963] Director [American]

Sensient Holdings UK
Incorporated: 20 July 1977
Net Worth: £30,338,972 *Total Assets:* £43,981,096
Registered Office: Bilton Road, Bletchley, Milton Keynes, Bucks, MK1 1HP
Activities: Other processing and preserving of fruit and vegetables
Parent: Sensient Technologies Corporation
Officers: Bradley Michael Conners [1977] Director/Senior Attorney [American]; Leroy Clark Watson [1973] Director of Taxation

Sensient Technologies Limited
Incorporated: 25 February 1981
Net Worth: £14,496,129 *Total Assets:* £14,496,129
Registered Office: Sensient Technologies, Bilton Road, Bletchley, Milton Keynes, Bucks, MK1 1HP
Activities: Activities of head offices
Parent: Sensient Technologies Corporation
Officers: David Joseph Farlee [1970] Benefits & Compensation Director [American]; Lori Marie Hauser [1980] Director/Treasury [American]

Sensitlive Limited
Incorporated: 26 August 2008
Net Worth: £190,999,648 *Total Assets:* £191,369,456
Registered Office: Sandford Gate, East Point Business Park, Sandy Lane West, Oxford, OX4 6LB
Activities: Distribution of electricity
Major Shareholder: Martin Strobl
Officers: Eva Maria de Almeida [1965] Director [Austrian]

Serasa Finance Limited
Incorporated: 8 November 2016
Net Worth: £194,519,664 *Total Assets:* £194,519,664
Registered Office: The Sir John Peace Building, Experian Way, NG2 Business Park, Nottingham, NG80 1ZZ
Activities: Fund management activities
Parent: Experian Finance PLC
Officers: Ronan Peter Hanna, Secretary; Paul Alan Atkinson [1960] Director; Antony Jonathan Ward Barnes [1964] Director; Karen Julia Greenwood [1967] Director/Chartered Accountant; Daniel Tristan Lilley [1961] Director; Mark Edward Pepper [1963] Director

Servelec Healthcare Limited
Incorporated: 27 July 1977 *Employees:* 110
Net Worth: £4,554,000 *Total Assets:* £11,778,000
Registered Office: The Straddle, Wharf Street, Sheffield, S2 5SY
Activities: Business and domestic software development
Parent: Servelec HSC Ltd
Officers: Michael Cane, Secretary; Michael Geoffrey Cane [1967] Director/Chartered Accountant; Paula Llewellyn [1975] Director; Alan Stubbs [1957] Director/Engineer; Christopher Sykes [1983] Director

Servelec Limited
Incorporated: 5 September 1995 *Employees:* 582
Previous: Servelec HSC Limited
Net Worth: £71,793,000 *Total Assets:* £113,405,000
Registered Office: The Straddle, Wharf Street, Sheffield, S2 5SY
Activities: Activities of head offices
Parent: Servelec Bidco Limited
Officers: Michael Cane, Secretary; Michael Geoffrey Cane [1967] Director/Chartered Accountant; Alan Stubbs [1957] Managing Director

Servelec Social Care Limited
Incorporated: 21 July 1999 *Employees:* 94
Previous: Servelec Corelogic Limited
Net Worth: £1,868,000 *Total Assets:* £9,956,000
Registered Office: The Straddle, Wharf Street, Sheffield, S2 5SY
Activities: Other information technology service activities
Parent: Servelec HSC Ltd
Officers: Michael Cane, Secretary; Michael Geoffrey Cane [1967] Director/Chartered Accountant; Garry McCord [1966] Director; Alan Stubbs [1957] Director/Engineer

Set Copyrights Limited
Incorporated: 28 March 1960 *Employees:* 4
Net Worth: £18,720,530 *Total Assets:* £19,075,584
Registered Office: The Pinnacle, 170 Midsummer Boulevard, Milton Keynes, Bucks, MK9 1BP
Activities: Book publishing
Officers: Judith Margaret Hooper [1962] Director/Tax and Finance Consultant; Laurence Peter Longe [1955] Director/Chartered Accountant; Clare Reihill [1962] Literary Director Set Copyrights [Irish]

Seth Bidco Limited
Incorporated: 15 June 2017
Net Worth: £24,582,400 *Total Assets:* £26,658,000
Registered Office: 15 Basset Court, Loake Close, Grange Park, Northampton, NN4 5EZ
Activities: Dental practice activities
Parent: Seth Midco Limited
Officers: Thomas Robert Biddle [1980] Director/Private Equity Investor; Dawn Farrell [1970] Director; Anand Jain [1976] Director/Private Equity Investor; Shalin Mehra [1961] Director; Richard Charles Smith [1957] Director

Seth Finco Limited
Incorporated: 15 June 2017
Net Worth: £24,582,400 *Total Assets:* £33,914,612
Registered Office: 15 Basset Court, Loake Close, Grange Park, Northampton, NN4 5EZ
Activities: Dental practice activities
Parent: Seth Topco Limited
Officers: Thomas Robert Biddle [1980] Director/Private Equity Investor; Dawn Farrell [1970] Director; Anand Jain [1976] Director/Private Equity Investor; Shalin Mehra [1961] Director; Richard Charles Smith [1957] Director

Seth Midco Limited
Incorporated: 15 June 2017
Net Worth: £24,582,400 *Total Assets:* £26,658,000
Registered Office: 15 Basset Court, Loake Close, Grange Park, Northampton, NN4 5EZ
Activities: Dental practice activities
Parent: Seth Finco Limited
Officers: Thomas Robert Biddle [1980] Director/Private Equity Investor; Dawn Farrell [1970] Director; Anand Jain [1976] Director/Private Equity Investor; Shalin Mehra [1961] Director; Richard Charles Smith [1957] Director

Seth Topco Limited
Incorporated: 15 June 2017 *Employees:* 902
Net Worth: £19,369,652 *Total Assets:* £71,326,544
Registered Office: 15 Basset Court, Loake Close, Grange Park, Northampton, NN4 5EZ
Activities: Dental practice activities
Parent: CBPE Capital LLP
Officers: Thomas Robert Biddle [1980] Director/Private Equity Investor; Dawn Farrell [1970] Director; Anand Jagdishchandra Jain [1976] Director/Private Equity Investor; Shalin Mehra [1961] Director; Richard Charles Smith [1957] Director

Sevco 5112 Limited
Incorporated: 19 August 2015 *Employees:* 283
Net Worth Deficit: £45,901,276 *Total Assets:* £131,623,352
Registered Office: Number One Pride Place, Pride Park, Derby, DE24 8QR
Activities: Other sports activities
Major Shareholder: Melvyn Morris
Officers: Christopher Mark Morris [1979] Director; Melvyn Morris [1956] Director

Severn Trent (W & S) Limited
Incorporated: 16 May 2000
Net Worth: £440,200,000 *Total Assets:* £2,257,999,872
Registered Office: Severn Trent Centre, 2 St John's Street, Coventry, Warwicks, CV1 2LZ
Activities: Other business support service activities n.e.c.
Parent: Severn Trent Holdings Limited
Officers: Gemma Eagle, Secretary; John Anthony Jackson [1960] Director; Bronagh Kennedy [1963] Director/General Counsel and Company Secretary; Robert Craig McPheely [1962] Director/Accountant

Severn Trent Carsington Limited
Incorporated: 18 March 2011
Net Worth: £3,129,200,128 *Total Assets:* £3,146,099,968
Registered Office: Severn Trent Centre, 2 St John's Street, Coventry, Warwicks, CV1 2LZ
Activities: Activities of other holding companies n.e.c.
Parent: Severn Trent (W & S) Limited
Officers: Gemma Eagle, Secretary; John Anthony Jackson [1960] Director; Bronagh Kennedy [1963] Director/General Counsel and Company Secretary; Robert Craig McPheely [1962] Director/Accountant

Severn Trent Corporate Holdings Limited
Incorporated: 15 March 2002
Net Worth: £10,194,000 *Total Assets:* £10,253,000
Registered Office: Severn Trent Centre, 2 St John's Street, Coventry, Warwicks, CV1 2LZ
Activities: Activities of other holding companies n.e.c.
Parent: Severn Trent Holdings Limited
Officers: Aline Anne Campbell, Secretary; John Anthony Jackson [1960] Director; Bronagh Kennedy [1963] Director/General Counsel and Company Secretary; Robert Craig McPheely [1962] Director/Accountant

Severn Trent Draycote Limited
Incorporated: 24 June 2011
Net Worth: £3,407,200,000 *Total Assets:* £6,453,899,776
Registered Office: Severn Trent Centre, 2 St John's Street, Coventry, Warwicks, CV1 2LZ
Activities: Activities of other holding companies n.e.c.
Parent: Severn Trent Investment Holdings Limited
Officers: Aline Anne Campbell, Secretary; John Anthony Jackson [1960] Director; Bronagh Kennedy [1963] Director/General Counsel and Company Secretary; Robert Craig McPheely [1962] Director/Accountant

Severn Trent Finance Holdings Limited
Incorporated: 8 January 2007
Net Worth: £516,108,000 *Total Assets:* £1,454,834,944
Registered Office: Severn Trent Centre, 2 St John's Street, Coventry, Warwicks, CV1 2LZ
Activities: Activities of other holding companies n.e.c.
Parent: Severn Trent Investment Holdings Limited
Officers: Gemma Eagle, Secretary; John Anthony Jackson [1960] Director; Bronagh Kennedy [1963] Director/General Counsel and Company Secretary; Robert Craig McPheely [1962] Director/Accountant

Severn Trent Finance Limited
Incorporated: 27 June 2007
Net Worth: £275,328,000 *Total Assets:* £276,087,008
Registered Office: Severn Trent Centre, 2 St John's Street, Coventry, Warwicks, CV1 2LZ
Activities: Activities of other holding companies n.e.c.
Parent: Severn Trent Carsington Limited
Officers: Aline Anne Campbell, Secretary; John Anthony Jackson [1960] Director; Bronagh Kennedy [1963] Director/General Counsel and Company Secretary; Robert Craig McPheely [1962] Director/Accountant

Severn Trent Green Power Limited
Incorporated: 1 August 2002
Net Worth Deficit: £907,000 *Total Assets:* £110,560,000
Registered Office: Severn Trent Centre, 2 St John's Street, Coventry, Warwicks, CV1 2LZ
Activities: Production of electricity
Parent: Severn Trent Holdings Limited
Officers: Gemma Eagle, Secretary; Neil Corrigall [1976] Director; Robert Craig McPheely [1962] Director/Accountant; Andrew Patrick Smith [1960] Director

Severn Trent Holdings Limited
Incorporated: 16 December 2005
Net Worth: £556,033,984 *Total Assets:* £749,216,000
Registered Office: Severn Trent Centre, 2 St John's Street, Coventry, Warwicks, CV1 2LZ
Activities: Activities of other holding companies n.e.c.
Parent: Severn Trent Finance Holdings Limited
Officers: Gemma Eagle, Secretary; John Anthony Jackson [1960] Director; Bronagh Kennedy [1963] Director/General Counsel and Company Secretary; Robert Craig McPheely [1962] Director/Accountant

Severn Trent Investment Holdings Limited
Incorporated: 10 March 2011
Net Worth: £3,160,800,000 *Total Assets:* £4,064,699,904
Registered Office: Severn Trent Centre, 2 St John's Street, Coventry, Warwicks, CV1 2LZ
Activities: Activities of other holding companies n.e.c.
Parent: Severn Trent PLC
Officers: Aline Anne Campbell, Secretary; John Anthony Jackson [1960] Director; Bronagh Kennedy [1963] Director/General Counsel and Company Secretary; Robert Craig McPheely [1962] Director/Accountant

Severn Trent LCP Limited
Incorporated: 9 February 2012
Net Worth: £110,454,000 *Total Assets:* £110,454,000
Registered Office: Severn Trent Centre, 2 St John's Street, Coventry, Warwicks, CV1 2LZ
Activities: Other business support service activities n.e.c.
Parent: Severn Trent Water Limited
Officers: Aline Anne Campbell, Secretary; John Anthony Jackson [1960] Director; Robert Craig McPheely [1962] Director/Accountant

Severn Trent Leasing Limited
Incorporated: 4 February 2009
Net Worth: £146,552,992 *Total Assets:* £422,240,992
Registered Office: Severn Trent Centre, 2 St John's Street, Coventry, Warwicks, CV1 2LZ
Activities: Other business support service activities n.e.c.
Parent: Severn Trent Water Limited
Officers: Aline Anne Campbell, Secretary; John Anthony Jackson [1960] Director; Robert Craig McPheely [1962] Director/Accountant

Severn Trent Overseas Holdings Limited
Incorporated: 27 December 1989
Net Worth: £46,816,000 *Total Assets:* £159,324,000
Registered Office: Severn Trent Centre, 2 St John's Street, Coventry, Warwicks, CV1 2LZ
Activities: Activities of other holding companies n.e.c.
Parent: Severn Trent Finance Limited
Officers: Gemma Eagle, Secretary; John Anthony Jackson [1960] Director; Bronagh Kennedy [1963] Director/General Counsel and Company Secretary; Robert Craig McPheely [1962] Director/Accountant

Severn Trent PLC
Incorporated: 1 April 1989 *Employees:* 6,633
Net Worth: £993,699,968 *Total Assets:* £9,421,800,448
Registered Office: Severn Trent Centre, 2 St John's Street, Coventry, Warwicks, CV1 2LZ
Activities: Activities of head offices
Officers: Bronagh Kennedy, Secretary; Kevin Stanley Beeston [1962] Director; James Bowling [1968] Director/Chartered Accountant; John Bernard Coghlan [1958] Director/Chartered Accountant [Irish]; Andrew James Duff [1959] Director; Olivia Ruth Garfield [1975] Director; Dominique Jacqueline Nicole Reiniche [1955] Director [French]; Philip John Remnant [1954] Director/Banker; Dr Angela Rosemary Emily Strank [1952] Oil Company Executive, Director

Severn Trent Reservoirs Limited
Incorporated: 18 October 1995
Net Worth Deficit: £34,918,000 *Total Assets:* £197,303,008
Registered Office: Severn Trent Centre, 2 St John's Street, Coventry, Warwicks, CV1 2LZ
Activities: Other business support service activities n.e.c.
Parent: Severn Trent Water Limited
Officers: Gemma Eagle, Secretary; John Anthony Jackson [1960] Director; Robert Craig McPheely [1962] Director/Accountant

Severn Trent Services Defence Limited
Incorporated: 26 April 2004
Net Worth: £10,568,000 *Total Assets:* £73,403,000
Registered Office: Severn Trent Centre, 2 St John's Street, Coventry, Warwicks, CV1 2LZ
Activities: Water collection, treatment and supply
Parent: Severn Trent Services Defence Holdings Limited
Officers: Gemma Eagle, Secretary; Robert Craig McPheely [1962] Director/Accountant; Adam Peter Stephens [1983] Director; Michael Alasdair Norval Williamson [1976] Director

Severn Trent Services Holdings Limited
Incorporated: 15 March 2002
Net Worth Deficit: £19,552,000 *Total Assets:* £30,814,000
Registered Office: Severn Trent Centre, 2 St John's Street, Coventry, Warwicks, CV1 2LZ
Activities: Activities of other holding companies n.e.c.
Parent: Severn Trent Holdings Limited
Officers: Gemma Eagle, Secretary; John Anthony Jackson [1960] Director; Bronagh Kennedy [1963] Director/General Counsel and Company Secretary; Robert Craig McPheely [1962] Director/Accountant

Severn Trent Services International (Overseas Holdings) Limited
Incorporated: 13 November 1995
Net Worth: £64,742,000 *Total Assets:* £65,367,000
Registered Office: Severn Trent Centre, 2 St John's Street, Coventry, Warwicks, CV1 2LZ
Activities: Activities of other holding companies n.e.c.
Parent: Severn Trent (W & S) Limited
Officers: Gemma Eagle, Secretary; John Anthony Jackson [1960] Director; Bronagh Kennedy [1963] Director/General Counsel and Company Secretary; Robert Craig McPheely [1962] Director/Accountant

Severn Trent Services Operations UK Limited
Incorporated: 9 August 2000 *Employees:* 224
Net Worth: £4,712,000 *Total Assets:* £20,565,000
Registered Office: Severn Trent Centre, 2 St John's Street, Coventry, Warwicks, CV1 2LZ
Activities: Water collection, treatment and supply
Parent: Severn Trent Services International (Overseas Holdings) Limited
Officers: Gemma Eagle, Secretary; Robert Craig McPheely [1962] Director/Accountant; Adam Peter Stephens [1983] Director; Michael Alasdair Norval Williamson [1976] Director

Severn Trent Trimpley Limited
Incorporated: 24 March 2017
Net Worth: £3,037,799,936 *Total Assets:* £3,046,700,032
Registered Office: 2 St Johns Street, Coventry, Warwicks, CV1 2LZ
Activities: Activities of other holding companies n.e.c.
Shareholders: Severn Trent Water Limited; Severn Trent Draycote Limited
Officers: Gemma Louise Eagle, Secretary; John Anthony Jackson [1960] Director; Robert Craig McPheely [1962] Director/Accountant

Severn Trent Utilities Finance PLC.
Incorporated: 25 March 1994
Net Worth: £100,000 *Total Assets:* £3,589,700,096
Registered Office: Severn Trent Centre, 2 St John's Street, Coventry, Warwicks, CV1 2LZ
Activities: Other business support service activities n.e.c.
Parent: Severn Trent Water Limited
Officers: Gemma Eagle, Secretary; John Anthony Jackson [1960] Director; Bronagh Kennedy [1963] Director/General Counsel and Company Secretary; Robert Craig McPheely [1962] Director/Accountant

Severn Trent Water Limited
Incorporated: 1 April 1989
Net Worth: £2,324,800,000 *Total Assets:* £10,590,300,160
Registered Office: Severn Trent Centre, 2 St John's Street, Coventry, Warwicks, CV1 2LZ
Activities: Water collection, treatment and supply
Parent: Severn Trent Draycote Limited
Officers: Bronagh Kennedy, Secretary; Kevin Stanley Beeston [1962] Director; James Bowling [1968] Director/Chartered Accountant; John Bernard Coghlan [1958] Director/Chartered Accountant [Irish]; Andrew James Duff [1959] Director; Olivia Ruth Garfield [1975] Director; Dominique Jacqueline Nicole Reiniche [1955] Director [French]; Philip John Remnant [1954] Director/Banker; Dr Angela Rosemary Emily Strank [1952] Oil Company Executive, Director

Severn Trent Wind Power Limited
Incorporated: 16 August 2011
Net Worth Deficit: £2,896,000 *Total Assets:* £23,152,000
Registered Office: Severn Trent Centre, 2 St John's Street, Coventry, Warwicks, CV1 2LZ
Activities: Production of electricity
Parent: Severn Trent Green Power Limited
Officers: Gemma Eagle, Secretary; Neil Corrigall [1976] Director; Robert Craig McPheely [1962] Director/Accountant; Andrew Patrick Smith [1960] Director

Seymour Distribution Limited
Incorporated: 27 July 1994 *Employees:* 77
Net Worth: £141,000 *Total Assets:* £22,586,000
Registered Office: Media House, Peterborough Business Park, Lynch Wood, Peterborough, Cambs, PE2 6EA
Activities: Retail sale of newspapers and stationery in specialised stores
Parent: Frontline Limited
Officers: Jonathan Mark Lambert [1965] Finance Director; Tracy Frances O'Sullivan [1967] Sales Director; Duncan Shearer [1975] Services Director; Dan Sims [1972] Director; Frank Carl Straetmans [1971] Managing Director [Belgian]

Seymour International Limited
Incorporated: 23 June 1994 *Employees:* 20
Net Worth: £811,000 *Total Assets:* £16,707,000
Registered Office: Media House, Peterborough Business Park, Lynch Wood, Peterborough, Cambs, PE2 6EA
Activities: Retail sale of newspapers and stationery in specialised stores
Parent: Frontline Limited
Officers: Jonathan Mark Lambert [1965] Finance Director; Tracy Frances O'Sullivan [1967] Sales Director; Duncan Shearer [1975] Services Director; Dan Sims [1972] Director; Frank Carl Straetmans [1971] Managing Director [Belgian]

SG International Holdings Limited
Incorporated: 3 July 2015 *Employees:* 2,182
Net Worth: £90,201,000 *Total Assets:* £482,303,008
Registered Office: Allen Ford, Tachbrook Park Drive, Warwick, CV34 6SY
Activities: Activities of other holding companies n.e.c.
Officers: Colin Alexander Brown [1969] Director/Chartered Accountant [South African]; Alan George Chambers [1967] Director/Lawyer [South African]; Peter William Mountford [1957] Director/Chartered Accountant; Paula Marie Wood [1969] Finance Director

SGBD Property Holdings Limited
Incorporated: 12 May 1926
Net Worth: £42,253,000 *Total Assets:* £181,168,992
Registered Office: Saint-Gobain House, Binley Business Park, Coventry, Warwicks, CV3 2TT
Activities: Other business support service activities n.e.c.
Shareholders: Compagnie de Saint-Gobain; Jewson Limited
Officers: Alun Roy Oxenham, Secretary; Nicholas James Cammack [1972] Director; Michael Strickland Chaldecott [1960] Managing Director; Michael David Newnham [1966] Director

SGP Holdings (UK) Limited
Incorporated: 1 March 2013 *Employees:* 71
Net Worth: £4,251,562 *Total Assets:* £19,143,714
Registered Office: 2 Pentagon South, Barton Lane, Abingdon, Oxon, OX14 3PZ
Activities: Wholesale of household goods (other than musical instruments) n.e.c
Major Shareholder: Paris Anthony Natar
Officers: Paris Anthony Natar [1955] Director/Businessman; Jonathan Richard Stobart [1961] Director

Sharing in Growth UK Limited
Incorporated: 23 October 2012
Total Assets: £36,358,000
Registered Office: P O Box 31, Moor Lane, Derby, DE24 8BJ
Activities: Management consultancy activities other than financial management
Officers: David Keith Rose, Secretary; Nicholas John Devey [1957] Director; Dr Bryan Samuel Jackson [1946] Director/Company Chairman; Jeffrey Philip Moore [1954] Director/Economic Development Consultancy; Andrew Norbert Page [1965] Director/Engineer; John Robert Thomson [1967] Director; Graham Robert Trevarthen [1955] Strategy Director

Sharmans Agricultural Limited
Incorporated: 16 July 1924 *Employees:* 91
Net Worth: £22,315,712 *Total Assets:* £26,210,172
Registered Office: College Farm, Gonerby Moor, Grantham, Lincs, NG32 2AB
Activities: Wholesale of agricultural machinery, equipment and supplies
Major Shareholder: Scott James Barclay
Officers: Guy Edward Kalijian Gasper, Secretary; Scott James Barclay [1981] Director; Francis John Disney [1950] Director; Sally-Anne Hazard [1977] Marketing Director; James David Madge [1980] Director/Business Executive

Sharnbrook Academy Federation
Incorporated: 20 January 2011 *Employees:* 523
Net Worth: £52,199,536 *Total Assets:* £58,341,944
Registered Office: Sharnbrook Upper School, Odell Road, Sharnbrook, Bedford, MK44 1JL
Activities: Other education n.e.c.
Officers: Tracy Bannister, Secretary; Jonathan Abbott [1971] Director/Retired; Alexander Kristian Ginns [1981] Director; Sean Hanson [1964] Director/Chief Executive, Local Partnerships LLP [Irish]; Alison Clare Horner [1964] Director/Partner at MHA MacIntyre Hudson; Tanja Kuveljic [1969] Director; Stelios Mores [1964] Director; Jeremy Francis Reynolds [1963] Director/Management Consultant; Marie-Chantal Thomas [1964] Director/Solicitor

Sharp Laboratories of Europe, Ltd.
Incorporated: 12 January 1990 *Employees:* 76
Net Worth: £16,683,554 *Total Assets:* £19,275,084
Registered Office: Edmund Halley Road, Oxford Science Park, Oxford, OX4 4GB
Activities: Other research and experimental development on natural sciences and engineering
Parent: Sharp Electronics (Europe) Limited
Officers: Jun Ashida [1966] Director [Japanese]; Mototaka Taneya [1958] Director/Group General Manager [Japanese]; Takayuki Yuasa [1960] Director [Japanese]

Ivor Shaw Limited
Incorporated: 29 March 1963 *Employees:* 265
Net Worth: £2,280,602 *Total Assets:* £9,485,436
Registered Office: City Gate, London Road, Derby, DE24 8WY
Activities: Manufacture of irradiation, electromedical and electrotherapeutic equipment
Parent: SP 225 Limited
Officers: Elizabeth Jane Fothergill [1953] Director; Luke Richard Fryer [1973] Director; David Nicholas Shaw [1960] Director; Ian Martin Shaw [1955] Director

Sheepy Magna Investments Ltd
Incorporated: 29 April 2014 *Employees:* 2
Net Worth Deficit: £7,452,687 *Total Assets:* £26,004,672
Registered Office: Rye Hills Barn, Watery Lane, Sheepy Magna, Atherstone, Warwicks, CV9 3RG
Activities: Fund management activities
Shareholders: John Charles Pennington Smith; Anna Sian Smith
Officers: Charles Smith [1965] Director; Sian Smith [1970] Director

Sheepy Magna Limited
Incorporated: 26 March 2014
Net Worth: £37,502,812 *Total Assets:* £38,377,512
Registered Office: Rye Hills Barn, Watery Lane, Sheepy Magna, Atherstone, Warwicks, CV9 3RG
Activities: Other credit granting n.e.c.
Shareholders: John Charles Pennington Smith; Anna Sian Smith
Officers: Anna Sian Smith [1970] Director; John Charles Pennington Smith [1965] Director

Sheermans Limited
Incorporated: 13 May 1993 *Employees:* 463
Net Worth: £9,991,256 *Total Assets:* £12,662,652
Registered Office: 1 Thornbury, West Ashland, Milton Keynes, Bucks, MK6 4BB
Activities: Take-away food shops and mobile food stands
Parent: Sheermans SS Limited
Officers: Adrian John Bushnell, Secretary; Scott Andrew Bush [1972] Operations Director [Australian]; Robin Keith Nigel Caley [1960] Director; Robert Michael Smith [1971] Director/Head of Partnerships

Sheetfed Holdings Limited
Incorporated: 31 January 2012
Net Worth: £7,596,377 *Total Assets:* £11,822,634
Registered Office: Unit 2 Enterprise Park, Enterprise Way, Retford, Notts, DN22 7HH
Activities: Wholesale of other machinery and equipment
Parent: Langley Holdings PLC
Officers: Anthony John Langley [1954] Director; Bernard James Langley [1993] Director

Sheffcare Limited
Incorporated: 11 September 1990 *Employees:* 460
Net Worth: £3,303,920 *Total Assets:* £12,373,644
Registered Office: Springwood House, 192 Penrith Road, Sheffield, S5 8UG
Activities: Residential care activities for the elderly and disabled
Officers: Peter Bradbury, Secretary; Anna Gailey [1987] Director/Executive Assistant; Brian Martin James [1953] Director/Retired; David Victor Johnson [1965] Director/Social Worker; Carole Janet Rainbird [1943] Director/Retired; Scott William Leslie Sanderson [1984] Director/Chartered Accountant; Dr Sarah Kate Smith [1969] Director/Research Doctor

Sheffield Business Park Limited
Incorporated: 7 July 1995 *Employees:* 9
Net Worth: £9,239,443 *Total Assets:* £10,834,924
Registered Office: Management Suite, Sheffield Business Centre, Europa Link, Sheffield, S9 1XZ
Activities: Buying and selling of own real estate
Parent: Tinsley Park Holdings Limited
Officers: James Spencer Matthews [1975] Director; Graham Michael Sadler [1957] Director/Chartered Surveyor; Thomas Berisford Sebire [1975] Director

Sheffield City Trust
Incorporated: 15 September 1987 *Employees:* 1,549
Net Worth: £24,915,000 *Total Assets:* £188,236,000
Registered Office: Riverside East, 2 Millsands, Sheffield, S3 8DT
Activities: Operation of sports facilities
Officers: Laurence Michael Gavin, Secretary; Helen Best [1966] Director/University Lecturer; Lynn Clarke [1954] Director/Managing Consultant; Justin Andrew Cole [1974] Director [British/Canadian/Australian]; David Grey Mbe [1956] Director; Jonathan Simon Parish [1965] Managing Director; John Warner [1955] Director/Chartered Accountant

Sheffield Diocesan Board of Finance
Incorporated: 29 February 1924 *Employees:* 55
Net Worth: £53,364,000 *Total Assets:* £58,928,000
Registered Office: Sheffield Diocesan, Church House, 95-99 Effingham Street, Rotherham, S Yorks, S65 1BL
Activities: Activities of religious organisations
Officers: Heidi Jane Adcock, Secretary; Neill Andrew Birchenall [1981] Director [American]; Reverend Peter Edward Bradley [1964] Director/Dean of Sheffield; The Right Reverend Peter Burrows [1955] Director/Bishop; Dr Jacqueline Anne Butcher [1965] Director/Foodbank Co-ordinator; Malcolm Leslie Chamberlain [1969] Director/Clerk in Holy Orders, Archdeacon; Revd Claire Louise Dawson [1968] Director/Clerk in Holy Orders; Ian Richard Downing [1939] Director/Retired; Revd Fiona Mary Kouble [1966] Director/Clerk in Holy Orders; Michael MacDonald [1966] Director/Negotiations Officer; Peter Martin Rainford [1948] Director/Town Planner; Revd Eleanor Elizabeth Mary Robertshaw [1977] Director/Clerk in Holy Orders; Reverend Ian Smith [1962] Director/Clerk in Holy Orders; Ian Geoffrey Walker [1958] Director; The Venerable Stephen Anthony Wilcockson [1951] Director/Archdeacon of Doncaster; Peter Jonathan Wilcox [1961] Director/Bishop of Sheffield

Sheffield Forgemasters Engineering Limited
Incorporated: 12 August 2003 *Employees:* 551
Net Worth Deficit: £5,737,000 *Total Assets:* £71,222,000
Registered Office: P O Box 286, Brightside Lane, Sheffield, S9 2RW
Activities: Manufacture of basic iron and steel and of ferro-alloys
Parent: Sheffield Forgemasters International Limited
Officers: Allan Geoffrey Skelton, Secretary; Gareth Keith Barker [1977] Director; Paul Alexander Cahill [1964] Director; Stephen Hammell [1973] Director

Sheffield Forgemasters International Limited
Incorporated: 1 September 2003 *Employees:* 666
Net Worth: £4,800,000 *Total Assets:* £82,537,000
Registered Office: P O Box 286, Brightside Lane, Sheffield, S9 2RW
Activities: Manufacture of basic iron and steel and of ferro-alloys
Shareholders: Sheffield Forgemasters Share Trustees Limited; Graham Aubrey Honeyman
Officers: Allan Geoffrey Skelton, Secretary; David Alan Bond [1962] Director; Paul Alexander Cahill [1964] Director; David Kenneth Duggins [1955] Director; Stephen Hammell [1973] Director; Janice Margaret Munday [1955] Director; Colin Peter Smith [1955] Director/Chairman

Sheffield Forgemasters Steel Limited
Incorporated: 5 June 1985 *Employees:* 86
Net Worth Deficit: £3,873,000 *Total Assets:* £41,696,000
Registered Office: P O Box 286, Brightside Lane, Sheffield, S9 2RW
Activities: Manufacture of basic iron and steel and of ferro-alloys
Parent: Sheffield Forgemasters International Limited
Officers: Allan Geoffrey Skelton, Secretary; Gareth Keith Barker [1977] Director; Paul Alexander Cahill [1964] Director; Stephen Hammell [1973] Director

Sheffield Galleries & Museums Trust
Incorporated: 10 March 1998 *Employees:* 96
Net Worth: £9,453,000 *Total Assets:* £11,097,000
Registered Office: Riverside East, 2 Millsands, Sheffield, S3 8DT
Activities: Operation of arts facilities
Officers: Charles Arnold John Biggin, Secretary; Charles Arnold John Biggin [1938] Director; Dr Antonia Bostrom [1957] Director/Curator; Lekisha Reshee Bradley [1992] Managing Director [American]; Darren Christopher Dryden Chouings [1986] Director/Artist and Events Manager; John Cowling [1954] Director/Retired; Maria Hanson [1967] Director/Academic; Councillor Dianne Lesley Hurst [1959] Director/Councillor; Neil Andrew MacDonald [1956] Director and Trustee; Patrick Paul Meleady [1965] Director/Manager; Ian Proctor [1966] Director/University of Sheffield; Peter Rippon [1943] Director/Councillor; Arun Thomas Singh [1980] Managing Director

Sheffield International Venues Limited
Incorporated: 2 March 1988 *Employees:* 694
Net Worth Deficit: £1,712,000 *Total Assets:* £13,028,000
Registered Office: Riverside East, 2 Millsands, Sheffield, S3 8DT
Activities: Operation of sports facilities
Parent: Sheffield City Trust
Officers: Andrew Edward Snelling, Secretary; Stuart George Britland [1950] Director; Neale Graham Gibson [1959] Director; Jonathan Simon Parish [1965] Managing Director; Andrew Edward Snelling [1963] Director of Finance

Sheffield South East Trust
Incorporated: 3 November 2016 *Employees:* 299
Net Worth: £16,314,000 *Total Assets:* £23,725,000
Registered Office: Manor Lodge Community Primary and Nursery School, Manor Lane, Sheffield, S2 1UF
Activities: Primary education
Officers: Michael Daniel Allen [1946] Director/Retired; Joanne Louise Bradshaw [1972] Director/Executive Headteacher; Keith Crawshaw [1951] Director/Retired; John Anthony Doyle [1961] Local Government Director; Derek James Langlands Grover [1949] Director/Retired Civil Servant; Marie Lowe [1949] Director/School Improvement Adviser; Mark Shipman [1976] Director/Teacher; Paul Stead [1954] Managing Director

Sheffield Theatres Crucible Trust
Incorporated: 21 December 2006
Net Worth: £6,382,211 *Total Assets:* £9,292,034
Registered Office: 55 Norfolk Street, Sheffield, S1 1DA
Activities: Performing arts
Officers: Neil Adleman [1973] Director/Solicitor; Matthew Byam Shaw [1963] Director/Theatre Producer; Richard Stuart Huntrods [1966] Director; Moji Adesola Kareem [1963] Artistic Director; The Lord Robert Walter Kerslake [1955] Director; Robert Frederick Strang Noble [1965] Deputy Managing Director

Sheffield Theatres Trust
Incorporated: 17 May 1968 *Employees:* 157
Net Worth: £8,214,889 *Total Assets:* £15,313,691
Registered Office: The Crucible Theatre, 55 Norfolk Street, Sheffield, S1 1DA
Activities: Artistic creation
Officers: Joan Carol Barton [1947] Director/Retired; Stephen David Betts [1972] Director; Ruth Elizabeth Bourne [1967] Director/Consultant; John Steven Cowling [1954] Director/Chartered Accountant; Mike Drabble [1971] Director/Trustee; Surriya Falconer [1961] Director; Mary Heyler [1954] Director; Mojisola Adesola Kareem [1963] Artistic Director; Julie Ann Kenny [1957] Director; The Lord Robert Walter Kerslake [1955] Director; Anne Marie Murphy [1964] Director/Councillor; Rosie Elisabeth Neave [1977] Communications Director; Giles Dominic Searby [1969] Director/Solicitor; Arun Thomas Singh [1980] Managing Director

Sheffield United Limited
Incorporated: 13 July 1945
Net Worth Deficit: £15,312,389 *Total Assets:* £27,309,348
Registered Office: Bramall Lane, Sheffield, S2 4SU
Activities: Activities of other holding companies n.e.c.
Parent: Scarborough United Group Limited
Officers: Kevin Charles McCabe [1948] Director/Chartered Surveyor; Scott Richard McCabe [1975] Managing Director; Simon Charles McCabe [1977] Director/Development Executive; Jeremy John Tutton [1966] Finance Director

The Sheffield UTC Academy Trust
Incorporated: 31 May 2011 *Employees:* 73
Net Worth: £18,881,000 *Total Assets:* £19,965,000
Registered Office: 111 Matilda Street, Sheffield, S1 4QF
Activities: Other education n.e.c.
Officers: Vivienne Martin, Secretary; Ian John Anniss [1949] Director/Retired; Nicholas John Crew [1965] Director/Principal of Sheffield UTC Academy Trust; Mike Drabble [1971] Director/Councillor; Christopher Charles Dymond [1968] Director/Digital Innovation Specialist; Daniel Fleetcroft [1975] Director/Engineer; Angela Foulkes [1969] Director/Principal; Professor Russell John Hand [1963] Director/University Professor; Kathryn Elizabeth Platts [1964] Finance & Resource Director; Mandy Scott [1964] Director/Nurse; Jonathan Blaise Stewart [1967] Director; Prof Christopher James Wigginton [1972] Director/Professor; Richard Kersey Wright [1956] Director

Sheffield Wednesday Football Club Limited
Incorporated: 8 June 1990 *Employees:* 274
Net Worth Deficit: £12,925,000 *Total Assets:* £47,511,000
Registered Office: Hillsborough, Sheffield, S6 1SW
Activities: Operation of sports facilities
Major Shareholder: Dejphon Chansiri
Officers: Dejphon Chansiri [1968] Director/Business Executive [Thai]

Sherwin-Williams Diversified Brands Limited
Incorporated: 16 September 1994 *Employees:* 412
Net Worth: £7,392,471 *Total Assets:* £70,249,040
Registered Office: Thorncliffe Park, Chapeltown, Sheffield, S35 2YP
Activities: Manufacture of paints, varnishes and similar coatings, mastics and sealants
Parent: Sherwin-Williams UK Holding Limited
Officers: Allen Mistysyn, Secretary; Ezio Nicola Giacomo Braggio [1956] Director/President EMEAI, Corporate Vice President [Italian]; Jeffrey James Miklich [1974] Director/Business Executive [American]; Allen Joseph Mistysyn [1968] Director/Business Executive [American]; Brian Edward Padden [1971] Director/General Manager [American]

Sherwin-Williams UK Holding Limited
Incorporated: 9 October 2009
Net Worth: £27,623,480 *Total Assets:* £78,390,672
Registered Office: The Sherwin-Williams Company, Thorncliffe Park, Chapeltown, Sheffield, S35 2YP
Activities: Activities of head offices
Parent: Sherwin-Williams Coatings S.A.R.L.
Officers: Ezio Nicola Giacomo Braggio [1956] Director/President EMEAI, Corporate Vice President [Italian]; Jeffrey James Miklich [1974] Director/Business Executive [American]; Allen Joseph Mistysyn [1968] Director/Business Executive [American]; Brian Edward Padden [1971] Director/General Manager [American]

Fred Sherwood & Sons (Transport) Limited
Incorporated: 20 May 1974 *Employees:* 44
Net Worth: £22,204,024 *Total Assets:* £35,150,764
Registered Office: 47 Ashby Road Central, Shepshed, Loughborough, Leics, LE12 9BS
Activities: Freight transport by road
Parent: Fred Sherwood Group Ltd
Officers: Andrew John Disney, Secretary; Alan Frederick Sherwood [1940] Director/Haulage Contractor; Ashley Paul Alan Sherwood [1969] Director/Haulage Contractor; Justin Anthony Sherwood [1973] Director/Manager; Sheila Irene Sherwood [1944] Director/Secretary; Belinda Hayley Sherwood Ratcliffe [1975] Director/Transport Administration

Fred Sherwood Group Limited
Incorporated: 5 November 2007 *Employees:* 452
Net Worth: £32,282,318 *Total Assets:* £52,873,620
Registered Office: 47 Ashby Road Central, Shepshed, Leics, LE12 9BS
Activities: Activities of head offices
Major Shareholder: Alan Frederick Sherwood
Officers: Andrew John Disney, Secretary; Alan Frederick Sherwood [1940] Director; Ashley Paul Alan Sherwood [1969] Director; Justin Anthony Sherwood [1973] Director; Sheila Irene Sherwood [1944] Director; Belinda Hayley Sherwood Ratcliffe [1975] Director

Sherwood Holdings Limited
Incorporated: 8 July 2016 *Employees:* 202
Net Worth Deficit: £57,372,000 *Total Assets:* £30,310,000
Registered Office: 1 Orchard Place, Nottingham Business Park, Nottingham, NG8 6PX
Activities: Activities of head offices
Shareholders: Stefano Bruno Serafino Camponovo; Benedetto Marti; North Atlantic Value GP 4 Limited; North Atlantic Smaller Companies Investment Trust PLC
Officers: James Douglas Agnew [1974] Director/Fund Manager; Marco Fumagalli [1970] Director/Manager [Italian]; Jay Charles Lecoque [1962] Director/Consultant [American]; Christopher Harwood Bernard Mills [1952] Director/Investment Manager; Trevor Frank Nolan [1973] Finance Director; Carlo Sgarbi [1964] Director/Manager [Italian]

Sherwood Homes Limited
Incorporated: 10 January 2013 *Employees:* 8
Net Worth Deficit: £11,679,488 *Total Assets:* £12,579,346
Registered Office: Houldsworth Mill Business and Arts Centre, Houldsworth Street, Stockport, Cheshire, SK5 6DA
Activities: Buying and selling of own real estate
Officers: David Burnett Scott [1946] Director

SHH 101 LLP
Incorporated: 5 July 2013 *Employees:* 188
Net Worth: £5,059,809 *Total Assets:* £12,196,185
Registered Office: St Helens House, King Street, Derby, DE1 3EE
Officers: James Oliver John Bagley [1982] Member; John Peter Farnsworth [1959] Member; Bruce James Montgomery [1964] Member; David Jonathan Nelson [1976] Member; Dean Anthony Nelson [1975] Member; Daniel Adam Bowtell [1976] LLP Member; James Charles Delve [1985] LLP Member; Catherine Desmond [1974] LLP Member; Sarah Flear [1972] LLP Member; Martin Alan Gadsby [1984] LLP Member; Jackie Hendley [1956] LLP Member; Darren Hodson [1974] LLP Member; Nicholas Charles Osborn Lee [1968] LLP Member; Janet Morgan [1957] LLP Member; Stephen Alexander Newman [1968] LLP Member; Michael Paul Roome [1980] LLP Member; Richard William Stanley [1963] LLP Member

Shield Engineering (Syston) Limited
Incorporated: 23 May 1951 *Employees:* 153
Net Worth: £12,654,657 *Total Assets:* £28,639,328
Registered Office: 365 Fosse Way, Syston, Leics, LE7 1NL
Activities: Machining
Major Shareholder: Christopher Richard Francis Shield
Officers: Christopher Richard Francis Shield, Secretary/Manager; Jonathan Cooper [1975] Director; Christopher Richard Francis Shield [1978] Director/Management

C R Shield Holdings Limited
Incorporated: 11 August 2016 *Employees:* 153
Net Worth: £17,207,742 *Total Assets:* £33,426,190
Registered Office: Third Floor, Two Colton Square, Leicester, LE1 1QH
Activities: Machining
Major Shareholder: Christopher Richard Francis Shield
Officers: Christopher Richard Francis Shield [1978] Director

Shield Properties Limited
Incorporated: 24 August 1998 *Employees:* 2
Net Worth: £12,410,520 *Total Assets:* £16,097,675
Registered Office: 365 Fosse Way, Syston, Leics, LE7 1NL
Activities: Buying and selling of own real estate
Parent: Shield Properties Holdings Limited
Officers: Jonathan Cooper [1975] Director; Christopher Richard Francis Shield [1978] Director/Engineer

Shima Seiki Europe Limited
Incorporated: 16 July 1985 *Employees:* 21
Net Worth: £5,914,068 *Total Assets:* £9,850,980
Registered Office: Sills Road, Willow Farm Business Park, Castle Donington, Derbys, DE74 2US
Activities: Agents involved in the sale of machinery, industrial equipment, ships and aircraft
Parent: Shima Seiki Manufacturing Limited
Officers: Hiroyuki Yamamoto, Secretary; Katsuyuki Hojo [1970] Director [Japanese]; Hiroshl Kato [1972] Director [Japanese]; Richard Webster [1963] Director; Hiroyuki Yamamoto [1969] Managing Director [Japanese]

Shipston High School
Incorporated: 9 August 2012 *Employees:* 68
Net Worth: £11,951,000 *Total Assets:* £12,785,000
Registered Office: Shipston High School, Darlingscote Road, Shipston on Stour, Warwicks, CV36 4DY
Activities: General secondary education
Officers: Yuhong Meads, Secretary; Robert Michael Armstrong [1943] Director/Retired; Richard Henry Baldwin [1936] Director/Retired; David George Ross Beeton [1948] Director/Teacher; Paul Gregory Chapman [1962] Director/Local Government Officer; Sarah Davies [1978] Director/Teacher; Frances Hudson [1962] Director/Teacher; Carolina Margaret Kovacs [1970] Director/Teacher; Brian Punt [1946] Director/Retired; Trevor William Joseph Russel [1941] Director/Retired; Christopher John Saint [1942] Director/Retired; Gavin Piers Saunders [1972] Director/Headteacher; David Richard Squires [1939] Director/Retired; Dr Richard Martin Willis [1973] Director/Manager; Timothy Wilson [1967] Director

Shire Foods Limited
Incorporated: 22 May 1970 *Employees:* 112
Net Worth: £6,181,000 *Total Assets:* £10,820,000
Registered Office: Tachbrook Road, Leamington Spa, Warwicks, CV31 3SF
Activities: Manufacture of other food products n.e.c.
Officers: Michael Andrew Tzirki, Secretary; Jonathan Edward Lander [1968] Director; Nicholas Paul Lander [1966] Director; Michael Andrew Tzirki [1961] Director/Chartered Engineer

Shoby Investments Limited
Incorporated: 20 March 2015
Net Worth: £91,144,808 *Total Assets:* £91,371,040
Registered Office: Northgate House, North Gate, New Basford, Nottingham, NG7 7BQ
Activities: Activities of distribution holding companies
Major Shareholder: David Edward Shelton
Officers: Alice Eleanor Shelton [1964] Director; David Edward Shelton [1953] Director; Samuel George Shelton [1990] Director

Shoby Properties Limited
Incorporated: 13 July 2000
Previous: Motorpoint Properties Limited
Net Worth: £13,868,037 *Total Assets:* £39,847,628
Registered Office: Northgate House, North Gate, New Basford, Nottingham, NG7 7BQ
Activities: Other letting and operating of own or leased real estate
Parent: Shoby Investments Limited
Officers: David Edward Shelton [1953] Director

Shoe Zone PLC
Incorporated: 26 March 2014 *Employees:* 3,521
Net Worth: £31,160,000 *Total Assets:* £67,555,000
Registered Office: Haramead Business Centre, Humberstone Road, Leicester, LE1 2LH
Activities: Retail sale of footwear in specialised stores
Shareholder: Slawston Investments Ltd
Officers: Jonathan Lee Fearn, Secretary; Charles Jerome Caminada [1957] Director; Malcolm James Collins [1955] Director; Nicholas John Davis [1978] Director; Jonathan Lee Fearn [1974] Director; Jeremy William Sharman [1963] Director; Anthony Edward Pennington Smith [1967] Director; John Charles Pennington Smith [1965] Director

Shoe Zone Retail Limited
Incorporated: 21 July 1917 *Employees:* 3,521
Net Worth: £31,696,000 *Total Assets:* £68,674,000
Registered Office: Haramead Business Centre, Humberstone Road, Leicester, LE1 2LH
Activities: Retail sale of footwear in specialised stores
Parent: Shoe Zone PLC
Officers: Nicholas John Davis [1978] Director/Chief Executive Officer; Jonathan Lee Fearn [1974] Director/Accountant; Clare Alison Howes [1965] Buying Director; Naomi Tamar Shefford-Thomas [1974] Marketing Director; Anthony Edward Pennington Smith [1967] Director/Chairman; John Charles Pennington Smith [1965] Director/Chief Operating Officer

Shoosmiths LLP
Incorporated: 4 May 2012 *Employees:* 1,337
Net Worth: £39,742,000 *Total Assets:* £82,722,000
Registered Office: Witan Gate House, 500-600 Witan Gate West, Milton Keynes, Bucks, MK9 1SH
Officers: Simon Andrew Boss [1964] Member; Melanie Chell [1975] Member; Stephen Mark Dawson [1977] Member; Peter Howarth Duff [1968] Member; Alastair Jonathan Taylor Peet [1974] Member; James Marlin Taylor [1972] Member; Sean Brian Wright [1966] Member; David Andrew Adams [1973] LLP Member; Bhavesh Amlani [1973] LLP Member; Craig Simon Armstrong [1975] LLP Member; Charles William Arrand [1969] LLP Member; Edell Mary Asquez [1976] LLP Member; Gary Dean Assim [1961] LLP Member; Richard Stephen Atha [1964] LLP Member; Melissa Kate Barker [1976] LLP Member; Philip Tudor Barnes [1975] LLP Member; Simon Timothy Barnes [1974] LLP Member; Steven Paul Barnett [1970] LLP Member; Paul James Peter Bachelor [1982] LLP Member; Richard Nicholas Bellamy [1974] LLP Member; Stephen Eric Belshaw [1961] LLP Member; Alexandra Elizabeth Bishop [1973] LLP Member; Angela Dawn Bowman [1971] LLP Member; Andrew John Brennan [1978] LLP Member; Anthony Crispin Bridges Webb [1962] LLP Member; Simon Matthew Briggs [1969] LLP Member; John Peter Buckley [1979] LLP Member; Helen Burgess [1980] LLP Member; Sean Robert Nicholas Patrick Burke [1962] LLP Member; Suzanne Ruth Burrell [1976] LLP Member; Jason Byrne [1979] LLP Member; Paul Bernard Carney [1965] LLP Member; Anna Lowri Cartledge [1980] LLP Member; Ruth Margaret Zanre Clare [1976] LLP Member; John Robert Cleaveley [1968] LLP Member; Stuart Alexander Clubb [1978] LLP Member; Alan Corcoran [1968] LLP Member; Hamish Richard Corner [1976] LLP Member; Gillian Elizabeth Crotty [1983] LLP Member; Philip Andrew Crowe [1980] LLP Member; Suman Dally [1969] LLP Member; Rosemary Donoghue [1957] LLP Member; Stephen Paul Dougherty [1961] LLP Member; Adam Draper [1976] LLP Member; Charlotte Dunn [1972] LLP Member; Mark Joseph Elder [1972] LLP Member; Angus Kenneth David Evers [1972] LLP Member; David Robert Farnell [1968] LLP Member; Vaqas Farooq [1977] LLP Member; Judy Anne Fawcett [1968] LLP Member; Kate Louise Featherstone [1977] LLP Member; Richard Thomas Follis [1956] LLP Member; James Alan Foster [1981] LLP Member; Andrew Joseph Foyle [1977] LLP Member; Heather Maxine Freeman [1966] LLP Member; Ellis Gardner-Browne [1972] LLP Member; Patrick Alan Garner [1973] LLP Member; Lisa Callen Gibbs [1971] LLP Member; Paul James Gidman [1974] LLP Member; Alison Mary Gilson [1978] LLP Member; Philip Edward Goldsborough [1969] LLP Member; Deborah Gordon Brown [1964] LLP Member; Thomas David Hall [1981] LLP Member; Daniel Edward Hargreaves [1979] LLP Member; Aaron Michael Harlow [1982] LLP Member; Laura Jayne Harper [1973] LLP Member; David Ian Harrison [1980] LLP Member; Kellie Hatton [1978] LLP Member; Adele Julie Hayfield [1982] LLP Member; Tracey Hemingway [1966] LLP Member; Kirsten Joanne Hewson [1971] LLP Member; Neil Hobden [1960] LLP Member; Catherine Elizabeth Hood [1974] LLP Member; William Ian Howard [1956] LLP Member; Charles Matthew Howarth [1968] LLP Member; Sara Mary Hunt [1973] LLP Member; Nicholas Patrick Iliff [1966] LLP Member; David Antony Jackson [1975] LLP Member; Jason Ronald Jackson [1969] LLP Member; Timothy David Jackson-Smith [1969] LLP Member; Alexander Francis Jones [1966] LLP Member; Kathryn Louise Jump [1972] LLP Member; James Laurence Keates [1970] LLP Member; Daniel John Kennedy [1978] LLP Member; Matthew William James Kenwood [1973] LLP Member; Alexander William Christopher Thompson Kirkhope [1979] LLP Member; James Klein [1970] LLP Member; Paul Russell Knight [1962] LLP Member; Stuart Owen Lawrenson [1973] LLP Member; Lynette Ann Lewis [1969] LLP Member; Stuart Little [1968] LLP Member; Katherine Livingston [1969] LLP Member; Matthew Jason Lonergan [1969] LLP Member; Roderick Gray MacPhail [1957] LLP Member; Sherif Malak [1980] LLP Member; Waine Gerard Mannix [1966] LLP Member; Melissa Mary Maple [1976] LLP Member; Rebecca Margaret Mauleverer [1975] LLP Member; Joseph Mazzucca [1973] LLP Member; Elizabeth Ann McArdle [1973] LLP Member

Shrubhill Farms Limited
Incorporated: 23 November 2006 *Employees:* 11
Net Worth: £3,706,665 *Total Assets:* £14,022,251
Registered Office: Colpmans Farm, Islip, Kettering, Northants, NN14 3LT
Activities: Growing of cereals (except rice), leguminous crops and oil seeds
Parent: Harrowden Farms Limited
Officers: Stuart Benjamin Ridd-Jones, Finance Director; Chantall Sylvette Florence Ridd-Jones [1974] Director; Stuart Benjamin Ridd-Jones [1972] Finance Director

SHV Energy Holdings UK Limited
Incorporated: 22 May 1987
Net Worth: £288,743,008 *Total Assets:* £634,246,016
Registered Office: Athena House, Athena Drive, Tachbrook Park, Warwick, CV34 6RL
Activities: Activities of head offices
Officers: Rowan Diane Marshall-Rowan, Secretary; Matthew Quentin Hickin [1967] Managing Director; Michael Kossack [1965] Director [Irish]; Adam Euan Thompson [1974] Operations Director; Jonathan Mark Wood [1968] Finance Director; Erich Franz Georg Zielinski [1971] Director/Legal Counsel [Dutch]

SHV Investments Limited
Incorporated: 22 September 2014 *Employees:* 2
Net Worth: £12,103,281 *Total Assets:* £12,103,281
Registered Office: Athena House, Athena Drive, Warwick, CV34 6RL
Activities: Other business support service activities n.e.c.
Officers: Matthew Quentin Hickin [1967] Managing Director; Jonathan Mark Wood [1968] Finance Director

Sibson Mill Properties Limited
Incorporated: 12 September 1961 *Employees:* 5
Net Worth: £21,828,010 *Total Assets:* £22,530,868
Registered Office: Sibson Mill Farm House, Wellsborough Road, Wellsborough, Nuneaton, Warwicks, CV13 6LR
Activities: Other letting and operating of own or leased real estate
Major Shareholder: Martin James Smith
Officers: Lesley Elaine Smith, Secretary; Benjamin James Smith [1975] Managing Director; Nicholas John Smith [1977] Director; Thomas Edward Smith [1978] Director

Siddall and Hilton,Limited
Incorporated: 17 August 1898 *Employees:* 9
Net Worth: £11,994,556 *Total Assets:* £13,692,284
Registered Office: Marland House, 13 Huddersfield Road, Barnsley, S Yorks, S70 2LW
Activities: Buying and selling of own real estate
Parent: Siddall Investments Limited
Officers: John Anthony Firth, Secretary; John Anthony Firth [1959] Finance Director; Adrienne Helen Siddall [1958] Director/Housewife; Andrew John Siddall [1959] Director/Group Chief Executive; Clive Philip Siddall [1962] Director; Jeremy Charles Siddall [1958] Project Director; Peter Robin Siddall [1946] Director/Group Executive Chairman; Susan Tracey Siddall [1962] Director/School Accounts Administrator

SIG European Holdings Limited
Incorporated: 17 December 2004
Net Worth: £580,000 *Total Assets:* £190,487,008
Registered Office: Adsetts House, 16 Europa View, Sheffield Business Park, Sheffield, S9 1XH
Activities: Non-trading company
Parent: SIG PLC
Officers: Richard Charles Monro, Chartered Secretary; Ian Jackson [1979] Director/Accountant; Nicholas William Maddock [1971] Director; Richard Charles Monro [1958] Director/Chartered Secretary

SIG European Investments Limited
Incorporated: 30 April 1984
Net Worth Deficit: £9,327,000 *Total Assets:* £635,296,000
Registered Office: Adsetts House, 16 Europa View, Sheffield Business Park, Sheffield, S9 1XH
Activities: Activities of head offices
Parent: SIG European Holdings Limited
Officers: Richard Charles Monro, Secretary; Christian Horn [1966] Director [Dutch]; Ian Jackson [1979] Director/Accountant; Nicholas William Maddock [1971] Director; Richard Charles Monro [1958] Director/Chartered Secretary

SIG Hillsborough Limited
Incorporated: 17 December 2009
Net Worth: £100,438,344 *Total Assets:* £101,552,032
Registered Office: Adsetts House, 16 Europa View, Sheffield Business Park, Sheffield, S9 1XH
Activities: Other specialised construction activities n.e.c.
Parent: SIG European Investments Limited
Officers: Richard Charles Monro, Secretary; Ian Jackson [1979] Director/Accountant; Richard Charles Monro [1958] Director

SIG Trading Limited
Incorporated: 27 September 1979 *Employees:* 4,428
Net Worth: £273,000,000 *Total Assets:* £676,000,000
Registered Office: Adsetts House, 16 Europa View, Sheffield Business Park, Sheffield, S9 1XH
Activities: Other building completion and finishing
Parent: SIG PLC
Officers: Richard Charles Monro, Secretary; Ian Jackson [1979] Director/Accountant; Nicholas William Maddock [1971] Director; Richard Charles Monro [1958] Director/Chartered Secretary

Sigma Components Holdings Limited
Incorporated: 17 February 2016 *Employees:* 854
Net Worth Deficit: £10,934,000 *Total Assets:* £68,678,000
Registered Office: Unit 1 Finch Way, Hemdale Business Park, Nuneaton, Warwicks, CV11 6GL
Activities: Activities of other holding companies n.e.c.
Officers: Kay Elizabeth Ashton [1965] Director/Investment Manager; Mark Stephen Johnson [1960] Director; David Arthur MacKenzie [1980] Director/Investment Manager; Edward John Riley [1957] Director/Chartered Accountant; Mark Rollins [1962] Director

Sigma Components Limited
Incorporated: 25 April 2016
Net Worth: £31,180,944 *Total Assets:* £66,051,704
Registered Office: Unit 1 Finch Way, Hemdale Business Park, Nuneaton, Warwicks, CV11 6GL
Activities: Activities of other holding companies n.e.c.
Parent: Sigma Components Midco 2 Limited
Officers: Mark Stephen Johnson [1960] Director; Edward John Riley [1957] Director/Chartered Accountant

Sigma Components Midco 1 Limited
Incorporated: 25 April 2016 *Employees:* 2
Net Worth: £35,420,424 *Total Assets:* £35,420,424
Registered Office: Unit 1 Finch Way, Hemdale Business Park, Nuneaton, Warwicks, CV11 6GL
Activities: Activities of other holding companies n.e.c.
Parent: Sigma Components Holdings Limited
Officers: Mark Stephen Johnson [1960] Director; Edward John Riley [1957] Director/Chartered Accountant

Sigma Components Midco 2 Limited
Incorporated: 25 April 2016 *Employees:* 2
Net Worth: £34,157,772 *Total Assets:* £35,420,424
Registered Office: Unit 1 Finch Way, Hemdale Business Park, Nuneaton, Warwicks, CV11 6GL
Activities: Activities of other holding companies n.e.c.
Parent: Sigma Components Midco 1 Limited
Officers: Mark Stephen Johnson [1960] Director; Edward John Riley [1957] Director/Chartered Accountant

Sigma Precision Components UK Limited
Incorporated: 15 November 1963 *Employees:* 315
Net Worth: £8,340,539 *Total Assets:* £20,150,360
Registered Office: Unit 1 Finch Way, Hemdale Business Park, Nuneaton, Warwicks, CV11 6GL
Activities: Machining
Parent: Sigma Components Limited
Officers: Thomas Noel Barrett [1964] Director; Mark Stephen Johnson [1960] Director; Edward John Riley [1957] Director/Chartered Accountant

Silbury Marketing Limited
Incorporated: 5 September 1985 *Employees:* 32
Net Worth: £4,932,133 *Total Assets:* £14,845,283
Registered Office: 9 Manor Park, Banbury, Oxon, OX16 3TB
Activities: Wholesale of dairy products, eggs and edible oils and fats
Shareholder: FMPP Group Limited
Officers: Adrian James Ashley Hall, Secretary/Commodity Trader; Adrian James Ashley Hall [1965] Director; Gary Lewis [1966] Director; John Mullen [1953] Director; David Page [1969] Director; David Savage [1957] Customer Services Director

Silentpride Limited
Incorporated: 28 June 2006
Net Worth: £6,053,077 *Total Assets:* £12,868,090
Registered Office: 1 Adelaide House, Corby Gate Business Park, Priors Haw Road, Corby, Northants, NN17 5JG
Activities: Development of building projects
Parent: JME Civils Limited
Officers: James Moore [1953] Managing Director

Silgan Closures UK Holdings Limited
Incorporated: 18 May 2003 *Employees:* 2
Previous: Portola Limited
Net Worth: £13,597,000 *Total Assets:* £23,894,000
Registered Office: 17-23 Thorne Road, Doncaster, S Yorks, DN1 2RP
Activities: Activities of head offices
Parent: Silgan Holdings Inc
Officers: Philip Crawley, Secretary; Glenn Heighington [1965] Managing Director; Richard Kirkland [1969] Financial Director

Silgan Closures UK Limited
Incorporated: 2 May 1991 *Employees:* 139
Previous: Portola Packaging Limited
Net Worth: £14,239,000 *Total Assets:* £29,489,000
Registered Office: 17-23 Thorne Road, Doncaster, S Yorks, DN1 2RP
Activities: Manufacture of other plastic products
Parent: Portola Limited
Officers: Philip Crawley, Secretary; Glenn Heighington [1965] Director; Richard Kirkland [1969] Finance Director

Silkstone Finance Limited
Incorporated: 12 August 1992 *Employees:* 328
Net Worth: £33,250,020 *Total Assets:* £44,639,096
Registered Office: 4 Hawthorne Grove, Silkstone, Barnsley, S Yorks, S75 4NS
Activities: Activities of other holding companies n.e.c.
Shareholders: Alfred Wilson Ellis; Clare Joan Ellis
Officers: Claire Joan Ellis, Secretary; Alfred Wilson Ellis [1947] Director

Silverstone Circuits Limited
Incorporated: 5 July 1966 *Employees:* 153
Net Worth Deficit: £6,543,000 *Total Assets:* £22,212,000
Registered Office: Silverstone Circuit, Towcester, Northants, NN12 8TN
Activities: Operation of sports facilities
Officers: Nicholas John Adams [1946] Director/Insurance Loss Adjuster; John Albert Martin Grant [1945] Director; Hannah Louise Irving [1973] Director/Accountant; Stuart Alexander MacKenzie Pringle [1971] Sporting Director Silverstone Circuits Ltd; Nicholas John Read [1970] Commercial Director

Simmerson Associates Ltd
Incorporated: 14 August 2002
Net Worth: £3,141,265 *Total Assets:* £18,951,592
Registered Office: Unit 2 Mallory Way, Gallagher Business Park, Coventry, Warwicks, CV6 6PB
Activities: Other information technology service activities
Parent: E-PPL Holdings Limited
Officers: Susan Simmerson, Secretary; John Thomas Birch [1964] Director; Paul Adrian Simmerson [1977] Director; David Taylor [1965] Director

Simoco Wireless Solutions Limited
Incorporated: 12 October 2009 *Employees:* 10
Previous: TTG Global Group Limited
Net Worth: £4,115,000 *Total Assets:* £31,566,000
Registered Office: Field House, Uttoxeter Old Road, Derby, DE1 1NH
Activities: Other telecommunications activities
Parent: TTG Global Limited
Officers: Philip Williams, Secretary; Peter Louis Burridge [1956] Director; Ian Carr [1963] Director; Michael Stewart Norfield [1963] Director; Paul Henry Brace Thomas [1961] Director; Philip Edward Williams [1968] Finance Director; Andrew Peter Woodhall [1964] Sales Director

Simons Construction Limited
Incorporated: 28 August 1969 *Employees:* 116
Net Worth: £6,336,171 *Total Assets:* £30,203,836
Registered Office: 991 Doddington Road, Lincoln, LN6 3AA
Activities: Construction of commercial buildings
Officers: Michael Harrison Kasher, Secretary; Paul Richard Hodgkinson [1956] Director/Chairman; Philip David Hodgkinson [1958] Director; Michael Harrison Kasher [1965] Director; Thomas Daniel Edwin Robinson [1970] Director

Simons Developments Limited
Incorporated: 28 October 1959 *Employees:* 3
Net Worth: £888,256 *Total Assets:* £12,663,268
Registered Office: 991 Doddington Road, Lincoln, LN6 3AA
Activities: Development of building projects
Officers: Michael Harrison Kasher, Secretary; Paul Richard Hodgkinson [1956] Director/Company Chairman; Philip David Hodgkinson [1958] Director/Company Chairman; Michael Harrison Kasher [1965] Director; Thomas Daniel Edwin Robinson [1970] Director

Simons Group Limited
Incorporated: 16 July 1987 *Employees:* 182
Net Worth: £3,604,000 *Total Assets:* £46,462,000
Registered Office: 991 Doddington Road, Lincoln, LN6 3AA
Activities: Construction of commercial buildings
Officers: Michael Harrison Kasher, Secretary; Paul Richard Hodgkinson [1956] Director/Architect; Philip David Hodgkinson [1958] Director/Property Surveyor; Michael Harrison Kasher [1965] Director; Philip James Kendall [1965] Director; Thomas Daniel Edwin Robinson [1970] Director

Simply Cartons Limited
Incorporated: 29 June 2006 *Employees:* 126
Net Worth: £6,635,000 *Total Assets:* £17,963,000
Registered Office: Perry Road, Nottingham, NG5 1GQ
Activities: Packaging activities
Parent: Simply Cartons Holdings Limited
Officers: Bethan Ceri Mather, Secretary; Karen Elizabeth Dinsmore [1961] Director; Craig Mather [1971] Director/Chief Executive Officer

Sims Group UK Holdings Limited
Incorporated: 3 March 1994 *Employees:* 2
Net Worth: £326,316,224 *Total Assets:* £326,428,768
Registered Office: Long Marston, Stratford upon Avon, Warwicks, CV37 8AQ
Activities: Activities of head offices
Officers: David Michael Williams, Chartered Secretary; Mark Ian Saunders [1968] Finance Director; David Michael Williams [1964] Director/Company Secretary

Sims Group UK Limited
Incorporated: 27 August 1996 *Employees:* 772
Net Worth: £186,774,000 *Total Assets:* £268,308,000
Registered Office: Long Marston, Stratford upon Avon, Warwicks, CV37 8AQ
Activities: Recovery of sorted materials
Parent: Sims Group UK Holdings Limited
Officers: David Michael Williams, Secretary; Mark Ian Saunders [1968] Finance Director; Stephen Michael Skurnac [1960] Director [American]; David Michael Williams [1964] Director/Company Secretary; Paul Michael Wright [1969] Director

J O Sims Holdings (1896) Limited
Incorporated: 9 November 2012 *Employees:* 129
Net Worth: £41,253,292 *Total Assets:* £93,618,784
Registered Office: Pudding Lane, Pinchbeck, Spalding, Lincs, PE11 3TJ
Activities: Activities of head offices
Shareholder: Christopher Oliver Sims
Officers: Andrew Bell, Secretary; Andrew James Bell [1972] Director; Alexander George Oliver Sims [1988] Director; Christopher Oliver Sims [1959] Director; James Victor Oliver Sims [1985] Director

J O Sims Holdings Limited
Incorporated: 1 March 1954 *Employees:* 129
Net Worth: £43,030,904 *Total Assets:* £94,023,232
Registered Office: Pudding Lane, Pinchbeck, Spalding, Lincs, PE11 3TJ
Activities: Wholesale of fruit and vegetables
Parent: J O Sims Holdings (1896) Limited
Officers: Andrew James Bell, Secretary; Andrew James Bell [1972] Director; Christopher Oliver Sims [1959] Director; James Victor Oliver Sims [1985] Director

J O Sims Limited
Incorporated: 15 December 1986 *Employees:* 87
Net Worth: £20,252,266 *Total Assets:* £65,364,976
Registered Office: Pudding Lane, Pinchbeck, Spalding, Lincs, PE11 3TJ
Activities: Wholesale of fruit and vegetables
Parent: J O Sims Holdings Limited
Officers: Andrew James Bell, Secretary; Andrew James Bell [1972] Director; Christopher Oliver Sims [1959] Director; James Victor Oliver Sims [1985] Director

John Sinclair (Sheffield) Limited
Incorporated: 12 August 1966 *Employees:* 50
Net Worth: £9,401,988 *Total Assets:* £12,012,599
Registered Office: 266 Glossop Road, Sheffield, S10 2HS
Activities: Retail sale of hardware, paints and glass in specialised stores
Shareholders: Rachel Emma Dodd; Cristian John Sinclair
Officers: Rachel Emma Dodd, Secretary; Cristian John Sinclair [1970] Retail Director; Janet Mary Louise Sinclair [1944] Director; John Christopher Lorne Sparre [1947] Director

Singleton Birch Limited
Incorporated: 23 April 1875 *Employees:* 131
Net Worth: £22,402,000 *Total Assets:* £52,426,000
Registered Office: Singleton Birch Limited, Melton Ross Quarries, Barnetby, N Lincs, DN38 6AE
Activities: Quarrying of ornamental and building stone, limestone, gypsum, chalk and slate
Officers: Ellen Patricia Tatterton, Secretary/Accountant; Stuart Robin Counsell [1950] Director/Chartered Accountant; Stephen William Foster [1962] Sales Director; Martyn John Gardiner [1946] Director; Martin David Haworth [1963] Technical Director; Richard Mark Stansfield [1967] Managing Director; Ellen Patricia Tatterton [1961] Director/Accountant

Sistine Properties (Westbury) Limited
Incorporated: 26 February 2008
Net Worth Deficit: £14,222,000 *Total Assets:* £69,596,000
Registered Office: Norcliffe House, Station Road, Wilmslow, Cheshire, SK9 1BU
Activities: Development of building projects
Parent: Brighterkind Health Care Group Limited
Officers: Abigail Mattison, Secretary; Jeremy Robert Arthur Richardson [1970] Director; Phillip Gary Thomas [1978] Director

Sitel Europe Limited
Incorporated: 12 October 1992 *Employees:* 151
Net Worth Deficit: £54,069,072 *Total Assets:* £105,102,560
Registered Office: Earlsdon Park, 53-55 Butts Road, Coventry, Warwicks, CV1 3BH
Activities: Other telecommunications activities
Officers: John William Hayward, Secretary/Solicitor; Karl Vernon Brough [1962] Director; Pedro Lozano de Castro [1963] Director [Spanish]

Sitel Solutions UK Limited
Incorporated: 5 May 2011
Net Worth Deficit: £2,040,995 *Total Assets:* £53,476,700
Registered Office: Earlsdon Park, 53-55 Butts Road, Coventry, Warwicks, CV1 3BH
Activities: Other business support service activities n.e.c.
Parent: Clientlogic Holding Limited
Officers: John William Hayward, Secretary; Karl Vernon Brough [1962] Director; Pedro Lozano de Castro [1963] Director [Spanish]

Sitel UK Finance
Incorporated: 23 November 2010
Net Worth: £65,893,396 *Total Assets:* £66,031,924
Registered Office: Earlsdon Park, 53-55 Butts Road, Coventry, Warwicks, CV1 3BH
Activities: Other business support service activities n.e.c.
Officers: John William Hayward, Secretary; Karl Vernon Brough [1962] Director; Pedro Lozano de Castro [1963] Director [Spanish]

Sitel UK Limited
Incorporated: 16 October 1997 *Employees:* 3,452
Net Worth: £14,959,000 *Total Assets:* £53,260,000
Registered Office: Earlsdon Park, 53-55 Butts Road, Coventry, Warwicks, CV1 3BH
Activities: Other telecommunications activities
Parent: Sitel Europe Limited
Officers: John William Hayward, Secretary/Solicitor; Karl Vernon Brough [1962] Director; Pedro Lozano de Castro [1963] Director [Spanish]

J.W.Sivil Limited
Incorporated: 6 September 1933 *Employees:* 2
Net Worth: £9,095,625 *Total Assets:* £9,331,207
Registered Office: Bank Farm, Barlow, Dronfield, Derbys, S18 7SE
Activities: Construction of domestic buildings
Major Shareholder: David John Sivil
Officers: Amanda Jane Sivil, Secretary; Amanda Jane Sivil [1953] Director/Interior Designer; David John Sivil [1950] Director

SJC 14 Limited
Incorporated: 29 May 1997 *Employees:* 11
Net Worth: £16,519,677 *Total Assets:* £29,847,156
Registered Office: 2 Lace Market Square, Nottingham, NG1 1PB
Activities: Other letting and operating of own or leased real estate
Parent: SJC 15 Limited
Officers: Sean Akins, Secretary; George Henry Akins [1974] Director; Sean Patrick Dennis Akins [1973] Director; David Paul McDerment [1981] Finance Director

SJC 15 Limited
Incorporated: 29 May 1997 *Employees:* 380
Net Worth: £31,583,170 *Total Assets:* £69,206,568
Registered Office: 2 Lace Market Square, Nottingham, NG1 1PB
Activities: Public houses and bars
Officers: Sean Akins, Secretary/Director; George Henry Akins [1974] Director; Sean Akins [1973] Director; David Paul McDerment [1981] Finance Director

SJH-All Plant Group Limited
Incorporated: 1 August 2002 *Employees:* 21
Net Worth: £3,983,893 *Total Assets:* £13,044,290
Registered Office: First Floor, 5 Doolittle Yard, Froghall Road, Ampthill, Beds, MK45 2NW
Activities: Wholesale of mining, construction and civil engineering machinery
Parent: SJH-All Plant Holdings Limited
Officers: David Gill [1966] Director [Irish]; Stephen John Hudson [1981] Director/Plant Sales [Irish]

SKF. Lo (Chemists) Limited
Incorporated: 24 April 2002 *Employees:* 154
Net Worth: £1,542,051 *Total Assets:* £14,086,791
Registered Office: Unit 5 Farfield Park, Manvers Way, Manvers, Rotherham, S Yorks, S63 5DB
Activities: Dispensing chemist in specialised stores
Major Shareholder: Steven Kwok Fu Lo
Officers: Iris Tung Wa Lo, Secretary; Iris Tung Wa Lo [1963] Director/Pharmacist; Steven Kwok Fu Lo [1965] Director/Pharmacist

Skills Leisure Limited
Incorporated: 22 April 1987 *Employees:* 356
Net Worth: £3,643,336 *Total Assets:* £22,085,128
Registered Office: White House, Clarendon Street, Nottingham, NG1 5GF
Activities: Travel agency activities
Shareholders: Nigel Stuart Arthur Skill; Simon Christopher Robert Skill
Officers: Simon Christopher Robert Skill, Secretary; Peter Roy Hallam [1963] Director/Engineer; Nigel Stuart Arthur Skill [1954] Director; Simon Christopher Robert Skill [1956] Director/Accountant

Skills Motor Coaches Limited
Incorporated: 3 October 1958 *Employees:* 269
Net Worth: £4,233,127 *Total Assets:* £18,607,370
Registered Office: Belgrave Business Park, Belgrave Road, Bulwell, Nottingham, NG6 8LY
Activities: Other passenger land transport
Parent: Skills Leisure Ltd
Officers: Simon Christopher Robert Skill, Secretary; Peter Roy Hallam [1963] Director/Engineer; Nigel Stuart Arthur Skill [1954] Director/Engineer; Simon Christopher Robert Skill [1956] Director/Chartered Accountant

Nigel Skinner Financial Advisers Limited
Incorporated: 6 November 2009 *Employees:* 1
Previous: Nigel Skinner Independent Financial Advisors Limited
Net Worth: £4,552,293 *Total Assets:* £10,129,492
Registered Office: The Old Vicarage, Church Close, Boston, Lincs, PE21 6NA
Activities: Financial intermediation not elsewhere classified
Major Shareholder: Nigel Darren Skinner
Officers: Nigel Darren Skinner [1962] Director

Skiptex Limited
Incorporated: 30 May 1984 *Employees:* 301
Net Worth: £26,518,000 *Total Assets:* £247,730,000
Registered Office: Saint-Gobain House, Binley Business Park, Coventry, Warwicks, CV3 2TT
Activities: Activities of head offices
Parent: Gypsum Investments Limited
Officers: Alun Roy Oxenham, Secretary; Nicholas James Cammack [1972] Director; Michael Strickland Chaldecott [1960] Managing Director

Skymark Packaging International Limited
Incorporated: 3 September 1987 *Employees:* 239
Net Worth: £19,740,772 *Total Assets:* £29,050,004
Registered Office: Manners Avenue, Manners Industrial Estate, Ilkeston, Derbys, DE7 8EF
Activities: Manufacture of other plastic products
Major Shareholder: Mehrdad Toofanian
Officers: Mehrdad Toofanian, Secretary; Mehrdad Toofanian [1952] Director; John Turner [1952] Director

Slack & Parr (Investments) Limited
Incorporated: 12 July 1917 *Employees:* 173
Net Worth: £5,647,000 *Total Assets:* £24,411,000
Registered Office: Long Lane, Kegworth, Derby, DE74 2FL
Activities: Manufacture of machinery for textile, apparel and leather production
Officers: Raymond Allan Howard, Secretary; Edward Pilsworth Barrington [1978] Project Director; Simon Lancaster Barrington [1946] Technical Director/Chief Engineer; Timothy Barwell Barrington [1949] Director/Chairman; Richard Edward Hallsworth [1967] Managing Director

Slack & Parr Limited
Incorporated: 1 September 1997 *Employees:* 169
Net Worth Deficit: £395,000 *Total Assets:* £9,466,000
Registered Office: Long Lane, Kegworth, Derby, DE74 2FL
Activities: Manufacture of machinery for textile, apparel and leather production
Officers: Raymond Allan Howard, Secretary; Edward Pilsworth Barrington [1978] Project Director; Simon Lancaster Barrington [1946] Technical Director/Chief Engineer; Timothy Barwell Barrington [1949] Director; Richard Edward Hallsworth [1967] Managing Director; Richard James Wilson [1966] Operations Director; Paul David Wykes [1972] Sales Director

Slater Hogg Mortgages Limited
Incorporated: 26 April 2001 *Employees:* 28
Net Worth: £2,249,000 *Total Assets:* £12,327,000
Registered Office: Countrywide House, 6 Caldecotte Lake Business Park, Caldecotte Lake Drive, Caldecotte, Milton Keynes, Bucks, MK7 8JT
Activities: Financial intermediation not elsewhere classified
Parent: Balanus Limited
Officers: Gareth Rhys Williams, Secretary; Paul Lewis Creffield [1954] Director; Peter Curran [1966] Director

Slawston Investments Ltd
Incorporated: 23 April 2014 *Employees:* 2
Net Worth Deficit: £9,470,643 *Total Assets:* £30,903,892
Registered Office: The Grange, Main Street, Slawston, Leics, LE16 7UF
Activities: Fund management activities
Shareholders: Catherine Lucy Smith; Anthony Edward Pennington Smith
Officers: Anthony Edward Pennington Smith [1967] Director; Catherine Lucy Smith [1971] Director

Slawston Limited
Incorporated: 26 March 2014 *Employees:* 2
Net Worth: £40,983,160 *Total Assets:* £41,656,812
Registered Office: The Grange, Main Street, Slawston, Market Harborough, Leics, LE16 7UF
Activities: Other credit granting n.e.c.
Shareholders: Anthony Edward Pennington Smith; Catherine Lucy Smith
Officers: Anthony Edward Pennington Smith [1967] Director/Chairman; Catherine Lucy Smith [1971] Director

Sleaford Quality Foods Limited
Incorporated: 27 November 1968 *Employees:* 130
Net Worth: £7,993,382 *Total Assets:* £32,638,272
Registered Office: Woodbridge Road, East Road Industrial Estate, Sleaford, Lincs, NG34 7JX
Activities: Manufacture of other food products n.e.c.
Shareholders: Jain Irrigation Systems Ltd; Sleaford Food Group Limited
Officers: Alan Philip Thomas, Secretary; James Patrick Arnold [1965] Production Director; Anil Bhavarlal Jain [1965] Managing Director [Indian]; Atul Bhavarial Jain [1969] Marketing Director [Indian]; Suvan Kumar Sharma [1972] Director/V P Food Products

Sleek International Limited
Incorporated: 17 January 1995 *Employees:* 20
Net Worth: £15,140,000 *Total Assets:* £20,647,000
Registered Office: 1 Thane Road West, Nottingham, NG2 3AA
Activities: Other business support service activities n.e.c.
Parent: The Boots Company PLC
Officers: Andrew Richard Thompson, Secretary; Rosemary Frances Counsell [1963] Director of Tax; Anne Louise Murphy [1967] Director; David Waller [1980] Director

Sleekmade Property Co. Limited
Incorporated: 20 June 1985
Net Worth: £20,158,144 *Total Assets:* £47,544,448
Registered Office: 18 The Ropewalk, Nottingham, NG1 5DT
Activities: Renting and operating of Housing Association real estate
Major Shareholder: Steven Singh
Officers: David Singh, Secretary; Steven Singh [1958] Director/Property Manager

SLM Fitness & Health Limited
Incorporated: 26 July 1999 *Employees:* 483
Net Worth: £8,676,682 *Total Assets:* £19,188,212
Registered Office: 2 Watling Drive, Sketchley Meadows, Hinckley, Leics, LE10 3EY
Activities: Fitness facilities
Officers: Martin Bell, Secretary/Managing Director; Martin Bell [1961] Managing Director; David John Bibby [1961] Director/Accountant; Joseph Mark Drysdale [1963] Finance Director

Sloane Helicopters Limited
Incorporated: 13 February 1989 *Employees:* 49
Net Worth: £4,854,949 *Total Assets:* £20,495,982
Registered Office: The Business Aviation Centre, Sywell Aerodrome, Sywell, Northampton, NN6 0BN
Activities: Non-scheduled passenger air transport
Major Shareholder: David Anthony George
Officers: William Jeremy Patrick Awenat [1958] Managing Director; David Anthony George [1947] Managing Director; George Jocelyn George [1986] Director/Trainee Solicitor; Simon Grant Underwood [1968] Finance Director

Slough Enterprise Limited
Incorporated: 14 November 2002
Net Worth: £15,694,000 *Total Assets:* £22,229,000
Registered Office: The Sherard Building, Edmund Halley Road, Oxford, OX4 4DQ
Activities: Other business support service activities n.e.c.
Parent: Accord Environmental Services Limited
Officers: Paul Birch, Secretary; James Stefan Haluch [1969] Highways Director; Andrew Latham Nelson [1959] Finance Director

SMA Estate Holdings Limited
Incorporated: 6 March 2012
Net Worth: £9,036,877 *Total Assets:* £21,203,602
Registered Office: The Stables, Station Drive, Kirby Muxloe, Leicester, LE9 2ET
Activities: Buying and selling of own real estate
Major Shareholder: Simeon Michael Alexander
Officers: Simeon Michael Alexander [1979] Director; Rebekah Totton [1980] Director/Businesswoman; Wayne Totton [1976] Director/Businessman; Jamileth Zapata-Alexander [1975] Director/Businesswoman [Colombian]

Smallpeice Trust (The)
Incorporated: 28 June 1966 *Employees:* 37
Net Worth: £25,028,352 *Total Assets:* £26,301,880
Registered Office: 74 Upper Holly Walk, Leamington Spa, Warwicks, CV32 4JL
Activities: Technical and vocational secondary education
Officers: Elizabeth Victoria Kavanagh, Secretary; Dr Alan Robert Begg [1954] Director/Retired; Paul Anthony Cyril Doble [1945] Director; Richard Folkson [1955] Director/Retired; Trevor Michael Gill [1956] Director/Retired; Prof Alison Halstead [1955] Director/Retired; Ian Michael Jess [1960] Director/Retired; Professor William Geraint Price [1943] Director/Retired; David Gavin Thompson [1965] Director; Rachael Warwick [1969] Director/Headteacher

Smart Currency Group Limited
Incorporated: 13 April 2012 *Employees:* 86
Net Worth: £4,552,517 *Total Assets:* £31,674,088
Registered Office: c/o Everyman Legal Limited, 1G Network Point, Range Road, Windrush Park, Witney, Oxon, OX29 0YN
Activities: Activities of other holding companies n.e.c.
Major Shareholder: John Charles Fairbairn Purdy
Officers: James Christopher Hunt, Secretary; Carl Anthony Hasty [1983] Director/Currency Trader; John Charles Fairbairn Purdy [1958] Director

Smart Garden Products Ltd
Incorporated: 7 November 2002 *Employees:* 71
Net Worth: £3,860,144 *Total Assets:* £17,709,296
Registered Office: 2 Pentagon South, Barton Lane, Abingdon, Oxon, OX14 3PZ
Activities: Wholesale of household goods (other than musical instruments) n.e.c
Parent: SGP Holdings (UK) Limited
Officers: Gary Ackers [1966] Director; Andrew Quinton Bestwick [1961] Director; Richard Alan Browne [1965] Finance Director; Xavier Faure [1971] Director [French]; Paul William Knott [1965] Sales Director; Fleur Morgan [1981] Category Management Director; Paris Anthony Natar [1955] Director/Businessman; Jonathan Richard Stobart [1961] Director; Philip John Tushingham [1957] Sales Director

Smartway Pharmaceuticals Limited
Incorporated: 9 April 2013 *Employees:* 62
Net Worth: £26,921,700 *Total Assets:* £36,737,676
Registered Office: The Old Mill, 9 Soar Lane, Leicester, LE3 5DE
Activities: Wholesale of pharmaceutical goods
Parent: Smartway PW Holdings Limited
Officers: Kirti Patel [1968] Director

Smartway PW. Holdings Limited
Incorporated: 16 January 2013 *Employees:* 76
Net Worth: £47,005,668 *Total Assets:* £60,983,800
Registered Office: The Old Mill, 9 Soar Lane, Leicester, LE3 5DE
Activities: Activities of head offices
Shareholders: Kirti Patel; Bhanumati Patel
Officers: Bhanumati Patel [1939] Director; Kirti Patel [1968] Director

SMC Pneumatics (U.K.) Limited
Incorporated: 14 February 1978 *Employees:* 369
Net Worth: £84,509,056 *Total Assets:* £100,994,928
Registered Office: Vincent Avenue, Crownhill, Milton Keynes, Bucks, MK8 0AN
Activities: Other manufacturing n.e.c.
Parent: SMC Corporation
Officers: Lewis John Williams, Secretary; Kevin Patrick O'Carroll [1960] Director; Yoshiyuki Takada [1926] Director/President [Japanese]; Ikuji Usui [1943] Director [Japanese]

John Smedley Limited
Incorporated: 28 November 1893 *Employees:* 350
Net Worth: £10,883,000 *Total Assets:* £13,545,000
Registered Office: Lea Mills, Lea Bridge, Matlock, Derbys, DE4 5AG
Activities: Manufacture of other wearing apparel and accessories n.e.c.
Officers: Jeremy Hope, Secretary; Jeremy Hope [1963] Finance Director; Bryan Jackson [1946] Director/Chairman; William John Philip Leach [1967] Director; Ian Lowry Cole MacLean [1967] Director/Sales [British/American]; Robert Andrew Huntsman Marsden-Smedley [1962] Director; Jess McGuire-Dudley [1985] Director

Smeg (UK) Limited
Incorporated: 28 March 1989 *Employees:* 112
Net Worth: £12,090,232 *Total Assets:* £39,357,496
Registered Office: The Magna Building, Wyndyke Furlong, Abingdon, Oxon, OX14 1DZ
Activities: Wholesale of radio, television goods & electrical household appliances (other than records, tapes, CDs)
Officers: Federico Ederle [1974] Director [Italian]; Michael Giddings [1963] Managing Director; Cesare Manotti [1965] Director [Italian]; Vanni Emanuele Treves [1940] Director/Solicitor

Smith & Brooks Limited
Incorporated: 13 November 1986
Net Worth: £9,639,805 *Total Assets:* £33,615,704
Registered Office: Unit A, Brook Park East, Shirebrook, Derbys, NG20 8RY
Activities: Wholesale of clothing and footwear
Parent: Smith and Brooks Holdings Limited
Officers: Cameron John Olsen, Secretary; Adedotun Ademola Adegoke [1973] Director/Senior Buyer; Rachel Isabel Lilian Stockton [1970] Director/Head of Customs and VAT

Smith & Sons (Bletchington) Limited
Incorporated: 4 March 1947 *Employees:* 121
Net Worth: £24,693,488 *Total Assets:* £33,740,144
Registered Office: Enslow, Kidlington, Oxon, OX5 3AY
Activities: Growing of cereals (except rice), leguminous crops and oil seeds
Shareholder: Andrew William Smith
Officers: Andrew William Smith, Secretary; Andrew William Smith [1960] Joint Managing Director; David John Smith [1933] Director; Simon Charles Smith [1958] Joint Managing Director

Ben Smith & Sons (Wantage) Limited
Incorporated: 20 March 1958 *Employees:* 30
Net Worth: £38,598,240 *Total Assets:* £42,205,732
Registered Office: Manor Road Farm, Manor Road, Wantage, Oxon, OX12 8NE
Activities: Mixed farming
Officers: Gilbert John Smith, Secretary; Caroline Kate Bridle [1930] Director/Consultant; Christopher Ian Bridle [1958] Director; Clifford Phillip Bridle [1955] Director; Angela Theresa Fowler [1966] Director; Helen Joanna Shepherd [1964] Director; Ben Smith [1962] Director; Gilbert John Smith [1936] Director; William John Smith [1969] Director

R.H. Smith & Sons (Wigmakers) Limited
Incorporated: 6 August 1974 *Employees:* 224
Net Worth: £11,223,788 *Total Assets:* £35,659,572
Registered Office: Peckett Plaza, Gainsborough Business Park, Gainsborough, Lincs, DN21 1FJ
Activities: Non-specialised wholesale trade
Shareholder: Raymond Peckett
Officers: Generaldine Ann Peckett, Secretary; Dominique Clugston [1974] Director; Elliott Peckett [1977] Director; Generaldine Ann Peckett [1949] Director; Raymond Peckett [1945] Director

A.W. Smith & Sons Limited
Incorporated: 26 March 1954 *Employees:* 19
Net Worth: £7,028,710 *Total Assets:* £12,671,540
Registered Office: Home Farm, Withcall, Louth, Lincs, LN11 9RL
Activities: Growing of cereals (except rice), leguminous crops and oil seeds
Shareholders: Alfred John Smith; Stanley Henry Smith
Officers: John William James Smith, Secretary; Andrew Alan Smith [1960] Director/Farmer; John William James Smith [1957] Director/Farmer; Martyn Craig Smith [1974] Director/Farmer; Nicholas Darren Smith [1972] Director/Farmer; Robert Gerrard Paul Smith [1959] Director/Farmer

F.P.Smith (Holdings) Limited
Incorporated: 14 March 1940 *Employees:* 147
Net Worth: £11,568,567 *Total Assets:* £19,659,640
Registered Office: Sturrock Way, Bretton Way, Bretton, Peterborough, Cambs, PE3 8YL
Activities: Sale of new cars and light motor vehicles
Major Shareholder: Jane Margaret Wisniewski
Officers: Mark Alan Edwards, Secretary; Mark Alan Edwards [1972] Finance Director; Daniel Fitzjohn [1972] Director; Sarah Jane Fitzjohn [1973] Director; Jane Margaret Wisniewski [1947] Director/Secretary; Matthew George Wisniewski [1976] Director

G.A.E. Smith (Holdings) Limited
Incorporated: 5 October 1972
Net Worth: £22,341,906 *Total Assets:* £31,067,378
Registered Office: Feldspar Close, Warren Industrial Park, Enderby, Leicester, LE19 4SD
Activities: Collection of non-hazardous waste
Shareholders: Mark Smith; Martin Smith; Maxine Woolley; Corinne Corser; Oceala Limited
Officers: Maxine Woolley, Secretary; Corinne Corser [1957] Director/Sales Executive; Georgina Cullen [1980] Director/Purchasing Executive; Mark Smith [1963] Director/Manager; Martin Smith [1964] Director/Commercial Representative; Maxine Woolley [1956] Director/Office Management

Paul Smith (Holdings) Ltd
Incorporated: 4 February 2002
Net Worth: £19,257,000 *Total Assets:* £40,505,000
Registered Office: The Poplars, Lenton Lane, Nottingham, NG7 2PW
Activities: Activities of head offices
Officers: Alison Margaret Bland, Secretary; Ashley James Snowden Long, Secretary; Ashley James Snowden Long [1963] Director/Chartered Accountant; Sir Paul Brierley Smith [1946] Director/Clothier Fashion Designer

Smith Bros.(Caerconan) Wholesale Limited
Incorporated: 15 July 1932 *Employees:* 58
Net Worth: £11,316,169 *Total Assets:* £12,442,139
Registered Office: Greyfriars House, Sidings Court, Doncaster, S Yorks, DN4 5NU
Activities: Wholesale of radio, television goods & electrical household appliances (other than records, tapes, CDs)
Shareholder: Ryszard Bielenica
Officers: Ryszard Bielenica [1951] Director; Mark Peter Jervis [1958] Director; Agnes Sheach [1944] Director

Smith Brothers (Leicester) Limited
Incorporated: 7 January 1907 *Employees:* 356
Net Worth: £60,207,000 *Total Assets:* £85,993,968
Registered Office: 295 Aylestone Road, Leicester, LE2 7QJ
Activities: Manufacture of other fabricated metal products n.e.c.
Shareholders: Stephen Woolfe; James Thomas Wilkinson; Margaret Jane Beasley; John Gregory Smith
Officers: Margaret Jane Beasley [1953] Director; Julie Diane Brooks [1963] Director; Martin Forbes Heatlie [1971] Director; Anthony David Smith [1960] Director; Christopher John Smith [1958] Director; Steven Richard Smith [1969] Director; Sally Rosamund White [1957] Director; James Thomas Wilkinson [1956] Director

Smith Brothers Stores Limited
Incorporated: 26 September 1969 *Employees:* 261
Net Worth: £1,968,761 *Total Assets:* £39,851,484
Registered Office: Unit V2, Blaby Industrial Park, Winchester Avenue, Blaby, Leicester, LE8 4GZ
Activities: Non-specialised wholesale trade
Parent: Smith Brothers (Leicester) Limited
Officers: Margaret Jane Beasley [1953] Director; David Allan Bryson [1963] Director; Martin Kinglsey Denton [1965] Director; Martin Forbes Heatlie [1971] Director; Anthony David Smith [1960] Director; Christopher John Smith [1958] Managing Director; Steven Richard Smith [1969] Director; David Craig Wildman [1968] Director

Smith Construction Group Limited
Incorporated: 4 January 1994 *Employees:* 83
Net Worth: £11,167,979 *Total Assets:* £16,854,484
Registered Office: Smith House, Maidstone Road, Kingston, Milton Keynes, Bucks, MK10 0BD
Activities: Construction of commercial buildings
Major Shareholder: Ian Christopher Smith
Officers: John Banks, Secretary/Quantity Surveyor; John Banks [1969] Director/Quantity Surveyor; Graham Scotney [1961] Director/Quantity Surveyor; Ian Christopher Smith [1966] Director/Engineer and Construction Expert

Smith Cooper Audit Limited
Incorporated: 30 July 1996 *Employees:* 5
Previous: Smith Cooper Limited
Net Worth: £1,239,181 *Total Assets:* £9,325,671
Registered Office: St Helen's House, King Street, Derby, DE1 3EE
Activities: Accounting and auditing activities
Shareholders: Smith Cooper Audit Services Holdings Limited; SHH 101 LPP
Officers: James Oliver John Bagley, Secretary; James Oliver John Bagley [1982] Director; James Charles Delve [1985] Director; Sarah Flear [1972] Director; Janet Morgan [1957] Director; David Jonathan Nelson [1976] Director; Stephen Alexander Newman [1968] Director

Paul Smith Group Holdings Limited
Incorporated: 12 August 2005 *Employees:* 1,137
Net Worth: £132,886,000 *Total Assets:* £190,391,008
Registered Office: The Poplars, Lenton Lane, Nottingham, NG7 2PW
Activities: Activities of head offices
Major Shareholder: Paul Brierley Smith
Officers: Alison Bland, Secretary; Ashley James Snowden Long, Secretary/Chartered Accountant; Ashley James Snowden Long [1963] Director/Chartered Accountant; Masahiro Morofuji [1960] Director [Japanese]; Sir Paul Brierley Smith [1946] Director

Paul Smith Limited
Incorporated: 17 May 1974 *Employees:* 940
Net Worth: £116,886,000 *Total Assets:* £222,534,000
Registered Office: The Poplars, Lenton Lane, Nottingham, NG7 2PW
Activities: Wholesale of clothing and footwear
Parent: Paul Smith (Holdings) Limited
Officers: Alison Margaret Bland, Secretary; Ashley James Snowden Long, Secretary; Glynn Ashley Chilton [1973] Director; Ashley James Snowden Long [1963] Director/Chartered Accountant; Masahiro Morofuji [1960] Director [Japanese]; Sir Paul Brierley Smith [1946] Director

Smiths Concrete Limited
Incorporated: 25 March 1957 *Employees:* 70
Net Worth: £9,982,433 *Total Assets:* £13,684,621
Registered Office: Enslow, Kidlington, Oxon, OX5 3AY
Activities: Operation of gravel and sand pits; mining of clays and kaolin
Shareholder: Hanson Quarry Products Ventures Limited
Officers: Wendy Fiona Rogers, Secretary; James Alexander Claydon [1960] Director; Andrew William Smith [1960] Director; David John Smith [1933] Director; Simon Charles Smith [1958] Director; Charles Andrew Stubbs [1952] Director

Smithy Wood Business Parks Development LLP
Incorporated: 10 November 2006
Net Worth: £4,991,450 *Total Assets:* £10,630,845
Registered Office: 6a Hall Annex, Thorncliffe Park, Chapeltown, Sheffield, S35 2PH

SML Europe Limited
Incorporated: 15 October 1998 *Employees:* 256
Net Worth Deficit: £6,263,000 *Total Assets:* £41,386,000
Registered Office: Corby Innovation Hub, Bangrave Road South, Corby, Northants, NN17 1NN
Activities: Manufacture of other wearing apparel and accessories n.e.c.
Major Shareholder: Siu Man Suen
Officers: Chin Sing Mak, Secretary; Shane Lee Clarke [1964] Director/General Manager; King Wah Ho [1959] Director/Manager [Chinese]; Chin Sing Mak [1955] Director/Manager [Chinese]

SMS Electronics Limited
Incorporated: 26 July 2002 *Employees:* 149
Net Worth: £4,485,000 *Total Assets:* £12,094,000
Registered Office: SMS House, Technology Drive, Beeston, Nottingham, NG9 1AD
Activities: Manufacture of other electrical equipment
Officers: Craig Lee Taylor, Secretary; Robert Walter Bridges [1949] Director; Michael William Harby [1955] Director; Christopher Hunt [1952] Director; Andrew Maddock [1973] Director; Graham Shaw [1953] Director; Craig Lee Taylor [1976] Director; John Wyles [1948] Director

The Snaith School Academy Trust
Incorporated: 3 March 2014 *Employees:* 127
Net Worth: £20,376,364 *Total Assets:* £21,135,268
Registered Office: The Snaith School, Pontefract Road, Snaith, Goole, E Yorks, DN14 9LB
Activities: General secondary education
Officers: Martin Robert Backhouse [1964] Director/Farmer; Lindsey Annette Bellamy [1959] Director/Staff Nurse; Celia Jane Evans [1954] Director/General and GP Outreach Manager; Graham Wragg [1953] Director/Clerk; Sheena Anne Young [1954] Director/Dentist

Snap-On Equipment Limited
Incorporated: 29 October 2001
Net Worth: £55,668,520 *Total Assets:* £55,747,728
Registered Office: 17 Denney Road, Hardwick Industrial Estate, King's Lynn, Norfolk, PE30 4HG
Activities: Wholesale of other machinery and equipment
Parent: Snap-On Business Solutions Ltd
Officers: William Bruno [1961] Director/Vice President Sales & Marketing [American]; David Ellingen [1957] Director/President - Mitchell Repair Information Company [American]

Snap-On Finance UK Limited
Incorporated: 26 February 1997 *Employees:* 28
Net Worth: £45,156,776 *Total Assets:* £104,269,560
Registered Office: Telford Way, Telford Way Industrial Estate, Kettering, Northants, NN16 8SN
Activities: Other credit granting n.e.c.
Parent: Snap-On U.K. Holdings Limited
Officers: William Brown [1971] Director/Certified Accountant; Joseph John Burger [1966] Director/Business Executive [American]; Stephen Hugh Jones [1962] Managing Director [Australian]; Julian Garnet Winch [1955] Director/General Manager; Barrie James Young [1957] Director/Business Executive [Australian]

Snap-On U.K. Holdings Limited
Incorporated: 25 September 1991 *Employees:* 544
Net Worth: £93,099,000 *Total Assets:* £164,792,992
Registered Office: Telford Way, Telford Way Industrial Estate, Kettering, Northants, NN16 8SN
Activities: Manufacture of other machine tools
Parent: Snap-On Equipment Limited
Officers: William Brown [1971] Director/Certified Accountant; Stephen Hugh Jones [1962] Managing Director [Australian]; Barrie James Young [1957] Director/Executive [Australian]

Snowmountain Enterprises Limited
Incorporated: 18 February 1964 *Employees:* 93
Net Worth: £32,410,184 *Total Assets:* £39,137,432
Registered Office: 36-38 King Street, Kings Lynn, Norfolk, PE30 1ES
Activities: Buying and selling of own real estate
Officers: John Michael Skoulding, Secretary; Amy Victoria Brown [1987] Director/Retail Manager; Amanda Jane Herring [1967] Director; Benjamin James Skoulding [1981] Director; Eric Peter Skoulding [1988] Director; John Michael Skoulding [1954] Director; Marjorie Joan Skoulding [1931] Director; Robert Frederick Skoulding [1957] Director; Cindy Ann Tufts [1963] Director; John Michael Tufts [1990] Director/Manager

C. Soar & Sons (UK) Limited
Incorporated: 29 October 2003 *Employees:* 47
Net Worth: £9,552,759 *Total Assets:* £11,085,835
Registered Office: Old Tank Row, off Grange Lane, Stairfoot, Barnsley, S Yorks, S71 5AD
Activities: Recovery of sorted materials
Shareholders: Michael Soar; Colin Soar
Officers: Tracey Evans, Secretary; Colin Soar [1952] Director; Michael Soar [1956] Director; Mollie Soar [1920] Director

Sobell House Hospice Charity Limited
Incorporated: 6 November 2006 *Employees:* 35
Net Worth: £15,634,043 *Total Assets:* £16,519,417
Registered Office: 30 St Giles, Oxford, OX1 3LE
Activities: Retail sale of antiques including antique books in stores
Officers: Diane Araxie Gardner, Secretary; William Couldrick [1935] Director/Retired Medical Practitioner; Julie Findley [1954] Director/Solicitor; Hugh Everard Duncan Fraser [1951] Director/Garage Proprietor; Maryrose Danvers Hodgson [1941] Director/Artist; Peter John Holloran [1944] Director; Ian David Miles [1957] Director/Chartered Accountant; Sandra Margaret Nash [1948] Director/Retired; Gillian Margaret Nineham [1954] Director; Kenneth John McEwing Smith [1939] Director/Retired; Vivienne Spurge [1959] Director/Surveyor; Dr Rachel Starer [1962] Director/General Practitioner

Social Justice and Human Rights Centre Limited
Incorporated: 11 May 2011
Net Worth: £9,792,873 *Total Assets:* £16,909,168
Registered Office: The Old Music Hall, 106-108 Cowley Road, Oxford, OX4 1JE
Activities: Other letting and operating of own or leased real estate
Shareholders: The Ethical Property Company Limited; Trust for London
Officers: Paul Neil Bellack [1955] Director of Commercial Property Company; Bharat Mehta [1956] Charity Director; Dr Deborah Frances Pippard [1960] Director/Manager Charitable Trust; Christopher Toye [1967] Director/Executive Headteacher

Society of The Sacred Mission (Europe)
Incorporated: 24 October 2003 *Employees:* 12
Net Worth: £12,070,431 *Total Assets:* £12,123,086
Registered Office: St Michael's Priory, Newport Road, Willen, Milton Keynes, Bucks, MK15 9AA
Activities: Activities of religious organisations
Officers: Allan Hargreaves, Secretary; Reverend Wendy Carey [1945] Director/Clerk in Holy Orders; Reverend Edward Sydney John Ewer [1936] Director/Retired [Australian]; Allan Hargreaves [1946] Director/Tax Consultant; Stephen William Hogg [1964] Director/Retired; Jeremy Stephen Frederick Hopkinson [1943] Director/Retired; Anthony Joseph Purivis [1957] Director/Religious; Anthony Joseph Purvis [1957] Director/Monk; Robert Scott-Biggs [1946] Director/Retired; Robert Stretton [1945] Director/Clerk in Holy Orders

Society of The Salutation of Mary The Virgin Limited (The)
Incorporated: 9 March 1950
Net Worth: £9,737,530 *Total Assets:* £9,840,483
Registered Office: c/o Critchleys LLP, Beaver House, 23-38 Hythe Bridge Street, Oxford, OX1 2EP
Activities: Activities of religious organisations
Officers: Thomas Gregory Quin, Secretary; Philip Dulson [1960] Director/Religious Brother; Revd Alison Jacquelyn Fry [1965] Director/Religious Sister; Sister Sally Anne Paley [1955] Director/Religious Sister; Thomas Gregory Quin [1961] Director/Religious Brother; Mossman Roueche [1947] Trustee Director [American]; Michael Edward Tavinor [1953] Director/Priest

Socotec UK Limited
Incorporated: 14 December 1993 *Employees:* 1,251
Previous: Environmental Scientifics Group Limited
Net Worth: £34,808,000 *Total Assets:* £99,547,000
Registered Office: Socotec House, Bretby Business Park, Ashby Road, Bretby, Burton on Trent, Staffs, DE15 0YZ
Activities: Technical testing and analysis
Parent: Inspicio Environmental Services Group Limited
Officers: Philip John Henry Ball [1959] Managing Director; Andrew Christopher Bolter [1970] Finance Director; James Robert Murphy [1958] Managing Director; Norman Sleeth [1968] Director; Ian Sparks [1961] Director

Sodexo Motivation Solutions U.K. Limited
Incorporated: 23 January 1992 *Employees:* 320
Net Worth: £21,951,000 *Total Assets:* £123,465,000
Registered Office: Avalon House, Breckland, Linford Wood, Milton Keynes, Bucks, MK14 6LD
Activities: Other professional, scientific and technical activities n.e.c.
Officers: Jean Armand Istasse [1972] Director [Belgian]; Nicolas Jean Baudouin Morel [1973] Director/CFO (Group BRS) [French]; Burcin Ressamoglu [1969] Director/Chief Executive Officer [Turkish]; Aurelien Marie Pascal Dominique Sonet [1975] Director [French]

Sodick Europe Holdings Limited
Incorporated: 16 December 2002 *Employees:* 2
Net Worth: £8,025,468 *Total Assets:* £10,723,477
Registered Office: Edm House, Rowley Drive, Baginton, Coventry, Warwicks, CV3 4FG
Activities: Wholesale of other machinery and equipment
Shareholders: Sodick Co. Ltd. (Japan); Sodick Co. Ltd.
Officers: Andrew Graham Chapple, Secretary; Peter Edward Capp [1954] Director; Kenichi Furukawa [1972] Director/Executive [Japanese]; Hirofumi Maejima [1961] Director [Japanese]

Sodick Europe Limited
Incorporated: 11 May 2000 *Employees:* 20
Net Worth: £8,611,440 *Total Assets:* £26,030,948
Registered Office: Edm House, Rowley Drive, Baginton, Coventry, Warwicks, CV3 4FG
Activities: Manufacture of other special-purpose machinery n.e.c.
Parent: Sodick Europe Holdings Limited
Officers: Peter Capp, Secretary; Peter Edward Capp [1954] Director; Kenichi Furukawa [1972] Director [Japanese]; Keisuke Takagi [1955] Director [Japanese]

Sofidel UK Limited
Incorporated: 19 April 1988 *Employees:* 503
Net Worth: £245,204,992 *Total Assets:* £338,875,008
Registered Office: Waterside Road, Hamilton Industrial Park, Leicester, LE5 1TZ
Activities: Manufacture of paper and paperboard
Officers: Natalie Morgan, Secretary; Luigi Lazzareschi [1963] Director [Italian]; Emi Stefani [1930] Director/Chairman [Italian]

Software (Europe) Limited
Incorporated: 26 October 2011
Previous: Selenity Limited
Net Worth: £2,314,800 *Total Assets:* £9,996,056
Registered Office: Nibley House, Low Moor Road, Lincoln, LN6 3JY
Activities: Business and domestic software development
Officers: Lesley Burlow [1952] Director; Peter Robert Burlow [1951] Director; Neil James Everatt [1965] Director; Darren Richard Newton [1983] Director; Deborah Louise Saunby [1976] Director; Andrew Graham Shettle [1981] Director; Jonathan Patrick Teer [1987] Finance Director

Software AG (UK) Limited
Incorporated: 27 April 1977 *Employees:* 185
Net Worth: £32,036,000 *Total Assets:* £77,714,000
Registered Office: Locomotive Way, Pride Park, Derby, DE24 8PU
Activities: Information technology consultancy activities
Parent: Software AG
Officers: Carol Holden, Secretary; Timothy Nigel Fox [1966] Director/Solicitor; Arnd Zinnhardt [1962] Director/Vorstand Member [German]

Solartron Metrology Limited
Incorporated: 21 May 2001 *Employees:* 109
Net Worth: £15,656,000 *Total Assets:* £18,010,000
Registered Office: P O Box 36, 2 New Star Road, Leicester, LE4 9JQ
Activities: Manufacture of electronic measuring, testing etc. equipment, not for industrial process control
Parent: Taylor Hobson Limited
Officers: Joy Atwell, Secretary; Timothy Charles Bache [1961] Managing Director; Bruce Peter Wilson [1956] Director; Pietro Luigi Enrico Zetti [1968] Finance Director [Italian]

Solenis UK Limited
Incorporated: 29 April 2014 *Employees:* 93
Net Worth: £3,098,140 *Total Assets:* £26,638,408
Registered Office: Alfreton Trading Estate, Wimsey Way, Somercotes, Derbys, DE55 4LR
Activities: Manufacture of other chemical products n.e.c.
Officers: Gary John Kingsley [1964] Sales Director; Cornelis Floor Saarloos [1969] Director/Businessman [Dutch]

Solidor Limited
Incorporated: 22 April 2005 *Employees:* 185
Net Worth: £10,493,230 *Total Assets:* £20,240,808
Registered Office: Birthwaite Business Park, Huddersfield Road, Darton, Barnsley, S Yorks, S75 5JS
Activities: Manufacture of other plastic products
Parent: Passivdor Limited
Officers: Rose Murphy, Secretary; Clare Doyle [1965] Managing Director [American]; Joanne Freiberger [1964] Director/Vice President and Treasurer [American]; Rose Murphy [1957] Director/Lawyer [American]

Solidus UK Solutions Ltd
Incorporated: 5 February 2015 *Employees:* 82
Net Worth Deficit: £1,745,935 *Total Assets:* £16,497,526
Registered Office: 2 Arnsley Road, Weldon North Industrial Estate, Corby, Northants, NN17 5QW
Activities: Manufacture of other paper and paperboard containers
Parent: Solidus Solutions Solid Board B.V
Officers: Nick Harding [1982] Sales Director; Graham Richard Hogben [1967] Director/Plant Manager; Richard Houben [1974] Director [Dutch]

Solo Cup (UK) Limited
Incorporated: 30 May 2000
Net Worth: £12,115,000 *Total Assets:* £41,692,000
Registered Office: 3 Flaxley Road, Kingston Park, Peterborough, Cambs, PE2 9EN
Activities: Activities of head offices
Parent: Solo Cup Finance Limited
Officers: Claire Theresa Dart [1929] Director/Businesswomen [American]; Robert Charles Dart [1958] Director/Businessman [Irish]; Thomas Lynn Jewell [1967] Director/Businessman [American]; James Donald Lammers [1959] Director/Businessman [American]

Solo Cup Finance Limited
Incorporated: 30 November 2010 *Employees:* 496
Net Worth: £67,697,000 *Total Assets:* £77,963,000
Registered Office: 3 Flaxley Road, Kingston Park, Peterborough, Cambs, PE2 9EN
Activities: Non-trading company
Major Shareholder: Robert Charles Dart
Officers: Claire Theresa Dart [1929] Director/Businesswoman [American]; Robert Charles Dart [1958] Director/Businessman [Irish]; Thomas Lynn Jewell [1967] Director/Businessman [American]; James Donald Lammers [1959] Director/Businessman [American]

Solpro Manufacturing Limited
Incorporated: 7 March 1967 *Employees:* 100
Net Worth: £10,228,720 *Total Assets:* £17,161,200
Registered Office: Royds Mills, Windsor Street, Sheffield, S4 7WB
Activities: Precious metals production
Major Shareholder: Paul James Tear
Officers: Malcolm Rathbone [1943] Director/Deputy Chairman; James Andrew Tear [1968] Group Managing Director; Paul James Tear [1937] Director/Chairman

Solutionhost Group Limited
Incorporated: 13 June 2017 *Employees:* 8
Net Worth: £13,520,004 *Total Assets:* £14,782,360
Registered Office: Kings Court, Water Lane, Wilmslow, Cheshire, SK9 5AR
Activities: Activities of other holding companies n.e.c.
Parent: Citation Limited
Officers: Christopher Paul Morris [1972] Director; James Matthew Murphy [1982] Director; Nicholas Alexander James Murphy [1962] Director; Eloise Wann [1977] Director/Chief Financial Officer

Somerset Equipment Finance (UK) Ltd
Incorporated: 15 December 2011 *Employees:* 5
Net Worth Deficit: £1,454,524 *Total Assets:* £22,412,556
Registered Office: The Pinnacle, 170 Midsummer Boulevard, Milton Keynes, Bucks, MK9 1FE
Activities: Renting and leasing of other machinery, equipment and tangible goods n.e.c.
Officers: Evan M Bokor [1962] Director/Chief Executive Officer [American]; Mark Fiorentino [1958] Director/Executive VP [American]; Adam Simon [1971] Director/Executive VP - Sales [American]

Soncell International Limited
Incorporated: 15 December 2005 *Employees:* 4
Net Worth Deficit: £3,560,801 *Total Assets:* £15,450,418
Registered Office: High Edge Court, Church Street, Heage, Belper, Derbys, DE56 2BW
Activities: Activities of head offices
Parent: Bowmer & Kirkland Ltd.
Officers: Michelle Ann Mucklestone, Secretary; Michael John Beale [1966] Director/Accountant; Kevin Daniel McDonald [1980] Director

Sonepar UK Limited
Incorporated: 4 September 2014 *Employees:* 5
Net Worth: £103,598,000 *Total Assets:* £137,339,008
Registered Office: Davy Avenue, Knowlhill, Milton Keynes, Bucks, MK5 8HJ
Activities: Activities of other holding companies n.e.c.
Parent: Otra NV
Officers: Marco Brunetti [1966] Director [Italian]; Eric Gerard Therese Joseph Coisne [1959] Director [French]; David George Gabriel [1958] Director [American]; Louise Garcia de Sola [1989] Director [French]; Andros Neocleous [1964] Director/Finance Executive [Cypriot]

Sonic Communications (International) Limited
Incorporated: 10 March 1976 *Employees:* 79
Net Worth: £12,413,988 *Total Assets:* £13,522,240
Registered Office: High Edge Court, Heage, Belper, Derbys, DE56 2BW
Activities: Other business support service activities n.e.c.
Shareholders: Soncell International Ltd.; Bowmer & Kirkland Ltd.
Officers: Michelle Ann Mucklestone, Secretary; Neil Barker [1957] Sales Director; Michael John Beale [1966] Director/Accountant; Mark Robert Wilbraham [1960] Production Director

Sophos Group PLC
Incorporated: 26 May 2015
Net Worth: £69,836,440 *Total Assets:* £1,022,746,304
Registered Office: The Pentagon, Abingdon Science Park, Abingdon, Oxon, OX14 3YP
Activities: Business and domestic software development
Officers: Eleanor Lacey, Secretary; Sandra England Bergeron [1958] Director [American]; Nicholas Paul Seaton Bray [1965] Director/Accountant; Peter Gyenes [1945] Director [American]; Kristof Peter Hagerman [1964] Director/Chief Executive Officer [American]; Charles Richard Kenneth Medlock [1960] Director; Vinodka Murria [1962] Director; Paul Ashton Walker [1957] Director

Sophos Holdings Limited
Incorporated: 16 April 2010
Net Worth: £507,856,480 *Total Assets:* £839,215,360
Registered Office: The Pentagon, Abingdon Science Park, Abingdon, Oxford, OX14 3YP
Activities: Activities of head offices
Parent: Sophos Group PLC
Officers: Nicholas Paul Seaton Bray [1965] Director/Accountant; Stuart Barry David Fillingham [1965] Director/VP Group and Commercial Finance; Alison Halliday Kennedy [1962] Director/Chartered Accountant; Jennifer Margaret Onslow [1955] Director/VP Financial Controller

Sophos Limited
Incorporated: 4 February 1987 *Employees:* 607
Net Worth: £119,369,000 *Total Assets:* £732,288,000
Registered Office: The Pentagon, Abingdon Science Park, Abingdon, Oxon, OX14 3YP
Activities: Business and domestic software development
Parent: Sophos Holdings Limited
Officers: Nicholas Paul Seaton Bray [1965] Director/Accountant; Stuart Barry David Fillingham [1965] Director/VP Group and Commercial Finance; Alison Halliday Kennedy [1962] Director/Chartered Accountant; Jennifer Margaret Onslow [1955] Director/VP Financial Controller

Sophos Treasury Limited
Incorporated: 27 May 2015
Net Worth: £677,509 *Total Assets:* £239,916,752
Registered Office: The Pentagon, Abingdon Science Park, Abingdon, Oxon, OX14 3YP
Activities: Activities of head offices
Parent: Sophos Holdings Limited
Officers: Nicholas Paul Seaton Bray [1965] Director/Accountant; Stuart Barry David Fillingham [1965] Director/Accountant; Alison Halliday Kennedy [1962] Director/Chartered Accountant; Jennifer Margaret Onslow [1955] Director/Accountant

Soufflet Malt UK Limited
Incorporated: 9 January 2015 *Employees:* 31
Net Worth: £2,845,000 *Total Assets:* £39,323,000
Registered Office: Shobnall Maltings, Wellington Road, Burton on Trent, Staffs, DE14 2AP
Activities: Manufacture of malt
Officers: Christophe Paul Alexandre Passelande [1965] Managing Director [French]

Source Bioscience Limited
Incorporated: 14 November 1903
Previous: Source Bioscience PLC
Net Worth: £30,280,000 *Total Assets:* £45,570,000
Registered Office: 1 Orchard Place, Nottingham Business Park, Nottingham, NG8 6PX
Activities: Activities of head offices
Parent: Sherwood Holdings Limited
Officers: James Douglas Agnew [1974] Director/Fund Manager; Jay Charles Lecoque [1962] Director/Consultant [American]; Trevor Frank Nolan [1973] Finance Director; Russell Steven Wheatcroft [1971] Commercial Director

Source Bioscience UK Limited
Incorporated: 26 September 2000 *Employees:* 116
Net Worth Deficit: £3,291,000 *Total Assets:* £20,967,000
Registered Office: 1 Orchard Place, Nottingham Business Park, Nottingham, NG8 6PX
Activities: Activities of head offices
Parent: Source Bioscience Limited
Officers: Jay Charles Lecoque [1962] Director/Executive Chairman [American]; Trevor Frank Nolan [1973] Finance Director; Russell Steven Wheatcroft [1971] Commercial Director

Sourcecircle Holdings Limited
Incorporated: 13 May 2016 *Employees:* 91
Net Worth: £9,251,069 *Total Assets:* £12,295,135
Registered Office: Swan Lake Glass Works, Upperton Road, Leicester, LE2 7AY
Activities: Activities of other holding companies n.e.c.
Major Shareholder: David Andrew King
Officers: Jennifer Anne King, Secretary; David Andrew King [1944] Director; Jennifer Anne King [1943] Director

South Coast Furnishing Company Limited
Incorporated: 13 March 1951 *Employees:* 4
Net Worth: £7,719,439 *Total Assets:* £11,110,070
Registered Office: 15 Station Road, St Ives, Cambs, PE27 5BH
Activities: Development of building projects
Shareholders: M & B Green Limited; DJS Browne Limited
Officers: Fruma Stephany Browne [1947] Director; Michael Green [1946] Director

South East London & Kent Bus Company Limited
Incorporated: 14 December 1988 *Employees:* 1,491
Net Worth: £63,708,000 *Total Assets:* £88,215,000
Registered Office: c/o Stagecoach Services Limited, One Stockport Exchange, 20 Railway Road, Stockport, Cheshire, SK1 3SW
Activities: Other urban, suburban or metropolitan passenger land transport (not underground, metro or similar)
Parent: Stagecoach Bus Holdings Limited
Officers: Michael John Vaux, Secretary; Colin Brown [1968] Director/Accountant; Paul Graham Lynch [1962] Director; Arnold Mark Threapleton [1954] Managing Director

South Lincolnshire Academies Trust
Incorporated: 10 March 2011 *Employees:* 302
Previous: South Lincolnshire Academies Trust Ltd
Net Worth: £24,890,628 *Total Assets:* £30,782,958
Registered Office: Bourne Academy, Edinburgh Crescent, Bourne, Lincs, PE10 9DT
Activities: General secondary education
Officers: Lucy Conley [1969] Director/Deputy Executive Headteacher; Stephen Alan Haigh [1958] Director/Vocational Learning Advisor; Will Hawkins [1967] Director/Business Manager; Robin Lee Immink [1974] Director/Governor; John Alfred Kirkman [1939] Director/Retired; Duncan Anthony Pickering [1965] Director/Solicitor; John Stokes [1958] Director/Head of Procurement

South Warwickshire Academy Trust
Incorporated: 8 January 2018 *Employees:* 132
Net Worth: £10,397,000 *Total Assets:* £12,312,000
Registered Office: Welcombe Hills School, Blue Cap Road, Stratford upon Avon, Warwicks, CV37 6TQ
Activities: Other education n.e.c.
Officers: Suzanne Ebrey [1965] Director/Nurse; Martin Grubb [1949] Director/Retired; Peter Robert Hearne [1955] Director/Retired Accountant; Judith Anne Humphry [1960] Director/Headteacher; Joyce Elizabeth James [1958] Director; Patricia Rita Knauff [1959] Director/Retired; Charlotte Williamson [1960] Director/Teacher

South Yorkshire Community Foundation Limited
Incorporated: 28 February 2011 *Employees:* 21
Net Worth: £12,813,969 *Total Assets:* £12,951,421
Registered Office: Unit 2, 9-12 Jessop's Riverside, 800 Brightside Lane, Sheffield, S9 2RX
Activities: Other professional, scientific and technical activities n.e.c.
Officers: Zaidah Ahmed [1969] Director/Schools Community Cohesion Officer; Paul Benington [1976] Director/Marketing and Business Development Consultant; Nigel Brewster [1973] Director; John Raymond Holt [1949] Director/Solicitor - Retired; Nicholas Anthony Kitchen [1959] Director/Retired; Yiannis Koursis [1975] Director/Deputy Principal; Melvyn Lunn [1948] Director/Chartered Accountant; Dr Julie MacDonald [1956] Director; Craig McKay [1970] Managing Director; James Henry Newman [1950] Director/Certified Chartered Accountant; Alex Pettifer Mbe [1951] Director/Retired; John Pickering [1955] Director/Retired; Roderick Howard Maxwell Plews [1952] Director/Chartered Accountant; Martin Ross [1954] Managing Director; Lord Richard Scarbrough [1973] Director/Landowner; Shahida Siddique [1976] Director/Chief Executive; Charles William Hugh Warrack [1950] Director/Property Development; Valerie Michele Wightman [1969] Director/Solicitor

South Yorkshire Investment Fund Limited
Incorporated: 29 February 2000 *Employees:* 4
Net Worth: £19,729,048 *Total Assets:* £22,558,688
Registered Office: 2nd Floor, Capitol Court, Dodworth, Barnsley, S Yorks, S75 3TZ
Activities: Activities of financial services holding companies
Officers: Trevor Walters, Secretary; Alexander James McWhirter [1958] Director/Public Servant; Challans Anthony Parsons [1949] Director/Consultant; Angela Stopforth [1952] Director; John Warner [1955] Director/Accountant

Southern Derbyshire Lift Project Company (No. 1) Limited
Incorporated: 8 October 2003
Net Worth Deficit: £4,282,000 *Total Assets:* £45,288,000
Registered Office: Unit G1, Ash Tree Court, Nottingham Business Park, Nottingham, NG8 6PY
Activities: Other business support service activities n.e.c.
Parent: Southern Derbyshire Lift (Midco) Limited
Officers: Michael George Duggan, Secretary; Richard John Coates [1966] CHP Investment Director; Charlotte Sophie Ellen Douglass [1978] Director/Chartered Surveyor; Brian Ibell [1949] Project Director; Gavin William MacKinlay [1957] Associate Director; Kirsty O'Brien [1982] Director/Operations Manager; Paddy Tipping [1949] Director

Southern Derbyshire Lift Project Company (No.2) Limited
Incorporated: 4 May 2006
Net Worth Deficit: £2,615,000 *Total Assets:* £29,718,000
Registered Office: Unit G1, Ash Tree Court, Nottingham Business Park, Nottingham, NG8 6PY
Activities: Other letting and operating of own or leased real estate
Parent: Southern Derbyshire Lift (Midco) (No.2) Limited
Officers: Michael George Duggan, Secretary; Richard John Coates [1966] CHP Investment Director; Charlotte Sophie Ellen Douglass [1978] Director/Chartered Surveyor; Brian Ibell [1949] Public Sector Director; Gavin William MacKinlay [1957] Associate Director; Kirsty O'Brien [1982] Director/Operations Manager; Paddy Tipping [1949] Director

Southern View Finance UK Limited
Incorporated: 4 March 2013
Net Worth: £81,483,920 *Total Assets:* £107,195,360
Registered Office: Witan Gate House, 500-600 Witan Gate West, Milton Keynes, Bucks, MK9 1SH
Activities: Financial intermediation not elsewhere classified
Parent: Steinhoff UK Holdings Limited
Officers: Harjinder Singh Sohal [1968] Director/Finance/Treasury Professional

Southgate Packaging Limited
Incorporated: 18 August 2006
Net Worth: £5,979,554 *Total Assets:* £13,991,731
Registered Office: Southgate Packaging Ltd, Hamlins Way, Hardwick, Narrows Industrial Estate, King's Lynn, Norfolk, PE30 4NG
Activities: Wholesale of other intermediate products
Parent: Arpo Global Limited
Officers: Stephen Richard Turner, Secretary/Purchasing Director; Charles David McIntyre [1974] Commercial Director; Clive Russell Turner [1977] Director/Manager; Craig Turner [1989] Director; Dale Turner [1991] Director; George Turner [1995] Director; Marcus James Turner [1970] Director/Sales Manager; Stephen Richard Turner [1972] Director/Manager

Southport Golf Complex Limited
Incorporated: 13 July 1987
Net Worth: £9,349,580 *Total Assets:* £16,220,996
Registered Office: 838 Ecclesall Road, Sheffield, S11 8TD
Activities: Other letting and operating of own or leased real estate
Shareholders: Keith John Wainman; Gillian Margaret Wainman
Officers: Joy Beverley Ferris [1972] Director/Data Manager; Gillian Margaret Wainman [1957] Director; Grace Wainman [1997] Director/Student; Ian James Wainman [1970] Director/Technical Assistant; Keith John Wainman [1950] Director/Salesman

Southwell and Nottingham Diocesan Board of Finance
Incorporated: 5 June 1891 *Employees:* 79
Net Worth: £73,923,000 *Total Assets:* £79,944,000
Registered Office: Jubilee House, Westgate, Southwell, Notts, NG25 0JH
Activities: Other business support service activities n.e.c.
Officers: Nigel Spraggins, Secretary; The Revd Canon Mark Adams [1967] Director/Vicar; Edward Michael Astley Arlington [1953] Director; Christopher Michael Bolton [1948] Director; Revd Colin Douglas Bourne [1956] Director/Minster; Frederick George Brand [1952] Director; The Venerable Sarah Elizabeth Clark [1965] Director/Minister of Religion; Susan Lesley Dunster [1944] Director; Revd Angela Fletcher [1959] Director/Minister of Religion; Jane Briony Gray [1952] Director; Professor Peter Richard Bloomfield Harris [1955] Director; Sarah Gillian Holt [1964] Director/Student; Revd Samantha Jane Hustwayte [1973] Director/Minister of Religion; Christopher James Perrett [1946] Director/Warden of Readers; The Venerable David Anthony Picken [1963] Director/Clergyman; Anthony Porter [1952] Director/Bishop of Sherwood; The Revd Canon Margaret Fiona Shouler [1955] Director/Minister of Religion; Revd Canon Stephen David Silvester [1959] Director/Minster of Religion; Colin Stuart Slater [1934] Director in Communications; Peter Vincent Stanley [1960] Director/IT Manager; Dean Nicola Ann Sullivan [1958] Director/Dean; Susan Waterston [1959] Director; Paul Gavin Williams [1968] Director/Bishop; Michael John Wilson [1950] Director/Retired School Teacher

Sovereign Crest Limited
Incorporated: 30 January 2004 *Employees:* 1
Net Worth: £1,568,047 *Total Assets:* £15,230,130
Registered Office: 3 Stadium Business Court, Millennium Way, Pride Park, Derby, DE24 8HP
Activities: Development of building projects
Major Shareholder: Neil Kenneth Smith
Officers: Mark Philby, Secretary; Mark Philby [1969] Director/Chartered Accountant; Neil Kenneth Smith [1968] Director

Spalding Grammar School
Incorporated: 11 January 2013 *Employees:* 118
Net Worth: £16,499,449 *Total Assets:* £18,386,160
Registered Office: Spalding Grammar School, Priory Lane, Spalding, Lincs, PE11 2XH
Activities: General secondary education
Officers: Keith John Bean [1943] Director/Retired; Philip Callow [1975] Director; Adrian Charles Cunnington [1960] Director/Head of Research; Craig Spencer Delaney [1971] Director/Solicitor; Sonya Yvonne Ely [1971] Director/Headteacher; Alan John Faulkner [1972] Director/Land Agent; Michael Paul John Flindall [1962] Director/School Caretaker; Debra Haslam [1961] Director/Personal Assistant; Anthony John Holdsworth [1942] Director/Retired; Sharon Ann Lynette Hoult [1954] Director/Science Technician; Jane Lutton [1965] Director/Teacher; Jane-Marie Mayne [1973] Director/Student Support Supervisor; Edward John Rees [1967] Director/Commercial Manager; Steve Wilkinson [1973] Director

Spaldings Holdings Limited
Incorporated: 12 September 2003 *Employees:* 1
Net Worth Deficit: £163,000 *Total Assets:* £11,138,000
Registered Office: 25-35 Sadler Road, Lincoln, LN6 3XJ
Activities: Support activities for crop production
Parent: Marubeni Agri Machinery Holdings Limited
Officers: Kevin Gissing, Secretary; Shuichi Kamizono [1965] Director [Japanese]; Susumu Wakamori [1967] Director [Japanese]; Noboru Yamamoto [1970] Director/Chairman [Japanese]

Spaldings Limited
Incorporated: 24 April 1981 *Employees:* 160
Net Worth: £16,790,000 *Total Assets:* £21,397,000
Registered Office: Sadler Road, Lincoln, LN6 3XJ
Activities: Support activities for crop production
Parent: Spaldings Holdings Limited
Officers: Kevin Gissing, Secretary; Shuichi Kamizono [1965] Director [Japanese]; Susumu Wakamori [1967] Director [Japanese]; Noboru Yamamoto [1970] Director/Chairman [Japanese]

Spark44 (JV) Limited
Incorporated: 18 February 2011 *Employees:* 1,104
Net Worth: £14,859,831 *Total Assets:* £44,516,328
Registered Office: Abbey Road, Whitley, Coventry, Warwicks, CV3 4LF
Activities: Management consultancy activities other than financial management
Shareholder: Jaguar Land Rover Limited
Officers: Susan Lesley Pearson, Secretary; Felix Brautigam [1967] Managing Director [German]; Dr Alex Buck [1961] Managing Director [German]; Brian Fraser [1965] Director; Fiona Pargeter [1969] Director; Avanesh Sharma [1968] Director; Ralf Specht [1962] Director/Manager [German]; Dr Ralf Dieter Speth [1955] Director/Chairman and CEO [German]

Sparken Hill Academy Trust
Incorporated: 6 October 2014 *Employees:* 97
Net Worth: £7,014,503 *Total Assets:* £9,547,181
Registered Office: Sparken Hill, Worksop, Notts, S80 1AW
Activities: Primary education
Shareholders: Marion Susan Cutts; John Hemshall; Phillip Gawthorpe
Officers: Vicky Marie Dashper, Secretary; Matthew Reece Burnell [1970] Director/Church Minister for The Southwell & Notts Diocese; Marion Susan Cutts [1950] Director; Phillip Gawthorpe [1952] Director/Education Advisor; John Hemshall [1946] Director; Richard Thomas Lilley [1970] Director/Headteacher; Clare Middleton [1972] Director; Annette Phillipson [1978] Director/Housewife; Emma Rodgers [1973] Director/Vice Principal; John Shephard [1957] Director/District Councillor; Susan Sparks [1958] Director/Senior Teacher

SPD Development Company Limited
Incorporated: 18 December 2006 *Employees:* 143
Net Worth: £15,126,000 *Total Assets:* £18,579,000
Registered Office: Stannard Way, Priory Business Park, Bedford, MK44 3UP
Activities: Other research and experimental development on natural sciences and engineering
Parent: SPD Swiss Precision Diagnostics GmbH
Officers: Dr Simon Alaluf [1970] Finance Director; Fiona Jane Clancy [1974] Scientific & Medical Affairs Director; Steven Christopher Hart [1975] R&D Director; Dr Sarah Rosemary Johnson [1971] Clinical Director

SPD Holdings Limited
Incorporated: 7 June 2004 *Employees:* 4
Net Worth: £8,741,680 *Total Assets:* £14,622,797
Registered Office: 6a Hall Annex, Thorncliffe Park Estate, Newton Chambers Road, Chapeltown, Sheffield, S35 2PH
Activities: Activities of head offices
Shareholders: Brian Malcolm Thomson; Brian Geoffrey Waldron
Officers: Antony Frederick Greasley, Secretary/Accountant; Antony Frederick Greasley [1959] Director/Accountant; Keith Michael Mellors [1955] Director; John David Newton [1963] Director

Spear & Jackson Group Limited
Incorporated: 25 May 2012 *Employees:* 462
Net Worth: £2,803,000 *Total Assets:* £67,154,000
Registered Office: Atlas Way, Atlas North, Sheffield, S4 7QQ
Activities: Activities of other holding companies n.e.c.
Major Shareholder: Simon Nai Cheng Hsu
Officers: John Maurice Dallman, Secretary; Simon Nai Cheng Hsu [1960] Director/Businessman [Chinese]; Alaina Shone [1962] Director/Chartered Accountant

Spear & Jackson Limited
Incorporated: 14 September 1989 *Employees:* 42
Net Worth: £20,290,000 *Total Assets:* £20,317,000
Registered Office: c/o James Neill Holdings Limited, Atlas Way, Atlas North Business Park, Sheffield, S4 7QQ
Activities: Activities of other holding companies n.e.c.
Parent: Spear & Jackson Group Limited
Officers: John Maurice Dallman, Company Secretary; John Broughton [1961] Director; Simon Nai Cheng Hsu [1960] Director/Businessman [Chinese]; Alaina Shone [1962] Director/Chartered Accountant

Special New Fruit Licensing Limited
Incorporated: 21 June 2004
Net Worth: £23,476,566 *Total Assets:* £37,458,324
Registered Office: Frans House, Fenton Way, Chatteris, Cambs, PE16 6UP
Activities: Other research and experimental development on natural sciences and engineering
Parent: Munoz Group Ltd
Officers: Amalio Fuster, Secretary; Fernando Juan de Lucas Lopez [1973] Director [Spanish]; David John Haresign [1963] Director; Josep Jove Estiarte [1978] Director [Spanish]; Ian Duncan MacIntyre [1954] Director; Alvaro Munoz Beraza [1966] Director/Chief Executive [Spanish]

Special Piping Materials Limited
Incorporated: 20 October 1988 *Employees:* 18
Net Worth: £8,389,175 *Total Assets:* £10,101,811
Registered Office: Unit 26 Globe Industrial Estate, Dukinfield, Cheshire, SK16 4UU
Activities: Non-specialised wholesale trade
Parent: Special Piping Materials (Holdings) Limited
Officers: Mary Linda Buckley, Secretary; Leslie Buckley [1950] Director; Mary Linda Buckley [1949] Director/Secretary; Paul Leslie Buckley [1975] Director

Special Quality Alloys Limited
Incorporated: 4 February 1986 *Employees:* 105
Net Worth: £22,212,622 *Total Assets:* £31,311,974
Registered Office: Bacon Lane, Sheffield, S9 3NH
Activities: Forging, pressing, stamping and roll-forming of metal; powder metallurgy
Major Shareholder: Alan Kenneth Beardshaw
Officers: Alan Christopher Beardshaw, Secretary; Alan Christopher Beardshaw [1974] Director; Alan Kenneth Beardshaw [1948] Steelworks Director; Bennett John Beardshaw [1977] Director; Simon Generald Scott Marshall [1965] Sales Director; Dean John Matthews [1971] Director/Operations Manager; Jason Miller [1973] Forge Director; Darren Michael Pryce [1969] Sales Director; Raymond Wood [1961] Technical Director

Special Steel Co.,Limited
Incorporated: 26 September 1925 *Employees:* 219
Net Worth: £45,453,536 *Total Assets:* £56,908,880
Registered Office: Bacon Lane, Sheffield, S9 3NH
Activities: Forging, pressing, stamping and roll-forming of metal; powder metallurgy
Major Shareholder: Alan Kenneth Beardshaw
Officers: Alan Christopher Beardshaw, Secretary; Alan Christopher Beardshaw [1974] Director/Metallurgist; Alan Kenneth Beardshaw [1948] Director; Bennett John Beardshaw [1977] Director

Specialised Fixings Limited
Incorporated: 10 June 2003
Net Worth: £525,000 *Total Assets:* £10,310,000
Registered Office: Adsetts House, 16 Europa View, Sheffield Business Park, Sheffield, S9 1XH
Activities: Dormant company
Parent: SIG Trading Limited
Officers: Richard Charles Monro, Secretary; Ian Jackson [1979] Director/Accountant; Richard Charles Monro [1958] Director/Chartered Secretary

Speedloan Finance Limited
Incorporated: 30 November 2001 *Employees:* 391
Net Worth Deficit: £3,503,082 *Total Assets:* £34,574,856
Registered Office: 164 Cowley Road, Oxford, OX4 1UE
Activities: Other credit granting n.e.c.
Officers: Taisuke Atsumi [1962] Director [Japanese]; Kohei Ogawa [1956] Director [Japanese]

Speeds (Burton) Limited
Incorporated: 29 October 2014 *Employees:* 1
Net Worth: £10,473,504 *Total Assets:* £10,664,374
Registered Office: Hallfield Farm, Hallfieldgate Lane, Shirland, Alfreton, Derbys, DE55 6AA
Activities: Other letting and operating of own or leased real estate
Officers: Martin Speed [1958] Director

Speeds Limited
Incorporated: 26 January 1973 *Employees:* 10
Net Worth: £23,963,996 *Total Assets:* £24,197,162
Registered Office: Hallfield Farm, Hallfieldgate Lane, Shirland, Alfreton, Derbys, DE55 6AA
Activities: Other letting and operating of own or leased real estate
Officers: Pauline Eva Speed, Secretary; Tracey Haggas [1961] Director; Martin Speed [1958] Director; Pauline Eva Speed [1932] Director; Kerry Elizabeth Strawson [1965] Director

The Spencer Academies Trust
Incorporated: 23 August 2010 *Employees:* 1,231
Net Worth: £133,365,000 *Total Assets:* £153,132,992
Registered Office: George Spencer School, Arthur Mee Road, Stapleford, Nottingham, NG9 7EW
Activities: Primary education
Officers: Kathryn Anna Godfrey, Secretary; Malcolm Clive Bachelor [1952] Director/Consultant; Nichola-Jane Beverly Kerr-Gilbert [1973] Director/Senior Lecturer; Donna Marie Kinderman [1971] Director/Teaching Assistant; Toby Benjamin Preston [1978] Director/Solicitor; James Adrian Smith [1973] Director; Michelle Thompson [1976] Director/HR Business Partner; Kelly Ann Vere [1981] Director/Higher Education Engagement Manager; Geoffrey Weightman [1950] Director/Examinations Officer; Paul Andrew West [1972] Director/Chief Executive Officer

Sperry Rail (International) Limited
Incorporated: 15 February 2002 *Employees:* 77
Net Worth: £15,552,000 *Total Assets:* £19,176,000
Registered Office: Derwent House, RTC Business Park, London Road, Derby, DE24 8UP
Activities: Technical testing and analysis
Parent: Sperry Rail Europe Holdings Limited
Officers: Bridgette Murphy, Secretary; Justin James Robert Stroud, Secretary; James Kevin O'Rourke [1961] Director/President [American]; Justin Stroud [1971] Director

A.E.Spink Limited
Incorporated: 25 June 1926 *Employees:* 81
Net Worth: £9,702,961 *Total Assets:* £13,764,359
Registered Office: A E Spink Ltd, Kelham Street, Doncaster, S Yorks, DN1 3RA
Activities: Wholesale of wood, construction materials and sanitary equipment
Shareholders: Nicholas Martin Harrison; Matthew Ian Harrison
Officers: Nicholas Martin Harrison, Secretary; Simon James Biltcliffe [1976] Plumbing Sales Director; Matthew Ian Harrison [1965] Director; Nicholas Martin Harrison [1962] Director; Pamela Harrison [1938] Director; Christopher James Meek [1982] Building Sales Director

Spire Homes (LG) Limited
Incorporated: 20 July 2000 *Employees:* 73
Net Worth: £142,207,008 *Total Assets:* £351,399,008
Registered Office: 1 Crown Court, Crown Way, Rushden, Northants, NN10 6BS
Activities: Renting and operating of Housing Association real estate
Officers: Rachel Heather Challinor, Secretary; Andrew Paul Bish [1961] Director/Consultant; Julie Carol Doyle [1966] Managing Director; Angela Frances Morris [1960] Director/Healthcare Consultant; Peter Raymond Oliver [1970] Director; Karen Anne Preece [1960] Director/Chartered Accountant; Manjula Sachdeva [1965] Director/Solicitor (Non Practising); Paul Smith [1971] Director/Company Manager; Lynn Marie Stubbs [1966] Executive Director of People and Performance; Stephen Wenham [1952] Director/Consultant

SPL II Acquisition Company (UK) Limited
Incorporated: 24 December 2014
Net Worth: £61,329,448 *Total Assets:* £69,358,280
Registered Office: Peckleton Lane, Desford, Leicester, LE9 9JT
Activities: Activities of other holding companies n.e.c.
Parent: Logistics Acquisition Company (UK) Limited
Officers: Zachary Green, Secretary; Zach Green [1960] Director/Attorney [American]; Nicholas Gerard Paterson [1966] Director, Operations; Terrance Glenn Sandlin [1968] Director/Executive VP and Chief Financial Officer [American]

SPL Logistics Holdings Acquisition Company (UK) Limited
Incorporated: 23 December 2014
Net Worth: £216,599,712 *Total Assets:* £246,895,648
Registered Office: Peckleton Lane, Desford, Leicester, LE9 9JT
Activities: Activities of other holding companies n.e.c.
Parent: Logistics Acquisition Company (UK) Limited
Officers: Zachary Green, Secretary; Zachary Carter Green [1960] Director/Attorney [American]; Nicholas Gerard Paterson [1966] Director, Operations; Terrance Glenn Sandlin [1968] Director/Executive VP and Chief Financial Officer [American]

SPL Logistics UK Holdings Limited
Incorporated: 23 May 2012
Net Worth Deficit: £488,000 *Total Assets:* £75,149,000
Registered Office: Peckleton Lane, Desford, Leicester, LE9 9JU
Activities: Activities of other holding companies n.e.c.
Parent: Logistics Acquisition Company (UK) Limited
Officers: Zach Green [1960] Director/Attorney [American]; Nicholas Gerard Paterson [1966] Director, Operations; Terrance Glenn Sandlin [1968] Director/Executive VP and Chief Financial Officer [American]

The Sports & Leisure Group Ltd
Incorporated: 24 August 2000 *Employees:* 345
Net Worth Deficit: £3,139,054 *Total Assets:* £27,546,556
Registered Office: Roko, Wilford Lane, West Bridgford, Nottingham, NG2 7RN
Activities: Operation of sports facilities
Parent: CSSC Properties Ltd
Officers: Nigel Raymond Maglione, Secretary; Raymond John Peter Haskell [1960] Director; Marian Holmes [1952] Director/Chief Executive; Barry Roy Hunter [1962] Director; Nigel Raymond Maglione [1956] Director; Richard Barry Simpson [1948] Director

Sports and Leisure Management Ltd
Incorporated: 9 December 1987 *Employees:* 6,837
Net Worth: £26,630,674 *Total Assets:* £81,214,368
Registered Office: 2 Watling Drive, Sketchley Meadows, Hinckley, Leics, LE10 3EY
Activities: Operation of sports facilities
Officers: Martin Bell, Secretary/Managing Director; Martin Bell [1961] Managing Director; David John Bibby [1961] Director/Accountant; Joseph Mark Drysdale [1963] Finance Director

Sports Direct International PLC
Incorporated: 21 December 2006 *Employees:* 17,559
Net Worth: £1,212,499,968 *Total Assets:* £2,849,600,000
Registered Office: Unit A, Brook Park East, Shirebrook, Derbys, NG20 8RY
Activities: Activities of head offices
Officers: Cameron John Olsen, Secretary; Richard John Bottomley [1953] Director; David Jameson Brayshaw [1953] Director/Banker; David John Daly [1959] Director; Nicola Julie Frampton [1966] Director; Jonathan Kempster [1963] Director/Accountant; Cally Jayne Price [1990] Director/Retail Manager

Sports Information Services (Holdings) Limited
Incorporated: 16 August 1985 *Employees:* 459
Previous: Satellite Information Services (Holdings) Limited
Net Worth: £81,100,000 *Total Assets:* £142,440,000
Registered Office: 2 Whitehall Avenue, Kingston, Milton Keynes, Bucks, MK10 0AX
Activities: Television programming and broadcasting activities
Officers: Richard Jonathan Ames [1970] Director; Trevor Kenneth Beaumont [1950] Director; Mark Russel Chambers [1972] Director/Retail COO; Fred Done [1943] Director; Sally Deborah Flanagan [1962] Director; Michael James Ford [1980] Director; John Michael Barry Gibson [1951] Director/Chairman; Duncan Edward Johnson [1970] Director; Paul James Kirszanek [1977] Director; Melvin Anthony Lawson [1958] Director; Christopher Harwood Bernard Mills [1952] Director/Investment Banker; Joseph Matthias Scanlon [1951] Managing Director

Sports Information Services Limited
Incorporated: 28 June 2001 *Employees:* 357
Previous: Satellite Information Services Limited
Net Worth: £77,600,000 *Total Assets:* £146,928,992
Registered Office: Unit 1-2 Whitehall Avenue, Kingston, Milton Keynes, Bucks, MK10 0AX
Activities: Television programming and broadcasting activities
Parent: Sports Information Services (Holdings) Limited
Officers: Richard Jonathan Ames [1970] Director; Nigel Stocks [1970] Director/Chief Financial Officer

Sportsdirect.Com Retail Limited
Incorporated: 21 July 1997 *Employees:* 14,780
Net Worth: £1,062,697,024 *Total Assets:* £2,566,496,000
Registered Office: Unit A, Brook Park East, Shirebrook, Derbys, NG20 8RY
Activities: Other retail sale of new goods in specialised stores (not commercial art galleries and opticians)
Parent: Sports Direct International PLC
Officers: Cameron John Olsen, Secretary; Karen Byers [1968] Director; Sean Matthew Nevitt [1970] Director/Buyer

Spraycon Limited
Incorporated: 2 June 1999 *Employees:* 114
Net Worth: £8,830,037 *Total Assets:* £9,182,106
Registered Office: 14 Park Row, Nottingham, NG1 6GR
Activities: Other business support service activities n.e.c.
Shareholders: Colin Griffith; Gillian Griffith
Officers: Martin Scott, Secretary; Colin Griffith [1954] Director/Contracts Manager; Gillian Griffith [1956] Director

Springfield Farm Limited
Incorporated: 13 March 1987 *Employees:* 14
Net Worth: £6,168,642 *Total Assets:* £10,782,044
Registered Office: The Estate Office, Wakefield Lodge Estate, Potterspury, Northants, NN12 7QX
Activities: Operation of gravel and sand pits; mining of clays and kaolin
Shareholders: Colin Woodrow Richmond-Watson; Stuart John Richmond-Watson
Officers: Stuart John Richmond Watson, Secretary; Daniel Thomas Richmond Watson [1977] Director; Stuart John Richmond Watson [1951] Director/Chartered Surveyor; Colin Woodrow Richmond-Watson [1951] Director; Julian Howard Richmond-Watson [1947] Director/Farmer

Springfield Park Properties Limited
Incorporated: 14 December 1993 *Employees:* 4
Net Worth: £9,545,201 *Total Assets:* £14,269,300
Registered Office: 3 Castlegate, Grantham, Lincs, NG31 6SF
Activities: Other letting and operating of own or leased real estate
Officers: Peter Sandham Townsend, Secretary/Chartered Accountant; Hugh Munro Bater Caseley [1960] Director/Chartered Surveyor; Geoffrey Ellwood Fearn [1937] Director/Farmer; David John Hindmarch [1965] Director; Peter Sandham Townsend [1948] Director/Chartered Accountant

SPS Aerostructures Limited
Incorporated: 9 September 1985 *Employees:* 643
Net Worth: £66,541,000 *Total Assets:* £108,337,000
Registered Office: Willow Drive, Sherwood Business Park, Annesley, Notts, NG15 0DP
Activities: Manufacture of metal structures and parts of structures
Parent: SPS Chevron Limited
Officers: Janet Freeman-Massey, Secretary; Anna Marie Armango [1981] Director [American]; Roger Paul Becker [1953] Director/Vice President-Taxes [American]; Ruth Ann Beyer [1955] Director/Senior VP, General Counsel and Assistant Secretary [American]; Shawn Hagel [1965] Director/Executive VP [American]; Inderjit Kumar Rattu [1967] Director; Joe Snowden [1956] Director/President [American]

SPS Technologies Limited
Incorporated: 9 August 1935 *Employees:* 582
Net Worth: £57,431,000 *Total Assets:* £103,205,000
Registered Office: 191 Barkby Road, Troon Industrial Area, Leicester, LE4 9HX
Activities: Manufacture of fasteners and screw machine products
Parent: Berkshire Hathaway Inc.
Officers: Paul Edelstyn, Secretary; Janet Freeman-Massey, Secretary; Jitesh Randeria, Secretary; Anna Marie Armagno [1981] Director [American]; Roger Paul Becker [1953] Director/VP Corporate Taxes [American]; Ruth Ann Beyer [1955] Director/Lawyer [American]; Shawn Hagel [1965] Director/Senior VP & Chief Financial Officer [American]; Jitesh Randeria [1972] Finance Director

Spurgeons
Incorporated: 11 May 2000 *Employees:* 75
Net Worth: £16,714,000 *Total Assets:* £17,722,000
Registered Office: 74 Wellingborough Road, Rushden, Northants, NN10 9TY
Activities: Child day-care activities
Officers: Alan Ross Hendry, Secretary; Simon Beresford [1982] Director/Charity Fundraiser; Andrew Howard Arthur Caplen [1958] Director/Solicitor; Natalie Therese Cronin [1967] Director - Fundraising; Sarah Elizabeth Powley [1973] Director/Accountant and Foster Carer; Safron Rose [1965] Director/Independent Consultant; Romaine Heather Thompson [1964] Director/Solicitor; Helen Jane Watson [1964] Director/Senior Manager

Squadron Medical Limited
Incorporated: 20 July 1995 *Employees:* 87
Net Worth: £7,165,000 *Total Assets:* £19,705,000
Registered Office: Unit A, Greaves Close, Markham Vale, Chesterfield, Derbys, S44 5TB
Activities: Retail sale of medical and orthopaedic goods in specialised stores (not incl. hearing aids) n.e.c.
Parent: Healthcare Acquisitions UK Limited
Officers: Leslie Deacon, Secretary; Conor Francis Costigan [1971] Director/Accountant [Irish]; Leslie Deacon [1963] Director/Chartered Accountant [Irish]; Harry Keenan [1959] Managing Director [Irish]; Redmond McEvoy [1964] Director [Irish]; Patrick Tracey [1958] Director [Irish]

SRC Transatlantic Limited
Incorporated: 16 April 2010 *Employees:* 256
Net Worth: £8,284,000 *Total Assets:* £22,400,000
Registered Office: First Floor, 30-34 Hounds Gate, Nottingham, NG1 7AB
Activities: Other credit granting n.e.c.
Officers: William Baker [1980] Director/Chief Operating Officer [American]; Julian Miles Graham-Rack [1967] Director/Chief Executive Officer; Duncan Peter Marrison [1981] Director/Chartered Accountant; Eugene Marvin Thomas IV [1976] Director/Chief Legal Officer [American]

SRS Rail System (Holdings) Limited
Incorporated: 18 April 1995 *Employees:* 101
Net Worth: £10,971,175 *Total Assets:* £13,155,518
Registered Office: Unit 3 Riverside Way, Gateway Business Park, Bolsover, Derbys, S44 6GA
Activities: Activities of head offices
Officers: John Denis Norie Rooke [1933] Director; Richard Mark Whatley [1968] Director; Simon John Whatley [1970] Director

SSCP Blink Bidco Limited
Incorporated: 19 April 2015 *Employees:* 31
Net Worth Deficit: £2,368,192 *Total Assets:* £10,881,720
Registered Office: Fernbank House, Springwood Way, Tytherington Business Park, Macclesfield, Cheshire, SK10 2XA
Activities: Wholesale of pharmaceutical goods
Officers: Ian Martin Snelson, Secretary; Roland Bruhin [1964] Director/Chief Executive [Swiss]; Ian Martin Snelson [1967] Director/Chartered Accountant

St Andrew's Healthcare
Incorporated: 12 July 2004 *Employees:* 4,203
Net Worth: £235,200,000 *Total Assets:* £293,900,000
Registered Office: St Andrew's Healthcare, Cliftonville Road, Northampton, NN1 5DG
Activities: Residential care activities for learning difficulties, mental health and substance abuse
Officers: Claire Carless, Secretary; Martin Francis Stafford Beer [1962] Director; Katie Fisher [1974] Director/Chief Executive; Jane Maude Foreman Hardy [1951] Director; Dr Michael Jeffrey Harris [1948] Clinical Non-Executive Director; Frances Miriam Jackson [1952] Director; Sanjith Kamath [1976] Director; Martin Kersey [1961] Director; Paul Thomas Serge Parsons [1955] Director/Farmer & Volunteer (Retired Solicitor); Stuart John Richmond Watson [1951] Director/Chartered Surveyor; Peter Anthony Winslow [1953] Director

St Andrew's Hospice Limited
Incorporated: 30 April 1992 *Employees:* 210
Net Worth: £10,490,796 *Total Assets:* £11,055,795
Registered Office: St Andrews Hospice, Peaks Lane, Grimsby, N E Lincs, DN32 9RP
Activities: Other human health activities
Officers: Stephen Alexander Oldridge, Secretary; Ian Jeffrey Hargreaves [1966] Director; David Raymond Hatfield [1945] Director/Chartered Accountant; Geoffrey Enoch Hirst [1939] Director/HR Adviser; Leslie Jones [1944] Director/Business Consultant; Andrew Kenneth North [1958] Director/Management Consultant; Stephen Alexander Oldridge [1975] Director/Solicitor; Steven Terence Parker [1966] Director/Businessman; John Scaife [1952] Director; Dr Anne Elizabeth Spalding [1961] Director/Doctor; Nigel Tranter [1959] Director/Retired

St Barnabas Hospice Trust (Lincolnshire)
Incorporated: 29 February 1996 *Employees:* 266
Net Worth: £18,058,240 *Total Assets:* £19,447,540
Registered Office: 36 Nettleham Road, Lincoln, LN2 1RE
Activities: Hospital activities
Officers: Anthony John Martin Maltby, Secretary; Paul John Banton [1970] Managing Director; Dr David Andrew Renwick Boldy [1954] Director/Doctor; Alan Graham Henderson [1949] Director/Retired; Charles Phillip Hoskins [1954] Director/Solicitor; Sylvia Knight [1969] Deputy Director of Nursing; Amanda Jane Legate [1978] Finance and Operations Director; David Libiszewski [1950] Director/Semi-Retired; Anthony John Martin Maltby [1953] Director/Retired; Robert Frederick Neilans [1942] Director/Retired; Karen Jane Rossdale [1958] Director/Retired

St George's Academy Trust
Incorporated: 26 November 2009 *Employees:* 314
Net Worth: £29,456,048 *Total Assets:* £31,681,502
Registered Office: St George's Academy, Westholme, Westgate, Sleaford, Lincs, NG34 7PS
Activities: General secondary education
Officers: Graham Leslie Arnold [1949] Retired Director; Wayne Russell William Birks [1959] Director/Principal; Roger William Burrell [1947] Director; Professor Harriet Gross [1954] Director/University Professor; Andrew Gibson Hagues [1951] Director; Jennifer Ann Harman [1957] Director/Teacher; Sue Harvey [1955] Director/Support Adviser; Brenda Hitchcock [1952] Director/Administrator; Revd Canon Christine Pennock [1948] Director/Clerk in Holy Orders

St Ivo School
Incorporated: 13 July 2011 *Employees:* 258
Net Worth: £14,854,199 *Total Assets:* £16,058,093
Registered Office: St Ivo School, High Leys, St Ives, Cambs, PE27 6RR
Activities: General secondary education
Officers: Emillie Louise Newell, Secretary; Judith Margaret Barnes [1947] Director/Retired; Daniel Gary Charles Coulson [1978] Director/Site Manager; Carol Anne Darnell [1965] Director/HR Consultant; Charles Walter Glanville [1959] Director/Medical Facilities; Samuel Barnaby Griffin [1972] Director/Headteacher; Claire Anne Lynn [1966] Director/Public Relations; Dr Martin Andrew McMahon [1969] Director/Senior Manager; Mark Ronald Newstead [1971] Executive Group Director - Property Services; Francis Craig Newton [1942] Director/Retired; Richard Carl Potter [1972] Director/Assistant Headteacher; Jonathan Anthony Read [1970] Director/Scientist; Adrian Mark Smith [1971] Director/Media; Philip Richard Speer [1952] Director/Solicitor; Anthony Ward [1985] Director/ICT Manager; Elaine Ruth Warriner [1975] Director/Teacher; Duncan Sidney Woodall [1953] Director/Retired

The St Lawrence Academy, Scunthorpe
Incorporated: 5 February 2008 *Employees:* 86
Net Worth: £22,308,496 *Total Assets:* £22,990,918
Registered Office: The Diocesan Education Centre, Edward King House, Minster Yard, Lincoln, LN2 1PU
Activities: General secondary education
Officers: Michael Iain Adnitt [1970] Director/Principal; Nasir Ahmed [1982] Director/Staff Training; Reverend Philip Brent [1968] Director/Vicar; Bishop David Eric Court [1958] Director/Bishop; David Anthony Esmond [1951] Director/Teacher; Lisa Gosling [1969] Director/Analyst; Simon Hardy [1953] Director/Retired; Ryan James Oates [1982] Director/Teacher; Leon Patrick Riley [1971] Director/Principal; Jenny Vincent [1976] Director/Careers Adviser

St Matthews Holdings Limited
Incorporated: 21 July 2011 *Employees:* 529
Net Worth: £10,288,516 *Total Assets:* £32,059,432
Registered Office: Peterbridge House, 3 The Lakes, Northampton, NN4 7HB
Activities: Activities of other holding companies n.e.c.
Shareholders: Kanwaljit Kaur Sandhu; Nisharn Singh Sidhu Brar
Officers: Amrit Sidhu Brar, Secretary; Kanwaljit Kaur Sandhu [1963] Director/Manager; Nisharn Singh Sidhu Brar [1957] Director/Barrister

The St Neots Learning Partnership
Incorporated: 13 July 2011 *Employees:* 396
Net Worth: £22,958,350 *Total Assets:* £26,849,380
Registered Office: Longsands Road, St Neots, Cambs, PE19 1LQ
Activities: General secondary education
Officers: Helen Bryson [1968] Director/Head Strategy Business Intelligence; Rev Thomas Roger Henthorne [1930] Director/Retired; Robert Alexander Law [1952] Director/Retired; Julie Ann Smith [1966] Director/Accountant; Karl David Wainwright [1964] Director/Business Development Manager; Graham Arthur Wright [1943] Director/Retired

St Therese of Lisieux Catholic Multi Academy Trust
Incorporated: 2 March 2012 *Employees:* 343
Previous: St Therese of Lisieux Catholic Multi Academy Trust Limited
Net Worth: £17,393,238 *Total Assets:* £20,240,432
Registered Office: Suite 4, The Lawn, Union Road, Lincoln, LN1 3BU
Activities: Other education n.e.c.
Officers: Tamer Elizabeth Hodgson, Secretary; Reverend Stephen Francis Durkin [1957] Director/Charity Retail Development and Property Manager; Simon Paul Gillespie [1975] Director/Roman Catholic Priest; Graham Green [1957] Retired Financial Director; Linda Generaldine Heaver [1952] Director/Retired Headteacher; Jerzy Kazimerz Michal Krawiec [1950] Director/Retired; David Lisle [1947] Director; John Arthur McGarel [1945] Director/Retired Headteacher; Anthony Kenneth Norton [1950] Director/Retired Headteacher

St. Ann's Hospice
Incorporated: 3 February 1969 *Employees:* 313
Net Worth: £14,579,157 *Total Assets:* £20,954,576
Registered Office: St Ann's Road North, Heald Green, Cheadle, Cheshire, SK8 3SZ
Activities: Hospital activities
Officers: Dr Paul Jarvis, Secretary; Alan John Bond [1943] Director/Accountant; Christopher Michael Brown [1946] Director/Management Consultant; Luke Dillon [1955] Director/Educational Consultant; Dr Stephanie Gomm [1950] Director/Retired Medical Doctor; Professor Jacqueline Oldham [1961] Director/Professor; Kate Squire [1962] Director/BBC Manager; Fiona Taylor [1964] Director/Chief Executive, NHS; Steve Wilson [1973] Director/Executive Lead

St. Clare's, Oxford.
Incorporated: 6 February 1986 *Employees:* 235
Net Worth: £36,340,000 *Total Assets:* £44,519,000
Registered Office: 139 Banbury Road, Oxford, OX2 7AL
Activities: General secondary education
Officers: Nicholas Paladina, Secretary; Ian Alexander Ashcroft [1968] Director; Bartholomew David Ashton [1969] Director/Bursar; John Edwin Church [1953] Director/Bursar; Mary Louise Dagenhart Culpepper [1967] Director/Housewife [American]; Moira Ellen Darlington [1952] Director/School Administrator; Charles Richard Dick [1950] Director; Dr Yao Su Hu [1946] Director/Academic; Ann Walford Lewis [1940] Director/Retired Civil Servant; Peter Morris Oppenheimer [1938] Director/Economist; Gordon Thomas Rankin [1954] Director/Marketing Consultant; Jens Jorgen Tholstrup [1955] Director/Business Analyst [Danish]

St. Luke's Hospice
Incorporated: 15 November 1967 *Employees:* 242
Net Worth: £8,233,025 *Total Assets:* £11,921,917
Registered Office: Little Common Lane, off Abbey Lane, Sheffield, S11 9NE
Activities: Other human health activities
Officers: Peter Conway Hartland, Secretary; Petra Billing [1969] Director/Solicitor; Professor Robert Edward Coleman [1955] Director/Consultant Medical Oncologist; Laurence Michael Gavin [1967] Director/Solicitor; Professor Diana Margaret Greenfield [1966] Director/Consultant Nurse; Susan Inglis [1952] Director/Retired; Neil Andrew MacDonald [1956] Director; Dr Toni Schwarz [1962] Director/Academic; Andrew Edward Snelling [1963] Director of Finance; Professor Sarah Elizabeth Thomas [1951] Director/Retired Doctor of Medicine

St. Matthews (North) Limited
Incorporated: 24 July 2009 *Employees:* 142
Net Worth: £491,780 *Total Assets:* £12,133,919
Registered Office: Peterbridge House, The Lakes, Northampton, NN4 7HB
Activities: Other human health activities
Parent: St Matthews (Holdings) Limited
Officers: Kanwaljit Kaur Sandhu [1963] Director/Manager; Nisharn Singh Sidhu Brar [1957] Director/Barrister

St. Matthews Limited
Incorporated: 6 December 2002 *Employees:* 311
Net Worth: £6,652,854 *Total Assets:* £14,593,752
Registered Office: 29-31 St Matthews Parade, Northampton, NN2 7HF
Activities: Other human health activities
Parent: St Matthews Holdings Limited
Officers: Kanwaljit Kaur Sandhu, Secretary/Manager; Kanwaljit Kaur Sandhu [1963] Director/Manager; Nisharn Singh Sidhu Brar [1957] Director/Barrister

St. Paul's Developments PLC
Incorporated: 7 March 1985 *Employees:* 4
Net Worth: £8,591,680 *Total Assets:* £14,622,797
Registered Office: 6a Hall Annex, Thorncliffe Park Estate, Newton Chambers Road, Chapeltown, Sheffield, S35 2PH
Activities: Development of building projects
Parent: SPD Holdings Ltd
Officers: Antony Frederick Greasley, Secretary/Accountant; Antony Frederick Greasley [1959] Director/Accountant; Keith Michael Mellors [1955] Director; John David Newton [1963] Director/Chartered Surveyor; Brian Geoffrey Waldron [1939] Director

St.Edward's School
Incorporated: 12 July 1911 *Employees:* 452
Net Worth: £78,047,000 *Total Assets:* £119,905,000
Registered Office: St Edwards School, Woodstock Road, Oxford, OX2 7NN
Activities: General secondary education
Officers: Stephen Withers Green, Secretary; Caroline Mary Baggs [1956] Director/Human Resources Business Partner; Georgina Arabella Sarah Dennis [1970] Director/Easel Paintings Conservator; Dr Louise L'estrange Fawcett Posada [1955] Director/University Lecturer; George Richard Ian Howe [1949] Director/Composer; David John Jackson [1953] Director/Company Secretary; Christopher Ian Montague Jones [1955] Director; Kenneth Macmillan Macritchie [1956] Director/Solicitor; The Very Reverend Martyn William Percy [1962] Director/Priest; Dr Clare Robertson [1960] Director/Doctor; Michael William Roulston [1956] Director/Headmaster; Michael Paul Stanfield [1942] Director; Edward Wilfrid Stephenson [1957] Director/Bursar

Stadco Holdings Ltd.
Incorporated: 14 May 2001
Net Worth: £18,733,000 *Total Assets:* £33,450,000
Registered Office: International House, Siskin Parkway East, Middlemarch Business Park, Coventry, Warwicks, CV3 4PE
Activities: Activities of head offices
Parent: Acertec Engineering Limited
Officers: Mark John Smith, Secretary; Christopher Paul Fisher [1962] Director; Mark John Smith [1968] Director

Stadco Limited
Incorporated: 31 July 1874 *Employees:* 838
Net Worth: £86,343,000 *Total Assets:* £208,258,000
Registered Office: International House, Siskin Parkway East, Middlemarch Business Park, Coventry, Warwicks, CV3 4PE
Activities: Manufacture of bodies (coachwork) for motor vehicles (except caravans)
Parent: Stadco Holdings Ltd
Officers: Matthew Richard Hawkin, Secretary; Christopher Paul Fisher [1962] Director; Matthew Richard Hawkin [1972] Director; Mark John Smith [1968] Director

Stadium MK Group Limited
Incorporated: 29 June 2007 *Employees:* 629
Previous: Inter MK Group Limited
Net Worth: £78,208,960 *Total Assets:* £113,836,768
Registered Office: Stadium MK, Stadium Way, Milton Keynes, Bucks, MK1 1ST
Activities: Activities of head offices
Major Shareholder: Peter John Winkelman
Officers: Anthony Neil Richens, Secretary; Mark Turner [1968] Director; Peter John Winkelman [1957] Director; Bernadette Winkleman [1958] Director

Staffline Group PLC
Incorporated: 25 October 2004 *Employees:* 2,357
Net Worth: £95,800,000 *Total Assets:* £263,500,000
Registered Office: 19-20 The Triangle, NG2 Business Park, Nottingham, NG2 1AE
Activities: Other business support service activities n.e.c.
Officers: Paul Simon Collins, Secretary; Edward Barker [1972] Director; John Rawcliffe Avery Crabtree [1949] Director; Tracy Lewis [1965] Director; Christopher Mark Pullen [1970] Director/Chief Financial Officer; Dawn Patricia Ward [1961] Director/Chief Executive, Burton & South Derbyshire College; Michael Robert Watts [1974] Director/Chief Financial Officer

Staffline Holdings Limited
Incorporated: 9 May 2014
Net Worth: £744,110 *Total Assets:* £65,210,100
Registered Office: 19-20 The Triangle, NG2 Business Park, Nottingham, NG2 1AE
Activities: Temporary employment agency activities
Parent: Staffline Group PLC
Officers: Paul Simon Collins, Secretary; Christopher Mark Pullen [1970] Director/Chief Executive Officer; Michael Robert Watts [1974] Director/Chief Financial Officer

Staffline Recruitment Limited
Incorporated: 18 May 2000 *Employees:* 852
Net Worth: £14,397,000 *Total Assets:* £168,884,992
Registered Office: 19-20 The Triangle, NG2 Business Park, Nottingham, NG2 1AE
Activities: Temporary employment agency activities
Parent: Staffline Group PLC
Officers: Paul Simon Collins, Secretary; John Rawcliffe Avery Crabtree [1949] Director; Mark Keegan [1979] Finance Director; Christopher Mark Pullen [1970] Director/Chief Executive Officer; Mark William Underwood [1977] Managing Director; Michael Robert Watts [1974] Director/Chief Financial Officer

Stagecoach (North West) Limited
Incorporated: 8 August 1912 *Employees:* 729
Net Worth: £8,943,000 *Total Assets:* £21,601,000
Registered Office: c/o Stagecoach Services Limited, One Stockport Exchange, 20 Railway Road, Stockport, Cheshire, SK1 3SW
Activities: Other urban, suburban or metropolitan passenger land transport (not underground, metro or similar)
Parent: Stagecoach Bus Holdings Limited
Officers: Michael John Vaux, Secretary; Colin Brown [1968] Director/Accountant; Arnold Mark Threapleton [1954] Managing Director; Mark Thomas Whitelocks [1982] Managing Director

Stagecoach (South) Limited
Incorporated: 22 October 1982 *Employees:* 1,250
Net Worth: £25,417,000 *Total Assets:* £45,054,000
Registered Office: c/o Stagecoach Services Limited, One Stockport Exchange, 20 Railway Road, Stockport, Cheshire, SK1 3SW
Activities: Other urban, suburban or metropolitan passenger land transport (not underground, metro or similar)
Parent: Stagecoach Bus Holdings Limited
Officers: Michael John Vaux, Secretary; Colin Brown [1968] Director/Accountant; Edward Leonard Hodgson [1970] Managing Director; Arnold Mark Threapleton [1954] Managing Director

Stagecoach Devon Limited
Incorporated: 21 December 1995 *Employees:* 1,248
Net Worth: £19,704,000 *Total Assets:* £41,835,000
Registered Office: c/o Stagecoach Services Limited, One Stockport Exchange, 20 Railway Road, Stockport, Cheshire, SK1 3SW
Activities: Other urban, suburban or metropolitan passenger land transport (not underground, metro or similar)
Parent: Stagecoach Bus Holdings Limited
Officers: Michael John Vaux, Secretary; Colin Brown [1968] Director/Accountant; Robert Dennison [1976] Managing Director [New Zealander]; Arnold Mark Threapleton [1954] Managing Director

Stagecoach Services Limited
Incorporated: 9 May 1989 *Employees:* 257
Net Worth Deficit: £6,034,000 *Total Assets:* £106,608,000
Registered Office: c/o Stagecoach Services Limited, One Stockport Exchange, 20 Railway Road, Stockport, Cheshire, SK1 3SW
Activities: Other transportation support activities
Parent: Stagecoach Bus Holdings Limited
Officers: Michael John Vaux, Secretary; Robert Gervase Andrew [1963] Director; Lesley Ashman [1961] Director; Colin Brown [1968] Director/Accountant; Mark Stuart Edwin Haberfield [1963] Managing Director; Ross John Paterson [1971] Director/Accountant; Arnold Mark Threapleton [1954] Managing Director

Stagecoach South Western Trains Limited
Incorporated: 21 October 2005 *Employees:* 4,887
Net Worth: £55,094,000 *Total Assets:* £97,544,000
Registered Office: 20 Railway Road, One Stockport Exchange, Stockport, Cheshire, SK1 3SW
Activities: Passenger rail transport, interurban
Parent: Stagecoach Rail Holdings Limited
Officers: Michael John Vaux, Secretary; Martin Andrew Griffiths [1966] Finance Director; Ross John Paterson [1971] Director/Accountant; Timothy Colin Shoveller [1972] Railway Director; Andrew Charles West [1956] Director/Accountant

Stagecoach Supertram Maintenance Ltd.
Incorporated: 30 June 1986 *Employees:* 85
Net Worth: £14,000 *Total Assets:* £9,952,000
Registered Office: c/o Stagecoach Services Limited, One Stockport Exchange, 20 Railway Road, Stockport, Cheshire, SK1 3SW
Activities: Repair and maintenance of other transport equipment n.e.c.
Parent: South Yorkshire Supertram Limited
Officers: Michael John Vaux, Secretary; Timothy David Bilby [1972] Director/Accountant; Martin Andrew Griffiths [1966] Finance Director; James Norton Stewart [1974] Director; Michael John Vaux [1971] Director/Solicitor; Nigel Wragg [1967] Director

Stainless Metalcraft (Chatteris) Limited
Incorporated: 29 May 1990 *Employees:* 158
Net Worth: £6,482,008 *Total Assets:* £17,824,544
Registered Office: Chatteris Engineering Works, 15 Honeysome Road, Chatteris, Cambs, PE16 6SA
Activities: Manufacture of metal structures and parts of structures
Parent: Avingtrans PLC
Officers: Christopher Lewis-Jones, Secretary; Austen Mark Adams [1965] Managing Director; Martin Robert Johnson [1969] Business Conformance Director; Stephen Michael King [1966] Director/Accountant; Martin Derrick Lawrence [1970] Customer Development Director

Staircraft Group Limited
Incorporated: 2 October 1995 *Employees:* 264
Previous: Staircraft (Midlands) Ltd
Net Worth: £5,745,597 *Total Assets:* £23,431,634
Registered Office: Dunns Close, Nuneaton, Warwicks, CV11 4NF
Activities: Manufacture of other builders' carpentry and joinery
Parent: P H Properties Limited
Officers: Andrew Melville Hamilton, Secretary; Francis Mark Elkins [1967] Director; Andrew Melville Hamilton [1965] Director; Dean Lucas [1968] Production Director

Stamford Group Limited (The)
Incorporated: 29 June 1982 *Employees:* 175
Net Worth: £7,769,000 *Total Assets:* £9,308,000
Registered Office: Stamford Works, Bayley Street, Stalybridge, Cheshire, SK15 1QQ
Activities: Activities of head offices
Parent: Navagator Ltd
Officers: Stephen Keith Picot, Secretary; Stephen Dubyl [1959] Director; Katie Jane Ferris [1971] Director/Teacher; Stephen Keith Picot [1950] Director/Chartered Accountant; Alan Reay [1938] Director

Stamford Property Company Limited
Incorporated: 25 January 1995 *Employees:* 7
Net Worth: £14,658,842 *Total Assets:* £16,482,476
Registered Office: 14 All Saints Street, Stamford, Lincs, PE9 2PA
Activities: Development of building projects
Shareholders: Simon Mark Caunt; Janet Mary Hindmarch; David John Hindmarch; Castlegate Trustees Limited
Officers: Kevin Glyn Williams, Secretary; Hugh Munro Bater Caseley [1960] Director/Chartered Surveyor; Simon Mark Caunt [1964] Director; Geoffrey Ellwood Fearn [1937] Director/Farmer; Peter Gaskell [1943] Director/Civil Engineer; David John Hindmarch [1965] Director; Mark Thomas Hindmarch [1963] Director/Accountant

Stampede Acquisition Limited
Incorporated: 29 December 2005 *Employees:* 1
Net Worth: £37,749,000 *Total Assets:* £81,993,000
Registered Office: 19 Jessops Riverside, 800 Brightside Lane, Sheffield, S9 2RX
Activities: Non-trading company
Parent: Danaher Corporation
Officers: Keith Graham Ward [1953] Director/Accountant

Standard Motor Products Europe Limited
Incorporated: 10 June 1969 *Employees:* 174
Net Worth: £10,555,981 *Total Assets:* £18,679,072
Registered Office: Unit 5b Little Oak Drive, Sherwood Park, Annesley, Notts, NG15 0DR
Activities: Manufacture of other parts and accessories for motor vehicles
Parent: Standard Motor Products Holdings Limited
Officers: Simon Thomas Hall [1964] Operations Director; Keith Hudson [1982] Finance Director; Ross Lloyd Toomey [1982] Director; Ian Leslie Turner [1955] Group Managing Director

Stanhope Partnership Limited
Incorporated: 8 November 2005
Net Worth: £23,643,376 *Total Assets:* £24,581,840
Registered Office: Victoria Mill, London Road, Wellingborough, Northants, NN8 2DT
Activities: Other professional, scientific and technical activities n.e.c.
Major Shareholder: Michael David George
Officers: Simone Louise Large, Secretary; Alison Mary Rachael George [1975] Director; Martin Francis George [1942] Director; Michael David George [1973] Director/Venture Capitalist

Stanley Black & Decker Finance Limited
Incorporated: 29 March 2016
Net Worth: £54,236,536 *Total Assets:* £54,236,536
Registered Office: 3 Europa Court, Sheffield Business Park, Sheffield, S9 1XE
Activities: Other professional, scientific and technical activities n.e.c.
Parent: Black & Decker Finance
Officers: Steven John Costello [1980] Director/Chartered Accountant; Mark Richard Smiley [1977] Director/General Manager UK & ROI; Amit Kumar Sood [1978] Director/Accountant

Stanley U.K. Holding Ltd.
Incorporated: 20 October 1997
Net Worth: £922,000 *Total Assets:* £541,169,984
Registered Office: 3 Europa Court, Sheffield Business Park, Europa Link, Sheffield, S9 1XE
Activities: Activities of head offices
Officers: Steven John Costello, Secretary; Steven John Costello [1980] Director/Chartered Accountant; Mark Richard Smiley [1977] Director/General Manager UK & ROI; Amit Kumar Sood [1978] Director/Accountant

Stanley UK Services Limited
Incorporated: 16 December 1999 *Employees:* 49
Net Worth Deficit: £8,361,000 *Total Assets:* £49,019,000
Registered Office: 3 Europa Court, Sheffield Business Park, Europa Link, Sheffield, S9 1XE
Activities: Other business support service activities n.e.c.
Parent: Stanley U.K. Holding Ltd.
Officers: Steven John Costello, Secretary; Erica Lynn Brennan [1974] Director/Chief Financial Officer [Canadian]; Mark Richard Smiley [1977] Director/General Manager UK & ROI

Stanley Works Limited (The)
Incorporated: 27 September 1920 *Employees:* 145
Net Worth Deficit: £9,605,000 *Total Assets:* £72,325,000
Registered Office: 3 Europa Court, Sheffield Business Park, Europa Link, Sheffield, S9 1XE
Activities: Manufacture of tools
Parent: Stanley UK Services Limited
Officers: Steven John Costello, Secretary; Erica Lynn Brennan [1974] Director/Chief Financial Officer [Canadian]; Mark Richard Smiley [1977] Director/General Manager UK & ROI

Stanton Bonna Concrete Limited
Incorporated: 1 June 1988 *Employees:* 168
Net Worth: £2,002,000 *Total Assets:* £21,693,000
Registered Office: Littlewell Lane, Stanton by Dale, Ilkeston, Derbys, DE7 4QW
Activities: Manufacture of concrete products for construction purposes
Parent: Consolis SAS
Officers: Amanda Louise Barlow, Secretary; Benoit Jean Rene Cattin-Martel [1968] Director [French]; Colin Charles Richardson [1963] Director; Nicolas Yatzimirsky [1966] Director [French]

Stanton Investments Limited
Incorporated: 5 August 1996
Net Worth: £15,185,959 *Total Assets:* £22,321,092
Registered Office: Towerfield, 66 Derngate, Northampton, NN1 1UH
Activities: Other letting and operating of own or leased real estate
Shareholders: Graham John Longden Stanton; Michael Philip Stanton
Officers: Michael Philip Stanton, Secretary/Chartered Accountant; Elaine Elizabeth Stanton [1953] Director/Secretary; Graham John Longden Stanton [1957] Director/Chartered Surveyor; Michael Philip Stanton [1953] Director/Chartered Accountant

Staples (Vegetables) Limited
Incorporated: 19 February 1952 *Employees:* 1,109
Net Worth: £10,187,764 *Total Assets:* £38,513,044
Registered Office: Station Farm, Station Road, Sibsey, Boston, Lincs, PE22 0SE
Activities: Other processing and preserving of fruit and vegetables
Officers: Vernon Edward Read, Secretary; George Read [1970] Director/Vegetable Merchant and Haulier; Janet Read [1945] Director; Vernon Edward Read [1968] Director/Farm Manager

Staples Brothers Limited
Incorporated: 16 July 1956 *Employees:* 2
Net Worth: £27,432,988 *Total Assets:* £47,718,688
Registered Office: Station Farm, Sibsey, Boston, Lincs, PE22 0SE
Activities: Growing of vegetables and melons, roots and tubers
Officers: George Read, Secretary; George Read [1970] Director/Farm Manager; Vernon Edward Read [1968] Director/Farm Manager

Star Bidco Limited
Incorporated: 17 July 2015 *Employees:* 25
Net Worth Deficit: £5,172,488 *Total Assets:* £27,972,588
Registered Office: 2nd Floor, Sir Wilfrid Newton House, Thorncliffe Park, Chapeltown, Sheffield, S35 2PH
Activities: Temporary employment agency activities
Parent: Star Midco 2 Limited
Officers: William John Etchell [1971] Director/Chief Financial Officer; Julian Edward Harley [1957] Director; Robyn Julieann Johnstone [1967] Director [British/Australian]; Robert Douglas King [1982] Director/Fund Manager

Star Mayan Limited
Incorporated: 11 June 2016 *Employees:* 806
Net Worth Deficit: £2,357,000 *Total Assets:* £52,524,000
Registered Office: Synergy LMS, Ascot Drive, Derby, DE24 8HE
Activities: Other human health activities
Officers: Laura Carballo Beautell [1976] Director/Manager [Spanish]; Sam Austin Benjamin Fletcher [1979] Director/Private Equity/Investment Professional; Paul Gough [1972] Director [New Zealander]; Andrew Darren Holdcroft [1970] Finance Director; Michael John Langhorn [1958] Director/Manager; Ian Theodore McNuff [1957] Director

Star Midco 1 Limited
Incorporated: 17 July 2015 *Employees:* 2
Net Worth Deficit: £1,652,351 *Total Assets:* £25,648,046
Registered Office: 2nd Floor, Sir Wilfrid Newton House, Thorncliffe Park, Chapeltown, Sheffield, S35 2PH
Activities: Temporary employment agency activities
Parent: Education Placement Group Limited
Officers: William John Etchell [1971] Director/Chief Financial Officer; Julian Edward Harley [1957] Director; Robyn Julieann Johnstone [1967] Director [British/Australian]; Robert Douglas King [1982] Director/Fund Manager

Starkey Laboratories Limited
Incorporated: 28 February 1992 *Employees:* 198
Net Worth: £9,900,508 *Total Assets:* £15,446,542
Registered Office: The Pinnacle, 170 Midsummer Boulevard, Milton Keynes, Bucks, MK9 1FE
Activities: Manufacture of medical and dental instruments and supplies
Major Shareholder: William Franklin Austin
Officers: Thomas Ting, Secretary; William Austin [1942] Director/President, Starkey Laboratories [American]; Roger Nigel Kent Lewin [1963] Director; Brandon L Sawalich [1975] Director/Senior Vice President, Starkey Laboratories Ltd [American]

Static Control Components (Europe) Limited
Incorporated: 30 September 1993 *Employees:* 109
Net Worth: £4,579,000 *Total Assets:* £15,291,000
Registered Office: Ashbrook House, Westbrook Street, Blewbury, Didcot, Oxon, OX11 9QA
Activities: Wholesale of other intermediate products
Parent: Static Control Components Limited
Officers: Simon Anthony Barrett, Secretary; William London [1957] Director/Attorney [American]

Staton Young (Anglesey) Limited
Incorporated: 16 May 2014
Net Worth: £2,740,285 *Total Assets:* £9,124,867
Registered Office: Derwent Business Centre, Clarke Street, Derby, DE1 2BU
Activities: Buying and selling of own real estate
Parent: Staton Young Holdings Limited
Officers: Marc Lee Brough [1984] Director; Rebecca Louise Brough [1983] Director

Stauff UK Limited
Incorporated: 26 April 1990 *Employees:* 197
Net Worth: £4,754,352 *Total Assets:* £17,187,892
Registered Office: 500 Carlisle Street East, Sheffield, S4 8BS
Activities: Non-specialised wholesale trade
Shareholders: Lutz Menshen; Dorle Tolle
Officers: Nicholas Deeks, Secretary; John Philip Morris [1965] Managing Director

Steel City Holdings Limited
Incorporated: 19 January 2016 *Employees:* 111
Net Worth: £17,969,592 *Total Assets:* £19,803,092
Registered Office: 1 Waterside Court, 3 Bold Street, Attercliffe, Sheffield, S9 2LR
Activities: Activities of other holding companies n.e.c.
Parent: City Taxis Holdings Limited
Officers: Arun Thomas Singh [1980] Director; Christopher Francis Turner [1953] Director/Self Employed

Steel City Schools Partnership
Incorporated: 11 January 2013 *Employees:* 227
Net Worth: £9,655,909 *Total Assets:* £14,578,163
Registered Office: Monteney Primary School, Monteney Crescent, Sheffield, S5 9DN
Activities: Primary education
Officers: Anita Dell [1979] Director/Communications Officer; Paul Martin Doherty [1954] Director/Retired; James Nicholas Glover [1969] Director/Solicitor; Sarah Ann Greenwood [1978] Director; Nicola Anne Shipman [1968] Director; Trevor Summerson [1951] Director/Retired

Steeple Bidco Limited
Incorporated: 25 November 2016
Net Worth Deficit: £6,068,000 *Total Assets:* £59,676,000
Registered Office: Brunel Business Park, Jessop Close, Newark, Notts, NG24 2AG
Activities: Other telecommunications activities
Parent: Steeple Holdco Limited
Officers: Simon John Hitchcock [1974] Director/Partner; Neil Keith Muller [1971] Director; Geoffrey Leslie Neville [1959] Director; Timothy Piers Radford [1960] Director

Steeple Group Limited
Incorporated: 4 February 2013 *Employees:* 106
Net Worth: £29,834,000 *Total Assets:* £35,401,000
Registered Office: Eterna Lighting, Huxley Close, Park Farm South, Wellingborough, Northants, NN8 6AB
Activities: Wholesale of furniture, carpets and lighting equipment
Major Shareholder: Arnold Geoffrey Denman
Officers: Andrew Freeman, Secretary; Susan Elizabeth Blatchford [1968] Director; Arnold Geoffrey Denman [1936] Director; Dorothy May Denman [1936] Director; Michael Dennis Denman [1970] Director; Andrew Jameson Freeman [1962] Finance Director; Martin John Stone [1963] Managing Director

Steeple Holdco Limited
Incorporated: 27 January 2017
Total Assets: £43,675,000
Registered Office: Brunel Business Park, Jessop Close, Newark, Notts, NG24 2AG
Activities: Other telecommunications activities
Parent: Steeple Midco Limited
Officers: Simon John Hitchcock [1974] Director/Partner; Neil Keith Muller [1971] Director; Geoffrey Leslie Neville [1959] Director

Steeple Midco Limited
Incorporated: 27 January 2017
Total Assets: £43,675,000
Registered Office: Brunel Business Park, Jessop Close, Newark, Notts, NG24 2AG
Activities: Other telecommunications activities
Parent: Steeple Topco Limited
Officers: Simon John Hitchcock [1974] Director/Partner; Neil Keith Muller [1971] Director; Geoffrey Leslie Neville [1959] Director

Steeple Topco Limited
Incorporated: 27 January 2017 *Employees:* 302
Net Worth Deficit: £10,506,000 *Total Assets:* £67,931,000
Registered Office: Brunel Business Park, Jessop Close, Newark, Notts, NG24 2AG
Activities: Other telecommunications activities
Parent: Lyceum Capital (GP3) Limited
Officers: Joe Edwards [1957] Director; Simon John Hitchcock [1974] Director/Partner; Neil Keith Muller [1971] Director; Geoff Neville [1959] Director/Partner; Timothy Piers Radford [1960] Director

Steetley Dolomite Limited
Incorporated: 14 September 2000 *Employees:* 58
Net Worth: £23,051,000 *Total Assets:* £30,918,000
Registered Office: Southfield Lane, Whitwell, Worksop, Notts, S80 3LJ
Activities: Manufacture of refractory products
Parent: CLEB Holdings Limited
Officers: Dirk Donck, Secretary; Axel Vincent Ampolini [1970] Vice President and Managing Director [American]; Cedric Joannes Rosa Georges de Vicq de Cumptich [1980] Director/Employee/Executive [Belgian]; Dirk Donck [1956] Director/General Counsel Europe [Belgian]

Stepan UK Limited
Incorporated: 17 October 1996 *Employees:* 116
Net Worth: £26,791,000 *Total Assets:* £51,685,000
Registered Office: Bridge House, Bridge Street, Stalybridge, Cheshire, SK15 1PH
Activities: Manufacture of soap and detergents
Parent: Stepan Europe S.A
Officers: Stephen David Smales, Secretary; Wojciech Mazurek [1966] Director [Polish]; Didier Ray [1962] Commercial Director [French]; Stephen Smales [1974] Director/Accountant

John A. Stephens Holdings Limited
Incorporated: 12 September 1984 *Employees:* 125
Net Worth: £16,514,948 *Total Assets:* £19,476,816
Registered Office: Castle Meadow Road, Nottingham, NG2 1AG
Activities: Agents involved in the sale of timber and building materials
Major Shareholder: Peter John Stephens
Officers: Alyce Stephens, Secretary; Jeremy Daniel [1960] Director/Builders Merchant; Paul Anthony Johns [1951] Director/Builders Merchant; Peter John Stephens [1942] Director/Builders Merchant

John A. Stephens Limited
Incorporated: 29 December 1966 *Employees:* 113
Net Worth: £13,422,796 *Total Assets:* £15,711,331
Registered Office: Castle Meadow Road, Nottingham, NG2 1AG
Activities: Agents involved in the sale of timber and building materials
Parent: John A Stephens Holdings Ltd
Officers: Susan Patricia Westwood, Secretary; Jeremy Daniel [1960] Director/Builders Merchant; Paul Anthony Johns [1951] Director/Builders Merchant; Stephen Paul Long [1962] Director/Builders Merchant; Andrew Peter Stephens [1972] Director/Builders Merchant; Peter John Stephens [1942] Director/Builders Merchant; Jon Alistair Taylor [1959] Director/Builders Merchant

Stephenson (MK) Trust
Incorporated: 23 January 2012 *Employees:* 123
Net Worth: £6,033,721 *Total Assets:* £9,613,879
Registered Office: Stephenson Academy, Crosslands, Stantonbury, Milton Keynes, Bucks, MK14 6AX
Activities: Other education n.e.c.
Officers: Nigel Handyside [1960] Director/Deputy Headteacher; Michael John Manley [1956] Director/Headteacher; John O'Donnell [1957] Director/Retired Headteacher; Christopher Sayles [1964] Director/School Governor; Kevin Scott [1949] Contract Director

Stepnell Developments Limited
Incorporated: 18 December 2008 *Employees:* 6
Net Worth: £22,610,832 *Total Assets:* £29,656,914
Registered Office: Stepnell House, Lawford Road, Rugby, Warwicks, CV21 2UU
Activities: Buying and selling of own real estate
Officers: James Richard Wakeford, Secretary; Catherine Elizabeth Wakeford [1948] Director; Edward Dudley Wakeford [1982] Director; James Richard Wakeford [1968] Director; Mark Robert Wakeford [1966] Director; Patricia Margaret Wakeford [1940] Director; Peter Guy Wakeford [1943] Director; Thomas Bosworth Wakeford [1977] Director

Stepnell Holdings Limited
Incorporated: 18 December 2008 *Employees:* 436
Net Worth: £67,950,600 *Total Assets:* £116,734,560
Registered Office: Stepnell House, Lawford Road, Rugby, Warwicks, CV21 2UU
Activities: Activities of head offices
Officers: Thomas Bosworth Wakeford, Secretary; Edward Dudley Wakeford [1982] Director; James Richard Wakeford [1968] Director; Mark Robert Wakeford [1966] Director; Peter Guy Wakeford [1943] Director; Thomas Bosworth Wakeford [1977] Director

Stepnell Limited
Incorporated: 10 January 1946 *Employees:* 422
Net Worth: £33,429,376 *Total Assets:* £65,024,176
Registered Office: Lawford Road, Rugby, Warwicks, CV21 2UU
Activities: Development of building projects
Parent: Stepnell Holdings Limited
Officers: Thomas Bosworth Wakeford, Secretary; Richard Bailey [1956] Director; William George Haynes [1956] Director; Robert Charles Speirs [1976] Director; James Richard Wakeford [1968] Director; Mark Robert Wakeford [1966] Director/Civil Engineer; Peter Guy Wakeford [1943] Director; Thomas Bosworth Wakeford [1977] Director

Sterigenics UK Limited
Incorporated: 1 March 1991 *Employees:* 47
Net Worth: £12,629,000 *Total Assets:* £15,163,000
Registered Office: Cotes Park Industrial Estate, Somercotes, Derbys, DE55 4NJ
Activities: Other human health activities
Officers: Adrian Wye [1956] Director/General Manager

Steris PLC
Incorporated: 9 October 2014 *Employees:* 12,258
Net Worth: £2,415,035,904 *Total Assets:* £3,917,389,056
Registered Office: Rutherford House, Stephensons Way, Chaddesden, Derby, DE21 6LY
Activities: Activities of other holding companies n.e.c.
Officers: John Adam Zangerle, Secretary; Richard C Breeden [1949] Director [American]; Cynthia Feldmann [1952] Director [American]; Jacqueline Kosecoff [1949] Director [American]; David Lewis [1944] Director [American]; Sir Duncan Kirkbride Nichol [1941] Director; Walter Rosebrough [1954] Director/Corporate Executive [American]; Dr Nirav Shah [1972] Director [American]; Mohsen Sohi [1959] Director [American]; Dr Richard Martin Steeves [1961] Director; John Wareham [1941] Director [American]; Loyal Wilson [1948] Director [American]; Michael Wood [1943] Director [American]

Steris Solutions Limited
Incorporated: 24 November 1992 *Employees:* 98
Previous: Steris Limited
Net Worth: £10,311,404 *Total Assets:* £21,630,576
Registered Office: Chancery House, Rayns Way, Watermead Business Park, Syston, Leicester, LE7 1PF
Activities: Non-specialised wholesale trade
Parent: Steris PLC
Officers: Ronald Snyder, Secretary; Julia Kipnis [1977] Director/Corporate Counsel [American]; Ronald E Snyder [1948] Director/Associate and Group General Counsel [American]; Michael Joseph Tokich [1968] Director/Chief Financial Officer [American]

Sterling Press Limited
Incorporated: 19 May 1989 *Employees:* 211
Net Worth: £3,332,938 *Total Assets:* £17,482,326
Registered Office: Kettering Venture Park, Kettering, Northants, NN15 6XU
Activities: Printing n.e.c.
Major Shareholder: Steven David Pizzey
Officers: Steven David Pizzey, Secretary; John Frederick Pizzey [1957] Director/Printer; Steven David Pizzey [1962] Director/Printer

Sterling Safetywear Limited
Incorporated: 20 January 1998 *Employees:* 32
Net Worth: £11,926,486 *Total Assets:* £24,940,996
Registered Office: Crown House, 310 Wellingborough Road, Rushden, Northants, NN10 6PP
Activities: Agents involved in the sale of textiles, clothing, fur, footwear and leather goods
Shareholder: Roger John Denton
Officers: Cynthia Minney, Secretary; Pauline Mary Campion [1944] Director; Richard James Campion [1943] Director/Heel Manufacturer; Amanda Jayne Denton [1966] Director; Roger John Denton [1967] Director; Tina Neal [1957] Director/Administrator; Darren Lee O'Dell [1965] Sales Director

Stertil UK Ltd.
Incorporated: 26 March 1973 *Employees:* 68
Net Worth: £5,364,636 *Total Assets:* £12,071,584
Registered Office: Unit A, Brackmills Business Park, Caswell Road, Northampton, NN4 7PW
Activities: Manufacture of lifting and handling equipment
Major Shareholder: Frits Kroijmans
Officers: William MacSweeney, Secretary; Ulbe Bijlsma [1958] Director [Dutch]; Martin Andrew Paynter [1964] Managing Director

Stillness 928 Limited
Incorporated: 1 February 2013 *Employees:* 212
Net Worth Deficit: £6,235,729 *Total Assets:* £13,753,404
Registered Office: 2 Christchurch Road, Abington, Northampton, NN1 5LL
Activities: Other human health activities
Parent: SC Management III LP
Officers: Professor Michael Philip Barnes [1952] Director/Medical Practitioner; David Jackson [1959] Finance Director; Richard William James McKenzie [1965] Director/Chief Executive

Stillness 930 Limited
Incorporated: 19 July 2013
Net Worth Deficit: £5,505,266 *Total Assets:* £11,716,485
Registered Office: 2 Christchurch Road, Abington, Northampton, NN1 5LL
Activities: Other human health activities
Parent: Stillness 928 Limited
Officers: Professor Michael Philip Barnes [1952] Director/Medical Practitioner; David Jackson [1959] Finance Director; Richard William James McKenzie [1965] Director/Chief Operating Officer; Paul Richard Preston [1955] Director

Stirling Management Group Limited
Incorporated: 10 September 1982
Net Worth: £7,914,115 *Total Assets:* £9,547,495
Registered Office: 24 Manchester Road, Wilmslow, Cheshire, SK9 1BG
Activities: Construction of domestic buildings
Shareholders: David Powell; Jonathan Nigel Ward; Judith Abercromby; Arthur John Abercromby
Officers: Arthur John Abercromby, Secretary; Arthur John Abercromby [1943] Director; Judith Abercromby [1941] Director; Marie-Louise Abercromby [1978] Director; Mark Lhind Abercromby [1975] Director

Stockcroft Limited
Incorporated: 12 October 2011 *Employees:* 14
Net Worth: £13,464,599 *Total Assets:* £17,105,530
Registered Office: Potters Farm, Ewelme, Wallingford, Oxon, OX10 6PX
Activities: Mixed farming
Major Shareholder: Sally Anne Stockings
Officers: Sally Anne Stockings [1955] Director

Stockport Grammar School
Incorporated: 29 May 2007 *Employees:* 221
Net Worth: £26,306,992 *Total Assets:* £28,237,524
Registered Office: Stockport Grammar School, Buxton Road, Stockport, Cheshire, SK2 7AF
Activities: Pre-primary education
Officers: Christopher Watson, Secretary; Philip John Britton [1969] Director/Headmaster; Anthony Paul Carr [1952] Director/Lawyer; Sarah Elizabeth Carroll [1965] Director/Banker; Philip Adrian Cuddy [1952] Director/Solicitor Consultant; Christopher Frank Dunn [1957] Director/Solicitor; Peter Laban Giblin [1949] Director/Retired; Samantha Lansbury [1970] Director/Solicitor; Jonathan Mark Round Lee [1964] Property Director; Paul Milner [1957] Director/Retired; Doctor Elizabeth Margaret Morris [1948] Director/Pediatrician; Christine Suzanne Muscutt [1954] Director/Retired; John Anthony Shackleton [1954] Director/Retired; Adrian Charles Simpson [1959] Finance Director

Stockport Homes Limited
Incorporated: 29 August 2002 *Employees:* 529
Net Worth: £12,488,000 *Total Assets:* £78,991,000
Registered Office: Cornerstone, 2 Edward Street, Stockport, Cheshire, SK1 3NQ
Activities: Management of real estate on a fee or contract basis
Parent: Stockport Metropolitan Borough Council
Officers: David Ronald Beckett [1970] Director/Chief Executive; Robin Barry Burman [1952] Director/Lawyer; Peter Fitzhenry [1958] Director/Consultant; Josephine Teresa Hague [1958] Director/Receptionist; Jamie MacLean Hirst [1978] Director/IT Professional; Sarah Leigh Keenan [1982] Director/Tenancy Enforcement Officer; Jenny Osbourne [1973] Director/Chief Executive; Stephen Brian Partridge [1963] Director/Management Consultant; Alanna Hourie Vine [1948] Director/Retired; Christine Woolridge [1945] Director/Retired

Stocksbridge Regeneration Company Limited
Incorporated: 27 October 2005
Net Worth: £10,340,709 *Total Assets:* £37,825,484
Registered Office: Dransfield House, 2 Fox Valley Way, Fox Valley, Sheffield, S36 2AB
Activities: Development of building projects
Parent: Dransfield Properties Ltd
Officers: Mark Dransfield [1962] Director; Steven John Stead [1978] Director

Stockshape Limited
Incorporated: 6 August 1999
Net Worth: £41,455,864 *Total Assets:* £77,925,192
Registered Office: Dene Park, Stratford Road, Wellesbourne, Warwicks, CV35 9RY
Activities: Other letting and operating of own or leased real estate
Officers: Patrick Tobin, Secretary; Angela O'Donoghue [1969] Director/Manager [Irish]; Gemma Ring [1976] Director [Irish]; Patrick Tobin [1941] Director/Accountant [Irish]

R.J.Stokes & Co. Limited
Incorporated: 4 June 1923 *Employees:* 55
Net Worth: £8,080,593 *Total Assets:* £9,897,273
Registered Office: Rother Valley Way, Holbrook Industrial Estate, Sheffield, S20 3RW
Activities: Non-specialised wholesale trade
Major Shareholder: Robert James Stokes
Officers: Darren Alan Large, Secretary; Richard James Askham [1971] Director; Richard Charles Stokes [1964] Director; Robert James Stokes [1936] Joint Managing Director; Timothy James Stokes [1961] Director; Mark Newman Yates [1963] Director

Stonbury (Holdings) Limited
Incorporated: 19 July 2016 *Employees:* 165
Net Worth: £6,483,353 *Total Assets:* £15,947,746
Registered Office: Chawston House, Chawston Lane, Chawston, Bedford, MK44 3BH
Activities: Activities of other holding companies n.e.c.
Shareholder: James Alexander Stonor
Officers: Jonathan Mark Featherstone [1963] Director; Neal Anthony Judd [1971] Director; Ian Geoffrey Mellor [1969] Director; Jonathan William Perryman [1975] Director; James Alexander Stonor [1977] Director; Peter Michael Stonor [1944] Director

Stone House Investments Limited
Incorporated: 11 June 2009
Net Worth: £6,099,287 *Total Assets:* £12,335,158
Registered Office: Pacioli House, 9 Brookfield, Duncan Close, Moulton Park, Northampton, NN3 6WL
Activities: Other letting and operating of own or leased real estate
Shareholders: Arthur Robert Heygate; Paul Michael Heygate
Officers: Stephen Chia, Secretary; Arthur Robert Heygate [1945] Director/Farmer and Flour Miller; Paul Michael Heygate [1943] Director/Farmer and Flour Miller

Stonebridge Homes Limited
Incorporated: 9 June 2010 *Employees:* 40
Previous: Stonebridge Projects Limited
Net Worth: £4,129,540 *Total Assets:* £28,854,764
Registered Office: Banner Cross Hall, Ecclesall Road South, Sheffield, S11 9PD
Activities: Development of building projects
Shareholders: Henry Boot Land Holdings Limited; Stonebridge Homes Limited
Officers: Darren Louis Littlewood [1975] Finance Director; Darren Stubbs [1968] Director; John Trevor Sutcliffe [1959] Director

Stoneleigh Abbey Limited
Incorporated: 13 September 1996 *Employees:* 12
Net Worth: £20,165,700 *Total Assets:* £20,390,164
Registered Office: The Estate Office, Stoneleigh Abbey, Kenilworth, Warwicks, CV8 2LF
Activities: Operation of historical sites and buildings and similar visitor attractions
Officers: Marcus Hugh Crofton Binney [1944] Director/Writer; Anthony Patrick Michael Bird [1935] Director; Dorothy Ingle [1951] Director; Roger John Beresford Pringle [1944] Director

Stonepit Limited
Incorporated: 20 June 2007
Net Worth: £26,162,766 *Total Assets:* £26,190,816
Registered Office: 3 Coventry Innovation Village, Cheetah Road, Coventry, Warwicks, CV1 2TL
Activities: Activities of head offices
Major Shareholder: Stewart Milne
Officers: David Colin Ingram-Moore, Secretary; William Neil Cordiner [1963] Director; Leslie Scott Dalgarno [1950] Director/Solicitor; David Colin Ingram-Moore [1957] Director/Chartered Accountant; Stewart Milne [1950] Director/Chairman and CEO; Ronald Russell [1956] Director

Stonewater Funding PLC
Incorporated: 24 August 2012
Net Worth: £52,000 *Total Assets:* £233,543,008
Registered Office: Suite C Lancaster House, Grange Business Park, Enderby Road, Whetstone, Leicester, LE8 6EP
Activities: Financial intermediation not elsewhere classified
Officers: Anne Louise Harling, Secretary; George Patrick Blunden [1952] Director/Board Member; John Philip Bruton [1957] Director of Finance at Raglan Housing Association; Peter John Hammond [1956] Director/Consultant; Nicholas Harris [1961] Director/Chief Executive; Tariq Kazi [1972] Director/Finance and Treasury Consultant; John Richard McLean Weguelin [1950] Director/Board Member of Raglan Housing/Raglan Homes

Storefield Group Limited
Incorporated: 28 March 2007 *Employees:* 54
Net Worth: £6,326,138 *Total Assets:* £16,427,610
Registered Office: Furnace Park, Old Telford Way, Telford Way Industrial Estate, Kettering, Northants, NN16 8UN
Activities: Activities of head offices
Major Shareholder: Douglas Alexander Wright
Officers: Douglas Alexander Wright [1961] Director

The Stowe House Preservation Trust
Incorporated: 30 June 1997 *Employees:* 3
Net Worth: £21,536,264 *Total Assets:* £21,734,460
Registered Office: Stowe House, Stowe, Buckingham, MK18 5EH
Activities: Operation of historical sites and buildings and similar visitor attractions
Officers: Mark Anthony Jackson Stops, Secretary; John Richard Charles Arkwright [1950] Director/Chartered Surveyor; Richard Broyd [1948] Director/Hotelier; Julie Christine Brunskill [1958] Director/Retired; Juliet Ursula Colman [1967] Director/Architect; Simon Charles Creedy Smith [1959] Director/Chartered Accountant; Andrew William Mildmay Fane [1949] Director/Chartered Accountant; Jeffrey Philip Haworth [1944] Director/Architect; Mark Anthony Jackson-Stops [1950] Director/Surveyor; Robert Charles Morley [1942] Director/Retired; Jeremy Gibson Dixon Musson [1965] Director/Writer; Duncan William Angus Stirling [1963] Director/Marketing Executive; Annabel Chaundy Westman [1953] Director/Textile Historian

Stowe School,Limited
Incorporated: 20 January 1923 *Employees:* 500
Net Worth: £43,479,320 *Total Assets:* £54,321,720
Registered Office: Stowe School, Stowe, Buckingham, MK18 5EH
Activities: General secondary education
Officers: Michael Beauchamp Mansel Porter, Secretary; Reverend Peter Michael Ackroyd [1960] Director/Clergyman; Jonathan Michael Arundell Bewes [1965] Director/Investment Banker; Julie Christine Brunskill [1958] Chartered Surveyor/Group Property Director; Sir James Michael Burnell Nugent [1949] Director; Geoffrey David Granville Carr [1959] Director; David Watson Cheyne [1948] Director/Solicitor; Juliet Ursula Colman [1967] Director/Architect; Simon Charles Creedy Smith [1959] Director/Accountant; Elizabeth Joy de Burgh Sidley [1951] Director/Retired Chartered Surveyor; John Philip Cardain Frost [1966] Director/Chartered Surveyor; Professor Guy Manning Goodwin [1947] Director/Professor of Psychiatry; Joanne Elizabeth Hastie-Smith [1960] Director/Vicar's Wife; Andrea Karen Johnson [1960] Director/Headmistress; Robert Anthony Lankester [1958] Director/Headmaster; Catriona Helen Lloyd [1967] Director/Solicitor; Elizabeth Mary Kirby Phillips [1940] Director/Education Consultant; Vanessa Jane Stanley [1966] Director/Teacher; Lady Jennifer Avril Kinmond Stringer [1952] Director/Doctor (Retired); Christopher John Tate [1953] Director

Stowe Valley Multi Academy Trust
Incorporated: 25 October 2016
Net Worth: £30,398,232 *Total Assets:* £38,118,504
Registered Office: Southam College, Welsh Road West, Southam, Warwicks, CV47 0JW
Activities: Primary education
Officers: David John Mark Billsborough [1972] Director/Manager; Karen Jane Boucher [1958] Director/Retired; Tracy Caroline Byrne [1967] Supply Chain Director; Claire Louise Chevassut [1965] Director; Lindsay Jane Dennish [1962] Director/Social Worker; Kyle Ferguson [1979] Director/Detective Constable; Iain Duncan Geddes [1974] Director/Bank Manager; Katherine Jane Latham [1971] Finance Director; Ranjit Singh Samra [1967] Director/Executive Headteacher; Richard Christopher Maurice Smart Mbe [1942] Director; Peter William Wain [1957] Director/Retired; Brian Thomas Wallace [1949] Director/Accountant; Nicole Joanne Wicks [1966] Director/Consultant

Straightset Limited
Incorporated: 19 November 1987 *Employees:* 86
Net Worth: £6,078,473 *Total Assets:* £11,497,240
Registered Office: Stadium Close, Dukeries Industrial Estate, Claylands Avenue, Worksop, Notts, S81 7BT
Activities: Other specialised construction activities n.e.c.
Major Shareholder: Paul Bates
Officers: Stephen Andrew Bates, Secretary; Paul Bates [1952] Managing Director; Stephen Andrew Bates [1959] Director; Nicholas Hopwood [1960] Finance Director; Terence Hornsby [1959] Projects Director

Strata Homes Holdings Limited
Incorporated: 18 July 2014 *Employees:* 191
Net Worth: £54,975,000 *Total Assets:* £121,086,000
Registered Office: Quay Point, Lakeside Boulevard, Doncaster, S Yorks, DN4 5PL
Activities: Activities of head offices
Shareholders: Andrew Richard Weaver; Richard Irving Weaver
Officers: Julian Nigel Davis, Secretary; Helen Jayne Browne [1975] Director; Julian Nigel Davis [1975] Finance Director; Andrew Richard Weaver [1973] Director; Dorothy Weaver [1950] Director; Richard Irving Weaver [1949] Director/Company Chairman; Simon Daniel Weaver [1977] Director

Strata Homes Limited
Incorporated: 23 March 1983 *Employees:* 191
Net Worth: £54,634,000 *Total Assets:* £121,086,000
Registered Office: Quay Point, Lakeside Boulevard, Doncaster, S Yorks, DN4 5PL
Activities: Construction of domestic buildings
Officers: Julian Nigel Davis, Secretary; Julian Nigel Davis [1975] Finance Director; Andrew Richard Weaver [1973] Director; Richard Irving Weaver [1949] Director

Strata Homes Yorkshire Limited
Incorporated: 10 November 1981 *Employees:* 153
Net Worth: £46,797,000 *Total Assets:* £132,049,000
Registered Office: Quay Point, Lakeside Boulevard, Doncaster, S Yorks, DN4 5PL
Activities: Construction of domestic buildings
Parent: Strata Homes Limited
Officers: Julian Nigel Davis, Secretary; Vernon Joseph Cunningham [1967] Director; Julian Nigel Davis [1975] Finance Director; Paul Dean Robinson [1964] Director; Nigel Robson [1973] Director; Gemma Smith [1984] Director; Andrew Richard Weaver [1973] Director; Richard Irving Weaver [1949] Director

Strata Products Limited
Incorporated: 31 March 1987 *Employees:* 165
Net Worth: £19,718,000 *Total Assets:* £33,964,000
Registered Office: Plymouth Avenue, Brookhill Industrial Estate, Pinxton, Notts, NG16 6NS
Activities: Manufacture of plastics in primary forms
Parent: RPC Packaging Holdings Ltd
Officers: Nicholas David Martin Giles, Secretary; Jay Ilsen [1983] Sales Director; Michael Anthony Ilsen [1958] Managing Director; Simon John Kesterton [1973] Director; Petrus Rudolf Maria Vervaat [1965] Director [Dutch]

Stratford Girls' Grammar School
Incorporated: 24 May 2011 *Employees:* 102
Net Worth: £12,880,000 *Total Assets:* £14,184,000
Registered Office: Shottery Manor, Shottery, Stratford upon Avon, Warwicks, CV37 9HA
Activities: General secondary education
Officers: Jane Wright, Secretary; Sarah Jane Recardo Bennett [1970] Director/Careers Coordinator; Daniel Robert Cale [1971] Director/Chartered Accountant; Jacqueline Anne Cornell [1969] Director/Headteacher; Richard Neal Cox [1966] Director/Solicitor; Anna Harvey [1957] Director; Ian Andrew Harwood [1966] Director; Natasha Male [1987] Director/Administrative Officer; Paul McAnaney [1973] Director/Teacher; John Millett [1946] Director/Retired; David Morse [1962] Director/University Lecturer; Clare Nicklin [1971] Director; Paul Offer [1963] Director; Christopher Harvey Pote [1969] Director/Consultant; Keith Richardson [1961] Director/Teacher; Janet Lucy Tomkinson [1966] Director/Educational Publisher; Dr Julie Marie Waters [1971] Director/Chief Executive D&T Association

Stratford-upon-Avon School
Incorporated: 4 July 2011 *Employees:* 234
Net Worth: £25,491,000 *Total Assets:* £28,498,000
Registered Office: Stratford upon Avon School, Alcester Road, Stratford upon Avon, Warwicks, CV37 9DH
Activities: General secondary education
Officers: Sally Ann Jones, Secretary; Susie Drummond [1972] Director/Manager; Trevor James Richard Handcock [1965] Director/Buyer; Philip James Heath [1956] Director/Solicitor; Tracy Irish [1964] Director/Doctoral Researcher/Education Practitioner; Wayne Mills [1968] Director/Bank Official; Sara Jane Mitchell [1965] Commercial Director; Anthony Simon Paxton [1975] Police Constable, Director and Governor; Jane Louise Price [1967] Director/Organisational Change Consultant; Christopher Strathie Rivett [1955] Director/Social Worker; Amanda Scott-Lee [1986] Director/IAC Lead; Neil Frederick Wallace [1970] Director/Headteacher; Nicola Clare Whan [1964] Director/Teacher - Secondary; Lucy Helen Wretham [1974] Director/Teacher

Stratford-upon-Avon Town Trust
Incorporated: 24 May 2001 *Employees:* 10
Net Worth: £60,005,144 *Total Assets:* £62,698,152
Registered Office: 14 Rother Street, Stratford upon Avon, Warwicks, CV37 6LU
Activities: Other business support service activities n.e.c.
Officers: Ian Duncan Campbell Andrew [1940] Director/Retired; Timothy Harry Bailey [1963] Director/Assistant Head of VI Form; Charles Henry Bates [1939] Director/Retired; Teresa Mary Bates [1947] Director/Retired; Anthony Jackson [1957] Director/Consultant; Dr Lindsay William MacDonald [1950] Director/Honorary Professor [British/Australian]; Matthew John MacDonald [1978] Director/Solicitor; Stephen Parker [1953] Director; Clive John Snowdon [1953] Director; Robert David Taylor [1953] Director/Architect; Quentin McDonald Willson [1957] Director/Journalist/Broadcaster

Stratstone Motor Holdings Limited
Incorporated: 3 September 1999
Previous: Stratstone Limited
Net Worth: £83,408,000 *Total Assets:* £136,032,992
Registered Office: Loxely House, 2 Oakwood Court, Little Oak Drive, Annesley, Nottingham, NG15 0DR
Activities: Other professional, scientific and technical activities n.e.c.
Parent: Pendragon PLC
Officers: Richard James Maloney, Secretary; Martin Shaun Casha [1960] Director; Trevor Garry Finn [1957] Director; Timothy Paul Holden [1964] Director/Chartered Accountant

R Stratton & Co Ltd.
Incorporated: 13 March 1992 *Employees:* 165
Net Worth: £20,141,000 *Total Assets:* £77,799,000
Registered Office: 2 Penman Way, Grove Park, Leicester, LE19 1ST
Activities: Sale of new cars and light motor vehicles
Parent: Sytner Group Limited
Officers: Adam Collinson, Secretary; Adam Collinson [1972] Finance Director; Darren Edwards [1968] Managing Director; Robert Harold Kurnick [1961] Director/Executive Vice President [American]; Jeremy Richard Mallett [1952] Director; Gerard Edward Nieuwenhuys [1960] Director; Laurence Edward William Vaughan [1963] Managing Director

Stratton-Streles Estates Limited
Incorporated: 17 January 1940 *Employees:* 29
Net Worth: £9,680,480 *Total Assets:* £11,583,180
Registered Office: Lower Lobbersdown Farm, Tetsworth, Thame, Oxon, OX9 7BB
Activities: Growing of cereals (except rice), leguminous crops and oil seeds
Officers: Penelope Ann Jarvis, Secretary; Vanessa Jane Burroughes [1960] Director/Textile Designer; Harry Hamlin-Wright [1989] Director/Veterinary Surgeon; Hugh William Jarvis [1986] Director/Accountant; Penelope Ann Jarvis [1951] Director/Housewife; Katherine Mary Taylor [1952] Director/Housewife and Aromatherapist; Paul Hugh Taylor [1987] Director/Senior Product Contractor; Hugh William Van Poortvliet [1944] Director/Farmer; Jeffrey William Van Poortvliet [1970] Director/Farmer; Matthew Anthony Van Poortvliet [1983] Director

Stratus (Holdings) Limited
Incorporated: 28 January 2011 *Employees:* 3
Net Worth Deficit: £23,618,190 *Total Assets:* £11,088,684
Registered Office: 3MC Middlemarch Business Park, Siskin Drive, Coventry, Warwicks, CV3 4FJ
Activities: Activities of head offices
Parent: Lloyds Development Capital (Holdings) Limited
Officers: Greg Clarke [1957] Business Director; Andrew Holman [1981] Director; John Morris [1965] Director

W. H. Strawson (Farms) Limited
Incorporated: 7 March 1968 *Employees:* 10
Net Worth: £9,399,402 *Total Assets:* £10,094,875
Registered Office: Broughton Grange, Wressle, Brigg, N Lincs, DN20 0BJ
Activities: Growing of cereals (except rice), leguminous crops and oil seeds
Parent: W.H. Strawson (Farms) Holdings Limited
Officers: Andrew Clive Severn [1959] Director/Accountant; William Robert Strawson [1965] Director/Farmer; Winifred Lucy Strawson [1931] Director

W. H. Strawson (Notts.) Limited
Incorporated: 7 March 1968 *Employees:* 2
Net Worth: £5,592,048 *Total Assets:* £10,272,617
Registered Office: The Farm Office, Blyborough Hall, Blyborough, Gainsborough, Lincs, DN21 4HB
Activities: Growing of cereals (except rice), leguminous crops and oil seeds
Parent: W.H. Strawson (Notts.) Holdings Limited
Officers: Andrew Clive Severn [1959] Director/Accountant; Richard Henry Strawson [1966] Director/Farmer; Sophie Strawson [1971] Director

C.A. Strawson Farming Limited
Incorporated: 17 March 1976 *Employees:* 2
Net Worth: £12,660,950 *Total Assets:* £19,231,838
Registered Office: Hexgreave Hall, Upper Hexgreave, Farnsfield, Newark, Notts, NG22 8LS
Activities: Growing of cereals (except rice), leguminous crops and oil seeds
Shareholders: Timothy Edward Shuldham; Charles Anthony Strawson; Graham Clive Holdich Smith
Officers: Charles Anthony Strawson, Secretary; Timothy Edward Shuldham [1958] Director/Chartered Surveyor; Charles Anthony Strawson [1939] Director/Farmer; Robert Mark Strawson [1967] Director/Farmer

Strawson Group Developments Limited
Incorporated: 21 February 2008 *Employees:* 16
Net Worth: £17,069,000 *Total Assets:* £49,445,000
Registered Office: Manor House Farm, East Drayton, Retford, Notts, DN22 0LG
Activities: Buying and selling of own real estate
Major Shareholder: George David Strawson
Officers: James Watson Eyre Wild, Secretary; Elizabeth Anne Bisson [1963] Director/Land Agent; George David Strawson [1937] Director/Farmer

Strawson Group Investments Limited
Incorporated: 21 February 2008
Net Worth: £37,173,000 *Total Assets:* £43,045,000
Registered Office: Manor House Farm, East Drayton, Retford, Notts, DN22 0LG
Activities: Other letting and operating of own or leased real estate
Major Shareholder: George David Strawson
Officers: James Watson Eyre Wild, Secretary; Elizabeth Anne Bisson [1963] Director/Land Agent; George David Strawson [1937] Director/Farmer

Strawson Holdings Limited
Incorporated: 29 September 1981 *Employees:* 16
Net Worth: £839,000 *Total Assets:* £22,640,000
Registered Office: Manor House Farm, East Drayton, Retford, Notts, DN22 0LG
Activities: Buying and selling of own real estate
Parent: Strawson Group Developments Limited
Officers: James Watson Eyre Wild, Secretary; Elizabeth Anne Bisson [1963] Director/Land Agent; George David Strawson [1937] Director/Farmer

Strawson Limited
Incorporated: 13 August 2001 *Employees:* 88
Net Worth: £8,968,806 *Total Assets:* £16,180,023
Registered Office: Featherstone House Farm, Bilsthorpe, Newark, Notts, NG22 8RD
Activities: Growing of cereals (except rice), leguminous crops and oil seeds
Major Shareholder: Robert Mark Strawson
Officers: Robert Mark Strawson, Secretary/Farmer; Annabel Jane Strawson [1996] Director; Harry Charles Strawson [1996] Director; Jane Strawson [1967] Director/Farmer; Robert Mark Strawson [1967] Director/Farmer

M.F. Strawson Limited
Incorporated: 8 November 1957 *Employees:* 40
Net Worth: £19,706,584 *Total Assets:* £23,236,514
Registered Office: Pyewipe Farm, Aylesby Road, Great Coates, Grimsby, N E Lincs, DN37 9NU
Activities: Growing of cereals (except rice), leguminous crops and oil seeds
Shareholders: Niel Andrew Strawson; Paul David Field Strawson
Officers: Niel Andrew Strawson, Secretary; Niel Andrew Strawson [1964] Director/Chartered Accountant; Paul David Field Strawson [1960] Director/Farmer

Strawson Management Limited
Incorporated: 2 July 1997 *Employees:* 4
Net Worth: £28,790,000 *Total Assets:* £29,667,000
Registered Office: Manor House Farm, East Drayton, Retford, Notts, DN22 0LG
Activities: Other letting and operating of own or leased real estate
Parent: Strawson Group Investments Limited
Officers: James Watson Eyre Wild, Secretary; Elizabeth Anne Bisson [1963] Director; George David Strawson [1937] Director

Stream Acquisitions Limited
Incorporated: 19 February 2014
Net Worth: £10,219,293 *Total Assets:* £22,336,624
Registered Office: Devonshire Green House, 14 Fitzwilliam Street, Sheffield, S1 4JL
Activities: Other telecommunications activities
Parent: Stream Midco Limited
Officers: Mark William Gerard Collins, Secretary; Jonathan James Burrows [1981] Director; Mark William Gerard Collins [1953] Director/Chartered Accountant

Stream Midco Limited
Incorporated: 16 May 2014 *Employees:* 2
Net Worth Deficit: £5,048,589 *Total Assets:* £14,210,268
Registered Office: Devonshire Green House, 14 Fitzwilliam Street, Sheffield, S1 4JL
Activities: Other telecommunications activities
Parent: Stream Topco Limited
Officers: Mark William Gerard Collins, Secretary; Jonathan James Burrows [1981] Director; Stephen Ross Delaney [1980] Director; Tom Shelford [1980] Director

Stream Topco Limited
Incorporated: 15 May 2014 *Employees:* 117
Net Worth Deficit: £7,121,206 *Total Assets:* £33,766,776
Registered Office: Devonshire Green House, 14 Fitzwilliam Street, Sheffield, S1 4JL
Activities: Other telecommunications activities
Parent: Ask4 (Buyco) Limited
Officers: Mark William Gerard Collins, Secretary; Jonathan James Burrows [1981] Director; Mark William Gerard Collins [1953] Director/Chartered Accountant

Streason Limited
Incorporated: 24 August 1962 *Employees:* 176
Net Worth: £10,927,575 *Total Assets:* £19,384,328
Registered Office: Townend Works, Chapel-en-le-Frith, Derbys, SK23 0PH
Activities: Activities of head offices
Officers: Jocelyn Sarah Street, Secretary; Martin Street, Secretary; Simon James Eastwood [1963] Director; Martin Street [1955] Director/Crane Manufacturer

Street Crane Company Limited
Incorporated: 2 May 1958 *Employees:* 176
Net Worth: £10,449,491 *Total Assets:* £18,906,432
Registered Office: Town End Works, Chapel-en-le-Frith, Derbys, SK23 0PH
Activities: Manufacture of lifting and handling equipment
Officers: Jocelyn Sarah Street, Secretary; Michael Andrew Husbands [1963] Finance Director; Christopher Mark Lindley-Smith [1972] Sales Director; Anthony Robert McClure [1961] Operations Director; Eric Andrew Pimblett [1953] Non-Executive - Director; Christopher Russell [1971] Director/Design Engineer; Martin Street [1955] Director; Augusto Zona [1971] Managing Director [Italian]

Strevens Vehicles Holdings Limited
Incorporated: 28 February 1992 *Employees:* 486
Net Worth: £20,333,000 *Total Assets:* £71,924,000
Registered Office: Hazel Drive, Narborough Road South, Leicester, LE3 2JG
Activities: Activities of head offices
Shareholders: Nigel Jeremy Strevens; Timothy Maxwell Strevens
Officers: Nigel Jeremy Strevens, Secretary; Janet Hyde Strevens [1944] Director; Nigel Jeremy Strevens [1971] Director/Chartered Accountant; Peter Alan Dawson Strevens [1938] Director; Timothy Maxwell Strevens [1974] Joint Managing Director

Sidney Stringer Multi Academy Trust
Incorporated: 14 August 2008 *Employees:* 410
Net Worth: £59,055,000 *Total Assets:* £70,521,000
Registered Office: Sidney Stringer Academy, 2 Primrose Hill Street, Coventry, Warwicks, CV1 5LY
Activities: General secondary education
Officers: Richard Edwin Kershaw, Secretary; John William Leslie Brodie [1949] Director/Retired; Ian Keith Dunn [1968] Director/University Lecturer; Barry Hastie [1969] Director/Accountant; Jocelyn Beryl Parry [1955] Director/Retired; Graham David Prebble [1964] Director/Chartered Engineer; Julienne Sullivan [1948] Director/Local Government Officer; Wendy Tomes [1961] Director/Principal

Stripestar Limited
Incorporated: 10 June 1999 *Employees:* 2,143
Net Worth: £57,940,000 *Total Assets:* £360,457,984
Registered Office: Loxley House, 2 Oakwood Court, Little Oak Drive, Annesley, Nottingham, NG15 0DR
Activities: Sale of new cars and light motor vehicles
Parent: Pendragon Motor Group Limited
Officers: Richard James Maloney, Secretary; Martin Shaun Casha [1960] Director; Trevor Garry Finn [1957] Director; Timothy Paul Holden [1964] Director/Chartered Accountant

STS Defence Limited
Incorporated: 1 May 1996 *Employees:* 157
Net Worth: £9,500,510 *Total Assets:* £13,059,036
Registered Office: 5 The Courtyard, Timothys Bridge Road, Stratford upon Avon, Warwicks, CV37 9NP
Activities: Manufacture of loaded electronic boards
Parent: Key Technologies Limited
Officers: Kevin Hilton, Secretary; Jonathan James Bowley [1967] Managing Director; Kevin Hilton [1958] Director; Trevor Middleton [1957] Director

Walter E. Sturgess & Sons Limited
Incorporated: 14 May 1938 *Employees:* 319
Net Worth: £14,180,000 *Total Assets:* £54,483,000
Registered Office: Almond Road, Leicester, LE2 7LP
Activities: Sale of new cars and light motor vehicles
Major Shareholder: Robin Patrick Greatorex Sturgess
Officers: Valerie Jane Sturgess, Secretary; Amanda Binner [1970] Operations Director; Geoffrey Page-Morris [1963] Director; Barnaby George Sturgess [1975] Director/Dealer Principal; Christopher Michael Greatorex Sturgess [1962] Director; Robin Patrick Greatorex Sturgess [1933] Director; Valerie Jane Sturgess [1940] Director

Suez Water Technologies & Solutions Services UK Limited
Incorporated: 13 February 2004
Previous: GE Mobile Water Limited
Net Worth: £17,546,000 *Total Assets:* £18,932,000
Registered Office: Hydrohouse, Newcombe Way, Orton Southgate, Peterborough, Cambs, PE2 6SE
Activities: Water collection, treatment and supply
Parent: Ionics Ventures Limited
Officers: Ana Rita Dias [1980] Director/Engineering Senior Leader [Portuguese]; Simon Gare [1975] Director/Commercial Engineering Leader, Mobile & Outsource; Jon Paul Hunt [1971] Director; Alexander Charles Ian Stewart [1964] Director

Summerfields School Trust,Limited
Incorporated: 12 August 1955 *Employees:* 137
Net Worth: £12,812,942 *Total Assets:* £15,052,345
Registered Office: Summer Fields School Trust Limited, Oxford, OX2 7EN
Activities: Primary education
Officers: Christopher Charles Burton, Secretary; Alastair Guy White Beor-Roberts [1958] Director/Chartered Surveyor; John Henry Chatfeild-Roberts [1962] Director/Fund Manager; Alastair John Chirnside [1976] Director/Teacher; Edward Alan Davidson [1943] Director/Queens Counsel; Tessa Gaisman [1954] Director; The Right Reverend David Willfred Michael Jennings [1944] Director/Bishop - Clerk in Holy Orders; Thomas Edmund Justin Nolan [1969] Director/School Master; Suzette Ray Peake [1961] Director/Estate Management; Andrew Edward Reekes [1950] Director/Schoolmaster; Jeremy Richard Michael Rooth [1971] Director; Roger Daniel Shaw [1970] Director/School Master; Diana Elizabeth Jane Sichel [1950] Director/Retired GP; Carole Marie Aleth Sweetnam [1963] Director/Account Manager; Philip Hugh Weaver [1957] Director/Solicitor

Summit (Oxford) Limited
Incorporated: 14 January 2003 *Employees:* 39
Net Worth Deficit: £86,308,496 *Total Assets:* £26,124,170
Registered Office: 136a Eastern Avenue, Milton Park, Milton, Abingdon, Oxon, OX14 4SB
Activities: Research and experimental development on biotechnology
Parent: Summit Therapeutics PLC
Officers: Melissa Claire Strange, Secretary; Glyn Owain Edwards [1955] Director

Summit Therapeutics PLC
Incorporated: 4 August 2004 *Employees:* 60
Previous: Summit Corporation PLC
Net Worth: £9,875,000 *Total Assets:* £53,962,000
Registered Office: 136a Eastern Avenue, Milton Park, Milton, Abingdon, Oxon, OX14 4SB
Activities: Research and experimental development on biotechnology
Officers: Melissa Claire Strange, Secretary; Valerie Andrews [1959] Director [American]; Frank Murdoch Armstrong [1957] Director; Glyn Owain Edwards [1955] Director; David Michael Wurzer [1958] Director [American]; Leopoldo Zambeletti [1968] Director [Spanish]

Sumo Digital Group Limited
Incorporated: 31 July 2014
Net Worth Deficit: £686,997 *Total Assets:* £15,620,764
Registered Office: 32 Jessops Riverside, Brightside Lane, Sheffield, S9 2RX
Activities: Management consultancy activities other than financial management
Parent: Sumo Digital Holdings Limited
Officers: Steven John Webb, Secretary; Carl Cavers [1967] Director; David Wilton [1962] Director

Sumo Digital Ltd.
Incorporated: 19 March 2003 *Employees:* 353
Net Worth: £21,761,468 *Total Assets:* £29,675,900
Registered Office: 32 Jessops Riverside, Brightside Lane, Sheffield, S9 2RX
Activities: Ready-made interactive leisure and entertainment software development
Parent: Sumo Digital Entertainment Limited
Officers: Steven John Webb, Secretary; Carl Cavers [1967] Director; Darren Richard Mills [1970] Director; Paul Reginald Porter [1971] Director; Christopher Mark Stockwell [1964] Director; David Charles Wilton [1962] Director

Sumo Group PLC
Incorporated: 20 November 2017 *Employees:* 444
Net Worth: £41,022,000 *Total Assets:* £53,101,000
Registered Office: 32 Jessops Riverside, Brightside Lane, Sheffield, S9 2RX
Activities: Ready-made interactive leisure and entertainment software development
Shareholder: Perwyn Bidco (UK) Limited
Officers: Steven Webb, Secretary; Kenneth Robert Beaty [1968] Director; Carl Cavers [1967] Director; Andrea Margaret Dunstan [1960] Director; Ian Livingstone [1949] Director; Michael Sherwin [1959] Director; David Charles Wilton [1962] Director

Sun Chemical Limited
Incorporated: 19 September 1991 *Employees:* 720
Net Worth: £18,425,000 *Total Assets:* £121,901,000
Registered Office: 3 High View Road, South Normanton, Derbys, DE55 2DT
Activities: Other business support service activities n.e.c.
Parent: DIC Corporation
Officers: Margaret Julia Pearce, Secretary; Sally Ann Foster [1965] HR Director (Northern Europe); Charles Allen Heynes [1958] Director; John Philip Law [1958] Managing Director Screen Circuits; Martjin Jan Charles Marie Schoonenberg [1977] Director/General Counsel [Dutch]

Sun Healthcare Limited
Incorporated: 21 May 2001 *Employees:* 392
Net Worth: £1,720,695 *Total Assets:* £16,277,444
Registered Office: Cockerham Hall, 17 Huddersfield Road, Barnsley, S Yorks, S70 2LT
Activities: Other residential care activities n.e.c.
Shareholders: Steven Garside; Alan James Tolan
Officers: Steven Garside, Secretary; Steven Garside [1955] Director; Alan James Tolan [1969] Director

Sundial Group Limited
Incorporated: 11 September 1997 *Employees:* 188
Net Worth: £7,225,621 *Total Assets:* £15,674,969
Registered Office: Highgate House, Creaton, Northants, NN6 8NN
Activities: Hotels and similar accommodation
Shareholder: Timothy Simon Chudley
Officers: Lee John Forskitt, Secretary; Joanna Elizabeth Chudley [1953] Director; Timothy Simon Chudley [1956] Director; Lee John Forskitt [1983] Finance Director; Lucy Margaret McGibbon [1961] Director; Jeremy Paul Toth [1964] Operations Director

Sunrise Eggs Holdings Limited
Incorporated: 9 October 2015 *Employees:* 59
Net Worth: £22,109,364 *Total Assets:* £26,953,262
Registered Office: Eltham House, 6 Forest Road, Loughborough, Leics, LE11 3NP
Activities: Activities of head offices
Shareholders: Adian Damian Crawley; Philip Anthony Crawley
Officers: Adian Damian Crawley [1971] Sales Director; Phillip Anthony Crawley [1969] Production Director

Sunrise Poultry Farms Limited
Incorporated: 20 September 1973 *Employees:* 59
Net Worth: £19,980,156 *Total Assets:* £23,902,944
Registered Office: 6 Forest Road, Loughborough, Leics, LE11 3NP
Activities: Raising of poultry
Shareholders: Phillip Anthony Crawley; Adian Damian Crawley
Officers: Adian Damian Crawley, Secretary; Adian Damian Crawley [1971] Director/Egg Farmer; Phillip Anthony Crawley [1969] Director/Egg Farmer

Sunrisestar Limited
Incorporated: 23 October 1995 *Employees:* 5
Net Worth: £6,604,151 *Total Assets:* £14,974,522
Registered Office: 10 Portland Lane, Sheffield, S1 4DG
Activities: Other letting and operating of own or leased real estate
Major Shareholder: Maxwell Dernie
Officers: Abigail Ansty Dernie, Secretary; Harry Maxwell Dernie [1992] Director; Maxwell Dernie [1946] Director/Builder

Sunshine Care Bidco Limited
Incorporated: 4 July 2017
Net Worth: £10,700,261 *Total Assets:* £11,278,274
Registered Office: Number Three, Siskin Drive, Middlemarch Business Park, Coventry, Warwicks, CV3 4FJ
Activities: Activities of head offices
Parent: Sunshine Care Midco Limited
Officers: Samuel James Caiger Gray [1977] Director/Investment Professional; Ford David Porter [1951] Director/Investment Professional [British/American]

Sunshine Care Midco Limited
Incorporated: 6 June 2017
Net Worth: £10,486,587 *Total Assets:* £19,000,000
Registered Office: Number Three, Siskin Drive, Middlemarch Business Park, Coventry, Warwicks, CV3 4FJ
Activities: Activities of head offices
Parent: Sunshine Care Topco Limited
Officers: Samuel James Caiger Gray [1977] Director/Investment Professional; Ford David Porter [1951] Director/Investment Professional [British/American]

Sunshine Care Topco Limited
Incorporated: 2 June 2017 *Employees:* 437
Net Worth Deficit: £2,763,830 *Total Assets:* £46,642,936
Registered Office: Number Three, Siskin Drive, Middlemarch Business Park, Coventry, Warwicks, CV3 4FJ
Activities: Activities of other holding companies n.e.c.
Parent: Apposite Healthcare II GP LLP
Officers: Samuel James Caiger Gray [1977] Director/Investment Professional; Ford David Porter [1951] Director/Investment Professional [British/American]

Sunway Travel (Coaching) Holdings Limited
Incorporated: 25 June 2013
Net Worth: £7,465,332 *Total Assets:* £32,882,400
Registered Office: Sunway House, Canklow Meadows Industrial Estate, West Bawtry Road, Rotherham, S Yorks, S60 2XR
Activities: Activities of head offices
Parent: Tours Abroad Group Limited
Officers: Andrew Oldfield, Secretary; Ian Duncan Henry [1963] Director; Kathleen Henry [1965] Director; Andrew Oldfield [1971] Finance Director

Sunway Travel (Coaching) Limited
Incorporated: 25 March 1987 *Employees:* 98
Net Worth: £1,363,372 *Total Assets:* £15,894,209
Registered Office: Sunway House, Canklow Meadows, Rotherham, S Yorks, S60 2XR
Activities: Tour operator activities
Parent: Sunway Travel (Coaching) Holdings Limited
Officers: Andrew Oldfield, Secretary; Ian Duncan Henry [1963] Director/Accountant; Kathleen Henry [1965] Director/Tour Operator; Andrew Oldfield [1971] Finance Director; Christopher Plummer [1969] Operations Director; Liam Race [1985] Commercial Director

Suon Limited
Incorporated: 15 August 1980 *Employees:* 10
Net Worth: £3,400,911 *Total Assets:* £25,656,334
Registered Office: Chander Hill Lane, Holymoorside, Chesterfield, Derbys, S42 7BW
Activities: Other letting and operating of own or leased real estate
Shareholders: John Lindley Wilson; Executors of The Estate of T Mulligan
Officers: Angela Suzanne Hunt, Secretary; Robert Arnold Veerman [1959] Director/Accountant [Dutch]; John Lindley Wilson [1943] Director/Civil Engineer

Supply Point Systems Limited
Incorporated: 14 January 1998 *Employees:* 68
Net Worth: £6,416,115 *Total Assets:* £9,808,176
Registered Office: Unit B, Swift Park, Swift Valley Industrial Estate, Rugby, Warwicks, CV21 1DZ
Activities: Manufacture of other special-purpose machinery n.e.c.
Officers: Andrew Jonathan Evans, Secretary; Paul Brown [1963] Director [American]; Douglas D. Macpherson [1966] Director [American]; Quintin Potgieter [1971] Finance Director

Supported Living Care Property Limited
Incorporated: 16 July 2015
Net Worth Deficit: £1,368,819 *Total Assets:* £37,538,520
Registered Office: Cedar House, Abingdon Road, Tubney, Oxon, OX13 5QQ
Activities: Other residential care activities n.e.c.
Shareholders: Dimitrios Hatzis; David Rae Wylde; Dimitrios Hatzis; David Rae Wylde
Officers: Dimitrios Hatzis [1961] Director [Greek]; David Rae Wylde [1950] Director

Supreme Concrete Limited
Incorporated: 19 January 1979 *Employees:* 227
Net Worth: £45,156,976 *Total Assets:* £58,081,888
Registered Office: Leicester Road, Ibstock, Leics, LE67 6HS
Activities: Manufacture of concrete products for construction purposes
Parent: Ibstock PLC
Officers: Robert Douglas, Secretary; Mark Whitfield Houghton [1961] Director; Joseph Henry Hudson [1969] Director; Kevin John Sims [1961] Director; Timothy William Wright [1972] Sales Director

Sureclean Holdco Limited
Incorporated: 18 February 2014 *Employees:* 78
Net Worth: £7,723,324 *Total Assets:* £9,686,074
Registered Office: NRC, Clarke Road, Bletchley, Milton Keynes, Bucks, MK1 1LG
Activities: Other service activities n.e.c.
Officers: David Leonard Rattner, Secretary; Neil Andrew Challis [1966] Director; Alexander Harman [1975] Director/Investor [American]

Surfpipe Limited
Incorporated: 13 August 1999
Net Worth: £8,234,282 *Total Assets:* £9,869,079
Registered Office: Dene Park, Stratford Road, Wellesbourne, Warwicks, CV35 9RY
Activities: Other letting and operating of own or leased real estate
Officers: Patrick Tobin, Secretary; Angela O'Donoghue [1969] Director/Manager [Irish]; Gemma Ring [1976] Director [Irish]; Patrick Tobin [1941] Director/Accountant [Irish]

Surfreset Limited
Incorporated: 13 August 1999
Net Worth: £2,043,030 *Total Assets:* £28,840,904
Registered Office: Dene Park, Stratford Road, Wellesbourne, Warwicks, CV35 9RN
Activities: Activities of other holding companies n.e.c.
Officers: Donal Ring, Secretary; Jerry Coffey [1947] Director [Irish]; Sean Michael Murphy [1975] Director/Accountant [Irish]; Donal Ring [1946] Director/Manager [Irish]; Patrick Tobin [1941] Director/Accountant [Irish]

Sutton Carter Investments Limited
Incorporated: 4 February 2015 *Employees:* 2
Net Worth: £3,277,702 *Total Assets:* £9,105,911
Registered Office: 8 Wolverton Road, Snitterfield, Stratford upon Avon, Warwicks, CV37 0HB
Activities: Buying and selling of own real estate
Officers: Violeta Ashraf [1985] Director/Accountant [Romanian]; Zahid Ashraf [1984] Director

Sutton Park Holdings Limited
Incorporated: 18 November 2003 *Employees:* 185
Net Worth: £10,161,850 *Total Assets:* £22,837,256
Registered Office: 37 Lichfield Street, Burton on Trent, Staffs, DE14 3RH
Activities: Sale of new cars and light motor vehicles
Major Shareholder: Dean Alfred Fulton
Officers: Joanne Louise Shannon, Secretary; Dean Alfred Fulton [1958] Managing Director; Jacqueline Fulton [1978] Director/Solicitor; Joanne Louise Shannon [1970] Director; Christine Thomas [1961] Financial Director; Mark Paul Yarwood [1971] Operations Director

Sutton Park Motor Company Limited
Incorporated: 25 June 1965 *Employees:* 185
Net Worth: £1,749,607 *Total Assets:* £13,144,376
Registered Office: 37 Lichfield Street, Burton on Trent, Staffs, DE14 3RH
Activities: Sale of new cars and light motor vehicles
Major Shareholder: Dean Alfred Fulton
Officers: Joanne Louise Shannon, Secretary; Dean Alfred Fulton [1958] Director; Jacqueline Fulton [1978] Director/Solicitor; Joanne Louise Shannon [1970] Director/Company Secretary; Christine Thomas [1961] Financial Director; Mark Paul Yarwood [1971] Director/General Manager

Suzuki GB PLC
Incorporated: 23 July 1963 *Employees:* 162
Net Worth: £50,296,000 *Total Assets:* £220,314,000
Registered Office: Steinbeck Crescent, Snelshall West, Milton Keynes, Bucks, MK4 4AE
Activities: Sale of new cars and light motor vehicles
Parent: Suzuki Motor Corporation
Officers: Junita Fernandez, Secretary; Nobuo Suyama [1958] Director [Japanese]; Takanori Suzuki [1957] Director [Japanese]

W.R.Swann & Co.Limited
Incorporated: 7 July 1948 *Employees:* 413
Net Worth: £20,038,352 *Total Assets:* £43,492,824
Registered Office: Owlerton Green, Sheffield, S6 2BJ
Activities: Activities of other holding companies n.e.c.
Shareholder: W R Swann & Co Trustee Ltd
Officers: Michael Ian Hirst, Secretary; Michael Ian Hirst [1959] Director/Chartered Accountant; Michael John McGinley [1942] Director/Retired; Christopher Lee Taylor [1962] Export Sales Director; Richard John Whiteley [1964] Managing Director

Swann-Morton Limited
Incorporated: 28 June 1961 *Employees:* 333
Net Worth: £11,099,349 *Total Assets:* £34,020,244
Registered Office: Owlerton Green, Sheffield, S6 2BJ
Activities: Manufacture of medical and dental instruments and supplies
Parent: W R Swann & Co Ltd
Officers: Michael Ian Hirst, Secretary; Michael Ian Hirst [1959] Director/Chartered Accountant; Christopher Lee Taylor [1962] Director/Sales Manager; Richard John Whiteley [1964] Director/Manager

Swanscombe Development LLP
Incorporated: 11 March 2015
Net Worth: £7,126,196 *Total Assets:* £16,347,991
Registered Office: Bardon Hall, Copt Oak Road, Markfield, Leics, LE67 9PJ

Swanton Care & Community (Andrew Frederick Care Homes) Limited
Incorporated: 5 June 1998 *Employees:* 347
Net Worth: £12,676,701 *Total Assets:* £14,298,532
Registered Office: Swanton Care & Community Limited, Number Three, Siskin Drive, Middlemarch Business Park, Coventry, Warwicks, CV3 4FJ
Activities: Residential care activities for the elderly and disabled
Parent: Swanton Care & Community Limited
Officers: Garry Anthony Cross [1961] Director; Andrew Dalton [1968] Director; Samuel James Caiger Gray [1977] Director/Investment Professional; Ford David Porter [1951] Director/Investment Professional [British/American]

Swanton Care & Community (Autism North) Limited
Incorporated: 16 September 2002 *Employees:* 269
Net Worth: £15,959,313 *Total Assets:* £16,547,625
Registered Office: Swanton Care & Community Limited, Number Three, Siskin Drive, Middlemarch Business Park, Coventry, Warwicks, CV3 4FJ
Activities: Residential care activities for the elderly and disabled
Parent: Swanton Care & Community (Glenpath Holdings) Limited
Officers: Garry Anthony Cross [1961] Director; Andrew Dalton [1968] Director; Samuel James Caiger Gray [1977] Director/Investment Professional; Ford David Porter [1951] Director/Investment Professional [British/American]

Swanton Care & Community (Glenpath Holdings) Limited
Incorporated: 5 March 1997
Net Worth: £18,064,480 *Total Assets:* £19,931,918
Registered Office: Swanton Care & Community Limited, Number Three, Siskin Drive, Middlemarch Business Park, Coventry, Warwicks, CV3 4FJ
Activities: Development of building projects
Parent: Swanton Care & Community Limited
Officers: Garry Anthony Cross [1961] Director; Andrew Dalton [1968] Director; Samuel James Caiger Gray [1977] Director/Investment Professional; Ford David Porter [1951] Director/Investment Professional [British/American]

Swanton Care & Community (Maesteilo Care Homes) Limited
Incorporated: 9 March 2000 *Employees:* 151
Net Worth: £15,836,062 *Total Assets:* £16,157,346
Registered Office: Swanton Care & Community Limited, Number Three, Siskin Drive, Middlemarch Business Park, Coventry, Warwicks, CV3 4FJ
Activities: Residential care activities for the elderly and disabled
Parent: Swanton Care & Community Limited
Officers: Garry Anthony Cross [1961] Director; Andrew Dalton [1968] Director; Samuel James Caiger Gray [1977] Director/Investment Professional; Ford David Porter [1951] Director/Investment Professional [British/American]; Gary David Thompson [1967] Director/Chief Operations Officer

Swanton Care & Community Limited
Incorporated: 21 April 2006 *Employees:* 877
Net Worth: £13,408,377 *Total Assets:* £48,266,264
Registered Office: Swanton Care & Community Limited, Number Three, Siskin Drive, Middlemarch Business Park, Coventry, Warwicks, CV3 4FJ
Activities: Other human health activities
Parent: Sunshine Care Bidco Limited
Officers: Dr Generald Michael Bereika [1947] Director [American]; Garry Anthony Cross [1961] Director; Andrew Dalton [1968] Director; Samuel James Caiger Gray [1977] Director/Investment Professional; Ford David Porter [1951] Director/Investment Professional [British/American]

Swiftbuild Properties Limited
Incorporated: 5 April 2004
Net Worth: £4,567,683 *Total Assets:* £9,066,489
Registered Office: Greenside House, Greenside Avenue, Staincross, Barnsley, S Yorks, S75 6BB
Activities: Construction of commercial buildings
Parent: Silk Healthcare Holdings Ltd
Officers: Mandy Joanne Mottram, Secretary; Simon Kirk Monaghan [1961] Director/Chief Executive; Mark Terry [1963] Finance Director

Swizzels Matlow Limited
Incorporated: 6 March 1956 *Employees:* 634
Net Worth: £41,499,000 *Total Assets:* £73,036,000
Registered Office: Carlton House, Albion Road, New Mills, High Peak, Derbys, SK22 3HA
Activities: Manufacture of sugar confectionery
Officers: Ian Walker, Secretary; Brian Neiman Dee [1945] Director/Manufacturing Confectioner; Jeremy Adam Dee [1975] Director; Jonathan Mark Dee [1976] Director; Trevor Jack Leslie William Matlow [1935] Director/Manufacturing Confectioner; Nicola Ruth Wertheim [1970] Director

SWK (U.K.) Holding Limited
Incorporated: 17 February 2004
Net Worth: £27,441,972 *Total Assets:* £27,441,972
Registered Office: 3 Europa Court, Sheffield Business Park, Europa Link, Sheffield, S9 1XE
Activities: Activities of head offices
Parent: Stanley U.K. Holding Ltd.
Officers: Steven John Costello, Secretary; Steven John Costello [1980] Director/Chartered Accountant; Mark Richard Smiley [1977] Director/General Manager UK & ROI; Amit Kumar Sood [1978] Director/Accountant

Sycamore (Peterborough) Limited
Incorporated: 1 October 1926 *Employees:* 99
Net Worth: £14,902,867 *Total Assets:* £29,750,804
Registered Office: c/o Grant Thornton UK LLP, Regent House, 80 Regent Road, Leicester, LE1 7NH
Activities: Sale of new cars and light motor vehicles
Parent: Central Garage (Uppingham) Limited
Officers: Ilse-Charlotte Hamblin [1940] Director [German]; Samantha Caroline Hamblin [1974] Director; Daniel Lee Stone [1968] Director/Chief Executive

Syita Properties Limited
Incorporated: 18 February 1986
Net Worth: £10,009,168 *Total Assets:* £14,622,854
Registered Office: First Floor, 11 Broad Street West, Sheffield, S1 2BQ
Activities: Other letting and operating of own or leased real estate
Parent: Sheffield City Region Combined Authority
Officers: Claire James, Secretary; Ruth Clare Adams [1967] Director; David Richard Corbett Phillips [1965] Director/Local Government Officer; Mike Thomas [1975] Director/Senior Finance Manager

Symm Group Limited
Incorporated: 18 August 1928 *Employees:* 158
Net Worth: £2,661,847 *Total Assets:* £9,013,413
Registered Office: Symm House, Osney Mead, Oxford, OX2 0EQ
Activities: Activities of head offices
Officers: Mark Wittet, Secretary; James John Axtell [1972] Director/Management Consultant; James Daniel Pike [1970] Director/Fund Manager; Mark Wittet [1960] Director/Chartered Accountant

Symmetry Medical Sheffield Ltd.
Incorporated: 18 October 1934 *Employees:* 276
Net Worth Deficit: £1,322,000 *Total Assets:* £33,580,000
Registered Office: Beulah Road, Sheffield, S6 2AN
Activities: Forging, pressing, stamping and roll-forming of metal; powder metallurgy
Officers: Adrian Robert Jones, Secretary; Ernest James Layland [1969] Finance Director; Kester Vaughan [1960] Director/General Manager

The Symphony Group PLC
Incorporated: 27 August 1971 *Employees:* 1,586
Net Worth: £59,397,000 *Total Assets:* £94,256,000
Registered Office: Pen Hill Estate, Park Spring Road, Barnsley, S Yorks, S72 7EZ
Activities: Manufacture of kitchen furniture
Parent: Symphony Holdings Limited
Officers: Adrienne Lee Murdoch, Secretary; Richard James Bunton [1968] Director; Martyn Royston Davis [1947] Director; Katherine May Gregory [1967] Director/Solicitor; Graham Smith [1960] Finance Director

Symphony Holdings Limited
Incorporated: 10 August 2005 *Employees:* 1,586
Net Worth: £59,703,000 *Total Assets:* £94,677,000
Registered Office: Pen Hill Estate, Park Spring Road, Barnsley, S Yorks, S72 7EZ
Activities: Activities of head offices
Officers: Adrienne Lee Murdoch, Secretary; Richard James Bunton [1968] Director; Martyn Royston Davis [1947] Director; Katherine May Gregory [1967] Director/Solicitor; Graham Smith [1960] Finance Director

Synarbor Limited
Incorporated: 4 March 2004
Previous: Synarbor PLC
Net Worth: £9,199,067 *Total Assets:* £19,371,122
Registered Office: Second Floor, Sir Wilfrid Newton House, Thorncliffe Park, Chapeltown, Sheffield, S35 2PH
Activities: Temporary employment agency activities
Parent: Star Bidco Limited
Officers: Katharine Irene Spedding, Secretary; William John Etchell [1971] Director/Chief Financial Officer; Julian Edward Harley [1957] Director; Robyn Julieann Johnstone [1967] Director [British/Australian]; Robert Douglas King [1982] Director/Fund Manager

Synchemicals Limited
Incorporated: 30 July 1941 *Employees:* 198
Net Worth: £26,556,000 *Total Assets:* £30,464,000
Registered Office: Owen Street, Coalville, Leics, LE67 3DE
Activities: Activities of head offices
Officers: Anja Gooding, Secretary; Anja Gooding [1984] Director/Finance; Paul Antony Gooding [1958] Director/Accountant; Julian Wesley Lee Plews [1955] Director/Accountant; Daniel Stephen Wilkinson [1971] Director/Sales & Marketing

Syncimage Limited
Incorporated: 31 August 1999
Net Worth: £16,931,972 *Total Assets:* £27,851,192
Registered Office: Dene Park, Stratford Road, Wellesbourne, Warwicks, CV35 9RY
Activities: Other letting and operating of own or leased real estate
Officers: Patrick Tobin, Secretary; Gemma O'Neill [1976] Director [Irish]; Angela O'Donoghue [1969] Director/Manager [Irish]; Patrick Tobin [1941] Director/Accountant [Irish]

Syncreon Automotive (UK) Ltd.
Incorporated: 23 January 1995 *Employees:* 491
Net Worth: £4,286,316 *Total Assets:* £19,824,850
Registered Office: Unit 5 Logix Road, R D Park, Watling Street, Hinckley, Leics, LE10 3BQ
Activities: Manufacture of other parts and accessories for motor vehicles
Officers: Kenneth Pocius, Secretary; Colin Michael Enright [1977] Director/Chief Operating Officer [Irish]; Patrick Joseph Brian Enright [1971] Director [Irish]; Carine Van Landschoot [1970] Director Finance and Administration [Belgian]

Syncreon Technology (UK) Ltd
Incorporated: 14 October 1983 *Employees:* 288
Net Worth: £4,583,291 *Total Assets:* £21,904,072
Registered Office: Unit 5 Logix Road, R D Park, Watling Street, Hinckley, Leics, LE10 3BQ
Activities: Freight transport by road
Officers: Kenneth Pocius, Secretary; Colin Michael Enright [1977] Director/Chief Operating Officer [Irish]; Patrick Joseph Brian Enright [1971] Director [Irish]; Carine Van Landschoot [1970] Director/Chief Financial Officer [Belgian]

Syncreon UK Holdings Limited
Incorporated: 25 September 2009
Net Worth Deficit: £30,325,476 *Total Assets:* £35,241,920
Registered Office: Unit 5 Logix Road, R D Park, Hinckley, Leics, LE10 3BQ
Activities: Activities of distribution holding companies
Officers: Kenneth Pocius, Secretary; Patrick Joseph Brian Enright [1971] Director [Irish]; Carine Van Landschoot [1970] Director [Belgian]

Synectic Systems Group Limited
Incorporated: 12 May 2006 *Employees:* 211
Net Worth: £5,816,000 *Total Assets:* £34,342,000
Registered Office: Synectics House, 3-4 Broadfield Close, Sheffield, S8 0XN
Activities: Security systems service activities
Parent: Synectics PLC
Officers: Simon Beswick, Secretary; Simon Beswick [1964] Finance Director; David Kerr Wilson Gavin [1977] Director/General Manager; Paul Anthony Webb [1965] Director

Synergy Fund LLP
Incorporated: 26 March 2009
Net Worth: £1,502 *Total Assets:* £16,264,006
Registered Office: The Old Rectory, Addington, Buckingham, MK18 2JR
Officers: Laurence Edward William Vaughan [1963] Member; Frank Goodman Sytner [1944] LLP Member

Synergy Health Managed Services Limited
Incorporated: 7 February 2013 *Employees:* 806
Net Worth: £27,541,000 *Total Assets:* £33,663,000
Registered Office: Synergylms, Ascot Drive, Derby, DE24 8HE
Activities: Other human health activities
Parent: Star Mayan Limited
Officers: Andrew Darren Holdcroft [1970] Finance Director; Michael John Langhorn [1958] Director

Synseal Extrusions Limited
Incorporated: 6 December 1991 *Employees:* 1,026
Net Worth: £25,998,000 *Total Assets:* £59,877,000
Registered Office: Synseal Extrusions, Common Road, Huthwaite, Notts, NG17 6AD
Activities: Manufacture of other plastic products
Parent: Allerford Intermediate Newco Limited
Officers: Leigh Daveran [1970] Director/Finance and Acquisition; Andrew Royston Jones [1968] Sales and Marketing Director; Rolf Peter Adrianus Nuijens [1969] Director/Investor & Advisor [Dutch]; Christian Reiner [1977] Investment Director [Swedish]

Synthetic Resins Limited
Incorporated: 15 December 1933
Net Worth: £439,000 *Total Assets:* £11,376,000
Registered Office: Wollaston Hall, Wollaston, Wellingborough, Northants, NN9 7RL
Activities: Manufacture of plastics in primary forms
Officers: Matthew Ian Collins, Secretary; Matthew Ian Collins [1972] Director; Jean-Claude Pierre [1964] Director/Group Chief Executive [French]

Synventive Acquisition UK Limited
Incorporated: 3 March 2005
Previous: 05381782 Limited
Net Worth Deficit: £20,389,376 *Total Assets:* £95,638,120
Registered Office: The Pinnacle, 160 Midsummer Boulevard, Milton Keynes, Bucks, MK9 1FF
Activities: Non-trading company
Parent: Barnes Group Inc
Officers: Michael Vincent Kennedy [1961] Director [American]; Douglas William McNeilly [1964] Director/Accountant; Klaus Peter Peya [1984] Director/Controller [German]

Synventive Acquisition Unlimited
Incorporated: 26 July 2005
Net Worth: £78,956,808 *Total Assets:* £79,989,104
Registered Office: The Pinnacle, 160 Midsummer Boulevard, Milton Keynes, Bucks, MK9 1FF
Activities: Manufacture of other plastic products
Parent: Barnes Group Inc
Officers: Michael Vincent Kennedy [1961] Director/Vice President of Tax [American]; Douglas William McNeilly [1964] Director/Accountant; Klaus Peter Peya [1984] Director/Controller [German]

Synventive Holding Limited
Incorporated: 16 July 2003
Net Worth Deficit: £1,464,957 *Total Assets:* £33,511,908
Registered Office: The Pinnacle, 160 Midsummer Boulevard, Milton Keynes, Bucks, MK9 1FF
Activities: Other manufacturing n.e.c.
Officers: Michael Vincent Kennedy [1961] Director/Vice President of Tax [American]; Douglas William McNeilly [1964] Director/Accountant; Klaus-Peter Peya [1984] Director/Controller [German]; Jason Todd Ulery [1975] Finance Director [American]

SYS8 Holding Limited
Incorporated: 26 August 2008
Net Worth: £30,365,272 *Total Assets:* £30,913,722
Registered Office: Sandford Gate, East Point Business Park, Sandy Lane West, Oxford, OX4 6LB
Activities: Distribution of electricity
Parent: Sensitlive Limited
Officers: Eva Maria de Almeida [1965] Director [Austrian]

Sysmex UK Limited
Incorporated: 5 April 1991 *Employees:* 147
Net Worth: £23,082,572 *Total Assets:* £37,554,648
Registered Office: Sysmex House, Garamonde Drive, Wymbush, Milton Keynes, Bucks, MK8 8DF
Activities: Hospital activities
Officers: Robert Victor Kaukis, Secretary; Seido Biwa [1972] Managing Director [Japanese]; Keith Lawrence Howes [1959] Managing Director; Nigel Pattinson [1963] Director of Sales & Marketing; Matthias Volkel [1967] Director/Senior Executive Officer EMEA [German]

System Q Limited
Incorporated: 7 January 1994 *Employees:* 33
Net Worth: £17,089,864 *Total Assets:* £17,646,988
Registered Office: McGregor's Way, Turnoaks Business Park, Hasland, Chesterfield, Derbys, S40 2WB
Activities: Manufacture of other electrical equipment
Officers: Philip Raymond Herrick, Secretary; Julia Anne Temple, Secretary; Paul David Goodwin [1965] Director/Sales; Generaldine Hitchen [1964] Director/General Manager; Julian Charles Hook [1963] Director; Julia Anne Temple [1971] Director/Marketing Manager

Sytner Cars Limited
Incorporated: 25 June 1993 *Employees:* 269
Net Worth: £33,933,000 *Total Assets:* £81,719,000
Registered Office: 2 Penman Way, Grove Park, Leicester, LE19 1ST
Activities: Sale of new cars and light motor vehicles
Parent: Sytner Group Limited
Officers: Adam Collinson, Secretary; Adam Collinson [1972] Finance Director; Darren Edwards [1968] Managing Director; Robert Harold Kurnick [1961] Director/Executive Vice President [American]; Jeremy Richard Mallett [1952] Director; Gerard Edward Nieuwenhuys [1960] Director; Laurence Edward William Vaughan [1963] Managing Director

Sytner Group Limited
Incorporated: 24 December 1993 *Employees:* 8,928
Net Worth: £350,820,000 *Total Assets:* £1,657,668,992
Registered Office: 2 Penman Way, Grove Park, Leicester, LE19 1ST
Activities: Sale of new cars and light motor vehicles
Parent: UAG UK Holdings Limited
Officers: Adam Collinson, Secretary; Adam Collinson [1972] Finance Director; Darren Edwards [1968] Managing Director; Robert Harold Kurnick [1961] Director/Executive Vice President [American]; Jeremy Richard Mallett [1952] Director; Gerard Edward Nieuwenhuys [1960] Director; Laurence Edward William Vaughan [1963] Managing Director; Jens Christian Werner [1964] Managing Director [German]

Sytner Limited
Incorporated: 23 July 1964 *Employees:* 2,068
Net Worth: £79,040,000 *Total Assets:* £484,305,984
Registered Office: 2 Penman Way, Grove Park, Leicester, LE19 1ST
Activities: Sale of new cars and light motor vehicles
Parent: Sytner Group Limited
Officers: Adam Collinson, Secretary; Adam Collinson [1972] Finance Director; Darren Edwards [1968] Managing Director; Robert Harold Kurnick [1961] Director/Executive Vice President [American]; Jeremy Richard Mallett [1952] Director; Gerard Edward Nieuwenhuys [1960] Director; Laurence Edward William Vaughan [1963] Managing Director

Sytner Vehicles Limited
Incorporated: 28 November 2009 *Employees:* 70
Net Worth: £7,586,000 *Total Assets:* £15,065,000
Registered Office: 2 Penman Way, Grove Park, Leicester, LE19 1ST
Activities: Sale of new cars and light motor vehicles
Parent: Sytner Group Limited
Officers: Adam Collinson, Secretary; Adam Collinson [1972] Finance Director; Darren Edwards [1968] Managing Director; Jeremy Richard Mallett [1952] Director; Gerard Edward Nieuwenhuys [1952] Director; Laurence Edward William Vaughan [1963] Managing Director

Sywell Aerodrome,Limited
Incorporated: 14 January 1933 *Employees:* 76
Net Worth: £10,132,868 *Total Assets:* £16,546,482
Registered Office: Hall Farm, Sywell Aerodrome, Sywell, Northampton, NN6 0BN
Activities: Mixed farming
Officers: Michael Harold Bletsoe Brown [1951] Director; Philip John Bletsoe Brown [1960] Director/Farmer; Amy Elizabeth Bletsoe-Brown [1985] Director; Jessica Conway [1990] Director; Meryl Findlay [1939] Director/Manager and Company Secretary; Philip Andrew Hall [1972] Director; Colin Bernard Heslop [1943] Director/Chartered Accountant; Anthony Clive Hewitt [1949] Director; Janet Jones [1967] Director/Chartered Accountant; Simon Durrant Shaw [1958] Director/Farmer

T & W Civil Engineering Limited
Incorporated: 17 January 1994 *Employees:* 42
Net Worth: £15,488,439 *Total Assets:* £26,154,290
Registered Office: 183 Fraser Road, Sheffield, S8 0JP
Activities: Construction of commercial buildings
Parent: T & W Holdings Limited
Officers: Martin David Burchnall [1967] Director; Adrian Timothy Norman [1966] Director

T & W Group Limited
Incorporated: 9 September 2015 *Employees:* 44
Net Worth: £6,038,128 *Total Assets:* £30,537,508
Registered Office: 183 Fraser Road, Sheffield, S8 0JP
Activities: Other business support service activities n.e.c.
Shareholders: Jill Penelope Wales; Peter Martin Wales
Officers: Nicola Ayres-Norman, Secretary; Martin David Burchnall [1967] Director; Adrian Timothy Norman [1966] Director

T N Capital Limited
Incorporated: 13 May 2014
Net Worth: £6,734,209 *Total Assets:* £15,755,569
Registered Office: 50 Woodgate, Leicester, LE3 5GF
Activities: Buying and selling of own real estate
Officers: Nitin Chouhan [1963] Director; Terry Grubb [1953] Director

T-Mobile Holdings Limited
Incorporated: 6 September 1999
Net Worth: £3,339,553,536 *Total Assets:* £3,339,591,936
Registered Office: Futura House, Bradbourne Drive, Tilbrook, Milton Keynes, Bucks, MK7 8AZ
Activities: Activities of head offices
Parent: CTA Holding GmbH
Officers: Jeevan D'Silva, Secretary; Jeremy Stuart Boorman [1972] Director; Jeevan D'Silva [1962] Director; Claire Sandra Hilton [1958] Director; Dr Uli Kuehbacher [1961] Director [German]

The T-Shirt Guy Holdings Limited
Incorporated: 11 September 2014
Net Worth: £11,598,658 *Total Assets:* £11,632,537
Registered Office: c/o Charnwood Accountants, The Point, Granite Way, Mountsorrel, Loughborough, Leics, LE12 7TZ
Activities: Activities of other holding companies n.e.c.
Shareholders: Susan Elizabeth Booth; Robert James Booth
Officers: Susan Elizabeth Booth, Secretary; Robert James Booth [1969] Director; Susan Elizabeth Booth [1978] Director

T. C. Landscapes Limited
Incorporated: 28 January 2003 *Employees:* 296
Net Worth: £5,509,078 *Total Assets:* £36,846,728
Registered Office: Covey Farm, Pitsford Road, Chapel Brampton, Northampton, NN6 8BE
Activities: Landscape service activities
Parent: T.C.L. Holdings Limited
Officers: Simon John Abley [1976] Director/Accountant; Joseph Anthony Cammiss [1970] Director; Simon John Cashmore [1970] Director/Accountant; Robert Chatwin [1984] Director

T. Quality Limited
Incorporated: 28 June 1947 *Employees:* 249
Net Worth: £8,091,241 *Total Assets:* £16,453,471
Registered Office: Ings Road, Doncaster, S Yorks, DN5 9TL
Activities: Wholesale of other food, including fish, crustaceans and molluscs
Parent: Saria Limited
Officers: Darren Creese, Secretary; Richard Graham Brooks [1965] Purchasing Director; Michael John Crees [1972] Sales Director; Darren Creese [1972] Director; Andrew Richard Smith [1962] Director/Group Commercial Manager

T.C. Landscapes Group Limited
Incorporated: 29 January 2007
Net Worth Deficit: £3,350,447 *Total Assets:* £33,204,140
Registered Office: TCL House, 7 Outrams Wharf, Little Eaton, Derby, DE21 5EL
Activities: Landscape service activities
Parent: T.C.L. Holdings Limited
Officers: Simon John Abley [1976] Director/Accountant; Simon John Cashmore [1970] Director/Accountant; Robert Chatwin [1984] Director

T.C.L. Holdings (Midco) Limited
Incorporated: 15 April 2014 *Employees:* 2
Net Worth Deficit: £1,772,688 *Total Assets:* £60,493,312
Registered Office: TCL House, 7 Outrams Wharf, Little Eaton, Derby, DE21 5EL
Activities: Landscape service activities
Parent: T.C.L. Holdings (Parent) Limited
Officers: Simon John Abley [1976] Director/Accountant; Simon John Cashmore [1970] Managing Director; Robert Chatwin [1984] Director

T.C.L. Holdings (Parent) Limited
Incorporated: 3 April 2014 *Employees:* 771
Net Worth Deficit: £12,682,628 *Total Assets:* £35,599,568
Registered Office: TCL House, 7 Outrams Wharf, Little Eaton, Derby, DE21 5EL
Activities: Activities of other holding companies n.e.c.
Shareholder: Business Growth Fund PLC
Officers: Simon John Abley [1976] Director/Accountant; Stuart John Black [1964] Director; Simon John Cashmore [1970] Managing Director; Robert Chatwin [1984] Director; Paul Oldham [1964] Investor Director; Mark Wood [1964] Director

T.C.L. Holdings Limited
Incorporated: 26 January 2007
Net Worth: £600,000 *Total Assets:* £26,528,968
Registered Office: TCL House, 7 Outrams Wharf, Little Eaton, Derby, DE21 5EL
Activities: Landscape service activities
Parent: T.C.L. Holdings (Midco) Limited
Officers: Simon John Abley [1976] Director/Accountant; Simon John Cashmore [1970] Director/Accountant; Robert Chatwin [1984] Director

T.D.P. Textiles Limited
Incorporated: 5 May 1982 *Employees:* 147
Net Worth: £13,262,674 *Total Assets:* £15,566,025
Registered Office: TDP House, Rawdon Road, Moira, Swadlincote, Derbys, DE12 6DT
Activities: Manufacture of other wearing apparel and accessories n.e.c.
Major Shareholder: Timothy James Goadby Dawson
Officers: Tony Myerscough, Secretary; Ann Marie Dawson [1954] Director; Timothy James Goadby Dawson [1953] Director; Dean Anthony Greasley [1964] Licensing Director; Neil Scotney Henfrey [1958] Director; Tony Alexander Myerscough [1968] Director; Brian Charles O'Connor [1973] Director

T.J.D. Trade Limited
Incorporated: 10 January 2003 *Employees:* 5
Net Worth Deficit: £235,333 *Total Assets:* £21,399,280
Registered Office: TJD Trade Ltd, Manton Lane, Manton Industrial Estate, Bedford, MK41 7TL
Activities: Development of building projects
Major Shareholder: Johanna Kesmin Marks
Officers: Johanna Kesmin Marks [1962] Director

T.L. Care Limited
Incorporated: 6 April 1994 *Employees:* 283
Net Worth: £13,763,300 *Total Assets:* £18,805,692
Registered Office: 91-97 Saltergate, Chesterfield, Derbys, S40 1LA
Activities: Other human health activities
Parent: Hill Care 2 Ltd
Officers: Alexandra Josephine Hill, Secretary; Ian Philip Mitchell, Secretary; John Hill [1975] Director/Care Home Proprietor; Wendy Jane Waddicor [1964] Operations Director

T.S.B. (Developments) Limited
Incorporated: 2 August 1996 *Employees:* 110
Net Worth: £9,495,127 *Total Assets:* £12,429,017
Registered Office: 29 Wood Street, Stratford upon Avon, Warwicks, CV37 6JG
Activities: Hotels and similar accommodation
Shareholders: Stuart Greville Moberley; Gavin Antony Lenthall
Officers: Dawn Sale, Company Secretary/Director; Dale Huckerby [1964] Director/Accountant; Daynor Moberley [1971] Director; Nicholas James Moberley [1971] Director; Dawn Sale [1963] Company Secretary/Director

Tadano UK Ltd
Incorporated: 18 October 2001 *Employees:* 18
Net Worth: £3,493,937 *Total Assets:* £15,308,765
Registered Office: 42 Pitt Street, Barnsley, S Yorks, S70 1BB
Activities: Wholesale of mining, construction and civil engineering machinery
Parent: Tadano Ltd
Officers: Andrew Plant [1967] Director/General Manager; Rolf Gottfried Sonntag [1965] Director [German]

TAG Partnership LLP
Incorporated: 10 February 2005
Net Worth: £8,559,873 *Total Assets:* £14,199,663
Registered Office: 2 Rutland Park, Sheffield, S10 2PD
Officers: Christopher James Green [1963] Member; Michael John Green [1958] Member; Gillian Elaine Green [1958] LLP Member; Helen Claire Green [1963] LLP Member; Rachel Lindsay Green [1969] LLP Member; Simon Green [1962] LLP Member; Sophie Rosanna Green [1991] LLP Member; Susan Humphrey [1960] LLP Member; Helen Whysall [1968] LLP Member

Talasey Ltd
Incorporated: 21 June 2004 *Employees:* 53
Previous: Natural Paving Products (UK) Ltd
Net Worth: £5,848,339 *Total Assets:* £15,637,078
Registered Office: Belton Road, Sandtoft, Doncaster, S Yorks, DN8 5SX
Activities: Non-specialised wholesale trade
Major Shareholder: Mark Wall
Officers: Duncan Weighill, Secretary; Malcolm Gough [1967] Business Development Director; Mark Wall [1972] Director/Chartered Engineer; Juliette Rose Yeardley [1976] Finance Director

Tallington Holdings Limited
Incorporated: 29 June 2004 *Employees:* 1
Net Worth: £6,367,809 *Total Assets:* £9,320,761
Registered Office: Barholm Road, Tallington, Stamford, Lincs, PE9 4RJ
Activities: Activities of head offices
Major Shareholder: Neil Morgan
Officers: Neil Morgan [1962] Director

Tamar (Selby) Limited
Incorporated: 25 October 2001
Net Worth: £3,759,149 *Total Assets:* £16,411,788
Registered Office: Euro Auctions Yard, Roall Lane, Kellington, Goole, N Humbers, DN14 0NY
Activities: Other letting and operating of own or leased real estate
Officers: Patricia Georgina Keys, Secretary; Derek Irwin Keys [1966] Director

Tamar Energy (Holdings) Limited
Incorporated: 16 June 2014 *Employees:* 75
Net Worth Deficit: £30,994,000 *Total Assets:* £9,912,000
Registered Office: c/o Biogen, Milton Parc, Milton Ernest, Bedford, MK44 1YU
Activities: Activities of other holding companies n.e.c.
Parent: Tamar Energy Limited
Officers: Adam Feneley [1980] Managing Director; Stuart Peter Greenfield [1962] Director/Financial Controller; Simon Musther [1958] Commercial Director; Andrew Mark Sibley [1978] Director; Graeme Kenneth Charles Vincent [1965] Operations Director

Tamar Energy Limited
Incorporated: 13 July 2011 *Employees:* 75
Net Worth: £22,962,000 *Total Assets:* £46,351,000
Registered Office: c/o Biogen, Milton Parc, Milton Ernest, Bedford, MK44 1YU
Activities: Construction of utility projects for electricity and telecommunications
Parent: Ancala Bioenergy Limited
Officers: Adam Feneley [1980] Managing Director; Simon Musther [1958] Commercial Director; Graeme Kenneth Charles Vincent [1965] Operations Director

Tamar Energy Operating Company (One) Limited
Incorporated: 17 June 2014
Net Worth Deficit: £23,563,000 *Total Assets:* £23,734,000
Registered Office: c/o Biogen, Milton Parc, Milton Ernest, Bedford, MK44 1YU
Activities: Activities of production holding companies
Parent: Tamar Energy (Hermes Holdings) Limited
Officers: Adam Feneley [1980] Managing Director; Stuart Peter Greenfield [1962] Director/Financial Controller; Simon Musther [1958] Commercial Director; Graeme Kenneth Charles Vincent [1965] Operations Director

Tamar Renewable Power (Essex) Limited
Incorporated: 23 February 2010 *Employees:* 9
Net Worth Deficit: £11,201,000 *Total Assets:* £10,384,000
Registered Office: c/o Biogen, Milton Parc, Milton Ernest, Bedford, MK44 1YU
Activities: Production of electricity
Parent: Tamar Energy Operating Company (One) Ltd
Officers: Adam Feneley [1980] Managing Director; Simon Musther [1958] Commercial Director; Andrew Mark Sibley [1978] Director/Operations Manager; Graeme Kenneth Charles Vincent [1965] Operations Director

Tamar Renewable Power (Hoddesdon) Limited
Incorporated: 18 June 2014
Net Worth Deficit: £18,515,000 *Total Assets:* £10,882,000
Registered Office: c/o Biogen, Milton Parc, Milton Ernest, Bedford, MK44 1YU
Activities: Production of electricity
Parent: Tamar Energy (Holdings) Limited
Officers: Adam Feneley [1980] Managing Director; Stuart Peter Greenfield [1962] Director/Financial Controller; Simon Musther [1958] Commercial Director; Graeme Kenneth Charles Vincent [1965] Operations Director

Tanglewood (Lincolnshire) Limited
Incorporated: 7 September 1988 *Employees:* 464
Net Worth: £21,395,156 *Total Assets:* £33,331,404
Registered Office: 2 Endeavour Park, Wyberton, Boston, Lincs, PE21 7TQ
Activities: Medical nursing home activities
Parent: Tanglewood Care Homes Limited
Officers: Jonathan Charles Griffin [1965] Director/Private Client Advisor; Tracy Ann Shelbourn [1959] Director

Tanglewood Care Homes Limited
Incorporated: 18 August 2011 *Employees:* 492
Net Worth: £14,212,713 *Total Assets:* £31,727,570
Registered Office: 2 Endeavour Park, Wyberton, Boston, Lincs, PE21 7TQ
Activities: Activities of head offices
Shareholders: Tracy Ann Shelbourn; Martin Shelbourn
Officers: Jonathan Charles Griffin [1965] Director/Private Client Advisor; Martin Shelbourn [1958] Director; Tracy Ann Shelbourn [1959] Director

Tanks and Vessels Industries Limited
Incorporated: 6 April 1977 *Employees:* 33
Net Worth: £6,716,022 *Total Assets:* £9,980,119
Registered Office: Bankwood Lane Trading Estate, Bankwood Lane, New Rossington, Doncaster, S Yorks, DN11 0PS
Activities: Manufacture of other tanks, reservoirs and containers of metal
Major Shareholder: Anthony Derrek Morris
Officers: George Arthur Smith, Secretary; Anthony Derrek Morris [1947] Director; George Arthur Smith [1950] Finance Director

Tansor (Cornbow) Limited
Incorporated: 6 June 2001 *Employees:* 3
Previous: Vale Retail (Cornbow) Limited
Net Worth: £7,340,480 *Total Assets:* £68,174,448
Registered Office: Nelson House, 2 Hamilton Terrace, Leamington Spa, Warwicks, CV32 4LY
Activities: Other letting and operating of own or leased real estate
Parent: Tansor (Halesowen) Limited
Officers: Anne Faherty, Secretary; Timothy Carswell [1954] Director; Anthony Robert Andrew Insall [1980] Director/Consultant; Robert Adrian Oliver [1954] Director/Chartered Surveyor

Tanvic Group Holdings Limited
Incorporated: 15 August 2016 *Employees:* 308
Net Worth: £32,386,672 *Total Assets:* £43,307,736
Registered Office: Granary Lodge, 96 Appleton Gate, Newark, Notts, NG24 1LS
Activities: Activities of other holding companies n.e.c.
Major Shareholder: Stephen David McCracken
Officers: Stephen David McCracken [1972] Director

Tanvic Group Limited
Incorporated: 28 July 1970 *Employees:* 308
Net Worth: £11,732,601 *Total Assets:* £21,664,816
Registered Office: Granary Lodge, 96 Appletongate, Newark, Notts, NG24 1LS
Activities: Maintenance and repair of motor vehicles
Officers: Stephen David McCracken, Secretary; Stephen David McCracken [1972] Director/Chief Executive; Andrew Zelos [1972] Wholesale Director

Tappex Thread Inserts Limited
Incorporated: 4 December 1956 *Employees:* 78
Net Worth: £11,406,252 *Total Assets:* £13,036,052
Registered Office: Masons Road, Stratford upon Avon, Warwicks, CV37 9NT
Activities: Manufacture of fasteners and screw machine products
Officers: Jennifer Susan Mary Bebbington, Secretary; Timothy John Roderick Barnsdale [1944] Director/Engineer; Jennifer Susan Mary Bebbington [1942] Director/Company Secretary

Tapton School Academy Trust
Incorporated: 7 July 2011 *Employees:* 807
Net Worth: £50,217,000 *Total Assets:* £66,791,000
Registered Office: Tapton School, Darwin Lane, Sheffield, S10 5RG
Activities: Pre-primary education
Officers: Julia Delaney, Secretary; Tom Ashford [1980] Director/Database Business Delivery; Caroline Bagley [1956] Director/Retired; Colin Beardmore [1949] Director/Business Consultant; David Beaumont [1956] Director/Educational Psychologist; Richard Dunlop [1961] Director/Financial Services; Navjeen Singh Kalkat [1985] Director/Property Professional; Peter Ronald Kearney [1987] Director/Solicitor; Kathryn Elizabeth Platts [1964] Director/Accountant; David Thorpe [1966] Director/Education Specialist

Tarka Controls Limited
Incorporated: 8 March 1971
Net Worth: £9,598,671 *Total Assets:* £9,860,631
Registered Office: Unit 12 Tongue Lane Industrial Estate, Dew Pond Lane, Fairfield, Buxton, Derbys, SK17 7LF
Activities: Activities of head offices
Parent: Otter Controls Limited
Officers: Michael Leonard Colling, Secretary; Michael Leonard Colling [1962] Director/Chartered Accountant; Dr David Andrew Smith [1964] Director

Tarras Park Properties Limited
Incorporated: 28 July 2003 *Employees:* 17
Net Worth: £93,658,752 *Total Assets:* £121,139,384
Registered Office: c/o Buccleuch Property Estate Office, Weekley, Kettering, Northants, NN16 9UP
Activities: Buying and selling of own real estate
Parent: Buccleuch Properties Ltd
Officers: James Alexander Kenneth MacLeod, Secretary/Accountant; Robert Edward Bowden [1942] Director/Surveyor; John Ronald Kerr Glen [1959] Director/Chief Executive; James Alexander Kenneth MacLeod [1975] Director/Chartered Accountant; David Howard Peck [1965] Director; Richard W J M Scott [1954] Director; Alexander Hay Laidlaw Smith [1972] Director/Surveyor; Nicholas Antony George Waugh [1960] Director/Property Manager

Tata Technologies Europe Limited
Incorporated: 2 May 1986 *Employees:* 649
Net Worth: £78,676,000 *Total Assets:* £125,621,000
Registered Office: European Innovation and Development Centre (EIDC), Olympus Avenue, Tachbrook Park, Warwick, CV34 6RJ
Activities: Information technology consultancy activities
Parent: Incat International PLC
Officers: Warren Kevin Harris [1963] Director; Praveen Purushottam Kadle [1957] Director [Indian]; Arun Krishnamurthi [1969] Director [Indian]

Tawnywood Limited
Incorporated: 23 August 1990
Net Worth: £8,518,435 *Total Assets:* £39,547,656
Registered Office: Capstone House, Prospect Park, Dunston Way, Dunston Road, Chesterfield, Derbys, S41 9RD
Activities: Buying and selling of own real estate
Shareholder: John Lindley Wilson
Officers: Angela Suzanne Hunt, Secretary; Robert Arnold Veerman [1959] Director/Accountant [Dutch]; John Lindley Wilson [1943] Director/Civil Engineer

O.A.Taylor & Sons Bulbs Limited
Incorporated: 2 February 1970 *Employees:* 105
Net Worth: £20,384,308 *Total Assets:* £23,232,678
Registered Office: Washway House Farm, Washway Road, Holbeach, Spalding, Lincs, PE12 7PP
Activities: Growing of cereals (except rice), leguminous crops and oil seeds
Parent: OAT 2012 Limited
Officers: Sam Roger Taylor, Secretary; The Hon Adam Edwin John Taylor [1975] Director; Roger David Taylor [1945] Director; Sam Roger Taylor [1977] Director

B Taylor & Sons Transport Limited
Incorporated: 8 February 1983 *Employees:* 213
Net Worth: £5,584,688 *Total Assets:* £12,731,083
Registered Office: Unit 3 Export Drive, Huthwaite, Sutton in Ashfield, Notts, NG17 6AF
Activities: Freight transport by road
Officers: Alan Taylor, Secretary; Alan Taylor [1962] Director

Taylor Bloxham Group Limited
Incorporated: 23 February 1939 *Employees:* 188
Previous: Taylor-Bloxham Limited
Net Worth: £1,325,982 *Total Assets:* £13,703,466
Registered Office: 17-21 Tolwell Road, Leicester, LE4 1BR
Activities: Other manufacturing n.e.c.
Parent: The Print People Group Limited
Officers: Robert Charles Lockwood [1958] Finance Director; April Jacqueline Sharpless [1975] Director; Jacqueline Sharpless [1943] Director/Admin Assistant; Wesley Mark Sykes [1964] Production Director; Matthew Wennington [1970] IT Director

Taylor Hobson Limited
Incorporated: 26 July 1996 *Employees:* 232
Net Worth: £34,323,000 *Total Assets:* £67,472,000
Registered Office: P O Box 36, 2 New Star Road, Leicester, LE4 9JQ
Activities: Manufacture of electronic measuring, testing etc. equipment, not for industrial process control
Parent: Ametek Instruments Group UK Limited
Officers: Joy Atwell, Secretary; Craig Timothy Howarth [1960] Managing Director; Bruce Peter Wilson [1956] Director; Pietro Luigi Enrico Zetti [1968] Finance Director [Italian]

Taylor Lindsey Limited
Incorporated: 21 May 1953 *Employees:* 41
Net Worth: £77,085,264 *Total Assets:* £90,420,832
Registered Office: 98 Searby Road, Lincoln, LN2 4DT
Activities: Development of building projects
Officers: Shirley Martha Taylor, Secretary; James Richard Stanton Taylor [1957] Director; Robin Charles Sandlant Taylor [1963] Director; Shirley Martha Taylor [1929] Director

C & S Taylor LLP
Incorporated: 18 October 2010
Net Worth: £6,703,902 *Total Assets:* £10,051,460
Registered Office: Taylor Group House, Wedgnock Lane, Warwick, CV34 5YA
Officers: Christopher John Taylor [1953] Member; Svetlana Taylor [1975] Member

John Taylor MAT
Incorporated: 27 October 2010 *Employees:* 382
Previous: John Taylor High School
Net Worth: £28,416,504 *Total Assets:* £34,726,560
Registered Office: John Taylor High School, Dunstall Road, Barton under Needwood, Burton on Trent, Staffs, DE13 8AZ
Activities: Pre-primary education
Officers: Barbara Frances Mahoney, Secretary; David John Beaty [1966] Director/Bank Manager; Michael Donoghue [1971] Director/Headteacher; Angela Helen Grandfield Mbe [1948] Director/Health & Safety Manager; Timothy Mark Hopkins [1983] Director/Teaching and Learning Development Manager; Amanda Lee [1961] Director/College Lecturer; Nicholas Lloyd [1951] Director/Retired; Gareth Brian Moss [1966] Director/Accountant; Barbara Vivienne Richardson [1952] Director/Company Secretary

Taylor Shaw Limited
Incorporated: 24 April 2008 *Employees:* 2,375
Net Worth Deficit: £2,295,406 *Total Assets:* £18,185,512
Registered Office: The Courtyard, Catherine Street, Macclesfield, Cheshire, SK11 6ET
Activities: Other food services
Parent: Waterfall Services Limited
Officers: Robin Givens [1962] Managing Director; Jim Lovett [1969] Director; Vincent John Pearson [1959] Director; Catherine Margaret Roe [1960] Managing Director; Eleni Savva [1972] Finance Director

Taylors Service Garages (Boston) Limited
Incorporated: 17 April 1974 *Employees:* 82
Net Worth: £5,757,962 *Total Assets:* £12,896,352
Registered Office: Taylors Peugeot, Ashton Hall Drive, Boston, Lincs, PE21 7TF
Activities: Sale of new cars and light motor vehicles
Shareholders: Nigel John Taylor; Timothy Charles Taylor
Officers: Nicholas Mark Graves, Secretary; Daphne Joyce Taylor [1933] Director; Nigel John Taylor [1958] Director/General Manager; Timothy Charles Taylor [1959] Director/General Manager

Tayto Group Limited
Incorporated: 17 June 2008 *Employees:* 1,376
Net Worth: £80,615,688 *Total Assets:* £173,737,056
Registered Office: Princewood Road, Earlstrees Industrial Estate, Corby, Northants, NN17 4AP
Activities: Manufacture of other food products n.e.c.
Parent: Manderley Food Group Limited
Officers: Stephen Thomas Alexander Hutchinson, Secretary; Paul Martin Allen [1968] Director; Raymond Latimer Hutchinson [1949] Director; Stephen Thomas Alexander Hutchinson [1958] Director; Anne Alexandra Hutchinson Kane [1947] Director

TCCT Holdings UK Limited
Incorporated: 21 July 2011
Net Worth: £243,995,008 *Total Assets:* £245,396,992
Registered Office: Westpoint, Peterborough Business Park, Lynch Wood, Peterborough, Cambs, PE2 6FZ
Activities: Other business support service activities n.e.c.
Shareholders: Thomas Cook Retail Limited; Co-operative Specialist Businesses Limited
Officers: Shirley Bradley, Secretary; Kathryn Louise Darbandi [1969] Director; Alan Charles Donald [1963] Director

TCCT Retail Limited
Incorporated: 5 October 2010 *Employees:* 4,005
Net Worth Deficit: £473,031,008 *Total Assets:* £247,055,008
Registered Office: Westpoint, Peterborough Business Park, Lynch Wood, Peterborough, Cambs, PE2 6FZ
Activities: Travel agency activities
Parent: TCCT Holdings UK Limited
Officers: Shirley Bradley, Secretary; Alan Charles Donald [1963] Director; Alice Hannah Marsden [1983] Director

TCGH Holdings Limited
Incorporated: 27 June 2013
Net Worth: £400,000,000 *Total Assets:* £400,000,000
Registered Office: Westpoint, Peterborough Business Park, Lynch Wood, Peterborough, Cambs, PE2 6FZ
Activities: Other business support service activities n.e.c.
Parent: Blue Sea Overseas Investments Limited
Officers: Christopher James Corner [1974] Director

TCI Renewables Limited
Incorporated: 10 February 2005 *Employees:* 9
Net Worth: £11,880,404 *Total Assets:* £12,076,373
Registered Office: Willow Court, Minns Business Park, 7 West Way, Oxford, OX2 0JB
Activities: Construction of utility projects for electricity and telecommunications
Officers: Terry Hutchins, Secretary; James Julian Cooney [1961] Director/Chartered Engineer [Australian]; Peter Cecil Craig [1971] Projects Director (NI); Wes Dickson [1966] Finance Director [Australian]; Brett O'Connor [1966] Director/Chartered Civil Engineer

TCL Tanker Rental Limited
Incorporated: 5 March 1993 *Employees:* 16
Net Worth: £5,245,818 *Total Assets:* £12,089,655
Registered Office: c/o Mitchell Diesel Limited, Fulwood Road, South Fulwood Industrial Estate, Sutton in Ashfield, Notts, NG17 2JZ
Activities: Renting and leasing of other machinery, equipment and tangible goods n.e.c.
Parent: Turner & Co (Glasgow) Ltd
Officers: Graham Bruce Knox [1967] Director; Ian Parrack [1961] Director; Michael Ashley Smith [1969] Director/Engineer; Alan Gerard Turner [1965] Director

TCS Biosciences Limited
Incorporated: 1 October 1987 *Employees:* 49
Net Worth: £5,799,439 *Total Assets:* £10,309,924
Registered Office: Botolph Farm, Botolph Claydon, Buckingham, MK18 2LR
Activities: Manufacture of basic pharmaceutical products
Major Shareholder: Lynda Jane Preston
Officers: Ruth Vanessa Toombs, Secretary; Dr Kate Langston [1973] Director/Doctor; James Eley Preston [1987] Director/Financial Analyst; Lynda Jane Preston [1947] Director/Farmer; Ruth Vanessa Toombs [1969] Director/Finance Manager; Emily Jane Utley [1971] Director/Solicitor; Gareth Arran Williams [1977] Sales and Marketing Director

TDY Holdings Limited
Incorporated: 29 January 1998
Net Worth Deficit: £30,029,000 *Total Assets:* £87,494,000
Registered Office: President Way Works, President Way, Sheffield, S4 7UR
Activities: Activities of head offices
Parent: Allegheny Technologies Incorporated
Officers: Elliot Staub Davis, Secretary; Elliot Staub Davis [1961] Director/Company Secretary/Vice President [American]; Patrick Decourcy [1962] Director/Chief Financial Officer [American]

TDY Limited
Incorporated: 8 February 1968
Net Worth: £39,306,036 *Total Assets:* £39,768,832
Registered Office: President Way Works, President Way, Sheffield, S4 7UR
Activities: Other business support service activities n.e.c.
Parent: TDY Holdings Limited
Officers: Elliot Staub Davis, Secretary; Elliot Staub Davis [1961] Director/Secretary/Vice President and General Counsel [American]; Patrick Decourccy [1962] Director/Chief Financial Officer [American]; Anthony Leonard Dudill [1958] Financial Director

Techman Engineering Ltd.
Incorporated: 11 January 1990 *Employees:* 91
Net Worth Deficit: £835,854 *Total Assets:* £15,040,766
Registered Office: Techman House, Broombank Park, Chesterfield Trading Estate, Sheepbridge, Chesterfield, Derbys, S41 9RT
Activities: Machining
Parent: Schoeller Bleckmann Oilfield Equipment (UK) Limited
Officers: Generald Grohmann [1953] Director [Austrian]; Campbell Mckay Macpherson [1974] Director; Klaus Hermann Mader [1970] Director/Chief Financial Officer [Austrian]; Simon John Oxspring [1956] Director

Technia Limited
Incorporated: 12 September 2001 *Employees:* 57
Previous: Intrinsys Limited
Net Worth: £7,058,650 *Total Assets:* £15,069,246
Registered Office: Nordic House, Brunleys, Kiln Farm, Milton Keynes, Bucks, MK11 3EW
Activities: Engineering related scientific and technical consulting activities
Officers: Johan Fredrik Andersson [1974] Director [Swedish]; Darren Christopher Cairns [1962] Director/Engineer; Karl Jonas Gejer [1963] Director [Swedish]; Jan Fredrik Isaksson [1967] Director [Swedish]

Technical Absorbents Limited
Incorporated: 5 April 1993 *Employees:* 46
Net Worth: £17,752,000 *Total Assets:* £19,025,000
Registered Office: P O Box 24, 1 Moody Lane, corner of Woad Lane, Great Coates, Grimsby, N E Lincs, DN31 2SS
Activities: Preparation and spinning of textile fibres
Parent: Bluestar Fibres Investment Company Limited
Officers: Michile Ann Riley, Secretary; Dr Zhigang Hao [1978] Director/Chemical Engineer [Chinese]; Michael Koenig [1963] Director/Chief Executive Officer [German]; Michael James Parkington [1969] Director/Engineer

Technical Consumer Products Limited
Incorporated: 8 December 2009 *Employees:* 30
Net Worth Deficit: £145,429 *Total Assets:* £15,464,194
Registered Office: Unit 1 Exchange Court, Cottingham Road, Corby, Northants, NN17 1TY
Activities: Wholesale of other intermediate products
Parent: TCP B.V.
Officers: Kevin Nolan [1972] Director

Technicut Limited
Incorporated: 24 April 1978 *Employees:* 154
Net Worth: £10,544,262 *Total Assets:* £22,813,464
Registered Office: 22 Hayhill Industrial Estate, Sileby Road, Barrow upon Soar, Loughborough, Leics, LE12 8LD
Activities: Manufacture of tools
Parent: KCT Holdings Limited
Officers: Christopher John Hart Hill, Secretary; Adrian Peter Allen [1959] Director; David John Fothergill [1980] Managing Director; Robert Derrick John Fothergill [1949] Director/Accountant; Paul Anthony Graham [1970] Director/Sales Engineer; Christopher John Hart Hill [1954] Director/Chartered Accountant; Mark Kirby [1954] Technical Director; Prof Keith Ridgway [1952] Director/University Professor; Warwick Simon Beaumont Spearing [1977] Director/Engineer; Paul James Webb [1967] Director/Sales Engineer

Technolog Group Limited
Incorporated: 4 April 1995 *Employees:* 110
Net Worth: £36,006,000 *Total Assets:* £60,842,000
Registered Office: Technolog House, Ravenstor Road, Wirksworth, Matlock, Derbys, DE4 4FY
Activities: Activities of other holding companies n.e.c.
Parent: Utilitec Limited
Officers: Jason Phillip Conley [1975] Finance Director [American]; Robert Christopher Crisci [1975] Finance Director [American]; Stephen Jason Drury [1969] Operations Director; Nigel Fearn [1963] Director; Paul Joseph Soni [1958] Director/Finance [American]; John Kenneth Stipancich [1968] Director/Vice President, General Counsel and Secretary [American]

Technolog Holdings Ltd
Incorporated: 3 July 2000 *Employees:* 276
Net Worth: £49,149,000 *Total Assets:* £68,348,000
Registered Office: Technolog House, Ravenstor Road, Wirksworth, Matlock, Derbys, DE4 4FY
Activities: Activities of other holding companies n.e.c.
Officers: Jason Phillip Conley [1975] Finance Director [American]; Robert Christopher Crisci [1975] Finance Director [American]; Stephen Jason Drury [1969] Operations Director; Nigel Charles Fearn [1963] Managing Director; Ben James [1976] Finance Director; John Kenneth Stipancich [1968] Director [American]

Technolog Limited
Incorporated: 14 July 1981 *Employees:* 95
Net Worth: £39,087,000 *Total Assets:* £58,735,000
Registered Office: Technolog House, Ravenstor Road, Wirksworth, Matlock, Derbys, DE4 4FY
Activities: Manufacture of electronic measuring, testing etc. equipment, not for industrial process control
Parent: Technolog Group Limited
Officers: Jason Phillip Conley [1975] Finance Director [American]; Robert Christopher Crisci [1975] Finance Director [American]; Stephen Jason Drury [1969] Operations Director; Nigel Charles Fearn [1963] Managing Director; Ben James [1976] Finance Director; John Kenneth Stipancich [1968] Director/Vice President, General Counsel and Secretary [American]

Techrete (U.K.) Limited
Incorporated: 20 June 1989 *Employees:* 151
Net Worth: £11,579,294 *Total Assets:* £18,584,350
Registered Office: Station Road, Scawby, Brigg, N Lincs, DN20 9DT
Activities: Construction of commercial buildings
Major Shareholder: Christopher O'Dea
Officers: Denis Farrell, Secretary; Denis Farrell [1966] Director/Chartered Accountant [Irish]; Mark O'Dea [1974] Director/Actuary [Irish]; Marcus Sweeney [1950] Director [Irish]

Teconnex Limited
Incorporated: 7 September 1979 *Employees:* 390
Net Worth: £15,166,000 *Total Assets:* £22,644,000
Registered Office: The Old Court House, 24 Market Street, Gainsborough, Lincs, DN21 2BE
Activities: Manufacture of other fabricated metal products n.e.c.
Parent: Hexadex Limited
Officers: Emma Joanne Shakespeare, Secretary; Ian Douglas Brown [1960] Director of Technologies; Kimberley Iverson [1973] HR Director; Michael John Love [1980] Operations Director; Stephen Douglas Evan Lucas [1966] Sales Director; Christopher Paul Marsden [1979] Director of Engineering; Andrew Joseph Meakin [1966] Director/Chartered Accountant; Steven David Pollard [1962] Deputy Managing Director; Paul Sleaford [1961] Managing Director; Darren Jason Spencer [1976] Finance and Commercial Director

TEG Holdings Limited
Incorporated: 22 February 2017
Net Worth: £38,635,000 *Total Assets:* £154,504,000
Registered Office: Aragon House, University Way, Cranfield Technology Park, Cranfield, Bedford, MK43 0EQ
Activities: Other amusement and recreation activities n.e.c.
Officers: Mark Simon Willis, Secretary; Nicolas Andrew Basing [1962] Director; Graham Edwin Blackwell [1969] Director; Dr Duncan Steven Garrood [1958] Director; Mark Simon Willis [1976] Director

Tegama Limited
Incorporated: 2 July 2003 *Employees:* 5
Net Worth: £20,407,746 *Total Assets:* £22,271,920
Registered Office: Braunston, Daventry, Northants, NN11 7HA
Activities: Other letting and operating of own or leased real estate
Parent: Matega Limited
Officers: Godfrey Alan Hall, Secretary/Director; Aaron Thomas Hall [1996] Director/Full Time Student; Amie Rachel Hall [1992] Director/Student; Eleanor Faith Hall [1994] Director/Student; Godfrey Alan Hall [1949] Director; Marie Hall [1965] Director; Tobias George Hall [1991] Director

Telent Communications Holdings Limited
Incorporated: 1 October 1936
Net Worth: £422,900,000 *Total Assets:* £717,699,968
Registered Office: Point 3 Haywood Road, Warwick, CV34 5AH
Activities: Activities of other holding companies n.e.c.
Parent: Telent Limited
Officers: Mark Andrew Webberley [1964] Director/Chartered Accountant

Telent Limited
Incorporated: 27 September 1900 *Employees:* 1,886
Net Worth: £906,400,000 *Total Assets:* £1,171,399,936
Registered Office: Point 3 Haywood Road, Warwick, CV34 5AH
Activities: Activities of other holding companies n.e.c.
Officers: Lucy May Barratt, Secretary; Heather Marie Green [1971] Director/Chief Financial Officer; Francis John McKay [1945] Director; David George Edward Naylor-Leyland [1955] Director; Mark Edward Plato [1959] Director/Chief Executive Officer

Telent Technology Services Limited
Incorporated: 14 September 1961 *Employees:* 1,865
Net Worth: £717,699,968 *Total Assets:* £868,499,968
Registered Office: Point 3 Haywood Road, Warwick, CV34 5AH
Activities: Repair of other equipment
Parent: Telent Communications Holdings Limited
Officers: Lucy May Barratt, Secretary; Stephen Russell Dalton [1969] Managing Director; John Paul Kimpton [1971] Director/Accountant; Janice Meade [1955] HR Director; Christopher Ellis Metcalfe [1967] Director; Peter William Alexander Moir [1973] Managing Director; Mark Edward Plato [1959] Director/Chief Executive Officer; Richard Worthington Welsby [1979] Managing Director

Teletrac Navman (UK) Ltd
Incorporated: 2 September 1988 *Employees:* 234
Previous: Trafficmaster Limited
Net Worth: £29,977,000 *Total Assets:* £58,012,000
Registered Office: First Floor, K1, Kents Hill Business Park, Milton Keynes, Bucks, MK7 6BZ
Activities: Other professional, scientific and technical activities n.e.c.
Parent: TGA Industries Ltd
Officers: Radomir Lalovic, Secretary; Radomir Lalovic [1960] Director/Accountant; Richard George Lilwall [1977] Managing Director; Mark David Schwarz [1965] Commercial Director

Templeborough Biomass Power Plant Limited
Incorporated: 29 April 2010
Previous: Brite Partnership (North East) Limited
Net Worth: £4,689,399 *Total Assets:* £155,686,960
Registered Office: River View, Sheffield Road, Rotherham, S Yorks, S60 1FA
Activities: Production of electricity
Parent: CI Brite Limited
Officers: Anna-Lena Jeppsson [1976] Director/Engineer [Swedish]; Rune Bro Roin [1972] Director [Danish]; Christina Grumstrup Sorensen [1972] Director [Danish]

Ten Albemarle Limited Liability Partnership
Incorporated: 13 July 2004
Net Worth: £34,856,240 *Total Assets:* £35,244,564
Registered Office: The Poplars, Lenton Lane, Nottingham, NG7 2PW
Officers: Pauline Hellenes Denyer Smith [1940] LLP Member; Sir Paul Brierley Smith [1946] LLP Member

Ten Cate Advanced Composites Limited
Incorporated: 27 June 1988 *Employees:* 79
Net Worth: £3,703,684 *Total Assets:* £9,319,386
Registered Office: Amber Drive, Langley Mill, Nottingham, NG16 4BE
Activities: Manufacture of plastics in primary forms
Officers: Shelley Palmer, Secretary; David Jon Bernard [1963] Director; Frank Johan Meurs [1967] Group Director [Dutch]; Nicholas Tiffin [1963] Director

Ten Cate UK Limited
Incorporated: 2 June 1987
Net Worth: £19,397,816 *Total Assets:* £19,402,068
Registered Office: 50 Osmaston Road, Derby, DE1 2HU
Activities: Activities of head offices
Officers: Paul Alec Langford [1969] Director; Steen Tanderup [1970] Director [Danish]

Ten Entertainment Group PLC
Incorporated: 15 March 2017 *Employees:* 1,134
Net Worth: £53,193,000 *Total Assets:* £72,000,000
Registered Office: Aragon House, University Way, Cranfield Technology Park, Cranfield, Bedford, MK43 0EQ
Activities: Other amusement and recreation activities n.e.c.
Parent: Harwood Capital Nominees Limited
Officers: Mark Willis, Secretary; Nicolas Andrew Basing [1962] Director; Graham Blackwell [1969] Director; Dr Duncan Steven Garrood [1958] Director/Chief Executive; Christopher Harwood Bernard Mills [1952] Director; Julie Mary Sneddon [1964] Director; David James Wild [1955] Director; Mark Simon Willis [1976] Director

Tenens Ede Limited
Incorporated: 7 September 1998 *Employees:* 5
Net Worth: £1,797,477 *Total Assets:* £12,866,569
Registered Office: Eden House, Two Rivers, Station Lane, Witney, Oxon, OX28 4BL
Activities: Development of building projects
Officers: Steven David Ingledew, Secretary; Daniel Robert Ede [1981] Director; Jonathan Ede [1949] Director; Steven David Ingledew [1959] Director; Daniel Peter Morris [1977] Director; Peter Ewan Morris [1944] Director/Chief Executive

Tennant Metallurgical Group Holdings Limited
Incorporated: 11 May 2017 *Employees:* 13
Net Worth: £4,869,045 *Total Assets:* £22,280,682
Registered Office: c/o Tennant Metallurgical Group Ltd, Dunston Innovation Centre, Dunston Road, Chesterfield, Derbys, S41 8NG
Activities: Other business support service activities n.e.c.
Major Shareholder: Ian Andrew Cunningham
Officers: William Francis Gilderoy Glossop, Secretary; Ian Andrew Cunningham [1966] Director; John James Cunningham [1940] Director; Michael Richard Cunningham [1976] Director; Jill Anne Snelling [1971] Director

Tennant Metallurgical Group Limited
Incorporated: 8 January 1960 *Employees:* 13
Net Worth: £4,793,606 *Total Assets:* £22,205,244
Registered Office: Room 111, Dunston Innovation Centre, Dunston Road, Chesterfield, Derbys, S41 8NG
Activities: Wholesale of metals and metal ores
Parent: Tennant Metallurgical Holdings Ltd
Officers: William Francis Gilderoy Glossop, Secretary/Accountant; Ian Andrew Cunningham [1966] Managing Director; William Francis Gilderoy Glossop [1966] Director/Accountant

Tenpin Limited
Incorporated: 6 June 2003 *Employees:* 1,126
Net Worth: £52,936,000 *Total Assets:* £75,270,000
Registered Office: Aragon House, Cranfield Technology Park, Cranfield, Bedford, MK43 0EQ
Activities: Other amusement and recreation activities n.e.c.
Parent: TEG Holdings Limited
Officers: George Jason Sheppard, Secretary; Nicholas Andrew Basing [1962] Director; Graham Edwin Blackwell [1969] Commercial Director; Dr Duncan Steven Garrood [1958] Director; George Jason Sheppard [1981] Director/Chartered Accountant; Mark Willis [1976] Director

Tensator Group Limited
Incorporated: 24 December 2001 *Employees:* 6
Net Worth: £10,026,000 *Total Assets:* £24,480,000
Registered Office: Unit 7 Danbury Court, Linford Wood, Milton Keynes, Bucks, MK14 6TS
Activities: Activities of head offices
Parent: Tensator Holdings Ltd
Officers: Alan Robert McPherson [1973] Director

Tensator Holdings Ltd
Incorporated: 11 July 2008 *Employees:* 165
Net Worth: £18,020,000 *Total Assets:* £38,924,000
Registered Office: Unit 7 Danbury Court, Linford Wood, Milton Keynes, Bucks, MK14 6TS
Activities: Activities of other holding companies n.e.c.
Parent: Prudential Financial Inc
Officers: Michael Philip Berry [1955] Director/Investment Manager; Marie Louise Fioramonti [1961] Managing Director [American]; Alan Robert McPherson [1973] Director; Stephen Rushworth Smith [1953] Director

Tensator Limited
Incorporated: 3 August 2000 *Employees:* 69
Net Worth: £26,957,000 *Total Assets:* £41,491,000
Registered Office: Unit 7 Danbury Court, Linford Wood, Milton Keynes, Bucks, MK14 6TS
Activities: Manufacture of other fabricated metal products n.e.c.
Parent: Tensator Group Limited
Officers: Alan Robert McPherson [1973] Director

Terberg Environmental UK Limited
Incorporated: 31 May 2017 *Employees:* 1
Net Worth: £32,100,152 *Total Assets:* £32,460,976
Registered Office: Dennis Eagle, Heathcote Way, Heathcote Industrial Estate, Warwick, CV34 6TE
Activities: Activities of other holding companies n.e.c.
Officers: Ian Roland Metcalfe [1958] Director/Businessman

Terberg Rosroca Group Limited
Incorporated: 9 February 2016 *Employees:* 1,538
Net Worth: £37,973,080 *Total Assets:* £273,034,624
Registered Office: Dennis Eagle, Heathcote Way, Heathcote Industrial Estate, Warwick, CV34 6TE
Activities: Activities of other holding companies n.e.c.
Parent: TRRG Holding Limited
Officers: Ian Roland Metcalfe [1958] Director/Businessman; Juan Puig Perez [1951] Director/Lawyer [Spanish]; Ramon Roca Enrich [1962] Director/Businessman [Spanish]; George Johannes Maria Terberg [1952] Director [Dutch]; Paulus Johannes Van Der Kroft [1960] Director/Businessman [Dutch]

Terex Pegson Limited
Incorporated: 13 August 1931 *Employees:* 85
Net Worth: £6,083,000 *Total Assets:* £27,317,000
Registered Office: The Pinnacle, 170 Midsummer Boulevard, Milton Keynes, Bucks, MK9 1FE
Activities: Manufacture of pumps
Parent: Pegson Group Limited
Officers: Eric I Cohen, Secretary/Lawyer [American]; Eric I Cohen [1958] Director/Lawyer [American]; John Daniel Sheehan [1960] Director/Chief Financial Officer [American]

Terrace Hills Farm LLP
Incorporated: 28 October 2010 *Employees:* 29
Net Worth: £32,848,172 *Total Assets:* £43,204,452
Registered Office: Bowden House, 36 Northampton Road, Market Harborough, Leics, LE16 9HE
Officers: Philip Dennis Burtt [1953] Member; Rachel Emma Duchess of Rutland [1963] Member; David Charles Robert Eleventh Duke of Rutland [1959] Member; Thomas Benjamin Roderick Sinclair [1962] Member

Tessella Holdings Limited
Incorporated: 2 July 2012
Net Worth: £4,520,875 *Total Assets:* £16,630,599
Registered Office: 26 The Quadrant, Abingdon Science Park, Abingdon, Oxon, OX14 3YS
Activities: Business and domestic software development
Parent: Altran UK Holding Limited
Officers: Stella Toresse, Secretary; Robert John Byrne [1964] Director; Mark Richard Kirwan [1961] Director; Michael John Simms [1961] Director

Tessella Limited
Incorporated: 12 December 1979 *Employees:* 219
Net Worth: £15,658,050 *Total Assets:* £25,563,326
Registered Office: 26 The Quadrant, Abingdon Science Park, Abingdon, Oxon, OX14 3YS
Activities: Business and domestic software development
Parent: Tessella Holdings Limited
Officers: Stella Toresse, Secretary; Robert John Byrne [1964] Director; Mark Richard Kirwan [1961] Director; Michael John Simms [1961] Director

TFHC 2015 Limited
Incorporated: 26 November 2014
Net Worth: £368,000 *Total Assets:* £15,302,000
Registered Office: Total Fitness, Wilmslow Way, Handforth, Cheshire, SK9 3PW
Activities: Management consultancy activities other than financial management
Officers: Jasvir Sanghera, Secretary; Sophie Lawler [1978] Director/Chief Executive; Warwick John Ley [1972] Director [Australian/British]; Keven David Parker [1969] Director/PE Partner; Jasvir Singh Sanghera [1966] Finance Director

TFHC Investments Limited
Incorporated: 3 February 2015 *Employees:* 596
Net Worth Deficit: £2,927,000 *Total Assets:* £24,940,000
Registered Office: Total Fitness, Wilmslow Way, Handforth, Wilmslow, Cheshire, SK9 3PE
Activities: Activities of head offices
Shareholders: Northedge Capital I GP LLP; Northedge Capital LLP
Officers: Jasvir Sanghera, Secretary; Sophie Lawler [1978] Director/Chief Executive; Warwick John Ley [1972] Director [Australian/British]; Keven David Parker [1969] Director/PE Partner; Jasvir Singh Sanghera [1966] Finance Director

TFS Holdings Limited
Incorporated: 4 April 2017
Net Worth: £10,062,000 *Total Assets:* £10,062,000
Registered Office: Lodge Way House, Lodge Way, Harlestone Road, Northampton, NN5 7UG
Activities: Non-trading company
Parent: Travis Perkins PLC
Officers: Andrew Cherrill [1969] Director; Francis Mark Elkins [1967] Director; Paul Joseph Lynott [1964] Director; Derek McMaster [1967] Director; Alan Richard Williams [1969] Director

TGH Acquisitions Limited
Incorporated: 6 February 2008
Net Worth: £299,060,992 *Total Assets:* £299,102,016
Registered Office: Whitley Lodge, Whitley Bridge, Doncaster, S Yorks, DN14 0HR
Activities: Activities of other holding companies n.e.c.
Parent: TGH Finance Limited
Officers: Jonathan Paul Furniss, Secretary; James Simon Edward Arnell [1969] Director/Investment Manager; Gunter Heinz Otto Dombrowe [1947] Director [German]; Lars Ernst Vilhelm Gatenbeck [1956] Director [Swedish]; Gerard Christopher Loftus [1960] Director; Craig Parsons [1970] Director; Thomas Spencer Patrick [1972] Director

TGH Finance Limited
Incorporated: 6 February 2008 *Employees:* 4
Net Worth Deficit: £1,088,786,048 *Total Assets:* £9,628,000
Registered Office: Whitley Lodge, Whitley Bridge, Doncaster, S Yorks, DN14 0HR
Activities: Activities of other holding companies n.e.c.
Parent: TGH Investments Limited
Officers: Jonathan Paul Furniss, Secretary; James Simon Edward Arnell [1969] Director/Investment Manager; Craig Parsons [1970] Director; Thomas Spencer Patrick [1972] Director

TGH Investments Limited
Incorporated: 6 February 2008
Net Worth Deficit: £1,024,868,992 *Total Assets:* £298,462,016
Registered Office: Whitley Lodge, Whitley Bridge, Doncaster, S Yorks, DN14 0HR
Activities: Activities of other holding companies n.e.c.
Parent: Tunstall Healthcare Group Limited
Officers: Jonathan Paul Furniss, Secretary; James Simon Edward Arnell [1969] Director/Investment Manager; Craig Parsons [1970] Director; Thomas Spencer Patrick [1972] Director/Solicitor

TGW (Holdings) Limited
Incorporated: 12 September 2002 *Employees:* 171
Net Worth: £13,288,669 *Total Assets:* £19,943,736
Registered Office: Clough Bank Works, Downgate Drive, Carlisle Street East, Sheffield, S4 8BT
Activities: Activities of head offices
Parent: BW TGW Holdings Limited
Officers: Steven John Corbett [1972] Group Manufacturing Director; Robert Groberg [1983] Director/Private Equity [American]; Michael Ranson [1972] Director/Private Equity [American]; John Julian Frederick Tattersfield [1963] Director/Operating Executive [American]

TGW Limited
Incorporated: 16 November 2006 *Employees:* 297
Net Worth: £1,732,481 *Total Assets:* £26,461,712
Registered Office: Falcon Court, Market Harborough, Leics, LE16 7FQ
Activities: Other construction installation
Major Shareholder: Ludwig Szinicz
Officers: Nathan Goudie [1975] Director; David Allan Hibbett [1975] Managing Director; David Malcolm Jenkinson [1961] Finance Director; Ian Maxwell Powell [1967] Operations Director; Andrew John Smith [1966] Managing Director

TH Finance Limited
Incorporated: 23 May 1997 *Employees:* 1
Previous: Tektronix U.K. Holdings Limited
Net Worth: £31,676,000 *Total Assets:* £31,681,000
Registered Office: 19 Jessops Riverside, 800 Brightside Lane, Sheffield, S9 2RX
Activities: Non-trading company
Parent: Danaher Corporation
Officers: Keith Graham Ward [1953] Director

Thame and London Limited
Incorporated: 7 August 2012 *Employees:* 6,740
Net Worth Deficit: £89,700,000 *Total Assets:* £706,400,000
Registered Office: Sleepy Hollow, Aylesbury Road, Thame, Oxon, OX9 3AT
Activities: Other business support service activities n.e.c.
Officers: Joanna Boydell, Secretary; Katherine Anna Ashford Thomas, Secretary; Joanna Boydell [1969] Director/Chief Financial Officer; Jonathan David Ford [1974] Director; Peter Darren Gowers [1972] Director/Chief Executive Officer; Paul Victor Harvey [1961] Director; Stephen John Shurrock [1971] Director; Brian Godman Wallace [1954] Director

Thame Partnership Academy Trust
Incorporated: 24 July 2012 *Employees:* 311
Net Worth: £15,213,004 *Total Assets:* £21,591,224
Registered Office: Lord Williams's School, Oxford Road, Thame, Oxon, OX9 2AQ
Activities: General secondary education
Officers: Dr Anne Clark [1941] Director/Medical Researcher; Stephen Anthony Duplock [1961] Director; Penelope Lowe [1979] Director/Teacher; Brian Jon Pridmore [1972] Director/Chartered Engineer; Roland Edward Tanner [1967] Director; Michael Underwood [1959] Director/Facilities Manager; Rebecca White [1971] Director/Teacher; Simon Hector Clive Whitfield [1955] Director; Sarah Wilson [1968] Director/Business Manager; David Lloyd Wybron [1959] Director/Teacher

Thames Land Limited
Incorporated: 18 September 1984
Net Worth: £16,876,714 *Total Assets:* £38,850,952
Registered Office: 9 Worton Park, Cassington, Oxon, OX29 4SX
Activities: Other letting and operating of own or leased real estate
Officers: Christopher Jeremy Guilbert [1963] Director; Mark Lyndon Jefferies [1970] Director

Thames Transit Limited
Incorporated: 28 June 1988 *Employees:* 540
Net Worth: £10,974,000 *Total Assets:* £31,199,000
Registered Office: c/o Stagecoach Services Limited, One Stockport Exchange, 20 Railway Road, Stockport, Cheshire, SK1 3SW
Activities: Other urban, suburban or metropolitan passenger land transport (not underground, metro or similar)
Parent: Stagecoach Bus Holdings Limited
Officers: Michael John Vaux, Secretary; Colin Brown [1968] Director/Accountant; Christopher Sean Lee Coleman [1970] Managing Director; Arnold Mark Threapleton [1954] Managing Director

Thames Valley Cambac Limited
Incorporated: 6 February 1975
Net Worth: £4,755,171 *Total Assets:* £15,238,503
Registered Office: First Floor, Pipe House, Lupton Road, Wallingford, Oxon, OX10 9BS
Activities: Support activities for animal production (other than farm animal boarding)
Officers: Geoffrey William Allen, Secretary; Charles Thomas Allen [1949] Director/Farmer; Geoffrey William Allen [1956] Director/Farmer; Robert Beckett [1968] Director; Richard William Lister [1963] Director/Farmer; Ian Rowland McFarlane [1974] Director/Farmer; Sally Anne Stockings [1955] Director; Robin Underwood Thompson [1958] Director/Farmer; Simon James Watchorn [1955] Director/Farmer

Thermasys CS UK Holding Limited
Incorporated: 8 December 2010 *Employees:* 149
Net Worth Deficit: £3,391,231 *Total Assets:* £21,252,936
Registered Office: Covrad, Sir Henry Parkes Road, Canley, Coventry, Warwicks, CV5 6BN
Activities: Activities of head offices
Officers: Michael Wayne Bremmer, Secretary; James Michael Laisure [1952] Director [American]; Thomas Gerard Strauss [1957] Director/Chief Finance Officer [American]

Thessco Limited
Incorporated: 29 May 1984 *Employees:* 84
Net Worth: £4,897,547 *Total Assets:* £11,367,347
Registered Office: Royds Mills, Windsor Street, Sheffield, S4 7WB
Activities: Precious metals production
Officers: Malcolm Rathbone [1943] Director/Deputy Chairman; James Andrew Tear [1968] Group Managing Director; Paul James Tear [1937] Director/Chairman

Thetford Limited
Incorporated: 29 January 1971 *Employees:* 202
Net Worth: £7,306,996 *Total Assets:* £14,357,571
Registered Office: Unit 6 Brookfields Way, Manvers, Rotherham, S Yorks, S63 5DL
Activities: Non-specialised wholesale trade
Shareholder: Robert Richard Dyson
Officers: Bartholomeus Anderson [1964] European P&O Director [Dutch]; Stephane Pascal Cordeille [1962] Director/Vice Senior President [French]; John Hamilton Fitzsimons [1948] Director/Lawyer [American]; Petrus Johannes Adriana Struijs [1968] European Financial Director [Dutch]

Thistle Insurance Services Limited
Incorporated: 31 March 1938 *Employees:* 229
Net Worth: £13,217,000 *Total Assets:* £24,635,000
Registered Office: Rossington's Business Park, West Carr Road, Retford, Notts, DN22 7SW
Activities: Other business support service activities n.e.c.
Parent: PIB Group Limited
Officers: Timothy Tracy Brooke [1960] Director; Ryan Christopher Brown [1973] Director; Adrian Colosso [1957] Director; Brendan James McManus [1959] Director; Jonathan Paul Stanley [1965] Director/Chief Risk Officer; Robert Alan Styring [1971] Director

Thistledown Investments Limited
Incorporated: 15 October 1998 *Employees:* 4
Net Worth: £5,153,586 *Total Assets:* £13,755,406
Registered Office: Brook House, Asher Lane Business Park, Asher Lane, Pentrich, Derbys, DE5 3SW
Activities: Financial leasing
Major Shareholder: Alexander Campbell Anderson
Officers: Jason John Melrose, Finance Director; Alexander Campbell Anderson [1954] Director; Georgina Belinda Anderson [1959] Director; Jason John Melrose [1968] Finance Director

B & K Thomas (Holdings) Limited
Incorporated: 24 March 1953 *Employees:* 3
Net Worth: £10,033,519 *Total Assets:* £10,920,678
Registered Office: Mill Farm, Mill Lane, Long Clawson, Melton Mowbray, Leics, LE14 4NU
Activities: Other letting and operating of own or leased real estate
Shareholders: Anthony Bernard Thomas; Timothy James Thomas
Officers: Anthony Bernard Thomas, Secretary; David Allwood [1967] Director/Chartered Accountant; Anthony Bernard Thomas [1951] Director; Timothy James Thomas [1957] Director

Charles Thompson (UK) Limited
Incorporated: 22 March 2012 *Employees:* 178
Net Worth: £9,536,955 *Total Assets:* £14,860,894
Registered Office: Glasshouse Road, Kilnhurst, Mexborough, S Yorks, S64 5TD
Activities: Activities of head offices
Major Shareholder: David Charles Thompson
Officers: David Thompson, Secretary; Peter James Coe [1968] Director; Paul Andrew Grainger [1962] Director; David Charles Thompson [1974] Director

Thoratec Europe Limited
Incorporated: 22 February 1995
Net Worth: £86,571,504 *Total Assets:* £87,681,592
Registered Office: Burnett House, Lakeview Court, Ermine Business Park, Huntingdon, Cambs, PE29 6UA
Activities: Other human health activities
Officers: Benjamin Edward Oosterbaan [1963] Director/Assistant Treasurer [American]; Karen Peterson [1965] Director/Business Executive [American]; Brian Bernard Yoor [1969] Director/Business Executive [American]

Thorneycroft Solicitors Limited
Incorporated: 15 October 2003 *Employees:* 143
Net Worth: £4,721,889 *Total Assets:* £11,927,345
Registered Office: Bridge Street Mills, Bridge Street, Macclesfield, Cheshire, SK11 6QA
Activities: Solicitors
Shareholders: TSG Professional Services Ltd; TSGroup Ltd
Officers: Mark David Belfield [1970] Director/Lawyer; Susan Patricia Carnwell [1966] Director/Chartered Accountant; Rachel Leonie Stow [1969] Director/Solicitor; Robert Patrick Thorneycroft [1958] Director

Thornhill Estates Limited
Incorporated: 7 November 1933 *Employees:* 5
Net Worth: £7,735,276 *Total Assets:* £9,829,936
Registered Office: The Granary, 24a The Street, Diddington, St Neots, Cambs, PE19 5XU
Activities: Other letting and operating of own or leased real estate
Major Shareholder: Edmund George William Thornhill
Officers: Kerry Lisa Simpson, Secretary; Kerry Lisa Simpson [1971] Director/Property Manager; Alison Clare Thornhill [1972] Director; Edmund George William Thornhill [1969] Director/Chartered Surveyor; Margaret Daughne Thornhill [1937] Director

Thornsett Properties Limited
Incorporated: 28 October 1999 *Employees:* 5
Net Worth: £15,077,897 *Total Assets:* £23,614,762
Registered Office: 195 Crookes Valley Road, Sheffield, S10 1BA
Activities: Development of building projects
Officers: Satnam Singh Choker, Secretary; Charanjit Singh Choker [1979] Director; Jaswinder Kaur Choker [1954] Director; Sarabjit Kaur Choker [1979] Director; Satnam Singh Choker [1955] Director

P.J. Thory Limited
Incorporated: 5 October 1976 *Employees:* 87
Net Worth: £5,339,257 *Total Assets:* £12,055,756
Registered Office: White Walls, Eldernell Lane, Coates, Whittlesey, Peterborough, PE7 2DD
Activities: Freight transport by road
Shareholders: James Peter Thory; Timothy David Thory
Officers: James Peter Thory [1961] Director/Manager; Timothy David Thory [1962] Director/Manager

ThruVision Group PLC
Incorporated: 8 February 2010 *Employees:* 100
Previous: Digital Barriers PLC
Net Worth: £19,479,000 *Total Assets:* £20,999,000
Registered Office: 121 Olympic Avenue, Milton Park, Milton, Abingdon, Oxon, OX14 4SA
Activities: Other information technology service activities
Officers: John Andrew Woollhead, Secretary; Thomas Joseph Black [1959] Director; Colin Michael Evans [1968] Director; Ian Alexander Robertson Lindsay [1979] Finance Director; Paul Ronald Taylor [1964] Director

Thwaites Limited
Incorporated: 13 May 1944 *Employees:* 223
Net Worth: £23,981,000 *Total Assets:* £40,656,000
Registered Office: Welsh Road, Cubbington, Leamington Spa, Warwicks, CV32 7NQ
Activities: Manufacture of lifting and handling equipment
Shareholder: Michael Dulverton
Officers: Simon Kimberley Hill, Secretary; Ian Charles Metcalfe Brown [1958] Managing Director; The Rt Hon The Lord Dulverton [1944] Director/Farmer; Simon Kimberley Hill [1971] Financial Director; Kevin Joseph Phelan [1954] Operations Director; The Hon. Robert Anthony Wills [1983] Director/Entrepreneur; Robert Ian Hamilton Wills [1948] Director/Farmer

Thyssenkrupp Elevator UK Limited
Incorporated: 5 April 1961
Net Worth: £3,489,000 *Total Assets:* £21,992,000
Registered Office: The Lookout, 4 Bull Close Road, Nottingham, NG7 2UL
Activities: Manufacture of other transport equipment n.e.c.
Officers: Mark James Adam Kalinowski, Secretary; Mark James Adam Kalinowski [1965] Director/Chartered Accountant; Kevin Paul Taylor [1952] Managing Director

TI Automotive (China) Limited
Incorporated: 2 October 2000
Net Worth: £63,438,228 *Total Assets:* £153,170,160
Registered Office: 4650 Kingsgate, Cascade Way, Oxford Business Park South, Oxford, OX4 2SU
Activities: Activities of head offices
Shareholders: TI Fluid Systems PLC; TI Automotive Holdings Limited
Officers: David Joseph Ludlow, Secretary; Simon Paul Howell [1968] Director/Accountant

TI Automotive Canada Holdings Limited
Incorporated: 25 August 2005
Net Worth: £9,140,219 *Total Assets:* £9,140,219
Registered Office: 4650 Kingsgate, Cascade Way, Oxford Business Park South, Oxford, OX4 2SU
Activities: Activities of head offices
Shareholders: TI Fluid Systems PLC; TI Automotive USA Holdings Limited
Officers: David Joseph Ludlow, Secretary/Legal Director; Simon Paul Howell [1968] Director/Accountant

TI Automotive Czech Holdings (UK) Limited
Incorporated: 9 May 2007
Previous: TI Automotive Czech Holdings 1 (UK) Limited
Net Worth: £103,670,432 *Total Assets:* £103,670,432
Registered Office: 4650 Kingsgate, Cascade Way, Oxford Business Park South, Oxford, OX4 2SU
Activities: Activities of head offices
Shareholders: TI Fluid Systems PLC; TI Group Automotive Systems (Belgium) SA
Officers: David Joseph Ludlow, Secretary; Simon Paul Howell [1968] Director/Accountant

TI Automotive Euro Holdings Limited
Incorporated: 20 October 2004
Net Worth: £123,633,672 *Total Assets:* £693,655,168
Registered Office: 4650 Kingsgate, Cascade Way, Oxford Business Park South, Oxford, OX4 2SU
Activities: Non-trading company
Shareholders: TI Fluid Systems PLC; TI Automotive Limited
Officers: David Joseph Ludlow, Secretary; Simon Paul Howell [1968] Director/Accountant

TI Automotive German Holdings (UK) Limited
Incorporated: 10 May 2007
Previous: TI Automotive German Holdings 2 (UK) Limited
Net Worth: £209,839,520 *Total Assets:* £247,134,656
Registered Office: 4650 Kingsgate, Cascade Way, Oxford Business Park South, Oxford, OX4 2SU
Activities: Activities of head offices
Shareholders: TI Fluid Systems PLC; TI Group Automotive Systems Spain Holdings S.L.
Officers: David Joseph Ludlow, Secretary; Simon Paul Howell [1968] Director/Accountant

TI Automotive Holdings Limited
Incorporated: 7 March 2001
Net Worth: £149,401,120 *Total Assets:* £610,521,792
Registered Office: 4650 Kingsgate, Cascade Way, Oxford Business Park South, Oxford, OX4 2SU
Activities: Activities of head offices
Shareholders: TI Fluid Systems PLC; TI Automotive Limited
Officers: David Joseph Ludlow, Secretary; Simon Paul Howell [1968] Director/Accountant

TI Automotive Korean Won Hedgeco Ltd
Incorporated: 3 November 2015
Net Worth: £205,107,584 *Total Assets:* £217,416,176
Registered Office: 4650 Kingsgate, Cascade Way, Oxford Business Park South, Oxford, OX4 2SU
Activities: Activities of head offices
Shareholders: TI Fluid Systems PLC; Omega Acquisition Bidco Limited
Officers: David Joseph Ludlow, Secretary; Robert Michael Allen [1964] Director/Accountant; Matthew Keats Paroly [1965] Director/Chief Legal Officer [American]

TI Automotive Limited
Incorporated: 27 October 2000
Net Worth: £64,371,528 *Total Assets:* £892,684,224
Registered Office: 4650 Kingsgate, Cascade Way, Oxford Business Park South, Oxford, OX4 2SU
Activities: Activities of head offices
Shareholders: TI Fluid Systems PLC; TIFS Holdings Limited
Officers: David Joseph Ludlow, Secretary; Robert Michael Allen [1964] Director/Accountant; Timothy James Knutson [1967] Director/Chief Financial Officer [American]; William Lawrence Kozyra [1957] Director/Chief Executive [American]; Matthew Keats Paroly [1965] Director/Chief Legal Officer [American]

TI Automotive USA Holdings Limited
Incorporated: 20 October 2004
Net Worth: £224,662,000 *Total Assets:* £427,924,512
Registered Office: 4650 Kingsgate, Cascade Way, Oxford Business Park South, Oxford, OX4 2SU
Activities: Non-trading company
Shareholders: TI Fluid Systems PLC; TI Automotive Limited
Officers: David Joseph Ludlow, Secretary; Simon Paul Howell [1968] Director/Accountant

TI Fluid Systems PLC
Incorporated: 22 January 2015 *Employees:* 24,562
Previous: TI Fluid Systems Limited
Net Worth: £806,000,192 *Total Assets:* £2,863,465,472
Registered Office: 4650 Kingsgate, Cascade Way, Oxford Business Park South, Oxford, OX4 2SU
Activities: Activities of head offices
Shareholders: BC Omega Holdco Limited; Bain Capital Fund XI, L.P.; Bain Capital Investors, LLC; Bain Capital Partners XI, L.P.
Officers: Matthew Keats Paroly, Secretary; Neil Andrew Patrick Carson [1957] Director; Paul Edgerley [1955] Director [American]; Timothy James Knutson [1967] Director [American]; William Lawrence Kozyra [1957] Director [American]; Elaine Anne Sarsynski [1955] Director [American]; John Frederick Smith [1950] Director [American]; Stephen Thomas [1974] Director/Private Equity [American]; Jeffrey Henry Vanneste [1959] Director; Manfred Heinrich Wennemer [1947] Director [German]

TI Group Automotive Systems (Deeside) Limited
Incorporated: 26 May 1995 *Employees:* 165
Net Worth: £1,086,606 *Total Assets:* £26,348,396
Registered Office: 4650 Kingsgate, Cascade Way, Oxford Business Park South, Oxford, OX4 2SU
Activities: Other business support service activities n.e.c.
Shareholders: TI Fluid Systems PLC; TI Automotive Limited
Officers: David Joseph Ludlow, Secretary; Robert Michael Allen [1964] Director/Accountant; Matthew Keats Paroly [1965] Director/Chief Legal Officer [American]

TI Group Automotive Systems (UK) Limited
Incorporated: 16 December 1963 *Employees:* 140
Net Worth: £244,162,624 *Total Assets:* £249,458,496
Registered Office: 4650 Kingsgate, Cascade Way, Oxford Business Park South, Oxford, OX4 2SU
Activities: Manufacture of tubes, pipes, hollow profiles and related fittings, of steel
Shareholders: TI Fluid Systems PLC; TI Automotive German Holdings (UK) Limited
Officers: David Joseph Ludlow, Secretary; Robert Michael Allen [1964] Director/Accountant; Matthew Keats Paroly [1965] Director/Chief Legal Officer [American]

TI Group Automotive Systems Limited
Incorporated: 5 April 1957 *Employees:* 32
Net Worth: £26,511,544 *Total Assets:* £59,523,980
Registered Office: 4650 Kingsgate, Cascade Way, Oxford Business Park South, Oxford, OX4 2SU
Activities: Other business support service activities n.e.c.
Shareholders: TI Fluid Systems PLC; TI Automotive Limited
Officers: David Joseph Ludlow, Secretary; Robert Michael Allen [1964] Director/Accountant; Matthew Keats Paroly [1965] Director/Chief Legal Officer [American]

The Tibbetts Group Limited
Incorporated: 15 August 2005 *Employees:* 103
Net Worth: £11,753,979 *Total Assets:* £23,296,296
Registered Office: Tibbetts House, Beaumont Road, Banbury, Oxon, OX16 1RH
Activities: Other business support service activities n.e.c.
Shareholders: Horace John Tibbetts; Jonathan Philip Tibbetts
Officers: Horace John Tibbetts [1948] Director; Jonathan Philip Tibbetts [1975] Director; Patricia Ann Tibbetts [1959] Director; Stephen Wilkinson [1959] Finance Director

Tickhill Engineering Company Limited
Incorporated: 16 June 1964 *Employees:* 71
Net Worth: £9,662,278 *Total Assets:* £12,829,847
Registered Office: Cow House Lane, Armthorpe, Doncaster, S Yorks, DN3 3EE
Activities: Manufacture of other special-purpose machinery n.e.c.
Major Shareholder: George Geoffrey Haith
Officers: Jennifer Susan Brindley, Secretary; Jennifer Susan Brindley [1963] Director; Christopher John Haith [1954] Director/Agricultural Engineer; David Ian Haith [1966] Director/Agricultural Engineer; George Geoffrey Haith [1925] Director/Agricultural Engineer; Michael Peter Haith [1959] Director/Agricultural Engineer; Nigel Geoffrey Haith [1956] Director/Agricultural Engineer; Stephen Phillip Haith [1952] Director/Agricultural Engineer

TIFS Holdings Limited
Incorporated: 29 October 2009
Previous: Omega Holdco II Limited
Net Worth: £365,877,696 *Total Assets:* £365,877,728
Registered Office: 4650 Kingsgate, Cascade Way, Oxford Business Park South, Oxford, OX4 2SU
Activities: Activities of head offices
Shareholders: TI Fluid Systems PLC; Omega Acquisition Bidco Limited
Officers: Matthew Keats Paroly, Secretary; Robert Michael Allen [1964] Director/Accountant; Timothy James Knutson [1967] Director [American]; William Lawrence Kozyra [1957] Director [American]

TII Technologies Limited
Incorporated: 6 November 1981 *Employees:* 2
Net Worth: £15,838,592 *Total Assets:* £16,569,326
Registered Office: Eagle House, 28 Billing Road, Northampton, NN1 5AJ
Activities: Other telecommunications activities
Major Shareholder: Parag Mehta
Officers: Parag Mehta [1968] Director/President and CEO [American]

Tilbrook Enterprise Limited
Incorporated: 20 April 2010 *Employees:* 19
Net Worth: £6,884,825 *Total Assets:* £20,511,400
Registered Office: Mirza House, Sherbourne Drive, Tilbrook, Milton Keynes, Bucks, MK7 8HY
Activities: Activities of other holding companies n.e.c.
Shareholder: Rashid Ahmed Mirza
Officers: Seemtab Ahmed [1969] Director/I T Consultant; Anwarul Habib [1977] Finance Director; Rashid Ahmed Mirza [1957] Director [Indian]

Tile Giant Limited
Incorporated: 19 October 2001 *Employees:* 562
Net Worth: £11,399,000 *Total Assets:* £22,856,000
Registered Office: Lodge Way House, Lodge Way, Harlestone Road, Northampton, NN5 7UG
Activities: Retail sale of hardware, paints and glass in specialised stores
Parent: Travis Perkins Finance Company Limited
Officers: John Peter Carter [1961] Director; Carol Kavanagh [1962] HR Director; Martin Richard Meech [1957] Director/Chartered Surveyor; Alan Richard Williams [1969] Director/Accountant

Tiles4less Limited
Incorporated: 12 December 2000
Net Worth: £661,000 *Total Assets:* £128,010,000
Registered Office: Tiles 4 Less Topps Tiles, Grove Park, Thorpe Way, Enderby, Leics, LE19 1SU
Activities: Retail sale of hardware, paints and glass in specialised stores
Parent: Topps Tiles PLC
Officers: Alistair Robert Hodder, Secretary; Robert Parker [1972] Director/Accountant; Matthew Thomas Mathieson Williams [1974] Director

Tillotts Pharma UK Limited
Incorporated: 11 March 2010 *Employees:* 28
Net Worth: £2,492,247 *Total Assets:* £13,840,558
Registered Office: Larbourne Suite, The Stables, Wellingore Hall, Wellingore, Lincs, LN5 0HX
Activities: Other business support service activities n.e.c.
Officers: Helen Louise Johnson, Secretary; Ingrid Eberle [1971] Director/General Counsel, Legal [Swiss]; Olof Mattias Norrman [1961] Director [Swedish]; Jeremy Thorpe [1963] Director/General Manager

Time Right Holdings Limited
Incorporated: 3 June 2014 *Employees:* 5
Net Worth Deficit: £4,156,256 *Total Assets:* £29,138,092
Registered Office: West Lodge Farm, West Haddon Road, Guilsborough, Northampton, NN6 8QE
Activities: Funeral and related activities
Parent: Time Right Group Limited
Officers: Johnathan Dudley [1963] Director/Chartered Accountant; David Timothy Lonsdale [1977] Director; Joanne Moore [1972] Director/Chief Financial Officer; David Taylor [1966] Director; Glenn Tuck [1965] Director

Timico Limited
Incorporated: 23 July 2003 *Employees:* 305
Net Worth: £1,189,000 *Total Assets:* £26,941,000
Registered Office: Brunel Business Park, Jessop Close, Newark, Notts, NG24 2AG
Activities: Other telecommunications activities
Parent: Timico Technology Group Limited
Officers: Neil Keith Muller [1971] Director; Geoffrey Leslie Neville [1959] Director

Timico Technology Group Limited
Incorporated: 2 November 2010
Net Worth: £2,237,000 *Total Assets:* £9,843,000
Registered Office: Brunel Business Park, Jessop Close, Newark, Notts, NG24 2AG
Activities: Other telecommunications activities
Parent: Steeple Bidco Limited
Officers: John Stuart Holt [1970] Director; Neil Keith Muller [1971] Director; Geoffrey Leslie Neville [1959] Director; Ben Savage [1973] Director

Tingdene (MJ) Limited
Incorporated: 25 April 2005 *Employees:* 160
Net Worth: £34,389,648 *Total Assets:* £104,960,488
Registered Office: Bradfield Road, Finedon Road Industrial Estate, Wellingborough, Northants, NN8 4HB
Activities: Other letting and operating of own or leased real estate
Major Shareholder: Matthew Charles Gibbard
Officers: Charles Richard Liebscher, Secretary/Director; Ian Charles Collier [1972] Director; Matthew Charles Gibbard [1969] Director; Charles Richard Liebscher [1964] Director; Jeremy Michael William Pearson [1967] Director

Tingdene Holdings Limited
Incorporated: 13 June 1989 *Employees:* 6
Net Worth: £12,141,939 *Total Assets:* £12,344,524
Registered Office: Bradfield Road, Finedon Road Industrial Estate, Wellingborough, Northants, NN8 4HB
Activities: Other letting and operating of own or leased real estate
Officers: Catherine Lucy Brown, Secretary; Lesley Ann Fry [1959] Director/Office Manager; Christopher James Gibbard [1963] Director; Matthew Charles Gibbard [1969] Director; Patricia Clare Gibbard [1961] Director/Property Manager; Sylvia Ann Gibbard [1939] Director

Tingdene Marinas Limited
Incorporated: 18 April 2005 *Employees:* 49
Net Worth: £8,795,755 *Total Assets:* £33,652,272
Registered Office: Bradfield Road, Finedon Road Industrial Estate, Wellingborough, Northants, NN8 4HB
Activities: Other letting and operating of own or leased real estate
Parent: Tingdene (MJ) Ltd
Officers: Charles Richard Liebscher, Secretary/Director; Stephen Charles Arber [1962] Director/Marina Manager; Ian Charles Collier [1972] Director; Matthew Charles Gibbard [1969] Director; Charles Richard Liebscher [1964] Director; Neil David Mallandain [1962] Director; Jeremy Michael William Pearson [1967] Director

Tingdene Parks Limited
Incorporated: 13 April 2000 *Employees:* 63
Net Worth: £16,624,705 *Total Assets:* £77,779,480
Registered Office: Bradfield Road, Finedon Road Industrial Estate, Wellingborough, Northants, NN8 4HB
Activities: Other letting and operating of own or leased real estate
Parent: Tingdene (MJ) Ltd
Officers: Charles Richard Liebscher, Secretary/Director; Ian Charles Collier [1972] Director; Matthew Charles Gibbard [1969] Director; Charles Richard Liebscher [1964] Director; Jeremy Michael William Pearson [1967] Director

R C Tinsley 2012 Limited
Incorporated: 23 February 2012
Net Worth: £10,488,498 *Total Assets:* £16,466,076
Registered Office: c/o Duncan & Toplis Limited, Enterprise Way, Pinchbeck, Spalding, Lincs, PE11 3YR
Activities: Activities of agricultural holding companies
Shareholders: Philippa Mary Ball; Annette Ruth White; Richard Paul Tinsley
Officers: Philippa Mary Ball [1956] Director/Farmer; Richard Paul Tinsley [1962] Director/Farmer

Tinsley Bridge Group Limited
Incorporated: 13 April 1987 *Employees:* 207
Previous: Tinsley Bridge (Holdings) Limited
Net Worth: £8,691,628 *Total Assets:* £16,053,001
Registered Office: 335 Shepcote Lane, Sheffield, S9 1TG
Activities: Activities of production holding companies
Shareholder: Mark Charles Webber
Officers: Barry Stuart Cunliffe, Secretary; David Ian Henderson Campbell [1956] Director; Kevin Charlesworth [1967] Production Director; Barry Stuart Cunliffe [1965] Director/Chartered Accountant; Michael Shield [1947] Director; Mark Charles Webber [1958] Managing Director

R. C. Tinsley Limited
Incorporated: 24 March 1955 *Employees:* 7
Net Worth: £9,781,070 *Total Assets:* £10,482,164
Registered Office: c/o Duncan & Toplis Limited, Enterprise Way, Pinchbeck, Spalding, Lincs, PE11 3YR
Activities: Growing of cereals (except rice), leguminous crops and oil seeds
Parent: R C Tinsley 2012 Limited
Officers: Eileen Theodora Tinsley, Secretary; Philippa Mary Ball [1956] Director/Farmer; Eileen Theodora Tinsley [1924] Director; Jennifer Gay Tinsley [1959] Director/Farmer; Richard Paul Tinsley [1962] Director/Farmer; Richard Cole Tinsley [1924] Director/Farmer; Annette Ruth White [1957] Director

Tinsley Park Holdings Limited
Incorporated: 11 March 1998
Net Worth: £8,474,896 *Total Assets:* £11,034,674
Registered Office: Management Suite, Sheffield Business Centre, Europa Link, Sheffield, S9 1XZ
Activities: Buying and selling of own real estate
Officers: James Spencer Matthews [1975] Director; Thomas Berisford Sebire [1975] Director

Tiny Tots Underwriting LLP
Incorporated: 10 September 2008
Net Worth: £728,690 *Total Assets:* £25,736,480
Registered Office: 3 Castlegate, Grantham, Lincs, NG31 6SF
Officers: Sylvia Anne Richards [1942] LLP Member; William Samuel Clive Richards [1937] LLP Member; William Samuel Clive Richards as Trustee of The Clive and Sylvia Richards Grandchildren's Sett [1937] LLP Member

Tioga Limited
Incorporated: 4 March 1996 *Employees:* 111
Net Worth: £4,154,871 *Total Assets:* £11,042,361
Registered Office: St Thomas House, St Mary's Wharf, Mansfield Road, Derby, DE1 3TN
Activities: Manufacture of loaded electronic boards
Parent: Simpatica Group Limited
Officers: Helen Catherine Higginbotham, Company Secretary; Warwick Adams [1960] Director/Electronic Engineer; Helen Catherine Higginbotham [1964] Director; John Alexander Hislop [1969] Director; Russell Blackburn Hoyle [1949] Director; Jeremy Andrew Darcy Mumby [1954] Director/Chartered Accountant

TMI Foods Limited
Incorporated: 23 October 2002 *Employees:* 217
Net Worth: £7,757,350 *Total Assets:* £34,009,152
Registered Office: Lodge Way, Lodge Farm Industrial Estate, Northampton, NN5 7US
Activities: Production of meat and poultry meat products
Parent: QDB Holdings Unlimited Company
Officers: Larry Murrin [1957] Director [Irish]; John Queally [1938] Director [Irish]; Michael Queally [1963] Director [Irish]; Peter Queally [1939] Director [Irish]; Alexander Ronald John Smith [1967] Director

TNS Transxpress Holding Company (U.K.) Limited
Incorporated: 14 August 1998
Net Worth: £10,345,841 *Total Assets:* £13,959,833
Registered Office: 5 Europa View, Sheffield Business Park, Sheffield, S9 1XH
Activities: Activities of head offices
Officers: Simon John Kershaw, Secretary; Mark John Collins [1962] Director [Irish]; Michael Quigley Keegan [1966] Director/Legal Counsel [American]; Simon John Kershaw [1968] Director/Solicitor

TNT Express ICS Limited
Incorporated: 19 January 2007 *Employees:* 323
Net Worth: £97,867,000 *Total Assets:* £164,754,000
Registered Office: TNT Express House, Holly Lane, Atherstone, Warwicks, CV9 2RY
Activities: Other information technology service activities
Parent: TNT Holdings (UK) Limited
Officers: Elizabeth Scott, Secretary; Frank Josef Jary [1971] Director Solutions Delivery [German]; Koen Vermeulen [1985] Finance Director [Dutch]

TNT Express Worldwide Investments Limited
Incorporated: 13 April 1982 *Employees:* 2
Net Worth: £51,239,308 *Total Assets:* £51,239,308
Registered Office: TNT Express House, Holly Lane, Atherstone, Warwicks, CV9 2RY
Activities: Freight transport by road
Parent: TNT Holdings (UK) Limited
Officers: Justin Neil Clarke, Secretary; Justin Neil Clarke [1976] Director/Solicitor; Robert James Peto [1967] Director of Finance

TNT GRS 2008 Limited
Incorporated: 18 August 2008 *Employees:* 2
Net Worth: £201,492,336 *Total Assets:* £412,756,608
Registered Office: TNT Express House, Holly Lane, Atherstone, Warwicks, CV9 2RY
Activities: Other business support service activities n.e.c.
Parent: TNT Holdings Luxembourg S.A.R.L
Officers: Justin Neil Clarke, Secretary; Justin Neil Clarke [1976] Director/Solicitor; Robert James Peto [1967] Director of Finance

TNT Holdings (UK) Limited
Incorporated: 26 July 1996
Net Worth: £343,200,288 *Total Assets:* £343,652,000
Registered Office: TNT Express House, Holly Lane, Atherstone, Warwicks, CV9 2RY
Activities: Other business support service activities n.e.c.
Parent: TNT GRS 2008 Limited
Officers: Justin Neil Clarke, Secretary; Justin Neil Clarke [1976] Director/Solicitor; Robert James Peto [1967] Director of Finance

TNT Transport Limited
Incorporated: 25 October 1973 *Employees:* 2
Net Worth: £63,234,140 *Total Assets:* £63,234,140
Registered Office: TNT Express House, Holly Lane, Atherstone, Warwicks, CV9 2RY
Activities: Freight transport by road
Parent: TNT Holdings (UK) Limited
Officers: Justin Neil Clarke, Secretary; Justin Neil Clarke [1976] Director/Solicitor; Robert James Peto [1967] Director of Finance

TNT UK Limited
Incorporated: 13 April 1982 *Employees:* 8,666
Net Worth: £151,092,992 *Total Assets:* £329,455,008
Registered Office: TNT Express House, Holly Lane, Atherstone, Warwicks, CV9 2RY
Activities: Freight transport by road
Parent: TNT Transport Limited
Officers: Justin Neil Clarke, Secretary; Lawrence Trevor Hoyle [1961] Director/Senior Vice President Northern Europe; Robert James Peto [1967] Director of Finance; Daniel John Vines [1976] Director of Sales & Customer Services

Today's Wholesale Services Limited
Incorporated: 3 August 2011 *Employees:* 29
Net Worth: £3,118,000 *Total Assets:* £12,075,000
Registered Office: 3 Carolina Court, Wisconsin Drive, Doncaster, S Yorks, DN4 5RA
Activities: Agents involved in the sale of food, beverages and tobacco
Officers: John Schofield, Secretary; John Charles Baines [1956] Trading Director; Darren Paul Goldney [1970] Managing Director; John FitzGenerald Kinney [1963] Retail Director; John Schofield [1954] Finance Director

Together Commercial Finance Limited
Incorporated: 26 September 1986
Previous: Lancashire Mortgage Corporation Limited
Net Worth: £101,500,000 *Total Assets:* £1,825,400,064
Registered Office: Lake View, Lakeside, Cheadle, Cheshire, SK8 3GW
Activities: Credit granting by non-deposit taking finance houses and other specialist consumer credit grantors
Parent: Together Financial Services Limited
Officers: Sarah Elizabeth Batt, Secretary; Gary Derek Beckett [1969] Director; Wayne Bowser [1952] Director; Marc Richard Goldberg [1971] Director; Robert Michael McTighe [1953] Director; Henry Neville Moser [1949] Director

Together Financial Services Limited
Incorporated: 15 June 1994 *Employees:* 663
Previous: Jerrold Holdings Limited
Net Worth: £711,900,032 *Total Assets:* £2,979,200,000
Registered Office: Lake View, Lakeside, Cheadle, Cheshire, SK8 3GW
Activities: Activities of head offices
Parent: Bracken Midco2 Limited
Officers: Sarah Elizabeth Batt, Secretary; Peter Simon Ball [1968] Director; Gary Derek Beckett [1969] Director; Wayne Bowser [1952] Non-Executive Director; Marcus John Joseph Reynolds Golby [1970] Director; Marc Richard Goldberg [1971] Director; John Lowe [1972] Director; Robert Michael McTighe [1953] Director; Henry Neville Moser [1949] Director; Joseph Michael Shaoul [1940] Director/Advisor

Together Personal Finance Limited
Incorporated: 22 May 1991
Previous: Cheshire Mortgage Corporation Limited
Net Worth: £41,100,000 *Total Assets:* £621,699,968
Registered Office: Lake View, Lakeside, Cheadle, Cheshire, SK8 3GW
Activities: Credit granting by non-deposit taking finance houses and other specialist consumer credit grantors
Parent: Together Financial Services Limited
Officers: Sarah Elizabeth Batt, Secretary; Peter Simon Ball [1968] Director; Ronald Baxter [1951] Director; Gary Derek Beckett [1969] Director; Wayne Bowser [1952] Director; Richard John Gregory [1954] Director; Henry Neville Moser [1949] Non-Executive Director; Paul Antony Wilson [1971] Director

The Together Trust
Incorporated: 12 June 1935 *Employees:* 829
Net Worth: £23,219,000 *Total Assets:* £29,063,000
Registered Office: Together Trust Centre, Schools Hill, Cheadle, Cheshire, SK8 1JE
Activities: Educational support services
Officers: Mark Robinson Lee, Secretary; Paul Adams [1962] Director/Photographer; Kirsteen Ann Atkinson [1976] Director/HR Consultant; Roger Bernard Bagguley [1941] Director/Retired Schools Inspector; Ralph John Ellerton [1944] Director/Accountant; Anthony John Farnworth [1961] Director/Chartered Accountant; Giles Hugh Joynson Gaddum [1973] Business Director; Lady Paula Doone Gilbart [1955] Director/Retired Solicitor; George David Herbert [1953] Director/Retired; Roger Anthony Horne [1947] Director/Solicitor; Ian Barry Johnson [1966] Commercial Director; Simon Christopher Lees-Jones [1966] Director; Sangam Mishra [1986] Director/Digital Transformation [Indian]; Hugh John Joseph Rylands [1954] Director; Robert John Stevenson [1952] Director/Chartered Insurance Broker

The Tolkien Estate Limited
Incorporated: 10 November 2011
Net Worth: £21,738,440 *Total Assets:* £24,328,696
Registered Office: Prama House, 267 Banbury Road, Oxford, OX2 7HT
Activities: Book publishing
Officers: Cathleen Blackburn, Secretary; Steven Andrew Maier [1961] Director/Solicitor; Baillie Jean Tolkien [1941] Director/Editor [Canadian/British]; Michael George Reuel Tolkien [1943] Director/Retired; Priscilla Mary Anne Reuel Tolkien [1929] Director/Retired; Simon Mario Reuel Tolkien [1959] Director/Writer

The Tolkien Trust
Incorporated: 10 January 2013
Net Worth: £29,085,598 *Total Assets:* £32,220,090
Registered Office: Prama House, 267 Banbury Road, Oxford, OX2 7HT
Activities: Book publishing
Officers: Cathleen Blackburn, Secretary; Baillie Jean Tolkien [1941] Director/Editor [Canadian/British]; Michael George Reuel Tolkien [1943] Director/Retired; Priscilla Mary Anne Reuel Tolkien [1929] Director/Retired

Tollbar Multi Academy Trust
Incorporated: 28 May 2012 *Employees:* 695
Net Worth: £115,345,000 *Total Assets:* £120,580,000
Registered Office: Tollbar Multi Academy Trust, Station Road, New Waltham, Grimsby, N E Lincs, DN36 4RZ
Activities: Primary education
Officers: Gill Margaret Alton [1962] Director/Chief Executive; Jane Cordelia Aukett [1956] Director; Philip Bond [1955] Director; Martyn Douglas Chilvers [1954] Director; Paul Antony Cornford [1959] Director; Michael Leslie Draper [1958] Director; Alec Else [1932] Director; Angela Heather Hampson [1955] Director/Chief Finance Officer; David John Hampson [1950] Director; Andrea Manders [1965] Director/Clerical Assistant; Stephen Geoffrey Woolsey [1956] Director

Tolsa UK Limited
Incorporated: 22 February 1996 *Employees:* 66
Net Worth: £6,302,000 *Total Assets:* £15,134,000
Registered Office: Second Avenue, Flixborough Industrial Estate, Scunthorpe, N Lincs, DN15 8SD
Activities: Manufacture of other non-metallic mineral products n.e.c.
Officers: David Simpson, Secretary; Ciaran Joseph Sullivan [1967] Director/Country Business Manager [Irish]

G F Tomlinson & Sons Ltd
Incorporated: 24 October 1979 *Employees:* 64
Net Worth: £2,713,493 *Total Assets:* £15,301,581
Registered Office: Tomlinson House, Duffield Road, Little Eaton, Derby, DE21 5DR
Activities: Construction of commercial buildings
Parent: G F Tomlinson Group Ltd
Officers: Stephen Dennis Parker, Secretary; Stephen Dennis Parker [1958] Director/Company Secretary; Andrew James Spencer Sewards [1968] Director/Manager

G.F. Tomlinson Building Limited
Incorporated: 6 January 1989 *Employees:* 148
Net Worth: £9,743,182 *Total Assets:* £22,930,102
Registered Office: Tomlinson House, Duffield Road, Little Eaton, Derby, DE21 5DR
Activities: Development of building projects
Parent: G F Tomlinson Group Ltd
Officers: Stephen Dennis Parker, Secretary; Christopher Flint [1967] Director/Commercial Manager; Andrew Mark Huges [1979] Director and General Manager; Stephen Dennis Parker [1958] Director/Company Secretary; Andrew James Spencer Sewards [1968] Director/Manager

G.F.Tomlinson Group Limited
Incorporated: 1 October 1928 *Employees:* 277
Net Worth: £13,450,535 *Total Assets:* £41,067,588
Registered Office: Tomlinson House, Duffield Road, Little Eaton, Derby, DE21 5DR
Activities: Development of building projects
Shareholders: Barry Edward Sewards; Andrew James Spencer Sewards
Officers: Stephen Dennis Parker, Secretary; Stephen Dennis Parker [1958] Director/Company Secretary; Andrew James Spencer Sewards [1968] Director/Manager

Toolstation Limited
Incorporated: 12 February 2002 *Employees:* 2,890
Net Worth: £45,367,000 *Total Assets:* £132,703,000
Registered Office: Lodge Way House, Lodge Way, Harlestone Road, Northampton, NN5 7UG
Activities: Retail sale of hardware, paints and glass in specialised stores
Parent: Travis Perkins PLC
Officers: David James Cox [1960] Director; Richard Lavin [1983] Director/Accountant; Lucy Jane Lynch [1972] Director; James Stuart MacKenzie [1976] Managing Director; Alan Richard Williams [1969] Director/Accountant

Top Tubes Limited
Incorporated: 12 December 1994 *Employees:* 140
Net Worth: £7,450,050 *Total Assets:* £26,687,120
Registered Office: 9 Hurst Road, Longford, Coventry, Warwicks, CV6 6EG
Activities: Other business support service activities n.e.c.
Shareholders: Matthew Bradley; Adam James Bradley
Officers: Matthew Bradley, Secretary; Adam James Bradley [1972] Director/Steel Stockholder; Matthew Bradley [1971] Director

Topalpha (Warehouse) Limited
Incorporated: 31 May 2002 *Employees:* 88
Net Worth Deficit: £8,402,000 *Total Assets:* £12,511,000
Registered Office: Topps Tiles, Thorpe Way, Grove Park, Enderby, Leics, LE19 1SU
Activities: Retail sale of hardware, paints and glass in specialised stores
Parent: Topalpha Limited
Officers: Alistair Robert Hodder, Secretary; Robert Parker [1972] Director/Accountant; Matthew Thomas Mathieson Williams [1974] Director

Topalpha Limited
Incorporated: 25 January 1996
Net Worth: £6,662,000 *Total Assets:* £10,638,000
Registered Office: Topps Tiles, Thorpe Way, Grove Park, Enderby, Leics, LE19 1SU
Activities: Other letting and operating of own or leased real estate
Parent: Topps Tiles PLC
Officers: Alistair Robert Hodder, Secretary; Robert Parker [1972] Director/Accountant; Matthew Thomas Mathieson Williams [1974] Director/Chief Operations Officer

R.H.Topham & Sons Limited
Incorporated: 6 September 1960 *Employees:* 4
Net Worth: £15,925,085 *Total Assets:* £29,288,316
Registered Office: Monks Hardwick, Priory Hill, St Neots, Huntingdon, Cambs, PE19 6ED
Activities: Growing of cereals (except rice), leguminous crops and oil seeds
Parent: Meltcrox Limited
Officers: Michael Raymond Topham [1953] Director/Accountant

Topps Europe Holdings Limited
Incorporated: 29 December 1988
Net Worth: £5,621,273 *Total Assets:* £12,536,490
Registered Office: 18 Vincent Avenue, Crownhill Business Centre, Milton Keynes, Bucks, MK8 0AW
Activities: Printing n.e.c.
Officers: Stephen Hancock, Secretary; Michael Neil Brandstaedter [1970] Director/Chief Executive [American]; David Leiner [1983] Director/Global General Manager [American]

Topps Europe Limited
Incorporated: 23 December 1991 *Employees:* 55
Net Worth Deficit: £16,543,446 *Total Assets:* £21,238,248
Registered Office: 18 Vincent Avenue, Crownhill Business Centre, Milton Keynes, Bucks, MK8 0AW
Activities: Printing n.e.c.
Parent: Topps Europe Holdings Limited
Officers: Stephen Hancock, Secretary; Michael Neil Brandstaedter [1970] Director/Chief Executive [American]; David Leiner [1983] Director/Global General Manager [American]

Topps Tile Kingdom Limited
Incorporated: 4 February 1983
Net Worth Deficit: £150,982,000 *Total Assets:* £53,822,000
Registered Office: Topps Tiles, Thorpe Way, Grove Park, Enderby, Leics, LE19 1SU
Activities: Retail sale of hardware, paints and glass in specialised stores
Parent: Topps Tiles Holdings Limited
Officers: Alistair Robert Hodder, Secretary; Robert Parker [1972] Director/Accountant; Matthew Thomas Mathieson Williams [1974] Director/Chief Executive Officer

Topps Tiles (UK) Limited
Incorporated: 29 May 2003 *Employees:* 1,672
Net Worth: £31,947,000 *Total Assets:* £344,991,008
Registered Office: Topps Tiles, Thorpe Way, Grove Park, Enderby, Leics, LE19 1SU
Activities: Retail sale of hardware, paints and glass in specialised stores
Parent: Topalpha Limited
Officers: Alistair Robert Hodder, Secretary; Robert Parker [1972] Director/Accountant; Matthew Thomas Mathieson Williams [1974] Director

Topps Tiles Distribution Limited
Incorporated: 20 September 2004 *Employees:* 37
Net Worth Deficit: £20,005,000 *Total Assets:* £16,904,000
Registered Office: Topps Tiles, Thorpe Way, Grove Park, Enderby, Leics, LE19 1SU
Activities: Retail sale of hardware, paints and glass in specialised stores
Parent: Topps Tile Kingdom Limited
Officers: Alistair Robert Hodder, Secretary; Robert Parker [1972] Director/Accountant; Matthew Thomas Mathieson Williams [1974] Director

Topps Tiles PLC
Incorporated: 19 June 1996 *Employees:* 2,030
Net Worth: £23,553,000 *Total Assets:* £99,372,000
Registered Office: Topps Tiles, Thorpe Way, Grove Park, Enderby, Leics, LE19 1SU
Activities: Retail sale of hardware, paints and glass in specialised stores
Officers: Alistair Robert Hodder, Secretary; Keith Down [1965] Director; Andrew James King [1961] Director/Retail CEO; Robert Parker [1972] Director/Accountant; Darren Shapland [1966] Director; Claire Tiney [1960] Director - HR Consultant; Matthew Thomas Mathieson Williams [1974] Director/Chief Operating Officer

Toray Textiles Europe Limited
Incorporated: 30 January 1989 *Employees:* 180
Net Worth: £17,675,708 *Total Assets:* £25,162,740
Registered Office: Crown Farm Way, Forest Town, Mansfield, Notts, NG19 0FT
Activities: Weaving of textiles
Parent: Toray Indutries Inc
Officers: Richard James Stephens, Secretary/Accountant; Tatsuo Amano [1967] Director [Japanese]; Takashi Kato [1957] Director [Japanese]; Colin Matthew Nicholson [1965] Director; Richard James Stephens [1970] Director/Accountant; Kazumine Torigoe [1960] Director [Japanese]

Total Computer Networks Limited
Incorporated: 10 November 2003 *Employees:* 111
Net Worth: £2,010,028 *Total Assets:* £16,062,277
Registered Office: Newspaper House, Rothwell Road, Kettering, Northants, NN16 8GA
Activities: Wholesale of computers, computer peripheral equipment and software
Shareholders: Aidan David Groom; Paul Howard Jones
Officers: Paul Howard Jones, Secretary/Computer Consultant; Aidan David Groom [1974] Director/IT Sales; Paul Howard Jones [1973] Director/Computer Consultant

Total Downstream UK PLC
Incorporated: 8 July 1927
Net Worth: £155,378,000 *Total Assets:* £155,406,000
Registered Office: Lindsey Oil Refinery, Eastfield Road, North Killingholme, Immingham, N E Lincs, DN40 3LW
Activities: Activities of production holding companies
Parent: Elf Petroleum UK Limited
Officers: Georgina Violet Crowhurst, Secretary; Olivier Jean-Luc Rene Alexandre [1958] Director/Engineer [French]; Jean-Marc Durand [1972] Director/General Manager of Total Lindsey Oil Refinery Limited [French]; Guillaume Eveno [1977] Director/Chemical Engineer [French]

Total Fitness Health Clubs Limited
Incorporated: 3 August 2010 *Employees:* 596
Net Worth Deficit: £2,498,000 *Total Assets:* £26,087,000
Registered Office: Total Fitness 2010 Ltd, Wilmslow Way, Handforth, Wilmslow, Cheshire, SK9 3PE
Activities: Fitness facilities
Officers: Jasvir Sanghera, Secretary; Sophie Lawler [1978] Director/Chief Executive; Jasvir Singh Sanghera [1966] Finance Director

Total Integrated Solutions (Holdings) Limited
Incorporated: 16 February 2016 *Employees:* 141
Net Worth: £4,171,576 *Total Assets:* £9,897,131
Registered Office: Hamilton Way, Oakham Business Park, Mansfield, Notts, NG18 5BU
Activities: Manufacture of other electrical equipment
Officers: Christopher Lewis [1958] Director; James John Twigg [1976] Director

Total Lindsey Oil Refinery Limited
Incorporated: 12 April 1956 *Employees:* 447
Net Worth: £294,468,000 *Total Assets:* £872,945,984
Registered Office: Lindsey Oil Refinery, Eastfield Road, North Killingholme, Immingham, N E Lincs, DN40 3LW
Activities: Mineral oil refining
Parent: Total Downstream UK PLC
Officers: Georgina Violet Crowhurst, Secretary; Olivier Jean-Luc Rene Alexandre [1958] Director/Engineer [French]; Jean-Marc Durand [1972] Director/General Manager [French]; Guillaume Eveno [1977] Director/Chemical Engineer [French]; Fabien Mornand [1973] Director/General Manager [French]

Total Motion Limited
Incorporated: 7 February 2003 *Employees:* 72
Net Worth: £3,654,268 *Total Assets:* £39,616,488
Registered Office: Southpoint House, Harcourt Way, Meridian Business Park, Leicester, LE19 1WP
Activities: Renting and leasing of cars and light motor vehicles
Shareholder: Simon John Hill
Officers: Caroline Louise Hill, Secretary/Director; Caroline Louise Hill [1964] Director; Simon John Hill [1968] Director; Kelly Jacqueline Longmuir [1975] Commercial Director; Claire Burnice Timms [1976] Director/Certified Chartered Accountant

Total Produce Holdings (UK) Limited
Incorporated: 9 August 2006
Net Worth: £31,756,000 *Total Assets:* £33,135,000
Registered Office: Total Produce, Enterprise Way, Pinchbeck, Spalding, Lincs, PE11 3YR
Activities: Activities of head offices
Parent: TPH (UK) Limited
Officers: Mark Christopher Owen, Secretary; Jacinta Frances Devine [1972] Director [Irish]; Francis Gerard McKernan [1962] Director; Mark Christopher Owen [1965] Director; Denis Leslie Punter [1953] Director

Total Produce Limited
Incorporated: 2 October 2006 *Employees:* 332
Net Worth: £11,940,000 *Total Assets:* £39,150,000
Registered Office: Total Produce, Enterprise Way, Pinchbeck, Spalding, Lincs, PE11 3YR
Activities: Wholesale of fruit and vegetables
Parent: Total Produce Holdings (UK) Limited
Officers: Mark Christopher Owen, Secretary; Andrew Roger Allmond [1944] Director; Jacinta Frances Devine [1972] Director [Irish]; Francis Gerard McKernan [1962] Director [Irish]; Mark Christopher Owen [1965] Director; Denis Leslie Punter [1953] Director; Stephen Mark Webster [1962] Director

Total Worldfresh Limited
Incorporated: 28 December 1987 *Employees:* 182
Net Worth: £6,463,000 *Total Assets:* £35,346,000
Registered Office: Total Produce, Enterprise Way, Pinchbeck, Spalding, Lincs, PE11 3YR
Activities: Wholesale of fruit and vegetables
Parent: Saybest Limited
Officers: Mark Christopher Owen, Secretary; Francis Gerard McKernan [1962] Director; Mark Christopher Owen [1965] Director; Denis Leslie Punter [1953] Managing Director

Totally Local Company Limited
Incorporated: 13 June 2006 *Employees:* 748
Previous: Solutions SK Limited
Net Worth Deficit: £5,516,000 *Total Assets:* £16,927,000
Registered Office: Enterprise House, Oakhurst Drive, off Bird Hall Lane, Cheadle Heath, Stockport, Cheshire, SK3 0XT
Activities: Collection of non-hazardous waste
Parent: Stockport Metropolitan Borough Council
Officers: Stephen Jallands, Secretary; Katherine Helen Cowell [1952] Director; Stephen Jallands [1963] Director/Chartered Accountant; Stephen Paul Morris [1952] Managing Director; Dermot Justin Power [1951] Director; Susan Webster [1950] Director

Totally PLC
Incorporated: 28 October 1999 *Employees:* 1,562
Net Worth: £27,338,000 *Total Assets:* £52,896,000
Registered Office: First Floor West, Cardinal Square, 10 Nottingham Road, Derby, DE1 3QT
Activities: Other human health activities
Officers: John William Charles Charlton, Secretary; Donald Ahelan Baladasan [1973] Director/Chartered Accountant; Lisa Barter-NG [1971] Finance Director; Anthony Rhys Bourne [1953] Director; Gloria Ann Cooke [1953] Clinical Quality Director; Robert Holt [1954] Director; Wendy Jayne Lawrence [1961] Director/Chief Executive; Michael Greig Rogers [1942] Director

Totemic (2014) Holdings Limited
Incorporated: 18 November 2010 *Employees:* 752
Net Worth: £12,027,744 *Total Assets:* £32,707,020
Registered Office: P O Box 9562, Kempton House, Kempton Way, Grantham, Lincs, NG31 0EA
Activities: Activities of head offices
Shareholder: Lesley Elizabeth Rann
Officers: Halina Briggs, Secretary; Lianne Estelle Firth [1966] HR Director; Andrew John Kirk [1981] Finance Director; Gordon Philip Dale Rann [1950] Managing Director; Lesley Elizabeth Rann [1959] Sales Director

Touchgold Limited
Incorporated: 11 September 2007
Net Worth Deficit: £70,872 *Total Assets:* £10,834,608
Registered Office: Juliette Suite, Unit 2 Lowes Lane Business Park, Lowes Lane, Wellesbourne, Warwicks, CV35 9RB
Activities: Production of electricity
Officers: Clive Ronald Hanley, Secretary; Richard Andrew Iain Evans [1966] Director/Engineer; John Martin Gardner [1950] Director; Patrick Joseph Albert Hansen [1972] Director [Luxembourger]; Dr Robert Evan Jones [1946] Director/Chartered Engineer; Mark Edward Petterson [1960] Director/Chartered Engineer; Graham Robinson [1944] Director; Jamie Samuel Rudkin [1972] Director; John Leslie Sulley [1951] Director/Chartered Engineer; Paul Andrew Vertigen [1967] Director/Consultant Engineer

Tours Abroad Group Limited
Incorporated: 11 June 2007 *Employees:* 98
Net Worth Deficit: £2,824,408 *Total Assets:* £10,849,663
Registered Office: Sunway House, Canklow Meadows, Rotherham, S Yorks, S60 2XR
Activities: Activities of head offices
Shareholders: Kathleen Henry; Ian Duncan Henry
Officers: Andrew Oldfield, Secretary; Ian Duncan Henry [1963] Director; Kathleen Henry [1965] Director; Andrew Oldfield [1971] Finance Director

Tove Learning Trust
Incorporated: 10 February 2011 *Employees:* 393
Previous: Sponne School
Net Worth: £60,335,272 *Total Assets:* £67,569,312
Registered Office: Brackley Road, Towcester, Northants, NN12 6DJ
Activities: General secondary education
Officers: Katherine Lindsay Fell, Secretary; Joanne Chitty [1969] Director/Support Practitioner; Jamie Richard Clarke [1961] Director/Headteacher; Timothy Martin Foster [1971] Director/Sales Manager; Graham John Rees [1947] Director/Retired; Susan Margaret Wagstaff [1969] Director/School Business Manager; Christopher Lawson Watt [1957] Director

Town and Country Petfoods Limited
Incorporated: 5 November 1974 *Employees:* 20
Net Worth: £10,634,561 *Total Assets:* £14,212,709
Registered Office: 3 Castlegate, Grantham, Lincs, NG31 6SF
Activities: Agents specialised in the sale of other particular products
Shareholders: Peter James Kenneth Parkinson; Julie Anne Bitowt; John Antony Winsor Parkinson
Officers: Julie Anne Bitowt, Secretary/Petfood Logistics; John Antony Winsor Parkinson [1962] Managing Director; John Andrew Parkinson [1936] Director/Chairman; Peter James Kenneth Parkinson [1969] Marketing Director

Toy Brokers Holdings Limited
Incorporated: 16 February 2009 *Employees:* 40
Net Worth: £18,674,628 *Total Assets:* £35,664,852
Registered Office: Hercules House, Pierson Road, Alconbury Weald, Huntingdon, Cambs, PE28 4YA
Activities: Manufacture of other games and toys, n.e.c.
Officers: Anthony Carson Shepherd, Secretary/Director; David Lytton Kremer [1964] Director; Michael Moody [1953] Director; Simon Richard Pilkington [1967] Managing Director; Anthony Carson Shepherd [1948] Director

Toymaster Limited
Incorporated: 10 October 1988 *Employees:* 17
Net Worth: £2,707,000 *Total Assets:* £15,969,000
Registered Office: Victoria House, Newport Pagnell Road West, Northampton, NN4 7JJ
Activities: Agents involved in the sale of a variety of goods
Officers: Colin Mark Farrow, Secretary; Christopher Bruce Blatcher [1970] Director; Roger Dyson [1947] Director/Vice Chairman; Ian Michael Edmunds [1964] Managing Director; Colin Mark Farrow [1949] Finance Director; Ciaran Pius Fitzpatrick [1954] Director/Shopkeeper [Irish]; Julian Owen Hartfield [1953] Director/Toy Retailer; Yogesh Parmar [1962] Operations Director; Andrew Charles Taylor [1964] Executive Director

Toyoda Gosei UK Ltd.
Incorporated: 1 April 1999 *Employees:* 896
Net Worth Deficit: £108,493,000 *Total Assets:* £37,513,000
Registered Office: Bessemer Way, Centurion Business Park, Templeborough, Rotherham, S Yorks, S60 1FB
Activities: Manufacture of other parts and accessories for motor vehicles
Parent: Toyoda Gosei Co Ltd
Officers: Gareth Mark Thraves, Secretary/Finance; Masahiko Ito [1960] Director [Japanese]; Shigenori Matsuo [1959] Managing Director [Japanese]; Katsumi Saito [1965] Director [Japanese]; Atsushi Sumida [1954] Director [Japanese]

Toyota Motor Manufacturing (UK) Limited
Incorporated: 24 February 1989 *Employees:* 2,698
Net Worth Deficit: £692,612,288 *Total Assets:* £392,552,576
Registered Office: Burnaston, Derby, DE1 9TA
Activities: Manufacture of motor vehicles
Parent: Toyota Motor Corporation
Officers: James Crosbie, Secretary; Marvin Lee Cooke [1966] Managing Director; James Crosbie [1967] Deputy Managing Director; Hiroyuki Hatakeyama [1962] Director [Japanese]; Akito Takami [1967] Director [Japanese]; Shigeru Teramoto [1955] Chairman & Director [Japanese]; Dr. Johannes Jacobus Van Zyl [1958] Director [South African]

TPH (UK) Limited
Incorporated: 6 November 2006
Net Worth: £20,341,000 *Total Assets:* £62,613,000
Registered Office: Total Produce, Enterprise Way, Pinchbeck, Spalding, Lincs, PE11 3YR
Activities: Activities of head offices
Parent: Total Produce PLC
Officers: Mark Christopher Owen, Secretary; Jacinta Frances Devine [1972] Director [Irish]; Francis Gerard McKernan [1962] Director; Seamus Mulvenna [1953] Director [Irish]; Mark Christopher Owen [1965] Director; Denis Leslie Punter [1953] Director

Trackwork Group Limited
Incorporated: 2 April 2008 *Employees:* 450
Net Worth: £26,759,000 *Total Assets:* £44,615,000
Registered Office: 2 Sandall Lane, Kirk Sandall Industrial Estate, Doncaster, S Yorks, DN3 1LL
Activities: Other specialised construction activities n.e.c.
Major Shareholder: Mark Jonathan Wilkinson Waind
Officers: Mark Jonathan Wilkinson Waind, Secretary; Mark Jonathan Wilkinson Waind [1961] Director

Trackwork Limited
Incorporated: 29 July 1976 *Employees:* 338
Net Worth: £26,924,000 *Total Assets:* £48,096,000
Registered Office: P O Box 139, Sandall Lane, Kirk Sandall Industrial Estate, Doncaster, S Yorks, DN3 1LL
Activities: Other specialised construction activities n.e.c.
Parent: Trackwork Holdings Limited
Officers: Gail Marie Rusling, Secretary; Simon Philip Lee [1962] Director/Quantity Surveyor; Mark Jonathan Wilkinson Waind [1961] Managing Director

Tradelink Direct Limited
Incorporated: 25 November 1991 *Employees:* 221
Net Worth: £7,370,957 *Total Assets:* £11,133,583
Registered Office: LHG House, Northside, Marwick Road, March, Cambs, PE15 8PH
Activities: Manufacture of other plastic products
Shareholder: Alan Manuel Greenberg
Officers: James William Moody, Secretary; James William Moody [1965] Managing Director; Anthony Charles Morley [1964] Business Director

Trafalgar Bidco Limited
Incorporated: 4 December 2014
Net Worth: £185,723,280 *Total Assets:* £348,429,120
Registered Office: 2 Des Roches Square, Witney, Oxon, OX28 4LE
Activities: Activities of other holding companies n.e.c.
Parent: Trafalgar Midco 2 Limited
Officers: Andrew James Galbraith, Secretary; Michael David Simon Edgeley [1966] Director; Andrew James Galbraith [1970] Director/Accountant; Carl Anthony Shuker [1961] Director

Trafalgar Court Northern Limited
Incorporated: 11 July 1994
Net Worth: £4,080,873 *Total Assets:* £16,004,016
Registered Office: Marchman House, 3a West Street, Mexborough, S Yorks, S64 9HZ
Activities: Other letting and operating of own or leased real estate
Major Shareholder: Fred Wilkinson Meggitt
Officers: Lisa Matilda Meggitt, Secretary; Fred Wilkinson Meggitt [1945] Director/Solicitor; Lisa Matilda Meggitt [1953] Director/Secretary

Trafalgar Midco 1 Limited
Incorporated: 4 December 2014
Net Worth Deficit: £556,373 *Total Assets:* £173,518,112
Registered Office: 2 Des Roches Square, Witney, Oxon, OX28 4LE
Activities: Activities of other holding companies n.e.c.
Parent: A-Plan Group Ltd
Officers: Andrew James Galbraith, Secretary; Michael David Simon Edgeley [1966] Director; Andrew James Galbraith [1970] Director/Accountant; Carl Anthony Shuker [1961] Director

Trafalgar Midco 2 Limited
Incorporated: 4 December 2014
Net Worth: £165,787,904 *Total Assets:* £168,054,896
Registered Office: 2 Des Roches Square, Witney, Oxon, OX28 4LE
Activities: Activities of other holding companies n.e.c.
Parent: Trafalgar Midco 1 Limited
Officers: Andrew James Galbraith, Secretary; Michael David Simon Edgeley [1966] Director; Andrew James Galbraith [1970] Director/Accountant; Carl Anthony Shuker [1961] Director

Leslie H. Trainer and Son Limited
Incorporated: 19 October 1973 *Employees:* 96
Net Worth: £994,000 *Total Assets:* £12,699,000
Registered Office: 2 Penman Way, Grove Park, Enderby, Leicester, LE19 1ST
Activities: Retail trade of motor vehicle parts and accessories
Parent: Trainer (Holdings) Limited
Officers: Adam Collinson [1972] Director; Darren Edwards [1968] Director

Transaction Network Services (UK) Limited
Incorporated: 26 July 1994 *Employees:* 163
Net Worth: £9,658,218 *Total Assets:* £22,297,696
Registered Office: 5 Europa View, Sheffield Business Park, Sheffield, S9 1XH
Activities: Other telecommunications activities
Parent: TNS Transxpress Holding Company (U.K.) Limited
Officers: Simon John Kershaw, Secretary; Mark John Collins [1962] Director [Irish]; Michael Quigley Keegan [1966] Director/Legal Counsel [American]; Simon John Kershaw [1968] Director/Solicitor

Transform Trust
Incorporated: 5 December 2012 *Employees:* 911
Net Worth: £43,722,920 *Total Assets:* £57,772,828
Registered Office: Unit 11 Castlebridge Office Village, Kirtley Drive, Nottingham, NG7 1LD
Activities: Primary education
Officers: Stephen Martin Patrick Cox, Secretary; Toby Michael Greany [1970] Director/Professor of Leadership & Innovation; Qing Gu [1973] Director/Educationalist; Vernon Lloyd [1977] Director/Emote Support Analyst; Joanna Luxton [1972] Director/Employment Law Consultant; Rebecca Meredith [1966] Director/Executive Headteacher; Peter Nicholas Munro [1947] Director/Retired; Roger John Periam [1958] Director/Financial Consultant; Alex Taylor [1975] Director/Teacher

Transforming Lives Educational Trust
Incorporated: 3 February 2011 *Employees:* 322
Previous: Ashlawn School Academy Trust
Net Worth: £14,404,644 *Total Assets:* £18,403,410
Registered Office: Ashlawn School, Ashlawn Road, Rugby, Warwicks, CV22 5ET
Activities: General secondary education
Officers: Sue Crosson [1956] Director/Professional Support Officer; Philip James Davis [1987] Director/Company Secretary; April Gold [1967] Deputy Diocesan Director of Education; Stewart Jardine [1957] Director/Consultant; Michael Howard Soley [1968] Director/Police Officer; Nichola Stacey Watson [1980] Director/Chief Executive

Transit 2017 Limited
Incorporated: 15 June 2017
Net Worth Deficit: £156,068 *Total Assets:* £11,631,073
Registered Office: Administration Building, Brigg Road, Scunthorpe, N Lincs, DN16 1BP
Activities: Other business support service activities n.e.c.
Parent: British Steel Limited
Officers: Damian Paul Hargreaves, Secretary; Roland Junck [1955] Director [Luxembourger]; Generald Reichmann [1976] Director [Austrian]

Trapoc Limited
Incorporated: 12 June 2007
Net Worth: £68,680,000 *Total Assets:* £73,593,000
Registered Office: Acrey Fields, Woburn Road, Wootton, Beds, MK43 9EJ
Activities: Buying and selling of own real estate
Parent: TRPC Limited
Officers: Aaron Jayson Adair [1969] Director/Chief Executive Officer [American]; Jonathan David Canning [1972] Director/General Counsel; Gregory Depasquale [1968] Director/SVP, General Counsel and Secretary of Copart, Inc [American]; William Easley Franklin [1956] Director/Chief Financial Officer [American]; Nigel James Paget [1966] Managing Director; Simon Sheldon-Wilson [1969] Director; Paul Anthony Styer [1956] Director/General Counsel [American]

Travelodge Hotels Limited
Incorporated: 29 July 1963 *Employees:* 6,671
Net Worth: £316,100,000 *Total Assets:* £689,699,968
Registered Office: Sleepy Hollow, Aylesbury Road, Thame, Oxon, OX9 3AT
Activities: Hotels and similar accommodation
Parent: Full Moon Holdco 7 Limited
Officers: Joanna Boydell, Secretary; Katherine Anna Ashford Thomas, Secretary; Joanna Boydell [1969] Director/Chief Financial Officer; Peter Darren Gowers [1972] Director; Paul Victor Harvey [1961] Director; Brian Godman Wallace [1954] Director

Travis Perkins (Properties) Limited
Incorporated: 2 May 1949
Net Worth: £332,700,000 *Total Assets:* £1,105,600,000
Registered Office: Lodge Way House, Lodge Way, Harlestone Road, Northampton, NN5 7UG
Activities: Development of building projects
Parent: Travis Perkins PLC
Officers: John Peter Carter [1961] Director; Martin Richard Meech [1957] Director/Chartered Surveyor; Darren Screen [1973] Director/Accountant; Alan Richard Williams [1969] Director/Accountant

Travis Perkins Finance Company Limited
Incorporated: 11 February 2008
Net Worth: £309,236,000 *Total Assets:* £310,095,008
Registered Office: Lodge Way House, Lodge Way, Harlestone Road, Northampton, NN5 7UG
Activities: Other business support service activities n.e.c.
Parent: Travis Perkins PLC
Officers: John Peter Carter [1961] Director; Alan Richard Williams [1969] Director/Accountant

Travis Perkins Financing Company No.2 Limited
Incorporated: 21 November 2008
Net Worth: £108,189,000 *Total Assets:* £108,600,000
Registered Office: Lodge Way House, Lodge Way, Harlestone Road, Northampton, NN5 7UG
Activities: Other business support service activities n.e.c.
Parent: Travis Perkins Acquisitions Company Limited
Officers: John Peter Carter [1961] Director; Alan Richard Williams [1969] Director/Accountant

Travis Perkins P & H Partner Limited
Incorporated: 7 October 2010
Net Worth: £743,900,032 *Total Assets:* £810,600,000
Registered Office: Lodge Way House, Lodge Way, Harlestone Road, Northampton, NN5 7UG
Activities: Non-trading company
Parent: Travis Perkins Acquisitions Company Limited
Officers: John Peter Carter [1961] Operations Director; Alan Richard Williams [1969] Director/Accountant

Travis Perkins PLC
Incorporated: 27 October 1964 *Employees:* 27,753
Net Worth: £2,848,600,064 *Total Assets:* £5,141,799,936
Registered Office: Lodge Way House, Lodge Way, Harleston Road, Northampton, NN5 7UG
Activities: Non-specialised wholesale trade
Officers: Robin Paul Miller, Secretary; Moreen Ruth Anderson [1953] Director; John Peter Carter [1961] Director; Stuart John Chambers [1956] Director; Coline Lucille McConville [1964] Director [Australian]; Peter Timothy Redfern [1970] Director; Christopher Charles Bevan Rogers [1960] Director; John Terence Rogers [1968] Director; Alan Richard Williams [1969] Director/Accountant

Travis Perkins Plumbing & Heating LLP
Incorporated: 31 October 2011 *Employees:* 5,423
Net Worth: £820,700,032 *Total Assets:* £1,277,200,000
Registered Office: Lodge Way House, Lodge Way, Harlestone Road, Northampton, NN5 7UG
Officers: John Peter Carter [1961] Member; Alan Richard Williams [1969] Member

Travis Perkins Trading Company Limited
Incorporated: 27 August 1962 *Employees:* 7,939
Net Worth: £553,600,000 *Total Assets:* £3,065,400,064
Registered Office: Lodgeway House, Lodgeway, Harlestone Road, Northampton, NN5 7UG
Activities: Agents involved in the sale of timber and building materials
Parent: Travis Perkins PLC
Officers: John Peter Carter [1961] Director; Martin Richard Meech [1957] Director/Chartered Surveyor; Ivan James Trevor [1979] Director; Alan Richard Williams [1969] Director/Accountant

TRB Technology Group Limited
Incorporated: 4 June 2007 *Employees:* 176
Previous: Amber Valley Holding Company Limited
Net Worth: £5,962,590 *Total Assets:* £12,663,954
Registered Office: 12 Clifton Road, St Peter's Hill, Huntingdon, Cambs, PE29 7EN
Activities: Activities of head offices
Major Shareholder: Jonathan McQueen
Officers: Richard Bernard Holland [1965] Director; Philip Martin [1953] Director/Accountant; Jonathan McQueen [1969] Director [American]

Trek Bicycle Corporation Limited
Incorporated: 6 March 1989 *Employees:* 85
Net Worth: £13,877,319 *Total Assets:* £25,287,584
Registered Office: 9 Sherbourne Drive, Tilbrook, Milton Keynes, Bucks, MK7 8HX
Activities: Retail sale of sports goods, fishing gear, camping goods, boats and bicycles
Parent: Trek Bicycle Corporation
Officers: Jennifer Lee Naeger, Secretary; Chad Robert Brown [1978] Director/Finance [American]; John Burke [1962] Director/President [American]; Jennifer Lee Naeger [1978] Director [American]

Trent Academies Group
Incorporated: 3 July 2012 *Employees:* 487
Net Worth: £42,081,000 *Total Assets:* £53,953,000
Registered Office: The Rushcliffe School, Boundary Road, West Bridgford, Nottingham, NG2 7BW
Activities: General secondary education
Officers: Geoffrey Charles Bail [1953] Director; Caroline Hudson [1968] Finance Director; Fiona Bianca Pearson [1966] Director/Property Manager; Andrew Jonathan Pickin [1958] Director/Solicitor; Matthew James Varley [1970] Director

Trent College Limited
Incorporated: 17 December 1890 *Employees:* 392
Net Worth: £32,148,000 *Total Assets:* £41,712,000
Registered Office: Trent College, Derby Road, Long Eaton, Nottingham, NG10 4AD
Activities: Primary education
Shareholders: Matthew Neil Hannah; Stephen Anelay; Gillian Hinks; Ian Francis Bowness; Andrew Gordon Crompton
Officers: Stephen Paul Burnham, Secretary; Stephen Charles Anelay [1946] Director/Chartered Surveyor; Gary John Bates [1969] Director; Ian Francis Bowness [1957] Director; Aidan Edward Butler [1971] Director/Private Client Head; Dr Glenn Crocker [1964] Director; Anthony Nicholas Doleman [1961] Director; Jennifer Anne Ellis [1972] Director/Solicitor; The Reverend Nicola Jane Fenton [1970] Director/Clergy; Dr Richard Field [1971] Director/Associate Professor; Neil David Finlay [1968] Director/Headteacher; Louise Ann Gray [1958] Director/Headmistress; Ian Richard Griffin [1969] Director/Deputy Headmaster; Dr Timothy Gardiner Hammond [1954] Director/Professor; Matthew Neil Hannah [1964] Director; Gillian Hinks [1976] Director/Accountant; Emma Justine Lindblom [1984] Director/Accountant; Dr Constantine Paul Nathanail [1964] Director/Geologist; Sally Anne Rosser [1961] Director/Deputy Head; Christopher David Swallow [1970] Managing Director

Trent Motor Traction Company Limited (The)
Incorporated: 31 October 1913 *Employees:* 798
Net Worth: £23,435,000 *Total Assets:* £63,894,000
Registered Office: Mansfield Road, Heanor, Derbys, DE75 7BG
Activities: Other passenger land transport
Officers: Graham Sutton, Secretary/Financial Director; Jeffrey Counsell [1958] Managing Director; Brian Robert King [1944] Director/Chairman; Richard Ian Morgan [1951] Director/Deputy Chairman; Graham Sutton [1960] Group Financial Director

Tresefir Limited
Incorporated: 13 February 1978 *Employees:* 3
Net Worth: £7,353,221 *Total Assets:* £10,351,061
Registered Office: 3 Isis Court, Wyndyke Furlong, Abingdon, Oxon, OX14 1DZ
Activities: Other letting and operating of own or leased real estate
Shareholders: Dawa Investments Ltd; Sanaga Investments Ltd
Officers: Duncan Spence [1943] Director/Printer & Publisher; Oliver James Stone [1988] Director/Management Accountant

Trewhiddle Village Limited
Incorporated: 19 February 2007 *Employees:* 4
Net Worth Deficit: £2,545,768 *Total Assets:* £10,147,474
Registered Office: Whitecroft House, 51 Water Lane, Wilmslow, Cheshire, SK9 5BQ
Activities: Other accommodation
Officers: Timothy Dennis [1975] Director; Ewan James Kearney [1971] Director; Matthew Dawson Spence [1963] Director; Anthony Wild [1974] Director

TRG Bonds IV Limited
Incorporated: 3 November 2015
Net Worth: £1 *Total Assets:* £16,685,557
Registered Office: 12a Melbourne Business Court, Pride Park, Derby, DE24 8LZ
Activities: Security dealing on own account
Major Shareholder: Charles Daniel King
Officers: Yasmin Reilly [1989] Operations Director

Trident 2020 Limited
Incorporated: 6 January 2014 *Employees:* 70
Net Worth: £6,583,085 *Total Assets:* £11,923,016
Registered Office: Unit 5 Gelders Hall Road, Shepshed, Leics, LE12 9NH
Activities: Management consultancy activities other than financial management
Major Shareholder: Paul Ippaso
Officers: Adriana Edy Ippaso [1938] Director; Paul Ippaso [1967] Director

Trigon Holdings Limited
Incorporated: 14 August 2008 *Employees:* 149
Net Worth: £5,417,190 *Total Assets:* £13,347,172
Registered Office: 5 Prospect Place, Millennium Way, Pride Park, Derby, DE24 8HG
Activities: Activities of other holding companies n.e.c.
Shareholders: Matthew John Eden; James Edwin Eden
Officers: Matthew John Eden, Secretary; James Edwin Eden [1974] Director; Matthew John Eden [1974] Director

Trimas Corporation Limited
Incorporated: 18 July 1996 *Employees:* 4
Net Worth: £2,778,000 *Total Assets:* £74,233,000
Registered Office: 44 Scudamore Road, Leicester, LE3 1UG
Activities: Activities of other holding companies n.e.c.
Parent: Rieke-Lamons International Holdings LLC
Officers: Mark Edward Box [1962] Managing Director; David John Pritchett [1966] Director; Joshua Alan Sherbin [1963] Director/Attorney [American]; Robert Joseph Zalupski [1959] Director/VP Finance [American]

Trimas UK Aerospace Holdings Limited
Incorporated: 7 August 2014 *Employees:* 2
Net Worth: £22,342,356 *Total Assets:* £297,526,912
Registered Office: 44 Scudamore Road, Leicester, LE3 1UG
Activities: Activities of production holding companies
Parent: Trimas Company LLC
Officers: Joshua Alan Sherbin, Secretary; Mark Edward Box [1962] Director; David John Pritchett [1966] Director

Trina Solar (UK) Limited
Incorporated: 13 March 2012 *Employees:* 3
Net Worth: £842,050 *Total Assets:* £11,224,088
Registered Office: Nottingham East Midlands Airport, Herald Way, Pegasus Business Park, Castle Donnington, Derbys, DE74 2TZ
Activities: Other manufacturing n.e.c.
Major Shareholder: Jifan Gao
Officers: Ye Chen [1969] Director/Assistant Vice President [Chinese]; Xiao Wu [1977] Credit Director [Chinese]

The Trinley Estate Limited
Incorporated: 9 July 2014 *Employees:* 5
Net Worth: £23,662,908 *Total Assets:* £23,888,188
Registered Office: Gasson Associates, Middle Hill, Hook Norton, Banbury, Oxon, OX15 5PL
Activities: Growing of cereals (except rice), leguminous crops and oil seeds
Major Shareholder: Bjorn Erik Saven
Officers: Peter Generald Baughen, Secretary; Peter Generald Baughen [1961] Director/Estates' Manager; Jonathan Edward McCalmont Harington [1955] Director/Property Buying Agent; Bjorn Erik Saven [1950] Director/Chairman [Swedish]; Isabel Saven [1985] Director's Associate [Swedish/British]

Tripal Group Limited
Incorporated: 5 September 2011 *Employees:* 31
Net Worth: £5,544,912 *Total Assets:* £9,734,422
Registered Office: 16 Don White Road, Ogee Business Park, Wellingborough, Northants, NN8 4FT
Activities: Activities of head offices
Officers: Simon Johnathon Poole, Secretary; Mark Burman [1974] Director; Simon Johnathon Poole [1974] Director; Michael Robert Turner [1970] Director

Tripal International Limited
Incorporated: 29 June 2004 *Employees:* 20
Net Worth: £5,386,370 *Total Assets:* £9,442,573
Registered Office: 16 Don White Road, Ogee Business Park, Wellingborough, Northants, NN8 4FT
Activities: Wholesale of clothing and footwear
Parent: Tripal Group Limited
Officers: Simon Johnathon Poole, Secretary; David Robert Guy Burman [1947] Director; Mark Burman [1974] Director; Simon Johnathon Poole [1974] Director; Michael Robert Turner [1970] Director; Michael John Turner [1940] Director

Tripleteam (Developments) Limited
Incorporated: 3 November 1995 *Employees:* 6
Net Worth: £14,506,962 *Total Assets:* £16,000,256
Registered Office: 1 Westmoreland Avenue, Thurmaston, Leicester, LE4 8PH
Activities: Other letting and operating of own or leased real estate
Parent: Charles Street Buildings (Leicester) Limited
Officers: Robert Henry Smith, Secretary; Winifred Mary Linnett [1950] Director; Mary Agnes Middleton [1981] Director; Hugh Patrick Murphy [1948] Director; Joseph John Murphy [1978] Director/Solicitor; Margaret Ann Murphy [1951] Director; Patrick Hugh Murphy [1977] Director

Triplex Lloyd Limited
Incorporated: 20 October 1936
Net Worth: £269,016,992 *Total Assets:* £277,272,000
Registered Office: Millennium Court, First Avenue, Burton on Trent, Staffs, DE14 2WH
Activities: Activities of head offices
Parent: Doncasters UK Holdings Limited
Officers: Ian Molyneux, Secretary; Duncan Andrew Hinks [1975] Director/Chief Financial Officer; Ian Molyneux [1964] Director/Solicitor; Lisa Marie Oxnard [1981] Director/Chief Financial Officer

Triplex Lloyd Properties Limited
Incorporated: 16 June 1887 *Employees:* 2
Net Worth: £8,798,000 *Total Assets:* £10,909,000
Registered Office: Millennium Court, First Avenue, Burton on Trent, Staffs, DE14 2WH
Activities: Development of building projects
Parent: Paralloy Limited
Officers: Ian Molyneux, Secretary; Duncan Andrew Hinks [1975] Director/Chief Financial Officer; Ian Molyneux [1964] Director/Solicitor; Lisa Marie Oxnard [1981] Director/Chief Financial Officer

Tripod Crest Group Limited
Incorporated: 30 June 2003 *Employees:* 170
Previous: McTaggart Limited
Net Worth: £10,235,673 *Total Assets:* £16,955,652
Registered Office: Tripod Crest House, The Business Centre, Ross Road, Weedon Road Industrial Estate, Northampton, NN5 5AX
Activities: Construction of roads and motorways
Major Shareholder: Eugene McTaggart
Officers: Eugene McTaggart [1957] Director [Irish]

Tripod Crest Limited
Incorporated: 28 January 1982 *Employees:* 74
Net Worth: £4,853,863 *Total Assets:* £11,764,127
Registered Office: Tripod Crest House, Ross Road, Weedon Road Industrial Estate, Northampton, NN5 5AX
Activities: Construction of roads and motorways
Officers: Eugene McTaggart [1957] Director [Irish]; Timothy Spencer Neal [1972] Finance Director; Cathal O'Boyle [1966] Director; Joanne Salmon [1974] Director

Trison Estates Limited
Incorporated: 5 March 2014 *Employees:* 2
Net Worth: £178,129 *Total Assets:* £26,725,196
Registered Office: Crown Crest, Desford Lane, Kirby Muxloe, Leics, LE9 2BJ
Activities: Other letting and operating of own or leased real estate
Major Shareholder: Abdul Aziz Tayub
Officers: Hemant Patel, Secretary; Hemant Patel [1961] Finance Director; Abdul Aziz Tayub [1955] Director

Triumph Designs Limited
Incorporated: 5 September 1983 *Employees:* 331
Net Worth: £19,495,000 *Total Assets:* £26,522,000
Registered Office: Ashby Road, Measham, Swadlincote, Derbys, DE12 7JP
Activities: Manufacture of motorcycles
Shareholders: John Stuart Bloor; Bloor Holdings Limited
Officers: Dinesh Kumar Ishwerlal Khushalbhai Mehta, Secretary; John Stuart Bloor [1943] Director/Builder; Nick Simon Bloor [1976] Director/Chief Executive Officer; John Lambert Eastham [1951] Director/Accountant; Geoffrey Charles Hurst [1968] Director/Chief Design Officer; Jamie Looker [1974] Director/Chief Operations Officer; Dinesh Kumar Ishwerlal Khushalbhai Mehta [1951] Director/Chartered Accountant; Adam Jody Samples [1976] Director/Chief Financial Officer

Triumph Motorcycles (Overseas) Limited
Incorporated: 9 February 1990 *Employees:* 4
Net Worth Deficit: £34,869,000 *Total Assets:* £43,245,000
Registered Office: Ashby Road, Measham, Swadlincote, Derbys, DE12 7JP
Activities: Activities of head offices
Shareholders: John Stuart Bloor; Bloor Holdings Limited
Officers: Dinesh Kumar Ishwerlal Khushalbhai Mehta, Secretary; John Stuart Bloor [1943] Director/Builder; John Lambert Eastham [1951] Director/Accountant; Dinesh Kumar Ishwerlal Khushalbhai Mehta [1951] Director/Chartered Accountant; Adam Jody Samples [1976] Director/Chief Financial Officer

Triumph Motorcycles Group Limited
Incorporated: 5 June 1987
Net Worth: £30,000,000 *Total Assets:* £43,020,000
Registered Office: Ashby Road, Measham, Swadlincote, Derbys, DE12 7JP
Activities: Activities of head offices
Shareholders: John Stuart Bloor; Bloor Holdings Limited
Officers: Dinesh Kumar Ishwerlal Khushalbhai Mehta, Secretary; John Stuart Bloor [1943] Director/Builder; John Lambert Eastham [1951] Director/Accountant; Dinesh Kumar Ishwerlal Khushalbhai Mehta [1951] Director/Chartered Accountant; Adam Jody Samples [1976] Director/Chief Financial Officer

Triumph Motorcycles Limited
Incorporated: 30 June 1983 *Employees:* 573
Net Worth: £37,007,000 *Total Assets:* £284,680,992
Registered Office: Ashby Road, Measham, Swadlincote, Derbys, DE12 7JP
Activities: Manufacture of motorcycles
Shareholders: John Stuart Bloor; Bloor Holdings Limited
Officers: Dinesh Kumar Ishwerlal Khushalbhai Mehta, Secretary; John Stuart Bloor [1943] Director; Nicholas Simon Bloor [1976] Director; John Lambert Eastham [1951] Director/Accountant; Paul John Graves [1958] Director; Geoffrey Charles Hurst [1968] Director; Lord Digby Marritt Jones [1955] Director/Solicitor; Jamie Looker [1974] Director/Chief Operations Officer; Dinesh Kumar Ishwerlal Khushalbhai Mehta [1951] Director/Chartered Accountant; Adam Jody Samples [1976] Director/Chief Financial Officer; Stephen John Sargent [1969] Director; Paul Anthony Stroud [1969] Sales and Marketing Director

Triumph Multi Academy Trust
Incorporated: 6 October 2016 *Employees:* 115
Net Worth: £10,527,791 *Total Assets:* £12,632,082
Registered Office: Courthouse Green Primary School, 736 Sewall Highway, Coventry, Warwicks, CV6 7JJ
Activities: Other education n.e.c.
Officers: Navejit Kaur Aujla [1979] Director/International Partner Relations Manager; William Bracken [1968] Director/Area Manager; Andrew John Norman Dewis [1977] Director/Financial Accountant; Carmen Hibbert [1956] Director/Retired Teacher; Mary Elizabeth Hoverd [1950] Director/Retired Headteacher; Mark James Adam Kalinowski [1965] Director/Accountant; Sarah Malam [1964] Director/Headteacher; Peter Bromley Richings [1951] Director/Professional Engineer; Frederick Paul Weston [1955] Director/Education Consultant

Trousdale Limited
Incorporated: 31 March 1998 *Employees:* 78
Net Worth: £2,935,705 *Total Assets:* £10,763,580
Registered Office: Wildmere Road, Banbury, Oxon, OX16 7TR
Activities: Manufacture of bread; manufacture of fresh pastry goods and cakes
Parent: Guenther Holdings Limited
Officers: Thomas McRae, Secretary; Melvyn Stewart Bugler [1956] Director; Thomas a McRae [1957] Director [American]; Janelle M Sykes [1964] Director [American]; Dale W Tremblay [1958] Director [American]

TRRG Holding Limited
Incorporated: 7 December 2015 *Employees:* 1,538
Net Worth: £37,947,400 *Total Assets:* £273,034,624
Registered Office: Dennis Eagle, Heathcote Way, Heathcote Industrial Estate, Warwick, CV34 6TE
Activities: Activities of other holding companies n.e.c.
Officers: Ramon Roca Enrich [1962] Director/Businessman [Spanish]; Ian Roland Metcalfe [1958] Director/Businessman; Juan Puig Perez [1951] Director/Lawyer [Spanish]; George Johannes Maria Terberg [1952] Director/Chairman [Dutch]; Paulus Johannes Van Der Kroft [1960] Director/Businessman [Dutch]

Trucast Limited
Incorporated: 20 November 2000 *Employees:* 183
Net Worth: £72,368,000 *Total Assets:* £76,343,000
Registered Office: Millennium Court, First Avenue, Burton on Trent, Staffs, DE14 2WH
Activities: Casting of other non-ferrous metals
Parent: Doncasters Limited
Officers: Ian Molyneux, Secretary; Duncan Andrew Hinks [1975] Director/Chief Financial Officer; Ian Molyneux [1964] Director/Solicitor; Lisa Marie Oxnard [1981] Director/Chief Financial Officer

Trueform Engineering Holdings Limited
Incorporated: 19 October 2011 *Employees:* 200
Net Worth Deficit: £1,447,762 *Total Assets:* £13,680,076
Registered Office: Unit 5 The Courtyard, Timothys Bridge Road, Stratford upon Avon, Warwicks, CV37 9NJ
Activities: Manufacture of other transport equipment n.e.c.
Shareholder: Kelman Limited
Officers: Richard Anton Banham [1979] Investment Director; Michael David Gillett [1951] Director/Chairman; Robert Ian MacNaughton [1978] Finance Director; Jonathan Morley [1970] Director

Truelove Property & Construction Ltd
Incorporated: 22 July 1968 *Employees:* 37
Net Worth: £15,144,526 *Total Assets:* £17,554,214
Registered Office: 4a Eastgate, Lincoln, LN2 1QB
Activities: Construction of domestic buildings
Officers: Jacqueline Patricia Truelove, Secretary; Barrie Michael Claude Kendal Truelove [1965] Director/House Builder; Paul Anthony John Truelove [1958] Director/Master Builder

Trust Estates (Clarence Street) Limited
Incorporated: 25 February 2014 *Employees:* 4
Net Worth: £707 *Total Assets:* £13,832,904
Registered Office: 19 King Street, King's Lynn, Norfolk, PE30 1HB
Activities: Other letting and operating of own or leased real estate
Shareholders: Rui Pan; Qinqin Song; Chengrun He
Officers: Honourable William John Cadogan [1973] Director/Chartered Surveyor; Weipeng Gu [1989] Director [Chinese]; Andrew David Jamieson [1956] Director; Rui Pan [1990] Director [Chinese]

Tsubakimoto UK Limited
Incorporated: 28 February 1975 *Employees:* 103
Net Worth: £12,639,000 *Total Assets:* £21,192,000
Registered Office: Osier Drive, Annesley, Nottingham, NG15 0DX
Activities: Other manufacturing n.e.c.
Officers: Philip Martin Shaw, Secretary; Bertus Rolf Hendrik Marinus Mellink [1957] Managing Director [Dutch]; Frank Rosmolen [1957] Director [Dutch]

TSYS Managed Services EMEA Limited
Incorporated: 26 September 2006 *Employees:* 1,006
Net Worth: £10,174,000 *Total Assets:* £18,133,000
Registered Office: Burystead Court, 120 Caldecotte Lake Drive, Caldecotte, Milton Keynes, Bucks, MK7 8LE
Activities: Financial intermediation not elsewhere classified
Parent: TSYS International Management Limited
Officers: David Leonard Chew [1963] Finance Director; Kelvin Dodd [1970] Director; Dennis Jones [1949] Director; Kelley Craig Knutson [1960] Managing Director

TTG Global Limited
Incorporated: 15 January 2009 *Employees:* 164
Net Worth Deficit: £8,600,000 *Total Assets:* £20,700,000
Registered Office: Field House, Uttoxeter Old Road, Derby, DE1 1NH
Activities: Non-trading company
Officers: Philip Williams, Secretary; Peter Louis Burridge [1956] Director; Michael Stewart Norfield [1963] Director; Paul Henry Brace Thomas [1961] Director; Philip Edward Williams [1968] Finance Director

TTKW Limited
Incorporated: 21 August 2015 *Employees:* 216
Net Worth: £8,192,353 *Total Assets:* £12,036,129
Registered Office: Northminster House, Northminster, Peterborough, Cambs, PE1 1YN
Activities: Activities of other holding companies n.e.c.
Shareholders: Adrian John George Jaggard; Antony Jaggard
Officers: John Ashley Bryant, Secretary; Simon Jeremy Banfield [1963] Director/Solicitor; Paul Allan Davis [1954] Director/Solicitor; Matthew David Hoe [1979] Director/Solicitor; Adrian John George Jaggard [1976] Director/Solicitor; Antony Jaggard [1978] Director/Solicitor

TTS Group Limited
Incorporated: 14 February 2002 *Employees:* 246
Net Worth: £4,742,000 *Total Assets:* £24,346,000
Registered Office: 140 Eastern Avenue, Milton Park, Milton, Abingdon, Oxon, OX14 4SB
Activities: Other software publishing
Parent: RM PLC
Officers: Gregory Davidson-Shrine, Secretary; Gregory Davidson-Shrine [1974] Director/Lawyer; Neil Thomas George Martin [1972] Director; Andrew Wilson [1965] Managing Director

Tubes Holdco Limited
Incorporated: 29 May 2012 *Employees:* 2
Net Worth: £16,270,000 *Total Assets:* £26,554,000
Registered Office: 2 New Star Road, Leicester, LE4 9JQ
Activities: Activities of other holding companies n.e.c.
Parent: Ametek Inc
Officers: Joy Atwell, Secretary; Emanuela Speranza [1968] Director [Italian]; Bruce Peter Wilson [1956] Director

Tucker Fasteners Limited
Incorporated: 7 July 1903
Net Worth: £173,824,992 *Total Assets:* £173,919,008
Registered Office: 3 Europa Court, Sheffield Airport Business Park, Sheffield, S9 1XE
Activities: Manufacture of fasteners and screw machine products
Parent: Black & Decker Europe
Officers: Steven John Costello [1980] Director/Chartered Accountant; Amit Kumar Sood [1978] Director/Accountant

Tudor Hall School
Incorporated: 28 November 1994 *Employees:* 233
Net Worth: £16,288,104 *Total Assets:* £21,283,540
Registered Office: Wykham Park, Banbury, Oxon, OX16 9UR
Activities: Pre-primary education
Officers: Neil Urquhart, Secretary; Duncan Bailey [1975] Director/Headmaster; Sally Elizabeth Ann Bowie [1961] Director/Governor/Trustee; Alison Darling [1968] Director/School Governor; John Andrew Elliot [1952] Director/Farmer; Kathleen Elizabeth Fidgeon [1958] Director/Chartered Accountant; John Gloag [1959] Director/Land Agent; Alice Victoria Harley [1960] Director; Mary Kinnear [1954] Director/Senior Mistress; Babak Lari [1996] Director/Property Development

Tulip International (UK) Limited
Incorporated: 16 September 1977
Net Worth: £189,711,008 *Total Assets:* £238,050,000
Registered Office: Seton House, Warwick Technology Park, Gallows Hill, Warwick, CV34 6DA
Activities: Activities of head offices
Officers: Erik Bredholt [1966] Director/Farmer [Danish]; Andrew Michael James Cracknell [1967] Director; Peter Fallesen Kjaer Ravn [1968] Director [Danish]; Preben Sunke [1961] Director [Danish]; Jais Stampe Li Valeur [1962] Director/Chairman [Danish]

Tulip Limited
Incorporated: 16 July 1958 *Employees:* 6,159
Net Worth: £74,985,000 *Total Assets:* £601,492,992
Registered Office: Seton House, Warwick Technology Park, Gallows Hill, Warwick, CV34 6DA
Activities: Production of meat and poultry meat products
Parent: Tulip International (UK) Limited
Officers: Erik Bredholt [1966] Director/Farmer [Danish]; Andrew Michael James Cracknell [1967] Director; Peter Fallesen Kjaer Ravn [1968] Director [Danish]; Preben Sunke [1961] Director [Danish]; Jais Stampe Li Valeur [1962] Director/Chairman [Danish]

Tullis Russell Coaters Limited
Incorporated: 8 June 1979 *Employees:* 97
Net Worth: £8,223,000 *Total Assets:* £16,359,000
Registered Office: Church Street, Bollington, Macclesfield, Cheshire, SK10 5QF
Activities: Manufacture of paper and paperboard
Parent: Tullis Russell Group Limited
Officers: Geoffrey Douglas Miller, Secretary; Frederick Alexander William Bowden [1947] Director; Julian Martyn Leek [1964] Finance Director; Geoffrey Douglas Miller [1962] Finance Director; Graeme David Milloy [1958] Managing Director; David Mark Roberts [1973] Operations Director; Hazel Jane Westwood [1976] Technology Director

Tunstall Group Acquisition Limited
Incorporated: 24 May 2005
Net Worth Deficit: £373,028,000 *Total Assets:* £377,736,992
Registered Office: Whitley Lodge, Whitley Bridge, N Yorks, DN14 0HR
Activities: Activities of other holding companies n.e.c.
Parent: Tunstall Group Finance Limited
Officers: Jonathan Paul Furniss, Secretary; Craig Parsons [1970] Director; John Lee Robinson [1958] Director

Tunstall Group Finance Limited
Incorporated: 23 May 2005 *Employees:* 2
Net Worth Deficit: £217,874,000 *Total Assets:* £205,084,992
Registered Office: Whitley Lodge, Whitley Bridge, N Yorks, DN14 0HR
Activities: Activities of other holding companies n.e.c.
Parent: Tunstall Group Holdings Limited
Officers: Jonathan Paul Furniss, Secretary; Craig Parsons [1970] Director; John Lee Robinson [1958] Director

Tunstall Group Holdings Limited
Incorporated: 23 May 2005 *Employees:* 3,081
Net Worth Deficit: £443,078,016 *Total Assets:* £367,240,992
Registered Office: Whitley Lodge, Whitley Bridge, N Yorks, DN14 0HR
Activities: Activities of other holding companies n.e.c.
Parent: TGH Acquisitions Limited
Officers: Jonathan Paul Furniss, Secretary; Craig Parsons [1970] Director; John Lee Robinson [1958] Director

Tunstall Group Limited
Incorporated: 20 March 1957 *Employees:* 1,787
Net Worth: £200,864,000 *Total Assets:* £399,606,016
Registered Office: Whitley Lodge, Whitley Bridge, N Yorks, DN14 0HR
Activities: Activities of other holding companies n.e.c.
Parent: Blythmore Limited
Officers: Jonathan Paul Furniss, Secretary; Craig Parsons [1970] Director; John Lee Robinson [1958] Director

Tunstall Healthcare (UK) Limited
Incorporated: 30 September 1977 *Employees:* 672
Net Worth: £250,740,000 *Total Assets:* £280,566,016
Registered Office: Whitley Bridge, N Yorks, DN14 0HR
Activities: Manufacture of communication equipment other than telegraph, and telephone apparatus and equipment
Parent: Tunstall Group Limited
Officers: Jonathan Paul Furniss, Secretary; Gavin Bashar [1963] Director; Katherine Heaton [1976] HR Director; Craig Parsons [1970] Director; Edward James Peck [1971] Finance Director; Elaine Quinn [1963] Director

Tunstall Healthcare Group Limited
Incorporated: 6 February 2008 *Employees:* 3,081
Net Worth Deficit: £1,559,382,016 *Total Assets:* £448,660,992
Registered Office: Whitley Lodge, Whitley Bridge, Doncaster, S Yorks, DN14 0HR
Activities: Activities of other holding companies n.e.c.
Officers: Jonathan Paul Furniss, Secretary; James Simon Edward Arnell [1969] Director; Craig Parsons [1970] Director; Thomas Spencer Patrick [1972] Director/Solicitor

Tunstall Holdings Limited
Incorporated: 22 September 1999
Net Worth Deficit: £74,244,000 *Total Assets:* £216,888,000
Registered Office: Whitley Lodge, Whitley Bridge, N Yorks, DN14 0HR
Activities: Activities of other holding companies n.e.c.
Parent: Tunstall Group Acquisition Limited
Officers: Jonathan Paul Furniss, Secretary; Craig Parsons [1970] Director; John Lee Robinson [1958] Director

Turbine Services Limited
Incorporated: 29 December 1980 *Employees:* 48
Net Worth: £31,144,692 *Total Assets:* £43,457,192
Registered Office: 10 Clover Nook Road, Cotes Park Industrial Estate, Somercotes, Alfreton, Derbys, DE55 4RF
Activities: Other engineering activities
Parent: Chromalloy United Kingdom Limited
Officers: David Kaplan, Secretary; Amanda Balog Sanders, Secretary; Derek Alexander Gartshore [1966] Director/Global Aftermarket Leader - Energy; Paul Anthony Jerram [1964] Director/General Manager; David Pert Phillips [1955] Director/Commercial Manager

Turbine Surface Technologies Limited
Incorporated: 25 July 2000 *Employees:* 377
Net Worth: £27,942,000 *Total Assets:* £39,413,000
Registered Office: Moor Lane, Derby, DE24 8BJ
Activities: Treatment and coating of metals
Shareholder: Rolls-Royce PLC
Officers: Jacqueline Marie Gentles, Secretary; Nigel Bird [1971] Director; Dave Alastair Deakin [1978] Director; Richard James Feely [1964] Director [American]; Craig Michael Haines [1972] Director [American]; Dr Peter Howard [1959] Director [American]; Dr Alan Partridge [1964] Director/Global Head of Materials Engineering

Turbo-Union Limited
Incorporated: 30 September 1969 *Employees:* 2
Net Worth: £244,202 *Total Assets:* £26,709,416
Registered Office: Moor Lane, Derby, DE24 8BJ
Activities: Activities of head offices
Shareholder: Rolls-Royce PLC
Officers: Simon Frederick Baldwin [1960] Director; Klaus Guenther [1967] Director [German]; Martin Majewski [1964] Director [German]; Piergiorgio Palmieri [1970] Director [Italian]; Matthew James Smith [1981] Director; Alberto Squillante [1974] Director [Italian]; Uwe Wehking [1958] Managing Director [German]

G.B.Turnbull Limited
Incorporated: 30 June 1958 *Employees:* 5
Net Worth: £16,408,705 *Total Assets:* £16,504,861
Registered Office: Burghwallis Grange, off Green Lane, Skellow, Doncaster, S Yorks, DN6 8JX
Activities: Growing of cereals (except rice), leguminous crops and oil seeds
Major Shareholder: William John Turnbull
Officers: William John Turnbull, Secretary; Jane Elizabeth Turnbull [1953] Director; William John Turnbull [1951] Director

Turner Investments Ltd.
Incorporated: 31 January 1961 *Employees:* 2
Net Worth: £3,998,343 *Total Assets:* £9,208,461
Registered Office: One Dunston Court, Dunston Road, Chesterfield, Derbys, S41 8NL
Activities: Other letting and operating of own or leased real estate
Officers: Ashley Ryck Turner [1968] Director; Jonathan James Vardy [1975] Property Director

Tuxford Exports Limited
Incorporated: 14 November 2001 *Employees:* 25
Previous: R C Tuxford Exports Limited
Net Worth: £3,032,026 *Total Assets:* £10,711,124
Registered Office: Old Colliery Site, Hollinwood Lane, Calverton, Nottingham, NG14 6NR
Activities: Sale of other motor vehicles
Officers: Roderick Charles Whitehead, Secretary; Richard Carlisle Tuxford [1967] Director/Exporter

TVCO Limited
Incorporated: 21 March 2006
Net Worth: £4,545,968 *Total Assets:* £13,182,188
Registered Office: Unicol House, Green Road, Headington, Oxford, OX3 8EU
Activities: Other letting and operating of own or leased real estate
Parent: Manxprop Ltd
Officers: Stephen Westhorpe, Secretary; Peter Ligertwood [1942] Director; Stephen Westhorpe [1958] Director

TVS Europe Distribution Limited
Incorporated: 9 November 2011 *Employees:* 179
Net Worth: £4,144,000 *Total Assets:* £22,953,000
Registered Office: Ashroyd Business Park, Ashroyds Way, Hoyland, Barnsley, S Yorks, S74 9SB
Activities: Wholesale trade of motor vehicle parts and accessories
Officers: Paul Roberts, Secretary; Rasesh Doshi [1962] Director [Indian]; Srinivasa Raghavan Gopalan [1969] Director [Indian]; David Richard Kernahan [1973] Managing Director; Srinivasavaradhan Padmanabhan [1963] Director [Indian]; Vijayaraghaven Parthasarathy [1948] Director [Indian]; Dinesh Ramachandran [1965] Managing Director [Indian]; Paul John Roberts [1968] Director/Accountant; Santhanagopalan Subramanian [1958] Director/President - Finance [Indian]

Twitten Trustees Limited
Incorporated: 18 March 1993
Net Worth: £2,317,252 *Total Assets:* £11,534,032
Registered Office: Nixon Mee Ltd, Unit 9 Whitwick Business Centre, Stenson Road, Coalville, Leics, LE67 4JP
Activities: Other letting and operating of own or leased real estate
Shareholders: Bradley John Kirkland; Simon Neville Chamberlain
Officers: Simon Neville Chamberlain, Secretary; Simon Neville Chamberlain [1967] Director/Stockbroker; Bradley John Kirkland [1968] Director/Stockbroker

The Two Counties Trust
Incorporated: 1 March 2012 *Employees:* 1,060
Previous: Ashfield School
Net Worth: £147,920,992 *Total Assets:* £165,092,000
Registered Office: Ashfield School, Sutton Road, Kirby-in-Ashfield, Notts, NG17 8HP
Activities: General secondary education
Officers: Alison Joan Chmiel [1964] Director at Mansfield Building Society; Suzanne Coffey [1952] Communications Officer and Director; Ian Paul Greenaway [1949] Director; Christopher John Hallam [1965] Director and Head of Innovation Portfolio; Gillian Lesley Haslam [1952] Director/Retired; Karen Lesley Potts [1964] Director of Procurement; Roman Paul Ruszczynski [1953] Director/Retired Headteacher; William Paul Unsworth [1976] Director/Engineer; Ruth Wheelhouse [1953] Director/Head of College

TWS Property Limited
Incorporated: 12 October 2012 *Employees:* 2
Net Worth: £2,195,930 *Total Assets:* £9,550,827
Registered Office: 33 Thorne Road, Doncaster, S Yorks, DN1 2HD
Activities: Other letting and operating of own or leased real estate
Shareholders: James Michael Barker; Anthony Ashton Woodhouse
Officers: James Michael Barker, Secretary; James Michael Barker [1980] Director; Anthony Ashton Woodhouse [1968] Director

Twycross Zoo - East Midland Zoological Society Limited
Incorporated: 10 July 1972 *Employees:* 165
Net Worth: £21,096,034 *Total Assets:* £27,768,468
Registered Office: Norton Grange, Burton Road, Norton-Juxta-Twycross, Atherstone, Warwicks, CV9 3PX
Activities: Botanical and zoological gardens and nature reserves activities
Officers: Louise Biffin, Secretary; Professor Gary Crane William England [1963] Director/Professor; John Peter Helas [1968] Director/Vice President of Operations and Technology; Geoffrey William Hoon [1953] Director/Consultant; Douglas John Keep [1947] Director/Retired; Gary Alan Middleton [1964] Director/Public Servant; Joanna Thornell [1968] Director; Liam Anthony Wall [1965] Finance Director

Tyler Packaging Holdings Limited
Incorporated: 16 March 2016 *Employees:* 16
Net Worth: £18,045,804 *Total Assets:* £25,677,138
Registered Office: Tyler Packaging Holdings Limited, Fosse Way, Chesterton, Leamington Spa, Warwicks, CV33 9JY
Activities: Activities of other holding companies n.e.c.
Shareholders: Howard Francis Woolley; Adam James Ford Kay
Officers: Adam James Ford Kay [1980] Sales Director; Mark Proffitt [1975] Director; Howard Francis Woolley [1946] Director

Tyler Packaging Limited
Incorporated: 19 August 1982 *Employees:* 16
Net Worth: £17,858,398 *Total Assets:* £20,931,750
Registered Office: Fosse Way, Chesterton, Leamington Spa, Warwicks, CV33 9JY
Activities: Non-specialised wholesale trade
Parent: Tyler Packaging Holdings Limited
Officers: Josephine Mary Hambidge, Secretary; Howard Francis Woolley [1946] Director

Tynemill Limited
Incorporated: 7 May 1975 *Employees:* 220
Net Worth: £5,002,969 *Total Assets:* £11,375,271
Registered Office: Castle Rock Brewery, Queens Bridge Road, Nottingham, NG2 1NB
Activities: Manufacture of beer
Major Shareholder: Christopher Roger Holmes
Officers: Neil Kellett, Secretary; Peter Robert Brettell [1943] Director; Anthony William Eastwood [1948] Director/Wholesaler; Geoffrey David Newton [1964] Director/Consultancy; Vicki Louise Saxby [1978] Finance & Administration Director; Colin Francis Wilde [1971] Commercial Director; Peter John Wilde [1944] Director/Wholesaler

Tytherington School
Incorporated: 3 March 2014 *Employees:* 161
Net Worth: £13,054,000 *Total Assets:* £15,030,000
Registered Office: Tytherington School, Manchester Road, Macclesfield, Cheshire, SK10 2EE
Activities: General secondary education
Officers: Stephen Acreman [1968] Director/Teacher; Sarah Bird [1968] Director; Emmanuel Botwe [1981] Director/Headteacher; Adam Brown [1983] Director/Teacher; Michael Charles Simon Brown [1962] Director; Jason Peter Gaunt [1987] Director; Kenneth George Gilliver [1947] Director/Retired Senior Civil Servant; Lynne Roose Jones [1959] Director; Dr David Dermot Patrick Laffan [1962] Director/Manager; Trevor David Langston [1970] Director; Charlotte Victoria Jean Lock [1972] Director/Lead Strategist; Derek Alan Ogden [1960] Director/Chartered Certified Accountant; Dr Simon Christopher Preston [1964] Director; Dr Peter Brian Simpson [1968] Director/Science Manager; Jane Louise Stairmand [1979] Director/Transformation Programme Manager; Jane Stephens [1965] Director/Management Consultant; David Thomas Sussex [1953] Director

U-Pol Bidco Limited
Incorporated: 29 July 2010 *Employees:* 2
Net Worth Deficit: £6,591,000 *Total Assets:* £55,250,000
Registered Office: U-Pol Tech Centre, Denington Road, Denington Industrial Estate, Wellingborough, Northants, NN8 2QH
Activities: Manufacture of paints, varnishes and similar coatings, mastics and sealants
Parent: U-Pol Finco Limited
Officers: Michael John Coombes [1963] Director; Guy Hampson Williams [1967] Director

U-Pol Bond Limited
Incorporated: 21 September 2005 *Employees:* 1
Net Worth Deficit: £30,077,000 *Total Assets:* £26,191,000
Registered Office: U-Pol Tech Centre, Denington Road, Denington Industrial Estate, Wellingborough, Northants, NN8 2QH
Activities: Manufacture of paints, varnishes and similar coatings, mastics and sealants
Parent: U-Pol Acquisition Limited
Officers: Michael John Coombes [1963] Director

U-Pol Finco Limited
Incorporated: 29 July 2010 *Employees:* 2
Net Worth Deficit: £65,490,000 *Total Assets:* £79,588,000
Registered Office: U-Pol Tech Centre, Denington Road, Denington Industrial Estate, Wellingborough, Northants, NN8 2QH
Activities: Manufacture of paints, varnishes and similar coatings, mastics and sealants
Parent: U-Pol Holdings Limited
Officers: Michael John Coombes [1963] Director; Guy Hampson Williams [1967] Director

U-Pol Limited
Incorporated: 23 February 1949 *Employees:* 278
Net Worth: £129,615,000 *Total Assets:* £172,368,000
Registered Office: U-Pol Tech Centre, Denington Road, Denington Industrial Estate, Wellingborough, Northants, NN8 2QH
Activities: Manufacture of paints, varnishes and similar coatings, mastics and sealants
Shareholder: Graphite Capital General Partner VII LLP
Officers: Michael John Coombes [1963] Director; Guy Hampson Williams [1967] Director

U-Pol Mezzanine Limited
Incorporated: 21 September 2005
Net Worth Deficit: £21,009,000 *Total Assets:* £43,669,000
Registered Office: U-Pol Tech Centre, Denington Road, Denington Industrial Estate, Wellingborough, Northants, NN8 2QH
Activities: Manufacture of paints, varnishes and similar coatings, mastics and sealants
Parent: U-Pol Bond Limited
Officers: Michael John Coombes [1963] Director

U-Pull-It Limited
Incorporated: 14 November 2008 *Employees:* 34
Net Worth: £2,565,000 *Total Assets:* £18,189,000
Registered Office: Acrey Fields, Woburn Road, Wootton, Beds, MK43 9EJ
Activities: Sale of other motor vehicles
Parent: Universal Salvage Limited
Officers: Aaron Jayson Adair [1969] Director/Chief Executive Officer [American]; Jonathan David Canning [1972] Director/General Counsel; Gregory Depasquale [1968] Director/SVP, General Counsel and Secretary of Copart, Inc [American]; William Easley Franklin [1956] Director/Chief Financial Officer [American]; Nigel James Paget [1966] Managing Director; Simon Sheldon-Wilson [1969] Director; Paul Anthony Styer [1956] Director/General Counsel [American]

UAV Tactical Systems Limited
Incorporated: 24 September 2004 *Employees:* 120
Net Worth: £13,635,000 *Total Assets:* £24,315,000
Registered Office: Unit F Meridian East, Meridian Business Park, Braunstone Town, Leicester, LE19 1WZ
Activities: Manufacture of electronic components
Shareholders: Elbit Systems UK Limited; Thales UK Limited
Officers: Moshe Carmon, Secretary/Legal Counsel [Israeli]; Elad Aharonson [1973] Director [Israeli]; Simona Akery [1973] Director; Richard Arthur David Applegate [1955] Director; Edwin Awang [1962] Director/Company Executive; Itzhak Dvir [1948] Director/General Manager [Israeli]; Suzanne Jayne Stratton [1972] Director

UBT (EU) Ltd
Incorporated: 21 October 2003 *Employees:* 139
Net Worth: £202 *Total Assets:* £17,639,492
Registered Office: Exchange Place, Poseidon Way, Warwick, CV34 6BY
Activities: Retail sale via mail order houses or via Internet
Parent: The Grace Trading Group Limited
Officers: John Nelson Abernethie [1965] Director; Roddy Neil Cox [1984] Director; Neil Hardwick [1976] Director; James Percy Hazell [1960] Director; Neil Richard Napthine [1971] Director; Peter Mark Wheatcroft [1971] Director

UCC Coffee UK Limited
Incorporated: 28 August 1987 *Employees:* 515
Net Worth: £35,989,268 *Total Assets:* £66,925,424
Registered Office: 2 Bradbourne Drive, Tilbrook, Milton Keynes, Bucks, MK7 8AT
Activities: Non-specialised wholesale trade
Parent: UCC Europe Ltd
Officers: Anthony Jessup, Secretary; Patrick David Cooke [1947] Director; Anthony Jessup [1977] Director; Elaine Swift [1967] Director; Marcus Richard Swift [1970] Director; Laura Turrell [1976] Director; Seisuke Ueshima [1973] Director [Japanese]

UDG Healthcare (UK) Holdings Limited
Incorporated: 10 June 1997
Previous: United Drug (UK) Holdings Limited
Net Worth: £196,727,280 *Total Assets:* £350,607,584
Registered Office: Ashfield House, Resolution Road, Ashby De La Zouch, Leics, LE65 1HW
Activities: Activities of head offices
Parent: UDG Healthcare UK (Holdco) Limited
Officers: Damien Moynagh, Secretary; Nicola Burns [1969] Director; Nigel Bernard John Clerkin [1973] Director/Chief Financial Officer [Irish]; Brendan McAtamney [1962] Director [Irish]; Clifford Alexander McConkey [1970] Director

UDG Healthcare UK (Holdco) Limited
Incorporated: 4 April 2016
Net Worth: £71,701,416 *Total Assets:* £225,719,872
Registered Office: Ashfield House, Resolution Road, Ashby De La Zouch, Leics, LE65 1HW
Activities: Activities of head offices
Parent: UDG Healthcare PLC
Officers: Damien Moynagh, Secretary; Nicola Burns [1969] Director; Nigel Bernard John Clerkin [1973] Director/Chief Financial Officer [Irish]; Brendan McAtamney [1962] Director [Irish]; Clifford Alexander McConkey [1970] Director

UGC Properties Limited
Incorporated: 23 July 2003
Net Worth: £31,589,000 *Total Assets:* £38,803,000
Registered Office: Unipart House, Garsington Road, Cowley, Oxford, OX4 2PG
Activities: Buying and selling of own real estate
Parent: Unipart Group of Companies Limited
Officers: Robert Paul David O'Brien, Secretary; Jonathan Chitty [1976] Director/Accountant; Alex Raymond Leung [1974] Director/Manager; Christopher James Weldon [1978] Director/Accountant

UGI Midlands Limited
Incorporated: 9 September 2011
Net Worth: £43,901,000 *Total Assets:* £43,916,000
Registered Office: UGI House, Gisborne Close, Staveley, Chesterfield, Derbys, S43 3JT
Activities: Distribution of gaseous fuels through mains
Officers: Monica Marie Gaudiosi [1962] Director/Attorney [American]; Donald Groth [1966] Director/Vice President, Finance [American]; Thaddeus J. Jastrzebski [1961] Director/Chief Financial Officer of UGI Corporation [American]; Neil Murphy [1961] Director/MD GM; John Walsh [1955] Director/President and Chief [American]

UK Biobank Limited
Incorporated: 28 November 2003 *Employees:* 155
Net Worth: £10,340,544 *Total Assets:* £16,678,800
Registered Office: Units 1 & 2 Spectrum Way, Adswood, Stockport, Cheshire, SK3 0SA
Activities: Other research and experimental development on natural sciences and engineering
Officers: Jonathan Michael Holmes Sellors, Secretary; Professor Martin Bobrow [1938] Director/Retired; Professor Ruth Elisabeth Gilbert [1958] Director/Professor of Clinical Epidemiology; Professor Andrew Hattersley [1958] Director/Medical Researcher; Professor Anneke Lucassen [1962] Director/University Professor/NHS Consultant [Dutch]; Sir Alexander Fred Markham [1950] Director/Physician, Professor of Medicine; Sara Elizabeth Farha Marshall [1962] Director/Doctor; Dr Joseph McNamara [1958] Director/Research Manager; Professor William Ollier [1952] Director/Professor; Sir Michael Rawlins [1941] Director; Jonathan Edward Simon Tross [1949] Director/Chair IPCC Audit and Risk Committee

UK Distributors (Footwear) Limited
Incorporated: 7 December 2000 *Employees:* 66
Net Worth: £15,890,174 *Total Assets:* £17,305,522
Registered Office: Marlow House, Churchill Way Industrial Estate, Saddington Road, Fleckney, Leics, LE8 8UD
Activities: Wholesale of clothing and footwear
Shareholders: James Periam Marlow; Guy Walter Marlow
Officers: Derek Periam Marlow, Secretary; Christopher Brown [1967] Operations Director; Derek Periam Marlow [1932] Director/Boot/Shoe Factor; Guy Walter Marlow [1960] Director/Boot/Shoe Factor; James Periam Marlow [1959] Director/Boot/Shoe Factor

UK Egg Centre Limited
Incorporated: 2 January 2007 *Employees:* 10
Net Worth: £2,053,721 *Total Assets:* £10,126,671
Registered Office: Dunston House, Dunston Road, Chesterfield, Derbys, S41 9QD
Activities: Agents specialised in the sale of other particular products
Shareholders: David John Edney; Neil Eric Carrington
Officers: David John Edney, Secretary; Neil Eric Carrington [1964] Director; David John Edney [1966] Director

UK Platforms Ltd
Incorporated: 15 February 2000 *Employees:* 119
Net Worth: £19,580,000 *Total Assets:* £37,753,000
Registered Office: 15 Midland Court, Central Park, Lutterworth, Leics, LE17 4PN
Activities: Renting and leasing of other machinery, equipment and tangible goods n.e.c.
Parent: Nationwide Platforms Limited
Officers: Jerome Sarragozi, Secretary; Thomas Donald Kenny [1954] Director [Irish]; Thomas Anthony Murray [1967] Director/Chartered Accountant

UK Steel Enterprise Limited
Incorporated: 21 July 1954 *Employees:* 29
Net Worth: £27,486,132 *Total Assets:* £31,765,700
Registered Office: The Innovation Centre, 217 Portobello, Sheffield, S1 4DP
Activities: Activities of venture and development capital companies
Parent: Tata Steel UK Ltd
Officers: Richard Thomas, Secretary; Simon Timothy Hamilton [1968] Managing Director; Colin Lloyd Harvey [1967] Director/Management Accountant; Christopher David Jaques [1971] Director Industrial Relations; Allan Jardine Johnston [1948] Director; Royston Rickhuss [1960] Director/Trade Union General Secretary

UK Ticketing Ltd
Incorporated: 19 December 2007 *Employees:* 2
Net Worth: £76,136,416 *Total Assets:* £76,136,416
Registered Office: Norfolk House, 47 Upper Parliament Street, Nottingham, NG1 2AB
Activities: Activities of head offices
Officers: Leanne Lipscombe, Secretary; Simon John Gillham [1956] Director/Senior Executive VP Comms Vivendi; Robert Ian Wilmshurst [1969] Director

UK Vast Holdco Limited
Incorporated: 14 July 2016
Net Worth Deficit: £124,138 *Total Assets:* £9,951,395
Registered Office: 2 Des Roches Square, Witney, Oxon, OX28 4LE
Activities: Other business support service activities n.e.c.
Shareholders: Trafalgar Midco 1 Limited; Trafalgar Midco 1 Limited
Officers: Andrew James Galbraith [1970] Director; Christopher Kindt [1984] Director/Investments Professional

UK Waste Solutions Limited
Incorporated: 15 December 2003 *Employees:* 169
Net Worth: £8,821,491 *Total Assets:* £13,206,633
Registered Office: Alexander House, Beacon Hill Business Park, Cafferata Way, Newark, Notts, NG24 2TN
Activities: Collection of non-hazardous waste
Shareholders: Christopher Giscombe; Garry David Johnson
Officers: Mr Christopher Giscombe [1960] Director; Mr Garry David Johnson [1967] Director; Jane Claire Mellor [1963] Director

UKKI Limited
Incorporated: 25 October 2012 *Employees:* 2
Net Worth: £39,530,940 *Total Assets:* £39,547,428
Registered Office: Cranford Terrace, 30 Harborough Road, Northampton, NN2 7AZ
Activities: Activities of open-ended investment companies
Officers: Marinus Cornelis Johannes Marie Krinkels [1961] Director [Dutch]; William Trotman [1953] Director

UKLS Acquisitions Limited
Incorporated: 4 July 2014 *Employees:* 477
Net Worth Deficit: £37,404,000 *Total Assets:* £51,828,000
Registered Office: Grant Hall, Parsons Green, St Ives, Cambs, PE27 4AA
Activities: Other business support service activities n.e.c.
Parent: UKLS Midco Ltd
Officers: Jean Michel Claude Bonnavion [1971] Director/Partner [French]; Gary Michael Pritchard [1970] Director/Chartered Accountant

UKMHPS Limited
Incorporated: 8 December 1989 *Employees:* 131
Previous: Terex MHPS (UK) Limited
Net Worth: £10,585,000 *Total Assets:* £11,002,000
Registered Office: c/o Konecranes Demag UK Limited, Unit 1 Charter Point Way, Ashby Business Park, Ashby De La Zouch, Leics, LE65 1NF
Activities: Manufacture of lifting and handling equipment
Officers: Teo Ottolla, Secretary; John Tomas Myntti [1963] Director [Finnish]; Teo Ottola [1968] Director [Finnish]; Marko Tapani Tulokas [1972] Director [Finnish]

ULS Technology PLC
Incorporated: 10 December 2010 *Employees:* 87
Net Worth: £9,340,000 *Total Assets:* £23,455,000
Registered Office: The Old Grammar School, Church Road, Thame, Oxon, OX9 3AJ
Activities: Other information technology service activities
Officers: John Sinclair Williams, Secretary; Elaine Bown [1969] Director; M Stephen Alan Goodall [1970] Director; Martin Christopher Rowland [1972] Director; Andrew John Weston [1967] Director; Geoffrey Alan Wicks [1949] Director; John Sinclair Williams [1967] Director/Accountant

Ultimate Packaging Limited
Incorporated: 30 March 1982 *Employees:* 252
Net Worth: £12,993,580 *Total Assets:* £24,737,268
Registered Office: Pegasus Way, Europarc, Grimsby, N E Lincs, DN37 9TS
Activities: Manufacture of plastic packing goods
Shareholders: Nigel Howard Tonge; Christopher Michael Tonge
Officers: Michael David Tonge, Secretary; Paul Best [1978] Sales Director; Jeremy Paul Hodson [1965] Director/Accountant; Jonathan Robert McCarthy [1968] Director; Christopher Michael Tonge [1960] Director; Justin Marc Tonge [1979] Director; Michael David Tonge [1962] Director; Nigel Tonge [1955] Director

Ulverscroft Group Limited
Incorporated: 18 October 1982 *Employees:* 126
Net Worth: £13,788,000 *Total Assets:* £16,066,000
Registered Office: The Green, Bradgate Road, Anstey, Leicester, LE7 7FU
Activities: Activities of head offices
Parent: The Ulverscroft Foundation
Officers: Mahomed Amin Aziz, Secretary; Anna Lee Gilbert [1956] Operation Director; Patricia Mary Henderson [1940] Director; Christopher John Mumby [1950] Director; Michele Linda Petty [1957] Director; Robert William Thirlby [1953] Managing Director

Umeco Composites Limited
Incorporated: 10 December 1990
Net Worth Deficit: £22,507,836 *Total Assets:* £9,734,633
Registered Office: Composites House, Sinclair Close, Heanor, Derbys, DE75 7SP
Activities: Other business support service activities n.e.c.
Officers: Alison Murphy, Secretary; Ad Schiebroek [1957] Tax and Treasury Director [Dutch]

Umeco Limited
Incorporated: 8 October 1917
Net Worth: £178,442,000 *Total Assets:* £180,368,992
Registered Office: Composites House, Sinclair Close, Heanor, Derbys, DE75 7SP
Activities: Activities of head offices
Parent: Cytec UK Holdings Limited
Officers: Alison Murphy, Secretary; David Shaun Clears [1957] Sales Director; Stephen Matthew Glennon [1967] Director/Business Analyst

Undercover Holdings Limited
Incorporated: 24 June 2009
Net Worth: £750,000 *Total Assets:* £9,902,000
Registered Office: Adsetts House, 16 Europa View, Sheffield, S9 1XH
Activities: Activities of other holding companies n.e.c.
Parent: SIG Trading Limited
Officers: Richard Charles Monro, Secretary; Ian Jackson [1979] Director; Christopher David Lodge [1978] Finance Director; Richard Charles Monro [1958] Director/Chartered Secretary

Undercover Roofing Supplies Limited
Incorporated: 16 July 2001
Net Worth: £20,000 *Total Assets:* £9,902,000
Registered Office: Adsetts House, 16 Europa View, Sheffield Business Park, Sheffield, S9 1XH
Activities: Wholesale of wood, construction materials and sanitary equipment
Parent: Undercover Holdings Limited
Officers: Richard Charles Monro, Secretary; Ian Jackson [1979] Director; Christopher David Lodge [1978] Finance Director; Richard Charles Monro [1958] Director/Chartered Secretary

Underwood Meat (Holdings) Limited
Incorporated: 23 October 2002 *Employees:* 252
Net Worth: £2,733,837 *Total Assets:* £11,413,887
Registered Office: Unit 15 Ashley Business Court, Rawmarsh Road, Rotherham, S Yorks, S60 1RU
Activities: Activities of head offices
Shareholders: Cora Bennett; John David Heeley; Tobias Matthew Smith Bennett; Anna Solveig Heeley
Officers: Cora Bennett, Secretary; Anna Solveig Heeley, Secretary; Tobias Matthew Smith Bennett [1972] Director/Butcher; John David Heeley [1959] Director/Butcher; Kevin Andrew Jones [1976] Director/Accountant; Richard Lloyd Mather [1955] Director

Underwood Meat Company Limited
Incorporated: 21 May 1992 *Employees:* 252
Net Worth: £4,859,572 *Total Assets:* £13,539,622
Registered Office: Unit 15 Ashley Business Court, Rawmarsh Road, Rotherham, S Yorks, S60 1RU
Activities: Wholesale of meat and meat products
Parent: Underwood Meat (Holdings) Limited
Officers: Cora Bennett, Secretary; Anna Solveig Heeley, Secretary; Tobias Matthew Smith Bennett [1972] Operations Director; John David Heeley [1959] Managing Director; Kevin Andrew Jones [1976] Director/Accountant; Richard Lloyd Mather [1955] Director

Unicarriers Leasing UK Limited
Incorporated: 31 October 1997
Net Worth: £8,720,732 *Total Assets:* £36,539,280
Registered Office: Jane Morbey Road, Thame, Oxon, OX9 3RR
Activities: Financial leasing
Parent: Unicarriers Europe AB
Officers: Kathryn Nicola Holden, Secretary; Mark Andrew Gibb [1958] Director; Kennerth Bjorn Magnus Lundgren [1966] Director [Swedish]; Masashi Takamatsu [1967] Director [Japanese]

Unicarriers UK Limited
Incorporated: 14 July 1969 *Employees:* 200
Net Worth: £16,505,593 *Total Assets:* £25,051,076
Registered Office: Jane Morbey Road, Thame, Oxon, OX9 3RR
Activities: Manufacture of lifting and handling equipment
Parent: Unicarriers Europe AB
Officers: Kathryn Nicola Holden, Secretary; Mark Andrew Gibb [1958] Managing Director; Masashi Takamatsu [1967] Director [Japanese]

Union Colours Limited
Incorporated: 9 October 2003 *Employees:* 24
Net Worth Deficit: £3,011,426 *Total Assets:* £11,279,744
Registered Office: Union House, Hempshaw Lane, Stockport, Cheshire, SK1 4LG
Activities: Wholesale of chemical products
Parent: Czna Group
Officers: Bo Zhu, Secretary; Phillip Ian Myles [1968] Operations Director; Hongbo Rui [1970] Director [Chinese]; Bo Zhu [1974] Director/Company Secretary

Union Papertech Limited
Incorporated: 6 June 2006 *Employees:* 112
Net Worth: £5,950,450 *Total Assets:* £12,699,487
Registered Office: Environment House, 6 Union Road, Nottingham, NG3 1FH
Activities: Manufacture of paper and paperboard
Shareholders: Purico Speciality Paper Company Limited; Purico Speciality Paper Company Limited
Officers: Roy Stewart Mochor [1950] Director; Anil Puri [1960] Director [Indian]; Stephen Todd [1959] Director/Accountant

Unipart Group Limited
Incorporated: 8 January 1957 *Employees:* 4,960
Net Worth Deficit: £252,600,000 *Total Assets:* £236,300,000
Registered Office: Unipart House, Garsington Road, Cowley, Oxford, OX4 2PG
Activities: Other business support service activities n.e.c.
Parent: Unipart Group of Companies Limited
Officers: Robert Paul David O'Brien, Secretary; Frank William Burns [1952] Director; Jonathan Chitty [1976] Director/Accountant; Alex Raymond Leung [1974] Director/Accountant; Christopher James Weldon [1978] Director/Accountant

Unipart Group of Companies Limited
Incorporated: 4 March 1986 *Employees:* 6,049
Net Worth Deficit: £171,300,000 *Total Assets:* £458,500,000
Registered Office: Unipart House, Cowley, Oxford, OX4 2PG
Activities: Activities of head offices
Shareholder: UGC Pension Funding LP
Officers: Robert Paul David O'Brien, Secretary; Frank William Burns [1952] Director; Jonathan Chitty [1976] Director/Accountant; Dr Bryan Samuel Jackson [1946] Director; Dr Hamid Ghafoor Mughal [1955] Director of Manufacturing; Noel James Travers [1969] Managing Director

Unipart International Holdings Limited
Incorporated: 22 October 1957
Net Worth: £16,125,000 *Total Assets:* £32,207,000
Registered Office: Unipart House, Cowley, Oxford, OX4 2PG
Activities: Activities of head offices
Parent: Unipart Group Limited
Officers: Robert Paul David O'Brien, Secretary; Jonathan Chitty [1976] Director/Accountant; Michael Glyn Ferris [1966] Managing Director; Christopher James Weldon [1978] Director/Accountant

Unipart Logistics Limited
Incorporated: 28 November 2001
Net Worth: £7,281,000 *Total Assets:* £34,718,000
Registered Office: Unipart House, Cowley, Oxford, OX4 2PG
Activities: Other business support service activities n.e.c.
Parent: Unipart Group Limited
Officers: Robert Paul David O'Brien, Secretary; Frank William Burns [1952] Director; Jonathan Chitty [1976] Director/Accountant; Alex Raymond Leung [1974] Director/Accountant; Christopher James Weldon [1978] Director/Accountant

Unipart Powertrain Applications Limited
Incorporated: 21 January 1998 *Employees:* 252
Previous: Unipart Eberspacher Exhaust Systems Limited
Net Worth: £6,641,000 *Total Assets:* £18,260,000
Registered Office: Unipart House, Garsington Road, Cowley, Oxford, OX4 2PG
Activities: Manufacture of other parts and accessories for motor vehicles
Parent: UGC (2015) Limited
Officers: Robert Paul David O'Brien, Secretary; Carol Burke [1967] Managing Director; Jonathan Chitty [1976] Director/Chartered Accountant; David Alistair Pound [1968] Managing Director; Nicola Squires [1971] Director/Accountant

Unipart Rail Holdings Limited
Incorporated: 29 July 1996
Net Worth: £25,220,000 *Total Assets:* £94,480,000
Registered Office: Unipart House, Cowley, Oxford, OX4 2PG
Activities: Activities of head offices
Parent: Unipart Group of Companies Limited
Officers: Robert Paul David O'Brien, Secretary; Jonathan Chitty [1976] Director/Accountant; Thomas George Johnstone [1960] Director/Accountant; Noel James Travers [1969] Managing Director; Christopher James Weldon [1978] Director/Accountant

Unipart Rail Limited
Incorporated: 22 March 1995 *Employees:* 692
Net Worth: £72,072,000 *Total Assets:* £132,317,000
Registered Office: Unipart House, Cowley, Oxford, OX4 2PG
Activities: Passenger rail transport, interurban
Parent: Unipart Rail Holdings Limited
Officers: Robert Paul David O'Brien, Secretary; Jonathan Chitty [1976] Director/Accountant; Graham Martin Jackson [1961] Managing Director; Thomas George Johnstone [1960] Director/Accountant; George James Tillier [1955] Managing Director; Noel James Travers [1969] Deputy Managing Director; Christopher James Weldon [1978] Director/Accountant

Unipath Limited
Incorporated: 14 August 1946 *Employees:* 82
Net Worth: £20,609,000 *Total Assets:* £41,001,000
Registered Office: Clearblue Innovation Centre, Priory Business Park, Stannard Way, Bedford, MK44 3UP
Activities: Other business support service activities n.e.c.
Parent: Alere UK Holdings Limited
Officers: David Bond [1971] Director/Accountant; Trevor Fellows [1969] Director/Chartered Accountant

Uniq (Holdings) Limited
Incorporated: 20 February 1959
Net Worth: £71,241,000 *Total Assets:* £81,129,000
Registered Office: Greencore Group UK Centre, Midland Way, Barlborough Links Business Park, Barlborough, Chesterfield, Derbys, S43 4XA
Activities: Activities of extraterritorial organisations and bodies
Parent: Hazlewood Foods Limited
Officers: Michael Evans, Secretary; Catherine Bradshaw [1975] Finance Director; Michael Evans [1967] Director/Group Communications Officer; Eoin Philip Tonge [1972] Director [Irish]

Uniq Limited
Incorporated: 24 January 2000
Net Worth: £89,474,000 *Total Assets:* £181,907,008
Registered Office: Greencore Group UK Centre, Midland Way, Barlborough Links Business Park, Barlborough, Chesterfield, Derbys, S43 4XA
Activities: Manufacture of prepared meals and dishes
Parent: Greencore Foods Limited
Officers: Michael Evans, Secretary; Michael Evans [1967] Director/Group Communications Officer; Eoin Philip Tonge [1972] Director [Irish]

Unique Window Systems Ltd
Incorporated: 2 March 2004 *Employees:* 178
Net Worth: £5,180,555 *Total Assets:* £12,308,379
Registered Office: 87 Parker Drive, Leicester, LE4 0JP
Activities: Manufacture of builders ware of plastic
Shareholders: Atul Jayantilal Patel; Sunil Jayantilal Patel
Officers: Sunil Jayantilal Patel, Secretary/Sales Manager; Steven James Birkin [1969] Director; Atul Jayantilal Patel [1968] Director/Production Manager; Sunil Jayantilal Patel [1970] Director/Sales Manager; James William Raven [1975] Director; David Charles Rowley [1976] Sales Director

United Carpets Holdings Limited
Incorporated: 24 January 1992 *Employees:* 8
Net Worth: £5,819,939 *Total Assets:* £14,820,013
Registered Office: Moorhead House, Moorhead Way, off Bawtry Road, Bramley, Rotherham, S Yorks, S66 1YY
Activities: Buying and selling of own real estate
Major Shareholder: Paul Robert Eyre
Officers: Deborah Grayson, Secretary; Paul Robert Eyre [1958] Director

United Cast Bar (UK) Limited
Incorporated: 18 January 1897 *Employees:* 103
Net Worth: £18,114,824 *Total Assets:* £30,568,852
Registered Office: Spital Lane, Chesterfield, Derbys, S41 0EX
Activities: Manufacture of basic iron and steel and of ferro-alloys
Parent: BI Group Limited
Officers: James Brand [1973] Director; Jonathon Paul Cripps [1969] Director; Yaseen Mohamed Jaafar Mohamed Mohsen [1960] Director [Bahraini]; Mark Anderson Penman [1970] Financial Director; Alessandro Bernardo Agostino Rottach [1963] Director [Italian]

United Church Schools Foundation Ltd
Incorporated: 12 July 1883 *Employees:* 7,739
Net Worth: £532,716,992 *Total Assets:* £739,315,008
Registered Office: Worldwide House, Thorpe Wood, Peterborough, PE3 6SB
Activities: Other letting and operating of own or leased real estate
Officers: Stephen John Whiffen, Secretary; Dr Stephen Richard Critchley [1951] Director/Retired; Richard Colin Neil Davidson [1951] Director; Michael David George [1973] Director; Joseph Benjamin Gordon [1959] Director and Chartered Civil Engineer; Richard Cecil Greenhalgh [1944] Director/Executive; Michael John Litchfield [1949] Director/Architect; Nigel Rhyl Robson [1951] Director/Retired Solicitor

United Church Schools Trust
Incorporated: 18 January 1993 *Employees:* 2,451
Net Worth: £20,535,000 *Total Assets:* £79,497,000
Registered Office: Worldwide House, Thorpe Wood, Peterborough, PE3 6SB
Activities: Primary education
Parent: United Church Schools Foundation Limited
Officers: Stephen John Whiffen, Secretary; Mary Elizabeth Curnock Cook [1958] Director/Educationalist; Dr Rosalind Margaret Given-Wilson [1955] Director/Doctor; Joseph Benjamin Gordon [1959] Director and Chartered Civil Engineer; Richard Cecil Greenhalgh [1944] Director/Executive; Michael John Litchfield [1949] Director/Retired; Sarah Laetitia Squire [1949] Director/University Senior Administrator

United Health Group Limited
Incorporated: 3 April 2006 *Employees:* 436
Net Worth: £9,200,805 *Total Assets:* £31,933,370
Registered Office: The Old Coach House, Gainsborough Road, Drinsey Nook, Lincoln, LN1 2JJ
Activities: Construction of commercial buildings
Major Shareholder: Philip John Pearson
Officers: Michael Ian Brown, Secretary; Mandy Teresa Cheriton-Metcalfe [1975] Director; Charles Richard Jackson [1951] Director; Philip John Pearson [1953] Director

United Health Limited
Incorporated: 24 May 2006 *Employees:* 372
Net Worth: £18,797,106 *Total Assets:* £37,737,496
Registered Office: The Old Coach House, Gainsborough Road, Drinsey Nook, Lincoln, LN1 2JJ
Activities: Residential nursing care facilities
Parent: United Health Group Limited
Officers: Michael Ian Brown, Secretary; Mandy Teresa Cheriton-Metcalfe [1975] Director; Charles Richard Jackson [1947] Director; Philip John Pearson [1953] Director

United Learning Trust
Incorporated: 15 May 2002 *Employees:* 5,145
Net Worth: £483,756,992 *Total Assets:* £550,627,968
Registered Office: Worldwide House, Thorpe Wood, Peterborough, PE3 6SB
Activities: Pre-primary education
Parent: United Church Schools Trust
Officers: Stephen John Whiffen, Secretary; Dame Yasmin Bevan [1953] Director/Executive Principal; Jonathan Andrew Coles [1972] Director/Chief Executive; Richard Colin Neil Davidson [1951] Director; Michael David George [1973] Director; Richard Cecil Greenhalgh [1944] Director/Executive; Dame Reena Keeble [1955] Director/Primary Headteacher - Retired; David Barrie Robinson [1966] Director/Chairman; Nigel Rhyl Robson [1951] Director/Retired Solicitor

United Rental Group America Limited
Incorporated: 29 May 2015
Net Worth: £21,021,776 *Total Assets:* £21,021,776
Registered Office: Durrant House, 47 Holywell Street, Chesterfield, Derbys, S41 7SJ
Activities: Other business support service activities n.e.c.
Parent: United Kenning Rental Group Limited
Officers: Tracey Howard, Secretary; Tracey Howard [1966] Finance Director; Ian Walter Lawrence [1959] Managing Director

United Rental Group Limited
Incorporated: 25 October 1990 *Employees:* 58
Net Worth: £53,435,000 *Total Assets:* £117,183,000
Registered Office: Durrant House, 47 Holywell Street, Chesterfield, Derbys, S41 7SJ
Activities: Renting and leasing of cars and light motor vehicles
Parent: United Kenning Rental Group Limited
Officers: Tracey Jane Howard, Secretary; Robert Baillie [1957] Director; Timothy Guy Bennett [1956] Development Director; Aaron Firth [1970] Sales & Marketing Director; Richard Hague [1964] Fleet Director; Tracey Howard [1966] Finance Director; Ian Walter Lawrence [1959] Director

Unity Property Holdings Limited
Incorporated: 6 January 2017
Net Worth: £5,343,852 *Total Assets:* £12,224,994
Registered Office: 31 Tentercroft Street, Lincoln, LN5 7DB
Activities: Other letting and operating of own or leased real estate
Officers: Simon William Dean Grace [1984] Director; Cameron Simon Jackson [1986] Director; Dominik Thomas Jackson [1984] Director; Simon Jackson [1957] Director

Universal Components UK Limited
Incorporated: 7 July 2004 *Employees:* 147
Net Worth: £6,479,000 *Total Assets:* £15,832,000
Registered Office: Ashroyd Business Park, Ashroyds Way, Hoyland, Barnsley, S Yorks, S74 9SB
Activities: Wholesale trade of motor vehicle parts and accessories
Parent: TVS Europe Distribution Limited
Officers: Paul Roberts, Secretary; Srinivasa Raghavan Gopalan [1969] Director [Indian]; David Kernahan [1973] Managing Director; Paul John Roberts [1968] Director/Accountant; Santhanagopalan Subramanian [1958] Director [Indian]

Universal Flexible Packaging Limited
Incorporated: 18 August 1995 *Employees:* 161
Net Worth: £4,625,762 *Total Assets:* £15,459,610
Registered Office: 61 Lunsford Road, Leicester, LE5 0HJ
Activities: Manufacture of other food products n.e.c.
Parent: Universal Developments (Leicester) Ltd
Officers: Mubushar Durrani, Secretary; Mubushar Durrani [1970] Director/Packaging; Nazia Awan Durrani [1980] Director; Ulfat Shahnaz Durrani [1934] Director

Universal Salvage Limited
Incorporated: 4 December 1979
Net Worth: £123,877,000 *Total Assets:* £138,166,000
Registered Office: Acrey Fields, Woburn Road, Wootton, Beds, MK43 9EJ
Activities: Sale of used cars and light motor vehicles
Parent: Copart Europe Limited
Officers: Aaron Jayson Adair [1969] Director/Chief Executive Officer [American]; Jonathan David Canning [1972] Director/General Counsel; Gregory Depasquale [1968] Director/SVP, General Counsel and Secretary of Copart, Inc [American]; William Easley Franklin [1956] Director/Senior VP & Chief Financial [American]; Nigel James Paget [1966] Managing Director; Simon Sheldon-Wilson [1969] Director; Paul Anthony Styer [1956] Director/General Counsel [American]

University of Derby
Incorporated: 7 July 1995 *Employees:* 2,156
Net Worth: £374,180,000 *Total Assets:* £517,323,008
Registered Office: Kedleston Road, Derby, DE22 1GB
Activities: Other research and experimental development on natural sciences and engineering
Officers: June Patricia Hughes, Secretary; Dr Sally Akehurst [1979] Director/Manager; Neil Douglas Calvert [1972] Director/Headteacher; Olivia Mary Dean [1947] Director/Education Consultant; James Eaglesfield [1975] Director/IT Governance Manager; Lesley Rebecca Giles [1968] Deputy Director; Gillian Howland [1956] Director/Retired; Gordon Alexander Lammie [1943] Director/Retired; Roohi Mehra [1986] Director/Clinical Pharmacist Trainer for The MOD; Professor Kathryn Mary Mitchell [1963] Director/Vice-Chancellor; Scarlet Rose Moss [1997] Director/Sabbatical Officer Union of Students; Elisabeth Louise Pigden [1971] Director/Head of Joint Honours Scheme; Dr Joanna Lai Kwan Poon [1974] Director/Academic Lecturer; Harindra Deepal Punchihewa [1961] Director of Finance; Stephen David Smith [1958] Director/Chief Executive; Stephen Jonathan Taylor [1957] Director/Business Consultant; Dr Ian Webster [1954] Director/Retired; Abby Wilson [1995] Director/President at The Union of Students

University of Warwick Science Park Limited
Incorporated: 20 August 1982 *Employees:* 25
Net Worth: £8,984,602 *Total Assets:* £14,060,089
Registered Office: University House, University of Warwick, Kirby Corner Road, Coventry, Warwicks, CV4 8UW
Activities: Other letting and operating of own or leased real estate
Officers: Jacob Mark Alexander Langlands, Secretary; Rosemary Ann Drinkwater [1960] Finance Director; Jennifer Greenway [1960] Corporate Director; Nigel Christopher Maris [1960] Managing Director; Professor Simon Charles Robert Swain [1961] Director/Pro-Vice Chancellor (External Engagement)

UOS LP Limited
Incorporated: 10 July 2015
Net Worth: £32,425,100 *Total Assets:* £33,700,136
Registered Office: University of Sheffield, Firth Court, Western Bank, Sheffield, S10 2TN
Activities: Activities of other holding companies n.e.c.
Officers: Ross Alexander McMaster, Secretary; Victoria Emma Louise Jackson [1974] Director/Accountant; Ian David Wright [1972] Associate Director of Human Resources

Uppingham School
Incorporated: 30 March 2012 *Employees:* 613
Net Worth: £69,242,008 *Total Assets:* £105,510,576
Registered Office: Uppingham School, High Street West, Uppingham, Rutland, LE15 9QD
Activities: General secondary education
Officers: Stephen Charles Taylor, Secretary; The Right Reverend Donald Spargo Allister [1952] Director/Bishop of Peterborough; Dr Priscilla Chadwick [1947] Director; Christopher Charles Dalliston [1956] Director/Dean; Sir Alan James Carter Duncan [1957] Director/Member of Parliament; Christopher Francis Ewbank [1961] Director/Senior Bursar; John Donald Read Fothergill [1961] Director; Dr Sarah Haddon Furness [1956] Director/Lord Lieutenant of Rutland; Dr Stephen John Goss [1952] Director/University Pro-Vice Chancellor; Sandra Ann Humphrey [1959] Director/Solicitor; Alasdair James Dougall Locke [1953] Director; Barbara Mary Matthews [1956] Director/University Dean; Roger Peel [1945] Director/Retired Headmaster; Russell Nicholas John Price [1966] Director/Farmer; David Peter John Ross [1965] Director/Businessman; Jonathan James Anthony Scott [1957] Director/University Pro-Vice-Chancellor; Dora Frieda Thornton [1961] Director/Museum Curator; Richard James Sunley Tice [1964] Director; Dominic Laurence Carden Wallis [1969] Director/Investment Banker

C.J. Upton Holdings Ltd.
Incorporated: 20 June 1997 *Employees:* 113
Net Worth: £10,463,843 *Total Assets:* £41,464,304
Registered Office: 21 Shaw Lane, Markfield, Leicester, LE67 9PU
Activities: Activities of head offices
Major Shareholder: Linda Kristin Upton
Officers: Linda Kristin Upton, Secretary/Director [Norwegian]; James Morten Timothy Upton [1972] Managing Director; Linda Kristin Upton [1954] Director [Norwegian]

URA Ventures Limited
Incorporated: 19 February 1997 *Employees:* 31
Net Worth: £14,510,000 *Total Assets:* £26,271,000
Registered Office: Centenary House, Bridge Business Centre, Beresford Way, Chesterfield, Derbys, S41 9FG
Activities: Sale of used cars and light motor vehicles
Officers: Carey Kenning, Secretary; Thomas William Kenning, Secretary; Michael Harry Wilson Canon [1943] Director of Quarrying Co; Michael Louis Leslie Higgins [1948] Director/Manager/Consultant; Richard Thomas Kenning [1951] Director; Robert Sayers [1955] Director/Chartered Accountant

Urgo Limited
Incorporated: 10 December 2001 *Employees:* 163
Net Worth: £7,461,353 *Total Assets:* £17,661,302
Registered Office: Shepshed Industrial Estate, Sullington Road, Shepshed, Loughborough, Leics, LE12 9JJ
Activities: Manufacture of other textiles n.e.c.
Parent: Laboratoires Urgo SAS
Officers: Graeme Charles Seymour Campbell Francis, Secretary; Gavin John Ashton [1980] Director and General Manager; Ronan Jean Louis Blanchard [1977] Director [French]; Laurent Antoine Francois Faugere [1974] Director [French]; Pierre Georges Andre Moustial [1963] Director [French]

Uris Central Administration Limited
Incorporated: 22 June 2007 *Employees:* 136
Previous: Direct Newco Limited
Net Worth: £9,020,000 *Total Assets:* £21,001,000
Registered Office: Quay Point, Lakeside Boulevard, Doncaster, S Yorks, DN4 5PL
Activities: Activities of financial services holding companies
Parent: Ryan Direct Group Limited
Officers: Derek John Coles [1960] Director; Scott William Hough [1971] Director

Uris Group Limited
Incorporated: 22 January 1990 *Employees:* 114
Previous: Direct Group Limited
Net Worth: £22,646,000 *Total Assets:* £59,545,000
Registered Office: Quay Point, Lakeside Boulevard, Doncaster, S Yorks, DN4 5PL
Activities: Activities auxiliary to financial intermediation n.e.c.
Parent: Ryan Direct Group Limited
Officers: Derek John Coles [1960] Director/Chief Executive Officer; Scott William Hough [1971] Director/Chief Finance Officer

Uris Topco Limited
Incorporated: 17 August 2012
Previous: Direct Group Topco Limited
Net Worth Deficit: £48,322,000 *Total Assets:* £52,830,000
Registered Office: Quay Point, Lakeside Boulevard, Doncaster, S Yorks, DN4 5PL
Activities: Activities of financial services holding companies
Parent: Nevada Investments 3 Limited
Officers: Derek John Coles [1960] Director; Scott William Hough [1971] Director

Urschel International Limited
Incorporated: 27 September 1972 *Employees:* 86
Net Worth: £14,627,501 *Total Assets:* £24,102,098
Registered Office: Tiber Way, Meridian Business Park, Leicester, LE19 1QP
Activities: Agents involved in the sale of machinery, industrial equipment, ships and aircraft
Parent: Urschel Laboratories Inc
Officers: Teresa Warburton, Secretary; Hans-Peter Bruendler [1954] Sales Director [Swiss]; Richard Andrew Cranefield [1966] Finance Director; Helena Cristina Gomes [1964] Marketing Director [Portuguese]; Florence Le Lay [1963] Marketing Director [French]; Alan Wayne Major [1964] Director [American]; Daniel Marchetti [1966] Director [American]; Timothy O'Brien [1958] Managing Director [American]; Patrick Charles Urschel [1978] Director/Corporate Secretary [American]; Robert R Urschel [1948] Director [American]

Richard Utley Limited
Incorporated: 2 May 1966 *Employees:* 6
Net Worth: £11,640,296 *Total Assets:* £13,258,401
Registered Office: Unit 12 Europark A5, Watling Street, Clifton upon Dunsmore, Rugby, Warwicks, CV23 0AL
Activities: Activities of head offices
Shareholders: John Holdsworth Stott Utley; Richard John Warburton Utley; James William Morris; Artemis Trustees Limited
Officers: Clifford Brian Cooper, Secretary/Solicitor; Chris James Utley [1973] Director/Chartered Surveyor; John Holdsworth Stott Utley [1938] Director; Richard John Warburton Utley [1935] Director

Utopia Holdings (Chesterfield) Limited
Incorporated: 30 May 2014 *Employees:* 107
Net Worth: £3,172,934 *Total Assets:* £21,612,812
Registered Office: Glassworks Park Road, Holmewood, Chesterfield, Derbys, S42 5UY
Activities: Activities of distribution holding companies
Shareholders: Mark Trevor Rammell; Fiona Rammell
Officers: Mark Trevor Rammell [1965] Director

Utopia Tableware Limited
Incorporated: 6 March 2000 *Employees:* 107
Net Worth: £6,342,841 *Total Assets:* £21,450,968
Registered Office: Glassworks Park Road, Holmewood, Chesterfield, Derbys, S42 5UY
Activities: Wholesale of household goods (other than musical instruments) n.e.c
Parent: Utopia Holdings (Chesterfield) Limited
Officers: Kathryn Ann Oldershaw [1971] Marketing Director [Irish]; Fiona Rammell [1973] Director; Mark Trevor Rammell [1965] Director

George Utz Limited
Incorporated: 24 February 1989 *Employees:* 70
Net Worth: £7,778,000 *Total Assets:* £15,862,000
Registered Office: Grange Close, Clover Nook Industrial Estate, Alfreton, Derbys, DE55 4QT
Activities: Manufacture of plastic packing goods
Parent: Georg Utz Holding AG
Officers: Barbara Mary Kapoor, Secretary; Bruno Josef Bucher [1963] Director [Swiss]; Axel Ritzberger [1965] Director [Swiss]

UYS Limited
Incorporated: 3 May 1996 *Employees:* 235
Net Worth: £4,399,000 *Total Assets:* £32,022,000
Registered Office: Garsington Road, Cowley, Oxford, OX4 2BW
Activities: Manufacture of other parts and accessories for motor vehicles
Officers: Nigel John Smith, Secretary; Kenji Ichikawa [1964] Director [Japanese]; Toshihide Kiriyama [1965] Director [Japanese]; Katsuhiro Kurokawa [1960] Director [Japanese]; Naoki Shiraishi [1960] Director [Japanese]

V Installations Mechanical Handling Limited
Incorporated: 12 February 2002 *Employees:* 44
Net Worth: £6,696,807 *Total Assets:* £9,837,701
Registered Office: 8 Jury Street, Warwick, CV34 4EW
Activities: Casting of steel
Shareholders: Gary James Fox; Paula Louise Ellen Fox
Officers: Paula Louise Ellen Fox, Secretary; Gary James Fox [1966] Director/Estimator Engineer; Stephen Craig Smith [1962] Commercial Director; Steven Jason Trow [1962] Director

V.I. Risk Capital LLP
Incorporated: 28 September 2006
Net Worth Deficit: £470,097 *Total Assets:* £33,276,152
Registered Office: 3 Castlegate, Grantham, Lincs, NG31 6SF

V12 Sports & Classics Ltd
Incorporated: 29 June 2006 *Employees:* 170
Net Worth: £7,650,067 *Total Assets:* £17,318,790
Registered Office: Unit 23 Harrowbrook Road, Hinckley, Leics, LE10 3DJ
Activities: Sale of used cars and light motor vehicles
Officers: Asiya Shaikh, Secretary [Indian]; Asiya Shaikh [1980] Director; Farhad Tailor [1977] Director; Gary Woods [1962] Director

Vacation Rental Group Holdings Limited
Incorporated: 16 May 1989
Net Worth: £25,090,000 *Total Assets:* £26,361,000
Registered Office: Haylock House, Kettering Parkway, Kettering, Northants, NN15 6EY
Activities: Activities of head offices
Parent: RCI Europe
Officers: Andrew Clarke [1976] Senior Director Finance; Andrew Liggins [1962] Director/VP Operations

Vacu-Lug Traction Tyres Limited
Incorporated: 1 December 1950 *Employees:* 136
Net Worth: £8,434,332 *Total Assets:* £13,736,509
Registered Office: Gonerby Road, Gonerby Hill Foot, Grantham, Lincs, NG31 8HE
Activities: Manufacture of rubber tyres and tubes; retreading and rebuilding of rubber tyres
Parent: Grantham Capital Limited
Officers: Timothy Rowland Hercock [1963] Managing Director; Harjeev Singh Kandhari [1975] Director [Indian]

Vaillant European Holdings Limited
Incorporated: 10 March 1900
Net Worth: £198,063,152 *Total Assets:* £217,426,960
Registered Office: Nottingham Road, Belper, Derbys, DE56 1JT
Activities: Activities of head offices
Parent: Vaillant Holdings Ltd
Officers: Alison Sarah Blincow, Secretary; Alison Sarah Blincow [1978] Director/Solicitor; Klaus Jesse [1959] Managing Director [German]

Vaillant Group UK Limited
Incorporated: 22 November 1934 *Employees:* 588
Net Worth: £56,116,000 *Total Assets:* £174,224,992
Registered Office: Nottingham Road, Belper, Derbys, DE56 1JT
Activities: Other business support service activities n.e.c.
Parent: Vaillant Home Products Ltd
Officers: Alison Sarah Blincow, Secretary; Dr Stefan Borchers [1969] Director [German]; Dr Andree Groos [1973] Director [German]; Klaus Jesse [1959] Managing Director [German]; Dr. Norbert SChiefeck [1965] Director [German]

Vaillant Holdings Limited
Incorporated: 30 October 1969 *Employees:* 5
Net Worth: £183,791,008 *Total Assets:* £515,036,000
Registered Office: Nottingham Road, Belper, Derbys, DE56 1JT
Activities: Activities of production holding companies
Parent: Vaillant Management Limited
Officers: Alison Sarah Blincow, Secretary; Klaus Jesse [1959] Managing Director [German]; Michael Weinholzer [1960] Director [German]

Vaillant Home Products Limited
Incorporated: 19 January 1955
Net Worth: £9,335,518 *Total Assets:* £14,586,199
Registered Office: Nottingham Road, Belper, Derbys, DE56 1JT
Activities: Activities of head offices
Parent: Vaillant Holdings Ltd
Officers: Alison Sarah Blincow, Secretary; Markus Schulz [1972] Director [German]

Vaillant Industrial UK Limited
Incorporated: 3 August 1972 *Employees:* 154
Net Worth: £33,450,000 *Total Assets:* £54,248,000
Registered Office: Nottingham Road, Belper, Derbys, DE56 1JT
Activities: Manufacture of central heating radiators and boilers
Parent: Vaillant Home Products Ltd
Officers: Alison Sarah Blincow, Secretary; Joseph Sidney Dunn [1974] Director; Klaus Jesse [1959] Director [German]; Karsten Kock [1966] Director [German]; Dr. Norbert SChiefeck [1965] Director [German]; Alexander Stark [1972] Director [German]

Vaillant Management Limited
Incorporated: 13 December 2000
Net Worth: £326,230,912 *Total Assets:* £503,779,200
Registered Office: Nottingham Road, Belper, Derbys, DE56 1JT
Activities: Activities of head offices
Officers: Alison Sarah Blincow, Secretary; Dr Stefan Borchers [1969] Director [German]; Klaus Jesse [1959] Director [German]

Vaillant Netherlands Holdings Limited
Incorporated: 16 November 1982
Net Worth: £195,795,168 *Total Assets:* £250,927,312
Registered Office: Nottingham Road, Belper, Derbys, DE56 1JT
Activities: Activities of head offices
Parent: Vaillant European Holdings Ltd
Officers: Alison Sarah Blincow, Secretary; Alison Sarah Blincow [1978] Director/Solicitor; Klaus Jesse [1959] Managing Director [German]

Valassis Limited
Incorporated: 17 February 2000 *Employees:* 334
Net Worth: £18,759,000 *Total Assets:* £32,708,000
Registered Office: Weldon House, Corby Gate Business Park, Priors Haw Road, Corby, Northants, NN17 5JG
Activities: Activities of head offices
Major Shareholder: Ronald Perelman
Officers: Charles Edward D'Oyly [1964] Director; Neil Owen Marks [1973] Finance Director

Vale Academy Trust
Incorporated: 20 June 2011 *Employees:* 541
Net Worth: £54,682,540 *Total Assets:* £71,740,968
Registered Office: Vale Academy Trust, The Studio, St Mary's Convent, Denchworth Road, Wantage, Oxon, OX12 9AU
Activities: Primary education
Officers: Victoria Mary-Ann Alice Roberts, Secretary; Christopher Richard Allen Ferguson [1966] Director; Philip David Harrison [1963] Director/Chartered Surveyor; Wendy Hart [1967] Director/Accountant; Gina Victoria Hocking [1964] Director/Charity Worker; Iain Anthony Littlejohn [1967] Director/Management Consultant; Dr Jeffrey Penfold [1948] Director/Retired; Joseph Charles Pillman [1952] Director/Solicitor; Kirsteen Caroline Susan Ross Roberts [1961] Assistant Director, Diocese of Oxford; Simon Anthony Spiers [1964] Director/Headteacher; Dr Elizabeth Helen Taylor [1950] Director/Retired; Christopher Paul Williams [1947] Director/Business Consultant

Vale Garden Houses Limited
Incorporated: 9 February 1994 *Employees:* 135
Net Worth: £11,806,135 *Total Assets:* £15,433,567
Registered Office: Belton Park, Londonthorpe, Grantham, Lincs, NG31 9SJ
Activities: Joinery installation
Shareholders: Dennis Herbert Morton; Simon Adrian Charles Morton
Officers: Denise Lesley Morton, Secretary; David Michael Cheney [1960] Director/Operations Manager; Steven Christopher John Hall [1964] Director; Denise Lesley Morton [1937] Director/Secretary; Dennis Herbert Morton [1931] Director/Manufacturer & Designer; Simon Adrian Charles Morton [1965] Director/Manufacturer; Lisa Catherine Moth [1962] Director/Sales & Account Coordinator

Valens Resources Group PLC
Incorporated: 16 June 2008 *Employees:* 78
Net Worth: £309,153 *Total Assets:* £9,314,632
Registered Office: Station Road, West Dereham, King's Lynn, Norfolk, PE33 9RR
Activities: Collection of non-hazardous waste
Shareholders: Simon Miles; Jonathan Miles
Officers: Jonathan Miles, Secretary/Director; Jonathan Miles [1963] Director; Simon David Miles [1960] Director/Chartered Accountant

Valpak Holdings Limited
Incorporated: 8 April 2011 *Employees:* 137
Net Worth: £16,320,000 *Total Assets:* £35,018,000
Registered Office: Unit 4 Stratford Business Park, Banbury Road, Stratford upon Avon, Warwicks, CV37 7GW
Activities: Activities of other holding companies n.e.c.
Parent: OS Phoenix Acquisition Limited
Officers: Philip Andrew Gale, Secretary; Ruth Susan Beckley [1979] Director; Paul Anthony Cox [1968] Director; Lord John Selwyn Deben [1939] Director; Philip Andrew Gale [1958] Finance Director; Steven Andrew Gough [1964] Director; Adrian Peter Hawkes [1959] Director; Alan Albert Price [1970] Director; John Terence Sullivan [1965] Director

Valpak Limited
Incorporated: 30 June 2011 *Employees:* 125
Net Worth: £5,941,000 *Total Assets:* £19,820,000
Registered Office: Unit 4 Stratford Business Park, Banbury Road, Stratford upon Avon, Warwicks, CV37 7GW
Activities: Environmental consulting activities
Parent: Valpak Holdings Limited
Officers: Philip Andrew Gale, Secretary; Ruth Susan Beckley [1979] Director; Paul Anthony Cox [1968] Director; Philip Andrew Gale [1958] Director; Steven Andrew Gough [1964] Director; Lord John Selwyn Gummer [1939] Director; Adrian Peter Hawkes [1959] Director; Andrew John McCaffery [1964] Director; Alan Albert Price [1970] Director; Duncan Simpson [1966] Director; John Terence Sullivan [1965] Director

The Valspar (UK) Corporation, Limited
Incorporated: 25 April 1995 *Employees:* 240
Net Worth Deficit: £1,280,854 *Total Assets:* £61,608,072
Registered Office: Station Lane, Witney, Oxon, OX28 4XR
Activities: Manufacture of other chemical products n.e.c.
Parent: The Valspar (UK) Holding Corporation Limited
Officers: Ezio Nicola Giacomo Braggio [1956] Director/Businessman [Italian]; Jeffrey James Miklich [1974] Director/Business Executive [American]; Allen Joseph Mistysyn [1968] Director/Business Executive [American]

The Valspar (UK) Holding Corporation Limited
Incorporated: 12 March 1996
Net Worth: £20,842,732 *Total Assets:* £163,723,424
Registered Office: Avenue One, Station Lane, Witney, Oxon, OX28 4XR
Activities: Other manufacturing n.e.c.
Parent: The Valspar Corporation
Officers: Ezio Nicola Giacomo Braggio [1956] Director/Businessman [Italian]; Jeffrey James Miklich [1974] Director/Business Executive [American]; Allen Joseph Mistysyn [1968] Director/Business Executive [American]

The Valspar (UK) Special Holding Corporation Ltd
Incorporated: 22 December 2016
Net Worth: £13,492,898 *Total Assets:* £13,519,590
Registered Office: Avenue One, Station Lane, Witney, Oxon, OX28 4XR
Activities: Other manufacturing n.e.c.
Parent: The Valspar (UK) Holding Corporation Limited
Officers: Ezio Nicola Giacomo Braggio [1956] Director/Businessman [Italian]; Jeffrey James Miklich [1974] Director/Business Executive [American]; Allen Joseph Mistysyn [1968] Director/Business Executive [American]

The Valve Partners Limited
Incorporated: 16 March 2004 *Employees:* 51
Net Worth: £6,700,787 *Total Assets:* £11,938,392
Registered Office: Unit 6 Interlink Way South, Bardon Hill, Coalville, Leics, LE67 1PH
Activities: Wholesale of other intermediate products
Parent: The Valve & Actuation Group Limited
Officers: Jessica Marguerite Findell, Secretary; Stephen Joseph Paul Craddock [1961] Director; Jessica Marguerite Findell [1984] Director; Nicholas Andrew Flint [1963] Director

Van Elle Holdings PLC
Incorporated: 2 April 2003 *Employees:* 575
Previous: Van Elle Holdings Limited
Net Worth: £41,366,000 *Total Assets:* £77,496,000
Registered Office: Kirkby Lane, Pinxton, Nottingham, NG16 6JA
Activities: Activities of head offices
Officers: Paul Michael Pearson, Secretary; Adrian Barden [1954] Director; Mark Lloyd Cutler [1968] Director/Chief Executive; David Stuart Hurcomb [1964] Director; Paul Michael Pearson [1968] Director; Robin George Walton Williams [1957] Director

Van Elle Limited
Incorporated: 11 March 1991 *Employees:* 575
Net Worth: £32,631,000 *Total Assets:* £75,390,000
Registered Office: Kirkby Lane, Pinxton, Nottingham, NG16 6JA
Activities: Construction of other civil engineering projects n.e.c.
Parent: Van Elle Holdings PLC
Officers: Paul Michael Pearson, Secretary; Christian Bosworth [1975] Director; Mark Lloyd Cutler [1968] Director/Chief Executive; Michael John Mason [1967] Director

Reg Vardy (VMC) Limited
Incorporated: 12 July 2002 *Employees:* 106
Net Worth: £8,603,000 *Total Assets:* £12,706,000
Registered Office: Loxley House, 2 Oakwood Court, Little Oak Drive, Annesley, Nottingham, NG15 0DR
Activities: Sale of new cars and light motor vehicles
Parent: Reg Vardy Limited
Officers: Richard James Maloney, Secretary; Trevor Garry Finn [1957] Director

Reg Vardy Limited
Incorporated: 12 September 1958 *Employees:* 398
Net Worth: £99,593,000 *Total Assets:* £132,349,000
Registered Office: Loxley House, 2 Oakwood Court, Little Oak Drive, Annesley, Notts, NG15 0DR
Activities: Sale of other motor vehicles
Officers: Richard James Maloney, Secretary; Martin Shaun Casha [1960] Director; Trevor Garry Finn [1957] Director; Timothy Paul Holden [1964] Director/Chartered Accountant

Varsity Design Limited
Incorporated: 28 February 1985
Net Worth: £10,379,510 *Total Assets:* £12,436,607
Registered Office: Unit 3 Bignell Park Barns, Chesterton, Bicester, Oxon, OX26 1TD
Activities: Other letting and operating of own or leased real estate
Major Shareholder: Howard Gordon Marshall
Officers: Paul Page, Secretary; Paul Page [1953] Director/Careers

Vectair Aviation (1995) Limited
Incorporated: 4 October 1995 *Employees:* 41
Net Worth: £5,394,723 *Total Assets:* £12,037,494
Registered Office: 7 Lakes Country Park, Wharf Road, Crowle, N Lincs, DN17 4JS
Activities: Other retail sale not in stores, stalls or markets
Major Shareholder: David Francis Keedy
Officers: David Francis Keedy [1944] Director; Jason Brian Keedy [1972] Managing Director; Rhodri John Marlow [1975] Director/Manager

Veeva U.K. Holdings Limited
Incorporated: 23 September 2015 *Employees:* 2
Net Worth: £17,190,790 *Total Assets:* £56,580,776
Registered Office: 4300 Nash Court, John Smith Drive, Oxford Business Park South, Oxford, OX4 2RU
Activities: Business and domestic software development
Parent: Veeva Systems Inc.
Officers: Timothy Stephen Cabral [1967] Director [American]; Jonathan Faddis [1971] Director/VP and General Counsel [American]

Vehicle Credit Limited
Incorporated: 8 February 2012 *Employees:* 21
Net Worth Deficit: £7,872,225 *Total Assets:* £16,302,764
Registered Office: No 1 The Osiers Business Centre, Leicester, LE19 1DX
Activities: Credit granting by non-deposit taking finance houses and other specialist consumer credit grantors
Parent: Ratesetter Motor Limited
Officers: Jolanta Bieda, Secretary; Peter William Edward Behrens [1977] Director; Jonathan Peter Shaw Hodge [1980] Director/Finance Professional

Velocys PLC
Incorporated: 16 February 2006 *Employees:* 60
Net Worth: £14,685,000 *Total Assets:* £19,460,000
Registered Office: Harwell Innovation Centre, 173 Curie Avenue, Harwell, Oxon, OX11 0QG
Activities: Engineering design activities for industrial process and production
Officers: Jeremy Philip Gorman, Secretary; Philip Malcolm Holland [1954] Director; Dr Pierre Jean Marie Henri Jungels [1944] Director [Belgian]; Darran Keith Messem [1966] Director; Andrew James Sinclair Morris [1962] Director; Sandra Nan Demby Shaw [1953] Director/Lawyer; Henrik Sven Gunnar Wareborn [1963] Director [Swedish]

Vencap International PLC
Incorporated: 13 October 1987 *Employees:* 20
Net Worth: £10,076,434 *Total Assets:* £11,054,859
Registered Office: Seacourt Tower, West Way, Oxford, OX2 0JJ
Activities: Financial intermediation not elsewhere classified
Major Shareholder: Michael Leslie Ashall
Officers: Simon Lyn Lasseter, Secretary; Ann Ruth Cooke [1952] Director/Chartered Accountant; Michael David Craig [1952] Director/Investment Manager; Timothy Paul Cruttenden [1968] Director/Chief Executive; David John Gamble [1944] Director/Chairman; Simon Lyn Lasseter [1966] Finance Director

Verder Holdings U.K. Limited
Incorporated: 25 June 1991 *Employees:* 1
Net Worth Deficit: £3,170,226 *Total Assets:* £25,466,856
Registered Office: Parsons Lane, Hope Valley, Derbys, S33 6RB
Activities: Activities of head offices
Officers: Dr Jurgen Pankratz [1965] Director [German]

Verdon Holdings Limited
Incorporated: 13 February 2017 *Employees:* 107
Net Worth: £3,484,342 *Total Assets:* £9,383,555
Registered Office: Charnwood House, Harcourt Way, Meridian Business Park, Leicester, LE19 1WP
Activities: Wholesale of wood, construction materials and sanitary equipment
Officers: John Terence Badham [1965] Director; Stephen Alfred Grady [1958] Director; Andrew William Jones [1969] Director; Jonathan Phillip Oram [1969] Director

Vernon Finance Limited
Incorporated: 20 June 2013 *Employees:* 3
Net Worth: £18,054,772 *Total Assets:* £22,111,988
Registered Office: 3 Castlegate, Grantham, Lincs, NG31 6SF
Activities: Activities of other holding companies n.e.c.
Officers: Christian James Roy Vernon [1971] Director; Dean John Vernon [1966] Director; John Michael Vernon [1945] Director

Vernon Holdings Limited
Incorporated: 24 March 2009 *Employees:* 5
Net Worth: £16,179,641 *Total Assets:* £43,320,692
Registered Office: 3 Castlegate, Grantham, Lincs, NG31 6SF
Activities: Other letting and operating of own or leased real estate
Shareholder: John Michael Vernon
Officers: Dean John Vernon, Secretary; Christian James Roy Vernon [1971] Director; Dean John Vernon [1967] Director; John Michael Vernon [1945] Director

Versalift Distributors (U.K.) Limited
Incorporated: 17 January 1994 *Employees:* 80
Net Worth: £4,118,380 *Total Assets:* £12,394,212
Registered Office: 1 Altendiez Way, Burton Latimer, Kettering, Northants, NN15 5YT
Activities: Installation of industrial machinery and equipment
Parent: Time Manufacturing Acquisition (UK) Limited
Officers: Andrew David Bray [1971] Commercial Director; Curt Howell [1962] Director [American]; Jay Jeffrey [1959] Director [American]; Kim Jensen [1969] Director [Danish]

Versus Arthritis
Incorporated: 13 January 1951 *Employees:* 255
Previous: Arthritis Research UK
Net Worth: £214,591,008 *Total Assets:* £230,559,008
Registered Office: Copeman House, St Marys Gate, Chesterfield, Derbys, S41 7TD
Activities: Other human health activities
Officers: Justin Parfitt, Secretary; Peter John Anscombe [1953] Director/Retired; Professor Jonathan Cohen [1949] Director/Retired; Phillip Henry Gray [1949] Director/Retired; Thomas Edward George Hayhoe [1956] Director; Alex Hesz [1982] Director/Advertising; Karin Kristina Hogsander [1972] Director/Head of M&A [Swedish]; Professor David Alan Isenberg [1949] Academic Director of Rheumatology; Dr Sylvia Jackson [1956] Director/University Lecturer; Professor Sarah Elizabeth Lamb [1965] Director/Professor; Dr Rodger Martin McMillan [1953] Director/Research and Development Consultant; Juliette Maria Scott [1967] Director; Professor Martijn Pieter Marie Steultjens [1972] Director/Medical Scientist [Dutch]; Dr Ian Walters [1943] Director/Retired

Vesso Limited
Incorporated: 12 October 2015 *Employees:* 2
Net Worth: £204,284 *Total Assets:* £18,647,436
Registered Office: Ferrymoor Way, Park Springs, Grimethorpe, Barnsley, S Yorks, S72 7BN
Activities: Activities of head offices
Parent: Carentan Holdings Limited
Officers: John Stewart Ross [1965] Director

Vesuvius UK Limited
Incorporated: 5 November 1897 *Employees:* 307
Net Worth: £78,543,000 *Total Assets:* £135,746,000
Registered Office: 1 Midland Way, Central Park, Barlborough Links, Chesterfield, Derbys, S43 4XA
Activities: Manufacture of refractory products
Parent: Vesuvius-Premier Refractories (Holdings) Limited
Officers: Michael Satterthwaite, Secretary; Henry James Knowles [1969] Director/Company Secretary; Ian James Lawson [1968] Director/Accountant; Michael Satterthwaite [1967] Finance Director; Sunderrajan Venkatraman [1960] Director/Vice President Finance - Advanced Refractories [Indian]

VGI Holdings Limited
Incorporated: 20 March 2017 *Employees:* 102
Net Worth: £7,551,001 *Total Assets:* £15,121,763
Registered Office: V Group International Limited, Unit 7 Erica Road, Stacey Bushes, Milton Keynes, Bucks, MK12 6HS
Activities: Activities of other holding companies n.e.c.
Major Shareholder: Martyn Derek Nash
Officers: James Nash [1985] Director; Martyn Derek Nash [1959] Director

Viad Service Companies Limited
Incorporated: 26 June 1974 *Employees:* 64
Net Worth: £10,250,000 *Total Assets:* £14,624,000
Registered Office: GES, Silverstone Drive, Gallagher Business Park, Coventry, Warwicks, CV6 6PA
Activities: Activities of head offices
Officers: Michael Stewart, Secretary; Ellen Marie Ingersoll [1964] Director/Financial Officer [American]; Steven Moster [1970] Director/Chairman, President and CEO of Viad Corp [American]; Jason Popp [1970] Director/Vice President [American]

Vicon Motion Systems Limited
Incorporated: 20 March 1984 *Employees:* 63
Net Worth: £9,283,000 *Total Assets:* £22,419,000
Registered Office: 6 Oxford Industrial Park, Yarnton, Oxon, OX5 1QU
Activities: Manufacture of electronic measuring, testing etc. equipment, not for industrial process control
Parent: Oxford Metrics PLC
Officers: Catherine Lindsay Robertson, Secretary; Nicholas Paul Bolton [1969] Director; David Anthony Deacon [1960] Director; Catherine Lindsay Robertson [1958] Director/Company Secretary; Thomas Michael Lawrence Shannon [1952] Director/Engineer

Victim Support
Incorporated: 28 August 1987 *Employees:* 1,057
Net Worth: £7,756,000 *Total Assets:* £11,649,000
Registered Office: 1 Bridge Street, Derby, DE1 3HZ
Activities: Other social work activities without accommodation n.e.c.
Officers: Anthony Gerard Silcock, Secretary; Kathryn Adkins [1980] Director/Certified Accountant; Joanne Cumbley [1972] Director/Barrister; Christopher Digby-Bell [1948] Director/Solicitor; Elizabeth Dymond [1966] Director/Chartered Accountant; Andrew Richard Edwards [1956] Director/University Teaching Fellow; Roger James Harding [1982] Director/Consultant; Leslie Mosco [1954] Director/Retired; Geoff Pollard [1945] Director/Retired; Lianne Smith [1983] Director/Banker; Andrew David Tivey [1958] Director/Chartered Accountant; Moyna Wilkinson [1950] Director/Trustee

Victoria (Bavaria) Limited
Incorporated: 20 November 1987 *Employees:* 79
Net Worth: £16,953,000 *Total Assets:* £34,087,000
Registered Office: Loxley House, 2 Oakwood Court, Little Oak Drive, Annesley, Nottingham, NG15 0DR
Activities: Sale of new cars and light motor vehicles
Parent: Reg Vardy Limited
Officers: Richard James Maloney, Secretary; Martin Shaun Casha [1960] Director; Trevor Garry Finn [1957] Director; Timothy Paul Holden [1964] Director/Chartered Accountant

Victoria Square Woking Limited
Incorporated: 26 March 2012
Previous: Bandstand Square Developments Limited
Net Worth Deficit: £11,457,234 *Total Assets:* £74,292,096
Registered Office: 5 Olympus Court, Olympus Avenue, Leamington Spa, Warwicks, CV34 6RZ
Activities: Development of building projects
Parent: Moyallen Holdings Limited
Officers: Paul Hearn, Secretary; David John Bittleston [1957] Director; Robert John Kingsbury [1963] Director/Retired; Raymond Nigel Morgan [1953] Director/Chief Executive; John Thomas Alexander Robinson [1964] Director; Peter Arthur Hayes Robinson [1961] Director

Vidal Group Holdings Ltd
Incorporated: 18 February 2013
Previous: Medica EMEA (Holdco) Limited
Net Worth Deficit: £3,503,552 *Total Assets:* £10,692,718
Registered Office: 2nd Floor, 20 Western Avenue, Milton Park, Milton, Abingdon, Oxon, OX14 4SH
Activities: Activities of head offices
Parent: Axio Medical Holdings Limited
Officers: Chris Thiele, Secretary; Anton Richter [1975] Director; Itaru Tanimura [1965] Director [Japanese]; Akihiko Tomaru [1972] Director [Japanese]

Videojet Technologies Limited
Incorporated: 6 December 2006 *Employees:* 117
Net Worth: £14,278,000 *Total Assets:* £29,508,000
Registered Office: 4 & 5 Ermine Centre, Lancaster Way, Huntingdon, Cambs, PE29 6XX
Activities: Manufacture of other special-purpose machinery n.e.c.
Parent: Launchchange Operations Limited
Officers: Pavan Khanna, Secretary; Ranjana Bhagwakar [1971] Director/VP Finance [American]; Stephen Hayes [1973] Director; Keith Graham Ward [1953] Director

Viewtone Limited
Incorporated: 30 October 1996 *Employees:* 2
Net Worth: £5,093,000 *Total Assets:* £15,516,000
Registered Office: Seebeck House, One Seebeck Place, Knowlhill, Milton Keynes, Bucks, MK5 8FR
Activities: Activities of head offices
Parent: Viewtone Trading Group Limited
Officers: Karen Mona Gunter [1963] Finance Director; Kevin Gunter [1961] Managing Director

Viewtone Trading Group Limited
Incorporated: 6 October 2010 *Employees:* 919
Net Worth: £3,318,000 *Total Assets:* £9,707,000
Registered Office: Unit 6 Bretton Point, Dearne Mills, Darton, Barnsley, S Yorks, S75 5NH
Activities: Activities of head offices
Shareholders: Karen Mona Gunter; Kevin Gunter
Officers: Karen Mona Gunter [1963] Finance Director; Kevin Gunter [1961] Managing Director; Carel Stassen [1950] Director/Self Employed

Viking Direct (Holdings) Limited
Incorporated: 27 February 1992
Net Worth: £48,320,000 *Total Assets:* £200,803,008
Registered Office: 501 Beaumont Leys Lane, Leicester, LE4 2BN
Activities: Activities of head offices
Parent: Office Depot (Holdings) Limited
Officers: Jacqueline Susan Hills, Secretary; Neil David Maslen [1972] Director/SVP Contract Europe; Michael William Walby [1973] Managing Director [Irish]

F. Vindis & Sons (Bedford) Limited
Incorporated: 23 September 1994 *Employees:* 387
Net Worth: £8,838,400 *Total Assets:* £55,199,932
Registered Office: Vindis House, Washingley Road, Huntingdon, Cambs, PE29 6WP
Activities: Sale of new cars and light motor vehicles
Parent: Vindis Group Ltd
Officers: Stephen Geoffrey Fossey, Secretary; Gary Frank Vindis [1945] Director; Jamie Francis Vindis [1976] Managing Director

F. Vindis & Sons (Sawston) Limited
Incorporated: 17 February 1984 *Employees:* 93
Net Worth: £7,417,160 *Total Assets:* £15,575,142
Registered Office: Vindis House, Washingley Road, Huntingdon, Cambs, PE29 6WP
Activities: Sale of new cars and light motor vehicles
Parent: Vindis Group Ltd
Officers: Stephen Geoffrey Fossey, Secretary; Gary Frank Vindis [1945] Director; Jamie Francis Vindis [1976] Managing Director

Vindis Developments Limited
Incorporated: 2 August 1983 *Employees:* 87
Net Worth: £4,144,902 *Total Assets:* £19,585,020
Registered Office: Vindis House, Washingley Road, Huntingdon, Cambs, PE29 6WP
Activities: Sale of new cars and light motor vehicles
Parent: Vindis Group Ltd
Officers: Stephen Geoffrey Fossey, Secretary; Gary Frank Vindis [1945] Director; Jamie Francis Vindis [1976] Managing Director

Vindis Group Limited
Incorporated: 18 January 1985 *Employees:* 887
Net Worth: £21,380,992 *Total Assets:* £111,467,584
Registered Office: Vindis House, Washingley Road, Huntingdon, Cambs, PE29 6WP
Activities: Sale of new cars and light motor vehicles
Shareholders: Gary Frank Vindis; Estate of Nigel Anthony Vindis
Officers: Stephen Geoffrey Fossey, Secretary; Gary Frank Vindis [1945] Director; Jamie Francis Vindis [1976] Managing Director

Vine Hotels Limited
Incorporated: 26 May 2015 *Employees:* 146
Net Worth: £3,217,149 *Total Assets:* £19,980,616
Registered Office: c/o Director of Finance, Kenwood Hall Hotel, Kenwood Road, Sheffield, S7 1NQ
Activities: Hotels and similar accommodation
Major Shareholder: Susan Howes
Officers: Andrew Gerard Rouse, Secretary; Garin James Davies [1967] Director; Gregory Dyke [1947] Director; Susan Howes [1949] Director; Andrew Gerard Rouse [1960] Director

Vine Kenwood Limited
Incorporated: 29 June 2016 *Employees:* 104
Net Worth: £4,574,816 *Total Assets:* £13,863,118
Registered Office: c/o Director of Finance, Kenwood Hall Hotel, Kenwood Road, Sheffield, S7 1NQ
Activities: Hotels and similar accommodation
Officers: Garin James Davies [1967] Director; Gregory Dyke [1947] Director; Susan Howes [1949] Director; Andrew Gerard Rouse [1960] Director

Vine Mill Limited
Incorporated: 24 July 2007
Net Worth: £46,025,000 *Total Assets:* £50,221,000
Registered Office: 5400 Lakeside, Cheadle Royal Business Park, Cheadle, Cheshire, SK8 3GQ
Activities: Agents involved in the sale of furniture, household goods, hardware and ironmongery
Parent: Pulse Home Products (Holdings) Limited
Officers: Ben Hartley [1976] Director/Attorney; Benjamin James Sturgell [1981] Director/Attorney [American]

Vinters Engineering Limited
Incorporated: 17 April 1867 *Employees:* 40
Net Worth Deficit: £800,000 *Total Assets:* £76,100,000
Registered Office: Rolls Royce PLC, Moor Lane, Derby, DE24 8BJ
Activities: Manufacture of other parts and accessories for motor vehicles
Parent: Vinters Limited
Officers: William Scott Mansfield [1964] Director/Group Chief Accountant

Vinters International Limited
Incorporated: 16 December 1954
Net Worth Deficit: £165,900,992 *Total Assets:* £2,652,931,072
Registered Office: Rolls Royce PLC, Moor Lane, Derby, DE24 8BJ
Activities: Activities of head offices
Parent: Vinters Engineering Limited
Officers: William Scott Mansfield [1964] Director/Group Chief Accountant

Vinyl Compounds Holdings Limited
Incorporated: 8 June 2015
Net Worth: £5,011,569 *Total Assets:* £15,127,357
Registered Office: c/o Mexichem, 8 Beler Way, Leicester Road Industrial Estate, Melton Mowbray, Leics, LE13 0DG
Activities: Activities of other holding companies n.e.c.
Parent: Mexichem Resinas Vinilicas S.A. de C.V.
Officers: Daniel Jean Delisle [1965] Director/General Manager [American]; Michael Ray Funderburg [1958] Director [American]; Gautam Nivarthy [1973] Director/Businessman [American]

Virani Food Products Limited
Incorporated: 6 July 1973 *Employees:* 51
Net Worth: £2,054,848 *Total Assets:* £10,288,916
Registered Office: 10-14 Stewarts Road, Finedon Road Industrial Estate, Wellingborough, Northants, NN8 4RJ
Activities: Grain milling
Shareholder: Naresh Shah
Officers: Milan Naresh Shah [1971] Director; Nareshbabu Devshi Shah [1946] Director; Tanoj Jivraj Shah [1963] Director

Vision Express (UK) Limited
Incorporated: 6 November 1987 *Employees:* 3,375
Net Worth: £106,943,000 *Total Assets:* £182,490,000
Registered Office: Ruddington Fields Business Park, Mere Way, Ruddington, Nottingham, NG11 6NZ
Activities: Other business support service activities n.e.c.
Parent: Vision Express Group Limited
Officers: Nicholas Dermott Vance Allen, Secretary; Ranald George Allan [1964] Director; Nicholas Dermott Vance Allen [1968] Director/Chief Financial Officer; Philip Martin Hyde [1966] Director/Head of Central Retail Operations; Onur Koksal [1976] Director/Chief Executive [Turkish]; Jonathan Mark Lawson [1971] Director

Vision Express Group Limited
Incorporated: 16 June 1994 *Employees:* 2
Net Worth: £88,671,000 *Total Assets:* £90,455,000
Registered Office: Mere Way, Ruddington Fields Business Park, Ruddington, Nottingham, NG11 6NZ
Activities: Other service activities n.e.c.
Parent: Vision Express Limited
Officers: Nicholas Dermott Vance Allen, Secretary; Nicholas Dermott Vance Allen [1968] Director/Chief Financial Officer; Onur Koksal [1996] Director/Chief Executive [Turkish]

Vision Express Limited
Incorporated: 22 November 2012
Net Worth: £49,166,964 *Total Assets:* £173,711,360
Registered Office: Mere Way, Ruddington Fields Business Park, Ruddington, Nottingham, NG11 6NZ
Activities: Other business support service activities n.e.c.
Officers: Nicholas Dermott Vance Allen, Secretary; Nicholas Dermott Vance Allen [1968] Director/Chief Financial Officer; Onur Koksal [1976] Director/Chief Executive [Turkish]

Vista Engineering Limited
Incorporated: 24 July 1979 *Employees:* 62
Net Worth: £7,979,460 *Total Assets:* £11,700,160
Registered Office: Carr Brook Works, Elnor Lane, Whaley Bridge, High Peak, Derbys, SK23 7JN
Activities: Manufacture of wire products, chain and springs
Shareholders: Gillian Travis; David Travis
Officers: Gillian Travis, Secretary; David Travis [1942] Director/Engineer; Gillian Travis [1943] Director/Secretary; Philip David Travis [1969] Director; Sarah Ann Travis [1969] Director

Vita First Street Limited
Incorporated: 13 October 2015
Net Worth: £7,435,000 *Total Assets:* £42,261,000
Registered Office: The Box, Horseshoe Lane, Alderley Edge, Cheshire, SK9 7QP
Activities: Other letting and operating of own or leased real estate
Parent: New Co (First Street) 2 Ltd
Officers: Giles Beswick, Secretary; Giles Peter Beswick [1974] Director; Mark Christopher Dawson [1973] Director; Michael Keith Slater [1974] Director; Mark David Stott [1972] Director

Vita Satellite 1 Limited
Incorporated: 16 December 2015
Net Worth: £10,445,000 *Total Assets:* £53,357,000
Registered Office: The Box, Horseshoe Lane, Alderley Edge, Cheshire, SK9 7QP
Activities: Activities of production holding companies
Parent: Vita Ventures Ltd
Officers: Giles Beswick, Secretary; Giles Peter Beswick [1974] Director; Mark Christopher Dawson [1973] Director; Kenneth John Knott [1959] Director; Michael Keith Slater [1974] Director

Vita Student Southampton Portswood Limited
Incorporated: 19 April 2016
Net Worth Deficit: £9,000 *Total Assets:* £39,417,000
Registered Office: The Box, Horseshoe Lane, Alderley Edge, Cheshire, SK9 7QP
Activities: Development of building projects
Parent: Vita Southampton Portswood Holdco 2 Limited
Officers: Giles Beswick, Secretary; Giles Peter Beswick [1974] Director; Mark Christopher Dawson [1973] Director; Mark David Stott [1972] Director

Vita Student York Holding Company Limited
Incorporated: 24 August 2015
Net Worth: £3,459,000 *Total Assets:* £11,699,000
Registered Office: The Box, Horseshoe Lane, Alderley Edge, Cheshire, SK9 7QP
Activities: Development of building projects
Parent: Vita Ventures Ltd
Officers: Giles Beswick, Secretary; Giles Peter Beswick [1974] Director; Mark Christopher Dawson [1973] Director; Mark David Stott [1972] Director

Vita York 1 Limited
Incorporated: 14 May 2014
Net Worth: £1,564,000 *Total Assets:* £13,538,000
Registered Office: The Box, Horseshoe Lane, Alderley Edge, Cheshire, SK9 7QP
Activities: Buying and selling of own real estate
Parent: Vita Ventures Limited
Officers: Giles Giles Beswick, Secretary; Giles Peter Beswick [1974] Director; Mark Christopher Dawson [1973] Director; Mark David Stott [1972] Director

Vital Pet Group Limited
Incorporated: 10 November 2004 *Employees:* 119
Previous: L. Batley Pet Products Limited
Net Worth: £7,829,854 *Total Assets:* £12,748,496
Registered Office: Unit 8 Pennine House, 35a Churchill Way, Sheffield, S35 2PY
Activities: Non-specialised wholesale trade
Parent: Paramount Retail Group Holdings Limited
Officers: Ravi Sharma [1986] Director; Sunny Sharma [1984] Director

Vivarail Ltd
Incorporated: 22 August 2013 *Employees:* 25
Net Worth: £17,201,238 *Total Assets:* £18,085,264
Registered Office: Quinton Rail Technology Centre, Station Road, Long Marston, Stratford upon Avon, Warwicks, CV37 8PL
Activities: Manufacture of railway locomotives and rolling stock
Parent: Railroad Development Corp
Officers: Ian David Wenman, Secretary; Neil William Bates [1955] Director; Colin Flack [1958] Director; John Hensler [1961] Director [American]; David Anthony King [1947] Director; William Berryman Morrow [1948] Director; Robert Pietrandrea [1952] Director [American]; Henry Posner [1955] Director [American]; Adrian Shooter [1948] Director; Ian David Wenman [1957] Director/Chartered Accountant

VJ Holdco UK Limited
Incorporated: 5 April 2016 *Employees:* 1
Net Worth: £49,529,000 *Total Assets:* £49,539,000
Registered Office: 19 Jessops Riverside, 800 Brightside Lane, Sheffield, S9 2RX
Activities: Activities of head offices
Parent: Danaher Corporation
Officers: Keith Graham Ward [1953] Director

VM Fabrics Limited
Incorporated: 2 June 2010 *Employees:* 134
Net Worth: £633,391 *Total Assets:* £12,739,089
Registered Office: 109 Coleman Road, Leicester, LE5 4LE
Activities: Weaving of textiles
Shareholders: Vincent McGee; Caroline McGee
Officers: Vince McGee, Secretary; Salim Mohammed Dadabhai [1976] Director; Vincent John McGee [1966] Director

Vocare Limited
Incorporated: 31 December 2015 *Employees:* 1,158
Net Worth: £1,692,012 *Total Assets:* £18,258,656
Registered Office: First Floor West, Cardinal Square, 10 Nottingham Road, Derby, DE1 3QT
Activities: General medical practice activities
Parent: Totally PLC
Officers: John William Charles Charlton, Secretary; Lisa Barter-NG [1971] Finance Director; Gloria Ann Cooke [1953] Director/Health Care Manager; Barry John Cooper [1978] Operations Director; Andrew John Gregory [1972] Managing Director; William James Heptinstall [1982] Medical Director; Wendy Jayne Lawrence [1961] Director; Heather Anne Maughan [1958] Director of Quality and Nursing

Volkswagen Financial Services (UK) Limited
Incorporated: 12 July 1993 *Employees:* 929
Net Worth: £1,245,260,032 *Total Assets:* £14,847,398,912
Registered Office: Brunswick Court, Yeomans Drive, Blakelands, Milton Keynes, Bucks, MK14 5LR
Activities: Financial intermediation not elsewhere classified
Parent: Volkswagen Aktiengesellschaft
Officers: Harald Hesske [1962] Director [German]; Jens Legenbauer [1965] Director [German]; Dr Michael Eberhard Reinhart [1963] Director [German]; Michael John Todd [1966] Director/Chief Executive; Albertus Antonius Maria Van Den Bergh [1961] Director [Dutch]; Patrick Ortwin Welter [1969] Director [German]

Volkswagen Group United Kingdom Limited
Incorporated: 1 January 1953 *Employees:* 1,028
Net Worth: £719,299,968 *Total Assets:* £3,532,100,096
Registered Office: Yeomans Drive, Blakelands, Milton Keynes, Bucks, MK14 5AN
Activities: Sale of new cars and light motor vehicles
Parent: Volkswagen Aktiengesellschaft
Officers: James Trainor, Secretary; Christian Dahlheim [1968] Director/Chairman [German]; Ulf Konrad Dierkesmann [1975] Director/Head of Sales Europe West/South [German]; Lukas Folc [1978] Finance Director [Czech]; Jaroslav Hercog [1973] Director [Slovak]; Manfred Kantner [1966] Director Sales Europe [Austrian]; Fintan Roger Knight [1971] Director/Audi Vice President Sales - Europe; Michael Alexander Obrowski [1969] Director [German]; Alexander James Campbell Smith [1974] Managing Director; Dr. Jan Utermarck [1967] Executive Director Sales Europe [German]

Volvo Group UK Limited
Incorporated: 10 November 1987 *Employees:* 1,693
Net Worth: £149,980,000 *Total Assets:* £693,393,024
Registered Office: Wedgnock Lane, Warwick, CV34 5YA
Activities: Sale of other motor vehicles
Parent: AB Volvo
Officers: Simon Villanueva, Secretary; Roger Alm [1962] Director [Swedish]; Arne Knaben [1958] Director [Norwegian]; Carlos Oliveira Rodrigues [1977] Director/Chief Financial Officer [Portuguese]; Simon Derek Villanueva [1973] Director

Vow Europe Limited
Incorporated: 20 March 1975 *Employees:* 1,430
Net Worth: £7,086,000 *Total Assets:* £202,806,000
Registered Office: K House, Sheffield Business Park, Europa Link, Sheffield, S9 1XU
Activities: Non-specialised wholesale trade
Parent: Vasanta Group Limited
Officers: Lorna Kathleen Mendelsohn, Secretary; Adrian Peter Butler [1972] Managing Director; Andrew Peter Gale [1970] Finance Director; Stephen Haworth [1970] Director/Group CEO; Jonathan Rolfe [1968] Group Operations Director

Vow Retail Limited
Incorporated: 4 March 2005 *Employees:* 27
Net Worth: £13,664,000 *Total Assets:* £22,300,000
Registered Office: K House, Sheffield Business Park, Europa Link, Sheffield, S9 1XU
Activities: Other business support service activities n.e.c.
Parent: Vow Europe Limited
Officers: Lorna Kathleen Mendelsohn, Secretary; Andrew Peter Gale [1970] Finance Director; Stephen Haworth [1970] Director/Group CEO; Cheryl Lamont [1976] Sales and Marketing Director

VR Finance Company
Incorporated: 28 August 1997 *Employees:* 1
Previous: Veeder-Root Finance Company
Net Worth: £3,677,701,888 *Total Assets:* £3,686,706,944
Registered Office: 19 Jessops Riverside, 800 Brightside Lane, Sheffield, S9 2RX
Activities: Financial intermediation not elsewhere classified
Parent: Launchchange Holding Company
Officers: Keith Graham Ward [1953] Director

VRES Holdings Limited
Incorporated: 17 March 1949
Previous: Veeder-Root Environmental Systems Limited
Net Worth: £13,767,000 *Total Assets:* £15,088,000
Registered Office: 19 Jessops Riverside, 800 Brightside Lane, Sheffield, S9 2RX
Activities: Activities of head offices
Parent: Launchchange Limited
Officers: Keith Graham Ward [1953] Director/Finance & Accounting

Vtech Electronics Europe PLC
Incorporated: 14 October 1987 *Employees:* 36
Net Worth: £13,427,000 *Total Assets:* £26,760,000
Registered Office: Napier Court, Abingdon Science Park, Abingdon, Oxon, OX14 3YT
Activities: Wholesale of electronic and telecommunications equipment and parts
Parent: VTech Electronics Europe B.V.
Officers: Stephen Mason, Secretary; Yu Wai Chang [1959] Director/Business Executive; Hon Kwong Andy Leung [1958] Director/Business Executive [Canadian]; King Fai Pang [1955] Director/Business Executive [American]; Ka Hung Tong [1968] Director/Business Executive [Chinese]; Chi Yun Allan Wong [1950] Director [Chinese]

Vulcan Engineering Limited
Incorporated: 14 September 1989 *Employees:* 86
Net Worth: £20,590,198 *Total Assets:* £22,233,164
Registered Office: Unit 3 South West Centre, Troutbeck Road, Sheffield, S8 0JR
Activities: Non-specialised wholesale trade
Shareholders: A.E.S Engineering Limted; A.E.S Engineerling Limited
Officers: Generald Peter Quinn, Secretary; Gordon Wilson Bridge [1944] Director; Michael James Carter [1967] Director; Stephen Martin Dodd [1956] Director; Generald Peter Quinn [1959] Director

Vulcan SFM Limited
Incorporated: 23 May 2003 *Employees:* 5
Net Worth: £7,181,000 *Total Assets:* £17,926,000
Registered Office: P O Box 286, Brightside Lane, Sheffield, S9 2RW
Activities: Casting of other non-ferrous metals
Parent: Sheffield Forgemasters International Limited
Officers: Allan Geoffrey Skelton, Secretary; Paul Alexander Cahill [1964] Director; Stephen Hammell [1973] Director; Ian Robert Nicholls [1963] Director

VWR Holdco Limited
Incorporated: 12 March 2008 *Employees:* 3
Net Worth: £22,774,000 *Total Assets:* £120,099,000
Registered Office: VWR Holdco Limited, Hunter Boulevard, Magna Park, Lutterworth, Leics, LE17 4XN
Activities: Activities of distribution holding companies
Parent: VWR Corporation
Officers: Karen Pulford, Secretary; Bernd Goell [1969] Director/VP Finance-Treasury [German]; William Patrick Hogan [1959] Managing Director [Irish]; Karen Jane Pulford [1968] Director/Chartered Accountant

VWR International Ltd
Incorporated: 23 July 1985 *Employees:* 412
Net Worth: £37,313,000 *Total Assets:* £70,478,000
Registered Office: Hunter Boulevard, Magna Park, Lutterworth, Leics, LE17 4XN
Activities: Wholesale of chemical products
Parent: VWR Holdco Limited
Officers: Karen Pulford, Secretary; Bernd Goell [1969] Director/VP Finance-Treasury [German]; Bill Hogan [1959] Managing Director [Irish]; Karen Jane Pulford [1968] Director/Chartered Accountant

W.& S.(Long Eaton) Limited
Incorporated: 29 May 1962 *Employees:* 14
Net Worth: £2,465,073 *Total Assets:* £11,475,749
Registered Office: Unit 1 Sheets Stores Industrial Estate, Long Eaton, Nottingham, NG10 1AU
Activities: Construction of domestic buildings
Shareholders: Matthew James Stanton; Andrew Paul Stanton
Officers: Andrew Paul Stanton, Secretary; Andrew Paul Stanton [1959] Director/Building Manager; Matthew James Stanton [1964] Director/Building Manager

W.L. Shareholding Company Limited
Incorporated: 23 July 1958 *Employees:* 1,353
Net Worth: £102,009,000 *Total Assets:* £275,150,016
Registered Office: 30 St Giles, Oxford, OX1 3LE
Activities: Activities of head offices
Officers: Fenella Mary Pearey, Secretary; Charles Richard Dick [1950] Director; Edward John Richard Dick [1989] Director/Solicitor; Ian Charles Dick [1979] Director/Estate Manager; Robert Ian Dick [1939] Director; Jonathan Charles Finch-Dick [1980] Director/Chartered Surveyor; Christopher Robert Levick [1948] Director

W.N. Developments Limited
Incorporated: 20 February 1987
Net Worth: £28,460,100 *Total Assets:* £36,522,976
Registered Office: 13 College Road, Bedford, MK42 9PL
Activities: Development of building projects
Shareholder: Seamus Neville
Officers: Therese Kelly, Secretary; Michelle Nolan, Secretary/Office Administrator [Irish]; Edmond William Daly [1963] Director/Surveyor [Irish]; Therese Kelly [1982] Director [Irish]; Brendan Neville [1960] Director [Irish]; Eoin Neville [1985] Director/Site Manager [Irish]; Seamus Neville [1952] Director [Irish]; William Neville [1980] Director [Irish]

WA Capital Investments Limited
Incorporated: 29 January 2014
Net Worth Deficit: £93,286,056 *Total Assets:* £201,000,880
Registered Office: Two Marlborough Court, Watermead Business Park, Syston, Leicester, LE7 1AD
Activities: Non-trading company
Parent: WA Capital Limited
Officers: William Lester Adderley [1972] Director; Darren Lee Wright [1977] Director/Chartered Accountant

WA Capital Limited
Incorporated: 6 July 2010 *Employees:* 6
Net Worth: £438,977,728 *Total Assets:* £466,599,200
Registered Office: Two Marlborough Court, Watermead Business Park, Syston, Leics, LE7 1AD
Activities: Non-trading company
Major Shareholder: William Lester Adderley
Officers: William Lester Adderley [1972] Director; Marion Jane Sears [1962] Director; Darren Lee Wright [1977] Director/Chartered Accountant

Wabtec Rail Limited
Incorporated: 27 April 1994 *Employees:* 1,328
Net Worth: £60,730,000 *Total Assets:* £233,163,008
Registered Office: Howard House, Graycar Business Park, Barton under Needwood, Staffs, DE13 8EN
Activities: Machining
Parent: Wabtec Air Brake Technologies Corporation
Officers: Michael James Isaac, Secretary; Raymond Theodore Betler [1955] Director/VP and Group Executive [American]; Christopher John Weatherall [1961] Managing Director

Wabtec UK Holdings Limited
Incorporated: 8 April 2011
Net Worth: £529,938,816 *Total Assets:* £1,011,732,352
Registered Office: Howard House, Graycar Business Park, Barton under Needwood, Staffs, DE13 8EN
Activities: Activities of head offices
Parent: Westinghouse Air Brake Technologies Corporation
Officers: Michael James Isaac, Secretary; Richard Mark Cox [1968] Director [American]; John a Mastalerz Jnr [1966] Director/Group Financial Controller [American]; David Seitz [1965] Director [American]; Christopher John Weatherall [1961] Director

Wabtec UK Investments Limited
Incorporated: 2 November 2011
Net Worth: £332,922,816 *Total Assets:* £707,272,064
Registered Office: Howard House, Graycar Business Park, Barton under Needwood, Staffs, DE13 8EN
Activities: Non-trading company
Parent: Wabtec Air Brake Technologies Corporation
Officers: Michael James Isaac, Secretary; John a Mastalerz Jnr [1966] Director/Group Financial Controller [American]; David Seitz [1965] Director [American]; Christopher John Weatherall [1961] Director

Wacoal EMEA Ltd
Incorporated: 1 November 1920 *Employees:* 395
Net Worth: £22,466,000 *Total Assets:* £56,953,000
Registered Office: The Corsetry Factory, Rothwell Road, Desborough, Kettering, Northants, NN14 2PG
Activities: Manufacture of women's underwear
Parent: Wacoal Europe Limited
Officers: Vaughan Peter Waylett, Secretary; Joanne Elizabeth Benton [1965] Director; Dean Terence Cooper [1971] Commercial Director; Geoffrey Michael Embley [1963] Director/Accountant; Simon Nicholls [1961] Logistics Director; Laura Sarah Simon [1976] Brand Director; Vaughan Peter Waylett [1969] Finance Director; Andrew Michael Yeomans [1967] Supply Chain Director

Wacoal Europe Ltd
Incorporated: 29 September 1993 *Employees:* 9
Net Worth: £15,400,000 *Total Assets:* £29,762,000
Registered Office: The Corsetry Factory, Rothwell Road, Desborough, Northants, NN14 2PG
Activities: Activities of head offices
Parent: Wacoal Holdings Corp
Officers: Vaughan Peter Waylett, Secretary; Geoffrey Michael Embley [1963] Director/Accountant; Masao Kawai [1959] Director [Japanese]; Takuya Miura [1962] Director [Japanese]; Mitsuru Sekiguchi [1965] Director [Japanese]; Yoshikata Tsukamoto [1948] Director and Chairman [Japanese]; Masaya Wakabayashi [1956] Director [Japanese]; Vaughan Peter Waylett [1969] Finance Director

Ernest V. Waddington Limited
Incorporated: 27 January 1949 *Employees:* 18
Net Worth: £52,338,144 *Total Assets:* £66,493,952
Registered Office: 68 Queen Street, Sheffield, S1 1WR
Activities: Wholesale of wood, construction materials and sanitary equipment
Officers: Anthony Edward Waddington [1960] Director/Manager

Wade Furniture Group Limited
Incorporated: 5 August 1986 *Employees:* 4
Net Worth: £12,366,110 *Total Assets:* £14,709,265
Registered Office: Estate Office, Ravenstone Hall, Ashby Road, Ravenstone, Leics, LE67 2AA
Activities: Combined office administrative service activities
Officers: Jemima Elizabeth Wade, Secretary; John Anthony Higton [1945] Finance Director; Daniel Anthony Lampugh Wade [1976] Director/Chairman; Jemima Elizabeth Wade [1952] Director

Wade Group Limited
Incorporated: 3 October 2002 *Employees:* 640
Net Worth: £11,361,000 *Total Assets:* £26,197,000
Registered Office: Estate Office, Ravenstone Hall, Ashby Road, Ravenstone, Leics, LE67 2AA
Activities: Activities of head offices
Major Shareholder: Charles Colin Wade
Officers: John Anthony Higton, Secretary; Anthony Joseph Eagle [1947] Director; John Anthony Higton [1945] Director; Daniel Anthony Lamplugh Wade [1976] Director/Linen Buyer; Jemima Elizabeth Wade [1952] Director

Wade Spring Limited
Incorporated: 4 September 1992 *Employees:* 97
Net Worth: £6,213,105 *Total Assets:* £14,906,894
Registered Office: Estate Office, Ravenstone Hall, Ashby Road, Ravenstone, Leics, LE67 2AA
Activities: Manufacture of wire products, chain and springs
Major Shareholder: Charles Colin Wade
Officers: John Anthony Higton, Secretary; Stephen Grainger [1955] Production Director; John Anthony Higton [1945] Director; Daniel Anthony Lampugh Wade [1976] Director/Chairman; Christopher Charles Woodcock [1958] Director/Chartered Accountant

Wake One Limited
Incorporated: 22 June 2015
Net Worth: £16,746,168 *Total Assets:* £16,787,068
Registered Office: Fourth Floor, The Pinnacle, 160 Midsummer Boulevard, Milton Keynes, Bucks, MK9 1FF
Activities: Activities of venture and development capital companies
Major Shareholder: Luigi Sala
Officers: Davide Pietro Chiesa [1976] Director [Italian]; Alberto Pons [1967] Director/Management Consultant; Luigi Sala [1957] Director/Manager [Italian]

Wakefield Waste Holdings Limited
Incorporated: 22 December 2015
Net Worth Deficit: £12,444,000 *Total Assets:* £112,236,000
Registered Office: Dunedin House, Auckland Park, Mount Farm, Bletchley, Milton Keynes, Bucks, MK1 1BU
Activities: Non-trading company
Shareholders: Equitix Infrastructure 4 Limited; Renewi PFI Investments Limited
Officers: Philip Bernard Griffin-Smith, Secretary; Alistair Daniel Brookes [1976] Director/Accountant; Andrew Keith Harmer [1964] Investment Director; Richard Daniel Knight [1974] Director; Adam Nathaniel Richford [1976] Director; William Spurr [1964] Contract Director; Nathan John Wakefield [1974] Director

Wakefield Waste PFI Limited
Incorporated: 28 August 2012
Net Worth Deficit: £12,444,000 *Total Assets:* £112,236,000
Registered Office: Dunedin House, Auckland Park, Mount Farm, Milton Keynes, Bucks, MK1 1BU
Activities: Other service activities n.e.c.
Parent: Wakefield Waste PFI Holdings Limited
Officers: Philip Bernard Griffin-Smith, Secretary; Alistair Daniel Brookes [1976] Director; Andrew Keith Harmer [1964] Investment Director; Richard Daniel Knight [1974] Director; Adam Nathaniel Richford [1976] Director; William Spurr [1964] Director; Nathan John Wakefield [1974] Director

Waldersey Farms Limited
Incorporated: 7 March 1980 *Employees:* 31
Net Worth: £5,725,621 *Total Assets:* £13,519,531
Registered Office: Northfield Farm, Lynn Road, Southery, Downham Market, Norfolk, PE38 0HT
Activities: Growing of cereals (except rice), leguminous crops and oil seeds
Parent: South Yorkshire Pensions Authority
Officers: Robert Brian Loxton, Secretary; David Andrew Gardner [1958] Director/CEO - Royal Agricultural Society of England; Pamela Mary Gladwin [1968] Director; John Nicholas Hattersley [1954] Director/Investment Manager; Alastair John Kerr [1973] Director/Farmer; Robert Brian Loxton [1954] Director/Farm Consultant; Cedric William Porter [1967] Director; Stephen Tom Ward [1959] Director/Farmer

Wales High School Academy Trust
Incorporated: 10 September 2010 *Employees:* 255
Net Worth: £9,713,192 *Total Assets:* £12,402,351
Registered Office: Wales High School, Storth Lane, Kiveton Park, Sheffield, S26 5QQ
Activities: General secondary education
Officers: Laura Frances Mytts Redmile, Secretary; Cllr Dominic Beck [1992] Director/Local Councillor; John William Carlill [1953] Director; Charlotte Louise Victoria Cooper [1983] Director/Teacher; John Day [1946] Director/Retired; Giuseppe Di'iasio [1968] Director/Headteacher; Rachel Habergham [1966] Director/NHS Programme Head; Jacqueline Ann Fox Holcombe [1965] Director/Pharmacist; Jane Hopkinson [1966] Director/Civil Servant; Tracey Anne Manson Jervis [1967] Director/Foster Carer; Martin John Lister [1958] Director/European Contracts Manager; Daniel Stephen Ramsden [1981] Director/Broadcaster; Thomas David Sorby [1977] Director/Solicitor; Alexandra Jane Stott [1965] Director/Sole Trader; Philip Whitaker [1966] Director/Environmental Health Officer

Walker & Son (Hauliers) Limited
Incorporated: 8 May 1954 *Employees:* 87
Net Worth: £39,426,576 *Total Assets:* £47,106,508
Registered Office: Ollerton Road, Tuxford, Newark, Notts, NG22 0PQ
Activities: Other letting and operating of own or leased real estate
Major Shareholder: Richard Edward Walker
Officers: Lee John Bartrop, Secretary; Daniel Richard Edward Walker [1985] Director; James Walker [1986] Director; Richard Edward Walker [1953] Director/Haulage Contractor

A N Wallis & Company Limited
Incorporated: 14 April 2000 *Employees:* 60
Net Worth: £9,584,239 *Total Assets:* £14,582,818
Registered Office: Greasley Street, Nottingham, NG6 8NG
Activities: Other manufacturing n.e.c.
Officers: Steven James Healy, Secretary; Adrian John Ferrari-Stanford [1959] Managing Director; Steven James Healy [1968] Finance Director; Derek Nesbitt [1956] Managing Director; Ishaque Noor [1955] Group Managing Director [Pakistani]; Mark Vincent Rimmington [1964] Sales Director

Wallis Farms Limited
Incorporated: 28 October 1988 *Employees:* 7
Net Worth: £11,339,478 *Total Assets:* £13,107,936
Registered Office: 2 Michaels Court, Hanney Road, Southmoor, Abingdon, Oxon, OX13 5HR
Activities: Raising of poultry
Shareholder: Helen Wallis
Officers: Helen Wallis [1976] Director; Linda Wallis [1952] Director

Walls and Floors Limited
Incorporated: 30 January 2003 *Employees:* 185
Net Worth: £3,913,261 *Total Assets:* £14,606,462
Registered Office: Garrard Way, Telford Industrial Estate, Kettering, Northants, NN16 8TD
Activities: Wholesale of hardware, plumbing and heating equipment and supplies
Shareholders: Richard William Greenbank; Duncan Edward Lewin
Officers: Duncan Edward Lewin, Secretary; Richard William Greenbank [1958] Director/Chairman; Duncan Edward Lewin [1974] Director; Thomas Murrell [1986] E-Commerce Director; Benjamin Smith [1987] Retail Sales Director; John Patrick Steel [1959] Managing Director

S.Walsh & Son Limited
Incorporated: 5 May 1972 *Employees:* 160
Net Worth: £8,833,474 *Total Assets:* £29,036,976
Registered Office: Unit 10 Goldsmith Way, Eliot Business Park, Nuneaton, Warwicks, CV10 7RJ
Activities: Construction of other civil engineering projects n.e.c.
Parent: S Walsh Holdings Limited
Officers: Kerry Louise Barnett [1979] Finance Director; Jonathan Gareth Fisher [1977] Director; Joseph Charles Gifford [1978] Director; Westley Mercer [1980] Director; Martin Paul Reid [1967] Director; Nicholas Sean Walsh [1970] Director; Richard Joseph Walsh [1975] Director

S Walsh Holdings Limited
Incorporated: 4 October 2013
Net Worth: £4,971,641 *Total Assets:* £12,973,705
Registered Office: Unit 10 Goldsmith Way, Nuneaton, Warwicks, CV10 7RJ
Activities: Collection of non-hazardous waste
Parent: GRS Roadstone Group Limited
Officers: Kerry Louise Barnett [1979] Financial Director; Jonathan Gareth Fisher [1977] Director; Joseph Charles Gifford [1978] Director; Westley Mercer [1980] Director; Martin Paul Reid [1967] Director; Nicholas Sean Walsh [1970] Director; Richard Joseph Walsh [1975] Director

C. Walton Limited
Incorporated: 28 December 1955 *Employees:* 81
Net Worth: £17,838,864 *Total Assets:* £26,185,036
Registered Office: Bruntingthorpe Airfield, Proving Ground, Bruntingthorpe, Lutterworth, Leics, LE17 5QS
Activities: Growing of cereals (except rice), leguminous crops and oil seeds
Officers: John Rees Walton, Secretary; David William Walton [1952] Director; Elizabeth Walton [1960] Director/Accountant; John Rees Walton [1954] Director; Peter Alfred Walton [1956] Director

Wanfeng (UK) Aviation Co., Ltd
Incorporated: 24 November 2015
Net Worth: £89,550,968 *Total Assets:* £319,532,864
Registered Office: Orchard Way, Calladine Park, Sutton in Ashfield, Notts, NG17 1JU
Activities: Manufacture of other transport equipment n.e.c.
Shareholder: Ailian Chen
Officers: Rong Chen, Secretary; Bin Chen [1979] Director [Chinese]

Wanfeng MLTH Holdings Co., Ltd
Incorporated: 6 November 2013
Net Worth: £58,965,360 *Total Assets:* £60,138,720
Registered Office: Orchard Way, Calladine Park, Sutton in Ashfield, Notts, NG17 1JU
Activities: Manufacture of other transport equipment n.e.c.
Parent: Zhejiang Wanfeng Auto Wheel Co., Ltd
Officers: Rong Chen, Secretary; Ailian Chen [1958] Director [Chinese]; Bin Chen [1979] Director [Chinese]; Weijun Chen [1964] Director [Chinese]; Jian Luo [1971] Director [Chinese]; Yahong Zhao [1970] Director [Chinese]

Wanzl Limited
Incorporated: 4 December 1978 *Employees:* 272
Net Worth: £27,264,604 *Total Assets:* £37,270,076
Registered Office: Europa House, Heathcote Lane, Warwick, CV34 6SP
Activities: Non-specialised wholesale trade
Officers: Bernhard Renzhofer [1968] Managing Director of Wanzl Metallwarenfabrik GmbH [German]; Dean Michael Rolland [1975] Director

R.H. Ward (Welton) Limited
Incorporated: 12 June 1959 *Employees:* 9
Net Worth: £10,286,470 *Total Assets:* £11,188,828
Registered Office: Holme Farm, Welton Cliff, Lincoln, LN2 3PU
Activities: Growing of cereals (except rice), leguminous crops and oil seeds
Major Shareholder: John Robert Ward
Officers: Kate Anne Ward, Secretary; Lucy Jane Haxton [1983] Director; Edith Margaret Ward [1920] Director/Housewife; John Robert Ward [1953] Director/Farmer; Kate Anne Ward [1981] Director/Developer

T.W. Ward C.N.C. Machinery Limited
Incorporated: 18 October 1983 *Employees:* 42
Net Worth: £7,426,402 *Total Assets:* £13,290,806
Registered Office: Albion Works, Savile Street, Sheffield, S4 7UD
Activities: Installation of industrial machinery and equipment
Major Shareholder: Simon Jeremy Whitworth
Officers: Simon Jeremy Whitworth, Secretary; Stephen Keith Bodsworth [1960] Director; Simon Jeremy Whitworth [1961] Director

Ward Hi-Tech Limited
Incorporated: 15 December 1983 *Employees:* 29
Net Worth: £6,725,724 *Total Assets:* £10,236,854
Registered Office: Number One, Atlas Way, Sheffield, S4 7QQ
Activities: Agents involved in the sale of machinery, industrial equipment, ships and aircraft
Major Shareholder: Stephen Alan Hill
Officers: Kim Sharron Birch, Secretary; Stephen Alan Hill [1956] Director

Donald Ward Limited
Incorporated: 24 December 1976 *Employees:* 287
Net Worth: £23,117,176 *Total Assets:* £48,229,512
Registered Office: Rawdon Works, Moira Road, Woodville, Burton on Trent, Staffs, DE11 8DG
Activities: Collection of non-hazardous waste
Shareholders: Michael Ward; David Ward
Officers: Janet Ward, Secretary; James Jonathan Balfour [1969] Director/Accountant; Dennis Michael Bell [1952] Director/Commercial Executive; Toby Potter [1975] Business Development Director; Malcolm Earl Richards [1963] Commercial Director; David Ward [1961] Director/Metal Merchant; Janet Ward [1937] Director/Secretary; Michael Ward [1957] Director/Metal Merchant

Warehouse Fashions Holdings Limited
Incorporated: 13 February 2009 *Employees:* 1,287
Net Worth Deficit: £13,000,000 *Total Assets:* £37,800,000
Registered Office: The Triangle, Stanton Harcourt Industrial Estate, Stanton Harcourt, Witney, Oxon, OX29 5UT
Activities: Activities of head offices
Parent: Oasis and Warehouse Limited
Officers: Hashim Ladha [1974] Director; Sanam Soufipour [1972] Director; Paula Stewart [1971] Director

Warehouse Fashions Limited
Incorporated: 17 February 2009 *Employees:* 1,193
Net Worth Deficit: £17,800,000 *Total Assets:* £31,800,000
Registered Office: The Triangle, Stanton Harcourt Industrial Estate, Stanton Harcourt, Witney, Oxon, OX29 5UT
Activities: Retail sale of clothing in specialised stores
Parent: Warehouse Fashions Holdings Limited
Officers: Hashim Ladha [1974] Director; Sanam Soufipour [1972] Director; Paula Stewart [1971] Director

Warm A Home Limited
Incorporated: 19 June 1997
Net Worth: £223,350 *Total Assets:* £9,682,973
Registered Office: Adsetts House, 16 Europa View, Sheffield Business Park, Sheffield, S9 1XH
Activities: Dormant company
Parent: Hillsborough Investments Limited
Officers: Richard Charles Monro, Secretary; Ian Jackson [1979] Director/Accountant; Richard Charles Monro [1958] Director/Chartered Secretary

Warners (Midlands) Public Limited Company
Incorporated: 28 July 1927 *Employees:* 240
Net Worth: £23,456,612 *Total Assets:* £29,143,580
Registered Office: The Maltings, Manor Lane, Bourne, Lincs, PE10 9PH
Activities: Printing n.e.c.
Shareholder: Philip Andrew Warner
Officers: Stephen Aquila Warner, Secretary; Jeannette Marie Warner [1965] Director; Philip Andrew Warner [1967] Director; Stephen Aquila Warner [1965] Director

Warners Group Publications PLC
Incorporated: 7 January 1991 *Employees:* 200
Net Worth: £7,218,525 *Total Assets:* £11,162,679
Registered Office: The Maltings, Manor Lane, Bourne, Lincs, PE10 9PH
Activities: Publishing of consumer and business journals and periodicals
Major Shareholder: Stephen Aquila Warner
Officers: Stephen Aquila Warner, Secretary; Lisa Maria Warner [1967] Director; Philip Andrew Warner [1967] Director; Stephen Aquila Warner [1965] Director

Roger Warnes Transport Limited
Incorporated: 23 October 1984 *Employees:* 12
Net Worth: £7,417,074 *Total Assets:* £9,884,686
Registered Office: Great Dunham Hall, Great Dunham, Kings Lynn, Norfolk, PE32 2LQ
Activities: Freight transport by road
Major Shareholder: Roger Guy Warnes
Officers: Anita Mary Warnes, Secretary; Neville Richard Alderton [1953] Director/Transport Manager; Ian Barclay [1960] Operations Director; Anita Mary Warnes [1950] Director/Company Secretary; Benjamin Roger Warnes [1988] Director; Roger Guy Warnes [1941] Director/Haulier; Timothy John Warnes [1982] Director

The Warriner Multi Academy Trust
Incorporated: 21 July 2015 *Employees:* 295
Net Worth: £18,842,988 *Total Assets:* £22,946,990
Registered Office: Warriner School, Bloxham, Oxon, OX15 4LJ
Activities: Primary education
Officers: Frances Mary Bartlett [1970] Director/ODBE School Link Adviser; Ian Colin Broome [1968] Director/Software Engineer; Roger Steven Corke [1955] Director/Television Journalist; Brian John Heather [1963] Director/Accountant; Mark Edward Howarth [1966] Director/Procurement Manager; Dr Annabel Natalie Kay [1967] Director/Headteacher; Jennie Anne Perry [1976] Director/Early Years Advisory Teacher; Duncan Raper [1956] Finance Director; Janet Elizabeth Watts [1959] Director/Support Manager - Gastro Pub Company; Stephen Wilson [1959] Director/Retired

Warth Developments Ltd
Incorporated: 5 October 2012
Net Worth: £7,796,657 *Total Assets:* £12,694,023
Registered Office: Emerson Farmhouse, Farm Court, Shenley Brook End, Milton Keynes, Bucks, MK5 7GY
Activities: Dormant company
Major Shareholder: Philip Leslie Seymour Milne
Officers: Philip Leslie Seymour Milne [1965] Director

Dare Warwick (Properties) Limited
Incorporated: 5 March 1955 *Employees:* 7
Net Worth: £30,663,724 *Total Assets:* £30,970,922
Registered Office: Richmead, Broadway, Didcot, Oxon, OX11 8DJ
Activities: Development of building projects
Officers: Juliet Claire Barwell, Secretary; Gillian Margaret Georgina Allen [1944] Director; Juliet Claire Barwell [1974] Director; Olivia Charlotte Ferrero [1978] Director; Lucy Gillian Ockenden [1968] Director; Sarah Kate Rose [1972] Director; James William Dare Warwick [1973] Director; Richard Dare Warwick [1941] Director

Warwick Care Limited
Incorporated: 26 February 2008 *Employees:* 239
Net Worth: £1,561,433 *Total Assets:* £11,132,863
Registered Office: Maranatha, Coventry Road, Cawston, Rugby, Warwicks, CV22 7RY
Activities: Activities of head offices
Shareholders: Rod Pettifer; Helen Teresa Pettifer
Officers: Helen Teresa Pettifer, Secretary; Helen Teresa Pettifer [1964] Director; Rod Pettifer [1960] Director/Manager

Warwick Energy Limited
Incorporated: 24 October 2000
Net Worth: £7,826,286 *Total Assets:* £15,839,028
Registered Office: Juliette Suite, Unit 2 Lowes Lane Business Park, Lowes Lane, Wellesbourne, Warwicks, CV35 9RB
Activities: Extraction of natural gas
Parent: Warwick Energy Holdings Limited
Officers: Dr Robert Evan Jones [1946] Director/Chartered Engineer; Mark Edward Petterson [1960] Director/Chartered Engineer; John Leslie Sulley [1951] Director

Warwick Independent Schools Foundation
Incorporated: 13 July 2001 *Employees:* 829
Net Worth: £62,074,000 *Total Assets:* £74,705,000
Registered Office: Warwick Independent Schools Foundation, Myton Road, Warwick, CV34 6PP
Activities: Other accommodation
Officers: Simon Jones, Secretary; Marie Bernadette Ashe [1969] Director/Chief Finance Officer [German]; Sally Margaret Austin [1976] Group HR Director; John Cavanagh [1960] Director/Barrister; Anthony David Cocker [1969] Director/Chief Executive; Timothy Blakiston Cox [1955] Director/Chartered Surveyor; Andrew Charles Firth [1965] Director/Businessman; Christopher Roy Gibbons [1974] Director/Project Manager/Consultant; Moira Ann Grainger [1956] Director/Retail; Professor Damian Russel Griffin [1965] Director/Professor of Medicine; Rupert Maxwell Braid Griffiths [1952] Director/Partner at Solicitors Firm; Nicholas Francis Keegan [1955] Director; Timothy Harold Keyes [1954] Director/Retired Headmaster; Elizabeth Jill Lillyman [1944] Director/Retired Teacher; Gillian Low [1955] Director/Retired Headmistress; Clare Anna Insull Sawdon [1956] Campaign Director; Pamela Ann Snape [1947] Director/HR Consultant; David Bennett Stevens [1955] Director/Franchise Development Manager; Jonathan Neil Wallis [1970] Development Director

Warwick International Group Limited
Incorporated: 25 October 1994 *Employees:* 159
Net Worth: £65,670,000 *Total Assets:* £84,749,000
Registered Office: The Knowle, Nether Lane, Hazelwood, Derby, DE56 4AN
Activities: Manufacture of other inorganic basic chemicals
Parent: Warwick International Intermediate Holdings Limited
Officers: Anthony Michael Smits [1972] Director [American]; Marc Martha Joseph Verthongen [1957] Finance Director [Belgian]

Warwick International Holdings Limited
Incorporated: 14 May 2008
Net Worth: £105,758,000 *Total Assets:* £118,097,000
Registered Office: The Knowle, Nether Lane, Hazelwood, Derby, DE56 4AN
Activities: Activities of head offices
Parent: Lubrizol Group, LLP
Officers: Anthony Michael Smits [1972] Director [American]; Marc Martha Joseph Verthongen [1957] Finance Director [Belgian]

Warwick International Intermediate Holdings Limited
Incorporated: 14 May 2008
Net Worth Deficit: £8,205,000 *Total Assets:* £108,401,000
Registered Office: The Knowle, Nether Lane, Hazelwood, Derby, DE56 4AN
Activities: Activities of head offices
Parent: Warwick International Holdings Limited
Officers: Anthony Michael Smits [1972] Director [American]; Marc Martha Joseph Verthongen [1957] Finance Director [Belgian]

Warwick Ward (Holdings) Limited
Incorporated: 7 July 2015 *Employees:* 85
Net Worth: £4,561,515 *Total Assets:* £19,458,414
Registered Office: Blacker Hill Sidings, Blacker Hill, Barnsley, S Yorks, S74 0RE
Activities: Agents involved in the sale of machinery, industrial equipment, ships and aircraft
Officers: Ashley Ward [1967] Director; Matthew Ward [1968] Director

Warwick Ward (Machinery) Limited
Incorporated: 7 September 1970 *Employees:* 85
Net Worth: £4,580,760 *Total Assets:* £19,477,660
Registered Office: Blacker Hill Sidings, Blacker Hill, Barnsley, S Yorks, S74 0RE
Activities: Repair of machinery
Parent: Warwick Ward (Holdings) Ltd
Officers: Ashley Ward, Secretary; Ashley Ward [1967] Director; Matthew Ward [1968] Director

Washbrook Capital Limited
Incorporated: 30 July 2013 *Employees:* 2
Net Worth: £1,000,003 *Total Assets:* £20,285,024
Registered Office: Grant Hall, Parsons Green, St Ives, Cambs, PE27 4AA
Activities: Other business support service activities n.e.c.
Parent: UKLS Acquisitions Limited
Officers: Robert Matson, Secretary; David Jeremy Grossman [1970] Director; Robert Matson [1970] Director/Chartered Accountant

Wasp Management Software Limited
Incorporated: 18 August 2011
Net Worth: £50,720,000 *Total Assets:* £51,981,000
Registered Office: c/o Workforce Software Ltd, Precedent Drive, Rooksley, Milton Keynes, Bucks, MK13 8PP
Activities: Other information technology service activities
Parent: Whistler Acquisitions Limited
Officers: Tammy Jones, Secretary; Denise Broady [1974] Director [American]; Robert Feller [1968] Director/CFO/Treasurer [American]; Mike Morini [1962] Director [American]

Wasps Finance PLC
Incorporated: 11 February 2015
Net Worth: £50,000 *Total Assets:* £34,908,000
Registered Office: Ricoh Arena, Judds Lane, Longford, Coventry, Warwicks, CV6 6AQ
Activities: Other credit granting n.e.c.
Major Shareholder: Derek Arthur Richardson
Officers: Nicholas John Eastwood, Secretary; Nicholas John Eastwood [1959] Director/Chief Executive; Derek Arthur Richardson [1961] Director [Irish]

Wasps Holdings Limited
Incorporated: 26 March 2001 *Employees:* 233
Previous: London Wasps Holdings Limited
Net Worth Deficit: £755,000 *Total Assets:* £86,389,000
Registered Office: Ricoh Arena, Judds Lane, Longford, Coventry, Warwicks, CV6 6AQ
Activities: Other sports activities
Major Shareholder: Derek Arthur Richardson
Officers: Nicholas John Eastwood, Secretary; David James Armstrong [1964] Director; Lawrence Bruno Nero Dallaglio [1972] Director; Robert Norman Dawbarn [1968] Director/Solicitor; Nicholas John Eastwood [1959] Director/Chief Executive; Robert William Gray [1960] Director [Irish]; Christopher John Holland [1954] Director; Derek Arthur Richardson [1961] Director [Irish]; Mark James Robertson [1974] Director

The Waste and Resources Action Programme
Incorporated: 11 December 2000 *Employees:* 183
Net Worth: £20,111,000 *Total Assets:* £45,361,000
Registered Office: 2nd Floor, Blenheim Court, 19 George Street, Banbury, Oxon, OX16 5BH
Activities: Other professional, scientific and technical activities n.e.c.
Officers: Philippa Foster, Secretary; Susan Noelle Corbett [1954] Director/Retired; Julie Elizabeth Hill [1961] Director/Environmental Consultant; Baroness Anne Caroline Jenkin [1955] Director/Parliamentarian; Robert Edward Longley-Cook [1958] Director/Charity Chief Executive; James William Oatridge [1944] Director; Dr Marc Timothy Richard Stephens [1962] Director/Management Consultant; Sophie Lysandra Thomas [1973] Director/Design Consultant

Waste Recycling Group (Central) Limited
Incorporated: 23 May 2000 *Employees:* 121
Net Worth: £182,943,008 *Total Assets:* £206,407,008
Registered Office: Ground Floor West, 900 Pavilion Drive, Northampton Business Park, Northampton, NN4 7RG
Activities: Other business support service activities n.e.c.
Parent: FCC Environment (UK) Limited
Officers: Carol Jayne Nunn, Secretary; Vicente Federico Orts-Llopis [1962] Director/Chief Financial Officer [Spanish]; Agustin Serrano Minchan [1959] Director/Technical Civil Engineer [Spanish]; Paul Taylor [1959] Director/Chief Executive Officer

Waste Recycling Group (UK) Limited
Incorporated: 29 November 1990
Net Worth: £6,101,000 *Total Assets:* £81,100,000
Registered Office: Ground Floor West, 900 Pavilion Drive, Northampton Business Park, Northampton, NN4 7RG
Activities: Other business support service activities n.e.c.
Parent: WRG Acquisitions 2 Limited
Officers: Carol Jayne Nunn, Secretary; Vicente Federico Orts-Llopis [1962] Director/Chief Financial Officer [Spanish]; Agustin Serrano Minchan [1959] Director/Technical Civil Engineer [Spanish]; Paul Taylor [1959] Director/Chief Executive Officer

Wastenotts (Reclamation) Limited
Incorporated: 24 December 1991 *Employees:* 6
Net Worth: £37,088,000 *Total Assets:* £60,319,000
Registered Office: Ground Floor West, 900 Pavilion Drive, Northampton Business Park, Northampton, NN4 7RG
Activities: Other business support service activities n.e.c.
Parent: Kent Energy Limited
Officers: Carol Jayne Nunn, Secretary; Vicente Federico Orts-Llopis [1962] Finance Director [Spanish]; Paul Taylor [1959] Director/Chief Financial Officer

Watch Bidco Limited
Incorporated: 20 November 2015 *Employees:* 8
Net Worth: £52,566,000 *Total Assets:* £191,430,000
Registered Office: Quotient Clinical Limited, Mere Way, Ruddington, Nottingham, NG11 6JS
Activities: Research and experimental development on biotechnology
Parent: Quotient Sciences Holdings Limited
Officers: Gordon Biggart Cameron [1966] Director; Dr Mark Egerton [1963] Director; Alan Browning MacKay [1962] Director/Private Equity Executive; Michael Irvine Mortimer [1960] Director/Private Equity Executive

Watch Shop Ltd
Incorporated: 25 July 2007
Net Worth: £15,110,706 *Total Assets:* £15,110,706
Registered Office: Aurum House, 2 Elland Road, Braunstone, Leicester, LE3 1TT
Activities: Dormant company
Parent: The Watches of Switzerland Group Limited
Officers: Anthony John Broderick [1958] Director; Hugh Brian Duffy [1954] Director; Lars Anders Ragnar Romberg [1963] Director [Swedish]

Watches of Switzerland Company Limited
Incorporated: 20 February 1917 *Employees:* 1,797
Previous: Aurum Group Limited
Net Worth: £169,446,000 *Total Assets:* £431,579,008
Registered Office: Aurum House, 2 Elland Road, Braunstone, Leicester, LE3 1TT
Activities: Retail sale of watches and jewellery in specialised stores
Parent: Aurum Acquisitions Limited
Officers: Gillian Oliff, Secretary; Ruth Georgina Benford [1973] Marketing and Communications Director; Craig Bolton [1972] Retail Director; Anthony John Broderick [1958] Director/Chief Operating Officer; James Smyth Crichton [1965] Merchandising Director; Hugh Brian Duffy [1954] Director/Chief Executive; Lars Anders Ragnar Romberg [1963] Director [Swedish]

The Watches of Switzerland Group Limited
Incorporated: 16 March 2004 *Employees:* 7
Previous: Aurum Holdings Limited
Net Worth: £84,551,336 *Total Assets:* £240,542,800
Registered Office: Aurum House, 2 Elland Road, Braunstone, Leicester, LE3 1TT
Activities: Retail sale of watches and jewellery in specialised stores
Parent: Jewel UK Bidco Limited
Officers: Gillian Oliff, Secretary; Anthony John Broderick [1958] Director/Chief Operating Officer; Teresa Colaianni [1968] Director [British/Italian]; Hugh Brian Duffy [1954] Director/Chief Executive; Dennis Henry Millard [1949] Director; The Hon. Rosamond Mary Monckton [1953] Director/Campaigner; Robert James Moorhead [1964] Director; Fabrice Nottin [1978] Director/Investment Professional [French]; Michele Raba [1984] Director/Investment Professional [Italian]; Lars Anders Ragnar Romberg [1963] Director [Swedish]

Waterfall Catering Group Limited
Incorporated: 13 August 2014
Net Worth: £737,383 *Total Assets:* £27,854,048
Registered Office: The Courtyard, Catherine Street, Macclesfield, Cheshire, SK11 6ET
Activities: Other manufacturing n.e.c.
Parent: Waterfall Elior Limited
Officers: Vincent John Pearson [1959] Director; Catherine Margaret Roe [1960] Managing Director; Eleni Savva [1972] Finance Director

Waterfall Elior Limited
Incorporated: 16 May 2016
Net Worth: £17,417,316 *Total Assets:* £50,053,480
Registered Office: The Courtyard, Catherine Street, Macclesfield, Cheshire, SK11 6ET
Activities: Other food services
Parent: Elior UK Holdings Limited
Officers: Esther Gaide [1961] Director/Group Chief Financial Officer [French]; Vincent John Pearson [1959] Director; Catherine Margaret Roe [1960] Managing Director; Eleni Savva [1972] Finance Director; Thierry Thonnier [1966] Director [French]

Waterfall Services Limited
Incorporated: 5 July 2006 *Employees:* 5
Net Worth: £1,222,696 *Total Assets:* £12,179,623
Registered Office: The Courtyard, Catherine Street, Macclesfield, Cheshire, SK11 6ET
Activities: Other manufacturing n.e.c.
Parent: Waterfall Catering Group Ltd
Officers: Vincent John Pearson [1959] Director; Catherine Margaret Roe [1960] Managing Director; Eleni Savva [1972] Finance Director

Waterline Limited
Incorporated: 3 February 1947 *Employees:* 173
Net Worth: £4,167,770 *Total Assets:* £16,854,604
Registered Office: Crown House, North Crawley Road, Newport Pagnell, Bucks, MK16 9TG
Activities: Wholesale of radio, television goods & electrical household appliances (other than records, tapes, CDs)
Parent: Waterline Group PLC
Officers: Adrian Cyril Davidson [1967] Director; Barry John Head [1968] Director; Michael John Head [1943] Director; Karen Elizabeth Sturgess [1970] Director; Robert Bryan Taylor [1967] Director/Salesman; Vadakke Vayante Valappil Zaheer [1966] Director

Waterloo Quay Properties Limited
Incorporated: 22 November 1993 *Employees:* 4
Net Worth: £3,402,027 *Total Assets:* £15,846,381
Registered Office: The Apex, 2 Sheriffs Orchard, Coventry, Warwicks, CV1 3PP
Activities: Other accommodation
Shareholders: Shaun Nigel Eardley; Anna-Marie Gale Eardley
Officers: Anna Marie Eardley, Secretary/Secretary and Administrator; Anna Marie Eardley [1964] Director; Shaun Nigel Eardley [1963] Director/Shipping Agent; Brian Richard Lewis [1963] Director/Shipping Agent

Watermill-CT Holdings Limited
Incorporated: 21 July 2017 *Employees:* 397
Net Worth: £11,085,000 *Total Assets:* £66,332,000
Registered Office: Templeborough Works, Sheffield Road, Sheffield, S9 1RS
Activities: Activities of production holding companies
Major Shareholder: Steven Edward Karol
Officers: Steven Edward Karol [1954] Director/Managing Partner [American]

Wathegar Wind Farm LLP
Incorporated: 23 July 2008
Net Worth: £204,321 *Total Assets:* £13,279,476
Registered Office: Glebe Barn, Great Barrington, Burford, Oxon, OX18 4US

Watling JCB Limited
Incorporated: 23 February 1976 *Employees:* 187
Net Worth: £15,672,000 *Total Assets:* £27,657,000
Registered Office: Dog & Gun Lane, Whetstone, Leicester, LE8 6LJ
Activities: Agents involved in the sale of machinery, industrial equipment, ships and aircraft
Parent: Hajco 199 Limited
Officers: Jason James King, Secretary; Jason James King [1971] Director/Accountant; Anthony Lees [1963] Product Support Director; Andrew Raine [1968] Sales Director; Michael David Roby [1980] National Accounts Director; Richard Edmund Telfer [1969] Director

Watts Industries UK Limited
Incorporated: 3 September 1991 *Employees:* 44
Net Worth: £5,117,731 *Total Assets:* £11,307,419
Registered Office: Ambuscade Road, Colmworth Business Park, Eaton Socon, St Neots, Cambs, PE19 8YX
Activities: Manufacture of taps and valves
Parent: Watts Industries Europe BV
Officers: Olivier Paul Jean Giverdon, Secretary; Olivier Paul Jean Giverdon [1978] Director [French]; Nigel Paul Wood [1966] Director

Wavin Limited
Incorporated: 8 March 1946 *Employees:* 875
Net Worth: £41,817,000 *Total Assets:* £353,940,992
Registered Office: Wavin, Edlington Lane, Edlington, Doncaster, S Yorks, DN12 1BY
Activities: Manufacture of builders ware of plastic
Parent: Wavin Hepworth Limited
Officers: Neil Robert John Douglas, Secretary; Neil Robert John Douglas [1964] Director; Paul Maclaurin [1967] Manufacturing Director; Alan Brent Nicholls [1961] Managing Director

Wavin UK (Holdings) Limited
Incorporated: 3 February 2005
Net Worth: £4,457,000 *Total Assets:* £220,024,000
Registered Office: Wavin, Edlington Lane, Edlington, Doncaster, S Yorks, DN12 1BY
Activities: Activities of head offices
Officers: Neil Robert John Douglas, Secretary; Neil Robert John Douglas [1964] Director; Paul Maclaurin [1967] Manufacturing Director; Alan Brent Nicholls [1961] Managing Director; Martinus Petrus Maria Roef [1964] Group Director [Dutch]

The Way Ahead Group Limited
Incorporated: 28 April 1998 *Employees:* 425
Net Worth: £44,602,000 *Total Assets:* £89,028,000
Registered Office: Norfolk House, 47 Upper Parliament Street, Nottingham, NG1 2AB
Activities: Other amusement and recreation activities n.e.c.
Officers: Leanne Lipscombe, Secretary; Simon John Gillham [1956] Director/Senior Executive VP Comms Vivendi; Robert Ian Wilmshurst [1969] Director

WCS Care Group Limited
Incorporated: 1 May 1992 *Employees:* 701
Net Worth: £15,096,000 *Total Assets:* £32,599,000
Registered Office: Head Office, 1st Floor, Newlands, Whites Row, Kenilworth, Warwicks, CV8 1HW
Activities: Residential care activities for the elderly and disabled
Officers: Paresh Chandrakant Parekh, Secretary; Mark Ronald Andrews [1961] Director/Retired; Tricia Mary Banks [1973] Director/Education Management; Barrie Christopher Cressey [1957] Director/Business Development - Utility Industry; Karl Wasyl Demian [1959] Director/Consultant; Alison Last [1958] Director/NHS Management Professional; Adrian Frederick Levett [1950] Director/Retired; Roger Leonard Merchant [1957] Director/Chartered Accountant; Lee Eamon Middleburgh [1956] Director/Chartered Surveyor; Keith Jon Nurcombe [1970] Director/Business Consultant; Patricia Jane Southeard [1949] Director/Retired; Rebecca Lynda Warwick [1979] Director/Management Consultant; Nicholas Keith Weatherburn [1973] Director/HR Management

WD-40 Company Limited
Incorporated: 26 September 1983 *Employees:* 200
Net Worth: £109,085,000 *Total Assets:* £126,676,000
Registered Office: Brick Close, Kiln Farm, Milton Keynes, Bucks, MK11 3LJ
Activities: Manufacture of other chemical products n.e.c.
Parent: WD-40 Holdings Limited
Officers: William Brian Noble [1958] Managing Director [Australian]; Garry Owen Ridge [1956] Director [Australian]

Weatherbys Bank Holdings Limited
Incorporated: 20 December 2005 *Employees:* 176
Net Worth: £39,506,744 *Total Assets:* £758,838,848
Registered Office: 52-60 Sanders Road, Wellingborough, Northants, NN8 4BX
Activities: Activities of other holding companies n.e.c.
Shareholders: Richard South Morse; Johnny Roger Weatherby; Roger Nicholas Weatherby; Jeremy Inglesby Francis
Officers: Adrian Stewart McGlynn, Company Secretary; Jonathan Roger Weatherby [1959] Director/Business Executive; Roger Nicholas Weatherby [1962] Director/Chief Executive

Weatherbys Bank Limited
Incorporated: 28 June 1994 *Employees:* 176
Net Worth: £39,201,432 *Total Assets:* £758,838,784
Registered Office: Sanders Road, Wellingborough, Northants, NN8 4BX
Activities: Banks
Parent: Weatherbys Bank Holdings Ltd
Officers: Adrian Stewart McGlynn, Secretary; David Charles Bellamy [1953] Director/Chairman; Brian Kenneth Bourne [1952] Director/Retired Bank Executive; Jonathan Lancelot Eddis [1960] Director/Banker; Carole Machell [1962] Director/Chartered Accountant; Quentin Noel John Marshall [1973] Director/Banker; Andrew Turberville Smith [1966] Finance Director; Jonathan Roger Weatherby [1959] Director/Chairman; Roger Nicholas Weatherby [1962] Director/Business Executive

Weatherbys Ltd
Incorporated: 5 December 1953 *Employees:* 206
Previous: Weatherbys Thoroughbred Limited
Net Worth Deficit: £10,299,252 *Total Assets:* £20,621,860
Registered Office: Sanders Road, Wellingborough, Northants, NN8 4BX
Activities: Other publishing activities
Parent: Weatherbys Thoroughbred Holdings Ltd
Officers: Adrian Stewart McGlynn, Secretary; Charles Graham Coles [1952] Director; Nicholas Dominic Craven [1964] Director/Business Executive; Patrick Simon Gronow Davis [1969] Director/Business Executive; Russell William Henry Ferris [1979] Director/Business Executive; Adrian Stewart McGlynn [1966] Director/Company Secretary; John Patrick O'Reilly [1960] Director; Jonathan Roger Weatherby [1959] Director/Business Executive; Roger Nicholas Weatherby [1962] Director/CEO - Weatherbys Bank

Weatherbys Thoroughbred Holdings Limited
Incorporated: 20 December 2005 *Employees:* 256
Net Worth Deficit: £4,185,683 *Total Assets:* £24,080,232
Registered Office: c/o Weatherbys, Sanders Road, Wellingborough, Northants, NN8 4BX
Activities: Activities of head offices
Shareholders: Richard South Morse; Johnny Roger Weatherby; Roger Nicholas Weatherby; Jeremy Inglesby Francis
Officers: Adrian Stewart McGlynn, Company Secretary; Jonathan Roger Weatherby [1959] Director/Business Executive; Roger Nicholas Weatherby [1962] Director/Chief Executive

Weatherford Eurasia Limited
Incorporated: 6 November 1989
Net Worth: £212,418,000 *Total Assets:* £323,007,008
Registered Office: Weatherford, Gotham Road, East Leake, Loughborough, Leics, LE12 6JX
Activities: Extraction of crude petroleum
Shareholders: Weatherford (G.B.) LLP; Weatherford International Public Limited Company
Officers: Richard Khalil Strachan, Secretary; Neil Alexander MacLeod [1966] Director/Region Tax Manager - Europe; Richard Khalil Strachan [1985] Director/Lawyer

Weatherford U.K. Limited
Incorporated: 1 November 1965 *Employees:* 764
Net Worth: £165,672,000 *Total Assets:* £402,358,016
Registered Office: Weatherford, Gotham Road, East Leake, Loughborough, Leics, LE12 6JX
Activities: Support activities for petroleum and natural gas mining
Parent: Weatherford Eurasia Limited
Officers: Richard Khalil Strachan, Secretary; Alexander Olsson [1977] Director/Geozone Vice President [Swedish]; Richard Khalil Strachan [1985] Director/Lawyer

Weavers Close Limited
Incorporated: 7 June 1973 *Employees:* 98
Net Worth: £2,949,501 *Total Assets:* £12,774,386
Registered Office: Gullivers Kingdom, Temple Walk, Matlock Bath, Derbys, DE4 3PG
Activities: Other service activities n.e.c.
Officers: Julie Hilary Dalton, Secretary/Director; Julie Hilary Dalton [1969] Director; Hilary Joan Phillips [1943] Director; Nicholas Gary Phillips [1975] Director; Dr Ramon Clarence Phillips [1943] Director

B. E. Webbe Removals (Derby) Limited
Incorporated: 25 November 1976 *Employees:* 49
Net Worth: £7,369,382 *Total Assets:* £13,850,542
Registered Office: Racecourse Industrial Park, Mansfield Road, Derby, DE21 4SX
Activities: Removal services
Officers: Andrew Mark Foulke, Secretary; Edward Anthony Blount [1975] Director/Removals Manager; John Samuel Blount [1944] Director; Nicholas John Blount [1971] Director; Richard Anthony Blount [1971] Director/General Manager

Webmart Limited
Incorporated: 9 January 1997 *Employees:* 44
Net Worth: £7,288,539 *Total Assets:* £11,824,170
Registered Office: Media Innovation Centre, 13-15 Wedgwood Road, Bicester, Oxon, OX26 4UL
Activities: Botanical and zoological gardens and nature reserves activities
Major Shareholder: Simon David William Watson Biltcliffe
Officers: Simon David William Watson Biltcliffe [1965] Director/Chief Executive Officer

Weddel Swift Distribution Limited
Incorporated: 19 June 1984 *Employees:* 241
Net Worth: £10,713,000 *Total Assets:* £30,156,000
Registered Office: The Old Rectory, Cold Higham, Towcester, Northants, NN12 8LR
Activities: Wholesale of meat and meat products
Parent: Randall Parker Food Group Limited
Officers: David Richard Brady, Secretary; David Richard Brady [1950] Director; Pragnesh Patel [1975] Director; Ronald Leslie Randall [1947] Director/Master Butcher

Weddel Swift Limited
Incorporated: 26 June 2000 *Employees:* 23
Net Worth: £5,657,000 *Total Assets:* £18,214,000
Registered Office: The Old Rectory, Banbury Lane, Cold Higham, Towcester, Northants, NN12 8LR
Activities: Wholesale of meat and meat products
Parent: Randall Parker Food Group Limited
Officers: David Richard Brady, Secretary; David Richard Brady [1950] Finance Director; Pragnesh Patel [1975] Director; Ronald Leslie Randall [1947] Director/Master Butcher

Weetabix Limited
Incorporated: 13 August 1932 *Employees:* 1,006
Net Worth: £388,903,008 *Total Assets:* £504,065,984
Registered Office: Weetabix Mills, Burton Latimer, Kettering, Northants, NN15 5JR
Activities: Manufacture of other food products n.e.c.
Parent: Westminster Acquisition Limited
Officers: Richard William Thomas Martin, Secretary; Sally Jane Abbott [1967] Director; Richard William Thomas Martin [1962] Director

Weidmuller Limited
Incorporated: 10 November 1959 *Employees:* 43
Net Worth: £8,088,000 *Total Assets:* £22,453,000
Registered Office: Klippon House, Centurion Court Office Park, Meridian East, Meridian Business Park, Leicester, LE19 1TP
Activities: Wholesale of electronic and telecommunications equipment and parts
Officers: Martin Leslie Finnegan, Secretary; Jose Carlos Alvarez-Tobar [1951] Director/Chief Marketing & Sales Officer [Spanish]; Volker Bibelhausen [1965] Director/Chief Technical Officer [German]; Simon John Goodwin [1965] Managing Director; Josef Gross [1970] Director/Executive Vice President Sales & Marketing [Czech]; Jorg Timmermann [1971] Director/Chief Financial Officer [German]

Welbeck Estates Company Limited (The)
Incorporated: 13 April 1961 *Employees:* 168
Net Worth: £210,115,008 *Total Assets:* £304,640,992
Registered Office: Portland Estate Office, Cavendish House, Welbeck, Whitwell, Worksop, Notts, S80 3LL
Activities: Other letting and operating of own or leased real estate
Major Shareholder: Nigel Timothy Bentley
Officers: Ian Goodwin, Secretary; Daisy Margharita Amelia Parente [1981] Director/Literary Agent; Henry Joseph Parente [1983] Director; William Henry Marcello Parente [1951] Director; Malcolm Peter Swan [1949] Director

Welbeck Waste Management Limited
Incorporated: 31 July 1992 *Employees:* 9
Net Worth: £460,000 *Total Assets:* £22,857,000
Registered Office: Ground Floor West, 900 Pavilion Drive, Northampton Business Park, Northampton, NN4 7RG
Activities: Other business support service activities n.e.c.
Parent: FCC Environment (UK) Limited
Officers: Carol Jayne Nunn, Secretary; Vicente Federico Orts-Llopis [1962] Director/Chief Financial Officer [Spanish]; Agustin Serrano Minchan [1959] Director/Technical Civil Engineer [Spanish]; Paul Taylor [1959] Director/Chief Executive Officer

Welcome Break Group Limited
Incorporated: 18 January 1996 *Employees:* 1,492
Net Worth: £20,947,000 *Total Assets:* £701,206,016
Registered Office: 2 Vantage Court, Tickford Street, Newport Pagnell, Bucks, MK16 9EZ
Activities: Retail sale in non-specialised stores with food, beverages or tobacco predominating
Parent: Welcome Break Holdings 1 Limited
Officers: Joseph James Barrett [1966] Director [Irish]; John Diviney [1979] Director/Chief Executive Officer [Irish]; Niall Dolan [1973] Director/Financial Controller [Irish]; Charles John Gore Hazelwood [1963] Director/Accountant; Surinder Singh Toor [1972] Director/Accountant

Welcome Break Holdings (1) Limited
Incorporated: 31 October 2000 *Employees:* 4,811
Net Worth Deficit: £83,611,000 *Total Assets:* £321,244,992
Registered Office: 2 Vantage Court, Tickford Street, Newport Pagnell, Bucks, MK16 9EZ
Activities: Activities of other holding companies n.e.c.
Parent: Welcome Break Holdings 2 Limited
Officers: Joseph James Barrett [1966] Director [Irish]; John Diviney [1979] Director/Chief Executive Officer [Irish]; Niall Dolan [1973] Director/Financial Controller [Irish]; Charles John Gore Hazelwood [1963] Director/Accountant; Surinder Singh Toor [1972] Director/Accountant

Welcome Break Holdings Limited
Incorporated: 11 December 1996 *Employees:* 4,951
Net Worth Deficit: £192,022,000 *Total Assets:* £342,236,992
Registered Office: 2 Vantage Court, Tickford Street, Newport Pagnell, Bucks, MK16 9EZ
Activities: Activities of other holding companies n.e.c.
Parent: Appia Europe Limited
Officers: Joseph James Barrett [1966] Director [Irish]; John Diviney [1979] Director/Chief Executive Officer [Irish]; Niall Dolan [1973] Director/Financial Controller [Irish]; Charles John Gore Hazelwood [1963] Director/Accountant; Surinder Singh Toor [1972] Director/Accountant

Welcome Break Limited
Incorporated: 30 June 1983 *Employees:* 2,531
Net Worth: £219,879,008 *Total Assets:* £423,462,016
Registered Office: 2 Vantage Court, Tickford Street, Newport Pagnell, Bucks, MK16 9EZ
Activities: Retail sale in non-specialised stores with food, beverages or tobacco predominating
Parent: Welcome Break Group Limited
Officers: Joseph James Barrett [1966] Director [Irish]; John Diviney [1979] Director/Chief Executive Officer [Irish]; Niall Dolan [1973] Director/Financial Controller [Irish]; Charles John Gore Hazelwood [1963] Director/Accountant; Surinder Singh Toor [1972] Director/Accountant

Welcome Break No. 1 Limited
Incorporated: 14 December 2012
Net Worth: £332,108,992 *Total Assets:* £466,100,000
Registered Office: 2 Vantage Court, Tickford Street, Newport Pagnell, Bucks, MK16 9EZ
Activities: Activities of other holding companies n.e.c.
Parent: Welcome Break No. 2 Limited
Officers: Joseph James Barrett [1966] Director [Irish]; John Diviney [1979] Director/Chief Executive Officer [Irish]; Niall Dolan [1973] Director/Financial Controller [Irish]; Charles John Gore Hazelwood [1963] Director/Accountant; Surinder Singh Toor [1972] Director/Accountant

Welcome Break No. 2 Limited
Incorporated: 14 December 2012
Net Worth: £339,100,992 *Total Assets:* £339,100,992
Registered Office: 2 Vantage Court, Tickford Street, Newport Pagnell, Bucks, MK16 9EZ
Activities: Activities of other holding companies n.e.c.
Parent: Welcome Break Holdings Limited
Officers: Joseph James Barrett [1966] Director [Irish]; John Diviney [1979] Director/Chief Executive Officer [Irish]; Niall Dolan [1973] Director/Financial Controller [Irish]; Charles John Gore Hazelwood [1963] Director/Accountant; Surinder Singh Toor [1972] Director/Accountant

Welcome Break Services Limited
Incorporated: 31 October 2000 *Employees:* 140
Net Worth Deficit: £22,701,000 *Total Assets:* £12,116,000
Registered Office: 2 Vantage Court, Tickford Street, Newport Pagnell, Bucks, MK16 9EZ
Activities: Retail sale in non-specialised stores with food, beverages or tobacco predominating
Parent: Welcome Break Holdings Limited
Officers: Joseph James Barrett [1966] Director [Irish]; John Diviney [1979] Director/Chief Executive Officer [Irish]; Niall Dolan [1973] Director/Financial Controller [Irish]; Charles John Gore Hazelwood [1963] Director/Accountant; Surinder Singh Toor [1972] Director/Accountant

Welcome Financial Services Limited
Incorporated: 23 January 1914 *Employees:* 106
Net Worth: £21,301,000 *Total Assets:* £74,201,000
Registered Office: Welcome Finance, Mere Way, Ruddington Fields Business Park, Ruddington, Nottingham, NG11 6NZ
Activities: Credit granting by non-deposit taking finance houses and other specialist consumer credit grantors
Shareholders: Cattles Holdings Limited; Compass Credit Limited
Officers: Roland Charles William Todd, Secretary; Jonathan Mark Briggs [1966] Director; James Robert Drummond Smith [1960] Director; Robert David East [1960] Director; Robin Simon Johnson [1954] Director

Welcomm Holdings Limited
Incorporated: 13 May 2014 *Employees:* 72
Net Worth: £5,629,692 *Total Assets:* £11,542,523
Registered Office: Welcomm House, 24 The Point, Rockingham Road, Market Harborough, Leics, LE16 7QU
Activities: Trade of electricity
Shareholder: Christopher Mark Stanton
Officers: Aidan John Piper [1956] Managing Director; Christopher Raymond Ruddle [1975] Finance Director; Rachel Williamson [1972] Operations Director

H.I.Weldrick Limited
Incorporated: 18 March 1959 *Employees:* 673
Net Worth: £18,624,468 *Total Assets:* £39,377,784
Registered Office: Leedale House, Railway Court, Doncaster, S Yorks, DN4 5FB
Activities: Dispensing chemist in specialised stores
Major Shareholder: Christopher William John Alcock
Officers: Paul Appleyard, Secretary; Christopher William John Alcock [1977] Director/Pharmacist; Lynne Hopwood Alcock [1947] Director/Secretary

Welland Park Community College Academy Trust
Incorporated: 20 June 2011 *Employees:* 101
Net Worth: £10,305,000 *Total Assets:* £11,725,000
Registered Office: Welland Park Community College, Welland Park Road, Market Harborough, Leics, LE16 9DR
Activities: General secondary education
Officers: Martin Peter Towers, Secretary; Caroline Mary Sarah Baker [1973] Director; Jim Harker [1973] Director; David John Hedley [1953] Director; John William Hill [1950] Director/Retired School Teacher; Frederique Lagarde [1967] Director [French]; Julie McBrearty [1969] Director/Principal; Julian Robert Oakland [1972] Director/Teacher; Julie Oakley [1962] Director/College Manager; Claire Parry [1972] Director/Civil Servant; Stephen Paul Peverett [1970] Director/Data Manager; David Robert Smith [1943] Director; Martin Peter Towers [1981] Finance Director; Dr Astrid Geertruida Maria Van Wilsem [1965] Director/Clinical Psychologist [Dutch]

Wellbeing Software Group Holdings Limited
Incorporated: 13 September 2013 *Employees:* 142
Previous: New Street Square Newco Limited
Net Worth Deficit: £19,883,240 *Total Assets:* £16,039,476
Registered Office: I2 Mansfield, Hamilton Court, Oakham Business Park, Mansfield, Notts, NG18 5FB
Activities: Activities of head offices
Parent: Elysian Capital GP (Scotland) Limited
Officers: Claire Christina White, Secretary; James Alan Cunningham [1964] Director; Christa Iris Echtle [1957] Director [German]; Richard Alexander Ramsey [1956] Director; Graham Paul Ridgway [1960] Director; Claire Christina White [1967] Director

Wellbeing Software Group Ltd
Incorporated: 26 January 2012 *Employees:* 3
Net Worth: £14,211,598 *Total Assets:* £29,837,228
Registered Office: Office Suite 0.1, I2 Mansfield, Hamilton Court, Oakham Business Park, Mansfield, Notts, NG18 5FB
Activities: Business and domestic software development
Officers: Claire Christina White, Secretary; Graham Paul Ridgway [1960] Director; Claire Christina White [1967] Director; Christopher Paul Yeowart [1976] Director

Wellbeing Software Holdings Limited
Incorporated: 4 December 2013
Previous: New Street Square Midco Limited
Net Worth Deficit: £1,689,513 *Total Assets:* £29,020,192
Registered Office: I2 Mansfield, Hamilton Court, Oakham Business Park, Mansfield, Notts, NG18 5FB
Activities: Other information technology service activities
Officers: Claire Christina White, Secretary; James Alan Cunningham [1964] Director; Richard Alexander Ramsey [1956] Director; Graham Paul Ridgway [1960] Director; Claire Christina White [1967] Director

Wellbeing Software Limited
Incorporated: 13 September 2013 *Employees:* 1
Previous: New Street Square Bidco Limited
Net Worth Deficit: £7,657,278 *Total Assets:* £31,602,076
Registered Office: I2 Mansfield, Hamilton Court, Oakham Business Park, Mansfield, Notts, NG18 5FB
Activities: Activities of head offices
Officers: Claire Christina White, Secretary; James Alan Cunningham [1964] Director; Richard Alexander Ramsey [1956] Director; Graham Paul Ridgway [1960] Director

Wellglade Holdings Limited
Incorporated: 26 January 2010 *Employees:* 1,552
Net Worth: £45,244,000 *Total Assets:* £66,095,000
Registered Office: Trent Barton Buses, Mansfield Road, Heanor, Derbys, DE75 7BG
Activities: Activities of head offices
Shareholders: Brian Robert King; Richard Ian Morgan
Officers: Graham Sutton, Secretary; Brian Robert King [1944] Director; Richard Ian Morgan [1951] Director; Graham Sutton [1960] Director

Wellglade Limited
Incorporated: 21 January 1986 *Employees:* 2
Net Worth: £3,902,000 *Total Assets:* £13,933,000
Registered Office: Mansfield Road, Heanor, Derbys, DE75 7BG
Activities: Activities of head offices
Shareholders: Brian Robert King; Richard Ian Morgan
Officers: Graham Sutton, Secretary/Financial Director; Brian Robert King [1944] Managing Director; Richard Ian Morgan [1951] Commercial Director; Graham Sutton [1960] Financial Director

Wellingborough School
Incorporated: 14 October 2003 *Employees:* 259
Net Worth: £21,833,228 *Total Assets:* £26,010,012
Registered Office: Wellingborough School, Wellingborough, Northants, NN8 2BX
Activities: General secondary education
Officers: Colin John Peter Evans, Secretary; Trevor Baldry [1951] Director/Consultant Accountant/Business Adviser; Ian Michael Cantelo [1967] Director/Chartered Engineer; Dr Jonathan Karll Cox [1968] Director/Doctor; Jeremy James Hale Higgins [1948] Director/Retired Marketing Manager; Dorothy Alice Line [1954] Director/Member of Institute Chartered Accountants of Scotland; Simon Michael Marriott [1952] Director/Developer; Lorna Pape [1974] Director/Barrister; Rajesh Haridas Thakrar [1970] Director; Peter Richard Tyldesley [1967] Director/Land Agent & Surveyor (Chief Executive); David Andrew Waller [1963] Director/Senior University Lecturer; Clive Alan Westley [1945] Director

Charles Wells Brewery Limited
Incorporated: 24 February 2006 *Employees:* 204
Previous: Wells & Young's Brewing Company Limited
Net Worth: £7,753,000 *Total Assets:* £65,067,000
Registered Office: The Brewery, Havelock Street, Bedford, MK40 4LU
Activities: Manufacture of beer
Parent: Charles Wells Limited
Officers: Anthony Robert Fryer [1973] Finance Director; William Andrew Justin Phillimore [1962] Director; Paul Richard Wells [1958] Director

John A.Wells Limited
Incorporated: 29 August 1961 *Employees:* 6
Net Worth: £43,768,060 *Total Assets:* £57,597,932
Registered Office: Granary House, Melton Road, Edwalton, Nottingham, NG12 4DR
Activities: Growing of cereals (except rice), leguminous crops and oil seeds
Shareholders: John Brian Wells; Jane Dorothy Robinson
Officers: John Brian Wells, Secretary/Director; Anthony Richard Robinson [1948] Director/Accountant; Jane Dorothy Robinson [1948] Director/Executive; John Brian Wells [1939] Director

Charles Wells,Limited
Incorporated: 7 January 1910 *Employees:* 365
Net Worth: £75,246,000 *Total Assets:* £141,250,000
Registered Office: Eagle Brewery, Havelock Street, Bedford, MK40 4LU
Activities: Manufacture of beer
Officers: Anthony Robert Fryer [1973] Finance Director; Robert Lewis Ivell [1952] Director; William Andrew Justin Phillimore [1962] Director/Chief Executive; Paul Stephen Rawlinson [1959] Director; Geoffrey Charles Vaughan Wells [1970] Director/Lawyer [Canadian]; Paul Richard Wells [1958] Director; Peter John Wells [1970] Director

Wellspring Academy Trust
Incorporated: 27 June 2012 *Employees:* 1,184
Net Worth: £29,493,778 *Total Assets:* £54,849,528
Registered Office: Digital Media Centre, County Way, Barnsley, S Yorks, S70 2JW
Activities: Pre-primary education
Officers: Karen Froggatt, Secretary; Molly Beever [1943] Director/Retired; Colin Booth [1959] Director/Principal; Neil Henry Clephan [1957] Director/Leadership and Education Consultant; Stewart Peter Harper [1979] Director/Deputy Secretary & Registrar; Cheryl Elizabeth Hobson [1964] Director/Head of Corporate & Business Services; Yiannis Koursis [1975] Director/Deputy Principal; Hearl Roger Lenton [1952] Director/Chartered Surveyor; Richard Owen [1970] Divisional Managing Director; Mark Wilson [1968] Director/Chief Executive

Welsh Slate Limited
Incorporated: 5 October 2007 *Employees:* 175
Net Worth: £13,402,256 *Total Assets:* £31,438,508
Registered Office: Pinnacle House, Breedon on the Hill, Derby, DE73 8AP
Activities: Quarrying of ornamental and building stone, limestone, gypsum, chalk and slate
Parent: Breedon Southern Limited
Officers: Ross Edward McDonald, Secretary; Mark Hodgkinson [1967] Director; Elizabeth Helen Lyon [1983] Director; Ross Edward McDonald [1961] Director; Michael Paul Pearce [1964] Director; Robert Wood [1966] Director

Welspun Home Textiles UK Limited
Incorporated: 20 June 2006 *Employees:* 262
Net Worth: £1,082,000 *Total Assets:* £18,003,000
Registered Office: Park Square, Bird Hall Lane, Stockport, Cheshire, SK3 0XF
Activities: Activities of head offices
Parent: Welspun Holdings Private Limited
Officers: Manish Bansal, Secretary; Manish Bansal [1972] Director/Accountant [Indian]; Balkrishan Gopiram Goenka [1965] Business Director [Indian]; Dipali Balkrishan Goenka [1969] Director [Indian]

Welspun UK Limited
Incorporated: 5 January 2000 *Employees:* 260
Net Worth: £5,062,000 *Total Assets:* £32,318,000
Registered Office: Park Square, Bird Hall Lane, Stockport, Cheshire, SK3 0XF
Activities: Wholesale of textiles
Parent: Christy Home Textiles Ltd
Officers: Manish Bansal, Secretary; Manish Bansal [1972] Director/Accountant [Indian]; Dipali Balkrishan Goenka [1969] Director [Indian]

H.K. Wentworth Limited
Incorporated: 21 August 1941 *Employees:* 231
Net Worth: £8,430,082 *Total Assets:* £18,610,020
Registered Office: Ashby Park, Coalfield Way, Ashby De La Zouch, Leics, LE65 1JR
Activities: Manufacture of paints, varnishes and similar coatings, mastics and sealants
Officers: Dr John Frank Humphries, Secretary; Dr John Frank Humphries [1941] Technical Director; Ronald Leslie Jakeman [1951] Managing Director; Generald Richard Charlemont Kingsbury [1945] Director; Thomas Jake Essex Charlemont Kingsbury [1977] Director/Sales Manager; Toby Bernard Richard Henry Kingsbury [1979] Director/Sales Manager

West Atlantic UK Limited
Incorporated: 1 March 2004 *Employees:* 249
Previous: Atlantic Airlines Limited
Net Worth: £47,034 *Total Assets:* £23,472,952
Registered Office: Ground Floor, East Wing, 2M, Middlemarch Office Park, Siskin Drive, Coventry, Warwicks, CV3 4FJ
Activities: Freight air transport
Shareholder: Goran Berglund
Officers: Paul James Huett, Secretary; William Anthony Auld [1959] Director; Nigel Hiorns [1962] Director/Engineer; Russell Ladkin [1970] Sales & Marketing Director

West Coventry Academy
Incorporated: 1 June 2011 *Employees:* 179
Previous: Tile Hill Wood School and Language College
Net Worth: £8,598,000 *Total Assets:* £12,194,000
Registered Office: West Coventry Academy, Nutbrook Avenue, Coventry, Warwicks, CV4 9PW
Activities: General secondary education
Officers: Malcolm Clive Gardner, Secretary; Helen Brookes [1971] Director; Christopher Denson [1981] Director; Mark Dodd [1970] Director; Ann Patricia Flavell [1941] Director/Senior Science Technician; Dave Jones [1967] Director/Teacher; Maxine Kelsall [1966] Director; Kevin Barry Maton [1957] Director/Business Consultant and Councillor; Gina Jayne Oconnor [1963] Director/Headteacher; Michele Palmer [1966] Director; Christopher Rose [1954] Director/Retired Headteacher; Tracey Sarjeant [1971] Director; Bryan William Sayers [1944] Director; Amanda Taylor [1969] Director/Commercial Traveller; Natalie Woodward [1975] Director/Teaching Assistant; Elaine Yates [1972] Director

The West Grantham Academies Trust
Incorporated: 11 January 2011 *Employees:* 154
Net Worth: £13,749,452 *Total Assets:* £15,876,771
Registered Office: St Hugh's Site, The Avenue, Dysart Road, Grantham, Lincs, NG31 7PX
Activities: Pre-primary education
Officers: Julie Annette Swatton, Secretary; Emma Jane Austen [1985] Director/Civil Servant; Janet Crook [1954] Director/Retired; Cherry Anne Edwards OBE [1951] Director/Education Consultant; Lee Mark Hulse [1983] Director/Teacher; Grace Amanda Morton [1985] Director/Self Employed; Jayne Elizabeth Robb [1967] Director

West Hill School
Incorporated: 7 July 2011 *Employees:* 106
Net Worth: £13,920,000 *Total Assets:* £14,258,000
Registered Office: West Hill School, Thompson Cross, Stamford Street, Stalybridge, Cheshire, SK15 1LX
Activities: General secondary education
Officers: Alan Frank Harrison [1970] Director/Headteacher; Peter Edward Holden [1957] Director/Solicitor; John William McElwee [1953] Director; Ian Saxon [1965] Director of Operations & Neighbourhoods (Council); Carolyn Joyce Wright [1975] Director/Office Manager

West Norfolk Academies Trust
Incorporated: 28 February 2011 *Employees:* 825
Net Worth: £52,415,592 *Total Assets:* £59,114,756
Registered Office: Queensway, Gaywood, King's Lynn, Norfolk, PE30 4AW
Activities: General secondary education
Officers: Roger Keeble Allflatt [1941] Director; Amanda Ann Arterton [1959] Director; Kevin Andrew Baldwin [1964] Director/Self Employed Evangelist; Lesley Bambridge [1948] Director/Retired; Paul Bland [1946] Director/Retired; Nicholas John Daubney [1950] Director/Retired; Peter David Harris [1940] Director/Retired; Andrew Michael Johnson [1973] Director/Headteacher; Roger Livesey [1947] Director/Retired Teacher; Susan Lunnun [1954] Director/Retired Headteacher; Anthony Robert Yates [1955] Director/Local Government Officer

West Park School
Incorporated: 10 March 2011 *Employees:* 162
Net Worth: £11,503,132 *Total Assets:* £13,809,351
Registered Office: West Road, Spondon, Derby, DE21 7BT
Activities: General secondary education
Officers: Robert Mousley, Secretary; Andrew Fooks [1968] Director/Audit Team Leader; Pauline Jennings [1948] Director/Retired; Richard Jennings [1973] Construction Director; Michael Owen Johnson [1973] Director/Football Coach; Kevin Lane [1984] Director/ICT Systems Network Manager; John Quintin Gillean MacLaine [1949] Director/Retired Technical Manager; Scott Alexander McGregor [1977] Director/Headteacher; Benjamin Hugh Paradise [1960] Director/Teacher; Iain Robert Pendry [1971] Director/Chief of Manufacturing Engineering Site Strategy; Sheena Ruth Ratcliffe [1960] Director/Assistant Bereavement Services Manager; Rebecca Jayne Smith [1982] Director/Counsellor; Neville Taylor [1948] Director/Retired Property Services Manager

The West Retail Group Limited
Incorporated: 20 February 2004 *Employees:* 4,188
Net Worth: £47,644,472 *Total Assets:* £230,448,112
Registered Office: The Nest, Falkland Way, Barton upon Humber, N Lincs, DN18 5RL
Activities: Activities of head offices
Major Shareholder: Malcolm Stanley Healey
Officers: Jane Marie Oldfield, Secretary; Malcolm Stanley Healey [1944] Director; William Stanley Healey [1987] Director; Jane Marie Oldfield [1964] Director/Chartered Accountant; Mark Jonathan Pullan [1972] Director/Chartered Accountant

Westbourne Leisure Limited
Incorporated: 19 December 2007 *Employees:* 164
Net Worth: £9,315,318 *Total Assets:* £22,258,310
Registered Office: Westbourne Head Office, Strawberry Bank Hotel, 72 Main Road, Meriden, Coventry, Warwicks, CV7 7NF
Activities: Public houses and bars
Major Shareholder: Paul Edward Owens
Officers: Paul Edward Owens, Secretary; Christine Owens [1966] Director; Paul Edward Owens [1968] Director

Westbridge Furniture Designs Limited
Incorporated: 9 June 2004 *Employees:* 1,371
Net Worth: £4,741,000 *Total Assets:* £22,186,000
Registered Office: Furnace Road, Ilkeston, Derbys, DE7 5EP
Activities: Manufacture of other furniture
Officers: Nigel George Holifield [1959] Operations Director; Paul Islip [1960] Director; Gary Lasham [1958] Director; Stephen Olds [1970] Design Director; Karl Ivor Stevens [1956] Finance Director

Westbrook Holdings Limited
Incorporated: 20 November 2007 *Employees:* 25
Net Worth: £4,548,564 *Total Assets:* £19,969,358
Registered Office: Westbrook House, Wreakes Lane, Dronfield, Sheffield, S18 1LY
Activities: Activities of head offices
Major Shareholder: Shaun Walton
Officers: Nicholas Lee Jones [1978] Finance Director; Shaun Walton [1966] Director

Westbrook Resources Limited
Incorporated: 22 August 2000 *Employees:* 25
Net Worth: £5,932,445 *Total Assets:* £21,379,606
Registered Office: Westbrook House, Wreakes Lane, Dronfield, Sheffield, S18 1LY
Activities: Wholesale of metals and metal ores
Parent: Westbrook Holdings Ltd
Officers: Mark Joseph Bradshaw [1972] Sales Director; Lee Graham Bruce [1971] Commercial Director; Ian Paul Howe [1963] Director; Nicholas Lee Jones [1978] Finance Director; Shaun Walton [1966] Managing Director

W.Westerman Limited
Incorporated: 15 March 1946 *Employees:* 27
Net Worth: £19,025,962 *Total Assets:* £34,427,560
Registered Office: 158 Bye-Pass Road, Chilwell, Nottingham, NG9 5HQ
Activities: Development of building projects
Shareholders: Louise Anne Roberts; Robert Brian Westerman; Nicola Marie Bethel; Benjamin David Shelton; Brian Walter Westerman
Officers: Louise Anne Roberts, Secretary; Nicola Marie Bethel [1978] Director; Michael John Freshney [1943] Director; Louise Anne Roberts [1970] Director/Accountant; Benjamin David Shelton [1976] Director; Brian Walter Westerman [1944] Director/Builder; Robert Brian Westerman [1967] Director/Builder and Developer

Western Bridge (Shipping) Limited
Incorporated: 31 May 2002
Net Worth: £24,074,984 *Total Assets:* £39,211,072
Registered Office: Bardon Hall, Copt Oak Road, Markfield, Leics, LE67 9PJ
Activities: Sea and coastal freight water transport
Parent: AB Shipping Holding B.V.
Officers: Abraham Willem Bontrup [1977] Director/Manager [Dutch]; Peter Franz Jozef Bontrup [1974] Director [Dutch]; John Ferguson Bowater [1949] Director/Deputy Group CEO; Stephen George Dryden [1976] Director Aggregate Industries Overseas

Western Buses Limited
Incorporated: 24 September 1913 *Employees:* 993
Net Worth: £19,462,000 *Total Assets:* £48,620,000
Registered Office: c/o Stagecoach Services Limited, One Stockport Exchange, 20 Railway Road, Stockport, Cheshire, SK1 3SW
Activities: Other urban, suburban or metropolitan passenger land transport (not underground, metro or similar)
Parent: Stagecoach Bus Holdings Limited
Officers: Michael John Vaux, Secretary; Robert Gervase Andrew [1963] Director; Colin Brown [1968] Director/Accountant; Samuel Derek Greer [1968] Director

Westernrange Limited
Incorporated: 22 September 1995 *Employees:* 2
Net Worth: £7,996,160 *Total Assets:* £15,335,072
Registered Office: 4-8 Kilwardby Street, Ashby-De-La-Zouch, Leics, LE65 2FU
Activities: Buying and selling of own real estate
Officers: David William Wilson [1941] Director; James David Wilson [1972] Director/Land Buyer

Westfield Contributory Health Scheme Limited
Incorporated: 27 July 1935 *Employees:* 214
Net Worth: £75,229,000 *Total Assets:* £84,999,000
Registered Office: Westfield House, 60 Charter Row, Sheffield, S1 3FZ
Activities: Non-life insurance
Officers: Kevin Bardsley [1959] Director/Solicitor; Patricia Ann Cantrill [1950] Director/Independent Consultant; David Andrew Capper [1978] Commercial Director; Philip Ashton Gregory [1952] Director/Professional Services; Jason Sidney Hogan [1970] Finance Director; Nicholas James Anthony Hutton [1948] Director; Graham Moore [1943] Director/Chairman; David Edward Palmer [1965] Director/Training/Management Consultant; Andrew Radi [1973] Executive Director of IT [Australian]; Lesley Welton [1958] Director/Consultant; David John Whitney [1950] Director

Westmoreland Investments Limited
Incorporated: 4 July 1968 *Employees:* 6
Net Worth: £172,512,304 *Total Assets:* £287,797,728
Registered Office: 1 Westmoreland Avenue, Thurmaston, Leicester, LE4 8PH
Activities: Other letting and operating of own or leased real estate
Parent: Charles Street Buildings (Leicester) Limited
Officers: Robert Henry Smith, Secretary; Winifred Mary Linnett [1950] Director; Mary Agnes Middleton [1981] Director; Hugh Patrick Murphy [1948] Director; Joseph John Murphy [1978] Director/Solicitor; Margaret Ann Murphy [1951] Director; Patrick Hugh Murphy [1977] Director

Westmoreland Properties Limited
Incorporated: 15 October 1967 *Employees:* 6
Net Worth: £38,994,260 *Total Assets:* £128,804,896
Registered Office: 1 Westmoreland Avenue, Thurmaston, Leicester, LE4 8PH
Activities: Other letting and operating of own or leased real estate
Parent: Charles Street Buildings (Leicester) Limited
Officers: Robert Henry Smith, Secretary; Winifred Mary Linnett [1950] Director; Mary Agnes Middleton [1981] Director; Hugh Patrick Murphy [1948] Director; Joseph John Murphy [1978] Director/Solicitor; Margaret Ann Murphy [1951] Director; Patrick Hugh Murphy [1977] Director

Weymead Holdings Limited
Incorporated: 21 February 2014
Net Worth: £580 *Total Assets:* £14,480,580
Registered Office: Adsetts House, 16 Europa View, Sheffield Business Park, Sheffield, S9 1XH
Activities: Roofing activities
Parent: SIG Trading Limited
Officers: Richard Charles Monro, Secretary; Ian Jackson [1979] Director/Accountant; Christopher David Lodge [1978] Director; Richard Charles Monro [1958] Director/Chartered Secretary

WFEL Holdings Limited
Incorporated: 29 April 2006 *Employees:* 75
Net Worth: £28,564,000 *Total Assets:* £54,214,000
Registered Office: WFEL, Sir Richard Fairey Road, Heaton Chapel, Stockport, Cheshire, SK4 5DY
Activities: Manufacture of other fabricated metal products n.e.c.
Parent: Krauss-Maffei Wegmann GmbH & Co. KG
Officers: Patrick Neill Grady, Secretary; Ian Anderton [1965] Director; Patrick Neill Grady [1965] Finance Director; Ralf Ketzel [1959] Director [German]; Horst Rieder [1965] Director [German]; Frank Peter Schnur [1965] Director [German]

WFEL Limited
Incorporated: 11 February 1936 *Employees:* 75
Net Worth: £41,444,000 *Total Assets:* £61,485,000
Registered Office: WFEL, Sir Richard Fairey Road, Heaton Chapel, Stockport, Cheshire, SK4 5DY
Activities: Manufacture of other fabricated metal products n.e.c.
Parent: WFEL Holdings Limited
Officers: Patrick Neill Grady, Secretary; Ian Anderton [1965] Director; Patrick Neill Grady [1965] Finance Director; Ralf Ketzel [1959] Director [German]; Horst Rieder [1965] Director [German]; Frank Peter Schnur [1965] Director [German]

J. Wharton (Agriculture) Limited
Incorporated: 26 June 1964
Net Worth: £8,425,493 *Total Assets:* £13,303,142
Registered Office: Valley House, Valley Farm, North Lane, Swaby, Alford, Lincs, LN13 0BD
Activities: Growing of cereals (except rice), leguminous crops and oil seeds
Shareholders: Peter Stuart Fearn; Ruth Brewin; John Steven Wharton; Fiona Lizbeth Wharton
Officers: Fiona Lizbeth Wharton, Secretary; Michael John Daniells [1945] Director/Farm Manager; Fiona Lizbeth Wharton [1955] Director; John Steven Wharton [1943] Director

J.Wharton (Shipping) Limited
Incorporated: 4 November 1938
Net Worth: £53,321,392 *Total Assets:* £59,687,212
Registered Office: Valley House, Valley Farm, North Lane, Swaby, Alford, Lincs, LN13 0BD
Activities: Other letting and operating of own or leased real estate
Shareholders: Peter Stuart Fearn; Ruth Brewin; John Steven Wharton; Fiona Lizbeth Wharton
Officers: John Steven Wharton, Secretary; Fiona Lizbeth Wharton [1955] Director; John Steven Wharton [1943] Director

WHC01 Limited
Incorporated: 25 July 2016 *Employees:* 594
Net Worth: £2,675,361 *Total Assets:* £11,949,275
Registered Office: Suite A, Fernbank House, Springwood Way, Tytherington Business Park, Macclesfield, Cheshire, SK10 2XA
Activities: Other activities of employment placement agencies
Shareholder: Andrew Healing
Officers: Michael McGowan, Secretary; Michael William Fell [1957] Director; Andrew Healing [1969] Director; Jacqueline Ann Lindsay [1964] Director; Michael McGowan [1970] Director; Roger Charles Queen [1964] Director

Wheatcroft (Group) Limited
Incorporated: 31 July 2012 *Employees:* 11
Net Worth: £34,319,716 *Total Assets:* £37,742,000
Registered Office: 4 Bank Court, Weldon Road, Loughborough, Leics, LE11 5RF
Activities: Activities of other holding companies n.e.c.
Major Shareholder: Kevin Wheatcroft
Officers: Alexandra Mary Wheatcroft, Secretary; Philip James O'Connor [1962] Director/Accountant; Alexandra Mary Wheatcroft [1968] Director; Kevin Wheatcroft [1959] Director

Wheatcroft Collections Limited
Incorporated: 11 December 1953 *Employees:* 11
Previous: Donington Park Racing Limited
Net Worth: £17,801,554 *Total Assets:* £24,349,758
Registered Office: 4 Bank Court, Weldon Road, Loughborough, Leics, LE11 5RF
Activities: Other amusement and recreation activities n.e.c.
Parent: Wheatcroft (Group) Limited
Officers: Alexandra Mary Wheatcroft, Secretary; Philip James O'Connor [1962] Director; Alexandra Mary Wheatcroft [1968] Director; Kevin Wheatcroft [1959] Director

Wheatcroft Properties Limited
Incorporated: 10 December 1953 *Employees:* 3
Net Worth: £16,469,163 *Total Assets:* £17,918,960
Registered Office: 4 Bank Court, Weldon Road, Loughborough, Leics, LE11 5RF
Activities: Other letting and operating of own or leased real estate
Parent: Wheatcroft (Group) Limited
Officers: Alexandra Mary Wheatcroft, Secretary; Philip James O'Connor [1962] Director; Alexandra Mary Wheatcroft [1968] Director; Kevin Wheatcroft [1959] Director

Wheeldon Brothers Limited
Incorporated: 8 November 1989 *Employees:* 42
Net Worth: £14,559,802 *Total Assets:* £20,020,234
Registered Office: Wheeldon House, Prime Enterprise Park, Prime Park Way, Derby, DE1 3QB
Activities: Development of building projects
Major Shareholder: Peter Wheeldon Parkin
Officers: David Brookes, Secretary; David Brookes [1966] Finance Director; Edward Peter Parkin [1976] Director/Surveyor; James Henry Parkin [1974] Director/Accountant; Peter Wheeldon Parkin [1946] Director

Whilton Marina Limited
Incorporated: 20 March 1987 *Employees:* 48
Net Worth: £16,705,483 *Total Assets:* £26,482,548
Registered Office: Whilton Locks, Daventry, Northants, NN11 2NH
Activities: Wholesale of other intermediate products
Shareholders: Nigel David Steele; Richard John Steele
Officers: Nigel David Steele, Secretary; Charles Richard Steele [1988] Director; Nigel David Steele [1957] Director/Boating Marina and Caravan Park Operator; Richard John Steele [1960] Director/Boating Marina and Caravan Park Operator; Robert James Pearson Steele [1986] Director

Whirlow Developments Limited
Incorporated: 20 July 2011
Net Worth: £12,619,100 *Total Assets:* £20,812,564
Registered Office: 91-97 Saltergate, Chesterfield, Derbys, S40 1LA
Activities: Activities of other holding companies n.e.c.
Parent: Heathcotes Group Limited
Officers: Simon John Maxwell Cobb [1958] Director; David Astill Harrison [1961] Director; John Andrew Hill [1965] Director

Whirlpool UK Appliances Limited
Incorporated: 30 December 1909 *Employees:* 2,840
Previous: Indesit Company UK Limited
Net Worth Deficit: £8,816,000 *Total Assets:* £341,740,000
Registered Office: Morley Way, Peterborough, Cambs, PE2 9JB
Activities: Manufacture of electric domestic appliances
Parent: General Domestic Appliances Holdings Limited
Officers: Tetiana Pidhaina, Secretary; Marco Bellinzona [1970] Director [Italian]; Lucianna Raffaini Carvalho [1973] Director [Italian]; Camila Perina [1982] Director [Brazilian]; Tetiana Pidhaina [1981] Director [Ukrainian]; Andrzej Tuleja [1973] Director [Polish]

Whistler Acquisitions Limited
Incorporated: 26 April 2016 *Employees:* 147
Net Worth: £23,674,000 *Total Assets:* £50,610,000
Registered Office: c/o Workforce Software Ltd, Precedent Drive, Rooksley, Milton Keynes, Bucks, MK13 8PP
Activities: Other information technology service activities
Parent: Workforce Software LLC
Officers: Tammy Jones, Secretary; Denise Broady [1974] Director [American]; Robert Feller [1968] Director [American]; Mike Morini [1962] Director [American]

White Capstan Limited
Incorporated: 3 September 1996 *Employees:* 2,391
Net Worth: £85,757,576 *Total Assets:* £253,486,640
Registered Office: Enviroment House, 6 Union Road, Nottingham, NG3 1FH
Activities: Non-trading company
Officers: Christian Falk [1976] Director [German]; Roy Stewart Mochor [1950] Director; Anil Puri [1960] Director [Indian]

The White Hills Park Federation Trust
Incorporated: 30 August 2012 *Employees:* 202
Net Worth: £19,066,000 *Total Assets:* £23,393,000
Registered Office: Bramcote College, Moor Lane, Bramcote, Nottingham, NG9 3GA
Activities: General secondary education
Officers: Karen Sims, Secretary; Adam Edward Bird [1972] Director; Frances Ruth Brittle [1970] Director; Clare Goodyear [1970] Childminder/Director-Breakfast/After School Club; Susan Elizabeth Headland [1967] Director/Teaching Assistant; Paul Heery [1963] Director/Executive Headteacher; Tina Launchbury [1955] Director/Lecturer; James MacDonald [1971] Director/Teacher; Cathy Peacock [1969] Director/Accountant; Graham Perry-Slack [1966] Director/IT Consultant; Sue Vasey [1967] Director/Senior School Improvement Officer

Thomas White Oxford Limited
Incorporated: 21 May 2015 *Employees:* 2
Net Worth: £18,893,074 *Total Assets:* £19,529,900
Registered Office: 8 King Edward Street, Oxford, OX1 4HL
Activities: Development of building projects
Parent: St John Baptist College in the University of Oxford
Officers: William Alan Donger [1953] Director/Chartered Surveyor; Mark Taylor [1955] Director/Lawyer/Consultant

Thomas White Properties Limited
Incorporated: 17 February 2012
Net Worth: £14,904,801 *Total Assets:* £15,020,046
Registered Office: Midland House, West Way, Botley, Oxford, OX2 0PH
Activities: Buying and selling of own real estate
Officers: Sally Jayne Layburn [1973] Director/Bursar; Professor Walter Mattli [1961] Director [Swiss]; Professor Andrew John Parker [1954] Director/Bursar; Professor Margaret Jean Snowling [1955] Director/College President

White Woods Primary Academy Trust
Incorporated: 28 June 2013 *Employees:* 507
Net Worth: £39,455,000 *Total Assets:* £47,991,000
Registered Office: The Hub, Wickersley Northfield Primary School, Northfield Lane, Wickersley, Rotherham, S Yorks, S66 2HL
Activities: Primary education
Officers: Michael David Jennings [1957] Director/Lawyer; Philip Marshall [1958] Director; Alan James Richards [1960] Director/Education & Training Consultant; Amy Elizabeth Skelton [1978] Director/CFO/Accountant; Julie Turner [1952] Director/Retired Headteacher

Whitecross@Stepnell Limited
Incorporated: 9 June 2004 *Employees:* 3
Net Worth Deficit: £855,005 *Total Assets:* £15,605,648
Registered Office: Stepnell House, Lawford Road, Rugby, Warwicks, CV21 2UU
Activities: Management of real estate on a fee or contract basis
Parent: Whitecross @ Stepnell Holdings Limited
Officers: Mark Robert Wakeford, Secretary; James Richard Wakeford [1968] Director/Civil Engineer; Mark Robert Wakeford [1966] Director/Civil Engineer; Thomas Bosworth Wakeford [1977] Director

Whitemeadow Furniture Limited
Incorporated: 1 October 2007 *Employees:* 473
Net Worth: £1,803,768 *Total Assets:* £15,265,425
Registered Office: Whitemeadow Furniture Limited, Orchard Way, Calladine Business Park, Sutton in Ashfield, Notts, NG17 1JU
Activities: Manufacture of other furniture
Major Shareholder: Ian Robert Oscroft
Officers: Paul Craig Ainley [1971] Design Director; Michael Stuart Clarridge [1970] Finance Director; Garfield Peter Garnett [1965] Director; Andrew Kitchen [1966] Director; Ian Robert Oscroft [1960] Director; Paul John Wesson [1964] Director

Whitemeadow Group Holdings Limited
Incorporated: 14 September 2010 *Employees:* 473
Net Worth: £7,892,443 *Total Assets:* £21,435,616
Registered Office: Whitemeadow Furniture Limited, Orchard Way, Calladine Business Park, Sutton in Ashfield, Notts, NG17 1JU
Activities: Manufacture of other furniture
Officers: Paul Craig Ainley [1971] Design Director; Michael Stuart Clarridge [1970] Finance Director; Garfield Peter Garnett [1965] Director; Andrew Kitchen [1966] Commercial Director; Ian Robert Oscroft [1960] Managing Director; Paul John Wesson [1964] Sales Director

Whites Engineering Limited
Incorporated: 20 November 1998 *Employees:* 150
Net Worth: £6,578,113 *Total Assets:* £12,663,090
Registered Office: The Mine Site, Mill Lane, South Witham, Grantham, Lincs, NG33 5QN
Activities: Manufacture of other transport equipment n.e.c.
Shareholders: Regen Holdings Limited; Regen Holdings Limited
Officers: Christopher John Odonoghue, Secretary; James Alexander Waldorf Astor [1965] Director; Roel Win Collier [1973] Director [Belgian]; Geoffrey Mark Duyk [1959] Director/United States [American]

Whitley Academy
Incorporated: 3 June 2011 *Employees:* 142
Net Worth: £9,291,148 *Total Assets:* £13,163,103
Registered Office: Whitley Academy, Abbey Road, Coventry, Warwicks, CV3 4BD
Activities: General secondary education
Officers: Sandra Rose Baker, Secretary; Catherine Black [1967] Director/Catering & Cleaning Manager; Sharon Chamberlain-Bates [1979] Director/Nursery Manager; Stuart Peter Davoile [1970] Director/School Games Organiser & Tennis Coach; Timothy Downing [1966] Director/Head of Research Team; Maureen Elizabeth Emms [1951] Director/Personnel Manager; Ian Thomas Jamie [1957] Director; Paul John Lapworth [1971] Director/Charity Worker; Mark John Richard Londesborough [1979] Director/Programme Manager, Education/Voluntary Sector; Denis James Anthony MacDaid [1944] Director/Retired; Adrian Noble [1961] Director/Electrical Engineer; Kathryn Lesley Wright [1971] Director/Senior Vice Principal

Whitworth Bros.Limited
Incorporated: 17 March 1949 *Employees:* 353
Net Worth: £48,742,000 *Total Assets:* £103,154,000
Registered Office: Victoria Mills, Wellingborough, Northampton, NN8 2DT
Activities: Grain milling
Major Shareholder: Martin Francis George
Officers: Simone Louise Large, Secretary; Roger William Butler [1960] Director; Michael David George [1973] Director; David James Goddard [1974] Director/Accountant; Horatio John Ewart Growdridge [1962] Director; Michael Grant Peters [1964] Director; Matthew Whiteside [1967] Director; David Keith Doake Wood [1957] Director

Whitworth Chemists Limited
Incorporated: 3 August 1999 *Employees:* 298
Net Worth: £11,574,893 *Total Assets:* £23,874,412
Registered Office: 54a Sunderland Street, Tickhill, Doncaster, S Yorks, DN11 9QJ
Activities: Dispensing chemist in specialised stores
Shareholders: Dorothy Ann Bradley; Sally Elizabeth Vernon
Officers: Dorothy Ann Bradley, Secretary; Jan Barend Badenhorst [1976] Director/Superintendent Pharmacist [British/South African]; Dorothy Ann Bradley [1941] Director; Richard Watson Bradley [1966] Managing Director; Sally Elizabeth Vernon [1973] Director/Fashion Manager

Whitworths Holdings Limited
Incorporated: 19 December 2003 *Employees:* 536
Net Worth: £68,594,000 *Total Assets:* £150,598,000
Registered Office: Victoria Mills, London Road, Wellingborough, Northants, NN8 2DT
Activities: Activities of head offices
Major Shareholder: Martin Francis George
Officers: Simone Louise Large, Secretary/Accountant; Roger William Butler [1960] Director/Flour Miller; Martin Francis George [1942] Director; Michael David George [1973] Director; Nicholas Steven Linney [1952] Director/Company Chairman; Jeremy Preston [1945] Director

Whitworths Limited
Incorporated: 26 October 2004 *Employees:* 344
Net Worth: £8,406,000 *Total Assets:* £43,284,000
Registered Office: Orchard House, Irthlingborough, Wellingborough, Northants, NN9 5DB
Activities: Manufacture of other food products n.e.c.
Parent: Whitworths Investments Limited
Officers: Daniel Jarman, Secretary; Ogan Ceryan [1972] Director [Turkish]; Mark Robert Fairweather [1962] Director; Koray Oz [1982] Director [Turkish]; Osman Oz [1953] Director/Chairman [Turkish]

Whizstock
Incorporated: 31 August 1999
Net Worth: £6,067,630 *Total Assets:* £15,294,905
Registered Office: Dene Park, Stratford Road, Wellesbourne, Warwicks, CV35 9RY
Activities: Other letting and operating of own or leased real estate
Major Shareholder: Donal Ring
Officers: Patrick Tobin, Secretary; Angela O'Donoghue [1969] Director/Manager [Irish]; Donal Ring [1946] Director [Irish]; Gemma Ring [1976] Director [Irish]; Patrick Tobin [1941] Director/Accountant [Irish]

WIC (1) Limited
Incorporated: 15 January 2001
Previous: The International Life Leisure Group Limited
Net Worth: £221,476,000 *Total Assets:* £16,552,205,312
Registered Office: Haylock House, Kettering Parkway, Kettering, Northants, NN15 6EY
Activities: Non-trading company
Parent: PointTravel Co. Ltd
Officers: Andrew Clarke [1976] Senior Director Finance; Andrew Liggins [1962] Director

Wickersley Partnership Trust
Incorporated: 6 January 2014 *Employees:* 1,027
Net Worth: £74,507,000 *Total Assets:* £95,214,560
Registered Office: Wickersley School and Sports College, Bawtry Road, Wickersley, Rotherham, S Yorks, S66 1JL
Activities: Primary education
Officers: David Michael Ashmore, Secretary; Stephen Calvert [1968] Director/Vice President - Logistics; Pippa Dodgshon [1964] Director/Principal; David Mathieson [1970] Director/Area Business Manager; Helen Claire O'Brien [1976] Director/Chief Executive Officer; Peter Charles Sadler [1967] Marketing Director; Vicky Elaine Whitehead [1961] Director/Locality Manager

Wickes Building Supplies Limited
Incorporated: 13 August 1984 *Employees:* 6,791
Net Worth: £258,800,000 *Total Assets:* £1,187,399,936
Registered Office: Lodge Way House, Lodge Way, Harlestone Road, Northampton, NN5 7UG
Activities: Other retail sale of new goods in specialised stores (not commercial art galleries and opticians)
Parent: Wickes Holdings Limited
Officers: John Peter Carter [1961] Director; Simon Theodore King [1959] Director; Martin Richard Meech [1957] Director/Chartered Surveyor; Alan Richard Williams [1969] Director/Accountant

Wickes Properties Limited
Incorporated: 28 December 1978
Net Worth: £5,957,000 *Total Assets:* £20,283,000
Registered Office: Lodge Way House, Lodge Way, Harlestone Road, Northampton, NN5 7UG
Activities: Real estate agencies
Parent: Wickes Holdings Limited
Officers: John Peter Carter [1961] Director; Martin Richard Meech [1957] Director/Chartered Surveyor; Alan Richard Williams [1969] Director/Accountant

Wicksteed Leisure Limited
Incorporated: 21 April 1958 *Employees:* 109
Net Worth: £9,708,015 *Total Assets:* £13,964,784
Registered Office: Digby Street, Kettering, Northants, NN16 8YJ
Activities: Manufacture of other fabricated metal products n.e.c.
Parent: Jardentome Ltd
Officers: Thomas James Falkner, Secretary; Jamie Alexander Gowans [1972] Director; Charles Edward John Howard [1986] Director; Greville Patrick Charles Howard [1941] Director/Landowner; Thomas Henry Greville Howard [1983] Director; Chen Kain Kwah [1956] Financial Director; Katherine Jane Perkins [1967] Administrative Director; Graham Richard Shatford [1959] Production Director; Stuart Nicholas Wetherell [1955] Sales Director

Wienerberger Limited
Incorporated: 29 November 2004 *Employees:* 1,166
Net Worth: £121,773,000 *Total Assets:* £315,228,000
Registered Office: Wienerberger House, Brooks Drive, Cheadle Royal Business Park, Cheadle, Cheshire, SK8 3SA
Activities: Manufacture of bricks, tiles and construction products, in baked clay
Officers: Michael Grace, Secretary; Keith Stuart Barker [1961] Managing Director; Paul Stevenson [1959] Finance Director; Johan Van Der Biest [1963] Director/Chief Operating Officer [Belgian]

Wight Building Materials Ltd
Incorporated: 30 May 2013 *Employees:* 38
Net Worth: £7,386,000 *Total Assets:* £11,901,000
Registered Office: Bardon Hall, Copt Oak Road, Markfield, Leics, LE67 9PJ
Activities: Operation of gravel and sand pits; mining of clays and kaolin
Shareholders: Aggregate Industries UK Limited; Eurovia UK Limited
Officers: Joanne Greene, Secretary; Mark Robert Billingham [1964] Director/Regional Financial Controller; Stephen Michael Davies [1962] Director/General Manager; Pablo Libreros [1978] Managing Director, Aggregates [French]; John Patrick Riley [1967] Director; Dale Colin Trigg [1981] Director/Financial Controller; Scott Alexander Wardrop [1966] Director

Wigley Contracts (Barby) Limited
Incorporated: 6 March 1964 *Employees:* 22
Net Worth: £13,449,781 *Total Assets:* £33,100,232
Registered Office: Stockton House, Rugby Road, Stockton, Southam, Warwicks, CV47 8LB
Activities: Development of building projects
Shareholder: Sea Rock Services Limited
Officers: Robert John Wigley, Secretary; James Maurice Davies [1979] Director/Estate Manager; Jane Ann Wigley [1962] Director/Administrative Assistant; John George Wigley [1967] Director/Estate Manager; Robert John Wigley [1960] Director/Estate Manager; Sarah Wigley [1965] Director/Administrative Assistant

Wigston Academies Trust
Incorporated: 5 March 2012 *Employees:* 332
Previous: Abington Academy Trust
Net Worth: £23,372,504 *Total Assets:* £28,690,486
Registered Office: Wigston Academy, Station Road, Wigston, Leics, LE18 2DU
Activities: General secondary education
Officers: Catherine Reeds, Secretary; Martin John Byrne [1960] Director/Business Consultant; Elizabeth Jane Coates [1957] Director/Retired; Colin Spencer Gore [1953] Director/Governance and Legal Advisor; Sheila Eileen Lamb [1944] Director/Retired; Pauline Munro [1949] Director; Gaynor Kathleen Swingler [1949] Director/Retired

Wilcox Commercial Vehicles Limited
Incorporated: 13 November 2000 *Employees:* 121
Net Worth: £5,927,229 *Total Assets:* £9,755,909
Registered Office: Blenheim Way, Market Deeping, Peterborough, Cambs, PE6 8LD
Activities: Manufacture of trailers and semi-trailers
Parent: Wilcox Holdings Limited
Officers: Vito Ronzano, Secretary/Production Director [Italian]; Christopher John Bartlett [1963] Sales Director; Vito Ronzano [1959] Production Director [Italian]

Wilcox Holdings Limited
Incorporated: 15 November 2001 *Employees:* 121
Previous: R & G Wilcox Limited
Net Worth: £7,781,749 *Total Assets:* £12,389,194
Registered Office: c/o Wilcox Commercial Vehicles Limited, Blenheim Way, Market Deeping, Peterborough, Cambs, PE6 8LD
Activities: Other letting and operating of own or leased real estate
Shareholders: Christopher John Bartlett; Vito Ronzano
Officers: Vito Ronzano, Secretary/Production Director [Italian]; Christopher John Bartlett [1963] Engineer/Sales Director; Vito Ronzano [1959] Production Director [Italian]

Thos. C. Wild Limited
Incorporated: 22 July 2005 *Employees:* 73
Net Worth: £3,281,408 *Total Assets:* £10,384,687
Registered Office: Vulcan Works, Tinsley Park Road, Sheffield, S9 5DP
Activities: Forging, pressing, stamping and roll-forming of metal; powder metallurgy
Shareholder: Irene Yvonne Hancock
Officers: Laura Jane Hetherington, Secretary; Anne Marie Bisby [1976] Director; Alexandra Margaret Elizabeth Hancock [1983] Director; John Hancock [1955] Director; Rachel Elizabeth Hancock [1990] Finance Director; Laura Jane Hetherington [1982] Director; Michael Howson [1959] Director; Martin Roy Justice [1959] Director; Stefan Sommefeldt [1962] Director

Wildgoose Construction Limited
Incorporated: 22 December 1921 *Employees:* 86
Net Worth: £4,149,476 *Total Assets:* £16,236,985
Registered Office: Horsefair House, 35 King Street, Alfreton, Derbys, DE55 7BY
Activities: Development of building projects
Shareholders: Jonathan Nigel Wildgoose; Laura Rebecca Harcourt
Officers: David Lawrence Withers, Secretary; Simon Alexander Carr [1958] Director; Laura Rebecca Harcourt [1963] Director; Andrew Tilford [1970] Director; Jonathan Nigel Wildgoose [1960] Director; Marjory Jean Wildgoose [1931] Director; Mark Winstanley [1963] Director; David Lawrence Withers [1966] Director/Accountant

Wilkin Chapman LLP
Incorporated: 12 February 2009 *Employees:* 354
Net Worth: £6,689,075 *Total Assets:* £16,247,229
Registered Office: Cartergate House, 26 Chantry Lane, Grimsby, N E Lincs, DN31 2LJ
Officers: James Mark Carlton [1960] Member; Andrew David Holt [1965] Member; Craig John McKay [1959] Member; Lesley Archer [1969] LLP Member; Edward James Atkin [1979] LLP Member; Flora Mary Bennett [1961] LLP Member; Lisa Michelle Boileau [1969] LLP Member; Paul Bowden [1984] LLP Member; Ruth Brewin [1959] LLP Member; Joshua Lee Briggs [1985] LLP Member; Andrew Peter Burnett [1975] LLP Member; Tean Miles Butcher [1966] LLP Member; Katie Jacqueline Davies [1982] LLP Member; Matthew Thomas George Dix [1977] LLP Member; Jane Eatock [1966] LLP Member; Russell John Eke [1967] LLP Member; Richard John Frogson [1966] LLP Member; Elizabeth Gilliatt [1981] LLP Member; Jonathan Thornes Goolden [1965] LLP Member; Christopher Richard Grocock [1968] LLP Member; Peter Hanson [1967] LLP Member; Catherine Elizabeth Harris [1974] LLP Member; Nikki Ann Hawkins [1984] LLP Member; Steven Paul Hennegan [1973] LLP Member; Imogen Fay Holmes [1974] LLP Member; Richard William Bruno Houltby [1958] LLP Member; Rupert Mark Houltby [1959] LLP Member; Lisa Jane Howes [1971] LLP Member; Jonathan James Judge [1971] LLP Member; James Michael Lloyd [1973] LLP Member; Adam Thomas Marham [1977] LLP Member; James Richard Marsden [1985] LLP Member; Claire Elizabeth Parker [1971] LLP Member; Jonty Sebastian Pearson [1982] LLP Member; Rachael Louise Perry [1981] LLP Member; Sharon Elaine Plumtree [1967] LLP Member; Mark Robinson [1966] LLP Member; Nasim Sharf [1970] LLP Member; Ian Sherburn [1969] LLP Member; Wendy Christina Spalding-Siracusa [1964] LLP Member; Michael James Squirrell [1984] LLP Member; Jonathan Edward Stork [1980] LLP Member; Oliver Richard Tasker [1985] LLP Member; Mark Taylor [1968] LLP Member; Teresa Lynne Thomas [1973] LLP Member; Jonathan Paul West [1972] LLP Member

The Wilkins Group Limited
Incorporated: 20 August 2003 *Employees:* 387
Net Worth: £12,619,261 *Total Assets:* £24,835,600
Registered Office: 1 Private Road, Colwick Industrial Estate, Nottingham, NG4 2JX
Activities: Other business support service activities n.e.c.
Officers: Ann Wilkins, Secretary; Andre Philip Wilkins [1947] Director/Printer; Ann Wilkins [1946] Director/Administrator; Margorie Peggy Wilkins [1927] Director/Lace Manufacturer

Ken Wilkins Print Limited
Incorporated: 21 February 1984 *Employees:* 270
Net Worth: £9,649,445 *Total Assets:* £21,734,280
Registered Office: Private Road Number One, Colwick Industrial Estate, Nottingham, NG4 2JQ
Activities: Printing n.e.c.
Officers: Ann Wilkins, Secretary; Andre Philip Wilkins [1947] Director/Printer; Ann Wilkins [1946] Director/Administrator; Marjorie Peggy Wilkins [1927] Director/Lace Manufacturer

Wilkinson Hardware Stores, Limited
Incorporated: 22 January 2014 *Employees:* 20,551
Net Worth: £104,949,000 *Total Assets:* £435,607,008
Registered Office: JK House, Roebuck Way, Manton Wood, Worksop, Notts, S80 3EG
Activities: Activities of other holding companies n.e.c.
Parent: Amalgamated Holdings Wilkinson Limited
Officers: Claire Phillips, Secretary; John Ellis Jackson [1947] Director; Andrew Jeffrey Moore [1957] Director; Timothy David Dalton Philips [1968] Director [Irish]; Alejandro Russo [1971] Director; Lisa Joanne Wilkinson [1968] Director/Solicitor

Wilko Retail Limited
Incorporated: 13 February 1941 *Employees:* 20,551
Net Worth: £104,949,000 *Total Assets:* £435,607,008
Registered Office: JK House, Roebuck Way, Manton Wood, Worksop, Notts, S80 3EG
Activities: Other retail sale in non-specialised stores
Parent: Wilkinson Hardware Stores, Limited
Officers: Claire Phillips, Secretary; Andrew John Green [1966] Director; Mark Jason Hale [1968] Director; Andrew Knowles [1969] Director; Duncan Craig McGregor [1970] Retail Director; Andrew Jeffrey Moore [1957] Director; Timothy David Dalton Philips [1968] Director [Irish]; Kate Price [1977] Director

Williams Grand Prix Engineering Limited
Incorporated: 8 February 1977 *Employees:* 624
Net Worth: £47,188,000 *Total Assets:* £118,575,000
Registered Office: Grove, Wantage, Oxon, OX12 0DQ
Activities: Manufacture of other electrical equipment
Parent: Williams Grand Prix Holdings PLC
Officers: Mark Biddle, Secretary; Mark Biddle [1966] Director/General Counsel; Douglas James Lafferty [1978] Director; Patrick Allen Lowe [1962] Director/Chief Technical Officer; Michael Patrick Odriscoll [1956] Director/Automotive Consultant; Claire Victoria Williams [1976] Director of Marketing and Communications; Sir Frank Owen Garbett Williams [1942] Director

Williams Grand Prix Holdings PLC
Incorporated: 21 December 2010 *Employees:* 793
Net Worth: £46,594,000 *Total Assets:* £124,703,000
Registered Office: Grove, Wantage, Oxon, OX12 0DQ
Activities: Activities of other holding companies n.e.c.
Major Shareholder: Francis Owen Garbett Williams
Officers: Mark Biddle, Secretary; Mark Biddle [1966] Director; Brad Eugene Hollinger [1954] Director/Health Care Executive [American]; Douglas James Lafferty [1978] Director; Patrick Allen Lowe [1962] Director/Chief Technical Officer; Michael Patrick O'Driscoll [1956] Director/Automotive Consultant; Nicholas Charles Rose [1957] Director; Claire Victoria Williams [1976] Director

Williams Jet Tenders (Holdings) Limited
Incorporated: 4 August 2017 *Employees:* 60
Net Worth: £8,225,765 *Total Assets:* £12,060,987
Registered Office: Unit 2 Vogue Business Park, Tower Road, Berinsfield, Wallingford, Oxon, OX10 7LN
Activities: Activities of other holding companies n.e.c.
Shareholders: Roy Parker; John Robert Hornsby; Mathew David Hornsby
Officers: Simon Mark Smith, Secretary; John Robert Hornsby [1970] Director; Mathew David Hornsby [1972] Director; Roy Parker [1943] Director

Williams Jet Tenders Limited
Incorporated: 10 September 2004 *Employees:* 60
Previous: Williams Performance Tenders Limited
Net Worth: £7,523,932 *Total Assets:* £10,292,524
Registered Office: Unit 2 Vogue Business Park, Tower Road, Berinsfield, Wallingford, Oxon, OX10 7LN
Activities: Building of pleasure and sporting boats
Shareholders: Mathew David Hornsby; John Robert Hornsby; Roy Parker
Officers: Simon Mark Smith, Secretary; Darren Kenneth Edwards [1963] Director/Production; John Robert Hornsby [1970] Director/Boat Builder; Mathew David Hornsby [1972] Director/Boat Builder; Roy Parker [1943] Director; Simon Mark Smith [1966] Director/Accountant

Willoughby (35) Limited
Incorporated: 12 September 1994 *Employees:* 10
Net Worth: £70,422,904 *Total Assets:* £212,965,952
Registered Office: Cabourn House, Station Street, Bingham, Notts, NG13 8AQ
Activities: Activities of other holding companies n.e.c.
Shareholders: Jill Brand; Sue Morris; Alan Philip Morris
Officers: Sue Morris, Secretary; Jill Brand [1953] Director; Alan Philip Morris [1951] Director; Sue Morris [1955] Director

Willoughby (396) Limited
Incorporated: 7 May 2002 *Employees:* 3
Net Worth: £19,343,844 *Total Assets:* £21,873,136
Registered Office: Navigation House, Mill Gate, Newark, Notts, NG24 4TS
Activities: Other letting and operating of own or leased real estate
Officers: Elizabeth Louise Coxe, Secretary; John Robert Coles [1946] Director/Chartered Surveyor

Willoughby 395 (EBK) Limited
Incorporated: 20 March 2014
Net Worth: £14,865,953 *Total Assets:* £14,960,616
Registered Office: North Lodge Farm, Widmerpool Lane, Widmerpool, Nottingham, NG12 5QE
Activities: Activities of other holding companies n.e.c.
Shareholders: Christopher Alan Butterfield; Julia Mary Butterfield
Officers: Julia Mary Butterfield, Secretary; Christopher Alan Butterfield [1951] Director/Chartered Accountant; Julia Mary Butterfield [1953] Director

Willoughby 395 Limited
Incorporated: 7 May 2002 *Employees:* 6
Net Worth: £9,863,348 *Total Assets:* £13,384,609
Registered Office: North Lodge Farm, Widmerpool Lane, Widmerpool, Nottingham, NG12 5QE
Activities: Growing of cereals (except rice), leguminous crops and oil seeds
Parent: Willoughby 395 (NLF) Limited
Officers: Julia Mary Butterfield, Secretary/Director; Christopher Alan Butterfield [1951] Director/Chartered Accountant; Julia Mary Butterfield [1953] Director

Willoughby Farms Limited
Incorporated: 13 May 1952 *Employees:* 14
Net Worth: £18,043,760 *Total Assets:* £19,291,736
Registered Office: The Estate Office, Elsom Farm, Bonthorpe, Alford, Lincs, LN13 9TD
Activities: Mixed farming
Shareholders: Peter Richard Brough; Roderick Mann
Officers: Susan Mary Needham, Secretary; Dianna Gay James [1954] Director; Nicholas Richard Givron Peck [1955] Director

Willowbrook Healthcare Debtco Limited
Incorporated: 24 July 2008 *Employees:* 3
Net Worth Deficit: £230,975 *Total Assets:* £58,756,492
Registered Office: 3 Cygnet Drive, Swan Valley, Northampton, NN4 9BS
Activities: Activities of other holding companies n.e.c.
Parent: Willowbrook Healthcare Limited
Officers: Matthew Frederick Proctor, Secretary; Ian Matthews [1948] Director; Matthew Frederick Proctor [1967] Director; John Michael Barrie Strowbridge [1967] Director

Willowbrook Healthcare Developments Limited
Incorporated: 24 July 2008 *Employees:* 3
Net Worth Deficit: £37,341 *Total Assets:* £10,361,659
Registered Office: 3 Cygnet Drive, Swan Valley, Northampton, NN4 9BS
Activities: Development of building projects
Parent: Willowbrook Healthcare Debtco Limited
Officers: Matthew Frederick Proctor, Secretary; Ian Matthews [1948] Director; Matthew Frederick Proctor [1967] Director; John Michael Barrie Strowbridge [1967] Director

Willowbrook Healthcare Group Limited
Incorporated: 18 March 2013 *Employees:* 3
Net Worth: £100,001 *Total Assets:* £14,117,978
Registered Office: 3 Cygnet Drive, Swan Valley, Northampton, NN4 9BS
Activities: Activities of other holding companies n.e.c.
Parent: Avery Healthcare Group Limited
Officers: Matthew Frederick Proctor, Secretary; Ian Matthews [1948] Director; Matthew Frederick Proctor [1967] Director; John Michael Barrie Strowbridge [1967] Director

Willowbrook Healthcare Limited
Incorporated: 24 July 2008 *Employees:* 154
Net Worth: £100,639 *Total Assets:* £31,573,242
Registered Office: 3 Cygnet Drive, Swan Valley, Northampton, NN4 9BS
Activities: Activities of head offices
Parent: Willowbrook Healthcare Group Limited
Officers: Matthew Frederick Proctor, Secretary; Ian Matthews [1948] Director; Matthew Frederick Proctor [1967] Director; John Michael Barrie Strowbridge [1967] Director

The H D H Wills 1965 Charitable Trust
Incorporated: 11 December 2006 *Employees:* 8
Net Worth: £93,433,256 *Total Assets:* £94,618,984
Registered Office: Henley Knapp Barn, Fulwell, Chipping Norton, Oxon, OX7 4EN
Activities: Non-trading company
Officers: Sue Trafford, Secretary; John Seton Burrell Carson [1952] Director/Chartered Accountant; Martin Guy Fiennes [1961] Director/Corporate Financier; Charles Philip Liell Francklin [1952] Director/Chartered Surveyor; Thomas Michael Nelson [1979] Director/Fund Manager; Anthony Richard Tulloch [1977] Director/Banking; Dr Catherine Mary Hamilton Wills [1950] Director/Art Historian/Freelance Writer

Wilson & Co. (Motor Sales) Limited
Incorporated: 28 January 1998 *Employees:* 239
Net Worth: £4,925,780 *Total Assets:* £21,434,108
Registered Office: Hewitts Avenue, Hewitts Circus, Grimsby, N E Lincs, DN36 4SE
Activities: Sale of new cars and light motor vehicles
Parent: RJTK Investments Ltd
Officers: Marcus Peter McVeigh, Secretary; Marcus Peter McVeigh [1971] Finance Director; Robin Wilson [1957] Managing Director; Thomas Robin Wilson [1987] Director

David Wilson Homes Limited
Incorporated: 8 December 1964
Net Worth: £143,316,000 *Total Assets:* £178,775,008
Registered Office: Barratt House, Cartwright Way, Forest Business Park, Bardon Hill, Coalville, Leics, LE67 1UF
Activities: Construction of commercial buildings
Parent: Wilson Bowden Limited
Officers: Steven John Boyes [1960] Group Executive Director; David Fraser Thomas [1963] Director; Jessica Elizabeth White [1978] Director/Chief Financial Officer

Winbro Group Technologies Limited
Incorporated: 16 April 1992 *Employees:* 188
Net Worth: £12,626,949 *Total Assets:* £22,369,476
Registered Office: Whitwick Business Park, Stenson Road, Coalville, Leics, LE67 4JP
Activities: Manufacture of other special-purpose machinery n.e.c.
Parent: Winbro Group UK Limited
Officers: Robert Michael Arbon [1965] Director [American]; Lloyd Philip Bromham [1973] Director; Mark Stewart Draisey [1967] Director; Robert James Folwell [1957] Director/Engineer; Andrew Marc Lawson [1971] Sales Director; Dr. Winfield Perry [1948] Director [American]

Winbro Group UK Limited
Incorporated: 29 March 1999 *Employees:* 188
Net Worth: £13,044,789 *Total Assets:* £22,369,476
Registered Office: Whitwick Business Park, Stenson Road, Coalville, Leics, LE67 4JP
Activities: Activities of head offices
Officers: Robert Michael Arbon [1965] Director [American]; Dr. Winfield Blount Perry [1948] Director [American]

Wind Port of Liverpool Limited
Incorporated: 12 February 2007 *Employees:* 2
Previous: Port of Liverpool Wind Farm Limited
Net Worth Deficit: £1,687,756 *Total Assets:* £11,840,643
Registered Office: Victoria House, 19-21 Ack Lane East, Bramhall, Stockport, Cheshire, SK7 2BE
Activities: Production of electricity
Parent: Wind Pol 2 Holding Limited
Officers: Derek Patrick Stewart Henderson, Secretary; Derek Patrick Henderson [1971] Director/Financial Controller; Duncan Andrew Levie [1963] Director/General Manager [Irish]

Windsor Vehicle Leasing Limited
Incorporated: 8 July 1958 *Employees:* 23
Net Worth: £2,688,825 *Total Assets:* £11,484,426
Registered Office: Centenary House, Beresford Way, Chesterfield, Derbys, S41 9FG
Activities: Sale of used cars and light motor vehicles
Parent: URA Ventures Limited
Officers: Philip Austin Smith, Secretary; Richard Thomas Kenning [1951] Director; Benjamin Philip Newton [1973] Marketing Director; Philip Austin Smith [1962] Director/Accountant

Wingfield Academy
Incorporated: 30 May 2013 *Employees:* 101
Net Worth: £7,779,590 *Total Assets:* £10,326,888
Registered Office: Wingfield Academy, Wingfield Road, Rotherham, S Yorks, S61 4AU
Activities: General secondary education
Officers: Andrew Stuart Winch, Secretary; Jeremy Brooke [1965] Director/Solicitor; Georgina Brown [1974] Director/Youth Worker; Zachary Aron Collingham [1991] Director/Solicitor; Nicholas John Davies [1967] Director/Chartered Surveyor; Phillip Davis [1978] Director/Headteacher; Susan Jayne Gladwin [1957] Director/Supply - Primary School Teacher; Jonathan Hamer [1967] Director; Julie Harris [1970] Director/Year Team Leader; Claire Louise Hartle [1978] Director/Mature Student; Lee Craig Morritt [1968] Director/Teacher; Allyson Mary Pearson [1967] Director/Receptionist; Michael James Richards [1989] Director/Teacher

Thos.Winnard & Sons Limited
Incorporated: 21 June 1945 *Employees:* 31
Net Worth: £7,136,874 *Total Assets:* £11,770,005
Registered Office: Barbot Hall Industrial Estate, Mangham Road, Rotherham, S Yorks, S62 6EF
Activities: Other manufacturing n.e.c.
Officers: Michael Barker, Secretary/Director; James Michael Barker [1980] Director; Michael Barker [1942] Director; Carl Jones [1967] Director/Sales; Anthony Ashton Woodhouse [1968] Director

Winslow Court Ltd
Incorporated: 5 June 1990 *Employees:* 197
Net Worth: £11,051,000 *Total Assets:* £11,781,000
Registered Office: 1 St George's House, Vernon Gate, Derby, DE1 1UQ
Activities: Other residential care activities n.e.c.
Parent: Qatar Investment Authority
Officers: James Richard Atkinson, Finance Director; James Richard Atkinson [1968] Finance Director; Brian James Jones [1950] Director/Chief Executive

Winter & Co. UK Limited
Incorporated: 1 January 1971 *Employees:* 31
Net Worth: £8,300,613 *Total Assets:* £9,825,453
Registered Office: Stonehill, Huntingdon, Cambs, PE29 6ED
Activities: Wholesale of textiles
Major Shareholder: Philippe Winter
Officers: Timothy James Stewart Edwards, Secretary; Christoph Peter Borer [1970] Director [Swiss]; Stephen Geoffrey Burdett [1956] Sales Director; Paul Davinson [1972] Sales Director; Timothy James Stewart Edwards [1964] Director/Accountant; Beat Paul Schreiber [1958] Director/Accountant [Swiss]

Winterhalter Ltd
Incorporated: 22 October 1970 *Employees:* 138
Net Worth: £6,201,795 *Total Assets:* £25,037,508
Registered Office: Winterhalter House, Roebuck Way, Knowlhill, Milton Keynes, Bucks, MK5 8WH
Activities: Repair of other equipment
Officers: David John Parsons, Secretary; Peter John Alsworth [1962] Director; Andrew Keith Blake [1957] Director; Viktor Faller [1964] Director [German]; Peter Huber [1957] Director [German]; Stephen Kinkead [1970] Director; Kieran Raymond Lynch [1960] Director [Irish]; David John Parsons [1961] Finance Director; Glenn Ernest Roberts [1960] Sales Director; David Smithson [1949] Director; Jurgen Winterhalter [1944] Director/Engineer [German]; Ralph Winterhalter [1978] Director [German]

Wintringham Newco1 Limited
Incorporated: 5 April 2017
Net Worth: £1 *Total Assets:* £27,856,380
Registered Office: University Offices, University of Oxford, Wellington Square, Oxford, OX1 2JD
Activities: Activities of other holding companies n.e.c.
Parent: 1 Wintringham LLP
Officers: Anne Malcolm Cowell [1948] Director; Sir Andrew William Dilnot [1960] Director; Dr Catherine Anne Grocock [1947] Director; Ian Michael Laing [1946] Director

Wintringham Newco2 Limited
Incorporated: 5 April 2017
Net Worth: £1 *Total Assets:* £9,900,001
Registered Office: University Offices, University of Oxford, Wellington Square, Oxford, OX1 2JD
Activities: Activities of other holding companies n.e.c.
Parent: 1 Wintringham LLP
Officers: Anne Malcolm Cowell [1948] Director; Sir Andrew William Dilnot [1960] Director; Dr Catherine Anne Grocock [1947] Director; Ian Michael Laing [1946] Director

Winvic Construction Limited
Incorporated: 4 January 2001 *Employees:* 203
Net Worth: £49,414,368 *Total Assets:* £157,117,424
Registered Office: Brampton House, 19 Tenter Road, Moulton Park, Northampton, NN3 6PZ
Activities: Construction of commercial buildings
Parent: Winvic Group Ltd
Officers: Simon Victor Girardier, Secretary; Christopher John Allsopp [1970] Director; Richard James Butler [1965] Director; Simon Victor Girardier [1964] Director/Commercial Manager; Simon Winston Hunt [1964] Director; Mark Idris Jones [1977] Director; Ivor Daniel Nelson [1980] Director; Timothy Simon Reeve [1972] Director; David Jonathan Ward [1961] Director

Winvic Group Limited
Incorporated: 20 July 2006 *Employees:* 204
Net Worth: £54,265,208 *Total Assets:* £162,869,024
Registered Office: Brampton House, 19 Tenter Road, Moulton Park, Northampton, NN3 6PZ
Activities: Construction of commercial buildings
Shareholders: Simon Victor Girardier; Simon Winston Hunt; David Jonathan Ward
Officers: Simon Victor Girardier, Secretary; Richard James Butler [1965] Director; Simon Victor Girardier [1964] Director; Simon Winston Hunt [1964] Director; David Jonathan Ward [1961] Director

Wipac Limited
Incorporated: 14 July 1969 *Employees:* 318
Net Worth: £20,100,048 *Total Assets:* £45,089,432
Registered Office: London Road, Buckingham, MK18 1BH
Activities: Manufacture of other parts and accessories for motor vehicles
Parent: Carclo PLC
Officers: Richard John Ottaway, Secretary; David Robert William Benton [1971] Director; Philip Dobbie [1966] Director/Chartered Engineer; Michael Terence Greenrod [1976] Director/Design; Christopher John Malley [1967] Director; Mark Andrew Ross [1965] Director/Accountant; Neil Sibley [1968] Sales Director

Wisbech Grammar School
Incorporated: 13 June 2001 *Employees:* 129
Net Worth: £9,537,042 *Total Assets:* £11,139,702
Registered Office: Wisbech Grammar School, North Brink, Wisbech, Cambs, PE13 1JX
Activities: Primary education
Officers: Natalie Jane Miller, Secretary; Dr Dennis Barter [1944] Director/Consultant Paediatrician; Judith Alison Bodger [1951] Director/Education; Christopher Mark Stephen Goad [1982] Director/Chartered Accountant; Karina Simonne Albertine Hart [1959] Director/Consultant Community Paediatrician [Belgian]; Ian MacLachlan [1964] Director/Building Surveyor; Catherine Rebecca Mair [1968] Director/Veterinary Surgeon; The Ven Hugh Kyle McCurdy [1958] Director/Church; Elizabeth Christine Morris [1950] Director/Solicitor; Professor James Russell Raven [1959] Director/University Professor; Dr Quintin Kwing Kee Wong [1962] Director/General Medical Practitioner

Wispington Farms Limited
Incorporated: 19 October 1995 *Employees:* 12
Net Worth: £5,989,857 *Total Assets:* £9,954,001
Registered Office: 18 Northgate, Sleaford, Lincs, NG34 7BJ
Activities: Mixed farming
Shareholders: Richard Frank Craven; Wendy Craven; Jarred Thomas Wright; John Russell Bowser Ward
Officers: Nicola Mary Frick, Secretary; Adam Richard Craven [1979] Director/Farmer; Richard Frank Craven [1951] Director/Farmer; Wendy Craven [1954] Director/Company Secretary; Nicola Mary Frick [1980] Director/Company Secretary

Witham (Specialist Vehicles) Limited
Incorporated: 2 August 1982 *Employees:* 33
Net Worth: £30,668,084 *Total Assets:* £41,702,196
Registered Office: Honeypot Lane, Colsterworth, Grantham, Lincs, NG33 5LY
Activities: Sale of other motor vehicles
Shareholders: Camilla Maria Pauline Southerington; Douglas Patrick Landy; Paul David Southerington
Officers: Camilla Maria Pauline Southerington, Secretary; Douglas Patrick Landy [1968] Director/Sales Manager [Irish]; Camilla Maria Pauline Southerington [1983] Director; Paul David Southerington [1951] Director

Wixams First Limited
Incorporated: 26 March 2002 *Employees:* 5
Net Worth: £1,004,249 *Total Assets:* £158,623,728
Registered Office: Gallagher House, Gallagher Way, Gallagher Business Park, Heathcote, Warwick, CV34 6AF
Activities: Buying and selling of own real estate
Officers: Edward Paul Farnsworth [1982] Director of Business Planning; Craig David Luttman [1975] Development Director; Martin Rowland Richmond [1953] Group Legal Director; Gregg Spencer Wilkinson [1973] Managing Director

WJ South Limited
Incorporated: 25 March 1994 *Employees:* 114
Previous: Linkline Maintenance Services Limited
Net Worth: £4,602,336 *Total Assets:* £9,525,391
Registered Office: Brook Farm, Drayton Road, Newton Longville, Milton Keynes, Bucks, MK17 0BH
Activities: Other specialised construction activities n.e.c.
Major Shareholder: Wayne Douglas Johnston
Officers: Nigel John Bayley, Secretary; Wayne Douglas Johnston [1967] Director

WJH Limited
Incorporated: 23 March 2005 *Employees:* 1,717
Net Worth: £125,353,000 *Total Assets:* £207,152,000
Registered Office: 7 Merseyway, Stockport, Cheshire, SK1 1PN
Activities: Non-trading company
Shareholder: John Coulter
Officers: Ann Jones, Secretary; John Coulter [1951] Director/Jeweller; Ann Jones [1954] Director/Jeweller

WLP Holdings Limited
Incorporated: 15 September 2008 *Employees:* 121
Net Worth: £3,579,941 *Total Assets:* £11,724,866
Registered Office: Wilds Lodge School, Stamford Road, Empingham, Oakham, Rutland, LE15 8QQ
Activities: Other education n.e.c.
Officers: Kevin Derbyshire, Secretary; Richard William Gamble [1946] Director; Robin Lee [1958] Director

Woburn Enterprises Limited
Incorporated: 12 November 1969
Net Worth: £21,235,352 *Total Assets:* £21,520,904
Registered Office: The Bedford Office, Woburn, Beds, MK17 9PQ
Activities: Other retail sale not in stores, stalls or markets
Shareholders: James Fitzroy Dean; Charles William Cayzer; Edmond Conolly Mahony; Paul Vere Lindon
Officers: Kevin Leslie Shurrock, Secretary; The Hon Charles William Cayzer [1957] Director; Timothy Francis How [1950] Director/Company Chairman; Paul Vere Lindon [1962] Director/Chartered Surveyor; Louise Rona Russell [1962] Director; Andrew Ian Henry Russell Fifteenth Duke of Bedford [1962] Director

Wolf Safety Lamp Company Limited (The)
Incorporated: 30 November 1916 *Employees:* 38
Net Worth: £11,269,961 *Total Assets:* £12,127,347
Registered Office: Saxon Road Works, Heeley, Sheffield, S8 0YA
Activities: Other manufacturing n.e.c.
Officers: Peter Raymond O'Connell, Secretary; Alexander William Maurice Jackson [1970] Managing Director; John Newton Maurice Jackson [1943] Director; Miles John Newton Jackson [1973] Director; Alasdair James Dunbar MacIntyre [1959] Sales & Marketing Director; Michael Charles Morley [1963] Technical Director; Peter Raymond O'Connell [1968] Director/Chartered Accountant; Grant Shires [1969] Operations Director

Wolf Systems Limited
Incorporated: 29 July 1987
Net Worth: £13,078,613 *Total Assets:* £14,717,805
Registered Office: Shilton Industrial Estate, Bulkington Road, Shilton, Coventry, Warwicks, CV7 9QL
Activities: Other specialised construction activities n.e.c.
Officers: Karl Foster, Secretary; Karl Foster [1967] Director/Sales & Marketing; Robert Joseph Harris [1971] Director; Christopher Derek Riches [1957] Technical Director; Heinz Stadler [1985] Director [Austrian]

Wollaston Motors Limited
Incorporated: 17 November 1961 *Employees:* 155
Net Worth: £4,303,622 *Total Assets:* £28,929,992
Registered Office: Bedford Road, Northampton, NN1 5SZ
Activities: Sale of new cars and light motor vehicles
Parent: William Morgan Group Ltd
Officers: Martin Huw Morgan Allard [1967] Director; Christian William Le Fevre [1967] Director

Wolseley UK Limited
Incorporated: 3 September 1959 *Employees:* 5,734
Net Worth: £599,481,024 *Total Assets:* £1,301,063,936
Registered Office: 2 Kingmaker Court, Warwick Technology Park, Gallows Hill, Warwick, CV34 6DY
Activities: Non-specialised wholesale trade
Parent: Wolseley Group Holdings Limited
Officers: Katherine Mary McCormick, Secretary; Simon Gray [1967] Director/Accountant; Sally-Anne Griffiths [1969] Director; Mark Vincent Higson [1956] Director

Wolseley Utilities Limited
Incorporated: 16 July 2012
Net Worth: £15,682,000 *Total Assets:* £17,374,000
Registered Office: 2 Kingmaker Court, Warwick Technology Park, Gallows Hill, Warwick, CV34 6DY
Activities: Other business support service activities n.e.c.
Parent: Wolseley UK Limited
Officers: Katherine Mary McCormick, Secretary; Simon Gray [1967] Director/Accountant

Wolstenholme Machine Knives Limited
Incorporated: 17 August 1990 *Employees:* 49
Net Worth: £10,713,025 *Total Assets:* £18,972,480
Registered Office: Clough Bank Works, Downgate Drive, Carlisle Street East, Sheffield, S4 8BT
Activities: Manufacture of other machine tools
Parent: T G Wolstenholme (Holdings) Limited
Officers: Ian Keith Brazewell [1967] Technical Director; Steven John Corbett [1972] Director/Chief Operations Officer; Robert Groberg [1983] Director/Private Equity [American]; Nicholas John Harrison [1960] Manufacturing Director; Michael Ranson [1972] Director/Private Equity [American]; John Julian Frederick Tattersfield [1963] Director/Operating Executive [American]

Wood Boilers LLP
Incorporated: 15 October 2012
Net Worth: £2,763,754 *Total Assets:* £13,193,122
Registered Office: Sterling House, Maple Court, Maple Road, Tankersley, S Yorks, S75 3DP
Officers: Anthony William Jude Cundall [1979] Member; Stewart James Davies [1951] Member; Simon Robert Duncan [1961] Member

Wood Green Animal Shelters
Incorporated: 13 November 1986 *Employees:* 208
Net Worth: £26,412,204 *Total Assets:* £27,560,376
Registered Office: Kings Bush Farm, London Road, Godmanchester, Peterborough, Cambs, PE29 2NH
Activities: Activities of other membership organisations n.e.c.
Officers: Colin Peter Alder [1944] Director/Retired; Angela Yin-Chiu Au [1967] Director/Chartered Accountant; Duncan Inglis Canney [1952] Director/Retired; Dr Steven James Carden [1972] Director/Partner; John Maurice Cousins [1945] Director/Retired; Joanne Day [1968] Human Resources Director; Pamela Lesley Gee [1940] Director/Kennel Cattery Proprietor; Dr Joanna Julia Lawton [1971] Director/Trustee; Lynee Povey [1961] Director/Accountant; Janet Mary South [1939] Director/Charity Executive; Jonathan Daniel Younger [1973] Director/Trustee

Wood Hill Heights Limited
Incorporated: 2 June 2009
Net Worth: £8,142,210 *Total Assets:* £16,709,396
Registered Office: Suite 1.16, Great House, off Rotherham Road, Dinnington, Sheffield, S25 3QA
Activities: Construction of domestic buildings
Officers: Laura Kathleen Higginbottom, Secretary; Carole Elizabeth Higginbottom [1957] Director; Laura Kathleen Higginbottom [1982] Director/Legal Advisor; Peter Higginbottom [1954] Director

Barry Wood Plant Hire Limited
Incorporated: 2 December 1994 *Employees:* 68
Net Worth: £7,062,837 *Total Assets:* £9,547,574
Registered Office: Field Farm, Batham Gate, Fairfield, Buxton, Derbys, SK17 7HS
Activities: Other specialised construction activities n.e.c.
Parent: Sustainable Quarrying and Tanker Services Group Ltd
Officers: Mark Ryall [1969] Managing Director; Ben Taft [1971] Director/Operations Manager; Graham Anthony Vaughan [1965] Finance Director

Woodard Schools (Nottinghamshire) Limited
Incorporated: 9 January 2004 *Employees:* 237
Net Worth: £6,406,143 *Total Assets:* £16,091,216
Registered Office: Worksop College, Worksop, Notts, S80 3AP
Activities: Pre-primary education
Parent: The Woodard Corporation
Officers: Robert John Dunmore, Secretary; Colin James Douglas Anderson [1950] Director/Barrister; Stephen Derek Armstrong [1962] Director; Jason Charles Barnsdale [1971] Director/Chartered Surveyor; Sara Jane Cundy [1969] Director; Alison Natasha Hurton [1973] Director/Solicitor; Kumar Muthukumarappan [1962] Director/Consultant Obstetrician & Gynaecologist [Malaysian]; Penelope Owston [1956] Director/Business Coach; Caroline Jane Peake [1956] Director/Retired; Andrew Mark Pepper [1970] Director; Professor Patricia Joan Sikes [1955] Director/University Professor; Richard Steel [1949] Director; Alan Clive Swain [1948] Retired Director; David Wilson [1944] Director/Chartered Accountant

Woodbury Residual Limited
Incorporated: 17 December 2010 *Employees:* 568
Previous: Quantel Holdings Limited
Net Worth Deficit: £81,857,000 *Total Assets:* £74,871,000
Registered Office: 3MC Middlemarch Business Park, Siskin Drive, Coventry, Warwicks, CV3 4FJ
Activities: Activities of head offices
Officers: Kevan Paul Leggett [1964] Director; Simon Rupert Staveley-Smith [1982] Director

Woodford Investment Management Limited
Incorporated: 11 April 2016 *Employees:* 45
Net Worth: £5,154,085 *Total Assets:* £12,727,758
Registered Office: 9400 Garsington Road, Oxford Business Park, Cowley, Oxford, OX4 2HN
Activities: Fund management activities
Shareholders: Craig Frederick Newman; Neil Russell Woodford
Officers: Craig Frederick Newman [1970] Director; Neil Russell Woodford [1960] Director

Robert Woodhead Holdings Limited
Incorporated: 29 June 1983 *Employees:* 170
Net Worth: £4,218,780 *Total Assets:* £14,078,079
Registered Office: Edwinstowe House, High Street, Edwinstowe, Mansfield, Notts, NG21 9PR
Activities: Activities of construction holding companies
Major Shareholder: David Paul Woodhead
Officers: Hilary Ailsa Cheshire, Secretary; Hilary Ailsa Cheshire [1960] Director; David Paul Woodhead [1955] Managing Director

The Woodland Buildings Investment Company Limited
Incorporated: 19 October 1901
Net Worth: £9,484,578 *Total Assets:* £11,407,371
Registered Office: Apex Court, Ruddington Lane, Nottingham, NG11 7DD
Activities: Other letting and operating of own or leased real estate
Officers: Jean Audrey Smith, Secretary; Duncan John Anderson Brown [1961] Director/Chartered Accountant; Jonathan Ernest Crammond [1965] Director; Jean Audrey Smith [1945] Director

Woodland Trust (The)
Incorporated: 27 January 1986 *Employees:* 445
Net Worth: £151,428,000 *Total Assets:* £156,468,000
Registered Office: The Woodland Trust, Kempton Way, Grantham, Lincs, NG31 6LL
Activities: Silviculture and other forestry activities
Officers: Helga Jane Edwards, Secretary; David Terence Babbs [1981] Director/Chief Executive; Humphrey William Battcock [1955] Director/Managing Partner; Sally Katherine Benthall [1962] Director/Retired; Dr Fay Margaret Cooke [1982] Director/Chartered Accountant; Michael Peter Greenwood [1959] Director; Patrick James MacDonald [1962] Director/Chief Executive/Chairman; Paul David Nevett [1964] Director/Marketing; James Fredrick Ogilvie [1957] Director/Chartered Forester; Julia Mary Smithies [1961] Director/Retired; Richard James Sykes [1956] Director/Chartered Accountant; Baroness Barbara Scott Young [1948] Director/Member of The House of Lords

Woodthorpe Hall Garden Centres Limited
Incorporated: 9 January 2002 *Employees:* 678
Net Worth: £15,430,271 *Total Assets:* £29,309,372
Registered Office: Woodthorpe Hall Garden Centre, Woodthorpe, Alford, Lincs, LN13 0DD
Activities: Other retail sale of new goods in specialised stores (not commercial art galleries and opticians)
Shareholders: Charles Edward Stubbs; Robert John Stubbs
Officers: Phillippa Marie Stubbs, Secretary; Charles Edward Stubbs [1965] Director; Robert John Stubbs [1967] Director

Woodway Holdings Limited
Incorporated: 5 February 1973 *Employees:* 42
Previous: Woodway Engineering Limited
Net Worth: £32,971,438 *Total Assets:* £35,296,592
Registered Office: Lower Road, Barnacle, Coventry, Warwicks, CV7 9LD
Activities: Other manufacturing n.e.c.
Major Shareholder: Raymond John Skelhon
Officers: Susan Ann Klesniks, Secretary; Raymond John Skelhon [1931] Director/Motor Engineer; Deborah Suzanne Taylor [1964] Director/Marketing

Woolley Bros. (Wholesale Meats) Limited
Incorporated: 20 February 1979 *Employees:* 93
Net Worth: £14,989,574 *Total Assets:* £16,480,908
Registered Office: Rother Valley Way, Holbrook, Sheffield, S20 3RW
Activities: Processing and preserving of meat
Parent: Woolley Bros Holdings Limited
Officers: Steven Richard Woolley, Secretary/Director; Paul Joseph Woolley [1971] Director; Steven Richard Woolley [1972] Director

Woolley GMC Engineering Holdings Limited
Incorporated: 11 August 2016 *Employees:* 93
Net Worth: £6,420,751 *Total Assets:* £10,882,082
Registered Office: Third Floor, Two Colton Square, Leicester, LE1 1QH
Activities: Machining
Major Shareholder: Christopher Richard Francis Shield
Officers: Christopher Richard Francis Shield [1978] Director

Wootton Academy Trust
Incorporated: 15 August 2011 *Employees:* 133
Net Worth: £34,535,824 *Total Assets:* £36,341,524
Registered Office: Wootton Upper School, Hall End Road, Wootton, Bedford, MK43 9HT
Activities: General secondary education
Officers: Jonathan Kimber Billington [1964] Director; David Clare [1959] Director/Electrical Engineer; Michael George Gleeson [1961] Director/Teacher; Peter Laurence Walby Haddon [1955] Director/Retired; Michael James Ridley [1967] Director/Department of Education; Ian Sibbald [1969] Director of Finance; Timothy Humphreys Williams [1953] Director/HR Consultant

Working Assets Limited
Incorporated: 7 October 1996 *Employees:* 3
Net Worth: £5,104,068 *Total Assets:* £9,870,008
Registered Office: Belmont House, 13 Upper Street, Thame, Oxon, OX9 3ER
Activities: Other letting and operating of own or leased real estate
Major Shareholder: Robert Loan Fraser Hamilton
Officers: Robert Loan Fraser Hamilton [1965] Director

Workplace Systems International Limited
Incorporated: 6 April 2000
Net Worth: £17,822,000 *Total Assets:* £23,886,000
Registered Office: c/o Workforce Software Ltd, Precedent Drive, Rooksley, Milton Keynes, Bucks, MK13 8PP
Activities: Other information technology service activities
Parent: Wasp Management Software Limited
Officers: Tammy Jones, Secretary; Denise Broady [1974] Director [American]; Robert Feller [1968] Director/CFO/Treasurer [American]; Mike Morini [1962] Director [American]

Worksop Manor Estates,Limited
Incorporated: 27 February 1930 *Employees:* 20
Net Worth: £1,510,647 *Total Assets:* £9,932,204
Registered Office: Worksop Manor, Worksop, Notts, S80 3DQ
Activities: Mixed farming
Major Shareholder: Henry John Philip Farr
Officers: Henry John Philip Farr, Secretary/Director; Henry John Philip Farr [1966] Director; Philippa Berain Elizabeth Plumptre Farr [1942] Director

World Habitat
Incorporated: 9 March 1976 *Employees:* 13
Previous: Building and Social Housing Foundation
Net Worth: £33,166,848 *Total Assets:* £33,282,272
Registered Office: Memorial Square, Coalville, Leics, LE67 3TU
Activities: Research and experimental development on social sciences and humanities
Officers: Patricia Agnes Elderfield [1947] Director/Retired; Dr Angus John Kennedy [1952] Director/Consultant; Stuart Keith MacDonald [1977] Director; Alan Pearson [1952] Director/Project Manager; Professor Joanna Richardson [1972] Director/University Professor

World of Sweets Limited
Incorporated: 3 May 2002 *Employees:* 24
Net Worth: £12,060,000 *Total Assets:* £22,201,000
Registered Office: 25 Jubilee Drive, Loughborough, Leics, LE11 5TX
Activities: Wholesale of sugar and chocolate and sugar confectionery
Parent: Hancocks Holdings Limited
Officers: Wayne Beedle [1970] Director; Stephen Edward Foster [1976] Director

World Vision UK
Incorporated: 3 November 1982 *Employees:* 301
Net Worth: £21,710,000 *Total Assets:* £30,207,000
Registered Office: World Vision House, Opal Drive, Fox Milne, Milton Keynes, Bucks, MK15 0ZR
Activities: Other social work activities without accommodation n.e.c.
Officers: Paul Jack James Hewitt Wratten, Secretary; Serena Marie Brown [1974] Director/Corporate Citizenship; Simon Shelford Burne [1954] Director/Fundraising and Marketing Specialist; Jennifer Mary Collins [1948] Executive Director; Linda Emery [1960] Talent & Diversity Director; Marcus James Frost [1969] Director/Partnership Leader Marketing & Resource Development; Richard Philip Izard [1963] Director/Consultant; Marcus William George Manuel [1962] Director/Senior Research Associate; John Douglas MacLean Millican [1964] Director/Chief Executive; Mark Richard Parsons [1977] Director/Banking; David Gareth Richards [1960] Director/Church Minister; Julian Clive Vaughan Thomas [1959] Director/Marketing Consultant

Worldwide Fruit Limited
Incorporated: 25 August 1999 *Employees:* 327
Net Worth: £6,097,000 *Total Assets:* £24,804,000
Registered Office: Worldwide Fruit, Apple Way, Wardentree Lane, Spalding, Lincs, PE11 3BB
Activities: Wholesale of fruit and vegetables
Shareholders: Fruition PO Limited; Enzafruit New Zealand International Limited
Officers: Robert Andrew Hinge [1963] Director/Farmer; Peter Hans Landon-Lane [1957] Director [New Zealander]; Paul Mansfield [1960] Director/Fruit Grower; Lancelot Peter Morrish [1956] Director/Farmer; Bastian Oliver Von Streit [1979] Director [German]

A H Worth and Company Limited
Incorporated: 17 March 1948 *Employees:* 383
Net Worth: £39,824,000 *Total Assets:* £61,458,000
Registered Office: Fleet Estate Office, Manor Farm, Holbeach Hurn, Holbeach, Spalding, Lincs, PE12 8LR
Activities: Activities of other holding companies n.e.c.
Officers: Mark Richard Henson, Secretary; Thomas Patrick Brennan [1975] Finance Director; Timothy John Cooper-Jones [1951] Director; Stephen John Ellwood [1957] Director; Martin John Taylor [1971] Director; Duncan Richard Worth [1965] Director; Stephen Tom Worth [1967] Director

M.J. Worth Limited
Incorporated: 20 March 1970 *Employees:* 11
Net Worth: £7,489,184 *Total Assets:* £10,008,585
Registered Office: Ivy House, Wainfleet, Lincs, PE24 4HJ
Activities: Growing of cereals (except rice), leguminous crops and oil seeds
Major Shareholder: Michael John Worth
Officers: Graham Scrimshaw, Secretary; Michael John Worth [1937] Director/Farmer

Wreake Valley Academy Trust
Incorporated: 13 March 2012 *Employees:* 108
Net Worth: £11,960,000 *Total Assets:* £15,255,000
Registered Office: Wreake Valley Academy, Parkstone Road, Syston, Leicester, LE7 1LY
Activities: General secondary education
Officers: Andrew Winter, Secretary; Mishelle Bennett [1973] Director/Student; Carol Chambers [1951] Director/Retired; Julie Patricia Dealey [1972] Director/Business Manager; Rita Mary Laughton [1947] Director/Retired; Mark Ronald Measures [1972] Director/Union Steward for Arriva; Jane Elizabeth Middleton [1966] Director; Antony Derek Pinnock [1964] Director/Headteacher; Matthew Reid [1969] Director/Teacher; Cassandra Jane Soulsby [1975] Director

Wren Kitchens Limited
Incorporated: 22 January 2009 *Employees:* 3,943
Previous: Wren Living Limited
Net Worth: £18,628,934 *Total Assets:* £183,475,712
Registered Office: The Nest, Falkland Way, Barton on Humber, N Lincs, DN18 5RX
Activities: Retail of furniture, lighting, and similar (not musical instruments or scores) in specialised store
Major Shareholder: Malcolm Stanley Healey
Officers: Jane Marie Oldfield, Secretary; Anthony Gerard Clay [1964] Engineering & Facilities Director; Craig Michael Douglas [1983] IT Director; Alexander David Grant [1971] Finance Director; Malcolm Stanley Healey [1944] Director/Chairman; Jason Anthony Hopper [1969] Southern Sales Director; Gemma Amanda Kerrigan [1981] Customer Service Director; Rafal Ryszard Klimek [1984] Manufacturing & Logistics Director [Polish]; Mohammed Tofiq Malik [1961] Northern Sales Director; Jane Marie Oldfield [1964] Director/Chartered Accountant; Mark Jonathan Pullan [1972] Managing Director; Kevin Selby [1962] Information & Compliance Director; Richard Birnie Durno Walker [1983] Marketing Director; Darren Watts [1971] Showroom Development Director

Wrendal Holdings Limited
Incorporated: 28 September 1959 *Employees:* 5
Net Worth: £12,670,268 *Total Assets:* £16,434,415
Registered Office: Unit 2 Second Avenue, Poynton Industrial Estate, Poynton, Cheshire, SK12 1ND
Activities: Activities of head offices
Officers: Edward Alexander Gifford Aspinall, Secretary; Edward Alexander Gifford Aspinall [1969] Director/Insurance Broker; Joanna Mary Babington Aspinall [1939] Director; Charlotte Ann Babington Kelly [1967] Director; Stephen Charles Vincent Kelly [1966] Director/Project Manager; Kate Mary Babington Titley [1966] Director

Wrengate Holdings Limited
Incorporated: 27 October 2010 *Employees:* 27
Net Worth: £24,943,248 *Total Assets:* £30,958,404
Registered Office: 10 Riverview, The Embankment, Vale Road, Heaton Mersey, Stockport, Cheshire, SK4 3GN
Activities: Activities of other holding companies n.e.c.
Shareholder: Alan Philip David Musry
Officers: Alan Philip David Musry [1963] Director/Chartered Accountant; Ronald Musry [1935] Director

Wrengate Limited
Incorporated: 6 June 1974 *Employees:* 3
Net Worth: £19,192,034 *Total Assets:* £27,391,848
Registered Office: 10 Riverview, The Embankment, Vale Road, Heaton Mersey, Stockport, Cheshire, SK4 3GN
Activities: Activities of other holding companies n.e.c.
Parent: Wrengate Holdings Limited
Officers: Alan Philip David Musry [1963] Director/Chartered Accountant; Ronald Musry [1935] Director

WRG Acquisitions 2 Limited
Incorporated: 26 February 2004
Net Worth Deficit: £130,818,000 *Total Assets:* £63,486,000
Registered Office: Ground Floor West, 900 Pavilion Drive, Northampton Business Park, Northampton, NN4 7RG
Activities: Other business support service activities n.e.c.
Parent: FCC Environment (UK) Limited
Officers: Carol Jayne Nunn, Secretary; Vicente Federico Orts-Llopis [1962] Finance Director [Spanish]; Agustin Serrano Minchan [1959] Director/Technical Civil Engineer [Spanish]; Paul Taylor [1959] Director/Chief Executive Officer

WRG Environmental Limited
Incorporated: 16 December 1987 *Employees:* 7
Net Worth Deficit: £941,000 *Total Assets:* £29,065,000
Registered Office: Ground Floor West, 900 Pavilion Drive, Northampton Business Park, Northampton, NN4 7RG
Activities: Other business support service activities n.e.c.
Parent: WRG Acquisitions 2 Limited
Officers: Carol Jayne Nunn, Secretary; Vicente Federico Orts-Llopis [1962] Director/Chief Financial Officer [Spanish]; Agustin Serrano Minchan [1959] Director/Technical Civil Engineer [Spanish]; Paul Taylor [1959] Director/Chief Executive Officer

P A Wright & Sons Limited
Incorporated: 15 February 1985 *Employees:* 190
Net Worth: £22,225,654 *Total Assets:* £40,778,684
Registered Office: Gopsall House Farm, Twycross, Atherstone, Warwicks, CV9 3PP
Activities: Mixed farming
Shareholders: Jarred Thomas Wright; Peter Alfred Wright
Officers: David Peter Wright [1956] Director/Farmer; James Alan Wright [1978] Director/Farmer; Peter Alfred Wright [1928] Director/Farmer; Robert Wright [1962] Director/Farmer

Wright Hassall LLP
Incorporated: 27 October 2005 *Employees:* 289
Net Worth: £5,368,807 *Total Assets:* £9,636,983
Registered Office: Olympus Avenue, Leamington Spa, Warwicks, CV34 6BF
Officers: Gemma Carson [1976] Member; John William Dormer [1974] Member; Lindsay Ellis [1965] Member; Steven Alexander Halkett [1981] Member; Anthony Rhys Jarman [1970] Member; Richard Lane [1960] Member; Robert James Lee [1966] Member; Peter Lowe [1965] Member; Peter John Maguire [1971] Member; Martin Stuart Oliver [1975] Member; Sarah Jane Perry [1966] Member; Paul Mathison Rice [1959] Member; Alexandra Janet Robinson [1973] Member; Claire Waring [1970] Member; Philip Albert Sutherland Formby Wilding [1972] Member

Frank Wright Limited
Incorporated: 30 August 1910 *Employees:* 202
Net Worth: £20,707,000 *Total Assets:* £61,443,000
Registered Office: Blenheim House, Blenheim Road, Ashbourne, Derbys, DE6 1HA
Activities: Manufacture of prepared feeds for farm animals
Parent: Nutreco Limited
Officers: Rob Binnekamp [1982] Managing Director [Dutch]; John Pritchard [1968] Finance Director

Wroxall Abbey Estate Limited
Incorporated: 29 December 2000 *Employees:* 68
Net Worth: £5,390,710 *Total Assets:* £10,155,555
Registered Office: Wroxall Abbey Estate, Birmingham Road, Wroxall, Warwicks, CV35 7NB
Activities: Hotels and similar accommodation
Shareholder: John Eric Clarkson
Officers: John Eric Clarkson [1949] Director; Grant Howlett [1957] Director/Hotel Consultant; John Michael Kent [1945] Director/Health Care

Wyboston Lakes Limited
Incorporated: 16 July 1973 *Employees:* 409
Net Worth: £35,141,404 *Total Assets:* £40,988,432
Registered Office: Wyboston Lakes Hotel, Great North Road, Wyboston, Beds, MK44 3AL
Activities: Development of building projects
Shareholders: Steve Richard Hutchinson; Jill Chapman
Officers: Julie Ireland, Secretary; David Howard Barford [1943] Director/Surveyor; Jill Chapman [1958] Director; Chelsey Rae Hutchinson [1986] Director; Steve Richard Hutchinson [1955] Director; Julie Ireland [1971] Director/Chartered Certified Accountant; Mark Charles Jones [1955] Director; Stephen Jones [1976] Managing Director; Craig Alfred Warner [1969] IT Director

Wycliffe Hall
Incorporated: 23 April 2014 *Employees:* 39
Net Worth: £9,655,456 *Total Assets:* £14,977,116
Registered Office: 54 Banbury Road, Oxford, OX2 6PW
Activities: Other education n.e.c.
Officers: Professor Nigel John Biggar [1955] Director/University Professor; Revd Emma Louise Coley [1976] Director/Clergy; Alison Jane Coulter [1964] Director/Leadership Associate; Peter Lawrence Doyle [1952] Director; Sarah Rosemary Ann Finch [1945] Director/Retired; Dr Philip James Giddings [1946] Director/Retired; Katrina Claire Hancock [1979] Director of Development; Julian Tudor Henderson [1954] Director/Church of England Bishop; John Dudley Irvine [1949] Director/Associate Vicar; Reverend James Edward Kennedy [1972] Director/Vicar; Frederick James Kilner [1943] Director/Clergyman; Alistair James Magowan [1955] Director/Anglican Bishop; Simon Robert McGuire [1957] Director; Rev Ann Joyce Templeman [1950] Director/Minister of Religion; Nigel Christopher Tinker [1960] Director/Chairman

Wykes Engineering Co. (Rushden) Limited
Incorporated: 17 September 1982 *Employees:* 71
Net Worth: £33,227,306 *Total Assets:* £43,396,360
Registered Office: Goosey Lodge, Wymington, Rushden, Northants, NN10 9LU
Activities: Manufacture of ovens, furnaces and furnace burners
Major Shareholder: David John Wykes
Officers: David John Wykes [1958] Director/Mechanical Engineer

Wyn Overseas Operations Limited
Incorporated: 24 December 2012
Net Worth: £1,160,009 *Total Assets:* £494,433,792
Registered Office: Haylock House, Kettering Parkway, Kettering, Northants, NN15 6EY
Activities: Other business support service activities n.e.c.
Parent: Wyndham Worldwide Corporation
Officers: Michael Brendan Cassidy [1966] Director/Treasurer [Irish]; Lee Rayson [1970] Director/Chartered Accountant

Wyndham Destination Network Europe Limited
Incorporated: 8 February 2010
Previous: Wyndham Exchange and Rentals Holdings Limited
Net Worth Deficit: £20,639,000 *Total Assets:* £234,663,008
Registered Office: Haylock House, Kettering Parkway, Kettering, Northants, NN15 6EY
Activities: Activities of head offices
Parent: Pointlux SARL
Officers: Andrew Clarke [1976] Senior Director Finance; Andrew Liggins [1962] Director/VP Operations

Wyndham Destination Network LLP
Incorporated: 5 February 2010
Previous: Wyndham Exchange and Rentals LLP
Net Worth: £23,012,000 *Total Assets:* £26,125,000
Registered Office: Haylock House, Kettering Parkway, Kettering Venture Park, Kettering, Northants, NN15 6EY

Wyndham Holdings
Incorporated: 4 January 2001
Previous: Wyndham Exchange and Rentals (UK) Holdings
Net Worth: £98,572,000 *Total Assets:* £483,704,992
Registered Office: Haylock House, Kettering Parkway, Kettering, Northants, NN15 6EY
Activities: Activities of head offices
Parent: Wyndham Destination Network Subsidiary, LLC
Officers: Michael Brendan Cassidy [1966] Director/Treasurer [Irish]; Lee Rayson [1970] Director/Chartered Accountant

X-Cel Superturn Ltd
Incorporated: 30 March 1983 *Employees:* 149
Previous: X-Cel Superturn (GB) Limited
Net Worth: £9,727,008 *Total Assets:* £19,232,348
Registered Office: Unit 3 R-Evolution@Amp, Brindley Way, Rotherham, S Yorks, S60 5FS
Activities: Manufacture of other fabricated metal products n.e.c.
Major Shareholder: Andrew Nicholas Taylor
Officers: Leanne Furniss-Plant, Secretary; David Barton-Phillips [1980] Director; Leanne Tracey Furniss-Plant [1980] Director; Tim Mark Heron [1977] Director; Andrew Nicholas Taylor [1956] Director & Engineer; Ben Grant Watson [1977] Director

Xanadu Investments Limited
Incorporated: 6 December 2010 *Employees:* 2
Net Worth: £1,612,462 *Total Assets:* £11,356,966
Registered Office: Keepers Lodge, Hollowell Reservoir, Hollowell, Northampton, NN6 8RL
Activities: Other business support service activities n.e.c.
Major Shareholder: John Michael Barrie Strowbridge
Officers: Matthew Frederick Proctor, Secretary; John Michael Barrie Strowbridge [1967] Director

Xeros Limited
Incorporated: 12 September 2006 *Employees:* 74
Net Worth Deficit: £23,702,350 *Total Assets:* £41,824,412
Registered Office: Unit 2 Evolution Advanced Manufacturing Park, Whittle Way, Catcliffe, Rotherham, S Yorks, S60 5BL
Activities: Other research and experimental development on natural sciences and engineering
Parent: Xeros Technology Group PLC
Officers: Paul Michael Denney, Secretary; Paul Michael Denney [1966] Director/Chief Financial Officer; Dr Stephen Derek Jenkins [1963] Technical Director; Mark James Nichols [1957] Director

Xeros Technology Group PLC
Incorporated: 10 September 2013 *Employees:* 146
Net Worth: £35,780,000 *Total Assets:* £40,356,000
Registered Office: Unit 2 Evolution Advanced Manufacturing Park, Whittle Way, Catcliffe, Rotherham, S Yorks, S60 5BL
Activities: Other research and experimental development on natural sciences and engineering
Shareholder: Woodford Investment Management LLP
Officers: Paul Michael Denney, Secretary; David Christopher Armfield [1961] Director; David Graham Baynes [1964] Director; Paul Michael Denney [1966] Director/Chief Financial Officer; Dr Simon Richard Ellis [1962] Director; Mark James Nichols [1957] Director

XMA Limited
Incorporated: 2 September 1986 *Employees:* 470
Net Worth: £18,671,000 *Total Assets:* £66,361,000
Registered Office: Wilford Industrial Estate, Ruddington Lane, Wilford, Nottingham, NG11 7EP
Activities: Wholesale of computers, computer peripheral equipment and software
Parent: Viglen Limited
Officers: Tajinder Singh Dhatt, Secretary; Christine Bachelor [1970] Director/Accountant; Ian Cunningham [1967] Sales Director; Tajinder Singh Dhatt [1974] Finance Director; Peter Heath [1960] Director; Leon Hemani [1971] Sales Director; Kelvin Lee [1980] Director; Sunil Jayantilal Madhani [1966] Director; Andrew Wright [1968] Director

XPO Bulk UK Limited
Incorporated: 6 October 1994 *Employees:* 825
Previous: Norbert Dentressangle Tankers Limited
Net Worth: £28,827,000 *Total Assets:* £59,554,000
Registered Office: XPO House, Lodge Way, New Duston, Northampton, NN5 7SL
Activities: Freight transport by road
Parent: XPO Transport Solutions UK Limited
Officers: Georgina Garratt, Secretary; Georgina Garratt [1981] Director/Head of Legal; Daniel Stephen Myers [1976] Managing Director

XPO Holdings UK and Ireland Limited
Incorporated: 25 June 1993 *Employees:* 73
Previous: Norbert Dentressangle Holdings Limited
Net Worth: £136,911,008 *Total Assets:* £616,729,024
Registered Office: XPO House, Lodge Way, New Duston, Northampton, NN5 7SL
Activities: Activities of head offices
Parent: XPO Logistics Europe SA
Officers: Georgina Garratt, Secretary; Richard Cawston [1973] Managing Director; Simon Gavin Evans [1971] Finance Director; Georgina Garratt [1981] Director/Head of Legal; Luis Angel Gomez [1971] Director [Spanish]

XPO Investment UK Limited
Incorporated: 23 August 1930
Previous: Christian Salvesen Investments Limited
Net Worth: £52,399,000 *Total Assets:* £141,300,992
Registered Office: XPO House, Lodge Way, New Duston, Northampton, NN5 7SL
Activities: Non-trading company
Parent: XPO Holdings UK and Ireland Limited
Officers: Georgina Garratt, Secretary; Simon Gavin Evans [1971] Finance Director; Georgina Garratt [1981] Director/Head of Legal

XPO Maintenance UK Limited
Incorporated: 1 July 2008 *Employees:* 90
Previous: Norbert Dentressangle Maintenance UK Limited
Net Worth: £2,909,000 *Total Assets:* £15,094,000
Registered Office: XPO House, Lodge Way, New Duston, Northampton, NN5 7SL
Activities: Other business support service activities n.e.c.
Parent: XPO Holdings UK and Ireland Limited
Officers: Georgina Garratt, Secretary; Georgina Garratt [1981] Director/Head of Legal; Daniel Stephen Myers [1976] Managing Director; Didier Raymond Antoine Tallaron [1959] Director [French]

XPO Transport Solutions UK Limited
Incorporated: 1 July 2008 *Employees:* 2,483
Previous: Norbert Dentressangle Transport UK Limited
Net Worth: £78,394,000 *Total Assets:* £187,542,000
Registered Office: XPO House, Lodge Way, New Duston, Northampton, NN5 7SL
Activities: Freight transport by road
Parent: XPO Holdings UK and Ireland Limited
Officers: Georgina Garratt, Secretary; Georgina Garratt [1981] Director/Head of Legal; Luis Angel Gomez [1971] Director [Spanish]; Daniel Stephen Myers [1976] Managing Director

Xtratherm UK Limited
Incorporated: 26 March 2002 *Employees:* 123
Net Worth: £27,907,248 *Total Assets:* £46,791,264
Registered Office: Park Road, Holmewood Industrial Park, Holmewood, Chesterfield, Derbys, S42 5UY
Activities: Other manufacturing n.e.c.
Parent: Mohawk Industries Inc
Officers: Generald Beggy, Secretary/Accountant [Irish]; Robert Bester [1970] Director of Finance [Irish]; Lieven Eric Gerard Malfait [1959] Director [Belgian]; Barry Rafferty [1971] Managing Director [Irish]

Xylem Water Solutions UK Ltd
Incorporated: 14 March 1950 *Employees:* 533
Net Worth: £36,882,000 *Total Assets:* £92,568,000
Registered Office: Private Road 1, Colwick, Nottingham, NG4 2AN
Activities: Manufacture of pumps
Parent: Xylem Water Solutions UK Holdings Ltd
Officers: Nicola Anne Tancred, Secretary; Martin Roy Greenhalgh [1966] Managing Director; Jason Howlett [1971] Managing Director; Claire Jane Rhodes [1972] Director/Accountant

Yara UK Limited
Incorporated: 2 August 1999 *Employees:* 225
Net Worth: £90,181,000 *Total Assets:* £225,638,000
Registered Office: Harvest House, Europarc, Grimsby, N E Lincs, DN37 9TZ
Activities: Manufacture of fertilizers and nitrogen compounds
Shareholder: Ministry of Trade, Industry and Fisheries, (Norway)
Officers: James Henry Domhnull Hancock, Secretary; Anne Grethe Dalane [1960] Director/Chief Financial Officer [Norwegian]; Charles Spenser Grey [1959] Director/Legal Counsel; David John Tomkinson [1965] Operations Director

Yarborough Limited
Incorporated: 30 May 1960 *Employees:* 121
Net Worth: £7,785,880 *Total Assets:* £9,683,637
Registered Office: Birley Vale Avenue, Sheffield, S12 2AX
Activities: Freight transport by road
Shareholders: Laurence Donal Abel; Ian Alexander Davis
Officers: Laurence Donal Abel [1970] Director; Ian Alexander Davis [1969] Director

Yardi Systems Limited
Incorporated: 24 February 2003 *Employees:* 90
Net Worth Deficit: £1,341,056 *Total Assets:* £22,411,498
Registered Office: Cranbrook House, 287-291 Banbury Road, Oxford, OX2 7JQ
Activities: Other information technology service activities
Parent: Yardi Systems Inc
Officers: Anant Madhukar Yardi [1946] Director/President [American]

Yasa Limited
Incorporated: 29 July 2009 *Employees:* 105
Previous: Yasa Motors Limited
Net Worth: £14,013,099 *Total Assets:* £18,436,236
Registered Office: 11-14 Oxford Industrial Park, Mead Road, Yarnton, Kidlington, Oxon, OX5 1QU
Activities: Manufacture of electric motors, generators and transformers
Shareholder: Parkwalk Advisors Limited
Officers: Nicola Jayne Johnson, Secretary; Arthur John Connelly [1958] Director/Businessman; Dr Christopher John Harris [1961] Director/Chief Executive; Paul Michael Mason [1953] Director; Stephen Parker [1953] Director/Businessman; Peter Terry Ward [1945] Commercial Director; Dr Timothy Woolmer [1981] Director/Chief Technical Officer

W S Yeates Limited
Incorporated: 22 October 1946 *Employees:* 2
Previous: W S Yeates Public Limited Company
Net Worth: £31,155,830 *Total Assets:* £32,846,200
Registered Office: 3rd Floor, St George's House, Leicester, LE1 1SH
Activities: Buying and selling of own real estate
Officers: Jonathan Charles Griffin [1965] Director; Mr Thomas James Shelbourn [1993] Director

Yeovil Developments Limited
Incorporated: 12 November 2004
Net Worth: £218,000 *Total Assets:* £12,782,000
Registered Office: Barratt House, Cartwright Way, Forest Business Park, Bardon Hill, Coalville, Leics, LE67 1UF
Activities: Development of building projects
Parent: BDW Trading Limited
Officers: Christopher Julian Burton [1962] Managing Director; David Fraser Thomas [1963] Director

Yew Lodge Limited
Incorporated: 28 March 1962 *Employees:* 141
Net Worth: £6,248,984 *Total Assets:* £10,266,694
Registered Office: Yew Lodge Hotel, 33 Packington Hill, Kegworth, Derby, DE74 2DF
Activities: Hotels and similar accommodation
Major Shareholder: Jeremy Derek Pick
Officers: Generaldine Pick, Secretary; Generaldine Pick [1939] Director/Manager; Jeremy Derek Pick [1963] Director/Hotelier; John Andrew Pick [1963] Director/Sales; Jo Anne Jessica Tilson [1966] Director/Training & Development Manager

The Yews Holding Company Limited
Incorporated: 10 August 2016
Net Worth Deficit: £174,135 *Total Assets:* £12,885,003
Registered Office: The Yews, Chapel End, Swerford, Chipping Norton, Oxon, OX7 4BQ
Activities: Financial management
Major Shareholder: Duncan Edward Ford
Officers: Duncan Edward Ford [1968] Director

YHA (England and Wales)
Incorporated: 12 December 1933 *Employees:* 1,212
Net Worth: £42,520,000 *Total Assets:* £102,297,000
Registered Office: Trevelyan House, Dimple Road, Matlock, Derbys, DE4 3YH
Activities: Youth hostels
Officers: William Edward Howarth, Secretary; Anthony Peter Gaines [1954] Director/Retired; Margaret Helen Hart [1954] Director; Cathryn Alice Hayhurst [1977] Director/Accountant; Marcus Holburn [1972] Director; Barbara Kasumu [1986] Director; Ian Philip Maginnis [1962] Transformation Director; Josephine Paula Murray [1963] Director/Heritage Adviser; Hannah Paterson [1987] Director; Simon Gareth Reeve [1965] Director; Christopher Charles Brining Roberts [1962] Director/Solicitor; Fiona Steggles [1969] Director; Graham Turnock [1968] Director of Finance

YLH Limited
Incorporated: 24 August 2015
Net Worth: £7,921,658 *Total Assets:* £17,850,864
Registered Office: 18 Prospect House, Colliery Close, Staveley, Chesterfield, Derbys, S43 3QE
Activities: Activities of other holding companies n.e.c.
Major Shareholder: Martyn Peter Steele
Officers: Amandip Singh Johal [1977] Director/Solicitor; Martyn Peter Steele [1976] Director/Solicitor

Yokohama H.P.T. Limited
Incorporated: 18 July 1988 *Employees:* 43
Net Worth: £5,137,716 *Total Assets:* £17,388,252
Registered Office: Yokohama House, Dawson Road, Mount Farm, Bletchley, Bucks, MK1 1QY
Activities: Wholesale trade of motor vehicle parts and accessories
Officers: Trevor Alan Melsom, Secretary; Yusaku Hanada [1975] Director/Office Manager [Japanese]; Keishi Hashimoto [1959] Director/Manager [Japanese]; Trevor Alan Melsom [1955] Director/Accountant; David Ronald Seward [1959] Sales Director

York Ward & Rowlatt Limited
Incorporated: 14 December 1912 *Employees:* 106
Net Worth: £4,891,122 *Total Assets:* £13,454,056
Registered Office: Balmoral House, Kettering Venture Park, Kettering, Northants, NN15 6XU
Activities: Sale of new cars and light motor vehicles
Parent: Grosvenor Contracts Leasing Limited
Officers: James Fleming Clark, Secretary; Shaun William Barritt [1957] Director; Clive Nicholas Hughes [1966] Director/Retail Operator; Brian Johnson [1945] Director; Peter Sidney Johnson [1937] Director/Sales Manager

Yorkshire Repak Holdings Limited
Incorporated: 23 September 2015 *Employees:* 576
Net Worth Deficit: £260,822 *Total Assets:* £9,890,873
Registered Office: Summer Lane, Barnsley, S Yorks, S70 2NP
Activities: Activities of head offices
Shareholders: Terence Malcolm Foy; Neil Askham
Officers: Diane Askham, Secretary; Neil Askham [1950] Director; Terence Malcolm Foy [1954] Director/Manager

Yorkshire Repak Limited
Incorporated: 11 March 1985 *Employees:* 541
Net Worth: £5,784,542 *Total Assets:* £11,849,973
Registered Office: Summer Lane, Barnsley, S Yorks, S70 2NP
Activities: Other manufacturing n.e.c.
Parent: Yorkshire Repak Holdings Limited
Officers: Neil Askham [1950] Managing Director; Terence Malcolm Foy [1954] Director

The Yorkshire Traction Company Limited
Incorporated: 17 October 1986 *Employees:* 1,147
Net Worth: £16,207,000 *Total Assets:* £44,991,000
Registered Office: c/o Stagecoach Services Limited, One Stockport Exchange, 20 Railway Road, Stockport, Cheshire, SK1 3SW
Activities: Other urban, suburban or metropolitan passenger land transport (not underground, metro or similar)
Parent: Stagecoach Bus Holdings Limited
Officers: Michael John Vaux, Secretary; Colin Brown [1968] Director/Accountant; Matthew Davies [1973] Managing Director; Arnold Mark Threapleton [1954] Managing Director

Yotta Limited
Incorporated: 7 February 1986 *Employees:* 48
Previous: Mayrise Limited
Net Worth: £5,971,286 *Total Assets:* £14,041,118
Registered Office: 6 Oxford Industrial Park, Mead Road, Yarnton, Kidlington, Oxon, OX5 1QU
Activities: Business and domestic software development
Parent: Oxford Metrics PLC
Officers: Catherine Lindsay Robertson, Secretary; Nicholas Paul Bolton [1969] Director; David Anthony Deacon [1960] Director; Catherine Lindsay Robertson [1958] Director

J. and A. Young (Leicester) Limited
Incorporated: 7 August 1975 *Employees:* 298
Net Worth: £21,626,000 *Total Assets:* £54,839,000
Registered Office: 15 Saxon Way East, Oakley Hay Industrial Estate, Corby, Northants, NN18 9EY
Activities: Non-specialised wholesale trade
Parent: J & A Young (Holdings) Limited
Officers: Anona Jane Young, Secretary; Anona Jane Young [1951] Director; Jeremy Robert Andrew Young [1949] Director

J & A Young Group Limited
Incorporated: 1 March 2008 *Employees:* 298
Net Worth: £34,629,000 *Total Assets:* £67,829,000
Registered Office: 15 Saxon Way East, Oakley Hay Industrial Estate, Corby, Northants, NN18 9EY
Activities: Other service activities n.e.c.
Officers: Anona Jane Young, Secretary; Jason James Graham Young, Secretary/Director; Anona Jane Young [1951] Director; Dominic Peter Robert Young [1975] Director; Jason James Graham Young [1970] Director; Jeremy Robert Andrew Young [1949] Director

Young's Seafood International Holdings Limited
Incorporated: 8 September 1998 *Employees:* 3
Previous: Findus UK Group Limited
Net Worth: £12,357,000 *Total Assets:* £80,273,000
Registered Office: Ross House, Wickham Road, Grimsby, N E Lincs, DN31 3SW
Activities: Other business support service activities n.e.c.
Parent: Lighthouse UKCo 6 (Treasury) Limited
Officers: Timothy Mark Busby [1964] Director; William John Showalter [1963] Director/Chief Financial Officer [American]

Young's Seafood Limited
Incorporated: 14 April 1999 *Employees:* 2,413
Net Worth: £42,920,000 *Total Assets:* £526,859,008
Registered Office: Ross House, Wickham Road, Grimsby, N E Lincs, DN31 3SW
Activities: Processing and preserving of fish, crustaceans and molluscs
Parent: Young's Seafood International Holdings Limited
Officers: Timothy Mark Busby [1964] Director; Stuart Ian Caborn [1975] Director; Dominic Eugene Kerrigan [1972] Director; William John Showalter [1963] Director/Group Chief Financial Officer [American]

Yourcash Europe Limited
Incorporated: 24 January 2013
Net Worth: £28,305,000 *Total Assets:* £28,639,000
Registered Office: Willow House, Woodland Business Park, Linford Wood, Milton Keynes, Bucks, MK14 6EU
Activities: Activities of financial services holding companies
Officers: Nikos Fountas [1963] Director/EVP & CEO EMEA [Greek]; Daniel James Entwistle Marland [1982] Director/Solicitor; Andrea Valacsay [1974] Finance Director [Hungarian]; Ricky Lee Weller [1957] Director [American]

Yourcash Holdings Limited
Incorporated: 6 April 2010
Net Worth: £9,059,000 *Total Assets:* £9,176,000
Registered Office: Willow House, Woodlands Business Park, Linford Wood, Milton Keynes, Bucks, MK14 6EU
Activities: Financial intermediation not elsewhere classified
Officers: Daniel James Entwistle Marland, Secretary; Nikos Fountas [1963] Director/EVP & CEO EMEA [Greek]; Daniel James Entwistle Marland [1982] Director/Solicitor; Andrea Valacsay [1974] Finance Director [Hungarian]; Ricky Lee Weller [1957] Director [American]

Yourcash Limited
Incorporated: 5 January 2000 *Employees:* 98
Net Worth: £7,154,000 *Total Assets:* £56,644,000
Registered Office: Willow House, Breckland, Linford Wood, Milton Keynes, Bucks, MK14 6EU
Activities: Financial intermediation not elsewhere classified
Officers: Nikos Fountas [1963] Director/EVP & CEO EMEA [Greek]; Daniel James Entwistle Marland [1982] Director/Solicitor; Andrea Valacsay [1974] Finance Director [Hungarian]; Ricky Lee Weller [1957] Director [American]

Yourcash Solutions Limited
Incorporated: 24 January 2013
Net Worth Deficit: £13,959,000 *Total Assets:* £23,115,000
Registered Office: Willow House, Woodland Business Park, Linford Wood, Milton Keynes, Bucks, MK14 6EU
Activities: Activities of financial services holding companies
Officers: Daniel James Entwistle Marland, Secretary; Nikos Fountas [1963] Director/EVP & CEO EMEA [Greek]; Daniel James Entwistle Marland [1982] Director/Solicitor; Andrea Valacsay [1974] Finance Director [Hungarian]; Ricky Lee Weller [1957] Director [American]

Yours Clothing Limited
Incorporated: 11 January 1994 *Employees:* 1,104
Net Worth: £9,660,510 *Total Assets:* £26,820,168
Registered Office: Unit B, Finmere Park, Southgate Road, Orton Southgate, Peterborough, Cambs, PE2 6YG
Activities: Retail sale of clothing in specialised stores
Parent: A K Retail Holdings Limited
Officers: David James Preece, Secretary; Saeed Hatteea [1950] Director; Anna Maria Heather [1965] Director; Andrew Robert Killingsworth [1962] Director; Richard James Thurlow [1955] Director/Chartered Accountant

Youth Sport Trust
Incorporated: 15 March 2001 *Employees:* 108
Net Worth: £8,078,872 *Total Assets:* £9,339,981
Registered Office: Sport Park, 3 Oakwood Drive, Loughborough, Leics, LE11 3QF
Activities: Sports and recreation education
Officers: Peter Jonathan Ellis, Secretary; Valerie Elizabeth Marie Copenhagen [1982] Director/Senior Manager; Richard Colin Neil Davidson [1951] Director; William Downie [1970] Director/Headteacher; Dr Paula Catherine Heather Franklin [1959] Medical Director; David John Gilbey [1964] Director; Denise Gladwell [1953] Director/Headteacher; Dr Katherine Jane Grainger [1975] Director/Chairman UK Sport; Melanie Beth Honnor [1971] Business Director [British/American]; Sally Elizabeth Munday [1972] Director/Chief Executive; Belinda Richards [1958] Non Executive Director; Benedict Ian Stimson [1971] Director

Yu Group PLC
Incorporated: 15 February 2016 *Employees:* 54
Net Worth: £8,813,000 *Total Assets:* £20,061,000
Registered Office: CPK House, Mellors Way, 2 Horizon Place, Nottingham Business Park, Nottingham, NG8 6PY
Activities: Activities of head offices
Major Shareholder: Bobby Kalar
Officers: Paul Rawson, Secretary; Ralph Leslie Cohen [1948] Director; John Colin Glasglow [1962] Director; Baljit Bobby Kalar [1975] Director; Garry Pickering [1974] Director; Paul Edwin Rawson [1975] Director/Chief Financial Officer

Yuill Family Properties Ltd
Incorporated: 11 December 2015
Net Worth: £3,562,341 *Total Assets:* £11,074,581
Registered Office: Barn 4 Yew Tree Farm, Upper Harlestone, Northampton, NN7 4EL
Activities: Other accommodation
Officers: Zoe Yuill, Secretary; Ian Trevor Yuill [1955] Director

Yusen Logistics (UK) Limited
Incorporated: 12 October 1990 *Employees:* 1,516
Net Worth: £21,464,000 *Total Assets:* £93,909,000
Registered Office: Grange Park, 1 Cheaney Drive, Northampton, NN4 5FB
Activities: Freight transport by road
Officers: Mark Bent, Secretary; Kevin Andrew Appleton [1960] Managing Director; John Fern [1980] Director; Andrew Charles Fitt [1959] Director; Masahiko Ishikawa [1961] Director [Japanese]; Kenichiro Miyamoto [1968] Director [Japanese]

Yutaka Giken (UK) Limited
Incorporated: 29 March 1996
Net Worth: £17,420,000 *Total Assets:* £17,631,000
Registered Office: Garsington Road, Cowley, Oxford, OX4 2BW
Activities: Wholesale trade of motor vehicle parts and accessories
Officers: Toshihide Kiriyama, Secretary; Toshihide Kiriyama [1965] Director [Japanese]; Katsuhiro Kurokawa [1960] Director [Japanese]

Zahawi & Zahawi Ltd
Incorporated: 16 June 2010 *Employees:* 5
Net Worth: £496,180 *Total Assets:* £29,038,650
Registered Office: Oaklands Stables, Shipston Road, Upper Tysoe, Warwick, CV35 0TR
Activities: Other business support service activities n.e.c.
Major Shareholder: Lana Fawsi Jamil Saib
Officers: Lana Fawsi Jamil Saib [1966] Director

Zapf Creation (UK) Limited
Incorporated: 15 October 1999 *Employees:* 3
Net Worth: £2,262,000 *Total Assets:* £9,425,000
Registered Office: Regent Business Park, 50 Presley Way, Crownhill, Milton Keynes, Bucks, MK8 0ES
Activities: Non-specialised wholesale trade
Parent: Zapf Creation Auslandsholding GmbH
Officers: Ian Peter Smith, Secretary; Thomas Eichhorn [1965] Director [German]; Andrew Howard Thomas Laughton [1965] Director; Hannelore Schalast [1958] Director [German]

Zapp (GB) Limited
Incorporated: 24 July 1984 *Employees:* 8
Net Worth: £3,671,796 *Total Assets:* £12,060,669
Registered Office: Unit 1 Thorncliffe Distribution Centre, Chapeltown, Sheffield, S35 2PW
Activities: Agents specialised in the sale of other particular products
Officers: Mark Richard Wragg, Secretary; Michael Franz Foidl [1957] Director [German]; Mark Richard Wragg [1973] Director

ZestBDW LLP
Incorporated: 22 July 2013
Net Worth: £73,986,000 *Total Assets:* £73,986,000
Registered Office: Barratt House, Cartwright Way, Forest Business Park, Bardon Hill, Coalville, Leics, LE67 1UF

ZF Services UK Limited
Incorporated: 3 October 1973 *Employees:* 180
Net Worth: £17,261,000 *Total Assets:* £42,787,000
Registered Office: Abbeyfield Road, Lenton, Nottingham, NG7 2SX
Activities: Wholesale trade of motor vehicle parts and accessories
Parent: Stadt Friedrichschafen
Officers: Gail Mansell, Secretary; Christopher Adcock [1965] Managing Director; Gail Mansell [1975] Finance Director; Martin Mueller [1961] Director/Head of Region Europe [German]

Zibrant Limited
Incorporated: 26 November 1987 *Employees:* 125
Net Worth: £3,586,807 *Total Assets:* £11,078,498
Registered Office: 2 Prospect Place, Pride Park, Derby, DE24 8HG
Activities: Other reservation service activities n.e.c.
Officers: Laura Everitt, Secretary; Darren Christer Boden [1971] Finance Director; Nigel Phillip Cooper [1963] Director; Geertjan Jan Jongeneel [1960] Director/Chief Financial Officer [Dutch]

Zinc Ahead Holdings Limited
Incorporated: 10 May 2011 *Employees:* 2
Net Worth: £35,117,548 *Total Assets:* £36,184,832
Registered Office: 4240 Nash Court, John Smith Drive, Oxford Business Park South, Oxford, OX4 2RU
Activities: Business and domestic software development
Parent: Mineral Newco Limited
Officers: Timothy Stephen Cabral [1967] Director [American]; Jonathan Faddis [1971] Director/Senior VP and General Counsel [American]

ZND (UK) Limited
Incorporated: 9 October 1997 *Employees:* 113
Net Worth: £21,363,260 *Total Assets:* £38,332,392
Registered Office: The Gateway, Parkgate, Rotherham, S Yorks, S62 6JL
Activities: Manufacture of metal structures and parts of structures
Shareholders: Hilde Johanna Martina Van Beek; Romy Lamberta Adriana Adriana Van Beek; Wilhelmus Josephus Van Beek
Officers: Wilhelmus Josephus Van Beek, Secretary/Director [Dutch]; James McLean [1964] Director; Wilhelmus Josephus Van Beek [1963] Director [Dutch]

Zonwering Holdings Limited
Incorporated: 4 May 2017
Net Worth: £304,537,984 *Total Assets:* £318,734,016
Registered Office: Unit 2 Churchill Park, Private Road No 2, Colwick, Nottingham, NG4 2JR
Activities: Activities of other holding companies n.e.c.
Parent: Hunter Douglas (UK) Limited
Officers: Craig Edwards [1974] Director; Ian Galpin [1974] Director; David Mathew Aubrey Lewis [1967] Director [Australian]; Darren Hansel Lock [1966] Director; John Risman [1965] Director; Andrew Richard Thomas [1972] Director/Business Executive; Susan Ann White [1976] Director

Zoo Digital Group PLC
Incorporated: 14 October 1999 *Employees:* 173
Net Worth: £2,076,209 *Total Assets:* £13,639,500
Registered Office: 7th Floor, Citygate, St Marys Gate, Sheffield, S1 4LW
Activities: Business and domestic software development
Officers: Phillip Blundell, Secretary; Phillip Robert Blundell [1961] Director/Chief Finance Officer; Stuart Antony Green [1965] Director; Roger David Jeynes [1952] Director; Maneck Minoo Kalifa [1967] Director

Zooom Holdings (UK) Limited
Incorporated: 26 June 2003
Net Worth: £98,051,000 *Total Assets:* £215,624,992
Registered Office: 15 Midland Court, Central Park, Lutterworth, Leics, LE17 4PN
Activities: Activities of head offices
Parent: Lavendon Holdings Limited
Officers: Jerome Sarragozi, Secretary; Thomas Donald Kenny [1954] Director/Group CEO [Irish]; Thomas Anthony Murray [1967] Director/Chartered Accountant

Zyox Limited
Incorporated: 22 June 1988 *Employees:* 9
Net Worth: £4,916,894 *Total Assets:* £32,231,810
Registered Office: Swallow House, Shilton Industrial Estate, Shilton, Coventry, Warwicks, CV7 9JY
Activities: Sale of used cars and light motor vehicles
Parent: Manxprop Ltd
Officers: Neil Edward Smith, Secretary; David Ellis Archer [1968] Finance Director; Peter Ligertwood [1942] Director; Irene de Los Angeles Reveco [1951] Director; Heather Juanita Sarah Smith [1954] Director; Neil Edward Smith [1957] Director/Engineer; Pauline Elizabeth Smith [1957] Director; Stephen Westhorpe [1958] Director

This page is intentionally left blank

Standard Industrial Classification

01110 Growing of cereals (except rice), leguminous crops and oil seeds [83]

Abbotsley Farms Limited
J.O.Adams & Son Limited
Agreserves Limited
Albanwise Limited
J.H. Bacon Limited
M.Baker Produce Limited
Bedfordia Farms Limited
Blankney Estates Limited
H.R Bourn & Sons (Linwood) Limited
R. Bratley (Quadring) Limited
Burrough Court Estate Limited
Bury Farm Sharpenhoe Limited
Joseph Camm Farms Limited
R.Caudwell (Produce) Limited
Caudwell Farms
W.S.Chapman & Sons Limited
K.J. Cherry & Sons Limited
J.R. Clark Limited
E.D. & A.D. Cooke, Bourne (Farms) Ltd
R.M. Cottingham Limited
Maurice Crouch (Growers) Limited
P.J. Duffy & Son (Farms) Limited
Earth Trust
Ellis Bros (Contractors) Limited
F.H. Farms Limited
Frickley Holdings.Limited
F & A George Limited
Gibbons (Holdings) Limited
R.A. Gibson (Colesden) Limited
J.C.M.Glassford Limited
Grainsby Farms Limited
J W Grant Co
Grantham Bros. Limited
Hague Farming Limited
Happy Days Farming Co Ltd
Hardys Farm Limited
Harrowden Farms Group Limited
Harrowden Farms Limited
Fred Hartley (Estates) Limited
J H & A J King Farms Limited
Knightwood Trust Farms Limited
LDC (Boston) Limited
R. H. Lamyman Limited
Lapwing Estate Limited
Leda Properties Limited
Limestone Farming Co Ltd
Lockwood Estates Limited
Geoffrey Mason Limited
Maurice Mason Limited
William F.Moore (Warplands) Limited
Morrells Farming Limited
M.C.Mountain and Son Limited
OAT 2012 Limited
G.H. Parker (North Cotes) Limited
C.W.Parker (Wainfleet) Limited
Pengethley Potatoes Limited
Proctor Bros. (Long Sutton) Limited
Rainthorpe Farms Limited
Richardson & Cock Limited
Rolleston Hall Estates Limited
D.H.Sanderson and Son Limited
John Saul Limited
Shrubhill Farms Limited
Smith & Sons (Bletchington) Limited
A.W. Smith & Sons Limited
Stratton-Streles Estates Limited
W. H. Strawson (Farms) Limited
W. H. Strawson (Notts.) Limited
C.A. Strawson Farming Limited
Strawson Limited
M.F. Strawson Limited
O.A.Taylor & Sons Bulbs Limited
R. C. Tinsley Limited
R.H.Topham & Sons Limited
Trinley Estate Limited
G.B.Turnbull Limited
Waldersey Farms Limited
C. Walton Limited
R.H. Ward (Welton) Limited
John A.Wells Limited
J. Wharton (Agriculture) Limited
Willoughby 395 Limited
M.J. Worth Limited

01130 Growing of vegetables and melons, roots and tubers [21]

Alan Bartlett & Sons (Chatteris) Ltd
Joseph Camm Farms Limited
T.H.Clements & Son Limited
Maurice Crouch (Growers) Limited
Emmett UK Limited
Glinwell PLC
Greenshoots Limited
Greenvale AP Limited
Harrowden Farms Limited
Keepstem Limited
R. H. Lamyman Limited
Lincolnshire Field Products Limited
M.C.Mountain and Son Limited
OAT 2012 Limited
J.E.Piccaver & Co. (Gedney Marsh)
Proctor Bros. (Long Sutton) Limited
Rowe Farming Limited
John Saul Limited
Staples Brothers Limited
Stratton-Streles Estates Limited
O.A.Taylor & Sons Bulbs Limited

01190 Growing of other non-perennial crops

APS Produce Limited
Florensis Flower Seeds UK Limited
Greenyard Flowers UK Ltd
Lockwood Estates Limited

01290 Growing of other perennial crops

Florensis Flower Seeds UK Limited
Greenyard Flowers UK Ltd
Harrowden Turf Limited
Shrubhill Farms Limited

01420 Raising of other cattle and buffaloes

Limestone Farming Co Ltd
J.G. Pears Limited

01430 Raising of horses and other equines

Old Road Securities PLC

01450 Raising of sheep and goats

J.G. Pears Limited
R. C. Tinsley Limited

01460 Raising of swine and pigs

Bedfordia Farms Limited
Easey Pigs Limited
Elsham Linc Limited
Hawkes Limited
Limestone Farming Co Ltd
Norfolk Free Range Limited

01470 Raising of poultry [11]

Aviagen Limited
Cherry Valley Farms Limited
L.J. Fairburn and Son Limited
Germany Farms Limited
P.D. Hook (Breeders) Limited
P.D.Hook (Hatcheries) Limited
P.D. Hook (Rearing) Limited
Hook 2 Sisters Limited
G.E. Porter & Sons Limited
Sunrise Poultry Farms Limited
Wallis Farms Limited

01490 Raising of other animals

Boden & Davies Limited

01500 Mixed farming [27]

Allen (Hanford) Limited
Averys (Radnage) Limited
The C. Alma Baker Trust
Berkshire Hops Limited
Cranford Asset Management Limited
A.R. Craven Farms Limited
Maurice Crouch (Growers) Limited
W. Cumber & Son (Theale) Limited
Davison & Co. (Barford) Limited
Patrick Dean Limited
Ducker Farming Limited
RE Evans Farms Limited
Everards Brewery Limited
Faccenda Farms Limited
Farnley Estates Limited
R.J. & A.E. Godfrey
J.H.& F.W.Green Limited
Magyar Farming Co Ltd
Mercer Farming Limited
Mark H Poskitt Limited
Ben Smith & Sons (Wantage) Limited
Stockcroft Limited
Sywell Aerodrome,Limited
Willoughby Farms Limited
Wispington Farms Limited
Worksop Manor Estates,Limited
P A Wright & Sons Limited

01610 Support activities for crop production

Agrovista UK Limited
FKB Limited
Hutchinson Group Limited
H.L. Hutchinson Limited
Karsten UK Limited
Marubeni Agro Machinery Holding Limited
Munks Agricultural Contractors Limited
Spaldings Holdings Limited
Spaldings Limited

01629 Support activities for animal production (other than farm animal boarding)

Addington Fund
Rycote Services Limited
Thames Valley Cambac Limited

01630 Post-harvest crop activities

A.B. Produce PLC
Bedfordia Farms Limited
Great Tew Grain Processing Limited
Greenvale AP Limited
Greenyard Flowers UK Ltd
Openfield Agriculture Limited
W. H. Strawson (Notts.) Limited

01640 Seed processing for propagation

Dunns (Long Sutton) Limited

01700 Hunting, trapping and related service activities

Rycote Services Limited

02100 Silviculture and other forestry activities

Forest of Marston Vale Trust
Grimsthorpe & Drummond Castle Trust Ltd
Woodland Trust
Worksop Manor Estates,Limited

03220 Freshwater aquaculture

Benchmark Genetics Limited

05102 Open cast coal working

Harworth Estates Group Limited
Harworth Services Limited

06100 Extraction of crude petroleum

British Drilling and Freezing Co Ltd
Dyas Exploration UK Limited
Dyas UK Limited
Dyon E & P Limited
Dyon UK Limited
International Logging Technology Limited
Regent Park Energy Limited
Roc Oil (Europe) Limited
Weatherford Eurasia Limited

06200 Extraction of natural gas

Dyas Exploration UK Limited
Dyon E & P Limited
Dyon UK Limited
Warwick Energy Limited

07290 Mining of other non-ferrous metal ores

Schoeller-Bleckmann Oilfield Equipment (UK) Ltd

08110 Quarrying of ornamental and building stone, limestone, gypsum, chalk and slate [13]

Aggregate Industries UK Limited
Ben Bennett Jr Limited
Breedon Cement Limited
Breedon Southern Limited
Bullimores Sand and Gravel Limited
Derbyshire Aggregates Limited
Mick George Limited
Johnston Quarry Group Limited
Lafarge Cauldon Limited
Longcliffe Quarries Limited
Singleton Birch Limited
Smith & Sons (Bletchington) Limited
Welsh Slate Limited

08120 Operation of gravel and sand pits; mining of clays and kaolin [15]

Aggregate Industries UK Limited
Breedon Cement Limited
Breedon Southern Limited
Bullimores Sand and Gravel Limited
Cemex UK Operations Limited
J. Curtis & Sons Limited
Frimstone Limited
Grundon Sand & Gravel Limited
Mansfield Sand Co Ltd
North Lincs Property Limited
Rotherham Sand and Gravel Co Ltd
Smith & Sons (Bletchington) Limited
Smiths Concrete Limited
Springfield Farm Limited
Wight Building Materials Ltd

08990 Other mining and quarrying n.e.c.

Duo Processing Limited
GRS (Roadstone) Limited
Gurney Slade Lime & Stone Co.Limited
Lafarge Cauldon Limited
Lafarge Ireland Limited
Long Rake Spar Co Ltd

09100 Support activities for petroleum and natural gas mining

Adams Challenge (UK) Limited
Energy Alloys UK Limited
RPS Energy Limited
Weatherford U.K. Limited

09900 Support activities for other mining and quarrying

CMS Cepcor Limited
GRS Roadstone Group Limited
Kal Tire (UK) Limited
Lafarge Cauldon Limited
O.T.R. Tyres Limited

10110 Processing and preserving of meat

CPC Foods Limited
Damika Limited
Giorgio's Continental Ltd.
Manifesto Foods Ltd
Meatsnacks Group Ltd.
Woolley Bros. (Wholesale Meats) Limited

10120 Processing and preserving of poultry meat

Rick Bestwick Limited
Faccenda Foods Limited
Magnavale Limited

10130 Production of meat and poultry meat products

CPC Foods Limited
Gafoor Pure Halal Ltd
OSI Food Solutions UK Limited
G W Padley Poultry Limited
Paragon Quality Foods Ltd
Pukka Pies Limited
TMI Foods Limited
Tulip Limited

10200 Processing and preserving of fish, crustaceans and molluscs

Caistor Seafoods Limited
Young's Seafood Limited

10310 Processing and preserving of potatoes

Branston Limited
Greenvale AP Limited
E.Park & Sons Limited

10320 Manufacture of fruit and vegetable juice

Alpro (UK) Limited
Orchard House Foods Limited

10390 Other processing and preserving of fruit and vegetables

Blue Skies Holdings Limited
Greenyard Frozen UK Limited
Moulton Bulb Co Ltd
Phytone Limited
Q V Foods Limited
Sensient Flavors Limited
Sensient Holdings UK
Staples (Vegetables) Limited

10410 Manufacture of oils and fats

BASF Pharma (Callanish) Limited
Nortech Foods Limited
Olam Food Ingredients UK Limited
Sarval (Hartshill) Limited
Sarval Limited
Secanim Limited

10511 Liquid milk and cream production

Alpro (UK) Limited

10512 Butter and cheese production

Giorgio's Continental Ltd.

10519 Manufacture of other milk products

Alpro (UK) Limited

10611 Grain milling

Carr's Flour Mills Limited
Heygates Limited
Wm. Nelstrop & Co. Ltd
Pioneer Foods (UK) Limited
Richardson Milling (UK) Limited
Virani Food Products Limited
Whitworth Bros.Limited

10612 Manufacture of breakfast cereals and cereals-based food

Pioneer Foods (UK) Limited

10620 Manufacture of starches and starch products

Roquette UK Limited

10710 Manufacture of bread; manufacture of fresh pastry goods and cakes

Brioche Pasquier U.K. Limited
Delifrance (UK) Limited
Fine Lady Bakeries Limited
Haywood and Padgett Limited
Lantmannen UK Holding Limited
Livwell Limited
New York Bakery Co Ltd
Santa Maria UK Limited
Trousdale Limited

10720 Manufacture of rusks and biscuits; manufacture of preserved pastry goods and cakes

Brioche Pasquier U.K. Limited
Gibbs Croft Limited
Kitchen Range Foods Limited

10821 Manufacture of cocoa and chocolate confectionery

Barry Callebaut Holding (UK) Limited
Barry Callebaut Manufacturing (UK) Ltd

10822 Manufacture of sugar confectionery

Swizzels Matlow Limited

10832 Production of coffee and coffee substitutes

Jacobs Douwe Egberts Ops GB Ltd
Lincoln & York Limited

10840 Manufacture of condiments and seasonings

Virani Food Products Limited

10850 Manufacture of prepared meals and dishes

Greencore Food To Go Limited
Greencore Foods Limited
Greencore Grocery Limited
Seachill UK Limited
Uniq Limited

10860 Manufacture of homogenized food preparations and dietetic food

Alpro (UK) Limited

10890 Manufacture of other food products n.e.c. [35]

Addo Food Group (Holdings) Ltd
Addo Food Group Limited
Birds (Derby) Limited
British Bakels Limited
Cambridge Weight Plan Limited
Daloon Foods (U.K.) Limited
Dri-Pak Limited
Elisabeth The Chef Limited
Fresh-Pak Chilled Foods Limited
Freshtime UK Limited
Frutarom (UK) Holdings Limited
Frutarom (UK) Limited
Greencore Prepared Meals Limited
Griffith Foods Limited
Haywood and Padgett Limited
Lakshmi & Son's Limited
Lighthouse UkCo 6 (Treasury) Limited
Manderley Food Group Limited
Naturex Limited
Noble Desserts Holdings Limited
Noble Foods Limited
Pedigree Wholesale Limited
Pork Farms Caspian Limited
Pork Farms Limited
Ryecroft Foods Limited
Samworth Brothers Limited
Sandwich Factory Holdings Limited
Seachill UK Limited
Shire Foods Limited
Sleaford Quality Foods Limited
Tayto Group Limited
Uniq Limited
Universal Flexible Packaging Limited
Weetabix Limited
Whitworths Limited

10910 Manufacture of prepared feeds for farm animals [13]

Cherwell Valley Silos Limited
Dodson & Horrell Limited
Elsham Linc Limited
GLW Feeds Limited
Heygate & Sons Limited
Natures Menu Limited
Pelagia (UK) Limited
J.E. Porter Limited
Rumenco Limited
Sarval (Hartshill) Limited
Sarval Limited
Secanim Limited
Frank Wright Limited

10920 Manufacture of prepared pet foods

Armitage Brothers Limited
Armitages Pet Products Limited
Butcher's Pet Care Limited
Fold Hill Foods Limited
Natures Menu Limited

11010 Distilling, rectifying and blending of spirits

Giorgio's Continental Ltd.

11050 Manufacture of beer [12]

George Bateman & Son Limited
Joseph Camm Farms Limited
Carlsberg Supply Company UK Limited
Carlsberg UK Limited
Cobra Beer Partnership Limited
Everards Brewery Limited
Hook Norton Brewery Co Ltd
Molson Coors Brewing Co (UK) Ltd
Frederic Robinson Limited
Tynemill Limited
Charles Wells Brewery Limited
Charles Wells,Limited

11060 Manufacture of malt

Soufflet Malt UK Limited

11070 Manufacture of soft drinks; production of mineral waters and other bottled waters

Refresco Drinks UK Limited
Rubicon Drinks Limited

13100 Preparation and spinning of textile fibres

A.T.C. Manufacturing Limited
Avery Dennison Retail Information Services UK Ltd
Technical Absorbents Limited

13200 Weaving of textiles

A.T.C. Manufacturing Limited
Bowmer-Bond Narrow Fabrics Limited
Toray Textiles Europe Limited
VM Fabrics Limited

13300 Finishing of textiles

A.T.C. Manufacturing Limited
Autofil Yarns Limited
Jandu Developments Limited
Toray Textiles Europe Limited

13910 Manufacture of knitted and crocheted fabrics

Fashion Fabric Transprinters Limited

13921 Manufacture of soft furnishings

Belfield Furnishings Limited

13931 Manufacture of woven or tufted carpets and rugs

Flair Flooring Supplies Limited

13939 Manufacture of other carpets and rugs

Flair Flooring Supplies Limited

13960 Manufacture of other technical and industrial textiles

Guilford Europe Limited
Toray Textiles Europe Limited

13990 Manufacture of other textiles n.e.c.

Fashion Fabric Transprinters Limited
Urgo Limited

14120 Manufacture of workwear

Ballyclare Limited
MWUK Limited

14131 Manufacture of other men's outerwear

Quantum Clothing Group Limited

14132 Manufacture of other women's outerwear

Crystal Martin Holdings Limited
Crystal Martin International Limited
David Nieper Limited

14142 Manufacture of women's underwear

Crystal Martin Holdings Limited
Crystal Martin International Limited
David Nieper Limited
Quantum Clothing Group Limited
Wacoal EMEA Ltd

14190 Manufacture of other wearing apparel and accessories n.e.c.

Christys By Design Limited
Douglas Gill International Limited
Outdoor & Sports Co Ltd
Quantum Clothing Group Limited
SML Europe Limited
John Smedley Limited
T.D.P. Textiles Limited

14310 Manufacture of knitted and crocheted hosiery

Quantum Clothing Group Limited

15200 Manufacture of footwear

Barker Shoes Limited
Cheaney Shoes Limited
Church & Co Limited
Crockett and Jones Limited
Loake Brothers Limited

16100 Sawmilling and planing of wood

Arbor Forest Products Limited
Etex (Exteriors) UK Limited
Harlow Bros. Limited
Jeld-Wen UK Limited
Linnell Brothers Limited
Metsa Wood UK Limited

16210 Manufacture of veneer sheets and wood-based panels

Bushboard Holdings Limited

16230 Manufacture of other builders' carpentry and joinery

Harlow Bros. Limited
Jeld-Wen UK Limited
Staircraft Group Limited

16240 Manufacture of wooden containers

Neal Brothers (Leicester) Limited

16290 Manufacture of other products of wood; manufacture of articles of cork, straw and plaiting materials

Dagless Limited
Harlow Bros. Limited
Premdor Crosby Limited

17120 Manufacture of paper and paperboard [10]

Consuma Holdings Limited
Consuma Paper Products Limited
Firstan Limited
John Hargreaves,(Collyhurst and Stalybridge) Ltd
Palm Paper Limited
Rigid Group Limited
Schades Limited
Sofidel UK Limited
Tullis Russell Coaters Limited
Union Papertech Limited

17211 Manufacture of corrugated paper and paperboard, sacks and bags

Corrboard UK Limited
Encase Holdings Limited
Encase Limited
Rigid Containers Limited

17219 Manufacture of other paper and paperboard containers

API Foils Limited
Cardboard Box Co Ltd
Firstan Holdings Limited
Multi Packaging Solutions Limited
Multi Packaging Solutions UK Limited
Printing & Packaging Co. Limited
Solidus UK Solutions Ltd

17220 Manufacture of household and sanitary goods and of toilet requisites

Northwood Tissue (Disley) Limited

17230 Manufacture of paper stationery

Adare SEC Limited
Bong UK Limited

17290 Manufacture of other articles of paper and paperboard n.e.c.

Darley Limited
IG Design Group UK Limited

18121 Manufacture of printed labels

Barcode Warehouse Limited
Leaworks Limited
Reflex Group Limited
Reflex Labels Limited

18129 Printing n.e.c. [13]

Adare International Limited
Buxton Press Limited
Coveris Flexibles UK Limited
Eclipse Colour Print Limited
FFP Packaging Solutions Limited
Fashion Fabric Transprinters Limited
W & J Linney Limited
Print People Group Limited
Sterling Press Limited
Topps Europe Holdings Limited
Topps Europe Limited
Warners (Midlands) PLC
Ken Wilkins Print Limited

18201 Reproduction of sound recording

Concentia Capital Limited
Imagesound Limited

19201 Mineral oil refining

Total Lindsey Oil Refinery Limited

19209 Other treatment of petroleum products (excluding petrochemicals manufacture)

Exol Lubricants (Rotherham) Limited

20120 Manufacture of dyes and pigments

Sensient Colors UK Ltd

20130 Manufacture of other inorganic basic chemicals

Apollo Scientific Ltd
Celanese Production UK Limited
Cristal Pigment UK Limited
Dow Chemical Co Ltd
Nippon Gases UK Limited
OQEMA Limited
Singleton Birch Limited
Warwick International Group Limited

20140 Manufacture of other organic basic chemicals

BASF PLC
EPC United Kingdom PLC
Evonik Chemicals Limited
Infineum International Limited
Infineum UK Ltd.

20150 Manufacture of fertilizers and nitrogen compounds

Omex Agriculture Limited
Omex Agrifluids Limited
Yara UK Limited

20160 Manufacture of plastics in primary forms [12]

Dynamic Cassette International Limited
Fusion Plastics Limited
Luxus Limited
Polynt Composites UK Limited
Polypipe Limited
Recticel Limited
Robimatic Limited
Scott Bader Co Ltd
Scott Bader UK Limited
Strata Products Limited
Synthetic Resins Limited
Ten Cate Advanced Composites Limited

20170 Manufacture of synthetic rubber in primary forms

Polytech International Limited

20200 Manufacture of pesticides and other agrochemical products

Croda Europe Limited

20301 Manufacture of paints, varnishes and similar coatings, mastics and sealants [10]

Dynamic Cassette International Limited
Inver UK Limited
Jotun Paints (Europe) Limited
Sherwin-Williams Diversified Brands Ltd
U-Pol Bidco Limited
U-Pol Bond Limited
U-Pol Finco Limited
U-Pol Limited
U-Pol Mezzanine Limited
H.K. Wentworth Limited

20302 Manufacture of printing ink

Perfectos Printing Inks Co Ltd.

20411 Manufacture of soap and detergents [10]

Coventry Chemicals Limited
Diversey Holdings Limited
Diversey Limited
Diversey UK Production Limited
Dri-Pak Limited
Evonik Goldschmidt UK Limited
Libra Speciality Chemicals Limited
SC Johnson Professional Limited
Selden Research Limited
Stepan UK Limited

20412 Manufacture of cleaning and polishing preparations

Diversey UK Production Limited
H.K. Wentworth Limited

20420 Manufacture of perfumes and toilet preparations

BCM Limited
CPL Aromas (Holdings) Limited
CPL Aromas Limited

20510 Manufacture of explosives

EPC United Kingdom PLC

20520 Manufacture of glues

Beardow and Adams (Adhesives) Limited

20590 Manufacture of other chemical products n.e.c. [27]

2K Polymer Systems Limited
AMG Superalloys UK Limited
Amega Sciences PLC
Basildon Chemical Co. Limited
Albert Browne Limited
Celanese Production UK Limited
Clark-Drain Limited
Croda Europe Limited
DSM Nutritional Products (UK) Limited
Datac Adhesives Limited
Foseco International Limited
HB Fuller UK Operations Limited
Leeson Chemicals Limited
Leeson Polyurethanes Limited
Lubrizol Limited
Miswa Chemicals Limited
Nexeon Limited
Nippon Gases UK Limited
Reabrook Ltd
Selden Research Limited
Sherwin-Williams Diversified Brands Ltd
Solenis UK Limited
Stepan UK Limited
U-Pol Limited
Valspar (UK) Corporation, Limited
WD-40 Co Ltd
H.K. Wentworth Limited

20600 Manufacture of man-made fibres

Lenzing Fibers Grimsby Limited

21100 Manufacture of basic pharmaceutical products [14]

AAH Pharmaceuticals Limited
Albumedix Ltd
Aspen Medical Europe Limited
BCM Specials Limited
Bio-Rad AbD Serotec Ltd
Brunel Healthcare Manufacturing Limited
Catalent UK Supply Chain Limited
Envigo RMS (UK) Limited
Hichrom Limited
Kent Pharmaceuticals Limited
Nova Laboratories Limited
Porvair PLC
Schering-Plough Limited
TCS Biosciences Limited

21200 Manufacture of pharmaceutical preparations [12]

Alliance Medical Radiopharmacy Limited
Aptuit (Oxford) Limited
BCM Limited
BCM Specials Limited
Circassia Pharmaceuticals PLC
Clinigen Group PLC
Intervet UK Production Limited
Morningside Pharmaceuticals Limited
Nova Laboratories Limited
Oxford Immunotec Global PLC
Oxford Immunotec Limited
Remedi Medical Holdings Limited

22110 Manufacture of rubber tyres and tubes; retreading and rebuilding of rubber tyres

Hankook Tyre U.K. Limited
Pirelli UK Tyres Limited
Vacu-Lug Traction Tyres Limited

22190 Manufacture of other rubber products

Aero Tec Laboratories Limited
Berwin Industrial Polymers Limited
Berwin Rubber Co Ltd
Dunlop Oil & Marine Limited
Edgetech (UK) Limited
Charles Lawrence Surfaces Limited
Metflex Precision Mouldings Limited
OSL Group Holdings Limited
Polytech International Limited

22210 Manufacture of plastic plates, sheets, tubes and profiles

API Foils Limited
API Laminates Limited
Coba Automotive (UK) Limited
JFC Plastics Limited
Brett Martin Daylight Systems Limited

22220 Manufacture of plastic packing goods [15]

Brayford Plastics Limited
Coveris Flexibles (Gainsborough) UK Ltd
Essentra Packaging & Security Limited
K.M. Packaging Services Limited
Massmould Limited
Maynard & Harris Plastics
Mondi Scunthorpe Limited
Nampak Plastics Europe Limited
Povoas Packaging Limited
Promens Packaging Limited
RPC Containers Limited
Schutz (U.K.) Limited
Sealed Air Limited
Ultimate Packaging Limited
George Utz Limited

22230 Manufacture of builders ware of plastic

Alumasc Limited
Freefoam Plastics (U.K.) Limited
Sash UK Limited
Unique Window Systems Ltd
Wavin Limited

22290 Manufacture of other plastic products [52]

Accuma Plastics Limited
Agema Engineering Limited
Amtico Co Ltd
Amtico Holdings Limited
Amtico International Limited
Artform International Limited
Bolton Plastic Components Limited
British Polythene Industries Limited
British Polythene Limited
Carpenter Limited
Cytec Industrial Materials (Derby) Ltd
Cytec Process Materials (Keighley) Ltd
Dart Products Europe Ltd.
Direct Leisure Supplies Limited
Dubois Limited
Dynamic Cassette International Limited
Essentra Components Limited
Essentra Packaging & Security Limited
Essentra Packaging Limited
Eurocell Profiles Limited
Global Closure Systems UK Limited
Goodfellow Cambridge Limited
Greene Tweed & Co Limited
Owen Greenings & Mumford (Holdings) Ltd
H L Plastics Limited
I.G. Industries PLC
R.A.Labone & Co Limited
Loadhog Limited
MacDermid Autotype Limited
Maneto (UK) 2 Limited
Maneto (UK) 3 Limited
Manthorpe Building Products Limited
Matrix Polymers Limited
Mexichem Specialty Compounds Limited
NP Aerospace Limited
Nenplas Limited
Oxford Plastic Systems Limited
Paccor (Mansfield) UK Limited
Plastek UK Ltd
Plastic Omnium Automotive Limited
Porvair Filtration Group Limited
RPC Containers Limited
Radius Systems Limited
Rieke Packaging Systems Limited
Rutland Plastics Limited
A. Schulman Gainsborough Ltd
Silgan Closures UK Limited
Skymark Packaging International Limited
Solidor Limited
Synseal Extrusions Limited
Synventive Acquisition Unlimited
Tradelink Direct Limited

23110 Manufacture of flat glass

Guardian Industries U.K. Limited

23120 Shaping and processing of flat glass

Potters-Ballotini Limited
Saint-Gobain Glass (United Kingdom) Ltd

23130 Manufacture of hollow glass

Beatson Clark Limited

23200 Manufacture of refractory products

Monocon International Refractories Ltd
Steetley Dolomite Limited
Vesuvius UK Limited

23320 Manufacture of bricks, tiles and construction products, in baked clay

Forterra Building Products Limited
Ibstock Brick Limited
Ibstock PLC
Wienerberger Limited

23440 Manufacture of other technical ceramic products

Goodfellow Cambridge Limited
Porvair PLC

23490 Manufacture of other ceramic products n.e.c.

Etex (Exteriors) UK Limited
Ross Ceramics Limited

23510 Manufacture of cement

Breedon Cement Limited
Cemex UK Operations Limited
Lafarge Cauldon Limited
Lafarge Ireland Limited

23520 Manufacture of lime and plaster

Lhoist UK Limited
Steetley Dolomite Limited

23610 Manufacture of concrete products for construction purposes

Aggregate Industries UK Limited
Cemex UK Operations Limited
Etex (Exteriors) UK Limited
Forticrete Limited
Monier Redland Limited
Stanton Bonna Concrete Limited
Supreme Concrete Limited
Wight Building Materials Ltd

23620 Manufacture of plaster products for construction purposes

Artex Limited

23630 Manufacture of ready-mixed concrete

Breedon Cement Limited
Cemex UK Operations Limited
Smiths Concrete Limited
Wight Building Materials Ltd

23640 Manufacture of mortars

Smiths Concrete Limited

23650 Manufacture of fibre cement

Etex (Exteriors) UK Limited

23690 Manufacture of other articles of concrete, plaster and cement

Anderton Concrete Products Limited
Stanton Bonna Concrete Limited

23910 Production of abrasive products

Icopal Limited

23990 Manufacture of other non-metallic mineral products n.e.c.

Ballast Phoenix Limited
CLEB Holdings Limited
Carbon International Limited
Coal Products Limited
James Durrans & Sons,Limited
LKAB Minerals Limited
Tolsa UK Limited

24100 Manufacture of basic iron and steel and of ferro-alloys [11]

AMG Superalloys UK Limited
AVK UK Limited
Abbey Forged Products Limited
British Steel Holdings Limited
British Steel Limited
Liberty Merchant Bar PLC
Outokumpu Stainless Limited
Sheffield Forgemasters Engineering Ltd
Sheffield Forgemasters International Ltd
Sheffield Forgemasters Steel Limited
United Cast Bar (UK) Limited

24200 Manufacture of tubes, pipes, hollow profiles and related fittings, of steel

Fine Tubes Limited
Lindab Limited
TI Group Automotive Systems (UK) Limited

24340 Cold drawing of wire

Lincoln Electric (U.K.) Limited

24410 Precious metals production

Select Alloys & Materials Limited
Solpro Manufacturing Limited
Thessco Limited

24420 Aluminium production [10]

AMG Alpoco UK Limited
AMG Aluminum UK Limited
Alanod Limited
Arconic Extruded Products (UK) Limited
Arconic Manufacturing (GB) Limited
Boal U.K. Limited
British Aluminium Limited
Hydro Extrusion UK Ltd
Kawneer U.K. Limited
Mil-Ver Metal Co Ltd

24440 Copper production

Lawton Tube Co Ltd
Mil-Ver Metal Co Ltd

24450 Other non-ferrous metal production

AMG Superalloys UK Limited
H. J. Enthoven Limited
RTI Advanced Forming Limited
Ross & Catherall Limited

24510 Casting of iron

William Lee Limited

24520 Casting of steel

William Cook Cast Products Limited
William Cook Stanhope Limited
V Installations Mechanical Handling Ltd

24530 Casting of light metals

Meridian Lightweight Technologies UK Ltd

24540 Casting of other non-ferrous metals

Alloy Technologies (UK) Limited
Doncasters Aerospace Limited
Howmet Limited
Paralloy Limited
Trucast Limited
Vulcan SFM Limited

25110 Manufacture of metal structures and parts of structures [13]

Alumasc Exterior Building Products Ltd
Alumet Systems (UK) Limited
Billington Structures Limited
Caunton Engineering Limited
Cullum Detuners Limited
Exlabesa Extrusions (Doncaster) Limited
Gardner Aerospace-Broughton Limited
Kaby Engineers Limited
Mosdorfer CCL Systems Limited
Qualter, Hall & Co Ltd
SPS Aerostructures Limited
Stainless Metalcraft (Chatteris) Limited
ZND (UK) Limited

25120 Manufacture of doors and windows of metal

Graham Holmes Astraseal Limited
Roof-Maker Ltd
Tradelink Direct Limited

25210 Manufacture of central heating radiators and boilers

Baxi Heating UK Limited
D D Heating Limited
Hoval Limited
Vaillant Industrial UK Limited

25290 Manufacture of other tanks, reservoirs and containers of metal

Stainless Metalcraft (Chatteris) Limited
Tanks and Vessels Industries Limited

25300 Manufacture of steam generators, except central heating hot water boilers

Rolls-Royce Submarines Limited

25500 Forging, pressing, stamping and roll-forming of metal; powder metallurgy [13]

Ben Bennett Jr Limited
Bifrangi UK Limited
Broadways Stampings Limited
Coverworld UK Limited
Firth Rixson Forgings Limited
Firth Rixson Metals Limited
Independent Forgings & Alloys Limited
Pegler Holdings Limited
Pegler Limited
Special Quality Alloys Limited
Special Steel Co.,Limited
Symmetry Medical Sheffield Ltd.
Thos. C. Wild Limited

25610 Treatment and coating of metals

Bodycote H.I.P. Limited
Bodycote Heat Treatments Limited
Bodycote Surface Technology Limited
ELG Utica Alloys Limited
Euramax Coated Products Limited
Oerlikon Balzers Coating UK Limited
Special Steel Co.,Limited
Turbine Surface Technologies Limited

25620 Machining [19]

Accrofab Limited
Ametek Airtechnology Group Limited
Bifrangi UK Limited
Dana Spicer Europe Limited
Deritend International Limited
Diamond Power Specialty Limited
Gardner Aerospace - Basildon Limited
Hyde Group Tooling Limited
L H Group Services Limited
Manthorpe Engineering Limited
Rolls-Royce Power Engineering PLC
Shield Engineering (Syston) Limited
C R Shield Holdings Limited
Sigma Precision Components UK Limited
Special Steel Co.,Limited
Stainless Metalcraft (Chatteris) Limited
Techman Engineering Ltd.
Wabtec Rail Limited
Woolley GMC Engineering Holdings Limited

25710 Manufacture of cutlery

Special Steel Co.,Limited

25730 Manufacture of tools

Artex Limited
Eclipse Magnetics Limited
I Holland Limited
Neill Tools Limited
Norbar Torque Tools Limited
Stanley Works Limited
Technicut Limited

25910 Manufacture of steel drums and similar containers

Stainless Metalcraft (Chatteris) Limited

25920 Manufacture of light metal packaging

Can-Pack UK Limited
Crown Aerosols UK Ltd

25930 Manufacture of wire products, chain and springs

Advanex Europe Limited
Arconic Global Fasteners Limited
Betafence Limited
Bridon International Ltd.
Hampton Steel Limited
Linread Limited
Vista Engineering Limited
Wade Spring Limited

25940 Manufacture of fasteners and screw machine products

Arconic Fastening Systems & Rings Ltd
Avdel UK Limited
Blanc Aero Industries UK Limited
Cooper & Turner Limited
Cooper and Turner Distribution Limited
SPS Technologies Limited
Sigma Precision Components UK Limited
Tappex Thread Inserts Limited
Tucker Fasteners Limited

25990 Manufacture of other fabricated metal products n.e.c. [45]

Abacus Lighting Limited
Alumasc Limited
Ancillary Components Limited
Ancon Limited
Arden Dies Limited
Ariens Co Ltd
Bodycote Surface Technology Limited
Bradgate Containers Limited
Cape Engineering Services Limited
Chromalloy United Kingdom Limited
Clarksteel Holdings Limited
Destec Engineering Limited
Doncasters Blaenavon Limited
Doncasters Limited
Electrosteel Castings (UK) Limited
Eminox Limited
Futaba Industrial U.K. Ltd.
Goodfellow Cambridge Limited
Gripple Limited
Hodge Clemco Limited
Howmet Limited
Kannegiesser UK Limited
Kaye Aluminium (Holdings) Limited
LTI Metaltech Limited
Manthorpe Engineering Limited
Mills CNC Limited
Multipanel UK Limited
NMB-Minebea UK Ltd
The Alan Nuttall Partnership Limited
Pegler Yorkshire Group Limited
Porvair PLC
Quartzelec Ltd
RTI Europe Limited
RTI Extrusions Europe Limited
Roe Bros. & Co Ltd.
Rotor Clip Limited
Sigma Precision Components UK Limited
Smith Brothers (Leicester) Limited
Special Quality Alloys Limited
Teconnex Limited
Tensator Limited
WFEL Holdings Limited
WFEL Limited
Wicksteed Leisure Limited
X-Cel Superturn Ltd

26110 Manufacture of electronic components [16]

A F Switchgear Limited
Axis Electronics Limited
BGB Engineering Limited
Cinch Connectors Limited
Dynex Semiconductor Limited
Glenair UK Limited
Huber + Suhner (UK) Limited
Jaybeam Limited
R.A.Labone & Co Limited
Landis + Gyr Limited
Murata Power Solutions (Milton Keynes) Ltd
Nexperia UK Ltd.
Pektron Group Limited
Pyronix Limited
Semelab Limited
UAV Tactical Systems Limited

26120 Manufacture of loaded electronic boards

Asteelflash (Bedford) Limited
Datapath Limited
Foundation Technology Limited
JJS Manufacturing Limited
STS Defence Limited
Tioga Limited

26200 Manufacture of computers and peripheral equipment

Abaco Systems Limited
Adder Technology Limited
CTDI Glenrothes Limited
Datapath Limited
Microlise Limited

26301 Manufacture of telegraph and telephone apparatus and equipment

BGB Engineering Limited
Oclaro Technology Limited

26309 Manufacture of communication equipment other than telegraph, and telephone apparatus and equipment

Industrial Control Distributors Limited
Tunstall Healthcare (UK) Limited

26400 Manufacture of consumer electronics

Drayson Technologies Limited
Meridian Audio Limited

26511 Manufacture of electronic measuring, testing etc. equipment, not for industrial process control [22]

Ametek (GB) Limited
Autologic Diagnostics Limited
Bowers Metrology Limited
Campbell Scientific Limited
Copley Scientific Limited
Crowcon Detection Instruments Limited
Curtis Instruments (U.K.) Limited
Druck Limited
Hach Lange Ltd
Horiba UK Limited
Land Instruments International Limited
Mettler-Toledo Limited
Micromass UK Limited
Nu Instruments Limited
Otter Controls Limited
Oxford Instruments Industrial Products Ltd
Oxford Instruments Nanotechnology Tools Ltd
Pico Technology (Holdings) Limited
Solartron Metrology Limited
Taylor Hobson Limited
Technolog Limited
Vicon Motion Systems Limited

26512 Manufacture of electronic industrial process control equipment

Blackburn Starling & Co Ltd
Bruker UK Limited
Diversey UK Services Limited
Krohne Limited
Mettler-Toledo Limited
Rockwell Automation Limited

26514 Manufacture of non-electronic industrial process control equipment

Diversey UK Services Limited

26600 Manufacture of irradiation, electromedical and electrotherapeutic equipment

Ivor Shaw Limited

26701 Manufacture of optical precision instruments

Laser Quantum Limited
Oclaro Technology Limited
Porvair PLC

26702 Manufacture of photographic and cinematographic equipment

Cooke Optics Group Limited
Cooke Optics Limited

27110 Manufacture of electric motors, generators and transformers

Crestchic Limited
Cummins Generator Technologies Limited
Northbridge Industrial Services PLC
Quartzelec Ltd
Yasa Limited

27120 Manufacture of electricity distribution and control apparatus

A F Switchgear Limited
BGB Engineering Limited
Lucy Group Ltd
PX Manufacturing Ltd
Pfisterer Limited

27200 Manufacture of batteries and accumulators

ABSL Power Solutions Ltd
MK Battery International Limited

27320 Manufacture of other electronic and electric wires and cables

Amnack Limited
OSL Group Holdings Limited
PX Manufacturing Ltd
STS Defence Limited

27400 Manufacture of electric lighting equipment

ASD Lighting PLC
Collingwood Lighting Limited
Dar Lighting Limited
Eaton Electrical Systems Limited
Holophane Europe Limited
Ritelite (Systems) Limited

27510 Manufacture of electric domestic appliances

CDA Group Limited
Jarden Consumer Solutions (Europe) Ltd
Whirlpool UK Appliances Limited

27900 Manufacture of other electrical equipment [16]

Axis EMS Group Limited
Axis Electronics Limited
CMD Limited
EMSC (UK) Limited
Eaton Electrical Products Limited
Eaton MEDC Limited
Guidance Marine Limited
Guided Ultrasonics Limited
ITM Power (Trading) Limited
ITM Power PLC
Lucy Electric UK Limited
Marshall Amplification PLC
SMS Electronics Limited
System Q Limited
Total Integrated Solutions (Holdings) Ltd
Williams Grand Prix Engineering Limited

28110 Manufacture of engines and turbines, except aircraft, vehicle and cycle engines

Allen Diesels Limited
Covrad Heat Transfer Limited
Ilmor Engineering Limited
Perkins Engines Co Ltd
Perkins Group Limited
Perkins Small Engines Limited
Rolls-Royce Power Engineering PLC

28120 Manufacture of fluid power equipment

Festo Limited
PMC Fluidpower Limited

28131 Manufacture of pumps

Clyde Union DB Limited
T. A. Savery & Co Limited
Terex Pegson Limited
Xylem Water Solutions UK Ltd

28140 Manufacture of taps and valves

Watts Industries UK Limited

28150 Manufacture of bearings, gears, gearing and driving elements

Cooper Roller Bearings Co Ltd
Koyo Bearings (Europe) Limited
Mahle Engine Systems UK Limited

28210 Manufacture of ovens, furnaces and furnace burners

Aga Rangemaster Limited
Carbolite Holdings Limited
Chinook Sciences Holdings Limited
Wykes Engineering Co. (Rushden) Limited

28220 Manufacture of lifting and handling equipment [16]

Ability Matters Group Limited
Caljan Rite-Hite Limited
Caterpillar (U.K.) Limited
Del Equipment (U.K.) Limited
Eclipse Magnetics Limited
Hi-Force Limited
Jungheinrich UK Limited
Kleemann Lifts UK Limited
Konecranes Demag UK Limited
Robson Handling Technology Limited
Rolls-Royce Power Engineering PLC
Stertil UK Ltd.
Street Crane Co Ltd
Thwaites Limited
UKMHPS Limited
Unicarriers UK Limited

28250 Manufacture of non-domestic cooling and ventilation equipment

Covrad Heat Transfer Limited

28290 Manufacture of other general-purpose machinery n.e.c.

A B Graphic International Limited
A.E.S. Engineering Limited
Adam Equipment Co. Limited
Atlas Converting Equipment Limited
Fusion Plastics Limited
G.H.B. (Holding) Limited

28301 Manufacture of agricultural tractors

AGCO Limited

28302 Manufacture of agricultural and forestry machinery other than tractors

Cimbria Holdings Limited
Grimme (U.K.) Limited

28490 Manufacture of other machine tools

DMG Mori UK Limited
Envisage Technologies Limited
Expert Tooling & Automation Limited
Snap-On U.K. Holdings Limited
Wolstenholme Machine Knives Limited

28921 Manufacture of machinery for mining

Caterpillar (U.K.) Limited
M.M.D. Mining Machinery Developments Ltd
Terex Pegson Limited

28922 Manufacture of earthmoving equipment

Caterpillar (U.K.) Limited

28923 Manufacture of equipment for concrete crushing and screening and roadworks

Parker Plant Limited

28930 Manufacture of machinery for food, beverage and tobacco processing

A.M. Packaging Limited
BW Integrated Systems UK Limited
Baker Perkins Limited
Briggs of Burton PLC
Flo-Mech. Limited

28940 Manufacture of machinery for textile, apparel and leather production

Slack & Parr (Investments) Limited
Slack & Parr Limited

28960 Manufacture of plastics and rubber machinery

Atlas Converting (UK Holdings) Limited
Engel U.K. Limited
Freudenberg Sealing Technologies Limited
Taylor Hobson Limited

28990 Manufacture of other special-purpose machinery n.e.c. [30]

Bearward Engineering Limited
Belle Engineering (Sheen) Limited
Beumer Group UK Limited
Bosch Packaging Technology Limited
Bosch Rexroth Limited
Chesterfield Special Cylinders Limited
Chinook Sciences Limited
Dematic Limited
Durr Limited
Erlson Precision Holdings Limited
Expert Tooling & Automation Limited
Fanuc UK Limited
Heraeus Electro-Nite (UK) Ltd
Linx Printing Technologies Limited
M.M.D. Mining Machinery Developments Ltd
Matthews Environmental Solutions Limited
Morgana Systems Limited
Napier Turbochargers Limited
Niftylift Limited
Nikon Metrology UK Limited
OSL Group Holdings Limited
Porvair Filtration Group Limited
Proseal UK Limited
Sodick Europe Limited
Supply Point Systems Limited
Tickhill Engineering Co Ltd
Videojet Technologies Limited
WFEL Holdings Limited
WFEL Limited
Winbro Group Technologies Limited

29100 Manufacture of motor vehicles [12]
Aston Martin Lagonda Limited
Jaguar Land Rover Holdings Limited
Jaguar Land Rover Limited
Leyland Trucks Limited
London EV Co Ltd
Mobius Motors Limited
Paccar Parts U.K. Limited
Paccar Trucks U.K. Ltd
Prodrive Group Limited
Radical Motorsport Limited
Toyota Motor Manufacturing (UK) Limited
Williams Grand Prix Engineering Limited

29201 Manufacture of bodies (coachwork) for motor vehicles (except caravans)
Cad Cam Automotive Limited
Dennis Eagle Limited
Magna Exteriors (Banbury) Limited
Premier Sheet Metal (Coventry) Limited
Stadco Limited

29202 Manufacture of trailers and semi-trailers
Boss Cabins Limited
Brian James Trailers Limited
Montracon Limited
Wilcox Commercial Vehicles Limited

29203 Manufacture of caravans
Auto-Trail V.R. Limited
Dunster House Limited

29310 Manufacture of electrical and electronic equipment for motor vehicles and their engines
Carwood Motor Units Limited
Kostal UK Limited
Snap-On U.K. Holdings Limited

29320 Manufacture of other parts and accessories for motor vehicles [34]
Adient Seating UK Ltd
Antolin Interiors UK Limited
Arlington Automotive Limited
Autocraft Drivetrain Solutions Limited
BBB Services Limited
BM Catalysts Limited
BPW Limited
Benteler Automotive UK Ltd
Bourbon Automotive Plastics Northampton Ltd
Brose Limited
Carwood Motor Units Limited
Dana UK Driveshaft Limited
Erlson Precision Components Limited
Faurecia Automotive Seating UK Limited
Grupo Antolin Leamington Limited
HBPO UK Limited
Harmor Limited
Hendrickson United Kingdom Ltd
Kab Seating Limited
Kautex Unipart Limited
I M Kelly Automotive Limited
Magna International Holding (UK) Limited
Mahle Filter Systems UK Limited
Mahle Powertrain Limited
Melett Limited
Pailton Engineering Limited
Standard Motor Products Europe Limited
Syncreon Automotive (UK) Ltd.
Toyoda Gosei UK Ltd.
UYS Limited
Unipart Powertrain Applications Limited
Vinters Engineering Limited
Williams Grand Prix Engineering Limited
Wipac Limited

30110 Building of ships and floating structures
Cathelco Limited
Vinters Engineering Limited

30120 Building of pleasure and sporting boats
Fairline Yachts Limited
Williams Jet Tenders Limited

30200 Manufacture of railway locomotives and rolling stock
Bombardier Transportation (Holdings) UK Ltd
Bombardier Transportation (Rolling Stock) UK Ltd
Bombardier Transportation UK Ltd
Crossfleet Limited
Vivarail Ltd

30300 Manufacture of air and spacecraft and related machinery
AEM Limited
Airbus Military UK Limited
Gardner Aerospace - Derby Limited
Gardner Aerospace - Hull Limited
Gardner Group Limited
ITP Engines UK Limited
Icon Aerospace Technology Ltd
Nasmyth Bulwell Limited

30400 Manufacture of military fighting vehicles
Lockheed Martin UK Ampthill Limited

30910 Manufacture of motorcycles
Norton Motorcycles (UK) Limited
Triumph Designs Limited
Triumph Motorcycles Limited

30990 Manufacture of other transport equipment n.e.c. [13]
Al-Ko Kober Limited
Dematic Limited
Dhollandia U.K. Limited
Gibbs Technologies Limited
Knott-Avonride Limited
Roubaix Bidco Limited
Thyssenkrupp Elevator UK Limited
Trueform Engineering Holdings Limited
Vinters Engineering Limited
Wanfeng (UK) Aviation Co., Ltd
Wanfeng MLTH Holdings Co., Ltd
Whites Engineering Limited
Wilcox Commercial Vehicles Limited

31010 Manufacture of office and shop furniture
Elite Office Furniture (UK) Ltd.
Ocee International Ltd

31020 Manufacture of kitchen furniture
Burbidge Holdings Limited
Bushboard Limited
Devol Kitchens Limited
East Coast Fittings Limited
Symphony Group PLC

31090 Manufacture of other furniture [12]
Belfield Furnishings Limited
Cycene Limited
Flair Flooring Supplies Limited
HFG Holdings Limited
Hammonds Furniture Limited
Home Decor GB Limited
JDP Furniture Group Limited
Lebus Upholstery Limited
Omega PLC
Westbridge Furniture Designs Limited
Whitemeadow Furniture Limited
Whitemeadow Group Holdings Limited

32300 Manufacture of sports goods
Acushnet Europe Ltd
Drennan International Limited
Ping Europe Limited

32409 Manufacture of other games and toys, n.e.c.
Bachmann Europe PLC
Games Workshop International Limited
Games Workshop Limited
Games Workshop US (Holdings) Limited
Games Workshop US Limited
Ravensburger Limited
Toy Brokers Holdings Limited

32500 Manufacture of medical and dental instruments and supplies [18]
Abbott Diabetes Care Limited
Alere Limited
Atlas Copco Medical Limited
Breas Medical Limited
Brightwake Limited
Cozart Limited
GN Hearing UK Ltd
Intermed Limited
JRI Orthopaedics Limited
Morningside Pharmaceuticals Limited
Owen Mumford Limited
Orchid Orthopedic Solutions Sheffield Ltd
Robinson Healthcare Group Limited
Robinson Healthcare Holdings Ltd
Robinson Healthcare Limited
Starkey Laboratories Limited
Swann-Morton Limited
Symmetry Medical Sheffield Ltd.

32990 Other manufacturing n.e.c. [104]

AESSEAL PLC
AFE Group Limited
AP Racing Limited
ARRK Europe Limited
AVK UK Limited
Advance Tapes Group Limited
Advance Tapes International Limited
Anpario PLC
Arconic Closure Systems International (UK) Ltd
Autins Limited
B.M. Polyco Limited
BASF Agricultural Specialities Limited
Bawtry Carbon International Limited
Beamglow Limited
Belle Holdings Limited
Benchmark Vaccines Limited
Binney & Smith (Europe) Limited
Boden & Davies Limited
CMI International Limited
Capital Refractories Limited
J.J.Churchill Limited
Classeq Limited
Clifton Packaging Group Limited
Coster Aerosols Limited
Cranford Asset Management Limited
DCS Group (UK) Limited
J.E. & V.M. Dalton Limited
Denby Potteries Limited
Diam UK Ltd.
Door-Stop International Limited
Dunster House Limited
E - Leather Limited
Edina UK Limited
Element Six Technologies Limited
Elliott Group Limited
Emerson Process Management Limited
Encocam Limited
Essentra Packaging & Security Limited
Euramax Solutions Limited
Everris Limited
Exaclair Limited
C.W.Fletcher & Sons,Limited
Flex-Seal Couplings Limited
Flo-Mech. Limited
Forbo Flooring UK Limited
GI Solutions Group Limited
Geely UK Limited
H & K Distribution Limited
W.E. Hewitt & Son Limited
Hillarys Blinds Limited
Hormann (U.K.) Limited
Hunter Douglas (UK) Limited
Insituform Linings Limited
Inspired Gaming (UK) Limited
Interfuse Limited
J & A (International) Limited
Jepson & Co Limited
Jepson Holdings Limited
Leadec Limited
Lincat Limited
Louver-Lite Limited
Usha Martin International Limited
Usha Martin UK Limited
Nationwide Windows Limited
Naylor Drainage Ltd
Naylor Industries PLC
OSL Group Holdings Limited
Oughtred & Harrison (Facilities) Ltd.
Oxford Products Limited
P2I Ltd
Padley & Venables Limited
Pal International Limited
Parex Ltd
Pollard Boxes Limited
Polyco (Group) Limited
Polyco Healthline Limited
Print-Rite Europe Ltd.
Pyrotek Engineering Materials Limited
RTI International Metals Limited
Red Bull Technology Limited
Reeves Wireline Technologies Limited
Rieke Packaging Systems Limited
Ritrama (U.K.) Limited
Rolls-Royce Controls and Data Services Ltd
Russell Building Products Limited
SEK Holdings Limited
SMC Pneumatics (U.K.) Limited
Solidor Limited
Synventive Holding Limited
Taylor Bloxham Group Limited
Trina Solar (UK) Limited
Tsubakimoto UK Limited
Valspar (UK) Holding Corporation Limited
Valspar (UK) Special Holding Corporation Ltd
Vinters Engineering Limited
A N Wallis & Co Ltd
Waterfall Catering Group Limited
Waterfall Services Limited
Wight Building Materials Ltd
Thos.Winnard & Sons Limited
Wolf Safety Lamp Co Ltd
Woodway Holdings Limited
Xtratherm UK Limited
Yorkshire Repak Limited

33120 Repair of machinery

Clyde Bergemann Materials Handling Ltd
Knapp U.K. Limited
MAN Energy Solutions UK Limited
Orona Limited
Warwick Ward (Machinery) Limited

33140 Repair of electrical equipment

GE Energy Power Conversion UK Holdings Ltd
GE Energy Power Conversion UK Limited
Genistics Limited
Muirhead Aerospace Limited
Quartzelec Ltd
Rolls-Royce Power Engineering PLC
Snap-On U.K. Holdings Limited

33150 Repair and maintenance of ships and boats

W.H.Munsey Limited

33160 Repair and maintenance of aircraft and spacecraft

Airbus Helicopters UK Limited

33170 Repair and maintenance of other transport equipment n.e.c. [10]

ALC (FMC) Limited
Balfour Beatty Plant & Fleet Services Ltd
Brecknell, Willis & Co. Limited
Daifuku Europe Limited
Gemini Rail Services UK Ltd
Johnson Bros (Tours) Limited
H.W. Martin (Plant) Limited
Stagecoach Supertram Maintenance Ltd.
Thyssenkrupp Elevator UK Limited
Wabtec Rail Limited

33190 Repair of other equipment

A Shade Greener Maintenance Limited
CTDI Repair Services Limited
Caljan Rite-Hite Limited
Cape Engineering Services Limited
Markem-Imaje Industries Limited
Mitchell Diesel Limited
Telent Technology Services Limited
Winterhalter Ltd

33200 Installation of industrial machinery and equipment [22]

ASSA ABLOY Entrance Systems Ltd
F G Alden Limited
Aroqua Power Services Ltd.
Biesse Group UK Limited
Bystronic UK Limited
Caljan Rite-Hite Limited
Cape Engineering Services Limited
Clyde Bergemann Materials Handling Ltd
Comex 2000 (UK) Limited
Daifuku Europe Limited
Dematic Limited
Fanuc UK Limited
Flo-Mech. Limited
Konecranes Demag UK Limited
Logistex Europe Ltd
MPAC Group PLC
Markem-Imaje Industries Limited
Motan Colortronic Limited
Rea Valley Tractors Limited
Satake Europe Limited
Versalift Distributors (U.K.) Limited
T.W. Ward C.N.C. Machinery Limited

35110 Production of electricity [55]

A Shade Greener Limited
Agrivert (Wallingford) Limited
Agrivert (West London) Limited
Agrivert Biogas Limited
Alauna Renewable Energy Limited
Alkane Energy CM Limited
Alkane Energy Limited
Alkane Energy UK Limited
Andina PLC
BESS Aylesford Limited
BWSC North Lincs Limited
Battery Energy Storage Solutions Limited
Bio Dynamic (UK) Limited
Biogen (UK) Limited
Blue Planet Solar Park II Limited
Citigen (London) Limited
Corby Power Limited
Coventry and Solihull Waste Disposal Co Ltd
E.On Climate & Renewables UK Biomass Ltd
E.On Climate & Renewables UK Developments Ltd
E.On Climate & Renewables UK Humber Wind Ltd
E.On Climate & Renewables UK London Array Ltd
E.On Climate & Renewables UK Offshore Wind Ltd
E.On Climate & Renewables UK Operations Ltd
E.On Climate & Renewables UK Robin Rigg East Ltd
E.On Climate & Renewables UK Robin Rigg West Ltd
E.On UK CHP Limited
E.On UK Cogeneration Limited

EDL (UK) LFG Generation Limited
Eggborough Power Limited
Energy Developments (UK) Limited
Enviroenergy Limited
Federal Estates Limited
Fswind Limited
Infinis (Re-Gen) Limited
Infinis Limited
Keadby Generation Limited
Lakeside Energy from Waste Limited
Lynn Wind Farm Limited
Novera Energy (Holdings 2) Limited
Novera Energy Generation No. 2 Limited
J G Pears Power Limited
Rampion Offshore Wind Limited
Refood UK Limited
Regent Park Energy Limited
Secanim Limited
Severn Trent Green Power Limited
Severn Trent Wind Power Limited
Tamar Renewable Power (Essex) Limited
Tamar Renewable Power (Hoddesdon) Ltd
Templeborough Biomass Power Plant Ltd
Touchgold Limited
Warwick Energy Limited
Wind Port of Liverpool Limited
Wykes Engineering Co. (Rushden) Limited

35130 Distribution of electricity

Andina PLC
SYS8 Holding Limited
Sensitlive Limited

35140 Trade of electricity

E.On Energy Solutions Limited
First Utility Limited
Flow Energy Limited
Hudson Energy Supply UK Limited
Impello Limited
Mayfourth Holdings Limited
Welcomm Holdings Limited

35210 Manufacture of gas

Refood UK Limited

35220 Distribution of gaseous fuels through mains

Cadent Gas Limited
Regent Park Energy Limited
UGI Midlands Limited

35230 Trade of gas through mains

Aster and Young Limited
E.On Energy Solutions Limited
Impello Limited
Mayfourth Holdings Limited

35300 Steam and air conditioning supply

Enviroenergy Limited
J G Pears Power Limited

36000 Water collection, treatment and supply [10]

Anglian Water Services Limited
Canal & River Trust
Envirogen Water Technologies Limited
Oxfam
SYS8 Holding Limited
Sensitlive Limited
Severn Trent Services Defence Limited
Severn Trent Services Operations UK Ltd
Severn Trent Water Limited
Suez Water Technologies & Solutions Services UK Ltd

37000 Sewerage

Ancala Water Services (Defence) Limited
Ancala Water Services (Estates) Limited
Anglian Water Services Limited

38110 Collection of non-hazardous waste [17]

ENVA England Limited
Mick George Limited
Grundon Waste Management Limited
Johnsons Aggregates and Recycling Ltd
Mid-UK Recycling Limited
Mulberry Waste Limited
Oceala Limited
J.G. Pears Limited
Regen Holdings Limited
Renewi UK Services Limited
Resource Recovery Solutions (Derbyshire) Ltd
G.A.E. Smith (Holdings) Limited
Totally Local Co Ltd
UK Waste Solutions Limited
Valens Resources Group PLC
S Walsh Holdings Limited
Donald Ward Limited

38120 Collection of hazardous waste

Grundon Waste Management Limited

38210 Treatment and disposal of non-hazardous waste [20]

Agrivert (Wallingford) Limited
Agrivert (West London) Limited
AmeyCespa (MK) ODC Limited
Ballast Phoenix Limited
Biogen (UK) Limited
C.F.Booth Limited
Coventry and Solihull Waste Disposal Co Ltd
ENVA England Limited
Glass Recycling (UK) Limited
Grantham Industries Limited
Grundon Waste Management Limited
H W Martin Waste Limited
Mid-UK Recycling Limited
Millennium EFW Limited
Monoworld Recycling Ltd
J.G. Pears Limited
Regen Holdings Limited
Ronald Hull Jnr. Limited
Singleton Birch Limited
Donald Ward Limited

38220 Treatment and disposal of hazardous waste

Grundon Waste Management Limited
Ronald Hull Jnr. Limited

38310 Dismantling of wrecks

Ronald Hull Jnr. Limited

38320 Recovery of sorted materials [25]

Ancillary Components Limited
Boden & Davies Limited
C.F.Booth Limited
Choice Packaging Solutions Limited
ELG Utica Alloys Limited
ENVA England Limited
Eurokey Recycling Limited
Mick George Limited
Green Meadow Limited
G.I. Hadfield & Son Limited
London Wiper Co Ltd
Luxus Limited
Mid-UK Recycling Limited
Oceala Limited
One51 ES Metals (UK) Limited
Palm Recycling Limited
Recresco Limited
Renewi UK Services Limited
Ronald Hull Jnr. Limited
Sims Group UK Limited
Smith & Sons (Bletchington) Limited
G.A.E. Smith (Holdings) Limited
C. Soar & Sons (UK) Limited
Valens Resources Group PLC
Donald Ward Limited

39000 Remediation activities and other waste management services

Aegion Rehabilitation Services Limited
Agrivert Limited
Ballast Phoenix Limited
Coventry and Solihull Waste Disposal Co Ltd
Regen Holdings Limited
G.A.E. Smith (Holdings) Limited
Smiths Concrete Limited
Valens Resources Group PLC
Donald Ward Limited

41100 Development of building projects [163]

Abbey Properties Cambridgeshire Limited
Abraham Investments Limited
Affinity Living Trinity Holdco Limited
Aintree Retail Park Limited
Allworks Properties Limited
Amak Property Investments (London) Ltd
Ambury Developments Limited
Aus-Bore Estates Limited
Avant Homes (Yorkshire) Limited
Avenuepoint Limited
B & S Hughes Limited
B.N.T. Properties Limited
BAJ 1 Limited
Barratt Wates (Lindfield) Limited
Beechcroft Developments Limited
Beechcroft Group Limited
Beechcroft UK Limited
Beechfield Estates Limited
Bildurn (Properties) Limited
Blue Deer Limited
Henry Boot Developments Limited
Brit de Vere Limited
Broadgate Homes Limited
Broadthorpe Limited
Cadent Services Limited
Callington's Construction Limited

Canal & River Trading CIC
Catesby Estates (Residential) Limited
Catesby Estates PLC
Catesby Strategic Land Limited
Cawrey Ltd
Cedar House Investments Limited
Chartmoor Estates Limited
Cintra Infrastructures SE
City Suites Manchester Limited
Clayson Country Homes Limited
Consolidated Property Wilmslow Limited
Corran (Wakefield) Limited
County Estates (Bakewell) Limited
Cranford Asset Management Limited
Ivor Crowson Developments (Stamford) Ltd
Custodian Real Estate (Leicester) Ltd
DP Group Developments Limited
DP Realty Limited
Davidsons Developments Limited
William Davis Limited
Deanbank Investments Limited
Dransfield Properties Limited
EOS Inc. Ltd
East Midlands Property Developments Ltd
Ebbsfleet Property Limited
Ede Holdings Limited
Ellis Bros (Contractors) Limited
Faccenda Property Limited
Factory (M1) Limited
J.F. Finnegan Limited
GPS Estates Limited
Gallagher Bathgate Limited
Gateway Plaza Limited
Gee Bee Investments Limited
Glanmoor Investments Limited
Grange Mill Developments Limited
Grantham Bros. Limited
Graystacks Exeter Limited
Grevayne Properties Limited
HM Estates Limited
Hallam Land Management Limited
Hanover Housing Developments Limited
Harworth Estates (Agricultural Land) Ltd
Harworth Estates (Waverley Prince) Ltd.
Harworth Estates Investments Limited
Hatchback Ltd
Holly Farm Limited
Horbury Building Systems Limited
Kalsi Properties (UK) Limited
Ashley King (Developments) Limited
Kingscrown Properties Limited
Lancer Properties Limited
Laver Regeneration Limited
A.C. Lloyd (Asset Management) Limited
Lochailort Fairfield Limited
Loxwood Holdings Limited
Lucy Developments Limited
M.J.C. Developments Limited
Maltgrade Limited
Manston Investments Limited
Marshall Street Regeneration Limited
John Martin-Hoyes (Holdings) Limited
Melbourne Holdings Limited
Memoria Limited
Morgan Industrial Properties Limited
Motspa Holdings Limited
Mulberry Commercial Developments Limited
New Co (Beith Street) Limited
New Co (Newcastle) Limited
New Co (Satellite) 2 Limited
New Co (Satellite) Limited
New Era Development (UK) Limited
North Lincs Property Limited
North West Portfolio (No.3) Limited
North West Portfolio Limited
Oakhill Group Limited
Orbit Developments (Manchester) Limited
Orbit Developments (Southern) Limited
Orbit Investments (Northern) Limited
Orbit Investments (Properties) Limited
Oxford Property Trading Ltd.
Oxford Science Park Limited
Oxford West End Development Limited
P H Property Holdings Limited
PTA Developments Limited
Palmer Family Trust PLC
H.B. Pearce (Contractors) Limited
Peartree Oxford Limited
Pelham Homes Limited
Peveril Securities Limited
Peveril Securities Long Lane Limited
Potomac Capital Limited
Primesite UK Limited
Princebuild Holdings Limited
Princebuild Limited.
REALL Limited
RH Development (Property) Limited
Radford Holdings Limited
Renco (Chesterfield) Limited
Rowlinson Constructions Limited
Roxhill Developments Group Limited
Salmon Harvester Properties Limited
Saul Construction Limited
Scott's Developments Limited
Select International Developments Ltd
Silentpride Limited
Simons Developments Limited
Sistine Properties (Westbury) Limited
South Coast Furnishing Co Ltd
Sovereign Crest Limited
St. Paul's Developments PLC
Stamford Property Co Ltd
Stepnell Limited
Stocksbridge Regeneration Co Ltd
Stonebridge Homes Limited
Swanton Care & Community (Glenpath Holdings) Ltd
T.J.D. Trade Limited
Taylor Lindsey Limited
Tenens Ede Limited
Thornsett Properties Limited
G.F. Tomlinson Building Limited
G.F.Tomlinson Group Limited
Travis Perkins (Properties) Limited
Triplex Lloyd Properties Limited
Victoria Square Woking Limited
Vita Student Southampton Portswood Ltd
Vita Student York Holding Co Ltd
W.N. Developments Limited
Dare Warwick (Properties) Limited
W.Westerman Limited
Wheeldon Brothers Limited
Thomas White Oxford Limited
Wigley Contracts (Barby) Limited
Wildgoose Construction Limited
Willowbrook Healthcare Developments Ltd
Wyboston Lakes Limited
Yeovil Developments Limited

41201 Construction of commercial buildings [60]

3 R Construction & Property Development Ltd
Avant Homes (England) Limited
B & K Building Services Limited
BDW Trading Limited
Bardsley Construction Limited
Barratt Developments P L C
Barratt Evolution Limited
Beeson Wright Limited
Henry Boot Construction Limited
Wilson Bowden Developments Limited
Bowmer and Kirkland Limited
Britcon (UK) Limited
Buckingham Group Contracting Limited
C3 Construction Limited
Chalcroft Limited
Clegg Construction Limited
Clegg Food Projects Limited
Clugston Construction Limited
DCS 452 Limited
Deeley Construction Limited
J.F. Finnegan Limited
Gelder Limited
M J Gleeson Group Limited
MJ Gleeson PLC
HID Estates Limited
Inter M.K. Limited
Investfront (Oxon) Limited
Ivygrove Developments Limited
Kingerlee Limited
Lincoln and London Holdings Limited
Lindum Group Limited
A.C. Lloyd (Asset Management) Limited
A.C. Lloyd Holdings Limited
M.J.S. Construction (March) Limited
MCS Build Limited
MCS Group Limited
Mulberry Property Developments Ltd
North Nottinghamshire Lift Project Company (No.1) Ltd
James O'Flanagan Limited
Orbit Developments (Manchester) Limited
Rowlinson Constructions Limited
Roxhill Developments Limited
S.D.C. Builders Limited
Saul Construction Limited
Simons Construction Limited
Simons Group Limited
Smith Construction Group Limited
Swiftbuild Properties Limited
T & W Civil Engineering Limited
Taylor Lindsey Limited
Techrete (U.K.) Limited
G F Tomlinson & Sons Ltd
G.F. Tomlinson Building Limited
United Health Group Limited
Victoria Square Woking Limited
W.Westerman Limited
Wheeldon Brothers Limited
David Wilson Homes Limited
Winvic Construction Limited
Winvic Group Limited

41202 Construction of domestic buildings [66]

Ablehomes Limited
Ackroyd & Abbott Limited
Alco Estates Limited
Ashford Riverside Park Limited
Barwood Homes Limited
Bewick Holdings Ltd
J.S.Bloor (Services) Limited
Bloor Holdings Limited
Bloor Homes Limited
Broadgate Builders (Spalding) Limited

Broadgate Homes Limited
Broadthorpe Limited
Broomgrove Properties Limited
Bushmead Homes Ltd
Chestnut Homes Limited
Clegg Construction Limited
Court Properties (Portugal) Limited
William Davis Limited
J.F. Finnegan Limited
Gelder Limited
Gleeson Developments Limited
Gleeson Regeneration Limited
Michael Goodall Quality Homes Limited
Hazelton Homes (Midlands) Limited
Francis Jackson Homes Limited
Jelson Limited
Jones Homes (Lancashire) Limited
Jones Homes (North West) Limited
Jones Homes (Southern) Limited
Jones Homes (Yorkshire) Limited
Keepmoat Homes Limited
Keigar Homes Limited
Keystone Developments (LG) Limited
Kingerlee Limited
Langridge Homes Limited
Larkfleet Limited
Lindum Group Limited
A C Lloyd Homes Limited
M.C.I. Developments Limited
Manor Crest Construction Limited
Manor Crest Homes Limited
Miller Wates (Didcot) Limited
Miller Wates (Southwater) Limited
Miller Wates (Wallingford) Limited
Morris Homes (Midlands) Limited
Morris Homes (North) Limited
Morris Homes Limited
Mulberry Property Developments Ltd
NMCN PLC
James O'Flanagan Limited
Paul John Construction (Leicester) Ltd
Peveril Homes Limited
J.A.Pye (Oxford) Limited
Pye Homes Limited
Rowlinson Constructions Limited
Saul Construction Limited
J.W.Sivil Limited
Stirling Management Group Limited
Strata Homes Limited
Strata Homes Yorkshire Limited
T.J.D. Trade Limited
Taylor Lindsey Limited
Truelove Property & Construction Ltd
W.& S.(Long Eaton) Limited
W.Westerman Limited
Wood Hill Heights Limited

42110 Construction of roads and motorways

Aggregate Industries UK Limited
Breedon Southern Limited
Buckingham Group Contracting Limited
Cintra Infrastructures SE
NMCN PLC
G F Tomlinson & Sons Ltd
Totally Local Co Ltd
Tripod Crest Group Limited
Tripod Crest Limited

42120 Construction of railways and underground railways

Amey Rail Limited
Bridgeway Consulting Limited
Buckingham Group Contracting Limited
Linbrooke Services Limited
Progress Rail Services UK Limited
S R S Rail System Limited

42220 Construction of utility projects for electricity and telecommunications

Clyde Bergemann Materials Handling Ltd
Comex 2000 (UK) Limited
Linbrooke Services Limited
NMCN PLC
TCI Renewables Limited
Tamar Energy Limited

42910 Construction of water projects

Dawson-Wam Ltd
NMCN PLC

42990 Construction of other civil engineering projects n.e.c. [10]

Bridgebank Limited
Buckingham Group Contracting Limited
Carmac (Building & Civil Engineering) Ltd
Dawson-Wam Ltd
Fox (Owmby) Limited
P. Hughes Construction Limited
M.P.B. Structures Ltd
Paul John Construction (Leicester) Ltd
Van Elle Limited
S.Walsh & Son Limited

43110 Demolition

Collins Earthworks Limited
Grantham Industries Limited

43120 Site preparation

Collins Earthworks Limited
Mick George Limited
O'Brien Contractors Limited
James O'Flanagan Limited

43130 Test drilling and boring

Bridgeway Consulting Limited
P R Marriott Drilling Limited

43210 Electrical installation [13]

Briggs & Forrester Engineering Services Ltd
Briggs & Forrester Living Limited
CEMA Group Ltd
Cape Industrial Services Limited
Derry Building Services Limited
Imtech Engineering Services Central Ltd
Walter Miles (Electrical Engineers) Ltd
Munro Building Services Limited
PWP Building Services (Holdings) Limited
PWP Building Services Limited
W.T. Parker Ltd.
Quartzelec Ltd
Rolec Services Limited

43220 Plumbing, heat and air-conditioning installation

Briggs & Forrester Engineering Services Ltd
Briggs & Forrester Living Limited
Coolair Equipment Limited
Derry Building Services Limited
FEL Group Limited
Imtech Engineering Services Central Ltd
Munro Building Services Limited
W.T. Parker Ltd.

43290 Other construction installation

Cape Industrial Services Limited
Gelder Limited
Key Property Solutions Limited
Munro Building Services Limited
Orona Limited
Ruddy Joinery Limited
TGW Limited

43310 Plastering

KJW Drylining Limited

43320 Joinery installation

Munster Joinery (U.K.) Limited
Ruddy Joinery Limited
Vale Garden Houses Limited

43330 Floor and wall covering

A C PLC
A.C.Flooring Ltd.
Axiom Group Limited
Designer Contracts Limited

43341 Painting

H.B. Pearce (Contractors) Limited
Saint-Gobain Glass (United Kingdom) Ltd

43342 Glazing

Graham Holmes Astraseal Limited
Inwido UK Limited

43390 Other building completion and finishing

CCF Limited
Emerson Management Services Limited
Gelder Limited
Oxford West End Development Limited
Ruddy Joinery Limited
SIG Trading Limited

43910 Roofing activities

A C PLC
Keyclad Limited
LR (UK) Limited
Langley UK Limited
M & J Group (Construction & Roofing) Ltd
Saint-Gobain Roofspace Limited
Weymead Holdings Limited

43999 Other specialised construction activities n.e.c. [51]

Aarsleff Ground Engineering Limited
Abbey Properties Cambridgeshire Limited
Abbeymill Homes Limited
Access Platform Sales Limited
Acorn Partitions & Storage Systems Ltd
Amey Power Services Limited
Apex Stainless Fasteners Limited
Banner Plant Limited
Bridgeway Consulting Limited
Roger Bullivant Limited
Byzak Limited
CNIM Clugston (Avonmouth) Limited
CRH Fencing & Security Group (UK) Ltd
Cape Industrial Services Limited
Combisafe International Limited
Crowland Cranes Limited
Danaher & Walsh Group Limited
Emerson Management Services Limited
Engie Fabricom UK Limited
GL Events UK Limited
Genie UK Limited
HTC Wolffkran Limited
Hague Plant Limited
Insituform Holdings (UK) Limited
Ischebeck Titan Limited
KNM Project Services Limited
Kaefer Limited
Keller Limited
Kendall Bros. (Portsmouth) Limited
Liberty Guard (U.K.) Limited
Linbrooke Services Limited
M.J.S. Holdings (March) Limited
M.S.W (UK) Limited
H.W. Martin (Traffic Management) Ltd
Measom (Dryline) Limited
Motherwell Bridge Limited
North West Steel Limited
Paragon Interiors Group PLC
W.T. Parker Ltd.
R U Estates Limited
R3 Polygon UK Ltd.
Rapidrop Global Limited
SCCS Survey Equipment Limited
SIG Hillsborough Limited
Straightset Limited
Trackwork Group Limited
Trackwork Limited
WJ South Limited
Warwick Energy Limited
Wolf Systems Limited
Barry Wood Plant Hire Limited

45111 Sale of new cars and light motor vehicles [84]

Alloy Racing Equipment Limited
Don Amott Parks Limited
Bells Motor Group Limited
C D Bramall Limited
Burrows Motor Co Ltd
Car Store Limited
Chandlers (Farm Equipment) Limited
Chatfields Limited
Citroen U.K. Limited
Cruickshank Motors Limited
Decidebloom Limited
Derwent Vehicles Limited
Drive Holdings 2015 Limited
Drive Motor Retail Limited
Martin Duckworth Limited
Falcon of Hull & Lincolnshire Limited
Allen Ford (UK) Limited
Goodman Retail Limited
Graypaul Motors Limited
Guy Salmon Limited
Halliwell Jones (Wilmslow) Limited
T. C. Harrison Group Limited
Tom Hartley Cars Limited
Hartwell Automotive Group Limited
Huntson Holdings Limited
Jaguar Land Rover (South Africa) Holdings Ltd
Listers Group Limited
Maranello Concessionaires Limited
Mercedes-Benz Cars UK Limited
Mercedes-Benz Retail Group UK Limited
Mill Garages North East Limited
William Morgan Group Limited
Motors (Coalville) Limited
N K Motors Limited
National Fleet Solutions Limited
C.John Norris (Cars & Caravans) Limited
Oakhill Group Limited
PSA Retail UK Limited
Pendragon Motor Group Limited
Pendragon PLC
Pendragon Premier Limited
Pendragon Sabre Limited
Pendragon Vehicle Management Limited
Pentagon Chrysler (Barnsley) Limited
Pentagon Motor Holdings Limited
Perrys East Midlands Limited
Perrys Group Limited
Perrys Motor Sales Limited
Peugeot Motor Company PLC
Progress Bedford Limited
Read Motor Group Limited
Reeve (Derby) Limited
Renault Truck Commercials Limited
Riverside Motors (Doncaster) Limited
Rowstock Limited
Rybrook Cars Limited
Rybrook Limited
Richard Sanders Limited
Sandicliffe Garage Limited
Sandicliffe Limited
Sandicliffe Motor Holdings Limited
F.P.Smith (Holdings) Limited
R Stratton & Co Ltd.
Stripestar Limited
Walter E. Sturgess & Sons Limited
Sutton Park Holdings Limited
Sutton Park Motor Co Ltd
Suzuki GB PLC
Sycamore (Peterborough) Limited
Sytner Cars Limited
Sytner Group Limited
Sytner Limited
Sytner Vehicles Limited
Taylors Service Garages (Boston) Limited
Reg Vardy (VMC) Limited
Victoria (Bavaria) Limited
F. Vindis & Sons (Bedford) Limited
F. Vindis & Sons (Sawston) Limited
Vindis Developments Limited
Vindis Group Limited
Volkswagen Group United Kingdom Limited
Wilson & Co. (Motor Sales) Limited
Wollaston Motors Limited
York Ward & Rowlatt Limited

45112 Sale of used cars and light motor vehicles [57]

Available Car Limited
Graham Bell Limited
Bells Motor Group Limited
C D Bramall Limited
Canei International Limited
Car People Limited
Car Shops Limited
Car Store Limited
Chatfields Limited
Citroen U.K. Limited
Copart UK Limited
Decidebloom Limited
Drive Holdings 2015 Limited
Drive Motor Retail Limited
Martin Duckworth Limited
Falcon of Hull & Lincolnshire Limited
Fleet Auction Group Limited
D Hales Limited
Halliwell Jones (Wilmslow) Limited
Harris Cars Limited
Tom Hartley Cars Limited
Hilton Garage Ltd
Huntson Holdings Limited
Listers Group Limited
Mercedes-Benz Retail Group UK Limited
William Morgan Group Limited
Motorpoint Group PLC
National Fleet Solutions Limited
PSA Retail UK Limited
Pendragon PLC
Pentagon Chrysler (Barnsley) Limited
Pentagon Motor Holdings Limited
Perrys East Midlands Limited
Perrys Group Limited
Perrys Motor Sales Limited
Rowstock Limited
Rybrook Cars Limited
Rybrook Limited
Sandicliffe Limited
Sandicliffe Motor Holdings Limited
Ben Smith & Sons (Wantage) Limited
Stripestar Limited
Sutton Park Motor Co Ltd
Sycamore (Peterborough) Limited
Taylors Service Garages (Boston) Limited
URA Ventures Limited
Universal Salvage Limited
V12 Sports & Classics Ltd
Victoria (Bavaria) Limited
F. Vindis & Sons (Bedford) Limited
F. Vindis & Sons (Sawston) Limited
Vindis Developments Limited
Vindis Group Limited
Windsor Vehicle Leasing Limited
Wollaston Motors Limited
York Ward & Rowlatt Limited
Zyox Limited

45190 Sale of other motor vehicles [31]

AEBI Schmidt UK Limited
Brownhills Motorhomes Limited
CPRT (Europe) Limited
Copart UK Limited
Brian Currie (Milton Keynes) Limited
Daf Trucks Limited
Evobus (UK) Limited
Ford & Slater Limited
Grosvenor Contracts Leasing Limited
D Hales Limited

John Hebb (Motor Engineers) Limited
Hexagon Leasing Limited
Intercounty Truck and Van Limited
JR Motorsports Limited
L Jackson & Co Limited
Lowdham Leisureworld Ltd
National Fleet Solutions Limited
Nesform Limited
North Oxford Garage Limited
Parkway Derby Limited
Pendragon PLC
Pentagon (Huddersfield) Limited
Scania (Great Britain) Limited
Stripestar Limited
Tuxford Exports Limited
U-Pull-It Limited
Universal Salvage Limited
Reg Vardy Limited
Victoria (Bavaria) Limited
Volvo Group UK Limited
Witham (Specialist Vehicles) Limited

45200 Maintenance and repair of motor vehicles [64]

AEBI Schmidt UK Limited
Alltruck PLC
Assured Group Investments Limited
Assured Group Limited
Aston Martin Works Limited
Bells Motor Group Limited
Belron UK Limited
Central Garage (Uppingham) Limited
Chandlers (Farm Equipment) Limited
Citroen U.K. Limited
Cruickshank Motors Limited
Brian Currie (Milton Keynes) Limited
Decidebloom Limited
Drive Holdings 2015 Limited
Drive Motor Retail Limited
Dunn Motor Traction Ltd
Electro-Motive Diesel Limited
Evobus (UK) Limited
Falcon of Hull & Lincolnshire Limited
Ford & Slater Limited
GB Fleetcare Limited
Gefco U.K. Limited
Goodman Retail Limited
Graypaul Motors Limited
Guy Salmon Limited
HRVS Group Limited
Halliwell Jones (Wilmslow) Limited
Listers Group Limited
Mercedes-Benz Retail Group UK Limited
William Morgan Group Limited
N K Motors Limited
National Fleet Solutions Limited
National Tyre Service Limited
Nationwide Accident Repair Services Ltd
Nationwide Crash Repair Centres Limited
PSA Retail UK Limited
Perrys East Midlands Limited
Perrys Group Limited
Perrys Motor Sales Limited
Renault Truck Commercials Limited
Rowstock Limited
Rybrook Cars Limited
Rybrook Limited
Richard Sanders Limited
Sandicliffe Garage Limited
Sandicliffe Limited
Sandicliffe Motor Holdings Limited
Sutton Park Motor Co Ltd
Sycamore (Peterborough) Limited
Sytner Cars Limited
Sytner Group Limited
Sytner Limited
Sytner Vehicles Limited
Tanvic Group Limited
Taylors Service Garages (Boston) Limited
URA Ventures Limited
Victoria (Bavaria) Limited
F. Vindis & Sons (Bedford) Limited
F. Vindis & Sons (Sawston) Limited
Vindis Developments Limited
Vindis Group Limited
C. Walton Limited
Wollaston Motors Limited
York Ward & Rowlatt Limited

45310 Wholesale trade of motor vehicle parts and accessories [37]

Allmakes Limited
Alpine Electronics of U.K. Limited
Apec Limited
BPW Limited
BTN Turbo Charger Service Limited
Bridgestone UK Limited
B.A.Bush & Son Limited
Car Electronics Limited
Caterpillar Logistics (UK) Limited
Cruickshank Motors Limited
Drive Holdings 2015 Limited
EGR Europe Limited
FPS Distribution Limited
Ferraris Piston Service Limited
First Line Limited
Freeman Automotive (UK) Ltd
Goodman Retail Limited
Graypaul Motors Limited
Guy Salmon Limited
Hella Limited
Mahle Aftermarket Limited
Pirelli Motorsport Services Limited
Charles Pugh (Glass) Limited
Renault Truck Commercials Limited
Sandicliffe Garage Limited
Sandicliffe Limited
Sandicliffe Motor Holdings Limited
Sytner Cars Limited
Sytner Group Limited
Sytner Limited
Sytner Vehicles Limited
TVS Europe Distribution Limited
Tanvic Group Limited
Universal Components UK Limited
Yokohama H.P.T. Limited
Yutaka Giken (UK) Limited
ZF Services UK Limited

45320 Retail trade of motor vehicle parts and accessories [33]

Central Garage (Uppingham) Limited
Chandlers (Farm Equipment) Limited
Citroen U.K. Limited
Decidebloom Limited
Drive Motor Retail Limited
Evobus (UK) Limited
Falcon of Hull & Lincolnshire Limited
Ford & Slater Limited
Huntson Holdings Limited
Leda Properties Limited
Listers Group Limited
National Tyre Service Limited
Nesform Limited
PSA Retail UK Limited
Perrys East Midlands Limited
Perrys Group Limited
Perrys Motor Sales Limited
Rowstock Limited
Rybrook Cars Limited
Rybrook Limited
Richard Sanders Limited
Sutton Park Holdings Limited
Sutton Park Motor Co Ltd
Sycamore (Peterborough) Limited
Tanvic Group Limited
Taylors Service Garages (Boston) Limited
Leslie H. Trainer and Son Limited
Tuxford Exports Limited
U-Pull-It Limited
F. Vindis & Sons (Bedford) Limited
F. Vindis & Sons (Sawston) Limited
Vindis Developments Limited
Vindis Group Limited

45400 Sale, maintenance and repair of motorcycles and related parts and accessories

Bramall Quicks Dealerships Limited
Central Garage (Uppingham) Limited
Ducati U.K. Limited
Harley-Davidson Europe Limited
Hi-Level Enterprises Limited
Huntson Holdings Limited
William Morgan Group Limited
Oxford Products Limited
Wollaston Motors Limited

46110 Agents selling agricultural raw materials, livestock, textile raw materials and semi-finished goods

Thomas Bell & Sons Limited
Elsoms (Spalding) Limited
Elsoms Seeds Limited
Fengrain Limited
GLW Feeds Limited
Limagrain UK Limited
Olmar Investments Limited

46120 Agents involved in the sale of fuels, ores, metals and industrial chemicals

Diamond Fuel Supplies Limited

46130 Agents involved in the sale of timber and building materials [18]

Arbor Forest Products Limited
Building and Plumbing Supplies Limited
Diamond Fuel Supplies Limited
Distinction Doors Limited
Harlow Bros Holdings Limited
Frank Key Group Limited
J.B.Kind Limited
Klober Limited
Arnold Laver & Co Ltd
M.Markovitz Limited
John Nicholls (Trading) Limited
PTS Group Limited
Red Arrow Trading Limited
Rudridge Limited
SIG Trading Limited
John A. Stephens Holdings Limited
John A. Stephens Limited
Travis Perkins Trading Co Ltd

46140 Agents involved in the sale of machinery, industrial equipment, ships and aircraft [16]

AGD Equipment Limited
Colortronic (U.K.) Limited
Cook Defence Systems Limited
Henton & Chattell Limited
Homag U.K. Ltd.
Karcher (U.K.) Limited
Manitowoc Crane Group (UK) Limited
Ney Limited
Peacock & Binnington
Reesink Turfcare UK Limited
Shima Seiki Europe Limited
Urschel International Limited
Ward Hi-Tech Limited
Warwick Ward (Holdings) Limited
Warwick Ward (Machinery) Limited
Watling JCB Limited

46150 Agents involved in the sale of furniture, household goods, hardware and ironmongery

Flair Flooring Supplies Limited
Miele Co Ltd
Pulse Home Products (Holdings) Limited
Vine Mill Limited

46160 Agents involved in the sale of textiles, clothing, fur, footwear and leather goods

Portwest Clothing Limited
Sterling Safetywear Limited

46170 Agents involved in the sale of food, beverages and tobacco

Landmark Wholesale Limited
Today's Wholesale Services Limited

46180 Agents specialised in the sale of other particular products

Central Glass Europe Limited
Cerealto UK Limited
Nexans Logistics Limited
Pirelli Motorsport Services Limited
John A. Stephens Holdings Limited
Town and Country Petfoods Limited
UK Egg Centre Limited
Zapp (GB) Limited

46190 Agents involved in the sale of a variety of goods

Axon Public Safety UK Limited
I.S. Group Limited
Toymaster Limited

46210 Wholesale of grain, unmanufactured tobacco, seeds and animal feeds

Fengrain (Services) Limited
Gleadell Agriculture Limited
Glencore Agriculture UK Ltd.
Kennelpak Limited
Olmar Investments Limited
Pedigree Wholesale Limited

46220 Wholesale of flowers and plants

Ball Colegrave Limited
Greenyard Flowers UK Ltd
MM Flowers Limited
OAT 2012 Limited
O.A.Taylor & Sons Bulbs Limited

46310 Wholesale of fruit and vegetables [19]

A.P.S. Salads Limited
AMT Fruit Limited
Bristol Fruit Sales (Market) Limited
Fesa (UK) Limited
Glinwell Marketing Limited
Greenyard Fresh UK Ltd
LDH (La Doria) Limited
A.E. Lenton Limited
MM (UK) Limited
Manor Fresh Limited
Mercian Limited
E.Park & Sons Limited
Produce World Group Ltd
Redbridge Produce & Flowers Limited
J O Sims Holdings Limited
J O Sims Limited
Total Produce Limited
Total Worldfresh Limited
Worldwide Fruit Limited

46320 Wholesale of meat and meat products [10]

CPC Foods Limited
Farmers Fresh Limited
Landmark Wholesale Limited
Meatsnacks Group Ltd.
Mutchmeats Limited
Randall Parker Foods Limited
Today's Wholesale Services Limited
Underwood Meat Co Ltd
Weddel Swift Distribution Limited
Weddel Swift Limited

46330 Wholesale of dairy products, eggs and edible oils and fats

C & P Bird Bros. Limited
Bradbury & Son (Buxton) Limited
Silbury Marketing Limited
Sunrise Poultry Farms Limited

46342 Wholesale of wine, beer, spirits and other alcoholic beverages [15]

Aspall Cyder Limited
Boutinot Limited
Cellar Trends Limited
Cobra Beer Partnership Limited
Concha y Toro UK Limited
Everards Brewery Limited
In Vino Bidco Limited
In Vino Limited
Landmark Wholesale Limited
Molson Coors Brewing Co (UK) Ltd
Origin Wine Limited
Remy Cointreau UK Distribution Limited
Today's Wholesale Services Limited
Charles Wells Brewery Limited
Charles Wells,Limited

46360 Wholesale of sugar and chocolate and sugar confectionery

World of Sweets Limited

46380 Wholesale of other food, including fish, crustaceans and molluscs

Freiberger (UK) Limited
Northcoast Seafoods Limited
Ritter-Courivaud Limited
T. Quality Limited

46390 Non-specialised wholesale of food, beverages and tobacco [14]

Barnack Estates UK Limited
Booker Retail Partners (GB) Limited
Delifrance (UK) Limited
Euro Food Brands Limited
Friar's Pride Limited
Hancock Cash & Carry Limited
Hyperama PLC
Natco Foods Limited
Noble Foods Limited
A.G. Parfett & Sons Limited
Pilgrim Foodservice Limited
D.B. Ramsden & Co Ltd
SCI-MX Nutrition Limited
T. Quality Limited

46410 Wholesale of textiles [10]

Adidas (U.K.) Limited
Atlas Textiles Ltd.
Fabrics & Yarns (Macclesfield) Ltd
M.& N.Textiles Limited
E J Orr Limited
Premier Textiles Limited
Romo (Holdings) Limited
Romo Limited
Welspun UK Limited
Winter & Co. UK Limited

46420 Wholesale of clothing and footwear [28]

Adidas (U.K.) Limited
Airwair International Limited
Bassi Fashions Limited
Bradshaw Taylor Ltd.
Bristol Novelty Limited
Burt Bros.(Hosiery) Limited
Charterhouse Holdings PLC
EOTH Limited
Equip Outdoor Technologies UK Limited
HPC Healthline UK Limited
Simon Jersey Ltd
Joules Group PLC
Joules Limited
Lipsy Limited
Loake Brothers Limited
Maggie Sottero Bridal (UK) Ltd.
Mirza (UK) Limited
Mori Lee Europe Limited
Moto Direct Limited
New Era Cap Co Ltd
E J Orr Limited
Oxford Products Limited
Panache Lingerie Limited
Prominent (Europe) Limited
Smith & Brooks Limited
Paul Smith Limited
Tripal International Limited
UK Distributors (Footwear) Limited

46431 Wholesale of audio tapes, records, CDs and video tapes and the equipment on which these are played

Anand International Limited

46439 Wholesale of radio, television goods & electrical household appliances (other than records, tapes, CDs) [11]

Anand International Limited
BSH Home Appliances Limited
ERF Electrical Wholesalers Ltd.
Fisher & Paykel Appliances Limited
Fujifilm UK Limited
Merloni Domestic Appliances Limited
Morphy Richards Limited
Roberts Radio Limited
Smeg (UK) Limited
Smith Bros.(Caerconan) Wholesale Limited
Waterline Limited

46450 Wholesale of perfume and cosmetics

Boots International Limited
Gojo Industries - Europe Limited
Meller Design Solutions Limited
Pricecheck Toiletries Limited

46460 Wholesale of pharmaceutical goods [21]

AAH Pharmaceuticals Limited
Alloga UK Limited
Amano Enzyme Europe Limited
Barclay Pharmaceuticals Limited
Boots International Limited
Clinigen Group PLC
Clinigen Healthcare Limited
Genzyme Therapeutics Limited
Idis Group Holdings Limited
Idis Limited
L & R Medical UK Ltd.
Lloyds Pharmacy Clinical Homecare Ltd
Morningside Pharmaceuticals Limited
Movianto UK Limited
Norbrook Laboratories (G.B.) Limited
Nova Laboratories Limited
Pricecheck Toiletries Limited
Remedi Medical Holdings Limited
SSCP Blink Bidco Limited
Ivor Shaw Limited
Smartway Pharmaceuticals Limited

46470 Wholesale of furniture, carpets and lighting equipment

Eterna Lighting Limited
Ikea Distribution Services Limited
Steeple Group Limited
Waterline Limited

46480 Wholesale of watches and jewellery

Fossil (UK) Limited

46499 Wholesale of household goods (other than musical instruments) n.e.c [17]

Apac Group Limited
Benchmarx Kitchens and Joinery Limited
Charles Bentley & Son Limited
Brita Water Filter Systems Limited
City Electrical Factors Limited
ERF Electrical Wholesalers Ltd.
Groves of Thame Limited
I.Grunwerg Limited
Ikea Distribution Services Limited
Richard Lang & Son Limited
Pricecheck Toiletries Limited
RFE International (Group) Ltd
Raleigh Holdings Ltd
Raleigh UK Ltd
SGP Holdings (UK) Limited
Smart Garden Products Ltd
Utopia Tableware Limited

46510 Wholesale of computers, computer peripheral equipment and software

Barcode Warehouse Limited
Ingram Micro (UK) Limited
Jigsaw Systems Limited
Millgate Limited
Total Computer Networks Limited
XMA Limited

46520 Wholesale of electronic and telecommunications equipment and parts [11]

Anglia Components Limited
BPX Electro-Mechanical Co Ltd
Fibrefab Limited
Ghekko Limited
Grass Valley Broadcast Solutions Limited
Ingram Micro (UK) Limited
Omron Electronics Limited
RS Components Limited
Salus Controls PLC
Vtech Electronics Europe PLC
Weidmuller Limited

46610 Wholesale of agricultural machinery, equipment and supplies

AGCO Limited
Chandlers (Farm Equipment) Limited
John W. Doubleday Limited
Farmstar Limited
Farol Limited
Interfood Technology Ltd.
Kubota (U.K.) Limited
G. & R. Pykett Limited
Sharmans Agricultural Limited

46620 Wholesale of machine tools

Evolution Power Tools Ltd
Matsuura Machinery Limited
Nikken Kosakusho Europe Limited

46630 Wholesale of mining, construction and civil engineering machinery [10]

B.T.E. Plant Sales Limited
Bell Equipment UK Limited
Hajco 199 Limited
T. C. Harrison Group Limited
Hikoki Power Tools (U.K.) Limited
Leica Geosystems Limited
Molson Compact Equipment Limited
SJH-All Plant Group Limited
Tadano UK Ltd
Watling JCB Limited

46640 Wholesale of machinery for the textile industry and of sewing and knitting machines

Monarch Knitting Machinery (U.K.) Ltd

46660 Wholesale of other office machinery and equipment

Evo Business Supplies Limited
Fellowes Ltd

46690 Wholesale of other machinery and equipment [26]

Acorn Industrial Services Group Ltd
Agrifac UK Ltd
Charterhouse Holdings PLC
Doosan Industrial Vehicle UK Ltd.
Eclipse Magnetics Limited
Eyre & Elliston Limited
Flowmax Limited
Fujifilm UK Limited
GEA Mechanical Equipment UK Limited
KSB Limited
Keyence (UK) Limited
Leica Geosystems Limited
Makita (UK) Limited
Neill Tools Limited
Pattonair (Derby) Limited
Pattonair Europe Limited
Pattonair UK Limited
Performance Health International Limited
Routeco Limited
S.I.P.(Industrial Products) Limited
Schueco UK Limited
Sharmans Agricultural Limited
Sheetfed Holdings Limited
Snap-On Equipment Limited
Sodick Europe Holdings Limited
Winterhalter Ltd

46711 Wholesale of petroleum and petroleum products

Flogas Britain Limited
Total Lindsey Oil Refinery Limited

46719 Wholesale of other fuels and related products

Avanti Gas Limited
Avro Energy Limited
CPL Distribution Limited
Calor Gas Limited
Moto Direct Limited
Oxbow Coal Limited
Total Lindsey Oil Refinery Limited

46720 Wholesale of metals and metal ores [13]

Asmet (UK) Limited
Asmet Limited
Clytha Holdings Limited
Cogne U.K. Limited
ELG Haniel Metals Ltd
ELG Utica Alloys Limited
Hall & Pickles 1812 Limited
Leen Gate Metals Limited
Neonickel (Blackburn) Limited
William Rowland Limited
Senior Architectural Systems Limited
Tennant Metallurgical Group Limited
Westbrook Resources Limited

46730 Wholesale of wood, construction materials and sanitary equipment [11]

Alumasc Limited
East Coast Fittings Limited
GRS (Bagging) Limited
Jewson Limited
Maccaferri Ltd
Novoferm Europe Limited
Saint-Gobain Building Distribution Ltd
A.E.Spink Limited

Undercover Roofing Supplies Limited
Verdon Holdings Limited
Ernest V. Waddington Limited

46740 Wholesale of hardware, plumbing and heating equipment and supplies [16]

Benchmarx Kitchens and Joinery Limited
Carl F Groupco Limited
Certikin International Limited
City Plumbing Supplies Holdings Limited
George Fischer Sales Limited
Fluidpower Limited
Fusion Plastics Limited
Geberit Sales Limited
John Nicholls (Trading) Limited
Michael Pavis Limited
Robert Pochin Limited
Primaflow Limited
Q.E.P. Co. U.K. Limited
Roca Limited
A.E.Spink Limited
Walls and Floors Limited

46750 Wholesale of chemical products [15]

BASF PLC
Belchim Crop Protection Limited
Caldic (UK) Ltd
Chemetall Limited
Elastomerics Limited
Evonik Goldschmidt UK Limited
Fluorochem Limited
Lehvoss UK Limited
OQEMA Limited
Phenomenex Limited
Plastribution Limited
Polydist (UK) Limited
Polydist Europe Holdings Limited
Union Colours Limited
VWR International Ltd

46760 Wholesale of other intermediate products [15]

Arpo Global Limited
Beaver-Visitec International Sales Ltd
Franke Sissons Limited
Fujifilm UK Limited
International Piping Products (Europe) Ltd
Larson-Juhl UK Limited
Monro Limited
Pattonair Limited
S.T.L. Trading Co Ltd
Southgate Packaging Limited
Static Control Components (Europe) Ltd
T. Quality Limited
Technical Consumer Products Limited
Valve Partners Limited
Whilton Marina Limited

46770 Wholesale of waste and scrap

Glazewing Limited
Lord & Midgley Limited
Mark Lyndon Paper Enterprises (UK) Ltd
G.A.E. Smith (Holdings) Limited

46900 Non-specialised wholesale trade [90]

ACESO Healthcare Group Holdings Limited
ACESO Healthcare Holdings Limited
ACESO Healthcare Limited
ADA Pacific Direct Limited
Accuride International Limited
Acorn Industrial Services Limited
John Adams Leisure Limited
Almadon Limited
Amscan International Limited
B.M. Polyco Limited
BRT (Wisbech) Limited
Baker & Taylor (UK) Ltd
Ball. Roller & Transmission Bearings Ltd
Battle,Hayward and Bower,Limited
Benchmarx Kitchens and Joinery Limited
Big Food Group Limited
Bio-Techne Ltd
Bonnington Plastics Limited
Booker Direct Limited
Booker Group Limited
Booker Limited
Boole's Tools & Pipe Fittings Limited
Buffaload Logistics Limited
Burton McCall Limited
Coloplast Limited
Consortium for Purchasing and Distribution Ltd
Cromwell Tools Limited
Crown Crest (Leicester) PLC
DCS Group (UK) Limited
DGS Group PLC
Ian Edgar (Liverpool) Limited
Eurocell Building Plastics Limited
Fairchild Fasteners (UK) Limited
Forever Living Products (U.K.) Limited
Giant U.K. Limited
Hafele U.K. Limited
W.E. Hewitt & Son Limited
History & Heraldry Limited
Alan Howard (Stockport) Limited
I.S. Group Limited
International Applications Limited
J & E Importers & Distributors Green Jem
Mfg Associates Co Ltd
JTF Wholesale Limited
Karcher (U.K.) Limited
Kelkay Limited
Kumho Tyre (U.K.) Limited
LC Packaging UK Ltd
Landmark Wholesale Limited
Richard Lang & Son Limited
Lesta Packaging PLC
Lindab Limited
MGA Entertainment (UK) Limited
MHH Contracting Limited
Makro Self Service Wholesalers Limited
Mistral Capital Management Limited
Mondottica Limited
Multipanel UK Limited
NUS Services Limited
Nottingham Rehab Limited
Office Depot UK Limited
PX Manufacturing Ltd
Pedigree Wholesale Limited
Ping Europe Limited
Pitacs Limited
Pricecheck Toiletries Limited
Pyramid Posters Limited
Resmed (UK) Limited
Resmed EPN Ltd
Salus Healthcare Limited
R.H. Smith & Sons (Wigmakers) Limited
Smith Brothers Stores Limited
Special Piping Materials Limited
Stauff UK Limited
Steris Solutions Limited
R.J.Stokes & Co. Limited
Talasey Ltd
Thetford Limited
Today's Wholesale Services Limited
Travis Perkins PLC
Tyler Packaging Limited
UCC Coffee UK Limited
VWR International Ltd
Vital Pet Group Limited
Vow Europe Limited
Vulcan Engineering Limited
Wanzl Limited
Waterline Limited
Wolseley UK Limited
J. and A. Young (Leicester) Limited
Zapf Creation (UK) Limited

47110 Retail sale in non-specialised stores with food, beverages or tobacco predominating [11]

Aldi Stores Limited
Company Shop Limited
A.E.Hewison Limited
James Convenience Retail Limited
K & S Buildings Limited
Motorway Services Limited
Papa John's (GB) Limited
Rippleglen Limited
Welcome Break Group Limited
Welcome Break Limited
Welcome Break Services Limited

47190 Other retail sale in non-specialised stores [13]

Argos Limited
Blue Cross
Boots UK Limited
Frasers Retail Limited
Habitat Retail Limited
JTF Wholesale Limited
LC Packaging UK Ltd
Lexden BH (Colchester) Limited
Machine Mart Limited
Magenta Storage Limited
Minorfern Limited
Oldrid & Co.,Limited
Wilko Retail Limited

47220 Retail sale of meat and meat products in specialised stores

Beckett's Foods Limited
CPC Foods Limited
Chesterfield Poultry Limited

47240 Retail sale of bread, cakes, flour confectionery and sugar confectionery in specialised stores

Brioche Pasquier U.K. Limited

47250 Retail sale of beverages in specialised stores

Holland & Barrett Retail Limited
James Convenience Retail Limited
Punch Partnerships (PML) Limited

47260 Retail sale of tobacco products in specialised stores
Rippleglen Limited

47290 Other retail sale of food in specialised stores
County Milk Products Limited
Frozen Value Limited
Holland & Barrett Retail Limited
James Convenience Retail Limited

47300 Retail sale of automotive fuel in specialised stores
Central Garage (Uppingham) Limited
Frasers Retail Limited
Jack Loggin Limited
M.P.K. Garages Limited
Motorway Services Limited
Welcome Break Group Limited
Welcome Break Limited
Welcome Break Services Limited

47410 Retail sale of computers, peripheral units and software in specialised stores
Compu B Ltd

47421 Retail sale of mobile telephones
A1 Comms Limited
Hopton Investment Holdings Limited
Hopton Retail Holdings Limited

47430 Retail sale of audio and video equipment in specialised stores
Anand International Limited

47510 Retail sale of textiles in specialised stores
CHT Holdings Limited
Dunelm (Soft Furnishings) Ltd

47520 Retail sale of hardware, paints and glass in specialised stores [12]
Lexden BH (Colchester) Limited
Multi-Tile Limited
John Sinclair (Sheffield) Limited
Tile Giant Limited
Tiles4less Limited
Toolstation Limited
Topalpha (Warehouse) Limited
Topps Tile Kingdom Limited
Topps Tiles (UK) Limited
Topps Tiles Distribution Limited
Topps Tiles PLC
Wilko Retail Limited

47530 Retail sale of carpets, rugs, wall and floor coverings in specialised stores
Fired Earth Limited
Minoli & Co Ltd

47540 Retail sale of electrical household appliances in specialised stores
Aga Rangemaster Limited
Argos Limited
Bodypower Sports PLC
Habitat Retail Limited
Lexden BH (Colchester) Limited
Mark's Electrical Limited
Toolstation Limited

47599 Retail of furniture, lighting, and similar (not musical instruments or scores) in specialised store
Argos Limited
DFS Trading Limited
Habitat Retail Limited
Ikea Limited
Lexden BH (Colchester) Limited
Wren Kitchens Limited

47610 Retail sale of books in specialised stores
Blackwell UK Limited

47620 Retail sale of newspapers and stationery in specialised stores
Blackwell UK Limited
Frontline Limited
James Convenience Retail Limited
Seymour Distribution Limited
Seymour International Limited

47640 Retail sale of sports goods, fishing gear, camping goods, boats and bicycles
Adidas (U.K.) Limited
Lillywhites Limited
Trek Bicycle Corporation Limited

47650 Retail sale of games and toys in specialised stores
Joules Limited

47710 Retail sale of clothing in specialised stores [16]
AK Retail Holdings Limited
Bradshaw Taylor Ltd.
Bravissimo Limited
Flannels Group Limited
Joules Group PLC
Joules Limited
Lipsy Limited
Karen Millen Fashions Limited
Next Retail Limited
Oasis Fashions Limited
S. & A. Drapers Limited
Selective Marketplace Limited
Paul Smith Limited
Trek Bicycle Corporation Limited
Warehouse Fashions Limited
Yours Clothing Limited

47721 Retail sale of footwear in specialised stores
Church UK Retail Limited
Crockett and Jones Limited
Deichmann-Shoes UK Limited
Joules Limited
Richard Lang & Son Limited
Loake Brothers Limited
Next Retail Limited
Shoe Zone PLC
Shoe Zone Retail Limited

47722 Retail sale of leather goods in specialised stores
Joules Group PLC
John Sinclair (Sheffield) Limited

47730 Dispensing chemist in specialised stores [11]
John Bell & Croyden Limited
Boots UK Limited
Daleacre Healthcare Limited
Dudley Taylor Pharmacies Limited
Jardines (U.K.) Limited
Lloyds Pharmacy Limited
Lo's Pharmacy Limited
SKF. Lo (Chemists) Limited
Saffron Apothecaries (Leicester) Limited
H.I.Weldrick Limited
Whitworth Chemists Limited

47749 Retail sale of medical and orthopaedic goods in specialised stores (not incl. hearing aids) n.e.c.
Ability Matters Group Limited
Arthrex Limited
Fannin (UK) Limited
Medical Equipment Supplies and Management Ltd
Squadron Medical Limited

47750 Retail sale of cosmetic and toilet articles in specialised stores
Avon Cosmetics Limited
Wilko Retail Limited

47760 Retail sale of flowers, plants, seeds, fertilizers, pet animals and pet food in specialised stores
Kennelpak Limited
Pennell's Holdings Limited
Wilko Retail Limited

47770 Retail sale of watches and jewellery in specialised stores [10]
Aurum Acquisitions Limited
Cranbrook (Jewellers) Ltd
Fossil (UK) Limited
Jewel UK Bidco Limited
Jewel UK Midco Limited
Jewel UK Topco Limited
Nimogen Limited
George Pragnell Limited
Watches of Switzerland Co Ltd
Watches of Switzerland Group Limited

47782 Retail sale by opticians
Boots Opticians Professional Services Ltd

47789 Other retail sale of new goods in specialised stores (not commercial art galleries and opticians) [15]
Aga Rangemaster Limited
Burford Garden Centre Limited
Fired Earth Limited
Frosts Garden Centre Restructuring Ltd
Go Outdoors Limited
Go Outdoors Topco Limited
Holland & Barrett Retail Limited
Warren James (Jewellers) Limited
Richard Lang & Son Limited
Lillywhites Limited
Next Retail Limited
Pets at Home Ltd
Sportsdirect.Com Retail Limited
Wickes Building Supplies Limited
Woodthorpe Hall Garden Centres Limited

47791 Retail sale of antiques including antique books in stores

Company of Master Jewellers Limited
George Pragnell Limited
Sobell House Hospice Charity Limited

47799 Retail sale of other second-hand goods in stores (not incl. antiques)

George Pragnell Limited
Salvation Army Trading Co Ltd
Sobell House Hospice Charity Limited

47910 Retail sale via mail order houses or via Internet [19]

Blinds 2 Go Limited
Dunelm (Soft Furnishings) Ltd
Ebuyer (UK) Limited
Entertainment Magpie Limited
Holland & Barrett Group Limited
Holland & Barrett Retail Limited
Ideal Shopping Direct Limited
Ikea Limited
Interflora British Unit
Lands' End Europe Limited
Lifeplus Europe Limited
NUS Services Limited
Next Retail Limited
OKA Direct Limited
Office Depot International (UK) Limited
QD Commercial Group Holdings Limited
Selective Marketplace Limited
UBT (EU) Ltd
Watches of Switzerland Co Ltd

47990 Other retail sale not in stores, stalls or markets [17]

A1 Comms Limited
Don Amott Parks Limited
Avon Cosmetics Limited
CPL Distribution Limited
Dunster House Limited
Everris Limited
Fischer Future Heat UK Limited
Ideal Shopping Direct Limited
Kartell UK Limited
Kumho Tyre (U.K.) Limited
Kybotech Limited
Lifeplus Europe Limited
Lister Wilder Limited
Motorpoint Limited
Robinsons Caravans Limited
Vectair Aviation (1995) Limited
Woburn Enterprises Limited

49100 Passenger rail transport, interurban

East Coast Main Line Co Ltd
East Midlands Trains Limited
Porterbrook Maintenance Limited
Stagecoach South Western Trains Limited
Unipart Rail Limited

49200 Freight rail transport

DB Cargo (UK) Holdings Limited
DB Cargo (UK) Limited
DB Cargo International Limited
Rail Express Systems Limited

49311 Urban and suburban passenger railway transportation by underground, metro and similar systems

Amey LUL 2 Limited

49319 Other urban, suburban or metropolitan passenger land transport (not underground, metro or similar) [22]

Barton Buses Limited
Busways Travel Services Limited
Cambus Limited
Cheltenham and Gloucester Omnibus Co Ltd
Cleveland Transit Ltd.
East Kent Road Car Co Ltd
East London Bus & Coach Co Ltd
First South Yorkshire Limited
Glenvale Transport Limited
Go Plant Fleet Services Ltd
Greater Manchester Buses South Limited
Lincolnshire Road Car Co Ltd
Midland Red (South) Limited
Nottingham City Transport Limited
Red & White Services Limited
South East London & Kent Bus Co Ltd
Stagecoach (North West) Limited
Stagecoach (South) Limited
Stagecoach Devon Limited
Thames Transit Limited
Western Buses Limited
Yorkshire Traction Co Ltd

49390 Other passenger land transport

Evobus (UK) Limited
GEO Amey PECS Limited
Go Plant Fleet Services Ltd
Skills Motor Coaches Limited
Trent Motor Traction Co Ltd
Mike de Courcey Travel Limited

49410 Freight transport by road [52]

Alltruck PLC
Ascott Transport Limited
Barton Petroleum (Holdings) Limited
Barton Petroleum Limited
Boden & Davies Limited
Bowring Transport Limited
Buffaload Logistics Limited
Bulk Freight (Midlands) Limited
Bullimores Sand and Gravel Limited
Cherwell Valley Silos Limited
H.W. Coates Limited
Cullingworth Commercials and Freight Services Ltd
DFDS Logistics Limited
DHL Supply Chain Limited
Dachser Limited
Davison & Co. (Barford) Limited
N.R. Evans and Son Limited
Freightroute Limited
Freshlinc Group Limited
Freshlinc Limited
GB Fleetcare Limited
Gefco U.K. Limited
Simon Gibson Transport Limited
R.J. & A.E. Godfrey
Hoban Limited
P.C. Howard Limited
Knights of Old,Limited
Knowles (Transport) Limited
Lomas Distribution Limited
Maxim Logistics Group Limited
Mid-UK Recycling Limited
Movianto UK Limited
NFT Distribution Operations Limited
Neal Brothers (Leicester) Limited
Pall-Ex (U.K.) Limited
Palletforce Limited
Park Industrial and Agricultural Holdings Ltd
Pinnacle International Freight Limited
Fred Sherwood & Sons (Transport) Ltd
Staples (Vegetables) Limited
Syncreon Technology (UK) Ltd
TNT Express Worldwide Investments Ltd
TNT Transport Limited
TNT UK Limited
B Taylor & Sons Transport Limited
P.J. Thory Limited
Roger Warnes Transport Limited
Frank Wright Limited
XPO Bulk UK Limited
XPO Transport Solutions UK Limited
Yarborough Limited
Yusen Logistics (UK) Limited

49420 Removal services

B. E. Webbe Removals (Derby) Limited

50100 Sea and coastal passenger water transport

Adams Challenge (UK) Limited
DFDS Seaways Newcastle Limited

50200 Sea and coastal freight water transport

DFDS Seaways Newcastle Limited
Graypen Limited
Princess International Sales and Service Ltd
Western Bridge (Shipping) Limited
Yusen Logistics (UK) Limited

50300 Inland passenger water transport

Salter Bros,Limited

50400 Inland freight water transport

Ernest V. Waddington Limited

51101 Scheduled passenger air transport

Bournemouth International Airport Ltd
Thomas Cook Airlines Limited
East Midlands International Airport Ltd

51102 Non-scheduled passenger air transport

Airtanker Services Limited
Sloane Helicopters Limited

51210 Freight air transport

Airtanker Services Limited
East Midlands International Airport Ltd
HAE Global Ltd
HAE Group Limited
Heavyweight Air Express Limited
West Atlantic UK Limited
Yusen Logistics (UK) Limited

52101 Operation of warehousing and storage facilities for water transport activities

Cygnia Logistics Limited
DFDS Seaways PLC
G.B. Terminals Limited
Ernest V. Waddington Limited

52102 Operation of warehousing and storage facilities for air transport activities

Cygnia Logistics Limited

52103 Operation of warehousing and storage facilities for land transport activities [28]

Ascott Transport Limited
Asfordby Storage & Haulage Limited
E.P.Barrus Limited
Rick Bestwick Limited
Bybox Field Support Limited
CML Limited
Chiltern Cold Storage Group Limited
H.W. Coates Limited
Cromwell Logistics Limited
Cygnia Logistics Limited
Dachser Limited
Freightroute Limited
Gefco U.K. Limited
HSH Cold Stores Limited
Michael I Holdsworth Limited
P.C. Howard Limited
Industrial Machinery Supplies Limited
Kuehne + Nagel Drinkflow Logistics Ltd
Kuehne + Nagel Drinks Logistics Limited
Maxim Logistics Group Limited
Meter Provida Limited
Moore Large & Co. Limited
Neovia Logistics Services (U.K.) Limited
Next Distribution Limited
Park Industrial and Agricultural Holdings Ltd
QD Commercial Group Holdings Limited
Syncreon Technology (UK) Ltd
Yusen Logistics (UK) Limited

52212 Operation of rail passenger facilities at railway stations

East Coast Main Line Co Ltd

52213 Operation of bus and coach passenger facilities at bus and coach stations

Johnson Bros (Tours) Limited

52219 Other service activities incidental to land transportation, n.e.c.

Amey Rail Limited
CEVA Freight (UK) Holding Co Ltd
Close Brothers Vehicle Hire Limited
Excel Parking Services Limited
Logistex Limited

52220 Service activities incidental to water transportation

Canal & River Trust
DFDS Seaways PLC
Xylem Water Solutions UK Ltd

52230 Service activities incidental to air transportation

Airtanker Services Limited
Gamston Aviation Limited

52241 Cargo handling for water transport activities

CEVA Freight (UK) Limited
G.B. Terminals Limited
Port of Boston Limited

52242 Cargo handling for air transport activities

Rolls-Royce Total Care Services Limited

52243 Cargo handling for land transport activities

Pall-Ex (U.K.) Limited

52290 Other transportation support activities [14]

Airtanker Services Limited
Amey Birmingham Highways Limited
Banks & Lloyd (Shipping) Limited
CEVA Container Logistics Limited
CEVA Logistics Limited
CEVA Supply Chain Solutions Limited
Chevron Traffic Management Limited
Cygnia Logistics Limited
Ford & Slater Limited
G.B. Terminals Limited
Magnavale Limited
Palletforce Limited
Rolls-Royce Total Care Services Limited
Stagecoach Services Limited

53202 Unlicensed carriers

Punch Partnerships (PML) Limited

55100 Hotels and similar accommodation [59]

A.B. Hotels Limited
Abacus Hotels Limited
Atlas Hotels (Bath) Limited
Atlas Hotels (Bristol North) Limited
Atlas Hotels (Bristol Property) Limited
Atlas Hotels (Chingford) Limited
Atlas Hotels (Derby) Limited
Atlas Hotels (Exeter) Limited
Atlas Hotels (Glasgow) Limited
Atlas Hotels (Greenwich) Limited
Atlas Hotels (Group 1) Limited
Atlas Hotels (Group 2) Limited
Atlas Hotels (Group 3 Property) Limited
Atlas Hotels (Group 4 Property 2) Ltd
Atlas Hotels (Inverness) Limited
Atlas Hotels (Lincoln) Limited
Atlas Hotels (Liverpool) Limited
Atlas Hotels (Salford Quays) Limited
Atlas Hotels (Stevenage) Limited
Atlas Hotels (Trading) Limited
Atlas Hotels (Warwick) Limited
Atlas Hotels Limited
Christian Conference Trust
Coombe Abbey Park Limited
Corus Hotels Limited
County Hotels Limited
Delaquest Limited
Eden Hotel Collection Limited
Flamepro Limited
Hotel MK Limited
Hundred Percent Holdings Limited
Imago @ Loughborough Limited
KRNS Properties Ltd
Kenwood Hotel Property Limited
London Vista Hotel Limited
Mallory Court Hotel Limited
Methodist Guild Holidays Limited
Mogford Hotels Limited
Mogford Limited
Motorway Services Limited
Patrolmake Limited
Plaza on Hyde Park Limited
Poste Holdings Limited
Poste Hotels Limited
Prahi Hotel Collection Limited
Prince Hotels Ltd
Ragdale Hall (1990) Limited
Rushton Hall Limited
Searles (Camping Ground) Limited
Sundial Group Limited
T.S.B. (Developments) Limited
Travelodge Hotels Limited
Vine Hotels Limited
Vine Kenwood Limited
Welcome Break Group Limited
Welcome Break Limited
Welcome Break Services Limited
Wroxall Abbey Estate Limited
Yew Lodge Limited

55201 Holiday centres and villages

Walter John Cook and Sons Limited
Pinelodge Holidays Limited
Searles (Camping Ground) Limited

55202 Youth hostels

YHA (England and Wales)

55209 Other holiday and other collective accommodation

Avon Estates Limited
Laver Leisure Limited

55300 Recreational vehicle parks, trailer parks and camping grounds [12]

Don Amott Parks Limited
Avondale Property (Holdings) Limited
Blue Anchor Leisure Limited
Camping and Caravanning Club Limited
Coastfields Leisure Limited
Hardys Farm Limited
A.E.Hewison Limited
Lifestyle Seeview Limited
Searles (Camping Ground) Limited
Seaside Leisure Parks Limited
Vectair Aviation (1995) Limited
Whilton Marina Limited

55900 Other accommodation [10]

Boston Mayflower Finance PLC
CP Woburn (Operating Company) Limited
Church Army
Glenco Limited
Natural Assets Investments Limited
Trewhiddle Village Limited
Warwick Independent Schools Foundation
Waterloo Quay Properties Limited
Whilton Marina Limited
Yuill Family Properties Ltd

56101 Licenced restaurants

Alchemist Bar & Restaurant Limited
Buttercup Bidco Limited
Buttercup Topco Limited
Domino's Pizza Group PLC
Methodist Guild Holidays Limited
Mogford Hotels Limited
Poste Holdings Limited
Poste Hotels Limited
T.J.D. Trade Limited

56102 Unlicenced restaurants and cafes

I & A Restaurants Ltd
Kyra Enterprises Limited
McLean Restaurants Limited
Motorway Services Limited
Premium Restaurants Limited
Welcome Break Group Limited
Welcome Break Limited
Welcome Break Services Limited

56103 Take-away food shops and mobile food stands

Bansols Beta Limited
Hertford Heath Limited
KL Ventures Limited
MSG Commercial Limited
MSG Sandhurst Limited
Sheermans Limited

56210 Event catering activities

Elior UK PLC

56290 Other food services

Bobby's Foods Limited
Harrison Catering Services Limited
Hopwells Ltd
Taylor Shaw Limited
Totally Local Co Ltd
Waterfall Elior Limited

56301 Licenced clubs

Deltic Group Limited

56302 Public houses and bars [13]

BCTI Holdings Limited
Bellcoin Holdings Limited
DHP Family Ltd.
Eaglebeam Limited
Everards Brewery Limited
McManus Pub Co. Limited
Punch Partnerships (PGRP) Limited
Punch Partnerships (PML) Limited
SJC 15 Limited
Tynemill Limited
Vectair Aviation (1995) Limited
Charles Wells,Limited
Westbourne Leisure Limited

58110 Book publishing [10]

Baker & Taylor (UK) Ltd
Igloo Books Group Holdings Limited
Igloo Books Limited
Imago Publishing Limited
Oxford Publishing Limited
Scholastic Limited
Scholastic UK Ltd
Set Copyrights Limited
Tolkien Estate Limited
Tolkien Trust

58130 Publishing of newspapers

Acredula Group Limited

58141 Publishing of learned journals

Oxford Publishing Limited

58142 Publishing of consumer and business journals and periodicals

Mortons Media Group Ltd
Mortons of Horncastle Limited
Warners Group Publications PLC

58190 Other publishing activities [10]

Belmont Press Limited
Imago Holdings Limited
Imago Publishing Limited
Myers-Briggs Company (Europe) Limited
Myers-Briggs Company Holdings (Europe) Ltd
Myers-Briggs Co Ltd
Oxford Pharmagenesis Holdings Limited
Oxford Pharmagenesis Limited
Scholastic Limited
Weatherbys Ltd

58210 Publishing of computer games

Rebellion Developments Limited

58290 Other software publishing [12]

Amtech Group Limited
Archipelago Learning Holdings UK Limited
Blue Chip Customer Engineering Limited
Codemasters Group Holdings PLC
Dassault Systemes UK Limited
Educationcity Limited
Experian Technology Limited
HBM United Kingdom Limited
IRESS FS Limited
IRESS Solutions Limited
New Blue Chip Limited
TTS Group Limited

59113 Television programme production activities

Bauer Digital Radio Limited
Orion Media Limited

59140 Motion picture projection activities

Natl. Amusements (UK) Limited
Reel Cinemas Limited
Savoy Cinemas Limited

60100 Radio broadcasting

Absolute Radio Limited
Bauer AR Holdings Limited

60200 Television programming and broadcasting activities

Ideal Shopping Direct Limited
Sports Information Services (Holdings) Ltd
Sports Information Services Limited

61100 Wired telecommunications activities

Comtec Cable Accessories Limited
Comtec Group (International) Limited
IX Reach Ltd

61200 Wireless telecommunications activities

Midland Communications Distribution Ltd
Park Air Systems Limited

61300 Satellite telecommunications activities

Hughes Network Systems Limited

61900 Other telecommunications activities [29]

Aster and Young Limited
Blancco Technology Group PLC
Chess Limited
Comex 2000 (UK) Limited
Commify UK Limited
GCI Managed Services Group Limited
GCI Network Solutions Limited
Gigaclear Limited
Impello Limited
Linbrooke Services Limited
London Internet Exchange Limited
Optilan (UK) Limited
Red Box Recorders Limited
Sawatch Limited
Simoco Wireless Solutions Limited
Sitel Europe Limited
Sitel UK Limited
Steeple Bidco Limited
Steeple Holdco Limited
Steeple Midco Limited
Steeple Topco Limited
Stream Acquisitions Limited
Stream Midco Limited
Stream Topco Limited
TII Technologies Limited
Telent Technology Services Limited
Timico Limited
Timico Technology Group Limited
Transaction Network Services (UK) Ltd

62011 Ready-made interactive leisure and entertainment software development

Mobica Limited
Project Republica Bidco Limited
Project Republica Topco Limited
Rebellion Developments Limited
Sumo Digital Ltd.
Sumo Group PLC

62012 Business and domestic software development [40]

Aareon UK Limited
Aptean Limited
Apteco Limited
Autologic Diagnostics Limited
Blackburn Starling & Co Ltd
ESKO Stonecube Limited
Electronic Data Processing Limited
Epyx Limited
Estate Computer Systems (Holdings) Ltd
Gladstone MRM Limited
HBM United Kingdom Limited
IRESS (UK) Limited
ITP Engines UK Limited
Ideagen PLC
Ingenta PLC
Jonas Computing (UK) Limited
KHL Newco Limited
Kirona Holdings Limited
Lablogic Group Holdings Limited
Microlise Holdings Limited
Microlise Limited
Netsupport Ltd.
Pinewood Technologies PLC

Prophet PLC
Red Box Recorders Group Limited
Red Box Recorders Limited
Resonate Group Limited
Respond Group Limited
Sanderson Group PLC
Servelec Healthcare Limited
Software (Europe) Limited
Sophos Group PLC
Sophos Limited
Tessella Holdings Limited
Tessella Limited
Veeva U.K. Holdings Limited
Wellbeing Software Group Ltd
Yotta Limited
Zinc Ahead Holdings Limited
Zoo Digital Group PLC

62020 Information technology consultancy activities [35]

ASK4 LIMITED
Aareon UK Limited
Business Control Solutions Group Limited
Business Control Solutions PLC
Business Management Software Limited
Codemasters Software Co Ltd
ENSEK Holdings Limited
Electronics for Imaging United Kingdom Ltd
Ellucian Global Limited
Ellucian SMS Ltd
European Electronique Limited
Experian Limited
Golflane Limited
Growth Partners Management Limited
IRESS (UK) Limited
IRESS FS Group Limited
IRESS Portal Limited
IRESS Solutions Limited
Ingenta PLC
Jigsaw Systems Limited
Lets Connect It Solutions Limited
W & J Linney Limited
Llamasoft Europe Holdings Limited
Mass Consultants Limited
Microlise Limited
Millgate Limited
PCMS Group Limited
PKF Cooper Parry Group Limited
Resonate Group Limited
Ricoh UK Limited
Software AG (UK) Limited
Tata Technologies Europe Limited
Telent Technology Services Limited
Yotta Limited
Zoo Digital Group PLC

62030 Computer facilities management activities

Ellucian Global Limited
Ellucian SMS Ltd
European Electronique Limited
MAM Software Limited

62090 Other information technology service activities [52]

Alphyra Payment Services Limited
Amey Group Information Services Limited
Apertio Limited
Art Systems Limited
Barron McCann Limited
Bibliotheca Limited
CCS Media Limited
CDL Group Holdings Limited
Cheshire Datasystems Limited
Drayson Technologies Limited
E.On IT UK Limited
Ellucian Global Limited
Ellucian SMS Ltd
Elsevier Limited
Epyx Limited
European Electronique Limited
Experian International Unlimited
Experian SURBS Investments Limited
Healthcare Software Solutions Ltd
IRESS (UK) Limited
Insight Direct (UK) Ltd
Insight Enterprises UK Limited
Insight Networking Solutions Limited
Jigsaw Systems Limited
MHR International UK Limited
Node 4 Limited
OCF PLC
PCS Business Systems Limited
Payzone UK Limited
Plusnet PLC
Proact IT (UK) Limited
Proact IT UK Limited
RM Education Ltd
Rightmove Group Limited
Rightmove PLC
Sanderson Limited
Sanderson Multi-Channel Retail Solutions Ltd
Servelec Social Care Limited
Simmerson Associates Ltd
Software (Europe) Limited
Sumo Digital Ltd.
Sumo Group PLC
TNT Express ICS Limited
Telent Technology Services Limited
ThruVision Group PLC
ULS Technology PLC
Wasp Management Software Limited
Wellbeing Software Holdings Limited
Whistler Acquisitions Limited
Workplace Systems International Limited
Yardi Systems Limited
Zoo Digital Group PLC

63110 Data processing, hosting and related activities

Axon Public Safety UK Limited
Co-operative Energy Limited
Microlise Holdings Limited
Nominet UK
Parseq Limited
Weatherbys Ltd

63120 Web portals

Rightmove Group Limited
Rightmove PLC

63990 Other information service activities n.e.c.

Experian (UK) Finance Limited
Experian Holdings (UK) Limited
ILI Limited
M3 (EU) Limited
Nominet UK
Premonition Analytics Limited
Radford Holdings Limited

64191 Banks

Aldermore Bank PLC
Bodycote America Treasury Limited
Cambridge & Counties Bank Limited
Kingdom Bank Limited
Weatherbys Bank Limited

64201 Activities of agricultural holding companies [15]

A.B. Produce Trading Limited
Aviagen European Holdings Limited
Aviagen International Finance Four Ltd
Aviagen International Finance Limited
Aviagen International Finance One Ltd
Aviagen International Finance Two Ltd
Aviagen International Holdings Ltd.
Aviagen Turkeys Holdings Limited
Beeswax Dyson Farming Limited
Grant Farming Limited
Jepco Limited
A.E. Lenton (Holdings) Limited
MDS Estates Limited
Marubeni Agrochemical Limited
R C Tinsley 2012 Limited

64202 Activities of production holding companies [41]

Anatis UK Limited
Anexhold Limited
Applied Composites Group Ltd
Baker Perkins Holdings Limited
Beardow Adams Holdings Ltd
Brayfour Limited
CI Brite Limited
Chilled Foods (UK) Ltd
Chromalloy UK Holdings Ltd
William Cook Holdings Limited
Cooke Optics Holdings Limited
Daisy UK Holdco Limited
Denby Holdings Limited
Gardner Aerospace Holdings Limited
Guardian Industries UK Holding Limited
Hexpol Finance UK Limited
J & A (International) Holdings Limited
K L Technologies Limited
MPAC Group PLC
Maynard & Harris Group Limited
Maynard & Harris Plastics (UK) Limited
Owen Mumford Holdings Limited
Phoenix Parker Holdings Limited
Pipe Holdings 1 PLC
Pipe Holdings 2 Limited
Pipe Holdings PLC
Polypipe Group PLC
Premier Group (Coventry) Limited
Promens Holding UK Limited
RPC 2017 Holding Co Ltd
RPC Asia Pacific Holdings Limited
RPC Packaging Holdings Limited
Radical Sportscars Limited
Radius Systems Limited
Tamar Energy Operating Company (One) Ltd
Tinsley Bridge Group Limited
Total Downstream UK PLC
Trimas UK Aerospace Holdings Limited
Vaillant Holdings Limited
Vita Satellite 1 Limited
Watermill-CT Holdings Limited

64203 Activities of construction holding companies [15]

Aggregate Industries Holdings Limited
Aggregate Industries Limited
Bardsley Construction Holdings Limited
Bardsley Group Limited
Chalcroft Holdings Limited
Dunamis Group Limited
Evans Leicester Limited
Experian US Holdings Unlimited
Foster Yeoman Limited
Miller Homes Group Holdings PLC
Novoferm Europe Limited
O'Brien (Group) Limited
P V H Holdings Limited
S D C (Holdings) Limited
Robert Woodhead Holdings Limited

64204 Activities of distribution holding companies [25]

B.I. (UK) Limited
Brady European Holdings Limited
Cromwell Group (Holdings) Limited
DNA (Holdings) Limited
Fluidpower Group Limited
Fluidpower Shared Services Limited
Forcefield Bidco Limited
Forcefield Midco Limited
Groves of Thame (Holdings) Limited
Homecrest Bidco Limited
Homecrest Midco Limited
Multi-Tile Distribution Limited
NFT Distribution Holdings Limited
Palletforce Holdings Limited
Pattonair Group Limited
Pattonair Holdings Limited
Quicksilver Dollar Loanco Limited
Quicksilver Euro Loanco Limited
Quicksilver Midco Limited
Stephen Sanderson Transport Holdings Ltd
Shoby Investments Limited
Syncreon UK Holdings Limited
TVS Europe Distribution Limited
Utopia Holdings (Chesterfield) Limited
VWR Holdco Limited

64205 Activities of financial services holding companies [36]

AG47 Limited
AU79 Limited
Alycidon Technologies Limited
Argos Business Solutions Limited
BFSL Limited
BGL (Holdings) Limited
BGL Group Limited
Barbon Holdings Limited
Beck Bidco Limited
Bracken Midco1 PLC
Bracken Midco2 Limited
Capital One Holdings Limited
Capital One Investments Limited
Digital House Group Ltd
Experian Finance 2012 Limited
Experian Finance PLC
Goldmore Asset Management Limited
Hagerty Holdings Limited
Hyde Industrial Holdings Limited
Jensten Group Limited
Jerrold Finco PLC
LGS Capital Limited
Lattice Trading Limited
Maxxia (UK) Limited
N.F.U. Mutual Management Co Ltd
Nirvana Holdings Limited
Porterbrook Holdings I Limited
Porterbrook Holdings II Limited
Quint Holdings Ltd
RDG Midas Holdings (NI) Limited
Redhill Famco Limited
South Yorkshire Investment Fund Limited
Uris Central Administration Limited
Uris Topco Limited
Yourcash Europe Limited
Yourcash Solutions Limited

64209 Activities of other holding companies n.e.c. [370]

A-Plan Group Ltd
A.F. Switchgear (Holdings) Limited
ALC (Superholdco) Limited
Achilles Group Holdings Limited
Achilles Group Limited
Achilles Holdco Limited
Achilles Subholdings Limited
Advanced Marketing (Europe) Limited
Advancis Holdings Limited
Advent Topco Limited
Aga-Rayburn Limited
Agrivert Holdings Limited
Alkane Energy Limited
Alvedius Ltd
Amey Belfast Schools Partnership Hold Co Ltd
Amey Hallam Highways Holdings Limited
Amey Holdings Limited
Amey Lighting (Norfolk) Holdings Limited
Amey Ventures Asset Holdings Limited
Amey Ventures Investments Limited
Amey Ventures Limited
Amey Ventures Management Services Ltd
AmeyCespa (AWRP) Holding Co Limited
AmeyCespa (MK) Holding Co Limited
Anglia Components Investments Limited
Apex Stainless Holdings Limited
Appia Europe Limited
Apted Holdings Limited
Armstrong Brooks Limited
Arugani Limited
Ascend Global Holdings, Ltd.
Ascend Global Intermediate Holdings, Ltd.
Aspall Holdings Limited
Autologic Diagnostics Holdings Limited
BHL (UK) Holdings Ltd
BWSC Power Corporation Limited
Bakkavor Estates Limited
Ballylynch Capital Limited
Bantham Holdings Ltd
Barron McCann Holdings Limited
Beachampton Group Limited
Belgium Bidco Limited
Belgium Midco Limited
Belgium Topco Limited
Graham Bell (Holdings) Limited
Bell Euro Finance Limited
Belvoir Lettings PLC
Bio Energy (UK) Limited
Blancco (Software) Services Limited
Bollington Wilson Group Limited
H C Bourn (Holdings) Limited
Brands Holdings Limited
Breas Technologies (UK) Limited
British Business Bank PLC
Russell Burgess Limited
Buxton Consortium Limited
C3 Construction Holdings Limited
CI Beatrice II Facility (BOWL) Limited
CI Beatrice II Facility (CI II) Limited
CI Brite (UK) Holdings Limited
CMS Cepcor (Holdings) Limited
CNH Bidco Limited
CPF Commercial Limited
Caesar Bidco Limited
Caesar Midco Limited
Caesar Topco Limited
Canaveral Bidco Limited
Canaveral Holdco Limited
Carden Croft (2012) Limited
Cavalier Marketing Holdings Limited
Cemex UK
Center Parcs (Holdings 1) Limited
Center Parcs (Holdings 3) Limited
Center Parcs Limited
Clarendon Office Group Ltd.
Codemasters Holdings Limited
Cognita BondCo Parent Limited
Cognita Financing PLC
Cognita Funding 1 Limited
Cognita Holdings Limited
Cognita International Holdings Limited
Cognita Limited
Cognita Midco Limited
Cognita UK Brazil Holdings Limited
Cognita UK Holdings Limited
Commify Limited
Commify Topco Limited
Conrad Energy Group Limited
Copart Europe Limited
Cosworth Group Holdings Limited
Country Attire Holdings Limited
Country Court Care Homes 3 MB Limited
Country Court Care Homes 3 SB Holdco Ltd
Country Court Care Homes 3 SB Limited
Coveris Flexibles Holdings UK Limited
Cristal Inorganic Chemicals UK Limited
Crown Crest Group Limited
DCS Inc Limited
DMWSL 631 Limited
DMWSL 632 Limited
DMWSL 633 Limited
DSS Group Limited
Dalepak Holdings Limited
Delgarth 2011 Limited
Deltic Group Holdings Limited
Desford Acquisition Company (UK) Limited
Doc Bidco Limited
Doc Debtco Limited
Doc Midco Limited
Doc Topco Limited
Donvale Holdings Limited
Dransfield Properties Investments Ltd
Durham & Co Holdings Limited
Dynamic Procurement Holdings Limited
E-PPL Holdings Limited
E.On Climate & Renewables UK Limited
E.On Climate & Renewables UK London Array Ltd
E.On Climate & Renewables UK Operations Ltd
E.On Energy Solutions Limited
E.Surv Limited
E4D & G Holdco Limited
EDL Holdings (UK) Limited
ENSEK Holdings Limited
ENVA Topco Limited
EPAL Holdings Limited

Eaton Holding (UK) II Limited
Eaton Industries (England) Limited
Eaton Industries (U.K.) Limited
Eaton Safety Limited
Eden Holdings Financing Limited
Edina Acquisitions Limited
Elsham Wold Estates Limited
Engineering Technology Group Limited
English Electric Co Ltd
Enterprise Holding Company No 1 Limited
Equity Solutions Lift Investments Ltd
Esendee Holdings Limited
Esland Group Limited
Exel Computer Systems (Holdings) PLC
Experian Group Limited
Experian Holdings Limited
Experian Latam Holdings Unlimited
F & G Holdings Limited
FSP Acquisition Limited
FTR Holdings Ltd
Faero UK Holding Limited
Falcon Bidco Limited
Falcon Equityco 2 Limited
Ferrovial Services UK Ltd.
First Carton Group Ltd
Forterra Holdings Limited
Forterra PLC
Fossil (UK) Holdings Limited
Friar 148 Limited
Funeral Partners Bidco Limited
Funeral Partners Holdco Limited
Funeral Partners Midco Limited
Funeral Services Partnership Limited
GBA Group Limited
GUS Catalogues Unlimited
GUS Holdings Unlimited
Games Workshop Group PLC
Gaming Acquisitions Limited
Gardeden Bidco Limited
Gardeden Midco Limited
Gardeden Topco Limited
ADP Gauselmann UK Limited
Gemsupa Limited
Genie International Holdings Limited
Genie Topco Limited
Go Inspire Group Limited
Green Planet Products Limited
HBVB
HD Holdings II Limited
Halcyon Acquisitions Limited
Halcyon Financing Limited
Halcyon Midco Limited
Halcyon Topco Limited
Hard 8 Limited
Harrison SD Holdings Limited
Roy Hatfield (Holdings) Limited
Hill-Rom UK (Holdings) Ltd
Hive Bidco Limited
Hive Topco Limited
Samuel Hodge Holdings Limited
Holcim Participations (UK) Limited
IRISNDT UK Holdings Limited
Impala Bidco Limited
Inclusion Care Holdings Limited
Indesit Company UK Holdings Limited
Industrial Control Distributors (Holdings) Ltd
Industrial Scientific Holdings UK Ltd
Infinis Energy Group Holdings Limited
Infinis Energy Management Limited
Integrated Bradford Hold Co One Limited
Integrated Bradford Hold Co Two Limited
Jakto Group Limited

Justrite Holdings Ltd
Kaystan Holdings Limited
Kelta Limited
Kent Power Corporation Limited
Kite Packaging Group Holdings Limited
Kite Packaging Group Limited
Knights of Old Group Limited
Lanai Medical Ltd
Launchchange Holding Company
Lenze U.K. Limited
Liberty Group Holdings Ltd
Limes Developments Limited
Lincoln Electric UK Holdings Limited
Logistics Acquisition Company (UK) Ltd
Longshaw Developments Limited
Loomis Investments US Limited
Loomis UK Finance Co Ltd
M & M (MK) Limited
M N Holdings Limited
Merkur Casino UK Ltd
Meter Provida Holdco Limited
Milehouse Foods Limited
Millennium Inorganic Chemicals Overseas Holdings
Millennium Inorganic Chemicals UK Holdings Ltd
Morningside Holdings Ltd
Multi Packaging Solutions Acquisitions 2 Ltd
Multi Packaging Solutions Asia Holdings Ltd
Multi Packaging Solutions GB Limited
Multi Packaging Solutions Global Holdings Ltd
Murley Limited
NAHL Group PLC
NSF International UK Limited
James Neill Holdings Limited
New Terex Holdings UK Limited
Niscayah Holdings Limited
Noble Foods Group Limited
Noble Foods Holdings Limited
Nu-Oval Acquisitions 1 Limited
Nu-Oval Acquisitions 2 Limited
Optimum Debtco Limited
Oxford Instruments UK 2013 Limited
PCMS Investments Holdings Limited
PCS Business Systems Group Limited
PMC Fluidpower Group Limited
Peach Pub Company (Holdings) Limited
J G Pears (Holdings) Limited
Performance Health Global Limited
Phoenix Advance Limited
Pickering Investments Limited
Polar Technology Management Group Ltd
Portbond Limited
Portugal Finco Limited
Powergen International Limited
Powerscreen International Limited
Praesepe Holdings Limited
Prahi (2017) Limited
Quartzinvest Limited
RMS Holdco Limited
RTFH Limited
RTL Bidco Limited
RTL Cleanco Limited
RTL Midco Limited
RTL Topco Limited
Red Box Recorders Group Limited
Regional & City Airports Holdings Ltd
Resmed European Holdings Limited
Richard's Pharma Limited
Rigby Group Finance Limited
Rigby Private Equity Limited

Rochmills (Holdings) Limited
Rotherwood Group Ltd
Rushcliffe Care Holdings Limited
Rushcliffe Specialist Schools (Mickleover) Ltd
Rushcliffe Specialist Schools Limited
S & W Design & Build (Group) Limited
SCGH Limited
SDI (LSL Holdings) Limited
SG International Holdings Limited
SPL II Acquisition Company (UK) Limited
SPL Logistics Holdings Acquisition Company (UK) Ltd
SPL Logistics UK Holdings Limited
Sape Group Holdings UK Ltd
Scantronic Holdings Limited
Sealord (Europe) Limited
Severn Trent Carsington Limited
Severn Trent Corporate Holdings Limited
Severn Trent Draycote Limited
Severn Trent Finance Holdings Limited
Severn Trent Finance Limited
Severn Trent Holdings Limited
Severn Trent Investment Holdings Limited
Severn Trent Overseas Holdings Limited
Severn Trent Services Holdings Limited
Severn Trent Services International (Overseas Holdings) Ltd
Severn Trent Trimpley Limited
Sheffield United Limited
Sigma Components Holdings Limited
Sigma Components Limited
Sigma Components Midco 1 Limited
Sigma Components Midco 2 Limited
Silkstone Finance Limited
Smart Currency Group Limited
Solutionhost Group Limited
Sonepar UK Limited
Sourcecircle Holdings Limited
Spear & Jackson Group Limited
Spear & Jackson Limited
St Matthews Holdings Limited
Steel City Holdings Limited
Steris PLC
Stonbury (Holdings) Limited
Sunshine Care Topco Limited
Surfreset Limited
W.R.Swann & Co.Limited
T-Shirt Guy Holdings Limited
T.C.L. Holdings (Parent) Limited
TGH Acquisitions Limited
TGH Finance Limited
TGH Investments Limited
TRRG Holding Limited
TTKW Limited
Tamar Energy (Holdings) Limited
Tanvic Group Holdings Limited
Technolog Group Limited
Technolog Holdings Ltd
Telent Communications Holdings Limited
Telent Limited
Tensator Holdings Ltd
Terberg Environmental UK Limited
Terberg Rosroca Group Limited
Tilbrook Enterprise Limited
Trafalgar Bidco Limited
Trafalgar Midco 1 Limited
Trafalgar Midco 2 Limited
Trigon Holdings Limited
Trimas Corporation Limited
Tubes Holdco Limited
Tunstall Group Acquisition Limited
Tunstall Group Finance Limited

Tunstall Group Holdings Limited
Tunstall Group Limited
Tunstall Healthcare Group Limited
Tunstall Holdings Limited
Tyler Packaging Holdings Limited
UOS LP Limited
Undercover Holdings Limited
VGI Holdings Limited
Valens Resources Group PLC
Valpak Holdings Limited
Vernon Finance Limited
Vinyl Compounds Holdings Limited
Waterfall Elior Limited
Weatherbys Bank Holdings Limited
Welcome Break Holdings (1) Limited
Welcome Break Holdings Limited
Welcome Break No. 1 Limited
Welcome Break No. 2 Limited
Wheatcroft (Group) Limited
Whirlow Developments Limited
Wilkinson Hardware Stores, Limited
Williams Grand Prix Holdings PLC
Williams Jet Tenders (Holdings) Limited
Willoughby (35) Limited
Willoughby 395 (EBK) Limited
Willowbrook Healthcare Debtco Limited
Willowbrook Healthcare Group Limited
Wintringham Newco1 Limited
Wintringham Newco2 Limited
A H Worth and Co Ltd
Wrengate Holdings Limited
Wrengate Limited
YLH Limited
Zonwering Holdings Limited

64303 Activities of venture and development capital companies [10]

Accelerated Digital Ventures Limited
Angel Cofund
Bell Rock Bidco Limited
Bell Rock Midco Limited
Bell Rock Topco Limited
Finance Yorkshire Limited
Northern Powerhouse Investments Limited
Oxford Sciences Innovation PLC
UK Steel Enterprise Limited
Wake One Limited

64304 Activities of open-ended investment companies

Blue Skies Investments Limited
Oxford Asset Management Co Ltd
Pergamon Finance Corporation Limited
UKKI Limited

64305 Activities of property unit trusts

Clayton (Lincoln) Limited

64306 Activities of real estate investment trusts

Custodian REIT PLC

64910 Financial leasing [17]

Arkle Finance Limited
Blackrock Secured Finance Limited
CVS Leasing Limited
County Asset Finance Limited
Jungheinrich Financial Services Limited
Jungheinrich Lift Truck Finance Limited
Kingsway Asset Finance Ltd
Kingsway Financial Group Holdings Ltd
Kingsway Leasing Limited
Lloyds Bank Commercial Finance Limited
Maxxia Finance Limited
Porterbrook Leasing Asset Co Ltd
Porterbrook Leasing Mid Co Ltd
Porterbrook March Leasing (4) Limited
Santander Asset Finance (December) Ltd
Thistledown Investments Limited
Unicarriers Leasing UK Limited

64921 Credit granting by non-deposit taking finance houses and other specialist consumer credit grantors [17]

Blemain Finance Limited
Bridging Finance Limited
Capital One (Europe) PLC
Cariole Limited
Charles Street Commercial Investments Ltd
First Response Finance Limited
Gemsupa Limited
HBB Bridging Loans Limited
Harpmanor Limited
Hartwell Finance Limited
Home Retail Group Card Services Limited
Mutual Clothing & Supply Co Ltd
Premium Plan Limited
Together Commercial Finance Limited
Together Personal Finance Limited
Vehicle Credit Limited
Welcome Financial Services Limited

64922 Activities of mortgage finance companies

Auction Finance Limited
Dransfield Properties Finance Limited
Godiva Mortgages Limited
ITL Mortgages Limited
MBS Lending Ltd

64929 Other credit granting n.e.c. [13]

Advancis Limited
Aurajoki Europe Limited
Aurajoki Romania Limited
Consolidated Property Wilmslow Limited
Cranbrook (Jewellers) Ltd
DHT Finance Limited
M.A.X. Funding Limited
SRC Transatlantic Limited
Sheepy Magna Limited
Slawston Limited
Snap-On Finance UK Limited
Speedloan Finance Limited
Wasps Finance PLC

64991 Security dealing on own account

Abel Investments Limited
BPHA Finance PLC
Bramah Limited
R Griggs & Co. Limited
Nibgreen
TRG Bonds IV Limited

64992 Factoring

Calverton Finance Limited

64999 Financial intermediation not elsewhere classified [74]

Adient Financing International Ltd
Adient Financing Ltd
Alliance & Leicester Personal Finance Ltd
Apex Credit Management Limited
Assemblies of God Property Trust
Ballyvesey Holdings Limited
Billing Finance Limited
Bodycote America Finance Limited
Brelade Estates Ltd
Brooklime Limited
CCN UK 2005 Limited
CCN UK Unlimited
CLS Finance Limited
Capital One Holdings Limited
Capital One Investments Limited
Centurion Finance (Lincoln) Limited
Chimneys Investment Co Ltd
Countrywide Principal Services Limited
Cullum Detuners Investments Limited
DSGPI 2015 Limited
Daimler Insurance Services UK Limited
Diligenta Limited
Donvale Holdings Limited
EHI 2005 Limited
EHI UK Unlimited
EIS 2005 Limited
EIS UK Unlimited
EMH Treasury PLC
Expatriate Advisory Services PLC
Experian (UK) Holdings 2006 Limited
Experian Investment Holdings Limited
Financial Funding Limited
GUS 1998 Unlimited
GUS 2000 Finance Unlimited
GUS 2004 Limited
Gallos Limited
Gilo Investments Limited
Grand Union Group Funding PLC
Home Retail Group Insurance Services Ltd
Horiba UK Finance Limited
JJC Investments Limited
Key Fund Investments Limited
Kingston Equity & Finance Limited
Lloyds Bank Commercial Finance Limited
Mercedes-Benz Financial Services UK Ltd
Midland Assured Finance Limited
Moorcroft Debt Recovery Limited
Moorcroft Group PLC
Mortgage Advice Bureau Limited
NFU Mutual Select Investments Limited
North Nottinghamshire Lift Project Company (No.1) Ltd
Norton Finance Group Limited
Norton Financial Services Limited
Norton Home Loans Limited
Oakbridge Financial Services Limited
Orbit Treasury Limited
Paccar Financial PLC
Perspective Financial Group Limited
Pirelli International PLC
Porterbrook Leasing Co Ltd
Praesepe Limited
Questport Limited
Rolls-Royce Overseas Holdings Limited
Nigel Skinner Financial Advisers Ltd
Slater Hogg Mortgages Limited
Southern View Finance UK Limited
Stonewater Funding PLC
TSYS Managed Services EMEA Limited
Thistledown Investments Limited

VR Finance Company
Vencap International PLC
Volkswagen Financial Services (UK) Ltd
Yourcash Holdings Limited
Yourcash Limited

65110 Life insurance

Amtrust Lloyd's Holdings (UK) Limited
National Farmers Union Mutual Insurance Society Ltd

65120 Non-life insurance [22]

Amtrust Europe Limited
Amtrust Lloyd's Holdings (UK) Limited
Avon Insurance PLC
BHIB Limited
BICL Limited
Barbon Insurance Group Limited
Brokerbility Holdings Limited
Citynet Insurance Brokers Limited
Croupier Underwriting Limited
Financial & Legal Insurance Co Ltd
Hadleigh Holdings Limited
Herts Insurance Consultants Limited
Ice House Street (No.1) Limited
MCE Insurance Limited
National Farmers Union Mutual Insurance Society Ltd
National House-Building Council
Oriana Underwriting Limited
PIB Risk Services Limited
Personal Assurance PLC
Ranquin Underwriting Limited
URA Ventures Limited
Westfield Contributory Health Scheme Ltd

65202 Non-life reinsurance

Amtrust Europe Limited

65300 Pension funding

DFDS Pension Limited

66120 Security and commodity contracts dealing activities

Forman Hardy Holdings Limited

66190 Activities auxiliary to financial intermediation n.e.c.

ACP Europe Limited
Experian Europe Unlimited
Uris Group Limited

66220 Activities of insurance agents and brokers

A-Plan Holdings
Berkeley Insurance Group Limited
Coversure Insurance Services Limited
I Go 4 Ltd.
Motorway Direct PLC
One Call Insurance Services Limited
PIB Group Limited
Policyfast Limited

66290 Other activities auxiliary to insurance and pension funding

Amey Finance Services Limited
PSV Claims Bureau Limited

66300 Fund management activities [12]

British Business Finance Ltd
British Business Investments Ltd
Howard & Hallam Limited
Investhom Limited
Jardines Finance Limited
N.F.U. Mutual Unit Managers Limited
RVB Investments
Riverleen Finance Unlimited
Serasa Finance Limited
Sheepy Magna Investments Ltd
Slawston Investments Ltd
Woodford Investment Management Limited

68100 Buying and selling of own real estate [161]

A Tiny Hamlet Limited
Aintree Retail Park Limited
B & P Properties Limited
BBHP Limited
Beckhall Properties Ltd
Beechwood Estates Co.Limited
Benchmark Leisure Limited
Binks Developments Limited
Bird Group of Companies Limited
Blenheim Land & Properties Ltd
Blue Anchor Leisure Holdings Limited
Henry Boot Estates Limited
Boughton Estates Limited
Bournemouth Airport Property Investments (Industrial) Ltd
Brighton Marina Block F1 Ltd
Brookhead Estate Limited
Buccleuch Property (Shawfair) Limited
Burbage Capital Limited
Cadent Services Limited
Cambridge Realty Limited
Castle Square Developments Limited
Catesby Estates PLC
Celus Holdings Limited
Cemex UK Properties Limited
Charles Street Buildings (Leicester) Ltd
Chatsworth Investments Limited
Chevin Homes Limited
Clowes Developments (North West) Limited
Clowes Developments (UK) Limited
Condie Investments Limited
Consolidated Property Wilmslow Limited
Cosma Casting UK R.E. Limited
Countywide Developments Limited
Court Properties (Portugal) Limited
Deanbank Investments Limited
Derbyshire Property Trust Limited
Dering Properties Finance Limited
Duncan Investments Limited
Dunelm Estates Limited
Dunkley Family Investments Limited
EOS Inc. Ltd
Eaglebeam Limited
East London Bus Group Property Investments Ltd
East Midlands Property Developments Ltd
Ede Holdings Limited
Emerson Developments (Holdings) Limited
Eraih Limited
Farmland Reserve UK Limited
Farnley Estates Limited
Fellside Estates Limited
GW 305 Limited
Gallagher Developments Holdco Limited
Gallagher Elstow Limited
Gallagher Estates Holdings Limited
Gallagher Estates Limited
Gallagher Estates No. 2 Limited
Gallagher Investments Holdco Limited
Gallagher Llanwern Limited
Gallagher Longstanton Limited
Gallagher Poole Limited
Georgetown Carr Limited
Glanmoor Investments Limited
Global Real Estate Portfolios Limited
Grantham Investments Limited
J.H.& F.W.Green Limited
Ground Group Limited
H.I. Limited
HBB Homes Limited
HBB Relocation Services Limited
HM Estates Limited
Hadrian (Residential) Limited
Hanover Housing Developments Limited
Harley (Winchester) Limited
Harworth Estates (Agricultural Land) Ltd
Harworth Estates (Waverley Prince) Ltd.
Harworth Estates Investments Limited
Harworth Estates Property Group Limited
Hatchback Ltd
Heyford Park Developments Limited
Hyde Investments Limited
Jaguar Estates Investments Limited
Jones Homes (Lancashire) Limited
Jones Homes (North West) Limited
Jones Homes (Southern) Limited
Jones Homes (Yorkshire) Limited
Kaystan Holdings Limited
Kenyon Forge Limited
Kindale Limited
T.H.Kingerlee & Sons Limited
Kingerlee Holdings Limited
Kingerlee Homes Limited
Leda Properties Limited
Jamie Lewis Residential Lettings Ltd
Limes Developments Limited
Lincoln Corn Exchange and Markets (1991) Ltd
Lincoln Diocesan Trust and Board of Finance Ltd
Lousada Investments Limited
Lousada PLC
Malco Holdings Limited
Marden Limited
Maro Developments Limited
Mercedes-Benz Brooklands Limited
Midlands Land Portfolio Limited
Moyallen Woking Limited
Mulberry Property Developments (HGP) Ltd
Newco (First Street) Limited
North West Portfolio Limited
Old Road Securities PLC
Orbit Developments (Manchester) Limited
Orbit Developments (Southern) Limited
Orbit Homes (2020) Limited
Orbit Investments (Northern) Limited
Orbit Investments (Properties) Limited
PTA Developments Limited
Partners in Property (U.K.) Limited
Pattonair Properties Limited
Pendragon Property Holdings Limited
Primesite UK Limited
QD Commercial Group (Property) Limited
Ragi Properties Limited
Reddil Properties Limited
Redlawn Land Limited
Redlawn Limited

Relta Limited
Rolls-Royce Power Development Limited
Roxhill (Peterborough) Limited
Roxhill (Tilbury) Limited
Rylston Road Limited
SMA Estate Holdings Limited
Sami Property Co Ltd
Saw Property Co Ltd
Scenic Land Developments Limited
Sheffield Business Park Limited
Sherwood Homes Limited
Shield Properties Limited
Siddall and Hilton,Limited
Snowmountain Enterprises Limited
Stamford Property Co Ltd
Staton Young (Anglesey) Limited
Stepnell Developments Limited
Strawson Group Developments Limited
Strawson Holdings Limited
M.F. Strawson Limited
Sutton Carter Investments Limited
T N Capital Limited
Tarras Park Properties Limited
Tawnywood Limited
Tenens Ede Limited
Tinsley Park Holdings Limited
G.F.Tomlinson Group Limited
Trapoc Limited
UGC Properties Limited
United Carpets Holdings Limited
Vita York 1 Limited
Westernrange Limited
Wheeldon Brothers Limited
Thomas White Properties Limited
Wixams First Limited
W S Yeates Limited
Yeovil Developments Limited
Zyox Limited

68201 Renting and operating of Housing Association real estate [29]

Acis Group Limited
Amak Property Investments (London) Ltd
B & S Hughes Limited
Bassi Properties Limited
Cranford Asset Management Limited
EOS Inc. Ltd
Extracare Charitable Trust
Framework Housing Association
Futures Homescape Limited
Futures Homeway Limited
Harworth Estates (Agricultural Land) Ltd
Harworth Estates (Waverley Prince) Ltd.
Harworth Estates Investments Limited
Lettings Room Limited
Libra (Longhurst Group) Treasury PLC
Loades PLC
Longleat Property Limited
Lucy Group Ltd
Map Property Investments Limited
Motspa Holdings Limited
Neal Brothers (Leicester) Limited
Principal Healthcare Finance (UK) No.1 Ltd
Principal Healthcare Finance (UK) No.2 Ltd
R.M.F. Properties Limited
Sleekmade Property Co. Limited
South Coast Furnishing Co Ltd
Spire Homes (LG) Limited
Swanton Care & Community (Glenpath Holdings) Ltd
Yeovil Developments Limited

68202 Letting and operating of conference and exhibition centres

Arena Coventry (2006) Limited
Arena Coventry Limited
Bicester Heritage Limited

68209 Other letting and operating of own or leased real estate [361]

107 Station Street Limited
A Tiny Hamlet Limited
A.M.S. Property Management Limited
AWG Land Holdings Limited
Aintree Retail Park Limited
Albanwise Limited
Alconbury Packing Solutions Limited
Arighi Bianchi Holdings Limited
Astrea Limited
Atlas Converting (UK Holdings) Limited
Aus-Bore Estates Limited
Autumnpark Limited
Avondale Property (Holdings) Limited
B & P Properties Limited
B.N.T. Properties Limited
BPI Limited
F.W. Baker Limited
Barrough Hospitality Limited
Baslow Holdings Developments Limited
Bassi Properties Limited
Beckhall Properties Ltd
Beechwood Estates Co.Limited
Belgrave Land (Wisbech) Limited
Charles Bentley Properties Limited
Bicester Heritage Limited
Blenheim Finance Limited
Blenheim Industrial Property Limited
Blenheim Land & Properties Ltd
E.E.Blyth & Co Limited
Bolsover Properties Limited
Boots Properties Limited
Boughton Estates Limited
Bramheath Limited
Branchwater Developments Limited
Breedon House Properties Limited
Brisbane House Limited
Brookhead Estate Limited
Broome Management Co. Limited
Broomgrove Properties Limited
Burbage Capital Limited
Burghley House Preservation Trust Ltd
Burrough Court Estate Limited
Bury's Dryanstore Limited
Business Village Limited
C Student Services Limited
CP Elveden Village Limited
CP Longleat Village Limited
CP Sherwood Village Limited
CP Whinfell Village Limited
CPG 2016 Limited
CRT Property Investments Limited
Camden Motors (Holdings) Limited
Camden Ventures Limited
Cannon Venture Finance Limited
Carlton Street Trading Limited
Castle Square Developments Limited
Caunton Investments Limited
Cavan Investments Limited
Cemex UK Properties Limited
Centurion Finance (Lincoln) Limited
Charles Street Buildings (Leicester) Ltd
Charles Street Buildings (U.K.) Limited
Church Growth Trust Limited
City Estates (UK) Limited
J.R. Clark Limited
Coastfields Leisure Limited
H.W. Coates Limited
Coleman Investments Limited
Colston Property Partners Limited
Community 1st Oldham (Chadderton) Ltd
Community 1st Oldham (Werneth and Shaw) Ltd
Community 1st Oldham Limited
Community 1st Oldham Tranche 2 Limited
Community 1st Sheffield (Tranche 2) Ltd
Community 1st Sheffield Limited
Community 1st Stockport Limited
Condie Investments Limited
Consolidated Property Wilmslow Limited
William Cook Properties Limited
Corby Land & Development Ltd
Country Court Care Homes 3 Propco Ltd
Coverland UK Limited
Crown Crest (Holdings) PLC
W. Cumber & Son (Theale) Limited
J. Curtis & Sons Limited
Cyden Homes Limited
DV Ventures Limited
Darby Group Ltd
Davison & Co. (Barford) Limited
Davison Property Investments Ltd
Patrick Dean Limited
Dean Property Group Limited
Deanbank Investments Limited
Derbyshire Property Trust Limited
Derbyshire Student Residences Limited
Devonshire Green (Broomgrove Road) Ltd
Devonshire Green (Commercial Properties) Ltd
Devonshire Green (Residential Investments) Ltd
Devonshire Green Holdings Limited
Symon Donovan Properties Limited
Draper Commercial Limited
Dunelm Estates Limited
E.I.R.P Limited
Eaglebeam Limited
Eamar Development (UK) Limited
East Midlands Property Developments Ltd
Eastern Counties Properties Limited
Easternrose Limited
Ede Holdings Limited
Edge Wear Properties Limited
Ellis Bros (Contractors) Limited
Elmsdale Estates Limited
Ely Cloisters Estate Limited
Emerson Developments (Holdings) Limited
Emerson Management Services Limited
Eraglow Building Limited
Estate Incomes Limited
Estates and Leisure Holdings Limited
Ethical Property Co Ltd
Extracare Charitable Trust
Fauxkin Limited
Federal Estates Limited
Fellside Estates Limited
Fields Property Limited
Fugro Properties Limited
G2M Unilets Limited
Gallagher Developments Caerphilly Ltd
Garner Holdings Limited
Gatecrasher Apartments Limited
Gemsupa Limited
Gibbons (Holdings) Limited
Glanmoor Investments Limited

Global Real Estate Portfolios Limited
R.J. & A.E. Godfrey
Goosebrook Limited
Grangefern Properties Limited
Grantham Bros. Limited
Grantham Industries Limited
Grantham Investments Limited
Great Tew Properties Limited
Grimsthorpe & Drummond Castle Trust Ltd
Ground Group Limited
HCH Property Limited
HM Estates Limited
Halgram Limited
Hammond Grange Limited
Hampton (Burlington Court) Ltd
Haramead
Harewood Moor Estates Limited
Harington Investments Limited
Harving Limited
Harworth Estates Property Group Limited
Hatchback Ltd
Haven Housing Limited
Hemswell Estates Limited
Heyford Residential Limited
Highcroft Investments PLC
Holding Holding Co Ltd
Homecome Limited
House & Home (Lettings) Ltd
Howard & Hallam Limited
Humphris (Banbury) Limited
John Hurt Estates (UK) Limited
Huttons Buildings Limited
Ikea Properties Investments Limited
Investco Limited
Ivygrove Developments Limited
Jaddu Ltd
A W James Limited
Adam James Limited
J.Jelley and Son Limited
Jennings of Garsington Limited
P.E.Jones (Properties) Limited
Jordan Developments (UK) Limited
Jx2 Limited
K & S Buildings Limited
Kadima Properties (UK) Limited
Kaystan Holdings Limited
Kelmarsh Trust
Kenyon Forge Limited
Keystone Developments (LG) Limited
Kidderminster Property Investments Ltd
Kindale Limited
Kingscrown Properties Limited
L. & M. Investment Co Ltd
Laen Limited
Land and Estates Commercial Properties Ltd
Larchsilver Properties Limited
Lazarus Properties Limited
Leda Properties Limited
Leicester Lettings Limited
Leicester Lift Project Company (No.2) Ltd
Jamie Lewis Residential Lettings Ltd
Lexitron Limited
Lifford Industrial Properties Ltd
Limes Developments Limited
Limes Estates Limited
Limestone Farming Co Ltd
London Clapham Investments and Developments Ltd
Loxton Developments Limited
Lukegate Limited
A.J.Mackaness Limited
Maltgrade Limited
Manston Investments Limited
Maplebeck Holdings Limited
Marlborough Property (Watermead) Limited
Marshalls Yard Limited
Maryland Securities Limited
Mays Properties Limited
McGowan Investments Limited
Megaclose Limited
Mellors Group Fantasy Island Holdings Ltd
Metlane Limited
Midcity Estates Limited
Midcity Investments Limited
Mira Land Limited
Mira Technology Park Limited
Morgan Industrial Properties Limited
Morpeth II Limited
Moyallen Woking Limited
Mumford's Mill Rentals Limited
W.H.Munsey Limited
Myton Investments Ltd
Nene Group PLC
New City Hotels Limited
North Lincs Property Limited
North West Portfolio Limited
Nottingham City Airport Limited
OM Properties Investment Co Ltd
Oakley Lorien Limited
Old Road Securities PLC
Omnitrade Limited
Openshaw Regeneration Limited
Orbit Developments (Manchester) Limited
Orbit Developments (Southern) Limited
Orbit Investments (Northern) Limited
Orbit Investments (Properties) Limited
Oxford Science Park Limited
Oxhold Limited
P V H Holdings Limited
P.A. Estates Management Limited
PEM 2000 Limited
Palmer Family Trust PLC
Paragon Property Investments Limited
Trevor Parr Associates Limited
Pauley Properties Limited
Pelham Homes Limited
Peppermint Grove Ltd
F. Perkins Limited
K. & O. Peros (Oxford) Limited
Pickering Developments Limited
Pickering Properties Limited
Pineapple Letting Ltd
Pinstone Securities Limited
Ponsford Investments Limited
H. Ponsford Limited
Prahi (2017) Limited
Pury Hill Limited
QD Commercial Group (Property) Limited
Quartzinvest Properties Ltd
R.T. Consultants Limited
Radford Holdings Limited
Ragi Properties Limited
Ransomwood Estates UK Limited
Ravent Limited
Raynsway Estates Limited
Raynsway Properties Limited
Real Estate Income Trust (SC) Limited
Real Estate Income Trust Limited
Reflex Group Limited
Rodenhurst Estates Limited
Romo (Holdings) Limited
Russell Acott Limited
Ryedale Estates Limited
SDI (Belfast) Limited
SDI (Edinburgh) Limited
SDI (Enfield) Limited
SDI (Jersey Holding) Limited
SDI (Liverpool) Limited
SDI (Manchester Cheetham Hill) Limited
SDI (Nottingham) Limited
SDI (Oxford Street) Limited
SDI (Thurrock) Limited
SJC 14 Limited
SJC 15 Limited
Samsons Limited
Scania Real Estate (UK) Limited
Selectkey Limited
Sheffield Business Park Limited
Shoby Properties Limited
Sibson Mill Properties Limited
Social Justice and Human Rights Centre Ltd
Southern Derbyshire Lift Project Company (No.2) Ltd
Southport Golf Complex Limited
Sovereign Crest Limited
Speeds (Burton) Limited
Speeds Limited
Springfield Park Properties Limited
Stamford Property Co Ltd
Stanton Investments Limited
Stepnell Developments Limited
Stockshape Limited
Stone House Investments Limited
Strawson Group Developments Limited
Strawson Group Investments Limited
Strawson Management Limited
Sunrisestar Limited
Suon Limited
Surfpipe Limited
Syita Properties Limited
Syncimage Limited
TVCO Limited
TWS Property Limited
Tamar (Selby) Limited
Tansor (Cornbow) Limited
Tawnywood Limited
Tegama Limited
Thames Land Limited
B & K Thomas (Holdings) Limited
Thornhill Estates Limited
Thornsett Properties Limited
Tingdene (MJ) Limited
Tingdene Holdings Limited
Tingdene Marinas Limited
Tingdene Parks Limited
Topalpha Limited
Trafalgar Court Northern Limited
Tresefir Limited
Trinley Estate Limited
Tripleteam (Developments) Limited
Trison Estates Limited
Trust Estates (Clarence Street) Limited
G.B.Turnbull Limited
Turner Investments Ltd.
Twitten Trustees Limited
UGC Properties Limited
United Church Schools Foundation Ltd
Unity Property Holdings Limited
University of Warwick Science Park Ltd
Varsity Design Limited
Vernon Holdings Limited
Vita First Street Limited
Walker & Son (Hauliers) Limited
Dare Warwick (Properties) Limited
Welbeck Estates Co Ltd
John A.Wells Limited

W.Westerman Limited
Westmoreland Investments Limited
Westmoreland Properties Limited
J.Wharton (Shipping) Limited
Wheatcroft Properties Limited
Wheeldon Brothers Limited
Whizstock
Wigley Contracts (Barby) Limited
Wilcox Holdings Limited
Willoughby (396) Limited
Woodland Buildings Investment Co Ltd
Working Assets Limited
Worksop Manor Estates,Limited
P A Wright & Sons Limited
Zyox Limited

68310 Real estate agencies

Avenue Lets Limited
Hall Contracts (Lakenheath) Limited
Oxcis Limited
Wickes Properties Limited
Yeovil Developments Limited

68320 Management of real estate on a fee or contract basis [54]

A Tiny Hamlet Limited
Abbey Properties Cambridgeshire Limited
Aintree Retail Park Limited
Amey Belfast Schools Partnership PFI Co Ltd
Amey Hallam Highways Limited
Beechfield Estates Limited
Bellrock Property & Facilities Management Ltd
Berneslai Homes Limited
Blue Support Services Limited
Henry Boot Land Holdings Limited
Breedon House Properties Limited
R.J.Brown & Sons Limited
Cadent Services Limited
Celus Holdings Limited
Ceylon Tea Growers Association,Limited
Community 1st Sheffield (Tranche 2) Ltd
Deanbank Investments Limited
Derby Homes Limited
Dunelm Estates Limited
E4D & G Project Co Limited
Education Solutions Speke Limited
Emerson Developments (Holdings) Limited
Emerson Management Services Limited
Ethical Property Co Ltd
First National Housing Trust Limited
Gallagher Projects Limited
Glanmoor Investments Limited
J.H.& F.W.Green Limited
Nell Gwynn Limited
Hunter Estates Limited
Integrated Bradford SPV One Limited
Integrated Bradford SPV Two Limited
Lancer Property Holdings Limited
Linford Properties (Leicester) Limited
Malco Holdings Limited
Marlborough Property Co Limited
Milltarn Limited
North West Portfolio Limited
Orbit Investments (Northern) Limited
Orbit Investments (Properties) Limited
PTA Developments Limited
Pelham Homes Limited
Primesite UK Limited
RMA Investments Limited
Red Primrose Ltd
Rotherwood Healthcare Limited
Santander Estates Limited
Staton Young (Anglesey) Limited
Stepnell Developments Limited
Stockport Homes Limited
Sywell Aerodrome,Limited
G.F.Tomlinson Group Limited
University of Warwick Science Park Ltd
Whitecross@Stepnell Limited

69102 Solicitors

Nelsons Solicitors Limited
Thorneycroft Solicitors Limited

69109 Activities of patent and copyright agents; other legal activities n.e.c.

Croner Group Limited

69201 Accounting and auditing activities

Bakkavor Central Finance Limited
Bakkavor Finance Limited
Emerson Process Management Shared Services Ltd
Hyde Group Holdings Limited
PKF Cooper Parry Group Limited
Smith Cooper Audit Limited

69203 Tax consultancy

PKF Cooper Parry Group Limited

70100 Activities of head offices [865]

2morrow Group Limited
AAH Limited
AGCO International Limited
AGCO Manufacturing Limited
AGCO Services Limited
APS Group Limited
ASG Group Associates Limited
AWG Group Limited
AWG Parent Co Limited
Aalberts Industries Limited
Aalberts Industries U.K. Ltd.
Abaco UK Holdco Limited
Abacus Lighting Holdings Limited
Abbey Group Cambridgeshire Limited
Abbeyfield V.E. Limited
Ability Matters Group Limited
Acentic Holdings Limited
Acertec Engineering Limited
Acertec UK Limited
Adenwood Limited
Adept Care Homes Limited
Adient Holding Germany Ltd
Adient Holding UK Ltd
Adient Properties UK Ltd
Admenta Holdings Limited
Admenta UK Limited
Aga Rangemaster Group Limited
Agellus Holdings Limited
Agellus Limited
Agritec Holdings Limited
Agriturf Holdings Limited
Agrivert Group Limited
Airline Investments Limited
Geo.Akins (Holdings) Limited
Aldi Stores Limited
Alere UK Holdings Limited
Alere as Holdings Limited
All Assist Limited
Allerford Intermediate Newco Limited
Alliance Medical Acquisitionco Limited
Alliance Medical Holdings Limited
Allied Textile Companies Limited
Alpha Holdco 1 Limited
Alumasc Group PLC
Alumax U.K. Limited
Ametek Aerospace and Defense Group UK Ltd
Ametek European Holdings Limited
Amey PLC
Amey UK PLC
AmeyCespa Limited
Amtech Group Limited
Amtrust International Limited
Anglian Venture Holdings Limited
Anglian Water Services Holdings Limited
Anglian Water Services Limited
Anisa Consolidated Holdings Limited
Anisa Group Holdings Limited
Anisa Supply Chain Solutions Limited
Arconic UK Finance
Arconic UK Holdings Limited
Arden Topco Limited
Argonaut Bidco Limited
Argos Holdings Limited
Ark Capital Limited
Artisan (UK) PLC
Asgard Group Ltd
Atlas Hotels (Borrowings 2) Limited
Atlas Hotels (Group 3 Property) Limited
Atlas Hotels (Property and Trading) Ltd
Aurora Fashions Finance Limited
Autins Group PLC
Avant Homes (No.2) Limited
Avant Homes Group Limited
Avant Homes Group No.2 Limited
Avant Homes Holdings Limited
Avant Homes Limited
Avdel Holding Limited
Avery Care (Cannock) Limited
Avery Healthcare Group Limited
Avery Healthcare Holdings Limited
Avingtrans PLC
Avon UK Holdings Limited
Axis Intermodal Limited
B.L. Marketing Limited
BBRG (Purchaser) Ltd
BBRG (Subsidiary) Ltd
BBRG Finance (UK) Ltd.
BBRG Holding (UK) Ltd
BBRG Operations (UK) Ltd.
BBRG Production (UK) Ltd.
BCA Marketplace PLC
BCHK UK Limited
BCN Holdco Limited
BDB Design Build Holdings Limited
BI Group Limited
BI Worldwide Holdings Limited
BPB Finance (No. 4) Limited
BPB Finance (No.2) Limited
BPB Group Finance Limited
BPB Group Operations Limited
BPB Investments Overseas Limited
BPB Limited
BPS Warwick Limited
F.W. Baker Limited
Ball Horticultural Europe Limited
Ballyvesey Holdings Limited
Barbara Limited
Barcode Warehouse Group Limited
Barons Eden Group Limited
Bassi Group (Nottingham) Limited

Battles Limited
Bauer Consumer Media Limited
Bauer Golden Square Limited
Bauer Radio Limited
Baxi Finance Limited
Baxi Group Limited
Baxi Holdings Limited
Baxi Overseas Holdings Limited
Baxi Potterton Limited
Bayard Metering (UK)
Bedfordia Group Limited
Belfield Group Limited
Bell Rock Workplace Management Limited
Bellotto Acquisition Limited
Bellotto Finance Limited
Bellotto Holdings Limited
Benchmark Holdings PLC
Bennie Holdings Limited
Billington Holdings PLC
Biogen (UK) Limited
Blackrow Corporation Limited
Blackwell Limited
Blancco Technology Group PLC
Bloor Holdings Limited
Bloor Investments Limited
Blue Skies Holdings Limited
Blugilt Holdings Limited
E.E.Blyth & Co Limited
Blythmore Limited
Bobby's Acquisition Limited
Bodycote Finance UK Limited
Bodycote Investments
Bodycote PLC
Bodypower Sports Holdings Limited
Bollin Group Limited
Henry Boot PLC
Boots Company PLC
Bourns (UK) Acquisition Limited
Wilson Bowden Limited
Bramptonia Limited
Branston Holdings Limited
Brayford Hotels Holdings Ltd
Breedon Holdings Limited
Bridge Leisure Bidco Limited
Bridge Leisure Finco Limited
Bridge Leisure Midco Limited
Bridge Leisure Topco Limited
Bridon Holdings Limited
Bridon Limited
Bridon-Bekaert Ropes Group (UK) Ltd
Bridon-Bekaert Ropes Group Ltd
Brigam Limited
Briggs & Forrester (UK) Limited
Briggs & Forrester Group Limited
Briggs & Forrester Limited
Brighterkind Limited
C Butt Holdings Limited
Buzz Entertainment Limited
Buzz Holdings Limited
Byrom PLC
CCS Media Limited
CEF Holdings Limited
CET Group Holdings Limited
CEVA Limited
CPL Industries Group Limited
CPL Industries Holdings Limited
CPL Industries Limited
Cad Cam Holdings Limited
Caledonia Bidco Limited
Caledonia Topco Limited
Caledonia Venus Acquisitions Limited
Caledonia Venus Group Limited
Caledonia Venus Holdings Limited
Calor Group Limited
Cambridge Nutritional Foods Limited
Canon Street Properties Limited
Cape UK Holdings Newco Limited
Capital One Holdings Limited
Capital One Investments Limited
Carbolite Holdings Limited
Carentan Holdings Limited
Carewatch Bidco Limited
Carewatch Holdings Limited
Carmelite Finance Limited
CarnaudMetalbox Group UK Ltd.
CarnaudMetalbox Overseas Ltd.
Carter Accommodation Holdings Limited
Carwood Holdings Limited
Castle 1 Limited
Castlegate 624 Limited
Caterpillar UK Engines Co Ltd
Caterpillar UK Group Limited
Ceetak Holdings Limited
Celixir PLC
Cemex Investments Limited
Center Parcs (Operating Company) Limited
Central Aggregates Ltd
Cespa UK Limited
Chargill (Holdings) Ltd
Charles Street Buildings (Leicester) Ltd
Chevron Traffic Management (Holdings) Ltd
Chiltern Distribution Ltd
Chivgate Limited
Christy Home Textiles Limited
Cintra Infrastructures SE
Clegg Group Limited
Clegg Holdings Limited
Clientlogic (UK) Holding Limited
Clientlogic Holding Limited
Clugston Group Limited
Coast Holdco 1 Limited
Coast Holdco 2 Limited
Coba International Limited
Colbert Wall Holdings Limited
Comet REFICO Limited
Commatone Limited
Compass Acquisitions Limited
Compass Community Ltd
Compass Holdco Limited
Complete Medical Group Worldwide Limited
Consumer Champion Group Limited
William Cook Cast Products Limited
Thomas Cook Group UK Limited
Cornshire Limited
Croda Europe Limited
Croda International PLC
Croda Investments No 3 Limited
Croda Overseas Holdings Limited
Crown UK Holdings Limited
W. Cumber & Son (Theale) Limited
J. Curtis & Sons (Holdings) Limited
Cuttech Limited
DFDS Seaways PLC
DFS Furniture Co Ltd
DFS Furniture Holdings PLC
DFS Furniture PLC
DH Alpha Limited
DH Omega Limited
DH UK Finance Limited
DK Group Investments Ltd.
DNC Holdings Limited
DPG Holdings Limited
DS John Holdings Limited
DTIL UK Limited
DW3 Products Group Limited
DW3 Products Holdings Limited
Dagless Holdings Limited
Daimler UK Limited
Datac Adhesives Limited
Datapath Group Limited
Davane Holding Co Ltd
Dawsongroup PLC
Deb Group Holdings Limited
Dee Valley Group Limited
Dee Valley Water (Holdings) Limited
Deeley Group Limited
Dematic (Services) Limited
Dematic Group Limited
Denby Pottery Co Ltd
Diamond Holdco 2 Limited
Diamond Holdco 7 Limited
Dippy Ridge Limited
Distinction Group Limited
Dodson & Horrell Group Limited
Dr Martens Airwair Group Limited
Drishaun Holdings Limited
Dry Mix Solutions UK Limited
Drybrough Trading Limited
Duki (2006) Finance Limited
Dunelm Group PLC
Dunstall Holdings Limited
Dyson Group PLC
E M Holdings UK Limited
E.A.T. (Holdings) Limited
E.F.B. Group Limited
E.I.R.P Limited
EMA Holdings UK Limited
EMB-Group Ltd
ESCO (UK) Holdings Limited
ESCO EMEA Holdings (UK) Limited
ESNT Holdings (No.1) Limited
ESNT Holdings (No.2) Limited
Eagle Hall Estates Limited
Earlham Trading Co Ltd
Eastgate Care Group Ltd
Echostar UK Holdings Limited
Eco-Bat Technologies Limited
Economy Energy Holdings Limited
Eden Care & Support Group Limited
Eden Care Solutions Limited
Elior UK Holdings Limited
Elli Finance (UK) PLC
C.S. Ellis (Holdings) Limited
Elmdene Group Limited
Emerson Developments (Holdings) Limited
Emerson International Limited
Emhart International Limited
English Electric Co Ltd
Ensco 1066 Limited
Ensco 645 Limited
Ensco 648 Limited
Enterprise PLC
Entertainment Magpie Group Limited
Envigo Developments Limited
Equita Limited
Esendex Bidco Limited
Esendex Holdings Limited
Esendex Midco Limited
Esendex Topco Limited
Essenden Limited
Essentra Filter Products International Ltd
Essentra International Limited
Essentra PLC
Euro E-Land Company PLC
Eurocell Group Limited
Eurocell Holdings Limited

Eurocell PLC
Evans Halshaw.Com Limited
Evo Group Services Limited
Evonik Speciality Organics Limited
Evonik UK Holdings Limited
FCL Organisation Ltd
FR Acquisitions Corporation (Europe) Ltd
FSHC (UK) Limited
FTD UK Holdings Limited
Faccenda Investments Limited
Fandstan Electric Limited
Farol Holdings Limited
Fernwood Group Limited
Fevore Limited
Fifthgrange Limited
Firth Rixson Limited
Flint Holdings Limited
Flocklynn Limited
Flowtech Fluidpower PLC
Fluidpower MIP Limited
Focus Solutions Group Limited
Forman Hardy Holdings Limited
Four Seasons Health Care (Capital) Ltd
Fox Lima Holdings Limited
Full Moon Holdings Limited
H.B. Fuller Group Limited
Futures Housing Group Limited
GHP Midco Limited
GL UK Holdings Limited
GRI Group Limited
GRI Libra Limited
Gamston Kennels & Farms Limited
Gands (U.K.)
Gapuma Group Limited
Gelder Group Holdings Limited
Gellaw 101 Limited
General Domestic Appliances Holdings Ltd
Generation Two Limited
Genistics Holdings Limited
Georgia GC Holdings Limited
Germanischer Lloyd Industrial Services Holdings (UK) Ltd
Ghekko Holdings Limited
Gill Marine Holdings Limited
Gilzoni Limited
Gladstone Limited
Glid Wind Farms Topco Limited
Global Derby (UK) Limited
Good 'n' Natural Limited
Granwood Holdings Limited
J.H.& F.W.Green Limited
Green Sky Energy Limited
Group GTI Ltd
Grove Industries (Holdings) Ltd
Guilbert UK Holdings Limited
Guilford Mills Europe Limited
Guilford Mills Limited
H (Lincs) Limited
HB Healthcare Limited
HBVB
HJE Limited
HLD Holdings Limited
Hadfield Properties Limited
Hancocks Acquisition Limited
Hancocks Group Holdings Limited
Hancocks Holdings Limited
Hancocks Midco Limited
Harting UK Limited
Hartwell Holdings Limited
Hartwell PLC
Harworth Group PLC
HaskoningDHV UK Holdings Limited
HaskoningDHV UK Limited
Health & Diet Group Limited
Heating Finance Limited
Hella UK Holdings Limited
Hexadex Limited
Hicks (1) Limited
Hillbridge Investments Limited
Hilton Food Group PLC
History & Heraldry Holdings Limited
Samuel Hodge Limited
Holland & Barrett Group Limited
Holland & Barrett Holdings Limited
Holland & Barrett International Limited
I Holland Holdings Limited
Home Retail Group Limited
P. D. Hook (Group) Limited
Horberg & Co Holdings Ltd
Horbury Group Limited
Hosting Developments Limited
Hostombe Group Limited
Hunt Group Limited
I.G. Industries Holdings Limited
IFA Metals International Limited
IG Design Group PLC
Ibstock Brick Holding Co Ltd
Ibstock Building Products Limited
Ibstock USA Limited
Ideal Industries Holdings Limited
Idverde Holdings Limited
Idverde UK Limited
Incat International PLC
Inclusion Care Group Limited
Indoor Bowling Acquisitions Limited
Indoor Bowling Equity Limited
Ingeus UK Holdings Limited
Ingleby (2016) Limited
Ingram Micro Holdings Limited
Inspired Gaming Group Limited
Interflora Group Limited
Interflora Holdings Limited
Interlevin Holdings Limited
Intermed Limited
Intrexon UK Insect Holdings Limited
Irth (19) Limited
J W D Holdings Limited
JFB Overseas Holdings Limited
JHC Finance Company
Jabco Capital Limited
Jaguar Land Rover Automotive PLC
Warren James Holdings Limited
A W James Limited
Jardentome Limited
Jaywing PLC
Jeld-Wen Europe Ltd.
Jelson Holdings Limited
Jenoptik Holdings UK Ltd
P.E.Jones (Properties) Limited
Joules Investments Holdings Limited
Jourdan PLC
K & A Merger Limited
K.M. Packaging Holdings Limited
KCI Holding UK Limited
KCT Holdings Limited
Kab Seating Limited
Kadima Holdings Limited
Kal Tire Southern African Holdings Ltd
Keepmoat Limited
I M Kelly Holdings Limited
William Kenyon & Sons Limited
Kermotion UK Holdings Limited
Key Technologies Limited
Keystone Bidco Limited
Keystone Financing PLC
Keystone JVCO Limited
Keystone Midco Limited
Keystone Topco Limited
Kinaxia Limited
Kinaxia Transport and Warehousing Ltd
Kuehne + Nagel Drinkflow Logistics Holdings Ltd
LTAG UK Limited
Lablogic Group Holdings Limited
Lakeside 1 Limited
Lakeside Energy from Waste Holdings Ltd
Langley Holdings PLC
Lapwing Estate Limited
Larkfleet Homes Limited
Launchchange Finance Limited
Launchchange Holdings Limited
Launchchange Instrumentation Limited
Launchchange Limited
Launchchange Operations Limited
Laurenglen Limited
Lavendon Access Services (International) Ltd
Lavendon Holdings Limited
Laver Regeneration Holdings Limited
Leaderflush + Shapland Holdings Limited
J.T. Leavesley Limited
Leicester Fancy Box Co Ltd
Lemac No.1 Limited
Lincat Group Limited
Linecross Group Limited
Linx Acquisition Limited
Lister Wilder Group Limited
Lloyd Fraser Holdings Co Ltd
Lockheed Martin UK Ampthill Group Ltd
Lockwood Group Limited
Longcliffe Group Limited
Loxwood Holdings Limited
Luxfab Limited
M.P.K. Group Limited
M3 Medical Holdings Ltd
MHR Global Holdings Limited
ML UK Holding Limited
MPS Care Group Limited
MS International PLC
MWUK Holding Co Ltd
MacIntyre Hudson Holdings Limited
A J Mackaness Holdings Limited
Manthorpe Limited
HW Martin Holdings Limited
Massarella Catering Group Limited
Maximus HHS Holdings Limited
McCann Health Medical Communications Ltd
Megaflo Limited
Melham Group Limited
Meller Group Limited
Mellors Group Limited
Metals & Materials Limited
Meter Provida Investments Limited
Micromass Holdings Limited
Micromass Limited
Middleby Holding UK Ltd
Middleby UK Residential Holding Ltd
Midland Assured Holdings Limited
Karen Millen Holdco 1 Limited
Karen Millen Holdings Limited
Minova International Limited
Mintridge Investments (Wikowo) Limited
Mintun 3 Limited
Mission Resources Group Limited
Monier (China) Holdings Limited
Monier (UK) Holdings Limited

J.H. Moore & Son (Rickmansworth) Ltd
Morgana Holdings Limited
Morrells Holdings Limited
Morris Group Limited
Mortgage Advice Bureau (Holdings) PLC
Motorhog Holdings Limited
Move Factory Holdings Limited
Moyallen Woking Limited
Multi Packaging Solutions Acquisitions 1 Ltd
Munro Building Services Holdings Limited
Murray Bidco Limited
My Home Move Ltd
NAH Group Limited
NAH Holdings Limited
NBCMH Holdings Limited
NBH Holdco Limited
NCL Holdings Limited
NIC Holdings (UK) Limited
NJDR Group Ltd
Nampak Holdings (UK) Limited
Nasmyth Group Limited
National Floorcoverings Group Limited
Nationwide Windows Holding Co Ltd
James Neill Holdings Limited
Nene Group Holdings PLC
Network Group Holdings Limited
New Testament Church of God
Newell and Wright (Holdings) Limited
Newincco 1382 Limited
Newincco 1386 Limited
Newtco Limited
Next Holdings Limited
Next PLC
Nicholas Associates Holdings Limited
John Nicholls (Holdings) Limited
Nickle Holdings Limited
Node 4 Holdings Limited
Norbar Torque Tools Holdings Limited
Norbrook Holdings Limited
Norcros Group (Holdings) Limited
Norcros PLC
North Bidco Limited
North Midco Limited
Northbridge Australia Limited
Nova Bio-Pharma Holdings Limited
Nuttall Group Limited
O & M-Movianto UK Holdings Ltd.
OGF Bidco Limited
OGF Topco Limited
OISE Holdings Limited
OSI International Holdings Limited
Oasis Fashions Holdings Limited
Oasis and Warehouse Holdco 1 Limited
Oasis and Warehouse Holdco 2 Limited
Office 1 Limited
Office Depot (Holdings) Limited
Office Depot Europe Holdings Limited
Omega Acquisition Bidco Limited
Omega Red Holdings Limited
On Line Group Limited
Oncimmune Holdings PLC
Optilan Group Limited
Optimum Debtco Limited
Orbital Education Limited
Orca Marine Leisure Limited
Orchid Orthopedic Solutions Ltd
Osprey Holdco Limited
Ossur UK Holding Limited
Oxford Instruments Nanotechnology Tools Holdings Ltd
Oxford Instruments Overseas Holdings 2008 Ltd
Oxford Instruments Overseas Holdings Ltd
Oxford Instruments PLC
Oxford Metrics PLC
P V H Holdings Limited
P. H. Properties Ltd
P3 Group Europe Limited
PAG International Limited
PCMS International Holdings Limited
PV Crystalox Solar PLC
G W Padley Holdings Limited
Pall UK Holdings Limited
Palma Bidco Limited
Paramount Holdings (UK) Limited
W. T. Parker Group Services Limited
W T Parker Holdings Limited
Parkers Motor Services (Syston) Limited
Parkers of Leicester Limited
Parseq Limited
Partnerships in Children's Services Ltd
Passionate About People Limited
Pauley Group Limited
Peacock & Binnington Holdings Limited
Peak Gen Top Co Limited
A Pearson Holdings Limited
Pendragon Management Services Limited
Pendragon Overseas Limited
Pendragon PLC
Penso Holdings Ltd
Perkins Holdings Limited
Personal Group Holdings PLC
Personal Group Limited
Pets at Home Group PLC
Peugeot Citroen Automobiles UK Limited
Pharos Group Limited
Philex Limited
Phoenix Oil & Marine Limited
Pinelog Group Limited
Pinnacle International Freight Holdings Ltd
Pirelli UK Limited
Polypearl Management Ltd
Ponsford Trading Limited
Premdor U.K. Holdings Limited
Premierfirst Vehicle Rental EMEA Holdings Ltd
Premierfirst Vehicle Rental Holdings Ltd
Pressure Technologies PLC
Prodrive (Holdings) Limited
Prodrive Investments Limited
Produce Investments Limited
Produce World Investments Ltd
Charles Pugh (Holdings) Limited
Punch Taverns (PGE) Limited
Punch Taverns Limited
Purico Limited
Purico Speciality Paper Co Ltd
Pye Homes Limited
QD Commercial Group Holdings Limited
Quadgas Holdco Limited
R Group Holdings Limited
RHS UK Holdings Limited
RM PLC
RMS Europe Group Limited
RMS Group Holdings Limited
RPC Group PLC
RPC Pisces Holdings Limited
RTC Group PLC
RVB Holding Co Ltd
Rain Dance Investments Limited
Rayfern Holdings Limited
Realpower Limited
Reconnaissance Ventures Limited
Reflex Group Limited
Regenersis (Depot) Services Ltd
Renewi Cumbria Holdings Limited
Resonate Holdings Limited
Revolve Group Limited
Richard's Pharma Limited
Rilmac Holdings Limited
Riverside Motors Holdings Limited
Robinson (Overseas) Limited
Robinson PLC
Rockwell Commercial Holdings Limited
E.M. Rogers Group Limited
Rohm Electronics Europe Limited
Rolls-Royce International Limited
Rolls-Royce Overseas Holdings Limited
F.H.Rowse Limited
Rybrook Holdings Limited
SAI Global CIS UK Limited
SCX Special Projects Holdings Limited
SDL Bigwood Limited
SDL Property Services Group Limited
SHV Energy Holdings UK Limited
SIG European Investments Limited
SMA Estate Holdings Limited
SPD Holdings Limited
SRS Rail System (Holdings) Limited
SWK (U.K.) Holding Limited
SYS8 Holding Limited
Saint-Gobain Construction Products UK Ltd
Saint-Gobain High Performance Materials UK Ltd
Saint-Gobain Isover UK Limited
Saint-Gobain Limited
Saint-Gobain Performance Plastics Rencol Ltd
Samworth Brothers (Holdings) Limited
Sandbrook Overseas Investments Limited
Saria Limited
Saybest Limited
Scoto Limited
Scott Bader Commonwealth Limited
Scusi Limited
Seckloe 297 Limited
Sector Aviation Holdings Limited
Select Group International Limited
Sensient Technologies Limited
Sensitlive Limited
Servelec Limited
Severn Trent PLC
Sherwin-Williams UK Holding Limited
Fred Sherwood Group Limited
Sherwood Holdings Limited
Silgan Closures UK Holdings Limited
Sims Group UK Holdings Limited
J O Sims Holdings (1896) Limited
Sitel Europe Limited
Skiptex Limited
Smartway PW. Holdings Limited
Paul Smith (Holdings) Ltd
Paul Smith Group Holdings Limited
Solo Cup (UK) Limited
Soncell International Limited
Sophos Holdings Limited
Sophos Treasury Limited
Source Bioscience Limited
Source Bioscience UK Limited
Southern Derbyshire Lift Project Company (No.2) Ltd
Spear & Jackson Group Limited
Spear & Jackson Limited
Sports Direct International PLC
Stadco Holdings Ltd.
Stadium MK Group Limited

Stamford Group Limited
Stanley U.K. Holding Ltd.
Stepnell Holdings Limited
Stonepit Limited
Storefield Group Limited
Strata Homes Holdings Limited
Stratus (Holdings) Limited
Strawson Group Developments Limited
Strawson Group Investments Limited
Streason Limited
Strevens Vehicles Holdings Limited
Sunrise Eggs Holdings Limited
Sunshine Care Bidco Limited
Sunshine Care Midco Limited
Sunway Travel (Coaching) Holdings Ltd
Swanton Care & Community (Glenpath Holdings) Ltd
Symm Group Limited
Symphony Holdings Limited
Synchemicals Limited
Sytner Group Limited
T-Mobile Holdings Limited
TDY Holdings Limited
TFHC Investments Limited
TGW (Holdings) Limited
TI Automotive (China) Limited
TI Automotive Canada Holdings Limited
TI Automotive Czech Holdings (UK) Ltd
TI Automotive German Holdings (UK) Ltd
TI Automotive Holdings Limited
TI Automotive Korean Won Hedgeco Ltd
TI Automotive Limited
TI Fluid Systems PLC
TIFS Holdings Limited
TNS Transxpress Holding Company (U.K.) Ltd
TPH (UK) Limited
TRB Technology Group Limited
Tallington Holdings Limited
Tanglewood Care Homes Limited
Tarka Controls Limited
Telent Communications Holdings Limited
Telent Limited
Ten Cate UK Limited
Tensator Group Limited
Thermasys CS UK Holding Limited
Thetford Limited
Charles Thompson (UK) Limited
Together Financial Services Limited
G.F.Tomlinson Group Limited
Total Produce Holdings (UK) Limited
Totemic (2014) Holdings Limited
Tours Abroad Group Limited
Tripal Group Limited
Triplex Lloyd Limited
Triumph Motorcycles (Overseas) Limited
Triumph Motorcycles Group Limited
Trueform Engineering Holdings Limited
Tulip International (UK) Limited
Turbo-Union Limited
UDG Healthcare (UK) Holdings Limited
UDG Healthcare UK (Holdco) Limited
UK Ticketing Ltd
Ulverscroft Group Limited
Umeco Limited
Underwood Meat (Holdings) Limited
Unipart Group of Companies Limited
Unipart International Holdings Limited
Unipart Rail Holdings Limited
C.J. Upton Holdings Ltd.
Richard Utley Limited
VJ Holdco UK Limited
VRES Holdings Limited
Vacation Rental Group Holdings Limited
Vaillant European Holdings Limited
Vaillant Home Products Limited
Vaillant Management Limited
Vaillant Netherlands Holdings Limited
Valassis Limited
Van Elle Holdings PLC
Verder Holdings U.K. Limited
Vesso Limited
Viad Service Companies Limited
Vidal Group Holdings Ltd
Viewtone Limited
Viewtone Trading Group Limited
Viking Direct (Holdings) Limited
Vinters International Limited
W.L. Shareholding Co Ltd
Wabtec UK Holdings Limited
Wacoal Europe Ltd
Wade Group Limited
Warehouse Fashions Holdings Limited
Warwick Care Limited
Warwick International Holdings Limited
Warwick International Intermediate Holdings Ltd
Wavin UK (Holdings) Limited
Weatherbys Thoroughbred Holdings Limited
Wellbeing Software Group Holdings Ltd
Wellbeing Software Limited
Wellglade Holdings Limited
Wellglade Limited
Welspun Home Textiles UK Limited
H.K. Wentworth Limited
West Retail Group Limited
Westbrook Holdings Limited
Whitworths Holdings Limited
Willoughby (396) Limited
Willowbrook Healthcare Limited
Winbro Group UK Limited
Woodbury Residual Limited
Wrendal Holdings Limited
Wyndham Destination Network Europe Ltd
Wyndham Holdings
XPO Holdings UK and Ireland Limited
Yorkshire Repak Holdings Limited
Yu Group PLC
Zooom Holdings (UK) Limited

70221 Financial management [10]

Bucks Investments Limited
Buster Jimmy Limited
CPRT European Investments Limited
Frutarom UK Investments Limited
Fugro Holdings Limited
Gregory Family Office Limited
Oakbrook Finance Limited
Potomac Capital Limited
SCR Financial Interventions Holding Co Ltd
Yews Holding Co Ltd

70229 Management consultancy activities other than financial management [37]

Toby Blackwell Limited
Blue Boar Holdings Limited
Business Control Solutions PLC
Byrom PLC
Citation Limited
Danetre Holdings Limited
Fresh Approach (UK) Holdings Limited
Gibbons (Holdings) Limited
Going Plural Limited
Growth Partners Management Limited
Hermitage Holdings (Wilmslow) Limited
Holding JDR Limited
Impero Developments Limited
Impero Holdings Limited
W & J Linney Limited
Loxwood Holdings Limited
Makita International Europe Limited
McGowan Investments Limited
NUS Holdings Limited
NUS Services Limited
Newton Europe Limited
Newton Industrial Consultants Holdings Ltd
Nicholas Associates Group Limited
Opal Ventures Limited
Oxford Policy Management Limited
R.T. Consultants Limited
Resonate Group Limited
Rycote Services Limited
Sape Group Holdings UK Ltd
Sharing in Growth UK Limited
Spark44 (JV) Limited
Sumo Digital Group Limited
TFHC 2015 Limited
Thistledown Investments Limited
Trident 2020 Limited
Trimas UK Aerospace Holdings Limited
University of Warwick Science Park Ltd

71111 Architectural activities

Benoy Limited
Pelham Homes Limited

71112 Urban planning and landscape architectural activities

Benoy Limited
REALL Limited

71121 Engineering design activities for industrial process and production

Atlas Converting (UK Holdings) Limited
Bucyrus Europe Limited
Bucyrus UK Limited
Clyde Bergemann Materials Handling Ltd
Danieli UK Holding Limited
ITP Engines UK Limited
S M C Design and Draughting Services Ltd
Velocys PLC

71122 Engineering related scientific and technical consulting activities

Amey OW Limited
Amey OWR Limited
GL Industrial Services UK Ltd
Integral Powertrain Limited
Technia Limited

71129 Other engineering activities [23]

Agema Engineering Limited
Amey Highways Limited
Amey Rail Limited
BWB Holdings Limited
Cintra Infrastructures SE
Comau U.K. Limited
Lawrence David Limited
Dematic Limited
Fichtner Consulting Engineers Limited
HaskoningDHV UK Limited
Hofer Powertrain UK Limited
Hyde Aero Products Limited

Hyde Details Limited
Hyde Group Limited
RM Property and Facilities Solutions Ltd
RPS Consulting Services Limited
RPS Environmental Management Limited
RPS Group US Holdings Limited
RPS US Holdings Limited
Romax Technology Ltd.
S.E.B. International Limited
Turbine Services Limited
Williams Grand Prix Engineering Limited

71200 Technical testing and analysis

ALS Environmental Limited
Millbrook Proving Ground Limited
Omega Red Group Limited
Orchid Cellmark Ltd
SYS8 Holding Limited
Sensitlive Limited
Socotec UK Limited
Sperry Rail (International) Limited

72110 Research and experimental development on biotechnology [23]

Adaptimmune Therapeutics PLC
Aghoco 1566 (Bidco) Limited
Aghoco 1578 (Midco) Limited
Aghoco 1579 (Topco) Limited
Celleron Therapeutics Limited
Circassia Limited
Circassia Pharmaceuticals PLC
Evotec (UK) Limited
Genzyme Therapeutics Limited
Green Biologics Limited
Oxford Biomedica (UK) Limited
Oxford Biomedica PLC
Oxford Gene Technology (Operations) Ltd
Oxford Gene Technology IP Limited
Plant Impact Limited
Psioxus Therapeutics Limited
Quotient Sciences Holdings Limited
Quotient Sciences Limited
Redx Pharma PLC
Replimune Limited
Summit (Oxford) Limited
Summit Therapeutics PLC
Watch Bidco Limited

72190 Other research and experimental development on natural sciences and engineering [47]

Adaptimmune Limited
Agri-Epi Centre Limited
Aircraft Research Association Limited
Bodycote H.I.P. Limited
CASP
Cambridge Display Technology Limited
Ceravision Limited
Datapath Limited
Diamond Light Source Limited
Drayson Technologies Limited
E - Leather Limited
E-Therapeutics PLC
Element Six (UK) Limited.
Envigo CRS Limited
GE Energy Power Conversion Technology Ltd
HR Wallingford Group Limited
HR Wallingford Limited
Horiba Mira Limited
ITP Engines UK Limited
Immunocore Limited
Intelligent Energy Limited
Intervet UK Limited
Juniper Pharma Services Limited
Lucy Electric (EMS) Limited
MTC Operations Limited
Manufacturing Technology Centre Limited
Mercedes AMG High Performance Powertrains Ltd
Metalysis Limited
Nu Instruments Limited
Oxford Gene Technology Limited
Oxford Nanopore Technologies Limited
Oxford Renewable Fuel Ltd
Oxford Trust
P2I Ltd
Pera International
Rolls-Royce Submarines Limited
SPD Development Co Ltd
Satra
Satra Technology Centre Limited
Scancell Holdings PLC
Sharp Laboratories of Europe, Ltd.
Special New Fruit Licensing Limited
UK Biobank Limited
University of Derby
Velocys PLC
Xeros Limited
Xeros Technology Group PLC

72200 Research and experimental development on social sciences and humanities

Lincoln Science and Innovation Park Ltd
Oncimmune Limited
Romax Technology Ltd.
World Habitat

73110 Advertising agencies

Lagardere Sports UK Ltd
McCann Manchester Limited
McCann-Erickson Network Limited
National Accident Helpline Limited

73120 Media representation services

Ingenta PLC

73200 Market research and public opinion polling

MMR Research Worldwide Limited
Mathematical Market Research Limited
A.C. Nielsen Co Ltd
Nielsen Holdings PLC
Rolls-Royce International Limited

74100 Specialised design activities

Accuride International Limited
Biogen (UK) Limited
DCA Design International Limited
Envisage Group Limited
W & J Linney Limited
Penso Consulting Ltd
Quest Global Engineering Limited

74209 Photographic activities not elsewhere classified

Picsolve International Limited

74901 Environmental consulting activities

Effective Energy Solutions Ltd
Valpak Limited

74909 Other professional, scientific and technical activities n.e.c. [55]

Accelerating Growth Fund Ltd
Agilent Technologies Lda UK Limited
Alere Toxicology PLC
Ashfield Healthcare Communications Group Ltd
Biocity Group Limited
Bridgstock Limited
CAE Aircrew Training Services PLC
CDT Holdings Limited
Cenduit Limited
Conservation Education & Research Trust
Coolsilk Property & Investment Limited
Cosworth Limited
Coventry University Enterprises Limited
Cozart Limited
E.On Control Solutions Limited
E.On Project Earth Limited
EResearchTechnology Limited
Envigo International Limited
Envigo RMS (UK) Limited
Envigo Research Limited
Focus100 Limited
Forest Commercial Services Limited
Fugro GB Marine Limited
Fugro Geos Limited
Fugro Geoservices Limited
Fusion Group Limited
Global Brands Limited
Horiba UK Limited
IMS Bidco Limited
IMS Topco Limited
In at the Side Limited
Inception Point Systems Ltd
Jazz Pharmaceuticals UK Limited
Leica Biosystems Newcastle Limited
Lincolnshire Wildlife Trust
Markem-Imaje Industries Limited
Meter Provida Limited
Mistras Group Limited
Nottingham Enterprise Zone Development Co Ltd
Oxford Economics Limited
Oxford Immunotec Limited
Pendragon Automotive Services Limited
Resonate Group Limited
SAI Global Assurance Services Ltd
SDL Surveying Limited
Satellite Applications Catapult Limited
Satra Technology Centre Limited
Sodexo Motivation Solutions U.K. Limited
South Yorkshire Community Foundation Ltd
Stanhope Partnership Limited
Stanley Black & Decker Finance Limited
Stratstone Motor Holdings Limited
Suon Limited
Teletrac Navman (UK) Ltd
Waste and Resources Action Programme

74990 Non-trading company [156]

3M Health Care Limited
ADA PD UK Limited
AGD Holdings Limited
AMPY Holdings Limited
API Overseas Holdings Limited
ASD Lighting Holdings Limited
Agrihold Limited
Alcaeus Holdings Limited
Alere UK Holdings Limited
Allmakes 4 X 4 Limited
Ames Companies UK Ltd.
Anglian Water Facilities Management Holdings (UK) Ltd
Argos SURBS Investments Limited
Asquith Court Holdings Limited
Aston Martin Holdings (UK) Limited
Aston Martin Investments Limited
Atlas Hotels (Property) Limited
Aurora Fashions Group Limited
Autofil Holdings Limited
Aven Tools Limited
Avon Products Holding Limited
BASF U.K. Holdings Limited
BCQ (Holdings) Limited
Bericote Holdings Limited
Booker Wholesale Holdings Limited
Bradgate Containers (Holdings) Limited
Bransby Horses
Burghley House Preservation Trust Ltd
Business By Technology (Holdings) Ltd
Caledonian Group Holdings Limited
Calor Properties Limited
Cape Industrial Services Group Limited
Carlsberg Chongqing Limited
Carlsberg UK Holdings Limited
Cedar 2015 Limited
Chestnutbay Acquisitionco Limited
Chiron Midco Limited
Citation Holdings Limited
Conchord Limited
Coolsilk Limited
Cristal Investments UK Limited
Croda Investments Limited
Croda Investments No 2 Limited
Cullum Detuners Investments Limited
Dawsongroup UK Limited
Diverseylever Limited
EJ UK Fabrication & Access Solutions Holdings Ltd
ELWA Holdings Limited
EOF Holdings Limited
EResearchTechnology UK 1 Limited
EResearchTechnology UK 2 Limited
ESNT Filter Products Limited
ESNT International Limited
ESNT Packaging & Securing Solutions Ltd
Eco-Bat Technologies GB
Element Six Limited
Elsevier Life Sciences IP Limited
Essentra Services Limited
FMC Corporation United Kingdom Limited
Field Boxmore II Limited
Florida Topco Limited
Forgings International Limited
GES Service Companies Limited
GRT Nottingham Lift Project Company (No.2) Ltd
Gamston Kennels & Farms Limited
Golden Acquisition
Growth LED Innovation Driven Employee Co Ltd
H.I.G. Europe-Dart III, Ltd
HS 524 Limited
Hallamshire Developments Limited
Harworth Estates Limited
Heathcotes Group Limited
Helford Land Limited
Idis Group Limited
Innspired (Cedar) Limited
Insanely Great Limited
Isotrak Group Limited
Isotrak Holdings Limited
Isotrak Midco Limited
Jeld-Wen Europe Ltd.
Knowledgepoint360 UK Acquisitionco Ltd
Langley Aviation Limited
Arnold Laver Holdings Limited
Luxury British Design 1 Limited
Luxury British Design 2 Limited
Luxury British Design Holdings Limited
MPAC Overseas Holdings Limited
MSW (Holdings) Limited
Manitowoc Crane Group (UK) Subco Limited
Millbrook European Holdings Limited
Karen Millen Group Limited
Monocon Overseas Limited
Moorhen Holdings Limited
Muslim Hands
Mytravel Pioneer Limited
Nationwide Fast Fit Plus Limited
Navagator Limited
Norcros Industry (International) Limited
Northampton Acquisition Ltd
Nottingham Industrial Group Limited
Oasis and Warehouse Limited
Pacific Direct Finance Limited
Pendragon Finance and Insurance Services Ltd
Pendragon Stock Finance Limited
Pet City Holdings Limited
Pets at Home Holdings Limited
Pets at Home No.1 Limited
Pets at Home Superstores Limited
Pets at Home Vet Group Limited
Pets at Home Veterinary Specialist Group Ltd
Picsolve Holdings Limited
Pointeuro V Limited
Pointtravel Co. Ltd
Porvair Filtration Limited
Precision Engineered Limited
Punch Taverns Holdco (B) Limited
Remy Cointreau UK Limited
Renewi Financial Management Limited
Renewi PFI Investments Limited
Richard's Pharma Limited
Rigby Group (RG) PLC
Right Digital Limited
Rigid Plastic Containers Finance Limited
Rigid Plastic Containers Holdings Ltd
Rigid Plastic Containers Packaging Ltd
Rittal Holdings Limited
Rugby Group Limited
SDI (Kingston) Limited
SDI (Market Road) Limited
SIG European Holdings Limited
Saint-Gobain Aldwych Limited
Salvesen Logistics Limited
Secure Holdings Limited
Silentpride Limited
Sistine Properties (Westbury) Limited
Solo Cup Finance Limited
Stagecoach Supertram Maintenance Ltd.
Stampede Acquisition Limited
Synventive Acquisition UK Limited
TFS Holdings Limited
TH Finance Limited
TI Automotive Euro Holdings Limited
TI Automotive USA Holdings Limited
TTG Global Limited
Terberg Environmental UK Limited
Travis Perkins P & H Partner Limited
VGI Holdings Limited
WA Capital Investments Limited
WA Capital Limited
WIC (1) Limited
WJH Limited
Wabtec UK Investments Limited
Wakefield Waste Holdings Limited
White Capstan Limited
The H D H Wills 1965 Charitable Trust
XPO Investment UK Limited

75000 Veterinary activities

Benchmark Animal Health Group Limited
Benchmark Animal Health Limited
Blue Cross
Intervet UK Limited
Intervet UK Production Limited
Schering-Plough Limited

77110 Renting and leasing of cars and light motor vehicles [20]

Amey Fleet Services Limited
Balfour Beatty Plant & Fleet Services Ltd
CCW 600 Limited
Dawsongroup Vans Limited
Europcar Group UK Limited
Europcar UK Limited
Global Self Drive Limited
Grosvenor Contracts Leasing Limited
Hanborough Enterprises Limited
T.C. Harrison 1960 Limited
Long Marsh Limited
Meynell Plant Hire Limited
Network Services (Nationwide) Limited
J G Pears Machinery Limited
Premierfirst Vehicle Rental Franchising Ltd
Reflex Vehicle Hire Limited
Total Motion Limited
URA Ventures Limited
United Rental Group Limited
Windsor Vehicle Leasing Limited

77120 Renting and leasing of trucks and other heavy vehicles [16]

Alltruck PLC
Amey Fleet Services Limited
Axis Fleet Management Limited
BRS Limited
Balfour Beatty Plant & Fleet Services Ltd
Dawsongroup Truck and Trailer Limited
Eurofleet Rental Limited
Fraikin Limited
Go Plant Fleet Services Ltd
Go Plant Limited
Hexagon Leasing Limited
Marcol Limited
Meynell Plant Hire Limited
Moran Commercials Ltd
J G Pears Machinery Limited
Rushlift Limited

77320 Renting and leasing of construction and civil engineering machinery and equipment [13]

Abba Plant Hire Limited
Balfour Beatty Plant & Fleet Services Ltd
Boels Rental Limited
Buckingham Plant Hire Limited
Bullimores Sand and Gravel Limited
Collins Earthworks Limited
Hall Contracts (Lakenheath) Limited
Ibstock Leasing Limited
Loxam Access Limited
N.M.T. Plant Hire Limited
PERI Limited
Scotts Hire Limited
Barry Wood Plant Hire Limited

77330 Renting and leasing of office machinery and equipment (including computers)

J G Pears Machinery Limited

77351 Renting and leasing of air passenger transport equipment

Rolls-Royce Leasing Limited
SDI Aviation Limited
Sector Aircraft Leasing Limited

77390 Renting and leasing of other machinery, equipment and tangible goods n.e.c. [24]

Alliance Medical Leasing Limited
Andaray (Holdings) Limited
BDF Plant Limited
Boels Rental Limited
Bridgstock Limited
Bybox Field Support Limited
Bybox Holdings Limited
Carter Accommodation Holdings Limited
Dawsongroup Bus and Coach Limited
Dawsongroup Material Handling Limited
Dawsongroup Temperature Control Solutions Ltd
Elliott Group Holdings (UK) Limited
Elliott Group Limited
Fusion Plastics Limited
Hydrainer Pump Hire Limited
L C & M Holdings Limited
Lavendon Group Limited
Loxam Access Limited
Nationwide Platforms Limited
J G Pears Machinery Limited
Somerset Equipment Finance (UK) Ltd
TCL Tanker Rental Limited
UK Platforms Ltd
Unicarriers Leasing UK Limited

77400 Leasing of intellectual property and similar products, except copyright works

Boots Company PLC
Experian Technology Limited
Fernbrook Investments (UK) Limited
Laurenglen Limited

78109 Other activities of employment placement agencies [12]

Ambitions Personnel Limited
Barker Ross Group Limited
Champion Employment Limited
E-PPL Limited
Education Placement Group Limited
GI Group Holdings Recruitment Limited
Grafton Recruitment Limited
Network Ventures Limited
P Investments Limited
Pertemps Jobshop Limited
Remploy Limited
WHC01 Limited

78200 Temporary employment agency activities [21]

Ambitions Personnel Limited
Champion Employment Limited
Draefern Limited
Education Placement Group Limited
Encore Personnel Services Limited
GI Group Recruitment Ltd
GI Recruitment Limited
Grafton Recruitment Limited
Hales Group Limited
Hexagon Investment Holdings Limited
ID Medical Group Limited
Interaction Recruitment PLC
Nicholas Associates Group Limited
PPF Limited
Pertemps Limited
Pertemps Recruitment Partnership Limited
Staffline Holdings Limited
Staffline Recruitment Limited
Star Bidco Limited
Star Midco 1 Limited
Synarbor Limited

78300 Human resources provision and management of human resources functions

Amey Services Limited
Dow Chemical Services UK Limited
Nicholas Associates Group Limited
Nicholas Associates Holdings Limited

79110 Travel agency activities [12]

AIAL Limited
Aferry Ltd
BI Worldwide Limited
Bolsover Cruise Club Limited
Thomas Cook Retail Limited
Thomas Cook Tour Operations Limited
Freedom Travel Group Limited
Future Travel Limited
Hotels4U.Com Limited
Johnson Bros (Tours) Limited
Skills Leisure Limited
TCCT Retail Limited

79120 Tour operator activities [10]

Audley Travel Group Limited
Boketto Bidco Limited
Boketto Holdco Limited
Boketto Midco Limited
Boketto Newco Limited
Broomco (3019) Limited
Rayburn Tours (Holdings) Limited
Rayburn Tours Limited
Riviera Tours Limited
Sunway Travel (Coaching) Limited

79909 Other reservation service activities n.e.c.

Forest Holidays Group Limited
Forest Holidays Limited
Zibrant Limited

80100 Private security activities

Loomis UK Limited

80200 Security systems service activities

Quadrant Security Group Limited
RM Property and Facilities Solutions Ltd
Synectic Systems Group Limited
Total Integrated Solutions (Holdings) Ltd
Totally Local Co Ltd

81100 Combined facilities support activities

Apollo Support Services Group Limited
Blue Support Services Limited
Leadec Limited
RM Property and Facilities Solutions Ltd

81210 General cleaning of buildings

Amey Community Limited
Cape Environmental Services Onshore Ltd
RM Property and Facilities Solutions Ltd
Regent Office Care Limited

81299 Other cleaning services

Clean Estates Limited

81300 Landscape service activities [10]

Continental Landscapes Limited
Dunlin Limited
Idverde Limited
Idverde UK Limited
Milton Keynes Parks Trust Limited
Quadron Services Limited
T. C. Landscapes Limited
T.C. Landscapes Group Limited
T.C.L. Holdings (Midco) Limited
T.C.L. Holdings Limited

82110 Combined office administrative service activities

Blenheim Agency Limited
Diversey UK Services Limited
Envigo Holdings Limited
R.J. & A.E. Godfrey
Northamptonshire Arts Management Trust
Ontex Healthcare UK Limited
Symm Group Limited
Wade Furniture Group Limited

82200 Activities of call centres

Argos Limited
Clientlogic Limited
Network Services (Nationwide) Limited
Parseq Limited

82301 Activities of exhibition and fair organisers

Freeman Company (UK) Limited

82302 Activities of conference organisers

BI Worldwide Limited

82920 Packaging activities

API Foils Limited
API Group PLC
API Laminates Limited
Board24 Ltd
Kite Packaging Limited
MacFarlane Group UK Limited
Simply Cartons Limited

82990 Other business support service activities n.e.c. [337]

3C Waste Limited
ACM ULR Limited
ALC (SPC) Limited
ARG Corporate Services Limited
Accord Limited
Ad Meliora Academy Trust
Adient UK Financing International Ltd
Adient UK Financing Ltd
Agrihold Limited
Airtanker Finance Limited
Airtanker Holdings Limited
Airtanker Limited
Allegheny Technologies Limited
Alliance Asset Management Limited
Allied Publicity Services (Manchester) Ltd
Allied Textiles Limited
Allington Waste Co Ltd
Alltruck PLC
Amey Belfast Schools Partnership PFI Co Ltd
Amey Community Limited
Amey Group Services Limited
Amey Investments Limited
Amey LG Limited
Amey Lighting (Norfolk) Limited
Amey Metering Limited
Amey Programme Management Limited
Amey Utility Services Limited
Amey Ventures Management Services Ltd
AmeyCespa (AWRP) SPV Limited
AmeyCespa (East) Limited
AmeyCespa (MK) SPV Limited
AmeyCespa WM (East) Limited
Anglian Water (Osprey) Financing PLC
Anglian Water Services Financing PLC
Anti-Waste (Restoration) Limited
Anti-Waste Limited
Arconic Limited
Arena Blinds Limited
Armitage Pet Care Limited
Ashfield Healthcare Limited
Ashfield Meetings & Events Limited
BCM Employment & Management Services Ltd
BDR Waste Disposal Limited
BI Worldwide Limited
BISL Limited
BPI International Limited
BV Holdings Limited
Banner Group Limited
Bartec Auto ID Limited
Baxi Global Limited
Beaver-Visitec International (UK) Ltd
Beeston Site Services Limited
Belling (1992) Limited.
Belron UK Limited
Berville Limited
Toby Blackwell Limited
Bloom Developments Limited
Blue Sea Overseas Investments Limited
Bodycote Finance Limited
Bodycote International Limited
Bodycote Treasury Services Limited
Boots Management Services Limited
Braeside Group Limited
Bridgebank Holdings Limited
Brophy Grounds Maintenance Limited
Buzzard Leisure Limited
Byrom PLC
CAME BPT UK Limited
Cadent Services Limited
Carpenter Holdings Limited
Caterpillar Overseas Limited
Caterpillar UK Holdings Limited
Cemex UK Services Limited
Central England Healthcare Limited
Centro Place Investments Limited
Century Health (Nottingham) Limited
Challenger Multi Academy Trust
Chartmoor Estates Limited
Chiron Bidco Limited
Citation Limited
City Furniture Hire Limited
Claypenny Property Services Limited
Clientlogic (UK) Limited
Co-op Group Travel 2 Holdings Limited
Coal Industry Social Welfare Organisation 2014
Commercial Legal Limited
Community 1st Sheffield (Holdco) Limited
Companion Care (Services) Limited
Compare The Market Limited
Conquest Bidco Limited
Thomas Cook Aircraft Engineering Ltd
Thomas Cook Continental Holdings Ltd
Thomas Cook Finance PLC
Thomas Cook Group Hedging Limited
Thomas Cook Group Treasury Limited
Thomas Cook Investments (2) Limited
Thomas Cook UK Limited
Thomas Cook UK Travel Limited
Thomas Cook West Investments Limited
Cosworth Electronics Limited
Cresta Court Hotel Holdings Limited
Cyprotex Discovery Limited
DHL Services Limited
DSI Construction Holdings UK Ltd
Dana UK Automotive Systems Limited
Dana UK Axle Limited
Darrington Quarries Limited
De Trafford and Palatine Estates Limited
Deb Holdings Limited
Deb IP Limited
Detrafford No1 Castlefield Ltd
Detrafford Sky Gardens Ltd
Dodson & Horrell (Holdings) Limited
Doncasters Group Limited
Doncasters UK Finance Limited
RR Donnelley UK Limited
Dundee Holdco 2 Limited
Dundee Holdco 3 Limited
Dundee Holdco 4 Limited
Dundee Pikco Limited
E S Management Services Limited
E.On Connecting Energies Limited
E4D & G Project Co Limited
EESL Energypro Assets Limited
East Worcester Water Limited
Elmwood Trading Limited
English Partnerships (LP) Limited
Enterprise Managed Services Limited
Environmental Scientifics Group Holdings Ltd
Enviropower Investments Limited
Equity Solutions Asset Management Ltd
Equity Solutions Lift Investments Cornwall Ltd
Equity Solutions Lift Investments Oldham Ltd
Equity Solutions Lift Investments Sheffield Ltd
Essential Supply Products Limited
Essentra Finance Limited
European Support Services (UK) Limited
Eyre & Elliston Holdings Limited
FCC (E & M) Holdings Limited
FCC Buckinghamshire Holdings Limited
FCC Buckinghamshire Limited
FCC Environment (Berkshire) Limited
FCC Environment (Lincolnshire) Limited
FCC Environment (UK) Limited
FCC Environment Developments Limited
FCC Environment Services (UK) Limited
FCC PFI Holdings Limited
FCC Recycling (UK) Limited
FCC Waste Services (UK) Limited
FCC Wrexham PFI Limited
Festino (Finance) Limited
Filta Group Holdings PLC
Fisher Scientific U.K., Limited
Flo-Mech Holdings Limited
Fluidone Holdings Limited
Fulcrum Infrastructure Services Limited
Fulcrum Pipelines Limited
Full Moon Holdco 4 Limited
Full Moon Holdco 5 Limited
Full Moon Holdco 6 Limited
Full Moon Holdco 7 Limited
H.B. Fuller U.K. Limited
GEO Amey PECS Limited
GRT Nottingham Lift Project Company (No. 1) Ltd
Gapuma (UK) Limited
Global Brands (GBL) Holdings Limited
Global Experience Specialists (GES) Holdings Ltd
Global Experience Specialists (GES) Ltd
Global Payments U.K. Ltd
Graven Hill Village Development Co Ltd
Grevayne Properties Limited
HC 1228 Limited
HC1221 Limited
HFG Holdings Limited
T.C. Harrison 1960 Limited
Haughton Textiles Limited
Hillco Investments (UK) Limited
Holdsworth Holdings Limited
Home Retail Group (UK) Limited
Horsforth Holdings Limited
John Hurt Estates (UK) Limited
IB Group Ltd
IMCI (Services) Limited
ISDC Developments (No2) Limited
ISN Europe Limited
ITC Enterprises Limited
Iceni Marine Services Limited
Infinity SDC Limited
Ingka Energy Services UK Limited
Ingleby (1981) Limited
Integrated Bradford SPV One Limited
Integrated Bradford SPV Two Limited
Integrated Waste Management Limited
Irth (15) Limited
Just A Bank Limited
K9 Midco Limited
Kent Energy, Ltd.
Kent Enviropower Limited

Keyence (UK) Limited
Kingston (City) Estates Trading Limited
Lamb-Weston/Meijer UK Limited
Landfill Management Limited
Latimer Associates (U.K) Limited
Leicester Lift Project Company (No. 1) Ltd
Levi Strauss (U.K.) Limited
Lexington Catering Limited
Lincwaste Limited
Lunette Properties Limited
Luxury for Less Limited
MRS Environmental Services Limited
MTU UK Limited
Mahle Industries UK Limited
Maintenance Management Limited
Makro Holding Limited
Mastercard Prepaid Management Services Ltd
Matrix SCM Limited
Mattioli Woods PLC
Stewart Milne Homes North West England Ltd
Stewart Milne Timber Systems Limited
Molson Coors Holdings Limited
E. Moss, Limited
Motor Insurers' Bureau
Mullahead Property Co Ltd
Myoderm Limited
Mytravel Group Limited
Mytravel North America Limited
NAHL Group PLC
NFU Mutual (Service Company) Limited
NHBC Building Control Services Limited
NUS Services Limited
Nasmyth Group Limited
National Accident Helpline Limited
Newlincs Development Limited
AC Nielsen Holdings UK Limited
Nottingham City Homes Limited
Nu Instruments Limited
Office Space in Town Limited
Orano UK Limited
Osprey Acquisitions Limited
Oxford Trust
Oxford University Innovation Limited
PAH Financial Services Limited
PFM Group Limited
PPL PRS Limited
Parkway Hellas Holdings Limited
Penmarric Limited
Peppermint Technology Holdings Limited
Peterborough Diocesan Board of Finance
Project Grace
Project Jupiter Limited
Punch Partnerships (PML) Limited
Pyvot Limited
QMS International Limited
Quadgas Midco Limited
R P S Group PLC
RE3 Limited
RRD GDS Limited
Rannoch Food Group Limited
Rigby Capital Investments Ltd
Rigby Real Estate Limited
Rockwell European Holdings Limited
Rockwell International
Rolls-Royce International Limited
Rolls-Royce Overseas Investments Limited
Roythornes Limited
Patrick Ruddy Homes Limited
Rycote Services Limited
SC Johnson Professional Group Limited
SGBD Property Holdings Limited
SHV Investments Limited
Saint-Gobain Glass (United Kingdom) Ltd
Senad Investments Limited
Severn Trent (W & S) Limited
Severn Trent LCP Limited
Severn Trent Leasing Limited
Severn Trent Reservoirs Limited
Severn Trent Utilities Finance PLC.
Sitel Europe Limited
Sitel Solutions UK Limited
Sitel UK Finance
Sitel UK Limited
Sleek International Limited
Slough Enterprise Limited
Solo Cup (UK) Limited
Sonic Communications (International) Ltd
Southern Derbyshire Lift Project Company (No. 1) Ltd
Southwell and Nottingham Diocesan Board of Finance
Spraycon Limited
Staffline Group PLC
Stanley UK Services Limited
Stratford-upon-Avon Town Trust
Sun Chemical Limited
T & W Group Limited
TCCT Holdings UK Limited
TCGH Holdings Limited
TDY Limited
TI Group Automotive Systems (Deeside) Ltd
TI Group Automotive Systems Limited
TNT GRS 2008 Limited
TNT Holdings (UK) Limited
Tennant Metallurgical Group Holdings Ltd
Thame and London Limited
Thistle Insurance Services Limited
Tibbetts Group Limited
Tillotts Pharma UK Limited
Top Tubes Limited
Transit 2017 Limited
Travis Perkins Finance Co Ltd
Travis Perkins Financing Company No.2 Ltd
UK Vast Holdco Limited
UKLS Acquisitions Limited
Umeco Composites Limited
Unipart Group Limited
Unipart Logistics Limited
Unipath Limited
United Rental Group America Limited
V Installations Mechanical Handling Ltd
Vaillant Group UK Limited
Vision Express (UK) Limited
Vision Express Limited
Vow Retail Limited
WRG Acquisitions 2 Limited
WRG Environmental Limited
C. Walton Limited
Washbrook Capital Limited
Waste Recycling Group (Central) Limited
Waste Recycling Group (UK) Limited
Wastenotts (Reclamation) Limited
Welbeck Waste Management Limited
Wilkins Group Limited
Wolseley Utilities Limited
Wyboston Lakes Limited
Wyn Overseas Operations Limited
XPO Maintenance UK Limited
Xanadu Investments Limited
Young's Seafood International Holdings Ltd
Zahawi & Zahawi Ltd

84110 General public administration activities [15]

ALC (FMC) Limited
ALC (SPC) Limited
Amey Community Limited
Amey Fleet Services Limited
Amey Group Information Services Limited
Amey Group Services Limited
Amey LUL 2 Limited
Amey OW Limited
Amey OWR Limited
Amey PLC
Amey Programme Management Limited
Amey Rail Limited
Amey Services Limited
Amey UK PLC
AmeyCespa Limited

84120 Regulation of health care, education, cultural and other social services, not incl. social security

First for Wellbeing CIC
Four CS MAT

84220 Defence activities

Affinity Capital Works Limited
Affinity Flying Training Services Ltd
Ancala Water Services (Defence) Limited
Ancala Water Services (Estates) Limited
Cook Defence Systems Limited
UAV Tactical Systems Limited

84230 Justice and judicial activities

Novo Community Ltd

84240 Public order and safety activities

Axon Public Safety UK Limited

85100 Pre-primary education [42]

Acorndrift Limited
Acorndrive Limited
Asquith Nurseries Limited
Aylesbury Vale Academy
BHCF2 Limited
BHFS One Limited
BHFS Two Limited
Boston Witham Academies Federation
Brigantia Learning Trust Limited
Bright Horizons Family Solutions Limited
Childbase Partnership Limited
Cognita Schools Limited
Cranford House School Trust Limited
De Ferrers Trust
Thomas Deacon Education Trust
Dragon School Trust Limited
Education Fellowship Trust
Fallibroome Trust
Forest Way School
Headington School Oxford Limited
Holy Spirit Catholic Multi Academy Company
Loughborough Schools Foundation
Maltby Learning Trust
Mount St Mary's
Pope Francis Catholic Multi Academy Company
Sir John Port's Charity
Princethorpe Foundation
Priory Federation of Academies
Quaker International Educational Trust

Ratcliffe College
Redhill Academy Trust
River Learning Trust
Rye St. Antony School Limited
Stockport Grammar School
Tapton School Academy Trust
John Taylor MAT
Tudor Hall School
United Learning Trust
Warwick Independent Schools Foundation
Wellspring Academy Trust
West Grantham Academies Trust
Woodard Schools (Nottinghamshire) Ltd

85200 Primary education [101]

Abingdon School
Archway Learning Trust
Aston Community Education Trust
Aylesbury Vale Academy
Believe Academy Trust
Bicester Learning Academy
Boston Witham Academies Federation
Brigantia Learning Trust Limited
Bright Tribe Trust
Brooke Weston Trust
Caroline Chisholm Education Trust
Cognita Schools Limited
Cokethorpe Educational Trust Limited
Community Schools Alliance Trust
Cothill Trust
Cranford House School Trust Limited
De Ferrers Trust
Thomas Deacon Education Trust
Derby Diocesan Academy Trust 2
Diocese of Coventry Multi-Academy Trust
Diocese of Sheffield Academies Trust
Discovery Schools Academies Trust Ltd
Dragon School Trust Limited
Duston Education Trust
Eastern Multi-Academy Trust
Education Fellowship Trust
Empowering Minds Academy Trust
Equals Trust
Fallibroome Trust
Flying High Trust
Forest Way School
Dorothy Goodman School
Hampton Academies Trust
Hatton Academies Trust
Headington School Oxford Limited
Healing Multi Academy Trust
Hill House School Limited
Holy Spirit Catholic Multi Academy Company
Innovate Multi Academy Trust
Inspire Education Trust
Inspire Trust
Isle Education Trust
Kimbolton School
King Edward VI Education Trust
L.E.A.D. Academy Trust
L.E.A.D. Trust
Lakes Academies Trust
Landau Forte Charitable Trust
Leicester Grammar School Trust
Link Education Trust
Loughborough Schools Foundation
Magdalen College School Oxford Limited
Maltby Learning Trust
Mayflower Specialist School Academy Trust
Mead Educational Trust
Mercia Learning Trust
Montsaye Community Learning Partnership
Moulsford Preparatory School Trust Ltd
Mount St Mary's
Mowbray Education Trust Limited
Mulberry Bush Organisation Limited
Northampton Primary Academy Trust
Northern House School Academy Trust
Nottingham High School
Peterborough Keys Academies Trust
Pope Francis Catholic Multi Academy Company
Sir John Port's Charity
Princethorpe Foundation
Priory Federation of Academies
Quaker International Educational Trust
Raleigh Learning Trust
Ratcliffe College
Reach2 Academy Trust
Redhill Academy Trust
River Learning Trust
The David Ross Education Trust
Rye St. Antony School Limited
Sheffield South East Trust
Sparken Hill Academy Trust
Spencer Academies Trust
Steel City Schools Partnership
Stockport Grammar School
Stowe Valley Multi Academy Trust
Summerfields School Trust,Limited
Tapton School Academy Trust
John Taylor MAT
Tollbar Multi Academy Trust
Transform Trust
Trent College Limited
Tudor Hall School
United Church Schools Trust
United Learning Trust
Vale Academy Trust
Warriner Multi Academy Trust
Warwick Independent Schools Foundation
Wellspring Academy Trust
West Grantham Academies Trust
White Woods Primary Academy Trust
Wickersley Partnership Trust
Wisbech Grammar School
Woodard Schools (Nottinghamshire) Ltd

85310 General secondary education [226]

5 Dimensions Trust
ACES Academies Trust
Abbey College, Ramsey
Abingdon School
Abney Trust
Academy @ Ridgewood Trust
Academy of Lincoln Trust
Acer Trust
Apollo Partnership Trust
Archway Learning Trust
Ashby School
Aspire Learning Trust (Whittlesey)
Aspire Schools Trust
Aspireplus Educational Trust
Aston Community Education Trust
Aylesbury Vale Academy
Aylesford School and Sixth Form College
Bicester Learning Academy
Birkdale School
Bishop Stopford School
Bloxham School Limited
Blue Coat Church of England Academy Ltd
Boston Witham Academies Federation
Bosworth Independent College Limited
Bourne Grammar School
Bradfield School
Branston Academy Trust
Brigantia Learning Trust Limited
Bright Tribe Trust
Brooke Weston Trust
Brookfield School Academy Trust
Burford School
CASP
Campion School & Language College
The Robert Carre Trust
Casterton College Rutland
Castle Phoenix Trust
Cavendish Learning Trust
Chenderit School Academy Trust
Chiltern Hills Academy
Caroline Chisholm Education Trust
Chorus Education Trust
Cognita Schools Limited
Cokethorpe Educational Trust Limited
Community Schools Alliance Trust
Coundon Court
Cranford House School Trust Limited
Cromwell Community College
De Aston School Academy Trust
De Ferrers Trust
Thomas Deacon Education Trust
Denbigh Alliance
Diocese of Coventry Multi-Academy Trust
Diverse Academies Trust
Dragon School Trust Limited
Duston Education Trust
East Midlands Education Trust
Eastern Multi-Academy Trust
Ecclesbourne School
Education Fellowship Trust
Elizabethan Academy Trust
Evolve Trust
Eynsham Partnership Academy
Fallibroome Trust
William Farr Church of England Comprehensive School
Fernwood Academy Trust
Ferrers School
Finham Park Multi-Academy Trust
Fir Vale School Academy Trust
Forest Way School
Four CS MAT
Gartree High School
Giles Academy
Gosford Hill School
Grammar School of King Edward VI at Stratford-upon-Avon
Greater Nottingham Education Trust
Greenwood Academies Trust
Guilsborough Multi Academy Trust
Hall Cross Academy Trust
Hampton Academies Trust
Hatton Academies Trust
Hayfield School
Hazeley Academy
Headington School Oxford Limited
Healing Multi Academy Trust
Heart of England School
Higham Lane School
Hill House School Limited
Holy Spirit Catholic Multi Academy Company
Horncastle Education Trust
Hungerhill Academy Trust
Huxlow Science College
Ibstock Community College
Inspire Trust
Instill Education Limited

Isle Education Trust
Kenilworth Multi Academy Trust
Kesteven and Grantham Girls' School Academy Trust
Kimbolton School
King Edward VI Education Trust
King's (The Cathedral) School, Peterborough
Kingham Hill Trust
L.E.A.D. Academy Trust
Landau Forte Charitable Trust
Laurus Trust
Lawrence Sheriff School Academy Trust
Learner Engagement and Achievement Partnership Multi-Academy Trust
Learning Without Limits Academy Trust
Leger Education Trust
Leicester Grammar School Trust
Life Multi-Academy Trust
Lincoln Christ's Hospital School
Lincoln College Academy Trust
Loughborough Schools Foundation
Lutterworth Academies Trust
Macclesfield Academy
Magdalen College School Brackley Academy Trust
Magdalen College School Oxford Limited
Maltby Learning Trust
Maplefields Academy
Market Bosworth School
Mead Educational Trust
Meadowhead School Academy Trust
Merchant Taylors' Oxfordshire Academy Trust Ltd
Mercia Learning Trust
Midland Academies Trust
Mill Academy
Milton Keynes Academy Trust
Milton Keynes Education Trust
Minerva Learning Trust
Montsaye Community Learning Partnership
Moulton School and Science College
Mount St Mary's
Mowbray Education Trust Limited
Myton School Trust
National Church of England Academy Trust
Nene Education Trust
New College Leicester Trust
North Kesteven Academy
Northampton School for Boys
Northworthy Trust
Nottingham High School
Nova Education Trust
Oakham School
Ousedale School
Oxford Said Business School Limited
Sir Robert Pattinson Academy
Peak Multi Academy Trust
Peterborough Keys Academies Trust
Pope Francis Catholic Multi Academy Company
Sir John Port's Charity
Princethorpe Foundation
Priory Federation of Academies
QED Academy Trust
QEGSMAT
Quaker International Educational Trust
Quarrydale Academy
Raleigh Learning Trust
Ratcliffe College
Rawlins Academy
Reach2 Academy Trust
Redborne Upper School and Community College
Redhill Academy Trust
Ridgeway Education Trust
River Learning Trust
The David Ross Education Trust
Royal Latin School
Mark Rutherford School Trust
Rutland and District Schools' Federation
Rye St. Antony School Limited
Samworth Church Academy
School of St. Helen and St. Katharine Trust
Sheffield South East Trust
Shipston High School
Snaith School Academy Trust
South Lincolnshire Academies Trust
Spalding Grammar School
Spencer Academies Trust
St George's Academy Trust
St Ivo School
St Lawrence Academy, Scunthorpe
St Neots Learning Partnership
St. Clare's, Oxford.
St.Edward's School
Stockport Grammar School
Stowe School,Limited
Stowe Valley Multi Academy Trust
Stratford Girls' Grammar School
Stratford-upon-Avon School
Sidney Stringer Multi Academy Trust
Summerfields School Trust,Limited
Tapton School Academy Trust
John Taylor MAT
Thame Partnership Academy Trust
Tollbar Multi Academy Trust
Tove Learning Trust
Transforming Lives Educational Trust
Trent Academies Group
Trent College Limited
Tudor Hall School
Two Counties Trust
Tytherington School
United Church Schools Trust
United Learning Trust
Uppingham School
Vale Academy Trust
Wales High School Academy Trust
Warriner Multi Academy Trust
Warwick Independent Schools Foundation
Welland Park Community College Academy Trust
Wellingborough School
Wellspring Academy Trust
West Coventry Academy
West Grantham Academies Trust
West Hill School
West Norfolk Academies Trust
West Park School
White Hills Park Federation Trust
Whitley Academy
Wickersley Partnership Trust
Wigston Academies Trust
Wingfield Academy
Wisbech Grammar School
Woodard Schools (Nottinghamshire) Ltd
Wootton Academy Trust
Wreake Valley Academy Trust

85320 Technical and vocational secondary education

Bright Tribe Trust
National Examination Board in Occupational Safety and Health
Sir Robert Pattinson Academy
Smallpeice Trust
Stowe Valley Multi Academy Trust
Woodard Schools (Nottinghamshire) Ltd

85410 Post-secondary non-tertiary education

Inspire Trust
Laurus Trust
Learndirect Limited
PIMCO 2909 Limited
Sir Robert Pattinson Academy
Pope Francis Catholic Multi Academy Company
Priory Federation of Academies
St. Clare's, Oxford.
University of Derby

85421 First-degree level higher education

Kingham Hill Trust
University of Derby

85422 Post-graduate level higher education

Oxford Centre for Hebrew and Jewish Studies
University of Derby

85510 Sports and recreation education

British Horse Society
Hungerhill Academy Trust
Youth Sport Trust

85530 Driving school activities

Radford Holdings Limited

85590 Other education n.e.c. [44]

Archway Learning Trust
Aspire Achieve Advance Group Limited
The Dominic Barberi Multi Academy Company
Bedford School Trust
Brigantia Learning Trust Limited
British Horse Society
British Journal of Anaesthesia
Cheadle Hulme School
Collaborative Academies Trust
Creating Tomorrow Multi Academy Trust
Diocese of Southwell and Nottingham Multi-Academy Trust
Ditchley Foundation
Djanogly Learning Trust
Evolve Trust
Heyfordian School Trust
Instill Education Limited
King Edward VI Education Trust
Kisimul Group Limited
Kisimul School Holdings Limited
The David Lewis Centre
Lincolnshire Wildlife Trust
Linkage Community Trust
Lionheart Academies Trust
Milton Keynes Education Trust
Nexus Multi Academy Trust
OISE Limited
Oxford Trust
Peopleplus Group Limited
Project Sinatra Midco Limited
Project Sinatra Topco Limited
Propeller Academy Trust
Rowden House School Limited
Ruskin College
Seashell Trust

Senad Group Limited
Senad Limited
Sharnbrook Academy Federation
Sheffield UTC Academy Trust
South Warwickshire Academy Trust
St Therese of Lisieux Catholic Multi Academy Trust
Stephenson (MK) Trust
Triumph Multi Academy Trust
WLP Holdings Limited
Wycliffe Hall

85600 Educational support services [10]

Bright Tribe Trust
East Midlands Academy Trust
Education Fellowship Trust
National Space Centre
Oxford Diocesan Schools Trust
Project Sinatra Bidco Limited
Protocol National Limited
RM Education Ltd
TTS Group Limited
Together Trust

86101 Hospital activities [10]

Alliance Medical Limited
Care Fertility Group Limited
Centres for Assisted Reproduction Ltd
Equilibrium Healthcare Limited
Life UK Healthcare Limited
Randomlight Limited
Sobell House Hospice Charity Limited
St Barnabas Hospice Trust (Lincolnshire)
St. Ann's Hospice
Sysmex UK Limited

86102 Medical nursing home activities

Ashberry Healthcare Limited
Evolution Homecare Services Limited
Healthcare at Home Ltd
Palms Row Health Care Limited
Tanglewood (Lincolnshire) Limited

86210 General medical practice activities

Air Ambulance Service
Evolution Homecare Services Limited
Healthcare at Home Ltd
Lima Orthopaedics UK Limited
Vocare Limited

86220 Specialists medical practice activities

Access Fertility Limited
Alliance Medical Limited
British Pregnancy Advisory Service
Care Fertility Group Limited
Care Fertility Holdings Limited
Centres for Assisted Reproduction Ltd
IVI UK Ltd
St Barnabas Hospice Trust (Lincolnshire)

86230 Dental practice activities

Mowbray Indigo Limited
Nationwide Healthcare Providers Limited
Rodericks Dental Limited
Seth Bidco Limited
Seth Finco Limited
Seth Midco Limited
Seth Topco Limited

86900 Other human health activities [76]

Ability Matters Group Limited
Action for Care Limited
Alliance Medical Group Limited
Alliance Medical Limited
Avery House Healthcare Limited
Bluebell Wood Children's Hospice
B. Braun Avitum UK Limited
B. Braun Medical Limited
B Braun Sterilog Limited
Brighterkind (CB) Limited
Brighterkind (MW) Limited
Brighterkind (PC) Limited
British Journal of Anaesthesia
Bush & Company Rehabilitation Limited
Care Fertility Group Limited
Centres for Assisted Reproduction Ltd
Christchurch Court Holdings Limited
Cope Children's Trust
Crabwall Claremont Limited
DMWSL 532 Limited
Evolution Homecare Services Limited
Extracare Charitable Trust
FSHC Developments (Properties) Limited
FSHC Properties (CH2) Limited
FSHC Properties (Manor) Limited
First for Wellbeing CIC
Four Seasons (Bamford) Limited
Four Seasons (DFK) Limited
Four Seasons Health Care Holdings Ltd
Four Seasons Homes No.4 Limited
Fresenius Medical Care (Holdings) Ltd
Fresenius Medical Care (UK) Limited
Fresenius Medical Care Renal Services Ltd
Granby Care Limited
Grandcross Limited
Healthcare at Home Ltd
Helen & Douglas House
Hill Care Limited
Hill-Rom Limited
Human Appeal
Huntercombe (BIR) Limited
Huntercombe (No 12) Limited
Huntercombe (SP) Limited
Huntercombe Properties (Frenchay) Ltd
Juice Master Limited
Kidney Research UK
Lawton Group Limited
Leicestershire & Rutland Organisation for The Relief of Suffering Ltd
Lloyds Pharmacy Clinical Homecare Ltd
Mediline Home Care Limited
Monarch Healthcare Limited
Motor Neurone Disease Association
Myton Hospices
North Nottinghamshire Lift Project Company (No.1) Ltd
Nottingham Citycare Partnership CIC
Pathfinders-Care (Ollerton) Limited
Pharmacy Care Plus Limited
Prime Life Limited
Proimmune Limited
Scancell Holdings PLC
Seashell Trust
St Andrew's Hospice Limited
St Barnabas Hospice Trust (Lincolnshire)
St. Luke's Hospice
St. Matthews (North) Limited
St. Matthews Limited
Star Mayan Limited
Sterigenics UK Limited
Stillness 928 Limited
Stillness 930 Limited
Swanton Care & Community Limited
Synergy Health Managed Services Limited
T.L. Care Limited
Thoratec Europe Limited
Totally PLC
Versus Arthritis

87100 Residential nursing care facilities [24]

Aaron Holdings Limited
Ashberry Healthcare Limited
Ashmere Derbyshire Limited
Astor Care Limited
CX Bidco Limited
CX Midco 2 Limited
CX Midco Limited
CX Topco Limited
Cairnwell Estates Limited
Castel Froma Neuro Care Limited
Country Court Care Homes 2 Limited
Country Court Care Homes Limited
Delano Birmingham 2009 Limited
Delano Sutton 2007 Limited
Eastgate Care Ltd
Exemplar Limited
Falcon Capital Investments Limited
Goldcrest Capital Investments Limited
HNB Care Limited
Hill Care 1 Limited
Methodist Homes
Orders of St. John Care Trust
Rushcliffe Care Limited
United Health Limited

87200 Residential care activities for learning difficulties, mental health and substance abuse

Coed du Hall Limited
Framework Housing Association
The David Lewis Centre
Quality Care (EM) Limited
St Andrew's Healthcare

87300 Residential care activities for the elderly and disabled [19]

Aaroncare Limited
Adara Group Limited
Avery Homes (Nelson) Limited
Country Court Care Homes 2 Limited
Country Court Care Homes Limited
Eden Supported Living Limited
Finbrook Limited
The David Lewis Centre
MacIntyre Care
Moriah House Limited
Orders of St. John Care Trust
Premier Nursing Homes Limited
Pride Care Homes Peterborough Limited
Ruddington Homes Limited
Sheffcare Limited
Swanton Care & Community (Andrew Frederick Care Homes) Ltd
Swanton Care & Community (Autism North) Ltd
Swanton Care & Community (Maesteilo Care Homes) Ltd
WCS Care Group Limited

87900 Other residential care activities n.e.c. [13]
Affinity Trust
Christchurch Court (UK) Limited
Hesley Care & Education Limited
Hesley Group Limited
Hesley Holdings Limited
Linkage Community Trust
PJ Care Group Limited
PJ Care Limited
Seashell Trust
Sun Healthcare Limited
Supported Living Care Property Limited
Together Trust
Winslow Court Ltd

88100 Social work activities without accommodation for the elderly and disabled
Carewatch Care Services Limited

88910 Child day-care activities
Breedon House Nurseries Limited
Spurgeons

88990 Other social work activities without accommodation n.e.c. [14]
Affinity Trust
Chartered Accountants' Benevolent Association
Country Court Care Homes Limited
Framework Housing Association
Lamport Hall Preservation Trust Limited
The David Lewis Centre
Lincoln Diocesan Trust and Board of Finance Ltd
Robert Luff Foundation Limited
Milton Keynes Community Foundation Ltd
Parallel Parents Ltd
Practical Action
Spurgeons
Victim Support
World Vision UK

90010 Performing arts
Belgrade Theatre Trust (Coventry) Ltd
Northampton Theatres Trust Limited
Sheffield Theatres Crucible Trust

90020 Support activities to performing arts
Belgrade Theatre Trust (Coventry) Ltd
Northamptonshire Arts Management Trust

90030 Artistic creation
Belgrade Theatre Trust (Coventry) Ltd
Dalziel & Pow Holdings Limited
Northampton Theatres Trust Limited
Set Copyrights Limited
Sheffield Theatres Trust

90040 Operation of arts facilities
Northampton Theatres Trust Limited
Sheffield Galleries & Museums Trust

91020 Museums activities
Bletchley Park Trust Limited
Canal & River Trading CIC
Canal & River Trust
National Memorial Arboretum Co Ltd
Sheffield Galleries & Museums Trust

91030 Operation of historical sites and buildings and similar visitor attractions [10]
Bicester Heritage Limited
Burghley House Preservation Trust Ltd
Canal & River Trust
Chatsworth House Trust
Grimsthorpe & Drummond Castle Trust Ltd
Kelmarsh Trust
National Memorial Arboretum Co Ltd
National Space Centre
Stoneleigh Abbey Limited
Stowe House Preservation Trust

91040 Botanical and zoological gardens and nature reserves activities
Banc D'Arguin, and Coastal and Marine Biodiversity Trust Fund Ltd
Cotswold Wild Life Park Limited
Lincolnshire Wildlife Trust
Twycross Zoo - East Midland Zoological Society Ltd
Webmart Limited
Woodland Trust

92000 Gambling and betting activities [10]
A & S Leisure Group Limited
Beacon Bingo Limited
Bellcoin Holdings Limited
Blueprint Operations Limited
Buzz Group Limited
Cashino Gaming Limited
Inspired Gaming (UK) Limited
Mark Jarvis Limited
Majestic Bingo Limited
RAL Limited

93110 Operation of sports facilities [15]
1LIFE Management Solutions Limited
Arena Coventry Limited
British Racing Drivers Club Limited
Everyone Active Administration Services Ltd
Midland Sports Centre for The Disabled Trust Ltd
Northampton Rugby Football Club Limited
Phoenix Sports Limited
Playfootball Ltd
Renault Sport Racing Limited
Sheffield City Trust
Sheffield International Venues Limited
Sheffield Wednesday Football Club Ltd
Silverstone Circuits Limited
Sports & Leisure Group Ltd
Sports and Leisure Management Ltd

93120 Activities of sport clubs
CFC 2001 Ltd
Leicester Football Club PLC
Northampton Saints PLC
Nottingham Forest Football Club Limited
Renault Sport Racing Limited

93130 Fitness facilities
1LIFE Management Solutions Limited
Roko Health Clubs Limited
SLM Fitness & Health Limited
Total Fitness Health Clubs Limited

93199 Other sports activities [14]
Arena Event Services Group Limited
British Horse Society
Derby County Football Club Limited
Haas Formula UK Ltd
Leicester City Football Club Limited
Leicester Racecourse Holdings Limited
Mercedes-Benz Grand Prix Ltd
Northamptonshire Association of Youth Clubs
Phoenix Sports Limited
Punch Promotions Limited
Red Bull Racing Limited
Seashell Trust
Sevco 5112 Limited
Wasps Holdings Limited

93210 Activities of amusement parks and theme parks
Blue Anchor Leisure Limited
Fantasy Island Operations Limited

93290 Other amusement and recreation activities n.e.c. [20]
1LIFE Management Solutions Limited
Bicester Heritage Limited
British Waterways Marinas Limited
Coaching Inn Group Ltd
Ellis Bros (Contractors) Limited
Georgica Limited
Glencalvie Estate
Inspired Gaming (UK) Limited
Magna Trust
Nene Park Trust
Plaza Investments Limited
Potter's Leisure Ltd.
See Group Limited
Sheffield City Trust
Sheffield International Venues Limited
TEG Holdings Limited
Ten Entertainment Group PLC
Tenpin Limited
Way Ahead Group Limited
Wheatcroft Collections Limited

94110 Activities of business and employers membership organisations
Horticultural Trades Association
Nisa Retail Limited

94120 Activities of professional membership organisations
College of Policing Limited

94910 Activities of religious organisations [17]
Baptist Union Corporation Limited
Church Army
Church Mission Society
Congregational & General Charitable Trust
Coventry Diocesan Board of Finance
Derby Diocesan Board of Finance Limited
Farmington Trust Limited
Farmland Reserve UK Limited

General Conference of The New Church
Kingsgate Community Church
Leicester Diocesan Board of Finance
Lincoln Diocesan Trust and Board of Finance Ltd
Oxford Diocesan Board of Finance
S L G Charitable Trust Limited
Sheffield Diocesan Board of Finance
Society of The Sacred Mission (Europe)
Society of The Salutation of Mary The Virgin Ltd

94990 Activities of other membership organisations n.e.c.

Berkshire, Buckinghamshire and Oxfordshire Wildlife Trust
British Horse Society
East Midlands Chamber (Derbyshire, Nottinghamshire, Leicestershire)
East of England Agricultural Society
Latvian Welfare Trust
Lincolnshire Agricultural Society
Lincolnshire Wildlife Trust
Wood Green Animal Shelters

95110 Repair of computers and peripheral equipment

Millgate Limited

95250 Repair of watches, clocks and jewellery

George Pragnell Limited
Watches of Switzerland Co Ltd

96010 Washing and (dry-)cleaning of textile and fur products

Micronclean Limited

96030 Funeral and related activities

Avalon (Europe) Limited
Avalon Trustee Co Ltd
Funeral Partners Limited
Lymn Funeral Services Limited
A.W.Lymn The Family Funeral Service Ltd
Nirvana Holdings Limited
Time Right Holdings Limited

96090 Other service activities n.e.c. [60]

3SE (Barnsley, Doncaster & Rotherham) Ltd
A4E Ltd
Amey Birmingham Highways Limited
Amey Defence Services (Housing) Limited
Amey Defence Services Limited
Aster and Young Limited
Blancco Technology Group PLC
Blitz Communications Limited
Blue Cross
T F Bowman & Son Limited
Brady Corporation Limited
Canal & River Trading CIC
Carrier Refrigeration UK Limited
Coalfields Regeneration Trust
Codemasters Group Limited
Corrpro Companies Engineering Limited
Denaro (UK) Limited
ELWA Limited
Enterprise (AOL) Limited
Equity Solutions Lift Investments Stockport Ltd
Jerry Green Dog Rescue
Guided Ultrasonics Limited
Harshl Limited
Headcrown Group PLC
T.P. Hopwell (Holdings) Limited
Infinis Energy Services Limited
International Brand Management Limited
MCL Group of Companies Limited
Manitowoc Crane Group (UK) Limited
Marmon Group Limited
Mertex UK Limited
Mobica Bidco Limited
Mobica Holdings Limited
MoveWithUs Conveyancing Limited
Normanby Estate Co Ltd
Novoferm UK Holdings Limited
Oxford University Trading Limited
People Potential Possibilities
Preci-Spark Limited
Profile Security Services Limited
Punch Taverns (Services) Limited
RCI Europe
RPS Group US Holdings Limited
Randall Parker Food Group Limited
Renewi Cumbria Limited
Renewi European Holdings Limited
Renewi Holdings Limited
Renewi UK Services Limited
Retail Merchant Finance Limited
Rittal Limited
Sansbury Bailey Holdings Limited
Sureclean Holdco Limited
Sywell Aerodrome,Limited
Vision Express (UK) Limited
Vision Express Group Limited
Vision Express Limited
Wakefield Waste PFI Limited
Weavers Close Limited
B. E. Webbe Removals (Derby) Limited
J & A Young Group Limited

97000 Activities of households as employers of domestic personnel

Burghley House Preservation Trust Ltd

98000 Residents property management

PTA Developments Limited

99000 Activities of extraterritorial organisations and bodies

Biogen Holdings Limited
Greencore Beechwood Limited
Greencore Northwood Limited
Greencore UK Holdings Limited
Hazlewood Foods Limited
Nottingham Roman Catholic Diocesan Trustees
Uniq (Holdings) Limited

99999 Dormant company [29]

Abbey Group UK Limited
BF Limited
BPI International (No 2) Limited
Carter Accommodation Group Limited
Caunton Holdings Limited
Cemex Seament Limited
H.W. Coates (Holdings) Limited
E. P. B. Holdings Limited
Essentra Filter Products Limited
Filtrona Limited
Giant Bidco Limited
Giant Booker Limited
Giant Midco Limited
Hazlewood (Blackditch) Limited
Heptagon Limited
Hillsborough Investments Limited
Hull Holdings Limited
IRESS UK Holdings Limited
Keelex 351 Limited
Moto Direct Holdings Limited
Northern Endeavour Limited
Omnico Plastics Limited
Phoenix Transworld Limited
Seaham Investments Limited
Fred Sherwood Group Limited
Specialised Fixings Limited
Warm A Home Limited
Warth Developments Ltd
Watch Shop Ltd

This page is intentionally left blank

Printed in 8pt Nimbus Sans L

Designed by URW++ Design and Development GmbH

Dellam Publishing Limited

2 Heath Drive, Sutton, Surrey, SM2 5RP

Fax: 020 8770 7478 email: enquiries@dellam.com

SAN: 0177881 EAN/GLN: 5030670177882

www.ingramcontent.com/pod-product-compliance
Lightning Source LLC
LaVergne TN
LVHW082005200926
848481LV00010B/2806